Baseball Prospectus 2007

THE ESSENTIAL GUIDE TO THE 2007 BASEBALL SEASON

Jim Baker • Maury Brown • Will Carroll

Clay Davenport • Neil de Mause • John Erhardt

Dan Fox • Steven Goldman • Kevin Goldstein

Derek Jacques • Jay Jaffe • Rany Jazayerli

Christina Kahrl • Ben Murphy • Rob Neyer

Marc Normandin • Nate Silver

Will Weiss • Keith Woolner

A Plume Book

PLUME
Published by Penguin Group
Penguin Group (USA) Inc., 375 Hudson Street, New York, New York 10014, U.S.A.
Penguin Group (Canada), 90 Eglinton Avenue East, Suite 700, Toronto, Ontario, Canada M4P 2Y3 (a division of Pearson Penguin Canada Inc.)
Penguin Books Ltd., 80 Strand, London WC2R 0RL, England
Penguin Ireland, 25 St. Stephen's Green, Dublin 2, Ireland (a division of Penguin Books Ltd.)
Penguin Group (Australia), 250 Camberwell Road, Camberwell, Victoria 3124, Australia (a division of Pearson Australia Group Pty. Ltd.)
Penguin Books India Pvt. Ltd., 11 Community Centre, Panchsheel Park, New Delhi—110 017, India
Penguin Group (NZ), 67 Apollo Drive, Mairangi Bay, Auckland 1311, New Zealand (a division of Pearson New Zealand Ltd.)
Penguin Books (South Africa) (Pty.) Ltd., 24 Sturdee Avenue, Rosebank, Johannesburg 2196, South Africa

Penguin Books Ltd., Registered Offices:
80 Strand, London WC2R 0RL, England

First published by Plume, a member of Penguin Group (USA) Inc.

First Printing (2007 edition), March 2007

10 9 8 7 6 5 4 3 2 1

Copyright © Prospectus Entertainment Ventures LLC, 2007
All rights reserved

 REGISTERED TRADEMARK—MARCA REGISTRADA

ISBN 978-0-452-28825-6

Printed in the United States of America
Set in Utopia
Designed by Pen & Palette Unlimited

Without limiting the rights under copyright reserved above, no part of this publication may be reproduced, stored in or introduced into a retrieval system, or transmitted, in any form, or by any means (electronic, mechanical, photocopying, recording, or otherwise), without the prior written permission of both the copyright owner and the above publisher of this book.

PUBLISHER'S NOTE
The scanning, uploading, and distribution of this book via the Internet or via any other means without the permission of the publisher is illegal and punishable by law. Please purchase only authorized electronic editions, and do not participate in or encourage electronic piracy of copyrighted materials. Your support of the author's rights is appreciated.

BOOKS ARE AVAILABLE AT QUANTITY DISCOUNTS WHEN USED TO PROMOTE PRODUCTS OR SERVICES. FOR INFORMATION PLEASE WRITE TO PREMIUM MARKETING DIVISION, PENGUIN GROUP (USA) INC., 375 HUDSON STREET, NEW YORK, NEW YORK 10014.

Contents

Fungoes

Foreword

Christina Kahrl and Steven Goldman

You hold in your hands the 12th edition of the Baseball Prospectus annual. The series is venerable, but it's far from static. One of the benefits of working with a group of supremely creative and inventive people is that there are always more ideas for each book than we can squeeze between two covers, yet we're bound to try. This is where we've typically alerted you, the reader, to the new things you will find within these pages. As Prospectus founder Gary Huckabay wrote with not a little poignance in the 1999 edition, "We've worked very hard to provide you with the finest baseball annual in the world. Please take a few minutes and read the introductory material."

The finest baseball annual has, as with all books, traditionally meant different things to different readers. For us it is simply this: a compendium of all the things we believe will happen in baseball this year and a review of much of what we have learned since last year, with the latter informing the former. That means more than the approximately two-thousand PECOTA projections contained herein, but also the player and manager comments and team essays themselves, each the product of knowing more about those players, managers, and teams and their scouting directors, general managers, and even owners than we did the year before. It's a continual education, one which we hope will never end.

That education is at the heart of what Baseball Prospectus is about. It's always informative to find out what people say about you when you're out of the room. Last year, Sam Walker published a book called *Fantasyland* about the culture of fantasy baseball. If you turn to the index, you'll find our entry: "Baseball Prospectus, arrogance of." It seems we think we know everything. Let's not play coy: we do know a lot about baseball. We also recognize that as much as any of us know, there is always more that we could know, and what we think we know can always be revised, reinterpreted, or even invalidated by new information.

That willingness to question assumptions about the game that are, in some cases, now over hundred years old is what marks Baseball Prospectus and has since the day that our five founders scratched out the first edition of this book back in the winter of 1995. It has continued through all the subsequent editions, daily on our web site, BaseballProspectus.com, where we publish a book's worth of new ideas and statistics roughly every few days, and in our other books, *Mind Game, Baseball Between the Numbers*, and the forthcoming *It Ain't Over*... Those five founders have since been joined by a long parade of some of the best young minds now working in the field of performance analysis, some of whom have gone on to careers in the front offices of your favorite ballclubs and as commentators on ESPN. If this be arrogance, let us make the most of it.

This year's book continues the expansion of last year. We've included more players than ever before, including more of the "Lineout" comments that we added last year. With the addition of prospect guru Kevin Goldstein to the BP team, we're also covering more prospects than ever before. Adding Kevin reflects Baseball Prospectus's commitment to the synergy between traditional player evaluation techniques and the quantitative performance analysis for which we're best known. We stand by our belief that, when you're talking about players, picking one method over another is a great way to miss the whole picture. In baseball, as in all things, informed analysis requires consideration of all of the information at your disposal. We're also making good on a promise we made in last year's book by adding to every team chapter a full-length manager comment complete with statistics that focus on that manager's player usage patterns, his tactics, and how successful he was with them.

This year, we have a new raft of outstanding "Fungoes" exploring issues of the importance to the game. Neil deMause and Maury Brown have teamed up their complementary areas of expertise to produce this year's wide-ranging discussion of the game off the field and in the boardrooms. Keith Woolner revisits one of BP's most controversial counting statistics, Pitcher Abuse Points. In a time when we see perhaps too many headlines on the subject of performance-enhancing drugs, Will Carroll and Jay Jaffe question the impact of the amphetamine ban on player performance. Finally, we're proud to present Will Weiss's look at the previously unexplored interaction between major league sports and the environment, with a focus on the initiatives that Major League Baseball is taking in this area. Thanks to the addition of Kevin Goldstein to the BP team, we've also doubled the size of our top prospects list. Kevin's expansive knowledge of every aspect of player development made him a major resource for this book and these pages are shot through with his observations. The Top 100 is entirely his show, and his place to shine.

The data that forms the core of this book results from our three resident statistical geniuses, Keith Woolner, Clay Davenport, and Nate Silver, working in concert. They and we received the indispensable aid of Ben Murphy, who single-handedly made it possible for us to integrate numbers and prose in a more timely manner than ever before, a combination that should reflect Baseball Prospectus at its very best. Beyond the genius of Nate's forecasting or Clay's ability to interpret performance across leagues and time, the patient cooperation of Keith Woolner and Jason Pare made possible much of the data you see within the team essays themselves. The work produced by the data team for this year's book was nothing short of Herculean.

As ever, we're glad for the opportunity to welcome a few rookies. This year, Derek Jacques, Dan Fox, and Marc Normandin got woven into a generally veteran crew. Much as we recognize that there is always more to learn, we also recognize that there are always new voices that must be heard, thus we are constantly looking to integrate young talented writers. As we make space for merit, you'll see more from all three in the years to come, in this book and on the BP website.

We are pleased to call Plume our new home. We'd like to thank Plume, and particularly our editor, Cliff Corcoran, for their enthusiasm for this project. Cliff's indefatigable, tireless work on behalf of the project has made a huge difference in the quality of the book. We have never had a better outside editor, and we tip our caps to Cliff. We're also glad for the assistance of Marie Coolman and Mary Pomponio, who have tackled the publicity for the book in our first year with Plume. We also remain extremely pleased with our agent, Sydelle Kramer, in her efforts to match Plume and Prospectus.

We'd also like to thank our design team, Don and Jan Rodgers at Pen & Palette, as this edition marks our tenth year together. The logistical challenge of assembling and publishing this book as late in the day as we do would border on the impossible without Don and Jan, not simply because of their professionalism, but because of the way in which they make delivering the best a point of pride. With-

out their tireless efforts, our ability to deliver this book would be severely compromised.

This is also an opportunity for us to point your towards the content we generate at BaseballProspectus.com. There, we've established an unparalleled reputation for regular columns devoted to performance analysis, injury reports, prospect evaluations, evaluations of trades and transactions, and other in-depth coverage of the great game. The vision for the site reflects the tireless efforts of Joe Sheehan and is the product of our regular rotation of contributors, including Joe, Will Carroll, and Kevin Goldstein among many others. A particularly fun addition has been BP Unfiltered, BP.com's new bloggier, off-the-cuff segment in which readers can catch our take on news as soon as it happens, including Nate's quick-fire PECOTA response to the latest player move, or Will's response to the latest positive test. Whereas several years ago the site might have gone dark for a month as we changed gears to create past editions of this book, we've grown to the point at which Joe is able to keep the mother ship humming along while we deliver this big book.

The site has also become a far more developed resource for fans and statheads as a result of the work of Keith Woolner, Clay Davenport, Ben Murphy, William Burke, and Tom Fontaine. Of particular note has been their introduction of custom sortable stat reports covering the full breadth of our play-by-play database (1960 to 2006). While we expected they'd be popular, we had no anticipation of how popular—as we go to press, our readers have generated almost 170,000 unique stat reports in less than a year. Looking forward to 2007, the tech team will continue to expand our offerings; by the time you read this, manager data similar to that which you'll find in this book will be on the site in a searchable form for you to play with.

Spring's rushing up on us, and anticipation is the name of the game. If you're one of our regular readers, you've no doubt anticipated getting this year's book. If you're a new reader, your decision to purchase this book is proof that you share our eager anticipation of the baseball season to come. Here's hoping you enjoy this book as much as you enjoy the season, because it's invariably a pleasure for us to put it together for your entertainment. If you have any observations about the book or baseball, feel free to take the time to start up a conversation with any or all of us through BaseballProspectus.com. Like you, we're fans, and nothing beats a great conversation about the game.

Steve Goldman
East Brunswick, New Jersey
Christina Kahrl
Fairfax, Virginia
January 22, 2007

Statistical Introduction

Clay Davenport, Nate Silver, and Keith Woolner

In this book, Baseball Prospectus presents the most advanced statistical summary of more than 16,000 major and minor league baseball players available anywhere, in print or on-line. In doing so, we employ some techniques unique to Baseball Prospectus. This section will serve as an introduction to those methods for the first-time reader, as well as a guide for returning readers to some of the changes introduced this year.

For each player, we present their statistics from every significant stint in the majors, minors, or prominent international leagues (Japanese and Mexican) over the previous three seasons. For an example, let's take the 2006 NL Rookie of the Year, Hanley Ramirez (see table 1).

The first line of the entry contains the player's name and some basic biographical information. The next line shows the headers for the columns of data that follow, where each horizontal line represents a player's season totals with a given team.

The first three columns of data show the year, team, and level at which that hitter played. Levels are designated as the major leagues (MLB), Triple-A, Double-A, Hi A-ball (A+), A-ball, Short-Season A-ball (A−), and Rookie ball (Rk) (this year, for the first time, we're including statistics and translations from the Gulf Coast League and Arizona League, baseball's lowest minor league levels). We also show the player's age for each season using his effective "baseball age," that is, his age as of July 1 of that year.

The next few columns—**PA, R, 2B, 3B, HR, RBI, BB, SO, SB,** and **CS**—show the actual and familiar statistical totals the player compiled in the following categories during this playing stint: plate appearances, runs, doubles, triples, home runs, runs batted in, bases on balls, strikeouts, stolen bases, and times caught stealing.

SPEED stands for Speed Score, which was originally the brainchild of Bill James. We have developed our own version of Speed Score that takes better advantage of play-by-play data. The BP version of SPEED is a composite metric that accounts for five characteristics related to a player's baseball speed: stolen base percentage, stolen base attempts as a percentage of opportunities (defined as times on first or second base while the next base is empty), triples, double plays grounded into as a percentage of opportunities (defined as times at-bat with a runner on first base and less than two outs), and runs scored as a percentage of times on base. Each of these five components is normalized to give them equal weight in the formula. An average SPEED score is exactly 5.0; Carl Crawford's SPEED last year was 8.4, while Mike Piazza's was 3.2.

The next three columns (**BA, OBP, SLG**) show the three most commonly used rate statistics in raw, unadjusted form: batting average (hits per at-bat), on-base percentage (hits + walks + hit-by-pitch / at-bats + walks + hit-by-pitch), and slugging average (total bases per at-bat).

The remaining columns contain Baseball Prospectus's most useful original statistics. The next column is Marginal Lineup Value Rate, or **MLVr.** Marginal Lineup Value estimates the value of a player by computing the change in expected run scoring between an average team, and a team with eight average players, plus our "hero." For example, if we were to substitute Travis Hafner for one

Table 1. Hitter Statistics Example

Hanley Ramirez   **SS**   **Bats: R**   **Throws: R**   Height: 6' 3"   Weight: 195   Born: December 23, 1983   Age: 23

YEAR	TM	LVL	AGE	PA	R	2B	3B	HR	RBI	BB	SO	SB	CS	SPEED	BA	OBP	SLG	MLVR	EQBA	EQOBP	EQSLG	EQA	VORP	DEFENSE	
2004	SAR	A+	20	263	33	8	4	1	24	17	39	12	7	6.4	.310	.364	.389	.118	.286	.328	.359	.244	5.9	60-SS	-7
2004	PME	AA	20	139	26	7	2	5	15	10	26	12	3	8.4	.310	.360	.512	.198	.277	.324	.454	.269	7.6	31-SS	0
2005	PME	AA	21	519	66	21	7	6	52	39	62	26	13	7.4	.271	.335	.385	.014	.250	.308	.356	.237	1.4	109-SS	-1
2006	FLO	MLB	22	700	119	46	11	17	59	56	128	51	15	8.0	.292	.353	.480	.150	.305	.366	.504	.294	54.9	149-SS	-4
2007	*FLO*	*MLB*	*23*	*663*	*104*	*36*	*8*	*15*	*66*	*52*	*102*	*47*	*17*	*7.1*	*.287*	*.349*	*.450*	*.034*	*.289*	*.347*	*.455*	*.276*	*37.7*	*155-SS*	*-1*

Breakout: 31% Improve: 54% Collapse: 12% Attrition: 0%   *Comparables: Mariano Duncan, Ryne Sandberg, Paul Molitor, Barry Larkin*

player in a lineup of nine identical average players, we would naturally expect his team to score more runs. Similarly, if you replaced one such player with Angel Berroa, expected run scoring would decrease.

Batting Order	Team A	Team B	Team C
1	Joe Average	Joe Average	Joe Average
2	Joe Average	Joe Average	Joe Average
3	Joe Average	Joe Average	Joe Average
4	Joe Average	Joe Average	Joe Average
5	Joe Average	TRAVIS HAFNER	ANGEL BERROA
6	Joe Average	Joe Average	Joe Average
7	Joe Average	Joe Average	Joe Average
8	Joe Average	Joe Average	Joe Average
9	Joe Average	Joe Average	Joe Average
Expected runs/game	4.939	5.457	4.607
Difference in runs/game versus Team A	0	+0.518	−0.332

Since the difference in expected run scoring between Team A and Team B is entirely due to having Travis Hafner in the lineup, we call this difference his Marginal Lineup Value Rate (MLVr). Marginal Lineup Value (MLV) is the total number of runs a player adds or subtracts over an entire season, while MLVr is his MLV divided by the number of games that the he participated in, or his MLV per game. MLV itself is not printed in this book, but it does form the basis for VORP, which is discussed below.

As you can see in the case of Angel Berroa, contributing a negative MLVr is certainly possible, and actually quite common. Any below average hitter will have a MLVr below zero.

The next three columns are **EqBA, EqOBP, EqSLG.** These are our "translated" rate statistics. Baseball Prospectus's Davenport Translations convert a player's statistics to a common baseline, adjusting for the player's home park, the offensive environment of the league he plays in, and, perhaps most importantly, the difficulty of the competition he plays against (thus compensating for the relative difficulty of the American and National Leagues). Slugging .512 against Eastern League competition, as Hanley Ramirez did in 2004, is not the same thing as slugging .512 in the majors. Similarly, good pitchers in the Eastern League will be able to post better ERAs and strikeout rates than they would in the majors because of the inferior hitters they're facing. The translation process adjusts for the lesser quality of opposition and converts the player's performance to an "equivalent" (hence, the Eq- prefix) major league performance. Thus, EqBA, EqOBP, and EqSLG can be used to make an apples-to-apples comparison of any two players in organized baseball.

EqA is Equivalent Average. Like MLVr, EqA is a rate statistic, and measures the player's total offensive value to his team, combining his abilities to reach base, hit for power, and steal bases. It is also a fully adjusted statistic: It takes into account park factors and a league's average offense. Unlike MLVr, the EqAs we show in BP 2006 are calculated from the player's translated statistics; they represent how a minor leaguer would perform in the major leagues as well as representing the performances of major leaguers in a completely neutral environment.

EqA is essentially runs produced per out made, although we've applied some mathematical trickery to make the result easier to understand. One problem shared by most "new" statistics is that casual fans have no intuitive feel for their scale; even if you know that a given score is above average, it takes time to learn how to distinguish "All-Star" good from "MVP" good. EqA sidesteps that problem by masquerading as batting average. An average player, by definition, will have a .260 EqA, which is close to the long-term norm for batting averages. You can think of a player's EqA as good or bad in exactly the same way you would consider a batting average to be good or bad. If .260 is average, an EqA of .300 makes you a legitimate star. Something like .350 is a typical league-leading total, as it was last year when Travis Hafner led the American League with a .367 EqA and Albert Pujols led the NL with a .356. A .400 EqA is exceptionally rare, but the greatest hitters in history—Ruth, Mantle, Williams, Bonds—have pulled it off. On the other hand, if your EqA is .220, you'd better be a great defensive player, or you'll be heading back to the minors.

The second-to-last column in the statistical record is **VORP,** which stands for Value Over Replacement Level. VORP is a cumulative stat that estimates total player value over a period of time. Built on MLVr, it measures value in runs, but rather than compare players to a single league-wide average, as MLVr does, it compares them to "replacement level" at their given position.

Replacement level is a concept discussed in great detail in the article "Understanding and Measuring Replacement Level" by Keith Woolner, which was published in *Baseball Prospectus 2002*, so we'll only summarize the main points here. We define replacement level as "the expected level of performance a major league team can receive from one or more of the best available players who substitute for a suddenly unavailable starting player at the same position and who can be (or were) obtained with minimal expenditure of team resources." Metrics such as MLVr, which compare a player to league-average offense, are incomplete because they do not account for the value of having a player healthy and in the lineup. Losing a starting player typically results in more starts being given to a bench player who is significantly below average. By comparing a player's production to the level of a typical bench player or "Quadruple-A" journeyman (a replacement player who thus plays at replacement level), we recognize the value of a player's durability. The concept of VORP is equally applicable to position players and pitchers.

VORP is available on the BP web site (www.baseball prospectus.com) for all players and seasons going back over 40 years, and is updated daily during the season. A couple of additional details about how VORP is presented for *minor* league players:

- VORP for minor leaguers is computed using their translated rates of production, and thus should be considered to be their major-league equivalent VORP, not their VORP relative to the minor league they actually played in.

- Minor league players are rated at their most frequently played position, rather than a weighted average across all positions they played in a given season (as is done with major leaguers). That is, if a minor league player plays 100 games at second base, and 20 at shortstop, he would be considered to be purely a second baseman in calculating his VORP. (This is *not* true for major league players. If a major league player played 100 games at second and 20 at shortstop, we would his compute his VORP on a weighted average basis, with second base having five times the weight of shortstop).

- Minor leagues have shorter seasons than the majors do, and as a result, even excellent translated rates of production may not produce as high a VORP as a player who had the benefit of a 162-game major league schedule would have had.

Although VORP looks at what position a player plays, it does not directly consider how well he fields that position. Thus we turn to the final column, **Defense,** to show the position, number of games, and fielding rating for the player at his primary position(s). The fielding rating is denominated in runs saved or allowed against average, thus Hanley Ramirez's 2006 line in Florida, which reads "149-SS -4," means he played the equivalent of 149 full games at shortstop with a defensive performance that would have allowed four more runs to score than an average shortstop over that same number of games.

The 2007 line is the PECOTA projection for the player in the upcoming season. Note that the player is projected into the league and park context indicated by his team abbreviation; Alfonso Soriano is now a Cub, and so forth. All PECOTAs represent a player's projected major league performance.

The numbers beneath the 2007 forecast line—*Breakout, Improve, Collapse,* and *Attrition*—are also a part of PECOTA and estimate the likelihood of changes in performance relative to a player's previously-established level of production. PECOTA differs from other projection systems in that it uses historically comparable data to generate a probability distribution, rather than just a single forecast line. History might tell us, for example, that an old, slow hitter will manage just fine eighty percent of the time, but will have a disastrous, career-ending season (a "collapse") twenty percent of the time. Conversely, a young pitcher with a high walk rate might show a sudden and marked improvement (a "breakout") fifteen percent of the time, while failing to improve much at all in his other seasons. The Breakout, Collapse, Improve, and Attrition numbers are an attempt to quantify these sorts of performance changes. To be more precise about it:

- **Breakout Rate** is the percent chance that a hitter's equivalent runs produced per plate appearance, or a pitcher's EqERA (see more on our pitcher stats below), will improve by at least 20 percent relative to the weighted average of his performance over the three seasons displayed (with 2006 performance weighted more heavily). High breakout rates are indicative of upside potential.

- **Improve Rate** is the percent chance that a hitter's equivalent runs produced per plate appearance, or a pitcher's EqERA, will improve *at all* relative to his baseline performance. A player who is expected to perform just the same as he has in the recent past will have an Improve Rate of 50%. Note that Breakout Rate is a subset of Improve Rate; Improve Rate is the chance that a player improves *at all*; Breakout Rate is the chance that he improves *a lot*.

- **Collapse Rate** is the percent chance that a position player's equivalent runs produced per plate appearance, or a pitcher's EqERA, will decline by at least 25 percent relative to his baseline performance over the three seasons displayed. High collapse rates are indicative of downside risk.

- **Attrition** Rate operates on playing time rather than performance. Specifically, it measures the likelihood that a hitter's plate appearances, or a pitcher's innings pitched, will decrease by at least 50 percent relative to his established level. Attrition Rate covers any reason for substantial playing time decline, including catastrophic injuries, but also a reduced role, midseason retirement, or anything similar.

Breakout Rate and Collapse Rate can sometimes be counterintuitive for players who have already experienced a radical change in their performance levels. For example, PECOTA gives Derrek Lee a Collapse Rate of 46%, even though it expects him to perform better than he did in 2006. This is because PECOTA is comparing its expectation for Lee's 2007 performance to a weighted average of the past *three* years, including his stupendous 2005, which boosts Lee's average.

Finally, note that these metrics do not necessarily represent a change in performance as a result of a change in underlying ability or skill and will also capture a player regressing to the mean after having had unusually good or bad luck. For example, Roy Oswalt's ERAs have tended to be much lower than his PERAs (see description below) over the past three seasons; this is almost always the result of favorable luck. Oswalt has a substantial Collapse Rate of 37%, but this may just mean that we expect his luck to return to normal, not that he's going to lose his fastball.

The final piece of information, listed just to the right of the hitter's Attrition Rate, are his four highest scoring comparable players as determined by PECOTA. PECOTA evaluates comparability by analyzing a number of quantifiable factors, including production metrics (batting average, isolated power), usage metrics (plate appearances, major league career length, minor league level), phenotypic attributes (handedness, height, and weight), and a player's defensive position. Although we list only a player's four best comparables here, PECOTA uses as many as a hundred comparables in producing a player's forecast in order to provide itself with a robust enough sample. Occasionally, a player's top comparables will not be representative of the larger sample that PECOTA uses.

Established major leaguers are compared to other major leaguers only. Minor league players may be compared to major league or minor league players, with PECOTA strongly preferring the latter (in fact, PECOTA prefers to compare a player at the same level of competition: a Double-A player versus other Double-A players, for example). All comparables represent a snapshot of how a historical player was performing at the age of the current player; being compared to a 23-year-old Sammy Sosa is much different than being compared to a 31-year-old Sammy Sosa, which is again different than being compared to a 36-year-old Sammy Sosa.

For the first time this season, the PECOTAs also incorporate an adjustment for league difficulty. That is, since the American League is quite a bit tougher than the National League (roughly 10 points worth of EqA, or 25 points of EqERA above and beyond the DH adjustment), a hitter migrating from the AL to the NL can expect a boost in his projection, and vice versa.

Now, let's take a look at a pitcher's entry, or in this case, Justin Verlander (see table 2). The first line and the **YEAR, TM, LVL,** and **AGE** columns are the same as in the hitter's example above, and should be self-explanatory. The next set of columns—**W, L, SV, G, GS, IP, H, BB, SO, HR**—are the actual, unadjusted totals compiled by the pitcher during the given season in the following categories: wins, loses, saves, games, games started, innings pitched, hits allowed, bases on balls, strikeouts, and home runs allowed.

Next is **GB%**, which is the percentage of all batted balls that were hit on the ground. For 2005 to 2006, we have ground/fly data for all batted balls, including both outs and base hits. For 2004, however, our data sources provided such data only for outs. Because ground balls are more likely to be turned into outs than fly balls are, the average GB% measured only from outs will be higher than for all batted balls. Furthermore, measuring GB% using just outs can be skewed by having an unusually good (or bad) infield or outfield defense. Therefore, we prefer to measure GB% using all batted balls, including both outs and hits.

To make sure that later GB% data matches that of previous seasons, we've gone back to the 2004 data, and esti-

Table 2. Pitcher Statistics Example

Justin Verlander | **Bats: R Throws: R** | Height: 6' 5" Weight: 200 Born: February 20, 1983 Age: 24

YEAR	TM	LVL	AGE	W	L	SV	G	GS	IP	H	BB	SO	HR	GB%	BABIP	STUFF	WHIP	ERA	PERA	EQERA	EQH9	EQBB9	EQSO9	EQHR9	VORP	WXRL
2005	LAK	A+	22	9	2	0	13	13	86	70	19	104	3	46%	.338	31	1.03	1.67	3.71	2.96	9.1	2.6	6.9	0.7	24.1	—
2005	ERI	AA	22	2	0	0	7	7	32²	11	7	32	1	43%	.135	30	0.55	0.28	3.26	0.84	3.4	2.2	6.2	0.3	16.9	—
2005	DET	MLB	22	0	2	0	2	2	11¹	15	5	7	1	49%	.350	0	1.76	7.17	4.58	6.94	11.6	3.9	5.4	0.8	-2.0	-0.1
2006	DET	MLB	23	17	9	0	30	30	186	187	60	124	21	43%	.297	14	1.33	3.63	4.27	3.77	9.0	2.8	5.7	0.9	47.5	6.1
2007	*DET*	*MLB*	*24*	*11*	*9*	*0*	*29*	*29*	*177²*	*183*	*59*	*128*	*22*	*44%*	*.294*	*15*	*1.36*	*4.28*	*4.31*	*4.19*	*8.8*	*2.9*	*6.0*	*1.0*	*26.8*	*4.1*

Breakout: 9%   Improve: 27%   Collapse: 36%   Attrition: 2%   Comparables: Bob Rush, Don Aase, Kevin Millwood, Stan Bahnsen

mated the likelihood that a given hit is a grounder, fly ball, line drive, or pop-up. For example, based on the complete 2006 data, a single may be a line drive 45 percent of the time, a ground ball 30 percent of the time, a fly ball 20 percent of the time, and a popup 5 percent of the time. We use these estimates for every hit that a pitcher gave up to create a truer picture of his groundball tendencies. Also note that traditional groundball-to-flyball ratios may exclude line drives and pop-ups. The GB% reported here is groundballs as a percentage of *all* batted balls put into play, including line drives and pop-ups, and not just ground balls and fly balls. The average GB% for a major league pitcher was about 45% in 2006; a pitcher with a GB% anywhere north of 50% can be considered a good groundball pitcher.

BABIP is batting average on balls in play, a statistic recently popularized by research indicating that pitchers exert a relatively small influence over the outcomes of balls in play (everything except home runs, strikeouts, walks, and times hit by pitch). A high BABIP is most likely due to a poor defense or bad luck, rather than a pitcher's own abilities, and may be a good indicator of a potential rebound. A typical league-average BABIP is about .290.

The next column is **STUFF**. STUFF is a shorthand rating of a pitcher's demonstrated skills relative to his age and level; its primary use is to evaluate prospects, not established major league pitchers. An average major league starter, or a minor league pitcher who has shown the talent to develop into an average major league starter, will score a 10. Pitchers who score above 20 are excellent prospects. Those above 30 belong the ranks of the truly elite. The largest single component of STUFF is strikeout rate, but walk rate, home run rate, hit rate, ERA, innings pitched per game, age, and age relative to league all figure into the final STUFF rating. Our definition of STUFF is a mathematical formula and not quite the same as the scouting term "stuff"; we aren't using radar guns or trying to evaluate the break on a curveball.

The **WHIP** and **ERA** columns are familiar to most fans, and fantasy owners in particular. WHIP is the number of baserunners allowed per inning [(**W**alks + **H**its) / **IP**], which makes it analogous to OBP. ERA is the pitcher's earned run average (earned runs allowed per nine innings). Both of these statistics are unadjusted and untranslated.

The next column is Peripheral ERA, abbreviated as **PERA**. PERA is the Equivalent ERA (EqERA) a pitcher would be expected to have given his Equivalent rate stats: EqH9, EqBB9, EqSO9, and EqHR9 (see below). A PERA lower than a pitcher's actual EqERA may indicate that he was somewhat unlucky, and could be expected to improve his EqERA next season even without substantial change in peripheral rates of production.

The next five columns, all starting with "Eq," are the pitcher's rates of production (hits allowed per nine innings, strikeouts per nine innings, etc.) based on his "translated" statistics. As with the hitter example above, a pitcher's raw statistics are adjusted and converted to a neutral-park major league equivalent performance. We present the translated (or equivalent) ERA **(EqERA)**, as well as the per-nine-inning rates of hits allowed **(EqH9)**, walks issued **(EqBB9)**, strikeouts recorded **(EqSO9)**, and home runs surrendered **(EqHR9)**.

VORP, again, is Value Over Replacement Player. A pitcher's VORP is the number of extra runs that a replacement level pitcher would have allowed to score if he pitched the same number of innings as this pitcher, based on the pitcher's translated statistics. Slightly different standards are applied for starting and relief pitchers because of the different replacement levels for the two roles.

The final column is **WXRL**, which refers to "Wins eXpected above Replacement and adjusted for Lineup faced." It is aggregated from each pitcher's actual outings, using the Win Expectation framework discussed in *Baseball Prospectus 2005* and *Baseball Prospectus 2006*. For those unfamiliar with Win Expectation, say a visiting team has a two run lead in the bottom of the ninth with the bases empty and one out. At that moment they have a 95.9 percent chance of winning that game, or 0.959 wins. If the pitcher gives up a home run in that situation, reducing his lead to one-run, he drops his team's Win Expectancy to 90.8 percent, or 0.908 wins, thus he's docked 0.051 wins. If he strikes out the batter in that situation to put his team one out from a win with a two-run lead, he improves his team's Win Expectancy to 99.6 percent, thus he's credited with 0.037 wins. WXRL credits a pitcher with his team's change in Win Expectancy, positive or negative, from the time he enters a game until he leaves and adjusts that total for the strength of the actual hitters faced, it then factors in the run expectancy of the runners left on base when he left the game (*not* the actual number of runs they score as a result of the following pitcher's performance), then compares everything to replacement level. WXRL is thus a measure of how many wins an average team would have been expected to win due to this pitcher's performance as compared to a replacement level pitcher facing the same batters. Like VORP, it is a cumulative, as opposed to rate, statistic. The similar statistic for starting pitchers is called SNLVAR (Support Neutral Lineup-adjusted Value Added over Replacement, which is derived from BP's longtime Support Neutral Win–Loss statistics). Although the heading remains WXRL, the figure shown for starting pitchers is SNLVAR. Both SNLVAR and WXRL are measured on the same scale, thus the figure shown for pitchers who both started and relieved during a given season is the sum of their SNLVAR as a starter and WXRL as a reliever. WXRL/ SNLVAR statistics are given for major league stints only.

A pitcher's 2007 line represents his PECOTA projection for the upcoming season. A pitcher's PECOTA, and the Breakout Rate, Collapse Rate, Improvement Rate, and comparables that accompany it, are determined by a parallel method to that used for hitters.

As a final point of reference, we have included the park factors used for the 2007 PECOTAs in table 3. The PECOTA park factor forecasts are calculated with nearly as much attention to detail as the PECOTAs themselves, and consider things such as park dimensions and altitude, as well as its historical performance. PECOTA park factors are cal-

culated separately for left- and right-handed hitters, and for each major component statistic. We have included the park factor for home runs, as well as the overall run-scoring factors, in the table.

We know that all these statistics and acronyms can appear to be alphabet soup, but we trust that they'll become familiar to you as you browse through the book. We also encourage you to check out our web site (www. base-ballprospectus.com), which includes daily updates on many of these categories throughout the season, and comprehensive PECOTA cards for each player (available to subscribers), which include five-year performance forecasts.

Table 3. Park Factors Used for 2007 PECOTA

Team	Ballpark	Runs			HR		
		LH	RH	Overall	LH	RH	Overall
ARI	Bank One Ballpark	1073	1056	1063	1145	1051	1089
ATL	Turner Field	993	1010	1003	953	1005	984
BAL	Camden Yards	975	1005	993	1001	1061	1037
BOS	Fenway Park	1020	1017	1018	903	953	933
CHA	U.S. Cellular Field	1048	1041	1043	1172	1137	1151
CHN	Wrigley Field	1014	1027	1022	1092	1070	1079
CIN	Great American Ball Park	1009	1025	1019	1090	1084	1087
CLE	Jacobs Field	1006	979	990	973	936	951
COL	Coors Field	1131	1151	1143	1053	1084	1071
DET	Comerica Park	987	975	980	963	934	945
FLO	Joe Robbie Stadium	976	979	978	986	924	949
HOU	Minute Maid Park	975	1002	991	993	1084	1047
KCA	Kaufmann Stadium	1001	1024	1015	941	948	945
LAA	Anaheim Stadium	961	979	972	940	966	956
LAN	Dodger Stadium	1007	997	1001	1045	1041	1043
MIL	Miller Park	997	999	998	987	1022	1008
MIN	Metrodome	985	988	986	934	976	960
NYA	Yankee Stadium II	989	988	988	1048	1024	1034
NYN	Shea Stadium	964	949	955	928	931	930
OAK	Oakland Coliseum	977	987	984	958	977	970
PHI	Citizens Bank Park	1026	1014	1019	1088	1081	1084
PIT	PNC Park	1037	991	1009	989	908	941
SDN	Petco Park	950	940	944	943	941	941
SEA	Safeco Field	1003	962	978	996	945	965
SFN	PacBell Park	962	979	972	836	931	893
SLN	New Busch Stadium	961	960	960	942	933	936
TBA	Tropicana Field	1015	979	993	1045	1004	1020
TEX	Ballpark at Arlington	1026	1030	1029	1059	1033	1043
TOR	Skydome	1012	1051	1036	1067	1105	1090
WAS	RFK Stadium (Nationals)	936	934	935	930	910	918

Manager Comments

Christina Kahrl and Ben Murphy

A new element to this year's book is an expansion of our initial attempt to provide managers data in *Baseball Prospectus 2006*. Space prevents us from providing every bit of information we have at our disposal, but, happily, that's what the Statistics section at www.base ballprospectus.com is for. Here, within the confines of print, we've restricted ourselves to several specific areas which reflect what sort of success managers enjoyed in employing their players to best effect. In keeping with our practice for hitters and pitchers, we've provided you with each manager's statistics for the last three years. That is, the last three calendar years, which may not necessarily be that manager's last three seasons as a major league skipper. For example, Jim Leyland's one-off with the Rockies is not included, but, again, you can find that information on our web site, where not so many trees take one for the team.

Let's use the manager of last year's World Champs as an example. Taking the columns from left to right, we start off with the year, team, and the team's actual record. **Pythag +/–** tells us by how many games the team under- or overperformed its Pythagenport record. Pythagenport record is a Baseball Prospectus adaptation of Bill James's original observation that you can infer a team's won-loss record from their total runs scored and runs allowed. James's version was called Pythagorean record due to the squares used in his formula $[RS^2/(RS^2+RA^2)]$. Pythagenport, partially named after its creator, our own Clay Davenport, replaces those squares with an exponent derived from each team's run environment. Pythag +/– suggests that a team was lucky or unlucky, but it also suggests that you might want to start digging into the reasons why a team failed to meet its expected won-loss record. Keep in mind

that Pythag +/– is not a number that tells you that Tony La Russa added three wins to the Cardinals' tally in 2004. It's a mathematical expression of team performance, not an interpretation of the manager's work.

Next come a group of statistics that measure a manager's use and success with his pitching staff. **Avg PC** is the average pitch count of his starting pitchers in that particular year, and **100+P** and **120+P** are the numbers of games in which a manager had his starter exceed 100 or 120 pitches. **QS** is the total number of quality starts a manager received from his starting pitchers. We define a quality start as any game in which the starter lasted a minimum of six innings pitched and allowed no more than three runs (*not* earned runs). We prefer to use runs instead of earned runs because the former are irrefutable fact—the runs scored—as opposed to a statistic dependent on judgment calls made by individual official scorers. **BQS** is Blown Quality Starts, a Baseball Prospectus invention. Blown Quality Stars are games in which the starter delivered a quality start through six innings, then lost it in the seventh inning or later by allowing a fourth run. It's always seemed strange to us to take a quality start off the board just because the manager chose to leave his pitcher in the game longer than proved optimal—the starter gave his team a quality start through six, after all. Of course, there are perfectly sound explanations for why a manager might leave his starter in a game long enough to "blow" a quality start—the bullpen might be tired, the starter might get into trouble faster than the manager expected, or, if the starter's a workhorse with a big lead, the manager might just give his pen the night off and accept a fourth run allowed as a matter of course. Whatever the individual decisions in any one game, the decision to "bank" a

Manager: Tony La Russa

Year	Team	W-L	Pythag +/–	Avg PC	100 +P	120 +P	QS	BQS	REL	REL w Zero R	IBB	SUBS	PH	PH Avg	PH HR	SB2	CS2	SB3	CS3	SAC Att	SAC %	POS SAC	Squeeze	Swing	In Play
2004	SLN	105-57	+3	97.6	82	6	87	9	469	336	24	99	272	.262	6	96	41	15	5	85	85.9%	43	5	178	118
2005	SLN	100-62	0	96.6	62	1	92	6	436	298	27	78	265	.226	6	69	28	13	4	104	74.0%	47	15	173	145
2006	SLN	83-78	+1	92.7	55	2	74	5	468	294	35	69	271	.235	7	53	26	6	5	93	76.3%	32	4	135	110

quality start by removing a pitcher who has accomplished one or to leave that pitcher in the game beyond that point reflects upon the manager's discretion.

Next up are **REL** and **REL w Zero R,** which count how many relievers the manager used over the season (REL) and how many of times the reliever called upon didn't allow any runs, be they his own or inherited runners, to score (REL w Zero R). Bequeathed runners also count against REL w Zero R, meaning if a reliever does not allow a run to score on his watch, but leaves the game with a man on base, and the pitcher who replaces him allows that runner to score, he does not earn his manager a tick in the REL w Zero R column. The **IBB** column should look familiar—it's the number of intentional walks the manager called for the given season. You'll see some pretty big differences here between, say, Frank Robinson, who called for a league-leading 93 free passes in 2006, and Buck Showalter, who gave his pitchers that particular order just 18 times. The final stat reflecting the manager's initiative on defense is **SUBS**, which is quite simply the number of substitutes the manager employed afield on the season.

Offensively, managers add themselves to the action to varying degrees. With **PH, PH Avg,** and **PH HR,** we're only reporting the number of pinch-hitters the manager used (PH), their combined batting average (PH Avg), and how many home runs they hit (PH HR). Again, these aren't reflective of any particular genius or lack of it; some managers simply like to pinch hit more than others. It's also important to keep in mind the differences between leagues; Ozzie Guillen calls for a lot of pinch-hitters for an American League manager, but calling for one 135 times, as he did last year, would still rank last in the National League where the pitcher hits, and is often hit for.

We then turn to the running game with a simple breakdown of the manager's team's successful steals of second base **(SB2)** and times caught **(CS2)** and third **(SB3 and CS3)**. What you won't find here, but can online, is similar information on double-steals and steals of home, as well as the number of times his runners were picked-off each of the three bases . . . basically, every flavor of basepath mayhem imaginable.

The sacrifice bunt remains a play that generates no end of controversy, in that some people believe in its general usefulness, others save it for specific situations, and some managers avoid it altogether, following Hall of Fame manager Earl Weaver's observation that "your most precious possessions on offense are your twenty-seven outs." We provide the number of sacrifices a team attempted **(SAC Att)** and their success rate **(SAC %)**. Again, be sure to keep in mind the differences between leagues, as National League sacrifice attempts are greatly inflated by those made by pitchers. To correct for this, we list the number of times a manager got a successful sacrifice from a position player, **(POS SAC)**, thus allowing for comparisons between the two leagues. This stat tells us that, Coors Field or no Coors Field, Clint Hurdle got a MLB-leading 64 sacrifices from non-pitchers, but also that American League managers Buddy Bell and Jim Leyland were among the top five in the game in getting sac bunts from their hitters. We finish up with **Squeeze,** which counts the number of successful squeeze plays the team executed over the season. Squeeze plays are pretty rare these days: Nine teams didn't have one at all in 2006, while former Cubs manager Dusty Baker led his managerial brethren with seven. That might mean we'll see fewer still, now that Dusty's no longer in a dugout.

Finally, we have a couple of statistics that attempt to count the manager's investment in hit-and-run tactics, and how well his team executed them. **Swing** is the number of times a hitter swung at a pitch while the runners were going, while **In Play** reflects how many times his hitters swung and made contact while those runners were off to the races.

Again, these represent small steps toward quantifying a manager's in-game tactics and resultant effect upon his team's fortunes. Much remains to be done, whether it's attempting to evaluate a manager's player usage patterns, how structured his bullpen usage is, how often he rests lineup regulars, what kinds of players he might favor in filling out his roster, or even how many games his team's roster is carrying twelve pitchers versus ten, eleven, or thirteen. In time, we hope to be able to reflect as much of the scope of a manger's job as possible, to give them their due, and to transcend the sabermetric canard that managers don't have that much impact.

Arizona Diamondbacks

In the first year of their regime, Diamondbacks General Manager Josh Byrnes and company proved that they aren't afraid to show expensive veterans the to the door or the bench in the service of giving full-time jobs to the team's coming wave of prospects. It started on opening day when Conor Jackson, not aging 2005 sensation Tony Clark, was installed as the starting first baseman, and continued from there as Russ Ortiz was designated for assignment in July, and Shawn Green was traded to the Mets in August. Following Jackson into the starting line-up were Carlos Quentin, who took over in right field just before Green's departure (something he could have done a year earlier had the previous regime not gone for broke with a last-ditch spending spree that included installing Green in right), and Stephen Drew, who took over shortstop in place of an injured Craig Counsell.

In the offseason, the last few guttering embers of the 2001 championship team—Luis Gonzalez and Prodigal Sons Craig Counsell and Miguel Batista—went gently into that good night, making room for the next wave of youngsters, including center fielder Chris Young and catcher Miguel Montero. Meanwhile, the minor leaguers who were supposed to improve in 2006 did just that, as second baseman Alberto Callaspo, outfielder Carlos Gonzalez, and shortstop Mark Reynolds have each crept that much closer to joining Jackson and company in the Diamondbacks' lineup.

All eight of the young players described above were brought into the organization under departed head of scouting Mike Rizzo, who left the team in July to become the Assistant GM of the Nationals—Callaspo and Young via trades, Montero and Gonzalez as international amateur free agents, and the other four via the amateur draft. While with Arizona, Rizzo oversaw seven drafts and helped stock

a farm system that has received many well-deserved accolades; it's so deep that you could assemble a pretty good major league team just out of the players who played in Tucson in 2005 and 2006—which is exactly what the D'backs are in the process of doing.

This is a new thing for Arizona, which not so long ago had a habit of avoiding players earning the league minimum. Just as Seth Godin argued that "small is the new big," so has "less is the new more" become the mantra in many front-offices, with more teams looking to exploit the three-year window before their players become arbitration eligible. A quick look at the Diamondbacks' Opening Day lineup shows just how much this philosophy has taken hold in Arizona, as the starters include four players who made their major league debuts last year, not counting Jackson, who was a rookie in 2006. The roots of this organizational shift pre-dated Josh Byrnes, but it has been Byrnes who has been charged with putting it into effect.

When Byrnes took office, he wisely retained the man who began building the 2007 Opening Day lineup all the way back in 2000. Mike Rizzo's fingerprints are all over the organization, and now that the book is closed on his time with the Diamondbacks, we can perform a quick draft audit on him (see table 1).

The numbers in table 1 are only for the players that Arizona *drafted* under Rizzo; the players who subsequently signed with the team are another matter entirely. It's also unknown how many of the high school picks here were draft-and-follows (or DFEs, for Draft, Follow, Evaluate); it's possible that Arizona made a few smart decisions by drafting players, but declining to offer them contracts after the evaluation period.

DIAMONDBACKS PROSPECTUS

2006 record: 76–86; Fourth place, NL West

Pythagenport record: 79–83

Runs scored per game: 4.77 (7th in NL)

Runs allowed per game: 4.86 (7th in NL)

Team EqA: .253 (14th in NL)

2006 Batters Age: 30.2 (6th oldest in NL)

2006 Pitchers Age: 29.3 (8th youngest in NL)

Ballpark: Chase Field; Severe hitter's park; Park Factor of 1.048

2006: Webb and the young talent comprise the best core in the division, which is something like being the best Applebee's in Baghdad.

2007: The best-run organization in the West will also be the best team in the division.

Table 1. Year-by-Year Breakdown of Rizzo's Drafts

Year	HS P	HS H	Coll P	Coll H	Juco P	Juco H	Other
2000	6	10	14	8	7	4	0
2001	8	9	10	11	7	5	0
2002	8	6	13	13	7	3	0
2003	5	5	15	19	6	1	0
2004	5	3	11	19	5	6	1
2005	3	6	17	8	13	4	1
2006	6	4	14	17	4	5	2
Total	**41**	**43**	**94**	**95**	**49**	**28**	**4**

NOTE: HS P: High School Pitcher; HS H: High School Hitter;Coll P: College Pitcher; Coll H: College Hitter;Juco P: Junior College Pitcher; Juco H: Junior College Hitter.

Rizzo built the farm system by doing some things we can see in the table, and some we can't. The most significant thing we can see is that his drafts were cumulatively college-heavy, with more than twice as many college players being taken as high schoolers. Though drafting college players is considered a conservative strategy, it is also the fastest way to build depth in a system; while you might wind up with a few lower-ceiling hitters such as Chris Carter, you'll also grab some cheap insurance policies and avoid having to pretend that Josh Booty is a hitter you can count on in an emergency. Rizzo stayed pretty far away from high school arms, far enough away that, to date, the most successful high school pitcher he drafted (and signed) is Brian Bruney. The junior college selections are a bit misleading, since most of them were never signed; the best out of the crop that were are Matt Chico and Doug Slaten, though Kyler Newby has had some recent success and is worth watching. (Side note: Rizzo drafted Ian Kinsler out of high school in 2000, and again out of Junior College in 2001; imagine the Arizona infield if Kinsler had signed with the D'backs and joined Drew and Jackson in the line-up last year.)

What we can't see from the table is that Rizzo would use his top draft slot on the best player available. Shortstop available? Take him. We took a shortstop last year? Doesn't matter: take this one too. Many position players move to a new position before they reach the majors, so drafting for need is folly in baseball.

Had Rizzo remained with Arizona, it's not certain that would have continued to do things the way he had, nor is it certain that Byrnes will be able to pick up where Rizzo left off. The new Collective Bargaining Agreement placed a strict two-month window on negotiations with new draft picks, so drafting the best available player isn't enough anymore. Under the new rules, 2006 first-rounder Max Scherzer, still unsigned at press time, would have been lost, as would have Stephen Drew and Justin Upton, both of whom took much longer than two months to sign. The new rule was intended to grant the clubs greater leverage (call it the Scott Boras Rule in honor of Drew and Scherzer's agent), but it's not clear that those players or their agents would have yielded under the new constraints. It's also worth noting that the new draft rules also effectively put an end to the draft-and-follow, though the implications of that are going to be hard to detect as there's no data on DFEs.

Though the offensive core of the next Arizona contender is already in place, those new rules could stymie the organization's attempts to build a pitching staff to carry it to glory. Here, finally, we get to the principle challenge facing the Byrnes regime. It's a petty criticism to lampoon an organization for not doing everything well in the player development department; none do, because failure is the ultimate destiny of the vast majority of amateur pickups. But Arizona's (and Rizzo's) struggle to develop pitching beyond Rizzo-drafted college hurler and reining NL Cy Young award winner Brandon Webb remains a problem spot that can't be ignored. The organization has always had low-minors arms who are long on promise and short on results, but then most organizations do. The issue is not that they haven't had any pitchers of note in the high minors—in recent years, they've had quite a few arms to choose from in the upper levels—the problem is that they've all had the same profile: they walk a lot, strike out a lot, and spend too much time hoping and praying that the ball will stay in the yard. As it stands, their promising pitchers of three years ago are still largely working through the same issues they were then, only now they're doing it in Phoenix.

The organization's rebuilding stage could have been on the verge of a brilliant conclusion in 2007 had they developed a few more pitchers alongside their offensive prospects. Instead, if the Diamondbacks are going to compete this year, it will have to be largely without the help of home-grown pitching. That isn't to say that they don't have any home-grown pitching; they just don't have home-grown pitching that can confidently and efficiently handle Triple-A hitters, let alone major leaguers. Most of the D'back pitchers worth watching are still a year or so away from making an impact in Phoenix, so Byrnes has had to invest in outsiders.

Webb gives Arizona a bona fide star to anchor its rotation; behind him are late-season acquisition Livan Hernandez and offseason pickups Doug Davis and Randy Johnson. Hernandez and Davis are durable above-average starters who should reliably provide the Snakes with innings. Johnson could be the same, but is a freakishly tall

43-year-old coming off back surgery, hardly the perennial Cy Young winner who left Arizona for the bitter cold of New York two winters ago. No one in this trio, not even Johnson himself, is going to join with Webb to form the 1-2 punch of the 2001 champions, but they will certainly take some of the burden off of the bullpen, which wasn't exactly dependable last year (finishing 16th in WXRL, 17th in Adjusted Runs Prevented). While building a bullpen on the cheap isn't necessarily hard, the D'backs could kill two birds with one stone by introducing their more promising youngsters to the big leagues the Earl Weaver way: by pitching them in long relief. Neither Edgar nor Enrique Gonzalez has ever tallied anything close to a full major league season's worth of innings, so expecting them both to make the leap to the majors *and* handle the workload of a full season is folly. But sticking them in the bullpen and working them up to a major league workload via long relief and spot starts increases the chances of those young pitchers staying healthy for the team's anticipated run of success and simultaneous financial flexibility. Ditto for the other pitchers the D'backs will be breaking in over the next few years: Micah Owings, Dustin Nippert, Matt Torra, and Greg Smith.

Still, Arizona's young offensive talent and solid top three in the rotation have the team poised to be a contender in the NL West, a division which has been eminently winnable the past few years. That they haven't been able to unseat the Padres of late isn't indicative of the shortcomings of your typical fourth-place finisher. This Arizona team is for real—they're young, they're run intelligently, and they're about to make their fans forget all about Matt Williams and Tony Womack.

HITTERS

Brian Barden 3B/2B Bats: R Throws: R Height: 5' 11" Weight: 185 Born: April 2, 1981 Age: 26

YEAR	TEAM	LVL	AGE	PA	R	2B	3B	HR	RBI	BB	SO	SB	CS	SPEED	AVG	OBP	SLG	MLVR	EQAVG	EQOBP	EQSLG	EQA	VORP	DEFENSE			
2004	ELP	AA	23	213	33	10	6	3	28	10	48	1	2	6.1	.303	.335	.462	.106	.258	.286	.394	.237	0.3	44-3B	-6		
2004	TUC	AAA	23	360	50	30	5	8	50	18	83	3	1	5.7	.283	.324	.476	-.074	.239	.279	.385	.230	-3.2	58-3B	8	22-2B	1
2005	TUC	AAA	24	576	78	36	5	15	85	38	111	14	5	5.4	.307	.363	.483	.059	.268	.317	.412	.253	14.4	112-3B	14	17-2B	0
2006	TUC	AAA	25	550	80	35	3	16	96	44	92	1	3	4.3	.298	.361	.478	.116	.271	.328	.438	.261	22.0	75-3B	7	20-2B	2
2007	ARI	MLB	26	467	54	27	3	13	57	30	93	3	2	4.8	.266	.320	.437	-.052	.256	.311	.416	.248	5.6	111-3B	4		

Breakout: 17% Improve: 38% Collapse: 35% Attrition: 13% Comparables: Mike Coolbaugh, J. J. Furmaniak, Trace Coquillette, Willis Otanez

Barden had a nice offensive year in his third go-round in Tucson—or so it appears at first glance. He played in an offensive park in an offensive league, which doesn't project well considering he's already 25. He did play every infield position, and managed a career-high walk rate. Left unprotected in the previous two Rule 5 drafts, Barden was finally added to the 40-man roster this winter. He'd make a decent offense-minded utility infielder for a team that doesn't need its primary reserve to play much short.

Eric Byrnes OF Bats: R Throws: R Height: 6' 2" Weight: 210 Born: February 16, 1976 Age: 31

YEAR	TEAM	LVL	AGE	PA	R	2B	3B	HR	RBI	BB	SO	SB	CS	SPEED	AVG	OBP	SLG	MLVR	EQAVG	EQOBP	EQSLG	EQA	VORP	DEFENSE			
2004	OAK	MLB	28	632	91	39	3	20	73	46	111	17	1	5.9	.283	.347	.467	.072	.283	.350	.470	.284	23.0	95-LF	3	23-CF	4
2005	OAK	MLB	29	215	30	15	2	7	24	14	27	2	2	6.1	.266	.336	.474	.077	.274	.350	.495	.281	6.9	43-LF	9		
2005	COL	MLB	29	60	2	2	0	0	5	7	11	2	0	4.5	.189	.283	.226	-.371	.151	.250	.189	.180	-3.8				
2005	BAL	MLB	29	181	17	7	1	3	11	11	33	3	0	4.9	.192	.246	.299	-.365	.189	.257	.299	.204	-11.8	43-LF	0		
2006	ARI	MLB	30	606	82	37	3	26	79	34	88	25	3	6.4	.267	.313	.482	.024	.260	.309	.471	.268	25.1	116-CF	2		
2007	ARI	MLB	31	547	76	32	4	20	72	39	84	17	5	5.7	.272	.332	.476	.026	.263	.323	.453	.265	12.8	129-CF	1		

Breakout: 23% Improve: 49% Collapse: 26% Attrition: 15% Comparables: Glenallen Hill, Al Cowens, Mike Devereaux, Joe Carter

Fans love his one-man-demolition-derby style of play, but Byrnes's overall line is less impressive than it appears. He hit .292/.352/.522 before the All-Star break but just .243/.274/.444 after; he also struggled against right-handed pitching, hitting .244/.287/.441 against righties. Neither of these issues is new to Byrnes—he's long been a streaky player who's had trouble with righties. He's a fourth outfielder/platoon player overtasked with starting. At the same time, his nascent career as a pre-game commentator during the postseason—during which his wet, sheepdog coiffure clearly intimidated Jeanie Zelasko's sinister Medusa 'do—should have fans looking forward to future tonsorial confrontations between commentators whose haircuts are more expressive than they are.

Alberto Callaspo   **2B**   **Bats: S**   **Throws: R**   Height: 5' 10"   Weight: 175   Born: April 19, 1983   Age: 24

YEAR	TEAM	LVL	AGE	PA	R	2B	3B	HR	RBI	BB	SO	SB	CS	SPEED	AVG	OBP	SLG	MLVR	EQAVG	EQOBP	EQSLG	EQA	VORP	DEFENSE	
2004	ARK	AA	21	612	76	29	2	6	48	47	25	15	14	4.9	.284	.338	.376	-.046	.244	.293	.323	.220	-11.9	122-SS	-3
2005	ARK	AA	22	385	53	9	0	10	49	28	17	9	8	4.3	.297	.346	.409	.019	.261	.310	.363	.236	0.4	87-2B	-2
2005	SLC	AAA	22	228	28	21	2	1	31	10	13	2	5	4.2	.316	.345	.448	-.023	.270	.295	.377	.229	0.1	46-2B	-5
2006	TUC	AAA	23	554	93	24	12	7	68	56	27	8	5	6.3	.337	.404	.478	.219	.306	.369	.443	.280	37.4	68-2B 3	22-SS -1
2006	ARI	MLB	23	47	2	1	1	0	6	4	6	0	1	5.6	.238	.298	.310	-.256	.214	.277	.286	.201	-1.8		
2007	*ARI*	*MLB*	*24*	*551*	*71*	*31*	*4*	*8*	*52*	*40*	*31*	*6*	*4*	*5.4*	*.293*	*.347*	*.418*	*-.008*	*.283*	*.337*	*.398*	*.255*	*14.6*	*129-2B 1*	

Breakout: 24% Improve: 54% Collapse: 18% Attrition: 11%   Comparables: Luis Rodriguez, Orlando Hudson, Tony Fernandez, Brent Abernathy

The hardest major league player to strike out in 2006 was Juan Pierre, who had .051 strikeouts per plate appearance. In the Pacific Coast League, Callaspo was even tougher, with just .049 strikeouts per PA at Tucson. As Pierre has proved repeatedly, not striking out does not guarantee that a player is a productive hitter. Still, Callaspo should be a passable regular for a middle infielder. He's looking at a year of being a utility infielder unless the D'backs do something with Orlando Hudson. He doesn't figure to get much better than this, so his future starts now.

Chris Carter   **1B**   **Bats: L**   **Throws: L**   Height: 5' 11"   Weight: 220   Born: September 16, 1982   Age: 24

YEAR	TEAM	LVL	AGE	PA	R	2B	3B	HR	RBI	BB	SO	SB	CS	SPEED	AVG	OBP	SLG	MLVR	EQAVG	EQOBP	EQSLG	EQA	VORP	DEFENSE	
2004	YAK	A-	21	305	47	15	1	15	63	46	35	2	3	3.7	.335	.436	.576	.468	.276	.344	.440	.268	10.2	26-LF -4	13-1B -1
2005	LNC	A+	22	470	71	26	2	21	85	46	66	0	0	2.9	.296	.370	.522	.074	.233	.296	.388	.238	-12.0	67-1B -9	23-LF -3
2005	TEN	AA	22	151	21	4	0	10	30	19	11	0	3	2.0	.297	.397	.563	.329	.265	.351	.515	.285	8.5	22-1B -3	
2006	TUC	AAA	23	588	87	30	3	19	97	78	69	10	4	5.1	.301	.395	.483	.178	.273	.362	.444	.278	20.0	118-1B -15	
2007	*ARI*	*MLB*	*24*	*508*	*66*	*27*	*2*	*17*	*70*	*49*	*65*	*3*	*2*	*4.2*	*.279*	*.353*	*.462*	*.049*	*.269*	*.343*	*.440*	*.268*	*8.6*	*120-1B -7*	

Breakout: 20% Improve: 56% Collapse: 21% Attrition: 6%   Comparables: Todd Helton, Dan Johnson, Mike O'Keefe, Jay Gibbons

Carter stalled this year, posting the lowest Isolated Power of his career (.176), though he had more walks than strikeouts, always a nice sign for a power hitter. He's an absolutely brutal first baseman, so you have to admire the Diamondbacks for trying him in the outfield. He won't displace Conor Jackson at first, so a move to the AL is the only way he'll get his career started.

Tony Clark   **1B**   **Bats: S**   **Throws: R**   Height: 6' 7"   Weight: 245   Born: June 15, 1972   Age: 35

YEAR	TEAM	LVL	AGE	PA	R	2B	3B	HR	RBI	BB	SO	SB	CS	SPEED	AVG	OBP	SLG	MLVR	EQAVG	EQOBP	EQSLG	EQA	VORP	DEFENSE	
2004	NYA	MLB	32	283	37	12	0	16	49	26	92	0	0	3.9	.221	.297	.459	-.071	.223	.304	.466	.260	1.1	75-1B	7
2005	ARI	MLB	33	393	47	22	2	30	87	37	88	0	0	3.6	.304	.366	.636	.384	.297	.363	.631	.319	39.0	72-1B	-5
2006	ARI	MLB	34	147	13	4	0	6	16	13	40	0	0	3.1	.197	.279	.364	-.246	.189	.277	.348	.220	-6.5	29-1B	-1
2007	*ARI*	*MLB*	*35*	*218*	*26*	*12*	*1*	*11*	*36*	*18*	*56*	*0*	*0*	*3.7*	*.258*	*.327*	*.489*	*.024*	*.249*	*.318*	*.466*	*.264*	*3.3*	*55-1B 0*	

Breakout: 11% Improve: 21% Collapse: 33% Attrition: 53%   Comparables: Walt Dropo, Mark Johnson, Deron Johnson, Dale Long

His 2005 was regal, impressive, and mighty, like the elegance of a trumpet voluntary. His 2006 season was more like a pack of fourth graders playing trombone for the very first time with no instruction during a locust infestation. Rumors of him being traded to the Cubs to fill in for the injured Derrek Lee never materialized; instead he remained in Arizona, injured his shoulder, and watched his EqA drop nearly 100 points from the year before. He had surgery just after the season, and should be healthy in time to reprise his reserve role.

Craig Counsell   **2B/SS**   **Bats: L**   **Throws: R**   Height: 6' 0"   Weight: 185   Born: August 21, 1970   Age: 36

YEAR	TEAM	LVL	AGE	PA	R	2B	3B	HR	RBI	BB	SO	SB	CS	SPEED	AVG	OBP	SLG	MLVR	EQAVG	EQOBP	EQSLG	EQA	VORP	DEFENSE
2004	MIL	MLB	33	545	59	19	5	2	23	59	88	17	4	6.6	.241	.330	.315	-.150	.236	.325	.309	.236	2.8	123-SS 17
2005	ARI	MLB	34	670	85	34	4	9	42	78	69	26	7	6.6	.256	.350	.375	-.024	.251	.347	.373	.260	15.9	138-2B 14
2006	ARI	MLB	35	415	56	14	4	4	30	31	47	15	8	6.8	.255	.327	.347	-.146	.252	.324	.343	.237	-0.6	81-SS 14
2007	*MIL*	*MLB*	*36*	*449*	*59*	*17*	*5*	*4*	*33*	*43*	*56*	*15*	*6*	*6.5*	*.257*	*.338*	*.352*	*-.140*	*.256*	*.334*	*.350*	*.243*	*4.8*	*107-SS 5*

Breakout: 9% Improve: 39% Collapse: 28% Attrition: 28%   Comparables: Jim Gantner, Walt Weiss, Omar Vizquel, Scott Fletcher

It was never clear when the transition between "Craig Counsell, Starting Shortstop" and "Craig Counsell, Tutor," would occur, but his shoulder injury officially kicked off the Stephen Drew era in mid-July. Counsell's walk rate took a nosedive in 2006. Without his plate discipline, Counsell contributes next to nothing offensively, which is now Milwaukee's problem, as the Brewers have signed him to back up J. J. Hardy and Rickie Weeks for the next two years.

Jamie D'Antona   3B/1B   Bats: R   Throws: R   Height: 6' 2"   Weight: 210   Born: May 12, 1982   Age: 25

YEAR	TEAM	LVL	AGE	PA	R	2B	3B	HR	RBI	BB	SO	SB	CS	SPEED	AVG	OBP	SLG	MLVR	EQAVG	EQOBP	EQSLG	EQA	VORP	DEFENSE		
2004	LNC	A+	22	295	45	18	1	13	57	16	36	2	3	3.8	.315	.353	.531	.148	.248	.281	.406	.233	0.5	64-3B	-6	
2004	ELP	AA	22	74	2	3	1	0	7	2	16	0	0	3.1	.211	.230	.282	-.394	.155	.176	.169	.130	-12.3	17-3B	-1	
2005	TEN	AA	23	458	58	25	2	9	49	44	67	5	6	4.2	.249	.322	.385	-.059	.227	.289	.360	.225	-7.6	96-3B	1	13-1B -2
2006	TEN	AA	24	521	72	29	0	17	67	54	88	2	1	3.9	.310	.382	.484	.269	.294	.357	.484	.285	29.5	70-1B	2	29-3B -2
2007	ARI	MLB	25	502	56	25	2	16	65	37	81	1	1	4.2	.263	.321	.428	-.063	.254	.312	.408	.245	-0.1	118-1B	0	

Breakout: 16% Improve: 41% Collapse: 30% Attrition: 3%   Comparables: Jeremy West, Tagg Bozied, Ryan Gripp, Andy Wilson

Prospect. No, wait: Not a prospect. No, no: Prospect again. Sort of. D'Antona saw a little time behind the plate in the Arizona Fall League, which isn't a bad idea; not much is expected out of NL catchers nowadays, and D'Antona's best tool on defense is his great arm. His AFL stint didn't go so well offensively, but his Tennessee time was promising, even if it was a do-over. D'Antona has a long swing that some scouts think is the main reason he wasn't able to build on his promising year in Lancaster. Those scouts failed to notice that Lancaster is a great place to hit.

Jeff DaVanon   OF   Bats: S   Throws: R   Height: 6' 0"   Weight: 200   Born: December 8, 1973   Age: 33

YEAR	TEAM	LVL	AGE	PA	R	2B	3B	HR	RBI	BB	SO	SB	CS	SPEED	AVG	OBP	SLG	MLVR	EQAVG	EQOBP	EQSLG	EQA	VORP	DEFENSE		
2004	ANA	MLB	30	337	41	11	4	7	34	46	54	18	3	6.6	.277	.372	.418	.034	.280	.381	.429	.290	13.3	32-CF	-3	19-LF 0
2005	ANA	MLB	31	271	42	10	1	2	15	39	44	11	6	6.0	.231	.347	.311	-.138	.244	.369	.339	.258	-3.0	15-RF	-1	15-CF 1
2006	ARI	MLB	32	256	38	12	4	5	35	31	42	10	4	6.6	.290	.371	.448	.091	.283	.369	.429	.279	12.0	29-CF	-2	13-RF -1
2007	ARI	MLB	33	296	47	15	3	6	29	39	49	11	4	6.3	.277	.373	.424	.031	.267	.362	.403	.271	7.1	72-DH		

Breakout: 10% Improve: 27% Collapse: 42% Attrition: 36%   Comparables: Billy North, Stan Javier, Delino DeShields, Russ Snyder

When healthy, DaVanon is almost the perfect backup outfielder; he can handle center in a pinch, is enough of a bat to handle a corner, can run, take a walk, and hit for a bit of power. A late-season ankle injury derailed what was shaping up to be a nice year, but his injury hastened the arrival of Chris Young, which isn't a bad thing. Originally in line for more playing time in 2007, particularly against righties, DaVanon won't be ready to start the season following September surgery to repair the split tendon in his ankle.

Stephen Drew   SS   Bats: L   Throws: R   Height: 6' 1"   Weight: 185   Born: March 16, 1983   Age: 24

YEAR	TEAM	LVL	AGE	PA	R	2B	3B	HR	RBI	BB	SO	SB	CS	SPEED	AVG	OBP	SLG	MLVR	EQAVG	EQOBP	EQSLG	EQA	VORP	DEFENSE	
2005	LNC	A+	22	177	33	16	3	10	39	26	25	1	1	4.5	.389	.486	.738	.670	.316	.401	.581	.323	25.3	37-SS	-5
2005	TEN	AA	22	113	11	5	0	4	13	12	24	2	3	3.4	.218	.301	.386	-.113	.184	.257	.330	.206	-5.4	26-SS	-1
2006	TUC	AAA	23	383	55	16	3	13	51	33	50	3	3	4.7	.284	.340	.462	.048	.257	.312	.425	.253	11.7	80-SS	-17
2006	ARI	MLB	23	226	27	13	7	5	23	14	50	2	0	6.2	.316	.357	.517	.191	.306	.351	.512	.291	18.1	54-SS	1
2007	ARI	MLB	24	527	73	30	6	21	75	44	89	4	3	5.0	.285	.347	.503	.101	.275	.338	.479	.275	29.1	124-SS	-4

Breakout: 28% Improve: 57% Collapse: 11% Attrition: 8%   Comparables: Chase Utley, Ian Kinsler, Mike Rouse, Josh Wilson

Despite hitting .316/.341/.474 in the PCL, Drew's EqA was a mere .253 thanks to the league's generous hitting environments. Installed at shortstop after Counsell's injury, Drew out-VORPed all but two Arizona batsmen. Still, his walk rate wasn't good when he was in the PCL, and got even worse in the bigs. Unless he refines his secondary skills, he'll be awfully dependent on his batting average to generate a lot of value, and with just a .273/.302/.391 line away from Arizona, he looks an awful lot like an impatient hitter taking advantage of a forgiving home ballpark. At this stage, these things are quibbles. His long-term outlook is still quite good.

Damion Easley   INF   Bats: R   Throws: R   Height: 5' 11"   Weight: 190   Born: December 31, 1969   Age: 37

YEAR	TEAM	LVL	AGE	PA	R	2B	3B	HR	RBI	BB	SO	SB	CS	SPEED	AVG	OBP	SLG	MLVR	EQAVG	EQOBP	EQSLG	EQA	VORP	DEFENSE		
2004	FLO	MLB	34	257	26	20	1	9	43	24	36	4	1	4.8	.238	.331	.457	.050	.246	.335	.473	.276	9.5	16-2B	1	15-1B 0
2005	FLO	MLB	35	304	37	19	1	9	30	26	47	4	1	4.9	.240	.312	.419	-.017	.247	.320	.446	.264	7.6	36-2B	-1	24-SS -1
2006	ARI	MLB	36	220	24	6	1	9	28	21	30	1	1	4.3	.233	.323	.418	-.069	.226	.317	.405	.251	2.4	23-SS	-2	14-3B -3
2007	NYN	MLB	37	243	28	11	1	6	27	21	37	2	1	4.5	.244	.321	.391	-.127	.247	.324	.404	.251	3.2			

Breakout: 10% Improve: 28% Collapse: 28% Attrition: 50%   Comparables: Mike Bordick, Chris Speier, Art Howe, Sal Bando

Easley's season could have been approximated by one of the many young middle infielders in the Arizona system (Brian Barden, for example). He's limited as a utility player since he doesn't play short well, but the Mets, who signed him to a one-year deal for 2007, don't need him for that. He'll be a desperate insurance policy at second, but if Jose Valentin goes up in flames, Easley's just gas on the fire.

Johnny Estrada   C   Bats: S   Throws: R   Height: 5' 11"   Weight: 215   Born: June 27, 1976   Age: 31

YEAR	TEAM	LVL	AGE	PA	R	2B	3B	HR	RBI	BB	SO	SB	CS	SPEED	AVG	OBP	SLG	MLVR	EQAVG	EQOBP	EQSLG	EQA	VORP	DEFENSE	
2004	ATL	MLB	28	517	56	36	0	9	76	39	66	0	0	3.2	.314	.378	.450	.165	.311	.373	.449	.286	34.7	123-C	-7
2005	ATL	MLB	29	383	31	26	0	4	39	20	38	0	0	3.3	.261	.303	.367	-.105	.256	.300	.369	.234	3.5	93-C	8
2006	ARI	MLB	30	443	43	26	0	11	71	13	40	0	0	3.2	.302	.328	.444	.028	.295	.321	.433	.260	14.3	103-C	-5
2007	MIL	MLB	31	419	41	27	1	9	50	23	45	0	0	3.5	.280	.326	.423	-.049	.280	.322	.420	.253	11.5	100-C	-2

Breakout: 24%   Improve: 44%   Collapse: 30%   Attrition: 13%   Comparables: Ben Molina, John Flaherty, Toby Hall, Tom Pagnozzi

Estrada had a nice year, rebounding from his weak final season with Atlanta. The dilemma for Josh Byrnes and Co. boiled down to this: Can the production that arbitration-eligible Estrada provided be approximated by the far cheaper tandem of Chris Snyder and Miguel Montero? One can only assume the answer they arrived at was "yes," since Estrada was shipped off to the Brewers for Doug Davis. Estrada was frustrated by the trade (and made public comments in the press about it), but he's about to get more expensive, and Arizona has the luxury of promoting from within at almost every position. If Snyder's rebound was for real, and if Montero can hit major league pitching the way some think he can, trading Estrada was the right call. Credit Josh Byrnes once again for letting the kids play.

Jerry Gil   UT   Bats: R   Throws: R   Height: 6' 3"   Weight: 195   Born: October 14, 1982   Age: 24

YEAR	TEAM	LVL	AGE	PA	R	2B	3B	HR	RBI	BB	SO	SB	CS	SPEED	AVG	OBP	SLG	MLVR	EQAVG	EQOBP	EQSLG	EQA	VORP	DEFENSE			
2004	TUC	AAA	21	443	53	31	8	11	58	12	94	12	1	7.2	.278	.299	.468	-.136	.231	.252	.377	.221	-9.3	107-SS	-14		
2004	ARI	MLB	21	88	3	2	1	0	8	0	33	2	0	5.7	.174	.182	.221	-.601	.105	.114	.140	.110	-8.8	27-SS	-1		
2005	TEN	AA	22	212	28	7	3	10	29	8	52	10	7	7.2	.256	.288	.472	.013	.232	.257	.429	.230	0.2	50-SS	2		
2006	TEN	AA	23	481	71	27	6	26	86	18	111	6	6	6.2	.269	.302	.531	.193	.267	.295	.546	.273	29.3	82-CF	-6	14-SS	-1
2006	TUC	AAA	23	49	6	1	0	1	3	0	15	1	0	6.7	.128	.146	.213	-.726	.083	.102	.083	.086	-11.4				
2007	CIN	MLB	24	495	58	26	3	22	68	19	118	9	5	5.8	.256	.292	.466	-.068	.255	.290	.461	.249	10.7	117-CF	-4		

Breakout: 39%   Improve: 61%   Collapse: 11%   Attrition: 8%   Comparables: Ray Sadler, Alfonso Soriano, Alex Ramirez, Brandon Larson

Gil had a nice little breakout of sorts at the plate last year, but his 111:18 strikeout-to-walk ratio in the Southern League was pretty gruesome. The Snakes were frustrated that Gil wasn't working on improving his approach to hitting and dealt him to the Reds for Abe Woody, but that power is tantalizing enough to make him a compelling utility alternative to the Juan Castros and the Quinton McCrackens of the world, particularly when faced with Cincinnati's reachable fences. Were it not for that power, Gil, gifted with one of the best arms on the planet, might have been moved to the mound by now.

Carlos Gonzalez   RF   Bats: L   Throws: L   Height: 6' 1"   Weight: 180   Born: October 17, 1985   Age: 21

YEAR	TEAM	LVL	AGE	PA	R	2B	3B	HR	RBI	BB	SO	SB	CS	SPEED	AVG	OBP	SLG	MLVR	EQAVG	EQOBP	EQSLG	EQA	VORP	DEFENSE	
2004	YAK	A-	18	329	44	15	2	9	44	22	69	2	0	4.9	.277	.330	.430	.067	.228	.260	.321	.204	-46.2	70-RF	1
2005	SBN	A	19	569	91	28	6	18	92	48	86	7	3	5.1	.307	.371	.489	.234	.287	.334	.453	.268	13.6	126-RF	0
2006	LNC	A+	20	452	82	35	4	21	94	30	104	15	8	6.2	.300	.356	.563	.185	.252	.294	.465	.256	0.3	95-RF	-4
2006	TEN	AA	20	69	11	6	0	2	5	7	12	1	0	4.7	.213	.294	.410	-.015	.194	.265	.403	.231	-3.6	15-RF	1
2007	ARI	MLB	21	519	67	32	3	20	71	33	107	8	4	5.2	.276	.326	.484	.031	.266	.317	.461	.262	6.4	122-RF	0

Breakout: 41%   Improve: 67%   Collapse: 14%   Attrition: 5%   Comparables: Chris Lubanski, Franklin Gutierrez, Laynce Nix, Brandon Moss

Gonzalez was supposed to follow up his strong Midwest League performance with a great year in the Cal League thanks to hitter-friendly Lancaster. He did, but not in the way most expected. He led the league in slugging, but had pronounced home/road splits, while just 23 of his walks were unintentional. Since he doesn't work the count much, comparisons to Bobby Abreu are premature. His 13 errors in right are mostly the product of a very strong arm, which he evidently can dial up to 11. As a 21 year old in Double-A, his future is still very, very bright.

Luis Gonzalez   LF   Bats: L   Throws: R   Height: 6' 2"   Weight: 200   Born: December 31, 1969   Age: 39

YEAR	TEAM	LVL	AGE	PA	R	2B	3B	HR	RBI	BB	SO	SB	CS	SPEED	AVG	OBP	SLG	MLVR	EQAVG	EQOBP	EQSLG	EQA	VORP	DEFENSE	
2004	ARI	MLB	36	451	69	28	5	17	48	68	58	2	2	5.1	.259	.373	.493	.146	.251	.366	.475	.286	15.9	93-LF	-3
2005	ARI	MLB	37	672	90	37	0	24	79	78	90	4	1	4.5	.271	.366	.459	.122	.265	.361	.458	.283	26.7	147-LF	2
2006	ARI	MLB	38	668	93	52	2	15	73	69	58	0	1	4.2	.271	.352	.444	.040	.264	.346	.432	.269	11.3	146-LF	2
2007	LAN	MLB	39	577	73	35	2	17	77	57	68	2	2	4.7	.268	.345	.446	.006	.269	.344	.448	.270	12.0	135-LF	-3

Breakout: 12%   Improve: 41%   Collapse: 25%   Attrition: 6%   Comparables: Steve Finley, Carl Yastrzemski, George Brett, Jose Cruz

Gonzalez is the best left fielder in team history, by far the franchise's most popular player, he has the most famous hit in team history, and he's generally regarded as a classy, respected guy. But he earned too much money for his declining production in 2006 and was blocking prospects who are younger and better. Still, some were howling at the thought of Josh Byrnes and his computer allowing Gonzalez to leave town, apparently unfamiliar with the harsh realities of outfielders in their decline phase on budget-conscious-yet-improving teams. Having signed a one-year deal with L.A., he'll get some nice ovations when the Dodgers visit Phoenix.

Andy Green   **UT**   **Bats: R**   **Throws: R**   Height: 5' 9"   Weight: 180   Born: July 7, 1977   Age: 29

YEAR	TEAM	LVL	AGE	PA	R	2B	3B	HR	RBI	BB	SO	SB	CS	SPEED	AVG	OBP	SLG	MLVR	EQAVG	EQOBP	EQSLG	EQA	VORP	DEFENSE			
2004	TUC	AAA	27	357	56	31	3	9	45	34	45	10	4	5.9	.327	.394	.534	.174	.271	.334	.429	.264	14.2	33-3B	1	27-2B	-1
2004	ARI	MLB	27	119	13	2	1	1	4	5	17	1	1	5.7	.202	.241	.266	-.425	.182	.222	.245	.173	-10.4	16-3B	0		
2005	TUC	AAA	28	609	125	46	13	19	80	68	82	9	6	6.6	.343	.422	.587	.340	.292	.360	.481	.284	45.9	58-2B	-7	40-LF	1
2005	ARI	MLB	28	39	5	1	0	0	2	7	3	0	0	4.2	.226	.359	.258	-.176	.194	.333	.226	.223	-0.7				
2006	ARI	MLB	29	102	15	4	0	1	6	13	20	1	0	5.9	.186	.293	.267	-.348	.172	.287	.241	.203	-4.9				
2007	*ARI*	*MLB*	*29*	*194*	*24*	*10*	*1*	*4*	*20*	*17*	*30*	*2*	*1*	*5.4*	*.258*	*.330*	*.406*	*-.081*	*.249*	*.321*	*.387*	*.245*	*0.6*	*49-DH*			

Breakout: 11% Improve: 31% Collapse: 32% Attrition: 52%   *Comparables: James Mouton, Chico Salmon, Jerry Royster, Kevin Sefcik*

The last man added to the 25-man roster out of spring training, Green was primarily used as a pinch-hitter, starting just five games all season. He's pursuing his career in Japan, having signed with Hokkaido, which is just as well; the D'backs' system is flush with middle infield prospects.

Scott Hairston   **LF**   **Bats: R**   **Throws: R**   Height: 6' 0"   Weight: 200   Born: May 25, 1980   Age: 27

YEAR	TEAM	LVL	AGE	PA	R	2B	3B	HR	RBI	BB	SO	SB	CS	SPEED	AVG	OBP	SLG	MLVR	EQAVG	EQOBP	EQSLG	EQA	VORP	DEFENSE			
2004	TUC	AAA	24	128	29	8	3	5	20	11	21	0	3	6.4	.313	.375	.565	.170	.267	.328	.466	.262	6.3	18-2B	-3		
2004	ARI	MLB	24	364	39	15	6	13	29	21	88	3	3	5.6	.248	.293	.442	-.057	.241	.288	.432	.242	5.3	81-2B	-11		
2005	TUC	AAA	25	237	45	8	3	16	40	21	40	3	0	5.5	.311	.384	.608	.273	.266	.329	.500	.280	7.1	31-LF	1	16-CF	-2
2006	TUC	AAA	26	440	83	22	1	26	81	52	78	3	0	5.6	.323	.407	.591	.362	.288	.365	.530	.300	27.1	85-LF	-1		
2006	ARI	MLB	26	16	2	2	0	0	2	1	5	0	0	2.9	.400	.438	.533	.454	.400	.438	.533	.331	2.0				
2007	*ARI*	*MLB*	*27*	*472*	*65*	*24*	*4*	*21*	*69*	*41*	*93*	*3*	*2*	*5.2*	*.272*	*.340*	*.496*	*.067*	*.262*	*.331*	*.472*	*.271*	*14.3*	*112-LF*	*-2*		

Breakout: 12% Improve: 30% Collapse: 34% Attrition: 9%   *Comparables: Brandon Berger, Chin-Feng Chen, Darren Burton, Jason Lane*

Consider for a moment the careers of Hairston and Florida's Dan Uggla. Both players were drafted by the Diamondbacks in 2001, Hairston in the third round, Uggla in the eleventh. Both played second base, and both had extended minor league careers. Hairston didn't have the glove for second or the bat for the outfield, and he's struggled to stay healthy. Uggla needed a Rule 5 selection to get his shot, and we know how that turned out. The Diamondbacks can't use all of their infield talent, so some of the surplus should be leveraged in trade lest they lose it for no return, as happened with Uggla. Hairston's career could go either way—he's a brutal fielder at any position, so he needs to catch a break just to be able to stick in left (or as a DH) with somebody, but his bat is too interesting to simply discard.

Orlando Hudson   **2B**   **Bats: S**   **Throws: R**   Height: 6' 0"   Weight: 185   Born: December 12, 1977   Age: 29

YEAR	TEAM	LVL	AGE	PA	R	2B	3B	HR	RBI	BB	SO	SB	CS	SPEED	AVG	OBP	SLG	MLVR	EQAVG	EQOBP	EQSLG	EQA	VORP	DEFENSE	
2004	TOR	MLB	26	551	73	32	7	12	58	51	98	7	3	6.1	.270	.341	.438	-.012	.264	.340	.435	.268	20.4	128-2B	24
2005	TOR	MLB	27	501	62	25	5	10	63	30	65	7	1	6.2	.271	.315	.412	-.043	.269	.323	.417	.260	11.4	120-2B	15
2006	ARI	MLB	28	650	87	34	9	15	67	61	78	9	6	5.6	.287	.354	.454	.072	.279	.350	.441	.271	30.8	150-2B	18
2007	*ARI*	*MLB*	*29*	*593*	*86*	*35*	*5*	*12*	*63*	*52*	*80*	*10*	*4*	*5.9*	*.294*	*.360*	*.450*	*.057*	*.284*	*.350*	*.428*	*.269*	*24.1*	*139-2B*	*9*

Breakout: 22% Improve: 55% Collapse: 19% Attrition: 5%   *Comparables: Tony Fernandez, Tom Herr, U. L. Washington, Len Randle*

Many analysts strongly suspected that the addition of Hudson would do wonders for Brandon Webb, and there's plenty of *post hoc ergo propter hoc* to go around in this case. Hudson got off to a terrible start, but had a blistering second half (.315/.389/.498) that vaulted him into the VORP lead among non-Cy-Young-winning Diamondbacks. His defense is preferable to Callaspo's, but his price tag is not. By the time you read this, he may be wearing a different uniform.

Conor Jackson **1B** **Bats: R** **Throws: R** Height: 6' 2" Weight: 225 Born: May 7, 1982 Age: 25

YEAR	TEAM	LVL	AGE	PA	R	2B	3B	HR	RBI	BB	SO	SB	CS	SPEED	AVG	OBP	SLG	MLVR	EQAVG	EQOBP	EQSLG	EQA	VORP	DEFENSE			
2004	LNC	A+	22	313	64	19	2	11	54	45	36	4	3	4.8	.345	.438	.562	.347	.280	.361	.446	.279	9.0	57-LF	0		
2004	ELP	AA	22	256	33	13	2	6	37	24	36	3	3	4.4	.301	.367	.456	.147	.255	.312	.394	.245	-5.3	40-LF	0		
2005	TUC	AAA	23	409	66	38	2	8	73	69	32	3	2	3.7	.354	.457	.553	.359	.302	.402	.463	.302	27.1	71-1B	2	17-LF	-2
2005	ARI	MLB	23	99	8	3	0	2	8	12	11	0	0	2.9	.200	.303	.306	-.225	.188	.293	.282	.213	-4.0	18-1B	-2		
2006	ARI	MLB	24	556	75	26	1	15	79	54	73	1	0	4.1	.291	.368	.441	.081	.283	.362	.430	.277	14.1	120-1B	-10		
2007	ARI	MLB	25	584	83	34	2	19	78	66	68	3	1	4.3	.293	.378	.483	.131	.282	.368	.460	.285	20.0	137-1B	-1		

Breakout: 26% Improve: 63% Collapse: 17% Attrition: 10% Comparables: Carmelo Martinez, Kevin Young, Paul Konerko, Joe Foy

The knock on Jackson has always been that his future value depended on his doubles eventually becoming home runs, something that doesn't actually happen with everybody. Jackson did turn some doubles into home runs in 2006, but his lack of power at a premium power position shows just how much a team was asking for when it wagered on the ol' doubles-to-homers transformation. In this case, the Diamondbacks actually got the unusual and it still wasn't enough. Still, Jackson's not overmatched, draws walks, covers the plate well, and hits the ball squarely to all fields, so he may have enough positive development left in him to become an above-average first baseman.

Miguel Montero **C** **Bats: L** **Throws: R** Height: 5' 11" Weight: 195 Born: July 9, 1983 Age: 23

YEAR	TEAM	LVL	AGE	PA	R	2B	3B	HR	RBI	BB	SO	SB	CS	SPEED	AVG	OBP	SLG	MLVR	EQAVG	EQOBP	EQSLG	EQA	VORP	DEFENSE			
2004	SBN	A	20	449	47	22	2	11	59	36	74	8	2	4.6	.263	.330	.409	.078	.243	.296	.369	.233	-3.7	78-C	2	13-1B	1
2005	LNC	A+	21	399	73	24	1	24	82	26	52	1	2	3.1	.349	.403	.625	.337	.278	.322	.474	.268	19.8	59-C	-1		
2005	TEN	AA	21	120	13	1	2	2	13	7	26	1	0	5.0	.250	.311	.352	-.122	.234	.283	.333	.218	-3.7	28-C	-1		
2006	TEN	AA	22	337	24	18	0	10	46	39	44	0	3	2.6	.270	.362	.436	.150	.255	.338	.442	.268	15.3	73-C	1		
2006	TUC	AAA	22	154	21	5	0	7	29	14	21	1	1	3.2	.321	.396	.515	.242	.292	.361	.474	.284	10.7	28-C	-2		
2006	ARI	MLB	22	17	0	1	0	0	3	1	3	0	0	3.8	.250	.294	.313	-.251	.250	.294	.312	.215	-0.5				
2007	ARI	MLB	23	490	56	23	1	19	67	38	74	1	1	3.8	.265	.330	.455	-.010	.256	.321	.433	.257	13.4	116-C	0		

Breakout: 25% Improve: 48% Collapse: 23% Attrition: 9% Comparables: John Roskos, Mike Jacobs, Jed Morris, Chris Carter

Montero went hitless in his big league debut, but so did the rest of the D'backs against Anibal Sanchez that night. By then Montero had already proven that his big year in Lancaster in 2005 wasn't just a park illusion. More importantly, Montero has improved his defense to the point that it's no longer a reason to keep him out of the lineup. His arm isn't so great that he'll win between-innings accuracy contests, but it's not Piazza-poor, either. He probably won't get much better than this, but with Johnny Estrada now in Milwaukee, he and Chris Snyder will form a productive, low-cost catching tandem for a few years.

Carlos Quentin **RF** **Bats: R** **Throws: R** Height: 6' 1" Weight: 225 Born: August 28, 1982 Age: 24

YEAR	TEAM	LVL	AGE	PA	R	2B	3B	HR	RBI	BB	SO	SB	CS	SPEED	AVG	OBP	SLG	MLVR	EQAVG	EQOBP	EQSLG	EQA	VORP	DEFENSE			
2004	LNC	A+	21	297	64	14	1	15	51	25	33	5	1	5.2	.310	.428	.562	.297	.252	.333	.450	.269	3.8	55-RF	1		
2004	ELP	AA	21	246	39	19	0	6	38	18	23	0	6	2.9	.357	.443	.533	.423	.291	.358	.441	.270	7.6	52-RF	3		
2005	TUC	AAA	22	561	98	28	4	21	89	72	71	9	1	5.2	.301	.422	.520	.205	.262	.370	.441	.284	16.0	73-RF	9	48-CF	-1
2006	TUC	AAA	23	396	66	30	3	9	52	45	46	5	0	5.1	.289	.424	.487	.220	.269	.384	.459	.294	16.0	73-RF	-4		
2006	ARI	MLB	23	191	23	13	3	9	32	15	34	1	0	4.7	.253	.342	.530	.123	.246	.332	.521	.284	8.4	42-RF	4		
2007	ARI	MLB	24	545	80	33	3	18	73	51	71	3	1	4.5	.285	.376	.483	.120	.275	.366	.460	.284	18.6	128-RF	4		

Breakout: 18% Improve: 48% Collapse: 19% Attrition: 7% Comparables: Marcus Thames, Carmelo Martinez, Ben Johnson, Dwight Evans

Between Tucson and Phoenix, Quentin got hit by 39 pitches in 2006, 18 more than MLB leader Reed Johnson. That wasn't a fluke year for Quentin, either: in 2005, he was plunked 29 times, and 2004 saw him get hit a whopping 43 times between High A and Double-A. Is getting hit by pitches a skill that translates to the majors? Arizona should hope so, because Quentin's OBP is pretty dependent on it. Though a .280 EqA isn't a bad way to start your career, he's even better than that; expect a higher average and a better strikeout-to-walk ratio this year. He may not have Chris Young's upside, but he's the safer bet for a solid career.

Mark Reynolds Rover **Bats: R** **Throws: R** Height: 6' 1" Weight: 200 Born: August 3, 1983 Age: 23

YEAR	TEAM	LVL	AGE	PA	R	2B	3B	HR	RBI	BB	SO	SB	CS	SPEED	AVG	OBP	SLG	MLVR	EQAVG	EQOBP	EQSLG	EQA	VORP	DEFENSE			
2004	YAK	A-	20	277	58	19	1	12	41	25	66	5	1	6.2	.274	.372	.517	.243	.225	.281	.399	.235	0.2	44-SS	-3	15-3B	-3
2005	SBN	A	21	484	65	26	2	19	76	37	107	4	1	3.9	.253	.319	.454	.064	.230	.278	.395	.230	-0.8	55-SS	-5	32-3B	-7
2006	LNC	A+	22	322	64	18	2	23	77	41	72	1	1	4.5	.337	.422	.670	.463	.285	.357	.556	.300	34.8	29-SS	-1	15-3B	-3
2006	TEN	AA	22	127	23	7	0	8	21	11	37	0	1	4.7	.272	.346	.544	.267	.267	.331	.543	.283	6.6	12-LF	2		
2007	*ARI*	*MLB*	*23*	*507*	*64*	*27*	*2*	*24*	*72*	*41*	*123*	*2*	*2*	*4.6*	*.260*	*.325*	*.483*	*.013*	*.250*	*.316*	*.460*	*.261*	*14.9*	*119-SS*	*-6*		

Breakout: 22% Improve: 47% Collapse: 25% Attrition: 6% Comparables: David Kelton, Ryan Ludwick, Jim Chamblee, Jonny Gomes

Just when you thought it was safe to ignore the D'backs' glut of middle infield prospects behind Drew and Callaspo, Reynolds went and dramatically raised his stock, improving across the board in 2006. He hit for Lancaster, for Tennessee, for Team USA, and in the AFL. Given his big step forward, it wouldn't make sense to expect another, and scouts kibitz over his unorthodox swing. While he'll have to start the season in Triple-A, he's reached the point at which the Snakes are going to have to decide whether to change his position or trade him.

Chris Snyder C **Bats: R** **Throws: R** Height: 6' 3" Weight: 230 Born: February 12, 1981 Age: 26

YEAR	TEAM	LVL	AGE	PA	R	2B	3B	HR	RBI	BB	SO	SB	CS	SPEED	AVG	OBP	SLG	MLVR	EQAVG	EQOBP	EQSLG	EQA	VORP	DEFENSE	
2004	ELP	AA	23	401	66	31	0	15	57	46	57	3	1	4.2	.301	.389	.520	.268	.244	.322	.433	.259	12.3	81-C	-3
2004	ARI	MLB	23	110	10	6	0	5	15	13	25	0	0	2.9	.240	.327	.458	.020	.229	.318	.438	.259	3.9	24-C	3
2005	ARI	MLB	24	373	24	14	0	6	28	40	87	0	1	3.6	.202	.297	.301	-.247	.193	.290	.294	.212	-9.5	102-C	-2
2006	ARI	MLB	25	213	19	9	0	6	32	22	39	0	0	3.3	.277	.349	.424	.013	.268	.343	.415	.268	6.1	54-C	7
2007	*ARI*	*MLB*	*26*	*367*	*42*	*19*	*1*	*11*	*46*	*36*	*67*	*0*	*0*	*3.8*	*.261*	*.338*	*.430*	*-.034*	*.251*	*.329*	*.409*	*.254*	*8.0*	*88-C*	*3*

Breakout: 32% Improve: 54% Collapse: 17% Attrition: 36% Comparables: Marc Hill, Glenn Borgmann, Charles Johnson, Harry Chiti

Snyder's 2006 season looks pretty mediocre, but keep in mind that it represented a huge step forward from 2005, when he looked totally overmatched at the plate. He knows the strike zone, and is a good defender, but if he's going to be the short side of a platoon, he could stand to be more of a lefty-masher. Because of his catch-and-throw skills (shooting down 38 percent of runners), he might force more of a job-sharing arrangement with Montero.

Chad Tracy 3B **Bats: L** **Throws: R** Height: 6' 2" Weight: 200 Born: May 22, 1980 Age: 27

YEAR	TEAM	LVL	AGE	PA	R	2B	3B	HR	RBI	BB	SO	SB	CS	SPEED	AVG	OBP	SLG	MLVR	EQAVG	EQOBP	EQSLG	EQA	VORP	DEFENSE			
2004	ARI	MLB	24	532	45	29	3	8	53	45	60	2	3	3.9	.285	.343	.407	.009	.277	.336	.398	.255	6.8	112-3B	10		
2005	ARI	MLB	25	553	73	34	4	27	72	35	78	3	1	4.8	.308	.359	.553	.268	.301	.353	.551	.300	39.6	73-1B	-2	42-RF	1
2006	ARI	MLB	26	662	91	41	0	20	80	54	129	5	1	4.7	.281	.343	.451	.043	.274	.338	.439	.269	16.3	142-3B	-19		
2007	*ARI*	*MLB*	*27*	*620*	*86*	*36*	*3*	*25*	*89*	*52*	*102*	*6*	*2*	*4.8*	*.289*	*.353*	*.499*	*.108*	*.278*	*.343*	*.475*	*.278*	*25.0*	*145-3B*	*-3*		

Breakout: 23% Improve: 51% Collapse: 14% Attrition: 2% Comparables: Pete Ward, Scott Cooper, Roy Howell, Todd Helton

Tracy suffers from Eric Chavez Disease, the only known cure of which is a good platoon partner. He signed a three-year contract extension worth $13.25 million; his MORP (Marginal Value Above Replacement Player) suggests this is a good deal for the D'backs, saving them on the order of three million dollars over the life of the deal. Since we're entering into a golden age of NL third basemen, Tracy figures to remain relatively obscure. He's not a star, but he's yet another bat with sock in what's shaping up to be a terrific D'back offense.

Justin Upton CF **Bats: R** **Throws: R** Height: 6' 1" Weight: 195 Born: August 25, 1987 Age: 19

YEAR	TEAM	LVL	AGE	PA	R	2B	3B	HR	RBI	BB	SO	SB	CS	SPEED	AVG	OBP	SLG	MLVR	EQAVG	EQOBP	EQSLG	EQA	VORP	DEFENSE	
2006	SBN	A	18	501	71	28	1	12	66	52	96	15	7	5.6	.263	.343	.413	.123	.238	.299	.374	.237	-6.4	103-CF	-8
2007	*ARI*	*MLB*	*19*	*526*	*62*	*31*	*3*	*12*	*53*	*41*	*95*	*10*	*5*	*5.3*	*.255*	*.318*	*.413*	*-.097*	*.246*	*.309*	*.393*	*.241*	*0.9*	*124-CF*	*-3*

Breakout: 49% Improve: 63% Collapse: 27% Attrition: 2% Comparables: Ben Johnson, Brandon Wood, Kimani Newton, Michael Hall

As Kevin Goldstein wrote on BP.com, Upton has "more tools than Home Depot." By all accounts, he had an awful pro debut, drawing criticism from scouts and coaches who didn't feel he was showing any effort; browsing his numbers to find some positive results in either cherry-picking or rationalizing. The Diamondbacks moved their High A affiliate from Lancaster to Visalia for 2007, so Upton won't get the park-effect boost so many young D'backs are accustomed to. He still has a ton of potential, but "potential" is a polite way of saying he hasn't done anything yet.

Chris Young   **CF**   **Bats: R**   **Throws: R**   Height: 6' 2"   Weight: 180   Born: September 5, 1983   Age: 23

YEAR	TEAM	LVL	AGE	PA	R	2B	3B	HR	RBI	BB	SO	SB	CS	SPEED	AVG	OBP	SLG	MLVR	EQAVG	EQOBP	EQSLG	EQA	VORP	DEFENSE
2004	KAN	A	20	554	83	31	5	24	56	67	146	31	9	6.7	.261	.365	.503	.197	.236	.313	.428	.256	8.3	133-CF -4
2005	BIR	AA	21	553	100	41	3	26	77	70	129	32	6	7.5	.277	.377	.545	.296	.261	.345	.516	.291	38.4	121-CF -6
2006	TUC	AAA	22	466	78	32	4	21	77	52	71	17	5	6.5	.276	.363	.532	.173	.252	.333	.489	.278	22.1	100-CF 6
2006	ARI	MLB	22	78	10	4	0	2	10	6	12	2	1	5.9	.243	.308	.386	-.120	.243	.308	.371	.240	0.0	17-CF 4
2007	*ARI*	*MLB*	*23*	*499*	*79*	*31*	*4*	*24*	*72*	*52*	*95*	*19*	*7*	*6.0*	*.280*	*.360*	*.532*	*.155*	*.270*	*.350*	*.507*	*.288*	*29.0*	*118-CF 2*

Breakout: 30% Improve: 61% Collapse: 13% Attrition: 6%   *Comparables: Don Baylor, Jonny Gomes, Cody Ross, Bob Coluccio*

Young's season began when he fell during spring workouts and broke his hand, and ended when he slipped while avoiding a ground ball and was ruled out at second on a reversed call that ended the Diamondbacks' season. Young managed to stand firm in between those spills, however, as his place on most prospect lists (whether scout-based or stat-based) will attest. He does a convincing Mike Cameron impression in just about every phase of the game, and approximated PECOTA's enthusiastic projection. Among a talented group of prospects, Young is the one with the most potential to bust out and have a truly outstanding career.

PITCHERS

Greg Aquino   **Bats: R**   **Throws: R**   Height: 6' 1"   Weight: 190   Born: January 11, 1979   Age: 29

YEAR	TEAM	LVL	AGE	W	L	SV	G	GS	IP	H	BB	SO	HR	GB%	BABIP	STUFF	WHIP	ERA	PERA	EQERA	EQH9	EQBB9	EQSO9	EQHR9	VORP	WXRL
2004	ARI	MLB	25	0	2	16	34	0	35¹	24	17	26	4	—	.213	0	1.16	3.06	4.85	3.25	6.0	3.8	5.8	1.0	7.6	1.13
2005	ARI	MLB	26	0	1	1	35	0	31¹	42	17	34	7	43.9%	.385	-8	1.88	7.76	5.72	7.44	11.6	4.4	8.5	1.9	-9.4	0.22
2006	ARI	MLB	27	2	0	0	42	0	48¹	54	24	51	8	49.3%	.348	5	1.61	4.47	4.61	4.29	9.7	3.8	8.4	1.3	6.2	0.53
2007	*MIL*	*MLB*	*29*	*3*	*3*	*2*	*48*	*1*	*56²*	*53*	*28*	*52*	*7*	*49.0%*	*.294*	*4*	*1.43*	*4.37*	*4.68*	*4.48*	*8.2*	*3.8*	*7.4*	*1.0*	*7.8*	*0.70*

Breakout: 26% Improve: 52% Collapse: 11% Attrition: 28%   *Comparables: Greg Harris, Darren Holmes, Joe Boever, Jeff Parrett*

One can understand the allure of converting hard-throwing infielders into pitchers; their arms haven't been abused and their coaches have more control over what habits they pick up. It's a risk worth taking to salvage a player's career, particularly if he has a cannon arm but a noodle bat. The downside is that having a good arm is the pitching equivalent of "toolsy." Aquino throws hard, but still has only a tenuous grasp of the strike zone. Dealt to Milwaukee, where quite a few pitchers shaved a quite a few walks off their game this past year, he appears to be in the right organization to try to work through his control problem.

Jeff Bajenaru   **Bats: R**   **Throws: R**   Height: 6' 1"   Weight: 200   Born: March 21, 1978   Age: 29

YEAR	TEAM	LVL	AGE	W	L	SV	G	GS	IP	H	BB	SO	HR	GB%	BABIP	STUFF	WHIP	ERA	PERA	EQERA	EQH9	EQBB9	EQSO9	EQHR9	VORP	WXRL
2004	BIR	AA	26	2	0	12	32	0	33²	19	11	51	3	—	.239	7	0.89	1.34	4.63	3.45	7.2	3.7	8.3	1.4	7.5	—
2004	CHR	AAA	26	1	2	10	16	0	20	12	3	16	2	—	.182	3	0.75	1.80	4.24	3.20	5.9	1.4	5.5	0.9	5.3	—
2005	CHR	AAA	27	4	6	19	61	0	70¹	45	29	83	4	35.2%	.263	22	1.05	1.41	3.64	2.08	6.0	4.0	8.0	0.6	27.1	—
2006	TUC	AAA	28	4	3	7	52	3	80	79	40	72	6	32.9%	.319	-4	1.49	4.50	4.81	5.33	8.9	4.4	6.0	0.9	2.4	—
2007	*ARI*	*MLB*	*29*	*3*	*4*	*2*	*48*	*5*	*59²*	*63*	*29*	*50*	*11*	*38.0%*	*.297*	*-5*	*1.54*	*5.43*	*5.45*	*5.08*	*8.9*	*4.0*	*6.7*	*1.4*	*3.9*	*0.50*

Breakout: 33% Improve: 59% Collapse: 15% Attrition: 10%   *Comparables: David Lee, Dave Tobik, Scott Cassidy, Alan Mills*

Bajenaru is not only a SABR member, but appears to be a member of the Society for Quadruple-A Pitchers, as well. Faced with another year of the Tucson nightlife, he elected to become free agent.

Miguel Batista   **Bats: R**   **Throws: R**   Height: 6' 1"   Weight: 195   Born: February 19, 1971   Age: 36

YEAR	TEAM	LVL	AGE	W	L	SV	G	GS	IP	H	BB	SO	HR	GB%	BABIP	STUFF	WHIP	ERA	PERA	EQERA	EQH9	EQBB9	EQSO9	EQHR9	VORP	WXRL
2004	TOR	MLB	33	10	13	5	38	31	198²	206	96	104	22	—	.293	-1	1.52	4.80	4.84	4.54	8.8	3.9	4.3	0.8	27.1	4.55
2005	TOR	MLB	34	5	8	31	71	0	74²	80	27	54	9	46.7%	.302	-3	1.43	4.10	4.35	4.46	9.4	3.2	6.3	0.9	9.5	0.85
2006	ARI	MLB	35	11	8	0	34	33	206¹	231	84	110	18	52.4%	.316	8	1.53	4.58	4.33	4.37	9.4	3.2	4.3	0.7	25.2	3.43
2007	*SEA*	*MLB*	*36*	*8*	*12*	*0*	*37*	*26*	*169¹*	*191*	*69*	*90*	*19*	*50.0%*	*.303*	*-5*	*1.54*	*5.00*	*4.92*	*4.94*	*9.8*	*3.3*	*4.5*	*0.9*	*8.9*	*2.10*

Breakout: 7% Improve: 28% Collapse: 35% Attrition: 6%   *Comparables: Bob Buhl, Bill Swift, Mike Morgan, Joe Niekro*

Batista throws half a dozen different pitches, induces a ton of groundballs, and gets three or four strikeouts per start. That has its value, but when attached to a 36-year-old arm, it's too risky to expect it to continue. Considering the price he was likely to command on the open market, the Diamondbacks wisely looked elsewhere to fill out their rotation. Bill Bavasi has his own priorities and handed Batista a three-year, $27-million contract to be the token veteran in the Mariner rotation.

Juan Cruz — Bats: R Throws: R | Height: 6' 2" | Weight: 155 | Born: October 15, 1978 | Age: 28

YEAR	TEAM	LVL	AGE	W	L	SV	G	GS	IP	H	BB	SO	HR	GB%	BABIP	STUFF	WHIP	ERA	PERA	EQERA	EQH9	EQBB9	EQSO9	EQHR9	VORP	WXRL
2004	ATL	MLB	25	6	2	0	50	0	72	59	30	70	7	—	.280	15	1.24	2.75	3.80	3.07	7.4	3.3	7.7	0.7	21.6	1.08
2005	OAK	MLB	26	0	3	0	28	0	32²	38	22	34	5	44.3%	.359	5	1.84	7.43	5.44	8.82	11.3	6.1	9.4	1.4	-12.1	-0.54
2005	SAC	AAA	26	5	1	0	13	13	75	51	28	90	4	49.5%	.273	36	1.05	2.40	3.56	2.88	6.4	3.2	8.0	0.6	22.7	—
2006	ARI	MLB	27	5	6	0	31	15	94²	80	47	88	7	42.3%	.289	22	1.34	4.18	4.06	3.70	7.5	3.8	7.5	0.6	19.8	2.94
2007	ARI	MLB	28	6	8	1	36	15	111¹	108	49	95	14	46.0%	.291	7	1.41	4.65	4.47	4.46	8.1	3.6	6.9	1.0	15.7	2.10

Breakout: 12% Improve: 36% Collapse: 31% Attrition: 10% Comparables: Wade Miller, John Tsitouris, Jose Guzman, Chan Ho Park

Cruz had a 2.65 ERA in April, which encouraged the D'backs to move him into the rotation. His rotation highlights included an outing in which he required 46 pitches to record two outs against the Padres (giving up nine earned runs in the process), a shoulder injury, and a month on the DL. He wasn't the same pitcher when he returned, so he was returned to the pen. The concerns that haunted Pedro Martinez's early career about a small-framed hurler consistently generating high velocities seem to be valid in Cruz's case, and the lesson of his 2006 adventure is that he'll be better off as a full-time reliever. He didn't reach his incentive clauses, so he'll do it again, cheaply, in 2007.

Casey Daigle — Bats: R Throws: R | Height: 6' 5" | Weight: 250 | Born: April 4, 1981 | Age: 26

YEAR	TEAM	LVL	AGE	W	L	SV	G	GS	IP	H	BB	SO	HR	GB%	BABIP	STUFF	WHIP	ERA	PERA	EQERA	EQH9	EQBB9	EQSO9	EQHR9	VORP	WXRL
2004	TUC	AAA	23	4	9	0	18	15	100²	154	24	51	21	—	.354	-27	1.77	6.88	5.90	6.79	12.1	2.1	3.4	1.8	-14.0	—
2004	ARI	MLB	23	2	3	0	10	10	49	63	27	17	9	—	.316	-23	1.84	7.16	6.31	6.00	10.8	4.2	2.6	1.4	-8.1	-0.15
2005	TEN	AA	24	9	3	19	58	2	64	75	18	50	3	51.6%	.350	-10	1.45	2.67	4.20	3.90	10.2	2.6	4.5	0.7	12.2	—
2006	TUC	AAA	25	3	5	4	42	0	48	60	17	41	6	53.5%	.342	-14	1.60	4.69	4.79	5.69	10.8	3.1	5.9	1.3	-0.5	—
2006	ARI	MLB	25	0	0	0	10	0	12¹	14	6	7	1	68.4%	.351	-10	1.62	3.66	4.29	2.84	9.2	3.6	4.3	0.7	3.5	0.03
2007	ARI	MLB	26	3	4	1	52	4	59²	71	25	39	8	51.0%	.322	-9	1.60	5.35	5.40	5.11	10.0	3.4	5.3	1.0	3.4	0.40

Breakout: 19% Improve: 48% Collapse: 11% Attrition: 33% Comparables: T. J. Tucker, Dave Lemanczyk, Mike Fetters, Gaylord Perry

Daigle still has an underwhelming assortment of stuff, but big guys who get groundballs get second chances, and he resurrected his career by enjoying some success as Tennessee's closer in 2005. That earned him a few trips on the Tucson shuttle last year. He's now outlasted guys such as Bajenaru, and he's still on the 40-man, so he'll be in the mix for one of the last slots in the pen this spring.

Edgar Gonzalez — Bats: R Throws: R | Height: 6' 0" | Weight: 225 | Born: February 23, 1983 | Age: 24

YEAR	TEAM	LVL	AGE	W	L	SV	G	GS	IP	H	BB	SO	HR	GB%	BABIP	STUFF	WHIP	ERA	PERA	EQERA	EQH9	EQBB9	EQSO9	EQHR9	VORP	WXRL
2004	TUC	AAA	21	5	5	0	15	15	94	99	25	66	15	—	.294	1	1.32	4.88	5.33	4.36	8.5	2.4	4.7	1.4	13.4	—
2004	ARI	MLB	21	0	9	0	10	10	46¹	72	18	31	15	—	.373	-18	1.94	9.33	6.90	8.19	13.2	3.0	5.2	2.4	-18.9	-0.64
2005	TUC	AAA	22	11	6	0	28	24	167	185	38	116	20	45.6%	.319	5	1.34	4.37	4.55	4.60	9.5	2.0	4.7	1.1	18.9	—
2006	TUC	AAA	23	3	8	0	24	24	138¹	142	27	107	11	46.0%	.319	15	1.22	3.91	4.16	4.49	9.1	1.7	5.3	0.8	17.3	—
2006	ARI	MLB	23	3	4	0	11	5	42²	45	9	28	7	38.7%	.292	5	1.27	4.22	4.60	3.68	8.8	1.6	5.3	1.2	8.6	0.82
2007	ARI	MLB	24	6	10	0	35	23	133	150	36	88	23	46.0%	.298	2	1.40	5.30	5.06	5.03	9.4	2.2	5.3	1.3	9.6	1.80

Breakout: 15% Improve: 56% Collapse: 5% Attrition: 0% Comparables: Sidney Ponson, Justin Germano, Shaun Marcum, Mike Saipe

For a few years, the most common refrain when discussing Diamondback pitchers was that they had high strikeout totals and high walk totals. Gonzalez is the complete opposite. Even though he's still just 24, his peripherals haven't improved much in the three years he's been shuttling between Phoenix and Tucson. This may be as good as it gets.

Enrique Gonzalez

Bats: R Throws: R   Height: 5' 10" Weight: 210 Born: July 14, 1982   Age: 24

YEAR	TEAM	LVL	AGE	W	L	SV	G	GS	IP	H	BB	SO	HR	GB%	BABIP	STUFF	WHIP	ERA	PERA	EQERA	EQH9	EQBB9	EQSO9	EQHR9	VORP	WXRL
2004	LNC	A+	21	13	6	0	42	17	142¹	128	44	110	13	—	.278	-14	1.21	3.23	5.65	4.32	7.9	3.4	4.4	1.4	20.2	—
2005	TEN	AA	22	11	8	0	27	27	161¹	160	52	146	8	48.9%	.336	18	1.31	3.46	4.08	4.48	8.7	2.9	5.6	0.7	20.2	—
2006	TUC	AAA	23	4	3	0	10	10	60²	61	14	35	2	53.0%	.303	15	1.25	2.24	3.62	3.48	8.4	2.0	3.9	0.3	14.6	—
2006	ARI	MLB	23	3	7	0	22	18	106¹	114	34	66	14	45.4%	.299	3	1.39	5.67	4.47	5.17	9.0	2.5	5.0	1.0	1.8	0.68
2007	ARI	MLB	24	9	12	0	34	30	178²	188	61	121	23	51.0%	.293	9	1.39	4.79	4.54	4.60	8.8	2.8	5.4	1.0	21.6	3.50

Breakout: 20% Improve: 53% Collapse: 11% Attrition: 0%   Comparables: Omar Olivares, Frank Rodriguez, Dick Drago, Bob Friend

There were two guys in the NHL a few years ago named Rich and Ron Sutter. When they played for the same team, both had to have their entire name spelled out on the back of their jersey to avoid confusion, because even "R. Sutter" wasn't specific enough. Enrique and Edgar (no relation) are going to have to deal with the same thing, but only if they both develop into major league pitchers. If we could create a single Gonzalez pitcher using each of their strengths, we'd take Enrique's velocity, and Edgar's command and mechanics. Enrique's translated rates aren't great, and for a guy who throws in the mid- to high-90s he should really have more strikeouts. Both Gonzalezes will be in the mix for the back of the rotation.

Livan Hernandez

Bats: R Throws: R   Height: 6' 2" Weight: 245 Born: February 20, 1975   Age: 32

YEAR	TEAM	LVL	AGE	W	L	SV	G	GS	IP	H	BB	SO	HR	GB%	BABIP	STUFF	WHIP	ERA	PERA	EQERA	EQH9	EQBB9	EQSO9	EQHR9	VORP	WXRL
2004	MON	MLB	29	11	15	0	35	35	255	234	83	186	26	—	.284	18	1.24	3.60	4.09	3.55	8.2	2.6	5.8	0.8	55.6	7.90
2005	WAS	MLB	30	15	10	0	35	35	246¹	268	84	147	25	41.7%	.315	7	1.43	3.98	4.52	4.40	9.7	2.8	4.9	0.9	33.6	5.24
2006	WAS	MLB	31	9	8	0	24	24	146²	176	52	89	22	39.3%	.322	-2	1.55	5.34	4.75	5.17	10.2	2.7	4.9	1.2	2.5	1.50
2006	ARI	MLB	31	4	5	0	10	10	69¹	70	26	39	7	35.3%	.290	8	1.38	3.77	4.37	3.52	8.4	2.9	4.5	0.8	16.1	1.66
2007	ARI	MLB	32	10	13	0	31	31	194¹	225	64	119	29	45.0%	.305	3	1.48	5.11	5.13	4.84	9.7	2.7	4.9	1.2	17.9	3.30

Breakout: 3% Improve: 26% Collapse: 25% Attrition: 1%   Comparables: Steve Trachsel, Mike Torrez, Jaime Navarro, Brett Tomko

With Livan Hernandez, the worrisome trend has always been his high pitch counts, but in terms of the number of pitches thrown per plate appearance (3.64), Hernandez had the most efficient year of his career. He's durable and lets the bullpen relax and put their feet up for seven or eight innings a night. He's lasted so long with such high work loads that there's no sense worrying about when his eventual breakdown will occur. Much like Pedro Martinez, he's already outlasted every prediction of his impending collapse. When it happens, it'll happen.

Steven Jackson

Bats: R Throws: R   Height: 6' 5" Weight: 215 Born: March 15, 1982   Age: 25

YEAR	TEAM	LVL	AGE	W	L	SV	G	GS	IP	H	BB	SO	HR	GB%	BABIP	STUFF	WHIP	ERA	PERA	EQERA	EQH9	EQBB9	EQSO9	EQHR9	VORP	WXRL
2004	YAK	A-	22	1	0	0	9	2	23²	24	6	18	4	—	.294	-37	1.27	4.56	9.38	5.96	10.3	3.2	3.2	3.6	-0.9	—
2005	SBN	A	23	10	5	0	28	28	158²	205	57	89	14	59.6%	.357	-37	1.65	5.33	6.41	7.78	11.7	4.0	3.0	1.7	-38.1	—
2006	TEN	AA	24	8	11	0	24	24	149²	131	45	125	6	57.6%	.300	14	1.18	2.65	4.05	4.13	8.3	2.9	4.9	0.7	24.2	—
2007	ARI	MLB	25	5	9	0	24	19	109²	130	44	64	17	57.0%	.312	-4	1.59	6.05	5.63	5.86	9.9	3.3	4.7	1.2	-2.8	0.50

Breakout: 16% Improve: 50% Collapse: 14% Attrition: 0%   Comparables: Mark Johnson, Josh Hall, Zach McClellan, Jim Brower

Drafted out of Clemson in 2004, Jackson posted the second-best ERA in the Southern League last year. His stuff isn't great, but he has a good slider and picked up a split-fingered fastball from former closing great Bryan Harvey, father of Jackson's college teammate (and current Marlins prospect) Kris Harvey. Dealt to the Yankees in the Randy Johnson deal, he joins what is becoming a long line of B/C grade starting pitching prospects waiting for a crack at the big league staff.

Jorge Julio

Bats: R Throws: R   Height: 6' 1" Weight: 235 Born: March 3, 1979   Age: 28

YEAR	TEAM	LVL	AGE	W	L	SV	G	GS	IP	H	BB	SO	HR	GB%	BABIP	STUFF	WHIP	ERA	PERA	EQERA	EQH9	EQBB9	EQSO9	EQHR9	VORP	WXRL
2004	BAL	MLB	25	2	5	22	65	0	69	59	39	70	11	—	.270	8	1.42	4.57	4.83	4.16	7.3	4.5	8.3	1.3	14.0	2.07
2005	BAL	MLB	26	3	5	0	67	0	71²	76	24	58	14	40.0%	.294	-11	1.41	5.90	5.05	5.84	9.1	2.9	7.1	1.6	-4.5	-0.61
2006	NYN	MLB	27	1	2	1	18	0	21¹	21	10	33	4	51.9%	.354	22	1.45	5.07	3.84	5.82	9.1	3.7	12.5	1.7	-1.2	-0.19
2006	ARI	MLB	27	1	2	15	44	0	44²	31	25	55	6	38.0%	.245	25	1.25	3.83	3.89	3.52	6.1	4.3	9.8	1.0	10.5	1.36
2007	ARI	MLB	28	3	5	22	52	0	61	53	29	65	7	44.0%	.289	12	1.35	4.29	3.99	4.11	7.3	3.9	8.6	0.9	11.4	1.40

Breakout: 30% Improve: 62% Collapse: 11% Attrition: 13%   Comparables: Don Robinson, Kyle Farnsworth, Bill Caudill, Mike Jackson

The Rob Deers and Russ Branyans always get a lot of BP ink because of their Three True Outcome prowess, but we never extend the same courtesy to those pitchers who pitch like they're alone on the field. In 2006, only Kansas City's Ambiorix Burgos had a higher Three True Outcome Percentage (combined walks, strikeouts, and homers per plate appearance) among pitchers who threw as much as Julio. Since walks and home runs are negative events for pitchers, his appearance on this leaderboard isn't exactly a positive thing. Curiously, the Mets disposed of Julio last year and picked up Burgos this winter.

Brandon Lyon
Bats: R Throws: R   Height: 6' 1"   Weight: 195   Born: August 10, 1979   Age: 27

YEAR	TEAM	LVL	AGE	W	L	SV	G	GS	IP	H	BB	SO	HR	GB%	BABIP	STUFF	WHIP	ERA	PERA	EQERA	EQH9	EQBB9	EQSO9	EQHR9	VORP	WXRL
2005	ARI	MLB	25	0	2	14	32	0	29¹	44	10	17	6	42.9%	.358	-24	1.84	6.45	5.65	6.75	12.6	2.6	4.7	1.8	-6.6	1.45
2006	ARI	MLB	26	2	4	0	68	0	69¹	68	22	46	7	44.0%	.289	1	1.30	3.90	3.90	3.64	8.2	2.4	5.3	0.8	15.4	1.64
2007	ARI	MLB	27	2	3	2	46	1	56²	64	18	37	9	47.0%	.301	-7	1.45	4.94	4.89	4.69	9.5	2.7	5.2	1.2	5.9	0.50

Breakout: 16% Improve: 40% Collapse: 27% Attrition: 36%   Comparables: Mike Lincoln, Ron Taylor, Travis Harper, Tom Buskey

Surprisingly, Lyon was one of the better Diamondback relievers in 2006 seeing as he was a question mark heading into the season after battling elbow trouble the year before. He managed to cut his walk rate to an exceptional 1.8 per nine (translated). A strikeout rate that hovers near league average isn't a huge deal if it's joined by a low walk rate and/or a good defense. Arizona's defense is improving, so as long as Lyon keeps his walk rate low, his strikeout rate can still play.

Brandon Medders
Bats: R Throws: R   Height: 6' 1"   Weight: 190   Born: January 26, 1980   Age: 27

YEAR	TEAM	LVL	AGE	W	L	SV	G	GS	IP	H	BB	SO	HR	GB%	BABIP	STUFF	WHIP	ERA	PERA	EQERA	EQH9	EQBB9	EQSO9	EQHR9	VORP	WXRL
2005	TUC	AAA	25	3	2	8	36	0	36¹	31	18	44	3	55.3%	.318	14	1.35	2.48	4.02	2.45	7.9	4.2	8.1	0.7	12.8	—
2005	ARI	MLB	25	4	1	0	27	0	30¹	21	11	31	2	48.1%	.253	24	1.05	1.78	3.26	1.74	6.1	2.9	8.4	0.6	12.6	0.73
2006	ARI	MLB	26	5	3	0	60	0	71²	76	28	47	5	43.6%	.310	2	1.45	3.64	3.87	4.01	8.9	3.0	5.2	0.5	12.0	0.92
2007	ARI	MLB	27	3	3	2	55	0	62²	65	26	52	8	45.0%	.301	1	1.45	4.38	4.58	4.15	8.6	3.4	6.6	1.0	10.6	0.90

Breakout: 8% Improve: 26% Collapse: 49% Attrition: 15%   Comparables: Vinnie Chulk, Jeff Brantley, Max Leon, Bob Reynolds

It's not entirely clear what a "tweaked scapula" is—we believe it's some sort of Madagascan weasel with a bent tail, that or something that only happens to Carl Pavano—but Medders began his 2006 spring training with one after having labrum trouble in 2005. The short-armer struggled with his command early on, but recovered to have a decent season, lasting more than an inning in 18 of his appearances, and being notably stingy with the home run. His eight unearned runs allowed all happened in a two-game span in early July, so that shouldn't be used as evidence of a problem. He doesn't have a lot of bullpen street cred, but he's an asset.

Dustin Nippert
Bats: R Throws: R   Height: 6' 8"   Weight: 225   Born: May 6, 1981   Age: 26

YEAR	TEAM	LVL	AGE	W	L	SV	G	GS	IP	H	BB	SO	HR	GB%	BABIP	STUFF	WHIP	ERA	PERA	EQERA	EQH9	EQBB9	EQSO9	EQHR9	VORP	WXRL
2004	ELP	AA	23	2	5	0	14	14	71²	77	40	73	0	—	.350	20	1.63	3.64	4.37	5.60	9.1	5.7	6.0	0.2	0.0	—
2005	TEN	AA	24	8	3	0	18	18	117¹	95	42	97	4	55.3%	.285	16	1.17	2.38	4.45	3.09	7.3	3.5	4.8	0.5	32.4	—
2005	ARI	MLB	24	1	0	0	3	3	14²	10	13	11	1	46.5%	.214	15	1.57	5.51	5.62	4.80	6.0	7.2	6.0	0.6	0.1	0.31
2006	TUC	AAA	25	13	8	0	25	24	140	161	52	130	11	47.0%	.353	12	1.52	4.89	4.14	5.41	10.1	3.2	6.3	0.9	3.0	—
2006	ARI	MLB	25	0	2	0	2	2	10	15	7	9	5	55.9%	.345	-10	2.20	11.70	8.62	10.12	11.8	5.1	6.8	3.4	-5.7	-0.41
2007	ARI	MLB	26	5	8	0	31	16	108	117	51	80	14	50.0%	.308	1	1.55	5.49	5.18	5.29	9.1	3.9	5.9	1.0	4.4	1.10

Breakout: 17% Improve: 48% Collapse: 16% Attrition: 1%   Comparables: Aaron Heilman, Jason Grilli, Brian Falkenborg, Rich Gale

Nippert was fully recovered from his 2004 Tommy John surgery last year, so his season should be considered a positive in that regard, but there was a pretty big disparity between what he did in the minors and what he did in his brief time in the majors. Nippert's a big boy who can pump gas in the 90s, but he has a reputation for being a nibbler, as well as someone who has problems repeating his delivery and retaining his command. The Diamondbacks are hoping he can build on his PCL playoff performance, in which he was pretty untouchable.

Ross Ohlendorf
Bats: R Throws: R   Height: 6' 4"   Weight: 235   Born: August 8, 1982   Age: 24

YEAR	TEAM	LVL	AGE	W	L	SV	G	GS	IP	H	BB	SO	HR	GB%	BABIP	STUFF	WHIP	ERA	PERA	EQERA	EQH9	EQBB9	EQSO9	EQHR9	VORP	WXRL
2004	YAK	A-	21	2	3	0	7	7	29	22	19	28	1	—	.259	4	1.41	2.79	6.96	5.86	7.5	8.1	4.2	0.7	-0.8	—
2005	SBN	A	22	11	10	0	27	26	157	181	48	144	10	59.6%	.357	-6	1.46	4.53	5.15	7.03	11.0	3.3	5.1	1.2	-24.6	—
2006	TEN	AA	23	10	8	0	27	27	177²	180	29	125	13	48.7%	.317	3	1.18	3.30	4.59	4.33	9.6	1.5	4.3	1.2	24.9	—
2007	ARI	MLB	24	5	10	0	25	21	122¹	142	41	74	19	53.0%	.306	1	1.50	5.80	5.30	5.60	9.7	2.8	4.8	1.2	0.6	1.00

Breakout: 10% Improve: 38% Collapse: 16% Attrition: 0%   Comparables: Mike Ziegler, Joshua Stevens, Scott Randall, Mark Johnson

(continued next page)

Ross Ohlendorf *(continued)*

Now with the Yankees thanks to the Randy Johnson deal, Princeton's Ross Ohlendorf is a big pitcher who suffers from a small repetoire, at least as a starter. He has a microscopic walk rate and a good sinking fastball, but currently lacks the secondary pitches to be more than an option for the back of the rotation. The sinker could cause the Yankees to look at him through Wang-colored glasses, but Wang is more of an exception than an example to be duplicated, and Ohlendorf is the kind of pitcher who could blossom in the bullpen and be something more than a middle reliever.

Micah Owings   Bats: R Throws: R   Height: 6' 5"   Weight: 220   Born: September 28, 1982   Age: 24

YEAR	TEAM	LVL	AGE	W	L	SV	G	GS	IP	H	BB	SO	HR	GB%	BABIP	STUFF	WHIP	ERA	PERA	EQERA	EQH9	EQBB9	EQSO9	EQHR9	VORP	WXRL
2005	LNC	A+	22	1	1	0	16	0	22	17	4	30	0	42.9%	.362	22	0.95	2.45	2.52	2.45	7.4	2.0	7.8	0.4	7.7	—
2006	TEN	AA	23	6	2	0	12	12	74	66	17	69	4	46.8%	.318	18	1.12	2.92	4.22	3.70	8.8	2.1	5.8	0.9	15.4	—
2006	TUC	AAA	23	10	0	0	15	15	87²	96	34	61	4	39.6%	.338	14	1.49	3.72	4.16	4.12	9.4	3.3	4.7	0.5	14.8	—
2007	*ARI*	*MLB*	*24*	*6*	*9*	*0*	*26*	*20*	*120²*	*134*	*42*	*88*	*19*	*45.0%*	*.304*	*7*	*1.46*	*5.26*	*5.11*	*4.99*	*9.3*	*2.9*	*5.8*	*1.2*	*9.0*	*1.80*

Breakout: 0%   Improve: 13%   Collapse: 62%   Attrition: 1%   Comparables: Cha-Seung Baek, Jin Cho, Rick Aguilera, Jose Silva

Owings promising but short pro career heralds very good things. It's slightly worrisome that his strikeout rate dropped and his walk rate rose as he ascended to Triple-A, but that he's there already is nice enough, and he was absolutely lights-out in the PCL championships. Performance aside, scouts get appropriately drooly over his mid-90s heat and sharp, high-velocity slider. Owings was also a terrific two-way player in college, and is a good bet to be one of the better hitting pitchers in the NL as soon as he arrives. TINSTAAPP aside, Owings is a promising young hurler who . . . oh, we'll say it: he's a pitching prospect.

Ramon Peña   Bats: R Throws: R   Height: 6' 1"   Weight: 220   Born: January 9, 1982   Age: 25

YEAR	TEAM	LVL	AGE	W	L	SV	G	GS	IP	H	BB	SO	HR	GB%	BABIP	STUFF	WHIP	ERA	PERA	EQERA	EQH9	EQBB9	EQSO9	EQHR9	VORP	WXRL
2004	ELP	AA	22	3	3	0	7	7	43	47	5	36	4	—	.333	10	1.21	5.44	4.26	5.28	8.9	1.2	5.1	1.2	1.6	—
2005	TEN	AA	23	7	13	0	25	25	148¹	165	40	95	17	42.3%	.314	-21	1.38	4.43	6.11	5.52	10.0	2.5	3.9	1.8	1.3	—
2006	TEN	AA	24	2	0	6	17	0	20²	18	5	17	0	60.3%	.295	1	1.14	0.89	3.48	1.80	8.6	2.2	4.9	0.4	8.4	—
2006	TUC	AAA	24	3	1	7	24	0	26²	17	2	21	1	48.5%	.212	13	0.73	1.72	3.05	2.36	5.7	0.7	5.4	0.3	9.6	—
2006	ARI	MLB	24	3	4	1	25	0	30²	36	8	21	6	40.8%	.309	-9	1.43	5.57	4.73	5.40	9.7	2.0	5.4	1.4	0.3	0.89
2007	*ARI*	*MLB*	*25*	*2*	*3*	*2*	*47*	*1*	*47²*	*52*	*14*	*31*	*7*	*49.0%*	*.295*	*-5*	*1.38*	*4.83*	*4.61*	*4.61*	*9.1*	*2.4*	*5.2*	*1.1*	*5.7*	*0.50*

Breakout: 20% Improve: 57% Collapse: 18% Attrition: 44%   Comparables: Mike Garman, Randy Moffitt, Max Leon, Steve Kealey

Peña is on his third name in two years, having moved to Ramon from Tony after previously aging five years when it was revealed he wasn't actually Adriano Rosario. A relatively hard thrower, Peña had a good season across three levels last year, including 30 promising MLB innings. Don't be too critical of his raw major league numbers; his Peripheral ERA is a bit more accurate, not to mention a little easier on the eyes. Like Medders, he'll be an important part of a quality pen made up of non-famous people.

Michael Schultz   Bats: R Throws: R   Height: 6' 7"   Weight: 220   Born: November 28, 1979   Age: 27

YEAR	TEAM	LVL	AGE	W	L	SV	G	GS	IP	H	BB	SO	HR	GB%	BABIP	STUFF	WHIP	ERA	PERA	EQERA	EQH9	EQBB9	EQSO9	EQHR9	VORP	WXRL
2005	TEN	AA	25	4	6	6	63	0	65¹	70	41	68	3	56.2%	.390	-3	1.70	3.58	5.12	5.04	9.8	6.3	5.9	0.8	4.0	—
2006	TEN	AA	26	1	0	3	9	0	11²	4	4	7	0	73.3%	.133	-13	0.71	1.61	4.07	2.45	3.3	3.3	3.3	0.0	3.9	—
2006	TUC	AAA	26	2	4	4	49	0	53²	58	19	41	1	56.0%	.322	2	1.45	3.55	3.53	3.79	9.2	3.1	5.1	0.2	11.0	—
2007	*ARI*	*MLB*	*27*	*2*	*4*	*1*	*30*	*5*	*58*	*67*	*35*	*38*	*6*	*57.0%*	*.323*	*-10*	*1.75*	*5.45*	*5.56*	*5.29*	*9.6*	*5.0*	*5.3*	*0.7*	*2.2*	*0.40*

Breakout: 8% Improve: 30% Collapse: 39% Attrition: 14%   Comparables: Rodney Ormond, Jason Standridge, Sean Green, Kevin Gryboski

Schultz doesn't appear to have earned a spot on the 40-man roster, but the new CBA allows teams to leave players unprotected until after their fourth year as a pro, creating room for guys such as Schultz, because they're big and they did draft him once upon a time, in the second round, no less. At 27, his time may be now, but he's been plagued by walk trouble. He has maybe one season left to make some sort of improvement.

Doug Slaten   Bats: L Throws: L   Height: 6' 5"   Weight: 200   Born: February 4, 1980   Age: 27

YEAR	TEAM	LVL	AGE	W	L	SV	G	GS	IP	H	BB	SO	HR	GB%	BABIP	STUFF	WHIP	ERA	PERA	EQERA	EQH9	EQBB9	EQSO9	EQHR9	VORP	WXRL
2004	SBN	A	24	5	2	2	5	36	0	44	44	13	40	2	—	.331	-20	1.30	2.25	5.07	4.04	10.2	3.8	4.3	1.1	7.3	—
2005	TEN	AA	25	2	2	1	58	0	61¹	61	26	72	2	53.8%	.371	-4	1.42	4.26	4.14	7.61	9.4	4.3	6.7	0.6	-13.5	—
2006	TEN	AA	26	2	3	8	40	0	43	31	15	59	1	46.2%	.341	14	1.07	1.88	3.30	3.64	7.7	3.4	7.9	0.4	9.1	—
2006	TUC	AAA	26	2	1	2	18	0	20²	10	7	21	0	51.0%	.222	18	0.84	0.45	2.95	1.33	4.4	3.1	7.1	0.0	9.6	—
2007	ARI	MLB	27	2	3	1	34	3	53	58	29	43	6	50.0%	.320	-4	1.64	5.40	5.33	5.19	9.2	4.5	6.5	0.9	2.7	0.30

Breakout: 9%   Improve: 32%   Collapse: 34%   Attrition: 18%   Comparables: Mike Bynum, Micah Bowie, Matt Smith, Jason Jimenez

Like Schultz, Slaten was a 2000 draft choice (17th round), and he's been an organizational soldier ever since. There's enough here to suggest he'd make a decent LOOGY, but that's a fairly common profile.

Jose Valverde   Bats: R Throws: R   Height: 6' 4"   Weight: 255   Born: July 24, 1979   Age: 27

YEAR	TEAM	LVL	AGE	W	L	SV	G	GS	IP	H	BB	SO	HR	GB%	BABIP	STUFF	WHIP	ERA	PERA	EQERA	EQH9	EQBB9	EQSO9	EQHR9	VORP	WXRL
2004	ARI	MLB	24	1	2	8	29	0	29²	23	17	38	7	—	.254	14	1.35	4.24	5.31	4.75	6.8	4.5	10.1	1.8	2.4	0.59
2005	ARI	MLB	25	3	4	15	61	0	66¹	51	20	75	5	35.9%	.284	31	1.07	2.44	3.00	2.51	6.6	2.4	9.1	0.7	21.9	2.91
2006	ARI	MLB	26	2	3	18	44	0	49¹	50	22	69	6	35.7%	.367	27	1.46	5.84	3.29	4.94	8.8	3.4	11.1	0.9	2.1	0.91
2007	ARI	MLB	27	2	3	5	46	0	51	47	22	58	6	42.0%	.308	17	1.35	3.99	4.08	3.77	7.7	3.6	9.2	1.0	11.0	1.00

Breakout: 33%   Improve: 55%   Collapse: 21%   Attrition: 17%   Comparables: Bobby Howry, Bob James, Kyle Farnsworth, Ron Davis

Valverde struggled so badly in the early going that he lost the closer role to Jorge Julio and was then demoted to Tucson in early July, ostensibly because he needed to work on his off-speed stuff. When he was on, he was pretty filthy and posted the best strikeout rate on the team. He was terribly inconsistent though, not the best quality to have if you're an aspiring closer. Though he's the early favorite to reclaim the job this season, his inconsistency and injury risk beg for a contingency plan.

Claudio Vargas   Bats: R Throws: R   Height: 6' 3"   Weight: 230   Born: May 19, 1979   Age: 29

YEAR	TEAM	LVL	AGE	W	L	SV	G	GS	IP	H	BB	SO	HR	GB%	BABIP	STUFF	WHIP	ERA	PERA	EQERA	EQH9	EQBB9	EQSO9	EQHR9	VORP	WXRL
2004	MON	MLB	25	5	5	0	45	14	118¹	120	64	89	26	—	.280	-21	1.55	5.25	6.18	5.36	9.1	4.3	6.0	1.8	-1.3	0.65
2005	NWO	AAA	26	2	2	0	5	5	28	24	12	35	4	41.1%	.308	19	1.29	4.18	4.76	4.55	8.5	3.9	8.5	1.6	3.2	—
2005	WAS	MLB	26	0	3	0	4	4	12²	22	7	5	4	29.6%	.360	-46	2.29	9.21	7.70	11.08	15.2	4.2	3.5	2.8	-7.0	-0.15
2005	ARI	MLB	26	9	6	0	21	19	119²	124	40	90	21	36.7%	.290	1	1.37	4.81	5.12	4.44	8.8	2.7	6.1	1.5	9.9	1.92
2006	ARI	MLB	27	12	10	0	31	30	167²	185	52	123	27	40.9%	.300	5	1.41	4.83	4.59	4.68	9.3	2.4	5.9	1.2	13.4	2.68
2007	MIL	MLB	29	9	10	0	32	25	160²	166	54	122	24	41.0%	.290	9	1.36	4.69	4.89	4.74	8.9	2.6	6.1	1.2	17.0	2.90

Breakout: 18%   Improve: 62%   Collapse: 14%   Attrition: 1%   Comparables: James Baldwin, Brett Tomko, Ken Johnson, Scott Elarton

Not a bad staff filler, Vargas is an example of what can happen when teams scour the waiver wire for some cheap talent. He isn't a bad back-of-the-rotation starter, but he averaged barely more than five innings per start last year, and that places a pretty heavy demand on a club's pen. Swapping him out in the Doug Davis deal is one way to solve that problem. Given his propensity to work high and give up a lot of deep flies, Miller should be kinder to him than Chase was.

Luis Vizcaino   Bats: R Throws: R   Height: 5' 11"   Weight: 185   Born: August 6, 1974   Age: 32

YEAR	TEAM	LVL	AGE	W	L	SV	G	GS	IP	H	BB	SO	HR	GB%	BABIP	STUFF	WHIP	ERA	PERA	EQERA	EQH9	EQBB9	EQSO9	EQHR9	VORP	WXRL
2004	MIL	MLB	29	4	4	1	73	0	72	61	24	63	12	—	.255	-1	1.18	3.75	4.52	4.17	7.5	2.7	6.9	1.3	10.0	2.76
2005	CHA	MLB	30	6	5	0	65	0	70	74	29	43	8	45.1%	.303	-8	1.47	3.73	4.69	3.80	9.8	3.7	5.5	1.0	15.2	0.29
2006	ARI	MLB	31	4	6	0	70	0	65¹	51	29	72	8	46.1%	.274	19	1.22	3.58	3.91	3.09	6.9	3.5	8.9	0.9	18.5	2.17
2007	NYA	MLB	32	3	2	2	52	0	58	57	22	48	9	42%	.287	2	1.36	4.08	4.19	3.94	8.8	3.2	7.0	1.2	10.9	0.9

Breakout: 16%   Improve: 39%   Collapse: 31%   Attrition: 22%   Comparables: Diego Segui, Dave Giusti, Steve Farr, Jeff Brantley

The best pure reliever on the team by both VORP (18.3) and WXRL (2.17) last year, Vizcaino figures to get a nice pay raise via arbitration. He's prone to the long ball, but he regained some of his ability to miss bats and has decent command of his repertoire. Dealt to the Yankees in the Randy Johnson deal, he'll have to contend with American League hitters again, who were less likely to swing and miss the last time around.

Brandon Webb Bats: R Throws: R   Height: 6' 2"   Weight: 230   Born: May 9, 1979   Age: 28

YEAR	TEAM	LVL	AGE	W	L	SV	G	GS	IP	H	BB	SO	HR	GB%	BABIP	STUFF	WHIP	ERA	PERA	EQERA	EQH9	EQBB9	EQSO9	EQHR9	VORP	WXRL
2004	ARI	MLB	25	7	16	0	35	35	208	194	119	164	17	—	.294	21	1.50	3.59	4.48	4.16	8.1	4.5	6.2	0.6	24.5	3.61
2005	ARI	MLB	26	14	12	0	33	33	229	229	59	172	21	65.9%	.310	23	1.26	3.54	3.63	3.46	8.3	2.1	6.1	0.8	46.2	5.33
2006	ARI	MLB	27	16	8	0	33	33	235	216	50	178	15	67.4%	.293	33	1.13	3.10	3.16	3.06	7.8	1.6	6.1	0.5	68.9	7.22
2007	ARI	MLB	28	14	11	0	33	33	225	221	68	177	15	63.0%	.303	21	1.28	3.67	3.60	3.59	8.2	2.5	6.3	0.5	54.4	7.10

Breakout: 10% Improve: 41% Collapse: 16% Attrition: 1%   Comparables: Rick Reuschel, Charles Nagy, Kevin Brown, Orel Hershiser

Webb was a popular breakout candidate before the season began, largely because he had finally gotten his walk rate under control. That only made up 50 percent of the wishlist for Webb watchers, as he also needed to handle lefties better. The addition of Orlando Hudson was intended to help, since lefty batters would presumably pull ground balls to the right side of the infield. It worked, with Webb holding lefties to a much-improved .261/.321/.386 line this past year, but Hudson's impact was mitigated by the fact that lefties put the ball in the air far more often against Webb than righties did (Webb recorded 3.64 ground outs per fly out overall, but only 2.62 ground outs per fly out against lefties). Thus the Arizona outfield also contributed to Webb's improvement against lefties. If this is indicative of something real—perhaps that lefties are more able to get under Webb's sinker and drive it to right field—then Webb should ask Carlos Quentin, not Orlando Hudson, to be his best friend in 2007.

Lineouts

PLAYER	TEAM	LVL	AGE	PA	R	2B	3B	HR	RBI	BB	SO	SB-CS	SPEED	AVG/OBP/SLG	MLVr	EqAVG/OBP/SLG	EqA	VORP
C P. Avlas	TEN	AA	23	334	43	17	0	7	29	46	50	3-5	4.6	.263/.373/.399	.115	.252/.351/.409	.263	12.9
2B E. Bonifacio#	LNC	A+	21	608	117	35	7	7	50	44	104	61-14	8.5	.321/.375/.449	.074	.267/.311/.377	.248	4.8
SS A. Gonzalez	TEN	AA	23	494	67	20	3	6	50	37	42	5-1	5.5	.290/.356/.392	.100	.282/.339/.403	.259	21.7
C R. Hammock	TUC	AAA	29	405	57	21	1	20	65	24	59	2-2	4.0	.290/.342/.515	.129	.249/.292/.435	.246	6.3
LF C. Hankerd	LNC	A+	21	78	15	4	0	8	23	8	9	0-0	4.0	.369/.474/.800	.740	.304/.385/.652	.330	9.1
	YAK	A-	21	236	24	17	0	4	38	13	54	0-0	3.6	.384/.424/.519	.490	.345/.370/.471	.290	26.3
CF C. Rahl	LNC	A+	22	613	101	44	8	13	83	35	119	19-10	6.6	.327/.369/.502	.145	.274/.307/.421	.249	10.4
RF J. Zeringue	LNC	A+	22	172	22	12	1	5	21	9	40	3-0	5.7	.278/.320/.462	-.031	.222/.256/.364	.219	-10.7
	TEN	AA	22	228	15	5	1	4	19	19	43	1-2	3.7	.217/.289/.310	-.143	.213/.274/.319	.210	-17.3

PLAYER	TEAM	LVL	AGE	W	L	SV	IP	H	BB	SO	HR	GB%	BABIP	STUFF	WHIP	ERA	PERA	EqERA	EqH9	EqBB9	EqSO9	EqHR9	VORP
A. Bass	TEN	AA	24	2	3	0	46	47	16	42	4	—	.328	-6	1.37	4.50	5.55	6.00	10.2	3.4	5.4	1.4	-2.0
	TUC	AAA	24	9	4	0	124	136	40	68	13	—	.310	-7	1.42	4.79	5.19	4.90	9.4	2.8	3.8	1.1	9.9
B. Brown	YAK	A-	21	0	2	0	23	23	12	30	2	—	.350	-7	1.52	3.52	7.84	6.00	12.0	6.9	6.9	2.1	-0.9
R. Choate*	TUC	AAA	30	6	0	8	45¹	39	10	44	0	—	.307	15	1.09	2.20	2.88	2.78	7.9	2.0	6.4	0.2	14.2
	ARI	MLB	30	0	1	0	16	21	3	12	0	—	.368	4	1.50	3.94	3.27	4.32	11.3	1.6	5.9	0.0	1.9
R. Doherty	SBN	A	22	9	1	5	62¹	50	20	76	2	—	.313	-3	1.13	2.61	4.63	5.52	8.7	4.1	6.3	0.9	0.5
M. Koplove	TUC	AAA	29	5	0	0	65	63	24	49	4	—	.311	-7	1.34	3.60	4.29	4.50	8.5	3.3	4.9	0.7	8.1
B. Murphy*	TEN	AA	25	0	1	0	21	22	9	26	2	—	.377	-3	1.48	5.57	5.58	7.08	11.1	4.4	7.1	1.8	-3.3
	TUC	AAA	25	5	4	0	80¹	86	38	72	5	—	.339	0	1.55	5.62	4.21	5.84	9.4	4.1	6.1	0.7	-2.2
K. Newby	SBN	A	21	6	1	11	44¹	22	19	64	0	—	.268	23	0.93	2.04	3.68	3.27	5.9	5.2	7.8	0.2	10.7
M. Torra	SBN	A	22	0	1	0	25²	24	5	20	0	—	.313	-2	1.15	1.79	3.56	3.96	9.0	2.5	4.0	0.4	4.6
B. White*	TEN	AA	27	0	1	12	63¹	59	33	76	6	—	.349	-11	1.46	3.57	6.28	5.10	10.2	5.4	7.2	1.6	3.3

His minor league numbers suggest that **Phil Avlas** wouldn't totally embarrass himself as an MLB backup. With Snyder, Montero, Hammock, and maybe D'Antona ahead of him, though, that might have to happen in another organization. **Emilio Bonifacio** is a fast slap hitter who doesn't walk much, and didn't do much of anything away from Lancaster. Venezuelan **Alberto Gonzalez** is an especially slick fielder who skipped a level and didn't get blown away by Double-A, though his bat is still nothing special. He went to the Yankees in the Big Unit deal. Perhaps in a year or two he'll be able to pry Miguel Cairo's cold, dead hands off of the utility infield job. **Robby Hammock** is a multi-position type who could make a neat third catcher/pinch hitter/third baseman. Sort of like Marty Castillo, except good. **Cyle Hankerd** won the Northwest League MVP thanks to his line-drive swing. His defense needs to improve, but he's worth watching. There are two things you should know about **Chris Rahl**. The first is that he hit .263/.349/.526 at Lancaster. The second is that he hit .190/.261/.381 everywhere else. More was expected of **Jon Zeringue** when he was picked out of LSU in the second round of the 2004, but he didn't hit in a return engagement in Lancaster, and didn't hit in Double-A.

The organization loves its big guys on the mound, and **Adam Bass** is yet another guy around six-and-a-half feet tall, though he's something of a gentle giant in terms of stuff. **Brooks Brown** is a sinker/slider pitcher who was moved to the bullpen after an extended college workload (he went to the College World Series with Georgia). He'll need a changeup if he's going to make a successful move back to the rotation. **Randy Choate** is your basic wandering LOOGY: something less than a *Seinfeld* gag, and something more persistent than a cough. **Ryan Doherty** is seven-foot-one. The former Notre Dame closer was dominant in his minor league return to South Bend last year. **Mike Koplove** is still trying to figure out why he fell out of favor after a nice 2004 season; leaving Phoenix should help him find a better park in which to pitch and a chance to stick in a right-handed situational role. **Bill Murphy** responded to being taken off of the 40-man roster by doing some good work both starting and relieving, but his fastball-curve combo doesn't seem suited for a situational job in the majors. In online parlance, a newbie is a newly-minted member of an internet forum, characterized by a tendency to make rookie mistakes, such as asking very common questions. **Kyler Newby**'s newbie mistakes typically involve ball four, but his strikeout, hit, and home run rates are all promising. Former UMass Minuteman and first-round pick **Matt Torra** should be getting more than a Lineout, but injury limited him to just 25 innings in 2006. They were excellent innings, though—all the more reason to keep an eye on him as he tries to stay healthy in his first full year. **Bill White** is a bit long in the tooth to be considered a prospect, but he does miss bats. His walk and homer trouble make him unlikely to take to Phoenix very well.

Manager: Bob Melvin

Year	Team	W-L	Pythag +/-	Avg PC	100 +P	120 +P	QS	BQS	REL	REL w Zero R	IBB	SUBS	PH	PH Avg	PH HR	SB2	CS2	SB3	CS3	SAC Att	SAC %	POS SAC	Squeeze	Swing	In Play
2004	SEA	63-99	+5	101.8	99	12	67	12	414	236	32	36	109	.271	4	92	33	18	9	64	71.9%	45	0	154	112
2005	ARI	77-85	+13	96.8	66	3	81	18	458	274	43	57	310	.231	9	64	21	3	4	104	68.3%	30	5	122	86
2006	ARI	76-86	-3	95.2	70	3	76	13	461	299	44	56	275	.193	7	64	26	11	4	84	72.6%	21	1	105	80

Maybe it's something to do with being an ex-catcher—Melvin has been in the top five managers in Blown Quality Starts in each of the last three years, finishing fourth last year behind fellow former backstops Jerry Narron, Eric Wedge, and Ned Yost. As far as offensive tactics, Melvin's pretty low-key, not going overboard on little-ball tactics, but willing to platoon players. He did solid work coping with the large number of young pitchers on last year's staff and got middle-of-the-pack results out of a relatively unknown relief crew after the previous season's disastrously bad bullpen performance. Look for this number to improve: Bob Melvin got a .193 average from his pinch hitters, the second-worst mark in the NL (the Mets were dead last).

Atlanta Braves

This past postseason found a new National League East champion in the mix for the first time since 1990. The Braves not only failed to win their division, they didn't even win the wild card. After 16 years, they simply, quietly, went home.

As the Yankees showed by keeping their dynasty alive from the 1940s through the early 1960s, and as various incarnations of the Philadelphia and Oakland A's demonstrated by failing to grow established mini-dynasties across the decades as the Yankees did, the maintenance of a sports dynasty requires more than just smarts, it takes money. Charles Finley was able to build his A's from the bottom up, but when free agency came along he couldn't compete with the big city boys and his green and gold champions scattered to the winds. Those pre-draft Yankees invested their profits in scouting and development and flourished. When they cut back prior to their sale to CBS, the dynasty died.

Like those 1960s Yankees, the Braves were transformed from a rich man's toy to a line on the ledger of a gigantic corporation. Ted Turner bought the Braves in January 1976, and whatever the positives or negatives of his unique style of leadership, he ran the Braves with a munificent largesse. Twenty years later, Turner's TBS, Inc. merged with Time Warner Inc. In 2001, the Time Warner execs debased their company by alloying it with the fool's gold of AOL stock, and as the corporation's profile suffered, the Braves would increasingly be run with one eye on the bottom line. Not only were the wild and crazy days gone when Turner would lavish huge contracts on mediocre free agents like Claudell Washington (a 1980 deal so disproportionate that then-Orioles owner Edward Bennett Williams suggested that it was the product of "madness"), but so, too, was much of the financial flexibility that allowed the Braves machine to run on year after year.

Time Warner has since proposed to sell the Braves to Liberty Media Corp. That deal, with its complex tax and stock implications, is stuck in a seemingly intractable limbo, further complicating the team's ability to spend and thus compete. It was inevitable that the Braves dynasty would pass, as all things must, but what was unexpected was the method of its extinction—gradual starvation.

That the Braves carried on as far into their corporate era as they did is a testament to the way John Schuerholz and Bobby Cox have run the team, and also a reflection on just how badly their competition in the division was run at the turn of the century and after. The never-ending Expos/Nationals saga reduced the question of contention in the NL East a four-team matter after 1996. Phillies management often seemed more absorbed with building its new ballpark than with putting a winning team on the field, letting players and managers consume each other in pointless personality clashes; make that a three-team division. The Marlins were sometimes committed to the idea of winning, but more often not, so call it a two-team division. That left the Mets, who tried gamely, but often shot themselves in the foot with unfortunate player valuations, like canonizing the likes of Rey Ordonez and Todd Zeile.

Meanwhile, the Braves system was rolling, producing top-quality reinforcements for the big league club. The worst-to-first 1991 edition of the Braves kicked things off with this lineup of old-style Bobby Cox improvisations and compromises, some as a reaction to the club's many injuries that year, some because, for many years, Cox's main managerial tool was the platoon:

C	Greg Olson
1B	Sid Bream/Brian Hunter
2B	Jeff Treadway/Mark Lemke

BRAVES PROSPECTUS

2006 record: 79–83; Third place, NL East

Pythagenport record: 85–77

Runs scored per game: 5.24 (2nd in NL)

Runs allowed per game: 4.97 (11th in NL)

Team EqA: .267 (4th in NL)

2006 Batters Age: 27.9 (2nd youngest in NL)

2006 Pitchers Age: 30.1 (6th oldest in NL)

Ballpark: Turner Field; Neutral park; Park Factor of .995

2006: Brian McCann's burgeoning stardom wasn't enough to compensate for the implosion of the pitching staff.

2007: Three or four more trades with the Mariners would really help the Braves start a new dynasty.

3B   Terry Pendleton
SS   Rafael Belliard/Jeff Blauser
LF   Lonnie Smith/Deion Sanders
CF   Ron Gant
RF   David Justice/Otis Nixon
SP: Tom Glavine, John Smoltz, Steve Avery, Charlie Leibrandt, Pete Smith
Closer: Juan Berenguer, Alejandro Pena

That lineup could not endure for more than a couple of years. Fortunately, the farm system, which had contributed so much to the team's renaissance, still had much to give, including Javy Lopez (signed as a non-drafted free agent in 1987), Ryan Klesko (fifth round, 1989), Chipper Jones (first overall pick, 1990), Andruw Jones (non-drafted free agent, 1993), and Kevin Millwood (11th round, 1993).

Simultaneously, a bevy of prospects were dealt away to gain the players the farm could not provide, including Melvin Nieves and Donnie Elliot to the Padres for Fred McGriff (1993), Tony Tarasco and Esteban Yan to the Expos for Marquis Grisson (1995), Ron Wright and Jason Schmidt to the Pirates for Denny Neagle (1996), and Jermaine Dye and Jamie Walker to the Royals for Keith Lockhart and Michael Tucker (1997).

By the late 1990s, the system was, if not dry, more likely to produce a good role player than another star. After the turn of the century, Rafael Furcal and Marcus Giles emerged in 2000 and 2001 respectively, and Brian McCann and perhaps Adam LaRoche established themselves in 2006, but by and large the Braves weren't getting the replacements they needed. Almost imperceptibly, a journeyman element began to overtake the roster. Ten years from now no one will remember Bobby Bonilla, Ken Caminiti, or Raul Mondesi as dynasty-era Braves, but they were there.

What sustained the Braves, more than anything else, was their historic trio of ace starting pitchers. The Braves' farm system produced lefty Tom Glavine; he was drafted in the second round of the 1984 amateur draft and made the majors in 1987. John Smoltz was acquired in the everybody-wins trade of Doyle Alexander to the Tigers in 1987, and reached the majors the next year. Greg Maddux established himself with the Cubs from 1986 to 1992, then joined the Braves as a free agent. The three of them were together from 1993 to 2002. All three pitchers would win Cy Young awards during that span: Glavine had already won the award in 1991, and would add another in 1998; Maddux had won one as a departing Cub in 1992, and added three more from 1993 to 1995; Smoltz joined the hardware club in 1996.

Five times in their ten seasons together, the trio represented three of the top ten pitchers in baseball as measured by VORP. Table 1 is each pitcher's National League VORP ranking during their time together. Note that Smoltz missed 2000 and was in the bullpen in 2001 and 2002.

Never had a team assembled three pitchers of such quality and kept them together for so long. As measured by WARP (Wins Above Replacement), Maddux, Glavine, and Smoltz are the most successful pitching trio of all time; see table 2, which depicts the top trios in major league history (pitchers are listed in order of their contribution to the total).

Table 1. The Elite Three

Year	Maddux	Glavine	Smoltz
1993	2	5	8
1994	1	15	49
1995	1	3	7
1996	2	5	3
1997	1	5	6
1998	1	3	10
1999	11	13	6
2000	3	4	—
2001	3	8	81
2002	5	6	61

Table 2. Three Bullets from the Same Gun

Rank	Pitchers	Team	Years	Combined Warp
1	Greg Maddux, Tom Glavine, John Smoltz	Braves	1993–2002	220.2
2	Hal Newhouser, Dizzy Trout, Virgil Trucks	Tigers	1941–1943, 1945–1952	203.2
3	Bob Lemon, Early Wynn, Mike Garcia	Indians	1949–1957	198.2
4	Don Drysdale, Sandy Koufax, Johnny Podres	Dodgers	1957–1966	192.2
5	Bob Lemon, Mike Garcia, Bob Feller	Indians	1948–1956	169.1
6	Warren Spahn, Lew Burdette, Bob Buhl	Braves	1953–1962	168.8
7	Hal Newhouser, Dizzy Trout, Fred Hutchinson	Tigers	1939–1940, 1946–1952	164.7
8	Christy Mathewson, Hooks Wiltse, Red Ames	Giants	1904–1913	162.2
9	Juan Marichal, Gaylord Perry, Bobby Bolin	Giants	1962–1969	141.1
10	Dolf Luque Eppa Rixey, Pete Donohue	Reds	1921–1929	136.8
11	Tom Seaver, Jon Matlack, Jerry Koosman	Mets	1971–1977	136.2
12	Frank Lary, Jim Bunning, Paul Foytack	Tigers	1955–1963	132.5

Table 2 leaves out certain permutations of the 1940s Tigers and 1950s Indians. In the case of the former, Newhouser was so dominant at his peak that he disproportionately elevates the entire trio; combinations such as Newhouser, Trout, and Stubby Overmire don't depict a dominant trio as much as they reflect a dominant pitcher, a very good pitcher, and the spare tire who went along for the ride. The Indians staff had four starters in Lemon, Wynn, Garcia, and Feller, each of whom could have been a number-one starter on another team. We could list every possible combination of the three depending on the year chosen as the starting point.

The Braves band was broken up after 2002, when Glavine decamped for New York and the Mets. Maddux followed him out the door after 2003. All other considerations aside, this was the key fracture in the Braves' dynasty. The club had enjoyed a historically rare advantage. It was unlikely that once the trio was split, whether by age, infirmity, or economic considerations, that the Braves would be able to recreate it. Indeed, given the prices that pitching now commands on the open market, it's prohibitive to keep even a homegrown trio of aces together beyond their pre-arbitration years, as was recently demonstrated by the Oakland A's. Though Smoltz had been retained, he was (temporarily, as it turned out) no longer a starter. Now the Braves were just like any other team, needing to find five reliable pitchers to man their rotation, rather than just two decent ones to support their three aces.

The timing of Glavine's departure was significant. Smoltz had become a free agent after the 2001 season and, though the 34-year-old had missed all of 2000 and parts of 2001, Schuerholz was allowed to re-sign him to a then-impressive three-year, $30-million contract. That appears to have been the end of the line for the Braves in terms of big-money free agent signings. Although Smoltz would sign an extension after 2004, the Braves would not compete to keep players such as Gary Sheffield, J. D. Drew, or Furcal. The Braves were beginning the slow process of ramping down the payroll (see table 3).

In 2006, the Braves raged against the dying of the light, though in truth it went dark pretty quickly with the Mets leading the Braves by 14.5 games on July 1. Smoltz, increasingly looking like the last living veteran of some ancient war, tied the second-best season of his career as measured by Support Neutral Lineup-adjusted Value Added over Replacement (SNLVAR). Injuries and ineffec-

tiveness claimed the rest of the starting rotation. The bullpen was a void, leading to late trades for Bob Wickman and Danys Baez, the latter of which cost the Braves Wilson Betemit, who the Braves had been nursing along for years and, at 24, finally seemed ready to blossom.

Simultaneously, some of the young players that had seemed so promising in 2005 went backwards. While McCann established himself as a top property and LaRoche became something like the new Tino Martinez, Jeff Francoeur's prideful insistence that he could hit any pitch turned him into one of baseball's biggest out machines, Ryan Langerhans went from potential platoon starter to fourth outfield fodder, and Kelly Johnson missed the entire season as he recovered from elbow surgery.

At this writing, further degradation of the roster seems inevitable. The Braves intend for their payroll to be closer to $80 million this year. The club has made no major acquisitions and is entertaining offers for LaRoche and Tim Hudson. Smoltz is turning 40. Marcus Giles was non-tendered after efforts to trade him proved fruitless. Chipper Jones is still a wonderful hitter, but is increasingly unlikely to play anything like a full campaign. Andruw Jones's contract is up after the season, making him a prime candidate to be dealt by the trading deadline. The question for 2007 is not if the Braves will resume their winning ways, but how much further they'll fall.

Table 3. No Fire Sale, but a Liquidation Nonetheless

Year	Braves Payroll (in millions)	Major League Average Payroll (in millions)	% of Major League Average
1991	$20.4	$24.2	84.3
1992	$33.0	$30.1	109.4
1993	$38.1	$30.6	124.6
1994	$40.5	$31.6	128.2
1995	$45.2	$31.5	143.5
1996	$47.9	$32.0	149.8
1997	$50.5	$38.0	132.8
1998	$59.5	$40.3	147.6
1999	$75.1	$48.2	155.9
2000	$82.7	$55.9	148.1
2001	$91.9	$65.4	140.5
2002	$93.5	$67.5	138.5
2003	$106.2	$70.9	149.8
2004	$90.2	$69.0	130.6
2005	$86.5	$73.1	118.3
2006	$90.2	$77.6	116.2

HITTERS

Elvis Andrus SS **Bats: R** **Throws: R** Height: 6' 0" Weight: 185 Born: August 26, 1988 Age: 18

YEAR	TEAM	LVL	AGE	PA	R	2B	3B	HR	RBI	BB	SO	SB	CS	SPEED	AVG	OBP	SLG	MLVR	EQAVG	EQOBP	EQSLG	EQA	VORP	DEFENSE	
2006	ROM	A	17	478	67	25	4	3	50	36	91	23	15	6.1	.265	.324	.362	.020	.247	.289	.332	.219	-8.6	104-SS	-2
2007	ATL	MLB	18	494	51	24	3	4	38	26	82	13	9	5.5	.249	.290	.341	-.248	.245	.286	.339	.212	-5.9	117-SS	-3

Breakout: 59% Improve: 75% Collapse: 17% Attrition: 11%   Comparables: Luis Rivas, Miguel Cabrera, Domingo Cuello, Kimani Newton

As toolsy as he is young, Andrus contributed little at the plate, his defense isn't all there yet, and his basestealing needs work, but the Venezuelan was playing full-season ball at 17. Most of us are wondering how many free fries we can filch on the job at that age. Opinions on his potential vary greatly, but even if he's only a speedy line-drive hitter with good glovework, that's still a potential All-Star, and there's a chance he'll be more than that.

Willy Aybar 2B/3B **Bats: S** **Throws: R** Height: 5' 11" Weight: 200 Born: March 9, 1983 Age: 24

YEAR	TEAM	LVL	AGE	PA	R	2B	3B	HR	RBI	BB	SO	SB	CS	SPEED	AVG	OBP	SLG	MLVR	EQAVG	EQOBP	EQSLG	EQA	VORP	DEFENSE			
2004	JAX	AA	21	537	56	27	0	15	77	50	77	8	10	3.8	.276	.346	.425	.107	.256	.316	.394	.245	8.6	123-2B	2		
2005	LVG	AAA	22	450	47	26	4	5	60	40	56	1	6	3.0	.297	.356	.419	-.057	.255	.310	.353	.232	-1.1	68-3B	6	25-2B	-2
2005	LAN	MLB	22	105	12	8	0	1	10	18	11	3	1	4.9	.326	.448	.453	.316	.337	.457	.488	.330	10.0	20-3B	-2		
2006	LVG	AAA	23	222	30	12	1	10	41	22	24	1	3	3.8	.315	.383	.538	.220	.281	.347	.497	.281	16.6	25-3B	3	20-2B	2
2006	LAN	MLB	23	151	15	12	0	3	22	18	17	1	0	3.9	.250	.356	.414	.008	.248	.353	.411	.269	3.5	24-3B	-3	11-2B	3
2006	ATL	MLB	23	127	17	6	0	1	8	10	19	0	2	3.7	.313	.373	.391	.051	.313	.378	.400	.268	2.1	27-3B	-5		
2007	ATL	MLB	24	508	60	26	2	13	59	46	66	3	3	4.3	.273	.343	.421	-.027	.269	.339	.419	.260	12.8	120-3B	-1		

Breakout: 22% Improve: 46% Collapse: 18% Attrition: 13%   Comparables: Bry Nelson, Garrett Atkins, Luis Rodriguez, Kurt Stillwell

Part of the return for trading Wilson Betemit, Aybar brought his batting average back up to 2005 levels with a flukish BABIP of .368—it's as if his line drives exert a gravitational force that makes outfielders fall down. With Giles out of the way, he's first in line to start at second. He's young enough to get better, but a lot of talented players get nicked up playing second base and don't pan out. He's a competent defender with good hands, iffy range, and is a solid hitter. If he can avoid injury, he'll be an inexpensive asset.

Gregor Blanco CF **Bats: L** **Throws: L** Height: 5' 11" Weight: 170 Born: December 12, 1983 Age: 23

YEAR	TEAM	LVL	AGE	PA	R	2B	3B	HR	RBI	BB	SO	SB	CS	SPEED	AVG	OBP	SLG	MLVR	EQAVG	EQOBP	EQSLG	EQA	VORP	DEFENSE	
2004	MYR	A+	20	495	73	17	9	8	41	47	114	25	9	8.0	.269	.342	.405	.096	.261	.320	.394	.250	5.5	97-CF	-15
2005	MIS	AA	21	486	64	11	12	6	37	73	124	28	12	7.6	.252	.367	.384	.030	.249	.346	.384	.260	9.4	108-CF	-2
2006	MIS	AA	22	302	45	16	3	0	9	43	57	17	6	6.7	.287	.397	.375	.143	.301	.397	.413	.288	20.5	66-CF	-3
2006	RIC	AAA	22	327	43	12	1	0	19	52	53	14	9	6.0	.294	.408	.346	.099	.285	.395	.339	.266	11.0	64-CF	-5
2007	ATL	MLB	23	537	82	23	6	5	39	59	108	23	9	6.8	.280	.364	.386	-.031	.276	.360	.384	.264	13.6	126-CF	-4

Breakout: 14% Improve: 43% Collapse: 31% Attrition: 6%   Comparables: Michael Bourn, Shin-Soo Choo, Scott Sollmann, Marcus Nettles

Blanco walks a great deal, having taken the free pass in 14.8 percent of his plate appearances across two levels in 2006. That's the one distinctive element to his otherwise water-bug skill set—he slaps and skitters, getting squashed on the bases more often than you'd like. Most players of this type don't pan out, but his patience could be the difference-maker.

Eric Campbell 3B **Bats: R** **Throws: R** Height: 6' 0" Weight: 195 Born: August 6, 1985 Age: 21

YEAR	TEAM	LVL	AGE	PA	R	2B	3B	HR	RBI	BB	SO	SB	CS	SPEED	AVG	OBP	SLG	MLVR	EQAVG	EQOBP	EQSLG	EQA	VORP	DEFENSE	
2005	DNV	Rk	19	298	77	26	2	18	64	28	64	15	4	7.3	.313	.383	.634	.538	.257	.302	.449	.257	18.9	64-3B	0
2006	ROM	A	20	480	83	27	3	22	77	23	68	18	4	5.6	.296	.335	.517	.277	.272	.299	.464	.260	19.5	106-3B	-11
2007	ATL	MLB	21	510	63	31	2	16	64	26	85	12	5	5.3	.270	.311	.447	-.050	.266	.307	.444	.254	10.0	120-3B	-4

Breakout: 35% Improve: 56% Collapse: 15% Attrition: 3%   Comparables: Edwin Encarnacion, Victor Diaz, Oscar Salazar, Brian Barden

Campbell led the Sally League in homers in 2006, then had a solid try-out at second base in the Hawaiian Winter League, making his potential trajectory to the majors especially interesting. He's a couple of years away, and by the time he's ready the Braves will have a better idea if they have more need for a second or a third baseman. Campbell needs to improve his walk totals and work on his tendency to try to pull everything, but he's got some serious pop in his bat.

Matt Diaz　　　　**OF**　　**Bats: R**　**Throws: R**　Height: 6′ 1″　Weight: 205　Born: March 3, 1978　　Age: 29

YEAR	TEAM	LVL	AGE	PA	R	2B	3B	HR	RBI	BB	SO	SB	CS	SPEED	AVG	OBP	SLG	MLVR	EQAVG	EQOBP	EQSLG	EQA	VORP	DEFENSE	
2004	DUR	AAA	26	548	81	47	5	21	93	26	96	15	4	6.2	.332	.377	.571	.302	.301	.342	.507	.286	28.9	123-RF	5
2005	OMA	AAA	27	277	48	22	4	14	56	12	49	10	3	6.4	.371	.408	.649	.555	.345	.372	.580	.311	28.9	58-LF	-1
2005	KCA	MLB	27	97	7	4	2	1	9	4	15	0	1	5.1	.281	.323	.404	-.030	.284	.333	.409	.255	0.6	16-LF	-1
2006	ATL	MLB	28	322	37	15	4	7	32	11	49	5	5	5.2	.327	.364	.475	.181	.332	.368	.483	.286	16.1	66-LF	11
2007	ATL	MLB	29	375	53	22	3	12	50	18	64	6	2	5.4	.302	.344	.486	.088	.297	.340	.483	.278	16.1	90-LF	4

Breakout: 6%　Improve: 32%　Collapse: 30%　Attrition: 14%　　Comparables: Alex Johnson, Rondell White, Brian Jordan, Aaron Rowand

After being discarded by two of the worst organizations of the decade, Diaz fell into a relationship with the Braves that left both parties ecstatic. The only drawback to his season was that he did most of his hitting in May and August, batting a combined .429/.467/.696 in those months and .265/.300/.341 in the others. It's not surprising that a player like Diaz slipped past the Royals and Devil Rays; bad teams are often so focused on their lack of star power that they miss the useful role players in their midst.

Yunel Escobar　　　**SS**　　**Bats: R**　**Throws: R**　Height: 6′ 2″　Weight: 200　Born: November 2, 1982　Age: 24

YEAR	TEAM	LVL	AGE	PA	R	2B	3B	HR	RBI	BB	SO	SB	CS	SPEED	AVG	OBP	SLG	MLVR	EQAVG	EQOBP	EQSLG	EQA	VORP	DEFENSE			
2005	ROM	A	22	214	30	13	3	4	19	14	30	0	2	4.3	.313	.358	.470	.243	.281	.315	.399	.244	6.5	47-SS	7		
2006	MIS	AA	23	501	55	21	4	2	45	59	77	7	9	4.5	.264	.361	.346	.041	.272	.356	.368	.257	19.1	60-SS	1	33-3B	1
2007	ATL	MLB	24	472	57	24	4	4	43	39	71	5	4	4.7	.281	.347	.384	-.064	.277	.342	.382	.252	12.1	112-SS	4		

Breakout: 20%　Improve: 45%　Collapse: 23%　Attrition: 12%　　Comparables: Joey Hammond, Dustin Carr, Mike Edwards, Tim Hummel

Escobar struggled in his Double-A debut, and, while he was relatively young for the level, he needs to slug better than .346 to keep moving up. His range is so-so at shortstop, but he has a strong arm. With Andrus coming up behind, and Renteria locked in for another two years in front, he could be a nice solution to the otherwise pointless choice between Peter Orr, Tony Peña, and the like for the utility job.

Jeff Francoeur　　　**RF**　　**Bats: R**　**Throws: R**　Height: 6′ 4″　Weight: 220　Born: January 8, 1984　Age: 23

YEAR	TEAM	LVL	AGE	PA	R	2B	3B	HR	RBI	BB	SO	SB	CS	SPEED	AVG	OBP	SLG	MLVR	EQAVG	EQOBP	EQSLG	EQA	VORP	DEFENSE			
2004	MYR	A+	20	367	56	26	0	15	52	22	70	10	6	5.2	.293	.346	.506	.265	.275	.314	.477	.265	8.0	82-RF	-3		
2005	MIS	AA	21	367	40	28	2	13	62	21	76	13	4	5.4	.275	.322	.487	.116	.261	.297	.466	.259	1.8	71-RF	-3	11-CF	0
2005	ATL	MLB	21	274	41	20	1	14	45	11	58	3	2	5.1	.300	.336	.549	.230	.301	.337	.562	.292	17.4	66-RF	1		
2006	ATL	MLB	22	686	83	24	6	29	103	23	132	1	6	4.3	.260	.293	.449	-.041	.262	.296	.454	.249	-1.0	160-RF	-8		
2007	ATL	MLB	23	598	80	32	4	26	91	29	110	6	4	5.2	.284	.327	.498	.060	.280	.323	.495	.272	16.0	140-RF	-4		

Breakout: 48%　Improve: 69%　Collapse: 10%　Attrition: 15%　　Comparables: Andre Dawson, Chili Davis, Larry Parrish, Albert Belle

Francoeur is a disparate blend of tremendous strengths and equally significant weaknesses. Though he would sometimes protest that he was temperamentally unsuited to taking pitches, Frenchy promised to work on his plate discipline during the 2006 season. Maybe he was right—despite his supposed commitment, he took fewer pitches per plate appearance than in 2005, and his walk rate actually dropped. Regardless of his RBI totals, he won't have real value to a lineup until he improves his approach at the plate. His Equivalent Average was 25 points below the average for right fielders, and his 473 outs tied for third in the majors; if he had been placed higher in the lineup, Francoeur almost certainly would have led the league. The good news is that part of his performance was attributable to a low BABIP, so it's probable that he'll bounce back with better luck. If ever does mature at the plate, he really will become the star right fielder that his RBIs and his arm have convinced so many he already is.

Marcus Giles　　　**2B**　　**Bats: R**　**Throws: R**　Height: 5′ 8″　Weight: 175　Born: May 18, 1978　Age: 29

YEAR	TEAM	LVL	AGE	PA	R	2B	3B	HR	RBI	BB	SO	SB	CS	SPEED	AVG	OBP	SLG	MLVR	EQAVG	EQOBP	EQSLG	EQA	VORP	DEFENSE	
2004	ATL	MLB	26	434	61	22	2	8	48	36	70	17	4	6.4	.311	.378	.443	.150	.310	.376	.438	.288	30.6	86-2B	12
2005	ATL	MLB	27	654	104	45	4	15	63	64	108	16	3	6.3	.291	.365	.461	.143	.290	.365	.467	.288	41.0	143-2B	10
2006	ATL	MLB	28	626	87	32	2	11	60	62	105	10	5	5.1	.262	.341	.387	-.040	.264	.345	.389	.258	14.5	129-2B	5
2007	SDN	MLB	29	600	78	29	3	13	59	58	100	12	5	5.7	.262	.341	.405	-.060	.269	.344	.418	.264	19.8	140-2B	3

Breakout: 9%　Improve: 33%　Collapse: 33%　Attrition: 5%　　Comparables: Davey Lopes, Charlie Neal, Mark Ellis, Bobby Avila

He disappointed many as Furcal's replacement at the top of the order, but Giles managed to rebound in the second half, hitting .289/.361/.427 from July 1 onward. Nevertheless, the Braves did not feel Giles was worth the cost of arbitration and non-tendered him in December. Giles underperformed his expected numbers by a great deal thanks to an unusually low BABIP; chances are good he's still in the peak period of his career, and that San Diego will get the benefit of something more than just brotherly love after signing him to an incentive-laden one-year deal.

Kelly Johnson   LF   Bats: L   Throws: R   Height: 6' 1"   Weight: 205   Born: February 22, 1982   Age: 25

YEAR	TEAM	LVL	AGE	PA	R	2B	3B	HR	RBI	BB	SO	SB	CS	SPEED	AVG	OBP	SLG	MLVR	EQAVG	EQOBP	EQSLG	EQA	VORP	DEFENSE			
2004	GRN	AA	22	534	70	35	3	16	50	49	102	9	9	4.9	.282	.350	.468	.141	.260	.318	.423	.253	-2.7	68-LF	-1	38-CF	-4
2005	RIC	AAA	23	192	35	12	3	8	22	34	22	7	1	6.9	.310	.438	.581	.411	.291	.411	.538	.321	17.4	15-LF	0	12-RF	0
2005	ATL	MLB	23	334	46	12	3	9	40	40	75	2	1	4.8	.241	.334	.397	-.029	.238	.335	.400	.257	1.4	73-LF	11		
2006	ROM	A	24	24	5	2	1	1	3	4	3	2	2	7.1	.474	.583	.842	1.191	.429	.500	.762	.389	6.8				
2006	RIC	AAA	24	47	3	4	0	1	7	6	6	1	0	4.3	.333	.426	.513	.366	.300	.396	.450	.305	3.3				
2007	ATL	MLB	25	366	58	21	2	13	50	41	58	7	2	5.4	.291	.375	.496	.142	.287	.371	.493	.293	20.7	88-LF	3		

Breakout: 18%   Improve: 43%   Collapse: 25%   Attrition: 15%   Comparables: Norm Miller, Mel Hall, Willie Crawford, J. D. Drew

Elbow surgery shelved Johnson for a considerable portion of the year, but he showed no ill effects once he made it back onto the field. As he did in 2005, Johnson will have likely have to contend with Francoeur and Langerhans for playing time, though with Giles non-tendered, his minor league experience at short and third could make him a candidate for the second base job this spring. Should the Braves find a spot for him, he'd provide some much-needed plate discipline in an offense that ranked tenth in the NL in walks last year.

Andruw Jones   CF   Bats: R   Throws: R   Height: 6' 1"   Weight: 210   Born: April 23, 1977   Age: 30

YEAR	TEAM	LVL	AGE	PA	R	2B	3B	HR	RBI	BB	SO	SB	CS	SPEED	AVG	OBP	SLG	MLVR	EQAVG	EQOBP	EQSLG	EQA	VORP	DEFENSE	
2004	ATL	MLB	27	646	85	34	4	29	91	71	147	6	6	4.5	.261	.345	.488	.116	.260	.345	.488	.278	28.6	150-CF	0
2005	ATL	MLB	28	672	95	24	3	51	128	64	112	5	3	4.4	.263	.347	.575	.243	.262	.345	.585	.301	52.8	153-CF	-5
2006	ATL	MLB	29	669	107	29	0	41	129	82	127	5	1	4.4	.262	.363	.531	.191	.263	.364	.536	.301	49.3	148-CF	-3
2007	ATL	MLB	30	622	96	30	2	35	103	68	120	5	2	4.6	.277	.363	.536	.162	.273	.358	.533	.296	40.6	145-CF	-4

Breakout: 17%   Improve: 46%   Collapse: 19%   Attrition: 7%   Comparables: Jesse Barfield, Greg Vaughn, Tom Brunansky, Chet Lemon

Jones's last two seasons are a testament to the MVP voters' overreliance on team performance and rounded counting stats. His 2006 was substantially similar in value to his 2005 campaign, which ended with him receiving 13 first-place votes for MVP, but the lack of team success and a shiny home run count buried him. Jones showed improved patience last year, though his increased walk rate may have been a function of pitchers giving him increased deference after his 51-homer campaign. After finishing right around his 2006 PECOTA forecast of .276/.353/.525, Jones should be essentially the same guy again at age 30 in 2007. Whether he's still a Brave is another question entirely, as he'll be a free agent following the season and could be traded beforehand.

Brandon Jones   RF   Bats: L   Throws: R   Height: 6' 2"   Weight: 195   Born: December 10, 1983   Age: 22

YEAR	TEAM	LVL	AGE	PA	R	2B	3B	HR	RBI	BB	SO	SB	CS	SPEED	AVG	OBP	SLG	MLVR	EQAVG	EQOBP	EQSLG	EQA	VORP	DEFENSE			
2004	DNV	Rk	20	235	35	6	5	3	33	23	33	4	2	5.7	.297	.366	.416	.187	.259	.302	.336	.227	-22.0	51-RF	2		
2005	ROM	A	21	189	37	12	3	8	27	29	29	4	1	6.6	.308	.423	.577	.473	.285	.370	.509	.296	12.1	35-RF	-5		
2005	MYR	A+	21	71	7	4	0	0	5	9	9	0	1	1.9	.350	.437	.417	.285	.333	.394	.381	.269	3.8				
2006	MYR	A+	22	255	27	10	3	7	35	25	49	11	6	5.8	.257	.329	.420	.061	.240	.295	.386	.236	-9.2	49-LF	-3		
2006	MIS	AA	22	194	18	9	3	7	25	15	38	4	2	5.6	.273	.326	.477	.165	.281	.326	.517	.281	8.9	30-RF	2	17-LF	2
2007	ATL	MLB	23	533	71	29	4	14	62	43	98	10	6	5.2	.278	.339	.444	.001	.274	.334	.442	.263	10.8	125-LF	2		

Breakout: 20%   Improve: 61%   Collapse: 20%   Attrition: 5%   Comparables: Rafael Alvarez, Curtis Granderson, Richard Brown, Kelly Johnson

Raw but toolsy, Jones is a long-limbed athlete with a decent idea of what he's doing at the plate to go along with his developing power, good speed, and strong range in the outfield corners. Unfortunately, he's not a center fielder, so his bat needs to continue to improve if he's going to have a future as more than a reserve. Jones is young enough that it could happen, and it's to his credit that he hasn't regressed despite some relatively aggressive promotions. If Jones can make it to the bigs before the Braves pull the trigger on an Andruw Jones deal, Bobby Cox will get the chance to play three Joneses in one game; it won't quite be like September 11, 1963, the day the Giants first had Felipe, Jesus, and Matty Alou appear in the same box score, but it will be as close as we're likely to get.

Chipper Jones | **3B** | **Bats: S** **Throws: R** Height: 6′ 4″ Weight: 230 Born: April 24, 1972 Age: 35

YEAR	TEAM	LVL	AGE	PA	R	2B	3B	HR	RBI	BB	SO	SB	CS	SPEED	AVG	OBP	SLG	MLVR	EQAVG	EQOBP	EQSLG	EQA	VORP	DEFENSE			
2004	ATL	MLB	32	567	69	20	1	30	96	84	96	2	0	4.2	.248	.362	.485	.130	.244	.358	.476	.286	23.5	84-3B	-3	18-LF	2
2005	ATL	MLB	33	432	66	30	0	21	72	72	56	5	1	4.8	.296	.412	.556	.347	.295	.414	.565	.327	43.4	93-3B	-9		
2006	ATL	MLB	34	477	87	28	3	26	86	61	73	6	1	5.4	.324	.409	.596	.417	.323	.411	.592	.332	53.8	100-3B	-12		
2007	ATL	MLB	35	474	79	25	2	22	73	65	72	6	2	4.9	.291	.390	.530	.209	.287	.384	.527	.307	35.7	112-3B	-8		

Breakout: 5% Improve: 26% Collapse: 40% Attrition: 19% Comparables: Ken Caminiti, Bobby Bonilla, Eddie Murray, Larry Walker

The other Jones had another injury-plagued yet productive campaign. Chipper certainly doesn't play like someone who's always hurting, but he misses the games just the same. Like Griffey in Cincinnati or Pavarotti on tour, he's something of a problem superstar—he's a centerpiece, but how often will he show up? Jones's defense has been much closer to league average during his second tour of duty at third, so his return to the hot corner hasn't been the disaster some expected.

Kala Kaaihue | **1B** | **Bats: R** **Throws: R** Height: 6′ 2″ Weight: 230 Born: March 29, 1985 Age: 22

YEAR	TEAM	LVL	AGE	PA	R	2B	3B	HR	RBI	BB	SO	SB	CS	SPEED	AVG	OBP	SLG	MLVR	EQAVG	EQOBP	EQSLG	EQA	VORP	DEFENSE	
2006	ROM	A	21	284	44	16	2	15	49	52	66	3	0	3.7	.329	.458	.614	.587	.310	.408	.554	.322	32.0	64-1B	-2
2006	MYR	A+	21	222	37	8	0	13	31	30	49	0	1	3.3	.223	.342	.473	.124	.204	.297	.418	.242	-4.8	49-1B	0
2007	ATL	MLB	22	518	62	26	1	22	71	54	134	1	1	3.7	.254	.336	.462	.000	.250	.332	.459	.267	7.7	122-1B	1

Breakout: 14% Improve: 28% Collapse: 44% Attrition: 5% Comparables: Hee-Seop Choi, Lance Berkman, Wes Bankston, Jonny Gomes

Hands down the greatest name in the organization, but not in the game, Kaaihue (pronounced kai-uh-HOO-ay), has a brother in the Royals system named Micah Kilakila Kaaihue. Kala showed real power at two levels, though he did most of his damage at Low-A Rome. Kaaihue drew a bunch of walks after his promotion, and his Isolated Power was a healthy .250, but his batting average cratered. A larger sample size should fix that, but he will need to work on making more contact to achieve more consistent results.

Ryan Langerhans | **LF** | **Bats: L** **Throws: L** Height: 6′ 3″ Weight: 205 Born: February 20, 1980 Age: 27

YEAR	TEAM	LVL	AGE	PA	R	2B	3B	HR	RBI	BB	SO	SB	CS	SPEED	AVG	OBP	SLG	MLVR	EQAVG	EQOBP	EQSLG	EQA	VORP	DEFENSE			
2004	RIC	AAA	24	538	103	34	3	20	72	70	113	5	9	5.1	.298	.397	.518	.266	.283	.377	.477	.288	41.6	71-CF	-5	28-LF	1
2005	ATL	MLB	25	373	48	22	3	8	42	37	75	0	2	4.8	.267	.348	.426	.051	.267	.349	.433	.269	7.8	43-LF	2	40-RF	-2
2006	ATL	MLB	26	369	46	16	3	7	28	50	91	1	2	3.6	.241	.350	.378	-.051	.242	.352	.385	.260	-0.8	79-LF	1	13-CF	2
2007	ATL	MLB	27	397	55	21	2	13	49	49	87	3	2	4.8	.265	.362	.449	.036	.261	.357	.446	.275	10.7	95-LF	-1		

Breakout: 24% Improve: 48% Collapse: 20% Attrition: 27% Comparables: Johnny Lewis, Joe Hague, Ryan Church, Scott Stahoviak

Harlan Ellison's collection *Deathbird Stories* contains the novella, "Adrift Just Off the Islets of Langerhans: Latitude 38° 54′ N, Longitude 77° 00′ 13″ W," the tale of a suicidal werewolf looking for the geographical coordinates for the location of his soul. The first sentence is, "When Moby Dick awoke one morning from unsettling dreams, he found himself changed in his bed of kelp into a monstrous Ahab." This happens to describe the Braves, transforming into the hunter having for so long been the hunted. Ryan Langerhans is a handy glove in the corners, but his performance at the plate last year was disappointing. He generated fewer line drives than in his rookie year, a development all the more irksome because it occurred concurrently with Kelly Johnson's injury and Jeff Francoeur's selfishness. He worked counts more, but there's a fine line between waiting on your pitch and passivity. The Islets of Langerhans are, of course, part of the pancreas, an organ that, if pressed, one can live without. Perhaps PECOTA was thinking of that very thing when it named Langerhans's top three comparables (above), all rapid flameouts who quickly vanished.

Adam LaRoche | **1B** | **Bats: L** **Throws: L** Height: 6′ 3″ Weight: 185 Born: November 6, 1979 Age: 27

YEAR	TEAM	LVL	AGE	PA	R	2B	3B	HR	RBI	BB	SO	SB	CS	SPEED	AVG	OBP	SLG	MLVR	EQAVG	EQOBP	EQSLG	EQA	VORP	DEFENSE	
2004	ATL	MLB	24	356	45	27	1	13	45	27	78	0	0	4.1	.278	.333	.488	.111	.274	.331	.480	.274	13.4	84-1B	-9
2005	ATL	MLB	25	502	53	28	0	20	78	39	87	0	2	3.2	.259	.320	.455	.038	.258	.320	.461	.265	7.7	114-1B	-4
2006	ATL	MLB	26	557	89	38	1	32	90	55	128	0	2	3.9	.285	.354	.561	.240	.284	.357	.561	.301	33.3	130-1B	8
2007	PIT	MLB	27	537	73	34	1	27	89	50	109	0	1	4.2	.283	.353	.526	.138	.276	.348	.524	.290	25.7	126-1B	2

Breakout: 22% Improve: 56% Collapse: 21% Attrition: 6% Comparables: Paul Sorrento, Greg Walker, Rico Brogna, Willie Upshaw

Adam LaRoche finally had a breakout season, but most of it took place in the second half, or around the time people were noting the end of an era in Atlanta. LaRoche hit .242/.323/.483 through June 30, but from that point forward he mashed at a .324/.383/.633 clip. Was it a three-month hot streak, or a new performance level? LaRoche started a prescription to combat his attention deficit disorder sometime during the season, and if his second half is any indication, it's working. The Braves sense that, even at his apparent peak, LaRoche may be more valuable as trade bait than as a player to rebuild around. That's why the winter was replete with rumors that he was being shopped. If he hasn't been dealt by the time you read this it's still likely he will be; the team would like to take this one decent player and turn him into two good ones.

Brian McCann   C   Bats: L   Throws: R   Height: 6′ 3″   Weight: 210   Born: February 20, 1984   Age: 23

YEAR	TEAM	LVL	AGE	PA	R	2B	3B	HR	RBI	BB	SO	SB	CS	SPEED	AVG	OBP	SLG	MLVR	EQAVG	EQOBP	EQSLG	EQA	VORP	DEFENSE	
2004	MYR	A+	20	421	45	35	0	16	66	31	54	2	2	3.2	.278	.337	.494	.219	.252	.301	.455	.255	13.4	69-C	7
2005	MIS	AA	21	198	27	13	2	6	26	25	26	2	3	4.4	.265	.359	.476	.147	.251	.328	.456	.267	9.1	43-C	2
2005	ATL	MLB	21	204	20	7	0	5	23	18	26	1	1	4.1	.278	.345	.400	.011	.276	.347	.403	.262	7.1	50-C	-3
2006	ATL	MLB	22	492	61	34	0	24	93	41	54	2	0	3.6	.333	.388	.572	.362	.332	.388	.575	.320	54.8	114-C	-2
2007	*ATL*	*MLB*	*23*	*536*	*76*	*33*	*1*	*24*	*85*	*47*	*61*	*2*	*1*	*3.9*	*.303*	*.367*	*.526*	*.181*	*.298*	*.362*	*.523*	*.295*	*41.9*	*126-C*	*0*

Breakout: 30%   Improve: 57%   Collapse: 20%   Attrition: 5%   Comparables: Ed Herrmann, Ed Kranepool, Barry Foote, Johnny Bench

Most of 2005's "Baby Braves" entered their terrible twos in 2006, but McCann was the gifted child, already annotating his leatherbound copy of *Hop on Pop*. He finished second to Joe Mauer in VORP among major league catchers; the two of them will vie for the top of the charts as long as they each remain behind the plate. McCann added some lift to his swing in 2006, pulling on more pitches and raising his line drive and fly ball rates to the level of other star major league hitters. Given his offensive profile, his .338 BABIP is not a fluke. As long as the power spike holds, he may become the Braves' most valuable property.

Pete Orr   INF   Bats: L   Throws: R   Height: 6′ 1″   Weight: 185   Born: June 8, 1979   Age: 28

YEAR	TEAM	LVL	AGE	PA	R	2B	3B	HR	RBI	BB	SO	SB	CS	SPEED	AVG	OBP	SLG	MLVR	EQAVG	EQOBP	EQSLG	EQA	VORP	DEFENSE				
2004	RIC	AAA	25	491	69	16	10	1	35	20	59	24	11	7.7	.320	.349	.404	.049	.303	.333	.377	.250	13.6	90-2B	8	12-3B	3
2005	ATL	MLB	26	162	32	8	1	1	8	6	23	7	1	7.6	.300	.331	.387	-.017	.303	.338	.388	.260	4.8	18-2B	0		
2006	ATL	MLB	27	164	22	3	4	1	8	5	30	2	4	7.1	.253	.277	.344	-.218	.256	.284	.346	.212	-5.0	18-2B	3		
2007	*ATL*	*MLB*	*28*	*225*	*27*	*8*	*3*	*2*	*18*	*10*	*33*	*6*	*2*	*7.0*	*.278*	*.313*	*.367*	*-.150*	*.274*	*.309*	*.365*	*.234*	*-0.7*				

Breakout: 20%   Improve: 36%   Collapse: 25%   Attrition: 40%   Comparables: John Morris, Ty Cline, Russ Snyder, Endy Chavez

His 2005 batting average was greatly assisted by a .349 average on balls in play, but Orr wasn't nearly so lucky in 2006. He led the Braves in pinch-hit appearances and batted .271/.283/.373, which explains why the Braves traded for Daryle Ward. Orr is a useful defensive fill-in and sometime pinch-runner, but he doesn't walk and lacks any semblance of power, so his average largely describes his value at the plate.

Brayan Peña   C   Bats: S   Throws: R   Height: 5′ 11″   Weight: 220   Born: January 7, 1982   Age: 25

YEAR	TEAM	LVL	AGE	PA	R	2B	3B	HR	RBI	BB	SO	SB	CS	SPEED	AVG	OBP	SLG	MLVR	EQAVG	EQOBP	EQSLG	EQA	VORP	DEFENSE	
2004	GRN	AA	22	299	30	10	4	2	30	15	29	3	5	4.5	.314	.349	.401	.076	.287	.319	.365	.238	3.4	73-C	-14
2005	RIC	AAA	23	319	27	21	2	0	25	28	19	3	1	3.5	.326	.383	.415	.120	.302	.359	.375	.261	12.3	60-C	-6
2005	ATL	MLB	23	40	2	2	0	0	4	1	7	0	0	4.0	.179	.200	.231	-.518	.103	.125	.128	.101	-3.5		
2006	RIC	AAA	24	352	32	18	1	1	33	21	28	6	6	4.8	.302	.342	.372	.034	.289	.330	.369	.246	6.7	80-C	-6
2006	ATL	MLB	24	43	9	2	0	1	5	2	5	0	0	5.1	.268	.302	.390	-.109	.268	.302	.390	.238	0.1		
2007	*ATL*	*MLB*	*25*	*409*	*44*	*19*	*2*	*2*	*37*	*24*	*34*	*4*	*2*	*4.6*	*.281*	*.325*	*.362*	*-.134*	*.276*	*.321*	*.360*	*.236*	*2.8*	*97-C*	*-4*

Breakout: 12%   Improve: 34%   Collapse: 33%   Attrition: 13%   Comparables: Koyie Hill, Bob Didier, Josh Bard, Einar Diaz

Peña's a groundball hitter, which is probably not ideal for a catcher—you don't get too many leg hits after you've been squatting for three hours. On offense, Peña doesn't stay at the plate very long, as evidenced by his 3.3 pitches per plate appearance in his short major league stint and the fact that he walked in 6 percent of his plate appearances at Richmond while striking out in only 8 percent. He's a decent enough backup in an organization with Saltalamacchia and McCann to its credit. Assuming one of them gets dealt, somebody has to inherit Eddie Perez's mantle.

Tony Peña SS **Bats: R** **Throws: R** Height: 6' 1" Weight: 180 Born: March 23, 1981 Age: 26

YEAR	TEAM	LVL	AGE	PA	R	2B	3B	HR	RBI	BB	SO	SB	CS	SPEED	AVG	OBP	SLG	MLVR	EQAVG	EQOBP	EQSLG	EQA	VORP	DEFENSE	
2004	GRN	AA	23	526	65	22	0	11	34	16	108	25	13	6.5	.255	.280	.366	-.125	.227	.249	.318	.204	-25.4	124-SS	6
2005	RIC	AAA	24	526	49	25	4	5	40	21	113	17	15	5.9	.249	.285	.347	-.208	.235	.272	.323	.210	-16.6	134-SS	9
2006	RIC	AAA	25	319	38	12	4	1	23	12	56	12	3	6.7	.282	.312	.359	-.044	.273	.304	.353	.234	1.2	81-SS	-1
2006	ATL	MLB	25	46	12	2	0	1	3	2	10	0	0	4.6	.227	.261	.341	-.273	.227	.261	.341	.209	-1.3		
2007	ATL	MLB	26	371	37	15	3	4	31	15	71	12	5	5.9	.247	.283	.341	-.262	.244	.279	.339	.213	-6.1	89-SS	1

Breakout: 34% Improve: 56% Collapse: 27% Attrition: 23% *Comparables: Aaron Holbert, Jason Bowers, Javy Rodriguez, Ed Rogers*

Peña's not really a prospect. His age-25 season at Richmond is right in line with his previous work in the minor leagues, which suggests that this is as far as his bat will go. Peña drew a free pass in fewer than 4 percent of his plate appearances in 2006, and he's nothing special defensively. If he limits his ambitions to winning a deathmatch with Pete Orr, he might end up happy.

Van Pope 3B **Bats: R** **Throws: R** Height: 6' 0" Weight: 200 Born: February 26, 1984 Age: 23

YEAR	TEAM	LVL	AGE	PA	R	2B	3B	HR	RBI	BB	SO	SB	CS	SPEED	AVG	OBP	SLG	MLVR	EQAVG	EQOBP	EQSLG	EQA	VORP	DEFENSE	
2004	DNV	Rk	20	261	39	18	2	5	39	11	44	5	1	5.5	.270	.333	.429	.131	.230	.257	.331	.208	-23.0	47-3B	5
2005	ROM	A	21	436	48	24	7	6	60	42	70	0	1	4.0	.277	.347	.422	.125	.255	.307	.373	.238	1.6	95-3B	-3
2005	MYR	A+	21	95	7	1	0	1	5	9	21	0	0	2.2	.167	.253	.214	-.427	.138	.200	.138	.140	-15.4	23-3B	0
2006	MYR	A+	22	544	78	31	1	15	74	58	92	7	4	4.7	.263	.353	.430	.115	.244	.311	.402	.247	8.1	120-3B	2
2007	ATL	MLB	23	491	53	26	2	12	53	34	92	3	2	4.7	.253	.311	.398	-.129	.249	.307	.396	.240	0.2	116-3B	1

Breakout: 39% Improve: 60% Collapse: 15% Attrition: 6% *Comparables: Tripper Johnson, Marshall McDougall, Jim Deschaine, Chris Bass*

The Braves love Pope, particularly for his athletic play at third. He doesn't have much power yet, but takes a free pass in over 10 percent of his plate appearances. If he can make the jump up Double-A, he'll rank as one of the organization's better prospects.

Martin Prado 2B **Bats: R** **Throws: R** Height: 6' 1" Weight: 170 Born: October 27, 1983 Age: 23

YEAR	TEAM	LVL	AGE	PA	R	2B	3B	HR	RBI	BB	SO	SB	CS	SPEED	AVG	OBP	SLG	MLVR	EQAVG	EQOBP	EQSLG	EQA	VORP	DEFENSE			
2004	ROM	A	20	467	68	25	6	3	38	30	47	14	10	5.8	.315	.363	.422	.172	.295	.330	.386	.247	13.3	99-2B	4		
2005	MYR	A+	21	326	44	13	3	4	34	24	48	9	6	5.8	.306	.353	.411	.105	.283	.317	.362	.239	2.9	72-2B	-4		
2005	MIS	AA	21	162	17	7	1	1	11	17	17	3	3	4.0	.280	.354	.364	.000	.265	.327	.347	.239	0.8	37-2B	3		
2006	MIS	AA	22	191	17	6	2	1	15	14	35	2	2	4.8	.278	.330	.352	.012	.287	.333	.382	.250	5.2	27-2B	0	16-3B	-1
2006	RIC	AAA	22	257	30	12	1	2	23	12	28	2	2	4.7	.282	.314	.365	-.033	.274	.309	.369	.236	1.4	45-2B	2	13-3B	-1
2006	ATL	MLB	22	49	3	1	1	1	9	5	7	0	0	4.3	.262	.340	.405	-.025	.256	.333	.395	.254	1.1				
2007	ATL	MLB	23	480	53	23	3	5	43	28	62	6	3	5.1	.276	.321	.375	-.127	.272	.316	.373	.238	3.7	113-2B	1		

Breakout: 16% Improve: 45% Collapse: 22% Attrition: 10% *Comparables: Ronny Cedeno, Brent Abernathy, Jack Wilson, Kevin Frandsen*

Considering his relative youth, Prado held his own in Triple-A, but the absence of any particularly impressive skill at the plate will keep him from being a productive regular. He hasn't cleared a .400 slugging percentage or an isolated power of .100 in the higher levels of the minors for any extended period of time. Called up for September, he performed adequately, but utility infielders who can't handle short are of little utility.

Todd Pratt C **Bats: R** **Throws: R** Height: 6' 3" Weight: 240 Born: December 31, 1969 Age: 40

YEAR	TEAM	LVL	AGE	PA	R	2B	3B	HR	RBI	BB	SO	SB	CS	SPEED	AVG	OBP	SLG	MLVR	EQAVG	EQOBP	EQSLG	EQA	VORP	DEFENSE	
2004	PHI	MLB	37	149	16	5	0	3	16	18	38	0	0	3.4	.258	.351	.367	-.044	.258	.351	.359	.255	2.8	41-C	-7
2005	PHI	MLB	38	196	17	4	0	7	23	19	50	0	0	3.8	.251	.332	.394	-.034	.246	.330	.400	.254	4.9	49-C	4
2006	ATL	MLB	39	152	14	6	0	4	19	12	43	1	0	3.7	.207	.272	.341	-.265	.200	.270	.341	.219	-5.0	40-C	-2
2007	ATL	MLB	40	212	22	9	1	7	28	17	57	1	1	4.1	.232	.303	.406	-.148	.228	.299	.404	.240	1.0	53-C	-3

Breakout: 26% Improve: 51% Collapse: 13% Attrition: 66% *Comparables: Walker Cooper, Bob Boone, Ruben Sierra, Tony Perez*

Charged with providing McCann a platoon partner, Pratt came up short, enduring his worst offensive campaign since the mid-nineties. With Brayan Pena providing evidence that he could adequately back up a major league catcher, you have to assume Pratt's as close to hanging it up as he is forty candles on the cake. Pratt's 14-year major league career had some nifty high points, and his .263 career EqA is sparkling in comparison to most reserve catchers of his era.

Atlanta Braves

Edgar Renteria   **SS**   **Bats: R**   **Throws: R**   Height: 6' 1"   Weight: 200   Born: August 7, 1975   Age: 31

YEAR	TEAM	LVL	AGE	PA	R	2B	3B	HR	RBI	BB	SO	SB	CS	SPEED	AVG	OBP	SLG	MLVR	EQAVG	EQOBP	EQSLG	EQA	VORP	DEFENSE
2004	SLN	MLB	28	642	84	37	0	10	72	39	78	17	11	5.6	.287	.327	.401	-.005	.288	.329	.404	.253	20.2	140-SS -7
2005	BOS	MLB	29	692	100	36	4	8	70	55	100	9	4	5.8	.276	.335	.385	-.048	.278	.347	.392	.260	19.6	147-SS -21
2006	ATL	MLB	30	673	100	40	2	14	70	62	89	17	6	5.7	.293	.361	.436	.087	.294	.364	.441	.278	37.6	142-SS -10
2007	ATL	MLB	31	622	85	32	3	10	59	50	82	16	6	5.8	.284	.346	.410	-.029	.280	.341	.407	.261	23.6	145-SS -7

Breakout: 11% Improve: 32% Collapse: 26% Attrition: 4%   Comparables: Dave Concepcion, Steve Sax, Mark Grudzielanek, Carney Lansford

One of the rare shortstops whose bat carries his glove instead of the other way around, Renteria posted his best EqA since 2003 upon returning to the NL, which must have been something of a relief for the Braves who gambled that his weak showings with the stick in back-to-back seasons didn't signal that he was no longer an asset at the position. Renty made a broad-based return to excellence, kicking his walk rate back up, knocking southpaws around, showing power away from the unfriendly Ted, and improving his stolen base efficiency. Still, he regressed in the second half, batting .264/.318/.404 after the break, even weaker than the combined .281/.331/.393 clip that got him run out of St. Louis and Boston in consecutive years. Renteria is signed through 2008, and the Braves are only on the hook for part of his salary, but it's entirely possible that the organization will soon see him as a player its rebuilding movement must overcome rather than embrace.

Jarrod Saltalamacchia   **C**   **Bats: S**   **Throws: R**   Height: 6' 4"   Weight: 195   Born: May 2, 1985   Age: 22

YEAR	TEAM	LVL	AGE	PA	R	2B	3B	HR	RBI	BB	SO	SB	CS	SPEED	AVG	OBP	SLG	MLVR	EQAVG	EQOBP	EQSLG	EQA	VORP	DEFENSE
2004	ROM	A	19	366	42	19	2	10	51	34	83	1	0	3.7	.272	.348	.437	.132	.257	.312	.388	.245	4.0	46-C -5
2005	MYR	A+	20	529	70	35	1	19	81	57	99	4	2	3.3	.314	.394	.519	.327	.289	.348	.456	.276	33.3	93-C -14
2006	MIS	AA	21	377	30	18	1	9	39	55	71	0	1	2.8	.230	.353	.380	.051	.237	.345	.409	.263	12.3	80-C 5
2007	ATL	MLB	22	451	51	23	1	15	59	46	84	0	0	3.7	.261	.342	.439	-.015	.257	.337	.437	.265	16.4	107-C -3

Breakout: 25% Improve: 41% Collapse: 28% Attrition: 10%   Comparables: Justin Huber, Guillermo Quiroz, Charles Alley, Wes Bankston

Salty suffered a setback at the plate in 2006 as a hand injury deepened an early slump, but he managed to pick it up as the season wore on, hitting .338/.474/.649 over the last two months. His BABIP was well below average, and should rebound this season, improving all of his numbers the way a rising tide raises all boats. Saltalamacchia also destroyed the ball in a short AFL stint, suggesting he's back to being one of the best catching prospects in the game. The other good news is that he improved behind the plate, throwing out 36 percent of opposing runners, so talk of moving him to first should be quieted. He's unlikely to displace McCann, but he gives the Braves options; it'll be interesting to see which way Schuerholz jumps.

Scott Thorman   **1B/LF**   **Bats: L**   **Throws: R**   Height: 6' 3"   Weight: 235   Born: January 6, 1982   Age: 25

YEAR	TEAM	LVL	AGE	PA	R	2B	3B	HR	RBI	BB	SO	SB	CS	SPEED	AVG	OBP	SLG	MLVR	EQAVG	EQOBP	EQSLG	EQA	VORP	DEFENSE	
2004	MYR	A+	22	176	20	11	1	4	29	12	19	1	0	4.1	.299	.358	.461	.224	.289	.331	.447	.269	4.6	43-1B 2	
2004	GRN	AA	22	387	31	14	3	11	51	39	73	5	3	4.3	.252	.326	.406	-.000	.233	.295	.366	.231	-14.5	90-1B -7	
2005	MIS	AA	23	383	49	21	2	15	65	28	76	2	2	3.4	.305	.360	.506	.228	.293	.339	.493	.280	20.2	90-1B 0	
2005	RIC	AAA	23	224	23	10	3	6	27	9	42	0	0	3.9	.276	.313	.438	-.012	.261	.298	.408	.242	-2.8	52-1B -1	
2006	RIC	AAA	24	344	38	16	2	15	48	31	48	4	2	4.8	.298	.360	.508	.238	.290	.352	.513	.288	21.4	49-1B -3	24-LF -3
2006	ATL	MLB	24	133	13	11	0	5	14	5	21	1	0	5.1	.234	.263	.438	-.133	.234	.269	.438	.238	-2.3	15-LF -2	13-1B 0
2007	ATL	MLB	25	482	59	25	2	16	66	34	79	3	2	4.4	.273	.328	.451	-.012	.269	.324	.449	.261	6.8	114-1B -2	

Breakout: 16% Improve: 39% Collapse: 28% Attrition: 11%   Comparables: Garrett Jones, Kurt Bierek, Jeff Liefer, Brant Colamarino

Slugging .508 with a .210 isolated power, as Thorman did at Richmond, might look impressive, but, for a first baseman, it really isn't. He might have been given more of a shot had LaRoche not broken out, or if Thorman had given the Braves anything inspiring in his brief trials. He's a below-average first base prospect, and while sometimes the Todd Benzinger or Scott Stahoviak types catch a break, Thorman's not even at that level. Still, he's the heir apparent should LaRoche be traded.

Daryle Ward   **1B**   **Bats: L   Throws: L**   Height: 6' 2"   Weight: 240   Born: June 27, 1975   Age: 32

YEAR	TEAM	LVL	AGE	PA	R	2B	3B	HR	RBI	BB	SO	SB	CS	SPEED	AVG	OBP	SLG	MLVR	EQAVG	EQOBP	EQSLG	EQA	VORP	DEFENSE	
2004	NAS	AAA	29	101	14	7	0	7	17	5	16	0	0	3.3	.281	.317	.573	.182	.237	.267	.443	.238	-2.1	21-1B	-1
2004	PIT	MLB	29	321	39	17	2	15	57	22	45	0	0	4.3	.249	.305	.474	.022	.246	.302	.468	.259	5.6	61-1B	-1
2005	PIT	MLB	30	453	46	21	1	12	63	37	60	0	2	3.1	.260	.318	.405	-.024	.260	.319	.416	.255	0.3	101-1B	-7
2006	WAS	MLB	31	123	15	9	0	6	19	14	21	0	1	2.5	.308	.390	.567	.340	.317	.403	.587	.324	11.9		
2006	ATL	MLB	31	27	2	1	0	1	7	1	6	0	0	4.1	.308	.333	.462	.081	.308	.333	.462	.269	1.1		
2007	*CHN*	*MLB*	*32*	*188*	*24*	*10*	*0*	*8*	*27*	*17*	*31*	*0*	*0*	*3.8*	*.274*	*.343*	*.486*	*.060*	*.269*	*.337*	*.472*	*.273*	*6.0*		

Breakout: 12% Improve: 37% Collapse: 26% Attrition: 41%   Comparables: Gordy Coleman, Sid Bream, Jim Spencer, George Crowe

Ward had the best season of his undistinguished career in 2006, but expecting a repeat would be naive. He's hit .277/.340/.492 against right-handed pitching the past three years, which might make him a solid platoon DH, but we don't see many of those anymore thanks to today's swollen pitching staffs. Ward seems to have settled into the pinch-hitter/reserve role well enough, going 8-for-14 (.571) with a home run pinch-hitting for the Braves and 21-for-60 (.350) with 4 home runs overall last year. Of course, pinch-hitters rarely have those kinds of seasons two years in a row. Signed to a one-year deal with the Cubs, he'll serve as a weak form of Derrek Lee insurance.

PITCHERS

Danys Baez   **Bats: R   Throws: R**   Height: 6' 1"   Weight: 230   Born: September 10, 1977   Age: 29

YEAR	TEAM	LVL	AGE	W	L	SV	G	GS	IP	H	BB	SO	HR	GB%	BABIP	STUFF	WHIP	ERA	PERA	EQERA	EQH9	EQBB9	EQSO9	EQHR9	VORP	WXRL
2004	TBA	MLB	26	4	4	30	62	0	68	60	29	52	6	—	.277	4	1.31	3.57	4.34	3.76	8.2	3.5	6.4	0.6	15.9	3.10
2005	TBA	MLB	27	5	4	41	67	0	72¹	66	30	51	7	47.9%	.278	2	1.33	2.86	4.34	3.23	7.5	3.6	6.1	0.8	19.1	4.47
2006	LAN	MLB	28	5	5	9	46	0	49²	53	11	29	3	40.5%	.323	0	1.29	4.35	3.81	4.73	9.1	1.8	4.7	0.5	4.1	-0.03
2006	ATL	MLB	28	0	1	0	11	0	10	7	6	10	0	37.0%	.259	7	1.30	5.40	3.62	5.23	6.1	4.4	7.8	0.0	0.6	0.07
2007	*BAL*	*MLB*	*29*	*3*	*3*	*5*	*49*	*0*	*57*	*63*	*19*	*35*	*7*	*44.0%*	*.302*	*-7*	*1.45*	*4.59*	*4.51*	*4.25*	*10.0*	*2.9*	*5.2*	*1.0*	*6.9*	*0.60*

Breakout: 17% Improve: 43% Collapse: 28% Attrition: 13%   Comparables: Bob Lee, Barry Jones, Lerrin LaGrow, Randy Moffitt

There's something intoxicating about the Proven Closer tag. Los Angeles paid a high price in young players for Proven Closer Baez and got nothing out of it. The Braves then rolled the same dice by dealing Wilson Betemit to L.A. and fared only slightly better before Baez hurt himself. Drunk on that label themselves, the Orioles threw a three-year, $19-million deal at Baez, a pitcher whose results have hewed close to league average throughout his career.

Kevin Barry   **Bats: R   Throws: R**   Height: 6' 2"   Weight: 235   Born: August 18, 1978   Age: 28

YEAR	TEAM	LVL	AGE	W	L	SV	G	GS	IP	H	BB	SO	HR	GB%	BABIP	STUFF	WHIP	ERA	PERA	EQERA	EQH9	EQBB9	EQSO9	EQHR9	VORP	WXRL
2004	GRN	AA	25	2	1	4	20	0	24²	15	10	31	0	—	.263	11	1.01	0.73	4.00	1.54	6.9	4.6	6.9	0.4	10.5	—
2004	RIC	AAA	25	3	3	2	30	0	35²	25	25	40	1	—	.279	23	1.40	2.52	4.25	4.08	6.4	6.9	7.9	0.3	6.0	—
2005	RIC	AAA	26	5	3	1	32	8	79	60	44	73	8	34.4%	.252	5	1.32	2.85	5.38	3.39	7.5	5.5	6.5	1.1	18.9	—
2006	RIC	AAA	27	4	5	0	18	15	95¹	87	36	73	5	39.6%	.290	9	1.29	3.31	4.41	4.14	8.1	3.7	5.2	0.8	15.5	—
2006	ATL	MLB	27	1	1	0	19	1	25²	24	14	19	2	32.9%	.297	-1	1.48	5.60	4.33	5.13	7.9	4.1	6.2	0.7	1.0	-0.46
2007	*ATL*	*MLB*	*28*	*5*	*6*	*1*	*38*	*12*	*95¹*	*98*	*49*	*70*	*14*	*39.0%*	*.289*	*-4*	*1.54*	*5.21*	*5.39*	*5.31*	*9.0*	*4.0*	*6.0*	*1.2*	*4.6*	*0.90*

Breakout: 1% Improve: 18% Collapse: 56% Attrition: 2%   Comparables: Luke Hudson, Steve McCatty, Sammy Stewart, Shawn Chacon

His numbers at Richmond look decent enough until you consider his age. Barry's an organizational arm whose greatest contribution to the Braves in 2006 was a pulse. He gave up a ton of fly balls, opponents slugged an unsurprising .442 against him, and he responded by nibbling and walking people. He's unlikely to see much time in Atlanta in the future, lest some apocalyptic pitching scenarios arise.

Lance Cormier   **Bats: R   Throws: R**   Height: 6' 1"   Weight: 200   Born: August 19, 1980   Age: 26

YEAR	TEAM	LVL	AGE	W	L	SV	G	GS	IP	H	BB	SO	HR	GB%	BABIP	STUFF	WHIP	ERA	PERA	EQERA	EQH9	EQBB9	EQSO9	EQHR9	VORP	WXRL
2004	ELP	AA	23	2	3	0	10	8	63	66	17	58	3	—	.341	18	1.32	2.29	3.94	2.78	8.6	2.6	5.3	0.7	20.3	—
2004	TUC	AAA	23	3	3	0	8	8	50¹	50	17	37	0	—	.321	19	1.33	2.68	3.59	2.77	8.0	3.1	5.0	0.2	16.4	—
2004	ARI	MLB	23	1	4	0	17	5	45¹	62	25	24	13	—	.329	-33	1.92	8.15	7.12	7.04	11.4	4.4	4.2	2.3	-12.9	-0.67
2005	ARI	MLB	24	7	3	0	67	0	79¹	86	43	63	7	49.8%	.341	1	1.63	5.11	4.51	5.12	9.1	4.4	6.3	0.8	-0.7	2.16
2006	RIC	AAA	25	4	3	0	9	9	54¹	65	14	27	4	58.5%	.330	-4	1.46	3.99	4.70	4.23	10.2	2.4	3.4	1.0	8.4	—
2006	ATL	MLB	25	4	5	0	29	9	73²	90	39	43	8	51.2%	.347	-9	1.75	4.88	4.79	4.91	10.2	4.1	4.7	0.8	4.9	1.32
2007	*ATL*	*MLB*	*26*	*4*	*5*	*1*	*41*	*10*	*87²*	*100*	*39*	*55*	*10*	*51.0%*	*.312*	*-7*	*1.58*	*5.01*	*5.35*	*5.19*	*10.0*	*3.5*	*5.1*	*0.9*	*5.4*	*0.90*

Breakout: 15% Improve: 30% Collapse: 31% Attrition: 13%   Comparables: Dave Weathers, Brian Williams, Omar Olivares, Ken Clay

Even after setting aside his unusually high number of intentional walks, Cormier walked nearly four batters per nine innings, and his strikeout rate dropped. He survived because he's a severe groundball pitcher and induced 16 double plays in only 73.2 innings, or almost two per per nine (league leader Miguel Batista induced a mere 1.4 GIDP/9). He's a bad bet to pitch this "well" in the future unless he starts fooling more of the batters more of the time, but he did notch four quality starts in seven at the tail end of the season.

Kyle Davies — Bats: R Throws: R — Height: 6' 2" Weight: 205 Born: September 9, 1983 Age: 23

YEAR	TEAM	LVL	AGE	W	L	SV	G	GS	IP	H	BB	SO	HR	GB%	BABIP	STUFF	WHIP	ERA	PERA	EQERA	EQH9	EQBB9	EQSO9	EQHR9	VORP	WXRL
2004	MYR	A+	20	9	2	0	14	14	75¹	55	32	95	3	—	.301	33	1.16	2.63	4.21	3.98	7.8	4.6	8.0	0.7	13.0	—
2004	GRN	AA	20	4	0	0	11	10	62	40	22	73	9	—	.225	15	1.00	2.32	5.97	3.34	7.1	3.5	7.1	2.0	14.9	—
2005	RIC	AAA	21	5	2	0	13	13	73¹	66	34	62	6	41.7%	.299	16	1.36	3.44	4.60	3.61	8.5	4.5	6.0	0.9	16.0	—
2005	ATL	MLB	21	7	6	0	21	14	87²	98	49	62	8	34.7%	.321	8	1.68	4.93	4.56	5.18	9.8	4.5	5.8	0.8	3.4	1.07
2006	ATL	MLB	22	3	7	0	14	14	63¹	90	33	51	14	37.7%	.369	-10	1.94	8.39	5.59	7.73	11.9	3.9	6.4	1.8	-18.2	-0.24
2007	ATL	MLB	23	6	8	0	27	21	119²	125	55	95	17	42.0%	.301	8	1.51	5.02	5.25	5.13	9.2	3.6	6.4	1.1	8.2	1.70

Breakout: 25% Improve: 63% Collapse: 12% Attrition: 11% Comparables: Steve Dunning, Rich Hand, Herm Wehmeier, Pete Smith

Pretty Young Thing Davies was supposed to be part of the Braves' reloading of their declining pitching staff, a cog that would help the Braves machine roll to yet another division title. Instead, he tore his groin in mid-May, an injury that required surgery and kept him off of the active roster until September. When he returned, the results were nightmarish—Davies got pounded for a 13.06 ERA in six September starts. The good news is that, unless the groin injury overly distorted Davies's mechanics, it shouldn't have affected his arm—he should still have the low-90s stuff that made him such a good prospect in the first place. Indeed, the Braves are counting on his being in the 2007 rotation.

Joey Devine — Bats: R Throws: R — Height: 6' 1" Weight: 225 Born: September 19, 1983 Age: 23

YEAR	TEAM	LVL	AGE	W	L	SV	G	GS	IP	H	BB	SO	HR	GB%	BABIP	STUFF	WHIP	ERA	PERA	EQERA	EQH9	EQBB9	EQSO9	EQHR9	VORP	WXRL
2005	MIS	AA	21	1	1	5	18	0	20	19	12	28	2	46.0%	.370	8	1.55	2.70	6.43	6.63	10.9	5.7	9.5	1.4	-2.2	—
2005	ATL	MLB	21	0	1	0	5	0	5	6	5	3	2	38.9%	.250	-19	2.20	12.60	10.25	10.12	10.1	8.4	5.1	3.4	-4.0	-0.31
2006	MYR	A+	22	1	3	0	13	2	18¹	13	11	28	1	30.8%	.343	17	1.33	5.97	4.73	7.27	8.3	6.2	9.9	1.0	-3.2	—
2006	MIS	AA	22	2	0	0	6	0	11¹	2	4	20	1	30.8%	.100	10	0.54	0.81	3.80	1.74	3.5	3.5	12.2	1.7	4.4	—
2006	ATL	MLB	22	0	0	0	10	0	6¹	8	9	10	1	12.5%	.467	7	2.68	10.00	5.95	9.00	10.3	10.3	11.6	1.3	-2.7	-0.35
2007	ATL	MLB	23	2	3	1	45	3	53²	50	40	60	9	35.0%	.303	5	1.68	5.57	5.83	5.63	8.3	5.8	9.0	1.3	0.5	0.20

Breakout: 47% Improve: 77% Collapse: 7% Attrition: 24% Comparables: Fernando Cabrera, Joshua Newman, Brad Baker, Justin Hedrick

The top relief prospect in the organization, Devine nearly made the Braves out of spring training last year. Recalled soon after the season started, he struggled mightily, and it was soon revealed that he was suffering from a degenerative disc in his back. Extensive rest and rehab followed as the Braves changed his pitching motion to cause less strain on his back. A rehab stint at Double-A Mississippi went quite well, and when Devine finally rejoined the big club in September he pitched 5.1 scoreless innings over eight outings, allowing three hits, walking four, and striking out eight. A subsequent AFL stint was less inspiring. He still has the plus fastball and slider that made him a first-round pick, but, still just 22 years old, he'd benefit from some time in Richmond before the Braves use him to rescue the inevitable Bob Wickman meltdown.

Mike Hampton — Bats: R Throws: L — Height: 5' 10" Weight: 195 Born: September 9, 1972 Age: 34

YEAR	TEAM	LVL	AGE	W	L	SV	G	GS	IP	H	BB	SO	HR	GB%	BABIP	STUFF	WHIP	ERA	PERA	EQERA	EQH9	EQBB9	EQSO9	EQHR9	VORP	WXRL
2004	ATL	MLB	31	13	9	0	29	29	172¹	198	65	87	15	—	.315	4	1.53	4.28	4.30	4.57	9.8	3.0	4.0	0.7	24.1	4.44
2005	ATL	MLB	32	5	3	0	12	12	69¹	74	18	27	5	51.3%	.299	3	1.33	3.51	4.06	3.91	9.1	2.1	3.2	0.6	15.0	2.23
2007	ATL	MLB	34	4	6	0	28	12	84¹	101	32	43	10	50.0%	.313	-11	1.57	5.15	5.49	5.33	10.6	2.9	4.1	0.9	3.6	0.80

Breakout: 1% Improve: 13% Collapse: 49% Attrition: 16% Comparables: Claude Osteen, Danny Jackson, Johnny Schmitz, Mike Flanagan

Remember him? Hampton pitched well in his short 2005 stint with the Braves, but lost an additional strikeout per nine innings he likely couldn't afford before a litany of injuries derailed his season. He eventually gave in to the Tommy John surgery that cost him all of 2006. Even against this winter's inflated pitching contracts, Hampton's not going to be worth the $14.5 million the Braves will dish out for him this year. If he reacquires his command, he's capable of league-average performance, but no more, and most likely less.

Matthew Harrison
Bats: L Throws: L   Height: 6' 4"   Weight: 221   Born: August 16, 1985   Age: 21

YEAR	TEAM	LVL	AGE	W	L	SV	G	GS	IP	H	BB	SO	HR	GB%	BABIP	STUFF	WHIP	ERA	PERA	EQERA	EQH9	EQBB9	EQSO9	EQHR9	VORP	WXRL
2004	DNV	Rk	18	4	4	0	13	12	66	72	10	49	3	—	.321	-2	1.24	4.09	4.51	7.30	10.5	1.8	3.0	1.0	-12.3	—
2005	ROM	A	19	12	7	0	27	27	167	151	30	118	17	43.1%	.270	-9	1.08	3.23	5.84	5.02	9.2	2.0	3.9	1.8	10.5	—
2006	MYR	A+	20	8	4	0	13	13	81	77	16	60	6	50.2%	.297	8	1.15	3.11	4.80	4.03	9.2	1.9	4.7	1.2	14.0	—
2006	MIS	AA	20	3	4	0	13	12	77	83	17	54	6	43.8%	.314	5	1.30	3.62	4.61	4.91	10.1	2.0	4.4	1.2	5.9	—
2007	ATL	MLB	21	7	9	0	26	21	127²	144	37	75	22	45.0%	.294	3	1.42	5.26	5.32	5.39	9.9	2.3	4.8	1.4	5.1	1.40

Breakout: 7%   Improve: 37%   Collapse: 25%   Attrition: 1%   Comparables: Derrin Ebert, Heath Phillips, Jake Kringen, Craig Anderson

Harrison's a big lefty with solid control and plus velocity for his handedness—he's touched 95 in the past, although he normally works in the low-90s. The North Carolina native throws a ton of strikes and supplements his heat with a plus curve and change. Harrison's problem is that he makes a few too many mistakes inside the strike zone. While he needs to pitch better to pan out, he's still one of the best arms in the system, and his numbers from his Double-A debut are encouraging.

Tim Hudson
Bats: R Throws: R   Height: 6' 1"   Weight: 170   Born: July 14, 1975   Age: 31

YEAR	TEAM	LVL	AGE	W	L	SV	G	GS	IP	H	BB	SO	HR	GB%	BABIP	STUFF	WHIP	ERA	PERA	EQERA	EQH9	EQBB9	EQSO9	EQHR9	VORP	WXRL
2004	OAK	MLB	28	12	6	0	27	27	188²	194	44	103	8	—	.305	23	1.29	3.53	3.51	3.87	9.1	1.9	4.6	0.3	46.2	4.79
2005	ATL	MLB	29	14	9	0	29	29	192	194	65	115	20	58.7%	.291	8	1.35	3.52	4.51	3.84	8.9	2.7	4.9	0.9	41.2	5.36
2006	ATL	MLB	30	13	12	0	35	35	218¹	235	79	141	25	58.4%	.303	9	1.44	4.86	4.38	4.82	9.0	2.8	5.2	0.9	17.0	3.48
2007	ATL	MLB	31	12	10	0	31	31	198	209	62	126	19	56.0%	.299	10	1.37	4.14	4.35	4.33	9.3	2.5	5.2	0.8	31.7	4.70

Breakout: 12%   Improve: 47%   Collapse: 9%   Attrition: 0%   Comparables: Joe Horlen, Larry Jackson, Mel Stottlemyre, Ken Hill

Hudson finally pitched a full season again, avoiding the various aches and pains that cost him four or five starts in each of the previous two years, but the results were the worst of his career. Outside of a solid stretch in May (2.79 ERA in 48⅓ innings), batters found Hudson to their liking all season long. Lefties batted .281/.353/.491 against him, and he was particularly vulnerable away from the pitcher-lovin' Ted. The collapse could have been expected; in 2005, Hudson stranded almost 80 percent of his baserunners. That was unlikely to happen again; the NL average over the last three seasons has been 69 percent. Indeed, Hudson stranded just 65 percent of his runners in 2006. Hudson is signed through 2009 and his contract is backloaded—he'll have made a total of just $10 million between last year and this, but in 2008 his salary jumps to $13 million. You can bet that the Braves will work hard to get another team to grab the fat end of Hudson's balloon.

Chuck James
Bats: L Throws: L   Height: 6' 0"   Weight: 190   Born: November 9, 1981   Age: 25

YEAR	TEAM	LVL	AGE	W	L	SV	G	GS	IP	H	BB	SO	HR	GB%	BABIP	STUFF	WHIP	ERA	PERA	EQERA	EQH9	EQBB9	EQSO9	EQHR9	VORP	WXRL
2004	ROM	A	22	10	5	0	26	22	132²	92	48	156	6	—	.272	15	1.06	2.24	4.66	3.88	7.3	4.2	5.9	0.8	24.4	—
2005	MYR	A+	23	3	3	0	7	7	41²	20	8	59	1	35.3%	.226	39	0.67	1.08	2.78	2.25	5.8	2.0	7.4	0.4	14.9	—
2005	MIS	AA	23	9	1	0	16	16	86	62	18	104	4	28.6%	.286	32	0.93	2.09	3.35	3.44	7.4	1.9	7.5	0.4	20.1	—
2005	RIC	AAA	23	1	3	0	6	6	33²	21	10	30	4	20.0%	.200	15	0.92	3.47	4.77	3.58	6.3	3.0	6.3	1.4	7.3	—
2006	RIC	AAA	24	1	0	0	7	6	33	30	6	25	3	37.5%	.273	9	1.09	2.73	4.30	2.97	8.1	1.6	5.1	1.1	9.7	—
2006	ATL	MLB	24	11	4	0	25	18	119	101	47	91	20	28.5%	.250	3	1.24	3.78	5.02	3.75	7.2	3.1	6.2	1.3	25.2	3.09
2007	ATL	MLB	25	8	9	0	34	23	142	136	54	114	22	33.0%	.275	10	1.33	4.49	4.61	4.54	8.4	3.0	6.5	1.2	19.8	2.90

Breakout: 2%   Improve: 13%   Collapse: 60%   Attrition: 3%   Comparables: Dan Schatzeder, Noah Lowry, Sterling Hitchcock, Jarrod Washburn

The Braves tried to bring James along slowly, ticketing him for middle relief despite an obvious need for viable starters. He had pitched just seven games when a strained hamstring sent him to the DL in early May. Rather than bring him back after his rehab period was up, the Braves sent him down to Richmond to buy more time. He finally returned in late June and spent the rest of the season in the rotation. But for a July game in which a Carlos Beltran grand slam helped the Mets pound James for seven runs in one inning, he was reasonably consistent the rest of the way. Outside of the lofty home run figures you'd expect, the gutty changeup artist fooled more people than most of the organization's scoutier arms. Given his current peripherals, you can see why PECOTA is skeptical of him—his incredibly low BABIP is going to be hard to sustain—but don't get worked up about the ominous collapse figure, and keep in mind that he's still being projected to be a useful starting pitcher.

Anthony Lerew

Bats: L Throws: R Height: 6' 3" Weight: 220 Born: October 28, 1982 Age: 24

YEAR	TEAM	LVL	AGE	W	L	SV	G	GS	IP	H	BB	SO	HR	GB%	BABIP	STUFF	WHIP	ERA	PERA	EQERA	EQH9	EQBB9	EQSO9	EQHR9	VORP	WXRL
2004	MYR	A+	21	8	9	0	27	27	144	145	46	125	12	—	.317	-7	1.33	3.75	5.38	6.09	10.2	3.4	5.4	1.5	-7.6	—
2005	MIS	AA	22	6	2	0	14	14	75²	70	32	64	6	46.7%	.299	0	1.35	3.92	5.22	4.82	8.9	3.9	5.4	1.2	6.5	—
2005	RIC	AAA	22	4	4	0	13	13	72¹	63	23	53	9	45.7%	.258	2	1.19	3.49	5.16	4.29	8.3	3.0	5.2	1.3	10.4	—
2006	MIS	AA	23	4	2	0	9	8	48¹	43	13	37	1	54.6%	.288	13	1.16	2.06	3.63	4.12	8.4	2.4	4.7	0.4	7.9	—
2006	RIC	AAA	23	3	5	0	16	15	71	92	36	69	12	43.1%	.379	-20	1.80	7.48	6.92	8.66	12.2	4.8	6.8	2.3	-24.0	—
2007	ATL	MLB	24	4	7	0	34	12	92²	104	43	67	14	46.0%	.309	-3	1.58	5.70	5.76	5.86	9.8	3.6	5.8	1.2	-1.4	0.30

Breakout: 22% Improve: 56% Collapse: 14% Attrition: 1%   Comparables: Michael Wuertz, Jason Ryan, Gary Glover, Jason Olsen

Lerew's an important young arm in the Braves system, hard as that might be to believe while looking at his performance with Richmond last year. That rough first half led to a return to Double-A and effectiveness. Lerew has average stuff coupled with good control, meaning he will most likely be a back of the rotation guy or middle reliever. The Braves could use assistance in either department, so he has a job waiting for him if he can just get past the International League.

Macay McBride

Bats: L Throws: L Height: 5' 11" Weight: 210 Born: October 24, 1982 Age: 24

YEAR	TEAM	LVL	AGE	W	L	SV	G	GS	IP	H	BB	SO	HR	GB%	BABIP	STUFF	WHIP	ERA	PERA	EQERA	EQH9	EQBB9	EQSO9	EQHR9	VORP	WXRL
2004	GRN	AA	21	1	7	0	38	12	103¹	113	46	102	9	—	.342	-8	1.54	4.44	4.94	6.11	10.4	4.3	5.8	1.2	-5.8	—
2005	MIS	AA	22	3	1	0	6	3	24²	21	12	16	2	64.0%	.264	-9	1.34	3.64	5.71	4.74	8.0	4.4	4.0	1.1	2.4	—
2005	RIC	AAA	22	1	5	2	25	1	43²	49	22	47	5	45.4%	.376	3	1.62	4.32	4.93	5.65	10.9	4.8	7.5	1.3	-0.2	—
2005	ATL	MLB	22	1	0	1	23	0	14	18	7	22	0	43.2%	.486	14	1.79	5.79	2.34	6.91	11.9	3.8	12.6	0.0	-2.4	1.08
2006	ATL	MLB	23	4	1	1	71	0	56²	53	32	46	2	47.6%	.307	10	1.50	3.65	3.67	4.14	8.0	4.3	6.4	0.3	9.9	1.19
2007	ATL	MLB	24	3	3	2	53	2	56	57	29	45	5	49.0%	.306	1	1.52	4.52	4.74	4.70	8.9	4.0	6.6	0.8	6.3	0.60

Breakout: 28% Improve: 56% Collapse: 17% Attrition: 32%   Comparables: Jeff Musselman, Kevin Saucier, Gerry Arrigo, Gary Ross

Short and squat, McBride's built for the bullpen. He usually works around 89 to 92 MPH, and his slider is fairly good at giving lefties fits (on his career, lefties have hit a mere .179/.245/.276 against him). You'd like to see better control from your LOOGY, but he's not giving up many big flies. Only 23, he has time to fix his control issues.

Peter Moylan

Bats: R Throws: R Height: 6' 3" Weight: 220 Born: November 30, 1999 Age: 28

YEAR	TEAM	LVL	AGE	W	L	SV	G	GS	IP	H	BB	SO	HR	GB%	BABIP	STUFF	WHIP	ERA	PERA	EQERA	EQH9	EQBB9	EQSO9	EQHR9	VORP	WXRL
2006	RIC	AAA		0	1	7	1	35	0	56²	61	38	54	4	63.4%	.343	-4	1.76	6.41	6.01	7.55	10.1	6.6	6.4	1.0	-12.1	—
2006	ATL	MLB		0	0	0	0	15	0	15	18	5	14	1	58.3%	.362	9	1.53	4.80	3.11	4.60	9.8	2.3	7.5	0.6	2.0	0.24
2007	ATL	MLB	28	3	4	1	62	3	66¹	74	38	49	7	57.0%	.324	-8	1.69	5.34	5.57	5.60	9.8	4.4	6.0	0.8	0.9	0.20

Breakout: 37% Improve: 67% Collapse: 14% Attrition: 9%   Comparables: Tyler Yates, Jeff Heaverlo, Steve Green, Rodney Ormond

Peter Moylan was an amazing comeback story in 2006. Spotted pitching for Australia in the World Baseball Classic, he was subsequently brought back to America for the first time since his days as a Twins farmhand in 1997. The sidearmer flings a decent fastball and slider, but he needs to dramatically improve his control or he'll be a go-back story in 2007.

Chad Paronto

Bats: R Throws: R Height: 6' 5" Weight: 250 Born: July 28, 1975 Age: 31

YEAR	TEAM	LVL	AGE	W	L	SV	G	GS	IP	H	BB	SO	HR	GB%	BABIP	STUFF	WHIP	ERA	PERA	EQERA	EQH9	EQBB9	EQSO9	EQHR9	VORP	WXRL
2004	MEM	AAA	28	5	3	4	47	0	55	46	25	38	3	—	.259	-6	1.29	2.13	4.99	3.58	7.2	4.4	4.6	0.5	12.4	—
2005	NAS	AAA	29	3	1	4	27	0	39¹	40	19	38	1	55.1%	.345	4	1.50	2.75	3.96	4.08	9.1	4.3	6.4	0.2	6.7	—
2005	RIC	AAA	29	3	1	0	26	0	41	43	17	28	4	51.6%	.322	-15	1.46	3.95	5.34	4.24	10.0	4.2	4.7	1.1	6.1	—
2006	RIC	AAA	30	1	1	4	12	0	17	17	3	15	1	56.6%	.308	5	1.18	1.06	3.88	2.08	8.8	1.6	5.7	1.0	6.8	—
2006	ATL	MLB	30	2	3	0	65	0	56²	53	19	41	5	43.2%	.293	4	1.27	3.17	3.92	3.39	7.9	2.6	5.9	0.6	14.8	-0.42
2007	ATL	MLB	31	2	2	2	48	0	49¹	52	20	34	5	48.0%	.302	-6	1.46	4.42	4.69	4.58	9.3	3.2	5.6	0.8	6.4	0.50

Breakout: 5% Improve: 24% Collapse: 59% Attrition: 22%   Comparables: Paul Reuschel, Tom Timmermann, Matt Karchner, Tony Fiore

Back in the majors for the first time since 2003, Paronto didn't merely peep in and play tourist, he managed to stick around and have a career year. He also managed to give up a significant number of line drives without suffering proportionate damage. If things even out in 2007, he'll be back in the minors but quick. Until then, he's the latest successful reclamation project from an organization with a good track record finding out-of-nowhere relief help.

Horacio Ramirez

Bats: L Throws: L　　Height: 6' 1"　Weight: 210　Born: November 24, 1979　Age: 27

YEAR	TEAM	LVL	AGE	W	L	SV	G	GS	IP	H	BB	SO	HR	GB%	BABIP	STUFF	WHIP	ERA	PERA	EQERA	EQH9	EQBB9	EQSO9	EQHR9	VORP	WXRL
2004	ATL	MLB	24	2	4	0	10	9	60¹	51	30	31	7	—	.234	1	1.34	2.39	5.10	3.65	7.3	3.9	4.1	0.9	14.6	1.90
2005	ATL	MLB	25	11	9	0	33	32	202¹	214	67	80	31	49.6%	.282	-16	1.39	4.63	5.41	4.91	9.2	2.7	3.3	1.3	17.5	3.38
2006	ATL	MLB	26	5	5	0	14	14	76¹	85	31	37	6	54.8%	.312	3	1.52	4.48	4.44	4.42	9.3	3.2	3.9	0.6	9.2	2.22
2007	SEA	MLB	27	5	9	0	30	20	118¹	142	44	53	14	52.0%	.309	-8	1.57	5.22	5.16	5.16	10.4	3.0	3.8	1.0	3.1	1.10

Breakout: 9%　Improve: 33%　Collapse: 31%　Attrition: 5%　　Comparables: Greg Hibbard, Paul Kilgus, John Curtis, Frank Baumann

Ramirez couldn't stay healthy through a second consecutive season in 2006, losing time to both a fatigued hamstring and torn ligament in his middle finger. When healthy, Ramirez tries to elicit weak ground balls from hitters, resulting in excessive nibbling and high pitch counts, which in turn result in high walk rates and short outings. This makes him a poor choice as a starter despite decent ERAs. The Mariners were expecting a fourth starter when they traded the electric Rafael Soriano for him, but considering his history of poor health, his lousy peripherals, and the move to a more challenging league, they'll be lucky to get someone who deserves to start at all.

Ken Ray

Bats: R Throws: R　　Height: 6' 2"　Weight: 200　Born: November 27, 1974　Age: 32

YEAR	TEAM	LVL	AGE	W	L	SV	G	GS	IP	H	BB	SO	HR	GB%	BABIP	STUFF	WHIP	ERA	PERA	EQERA	EQH9	EQBB9	EQSO9	EQHR9	VORP	WXRL
2004	WNS	A+	29	12	8	1	29	18	123²	124	43	99	12	—	.309	-33	1.35	4.07	6.58	6.08	10.4	4.2	4.6	1.9	-6.2	—
2005	RIC	AAA	30	2	4	0	17	10	67	68	35	40	6	45.2%	.307	-10	1.54	3.90	5.88	4.93	9.6	5.3	4.0	1.0	4.9	—
2006	ATL	MLB	31	1	1	5	69	0	67²	66	38	50	9	38.0%	.291	-5	1.54	4.52	4.86	4.37	8.2	4.4	5.9	1.0	9.1	0.59
2007	KCA	MLB	32	2	3	1	44	1	51²	63	30	33	8	43.0%	.322	-17	1.78	6.21	5.92	5.60	10.0	4.9	5.3	1.1	-2.7	0.20

Breakout: 13%　Improve: 28%　Collapse: 41%　Attrition: 34%　　Comparables: Dave Madison, Brian Boehringer, Mel Queen, Juan Acevedo

The last time Kenny Ray hit the majors, he was throwing a popgun fastball for one of the worst relief corps in major league history. Seven years later, he returned with slightly better command, and had his first-ever taste of big league success, including a brief stint as the Braves closer. That's great for Ken Ray, but not so great for the Braves. Fortunately, their suspension of disbelief only stretched so far, and they allowed Ray to be reunited with the Royals via the waiver wire.

Chris Reitsma

Bats: R Throws: R　　Height: 6' 5"　Weight: 235　Born: December 31, 1977　Age: 29

YEAR	TEAM	LVL	AGE	W	L	SV	G	GS	IP	H	BB	SO	HR	GB%	BABIP	STUFF	WHIP	ERA	PERA	EQERA	EQH9	EQBB9	EQSO9	EQHR9	VORP	WXRL
2004	ATL	MLB	26	6	4	2	84	0	79²	89	20	60	9	—	.328	1	1.37	4.07	3.92	4.30	9.7	2.0	6.0	0.9	12.4	0.94
2005	ATL	MLB	27	3	6	15	76	0	73¹	79	14	42	3	54.0%	.310	6	1.27	3.93	3.16	4.06	9.3	1.6	4.7	0.4	12.9	0.66
2006	ATL	MLB	28	1	2	8	27	0	28	46	8	13	7	51.8%	.364	-32	1.93	8.68	6.07	7.67	13.8	2.1	3.7	1.8	-8.4	-0.23
2007	SEA	MLB	29	2	3	6	36	0	43²	51	11	22	5	51%	.307	-9	1.41	4.32	4.44	4.25	10.2	2.0	4.2	0.9	5.7	0.6

Breakout: 39%　Improve: 65%　Collapse: 18%　Attrition: 33%　　Comparables: Tom Morgan, Antonio Alfonseca, Steve Crawford, Tom Buskey

In an awful snippet of a season, Reitsma somehow induced infield flies on over 20 percent of his fly balls, but saw another 25 percent clear the outfield wall. As Freddy Mercury in "Bohemian Rapsody," "Any way the wind blows . . ." Shut down in July for ulnar transposition surgery, it's not clear when he'll be ready to pitch, or for whom. Reitsma was rumored to be in high demand after the Braves non-tendered him, but no one could really say why.

Dan Smith

Bats: L Throws: L　　Height: 6' 5"　Weight: 250　Born: September 9, 1983　Age: 23

YEAR	TEAM	LVL	AGE	W	L	SV	G	GS	IP	H	BB	SO	HR	GB%	BABIP	STUFF	WHIP	ERA	PERA	EQERA	EQH9	EQBB9	EQSO9	EQHR9	VORP	WXRL
2004	DNV	Rk	20	3	1	1	14	2	39²	24	16	52	2	—	.256	0	1.01	2.27	6.14	4.00	7.8	5.8	5.5	1.2	6.4	—
2005	ROM	A	21	3	2	5	19	0	33¹	24	18	45	1	41.3%	.324	15	1.26	1.89	4.69	3.45	8.0	6.3	7.2	0.6	7.5	—
2005	MYR	A+	21	2	2	6	25	0	38	33	17	32	1	30.9%	.294	-3	1.32	2.61	4.30	3.35	8.1	4.3	4.8	0.5	9.4	—
2006	MIS	AA	22	3	6	0	28	8	60	41	32	86	3	36.6%	.317	24	1.22	3.15	4.09	4.88	7.5	4.7	9.2	0.8	4.7	—
2007	ATL	MLB	23	3	4	1	26	8	65¹	64	37	59	10	37.0%	.292	5	1.55	4.98	5.41	5.03	8.6	4.5	7.4	1.3	4.9	0.80

Breakout: 9%　Improve: 25%　Collapse: 48%　Attrition: 12%　　Comparables: Fernando Cabrera, Scott Sobkowiak, Dan Meyer, Chad Hutchinson

Smith's got a good breaking ball and strikes out a ton of batters, but, like everyone else in the upper levels of the organization, he walks around five batters per nine innings. He doesn't allow a lot of balls out of the infield, but the free passes are worrisome. Still, considering the state of the Braves pen, he might be worth a flyer after gaining some experience in Triple-A.

John Smoltz   Bats: R   Throws: R   Height: 6′ 3″   Weight: 220   Born: December 31, 1969   Age: 40

YEAR	TEAM	LVL	AGE	W	L	SV	G	GS	IP	H	BB	SO	HR	GB%	BABIP	STUFF	WHIP	ERA	PERA	EQERA	EQH9	EQBB9	EQSO9	EQHR9	VORP	WXRL
2004	ATL	MLB	37	0	1	44	73	0	81²	75	13	85	8	—	.315	26	1.08	2.75	2.90	2.82	8.0	1.3	8.2	0.8	26.7	7.00
2005	ATL	MLB	38	14	7	0	33	33	229²	210	53	169	18	48.9%	.284	26	1.15	3.06	3.44	3.42	8.0	1.9	6.0	0.7	60.1	6.80
2006	ATL	MLB	39	16	9	0	35	35	232	221	55	211	23	48.0%	.306	33	1.19	3.49	3.39	3.36	8.1	1.9	7.3	0.8	61.9	7.51
2007	ATL	MLB	40	14	10	0	36	31	212	207	54	166	21	47.0%	.293	17	1.23	3.68	3.81	3.81	8.6	2.0	6.4	0.8	45.2	6.30

Breakout: 4%   Improve: 21%   Collapse: 28%   Attrition: 2%   Comparables: Gaylord Perry, Roger Clemens, Don Sutton, Dennis Martinez

Smoltz turns 40 in May. Note that PECOTA picked some real greats as comparables for him. All of them kept rolling past 40 with varying degrees of success. Clemens, of course, is the most dominant quatrogenarian pitcher of all time, with a cumulative ERA of 2.83 from his 40th year onwards. Perry threw his spitter into his 44th year, declining towards the league average in his last three seasons. Sutton, who might have done a little doctoring of the ball to keep his edge, lasted until Tommy Lasorda ran him off the Dodgers at age 43. He, too, was roughly league average in his forties. Martinez also made it to 43. He was spectacular at 40, but rapidly declined after that. To put the lessons of these three in clearer perspective, 43 pitchers have thrown 150 or more innings in a season at age 40. Twenty-seven have done it at 41. Fourteen have done it at 42. Just six of them had an ERA below league average. Just eight have done it at 43, and that group included two spitballers, two knuckleballers, Cy Young, Nolan Ryan, and Jamie Moyer. You know—freaks. Smoltz is signed through 2007, and he's probably a safe bet for this year. Assuming he wants to pitch beyond that, perhaps to build up his counting stats for the shallower Hall of Fame voters, the team that signs him will be rolling the dice.

Phil Stockman   Bats: R   Throws: R   Height: 6′ 8″   Weight: 250   Born: January 25, 1980   Age: 27

YEAR	TEAM	LVL	AGE	W	L	SV	G	GS	IP	H	BB	SO	HR	GB%	BABIP	STUFF	WHIP	ERA	PERA	EQERA	EQH9	EQBB9	EQSO9	EQHR9	VORP	WXRL
2004	ELP	AA	24	1	3	0	6	6	27	17	20	21	1	—	.213	9	1.37	2.67	7.01	4.44	5.5	8.2	4.4	0.7	3.4	—
2004	TUC	AAA	24	3	2	0	12	12	56¹	60	36	35	6	—	.302	-4	1.71	5.75	6.05	5.43	8.5	5.9	4.2	0.9	1.1	—
2005	TEN	AA	25	1	3	1	47	1	36	31	24	30	2	33.3%	.293	-12	1.53	3.25	6.68	4.67	8.3	7.0	4.9	1.0	3.6	—
2005	TUC	AAA	25	1	1	0	17	4	31²	35	27	16	4	40.7%	.301	-21	1.96	6.25	6.98	7.52	9.5	7.2	3.3	1.1	-6.9	—
2006	RIC	AAA	26	0	0	2	18	0	33	13	10	41	0	31.8%	.200	33	0.70	0.82	2.59	1.38	3.9	3.0	8.5	0.3	15.3	—
2007	ATL	MLB	27	3	3	1	28	4	54¹	50	35	50	7	37.0%	.285	1	1.58	4.96	5.27	5.04	8.2	5.1	7.4	1.1	4.0	0.50

Breakout: 9%   Improve: 25%   Collapse: 49%   Attrition: 37%   Comparables: Jim Britton, Blake Stein, Jim Kern, Bill Wertz

A big Aussie rescued from the Snakes, Stockman managed to sneak up on baseball even more successfully than his countryman Moylan did. He can dial up a low-to-mid-90s fastball and tie hitters up with a nice curve. Poised to help the Braves fix their pen problems, he suffered a season-ending hamstring injury four games into his major league career. He'll be back this year as something of a high up-side dark horse behind more familiar names such as Paronto or Yates.

John Thomson   Bats: R   Throws: R   Height: 6′ 3″   Weight: 220   Born: October 1, 1973   Age: 33

YEAR	TEAM	LVL	AGE	W	L	SV	G	GS	IP	H	BB	SO	HR	GB%	BABIP	STUFF	WHIP	ERA	PERA	EQERA	EQH9	EQBB9	EQSO9	EQHR9	VORP	WXRL
2004	ATL	MLB	30	14	8	0	33	33	198¹	210	52	133	20	—	.313	15	1.32	3.72	3.95	4.27	9.2	2.1	5.3	0.8	33.8	4.96
2005	ATL	MLB	31	4	6	0	17	17	98²	111	28	61	6	47.6%	.324	17	1.41	4.47	3.63	4.80	9.8	2.3	5.1	0.5	9.7	1.64
2006	ATL	MLB	32	2	7	0	18	15	80¹	93	32	46	11	45.0%	.318	-7	1.56	4.82	4.82	5.51	9.6	3.0	4.6	1.1	-1.8	0.93
2007	TOR	MLB	33	4	5	0	25	12	81¹	99	25	42	12	47%	.309	-9	1.52	5.53	5.00	5.22	9.9	2.6	4.3	1.2	2.7	0.7

Breakout: 10%   Improve: 34%   Collapse: 46%   Attrition: 28%   Comparables: Duane Pillette, Dock Ellis, Don Cardwell, Bob Walk

Thomson is a reminder that not every veteran starter comes to Atlanta, takes a sprinkle of fairy dust, and becomes a world-beater forever after. Hits, homers, walks, runs, earned or unearned, you name it, Thomson surrendered them with an alacrity that made him an honorary French citizen. He also got hurt frequently enough to get sympathy cards from Super Dave Osborne. As of late December, there's talk of his signing with the Mariners, which seems like a perfect match of low expectations and unhappy outcomes.

Oscar Villarreal   Bats: L   Throws: R   Height: 6′ 0″   Weight: 215   Born: November 22, 1981   Age: 25

YEAR	TEAM	LVL	AGE	W	L	SV	G	GS	IP	H	BB	SO	HR	GB%	BABIP	STUFF	WHIP	ERA	PERA	EQERA	EQH9	EQBB9	EQSO9	EQHR9	VORP	WXRL
2004	ARI	MLB	22	0	2	0	17	0	18	25	7	17	3	—	.415	1	1.78	7.00	4.49	5.79	12.1	2.9	7.2	1.4	-2.3	-0.26
2005	ARI	MLB	23	2	0	0	11	0	13²	11	6	5	2	33.3%	.225	-26	1.24	5.26	6.18	4.50	7.1	3.9	3.2	1.3	0.7	0.14
2006	ATL	MLB	24	9	1	0	58	4	92¹	93	27	55	13	47.8%	.278	-8	1.30	3.61	4.68	3.68	8.4	2.3	4.8	1.1	20.7	1.52
2007	ATL	MLB	25	4	4	2	51	3	77¹	83	26	49	10	47.0%	.293	-5	1.40	4.57	4.70	4.72	9.4	2.6	5.1	1.0	9.2	0.90

Breakout: 9%   Improve: 28%   Collapse: 43%   Attrition: 14%   Comparables: Willie Fraser, Howie Judson, Bill Stafford, Jeff Russell

(continued next page)

Oscar Villarreal *(continued)*

Villarreal mostly worked out of the bullpen after arriving from Arizona, but was thrown into the breach as a starter in a moment of need in late August. It's a bit difficult to determine what his role might be this year, but he's a hard thrower, doesn't walk many batters, and put close to 50 percent of his batted balls on the ground. He's not yet a key cog in the bullpen, but he could be.

Tyler Yates — Bats: R Throws: R — Height: 6′ 4″ Weight: 240 Born: August 7, 1977 Age: 29

YEAR	TEAM	LVL	AGE	W	L	SV	G	GS	IP	H	BB	SO	HR	GB%	BABIP	STUFF	WHIP	ERA	PERA	EQERA	EQH9	EQBB9	EQSO9	EQHR9	VORP	WXRL
2004	NOR	AAA	26	6	2	4	30	1	39²	28	22	43	2	—	.257	13	1.26	3.17	4.56	4.62	6.9	5.5	7.6	0.5	4.2	—
2004	NYN	MLB	26	2	4	0	21	7	46²	61	25	35	6	—	.355	-12	1.84	6.36	4.95	6.56	11.6	4.3	5.8	1.1	-6.8	0.03
2006	ATL	MLB	28	2	5	1	56	0	50	42	31	46	6	41.3%	.273	8	1.46	3.96	4.54	3.83	7.1	4.7	7.3	0.9	10.4	-0.63
2007	ATL	MLB	29	2	2	2	45	0	46²	46	27	40	5	48.0%	.300	-1	1.55	4.48	4.87	4.64	8.6	4.5	7.0	0.9	5.6	0.50

Breakout: 23% Improve: 50% Collapse: 24% Attrition: 28% Comparables: Matt Karchner, Fred Lasher, Frank Wills, Turk Wendell

Yates was much better with the Braves than he had been with the Mets in 2004, but he still wasn't all that good. Bobby Cox called for a lot of intentional passes in 2006, but even allowing for his, Yates was pretty wild. His sub-4.00 ERA was largely the result of a very high rate of stranding baserunners. Like Paronto, he's due for a major correction.

Lineouts

PLAYER	TEAM	LVL	AGE	PA	R	2B	3B	HR	RBI	BB	SO	SB-CS	SPEED	AVG/OBP/SLG	MLVr	EqAVG/OBP/SLG	EqA	VORP
SS R. Fontaine*	DNV	Rk	20	241	42	11	0	4	25	37	45	4-2	4.8	.296/.411/.412	.278	.265/.339/.349	.245	9.8
SS L. Hernandez#	MIS	AA	22	413	39	12	4	1	29	20	46	4-4	5.1	.268/.308/.329	-.057	.271/.305/.344	.228	0.2
	RIC	AAA	22	74	3	4	0	1	5	0	8	0-1	4.0	.192/.192/.288	-.389	.178/.189/.260	.156	-8.2
LF J. Johnson*	BRA	Rk	17	127	13	6	1	1	16	12	49	2-0	25.4	.184/.260/.281	-.182	.144/.203/.195	.155	-61.7
1B B. Jordan	ATL	MLB	39	101	11	2	0	3	10	7	23	0-0	3.5	.231/.287/.352	-.203	.231/.287/.352	.227	-3.5
OF C. Loadenthal*	MYR	A+	24	434	64	13	2	7	48	62	67	25-10	5.9	.323/.425/.427	.265	.296/.373/.392	.272	8.5
	MIS	AA	24	56	7	2	0	1	4	6	5	5-0	7.6	.167/.268/.271	-.240	.163/.250/.265	.210	-5.6
RF J. Romak	ROM	A	20	420	55	26	2	16	68	59	102	3-1	3.4	.247/.369/.471	.216	.228/.316/.417	.253	-5.1
C C. Sammons	MYR	A+	23	407	36	21	0	8	56	32	65	4-4	3.2	.258/.323/.383	.002	.227/.272/.331	.213	-15.7

PLAYER	TEAM	LVL	AGE	W	L	SV	IP	H	BB	SO	HR	GB%	BABIP	STUFF	WHIP	ERA	PERA	EqERA	EqH9	EqBB9	EqSO9	EqHR9	VORP
N. Feliz	BRA	Rk	18	0	2	2	29¹	20	14	42	0	—	.346	25	1.17	4.02	3.80	5.53	8.1	5.5	7.5	0.3	0.2
W. Franklin*	RIC	AAA	32	2	3	4	53	39	17	52	2	—	.266	7	1.06	2.38	3.69	3.25	6.8	3.2	6.3	0.5	13.8
B. Jones*	ROM	A	19	5	5	1	110²	125	83	101	8	—	.357	-11	1.89	5.64	7.16	8.29	11.1	8.3	5.0	1.5	-31.8
J. Locke*	BRA	Rk	18	4	3	0	32	38	5	38	4	—	.427	-5	1.34	4.22	8.36	6.52	15.2	1.9	6.5	4.3	-3.0
M. Remlinger*	ATL	MLB	40	2	4	2	22¹	27	9	19	2	—	.352	2	1.61	4.04	3.98	3.91	10.6	3.1	7.0	0.8	3.9
Z. Schreiber	MYR	A+	24	0	0	3	16	13	8	18	1	—	.286	1	1.31	1.13	5.37	1.76	8.8	5.3	6.5	1.2	6.5
	MIS	AA	24	1	2	21	39	26	28	45	3	—	.253	3	1.38	2.54	6.50	3.62	7.5	7.0	7.0	1.4	8.2
J. Shiell	RIC	AAA	29	2	4	0	52²	51	16	34	3	—	.306	1	1.28	4.48	4.59	4.78	8.5	3.1	4.3	0.9	4.8
	ATL	MLB	29	0	2	0	15²	23	9	14	5	—	.375	-10	2.04	8.60	6.74	7.71	12.7	4.4	7.2	2.2	-4.4
W. Startup*	MIS	AA	21	3	0	4	25¹	18	6	29	0	—	.300	25	0.96	0.72	2.61	1.44	7.2	2.2	7.2	0.4	11.6
	RIC	AAA	21	5	2	0	42¹	45	11	38	3	—	.341	5	1.33	3.42	3.90	4.01	9.5	2.5	6.1	0.8	7.5
J. Stevens*	ROM	A	21	2	4	3	62	56	19	48	4	—	.289	-18	1.21	4.06	5.81	6.79	8.9	3.4	4.0	1.3	-8.1
	MYR	A+	21	1	6	0	60²	69	30	33	5	—	.337	-23	1.64	6.43	6.55	8.10	10.9	4.7	3.5	1.5	-16.7

Picked in the second round out of a Florida juco, **Chase Fontaine** made a nice debut last summer. He's a consummate baseball rat whose tools will likely take him to second base eventually. Even the Braves have their limits when it comes to light-hitting middle infielders, as they proved by letting **Luis Hernandez** slip away to the Orioles. **John Johnson** struck out in almost 40 percent of his plate appearances. He gets a mulligan because he was a virginal pro of 17, but until he learns to make better contact he won't be able to exploit his power potential. Given **Brian Jordan**'s fragility, he's probably a couple of years overdue on his retirement. **Carl Loadenthal** hit .368/.459/.510 against right-handers, but he was a 24-year-old in High-A. Predictably, he greeted Double-A Mississippi with a dull thud. A very raw Canadian amateur, **Jamie Romak** is just coming into his own at the plate in his third year as a pro; the other phases of his game are still lagging behind. Clint Sammons is a popular organizational soldier and a heads-up catch-and-throw guy; he might wind up getting Ken Huckaby-style service time someday.

Blaine Boyer had a diagnostic arthroscopy on his right shoulder in April and never made it back to the Braves in 2006. The pen could use his sinker/curve mix. **Neftali Feliz** is a Dominican import who can hit 98 on any gun, and just put the fear of sweet Jeebus into the Gulf Coast League. **John Foster**'s late-2005 elbow injury turned into mid-2006 Tommy John surgery after a failed rehab stint. Released by the Braves, this solid LOOGY could turn up anywhere at any time. On the list of in-season apocalyptic events that tell you it's time to start thinking about next year, calling up **Wayne Franklin** has to rank pretty close to the top. A power lefty arm picked up in the first round of the 2005 draft, **Beau Jones** hasn't shown any more control than Jimmy Walker, a.k.a. "Beau James," the wild and crazy mayor of 1920s New York. Beau James fled to Europe to avoid prosecution for corruption; Beau Jones won't have to do anything more extreme than learn to throw the ball over the plate. **Jeff Locke**, another lefty with low-90s heat, was picked in the second round of the 2006 draft, the rare high school pitcher taken by the Braves from outside the state of Georgia. Brought to be the situational lefty greybeard, **Mike Remlinger** didn't find renewed vigor upon returning to the scene of his previous rebirth and earned his release in June. A bit old for his level, **Zach Schreiber** nevertheless managed to impress with low-90s heat and a can-do bulldoggy sensibility. He could make it. Three years after last pitching in the majors, **Jason Shiell** was plucked out of the independent Atlantic League in a desperate attempt to put bodies in the Atlanta bullpen. The way he pitched, he'll be back in a Somerset Patriots uniform this summer. A college hurler in an organization full of high school products, **Will Startup** has been on an aggressive timetable. A lefty, but not a LOOGY, he may end up as a short reliever with his low-90s heat and hard slider. Of course, he'll have to change his name to Will Setup. There was a time not so long ago when **Jake Stevens** was seen as a top prospect, but he's lost velocity and command, and has fallen far from his teenage glory days. Welcome to the club, Jake.

Manager: Bobby Cox

Year	Team	W-L	Pythag +/-	Avg PC	100 +P	120 +P	QS	BQS	REL	REL w Zero R	IBB	SUBS	PH	PH Avg	PH HR	SB2	CS2	SB3	CS3	SAC Att	SAC %	POS SAC	Squeeze	Swing	In Play
2004	ATL	96-66	0	94.2	64	4	94	8	481	317	50	53	242	.277	5	83	27	3	3	95	79.0%	35	2	125	84
2005	ATL	90-72	-2	93.9	69	1	75	14	483	319	52	54	245	.226	3	81	31	11	1	107	70.1%	29	3	109	84
2006	ATL	79-83	-6	92.6	61	8	70	6	522	342	69	51	299	.277	8	49	34	4	1	105	74.3%	25	6	106	78

Bobby Cox has been at the helm throughout the Braves division title run and, like a literal-minded sea captain, is now going down with the ship. It's not Cox's fault that there was little to work with in the bullpen, though he kept trying, using the most relievers of his career and the second-most in the majors. Cox was caught in something of a vicious cycle. He had just six blown quality starts (that is, after getting a good game out of his starters, he didn't push them until they broke), but getting the best out of his starters meant getting the worst of his pen, a group that was fourth worst in the majors with just 1.24 WXRL. Trying to manage his way past this pen's limitations, Cox tied his career high for intentional walks. On offense, he often pushed the right buttons when going to his bench. He set a career high in pinch-hitters used and—primarily using Pete Orr, Matt Diaz, and Wilson Betemit, with some late-season help from Daryle Ward—was rewarded with the best pinch-hit average in the majors. That aside, Cox did little to force the offense; on a team without much speed he didn't try to run, and he has always disdained the hit and run.

Baltimore Orioles

Has Peter Angelos lost Baltimore?

Not the team, but the city. It seems hard to imagine now, but there was a time when Angelos was regarded as the savior for Baltimore baseball. It was Angelos, native Baltimorean, newly rich from asbestos litigation, who bought the Orioles from out-of-town ownership in 1992, ending the threat of relocation once and for all. Don't underestimate how painful a threat that was to Charm City; this was a town that had lost its NBA franchise in the seventies and its NFL franchise in the eighties. There was a real fear that previous owners would carry the MLB franchise to Northern Virginia, so close that they wouldn't necessarily need the permission of another team to do it. It was quelling that fear that made Angelos the local hero, and got the Maryland General Assembly to fund Camden Yards.

Angelos started out well, hiring good people—Davey Johnson, Pat Gillick—to run the team. His opposition to the other owners during the big strike of 1994–95—questioning their business acumen, refusing to field replacement players—garnered him positive press and helped avoid the public antagonism that followed other teams out of the strike. The combination of good press, good management, a new standard-setting stadium, and the culmination of Cal Ripken's epic quest to surpass Lou Gehrig, drove Oriole attendance to the top of the majors. That success carried over into total revenue, in which the Orioles were second in all of baseball (to the Yankees) from 1995 to 1997, and onto the field, where they won a wild card in 1996 and a division title in 1997.

Those good times ended in the decisive Game Six of the 1997 League Championship Series, when the Indians'

> ## ORIOLES PROSPECTUS
>
> **2006 record:** 70–92; Fourth place, AL East
>
> **Pythagenport record:** 68–94
>
> **Runs scored per game:** 4.74 (10th in AL)
>
> **Runs allowed per game:** 5.55 (13th in AL)
>
> **Team EqA:** .259 (8th in AL)
>
> **2006 Batters Age:** 30.7 (3rd oldest in AL)
>
> **2006 Pitchers Age:** 28.4 (4th youngest in AL)
>
> **Ballpark:** Oriole Park; Slight pitcher's park; Park Factor of .985
>
> **2006:** Following their eighth fourth-place finish in nine years, Peter Angelos is insisting the O's control all rights to the number four throughout baseball.
>
> **2007:** Papa's got a brand new bullpen and some fresh free agent mediocrities, but the ballpark remains the attraction, not the team.

Tony Fernandez hit a two-out solo homer off Armando Benitez in the top of the eleventh inning. Soon after, the manager and owner got into an argument over who deserved credit for the Oriole resurgence, and Davey Johnson was gone. The '97 Orioles under Johnson won 98 games; none of his successors have been able to win 80. Upper management also changed, most notably and egregiously to Syd Thrift, who became general manager after the 1999 season. Years of bad drafts and bad signings have crippled the team, and while there are some signs of improvement, chronic mismanagement has caused fundamental problems that will linger for years to come.

The Orioles have since lost several of the advantages that that they had in the nineties. In 1996, when the NFL's Cleveland Browns moved to Baltimore and became the Ravens, the Orioles were no longer the only game in town; gone was the sentiment among locals that "win or lose, we have to be support the Orioles because they're all we have." Camden Yards lost its novelty, as imitations sprang up all around the country. The hard feelings from the strike slowly evaporated in other cities, giving them a relative boost that the Orioles, having avoided those hard feelings in the first place, did not share.

Finally, there are the Nationals. Angelos fought the move of any team to Washington for years, arguing that a substantial portion—he claimed 25 percent—of his attendance came from the Washington, D.C. market. When he finally lost that battle after the 2004 season, he got a lucrative package of consolation prizes from MLB, the most important being control over the regional sports network, MASN, which will televise both Oriole and Nationals games. A dispute between Angelos and Comcast, the dominant cable provider in the D.C. area, kept Nationals game untelevised through most of the 2006 season. While the dispute was as much Comcast's fault, the acrimony created by the years he spent obstructing D.C. baseball meant that Angelos received the most blame. Now that they have a team of their own, the Washington-area fans that used to attend Oriole games have turned on Angelos for good. Even if the Nationals were to move to Las Vegas tomorrow, those fans would be lost.

Nine years of losing have generated those same dangerous feelings in Baltimore itself. Attendance has been slipping ever since 1997, despite the fact that baseball as a whole enjoyed a measured growth. In 2006 Baltimore's attendance crashed to its lowest level since the 1988, when Birds started the season 0–21, dropping by 18 percent from 2005. Revenues have stagnated. By 1997, at a time when the average major league team earned only $79 million, Oriole revenues had reached $135 million, but they stayed fixed for the next six years. The average team saw their revenues double between 1997 and 2005, but the Orioles experienced a mere 16 percent increase over that period. Once second in baseball, their revenues now rank 15th, smack in the middle of the major league pack.

Peter Angelos controls the team in a way beyond all other owners in the game right now, even the famously autocratic George Steinbrenner. In one of his early years as owner, Angelos overruled his baseball men on a proposed trade; the players not dealt were instrumental in the late run that carried Baltimore to the wild card in 1996. Angelos seems to have taken away the lesson that he was more prescient than his baseball men, and ever since has capriciously wielded his owner's veto on free agent signings, trades, and even draft picks, robbing team management of its initiative.

Last September, during another meaningless stretch drive in Baltimore, a thousand fans, egged on by a local DJ, staged a mass walkout in the middle of a game to protest Angelos's ownership. It may have been a meaningless stunt, but such stunts can only happen when there is a real current of frustration, anger, and lost hope. That last is Angelos's biggest problem. Fans buy tickets because they hope to see the home team win. If you lose that hope, you lose the fans. By repeatedly failing to deliver a useful product, the Orioles wore down even their most loyal supporters; there is absolutely no belief that things will ever change under the current ownership.

The Orioles did little in the offseason to alleviate local feelings of despair and apathy. They committed $40 million over the next three years to Danys Baez, Chad Bradford, and Jamie Walker, a trio of arms meant to stabilize the bullpen. The Orioles correctly identified a problem with the bullpen (they were eleventh in the AL in WXRL, about 3.5 wins below average) and moved to fix it. Trading away Chris Britton, the second-best reliever on the team a year ago, cuts into some of the value gained. Still, these moves should yield a gain of about four wins, a solid improvement. The only problem is that they stopped there, acting as if this was *the* problem, instead of *a* problem.

The starting rotation was actually worse than the bullpen last year, ranking 13th in the American League in expected wins for starting pitchers (SNLVAR); only the Royals were worse. The only move made here was to replace Rodrigo Lopez with Jaret Wright, for whom Britton was traded. The Orioles' ranking here is a little misleading, since the returning pitchers (Erik Bedard, Daniel Cabrera, Adam Loewen, and Kris Benson) had respectable figures; the team total was dragged down by some awesomely bad performances from Bruce Chen, Jim Johnson, Hayden Penn, and Russ Ortiz, all of whom were below zero in SNLVAR. The Orioles gave 24 starts to this quartet, who combined for −2.2 wins, a total unmatched by any group of sub-zeroes elsewhere (only the Royals and Cubs gave more starts to below-zero pitchers). The four produced a real-life record of 0–15, and gave up 161 runs in 162 innings of work. Simply replacing them with "normal" bad performances is going to save the Orioles another couple of wins.

The Orioles were also damaged, more than any other team, by the World Baseball Classic. There was a lot of concern last spring that the tournament would interfere with spring training, especially for the pitchers. The O's were especially worried because they were trying to break in a new catcher (Ramon Hernandez) and a new pitching coach (Leo Mazzone), and thus already had more than the usual concerns about getting pitchers ready. Baltimore sent 11 players to the WBC, more than any other team in the majors, including Erik Bedard, Daniel Cabrera, Adam Loewen, Rodrigo Lopez, and Bruce Chen, pitchers who would ultimately start 119 of Baltimore's 162 games; Kris Benson was the only regular starter who stayed put in Ft. Lauderdale. Our own Nate Silver did a study last May showing that the WBC seemed to have a brutal effect on starting pitchers. Starters that participated went on to post regular season ERAs about a run and a half higher than expected (relief pitchers and position players were mostly unaffected). Consider the ERAs of Oriole starters before and after the All-Star break (see table 1).

All of the WBC pitchers except Chen (who won't be back) were substantially better after the break, another part of the reason the Orioles felt reasonably comfortable staying with essentially the same rotation. If these pitchers

Table 1. Pitcher Performance Before and After the All-Star break

Pitcher	Before	After	Change
Bedard	4.28	3.10	−1.18
Cabrera	5.15	4.26	−0.89
Lopez	6.77	4.76	−2.01
Chen	6.78	7.24	+0.46
Loewen	7.12	4.72	−2.40
Benson	4.79	4.86	+0.07

had pitched all year like they did after the All-Star break, the Orioles would have saved more than 50 run and likely gained five games in the standings—and perhaps more, since without the rotation struggles they might never have experimented with Russ Ortiz.

The only offensive changes this winter were the signings of Jay Payton, who will presumably take over as the regular left fielder, and Aubrey Huff, who will split time at several positions. Huff will be a useful addition to the extent that his versatility is used aggressively to keep the Orioles from using replacement-level substitutes at any of the corner positions and designated hitter, but his second-tier bat won't make a significant dent in the team's offensive shortcomings. The addition of Payton was a good move in the sense that the Orioles recognized a problem. Orioles left fielders had an EqA of just .249, easily the worst mark in the major leagues. The trouble is that Payton's EqA over the last four years has only been about .260, meaning the position is still broken from any reasonable standpoint, and in desperate need of an upgrade.

The same is true of all of the traditional power positions, except for right field, where Nick Markakis emerged as a burgeoning star. Orioles first basemen were 20th in the majors in EqA, their third basemen were 23rd, and their designated hitters were 10th among the 14 AL teams. For the last several years, the team has relied on a series of similar players for these spots, mediocrities such as Jay Gibbons, Kevin Millar, and Jeff Conine. The farm system has added some very promising players in the last two drafts, but they are still way down in the minors. Jeff Fiorentino, who projects as another Conine-type player, is really the only hitter in the organization positioned to move into the majors this year.

Nor can they count on any help from the bench. Orioles' pinch-hitters have been abysmal for five years running, compiling a .146/.224/.202 batting line over that time, but last year's crew (5-57, no extra base hits, two walks) set new lows for pinch-hitting. Within the 1960-present timeframe presently covered by Retrosheet, the 2006 Orioles set an entire constellation of all-time worst records for pinch-hitters: worst batting average (.088), worst slugging average (.088), worst isolated power (.000, shared with three other teams), worst OBP (.131; interestingly enough, the second- and third-worst OBPs for pinch-hitters also belong to Oriole teams, from 1994 and 2002), fewest total bases (five, shared with two other teams). In 2006, failure was a true team effort, spread over 16 players, led by Luis Matos and Ramon Hernandez each going 0-for-8.

One could look at the Orioles optimistically and say that the pitching in 2007 is likely to improve by 100 runs over 2006, but that's only half the picture. There is no reason to expect a significant improvement on offense. Without that improvement—or, alternatively, an improvement in pitching closer to 200 runs—the Orioles will not contend for a playoff spot. Instead, the current lineup suggests the Orioles will once again be contending for, at best, a .500 record and their ninth fourth-place finish in ten years. If you check another set of standings, the one that tracks the downward spiral from despair to apathy, you'll find the Orioles on top by a wide margin. Or is that on the bottom?

HITTERS

Danny Ardoin C **Bats: R** **Throws: R** Height: 6' 0" Weight: 215 Born: July 8, 1974 Age: 32

YEAR	TEAM	LVL	AGE	PA	R	2B	3B	HR	RBI	BB	SO	SB	CS	SPEED	AVG	OBP	SLG	MLVR	EQAVG	EQOBP	EQSLG	EQA	VORP	DEFENSE	
2004	OKL	AAA	30	291	50	12	0	10	44	41	66	1	1	3.9	.308	.422	.485	.260	.278	.372	.407	.276	14.0	67-C	3
2005	CSP	AAA	31	170	27	12	2	6	24	20	38	3	1	4.9	.338	.438	.577	.363	.289	.371	.456	.284	11.8	39-C	6
2005	COL	MLB	31	248	28	10	0	6	22	20	69	1	1	3.9	.229	.320	.362	-.144	.220	.310	.350	.235	-0.3	68-C	15
2006	COL	MLB	32	120	12	5	1	0	2	8	27	0	0	4.0	.193	.261	.257	-.431	.165	.242	.220	.173	-8.8	32-C	0
2006	BAL	MLB	32	15	2	0	0	0	1	1	6	0	0	3.9	.077	.200	.077	-.849	.000	.133	.000	.083	-2.5		
2007	WAS	MLB	32	309	27	12	1	5	28	27	82	1	1	4.0	.214	.301	.327	-.266	.219	.305	.337	.224	-4.2	75-C	4

Breakout: 31% Improve: 56% Collapse: 20% Attrition: 43%   Comparables: Phil Roof, Haywood Sullivan, Ron Tingley, Dixie Howell

Ardoin's been around practically forever; he made his first appearance in these pages in 1998, when we described him as, "a highly-touted defender" who "can't hit." That's still true today. He hit over .500 last spring, which, combined with a Yorvit Torrealba injury, made him the Opening Day starter for the Rockies. That lasted as long as it takes to say "0 for his first 13." A knee injury knocked him out and he was waived to make room for Chris Iannetta. Picked up by Baltimore, he improved to 1 for his first 13 as an Oriole before getting waived again. He's signed with the Nationals.

Brandon Fahey   UT   Bats: L   Throws: R   Height: 6' 2"   Weight: 160   Born: January 18, 1981   Age: 26

YEAR	TEAM	LVL	AGE	PA	R	2B	3B	HR	RBI	BB	SO	SB	CS	SPEED	AVG	OBP	SLG	MLVR	EQAVG	EQOBP	EQSLG	EQA	VORP	DEFENSE			
2004	FRD	A+	23	212	20	7	0	3	19	22	20	3	3	3.5	.271	.354	.359	.002	.233	.301	.307	.219	-4.8	53-SS	-2		
2004	BOW	AA	23	232	20	7	1	1	15	17	27	3	1	4.4	.236	.293	.293	-.210	.226	.278	.278	.204	-11.1	63-SS	10		
2005	BOW	AA	24	578	63	21	4	3	47	44	71	17	8	5.5	.291	.349	.367	.051	.279	.330	.346	.244	8.9	139-SS	12		
2006	OTT	AAA	25	84	8	1	1	0	3	10	5	4	3	5.9	.279	.402	.324	.046	.257	.373	.300	.249	1.5	19-SS	2		
2006	BAL	MLB	25	286	36	8	2	2	23	23	48	3	3	6.0	.235	.307	.307	-.265	.234	.314	.306	.224	-11.2	43-LF	-1	12-2B	1
2007	BAL	MLB	26	386	41	13	2	2	29	28	50	6	3	5.8	.254	.314	.324	-.214	.252	.317	.329	.236	-4.5	92-SS	3		

Breakout: 30%   Improve: 57%   Collapse: 23%   Attrition: 28%   Comparables: Ramon Vazquez, Jeff Huson, Sonny Jackson, Mickey Morandini

Fahey is one of the skinniest major league players in the game; of the handful of players at or below his 160 pounds, only Arizona's Juan Cruz is as tall as Fahey. As you'd expect from a stick figure, he has absolutely no power. The Orioles used him primarily as a left fielder last year because they didn't really have a better option; that tells you a lot about the state of their minor league system. He should take over the role that the non-tendered David Newhan has filled the last three years. Note that all four of his comps are middle infielders.

Jeff Fiorentino   LF   Bats: L   Throws: R   Height: 6' 1"   Weight: 180   Born: April 14, 1983   Age: 24

YEAR	TEAM	LVL	AGE	PA	R	2B	3B	HR	RBI	BB	SO	SB	CS	SPEED	AVG	OBP	SLG	MLVR	EQAVG	EQOBP	EQSLG	EQA	VORP	DEFENSE			
2004	DEL	A	21	203	40	15	2	10	36	20	50	2	2	5.4	.296	.374	.570	.339	.269	.325	.484	.270	10.4	41-CF	-5		
2005	FRD	A+	22	455	70	18	4	22	66	34	90	12	6	6.1	.286	.346	.508	.164	.251	.296	.430	.247	4.7	70-CF	-7	18-LF	-1
2005	BAL	MLB	22	47	7	2	0	1	5	2	10	1	0	6.5	.250	.277	.364	-.182	.256	.298	.372	.240	-0.4	11-CF	1		
2006	BOW	AA	23	450	63	14	0	13	62	53	58	9	3	5.1	.275	.365	.413	.140	.269	.349	.416	.268	4.7	59-LF	-5	37-CF	5
2006	BAL	MLB	23	50	8	2	0	0	7	7	3	1	0	5.2	.256	.375	.308	-.111	.263	.396	.316	.274	-0.2	12-LF	2		
2007	BAL	MLB	24	506	61	24	2	14	59	42	85	6	3	5.3	.262	.326	.416	-.063	.260	.330	.423	.266	7.0	119-LF	1		

Breakout: 22%   Improve: 54%   Collapse: 20%   Attrition: 10%   Comparables: Curtis Granderson, Kevin Burford, Eric Valent, Ryan Langerhans

Is the real Fiorentino the one who hit .205/.286/.351 in the first three months of 2006 while twice going down with ankle and hamstring injuries, or is he the guy who healed up and hit .358/.450/.495 over the last two months? The answer to questions such as this is almost always somewhere between, which gives us a more or less average ballplayer, without glaring strengths or weaknesses, capable of playing all three outfield positions, but without the bat to justify a starting role.

Jay Gibbons   RF   Bats: L   Throws: L   Height: 6' 0"   Weight: 205   Born: March 2, 1977   Age: 30

YEAR	TEAM	LVL	AGE	PA	R	2B	3B	HR	RBI	BB	SO	SB	CS	SPEED	AVG	OBP	SLG	MLVR	EQAVG	EQOBP	EQSLG	EQA	VORP	DEFENSE			
2004	BAL	MLB	27	380	36	14	1	10	47	29	64	1	1	3.7	.246	.303	.379	-.174	.245	.309	.385	.242	-7.5	57-RF	1	13-1B	0
2005	BAL	MLB	28	518	72	33	3	26	79	28	56	0	0	4.3	.277	.317	.516	.121	.283	.334	.542	.289	24.4	63-RF	6	19-1B	-2
2006	BAL	MLB	29	378	34	23	0	13	46	32	48	0	0	3.2	.277	.341	.458	.042	.277	.349	.472	.279	11.8	40-RF	2		
2007	BAL	MLB	30	463	52	24	1	17	69	35	68	0	0	4.0	.263	.321	.443	-.036	.261	.324	.451	.270	7.2	110-RF	-1		

Breakout: 11%   Improve: 42%   Collapse: 25%   Attrition: 18%   Comparables: Troy O'Leary, Robert Fick, Jim Spencer, Wes Covington

It has been three years since Gibbons stayed healthy through an entire season; this past year it was knees, back, and a pinched nerve that put him out of action. Chronologically he may be 30, but his skills and his injury record are those of a player several years older. There's talk, on and off again, about making him a first baseman, which would finally give the Orioles something more than a non-entity at the position, but Gibbons can't be expected to hold up well, which makes the contract he signed last year ($21 million for 2006 through 2009) look like a bad risk.

Chris Gomez   INF   Bats: R   Throws: R   Height: 6' 1"   Weight: 190   Born: June 16, 1971   Age: 36

YEAR	TEAM	LVL	AGE	PA	R	2B	3B	HR	RBI	BB	SO	SB	CS	SPEED	AVG	OBP	SLG	MLVR	EQAVG	EQOBP	EQSLG	EQA	VORP	DEFENSE			
2004	TOR	MLB	33	377	41	11	1	3	37	28	41	3	2	5.1	.282	.337	.346	-.136	.274	.336	.336	.242	2.5	74-SS	-8	16-1B	-2
2005	BAL	MLB	34	254	27	11	0	1	18	27	17	2	1	3.8	.279	.359	.342	-.057	.288	.379	.358	.267	2.1	27-1B	-1	14-3B	-1
2006	BAL	MLB	35	142	14	7	0	2	17	7	11	1	2	3.3	.341	.387	.439	.156	.344	.399	.450	.288	8.1	16-1B	0	14-2B	-1
2007	BAL	MLB	36	247	26	10	0	3	24	17	23	2	1	4.3	.280	.336	.366	-.101	.278	.339	.371	.256	2.8	61-1B	-3		

Breakout: 13%   Improve: 44%   Collapse: 23%   Attrition: 51%   Comparables: Jack Phillips, Billy Hitchcock, Mark Grudzielanek, Jim Piersall

(continued next page)

Chris Gomez *(continued)*

At the end of August, Gomez was hitting .237. He had disappeared for almost four months after a Joel Zumaya pitch broke his hand, and he struggled to get playing time after returning. Then, in yet another meaningless September for the Orioles, he hit .437, played almost every day, and made it look like he'd had a good year instead of just a good month. The hot September amounts to nice résumé-padding for an otherwise generic utility player; easily-impressed, the Orioles took him back.

Ramon Hernandez   **C**   **Bats: R**   **Throws: R**   Height: 6' 0"   Weight: 225   Born: May 20, 1976   Age: 31

YEAR	TEAM	LVL	AGE	PA	R	2B	3B	HR	RBI	BB	SO	SB	CS	SPEED	AVG	OBP	SLG	MLVR	EQAVG	EQOBP	EQSLG	EQA	VORP	DEFENSE	
2004	SDN	MLB	28	432	45	23	0	18	63	35	45	1	0	3.7	.276	.341	.477	.121	.285	.348	.492	.285	25.0	99-C	5
2005	SDN	MLB	29	392	36	19	2	12	58	18	40	1	0	4.0	.290	.322	.450	.080	.300	.334	.474	.275	20.7	90-C	-2
2006	BAL	MLB	30	560	66	29	2	23	91	43	79	1	0	4.1	.275	.343	.479	.074	.276	.350	.490	.285	28.8	125-C	2
2007	BAL	MLB	31	495	59	25	1	16	68	35	65	1	0	4.0	.276	.333	.445	-.001	.274	.337	.453	.276	20.0	117-C	-1

Breakout: 14%   Improve: 31%   Collapse: 35%   Attrition: 11%   Comparables: Javy Lopez, Bob Brenly, Del Crandall, Terry Steinbach

There was considerable moaning about Hernandez's contract last year, but he made Year One of his four-year deal look awfully good, setting or matching career highs in at-bats, hits, doubles, homers, RBIs, and stolen bases (this was one of the years in which he stole one). That said, setting a career high in at-bats is not a good indicator of future value when you're talking about a 30-year-old catcher. He's been a very steady player for the last four years, so he gets the benefit of the doubt for now.

Val Majewski   **OF**   **Bats: L**   **Throws: L**   Height: 6' 2"   Weight: 215   Born: June 19, 1981   Age: 26

YEAR	TEAM	LVL	AGE	PA	R	2B	3B	HR	RBI	BB	SO	SB	CS	SPEED	AVG	OBP	SLG	MLVR	EQAVG	EQOBP	EQSLG	EQA	VORP	DEFENSE			
2004	BOW	AA	23	476	71	24	5	15	80	33	68	14	4	6.2	.307	.359	.490	.231	.302	.346	.475	.280	19.2	52-LF	-3	41-CF	-2
2006	OTT	AAA	25	366	44	15	6	4	39	37	72	7	8	5.8	.260	.344	.381	.012	.252	.331	.380	.246	-6.1	41-LF	-5	25-RF	1
2007	BAL	MLB	26	399	45	19	3	8	41	28	76	5	4	5.5	.252	.309	.385	-.141	.251	.313	.391	.249	-4.6	95-LF	-3		

Breakout: 10%   Improve: 31%   Collapse: 41%   Attrition: 15%   Comparables: Luke Allen, Raul Ibanez, Len Gabrielson, Mike Frank

At one time seen as one of the organization's top prospects, Majewski's bat couldn't recover from his 2004 shoulder surgery. He did slightly better in the second half of 2006, but showed next to no power. At this point, his prospect status is dead until he does something beyond just showing up for work.

Nick Markakis   **RF**   **Bats: L**   **Throws: L**   Height: 6' 2"   Weight: 195   Born: November 17, 1983   Age: 23

YEAR	TEAM	LVL	AGE	PA	R	2B	3B	HR	RBI	BB	SO	SB	CS	SPEED	AVG	OBP	SLG	MLVR	EQAVG	EQOBP	EQSLG	EQA	VORP	DEFENSE			
2004	DEL	A	20	406	57	22	3	11	64	42	66	12	3	5.5	.299	.371	.470	.203	.272	.328	.410	.258	0.3	62-RF	-4		
2005	FRD	A+	21	401	59	25	1	12	62	43	65	2	1	3.7	.300	.379	.480	.189	.262	.322	.405	.252	-2.6	86-RF	-5		
2005	BOW	AA	21	143	19	16	2	3	30	18	30	0	1	4.2	.339	.420	.573	.476	.333	.406	.563	.322	19.8	19-CF	2	15-RF	-1
2006	BAL	MLB	22	542	72	25	2	16	62	43	72	2	0	4.8	.291	.351	.448	.059	.293	.360	.460	.282	19.4	105-RF	6	23-LF	2
2007	BAL	MLB	23	537	70	28	2	15	68	43	77	4	2	5.2	.289	.348	.446	.036	.287	.352	.453	.283	15.8	126-RF	4		

Breakout: 27%   Improve: 61%   Collapse: 15%   Attrition: 9%   Comparables: Carl Yastrzemski, Carlos May, Rick Manning, Gus Bell

In another year, Markakis's debut performance might have won the Rookie of the Year award, but with all of the young pitching that emerged in the American League in 2006, he had to settle for a distant sixth despite a .311/.364/.532 second-half surge. Of course, most of that power came in a 14-game stretch in August in which he hit 9 of his season total of 16 home runs. The rest of the year he didn't show much pop at all, particularly against lefties (one homer in 119 AB). He may still be catching up from development time lost to being a pitcher-slash-outfielder, and it is certainly true that he has had better-than-average improvement each year, but how far he goes depends on how much sustainable power he develops. The Orioles have nothing to lose by finding out who the real Markakis is.

Kevin Millar   **1B**   **Bats: R**   **Throws: R**   Height: 6' 0"   Weight: 215   Born: September 24, 1971   Age: 35

YEAR	TEAM	LVL	AGE	PA	R	2B	3B	HR	RBI	BB	SO	SB	CS	SPEED	AVG	OBP	SLG	MLVR	EQAVG	EQOBP	EQSLG	EQA	VORP	DEFENSE			
2004	BOS	MLB	32	588	74	36	0	18	74	57	91	1	1	3.6	.297	.383	.474	.136	.292	.379	.470	.293	28.5	57-1B	-1	49-RF	-1
2005	BOS	MLB	33	519	57	28	1	9	50	54	74	0	1	3.4	.272	.355	.399	.005	.274	.365	.410	.274	7.1	90-1B	9	14-LF	-3
2006	BAL	MLB	34	503	64	26	0	15	64	59	74	1	1	3.2	.272	.374	.437	.068	.273	.382	.447	.288	15.5	91-1B	6		
2007	BAL	MLB	35	431	51	20	1	12	55	48	64	1	1	3.9	.262	.353	.420	-.012	.260	.356	.426	.279	8.0	102-1B	0		

Breakout: 13%   Improve: 37%   Collapse: 27%   Attrition: 20%   Comparables: Jeff Conine, Chet Lemon, Todd Zeile, Gil Hodges

When the Orioles signed Millar, they weren't sure if they'd get the "Cowboy Up" Millar of the 2004, or the "Cowboy Down" version from 2005 whose power had completely evaporated. Part of a logjam of Orioles—principally Jeff Conine, Jay Gibbons, and Javy Lopez—vying for playing time at first base and DH last year, Millar started out very weakly but improved as the season went on. Gradually taking over full-time as trades thinned his competition, Millar closed out the year at an All-Star level. Re-signed for 2007, he'll once again have to earn his at-bats thanks to the addition of Aubrey Huff.

Melvin Mora   **3B**   **Bats: R**   **Throws: R**   Height: 5' 11" Weight: 200 Born: February 2, 1972   Age: 35

YEAR	TEAM	LVL	AGE	PA	R	2B	3B	HR	RBI	BB	SO	SB	CS	SPEED	AVG	OBP	SLG	MLVR	EQAVG	EQOBP	EQSLG	EQA	VORP	DEFENSE
2004	BAL	MLB	32	636	111	41	0	27	104	66	95	11	6	5.1	.340	.419	.562	.359	.342	.424	.570	.329	64.3	137-3B -10
2005	BAL	MLB	33	664	86	30	1	27	88	50	112	7	4	4.7	.283	.348	.474	.115	.291	.364	.497	.290	32.6	146-3B -1
2006	BAL	MLB	34	705	96	25	0	16	83	54	99	11	1	5.7	.274	.342	.391	-.053	.276	.350	.397	.266	8.9	151-3B -18
2007	BAL	MLB	35	610	80	28	2	18	75	51	92	8	3	5.3	.276	.344	.431	-.002	.274	.348	.438	.278	20.3	143-3B -8

Breakout: 6%   Improve: 24%   Collapse: 37%   Attrition: 4%   Comparables: Al Smith, Ken Boyer, Craig Biggio, Phil Garner

Back in 2003, Mora took a great leap forward in productivity almost unrivaled in major league history. He reached an even higher peak in 2004, but since then he's been going down the other side of the mountain. Mora signed a three-year contract extension for $25 million in late May. Immediately afterwards, his power decreased—having hit 13 doubles and 8 home runs in the first two months of the season, he hit only 12 more doubles and 8 more home runs over the remaining four. Given that he's 35 years old, we should not expect to see Mora's power to return to its previous levels, and without that level of power he isn't an $8-million player.

David Newhan   **UT**   **Bats: L**   **Throws: R**   Height: 5' 10" Weight: 170 Born: September 7, 1973   Age: 33

YEAR	TEAM	LVL	AGE	PA	R	2B	3B	HR	RBI	BB	SO	SB	CS	SPEED	AVG	OBP	SLG	MLVR	EQAVG	EQOBP	EQSLG	EQA	VORP	DEFENSE		
2004	OKL	AAA	30	292	57	21	6	9	38	26	55	10	0	7.9	.328	.387	.557	.329	.291	.342	.455	.276	16.4	35-2B -1		
2004	BAL	MLB	30	412	66	15	7	8	54	27	72	11	1	7.6	.311	.361	.453	.079	.313	.366	.461	.288	18.0	19-LF 0	19-RF	-1
2005	BAL	MLB	31	249	31	9	0	5	21	22	45	9	2	6.8	.202	.279	.312	-.287	.206	.295	.318	.228	-9.9	27-CF -2	15-LF	-3
2006	BAL	MLB	32	143	14	4	0	4	18	7	22	4	2	4.8	.252	.294	.374	-.185	.254	.301	.392	.241	-2.2	18-CF -5	14-LF	-3
2007	NYN	MLB	33	214	28	9	2	4	21	16	35	7	2	6.3	.269	.329	.394	-.092	.272	.332	.406	.257	5.6	54-CF -3		

Breakout: 24% Improve: 43% Collapse: 36% Attrition: 34%   Comparables: Marvin Benard, Bill Bruton, Wayne Kirby, Milt Thompson

Somebody has to be the last man on the bench, and Newhan's mostly an outfielder who only moonlights at first, second or third on occasion. He's not going to hit .311 again, but that's not the end of the world. After he was non-tendered, the Mets gave Newhan a new home. He'll be used in both the infield and the outfield. Unless the Mets roster is struck by some kind of highly communicable disease, he should play a good deal less than he did with the Orioles.

Corey Patterson   **CF**   **Bats: L**   **Throws: R**   Height: 5' 9" Weight: 175 Born: August 13, 1979   Age: 27

YEAR	TEAM	LVL	AGE	PA	R	2B	3B	HR	RBI	BB	SO	SB	CS	SPEED	AVG	OBP	SLG	MLVR	EQAVG	EQOBP	EQSLG	EQA	VORP	DEFENSE
2004	CHN	MLB	24	687	91	33	6	24	72	45	168	32	9	7.4	.266	.320	.452	.006	.262	.316	.445	.261	19.4	147-CF 2
2005	IOW	AAA	25	102	16	4	0	5	12	8	19	6	1	5.7	.297	.366	.505	.159	.280	.337	.473	.276	5.5	23-CF 5
2005	CHN	MLB	25	481	47	15	3	13	34	23	118	15	5	6.8	.215	.254	.348	-.254	.208	.251	.344	.211	-17.0	111-CF 0
2006	BAL	MLB	26	498	75	19	5	16	53	21	94	45	9	8.6	.276	.314	.443	-.027	.279	.324	.459	.273	23.3	123-CF 3
2007	BAL	MLB	27	486	61	22	3	14	52	26	98	31	11	7.4	.259	.304	.412	-.110	.257	.307	.419	.260	6.1	115-CF 0

Breakout: 16% Improve: 33% Collapse: 32% Attrition: 23%   Comparables: Gil Coan, Deion Sanders, Devon White, Oddibe McDowell

Patterson was in the Cubs'—and especially Dusty Baker's—doghouse after a disastrous 2005, which meant the Orioles were able buy low, for a change, picking him up for two players (Nate Spears and Carlos Perez) who turned in awful seasons for the Cubs' High-A team in Daytona. Patterson is a former favorite of scouts and statheads alike, but he turned out to be one of those players who, at age 20, was about as good as he was ever going to be. The idea that the average player improves through his twenties to age 27 is mistaken, as that trend really only applies to the average *major leaguer*. What distinguishes a typical major leaguer from a typical minor leaguer is the ability to learn and improve. Patterson doesn't have that talent, but his basic skills are good enough to keep him in the majors for years to come. Just keep him away from left-handed pitchers.

Nolan Reimold RF **Bats: R Throws: R** Height: 6' 4" Weight: 207 Born: October 12, 1983 Age: 23

YEAR	TEAM	LVL	AGE	PA	R	2B	3B	HR	RBI	BB	SO	SB	CS	SPEED	AVG	OBP	SLG	MLVR	EQAVG	EQOBP	EQSLG	EQA	VORP	DEFENSE		
2005	FRD	A+	21	97	17	6	0	6	11	12	27	3	0	4.8	.265	.371	.554	.242	.230	.309	.448	.257	1.8	13-CF	-1	
2005	ABE	A-	21	212	33	15	2	9	30	29	44	2	0	4.5	.294	.392	.550	.376	.245	.311	.432	.256	-2.1	29-RF	1	15-CF -2
2006	FRD	A+	22	504	73	26	0	19	75	76	107	14	8	4.7	.255	.379	.455	.146	.225	.323	.406	.254	-6.6	94-RF	-11	19-CF -1
2007	BAL	MLB	23	474	55	22	1	17	59	46	109	5	3	4.8	.236	.316	.414	-.103	.234	.319	.421	.260	-0.9	112-RF	-5	

Breakout: 31% Improve: 62% Collapse: 20% Attrition: 6%   Comparables: Ryan Ludwick, Jonny Gomes, Mike Glendenning, Lamont Matthews

If you're going to be one-dimensional, you need to be great in that dimension, not just good. Reimold a poor defender, doesn't hit for average at all, and has good power, maybe very good, but definitely not great. He has had back problems, which one could plausibly argue sapped some of his power, but that's about the only way to spin back problems in a 22 year old as a positive.

Brian Roberts 2B **Bats: S Throws: R** Height: 5' 9" Weight: 175 Born: October 9, 1977 Age: 29

YEAR	TEAM	LVL	AGE	PA	R	2B	3B	HR	RBI	BB	SO	SB	CS	SPEED	AVG	OBP	SLG	MLVR	EQAVG	EQOBP	EQSLG	EQA	VORP	DEFENSE	
2004	BAL	MLB	26	734	107	50	2	4	53	71	95	29	12	6.9	.273	.344	.376	-.094	.274	.350	.381	.261	13.4	145-2B	1
2005	BAL	MLB	27	640	92	45	7	18	73	67	83	27	10	6.9	.314	.387	.515	.265	.325	.408	.544	.317	61.9	137-2B	4
2006	BAL	MLB	28	629	85	34	3	10	55	55	66	36	7	6.7	.286	.347	.410	-.008	.288	.356	.421	.277	31.3	133-2B	-2
2007	BAL	MLB	29	641	88	29	4	11	58	62	75	33	10	6.9	.263	.336	.390	-.079	.261	.340	.396	.269	17.1	150-2B	1

Breakout: 1% Improve: 9% Collapse: 56% Attrition: 3%   Comparables: Ray Durham, Don Buford, Bill Doran, Roberto Alomar

Roberts was slow to recover from the awful elbow injury that ended his 2005 season; even though he was on the field to start 2006, he wasn't really *back*. For the first half of the season, Roberts was little more than a slap-hitter, albeit an effective one—a .330 average with nine steals, like he had in April, is plenty valuable, even without any power. He was still hitting .309/.376/.395 when he popped his first dinger near the end of June, compared to .271/.327/.420 afterwards. Chicks may dig the long ball, but Roberts was a more valuable player when the injury forced him to ignore it.

Billy Rowell 3B **Bats: L Throws: R** Height: 6' 5" Weight: 205 Born: September 10, 1988 Age: 18

YEAR	TEAM	LVL	AGE	PA	R	2B	3B	HR	RBI	BB	SO	SB	CS	SPEED	AVG	OBP	SLG	MLVR	EQAVG	EQOBP	EQSLG	EQA	VORP	DEFENSE	
2006	ABE	A-	17	49	8	4	0	1	6	4	12	0	0	4.8	.326	.388	.488	.351	.311	.347	.511	.287	8.4	11-3B	-2
2006	BLU	Rk	17	180	38	15	3	2	26	25	47	3	0	5.7	.329	.422	.507	.354	.284	.344	.432	.269	19.7	36-3B	0
2007	BAL	MLB	18	516	59	33	3	14	54	37	125	6	3	5.7	.249	.304	.421	-.105	.247	.308	.428	.257	5.3	121-3B	0

Breakout: 9% Improve: 45% Collapse: 28% Attrition: 3%   Comparables: Ian Stewart, Billy Butler, Ben Johnson, Wilson Betemit

Taken as the ninth overall pick in last year's draft, Rowell didn't turn 18 until the minor league season was over. He's already six-foot-five and still growing, so there's some concern that he'll outgrow third base, just as he outgrew shortstop (his high school position), but the Orioles could move him just about anywhere, because the young man can flat out hit. Rowell also gets high marks for his work ethic—he's not simply relying on his talent, he works at honing it.

Brandon Snyder C **Bats: R Throws: R** Height: 6' 2" Weight: 205 Born: November 23, 1986 Age: 20

YEAR	TEAM	LVL	AGE	PA	R	2B	3B	HR	RBI	BB	SO	SB	CS	SPEED	AVG	OBP	SLG	MLVR	EQAVG	EQOBP	EQSLG	EQA	VORP	DEFENSE	
2005	ABE	A-	18	31	4	2	0	0	6	2	7	0	0	2.6	.393	.419	.464	.398	.345	.355	.414	.275	2.9		
2005	BLU	Rk	18	180	26	8	0	8	35	28	36	7	2	4.1	.271	.380	.493	.191	.197	.274	.299	.212	-20.1	19-C	1
2006	DEL	A	19	159	12	12	0	3	20	9	55	0	0	3.5	.194	.237	.340	-.208	.142	.177	.216	.152	-24.0	23-C	-2
2006	ABE	A-	19	131	14	8	1	1	11	5	43	2	1	4.8	.234	.267	.339	-.047	.214	.237	.310	.191	-16.9	26-C	-4
2007	BAL	MLB	20	392	27	17	1	7	35	19	107	3	2	4.4	.198	.239	.306	-.408	.197	.242	.311	.189	-19.2	94-C	-3

Breakout: 61% Improve: 64% Collapse: 30% Attrition: 19%   Comparables: Josh McAffee, Josh Phelps, Gabe Johnson, Matthew Spring

In 2005, Snyder had a 43:30 strikeout-to-walk ratio, but in 2006 it was 98:14. That is indicative about how much worse he was last year, offensively and defensively, than the player the O's drafted in the first round in 2005. In his defense, he was playing with a torn rotator cuff. He should make it back around the start of the 2007 season, and, even though it was not his throwing shoulder that was hurt, the injury may end his catching career. Snyder is regarded as having enough hitting talent to move elsewhere, but this is an as-yet-unproven assertion.

Fernando Tatis **1B/3B** **Bats: R** **Throws: R** Height: 5' 10" Weight: 195 Born: January 1, 1975 Age: 32

YEAR	TEAM	LVL	AGE	PA	R	2B	3B	HR	RBI	BB	SO	SB	CS	SPEED	AVG	OBP	SLG	MLVR	EQAVG	EQOBP	EQSLG	EQA	VORP	DEFENSE	
2006	OTT	AAA	31	368	44	15	2	7	37	36	56	8	2	5.7	.298	.372	.420	.132	.269	.333	.386	.253	9.5	83-3B	-8
2006	BAL	MLB	31	64	7	6	1	2	8	6	17	0	0	4.8	.250	.313	.500	.024	.255	.328	.509	.282	1.7		
2007	BAL	MLB	32	378	45	19	2	8	42	27	69	4	3	5.1	.267	.324	.409	-.072	.265	.328	.416	.262	5.6	90-3B	-1

Breakout: 24% Improve: 48% Collapse: 22% Attrition: 28% Comparables: Raul Gonzalez, Mike McCormick, Hector Lopez, Damian Jackson

Tatis's return to the majors was a nice story, but like cotton candy, beyond the sweetness there was almost nothing of substance. The Orioles had an especially difficult time attracting minor league free agents in 2006—it seems nobody wants to go Ottawa—and that left them with reclamation projects such as Tatis, who had been out of pro ball completely for two years. He showed that he could still hit in the majors, but fielded like someone who hadn't worn a glove in a decade.

Miguel Tejada **SS** **Bats: R** **Throws: R** Height: 5' 9" Weight: 215 Born: May 25, 1976 Age: 31

YEAR	TEAM	LVL	AGE	PA	R	2B	3B	HR	RBI	BB	SO	SB	CS	SPEED	AVG	OBP	SLG	MLVR	EQAVG	EQOBP	EQSLG	EQA	VORP	DEFENSE	
2004	BAL	MLB	28	725	107	40	2	34	150	48	73	4	1	4.5	.311	.360	.534	.202	.311	.363	.542	.303	65.1	159-SS	23
2005	BAL	MLB	29	704	89	50	5	26	98	40	83	5	1	4.6	.304	.349	.515	.201	.311	.365	.540	.302	62.9	158-SS	4
2006	BAL	MLB	30	709	99	37	0	24	100	46	79	6	2	4.5	.330	.379	.498	.219	.332	.387	.510	.304	65.9	148-SS	6
2007	BAL	MLB	31	655	90	37	2	22	96	39	74	4	2	4.7	.308	.355	.484	.116	.306	.359	.492	.295	49.2	153-SS	5

Breakout: 11% Improve: 37% Collapse: 25% Attrition: 2% Comparables: Hubie Brooks, Alvin Dark, Kirby Puckett, Buddy Bell

Tejada remains one of the foremost targets of the Steroid Police, having been fingered by both Rafael Palmeiro and Jason Grimsley. He has passed all the tests given him so far, though, and just keeps turning in the same great season year after year. He still has three years left on his contract, and the Orioles need to consider whether or not they'll be a serious contender within that time frame (possible, but not likely). Both player and team might be better off if Baltimore were to attempt to restock their farm system by trading Tejada to a contender. It was discussed and almost consummated last year (with the Angels), and will be a hot topic again this year.

Luis Terrero **CF** **Bats: R** **Throws: R** Height: 6' 3" Weight: 225 Born: May 18, 1980 Age: 27

YEAR	TEAM	LVL	AGE	PA	R	2B	3B	HR	RBI	BB	SO	SB	CS	SPEED	AVG	OBP	SLG	MLVR	EQAVG	EQOBP	EQSLG	EQA	VORP	DEFENSE			
2004	TUC	AAA	24	240	36	9	6	9	35	17	48	15	3	8.0	.313	.374	.535	.126	.264	.322	.432	.263	6.1	40-CF	1	13-RF	0
2004	ARI	MLB	24	255	21	14	0	4	14	20	78	10	2	5.4	.245	.319	.358	-.129	.235	.307	.339	.235	-0.8	55-CF	-5		
2005	ARI	MLB	25	184	23	6	1	4	20	14	40	3	2	5.2	.230	.313	.354	-.138	.228	.311	.370	.240	-2.3	47-CF	1		
2006	OTT	AAA	26	329	52	21	2	16	44	16	61	18	9	6.7	.318	.367	.560	.325	.302	.348	.541	.291	30.8	55-CF	4	22-LF	4
2006	BAL	MLB	26	42	4	1	0	1	6	1	7	0	3	5.9	.200	.238	.300	-.437	.175	.214	.275	.160	-4.9				
2007	CHA	MLB	27	418	54	19	2	13	52	23	87	11	5	5.7	.267	.318	.431	-.054	.262	.316	.424	.261	5.7	100-CF	1		

Breakout: 16% Improve: 40% Collapse: 26% Attrition: 19% Comparables: Nick Gorneault, Barry Wesson, Brian Buchanan, Mike Hill

Terrero had the best season of his career last year; too bad it was all at Triple-A. When Terrero was a prospect, his statistics were never as good as his scouting reports, and, after three stints in the Show, we can say with some confidence that his major league stats aren't measuring up to his minor league performance. Released by Arizona last spring, Terrero had two futile stints in Camden Yards before signing with the White Sox for 2007.

Christopher Vinyard **1B** **Bats: R** **Throws: R** Height: 6' 4" Weight: 230 Born: December 15, 1985 Age: 21

YEAR	TEAM	LVL	AGE	PA	R	2B	3B	HR	RBI	BB	SO	SB	CS	SPEED	AVG	OBP	SLG	MLVR	EQAVG	EQOBP	EQSLG	EQA	VORP	DEFENSE	
2006	ABE	A-	20	306	40	26	2	8	47	28	62	0	0	3.2	.284	.366	.489	.292	.256	.314	.458	.263	7.7	61-1B	-4
2007	BAL	MLB	21	505	44	33	1	14	65	31	101	0	0	3.3	.247	.296	.413	-.131	.246	.300	.419	.251	-5.3	119-1B	-5

Breakout: 18% Improve: 33% Collapse: 34% Attrition: 6% Comparables: Brian Dopirak, Jason Stokes, Jeremy Cotten, Scott Thorman

A 38th-round draft-and-follow from 2005, Vinyard came from a community college in Arizona that used wooden bats, and thus had no trouble adjusting to pro ball. He led the New York-Penn league in doubles and homers with a short, strong swing that should carry him upwards. Even at first base he'll be a defensive liability, which will hold him back, but in a thin system, he's one of the prospects.

PITCHERS

Winston Abreu

Bats: R Throws: R   Height: 6' 2"   Weight: 170   Born: April 5, 1977   Age: 30

YEAR	TEAM	LVL	AGE	W	L	SV	G	GS	IP	H	BB	SO	HR	GB%	BABIP	STUFF	WHIP	ERA	PERA	EQERA	EQH9	EQBB9	EQSO9	EQHR9	VORP	WXRL
2004	LVG	AAA	27	1	2	0	14	1	23	20	20	23	5	—	.250	-2	1.74	7.83	8.27	7.04	7.4	8.2	6.7	2.0	-3.7	—
2004	TUC	AAA	27	1	0	3	28	0	44¹	44	25	41	10	—	.281	-16	1.56	5.69	7.05	5.00	8.4	5.4	6.2	2.0	3.0	—
2005	TUC	AAA	28	2	3	2	27	0	33¹	37	15	42	6	38.7%	.356	-5	1.56	6.49	5.15	5.94	10.3	4.1	8.4	1.9	-1.3	—
2005	OAX	MX	28	4	0	10	18	0	20	10	5	32	0	46.2%	.256	20	0.75	1.35	1.43	1.77	4.0	2.2	14.2	0.0	8.6	—
2006	OTT	AAA	29	9	4	1	46	0	65¹	54	20	78	4	39.9%	.307	13	1.14	2.49	3.85	3.80	8.3	3.1	8.0	0.8	12.8	—
2006	BAL	MLB	29	0	0	0	7	0	8	10	6	6	1	17.9%	.333	-13	2.00	10.13	5.83	9.72	10.8	6.5	6.5	1.1	-4.7	0.01
2007	*WAS*	*MLB*	*30*	*3*	*3*	*1*	*34*	*3*	*57¹*	*55*	*27*	*52*	*9*	*37.0%*	*.282*	*2*	*1.43*	*4.63*	*5.28*	*4.97*	*8.6*	*3.8*	*7.4*	*1.3*	*4.4*	*0.50*

Breakout: 32% Improve: 65% Collapse: 16% Attrition: 14%   Comparables: Dwayne Henry, Luis Vizcaino, Alan Mills, Brian Boehringer

After ten years in the minors, the former Braves/Royals/Cubs/Dodgers/Diamondbacks farmhand finally made it to the majors. The first batter he faced was the reigning MVP. In true fairy-tale fashion, Abreu struck him out. Best to fade to black right there, as it went downhill after that. An unusually good year at Triple-A bought him a chance with the Nationals this spring.

Pedro Beato

Bats: R Throws: R   Height: 6' 5"   Weight: 210   Born: October 27, 1986   Age: 20

YEAR	TEAM	LVL	AGE	W	L	SV	G	GS	IP	H	BB	SO	HR	GB%	BABIP	STUFF	WHIP	ERA	PERA	EQERA	EQH9	EQBB9	EQSO9	EQHR9	VORP	WXRL
2006	ABE	A-	19	3	2	0	14	10	57	47	23	52	6	53.3%	.266	-35	1.23	3.63	10.43	7.25	11.4	5.6	5.3	4.2	-9.1	—
2007	*BAL*	*MLB*	*20*	*3*	*7*	*0*	*23*	*15*	*84*	*101*	*51*	*49*	*22*	*47.0%*	*.290*	*-15*	*1.80*	*6.50*	*6.95*	*5.88*	*10.8*	*5.2*	*4.9*	*2.2*	*-7.1*	*0.20*

Breakout: 44% Improve: 71% Collapse: 3% Attrition: 5%   Comparables: Ben Hendrickson, Carlos De La Cruz, Dan Curtis, Neomar Flores

Beato's more of a scout's pick right now than a sabermetric one. He had TJ surgery in 2004, which caused him to drop in the following year's draft. The Mets ultimately picked him in the seventeenth round, but didn't want to give him above-slot money, so he went back into the draft last year and the Orioles got him with the 32nd overall pick. He claims to throw six pitches, but he should work on controlling at least one of them well before trying the rest. He'll be popular if he gets it worked out; Beato's outgoing, demonstrative, works quickly, and just generally looks like he's having fun playing baseball.

Erik Bedard

Bats: L Throws: L   Height: 6' 1"   Weight: 190   Born: March 6, 1979   Age: 28

YEAR	TEAM	LVL	AGE	W	L	SV	G	GS	IP	H	BB	SO	HR	GB%	BABIP	STUFF	WHIP	ERA	PERA	EQERA	EQH9	EQBB9	EQSO9	EQHR9	VORP	WXRL
2004	BAL	MLB	25	6	10	0	27	26	137¹	149	71	121	13	—	.326	19	1.60	4.59	4.17	4.92	9.3	4.1	7.3	0.8	13.0	2.16
2005	BAL	MLB	26	6	8	0	24	24	141²	139	57	125	10	41.5%	.323	31	1.38	4.00	3.65	3.95	8.5	3.6	7.6	0.6	24.7	3.74
2006	BAL	MLB	27	15	11	0	33	33	196¹	196	69	171	16	49.7%	.314	30	1.35	3.76	3.57	3.80	8.2	2.9	7.2	0.7	40.2	5.42
2007	*BAL*	*MLB*	*28*	*11*	*10*	*0*	*30*	*30*	*184²*	*189*	*69*	*149*	*20*	*46.0%*	*.304*	*18*	*1.39*	*4.32*	*4.18*	*4.03*	*9.2*	*3.2*	*6.8*	*0.9*	*26.6*	*4.20*

Breakout: 16% Improve: 53% Collapse: 13% Attrition: 4%   Comparables: Gary Peters, Bob Ojeda, Cliff Chambers, Bob Kuzava

Bedard is one of the best pitchers in the majors right now. In terms of rate stats, he basically repeated his very good 2005 last year, but what made 2006 even better was that he stayed healthy, throwing more than 150 innings for the first time in his professional career. Staying healthy is a skill; now that Bedard has done it once, the chances of his doing it again are better. Even so, the odds still favor more injury time. Another encouraging sign was that Bedard got better as the season went on, perhaps having shaken off some World Baseball Classic fatigue.

Kris Benson

Bats: R Throws: R   Height: 6' 4"   Weight: 205   Born: November 7, 1974   Age: 32

YEAR	TEAM	LVL	AGE	W	L	SV	G	GS	IP	H	BB	SO	HR	GB%	BABIP	STUFF	WHIP	ERA	PERA	EQERA	EQH9	EQBB9	EQSO9	EQHR9	VORP	WXRL
2004	NYN	MLB	29	4	4	0	11	11	68	65	17	51	8	—	.275	15	1.21	4.50	4.12	4.72	8.7	2.0	6.0	0.9	6.6	1.45
2005	NYN	MLB	30	10	8	0	28	28	174¹	171	49	95	24	45.4%	.264	-2	1.26	4.13	4.84	4.53	8.9	2.3	4.5	1.2	20.9	3.38
2006	BAL	MLB	31	11	12	0	30	30	183	199	58	88	33	44.6%	.290	-11	1.40	4.82	5.49	4.49	8.8	2.6	4.0	1.4	17.8	3.56
2007	*BAL*	*MLB*	*32*	*9*	*12*	*0*	*30*	*29*	*173²*	*204*	*53*	*88*	*27*	*43.0%*	*.299*	*-1*	*1.47*	*5.19*	*5.01*	*4.79*	*10.6*	*2.6*	*4.3*	*1.3*	*8.6*	*2.20*

Breakout: 11% Improve: 42% Collapse: 23% Attrition: 1%   Comparables: Dave Mlicki, Dock Ellis, Brett Tomko, Steve Trachsel

One of MLB.com's reporters described Kris Benson as an average major league pitcher signed for an average salary through 2007. What that reporter didn't realize was that paying average players average salaries is typical of a losing team. Good teams pay big bucks for big performers, but make up for it by going cheap on the average guys, which they get via their minor league system or canny scouting. The Orioles traded John Maine, a young major league pitcher at a stage in his career when he was still likely to improve, and still-serviceable reliever Jorge Julio to get Benson, an average major league pitcher with a long injury history at an age at which he was most likely to experience a decline, and dramatically increased their payroll in the process. It was dumb then, and it still is a year later.

Kurt Birkins   Bats: L   Throws: L   Height: 6' 2"   Weight: 190   Born: August 11, 1980   Age: 26

YEAR	TEAM	LVL	AGE	W	L	SV	G	GS	IP	H	BB	SO	HR	GB%	BABIP	STUFF	WHIP	ERA	PERA	EQERA	EQH9	EQBB9	EQSO9	EQHR9	VORP	WXRL
2004	FRD	A+	23	5	2	2	27	6	68	70	22	55	9	—	.305	-39	1.35	4.50	7.35	5.65	10.2	3.7	4.7	2.5	-0.4	—
2005	BOW	AA	24	7	11	0	26	24	129	134	42	114	8	55.9%	.336	-2	1.36	3.91	4.91	6.30	10.6	3.7	5.1	0.9	-9.7	—
2006	OTT	AAA	25	1	3	0	5	5	25²	20	11	19	2	64.3%	.265	3	1.23	3.21	5.24	4.26	7.5	4.3	5.0	1.1	3.8	—
2006	BAL	MLB	25	5	2	0	35	0	31	25	16	27	4	41.9%	.256	2	1.32	4.94	5.02	5.06	6.8	4.2	7.3	1.1	1.9	0.22
2007	*BAL*	*MLB*	*26*	*3*	*4*	*1*	*52*	*4*	*66²*	*72*	*31*	*43*	*9*	*48.0%*	*.298*	*-9*	*1.55*	*5.18*	*4.95*	*4.84*	*9.8*	*4.0*	*5.4*	*1.1*	*3.0*	*0.40*

Breakout: 33%   Improve: 63%   Collapse: 13%   Attrition: 28%   Comparables: Dave Tomlin, Tim Van Egmond, Frank Kreutzer, Xavier Hernandez

Up until last year, Birkins was a slop-throwing starter making steady but unspectacular progress through the weak Oriole system. Last year started exactly the same way. Birkins is left-handed, though, so the Orioles called him up to be a situational lefty. It worked for about three weeks, when either the scouting reports caught up to him, or his elbow started to give out—we can't be certain which. All we know is that he pitched terribly for the next two months, then went on the DL for the rest of the season with an inflamed elbow nerve.

Chris Britton   Bats: R   Throws: R   Height: 6' 3"   Weight: 280   Born: December 16, 1982   Age: 24

YEAR	TEAM	LVL	AGE	W	L	SV	G	GS	IP	H	BB	SO	HR	GB%	BABIP	STUFF	WHIP	ERA	PERA	EQERA	EQH9	EQBB9	EQSO9	EQHR9	VORP	WXRL
2004	DEL	A	21	9	4	1	27	8	84	76	31	80	11	—	.286	-26	1.27	3.75	6.73	4.97	9.8	4.2	5.1	2.1	5.6	—
2005	FRD	A+	22	6	0	6	46	0	78²	47	23	110	5	50.0%	.264	17	0.89	1.60	3.89	2.39	6.8	3.1	7.8	1.0	26.9	—
2006	BOW	AA	23	1	0	2	13	0	16¹	14	6	24	0	35.1%	.389	16	1.24	2.80	2.86	3.45	9.2	4.0	9.2	0.0	3.8	—
2006	BAL	MLB	23	0	2	1	52	0	53²	46	17	41	4	34.2%	.268	10	1.17	3.35	3.49	3.40	7.0	2.6	6.3	0.6	14.2	0.50
2007	*NYA*	*MLB*	*24*	*3*	*2*	*3*	*51*	*0*	*55²*	*53*	*21*	*48*	*8*	*39.0%*	*.282*	*7*	*1.32*	*4.02*	*4.00*	*3.83*	*8.4*	*3.1*	*7.2*	*1.2*	*10.1*	*0.90*

Breakout: 9%   Improve: 33%   Collapse: 32%   Attrition: 28%   Comparables: Ron Robinson, Edwin Nunez, Cecilio Guante, Eric King

Britton burst on the scene in 2005 with a dominating relief season at High-A Frederick; when he continued to impress, striking out six of the first ten batters faced at Bowie last year, the Orioles brought him up to the majors. Britton was a lucky accident for the Orioles, an eighth-round pick from 2001 who was nearly written off after injuries wiped out his 2003 season, then moved to the bullpen in 2004 to pitch himself back into shape. "Shape" is going to be a problem with Britton, who was rather generously listed at only 280 last year. The Orioles let that scare them into trading him to the Yankees for Jaret Wright; see the Kris Benson comment.

Brian Burres   Bats: L   Throws: L   Height: 6' 1"   Weight: 180   Born: April 8, 1981   Age: 26

YEAR	TEAM	LVL	AGE	W	L	SV	G	GS	IP	H	BB	SO	HR	GB%	BABIP	STUFF	WHIP	ERA	PERA	EQERA	EQH9	EQBB9	EQSO9	EQHR9	VORP	WXRL
2004	SJO	A+	23	12	1	0	36	15	123²	115	30	114	10	—	.303	-16	1.17	2.84	5.51	4.84	9.5	2.9	5.0	1.5	10.0	—
2005	NRW	AA	24	9	6	0	26	24	128²	130	57	105	13	39.3%	.312	-15	1.45	4.20	6.34	5.81	9.9	5.1	4.7	1.5	-2.9	—
2006	OTT	AAA	25	10	6	0	26	26	139²	133	57	110	14	42.9%	.300	-6	1.36	3.75	5.56	4.68	9.0	4.0	5.5	1.4	14.1	—
2006	BAL	MLB	25	0	0	0	11	0	8	6	1	6	1	54.2%	.217	8	0.88	2.25	3.52	2.16	6.5	1.1	6.5	1.1	3.4	0.50
2007	*BAL*	*MLB*	*26*	*4*	*7*	*0*	*33*	*13*	*93*	*112*	*45*	*55*	*17*	*43.0%*	*.309*	*-12*	*1.69*	*6.11*	*6.05*	*5.62*	*10.9*	*4.1*	*5.0*	*1.6*	*-4.9*	*0.00*

Breakout: 6%   Improve: 30%   Collapse: 40%   Attrition: 1%   Comparables: Brent Billingsley, Mike Riley, Mario Ramos, Steve Smyth

Burres was waived by the Giants after 2005, and the Orioles took a chance on him, eventually bringing him up for a September look-see. A lefty medium-tosser, Burres works up in the zone and gets a lot of pop-ups and fly balls, the latter of which tend to leave the yard. The O's used him as a situational lefty, something his repertoire is not really suited for.

Daniel Cabrera   Bats: R   Throws: R   Height: 6' 7"   Weight: 260   Born: May 28, 1981   Age: 26

YEAR	TEAM	LVL	AGE	W	L	SV	G	GS	IP	H	BB	SO	HR	GB%	BABIP	STUFF	WHIP	ERA	PERA	EQERA	EQH9	EQBB9	EQSO9	EQHR9	VORP	WXRL
2004	BOW	AA	23	0	1	0	5	5	27¹	11	12	35	1	—	.169	27	0.84	2.64	3.87	4.05	4.7	4.4	8.1	0.3	4.6	—
2004	BAL	MLB	23	12	8	1	28	27	147²	145	89	76	14	—	.279	4	1.58	5.00	5.08	4.64	8.3	4.8	4.2	0.8	18.0	2.89
2005	BAL	MLB	24	10	13	0	29	29	161¹	144	87	157	14	52.4%	.294	31	1.43	4.52	4.22	4.84	7.8	4.8	8.5	0.7	11.4	2.88
2006	OTT	AAA	25	3	1	0	4	4	24¹	20	9	27	1	40.9%	.302	22	1.20	4.11	3.63	5.62	7.9	3.8	7.9	0.4	-0.1	—
2006	BAL	MLB	25	9	10	0	26	26	148	130	104	157	11	42.6%	.320	40	1.58	4.74	4.19	4.52	7.3	5.8	8.8	0.6	18.0	3.33
2007	*BAL*	*MLB*	*26*	*10*	*11*	*0*	*30*	*30*	*177*	*163*	*94*	*169*	*18*	*45.0%*	*.296*	*22*	*1.45*	*4.45*	*4.19*	*4.18*	*8.3*	*4.6*	*8.0*	*0.9*	*22.1*	*3.70*

Breakout: 36%   Improve: 63%   Collapse: 11%   Attrition: 3%   Comparables: J. R. Richard, Jose Deleon, Stan Williams, Kerry Wood

(continued next page)

Daniel Cabrera *(continued)*

Cabrera was supposed to be the one guy above all who would be helped by the arrival of Leo Mazzone. It didn't happen, at least not at first. You can lay some blame on the World Baseball Classic, which seemed to wear down just about everyone who pitched in it, but through the first half of the season, Cabrera couldn't find the plate with a GPS unit. It got so bad that the Orioles had to send him back to Ottawa to work on his control. Cabrera could have sulked at the demotion, but, to his credit, he worked on his control and earned a recall. Before going to Ottawa, Cabrera had walked just under 8 men per nine innings; after returning, he cut it down to 4.2, and his second-half ERA was a manageable 4.26. Maybe it was Mazzone, maybe it was the minors, maybe it was the glasses he started wearing, a la Rick "Wild Thing" Vaughn. PECOTA doesn't know about the glasses, but it's optimistic nonetheless.

Bruce Chen Bats: L Throws: L Height: 6' 1" Weight: 215 Born: June 19, 1977 Age: 30

YEAR	TEAM	LVL	AGE	W	L	SV	G	GS	IP	H	BB	SO	HR	GB%	BABIP	STUFF	WHIP	ERA	PERA	EQERA	EQH9	EQBB9	EQSO9	EQHR9	VORP	WXRL
2004	OTT	AAA	27	4	3	0	22	17	95	85	30	108	12	—	.297	10	1.21	3.22	4.47	4.01	8.2	3.1	7.7	1.3	16.7	—
2004	BAL	MLB	27	2	1	0	8	7	47²	39	16	32	7	—	.232	11	1.15	3.02	4.58	3.31	6.8	2.8	5.5	1.1	14.3	1.42
2005	BAL	MLB	28	13	10	0	34	32	197¹	187	63	133	33	38.8%	.262	2	1.27	3.83	5.08	3.99	8.2	2.8	5.9	1.4	32.4	4.42
2006	BAL	MLB	29	0	7	0	40	12	98²	137	35	70	28	33.5%	.349	-36	1.74	6.93	6.00	6.53	11.2	3.0	5.8	2.3	-14.8	-0.73
2007	*BAL*	*MLB*	*30*	*4*	*6*	*1*	*43*	*10*	*92*	*103*	*33*	*65*	*16*	*40.0%*	*.301*	*-4*	*1.48*	*5.25*	*5.15*	*4.80*	*10.2*	*3.1*	*5.9*	*1.5*	*4.8*	*0.80*

Breakout: 24% Improve: 50% Collapse: 18% Attrition: 12% Comparables: Randy Wolf, Pete Schourek, Bob Shirley, Dan Plesac

Absence certainly did not make the heart grow fonder for Chen, who chafed under Mazzone as a Brave prospect years ago and fell apart on him upon their reacquaintance this year. Chen didn't really pitch much differently last year than in the past; he's been getting away with nothing but finesse for two years, and last year it caught up with him. Proof that not everybody has a career year in their walk year, Chen lost his starting job in May and didn't do anything in relief to merit getting it back.

Brandon Erbe Bats: R Throws: R Height: 6' 4" Weight: 180 Born: December 25, 1987 Age: 19

YEAR	TEAM	LVL	AGE	W	L	SV	G	GS	IP	H	BB	SO	HR	GB%	BABIP	STUFF	WHIP	ERA	PERA	EQERA	EQH9	EQBB9	EQSO9	EQHR9	VORP	WXRL
2005	BLU	Rk	17	1	1	1	11	3	23¹	8	10	48	1	33.3%	.241	21	0.77	3.09	5.54	5.23	6.5	6.5	9.1	0.9	0.9	—
2006	DEL	A	18	5	9	0	28	27	114¹	88	47	133	2	36.0%	.319	35	1.18	3.23	3.97	4.70	7.9	4.5	6.3	0.3	11.1	—
2007	*BAL*	*MLB*	*19*	*5*	*8*	*0*	*28*	*18*	*107*	*112*	*72*	*93*	*19*	*38.0%*	*.302*	*4*	*1.72*	*6.06*	*5.88*	*5.59*	*9.5*	*5.7*	*7.3*	*1.5*	*-4.7*	*0.20*

Breakout: 8% Improve: 35% Collapse: 34% Attrition: 0% Comparables: Francisco Rodriguez, Joel Zumaya, Alan Webb, Matt Cain

Erbe, like third baseman Billy Rowell last year, was just 17 when he was drafted, giving the generally over-age Birds a pair of extremely young and talented prospects. The slightly-built Erbe throws in the mid- to upper-90s and was kept on a tight leash all season as the O's want to bring him along slowly, to allow him to work on his pitches and command and polish up his delivery. Above all, they want to keep him healthy. Erbe's biggest challenge might be learning to work from the stretch; he was far less effective with men on.

La Troy Hawkins Bats: R Throws: R Height: 6' 5" Weight: 215 Born: December 21, 1972 Age: 34

YEAR	TEAM	LVL	AGE	W	L	SV	G	GS	IP	H	BB	SO	HR	GB%	BABIP	STUFF	WHIP	ERA	PERA	EQERA	EQH9	EQBB9	EQSO9	EQHR9	VORP	WXRL
2004	CHN	MLB	31	5	4	25	77	0	82	72	14	69	10	—	.270	12	1.05	2.63	3.61	2.93	7.8	1.4	6.7	1.0	25.4	2.27
2005	CHN	MLB	32	1	4	4	21	0	19	18	7	13	4	45.8%	.255	-11	1.32	3.32	5.66	4.19	8.4	2.8	5.6	1.9	2.6	-0.52
2005	SFN	MLB	32	1	4	2	45	0	37¹	40	17	30	3	46.2%	.325	0	1.53	4.10	3.91	4.23	9.4	3.8	6.6	0.7	4.9	-0.06
2006	BAL	MLB	33	3	2	0	60	0	60¹	73	15	27	4	46.8%	.325	-6	1.46	4.48	3.77	3.71	9.7	2.0	3.7	0.6	10.8	1.81
2007	*COL*	*MLB*	*34*	*2*	*3*	*1*	*45*	*0*	*51*	*60*	*15*	*32*	*8*	*47.0%*	*.312*	*-10*	*1.49*	*5.17*	*4.71*	*4.67*	*9.7*	*2.6*	*4.9*	*1.1*	*5.8*	*0.50*

Breakout: 6% Improve: 17% Collapse: 60% Attrition: 26% Comparables: Ron Kline, Phil Regan, Eddie Fisher, Rick White

The Orioles thought they were getting the Hawk that throttled hitters from 2002–04, but it looks as though his 2005 drop-off was real and ongoing. The erosion in his strikeout rates, starting from 8.4 K/9 in 2003, turned into a landslide collapse in 2006. He can't throw the ball past anyone anymore, although he can still get hitters to pound his splitter into the dirt. Hawkins's numbers were decent, especially by the standards of the Oriole bullpen, but his prospective employers should be sure they're not paying for his glamorous past. If dogs come home to die, and cats leave, pitchers go to Colorado. The $3.5 million the Rockies will pay for the privilege seems like a lot for a shovel and a hole.

James Hoey   Bats: R Throws: R   Height: 6' 6"   Weight: 200   Born: December 30, 1982   Age: 24

YEAR	TEAM	LVL	AGE	W	L	SV	G	GS	IP	H	BB	SO	HR	GB%	BABIP	STUFF	WHIP	ERA	PERA	EQERA	EQH9	EQBB9	EQSO9	EQHR9	VORP	WXRL
2005	ABE	A-	22	1	1	0	9	0	15	11	10	15	1	46.2%	.286	-17	1.40	4.80	10.19	8.31	9.0	9.7	4.8	2.1	-3.9	—
2006	DEL	A	23	2	1	18	27	0	28²	17	10	46	2	54.4%	.306	4	0.96	2.55	5.26	3.81	8.0	4.5	8.3	1.7	5.2	—
2006	FRD	A+	23	0	0	11	14	0	14	13	5	16	0	43.9%	.317	3	1.29	0.64	3.59	2.63	9.2	4.0	6.6	0.0	4.5	—
2006	BOW	AA	23	0	0	4	8	0	9²	9	3	11	1	44.4%	.320	-2	1.30	3.91	4.92	6.00	10.0	3.0	7.0	2.0	-0.4	—
2006	BAL	MLB	23	0	1	0	12	0	9²	14	5	6	1	54.5%	.406	-21	1.97	10.21	5.36	8.71	12.2	4.4	5.2	0.9	-4.6	-0.57
2007	BAL	MLB	24	2	4	2	65	2	62²	77	32	44	12	46.0%	.322	-13	1.74	6.43	6.29	5.94	11.1	4.4	5.9	1.7	-5.6	0.50

Breakout: 28%   Improve: 60%   Collapse: 23%   Attrition: 12%   Comparables: Andy Shipman, Brett Evert, Talley Haines, J. D. Brammer

Hoey finished 2005 in Aberdeen, still recovering from a 2004 date with TJ surgery, but a year later he'd jumped all the way to Baltimore. He was snapping off a nifty slider and consistently working in the upper-90s in the minors (even reaching 100 on a generous gun in Bowie), but had a sore shoulder by the time he got to Baltimore and got clobbered. The injury is not supposed to be structural; Hoey should be fine for 2007. Given the crowd of veteran relievers brought in over the winter, if Hoey makes the staff it will be in a middle relief role.

Jim Johnson   Bats: R Throws: R   Height: 6' 5"   Weight: 225   Born: June 27, 1983   Age: 24

YEAR	TEAM	LVL	AGE	W	L	SV	G	GS	IP	H	BB	SO	HR	GB%	BABIP	STUFF	WHIP	ERA	PERA	EQERA	EQH9	EQBB9	EQSO9	EQHR9	VORP	WXRL
2004	DEL	A	21	8	7	0	20	17	106²	97	30	93	9	—	.291	-6	1.19	3.29	5.49	4.62	9.5	3.0	4.5	1.4	11.2	—
2005	FRD	A+	22	12	9	1	28	27	159²	139	64	168	11	52.1%	.303	7	1.27	3.49	5.30	5.10	8.9	4.2	5.8	1.0	8.6	—
2006	BOW	AA	23	13	6	0	27	26	156²	165	57	124	13	53.0%	.327	-8	1.42	4.44	5.42	5.67	10.3	3.7	4.8	1.2	-1.2	—
2007	BAL	MLB	24	5	9	0	28	19	112¹	134	53	64	17	48.0%	.312	-7	1.66	6.11	5.68	5.72	10.8	4.0	4.8	1.3	-7.6	0.00

Breakout: 19%   Improve: 49%   Collapse: 17%   Attrition: 0%   Comparables: Zach Day, Josh Hancock, Matt Wright, Mark Johnson

Johnson's fastball-curve mix didn't work quite so well in his jump up to Double-A, and he further failed to build on his breakthrough 2005 season by getting crushed in his one major league start. He generates nearly twice as many ground-ball outs as fly balls and could benefit from better glovework as he moves up, but for now his focus should be regrouping from his rough 2006.

Radhames Liz   Bats: R Throws: R   Height: 6' 2"   Weight: 170   Born: June 10, 1983   Age: 24

YEAR	TEAM	LVL	AGE	W	L	SV	G	GS	IP	H	BB	SO	HR	GB%	BABIP	STUFF	WHIP	ERA	PERA	EQERA	EQH9	EQBB9	EQSO9	EQHR9	VORP	WXRL
2005	DEL	A	22	2	3	0	10	10	38¹	33	23	55	2	36.3%	.360	13	1.46	4.46	5.62	7.00	9.0	7.5	7.5	1.0	-5.6	—
2005	ABE	A-	22	5	4	0	11	11	56	36	19	82	1	45.0%	.324	19	0.98	1.77	4.24	3.78	7.6	4.6	6.5	0.5	10.6	—
2006	FRD	A+	23	6	5	0	16	16	83²	57	44	95	8	41.6%	.261	2	1.21	2.81	6.69	4.35	7.9	5.6	6.9	1.8	10.9	—
2006	BOW	AA	23	3	1	0	10	10	50²	55	31	54	9	42.0%	.346	-11	1.71	5.38	7.98	6.80	11.7	6.4	6.8	2.8	-6.4	—
2007	BAL	MLB	24	4	8	0	26	18	100	110	67	78	20	39.0%	.300	-4	1.77	6.27	6.26	5.75	10.0	5.7	6.6	1.7	-6.8	0.00

Breakout: 9%   Improve: 34%   Collapse: 32%   Attrition: 0%   Comparables: Justin Echols, Winston Abreu, Carlos Marmol, Juan Cruz

The slender Liz has a truly live arm, with a moving fastball in the upper-90s and a plus curve, but lacks stamina, both within a game (opposing batters hit him for much better average and power after the fourth inning) and season (after striking out 33 in his first 15 innings he steadily declined across the entire season). Although he's working on adding a changeup, if he can't go deeper into games he'll have to move into relief work.

Adam Loewen   Bats: L Throws: L   Height: 6' 5"   Weight: 235   Born: April 9, 1984   Age: 23

YEAR	TEAM	LVL	AGE	W	L	SV	G	GS	IP	H	BB	SO	HR	GB%	BABIP	STUFF	WHIP	ERA	PERA	EQERA	EQH9	EQBB9	EQSO9	EQHR9	VORP	WXRL
2004	DEL	A	20	4	5	0	20	19	85¹	77	58	82	3	—	.323	14	1.58	4.11	5.48	5.79	9.1	7.2	5.2	0.5	-1.7	—
2005	FRD	A+	21	10	8	0	28	27	142	130	86	146	8	62.0%	.324	13	1.52	4.12	5.52	5.57	9.1	6.0	5.8	0.8	0.5	—
2006	BOW	AA	22	4	2	0	9	8	49²	46	26	55	3	55.3%	.341	19	1.46	2.74	4.75	3.91	9.3	5.2	7.1	0.9	9.1	—
2006	OTT	AAA	22	2	0	0	3	3	21¹	10	3	21	0	69.4%	.204	21	0.62	1.28	2.37	1.71	4.7	1.3	6.9	0.0	9.1	—
2006	BAL	MLB	22	6	6	0	22	19	112¹	111	62	98	8	50.5%	.319	26	1.54	5.37	4.23	5.18	8.3	4.6	7.3	0.5	3.5	1.66
2007	BAL	MLB	23	10	12	0	35	32	182¹	180	97	148	14	53.0%	.305	15	1.52	4.59	4.37	4.35	8.9	4.6	6.8	0.7	20.0	3.30

Breakout: 43%   Improve: 69%   Collapse: 1%   Attrition: 0%   Comparables: Jerry Reuss, Chuck Dobson, Steve Barber, Jim Abbott

Loewen was rushed to the majors last year, but the Orioles' rotation was a shambles by May, he was too good for either Bowie or Ottawa, and his contract mandates that he be in the majors for good by 2007 anyway. His two biggest problems are

(continued next page)

Adam Loewen *(continued)*

control and endurance, although the two are closely related for him. His batting and slugging averages against increased last year as a direct result of his pitching from behind more often. It is possible that the problem is temporary, a result of a partially torn labrum two years ago; it is also possible that he's only going to become the monster he was drafted to be by switching to relief.

Rodrigo Lopez　　Bats: R　Throws: R　　Height: 6' 1"　Weight: 185　Born: December 14, 1975　Age: 31

YEAR	TEAM	LVL	AGE	W	L	SV	G	GS	IP	H	BB	SO	HR	GB%	BABIP	STUFF	WHIP	ERA	PERA	EQERA	EQH9	EQBB9	EQSO9	EQHR9	VORP	WXRL
2004	BAL	MLB	28	14	9	0	37	23	170²	164	54	121	21	—	.281	12	1.28	3.59	4.15	3.42	8.1	2.6	5.9	1.0	49.0	6.42
2005	BAL	MLB	29	15	12	0	35	35	209¹	232	63	118	28	44.0%	.294	1	1.41	4.90	4.72	4.91	9.5	2.7	4.9	1.1	8.0	3.83
2006	BAL	MLB	30	9	18	0	36	29	189	234	59	136	32	44.7%	.333	0	1.55	5.90	4.67	5.37	10.1	2.6	5.9	1.3	-2.0	1.43
2007	COL	MLB	31	8	11	0	36	23	158²	177	51	116	21	51%	.312	6	1.44	4.99	4.50	4.52	9.1	2.7	5.8	1.0	20.4	3.2

Breakout: 18%　Improve: 55%　Collapse: 20%　Attrition: 22%　Comparables: Milt Wilcox, Joaquin Andujar, Ray Herbert, Jack Kramer

Lopez led the AL in earned runs allowed last year, joining past winners such as Jose Lima, Sidney Ponson, and Tanyon Sturtze. When the slider doesn't bite anymore, you've got problems; when you've always relied on it as your out-pitch, those problems potentially become career-ending.

Julio Mañon　　Bats: R　Throws: R　　Height: 6' 0"　Weight: 200　Born: June 10, 1973　　Age: 34

YEAR	TEAM	LVL	AGE	W	L	SV	G	GS	IP	H	BB	SO	HR	GB%	BABIP	STUFF	WHIP	ERA	PERA	EQERA	EQH9	EQBB9	EQSO9	EQHR9	VORP	WXRL
2006	OTT	AAA	33	0	2	30	47	0	50	35	20	61	4	35.0%	.277	8	1.10	2.16	4.62	3.17	7.3	4.3	7.8	1.1	13.0	—
2006	BAL	MLB	33	0	1	0	22	0	20	23	16	22	5	32.3%	.316	7	1.95	5.40	6.63	5.14	9.9	6.4	9.0	2.1	0.5	-0.65
2007	BAL	MLB	34	2	3	3	50	1	47²	48	25	42	9	35.0%	.288	-5	1.55	5.13	5.26	4.64	9.2	4.6	7.5	1.7	3.2	0.30

Breakout: 4%　Improve: 28%　Collapse: 30%　Attrition: 35%　Comparables: Doug Creek, Rich Delucia, Tom Martin, Aurelio Lopez

The well-traveled Mañon—he pitched for Ottawa, then affiliated with the Expos, back in 2001–02, and spent 2004–2005 pitching in Korea—had an outstanding year in Ottawa for the Orioles last year except for two September outings in which he allowed a total of six runs in ⅓ of an inning. He also pitched well in three stints with the major league club. He then spent the offseason looking for another team to give him a chance.

Garrett Olson　　Bats: R　Throws: L　　Height: 6' 1"　Weight: 200　Born: October 18, 1983　Age: 23

YEAR	TEAM	LVL	AGE	W	L	SV	G	GS	IP	H	BB	SO	HR	GB%	BABIP	STUFF	WHIP	ERA	PERA	EQERA	EQH9	EQBB9	EQSO9	EQHR9	VORP	WXRL
2005	ABE	A-	21	2	1	1	11	6	40	22	13	40	1	61.2%	.226	1	0.88	1.58	5.06	2.84	5.9	4.3	4.5	0.7	11.7	—
2005	FRD	A+	21	0	0	0	3	3	14¹	10	7	19	0	63.6%	.303	14	1.19	3.15	4.16	3.95	7.9	5.3	7.9	0.0	2.5	—
2006	FRD	A+	22	4	4	0	14	14	81	81	19	77	7	46.4%	.336	4	1.23	2.78	5.30	4.08	10.3	2.3	5.8	1.6	13.4	—
2006	BOW	AA	22	6	5	0	14	14	84	78	31	85	5	46.8%	.327	16	1.30	3.43	4.46	4.34	9.2	3.6	6.3	0.9	11.6	—
2007	BAL	MLB	23	6	9	0	27	22	130¹	146	52	84	22	45.0%	.299	2	1.52	5.39	5.25	4.98	10.2	3.4	5.4	1.4	3.7	1.30

Breakout: 4%　Improve: 19%　Collapse: 46%　Attrition: 0%　Comparables: Tom Gorzelanny, Corey Lee, Jon Switzer, Glen Perkins

A polished college pitcher drafted in 2005, Olson relies on one of the best curveballs in the minors. He could probably step in as a lefty specialist in the majors right now. That's a position he could fall back on if his changeup doesn't continue to develop and he can't make it as a starter, but right now, he's the guy most likely to get called up in September prior to taking a shot at the 2008 rotation.

Russ Ortiz　　Bats: R　Throws: R　　Height: 6' 1"　Weight: 220　Born: June 5, 1974　　Age: 33

YEAR	TEAM	LVL	AGE	W	L	SV	G	GS	IP	H	BB	SO	HR	GB%	BABIP	STUFF	WHIP	ERA	PERA	EQERA	EQH9	EQBB9	EQSO9	EQHR9	VORP	WXRL
2004	ATL	MLB	30	15	9	0	34	34	204²	197	112	143	23	—	.291	10	1.51	4.13	4.81	4.29	8.4	4.3	5.5	0.9	32.3	5.31
2005	ARI	MLB	31	5	11	0	22	22	115	147	65	46	18	37.8%	.319	-23	1.84	6.89	6.05	6.27	10.6	4.5	3.2	1.3	-18.3	-1.04
2006	ARI	MLB	32	0	5	0	6	6	22²	27	22	21	3	39.7%	.369	12	2.16	7.53	5.57	7.12	10.1	7.1	7.1	1.1	-5.1	-0.10
2006	BAL	MLB	32	0	3	0	20	5	40¹	59	18	23	15	34.2%	.336	-42	1.91	8.49	7.81	7.65	11.9	3.6	4.7	3.0	-11.6	-0.82
2007	SFN	MLB	33	2	4	0	26	7	58	63	31	40	8	41%	.300	-11	1.61	5.43	5.82	5.70	9.1	4.2	5.4	1.0	0.0	0.2

Breakout: 19%　Improve: 36%　Collapse: 40%　Attrition: 44%　Comparables: Bob Turley, Pat Mahomes, Cal Eldred, Paul Foytack

Ortiz pitched so badly in early 2006 that the Diamondbacks chose to eat the remaining two years and $20 million left on his contract and spare themselves and their fans anymore pain. The Orioles picked him up, reasoning that he had pitched well under Mazzone in the past and might do so again, a nice thought, but wrong. American League batters played Home

Run Derby with Ortiz's offerings. You would think that the resounding success of this move would have influenced the decision to pick up Jaret Wright. A free agent at this writing, Ortiz will no doubt be offered at least a spring training invite by some team hoping to recapture the glorious spirit of 2001.

Hayden Penn   Bats: R Throws: R   Height: 6′ 3″   Weight: 195   Born: October 13, 1984   Age: 22

YEAR	TEAM	LVL	AGE	W	L	SV	G	GS	IP	H	BB	SO	HR	GB%	BABIP	STUFF	WHIP	ERA	PERA	EQERA	EQH9	EQBB9	EQSO9	EQHR9	VORP	WXRL
2004	DEL	A	19	4	1	1	13	6	43¹	30	19	41	4	—	.234	-2	1.13	3.33	6.18	4.57	7.6	4.8	5.2	1.5	4.7	—
2004	FRD	A+	19	6	5	0	13	13	73¹	59	20	61	7	—	.260	6	1.08	3.81	5.64	4.62	7.6	2.9	5.1	1.6	7.8	—
2004	BOW	AA	19	3	0	0	4	4	20¹	22	9	20	0	—	.379	20	1.53	4.88	3.68	5.66	10.0	3.9	6.1	0.4	-0.1	—
2005	BOW	AA	20	7	6	0	20	19	110¹	101	37	120	11	47.8%	.326	13	1.25	3.84	4.74	5.06	9.4	3.5	6.8	1.4	6.4	—
2005	BAL	MLB	20	3	2	0	8	8	38¹	46	21	18	6	44.2%	.303	-10	1.75	6.34	5.84	6.35	10.2	4.8	4.1	1.4	-5.4	0.13
2006	OTT	AAA	21	7	4	0	14	14	87	71	27	85	5	47.3%	.286	30	1.13	2.28	3.74	3.10	7.6	2.9	6.7	0.7	24.2	—
2006	BAL	MLB	21	0	4	0	6	6	19²	38	13	8	8	37.1%	.370	-41	2.59	15.08	8.97	13.94	16.1	5.7	3.5	3.0	-20.0	-0.89
2007	*BAL*	*MLB*	*22*	*6*	*9*	*0*	*32*	*23*	*123*	*136*	*55*	*85*	*19*	*45.0%*	*.301*	*1*	*1.55*	*5.54*	*5.21*	*5.15*	*10.0*	*3.9*	*5.8*	*1.3*	*0.8*	*0.90*

Breakout: 50% Improve: 83% Collapse: 4%   Attrition: 0%   Comparables: Sean Douglass, Jason Marquis, Joel Hanrahan, John Roper

Major league hitters were just one hit shy of .400 against Penn last year. That makes two major league trials with results far below what the Orioles could have expected from his minor league lines. Still, Penn did well at Triple-A last year, despite missing two months to appendicitis. He has most of the assortment to succeed (low-90s heat, a plus change), but needs to tighten up his curve to keep big league hitters honest. It also appears that he needs further seasoning, and quite possibly the confidence to keep doing what got him to the majors in the first place.

Chris Ray   Bats: R Throws: R   Height: 6′ 3″   Weight: 225   Born: January 12, 1982   Age: 25

YEAR	TEAM	LVL	AGE	W	L	SV	G	GS	IP	H	BB	SO	HR	GB%	BABIP	STUFF	WHIP	ERA	PERA	EQERA	EQH9	EQBB9	EQSO9	EQHR9	VORP	WXRL
2004	DEL	A	22	2	3	0	10	9	50	43	17	46	3	—	.286	-4	1.20	3.42	5.39	4.88	9.2	3.9	4.7	0.9	3.8	—
2004	FRD	A+	22	6	3	0	14	14	73¹	82	20	74	6	—	.362	2	1.39	3.81	4.92	4.48	10.6	3.0	6.0	1.5	9.0	—
2005	BOW	AA	23	1	2	18	31	0	37¹	17	7	40	3	51.2%	.179	10	0.64	0.97	4.44	2.02	5.6	2.0	6.6	1.0	14.2	—
2005	BAL	MLB	23	1	3	0	41	0	40²	34	18	43	5	34.5%	.276	18	1.28	2.65	4.00	3.21	7.3	3.9	9.2	1.1	10.9	-0.33
2006	BAL	MLB	24	4	4	33	61	0	66	45	27	51	10	37.4%	.203	0	1.09	2.73	4.85	2.79	5.6	3.5	6.5	1.2	22.7	4.25
2007	*BAL*	*MLB*	*25*	*3*	*4*	*20*	*49*	*0*	*55*	*52*	*22*	*46*	*7*	*41.0%*	*.282*	*5*	*1.35*	*3.99*	*3.98*	*3.66*	*8.5*	*3.5*	*7.1*	*1.1*	*11.1*	*1.40*

Breakout: 11% Improve: 34% Collapse: 36%   Attrition: 13%   Comparables: Cecilio Guante, Frank Smith, Stan Belinda, Joe Price

Ray allowed 18 fewer hits than expected last year based on his balls in play, a staggering number given the relatively small number of innings he pitched. Since 1997, 14 relievers had similar seasons. As a group, in the year they exceeded expectations, they allowed 6.1 hits per nine innings and had an ERA of 2.87. The year after, their hits per nine innings rose to 8.3 and their ERA followed it northward, landing at 3.76. If you intuit from this that Ray had some good luck on balls in play last year, and that he's likely to experience a regression that will probably send his ERA to somewhere between 3.50 and 4.00, you're right.

Sendy Rleal   Bats: R Throws: R   Height: 6′ 1″   Weight: 180   Born: June 21, 1980   Age: 27

YEAR	TEAM	LVL	AGE	W	L	SV	G	GS	IP	H	BB	SO	HR	GB%	BABIP	STUFF	WHIP	ERA	PERA	EQERA	EQH9	EQBB9	EQSO9	EQHR9	VORP	WXRL
2004	BOW	AA	24	4	0	3	39	0	47¹	41	12	60	7	—	.304	-4	1.12	2.66	5.53	3.94	9.3	2.6	7.9	2.0	8.4	—
2005	BOW	AA	25	4	4	16	56	0	70²	46	18	75	4	45.1%	.252	1	0.91	2.04	4.15	3.48	7.1	3.1	6.0	0.8	15.9	—
2006	OTT	AAA	26	2	2	0	19	0	23¹	29	5	14	4	37.0%	.338	-32	1.47	6.62	6.34	7.94	11.9	2.0	4.4	2.4	-5.9	—
2006	BAL	MLB	26	1	1	0	42	0	46²	48	23	19	10	42.3%	.260	-30	1.52	4.43	6.53	4.25	8.3	4.1	3.3	1.7	6.5	0.36
2007	*BAL*	*MLB*	*27*	*2*	*2*	*1*	*43*	*0*	*46²*	*50*	*18*	*28*	*8*	*41.0%*	*.283*	*-11*	*1.47*	*4.76*	*4.82*	*4.34*	*9.7*	*3.4*	*5.0*	*1.4*	*4.9*	*0.40*

Breakout: 19% Improve: 43% Collapse: 18%   Attrition: 47%   Comparables: Bill Kunkel, Floyd Chiffer, Mark Portugal, Dave Stevens

Rleal (silent "r") skated by this past season, allowing many fewer runs than he should have and lowering his ERA by about two runs over what would have been expected given his peripherals. That was partly because he pitched so well with men on base, a characteristic that doesn't usually carry over from one year to the next. Rleal has a reverse platoon split thanks to a changeup that works especially well against lefties, but it's a dangerous pitch, inducing harmless pop-ups when it's on, but deep flies when it misses.

Eddy Rodriguez Bats: R Throws: R   Height: 6′ 1″   Weight: 215   Born: August 8, 1981   Age: 25

YEAR	TEAM	LVL	AGE	W	L	SV	G	GS	IP	H	BB	SO	HR	GB%	BABIP	STUFF	WHIP	ERA	PERA	EQERA	EQH9	EQBB9	EQSO9	EQHR9	VORP	WXRL
2004	OTT	AAA	22	1	0	3	28	0	31²	34	18	31	4	—	.319	-1	1.64	5.11	5.77	5.40	9.7	5.4	6.8	1.4	0.7	—
2004	BAL	MLB	22	1	0	0	29	0	43¹	36	30	37	5	—	.272	9	1.52	4.78	5.33	4.40	7.4	5.6	7.0	0.8	7.7	0.49
2005	OTT	AAA	23	2	3	3	50	0	62	57	36	51	2	35.2%	.311	6	1.50	3.77	4.48	4.52	8.3	5.5	5.8	0.3	7.4	—
2006	OTT	AAA	24	3	1	12	42	0	47	33	18	55	0	40.0%	.280	21	1.09	1.72	3.04	3.09	6.8	3.7	8.1	0.2	13.0	—
2006	BAL	MLB	24	1	1	0	9	0	15	17	10	11	5	30.6%	.273	-13	1.80	7.20	7.79	7.47	9.2	5.7	6.3	2.9	-3.9	-0.50
2007	FLO	MLB	25	2	3	2	43	2	50	49	27	45	7	36.0%	.292	1	1.50	4.96	5.26	5.03	8.5	4.1	7.3	1.1	3.1	0.40

Breakout: 19% Improve: 41% Collapse: 21% Attrition: 35%   Comparables: Jeff Jones, Brandon Backe, Chad Orvella, Francisco Cordero

Having struggled in Baltimore's pen last year, Rodriguez was called up and sent down three times, a process that will be a little easier on the Orioles' farmhands in coming years now that the team's Triple-A affiliate has moved from Ottawa (525 miles away) to Norfolk (240 miles). Clearly discouraged by the resulting effect on his frequent flier mileage, Rodriguez has signed a minor league deal with the Marlins', whose Triple-A affiliate, the Albuquerque Isotopes, is more than 1,600 miles from Miami as the crow flies.

Todd Williams Bats: R Throws: R   Height: 6′ 3″   Weight: 220   Born: February 13, 1971   Age: 36

YEAR	TEAM	LVL	AGE	W	L	SV	G	GS	IP	H	BB	SO	HR	GB%	BABIP	STUFF	WHIP	ERA	PERA	EQERA	EQH9	EQBB9	EQSO9	EQHR9	VORP	WXRL
2004	BAL	MLB	33	2	0	0	29	0	31¹	26	9	13	2	—	.247	-9	1.12	2.88	4.66	2.53	7.3	2.2	3.4	0.6	12.2	0.84
2005	BAL	MLB	34	5	5	1	72	0	76¹	72	26	38	5	65.7%	.276	-4	1.28	3.30	4.20	3.66	8.1	3.0	4.3	0.6	14.6	1.74
2006	BAL	MLB	35	2	4	1	62	0	57	76	19	24	8	59.2%	.335	-23	1.67	4.74	5.03	4.80	10.8	2.7	3.5	1.0	2.4	-0.43
2007	BAL	MLB	36	2	3	2	53	0	57¹	65	17	25	5	56.0%	.299	-15	1.42	4.29	4.13	4.04	10.3	2.5	3.7	0.8	8.1	0.70

Breakout: 32% Improve: 56% Collapse: 33% Attrition: 15%   Comparables: Fred Gladding, Dixie Howell, Dan Osinski, Mike Timlin

Either the league's catching up or he's winding down, but Williams's days fulfilling an important role in the bullpen are numbered. He's essentially a one-pitch pitcher, tossing a steady diet of low fastballs, hoping hitters will beat them into the ground. Williams himself was non-tendered into the ground by the Orioles and is still looking to be exhumed as we go to press.

Lineouts

PLAYER	TEAM	LVL	AGE	PA	R	2B	3B	HR	RBI	BB	SO	SB-CS	SPEED	AVG/OBP/SLG	MLVr	EqAVG/OBP/SLG	EqA	VORP
SS A. Chavez	SWB	AAA	24	231	27	22	1	6	28	13	41	6-0	5.7	.276/.317/.476	.125	.269/.313/.481	.270	13.5
C R. Chavez	BOW	AA	33	213	18	10	0	2	21	11	19	0-0	3.6	.255/.290/.337	-.086	.204/.232/.239	.174	-21.7
1B M. Fleisher	DEL	A	22	478	51	29	1	16	67	47	84	2-1	2.7	.261/.343/.449	.138	.223/.282/.371	.228	-21.6
OF K. Pope	ABE	A-	19	81	9	0	0	0	7	2	33	1-0	5.8	.107/.160/.107	-.520	.103/.134/.103	.100	-37.2
	BLU	Rk	19	151	20	16	1	5	29	10	36	4-3	4.5	.341/.411/.585	.456	.280/.318/.469	.266	5.6
2B E. Rogers	OTT	AAA	27	359	40	18	1	5	30	13	52	12-7	5.5	.298/.324/.401	.034	.279/.305/.384	.238	6.6
C E. Whiteside	OTT	AAA	26	340	37	18	1	11	47	10	73	1-3	4.1	.244/.278/.413	-.060	.230/.263/.397	.227	-5.8
C C. Widger	CHA	MLB	35	87	6	3	0	1	7	9	20	0-0	3.1	.184/.264/.263	-.445	.160/.253/.227	.186	-6.0

PLAYER	TEAM	LVL	AGE	W	L	SV	IP	H	BB	SO	HR	GB%	BABIP	STUFF	WHIP	ERA	PERA	EqERA	EqH9	EqBB9	EqSO9	EqHR9	VORP
J. Berken	ABE	A-	22	1	4	0	45¹	39	5	46	4	—	.299	-24	0.98	2.79	8.50	6.69	12.3	1.8	5.1	3.8	-4.9
E. Dubose*	BOW	AA	30	7	1	0	84¹	70	34	67	7	—	.273	-13	1.24	3.10	5.92	4.78	8.4	4.6	4.6	1.3	7.4
	OTT	AAA	30	3	4	0	39²	44	23	30	3	—	.350	-2	1.71	5.51	5.61	6.92	10.4	6.0	5.1	1.2	-5.7
J. Halama*	BAL	MLB	34	3	1	0	29¹	38	13	12	6	—	.323	-31	1.74	6.45	6.05	5.58	10.6	3.8	3.5	1.5	-1.4
R. Keefer	ABE	A-	24	2	0	0	16²	14	11	17	0	—	.326	-2	1.54	2.22	6.53	5.02	10.0	10.7	5.0	0.6	0.9
L. Gustavo	ABE	A-	21	0	2	20	30	17	15	46	2	—	.268	3	1.07	1.20	8.60	3.24	9.4	7.9	8.3	2.9	6.6
M. Salas	BOW	AA	25	2	6	19	49	39	16	46	3	—	.273	-11	1.12	2.94	4.77	4.15	8.1	3.6	5.3	0.9	7.7

Angel Chavez came to the Orioles when they swapped Jeff Conine to the Phillies. He's a solid defensive player who can't hit, so don't expect him to play in the majors. A third-string catcher, **Raul Chavez** is the kind of "just in case" guy who doesn't help at the plate, but behind it is an improvement on just about anybody but the Gold Glove winners. He'll try to move up to second-string with the Yankees. A big slugger picked out of Radford in the fourteenth round in 2005, **Mark Fleisher** is one of the Orioles' few hitter picks from that draft who didn't fall flat on his face. That's doesn't mean he's a prospect, but that's the state of this system. Fourth rounder **Kieron Pope** joined the O's after last summer's draft; he's such a free swinger that he'd make Austin Powers blush, but he's got big-time power potential. Long one of the system's top prospects, **Ed Rogers** finally peaked—in Ottawa. He signed with Boston as a minor league free agent. There's talk that **Sammy Sosa** is working out and trying to elicit offers from the majors as well as the Japanese Leagues. We'll see where he winds up; his gameday uniform could still be his pajamas by the time you read this. **Eli Whiteside** is probably wondering if he accidentally ran over the Angelos family cat or something; he didn't pan out as a prospect, but c'mon, **Chris Widger**? In his last two months with the White Sox before his release, Widger went 2-for-35; after joining the Orioles, he went 2-for-17, convincing them they'd be better off with Ardoin. He's a free agent and likely retiree.

A sixth-round pick out of Clemson last year, **Jason Berken** showed excellent control, but when opponents hit the ball they hit it hard. **Tim Byrdak** was okay in a situational role in 2005, but he wasn't a lock to make the team as the Orioles brought in every lefty from Driesell to Loosey to challenge him. Maybe that's why he hid the fact that his elbow hurt last year. The results were unbelievably ugly before he was mercifully sent to the DL for bone chip surgery, and he only improved to believably ugly when he came back three months later. Cut, he's signed on with the Tigers. **Eric DuBose** won a bullpen job out of spring training and lost it in two weeks. He signed with those famous rehabilitators of pitchers, the Rockies. The definition of a replacement-level pitcher, **John Halama** was released by the Orioles in June and couldn't find another team to pick him up . . . not that anyone should have. **Ryan Keefer** was hampered all season by a sore elbow which probably cost him a shot at the big league bullpen. He had a solid AFL campaign and should be dealing his low-90s heat in Bowie or Norfolk this season in an attempt to get back on track. **Luis Lebron**, a.k.a. Luis Gustavo, throws 98 miles per hour under any name, albeit in random directions. **John Parrish** missed the entire 2006 season after yet another elbow surgery (cleaning up some of the mess left over from his TJ in 2005), but he's on the 40-man, and the Orioles understandably want to see if he can still throw hard. Dominican **Marino Salas** is entering his tenth season in the organization, but he's still only 26, and his low-90s heat and slider seem to have finally propelled him past Double-A.

Manager: Sam Perlozzo

Year	Team	W-L	Pythag +/-	Avg PC	100 +P	120 +P	QS	BQS	REL	REL w Zero R	IBB	SUBS	PH	PH Avg	PH HR	SB2	CS2	SB3	CS3	SAC Att	SAC %	POS SAC	Squeeze	Swing	In Play
2005	BAL	23-32	0	93.4	22	0	22	2	180	114	3	35	28	.130	0	20	15	4	2	26	73.1%	19	0	28	22
2006	BAL	70-92	+2	95.9	74	2	58	9	470	275	26	65	72	.092	0	100	27	21	4	65	61.5%	38	0	113	91

The most that can be said for Perlozzo is that he provided the Orioles their lifeline to pitching coach Leo Mazzone, and he's aggressive when it comes to the running game—not as aggressive as Mike Scioscia, but then he doesn't have as many weapons at his disposal. Perlozzo is more partial to using pinch-runners than most. He's also bunt-happy for a manager in the DH league, finishing fourth among AL managers in calling for position-player sac bunts. All tactical considerations aside, the bigger issue is that for someone who was supposed to be instilling discipline, the O's have faded pretty badly at the end of both seasons he's managed them. There's a distinct phoning-it-in quality to his team's performances. If Perlozzo has taken steps to up the team's level of professionalism, it's not visible on the field.

Boston Red Sox

July 30 was not a good day for the 2006 Red Sox. That afternoon, the Yankees acquired right fielder Bobby Abreu and starter Cory Lidle from the Phillies, shoring up two trouble spots without surrendering any of the team's top prospects. Boston had pursued both, but an unwillingness to part with rookie Jon Lester and/or pick up the balance of Abreu's contract in a deal for Trot Nixon left the Sox unable to complete a trade. That same night, Nixon, already hampered by an April groin injury, sustained a Grade 2 biceps strain. He would miss five weeks.

July 31 was not a good day for the Sox, either. Despite rumors involving Andruw Jones, Julio Lugo, and more three-ways than a night at Plato's Retreat, the Sox completed just one deal before the trade deadline passed—the minor acquisition of Texas reliever Bryan Corey. That same night, Jason Varitek suffered a torn medial meniscus in his left knee, an injury requiring minor arthroscopic surgery. Like Nixon, Varitek wouldn't return for five weeks.

The Sox were 63–41 at the close of play on July 31, one game ahead of the Yankees in the AL East, but the injuries to Nixon and Varitek were far from the team's only maladies. Injuries had reduced the rotation to a resurgent Curt Schilling, a very erratic Josh Beckett, Lester, Royals retread Kyle Snyder, and the thrice-disabled David Wells, with nonprospect Kason Gabbard and the utterly hittable Jason Johnson filling in when needed. Tim Wakefield had fractured a rib two weeks prior, and a sore-shouldered and ineffective Matt Clement had just been shifted to the 60-day DL, ending his season. The bullpen was shaky, too; though Jonathan Papelbon had surprised with his dominance at closer, Keith Foulke was on the DL, Mike Timlin had served time there, free-agent signings Julian Tavarez and Rudy

Seanez had been busts, and rookies Craig Hansen and Manny Delcarmen appeared unready for high-leverage roles. As for the offense, new outfield acquisitions Wily Mo Peña and Coco Crisp both had missed considerable time with hand injuries; while the former had recovered thanks to minor surgery, the latter had disappointed since returning from the DL.

The Sox had real needs at the deadline, but they were unable to fill any of them. Reeling from their injuries, the team quickly plummeted out of contention, going 9–21 in August including losing a humiliating five times in four days to the Yankees by a combined score of 49–26. The pitching staff yielded a 5.81 ERA that month, the offense slowed to 4.4 runs per game, and from there the situation would be further exacerbated by injuries to Manny Ramirez, David Ortiz, Schilling, and Papelbon, who was shut down just before Labor Day due to fatigue.

If, as sabermetric godfather Branch Rickey asserted, luck is the residue of design, it follows that bad luck is the residue of bad design. The Sox had the ingredients at hand to contend for another pennant—talent, prospects, money—yet squandered their season through a series of poor choices that invited misfortune. The unsuccessful championship defense of 2005 had scarcely ended when their troubles began, as Theo Epstein left his GM job upon the expiration of his contract on October 31. Amid a flurry of rumors that he was still involved in the team's decision-making process, Boston didn't exactly replace him, opting for a co-GM alignment involving Jed Hoyer, who had been Epstein's assistant, and Director of Player Development Ben Cherington overseen by team President Larry Lucchino. Epstein's shadow hovered over

---

RED SOX PROSPECTUS

2006 record: 86–76; Third place, AL East

Pythagenport record: 80–82

Runs scored per game: 5.06 (6th in AL)

Runs allowed per game: 5.09 (11th in AL)

Team EqA: .263 (5th in AL)

2006 Batters Age: 31.0 (2nd oldest in AL)

2006 Pitchers Age: 32.0 (2nd oldest in AL)

Ballpark: Fenway Park; Slight hitter's park; Park Factor of 1.017

2006: Welcome to the Boston Zoo: they pancaked in August after an offseason spent squabbling, and several bold moves failed boldly.

2007: Between the Matsuzaka and Drew contracts, they committed roughly the GDP of Luxembourg, but that dough didn't buy them a bullpen.

---

this ad hoc front office's moves, which included trades for Beckett, Mark Loretta, and Andy Marte, the departure of Johnny Damon (the sole free agent from the 2004 champs who still had life in his bat) and the signings of Tavarez and Seanez. "What Would Theo Do?" became a popular refrain in Red Sox Nation.

When Epstein returned in late January, his team still needed a starting center fielder and a shortstop. His first major move upon returning was to ship third base prospect Marte—acquired from Atlanta in a December deal for 2005 free-agent mistake Edgar Renteria—catching prospect Kelly Shoppach, and reliever Guillermo Mota to Cleveland for Crisp, a tweener considered not fast enough to man center, but not productive enough to carry a corner outfield position. Epstein's second move was signing Alex Gonzalez, the former Marlin (as opposed to the former player) to play short. Neither was a bad move. Gonzalez would provide a major defensive upgrade over the disappointing Renteria. Crisp's PECOTA projection was very similar to Damon's; his underperformance would be due to freak injury—no one could have predicted that he'd fracture a finger on a hit-by-pitch.

On the other hand (no pun intended), predicting that a gaggle of aged pitchers with demonstrably creaky joints might fail to perform is not that difficult—which is what made Epstein's next move the real clunker. In late March, he shipped Bronson Arroyo to Cincinnati for Peña, breaking up an apparent rotation logjam for some needed outfield depth. A closer look reveals the sheer hubris of the move; even though the Red Sox hadn't anointed Papelbon as closer yet, parting with a 200-inning horse, who would go on to lead the NL in innings pitched, on the assumption that they had enough pitching elsewhere was quite a risk. Before the trade, the Sox's rotation consisted of the very durable but nonetheless 39-year-old Wakefield; Schilling, also 39 and coming off of an injury-plagued campaign; Wells, 43, who had undergone arthroscopic surgery and requested a trade; Clement, 31, coming into the year off a second-half ERA of 5.72; Beckett, 26, having never topped 180 innings; and Arroyo, 29, who, for all of his flaws, was a league-average innings-muncher in 2005. Pile all that on top of the expectation that the injury-prone Foulke would remain the closer without accompanying reinforcements, and you've got a staff begging for trouble.

If the Arroyo deal smacked of hubris, then the Doug Mirabelli situation smelled of panic. Needing a second baseman to replace free agent Tony Graffanino, the Sox shipped Mirabelli to San Diego for Loretta. Perennial prospect Shoppach was then flipped for Josh Bard in the Crisp deal. Bard seemed an acceptable backup for Varitek, but when he proved incapable of handling Wakefield's knuckler, Epstein hastily reacquired Mirabelli, but only after San Diego GM Kevin Towers forced the Sox into a bidding war with the Yanks. For his troubles, Towers wound up prying away Bard, reliever Cla Meredith, and cash. Both players contributed mightily to the Pads' NL West title run; Bard hit .338/.406/.537 in a platoon with Mike Piazza, while Meredith reeled off a 34-inning scoreless streak. Mirabelli gloved those knucklers, but never got his average above .200, and when Varitek went down, his inadequacy forced Epstein to make a waiver deal for D.O.A. Baltimore "catcher" Javy Lopez. Epstein fared better in another backstop-related deal with the Padres at the end of August, when he acquired prospect George Kottaras for one month of the finally-healthy Wells, though even that move—Boston's white flag—was tainted by the identity of Wells's utterly uninspiring replacement, Kevin Jarvis. Enough said.

If Boston's pennywise pound-foolishness at the deadline helped create a $142 million bust of a ballclub—the most expensive team ever to miss the playoffs—they could not be accused of such frugality over the winter. In mid-November, they bid an astounding $51.1 million dollars to win the posting rights to Japanese hurler Daisuke Matsuzaka. Extending negotiations right up to the one-month deadline, they signed him to a six-year, $52-million deal with escalator clauses that, despite the burden of the high bid, looks like a stroke of brilliance in a market in which Gil Meche is worth $55 million and Barry Zito $126 million. No other free agent hurler could approach the upside of Matsuzaka, whose comparables (according to Clay Davenport's translations) include true right-handed aces such as Roger Clemens, Roy Halladay, Brandon Webb, and Chris Carpenter. The addition of Matsuzaka and the shift of Papelbon back to starting make the Sox's rotation significantly younger than it was last year, with Lester—hopefully free of cancer—able to provide additional youth and depth.

Boston also upgraded in the outfield by signing J. D. Drew. After the new Collective Bargaining Agreement set teams awash in cash, Drew, already guaranteed $33 million over the last three years of his five-year deal with the Dodgers, exercised his out clause—an option he'd claimed he would forego just weeks earlier. The Sox then signed him to a five-year, $70-million deal, prompting them once again to explore the market for a Manny Ramirez trade. In one of the winter's least surprising moves, they also signed Julio Lugo to a four-year, $36-million deal. Taken together, the Matsuzaka, Drew, and Lugo acquisitions represent the Sox brass's hardnosed determination to rebound from a season filled with mistakes and indecision.

These free agent moves also allowed the Sox to keep their core of young pitching intact—not just Papelbon, Hansen, Lester, and Delcarmen, but also high-impact arms lower down in the system, such as Michael Bowden and Clay Buchholz. This team still has its issues, however, which threaten to endanger its return to October baseball. The Papelbon shift leaves them without a closer at this writing—pursuits of such pitchers as Eric Gagne, Jonathan Broxton, Scott Linebrink, and Mike Gonzalez, either as free agents or in trade, have all failed, and it's apparent that the in-house youngsters aren't ready for the job. Additionally, the team is still banking on a relatively old lineup; aside from 23-year-old Dustin Pedroia (slated to take over at second base), only Crisp (27), Peña (25), and Youkilis (28) are below 30, and none of them are among the offense's big movers and shakers.

The addition of Matsuzaka alone leaves them in a better spot than they were a year ago. Even so, beyond relying as heavily as ever on their key hitters, they're going to have to exercise some better decision-making to get better breaks than they got in 2006 and return to the postseason.

HITTERS

Alex Cora　SS　Bats: L　Throws: R　Height: 6' 0"　Weight: 200　Born: October 18, 1975　Age: 31

YEAR	TEAM	LVL	AGE	PA	R	2B	3B	HR	RBI	BB	SO	SB	CS	SPEED	AVG	OBP	SLG	MLVR	EQAVG	EQOBP	EQSLG	EQA	VORP	DEFENSE			
2004	LAN	MLB	28	484	47	9	4	10	47	47	41	3	4	4.7	.264	.364	.380	.003	.269	.364	.390	.265	13.4	122-2B	-4		
2005	CLE	MLB	29	157	11	5	2	1	8	5	18	6	0	6.4	.205	.250	.288	-.357	.208	.258	.292	.209	-5.7	22-SS	4	13-2B	2
2005	BOS	MLB	29	116	14	3	2	2	16	6	12	1	2	6.0	.269	.310	.394	-.094	.275	.327	.402	.249	0.1	24-2B	-1		
2006	BOS	MLB	30	264	31	7	2	1	18	19	29	6	2	6.2	.238	.312	.298	-.272	.232	.312	.288	.221	-5.4	49-SS	4	11-2B	-3
2007	BOS	MLB	31	306	34	10	2	2	25	19	35	6	2	5.8	.255	.314	.335	-.197	.243	.309	.331	.233	-2.3	74-SS	2		

Breakout: 23%　Improve: 48%　Collapse: 28%　Attrition: 31%　Comparables: Marlon Anderson, Rob Wilfong, Jeff Huson, Tim Bogar

After coming over from the Indians in a mid-2005 trade, Cora hit well enough that some thought he might win the starting job at short. Then the Sox signed Alex Gonzalez, relegating Cora to the backup role. Despite a shortage of at-bats, he hit well enough through the first four months of the season (.293/.383/.358), but turned into an offensive cipher from August 1 onward (.179/.227/.232). Still a reasonably adept fielder, the Red Sox brought him back on a two-year contract.

Coco Crisp　CF　Bats: S　Throws: R　Height: 6' 0"　Weight: 180　Born: November 1, 1979　Age: 27

YEAR	TEAM	LVL	AGE	PA	R	2B	3B	HR	RBI	BB	SO	SB	CS	SPEED	AVG	OBP	SLG	MLVR	EQAVG	EQOBP	EQSLG	EQA	VORP	DEFENSE			
2004	CLE	MLB	24	538	78	24	2	15	71	36	69	20	13	6.2	.297	.344	.446	.057	.305	.357	.459	.275	17.2	87-CF	-10	37-LF	4
2005	CLE	MLB	25	656	86	42	4	16	69	44	81	15	6	6.3	.300	.345	.465	.119	.312	.366	.494	.291	30.2	134-LF	11		
2006	BOS	MLB	26	452	58	22	2	8	36	31	67	22	4	7.1	.264	.317	.385	-.125	.260	.321	.385	.253	7.5	101-CF	-1		
2007	BOS	MLB	27	561	84	27	3	13	63	40	76	21	7	6.6	.310	.361	.452	.084	.296	.355	.447	.285	23.3	132-CF	0		

Breakout: 23%　Improve: 57%　Collapse: 15%　Attrition: 9%　Comparables: R. J. Reynolds, Mitch Webster, Brian McRae, Marquis Grissom

In trading for Crisp, the Sox appeared to get a younger, cheaper version of Johnny Damon. PECOTA saw it that way, projecting .295/.347/.445 (.276 EqA) for Crisp, compared to .290/.352/.423 (.274 EqA) for Damon. Legitimate comparison of the two players' 2006 campaigns was scuttled when Crisp broke a bone in his left index finger during the season's opening week, and severe kidney stones prolonged his absence to seven weeks. His return was another data point in the annals of hitter drop-offs after hand injuries—despite putting the ball into play with about the same frequency, Crisp's line-drive percentage dropped from 19.6 to 15.9, and the percentage of his fly balls that left the park dropped from 10.1 to 6.7. Late September X-rays showed that his fracture had regressed to where it was in mid-April, and Crisp underwent season-ending surgery. The perception that he was a disappointment in Boston, coupled with his cost certainty ($15.5 million over the next three years) ensured that his availability would be a hot topic over the winter, but the Sox should avoid the temptation to sell low because of one season derailed by a relatively random injury.

Jacoby Ellsbury　CF　Bats: L　Throws: L　Height: 6' 1"　Weight: 185　Born: September 11, 1983　Age: 23

YEAR	TEAM	LVL	AGE	PA	R	2B	3B	HR	RBI	BB	SO	SB	CS	SPEED	AVG	OBP	SLG	MLVR	EQAVG	EQOBP	EQSLG	EQA	VORP	DEFENSE	
2005	LOW	A-	21	165	28	3	5	1	19	24	20	23	3	8.9	.317	.418	.432	.256	.268	.333	.356	.255	1.2	26-CF	-1
2006	WIL	A+	22	281	35	7	5	4	32	25	28	25	9	7.3	.299	.379	.418	.169	.286	.342	.404	.261	8.6	58-CF	0
2006	PME	AA	22	225	29	10	3	3	19	24	25	16	8	7.1	.308	.387	.434	.195	.299	.369	.443	.280	14.6	47-CF	7
2007	BOS	MLB	23	522	77	25	7	5	44	35	63	25	10	6.8	.300	.351	.410	.002	.287	.345	.406	.271	15.1	123-CF	5

Breakout: 26%　Improve: 59%　Collapse: 10%　Attrition: 11%　Comparables: Chris Duffy, Josh Anderson, McKay Christensen, Mike Rodriguez

This speedy center fielder was the first of Boston's five first-round picks in 2005. Thus far, he's fully justified both the team's investment and the inevitable Damon comparisons. Ellsbury has climbed through the system rapidly, showing significant improvement at each stop, excellent on-base skills, developing power, and outstanding range in the field; he was honored as both the organization's defensive player and baserunner of the year. Coco Crisp may be signed through 2009, but bet on the Sox to offload him when Ellsbury is ready.

Alex Gonzalez   **SS**   **Bats: R**   **Throws: R**   Height: 6' 0"   Weight: 200   Born: February 15, 1977   Age: 30

YEAR	TEAM	LVL	AGE	PA	R	2B	3B	HR	RBI	BB	SO	SB	CS	SPEED	AVG	OBP	SLG	MLVR	EQAVG	EQOBP	EQSLG	EQA	VORP	DEFENSE	
2004	FLO	MLB	27	599	67	30	3	23	79	27	126	3	1	4.5	.232	.270	.419	-.115	.235	.273	.425	.237	5.5	153-SS	-6
2005	FLO	MLB	28	478	45	30	0	5	45	31	81	5	3	4.6	.264	.319	.368	-.058	.274	.328	.386	.249	9.5	122-SS	-1
2006	BOS	MLB	29	429	48	24	2	9	50	22	67	1	0	5.0	.255	.299	.397	-.151	.251	.302	.397	.244	3.2	109-SS	-3
2007	CIN	MLB	30	461	51	25	2	14	56	28	78	4	2	5.0	.257	.308	.424	-.097	.255	.306	.419	.247	10.6	109-SS	-3

Breakout: 23% Improve: 51% Collapse: 19% Attrition: 22%   Comparables: Pat Meares, Pete Mackanin, Greg Gagne, Andy Carey

Thanks to the midseason retirement of his eponymous counterpart, here's the winner of the Last Alex Gonzalez Standing award, a boon to anyone incapable of remembering which was which. Sox fans were simply excited that he was anyone but Edgar Renteria. While Gonzalez anchored an infield defense that was much improved by Renteria's departure—from −16 to +6 runs, according to the Davenport Translations—he was actually a few runs below average. His bat was a net loss as well, though as late as August 3 he was hitting a useful .291/.335/.444; injuries, pregnancy leave, and general Alex Gonzalez-ness held him to an anemic .122/.159/.220 showing the rest of the way. He signed a three-year, $14-million deal with the Reds, allowing the Sox to consummate their lust for Julio Lugo.

Eric Hinske   **1B/OF**   **Bats: L**   **Throws: R**   Height: 6' 2"   Weight: 235   Born: August 5, 1977   Age: 29

YEAR	TEAM	LVL	AGE	PA	R	2B	3B	HR	RBI	BB	SO	SB	CS	SPEED	AVG	OBP	SLG	MLVR	EQAVG	EQOBP	EQSLG	EQA	VORP	DEFENSE	
2004	TOR	MLB	26	634	66	23	3	15	69	54	109	12	8	5.1	.246	.312	.375	-.161	.240	.312	.373	.241	-11.8	146-3B	3
2005	TOR	MLB	27	537	79	31	2	15	68	46	121	8	4	5.7	.262	.333	.430	.003	.262	.343	.441	.270	9.0	96-1B	0
2006	TOR	MLB	28	224	35	9	2	12	29	27	49	1	1	4.7	.264	.353	.513	.109	.258	.357	.505	.289	10.4	24-RF	0
2006	BOS	MLB	28	88	8	8	0	1	5	8	30	1	1	3.7	.288	.352	.425	.018	.278	.352	.405	.263	1.6		
2007	BOS	MLB	29	351	45	20	2	11	45	33	77	5	2	5.4	.261	.334	.441	-.017	.250	.328	.435	.270	5.0		

Breakout: 10% Improve: 39% Collapse: 30% Attrition: 28%   Comparables: Mark Johnson, Raul Ibanez, Ben Broussard, Cliff Mapes

After three seasons of diminishing returns on Hinske's Rookie of the Year campaign, the Blue Jays bolstered their corner infield by acquiring Troy Glaus and Lyle Overbay, forcing Hinkse to learn the outfield. He chipped in regularly off the bench, but by mid-August, Hinkse was a Red Sock, arriving just in time for the team's collapse, despite his own efforts. Cheap (the Jays will pay half of his $5.6 million salary for 2007) and nominally capable of manning all four corners, he's an asset so long as the Sox shield him from southpaws.

George Kottaras   **C**   **Bats: L**   **Throws: R**   Height: 6' 0"   Weight: 185   Born: May 16, 1983   Age: 24

YEAR	TEAM	LVL	AGE	PA	R	2B	3B	HR	RBI	BB	SO	SB	CS	SPEED	AVG	OBP	SLG	MLVR	EQAVG	EQOBP	EQSLG	EQA	VORP	DEFENSE	
2004	FTW	A	21	326	40	18	1	7	46	51	41	0	0	3.0	.310	.415	.461	.314	.290	.375	.428	.281	21.4	49-C	-9
2005	LEL	A+	22	394	54	29	0	9	50	50	60	2	1	2.9	.303	.390	.469	.115	.249	.324	.370	.246	3.1	81-C	-6
2005	MOB	AA	22	121	16	7	0	2	15	19	23	0	0	2.7	.287	.397	.416	.140	.260	.355	.394	.267	4.4	24-C	-5
2006	MOB	AA	23	310	40	19	1	8	33	50	68	0	1	3.0	.276	.394	.451	.223	.275	.381	.473	.293	26.4	67-C	-10
2006	POR	AAA	23	133	14	10	1	2	17	12	30	0	0	3.9	.210	.286	.361	-.193	.198	.269	.339	.216	-5.2	28-C	-4
2007	BOS	MLB	24	457	48	26	1	10	54	47	88	0	0	3.9	.258	.337	.404	-.063	.246	.331	.400	.261	8.9	108-C	-8

Breakout: 21% Improve: 45% Collapse: 24% Attrition: 17%   Comparables: Mario Valdez, Nick Leach, Jeff Bailey, Chris Richard

For five starts worth of a revitalized David Wells, Theo Epstein scored a nice haul with the fourth catcher to change hands between the Red Sox and Padres within a year. Kottaras's size, durability, and will to endure the daily grind of catching are all concerns, but he offers a nice mix of line-drive power and good plate discipline; his bat could support a position change if necessary. He'll likely spend the season in Pawtucket, but could see Boston if Varitek is sidelined again.

Javy Lopez   C   Bats: R   Throws: R   Height: 6' 3"   Weight: 220   Born: November 5, 1970   Age: 36

YEAR	TEAM	LVL	AGE	PA	R	2B	3B	HR	RBI	BB	SO	SB	CS	SPEED	AVG	OBP	SLG	MLVR	EQAVG	EQOBP	EQSLG	EQA	VORP	DEFENSE	
2004	BAL	MLB	33	638	83	33	3	23	86	47	97	0	0	4.0	.316	.370	.503	.177	.317	.374	.511	.300	48.2	124-C	-5
2005	BAL	MLB	34	423	47	24	1	15	49	19	68	0	1	3.8	.278	.322	.458	.052	.285	.336	.483	.276	19.7	71-C	-6
2006	BAL	MLB	35	299	30	15	1	8	31	18	60	0	0	3.9	.265	.314	.412	-.079	.264	.321	.420	.254	2.0	20-C	-4
2006	BOS	MLB	35	65	6	5	0	0	4	2	16	0	0	3.5	.190	.215	.270	-.530	.161	.200	.226	.156	-5.6	15-C	-3
2007	COL	MLB	36	267	33	15	1	9	39	18	46	1	1	4.0	.287	.339	.472	.047	.265	.321	.436	.258	9.5	66-C	-3

Breakout: 10% Improve: 30% Collapse: 40% Attrition: 47%   Comparables: Damian Miller, Mike Heath, Terry Steinbach, Joe Torre

Lopez entered the season already disgruntled by the Orioles' signing of Ramon Hernandez. When the O's asked him to learn first base but didn't accompany the request with a contract extension, Lopez allowed a slow start at the plate to distract him from breaking in that new mitt; he never played a regular-season game at first. Confined to a DH/backup backstop role and troubled by back and neck problems, his misery was such a perfect fit within the general Orioles malaise that it came as a surprise when the Sox traded for him in the wake of Varitek's injury. The move was a disaster; Lopez didn't hit, and the Sox didn't win. When Varitek returned, the team promptly pulled the plug. The market for recalcitrant 36-year-old catchers with declining skills on both sides of the ball being what it is, Lopez is still looking for a job at this writing.

Mark Loretta   2B   Bats: R   Throws: R   Height: 6' 0"   Weight: 185   Born: August 14, 1971   Age: 35

YEAR	TEAM	LVL	AGE	PA	R	2B	3B	HR	RBI	BB	SO	SB	CS	SPEED	AVG	OBP	SLG	MLVR	EQAVG	EQOBP	EQSLG	EQA	VORP	DEFENSE	
2004	SDN	MLB	32	707	108	47	2	16	76	58	45	5	3	5.0	.335	.391	.495	.286	.346	.399	.510	.311	67.6	145-2B	22
2005	SDN	MLB	33	463	54	16	1	3	38	45	34	8	4	4.8	.280	.360	.347	-.001	.295	.372	.369	.266	11.0	101-2B	2
2006	BOS	MLB	34	703	75	33	0	5	59	49	63	4	1	4.5	.285	.345	.361	-.093	.282	.349	.361	.254	12.3	132-2B	-9
2007	HOU	MLB	35	481	58	24	2	7	47	39	41	5	2	5.0	.276	.341	.388	-.073	.275	.340	.383	.252	12.7	114-2B	-3

Breakout: 3% Improve: 17% Collapse: 47% Attrition: 24%   Comparables: Dick Groat, Eric Young, Johnny Temple, Bill Madlock

Loretta unfortunately showed that his 2005 falloff wasn't solely attributable to his thumb injury. Acquired in the Mirabelli deal, his move from pitcher-friendly PETCO to hitter-friendly Fenway should have pumped some air into his rate stats, but his OBP fell by 15 points, and his slight up-tick in SLG was all park, not performance (.308/.376/.411 at home, .261/.313/.309 on the road). He's 35 and below average with both the glove and the bat, but versatile enough to go back to the utility role with the Astros now that he's inked a one-year, $2.5-million deal.

Mike Lowell   3B   Bats: R   Throws: R   Height: 6' 3"   Weight: 210   Born: February 24, 1974   Age: 33

YEAR	TEAM	LVL	AGE	PA	R	2B	3B	HR	RBI	BB	SO	SB	CS	SPEED	AVG	OBP	SLG	MLVR	EQAVG	EQOBP	EQSLG	EQA	VORP	DEFENSE	
2004	FLO	MLB	30	671	87	44	1	27	85	64	77	5	1	4.5	.293	.365	.505	.217	.298	.370	.515	.299	43.9	146-3B	13
2005	FLO	MLB	31	558	56	36	1	8	58	46	58	4	0	4.4	.236	.298	.360	-.119	.241	.305	.380	.243	-4.8	127-3B	15
2006	BOS	MLB	32	631	79	47	1	20	80	47	61	2	2	4.0	.284	.339	.475	.058	.279	.342	.479	.278	20.7	146-3B	19
2007	BOS	MLB	33	559	66	34	1	16	76	44	62	2	1	4.3	.272	.332	.439	-.016	.260	.326	.434	.268	11.4	131-3B	6

Breakout: 13% Improve: 42% Collapse: 26% Attrition: 9%   Comparables: Brooks Robinson, Tim Wallach, Matt Williams, John Valentin

Lowell was supposed to be the poison pill in the Josh Beckett trade, with the Sox taking on the remaining two years and $18 million of his contract. Moving to Fenway, he figured to improve superficially, and with Kevin Youkilis still available to slot in across the diamond, the Sox might have leveraged Lowell's resuscitated value into a midseason trade. But after a hot start (.317/.373/.565 through May), Lowell cooled off considerably (.269/.323/.432) and was left to play out the string far from any pennant race. Still, he posted a stellar season in the field; even if he continues his more modest hitting, the leather helps him maintain some value.

Jed Lowrie   SS   Bats: S   Throws: R   Height: 6' 0"   Weight: 180   Born: April 17, 1984   Age: 23

YEAR	TEAM	LVL	AGE	PA	R	2B	3B	HR	RBI	BB	SO	SB	CS	SPEED	AVG	OBP	SLG	MLVR	EQAVG	EQOBP	EQSLG	EQA	VORP	DEFENSE			
2005	LOW	A-	21	240	36	12	0	4	32	34	30	7	5	4.1	.328	.429	.448	.300	.265	.335	.349	.242	7.5	40-SS	-5	11-2B	-1
2006	WIL	A+	22	438	43	21	6	3	50	54	65	2	2	4.4	.262	.352	.374	.041	.249	.320	.357	.240	4.1	88-SS	-9		
2007	BOS	MLB	23	448	51	22	3	7	44	37	73	2	2	4.7	.278	.340	.396	-.053	.266	.334	.392	.259	13.3	106-SS	-6		

Breakout: 55% Improve: 80% Collapse: 9% Attrition: 11%   Comparables: Drew Sutton, Jake Thrower, Carlos Mendoza, Andrew Beattie

A 2005 first-round supplemental pick, Lowrie led the New York–Penn League in OBP while surviving the switch from second base to shortstop. His Carolina League stint didn't go as well. Already off to a slow start, Lowrie missed five weeks due to a high ankle sprain, and was nearly demoted back to Lowell when he struggled upon returning. As late as August 4 he was hitting just .233/.330/.305, but he closed the season with a .327/.380/.529 month, and maintained good plate discipline all year despite his woes. He's got the arm for shortstop, but his speed is only average, and he may not have enough range; a move back to second wouldn't surprise anyone, but you can't fault the Sox for challenging him.

Doug Mirabelli		C					Bats: R		Throws: R			Height: 6' 1"		Weight: 220		Born: October 18, 1970			Age: 36	
YEAR	TEAM	LVL	AGE	PA	R	2B	3B	HR	RBI	BB	SO	SB	CS	SPEED	AVG	OBP	SLG	MLVR	EQAVG	EQOBP	EQSLG	EQA	VORP	DEFENSE
2004	BOS	MLB	33	182	27	12	0	9	32	19	46	0	0	3.1	.281	.368	.525	.165	.277	.368	.522	.298	13.4	48-C -14
2005	BOS	MLB	34	152	16	7	0	6	18	14	48	2	0	4.5	.228	.309	.412	-.088	.224	.316	.418	.255	3.1	35-C 2
2006	SDN	MLB	35	26	1	1	0	0	0	4	5	0	0	4.1	.182	.308	.227	-.327	.182	.308	.227	.205	-1.2	
2006	BOS	MLB	35	176	12	6	0	6	25	11	54	0	0	3.2	.193	.261	.342	-.339	.181	.260	.319	.205	-7.6	45-C -5
2007	BOS	MLB	36	257	24	13	0	9	32	22	70	0	0	3.8	.221	.296	.392	-.177	.211	.290	.388	.239	-1.8	63-C -1

Breakout: 9% Improve: 28% Collapse: 40% Attrition: 56%   Comparables: Steve Yeager, Lance Parrish, Jim Hegan, Jim Sundberg

Attempting to shed Tim Wakefield's personal valet, the Sox swapped Mirabelli to San Diego in exchange for Mark Loretta. The Padres scrapped plans to start him when they snagged Mike Piazza on the cheap; Mirabelli sulked, and started agitating Kevin Towers for a deal. Meanwhile, back in Boston, Josh Bard's monumental struggles to catch Wakefield's knuckleball (10 passed balls in five starts) induced Epstein to hastily reacquire Mirabelli, but Theo drastically overpaid by parting with Bard, Cla Meredith, and $100,000 cash. Once Wakefield and then Jason Varitek went down, the Sox were left with a sub-Mendozoid backup of decreased utility, while the Pads had obtained key ingredients for their NL West title run. Showing little imagination, the Sox re-signed Mirabelli to a one-year deal in December.

Brandon Moss		RF					Bats: L		Throws: R			Height: 6' 0"		Weight: 180		Born: September 16, 1983			Age: 23	
YEAR	TEAM	LVL	AGE	PA	R	2B	3B	HR	RBI	BB	SO	SB	CS	SPEED	AVG	OBP	SLG	MLVR	EQAVG	EQOBP	EQSLG	EQA	VORP	DEFENSE	
2004	AUG	A	20	490	66	25	6	13	101	46	75	19	8	5.6	.339	.402	.515	.358	.312	.360	.458	.282	22.1	90-RF 2	12-LF 1
2004	SAR	A+	20	91	16	2	1	2	10	7	15	2	0	5.3	.422	.462	.542	.569	.388	.424	.506	.324	11.3	21-RF -1	
2005	PME	AA	21	568	87	31	4	16	61	53	129	6	3	5.6	.268	.337	.441	.089	.251	.315	.409	.252	-6.1	126-RF 0	
2006	PME	AA	22	573	76	36	3	12	83	56	108	8	5	4.8	.285	.357	.439	.142	.275	.340	.434	.267	9.9	128-RF -9	
2007	BOS	MLB	23	529	64	34	3	13	64	42	104	5	2	5.0	.276	.336	.437	-.007	.264	.330	.432	.269	4.2	124-RF -1	

Breakout: 17% Improve: 55% Collapse: 21% Attrition: 1%   Comparables: Kevin Burford, Curtis Granderson, Kelly Johnson, Doug Deeds

The 2004 Sally League MVP's career stalled at Portland in 2005. The Sox made him repeat the level last year, and, despite a slow start (.222/.266/.356 through May), he improved his strike zone judgment and rate of contact. Though his power didn't develop accordingly, he homered five times in nine playoff games, winning postseason MVP honors and helping Portland to its first Eastern League title. If he can carry that progress up to Pawtucket, he could find himself in the big club's plans before too long.

David Murphy		RF					Bats: L		Throws: L			Height: 6' 4"		Weight: 190		Born: October 18, 1981			Age: 25	
YEAR	TEAM	LVL	AGE	PA	R	2B	3B	HR	RBI	BB	SO	SB	CS	SPEED	AVG	OBP	SLG	MLVR	EQAVG	EQOBP	EQSLG	EQA	VORP	DEFENSE	
2004	SAR	A+	22	297	35	11	0	4	38	25	46	3	5	4.0	.261	.323	.346	-.034	.231	.283	.307	.208	-15.3	56-CF -5	
2005	PME	AA	23	535	71	25	4	14	75	46	83	13	6	5.7	.275	.337	.430	.079	.256	.316	.404	.250	6.1	129-CF -15	
2006	PME	AA	24	184	22	17	1	3	25	11	29	4	2	5.4	.273	.315	.436	.069	.254	.293	.410	.244	0.3	41-CF -3	
2006	PAW	AAA	24	366	45	23	5	8	44	45	53	3	3	4.8	.267	.355	.447	.120	.259	.344	.447	.270	15.5	61-CF -8	15-RF -4
2006	BOS	MLB	24	26	4	1	0	1	2	4	4	0	0	3.5	.227	.346	.409	-.062	.227	.346	.409	.264	0.4		
2007	BOS	MLB	25	498	53	28	3	8	54	37	83	4	2	4.8	.257	.314	.383	-.131	.246	.308	.379	.244	-2.8	118-CF -8	

Breakout: 18% Improve: 41% Collapse: 30% Attrition: 9%   Comparables: Luke Wilcox, Brett Roneberg, David Miller, Mike Lockwood

The Sox passed over Conor Jackson, Chad Cordero, Chad Billingsley, and Carlos Quentin to take Murphy with the 17th pick in the 2003 draft. Oops. This modestly-developing center fielder is already regarded as MLB-caliber with the glove, but he's got a way to go with the lumber. Despite a slow start in Portland—the entire team hit .219/.299/.322 in a chilly April—Murphy was promoted to Pawtucket in late May, possibly to be showcased as trade bait. Nobody bit, though Murphy improved his plate discipline and earned a cup of coffee in the Show. He'll probably start the season in Triple-A, but his defensive skills could earn him a spot on the Red Sox roster. The development of Jacob Ellsbury suggests that Murphy's window of opportunity in this organization isn't very wide.

Jeffrey Natale   2B   **Bats: R**   **Throws: R**   Height: 5' 9"   Weight: 180   Born: August 24, 1982   Age: 24

YEAR	TEAM	LVL	AGE	PA	R	2B	3B	HR	RBI	BB	SO	SB	CS	SPEED	AVG	OBP	SLG	MLVR	EQAVG	EQOBP	EQSLG	EQA	VORP	DEFENSE
2005	LOW	A-	22	46	9	5	0	0	9	3	3	2	0	4.4	.488	.522	.610	.815	.395	.413	.488	.321	10.0	
2005	GRN	A	22	202	35	19	4	2	35	28	14	1	0	5.5	.338	.463	.544	.458	.291	.376	.463	.291	15.4	39-2B -1
2006	GRN	A	23	231	38	10	0	10	41	41	20	2	1	3.5	.343	.487	.571	.509	.289	.391	.464	.295	18.7	27-2B -6
2006	WIL	A+	23	353	46	13	0	7	46	62	54	1	0	3.8	.278	.419	.403	.194	.253	.361	.362	.264	9.0	57-2B -10
2007	BOS	MLB	24	521	63	28	2	10	56	55	73	2	1	4.5	.269	.354	.402	-.026	.257	.348	.398	.269	15.2	123-2B -10

Breakout: 9%   Improve: 35%   Collapse: 34%   Attrition: 7%   Comparables: Keith Luuloa, Keith Ginter, Rob Ryan, Tony Schrager

Natale picked up where he left off in 2006, tearing up Sally League pitching. He didn't dominate once promoted to Wilmington—a 29-game stretch with just one extra-base hit caused some alarm—but did reached base in his first 22 games at the new level. That plate discipline was no fluke; overall he hit .304/.446/.469, and was named the organization's Minor League Hitter of the Year. Undersized, below average at second, and old for his league at every stop, the former 32nd-rounder won't win many believers until he succeeds in Double-A, but he is in an organization that will give him that chance.

Trot Nixon   RF   **Bats: L**   **Throws: L**   Height: 6' 2"   Weight: 210   Born: April 11, 1974   Age: 33

YEAR	TEAM	LVL	AGE	PA	R	2B	3B	HR	RBI	BB	SO	SB	CS	SPEED	AVG	OBP	SLG	MLVR	EQAVG	EQOBP	EQSLG	EQA	VORP	DEFENSE
2004	BOS	MLB	30	167	24	9	1	6	23	15	24	0	0	4.6	.315	.377	.510	.193	.311	.377	.500	.299	10.6	28-RF 2
2005	BOS	MLB	31	470	64	29	1	13	67	53	59	2	1	4.8	.275	.357	.446	.073	.274	.367	.454	.285	15.2	106-RF 10
2006	BOS	MLB	32	452	59	24	0	8	52	60	55	0	2	3.8	.268	.374	.395	-.002	.264	.377	.397	.275	8.0	100-RF 6
2007	BOS	MLB	33	449	56	25	1	10	53	51	60	1	1	4.5	.267	.355	.417	-.009	.255	.348	.412	.273	3.4	106-RF 2

Breakout: 3%   Improve: 28%   Collapse: 36%   Attrition: 14%   Comparables: Roger Maris, Gene Woodling, Greg Brock, Wally Joyner

For a fan favorite in his walk year, Nixon had a rough go. Slowed by a groin strain, he still hit .311/.415/.455 in the first half—short in the power department, the result of less leg in his swing, but still a performance to be reckoned with. Things fell apart from there; Nixon missed all of August with a Grade 2 biceps strain and a scary staph infection. Upon returning, he hit just .147/.266/.250 in September, hardly an advertisement for his next contract. Whether he returns to Boston for a farewell tour or signs elsewhere, he won't be critical to anyone's plans given his injury history, but he can still be useful in a reduced role.

David Ortiz   DH   **Bats: L**   **Throws: L**   Height: 6' 4"   Weight: 230   Born: November 18, 1975   Age: 31

YEAR	TEAM	LVL	AGE	PA	R	2B	3B	HR	RBI	BB	SO	SB	CS	SPEED	AVG	OBP	SLG	MLVR	EQAVG	EQOBP	EQSLG	EQA	VORP	DEFENSE
2004	BOS	MLB	28	669	94	47	3	41	139	75	133	0	0	4.0	.301	.380	.603	.305	.293	.377	.594	.318	60.8	30-1B -2
2005	BOS	MLB	29	713	119	40	1	47	148	102	124	1	0	3.9	.300	.397	.604	.366	.298	.406	.614	.333	75.6	
2006	BOS	MLB	30	686	115	29	2	54	137	119	117	1	0	4.2	.287	.413	.636	.400	.280	.415	.633	.339	76.8	
2007	BOS	MLB	31	695	116	37	1	40	133	116	130	0	0	3.6	.289	.410	.573	.300	.276	.402	.567	.331	58.8	162-DH

Breakout: 2%   Improve: 22%   Collapse: 50%   Attrition: 3%   Comparables: Willie McCovey, Carlos Delgado, Jason Giambi, Barry Bonds

It may be heresy to suggest that Big Papi enjoyed his finest season in a Red Sox uniform in 2006, but he set personal bests in OBP, SLG, and EqA, broke the franchise single-season home run record (besting Jimmie Foxx's 50 in 1938), and tied the AL record for home runs in road games (32, matching Babe Ruth's 1927 mark). For those arguing that he's got that special clutch goodness, he also led the AL in hitter Win Expectancy (8.14) for the second year in a row. Nonetheless, the final stretch of Ortiz's season left a bitter aftertaste beyond the Sox's ignominious fate. Just after Manny Ramirez went down in late August, Ortiz was hospitalized due to an irregular heartbeat, missing a week. His return to the lineup underscored the fact that Ortiz benefits considerably from having an all-time great batting behind him; in 23 Manny-less games following his return, opposing pitchers walked Ortiz 31 times, all but one of the slugger's nine homers were solo shots, and he drove in just five additional runners. His mid-September comments regarding the upcoming MVP voting—including a petty dismissal of Derek Jeter's candidacy—and his reaction to the fallout made him appear more focused on individual glory than team success. All in all, the fairytale of 2004 seems a long way away, but as long as he has Ramirez protecting him, there's no reason he can't continue his heroics.

Dustin Pedroia   2B   Bats: R   Throws: R   Height: 5' 9"   Weight: 180   Born: August 17, 1983   Age: 23

YEAR	TEAM	LVL	AGE	PA	R	2B	3B	HR	RBI	BB	SO	SB	CS	SPEED	AVG	OBP	SLG	MLVR	EQAVG	EQOBP	EQSLG	EQA	VORP	DEFENSE	
2004	AUG	A	20	57	11	5	0	1	5	6	3	2	0	4.6	.400	.474	.560	.586	.365	.421	.500	.314	8.2	12-SS	1
2004	SAR	A+	20	128	23	8	3	2	14	13	4	0	2	5.5	.336	.417	.523	.393	.321	.386	.518	.301	15.6	30-SS	-1
2005	PME	AA	21	298	39	19	2	8	40	34	26	7	3	4.7	.324	.409	.508	.330	.303	.378	.479	.293	26.4	56-2B	-3
2005	PAW	AAA	21	240	39	9	1	5	24	24	17	1	0	4.7	.255	.356	.382	-.031	.240	.331	.361	.246	1.6	38-2B	2
2006	PAW	AAA	22	493	55	30	3	5	50	48	27	1	4	4.2	.305	.384	.426	.165	.295	.370	.430	.277	34.2	74-SS 5	32-2B 3
2006	BOS	MLB	22	98	5	4	0	2	7	7	7	0	1	3.3	.191	.258	.303	-.396	.170	.247	.273	.187	-5.5	19-2B	1
2007	*BOS*	*MLB*	*23*	*529*	*66*	*33*	*2*	*9*	*57*	*45*	*37*	*1*	*1*	*4.7*	*.291*	*.357*	*.424*	*.022*	*.278*	*.350*	*.419*	*.274*	*21.7*	*124-2B*	*4*

Breakout: 13% Improve: 34% Collapse: 25% Attrition: 8%   *Comparables: Ronnie Belliard, Carlos Villalobos, Buddy Bell, Aaron Hill*

This PECOTA favorite tends to excite statheads more than scouts. The former cite his impressive plate discipline and gap power—a good offensive package for a middle infielder—while the latter caution against his small size, unimpressive speed, and lack of the arm strength or range to play shortstop. But really, it's a question of degree; he should be a very good middle infielder in the majors for years to come. Overcoming a slow start (.261/.352/.359 through May), Pedroia put up very good numbers in Pawtucket, walking nearly twice as often as he struck out and continuing to show gap power. With Hanley Ramirez traded to Florida, he moved back to shortstop and didn't embarrass himself there; he also saw considerable time at second base, his likely role with the Sox in 2007.

Carlos Peña   1B   Bats: L   Throws: L   Height: 6' 2"   Weight: 210   Born: May 17, 1978   Age: 29

YEAR	TEAM	LVL	AGE	PA	R	2B	3B	HR	RBI	BB	SO	SB	CS	SPEED	AVG	OBP	SLG	MLVR	EQAVG	EQOBP	EQSLG	EQA	VORP	DEFENSE
2004	DET	MLB	26	561	89	22	4	27	82	70	146	7	1	5.9	.241	.338	.472	.046	.245	.347	.486	.284	18.6	132-1B -6
2005	TOL	AAA	27	309	43	17	1	12	45	45	65	3	4	3.4	.311	.424	.525	.372	.303	.401	.492	.303	24.1	63-1B -4
2005	DET	MLB	27	295	37	9	0	18	44	31	95	0	1	3.1	.235	.325	.477	.051	.242	.342	.508	.283	8.0	48-1B 0
2006	COH	AAA	28	462	65	17	0	19	66	63	89	4	0	4.9	.260	.370	.454	.182	.253	.348	.445	.277	11.3	86-1B -7
2006	PAW	AAA	28	44	7	3	0	4	8	5	5	0	0	3.5	.459	.523	.865	1.100	.421	.477	.789	.394	11.9	
2006	BOS	MLB	28	37	3	2	0	1	3	4	10	0	0	3.2	.273	.351	.424	.002	.273	.351	.424	.269	0.5	
2007	*BOS*	*MLB*	*29*	*451*	*58*	*22*	*2*	*18*	*62*	*52*	*106*	*2*	*1*	*4.6*	*.252*	*.344*	*.457*	*.013*	*.241*	*.338*	*.452*	*.278*	*6.3*	*107-1B -5*

Breakout: 9% Improve: 21% Collapse: 38% Attrition: 14%   *Comparables: Don Mincher, Wayne Gross, Greg Brock, Marcus Thames*

Despite Peña's .286/.345/.662 showing over the final six weeks of 2005, he failed to win over new Tiger skipper Jim Leyland in spring training, resulting in his release. A stint with the Yankees' Columbus affiliate didn't win him a roster spot, so he exercised a contractual out clause in mid-August and caught on with his hometown team. Recalled at month's end, he hit a walk-off homer at Fenway against the White Sox on September 4, but saw only sporadic action the rest of the way. He'll never live up to that first-round pedigree, but he should still catch on somewhere.

Wily Mo Peña   RF   Bats: R   Throws: R   Height: 6' 3"   Weight: 245   Born: January 23, 1982   Age: 25

YEAR	TEAM	LVL	AGE	PA	R	2B	3B	HR	RBI	BB	SO	SB	CS	SPEED	AVG	OBP	SLG	MLVR	EQAVG	EQOBP	EQSLG	EQA	VORP	DEFENSE	
2004	CIN	MLB	22	364	45	10	1	26	66	22	108	5	2	4.6	.259	.316	.527	.145	.258	.315	.522	.275	18.8	46-CF 8	37-RF -7
2005	CIN	MLB	23	335	42	17	0	19	51	20	116	2	1	4.3	.254	.304	.492	.062	.252	.304	.503	.268	9.5	46-RF -2	22-CF -2
2006	BOS	MLB	24	305	36	15	2	11	42	20	91	0	1	4.3	.300	.348	.487	.105	.296	.351	.493	.285	14.3	32-RF -1	22-CF 1
2007	*BOS*	*MLB*	*25*	*431*	*57*	*24*	*2*	*20*	*68*	*32*	*114*	*3*	*1*	*4.7*	*.275*	*.335*	*.501*	*.075*	*.263*	*.329*	*.495*	*.283*	*14.6*	*102-RF 0*	

Breakout: 22% Improve: 56% Collapse: 13% Attrition: 18%   *Comparables: Frank Howard, Matt Holliday, Pete Incaviglia, Charlie Spikes*

Peña didn't perform badly in 2006, but continued to be the same maddening collection of raw talent and bad habits that he was in Cincy. Davenport numbers to the contrary, Peña is a fright to behold in the field, the athleticism which tempts managers to spot him in centerfield is trumped by bad routes to the ball, which result in some brutal misplays. At the plate, though his isolated power dropped significantly, it was likely the result of the fractured hamate bone which cost him two months; he showed more power upon returning from surgery than prior. Still, the career highs in OBP and EqA he posted were the byproduct of a .411 BABIP—tops among AL hitters with 250+ PA—rather than an improved approach. In all, one should probably take Peña's first year in Boston with a grain of salt; a regression towards the 2004–2005 model is hardly out of the question, but a fully healthy Peña could drive a whole lot of baseballs over (or even through) the Green Monster.

Manny Ramirez LF **Bats: R** **Throws: R** Height: 6′ 0″ Weight: 200 Born: May 30, 1972 Age: 35

YEAR	TEAM	LVL	AGE	PA	R	2B	3B	HR	RBI	BB	SO	SB	CS	SPEED	AVG	OBP	SLG	MLVR	EQAVG	EQOBP	EQSLG	EQA	VORP	DEFENSE
2004	BOS	MLB	32	663	108	44	0	43	130	82	124	2	4	3.3	.308	.397	.613	.352	.300	.395	.602	.323	57.7	112-LF -2
2005	BOS	MLB	33	650	112	30	1	45	144	80	119	1	0	4.0	.292	.388	.594	.333	.292	.396	.609	.328	59.9	139-LF -10
2006	BOS	MLB	34	558	79	27	1	35	102	100	102	0	1	3.1	.321	.439	.619	.456	.312	.440	.615	.347	66.1	116-LF -14
2007	*BOS*	*MLB*	*35*	*598*	*96*	*32*	*1*	*34*	*109*	*85*	*116*	*0*	*1*	*3.6*	*.297*	*.399*	*.566*	*.283*	*.284*	*.392*	*.560*	*.324*	*43.9*	*140-LF -9*

Breakout: 0% Improve: 3% Collapse: 41% Attrition: 12% Comparables: Frank Robinson, Sammy Sosa, Ted Williams, Sid Gordon

Babe Ruth (.366), Ted Williams (.364), Barry Bonds (.356), Lou Gehrig (.345), Albert Pujols (.343), Frank Thomas (.342), Mickey Mantle (.341), Rogers Hornsby (.335), Mark McGwire (.335). Those are the top nine hitters in major league baseball history according to Equivalent Average. Number ten is Manny Ramirez (.334). For all the bitching about his indifference in the field and the legitimacy of the patellar tendonitis that limited him to 33 PA over the season's final six weeks, he's still as good a hitter as any team could possibly hope for, and his role of protecting David Ortiz in the lineup is part of what enables Big Papi's heroics. Still, the annual "Trade Manny" melodrama began during his absence from the lineup, and continued unabated through the Winter Meetings. With "only" $40 million due him over the next two years and a ton of new money being tossed around, chances are better than ever that he finally leaves Beantown, but Sox fans tired of Manny Being Manny should be careful what they wish for.

Chad Spann 3B **Bats: R** **Throws: R** Height: 6′ 1″ Weight: 195 Born: October 25, 1983 Age: 23

YEAR	TEAM	LVL	AGE	PA	R	2B	3B	HR	RBI	BB	SO	SB	CS	SPEED	AVG	OBP	SLG	MLVR	EQAVG	EQOBP	EQSLG	EQA	VORP	DEFENSE
2004	SAR	A+	20	228	26	9	0	4	22	9	53	6	2	5.2	.252	.291	.350	-.083	.229	.259	.326	.208	-10.8	50-3B 0
2005	WIL	A+	21	455	55	23	4	13	48	39	106	1	4	3.8	.248	.322	.423	.007	.224	.278	.359	.222	-10.5	71-3B 2
2006	PME	AA	22	399	53	28	3	10	50	29	85	3	3	5.0	.294	.361	.472	.197	.287	.343	.470	.275	27.3	95-3B 1
2007	*BOS*	*MLB*	*23*	*471*	*47*	*29*	*1*	*11*	*55*	*27*	*107*	*3*	*2*	*4.6*	*.252*	*.302*	*.403*	*-.131*	*.241*	*.296*	*.398*	*.243*	*-2.4*	*111-3B 1*

Breakout: 24% Improve: 42% Collapse: 28% Attrition: 4% Comparables: Tripper Johnson, Josh Fields, Travis Metcalf, Tony Darden

After an impressive pro debut in 2003 (.312/.379/.413 as a 19 year old in the Sally League), Spann couldn't do anything like it in two years of High-A ball, though a lingering knee injury certainly played a part. A Portland reunion with hitting coach Russ Morman, who tutored him at Augusta in 2003, helped Spann regain his stroke and earn Eastern League All-Star honors. As his K/BB ratio shows, his approach at the plate still needs refinement, but he's back on the right path.

Adam Stern CF **Bats: L** **Throws: R** Height: 5′ 11″ Weight: 180 Born: February 12, 1980 Age: 27

YEAR	TEAM	LVL	AGE	PA	R	2B	3B	HR	RBI	BB	SO	SB	CS	SPEED	AVG	OBP	SLG	MLVR	EQAVG	EQOBP	EQSLG	EQA	VORP	DEFENSE	
2004	GRN	AA	24	435	64	26	6	8	47	35	58	27	10	7.3	.322	.378	.480	.233	.293	.338	.427	.266	17.8	88-CF 1	
2005	PAW	AAA	25	92	16	8	0	2	14	8	10	3	1	5.5	.321	.385	.494	.221	.293	.359	.439	.276	4.7	15-CF -1	
2006	PAW	AAA	26	421	59	21	3	8	34	23	78	23	7	7.4	.258	.300	.388	-.047	.246	.289	.381	.235	-5.6	46-CF 0	30-RF -1
2006	BOS	MLB	26	21	3	1	0	0	4	0	4	1	0	7.4	.150	.190	.200	-.697	.100	.143	.100	.118	-2.3		
2007	*BOS*	*MLB*	*27*	*401*	*48*	*23*	*2*	*6*	*41*	*21*	*68*	*14*	*5*	*6.5*	*.270*	*.313*	*.396*	*-.108*	*.259*	*.307*	*.391*	*.250*	*-0.9*	*96-CF 2*	

Breakout: 27% Improve: 46% Collapse: 21% Attrition: 20% Comparables: McKay Christensen, Scott Podsednik, Kory Dehaan, Bubba Crosby

After an injury-addled 2005 campaign that served as a primer on Rule 5 loopholes, Stern underwent surgery to repair a torn labrum in his right shoulder. His Rule 5 obligations finished, he struggled immensely at Pawtucket this season and was sent to Baltimore in October as the PTBNL in the Lopez trade. He's lost much of the last two years developmentally, and though his speed and solid defense are assets, he looks more like a spare part—and poster child for roster shenanigans—than ever.

Jason Varitek C **Bats: S** **Throws: R** Height: 6′ 2″ Weight: 230 Born: April 11, 1972 Age: 35

YEAR	TEAM	LVL	AGE	PA	R	2B	3B	HR	RBI	BB	SO	SB	CS	SPEED	AVG	OBP	SLG	MLVR	EQAVG	EQOBP	EQSLG	EQA	VORP	DEFENSE
2004	BOS	MLB	32	536	67	30	1	18	73	62	126	10	3	4.5	.296	.390	.482	.155	.289	.388	.478	.299	39.5	111-C 10
2005	BOS	MLB	33	539	70	30	1	22	70	62	117	2	0	4.6	.281	.366	.489	.151	.281	.377	.500	.298	39.8	124-C 3
2006	BOS	MLB	34	416	46	19	2	12	55	46	87	1	2	4.0	.238	.325	.400	-.109	.233	.330	.400	.253	2.8	92-C 3
2007	*BOS*	*MLB*	*35*	*449*	*59*	*21*	*2*	*15*	*60*	*48*	*102*	*3*	*1*	*4.4*	*.272*	*.354*	*.448*	*.035*	*.260*	*.348*	*.443*	*.279*	*17.5*	*106-C -1*

Breakout: 12% Improve: 31% Collapse: 40% Attrition: 21% Comparables: Lance Parrish, Carlton Fisk, Johnny Edwards, Chris Chambliss

Awash in their championship afterglow, the Sox signed Varitek to a four-year, $40-million contract knowing they'd be paying for his decline; they just didn't expect it to start in Year Two of the deal. Varitek never got on track in 2006. His

.243/.331/.411 line through July 31 would have been his worst since 2002, but a torn medial meniscus gave "worst" a whole new meaning. In the captain's absence, the team went 10–23, plunging out of the playoff picture with the grace of a Boomer Wells cannonball. Upon returning, Varitek struck out an alarming 29 times in 61 AB, suggesting he still wasn't right. He'll have the winter to recuperate, but the Sox must reckon with owning a 35-year-old catcher whose body is no longer under warranty.

Mark Wagner   **C**   **Bats: R**   **Throws: R**   Height: 6' 1"   Weight: 205   Born: June 11, 1984   Age: 23

YEAR	TEAM	LVL	AGE	PA	R	2B	3B	HR	RBI	BB	SO	SB	CS	SPEED	AVG	OBP	SLG	MLVR	EQAVG	EQOBP	EQSLG	EQA	VORP	DEFENSE
2005	LOW	A-	21	81	10	2	1	0	6	9	7	1	1	4.9	.203	.309	.261	-.191	.135	.207	.135	.144	-22.9	21-C	-3
2006	GRN	A	22	407	49	32	1	7	45	42	52	1	3	2.9	.301	.386	.456	.205	.258	.317	.387	.243	5.1	64-C	-4
2006	WIL	A+	22	74	8	4	0	1	5	7	9	0	0	4.3	.169	.243	.277	-.317	.134	.189	.209	.156	-10.6	13-C	-4
2007	*BOS*	*MLB*	*23*	*451*	*33*	*25*	*0*	*7*	*47*	*28*	*64*	*0*	*1*	*3.6*	*.231*	*.285*	*.343*	*-.255*	*.221*	*.280*	*.339*	*.218*	*-10.5*	*107-C*	*-4*

Breakout: 49%   Improve: 63%   Collapse: 16%   Attrition: 9%   *Comparables: Jason Hill, Javi Herrera, Bobby Wilson, Neil Wilson*

A ninth-round pick in 2005, Wagner broke out in his first full year as a pro at Greenville, both at the plate—showing on-base skills and gap power—and behind it, where he threw out 32 percent of baserunners. That earned him Sally League All-Star honors and a promotion to Wilmington. Though he didn't hit there, he's bound for a return engagement to start the season, and could reach Double-A by midsummer. He and Kotteras give the Red Sox two more catching prospects than most teams have.

Kevin Youkilis   **1B**   **Bats: R**   **Throws: R**   Height: 6' 1"   Weight: 220   Born: March 15, 1979   Age: 28

YEAR	TEAM	LVL	AGE	PA	R	2B	3B	HR	RBI	BB	SO	SB	CS	SPEED	AVG	OBP	SLG	MLVR	EQAVG	EQOBP	EQSLG	EQA	VORP	DEFENSE			
2004	PAW	AAA	25	178	25	12	0	3	18	19	28	2	0	4.7	.266	.350	.403	.001	.237	.316	.359	.243	-0.0	34-3B	1		
2004	BOS	MLB	25	248	38	11	0	7	35	33	45	0	1	4.1	.260	.367	.413	-.002	.252	.364	.408	.272	4.3	57-3B	2		
2005	PAW	AAA	26	194	30	15	1	8	27	35	29	1	2	3.4	.322	.459	.592	.464	.293	.418	.522	.317	22.0	22-3B	-2	16-1B	2
2005	BOS	MLB	26	95	11	7	0	1	9	14	19	0	1	4.7	.278	.400	.405	.096	.282	.417	.397	.290	3.5	16-3B	1		
2006	BOS	MLB	27	680	100	42	2	13	72	91	120	5	2	4.8	.279	.381	.429	.064	.275	.384	.428	.287	19.6	116-1B	1	15-LF	3
2007	*BOS*	*MLB*	*28*	*639*	*92*	*38*	*2*	*19*	*78*	*86*	*109*	*4*	*3*	*5.0*	*.270*	*.375*	*.455*	*.078*	*.258*	*.368*	*.450*	*.291*	*18.8*	*149-1B*	*4*		

Breakout: 11%   Improve: 44%   Collapse: 20%   Attrition: 3%   *Comparables: Carmelo Martinez, Joe Foy, Bob Allison, Edgar Martinez*

The Greek God of Walks finally spent a full year in the majors in 2006, three years after becoming a cause célèbre among statheads, and hit in the vicinity of his 60th percentile PECOTA projection. Factor in above-average defense and a salary just above $350,000, and it's tempting to pat the Red Sox on the back here and focus on other concerns. However, Youkilis is already 28, and the move to first base raised the offensive bar; that .381 OBP was tasty, but due to a lack of power, his Positional Marginal Lineup Value rate was negative (–0.052), even below that of Kevin Millar (–0.030), the man he replaced. In other words, relative to other AL first basemen, he costs his team runs. His bat fits in better across the diamond, but with Mike Lowell, the Sox have that base covered. There's no reason to punt Youkilis while he's cheap, but the Sox needn't become overly enamored.

PITCHERS

Abe Alvarez   **Bats: L**   **Throws: L**   Height: 6' 2"   Weight: 190   Born: October 17, 1982   Age: 24

YEAR	TEAM	LVL	AGE	W	L	SV	G	GS	IP	H	BB	SO	HR	GB%	BABIP	STUFF	WHIP	ERA	PERA	EQERA	EQH9	EQBB9	EQSO9	EQHR9	VORP	WXRL
2004	PME	AA	21	10	9	0	26	26	135¹	132	32	108	13	—	.292	8	1.21	3.59	4.52	4.19	8.6	2.2	5.1	1.1	21.5	—
2005	PAW	AAA	22	11	6	0	26	26	144²	143	31	109	17	39.8%	.290	5	1.20	4.85	4.52	5.36	8.7	2.0	5.2	1.2	3.9	—
2006	PAW	AAA	23	6	9	0	22	21	118¹	136	40	71	22	39.7%	.300	-42	1.49	5.64	7.18	6.69	10.9	3.2	4.2	2.5	-14.2	—
2006	BOS	MLB	23	0	0	0	1	0	3	5	2	2	2	18.2%	.333	-29	2.33	12.00	10.83	10.80	13.5	5.4	5.4	5.4	-1.8	-0.05
2007	*BOS*	*MLB*	*24*	*4*	*7*	*0*	*33*	*13*	*95*	*120*	*35*	*53*	*18*	*41.0%*	*.315*	*-9*	*1.63*	*6.40*	*5.96*	*5.76*	*9.9*	*3.2*	*4.7*	*1.4*	*-6.0*	*0.10*

Breakout: 18%   Improve: 49%   Collapse: 7%   Attrition: 4%   *Comparables: Phil Seibel, Jake Woods, Brent Billingsley, Chris Narveson*

The lanky lefty with the skewed hat (which compensates for the legal blindness in his left eye by adjusting the light), Alvarez climbed the ladder quickly in his first two years out of Long Beach State. Last year's fast start (2.18 ERA, 30 hits in 41⅓ innings) was interrupted a brief stint in Boston in late May. Upon returning to Triple-A, he was beaten like a rented mule (7.51 ERA and 2.11 HR/9) before a season-ending ankle fracture. With stuff as fringy as a Dolly Parton outfit, he's in danger of becoming organizational fodder.

Josh Beckett

Bats: R **Throws: R**   Height: 6' 5"   Weight: 220   Born: May 15, 1980   Age: 27

YEAR	TEAM	LVL	AGE	W	L	SV	G	GS	IP	H	BB	SO	HR	GB%	BABIP	STUFF	WHIP	ERA	PERA	EQERA	EQH9	EQBB9	EQSO9	EQHR9	VORP	WXRL
2004	FLO	MLB	24	9	9	0	26	26	156²	137	54	152	16	—	.292	28	1.22	3.79	3.74	4.26	8.0	2.7	7.7	0.9	26.2	3.84
2005	FLO	MLB	25	15	8	0	29	29	178²	153	58	166	14	43.1%	.294	33	1.18	3.37	3.52	3.86	7.3	2.6	7.5	0.7	34.0	5.25
2006	BOS	MLB	26	16	11	0	33	33	204²	191	73	158	36	46.5%	.265	6	1.29	5.01	5.00	4.62	7.6	3.0	6.4	1.4	19.9	3.87
2007	BOS	MLB	27	11	10	0	30	30	189	193	64	151	22	46.0%	.302	19	1.36	4.49	4.12	4.11	8.0	2.9	6.7	0.8	26.6	4.20

Breakout: 24%   Improve: 57%   Collapse: 8%   Attrition: 1%   Comparables: Don Wilson, Freddy Garcia, Joey Jay, Andy Benes

The centerpiece of last winter's master plan, Beckett was expected to front the Sox's rotation. While he avoided the blister problems that have disabled him six times so far—enabling his first 200-inning campaign—the solution was a costly one. Beckett covered his middle finger with a Band-Aid between starts, but the remedy prevented him from throwing his curve during bullpen sessions. He then struggled to locate it during games and was forced to over-rely on a very straight fastball. The results were predictable; his 36 homers allowed tied for second in the majors, and his 10 first-pitch homers tied for first. Despite his troubles, the Sox signed him to a three-year, $30-million extension in July, a smart move in light of the winter's drastic salary inflation. Beckett has the talent to justify that faith, but he'll need to adjust to succeed in the AL.

Michael Bowden

Bats: R **Throws: R**   Height: 6' 3"   Weight: 215   Born: September 9, 1986   Age: 20

YEAR	TEAM	LVL	AGE	W	L	SV	G	GS	IP	H	BB	SO	HR	GB%	BABIP	STUFF	WHIP	ERA	PERA	EQERA	EQH9	EQBB9	EQSO9	EQHR9	VORP	WXRL
2006	GRN	A	19	9	6	0	24	24	107²	91	31	118	9	52.7%	.293	0	1.14	3.53	5.40	5.40	9.7	3.2	6.1	1.7	2.3	—
2007	BOS	MLB	20	6	8	0	27	19	115¹	135	47	82	17	48.0%	.319	7	1.58	5.60	5.31	5.10	9.1	3.5	5.9	1.1	2.1	1.00

Breakout: 28%   Improve: 64%   Collapse: 3%   Attrition: 2%   Comparables: Anthony Swarzak, William Martinez, Aaron Dean, Beltran Perez

A highly-touted high schooler, Bowden's impressive arsenal includes a curve considered one of the best of the 2005 prep class. His unorthodox delivery generated concern—"He takes a long time to short-arm the ball," says one observer—but analysis at the American Sports Medicine Institute concluded that he's not unduly taxing his arm. After a limited debut in the Gulf Coast League in 2005, Bowden skipped to Low-A Greenville, where he was the team's youngest player. He justified the move, pitching nearly as well as fellow 2005 supplemental first rounder Clay Buchholz, who's two years his senior. Definitely one to watch.

Craig Breslow

Bats: L **Throws: L**   Height: 6' 1"   Weight: 180   Born: August 8, 1980   Age: 26

YEAR	TEAM	LVL	AGE	W	L	SV	G	GS	IP	H	BB	SO	HR	GB%	BABIP	STUFF	WHIP	ERA	PERA	EQERA	EQH9	EQBB9	EQSO9	EQHR9	VORP	WXRL
2004	HDS	A+	23	1	3	0	23	0	41¹	54	24	41	5	—	.383	-23	1.89	7.19	7.49	8.19	11.3	6.9	5.3	2.0	-11.7	—
2005	MOB	AA	24	2	1	0	40	0	52¹	38	17	47	3	44.5%	.271	-6	1.05	2.75	4.63	3.51	6.8	3.2	5.3	0.9	11.9	—
2005	SDN	MLB	24	0	0	0	14	0	16¹	15	13	14	1	46.9%	.292	6	1.71	2.21	4.83	3.71	7.9	6.4	6.9	0.5	3.9	0.06
2006	PAW	AAA	25	7	1	7	39	0	67²	49	24	77	3	46.8%	.279	19	1.09	2.68	3.70	3.38	7.2	3.4	8.0	0.5	16.5	—
2006	BOS	MLB	25	0	2	0	13	0	12	12	6	12	0	38.2%	.353	12	1.50	3.75	3.44	3.65	8.8	4.4	8.0	0.0	3.2	-0.05
2007	BOS	MLB	26	3	4	2	74	3	63	69	32	50	7	45.0%	.316	-3	1.59	5.10	4.95	4.65	8.5	4.4	6.5	0.9	4.7	0.50

Breakout: 13%   Improve: 36%   Collapse: 33%   Attrition: 14%   Comparables: Mike Stanton, John Parrish, Chuck McElroy, Travis Miller

If lefty hitters were vulnerable to Yalies with biochemistry degrees, then Breslow would already have a spot in the Boston pen. As it is, he's not far off but don't expect Jason Giambi to cower in fear of Breslow's command of the Krebs cycle. Last year, Breslow added a cut fastball to a repertoire that stars a plus overhand curve and handled righties (.200/.269/.284) as well as lefties (.200/.323/.236) in winning International League All-Star honors. He'll still have to beat out J. C. Romero and/or Javier Lopez to stick.

Clay Buchholz

Bats: L **Throws: R**   Height: 6' 3"   Weight: 190   Born: August 14, 1984   Age: 22

YEAR	TEAM	LVL	AGE	W	L	SV	G	GS	IP	H	BB	SO	HR	GB%	BABIP	STUFF	WHIP	ERA	PERA	EQERA	EQH9	EQBB9	EQSO9	EQHR9	VORP	WXRL
2005	LOW	A-	20	0	1	0	15	15	41¹	34	9	45	2	51.4%	.296	-2	1.04	2.62	4.92	4.54	8.8	2.7	5.0	1.4	4.7	—
2006	GRN	A	21	9	4	0	21	21	103	78	29	117	10	46.5%	.281	-10	1.04	2.62	6.14	4.11	9.3	3.3	6.2	2.1	15.9	—
2006	WIL	A+	21	2	0	0	3	3	16¹	10	4	23	0	53.3%	.302	16	0.87	1.12	2.39	2.87	6.9	2.3	9.2	0.0	4.8	—
2007	BOS	MLB	22	6	8	0	27	21	121	139	51	86	20	46.0%	.311	6	1.56	5.48	5.35	4.96	9.0	3.6	6.0	1.2	4.5	1.30

Breakout: 2%   Improve: 16%   Collapse: 46%   Attrition: 1%   Comparables: Mark Brownson, Bobby Basham, Ryan Vogelsong, Steven Shell

The younger brother of Rockies pitcher Taylor, Buchholz gained notoriety for a 2004 arrest after stealing 29 laptops from a middle school, but the Sox drafted him in the 2005 supplemental round after deciding his actions were an isolated incident. Buchholz pitched well in Lowell despite a short leash, exhibiting a low-90s fastball that tended to gain steam later in the game, a good changeup, and a nasty curve. In 2006, he dominated Sally and Carolina League hitters while pushing his velocity into the mid-90s. The organization's Minor League Pitcher of the Year, he should continue his rapid rise.

Matt Clement   **Bats: R Throws: R**   Height: 6' 3"   Weight: 210   Born: August 12, 1974   Age: 32

YEAR	TEAM	LVL	AGE	W	L	SV	G	GS	IP	H	BB	SO	HR	GB%	BABIP	STUFF	WHIP	ERA	PERA	EQERA	EQH9	EQBB9	EQSO9	EQHR9	VORP	WXRL
2004	CHN	MLB	29	9	13	0	30	30	181	155	77	190	23	—	.284	26	1.28	3.68	4.18	3.82	7.8	3.4	8.3	1.0	38.4	4.49
2005	BOS	MLB	30	13	6	0	32	32	191	192	68	146	18	47.1%	.303	21	1.36	4.57	4.18	4.39	8.4	3.1	6.6	0.8	23.7	4.20
2006	BOS	MLB	31	5	5	0	12	12	65¹	77	38	43	8	48.2%	.322	3	1.76	6.62	5.38	5.96	9.8	4.8	5.4	0.9	-5.2	0.28
2007	BOS	MLB	32	7	8	0	29	20	125	140	56	91	14	47.0%	.318	4	1.57	5.30	4.95	4.88	8.8	3.8	6.1	0.8	6.0	1.50

Breakout: 10% Improve: 36% Collapse: 28% Attrition: 8%   Comparables: Walt Masterson, Bob Buhl, Milt Wilcox, Mike Moore

In retrospect, Clement's late 2005 woes may not have been attributable to being drilled by a Carl Crawford line drive in July (his ERA rose just 0.43 runs via that split), but rather to the shoulder termites that were confirmed when Dr. Jim Andrews performed surgery in late September. Tagged in three of his final four 2005 appearances, Clement started 2006 slowly, never getting his ERA below 5.35 before things went from bad to worse. With significant damage to both his rotator cuff and labrum, his 2007 is likely shot, setting the cost of Clement's three-year deal at roughly $4.8 million per marginal win. Ouch.

Manny Delcarmen   **Bats: R Throws: R**   Height: 6' 2"   Weight: 190   Born: February 16, 1982   Age: 25

YEAR	TEAM	LVL	AGE	W	L	SV	G	GS	IP	H	BB	SO	HR	GB%	BABIP	STUFF	WHIP	ERA	PERA	EQERA	EQH9	EQBB9	EQSO9	EQHR9	VORP	WXRL
2004	SAR	A+	22	3	6	0	19	18	73	84	20	76	10	—	.356	-26	1.42	4.68	6.94	6.62	12.5	3.0	6.2	2.9	-7.9	—
2005	PME	AA	23	4	4	3	31	0	39	31	20	49	3	58.0%	.298	5	1.31	3.23	4.87	6.03	8.4	5.5	7.7	1.0	-1.8	—
2005	PAW	AAA	23	3	1	2	15	0	21	17	13	23	0	34.5%	.309	21	1.43	1.29	3.99	1.71	7.7	6.0	7.7	0.4	9.1	—
2005	BOS	MLB	23	0	0	0	10	0	9	8	7	9	0	62.5%	.333	9	1.67	3.00	4.36	2.89	7.7	6.8	8.7	0.0	2.8	-0.07
2006	PAW	AAA	24	0	1	0	10	0	17²	9	6	19	0	41.0%	.231	17	0.87	2.09	3.18	2.65	5.3	3.2	7.9	0.0	5.6	—
2006	BOS	MLB	24	2	0	0	50	0	53¹	68	17	45	2	46.3%	.382	12	1.59	5.07	3.13	4.69	10.5	2.6	7.0	0.3	4.3	0.60
2007	BOS	MLB	25	3	3	2	51	1	57²	63	23	50	6	48.0%	.326	6	1.49	4.74	4.47	4.35	8.5	3.4	7.2	0.8	6.5	0.60

Breakout: 26% Improve: 67% Collapse: 11% Attrition: 25%   Comparables: Tom Walker, Pep Harris, Mike Garman, Joey Mclaughlin

This West Roxbury High product has missed bats at every level, both before and after his 2003 Tommy John surgery. Moving to the bullpen has pushed his fastball into the high-90s. Good stuff aside, his 2006 season was a mixed bag. His peripherals considerably outpaced his ERA, but his BABIP was the third-highest in the majors among pitchers with at least 50 innings. He also allowed 19 out of 31 inherited runners to score; at 10.1 runs below expectation, that was the worst in baseball. Much of the damage to his stat line occurred in September, suggesting fatigue was a factor. He's still young and gifted enough that the Sox aren't panicking, so expect him to retain a key role in the bullpen.

Lenny DiNardo   **Bats: L Throws: L**   Height: 6' 4"   Weight: 190   Born: September 19, 1979 Age: 27

YEAR	TEAM	LVL	AGE	W	L	SV	G	GS	IP	H	BB	SO	HR	GB%	BABIP	STUFF	WHIP	ERA	PERA	EQERA	EQH9	EQBB9	EQSO9	EQHR9	VORP	WXRL
2004	BOS	MLB	24	0	0	0	22	0	27²	34	12	21	1	—	.359	1	1.66	4.22	3.61	5.02	10.7	3.5	6.3	0.3	3.0	-0.18
2005	PAW	AAA	25	6	3	0	23	22	108²	109	35	93	7	67.2%	.328	14	1.32	3.15	4.18	4.43	9.0	3.0	5.9	0.7	14.3	—
2005	BOS	MLB	25	0	1	0	8	1	14²	13	5	15	1	67.5%	.308	15	1.23	1.84	3.02	3.52	7.0	2.9	8.8	0.6	3.6	-0.01
2006	BOS	MLB	26	1	2	0	13	6	39	61	20	17	6	60.3%	.379	-26	2.08	7.85	5.48	6.91	12.3	4.1	3.5	1.1	-8.0	-0.22
2007	BOS	MLB	27	4	5	0	33	11	83¹	102	33	48	8	57.0%	.331	-6	1.62	5.36	5.08	4.99	9.6	3.4	4.8	0.7	2.6	0.60

Breakout: 32% Improve: 60% Collapse: 17% Attrition: 22%   Comparables: Heath Murray, Tom Bolton, Jim Shellenback, Ted Bowsfield

DiNardo's led a double life in the Sox organization, starting in the minors, but pitching out of the Bosox bullpen when he's been up. The early-season injury to David Wells pressed him into Boston's rotation with generally poor results. A late-May neck strain—perhaps induced by watching hitters launch his pedestrian offerings into the stratosphere—cost him most of the summer, but if his 2006 campaign was less a manifestation of injury than an indication that his already fringy stuff is getting fringier, the Sox need to look elsewhere.

Keith Foulke   **Bats: R Throws: R**   Height: 6' 0"   Weight: 210   Born: October 19, 1972   Age: 34

YEAR	TEAM	LVL	AGE	W	L	SV	G	GS	IP	H	BB	SO	HR	GB%	BABIP	STUFF	WHIP	ERA	PERA	EQERA	EQH9	EQBB9	EQSO9	EQHR9	VORP	WXRL
2004	BOS	MLB	31	5	3	32	72	0	83	63	15	79	8	—	.251	27	0.94	2.17	3.23	2.24	6.7	1.5	8.0	0.7	36.7	4.42
2005	BOS	MLB	32	5	5	15	43	0	45²	53	18	34	8	27.3%	.317	-11	1.55	5.91	5.41	5.48	9.8	3.4	6.4	1.5	-0.1	-0.99
2006	BOS	MLB	33	3	1	0	44	0	49²	52	7	36	9	25.0%	.293	0	1.19	4.35	4.42	3.83	8.4	1.2	5.9	1.4	10.0	1.53
2007	CLE	MLB	34	3	2	2	41	0	48	49	13	36	8	33%	.282	0	1.28	4.15	4.18	3.90	8.8	2.3	6.3	1.3	9.1	0.7

Breakout: 16% Improve: 35% Collapse: 43% Attrition: 25%   Comparables: Jeff Reardon, Bob Wells, Alejandro Pena, Dave LaRoche

(continued next page)

Keith Foulke *(continued)*

Foulke's balky knees—both surgically repaired in 2005—were expected to heal by spring training, but Synvisc injections delayed his Grapefruit League debut. The nominal closer on Opening Day, he was passed over in favor of Jonathan Papelbon by the season's third game. Initial returns in a setup role weren't good; he carried a 5.63 ERA to the DL in mid-June, and elbow tendonitis and back trouble kept him out for two months. His results upon returning were cause for optimism; Foulke was scored upon in just one of his final 15 appearances (17 2/3 IP, 13/3 K/BB). Foulke opted to look elsewhere for 2007 employment, eventually landing another chance to close in Cleveland, where he'll have to beat out Joe Borowski; telling that that's what we're talking about, considering where Foulke was a couple of years ago.

Kason Gabbard								Bats: L		Throws: L				Height: 6' 3"		Weight: 200		Born: April 8, 1982			Age: 25	
YEAR	TEAM	LVL	AGE	W	L	SV	G	GS	IP	H	BB	SO	HR	GB%	BABIP	STUFF	WHIP	ERA	PERA	EQERA	EQH9	EQBB9	EQSO9	EQHR9	VORP	WXRL
2004	SAR	A+	22	3	2	1	10	7	43¹	43	16	30	2	—	.293	-8	1.36	2.70	5.38	4.46	9.6	3.8	4.0	0.9	5.4	—
2004	PME	AA	22	3	6	0	14	14	53	61	26	35	5	—	.311	-14	1.64	5.77	5.52	6.83	10.0	4.5	4.2	1.2	-7.4	—
2005	PME	AA	23	9	11	0	27	25	132²	128	65	96	10	55.9%	.298	-5	1.45	4.61	5.65	6.28	9.3	5.3	4.4	1.0	-9.7	—
2006	PME	AA	24	9	2	0	13	13	73¹	51	25	68	4	61.8%	.242	8	1.04	2.59	4.88	4.24	7.7	3.7	5.5	0.9	10.6	—
2006	PAW	AAA	24	1	7	0	9	8	51¹	51	26	48	8	64.4%	.321	-5	1.51	5.28	6.43	6.08	9.7	4.8	6.6	2.1	-2.7	—
2006	BOS	MLB	24	1	3	0	7	4	25²	24	16	15	0	60.8%	.304	6	1.56	3.50	4.20	3.38	7.8	5.1	4.7	0.3	6.3	0.86
2007	BOS	MLB	25	5	8	0	34	22	112	131	66	74	13	54.0%	.325	-6	1.76	6.04	5.60	5.63	9.2	5.0	5.5	0.8	-5.3	0.20

Breakout: 6%   Improve: 37%   Collapse: 24%   Attrition: 1%   Comparables: Lance Caraccioli, Andy Hassler, Alex Graman, Zach Day

Gabbard Gabbard Hey! Improved command helped this unprepossessing lefty finally break out of Double-A, and with Boston's injury woes, it wasn't long before he was making big league cameos. While he had trouble staying in the strike zone, Gabbard was a worm-killing machine, generating a ton of grounders and escaping jams with double plays. In a system that doesn't lack for pitching prospects, he'll remain a sleeper, but there are worse things the Sox could have stashed away.

Devern Hansack								Bats: R		Throws: R				Height: 6' 2"		Weight: 185		Born: August 5, 1982			Age: 29	
YEAR	TEAM	LVL	AGE	W	L	SV	G	GS	IP	H	BB	SO	HR	GB%	BABIP	STUFF	WHIP	ERA	PERA	EQERA	EQH9	EQBB9	EQSO9	EQHR9	VORP	WXRL
2006	PME	AA	23	8	7	1	31	18	132	122	36	124	14	40.4%	.287	-18	1.20	3.27	5.78	5.01	10.1	3.1	5.4	1.7	8.2	—
2006	BOS	MLB	23	1	1	0	2	2	10	6	1	8	2	48.1%	.160	10	0.70	2.70	4.31	2.61	4.4	0.9	7.0	1.7	3.9	0.44
2007	BOS	MLB	29	4	6	0	30	13	91²	114	30	56	16	41.0%	.317	-6	1.57	5.91	5.61	5.32	9.7	2.8	5.1	1.3	-0.8	0.40

Breakout: 6%   Improve: 27%   Collapse: 37%   Attrition: 7%   Comparables: Dan Carlson, Steve Schrenk, Jeremy Cummings, Shane Bowers

The ninth Nicaraguan ever to play in the majors took some strange detours en route. After two years with the Astros' Venezuelan Summer League affiliate and two in their stateside system, he was released when Agegate altered his birth certificate by 4.5 years. Returning to play in a Nicaraguan league, he supplemented his income as a lobsterman and caught the eye of the Sox's VP of Scouting Craig Shipley while pitching in a tournament in Holland. He cracked the Portland rotation in mid-June and by September's end had starred in the Eastern League finals, debuted in the majors, and tossed five no-hit innings in a rain-shortened season finale. Hansack really isn't a prospect, but he throws strikes. He'll bide his time at Pawtucket awaiting the opportunity to continue his saga.

Craig Hansen								Bats: R		Throws: R				Height: 6' 5"		Weight: 185		Born: November 15, 1983			Age: 23	
YEAR	TEAM	LVL	AGE	W	L	SV	G	GS	IP	H	BB	SO	HR	GB%	BABIP	STUFF	WHIP	ERA	PERA	EQERA	EQH9	EQBB9	EQSO9	EQHR9	VORP	WXRL
2005	PME	AA	21	0	0	0	8	0	9²	9	1	10	0	55.6%	.333	10	1.03	0.00	2.50	0.93	9.3	0.9	6.5	0.0	5.0	—
2005	BOS	MLB	21	0	0	0	4	0	3	6	1	3	1	54.5%	.500	2	2.33	6.00	5.79	9.00	18.0	3.0	9.0	3.0	-0.1	-0.29
2006	PME	AA	22	1	0	0	5	0	11	4	4	12	0	53.8%	.154	11	0.73	0.82	4.37	1.69	5.1	3.4	6.8	0.0	4.6	—
2006	PAW	AAA	22	1	2	0	14	4	36²	31	19	26	0	52.3%	.298	3	1.38	2.73	4.11	3.96	7.7	5.0	5.0	0.2	6.6	—
2006	BOS	MLB	22	2	2	0	38	0	38	46	15	30	5	46.3%	.353	-4	1.61	6.63	4.71	6.64	10.1	3.2	6.6	0.9	-6.0	-0.68
2007	BOS	MLB	23	3	3	1	43	3	57	65	24	43	6	48.0%	.325	1	1.55	5.23	4.79	4.83	8.9	3.7	6.3	0.8	3.0	0.40

Breakout: 31%   Improve: 70%   Collapse: 7%   Attrition: 37%   Comparables: Ryan Wagner, Joe Kerrigan, Rick Baldwin, Howie Judson

A 2005 first-rounder out of St. John's, this college closer reached the majors quickly thanks to Boston's Foulked-up bullpen situation. Last year, the team made it clear he'll have to earn the closer job, testing Hansen in starting and non-closing relief situations to acclimate him to working out of jams, pitching out of a windup, and developing a changeup to augment his high-90s fastball and wicked slider. He struggled with mechanics and command, and those familiar with his stuff swore his slider wasn't the same. Hit hard, he allowed 19 earned runs in his last 18 innings. There's no shame in a pitcher of his vintage not being ready; the Sox brass needs to stay the course with his development rather then plugging him in every time the staff springs a leak.

Jon Lester

Bats: L Throws: L   Height: 6' 2" Weight: 190 Born: January 7, 1984   Age: 23

YEAR	TEAM	LVL	AGE	W	L	SV	G	GS	IP	H	BB	SO	HR	GB%	BABIP	STUFF	WHIP	ERA	PERA	EQERA	EQH9	EQBB9	EQSO9	EQHR9	VORP	WXRL
2004	SAR	A+	20	7	6	0	21	20	90¹	82	37	97	2	—	.329	23	1.32	4.29	3.89	5.60	9.0	4.2	6.5	0.4	0.0	—
2005	PME	AA	21	11	6	0	26	26	148¹	114	57	163	10	47.9%	.291	23	1.15	2.61	4.36	3.69	7.8	4.0	6.9	0.9	30.6	—
2006	PAW	AAA	22	3	4	0	11	11	46	43	25	43	5	43.9%	.290	6	1.48	2.74	5.62	3.94	8.9	5.1	6.5	1.4	8.4	—
2006	BOS	MLB	22	7	2	0	15	15	81¹	91	43	60	7	41.4%	.347	17	1.65	4.76	4.50	4.13	9.1	4.3	6.0	0.6	12.3	1.73
2007	BOS	MLB	23	7	9	0	29	25	134	145	64	110	15	44.0%	.319	12	1.56	5.09	4.87	4.64	8.5	4.1	6.8	0.8	10.5	2.00

Breakout: 6%   Improve: 33%   Collapse: 34%   Attrition: 6%   Comparables: Les Cain, Jim O'Toole, Pete Smith, Dick Ruthven

After dominating the Eastern League in 2005, Lester was held in higher regard than even Jonathan Papelbon. Nonetheless, expectations that he would contribute in 2006 were tempered by his lack of experience above Double-A and concerns about overtaxing his arm. Pitching well on a short leash at Pawtucket, he got the call when the injury bug bit in June, and ran off a string of seven starts in which he allowed no more than two runs, lowering his ERA to 2.38 with eight shutout innings in the last of them. Then things unraveled; he was shellacked in five of his next six starts before sustaining a back strain in a car accident. While treating the injury, doctors diagnosed Lester with anaplastic large cell lymphoma, a treatable type of cancer. Thanks to chemotherapy, he was in remission by mid-December and planning to be ready for spring training. Like the rest of the baseball world, we wish him good health and eagerly await his return, no matter the timeframe.

Javier Lopez

Bats: L Throws: L   Height: 6' 4" Weight: 220 Born: July 11, 1977   Age: 29

YEAR	TEAM	LVL	AGE	W	L	SV	G	GS	IP	H	BB	SO	HR	GB%	BABIP	STUFF	WHIP	ERA	PERA	EQERA	EQH9	EQBB9	EQSO9	EQHR9	VORP	WXRL
2004	COL	MLB	26	1	2	0	64	0	40²	45	26	20	1	—	.324	-14	1.75	7.52	4.61	6.54	9.1	4.9	3.8	0.2	-5.8	0.73
2005	TUC	AAA	27	0	1	2	27	0	24¹	17	12	16	0	70.6%	.266	-6	1.19	2.22	4.28	2.59	6.3	4.4	4.4	0.4	8.1	—
2005	ARI	MLB	27	1	1	2	29	0	14¹	19	11	11	2	52.0%	.354	-11	2.09	9.44	5.70	8.40	11.4	6.0	6.0	1.2	-5.8	0.26
2006	CHR	AAA	28	2	1	12	26	0	33	28	6	26	1	73.1%	.293	8	1.03	0.55	3.34	1.11	8.6	1.9	5.3	0.6	16.1	—
2006	PAW	AAA	28	0	0	4	13	0	16	20	8	12	1	61.4%	.352	-15	1.75	5.06	5.15	6.19	11.2	5.1	5.1	1.1	-1.0	—
2006	BOS	MLB	28	1	0	1	27	0	16²	13	10	11	1	68.9%	.273	-6	1.38	2.69	5.04	4.76	6.9	5.3	5.8	0.5	1.4	0.82
2007	BOS	MLB	29	2	3	2	59	2	50¹	60	24	31	4	58.0%	.326	-11	1.65	5.33	4.96	4.99	9.2	4.1	5.1	0.6	1.5	0.20

Breakout: 20% Improve: 59% Collapse: 19% Attrition: 41%   Comparables: Hal Woodeshick, Dennis Powell, Russ Swan, Mike Fetters

From the department of *"Wha?"* comes the mid-June exchange in which the Red Sox sent serviceable reliever David Riske to the White Sox for sidearming LOOGY Lopez. Despite a paucity of innings with the Bosox, Lopez's WXRL was fourth on the team. On his career, he's held lefties to a .246/.326/.335 showing, but righties have bombed him to the tune of .310/.400/.460, which proves that he's unsuited for broader responsibilities. Brilliant.

Edgar Martinez

Bats: R Throws: R   Height: 6' 0" Weight: 220 Born: October 23, 1981   Age: 25

YEAR	TEAM	LVL	AGE	W	L	SV	G	GS	IP	H	BB	SO	HR	GB%	BABIP	STUFF	WHIP	ERA	PERA	EQERA	EQH9	EQBB9	EQSO9	EQHR9	VORP	WXRL
2005	WIL	A+	23	1	1	7	28	0	34¹	20	12	46	3	45.9%	.239	-1	0.93	2.10	5.31	3.66	7.3	3.9	7.3	1.4	6.9	—
2005	PME	AA	23	0	0	1	15	0	18	12	8	13	0	37.3%	.240	-6	1.11	1.50	4.29	2.08	6.2	4.7	4.2	0.0	6.8	—
2006	PME	AA	24	5	3	12	49	0	69²	51	18	59	9	41.7%	.237	-27	1.00	2.60	6.43	3.95	8.3	2.9	5.0	2.0	12.1	—
2007	BOS	MLB	25	3	4	1	30	5	61	72	26	37	13	40.0%	.297	-11	1.61	5.81	5.82	5.18	9.2	3.7	5.1	1.5	0.5	0.20

Breakout: 4%   Improve: 9%   Collapse: 69%   Attrition: 13%   Comparables: Mike Nannini, Jason Anderson, Jason Arnold, Francisco Rosario

After six years as a no-hit catcher (.223/.282/.298), this Venezuelan underwent a mid-2004 conversion to the mound. He caught on quickly (again, no pun intended), showing a willingness to pound the strike zone and, with a mid-90s fastball and decent slider, the stuff to get away with it; he even closed effectively. This past year he got a little gopher-happy when he failed to locate the heater; in pitcher-friendly Portland, opponents slugged .283 against him, but on the road they managed a more robust .423. Above all, he needs innings, so expect him to get plenty in Pawtucket as he works on his command.

Justin Masterson

Bats: R Throws: R   Height: 6' 6" Weight: 250 Born: March 22, 1985   Age: 22

YEAR	TEAM	LVL	AGE	W	L	SV	G	GS	IP	H	BB	SO	HR	GB%	BABIP	STUFF	WHIP	ERA	PERA	EQERA	EQH9	EQBB9	EQSO9	EQHR9	VORP	WXRL
2006	LOW	A-	21	3	1	0	14	0	31	20	2	33	0	74.4%	.244	13	0.71	0.87	3.16	2.37	7.1	0.9	5.0	0.3	10.9	—
2007	BOS	MLB	22	4	4	1	27	7	70²	75	11	39	5	63.0%	.298	7	1.22	3.79	3.41	3.56	8.3	1.3	4.6	0.5	14.2	1.70

Breakout: 4%   Improve: 6%   Collapse: 77%   Attrition: 21%   Comparables: Chien-Ming Wang, Brandon League, Denny Bautista, Manuel Parra

The 71st pick in the 2006 draft, this behemoth came to the team's attention a closer in the Cape Cod League in 2005. Having already thrown 116 innings prior to the draft, he worked out of the bullpen in Lowell. Adding a few MPH to a low-90s

(continued next page)

Justin Masterson *(continued)*

two-seam fastball that he continued to located very well, he made mincemeat out of opposing hitters, holding them to a .174/.208/.200 showing. The Sox will move him back into the rotation in 2007; the development of his secondary pitches will determine if he stays there.

Daisuke Matsuzaka　Bats: R　Throws: R　Height: 6' 0"　Weight: 190　Born: September 13, 1980　Age: 26

YEAR	TEAM	LVL	AGE	W	L	SV	G	GS	IP	H	BB	SO	HR	GB%	BABIP	STUFF	WHIP	ERA	PERA	EQERA	EQH9	EQBB9	EQSO9	EQHR9	VORP	WXRL
2004	SEI	JPL	23	10	6	0	23	0	146	127	42	127	7	—	.278	33	1.16	2.90	3.41	3.26	7.9	2.5	6.3	0.4	38.7	—
2005	SEI	JPL	24	14	13	0	28	28	215	172	49	226	13	—	.275	36	1.03	2.30	3.22	3.22	7.2	2.4	7.5	0.6	56.9	—
2006	SEI	JPL	25	17	5	0	25	25	186¹	138	34	200	13	—	.258	31	0.92	0.14	3.52	3.46	7.4	2.1	7.7	0.9	42.7	—
2007	BOS	MLB	26	12	9	0	29	29	187²	188	52	168	19	45%	.308	27	1.28	3.99	3.71	3.65	7.8	2.4	7.4	0.7	35.9	5.2

Breakout: 8%　Improve: 28%　Collapse: 23%　Attrition: 4%　　Comparables: Kevin Appier, Jose Rijo, Dennis Leonard, Dave Stieb

For all the drama surrounding the record-setting posting fee and tense deadline negotiations, the Sox secured the best pitcher on the winter market at a price that was hardly out of line. Matsuzaka's PECOTA EqERA [3.65] compares favorably to free agents Barry Zito (4.45), Jason Schmidt (4.13), Ted Lilly (4.30) and—guffaw—Gil Meche (4.86),and holds its own with front-liners like Roy Halladay (3.48), Brandon Webb (3.59) Chris Carpenter (3.62), and Roy Oswalt (3.84), not to mention his rotation mates and new pinstriped rivals. Matsuzaka's transition to stateside ball should be fascinating to behold, particularly with regards to the gyroball, the much-ballyhooed side-spinning pitch whose very existence is disputed (according to Will Carroll, Matsuzaka throws several variants of the gyro but doesn't know which is coming out of his hand when he does). Thirty-odd starts in high-definition TV might settle the matter, quite possibly offering the 2007 season's most compelling spectacle.

Jonathan Papelbon　Bats: R　Throws: R　Height: 6' 4"　Weight: 230　Born: November 23, 1980　Age: 26

YEAR	TEAM	LVL	AGE	W	L	SV	G	GS	IP	H	BB	SO	HR	GB%	BABIP	STUFF	WHIP	ERA	PERA	EQERA	EQH9	EQBB9	EQSO9	EQHR9	VORP	WXRL
2004	SAR	A+	23	12	7	0	24	24	129²	97	43	153	6	—	.287	13	1.08	2.64	4.65	4.16	8.2	3.8	6.7	1.0	19.7	—
2005	PME	AA	24	5	2	0	14	14	87	59	23	83	9	44.8%	.234	1	0.94	2.48	5.48	3.69	7.4	3.0	5.5	1.4	17.6	—
2005	PAW	AAA	24	1	2	1	7	4	27²	21	3	27	2	44.7%	.264	24	0.87	2.92	3.18	3.25	6.8	1.0	6.8	0.7	7.2	—
2005	BOS	MLB	24	3	1	0	17	3	34	33	17	34	4	35.5%	.326	17	1.47	2.65	4.46	2.80	8.2	4.3	8.7	1.0	11.0	1.10
2006	BOS	MLB	25	4	2	35	59	0	68¹	40	13	75	3	38.8%	.228	45	0.78	0.92	2.28	1.02	4.7	1.5	9.1	0.4	38.6	6.61
2007	BOS	MLB	26	4	4	27	55	0	62¹	57	21	61	6	40.0%	.295	17	1.25	3.33	3.37	2.99	7.2	2.9	8.2	0.8	18.0	2.60

Breakout: 13%　Improve: 37%　Collapse: 51%　Attrition: 3%　　Comparables: Jose Valverde, Ron Davis, Bobby Howry, Dan Plesac

YEAR	TEAM	LVL	AGE	W	L	SV	G	GS	IP	H	BB	SO	HR	GB%	BABIP	STUFF	WHIP	ERA	PERA	EQERA	EQH9	EQBB9	EQSO9	EQHR9	VORP	WXRL
2007	BOS	MLB	26	9	7	0	25	25	146	153	44	124	19	39%	.308	22	1.35	4.28	4.22	3.85	8.2	2.6	7.1	1.0	26.5	3.7

Breakout: 4%　Improve: 10%　Collapse: 71%　Attrition: 4%　　Comparables: Jose Valverde, Dan Plesac, Ron Davis, Bobby Howry

Even after the Arroyo trade, a surplus of starters ticketed Papelbon for a setup role, his success out of the bullpen down the 2005 stretch having made such an impression on Terry Francona. When Foulke's knees prevented the nominal closer from getting enough innings in spring training, Francona called Papelbon's number, and after 10 saves in 10 April chances, there was no going back. Papelbon didn't give up his first run until May 3, and by the time he gave up his fourth, he'd racked up 30 saves with the calendar showing August. Fatigue soon compromised his mechanics, and the team shut him down before Labor Day when an MRI showed a "transient subluxation event" (a.k.a. a tired rotator cuff). Amid much debate about his future role, Papelbon expressed a strong desire to return to the rotation in 2007 and the Sox brass concurred. Nothing less than the outcome of the AL East may ride on this decision. If Papelbon was guaranteed to be as dominant as a starter, the move would be a no-brainer, but all signs (including the dual PECOTAs above) suggest he would be greatly diminished by changing roles. Then again, the health of Papelbon's shoulder may force the Red Sox's hand.

David Pauley　Bats: R　Throws: R　Height: 6' 2"　Weight: 185　Born: June 17, 1983　Age: 24

YEAR	TEAM	LVL	AGE	W	L	SV	G	GS	IP	H	BB	SO	HR	GB%	BABIP	STUFF	WHIP	ERA	PERA	EQERA	EQH9	EQBB9	EQSO9	EQHR9	VORP	WXRL
2004	LEL	A+	21	7	12	0	27	26	153¹	155	60	128	8	—	.319	4	1.40	4.17	5.01	5.91	9.4	4.4	4.8	0.8	-5.2	—
2005	PME	AA	22	9	7	0	27	27	156	169	34	104	18	54.0%	.306	-10	1.30	3.81	5.22	5.60	10.3	2.3	4.1	1.5	0.0	—
2006	PME	AA	23	2	3	0	10	10	60²	54	17	47	6	54.7%	.291	-1	1.18	2.39	5.39	3.84	9.2	2.9	4.8	1.5	11.5	—
2006	PAW	AAA	23	1	3	0	9	9	50²	60	18	25	10	50.3%	.307	-35	1.55	5.56	8.01	7.97	11.4	3.4	3.4	2.7	-13.1	—
2006	BOS	MLB	23	0	2	0	3	3	16	31	6	10	1	46.9%	.476	0	2.31	7.88	4.08	6.75	15.6	3.1	5.2	0.5	-3.1	-0.07
2007	BOS	MLB	24	5	9	0	30	19	117²	150	46	60	17	50.0%	.323	-7	1.66	6.24	5.75	5.73	10.0	3.4	4.3	1.1	-7.5	0.10

Breakout: 18%　Improve: 53%　Collapse: 11%　Attrition: 0%　　Comparables: Dan Perkins, Tom Farmer, Jonathan Johnson, Jay Yennaco

Not ready for prime time yet, this unheralded righty was acquired from the Padres in the Jay Payton-Dave Roberts deal. Pauley has no dominant out-pitch, but he mixes an excellent sinker with a moving low-90s fastball, a good curve, and a pretty good changeup, all of which he throws for strikes. Too many strikes, in fact; he doesn't miss enough bats, and for a pitcher with groundball tendencies, his stat line suffers from a serious gopher infestation. He'll try to work it out at Pawtucket.

Curt Schilling   Bats: R Throws: R   Height: 6' 5"   Weight: 235   Born: December 31, 1969   Age: 40

YEAR	TEAM	LVL	AGE	W	L	SV	G	GS	IP	H	BB	SO	HR	GB%	BABIP	STUFF	WHIP	ERA	PERA	EQERA	EQH9	EQBB9	EQSO9	EQHR9	VORP	WXRL
2004	BOS	MLB	37	21	6	0	32	32	226²	206	35	203	23	—	.288	36	1.06	3.26	3.12	3.06	7.9	1.2	7.4	0.8	76.2	7.77
2005	BOS	MLB	38	8	8	9	32	11	93¹	121	22	87	12	36.2%	.381	14	1.53	5.69	3.63	5.14	10.7	2.0	7.9	1.0	2.1	0.03
2006	BOS	MLB	39	15	7	0	31	31	204	220	28	183	28	40.9%	.328	28	1.22	3.97	3.44	3.51	8.7	1.1	7.4	1.1	48.6	5.08
2007	BOS	MLB	40	12	9	0	31	29	192¹	205	36	155	23	41.0%	.310	20	1.26	4.11	3.85	3.73	8.3	1.6	6.7	0.9	36.2	5.20

Breakout: 19% Improve: 49% Collapse: 8%   Attrition: 4%   Comparables: Gaylord Perry, Roger Clemens, Don Sutton, Fergie Jenkins

Though he didn't reach the heights of 2004, Schilling sufficiently recovered from his famous ankle injury to reassert himself as a frontline starter in 2006, posting the top K/BB ratio of any ERA qualifier. That said, he showed some wear and tear. Early in the year, instability shortened his stride, causing his pitches to stay higher in the strike zone and offering clues that his ankle was still bothering him. A strained lat cost him a few September starts and may have factored into some second-half struggles (5.04 ERA over his final 11 starts). Still, simply by proving that reports of his demise were greatly exaggerated, Schilling's 2006 has to be counted as a success, and while the normal precautions apply to a 40-year-old pitcher, he should be capable of a repeat in the finale of his four-year, $50.5-million deal.

Kyle Snyder   Bats: S Throws: R   Height: 6' 8"   Weight: 215   Born: September 9, 1977   Age: 29

YEAR	TEAM	LVL	AGE	W	L	SV	G	GS	IP	H	BB	SO	HR	GB%	BABIP	STUFF	WHIP	ERA	PERA	EQERA	EQH9	EQBB9	EQSO9	EQHR9	VORP	WXRL
2005	OMA	AAA	27	2	3	0	15	12	66	61	22	48	3	56.9%	.291	8	1.26	3.55	3.97	4.43	7.9	3.0	4.8	0.4	8.7	—
2005	KCA	MLB	27	1	3	0	13	3	36	55	10	19	3	46.7%	.388	-7	1.81	6.75	3.96	5.82	11.9	2.3	4.4	0.7	-6.1	-0.47
2006	OMA	AAA	28	0	4	1	10	9	60¹	63	9	43	4	56.0%	.307	11	1.20	3.89	3.73	5.46	9.0	1.3	4.7	0.7	0.9	—
2006	PAW	AAA	28	1	1	0	3	3	20¹	24	2	7	1	59.7%	.324	-4	1.29	3.58	4.14	4.43	10.6	0.9	2.2	0.9	2.6	—
2006	BOS	MLB	28	4	5	0	16	10	58¹	77	19	55	11	42.6%	.369	6	1.65	5.87	4.47	5.58	10.7	2.6	7.8	1.5	-1.6	0.28
2007	BOS	MLB	29	7	8	0	35	20	122¹	147	31	77	15	48.0%	.323	3	1.46	5.14	4.70	4.72	9.4	2.2	5.3	0.9	8.3	1.50

Breakout: 48% Improve: 78% Collapse: 7%   Attrition: 8%   Comparables: Doc Medich, Mike Smithson, Gene Conley, John Halama

It's tempting to upbraid the Sox for installing a guy who couldn't crack the Royals rotation as a stopgap at a time when the outcome of Boston's season wasn't a foregone conclusion. But despite the grisly ERA and home run rate, Snyder's strikeout rate and K/BB ratio suggest more going on than a simple case of the Sucks. Though 2004 labrum surgery cost him velocity, his sinking fastball can still top 90, and he has a decent changeup and a slow curveball (68 to 71 MPH) to boot. Fatigue and exposure appear to be issues (pitches 1 to 30: .245/.304/.443; pitches 31 to 100: .389/.435/.611), suggesting he's worth a shot in the bullpen.

Julian Tavarez   Bats: L Throws: R   Height: 6' 2"   Weight: 195   Born: May 22, 1973   Age: 34

YEAR	TEAM	LVL	AGE	W	L	SV	G	GS	IP	H	BB	SO	HR	GB%	BABIP	STUFF	WHIP	ERA	PERA	EQERA	EQH9	EQBB9	EQSO9	EQHR9	VORP	WXRL
2004	SLN	MLB	31	7	4	4	77	0	64¹	57	19	48	1	—	.295	15	1.18	2.38	3.24	3.22	8.5	2.4	6.0	0.1	19.2	1.77
2005	SLN	MLB	32	2	3	4	74	0	65²	68	19	47	6	52.0%	.323	1	1.32	3.42	4.28	4.09	9.8	2.3	6.0	0.8	12.0	2.27
2006	BOS	MLB	33	5	4	1	58	6	98²	110	44	56	10	58.6%	.324	-7	1.56	4.56	4.79	4.35	9.1	3.7	4.7	0.8	12.4	0.35
2007	BOS	MLB	34	4	4	2	54	3	74¹	91	29	47	8	53.0%	.332	-9	1.60	5.19	5.03	4.78	9.5	3.3	5.2	0.8	4.4	0.50

Breakout: 6% Improve: 23% Collapse: 39% Attrition: 9%   Comparables: Kirk McCaskill, Clay Carroll, Tom Hume, Dave Weathers

Still crazy after all these years, Tavarez earned a 10-day suspension for sucker-punching Joey Gathright after landing on him in a close play at home plate—in a spring training game. Scored upon in 18 of his first 33 appearances, Tavarez trudged through an unhappy summer, but in an Alamo moment in late August, the Sox inserted him into the rotation. The results were compelling, if not revelatory; as a starter he posted a 4.01 ERA in 33.2 IP, generated a ton of groundballs, and yielded only two homers. He also won over a hostile Fenway crowd that had booed him lustily all season long, paving the way for a return for Year Two of his $6.7-million deal and perhaps a job as a back-end starter or swingman, a role in which his salary might suddenly seem like a bargain.

Mike Timlin   Bats: R Throws: R   Height: 6' 4"   Weight: 210   Born: December 31, 1969   Age: 41

YEAR	TEAM	LVL	AGE	W	L	SV	G	GS	IP	H	BB	SO	HR	GB%	BABIP	STUFF	WHIP	ERA	PERA	EQERA	EQH9	EQBB9	EQSO9	EQHR9	VORP	WXRL
2004	BOS	MLB	38	5	4	1	76	0	76¹	75	19	56	8	—	.294	6	1.23	4.13	3.88	3.68	8.6	2.1	6.1	0.8	19.1	2.68
2005	BOS	MLB	39	7	3	13	81	0	80¹	86	20	59	2	46.4%	.336	22	1.32	2.24	2.94	2.46	8.8	2.1	6.3	0.2	28.9	2.25
2006	BOS	MLB	40	6	6	9	68	0	64	78	17	30	7	38.9%	.324	-11	1.48	4.36	4.37	3.88	9.8	2.1	3.9	0.8	10.6	1.56
2007	BOS	MLB	41	2	2	3	31	0	35¹	43	9	20	4	47.0%	.319	-9	1.45	4.45	4.40	4.05	9.4	2.2	4.8	0.8	6.5	0.50

Breakout: 4%   Improve: 12%   Collapse: 36%   Attrition: 47%   Comparables: Ron Reed, Kent Tekulve, Gerry Staley, Al Benton

With a cheekful of chaw and the disdainful sneer of a well-traveled relief pitcher, the straight-from-central-casting Timlin averaged 76 appearances and 80 innings of 3.88 ERA ball from 2003 to 2005, while striking out 6.7 per nine innings. That ended in 2006. His effectiveness took a sharp downturn after a late-May shoulder strain; Timlin posted a 1.40 ERA and 5.6 K/9 before, but a 5.64 ERA and 3.6 K/9 afterwards. For a 41-year-old, that isn't a sign of good things to come. Still, the Sox inked him to a $2.8-million deal with incentives that could escalate it to $3.3 million with 70 appearances.

Jermaine Van Buren   Bats: R Throws: R   Height: 6' 1"   Weight: 220   Born: July 2, 1980   Age: 26

YEAR	TEAM	LVL	AGE	W	L	SV	G	GS	IP	H	BB	SO	HR	GB%	BABIP	STUFF	WHIP	ERA	PERA	EQERA	EQH9	EQBB9	EQSO9	EQHR9	VORP	WXRL
2004	WTN	AA	24	3	2	21	51	0	53	23	24	64	2	—	.194	15	0.89	1.87	4.14	2.68	5.0	4.6	7.2	0.5	16.3	—
2005	IOW	AAA	25	2	3	25	52	0	54²	33	22	65	5	45.5%	.250	16	1.01	1.97	4.09	2.14	5.8	3.5	8.1	0.8	21.0	—
2005	CHN	MLB	25	0	2	0	6	0	6	2	9	3	0	42.9%	.143	6	1.83	3.00	7.43	2.84	2.8	11.4	4.3	0.0	1.7	0.09
2006	PAW	AAA	26	4	0	16	33	0	45²	37	18	46	2	42.4%	.315	7	1.22	2.99	3.94	3.80	7.8	3.8	7.0	0.6	9.0	—
2006	BOS	MLB	26	1	0	0	10	0	13	14	15	8	1	45.0%	.333	-2	2.23	11.77	6.25	10.54	8.6	9.2	5.3	0.7	-8.0	0.13
2007	WAS	MLB	26	2	3	2	45	2	47	43	27	40	5	42%	.280	-2	1.48	4.56	4.96	5.00	8.2	4.6	6.9	0.9	3.9	0.4

Breakout: 22%   Improve: 48%   Collapse: 35%   Attrition: 25%   Comparables: Ken Wright, Bob Gibson, Preston Hanna, Jack Lamabe

Martin Van Buren was elected eighth president of the United States in 1836 and immediately had to deal with a collapsing economy. Exactly 170 years later, Jermaine Van Buren was elected to the Boston Red Sox and immediately became part of a collapsing bullpen. Desperate for roster space leading up to the Rule 5 Draft, the Cubs traded Van Buren, their 2005 Minor League Baseball Relief Pitcher of the Year, to the Red Sox. Shuttling between Pawtucket and Boston six times as Warm Body No. 11, he didn't do nearly as much damage as his line would indicate; his WXRL was seventh out of 18 Sox relievers, and his minor league numbers (2.22 ERA and 2.7 K/BB over the past three seasons) and repertoire (a power slider and a low-90s fastball) suggest he deserves another shot. Appropriately, he'll get it in Washington, where he happened to land in November.

Tim Wakefield   Bats: R Throws: R   Height: 6' 2"   Weight: 210   Born: December 31, 1969   Age: 40

YEAR	TEAM	LVL	AGE	W	L	SV	G	GS	IP	H	BB	SO	HR	GB%	BABIP	STUFF	WHIP	ERA	PERA	EQERA	EQH9	EQBB9	EQSO9	EQHR9	VORP	WXRL
2004	BOS	MLB	37	12	10	0	32	30	188¹	197	63	116	29	—	.280	0	1.38	4.88	5.01	5.16	9.2	2.7	5.1	1.2	13.3	2.18
2005	BOS	MLB	38	16	12	0	33	33	225¹	210	68	151	35	43.9%	.261	6	1.23	4.15	4.86	4.15	7.7	2.7	5.8	1.3	34.5	4.50
2006	BOS	MLB	39	7	11	0	23	23	140	135	51	90	19	40.2%	.266	6	1.33	4.63	4.91	4.46	7.9	3.0	5.3	1.1	15.2	2.06
2007	BOS	MLB	40	10	10	0	29	27	167	176	61	106	22	43.0%	.289	4	1.41	4.78	4.43	4.36	8.2	3.1	5.3	1.0	17.7	3.10

Breakout: 11%   Improve: 65%   Collapse: 3%   Attrition: 15%   Comparables: Joe Niekro, Tom Seaver, Charlie Hough, Don Sutton

Wakefield's injury—a stress fracture at the attachment of a rib, an injury nowhere in BP's database—reduced the rotation to Schilling, Beckett, Lester, Famine, and Pestilence; in this case, two horsemen were enough to herald the apocalypse in Boston. The Sox went 22–31 during Wakefield's two-month absence, dropping 11 games in the standings. Wakefield's the leading practitioner of a dying art, and the Sox hold a perpetual option on his services, but 2006 served as a warning that, now that he's past 40, a big chunk of his innings could quickly disappear off the ledger.

Lineouts

PLAYER	TEAM	LVL	AGE	PA	R	2B	3B	HR	RBI	BB	SO	SB-CS	SPEED	AVG/OBP/SLG	MLVr	EqAVG/OBP/SLG	EqA	VORP
1B H. Choi*	PAW	AAA	27	277	35	9	1	8	27	47	56	0-0	4.2	.207/.347/.361	-.036	.194/.319/.341	.238	-10.7
3B A. Granadillo#	GRN	A	21	486	70	29	2	13	68	43	79	3-0	4.8	.283/.360/.455	.153	.252/.305/.400	.245	5.8
UT W. Harris*	PAW	AAA	28	253	32	6	1	8	17	29	56	11-3	6.1	.220/.319/.367	-.067	.206/.294/.345	.231	-6.0
	BOS	MLB	28	52	17	2	0	0	1	4	11	6-3	7.3	.156/.250/.200	-.568	.133/.245/.178	.183	-5.1
C K. Huckaby	PAW	AAA	35	305	18	10	0	2	23	9	72	4-0	4.1	.219/.239/.274	-.317	.165/.185/.179	.143	-45.8
INF A. Machado#	PAW	AAA	24	437	46	12	4	4	32	52	51	21-6	6.1	.260/.356/.346	-.010	.251/.343/.344	.251	7.3
CF J. Place	RSX	Rk	18	132	14	3	1	4	21	17	35	3-3	4.0	.292/.386/.442	.249	.269/.333/.437	.263	12.8

PLAYER	TEAM	LVL	AGE	W	L	SV	IP	H	BB	SO	HR	GB%	BABIP	STUFF	WHIP	ERA	PERA	EqERA	EqH9	EqBB9	EqSO9	EqHR9	VORP
B. Corey	TEX	MLB	32	1	1	0	17^1	15	8	13	0	36.5%	.288	5	1.33	2.60	3.37	2.50	7.0	4.0	6.0	0.0	6.9
	BOS	MLB	32	1	0	0	21^2	20	7	15	1	46.2%	.297	4	1.25	4.56	3.71	3.97	7.5	2.8	5.6	0.4	3.8
B. Cox	WIL	A+	21	2	0	0	24	14	9	25	0	—	.215	15	0.96	0.75	3.45	2.28	6.1	3.4	6.5	0.4	8.7
T. Hottovy*	WIL	A+	24	8	6	0	122^2	109	35	91	3	—	.290	11	1.18	2.80	4.13	4.76	8.5	3.0	4.2	0.4	11.3
	PME	AA	24	2	4	0	41^1	28	15	31	1	—	.252	5	1.05	4.16	4.47	5.67	7.0	3.9	4.5	0.5	-0.3
K. Jarvis	TUC	AAA	36	3	6	0	83^2	76	22	58	7	—	.274	-1	1.18	3.46	4.80	4.86	8.2	2.6	4.3	1.1	6.8
	ARI	MLB	36	0	1	0	11^1	18	5	6	2	—	.381	-28	2.03	11.95	5.42	10.50	13.5	3.0	4.5	1.5	-6.9
	BOS	MLB	36	0	1	0	16^2	22	6	7	1	—	.350	-10	1.68	4.85	4.32	5.19	10.9	3.1	3.6	0.5	-0.6
K. Johnson*	LOW	A-	21	0	2	0	30^2	25	7	27	0	—	.305	-5	1.06	0.89	4.17	3.68	8.6	3.1	4.3	0.3	6.3
P. Seibel*	GRN	A	27	2	0	0	20	12	0	19	2	—	.213	5	0.60	1.35	6.17	2.45	7.9	1.0	4.9	2.5	6.4
	PME	AA	27	2	3	0	45^2	24	12	42	5	—	.173	-2	0.80	1.19	6.11	3.16	6.5	3.0	5.5	1.9	11.6
	PAW	AAA	27	2	0	0	15	6	3	22	1	—	.179	15	0.60	1.20	2.88	1.84	4.3	1.8	9.8	0.6	6.1
C. Zink	PAW	AAA	26	9	4	0	109^1	100	60	58	7	—	.274	-5	1.47	4.04	5.85	5.13	8.4	5.3	3.6	0.8	5.7

Bad luck and trouble are apparently **Hee Seop Choi**'s only friends; though the Sox seemed the ideal organization to appreciate his skills, hamstring, knee, and back strains prevented him from ever getting going. He'll try his luck as a non-roster invitee with the Devil Rays this spring. In his repeat engagement in Greenville, pint-sized **Tony Granadillo** recaptured the power that prompted the Sox to draft him away from the Cardinals in the Triple-A Rule 5 draft in 2004. **Willie Harris**'s speed off the bench provided decent utility for the World Champion White Sox in 2005, and while he had his uses as a pinch-runner with the Red Sox, their absence from the postseason prevented his turn as the next Dave Roberts. His apparent inability to hit makes him a 25th man at best; the Braves will consider him for that spot in 2007. As a Blue Jay, **Ken Huckaby** infamously fell on top of Derek Jeter while covering third base, separating the star's shoulder, but he hasn't made solid contact like that in four years. A utilityman who can actually get on base, **Alejandro Machado** deserves better in a world full of Neifis. He'll fight for a spot on the Twins' roster in 2007. A five-tool high schooler out of South Carolina, **Jason Place** was the first of the team's four first-round picks in the 2006 draft. He had a solid debut in pro ball, despite significant contact problems.

Bryan Corey puts the journey in journeyman. Drafted by Detroit as an infielder in 1993, he accumulated just five major league innings while passing through eight organizations plus the Yomiuri Giants before signing with Texas last year. Flipped to the desperate Sox at the deadline, he gained Francona's favor, but whether he can repeat that is unknown. As a junior at Rice, **Bryson Cox** suffered a case of the strike-zone yips, but straightened out during his senior year to become one of the best relievers in college baseball on the strength of 96- to 98-MPH heat and a sharp-breaking slider. Some consider this third-rounder the steal of the 2006 draft. **Tommy Hottovy** fared better in a repeat of Wilmington after the Sox devoted a season to remaking the 2004 fourth-rounder's delivery. The extremely His extremely low percentage of his fly balls that become home runs (2.3) screams for a correction, though. On August 31, Theo Epstein raised the white flag over Fenway Park by trading David Wells to the Padres and acquiring 37-year-old journeyman **Kevin Jarvis**, who'd spent parts of twelve seasons with nine different teams, accumulating an ERA above 6.00. We have to assume it was done for the sake of amusement. The alternative is nightmarish: if Jarvis is your final answer, you haven't just asked the wrong question, you've shown up naked for the test. A draft-eligible Wichita State sophomore who underwent Tommy John surgery in 2005, **Kristofer Johnson** healed quickly and was the 40th overall pick last June. Limited to short stints, he made a nice debut at Lowell, generating a ton of groundballs and missing a fair share of bats while showing good velocity for a lefty. Younger brother of Jonathan and twin of the Cubs' 19th-round draft pick Jeremy, **Josh Papelbon** is considered the least gifted of the three, but bears watching thanks to his pedigree, a submarine delivery, and a good pro debut. A soft-tossing U. of Texas product who hadn't distinguish himself prior to undergoing Tommy John surgery in late 2004, **Phil Seibel** threw a ton of strikes while working his way back to Triple-A. It may have been the level of competition, but K/BB ratios like that bear watching. The Red Sox dealt him to the Angels for reliever Brendan Donnelly in December. If you squint, you can see a replacement-level pitcher emerging from the statistical fog, but knuckleballer **Charlie Zink** needs another breakthrough to merit a shot at the majors. For now, he remains a curiosity.

Manager: Terry Francona

Year	Team	W-L	Pythag +/-	Avg PC	100 +P	120 +P	QS	BQS	REL	REL w Zero R	IBB	SUBS	PH	PH Avg	PH HR	SB2	CS2	SB3	CS3	SAC Att	SAC %	POS SAC	Squeeze	Swing	In Play
2004	BOS	98-64	0	99.0	89	3	81	14	436	276	28	73	112	.263	2	64	27	4	2	20	60.0%	10	0	117	78
2005	BOS	95-67	+4	99.9	93	3	74	7	442	255	28	59	108	.202	1	42	12	3	0	24	58.3%	13	0	139	98
2006	BOS	86-76	+5	95.6	64	2	67	11	453	263	25	71	93	.221	0	46	22	5	1	39	56.4%	22	0	126	106

Terry Francona's first season in Boston was the team's most successful in 86 years. As such, Francona holds a huge advantage over his predecessors, and has drawn relatively little flak or the kind of second-guessing-from-within that characterized the Grady Little and Jimy Williams regimes. That's a product of his bosses; the Henry-Epstein Sox are devoted to rational decision-making and statistical analysis, and Francona is in place because he's bought into the system. A major facet of that is eschewing unproductive one-run strategies. The Sox tied for last with just 83 sacrifice bunts from 2004 to 2006. They ranked last in the AL stolen bases in 2006, and second-to-last in 2005. Francona does value speed off the bench, using an MLB-leading 165 pinch-runners—Dave Roberts, Willie Harris, et al.—from 2004 to 2006, but the loss of Johnny Damon (18-for-19 in '05) turned them from efficient thieves (79 percent) to inefficient ones (69 percent). As for the pitching staff, Francona tends to push his starters, but only up to a point. They ranked fifth among all teams in pitches per start from 2004 to 2006, but tied for 19th with just eight starts of 120 or more pitches. Francona's generally mid-pack in terms of reliever usage; last year he used the fifth-most in the AL, owing to the staff's injury situation. Like Joe Torre in New York, he's got the horses to compete, and the stability he provides amid the tumult may be as valuable as his ability to carry out management's program.

Chicago Cubs

The Dusty Baker era almost got off on the right foot in 2003 only to have its moment of triumph interrupted by the now-infamous Bartman game. Despite falling short of 90 wins, Baker's first Cubs team won both its division and the first postseason series by any Cubs contingent since 1908. But after winning 90 games five times in his eight full seasons steering the Giants, Baker failed to reach the mark even once in his four-years in Chicago. Instead of winning big on the diamond, Baker's victories in the Windy City were of a more pyrrhic and petty variety; cutting Sammy Sosa down to size was one of his first orders of business, and, after promising to keep his young son out of the way, he had Darren working as a bat boy and performing human shield missions in postgame press conferences long before the bitter end.

It remains to be seen if Dusty Baker is more than just a manager who made a name for himself by having had the good fortune to manage one of the game's greatest players through his best seasons. The only thing that his stint with the Cubs has made clear is that he's exceedingly ill-suited to guide a team that's not in contention. Having skippered a Giants team that was in a perpetual win-now mode, Baker hadn't had a lot of experience in building when he came to Chicago. When his new team made it to the playoffs in his first year, he continued on with that win-now mentality, ultimately costing the organization a regrettable amount of talent without producing another trip to the postseason. One of the core tasks a manager must perform is identifying talent and putting it to work in roles that best exploit it. That aspect of the job seemed to hold little appeal for Baker, who preferred to discard people because he couldn't figure out what to do with them. By

2006, Baker had run off a goodly amount of established talent, completely giving up on players with demonstrated ability, such as Mark Bellhorn, Kyle Farnsworth, Corey Patterson, Juan Cruz, and LaTroy Hawkins.

In 2006, General Manager Jim Hendry forced Baker to give starting jobs to youngsters Matt Murton and Ronny Cedeño. It didn't go well for anyone involved. Cedeño failed badly, while Murton was under constant threat of platoon and lost playing time to Angel Pagan, Freddie Bynum, and even fellow righty Phil Nevin. Due in part to a lack of talent coming up through the Giants' and Cubs' systems, and in part to his own distaste for young players, Baker hadn't successfully established a position player since Rich Aurilia in 1998, and it showed.

There was at least reason for optimism on the pitching side of the equation. Baker had gotten good results from prospects Shawn Estes and Russ Ortiz in San Francisco and was armed with phenoms Mark Prior and Kerry Wood in 2003, but repeated injuries to the two young hurlers put the Cubs' hopes on pause for four years. That's not all Baker's fault. Both were damaged goods before he arrived and many managers would have been overwhelmed by the resulting degeneration of the Cubs staff. Whereas in 2003 the Cubs had all but eight starts made by their five primary starting pitchers, by 2006 they were forced to use 15 different starters. In the end, Baker was overcome by the rotation's overlapping problems of injuries and ineffectiveness. In 2006, Wood and Prior combined to make just 13 starts, with Wood recording the duo's only quality start, while Baker indecisively lurched back and forth on the virtues of young arms such as Rich Hill and Angel Guzman rather than committing to their young talent. As management

---

CUBS PROSPECTUS

2006 record: 66–96; Sixth place, NL Central

Pythagenport record: 68–94

Runs scored per game: 4.40 (15th in NL)

Runs allowed per game: 5.15 (15th in NL)

Team EqA: .250 (15th in NL)

2006 Batters Age: 29.1 (6th youngest in NL)

2006 Pitchers Age: 28.2 (3rd youngest in NL)

Ballpark: Wrigley Field; Moderate hitter's park; Park Factor of 1.026

2006: Overrated talent and some bad breaks lead to a disastrous season, spiced with heapin' helpin's of Dusty defensiveness.

2007: There's no limit to how .480 this team could be, even a healthy Derrek Lee and Soriano's arrival won't be enough to fix the offense's inability to get on base.

---

became increasingly punch-drunk, the wave of rookie hurlers who pitched for the 2006 Cubs became something of a blur.

Some of that was anticipated by Hendry—the organization did, after all, have the kind of pitching depth to send all of those youngsters to the mound. Hendry also tried to compensate for his fragile rotation by making major outlays for relief help, spending a combined $38.5 million over three years to retain Ryan Dempster and add veterans Scott Eyre and Bobby Howry. Unfortunately, those additions didn't compensate nearly enough. Dempster was a risky proposition from the start and Dusty Baker's bullpen management—never a strong suit—didn't help. At least Howry and Eyre were relatively Baker-proof, since he couldn't put them on the Iowa shuttle as readily as Michael Wuertz, Todd Wellemeyer, or Rafael Novoa.

Baker set at least one record while managing the Cubs. Although our play-by-play database goes back only as far as the 1960 season, it is almost certain that Baker used his relievers in back-to-back games more often in 2006 than any manager in the history of baseball, a total of 166 appearances without rest. Baker is merely the tip of the iceberg, as reliever usage has become so frenetic that four of the top six totals in table 1 were amassed by National League managers in 2006. Still, the impact on the Cubs pen should not be underestimated and it's worth noting that Baker appears twice more in the top 16 single-season totals.

For all the tedium of those multiple late-game pitching changes, they neither fixed the rotation, nor helped the

Cubs win games. Overall, the Cubs' reliever performance with zero days of rest ranked 16th in baseball in WXRL and 14th in ARP. That seems like a respectable showing considering how often they were asked to do it, but then only three teams in table 1 posted a lower ARP total. Disastrously, in the first season of his three-year, $15.5-million contract, closer Ryan Dempster, already limited to single-inning Eckersley-style usage, proved to be the one guy who very clearly couldn't handle back-to-back assignments (see table 2).

Table 2. Cub Pen Performance on Consecutive Days

Pitcher	G	ARP	WXRL
Bob Howry	31	3.956	.911
Will Ohman	28	2.461	.538
Ryan Dempster	28	−6.242	−.151
Scott Eyre	26	2.458	−.051
Roberto Novoa	17	−0.970	.008
Mike Wuertz	13	1.551	.106
Dave Aardsma	11	3.849	.165
Others	12	−1.951	.021

Rather than feel burned by the Baker experience, Jim Hendry's gone double-down on celebrity managers by bringing in Lou Piniella. Replacing one high-priced dugout diva who's made his name someplace else with another hasn't always been a great play; whether it was the Red Sox ditching Joe Cronin for Joe McCarthy in 1948, or, more recently, the Mets' utterly pointless exercise of replacing Bobby Valentine with Art Howe. There is reason for hope with Piniella, though you have to look past his unhappy sojourn with the Devil Rays to see it. Piniella's time working with Pat Gillick in Seattle was a model for how a larger-than-life field manager can work hand-in-glove with a general manager who would rather keep a lower profile. Just because Hendry-Baker didn't work, doesn't mean that Hendry-Piniella won't.

To assess Hendry fairly, one must recognize that not every general manager is gunning to become the Ayn Rand-style superman that contemporaries ranging from Billy Beane to Omar Minaya are billed as. Hendry has his strengths as a GM, particularly in player development, and especially in assembling a worthwhile crowd of pitching prospects. If things haven't always worked out on the major league level, remember that under Hendry the Cubs have identified problems and pursued defensible courses of action to fix them. Having built up a reservoir of desirable pitching talent but finding himself short a leadoff hitter, Hendry dealt young pitching to get one. That's a rea-

Table 1. Back to Work, Boys—Relief Appearances on Consecutive Days

Year	Team	Manager	G	ARP
2006	Cubs	Dusty Baker	166	5.113
2004	Giants	Felipe Alou	159	7.370
2006	Astros	Phil Garner	157	15.362
2006	Pirates	Jim Tracy	156	11.050
2003	Dodgers	Jim Tracy	148	36.622
2006	Braves	Bobby Cox	146	11.065
2005	Giants	Felipe Alou	145	19.302
2005	Nationals	Frank Robinson	141	10.287
1987	Phillies	Felske/Elia	139	46.166
2001	Cardinals	Tony La Russa	139	36.745
2006	Nationals	Frank Robinson	138	-2.560
2004	Pirates	Lloyd McClendon	137	12.518
1998	Cubs	Jim Riggleman	136	25.851
1997	Giants	Dusty Baker	134	-4.660
2003	D'backs	Bob Brenly	134	16.610
2004	Cubs	Dusty Baker	130	3.262
2004	Braves	Bobby Cox	130	15.596

NOTE: ARP: Adjusted Runs Prevented.

sonable course of action; the problem is that the leadoff hitter he acquired was Juan Pierre.

Among his happier master strokes, Hendry deserves credit for his stretch-drive pickups, particularly the 2003 deal that brought in Aramis Ramirez and Kenny Lofton for Bobby Hill, Jose Hernandez, and Matt Bruback, as well as the 2004 deal that drew Nomar Garciaparra and Matt Murton for Alex Gonzalez, Brendan Harris, and Francis Beltran. That's a pair of very similarly-structured deals—getting top talent for two packages of a generic veteran infielder, a middling middle-infield prospect, and a token arm with 90-plus velocity. Both deals provided high-end talent at minimal loss.

Less defensible has been the organization-wide failure to develop position players. If there's an area in which Hendry can be blamed for the team's lack of progress, it's this. Baker's lack of experience in turning around struggling youngsters can be blamed for the dead end the club reached with Corey Patterson, but the other homegrown goodies simply aren't very good. Felix Pie might at least give the Cubs a direct one-for-one replacement for Patterson, but beyond him there's only Corey's little brother, second baseman Eric Patterson, and a parade of players with significant problems.

This lack of position prospects helps explain Hendry's turn towards the free agent market this winter. The Cubs made a huge splash during the offseason, doling out a whopping $224 million to re-sign Ramirez and add Mark DeRosa and Alfonso Soriano, then invested an additional $61 million to have reliable veteran starters Ted Lilly and Jason Marquis shore up the rotation in the wake of Prior and Wood's injuries. Rather than tear down after last season's debacle, the Cubs are going for broke. If that's a matter of self-preservation for Hendry and/or part of ownership's desire to pump up franchise value before a sale, then everyone involved can accept a short-term grasp for expensive glory—especially if footing the bill becomes somebody else's problem.

The larger question is whether or not the Cubs have done enough to challenge for a division title, even in the weak NL Central. Tilting towards fixing the offense is just as well given the problems that have afflicted it. Slightly less historic than Baker's record for placing a heavy workload on his pen but equally significant, the 2006 Cubs became the first team to fail to draw 400 unintentional walks in consecutive years since the 1992–93 Cubs. If they repeat the trick a third time in 2007, they'll be the first to do it since the Cubs of 1988–90. Baker openly deplored players who walk as base-cloggers. His charges got the message. It's going to take some time to undo the culture of self-defeating impatience that has been the team's credo for the last few years.

This winter's changes—swapping out Juan Pierre for Alfonso Soriano, replacing the remarkably awful Neifi Perez and his like with Mark DeRosa—plus the anticipated return of a healthy Derek Lee should portend good things, but it is far from certain that they will erase all of the club's offensive shortcomings. Soriano, Lee, and DeRosa should generate more extra-base hits than the men they're replacing, but far as creating baserunners by every possible means, including taking ball four, that's not quite as certain. DeRosa had a nice two-month run in 2006 before going to back to hitting like Mark DeRosa, while both Lee in 2005 and Soriano in 2006 saw their walk totals get big boosts from intentional passes, as opposing managers sensibly identified them as the singular game-breaking talent in their respective lineups. Put in the same lineup, neither is as likely to get as many free passes. However, as the White Sox demonstrated in 2005, and the Tigers did in 2006, a lineup with wall-to-wall power can propel a team deep into October despite a low OBP, and the only offensive zero in 2007 Cubs' projected lineup looks to be shortstop Cesar Izturis.

Of course one thing the 2005 White Sox and 2006 Tigers had in common was a league-leading pitching staff. That brings us back to asking whether or not a rotation built around Carlos Zambrano, Lilly, Marquis, Rich Hill, and either Wade Miller or Prior can win the 85 games or so it should take to contend in this division. It's certainly within the realm of possibility, and while that may not sound like much to go on, it's a better scenario than the two equally unhealthy articles of faith the Cubs were relying on entering 2006: the arms of Mark Prior and Kerry Wood, and Dusty Baker's leadership.

HITTERS

Michael Barrett   C   Bats: R   Throws: R   Height: 6' 3"   Weight: 210   Born: October 22, 1976   Age: 30

YEAR	TEAM	LVL	AGE	PA	R	2B	3B	HR	RBI	BB	SO	SB	CS	SPEED	AVG	OBP	SLG	MLVR	EQAVG	EQOBP	EQSLG	EQA	VORP	DEFENSE	
2004	CHN	MLB	27	506	55	32	6	16	65	33	64	1	4	4.5	.287	.337	.489	.102	.282	.331	.484	.273	24.8	117-C	-1
2005	CHN	MLB	28	477	48	32	3	16	61	40	61	0	3	3.7	.276	.345	.479	.122	.274	.345	.487	.279	28.1	115-C	-11
2006	CHN	MLB	29	418	54	25	3	16	53	33	41	0	1	3.8	.307	.368	.517	.209	.301	.365	.509	.294	31.3	96-C	-19
2007	CHN	MLB	30	468	64	28	3	15	64	37	55	1	2	4.3	.293	.355	.479	.088	.287	.349	.465	.276	24.5	111-C	-8

Breakout: 12%   Improve: 40%   Collapse: 27%   Attrition: 8%   Comparables: Del Crandall, Sandy Alomar, Bob Boone, Bob Brenly

Protective gear in baseball has come a long way, but it wasn't enough to save Barrett from a foul tip. Barrett took a hit that broke his cup, leaving him with an interscrotal hematoma that ended his season in early September. The shame of it was that he was on his way to a career year at the plate. His already poor defense took a turn for the worse in 2006, though much of that may have been related to turnover on the pitching staff. He threw out only 15 percent of opposing baserunners, and he's had his problems handling power stuff. Another poor year behind the plate could put a big dent in his 2008 date with free agency.

Henry Blanco   C   Bats: R   Throws: R   Height: 5' 11"   Weight: 220   Born: August 29, 1971   Age: 35

YEAR	TEAM	LVL	AGE	PA	R	2B	3B	HR	RBI	BB	SO	SB	CS	SPEED	AVG	OBP	SLG	MLVR	EQAVG	EQOBP	EQSLG	EQA	VORP	DEFENSE	
2004	MIN	MLB	32	353	36	19	1	10	37	21	56	0	3	3.9	.206	.260	.368	-.318	.201	.257	.366	.216	-14.1	91-C	17
2005	CHN	MLB	33	178	16	6	0	6	25	11	24	0	0	3.3	.242	.287	.391	-.127	.235	.284	.389	.233	0.7	48-C	11
2006	CHN	MLB	34	261	23	15	2	6	37	14	38	0	0	3.8	.266	.304	.419	-.076	.260	.301	.421	.247	1.7	59-C	10
2007	CHN	MLB	35	315	31	16	1	9	37	19	48	0	1	3.8	.254	.302	.407	-.134	.249	.296	.395	.235	0.8	76-C	4

Breakout: 28%   Improve: 53%   Collapse: 22%   Attrition: 46%   Comparables: Gary Carter, John Flaherty, Joe Oliver, Jim Hegan

It used to be that Blanco was an outstanding defensive catcher who couldn't hit, in part because he never singled. He can still do the outstanding catcher thing, but a few more base hits last year made him into something of gray hole offensively, rather than a black one. Keep in mind his age and track record—when backup catchers get this old, they start falling and can't get back up.

Freddie Bynum   UT   Bats: L   Throws: R   Height: 6' 1"   Weight: 185   Born: March 15, 1980   Age: 27

YEAR	TEAM	LVL	AGE	PA	R	2B	3B	HR	RBI	BB	SO	SB	CS	SPEED	AVG	OBP	SLG	MLVR	EQAVG	EQOBP	EQSLG	EQA	VORP	DEFENSE			
2004	MID	AA	24	297	38	13	4	1	22	24	56	18	7	7.3	.268	.332	.358	-.074	.239	.293	.316	.222	-10.8	61-CF	-8		
2004	SAC	AAA	24	291	42	11	3	2	26	19	61	21	4	7.8	.287	.343	.376	-.082	.273	.324	.348	.247	-7.3	21-LF	0	18-SS	-1
2005	SAC	AAA	25	428	56	16	9	2	40	38	83	23	7	8.0	.278	.347	.384	-.083	.268	.325	.361	.247	0.7	51-CF	1	21-SS	-5
2006	CHN	MLB	26	148	20	5	5	4	12	9	44	8	4	7.8	.257	.308	.456	-.017	.255	.311	.460	.258	3.3	13-2B	-2		
2007	BAL	MLB	27	260	31	10	2	4	23	16	55	11	4	7.0	.254	.306	.361	-.179	.252	.309	.367	.245	-1.7				

Breakout: 22%   Improve: 42%   Collapse: 24%   Attrition: 36%   Comparables: Ty Cline, Cory Sullivan, Herm Winningham, Jeff Stone

Bynum was out of options with the A's last spring, and a three-team deal before Opening Day made him a Cub. Dusty loves guys that can be shoved all over the lineup and field, and that's Bynum in a nutshell—versatility and speed are about all he offers. He had a relapse of a clot problem in his arm last year and missed about four months. Traded to the Orioles for a non-prospect pitcher after the season, he'll challenge Brandon Fahey and Chris Gomez for a utility spot.

Ronny Cedeño   SS   Bats: R   Throws: R   Height: 6' 0"   Weight: 180   Born: February 2, 1983   Age: 24

YEAR	TEAM	LVL	AGE	PA	R	2B	3B	HR	RBI	BB	SO	SB	CS	SPEED	AVG	OBP	SLG	MLVR	EQAVG	EQOBP	EQSLG	EQA	VORP	DEFENSE			
2004	WTN	AA	21	432	39	19	5	6	48	24	74	10	10	5.1	.279	.328	.401	.031	.266	.304	.380	.239	5.8	112-SS	4		
2005	IOW	AAA	22	275	42	14	1	8	36	20	31	11	3	5.4	.355	.403	.518	.307	.331	.373	.470	.290	27.0	64-SS	5		
2005	CHN	MLB	22	89	13	3	0	1	6	5	11	1	0	4.7	.300	.356	.375	.012	.296	.360	.370	.261	3.6	18-SS	-1		
2006	CHN	MLB	23	572	51	18	7	6	41	17	109	8	8	5.5	.245	.271	.339	-.258	.241	.269	.335	.210	-17.8	127-SS	-2	14-2B	-1
2007	CHN	MLB	24	524	61	24	4	10	50	24	80	11	6	5.7	.269	.307	.399	-.123	.264	.302	.387	.236	6.7	123-SS	2		

Breakout: 16%   Improve: 44%   Collapse: 23%   Attrition: 12%   Comparables: Julio Gotay, Hal Lanier, Woody Woodward, Chico Carrasquel

Cedeño won the starting shortstop job on the strength of his .300 batting average in 80 at-bats in 2005 and strong winter ball and spring training performances. He made Dusty look smart for about a month. Thereafter, teams started recognizing his faults, such as his total inability to hit breaking pitches from lefties. He also had too many throwing errors. When the Cubs got Cesar Izturis at the end of July, Cedeño's days as the starting shortstop were done. He'll try to hang on as a second baseman or maybe a utility guy.

Buck Coats UT   Bats: L   Throws: R   Height: 6′ 3″   Weight: 195   Born: June 6, 1982   Age: 25

YEAR	TEAM	LVL	AGE	PA	R	2B	3B	HR	RBI	BB	SO	SB	CS	SPEED	AVG	OBP	SLG	MLVR	EQAVG	EQOBP	EQSLG	EQA	VORP	DEFENSE			
2004	DAY	A+	22	457	64	23	4	8	56	32	91	28	9	7.2	.292	.341	.423	.093	.265	.308	.397	.248	11.5	84-SS	-15	21-3B	-1
2005	WTN	AA	23	484	47	32	6	1	49	38	80	17	5	5.9	.282	.340	.390	.014	.268	.315	.374	.243	8.3	90-SS	-20	23-CF	3
2006	IOW	AAA	24	498	60	21	0	7	51	38	87	17	4	5.6	.282	.342	.376	-.017	.270	.325	.368	.247	-8.6	67-RF	2	21-CF	-3
2006	CHN	MLB	24	18	2	1	0	1	1	0	6	0	0	3.8	.167	.167	.389	-.436	.167	.167	.389	.185	-1.2				
2007	CHN	MLB	25	442	55	22	3	8	43	31	86	14	4	5.8	.261	.317	.394	-.118	.256	.312	.383	.242	0.0	105-RF	-3		

Breakout: 17% Improve: 43% Collapse: 23% Attrition: 15%   Comparables: Garry Maddox, Doug Clark, Chris Stowers, Alexis Gomez

Coats has failed to show any development as a hitter, having had essentially the same season four years in a row. He wasn't a good enough hitter to overcome his awful defense as an infielder, and his bat isn't enough to justify an outfield spot either. Has the name in baseball most likely to be mistaken for that of a performer in an old Western serial ("Buck Coats in . . . *The Yodeling Mesquiteer!*") or adult films ("Buck Coats in . . ." well, we won't say).

Tyler Colvin OF   Bats: L   Throws: L   Height: 6′ 3″   Weight: 190   Born: September 5, 1985   Age: 20

YEAR	TEAM	LVL	AGE	PA	R	2B	3B	HR	RBI	BB	SO	SB	CS	SPEED	AVG	OBP	SLG	MLVR	EQAVG	EQOBP	EQSLG	EQA	VORP	DEFENSE			
2006	BOI	A-	20	288	50	12	6	11	53	17	55	12	5	7.2	.268	.313	.483	.138	.232	.266	.408	.230	-23.1	46-LF	-5	18-CF	0

The Cubs' first-round pick in 2006 had a lackluster pro debut, but the predictive power of a player's first exposure to wooden bats is exceptionally low. He's more toolsy and less polished than your typical collegiate first-rounder; then again, most scouts thought he was more of a third-round pick than a first. He's seen as above average in the traditional five tools, but his plate discipline last year was dismal.

Brian Dopirak 1B   Bats: R   Throws: R   Height: 6′ 4″   Weight: 230   Born: December 20, 1983   Age: 23

YEAR	TEAM	LVL	AGE	PA	R	2B	3B	HR	RBI	BB	SO	SB	CS	SPEED	AVG	OBP	SLG	MLVR	EQAVG	EQOBP	EQSLG	EQA	VORP	DEFENSE	
2004	LNS	A	20	597	94	38	0	39	120	48	123	4	3	3.7	.307	.363	.593	.396	.273	.318	.514	.276	25.1	114-1B	-10
2005	DAY	A+	21	553	53	26	0	16	76	37	107	1	4	1.9	.235	.289	.381	-.091	.198	.246	.321	.200	-51.5	116-1B	-14
2006	WTN	AA	22	199	16	12	0	1	23	16	41	0	0	3.2	.257	.322	.341	-.021	.249	.303	.337	.228	-8.2	40-1B	0
2007	CHN	MLB	23	357	35	17	0	11	44	24	72	0	0	3.7	.249	.303	.408	-.133	.244	.298	.396	.236	-6.7	86-1B	-4

Breakout: 34% Improve: 53% Collapse: 18% Attrition: 19%   Comparables: Ramon Castro, Brandon Sing, Ron Wright, Doug Gredvig

Dopirak's lone home run last year was quite a letdown for a guy who hit 39 in the Midwest League two years ago and two in 30 at-bats during spring training. Dopirak broke his foot in the first game of the season, missed more than two months, and wasn't right when he came back. Having made extensive changes to his swing, he now hits ground balls at a rate to rival Juan Pierre. It's an approach ridiculously unsuited for someone with his power. At this point, his prospect status is about the same as Taylor Hicks's.

Mike Fontenot 2B   Bats: L   Throws: R   Height: 5′ 8″   Weight: 160   Born: June 9, 1980   Age: 27

YEAR	TEAM	LVL	AGE	PA	R	2B	3B	HR	RBI	BB	SO	SB	CS	SPEED	AVG	OBP	SLG	MLVR	EQAVG	EQOBP	EQSLG	EQA	VORP	DEFENSE			
2004	OTT	AAA	24	590	73	30	10	8	49	48	111	14	7	6.5	.279	.346	.420	.009	.260	.325	.387	.250	10.3	133-2B	-18		
2005	IOW	AAA	25	449	60	22	10	6	39	59	77	3	2	5.2	.272	.377	.430	.047	.251	.342	.379	.255	9.9	58-2B	-5	35-3B	-3
2006	IOW	AAA	26	418	54	28	2	8	36	47	64	5	4	5.1	.296	.375	.450	.155	.284	.353	.432	.272	22.4	87-2B	-6		
2007	CHN	MLB	27	430	54	22	4	8	39	41	75	5	2	5.5	.259	.336	.397	-.082	.254	.330	.386	.249	6.9	102-2B	-5		

Breakout: 7% Improve: 28% Collapse: 37% Attrition: 16%   Comparables: Stubby Clapp, John Powers, David Newhan, Marty Malloy

In a just world, Fontenot would have gotten the opportunity that went to Ryan Theriot; he's a better hitter and more experienced at second base. Fontenot wasn't on the 40-man roster, though, which was one strike against him. He's limited to second base; that's another. And he's not fast enough to use as a pinch-runner, which on a Dusty Baker-led team makes three. He'll be hard-pressed to have a career, as he'll have to wait for minor league free agency—another year away— before he gets a chance.

Jake Fox   C   Bats: R   Throws: R   Height: 6' 0"   Weight: 210   Born: July 20, 1982   Age: 24

YEAR	TEAM	LVL	AGE	PA	R	2B	3B	HR	RBI	BB	SO	SB	CS	SPEED	AVG	OBP	SLG	MLVR	EQAVG	EQOBP	EQSLG	EQA	VORP	DEFENSE	
2004	LNS	A	21	395	49	19	3	14	55	17	75	2	1	4.1	.287	.331	.470	.168	.262	.293	.422	.243	5.9	77-C	6
2005	DAY	A+	22	309	37	20	0	9	40	26	48	5	2	3.5	.281	.357	.456	.141	.245	.308	.403	.247	3.9	60-C	-3
2006	DAY	A+	23	291	45	15	1	16	61	27	49	4	1	4.3	.313	.383	.574	.361	.283	.338	.527	.290	24.6	48-C	-3
2006	WTN	AA	23	204	20	17	0	5	25	9	44	0	0	2.7	.269	.304	.435	.085	.258	.289	.443	.248	4.4	41-C	0
2007	CHN	MLB	24	485	55	25	1	20	69	29	93	2	1	3.9	.262	.314	.455	-.040	.257	.309	.442	.254	11.9	115-C	-1

Breakout: 23% Improve: 44% Collapse: 30% Attrition: 7%   Comparables: Javier Cardona, Matthew LeCroy, Ryan Garko, Wiki Gonzalez

A power surge in A-ball gave Fox a glimmer of prospect status. Until last year's performance at Daytona, his numbers were consistently on the low side for a major league prospect. He has legitimate power but doesn't get on base enough. His offense is more than adequate for a backup, but most teams prefer would prefer a better defender. Another year slugging better than .500 will do wonders in creating believers.

Sam Fuld   CF   Bats: L   Throws: L   Height: 5' 10"   Weight: 180   Born: November 20, 1981   Age: 25

YEAR	TEAM	LVL	AGE	PA	R	2B	3B	HR	RBI	BB	SO	SB	CS	SPEED	AVG	OBP	SLG	MLVR	EQAVG	EQOBP	EQSLG	EQA	VORP	DEFENSE	
2005	PEO	A	23	508	82	32	6	5	37	50	44	18	11	6.4	.300	.377	.433	.162	.261	.315	.366	.239	-1.4	118-CF	3
2006	DAY	A+	24	405	63	19	6	4	40	40	54	22	3	7.0	.300	.378	.422	.151	.268	.329	.383	.254	5.2	84-CF	8
2007	CHN	MLB	25	442	59	24	5	5	36	31	58	13	5	6.2	.280	.336	.402	-.059	.275	.330	.391	.251	6.9	105-CF	6

Breakout: 23% Improve: 52% Collapse: 21% Attrition: 11%   Comparables: Dave Roberts, Kevan Burns, Adam Stern, Mike Rodriguez

Fuld posted encouraging numbers again, but as he's a bit too old to be playing in A-ball, no one's ready to referring to him as a prospect. Still, he's a scrapper and he has yet to fail. That's been enough to get some people up to the Show.

Ryan Harvey   RF   Bats: R   Throws: R   Height: 6' 5"   Weight: 220   Born: August 30, 1984   Age: 22

YEAR	TEAM	LVL	AGE	PA	R	2B	3B	HR	RBI	BB	SO	SB	CS	SPEED	AVG	OBP	SLG	MLVR	EQAVG	EQOBP	EQSLG	EQA	VORP	DEFENSE	
2004	BOI	A-	19	257	42	8	0	14	43	20	77	2	2	4.4	.268	.331	.485	.100	.211	.249	.343	.205	-37.6	37-RF	0
2005	PEO	A	20	507	71	30	2	24	100	24	137	8	4	4.6	.257	.302	.484	.084	.227	.257	.417	.228	-21.4	94-RF	-10
2006	DAY	A+	21	507	64	25	1	20	84	25	125	7	0	5.1	.248	.290	.432	-.000	.223	.258	.392	.224	-27.9	116-RF	-10
2007	CHN	MLB	22	471	50	24	1	18	60	22	128	4	2	4.7	.242	.283	.421	-.157	.237	.278	.409	.231	-11.5	111-RF	-5

Breakout: 46% Improve: 70% Collapse: 16% Attrition: 7%   Comparables: Thomas Collaro, John Adams, Jamar Hill, Dustan Mohr

Harvey was the sixth overall pick in 2003, a high school monster-masher whose tools—particularly his power and his arm—still generate puddles under the chairs in the scout's section at the ballpark. Unfortunately, he doesn't appear to have any pitch recognition skills at all, and with a swing longer than a Bill Clinton speech they're an absolute necessity. The potential payoff is large, but so are the odds against ever collecting.

Cesar Izturis   SS   Bats: S   Throws: R   Height: 5' 7"   Weight: 190   Born: February 10, 1980   Age: 27

YEAR	TEAM	LVL	AGE	PA	R	2B	3B	HR	RBI	BB	SO	SB	CS	SPEED	AVG	OBP	SLG	MLVR	EQAVG	EQOBP	EQSLG	EQA	VORP	DEFENSE	
2004	LAN	MLB	24	728	90	32	9	4	62	43	70	25	9	7.1	.288	.330	.381	-.036	.290	.332	.384	.252	21.7	153-SS	-6
2005	LAN	MLB	25	478	48	19	2	2	31	25	51	8	8	5.0	.257	.302	.322	-.162	.259	.305	.331	.223	-4.2	104-SS	10
2006	LAN	MLB	26	129	10	7	1	1	12	7	6	1	3	4.9	.252	.302	.353	-.163	.252	.308	.353	.225	-4.4	28-3B	-1
2006	CHN	MLB	26	79	4	2	0	0	6	5	8	0	1	3.1	.233	.282	.260	-.360	.205	.256	.233	.177	-4.6	18-SS	-1
2007	CHN	MLB	27	382	48	16	3	2	29	26	34	8	4	6.0	.278	.331	.358	-.130	.273	.325	.348	.235	3.4	92-SS	3

Breakout: 18% Improve: 46% Collapse: 22% Attrition: 28%   Comparables: Rafael Landestoy, Onix Concepcion, Terry Pendleton, Cristian Guzman

Izturis has been injured more or less constantly since the middle of 2005, and not with little, one-off injuries—he's had back problems, which tend to be chronic; multiple hamstring problems, which tend to be chronic; and he lost close to a full year to TJ surgery. A nimble shortstop when his health permits it, the Cubs got him from the Dodgers in the Greg Maddux trade. He fits right in with the Neifi Perez, Rey Ordoñez, and Ronny Cedeño line of punchless Cub shortstops. For everyone who ever wanted Bowa over Dunston, congratulations, you got your wish.

Jacque Jones RF **Bats: L** **Throws: L** Height: 5' 10" Weight: 200 Born: April 25, 1975 Age: 32

YEAR	TEAM	LVL	AGE	PA	R	2B	3B	HR	RBI	BB	SO	SB	CS	SPEED	AVG	OBP	SLG	MLVR	EQAVG	EQOBP	EQSLG	EQA	VORP	DEFENSE	
2004	MIN	MLB	29	608	69	22	1	24	80	40	117	13	10	5.0	.254	.315	.427	-.058	.251	.315	.425	.252	1.8	132-RF	9
2005	MIN	MLB	30	585	74	22	4	23	73	51	120	13	4	5.7	.249	.319	.438	-.013	.251	.332	.451	.269	9.6	120-RF	13
2006	CHN	MLB	31	577	73	31	1	27	81	35	116	9	1	5.0	.285	.334	.499	.108	.282	.333	.494	.280	24.6	136-RF	0
2007	CHN	MLB	32	448	63	22	2	17	60	33	88	8	3	5.1	.281	.340	.467	.037	.276	.334	.454	.268	8.9	106-RF	0

Breakout: 17% Improve: 39% Collapse: 27% Attrition: 17% Comparables: Claudell Washington, Del Unser, Jim Eisenreich, Marvin Benard

Jones started the year just 2 for 22, provoking the ire of the Wrigley faithful, but eventually found the Friendly Confines very much to his liking, putting up his best season in five years. He still couldn't hit lefties, a continuing problem that begs for a platoon partner, though the Twins didn't do anything about that either. With Baker out as manager, Jones was reportedly asking to go elsewhere this off-season. The combination of his trade-friendly price tag—$9 million for the next two years looks cheap after this winter—and potential to decline should make moving him equally attractive to the Cubs.

Derrek Lee 1B **Bats: R** **Throws: R** Height: 6' 5" Weight: 245 Born: September 6, 1975 Age: 31

YEAR	TEAM	LVL	AGE	PA	R	2B	3B	HR	RBI	BB	SO	SB	CS	SPEED	AVG	OBP	SLG	MLVR	EQAVG	EQOBP	EQSLG	EQA	VORP	DEFENSE	
2004	CHN	MLB	28	688	90	39	1	32	98	68	128	12	5	5.0	.278	.356	.504	.148	.272	.350	.495	.285	32.1	158-1B	18
2005	CHN	MLB	29	691	120	50	3	46	107	85	109	15	3	5.8	.335	.418	.662	.534	.330	.415	.667	.347	95.6	156-1B	15
2006	CHN	MLB	30	204	30	9	0	8	30	25	41	8	4	4.5	.286	.368	.474	.127	.282	.368	.471	.286	7.5	44-1B	3
2007	CHN	MLB	31	451	74	25	1	22	68	49	84	14	4	4.8	.288	.369	.528	.173	.283	.363	.513	.296	21.8	107-1B	7

Breakout: 5% Improve: 19% Collapse: 46% Attrition: 14% Comparables: Cliff Floyd, Jose Canseco, Eric Karros, Glenn Davis

We have a statistic on our site called WARP, which stands for Wins Above Replacement Player. It represents the number of wins a given player generated for his team above or below that which could have been generated by a replacement level player in the same amount of playing time. Lee dropped from 12.8 WARP in his super-duper 2005 to just 2.1 last year. That's the 16th-largest drop from one year to the next in major league history. It moves up to fourth-largest if we ignore pitchers (Ed Walsh 1912–13, the retired Sandy Koufax 1966–67), nineteenth-century players (Ross Barnes 1876–77), and nineteenth century pitchers (John Clarkson 1887–88, Pud Galvin 1884–85). That leaves three players who had larger drops than Lee, all of them injury-related: Barry Bonds (whose knees gave out on him in 2005) holds the top spot, followed by Rogers Hornsby (whose broken ankle in April 1930 essentially ended his career), and Dickie Thon (hit in the eye with a pitch in April 1984). Lee did not recover well from what was originally thought to be a fairly simple broken wrist, although in hindsight it's clear that he was trying to come back too quickly. A full offseason of rest should help, but the injury has only increased the likelihood that 2005 will remain an outlier on Lee's record. Lee should come back at his 2000–2004 level, when he was a very good player, but not a great one.

Scott Moore 3B **Bats: L** **Throws: R** Height: 6' 2" Weight: 180 Born: November 17, 1983 Age: 23

YEAR	TEAM	LVL	AGE	PA	R	2B	3B	HR	RBI	BB	SO	SB	CS	SPEED	AVG	OBP	SLG	MLVR	EQAVG	EQOBP	EQSLG	EQA	VORP	DEFENSE	
2004	LAK	A+	20	453	52	13	4	14	56	49	125	2	4	4.2	.223	.322	.384	-.020	.204	.283	.347	.221	-14.1	114-3B	-20
2005	DAY	A+	21	536	77	31	2	20	82	55	134	22	7	5.7	.281	.358	.485	.180	.253	.318	.436	.263	19.1	116-3B	-19
2006	WTN	AA	22	532	52	28	0	22	75	55	126	12	7	4.3	.276	.360	.479	.223	.274	.347	.495	.284	40.7	121-3B	-4
2006	CHN	MLB	22	42	6	2	0	2	5	2	10	0	0	4.3	.263	.317	.474	.015	.256	.310	.462	.260	0.7		
2007	CHN	MLB	23	545	76	28	2	25	74	53	132	11	4	4.8	.266	.343	.486	.053	.261	.337	.472	.273	20.7	128-3B	-5

Breakout: 33% Improve: 66% Collapse: 14% Attrition: 2% Comparables: Carlos Pena, Eric Valent, David Kelton, Nate Dishington

Moore has added 35 to 40 points of isolated power to his translation in each of the last three years and made major improvements in his batting average, strikeout rate, and fielding. Unfortunately for Moore, these improvements have coincided with the Cubs signing Aramis Ramirez to a long-term deal. That puts Moore in the position of hoping for an injury, a trade, or a new role as a four-corners utility man. Given the shortage of quality third basemen, he's a commodity Jim Hendry could and should use in high-stakes barter.

Matt Murton LF Bats: R Throws: R Height: 6' 1" Weight: 220 Born: October 3, 1981 Age: 25

YEAR	TEAM	LVL	AGE	PA	R	2B	3B	HR	RBI	BB	SO	SB	CS	SPEED	AVG	OBP	SLG	MLVR	EQAVG	EQOBP	EQSLG	EQA	VORP	DEFENSE			
2004	DAY	A+	22	89	13	1	1	2	8	8	10	2	0	5.8	.253	.326	.367	-.030	.222	.281	.333	.223	-6.8	19-LF	-3		
2004	SAR	A+	22	425	60	16	4	11	55	42	61	5	4	5.0	.301	.372	.452	.206	.282	.341	.440	.268	8.2	96-LF	2		
2005	WTN	AA	23	350	46	17	4	8	46	29	42	18	5	6.1	.342	.403	.498	.316	.321	.372	.486	.295	21.6	61-LF	3	14-RF	-2
2005	CHN	MLB	23	160	19	3	2	7	14	16	22	2	1	5.3	.321	.386	.521	.280	.314	.384	.536	.308	12.5	37-LF	-1		
2006	CHN	MLB	24	508	70	22	3	13	62	45	62	5	2	5.0	.297	.365	.444	.092	.293	.363	.438	.278	16.2	118-LF	6		
2007	CHN	MLB	25	514	78	26	4	15	62	42	66	7	3	5.4	.303	.365	.475	.108	.298	.358	.461	.281	19.2	121-LF	2		

Breakout: 18% Improve: 45% Collapse: 27% Attrition: 11%   Comparables: Rondell White, Rick Reichardt, Chad Allen, Alex Ochoa

Murton's debut generated some fairly lofty expectations for 2006, and, except for a miserable stretch in June, he fully met them. Being a rookie and hitting a wall while playing for Dusty Baker meant that he lost his job for a while, of course, but his resurgence and the team's losing guaranteed him a spot in the second half. He has more power than comes through in his stats because his swing is so level; if he ever decides to alter it to add a little loft, he's liable to go from 10 to 30 HR in a flash, which will likely result in some unfortunate accusations given the tenor of the times.

Angel Pagan LF Bats: S Throws: R Height: 6' 1" Weight: 180 Born: July 2, 1981 Age: 25

YEAR	TEAM	LVL	AGE	PA	R	2B	3B	HR	RBI	BB	SO	SB	CS	SPEED	AVG	OBP	SLG	MLVR	EQAVG	EQOBP	EQSLG	EQA	VORP	DEFENSE			
2004	BIN	AA	23	501	71	25	8	4	63	42	96	29	5	7.9	.288	.346	.406	.037	.272	.325	.377	.253	-8.1	56-LF	5	51-CF	5
2005	NOR	AAA	24	579	69	20	10	8	40	49	111	27	15	7.5	.271	.333	.395	.024	.278	.338	.395	.256	13.4	102-CF	13		
2006	CHN	MLB	25	187	28	6	2	5	18	15	28	4	2	6.4	.247	.306	.394	-.119	.241	.305	.388	.242	-2.7	24-LF	0	15-RF	3
2007	CHN	MLB	25	325	47	15	4	7	31	28	56	11	4	6.8	.279	.343	.426	-.015	.274	.337	.414	.261	5.8	79-LF	5		

Breakout: 28% Improve: 53% Collapse: 20% Attrition: 25%   Comparables: Milt Cuyler, Dave Collins, Stan Javier, Wes Parker

Picked up from the Mets last January, Pagan's best weapon was supposed to be speed, but he jeopardized that by badly tearing his hamstring in April. He didn't come back until the last day of June, but a two-homer day on his birthday convinced Dusty he had unrevealed talents. This led to too much playing time. If Pagan can't run, he's not a good choice for fourth outfielder.

Eric Patterson 2B Bats: L Throws: R Height: 5' 11" Weight: 170 Born: April 8, 1983 Age: 24

YEAR	TEAM	LVL	AGE	PA	R	2B	3B	HR	RBI	BB	SO	SB	CS	SPEED	AVG	OBP	SLG	MLVR	EQAVG	EQOBP	EQSLG	EQA	VORP	DEFENSE	
2005	PEO	A	22	500	90	26	11	13	71	53	94	40	11	8.6	.333	.405	.535	.371	.299	.354	.470	.284	36.7	103-2B	6
2005	WTN	AA	22	37	5	2	0	0	2	6	7	3	2	6.0	.200	.324	.267	-.223	.194	.297	.258	.216	-2.6		
2006	WTN	AA	23	501	66	22	9	8	48	46	89	38	12	8.5	.263	.330	.408	.081	.264	.323	.424	.263	16.3	111-2B	-1
2006	IOW	AAA	23	76	14	1	1	2	12	6	9	8	0	7.2	.358	.395	.493	.313	.353	.382	.485	.310	7.9	17-2B	0
2007	CHN	MLB	24	560	88	31	9	14	56	48	100	32	12	7.2	.289	.353	.475	.076	.284	.347	.461	.277	29.3	131-2B	3

Breakout: 12% Improve: 49% Collapse: 16% Attrition: 6%   Comparables: Jason Conti, Julio Lugo, Adam Greenberg, Willie Harris

Taken in the eighth round of the 2004 draft, Eric Patterson was initially known only as Corey's slower, weaker little brother. Comparing their translated stats at ages 22 and 23, and granting that Corey was in the majors for those two years, Eric does have a little less power, although he still has good sock for a second baseman. The biggest difference is that Eric takes about 30 of Corey's strikeouts and turns them into walks, giving him a 40-point edge in OBP and putting him in position to steal more bases than his faster sibling. The Cubs' signing of Mark DeRosa gives them time to bring Patterson along, but his successful jump past High-A Daytona indicates that Patterson has the talent to accelerate at his own pace.

Felix Pie CF Bats: L Throws: L Height: 6' 2" Weight: 170 Born: February 8, 1985 Age: 22

YEAR	TEAM	LVL	AGE	PA	R	2B	3B	HR	RBI	BB	SO	SB	CS	SPEED	AVG	OBP	SLG	MLVR	EQAVG	EQOBP	EQSLG	EQA	VORP	DEFENSE			
2004	DAY	A+	19	467	79	17	9	8	47	38	113	31	16	8.4	.299	.361	.442	.149	.273	.324	.414	.257	12.2	98-CF	2		
2005	WTN	AA	20	262	41	17	5	11	25	16	53	13	9	7.7	.304	.349	.554	.280	.282	.317	.514	.273	16.2	55-CF	-6		
2006	IOW	AAA	21	623	78	33	8	15	57	46	126	17	11	5.9	.283	.341	.451	.088	.276	.327	.438	.261	21.0	122-CF	8	13-RF	5
2007	CHN	MLB	22	543	78	32	5	17	65	37	110	17	8	6.2	.286	.339	.477	.053	.281	.333	.463	.269	20.5	128-CF	4		

Breakout: 20% Improve: 56% Collapse: 19% Attrition: 6%   Comparables: Brandon Moss, Tony Mota, Claudell Washington, Gus Bell

Pie is statistically similar to Corey Patterson, which is not something Cub fans are going to want to hear. Both came from the minors with good power and speed (though Patterson was better in both departments) and poor strike-zone judgment. Corey's stats translated to a 118/36 K/BB ratio through age 21, Pie is at 129/40. Unlike Patterson, however, Pie has shown a remarkable ability to get hits in spite of the strikeouts, causing scouts to praise his "bad-ball" contact ability. Pie still has ample room to fill out and get stronger, but, like Murton, he has a groundball-oriented swing that suppresses his power. He needs more polish with his base-stealing technique, something he can work on in Iowa to start the season, but he's already a plus center fielder.

Juan Pierre — CF — Bats: L — Throws: L — Height: 6' 0" — Weight: 180 — Born: August 14, 1977 — Age: 29

YEAR	TEAM	LVL	AGE	PA	R	2B	3B	HR	RBI	BB	SO	SB	CS	SPEED	AVG	OBP	SLG	MLVR	EQAVG	EQOBP	EQSLG	EQA	VORP	DEFENSE	
2004	FLO	MLB	26	748	100	22	12	3	49	45	35	45	24	7.6	.326	.374	.407	.114	.337	.383	.423	.277	35.1	162-CF	-9
2005	FLO	MLB	27	718	96	19	13	2	47	41	45	57	17	8.2	.276	.326	.354	-.061	.288	.339	.375	.257	12.1	155-CF	-6
2006	CHN	MLB	28	750	87	32	13	3	40	32	38	58	20	7.7	.292	.330	.388	-.051	.292	.330	.390	.254	18.0	161-CF	0
2007	LAN	MLB	29	676	98	23	9	4	43	41	39	45	15	7.9	.291	.338	.374	-.086	.292	.337	.375	.253	11.7	157-CF	-3

Breakout: 3% Improve: 30% Collapse: 41% Attrition: 1% Comparables: Lance Johnson, Tom Goodwin, Willie Wilson, Scott Podsednik

Without his legs, Pierre is nothing. He has no power and rarely walks, so his value is entirely tied up in his stolen bases and batting average—an average held up by infield hits. The Dodgers made a very large bet that Pierre's legs will hold up from ages 29 to 33. Looking at all of the players who stole 50 bases in season during the 1990s, the average age at which they last stole 35 was just 29.4, but 32 was the most common. Why anyone ever throws him a fastball (he hits them about 100 points better than he does breaking balls) is a mystery the Dodgers hope continues to go unsolved.

Aramis Ramirez — 3B — Bats: R — Throws: R — Height: 6' 1" — Weight: 215 — Born: June 25, 1978 — Age: 29

YEAR	TEAM	LVL	AGE	PA	R	2B	3B	HR	RBI	BB	SO	SB	CS	SPEED	AVG	OBP	SLG	MLVR	EQAVG	EQOBP	EQSLG	EQA	VORP	DEFENSE
2004	CHN	MLB	26	606	99	32	1	36	103	49	62	0	2	2.9	.318	.373	.578	.316	.311	.367	.566	.307	50.8	129-3B -11
2005	CHN	MLB	27	506	72	30	0	31	92	35	60	0	1	3.4	.302	.358	.568	.288	.299	.356	.571	.303	42.3	115-3B -14
2006	CHN	MLB	28	660	93	38	4	38	119	50	63	2	1	4.4	.291	.352	.561	.227	.287	.348	.552	.298	44.5	152-3B -5
2007	CHN	MLB	29	607	93	35	2	35	108	49	68	2	1	4.1	.299	.361	.562	.217	.293	.355	.546	.298	43.1	142-3B -6

Breakout: 23% Improve: 49% Collapse: 13% Attrition: 4% Comparables: Bob Horner, Tim Wallach, Mike Lowell, Matt Williams

Ramirez cleaned up this offseason with a $75-million deal that will keep him in Wrigleyville until at least 2011. Make no mistake, this should be a better deal than, Juan Pierre's Dodger contract, but Ramirez and his former teammate make an interesting comparison. Players with either no power (like Pierre) or no speed (like Ramirez) don't tend to age as well as players who have some of each. Of the four PECOTA comparables above, only Tony Perez aged gracefully, and Perez's did it after moving to first base following an age-28 season in 1970 was arguably his best. Still, Ramirez has a decent chance to hold his value as well as Perez did. He's worked on his defense, he has good strikezone coverage, and his three-year run with the Cubs has been remarkable for its consistency at the plate.

Michael Restovich — OF — Bats: R — Throws: R — Height: 6' 4" — Weight: 250 — Born: January 3, 1979 — Age: 28

YEAR	TEAM	LVL	AGE	PA	R	2B	3B	HR	RBI	BB	SO	SB	CS	SPEED	AVG	OBP	SLG	MLVR	EQAVG	EQOBP	EQSLG	EQA	VORP	DEFENSE			
2004	ROC	AAA	25	454	65	20	3	20	63	25	104	4	3	5.4	.247	.291	.449	-.076	.223	.267	.390	.224	-21.5	58-RF	-2	38-LF	-2
2004	MIN	MLB	25	51	9	3	0	2	6	4	10	0	0	5.6	.255	.314	.447	.048	.255	.314	.447	.258	1.4				
2005	COL	MLB	26	34	5	2	0	1	3	3	5	0	0	3.5	.290	.353	.452	.079	.258	.324	.419	.255	1.1				
2005	PIT	MLB	26	92	10	3	1	2	5	8	24	0	0	4.8	.214	.283	.345	-.201	.214	.283	.345	.220	-3.0				
2006	IOW	AAA	27	506	75	29	4	27	85	52	121	2	1	4.5	.293	.374	.560	.304	.278	.347	.517	.289	26.2	56-RF	-6	38-LF	-8
2006	CHN	MLB	27	13	0	1	0	0	1	1	5	0	0	3.8	.167	.231	.250	-.495	.083	.154	.167	.126	-1.1				
2007	WAS	MLB	28	457	50	23	2	17	60	36	119	2	1	4.4	.246	.311	.431	-.091	.251	.315	.444	.256	3.0	108-RF	-4		

Breakout: 13% Improve: 39% Collapse: 32% Attrition: 14% Comparables: Scott Morgan, Bucky Jacobsen, Bubba Smith, Mitch Jones

Having fallen from touted Twins prospect to journeyman outfielder, Restovich is basically good for a .270 average and 20 homers at a Triple-A club near you. In 2007 that looks to be Columbus, Washington's new affiliate. Restovich was put on the 40-man roster and might have a shot at a platoon role with the Nats, but remember, that's his upside.

Brandon Sing   **1B**   **Bats: R**   **Throws: R**   Height: 6' 5"   Weight: 215   Born: March 13, 1981   Age: 26

YEAR	TEAM	LVL	AGE	PA	R	2B	3B	HR	RBI	BB	SO	SB	CS	SPEED	AVG	OBP	SLG	MLVR	EQAVG	EQOBP	EQSLG	EQA	VORP	DEFENSE		
2004	DAY	A+	23	504	86	27	0	32	94	84	101	1	3	3.4	.270	.399	.571	.335	.233	.337	.493	.279	18.9	110-1B	-15	
2005	WTN	AA	24	508	74	29	0	26	71	91	110	2	5	2.4	.276	.404	.538	.303	.246	.356	.474	.281	19.5	75-1B	0	31-RF -2
2006	IOW	AAA	25	114	10	4	0	4	11	13	33	0	1	2.3	.177	.307	.344	-.192	.172	.281	.323	.211	-7.6	25-1B	0	
2006	WTN	AA	25	295	26	9	0	8	39	49	76	1	0	3.3	.203	.339	.340	-.025	.192	.305	.324	.230	-16.1	53-1B	2	12-RF 0
2007	CHN	MLB	26	394	47	18	1	18	54	48	97	0	0	3.6	.242	.340	.458	-.008	.237	.334	.445	.266	3.5	94-1B	-1	

Breakout: 26%   Improve: 67%   Collapse: 14%   Attrition: 17%   Comparables: Bobby Estalella, Shane Spencer, Adam Hyzdu, Ron Wright

After two strong years and a hot spring training, Sing looked like a good bet to get a callup sometime last year. He flopped at Triple-A, though, and kept flopping when sent back to Double-A, looking nothing like the guy who hit 26 home runs there the year before. He signed with the Orioles as a minor league free agent.

Geovany Soto   **C**   **Bats: R**   **Throws: R**   Height: 6' 1"   Weight: 230   Born: January 20, 1983   Age: 24

YEAR	TEAM	LVL	AGE	PA	R	2B	3B	HR	RBI	BB	SO	SB	CS	SPEED	AVG	OBP	SLG	MLVR	EQAVG	EQOBP	EQSLG	EQA	VORP	DEFENSE	
2004	WTN	AA	21	381	47	16	0	9	48	40	71	1	2	3.5	.271	.355	.401	.068	.249	.320	.367	.243	2.1	100-C	2
2005	IOW	AAA	22	345	30	14	0	4	39	48	77	0	1	1.8	.253	.357	.342	-.127	.231	.324	.304	.229	-6.8	86-C	2
2006	IOW	AAA	23	391	34	21	0	6	38	41	74	0	1	3.2	.272	.353	.386	.009	.253	.328	.359	.244	2.7	96-C	-3
2006	CHN	MLB	23	26	1	1	0	0	2	0	5	0	0	4.3	.200	.231	.240	-.499	.160	.192	.200	.146	-2.3		
2007	CHN	MLB	24	410	36	16	0	7	39	36	81	0	0	3.6	.240	.313	.346	-.204	.236	.307	.336	.223	-4.7	98-C	-1

Breakout: 26%   Improve: 37%   Collapse: 32%   Attrition: 16%   Comparables: Carlos Maldonado, Dusty Wathan, David Parrish, Trey Lunsford

Soto got the barest look-see from the Cubs last September, as Baker chose to run Blanco out there every day after Barrett's injury rather than give Soto a chance. Soto didn't show much and really shouldn't have been expected to, but it would have been nice to see the Cubs at least try to evaluate young guys like him while playing out the string. If Henry Blanco goes 10-for-20 in the last week of September, it's fun for his family but does nothing for the future of the franchise.

Ryan Theriot   **2B**   **Bats: R**   **Throws: R**   Height: 5' 11"   Weight: 175   Born: December 7, 1979   Age: 27

YEAR	TEAM	LVL	AGE	PA	R	2B	3B	HR	RBI	BB	SO	SB	CS	SPEED	AVG	OBP	SLG	MLVR	EQAVG	EQOBP	EQSLG	EQA	VORP	DEFENSE		
2004	DAY	A+	24	390	47	14	3	1	34	48	43	13	11	5.4	.273	.367	.342	.013	.234	.308	.292	.219	-14.2	64-2B	2	37-SS -4
2005	WTN	AA	25	503	52	28	4	1	53	45	38	24	10	5.6	.304	.365	.391	.072	.273	.321	.351	.240	2.2	82-2B	-1	31-SS -4
2006	IOW	AAA	26	312	41	11	5	0	22	27	34	14	3	6.6	.304	.367	.379	.047	.288	.343	.354	.252	8.5	40-SS	-5	19-2B -2
2006	CHN	MLB	26	159	34	11	3	3	16	17	18	13	2	8.2	.328	.412	.522	.298	.321	.408	.511	.316	19.2	32-2B	-5	
2007	CHN	MLB	27	444	58	20	4	2	32	34	49	20	6	6.0	.269	.330	.354	-.144	.264	.324	.343	.239	2.0	105-2B	-3	

Breakout: 11%   Improve: 30%   Collapse: 35%   Attrition: 21%   Comparables: Eric Owens, Esteban German, Craig Wilson, Luis Ordaz

After Neifi left, Izturis got hurt, and Cedeño stopped hitting, so Theriot got a chance at the second base job and ran with it. His performance was way out of line with anything he's ever done before, making him this year's David Newhan. Remember, anyone who can play in the majors can hit .400 for a month, especially if that month is September.

PITCHERS

David Aardsma   **Bats: R**   **Throws: R**   Height: 6' 4"   Weight: 205   Born: December 27, 1981   Age: 25

YEAR	TEAM	LVL	AGE	W	L	SV	G	GS	IP	H	BB	SO	HR	GB%	BABIP	STUFF	WHIP	ERA	PERA	EQERA	EQH9	EQBB9	EQSO9	EQHR9	VORP	WXRL
2004	FRE	AAA	22	6	4	11	44	0	55¹	46	30	53	2	—	.284	14	1.37	3.09	4.17	3.38	7.2	5.0	6.6	0.3	13.8	—
2004	SFN	MLB	22	1	0	0	11	0	10²	20	10	5	1	—	.452	-20	2.81	6.73	6.33	6.55	16.4	7.4	4.1	0.8	-1.2	-0.81
2005	NRW	AA	23	6	2	0	9	8	46	44	13	30	2	51.4%	.300	1	1.24	2.93	4.18	4.14	8.7	3.0	3.9	0.6	7.4	—
2005	WTN	AA	23	4	1	2	33	3	50²	48	32	43	3	55.5%	.324	-7	1.58	3.91	5.88	4.74	9.3	6.0	5.3	0.9	4.7	—
2006	IOW	AAA	24	2	3	8	29	0	36	31	15	36	1	55.6%	.326	9	1.28	3.25	3.33	3.93	7.6	3.7	6.9	0.2	6.8	—
2006	CHN	MLB	24	3	0	0	45	0	53	41	28	49	9	38.5%	.239	5	1.30	4.08	4.94	3.67	7.0	4.2	7.5	1.3	11.0	1.32
2007	CHA	MLB	25	3	3	1	48	1	53¹	55	29	42	7	45.0%	.296	-3	1.58	5.12	4.73	4.71	9.2	4.6	6.6	1.2	4.4	0.40

Breakout: 7%   Improve: 26%   Collapse: 39%   Attrition: 30%   Comparables: Sammy Stewart, Jeff Jones, Elias Sosa, Gene Pentz

Aardsma made four separate trips between Chicago and Des Moines last year, repeatedly being called up and sent back as other pitchers went on and off the DL. He kept an even keel throughout, a task simplified by his limited-though-potent repertoire—virtually all fastballs, reaching up to 97 MPH. Facing a crowded bullpen, the Cubs traded him to the White Sox for Neal Cotts; he'll have a better chance of sticking on the South Side.

Chicago Cubs

Ryan Dempster   Bats: R   Throws: R   Height: 6' 2"   Weight: 215   Born: May 3, 1977   Age: 30

YEAR	TEAM	LVL	AGE	W	L	SV	G	GS	IP	H	BB	SO	HR	GB%	BABIP	STUFF	WHIP	ERA	PERA	EQERA	EQH9	EQBB9	EQSO9	EQHR9	VORP	WXRL
2004	CHN	MLB	27	1	1	1	2	23	0	20²	16	13	18	1	—	.259	6	1.40	3.91	4.30	3.80	7.2	5.1	6.8	0.4	4.3	0.99
2005	CHN	MLB	28	5	3	33	63	6	92	83	49	89	4	59.1%	.316	24	1.43	3.13	3.59	3.35	8.2	4.3	7.9	0.4	21.8	5.54
2006	CHN	MLB	29	1	9	24	74	0	75	77	36	67	5	55.1%	.324	10	1.51	4.80	3.69	4.81	9.2	3.8	7.3	0.5	3.9	-1.26
2007	*CHN*	*MLB*	*30*	*3*	*4*	*19*	*48*	*0*	*54¹*	*54*	*27*	*47*	*4*	*53.0%*	*.311*	*3*	*1.48*	*4.14*	*4.35*	*4.35*	*8.6*	*3.8*	*7.0*	*0.6*	*9.5*	*1.20*

Breakout: 16%   Improve: 39%   Collapse: 25%   Attrition: 7%   Comparables: Bob Wickman, Heathcliff Slocumb, Todd Jones, Jay Powell

It wasn't just that he blew nine saves, but how he blew them. Other pitchers who blow a save might give up a run, allowing the other team to tie, then vulture a win out of it when their team comes back. Not Dempster—when he blew a save last year, it tended to stay blown. The Cubs lost seven of those nine games; Dempster took all seven losses, giving up 19 runs, but the two times he blew a save giving up just one run, the Cubs came back to win. Dempster had 17 appearances in which he gave up two or more runs; Brad Lidge had an awful year, and he had only nine. Mariano Rivera, Trevor Hoffman, and B. J. Ryan had 10 *combined*. Jon Papelbon only had one *month* in which he gave up two runs. Dempster's hold on the closer's job is only as strong as Kerry Wood's shoulder is weak.

Scott Eyre   Bats: L   Throws: L   Height: 6' 1"   Weight: 215   Born: May 30, 1972   Age: 35

YEAR	TEAM	LVL	AGE	W	L	SV	G	GS	IP	H	BB	SO	HR	GB%	BABIP	STUFF	WHIP	ERA	PERA	EQERA	EQH9	EQBB9	EQSO9	EQHR9	VORP	WXRL
2004	SFN	MLB	32	2	2	1	83	0	52²	43	27	49	8	—	.252	0	1.33	4.10	4.70	4.33	7.2	4.0	7.3	1.2	7.7	1.20
2005	SFN	MLB	33	2	2	0	86	0	68¹	48	26	65	3	38.3%	.262	23	1.10	2.64	3.29	2.86	6.5	3.1	7.8	0.4	20.9	3.81
2006	CHN	MLB	34	1	3	0	74	0	61¹	61	30	73	11	45.2%	.342	12	1.48	3.38	4.25	3.30	8.9	3.7	9.6	1.4	16.5	1.26
2007	*CHN*	*MLB*	*35*	*3*	*3*	*3*	*63*	*0*	*58*	*54*	*29*	*59*	*8*	*42.0%*	*.293*	*5*	*1.42*	*4.23*	*4.54*	*4.32*	*8.0*	*3.9*	*8.1*	*1.1*	*9.8*	*0.90*

Breakout: 7%   Improve: 21%   Collapse: 56%   Attrition: 13%   Comparables: Randy Myers, Mike Remlinger, Juan Berenguer, Dennis Cook

In four years, Eyre's platoon split has gone from strong against lefties (making him a nifty LOOGY) to strongly bass-ackwards. The conventional wisdom for hitters is that they're done when they can't recognize the curve ball anymore, which makes sense (their eyes are going), and tends to show up in their platoon splits. It's tough to find an analogous mechanism for pitchers to decide what kind of significance to attach to Eyre's disappearing split, but however valuable he's been these last couple of years, PECOTA's expecting Eyre to revert to the pedestrian form he displayed before earning his big contract.

Sean Gallagher   Bats: R   Throws: R   Height: 6' 1"   Weight: 210   Born: December 30, 1985   Age: 21

YEAR	TEAM	LVL	AGE	W	L	SV	G	GS	IP	H	BB	SO	HR	GB%	BABIP	STUFF	WHIP	ERA	PERA	EQERA	EQH9	EQBB9	EQSO9	EQHR9	VORP	WXRL
2005	PEO	A	19	14	5	0	26	26	146	107	55	139	10	48.6%	.262	15	1.11	2.71	5.46	3.91	7.6	3.8	5.7	1.2	26.8	—
2006	DAY	A+	20	4	0	0	13	13	78¹	75	21	80	5	58.8%	.345	20	1.23	2.30	4.50	3.49	9.5	2.8	6.1	1.0	18.1	—
2006	WTN	AA	20	7	5	0	15	15	86²	74	55	91	4	51.5%	.326	27	1.50	2.71	4.69	4.01	8.5	5.7	6.8	0.7	15.1	—
2007	*CHN*	*MLB*	*21*	*7*	*9*	*0*	*28*	*22*	*135*	*132*	*68*	*108*	*18*	*50.0%*	*.289*	*11*	*1.48*	*4.60*	*4.93*	*4.73*	*8.5*	*3.9*	*6.4*	*1.0*	*16.9*	*2.60*

Breakout: 2%   Improve: 15%   Collapse: 49%   Attrition: 0%   Comparables: Ricky Nolasco, Kyle Davies, Alberto Garza, Chad Billingsley

Gallagher ended 2005 with a reputation for a great curveball, a bad body, and no projectability. He got serious in his off-season workouts and added three miles per hour to his fastball, elevating it from a C–/D+ to a B/B– pitch. Part of what makes his stats look so good is that he allowed about 20 fewer runs than expected from his other numbers; whereas most pitchers are a little worse with men on base, Gallagher did far better (200 OPS points) from the stretch. That's usually not sustainable, but Gallagher's already surprised people once.

Angel Guzman   Bats: R   Throws: R   Height: 6' 3"   Weight: 195   Born: December 14, 1981   Age: 25

YEAR	TEAM	LVL	AGE	W	L	SV	G	GS	IP	H	BB	SO	HR	GB%	BABIP	STUFF	WHIP	ERA	PERA	EQERA	EQH9	EQBB9	EQSO9	EQHR9	VORP	WXRL
2004	DAY	A+	22	3	1	0	7	7	30	27	0	40	2	—	.347	24	0.90	4.20	3.63	5.40	9.8	0.6	7.9	1.3	0.6	—
2004	WTN	AA	22	0	3	0	4	4	17²	20	4	13	2	—	.321	-8	1.36	5.59	5.13	7.27	10.9	2.1	4.2	1.6	-3.2	—
2006	IOW	AAA	24	4	4	0	15	15	75²	72	24	77	5	40.6%	.328	21	1.28	4.07	3.69	4.48	8.5	2.7	7.1	0.7	9.5	—
2006	CHN	MLB	24	0	6	0	15	10	56	68	37	60	9	33.5%	.388	9	1.88	7.39	5.03	6.67	10.9	5.1	8.5	1.2	-9.7	0.26
2007	*CHN*	*MLB*	*25*	*6*	*8*	*1*	*32*	*20*	*122*	*124*	*51*	*109*	*17*	*43.0%*	*.301*	*12*	*1.43*	*4.88*	*4.86*	*5.00*	*8.7*	*3.2*	*7.1*	*1.1*	*12.0*	*1.90*

Breakout: 41%   Improve: 77%   Collapse: 7%   Attrition: 8%   Comparables: Charlie Lea, Alan Benes, Tim Redding, Wynn Hawkins

Once the top pitching prospect in the Cubs' system, Guzman suffered a series of arm injuries that set him back years—a torn labrum in 2003, more shoulder trouble in 2004, and a stiff forearm in 2005. His velocity is back in the 90s, but he's lost command of what used to be a plus curve and changeup, allowing hitters to sit on his fastball. He's been an extreme fly-ball pitcher throughout his career, making him a poor fit for Wrigley Field.

Rich Hill Bats: L Throws: L Height: 6' 5" Weight: 205 Born: March 11, 1980 Age: 27

YEAR	TEAM	LVL	AGE	W	L	SV	G	GS	IP	H	BB	SO	HR	GB%	BABIP	STUFF	WHIP	ERA	PERA	EQERA	EQH9	EQBB9	EQSO9	EQHR9	VORP	WXRL
2004	DAY	A+	24	7	6	0	28	19	109¹	88	72	136	9	—	.296	-10	1.46	4.03	8.08	6.91	9.7	8.1	7.3	1.9	-14.4	—
2005	WTN	AA	25	4	3	0	10	10	57²	42	21	90	9	43.0%	.297	3	1.09	3.28	6.76	4.42	9.3	3.9	9.5	2.9	6.9	—
2005	IOW	AAA	25	6	1	0	11	10	65	53	14	92	11	44.1%	.300	29	1.03	3.60	4.31	3.76	7.9	1.8	9.6	1.7	13.2	—
2005	CHN	MLB	25	0	2	0	10	4	23²	25	17	21	3	38.7%	.306	2	1.77	9.11	5.24	8.88	9.6	5.9	7.0	1.1	-9.1	-0.41
2006	IOW	AAA	26	7	1	0	15	15	100²	62	21	135	3	48.4%	.282	59	0.83	1.80	2.52	2.33	6.0	1.9	9.1	0.4	36.4	—
2006	CHN	MLB	26	6	7	0	17	16	99¹	83	39	90	16	31.6%	.259	15	1.23	4.17	4.46	4.01	7.4	3.0	7.4	1.2	16.8	2.50
2007	*CHN*	*MLB*	*27*	*9*	*10*	*0*	*30*	*28*	*159*	*144*	*66*	*157*	*23*	*41.0%*	*.283*	*22*	*1.31*	*4.28*	*4.29*	*4.37*	*7.8*	*3.2*	*7.9*	*1.1*	*26.6*	*3.80*

Breakout: 16% Improve: 50% Collapse: 9% Attrition: 2% Comparables: Dick Stigman, Jim Deshaies, Cliff Lee, Dennis Rasmussen

In four April starts for Iowa, Hill threw 25 innings, allowing 13 hits, issuing 7 walks, and recording 33 strikeouts. That earned him a call to replace Glendon Rusch in the Cubs rotation. He was horrible. In four May starts for Chicago, Hill went 19 innings, allowing 23 hits, walked 15, and struck out just 11. Sent back down, Hill continued to carve up the PCL, posting lines like 7 IP, 1 H, 14 K, resulting in another callup. His third call to the majors was the charm. After one more bad start, he began to pitch like he did in the minors, posting a 2.58 ERA over his last dozen starts. No one ever doubted that Hill's power fastball/curve mix could beat major league hitters, but now that he's actually done it, he should breathe a bit easier.

Bob Howry Bats: L Throws: R Height: 6' 5" Weight: 220 Born: August 4, 1973 Age: 33

YEAR	TEAM	LVL	AGE	W	L	SV	G	GS	IP	H	BB	SO	HR	GB%	BABIP	STUFF	WHIP	ERA	PERA	EQERA	EQH9	EQBB9	EQSO9	EQHR9	VORP	WXRL
2004	CLE	MLB	30	4	2	0	37	0	42²	37	12	39	5	—	.271	15	1.15	2.74	3.74	2.86	7.4	2.2	7.6	1.0	15.6	0.25
2005	CLE	MLB	31	7	4	3	79	0	73	49	16	48	4	40.4%	.221	14	0.89	2.47	3.22	3.04	6.2	1.9	5.8	0.5	23.3	3.12
2006	CHN	MLB	32	4	5	5	84	0	76²	70	17	71	8	39.1%	.300	18	1.13	3.17	3.36	2.88	8.1	1.7	7.5	0.8	23.8	2.17
2007	*CHN*	*MLB*	*33*	*3*	*3*	*5*	*60*	*0*	*64¹*	*66*	*18*	*49*	*9*	*41.0%*	*.290*	*0*	*1.30*	*4.08*	*4.22*	*4.18*	*8.8*	*2.2*	*6.1*	*1.1*	*12.2*	*1.10*

Breakout: 5% Improve: 16% Collapse: 65% Attrition: 6% Comparables: Jeff Russell, Jim Brosnan, Carl Willis, Rick Aguilera

Fastball, fastball, fastball . . . a boring pitch selection, but, when it's thrown 95 MPH with pinpoint control, one hardly needs to bother with a slider. Howry was far and away the Cubs' best reliever in 2006, something Baker finally figured out in August. Howry has probably earned the closer's job, but there's a groundswell of support promoting Wood for the role. There's a good chance that Howry will once again settle for setting up a lesser pitcher.

Carlos Marmol Bats: R Throws: R Height: 6' 2" Weight: 180 Born: October 14, 1982 Age: 24

YEAR	TEAM	LVL	AGE	W	L	SV	G	GS	IP	H	BB	SO	HR	GB%	BABIP	STUFF	WHIP	ERA	PERA	EQERA	EQH9	EQBB9	EQSO9	EQHR9	VORP	WXRL
2004	LNS	A	21	14	8	0	26	24	154²	131	53	154	15	—	.286	-16	1.19	3.20	6.72	5.14	9.7	4.1	5.2	1.9	7.4	—
2005	DAY	A+	22	6	2	0	13	13	72¹	60	37	71	7	42.1%	.285	1	1.34	2.99	6.83	4.43	8.2	6.0	5.6	1.7	9.0	—
2005	WTN	AA	22	3	4	0	14	14	81¹	70	40	70	10	47.2%	.282	-8	1.35	3.65	6.91	4.35	8.9	4.6	5.6	1.9	10.9	—
2006	WTN	AA	23	3	2	0	11	11	58	42	25	67	1	46.8%	.304	28	1.16	2.33	3.43	3.79	7.4	3.9	7.1	0.3	11.5	—
2006	CHN	MLB	23	5	7	0	19	13	77	71	59	59	14	31.6%	.270	0	1.69	6.08	6.23	5.45	8.3	5.9	6.1	1.4	-1.3	0.46
2007	*CHN*	*MLB*	*24*	*7*	*11*	*0*	*35*	*25*	*144²*	*141*	*84*	*119*	*24*	*42.0%*	*.280*	*3*	*1.56*	*5.28*	*5.51*	*5.35*	*8.4*	*4.5*	*6.6*	*1.3*	*7.9*	*1.80*

Breakout: 8% Improve: 40% Collapse: 23% Attrition: 0% Comparables: Ben Howard, Darryl Kile, Brian Sikorski, Seung Song

When you hit .149 in the Midwest League, as Marmol did in 2002, you need to think about changing your career. Marmol did, moving from the outfield to the mound. He blossomed at Double-A last year, but letting someone who has 60 professional starts in his entire career skip Triple-A seems precipitous. He did well in the majors initially, showing a nearly unhittable curve, but he also kept showing lefties a very hittable changeup. He was pounded hard over the last two months, but that's more reflective of a biceps injury than any lack of ability. After some steady work at Iowa, he'll be back in the rotation mix.

Sean Marshall
Bats: L Throws: L Height: 6' 7" Weight: 205 Born: August 30, 1982 Age: 24

YEAR	TEAM	LVL	AGE	W	L	SV	G	GS	IP	H	BB	SO	HR	GB%	BABIP	STUFF	WHIP	ERA	PERA	EQERA	EQH9	EQBB9	EQSO9	EQHR9	VORP	WXRL
2004	LNS	A	21	2	0	0	7	7	48²	29	4	51	1	—	.235	32	0.68	1.11	2.88	2.27	6.4	0.9	5.3	0.4	17.6	—
2004	WTN	AA	21	2	2	0	6	6	29	36	12	23	2	—	.362	-7	1.66	5.90	5.05	7.53	11.6	4.1	4.7	0.9	-6.2	—
2005	DAY	A+	22	4	4	0	12	12	69	63	26	61	7	59.7%	.298	-7	1.29	2.74	6.27	3.76	8.7	4.4	5.0	1.7	13.7	—
2005	WTN	AA	22	0	1	0	4	4	25	16	5	24	1	47.0%	.234	24	0.84	2.52	3.50	3.33	6.3	1.8	6.3	0.7	6.1	—
2006	IOW	AAA	23	0	2	0	4	4	21²	17	14	21	1	57.9%	.291	22	1.46	3.40	4.41	4.15	7.1	5.8	6.6	0.4	3.5	—
2006	CHN	MLB	23	6	9	0	24	24	125²	132	59	77	20	47.8%	.286	-7	1.52	5.58	5.34	5.18	9.3	3.6	5.0	1.3	-0.2	1.58
2007	CHN	MLB	24	7	10	0	29	23	139	143	62	98	18	50.0%	.292	5	1.48	4.89	4.94	5.07	8.9	3.4	5.6	1.0	12.0	2.20

Breakout: 9%   Improve: 38%   Collapse: 21%   Attrition: 8%   Comparables: A. J. Burnett, Randy Lerch, Andy Hassler, Rick Waits

Marshall was one of the many young, unready hurlers pressed into action by the Cubs in 2006. Despite having only 10 starts at Double-A or above, Marshall's camp performance put him in contention for the fifth starter's spot. He then beat out Jerome Williams for number four. The tall lefty was probably a little better than his final statistics would lead you to believe; he didn't pitch well at all after returning from an oblique strain in August, serving up seven of his 20 homers in his last five starts.

Juan Mateo
Bats: R Throws: R Height: 6' 2" Weight: 180 Born: December 17, 1982 Age: 24

YEAR	TEAM	LVL	AGE	W	L	SV	G	GS	IP	H	BB	SO	HR	GB%	BABIP	STUFF	WHIP	ERA	PERA	EQERA	EQH9	EQBB9	EQSO9	EQHR9	VORP	WXRL
2004	LNS	A	21	4	1	9	53	1	74¹	61	19	60	3	—	.270	-11	1.08	3.27	4.50	4.88	8.2	3.0	4.1	0.8	5.8	—
2005	DAY	A+	22	10	5	2	32	16	109¹	99	27	123	9	39.8%	.321	-2	1.15	3.21	4.85	4.64	8.9	2.9	6.2	1.4	11.4	—
2006	WTN	AA	23	7	4	0	18	17	92	78	26	70	6	35.1%	.272	2	1.13	2.84	4.73	4.18	8.5	2.6	4.7	1.1	14.2	—
2006	CHN	MLB	23	1	3	0	11	10	45²	51	23	35	6	43.0%	.331	2	1.62	5.32	4.80	5.21	10.0	3.9	6.2	1.0	0.1	0.64
2007	CHN	MLB	24	6	10	0	33	25	135¹	141	54	95	23	43.0%	.285	2	1.44	5.23	5.17	5.34	9.0	3.1	5.6	1.3	7.6	1.70

Breakout: 3%   Improve: 26%   Collapse: 27%   Attrition: 0%   Comparables: Brian Sikorski, Seung Song, Mark Brownson, Felix Diaz

The Cardinals took Mateo in the 2005 Rule 5 draft, but returned him at the end of spring training. Back in Double-A, he posted a 2.62 ERA, earning a call-up. The Southern League was insanely pitcher-friendly last year, with a league ERA more than a run below that of the National League; Mateo wasn't the only pitcher overrated as a result (see also Marmol and Gallagher). A good slider allows him to finish off right-handed hitters, but he struggles badly against lefties.

Wade Miller
Bats: R Throws: R Height: 6' 2" Weight: 210 Born: September 13, 1976 Age: 30

YEAR	TEAM	LVL	AGE	W	L	SV	G	GS	IP	H	BB	SO	HR	GB%	BABIP	STUFF	WHIP	ERA	PERA	EQERA	EQH9	EQBB9	EQSO9	EQHR9	VORP	WXRL
2004	HOU	MLB	27	7	7	0	15	15	88²	76	44	74	11	—	.262	16	1.35	3.35	4.49	3.36	7.3	4.0	6.5	1.0	21.8	2.95
2005	BOS	MLB	28	4	4	0	16	16	91	96	47	64	8	46.4%	.307	15	1.57	4.95	4.51	4.74	8.7	4.5	6.1	0.8	6.9	0.79
2006	CHN	MLB	29	0	2	0	5	5	21²	19	18	20	4	32.3%	.259	14	1.71	4.56	6.08	4.43	8.1	6.4	7.3	1.6	2.8	0.69
2007	CHN	MLB	30	5	8	0	29	19	107	109	54	84	17	40.0%	.289	0	1.53	5.15	5.38	5.22	8.8	3.9	6.3	1.3	7.6	1.40

Breakout: 1%   Improve: 17%   Collapse: 55%   Attrition: 12%   Comparables: Russ Ortiz, Chan Ho Park, Don Larsen, Cal Eldred

Miller has had a multitude of shoulder problems since the middle of 2004, but he keeps coming back to chase the dream. Admirable as that is, just about the only positive thing we can say about Miller's 2006 is that he did come back. He's a slop-baller now and unlikely to ever throw in the nineties again. Signed for another year in Wrigley, he'll contend for the last spot in the rotation.

Roberto Novoa
Bats: R Throws: R Height: 6' 5" Weight: 200 Born: August 15, 1979 Age: 27

YEAR	TEAM	LVL	AGE	W	L	SV	G	GS	IP	H	BB	SO	HR	GB%	BABIP	STUFF	WHIP	ERA	PERA	EQERA	EQH9	EQBB9	EQSO9	EQHR9	VORP	WXRL
2004	ERI	AA	24	7	0	4	41	0	79	63	18	59	7	—	.240	-12	1.03	2.96	4.73	4.40	7.8	2.3	4.5	1.2	10.4	—
2004	DET	MLB	24	1	1	0	16	0	21	25	6	15	4	—	.350	-8	1.55	5.57	5.16	5.82	10.4	2.5	5.8	1.7	-1.2	-0.13
2005	IOW	AAA	25	2	2	4	19	0	27¹	20	11	18	1	60.3%	.260	-7	1.14	3.30	4.64	3.58	6.5	3.6	4.6	0.3	6.2	—
2005	CHN	MLB	25	4	5	0	49	0	44²	47	25	47	4	38.2%	.339	11	1.61	4.43	3.86	4.34	9.5	4.5	8.7	0.8	5.4	-0.18
2006	CHN	MLB	26	2	1	0	66	0	76	77	32	53	15	44.4%	.274	-18	1.43	4.26	5.59	4.75	9.0	3.2	5.7	1.5	4.6	0.55
2007	CHN	MLB	27	3	4	2	54	2	68²	70	27	47	10	44.0%	.282	-6	1.42	4.67	4.81	4.80	8.8	3.1	5.5	1.2	8.1	0.70

Breakout: 15%   Improve: 41%   Collapse: 26%   Attrition: 21%   Comparables: Jeff Shaw, Travis Harper, Frank Reberger, Matt Guerrier

Novoa's season was sidetracked in spring training by Valley Fever, a lung infection he contracted by inhaling the spores of a fungus found in the soil of the Southwest. He recovered and settled into his generic bullpen role; he can throw in the 90s, but pipes it down the middle way too often.

Will Ohman   Bats: L   Throws: L   Height: 6′ 2″   Weight: 195   Born: August 13, 1977   Age: 29

YEAR	TEAM	LVL	AGE	W	L	SV	G	GS	IP	H	BB	SO	HR	GB%	BABIP	STUFF	WHIP	ERA	PERA	EQERA	EQH9	EQBB9	EQSO9	EQHR9	VORP	WXRL
2004	IOW	AAA	26	3	3	3	0	45	1	52¹	53	29	75	6	—	.379	16	1.57	4.30	4.48	4.67	9.5	5.2	9.9	1.0	5.4	—
2005	CHN	MLB	27	2	2	0	69	0	43¹	32	24	45	6	51.8%	.241	12	1.29	2.91	4.88	2.86	7.0	4.5	8.6	1.2	12.6	0.12
2006	CHN	MLB	28	1	1	0	78	0	65¹	51	34	74	6	34.5%	.273	21	1.30	4.13	3.80	3.65	7.2	4.1	9.2	0.7	14.2	1.70
2007	CHN	MLB	29	3	3	3	64	0	58²	55	32	60	8	42.0%	.296	6	1.47	4.43	4.67	4.52	8.0	4.2	8.2	1.0	8.8	0.70

Breakout: 5%   Improve: 19%   Collapse: 57%   Attrition: 13%   Comparables: Bill Kennedy, Joe Hesketh, Yorkis Perez, Dave Hamilton

A designated lefty-killer, and very good at it, Ohman has the added benefit of being competent against right-handers. The Cubs recognized this and expanded his use beyond a strict LOOGY role last year, using him for two innings with some regularity. Ohman was also one of the few guys given the chance to overcome a horrible April (11 runs in 10 outings, including a game in which all five batters he faced came around to score). Where he fits in now, with Eyre still around and Cotts in the picture, is a bit of a pickle.

Carmen Pignatiello   Bats: R   Throws: L   Height: 6′ 0″   Weight: 190   Born: September 12, 1982   Age: 24

YEAR	TEAM	LVL	AGE	W	L	SV	G	GS	IP	H	BB	SO	HR	GB%	BABIP	STUFF	WHIP	ERA	PERA	EQERA	EQH9	EQBB9	EQSO9	EQHR9	VORP	WXRL
2004	WTN	AA	21	9	7	0	27	27	148	167	39	137	16	—	.341	-4	1.39	4.56	5.12	6.66	11.1	2.6	5.5	1.5	-17.0	—
2005	WTN	AA	22	5	4	0	16	10	80²	67	28	77	3	58.3%	.299	21	1.18	2.68	3.81	3.62	8.0	3.2	6.1	0.6	17.5	—
2005	IOW	AAA	22	1	5	0	22	5	47¹	52	20	43	6	48.6%	.326	-6	1.52	5.52	4.95	6.14	9.5	3.5	6.1	1.3	-2.9	—
2006	WTN	AA	23	3	1	0	38	1	60¹	52	19	74	3	58.7%	.329	13	1.18	2.70	3.98	3.70	9.3	2.9	7.7	0.8	12.3	—
2007	CHN	MLB	24	3	4	1	31	6	62²	67	25	49	8	53.0%	.309	2	1.47	4.68	4.87	4.85	9.2	3.1	6.2	1.0	6.7	0.80

Breakout: 25%   Improve: 55%   Collapse: 10%   Attrition: 14%   Comparables: Ricardo Palma, Mike Koplove, Aaron Fultz, Alan Mahaffey

A twentieth-round draft pick from way back in 2000, Pignatiello has always been about command, not power. His fastball that won't crack 90, but his curve dives towards the ground, forcing a ton of ground balls. The switch to relief may keep him from getting tired and hanging so many of them.

Mark Prior   Bats: R   Throws: R   Height: 6′ 5″   Weight: 230   Born: September 7, 1980   Age: 26

YEAR	TEAM	LVL	AGE	W	L	SV	G	GS	IP	H	BB	SO	HR	GB%	BABIP	STUFF	WHIP	ERA	PERA	EQERA	EQH9	EQBB9	EQSO9	EQHR9	VORP	WXRL
2004	CHN	MLB	23	6	4	0	21	21	118²	112	48	139	14	—	.333	34	1.35	4.02	3.61	3.87	8.5	3.2	9.2	1.0	25.6	3.60
2005	CHN	MLB	24	11	7	0	27	27	166²	143	59	188	25	38.5%	.283	27	1.21	3.67	4.00	3.83	7.9	2.9	9.3	1.3	31.8	4.17
2006	CHN	MLB	25	1	6	0	9	9	43²	46	28	38	9	37.6%	.298	1	1.69	7.21	6.33	7.05	9.7	5.0	7.1	1.6	-9.5	-0.48
2007	CHN	MLB	26	6	8	1	30	18	113	104	49	105	17	40.0%	.280	13	1.36	4.50	4.49	4.59	8.0	3.4	7.4	1.2	15.5	2.30

Breakout: 16%   Improve: 45%   Collapse: 18%   Attrition: 12%   Comparables: Bobby Bolin, Jim Lonborg, Tom Griffin, Wayne Twitchell

Prior was hurt last year from the beginning, regardless of how many or which messengers Cub management (and their fellow travelers in the Tribune Company) tried to shoot. His injury is similar to Wood's in 2005, which was repaired but did not hold for long. Prior is the candidate of preference for the fifth slot in the rotation as he's still a guy with big upside. We certainly hope for Prior's sake that his results are more enduring than Wood's.

Glendon Rusch   Bats: L   Throws: L   Height: 6′ 1″   Weight: 225   Born: November 7, 1974   Age: 32

YEAR	TEAM	LVL	AGE	W	L	SV	G	GS	IP	H	BB	SO	HR	GB%	BABIP	STUFF	WHIP	ERA	PERA	EQERA	EQH9	EQBB9	EQSO9	EQHR9	VORP	WXRL
2004	CHN	MLB	29	6	2	2	32	16	129²	127	33	90	10	—	.295	17	1.23	3.47	3.63	3.69	8.7	2.1	5.5	0.6	28.7	3.27
2005	CHN	MLB	30	9	8	0	46	19	145¹	175	53	111	14	40.0%	.355	7	1.57	4.52	3.94	4.78	10.7	3.0	6.2	0.8	11.5	2.38
2006	CHN	MLB	31	3	8	0	25	9	66¹	86	33	59	21	36.7%	.344	-26	1.79	7.47	6.36	6.72	11.2	3.8	7.1	2.5	-11.9	-0.48
2007	CHN	MLB	32	4	6	1	41	9	92²	101	36	68	15	42.0%	.301	-4	1.48	5.10	5.24	5.19	9.4	3.0	5.9	1.3	6.7	1.00

Breakout: 9%   Improve: 47%   Collapse: 18%   Attrition: 18%   Comparables: Johnny Podres, Alex Kellner, Sterling Hitchcock, Greg Swindell

Rusch was never completely healthy in 2006. He was sidelined by back spasms, tennis elbow, and a pulmonary embolism. The first two are merely painful, the last is potentially fatal. Hockey player Jed Ortmeyer of the New York Rangers had the same thing last year and was able to return to playing after about four months; if Rusch's case is at all similar, he could be back by the start of the season.

Jae-Kuk Ryu

Bats: R Throws: R   Height: 6' 3"   Weight: 220   Born: May 30, 1983   Age: 24

YEAR	TEAM	LVL	AGE	W	L	SV	G	GS	IP	H	BB	SO	HR	GB%	BABIP	STUFF	WHIP	ERA	PERA	EQERA	EQH9	EQBB9	EQSO9	EQHR9	VORP	WXRL
2004	WTN	AA	21	1	0	0	14	0	18¹	22	10	19	0	—	.379	-1	1.75	2.95	4.16	5.00	11.5	5.5	6.0	0.5	1.2	—
2005	WTN	AA	22	11	8	0	27	27	169²	154	49	133	12	47.2%	.295	7	1.20	3.34	4.69	4.30	8.7	2.6	5.0	1.1	24.2	—
2006	IOW	AAA	23	8	8	0	24	23	139	123	51	114	12	52.1%	.282	11	1.25	3.24	4.55	3.64	7.8	3.2	5.7	1.0	30.7	—
2006	CHN	MLB	23	0	1	0	10	1	15	23	6	17	7	36.7%	.381	-1	1.93	8.40	7.58	7.04	13.5	2.9	9.4	3.5	-3.6	-0.56
2007	*CHN*	*MLB*	*24*	*5*	*8*	*1*	*35*	*15*	*108*	*114*	*44*	*80*	*18*	*46.0%*	*.291*	*1*	*1.46*	*5.08*	*5.23*	*5.18*	*9.1*	*3.1*	*5.9*	*1.3*	*7.9*	*1.40*

Breakout: 6%   Improve: 22%   Collapse: 37%   Attrition: 0%   Comparables: Dustin McGowan, Anthony Lerew, Pete Munro, Jason Ryan

Ryu survived elbow trouble in 2004 and has made a compelling case since then that he can handle the minor leagues. He had a rather disastrous introduction to the majors, however, yielding four home runs in his May 28 start against the Braves. In spite of all the maneuvering in the Cubs' rotation, he never got another chance to start, even after returning to the majors in late August. Between returning starters and newly signed ones, there will be a crowded mound in Mesa, making Iowa his most likely destination at the end of camp.

Donald Veal

Bats: L Throws: L   Height: 6' 4"   Weight: 215   Born: September 18, 1984   Age: 22

YEAR	TEAM	LVL	AGE	W	L	SV	G	GS	IP	H	BB	SO	HR	GB%	BABIP	STUFF	WHIP	ERA	PERA	EQERA	EQH9	EQBB9	EQSO9	EQHR9	VORP	WXRL
2005	BOI	A-	20	1	2	0	7	6	29	18	15	34	2	44.1%	.250	9	1.14	2.48	6.97	4.39	7.1	6.8	5.7	1.7	3.6	—
2006	PEO	A	21	5	3	0	14	14	73²	45	40	86	4	36.3%	.255	13	1.16	2.70	6.45	4.70	7.5	6.9	6.4	1.3	6.7	—
2006	DAY	A+	21	6	2	0	14	14	80²	46	42	88	3	41.1%	.240	31	1.10	1.68	4.70	2.65	5.9	5.4	6.6	0.6	25.6	—
2007	*CHN*	*MLB*	*22*	*6*	*8*	*0*	*24*	*22*	*115*	*100*	*95*	*110*	*17*	*39.0%*	*.271*	*8*	*1.69*	*5.19*	*5.66*	*5.25*	*7.5*	*6.4*	*7.7*	*1.2*	*7.0*	*1.60*

Breakout: 0%   Improve: 5%   Collapse: 77%   Attrition: 3%   Comparables: Brian Fuentes, Radhames Liz, Junior Guerrero, Chris Capuano

Veal has the makings of a front-line lefty, but let's not get too hasty. He's mostly fastball right now; his changeup is good, his curve not so much, but control is a problem for both pitches. He had to overcome a torn labrum in college, which is another worry point. On the mound, Veal comes out of a high leg kick, making the ball tough to pick up. That's why he has those exceptionally low BABIPs; other pitchers who hide the ball well, such as Dontrelle Willis, share that trait.

Les Walrond

Bats: L Throws: L   Height: 6' 3"   Weight: 205   Born: November 7, 1976   Age: 30

YEAR	TEAM	LVL	AGE	W	L	SV	G	GS	IP	H	BB	SO	HR	GB%	BABIP	STUFF	WHIP	ERA	PERA	EQERA	EQH9	EQBB9	EQSO9	EQHR9	VORP	WXRL
2004	WIC	AA	27	3	3	0	8	6	39	30	17	34	2	—	.255	2	1.21	4.38	5.54	5.50	7.4	5.0	5.0	1.0	0.4	—
2004	OMA	AAA	27	11	5	0	19	19	123²	114	41	107	12	—	.288	13	1.25	3.06	4.45	3.47	8.0	3.2	5.8	0.9	29.5	—
2005	ABQ	AAA	28	4	5	0	15	15	86²	97	37	61	13	50.0%	.324	-13	1.55	4.57	5.58	4.93	9.8	3.8	4.6	1.4	6.5	—
2006	IOW	AAA	29	10	5	0	31	20	133¹	134	59	104	11	53.7%	.315	-3	1.45	3.99	5.07	5.16	9.0	4.0	5.2	1.0	6.6	—
2006	CHN	MLB	29	0	1	0	10	2	17¹	19	12	21	2	55.1%	.362	15	1.79	6.24	4.03	6.11	9.7	5.6	9.7	1.0	-1.2	-0.33
2007	*CHN*	*MLB*	*30*	*4*	*6*	*1*	*45*	*10*	*84*	*89*	*42*	*59*	*12*	*49.0%*	*.295*	*-8*	*1.55*	*5.21*	*5.35*	*5.36*	*9.1*	*3.8*	*5.7*	*1.2*	*4.5*	*0.80*

Breakout: 6%   Improve: 32%   Collapse: 31%   Attrition: 3%   Comparables: Bo Belinsky, Terry Burrows, Cliff Chambers, Woodie Fryman

Walrond makes sense as a LOOGY, since he has an assortment of the off- and further off-speed pitches that lefties hate and righties kill. He also has a fastball that every hitter loves. His two starts were bad jokes.

Jerome Williams

Bats: R Throws: R   Height: 6' 3"   Weight: 240   Born: December 4, 1981   Age: 25

YEAR	TEAM	LVL	AGE	W	L	SV	G	GS	IP	H	BB	SO	HR	GB%	BABIP	STUFF	WHIP	ERA	PERA	EQERA	EQH9	EQBB9	EQSO9	EQHR9	VORP	WXRL
2004	SFN	MLB	22	10	7	0	22	22	129¹	123	44	80	14	—	.279	10	1.29	4.25	4.85	4.59	8.6	2.7	4.9	0.9	14.8	2.38
2005	SFN	MLB	23	0	2	0	4	3	16²	21	4	11	2	48.2%	.352	2	1.50	6.47	4.27	6.35	11.1	2.1	5.3	1.1	-1.7	0.03
2005	FRE	AAA	23	1	4	0	6	6	30²	47	17	15	3	53.0%	.396	-22	2.08	9.38	5.67	9.95	13.1	4.5	3.4	0.9	-15.3	—
2005	IOW	AAA	23	1	1	0	4	4	24¹	27	6	17	2	62.8%	.301	10	1.36	2.22	4.31	3.60	9.4	2.2	4.7	0.7	5.6	—
2005	CHN	MLB	23	6	8	0	18	17	106	98	45	59	12	45.4%	.272	2	1.35	3.91	5.17	4.18	8.5	3.5	4.6	1.0	16.4	2.42
2006	CHN	MLB	24	0	2	0	5	2	12¹	15	11	5	2	53.7%	.333	-23	2.11	7.32	6.95	7.62	10.4	6.9	3.5	1.4	-3.6	-0.06
2006	IOW	AAA	24	5	7	0	29	16	111²	145	35	52	17	45.9%	.339	-33	1.62	4.78	5.96	5.35	11.1	2.7	3.2	1.7	3.2	—
2007	*WAS*	*MLB*	*25*	*4*	*7*	*0*	*27*	*14*	*93*	*105*	*38*	*50*	*12*	*46%*	*.297*	*-9*	*1.53*	*5.36*	*5.89*	*5.85*	*10.1*	*3.3*	*4.3*	*1.1*	*-2.3*	*0.3*

Breakout: 5%   Improve: 32%   Collapse: 35%   Attrition: 24%   Comparables: Willis Roberts, Kent Bottenfield, Matt Hensley, Arnold Gooch

(continued next page)

Jerome Williams *(continued)*

Williams pitched poorly last year, from spring training, through an April demotion and a full season at Triple-A. Baseball isn't the only thing in players' lives, and it was almost certainly not Williams's top priority in 2006. Still, it's not hard to understand that your manager is going to be royally ticked when you put family issues above baseball. Williams was claimed by Oakland in September and released in December without ever wearing their uniform. At this point, it's worth asking if he was ever that much of a prospect. With one foot in the washout bucket, he can't afford another failure.

Kerry Wood   **Bats: R Throws: R**   Height: 6' 5" Weight: 225 Born: June 16, 1977 Age: 30

YEAR	TEAM	LVL	AGE	W	L	SV	G	GS	IP	H	BB	SO	HR	GB%	BABIP	STUFF	WHIP	ERA	PERA	EQERA	EQH9	EQBB9	EQSO9	EQHR9	VORP	WXRL
2004	CHN	MLB	27	8	9	0	22	22	140¹	127	51	144	16	—	.307	29	1.27	3.72	3.94	3.86	8.3	2.9	8.2	0.9	28.8	3.67
2005	CHN	MLB	28	3	4	0	21	10	66	52	26	77	14	36.4%	.252	13	1.18	4.23	4.93	4.18	7.3	3.2	9.6	1.9	9.2	1.03
2006	CHN	MLB	29	1	2	0	4	4	19²	19	8	13	5	43.5%	.246	-5	1.37	4.11	6.22	5.31	8.4	3.1	5.3	1.8	0.2	0.17
2007	*CHN*	*MLB*	*30*	*4*	*6*	*1*	*28*	*11*	*85*	*82*	*36*	*75*	*13*	*43.0%*	*.286*	*7*	*1.38*	*4.45*	*4.72*	*4.52*	*8.3*	*3.3*	*7.0*	*1.2*	*12.5*	*1.70*

Breakout: 7% Improve: 32% Collapse: 33% Attrition: 12% Comparables: Wayne Twitchell, Joey Jay, Larry Dierker, Kevin Gross

Wood hurt his shoulder in the summer of 2005. He got it fixed, but the fix only held for five starts in 2006 and blew out again in a sixth. Wood opted not to have surgery for what is now a partially torn rotator cuff. If he's able to pitch in 2007, it will be as a reliever; there was some indication that he could throw about 50 pitches before starting to feel pain, and the plans are to let him do that, possibly as the closer. This assumes that his shoulder has healed to some degree. There is a solid chance that it will blow out again, requiring surgery. If the partial tear ends up going completely through, his career may be over.

Michael Wuertz   **Bats: R Throws: R**   Height: 6' 3" Weight: 205 Born: December 15, 1978 Age: 28

YEAR	TEAM	LVL	AGE	W	L	SV	G	GS	IP	H	BB	SO	HR	GB%	BABIP	STUFF	WHIP	ERA	PERA	EQERA	EQH9	EQBB9	EQSO9	EQHR9	VORP	WXRL
2004	IOW	AAA	25	1	1	19	37	0	44²	30	15	59	4	—	.260	23	1.01	2.42	3.44	2.62	6.2	3.2	9.1	0.8	14.8	—
2004	CHN	MLB	25	1	0	1	31	0	29	22	17	30	4	—	.269	12	1.34	4.34	4.53	4.25	6.7	4.6	8.2	1.2	4.6	0.30
2005	CHN	MLB	26	6	2	0	75	0	75²	60	40	89	6	43.2%	.302	25	1.32	3.80	3.46	4.21	7.2	4.3	9.6	0.7	10.4	1.21
2006	IOW	AAA	27	6	0	10	30	0	41	30	9	67	2	44.0%	.318	41	0.95	1.76	2.40	2.43	7.3	2.0	11.1	0.7	14.3	—
2006	CHN	MLB	27	3	1	0	41	0	40²	35	16	42	5	54.0%	.278	16	1.25	2.65	3.79	2.83	7.6	3.0	8.5	0.9	13.5	0.26
2007	*CHN*	*MLB*	*28*	*3*	*3*	*4*	*53*	*1*	*58¹*	*51*	*25*	*60*	*6*	*46.0%*	*.287*	*14*	*1.29*	*3.69*	*3.72*	*3.82*	*7.5*	*3.3*	*8.3*	*0.8*	*13.3*	*1.20*

Breakout: 21% Improve: 31% Collapse: 41% Attrition: 12% Comparables: Paul Shuey, Ricky Bottalico, Xavier Hernandez, T. J. Mathews

After a solid year and a half with the Cubs, Wuertz should have been assured of a job in 2006, but giving up 15 runs in eight spring innings put him on thin ice, and when he imploded in his third April outing he was banished to Iowa via another Dusty fiat. Triple-A hitters couldn't touch his fastball-slider combination, and neither could major leaguers when he was finally called back in late July. He's had no trouble closing in Iowa, but Wood, Howry, and Dempster would all seem to be in line ahead of him for that job.

Carlos Zambrano   **Bats: S Throws: R**   Height: 6' 5" Weight: 255 Born: June 1, 1981 Age: 26

YEAR	TEAM	LVL	AGE	W	L	SV	G	GS	IP	H	BB	SO	HR	GB%	BABIP	STUFF	WHIP	ERA	PERA	EQERA	EQH9	EQBB9	EQSO9	EQHR9	VORP	WXRL
2004	CHN	MLB	23	16	8	0	31	31	209²	174	81	188	14	—	.280	34	1.22	2.75	3.80	3.14	7.7	3.1	7.1	0.6	62.8	6.94
2005	CHN	MLB	24	14	6	0	33	33	223¹	170	86	202	21	52.4%	.258	28	1.15	3.26	3.90	3.50	7.0	3.1	7.4	0.8	51.2	6.78
2006	CHN	MLB	25	16	7	0	33	33	214	162	115	210	20	48.6%	.259	33	1.29	3.41	4.03	3.39	6.9	4.2	8.0	0.7	53.8	6.31
2007	*CHN*	*MLB*	*26*	*13*	*11*	*0*	*32*	*32*	*213¹*	*179*	*87*	*208*	*21*	*49.0%*	*.276*	*27*	*1.25*	*3.66*	*3.62*	*3.81*	*7.2*	*3.2*	*7.8*	*0.8*	*49.0*	*6.60*

Breakout: 6% Improve: 28% Collapse: 28% Attrition: 0% Comparables: Mark Gubicza, Kerry Wood, Stan Williams, John Smoltz

Zambrano has seemingly been the model of consistency for the Cubs, delivering high-value innings for 30-plus starts a year, pumping in fastball after fastball. Unfortunately, there were a couple of worrisome notes in 2006—his walk rate jumped up to an unhealthy level, and his groundball-flyball ratio took a sharp downward turn. It's might be nothing, but it could be the first warning sign that his years of hard pitching at tender ages are catching up to him.

Lineouts

PLAYER	TEAM	LVL	AGE	PA	R	2B	3B	HR	RBI	BB	SO	SB-CS	SPEED	AVG/OBP/SLG	MLVr	EqAVG/OBP/SLG	EqA	VORP
1B M. Craig#	DAY	A+	25	527	67	35	3	12	76	68	107	6-1	4.7	.287/.384/.458	.193	.246/.321/.386	.248	-6.9
OF J. Mabry*	CHN	MLB	35	237	16	8	1	5	25	23	57	0-0	3.5	.205/.283/.324	-.280	.196/.278/.311	.213	-12.8
INF R. Malone*	PEO	A	21	213	26	16	2	2	29	27	34	6-3	5.5	.284/.385/.426	.201	.262/.338..387	.252	6.0
3B C. McGehee	IOW	AAA	23	546	56	28	1	11	68	41	70	0-3	3.3	.280/.336/.406	.014	.267/.317/.394	.246	10.5
C J. Reyes#	WTN	AA	22	156	15	3	0	0	11	9	25	0-1	3.5	.229/.275/.250	-.225	.224/.265/.245	.184	-12.2
	IOW	AAA	22	126	10	6	0	0	11	14	11	0-1	3.4	.250/.347/.306	-.127	.234/.320/.279	.218	-3.7
CF C. Walker	WTN	AA	26	566	70	22	11	2	35	40	102	50-23	7.7	.292/.351/.390	.108	.284/.332/.389	.254	11.4
2B T. Womack*	CIN	MLB	36	23	1	2	0	0	3	4	3	0-0	4.1	.222/.364/.333	-.112	.222/.364/.333	.255	0.2
	CHN	MLB	36	57	6	1	0	1	2	4	4	1-1	4.6	.280/.333/.360	-.094	.275/.327/.353	.238	0.3

PLAYER	TEAM	LVL	AGE	W	L	SV	IP	H	BB	SO	HR	GB%	BABIP	STUFF	WHIP	ERA	PERA	EqERA	EqH9	EqBB9	EqSO9	EqHR9	VORP
M. Atkins	PEO	A	20	13	4	0	138	110	53	127	10	—	.267	-10	1.18	2.41	6.34	4.38	9.0	4.6	5.1	1.7	17.5
E. Campusano*	PEO	A	23	0	0	21	29	16	9	47	0	—	.276	17	0.86	1.24	3.55	2.70	7.4	4.1	8.1	0.3	8.6
	WTN	AA	23	2	1	4	25²	22	8	34	2	—	.328	14	1.19	1.79	4.08	2.92	9.1	2.9	8.4	1.5	7.4
J. Ceda	PDR	Rk	19	2	0	0	23¹	20	13	31	1	—	.358	-4	1.43	5.06	7.13	7.17	10.5	6.8	6.3	2.1	-3.7
	CUB	Rk	19	0	0	0	12²	6	7	21	0	—	.333	12	1.07	0.74	4.11	2.31	6.2	6.2	7.7	0.0	4.3
	BOI	A-	19	1	0	0	11²	5	2	11	1	—	.250	11	0.63	3.21	6.97	4.09	6.5	2.5	4.9	1.6	1.8
A. Harben	NBR	AA	22	4	9	1	122²	118	67	74	5	—	.294	1	1.51	3.98	5.62	5.20	8.9	5.3	3.7	0.6	5.5
C. Huseby	CUB	Rk	18	0	2	0	17²	21	6	14	1	—	.357	-15	1.57	5.23	7.17	6.35	12.2	3.7	3.7	2.6	-1.4
R. O'Malley*	IOW	AAA	26	7	7	0	123²	135	30	71	9	39%	.318	0	1.34	4.09	4.38	4.63	9.3	2.1	3.8	0.9	13.6
M. Pawelek*	BOI	A-	19	3	5	0	61¹	54	23	52	1	—	.283	8	1.26	2.50	4.92	4.83	9.2	4.4	4.4	0.3	5.1
J. Samardzija	PEO	A	21	0	1	0	11¹	6	6	4	1	—	.161	-14	1.08	3.24	9.52	6.10	6.1	7.0	1.7	2.6	-0.6
	BOI	A-	21	1	1	0	19	18	6	13	1	—	.288	-17	1.26	2.37	6.84	4.00	10.5	4.0	3.5	1.5	3.2
C. Vasquez*	DAY	A+	23	3	0	0	34²	24	10	31	0	—	.267	2	0.99	1.58	3.56	2.65	6.6	3.2	4.8	0.3	11.1
	WTN	AA	23	3	5	3	50	41	32	60	2	—	.315	11	1.46	3.60	4.87	5.55	8.7	5.9	7.6	0.7	0.3
R. Wells	WTN	AA	23	4	2	0	62¹	45	13	54	2	—	.253	21	0.93	1.59	3.61	2.80	7.2	1.9	5.5	0.6	19.0
	IOW	AAA	23	5	5	0	69²	87	23	59	7	—	.370	4	1.59	4.94	4.43	5.45	10.9	2.8	5.8	1.1	1.2

There was some hope for **Matt Craig** after his big 2004, but that now looks like a bit of a fluke, and he's been bucked down to organizational soldiery. **John Mabry**'s made a career as a left-handed pinch-hitter, but it should be over; he simply can't handle breaking pitches any more, whoever's throwing them. Arriving in the right organization for a man with his name, **Ryne Malone** was a 49th-round draft pick out of Florida State in June, and had a better debut than first-rounder Colvin. The trick will be finding a position for him. **Casey McGehee** has Gold-Glove potential as a third baseman, but hitting enough to force Aramis Ramirez out of the picture is a wee bit beyond his ability. **Jose Reyes** will only be confused with the Mets' shortstop in alphabetical listings; he's your basic catch-and-throw type. **Chris Walker** is your basic crazy-fast speedster. He's here because fantasy players love steals, fifth-outfielder candidacies are unpredictable, and, hey, younever-know. Picking up **Tony Womack** was one of the symptoms of Dusty's disconnect from reality; he's not the speedster from days of yore, and, without a position, he's Lenny Harris without the cachet of being Lenny Harris.

Mitch Atkins is a good example of why you shouldn't jump to conclusions with high school pitchers. He struggled for two years before jumping all over the Midwest League last year. His middling assortment won't make people believers, but continued success will. Through the chicanery of the Rule 5 draft, Venezuelan lefty **Edward Campusano** was swiped from the Cubs by the Brewers and sent to the Tigers. He throws harder than a lot of lefties and also has a solid slider, so he has a better-than-average chance to stick. **Jose Ceda** is a big, big guy, more like 250 pounds than his listed 205, and he can bring 96-MPH heat. Part of the Todd Walker deal, he has no control or breaking pitches to speak of, and seems ultimately destined for relief. The Cubs got something of value in return for Phil Nevin when they received **Adam Harben** as the PTBNL from the Twins. He's a big guy with a good fastball. He needs to refine his other pitches, but that's true of a lot of pitchers at his stage of development. **Chris Huseby** was drafted by the Cubs in the eleventh round of the 2006 draft, but the team gave him $1.3 million—the slot value of a late first-rounder—to pry him away from college ball at Auburn. He fell that far in the draft because of an elbow injury and TJ surgery in high school, but the medical reports say he's doing fine. At six-foot-seven and 210 pounds, he's a big guy with an excellent fastball and curve. His potential is unlimited, but questions—youth, inexperience, already having major surgery—are there too. **Ryan O'Malley** made the most of what is likely to be his only big league chance, having seriously injured his elbow. The Cubs' first-round pick from 2005, **Mark Pawelek** apparently took it a little too easy in his first professional off-season and reported to camp out of shape. He had enough talent to put up good numbers in Boise without even trying, but his mechanics were off, his velocity was down; if he'd pitched like that the year before, he wouldn't have been a first-round pick. Based on what we've actually seen—30 okay innings in the low minors, with pitiful translated strikeout rates—there's no way **Jeff Samardzija** should be in this book. He throws 96, which is why baseball wants him, but at this point his fastball is laser-straight and hittable for all its speed. His breaking pitches are all over the place, and he doesn't have the experience or training in baseball to make adjustments. Still, this may be his only chance to be in a baseball book, especially if an NFL team makes him a better offer to play wideout than the $7.5 million signing bonus the Cubs have offered him to commit to baseball. **Carlos Vasquez** is a hard-throwing lefty sinker-slider guy; when batters aren't whiffing, they're pounding the ball into the ground. Thrown to the White Sox in the Cotts deal. **Randy Wells** looked good in the pitcher-friendly Southern League only to get beat with the reality stick outside of it. Only three years removed from catching, he sprouted from six-foot upon drafting to six-four now, but a modest fastball-slider-change mix makes him more the moxie-dependent type.

Manager: Dusty Baker

Year	Team	W-L	Pythag +/-	Avg PC	100 +P	120 +P	QS	BQS	REL	REL w Zero R	IBB	SUBS	PH	PH Avg	PH HR	SB2	CS2	SB3	CS3	SAC Att	SAC %	POS SAC	Squeeze	Swing	In Play
2004	CHN	89-73	-6	99.1	81	13	92	7	459	302	33	44	254	.236	4	64	24	2	4	97	80.4%	37	0	108	81
2005	CHN	79-83	0	97.7	80	10	88	4	457	284	48	49	240	.195	2	60	34	5	3	93	74.2%	42	2	123	105
2006	CHN	66-96	-3	91.9	57	7	55	5	542	357	44	40	270	.216	5	107	41	13	5	117	71.8%	56	7	145	117

Dusty's last stand was a testament to TribCorp's desire to wring every last dollar out of the man, as Dusty had pretty much lost the generally friendly local media at least a year beforehand. Charged with guiding the club through a rebuilding year, Baker's loyalties to the team's various rookies proved fickle and the entire pitching staff seemed to get stood on its head out of a misplaced, wheel-spinning impatience. With Dusty gone, the Cubs get to see how much Lou Piniella has mellowed with age. Sweet Lou has fled a rebuilding situation in Tampa for one in Chicago, and, though this one may prove more tractable, he's still going to need to show more patience than has been his wont. The good news is that Piniella is more supple tactically than Baker—don't be surprised if Mark DeRosa plays all over the place—and a little more stable in picking his relievers and sticking with them.

Chicago White Sox

The problem with the White Sox in 2006 was not that the team they fielded was fundamentally worse than the one that brought home the big trophy the year before. The problem was that the 2005 team won despite of its inherent quality—as measured by either runs scored and allowed, or run elements such as walks, home runs, batting average, and stolen bases—not because of it.

As detailed in this space last year, the 2005 White Sox won 99 games despite outscoring their opponents by just 96 runs; only three teams in history have won more games with a worse run differential: The 1970 Reds, 2004 Yankees, and 1969 Mets. The World Champs also allowed fewer runs than would have been expected based on how their opponents performed offensively. Some of that may have been attributable to Ozzie Guillen's in-game management and savvy bullpen usage, or to clutch performance on the part of his players, but because teams have essentially no repeatable ability to outperform their projected records or their run expectations, we can label all of it "luck" when weighing its impact on future performance. In the case of the 2005 White Sox, it was good luck layered upon good luck.

Indeed, Sox pitching gave up nearly an extra run per game in 2006 despite an improvement in the staff's strikeout-to-walk ratio from 2.27 K/BB in 2005 to 2.34 K/BB in 2006. In the last 70 years, only two other teams have seen their runs allowed per game increase by a greater amount from one non-strike season to the next despite improving their staff strikeout-to-walk ratio (see table 1).

The difference in run prevention can be explained by two factors. The first is what happened to balls after contact. After allowing only 167 homers in 2005, a better than league-average figure, the Sox gave up 200 last season. Research by Nate Silver has shown that a pitcher's home

run rate is only partially attributable to skill in that it is largely a product of his ratio of ground balls to fly balls—the more fly balls, the more home runs.

The White Sox gave up more fly balls in 2006 than they did in 2005, but just barely. The difference amounted to about 1 percent of their balls in play, or about 45 fly balls. That alone should have resulted in approximately 6 more homers being surrendered by White Sox pitching in 2006. An additional 8 home runs can be attributed to the league-wide increase in homers (12.93 percent of fly balls became home runs in 2005 vs. 13.53 percent in 2006), bringing their expected increase to 14. That leaves 19 of the 33 additional home runs the Sox allowed in 2006 unaccounted for. Indeed, the percentage of fly balls allowed by White Sox pitching that left the park jumped considerably from a below-average 12.5 percent in 2005 to an above-average 14.1 percent in 2006. In other words, those 19 extra homers were the result of, if not bad luck, then at least a non-repeatable trend.

The Sox didn't just give up more home runs, they gave up more hits on the field of play (see table 2). In 2005, the team's defensive efficiency—its rate of turning balls in play into outs—was .710. Park-Adjusted Defensive Efficiency (PADE) pegs the 2005 White Sox as 2.78 standard deviations above the mean, easily the best figure in the majors. In 2006, those numbers dropped, to .694 and −0.14 standard deviations. In plain English, that means the White Sox went from league-best to league-average in one year, even though they had the same primary starter at every position on the field in both seasons, save for center field, where Aaron Rowand (+6 fielding runs in 2005) was replaced by Brian Anderson, who, at +12, was the Sox's best fielder last season. Some of the defensive decline was real, no doubt,

WHITE SOX PROSPECTUS

2006 record: 90–72; Third place, AL Central

Pythagenport record: 87–75

Runs scored per game: 5.36 (3rd in AL)

Runs allowed per game: 4.90 (10th in AL)

Team EqA: .264 (4th in AL)

2006 Batters Age: 30.3 (4th oldest in AL)

2006 Pitchers Age: 28.8 (3rd oldest in AL)

Ballpark: U.S. Cellular Field; Moderate hitter's park; Park Factor of 1.028

2006: The reason they call it overachieving is that it tends not to happen in consecutive years.

2007: Despite having a win-now team, Kenny Williams failed to make any win-now acquisitions. Chances are they won't win now.

Table 1. It Wasn't Supposed to Be This Way

Team	Year	K/BB	RA/G	Year	K/BB	RA/G	RA/G Increase
San Diego	1976	1.20	4.09	1977	1.23	5.15	1.06
Pittsburgh	1946	0.82	4.31	1947	0.90	5.24	0.93
Chicago (AL)	2005	2.27	3.98	2006	2.34	4.90	0.92
St. Louis	2002	1.84	4.00	2003	1.91	4.91	0.91
Milwaukee (NL)	1963	1.89	3.70	1964	2.00	4.59	0.89

Table 2. Taking a Turn for the Worse

Category	2005	2006
UIBB/9	2.73	2.32
K/9	6.58	6.29
H/9	8.75	9.53
HR/9	1.07	1.24

NOTE: All stats adjusted for league effects.

but given the largely random nature of balls in play, it's likely that luck played a part here as well.

The second factor in the change in the White Sox's run prevention from 2005 to 2006 is what happened with runners on base. The 2005 pitching staff surrendered far fewer runs—40 fewer, to be exact—than would have been expected based on their walks, hits, home runs, and so on. Again, when a team allows fewer runs than can be expected from their run elements, the discrepancy is largely due to luck. In this case, "luck" can be more precisely defined as "performance with runners in scoring position." As table 3 shows, the 2005 White Sox pitched phenomenally well in those key situations—their opponents had a mere 658 OPS with runners in scoring position, the lowest mark against any AL pitching staff since 1989. That performance could not be sustained, and wasn't, and last year the Sox allowed only 10 more runs than expected.

Table 3. Rising to the Occasion

Year	RISP	All Other PA
2005	.222/.309/.349	.258/.311/.412
2006	.270/.358/.438	.271/.315/.441

Finally, the 2005 White Sox won significantly more games than expected for a team that only outscored its opponents by 96 runs largely because they went 35–19 in games decided by one run, another luck-dependent showing. Last season, the White Sox were just 24–21 in one-run games.

So if you're looking to scapegoat the team's inability to defend their title, blame luck—not *bad* luck, but simply the absence of good luck, the kind that propelled a good but flawed team to a championship. Based purely on runs scored and runs allowed, the White Sox actually fought regression to the mean better than the average defending champion: the Sox's 22-run drop in run differential was less than the average drop of 51 runs by all defending World Champions in the expansion era. In fact, since 1960 only two reigning World Champions completely missed the postseason the following year despite maintaining their run differential as well as the White Sox did: the 1987 Twins, who were actually outscored the year they won the World Series, and the 1981 Dodgers, who missed the playoffs by a single game in 1982.

Indeed, counteracting the problems on the mound, the offense was a force to be reckoned with all season, and, despite terrible production from the 8-9-1 third of their lineup, was substantially more productive than the one that took home the ring. The 2006 White Sox scored 868 runs, 127 more than in 2005 and good for third in the AL. Even after adjusting for the league-wide increase in offense, the team's run production went up over 12 percent. Replacing Carl Everett with Jim Thome was worth 50 runs alone. Thus, the White Sox's failure to repeat should not reflect poorly on Kenny Williams, or Ozzie Guillen, or the players. Last season, we wrote in these pages that the "true" record of the 2005 White Sox, once all the non-repeatable factors were stripped out, was 90–72, and that is exactly how the 2006 White Sox finished.

The potential absence of past good luck continues to loom as the White Sox are likely to suffer the ravages of injuries more than they have the last two years, simply because they have been unusually healthy. The rotation has been particularly injury-free; aside from a single start from knuckleballer Chuck Haeger, the White Sox have used just six starters (counting the swapped Orlando Hernandez and Javier Vazquez as one) in the last two years combined. In only having to place four players on the DL all last season, the Sox won Baseball Prospectus's Dick Martin Award for the best training staff in the game.

The good news is that the White Sox do not have a particularly old roster. Weighted for playing time, the average age of last year's team was just two months older than the AL average. Virtually the entire squad is in its prime. By the end of the coming season, Jim Thome will be 37 and Anderson will be 25, but every other projected starter and key bench player will be between 28 and 33. The rotation is similarly positioned. Jose Contreras is 35—well, he's listed at 35—and the eventual fifth starter will come from a pool of youngsters, the oldest being newly acquired Nick Masset who turns 25 in May, but Mark Buehrle, Jon Garland, and Javier Vazquez are all in that 28–31 range.

Among the club's other standing assets, Ozzie Guillen has proven to be one of the game's most adept handlers of a pitching staff. Guillen would probably tell us to stick our PAP numbers somewhere inappropriate, but he nonetheless uses his starting pitchers in a statistically optimal manner as far as managing workloads. With a largely veteran rotation at his disposal, Guillen has been unflinchingly aggressive about insisting that his starters work deep into games. They cross the 100-pitch barrier as much as any team in baseball, but they rarely do they go over the dangerous 120-pitch mark (just four times last season). In this way, Guillen keeps his pitchers in long enough to save his bullpen, but not so long that they risk injury; table 4 lists the teams with the most starts that lasted between 100 and 120 pitches since 1988.

Table 4. Welcome to Conditioning

Year	Team	GS
2005	Chicago (AL)	107
2003	Seattle	105
2004	Chicago (AL)	100
2005	Boston	95
2006	Chicago (AL)	94

We only have pitch count data back to 1988, but pitch counts have been trending towards this 100–120 pitch window for decades, as is evidenced by the absence of teams from before 2003 in table 4. It is likely that no team has ever maximized its starting pitchers innings while minimizing their injury risk as well as Ozzie Guillen's White Sox.

Though the Sox are well positioned to stave off the ravages of age and injuries, the ravages of free agency threaten the club's immediate future. Whether by foresight or happenstance, the Sox went into the 2006–2007 offseason with every significant contributor under contract for another year. But Vazquez, Buehrle, Dye, and Podsednik are all free agents after 2007; Garland, Pierzynski, Uribe, and Crede follow in 2008. In two years, the Sox will have had to either re-sign or replace more than half of their lineup and starting rotation.

The time to strike is now, which is what makes Chicago's big winter meetings move—trading Freddy Garcia for Gio Gonzalez and Gavin Floyd—so perplexing, especially given that it was followed by trading Garcia's apparent replacement, Brandon McCarthy, to Texas in exchange for John Danks and two other prospects. It's not that Gonzalez and Floyd don't represent a reasonable haul for a pitcher a year away from free agency, although Floyd is less a prospect than a reject at this point in his career, and Garcia is likely to be a Type A free agent a year from now, which means even under the new CBA he would have fetched a pair of draft picks had they kept him. It's not that Danks and company might not prove to be a better haul of talent in the long term than McCarthy, or that Charlie Haeger won't do a fine job in the rotation if he gets a shot. It's that stockpiling minor leaguers for the future should not be the team's highest priority. The priority should be to maximize the talent on the field this year and next by finding solutions for the sub-optimal production they're getting at multiple lineup positions, particularly left field.

Kenny Williams had the enviable position of having starting pitching to trade in a market that has become completely unhinged for even mediocre pitchers. For two above-average major league starters, one of whom is 23 years old and not yet arbitration-eligible, Williams could have easily added a thumper or two for the outfield and still snagged a few decent prospects. Instead of using his excess to place a better team on the field this year, he punted all of his leverage to a future which may or may not involve a competitive Sox team.

There's still time to rectify this mistake, but the clock is ticking. The White Sox are at a point on the competitive curve at which a small improvement in team quality may lead to a dramatic improvement in their chances of making the playoffs. No matter what happens between now and the time the White Sox need to scrap their roster and start over, the current run can hardly be considered a disappointment; far more talented teams have finished with far less to show for their ability than these White Sox. But if the White Sox miss the playoffs again because they failed to show the same proactive mindset that they displayed last winter, neither can it be considered an unqualified success.

HITTERS

Brian Anderson — CF — Bats: R — Throws: R — Height: 6' 2" — Weight: 215 — Born: March 11, 1982 — Age: 25

YEAR	TEAM	LVL	AGE	PA	R	2B	3B	HR	RBI	BB	SO	SB	CS	SPEED	AVG	OBP	SLG	MLVR	EQAVG	EQOBP	EQSLG	EQA	VORP	DEFENSE	
2004	WNS	A+	22	287	43	22	4	8	46	29	44	10	1	6.8	.319	.394	.532	.307	.284	.345	.483	.282	18.6	63-CF	-2
2004	BIR	AA	22	209	26	9	3	4	27	19	30	3	2	5.4	.270	.346	.416	.084	.258	.321	.389	.248	1.8	41-CF	-5
2005	CHR	AAA	23	501	71	24	3	16	57	44	115	4	2	4.6	.295	.360	.469	.124	.279	.342	.437	.269	20.8	111-CF	-2
2006	CHA	MLB	24	406	46	23	1	8	33	30	91	4	7	5.2	.224	.290	.358	-.247	.218	.292	.354	.223	-11.3	108-CF	12
2007	CHA	MLB	25	450	58	23	2	15	56	33	88	6	3	5.4	.263	.323	.442	-.032	.258	.322	.435	.265	9.6	107-CF	3

Breakout: 34% Improve: 66% Collapse: 13% Attrition: 23%   Comparables: Dave Engle, Lee Walls, Ivan Calderon, Gabe Kapler

It's tempting to praise the White Sox's stick-to-itiveness for letting Anderson keep his job all season despite the fact that it took him until July 16 to get his batting average over the .200 mark. Truth be told, his job security had more to do with the lack of worthwhile alternatives. Jerry Owens offered the same light bat with less upside, Rob Mackowiak's outfield defense wasn't up to snuff, Ryan Sweeney didn't become tempting until late in the season, and Chris Young was busy making Kenny Williams look bad in Tucson. PECOTA insists that the Sox will be rewarded for their determination. If Anderson can get his batting average up to the .270 mark, he'll bring enough secondary skills to the table to be a B/B– alternative in center field. He'll have to learn to hit a breaking pitch first, though—according to ESPN's Inside Edge data, Anderson batted just .125 against curveballs. With that kind of deficiency in play, Anderson has more work left to do than overcoming the usual growing pains.

Christopher Carter — Bats: R — Throws: R — Height: 6' 4" — Weight: 210 — Born: December 18, 1986 — Age: 20

YEAR	TEAM	LVL	AGE	PA	R	2B	3B	HR	RBI	BB	SO	SB	CS	SPEED	AVG	OBP	SLG	MLVR	EQAVG	EQOBP	EQSLG	EQA	VORP	DEFENSE			
2005	BRI	Rk	18	262	33	17	0	10	37	17	64	2	1	2.8	.283	.350	.485	.180	.212	.254	.318	.203	-29.0	36-3B	-6	20-1B	-1
2006	GRF	Rk	19	294	37	21	1	15	59	34	70	4	4	3.6	.299	.398	.570	.387	.253	.315	.454	.259	6.4	59-1B	-11		
2006	KAN	A	19	52	4	3	0	1	5	5	17	0	0	3.6	.130	.231	.261	-.353	.042	.115	.042	.083	-14.7				
2007	CHA	MLB	20	479	42	22	1	15	53	29	114	2	2	4.0	.223	.275	.375	-.235	.218	.274	.369	.224	-17.3	113-1B	-8		

Breakout: 44% Improve: 60% Collapse: 26% Attrition: 7%   Comparables: Dusty Gomon, Brandon Sing, Josh Gray, Ryan Darr

After flopping in extended spring training, Carter returned to Rookie-ball and recovered to have a nice season, flashing power potential that shines through the harsh translations for league and altitude effects. It will be power that pushes Carter to the big leagues; his swing is too long to provide for much contact hitting ability, and he isn't much of an athlete. He'll get his chances in a thin system. His short-term goal will be reaching Winston-Salem by year's end.

Alex Cintron — SS/2B — Bats: S — Throws: R — Height: 6' 1" — Weight: 205 — Born: December 17, 1978 — Age: 28

YEAR	TEAM	LVL	AGE	PA	R	2B	3B	HR	RBI	BB	SO	SB	CS	SPEED	AVG	OBP	SLG	MLVR	EQAVG	EQOBP	EQSLG	EQA	VORP	DEFENSE			
2004	ARI	MLB	25	613	56	31	7	4	49	31	59	3	3	5.1	.262	.301	.363	-.150	.253	.293	.351	.226	-1.1	119-SS	4	16-2B	-2
2005	ARI	MLB	26	348	36	19	2	8	48	12	33	1	2	4.5	.273	.298	.415	-.051	.267	.296	.416	.242	4.2	30-SS	-2	21-3B	-1
2006	CHA	MLB	27	304	35	10	3	5	41	10	35	10	3	6.2	.285	.310	.392	-.118	.281	.314	.396	.248	4.6	36-SS	-1	23-2B	-3
2007	CHA	MLB	28	363	37	13	2	5	33	17	40	6	3	5.3	.252	.291	.352	-.220	.247	.289	.346	.226	-4.9	87-SS	0		

Breakout: 8% Improve: 24% Collapse: 45% Attrition: 21%   Comparables: Garry Templeton, Marlon Anderson, Tony Kubek, Alex Cora

Cintron Añejo? Picked up for the low, low price of Jeff Bajenaru like some knock-off brand tequila at the discount liquor warehouse, Cintron has emerged as a good utility player who hints at the promise of something more. PECOTA reminds us that he's played in some very good hitters' parks, and that he's now four years removed from the .317/.359/.489 line of his age-24 season, but he's flashed every skill except plate discipline at different times in his career. In another life, he'd be the starting shortstop for a second-division club.

Joe Crede — 3B — Bats: R — Throws: R — Height: 6' 2" — Weight: 220 — Born: April 26, 1978 — Age: 29

YEAR	TEAM	LVL	AGE	PA	R	2B	3B	HR	RBI	BB	SO	SB	CS	SPEED	AVG	OBP	SLG	MLVR	EQAVG	EQOBP	EQSLG	EQA	VORP	DEFENSE	
2004	CHA	MLB	26	543	67	25	0	21	69	34	81	1	2	3.8	.239	.299	.418	-.135	.236	.299	.418	.245	-6.8	138-3B	-5
2005	CHA	MLB	27	471	54	21	0	22	62	25	66	1	1	3.3	.252	.303	.454	-.022	.251	.311	.462	.262	7.8	123-3B	9
2006	CHA	MLB	28	586	76	31	0	30	94	28	58	0	2	3.1	.283	.323	.506	.067	.277	.323	.506	.276	20.2	141-3B	23
2007	CHA	MLB	29	549	65	27	1	25	85	33	69	0	1	3.9	.267	.317	.475	.004	.261	.316	.467	.270	14.4	129-3B	4

Breakout: 33% Improve: 59% Collapse: 15% Attrition: 9%   Comparables: Charlie Hayes, Mike Lowell, Ed Sprague, Tim Wallach

This winter's trade talk about Joe Crede was a little bit perplexing—the third baseman won't hit the free agent market until after the 2008 season—but this is how an organization that prides itself on cost certainty reacts to a bubble economy. Indeed, a trade makes a certain amount of sense. Though he's a fine two-way player and perhaps the most popular Sock after Paul Konerko, Crede has exactly the sort of skill set—heavy on Cell-powered triple-crown stats but light on walk rate and baserunning value—that is likely to be overvalued by the market. On the other hand, third basemen tend to peak a bit late, his defense is as good as advertised, and Crede has found an aggressive plate approach that really works for him; 19 of his 30 home runs came on one of the first two pitches of an at-bat. Crede should remain a blue-chip commodity at the trade deadline; whether he's in Chicago on August 1 could be the bellwether for the sort of season that the White Sox are having.

Aaron Cunningham   OF   Bats: R   Throws: R   Height: 5′ 11″   Weight: 195   Born: April 24, 1986   Age: 21

YEAR	TEAM	LVL	AGE	PA	R	2B	3B	HR	RBI	BB	SO	SB	CS	SPEED	AVG	OBP	SLG	MLVR	EQAVG	EQOBP	EQSLG	EQA	VORP	DEFENSE			
2005	BRI	Rk	19	255	41	10	2	5	25	16	45	6	5	4.6	.315	.392	.446	.220	.256	.301	.324	.223	-25.8	36-RF	-4	14-LF	-2
2006	KAN	A	20	402	58	26	3	11	41	34	72	19	10	5.3	.305	.386	.496	.285	.280	.334	.452	.268	7.8	79-LF	-6		
2007	CHA	MLB	21	485	56	25	2	11	51	27	91	11	6	5.2	.263	.312	.405	-.101	.258	.311	.399	.250	-4.3	115-LF	-5		

Breakout: 27%   Improve: 52%   Collapse: 27%   Attrition: 9%   Comparables: Laynce Nix, Lastings Milledge, Cody Ross, Neesan Zieour

In an organization whose better prospects are a bit overrated, Cunningham is something of a sleeper; any player who posts a .254 EqA as a 20 year old has a good chance of becoming a major league regular. Still, Cunningham has a long way to go, and while scouts praise his hitting mechanics, he is both undersized and underathletic. His upside involves some combination of power and contact hitting.

Jermaine Dye   RF   Bats: R   Throws: R   Height: 6′ 5″   Weight: 235   Born: January 28, 1974   Age: 33

YEAR	TEAM	LVL	AGE	PA	R	2B	3B	HR	RBI	BB	SO	SB	CS	SPEED	AVG	OBP	SLG	MLVR	EQAVG	EQOBP	EQSLG	EQA	VORP	DEFENSE	
2004	OAK	MLB	30	590	87	29	4	23	80	49	128	4	2	5.0	.265	.329	.464	.004	.263	.332	.466	.272	12.0	131-RF	-1
2005	CHA	MLB	31	579	74	29	2	31	86	39	99	11	4	4.9	.274	.333	.512	.128	.273	.342	.520	.287	27.7	136-RF	-1
2006	CHA	MLB	32	611	103	27	3	44	120	59	118	7	3	4.8	.315	.385	.622	.367	.308	.385	.622	.325	64.6	139-RF	9
2007	CHA	MLB	33	583	88	27	2	31	96	52	115	7	3	4.8	.285	.354	.524	.145	.279	.352	.515	.298	25.2	137-RF	0

Breakout: 4%   Improve: 35%   Collapse: 28%   Attrition: 7%   Comparables: Dave Henderson, Cliff Floyd, Dave Winfield, Jim Rice

You might assume that Dye was lighting-fast before his leg injury in 2001 ALDS, but that wasn't the case. While always a competent baserunner, he stole just 16 bags over his first six big league seasons, and had just 11 triples. What is true, however, is that Dye is a fine athlete who keeps himself in suburb physical condition. That helps to explain not only his recovery from the injury, but also the late peak he's experienced. Dye is also a good defensive player, making up for diminishing lateral range with hustle, good route selection, and a plus arm. Okay, we have a little bit of a man-crush on Jermaine Dye. The White Sox are getting a great deal on his $6.75 million option for 2007, even if PECOTA is right that his future output will look more like 2005 than 2006.

Josh Fields   3B   Bats: R   Throws: R   Height: 6′ 1″   Weight: 215   Born: December 14, 1982   Age: 24

YEAR	TEAM	LVL	AGE	PA	R	2B	3B	HR	RBI	BB	SO	SB	CS	SPEED	AVG	OBP	SLG	MLVR	EQAVG	EQOBP	EQSLG	EQA	VORP	DEFENSE	
2004	WNS	A+	21	279	36	12	4	7	39	18	74	0	0	5.1	.285	.333	.445	.081	.253	.294	.398	.237	1.8	55-3B	-1
2005	BIR	AA	22	560	76	27	0	16	79	55	142	7	6	4.0	.252	.341	.409	.036	.240	.312	.397	.247	6.9	127-3B	-6
2006	CHR	AAA	23	526	85	32	4	19	70	54	136	28	5	6.8	.305	.379	.515	.279	.300	.372	.524	.304	55.7	113-3B	-15
2006	CHA	MLB	23	25	4	2	0	1	2	5	8	0	0	5.4	.150	.320	.400	-.168	.150	.320	.350	.241	-0.4		
2007	CHA	MLB	24	528	70	26	2	21	68	45	143	11	5	5.5	.260	.329	.460	-.002	.255	.327	.452	.272	13.9	124-3B	-5

Breakout: 18%   Improve: 41%   Collapse: 23%   Attrition: 12%   Comparables: David Kelton, Bobby Crosby, Michael Coleman, Nick Esasky

Put him on the big league stage right now, and Fields probably provides 85 percent of Joe Crede's bat and 75 percent of his defense. That isn't a bad thing, but the White Sox remain hopeful that there's another leap forward coming, as Fields's football background means that he's relatively unrefined for a player of his age. There are rumors that Fields will be in the left field mix this season, but he's more likely to be returned to Charlotte, where he can work on his defense while the White Sox figure out to do with Crede. At the very least, Fields should turn out better than Josh Booty.

Ross Gload   **1B**   **Bats: L**   **Throws: L**   Height: 6' 1"   Weight: 190   Born: April 5, 1976   Age: 31

YEAR	TEAM	LVL	AGE	PA	R	2B	3B	HR	RBI	BB	SO	SB	CS	SPEED	AVG	OBP	SLG	MLVR	EQAVG	EQOBP	EQSLG	EQA	VORP	DEFENSE			
2004	CHA	MLB	28	260	28	16	0	7	44	20	37	0	3	2.5	.321	.375	.479	.141	.315	.375	.478	.288	11.8	32-1B	-3	20-RF	-2
2005	CHR	AAA	29	263	45	22	1	15	45	22	37	0	1	3.3	.364	.416	.657	.549	.325	.375	.571	.311	27.2	37-1B	3		
2005	CHA	MLB	29	44	2	2	0	0	5	2	9	0	0	3.5	.167	.205	.214	-.564	.098	.159	.122	.116	-5.2				
2006	CHA	MLB	30	167	22	8	2	3	18	6	15	6	0	6.5	.327	.354	.462	.099	.318	.354	.448	.282	8.6	28-1B	1		
2007	KCA	MLB	31	277	36	16	1	7	37	18	33	3	1	4.4	.305	.353	.456	.071	.295	.348	.456	.283	9.4	68-1B	0		

Breakout: 12% Improve: 37% Collapse: 33% Attrition: 24%   *Comparables: Jim Holt, Glenn Adams, Scott Livingstone, Dane Iorg*

Gload has always been something of a square peg. Over the course of his brief major league career, he's posted a 958 OPS as a first baseman, but a 635 OPS at all other positions. That makes enough sense, considering that Gload has never looked comfortable in the outfield, and that coming off the bench as a pinch-hitter is hard for just about anyone. A regular role as the platoon first baseman for his new employer in Kansas City might serve him well; whether it would serve the Royals as well remains to be seen.

Tadahito Iguchi   **2B**   **Bats: R**   **Throws: R**   Height: 5' 10"   Weight: 200   Born: November 30, 1999   Age: 32

YEAR	TEAM	LVL	AGE	PA	R	2B	3B	HR	RBI	BB	SO	SB	CS	SPEED	AVG	OBP	SLG	MLVR	EQAVG	EQOBP	EQSLG	EQA	VORP	DEFENSE	
2004	FKU	JP	29	566	96	34	2	24	89	47	90	18	0	6.2	.333	.399	.549	.310	.331	.390	.477	.297	51.0		
2005	CHA	MLB	30	581	74	25	6	15	71	47	114	15	5	5.8	.278	.342	.438	.034	.277	.350	.450	.277	23.8	129-2B	-14
2006	CHA	MLB	31	627	97	24	0	18	67	59	110	11	5	5.7	.281	.352	.422	-.001	.274	.354	.422	.269	25.5	135-2B	-12
2007	CHA	MLB	32	578	83	25	3	15	62	52	100	11	4	5.8	.287	.356	.435	.032	.281	.354	.428	.278	24.3	135-2B	-10

Breakout: 16% Improve: 43% Collapse: 26% Attrition: 9%   *Comparables: Bobby Avila, Chuck Knoblauch, Phil Garner, Barry Larkin*

Among the 18 major league players to record at least 1,000 defensive innings at second base last season, Iguchi was involved in the fewest double plays by far, turning the deuce just .56 times per 9 innings (Adam Kennedy was the next-lowest at .60, while Mark Grudzielanek led the league at .87). The White Sox's pitching staff generates its fair share of groundballs, and Iguchi has good defensive partners in Joe Crede and Juan Uribe, so this really does point toward Iguchi as the source of the sort of missed opportunities that might cost the White Sox a win or two over the course of the season. That's the bad, but the good is everything else. Iguchi has a robust and underrated offensive skill set that can be useful virtually anywhere in the batting order and helps to compensate for his defensive limitations.

Paul Konerko   **1B**   **Bats: R**   **Throws: R**   Height: 6' 2"   Weight: 220   Born: March 5, 1976   Age: 31

YEAR	TEAM	LVL	AGE	PA	R	2B	3B	HR	RBI	BB	SO	SB	CS	SPEED	AVG	OBP	SLG	MLVR	EQAVG	EQOBP	EQSLG	EQA	VORP	DEFENSE	
2004	CHA	MLB	28	643	84	22	0	41	117	69	107	1	0	2.9	.277	.359	.535	.166	.272	.359	.531	.297	38.0	126-1B	11
2005	CHA	MLB	29	664	98	24	0	40	100	81	109	0	0	3.1	.283	.375	.534	.232	.281	.383	.542	.309	46.1	140-1B	15
2006	CHA	MLB	30	643	97	30	0	35	113	60	104	1	0	3.4	.313	.381	.551	.259	.304	.379	.546	.310	47.7	132-1B	5
2007	CHA	MLB	31	614	87	27	1	33	102	66	101	1	0	3.7	.283	.364	.518	.152	.277	.362	.510	.301	28.0	144-1B	5

Breakout: 9% Improve: 35% Collapse: 35% Attrition: 6%   *Comparables: Jeff Conine, Gil Hodges, Tino Martinez, Orlando Cepeda*

One year and another fine season later, the five-year, $60-million deal the White Sox signed Konerko to last winter looks more like an asset than a liability. That's Gary Matthews Jr. money, after all, and Konerko can not only turn on a fastball with the best of them, he's improved his positioning and throw-scooping abilities enough to make himself at least an average defensive first baseman. Still, the Tino Martinez comparison that PECOTA cites works on a number of levels, and it's worth noting that Martinez's production declined markedly as of his age-31 season.

Pedro Lopez   **SS/2B**   **Bats: R**   **Throws: R**   Height: 6' 1"   Weight: 160   Born: April 28, 1984   Age: 23

YEAR	TEAM	LVL	AGE	PA	R	2B	3B	HR	RBI	BB	SO	SB	CS	SPEED	AVG	OBP	SLG	MLVR	EQAVG	EQOBP	EQSLG	EQA	VORP	DEFENSE			
2004	WNS	A+	20	478	62	13	0	4	35	23	35	12	9	5.1	.292	.331	.350	-.046	.245	.279	.299	.208	-17.1	99-SS	8		
2005	BIR	AA	21	271	26	7	1	3	24	13	29	0	2	3.0	.238	.287	.314	-.195	.220	.259	.288	.198	-14.3	68-SS	6		
2005	CHR	AAA	21	208	14	6	0	3	17	7	24	1	1	2.9	.202	.236	.282	-.417	.178	.213	.241	.172	-20.3	44-SS	-1	10-2B	0
2006	BIR	AA	22	284	30	15	2	5	34	16	32	3	6	4.5	.322	.358	.453	.253	.327	.358	.483	.283	27.7	62-SS	0		
2006	CHR	AAA	22	228	32	12	0	5	24	11	28	4	0	5.4	.274	.320	.404	.021	.256	.302	.393	.243	1.7	36-2B	-3	19-SS	2
2007	CHA	MLB	23	483	49	20	1	7	45	22	51	4	3	4.9	.271	.309	.372	-.147	.266	.307	.366	.239	3.8	114-SS	1		

Breakout: 40% Improve: 64% Collapse: 19% Attrition: 8%   *Comparables: Luis Ordaz, Martin Prado, Jhonny Perez, Dan Cey*

Pedro Lopez is dangerous. He almost certainly has the fielding chops and just enough stick to hang around as a plus utility infielder, but the risk is that he'll hit .310 over some 200-at-bat sample and some organization will decide he's their Shortstop of the Future. The Cubs, faced with a parallel situation a year ago, talked Ronny Cedeño up as though he was the next Barry Larkin, then panicked and dealt for Cesar Izturis. Happily, the White Sox have historically been more sensible than this, and are more likely to deploy Lopez correctly.

Rob Mackowiak   **UT**   **Bats: L**   **Throws: R**   Height: 6' 0"   Weight: 200   Born: June 20, 1976   Age: 31

YEAR	TEAM	LVL	AGE	PA	R	2B	3B	HR	RBI	BB	SO	SB	CS	SPEED	AVG	OBP	SLG	MLVR	EQAVG	EQOBP	EQSLG	EQA	VORP	DEFENSE			
2004	PIT	MLB	28	555	65	22	6	17	75	50	114	13	4	6.5	.246	.319	.420	-.021	.244	.317	.422	.257	5.9	51-3B	-1	51-RF	-4
2005	PIT	MLB	29	512	57	21	3	9	58	43	100	8	4	5.7	.272	.337	.389	-.007	.273	.339	.394	.256	8.7	50-3B	5	32-CF	-4
2006	CHA	MLB	30	290	31	12	1	5	23	28	59	5	2	5.4	.290	.365	.404	.005	.282	.365	.405	.271	10.0	49-CF	-3	11-RF	0
2007	CHA	MLB	31	339	44	14	2	8	35	30	66	6	3	6.1	.260	.328	.403	-.078	.255	.327	.396	.258	2.4	82-CF	-1		

Breakout: 10%   Improve: 35%   Collapse: 30%   Attrition: 24%   Comparables: Wayne Kirby, Russ Snyder, Pat Sheridan, Todd Hollandsworth

Mackowiak deserves praise for his extraordinarily consistent performances despite constant shifts in his position and role. Nevertheless, with his defense becoming more problematic, Mackowiak's opportunities for playing time are more a barometer for his team's performance than him own. If Rob Mackowiak gets 150 at-bats, all went according to plan. If gets 450 at-bats, something went horribly wrong. Last year, Mackowiak finished in the bottom half of that range with 255 ABs; accordingly, the White Sox's offense had a year that met, but did not exceed expectations.

Jerry Owens   **CF**   **Bats: L**   **Throws: L**   Height: 6' 3"   Weight: 195   Born: February 16, 1981   Age: 26

YEAR	TEAM	LVL	AGE	PA	R	2B	3B	HR	RBI	BB	SO	SB	CS	SPEED	AVG	OBP	SLG	MLVR	EQAVG	EQOBP	EQSLG	EQA	VORP	DEFENSE			
2004	SAV	A	23	470	69	17	2	1	37	46	59	30	13	6.3	.292	.365	.349	.030	.257	.309	.299	.221	-29.1	47-LF	-6	17-CF	-4
2005	BIR	AA	24	587	99	21	6	2	52	52	72	38	20	7.3	.331	.393	.406	.178	.309	.358	.379	.260	5.3	116-LF	3		
2006	CHR	AAA	25	493	75	15	5	4	48	45	61	40	12	7.9	.262	.330	.346	-.046	.253	.318	.343	.242	-5.8	83-CF	-1	26-LF	3
2006	CHA	MLB	25	9	4	1	0	0	0	0	2	1	0	7.4	.333	.333	.444	.074	.333	.333	.444	.283	0.8				
2007	CHA	MLB	26	438	58	16	3	3	29	31	57	25	9	6.8	.269	.322	.347	-.157	.263	.321	.342	.244	-4.8	104-CF	-1		

Breakout: 27%   Improve: 47%   Collapse: 28%   Attrition: 18%   Comparables: Kerry Robinson, Peter Bergeron, Rich Thompson, Tyrell Godwin

Owens has always been a slow starter, but last year his bat never did come around. That should kill any talk of his becoming a big league regular. The White Sox might use him to make some hollow threats about Brian Anderson's job security, but if Anderson can't improve his offense, the center field job will go to Ryan Sweeney or Luis Terrero before it goes to Owens. Owens probably has a future as a fifth outfielder, but his defense is surprisingly uninspired for a player with his wheels.

Pablo Ozuna   **UT**   **Bats: R**   **Throws: R**   Height: 5' 11"   Weight: 195   Born: August 25, 1974   Age: 32

YEAR	TEAM	LVL	AGE	PA	R	2B	3B	HR	RBI	BB	SO	SB	CS	SPEED	AVG	OBP	SLG	MLVR	EQAVG	EQOBP	EQSLG	EQA	VORP	DEFENSE			
2004	SWB	AAA	29	516	77	27	3	6	76	22	43	31	12	7.4	.307	.343	.415	.032	.275	.308	.360	.239	0.7	57-2B	0	56-SS	4
2005	CHA	MLB	30	217	27	7	2	0	11	7	26	14	7	7.3	.276	.313	.330	-.162	.280	.324	.335	.235	-2.8	29-3B	2	11-SS	1
2006	CHA	MLB	31	203	25	12	2	2	17	7	16	6	6	6.1	.328	.365	.444	.097	.326	.370	.444	.271	6.9	30-LF	-4		
2007	CHA	MLB	32	276	32	11	1	2	21	10	25	8	4	6.1	.278	.312	.349	-.167	.272	.311	.343	.236	-3.5	68-LF	-1		

Breakout: 3%   Improve: 17%   Collapse: 62%   Attrition: 30%   Comparables: Eric Owens, Craig Shipley, Tommy Davis, Henry Cotto

A true utility player, Ozuna's out-of-character offensive numbers in 2006 led Ozzie Guillen to misuse him as Scott Podsednik's platoon partner in left. Re-signed for 2007, Ozuna has his fans within the organization, but if the White Sox can identify a more reliable solution for right-handed pop off the bench, he could be squeezed by mid-season.

A. J. Pierzynski   **C**   **Bats: L**   **Throws: R**   Height: 6' 3"   Weight: 235   Born: December 30, 1976   Age: 30

YEAR	TEAM	LVL	AGE	PA	R	2B	3B	HR	RBI	BB	SO	SB	CS	SPEED	AVG	OBP	SLG	MLVR	EQAVG	EQOBP	EQSLG	EQA	VORP	DEFENSE	
2004	SFN	MLB	27	510	45	28	2	11	77	19	27	0	1	3.2	.272	.319	.410	-.043	.271	.316	.412	.250	9.1	104-C	5
2005	CHA	MLB	28	497	61	21	0	18	56	23	68	0	2	3.7	.257	.308	.420	-.055	.256	.315	.425	.252	12.1	123-C	5
2006	CHA	MLB	29	543	65	24	0	16	64	22	72	1	0	4.2	.295	.333	.436	-.005	.288	.332	.437	.263	18.3	126-C	-5
2007	CHA	MLB	30	496	54	22	1	14	62	23	59	1	1	4.0	.274	.315	.414	-.076	.268	.314	.407	.253	8.3	117-C	-3

Breakout: 16%   Improve: 55%   Collapse: 20%   Attrition: 13%   Comparables: Terry Kennedy, John Bateman, Bill Fahey, Brian Johnson

(continued next page)

A. J. Pierzynski *(continued)*

Pierzynski is best known for his Zelig-like propensity to find himself in situations where he just doesn't belong, such as on the receiving end of Michael Barrett's right hook, or on Joe Cowley's MVP ballot. He's perhaps more remarkable, though, for an extremely unusual statistical profile. Most players who put the ball in play as often as Pierzynski tend to be Juan Pierre types who run pretty well. Pierzynski, on the other hand, runs like Juan Berenguer... after a big meal. He remains a valuable asset to the White Sox, but may need to work deeper into the count as he ages, as his profile is not very well hedged against any decline in bat speed.

Scott Podsednik		OF			Bats: L		Throws: L			Height: 6′ 1″		Weight: 190		Born: March 18, 1976					Age: 31			
YEAR	TEAM	LVL	AGE	PA	R	2B	3B	HR	RBI	BB	SO	SB	CS	SPEED	AVG	OBP	SLG	MLVR	EQAVG	EQOBP	EQSLG	EQA	VORP	DEFENSE
2004	MIL	MLB	28	712	85	27	7	12	39	58	105	70	13	7.7	.244	.313	.364	-.106	.241	.310	.364	.250	10.4	150-CF -2
2005	CHA	MLB	29	568	80	28	1	0	25	47	75	59	23	7.2	.290	.351	.349	-.058	.293	.363	.355	.262	5.8	117-LF 12
2006	CHA	MLB	30	591	86	27	6	3	45	54	95	40	19	7.4	.262	.331	.354	-.150	.260	.337	.357	.248	-9.9	122-LF -4
2007	CHA	MLB	31	557	80	24	5	6	41	47	78	42	14	7.4	.260	.326	.365	-.132	.255	.324	.359	.253	-5.1	131-LF 0

Breakout: 7% Improve: 24% Collapse: 34% Attrition: 12% Comparables: Tom Goodwin, Dave Roberts, Pat Kelly, Alex Cole

A year ago, we fretted about the White Sox getting locked into Podsednik on the basis of his feel-good role on the 2005 championship team. Speed-only players don't tend to survive long into their thirties, and even Podsednikñs speed is in question given his on-again, off-again relationship with his hamstrings. Thankfully, it appears that those sort of self-destructive commitments are something the White Sox will leave for the team that plays on the other side of town. Podsednik had been reduced to a platoon player and number-eight hitter by September of last year, and while he might or might not be the left fielder on Opening Day, the White Sox no longer view him as anything more than a stopgap.

Casey Rogowski		1B			Bats: L		Throws: L			Height: 6′ 3″		Weight: 230		Born: May 1, 1981					Age: 26				
YEAR	TEAM	LVL	AGE	PA	R	2B	3B	HR	RBI	BB	SO	SB	CS	SPEED	AVG	OBP	SLG	MLVR	EQAVG	EQOBP	EQSLG	EQA	VORP	DEFENSE
2004	WNS	A+	23	566	88	28	2	18	90	91	94	16	9	5.3	.286	.401	.471	.211	.248	.343	.413	.264	5.5	107-1B 1 13-LF 0
2005	BIR	AA	24	583	83	37	6	9	78	58	111	20	12	6.1	.293	.374	.444	.169	.279	.344	.426	.266	12.5	129-1B -4
2006	CHR	AAA	25	525	69	32	2	13	76	53	97	26	9	6.0	.272	.351	.436	.109	.265	.340	.440	.270	11.4	124-1B 3
2007	CHA	MLB	26	465	62	24	2	14	56	43	91	12	5	5.1	.261	.333	.429	-.034	.256	.332	.422	.268	2.4	110-1B 2

Breakout: 21% Improve: 46% Collapse: 23% Attrition: 12% Comparables: Corey Koskie, Todd Self, Kevin Burns, Jason Grabowski

Rogowski hit just enough at Charlotte to keep himself from being voted off the island, but if a six-foot-three, 230-pound guy can't hit more than 13 home runs while playing half his games at Knights Stadium, he'll probably never have the power bat to be more than bench filler. On the other hand, he could be the new Ross Gload, which is why Kenny Williams will keep Dayton Moore's cell-phone number in his Friends & Family plan.

John Shelby		2B			Bats: R		Throws: R			Height: 5′ 10″		Weight: 185		Born: August 6, 1985					Age: 21				
YEAR	TEAM	LVL	AGE	PA	R	2B	3B	HR	RBI	BB	SO	SB	CS	SPEED	AVG	OBP	SLG	MLVR	EQAVG	EQOBP	EQSLG	EQA	VORP	DEFENSE
2006	GRF	Rk	20	279	37	12	3	8	36	18	55	8	4	4.8	.272	.332	.440	.086	.232	.264	.354	.216	-16.3	42-2B 2 23-SS -3
2007	CHA	MLB	21	416	34	18	2	8	40	15	82	5	3	4.6	.230	.263	.344	-.295	.225	.262	.338	.209	-12.2	99-2B 2

Breakout: 38% Improve: 52% Collapse: 26% Attrition: 13% Comparables: German Duran, Dan Uggla, Josh Arteaga, Amaury Pena

Despite being the son of a big leaguer, Shelby hasn't received many favors. Undrafted out of high school, he had to settle for a second-tier NCAA program in Kentucky, before finally being claimed in the sixth round of the 2006 draft. How much you believe in his prospect status depends on how much you believe in bloodlines. Shelby has no one skill that projects as a major league plus, but the hope is that he can develop into a well-rounded player along the lines of Josh Barfield. Otherwise, he may need to take more balls at shortstop to prepare himself for life as a utility player.

Ryan Sweeney		OF			Bats: L		Throws: L			Height: 6′ 4″		Weight: 200		Born: February 20, 1985					Age: 22				
YEAR	TEAM	LVL	AGE	PA	R	2B	3B	HR	RBI	BB	SO	SB	CS	SPEED	AVG	OBP	SLG	MLVR	EQAVG	EQOBP	EQSLG	EQA	VORP	DEFENSE
2004	WNS	A+	19	567	71	22	3	7	66	40	65	8	6	4.9	.284	.342	.379	.004	.249	.296	.340	.224	-27.7	124-RF 3
2005	BIR	AA	20	483	64	22	3	1	47	35	53	6	6	4.5	.298	.357	.371	.044	.285	.333	.360	.244	-6.5	107-RF 0
2006	CHR	AAA	21	492	64	25	3	13	70	35	73	7	7	5.1	.296	.350	.452	.147	.288	.341	.459	.270	26.2	57-CF -2 42-RF 0
2006	CHA	MLB	21	35	1	0	0	0	5	0	7	0	0	2.8	.229	.229	.229	-.549	.171	.171	.171	.127	-3.4	
2007	CHA	MLB	22	507	64	26	2	12	58	32	68	5	4	5.2	.284	.332	.427	-.021	.278	.331	.420	.264	6.4	120-RF 1

Breakout: 38% Improve: 71% Collapse: 11% Attrition: 8% Comparables: Alex Romero, Casey Kotchman, Alex Fernandez, Robinson Cano

Perhaps no player creates more dissension in the prospect community than Ryan Sweeney. Many scouts take one look at his picture-perfect swing, his Abercrombie & Fitch-catalog physique, and his tender age for his levels and insist that he's a future stud. Statheads—and a silent minority of scouts—look at his statistical record and see a fourth outfielder. These sorts of debates often rage over pitching prospects or players in the very low minors, but rarely over a corner outfielder who has already hit Triple-A. The wrench in the stathead argument is that Sweeney has actually started to hit. Whether he'll develop the power to work in a corner outfield spot remains to be seen, but the upside is there, and one benefit of Sweeney's athleticism is that he should be able to handle center field, at least early in his career. Even PECOTA has come around on him, citing Nick Markakis as a positive precedent.

Jim Thome DH **Bats: L** **Throws: R** Height: 6' 4" Weight: 245 Born: August 27, 1970 Age: 36

YEAR	TEAM	LVL	AGE	PA	R	2B	3B	HR	RBI	BB	SO	SB	CS	SPEED	AVG	OBP	SLG	MLVR	EQAVG	EQOBP	EQSLG	EQA	VORP	DEFENSE	
2004	PHI	MLB	33	618	97	28	1	42	105	104	144	0	2	3.6	.274	.396	.581	.320	.270	.393	.574	.318	50.6	125-1B	4
2005	PHI	MLB	34	242	26	7	0	7	30	45	59	0	0	3.8	.207	.360	.352	-.059	.203	.360	.354	.260	-1.1	49-1B	3
2006	CHA	MLB	35	610	108	26	0	42	109	107	147	0	0	4.3	.288	.416	.598	.351	.277	.415	.588	.332	62.6		
2007	CHA	MLB	36	478	76	19	1	27	75	77	111	1	1	4.3	.264	.385	.522	.173	.259	.383	.513	.310	26.7	113-DH	

Breakout: 14% Improve: 37% Collapse: 37% Attrition: 28% Comparables: Willie McCovey, Jose Canseco, Cliff Johnson, Frank Thomas

That went well. Thome's numbers speak for themselves, and the Peoria native looked as natural in Chicago as mustard (not ketchup!) on a Vienna Beef hot dog. That said, Thome has one of the more bipolar PECOTA profiles around. Half of his comparables, such as Willie McCovey, remained productive into their forties, while the other half, such as Jose Canseco, got injured one too many times and fell off the face of the earth. Then you have Frank Thomas, who has done a little bit of both. Both Thome and Thomas are as likely to hit 12 home runs this year as they are to hit 40.

Juan Uribe SS **Bats: R** **Throws: R** Height: 6' 0" Weight: 220 Born: July 22, 1979 Age: 28

YEAR	TEAM	LVL	AGE	PA	R	2B	3B	HR	RBI	BB	SO	SB	CS	SPEED	AVG	OBP	SLG	MLVR	EQAVG	EQOBP	EQSLG	EQA	VORP	DEFENSE			
2004	CHA	MLB	24	553	82	31	6	23	74	32	96	9	11	5.6	.283	.327	.506	.064	.281	.328	.507	.273	25.0	72-2B	-1	35-SS	5
2005	CHA	MLB	25	540	58	23	3	16	71	34	77	4	6	4.7	.252	.301	.412	-.093	.250	.309	.422	.250	7.5	142-SS	6		
2006	CHA	MLB	26	495	53	28	2	21	71	13	82	1	1	4.3	.235	.257	.441	-.184	.229	.259	.437	.236	-0.6	126-SS	6		
2007	CHA	MLB	28	550	67	29	2	21	74	30	86	5	3	5.1	.265	.309	.457	-.036	.260	.307	.449	.262	16.8	129-SS	4		

Breakout: 28% Improve: 60% Collapse: 21% Attrition: 13% Comparables: Gary Gaetti, Kevin Elster, Charlie Hayes, Aaron Boone

One has to wonder what Juan Uribe does with his offseasons. Last year, he skipped winter ball and came into the season looking out of shape. This winter, he was implicated in a double homicide in the Dominican Republic, ultimately avoiding prosecution. He hit just .167 last April and appeared to be playing Home Run Derby at the plate all year, hitting 21 dingers while drawing just 13 walks and struggling intermittently with a back injury. On the season, Uribe combined a .257 OBP with a .441 slugging average. A major leaguer had combined an OBP under .260 with a slugging average over .440 in a season of 350 or more plate appearances just once before, in 1983, when Tony Armas did it. Of course, the White Sox are relatively used to this sort of thing—the man Uribe replaced, Jose Valentin, hit .216/.287/.473 in his last season in Chicago. The good news, particularly to those concerned about his conditioning, is that Uribe will have to earn his $5 million team option for 2008 this season. That and his defense, which has been decidedly slump-proof, portend a rebound in 2007.

PITCHERS

Lance Broadway **Bats: R** **Throws: R** Height: 6' 2" Weight: 210 Born: August 20, 1983 Age: 23

YEAR	TEAM	LVL	AGE	W	L	SV	G	GS	IP	H	BB	SO	HR	GB%	BABIP	STUFF	WHIP	ERA	PERA	EQERA	EQH9	EQBB9	EQSO9	EQHR9	VORP	WXRL
2005	WNS	A+	21	1	3	0	11	11	55	68	20	58	4	53.0%	.400	5	1.60	4.58	4.89	5.73	11.6	3.6	5.9	1.0	-0.8	—
2006	BIR	AA	22	8	8	0	25	25	154²	160	40	111	10	48.6%	.316	6	1.30	2.74	4.68	4.08	9.7	2.3	4.5	1.0	26.1	—
2007	CHA	MLB	23	6	9	0	27	21	126	152	42	69	20	50.0%	.310	0	1.54	5.68	5.11	5.23	10.7	2.8	4.6	1.3	2.5	1.10

Breakout: 0% Improve: 21% Collapse: 36% Attrition: 0% Comparables: Beau Hale, Matt Belisle, Brian Bannister, Tony Pena

Don't be fooled by that gaudy ERA in Birmingham; it came in one of the best pitchers' parks in the minor leagues and was accompanied by less-than-impressive strikeout numbers. Broadway should get to the big leagues on the strength of a plus curveball and good mechanics, but he doesn't miss enough bats to project as more than a fourth starter. What chance he has to be more than that probably depends on his developing something with a little sink on it, because hitters are going to tee off on his middling fastball in the Cell. Failing that, he looks like more of an Off-Broadway production.

Mark Buehrle

Bats: L   Throws: L   Height: 6' 2"   Weight: 225   Born: March 23, 1979   Age: 28

YEAR	TEAM	LVL	AGE	W	L	SV	G	GS	IP	H	BB	SO	HR	GB%	BABIP	STUFF	WHIP	ERA	PERA	EQERA	EQH9	EQBB9	EQSO9	EQHR9	VORP	WXRL
2004	CHA	MLB	25	16	10	0	35	35	245¹	257	51	165	33	—	.299	14	1.26	3.89	4.07	4.01	9.1	1.7	5.6	1.0	55.3	5.92
2005	CHA	MLB	26	16	8	0	33	33	236²	240	40	149	20	47.8%	.295	22	1.18	3.12	3.49	3.78	9.3	1.5	5.5	0.7	54.8	5.73
2006	CHA	MLB	27	12	13	0	32	32	204	247	48	98	36	46.0%	.313	-9	1.45	4.99	5.04	4.96	10.2	2.0	4.0	1.4	16.1	2.41
2007	CHA	MLB	28	11	11	0	31	31	192¹	225	43	108	27	47.0%	.306	8	1.39	4.74	4.37	4.36	10.4	1.9	4.8	1.2	24.6	4.00

Breakout: 12% Improve: 50% Collapse: 14% Attrition: 0%   Comparables: Jerry Reuss, Jim Kaat, Jim Abbott, Ken Holtzman

There's no neat capsule summary to explain what happened to Mark Buehrle in 2006. It was part fatigue (including the postseason, Buehrle pitched more than 500 innings between 2004 and 2005), part regression to the mean, and perhaps partly a bit of premature graying for a guy that could never really afford to lose much off his fastball. It might also be part conditioning. Buehrle's paunch wasn't discussed when he was an annual 16-game-winner, but 2006 changed that. The organization expects that Buehrle will undergo a vastly more strenuous offseason regimen this winter. Top comps Jim Kaat and Jerry Reuss resurrected themselves as crafty lefties after down seasons, but the specter of a Jim Abbott-style fade looms.

Jose Contreras

Bats: R   Throws: R   Height: 6' 4"   Weight: 245   Born: December 12, 1971   Age: 35

YEAR	TEAM	LVL	AGE	W	L	SV	G	GS	IP	H	BB	SO	HR	GB%	BABIP	STUFF	WHIP	ERA	PERA	EQERA	EQH9	EQBB9	EQSO9	EQHR9	VORP	WXRL
2004	NYA	MLB	32	8	5	0	18	18	95²	93	42	82	22	—	.265	-7	1.41	5.64	5.73	5.64	8.3	3.5	7.1	1.8	0.0	1.52
2004	CHA	MLB	32	5	4	0	13	13	74²	73	42	68	9	—	.332	19	1.67	5.30	4.45	5.14	8.5	4.6	7.5	0.9	-0.5	0.62
2005	CHA	MLB	33	15	7	0	32	32	204²	177	75	154	23	45.5%	.263	18	1.23	3.61	4.33	3.87	8.1	3.3	6.7	1.0	42.1	5.04
2006	CHA	MLB	34	13	9	0	30	30	196	194	55	134	20	46.2%	.288	18	1.27	4.27	4.04	4.21	8.5	2.4	5.7	0.8	33.1	4.19
2007	CHA	MLB	35	11	11	0	32	29	181	192	63	123	28	46.0%	.290	7	1.41	4.84	4.39	4.45	9.4	2.9	5.7	1.3	20.7	3.50

Breakout: 14% Improve: 48% Collapse: 16% Attrition: 0%   Comparables: Jim Bibby, Dave Burba, Tom Candiotti, Vic Raschi

After finishing 2005 as one of the most dominant right-handers in baseball, Contreras started out 2006 well enough, but even in the early going, he wasn't the same pitcher. His strikeout rate declined from 7.0 K/9 in August and September of 2005 to 4.3 K/9 in April and May 2006. A series of nagging injuries helped to explain the regression to the mean—at various points during the season, Contreras had issues with his triceps, back, hamstrings, hip, and push leg—but those injuries were troubling enough in their own right for a pitcher who looks old enough to remember the Cuban Revolution. Going forward, he'll likely need to rely more on guile than on raw stuff.

Neal Cotts

Bats: L   Throws: L   Height: 6' 1"   Weight: 195   Born: March 25, 1980   Age: 27

YEAR	TEAM	LVL	AGE	W	L	SV	G	GS	IP	H	BB	SO	HR	GB%	BABIP	STUFF	WHIP	ERA	PERA	EQERA	EQH9	EQBB9	EQSO9	EQHR9	VORP	WXRL
2004	CHA	MLB	24	4	4	0	56	1	65¹	61	30	58	13	—	.273	-8	1.39	5.65	5.23	5.51	8.2	3.8	7.4	1.5	2.2	-0.46
2005	CHA	MLB	25	4	0	0	69	0	60¹	38	29	58	1	47.4%	.242	30	1.11	1.94	3.26	2.23	6.1	4.3	8.5	0.1	23.8	2.03
2006	CHA	MLB	26	1	2	1	70	0	54	64	24	43	12	42.9%	.315	-15	1.63	5.17	5.67	4.85	10.2	3.7	6.6	1.8	4.1	0.06
2007	CHN	MLB	27	2	2	3	55	0	52	50	22	44	7	46.0%	.283	2	1.37	4.01	4.28	4.13	8.3	3.2	6.8	1.1	9.7	0.90

Breakout: 26% Improve: 49% Collapse: 20% Attrition: 14%   Comparables: Mike Stanton, Paul Assenmacher, Mike Magnante, Ted Davidson

As home run numbers go, so goes ERA. The dozen jacks hit off of Cotts last year account for nearly the entire decline in his output from 2005, and an ugly reversion to his struggles in 2004. It may have been a case of hitters figuring him out: opponents laid off Cotts's first offering more often in 2006 and were rewarded with a .308/.438/.648 line after getting ahead 1–0, as Cotts was unable to make good use of his slider after falling behind. Adjustments are difficult to make in mere fractions of high leverage innings, but, shipped to the Cubs in a rare cross-town challenge trade, Cotts could run ahead of his projection in the early going before a new league of hitters learns to lay off his early offerings. Not an easy lefty to employ to advantage, Cotts has had a reverse platoon split each of the last three years and joins a pen that already features two veteran lefties.

John Egbert

Bats: L   Throws: R   Height: 6' 3"   Weight: 205   Born: May 12, 1983   Age: 24

YEAR	TEAM	LVL	AGE	W	L	SV	G	GS	IP	H	BB	SO	HR	GB%	BABIP	STUFF	WHIP	ERA	PERA	EQERA	EQH9	EQBB9	EQSO9	EQHR9	VORP	WXRL
2004	GRF	Rk	21	4	1	0	17	9	58²	51	33	52	2	—	.308	-6	1.43	3.37	6.10	4.92	8.4	6.4	3.7	0.8	4.3	—
2005	KAN	A	22	10	5	0	30	24	147	127	48	107	5	56.8%	.286	-3	1.19	3.12	5.17	5.57	9.0	4.0	3.7	0.6	0.5	—
2006	WNS	A+	23	9	8	0	25	25	140	131	46	120	2	58.3%	.315	20	1.26	2.96	3.73	4.43	9.1	3.4	5.0	0.3	17.9	—
2006	BIR	AA	23	0	2	0	4	4	21¹	17	8	24	0	50.0%	.309	21	1.18	0.85	3.16	2.57	7.7	3.4	6.9	0.4	7.1	—
2007	CHA	MLB	24	6	8	0	26	20	116	130	58	65	15	54.0%	.300	-4	1.62	5.66	5.02	5.29	9.9	4.1	4.7	1.1	1.5	1.00

Breakout: 5% Improve: 28% Collapse: 30% Attrition: 1%   Comparables: Zach Day, Nate Bump, Brian Bannister, Tom Mastny

Egbert has a few things to recommend him. He's a big guy who keeps hitters off-balance with his changeup and does an excellent job of keeping the ball on the ground. Still, the combination of his off-speed repertoire and mediocre walk rate suggests a pitcher who is working around batters rather than working at them, and that could mean trouble as he faces more advanced hitters. Egbert hasn't been young for his levels, so it might be worth the Sox forcing the issue and getting him to Charlotte by June.

Freddy Garcia Bats: R Throws: R

Height: 6' 4"   Weight: 250   Born: June 10, 1976   Age: 31

YEAR	TEAM	LVL	AGE	W	L	SV	G	GS	IP	H	BB	SO	HR	GB%	BABIP	STUFF	WHIP	ERA	PERA	EQERA	EQH9	EQBB9	EQSO9	EQHR9	VORP	WXRL
2004	SEA	MLB	28	4	7	0	15	15	107	96	32	82	8	—	.278	29	1.20	3.20	3.49	3.29	8.0	2.5	6.4	0.6	33.9	3.61
2004	CHA	MLB	28	9	4	0	16	16	103	96	32	102	14	—	.300	27	1.24	4.46	3.84	4.19	8.2	2.5	8.3	1.0	20.4	2.30
2005	CHA	MLB	29	14	8	0	33	33	228	225	60	146	26	50.4%	.285	14	1.25	3.87	4.10	3.97	9.1	2.4	5.6	0.9	45.7	5.07
2006	CHA	MLB	30	17	9	0	33	33	216¹	228	48	135	32	42.1%	.285	7	1.28	4.54	4.42	4.37	8.9	1.9	5.2	1.2	32.3	3.71
2007	PHI	MLB	31	12	11	0	31	31	198	204	53	142	27	47.0%	.290	13	1.30	4.30	4.40	4.25	9.0	2.1	5.8	1.1	31.5	4.70

Breakout: 11% Improve: 40% Collapse: 18% Attrition: 0%   Comparables: Chris Bosio, Jim Clancy, Turk Farrell, Aaron Sele

It's hard to understand why Garcia gets pigeonholed as an underachiever. He's made at least 31 starts in all but one of his eight big league seasons, has never had an ERA materially worse than league average, and has won 62 percent of his lifetime decisions. Owed $10 million in 2007, the last year of his current contract, he projects to provide a performance comparable to those of Jason Schmidt and Barry Zito at a relative discount. Whether the White Sox were right to move him remains to be seen, but this was clearly a good buy for the Phillies. There's been some grumbling about Garcia's declining strikeout rate, but he's always been a guy that mixed different pitches and approaches; we see no red flags in the near term.

Jon Garland Bats: R Throws: R

Height: 6' 6"   Weight: 215   Born: September 27, 1979 Age: 27

YEAR	TEAM	LVL	AGE	W	L	SV	G	GS	IP	H	BB	SO	HR	GB%	BABIP	STUFF	WHIP	ERA	PERA	EQERA	EQH9	EQBB9	EQSO9	EQHR9	VORP	WXRL
2004	CHA	MLB	24	12	11	0	34	33	217	223	76	113	34	—	.280	-5	1.40	4.89	5.03	4.76	8.9	2.8	4.4	1.2	23.4	2.90
2005	CHA	MLB	25	18	10	0	32	32	221	212	47	115	26	47.6%	.270	8	1.17	3.50	4.33	3.82	8.9	1.9	4.6	1.0	50.7	6.00
2006	CHA	MLB	26	18	7	0	33	32	211¹	247	41	112	26	43.5%	.315	7	1.36	4.51	4.19	4.34	9.9	1.6	4.4	1.0	32.4	3.90
2007	CHA	MLB	27	12	11	0	31	31	195¹	225	50	106	29	47.0%	.299	6	1.41	4.74	4.46	4.34	10.2	2.1	4.6	1.2	25.7	4.10

Breakout: 12% Improve: 50% Collapse: 9%   Attrition: 0%   Comparables: Jeff Weaver, Brad Penny, Larry Dierker, Rick Wise

Ignore the fluctuating ERAs and focus on the peripheral stats. You'll see that Jon Garland has transitioned from a power approach that wasn't really suited to his repertoire to a command, control, and speed-changing strategy, the upshot being that he's trimmed a walk per game off of his ledger without any tradeoff in his strikeout rate. If anything, Garland has become too willing to challenge hitters when he has an edge: hitters slugged just as well against him following first-pitch strikes (.448) as first-pitch balls (.446). It would be fun to see what he could do with a hammer curve or a splitter, but the greater theme here is that this is a pitcher who has learned to pitch to his strengths.

Charlie Haeger Bats: R Throws: R

Height: 6' 1"   Weight: 200   Born: September 19, 1983 Age: 23

YEAR	TEAM	LVL	AGE	W	L	SV	G	GS	IP	H	BB	SO	HR	GB%	BABIP	STUFF	WHIP	ERA	PERA	EQERA	EQH9	EQBB9	EQSO9	EQHR9	VORP	WXRL
2004	KAN	A	20	1	3	0	5	5	31¹	31	12	21	0	—	.307	1	1.37	2.01	4.45	5.52	9.6	4.1	3.5	0.3	0.3	—
2004	BRI	Rk	20	1	6	0	10	10	57¹	70	22	23	6	—	.315	-44	1.61	5.03	9.06	8.94	12.6	5.1	1.7	2.5	-20.2	—
2005	WNS	A+	21	8	2	0	14	13	81²	82	40	64	3	53.2%	.329	11	1.49	3.19	4.82	4.15	8.9	4.7	4.4	0.5	13.3	—
2005	BIR	AA	21	6	3	0	13	13	85²	84	45	48	1	51.1%	.307	11	1.51	3.78	4.56	5.38	8.3	4.7	3.5	0.2	2.1	—
2006	CHR	AAA	22	14	6	0	26	25	170²	143	78	130	9	47.0%	.279	14	1.30	3.07	4.87	4.65	8.5	4.4	5.4	0.7	17.6	—
2006	CHA	MLB	22	1	1	1	7	1	18¹	12	13	19	0	46.8%	.255	19	1.36	3.44	3.60	4.34	5.8	5.8	8.7	0.0	2.7	0.00
2007	CHA	MLB	23	5	8	0	31	18	111¹	127	62	70	18	49.0%	.305	-6	1.70	6.10	5.49	5.63	10.1	4.6	5.3	1.3	-3.4	0.40

Breakout: 7% Improve: 30% Collapse: 28% Attrition: 1%   Comparables: Juan Rincon, Jose Garcia, Mike Moore, Pedro Liriano

Although there is no official list of knuckleball pitchers, you probably have to go back to Charlie Hough in 1970 to find a true knuckleballer who made his major league debut at a younger age than Charlie Haeger. Hough was 22 years and 219 days old when he pitched in his first game for the Dodgers; Haeger was 22 years and 233 days old when he made a surprise start against the Angels in May. Hough is now mentoring Haeger, though the apprentice might do just as well to study tape of Tim Wakefield. When he's on, Wakefield will vary the speed of his knuckler—from about 60 MPH to 69 MPH, the slower version having correspondingly more break—to the point where he's almost throwing two different pitches. When we watched him, Haeger almost always kept the pitch in the 70 to 72 MPH range, alleviating the hitter of a certain

(continued next page)

Charlie Haeger *(continued)*

amount of guesswork. In any event, the lack of precedent makes Haeger's PECOTA almost useless. He's in the White Sox's plans for 2007 as either as a fifth starter or a set-up man. In the latter case, the contrast between his knuckler and the hard heat of Bobby Jenks and Matt Thornton could leave hitters truly baffled.

Dustin Hermanson   Bats: R Throws: R   Height: 6' 2" Weight: 205 Born: December 21, 1972 Age: 34

YEAR	TEAM	LVL	AGE	W	L	SV	G	GS	IP	H	BB	SO	HR	GB%	BABIP	STUFF	WHIP	ERA	PERA	EQERA	EQH9	EQBB9	EQSO9	EQHR9	VORP	WXRL
2004	SFN	MLB	31	6	9	17	47	18	131	132	46	102	15	—	.302	5	1.36	4.53	4.13	4.65	8.9	2.8	6.2	0.9	14.3	2.62
2005	CHA	MLB	32	2	4	34	57	0	57¹	46	17	33	4	39.1%	.247	2	1.10	2.04	3.86	2.64	7.4	2.6	5.1	0.6	19.9	3.87
2006	CHA	MLB	33	0	0	0	6	0	6²	6	1	5	2	50.0%	.222	2	1.05	4.03	6.48	4.05	8.1	1.4	6.8	2.7	1.6	0.06
2007	*CHA*	*MLB*	*34*	*3*	*3*	*1*	*39*	*3*	*53*	*59*	*20*	*36*	*9*	*44.0%*	*.294*	*-9*	*1.48*	*5.19*	*4.79*	*4.73*	*9.8*	*3.1*	*5.7*	*1.4*	*3.9*	*0.50*

Breakout: 12% Improve: 24% Collapse: 47% Attrition: 30%   Comparables: Tom Sturdivant, Dick Tidrow, Bill Campbell, Kirk McCaskill

Hermanson lost his closer's job at the end of the 2005 season to Bobby Jenks and back pain, the latter of which looked like it might have cost him his career as well when the White Sox were openly pessimistic about his return in 2006. Happily, Hermanson came back in September to turn in a series of relatively healthy and encouraging outings with the big league club. That should be enough to earn him a meal ticket for 2007, though it won't be with the White Sox, who declined his option. Prospective suitors would be wise to review his 2005 season in detail, including his mediocre K/BB numbers. Hermanson is high risk, but he might not be high reward.

Bobby Jenks   Bats: R Throws: R   Height: 6' 3" Weight: 280 Born: March 14, 1981 Age: 26

YEAR	TEAM	LVL	AGE	W	L	SV	G	GS	IP	H	BB	SO	HR	GB%	BABIP	STUFF	WHIP	ERA	PERA	EQERA	EQH9	EQBB9	EQSO9	EQHR9	VORP	WXRL
2005	BIR	AA	24	1	2	19	35	0	41	34	20	48	1	61.3%	.320	5	1.32	2.85	4.37	4.72	8.3	4.7	7.0	0.4	3.9	—
2005	CHA	MLB	24	1	1	6	32	0	39¹	34	15	50	3	46.5%	.316	34	1.25	2.75	2.90	3.18	7.9	3.4	11.1	0.7	10.4	1.41
2006	CHA	MLB	25	3	4	41	67	0	69²	66	31	80	5	60.2%	.347	26	1.39	4.00	3.24	3.66	8.2	3.8	9.6	0.5	15.9	3.94
2007	*CHA*	*MLB*	*26*	*4*	*5*	*27*	*58*	*0*	*64*	*58*	*28*	*67*	*5*	*56.0%*	*.307*	*18*	*1.34*	*3.70*	*3.30*	*3.49*	*8.1*	*3.6*	*8.8*	*0.7*	*15.0*	*2.10*

Breakout: 31% Improve: 62% Collapse: 8% Attrition: 12%   Comparables: Gene Brabender, Ken Ryan, Duane Ward, Bobby Ayala

Perhaps the biggest indication of how far Bobby Jenks has come is that his 2006 season was a little . . . boring. His ERA was somewhat higher than expected, but the save total and peripherals were spot on. He slumped in July and again in September, but there was no sign of a mental or physical breakdown. Jenks will never move into the Rivera-Wagner-Hoffman class of relievers without some radical improvement to his command, but he significantly improved his ground ball rate last season, which helps keep those walks from doing damage via three-run homers. He should remain a good closer, provided one remembers that "good" in this division and this ballpark can mean a 3.60 ERA.

Boone Logan   Bats: R Throws: L   Height: 6' 5" Weight: 200 Born: August 13, 1984 Age: 22

YEAR	TEAM	LVL	AGE	W	L	SV	G	GS	IP	H	BB	SO	HR	GB%	BABIP	STUFF	WHIP	ERA	PERA	EQERA	EQH9	EQBB9	EQSO9	EQHR9	VORP	WXRL
2004	GRF	Rk	19	3	7	1	18	9	64¹	74	31	48	7	—	.327	-36	1.63	5.60	7.54	8.04	11.1	5.0	3.3	2.2	-17.0	—
2005	GRF	Rk	20	1	1	2	21	0	35¹	34	4	29	1	54.3%	.324	-8	1.08	3.31	4.02	4.33	8.9	1.3	3.3	0.5	5.0	—
2006	CHR	AAA	21	3	1	11	38	0	42¹	35	12	57	1	44.7%	.340	30	1.12	3.42	3.40	4.65	9.3	2.9	9.7	0.2	4.3	—
2006	CHA	MLB	21	0	0	1	21	0	17¹	21	15	15	2	46.6%	.339	3	2.08	8.32	6.06	8.15	10.7	7.1	7.1	1.0	-6.3	-0.55
2007	*CHA*	*MLB*	*22*	*3*	*4*	*2*	*74*	*2*	*64¹*	*75*	*32*	*46*	*11*	*45.0%*	*.317*	*-8*	*1.67*	*6.33*	*5.49*	*5.82*	*10.4*	*4.2*	*6.1*	*1.4*	*-3.3*	*0.30*

Breakout: 35% Improve: 64% Collapse: 7% Attrition: 12%   Comparables: Johan Santana, Bobby Seay, Rich Gossage, Jung Bong

Perhaps unfairly, Logan's big league future is staked on the prospect of his becoming a LOOGY—that's what lefty relievers get asked to do. In 2006, he came up short, as his combined major league and minor league numbers from last year attest: his K/BB ratio was 2.62 against left-handed hitters and 2.68 against righties, and lefties hit him for higher batting and slugging averages. The big disparity between his major and minor league numbers can probably be excused as jitters; it's not often that a pitcher jumps from the Pioneer League to the bigs in the span of a single winter.

Mike MacDougal

Bats: S Throws: R   Height: 6' 4"   Weight: 185   Born: March 5, 1977   Age: 30

YEAR	TEAM	LVL	AGE	W	L	SV	G	GS	IP	H	BB	SO	HR	GB%	BABIP	STUFF	WHIP	ERA	PERA	EQERA	EQH9	EQBB9	EQSO9	EQHR9	VORP	WXRL
2004	KCA	MLB	27	1	1	1	13	0	11¹	16	9	14	2	—	.452	11	2.36	5.58	5.09	5.25	12.0	6.0	9.8	1.5	-1.5	-0.87
2005	KCA	MLB	28	5	6	21	68	0	70¹	69	24	72	6	55.8%	.330	22	1.34	3.33	3.38	3.65	7.8	2.9	8.6	0.7	13.0	1.24
2006	KCA	MLB	29	0	0	1	4	0	4	2	0	2	0	72.7%	.182	4	0.50	0.00	2.47	0.00	4.2	0.0	4.2	0.0	2.7	0.24
2006	CHA	MLB	29	1	1	0	25	0	25	19	6	19	1	62.9%	.261	15	1.00	1.80	3.09	1.78	6.8	2.1	6.4	0.4	12.1	0.88
2007	CHA	MLB	30	3	2	3	47	1	51¹	50	23	43	5	58.0%	.303	5	1.43	3.87	3.79	3.62	8.7	3.7	7.0	0.7	11.5	1.00

Breakout: 13% Improve: 31% Collapse: 28% Attrition: 18%   Comparables: *Mike Timlin, Jim Mecir, Scot Shields, Todd Jones*

The White Sox have gotten something for nothing in MacDougal, first picking him up from the Royals for two minor league nobodies, then signing him to a three-year extension at well below market rate-the pitcher apparently preferring some measure of security after an up-and-down career and a season half-lost to injury. MacDougal is older than you'd think, having taken until 26 to establish himself, but he's still developing as a pitcher, most recently by pinning his slider down in the zone to generate some huge groundball numbers. If the progress continues, there's a chance that he could supplant Bobby Jenks as closer by year's end. The Sox are happy with Jenks and aren't looking to force anything, but they're also an organization that lets performance dictate.

Jay Marshall

Bats: L Throws: L   Height: 6' 5"   Weight: 185   Born: February 25, 1983   Age: 24

YEAR	TEAM	LVL	AGE	W	L	SV	G	GS	IP	H	BB	SO	HR	GB%	BABIP	STUFF	WHIP	ERA	PERA	EQERA	EQH9	EQBB9	EQSO9	EQHR9	VORP	WXRL
2004	BRI	Rk	21	1	6	0	11	11	57²	63	8	52	8	—	.318	-36	1.23	3.59	8.17	7.04	12.7	2.0	3.5	3.4	-8.6	—
2004	GRF	Rk	21	2	0	0	4	2	15²	19	6	17	2	—	.386	-20	1.59	3.44	7.60	6.75	12.9	4.3	4.3	3.1	-1.9	—
2005	GRF	Rk	22	2	0	6	29	0	43¹	35	7	43	3	60.3%	.274	-20	0.97	2.70	5.48	5.14	8.4	2.1	4.1	1.5	2.1	—
2006	WNS	A+	23	5	1	4	58	0	62	46	8	44	2	71.7%	.254	0	0.87	1.02	3.69	2.21	7.4	1.3	4.1	0.6	23.0	—
2007	OAK	MLB	24	3	4	1	33	5	62¹	72	15	27	10	54.0%	.291	-12	1.41	4.97	4.83	4.84	9.9	2.2	3.6	1.3	3.9	0.50

Breakout: 11% Improve: 40% Collapse: 27% Attrition: 19%   Comparables: *Chris Key, Mitch Stetter, Christopher Young, Edwin Almonte*

Jay Marshall is Tony La Russa's wet dream. Left-handed hitters went 10-for-104 against him in 2006 with two doubles and eight singles. His groundball-to-flyball ratio against lefties was 61-to-11. Marshall generates those numbers with a sidearm motion that starts almost completely behind left-handed hitters thanks to his long arms; lefties may lose ten feet worth of reaction time before they pick up the baseball. The flip side is that Marshall is as bad against righties as he is good against lefties. The A's acquired him in the Rule 5 draft, and he has a good chance to contribute in the big leagues, but he'll need to be platooned as carefully as Manny Mota's 1975 Strat card.

Brandon McCarthy

Bats: R Throws: R   Height: 6' 7"   Weight: 195   Born: July 7, 1983   Age: 23

YEAR	TEAM	LVL	AGE	W	L	SV	G	GS	IP	H	BB	SO	HR	GB%	BABIP	STUFF	WHIP	ERA	PERA	EQERA	EQH9	EQBB9	EQSO9	EQHR9	VORP	WXRL
2004	KAN	A	21	8	5	0	15	15	94	80	21	113	10	—	.313	11	1.07	3.64	5.12	4.57	9.4	2.4	6.6	1.7	10.4	—
2004	WNS	A+	21	6	0	0	8	8	52	31	3	60	3	—	.230	42	0.65	2.08	3.22	2.84	6.4	0.5	7.1	1.1	15.5	—
2004	BIR	AA	21	3	1	0	4	4	26	23	6	29	2	—	.309	25	1.12	3.46	4.29	4.32	9.4	2.2	6.8	1.1	3.6	—
2005	CHR	AAA	22	7	7	0	20	19	119¹	104	32	130	16	40.8%	.292	21	1.14	3.92	4.37	4.08	8.0	2.6	7.6	1.4	20.1	—
2005	CHA	MLB	22	3	2	0	12	10	67	62	17	48	13	37.5%	.251	11	1.18	4.03	5.01	3.97	8.5	2.2	6.4	1.6	13.6	1.56
2006	CHA	MLB	23	4	7	0	53	2	84²	77	33	69	17	38.7%	.260	-5	1.30	4.68	5.08	4.24	7.7	3.3	6.8	1.6	14.1	1.05
2007	TEX	MLB	23	7	9	0	31	23	138¹	159	48	100	26	40.0%	.306	7	1.49	5.53	5.15	4.96	9.6	3.0	6.0	1.5	5.1	1.50

Breakout: 7% Improve: 23% Collapse: 54% Attrition: 21%   Comparables: *Dave Beard, Jim Donohue, Frank Smith, Bobby Bolin*

This is the year Brandon McCarthy is supposed to break out. The White Sox traded Freddy Garcia to make room for McCarthy in their rotation, then dealt McCarthy to Texas where he's being counted on to anchor the Rangers' starting five. Buyer beware: he'll first need a cure for his gopheritis. McCarthy gave up 31 home runs per 650 plate appearances in 2006, the fifth-highest rate in the big leagues (minimum 70 IP). Worse yet, this does not appear to be an isolated problem. McCarthy's home run rates were fairly high throughout his minor league career, as well as in his big league debut in 2005. The reason is that he pitches up in the zone fairly often, sometimes intentionally and sometimes not. McCarthy's mechanics are reasonably well-regarded, but his tall, lanky frame can cause him to miss his landing point at times, resulting in flat, off-balance pitches. It's possible that the problem can be resolved through mechanical adjustments—a job which falls to veteran pitching coach Mark Connor, just promoted from the Rangers' bullpen. PECOTA is probably too pessimistic, but, despite the hype, McCarthy's not a sure-fire success, and his relocation to the Ballpark in Arlington casts even more doubt.

Kyle McCulloch Bats: R Throws: R Height: 6' 3" Weight: 180 Born: March 20, 1985 Age: 22

YEAR	TEAM	LVL	AGE	W	L	SV	G	GS	IP	H	BB	SO	HR	GB%	BABIP	STUFF	WHIP	ERA	PERA	EQERA	EQH9	EQBB9	EQSO9	EQHR9	VORP	WXRL
2006	WNS	A+	21	2	5	0	7	7	35¹	37	17	21	4	53.3%	.289	-16	1.54	4.10	7.06	5.50	10.5	4.7	3.9	1.8	0.4	—
2006	GRF	Rk	21	1	1	0	6	5	22²	19	7	27	1	61.3%	.295	-6	1.17	1.62	5.18	7.48	8.7	3.7	5.4	1.2	-4.5	—
2007	CHA	MLB	22	4	7	0	24	16	90¹	112	49	50	21	50.0%	.302	-14	1.78	7.08	6.46	6.44	11.0	4.5	4.6	2.0	-11.4	0.60

Breakout: 13% Improve: 42% Collapse: 17% Attrition: 2% Comparables: John Bannister, Brian Lockwood, Aaron Akin, Ben Shaffar

The White Sox's top pick in the 2006 draft, McCulloch might be the player who changes the organization's drafting philosophy once and for all. PECOTA looks at his mediocre peripherals and concludes that McCulloch has virtually no chance to become a plus major league pitcher. Scouts look at a fastball that tops out at 91 MPH and a curve that's just okay and reach the same verdict. Coming on the heels of similarly low-risk, low-reward selections such as Lance Broadway, Royce Ring, and perhaps Brian Anderson, there's an increasing sense of buyer's remorse down at 35th and Shields.

Oneli Perez Bats: R Throws: R Height: 6' 2" Weight: 163 Born: May 26, 1983 Age: 24

YEAR	TEAM	LVL	AGE	W	L	SV	G	GS	IP	H	BB	SO	HR	GB%	BABIP	STUFF	WHIP	ERA	PERA	EQERA	EQH9	EQBB9	EQSO9	EQHR9	VORP	WXRL
2005	KAN	A	22	4	2	2	36	2	80	84	32	62	7	38.6%	.310	-32	1.45	3.71	6.76	6.24	11.3	5.0	4.1	1.7	-5.3	—
2006	KAN	A	23	3	1	8	30	0	36	23	8	42	1	35.9%	.242	3	0.86	1.00	3.99	2.08	6.7	2.6	5.7	0.5	13.6	—
2006	WNS	A+	23	1	0	0	17	0	25¹	17	5	29	1	48.5%	.250	11	0.88	0.72	3.88	2.59	7.8	2.2	6.7	0.7	8.1	—
2006	BIR	AA	23	0	1	1	7	0	16²	6	6	20	1	57.6%	.161	16	0.74	0.56	5.24	1.15	5.2	3.4	7.5	1.1	7.8	—
2007	CHA	MLB	24	3	4	1	29	5	59²	71	26	39	14	41.0%	.297	-9	1.61	5.79	5.76	5.17	10.5	3.6	5.5	2.0	1.5	0.30

Breakout: 3% Improve: 16% Collapse: 57% Attrition: 13% Comparables: David Shafer, Jason Anderson, Jeff Harris, Ralph Roberts

Minor league middle relievers don't usually make our book, but a 0.81 ERA across three minor league levels warrants an exception. Scouts remain unimpressed by Perez's fastball, which tops out in the high-80s, but his breaking ball gets good reviews. Having originally been signed by the Padres as a position player, he deserves the benefit of the doubt as a late bloomer.

Cliff Politte Bats: R Throws: R Height: 5' 10" Weight: 195 Born: February 27, 1974 Age: 33

YEAR	TEAM	LVL	AGE	W	L	SV	G	GS	IP	H	BB	SO	HR	GB%	BABIP	STUFF	WHIP	ERA	PERA	EQERA	EQH9	EQBB9	EQSO9	EQHR9	VORP	WXRL
2004	CHA	MLB	30	0	3	1	54	0	51¹	52	22	48	6	—	.317	8	1.44	4.39	4.01	4.08	8.8	3.4	7.6	0.8	10.6	0.57
2005	CHA	MLB	31	7	1	1	68	0	67¹	42	21	57	7	33.1%	.208	17	0.94	2.01	3.90	1.99	6.0	2.8	7.5	0.9	28.3	3.85
2006	CHA	MLB	32	2	2	0	30	0	30	47	15	15	9	33.9%	.349	-42	2.07	8.70	7.03	8.13	13.4	4.1	4.1	2.3	-9.2	-0.70
2007	CHA	MLB	33	2	2	1	32	0	38²	42	14	27	7	38.0%	.285	-6	1.42	4.81	4.50	4.36	9.5	2.9	5.9	1.5	5.0	0.40

Breakout: 25% Improve: 56% Collapse: 11% Attrition: 41% Comparables: Shigetoshi Hasegawa, Dan Miceli, Don Elston, Bob Wells

The Sox deserve credit for working around some terrible declines in the bullpen. Cliff Politte, Dustin Hermanson, and Neal Cotts combined for 53.3 Adjusted Runs Prevented (ARP) in 2005, but slumped to −21.0 in 2006, a decline which amounts to seven or eight fewer wins. Politte was the largest part of the problem, going from the fourth-best reliever in baseball in 2005 (25.1 ARP), to the second worst in 2006 (−16.1 ARP). Rather than sit on their hands, the Sox almost completely turned the bullpen over by midseason, bringing in Mike MacDougal and David Riske to complement the offseason acquisition of Matt Thornton. For his part, Politte was released in July, and had rotator cuff surgery in August. He'll get a look somewhere if his arm heals up, but having never been a favorite of baseball people, he might need to settle for a minor league deal.

Tim Redding Bats: R Throws: R Height: 6' 0" Weight: 205 Born: February 12, 1978 Age: 29

YEAR	TEAM	LVL	AGE	W	L	SV	G	GS	IP	H	BB	SO	HR	GB%	BABIP	STUFF	WHIP	ERA	PERA	EQERA	EQH9	EQBB9	EQSO9	EQHR9	VORP	WXRL
2004	NWO	AAA	26	1	3	0	5	5	28¹	30	12	26	2	—	.326	5	1.48	6.04	4.48	6.99	9.5	4.1	6.4	0.6	-4.4	—
2004	HOU	MLB	26	5	7	0	27	17	100²	125	43	56	15	—	.330	-16	1.67	5.72	5.23	5.88	10.6	3.4	4.3	1.2	-9.3	0.66
2005	SDN	MLB	27	0	5	0	9	6	29²	40	13	17	7	46.7%	.337	-31	1.79	9.09	6.61	10.57	11.7	3.5	4.7	2.1	-18.0	-0.65
2005	COH	AAA	27	3	4	0	10	10	51¹	62	13	47	5	43.0%	.361	8	1.46	5.09	4.19	5.40	10.8	2.4	6.1	1.0	1.1	—
2006	CHR	AAA	28	12	10	0	29	28	187	168	56	148	21	46.4%	.272	-8	1.20	3.42	5.47	4.77	9.3	3.0	5.5	1.6	16.7	—
2007	WAS	MLB	29	6	9	0	25	21	126²	135	47	85	17	44.0%	.294	3	1.44	5.11	5.40	5.59	9.5	3.0	5.4	1.1	1.0	1.00

Breakout: 27% Improve: 65% Collapse: 7% Attrition: 0% Comparables: Brandon Duckworth, Wayne Garland, Brian Sweeney, Kerry Taylor

Yes, this is the same old Tim Redding, and he's still trucking along with the same old level of performance, right along the major league fringe. The Nationals signed him in November, which is perhaps the best possible destination for him: not only does the nation's capital desperately need a few good arms, but RFK Stadium should help counteract his problems with the home run ball. Don't be surprised if he wins a rotation slot in camp.

David Riske   Bats: R Throws: R   Height: 6' 2"   Weight: 180   Born: October 23, 1976   Age: 30

YEAR	TEAM	LVL	AGE	W	L	SV	G	GS	IP	H	BB	SO	HR	GB%	BABIP	STUFF	WHIP	ERA	PERA	EQERA	EQH9	EQBB9	EQSO9	EQHR9	VORP	WXRL
2004	CLE	MLB	27	7	3	5	72	0	77¹	69	41	78	11	—	.291	10	1.42	3.73	4.47	3.47	7.5	4.3	8.3	1.1	21.9	1.17
2005	CLE	MLB	28	3	4	1	58	0	72²	55	15	48	11	42.4%	.214	-2	0.96	3.09	4.68	3.68	7.1	1.8	5.9	1.3	17.9	0.20
2006	BOS	MLB	29	0	1	0	8	0	9²	8	3	5	2	41.9%	.207	-13	1.14	3.71	6.73	3.60	7.2	2.7	4.5	1.8	2.6	-0.05
2006	CHA	MLB	29	1	1	0	33	0	34¹	32	14	23	4	37.4%	.272	-5	1.34	3.94	4.55	3.82	7.9	3.3	5.6	1.0	7.6	0.05
2007	*KCA*	*MLB*	*30*	*2*	*3*	*2*	*45*	*0*	*52*	*56*	*20*	*38*	*8*	*40.0%*	*.297*	*-4*	*1.46*	*4.78*	*4.76*	*4.24*	*8.9*	*3.3*	*6.1*	*1.2*	*6.0*	*0.50*

Breakout: 10% Improve: 32% Collapse: 41% Attrition: 19%   Comparables: T. J. Mathews, Dave Tobik, John Johnstone, John Wyatt

Riske's fastball is no longer overpowering, and he's regressed into a defensive style of pitching that involves working the inside portion of the plate and hoping that hitters won't tee off on anything. That worked well enough in 2006, but between the decline in his strikeout rate in 2005, the decline in his command in 2006, and his lack of a breaking ball, he doesn't have much left to work with.

Adam Russell   Bats: R Throws: R   Height: 6' 8"   Weight: 250   Born: April 14, 1983   Age: 24

YEAR	TEAM	LVL	AGE	W	L	SV	G	GS	IP	H	BB	SO	HR	GB%	BABIP	STUFF	WHIP	ERA	PERA	EQERA	EQH9	EQBB9	EQSO9	EQHR9	VORP	WXRL
2004	GRF	Rk	21	4	0	0	15	4	38	31	18	33	2	—	.274	-16	1.29	2.37	6.04	3.68	7.9	5.4	3.4	1.2	7.8	—
2004	KAN	A	21	0	2	0	2	2	10	18	7	3	3	—	.366	-34	2.50	9.00	12.47	11.57	18.3	7.7	1.9	4.8	-6.2	—
2005	KAN	A	22	9	7	0	24	24	126¹	116	55	82	10	51.6%	.279	-22	1.35	3.78	6.86	5.97	9.7	5.4	3.3	1.5	-4.9	—
2006	WNS	A+	23	7	3	0	17	17	94	80	39	61	5	60.8%	.273	-5	1.27	2.68	5.66	4.03	8.5	4.3	3.8	1.0	16.0	—
2006	BIR	AA	23	3	3	0	10	10	55²	59	19	47	5	49.7%	.323	-6	1.41	4.73	5.46	6.42	10.4	3.1	5.3	1.5	-5.0	—
2007	*CHA*	*MLB*	*24*	*5*	*8*	*0*	*25*	*18*	*101*	*121*	*60*	*52*	*19*	*50.0%*	*.301*	*-15*	*1.79*	*6.66*	*6.12*	*6.10*	*10.7*	*4.9*	*4.3*	*1.6*	*-9.1*	*0.20*

Breakout: 5% Improve: 27% Collapse: 35% Attrition: 1%   Comparables: Jon Pridie, Chad Paronto, Jamie Merchant, Mark Michael

Having finished his NCAA ball with a 6.28 intercollegiate ERA, Russell has been a projection pick from the very get-go. He remains very raw, having yet to find a reliable secondary pitch to match his plus fastball that comes straight over the top from his jumbo six-foot-eight-inch frame. The organization likes Russell, and he's been moved pretty fast, but with that body of his, he looks more like someone who is being groomed for a career in the Arena Football League.

Matt Thornton   Bats: L Throws: L   Height: 6' 6"   Weight: 235   Born: September 15, 1976   Age: 30

YEAR	TEAM	LVL	AGE	W	L	SV	G	GS	IP	H	BB	SO	HR	GB%	BABIP	STUFF	WHIP	ERA	PERA	EQERA	EQH9	EQBB9	EQSO9	EQHR9	VORP	WXRL
2004	TAC	AAA	27	7	5	0	16	15	83	86	63	74	4	—	.332	19	1.80	5.42	5.37	6.51	9.2	7.3	6.1	0.5	-8.4	—
2004	SEA	MLB	27	1	2	0	19	1	32²	30	25	30	2	—	.326	18	1.76	4.13	4.29	4.01	8.3	6.1	7.5	0.5	6.2	0.27
2005	SEA	MLB	28	0	4	0	55	0	57	54	42	57	13	45.3%	.277	1	1.68	5.21	6.38	5.12	8.4	6.5	8.7	2.0	2.8	-0.35
2006	CHA	MLB	29	5	3	2	63	0	54	46	21	49	5	50.7%	.279	13	1.24	3.33	3.69	3.09	7.3	3.3	7.6	0.7	17.0	1.74
2007	*CHA*	*MLB*	*30*	*3*	*3*	*2*	*53*	*0*	*52¹*	*52*	*29*	*47*	*7*	*46.0%*	*.301*	*2*	*1.54*	*4.67*	*4.45*	*4.29*	*8.8*	*4.6*	*7.6*	*1.1*	*7.0*	*0.60*

Breakout: 34% Improve: 54% Collapse: 18% Attrition: 14%   Comparables: Tim Stoddard, Andy Hassler, Greg Cadaret, Mike Munoz

Thornton never had a large platoon split with the Mariners, but limited left-handed hitters to a .211/.253/.316 line last season with more aggressive use of his slider, which has an awful lot of lateral break. Like a lot of pitchers, he needs to get his fastball across to set up the breaking pitch, and so he tends toward all-or-nothing outings. If this profile sounds a lot like Neal Cotts, that's because it is. Having fully assumed Cotts's job, Thornton will likely take the Sox on that same roller coaster of fixation and frustration.

Javier Vazquez   Bats: R Throws: R   Height: 6' 2"   Weight: 215   Born: July 25, 1976   Age: 30

YEAR	TEAM	LVL	AGE	W	L	SV	G	GS	IP	H	BB	SO	HR	GB%	BABIP	STUFF	WHIP	ERA	PERA	EQERA	EQH9	EQBB9	EQSO9	EQHR9	VORP	WXRL
2004	NYA	MLB	27	14	10	0	32	32	198	195	60	150	33	—	.279	8	1.29	4.91	4.72	4.69	8.3	2.4	6.2	1.3	21.9	3.90
2005	ARI	MLB	28	11	15	0	33	33	215²	223	46	192	35	43.7%	.308	16	1.25	4.42	4.15	4.20	8.7	1.7	7.2	1.4	22.7	4.08
2006	CHA	MLB	29	11	12	0	33	32	202²	206	56	184	23	41.7%	.311	27	1.29	4.84	3.82	4.59	8.8	2.3	7.6	0.9	22.8	3.29
2007	*CHA*	*MLB*	*30*	*12*	*10*	*0*	*32*	*31*	*199*	*205*	*54*	*153*	*31*	*44.0%*	*.289*	*17*	*1.30*	*4.48*	*4.05*	*4.10*	*9.2*	*2.2*	*6.5*	*1.3*	*31.3*	*4.70*

Breakout: 24% Improve: 71% Collapse: 6% Attrition: 4%   Comparables: Pedro Astacio, Don Sutton, Burt Hooton, Bob Welch

(continued next page)

Javier Vazquez *(continued)*

Luck comes in many different forms for pitchers. In 2006, Vazquez was lucky to give up only 23 home runs in spite of being a fly-ball pitcher in U.S. Cellular Field, but was unlucky enough to yield a .311 BABIP in front of a pretty good defense and post an ERA that was more than 75 points higher than his PERA. Add it all up and two out of three indicators point toward a rebound in 2007. No Shane Reynolds or Eric Milton case in which a pitcher has strong K/BB numbers that aren't very well supported by his stuff, Vazquez throws four pretty good pitches and remains one of the more underrated pitchers in his league.

Lineouts

PLAYER	TEAM	LVL	AGE	PA	R	2B	3B	HR	RBI	BB	SO	SB-CS	SPEED	AVG/OBP/SLG	MLVr	EqAVG/OBP/SLG	EqA	VORP
C S. Alomar	LAN	MLB	40	62	3	5	0	0	9	0	7	0-0	3.3	.323/.323/.403	-.006	.323/.323/.403	.249	1.6
	CHA	MLB	40	51	5	3	0	1	8	3	7	0-0	4.9	.217/.255/.348	-.330	.200/.255/.333	.213	-2.2
2B A. Gonzalez	CHR	AAA	24	462	48	27	0	6	51	46	77	16-8	5.1	.271/.354/.383	.046	.256/.336/.378	.252	9.0
C F. Hernandez#	KAN	A	20	351	29	16	1	6	34	22	31	3-1	3.8	.247/.305/.361	-.051	.217/.256/.318	.205	-19.8
3B M. Schnurstein	BIR	AA	21	518	48	25	2	9	46	24	100	8-6	4.7	.219/.264/.335	-.118	.225/.264/.359	.216	-16.0
C C. Stewart	CHR	AAA	24	301	40	17	3	4	28	15	35	3-0	5.8	.265/.314/.393	-.009	.257/.306/.395	.245	3.0
SS R. Valido	BIR	AA	21	192	15	9	3	1	11	13	24	8-3	7.1	.208/.269/.315	-.142	.223/.277/.354	.224	-3.7
OF E. Young	CHR	AAA	37	417	52	26	0	13	68	55	85	2-2	3.4	.300/.405/.486	.272	.253/.335/.399	.257	-1.6

PLAYER	TEAM	LVL	AGE	W	L	SV	IP	H	BB	SO	HR	GB%	BABIP	STUFF	WHIP	ERA	PERA	EqERA	EqH9	EqBB9	EqSO9	EqHR9	VORP
L. Harrell	WNS	A+	21	7	2	0	91²	58	44	70	3	—	.224	17	1.12	2.47	4.88	3.30	6.4	4.6	4.8	0.6	23.0
	BIR	AA	21	0	2	0	9²	12	14	4	1	—	.333	-14	2.83	10.76	9.60	13.50	11.6	13.5	2.9	1.9	-8.2
R. Liotta*	WNS	A+	23	1	6	0	42	62	19	30	5	—	.407	-38	1.93	8.14	7.03	12.39	14.8	4.6	4.2	2.2	-30.7
	BIR	AA	23	3	8	0	96	109	46	52	3	—	.330	-2	1.61	4.97	4.73	6.20	10.0	4.3	3.2	0.5	-6.5
A. Montero	CHR	AAA	28	2	3	1	59	54	20	55	8	—	.279	-20	1.25	4.88	6.06	6.19	9.8	3.5	6.5	1.9	-3.7
	CHA	MLB	28	1	0	0	14	15	2	7	3	—	.273	-14	1.21	5.14	5.08	5.65	8.8	1.3	4.4	1.9	-0.3
A. Munoz*	BIR	AA	24	2	4	2	46	38	14	48	4	—	.291	-9	1.13	3.72	5.27	5.24	8.7	3.0	6.2	1.6	1.8
	CHR	AAA	24	0	1	0	6	10	7	5	1	—	.409	-29	2.83	15.00	9.21	17.47	17.5	11.1	6.4	1.6	-7.5
P. Reynoso*	CHR	AAA	25	3	3	0	59²	48	45	59	3	—	.279	10	1.57	4.41	5.62	5.18	8.5	7.5	7.1	0.6	2.7
S. Tracey	CHR	AAA	25	8	9	0	129²	111	76	102	17	—	.271	-18	1.45	4.32	7.47	5.60	9.4	5.9	5.7	1.8	0.0
	CHA	MLB	25	0	0	0	8	4	5	3	2	—	.087	-21	1.13	3.38	8.83	3.38	4.5	5.6	3.4	2.2	2.5

Sandy Alomar never quite lived up to expectations, but he trudged on quietly and honorably, not being too proud to adjust to life as a role player. That role is becoming ever more limited with what's left of the 40-year-old Alomar's power fizzing away. Toby Hall takes his place as the Sox's backup catcher. **Andy Gonzalez** isn't seen as a prospect, but middle infielders who do a few things well and survive can drift into major league utility roles, and he's on the 40-man. **Francisco Hernandez** is probably the best prospect listed in this paragraph due to his youth and defensive abilities, but his bat has failed to progress after a promising 250-PA stretch at Great Falls in the first half of 2005. Young for his level, **Micah Schnurstein** made defensive strides at third base, but Sox fans will probably never experience the joy of listening to Hawk Harrelson try to pronounce his name. **Chris Stewart** is a catching prospect with a slingshot of an arm and a BB gun of a bat. There's not much to get excited about here, but there's also no reason that Stewart can't be a perfectly adequate second-string catcher in the big leagues. **Rob Valido**'s star dimmed significantly after a steroid suspension to start the 2005 season; like Hernandez, he's young, but looks increasingly like a good-field, no-hit player. Perhaps the greatest Triple-A outfielder of his generation, we list **Ernie Young** to highlight the shortage of actual prospects in this system as well as tip our caps to him; other major league vets getting significant playing time in the system included Ruben Rivera, Mark Quinn, and Jorge Velandia.

Lucas Harrell already has a plus sinker, which he uses to generate a lot of groundball outs, and the potential to develop a plus curveball, but for the time being he lacks sufficient command of either pitch. Check back in a year. **Ray Liotta** scuffled badly after being one of the organization's rising stars a year ago, but he gets a mulligan: his family's home in Kenner, Louisiana was devastated by Hurricane Katrina, and his focus was understandably not on the diamond. **Agustin Montero**

has been re-gifted as often as a George Foreman Grill, having passed through four organizations on account of a big pitcher's body and a big fastball; he is best known for being the third player suspended under MLB's steroid testing policy that went into effect in 2005. He remains in the system, but is off the 40-man roster. **Arnie Muñoz** had a poor spring training, which led Ozzie Guillen to question his *juevos,* and was dispatched down to Birmingham to adjust to life as a full-time reliever. He fared reasonably well in that role and, as a lefty with a good curveball, he retains a shot at a major league career. Tall and wild, **Paulino Reynoso** is a Dominican lefty who's on the 40-man roster on the off chance he figures out where home plate is. Like Muñoz, **Sean Tracey** also ran into trouble with Guillen, drawing his ire after refusing an order to bean Hank Blalock in a June game against the Rangers. He was returned to Charlotte the next day, although the Sox did have the good grace to recall him in September. He'll be back in Chicago when injuries and doubleheaders strike.

Manager: Ozzie Guillen

Year	Team	W-L	Pythag +/-	Avg PC	100 +P	120 +P	QS	BQS	REL	REL w Zero R	IBB	SUBS	PH	PH Avg	PH HR	SB2	CS2	SB3	CS3	SAC Att	SAC %	POS SAC	Squeeze	Swing	In Play
2004	CHA	83-79	-1	101.6	102	5	64	8	401	243	36	34	130	.283	4	71	46	7	5	85	68.2%	55	3	125	94
2005	CHA	99-63	+7	101.9	105	3	89	13	410	272	42	36	100	.205	2	115	61	21	5	78	68.0%	51	4	159	121
2006	CHA	90-72	+2	100.9	93	4	76	12	398	222	59	51	135	.225	6	83	43	10	4	72	61.1%	39	2	127	100

Ozzie Guillen is sometimes described as a modern day Billy Martin, but the comparison doesn't really hold water. Guillen's fights are with snarky columnists and opposing managers; Martin's were with the bottle and his own players. Guillen is candid and quotable, but unlike Martin, there's no evidence that he is unstable. He enjoys a certain co-dependency with the Chicago press corps, which is at once indebted to him for the column inches that he fills, and disdainful of his political incorrectness. How much of this is Ozzie being Ozzie, versus Ozzie being *Ozzie!,* the self-caricature, is hard to say. Perhaps Guillen deliberately makes himself a lighting rod for attention to shield his clubhouse from it, or perhaps his candor is read by his players as honesty. However he goes about it, Guillen's tenure has been characterized by players who play relaxed, professional baseball toward the upper end of their ability, and that's really the bottom line.

Tactically, Guillen shows little of the tendency toward low-percentage baseball that he exhibited as a player. His frequency of sacrifice attempts, pitchouts, and intentional walks are all very close to the norm; he gives his runners the green light a little bit more than average, and pinch hits a little bit less. More notable is his handling of the pitching staff, where he and Don Cooper have developed a centrist philosophy of working the starter past the century mark, but almost never beyond the truly dangerous 120-pitch threshold. The bullpen has been equally well-managed, as Guillen's tendency to ride the hot hand usually works out well.

Cincinnati Reds

The 2006 season wound up being particularly memorable in Cincinnati for all sorts of reasons, but the most important events didn't happen on the diamond, but in the boardrooms. If the subsequent excitement on the field seemed to spring from a happy resolution to the years of disappointment and embarrassment off of it, who are we to argue with karma? Now, having given Reds fans their most exciting season since 1999, the team's future seems more promising than it has in years, and it isn't implausible to suggest that Cincinnati might again become a baseball town that rivals St. Louis.

The foundation event was the takeover of the team by a new ownership group headed by Bob Castellini and Joe Williams, at long last exorcising the specter of Carl Lindner's failed antidote to the Schott era. Both Castellini and Williams have plenty of experience inside the industry, having previously been minority stakeholders in first the Orioles and then the Cardinals. If this sounds remarkably similar to the Seligian owner recruiting process that saw both John Henry and Jeffrey Loria calved from the Yankee mothership to teams of their own, that's the way things get done these days—random rich guys do not just drop in and buy a luxury item like a baseball team. We may no longer have owners such as Marge Schott or Gussie Busch or Charlie Finley, but that's progress—the industry is a business, increasingly run like one by businessmen. The Castellini-Williams group is just the latest sign of that kind of progress.

Four days after taking over the team in January, the new owners fired incumbent general manager Dan O'Brien. History might be more kind to O'Brien than the present was, depending on how well top picks Homer Bailey, Jay Bruce, and Travis Wood pan out. Certainly, two years is far

REDS PROSPECTUS

2006 record: 80–82; Third place, NL Central

Pythagenport record: 75–87

Runs scored per game: 4.62 (10th in NL)

Runs allowed per game: 4.94 (10th in NL)

Team EqA: .259 (9th in NL)

2006 Batters Age: 29.9 (8th oldest in NL)

2006 Pitchers Age: 29.5 (7th oldest in NL)

Ballpark: Great American Ball Park; Moderate hitter's park; Park Factor of 1.038

2006: Reds being labeled contenders late in the season a function of division's pedestrian nature, not Reds' high quality.

2007: Kyle Lohse and Eric Milton on the same staff? Didn't Wayne Krivsky spend some time in Minnesota? How well *did* that work out?

too little time to determine whether or not O'Brien could really handle the job. He clearly wasn't Hawk Harrelson-bad, but overpaying for Eric Milton, blowing $8.2 million to get two starts from a sore-armed Paul Wilson, and getting worked up over bringing in players such as Ramon Ortiz and Tony Womack didn't constitute evidence of any particular brand of genius.

After two weeks of hasty deliberations, ownership brought in Wayne Krivsky as O'Brien's replacement in early February. Krivsky had been the Assistant GM of the Twins for the previous eight years, just about the perfect association for a club seeking some old-school player development know-how. Krivsky had also played a major role in the Twins' arbitration cases and contract negotiations, no small thing in today's game, and perhaps particularly important to a team with an eye on the bottom line.

Coming into the job with camps just about to open, Krivsky didn't have much opportunity to shore up the team with any late shopping. Instead, he made a point of cutting a lot of dreck and wound up plugging the hole at second base with a roster-juggling move during the season's first week, acquiring Brandon Phillips from the Indians, thereby landing a middle infielder with real promise to replace Tony Womack's counterfeit.

Krivsky's biggest preseason move finally resolved the problem that had been hanging over this team for two years: what to do with their four legitimate star-caliber starting outfielders in the non-DH league. Krivsky made the decisive deal-from-depth Reds fans have been anticipating for years, addressing his rotation problems by picking up Bronson Arroyo—who had just signed a three-year deal to stay in Boston in January—for Wily Mo Peña, the youngest of the Reds' outfield quartet. Getting a pitcher with Arroyo's relative durability who was already inked for years to come was critical, as it would spare the club the need to shop for at least one starter for the next two offseasons. The deal was not without considerable risk: Wily Mo Peña had the potential to flower into a premium hitter, while Arroyo's track record up to this point was relatively mediocre. To the surprise of many, it worked out far better than expected. Arroyo came into his own in the National League, and combined with Aaron Harang's continued development and Eric Milton's relatively modest return to effectiveness to give the Reds a trio of starters they could rely on.

Even more surprising, the rotation and a relatively strong offense were enough to keep the Reds in the wild card chase, although killjoys would note that with only three teams really out of it at the All-Star break, contention was a product of the NL's weak competitive environment. Under the circumstances, Krivsky couldn't help but go for it, especially considering the low expectations with which the team had entered the year. He correctly identified two basic problems with his ballclub—his bullpen wasn't very good, and Felipe Lopez wasn't a good shortstop. To initially address the former problem, he took a chance on an aging Eddie Guardado's elbow, picking him up cheaply from the Mariners. But Krivsky couldn't resist doing something more, and his dissatisfaction with Lopez's limitations in the field had gotten to the point that he'd picked good-field/no-hit ex-Twin Juan Castro off the scrapheap.

Enter Jim Bowden, no longer the boy genius, but perhaps now Cincinnati's Dr. Caligari, the evil genius whose schemes seem defined by a hyperactive creativity, if nothing else. The ultimate transactions addict, Bowden couldn't help but be drawn in by the prospect of providing whatever Krivsky thought the Reds might need in order to bring a couple of his former Cincy projects and prospects to D.C. Krivsky wound up dealing away a quarter of his lineup (Lopez and Austin Kearns) and former relief prospect Ryan Wagner for another no-hit shortstop in Royce Clayton, young relievers Bill Bray and Gary Majewski, and aspiring utility infielder Brendan Harris.

The deal was an unmitigated disaster for the Reds. From having one outfielder too many in February, the team had one too few in July, and that's if you give them full credit for the oft-absent Griffey. The lineup slumped from scoring five runs per game before the All-Star break to 4.1 runs after, while the pitching staff, which had been allowing 5.2 runs per game before the deal, only cut its runs allowed to 4.6 per. The club's run differential actually increased after the deal, but the improvement in the pitching staff had more to do with getting rid of bad ideas in the rotation such as Dave Williams and Joe Mays than with Clayton's fading fielding

skills or Krivsky's reworked pen. Indeed, the need to rework the pen became his consuming project for the remainder of the summer, as Majewski proved to be damaged goods after carrying one of the heaviest relief workloads in baseball for the Nats in the early going, and Guardado's elbow blew out after all. Krivsky spent the rest of July and August acquiring assorted relief junk from other people's rosters, none of which helped erase the now more pressing problem, the club's enfeebled lineup. The Cardinals would come back to the pack in the Central over the season's final two months, but the Reds had already shot their bolt.

As unhappy as the ending was, 2006 was still an outstanding season for the franchise. Local interest revived, and the Krivsky era was launched with a penumbra of success. The rotation that came together so well last season will be the basis for the team's subsequent shot at contention. If Homer Bailey winds up joining Milton in it this summer, for at least one year it will contain as many significant O'Brien pickups as Krivsky's. (Harang is to the credit of departed interim GM Brad Kullman.) Kyle Lohse makes a serviceable fourth starter, and between Elizardo Ramirez, Matt Belisle, and Bobby Livingston (claimed off of waivers from the Mariners in December) they should have a serviceable fifth until Bailey's ready.

The real threat to the team's ability to contend right now is that the lineup's stars come up just short of being the players you really want to build your lineup around. To be sure, Adam Dunn and Ken Griffey Jr. have both been major-impact hitters, but in the last year or two, they've become something less. Griffey's problems with staying healthy have been the rule instead of the exception over the last six years; he hasn't played in 140 games since 2000, his first year as a Red. He also just went through his worst year at the plate, posting career-lows in OBP and EqA and slugging less than .500 for only the second time in eleven years. Dunn is the posterboy for the virtues of what are jokingly referred to by some as the Three True Outcomes (homers, walks, and strikeouts, see table 1), having just generated that trio of results in a league-leading 50.7% of his plate appearances in 2006.

Unfortunately, Dunn has slipped significantly in a more basic area of responsibility when it comes to delivering with men on base. In each of the last two seasons, he has failed to hit safely in more than 80 percent of his plate appearances. That's not the end of the world by itself—taking walks creates opportunities for the hitters behind him, and Dunn's power can and does make a difference. The problem is that if you're counting on Dunn's low frequency of delivering hits and Griffey's occasional attendance to carry your offense, you're building on a faulty foundation. Indeed, the

Table 1. The 2006 Three True Outcomes Leaderboard

Rnk	Player	PA	HR	BB	SO	TTO	TTO%
1	Adam Dunn	683	40	112	194	346	50.7%
2	Russell Branyan	282	18	34	89	141	50.0%
3	Ryan Howard	704	58	108	181	347	49.3%
4	Jim Thome	610	42	107	147	296	48.5%
5	Mike Napoli	325	16	51	90	157	48.3%
6	Brad Wilkerson	365	15	37	116	168	46.0%
7	Pat Burrell	567	29	98	131	258	45.5%
8	Mark Bellhorn	288	8	32	90	130	45.1%
9	David Ross	296	21	37	75	133	44.9%
10	Travis Hafner	564	42	100	111	253	44.9%

NOTE: TTO: Three True Outcomes; TTO%: Three True Outcome Percentage (of all PA).

2005 Reds' were abysmal when it came to plating baserunners, with only the ever-pathetic Pirates doing a worse job (see tables 2 and 3). The average rate of driving runners home for major league non-pitchers in 2006 was 14.7 percent. The Reds did it successfully just 13.12 percent of the time.

Because the Reds are paying Griffey $12.5 million and Dunn $10.5 million, they don't have the flexibility to add a third high-impact bat through free agency, which puts the onus on younger talent. Scott Hatteberg will not top his 2006 performance at first base, further increasing the need for improvement elsewhere in the lineup. Brandon Phillips and Alex Gonzalez give the team a middle infield combo that will deliver a modest amount of sock, all the more helpful in the bandbox the Reds now call home, but barring a major surprise, they'll only contribute, not lead. In this atmosphere, Edwin Encarnacion's potential as a high-impact bat takes on particular significance, as does finding the right outfielder to plug into the lineup to replace the departed Kearns.

As a result, the Reds problems entering 2007 all come back to the outfield and the team's pair of stars: can they get Dunn to make better contact, can Griffey find the fountain of youth, and can Krivksy find that third outfielder who can deliver? Dunn might get back to where he was in

2004 as a hitter, and he will be turning 27 this season, the age at which talent often peaks. Griffey might take heart from Frank Thomas's reappearance on the starscape in 2006; perhaps if he's put in an outfield corner and asked to do less on defense, he can deliver another season to be proud of. Although Kearns would certainly have provided a better answer to the self-inflicted third outfielder question, barring a late winter pickup, Chris Denorfia might give the club someone who can get Griffey into a corner while providing offensive value as a hitter with a good balance of plate coverage and power.

That's a lot of maybes, but nobody in the division looks like a 90-game winner on paper. If the Reds can get two of those maybes to go their way, they could be the team to beat. If Krivsky learned from the disastrous trade with the Nats and the subsequent pointless hyperactivity of assembling a pen out of other people's veteran chaff, he'll be ahead of where a lot of GMs are after a year on the job.

Happily, tomorrow holds a lot of promise for home-grown improvements, because what the Reds' system lacks in depth, it's making up for with quality. In the immediate future, the hope is that first baseman Joey Votto will join Encarnacion to give the Reds a pair of low-cost/high-yield hitters to complement Griffey and Dunn. Further away,

Table 3. Seeing Red—Individual Cincy OBI% (200 PA minimum)

Edwin Encarnacion	16.9%
Rich Aurilia	16.3%
David Ross	15.9%
Ken Griffey Jr.	15.5%
Brandon Phillips	14.5%
Royce Clayton (combined)	12.8%
Adam Dunn	12.7%
Scott Hatteberg	12.3%
Javier Valentin	11.7%
Ryan Freel	8.9%
Jason LaRue	7.9%

Table 2. Getting Those Ducks on the Pond Home

Team	ROB	OBI	OBI%	Team	ROB	OBI	OBI%	Team	ROB	OBI	OBI%	Team	ROB	OBI	OBI%
Indians	4114	643	15.63%	Royals	3893	594	15.26%	Cubs	3597	511	14.21%	Astros	3972	534	13.44%
Tigers	3731	582	15.60%	Twins	4018	611	15.21%	Marlins	3745	531	14.18%	A's	4190	560	13.37%
Angels	3726	578	15.51%	Dodgers	4212	634	15.05%	Mariners	3748	531	14.17%	Nationals	4000	531	13.28%
White Sox	3912	603	15.41%	Blue Jays	3924	579	14.76%	Cardinals	3968	562	14.16%	Red Sox	4411	585	13.26%
Rangers	4013	616	15.35%	Rockies	4110	604	14.70%	Orioles	4077	563	13.81%	Reds	3820	501	13.12%
Mets	3911	600	15.34%	D'backs	3993	583	14.60%	Brewers	3768	515	13.67%	Pirates	3950	515	13.03%
Yankees	4518	692	15.32%	Giants	3783	548	14.49%	Padres	3932	537	13.66%				
Braves	3896	596	15.30%	Phillies	4227	607	14.36%	Devil Rays	3373	460	13.64%				

NOTE: ROB: Runners On Base; OBI: On-Base Runners Batted In; OBI%: Percentage of On-Base Runners Batted In.

young outfielders Jay Bruce and Drew Stubbs are among the top prospects in all of baseball, true blue-chippers. Similarly, on the pitching side of the equation an already-good rotation can look forward to Homer Bailey at some point this season, with promising arms such as Travis Wood and Sam LeCure on the way. Beyond them, the organization has a passel of homegrown relief talent, some of which may stick. If Krivsky can use the talent he inherited to keep enough people happy in the near term on the major league level, he'll get the opportunity to extend his Minnesota branch campus approach to player development.

HITTERS

Drew Anderson — 2B — Bats: S — Throws: R — Height: 5' 9" — Weight: 170 — Born: February 2, 1983 — Age: 24

YEAR	TEAM	LVL	AGE	PA	R	2B	3B	HR	RBI	BB	SO	SB	CS	SPEED	AVG	OBP	SLG	MLVR	EQAVG	EQOBP	EQSLG	EQA	VORP	DEFENSE			
2004	BIL	Rk	21	243	40	10	4	2	29	39	42	14	4	7.0	.254	.377	.376	-.065	.181	.255	.222	.186	-55.3	30-RF	-5		
2005	DYT	A	22	443	59	15	9	6	37	31	96	15	9	7.5	.246	.298	.371	-.087	.209	.248	.305	.198	-28.6	36-2B	-6	31-RF	2
2006	SAR	A+	23	361	48	19	9	4	31	29	51	7	4	6.5	.300	.360	.450	.180	.278	.329	.428	.259	15.1	67-2B	-9		
2006	CHT	AA	23	168	19	9	3	2	15	14	25	2	2	5.7	.277	.337	.419	.108	.276	.331	.441	.264	7.6	31-2B	-2		
2007	CIN	MLB	24	492	49	19	6	7	42	32	88	7	4	5.9	.236	.289	.352	-.244	.235	.286	.348	.217	-10.3	116-2B	-6		

Breakout: 21% Improve: 46% Collapse: 33% Attrition: 7% — Comparables: Chris Dean, Mickey Lopez, Brooks Conrad, Andrew Beattie

A stubby, scrappy little Hoosier who played his college ball at Ohio State before getting picked in the 13th round of the 2004 draft, Anderson isn't seen as the sort of gloveman that could be a future utility infielder. To make it as a strict second baseman, Anderson will have to hit for average with decent pop as he clambers up the chain, and that won't be easy.

Rich Aurilia — INF — Bats: R — Throws: R — Height: 6' 1" — Weight: 190 — Born: September 2, 1971 — Age: 35

YEAR	TEAM	LVL	AGE	PA	R	2B	3B	HR	RBI	BB	SO	SB	CS	SPEED	AVG	OBP	SLG	MLVR	EQAVG	EQOBP	EQSLG	EQA	VORP	DEFENSE			
2004	SEA	MLB	32	292	27	13	0	4	28	22	43	1	0	3.5	.241	.304	.337	-.206	.246	.314	.350	.236	-0.8	72-SS	-4		
2004	SDN	MLB	32	158	22	8	2	2	16	15	28	0	0	5.5	.254	.331	.384	-.038	.261	.338	.391	.257	1.4	25-3B	-3		
2005	CIN	MLB	33	468	61	23	2	14	68	37	67	2	0	4.8	.282	.338	.444	.074	.278	.338	.450	.271	20.6	62-2B	0	27-SS	-1
2006	CIN	MLB	34	481	61	25	1	23	70	34	51	3	0	4.5	.300	.349	.518	.169	.294	.346	.508	.288	27.4	40-3B	-1	37-1B	-1
2007	SFN	MLB	35	424	51	22	2	12	55	32	52	3	1	4.6	.276	.334	.438	-.018	.274	.331	.442	.264	13.2	101-3B	-2		

Breakout: 8% Improve: 34% Collapse: 30% Attrition: 22% — Comparables: Ken Boyer, Brooks Robinson, Bill Madlock, Art Howe

Aurilia seems to favor imbalance. After struggling to hit outside of Cincy in 2005, his home-road splits balanced out last year only for his lefty/righty splits to take a big tilt. But he doesn't just hit in hitter's parks, and he doesn't just hit lefties, and an infielder who hits for power and plays all four infield positions well enough has value. Back in San Francisco on a two-year deal, the 35-year-old Aurilia will fit right in on a team that might make MLB ask whether or not Geritol needs to become a banned performance-enhancing substance.

Jay Bruce — OF — Bats: L — Throws: L — Height: 6' 3" — Weight: 195 — Born: April 3, 1987 — Age: 20

YEAR	TEAM	LVL	AGE	PA	R	2B	3B	HR	RBI	BB	SO	SB	CS	SPEED	AVG	OBP	SLG	MLVR	EQAVG	EQOBP	EQSLG	EQA	VORP	DEFENSE			
2005	BIL	Rk	18	81	16	2	0	4	13	11	22	2	2	4.5	.257	.358	.457	.083	.203	.272	.297	.203	-12.6	10-RF	2		
2006	DYT	A	19	498	69	42	5	16	81	44	106	19	9	6.1	.291	.355	.516	.261	.258	.309	.456	.260	3.0	52-RF	-3	41-CF	5
2007	CIN	MLB	20	514	64	35	2	17	61	36	113	12	6	5.4	.263	.318	.459	-.028	.262	.315	.454	.259	8.4	121-RF	5		

Breakout: 44% Improve: 61% Collapse: 9% Attrition: 2% — Comparables: Ian Stewart, Carlos Gonzalez, Chris Lubanski, Eric Duncan

Bruce is a prime example of what you can get when you go for high-yield high school talent in the first round. Nabbed out of a Texas high school in the 2005 draft, Bruce did fine work in his full-season debut, showing off a full range of tools afield and at the plate. His range might not play in center, but he has the arm for right, so a destination in the outfield already suggests itself. The power generated by his quick-wristed stroke is already impressive. With improved command of the strike zone he'll deliver on his status as one of the best prospects in baseball.

Juan Castro SS **Bats: R** **Throws: R** Height: 5' 11" Weight: 195 Born: June 20, 1972 Age: 35

YEAR	TEAM	LVL	AGE	PA	R	2B	3B	HR	RBI	BB	SO	SB	CS	SPEED	AVG	OBP	SLG	MLVR	EQAVG	EQOBP	EQSLG	EQA	VORP	DEFENSE			
2004	CIN	MLB	32	316	36	21	2	5	26	14	51	1	0	4.8	.244	.277	.378	-.145	.240	.273	.370	.223	-3.5	42-3B	-3	23-SS	2
2005	MIN	MLB	33	292	27	18	1	5	33	9	39	0	1	4.0	.257	.279	.386	-.160	.258	.291	.397	.237	-0.9	63-SS	14	14-3B	-3
2006	MIN	MLB	34	164	10	5	2	1	14	6	23	1	1	4.5	.231	.258	.308	-.368	.221	.258	.292	.197	-7.5	46-SS	2		
2006	CIN	MLB	34	100	8	5	1	2	14	5	13	0	1	4.9	.284	.320	.421	-.027	.274	.310	.411	.243	1.7	16-SS	0		
2007	CIN	MLB	35	266	25	13	1	4	27	13	35	1	2	4.7	.256	.296	.369	-.195	.255	.293	.365	.223	-0.6	65-SS	1		

Breakout: 25% Improve: 47% Collapse: 31% Attrition: 49% Comparables: Alvaro Espinoza, Luis Sojo, Tim Foli, Billy Gardner

After starting the year playing to Batista's left in Minnesota, *Castro libre* landed in a town not nearly so disappointed to have him as the Twin Cities had become. Slick in the field and slack at the plate, the Reds happily haven't taken his 100 uncharacteristically robust plate appearances as reason to make him their starting shortstop.

Royce Clayton SS **Bats: R** **Throws: R** Height: 6' 0" Weight: 200 Born: January 2, 1970 Age: 37

YEAR	TEAM	LVL	AGE	PA	R	2B	3B	HR	RBI	BB	SO	SB	CS	SPEED	AVG	OBP	SLG	MLVR	EQAVG	EQOBP	EQSLG	EQA	VORP	DEFENSE	
2004	COL	MLB	34	652	95	36	4	8	54	48	125	10	5	6.2	.279	.338	.397	-.084	.263	.323	.376	.246	10.1	138-SS	-10
2005	ARI	MLB	35	573	59	28	4	2	44	38	105	13	3	5.9	.270	.320	.351	-.111	.265	.319	.345	.238	6.7	131-SS	-7
2006	WAS	MLB	36	338	36	22	1	0	27	19	53	8	3	5.5	.269	.315	.348	-.129	.278	.324	.363	.245	1.9	82-SS	-4
2006	CIN	MLB	36	164	13	8	0	2	13	11	32	6	3	4.9	.235	.290	.329	-.245	.228	.288	.322	.219	-3.8	38-SS	-3
2007	TOR	MLB	37	452	51	21	3	4	38	27	81	11	5	5.8	.262	.310	.356	-.173	.252	.306	.345	.235	0.2	107-SS	-7

Breakout: 15% Improve: 53% Collapse: 15% Attrition: 16% Comparables: Dave Concepcion, Alvin Dark, Jim Gantner, Ron Washington

A shadow of a once useful player, and now the second entry under "Mostly Harmless" in *The Hitchhiker's Guide to the Galaxy*. At this point, his skills are limited to running the bases well, dropping bunts on command, and playing a merely functional short. Bound for Toronto and a battle for playing time, at least he'll not be in any danger of being tarred and feathered for being part of the Kearns/Lopez deal.

Chris Denorfia OF **Bats: R** **Throws: R** Height: 6' 0" Weight: 195 Born: July 15, 1980 Age: 26

YEAR	TEAM	LVL	AGE	PA	R	2B	3B	HR	RBI	BB	SO	SB	CS	SPEED	AVG	OBP	SLG	MLVR	EQAVG	EQOBP	EQSLG	EQA	VORP	DEFENSE			
2004	POT	A+	23	321	52	18	4	11	51	48	66	10	6	6.3	.312	.416	.532	.355	.278	.361	.466	.283	20.4	72-CF	5		
2004	CHT	AA	23	256	30	10	2	6	27	30	42	5	2	5.2	.249	.340	.394	-.001	.228	.306	.355	.235	-4.5	61-CF	3		
2005	CHT	AA	24	209	40	17	3	7	26	17	38	4	3	6.4	.330	.391	.564	.379	.301	.351	.513	.285	17.4	28-CF	-4	17-RF	1
2005	LOU	AAA	24	374	50	12	6	13	61	41	54	8	3	5.8	.310	.391	.505	.245	.297	.374	.480	.291	28.8	69-CF	-5	11-RF	-1
2005	CIN	MLB	24	44	8	3	0	1	2	6	9	1	0	5.5	.263	.364	.421	.074	.263	.364	.421	.278	1.9				
2006	LOU	AAA	25	353	46	19	1	7	45	34	41	15	1	5.6	.349	.409	.484	.353	.347	.405	.497	.313	40.7	59-CF	1	12-RF	2
2006	CIN	MLB	25	120	14	6	0	1	7	11	21	1	1	4.4	.283	.356	.368	-.040	.280	.358	.355	.254	1.1	13-RF	3		
2007	CIN	MLB	26	461	65	24	2	11	54	42	72	9	3	5.3	.291	.359	.445	.046	.289	.355	.440	.274	17.9	109-CF	0		

Breakout: 6% Improve: 26% Collapse: 35% Attrition: 15% Comparables: Carl Furillo, Rontrez Johnson, Mike Edwards, Raul Gonzalez

Denorfia's trying to avoid the organizational cul-de-sac that sucked up Brady Clark and made him a Brewer, but so far, no dice. He has the skills to be a solid outfield regular, and if, like Clark, he can hack it in center, he'll be a valuable player. If he can't, he'll have to either luck into a job somewhere, or wind up in the pool of very good fourth outfielders. If the Reds move Griffey to a corner to play him in center, everyone comes out ahead, but Denorfia has little to no star potential.

Adam Dunn LF **Bats: L** **Throws: R** Height: 6' 6" Weight: 275 Born: November 9, 1979 Age: 27

YEAR	TEAM	LVL	AGE	PA	R	2B	3B	HR	RBI	BB	SO	SB	CS	SPEED	AVG	OBP	SLG	MLVR	EQAVG	EQOBP	EQSLG	EQA	VORP	DEFENSE			
2004	CIN	MLB	24	681	105	34	0	46	102	108	195	6	1	4.6	.266	.388	.569	.320	.264	.386	.565	.315	53.4	147-LF	-15		
2005	CIN	MLB	25	671	107	35	2	40	101	114	168	4	2	5.1	.247	.387	.540	.245	.245	.387	.546	.310	45.0	124-LF	-8	29-1B	-1
2006	CIN	MLB	26	683	99	24	0	40	92	112	194	7	0	4.3	.234	.365	.490	.098	.225	.362	.478	.288	23.5	148-LF	-15		
2007	CIN	MLB	27	632	108	30	1	43	110	99	161	6	2	4.6	.267	.390	.578	.249	.265	.387	.572	.315	46.1	148-LF	-9		

Breakout: 41% Improve: 66% Collapse: 8% Attrition: 4% Comparables: Troy Glaus, Mike Epstein, Kevin Maas, Rob Deer

As you'd expect from a player with old-player skills (walks and power with a healthy dose of strikeouts), Dunn isn't getting better at an age when players are supposed to be rising to their peak. Add in that he's a bit of a klutz in the outfield—a problem that's exacerbated by Griffey's decline in center—and a plodder on the bases, and you can understand why the Reds might not want to pick up their $13 million option for 2008.

Edwin Encarnacion   **3B**   **Bats: R**   **Throws: R**   Height: 6' 1"   Weight: 195   Born: January 7, 1983   Age: 24

YEAR	TEAM	LVL	AGE	PA	R	2B	3B	HR	RBI	BB	SO	SB	CS	SPEED	AVG	OBP	SLG	MLVR	EQAVG	EQOBP	EQSLG	EQA	VORP	DEFENSE	
2004	CHT	AA	21	526	73	35	1	13	76	53	79	17	3	6.0	.281	.352	.444	.106	.251	.312	.392	.248	6.8	116-3B	-15
2005	LOU	AAA	22	330	44	23	0	15	54	33	53	7	2	4.0	.314	.388	.548	.304	.294	.364	.519	.297	31.7	75-3B	3
2005	CIN	MLB	22	234	25	16	0	9	31	20	60	3	0	4.0	.232	.308	.436	-.019	.232	.308	.445	.258	3.8	54-3B	4
2006	CIN	MLB	23	463	60	33	1	15	72	41	78	6	3	4.9	.276	.359	.473	.099	.271	.353	.466	.279	17.0	104-3B	-7
2007	*CIN*	*MLB*	*24*	*519*	*73*	*31*	*2*	*20*	*69*	*47*	*88*	*8*	*2*	*5.2*	*.277*	*.350*	*.482*	*.070*	*.276*	*.347*	*.476*	*.279*	*22.7*	*122-3B*	*-1*

Breakout: 25% Improve: 55% Collapse: 12% Attrition: 17%   *Comparables: Ron Jackson, Ken McMullen, Don Money, Willie Jones*

Encarnacion lost most of June to an ankle injury and a good chunk of July to Jerry Narron's disgust over his defense. He was the Reds' leading regular in RBI percentage, plating almost 17 percent of the guys on board when he hit, but like a lot of Reds, you have to wonder how much of his production is the hitter and how much is the ballpark. He hit .323/.419/.526 at the Gap, but just .234/.301/.425 on the road. That's the difference between earning comparisons to David Wright or to Jim Presley. In the field, Encarnacion is athletic, but his glovework at third is inconsistent enough to be career-altering. The Reds need him at third for the time being, but barring improvement, there will come a time when they'll have to decide if first is his destiny or Joey Votto's.

Ryan Freel   **UT**   **Bats: R**   **Throws: R**   Height: 5' 10"   Weight: 180   Born: March 8, 1976   Age: 31

YEAR	TEAM	LVL	AGE	PA	R	2B	3B	HR	RBI	BB	SO	SB	CS	SPEED	AVG	OBP	SLG	MLVR	EQAVG	EQOBP	EQSLG	EQA	VORP	DEFENSE			
2004	CIN	MLB	28	592	74	21	8	3	28	67	88	37	10	7.4	.277	.375	.368	.038	.278	.374	.369	.271	19.1	48-3B	-2	36-RF	0
2005	CIN	MLB	29	431	69	19	3	4	21	51	59	36	10	7.1	.271	.372	.371	.021	.273	.373	.381	.274	15.2	44-2B	0	19-LF	5
2006	CIN	MLB	30	523	67	30	2	8	27	57	98	37	11	6.7	.271	.363	.399	.007	.268	.362	.398	.271	16.4	45-CF	2	40-RF	5
2007	*CIN*	*MLB*	*31*	*487*	*77*	*22*	*4*	*8*	*38*	*54*	*79*	*34*	*11*	*7.1*	*.267*	*.357*	*.396*	*-.039*	*.266*	*.354*	*.392*	*.267*	*9.7*	*115-CF*	*6*		

Breakout: 7% Improve: 25% Collapse: 32% Attrition: 20%   *Comparables: Lonnie Smith, Jacob Brumfield, Calvin Murray, Alan Bannister*

Freel's a good example of the difference between an athletic player who can actually handle a variety of positions and your more standard-issue ex-second baseman who plays elsewhere to survive. Unlike a lot of minor league journeymen who wind up in a major league utility role, Freel's a good outfielder as well as a decent enough second or third baseman, he gets on base regularly, and runs well when he does. Floating between four or five spots around the lineup, his real position is utility leadoff man.

Ken Griffey   **CF**   **Bats: L**   **Throws: L**   Height: 6' 3"   Weight: 220   Born: December 31, 1969   Age: 37

YEAR	TEAM	LVL	AGE	PA	R	2B	3B	HR	RBI	BB	SO	SB	CS	SPEED	AVG	OBP	SLG	MLVR	EQAVG	EQOBP	EQSLG	EQA	VORP	DEFENSE	
2004	CIN	MLB	34	348	49	18	0	20	60	44	67	1	0	4.1	.253	.351	.513	.181	.250	.348	.513	.289	22.1	68-CF	0
2005	CIN	MLB	35	555	85	30	0	35	92	54	93	0	1	3.6	.301	.369	.576	.319	.299	.368	.584	.312	52.3	121-CF	-15
2006	CIN	MLB	36	472	62	19	0	27	72	39	78	0	0	3.8	.252	.316	.486	.026	.246	.314	.474	.265	16.0	98-CF	-14
2007	*CIN*	*MLB*	*37*	*474*	*64*	*23*	*1*	*24*	*78*	*43*	*81*	*0*	*1*	*4.0*	*.275*	*.344*	*.505*	*.088*	*.274*	*.341*	*.499*	*.281*	*23.0*	*112-CF*	*-10*

Breakout: 16% Improve: 38% Collapse: 21% Attrition: 17%   *Comparables: Dave Parker, Fred Lynn, George Crowe, Paul O'Neill*

Let's pretend we know who was and wasn't taking something stronger than their multivitamins in recent years, and let's also say we're absolutely certain that Griffey is one of the good kids. He can't really play center any more, he can't run, the odds of his bat snapping back don't seem great. But what has happened to him is what used to happen to great players. Perhaps more than any other contemporary, Griffey has seen his standing as an all-time great suffer from the context of the juiced era. It's worth remembering that some modern players don't require caveats when you want to compare them to Mays or Mantle.

Brendan Harris　　　　**INF**　　　**Bats: R**　**Throws: R**　　Height: 6' 1"　　Weight: 200　　Born: August 26, 1980　　　Age: 26

YEAR	TEAM	LVL	AGE	PA	R	2B	3B	HR	RBI	BB	SO	SB	CS	SPEED	AVG	OBP	SLG	MLVR	EQAVG	EQOBP	EQSLG	EQA	VORP	DEFENSE			
2004	IOW	AAA	23	275	48	21	1	11	35	16	40	0	2	4.1	.311	.353	.532	.179	.280	.321	.459	.262	13.2	48-2B	6		
2004	EDM	AAA	23	145	20	6	0	6	24	10	21	0	0	3.7	.269	.317	.454	-.066	.250	.295	.394	.239	0.6	34-3B	-4		
2004	MON	MLB	23	53	4	2	0	1	2	2	11	0	0	4.2	.160	.208	.260	-.486	.120	.170	.200	.140	-4.7				
2005	NWO	AAA	24	519	67	22	4	13	81	40	77	9	5	4.9	.270	.329	.417	-.075	.266	.315	.395	.247	8.8	81-2B	1	42-3B	3
2006	NWO	AAA	25	257	37	14	0	5	32	26	56	3	2	4.6	.283	.379	.416	.139	.284	.366	.422	.274	14.5	34-3B	-1	14-SS	-2
2006	WAS	MLB	25	36	3	2	0	0	2	3	3	0	0	3.3	.250	.333	.313	-.148	.250	.333	.312	.234	-0.2				
2006	LOU	AAA	25	165	22	14	1	5	28	14	29	2	0	4.4	.324	.384	.534	.361	.322	.382	.544	.311	20.7	20-3B	-1		
2006	CIN	MLB	25	11	2	0	0	1	1	1	4	0	0	3.7	.200	.273	.500	-.071	.200	.273	.500	.254	0.2				
2007	TBA	MLB	26	500	54	23	2	11	54	33	91	3	2	4.6	.259	.314	.390	-.120	.256	.316	.392	.251	2.9	118-3B	-3		

Breakout: 12%　Improve: 27%　Collapse: 40%　Attrition: 7%　　　*Comparables: Marshall McDougall, Lou Merloni, Ramon Martinez, Jose Leon*

Sort of the antithesis to Freel, in that, while Harris can hit for a bit more power than most minor league second basemen looking for work, he really isn't much of an asset at any infield position. It will take a well-timed injury or a manager deciding "I *must* have that guy" for Harris to get much of a chance. Traded to the D-Rays, where he might stick in a utility role; maybe Joe Maddon's that manager.

Scott Hatteberg　　　　**1B**　　　**Bats: L**　**Throws: R**　　Height: 6' 1"　　Weight: 210　　Born: December 31, 1969　Age: 37

YEAR	TEAM	LVL	AGE	PA	R	2B	3B	HR	RBI	BB	SO	SB	CS	SPEED	AVG	OBP	SLG	MLVR	EQAVG	EQOBP	EQSLG	EQA	VORP	DEFENSE	
2004	OAK	MLB	34	638	87	30	0	15	82	72	48	0	0	4.2	.284	.367	.420	.048	.283	.370	.422	.279	19.1	135-1B	-1
2005	OAK	MLB	35	523	52	19	0	7	59	51	54	0	1	3.2	.256	.334	.343	-.107	.261	.348	.353	.251	-3.6	49-1B	-2
2006	CIN	MLB	36	539	62	28	0	13	51	74	41	2	2	3.9	.289	.389	.436	.114	.281	.385	.424	.284	16.9	122-1B	-7
2007	CIN	MLB	37	452	59	22	1	9	51	54	41	2	1	4.2	.285	.374	.415	.028	.284	.370	.411	.273	10.0	107-1B	-4

Breakout: 14%　Improve: 43%　Collapse: 25%　Attrition: 14%　　　*Comparables: Mark Grace, Wally Joyner, Dave Bergman, Tino Martinez*

An occasionally functional filler at first base, and as much a potential problem as a real solution if your team makes the mistake of latching on to him for any great length of time. He'll stand in and take his cuts (or just take) in any at-bat, but this latest resurrection was all about being hidden from lefties and loving life in his new ballpark (he hit .329/.428/.507 at the Gap). Krivsky sensibly gave him a low-cost one-year deal (plus a one-year option), but he's just keeping the seat warm for Joey Votto.

Todd Hollandsworth　　　**OF**　　　**Bats: L**　**Throws: L**　　Height: 6' 2"　　Weight: 225　　Born: April 20, 1973　　　Age: 34

YEAR	TEAM	LVL	AGE	PA	R	2B	3B	HR	RBI	BB	SO	SB	CS	SPEED	AVG	OBP	SLG	MLVR	EQAVG	EQOBP	EQSLG	EQA	VORP	DEFENSE			
2004	CHN	MLB	31	167	28	6	2	8	22	17	26	1	1	5.6	.318	.392	.547	.299	.311	.386	.541	.308	13.5	27-RF	2		
2005	CHN	MLB	32	290	23	17	2	5	35	18	53	4	4	5.4	.254	.301	.388	-.088	.251	.301	.393	.237	-3.6	64-LF	-4		
2005	ATL	MLB	32	40	3	0	0	1	1	5	13	0	1	2.8	.171	.275	.257	-.341	.143	.250	.229	.175	-3.0				
2006	CLE	MLB	33	162	21	12	1	6	27	4	33	0	1	5.2	.237	.253	.442	-.168	.240	.265	.461	.241	-3.6	24-LF	3	11-RF	-2
2006	CIN	MLB	33	74	6	6	0	1	8	6	19	0	1	4.2	.265	.324	.397	-.069	.250	.311	.368	.233	-0.4	13-RF	-2		
2007	CIN	MLB	34	262	33	15	1	9	37	19	52	3	2	5.1	.272	.326	.456	-.010	.271	.323	.451	.260	4.4	65-LF	-2		

Breakout: 21%　Improve: 46%　Collapse: 30%　Attrition: 42%　　　*Comparables: George Altman, Jim Beauchamp, Claudell Washington, Franklin Stubbs*

Historians reviewing Hollandsworth's career might make the mistake of seeing him as a gritty, dirty-shirted underdog who won hearts and minds on his way to the 1996 NL Rookie of the Year award. Not that Hollandsworth isn't that sort of player, but the fact that he came up at a time when beat writers were mailing in votes for anyone in Dodger blue sort of takes the starch out of the honor. Meanwhile, Ryan Zimmerman was left high and dry for last year's award despite being a far more deserving candidate than Hollandsworth ever was. Zimmerman's legacy should survive without the ROY; Hollandsworth's will be distorted by it. He's never been more than what he is, a line-drive hitter with modest power who can handle pinch-hitting chores.

Paul Janish
SS **Bats: R** **Throws: R** Height: 6' 2" Weight: 185 Born: October 12, 1982 Age: 24

YEAR	TEAM	LVL	AGE	PA	R	2B	3B	HR	RBI	BB	SO	SB	CS	SPEED	AVG	OBP	SLG	MLVR	EQAVG	EQOBP	EQSLG	EQA	VORP	DEFENSE	
2004	BIL	Rk	21	263	39	11	0	2	22	45	45	7	3	4.4	.263	.406	.346	-.042	.191	.275	.213	.189	-36.5	63-SS	8
2005	DYT	A	22	254	30	10	2	5	29	29	38	5	2	4.4	.245	.346	.385	.007	.209	.283	.314	.220	-8.1	55-SS	8
2006	DYT	A	23	108	19	6	0	5	18	7	10	0	0	4.6	.398	.435	.612	.597	.337	.361	.525	.298	12.9	24-SS	4
2006	SAR	A+	23	393	53	17	2	9	55	38	39	8	2	5.2	.278	.355	.421	.118	.256	.319	.394	.251	9.7	83-SS	10
2007	*CIN*	*MLB*	*24*	*484*	*50*	*21*	*1*	*8*	*47*	*38*	*68*	*4*	*2*	*4.9*	*.251*	*.315*	*.366*	*-.167*	*.250*	*.312*	*.362*	*.235*	*4.3*	*114-SS*	*9*

Breakout: 23% Improve: 52% Collapse: 28% Attrition: 8% Comparables: *Tyler Turnquist, Angel Gonzalez, Rick Gama, Dustin Carr*

Drafted out of Rice in the fifth round of the 2004 draft, Janish lost a good chunk of 2005 to Tommy John surgery, so he's already behind the curve for his age. That said, he's a plus defender with an acceptable range of hitting skills. Sometimes these guys wind up with opportunities, but more often they don't—anyone remember Nate Frese? If Janish adapts well to Double-A, he'll have a chance.

Jason LaRue
C **Bats: R** **Throws: R** Height: 5' 11" Weight: 205 Born: March 19, 1974 Age: 33

YEAR	TEAM	LVL	AGE	PA	R	2B	3B	HR	RBI	BB	SO	SB	CS	SPEED	AVG	OBP	SLG	MLVR	EQAVG	EQOBP	EQSLG	EQA	VORP	DEFENSE	
2004	CIN	MLB	30	445	46	24	2	14	55	26	108	0	2	3.7	.251	.334	.431	.037	.254	.331	.437	.262	15.7	101-C	-2
2005	CIN	MLB	31	422	38	27	0	14	60	41	101	0	0	3.2	.260	.355	.452	.088	.261	.353	.462	.279	22.7	104-C	-1
2006	CIN	MLB	32	230	22	5	0	8	21	27	51	1	0	4.0	.194	.317	.346	-.197	.192	.311	.337	.234	-4.3	57-C	8
2007	*KCA*	*MLB*	*33*	*321*	*31*	*14*	*1*	*8*	*35*	*27*	*70*	*1*	*1*	*3.9*	*.233*	*.314*	*.369*	*-.166*	*.225*	*.311*	*.369*	*.243*	*-0.7*	*78-C*	*1*

Breakout: 9% Improve: 33% Collapse: 33% Attrition: 36% Comparables: *Kelly Stinnett, Duffy Dyer, Jim Hegan, Dixie Howell*

The combination of a preseason knee injury and the incredible hot streak of David Ross reduced the five-year incumbent backstop to "what have you done for me lately" status. If he's healthy and gets a larger share of playing time in Kansas City at John Buck's expense, he might reward the Royals' decision to take on $2.5 million of what he's owed for 2007, especially if he thrives in the first three or four months and Dayton Moore sensibly flips him at the deadline.

Javon Moran
OF **Bats: R** **Throws: R** Height: 5' 11" Weight: 175 Born: September 30, 1982 Age: 24

YEAR	TEAM	LVL	AGE	PA	R	2B	3B	HR	RBI	BB	SO	SB	CS	SPEED	AVG	OBP	SLG	MLVR	EQAVG	EQOBP	EQSLG	EQA	VORP	DEFENSE			
2004	DYT	A	21	106	11	2	0	0	7	10	15	11	3	5.3	.383	.448	.404	.282	.330	.381	.351	.269	4.3	22-CF	-3		
2004	LWD	A	21	467	73	18	9	2	38	24	78	41	17	8.4	.285	.340	.385	.061	.272	.307	.355	.236	-4.2	81-CF	-3	18-RF	-2
2005	SAR	A+	22	231	35	4	2	2	23	14	32	13	7	6.4	.329	.378	.395	.148	.299	.342	.364	.250	4.5	25-CF	-4	24-LF	3
2005	CHT	AA	22	88	14	5	1	0	2	5	21	7	4	7.7	.301	.341	.386	.025	.274	.307	.357	.233	-0.7	17-CF	5		
2006	SAR	A+	23	46	5	2	0	0	3	2	5	4	4	5.8	.372	.413	.419	.273	.341	.383	.386	.253	2.5				
2006	CHT	AA	23	269	34	11	3	1	12	11	26	16	7	6.8	.320	.355	.400	.139	.315	.345	.413	.264	5.5	34-RF	5	12-CF	-1
2007	*PHI*	*MLB*	*24*	*428*	*53*	*17*	*4*	*3*	*34*	*18*	*55*	*19*	*8*	*6.6*	*.280*	*.317*	*.366*	*-.144*	*.276*	*.314*	*.358*	*.235*	*-4.7*	*102-CF*	*2*		

Breakout: 6% Improve: 21% Collapse: 48% Attrition: 12% Comparables: *Ramon Moreta, Wilkin Ruan, Carlos Mendoza, Eric Reed*

The Reds have a sweet-tooth for the slap-happy, run-like-hell class of hitters. If you had to pick, Moran's probably not the best of the bunch, and his hitting from the right side and weak arm in center make him look like someone doomed to spare part possibilities. Dealt to the Phillies for Jeff Conine, his opportunities are no better there.

Ray Olmedo
SS **Bats: S** **Throws: R** Height: 5' 11" Weight: 155 Born: May 31, 1981 Age: 26

YEAR	TEAM	LVL	AGE	PA	R	2B	3B	HR	RBI	BB	SO	SB	CS	SPEED	AVG	OBP	SLG	MLVR	EQAVG	EQOBP	EQSLG	EQA	VORP	DEFENSE			
2004	LOU	AAA	23	327	33	13	7	2	26	23	40	2	3	5.1	.286	.342	.398	-.024	.265	.320	.366	.240	2.6	59-2B	6	23-SS	-3
2005	LOU	AAA	24	60	8	3	0	1	5	1	11	2	2	5.8	.276	.300	.379	-.113	.259	.283	.345	.214	-1.2	13-2B	2		
2005	CIN	MLB	24	88	10	4	1	1	4	6	22	4	0	7.6	.221	.282	.338	-.223	.218	.287	.333	.232	-1.1	16-2B	-1		
2006	LOU	AAA	25	430	47	20	3	3	29	34	71	17	6	6.1	.282	.344	.373	.049	.284	.341	.384	.257	16.2	94-SS	6		
2006	CIN	MLB	25	48	5	2	0	1	4	4	4	1	0	5.5	.205	.271	.318	-.315	.182	.250	.295	.200	-1.6				
2007	*CIN*	*MLB*	*26*	*446*	*53*	*16*	*4*	*5*	*34*	*33*	*72*	*15*	*6*	*6.1*	*.260*	*.320*	*.356*	*-.166*	*.258*	*.317*	*.352*	*.236*	*1.5*	*106-SS*	*2*		

Breakout: 12% Improve: 36% Collapse: 33% Attrition: 10% Comparables: *Alfredo Amezaga, Marty Malloy, Kevin Estrada, Henry Mateo*

A superb defender in an organization that seems to prefer old-timers like Juan Castro in that sort of job, Olmedo's really in a bad spot. He wouldn't be the worst starting shortstop in baseball, but he also doesn't have a lot of potential to blossom into a significantly better hitter. With Alex Gonzalez locked up for three years and Juan Castro for two, Olmedo's only trade bait now.

Brandon Phillips | **2B** | **Bats: R** | **Throws: R** | Height: 6' 0" | Weight: 195 | Born: June 28, 1981 | Age: 26

YEAR	TEAM	LVL	AGE	PA	R	2B	3B	HR	RBI	BB	SO	SB	CS	SPEED	AVG	OBP	SLG	MLVR	EQAVG	EQOBP	EQSLG	EQA	VORP	DEFENSE	
2004	BUF	AAA	23	588	83	34	4	8	50	44	56	14	11	5.6	.303	.363	.430	.085	.284	.342	.398	.258	19.9	69-2B 3	65-SS -7
2005	BUF	AAA	24	518	79	24	1	15	46	39	90	7	5	5.1	.256	.326	.409	-.059	.236	.302	.377	.236	2.5	109-SS 3	
2006	CIN	MLB	25	587	65	28	1	17	75	35	88	25	2	5.8	.276	.324	.427	-.020	.271	.321	.416	.262	22.6	136-2B -15	
2007	CIN	MLB	26	552	71	27	2	13	58	38	75	16	6	5.3	.273	.330	.417	-.055	.271	.327	.413	.256	15.1	130-2B -4	

Breakout: 27% Improve: 56% Collapse: 21% Attrition: 10%   Comparables: Damion Easley, Reno Bertoia, Rafael Ramirez, Andy Carey

A perfect free-talent pickup, Phillips was obviously frustrated and spinning his wheels in the Indians' organization. Given a shot at playing somewhere besides Buffalo, he hit more like he can. He can stand in and drive the ball, so he's not your usual placeholding patsy, and getting power out of all eight lineup slots has its benefits, especially in Cincy's power-friendly park. Although the Reds flirted with the possibility of making him a shortstop again at the end of the season, he's better off seeing if he can settle in at second, which the signing of Alex Gonzalez should allow him to do. There's potential for improvement, but he's not that young anymore. He'll give the Reds a nice three- or four-year run before arbitration encourages them to make him somebody else's second baseman.

Dave Ross | **C** | **Bats: R** | **Throws: R** | Height: 6' 2" | Weight: 225 | Born: March 19, 1977 | Age: 30

YEAR	TEAM	LVL	AGE	PA	R	2B	3B	HR	RBI	BB	SO	SB	CS	SPEED	AVG	OBP	SLG	MLVR	EQAVG	EQOBP	EQSLG	EQA	VORP	DEFENSE
2004	LAN	MLB	27	190	13	3	1	5	15	15	62	0	0	4.0	.170	.253	.291	-.357	.158	.237	.279	.193	-10.2	48-C 0
2005	PIT	MLB	28	119	9	8	0	3	15	6	24	0	0	3.2	.222	.263	.380	-.183	.222	.267	.389	.230	-1.1	31-C 6
2005	SDN	MLB	28	19	2	0	1	0	0	0	4	0	0	6.2	.353	.389	.471	.255	.333	.368	.444	.280	1.8	
2006	CIN	MLB	29	296	37	15	1	21	52	37	75	0	0	3.2	.255	.353	.579	.215	.246	.346	.560	.298	22.6	70-C 5
2007	CIN	MLB	30	306	35	14	1	14	42	31	76	0	0	3.9	.238	.322	.455	-.046	.237	.320	.450	.260	8.4	74-C 4

Breakout: 26% Improve: 55% Collapse: 17% Attrition: 48%   Comparables: Ramon Castro, Tim Laudner, Sal Fasano, Dave Duncan

Although Ross's season might seem ridiculously out of character, he did hit .258/.336/.556 backing up Paul Lo Duca for the Dodgers in 2003. Ross also played more in 2006 than in any season since he was in Triple-A Las Vegas in 2002, and he hasn't been an everyday player since 1999, in High-A Vero Beach. Which is all to say that Ross has had a pretty unusual career path already, and it isn't inconceivable that, after being constantly overlooked, he could be the new Tim Laudner. He's a good backstop and deters the running game, he'll take a walk if played regularly, and he can bust a cookie to crumbs when a pitcher makes a mistake. Sharing the job with Valentin, he'll give the Reds a cheap and effective catching set-up at a time when teams are throwing millions of dollars at Rod Barajas.

Drew Stubbs | **OF** | **Bats: R** | **Throws: R** | Height: 6' 5" | Weight: 190 | Born: October 4, 1984 | Age: 22

YEAR	TEAM	LVL	AGE	PA	R	2B	3B	HR	RBI	BB	SO	SB	CS	SPEED	AVG	OBP	SLG	MLVR	EQAVG	EQOBP	EQSLG	EQA	VORP	DEFENSE
2006	BIL	Rk	21	252	39	7	3	6	24	32	64	19	4	7.1	.252	.368	.400	.065	.211	.279	.298	.213	-25.0	52-CF 5
2007	CIN	MLB	22	392	40	14	2	6	30	29	107	13	6	5.8	.223	.287	.324	-.293	.222	.284	.320	.210	-12.8	94-CF 6

Breakout: 41% Improve: 55% Collapse: 32% Attrition: 32%   Comparables: Darwinson Salazar, Jeremy Owens, Billy Brown, Timi Moni-Erigbali

Tabbed out of the University of Texas, Stubbs is Krivsky's first first-rounder. He has the full assortment of tools, with defensive skills in center that already rank him among the best at any level. Scouts also give him high marks for his power potential, and he can run. He'll be given plenty of time to develop and address concerns about his ability to handle pro pitching given some plate coverage issues, but the upside is considerable.

B. J. Szymanski | **OF** | **Bats: S** | **Throws: R** | Height: 6' 5" | Weight: 210 | Born: October 1, 1982 | Age: 24

YEAR	TEAM	LVL	AGE	PA	R	2B	3B	HR	RBI	BB	SO	SB	CS	SPEED	AVG	OBP	SLG	MLVR	EQAVG	EQOBP	EQSLG	EQA	VORP	DEFENSE	
2004	BIL	Rk	21	92	13	4	2	3	17	9	26	2	1	5.9	.259	.330	.469	-.005	.186	.220	.267	.179	-17.7	12-CF 2	
2005	DYT	A	22	214	32	8	1	10	26	21	57	7	1	5.3	.262	.332	.471	.113	.228	.282	.396	.234	-3.2	42-CF -4	
2006	DYT	A	23	534	68	31	3	16	59	46	191	22	10	6.5	.239	.309	.415	.031	.197	.249	.323	.204	-36.1	92-CF 0	31-RF -3
2007	CIN	MLB	24	444	41	17	3	12	45	27	161	10	4	5.5	.210	.262	.351	-.309	.209	.260	.348	.205	-18.2	105-CF 2	

Breakout: 39% Improve: 56% Collapse: 31% Attrition: 17%   Comparables: Benny Craig, Darron Ingram, Scott Whitrock, Charlton Jimerson

Almost a caricature of the tool-time guy who really just doesn't deliver, Szymanski had the benefits of all of the little things that help make a cipher get touted as a top prospect. He looks good in a uniform, appeasing scouts, and he went to Princeton, impressing the Fourth Estate. Did we mention he's big and strapping? The real story is that he's already earned a reputation for fragility and didn't hit in the Midwest League. In an organization with better depth, he'd be a footnote.

Cincinnati Reds

Javier Valentin   **C**   **Bats: S**   **Throws: R**   Height: 5′ 10″   Weight: 210   Born: September 19, 1975   Age: 31

YEAR	TEAM	LVL	AGE	PA	R	2B	3B	HR	RBI	BB	SO	SB	CS	SPEED	AVG	OBP	SLG	MLVR	EQAVG	EQOBP	EQSLG	EQA	VORP	DEFENSE	
2004	CIN	MLB	28	222	18	10	1	6	20	17	36	0	0	3.8	.233	.293	.381	-.116	.228	.288	.371	.230	0.3	50-C	0
2005	CIN	MLB	29	254	36	11	0	14	50	30	37	0	0	3.6	.281	.362	.520	.213	.277	.361	.518	.296	20.8	58-C	-3
2006	CIN	MLB	30	201	24	6	1	8	27	13	29	0	0	3.9	.269	.313	.441	-.027	.265	.313	.432	.256	4.5	35-C	3
2007	*CIN*	*MLB*	*31*	*224*	*25*	*8*	*1*	*8*	*28*	*21*	*34*	*0*	*0*	*4.1*	*.246*	*.319*	*.413*	*-.101*	*.245*	*.316*	*.409*	*.248*	*2.3*	*56-C*	*0*

Breakout: 8%   *Improve: 25%*   *Collapse: 44%*   *Attrition: 39%*   *Comparables: Ed Herrmann, Todd Benzinger, Damon Berryhill, Ebba St. Claire*

Rescued from the scrapheap, in three years as a Reds reserve, Valentin's hit .286/.340/.501 against right-handed pitching, and he's effective against the running game. He wouldn't quite hit that well if he was playing full-time in a platoon, but he won't do too much worse if he simply gets to share the job with Ross.

Joey Votto   **1B**   **Bats: L**   **Throws: R**   Height: 6′ 3″   Weight: 220   Born: September 10, 1983   Age: 23

YEAR	TEAM	LVL	AGE	PA	R	2B	3B	HR	RBI	BB	SO	SB	CS	SPEED	AVG	OBP	SLG	MLVR	EQAVG	EQOBP	EQSLG	EQA	VORP	DEFENSE	
2004	DYT	A	20	473	60	26	2	14	73	79	110	9	2	4.6	.302	.419	.486	.279	.267	.362	.423	.276	13.1	87-1B	-10
2004	POT	A+	20	96	11	7	0	5	20	11	21	1	1	3.0	.298	.385	.560	.338	.264	.333	.494	.272	3.8	18-1B	0
2005	SAR	A+	21	529	64	23	2	17	83	52	122	4	5	3.4	.256	.330	.425	.058	.236	.297	.385	.237	-15.8	105-1B	-4
2006	CHT	AA	22	590	85	46	2	22	77	78	109	24	7	5.5	.319	.408	.547	.398	.312	.393	.564	.319	64.9	134-1B	6
2007	*CIN*	*MLB*	*23*	*582*	*88*	*33*	*2*	*26*	*86*	*65*	*123*	*16*	*5*	*4.7*	*.284*	*.366*	*.510*	*.139*	*.283*	*.363*	*.504*	*.293*	*28.0*	*136-1B*	*2*

Breakout: 21%   *Improve: 53%*   *Collapse: 9%*   *Attrition: 5%*   *Comparables: Carlos Pena, Brad Hawpe, Nate Dishington, Travis Hafner*

In order to refresh his prospect status after a disappointing 2005, Votto needed bounce back while rising to the challenge of Double-A last year. After a slow start, he more than managed it. Although he's more likely to become Votto the Very Good as opposed to Joey the Great, he generates a lot of flyballs, and those can do major damage in the Gap, and while he has problems with lefties, he did just slug .631 against right-handers. Votto can press at times, but he has the all-round hitting skill to exploit his environment. There's more breakout potential here than you might see at first glance.

Brandon Watson   **CF**   **Bats: L**   **Throws: R**   Height: 6′ 1″   Weight: 170   Born: September 30, 1981   Age: 25

YEAR	TEAM	LVL	AGE	PA	R	2B	3B	HR	RBI	BB	SO	SB	CS	SPEED	AVG	OBP	SLG	MLVR	EQAVG	EQOBP	EQSLG	EQA	VORP	DEFENSE			
2004	EDM	AAA	22	566	74	17	3	2	41	31	68	22	10	6.1	.293	.332	.348	-.174	.282	.320	.330	.232	-5.7	116-CF	-8		
2005	HAR	AA	23	156	13	1	0	0	6	7	21	7	5	4.9	.247	.290	.253	-.255	.224	.265	.231	.188	-13.8	33-CF	-5		
2005	NWO	AAA	23	408	69	15	3	1	25	28	33	31	13	7.1	.355	.400	.419	.135	.356	.394	.414	.283	31.6	68-CF	-1	15-RF	4
2005	WAS	MLB	23	48	8	1	1	1	5	4	8	0	2	8.0	.175	.250	.325	-.339	.190	.261	.333	.201	-4.3				
2006	NWO	AAA	24	87	11	3	1	0	13	3	10	2	1	5.8	.305	.326	.366	-.009	.313	.333	.373	.246	1.7	11-CF	-2		
2006	WAS	MLB	24	29	0	0	0	0	0	1	3	0	2	4.9	.179	.207	.179	-.619	.000	.034	.000	.038	-4.5				
2006	LOU	AAA	24	152	16	3	0	0	8	11	12	6	2	6.0	.270	.324	.292	-.099	.266	.320	.288	.224	-4.5	21-CF	-1		
2007	*CIN*	*MLB*	*25*	*348*	*42*	*11*	*2*	*0*	*21*	*21*	*37*	*15*	*5*	*6.5*	*.279*	*.325*	*.327*	*-.184*	*.277*	*.322*	*.323*	*.230*	*-4.4*	*84-CF*	*-1*		

Breakout: 20%   *Improve: 41%*   *Collapse: 34%*   *Attrition: 21%*   *Comparables: Kerry Robinson, Carlos Mendoza, Chaz Lytle, Alex Sanchez*

Watson might suffer some guilt by association for coming over form the Nats as a waiver claim in the aftermath of the Kearns trade. Like most aspiring fifth outfield types, he hits lefty, runs well, can handle playing in center, and lights a candle every week praying to Tom Goodwin, their patron saint, that he, too, will someday luck into an everyday job.

PITCHERS

Bronson Arroyo   **Bats: R**   **Throws: R**   Height: 6′ 5″   Weight: 190   Born: February 24, 1977   Age: 30

YEAR	TEAM	LVL	AGE	W	L	SV	G	GS	IP	H	BB	SO	HR	GB%	BABIP	STUFF	WHIP	ERA	PERA	EQERA	EQH9	EQBB9	EQSO9	EQHR9	VORP	WXRL
2004	BOS	MLB	27	10	9	0	32	29	178²	171	47	142	17	—	.291	24	1.22	4.03	3.87	4.47	8.5	2.1	6.6	0.7	27.7	3.81
2005	BOS	MLB	28	14	10	0	35	32	205¹	213	54	100	22	40.0%	.281	5	1.30	4.52	4.57	4.57	8.6	2.3	4.2	0.9	18.7	2.89
2006	CIN	MLB	29	14	11	0	35	35	240²	222	64	184	31	39.3%	.274	20	1.19	3.29	3.98	3.16	7.7	2.1	6.2	1.0	64.9	7.35
2007	*CIN*	*MLB*	*30*	*13*	*11*	*0*	*32*	*32*	*212*	*215*	*59*	*157*	*30*	*43.0%*	*.286*	*14*	*1.29*	*4.31*	*4.37*	*4.19*	*9.3*	*2.2*	*6.0*	*1.2*	*34.2*	*5.00*

Breakout: 5%   *Improve: 33%*   *Collapse: 20%*   *Attrition: 0%*   *Comparables: John Thomson, Jack McDowell, Matt Morris, Pat Dobson*

Put on the spot to be a workhorse following a high-stakes challenge trade, Arroyo rose to the challenge, posting career highs in starts and innings pitched. He was news early on, getting off to a 9–3 start, but poor run support and a bumpy

(continued next page)

Bronson Arroyo *(continued)*

stretch in which he posted only a pair of quality starts in eight appearances from July 4 to August 10 seemed to erase him from mainstream memory. Perhaps equally important, his groundball-to-flyball ratio dropped from roughly 1:1 to 1:2 during that stretch, and he gave up 14 home runs in 51.2 innings. Arroyo's season didn't end there, though, as he logged eight quality starts (one blown) in his remaining ten games, finishing with a year among the best five or six pitchers in baseball. Not that he doesn't have work to do: his platoon splits are massive and getting worse, and lefties have pumped their slugging against him from .429 to .488 to .498 in the last three years. Legit four-pitch assortment or no, something clearly isn't working. If Arroyo and new pitching coach Dick Pole can find something to freeze lefties, the Reds' current ace will be that much more likely to stick as a premier starter.

Homer Bailey   Bats: R   Throws: R   Height: 6' 4"   Weight: 205   Born: May 3, 1986   Age: 21

YEAR	TEAM	LVL	AGE	W	L	SV	G	GS	IP	H	BB	SO	HR	GB%	BABIP	STUFF	WHIP	ERA	PERA	EQERA	EQH9	EQBB9	EQSO9	EQHR9	VORP	WXRL
2005	DYT	A	19	8	4	0	28	21	103²	89	62	125	5	49.3%	.332	21	1.46	4.43	4.91	6.24	8.7	6.1	7.3	0.8	-7.2	—
2006	SAR	A+	20	3	5	0	13	13	70²	49	22	79	6	44.8%	.247	14	1.01	3.33	5.26	5.29	7.8	3.3	6.8	1.5	2.3	—
2006	CHT	AA	20	7	1	0	13	13	68¹	50	28	77	1	52.4%	.298	40	1.15	1.59	3.28	2.53	7.3	3.6	7.2	0.3	23.1	—
2007	CIN	MLB	21	7	8	0	28	19	119	113	65	112	16	46.0%	.292	14	1.49	4.76	4.97	4.67	8.7	4.4	7.6	1.2	12.5	2.10

Breakout: 21%   Improve: 53%   Collapse: 19%   Attrition: 0%   Comparables: *Edwin Jackson, Rich Harden, Chad Billingsley, Jake Peavy*

Cocky and talented, Bailey's the classic Texas amateur power pitcher. Consistently delivering heat in the mid-90s and touching 98 MPH, he also features a sledgehammer 12-to-6 curve and a solid change. Bailey was handled carefully in his first two years as a pro, and Krivsky followed suit last year, resisting the temptation to bring him up into the middle of a faltering stretch drive. Bailey will get a good look in camp. Bet on his making the rotation before the All-Star break.

Matt Belisle   Bats: R   Throws: R   Height: 6' 3"   Weight: 195   Born: June 6, 1980   Age: 27

YEAR	TEAM	LVL	AGE	W	L	SV	G	GS	IP	H	BB	SO	HR	GB%	BABIP	STUFF	WHIP	ERA	PERA	EQERA	EQH9	EQBB9	EQSO9	EQHR9	VORP	WXRL
2004	LOU	AAA	24	9	11	0	28	28	162²	192	51	106	16	—	.331	-2	1.49	5.26	4.88	5.63	10.3	3.0	4.5	1.0	-0.5	—
2005	CIN	MLB	25	4	8	1	60	5	85²	101	26	59	11	53.5%	.330	-6	1.48	4.41	4.57	4.72	9.7	2.4	5.5	1.1	3.5	0.63
2006	CIN	MLB	26	2	0	0	30	2	40	43	19	26	5	50.4%	.306	-8	1.55	3.60	4.92	3.46	9.1	3.7	5.2	0.9	9.0	0.39
2007	CIN	MLB	27	3	3	1	47	3	63²	70	25	42	7	52.0%	.307	-6	1.49	4.64	4.90	4.58	10.2	3.1	5.3	1.0	7.0	0.70

Breakout: 16%   Improve: 40%   Collapse: 26%   Attrition: 14%   Comparables: *Cal Koonce, Randy O'Neal, Jose Santiago, Jeff Dedmon*

In Old Testament Hebrew, *belial* means "without worth." While Matt's not that bad, it's time to cue up Peggy Lee and accept that this is all that there is. You could cut him some slack over the back injury that cost him more than two months in 2006, but he wasn't all that good in 2005, and that wasn't the first major back injury he's endured. With pedestrian stuff, he's in danger of falling into the dreaded Quadruple-A class of pitching talent, perpetually hoping for a fifth starter's job or garbage time out of the pen.

Bill Bray   Bats: L   Throws: L   Height: 6' 3"   Weight: 215   Born: June 5, 1983   Age: 24

YEAR	TEAM	LVL	AGE	W	L	SV	G	GS	IP	H	BB	SO	HR	GB%	BABIP	STUFF	WHIP	ERA	PERA	EQERA	EQH9	EQBB9	EQSO9	EQHR9	VORP	WXRL
2005	POT	A+	22	1	0	3	8	0	12²	8	3	18	1	44.8%	.250	12	0.87	2.13	3.98	3.00	7.5	2.2	8.2	1.5	3.5	—
2005	NWO	AAA	22	1	4	2	23	0	21¹	23	9	25	3	39.1%	.351	1	1.50	5.07	4.99	6.75	10.1	3.8	8.0	1.3	-2.7	—
2006	NWO	AAA	23	4	1	5	21	0	31²	26	9	45	5	41.3%	.300	19	1.12	4.04	4.71	4.40	8.5	2.6	10.3	1.8	4.1	—
2006	WAS	MLB	23	1	1	0	19	0	23	24	9	16	2	50.0%	.314	-2	1.43	3.91	4.11	3.86	9.3	3.1	5.8	0.8	4.2	0.41
2006	CIN	MLB	23	2	1	2	29	0	27²	33	9	23	3	40.0%	.345	4	1.52	4.22	3.66	4.40	10.0	2.5	6.6	0.9	2.9	0.69
2007	CIN	MLB	24	3	3	3	50	2	53¹	57	20	43	7	44.0%	.306	2	1.43	4.45	4.69	4.33	9.8	3.0	6.5	1.1	7.9	0.70

Breakout: 16%   Improve: 43%   Collapse: 21%   Attrition: 31%   Comparables: *Bob Sykes, Esteban Yan, Will McEnaney, Dave LaRoche*

Setting aside what it took to get him here, Bray's about as worthwhile a young lefty reliever as you could imagine. Boasting a high-velocity fastball/slider combo that can fool most of the people most of the time, he combines with Todd Coffey to give the Reds a lefty-righty tandem that might soon conjure up comparisons to the Nasty Boys. There's some speculation that he might wind up a starter at some point, but there are plenty of candidates for the fifth slot this spring. Barring a serious commitment to the experiment, his ability as a reliever might provide too strong a disincentive to mess with success.

Brandon Claussen

Bats: R Throws: L Height: 6' 1" Weight: 200 Born: May 1, 1979 Age: 28

YEAR	TEAM	LVL	AGE	W	L	SV	G	GS	IP	H	BB	SO	HR	GB%	BABIP	STUFF	WHIP	ERA	PERA	EQERA	EQH9	EQBB9	EQSO9	EQHR9	VORP	WXRL
2004	LOU	AAA	25	8	6	0	18	18	100¹	98	47	111	10	—	.325	16	1.45	4.67	4.70	5.06	9.0	4.6	7.7	1.1	6.0	—
2004	CIN	MLB	25	2	8	0	14	14	66	80	35	45	9	—	.332	-6	1.74	6.14	5.05	6.19	10.3	4.2	5.3	1.1	-8.9	0.53
2005	CIN	MLB	26	10	11	0	29	29	166²	178	57	121	24	36.3%	.303	5	1.41	4.21	4.73	4.46	8.8	2.7	5.8	1.2	14.9	3.30
2006	CIN	MLB	27	3	8	0	14	14	77	93	28	57	14	38.9%	.332	-1	1.57	6.19	5.04	5.51	10.1	2.8	6.0	1.4	-2.7	0.65
2007	WAS	MLB	28	3	5	1	25	9	67²	72	26	48	10	40%	.293	-2	1.44	4.83	5.51	5.20	9.5	3.0	5.8	1.2	4.3	0.7

Breakout: 18% Improve: 43% Collapse: 32% Attrition: 45% Comparables: Woodie Fryman, Rick Krivda, Lance Painter, Andrew Lorraine

Claussen logged only four quality starts in fourteen tries before hitting the shelf with shoulder problems that ended in surgery to repair a labrum tear. Since he was already slipping toward junkballer status, the shoulder damage might not derail his career, but he was dumped from the roster in December, in part because he isn't going to be ready to pitch at the start of the year. The sooner he can get a new start as somebody else's retread the better, because this is the wrong park and the wrong division for him.

Todd Coffey

Bats: R Throws: R Height: 6' 5" Weight: 230 Born: September 9, 1980 Age: 26

YEAR	TEAM	LVL	AGE	W	L	SV	G	GS	IP	H	BB	SO	HR	GB%	BABIP	STUFF	WHIP	ERA	PERA	EQERA	EQH9	EQBB9	EQSO9	EQHR9	VORP	WXRL
2004	CHT	AA	23	4	1	20	40	0	45¹	36	4	53	3	—	.284	12	0.88	2.38	3.24	3.48	8.4	0.8	6.8	1.0	10.4	—
2005	CIN	MLB	24	4	1	1	57	0	58	84	11	26	5	53.7%	.371	-11	1.64	4.50	4.18	4.40	11.7	1.5	3.5	0.7	2.4	0.56
2006	CIN	MLB	25	6	7	8	81	0	78	85	26	60	7	52.0%	.321	8	1.42	3.46	3.71	3.22	9.1	2.6	6.1	0.7	19.8	2.59
2007	CIN	MLB	26	3	3	4	58	0	64²	74	21	43	8	50.0%	.315	-4	1.46	4.36	4.80	4.25	10.6	2.6	5.4	1.0	9.8	0.80

Breakout: 14% Improve: 30% Collapse: 42% Attrition: 18% Comparables: T. J. Tucker, Chris Reitsma, Dave Heaverlo, Rich Loiselle

If the decision to press Coffey into action in 2005 amounted to a trial by fire, the good news is that Coffey came out of it ready to reply in kind with velocity that is now up into the mid-90s. He's still got a good slider, but experiments with a revived splitter didn't give him a reliably effective weapon against lefties. If Dick Pole helps him with that, Coffey could either blossom into a star closer or settle in as slightly more equal among equals in a bullpen by committee.

Rheal Cormier

Bats: L Throws: L Height: 5' 10" Weight: 195 Born: December 31, 1969 Age: 40

YEAR	TEAM	LVL	AGE	W	L	SV	G	GS	IP	H	BB	SO	HR	GB%	BABIP	STUFF	WHIP	ERA	PERA	EQERA	EQH9	EQBB9	EQSO9	EQHR9	VORP	WXRL
2004	PHI	MLB	37	4	5	0	84	0	81	70	26	46	7	—	.260	-4	1.19	3.56	4.35	3.64	7.8	2.5	4.5	0.7	19.8	2.40
2005	PHI	MLB	38	4	2	0	57	0	47¹	56	16	34	9	52.3%	.322	-17	1.52	5.90	5.27	6.33	10.6	2.8	6.0	1.7	-3.4	0.33
2006	PHI	MLB	39	2	2	0	43	0	34	27	13	13	2	46.7%	.238	-12	1.18	1.59	4.59	1.54	6.7	3.1	3.1	0.5	16.9	0.42
2006	CIN	MLB	39	0	1	0	21	0	14	21	4	6	3	44.4%	.353	-22	1.79	4.50	5.41	3.68	12.3	2.5	3.7	1.8	2.5	-0.46
2007	CIN	MLB	40	2	2	1	40	0	38	45	15	19	6	50.0%	.303	-22	1.58	5.31	5.62	5.20	10.9	3.2	4.1	1.3	1.5	0.10

Breakout: 4% Improve: 25% Collapse: 67% Attrition: 48% Comparables: Chris Hammond, Mike Flanagan, Gerry Staley, Grant Jackson

He's not really an effective situational lefty anymore, just a guy with a pretty good move to first, but the Reds saw that shiny ERA and just had to have him. He parlayed waiving his 10-and-5 rights into a guaranteed $2.25 million for 2007 and an option for '08, securing his faltering career a little while longer. He's now the occupant of the Chris Hammond chair in the pen. You know, the one with the ejector seat.

Jonathan Coutlangus

Bats: L Throws: L Height: 6' 1" Weight: 185 Born: October 21, 1980 Age: 26

YEAR	TEAM	LVL	AGE	W	L	SV	G	GS	IP	H	BB	SO	HR	GB%	BABIP	STUFF	WHIP	ERA	PERA	EQERA	EQH9	EQBB9	EQSO9	EQHR9	VORP	WXRL
2005	SJO	A+	24	4	0	3	50	0	77	64	29	79	3	55.9%	.318	0	1.21	3.04	4.49	4.22	8.2	4.3	5.5	0.6	11.5	—
2006	CHT	AA	25	1	3	9	49	0	63	40	32	56	0	59.3%	.250	3	1.14	2.86	5.06	4.77	6.9	5.2	5.2	0.3	5.6	—
2007	CIN	MLB	26	3	4	1	31	5	58¹	62	37	41	6	53.0%	.309	-8	1.69	5.27	5.47	5.26	9.8	5.0	5.7	0.8	2.0	0.40

Breakout: 12% Improve: 28% Collapse: 41% Attrition: 13% Comparables: Sean Fesh, Matt Jarvis, J. J. Trujillo, Tim Byrdak

Normally, when you get some Coutlangus from San Francisco, you might wonder what "waiver bait" really involves, but this isn't just your standard lefty with a nice breaking pitch—he's a converted outfielder, still learning his craft. He was more than a mere situational lefty in Chattanooga and had a nice AFL campaign during the winter. The Reds have him on their 40-man, so he bears watching.

Johnny Cueto **Bats: R Throws: R** Height: 5' 11" Weight: 174 Born: February 15, 1986 Age: 21

YEAR	TEAM	LVL	AGE	W	L	SV	G	GS	IP	H	BB	SO	HR	GB%	BABIP	STUFF	WHIP	ERA	PERA	EQERA	EQH9	EQBB9	EQSO9	EQHR9	VORP	WXRL
2006	DYT	A	20	8	1	0	14	14	76¹	52	15	82	5	53.4%	.254	12	0.88	2.60	5.14	3.73	8.0	2.4	6.0	1.5	15.0	—
2006	SAR	A+	20	7	2	0	12	12	61	48	23	61	6	37.0%	.268	4	1.16	3.54	6.16	4.45	8.6	4.0	6.0	1.7	7.5	—
2007	CIN	MLB	21	7	8	0	29	21	127²	130	51	99	22	44.0%	.284	9	1.41	4.89	5.10	4.74	9.4	3.2	6.3	1.5	12.3	2.10

Breakout: 5%   Improve: 20%   Collapse: 39%   Attrition: 1%   Comparables: Juan Pena, Ian Snell, Alberto Garza, Kyle Davies

Signed out of the Dominican in 2004, Cueto was undersized and under the radar until he started dialing up mid-90s heat and mixing in a crisp slider in his full-season debut last year. Concerns over his stature dog him almost as much as questions about whether or not he'll add the changeup which will give him the three-pitch mix he needs to make it as a starter. Considering how young he is, he might, but the more reasonable expectation is that he'll grow up to be a quality big league reliever.

Phil Dumatrait **Bats: R Throws: L** Height: 6' 2" Weight: 170 Born: July 12, 1981 Age: 25

YEAR	TEAM	LVL	AGE	W	L	SV	G	GS	IP	H	BB	SO	HR	GB%	BABIP	STUFF	WHIP	ERA	PERA	EQERA	EQH9	EQBB9	EQSO9	EQHR9	VORP	WXRL
2005	CHT	AA	23	4	12	0	24	24	127²	115	70	101	4	54.2%	.305	15	1.45	3.17	4.65	4.64	7.9	5.1	4.8	0.5	13.7	—
2006	CHT	AA	24	3	4	0	10	10	49²	39	22	45	4	43.5%	.269	-4	1.24	3.66	5.65	5.81	8.2	4.3	5.4	1.3	-1.1	—
2006	LOU	AAA	24	5	7	0	16	15	87²	104	36	58	10	48.8%	.338	-20	1.61	4.75	5.74	6.10	11.1	3.9	4.7	1.6	-4.8	—
2007	CIN	MLB	25	4	7	0	25	16	95¹	109	51	62	16	47.0%	.303	-7	1.67	5.93	6.11	5.81	10.5	4.2	5.3	1.4	-2.7	0.40

Breakout: 9%   Improve: 39%   Collapse: 28%   Attrition: 0%   Comparables: Lindsay Gulin, Andy Beal, Lance Caraccioli, Charlie Manning

Although not a junkballer per se—he'll nudge a fastball over 90 once in a while—Dumatrait's problem is the absence of a true out-pitch. Without one, he was easy meat in the veteran-heavy International League. Another year removed from the Tommy John surgery that cost him 2004, his poor command of a modest assortment no longer looks like a recovery issue, rather he looks more like a journeyman in the making. He's a little tougher on lefties, so a move to the pen might make sense.

Carlos Fisher **Bats: R Throws: R** Height: 6' 4" Weight: 220 Born: February 22, 1983 Age: 24

YEAR	TEAM	LVL	AGE	W	L	SV	G	GS	IP	H	BB	SO	HR	GB%	BABIP	STUFF	WHIP	ERA	PERA	EQERA	EQH9	EQBB9	EQSO9	EQHR9	VORP	WXRL
2005	BIL	Rk	22	4	4	1	15	8	53²	56	19	45	3	58.4%	.329	-23	1.40	4.19	6.13	7.14	10.1	4.7	3.3	1.2	-8.8	—
2006	DYT	A	23	12	5	0	27	27	150	133	38	122	5	57.9%	.295	-2	1.14	2.76	4.85	4.83	9.2	3.3	4.0	0.9	12.3	—
2007	CIN	MLB	24	5	9	0	26	19	111²	127	51	61	16	53.0%	.301	-7	1.60	5.91	5.68	5.91	10.5	3.6	4.4	1.2	-4.5	0.30

Breakout: 5%   Improve: 28%   Collapse: 32%   Attrition: 0%   Comparables: Jordan Tata, Brian Finch, Bobby Rodgers, Scott Macrae

No, this isn't some new mall-bound Mexican seafood chain, but yes, he does pitch with flair. Picked in the 11th round in 2005, Fisher's a former high school outfielder who started pitching at Lewis-Clark State College. He was a tad old for the lowest rung of full-season ball last year, but he's athletic, has clean mechanics and good control, keeps the ball on the ground, and throws in the low-90s with good movement. His spotty secondary stuff is what might push him into the bullpen, but he has promise.

Ryan Franklin **Bats: R Throws: R** Height: 6' 3" Weight: 190 Born: March 5, 1973 Age: 34

YEAR	TEAM	LVL	AGE	W	L	SV	G	GS	IP	H	BB	SO	HR	GB%	BABIP	STUFF	WHIP	ERA	PERA	EQERA	EQH9	EQBB9	EQSO9	EQHR9	VORP	WXRL
2004	SEA	MLB	31	4	16	0	32	32	200¹	224	61	104	33	—	.294	-7	1.42	4.90	5.16	5.04	9.9	2.5	4.3	1.3	20.3	3.40
2005	SEA	MLB	32	8	15	0	32	30	190²	212	62	93	28	42.0%	.289	-8	1.44	5.10	5.18	5.11	9.8	2.9	4.3	1.2	11.5	2.93
2006	PHI	MLB	33	1	5	0	46	0	53	59	17	25	10	48.4%	.278	-22	1.43	4.58	5.64	4.25	9.2	2.5	3.8	1.5	7.9	0.10
2006	CIN	MLB	33	5	2	0	20	0	24¹	27	17	18	3	47.9%	.343	-5	1.81	4.81	5.04	4.62	9.2	5.3	6.0	1.1	1.5	-0.36
2007	SLN	MLB	34	2	3	1	33	2	51¹	56	18	28	8	43%	.286	-15	1.44	4.71	5.26	5.25	10.2	2.9	4.4	1.3	4.5	0.4

Breakout: 8%   Improve: 40%   Collapse: 37%   Attrition: 41%   Comparables: Tom Hume, Tanyon Sturtze, Dave Schmidt, Eddie Fisher

What's sillier, that Franklin was given a one-year, $2.6-million deal by Pat Gillick for 2006, or that he became another example of Krivksy's speed-dating approach to shoring up his bullpen? Franklin might still have value as a utility pitcher pickup for a club looking to make sure it's fielding a full team in 2007, but even that's a best-case scenario. Given his guile and willingness to try anything for a strike, he's more likely to turn up as a pitching coach who can work with non-star talent.

Eddie Guardado   Bats: R Throws: L   Height: 6' 0"   Weight: 205   Born: October 2, 1970   Age: 36

YEAR	TEAM	LVL	AGE	W	L	SV	G	GS	IP	H	BB	SO	HR	GB%	BABIP	STUFF	WHIP	ERA	PERA	EQERA	EQH9	EQBB9	EQSO9	EQHR9	VORP	WXRL
2004	SEA	MLB	33	2	2	18	41	0	45¹	31	14	45	8	—	.215	15	0.99	2.78	4.32	2.72	6.0	2.5	8.4	1.4	17.3	2.00
2005	SEA	MLB	34	2	3	36	58	0	56¹	52	15	48	7	34.7%	.276	9	1.19	2.72	3.80	3.75	8.1	2.3	7.5	1.1	12.7	2.71
2006	SEA	MLB	35	1	3	5	28	0	23	29	11	22	8	34.7%	.328	-12	1.74	5.48	6.74	5.25	10.5	4.1	7.9	2.6	1.2	-1.17
2006	CIN	MLB	35	0	0	8	15	0	14	15	2	17	2	35.1%	.371	14	1.21	1.29	3.16	2.51	9.4	1.3	10.0	1.3	4.5	0.55
2007	CIN	MLB	36	2	2	3	41	0	40²	42	14	39	6	38.0%	.310	5	1.38	4.31	4.67	4.13	9.5	2.7	7.7	1.3	6.5	0.60

Breakout: 13%   Improve: 34%   Collapse: 51%   Attrition: 41%   Comparables: Don Mossi, Jeff Reardon, Alan Embree, Bob Patterson

The supposed bullpen savior and part of Krivsky's attempted reassembly of the 2003 Twins staff, Everyday Eddie's elbow went sproing a month into his late-game heroics gig. For that brief moment, he provided a nice reminder of what a guy can do with a sneaky delivery and guts, but now he's recovering from a torn ligament and expected to miss a considerable chunk of 2007. There's talk that the Reds might bring him back as a non-roster invitee, but retirement's a possibility.

Aaron Harang   Bats: R Throws: R   Height: 6' 7"   Weight: 270   Born: May 9, 1978   Age: 29

YEAR	TEAM	LVL	AGE	W	L	SV	G	GS	IP	H	BB	SO	HR	GB%	BABIP	STUFF	WHIP	ERA	PERA	EQERA	EQH9	EQBB9	EQSO9	EQHR9	VORP	WXRL
2004	CIN	MLB	26	10	9	0	28	28	161	177	53	125	26	—	.313	5	1.43	4.86	4.65	4.63	9.4	2.6	6.1	1.3	9.1	2.79
2005	CIN	MLB	27	11	13	0	32	32	211²	217	51	163	22	40.4%	.311	21	1.27	3.83	3.83	3.72	8.4	1.9	6.2	0.9	38.9	4.86
2006	CIN	MLB	28	16	11	0	36	35	234¹	242	56	216	28	41.5%	.326	29	1.27	3.76	3.54	3.58	8.7	1.8	7.4	0.9	50.2	6.11
2007	CIN	MLB	29	13	11	0	32	32	215²	221	53	183	30	45.0%	.300	21	1.27	4.11	4.26	4.00	9.4	2.0	6.8	1.2	38.9	5.60

Breakout: 5%   Improve: 43%   Collapse: 9%   Attrition: 0%   Comparables: Freddy Garcia, Don Newcombe, Paul Wilson, Mark Clark

While Arroyo got the headlines, the completion of Harang's slow development into a quality starter was equally satisfying; credit former Assistant GM Brad Kullman with landing Harang as the prize in the Jose Guillen deal of 2003. Harang had already taken a big step forward in 2005, but he showed improved command of his five-pitch arsenal in 2006. One of the penalties of becoming a trustworthy workhorse on a team with a bad pen is that you're asked to go deep into games, and the fatigue showed. Harang took 24 quality starts through six innings, which would have put him among the league leaders, but blew nine of them after that point by pushing his earned run total past three. Four of those blown quality starts came in September. In his other two starts that month, he held his opponents to four total runs in a pair of complete-game wins.

Steve Kelly   Bats: R Throws: R   Height: 6' 1"   Weight: 195   Born: September 30, 1979 Age: 27

YEAR	TEAM	LVL	AGE	W	L	SV	G	GS	IP	H	BB	SO	HR	GB%	BABIP	STUFF	WHIP	ERA	PERA	EQERA	EQH9	EQBB9	EQSO9	EQHR9	VORP	WXRL
2004	CHT	AA	24	12	7	0	28	28	161¹	156	48	116	12	—	.283	-8	1.26	2.96	5.09	5.24	9.5	3.2	4.0	1.1	6.3	—
2005	LOU	AAA	25	5	5	0	19	19	104²	108	41	67	10	55.1%	.306	-5	1.42	4.81	5.08	5.42	8.6	3.7	4.4	1.0	2.1	—
2006	CHT	AA	26	9	4	0	15	14	83¹	88	24	63	4	48.5%	.329	1	1.35	2.82	4.60	5.18	10.2	2.9	4.4	0.9	3.8	—
2006	LOU	AAA	26	4	7	0	12	10	68¹	68	29	46	7	50.5%	.298	-8	1.42	3.17	5.89	4.41	9.5	4.1	4.7	1.5	8.9	—
2007	CIN	MLB	27	5	7	0	27	16	99¹	115	42	58	15	50.0%	.305	-7	1.58	5.74	5.73	5.66	10.7	3.3	4.8	1.3	-1.2	0.50

Breakout: 8%   Improve: 25%   Collapse: 34%   Attrition: 1%   Comparables: Reid Cornelius, Clay Condrey, Jeff D'Amico, Chris Baker

Kelly had great promise as a high school hurler, but his career has merely poked along since he elected to go to Georgia Tech instead of turning pro. He can throw his breaking and off-speed stuff for strikes, but he doesn't throw especially hard. If the good news is that he shrugged off elbow troubles in 2005, the bad is that he turned into a nondescript organizational soldier in 2006.

Sam LeCure   Bats: R Throws: R   Height: 6' 1"   Weight: 190   Born: May 4, 1984   Age: 23

YEAR	TEAM	LVL	AGE	W	L	SV	G	GS	IP	H	BB	SO	HR	GB%	BABIP	STUFF	WHIP	ERA	PERA	EQERA	EQH9	EQBB9	EQSO9	EQHR9	VORP	WXRL
2005	BIL	Rk	21	5	1	0	13	6	41¹	43	15	44	2	51.3%	.366	-14	1.40	3.27	5.51	5.49	10.5	4.8	4.3	1.1	0.5	—
2006	SAR	A+	22	7	12	0	27	27	141¹	130	46	115	12	40.9%	.290	-13	1.25	3.44	5.75	4.99	9.5	3.5	4.7	1.5	9.3	—
2007	CIN	MLB	23	5	8	0	24	19	108	124	50	70	21	43.0%	.298	-3	1.61	5.96	6.11	5.79	10.5	3.7	5.2	1.6	-2.9	0.50

Breakout: 4%   Improve: 32%   Collapse: 34%   Attrition: 0%   Comparables: Nick Regilio, Shane Bazzell, Ruddy Lugo, Travis Phelps

The academic issues that kept LeCure from pitching as a junior at the University of Texas helped drop him to the fourth round in the 2005 draft. The Reds jumped him up to High-A in his full-season debut in 2006 and LeCure didn't disappoint. Flashing an ability to mix low-90s heat with good sliders and changeups, a successful jump to Double-A this year would put him into the picture for the back end of the big league rotation in 2008.

Kyle Lohse

Bats: R Throws: R Height: 6' 2" Weight: 200 Born: October 4, 1978 Age: 28

YEAR	TEAM	LVL	AGE	W	L	SV	G	GS	IP	H	BB	SO	HR	GB%	BABIP	STUFF	WHIP	ERA	PERA	EQERA	EQH9	EQBB9	EQSO9	EQHR9	VORP	WXRL
2004	MIN	MLB	25	9	13	0	35	34	194	240	76	111	28	—	.327	-4	1.64	5.34	4.89	5.20	10.3	3.1	4.7	1.1	7.9	1.95
2005	MIN	MLB	26	9	13	0	31	30	178²	211	44	86	22	45.8%	.316	1	1.43	4.18	4.62	4.33	10.6	2.2	4.2	1.0	30.9	3.75
2006	MIN	MLB	27	2	5	0	22	8	63²	80	25	46	8	39.3%	.350	-4	1.65	7.06	4.69	6.51	10.6	3.3	6.0	0.9	-6.7	-0.44
2006	ROC	AAA	27	2	1	0	4	4	24¹	15	6	12	1	36.8%	.194	3	0.87	1.49	4.13	3.00	6.0	2.2	3.4	0.8	6.9	—
2006	CIN	MLB	27	3	5	0	12	11	63	70	19	51	7	47.9%	.341	18	1.41	4.57	3.68	3.99	9.2	2.3	6.5	0.8	9.5	1.45
2007	CIN	MLB	28	8	9	1	39	21	144	162	46	99	20	46.0%	.309	3	1.44	4.85	4.99	4.74	10.3	2.5	5.6	1.2	13.6	2.20

Breakout: 20% Improve: 54% Collapse: 15% Attrition: 2% Comparables: Todd Stottlemyre, Stan Bahnsen, Dick Drago, Reggie Cleveland

Another of Krivsky's resurrected former charges, Lohse bounced back relatively nicely from his early meltdown with the Twins after coming over in a deadline deal. He gave the Reds six quality starts (one blown) in eleven tries, the sort of performance from a fourth or fifth starter that could allow a team to go places. Lohse will have his bad days at the office as a flyball pitcher in this ballpark, and it might help if he was less given to grousing over close calls, but he's a solid command pitcher and probably someone the Reds couldn't have afforded in this past winter's free agent market.

Gary Majewski

Bats: R Throws: R Height: 6' 1" Weight: 215 Born: February 26, 1980 Age: 27

YEAR	TEAM	LVL	AGE	W	L	SV	G	GS	IP	H	BB	SO	HR	GB%	BABIP	STUFF	WHIP	ERA	PERA	EQERA	EQH9	EQBB9	EQSO9	EQHR9	VORP	WXRL
2004	CHR	AAA	24	3	3	14	35	0	42¹	30	16	41	2	—	.262	7	1.09	3.19	3.93	3.67	7.1	3.7	6.9	0.4	8.9	—
2004	EDM	AAA	24	1	2	1	15	0	16¹	18	8	17	0	—	.383	6	1.60	3.87	3.50	4.41	9.9	4.4	7.2	0.0	2.2	—
2004	MON	MLB	24	0	1	1	16	0	21	28	5	12	2	—	.361	-10	1.57	3.86	4.18	5.82	11.6	2.1	4.6	0.8	-2.1	-0.74
2005	WAS	MLB	25	4	4	1	79	0	86	80	37	50	2	46.9%	.288	6	1.36	2.93	3.95	3.59	8.4	3.5	4.8	0.2	19.7	3.13
2006	WAS	MLB	26	3	2	0	46	0	55¹	49	25	34	4	55.7%	.262	-3	1.34	3.58	4.18	3.65	7.6	3.5	4.9	0.6	12.7	0.07
2006	CIN	MLB	26	1	2	0	19	0	15	30	4	9	1	58.3%	.492	-14	2.27	8.40	4.07	6.89	17.2	2.3	4.6	0.6	-3.7	-1.67
2007	CIN	MLB	27	3	3	2	58	0	65²	71	28	40	8	51.0%	.298	-10	1.51	4.60	4.91	4.52	10.0	3.4	4.9	1.0	7.7	0.60

Breakout: 15% Improve: 36% Collapse: 40% Attrition: 17% Comparables: Danny Graves, Joe Grahe, Rick Camp, Jeff Dedmon

The wheels of justice are a few sprockets shy of a full gear in Pax Seliga, but even so, the Reds' grievance seems dicey. The Nats are insisting all relevant medical reports were turned over, and doctors described Majewski's injury as nothing more than tendonitis, even if it did force him to the DL. Whether or not Jim Bowden committed an error of ommission by not directly mentioning that Majewski had a cortisone shot in July, the Reds ought to have to prove that information would have encouraged Krivsky not to make the deal. Since Krivsky overlooked both Majewski's workload (he ranked second in the majors in relief innings pitched at the time of the deal) and the medical reports, that's not going to be an easy case to make. As for Majewski himself, he's a decent enough sinker-slider guy. The real problem wasn't that he was hurting, it was that he isn't the second coming of Goose Gossage—getting Gary Majewski was not going to put the Reds in the playoffs, though Krivksy acted like it would. Whining about it after the fact is just so much face-saving nonsense.

Calvin Medlock

Bats: R Throws: R Height: 5' 10" Weight: 175 Born: November 8, 1982 Age: 24

YEAR	TEAM	LVL	AGE	W	L	SV	G	GS	IP	H	BB	SO	HR	GB%	BABIP	STUFF	WHIP	ERA	PERA	EQERA	EQH9	EQBB9	EQSO9	EQHR9	VORP	WXRL
2004	DYT	A	21	8	3	0	22	15	94²	74	21	111	5	—	.285	12	1.00	2.57	4.37	3.91	8.1	2.6	5.9	1.0	17.3	—
2004	POT	A+	21	3	4	1	11	9	46²	49	22	46	8	—	.301	-19	1.52	6.36	8.31	8.18	11.2	5.1	6.3	3.1	-12.6	—
2005	SAR	A+	22	6	3	0	25	17	108²	95	22	98	6	37.8%	.295	6	1.08	3.06	4.27	4.29	8.3	2.4	5.0	0.9	15.6	—
2006	CHT	AA	23	7	2	2	42	0	63²	54	28	70	4	48.9%	.306	1	1.30	2.99	4.72	4.35	8.9	4.1	6.8	1.0	8.6	—
2007	CIN	MLB	24	3	4	1	29	5	60¹	68	28	45	10	42.0%	.307	-5	1.58	5.59	5.83	5.43	10.3	3.7	6.1	1.5	1.0	0.30

Breakout: 9% Improve: 31% Collapse: 42% Attrition: 8% Comparables: Micheal Nakamura, Jeff Harris, Manny Barrios, Gabe Molina

Medlock's a diminutive flamethrower picked as a draft-and-follow out of a Texas juco in 2002. He can consistently deal in the 90s, then exasperate hitters with an equally effective change. The decision to move him into the pen full-time in 2006 opened up the possibility of his becoming part of the bullpen picture after some of the veterans crater this summer, but to stay he'll have to overcome the general bias against short right-handers.

Eric Milton Bats: L Throws: L   Height: 6' 3"   Weight: 205   Born: August 4, 1975   Age: 31

YEAR	TEAM	LVL	AGE	W	L	SV	G	GS	IP	H	BB	SO	HR	GB%	BABIP	STUFF	WHIP	ERA	PERA	EQERA	EQH9	EQBB9	EQSO9	EQHR9	VORP	WXRL
2004	PHI	MLB	28	14	6	0	34	34	201	196	75	161	43	—	.271	-5	1.35	4.75	5.32	4.90	8.7	3.0	6.4	1.7	19.4	3.05
2005	CIN	MLB	29	8	15	0	34	34	186¹	237	52	123	40	33.6%	.317	-16	1.55	6.47	5.48	6.23	10.4	2.2	5.3	1.8	-24.3	-0.01
2006	CIN	MLB	30	8	8	0	26	26	152²	163	42	90	29	32.0%	.275	-5	1.34	5.19	5.10	4.61	8.8	2.1	4.7	1.5	10.2	2.20
2007	CIN	MLB	31	8	11	0	31	25	158¹	175	48	99	31	37.0%	.286	0	1.41	5.27	5.33	5.07	10.2	2.4	5.1	1.6	8.6	2.00

Breakout: 19% Improve: 54% Collapse: 17% Attrition: 8%   Comparables: Brian Anderson, Pete Harnisch, Terry Mulholland, Bobby Bolin

Not every former Twin came in after Krivsky—some of them got big money beforehand. Although it doesn't look all that hot, compared to the disaster of his first season with the Reds, Milton's 2006 campaign provided the team with some good work. Milton lost time to a knee injury early on and injured his elbow in his next-to-last start, but by that point he'd made 16 quality starts (through the sixth inning) in 25 attempts, and his ERA on the year was 4.84. Asked to go out one last time, he only succeeded in proving he was hurt. Chased in the first, he subsequently underwent season-ending surgery on his elbow. He's expected to be healthy in camp. While his flyballing tendencies mean he'll never be a perfect fit with the Reds, he's still got a solid combination of good heat and a nice curve. Milton could help a club with better middle relief help and a larger ballpark if managed carefully. That may seem like a lot of qualifiers, but it's a far cry from being useless.

Tyler Pelland Bats: R Throws: L   Height: 6' 0"   Weight: 198   Born: October 9, 1983   Age: 23

YEAR	TEAM	LVL	AGE	W	L	SV	G	GS	IP	H	BB	SO	HR	GB%	BABIP	STUFF	WHIP	ERA	PERA	EQERA	EQH9	EQBB9	EQSO9	EQHR9	VORP	WXRL
2004	DYT	A	20	1	7	0	14	10	44²	66	20	38	6	—	.390	-33	1.92	8.66	7.56	10.92	14.2	5.2	4.5	2.5	-25.8	—
2004	BIL	Rk	20	9	3	0	18	12	73¹	67	39	81	3	—	.328	-1	1.45	3.44	5.68	5.58	9.9	6.0	4.7	0.9	0.2	—
2005	SAR	A+	21	5	8	0	30	15	102¹	103	63	103	5	43.5%	.359	9	1.62	4.05	5.74	5.45	9.6	6.9	5.9	0.8	1.7	—
2006	CHT	AA	22	9	5	0	28	28	142	144	89	107	11	42.7%	.331	-5	1.64	3.99	6.07	6.00	9.8	5.6	4.8	1.2	-6.3	—
2007	CIN	MLB	23	4	8	0	23	17	92¹	109	63	61	17	45.0%	.311	-12	1.87	6.79	7.03	6.64	10.8	5.5	5.3	1.5	-11.6	0.50

Breakout: 14% Improve: 38% Collapse: 30% Attrition: 2%   Comparables: Justin Carter, Mike Gonzalez, Adrian Burnside, Tim Bittner

Pelland might yet live up to his former billing as a prospect, but he gets speed-happy, which costs his fastball the movement that makes it effective, and then his curve flattens out, and then he gets tentative, and the results end up getting Verhoeven-gory. Still, lefties who throw over 90 are commodities. The question is whether he can improve his secondary pitches to help him mix it up against right-handers and thereby escape the situational relief role that might otherwise claim his future.

Elizardo Ramirez Bats: L Throws: R   Height: 6' 0"   Weight: 180   Born: January 28, 1983   Age: 24

YEAR	TEAM	LVL	AGE	W	L	SV	G	GS	IP	H	BB	SO	HR	GB%	BABIP	STUFF	WHIP	ERA	PERA	EQERA	EQH9	EQBB9	EQSO9	EQHR9	VORP	WXRL
2004	CLR	A+	21	5	1	0	9	9	59	55	8	33	3	—	.278	5	1.07	2.44	4.60	3.39	8.9	1.4	3.4	0.9	14.3	—
2004	REA	AA	21	2	5	0	8	8	33²	51	14	20	4	—	.367	-23	1.93	6.68	5.57	9.96	13.4	3.9	3.7	1.3	-16.6	—
2004	PHI	MLB	21	0	0	0	7	0	15	17	5	9	3	—	.292	-7	1.47	4.80	5.62	4.70	10.0	2.9	4.7	1.8	1.6	-0.04
2004	CHT	AA	21	1	0	0	5	5	31	35	4	23	6	—	.305	-1	1.26	3.19	6.65	4.20	11.4	1.2	4.5	2.7	4.7	—
2005	LOU	AAA	22	7	7	0	21	21	131¹	150	18	82	14	53.1%	.319	7	1.28	3.77	4.24	4.33	9.5	1.3	4.3	1.1	19.1	—
2005	CIN	MLB	22	0	3	0	6	4	22¹	33	10	9	5	41.4%	.341	-26	1.93	8.48	6.68	7.99	12.2	3.4	3.0	1.9	-7.7	-0.51
2006	CIN	MLB	23	4	9	0	21	19	104	123	29	69	14	45.0%	.323	5	1.46	5.37	4.43	5.10	9.9	2.2	5.3	1.0	1.0	0.79
2007	CIN	MLB	24	7	9	0	31	22	136¹	154	38	83	21	46.0%	.298	2	1.40	5.05	5.03	4.95	10.4	2.2	4.9	1.3	9.7	1.90

Breakout: 19% Improve: 60% Collapse: 17% Attrition: 12%   Comparables: Joe Johnson, Ricky Bones, Johnny Kucks, John Snyder

Although not gifted with any particularly strong pitch, "Easy E" is relatively young and throws strikes with his fastball, curve, and change. Called up to fill the rotation slot David Williams couldn't hold onto, he gave the Reds ten quality starts in his first sixteen, only to go to pieces in August. Scouts might sniff that that was the league catching up to him, but in getting rocked by two playoff teams, then having to start the day after having to come into an extra-inning loss in relief, then hitting the DL with a sore shoulder, Ramirez was contending with more than familiarity breeding contempt. He'll be in the running for the fifth slot in the rotation in the spring. If he can continue to improve his strikeout rate, he'll continue to be more successful than expected.

Brad Salmon　　　　**Bats: L　Throws: R**　　　Height: 6' 4"　Weight: 220　Born: January 3, 1980　　Age: 27

YEAR	TEAM	LVL	AGE	W	L	SV	G	GS	IP	H	BB	SO	HR	GB%	BABIP	STUFF	WHIP	ERA	PERA	EQERA	EQH9	EQBB9	EQSO9	EQHR9	VORP	WXRL
2004	POT	A+	24	1	0	0	5	1	16²	12	3	16	0	—	.250	13	0.90	0.54	3.37	1.10	7.2	2.2	5.5	0.0	8.2	—
2004	CHT	AA	24	4	2	3	39	1	65¹	68	22	53	3	—	.322	-15	1.38	4.27	4.46	6.36	10.2	3.5	4.5	0.7	-5.4	—
2005	CHT	AA	25	3	8	4	38	0	72²	66	31	71	3	49.8%	.326	-3	1.33	3.34	4.65	4.69	8.6	4.3	5.6	0.8	7.2	—
2005	LOU	AAA	25	0	0	0	9	0	16¹	14	5	8	2	59.3%	.231	-19	1.17	3.31	5.39	3.24	7.0	2.7	3.2	1.1	4.4	—
2006	CHT	AA	26	2	1	2	16	0	23¹	18	16	24	0	55.6%	.300	6	1.47	2.73	4.60	4.03	8.1	6.9	6.0	0.4	3.9	—
2006	LOU	AAA	26	5	1	3	39	0	57¹	36	27	72	3	39.7%	.273	21	1.10	2.36	4.04	3.56	6.5	4.7	8.7	0.8	12.6	—
2007	*CIN*	*MLB*	*27*	*3*	*4*	*1*	*29*	*5*	*57¹*	*61*	*34*	*47*	*8*	*46.0%*	*.307*	*-4*	*1.64*	*5.47*	*5.68*	*5.38*	*9.8*	*4.7*	*6.6*	*1.2*	*1.2*	*0.30*

Breakout: 8%　Improve: 21%　Collapse: 53%　Attrition: 14%　Comparables: Mark Corey, Roy Smith, Jesus Colome, Brandon Kolb

Having spent much of the last four seasons pitching for Chattanooga, Salmon's a little older than you might otherwise expect a pitcher just added to the 40-man roster to be. He's big and he throws hard, but his command comes and goes. Without a working second pitch, he ends up walking lefties who won't go fishing. That said, he doesn't rattle, and there's always the possibility that he could stick as a rare situational righty.

Scott Schoeneweis　　　　**Bats: L　Throws: L**　　　Height: 6' 0"　Weight: 190　Born: October 2, 1973　　Age: 33

YEAR	TEAM	LVL	AGE	W	L	SV	G	GS	IP	H	BB	SO	HR	GB%	BABIP	STUFF	WHIP	ERA	PERA	EQERA	EQH9	EQBB9	EQSO9	EQHR9	VORP	WXRL
2004	CHA	MLB	30	6	9	0	20	19	112²	129	49	69	17	—	.314	-4	1.58	5.59	4.99	5.34	9.9	3.5	5.1	1.2	5.9	1.34
2005	TOR	MLB	31	3	4	1	80	0	57	54	25	43	2	59.9%	.297	9	1.39	3.32	3.73	3.55	8.5	3.9	6.6	0.3	12.9	0.69
2006	TOR	MLB	32	2	2	1	55	0	37¹	39	16	18	3	57.6%	.295	-19	1.47	6.51	4.55	5.87	8.9	3.5	4.0	0.7	-1.2	0.06
2006	CIN	MLB	32	2	0	3	16	0	14¹	9	8	11	1	60.0%	.205	11	1.19	0.63	4.35	0.60	5.4	4.2	6.0	0.6	8.6	0.95
2007	*NYN*	*MLB*	*33*	*2*	*2*	*3*	*52*	*0*	*46²*	*48*	*21*	*31*	*4*	*53%*	*.300*	*-9*	*1.48*	*4.30*	*4.67*	*4.76*	*9.3*	*3.6*	*5.4*	*0.7*	*5.1*	*0.4*

Breakout: 15%　Improve: 44%　Collapse: 30%　Attrition: 28%　Comparables: Ron Perranoski, Mike Magnante, Juan Agosto, Steve Kline

Once good for almost anything you asked him to do, he's left behind his utility pitcher rep to ascend to the luxuries of LOOGYdom. Now a free agent, his ugly ERA might end up making him a bargain for a team looking for a veteran lefty with postseason experience who can handle the challenge of a situational workload.

Brian Shackelford　　　　**Bats: L　Throws: L**　　　Height: 6' 1"　Weight: 195　Born: August 30, 1976　　Age: 30

YEAR	TEAM	LVL	AGE	W	L	SV	G	GS	IP	H	BB	SO	HR	GB%	BABIP	STUFF	WHIP	ERA	PERA	EQERA	EQH9	EQBB9	EQSO9	EQHR9	VORP	WXRL
2004	LOU	AAA	27	8	1	0	59	0	73	58	42	63	6	—	.263	2	1.37	3.58	5.28	3.98	7.1	5.7	5.8	0.9	13.0	—
2005	LOU	AAA	28	1	6	1	31	0	32²	35	10	21	1	56.6%	.333	-11	1.38	5.23	3.94	5.40	8.9	3.0	4.3	0.3	0.7	—
2005	CIN	MLB	28	1	0	0	37	0	29²	21	9	17	2	45.3%	.226	-2	1.01	2.42	4.79	2.67	6.2	2.4	4.7	0.6	9.1	0.39
2006	LOU	AAA	29	1	0	1	34	0	29²	29	14	23	0	45.7%	.326	-1	1.47	1.85	4.30	2.79	9.3	4.7	5.3	0.3	9.1	—
2006	CIN	MLB	29	1	0	0	26	0	16¹	18	10	15	4	36.5%	.292	-6	1.71	7.18	6.31	6.35	9.5	4.8	7.4	2.1	-1.8	0.16
2007	*CIN*	*MLB*	*30*	*2*	*3*	*1*	*59*	*1*	*48²*	*53*	*26*	*35*	*6*	*46.0%*	*.309*	*-11*	*1.63*	*5.27*	*5.55*	*5.17*	*10.0*	*4.3*	*5.8*	*1.1*	*2.1*	*0.20*

Breakout: 4%　Improve: 19%　Collapse: 47%　Attrition: 37%　Comparables: Paul Mirabella, Mike Matthews, Mike Munoz, Rich Rodriguez

Between getting smacked around in the Show and a having a run-in with John Law, 2006 wasn't the year for the former outfielder to break through and stick. He's a functional lefty specialist, but so are a lot of guys. Shackelford is a good candidate to be outrighted or dealt before Opening Day in light of the addition of Mike Stanton to a collection of lefties that already included Bray and Cormier.

David Shafer　　　　**Bats: R　Throws: R**　　　Height: 6' 3"　Weight: 185　Born: March 7, 1982　　Age: 24

YEAR	TEAM	LVL	AGE	W	L	SV	G	GS	IP	H	BB	SO	HR	GB%	BABIP	STUFF	WHIP	ERA	PERA	EQERA	EQH9	EQBB9	EQSO9	EQHR9	VORP	WXRL
2004	DYT	A	22	5	3	5	31	7	77	60	16	84	8	—	.268	-20	0.99	2.92	6.19	4.66	8.6	2.6	5.4	2.1	7.7	—
2005	SAR	A+	23	1	0	5	10	0	13²	9	2	18	0	18.8%	.300	13	0.80	0.00	2.92	0.68	7.4	2.0	6.8	0.0	7.3	—
2005	CHT	AA	23	1	6	6	34	0	39²	31	24	41	3	49.1%	.283	-4	1.39	4.08	5.94	5.35	7.7	5.8	6.5	1.2	1.1	—
2006	CHT	AA	24	1	2	26	44	0	49²	37	16	52	2	43.2%	.276	3	1.08	2.38	4.16	3.56	7.9	3.2	6.4	0.8	10.9	—
2007	*CIN*	*MLB*	*25*	*2*	*3*	*1*	*22*	*4*	*47²*	*48*	*18*	*38*	*7*	*42%*	*.288*	*3*	*1.39*	*4.63*	*4.72*	*4.50*	*9.2*	*3.1*	*6.4*	*1.2*	*6.5*	*0.7*

Breakout: 17%　Improve: 35%　Collapse: 47%　Attrition: 35%　Comparables: Al Widmar, Dick Woodson, Brian Williams, George Susce

Drafted during the Bowden regime like Salmon, Shafer's another longtime relief farmhand who was added to the 40-man over the winter. Shafer's virtues are a particularly sharp slider and command, a combination that promises a slightly better upside than Salmon, in that Shafer might be able to cut it as a reliable middle-innings guy.

Cincinnati Reds

Dave Weathers

Bats: R Throws: R   Height: 6' 3"   Weight: 230   Born: December 31, 1969   Age: 37

YEAR	TEAM	LVL	AGE	W	L	SV	G	GS	IP	H	BB	SO	HR	GB%	BABIP	STUFF	WHIP	ERA	PERA	EQERA	EQH9	EQBB9	EQSO9	EQHR9	VORP	WXRL
2004	NYN	MLB	34	5	3	0	32	0	33²	41	15	25	5	—	.343	-10	1.66	4.27	4.97	4.72	11.0	3.4	5.8	1.3	2.1	-0.44
2004	HOU	MLB	34	1	4	0	26	0	32	31	13	26	5	—	.295	-5	1.38	4.78	5.03	5.18	8.5	3.3	6.3	1.4	0.2	-0.42
2004	FLO	MLB	34	1	0	0	8	2	16²	13	7	10	2	—	.250	-6	1.20	2.69	4.74	3.18	6.9	3.2	4.8	1.1	5.5	0.72
2005	CIN	MLB	35	7	4	15	73	0	77²	71	29	61	7	51.9%	.283	6	1.29	3.94	3.97	3.89	7.4	3.0	6.3	0.8	11.6	2.61
2006	CIN	MLB	36	4	4	12	67	0	73²	61	34	50	12	45.9%	.236	-10	1.29	3.54	5.21	3.20	6.9	3.6	5.4	1.3	18.9	2.57
2007	CIN	MLB	37	3	3	5	54	0	62¹	67	27	42	8	47.0%	.298	-11	1.50	4.65	5.01	4.55	9.9	3.4	5.4	1.1	7.3	0.60

Breakout: 13% Improve: 33% Collapse: 46% Attrition: 16%   Comparables: Dave Burba, Jose Mesa, Tim Worrell, Mike Fetters

Having gone fourteen years without suffering a significant injury, Stormy is as durable as they get and pretty much the perfect utility reliever, able to close, set up, or work multiple innings as needed. He pitched around some of his weaknesses in 2006, showing a pronounced tendency to walk lefties and not give in to hitters in the Gap, while generally challenging them on the road. That said, he's fooling fewer people than he used to, and there's a chance he'll lose it completely before the end of his new two-year contract.

Travis Wood

Bats: R Throws: L   Height: 6' 0"   Weight: 165   Born: February 6, 1987   Age: 20

YEAR	TEAM	LVL	AGE	W	L	SV	G	GS	IP	H	BB	SO	HR	GB%	BABIP	STUFF	WHIP	ERA	PERA	EQERA	EQH9	EQBB9	EQSO9	EQHR9	VORP	WXRL
2005	BIL	Rk	18	2	0	0	6	4	24²	15	13	22	0	36.9%	.234	7	1.13	1.82	5.72	3.04	6.1	6.1	4.2	0.4	6.7	—
2006	DYT	A	19	10	5	0	27	27	140	108	56	133	14	37.9%	.265	-24	1.17	3.66	7.69	5.55	9.2	4.9	5.3	2.4	0.7	—
2007	CIN	MLB	20	5	8	0	25	20	111¹	114	63	81	23	39.0%	.274	-1	1.59	5.63	6.05	5.40	9.4	4.5	5.9	1.7	2.2	1.00

Breakout: 18% Improve: 51% Collapse: 22% Attrition: 3%   Comparables: Juan Cedeno, Jacob McGee, Onan Masaoka, Abel Gomez

Wood is already showing a refined trio of pitches, topping 90 now and again, and using the heat to set up an outstanding changeup. His curve doesn't, and it gets flatter as he starts working up a sweat. The hope is that he'll show improved velocity and control as he adapts to heavier professional workloads. Considering he'll need his fake ID for another year, he's young enough to have plenty of time to fill out and develop.

Lineouts

PLAYER	TEAM	LVL	AGE	PA	R	2B	3B	HR	RBI	BB	SO	SB-CS	SPEED	AVG/OBP/SLG	MLVr	EqAVG/OBP/SLG	EqA	VORP
OF C. Dickerson*	CHT	AA	24	465	65	21	7	12	48	65	129	21-6	7.7	.242/.355/.424	.114	.242/.340/.434	.271	15.1
OF N. Hopper	CHT	AA	27	52	7	2	1	0	10	6	3	3-0	6.0	.283/.365/.370	.088	.250/.321/.333	.244	-1.1
	LOU	AAA	27	410	47	11	3	0	26	20	25	25-7	6.4	.347/.378/.392	.178	.335/.366/.384	.269	8.7
	CIN	MLB	27	47	6	1	0	1	5	6	4	2-2	4.9	.359/.435/.462	.284	.359/.435/.462	.305	3.4
SS M. Loo	RDS	Rk	20	46	10	6	0	1	7	1	5	0-1	4.5	.372/.413/.581	.536	.333/.362/.578	.303	14.5
C M. Perez	CHT	AA	22	434	33	16	0	3	33	19	88	5-1	4.8	.241/.290/.305	-.131	.231/.271/.301	.207	-21.4
RF C. Strait	SAR	A+	23	544	85	36	4	17	74	36	108	50-9	7.5	.258/.325/.452	.100	.237/.287/.417	.248	-14.0
INF C. Valaika	BIL	Rk	20	315	58	22	4	8	60	24	61	2-2	4.7	.324/.387/.520	.323	.277/.312/.421	.253	19.6

PLAYER	TEAM	LVL	AGE	W	L	SV	IP	H	BB	SO	HR	GB%	BABIP	STUFF	WHIP	ERA	PERA	EqERA	EqH9	EqBB9	EqSO9	EqHR9	VORP
C. Alvarado	SAR	A+	28	1	1	2	15	6	4	20	1	—	.167	11	0.67	1.20	4.57	1.88	5.0	3.1	6.9	1.3	5.9
	CHT	AA	28	5	1	0	49²	38	25	58	1	—	.301	8	1.28	3.29	4.13	4.91	8.1	5.1	6.8	0.4	3.7
S. Chiasson	LOU	AAA	28	3	2	29	61²	40	29	49	3	—	.242	1	1.13	1.91	5.04	2.85	6.4	4.8	5.4	0.8	18.3
M. Gosling*	LOU	AAA	25	6	8	0	118	118	53	100	12	—	.315	-8	1.45	4.58	5.57	6.25	9.6	4.3	5.9	1.4	-8.4
C. Guevara	CHT	AA	24	2	3	1	77²	74	27	89	6	—	.335	-8	1.31	3.73	4.78	5.40	10.0	3.4	6.8	1.3	1.7
J. Hall	CHT	AA	25	9	6	0	116	130	34	69	11	—	.310	-27	1.41	3.41	6.01	6.51	11.0	2.9	3.4	1.7	-11.5
	LOU	AAA	25	1	3	0	35²	34	14	22	3	—	.284	-11	1.36	4.09	5.68	6.17	9.3	3.9	4.4	1.3	-2.2
K. Mercker*	CIN	MLB	38	1	1	1	28¹	28	11	17	6	—	.259	-17	1.38	4.13	5.56	3.99	8.0	3.1	4.9	1.5	4.3
C. Michalak*	LOU	AAA	35	9	5	0	132	142	28	61	17	—	.289	-35	1.29	3.00	6.67	5.37	10.5	2.3	2.9	2.0	3.3
	CIN	MLB	35	2	4	0	35	42	16	10	6	—	.295	-24	1.66	4.89	6.20	4.46	9.9	3.5	2.2	1.2	2.9
J. Rojas	DYT	A	23	3	1	4	42²	27	22	63	2	—	.305	10	1.16	1.07	6.15	2.63	8.4	7.2	7.9	1.4	12.4
J. Standridge	LOU	AAA	27	2	2	0	46²	40	15	43	2	—	.299	3	1.19	2.92	3.90	4.11	8.2	3.1	6.3	0.6	7.6
	CIN	MLB	27	1	1	0	18²	17	14	18	2	—	.294	6	1.66	4.81	4.79	5.95	7.8	5.5	7.8	0.9	-1.2
D. Thompson	RDS	Rk	20	0	0	0	14¹	10	4	16	1	—	.321	4	0.99	2.55	7.21	3.38	8.8	3.4	6.1	2.7	3.3
C. Vazquez*	SAR	A+	22	4	5	0	83²	84	32	79	10	—	.318	-19	1.39	4.00	6.62	5.54	10.7	4.2	5.5	2.1	0.5
	CHT	AA	22	3	5	0	60	66	25	56	6	—	.351	-4	1.52	4.35	5.33	7.13	10.8	3.6	5.9	1.5	-10.1
S. Watson	DYT	A	20	1	2	0	14	22	5	16	2	—	.444	-20	1.93	9.00	8.43	11.08	18.0	4.2	6.2	3.5	-7.9
	BIL	Rk	20	0	0	1	23²	16	5	19	0	—	.246	-1	0.91	1.55	3.80	4.76	7.5	2.4	3.6	0.4	2.1
P. Wilson	LOU	AAA	33	0	2	0	11²	15	1	3	4	—	.256	-49	1.43	4.82	12.68	11.81	14.3	0.8	1.7	5.9	-7.4
A. Woody	SAR	A+	23	5	5	12	83¹	80	38	62	1	—	.316	-2	1.42	2.92	4.69	5.11	9.2	5.2	4.1	0.2	4.4

Chris Dickerson is a big, athletic outfielder who seems to leave the tool belt in the dugout when he comes to the plate, but he's solid enough in center that he might help somebody win the International League. **Norris Hopper** drives the ball with about as much authority as a badminton player, but he covers the plate well, and he can run. Fifth outfielderdom beckons. Nabbed in 2005's the ninth round as a high-risk draft-and-follow, **Milton Loo** is aggressive and unpolished, but has the tools to become a plus hitter at short. **Miguel Perez** can't hit and won't, but the game always has space for its catch-and-throw types. **Cody Strait** is the toolsy outfielder who delivers power and speed, but he'll have to show better command of the strike zone as he advances to Double-A, no easy feat. **Chris Valaika** is a 2006 third-rounder picked out of UCSB; he's a scrapper with solid fundamentals, but he's not likely to stick at short, making his bat the tool that will have to shine.

A survivor, **Carlos Alvarado** washed out of the Pirates' organization, marked time in the Central, Atlantic, and Mexican leagues, and has now resurfaced as a greybeard in the Reds system. You have to admire the commitment, and he also has decent stuff. **Scott Chiasson** lost his best shot at a career to elbow surgery, but he's still snapping off enough strikes to merit a peek somewhere. **Mike Gosling** is a lefty, and that's usually enough to encourage people to take a gander. **Carlos Guevara** is an undersized college reliever picked up in the 2004 draft; given his unexceptional assortment, he's unlikely to ever stick in a middle relief role. **Josh Hall** keeps trying to reassemble a career after two shoulder surgeries, but his future is limited at best. His former GM, Jim Bowden, signed him to a minor league deal with the Nats. **Kent Mercker** considered calling it a career, but he'll be in camp one more time to see if his elbow will hold up. **Chris Michalak** gave the Reds a nifty emergency long relief appearance in his season debut, then resumed being the same journeyman lefty Triple-A fans know and love. He'll also be in the Nats' camp. A former Pirates outfield suspect, **Jose Rojas** surprised people with consistent mid-90s heat; his violent mechanics make him more of a thrower than a pitcher, but iron those out and the Reds may have something. **Jason Standridge** did well enough in some garbage time in the Reds pen for the Mets to pick the former D-Ray first-rounder off waivers in November. **Darryl Thompson** is the prospect whose lot might be that he's expected to become the first or second-best player acquired in the Kearns deal. Initially seen as a sleeper in the weak Nationals system because he throws in the low-90s and has a nice curve, he needs reps to master a change he can throw for strikes. "Non-serious" shoulder trouble kept him shelved much of the year, but he's supposed to be fine by spring training. At his age, anything's possible, and it will reflect well on Krivsky's scouting if he pans out. **Camillo Vazquez** is that less-exotic variety of Cuban pitcher, one who grew up in the States and got drafted out of a Florida high school (fourth round, 2002). He needs to continue to improve his command of his pedestrian assortment. Nabbed in the second round of the 2006 draft, former University of Tennessee relief ace **Sean Watson** has both mid-90s heat and a hard, nasty curve; he's a good bet to move up fast. **Paul Wilson** couldn't come back from his torn labrum in 2006, but will try again for somebody in 2007. Assuming he can pitch at all, the above is PECOTA's best guess as to what to expect. **Abe Woody** is a short, right-handed sinkerballer sent to Arizona for Jerry Gil in October. His control leaves a bit to be desired, but he'll get a groundball for you.

Manager: Jerry Narron

Year	Team	W-L	Pythag +/-	Avg PC	100 +P	120 +P	QS	BQS	REL	REL w Zero R	IBB	SUBS	PH	PH Avg	PH HR	SB2	CS2	SB3	CS3	SAC Att	SAC %	POS SAC	Squeeze	Swing	In Play
2005	CIN	46-46	0	94.5	37	1	45	6	287	189	25	26	156	.218	4	36	6	4	3	48	62.5%	13	0	73	50
2006	CIN	80-82	+4	97.3	74	4	75	15	474	288	55	64	272	.270	13	98	24	26	5	91	72.5%	33	2	149	105

Some interesting things happened during Narron's first full season. His club led the league in pinch-hit homers, which you'd expect from a team in a hitter's park, but finished second in the league in attempted double steals, which you wouldn't. The Reds led the league in blown quality starts, or quality starts through six innings that saw the starter ultimately surrender more than four earned runs because of what happened in the seventh or beyond. That says a lot about the bullpen, of course, but it will be interesting to see if Narron pushes his starters as far this year.

Cleveland Indians

Much was expected of the Cleveland Indians in 2006—contention, victory, possibly even the beginning of a new Tribe mini-dynasty in the AL Central. Sabermetric darlings coming into the season, it was the Indians—not the White Sox, not the Twins, and certainly not the Tigers—who were thought to have staying power in their increasingly competitive division. Reality has a nasty habit of upsetting analysts' applecarts, but in the case of the Indians, the 2006 season provided a rude reminder that, despite the lofty expectations, the team was not yet fully rebuilt.

As we documented in the previous edition of this book, the 2005 Indians had the fourth worst differential in the history of the game between their winning percentage in games decided by a single run and their winning percentage in all other games. The assumption was that the Tribe's lousy .379 winning percentage in one-run contests would automatically snap back toward .500, as one-run records are prone do to, giving the otherwise excellent Indians the extra kick they needed to make the postseason. To the surprise of math-heads everywhere, the Indians finished well below .500 in one-run games again last year, going 18–26 for a .409 winning percentage in those games.

That the Indians posted losing one-run records in consecutive seasons is, on it's face, not terribly significant. Since 1960, a team has posted a losing record in one-run games in back-to-back seasons 265 times, however the severity of the Indians' losing one-run records placed them in the 88th percentile of that group. Only 32 of the 265 teams who have had losing one-run records in consecutive years over that span have had lower combined one-run winning percentages over those two seasons than the

INDIANS PROSPECTUS

2006 record: 78–84; Fourth place, AL Central

Pythagenport record: 89–73

Runs scored per game: 5.37 (2nd in AL)

Runs allowed per game: 4.83 (7th in AL)

Team EqA: .273 (2nd in AL)

2006 Batters Age: 28.1 (2nd youngest in AL)

2006 Pitchers Age: 28.8 (3rd oldest in AL)

Ballpark: Jacobs Field; Moderate pitcher's park; Park Factor of .961

2006: Every reliever this side of Ernie Camacho was found wanting, but at least Hafner and Sizemore were among baseball's best players.

2007: They've turned over a good deal of the lineup and bought another bullpen; they'll be back in the hunt in the Central.

2005–2006 Indians, and most of them were awful. Of those 32 teams, only four, including the 2005 Indians, posted a winning record in either of those two seasons. The other three teams to do so were the 1974–1975 Mets, who went 82–80 in 1975 after losing 91 games the year before and would only post one more winning record over the next eight seasons, the 1988–1989 Red Sox, who won the AL East in 1988 and then again in 1990, and the 1963–1964 Minnesota Twins, who dropped from 91 wins in 1963 to 79 in 1964, then won the pennant in 1965.

Those Red Sox and Twins also appear on another list with the 2005–2006 Indians, that is the list of the teams with the largest two-year differential between their winning percentage in one-run games and their winning percentage in all other games. In fact, these three teams finish two, three, and four on that list (number one is the 1962–1963 Twins, who, like the second place 1963–1964 Twins, are there largely because of the Twins' 1963 differential). Of the three, the fourth-place Red Sox were comparatively consistent, winning 89 games on their way to that 1988 division title, dropping six wins and finishing exactly that many games out of first in 1989, then winning 88 games and another division title in 1990. The six wins the Sox lost between 1988 and 1989 were entirely the result of a six-win dip in their one-run record.

The Twins and Indians, on the other hand, charted parallel courses. In Year One, the 1963 Twins and 2005 Indians both won over 90 games while posting the third and fourth largest one-run/multi-run winning percentage differentials of all-time respectively. In Year Two, they experienced only slight corrections in their still-losing one-run records, but saw huge drops in their records in all other games resulting in net losses of 12 and 15 wins and nearly identical win totals of 79 and 78 wins respectively. In Year Three, the Twins finally got the expected rebound in their one-run decisions, going 30–21 in those games and winning Minnesota's first American League pennant. Similarly, when the Red Sox bounced back to win the 1990 AL East title in their Year Three, they did so on the strength of an eerily similar 31–22 record in one-run games.

That's the long way around of saying that Cleveland GM Mark Shapiro should feel good about his team being a wee bit better than your run of the mill 78-game winner. It generally takes a very good team to generate those sorts of differentials in the first place, but with good teams come the sort of expectations that the above history once again places on the Indians. Those expectations will be even harder to meet in 2007, coming off a 78-win season and the ignominy of looking up at everyone but Kansas City, than they were for the 2006 team that came off a 93-wins campaign that ended with the club just barely missing the playoffs.

Hidden in the above breakdown is that, even if the Indians had pulled their one-run record back up to .500 last year, it wouldn't have put them in the playoffs. In fact, they would have finished 82–80 and in exactly the same no-man's land between the 90-win White Sox and 62-win Royals that they were with their .409 one-run winning percentage. In other words, they *still* would have been considered a major disappointment. The real disaster of the 2006 Indians' season was their drop from winning almost 70 percent of their non-one-run games in 2005 to barely more than half of them last year. That drop was the result of several fundamental problems: The Indians' reliance on second-tier players to patch the rotation and the lineup, the bitterly

disappointing seasons they received from two homegrown stars, their unhealthy collection of defensive problems (especially in the early going), and their failure to field a reliable bullpen at any point during the season.

The Indians were particularly ill-starred in that last regard as they thrashed about trying to find a winning combination, but between injury-prone or used-up veterans and inconsistent kids, nothing worked. The Tribe's pen shared the ignominious distinction of being one of four teams in the majors to lose seven games in which they held a lead after eight innings (joining the Marlins, Giants, and Royals). In 2006, major league teams won 94.7 percent of the time when they held the lead after eight innings, while the Twins and Blue Jays were a perfect 83-for-83 and 80-for-80 respectively. The Indians won just 90.9 percent of their 77 times in that situation; a league-average success rate would have been worth three extra wins. Narrow the margin to a one-run lead after eight and the only two teams that did worse than the Indians' 9–4 were, once again, those hapless Royals (8–4) and the surprising Fish (14–7).

In addition to its propensity to blow late-game leads, the Indians' bullpen also suffered for a lack of anyone who could help finish an inning the starter couldn't thereby extracting the team from a potentially dangerous situation with a minimum of damage. Table 1 reflects what happened in these "Transition Inning," in which relievers had to come in to finish the starter's final frame, usually with runners on base. The lack of a reliable middle innings fireman was exacerbated by Rafael Betancourt's early injury, and manager Eric Wedge reacted to his pen's failings like the subject of a negative reinforcement experiment. His

Table 1. Reliever Performance in Transition Innings: A Fine Mess You've Made of Things

Team	G	IP	R	BR/9	ROB	ROBS	ROBS%	TRA/9	Team	G	IP	R	BR/9	ROB	ROBS	ROBS%	TRA/9
Athletics	60	33.1	7	12.2	85	22	25.9%	7.8	Royals	96	60.1	30	11.5	145	49	33.8%	11.8
Blue Jays	77	46.2	15	12.7	108	33	30.6%	9.3	Rangers	75	43.2	24	14.6	108	34	31.5%	11.9
D'backs	44	25.2	9	9.8	78	19	24.4%	9.8	Astros	60	35.1	14	11.2	100	33	33.0%	11.9
Braves	60	38.0	15	13.3	82	28	34.1%	10.2	Rockies	73	42.0	13	13.3	120	44	36.7%	12.2
Mets	57	38.1	12	13.1	87	32	36.8%	10.3	Reds	58	36.0	21	15.8	78	28	35.9%	12.2
Marlins	62	36.2	15	15.7	95	28	29.5%	10.6	Phillies	70	42.2	18	15.0	104	42	40.4%	12.7
Twins	56	29.2	8	12.4	75	27	36.0%	10.6	Angels	59	32.2	7	11.8	83	29	34.9%	12.7
Cardinals	70	46.1	25	13.8	93	31	33.3%	10.9	Padres	55	34.0	20	13.2	81	28	34.6%	12.7
D-Rays	74	45.0	27	18.2	81	28	34.6%	11.0	Yankees	75	48.2	19	12.0	111	41	36.9%	12.9
Dodgers	47	29.1	9	11.0	75	27	36.0%	11.0	White Sox	74	49.0	25	15.8	96	45	46.9%	12.9
Red Sox	60	38.0	13	13.0	89	34	38.2%	11.1	Cubs	68	39.0	20	16.8	107	37	34.6%	13.2
Nationals	74	42.2	15	17.7	106	39	36.8%	11.4	Mariners	72	42.2	22	15.6	121	44	36.4%	13.9
Tigers	73	41.2	17	15.1	85	36	42.4%	11.4	Giants	62	37.1	16	18.3	94	47	50.0%	15.2
Pirates	57	32.2	9	13.2	85	33	38.8%	11.6	Indians	51	28.1	14	14.9	74	34	45.9%	15.2
Brewers	50	33.1	18	11.1	69	25	36.2%	11.6	Orioles	67	40.1	28	19.9	96	44	45.8%	16.1

NOTE: ROB: inherited Runners On Base; ROBS: Runners On Base-Scored; ROBS%: Percentage of Runners On Base who Scored; TRA/9: Transition inning Runs Allowed per 9 IP.

relievers were collectively among the worst in baseball in allowing inherited baserunners to score, and Wedge, perhaps wisely, became one of the managers least likely to try to bring his pen into such situations.

Something else that hurt the Indians attempt to build on their 2005 breakout was that their roster reflected a certain willingness to settle. The "solutions" dug up for 2006 generally weren't top-shelf pickups, or guys who could step up if someone from the team's talented core faltered. This approach to team-building proved to be particularly problematic in both the rotation and the lineup.

In the rotation, in addition to expecting good works from their big three of C. C. Sabathia, Jake Westbrook, and Cliff Lee, the team imported free agents Paul Byrd and Jason Johnson. Neither Byrd nor Johnson are really good starting pitchers—they were simply the guys the Indians could afford to employ when Kevin Millwood left—but the Indians took the reasonable gamble that they'd be better than the team's homegrown options. Instead, Johnson completely imploded. Byrd took his regular turns, but, at 35, didn't look like somebody who should have—only once in the season was he able to follow a quality start with another on a standard four days' rest. Not only could neither pitcher fill Millwood's shoes, neither was able to help the team compensate for Cliff Lee's return to mediocrity. Eventually, the arrival of Jeremy Sowers gave the Tribe a reliable third starter behind Sabathia and Westbrook, but by the time of his late-June arrival, it was much too late to save the team's season.

Similarly, the Curse of the Weak Second Fiddles handicapped the offense in 2006. This might seem like a strange thing to say, since the Indians scored the second-most runs in baseball, trailing only the Yankees. But team strength is not the same as the absence of weakness. A lot of excuses were made for Aaron Boone in 2005; he'd need even grander excuses in 2006. Jason Michaels was a nice low-end pickup, but instead of being seen for what he was and is (a nice part-timer and lefty-masher), the Indians expected him to blossom into a full-time contributor once freed from the Phillies bench. To be fair to Shapiro, Michaels was acquired from the Phillies on the same day that Cleveland shipped Coco Crisp to the Red Sox for blue-chip third base prospect Andy Marte. In the years to come, Marte may be the offensive star that neither Crisp, Boone, nor Michaels could ever be, but for the team's prospects in 2006, this exchange represented a bit of a risk. It was even more of one given that the Cleveland outfield was already employing the only adequate Casey Blake in the opposite corner, making the club that much more reliant on the production of its core players.

Unfortunately, just as the team had to endure Lee's shortcomings in the rotation, the Indians would wind up with the production of one major lineup regular going AWOL. Jhonny Peralta's breakout in 2005 promised the team a future armed with one of the league's best-hitting shortstops, but his age-24 season last year made it plain that he's still a work in progress. Peralta's 43-point drop in on-base percentage and 135-point drop in slugging were equally debilitating to an offense that had anticipated his being the fourth star in a firmament also featuring Travis Hafner, Victor Martinez, and Grady Sizemore. Although the Indians would nevertheless wind up with the best offense in baseball not wearing pinstripes, Peralta's struggles, combined with the club's lack of a star in either outfield corner, helped keep the offense from building up leads even this team's staff couldn't blow.

Perhaps even more troubling than Peralta's decline at the plate were the complaints about his defense. Although reliable at starting the double play, concerns about Peralta's range called into question whether his future is even at shortstop. To some extent, the problem may have been overstated. Both Clay Davenport's defensive statistics and Dave Pinto's Probabilistic Model of Range (for more, check out www.baseballmusings.com) suggest that there wasn't that much of a problem with what Peralta was doing with balls in play. Rather, it's worth noting that Peralta didn't have the benefit of great support to his right and left; Boone lost almost as much ground in the field as he did at the plate (according to both scouts and metrics), while Ronnie Belliard's range at second left a lot to be desired.

As if the pitching staff didn't have enough problems already, they also had to deal with the difficulties that came with having Victor Martinez behind the plate. Martinez's basic catching skills aren't seen as a problem—the club gives Martinez good marks for his game-calling, receiving, and plate-blocking. The problem is Martinez's throwing. Opposing base thieves went from being successful around 75 percent of the time in Martinez's first two years to better than 80 percent last year. However, things did change for the better within the season: After allowing an ugly 61 of 70 steal attempts to succeed in the first half, capped by the Yankees going six-for-six on July 5th, Martinez rallied to throw out 13 of 52 runners after the All-Star break. That second-half performance is back in line with the 25 percent caught-stealing rate he achieved in his first two full seasons. As a result, his throwing is not going to force him out from behind the plate; the Indians understand what having him catch does towards helping them field the league's best lineup.

Generally speaking, Martinez's second-half improvement reflects how things get done in Cleveland. To their credit, the Indians have been aggressive in fixing their guys, instead of just hoping they'll get better. Lee, Peralta, and Martinez have all gotten specific attention to help them fix the weak spots in their games. In Peralta's case, the questions about his fielding should be mitigated by the pair of significant defensive upgrades to his left and right. The additions of younger, more athletic players at second (Josh Barfield) and third (Marte) should help cover for Peralta's range, assuming he doesn't improve himself. Rather than settle for near-adequacy in the outfield corners, the Indians have improved their offense with the additions of Shin-Soo Choo and David Dellucci. A full season of Jeremy Sowers will help push Paul Byrd into the fifth slot in the rotation, and, if Cliff Lee gets ironed out, the Tribe will have a starting five that stacks up pretty nicely against anyone else's in the division.

Which brings us back to the action item that demanded the most attention this past winter, the part of the team which is most in need of significant improvement, and the area that may determine how long Eric Wedge remains the Cleveland manager—the bullpen. The Twins teams that kept coming up short in one-run ballgames also lacked a settled pen until they dug up veterans Al Worthington and Johnny Klippstein during the 1964 season. Similarly, the Tribe has restocked its pen with veteran help, rolling the dice on closers past and present Keith Foulke, Roberto Hernandez, and Joe Borowski, and well-traveled situa-

tional lefty Aaron Fultz. None of that quartet were top performers in 2006—however many saves he logged, Borowski contributed to the Marlins' aforementioned late-game failures, while Hernandez and Fultz are both suited for limited situational roles at best. On the other hand, Foulke finished 2006 strong after finally getting healthy, and comes to the Tribe with something to prove after the disintegration of his relationship with the Red Sox and their fans. Whether or not Foulke and company are improvements over Bob Wickman, Guillermo Mota, and the rest of last year's class of vets remains to be seen, but the hope is that they're here to help youngsters such as Fernando Cabrera and Jason Davis adapt their talent to the challenge of delivering on demand in a big league bullpen, and will take a back seat once their mentoring missions are complete.

If Wedge can find the best combination of relievers and the best ways to deploy them early on, he's in a position to strap in and win with a tremendously talented ballclub. But if key players such as Peralta and Lee keep struggling, and the Indians start losing more one-run games early on, it won't be long before everyone starts wondering just when newly hired senior advisor Buck Showalter will descend from the front office.

HITTERS

Brian Barton　CF　Bats: R　Throws: R　Height: 6' 3"　Weight: 187　Born: April 25, 1982　Age: 25

YEAR	TEAM	LVL	AGE	PA	R	2B	3B	HR	RBI	BB	SO	SB	CS	SPEED	AVG	OBP	SLG	MLVR	EQAVG	EQOBP	EQSLG	EQA	VORP	DEFENSE			
2005	LKC	A	23	160	31	14	1	4	32	18	21	7	2	5.4	.414	.506	.624	.705	.361	.422	.528	.322	17.8	25-RF	1		
2005	KIN	A+	23	273	42	15	6	3	32	34	57	13	8	7.4	.274	.404	.435	.177	.246	.337	.367	.249	1.7	32-CF	2	23-LF	0
2006	KIN	A+	24	359	56	16	3	13	57	39	83	26	3	6.7	.308	.410	.515	.346	.284	.353	.454	.282	18.8	24-CF	-2	21-RF	1
2006	AKR	AA	24	171	32	5	0	6	26	13	26	15	5	6.5	.351	.415	.503	.366	.329	.384	.490	.301	16.1	23-CF	0		
2007	CLE	MLB	25	506	67	25	3	12	52	37	117	17	7	5.9	.267	.332	.411	-.056	.265	.333	.421	.268	7.9	119-CF	2		

Breakout: 5%　Improve: 22%　Collapse: 36%　Attrition: 8%　Comparables: Mike Zywica, Jason Bay, Carlos Valderrama, Pat Bryant

Always more of an athlete than a baseball player, Barton hit .326/.424/.506 between Cleveland's two A-level teams in 2005 . . . and a nation yawned. Last year, he kept hitting, and people began to take notice. He hit for average, he hit for power, he stole 41 bases at a better than 80 percent success rate, he drew walks, and he even proved to be capable in center field. What else do you want, a trip to Europe? The only real negative for Barton is his age—because he spent a full four years at the University of Miami, he'll turn 25 a month into the 2007 season. Still, this is an undrafted college player who almost certainly is going to have some semblance of a big league career, and that's a rare thing.

Casey Blake　RF　Bats: R　Throws: R　Height: 6' 2"　Weight: 210　Born: August 23, 1973　Age: 33

YEAR	TEAM	LVL	AGE	PA	R	2B	3B	HR	RBI	BB	SO	SB	CS	SPEED	AVG	OBP	SLG	MLVR	EQAVG	EQOBP	EQSLG	EQA	VORP	DEFENSE	
2004	CLE	MLB	30	668	93	36	3	28	88	68	139	5	8	4.1	.271	.354	.486	.120	.278	.363	.501	.288	27.8	149-3B	-9
2005	CLE	MLB	31	583	72	32	1	23	58	43	116	4	5	4.3	.241	.308	.438	-.023	.250	.326	.464	.266	4.3	133-RF	7
2006	CLE	MLB	32	456	63	20	1	19	68	45	93	6	0	4.7	.282	.356	.479	.109	.285	.367	.492	.295	22.4	93-RF	3
2007	CLE	MLB	33	487	61	23	2	18	68	43	100	4	2	4.6	.259	.330	.444	-.021	.256	.332	.455	.275	7.6	115-RF	-3

Breakout: 3%　Improve: 25%　Collapse: 37%　Attrition: 23%　Comparables: Ellis Burks, Jim Lemon, Dave Henderson, Sam Chapman

(continued next page)

Casey Blake *(continued)*

Blake blossomed into a big leaguer in 2003 at the advanced age of 29, but the bloom seemed to be off the rose after a 2005 season that was just plain bad. After pushing off speculation that his job was in jeopardy with a torrid start to 2006, hitting .330/.411/.566 through early June, Blake was already cooling when a strained left oblique sent him to the DL for a month. He continued to hit well upon returning in mid-July, but an ankle injury that shelved him for twenty days in August finally derailed his momentum. From his August 25 return until the end of the season, he batted .211/.268/.325 with just 3 home runs in 114 at-bats. For the season, he was a league-average right fielder—not great, not bad, but good enough for the Indians to pick up his $3.75 million extension for 2007. He'll get plenty of at-bats as a platoon option at both corner outfield positions and as a back-up first baseman.

Aaron Boone **3B** **Bats: R** **Throws: R** Height: 6' 2" Weight: 200 Born: March 9, 1973 Age: 34

YEAR	TEAM	LVL	AGE	PA	R	2B	3B	HR	RBI	BB	SO	SB	CS	SPEED	AVG	OBP	SLG	MLVR	EQAVG	EQOBP	EQSLG	EQA	VORP	DEFENSE	
2005	CLE	MLB	32	565	61	19	1	16	60	35	92	9	3	4.8	.243	.299	.378	-.121	.250	.316	.396	.250	-2.7	139-3B	3
2006	CLE	MLB	33	392	50	19	1	7	46	27	62	5	4	5.2	.251	.314	.370	-.146	.257	.326	.380	.246	-5.8	96-3B	-7
2007	FLO	MLB	34	429	51	21	2	9	46	34	70	7	4	5.3	.255	.325	.396	-.107	.256	.322	.400	.248	3.5	102-3B	-2

Breakout: 16% Improve: 38% Collapse: 28% Attrition: 31% Comparables: Scott Brosius, Gary Gaetti, Jim Davenport, Tom Brookens

The Tribe tried to deal Boone at the trading deadline to make room for Andy Marte, and when they found no takers they simply benched him. After two years of little production, he's in line for no more than a non-roster invite to somebody's spring training site. He'll always have that cold night in New York a few years back, just like Bogie and Bergman always had Paris, but here in Cleveland, Louis, this is the end of a forgettable friendship. Signed by the Marlins to step into Wes Helms's corner infield utility role, which he'll struggle to fulfill.

Asdrubal Cabrera **SS** **Bats: S** **Throws: R** Height: 6' 0" Weight: 170 Born: November 13, 1985 Age: 21

YEAR	TEAM	LVL	AGE	PA	R	2B	3B	HR	RBI	BB	SO	SB	CS	SPEED	AVG	OBP	SLG	MLVR	EQAVG	EQOBP	EQSLG	EQA	VORP	DEFENSE			
2004	EVE	A-	18	274	44	16	3	5	41	21	43	7	5	6.5	.272	.330	.427	.024	.210	.248	.306	.199	-26.7	40-SS	-1	16-2B	-2
2005	WIS	A	19	228	26	12	3	4	30	30	32	2	6	3.4	.318	.407	.474	.283	.294	.363	.433	.271	13.7	28-2B	1		
2005	SBR	A+	19	244	31	15	6	1	26	15	47	3	1	6.3	.284	.325	.418	-.102	.253	.287	.354	.225	-2.0	54-SS	-4		
2006	TAC	AAA	20	233	27	12	2	3	22	24	51	7	5	5.3	.236	.323	.360	-.075	.242	.318	.362	.240	2.0	60-SS	3		
2006	BUF	AAA	20	211	26	11	0	1	14	8	39	5	4	5.8	.263	.295	.337	-.132	.241	.274	.314	.215	-6.8	52-SS	-9		
2007	CLE	MLB	21	469	48	20	3	7	42	29	84	8	5	5.6	.249	.299	.357	-.199	.247	.301	.365	.237	1.2	111-SS	-4		

Breakout: 37% Improve: 69% Collapse: 16% Attrition: 12% Comparables: Felipe Lopez, Ray Olmedo, Luis Hernandez, Angel Santos

Cabrera is an outstanding defender who was acquired from Seattle in the same deal that netted the organization Shin-Soo Choo. He's been rushed through both systems, but even if his bat doesn't catch up, he'll make a glovely utility player.

Shin-Soo Choo **RF** **Bats: L** **Throws: L** Height: 5' 11" Weight: 210 Born: July 13, 1982 Age: 24

YEAR	TEAM	LVL	AGE	PA	R	2B	3B	HR	RBI	BB	SO	SB	CS	SPEED	AVG	OBP	SLG	MLVR	EQAVG	EQOBP	EQSLG	EQA	VORP	DEFENSE			
2004	SAN	AA	21	579	89	17	7	15	84	56	97	40	8	7.3	.315	.382	.462	.262	.311	.366	.453	.286	27.8	80-RF	-3	44-LF	-1
2005	TAC	AAA	22	502	73	21	5	11	54	69	97	20	10	6.1	.282	.382	.431	.125	.282	.371	.415	.274	11.6	112-LF	14		
2006	TAC	AAA	23	427	71	21	3	13	48	45	73	26	4	7.4	.323	.394	.499	.323	.329	.392	.513	.310	35.4	50-LF	-6	30-RF	-6
2006	CLE	MLB	23	167	23	11	3	3	22	18	46	5	3	7.1	.295	.373	.473	.138	.299	.386	.500	.296	8.4	29-RF	1		
2007	CLE	MLB	24	545	80	26	4	12	56	49	110	19	7	6.5	.286	.354	.427	.018	.283	.355	.437	.282	15.0	128-LF	-2		

Breakout: 12% Improve: 32% Collapse: 27% Attrition: 7% Comparables: Bobby Abreu, Jacob Cruz, Nate McLouth, Gene Richards

The Mariners thought they had too many outfielders, and the Indians knew they had too many first basemen, so the latter traded Ben Broussard to the former at the deadline for Shin-Soo Choo. Choo did well in Cleveland as a platoon outfielder, but that's the extent of his potential—he has too many weaknesses to be an every day player, including below-average power and an inability to hit lefties. Still, he's a stud defender with a rocket arm, runs well, and swings a decent bat against right-handers. While it's hard to see him as an impact player, he'll be around for a long time and can help a team win ballgames as a non-starring semi-regular.

Jason Cooper   LF   Bats: L   Throws: L   Height: 6' 2"   Weight: 215   Born: December 6, 1980   Age: 26

YEAR	TEAM	LVL	AGE	PA	R	2B	3B	HR	RBI	BB	SO	SB	CS	SPEED	AVG	OBP	SLG	MLVR	EQAVG	EQOBP	EQSLG	EQA	VORP	DEFENSE			
2004	AKR	AA	23	477	54	24	6	14	69	47	106	2	2	4.6	.239	.321	.424	-.034	.219	.289	.379	.232	-21.4	91-LF	-6		
2004	BUF	AAA	23	60	6	1	0	3	7	9	15	1	1	3.6	.176	.300	.373	-.192	.173	.295	.365	.231	-3.2	14-LF	0		
2005	AKR	AA	24	245	41	9	2	11	42	30	67	3	2	5.6	.254	.359	.478	.140	.237	.327	.436	.264	-0.1	50-LF	5		
2005	BUF	AAA	24	285	43	12	3	14	58	23	76	1	4	5.0	.257	.317	.494	.041	.239	.298	.447	.250	-2.9	69-LF	-4		
2006	BUF	AAA	25	462	56	23	4	13	61	41	126	5	2	5.1	.228	.303	.398	-.062	.214	.287	.378	.233	-21.9	67-LF	-2	30-RF	-1
2007	CLE	MLB	26	406	39	19	2	11	46	33	112	3	2	4.7	.216	.284	.368	-.233	.214	.285	.377	.233	-13.1	97-LF	-3		

Breakout: 21% Improve: 38% Collapse: 32% Attrition: 18%   Comparables: Ryan Radmanovich, John-Ford Griffin, Luke Scott, Cory Aldridge

The Indians have the worst luck with Stanford guys. Cooper has a ton of power, but he's proven to be utterly unable to hit for any kind of average at the upper levels. Low averages and lots of strikeouts seem to be something he's doomed to at this point, and he's pretty much out of chances.

Trevor Crowe   CF   Bats: S   Throws: R   Height: 6' 0"   Weight: 190   Born: November 17, 1983   Age: 23

YEAR	TEAM	LVL	AGE	PA	R	2B	3B	HR	RBI	BB	SO	SB	CS	SPEED	AVG	OBP	SLG	MLVR	EQAVG	EQOBP	EQSLG	EQA	VORP	DEFENSE	
2005	MHV	A-	21	58	9	2	1	1	6	6	8	4	3	7.2	.255	.345	.392	.061	.222	.276	.352	.221	-3.8	12-CF	-2
2005	LKC	A	21	199	18	8	2	0	23	18	25	7	5	5.0	.258	.327	.326	-.094	.212	.261	.250	.191	-16.9	37-CF	4
2006	KIN	A+	22	273	51	15	2	4	31	48	46	29	6	6.6	.329	.449	.470	.358	.317	.415	.465	.311	26.5	59-CF	-10
2006	AKR	AA	22	176	20	7	2	1	13	20	24	16	6	7.3	.234	.318	.325	-.086	.224	.301	.314	.229	-6.5	22-CF	1
2007	CLE	MLB	23	482	62	20	4	5	37	44	81	23	10	6.1	.254	.324	.351	-.158	.252	.325	.359	.250	0.2	114-CF	-6

Breakout: 28% Improve: 60% Collapse: 23% Attrition: 18%   Comparables: Chris Magruder, Jarred Ball, Rashad Eldridge, Reggie Willits

The team's first-round pick in 2005, Crowe's full-season debut was pretty stunning. He reached base 122 times in 60 games for Kinston before an ankle injury, a muscle strain in his rib cage, and a very short-lived (six errors in six games) move to second base limited him at Akron. More than just an on-base machine, Crowe should be good for 10 to 15 home runs a year. The only problem is that Sizemore is this organization's center fielder, so Crowe will have to provide enough production for left field, where offensive expectations are much higher.

Ben Francisco   OF   Bats: R   Throws: R   Height: 6' 1"   Weight: 190   Born: October 23, 1981   Age: 25

YEAR	TEAM	LVL	AGE	PA	R	2B	3B	HR	RBI	BB	SO	SB	CS	SPEED	AVG	OBP	SLG	MLVR	EQAVG	EQOBP	EQSLG	EQA	VORP	DEFENSE			
2004	AKR	AA	22	563	72	29	3	15	71	50	86	21	5	6.2	.254	.326	.414	-.029	.230	.293	.372	.236	-22.5	72-RF	1	42-CF	0
2005	AKR	AA	23	352	45	19	7	7	46	24	59	15	4	7.4	.307	.357	.474	.175	.288	.336	.448	.270	8.2	38-RF	-3	31-LF	-3
2006	BUF	AAA	24	579	80	32	4	17	59	45	72	25	5	6.6	.278	.345	.454	.106	.262	.326	.444	.267	19.0	38-CF	0	34-RF	0
2007	CLE	MLB	25	488	60	26	2	11	53	33	74	13	4	5.8	.264	.320	.407	-.084	.262	.322	.416	.263	3.5	115-RF	0		

Breakout: 12% Improve: 47% Collapse: 20% Attrition: 10%   Comparables: Eric Byrnes, Craig Monroe, Emil Brown, Rontrez Johnson

Francisco is one of those college outfielders who do many things well, but nothing well enough to have a long big league career. Francisco split his time evenly between all three outfield positions in 2006, so when the Tribe needs an extra outfielder in 2007 because of a trade or a DL move, he could be the guy who gets the call.

Ryan Garko   1B   Bats: R   Throws: R   Height: 6' 2"   Weight: 225   Born: January 2, 1981   Age: 26

YEAR	TEAM	LVL	AGE	PA	R	2B	3B	HR	RBI	BB	SO	SB	CS	SPEED	AVG	OBP	SLG	MLVR	EQAVG	EQOBP	EQSLG	EQA	VORP	DEFENSE			
2004	KIN	A+	23	280	44	17	1	16	58	26	34	4	1	4.5	.328	.425	.609	.511	.299	.368	.558	.305	24.9	25-1B	1	19-C	3
2004	AKR	AA	23	194	29	15	0	6	38	14	28	1	0	3.9	.331	.397	.523	.293	.295	.347	.472	.281	13.2	23-C	0	16-1B	0
2005	BUF	AAA	24	520	75	25	3	19	77	44	92	1	3	3.5	.303	.384	.498	.198	.285	.358	.461	.279	21.6	63-1B	-1	55-C	-8
2006	BUF	AAA	25	437	43	18	0	15	59	45	67	4	5	3.6	.247	.352	.420	.053	.232	.326	.410	.256	-1.5	85-1B	4		
2006	CLE	MLB	25	209	28	12	0	7	45	14	37	0	0	3.9	.292	.359	.470	.105	.295	.365	.492	.292	8.0	45-1B	-2		
2007	CLE	MLB	26	505	60	26	1	16	68	41	86	1	1	4.1	.268	.339	.437	-.009	.265	.340	.447	.276	10.1	119-1B	0		

Breakout: 18% Improve: 44% Collapse: 20% Attrition: 9%   Comparables: John Ellis, Ryan Shealy, Matthew LeCroy, Derrek Lee

The Broussard trade gave Garko a 50-game audition for the first base job after he moped a bit through his summer in Buffalo. He responded to the challenge and hit well enough to make the Indians comfortable with him there to open the season. He's a good hitter, but whether he's good enough to be anything more than an average bat among first basemen remains to be seen. At age 26, he's more of an "is what he is" guy than a high-ceiling prospect.

Ryan Goleski　OF　Bats: R　Throws: R　Height: 6' 3"　Weight: 225　Born: March 19, 1982　Age: 25

YEAR	TEAM	LVL	AGE	PA	R	2B	3B	HR	RBI	BB	SO	SB	CS	SPEED	AVG	OBP	SLG	MLVR	EQAVG	EQOBP	EQSLG	EQA	VORP	DEFENSE	
2004	LKC	A	22	581	83	22	5	28	104	55	100	6	7	4.1	.297	.372	.527	.265	.259	.313	.434	.255	-0.2	117-RF	-6
2005	KIN	A+	23	507	59	27	0	17	67	39	134	6	4	4.1	.212	.276	.382	-.150	.171	.217	.281	.182	-64.4	110-RF	-5
2006	KIN	A+	24	153	28	7	0	10	43	25	30	2	2	4.3	.331	.441	.636	.566	.292	.379	.538	.307	11.8	37-RF	1
2006	AKR	AA	24	370	48	24	0	17	63	36	87	4	2	4.1	.296	.370	.528	.287	.278	.342	.502	.284	15.3	82-LF	2
2007	OAK	MLB	25	506	48	23	1	16	64	37	119	2	1	4.3	.235	.295	.391	-.170	.232	.297	.398	.244	-10.3	119-RF	0

Breakout: 24%　Improve: 47%　Collapse: 28%　Attrition: 7%　　Comparables: Kevin West, Ryan Mulhern, Ben Johnson, Kirk Asche

At some point, we have to start taking this guy seriously as a prospect. We didn't do it when he had a monster year in 2004 because he was a little old for the Sally League. Most of the few believers subsequently wrote him off as a injuries and a crisis of confidence combined to wreck his 2005. But Goleski came back with a vengeance this year, passing the big test at Double-A with flying colors thanks to much-improved plate discipline. Goleski's power is for real, but in scouting terms it's really his only plus offensive tool. He strikes out a lot, isn't especially athletic, and bats right-handed. That limits his options as a bench player, but Oakland liked him enough the take him with the first pick in the Rule 5 draft; they'll try him as a platoon outfielder.

Franklin Gutierrez　OF　Bats: R　Throws: R　Height: 6' 2"　Weight: 180　Born: February 21, 1983　Age: 24

YEAR	TEAM	LVL	AGE	PA	R	2B	3B	HR	RBI	BB	SO	SB	CS	SPEED	AVG	OBP	SLG	MLVR	EQAVG	EQOBP	EQSLG	EQA	VORP	DEFENSE		
2004	AKR	AA	21	298	38	24	2	5	35	23	77	6	3	5.1	.302	.372	.466	.151	.283	.339	.435	.268	11.9	46-CF	-4	
2005	AKR	AA	22	426	70	25	2	11	42	30	77	14	4	7.0	.261	.322	.423	.020	.245	.300	.399	.245	-0.4	82-CF	-1	
2005	BUF	AAA	22	75	10	6	2	0	7	6	13	2	2	7.5	.254	.320	.403	-.078	.235	.303	.368	.231	-1.0	16-CF	4	
2006	BUF	AAA	23	413	63	27	0	9	38	49	84	13	8	5.8	.278	.373	.433	.120	.259	.352	.425	.268	15.6	56-CF	4	18-LF 1
2006	CLE	MLB	23	141	21	9	0	1	8	3	28	0	0	4.8	.272	.288	.360	-.201	.274	.295	.370	.230	-3.6	24-RF	-2	
2007	CLE	MLB	24	480	57	28	2	12	53	37	105	8	4	5.6	.257	.320	.410	-.086	.254	.321	.420	.261	4.2	114-CF	2	

Breakout: 26%　Improve: 57%　Collapse: 14%　Attrition: 10%　　Comparables: Prentice Redman, Ben Francisco, Damon Hollins, Brian Anderson

He's become a bit of an annoyance in the system, really. The prize of 2004's Milton Bradley deal, Gutierrez is a five-tool athlete who has never translated those tools into baseball skills. He hits for a decent average, he hits doubles but not many home runs, he draws a few walks, he steals a few bases, all nice things, but collectively they add up to a prototypical fourth outfielder, not the future star he was supposed to be. He spent 2006 shuttling back and forth between Buffalo and Cleveland, and that will probably continue this year.

Travis Hafner　DH　Bats: L　Throws: R　Height: 6' 3"　Weight: 240　Born: June 3, 1977　Age: 30

YEAR	TEAM	LVL	AGE	PA	R	2B	3B	HR	RBI	BB	SO	SB	CS	SPEED	AVG	OBP	SLG	MLVR	EQAVG	EQOBP	EQSLG	EQA	VORP	DEFENSE
2004	CLE	MLB	27	573	96	41	3	28	109	68	111	3	2	4.7	.311	.410	.583	.373	.321	.419	.608	.337	61.8	
2005	AKR	AA	28	11	0	0	0	0	0	1	0	0	0	1.7	.000	.182	.000	-.807	.000	.091	.000	.068	-3.0	
2005	CLE	MLB	28	578	94	42	0	33	108	79	123	0	0	4.1	.305	.408	.595	.410	.316	.427	.634	.345	68.7	
2006	CLE	MLB	29	563	100	31	1	42	117	100	111	0	0	3.7	.308	.439	.659	.518	.313	.450	.680	.362	79.7	
2007	CLE	MLB	30	623	109	33	1	39	112	92	119	1	0	4.3	.296	.407	.588	.322	.293	.409	.602	.339	64.1	146-DH

Breakout: 0%　Improve: 26%　Collapse: 35%　Attrition: 2%　　Comparables: Willie McCovey, David Ortiz, Boog Powell, Fred McGriff

Per plate appearance, Hafner was the best hitter in the American League in 2006, with a broken right hand on September 1st possibly costing him an MVP award. The Rangers had let Hafner stagnate in their system, but not even the Indians dreamed he'd be this good when they acquired him for what basically amounts to the immortal Einar Diaz. Hafner's track record suggests he can continue at this level, but it's important to note that he's not a young, budding superstar—he turns 30 in June and has those dreaded "old player skills."

Joe Inglett　UT　Bats: L　Throws: R　Height: 5' 10"　Weight: 180　Born: June 29, 1978　Age: 29

YEAR	TEAM	LVL	AGE	PA	R	2B	3B	HR	RBI	BB	SO	SB	CS	SPEED	AVG	OBP	SLG	MLVR	EQAVG	EQOBP	EQSLG	EQA	VORP	DEFENSE		
2004	AKR	AA	26	300	49	19	7	1	20	31	28	3	5	6.0	.320	.393	.455	.183	.277	.338	.387	.250	8.5	51-2B	-6	
2005	BUF	AAA	27	366	57	20	9	2	40	17	41	13	6	7.7	.330	.376	.465	.166	.301	.342	.418	.264	16.5	54-2B	-1	20-CF 3
2006	AKR	AA	28	77	20	9	0	3	9	11	4	7	3	6.9	.516	.587	.797	1.140	.441	.500	.662	.371	20.5	16-SS	0	
2006	BUF	AAA	28	181	21	7	2	1	13	13	24	3	2	5.0	.299	.358	.389	.058	.278	.330	.364	.242	2.6	15-2B	1	12-SS -2
2006	CLE	MLB	28	222	26	8	3	2	21	14	39	5	1	6.5	.284	.332	.383	-.072	.288	.343	.389	.260	5.9	47-2B	4	
2007	CLE	MLB	29	451	55	23	3	6	40	28	59	8	4	5.8	.282	.331	.396	-.067	.279	.332	.405	.262	12.1	107-2B	2	

Breakout: 9%　Improve: 33%　Collapse: 35%　Attrition: 21%　　Comparables: Adam Kennedy, Mickey Morandini, Jerry Remy, Dave Martinez

Cleveland Indians

Inglett took a slow route to the majors, not making his debut until he was 28. His big league performance showed why. Inglett can hit for a decent average, but he has no secondary skills as a hitter. He was the primary second baseman after Ron Belliard was dealt, but his days as a starter ended with the arrival of Josh Barfield.

Kevin Kouzmanoff   3B   Bats: R   Throws: R   Height: 6′ 1″   Weight: 210   Born: July 25, 1981   Age: 25

YEAR	TEAM	LVL	AGE	PA	R	2B	3B	HR	RBI	BB	SO	SB	CS	SPEED	AVG	OBP	SLG	MLVR	EQAVG	EQOBP	EQSLG	EQA	VORP	DEFENSE	
2004	LKC	A	22	531	74	35	5	16	87	44	75	5	4	4.3	.330	.394	.526	.329	.291	.335	.447	.267	29.3	114-3B	-3
2005	KIN	A+	23	287	47	20	4	12	58	24	51	3	1	5.6	.339	.401	.591	.446	.303	.346	.496	.285	23.8	55-3B	3
2006	AKR	AA	24	276	46	19	1	15	55	23	34	2	3	4.3	.389	.449	.660	.655	.368	.417	.636	.340	52.1	54-3B	4
2006	BUF	AAA	24	115	22	9	0	7	20	10	12	2	1	5.2	.353	.409	.647	.515	.324	.383	.618	.322	17.7	19-3B	3
2006	CLE	MLB	24	61	4	2	0	3	11	5	12	0	0	2.6	.214	.279	.411	-.195	.218	.295	.418	.243	-1.4		
2007	SDN	MLB	25	533	73	30	3	22	82	39	83	4	2	4.7	.291	.348	.500	.103	.298	.351	.516	.289	33.6	125-3B	4

Breakout: 9%   Improve: 28%   Collapse: 37%   Attrition: 5%   Comparables: Mark Quinn, Jorge Toca, Tony Perez, Gary Sheffield

Hero of the Macedonian-American community, Kouzmanoff has two primary modes: hitting and hurting. Kouz (hey, that's what his friends call him) has a career batting line of .332/.395/.556 in the minors, but he's only played in 181 games over the past two seasons because of a back injury—one that some fear is chronic. He's not a very good defender, and a back injury won't help him improve at the hot corner, which is why he spent some time at first base in the Arizona Fall League. Shipped to San Diego, he'll get a shot at the Padres' third base job. As always, he'll hit if he's healthy.

Hector Luna   UT   Bats: R   Throws: R   Height: 6′ 1″   Weight: 170   Born: February 1, 1980   Age: 27

YEAR	TEAM	LVL	AGE	PA	R	2B	3B	HR	RBI	BB	SO	SB	CS	SPEED	AVG	OBP	SLG	MLVR	EQAVG	EQOBP	EQSLG	EQA	VORP	DEFENSE				
2004	SLN	MLB	24	192	25	7	2	3	22	13	37	6	3	6.6	.249	.304	.364	-.128	.249	.304	.364	.236	-0.7	22-SS	-4	10-2B	0
2005	MEM	AAA	25	247	24	13	1	3	21	20	38	11	4	5.8	.224	.294	.332	-.298	.215	.272	.298	.207	-12.8	43-2B	-1	11-SS	0
2005	SLN	MLB	25	153	26	10	2	1	18	9	25	10	2	8.0	.285	.344	.409	.041	.290	.349	.413	.271	6.2	16-2B	0	13-RF	2
2006	SLN	MLB	26	245	27	14	1	4	21	21	34	5	3	5.1	.291	.355	.417	.045	.293	.359	.414	.267	8.6	34-2B	-6	13-LF	0
2006	CLE	MLB	26	134	14	7	1	2	17	6	26	0	1	4.2	.276	.306	.394	-.122	.278	.313	.397	.243	0.8	19-2B	-1		
2007	CLE	MLB	27	359	43	18	2	6	33	25	59	8	4	6.1	.262	.318	.382	-.122	.259	.320	.391	.253	4.3	86-2B	-1		

Breakout: 25%   Improve: 51%   Collapse: 25%   Attrition: 25%   Comparables: Jerry Coleman, Fred Manrique, Bill Russell, Nick Green

After trading Ron Belliard for him, the Indians found that Luna isn't the kind of guy they want to have in the lineup every day because of his offensive limitations. Still, they loved having him on the roster. Because Moon Man laces some singles, has a knack for making contact, and can play six positions, the two-time Rule 5 selection has significant real-world value as a utility man, especially on planets where seven-man bullpens are increasingly common.

Andy Marte   3B   Bats: R   Throws: R   Height: 6′ 1″   Weight: 190   Born: October 21, 1983   Age: 23

YEAR	TEAM	LVL	AGE	PA	R	2B	3B	HR	RBI	BB	SO	SB	CS	SPEED	AVG	OBP	SLG	MLVR	EQAVG	EQOBP	EQSLG	EQA	VORP	DEFENSE	
2004	GRN	AA	20	450	52	28	1	23	68	58	105	1	1	3.4	.269	.364	.525	.223	.244	.324	.467	.268	21.2	101-3B	7
2005	RIC	AAA	21	460	51	26	2	20	74	64	83	0	3	2.2	.275	.372	.506	.179	.257	.351	.466	.279	28.4	108-3B	6
2005	ATL	MLB	21	66	3	2	1	0	4	7	13	0	1	4.0	.140	.227	.211	-.508	.107	.200	.179	.153	-7.3	15-3B	-5
2006	BUF	AAA	22	394	49	23	0	15	46	34	81	1	0	3.6	.261	.322	.451	.056	.243	.305	.444	.255	11.0	91-3B	7
2006	CLE	MLB	22	178	20	15	1	5	23	13	38	0	0	3.6	.226	.287	.421	-.151	.228	.298	.438	.249	-2.5	49-3B	2
2007	CLE	MLB	23	496	54	27	1	19	66	46	105	0	1	3.9	.247	.320	.439	-.056	.245	.321	.449	.268	10.7	117-3B	1

Breakout: 36%   Improve: 56%   Collapse: 17%   Attrition: 9%   Comparables: Tom Evans, Edwin Encarnacion, Rico Petrocelli, Juan Tejeda

There is still a lot to like here. Marte remains a very good hitter with above-average power. At the same time, those projections for future superstardom are starting to fade away. Future superstars don't get traded twice within 45 days. Future superstars don't wait 33 games to hit their first Triple-A home run. Despite the tough MLB debut, Marte looks like a lock to be the Tribe's every-day third baseman in 2007, with hopes to stay on the future star track. Let's forget about that "super" prefix for now.

Victor Martinez   **C**   **Bats: S   Throws: R**   Height: 6' 2"   Weight: 195   Born: December 23, 1978   Age: 28

YEAR	TEAM	LVL	AGE	PA	R	2B	3B	HR	RBI	BB	SO	SB	CS	SPEED	AVG	OBP	SLG	MLVR	EQAVG	EQOBP	EQSLG	EQA	VORP	DEFENSE	
2004	CLE	MLB	25	591	77	38	1	23	108	60	69	0	1	3.3	.283	.359	.492	.141	.289	.368	.508	.296	39.8	126-C -10	
2005	CLE	MLB	26	622	73	33	0	20	80	63	78	0	1	3.4	.305	.378	.475	.204	.316	.395	.504	.307	53.2	138-C -2	
2006	CLE	MLB	27	652	82	37	0	16	93	71	78	0	0	3.3	.316	.391	.465	.182	.320	.402	.478	.305	47.8	126-C -16	19-1B -3
2007	CLE	MLB	28	609	78	28	1	19	81	63	73	0	1	3.7	.288	.365	.452	.072	.286	.367	.462	.292	33.4	142-C -6	

Breakout: 10% Improve: 34% Collapse: 31% Attrition: 6%   *Comparables: Ted Simmons, Joe Torre, Jason Varitek, Thurman Munson*

Martinez's been a reliable offensive asset in his three years as a regular, yet people somehow aren't as excited about him as they once were. His interesting trends are an on-base percentage that continues to rise thanks to a slowly increasing walk rate and a slugging percentage that continues to fall due to a slowly dropping home run rate. They've basically balanced each other out, giving Martinez roughly equal offensive value over those three years. His defense, on the other hand, is continuing to regress. Baserunners stole on Martinez at will in 2006, racking up a major-league-leading 100 steals against him despite his second half improvement. There have been calls to move him to first base, but his bat wouldn't be nearly the asset it is now if he is relocated from one of the weakest offensive position in the game to one of the strongest.

Jason Michaels   **OF**   **Bats: R   Throws: R**   Height: 6' 0"   Weight: 205   Born: May 4, 1976   Age: 31

YEAR	TEAM	LVL	AGE	PA	R	2B	3B	HR	RBI	BB	SO	SB	CS	SPEED	AVG	OBP	SLG	MLVR	EQAVG	EQOBP	EQSLG	EQA	VORP	DEFENSE	
2004	PHI	MLB	28	346	44	12	0	10	40	42	80	2	2	4.6	.274	.364	.415	.059	.271	.361	.411	.270	8.9	38-CF -3	27-LF 2
2005	PHI	MLB	29	343	54	16	2	4	31	44	45	3	3	5.5	.305	.399	.415	.144	.301	.397	.422	.288	17.5	61-CF 11	
2006	CLE	MLB	30	548	77	32	1	9	55	43	101	9	5	5.7	.267	.326	.391	-.083	.273	.339	.402	.258	-1.7	115-LF -7	
2007	CLE	MLB	31	523	68	26	2	12	53	51	94	7	4	5.6	.263	.339	.406	-.054	.261	.340	.415	.269	5.7	123-LF -1	

Breakout: 13% Improve: 37% Collapse: 30% Attrition: 11%   *Comparables: Chuck Hinton, Al Smith, Al Cowens, Bill Tuttle*

It's one of those mistakes that gets made every year. Bench player establishes himself as a good bench player; bench player gets a chance to play every day; bench player proves why he was a bench player in the first place. Predictably, Michaels hit lefties well in 2006 but did nothing at all with righties. Sorry, Jason, back to the bench. He'll make a nice complementary player to either David Dellucci or Shin-Soo Choo in one of the outfield corners.

Ryan Mulhern   **1B/LF**   **Bats: R   Throws: R**   Height: 6' 2"   Weight: 205   Born: November 29, 1980   Age: 26

YEAR	TEAM	LVL	AGE	PA	R	2B	3B	HR	RBI	BB	SO	SB	CS	SPEED	AVG	OBP	SLG	MLVR	EQAVG	EQOBP	EQSLG	EQA	VORP	DEFENSE	
2004	LKC	A	23	415	48	28	1	7	43	32	87	3	2	3.9	.255	.319	.392	-.031	.210	.254	.301	.198	-36.3	94-1B 3	
2005	KIN	A+	24	185	32	11	0	17	48	19	50	2	2	3.0	.321	.395	.711	.583	.275	.326	.557	.288	11.6	34-1B -3	
2005	AKR	AA	24	277	40	18	3	15	46	28	64	4	2	4.9	.311	.386	.594	.377	.285	.353	.526	.294	18.2	46-1B 1	
2006	AKR	AA	25	501	65	26	3	15	69	40	123	1	0	4.3	.268	.335	.438	.102	.249	.305	.403	.245	-6.9	86-1B -6	22-LF -1
2007	CLE	MLB	26	449	40	23	1	13	54	30	123	1	1	4.1	.227	.284	.380	-.211	.224	.285	.389	.236	-12.9	106-1B -1	

Breakout: 9% Improve: 27% Collapse: 41% Attrition: 10%   *Comparables: Shelley Duncan, Mike Hessman, Earl Snyder, T.R. Marcinczyk*

After hitting 32 home runs and slugging .640 in 2005, Mullhern came back down to earth last year. It was the kind of regression that he just couldn't afford as a 26-year-old Double-A first baseman whose bat has to carry him. If you have him on a prospect list, put down the Kool-Aid and check out how guys are ahead of him at the position in this system.

Jhonny Peralta   **SS**   **Bats: R   Throws: R**   Height: 6' 1"   Weight: 195   Born: May 28, 1982   Age: 25

YEAR	TEAM	LVL	AGE	PA	R	2B	3B	HR	RBI	BB	SO	SB	CS	SPEED	AVG	OBP	SLG	MLVR	EQAVG	EQOBP	EQSLG	EQA	VORP	DEFENSE	
2004	BUF	AAA	22	623	109	44	2	15	86	54	126	8	4	5.5	.326	.384	.493	.229	.308	.366	.460	.285	51.0	77-SS -1	59-3B -1
2005	CLE	MLB	23	570	82	35	4	24	78	58	128	0	2	4.3	.292	.366	.520	.231	.303	.387	.549	.311	52.1	137-SS 13	
2006	CLE	MLB	24	632	84	28	3	13	68	56	152	0	1	4.2	.257	.323	.385	-.105	.258	.332	.395	.254	10.5	145-SS 25	
2007	CLE	MLB	25	624	80	33	2	19	80	57	135	3	2	4.8	.272	.342	.444	.010	.269	.344	.455	.279	30.3	146-SS 9	

Breakout: 14% Improve: 45% Collapse: 20% Attrition: 6%   *Comparables: Chris Speier, Travis Fryman, Denis Menke, Jim Fregosi*

While various defensive metrics suggest that Peralta was pretty good defensively, the Indians sure didn't think so, with manager Eric Wedge being a particularly vocal critic. At the plate, PECOTA expects something in between last year's low and the high of 2005, and more in keeping with his minor league track record, meaning he'll once again be one of the top hitters at his position. The Indians know they can't really deal him just one disappointing year after signing him to an arbitration-erasing extension through 2010, and with the defensive upgrades to his right and left, and the equally reasonable expectation that his bat will bounce back, sticking with him isn't just the path of least resistance, it's a good idea.

Kelly Shoppach   C   Bats: R   Throws: R   Height: 6′ 0″   Weight: 220   Born: April 29, 1980   Age: 27

YEAR	TEAM	LVL	AGE	PA	R	2B	3B	HR	RBI	BB	SO	SB	CS	SPEED	AVG	OBP	SLG	MLVR	EQAVG	EQOBP	EQSLG	EQA	VORP	DEFENSE	
2004	PAW	AAA	24	454	62	25	0	22	64	46	138	0	0	3.6	.233	.320	.461	-.000	.216	.300	.419	.247	3.4	95-C	0
2005	PAW	AAA	25	432	60	16	0	26	75	46	116	0	0	2.6	.253	.352	.507	.122	.238	.326	.466	.269	17.2	83-C	9
2006	BUF	AAA	26	87	11	8	0	4	9	6	25	0	1	4.0	.282	.356	.538	.233	.266	.333	.532	.280	6.7	21-C	2
2006	CLE	MLB	26	120	7	6	0	3	16	8	45	0	0	2.8	.245	.297	.382	-.170	.248	.305	.404	.244	-0.6	32-C	6
2007	CLE	MLB	27	346	36	16	1	14	46	31	102	0	0	3.5	.231	.309	.422	-.107	.229	.311	.432	.259	6.4	83-C	5

Breakout: 22% Improve: 49% Collapse: 28% Attrition: 37%   Comparables: Tim Laudner, George Mitterwald, Dave Duncan, Randy Knorr

At this point, Shoppach is officially on the backup catcher career path. He's a pretty good defender, has decent power, doesn't hit for average, and strikes out a lot. He'll get a couple of everyday assignments during his career due to positional scarcity, but in the end he'll have played thirteen years for eight different teams.

Grady Sizemore   CF   Bats: L   Throws: L   Height: 6′ 2″   Weight: 200   Born: August 2, 1982   Age: 24

YEAR	TEAM	LVL	AGE	PA	R	2B	3B	HR	RBI	BB	SO	SB	CS	SPEED	AVG	OBP	SLG	MLVR	EQAVG	EQOBP	EQSLG	EQA	VORP	DEFENSE	
2004	BUF	AAA	21	473	73	23	8	8	51	42	72	15	10	6.9	.287	.360	.438	.078	.270	.339	.405	.259	11.9	99-CF	1
2004	CLE	MLB	21	159	15	6	2	4	24	14	34	2	0	5.6	.246	.333	.406	-.118	.254	.340	.413	.266	0.9	42-CF	-4
2005	CLE	MLB	22	706	111	37	11	22	81	52	132	22	10	6.8	.289	.348	.484	.149	.302	.369	.517	.295	44.2	153-CF	-3
2006	CLE	MLB	23	751	134	53	11	28	76	78	153	22	6	8.0	.290	.375	.533	.224	.295	.386	.555	.312	69.1	157-CF	1
2007	CLE	MLB	24	685	105	42	6	25	92	67	127	16	7	6.9	.287	.364	.501	.132	.284	.365	.512	.302	46.1	160-CF	0

Breakout: 12% Improve: 43% Collapse: 12% Attrition: 0%   Comparables: Duke Snider, J. D. Drew, Barry Bonds, Ellis Burks

In June of 2000, a guy named Dave Malpass, a regional crosschecker for the Expos (remember them?), fought hard to get the Montreal brass to draft Grady Sizemore in the second round, and then again to convince the club to give him $2 million to lure him away from playing college football. The industry mocked both the selection and the bonus. A couple of years later, Malpass found himself with the Indians. When the time for the club to trade Bartolo Colon came and the Expos were interested, Malpass told the Indians about the kid he was still convinced would be an impact player and perennial All-Star, despite Sizemore's .258/.351/.348 line in the Florida State League at the time. The next time somebody portrays scouts as a bunch of cigar-chomping, Panama-hat-wearing know-nothings, tell them about Dave Malpass and the franchise player he brought to Cleveland.

Brad Snyder   OF   Bats: L   Throws: L   Height: 6′ 3″   Weight: 200   Born: May 25, 1982   Age: 25

YEAR	TEAM	LVL	AGE	PA	R	2B	3B	HR	RBI	BB	SO	SB	CS	SPEED	AVG	OBP	SLG	MLVR	EQAVG	EQOBP	EQSLG	EQA	VORP	DEFENSE			
2004	LKC	A	22	361	52	15	5	10	54	48	78	11	4	5.9	.280	.382	.461	.178	.247	.324	.384	.250	2.2	55-CF	-2	16-LF	-1
2004	KIN	A+	22	125	20	7	1	6	21	13	28	4	2	5.4	.355	.424	.600	.531	.336	.392	.575	.318	17.6	25-CF	-3		
2005	KIN	A+	23	241	36	10	2	6	28	24	64	12	1	7.1	.278	.365	.431	.111	.256	.315	.384	.250	0.8	47-CF	-3		
2005	AKR	AA	23	337	56	21	5	16	54	25	94	5	3	6.7	.280	.345	.539	.219	.266	.324	.503	.275	11.2	37-RF	5	17-LF	-1
2006	AKR	AA	24	594	86	28	5	18	72	62	158	20	2	6.4	.270	.351	.446	.135	.258	.328	.425	.264	2.1	124-RF	0		
2007	CLE	MLB	25	502	60	26	3	14	59	41	137	8	3	5.7	.251	.316	.415	-.090	.249	.318	.425	.262	1.1	118-RF	1		

Breakout: 13% Improve: 49% Collapse: 28% Attrition: 8%   Comparables: Doug Deeds, Jason Cooper, Jon Hamilton, Chin-Feng Chen

A first-round pick out of Ball State in 2003, Snyder is a terrific athlete with solid or better tools across the board, but his continued inability to make contact is squashing any hope of a sustained big league career. He's struck out 158 times in each of the last two seasons, and his career rate of striking out once every 3.32 at-bats needs to be addressed before anyone can get excited about his raw power.

Eider Torres   2B/SS   Bats: S   Throws: R   Height: 5′ 9″   Weight: 175   Born: January 16, 1983   Age: 24

YEAR	TEAM	LVL	AGE	PA	R	2B	3B	HR	RBI	BB	SO	SB	CS	SPEED	AVG	OBP	SLG	MLVR	EQAVG	EQOBP	EQSLG	EQA	VORP	DEFENSE			
2004	KIN	A+	21	477	68	24	3	3	46	22	46	48	6	8.2	.302	.337	.391	.069	.281	.309	.367	.247	2.9	107-2B	-4		
2005	AKR	AA	22	503	73	27	5	6	57	16	66	33	9	8.5	.285	.322	.407	.017	.267	.300	.381	.243	1.9	101-2B	-4		
2006	AKR	AA	23	475	49	12	2	2	42	32	54	41	12	6.6	.273	.325	.325	-.053	.257	.305	.307	.230	-11.4	90-2B	-4	13-SS	0
2006	BUF	AAA	23	48	5	0	0	0	2	2	4	3	1	6.8	.205	.239	.205	-.423	.178	.213	.178	.163	-6.4	11-2B	1		
2007	BAL	MLB	24	460	49	16	3	3	33	19	52	27	8	6.8	.247	.282	.320	-.281	.245	.285	.325	.226	-8.2	109-2B	-2		

Breakout: 18% Improve: 47% Collapse: 40% Attrition: 9%   Comparables: Carlos Leon, Alfredo Amezaga, Danny Sandoval, Juan Francia

(continued next page)

Eider Torres *(continued)*

Torres is a small, switch-hitting second baseman who hits singles and steals bases, but doesn't have any power or draw many walks. As importantly, he can't really play on the left side of the infield. Signed by the Orioles as a minor league free agent and deposited directly onto their 40-man roster, he'll get a chance to stick, but to be a utility guy in the majors, you have to be able to play more than one skill position.

Ramon Vazquez INF **Bats: L Throws: R** Height: 5′ 11″ Weight: 170 Born: August 21, 1976 Age: 30

YEAR	TEAM	LVL	AGE	PA	R	2B	3B	HR	RBI	BB	SO	SB	CS	SPEED	AVG	OBP	SLG	MLVR	EQAVG	EQOBP	EQSLG	EQA	VORP	DEFENSE	
2004	POR	AAA	27	223	36	21	1	8	34	33	28	2	0	4.7	.299	.402	.554	.304	.262	.353	.455	.279	12.5	41-2B	-3
2004	SDN	MLB	27	132	12	3	2	1	13	11	24	1	1	5.7	.235	.297	.322	-.203	.239	.300	.325	.225	-2.7	18-SS	-3
2005	BUF	AAA	28	92	13	3	1	0	4	7	16	1	1	6.1	.214	.275	.274	-.356	.188	.242	.235	.178	-8.1	16-SS	1
2005	CLE	MLB	28	26	1	3	0	0	1	2	3	0	0	2.4	.250	.308	.375	-.098	.250	.308	.375	.237	0.3		
2005	BOS	MLB	28	66	6	2	0	0	4	3	14	0	0	5.3	.197	.234	.230	-.497	.167	.219	.200	.162	-5.5		
2006	BUF	AAA	29	123	19	2	1	2	11	22	27	2	1	5.7	.242	.377	.343	-.003	.225	.344	.324	.242	0.8	14-SS	-2
2006	CLE	MLB	29	77	11	2	0	1	8	6	18	0	0	4.5	.209	.267	.284	-.385	.197	.267	.273	.204	-4.4	11-3B	-1
2007	*TEX*	*MLB*	*30*	*173*	*19*	*7*	*1*	*3*	*15*	*16*	*34*	*1*	*1*	*5.2*	*.242*	*.313*	*.356*	*-.180*	*.234*	*.310*	*.350*	*.238*	*-1.3*	*45-SS*	*0*

Breakout: 33% Improve: 60% Collapse: 22% Attrition: 41%   *Comparables: Rob Wilfong, Frank Quilici, Tim Jones, Jeff Huson*

Vazquez would like to be like Hector Luna, only he's a few years older and an even weaker hitter. Still, a left-handed bat with a patient approach and defensive versatility can pick up Triple-A contracts for years to come. It sure beats working at Sears—something that Vazquez perhaps failed to consider when he bitched after being optioned by the Indians. Signed to a minor league contract by the Rangers with an invite to spring training, Vazquez can put off showcasing those Kenmores for another year.

PITCHERS

Bear Bay **Bats: R Throws: R** Height: 6′ 3″ Weight: 155 Born: August 7, 1983 Age: 23

YEAR	TEAM	LVL	AGE	W	L	SV	G	GS	IP	H	BB	SO	HR	GB%	BABIP	STUFF	WHIP	ERA	PERA	EQERA	EQH9	EQBB9	EQSO9	EQHR9	VORP	WXRL
2004	LNS	A	20	11	9	0	28	28	168¹	166	30	139	7	—	.310	13	1.16	3.10	4.07	5.27	9.7	2.0	4.3	0.8	6.1	—
2005	KIN	A+	21	6	5	0	15	15	85¹	82	15	85	14	43.0%	.304	-10	1.14	3.38	6.23	4.61	10.3	1.8	5.7	2.4	9.0	—
2005	AKR	AA	21	3	3	0	8	8	45¹	45	13	40	5	50.4%	.320	4	1.28	4.77	5.14	5.52	10.0	3.1	5.5	1.4	0.4	—
2006	AKR	AA	22	7	8	0	27	19	133¹	126	48	114	24	43.8%	.287	-34	1.31	4.33	7.20	5.95	9.9	3.6	5.5	2.6	-5.0	—
2007	*CLE*	*MLB*	*23*	*5*	*7*	*0*	*27*	*16*	*98*	*118*	*40*	*58*	*20*	*43.0%*	*.304*	*-7*	*1.61*	*6.05*	*5.93*	*5.72*	*10.4*	*3.5*	*4.9*	*1.6*	*-4.6*	*0.20*

Breakout: 7% Improve: 39% Collapse: 18% Attrition: 1%   *Comparables: Johann Lopez, Jason Olsen, Michael Howell, Brett Evert*

While Bear Bay sounds like a 19th-century explorer who helped conquer the Wild West, in reality he's a skinny right-hander from Texas whose first name is Ronald. Bay has a decent fastball and a very good slider, and could end up making some noise in the Cleveland bullpen in the end; he just doesn't have the arsenal to start in the big leagues.

Rafael Betancourt **Bats: R Throws: R** Height: 6′ 2″ Weight: 200 Born: April 29, 1975 Age: 32

YEAR	TEAM	LVL	AGE	W	L	SV	G	GS	IP	H	BB	SO	HR	GB%	BABIP	STUFF	WHIP	ERA	PERA	EQERA	EQH9	EQBB9	EQSO9	EQHR9	VORP	WXRL
2004	CLE	MLB	29	5	6	4	68	0	66²	71	18	76	7	—	.352	24	1.34	3.91	3.01	4.04	9.0	2.2	9.4	0.8	14.5	1.36
2005	CLE	MLB	30	4	3	1	54	0	67²	57	17	73	5	34.8%	.295	31	1.09	2.79	2.77	3.28	7.7	2.2	9.4	0.7	19.9	1.15
2006	CLE	MLB	31	3	4	3	50	0	56²	52	11	48	7	25.0%	.280	12	1.11	3.81	3.53	3.81	7.3	1.7	7.0	0.9	13.2	1.62
2007	*CLE*	*MLB*	*32*	*3*	*2*	*4*	*44*	*0*	*51²*	*50*	*12*	*49*	*7*	*35.0%*	*.293*	*14*	*1.18*	*3.49*	*3.45*	*3.30*	*8.3*	*1.9*	*7.9*	*1.1*	*13.1*	*1.20*

Breakout: 35% Improve: 62% Collapse: 16% Attrition: 12%   *Comparables: Steve Reed, Justin Speier, Alejandro Pena, Stan Belinda*

One of those nice scrapheap finds, Betancourt was moved from shortstop to the mound by the Red Sox, but didn't develop all that fast and wound up spending some time in Japan before the Indians gave him a look. In return, he's given them three and a half seasons of solid bullpen work with nice ERAs and ratios. "Consistent middle reliever" sounds like an oxymoron, but Betancourt is the exception to the rule. Of course, health is part of consistency and he's also spent time on the DL in each of his three full seasons.

Andrew Brown

Bats: R Throws: R   Height: 6' 6"   Weight: 230   Born: February 17, 1981   Age: 26

YEAR	TEAM	LVL	AGE	W	L	SV	G	GS	IP	H	BB	SO	HR	GB%	BABIP	STUFF	WHIP	ERA	PERA	EQERA	EQH9	EQBB9	EQSO9	EQHR9	VORP	WXRL
2004	AKR	AA	23	3	6	0	17	17	77¹	66	36	67	7	—	.262	0	1.32	4.66	5.38	5.28	8.0	4.6	5.5	1.1	2.7	—
2004	JAX	AA	23	1	3	0	8	8	40¹	36	14	58	5	—	.326	11	1.24	4.02	5.29	6.34	9.9	3.5	8.5	1.9	-3.1	—
2005	BUF	AAA	24	4	2	4	49	0	69²	52	19	81	7	38.1%	.269	15	1.02	3.36	3.85	3.75	6.8	2.6	8.1	1.0	14.3	—
2006	BUF	AAA	25	5	4	5	39	0	62	52	36	53	5	46.4%	.276	-1	1.42	2.61	5.74	3.56	8.3	5.6	5.9	1.0	13.8	—
2006	CLE	MLB	25	0	0	0	9	0	10	6	8	7	0	39.3%	.214	9	1.40	3.60	5.13	3.48	5.2	7.0	6.1	0.0	2.7	-0.17
2007	SDN	MLB	26	3	3	1	37	3	62²	59	37	50	8	41.0%	.281	-4	1.54	4.84	5.52	5.28	8.6	4.6	6.5	1.1	3.2	0.40

Breakout: 5%   Improve: 19%   Collapse: 49%   Attrition: 10%   Comparables: Aaron Myette, Brian Bowles, Chris Gissell, Bart Miadich

The stuff to get big league hitters out is there—Brown can consistently get it into the mid-90s—but poor command has handicapped his progress. Some within the Indians' organization questioned if Brown has the, shall was say, gonads to pitch in the late innings. It's San Diego's problem now, if getting a 26-year-old reliever with more than a strikeout per inning in the minor leagues can be considered a problem. Maybe they'll find the secret to unleash the genie from this bottle—if Brown has a, shall we say, genie.

Paul Byrd

Bats: R Throws: R   Height: 6' 1"   Weight: 190   Born: December 3, 1970   Age: 36

YEAR	TEAM	LVL	AGE	W	L	SV	G	GS	IP	H	BB	SO	HR	GB%	BABIP	STUFF	WHIP	ERA	PERA	EQERA	EQH9	EQBB9	EQSO9	EQHR9	VORP	WXRL
2004	ATL	MLB	33	8	7	0	19	19	114¹	123	19	79	18	—	.293	7	1.24	3.94	4.25	4.47	9.3	1.3	5.5	1.2	15.8	2.60
2005	ANA	MLB	34	12	11	0	31	31	204¹	216	28	102	22	39.4%	.290	10	1.19	3.74	4.03	4.28	9.2	1.2	4.4	0.9	35.4	4.10
2006	CLE	MLB	35	10	9	0	31	31	179	232	38	88	26	41.6%	.322	-4	1.51	4.88	4.62	5.56	10.4	1.8	4.1	1.2	-0.5	1.98
2007	CLE	MLB	36	9	10	0	31	25	159²	190	34	80	25	41.0%	.301	-2	1.41	5.00	4.84	4.76	10.3	1.8	4.2	1.3	11.7	2.30

Breakout: 18%   Improve: 53%   Collapse: 8%   Attrition: 5%   Comparables: Mark Portugal, Kevin Tapani, Vern Law, Hal Brown

The Indians couldn't have expected more than a solid innings eater when they signed Byrd to a two-year, $14.25-million contract last December, but he failed to live up to even that modest standard in the first year of his deal. Byrd always gave up a lot of hits, but his pinpoint control typically made up for it. That worked when opposing batters hit .270 or so against him, but proved to be more difficult when they hit .308, as in 2006. It's hard to figure out what's a fluke season and what's an actual downturn with these Bob Tewksbury types; Byrd allowed a goodly number of line drives in 2006, but the Indians defense didn't do him any favors. He should get closer to a league-average ERA in 2007, but another 2005 seems unlikely.

Fernando Cabrera

Bats: R Throws: R   Height: 6' 4"   Weight: 220   Born: November 16, 1981   Age: 25

YEAR	TEAM	LVL	AGE	W	L	SV	G	GS	IP	H	BB	SO	HR	GB%	BABIP	STUFF	WHIP	ERA	PERA	EQERA	EQH9	EQBB9	EQSO9	EQHR9	VORP	WXRL
2004	BUF	AAA	22	4	3	5	45	0	76	57	43	93	9	—	.268	14	1.32	3.79	5.17	4.68	7.1	5.5	8.6	1.2	7.7	—
2005	BUF	AAA	23	6	1	3	30	0	51¹	36	11	68	3	35.0%	.292	36	0.92	1.23	2.69	1.75	6.5	2.1	9.1	0.5	21.9	—
2005	CLE	MLB	23	2	1	0	15	0	30²	24	11	29	1	38.1%	.277	26	1.14	1.47	2.87	2.32	7.3	3.2	8.4	0.3	12.4	0.56
2006	CLE	MLB	24	3	3	0	51	0	60²	53	32	71	12	35.4%	.304	10	1.40	5.19	4.86	5.03	7.2	4.3	9.8	1.6	4.7	0.02
2007	CLE	MLB	25	3	3	3	52	1	62	55	29	69	8	38.0%	.296	18	1.35	3.91	3.94	3.72	7.6	4.0	9.3	1.0	13.3	1.10

Breakout: 30%   Improve: 63%   Collapse: 12%   Attrition: 11%   Comparables: Stan Belinda, Doug Bochtler, John Wetteland, Jeff Reardon

Other than the ERA, those final numbers are actually pretty good. Cabrera dealt with a bruised heel early in the season and had some mechanical issues later on, but he was very effective in the second half once he was healthy and straightened out. His fastball/splitter combination leaves him susceptible to left-handed hitters at times, but he'll get some late-innings work and could assume the closer role if something goes wrong with Joe Borowski.

Fausto Carmona

Bats: R Throws: R   Height: 6' 4"   Weight: 220   Born: December 7, 1983   Age: 23

YEAR	TEAM	LVL	AGE	W	L	SV	G	GS	IP	H	BB	SO	HR	GB%	BABIP	STUFF	WHIP	ERA	PERA	EQERA	EQH9	EQBB9	EQSO9	EQHR9	VORP	WXRL
2004	KIN	A+	20	5	2	0	13	13	70	68	20	57	6	—	.292	1	1.26	2.83	5.47	4.92	9.8	3.1	5.1	1.6	5.1	—
2004	AKR	AA	20	4	8	0	15	15	87	114	21	63	3	—	.369	21	1.55	4.76	3.52	5.04	11.2	2.2	4.6	0.4	5.6	—
2005	AKR	AA	21	6	5	0	14	14	90²	100	20	57	7	57.4%	.312	2	1.32	4.07	4.78	5.44	10.7	2.3	3.9	1.0	1.6	—
2005	BUF	AAA	21	7	4	0	13	12	83	76	15	49	10	53.5%	.261	5	1.10	3.25	4.79	3.52	7.8	1.7	4.1	1.2	19.5	—
2006	BUF	AAA	22	1	3	0	6	5	27¹	28	8	28	2	49.4%	.342	11	1.33	5.65	4.00	7.76	10.1	2.7	7.4	1.0	-6.4	—
2006	CLE	MLB	22	1	10	0	38	7	74²	88	31	58	9	60.8%	.346	1	1.59	5.42	4.65	5.21	9.7	3.5	6.5	0.9	3.8	-0.91
2007	CLE	MLB	23	6	6	1	42	13	103²	115	35	71	10	52.0%	.314	4	1.44	4.57	4.40	4.45	9.5	2.9	5.7	0.8	12.4	1.60

Breakout: 30%   Improve: 72%   Collapse: 8%   Attrition: 10%   Comparables: Kevin Gross, Jaime Navarro, John Denny, Brett Myers

(continued next page)

Fausto Carmona *(continued)*

Maybe we should give Carmona a mulligan, because he was certainly jerked around in 2006. He was put into the rotation in April when C. C. Sabathia got hurt, but went back to Triple-A after just three starts. He got called up to the bullpen a couple of weeks later, and pitched well enough to be installed as the closer when the organization dealt Bob Wickman to the Braves in late July. Two weeks and three straight blown saves later, he was back to a long relief role, and two weeks after that it was back to Triple-A. Eight days later, he was called back up again and finished the year with four more starts, looking pretty good in the last three. He has the stuff to succeed as a starter if the Indians give him the opportunity to do so.

Jason Davis   Bats: R Throws: R   Height: 6' 6"   Weight: 225   Born: May 8, 1980   Age: 27

YEAR	TEAM	LVL	AGE	W	L	SV	G	GS	IP	H	BB	SO	HR	GB%	BABIP	STUFF	WHIP	ERA	PERA	EQERA	EQH9	EQBB9	EQSO9	EQHR9	VORP	WXRL
2004	BUF	AAA	24	3	2	0	9	9	54	53	18	39	4	—	.301	7	1.31	3.00	4.41	4.64	8.4	3.1	5.0	0.8	5.8	—
2004	CLE	MLB	24	2	7	0	26	19	114¹	148	51	72	13	—	.348	-2	1.74	5.51	4.58	5.78	10.7	3.5	5.2	0.9	-2.6	0.66
2005	BUF	AAA	25	8	5	0	16	16	95²	106	27	77	9	57.6%	.336	7	1.39	4.61	4.34	6.12	9.6	2.7	5.5	0.9	-5.6	—
2005	CLE	MLB	25	4	2	0	11	4	40¹	44	20	32	4	51.6%	.333	7	1.59	4.69	4.60	5.05	10.1	4.4	7.0	0.9	3.8	0.01
2006	BUF	AAA	26	0	2	4	11	0	16²	8	3	15	0	63.6%	.186	16	0.68	0.56	2.64	1.65	5.0	1.7	6.1	0.0	7.2	—
2006	CLE	MLB	26	3	2	1	39	0	55¹	67	14	37	1	50.8%	.359	10	1.46	3.74	3.12	4.21	9.8	2.0	5.5	0.2	9.1	0.05
2007	*CLE*	*MLB*	*27*	*3*	*3*	*2*	*47*	*1*	*63²*	*71*	*23*	*43*	*7*	*52.0%*	*.313*	*-3*	*1.47*	*4.55*	*4.47*	*4.42*	*9.6*	*3.0*	*5.6*	*0.9*	*7.1*	*0.70*

Breakout: 33% Improve: 67% Collapse: 9%   Attrition: 16%   Comparables: Adrian Devine, Bob Anderson, Rich Bordi, Jay Powell

The Indians gave Davis a couple of closing opportunities toward the end of the season. That's understandable considering how hard he throws, but not so understandable considering his inability to miss bats despite power stuff. He'll stick around in a middle-innings role, but it's hard to expect much more.

Dan Denham   Bats: R Throws: R   Height: 6' 2"   Weight: 195   Born: December 24, 1982   Age: 23

YEAR	TEAM	LVL	AGE	W	L	SV	G	GS	IP	H	BB	SO	HR	GB%	BABIP	STUFF	WHIP	ERA	PERA	EQERA	EQH9	EQBB9	EQSO9	EQHR9	VORP	WXRL
2004	KIN	A+	21	7	4	0	13	13	71	73	29	62	6	—	.332	-4	1.44	4.18	6.09	5.66	10.5	4.3	5.5	1.4	-0.5	—
2004	AKR	AA	21	5	3	0	14	13	76	84	30	50	12	—	.296	-19	1.50	4.74	6.63	6.01	10.1	3.7	4.2	1.9	-3.5	—
2005	AKR	AA	22	9	7	0	21	21	140	115	30	108	6	48.6%	.270	20	1.04	3.15	4.01	4.26	8.3	2.2	4.8	0.5	20.4	—
2006	AKR	AA	23	6	2	0	23	10	66¹	66	39	40	3	53.1%	.304	-11	1.59	4.90	5.69	6.51	9.6	6.1	3.7	0.7	-6.6	—
2006	BUF	AAA	23	1	2	0	9	4	25²	41	11	14	3	54.6%	.404	-32	2.06	8.21	5.67	9.59	14.9	4.3	3.9	1.4	-11.2	—

A first round pick in 2001, Denham has always been healthy, taking his turn on the mound every five days throughout his first five professional seasons. The problem is that, despite all that work, he never really developed. Moved to the bullpen last year for the first time, Denham has become a marginal right-hander with a slender chance at a big league career.

Jake Dittler   Bats: R Throws: R   Height: 6' 4"   Weight: 220   Born: November 24, 1982   Age: 24

YEAR	TEAM	LVL	AGE	W	L	SV	G	GS	IP	H	BB	SO	HR	GB%	BABIP	STUFF	WHIP	ERA	PERA	EQERA	EQH9	EQBB9	EQSO9	EQHR9	VORP	WXRL
2004	AKR	AA	21	5	12	0	21	20	107²	119	40	85	7	—	.323	7	1.48	5.01	4.53	5.94	9.8	3.5	5.0	0.7	-4.1	—
2005	AKR	AA	22	10	9	0	28	27	173	187	61	107	12	64.8%	.305	-4	1.43	3.64	4.99	5.82	10.4	3.7	3.8	0.8	-4.2	—
2006	BUF	AAA	23	5	12	0	25	24	130	152	50	54	6	61.7%	.314	-9	1.55	4.71	4.83	6.84	10.6	3.7	2.9	0.6	-18.0	—
2007	*CLE*	*MLB*	*24*	*5*	*7*	*0*	*26*	*16*	*96²*	*119*	*45*	*41*	*10*	*58.0%*	*.318*	*-12*	*1.69*	*5.97*	*5.44*	*5.91*	*10.6*	*3.9*	*3.5*	*0.8*	*-6.7*	*0.00*

Breakout: 25% Improve: 62% Collapse: 7%   Attrition: 3%   Comparables: Shane Loux, Preston Larrison, Dan Kolb, Mike LaCoss

Once highly regarded, Dittler has gone backward in each of the last two seasons. It doesn't take a statistical genius to figure out that 54 strikeouts in 130 ⅓ Triple-A innings isn't very good. How far has his star sunk? He was outrighted at the end of the season, and nobody bit.

Teams   **147**

Jeremy Guthrie   **Bats: R Throws: R**   Height: 6' 1"   Weight: 200   Born: April 8, 1979   Age: 28

YEAR	TEAM	LVL	AGE	W	L	SV	G	GS	IP	H	BB	SO	HR	GB%	BABIP	STUFF	WHIP	ERA	PERA	EQERA	EQH9	EQBB9	EQSO9	EQHR9	VORP	WXRL
2004	AKR	AA	25	8	8	0	23	21	130¹	145	42	94	16	—	.309	-22	1.44	4.21	6.37	5.75	10.6	3.4	4.3	1.6	-2.1	—
2004	BUF	AAA	25	1	2	0	4	4	19¹	23	18	10	0	—	.343	-3	2.12	7.93	6.88	9.47	10.9	9.5	3.8	0.5	-8.2	—
2004	CLE	MLB	25	0	0	0	6	0	11²	9	6	7	1	—	.235	-9	1.29	4.62	4.89	4.50	6.8	4.5	5.2	0.8	2.0	0.01
2005	BUF	AAA	26	12	10	0	25	25	136¹	152	49	100	15	44.0%	.329	-5	1.47	5.08	5.21	5.82	9.8	3.5	5.0	1.1	-3.4	—
2006	BUF	AAA	27	9	5	0	21	20	123	104	48	88	6	53.0%	.271	10	1.24	3.15	4.69	4.30	8.2	3.9	4.9	0.7	17.5	—
2006	CLE	MLB	27	0	0	0	9	1	19¹	24	15	14	2	48.4%	.367	-2	2.02	6.99	5.62	6.64	10.2	6.2	5.8	0.9	-2.2	-0.16
2007	CLE	MLB	28	5	7	0	32	13	98¹	114	47	59	14	47.0%	.309	-8	1.63	5.79	5.51	5.58	10.0	4.0	5.0	1.2	-2.9	0.20

Breakout: 15% Improve: 39% Collapse: 18% Attrition: 1%   Comparables: Erv Palica, Sean Lowe, Cloyd Boyer, Fred Talbot

Well, that's $3 million down the drain—that was Guthrie's bonus as a first-round pick out of Stanford. He did a Mormon mission during his amateur days, so he was almost 23 when he signed, and it's just never come together for him. He showed some signs of life at Triple-A in 2006, pitching well for the first time in three years, but it was probably too little, too late. He's out of options, and could be out of the organization this spring.

Juan Lara   **Bats: R Throws: L**   Height: 6' 2"   Weight: 190   Born: January 26, 1981   Age: 26

YEAR	TEAM	LVL	AGE	W	L	SV	G	GS	IP	H	BB	SO	HR	GB%	BABIP	STUFF	WHIP	ERA	PERA	EQERA	EQH9	EQBB9	EQSO9	EQHR9	VORP	WXRL
2004	KIN	A+	23	4	3	1	35	8	84¹	106	38	74	6	—	.368	-24	1.71	5.66	5.91	8.74	12.7	5.3	5.2	1.5	-28.0	—
2005	KIN	A+	24	0	1	0	26	0	42¹	40	15	46	4	61.3%	.316	-19	1.30	4.04	5.51	6.25	10.0	4.0	5.6	1.6	-2.9	—
2005	AKR	AA	24	1	2	5	18	0	23²	27	14	16	1	51.9%	.342	-17	1.73	4.56	5.65	7.15	11.1	6.8	4.0	0.4	-3.9	—
2006	AKR	AA	25	4	2	7	40	0	46²	32	21	48	2	55.2%	.254	1	1.15	2.73	4.87	3.86	7.3	5.1	5.9	0.6	8.6	—
2006	BUF	AAA	25	1	1	1	13	0	15²	17	3	15	1	63.0%	.356	4	1.32	2.96	3.79	4.20	10.8	1.8	6.6	0.6	2.3	—
2007	CLE	MLB	26	2	3	0	35	3	54¹	66	31	36	7	51.0%	.328	-13	1.78	5.92	5.94	5.71	10.5	4.9	5.5	1.1	-2.3	0.10

Breakout: 33% Improve: 57% Collapse: 16% Attrition: 5%   Comparables: Jonathon Rouwenhorst, Doug Slaten, Carmen Cali, Jose Rodriguez

Because the lefty Lara throws pretty hard and boasts a decent breaking ball, opposing left-handed batters can't touch him. He could be vying for various LOOGY jobs against Borg Orosco ("Second of Two") and zombie Everynight Eddie Guardado until 2020 if he stays healthy.

Cliff Lee   **Bats: L Throws: L**   Height: 6' 3"   Weight: 190   Born: August 30, 1978   Age: 28

YEAR	TEAM	LVL	AGE	W	L	SV	G	GS	IP	H	BB	SO	HR	GB%	BABIP	STUFF	WHIP	ERA	PERA	EQERA	EQH9	EQBB9	EQSO9	EQHR9	VORP	WXRL
2004	CLE	MLB	25	14	8	0	33	33	179	188	81	161	30	—	.314	7	1.53	5.43	4.88	5.27	8.9	3.6	7.4	1.3	7.4	2.66
2005	CLE	MLB	26	18	5	0	32	32	202	194	52	143	22	36.1%	.282	17	1.22	3.79	3.88	4.26	8.8	2.3	6.2	0.9	37.2	4.65
2006	CLE	MLB	27	14	11	0	33	33	200²	224	58	129	29	33.9%	.300	5	1.41	4.39	4.62	4.77	9.0	2.4	5.3	1.2	20.0	2.95
2007	CLE	MLB	28	11	10	0	30	30	186²	205	55	128	27	38.0%	.300	11	1.39	4.74	4.62	4.50	9.5	2.5	5.7	1.2	19.8	3.40

Breakout: 23% Improve: 63% Collapse: 7% Attrition: 0%   Comparables: Doug Rau, Don Carman, Jarrod Washburn, Tom Browning

Lee was pretty bad in 2004 and awfully good in 2005. Any sensible projection will say that the median performance we saw in 2006 is the real deal. That performance is a bit misleading, however, as Lee was a particular victim of the club's lack of a quality middle-inning fireman. In the middle four months of 2006, nearly half of Lee's quality starts were blown by the bullpen after the sixth inning (five of 12, in 23 starts overall). His ability to get back to where he was in 2005 will play a major part of the Indians' chances in 2007, but his career-high rate in hits allowed and career-low strikeout rate in 2006 leave us less than optimistic.

Scott Lewis   **Bats: S Throws: L**   Height: 6' 0"   Weight: 185   Born: September 26, 1983 Age: 23

YEAR	TEAM	LVL	AGE	W	L	SV	G	GS	IP	H	BB	SO	HR	GB%	BABIP	STUFF	WHIP	ERA	PERA	EQERA	EQH9	EQBB9	EQSO9	EQHR9	VORP	WXRL
2005	MHV	A-	21	0	1	0	7	6	15²	13	6	24	2	41.2%	.344	-6	1.21	4.59	9.72	6.75	12.2	5.4	7.4	4.1	-1.7	—
2006	KIN	A+	22	3	3	0	27	26	115¹	84	28	123	3	43.4%	.277	30	0.97	1.49	3.21	2.88	7.5	2.4	6.6	0.5	34.1	—
2007	CLE	MLB	23	7	7	0	29	18	117	121	43	91	17	42.0%	.294	10	1.40	4.61	4.52	4.40	8.9	3.1	6.5	1.2	13.7	2.10

Breakout: 0% Improve: 14% Collapse: 64% Attrition: 3%   Comparables: Ted Lilly, Jon Switzer, Allen Davis, Jesus Sanchez

Lewis led the minor leagues with a 1.48 ERA, but he's more of a crafty left-hander than any sort of future star. Lewis had Tommy John surgery in college, and a sore arm since signing has kept him on a limited pitch count as a pro. A strike-thrower who sits in the mid-80s with outstanding command and a plus curveball, Lewis has the perfect formula to succeed in High A-ball, but pitchers with his profile often hit a wall at the upper levels, long before they reach the majors.

Cleveland Indians

Chuck Lofgren **Bats: L Throws: L** Height: 6′ 3″ Weight: 205 Born: January 29, 1986 Age: 21

YEAR	TEAM	LVL	AGE	W	L	SV	G	GS	IP	H	BB	SO	HR	GB%	BABIP	STUFF	WHIP	ERA	PERA	EQERA	EQH9	EQBB9	EQSO9	EQHR9	VORP	WXRL
2004	BNC	Rk	18	0	0	0	9	9	22¹	25	13	23	4	—	.344	-25	1.70	6.05	11.02	8.10	13.5	7.7	4.5	4.1	-5.6	—
2005	LKC	A	19	5	5	0	18	18	93	73	43	89	6	43.7%	.279	7	1.25	2.81	5.90	3.96	8.5	5.3	5.3	1.1	16.2	—
2006	KIN	A+	20	17	5	0	25	25	139	108	54	125	5	38.0%	.276	22	1.17	2.33	4.28	4.47	7.9	3.7	5.6	0.7	17.2	—
2007	CLE	MLB	21	6	8	0	26	20	115¹	124	63	82	20	40.0%	.294	1	1.62	5.53	5.60	5.22	9.3	4.6	5.9	1.4	1.8	1.00

Breakout: 5% Improve: 28% Collapse: 33% Attrition: 1% Comparables: Jon Lester, Travis Blackley, Wilfredo Rodriguez, Ryan Ketchner

Stud. Lofgren led the Carolina League in wins, while finishing second in ERA and strikeouts. The good news is that, unlike Lewis, Lofgren has the stuff to match the stats. Pitchers who are barely able to drink legally (he turned 21 in January) yet have a fastball, two breaking balls, and a changeup that are all quality pitches are hard to find. The scariest part? The Indians think he is just starting to scratch the surface of his potential.

Tom Mastny **Bats: R Throws: R** Height: 6′ 6″ Weight: 220 Born: February 4, 1981 Age: 26

YEAR	TEAM	LVL	AGE	W	L	SV	G	GS	IP	H	BB	SO	HR	GB%	BABIP	STUFF	WHIP	ERA	PERA	EQERA	EQH9	EQBB9	EQSO9	EQHR9	VORP	WXRL
2004	CWV	A	23	10	3	0	27	27	149	123	41	143	4	—	.292	15	1.10	2.17	3.98	3.87	8.4	3.2	4.6	0.4	27.7	—
2005	KIN	A+	24	7	3	2	29	11	88	78	26	94	4	57.4%	.320	2	1.18	2.35	4.40	4.07	9.4	3.3	5.6	0.8	14.3	—
2005	AKR	AA	24	1	1	0	5	3	20²	18	5	18	0	32.3%	.290	5	1.11	2.17	3.80	4.12	9.2	2.7	5.0	0.5	3.2	—
2006	AKR	AA	25	0	1	1	12	1	24¹	15	8	30	0	60.7%	.254	13	0.95	1.12	3.39	2.74	7.0	3.9	7.0	0.4	7.3	—
2006	BUF	AAA	25	2	1	0	24	0	38²	25	16	46	0	46.7%	.278	20	1.07	2.59	3.48	3.11	6.9	4.1	8.4	0.2	10.4	—
2006	CLE	MLB	25	0	1	5	15	0	16¹	17	8	14	1	51.1%	.348	1	1.53	5.52	3.90	5.29	8.5	4.2	6.9	0.5	1.0	0.09
2007	CLE	MLB	26	3	3	4	58	2	60¹	62	28	45	6	49.0%	.306	-1	1.49	4.54	4.39	4.42	8.9	3.9	6.3	0.7	6.8	0.70

Breakout: 12% Improve: 30% Collapse: 33% Attrition: 16% Comparables: Roy Smith, Ryan Speier, Jay Powell, Brian Bowles

How many people foresaw Mastny picking up five major league saves last year? Acquired from the Blue Jays a couple of years back for John McDonald, Mastny was always seen as a fringy right-hander. He throws strikes, has a good curve, and his mechanics, aided by a long, six-foot-six frame, create plenty of deception. With a fastball that sits at 88–90 MPH, he doesn't deserve many more save opportunities, but he's proven to be good enough to get big league hitters out.

Adam Miller **Bats: R Throws: R** Height: 6′ 4″ Weight: 175 Born: November 26, 1984 Age: 22

YEAR	TEAM	LVL	AGE	W	L	SV	G	GS	IP	H	BB	SO	HR	GB%	BABIP	STUFF	WHIP	ERA	PERA	EQERA	EQH9	EQBB9	EQSO9	EQHR9	VORP	WXRL
2004	LKC	A	19	7	4	0	19	19	91	79	28	106	7	—	.320	16	1.18	3.36	4.69	4.55	8.8	3.2	6.3	1.2	10.4	—
2004	KIN	A+	19	3	2	0	8	8	43¹	29	12	46	1	—	.252	33	0.95	2.08	3.67	4.71	7.1	3.0	6.6	0.4	4.2	—
2005	KIN	A+	20	2	4	0	12	12	59²	76	17	45	5	47.7%	.376	-7	1.56	4.82	5.14	7.98	12.4	2.8	4.3	1.2	-15.5	—
2006	AKR	AA	21	15	6	0	26	24	153²	129	43	157	9	55.6%	.301	24	1.12	2.76	4.19	4.17	8.6	2.7	6.4	0.8	24.0	—
2007	CLE	MLB	22	7	8	0	26	20	122¹	135	48	86	15	48.0%	.309	8	1.49	5.05	4.82	4.88	9.5	3.4	5.8	1.0	7.2	1.60

Breakout: 20% Improve: 56% Collapse: 13% Attrition: 1% Comparables: Pete Munro, Mark Brownson, Kurt Ainsworth, Josh Hall

Miller was consistently touching triple digits with his heat at the end of 2004, but 2005 was something of a lost season as he battled arm soreness that never really went away. Finally healthy in 2006, Miller didn't throw as hard as he used to (though at 94–97 MPH he still has plenty of stuff), but a funny thing happened: he became a much better *pitcher*. His slider is now a true major league out-pitch, and he made dramatic improvements with his command and control. The Indians would like to give him some Triple-A experience in 2007, but he's very close to ready.

Edward Mujica **Bats: R Throws: R** Height: 6′ 2″ Weight: 220 Born: May 10, 1984 Age: 23

YEAR	TEAM	LVL	AGE	W	L	SV	G	GS	IP	H	BB	SO	HR	GB%	BABIP	STUFF	WHIP	ERA	PERA	EQERA	EQH9	EQBB9	EQSO9	EQHR9	VORP	WXRL
2004	LKC	A	20	7	7	2	26	19	124	130	32	89	18	—	.293	-30	1.31	4.65	6.86	6.53	10.2	2.7	3.8	2.2	-12.7	—
2005	KIN	A+	21	1	0	14	25	0	26	17	2	32	3	40.3%	.241	15	0.73	2.08	4.41	2.88	7.6	0.7	7.2	1.8	7.6	—
2005	AKR	AA	21	2	1	10	27	0	34¹	36	5	33	2	44.7%	.351	8	1.20	2.89	3.38	3.48	10.4	1.6	5.9	0.8	7.9	—
2006	AKR	AA	22	1	0	8	12	0	19²	11	9	17	0	54.0%	.229	8	1.04	0.00	4.11	0.95	5.7	4.7	5.7	0.0	9.8	—
2006	BUF	AAA	22	3	1	5	22	0	32¹	31	5	29	1	37.9%	.333	13	1.12	2.52	3.03	3.41	9.4	1.4	6.3	0.3	7.7	—
2006	CLE	MLB	22	0	1	0	10	0	18¹	25	0	12	1	25.4%	.387	11	1.36	2.95	3.01	2.84	10.9	0.5	5.7	0.5	6.3	-0.24
2007	CLE	MLB	23	4	4	3	63	3	72²	82	20	47	12	38.0%	.295	-4	1.39	4.73	4.75	4.46	9.7	2.3	5.3	1.4	8.1	0.80

Breakout: 12% Improve: 40% Collapse: 25% Attrition: 6% Comparables: Dan Wheeler, Brian Rose, Jeff Suppan, Jarod Matthews

Yet another young arm that got a look in the major league pen in 2006, the Venezuelan has thrived since a move to the bullpen in late 2004. The secret of his success is his excellent command of a solid fastball/slider combination, as evidenced by the zero free passes he handed out to the 78 big league hitters he faced. If anything, he might throw a few too many strikes, which makes him hittable. He's definitely a prospect, although slightly behind some others in the Indians' pecking order. And remember, when you hear "Strike three!" the hills are alive with the sound of Mujica.

Rafael Perez Bats: L Throws: L   Height: 6' 3" Weight: 185 Born: May 15, 1982   Age: 25

YEAR	TEAM	LVL	AGE	W	L	SV	G	GS	IP	H	BB	SO	HR	GB%	BABIP	STUFF	WHIP	ERA	PERA	EQERA	EQH9	EQBB9	EQSO9	EQHR9	VORP	WXRL
2004	LKC	A	22	7	6	0	23	22	115	121	47	99	9	—	.326	-16	1.46	4.85	5.97	7.31	10.2	4.7	4.3	1.3	-21.3	—
2005	KIN	A+	23	8	5	0	14	14	77²	54	32	48	6	65.7%	.213	-12	1.11	3.36	6.20	5.18	7.0	4.5	3.3	1.2	3.5	—
2005	AKR	AA	23	4	3	1	15	8	66²	53	12	46	5	61.1%	.245	1	0.97	1.75	4.48	3.88	7.9	1.9	4.2	1.0	12.4	—
2006	AKR	AA	24	4	5	0	12	12	67¹	53	22	53	3	61.2%	.267	4	1.12	2.82	4.57	4.68	8.0	3.6	4.7	0.7	6.7	—
2006	BUF	AAA	24	0	3	0	13	0	27¹	20	8	33	0	71.0%	.303	23	1.03	2.66	2.93	4.10	7.5	2.7	8.5	0.3	4.4	—
2006	CLE	MLB	24	0	0	0	18	0	12¹	10	6	15	2	58.8%	.250	13	1.30	4.39	4.17	4.26	6.4	4.3	9.9	1.4	2.3	0.11
2007	*CLE*	*MLB*	*25*	*4*	*5*	*1*	*57*	*8*	*82*	*90*	*38*	*52*	*8*	*56.0%*	*.308*	*-8*	*1.56*	*5.25*	*4.85*	*5.17*	*9.5*	*4.0*	*5.3*	*0.8*	*1.8*	*0.50*

Breakout: 16% Improve: 53% Collapse: 12% Attrition: 8%   *Comparables: Steve Green, Andy Hassler, Lance Caraccioli, Zach Day*

Perez is left-handed and throws hard, and he'll get plenty off chances because of it. With a low-90s fastball that touches 95 and a nasty slider, Perez has strong stuff and combines it with excellent control. He got a quick cameo in 2006 and has an outside shot at a career something like Mike Stanton's or Alan Embree's, that rare high-velocity southpaw set-up man who might even hold his own in a closer role somewhere down the road.

C. C. Sabathia Bats: L Throws: L   Height: 6' 7" Weight: 290 Born: July 21, 1980   Age: 26

YEAR	TEAM	LVL	AGE	W	L	SV	G	GS	IP	H	BB	SO	HR	GB%	BABIP	STUFF	WHIP	ERA	PERA	EQERA	EQH9	EQBB9	EQSO9	EQHR9	VORP	WXRL
2004	CLE	MLB	23	11	10	0	30	30	188	176	72	139	20	—	.289	18	1.32	4.12	4.21	3.98	7.9	3.1	6.1	0.8	39.7	4.74
2005	CLE	MLB	24	15	10	0	31	31	196²	185	62	161	19	49.8%	.294	24	1.26	4.03	3.83	4.38	8.7	2.8	7.2	0.8	32.8	4.48
2006	CLE	MLB	25	12	11	0	28	28	192²	182	44	172	17	46.3%	.301	34	1.17	3.22	3.31	3.69	7.7	1.9	7.4	0.7	46.5	5.99
2007	*CLE*	*MLB*	*26*	*14*	*9*	*0*	*31*	*31*	*209*	*206*	*57*	*172*	*22*	*47.0%*	*.297*	*24*	*1.26*	*3.91*	*3.67*	*3.79*	*8.5*	*2.3*	*6.9*	*0.9*	*39.9*	*5.70*

Breakout: 12% Improve: 52% Collapse: 4% Attrition: 1%   *Comparables: Andy Benes, Freddy Garcia, Andy Pettitte, Wilson Alvarez*

Year after year, people have expected a breakout campaign from Sabathia, and last year they got it—maybe now it's time to accept Sabathia for what he is. He cut his walk rate and raised his strikeout rate for the second year in a row, and posted a career-low ERA that was third-best in the AL. The result was only a 12–11 record, but poor run support and even weaker defensive support will do that. He looks the part of an ace power pitcher, and his raw stuff leaves nothing to complain about, but his size is an impediment, sometimes creating problems with an inconsistent release point. Accept him for what he is now, because if what you see is what you get, it's pretty damned good; Sabathia should remain at this level for the next few years.

Tony Sipp Bats: L Throws: L   Height: 6' 0" Weight: 190 Born: July 12, 1983   Age: 23

YEAR	TEAM	LVL	AGE	W	L	SV	G	GS	IP	H	BB	SO	HR	GB%	BABIP	STUFF	WHIP	ERA	PERA	EQERA	EQH9	EQBB9	EQSO9	EQHR9	VORP	WXRL
2004	MHV	A-	20	3	1	0	10	10	42²	33	13	74	5	—	.326	5	1.08	3.16	7.28	6.69	11.0	4.3	8.8	3.1	-4.6	—
2005	LKC	A	21	4	1	0	13	12	69	47	19	71	5	43.4%	.256	7	0.96	2.22	5.00	3.43	7.5	3.3	5.5	1.4	15.8	—
2005	KIN	A+	21	2	2	2	22	5	47¹	34	23	59	4	39.3%	.291	6	1.21	2.66	5.27	4.57	7.9	5.0	7.1	1.2	5.2	—
2006	AKR	AA	22	4	2	3	29	4	60²	44	21	80	2	38.2%	.309	24	1.08	3.14	3.16	4.27	7.6	3.5	8.4	0.5	8.7	—
2007	*CLE*	*MLB*	*23*	*3*	*4*	*1*	*25*	*7*	*59²*	*61*	*28*	*51*	*10*	*38.0%*	*.294*	*6*	*1.48*	*4.96*	*4.94*	*4.69*	*8.8*	*4.0*	*7.2*	*1.4*	*4.8*	*0.70*

Breakout: 14% Improve: 33% Collapse: 33% Attrition: 18%   *Comparables: Dan Meyer, P. J. Bevis, Ted Lilly, Kent Mercker*

Entering the 2004 amateur draft, Sipp indicated to that he wanted big money to prevent a return to college. The Indians decided to draft him in the 45th round and watch him pitch in the Cope Cod League. Sipp's performance there netted him a $130,000 bonus, which looks like a bargain so far. With a low-90s fastball, a devastating slider, and a very good changeup, Sipp has 284 strikeouts in 219.1 pro innings and late-innings potential out of the bullpen. He could get his first look by midseason, a nice coup for Indians scouting director John Mirabelli.

Brian Slocum Bats: R Throws: R   Height: 6′ 4″ Weight: 200 Born: March 27, 1981   Age: 26

YEAR	TEAM	LVL	AGE	W	L	SV	G	GS	IP	H	BB	SO	HR	GB%	BABIP	STUFF	WHIP	ERA	PERA	EQERA	EQH9	EQBB9	EQSO9	EQHR9	VORP	WXRL
2004	KIN	A+	23	15	6	0	25	25	135	136	41	102	13	—	.304	-28	1.31	4.33	6.40	6.26	10.5	3.6	4.4	1.9	-9.4	—
2005	AKR	AA	24	7	5	0	21	18	102¹	98	36	95	9	47.8%	.317	-8	1.31	4.40	5.37	5.71	10.0	4.1	5.4	1.2	-1.2	—
2006	BUF	AAA	25	6	3	1	27	15	94¹	78	37	91	5	51.4%	.294	12	1.22	3.35	4.42	4.58	8.3	3.8	6.7	0.7	10.5	—
2006	CLE	MLB	25	0	0	0	8	2	17²	27	9	11	3	31.3%	.393	-16	2.04	5.59	5.50	5.30	12.5	4.3	5.3	1.4	1.0	0.46
2007	CLE	MLB	26	4	5	0	35	9	82	97	40	54	13	45.0%	.315	-8	1.66	5.78	5.78	5.51	10.2	4.1	5.5	1.3	-1.5	0.20

Breakout: 14% Improve: 42% Collapse: 21% Attrition: 5%   Comparables: Josh Karp, Eric Schmitt, Aaron Heilman, Brett Hinchliffe

The pitching version of a tweener, Slocum might not have the off-speed stuff to start, but also lacks the power arsenal to be a late-innings reliever. Accordingly, the Indians aren't sure what to do with him and have moved him back and forth between the rotation and the bullpen over the past two seasons.

Jeremy Sowers Bats: L Throws: L   Height: 6′ 1″ Weight: 180 Born: May 17, 1983   Age: 24

YEAR	TEAM	LVL	AGE	W	L	SV	G	GS	IP	H	BB	SO	HR	GB%	BABIP	STUFF	WHIP	ERA	PERA	EQERA	EQH9	EQBB9	EQSO9	EQHR9	VORP	WXRL
2005	KIN	A+	22	8	3	0	13	13	71¹	60	19	75	5	54.9%	.291	11	1.11	2.78	4.50	4.17	8.9	2.7	5.9	1.0	11.0	—
2005	AKR	AA	22	5	1	0	13	13	82¹	74	9	70	8	49.0%	.288	13	1.01	2.08	4.25	3.46	9.0	1.1	5.2	1.2	19.2	—
2006	BUF	AAA	23	9	1	0	15	15	97²	78	29	54	1	53.5%	.263	24	1.10	1.39	3.54	2.40	7.3	2.9	3.9	0.1	34.7	—
2006	CLE	MLB	23	7	4	0	14	14	88¹	85	20	35	10	49.0%	.257	3	1.19	3.57	4.55	3.52	7.6	1.9	3.3	0.9	23.0	2.78
2007	CLE	MLB	24	11	10	0	34	31	177²	199	53	93	23	49.0%	.295	3	1.41	4.66	4.53	4.50	9.6	2.5	4.4	1.0	18.7	3.20

Breakout: 1% Improve: 9% Collapse: 65% Attrition: 0%   Comparables: Claude Osteen, Tom Glavine, Dave Fleming, Brad Halsey

There's been much discussion about Yankee Chien-Ming Wang's ability to maintain his effectiveness despite his very low strikeout rate, which seems like a once-in-a-generation anomaly. Sowers is test case number two. Can he match Wang's success? It's highly doubtful. Sowers's command and control are beyond outstanding, but, unlike Wang, he's not really a power pitcher in any sense of the term. His groundball-to-flyball ratio is good, but not nearly as extreme as Wang's. Sowers has a chance to become Jaime Moyer, but stardom with these kind of ratios seems downright impossible.

Jake Westbrook Bats: R Throws: R   Height: 6′ 3″ Weight: 200 Born: September 29, 1977 Age: 29

YEAR	TEAM	LVL	AGE	W	L	SV	G	GS	IP	H	BB	SO	HR	GB%	BABIP	STUFF	WHIP	ERA	PERA	EQERA	EQH9	EQBB9	EQSO9	EQHR9	VORP	WXRL
2004	CLE	MLB	26	14	9	0	33	30	215²	208	61	116	19	—	.277	13	1.25	3.38	4.05	3.63	8.0	2.3	4.4	0.7	53.5	5.58
2005	CLE	MLB	27	15	15	0	34	34	210²	218	56	119	19	61.9%	.291	10	1.30	4.49	4.09	5.43	9.5	2.4	5.0	0.8	12.2	3.08
2006	CLE	MLB	28	15	10	0	32	32	211¹	247	55	109	15	62.5%	.326	14	1.43	4.17	3.82	4.23	9.4	2.2	4.3	0.6	35.6	5.02
2007	CLE	MLB	29	13	10	0	32	32	206	226	55	110	17	59.0%	.302	8	1.36	4.15	3.99	4.10	9.4	2.3	4.4	0.7	31.6	4.80

Breakout: 24% Improve: 68% Collapse: 3% Attrition: 0%   Comparables: Kevin Brown, Scott Erickson, Dennis Lamp, Albie Lopez

Westbrook's $6.1-million option for 2007 looks like an absolute bargain given the inflation that hit the offseason pitching market. At the very least, Westbrook is a proven workhorse, having exceeded 210 innings in each of the last three seasons. That's really all he is, a guy who can keep you in the ballgame and give the bullpen some rest. That's not such a bad thing, and if the Indians support his groundball stuff with some better, younger defenders in the infield, as it appears they will this year, he could see even better results.

Lineouts

PLAYER	TEAM	LVL	AGE	PA	R	2B	3B	HR	RBI	BB	SO	SB-CS	SPEED	AVG/OBP/SLG	MLVr	EqAVG/OBP/SLG	EqA	VORP
1B M. Aubrey*	KIN	A+	24	36	8	3	0	2	10	5	5	0-0	5.3	.286/.417/.607	.449	.226/.324/.484	.281	1.1
	AKR	AA	24	29	3	2	0	1	2	2	4	0-0	4.4	.269/.345/.462	.146	.259/.333/.444	.262	0.9
LF J. Brown*	KIN	A+	22	533	71	26	7	15	87	51	59	4-0	5.0	.290/.362/.469	.202	.270/.325/.440	.263	4.0
RF J. Constanza#	LKC	A	22	191	31	5	3	1	9	30	30	19-4	8.2	.277/.395/.365	.090	.238/.326/.310	.239	-8.8
	KIN	A+	22	321	55	15	6	1	27	42	50	20-4	7.5	.327/.419/.436	.271	.315/.386/.423	.287	14.4
CF J. Drennen*	LKC	A	19	277	33	12	3	6	30	31	52	6-6	4.8	.321/.409/.471	.276	.287/.351/.422	.264	12.1
	KIN	A+	19	128	15	6	2	0	8	12	21	2-1	4.8	.239/.328/.327	-.075	.222/.283/.299	.207	-6.6
LF J. Dubois	BUF	AAA	27	512	65	31	1	22	87	45	131	4-1	4.1	.275/.342/.492	.149	.250/.313/.454	.262	2.7
1B S. Head*	KIN	A+	22	545	65	26	0	14	73	54	73	2-1	3.9	.235/.319/.377	-.028	.210/.274/.337	.216	-33.6
2B L. Merloni	BUF	AAA	35	374	33	22	0	7	38	29	49	0-2	3.1	.285/.361/.415	.086	.228/.288/.325	.217	-20.7
C M. Ramirez	ROM	A	21	326	50	17	0	9	37	54	72	2-0	4.1	.285/.408/.449	.274	.262/.356/.411	.271	14.5
	LKC	A	21	161	19	6	1	4	26	30	27	0-0	3.3	.307/.435/.465	.290	.274/.373/.422	.283	9.5
C W. Toregas	KIN	A+	23	171	25	14	0	4	23	20	28	0-0	3.7	.336/.418/.514	.382	.301/.363/.458	.282	12.4
	AKR	AA	23	184	21	10	0	4	29	14	33	1-3	3.4	.258/.319/.393	.013	.241/.295/.373	.231	-1.3

PLAYER	TEAM	LVL	AGE	W	L	SV	IP	H	BB	SO	HR	GB%	BABIP	STUFF	WHIP	ERA	PERA	EqERA	EqH9	EqBB9	EqSO9	EqHR9	VORP
C. Bunkelman	LKC	A	21	1	2	0	44²	26	28	48	2	—	.231	5	1.22	2.85	6.30	4.35	7.0	7.4	5.9	0.9	5.7
	KIN	A+	21	3	1	0	23²	23	19	23	3	—	.323	-11	1.81	6.59	9.01	8.46	11.3	8.1	6.4	2.4	-7.1
E. Buzachero	AKR	AA	25	8	3	4	79²	74	25	71	2	—	.326	0	1.25	2.73	4.23	4.42	9.4	3.5	5.1	0.3	10.1
H. Choi	BUF	AAA	35	8	5	0	106¹	95	35	103	5	—	.307	9	1.23	2.38	4.20	3.58	9.0	3.6	6.2	0.7	23.1
D. Graves	BUF	AAA	32	1	1	1	51	55	13	27	5	—	.301	-28	1.33	4.06	5.56	5.54	10.4	2.7	3.4	1.4	0.3
	CLE	MLB	32	2	1	0	14	18	5	3	3	—	.283	-42	1.64	5.79	6.39	6.75	10.4	3.1	1.8	1.8	-2.7
J. Martin	LKC	A	23	0	1	0	15	13	3	16	2	—	.306	-13	1.07	4.20	7.67	5.93	11.2	2.6	5.3	3.3	-0.5
	KIN	A+	23	1	0	0	11¹	6	1	11	0	—	.212	11	0.63	0.00	2.58	0.84	5.9	0.8	5.9	0.0	5.7
	MHV	A-	23	0	1	0	18¹	11	1	13	1	—	.196	-11	0.66	1.49	6.58	2.65	7.9	1.1	3.2	2.1	5.6
M. Miller	CLE	MLB	34	1	0	0	15²	10	9	12	2	—	.211	2	1.21	2.87	5.78	3.38	5.6	5.1	6.2	1.1	4.6
B. Sikorski	POR	AAA	31	2	3	7	28¹	25	7	44	3	—	.344	22	1.14	3.20	3.51	4.23	8.8	2.3	10.4	1.3	4.2
	SDN	MLB	31	1	1	0	14¹	16	3	14	4	—	.308	4	1.33	5.66	5.22	5.65	10.0	1.9	8.2	2.5	0.1
	CLE	MLB	31	2	1	0	19²	20	4	24	4	—	.340	20	1.22	4.57	3.94	4.43	8.4	1.8	10.2	1.8	3.2
J. Stanford*	BUF	AAA	29	6	6	0	112²	102	38	81	11	—	.277	-11	1.25	4.01	5.89	4.94	9.2	3.5	4.9	1.4	8.0
N. Wagner	MHV	A-	22	0	1	17	32²	16	9	50	1	—	.246	7	0.78	1.40	4.89	2.79	7.4	4.3	7.4	1.2	9.1
J. Warden	AKR	AA	27	5	2	11	59²	35	29	47	3	—	.218	-11	1.08	2.89	6.43	5.11	6.6	5.6	4.6	0.8	3.1

When **Mike Aubrey** is healthy, he's really good. The only problem is he's absolutely never healthy. The back problems are officially chronic, the center cannot hold, mere anarchy is loosed upon the world. **Jordan Brown** is one of those unathletic college hitters who has proven he can put up decent numbers in A-ball, but little else; as a 23-year-old bat who is limited to first or left, that's good, but not nearly good enough. **Jose Constanza** is the fastest player in the Cleveland system, but unlike many minor league burners, he actually has an idea of what to do at the plate and features some solid on-base skills. Unfortunately, he's shaky in center, and won't hit enough for a corner. **John Drennen** made national headlines when he took Roger Clemens deep in the Rocket's first minor league warm-up start of the season, but it's his ability to hit for average that will play a bigger role in ensuring that he has more than fifteen minutes of fame. A center fielder, he'll probably have to move to an outfield corner. **Jason DuBois** finished among the International League leaders in home runs and RBI, which is probably what he'll do for someone else this year. He's trapped in the Quadruple-A zone without Rod Serling to give him directions. **Stephen Head** hit six home runs in his first ten pro games, and everyone got a little too excited. Since then, he's done very little to prove he can even handle Carolina League pitching, and his stock is plummeting. If you're a college first baseman who can't get it done in A-ball, you probably have a bright future in insurance. Despite not being blessed with an abundance of talent, **Lou Merloni** keeps getting looks. There's a lesson here for surly types such as Elijah Dukes: if you're perceived as a nice guy, teams will make a point of working with you; if you like playing baseball, you get to do it for longer, even if you're relatively untalented. Acquired from the Braves in the Bob Wickman deal, **Max Ramirez** instantly became the Indians' best catching prospect thanks to very good on-base skills and a little bit of power. On paper, he's the heir apparent to Victor Martinez, but in reality, he has defensive issues of his own. **Wyatt Toregas** went from organizational catcher to actual prospect by transforming from great glove/no hit to great glove/hit a little. The package is enough for a career as a backup, and the Indians think so highly of him as a person that they already speak of him as a future manager.

A big guy with a big fastball, **Cody Bunkelman** could be the next young reliever angling for a look by the end of the year. Contrary to the popular misconception, he was not the co-host on the first season of "American Idol." As if Bunkelman's name isn't good enough, **Edward Buzachero** goes by "Bubbie." An undersized right-hander who depends on a very good slider more than an overpowering fastball, Buzachero has moved slowly through the minors, but might be close to the majors, although perhaps as nothing more than an extra arm. **Hyang-Nam Choi** posted outstanding numbers in his American debut at Triple-A after more than a decade in the Korean League. He's a command and control type who throws in the 80s and mixes in a slider and changeup; basically, he's succeeded on moxie more than anything else. With 182 career saves despite never really pitching like a closer, **Danny Graves** spent the offseason looking for a spring training invite. In 2005 and 2006 combined, his major league ERA was 6.32 and he allowed 12 home runs in 52.2 innings—the sort of performance that makes a team send a guy invites to other people's camps. Just when he seemed to be emerging as a prospect, **J. D. Martin** succumbed to Tommy John surgery. He looked good in his late-season return, so keep an eye on this one—he was on the verge of a big league look as a starter. For former indie leaguer **Matt Miller** to reach the majors at all is a huge accomplishment, but also a point in favor of the situational value of sidearmers. He's supposedly all the way back from elbow surgery, but the Cleveland pen will be crowded with possibilities this year. **Brian Sikorski** returned from Japan and proved to be a competent relief arm and as generic an example of a relief pitcher as they come. DFA'd once Keith Foulke was signed. **Jason Stanford** is your classic Quadruple-A lefthander. He's appeared in 15 major league games, and might get a couple more here and there. Not bad for a player undrafted out of college, though a late-season tantrum might handicap his finding his next gig. **Neil Wagner** put up dominating numbers in his pro debut thanks to an upper-90s fastball, but his ability to find a quality off-speed pitch will define his future. A towering Rule 5 selection by the Phillies, **Jim Warden** turned himself into something of a prospect when former Indians farm director and new Red Sox pitching coach John Farrell suggested a sidearm delivery.

Manager: Eric Wedge

Year	Team	W-L	Pythag +/-	Avg PC	100 +P	120 +P	QS	BQS	REL	REL w Zero R	IBB	SUBS	PH	PH Avg	PH HR	SB2	CS2	SB3	CS3	SAC Att	SAC %	POS SAC	Squeeze	Swing	In Play
2004	CLE	80-82	-1	95.8	81	2	69	6	477	277	47	34	89	.264	4	83	46	11	7	57	82.5%	46	1	134	106
2005	CLE	93-69	-5	96.7	72	0	83	12	409	281	20	33	87	.213	0	55	30	6	5	54	72.2%	38	0	126	97
2006	CLE	78-84	-12	97.4	81	2	77	14	379	221	35	26	97	.232	2	50	19	5	4	44	68.2%	27	0	121	87

Four seasons into his young career, Wedge has no playoff appearances, three losing seasons, and his most recent campaign represented the largest gap between what was expected of his team and what actually happened. By most measurements, Wedge is a very conservative manager; he rarely calls for a pinch-runner or defensive sub. Last season he went to the bullpen fewer times than any manager in baseball. Though it's hard to criticize Wedge for that given his bullpen, he also saw his starting pitchers allow more quality starts to slip away after six innings than anyone not named Jerry Narron. Buck Showalter was hired during the offseason as the dreaded "Special Assistant to the General Manager," so the shadow is looming.

Colorado Rockies

I think as long as people are talking in that vein and that avenue, it can do nothing but work for us. We're not allowed to cheat. And the balls that we send in are tested. And the humidor's regulated. You know, Jeff's always been a very creative thinker. He's always been able to think outside the box.

—Rockies Manager Clint Hurdle responding to accusations of humidor shenanigans by former Rocky Jeff Cirillo

A spate of early season stories led many observers to conclude that the Rockies were using their league-sanctioned humidor to water down baseballs and turn longtime pitcher's nightmare Coors Field into a soggy pitcher's haven. Protestations to the contrary by the front office, which asserted that baseballs stored in the humidor were under the same conditions as in previous seasons, 70 degrees Fahrenheit and 50 percent humidity, did little to cool the controversy.

Whatever was involved, Coors Field did indeed play as more of a pitcher's park in 2006 than ever before. The ballpark hosted 12 shutouts, by far the most in its history (see table 1) and only two less than in previous four "humidor years" combined. Eight of those 12 shutouts occurred before the end of June, provoking the early season press coverage. Two of the shutouts came back-to-back on June 24 and 25 when the Rockies blanked the A's 7–0 and 6–0, with three Rocky hurlers combining on a one-hitter in the latter contest.

A more complete analysis shows that the ratio of runs scored per out at Coors versus runs scored per out in Rockies road games fell to just 1.15, its lowest point ever (see figure 1). At the same time, the ratio of home runs hit at Coors versus those in Rockies road games actually increased slightly, rebounding from three straight years in decline. However, much of that apparent rebound can be attributed to the Rockies' trio of sinkerballers, Aaron Cook, Jason Jennings, and Josh Fogg. Led by the worm-killing trio, the pitching staff yielded just 62 home runs on the road—the fewest in the majors.

ROCKIES PROSPECTUS

2006 record: 76–86; Fourth place, NL West

Pythagenport record: 81–81

Runs scored per game: 5.02 (5th in NL)

Runs allowed per game: 5.01 (12th in NL)

Team EqA: .255 (10th in NL)

2006 Batters Age: 28.2 (3rd youngest in NL)

2006 Pitchers Age: 28.7 (5th youngest in NL)

Ballpark: Coors Field; Severe hitter's park; Park Factor of 1.083

2006: Todd Helton's early aging syndrome was a more powerful downward drag than the young hitters' development was a lift.

2007: Lots of projects on the roster; if half of them pan out, they'll be in the running. If not, they could be the NL West version of the Orioles.

Even in these perhaps soggier times, Coors Field remained one of the premier hitter's parks in baseball along with Cincinnati's Great American Ballpark, Kauffman Stadium in Kansas City, and Chase Field in Phoenix. Fifteen percent more runs were scored and 17 percent more home runs were hit in Coors than in the Rockies' road games. It should also be noted that the humidor spell was broken on the homestand immediately following Cirillo's comments as an *average* of 14.25 runs were scored per game in the park's final 27 contests. Whether that resulted from the Rockies' front office dialing down the humidor settings or the vagaries of a small sample, conspiracy theorists found it hard to overlook the timing.

Park factors are notoriously prone to single-year fluctuations. We can't be sure if Coors will continue to play the way it did over the first two-thirds of 2006, when it was a neutral park with 8.96 runs scored per game against a league average of 9.00, or over the final third, when it played like it did before the humidor was introduced in 2002. It's entirely possible that it will settle down somewhere in between, but even if Coors Field isn't the launching pad it once was, it's likely that the Rockies will continue to have to grapple with playing in a relatively high run-scoring environment.

A large part of that will continue to be avoiding over-valuing hitters who post raw offensive statistics in Coors that make them look better than they actually are. General Manager Dan O'Dowd and company were rewarded for

Table 1. Shutouts at Coors

1995	2	2001	3
1996	3	2002	3
1997	6	2003	4
1998	1	2004	2
1999	2	2005	5
2000	0	2006	12

Table 2. NL VORP Up the Middle, 2006

Team	VORP	Team	VORP
Phillies	153.8	Marlins	76.3
Braves	151.1	Brewers	61.2
Mets	148.1	Nationals	47.3
Padres	130.0	Cubs	37.8
Dodgers	127.7	Pirates	14.4
Diamondbacks	105.5	Cardinals	9.5
Reds	86.1	Astros	-2.8
Giants	85.6	Rockies	-13.1

Figure 1. Coors Field Home vs. Road Ratios per Out Consumed

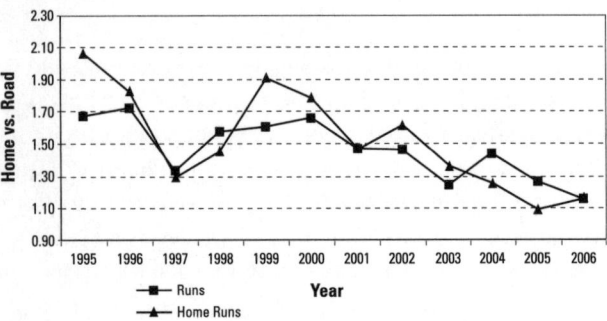

sticking with Garrett Atkins and Matt Holliday in 2006, but the overall offense was once again a shade under league average, turning in a team EqA of .259. That poor showing can be laid squarely at the feet of O'Dowd for his construction of the 2006 roster.

Despite obvious offensive problems at catcher, second base, shortstop, and centerfield, O'Dowd prioritized his bullpen in the 2005–2006 offseason. Pitching wins in hitter's parks—no team from an extreme hitter's park has ever gone to the postseason while finishing in the lower half of their league in park-adjusted ERA—but "pitching wins" means good pitching, not any pitching. O'Dowd overspent on veteran relievers Jose Mesa, Ray King, and Mike DeJean and then watched as they failed to meet even their projected performances levels, which could easily have been delivered by less familiar names at a fraction of the cost. Instead, those acquisitions left the Rockies little budget room to address their more pressing offensive needs, costing them a run at the NL West title.

An old baseball axiom contends that a good team has to be strong up the middle. It's no less true offensively than it is defensively. The Rockies' up-the-middle offense was once again crippling in 2006, as the combination of catchers Danny Ardoin, J. D. Closser, and Yorvit Torrealba, second baseman Jamey Carroll, shortstop Clint Barmes, and center fielders Cory Sullivan and Choo Freeman effectively took runs off the board. In 2006, the average NL team received a combined VORP of 76.2 runs from its players whose primary positions were catcher, second base, short-

stop, and center field. The Rockies up-the-middle contingent was dead last in the league, a dismal 13.1 runs *below* replacement (see table 2).

Since at least 1960, no team with a combined negative VORP from its four up-the-middle defensive positions has reached the postseason, and only the 1973 Mets, 1974 A's, and the 2006 Cardinals did so with a VORP of less than 15.0. Further, teams that exceed the average VORP up the middle were more than two and a half times more likely to make it to the postseason than those who did not.

Fortunately, the Rockies appear to have found a remedy for their "middling" problem. Chris Iannetta appeared to be more than capable both as a receiver and a hitter in his September trial and should be ensconced behind the plate as the season starts. Kaz Matsui looked surprisingly able in a late-season trial, earning a return engagement, though the O'Dowd was savvy enough to hedge against Matsui's small sample size and very high batting average on balls in play (.391) by signing the second baseman to an incentive-laden one-year contract. Shortstop Troy Tulowitzki, who debuted along with Iannetta last season, has the upside of an elite player, and with Matsui and Tulowitzki in place, Jamey Carroll is freed to play the utility role for which he is best suited and act as insurance should Tulowitzki or Matsui falter.

To complete the up-the-middle makeover and meet his stated goal of increasing team speed, O'Dowd acquired Willy Taveras from the Astros to fill the center-field void. As was the case with fellow speedster and groundball-masher Juan Pierre, Taveras won't be helped much by Coors, so the offensive problem in center likely remains; O'Dowd could have gotten as much out of in-house candidates Ryan Spilborghs and Jeff Salazar, both of whom played respectably in limited appearances. But the Rockies could still benefit from Taveras's presence on the bases and in the field—his speed may make Clint Hurdle feel less obligated to bunt, bunt, and bunt again, and on defense that same speed will take on increased value in the wide open spaces of Coors's center field. All of these moves bode well for the Rockies' chances in 2007 as simply league-average offensive performances up the middle could allow the Rox to improve by around a half-dozen games.

We say "could" because that improvement will be moot if what was the best pitching staff in team history doesn't continue to perform. For the first time ever, the Rockies did not finish last or second to last in ERA, and the improvement was not simply a byproduct of the reduced offensive environment at Coors. Jeff Jennings, Aaron Cook, and Jeff Francis combined for an SNLVAR of 14.4, far outpacing the efforts of any other trio of Rockies starters in team history (the previous high was 9.0 set by immortals Pedro Astacio, Brian Bohanon, and Masato Yoshii in 2000). That 2006 tally was also good for fifth in the National League last year, but the final two starting spots were a glaring weakness, and Jennings is now an Astro, having been dealt in the Taveras deal.

Taylor Buchholz and Jason Hirsh, the pitchers received in exchange for Jennings, will have to pick up the slack. The six-foot-eight Hirsh projects as a solid middle of the rotation starter, and his hard, sinking fastball is consistent with the kind of approach that seems to best cope with Coors as evidenced by the success of Cook and Jennings himself. The performance of these pitchers will help resolve whether O'Dowd fully leveraged Jennings in a winter in which baseball was convulsed by a kind of pitching tulip mania, or if he prematurely yielded to the pressure of Jennings's impending free agency.

As for the bullpen, burdened by O'Dowd's overpriced acquisitions, the Rockies' pen ranked 23rd in baseball last year with a WXRL of just 2.36, sending O'Dowd back out to troll for relievers this winter. This time he threw $3.5 million at LaTroy Hawkins for one year with a mutual option for 2008. At best, Hawkins will provide a bevy of league average-innings, but his declining effectiveness in recent years makes even that questionable. O'Dowd would be well served to be as thrifty with his pen as he is with the rest of his club.

O'Dowd and Hurdle have had a long run in Colorado—the GM was hired in 2000, the manager in 2002—and both had their contracts extended through 2007 despite a dismal second half in 2006. Save for his bullpen misadventures, O'Dowd has done well to stick to his rebuilding plan in a market flush with irrational exuberance in the wake of labor peace and rising revenues. Even with the loss of Jennings, his moves this offseason should yield a team that is at least marginally improved in 2007. But all signs from ownership indicate that, unless the young Rockies show *more* than marginal improvement this year, further extensions won't be forthcoming, nor should they be.

HITTERS

Garrett Atkins   **3B**   **Bats: R**   **Throws: R**   Height: 6' 3"   Weight: 215   Born: December 12, 1979   Age: 27

YEAR	TEAM	LVL	AGE	PA	R	2B	3B	HR	RBI	BB	SO	SB	CS	SPEED	AVG	OBP	SLG	MLVR	EQAVG	EQOBP	EQSLG	EQA	VORP	DEFENSE
2004	CSP	AAA	24	516	88	43	3	15	94	57	45	0	0	4.0	.366	.434	.578	.366	.313	.381	.481	.297	47.7	104-3B -5
2005	COL	MLB	25	573	62	31	1	13	89	45	72	0	2	3.4	.287	.347	.426	.040	.275	.338	.414	.260	13.6	133-3B -12
2006	COL	MLB	26	695	117	48	1	29	120	79	76	4	0	4.6	.329	.409	.556	.328	.314	.396	.529	.314	62.7	155-3B -14
2007	COL	MLB	27	668	102	41	2	25	99	71	75	3	2	4.2	.314	.391	.523	.225	.289	.369	.484	.292	37.3	156-3B -4

Breakout: 23% Improve: 56% Collapse: 15% Attrition: 3%   Comparables: Cal Ripken, Jeff Cirillo, Tony Perez, Ken McMullen

After launching his big league career with younger, more heralded prospects looming behind him, Atkins made a name for himself with a mammoth 2006 campaign in which he ranked second in VORP among major league third basemen behind Miguel Cabrera. Atkins was steady from start to finish in 2006, even hitting .313/.402/.531 on the road, a marked improvement from 2005. He still plays defense like a converted first baseman, but between Ian Stewart's struggles and his own breakthrough at the plate, Atkins should be the Rockies third baseman for the foreseeable future.

Jeff Baker   **RF**   **Bats: R**   **Throws: R**   Height: 6' 2"   Weight: 220   Born: June 21, 1981   Age: 26

YEAR	TEAM	LVL	AGE	PA	R	2B	3B	HR	RBI	BB	SO	SB	CS	SPEED	AVG	OBP	SLG	MLVR	EQAVG	EQOBP	EQSLG	EQA	VORP	DEFENSE
2004	VIS	A+	23	321	60	23	1	11	64	47	70	1	0	4.1	.330	.439	.547	.385	.280	.366	.454	.283	21.4	68-3B -7
2004	TUL	AA	23	99	10	5	1	4	20	7	22	1	0	3.9	.297	.343	.505	.188	.272	.313	.467	.267	4.8	20-3B 1
2005	CSP	AAA	24	248	40	16	1	10	41	16	44	3	1	4.6	.303	.348	.513	.088	.268	.310	.450	.258	9.2	57-3B -8
2005	COL	MLB	24	43	6	4	0	1	4	5	12	0	0	4.7	.211	.302	.395	-.145	.184	.279	.342	.219	-0.7	
2006	CSP	AAA	25	538	71	30	4	20	108	46	110	7	1	5.1	.305	.369	.508	.161	.276	.333	.466	.272	13.6	119-RF -3
2006	COL	MLB	25	58	13	7	2	5	21	1	14	2	0	8.2	.368	.379	.825	.699	.351	.362	.789	.353	10.8	
2007	COL	MLB	26	508	71	30	3	21	78	41	102	7	2	4.7	.292	.352	.507	.121	.269	.333	.469	.272	12.9	120-RF -4

Breakout: 14% Improve: 41% Collapse: 13% Attrition: 12%   Comparables: Nelson Cruz, Jason Lane, Stephen Smitherman, Craig Monroe

(continued next page)

Jeff Baker *(continued)*

Baker's plate discipline has derailed a once-promising career, dropping him from prospect to potentially handy reserve. No longer a third baseman, the former Clemson star is now angling to stick as the right-handed half of an outfield platoon. He hit a ton upon his September callup. That doesn't totally negate a mediocre season in Colorado Springs, but he did hit .347/.413/.636 against Pacific Coast League southpaws.

Sean Barker		OF					Bats: R		Throws: R		Height: 6' 3"		Weight: 220		Born: May 26, 1980						Age: 27	

YEAR	TEAM	LVL	AGE	PA	R	2B	3B	HR	RBI	BB	SO	SB	CS	SPEED	AVG	OBP	SLG	MLVR	EQAVG	EQOBP	EQSLG	EQA	VORP	DEFENSE			
2004	VIS	A+	24	468	75	29	5	20	97	40	89	11	3	5.7	.308	.373	.549	.266	.254	.304	.422	.250	-4.7	53-RF	-2	36-LF	0
2004	TUL	AA	24	91	9	3	0	2	12	7	24	2	0	4.1	.229	.289	.337	-.192	.200	.253	.294	.202	-9.1	23-RF	2		
2005	TUL	AA	25	513	72	24	8	14	76	37	133	15	7	7.2	.261	.319	.436	.006	.227	.278	.364	.225	-27.2	110-RF	-14		
2006	CSP	AAA	26	365	53	14	9	13	55	29	104	17	7	7.3	.297	.362	.512	.148	.269	.324	.466	.267	6.0	52-LF	1	17-CF	0
2007	COL	MLB	27	413	54	20	4	13	52	27	108	10	4	5.6	.275	.327	.454	-.009	.254	.309	.420	.249	-0.9	98-RF	-3		

Breakout: 19% Improve: 52% Collapse: 21% Attrition: 21%   Comparables: Nick Gorneault, Mario Encarnacion, Anthony Sanders, Barry Wesson

Drafted out of LSU in 2002, the big corner outfielder has made steady if unspectacular progress through the Rockies' system. He caught some attention last year with a big August, hitting seven home runs, but showed no power and even worse plate discipline against lefties. His window of opportunity as a pinch hitter—usually a job that goes to hitters who put the ball in play much more consistently than Barker does—is closing fast.

Clint Barmes		SS					Bats: R		Throws: R		Height: 6' 0"		Weight: 210		Born: March 6, 1979						Age: 28	

YEAR	TEAM	LVL	AGE	PA	R	2B	3B	HR	RBI	BB	SO	SB	CS	SPEED	AVG	OBP	SLG	MLVR	EQAVG	EQOBP	EQSLG	EQA	VORP	DEFENSE	
2004	CSP	AAA	25	589	104	42	2	16	51	28	61	20	8	6.2	.328	.376	.505	.121	.276	.319	.414	.254	20.2	117-SS	5
2004	COL	MLB	25	77	14	3	1	2	10	3	10	0	1	5.1	.282	.320	.437	-.043	.264	.303	.417	.241	1.2		
2005	COL	MLB	26	377	55	19	1	10	46	16	36	6	4	5.4	.289	.330	.434	.013	.279	.323	.425	.255	13.4	78-SS	-5
2006	COL	MLB	27	535	57	26	4	7	56	22	72	5	4	5.9	.220	.264	.335	-.304	.207	.252	.318	.205	-20.5	120-SS	-5
2007	COL	MLB	28	538	65	28	4	12	59	26	62	9	5	5.5	.276	.321	.420	-.064	.255	.304	.389	.238	6.5	127-SS	0

Breakout: 36% Improve: 63% Collapse: 14% Attrition: 11%   Comparables: Pat Meares, Eddie Miksis, Rafael Ramirez, Frank Duffy

Barmes's –20.5 VORP represents the ninth-worst single-season offensive performance in baseball since 1960 among players with 500 or more plate appearances, an indictment both of Barmes and Rockies management. Barmes proved that his performance after returning from a venison-related injury in 2005 was no fluke. He combines the uncanny ability to get jammed on almost any pitch with a distressing lack of patience—Barmes saw just 3.44 pitches per PA. Although an adequate defender, he developed the habit of throwing off of his right foot, even on routine grounders. He finally lost his job to Troy Tulowitzki at the end of the season, so expect the regular lineup to be relatively Barmes-free in 2007. The league lead in sacrifice bunts is hereby up for grabs.

Jamey Carroll		INF					Bats: R		Throws: R		Height: 5' 9"		Weight: 170		Born: February 18, 1974						Age: 33	

YEAR	TEAM	LVL	AGE	PA	R	2B	3B	HR	RBI	BB	SO	SB	CS	SPEED	AVG	OBP	SLG	MLVR	EQAVG	EQOBP	EQSLG	EQA	VORP	DEFENSE			
2004	MON	MLB	30	256	36	14	2	0	16	32	21	5	1	6.0	.289	.378	.372	.051	.283	.373	.356	.267	11.2	37-2B	-2	12-3B	0
2005	WAS	MLB	31	358	44	8	1	0	22	34	55	3	4	5.5	.251	.333	.284	-.174	.260	.341	.295	.233	-6.5	48-2B	4	27-SS	-2
2006	COL	MLB	32	534	84	23	5	5	36	56	66	10	12	5.4	.300	.377	.404	.044	.290	.371	.394	.264	18.2	101-2B	26		
2007	COL	MLB	33	433	62	19	4	3	34	43	53	8	5	6.0	.294	.369	.394	-.001	.271	.349	.365	.252	8.0	103-2B	4		

Breakout: 15% Improve: 39% Collapse: 33% Attrition: 27%   Comparables: Bobby Adams, Rich Amaral, Eric Young, Danny Murtaugh

Parlayed a fast April start (.351/.455/.378), a Luis Gonzalez injury, and an enormous home/road split (.371/.440/.485 at Coors, .219/.302/.320 on the road) into a starting gig that lasted almost the entire year, then regressed to his normal levels in the second half. Although not the top-of-the-order hitter Hurdle used him as, Carroll will take a walk. With that and his ability to play all three infield positions, he can be a productive utility man for the next few years.

J. D. Closser C Bats: S Throws: R Height: 5′ 10″ Weight: 200 Born: January 15, 1980 Age: 27

YEAR	TEAM	LVL	AGE	PA	R	2B	3B	HR	RBI	BB	SO	SB	CS	SPEED	AVG	OBP	SLG	MLVR	EQAVG	EQOBP	EQSLG	EQA	VORP	DEFENSE
2004	CSP	AAA	24	348	53	19	1	7	54	41	47	0	2	3.6	.299	.384	.440	.016	.257	.336	.372	.249	5.7	73-C -1
2004	COL	MLB	24	124	5	6	0	1	10	6	22	0	0	2.9	.319	.364	.398	.005	.304	.350	.374	.254	3.8	32-C 0
2005	COL	MLB	25	272	31	12	2	7	27	32	48	1	0	4.4	.219	.314	.376	-.134	.208	.306	.373	.239	0.9	65-C -13
2006	CSP	AAA	26	258	32	15	1	8	30	31	38	8	2	5.3	.298	.384	.480	.140	.266	.345	.437	.270	12.2	53-C 2
2006	COL	MLB	26	112	10	3	1	2	11	12	23	0	1	4.5	.196	.288	.309	-.297	.175	.277	.289	.205	-5.3	26-C 2
2007	MIL	MLB	27	388	45	20	2	9	43	40	66	4	2	4.3	.254	.335	.397	-.087	.253	.332	.395	.252	7.2	93-C -1

Breakout: 33% Improve: 59% Collapse: 20% Attrition: 21%   Comparables: Mike Rose, Chris Bando, Alan Ashby, Buck Martinez

The promise of 2004 appears to be gone despite a new hairdo and improved defense. For some idea of how far out of favor he fell in Colorado, realize that he was only called up in September after the team had given up on *Danny Ardoin*, of all people. Closser is a better hitter than he's shown so far, but not so much that you'd want him to be your starter. Waived after the season and picked up by Milwaukee, he'll spend 2007 waiting for an injury or trade to bring him back to the majors.

Dexter Fowler CF Bats: R Throws: R Height: 6′ 4″ Weight: 173 Born: March 22, 1986 Age: 21

YEAR	TEAM	LVL	AGE	PA	R	2B	3B	HR	RBI	BB	SO	SB	CS	SPEED	AVG	OBP	SLG	MLVR	EQAVG	EQOBP	EQSLG	EQA	VORP	DEFENSE
2005	CAS	Rk	19	252	43	10	4	4	23	27	73	18	6	7.8	.273	.357	.409	-.013	.216	.272	.289	.206	-28.8	57-CF -1
2006	ASH	A	20	458	92	31	6	8	46	43	79	43	23	7.7	.296	.373	.462	.146	.245	.302	.378	.237	-3.8	97-CF -1
2007	COL	MLB	21	500	72	28	6	8	45	34	90	34	16	6.7	.280	.333	.418	-.043	.258	.315	.386	.243	2.1	118-CF 2

Breakout: 54% Improve: 78% Collapse: 11% Attrition: 12%   Comparables: Willy Taveras, Kenny Kelly, Choo Freeman, Dave Krynzel

Fowler's an extremely intelligent, socially conscious guy, so much so that if word of his potential Ivy League exploits (he was recruited to play basketball at Harvard) got out, fans might start calling him Poindexter. Drafted for his raw athletic talents, Fowler showed an unexpectedly keen eye and an incipient power stroke both with Asheville and in the Hawaiian League. Key word: incipient. Whether that power continues to develop will determine if Fowler becomes an all-around star or a highly athletic ballhawk who makes a living with his legs.

Choo Freeman CF Bats: R Throws: R Height: 6′ 2″ Weight: 200 Born: October 20, 1979 Age: 27

YEAR	TEAM	LVL	AGE	PA	R	2B	3B	HR	RBI	BB	SO	SB	CS	SPEED	AVG	OBP	SLG	MLVR	EQAVG	EQOBP	EQSLG	EQA	VORP	DEFENSE
2004	CSP	AAA	24	400	58	21	7	10	50	26	84	7	3	6.3	.297	.350	.478	.006	.258	.307	.400	.245	2.2	101-CF -4
2004	COL	MLB	24	105	15	3	2	1	11	14	21	1	1	5.8	.189	.298	.300	-.297	.167	.279	.278	.205	-5.3	28-CF 0
2005	CSP	AAA	25	390	46	10	6	10	59	29	78	4	3	4.7	.280	.334	.427	-.081	.247	.293	.369	.231	-6.1	80-CF -3
2006	COL	MLB	26	191	24	6	3	2	18	14	42	5	6	6.3	.237	.298	.341	-.228	.224	.289	.328	.213	-6.6	36-CF 2
2007	COL	MLB	27	264	35	13	3	6	30	19	51	5	3	5.6	.277	.335	.437	-.018	.256	.316	.404	.247	1.7	65-CF 1

Breakout: 54% Improve: 74% Collapse: 13% Attrition: 48%   Comparables: Reggie Williams, Jerry Martin, Clyde Mashore, Tommie Reynolds

In July, Clint Hurdle said, "I want to give Choo an opportunity so at the end of the season we don't have any more questions about Choo." Freeman got just ten more starts over the remainder of the season. Apparently finding out if moss would grow on Choo if he sat really still for three hours a day was one of the questions that Hurdle was intent on answering. With the winter acquisition of Willy Taveras, Freeman may get mistaken for the team Chia Pet. If Choo ever becomes a free man, he could catch on somewhere as a defensive outfielder who can hit southpaws a little, but even that might be too much to expect.

Joe Gaetti OF Bats: R Throws: R Height: 5′ 11″ Weight: 205 Born: October 16, 1981 Age: 25

YEAR	TEAM	LVL	AGE	PA	R	2B	3B	HR	RBI	BB	SO	SB	CS	SPEED	AVG	OBP	SLG	MLVR	EQAVG	EQOBP	EQSLG	EQA	VORP	DEFENSE	
2004	ASH	A	22	441	62	24	1	16	55	55	107	16	6	5.1	.257	.370	.457	.061	.204	.286	.344	.224	-25.8	43-RF -4	34-CF -1
2005	MOD	A+	23	463	90	29	8	21	87	52	114	5	7	6.0	.332	.418	.605	.415	.286	.353	.477	.280	29.1	75-CF -2	21-LF -3
2006	TUL	AA	24	446	68	23	4	16	62	38	99	5	2	5.4	.296	.369	.497	.185	.272	.329	.442	.265	4.7	41-LF 1	26-CF -5
2007	COL	MLB	25	464	61	25	4	15	60	39	109	6	3	5.1	.275	.343	.463	.031	.254	.325	.428	.258	5.0	110-CF -2	

Breakout: 13% Improve: 47% Collapse: 26% Attrition: 14%   Comparables: Brandon Berger, Jason Michaels, Mike Vento, Cody Ross

After a stellar 2005 campaign in High A-ball that put him back on the prospect map, Gaetti continued his quest to become a fourth outfielder in Tulsa by nailing his PECOTA forecast and raking against lefties (.381/.465/.548). He has always had a high strikeout rate, but his walk rate fell as he moved up a level. Although he played all three outfield slots, he projects as a left fielder since neither his range nor arm is above average.

Luis A. Gonzalez UT **Bats: R** **Throws: R** Height: 5' 11" Weight: 205 Born: June 26, 1979 Age: 28

YEAR	TEAM	LVL	AGE	PA	R	2B	3B	HR	RBI	BB	SO	SB	CS	SPEED	AVG	OBP	SLG	MLVR	EQAVG	EQOBP	EQSLG	EQA	VORP	DEFENSE			
2004	COL	MLB	25	351	42	17	2	12	40	15	67	1	5	4.3	.292	.330	.469	.018	.278	.317	.450	.254	6.5	34-2B	-3	11-3B	0
2005	COL	MLB	26	441	51	25	0	9	44	20	63	3	4	4.5	.292	.333	.421	-.000	.283	.325	.416	.254	9.0	66-2B	5	15-SS	-3
2006	CSP	AAA	27	110	15	4	2	2	10	6	11	1	0	4.6	.268	.345	.412	-.035	.240	.300	.380	.239	-1.6				
2006	COL	MLB	27	158	7	9	1	2	14	4	27	1	1	4.2	.242	.269	.356	-.256	.227	.259	.333	.208	-5.4	24-2B	-1		
2007	COL	MLB	28	264	32	14	2	7	33	13	39	2	2	4.6	.282	.329	.440	-.019	.260	.311	.406	.244	2.4	65-2B	-1		

Breakout: 31% Improve: 57% Collapse: 22% Attrition: 39% Comparables: Vinny Castilla, Billy Ripken, Billy Moran, Pedro Feliz

Handed the starting second base job last year, Gonzalez lost the opportunity when he injured his left wrist in early April. As is typical of wrist injuries, when Gonzalez came back he showed little power and even less patience—not that power was ever a strength. Sent down at the end of August to make room for Tulowitzki, Gonzalez didn't fare much better south of Denver. With the solid play of Carroll and the possibility that Matsui will succeed, he could find himself filling a super-utility role on another team in 2007.

Brad Hawpe RF **Bats: L** **Throws: L** Height: 6' 3" Weight: 205 Born: June 22, 1979 Age: 28

YEAR	TEAM	LVL	AGE	PA	R	2B	3B	HR	RBI	BB	SO	SB	CS	SPEED	AVG	OBP	SLG	MLVR	EQAVG	EQOBP	EQSLG	EQA	VORP	DEFENSE			
2004	CSP	AAA	25	388	62	19	1	31	86	36	91	3	2	4.0	.322	.384	.652	.339	.274	.333	.527	.284	18.5	76-RF	7	10-LF	2
2004	COL	MLB	25	118	12	3	2	3	9	11	34	1	1	5.1	.248	.322	.400	-.098	.238	.314	.390	.245	-1.4	28-RF	1		
2005	COL	MLB	26	351	38	10	3	9	47	43	70	2	2	5.1	.262	.350	.403	-.004	.251	.342	.399	.260	3.0	79-RF	1		
2006	COL	MLB	27	575	67	33	6	22	84	74	123	5	5	4.9	.293	.383	.515	.197	.278	.374	.490	.291	32.0	134-RF	13		
2007	COL	MLB	28	536	77	28	4	23	80	56	120	4	3	4.7	.282	.360	.502	.117	.260	.340	.464	.273	10.2	126-RF	3		

Breakout: 12% Improve: 38% Collapse: 28% Attrition: 12% Comparables: Paul O'Neill, Eric Anthony, Michael Tucker, George Altman

Hawpe credited a minor repositioning of his hands for the fast start that had him at 15 home runs and .310/.392/.562 before the break. He then slumped in the second half and lost playing time to Baker before finishing strong, ending the season with better numbers on the road than in Coors. Hawpe is a patient hitter (his 3.95 pitches per PA ranked 44th among qualified hitters), but he continues to be among the leaders in swinging through pitches. He also struggles against southpaws (.227/.309/.400 over the last three seasons), and Hurdle often kept him out of the lineup against them, starting him in just nine of the Rockies' 29 games against lefty starting pitchers, none of them coming after mid-July. Although once a first baseman, Hawpe's transition to the outfield has panned out pretty well; his strong, accurate arm notched 16 assists on baserunners that will now know better.

Todd Helton 1B **Bats: L** **Throws: L** Height: 6' 2" Weight: 210 Born: August 20, 1973 Age: 33

YEAR	TEAM	LVL	AGE	PA	R	2B	3B	HR	RBI	BB	SO	SB	CS	SPEED	AVG	OBP	SLG	MLVR	EQAVG	EQOBP	EQSLG	EQA	VORP	DEFENSE	
2004	COL	MLB	30	683	115	49	2	32	96	127	72	3	0	4.8	.347	.469	.620	.477	.324	.449	.581	.347	83.8	144-1B	22
2005	COL	MLB	31	626	92	45	2	20	79	106	80	3	0	4.7	.320	.445	.534	.355	.303	.432	.514	.325	57.9	140-1B	13
2006	COL	MLB	32	649	94	40	5	15	81	91	64	3	2	4.8	.302	.404	.476	.186	.287	.393	.457	.296	31.1	142-1B	3
2007	COL	MLB	33	608	96	35	3	20	86	79	74	3	1	4.5	.301	.396	.497	.186	.278	.374	.459	.289	21.4	142-1B	4

Breakout: 3% Improve: 15% Collapse: 43% Attrition: 4% Comparables: Wally Joyner, Ryan Klesko, John Olerud, Will Clark

Helton missed 14 games in late April and early May with what was diagnosed as "acute terminal ileitis," or, in layman's terms, one helluva stomachache. Upon his return, Helton played in 48 straight games, which may have been too much, too soon. The result was a loss of power and an EqA under .300 for the first time since 1999. By year's end, Hurdle was batting him second a la Brian Giles. It's difficult to disentangle Helton's ailment from natural skill erosion. Helton is owed $16.6 million annually through 2010 and $23.7 million in 2011. That's a lot to pay for a five- to seven-win player. The Rockies and Angels labored throughout the winter to find a formula that would allow Colorado to shift some portion of Helton's salary—which by itself could make up about a third of the team's 2007 payroll—to Los Angeles.

Jonathan Herrera **SS** **Bats: S** **Throws: R** Height: 5′ 9″ Weight: 155 Born: November 3, 1984 Age: 22

YEAR	TEAM	LVL	AGE	PA	R	2B	3B	HR	RBI	BB	SO	SB	CS	SPEED	AVG	OBP	SLG	MLVR	EQAVG	EQOBP	EQSLG	EQA	VORP	DEFENSE	
2004	ASH	A	19	418	71	20	2	6	35	26	80	21	12	6.7	.279	.335	.389	-.061	.224	.266	.301	.205	-19.0	91-SS -2	
2005	ASH	A	20	99	17	2	0	0	5	8	11	6	6	6.0	.310	.384	.333	-.028	.242	.293	.253	.200	-4.5	16-SS -3	
2005	MOD	A+	20	345	48	9	4	2	30	23	52	9	4	6.8	.258	.315	.332	-.257	.223	.266	.264	.196	-20.0	51-SS 6	19-2B -1
2006	MOD	A+	21	568	87	20	8	7	77	58	67	34	15	7.2	.310	.382	.427	.128	.281	.338	.383	.256	19.4	121-SS 10	
2007	*COL*	*MLB*	*22*	*534*	*67*	*24*	*4*	*4*	*44*	*34*	*73*	*19*	*9*	*6.2*	*.283*	*.333*	*.379*	*-.096*	*.261*	*.314*	*.350*	*.234*	*3.8*	*126-SS 5*	

Breakout: 41% Improve: 59% Collapse: 16% Attrition: 5%   Comparables: *Ramon Santiago, Maicer Izturis, Callix Crabbe, Anderson Hernandez*

An athletic middle infielder, Herrera has limited secondary skills, but he is still one to watch for more reasons than his presence on the 40-man roster. The little Venezuelan has the tools to play a good short, although he's still learning to avoid trying to make the impossible play, and he's not just a slap-and-dash speed guy at the plate.

Matt Holliday **LF** **Bats: R** **Throws: R** Height: 6′ 4″ Weight: 235 Born: January 10, 1980 Age: 27

YEAR	TEAM	LVL	AGE	PA	R	2B	3B	HR	RBI	BB	SO	SB	CS	SPEED	AVG	OBP	SLG	MLVR	EQAVG	EQOBP	EQSLG	EQA	VORP	DEFENSE
2004	COL	MLB	24	439	65	31	3	14	57	31	86	3	3	5.0	.290	.349	.488	.078	.274	.335	.466	.270	8.0	101-LF -2
2005	COL	MLB	25	526	68	24	7	19	87	36	79	14	3	6.5	.307	.361	.505	.180	.294	.350	.488	.285	30.3	120-LF -4
2006	COL	MLB	26	667	119	45	5	34	114	47	110	10	5	5.5	.326	.387	.586	.333	.312	.375	.566	.309	56.8	149-LF 3
2007	*COL*	*MLB*	*27*	*619*	*105*	*37*	*6*	*28*	*100*	*49*	*101*	*13*	*5*	*5.6*	*.320*	*.382*	*.557*	*.264*	*.295*	*.361*	*.515*	*.295*	*32.7*	*145-LF -3*

Breakout: 24% Improve: 61% Collapse: 7% Attrition: 1%   Comparables: *Rick Reichardt, Ellis Burks, Torii Hunter, Marty Cordova*

After a slow April, Holliday hit .338/.407/.607 the rest of the way and edged Jason Bay for the highest VORP among NL left fielders. Holliday has now twice made significant improvements to his game over an offseason. Although he'll always have better offensive stats at Coors, his power travels everywhere, as evinced by a notable September blast that cleared Dodger Stadium entirely. As the league has learned to fear him, Holliday has received a few more walks and been hit with almost twice as many pitches, but he remains an aggressive hitter who excels at squaring up the ball. In the field, he's still learning that the shortest route between two points is a straight line, but as long as he can hit 500-foot home runs, Holliday's in.

Chris Iannetta **C** **Bats: R** **Throws: R** Height: 5′ 11″ Weight: 195 Born: April 8, 1983 Age: 24

YEAR	TEAM	LVL	AGE	PA	R	2B	3B	HR	RBI	BB	SO	SB	CS	SPEED	AVG	OBP	SLG	MLVR	EQAVG	EQOBP	EQSLG	EQA	VORP	DEFENSE
2004	ASH	A	21	152	23	5	1	5	17	27	29	0	1	3.4	.314	.454	.496	.273	.264	.375	.411	.275	8.1	32-C 5
2005	MOD	A+	22	312	51	17	3	11	58	45	61	1	2	4.2	.276	.381	.490	.121	.236	.325	.387	.249	3.9	68-C -2
2005	TUL	AA	22	70	7	3	1	2	11	8	15	0	0	4.0	.233	.329	.417	-.024	.230	.314	.410	.248	1.0	14-C 1
2006	TUL	AA	23	185	38	10	2	11	26	24	26	1	0	5.5	.321	.418	.622	.454	.298	.384	.565	.313	22.7	37-C -3
2006	CSP	AAA	23	180	23	12	1	3	22	24	29	0	0	3.3	.351	.447	.503	.316	.325	.413	.474	.307	19.1	36-C 3
2006	COL	MLB	23	93	12	4	0	2	10	13	17	0	1	4.6	.260	.370	.390	-.023	.247	.366	.364	.260	1.3	22-C -2
2007	*COL*	*MLB*	*24*	*496*	*69*	*27*	*3*	*16*	*64*	*56*	*85*	*1*	*1*	*4.2*	*.290*	*.377*	*.476*	*.117*	*.267*	*.356*	*.440*	*.275*	*22.0*	*117-C -1*

Breakout: 13% Improve: 37% Collapse: 24% Attrition: 14%   Comparables: *Justin Huber, Joe Lawrence, Jim Pagliaroni, Justin Towle*

The organization's first true catching prospect, Iannetta earned his call-up on August 26 by hitting a combined .336/.433/.567 at Double- and Triple-A. After starting out 2-for-22 with the big club, he had a nice September showing, hitting .261/.381/.406. Those rates reflect his skills; his ability to get on base is more developed than his power, which leads to some odd comps in PECOTA; you might be better off thinking of him as the new Jim Sundberg. Given the traditional low standards of Rockies backstops, he'll be a Denver revelation.

Joe Koshansky **1B** **Bats: L** **Throws: L** Height: 6′ 4″ Weight: 225 Born: May 26, 1982 Age: 25

YEAR	TEAM	LVL	AGE	PA	R	2B	3B	HR	RBI	BB	SO	SB	CS	SPEED	AVG	OBP	SLG	MLVR	EQAVG	EQOBP	EQSLG	EQA	VORP	DEFENSE
2004	TRI	A-	22	278	41	18	0	12	43	31	84	1	0	4.2	.234	.330	.460	.128	.168	.227	.273	.184	-59.4	63-1B 3
2005	ASH	A	23	525	92	31	1	36	103	53	122	6	6	4.0	.291	.373	.603	.282	.217	.274	.418	.236	-15.8	115-1B 1
2005	TUL	AA	23	48	5	3	0	2	12	2	15	0	0	2.3	.267	.292	.467	.008	.244	.271	.422	.234	-1.2	12-1B 1
2006	TUL	AA	24	573	84	28	0	31	109	64	134	3	2	3.9	.284	.371	.526	.214	.254	.325	.460	.267	11.1	125-1B 8
2007	*COL*	*MLB*	*25*	*507*	*56*	*25*	*2*	*21*	*75*	*38*	*144*	*1*	*1*	*4.0*	*.253*	*.312*	*.452*	*-.056*	*.233*	*.295*	*.418*	*.242*	*-7.8*	*120-1B 5*

Breakout: 31% Improve: 56% Collapse: 18% Attrition: 10%   Comparables: *Eric Munson, Derek Michaelis, Andy Tracy, Kevin Witt*

(continued next page)

Joe Koshansky *(continued)*

Coming into 2006, Koshansky needed to prove he was something more than a product of Asheville's McCormick Field. Mission accomplished. He moved up to Double-A and retained his power and walk rate, albeit with the help of Texas League inflation. He's a left-handed version of Ryan Shealy, with the difference being that he's a better defender. Koshansky's slow and can't hit southpaws (he hit just .205/.297/.321 against them), but, with Helton dug in at first, the Rockies must hope Koshansky can fetch more in the inevitable trade than the Royals pitching castoffs that Ryan Shealy yielded.

Kazuo Matsui **2B** **Bats: S** **Throws: R** Height: 5' 10" Weight: 185 Born: October 23, 1975 Age: 31

YEAR	TEAM	LVL	AGE	PA	R	2B	3B	HR	RBI	BB	SO	SB	CS	SPEED	AVG	OBP	SLG	MLVR	EQAVG	EQOBP	EQSLG	EQA	VORP	DEFENSE	
2004	NYN	MLB	28	509	65	32	2	7	44	40	97	14	3	6.2	.272	.331	.396	-.021	.273	.333	.400	.258	18.0	104-SS	1
2005	NYN	MLB	29	295	31	9	4	3	24	14	43	6	1	6.9	.255	.300	.352	-.136	.257	.304	.366	.240	-1.0	63-2B	2
2006	NYN	MLB	30	139	10	6	0	1	7	6	19	2	0	5.2	.200	.235	.269	-.429	.183	.225	.237	.173	-8.7	31-2B	4
2006	CSP	AAA	30	129	26	4	0	3	16	9	20	3	1	6.3	.278	.328	.391	-.086	.237	.281	.339	.221	-2.5	26-SS	-3
2006	COL	MLB	30	126	22	6	3	2	19	10	27	8	1	8.4	.345	.392	.504	.243	.327	.381	.487	.304	12.9	20-2B	5
2007	COL	MLB	31	360	44	18	4	5	36	21	63	9	3	6.5	.275	.322	.402	-.089	.254	.304	.372	.236	0.9	86-2B	2

Breakout: 10% Improve: 34% Collapse: 32% Attrition: 23% Comparables: U. L. Washington, Jose Uribe, Jose Macias, Dennis Hocking

When you combine his copious badness in New York with his Denver comeback, you end up with a season that almost perfectly matches his 2004–2005 totals. Though several Japanese teams showed interest in reclaiming their nation's tarnished star, Matsui elected to sign a one-year contract with the Rockies with a base value of $1.5 million and another $950,000 of possible incentives. That's quite a comedown from his previous $6.7 million contract, though not a bad reward for 125 Denver-ized plate appearances. He'll split time at second with Carroll.

Chris Nelson **SS** **Bats: R** **Throws: R** Height: 5' 11" Weight: 176 Born: September 3, 1985 Age: 21

YEAR	TEAM	LVL	AGE	PA	R	2B	3B	HR	RBI	BB	SO	SB	CS	SPEED	AVG	OBP	SLG	MLVR	EQAVG	EQOBP	EQSLG	EQA	VORP	DEFENSE	
2004	CAS	Rk	18	169	36	6	3	4	20	20	42	6	5	6.3	.347	.432	.510	.282	.272	.324	.367	.241	6.0	16-SS	-1
2005	ASH	A	19	349	51	13	3	3	38	25	88	7	4	6.5	.241	.304	.330	-.197	.187	.232	.245	.178	-31.8	67-SS	-12
2006	ASH	A	20	517	69	38	1	11	76	32	101	14	2	5.5	.260	.313	.416	-.019	.206	.245	.326	.205	-26.4	109-SS	-22
2007	COL	MLB	21	480	50	26	3	9	47	26	93	9	4	5.5	.253	.297	.388	-.169	.233	.281	.358	.219	-3.8	113-SS	-9

Breakout: 65% Improve: 81% Collapse: 8% Attrition: 9% Comparables: Carlos Casimiro, Jason Repko, Jon Helquist, Felix Escalona

Remember, if Nelson had gone to college, he'd still be a potential top draft pick this season. After a great 2004 and terrible 2005, he may have found his level this year, but it's still well short of actual prospectdom.

Omar Quintanilla **SS/2B** **Bats: L** **Throws: R** Height: 5' 9" Weight: 190 Born: October 24, 1981 Age: 25

YEAR	TEAM	LVL	AGE	PA	R	2B	3B	HR	RBI	BB	SO	SB	CS	SPEED	AVG	OBP	SLG	MLVR	EQAVG	EQOBP	EQSLG	EQA	VORP	DEFENSE			
2004	MOD	A+	22	503	75	32	5	11	72	37	54	1	3	4.0	.315	.370	.481	.195	.278	.323	.416	.254	18.6	103-SS	-4		
2004	MID	AA	22	105	20	10	0	2	20	10	9	2	0	4.8	.351	.419	.521	.362	.312	.371	.479	.289	9.9	23-SS	4		
2005	MID	AA	23	321	46	14	2	4	25	23	40	2	3	4.3	.293	.347	.395	.023	.267	.319	.358	.237	3.9	70-SS	1		
2005	CSP	AAA	23	57	14	3	2	1	7	3	8	0	0	5.9	.346	.375	.538	.218	.321	.351	.509	.289	5.6	13-SS	2		
2005	COL	MLB	23	143	16	1	1	0	7	9	15	2	1	5.9	.219	.270	.242	-.394	.200	.257	.223	.183	-8.5	31-SS	-3		
2006	CSP	AAA	24	349	48	23	2	4	29	28	55	4	1	5.3	.276	.342	.403	-.048	.251	.312	.371	.241	3.6	47-SS	-5	30-2B	4
2006	COL	MLB	24	38	3	1	1	0	3	3	9	1	1	5.9	.176	.243	.265	-.463	.147	.216	.235	.169	-3.1				
2007	COL	MLB	25	410	47	21	3	6	40	26	59	4	2	5.2	.277	.328	.400	-.079	.256	.310	.370	.236	3.7	98-SS	0		

Breakout: 17% Improve: 36% Collapse: 27% Attrition: 17% Comparables: Joe Thurston, Scott Hodges, Dominic Rich, Alejandro Prieto

Quintanilla needed a full season at Triple-A after playing only 13 games there in 2005. He started out slowly but found his groove in May, hitting .347/.405/.500 that month. He was immediately called up, but only played sporadically spelling Barmes and Carroll before a foul ball off his right shin put him on the DL in July. By the time he returned, his bat had gone cold. He has not yet shown the gap power that scouts have predicted, but the Rockies would be well served to put him above Barmes on the depth chart.

Jeff Salazar CF Bats: L Throws: L Height: 6′ 0″ Weight: 190 Born: November 24, 1980 Age: 26

YEAR	TEAM	LVL	AGE	PA	R	2B	3B	HR	RBI	BB	SO	SB	CS	SPEED	AVG	OBP	SLG	MLVR	EQAVG	EQOBP	EQSLG	EQA	VORP	DEFENSE			
2004	VIS	A+	23	358	79	18	9	13	44	38	33	17	2	8.1	.347	.419	.586	.431	.291	.350	.472	.284	21.5	72-CF	2		
2004	TUL	AA	23	270	39	13	2	1	17	35	31	10	3	6.5	.223	.331	.313	-.152	.202	.293	.275	.216	-15.9	43-CF	2	15-LF	1
2005	TUL	AA	24	319	47	13	2	6	35	44	49	12	8	5.6	.278	.381	.410	.088	.248	.340	.354	.249	1.1	50-CF	2	17-LF	1
2005	CSP	AAA	24	272	42	17	3	6	26	32	58	5	2	5.8	.263	.349	.436	-.053	.232	.311	.373	.241	-2.0	51-CF	6		
2006	CSP	AAA	25	381	62	14	7	9	39	46	64	12	5	7.1	.265	.357	.433	.009	.236	.319	.385	.248	0.7	82-CF	-5		
2006	COL	MLB	25	67	13	4	0	1	8	11	16	2	0	6.2	.283	.409	.415	.083	.264	.394	.377	.287	3.8	12-CF	-2		
2007	COL	MLB	26	431	57	23	4	10	46	40	75	8	4	5.9	.266	.337	.428	-.034	.245	.319	.396	.248	2.4	102-CF	0		

Breakout: 17% Improve: 46% Collapse: 34% Attrition: 21% Comparables: Brian Sellier, Brady Anderson, Billy McMillon, Terrmel Sledge

Unlike Koshansky, Salazar has unfortunately proven that his 29-homer barrage in 2003 was indeed a product of Asheville's cozy confines. Still, he's a patient hitter and a good baserunner despite merely decent speed, though his defense seemed to regress a bit in 2006, and his arm remains below-average. Taveras's arrival will leave Salazar scrambling for a role with the team, but he could capably fill the larger side of a center-field platoon.

Jason Smith INF Bats: L Throws: R Height: 6′ 3″ Weight: 200 Born: July 24, 1977 Age: 29

YEAR	TEAM	LVL	AGE	PA	R	2B	3B	HR	RBI	BB	SO	SB	CS	SPEED	AVG	OBP	SLG	MLVR	EQAVG	EQOBP	EQSLG	EQA	VORP	DEFENSE			
2004	TOL	AAA	26	130	18	8	2	3	13	6	26	5	1	7.4	.270	.300	.443	-.007	.262	.292	.426	.249	2.4	32-3B	-1		
2004	DET	MLB	26	169	20	7	4	5	19	8	37	1	2	6.4	.239	.280	.432	-.154	.245	.291	.458	.249	-0.3	28-2B	0		
2005	TOL	AAA	27	207	24	11	2	6	25	11	53	8	4	7.2	.230	.269	.406	-.132	.216	.255	.358	.219	-12.5	16-1B	-1	11-3B	1
2005	DET	MLB	27	63	4	1	2	0	2	0	16	2	1	8.0	.190	.203	.276	-.500	.175	.203	.263	.179	-5.4				
2006	CSP	AAA	28	159	26	9	5	4	23	15	41	3	1	6.2	.291	.354	.511	.129	.257	.314	.451	.261	5.9	27-3B	3		
2006	COL	MLB	28	108	9	1	0	5	13	7	29	3	0	4.7	.263	.324	.424	-.039	.253	.315	.414	.256	2.8	13-2B	2		
2007	COL	MLB	29	372	44	18	4	10	44	22	100	8	4	6.0	.258	.308	.428	-.091	.238	.291	.396	.235	-2.3	89-2B	2		

Breakout: 18% Improve: 47% Collapse: 30% Attrition: 22% Comparables: Rob Lukachyk, Colin Porter, Todd Dunwoody, Marc Sagmoen

Smith made the team out of spring training and was in line for the second-base job when Gonzalez got hurt. Though he hit well, he was quickly deselected in favor of Carroll and demoted. He's always had good power for a middle infielder, but lacks the patience or tools to really play short regularly. Taken by the Blue Jays in the Rule 5 draft, he'll vie for a utility role on a team without a regular shortstop.

Seth Smith RF Bats: L Throws: L Height: 6′ 3″ Weight: 215 Born: September 30, 1982 Age: 24

YEAR	TEAM	LVL	AGE	PA	R	2B	3B	HR	RBI	BB	SO	SB	CS	SPEED	AVG	OBP	SLG	MLVR	EQAVG	EQOBP	EQSLG	EQA	VORP	DEFENSE			
2004	TRI	A-	21	29	6	1	1	2	5	1	3	0	0	6.7	.259	.276	.593	.265	.214	.233	.429	.226	-1.9				
2004	CAS	Rk	21	260	46	21	3	9	61	25	47	9	1	5.7	.369	.427	.601	.447	.283	.315	.421	.254	0.5	40-RF	-3		
2005	MOD	A+	22	585	87	45	6	9	72	44	115	5	3	5.2	.300	.353	.458	.044	.259	.302	.373	.236	-17.2	106-RF	1	17-CF	-4
2006	TUL	AA	23	582	79	46	4	15	71	51	74	4	4	4.8	.294	.361	.483	.149	.269	.326	.436	.259	5.4	107-RF	3		
2007	COL	MLB	24	523	62	33	3	12	65	33	91	4	2	4.8	.283	.331	.443	-.010	.261	.313	.410	.248	-2.7	123-RF	0		

Breakout: 19% Improve: 47% Collapse: 30% Attrition: 4% Comparables: Luke Allen, Mike Ryan, Doug Deeds, Brian Stavisky

Seth Smith was born in Beverly Hills, California but wound up going to high school in Jackson, Mississippi. The former backup quarterback at Ole Miss had LASIK surgery before last season, and it appears to have paid dividends. He improved as the season went along, cutting his strikeouts by more than a third while ratcheting up his home runs, all while moving up a level. Smith is probably still a little short of the power and patience needed to be an everyday player at an outfield corner, but he could have a nifty career as a reserve.

Ryan Spilborghs OF Bats: R Throws: R Height: 6′ 1″ Weight: 190 Born: September 5, 1979 Age: 27

YEAR	TEAM	LVL	AGE	PA	R	2B	3B	HR	RBI	BB	SO	SB	CS	SPEED	AVG	OBP	SLG	MLVR	EQAVG	EQOBP	EQSLG	EQA	VORP	DEFENSE			
2004	VIS	A+	24	520	59	26	3	8	57	64	98	8	6	4.2	.259	.357	.385	-.032	.206	.279	.281	.205	-31.5	61-CF	2	39-LF	0
2005	TUL	AA	25	301	52	23	3	6	54	42	49	10	3	6.1	.341	.435	.525	.381	.304	.385	.460	.295	16.2	28-LF	7	22-RF	0
2005	CSP	AAA	25	253	49	23	5	5	30	22	53	7	3	7.3	.339	.405	.551	.275	.302	.360	.470	.281	11.7	29-RF	-5	25-LF	3
2006	CSP	AAA	26	306	50	20	1	5	34	30	49	8	2	5.6	.338	.400	.476	.196	.303	.361	.431	.276	8.8	40-LF	4	27-CF	0
2006	COL	MLB	26	186	26	6	3	4	21	14	30	5	2	6.3	.287	.337	.431	.002	.275	.330	.407	.259	4.6	19-CF	0	11-RF	-1
2007	COL	MLB	27	442	60	25	3	9	49	36	78	10	4	5.3	.291	.352	.436	.024	.269	.333	.403	.256	4.7	105-CF	2		

Breakout: 17% Improve: 34% Collapse: 32% Attrition: 22% Comparables: Paul Dade, Chad Allen, Adam Piatt, Kenny Kelly

(continued next page)

Ryan Spilborghs *(continued)*

Spilborghs proved that his leap forward in 2005 was no fluke as he repeated his performance at Triple-A and performed adequately in his opportunities in Denver. With the Rockies, he showed good control of the strike zone and handled lefties well, important since he often caddied for Hawpe against portsiders. Spilborghs can play all three outfield spots and sports an accurate if average arm. Like Salazar, Spilborghs finds his career aspirations suffering from a Taveras problem.

Ian Stewart 3B **Bats: L Throws: R** Height: 6' 3" Weight: 205 Born: April 5, 1985 Age: 22

YEAR	TEAM	LVL	AGE	PA	R	2B	3B	HR	RBI	BB	SO	SB	CS	SPEED	AVG	OBP	SLG	MLVR	EQAVG	EQOBP	EQSLG	EQA	VORP	DEFENSE		
2004	ASH	A	19	581	92	31	9	30	101	66	112	19	9	6.0	.319	.398	.594	.323	.261	.327	.468	.269	30.4	113-3B	16	
2005	MOD	A+	20	499	83	32	7	17	86	52	113	2	2	5.4	.274	.353	.497	.074	.236	.301	.399	.242	3.3	106-3B	-3	
2006	TUL	AA	21	528	75	41	7	10	71	50	103	3	8	5.1	.268	.351	.452	.068	.250	.316	.416	.249	12.5	113-3B	15	
2007	COL	MLB	22	530	70	33	4	17	70	41	111	5	3	5.0	.281	.342	.472	.046	.259	.323	.436	.259	10.9	125-3B	7	

Breakout: 25% Improve: 59% Collapse: 17% Attrition: 3%   Comparables: Kelly Johnson, Scott Moore, David Kelton, Edwin Encarnacion

Stewart rocketed to the top of prospect lists with a stunning full-season debut in 2004, but since then has turned in two disappointing years in a row. Stewart got a mulligan in 2005 because of some nagging injuries, but his Texas League performance last season is of far greater concern. Scouts are no longer enamored with his swing, which has become long, and his power has nearly fallen off the map. From the Department of Cruel Coincidence: The only part of Stewart's game that has improved in the past two years is his defense, but just as he was finally being taken seriously by scouts as a major league-caliber third baseman, the door to that position was slammed shut in Colorado for years to come by the emergence of Garrett Atkins.

Cory Sullivan CF **Bats: L Throws: L** Height: 6' 0" Weight: 190 Born: August 20, 1979 Age: 27

YEAR	TEAM	LVL	AGE	PA	R	2B	3B	HR	RBI	BB	SO	SB	CS	SPEED	AVG	OBP	SLG	MLVR	EQAVG	EQOBP	EQSLG	EQA	VORP	DEFENSE			
2005	COL	MLB	25	424	64	15	4	4	30	28	83	12	3	6.9	.294	.343	.386	-.027	.281	.332	.378	.253	7.6	71-CF	-1	17-LF	0
2006	COL	MLB	26	443	47	26	10	2	30	32	100	10	6	6.7	.267	.321	.402	-.079	.257	.315	.384	.245	3.9	94-CF	-3		
2007	COL	MLB	27	453	60	24	8	7	43	29	98	13	6	6.8	.283	.333	.430	-.025	.261	.315	.397	.246	2.8	107-CF	-1		

Breakout: 28% Improve: 47% Collapse: 25% Attrition: 31%   Comparables: Gil Coan, Larry Stahl, Tom Goodwin, Omar Moreno

Sullivan began the season as the starting center fielder. After a hot April (.327/.377/.541), he collapsed in May and lost playing time the rest of the way—though he played enough to record 19 sacrifice bunts. Always stretched as an offensive regular, Sullivan has trouble with inside pitches, leading to a strikeout every four plate appearances. Although a better defender than Spilborghs and Salazar, he's likely to be the odd man out this season.

Yorvit Torrealba C **Bats: R Throws: R** Height: 5' 11" Weight: 200 Born: July 19, 1978 Age: 28

YEAR	TEAM	LVL	AGE	PA	R	2B	3B	HR	RBI	BB	SO	SB	CS	SPEED	AVG	OBP	SLG	MLVR	EQAVG	EQOBP	EQSLG	EQA	VORP	DEFENSE	
2004	SFN	MLB	25	196	19	7	3	6	23	17	31	2	0	5.3	.227	.302	.407	-.116	.224	.299	.402	.245	1.1	57-C	0
2005	SFN	MLB	26	105	18	8	0	1	7	9	25	1	0	5.6	.226	.301	.344	-.177	.223	.305	.362	.236	-0.6	24-C	3
2005	SEA	MLB	26	119	14	4	0	2	8	7	25	0	0	3.2	.241	.293	.333	-.212	.245	.310	.358	.236	-1.2	36-C	1
2006	COL	MLB	27	241	23	16	3	7	43	11	49	4	3	5.7	.247	.293	.439	-.095	.237	.283	.429	.239	0.4	60-C	7
2007	COL	MLB	28	332	40	16	3	8	40	23	63	5	2	4.8	.268	.325	.421	-.063	.247	.307	.390	.239	2.0	80-C	4

Breakout: 54% Improve: 73% Collapse: 12% Attrition: 45%   Comparables: Bob Montgomery, Robert Machado, Marc Sullivan, Phil Roof

Fished out of the teeming pool of backup catchers, Torrealba started the season on the DL, but when he finally did play from June through August he did well, at least by backup catcher standards. The shoulder that had troubled him from the start finally shelved him for good in September. A good defensive catcher with a very strong arm, Torrealba should make a satisfactory backup to Iannetta this year.

Troy Tulowitzki SS **Bats: R Throws: R** Height: 6' 3" Weight: 205 Born: October 10, 1984 Age: 22

YEAR	TEAM	LVL	AGE	PA	R	2B	3B	HR	RBI	BB	SO	SB	CS	SPEED	AVG	OBP	SLG	MLVR	EQAVG	EQOBP	EQSLG	EQA	VORP	DEFENSE	
2005	MOD	A+	20	105	17	6	0	4	14	9	18	1	0	3.9	.266	.343	.457	-.009	.216	.276	.340	.217	-2.7	19-SS	0
2006	TUL	AA	21	485	75	34	2	13	61	46	71	6	5	5.1	.291	.370	.473	.147	.271	.335	.438	.264	25.2	102-SS	-11
2006	COL	MLB	21	108	15	2	0	1	6	10	25	3	0	5.8	.240	.318	.292	-.251	.229	.315	.281	.225	-1.7	25-SS	0
2007	COL	MLB	22	553	74	34	4	14	68	41	90	7	4	5.0	.290	.349	.460	.049	.268	.330	.425	.259	20.5	130-SS	-4

Breakout: 34% Improve: 62% Collapse: 10% Attrition: 5%   Comparables: Ramon Castro, Rickie Weeks, Edwin Encarnacion, Jhonny Peralta

After suffering through a torn quad and a broken hamate bone in 2005, the tenth overall pick of the 2005 draft showed he could handle the jump to Double-A in his full-season debut. That's quite an accomplishment in itself, but he also earned a callup to the Show on August 30. He held his own on the big stage despite understandably appearing overmatched at times at the plate and in the field. There are still some adjustments to made, especially given how little power Tulowitzki displayed in his first major league go-round—just three extra-base hits in 96 at-bats. The power should come eventually, and, given the park, he should easily reach 20 home runs annually at his peak. Expected to be the Rockies' starting short-stop on Opening Day, he'll get the chance to make those strides at the major league level.

PITCHERS

Jeremy Affeldt

Bats: L Throws: L   Height: 6' 4"   Weight: 225   Born: June 6, 1979   Age: 28

YEAR	TEAM	LVL	AGE	W	L	SV	G	GS	IP	H	BB	SO	HR	GB%	BABIP	STUFF	WHIP	ERA	PERA	EQERA	EQH9	EQBB9	EQSO9	EQHR9	VORP	WXRL
2004	KCA	MLB	25	3	4	13	38	8	76¹	91	32	49	6	—	.348	0	1.63	4.95	4.10	4.82	9.7	3.4	5.3	0.6	2.9	0.30
2005	KCA	MLB	26	0	2	0	49	0	49²	56	29	39	3	54.0%	.331	6	1.71	5.25	4.08	5.47	8.7	5.0	6.7	0.5	-3.3	1.35
2006	KCA	MLB	27	4	6	0	27	9	70	71	42	28	9	49.8%	.265	-18	1.61	5.91	5.82	5.65	8.1	4.9	3.3	1.0	-3.2	0.11
2006	COL	MLB	27	4	2	1	27	0	27¹	31	13	20	4	54.3%	.307	-13	1.61	6.92	4.81	6.67	9.5	3.8	5.7	1.0	-3.6	0.25
2007	COL	MLB	28	3	5	1	52	5	73	86	36	47	9	52.0%	.322	-12	1.67	5.76	5.14	5.26	9.7	4.2	5.1	0.9	3.7	0.50

Breakout: 27%   Improve: 50%   Collapse: 22%   Attrition: 27%   Comparables: Jim Shellenback, Vaughn Eshelman, Kenny Rogers, Chris Nabholz

Affeldt began the season in the Royals' rotation, but after 84 baserunners in 43.2 innings was headed back to the pen. He fixed a mechanical problem in late May and tightened up his peripherals with Colorado after being dealt with Denny Bautista for Ryan Shealy and Scott Dohmann. Even so, the use of Affeldt and other marginal pitchers in critical situations was one clear cause of the Rockies' September fade. The team now plans to re-reconvert him to starting despite his fragility (blisters, oblique, groin). Maybe the sixth time will be the charm.

Denny Bautista

Bats: R Throws: R   Height: 6' 5"   Weight: 190   Born: October 23, 1982   Age: 24

YEAR	TEAM	LVL	AGE	W	L	SV	G	GS	IP	H	BB	SO	HR	GB%	BABIP	STUFF	WHIP	ERA	PERA	EQERA	EQH9	EQBB9	EQSO9	EQHR9	VORP	WXRL
2005	KCA	MLB	22	2	2	0	7	7	35²	36	17	23	2	65%	.298	9	1.46	5.80	4.24	5.02	7.9	4.1	5.5	0.5	-0.3	0.4
2006	KCA	MLB	23	0	2	0	8	7	35	38	17	22	5	51%	.300	-3	1.57	5.66	5.53	5.40	8.8	3.9	5.2	1.0	-0.2	0.2
2006	OMA	AAA	23	2	5	0	10	10	44²	52	32	28	3	60%	.350	-7	1.90	7.33	5.57	7.69	9.9	6.3	4.3	0.8	-10.6	—
2006	CSP	AAA	23	1	4	0	6	6	36²	46	16	35	2	57%	.396	12	1.71	4.48	4.23	5.73	10.8	3.8	6.5	0.5	-0.5	—
2006	COL	MLB	23	0	1	0	4	1	6²	9	4	5	0	42%	.375	-21	1.95	5.37	3.64	11.57	11.6	5.1	6.4	0.0	-5.0	-0.2
2007	COL	MLB	26	5	9	0	35	20	117²	134	60	84	12	57%	.324	-1	1.64	5.73	4.97	5.29	9.3	4.3	5.6	0.8	6.0	1.3

Breakout: 37%   Improve: 68%   Collapse: 10%   Attrition: 0%   Comparables: Don Schwall, Steve Green, Jason Grimsley, Ariel Prieto

Bautista started the season as the Royals' fifth starter, but a trip to the DL after two starts and poor performance upon his return got him demoted to the pen and then to Omaha. He wasn't any better there; he wasn't any better anywhere. Still, the Rockies may give him another chance to start as his low-90s sinking fastball can be devastating when he's on. In one of his rare good starts in 2006, he induced 16 groundball outs in six innings. That's what the Rockies are after, but they might as well try to catch love in a butterfly net or spend 60 years teaching a pigeon to peck out "Turkey in the Straw" on the xylophone in the hopes that it might one day play *The Goldberg Variations*.

Aaron Cook

Bats: R Throws: R   Height: 6' 3"   Weight: 215   Born: February 8, 1979   Age: 28

YEAR	TEAM	LVL	AGE	W	L	SV	G	GS	IP	H	BB	SO	HR	GB%	BABIP	STUFF	WHIP	ERA	PERA	EQERA	EQH9	EQBB9	EQSO9	EQHR9	VORP	WXRL
2004	CSP	AAA	25	3	1	0	7	7	46	34	8	25	1	—	.236	16	0.91	2.74	3.51	3.06	5.9	1.5	3.6	0.2	13.3	—
2004	COL	MLB	25	6	4	0	16	16	96²	112	39	40	7	—	.314	4	1.56	4.28	4.62	3.83	9.4	3.1	3.2	0.5	18.3	2.18
2005	COL	MLB	26	7	2	0	13	13	83¹	101	16	24	8	61.1%	.307	-1	1.40	3.67	4.39	3.27	9.5	1.5	2.2	0.8	15.7	2.50
2006	COL	MLB	27	9	15	0	32	32	212²	242	55	92	17	58.6%	.308	9	1.40	4.23	4.04	4.17	9.4	2.0	3.5	0.6	40.6	4.58
2007	COL	MLB	28	10	12	0	31	29	183²	226	47	88	19	60.0%	.320	3	1.49	4.84	4.51	4.46	10.0	2.2	3.8	0.8	27.1	4.10

Breakout: 2%   Improve: 28%   Collapse: 20%   Attrition: 1%   Comparables: Dennis Lamp, Jake Westbrook, Brian Moehler, Chris Holt

(continued next page)

Aaron Cook *(continued)*

The National League's answer to Chien-Ming Wang, Cook also relies heavily on a mid-90s sinking fastball to force hitters to beat the ball into the ground nearly 60 percent of the time. Also like Wang, Cook had a strong season despite a strike-out rate that ranked lowest among qualifiers in the league. His unusual control for a sinkerballer and ability to induce groundballs allows him to succeed even with a STUFF score that bears little resemblance to the actual quality of his pitches. Also like Wang, Cook is dancing at the edge of a precipice, and any loss of velocity or command will be unusually destructive.

Manny Corpas Bats: R Throws: R   Height: 6' 3" Weight: 170 Born: December 3, 1982 Age: 24

YEAR	TEAM	LVL	AGE	W	L	SV	G	GS	IP	H	BB	SO	HR	GB%	BABIP	STUFF	WHIP	ERA	PERA	EQERA	EQH9	EQBB9	EQSO9	EQHR9	VORP	WXRL
2004	ASH	A	21	2	2	3	43	0	44¹	48	13	52	3	—	.357	-4	1.38	3.05	4.74	4.57	11.2	3.1	6.0	1.0	5.0	—
2005	MOD	A+	22	3	2	2	47	0	69	83	14	52	2	60.9%	.362	-1	1.41	3.78	3.59	4.77	9.8	2.0	4.0	0.4	6.6	—
2006	TUL	AA	23	2	1	19	34	0	36²	22	4	35	0	63.0%	.247	19	0.72	0.99	2.78	2.27	6.3	1.0	6.3	0.3	13.2	—
2006	COL	MLB	23	1	2	0	35	0	32¹	36	8	27	3	45.5%	.344	10	1.36	3.62	3.52	3.24	9.5	1.9	6.8	0.8	9.2	0.20
2007	COL	MLB	24	2	3	3	56	1	54¹	62	16	41	6	53.0%	.326	2	1.44	4.56	4.26	4.16	9.4	2.5	5.9	0.8	9.2	0.90

Breakout: 10% Improve: 24% Collapse: 47% Attrition: 26%   Comparables: Tom Walker, Ron Davis, Bobby Thigpen, Julian Tavarez

Signed as a 16 year old out of Panama, "Habeas" Corpas dominated as Tulsa's closer and looked good in a short stint in Triple-A before being called up on July 17. Corpas throws his 95 to 97-MPH sinking fastball sidearm and also packs a hard slider. With improving control and risking strikeout rates, he should be the primary setup man in 2007.

David Cortes Bats: R Throws: R   Height: 5' 11" Weight: 225 Born: October 15, 1973 Age: 33

YEAR	TEAM	LVL	AGE	W	L	SV	G	GS	IP	H	BB	SO	HR	GB%	BABIP	STUFF	WHIP	ERA	PERA	EQERA	EQH9	EQBB9	EQSO9	EQHR9	VORP	WXRL
2005	CSP	AAA	31	1	0	1	12	0	15²	15	7	15	3	42.6%	.286	-14	1.40	4.01	6.12	5.06	7.9	3.9	6.2	1.7	1.0	—
2005	COL	MLB	31	2	0	2	50	0	52²	50	10	36	9	33.1%	.266	-4	1.14	4.10	4.59	3.46	7.6	1.5	5.4	1.5	9.4	0.26
2006	CSP	AAA	32	1	1	2	18	0	18	22	9	16	2	33.9%	.333	-13	1.72	5.00	5.31	4.91	10.3	4.4	5.4	1.5	1.4	—
2006	COL	MLB	32	3	1	0	30	0	29¹	35	6	14	3	42.4%	.333	-10	1.40	4.30	4.05	3.86	9.8	1.5	3.9	0.9	6.1	0.49
2007	SFN	MLB	33	2	2	2	43	0	45	49	14	28	6	39.0%	.297	-10	1.41	4.57	4.97	4.83	9.2	2.5	5.0	1.0	4.3	0.40

Breakout: 5% Improve: 20% Collapse: 53% Attrition: 41%   Comparables: Jose Cabrera, Joe Borowski, Ron Taylor, Chuck Taylor

Cortes held his own in 2005, but Hurdle soured on him for relying on his fastball too much; he recorded fewer appearances each month before being sent down on July 17th. He signed with the Giants for 2007, but, like Santa Anna or Paulina Rubio, he's more likely to return to Mexico after leaving a brief impression upon the United States.

Samuel Deduno Bats: R Throws: R   Height: 6' 1" Weight: 156 Born: July 2, 1983 Age: 23

YEAR	TEAM	LVL	AGE	W	L	SV	G	GS	IP	H	BB	SO	HR	GB%	BABIP	STUFF	WHIP	ERA	PERA	EQERA	EQH9	EQBB9	EQSO9	EQHR9	VORP	WXRL
2004	CAS	Rk	21	6	4	0	15	15	76¹	62	32	118	3	—	.349	16	1.23	3.18	4.93	5.28	8.2	4.6	6.4	0.7	2.7	—
2005	ASH	A	22	8	8	0	20	20	89²	82	65	110	9	54.5%	.346	-2	1.64	5.62	7.80	7.71	9.8	8.6	6.6	1.7	-19.7	—
2006	MOD	A+	23	5	8	0	27	26	146¹	121	92	167	3	63.6%	.315	30	1.46	4.80	4.99	5.86	7.7	6.3	6.3	0.3	-4.2	—
2007	COL	MLB	23	5	9	0	24	20	110²	114	79	93	11	61.0%	.318	5	1.75	5.68	5.14	5.26	8.4	6.1	6.7	0.7	6.2	1.40

Breakout: 37% Improve: 77% Collapse: 5% Attrition: 1%   Comparables: Vince Perkins, Mike MacDougal, Denny Bautista, Dan Reichert

Deduno stayed healthy all season despite concerns that he was an injury risk due to past shoulder soreness. He faded in July and August as his walk rate shot up (52 in 66.1 innings). Despite this, his excellent stuff allowed him some margin for error: Deduno has a nasty 92 to 94-MPH cut fastball and uses his curve as an out-pitch. The Rockies will have a better idea what they've got after Deduno spends a year in the Texas League.

Mike DeJean Bats: R Throws: R   Height: 6' 2" Weight: 220 Born: September 28, 1970 Age: 36

YEAR	TEAM	LVL	AGE	W	L	SV	G	GS	IP	H	BB	SO	HR	GB%	BABIP	STUFF	WHIP	ERA	PERA	EQERA	EQH9	EQBB9	EQSO9	EQHR9	VORP	WXRL
2004	BAL	MLB	33	0	5	0	37	0	39²	49	28	36	2	—	.388	6	1.94	6.12	4.47	5.83	10.8	5.6	7.3	0.4	-0.6	-1.69
2004	NYN	MLB	33	0	0	0	17	0	21¹	21	5	24	0	—	.362	21	1.22	1.69	2.61	2.11	9.3	1.7	8.9	0.0	8.5	0.65
2005	COL	MLB	34	2	3	0	38	0	36²	26	12	35	0	48.0%	.265	23	1.04	3.19	2.85	3.08	5.9	2.6	7.6	0.2	8.9	0.93
2005	NYN	MLB	34	3	1	0	28	0	25²	36	18	17	3	60.2%	.367	-16	2.10	6.30	5.35	6.75	12.5	5.7	5.4	1.0	-3.5	-0.05
2007	COL	MLB	36	2	2	1	30	1	38¹	43	22	26	4	55.0%	.318	-13	1.68	5.28	4.91	4.86	9.2	4.8	5.4	0.8	3.9	0.30

Breakout: 16% Improve: 47% Collapse: 33% Attrition: 27%   Comparables: Ted Abernathy, Greg Minton, Joe Gibbon, Norm Charlton

DeJean injured his shoulder right out of the gate and underwent season-ending arthroscopic surgery in mid-June. He's expected to be ready for spring training, but the Rockies did not pick up his $1.5-million option. DeJean has made it known that he wants to retire as a Rocky, marking him as a man of singularly low ambition.

Nate Field — Bats: R Throws: R   Height: 6' 2" Weight: 205 Born: December 11, 1975 Age: 31

YEAR	TEAM	LVL	AGE	W	L	SV	G	GS	IP	H	BB	SO	HR	GB%	BABIP	STUFF	WHIP	ERA	PERA	EQERA	EQH9	EQBB9	EQSO9	EQHR9	VORP	WXRL
2004	KCA	MLB	28	2	3	3	43	0	44¹	40	19	30	5	—	.267	-5	1.33	4.27	4.55	4.27	7.4	3.5	5.6	0.8	5.6	-0.03
2005	OMA	AAA	29	1	0	0	16	0	22	26	14	24	1	26.9%	.397	4	1.82	4.91	4.12	4.84	10.5	5.6	6.9	0.4	1.9	—
2006	CSP	AAA	30	3	3	25	49	0	49	63	9	55	7	40.5%	.403	-4	1.47	4.78	4.42	5.04	11.3	1.6	7.2	1.6	3.1	—
2006	COL	MLB	30	1	1	0	14	0	9	9	5	14	2	28.6%	.368	9	1.56	4.00	4.15	2.89	8.7	3.9	12.5	1.9	2.1	0.19
2007	FLO	MLB	31	2	3	3	43	2	47²	52	20	41	7	39.0%	.315	-1	1.49	4.95	5.36	5.01	9.6	3.2	6.9	1.1	3.0	0.30

Breakout: 14% Improve: 32% Collapse: 34% Attrition: 38%   Comparables: Bob Johnson, Terry Mathews, Rodney Myers, Don McMahon

Signed to a minor league contract before the season, Field closed for the Sky Sox in 2006, leading the PCL with 25 saves despite being raked by lefties (.344/.372/.500). Called up in September, he pitched well in limited action. He was signed by the Marlins as a minor league free agent and seems to have a good chance to make what is shaping up to be a no-name pen provided the Fish don't confuse him with Nate Bump.

Josh Fogg — Bats: R Throws: R   Height: 6' 0" Weight: 205 Born: December 13, 1976 Age: 30

YEAR	TEAM	LVL	AGE	W	L	SV	G	GS	IP	H	BB	SO	HR	GB%	BABIP	STUFF	WHIP	ERA	PERA	EQERA	EQH9	EQBB9	EQSO9	EQHR9	VORP	WXRL
2004	PIT	MLB	27	11	10	0	32	32	178¹	193	66	82	17	—	.302	0	1.45	4.64	4.67	4.70	9.2	2.9	3.6	0.8	13.8	3.70
2005	PIT	MLB	28	6	11	0	34	28	169¹	196	53	85	27	41.2%	.301	-15	1.47	5.05	5.27	5.57	10.2	2.5	4.1	1.4	-0.9	1.75
2006	COL	MLB	29	11	9	0	31	31	172	206	60	93	24	43.3%	.319	-3	1.55	5.49	4.72	5.34	9.9	2.7	4.3	1.1	4.6	1.47
2007	COL	MLB	30	8	12	0	29	27	160¹	196	51	92	26	48.0%	.314	0	1.54	5.47	5.07	4.91	10.0	2.7	4.5	1.2	15.0	2.70

Breakout: 28% Improve: 65% Collapse: 10% Attrition: 2%   Comparables: Jim Colborn, Early Wynn, James Baldwin, Art Ditmar

A danger at any altitude, Fogg was a workmanlike, uninteresting, garden-variety failure in Denver. He was pummeled at Coors to the tune of .323/.381/.557, surrendering 16 home runs in 341 at bats. He was somewhat more successful on the road, though his ERA in neutral parks was a still-high 4.80. Fogg's disastrous second half (6.94 ERA after the All-Star break) could be partially blamed on bone chips in his pitching elbow, but the fact remains that he's just not any good. For what it's worth, the bone chips were removed in November, and Fogg is expected to make a full recovery by spring training.

Jeff Francis — Bats: L Throws: L   Height: 6' 5" Weight: 205 Born: January 8, 1981 Age: 26

YEAR	TEAM	LVL	AGE	W	L	SV	G	GS	IP	H	BB	SO	HR	GB%	BABIP	STUFF	WHIP	ERA	PERA	EQERA	EQH9	EQBB9	EQSO9	EQHR9	VORP	WXRL
2004	TUL	AA	23	13	1	0	17	17	113²	73	22	147	9	—	.253	28	0.84	1.98	4.01	2.75	7.5	2.1	8.1	1.2	34.2	—
2004	CSP	AAA	23	3	2	0	7	7	41	35	7	49	3	—	.320	38	1.02	2.85	3.26	3.27	7.6	1.5	8.3	0.7	10.7	—
2004	COL	MLB	23	3	2	0	7	7	36²	42	13	32	8	—	.318	9	1.50	5.15	5.05	4.70	9.4	2.8	6.8	1.6	2.4	0.64
2005	COL	MLB	24	14	12	0	33	33	183²	228	70	128	26	38.8%	.349	2	1.62	5.68	4.73	4.97	10.0	3.0	5.5	1.2	0.1	0.99
2006	COL	MLB	25	13	11	0	32	32	199	187	69	117	18	46.0%	.276	13	1.29	4.16	4.27	4.03	7.9	2.7	4.7	0.7	35.5	4.18
2007	COL	MLB	26	10	12	0	30	30	185	207	59	128	27	46.0%	.306	11	1.43	4.87	4.51	4.38	9.1	2.7	5.5	1.1	29.1	4.30

Breakout: 12% Improve: 42% Collapse: 20% Attrition: 0%   Comparables: Joe Kennedy, John Smiley, Bob Knepper, Scott Karl

On September 17, Francis threw eight innings of one-run ball against the Diamondbacks, lowering his ERA to 3.88. Had the season ended at that moment, he would have become just the third starter in team history to post a sub-4.00 ERA (Joe Kennedy and Jason Jennings were the others). As in 2005, Francis pitched well at Coors Field (4.05 ERA), but this time around he was equally good on the road (4.30 ERA). Francis saw a marked reduction in BABIP while decreasing his strikeout rate, which raises the question of whether he'll be able to repeat his 2006 performance. It's almost certain he's going to give back some of the progress he made this year. The Rockies believed he'd hold onto enough of it to justify signing him to a four-year extension (with a team option for 2011) in November.

Brian Fuentes | | | **Bats: L Throws: L** | | | Height: 6' 4" | Weight: 230 | Born: August 9, 1975 | | Age: 31

YEAR	TEAM	LVL	AGE	W	L	SV	G	GS	IP	H	BB	SO	HR	GB%	BABIP	STUFF	WHIP	ERA	PERA	EQERA	EQH9	EQBB9	EQSO9	EQHR9	VORP	WXRL
2004	COL	MLB	28	2	4	0	47	0	44²	46	19	48	5	—	.347	10	1.46	5.64	3.96	5.24	8.7	3.3	8.4	0.8	0.6	1.42
2005	COL	MLB	29	2	5	31	78	0	74¹	59	34	91	6	40.0%	.305	29	1.25	2.91	3.71	2.70	6.9	3.6	9.9	0.7	21.8	5.39
2006	COL	MLB	30	3	4	30	66	0	65¹	50	26	73	8	34.9%	.266	21	1.16	3.45	3.86	2.96	6.7	3.1	9.0	0.9	19.8	2.18
2007	COL	MLB	31	3	4	27	55	0	55	51	21	59	7	41.0%	.299	13	1.31	3.71	3.67	3.31	7.5	3.2	8.5	1.0	15.6	2.20

Breakout: 27% Improve: 52% Collapse: 21% Attrition: 8%   Comparables: Arthur Rhodes, Joe Page, Jim Brewer, Paul Assenmacher

The first Rockies closer with two 30-save seasons, Fuentes uses his slider on the outer half of the plate with devastating effect on left-handed hitters (.186/.250/.390) and locates his fastball and changeup against right-handers (.217/.317/.367) in combination with a deceptive motion and release. Despite a climbing home run rate, he should be equally effective in his third year as the team's closer.

Justin Hampson | | | **Bats: L Throws: L** | | | Height: 6' 1" | Weight: 200 | Born: May 24, 1980 | | Age: 27

YEAR	TEAM	LVL	AGE	W	L	SV	G	GS	IP	H	BB	SO	HR	GB%	BABIP	STUFF	WHIP	ERA	PERA	EQERA	EQH9	EQBB9	EQSO9	EQHR9	VORP	WXRL
2004	TUL	AA	24	10	9	0	27	27	170¹	176	63	104	22	—	.287	-38	1.40	3.49	7.20	5.80	10.8	4.2	3.7	2.1	-3.6	—
2005	CSP	AAA	25	5	13	0	27	26	144¹	167	71	93	18	48.1%	.317	-12	1.65	5.99	5.72	5.96	9.1	4.1	4.2	1.1	-6.0	—
2006	CSP	AAA	26	8	4	0	31	13	121¹	121	39	95	10	44.9%	.314	4	1.32	3.34	4.42	4.13	8.3	2.8	5.3	0.9	20.3	—
2006	COL	MLB	26	1	0	0	5	1	12	19	5	9	3	31.1%	.381	-11	2.00	7.50	5.71	6.39	12.8	2.8	5.7	2.1	-1.3	-0.22
2007	SDN	MLB	27	4	5	1	32	8	72²	76	30	47	10	44%	.288	-6	1.47	4.85	5.49	5.29	9.5	3.2	5.3	1.2	3.9	0.7

Breakout: 14% Improve: 45% Collapse: 26% Attrition: 26%   Comparables: Matt Blank, Chris George, Mike McCormick, Mike Kekich

A lefty with fringy stuff who pitched himself back into relevance this year, Hampson can be distinguished from most Rockies prospects because he doesn't throw hard and usually can tell where the ball is going. He can also be distinguished from most Rockies prospects by the fact that he was waived after the season, and is now a Padre.

Jason Jennings | | | **Bats: L Throws: R** | | | Height: 6' 2" | Weight: 235 | Born: July 17, 1978 | | Age: 28

YEAR	TEAM	LVL	AGE	W	L	SV	G	GS	IP	H	BB	SO	HR	GB%	BABIP	STUFF	WHIP	ERA	PERA	EQERA	EQH9	EQBB9	EQSO9	EQHR9	VORP	WXRL
2004	COL	MLB	25	11	12	0	33	33	201	241	101	133	27	—	.332	1	1.70	5.51	4.93	4.83	9.8	3.9	5.1	1.0	12.8	2.36
2005	COL	MLB	26	6	9	0	20	20	122	130	62	75	11	49.5%	.306	8	1.57	5.02	4.69	4.63	8.6	4.0	4.9	0.7	6.4	1.26
2006	COL	MLB	27	9	13	0	32	32	212	206	85	142	17	45.1%	.295	19	1.37	3.78	3.93	3.53	8.1	3.1	5.4	0.6	50.8	5.68
2007	HOU	MLB	28	11	11	0	30	30	192²	191	73	137	21	46.0%	.287	12	1.37	4.20	4.49	4.43	8.6	3.0	5.8	0.9	29.8	4.50

Breakout: 6% Improve: 39% Collapse: 19% Attrition: 0%   Comparables: Russ Ortiz, Aaron Sele, Joey Jay, Jim Clancy

Last year, Jennings had the highest single-season VORP of any starting pitcher in Rockies' history, good for eleventh-best in the majors, and posted the lowest ERA for any starter in club history. His ERA at Coors was 3.56, impressive even in the humidor era, but, because the Rockies averaged a scant 4.03 runs of support (the third-lowest in baseball) in his starts, they threw a good deal of that performance away. Jennings's hard sinker keeps the ball in the park, and he has improved his change and slider. The Astros did not get great value on a single year of his services, but, make no mistake, Jennings is a talented NL starter. A move from Coors Field to Minute Maid Park will not only lower the blood alcohol content of his home stadium, it will also allow Jennings's counting stats to flourish in a more earthbound environment.

Ubaldo Jimenez | | | **Bats: R Throws: R** | | | Height: 6' 4" | Weight: 200 | Born: January 22, 1984 | | Age: 23

YEAR	TEAM	LVL	AGE	W	L	SV	G	GS	IP	H	BB	SO	HR	GB%	BABIP	STUFF	WHIP	ERA	PERA	EQERA	EQH9	EQBB9	EQSO9	EQHR9	VORP	WXRL
2004	VIS	A+	20	4	1	0	9	9	44¹	29	12	61	1	—	.289	40	0.93	2.23	3.22	3.48	6.3	3.1	7.8	0.4	10.4	—
2005	MOD	A+	21	5	3	0	14	14	72¹	61	40	78	5	38.7%	.311	18	1.40	3.98	5.23	4.50	7.6	5.6	6.2	0.9	8.8	—
2005	TUL	AA	21	2	5	0	12	11	63	58	31	53	12	30.9%	.264	-12	1.41	5.43	7.74	6.30	9.4	5.4	5.8	2.4	-4.7	—
2006	TUL	AA	22	9	2	0	13	13	73²	49	40	86	2	43.2%	.287	40	1.22	2.46	3.81	2.99	7.0	5.0	7.8	0.4	21.0	—
2006	CSP	AAA	22	5	2	0	13	13	78¹	74	43	64	7	43.2%	.300	9	1.50	5.07	5.38	5.29	8.1	4.7	5.6	0.9	2.8	—
2006	COL	MLB	22	0	0	0	2	1	7²	5	3	3	1	45.8%	.174	-12	1.04	3.51	5.11	4.50	5.6	3.4	3.4	1.1	1.3	0.25
2007	COL	MLB	23	6	9	0	29	19	117¹	122	65	98	19	43.0%	.300	5	1.59	5.52	5.09	4.95	8.5	4.7	6.6	1.2	10.5	1.80

Breakout: 12% Improve: 31% Collapse: 28% Attrition: 2%   Comparables: Mike Meyers, Adam Johnson, Thomas Diamond, Aaron Myette

A stress fracture in Jimenez's shoulder shelved him for most of 2004, but he appears to have put that well behind him. One result of the injury was a tendency to hook his arm behind him, pausing his delivery and exposing his grip. Jimenez corrected that problem last year and dominated the Texas League, earning a promotion to Triple-A in late June. He still needs to improve his command, but his mid-90s fastball and big curve are ready now. His progress was rewarded with a start on the final day of the 2006 season, and he should be back at Coors by midyear.

Byung-Hyun Kim   Bats: R Throws: R   Height: 5' 9"   Weight: 175   Born: January 21, 1979   Age: 28

YEAR	TEAM	LVL	AGE	W	L	SV	G	GS	IP	H	BB	SO	HR	GB%	BABIP	STUFF	WHIP	ERA	PERA	EQERA	EQH9	EQBB9	EQSO9	EQHR9	VORP	WXRL
2004	PAW	AAA	25	2	6	0	22	19	60²	71	12	39	6	—	.319	-11	1.37	5.34	4.70	6.79	10.5	1.9	4.4	1.0	-8.1	—
2004	BOS	MLB	25	2	1	0	7	3	17¹	17	7	6	1	—	.271	-22	1.38	6.24	4.80	7.00	8.5	3.0	3.0	0.5	-2.6	0.26
2005	COL	MLB	26	5	12	0	40	22	148	156	71	115	17	42.7%	.320	5	1.54	4.86	4.82	4.35	8.7	3.8	6.2	0.9	13.3	0.66
2006	COL	MLB	27	8	12	0	27	27	155	179	61	129	18	42.9%	.350	16	1.55	5.57	4.09	5.15	9.7	3.0	6.7	0.8	4.9	1.71
2007	*COL*	*MLB*	*28*	*8*	*11*	*0*	*31*	*27*	*159*	*179*	*54*	*122*	*22*	*47.0%*	*.317*	*11*	*1.47*	*5.03*	*4.59*	*4.54*	*9.2*	*2.9*	*6.1*	*1.0*	*21.5*	*3.40*

Breakout: 34% Improve: 68% Collapse: 5% Attrition: 1%   Comparables: Jim Slaton, Tom Brewer, Ned Garver, Richard Dotson

For the first time since Kim began starting games, he was able to stay in the rotation for an entire season. That might have been three months too long—he put up a 6.20 ERA after the break. Typical of sidearmers, lefties get a very good look at him (they tagged him to the tune of .325/.414/.534). He's probably better suited to the relief role he abandoned, yet he shows signs of anxiety when pitching out of the pen, losing control and working too fast with runners on base. He's an enigma inside a riddle wrapped in a chalupa, but for the second year in a row he's pitched better at Coors Field (4.57 home ERA, 6.78 road), so the Rockies think is still a puzzle worth frying their brains over.

Ray King   Bats: L Throws: L   Height: 6' 1"   Weight: 240   Born: January 15, 1974   Age: 33

YEAR	TEAM	LVL	AGE	W	L	SV	G	GS	IP	H	BB	SO	HR	GB%	BABIP	STUFF	WHIP	ERA	PERA	EQERA	EQH9	EQBB9	EQSO9	EQHR9	VORP	WXRL
2004	SLN	MLB	30	5	2	0	86	0	62	43	24	40	1	—	.237	8	1.08	2.61	3.50	3.05	6.7	3.2	5.2	0.1	19.9	3.13
2005	SLN	MLB	31	4	4	0	77	0	40	46	16	23	4	50.0%	.323	-13	1.55	3.38	4.76	4.20	10.6	3.3	4.6	0.9	7.3	-1.10
2006	COL	MLB	32	1	4	1	67	0	44²	56	21	23	6	52.7%	.352	-20	1.72	4.43	5.06	4.63	10.4	3.7	4.0	1.0	4.9	0.01
2007	*WAS*	*MLB*	*33*	*2*	*2*	*1*	*49*	*0*	*43*	*48*	*20*	*25*	*4*	*48.0%*	*.305*	*-15*	*1.56*	*4.70*	*5.47*	*5.15*	*9.9*	*3.7*	*4.7*	*0.8*	*2.2*	*0.20*

Breakout: 4% Improve: 12% Collapse: 61% Attrition: 34%   Comparables: Juan Agosto, Buddy Groom, Mike Munoz, Mark Guthrie

With a plethora of lefties in the pen and the deadline acquisition of Jeremy Affeldt, not to mention King's own putrid performance, it boggles the mind as to how the hefty lefty remained a Rocky into October despite the Astros, Red Sox, and Braves all reportedly expressing interest at the trade deadline. For mediocre teams such as the Rockies, one of the primary reasons to sign free agent relievers such as King is the opportunity they provide to fleece a desperate contender for a juicy prospect—an opportunity Dan O'Dowd wasted. The Nationals get the next crack at shopping King midseason.

Tom Martin   Bats: L Throws: L   Height: 6' 1"   Weight: 205   Born: May 21, 1970   Age: 37

YEAR	TEAM	LVL	AGE	W	L	SV	G	GS	IP	H	BB	SO	HR	GB%	BABIP	STUFF	WHIP	ERA	PERA	EQERA	EQH9	EQBB9	EQSO9	EQHR9	VORP	WXRL
2004	LAN	MLB	34	0	1	1	47	0	28¹	32	14	18	3	—	.326	-14	1.62	4.13	5.05	4.40	10.7	4.1	5.0	0.9	4.8	-0.26
2004	ATL	MLB	34	0	1	0	29	0	17	17	5	12	4	—	.277	-9	1.29	3.71	5.57	3.63	8.8	2.1	5.7	2.1	3.7	-0.02
2005	ROU	AAA	35	0	0	5	20	0	27¹	33	13	13	4	60.8%	.322	-35	1.68	3.63	6.75	4.67	11.0	4.7	3.0	1.7	2.8	—
2006	COL	MLB	36	2	0	0	68	0	60¹	62	25	46	4	49.7%	.314	4	1.44	5.07	3.83	4.76	8.8	3.2	6.1	0.4	5.0	0.58
2007	*COL*	*MLB*	*37*	*2*	*2*	*1*	*50*	*0*	*47*	*58*	*20*	*31*	*6*	*50.0%*	*.330*	*-13*	*1.65*	*5.43*	*5.19*	*4.90*	*10.0*	*3.7*	*5.3*	*1.0*	*3.9*	*0.40*

Breakout: 27% Improve: 49% Collapse: 31% Attrition: 36%   Comparables: Rich Rodriguez, Giovanni Carrara, Grant Jackson, Darold Knowles

A testament to just how long a southpaw's career can last, Martin signed a minor league deal with the Rockies last January, made the team, and eventually took over the LOOGY role more by default than through his own performance, which included better success against right-handers and a dismal 6.23 ERA after the break. With the departure of King and Affeldt's possible return to a starting role, the Rockies will bring back Martin for his age-37 season.

Jose Mesa   Bats: R Throws: R   Height: 6' 3"   Weight: 235   Born: December 31, 1969   Age: 41

YEAR	TEAM	LVL	AGE	W	L	SV	G	GS	IP	H	BB	SO	HR	GB%	BABIP	STUFF	WHIP	ERA	PERA	EQERA	EQH9	EQBB9	EQSO9	EQHR9	VORP	WXRL
2004	PIT	MLB	38	5	2	43	70	0	69¹	78	20	37	6	—	.320	-5	1.41	3.25	4.04	3.28	9.5	2.3	4.2	0.8	17.2	3.66
2005	PIT	MLB	39	2	8	27	55	0	56²	61	26	37	7	45.8%	.318	-13	1.54	4.76	5.00	4.66	9.6	3.7	5.3	1.1	4.5	-1.16
2006	COL	MLB	40	1	5	1	79	0	72¹	73	35	39	9	47.2%	.288	-15	1.49	3.86	5.14	3.48	8.5	3.7	4.3	1.0	17.7	0.93
2007	*DET*	*MLB*	*41*	*2*	*2*	*1*	*48*	*0*	*53¹*	*61*	*23*	*29*	*6*	*46.0%*	*.306*	*-17*	*1.56*	*4.66*	*4.81*	*4.59*	*9.7*	*3.7*	*4.5*	*0.8*	*5.9*	*0.40*

Breakout: 2% Improve: 21% Collapse: 56% Attrition: 39%   Comparables: Roberto Hernandez, Harry Gumbert, Virgil Trucks, Jeff Fassero

(continued next page)

Jose Mesa *(continued)*

Although he's aging far more gracefully than any early-nineties Baltimore Orioles fan would have ever thought possible, 2006 was not a success for Mesa. His relatively low ERA was a mirage caused by stranding an unusually high number of runners on base, and he routinely harmed the team in his high-leverage setup role. His otherwise uniformly declining peripherals mean that the Tigers have needlessly acquired a remarkable booby prize. Say goodbye to that hideous purple pitching glove, and hello to an orange road mitt.

Franklin Morales   Bats: L Throws: L   Height: 6' 0"   Weight: 175   Born: January 24, 1986   Age: 21

YEAR	TEAM	LVL	AGE	W	L	SV	G	GS	IP	H	BB	SO	HR	GB%	BABIP	STUFF	WHIP	ERA	PERA	EQERA	EQH9	EQBB9	EQSO9	EQHR9	VORP	WXRL
2004	CAS	Rk	18	6	4	0	15	15	65	92	39	82	8	—	.447	-15	2.02	7.62	7.10	8.24	12.3	5.8	5.4	2.2	-19.6	—
2005	ASH	A	19	8	4	1	21	15	96¹	73	48	108	6	54.9%	.295	15	1.26	3.08	5.60	4.24	7.6	5.6	6.1	1.0	14.1	—
2006	MOD	A+	20	10	9	0	27	26	154²	126	89	179	9	54.5%	.310	24	1.39	3.68	5.18	4.72	7.6	5.6	6.7	0.9	15.1	—
2007	*COL*	*MLB*	*21*	*5*	*9*	*0*	*26*	*21*	*116²*	*122*	*79*	*97*	*16*	*53.0%*	*.308*	*5*	*1.72*	*5.67*	*5.37*	*5.13*	*8.5*	*5.7*	*6.6*	*1.0*	*8.0*	*1.70*

Breakout: 20% Improve: 49% Collapse: 16% Attrition: 0%   Comparables: Chi-Hung Cheng, Jon Lester, Clayton Andrews, Wilfredo Rodriguez

Morales has the highest ceiling of any Rockies pitching prospect. If he stays on track, he projects as a number-one starter. He sports a heavy fastball that has some sink and a tough breaking ball that has tremendous torque. Like other Rockies pitching prospects, he's battled control problems, but a lefty that throws as hard as he does is a once-per-generation thing for an organization.

Juan Morillo   Bats: R Throws: R   Height: 6' 3"   Weight: 190   Born: November 5, 1983   Age: 23

YEAR	TEAM	LVL	AGE	W	L	SV	G	GS	IP	H	BB	SO	HR	GB%	BABIP	STUFF	WHIP	ERA	PERA	EQERA	EQH9	EQBB9	EQSO9	EQHR9	VORP	WXRL
2004	TRI	A-	20	3	2	0	14	14	66¹	56	41	73	0	—	.315	16	1.46	2.99	5.37	6.39	9.3	7.5	5.4	0.4	-5.4	—
2005	ASH	A	21	1	3	0	7	7	33²	40	13	43	2	55.8%	.409	3	1.57	4.54	4.63	7.44	11.6	4.4	6.6	1.1	-6.7	—
2005	MOD	A+	21	6	5	0	20	20	112¹	107	65	101	10	52.7%	.319	5	1.53	4.41	5.94	5.65	8.3	5.8	5.2	1.0	-0.6	—
2006	TUL	AA	22	12	8	0	27	27	140	128	80	132	13	47.9%	.307	7	1.49	4.63	5.38	5.74	9.1	5.2	6.3	1.1	-2.1	—
2007	*COL*	*MLB*	*23*	*4*	*8*	*0*	*28*	*17*	*103¹*	*119*	*66*	*81*	*16*	*51.0%*	*.324*	*-2*	*1.78*	*6.32*	*5.80*	*5.71*	*9.4*	*5.4*	*6.2*	*1.1*	*0.3*	*0.70*

Breakout: 32% Improve: 66% Collapse: 7% Attrition: 1%   Comparables: Justin Echols, Joel Hanrahan, Scott Dunn, Russ Ortiz

If you took him to a carnival and had him throw for the speed guns there, he could win you a lot of teddy bears. In the real world, he's far too wild to stick as a starting pitcher. The Rockies will likely try him in the bullpen to see if they can harness his arm for more than just an array of stuffed octopodes.

Ramon Ramirez   Bats: R Throws: R   Height: 5' 11"   Weight: 190   Born: August 31, 1981   Age: 25

YEAR	TEAM	LVL	AGE	W	L	SV	G	GS	IP	H	BB	SO	HR	GB%	BABIP	STUFF	WHIP	ERA	PERA	EQERA	EQH9	EQBB9	EQSO9	EQHR9	VORP	WXRL
2004	TRN	AA	22	4	6	0	18	18	114	115	32	128	11	—	.333	18	1.29	4.66	4.15	5.03	8.8	2.6	7.1	1.2	7.4	—
2005	TRN	AA	23	6	5	0	15	15	89	79	35	82	10	44.4%	.284	-5	1.28	3.84	5.74	5.42	8.7	4.3	5.5	1.6	1.7	—
2005	COH	AAA	23	1	3	0	6	6	27	32	9	26	3	48.1%	.382	7	1.52	5.33	4.45	5.60	10.5	3.3	6.6	1.0	0.0	—
2005	TUL	AA	23	2	1	0	9	3	25¹	27	8	23	6	41.0%	.300	-18	1.38	5.34	7.89	6.75	11.2	3.4	6.4	3.4	-3.1	—
2006	COL	MLB	24	4	3	0	61	0	67²	58	27	61	5	41.4%	.285	16	1.26	3.46	3.46	3.23	7.2	3.1	7.2	0.5	18.8	0.89
2007	*COL*	*MLB*	*25*	*3*	*3*	*2*	*48*	*1*	*59²*	*61*	*25*	*54*	*8*	*44.0%*	*.304*	*6*	*1.42*	*4.75*	*4.24*	*4.28*	*8.3*	*3.5*	*7.2*	*1.0*	*10.5*	*0.90*

Breakout: 28% Improve: 53% Collapse: 17% Attrition: 19%   Comparables: Chad Orvella, Juan Rincon, Marty Pattin, Cecilio Guante

Yeah, he was probably worth a year of Shawn Chacon. After an unimpressive run in the minors with both Yankee and Rocky affiliates, the righty with the hard slider started the year like a house afire, holding the opposition scoreless over his first 15 ⅓ major league innings and allowing a run in just one of his first 22 appearances. Once the damn broke, however, Hurdle exiled him to the back of the bullpen queue. Late season wildness and his fly-ball tendencies may catch up to him in the short run, but his success in longer relief stints in 2006 could augur another role for this Colorado find.

Lineouts

PLAYER	TEAM	LVL	AGE	PA	R	2B	3B	HR	RBI	BB	SO	SB-CS	SPEED	AVG/OBP/SLG	MLVr	EqAVG/OBP/SLG	EqA	VORP
SS M. Macri	TUL	AA	24	326	35	12	2	8	35	22	66	2-4	4.4	.233/.294/.372	-.168	.208/.257/.319	.206	-17.0
LF M. Miller	MOD	A+	23	415	52	20	2	12	77	31	37	4-9	3.6	.323/.381/.486	.226	.285/.328/.424	.257	3.7
	TUL	AA	23	97	14	1	1	1	7	11	13	1-1	4.8	.229/.330/.301	-.198	.209/.289/.279	.212	-8.1
2B J. Nix	CSP	AAA	23	397	39	14	1	2	26	32	61	15-3	5.9	.251/.317/.313	-.227	.223/.284/.278	.210	-20.2
OF J. Piedra*	CSP	AAA	27	156	15	8	0	6	18	15	31	0-2	3.5	.239/.314/.428	-.089	.199/.268/.340	.211	-11.3
	COL	MLB	27	63	4	2	0	3	10	3	22	1-0	2.8	.169/.222/.356	-.371	.153/.206/.339	.193	-3.4
INF J. Wilson	CSP	AAA	25	384	61	18	4	10	45	37	41	15-4	6.1	.307/.376/.475	.129	.276/.339/.431	.269	19.6
2B C. Wimberly#	MOD	A+	22	399	72	6	4	2	24	30	42	50-16	8.0	.325/.404/.383	.115	.292/.346/.342	.255	6.7
2B E. Young#	ASH	A	21	569	92	28	6	5	49	67	75	87-31	7.9	.295/.391/.409	.105	.244/.316/.341	.240	-4.3

PLAYER	TEAM	LVL	AGE	W	L	SV	IP	H	BB	SO	HR	GB%	BABIP	STUFF	WHIP	ERA	PERA	EqERA	EqH9	EqBB9	EqSO9	EqHR9	VORP
M. Asencio	CSP	AAA	25	8	7	1	111¹	127	41	71	13	—	.328	-19	1.51	5.02	5.28	5.26	9.4	3.1	4.3	1.3	4.3
D. Clarke	MOD	A+	25	1	1	5	26²	13	7	37	1	—	.218	12	0.76	1.37	3.64	2.49	5.3	2.8	7.5	0.7	8.7
S. Lindsay	ASH	A	21	2	1	0	33¹	26	27	43	2	—	.308	20	1.60	2.72	6.89	4.99	8.5	9.7	7.0	1.2	2.1
	TRI	A-	21	2	2	0	29¹	18	17	48	0	—	.333	26	1.20	2.78	4.63	4.85	8.3	8.0	8.7	0.3	2.2
J. Miller	TUL	AA	24	0	3	12	44¹	50	14	41	10	—	.316	-35	1.45	3.88	7.77	5.53	12.1	3.2	6.0	3.0	0.3
J. Newman*	TUL	AA	24	9	5	2	77	56	24	77	8	—	.251	-9	1.04	3.16	5.05	3.87	7.7	3.1	6.3	1.3	14.3
S. Nin	CSP	AAA	25	1	3	0	31¹	32	8	26	3	—	.330	9	1.29	4.63	4.25	4.78	8.7	2.2	5.6	1.1	2.9
G. Reynolds	MOD	A+	21	2	1	0	48¹	51	14	29	1	—	.316	5	1.35	3.37	4.01	3.96	8.5	2.7	3.4	0.4	9.1
C. Roe	ASH	A	19	7	4	0	99²	105	47	80	4	—	.336	4	1.53	4.08	5.47	5.64	9.9	5.0	4.3	0.7	-0.4
M. Venafro*	LOU	AAA	32	0	0	2	22²	19	8	18	0	—	.297	-7	1.22	2.43	3.88	3.27	8.2	3.7	5.3	0.4	5.7
	CSP	AAA	32	3	1	0	16	10	5	10	1	—	.196	-12	0.94	2.25	4.82	2.20	5.0	2.8	3.9	0.6	6.2

Life away from the Golden Dome has been hard on **Matt Macri**; once he made it to an age-appropriate minor league level, he stopped hitting. Sometimes talked up as a sleeper prospect, **Matt Miller** is a minor-league slugger with a long swing who's unlikely to make it. **Jayson Nix** has never adjusted to hitting in the upper levels of the minors. He and brother Laynce are both in danger of washing out of baseball due to a lack of strike zone recognition, but once they do, they could always donate their extra Ys to needy minor leaguers. The Rockies never found a use for **Jorge Piedra** beyond designated hitter during interleague play, and his *manos de piedra* and prior steroid suspension certainly didn't help matters. He's still useful, but he's long past due for a change of scenery. **Josh Wilson** has always been highly regarded defensively, but, although he's made some progress with his plate discipline, he's probably not going to get much further. Now with Washington, he'll suffer the indignity of playing behind Cristian Guzman. **Corey Wimberly** is a tiny, insanely fast second baseman. He has no other skills of note, but he may be able to beat out enough infield grounders to irritate opponents. **Eric Young Jr.** led organized baseball in stolen bases in 2006, which will win him a Non-Prize delivered personally by Esix Snead.

Miguel Asencio is a former Rule 5er and Tommy John survivor who was the vigorish in the Jason Jennings trade. He's mostly indistinct from Ezequiel Astacio or Wandy Rodriguez, but he could possibly become a relief asset for the Astros. Despite the Rockies' love of multi-sport athletes, this **Darren Clarke** is not the golfer. The hard-throwing big boy had better get out of A-ball, or he won't be the baseball player either. **Shane Lindsay** had a power profile, but surgery to repair a torn labrum will knock the hard-luck Aussie out indefinitely. It's a shame, because he's a firecracker when healthy. **Jim Miller** has battled injuries since his impressive 2004 showing, but his slider has allowed him to build impressive strikeout totals when healthy. He still has a shot, but he'll likely be repeating Double-A at age 25. This year is make or break for him. A 2004 19th rounder out of Ohio State, **Josh Newman** put himself on the future LOOGY map with his work at Tulsa, limiting lefties to .179/.248/.239 before doing good winter work in the AFL. In addition to feminist theory and highly-charged erotica, the diary of **Sandy Nin** would likely include odes to Dan O'Dowd and slams against most of his fellow marginal relief candidates. **Greg Reynolds** is baseball's answer to Sam Bowie. The second selection in the 2006 draft, he was a safe choice who stands to settle in quickly as a back-of-the-rotation starter, but has no chance at stardom. For a pick that high in a seemingly loaded draft, the Rockies had to do better. Like many top Rockies pitching prospects, **Chaz Roe** is a power pitcher who induces groundouts. "Skid" struggled mechanically in 2006, but last year's first round supplemental pick is still very young. **Ryan Speier**'s low three-quarters delivery and solid fastball result in plenty of ground balls; however, the torn labrum he suffered last year is a major setback at a critical juncture in his career. Reports from the Arizona Fall League were encouraging, but check back in the spring to see how he withstands a major league schedule. We once called

Chin-Hui Tsao a "lulu" of an international free agent signing, but after years of shifting roles, heavy workloads, and several major arm injuries, he's become a long shot, begging the question, Is it better to have had great talent once, even if you have to leave most of it on the surgeon's table, or to never have had it at all? **Mike Venafro**, now with the Twins, is not likely to get his own chapter in *Moneyball II*.

Manager: Clint Hurdle

Year	Team	W-L	Pythag +/-	Avg PC	100 +P	120 +P	QS	BQS	REL	REL w Zero R	IBB	SUBS	PH	PH Avg	PH HR	SB2	CS2	SB3	CS3	SAC Att	SAC %	POS SAC	Squeeze	Swing	In Play
2004	COL	68-94	-5	95.9	60	3	62	12	473	280	84	59	287	.253	11	36	31	8	2	125	77.6%	55	1	134	87
2005	COL	67-95	-2	94.2	52	1	63	6	459	283	54	61	272	.224	4	61	26	4	5	123	71.5%	52	3	142	116
2006	COL	76-86	-5	95.9	56	2	74	11	498	310	81	34	259	.214	6	80	44	4	3	162	73.5%	64	0	145	111

By all accounts, Hurdle works well with young players and is a good communicator. He generally left disciplinary issues to first base coach Dave Collins, who often had to prompt Hurdle to follow through on consequences for baserunning blunders. The effect Collins's departure will have on the clubhouse atmosphere remains to be seen. A poor tactical manager, Hurdle doesn't think twice about putting low on-base guys in the top two spots of his lineup, preferring a traditional bat control specialist in the two-hole. He bunts indiscriminately, racking up the most sacrifice hits in the majors. His approach to the bullpen is formulaic, compulsively seeking the platoon advantage to the point that, in one game last season, he brought in five different pitchers to face five consecutive hitters. The Rockies extended Hurdle's contract through the 2007 season, but if the team doesn't play .500 ball this summer it's unlikely another extension will be forthcoming.

Detroit Tigers

On September 14th, 2003, a typhoon hit South Korea and killed 42 people. Sweden decided not to adopt the Euro. The Ravens' Jamal Lewis rushed for 295 yards, breaking the NFL's single-game rushing record. And, at Comerica Park, the Detroit Tigers lost to the Royals, making them the first team in the Free Agency Era to cross the 110-loss threshold.

General Manager Dave Dombrowski couldn't have expected much from his team that season. He'd traded away Jeff Weaver, their best pitcher, in a three-team deal a year earlier. Players such as Warren Morris, Ramon Santiago, and Adam Bernero were regulars, and Shane Halter accumulated almost 400 plate appearances in a utility role. PECOTA had forecast the Tigers to lose 107 games.

Teams in the free agency era are expected to compete; rebuilding is only tolerated for a year or two at a time, and then only if there is a clear development plan in place and some Grade-A prospects to get excited about. The 2003 Tigers didn't appear to have either, and hadn't since before Kurt Cobain became a household name. They would go on to compile a 43–119 record, finishing a full 47 games out of first place in the AL Central. Alex Rodriguez was the league's MVP that season; he produced 10.7 wins for the Rangers according to our WARP (Wins Above Replacement Player) statistic. Roy Halladay won the Cy Young with a 10.6-win season. Barry Bonds (12.8 WARP) and Eric Gagne (10.2) took home the hardware in the National League. The Tigers could have added all four of them and still finished three games behind the Twins.

*   *   *

Both conventional wisdom and sabermetric orthodoxy warn not to invest money in a failing product. When the Royals sign Gil Meche or the Orioles go after Jay Payton, they are ridiculed both by *Baseball Prospectus* and *Pardon the Interruption*. What's the point of winning 75 games rather than 70, the argument goes, when the fans want to see a winner, and neither one is going to get you into the playoffs?

It turns out that this argument has a good deal of economic backing. Our research for *Baseball Between the Numbers* discovered that there is a very substantial premium associated with reaching the playoffs—a single postseason appearance results in about $25 million in revenue. The price for free agent talent is going to be dictated by the highest bidder, and the highest bidder will usually be a team that can hope to push itself over the playoff hump by signing the player. By extension, a team that doesn't have playoff aspirations is almost always making a mistake when they sign a free agent, because they're paying a premium price for something that can't enhance their overall value. It's the equivalent of putting a jet engine on a pack mule.

Teams largely abide by this principle in practice. figure 1 presents the distribution of regular-season win totals for all major league clubs since 2000, when teams really began to understand the dynamics of what it means to compete in the wild card era. This is compared to the expected distribution of win totals over the same period, using a normal distribution.

What we see is that there are fewer teams than expected in the range between about 70 and 85 wins–the no-man's land in which a team is not competing, but probably still has a few leftover assets that could cashed in or leveraged as part of a rebuilding process. Conversely, there are quite a few more teams than expected in the range of 65–69 wins, where a team is putting little more than a replacement-level product on the field, and again between 90–99

TIGERS PROSPECTUS

2006 record: 95–67; Second place, AL Central; Lost to Cardinals in World Series

Pythagenport record: 96–66

Runs scored per game: 5.07 (5th in AL)

Runs allowed per game: 4.17 (1st in AL)

Team EqA: .259 (9th in AL)

2006 Batters Age: 29.8 (7th oldest in AL)

2006 Pitchers Age: 28.8 (3rd oldest in AL)

Ballpark: Comerica Park; Slight pitcher's park; Park Factor of .981

2006: Just a little pitcher fatigue and a few timely hits away from a World Championship.

2007: A deep team full of young veterans and power arms will keep them competing for the postseason.

Figure 1. Distribution of MLB Regular Season Win Totals, 2000–2006

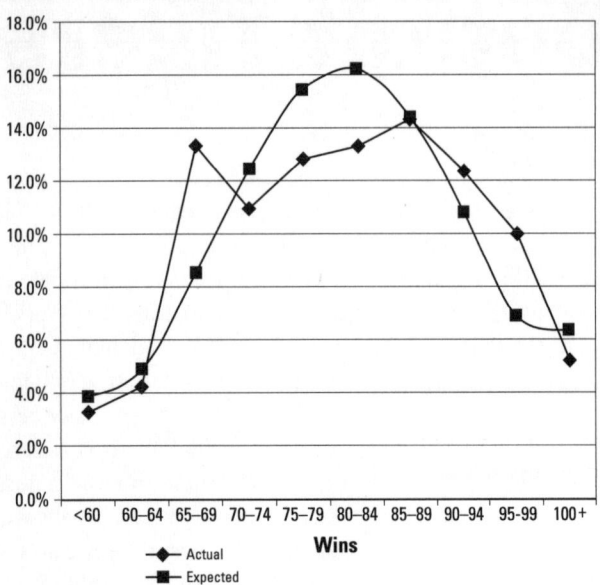

Figure 2. Hypothesized Equilibria for MLB Win Totals

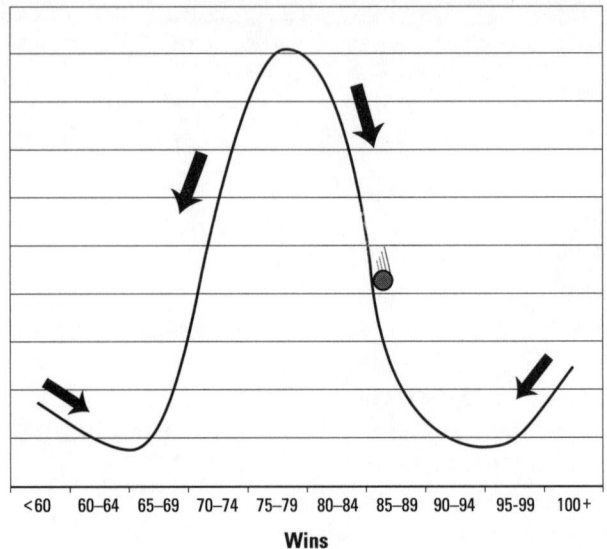

wins, where a team is in the thick of the pennant race. There is not, on the other hand, an excess of 100-plus game winners, where wins can become superfluous. Nor is there an excess of teams winning fewer than 60 games, where upgrading the product is usually very cheap; a good farm system or the mass acquisition of some young talent can produce a 70-game winner (witness last year's Marlins).

In other words, teams are gravitating toward one of two equilibria: The first is at about 95 wins and represents a full-fledged effort to win a championship; the second is at about 65 wins and represents punting on the season. Teams don't like to get stuck in the middle.

We can visualize this in terms of gravity: the process of a ball rolling down a warped track (see figure 2). There is an inflection point at about 75 wins, where a decision must be made between competing and rebuilding. If a team decides to compete, they'll find—like the ball picking up momentum as it rolls down the track—that it gets closer and closer to the Promised Land with every subsequent acquisition, making each investment progressively more attractive. It's not unusual to see this pattern in practice, such as in the Mets' talent grabs of past few seasons, or the Blue Jays' massive reinvestments in their franchise. If a team starts down the rebuilding path, on the other hand, a fire sale may soon be at hand.

Dave Dombrowski must have had a pretty thorough understanding of this process from his days with the Marlins. The same is true of team owner Mike Ilitch, whose NHL Red Wings endured some awfully lean years in the early 1980s before a decade-long rebuilding effort transformed

them into a perennial high-revenue contender. So what happens, they must have been asking themselves that day in September 2003, if a team finds that it's on the wrong side of the track? What happens if a team wants to go from the 65-win equilibrium to the 95-win equilibrium? How does it accomplish that? The answer turns out to be hold your nose, throw caution to the wind, and spend a lot of money.

Enter Ivan Rodriguez, who was signed to a four-year, $40-million deal in the 2003–2004 offseason. The deal, coming on the heels of the patch-up acquisitions of Rondell White and Fernando Viña, was largely regarded as a public relations move. That's how it looked after 2004, too: Rodriguez had a fantastic season, the Tigers finished with a respectable 72–90 record, and attendance at Comerica Park increased by 40 percent.

What's forgotten about the Rodriguez deal is that it came about, at least partially, by accident. Rodriguez, perhaps overestimating his asking price after leading the Marlins to a championship, was left unemployed very late into the free agency cycle, and was not signed by the Tigers until early February. Looking back on the deal now, the Tigers remember Rodriguez as having been too cheap to pass up (a slightly rose-colored perception). His deal contained an array of injury-related out-clauses and deferred money that brought the guaranteed value of the contract down to about $19 million in present value. Even still, had Juan Gonzalez not turned down Randy Smith's eight-year, $140-million offer three winters earlier, Ilitch might not have had the appetite for anything more than a Little Caesars Pizza on the house.

However the Pudge deal came about, it is clear based on the Tigers' subsequent behavior that they took a very explicit message from the results: our return on investment is high. Detroit fans will come out to see a team that provides them with hope and faith, and maybe we're not that far from being a contender. Thus, the Tigers repeated the process in 2005 with Magglio Ordoñez, another player who had trouble finding a contract to his liking, and again last winter with Kenny Rogers and Todd Jones.

Indeed, the Tigers weren't that far from being a contender, but this was largely based on the good work that Dombrowski was doing through other channels. The trades for Carlos Guillen and Placido Polanco came at little cost and gave the Tigers one of the best middle infields in baseball. The farm system, after years of neglect, began turning out products such as Curtis Granderson, Justin Verlander, and Joel Zumaya. And, to his credit, Dombrowski has had a particular knack for finding talent where few others were looking, such as through minor league free agency (Marcus Thames), the waiver wire (Craig Monroe), or the Rule 5 draft (Wil Ledezma and Chris Shelton).

A more complete reckoning of the Tigers' rebuilding process is included in table 1. Each player on a hypothesized 25-man roster is included, which represents the 11 pitchers and 14 position players who received the most playing time with the Tigers in 2006. Rookies are listed not by the year in which they came into the franchise, but by the year in which they graduated to the majors, as signified by losing their rookie eligibility. Players are listed with their associated WARP totals, which measures their relative contribution to the team's success last season.

One thing that's abundantly clear is just how much of the heavy lifting Dombrowski since taking over the GM chair from Randy Smith in the early days of the 2002 regular season. Of the players above, only Inge, Walker, and Dmitri Young were on the Tigers' major league roster when Dombrowski took over, and only Fernando Rodney, Omar Infante, and Craig Monroe were elsewhere within the organization. Collectively, these six players represent 13.8 wins, or about 17 percent of the Tigers' talent stock in 2006; Dombrowski is directly responsible for finding the remaining 83 percent. Nearly twice as much talent (21.9 wins) was added to the major league roster during the 2006 season as was left over from the entire six-year run of the Randy Smith administration.

It also is apparent that major league free agency is a relatively small part of the Tigers' rebuilding story. Players generally come into an organization by one of three means: Free agency, trade, or the June amateur draft (and the concomitant process of Latin American player development). In Dombrowski's case, however, it is necessary to add a fourth category: A&D, or Acquire and Develop (see table 2). This category includes all players who were

Table 1. Tigers Rebuilding Process, with 2006 WARP Totals

WARP Total	Player Acquisition
	2001
6.0	Brandon Inge, graduation (June draft, 1998)
	2002
1.2	Jamie Walker, minor league free agent
0.0	Dmitri Young, trade
	2003
5.5	Nate Robertson, graduation (trade, 2003)
5.3	Jeremy Bonderman, graduation (trade, 2002)
2.8	Fernando Rodney, graduation (Latin America, 1997)
2.5	Craig Monroe, graduation (waivers, 2002)
1.7	Wil Ledezma, graduation (Rule 5 draft, 2003)
1.3	Omar Infante, graduation (Latin America, 1999)
	2004
6.3	Carlos Guillen, trade
5.8	Ivan Rodriguez, free agent
2.5	Marcus Thames, graduation (minor league free agent, 2004)
	2005
6.5	Curtis Granderson, graduation (June draft, 2002)
4.1	Magglio Ordonez, free agent
2.8	Placido Polanco, trade
2.2	Chris Shelton, graduation (Rule 5 draft, 2004)
1.4	Vance Wilson, trade
1.4	Jason Grilli, minor league free agent
	2006
6.5	Justin Verlander, graduation (June draft, 2005)
5.3	Kenny Rogers, free agent
4.6	Joel Zumaya, graduation (June draft, 2002)
3.3	Todd Jones, free agent
1.8	Zach Miner, graduation (trade, 2005)
0.5	Alexis Gomez, graduation (waivers, 2004)
-0.1	Sean Casey, trade
??	Jim Leyland, manager

Table 2. Tigers' 2006 WARP by Acquisition Type

Acquisition Type	WARP	Distribution
Free Agent	21.1	26%
Trade	10.4	13%
Draft/Latin America	27.7	34%
Acquire & Develop	22.0	27%

Detroit Tigers

brought into the system from other organizations by any means while still rookies, a group that includes players such as Thames and Ledezma, as well as Jeremy Bonderman, Zach Miner, and Nate Robertson, all of whom were acquired as prospects in trade.

The free agency group was responsible for only about a quarter of the Tigers' 2006 output. The A&D route alone accounted for more than that, with the largest contribution coming from players developed entirely within the organization. In fact, the Tigers' free agent acquisitions during Dombrowski's tenure have not been tremendous. While the Tigers will get at least one MVP-caliber season and one pennant out of Rodriguez' four-year deal, they would happily do away with the remaining money owed to Magglio Ordoñez and Todd Jones, and they were probably lucky to get as much as they did out of Kenny Rogers. There were also deals with Rondell White, Viña, and Troy Percival, who collectively contributed just 5.2 wins to the club before departing.

Free agency is a necessary evil. For all the tremendous work that Dombrowksi and his organization's scouting and development staff has done, the Tigers would have struggled to reach .500 without the high-priced acquisitions of Rodriguez, Ordoñez, and Rogers. But the difference between what the Tigers and Mets have done, and what teams such as the Giants and the Orioles have tried to do, is that in the former two cases the surgical strikes into the free agent market have been supplemented with production from the farm system and a core competency for talent evaluation, while in the latter it exists on its own. If building a winner entirely from development and trade channels is impossible, than buying one is very nearly so, unless you're willing to grow accustomed to $200 million payrolls. The Orioles, for example, seem to be engaged in a Sisyphean process in which their payroll never goes below $75 million, and their win total never above 75.

*　　　*　　　*

Gary Sheffield, the Tigers' major acquisition this winter, was not a free agent, but he might as well have been. Sheffield's $13-million option for 2007 was not picked up by the Yankees until just days before he was dealt to the Tigers, and the Tigers were quick to append two additional years to Sheffield's contract.

Just like they did with Ordoñez and I-Rod, the Tigers have overpaid for Sheffield. While the prospects moved in the deal are not much—Humberto Sanchez has serious health and conditioning issues, Kevin Whelan is a minor league reliever, and Anthony Claggett has little track record to speak of—Sheffield is not a great bet to earn his salary.

PECOTA has a very bearish .276/.347/.433 line projected for Sheffield in 2007, with things only getting worse from there.

That said, Sheffield's fortunes for the next few seasons are very hard to project, and the Tigers have a track record of getting surprising performances from their veterans. There is a due diligence process that goes on any time that a big-budget player is acquired, one that's likely to be especially important in the case of the moody Sheffield. The Tigers' feeling is that Sheffield passed through this process with flying colors. Although Sheffield did not have a no-trade clause, the Tigers were one of a handful of teams that he was happy to be traded to, and the team expects him to be more comfortable knowing that he's locked into a DH role instead of having to play the outfield or first base. Sheffield also has a history with both Dombrowski and Jim Leyland going back to their Marlins days a decade ago, and Sheffield's patience at the plate certainly fits an area of need.

Besides, if the Tigers are paying too much for Sheffield, they'll make a great deal of that back with the extensions to Brandon Inge and Jeremy Bonderman, each of which locked up key players at well below market rates. It might seem easy to leverage a feel-good season like 2006 into good deals with established talent, but this is not always the case: consider the Red Sox' ill-advised deal with Jason Varitek following their 2004 championship, or the mixed bag of contracts that the White Sox signed after they won it all the following year

Win it all, that's the one thing Detroit did not do in 2006, though when the history of the season is written, it will surely be remembered as the Year of the Tiger. A cursory look forward to next October reveals the Tigers as one of several co-favorites for the title. For a team that made a 26-win leap, the 2006 Tigers did not have a tremendous number of players who performed over their heads—exceptions being Rogers and several other pitchers such as rookies Justin Verlander and Joel Zumaya who finished with ERAs that were ahead of their peripherals. The Tigers also stayed extremely healthy in 2006, something which is never a *fait accompli* when you're counting on so many young arms. On the other hand, the Tigers might well expect improvement from Jeremy Bonderman, Curtis Granderson, and possibly Placido Polanco, and there are scenarios under which Andrew Miller and perhaps even Cameron Maybin could become important parts of their 2007 story. Certainly, the Tigers will need a little bit of luck to win the championship, as will any team emerging from the American League bracket. But the job of a good general manager is to put his team in a position to get lucky. That's what Dave Dombrowski has done.

HITTERS

Sean Casey 1B   Bats: L   Throws: R   Height: 6′ 4″   Weight: 235   Born: July 2, 1974   Age: 32

YEAR	TEAM	LVL	AGE	PA	R	2B	3B	HR	RBI	BB	SO	SB	CS	SPEED	AVG	OBP	SLG	MLVR	EQAVG	EQOBP	EQSLG	EQA	VORP	DEFENSE
2004	CIN	MLB	30	633	101	44	2	24	99	46	36	2	0	4.7	.324	.381	.534	.326	.322	.378	.534	.307	55.9	139-1B -12
2005	CIN	MLB	31	587	75	32	0	9	58	48	48	2	0	4.3	.312	.371	.423	.126	.311	.372	.433	.282	22.6	130-1B 1
2006	PIT	MLB	32	244	30	15	0	3	29	23	22	0	0	3.9	.296	.377	.408	.069	.296	.377	.413	.279	5.5	52-1B -3
2006	DET	MLB	32	196	17	7	0	5	30	10	21	0	1	3.7	.245	.286	.364	-.221	.242	.291	.368	.228	-8.0	46-1B -2
2007	DET	MLB	32	429	50	21	1	7	46	31	41	1	1	4.4	.281	.337	.396	-.057	.278	.340	.404	.265	2.6	102-1B -3

Breakout: 4% Improve: 34% Collapse: 33% Attrition: 27%   Comparables: Hal Morris, Ed Kranepool, Larry Biittner, Dick Sisler

Casey made up for an uninspired stretch run with a strong postseason; he was one of the few Tigers to hit his weight in the World Series. The team likes his track record of professionalism and high on-base percentages, but the latter will be harder to come now that the Mayor is no longer playing his home games in hitters havens (though generally neutral, PNC Park is perhaps the most favorable environment for a left-handed line-drive hitter in the majors). The problem is not so much that Casey will be the starting first baseman in April—it's that he might retains his hold on the position while putting up numbers like the PECOTA line you see above.

Brent Clevlen OF   Bats: R   Throws: R   Height: 6′ 2″   Weight: 190   Born: October 27, 1983   Age: 23

YEAR	TEAM	LVL	AGE	PA	R	2B	3B	HR	RBI	BB	SO	SB	CS	SPEED	AVG	OBP	SLG	MLVR	EQAVG	EQOBP	EQSLG	EQA	VORP	DEFENSE
2004	LAK	A+	20	474	49	23	6	6	50	44	127	2	1	5.0	.223	.300	.349	-.097	.206	.266	.324	.210	-41.1	116-RF -12
2005	LAK	A+	21	568	77	28	4	18	102	65	118	14	5	4.9	.302	.387	.484	.240	.274	.346	.440	.271	13.0	128-RF 8
2006	ERI	AA	22	451	47	17	0	11	45	47	138	6	2	4.5	.230	.313	.357	-.049	.224	.299	.352	.232	-21.3	100-RF -1
2006	DET	MLB	22	42	9	1	2	3	6	2	15	0	0	7.2	.282	.317	.641	.270	.282	.317	.641	.302	4.0	
2007	DET	MLB	23	457	46	19	2	11	48	35	122	4	2	4.6	.237	.299	.375	-.183	.234	.302	.383	.242	-9.9	108-RF -1

Breakout: 32% Improve: 50% Collapse: 30% Attrition: 10%   Comparables: Hipolito Martinez, Jason Michaels, Jonathan Rivers, Mike Zywica

Brent Clevlen (pronounced like Cleveland without the D) is a tough nut to crack. He mauled the ball in 2005 and was named the Florida State League MVP, but started out 2006 hitting like Willie Mays Hayes, with just four home runs in his first three months at Erie. His bat finally came around in July, with a six-homer month that precipitated a successful big league call-up. Just to confuse matters further, he had an unusual .250/.384/.326 campaign in the Arizona Fall League, in which nearly half his plate appearances ended in walks or strikeouts. This may be nothing more than the natural ebb and flow of a player with an extremely high strikeout rate who is doing his damnedest to find an approach at the plate that works for him, but, for now, Clevlen projects as nothing more than a fourth outfielder.

David Espinosa RF   Bats: S   Throws: R   Height: 6′ 2″   Weight: 190   Born: December 16, 1981   Age: 25

YEAR	TEAM	LVL	AGE	PA	R	2B	3B	HR	RBI	BB	SO	SB	CS	SPEED	AVG	OBP	SLG	MLVR	EQAVG	EQOBP	EQSLG	EQA	VORP	DEFENSE	
2004	ERI	AA	22	603	89	23	5	19	52	80	134	20	7	6.2	.264	.366	.440	.076	.246	.336	.404	.259	-1.7	123-RF 0	
2005	ERI	AA	23	506	66	21	8	9	40	66	109	11	6	6.4	.262	.362	.411	.086	.248	.339	.390	.258	-3.1	84-RF -9	23-LF -3
2006	TOL	AAA	24	349	50	13	7	9	27	43	70	12	6	6.7	.266	.362	.451	.192	.279	.368	.485	.290	16.2	33-LF 2	
2007	DET	MLB	25	432	59	23	4	11	46	45	92	9	4	6.3	.259	.339	.430	-.024	.256	.342	.439	.276	6.8	103-RF -1	

Breakout: 21% Improve: 50% Collapse: 21% Attrition: 16%   Comparables: Brian Simmons, Cesar Crespo, Chip Ambres, Abraham Nunez

Espinosa was the high school shortstop and Scott Boras client who forsook a bonus to sign a major league contract with the Reds following the 2000 draft. Six years, one organization, and several position switches later, his bat has finally begun to come around; a .290 EqA in pitcher-friendly Toledo is no easy feat. He's not on the 40-man roster and will need a break to find playing time in Detroit, but some budget-conscious club such as the Marlins or Nationals could give him a big league trial, proving once again that freely-available talent is not extinct.

Alexis Gomez   OF   Bats: L   Throws: L   Height: 6′ 2″   Weight: 180   Born: August 6, 1980   Age: 28

YEAR	TEAM	LVL	AGE	PA	R	2B	3B	HR	RBI	BB	SO	SB	CS	SPEED	AVG	OBP	SLG	MLVR	EQAVG	EQOBP	EQSLG	EQA	VORP	DEFENSE			
2004	OMA	AAA	23	411	45	17	8	7	34	19	96	8	6	6.4	.251	.285	.392	-.202	.227	.261	.328	.209	-29.8	103-RF	-6		
2005	TOL	AAA	24	460	51	28	6	7	55	27	91	21	7	6.7	.307	.348	.450	.139	.302	.342	.436	.270	11.2	100-RF	-12		
2006	TOL	AAA	25	251	36	18	3	11	36	18	48	8	4	5.7	.288	.343	.540	.305	.288	.337	.546	.291	15.4	30-RF	1	20-CF	-2
2006	DET	MLB	25	111	17	5	2	1	6	6	21	4	0	7.5	.272	.318	.388	-.102	.275	.327	.392	.257	0.9	13-RF	-1	12-LF	2
2007	DET	MLB	28	422	49	21	3	9	44	23	89	12	5	5.8	.258	.300	.398	-.136	.255	.303	.406	.251	-3.5	100-RF	-2		

Breakout: 10%   Improve: 25%   Collapse: 37%   Attrition: 19%   Comparables: Reggie Taylor, Adam Shabala, Colin Porter, Lee Maye

Gomez used up 14 minutes of fame with a four-homer game at Toledo in August, and another 57 seconds with a four-RBI day in Game Two of the ALCS. The Tigers were not endeared enough to tender him a contract. Gomez's power has come around just a little bit, but his plate discipline hasn't, and his utility as a bench guy is limited because he's struggled whenever he's tried to play center field.

Curtis Granderson   CF   Bats: L   Throws: R   Height: 6′ 1″   Weight: 185   Born: March 16, 1981   Age: 26

YEAR	TEAM	LVL	AGE	PA	R	2B	3B	HR	RBI	BB	SO	SB	CS	SPEED	AVG	OBP	SLG	MLVR	EQAVG	EQOBP	EQSLG	EQA	VORP	DEFENSE	
2004	ERI	AA	23	553	89	19	8	21	94	80	95	14	8	6.1	.301	.405	.513	.260	.276	.368	.463	.284	34.7	121-CF	10
2004	DET	MLB	23	28	2	1	1	0	0	3	8	0	0	4.2	.240	.321	.360	-.134	.240	.321	.360	.240	-0.0		
2005	TOL	AAA	24	503	79	29	13	15	65	48	129	22	6	8.2	.290	.359	.515	.232	.288	.355	.498	.291	36.6	105-CF	11
2005	DET	MLB	24	174	18	6	3	8	20	10	43	1	1	5.4	.272	.314	.494	.083	.283	.337	.528	.285	7.7	36-CF	9
2006	DET	MLB	25	679	90	31	9	19	68	66	174	8	5	6.4	.260	.335	.438	-.012	.259	.341	.444	.269	22.7	147-CF	19
2007	DET	MLB	26	615	87	28	6	22	75	62	142	11	5	6.1	.264	.341	.459	.020	.261	.344	.469	.284	25.4	144-CF	10

Breakout: 19%   Improve: 47%   Collapse: 18%   Attrition: 2%   Comparables: Irv Noren, Ray Lankford, Rick Miller, Larry Doby

Granderson will have plenty of opportunities to outlive his slip-and-slide on the wet Busch Stadium turf in Game Four of the World Series, an incident that brought back memories of a similar misstep from Curt Flood 38 years earlier. Granderson actually profiles quite a bit like Flood, a player who was not a burner, but a natural in center field nevertheless. The more immediate concern is getting him to cut down on his strikeouts; they became a real problem during the stretch run and again in October as teams took advantage of his propensity to chase breaking pitches. At 26, Granderson has reached the age at which a player typically doesn't have a lot of development time left, but he comes from a northern state and an obscure college program (Illinois-Chicago), so he could be younger than that in baseball years. In the worst case scenario, he'll be the Tigers' version of Mike Cameron.

Carlos Guillen   SS   Bats: S   Throws: R   Height: 6′ 1″   Weight: 215   Born: September 30, 1975   Age: 31

YEAR	TEAM	LVL	AGE	PA	R	2B	3B	HR	RBI	BB	SO	SB	CS	SPEED	AVG	OBP	SLG	MLVR	EQAVG	EQOBP	EQSLG	EQA	VORP	DEFENSE	
2004	DET	MLB	28	583	97	37	10	20	97	52	87	12	5	6.7	.318	.379	.542	.278	.324	.390	.558	.314	63.9	132-SS	15
2005	DET	MLB	29	361	48	15	4	5	23	24	45	2	3	5.1	.320	.368	.434	.140	.331	.388	.456	.289	24.8	71-SS	2
2006	DET	MLB	30	622	100	41	5	19	85	71	87	20	9	6.0	.320	.400	.519	.274	.321	.408	.528	.314	66.3	138-SS	-11
2007	DET	MLB	31	567	90	39	3	18	73	53	79	12	4	5.8	.303	.371	.497	.155	.299	.374	.508	.306	48.7	133-SS	1

Breakout: 7%   Improve: 35%   Collapse: 27%   Attrition: 2%   Comparables: Roberto Alomar, Ken Boyer, Jackie Robinson, Barry Larkin

Guillen is perhaps the most underrated player in baseball, and the crown jewel of Dave Dombrowski's rebuilding job. Guillen's strength is his ability to take multiple approaches at the plate, taking power cuts early in an at-bat, choking up and leveraging his slap-hitting ability when behind in the count, and working a walk when ahead. The only catch is that he's lost a step in the field; note the 26-run decline in his fielding runs in the span of just two years. The feeling that Guillen's destined for first base might have been behind the team's decision to re-up Sean Casey for one year, rather than pursue a longer-term solution at the position.

Gorkys Hernandez   CF   Bats: R   Throws: R   Height: 6′ 0″   Weight: 175   Born: September 7, 1987   Age: 19

YEAR	TEAM	LVL	AGE	PA	R	2B	3B	HR	RBI	BB	SO	SB	CS	SPEED	AVG	OBP	SLG	MLVR	EQAVG	EQOBP	EQSLG	EQA	VORP	DEFENSE	
2006	TGR	Rk	18	217	41	9	2	5	23	10	27	20	4	7.5	.327	.356	.463	.270	.292	.313	.431	.259	18.2	49-CF	0
2007	DET	MLB	19	470	56	24	3	7	41	14	61	19	8	6.3	.279	.301	.393	-.125	.276	.304	.402	.250	4.0	111-CF	1

Breakout: 26%   Improve: 57%   Collapse: 13%   Attrition: 17%   Comparables: Warner Madrigal, Jason Pridie, James Tomlin, Jhensy Sandoval

Hernandez has not received the press clippings of the Mets' Fernando Martinez or the Yankees' Jose Tabata, but as barely legal outfielders go, he isn't far behind. Hernandez has everything it should take to become a .300 hitter in the big leagues: Outstanding hitting reflexes, speed that rates as a 70 or 75 on the scouting scale, and a relatively low strikeout rate. He could go in a couple of directions as a prospect, either improving his walk rate to the point that he becomes a viable lead-off hitter, or filling out and developing 15–20 home run power—or both, in which case we could be talking about the next Bobby Abreu.

| **Michael Hollimon** | | **SS** | | | | **Bats: S** | | **Throws: R** | | | Height: 6' 1" | | Weight: 185 | | Born: June 14, 1982 | | | Age: 25 | |

YEAR	TEAM	LVL	AGE	PA	R	2B	3B	HR	RBI	BB	SO	SB	CS	SPEED	AVG	OBP	SLG	MLVR	EQAVG	EQOBP	EQSLG	EQA	VORP	DEFENSE	
2005	ONE	A-	23	313	66	13	10	13	53	48	76	8	3	7.5	.277	.389	.559	.314	.204	.279	.366	.227	-9.7	67-SS	5
2006	WMI	A	24	537	69	29	13	15	54	77	124	19	5	6.5	.278	.386	.501	.297	.236	.312	.400	.249	10.2	123-SS	8
2007	DET	MLB	25	477	53	28	5	11	47	40	137	7	3	5.9	.229	.297	.395	-.167	.226	.299	.404	.248	5.8	113-SS	8

Breakout: 30%   Improve: 53%   Collapse: 17%   Attrition: 7%   Comparables: Blake Whealy, Rod Smith, Brooks Conrad, Darren Blakely

The dilemma that lower-round college picks face is that their biological clocks start ticking before they reach a level of competition sufficient to prove if they have big league upside. A sixteenth-round pick in 2005, Hollimon is the case in point: His raw numbers at West Michigan reveal a very interesting combination of power, speed, walks, and defense, but he'll be 25 next year without having spent a day above the Midwest League. Hollimon's amateur background is just as perplexing—he was a star prospect as a high schooler, but hit just .243 at the University of Texas before losing his starting job and transferring to Oral Roberts, where he put himself back on the radar with an excellent senior season. The Tigers need to skip him a level and start him at Erie this year to see if he has a future.

| **Omar Infante** | | **2B/SS** | | | | **Bats: R** | | **Throws: R** | | | Height: 6' 0" | | Weight: 180 | | Born: December 26, 1981 | | Age: 25 | | |

YEAR	TEAM	LVL	AGE	PA	R	2B	3B	HR	RBI	BB	SO	SB	CS	SPEED	AVG	OBP	SLG	MLVR	EQAVG	EQOBP	EQSLG	EQA	VORP	DEFENSE			
2004	DET	MLB	22	556	69	27	9	16	55	40	112	13	7	6.6	.264	.317	.449	-.024	.271	.328	.467	.269	18.2	98-2B	-5	20-SS	2
2005	DET	MLB	23	434	36	28	2	9	43	16	73	8	0	5.6	.222	.254	.367	-.242	.226	.268	.378	.228	-7.7	67-2B	-4	44-SS	4
2006	DET	MLB	24	245	35	11	4	4	25	14	45	3	2	6.2	.277	.325	.415	-.048	.275	.332	.423	.259	5.5	34-2B	2		
2007	DET	MLB	25	385	47	19	3	10	43	23	64	6	2	6.0	.264	.311	.423	-.078	.261	.314	.432	.262	10.1	92-2B	4		

Breakout: 23%   Improve: 52%   Collapse: 18%   Attrition: 24%   Comparables: Pat Kelly, Frank Bolling, Terry Shumpert, Luis Rivas

Infante seems to have gotten himself pigeonholed as a utility infielder, which reflects a failure to manage expectations following his premature promotion to the big leagues in 2003. His profile is not dissimilar to what Juan Uribe or Carlos Guillen looked like after their age-24 seasons, and, in the abstract, it's worth giving him a full season's worth of playing time to see if he can replicate their development. The trouble is that the price for that information is much higher for a team hoping to contend for a title. The Tigers have a lot of players in their system whose track records provoke this sort of cognitive dissonance.

| **Brandon Inge** | | **3B** | | | | **Bats: R** | | **Throws: R** | | | Height: 5' 11" | | Weight: 190 | | Born: May 19, 1977 | | | Age: 30 | |

YEAR	TEAM	LVL	AGE	PA	R	2B	3B	HR	RBI	BB	SO	SB	CS	SPEED	AVG	OBP	SLG	MLVR	EQAVG	EQOBP	EQSLG	EQA	VORP	DEFENSE			
2004	DET	MLB	27	458	43	15	7	13	64	32	72	5	4	5.6	.287	.340	.453	.037	.293	.348	.466	.277	15.0	61-3B	2	29-C	9
2005	DET	MLB	28	694	75	31	9	16	72	63	140	7	6	4.9	.261	.330	.419	-.004	.271	.349	.446	.272	13.3	158-3B	21		
2006	DET	MLB	29	601	83	29	2	27	83	43	128	7	4	5.3	.253	.313	.463	-.022	.252	.319	.470	.266	9.4	156-3B	22		
2007	DET	MLB	30	575	74	27	4	20	73	47	118	6	4	5.2	.261	.327	.444	-.026	.258	.330	.454	.273	15.4	135-3B	9		

Breakout: 16%   Improve: 38%   Collapse: 28%   Attrition: 6%   Comparables: Travis Fryman, Damion Easley, Aaron Boone, Randy Jackson

That the Tigers managed to sign Inge on the heels of a breakout season to an extension below-market rate (four years, $24 million) is a testament to the sense of loyalty engendered by the front office. Inge represents the Tigers in microcosm: A gamer who has sat out just five games over the past two seasons, a late-bloomer who converted from college shortstop to minor league catcher to major league third baseman without missing a beat, a defensive wizard whose glove went cold on him during the World Series, and an all-or-nothing hitter who swings for power first and asks questions later.

Kody Kirkland   3B   Bats: R   Throws: R   Height: 6' 4"   Weight: 200   Born: June 9, 1983   Age: 24

YEAR	TEAM	LVL	AGE	PA	R	2B	3B	HR	RBI	BB	SO	SB	CS	SPEED	AVG	OBP	SLG	MLVR	EQAVG	EQOBP	EQSLG	EQA	VORP	DEFENSE	
2004	WMI	A	21	529	50	30	11	10	61	15	149	6	8	5.4	.236	.276	.401	-.038	.213	.241	.345	.203	-26.7	119-3B	-6
2005	LAK	A+	22	497	78	24	9	16	65	36	102	12	3	7.2	.266	.342	.470	.129	.243	.303	.428	.250	10.4	120-3B	6
2006	ERI	AA	23	478	61	25	5	22	65	26	157	9	10	6.1	.217	.290	.453	.026	.217	.275	.447	.240	3.7	111-3B	-13
2007	DET	MLB	24	453	44	22	3	14	51	22	125	5	4	5.5	.222	.271	.385	-.232	.219	.273	.393	.231	-9.1	107-3B	-2

Breakout: 28% Improve: 48% Collapse: 36% Attrition: 9%   Comparables: Mike Hessman, Kelly Dransfeldt, Anthony Sanders, Justin Sherrod

Kody Kirkland is a name for a quarterback, not a baseball player, but that's the least of his concerns: The kid can't hit right-handed pitching. At Erie last year, Kirkland's line against righties was .190/.253/.366, with 117 strikeouts against 12 walks. Kirkland is a big, physical player with a great arm at third base, but unless he starts channeling the platoon splits of John Lowenstein instead of Mickey Klutts, he isn't going to make it.

Jeff Larish   1B   Bats: L   Throws: R   Height: 6' 2"   Weight: 200   Born: October 11, 1982   Age: 24

YEAR	TEAM	LVL	AGE	PA	R	2B	3B	HR	RBI	BB	SO	SB	CS	SPEED	AVG	OBP	SLG	MLVR	EQAVG	EQOBP	EQSLG	EQA	VORP	DEFENSE	
2005	ONE	A-	22	79	16	3	0	6	13	13	6	0	0	3.0	.297	.430	.625	.460	.214	.304	.414	.249	-2.5	16-1B	2
2006	LAK	A+	23	552	76	34	2	18	65	81	101	9	7	4.3	.258	.379	.460	.170	.231	.329	.413	.257	-0.7	131-1B	0
2007	DET	MLB	24	490	53	24	2	13	55	47	94	2	2	4.3	.235	.315	.390	-.136	.233	.318	.398	.253	-6.5	116-1B	2

Breakout: 21% Improve: 49% Collapse: 25% Attrition: 10%   Comparables: Eddy Furniss, Eric Munson, Dan Meier, Nick Leach

The phrase "Moneyball Player" has become a cliché, but, alas, it's an effective shorthand to describe Larish, who drew 78 walks in just 65 games in his sophomore year at Arizona State. Larish isn't considered a bad-body guy, but he's not athletic enough to have any defensive value. Drafted as a college senior, he's been old for his levels. PECOTA thinks his long swing and inability to make contact will limit him to an Eric Munson career path.

Cameron Maybin   CF   Bats: R   Throws: R   Height: 6' 3"   Weight: 200   Born: April 4, 1987   Age: 20

YEAR	TEAM	LVL	AGE	PA	R	2B	3B	HR	RBI	BB	SO	SB	CS	SPEED	AVG	OBP	SLG	MLVR	EQAVG	EQOBP	EQSLG	EQA	VORP	DEFENSE	
2006	WMI	A	19	445	59	20	6	9	69	50	116	27	7	7.1	.304	.387	.457	.265	.285	.347	.430	.272	19.4	87-CF	-1
2007	DET	MLB	20	500	65	25	4	11	45	35	127	15	6	6.2	.267	.321	.409	-.077	.264	.324	.418	.263	10.0	118-CF	2

Breakout: 30% Improve: 47% Collapse: 25% Attrition: 3%   Comparables: Delmon Young, Steve Moss, Gregor Blanco, Xavier Paul

Monster. Maybin's numbers, impressive enough on their own, become even more remarkable in the context of the pitcher-friendly Midwest League and the obscure North Carolina high school program that he emerged from, which didn't afford him much opportunity to play against tough competition. His physical tools are supreme, and he's shown an advanced capacity for pitch recognition, even if he sometimes can't help himself from swinging at the breaking ones. Center fielders with true 30-30 potential are fairly rare in today's game, but Maybin both looks and plays a little bit like Eric Davis.

Craig Monroe   OF   Bats: R   Throws: R   Height: 6' 1"   Weight: 205   Born: February 27, 1977   Age: 30

YEAR	TEAM	LVL	AGE	PA	R	2B	3B	HR	RBI	BB	SO	SB	CS	SPEED	AVG	OBP	SLG	MLVR	EQAVG	EQOBP	EQSLG	EQA	VORP	DEFENSE			
2004	DET	MLB	27	481	65	27	3	18	72	29	79	3	4	5.1	.293	.337	.488	.114	.300	.347	.507	.284	19.5	56-LF	-9	49-RF	3
2005	DET	MLB	28	623	69	30	3	20	89	40	95	8	3	5.0	.277	.322	.446	.036	.285	.339	.472	.278	17.1	71-RF	-3	57-LF	0
2006	DET	MLB	29	585	89	35	2	28	92	37	126	2	2	4.6	.255	.301	.482	-.012	.254	.308	.493	.267	8.6	104-LF	-1		
2007	DET	MLB	30	553	68	29	2	21	79	37	104	3	2	4.8	.265	.316	.458	-.022	.262	.319	.468	.272	9.9	130-LF	-2		

Breakout: 6% Improve: 36% Collapse: 33% Attrition: 7%   Comparables: Jeff Leonard, Gary Ward, Rip Repulski, Torii Hunter

The hundreds of outfielders who have been tagged with the Quadruple-A label would do well to look at Craig Monroe's career. Monroe didn't earn a big league job until the age of 26, and then only because he happened to be around on a 119-loss team. Nevertheless, he managed to become an important contributor on a pennant-winner, mashing five home runs in last year's playoffs. Monroe's play will come under greater scrutiny now that arbitration will make him more expensive; the truth is that the Tigers might have outgrown him.

Magglio Ordoñez RF Bats: R Throws: R Height: 6' 0" Weight: 215 Born: January 28, 1974 Age: 33

YEAR	TEAM	LVL	AGE	PA	R	2B	3B	HR	RBI	BB	SO	SB	CS	SPEED	AVG	OBP	SLG	MLVR	EQAVG	EQOBP	EQSLG	EQA	VORP		DEFENSE	
2004	CHA	MLB	30	222	32	8	2	9	37	16	22	0	2	4.8	.292	.351	.485	.092	.289	.351	.478	.278	8.3		43-RF	1
2005	DET	MLB	31	343	38	17	0	8	46	30	35	0	0	3.9	.302	.359	.436	.109	.311	.376	.462	.291	14.4		76-RF	-1
2006	DET	MLB	32	646	82	32	1	24	104	45	87	1	4	3.8	.298	.350	.477	.106	.299	.358	.485	.283	27.6		142-RF	-4
2007	DET	MLB	33	557	72	28	2	17	73	42	72	1	2	4.3	.291	.346	.453	.045	.288	.349	.463	.283	15.8		131-RF	-4

Breakout: 5% Improve: 38% Collapse: 25% Attrition: 8% Comparables: Andy Pafko, Carl Furillo, Jim Rice, Brian Jordan

This was pretty much the best-case scenario for Ordoñez: an excellent, healthy season that helped push his team toward the AL pennant, capped off by the most famous Tiger home run since Cecil Fielder hit number 50. Even so, the Tigers owe him $60 million over the next three seasons, an absurd amount even in an absurd market. Ordoñez has managed to endear himself to Tiger fans on the strength of that home run and the best baseball hair since Oscar Gamble, but the griping about his contract will resurface if he can't sustain this level of performance.

Neifi Perez 2B/SS Bats: S Throws: R Height: 6' 0" Weight: 195 Born: June 2, 1973 Age: 34

YEAR	TEAM	LVL	AGE	PA	R	2B	3B	HR	RBI	BB	SO	SB	CS	SPEED	AVG	OBP	SLG	MLVR	EQAVG	EQOBP	EQSLG	EQA	VORP	DEFENSE			
2004	SFN	MLB	31	353	28	12	1	2	33	21	35	0	1	3.9	.232	.276	.295	-.315	.220	.266	.279	.199	-14.4	49-SS	2	36-2B	-1
2004	CHN	MLB	31	67	12	5	0	2	6	3	6	1	0	5.0	.371	.400	.548	.385	.365	.394	.524	.311	8.6	14-SS	0		
2005	CHN	MLB	32	609	59	33	1	9	54	18	47	8	4	4.6	.274	.298	.383	-.094	.271	.297	.381	.235	6.6	120-SS	17	18-2B	-1
2006	CHN	MLB	33	246	27	13	1	2	24	5	21	0	1	4.6	.254	.266	.343	-.254	.246	.261	.331	.207	-7.6	37-2B	0	15-SS	-1
2006	DET	MLB	33	70	4	1	0	0	5	3	4	1	0	3.8	.200	.235	.215	-.554	.156	.206	.172	.154	-6.0	13-2B	2		
2007	DET	MLB	34	335	29	17	1	4	30	11	30	2	1	4.9	.247	.275	.342	-.265	.245	.277	.349	.220	-4.8	81-SS	1		

Breakout: 33% Improve: 56% Collapse: 23% Attrition: 35% Comparables: Tim Foli, Garry Templeton, Paul Popovich, Rafael Ramirez

Five years ago, the Neifi Perez comment space is where BP would have made some ill-considered joke about SARS, or e-coli, or David Gest. We've mellowed out now, and can admit that Perez's nifty glovework makes him a helpful guy to have around on the 25-man roster. The problem is that he and Ramon Santiago are redundant, and Omar Infante should be playing before either of them.

Josh Phelps DH Bats: R Throws: R Height: 6' 3" Weight: 225 Born: May 12, 1978 Age: 29

YEAR	TEAM	LVL	AGE	PA	R	2B	3B	HR	RBI	BB	SO	SB	CS	SPEED	AVG	OBP	SLG	MLVR	EQAVG	EQOBP	EQSLG	EQA	VORP		DEFENSE	
2004	TOR	MLB	26	321	38	13	2	12	51	18	73	0	0	4.5	.237	.296	.417	-.142	.235	.296	.422	.245	-2.9		11-1B	-1
2004	CLE	MLB	26	80	13	6	0	5	10	4	20	0	0	3.0	.303	.338	.579	.322	.303	.346	.605	.307	6.8			
2005	DUR	AAA	27	243	35	14	3	14	33	15	53	0	1	4.3	.270	.329	.550	.166	.240	.292	.471	.254	0.9		19-1B	-1
2005	TBA	MLB	27	177	21	10	0	5	26	12	48	0	0	3.3	.266	.328	.424	.009	.276	.345	.436	.271	4.6			
2006	TOL	AAA	28	522	60	26	3	24	90	38	124	6	1	4.5	.308	.370	.532	.354	.312	.365	.541	.303	43.2		87-1B	2
2007	NYA	MLB	29	478	54	24	2	20	74	28	121	2	1	4.1	.261	.312	.461	-.028	.259	.315	.466	.270	7.8		113-1B	-1

Breakout: 11% Improve: 31% Collapse: 39% Attrition: 10% Comparables: Bucky Jacobsen, Randy Ruiz, Adam Hyzdu, Izzy Alcantara

One of the bigger marketing flubs in the last quarter century was the McDLT, the McDonald's sandwich whose meat was packaged separately from its veggies. The gimmick backfired because the design required customers to actually examine the contents of the sandwich, at which point they discovered that the tomato, iceberg lettuce, and beef patty were all the same pallid shade of brown. Phelps is like a McDLT—the power's stayed hot, and the plate discipline's stayed cool. Put him in a styrofoam package, and he might satiate the Yankees for three months or so, but they'll be looking for Richie Sexson and a bottle of Tums by August.

Placido Polanco 2B Bats: R Throws: R Height: 5' 10" Weight: 195 Born: October 10, 1975 Age: 31

YEAR	TEAM	LVL	AGE	PA	R	2B	3B	HR	RBI	BB	SO	SB	CS	SPEED	AVG	OBP	SLG	MLVR	EQAVG	EQOBP	EQSLG	EQA	VORP	DEFENSE			
2004	PHI	MLB	28	555	74	21	0	17	55	27	39	7	4	4.9	.298	.345	.441	.077	.298	.342	.444	.270	24.7	108-2B	13	13-3B	1
2005	PHI	MLB	29	173	26	7	0	3	20	12	9	0	0	4.6	.316	.376	.418	.127	.310	.370	.418	.275	8.8	26-2B	3		
2005	DET	MLB	29	378	58	20	2	6	36	21	16	4	3	4.8	.338	.386	.461	.214	.352	.407	.485	.305	30.0	81-2B	-1		
2006	DET	MLB	30	495	58	18	1	4	52	17	27	1	2	4.3	.295	.329	.364	-.100	.296	.335	.371	.247	7.9	106-2B	7		
2007	DET	MLB	31	529	63	23	2	5	48	24	32	4	2	4.9	.295	.334	.381	-.071	.292	.337	.390	.260	13.8	124-2B	4		

Breakout: 9% Improve: 31% Collapse: 27% Attrition: 9% Comparables: Glenn Beckert, Mark Grudzielanek, Steve Sax, Felix Millan

(continued next page)

Placido Polanco (*continued*)

Polanco puts the ball in play more often than any hitter in the big leagues, so even a slight decline in foot speed could mean that he's on his way to a second career as the long-lost member of the Three Tenors. Unfortunately, that's exactly what appears to be happening: Polanco grounded into 18 double plays in just 110 games last season, he no longer steals bases, and his SPEED score has declined for three straight years. His outstanding defense and extremely low strikeout rate should buy him a couple of years as a league-average player, but the Tigers need to move him to the bottom of the order.

Ryan Raburn　　　　　　**2B**　　　　**Bats: R**　**Throws: R**　　Height: 6′ 0″　　Weight: 185　　Born: April 17, 1981　　　　Age: 26

YEAR	TEAM	LVL	AGE	PA	R	2B	3B	HR	RBI	BB	SO	SB	CS	SPEED	AVG	OBP	SLG	MLVR	EQAVG	EQOBP	EQSLG	EQA	VORP	DEFENSE			
2004	ERI	AA	23	422	66	29	4	16	63	47	96	3	0	5.3	.301	.390	.533	.262	.277	.354	.483	.284	30.0	93-2B	-4		
2005	TOL	AAA	24	524	62	22	4	19	64	45	109	8	3	4.9	.253	.323	.437	.028	.249	.315	.418	.253	11.5	96-2B	-4		
2006	TOL	AAA	25	512	68	29	4	20	79	51	120	16	4	5.6	.275	.352	.490	.238	.284	.355	.514	.293	27.4	73-LF	5	32-2B	-3
2007	DET	MLB	26	480	58	24	3	15	58	39	115	8	3	5.0	.252	.318	.424	-.074	.249	.321	.434	.266	8.1	113-2B	-1		

Breakout: 3%　Improve: 27%　Collapse: 30%　Attrition: 15%　　Comparables: *Chin-Feng Chen, Keith Ginter, Bruce Aven, Prentice Redman*

We've called Rip Van Raburn a sleeper before, but he's coming off a career-high .293 EqA at Toledo. Many players would be discouraged after being shuffled between third base, second base, and the outfield, but Rayburn has adapted reasonably well to each position. There are no particular scouting red flags concerning his bat, and while he's too old to have enormous upside, he could wind up somewhere between Rob Mackowiak and Todd Walker. That would be a heck of a return for the league minimum salary; the Tigers were both relieved and fortunate not to lose him in the Rule 5 draft.

Ivan Rodriguez　　　　　**C**　　　　　**Bats: R**　**Throws: R**　　Height: 5′ 9″　　Weight: 195　　Born: November 30, 1971　Age: 35

YEAR	TEAM	LVL	AGE	PA	R	2B	3B	HR	RBI	BB	SO	SB	CS	SPEED	AVG	OBP	SLG	MLVR	EQAVG	EQOBP	EQSLG	EQA	VORP	DEFENSE	
2004	DET	MLB	32	575	72	32	2	19	86	41	91	7	4	4.6	.334	.383	.510	.260	.340	.392	.526	.308	55.9	122-C	-5
2005	DET	MLB	33	525	71	33	5	14	50	11	93	7	3	5.9	.276	.290	.444	-.021	.284	.309	.466	.262	18.5	117-C	10
2006	DET	MLB	34	580	74	28	4	13	69	26	86	8	3	5.7	.300	.332	.437	.016	.299	.339	.445	.268	22.0	118-C	16
2007	DET	MLB	35	512	62	26	3	11	59	22	77	8	3	5.4	.286	.319	.420	-.050	.283	.322	.429	.264	15.1	121-C	5

Breakout: 4%　Improve: 25%　Collapse: 28%　Attrition: 15%　　Comparables: *Mike Heath, Steve Garvey, Bill Skowron, Vic Power*

Catchers do not age gracefully; the position takes too high a toll on their knees and backs. The one saving grace is that catching does not require a lot of mobility, so they can remain extremely valuable defensive players late into their careers. Rodriguez was well-deserving of his twelfth Gold Glove last year, limiting opposing base-stealers to 25 swipes in 51 tries and allowing only 4 passed balls while catching one of the harder-throwing staffs in baseball. His bat will never recover to 2004 levels, but if I-Rod is the fourth- or fifth-best player on your team, you can win a few pennants.

Chris Shelton　　　　　**1B**　　　　**Bats: R**　**Throws: R**　　Height: 6′ 0″　　Weight: 215　　Born: June 26, 1980　　　Age: 27

YEAR	TEAM	LVL	AGE	PA	R	2B	3B	HR	RBI	BB	SO	SB	CS	SPEED	AVG	OBP	SLG	MLVR	EQAVG	EQOBP	EQSLG	EQA	VORP	DEFENSE	
2004	TOL	AAA	24	73	5	2	0	0	7	10	13	0	0	2.6	.339	.425	.371	.172	.333	.419	.365	.291	4.4		
2004	DET	MLB	24	56	6	1	0	1	3	9	14	0	0	2.8	.196	.321	.283	-.240	.196	.333	.283	.234	-1.6		
2005	TOL	AAA	25	211	34	19	0	8	39	25	33	0	2	2.9	.331	.417	.569	.444	.310	.392	.527	.308	18.7	31-1B	0
2005	DET	MLB	25	431	61	22	3	18	59	34	87	0	0	3.9	.299	.360	.510	.210	.309	.377	.537	.306	28.1	83-1B	4
2006	DET	MLB	26	412	50	16	4	16	47	34	107	1	2	3.7	.273	.340	.466	.049	.271	.346	.469	.275	9.5	102-1B	0
2006	TOL	AAA	26	129	20	6	2	3	14	18	37	1	0	5.3	.266	.372	.440	.195	.279	.377	.477	.296	7.3	24-1B	0
2007	DET	MLB	27	523	68	25	3	21	73	56	117	2	1	4.1	.266	.349	.470	.049	.263	.352	.480	.290	16.2	123-1B	0

Breakout: 14%　Improve: 36%　Collapse: 28%　Attrition: 12%　　Comparables: *Deron Johnson, Pancho Herrera, Craig Wilson, Johnny Romano*

There's a working theory that Shelton's hot start—he hit .326/.404/.783 with 10 home runs in April—was the worst thing that could have happened to him. Shelton struck out in 26 percent of his plate appearances from May 1 onward, swinging at any breaking ball in the 313 area code. Although he'll be 27 next year, the organization regards him more as a prospect than a short-term fix, which means he might stay in the minors rather than sit on the bench as Sean Casey's platoon partner. The Tigers haven't given up on him, rather they want him to use the whole field and become a well-rounded hitter. It's worth remembering that Shelton's career minor league batting average is .327.

Scott Sizemore　　2B　　Bats: R　Throws: R　Height: 6' 0"　Weight: 185　Born: January 4, 1985　Age: 22

YEAR	TEAM	LVL	AGE	PA	R	2B	3B	HR	RBI	BB	SO	SB	CS	SPEED	AVG	OBP	SLG	MLVR	EQAVG	EQOBP	EQSLG	EQA	VORP	DEFENSE	
2006	ONE	A-	21	333	49	15	4	3	37	32	47	7	5	5.5	.327	.394	.435	.251	.282	.335	.393	.254	22.7	63-SS	-10
2007	DET	MLB	22	520	56	25	4	5	44	33	81	6	5	5.3	.257	.307	.361	-.174	.254	.310	.369	.241	4.7	122-SS	-9

Breakout: 18%　Improve: 40%　Collapse: 30%　Attrition: 6%　　Comparables: Josh Asanovich, Jason Bartlett, Chris Basak, Aaron Hill

Drafted out of Virginia Commonwealth with the expectation that he'd be a second baseman, Sizemore was played primarily at shortstop last year. While he wasn't clumsy out there, he lacks the raw range to project as a big leaguer at the position. As a second baseman, he'll need to get more out of his bat, but there's a reasonable chance that he could grow up to be Adam Kennedy.

Matt Stairs　　DH　　Bats: L　Throws: R　Height: 5' 9"　Weight: 215　Born: December 31, 1969　Age: 39

YEAR	TEAM	LVL	AGE	PA	R	2B	3B	HR	RBI	BB	SO	SB	CS	SPEED	AVG	OBP	SLG	MLVR	EQAVG	EQOBP	EQSLG	EQA	VORP	DEFENSE			
2004	KCA	MLB	36	496	48	21	3	18	66	49	92	1	0	3.8	.267	.345	.451	.074	.264	.347	.452	.275	18.7	51-RF	-3	27-1B	-4
2005	KCA	MLB	37	466	55	26	1	13	66	60	69	1	2	3.9	.275	.373	.444	.112	.280	.386	.460	.292	19.9	58-1B	-5	11-RF	-2
2006	KCA	MLB	38	261	31	14	0	8	32	31	52	0	0	3.8	.261	.352	.429	.000	.256	.356	.435	.275	5.6				
2006	TEX	MLB	38	88	6	4	0	3	11	6	22	0	0	3.4	.210	.273	.370	-.268	.200	.273	.350	.218	-3.5				
2006	DET	MLB	38	44	5	3	0	2	8	3	12	0	0	2.7	.244	.295	.463	-.063	.244	.311	.439	.255	0.3				
2007	TOR	MLB	39	363	44	18	1	13	49	39	76	1	1	3.9	.260	.344	.442	.001	.250	.340	.429	.272	6.2	87-DH			

Breakout: 8%　Improve: 25%　Collapse: 37%　Attrition: 39%　　Comparables: Ellis Burks, George Brett, Dave Bergman, Harmon Killebrew

The One-Ton Human Hamster Wheel is slowing to a stop. Stairs probably has 200 decent platoon at-bats left in his stick, but he's having more trouble drawing walks as his power fades; pitchers can challenge him without fear of reprisal. He's fully into the itinerant phase that often marks the end of an average player's career; the minor league deal he signed with the Blue Jays in December marks his fourth club since the July trading deadline.

Marcus Thames　　LF　　Bats: R　Throws: R　Height: 6' 2"　Weight: 220　Born: March 6, 1977　Age: 30

YEAR	TEAM	LVL	AGE	PA	R	2B	3B	HR	RBI	BB	SO	SB	CS	SPEED	AVG	OBP	SLG	MLVR	EQAVG	EQOBP	EQSLG	EQA	VORP	DEFENSE			
2004	TOL	AAA	27	274	57	21	1	24	59	33	40	4	1	5.3	.329	.410	.735	.644	.301	.377	.657	.329	34.8	60-RF	-10		
2004	DET	MLB	27	184	24	12	0	10	33	16	42	0	1	3.7	.255	.326	.509	.088	.262	.337	.518	.283	5.7	39-LF	0		
2005	TOL	AAA	28	314	53	18	3	22	56	41	59	4	1	4.9	.340	.427	.679	.622	.324	.401	.610	.330	37.7	31-LF	-2	23-RF	-5
2005	DET	MLB	28	118	11	2	0	7	16	9	38	0	0	3.6	.196	.263	.411	-.176	.200	.280	.419	.239	-2.9	17-LF	-1		
2006	DET	MLB	29	390	61	20	2	26	60	37	92	1	1	5.6	.256	.333	.549	.134	.253	.338	.561	.293	19.7	45-LF	-5		
2007	DET	MLB	30	452	64	21	2	27	73	49	98	1	1	4.6	.257	.342	.521	.098	.254	.345	.533	.298	21.6	107-LF	-3		

Breakout: 4%　Improve: 21%　Collapse: 43%　Attrition: 14%　　Comparables: Kevin Mitchell, Jose Canseco, Greg Luzinski, Franklin Stubbs

Though most of the work had been done in Toledo, Thames has been crushing the ball ever since joining the Tigers organization in 2004, so his major league "breakout" shouldn't be considered too much of a surprise. Indeed, it's now his uninspired performances of 2002 and 2003 that look like outliers, and those can perhaps be excused on account of his being with the Yankees, an organization that was never going to give him a chance. Thames really should be playing every day. The Tigers were uncomfortable trying him at first base in the heat of a pennant race, but that could change in 2007 after he's had an offseason to prepare.

Vance Wilson　　C　　Bats: R　Throws: R　Height: 5' 11"　Weight: 215　Born: March 17, 1973　Age: 34

YEAR	TEAM	LVL	AGE	PA	R	2B	3B	HR	RBI	BB	SO	SB	CS	SPEED	AVG	OBP	SLG	MLVR	EQAVG	EQOBP	EQSLG	EQA	VORP	DEFENSE	
2004	NYN	MLB	31	177	18	10	1	4	21	11	24	1	0	4.3	.274	.335	.427	.025	.278	.335	.430	.267	6.6	55-C	-5
2005	DET	MLB	32	173	18	4	0	3	19	11	26	0	0	3.7	.197	.275	.283	-.328	.200	.287	.300	.215	-6.6	46-C	-1
2006	DET	MLB	33	168	18	9	0	5	18	2	33	0	4	4.4	.283	.304	.441	-.044	.287	.312	.447	.248	1.7	44-C	3
2007	DET	MLB	34	261	26	12	1	6	30	11	46	1	1	4.3	.256	.299	.395	-.142	.254	.302	.404	.247	2.4	64-C	0

Breakout: 15%　Improve: 40%　Collapse: 30%　Attrition: 44%　　Comparables: Jerry McNertney, Matt Batts, Bill Haselman, Del Wilber

The Tigers took the unusual step of signing Wilson to a two-year contract extension in August, a sign of just how much his pitchers like throwing to him. He hits enough that the Tigers aren't tempted to push Ivan Rodriguez's playing time more than they really should, which has its own intangible benefits.

Dmitri Young　　　　**DH**　　**Bats: S**　**Throws: R**　　Height: 6′ 2″　　Weight: 220　　Born: October 11, 1973　　Age: 33

YEAR	TEAM	LVL	AGE	PA	R	2B	3B	HR	RBI	BB	SO	SB	CS	SPEED	AVG	OBP	SLG	MLVR	EQAVG	EQOBP	EQSLG	EQA	VORP	DEFENSE			
2004	DET	MLB	30	432	72	23	2	18	60	33	71	0	1	4.6	.272	.336	.481	.072	.279	.345	.501	.284	16.6	22-1B	0		
2005	DET	MLB	31	508	61	25	3	21	72	29	100	1	0	4.4	.271	.325	.471	.069	.279	.342	.499	.283	18.9	29-1B	0	16-LF	1
2006	DET	MLB	32	184	19	4	1	7	23	11	39	1	1	4.8	.250	.293	.407	-.141	.247	.299	.424	.246	-2.4				
2007	DET	MLB	33	352	43	19	1	12	50	24	71	1	1	4.4	.269	.322	.451	-.019	.266	.324	.461	.273	8.6	85-DH			

Breakout: 11%　Improve: 41%　Collapse: 28%　Attrition: 33%　　Comparables: David Segui, Rondell White, Jim Beauchamp, Lee Stevens

Young carried the Tigers during their troubled days of 2003, both on the field and as the public face of the franchise, so perhaps there's some karmic justice in the team's meteoric rise helping to bury his off-the-field problems in the sports pages. Those problems included an arrest and no-contest plea on domestic violence charges and a 30-day stint at the Betty Ford Center. The Tigers claimed that his September release was for performance reasons, but comments made by Sean Casey made it clear that Young wasn't ready to contribute 100 percent on the baseball field or in the clubhouse. The sad truth is that Young would have no trouble landing a major league job if he was still a .300 hitter, but with his personal issues on top of the usual age-related decline, he may be left to get his life sorted out without baseball.

PITCHERS

Jeremy Bonderman　　　　**Bats: R　Throws: R**　　　Height: 6′ 2″　　Weight: 220　　Born: October 28, 1982　　Age: 24

YEAR	TEAM	LVL	AGE	W	L	SV	G	GS	IP	H	BB	SO	HR	GB%	BABIP	STUFF	WHIP	ERA	PERA	EQERA	EQH9	EQBB9	EQSO9	EQHR9	VORP	WXRL
2004	DET	MLB	21	11	13	0	33	32	184	168	73	168	24	—	.286	24	1.31	4.89	4.25	4.60	7.8	3.2	7.5	1.0	26.3	4.20
2005	DET	MLB	22	14	13	0	29	29	189	199	57	145	21	48.4%	.313	20	1.35	4.57	3.97	4.77	9.2	2.7	6.7	0.9	19.8	3.95
2006	DET	MLB	23	14	8	0	34	34	214	214	64	202	18	50.6%	.323	35	1.30	4.08	3.28	4.22	9.0	2.5	8.0	0.7	39.8	5.33
2007	DET	MLB	24	14	9	0	32	32	211²	201	61	182	20	48.0%	.295	26	1.24	3.62	3.52	3.58	8.1	2.5	7.1	0.8	47.8	6.40

Breakout: 44%　Improve: 90%　Collapse: 2%　Attrition: 0%　　Comparables: Bill Gullickson, Jose Rijo, Jake Peavy, Bert Blyleven

Bonderman is as good a bet as any pitcher in the American League to win a Cy Young Award, provided that Johan Santana gets hit by a bus or something. His peripherals last year pointed toward an ERA in the low 3.00s, and opponents hit just .169 against his deadly slider, remarkable for a pitch that he throws as often as one third of the time. He's young, healthy, has been handled carefully, and his trends are improving; he just needs to settle down a bit. Hitters leading off innings hit .286/.315/.469 against Bonderman last year (versus the .249/.311/.382 compiled by subsequent batters), and he's struggled in the first inning. He's also had a couple of dugout temper tantrums following frustrating outings. The Tigers think that his new contract extension will calm him down. Even without it, natural maturation combined with some good luck should make him a very good pitcher for a very long time.

Roman Colon　　　　**Bats: R　Throws: R**　　　Height: 6′ 6″　　Weight: 225　　Born: August 13, 1979　　Age: 27

YEAR	TEAM	LVL	AGE	W	L	SV	G	GS	IP	H	BB	SO	HR	GB%	BABIP	STUFF	WHIP	ERA	PERA	EQERA	EQH9	EQBB9	EQSO9	EQHR9	VORP	WXRL
2004	RIC	AAA	24	4	1	0	51	0	74	72	22	64	4	—	.318	5	1.27	3.65	3.77	4.38	8.8	2.9	6.0	0.6	10.0	—
2004	ATL	MLB	24	2	1	0	18	0	19	18	8	15	0	—	.321	3	1.37	3.32	3.22	4.19	8.4	3.3	6.1	0.0	3.0	0.23
2005	ATL	MLB	25	1	5	0	23	4	44¹	47	14	30	10	48.3%	.278	-17	1.38	5.28	5.71	5.76	9.3	2.6	5.6	2.0	-0.9	0.21
2005	DET	MLB	25	1	1	0	12	3	25	35	7	17	7	54.4%	.337	-15	1.68	6.12	5.92	5.88	12.1	2.4	5.9	2.4	-1.2	0.03
2006	DET	MLB	26	2	0	1	20	1	38²	46	14	25	6	42.5%	.331	-9	1.55	4.88	4.86	4.81	10.5	3.0	5.5	1.1	5.1	0.13
2007	DET	MLB	27	4	4	2	38	6	75	83	24	47	11	46.0%	.299	-4	1.42	4.65	4.70	4.55	9.5	2.7	5.2	1.1	8.0	0.90

Breakout: 28%　Improve: 62%　Collapse: 15%　Attrition: 23%　　Comparables: Doug Brocail, Greg Hansell, J. J. Putz, Don Johnson

Colon had surgery in November to repair a herniated disk in his neck. That sounds scarier than it really is in baseball terms; he's expected to be back for the start of the season, though he might need extended spring training. On the mound, he's had trouble missing bats with his fastball, but there are 30 pitching coaches in the league who will tell you they can turn him into a plus reliever. His stature and overall approach are reminiscent of Antonio Alfonseca.

Eulogio de la Cruz   Bats: R   Throws: R   Height: 5' 11"   Weight: 175   Born: March 12, 1984   Age: 23

YEAR	TEAM	LVL	AGE	W	L	SV	G	GS	IP	H	BB	SO	HR	GB%	BABIP	STUFF	WHIP	ERA	PERA	EQERA	EQH9	EQBB9	EQSO9	EQHR9	VORP	WXRL
2004	WMI	A	20	2	4	17	54	0	54	51	33	44	2	—	.292	-11	1.56	3.83	5.94	6.62	9.4	7.1	4.4	0.7	-5.9	—
2005	LAK	A+	21	4	3	5	40	10	95²	66	36	97	5	58.4%	.250	3	1.07	3.39	4.83	5.54	7.6	4.4	6.0	0.9	0.6	—
2006	ERI	AA	22	5	6	2	38	12	105¹	103	45	87	3	56.1%	.324	8	1.41	3.43	4.12	4.60	8.9	4.2	5.1	0.4	11.7	—
2007	DET	MLB	23	3	5	0	27	10	75	86	42	45	9	52.0%	.313	-10	1.71	5.90	5.59	5.87	9.8	4.9	5.0	0.9	-4.4	0.00

Breakout: 10%   Improve: 36%   Collapse: 28%   Attrition: 7%   Comparables: Franklin Nunez, Nick Stocks, Jason Marquis, Juan Rincon

De la Cruz's strikeout numbers have been merely average, but it's not for lack of stuff. He gets rave reviews for three pitches—a heater that stays in the high-90s, as well as his curve and change—but he has had command problems. Sometimes pitchers like that have trouble leveraging their arsenal into Ks because they're often working from behind in the count. This profile would ordinarily be targeted for the bullpen, where it's easier to maintain consistent mechanics, but de la Cruz's numbers improved once he was moved to the rotation mid-season, and that's where he'll start 2007.

Jason Grilli   Bats: R   Throws: R   Height: 6' 5"   Weight: 225   Born: November 11, 1976   Age: 30

YEAR	TEAM	LVL	AGE	W	L	SV	G	GS	IP	H	BB	SO	HR	GB%	BABIP	STUFF	WHIP	ERA	PERA	EQERA	EQH9	EQBB9	EQSO9	EQHR9	VORP	WXRL
2004	CHR	AAA	27	9	9	0	25	25	152²	163	58	101	22	—	.295	-20	1.45	4.83	6.09	6.21	10.3	3.9	4.6	1.6	-10.1	—
2004	CHA	MLB	27	2	3	0	8	8	45	52	20	26	11	—	.293	-17	1.60	7.40	6.39	6.80	10.1	3.7	4.9	1.9	-5.9	-0.46
2005	TOL	AAA	28	12	9	0	28	28	167¹	170	58	120	21	51.7%	.294	-10	1.36	4.09	5.53	5.51	9.6	3.5	4.9	1.4	1.7	—
2005	DET	MLB	28	1	1	0	3	2	16	14	6	5	1	46.0%	.265	-10	1.25	3.38	4.52	3.78	7.6	3.2	2.7	0.5	4.2	0.35
2006	DET	MLB	29	2	3	0	51	0	62	61	25	31	6	49.3%	.279	-13	1.39	4.21	4.92	4.45	9.0	3.4	4.3	0.7	10.8	0.08
2007	DET	MLB	30	2	2	1	42	0	52²	57	22	32	7	46.0%	.296	-11	1.51	4.83	4.85	4.74	9.3	3.7	5.0	1.0	4.1	0.30

Breakout: 33%   Improve: 64%   Collapse: 16%   Attrition: 33%   Comparables: Randy Veres, Doug Brocail, Bob Lee, Mike DeJean

There's something to be said for a player like Grilli, the fourth overall pick in the 1997 draft, who has lived down the stigma of being a bust and pitched professionally for a decade. While Grilli's slider can freeze batters from time to time, there's not much else keeping him in the major leagues. He'll be fighting for a job in March.

Todd Jones   Bats: L   Throws: R   Height: 6' 3"   Weight: 230   Born: December 31, 1969   Age: 39

YEAR	TEAM	LVL	AGE	W	L	SV	G	GS	IP	H	BB	SO	HR	GB%	BABIP	STUFF	WHIP	ERA	PERA	EQERA	EQH9	EQBB9	EQSO9	EQHR9	VORP	WXRL
2004	PHI	MLB	36	3	3	1	27	0	25¹	35	8	22	3	—	.395	0	1.70	4.98	4.54	4.91	13.0	2.5	7.0	1.1	2.0	0.35
2004	CIN	MLB	36	8	2	1	51	0	57	49	25	37	4	—	.280	-2	1.30	3.79	4.11	3.68	7.4	3.5	5.1	0.6	9.9	3.13
2005	FLO	MLB	37	1	5	40	68	0	73	61	14	62	2	53.7%	.294	27	1.03	2.10	2.72	2.51	7.0	1.6	6.9	0.2	24.9	4.85
2006	DET	MLB	38	2	6	37	62	0	64	70	11	28	4	55.3%	.297	-5	1.27	3.94	3.74	4.57	9.8	1.5	3.7	0.6	12.2	2.30
2007	DET	MLB	39	3	4	17	46	0	53	60	12	28	4	49.0%	.306	-10	1.36	4.20	4.01	4.20	9.7	2.0	4.3	0.7	6.9	1.00

Breakout: 24%   Improve: 34%   Collapse: 42%   Attrition: 28%   Comparables: Dennis Lamp, Steve Reed, Terry Leach, Doug Jones

The theoretical benefit of Jones's approach, which involves avoiding walks and fly balls at all costs, is that it should prevent the multi-run innings that cost teams ballgames. In practice, Jones had eight outings in which he allowed two or more runs, six of which resulted in him taking the loss. With that said, Jones was much better in the second half after his hamstring quit bothering him, and the difference between his PERA (3.74) and Joel Zumaya's (3.38) was much less than their raw ERAs would indicate. He'll go into camp as the Tigers' closer and probably won't have to endure a spring training battle.

Jair Jurrjens   Bats: R   Throws: R   Height: 6' 1"   Weight: 160   Born: January 29, 1986   Age: 21

YEAR	TEAM	LVL	AGE	W	L	SV	G	GS	IP	H	BB	SO	HR	GB%	BABIP	STUFF	WHIP	ERA	PERA	EQERA	EQH9	EQBB9	EQSO9	EQHR9	VORP	WXRL
2004	ONE	A-	18	1	5	0	7	7	39	50	10	31	0	—	.382	8	1.54	5.31	4.06	7.15	11.8	3.0	3.7	0.2	-6.7	—
2005	WMI	A	19	12	6	0	26	26	142²	132	36	108	5	56.7%	.300	20	1.18	3.41	4.05	4.99	9.1	2.6	4.5	0.6	9.5	—
2006	LAK	A+	20	5	0	0	12	12	73²	53	10	59	4	54.8%	.239	20	0.86	2.09	4.01	3.62	7.5	1.4	4.8	0.9	15.8	—
2006	ERI	AA	20	4	3	0	12	12	67¹	71	21	53	7	51.7%	.327	2	1.37	3.35	5.44	4.68	9.9	3.1	4.9	1.5	6.9	—
2007	DET	MLB	21	7	8	0	27	21	128²	145	38	70	18	49.0%	.297	3	1.42	5.05	4.76	4.99	9.6	2.6	4.5	1.1	6.6	1.60

Breakout: 12%   Improve: 39%   Collapse: 19%   Attrition: 0%   Comparables: Edwin Gonzalez, Ronald Bay, Dustin Moseley, Mike Kusiewicz

A Curacao product who represented the Dutch in the World Baseball Classic, Jurrjens has moved through the system quickly by attacking the strike zone, relying on a low-90s fastball that moves well and generates its share of ground balls. He's not really a stuff guy, and his PECOTA comps consist mostly of guys who got caught up to by the time they reached the majors, but his youth should give him time to work on his secondary pitches and perhaps emerge as a number-four starter.

Wil Ledezma
Bats: L Throws: L   Height: 6' 4"   Weight: 210   Born: January 21, 1981   Age: 26

YEAR	TEAM	LVL	AGE	W	L	SV	G	GS	IP	H	BB	SO	HR	GB%	BABIP	STUFF	WHIP	ERA	PERA	EQERA	EQH9	EQBB9	EQSO9	EQHR9	VORP	WXRL
2004	ERI	AA	23	10	3	0	17	16	111²	95	24	98	8	—	.276	18	1.07	2.42	4.05	3.43	8.2	2.1	5.5	0.9	26.6	—
2004	DET	MLB	23	4	3	0	15	8	53¹	55	18	29	3	—	.306	4	1.37	4.39	3.87	4.39	8.6	2.8	4.6	0.5	9.1	0.98
2005	TOL	AAA	24	5	3	0	11	10	51	52	27	44	3	46.5%	.320	10	1.55	5.29	4.50	5.86	9.4	5.2	6.0	0.7	-1.5	—
2005	DET	MLB	24	2	4	0	10	10	49²	61	24	30	10	44.4%	.317	-18	1.71	7.06	6.05	8.29	10.8	4.2	5.3	1.8	-14.4	-0.79
2006	TOL	AAA	25	4	3	0	12	12	71²	60	23	66	6	39.4%	.295	12	1.17	2.53	4.71	3.75	8.5	3.1	6.5	1.2	14.3	—
2006	DET	MLB	25	3	3	0	24	7	60¹	60	23	39	5	36.0%	.286	2	1.38	3.58	4.14	4.11	9.0	3.2	5.4	0.7	12.6	1.00
2007	DET	MLB	26	5	6	1	40	12	91²	99	36	60	12	42.0%	.298	-4	1.48	5.03	4.80	4.93	9.2	3.4	5.5	1.0	5.3	0.90

Breakout: 15% Improve: 42% Collapse: 22% Attrition: 10%   Comparables: Jeremy Affeldt, Chris Haney, Chris Nabholz, Ross Baumgarten

Ledezma throws hard enough for a left-handed pitcher, but he's really at his best when he's not trying to blow the ball by people and instead focuses on changing speeds and getting strikeouts of the caught-looking variety. There are ample signs that he can accomplish that better as a relief pitcher—he had a fairly large starter-reliever ERA split last year (4.29 versus 2.55), and when he did start, he lost effectiveness after the 30th pitch. If the Tigers' give him the left-handed setup job vacated by Jamie Walker, Ledezma should beat his PECOTA, perhaps by a good margin.

Mike Maroth
Bats: L Throws: L   Height: 6' 0"   Weight: 190   Born: August 17, 1977   Age: 29

YEAR	TEAM	LVL	AGE	W	L	SV	G	GS	IP	H	BB	SO	HR	GB%	BABIP	STUFF	WHIP	ERA	PERA	EQERA	EQH9	EQBB9	EQSO9	EQHR9	VORP	WXRL
2004	DET	MLB	26	11	13	0	33	33	217	244	59	108	25	—	.307	4	1.40	4.31	4.41	4.27	9.4	2.2	4.1	0.9	39.3	5.23
2005	DET	MLB	27	14	14	0	34	34	209	235	51	115	30	48.1%	.306	-1	1.37	4.74	4.73	5.32	9.9	2.2	4.8	1.2	10.0	1.98
2006	DET	MLB	28	5	2	0	13	9	53²	64	16	24	11	42.0%	.291	-18	1.49	4.19	5.67	4.45	10.5	2.5	3.8	1.6	10.0	1.44
2007	DET	MLB	29	6	7	0	34	16	108²	127	31	55	15	46.0%	.302	-7	1.46	4.94	4.93	4.83	10.0	2.5	4.2	1.1	7.5	1.40

Breakout: 14% Improve: 45% Collapse: 23% Attrition: 9%   Comparables: John Cerutti, Greg Hibbard, Curt Young, Bud Daley

Even in an environment that's forgiving to finesse pitchers, Maroth's strikeout rate is hitting an intolerably low level, especially when coupled with his elbow problems. There's been some speculation that the Tigers will trade him if he gets off to a hot and healthy start. That strikes us as a good idea; few of his PECOTA comparables had much to contribute after their 30th birthday.

Andrew Miller
Bats: R Throws: L   Height: 6' 6"   Weight: 210   Born: November 30, 1999   Age: 22

YEAR	TEAM	LVL	AGE	W	L	SV	G	GS	IP	H	BB	SO	HR	GB%	BABIP	STUFF	WHIP	ERA	PERA	EQERA	EQH9	EQBB9	EQSO9	EQHR9	VORP	WXRL
2006	DET	MLB	0	0	1	0	8	0	10¹	8	10	6	0	69.7%	.242	-5	1.74	6.12	6.34	6.97	7.8	8.7	5.2	0.0	-2.0	-0.04
2007	DET	MLB	22	2	3	1	35	3	50	45	38	39	2	64.0%	.294	-3	1.65	4.82	4.43	4.96	7.8	6.5	6.5	0.3	2.7	0.30

Breakout: 48% Improve: 65% Collapse: 10% Attrition: 37%   Comparables: Dave Cole, Dennis Blair, Tommie Sisk, Gil Meche

Miller is a six-foot-six-inch lefty who can hit the upper-90s on radar guns. Detroit offered above-slot money in order to get him signed, and he was retiring big league hitters by Labor Day. He leverages his height extremely well, throwing in on batters' hands so effectively he generated a 22:3 groundball-to-flyball ratio in his time with the Tigers. Nevertheless, he isn't quite a finished product; his walk rate was relatively high at North Carolina (4.1 per nine innings), something that carried over into his major league trial, and he lacks an effective third pitch. The upside here is along the lines of a left-handed Carlos Zambrano. Last year's bullpen stint notwithstanding, the next time Miller pitches in the major leagues it will be as a starter. The Tigers are unlikely to press him to compete for a job in spring training, but the stretch run could be another story.

Zach Miner
Bats: R Throws: R   Height: 6' 3"   Weight: 200   Born: March 12, 1982   Age: 25

YEAR	TEAM	LVL	AGE	W	L	SV	G	GS	IP	H	BB	SO	HR	GB%	BABIP	STUFF	WHIP	ERA	PERA	EQERA	EQH9	EQBB9	EQSO9	EQHR9	VORP	WXRL
2004	GRN	AA	22	6	10	0	27	22	129¹	132	55	111	14	—	.316	-15	1.45	5.22	5.74	7.18	9.9	4.1	5.1	1.4	-22.2	—
2005	RIC	AAA	23	2	7	0	17	17	89¹	97	45	63	6	51.4%	.320	7	1.59	4.23	4.78	4.87	10.0	4.9	5.0	0.7	7.2	—
2005	TOL	AAA	23	3	1	0	6	6	34¹	28	20	20	4	59.0%	.245	1	1.40	2.36	6.52	3.21	7.8	5.6	4.3	1.3	8.9	—
2006	TOL	AAA	24	6	0	0	9	9	51²	43	21	40	2	57.9%	.287	12	1.25	2.81	4.09	4.26	8.0	3.9	5.5	0.5	7.5	—
2006	DET	MLB	24	7	6	0	27	16	93	100	32	59	11	49.2%	.305	-1	1.42	4.84	4.30	5.04	9.5	2.9	5.4	1.0	9.6	1.51
2007	DET	MLB	25	7	8	1	39	19	121¹	130	51	79	14	49.0%	.300	-1	1.49	4.88	4.69	4.84	9.2	3.7	5.4	0.9	8.8	1.60

Breakout: 28% Improve: 60% Collapse: 15% Attrition: 6%   Comparables: Charlie Lea, Jerry Johnson, Bill Gogolewski, Brian Williams

One of an increasing number of good arms that got away from the Braves organization, Miner brought back memories of Mark Fidrych with a six-start win streak in June and July before faring less impressively his second time through the league. He pitches older than his age, relying heavily on his change and throwing an awful lot of pitches in the dirt, something which his opponents might have caught onto in his scouting reports. He should have a good five-year run as a number-four starter.

Nate Robertson Bats: R Throws: L   Height: 6' 2" Weight: 225 Born: September 3, 1977   Age: 29

YEAR	TEAM	LVL	AGE	W	L	SV	G	GS	IP	H	BB	SO	HR	GB%	BABIP	STUFF	WHIP	ERA	PERA	EQERA	EQH9	EQBB9	EQSO9	EQHR9	VORP	WXRL
2004	DET	MLB	26	12	10	1	34	32	196²	210	66	155	30	—	.302	9	1.39	4.90	4.41	4.90	9.0	2.7	6.5	1.2	21.4	3.68
2005	DET	MLB	27	7	16	0	32	32	196²	202	65	122	28	52.7%	.285	1	1.36	4.48	4.85	5.17	9.0	2.9	5.4	1.2	13.3	3.32
2006	DET	MLB	28	13	13	0	32	32	208²	206	67	137	29	48.2%	.281	7	1.31	3.84	4.65	4.13	8.9	2.7	5.6	1.1	42.4	5.61
2007	*DET*	*MLB*	*29*	*12*	*10*	*0*	*30*	*30*	*193*	*202*	*63*	*127*	*22*	*48.0%*	*.294*	*11*	*1.37*	*4.34*	*4.28*	*4.28*	*8.9*	*2.8*	*5.5*	*0.9*	*27.1*	*4.20*

Breakout: 19% Improve: 71% Collapse: 2%   Attrition: 0%   Comparables: Kenny Rogers, Gary Peters, Atlee Hammaker, Brian Bohanon

PECOTA reckons Kenny Rogers as a good comparable for Robertson. Neither pitcher is without his stuff, but each depends heavily on pitch selection and a philosophy of staying within their limits on the mound. Both are partial to their foreign substances, Rogers his pine tar and Robertson his Big League Chew—he stuffs fistfuls into his mouth at a time in a ritualized attempt to instigate Tiger rallies. Robertson's ERA was a little ahead of his peripherals last season, but he's a legitimate number-three starter.

Fernando Rodney Bats: R Throws: R   Height: 5' 11" Weight: 220 Born: March 18, 1977   Age: 30

YEAR	TEAM	LVL	AGE	W	L	SV	G	GS	IP	H	BB	SO	HR	GB%	BABIP	STUFF	WHIP	ERA	PERA	EQERA	EQH9	EQBB9	EQSO9	EQHR9	VORP	WXRL
2005	DET	MLB	28	2	3	9	39	0	44	39	17	42	5	40.2%	.291	14	1.27	2.86	4.03	3.02	7.9	3.4	8.5	1.0	13.9	0.73
2006	DET	MLB	29	7	4	7	63	0	71²	51	34	65	6	57.9%	.238	13	1.19	3.51	4.34	4.25	6.8	4.0	7.8	0.6	12.3	2.22
2007	*DET*	*MLB*	*30*	*3*	*3*	*5*	*55*	*0*	*64*	*61*	*27*	*57*	*6*	*50.0%*	*.296*	*6*	*1.36*	*3.84*	*3.90*	*3.80*	*8.1*	*3.6*	*7.4*	*0.8*	*13.0*	*1.20*

Breakout: 22% Improve: 60% Collapse: 13% Attrition: 10%   Comparables: Darren Holmes, Steve Farr, Doug Bair, Jim Mecir

Rodney is one of the few big league pitchers who both hits the upper-90s and relies heavily on a changeup. When he's outguessing his opponents, he can make them look even more foolish than they do against Justin Verlander or Joel Zumaya. His changeup breaks a fair bit, which leads to intermittent walk problems, but he has learned not to put it in places where it might wind up traveling 400 feet. Rodney is older than you'd think, having lost four years to a falsified birth certificate, but his best days may nevertheless be ahead of him.

Kenny Rogers Bats: L Throws: L   Height: 6' 1" Weight: 190 Born: December 31, 1969   Age: 42

YEAR	TEAM	LVL	AGE	W	L	SV	G	GS	IP	H	BB	SO	HR	GB%	BABIP	STUFF	WHIP	ERA	PERA	EQERA	EQH9	EQBB9	EQSO9	EQHR9	VORP	WXRL
2004	TEX	MLB	39	18	9	0	35	35	211²	248	66	126	24	—	.321	10	1.48	4.76	4.27	4.17	9.8	2.5	4.9	0.9	34.2	3.66
2005	TEX	MLB	40	14	8	0	30	30	195¹	205	53	87	15	46.8%	.291	11	1.32	3.46	4.18	3.29	8.5	2.4	3.8	0.6	41.4	3.97
2006	DET	MLB	41	17	8	0	34	33	204	195	62	99	23	50.5%	.265	3	1.26	3.84	4.68	4.27	8.6	2.6	4.1	0.9	40.6	5.24
2007	*DET*	*MLB*	*42*	*9*	*11*	*0*	*41*	*25*	*170¹*	*201*	*51*	*77*	*20*	*48.0%*	*.304*	*-10*	*1.48*	*4.86*	*4.84*	*4.79*	*10.1*	*2.6*	*3.8*	*1.0*	*11.9*	*2.40*

Breakout: 0% Improve: 12% Collapse: 36% Attrition: 13%   Comparables: Warren Spahn, Jamie Moyer, Don Sutton, Jerry Koosman

The Tigers couldn't get the World Series back to Detroit, so we never did get to see how Rogers would perform in his first start in the post-smudgegate universe. He's had some fairly profound home-road splits for a long time, not just as a Tiger, but also in places such as Texas and Minnesota where the home park would ordinarily work against a pitcher. We don't mean to make too much of the pine tar issues, but when coupled with his age and his very low strikeout numbers, they suggest that he's likely to flame out at some point this season.

Humberto Sanchez   Bats: R   Throws: R

Height: 6' 6"   Weight: 230   Born: May 28, 1983   Age: 24

YEAR	TEAM	LVL	AGE	W	L	SV	G	GS	IP	H	BB	SO	HR	GB%	BABIP	STUFF	WHIP	ERA	PERA	EQERA	EQH9	EQBB9	EQSO9	EQHR9	VORP	WXRL
2004	LAK	A+	21	7	11	0	19	19	105¹	103	51	115	9	—	.333	-3	1.46	5.21	5.82	7.02	10.1	5.1	6.8	1.6	-16.0	—
2005	ERI	AA	22	3	5	0	15	11	64²	72	27	65	10	49.2%	.346	-12	1.53	5.56	6.16	6.54	10.7	4.4	6.3	2.0	-6.6	—
2006	ERI	AA	23	5	3	0	11	11	71	47	27	86	2	51.8%	.281	34	1.04	1.77	3.63	2.97	6.7	3.9	7.4	0.4	20.4	—
2006	TOL	AAA	23	5	3	0	9	9	51¹	50	20	43	2	41.1%	.327	12	1.37	3.87	4.16	5.19	9.5	3.8	5.9	0.5	2.3	—
2007	NYA	MLB	24	6	7	0	26	19	111	122	56	82	17	46.0%	.306	3	1.60	5.64	5.44	5.41	9.7	4.3	6.2	1.3	-1.0	0.70

Breakout: 19%   Improve: 45%   Collapse: 18%   Attrition: 0%   Comparables: Clint Nageotte, Jason Young, John Sneed, Kurt Ainsworth

Sanchez is probably an overrated prospect. He has never thrown more than 123 innings in a season, and he missed the last two months of 2006 with an inflamed elbow. His large frame raises questions about his conditioning. Let's stop being polite: The kid is fat. Both his fastball and his curve are major-league ready, and he turned in one of the most impressive performances of last year's Futures Game, but the Yankees would be smarter to convert him to relief than to hope he's the second coming of Bartolo Colon.

Jordan Tata   Bats: R   Throws: R

Height: 6' 6"   Weight: 220   Born: September 20, 1981   Age: 25

YEAR	TEAM	LVL	AGE	W	L	SV	G	GS	IP	H	BB	SO	HR	GB%	BABIP	STUFF	WHIP	ERA	PERA	EQERA	EQH9	EQBB9	EQSO9	EQHR9	VORP	WXRL
2004	WMI	A	22	8	11	0	28	28	166¹	167	68	116	7	—	.311	-5	1.41	3.36	5.70	6.11	10.0	5.1	3.4	0.8	-9.0	—
2005	LAK	A+	23	13	2	0	25	25	155	138	41	134	12	51.2%	.292	-8	1.15	2.79	5.56	4.74	9.7	3.3	4.7	1.4	14.0	—
2006	TOL	AAA	24	10	6	0	21	21	122²	117	49	86	11	46.4%	.288	-8	1.36	3.83	5.50	5.53	9.4	3.9	4.9	1.3	0.9	—
2006	DET	MLB	24	0	0	0	8	0	14²	14	7	6	1	46.0%	.265	-24	1.43	6.12	4.60	6.60	8.4	4.2	3.6	0.6	-1.0	0.13
2007	DET	MLB	25	5	7	0	34	14	101²	120	47	54	14	48.0%	.306	-11	1.64	5.73	5.61	5.62	10.1	4.0	4.4	1.1	-2.9	0.30

Breakout: 14%   Improve: 46%   Collapse: 14%   Attrition: 0%   Comparables: Josh Karp, Jason Standridge, Steve Watkins, Jason Young

One of the few finesse pitchers in the system, Tata throws a knucklecurve and an 88- to 92-MPH fastball with good downward break. The catch is that his walk rates are fairly high in spite of his ability to locate. It may be that his lack of an outpitch is forcing him to work around minor league hitters, which isn't a positive developmental sign. He also fatigues easily, posting a 5.16 ERA from the fourth inning onward. Add that all up, and Tata will probably need to develop a third pitch to find success in the major leagues.

Dallas Trahern   Bats: R   Throws: R

Height: 6' 3"   Weight: 190   Born: November 29, 1985   Age: 21

YEAR	TEAM	LVL	AGE	W	L	SV	G	GS	IP	H	BB	SO	HR	GB%	BABIP	STUFF	WHIP	ERA	PERA	EQERA	EQH9	EQBB9	EQSO9	EQHR9	VORP	WXRL
2005	WMI	A	19	7	11	0	26	26	156	158	50	66	9	62.8%	.286	-8	1.33	3.58	5.46	5.96	9.8	3.2	2.6	1.0	-6.2	—
2006	LAK	A+	20	6	11	0	25	25	144¹	129	41	86	9	65.7%	.269	-2	1.18	3.31	5.38	5.09	9.0	3.0	3.6	1.0	8.0	—
2007	DET	MLB	21	6	9	0	28	20	123	143	46	51	14	57.0%	.299	-7	1.53	5.43	5.04	5.44	9.9	3.2	3.4	0.9	-0.8	0.80

Breakout: 8%   Improve: 44%   Collapse: 15%   Attrition: 1%   Comparables: Brandon League, Sergio Mitre, Mitch Talbot, Denny Bautista

Trahern is very young, and he does everything well except generate strikeouts, compensating by locating his sinking fastball to produce lots of ground balls. The odds are against any pitcher with this kind of strikeout rate, but there's some positive precedent in Jon Garland, who had similar numbers and a similar approach.

Justin Verlander   Bats: R   Throws: R

Height: 6' 5"   Weight: 200   Born: February 20, 1983   Age: 24

YEAR	TEAM	LVL	AGE	W	L	SV	G	GS	IP	H	BB	SO	HR	GB%	BABIP	STUFF	WHIP	ERA	PERA	EQERA	EQH9	EQBB9	EQSO9	EQHR9	VORP	WXRL
2005	LAK	A+	22	9	2	0	13	13	86	70	19	104	3	45.7%	.338	31	1.03	1.67	3.71	2.96	9.1	2.6	6.9	0.7	24.1	—
2005	ERI	AA	22	2	0	0	7	7	32²	11	7	32	1	43.4%	.135	30	0.55	0.28	3.26	0.84	3.4	2.2	6.2	0.3	16.9	—
2005	DET	MLB	22	0	2	0	2	2	11¹	15	5	7	1	48.8%	.350	0	1.76	7.17	4.58	6.94	11.6	3.9	5.4	0.8	-2.0	-0.13
2006	DET	MLB	23	17	9	0	30	30	186	187	60	124	21	42.7%	.297	14	1.33	3.63	4.27	3.77	9.0	2.8	5.7	0.9	47.5	6.15
2007	DET	MLB	24	11	9	0	29	29	177²	183	59	128	22	44.0%	.294	15	1.36	4.28	4.31	4.19	8.8	2.9	6.0	1.0	26.8	4.10

Breakout: 9%   Improve: 27%   Collapse: 36%   Attrition: 2%   Comparables: Bob Rush, Don Aase, Kevin Millwood, Stan Bahnsen

Verlander is something of an enigma. He can hit triple digits on the radar gun, but his strikeout rate was about league average. He was 23 last year, but pitched with a veteran's savvy. His mechanics are well-regarded, but there were times, such as his World Series start against the Cardinals, when it looked like he was pitching uphill. His 17–9 record and 3.63 ERA probably overstate his ability to some extent, but he's adept at pitching to the situation, with his strikeout rate going way up with runners in scoring position. Postseason included, Verlander threw nearly 60 percent more innings in 2006 than in his pro debut in 2005 and looked tired toward the end of the year, particularly in the playoffs. There are arguments for doing something creative with him this year, such as using him out of the bullpen for a month at the start of the season. At the very least, the Tigers need to err on the side of caution, because his arm is much too valuable to put in any long-term jeopardy.

Jamie Walker   Bats: L   Throws: L   Height: 6' 2"   Weight: 185   Born: July 1, 1971   Age: 35

YEAR	TEAM	LVL	AGE	W	L	SV	G	GS	IP	H	BB	SO	HR	GB%	BABIP	STUFF	WHIP	ERA	PERA	EQERA	EQH9	EQBB9	EQSO9	EQHR9	VORP	WXRL
2004	DET	MLB	33	3	4	1	70	0	64²	69	12	53	8	—	.307	9	1.27	3.20	3.58	3.65	9.0	1.5	6.8	0.9	16.5	-0.12
2005	DET	MLB	34	4	3	0	66	0	48²	49	13	30	5	43.5%	.282	-4	1.27	3.70	4.18	4.14	8.8	2.3	5.4	0.9	8.9	1.11
2006	DET	MLB	35	0	1	0	56	0	48	47	8	37	8	33.3%	.275	5	1.15	2.81	4.08	2.77	8.7	1.5	6.5	1.3	17.5	0.75
2007	BAL	MLB	35	2	2	3	54	0	51²	58	10	39	8	38.0%	.309	0	1.32	4.32	4.29	3.92	10.2	1.7	6.3	1.3	7.9	0.70
Breakout: 15%	*Improve: 32%*	*Collapse: 50%*	*Attrition: 17%*						*Comparables: Alan Embree, Bob Patterson, Joe Hoerner, Bob Wells*																

Walker's major fault is giving up the home run ball, which usually happens when he's behind in the count and has to attack the batter with his mediocre fastball. He's been lucky on that front; the eight home runs he gave up in 2006 resulted in just nine RBI, the primary reason that his ERA ran well ahead of his PERA. The Tigers got a heck of a lot of value out of Walker, who was signed as a minor league free agent five years ago, but they made a good decision not to match the Orioles' three-year, $11-million offer.

Kevin Whelan   Bats: R   Throws: R   Height: 6' 0"   Weight: 200   Born: January 8, 1984   Age: 23

YEAR	TEAM	LVL	AGE	W	L	SV	G	GS	IP	H	BB	SO	HR	GB%	BABIP	STUFF	WHIP	ERA	PERA	EQERA	EQH9	EQBB9	EQSO9	EQHR9	VORP	WXRL
2006	LAK	A+	22	4	1	27	51	0	54²	33	29	69	1	37.7%	.278	18	1.14	2.66	4.09	4.18	6.8	5.9	7.5	0.3	8.2	—
2007	NYA	MLB	23	3	3	1	25	5	53¹	48	36	50	7	37.0%	.280	5	1.58	4.87	4.81	4.64	8.0	5.8	7.9	1.1	4.4	0.60
Breakout: 14%	*Improve: 25%*	*Collapse: 41%*	*Attrition: 19%*						*Comparables: Joe Valentine, Eric Cammack, P. J. Bevis, Brian Bruney*																

One of the three pitching prospects dealt to the Yankees in the Gary Sheffield trade, Whelan began his career at Texas A&M as a catcher before showing off his 96-MPH heat in summer league competition and eventually becoming the team's closer. His strikeout rates have been tremendous, and he's allowed just two homers in his minor league career on the strength of his tough splitter, though he leaves his fastball up in the zone enough that he grades out as a fly ball pitcher. His command needs work and his stocky body is a bit nontraditional, but he projects as a good setup man along the lines of Scott Williamson.

Joel Zumaya   Bats: R   Throws: R   Height: 6' 3"   Weight: 210   Born: November 9, 1984   Age: 22

YEAR	TEAM	LVL	AGE	W	L	SV	G	GS	IP	H	BB	SO	HR	GB%	BABIP	STUFF	WHIP	ERA	PERA	EQERA	EQH9	EQBB9	EQSO9	EQHR9	VORP	WXRL
2004	LAK	A+	19	6	4	0	16	16	94	65	43	92	8	—	.245	4	1.15	3.54	6.40	4.92	7.5	4.8	6.1	1.6	6.8	—
2004	ERI	AA	19	2	2	0	4	4	20	19	10	29	6	—	.289	19	1.45	6.30	8.35	9.78	10.2	4.7	9.8	3.7	-9.0	—
2005	ERI	AA	20	8	3	0	18	18	107¹	71	52	143	8	40.7%	.276	36	1.15	2.77	4.52	3.91	6.9	5.1	8.3	1.0	19.5	—
2005	TOL	AAA	20	1	2	0	8	8	44	30	24	56	2	37.6%	.289	43	1.23	2.66	4.11	3.12	7.1	5.2	8.9	0.4	11.9	—
2006	DET	MLB	21	6	3	1	62	0	83¹	56	42	97	6	35.0%	.254	39	1.18	1.94	3.38	2.14	6.2	4.3	9.9	0.5	36.5	5.01
2007	DET	MLB	22	4	4	4	58	2	79²	65	41	91	9	38.0%	.280	21	1.32	3.66	3.71	3.56	6.9	4.4	9.5	0.9	18.7	1.70
Breakout: 15%	*Improve: 30%*	*Collapse: 30%*	*Attrition: 14%*						*Comparables: Ambiorix Burgos, Victor Cruz, Billy McCool, Byung-Hyun Kim*																

One of the happy accidents resulting from Justin Verlander winning a rotation spot in spring training was that Zumaya found his way to the bullpen. That's probably where he should have been all along; his high-effort mechanics hold up better given short outings, and our research indicates that pitchers with some command problems often make successful starter-to-reliever conversions. It's those command issues that will probably cause Zumaya's ERA to go north, but it's hard to imagine that a pitcher with stuff this nasty won't beat that PECOTA projection, provided that he stays away from *Guitar Hero II*. And, man, that stuff is nasty. While the FOX radar guns can be misleading, we received independent confirmation that during the ALDS against the Yankees, Zumaya really was hitting at least 102 MPH . . . with movement.

Lineouts

PLAYER	TEAM	LVL	AGE	PA	R	2B	3B	HR	RBI	BB	SO	SB-CS	SPEED	AVG/OBP/SLG	MLVr	EqAVG/OBP/SLG	EqA	VORP
SS T. Giarratano#	ERI	AA	23	295	35	19	5	0	19	22	45	16-4	7.2	.283/.340/.390	.067	.276/.327/.393	.255	9.9
3B J. Hannahan*	TOL	AAA	26	494	59	27	0	9	62	61	114	9-6	4.9	.282/.379/.412	.181	.286/.373/.435	.282	31.7
OF R. Ludwick	TOL	AAA	27	571	81	34	2	28	80	48	167	2-6	4.2	.266/.342/.506	.236	.266/.333/.505	.278	21.6
C M. Rabelo#	ERI	AA	26	242	31	13	1	6	28	19	38	2-1	4.5	.277/.361/.432	.146	.253/.315/.385	.242	2.5
	TOL	AAA	26	153	19	12	0	3	22	11	33	1-1	3.9	.270/.333/.423	.116	.268/.327/.442	.264	6.2
SS R. Santiago#	TOL	AAA	26	100	13	6	0	2	12	9	18	2-1	5.8	.253/.333/.398	.068	.256/.333/.419	.261	3.1
	DET	MLB	26	86	9	1	1	0	3	1	14	2-0	6.9	.225/.244/.263	-.461	.203/.232/.241	.183	-5.1

PLAYER	TEAM	LVL	AGE	W	L	SV	IP	H	BB	SO	HR	GB%	BABIP	STUFF	WHIP	ERA	PERA	EqERA	EqH9	EqBB9	EqSO9	EqHR9	VORP
C. Durbin	TOL	AAA	28	11	8	0	185	169	46	149	17	—	.283	1	1.16	3.11	5.05	4.78	9.3	2.5	5.5	1.3	16.5
B. Jensen	ONE	A-	22	1	0	17	26¹	17	5	31	0	—	.262	1	0.84	0.69	3.49	2.92	7.3	2.9	5.5	0.4	7.4
P. Larrison	ERI	AA	25	4	10	1	105	108	40	48	10	—	.289	-35	1.41	3.94	6.71	5.12	9.5	4.2	2.6	1.5	5.5
	TOL	AAA	25	1	0	0	10	12	5	3	1	—	.295	-27	1.70	1.80	7.38	3.60	11.7	4.5	1.8	1.8	2.2
C. Lewis	TOL	AAA	26	6	7	0	147²	154	36	104	13	—	.311	-3	1.29	3.97	4.89	5.70	10.2	2.4	4.9	1.2	-1.6
B. Seay*	TOL	AAA	28	1	2	0	24²	25	6	14	3	—	.313	-29	1.28	4.83	5.98	7.50	10.1	2.6	3.8	1.9	-5.1
	DET	MLB	28	0	0	0	15¹	14	9	12	1	—	.295	-1	1.50	6.47	5.11	5.87	8.8	5.3	6.5	0.6	-0.7
K. Sleeth	TGR	Rk	24	1	0	1	17	22	3	17	0	—	.423	-3	1.47	3.71	3.54	6.88	13.2	2.1	4.8	0.5	-2.4
	LAK	A+	24	1	4	0	19²	23	21	7	2	—	.300	-35	2.29	12.19	11.50	16.10	12.5	14.0	2.1	2.1	-20.2
V. Vasquez	ERI	AA	24	7	12	0	173²	174	50	129	21	—	.302	-24	1.29	3.74	6.58	5.08	10.0	3.1	4.3	1.9	9.8

Tony Giarratano had another ho-hum year at Erie interrupted by a knee injury that required surgery; his glove is major-league caliber, but his window to become a big league utility player is closing quickly. **Jack Hannahan**'s principal asset is that he's one of the better defensive third basemen in professional baseball, so the fact that the Tigers gave him nearly half his plate appearances as a second baseman last year gives tells you something about what they think of his future. His year at Toledo wasn't bad, but for a 26-year-old repeater at Triple-A, the upside here is Scott Cooper. **Ryan Ludwick** was one of a number of "in case of emergency" players that the Tigers signed last winter; he had a pretty good year at Toledo, but the emergency never came. There's nothing to suggest that he can't be an effective fourth outfielder in the big leagues, and nothing to suggest he'll be better than that either. A 2001 fourth-rounder, **Mike Rabelo** isn't really a prospect, but he's on the 40-man as the homegrown third catcher-designate. **Ramon Santiago** is a good-field, no-hit infielder, exactly as meets the eye, although his career FRAA (-1) suggests that his defense is closer to solid than superlative. The Tigers signed him to a major league deal for 2007, but would be better served by giving his roster spot to someone like Ryan Raburn.

Chad Durbin made 45 starts in the major leagues before his 24th birthday, but was largely forgotten about after undergoing reconstructive elbow surgery in 2002. He's made a full recovery. Unfortunately, 100 percent of Chad Durbin is still Chad Durbin. The Tigers' fourteenth-round pick in the June draft, **Brett Jensen** is a sidearm pitcher and former college closer who made a flawless debut at Oneonta. The organization takes him pretty seriously; he could reach Double-A this year. **Preston Larrison** came back from repeated elbow problems (and Tommy John surgery) to show he still throws a nifty sinker, but that likely won't be enough to keep him on the 40-man. The former Rangers pitching prospect may have lost all of 2005 recovering from shoulder surgery, but **Colby Lewis** didn't look entirely done as a Mudhen last summer. Now that he's with the Nationals, he might stick. **Bobby Seay**'s strikeout rates haven't been bad, and it's a little surprising that he hasn't gotten a longer look at as a left-handed set-up option, but one suspects that his reputation as a busted bonus baby doesn't do him any favors. Speaking of bonus babies, **Kyle Sleeth**'s career is spoiled, as in ruined. He did stay on the mound a year removed from Tommy John surgery, but once he got out of the rookie league complex, the results were disastrous. A member in good standing of the Tigers' All-Alliteration Team, **Virgil Vasquez** mixed his pitches well enough to secure a spot on Detroit's 40-man roster. He throws strikes and has a reputation as a hard worker, but his stuff doesn't do more than tread water.

Manager: Jim Leyland

Year	Team	W-L	Pythag +/-	Avg PC	100 +P	120 +P	QS	BQS	REL	REL w Zero R	IBB	SUBS	PH	PH Avg	PH HR	SB2	CS2	SB3	CS3	SAC Att	SAC %	POS SAC	Squeeze	Swing	In Play
2006	DET	95-67	-2	94.0	68	2	83	9	390	238	35	51	81	.222	2	49	32	11	6	60	75.0%	44	2	151	116

If we tried to develop some sort of überstat to evaluate managers, Jim Leyland would probably fare rather poorly. The decision to stick with Todd Jones in the closer role last year was especially hard to stomach, though, in Leyland's defense, Joel Zumaya wasn't far behind Jones in terms of leverage. It was a shame that he couldn't find more playing time for Marcus Thames, particularly during the World Series, when the Tigers could desperately have used his bat. And his lineup construction would have lost him points, particularly when it involved using Neifi Perez as the leadoff hitter. The truth is that Leyland is not a guy to sweat the small stuff. His modus operandi is to keep his players in well-defined roles they'll be comfortable with over the course of a 162-game season. It wasn't worth creating a clubhouse controversy to depose Jones from the closer's role, or to do something like ask Thames to play first base for the first time in his career in the heat of a pennant race. Leyland will play hunches, but he won't yank players out of the lineup willy-nilly; he endured Chris Shelton's horrible slump, for example, until the organization acted and brought in Sean Casey. This speaks to Leyland's greatest strength, managing expectations and egos, something that jibes well with the Tigers' working-class personality. It's hard to think of a more important task in twenty-first century Major League Baseball, and it's hard to think of a more egoless pennant winner than the 2006 Tigers.

Florida Marlins

On September 6, 2006, Marlins rookie Anibal Sanchez no-hit the Arizona Diamondbacks it Miami. As the young Marlin squad carried Sanchez around the field as if they had won the World Series, television cameras took in the bold color contrasts around Dolphin Stadium: the home team's white pin-striped uniforms standing out against both the solid green of the field and the solid orange of the stadium's most empty seats. That just 12,561 fans were in attendance to see one of the highlights of the season managed was, sadly, unsurprising.

If it's possible to stay away in droves, then Marlins fans did just that; just 1,164,134 fans (a mere 14,372 per game) turned out to see the Marlins play in person in 2006. That was far and away the lowest attendance in the majors, almost 200,000 fewer people than saw the runner-up in being ignored, fellow Floridi-ans the Devil Rays. The fans who stayed at home missed out on some exciting baseball, but it's hard to blame them. The Marlins' front office had its anti-marketing campaign in full-gear all offseason. It began with a "woe is us" Fire Sale (version 2.0), in which the team plead poverty, gutted payroll to an almost comical degree (see table 1), and effectively took the team on a cross-country sales trip. After failing to find a new home in Port-land, San Antonio, and Las Vegas, the team returned to Miami and went about its business, but not before having to answer to irate season-ticket holders who were none too pleased at the prospect of paying to see the Cleveland Spi-ders of the twenty-first century.

The Magical Misery Tour was real enough, whether the goal was actually to move the team or pressure Sunshine State pols or both, but the Cleveland Spiders aspect was overstated. Had the front office traded Carlos Delgado for Eric Valent, Juan Padilla, and Chris Woodward, then fans would have been right to assume the team was deliberately tanking, *Major League*-style. But the Marlins were instead flipping veterans for high-ceiling prospects years away from being arbitration-eligible. They also watched the waiver wire for cheap, short-term insurance at several positions.

This was very different from the original Marlins fire sale of 1997–1998. The first tear-down came after the team won its first World Championship and resulted in a 38-win decline in 1998. Teardown II followed a pair of 83-win, third-place fin-ishes, and the collection of youngsters who made up the replacement team came pretty close to matching that. More importantly, General Manager Larry Beinfest did a canny job of acquiring baseball's most pre-cious commodity, pitching. If anything, his focus was almost too obsessive; the Marlins ended up with a congeries of promis-ing, inexpensive arms, but the team went through the 2006 sea-son without a viable center fielder, and during spring train-ing it appeared the same would be true for second base (no one saw Dan Uggla coming).

Thus, 2006 just wasn't your father's fire sale, but an honest-to-gosh attempt at rebuilding. The question becomes what kind of team Florida will be in 2007. Most obviously, the team still lacks a center fielder. Last year, National League center fielders batted .264/.335/.418, AL center fielders batted .275/.334/.437, and Marlins center fielders batted .228/.298/.344. Center isn't the only prob-lem. At least two of their promising younger pitchers need to start throwing more strikes. Dan Uggla was a great story in 2006, but the jury is still out on whether he's a keeper or just a flash in the pan. Josh Willingham was held in the minors for so long that, just a year after being eligible for the Rookie of the Year award, he's at the age at which most players stop developing. Mike Jacobs is older than Willing-

MARLINS PROSPECTUS

2006 record: 78–84; Fourth place, NL East

Pythagenport record: 79–83

Runs scored per game: 4.68 (8th in NL)

Runs allowed per game: 4.77 (6th in NL)

Team EqA: .266 (5th in NL)

2006 Batters Age: 25.9 (Youngest in NL)

2006 Pitchers Age: 25.7 (Youngest in NL)

Ballpark: Dolphin Stadium; Severe pitcher's park; Park Factor of .944

2006: What was supposed to be a laughingstock became a team no one wanted to play by season's end.

2007: Young, scary-good talent. If it all comes together at once, look out. It won't, but the rest of the division should worry.

Table 1. Opening Day Payroll, 2006

Rank	Team	Payroll
1	New York Yankees	$194,663,079
2	Boston Red Sox	$120,099,824
3	Los Angeles Angels	$103,472,000
4	Chicago White Sox	$102,750,667
5	New York Mets	$101,084,963
25	Cleveland Indians	$56,031,500
26	Kansas City Royals	$47,294,000
27	Pittsburgh Pirates	$46,717,750
28	Colorado Rockies	$41,233,000
29	Tampa Bay Devil Rays	$35,417,967
30	Florida Marlins	$14,998,500

SOURCE: USA Today.

ham and his new platoon partner is Aaron Boone, who's never done anything exceptional against lefties. There are also questions surrounding Jeremy Hermida, who at least has an injury excuse to account for some of his struggles in 2006, but who clearly didn't resemble the player many were expecting to see in right field last year.

These position player questions are significant, because the Marlins don't have anyone in their system who could arrive in the next year or so to be another Rookie of the Year contender; it was fun watching the kids for a year, but there are no more kids. A common misconception when talking about the Marlins and their fire sale is that they rebuilt their farm system—they didn't. They rebuilt their major-league roster and added a plethora of pitching prospects, but the offensive side of the equation was neglected, demonstrating the near-term limits of Beinfest's strategy.

Still, there's a method to Beinfest's madness. As the cliché about young pitcher attrition goes, the best way to develop a starting pitcher is to try to develop five; Florida now has many more interesting arms than they can profitably use on the major league squad. While 2006's pitching staff seemed like an endless parade of 22-year-old pitchers,

the Marlins have a few more hurlers who can provide big league innings next year, a few, such as Gaby Hernandez and Brett Sinkbeil, who need another year or so of seasoning, and then a third grouping of mostly teenage arms that looks promising, but represent a more distant solution. Pitchers such as Ryan Tucker, Aaron Thompson, and Sean West won't impact 2007 in any meaningful way, but they're on the way.

All that remains is for Beinfest to sort through them and use the surplus to acquire the position players the team needs. That's why it was more than a little curious that one of the first transactions of the offseason for the Marlins was to take a live, young arm (Chris Resop) and exchange him for a veteran reliever (Kevin Gregg). It got even stranger when the follow-up transaction was to flip two other young arms (Adam Bostick and Jason Vargas) to intradivision rivals the Mets in exchange for two older pitchers (Henry Owens and Matt Lindstrom). Ultimately, this is small beer; the Marlins can live without all three of the players they traded because there's plenty more where that came from. But it's also a case of the Fish treading water instead of addressing their real problems.

The first time the Marlins started over from scratch, the on-field results turned out just fine, climaxing in a second championship just six years later, but following some extremely harsh immediate criticism, they never did recover their attendance figures from 1997 despite the latter title. This time around, they're more likely to get the benefit of the doubt when it comes to appropriate team-building strategies. At the same time, it's not clear how many times the Marlins will pursue this strategy and how many times the franchise's credibility can recover no matter how well-executed the policy. A retreat is still a retreat, even if conducted in an orderly fashion. If the Marlins were to deal Miguel Cabrera or Dontrelle Willis, two of the best young players in the game, it's hard to imagine that there would be anyone left who would take the franchise seriously.

HITTERS

Reggie Abercrombie   **CF**   **Bats: R**   **Throws: R**   Height: 6' 3"   Weight: 220   Born: July 15, 1980   Age: 26

YEAR	TEAM	LVL	AGE	PA	R	2B	3B	HR	RBI	BB	SO	SB	CS	SPEED	AVG	OBP	SLG	MLVR	EQAVG	EQOBP	EQSLG	EQA	VORP	DEFENSE		
2004	LNC	A+	23	123	24	10	2	3	19	2	24	8	1	7.9	.342	.358	.533	.187	.273	.285	.405	.236	-0.0	31-CF	-2	
2004	VRO	A+	23	143	18	4	5	5	12	6	33	16	5	8.4	.271	.305	.489	.108	.235	.266	.419	.240	-2.0	28-CF	-2	
2004	JAX	AA	23	177	17	6	4	4	20	4	66	3	3	7.5	.173	.193	.327	-.348	.147	.164	.247	.155	-31.5	26-RF -2	16-CF	0
2005	JUP	A+	24	321	51	12	3	15	45	14	87	19	6	7.9	.274	.317	.485	.192	.260	.292	.441	.250	4.8	73-CF	2	
2005	CAR	AA	24	197	28	7	2	10	23	11	40	7	5	6.3	.253	.315	.483	.081	.230	.278	.437	.242	-0.2	46-CF	2	
2006	FLO	MLB	25	281	39	12	2	5	24	18	78	6	5	6.7	.212	.271	.333	-.264	.219	.277	.352	.219	-10.7	67-CF	-1	
2007	*FLO*	*MLB*	*26*	*352*	*43*	*16*	*3*	*11*	*40*	*19*	*91*	*14*	*5*	*6.7*	*.248*	*.297*	*.421*	*-.126*	*.249*	*.295*	*.426*	*.246*	*2.4*	*85-CF*	*0*	

Breakout: 49%   Improve: 75%   Collapse: 14%   Attrition: 35%   Comparables: Ivan Murrell, Jose Gonzalez, Bobby Brown, Luis Matos

(continued next page)

Reggie Abercrombie *(continued)*

Getting Reggie Abercrombie out in 2006 was as easy as shooting fish in a barrel, a shallow, fish-shaped barrel that contains no water. Last year we didn't even bother putting Abercrombie in the book; we saw a 25-year-old with career minor league rates of .258/.303/.418 and concluded that he was not ready to hit, likely never would be, and that the Marlins wouldn't be foolish enough to play him. Either we underestimated the Marlins, or the Marlins underestimated us. Either way, Abercrombie remains a player with as little upside, even as a reserve, as any player in the majors, last year or this.

Alfredo Amezaga   **UT**   **Bats: S**   **Throws: R**   Height: 5' 10"   Weight: 165   Born: January 16, 1978   Age: 29

YEAR	TEAM	LVL	AGE	PA	R	2B	3B	HR	RBI	BB	SO	SB	CS	SPEED	AVG	OBP	SLG	MLVR	EQAVG	EQOBP	EQSLG	EQA	VORP	DEFENSE			
2004	SLC	AAA	26	150	15	5	2	2	14	13	18	7	0	6.3	.259	.329	.370	-.231	.204	.268	.270	.206	-8.5	32-SS	5		
2004	ANA	MLB	26	105	12	2	0	2	11	3	24	3	2	6.4	.161	.212	.247	-.633	.149	.200	.234	.171	-10.7	25-SS	-2		
2005	IND	AAA	27	211	28	12	2	1	12	17	27	14	7	6.7	.341	.398	.443	.204	.323	.375	.418	.275	15.4	21-SS	0	14-2B	0
2006	FLO	MLB	28	378	43	9	3	3	19	33	46	20	12	6.5	.260	.332	.332	-.117	.274	.345	.354	.247	-0.5	59-CF	-1	14-2B	1
2007	FLO	MLB	29	370	49	14	4	3	28	28	47	18	8	6.7	.267	.329	.357	-.143	.268	.326	.361	.242	2.1	89-CF	0		

Breakout: 14%   Improve: 41%   Collapse: 25%   Attrition: 26%   Comparables: *Chuck Carr, John Moses, Doug Dascenzo, Pat Listach*

Among the 35 players to play regularly or semi-regularly as center fielders in the NL last year, Florida had the bottom two in VORP: Abercrombie and Eric Reed. It was such a persistent problem that they eventually turned to career utility infielder Amezaga, who had never before played center in the majors. He wound up being the best of the bunch, which is sort of like being the tallest midget in the circus. Amezaga is on the wrong side of 27 and has a career line of .240/.306/.325. His now-enhanced versatility makes him an even more useful last man off the bench, but any team that starts him for more than a day at a time really isn't serious about its chances.

Robert Andino   **SS**   **Bats: R**   **Throws: R**   Height: 6' 0"   Weight: 170   Born: April 25, 1984   Age: 23

YEAR	TEAM	LVL	AGE	PA	R	2B	3B	HR	RBI	BB	SO	SB	CS	SPEED	AVG	OBP	SLG	MLVR	EQAVG	EQOBP	EQSLG	EQA	VORP	DEFENSE	
2004	GRB	A	20	324	27	10	1	8	46	18	83	9	2	4.3	.281	.321	.403	.007	.255	.283	.351	.225	-3.9	74-SS	0
2004	JUP	A+	20	208	18	7	2	0	15	7	43	6	2	5.5	.281	.304	.337	-.030	.271	.291	.317	.218	-4.0	46-SS	2
2005	CAR	AA	21	570	63	30	0	5	48	37	111	22	7	5.3	.269	.324	.357	-.067	.242	.286	.329	.221	-12.5	124-SS	-7
2005	FLO	MLB	21	50	4	4	0	0	1	5	8	1	0	4.4	.159	.245	.250	-.409	.136	.224	.227	.175	-2.8	14-SS	-3
2006	ABQ	AAA	22	549	70	18	6	8	46	33	100	13	11	5.7	.255	.303	.363	-.210	.219	.264	.314	.206	-22.3	113-SS	7
2006	FLO	MLB	22	28	0	1	0	0	2	1	6	1	0	5.1	.167	.185	.208	-.630	.125	.148	.167	.149	-2.9		
2007	FLO	MLB	23	436	41	18	2	5	36	25	83	8	4	5.3	.243	.292	.340	-.249	.244	.290	.344	.218	-3.6	104-SS	0

Breakout: 43%   Improve: 64%   Collapse: 22%   Attrition: 13%   Comparables: *Teuris Olivares, Jhonny Perez, Enohel Polanco, Luis Ordaz*

One morning, Robert Andino woke up from troubled dreams and found he had been transformed into a giant glove. In the field, he was a vacuum—there was no way a batted ball could sneak past him, no matter how hard it was hit. It was impossible, however, for him to hold a baseball bat. Even when he propped it up a bit with his webbing and turned his glove heel into a crude lever, he couldn't generate any power and wound up slugging just .370 in Albuquerque. It was all very existential, sort of like question of whether or not he'll ever hit enough to play regularly in the majors.

Joe Borchard   **OF**   **Bats: S**   **Throws: R**   Height: 6' 4"   Weight: 230   Born: November 25, 1978   Age: 28

YEAR	TEAM	LVL	AGE	PA	R	2B	3B	HR	RBI	BB	SO	SB	CS	SPEED	AVG	OBP	SLG	MLVR	EQAVG	EQOBP	EQSLG	EQA	VORP	DEFENSE			
2004	CHR	AAA	25	336	44	21	0	16	48	30	68	4	3	4.2	.266	.333	.495	.091	.238	.304	.432	.251	-3.5	65-RF	0	12-CF	1
2004	CHA	MLB	25	222	26	4	1	9	20	19	57	1	0	4.5	.174	.249	.338	-.453	.165	.248	.325	.204	-18.3	50-RF	-2		
2005	CHR	AAA	26	550	69	20	0	29	67	50	143	6	4	3.4	.263	.335	.480	.070	.244	.311	.435	.253	-2.4	109-RF	-10	13-CF	-2
2006	FLO	MLB	27	261	30	7	1	10	28	28	66	0	2	3.7	.230	.322	.400	-.065	.240	.331	.424	.257	-0.8	36-RF	4		
2007	FLO	MLB	28	281	33	12	1	11	38	26	71	1	1	4.4	.247	.323	.436	-.063	.248	.320	.440	.257	2.4	69-RF	0		

Breakout: 31%   Improve: 57%   Collapse: 16%   Attrition: 53%   Comparables: *Jeff Liefer, Norm Zauchin, Brian Buchanan, Charlie Spikes*

Out of options, the former first-round pick failed to win a job with the White Sox in spring training and was dealt to the Mariners for reliever Matt Thornton, another busted first-rounder. The M's gave Borchard a month of mostly bench time before waiving him. The Marlins claimed him as part of their Take an Outfielder (Any Outfielder) to Work program. The Fish never gave Borchard a shot at their center field job, but with Jeremy Hermida on the DL he got some time in right. Borchard did little when batting right-handed, but hit .256/.354/.453 batting lefty. He also played well in right, and between his defense and his modest offensive abilities, he'll make a fine spare part.

Miguel Cabrera — 3B — Bats: R — Throws: R — Height: 6' 2" — Weight: 210 — Born: April 18, 1983 — Age: 24

YEAR	TEAM	LVL	AGE	PA	R	2B	3B	HR	RBI	BB	SO	SB	CS	SPEED	AVG	OBP	SLG	MLVR	EQAVG	EQOBP	EQSLG	EQA	VORP	DEFENSE			
2004	FLO	MLB	21	685	101	31	1	33	112	68	148	5	2	4.5	.294	.366	.512	.231	.299	.371	.525	.301	43.5	91-RF	-7	52-LF	3
2005	FLO	MLB	22	685	106	43	2	33	116	64	125	1	0	4.3	.323	.385	.561	.372	.332	.396	.588	.325	68.2	124-LF	-5	27-3B	1
2006	FLO	MLB	23	676	112	50	2	26	114	86	108	9	6	4.4	.339	.430	.568	.443	.352	.443	.591	.341	78.7	150-3B	1		
2007	FLO	MLB	24	672	115	41	3	32	107	80	112	7	3	4.8	.317	.404	.566	.305	.318	.400	.572	.322	65.9	156-3B	-2		

Breakout: 7% Improve: 48% Collapse: 17% Attrition: 0% Comparables: Jim Ray Hart, Jack Clark, Ellis Valentine, Cal Ripken

Overall, in the National League, there's Pujols, then Ryan Howard, and then Cabrera, who fell just shy of a batting title. Keep in mind that Cabrera spends a lot of time in cavernous pitcher's parks, that he's just 24—still several years away from his peak and three and a half years Howard's junior—and that, unlike the other two, he plays a skill position. If you wanted to start from scratch with one hitter, you couldn't do better than Cabrera right now.

Brett Carroll — OF — Bats: R — Throws: R — Height: 6' 0" — Weight: 190 — Born: October 3, 1982 — Age: 24

YEAR	TEAM	LVL	AGE	PA	R	2B	3B	HR	RBI	BB	SO	SB	CS	SPEED	AVG	OBP	SLG	MLVR	EQAVG	EQOBP	EQSLG	EQA	VORP	DEFENSE			
2004	JAM	A-	21	236	27	16	1	6	28	15	57	1	0	4.0	.251	.321	.422	.029	.200	.250	.327	.204	-23.4	33-3B	-6	10-2B	0
2005	GRB	A	22	449	57	28	1	18	54	17	108	10	10	4.7	.243	.296	.447	.007	.190	.221	.321	.190	-47.3	76-RF	0	20-CF	1
2006	JUP	A+	23	244	31	12	1	8	30	18	48	9	3	5.5	.241	.324	.417	.120	.246	.306	.415	.249	-3.6	52-RF	-7		
2006	CAR	AA	23	280	29	15	3	9	30	18	62	4	1	5.0	.231	.303	.422	.029	.230	.290	.436	.247	1.4	46-CF	8	27-RF	4
2007	FLO	MLB	24	481	49	25	3	13	56	26	113	8	4	5.0	.234	.287	.393	-.192	.235	.285	.397	.231	-9.3	114-RF	2		

Breakout: 35% Improve: 56% Collapse: 16% Attrition: 7% Comparables: Kirk Asche, Andy Bevins, Eric Cole, Matt Carson

While he's never had the numbers to go along with his skills (power, great arm), Carroll may yet find himself in the mix for the center field vacancy should Florida fail to acquire someone else to fill it. Coming soon on Bravo: "Center Fielders of Miami," the reality TV show where a dozen catty professionals squabble over their relatively slender merits, and Tim Gunn teaches them how to properly wear stirrups.

Kris Harvey — RF/3B — Bats: R — Throws: R — Height: 6' 2" — Weight: 195 — Born: January 5, 1984 — Age: 23

YEAR	TEAM	LVL	AGE	PA	R	2B	3B	HR	RBI	BB	SO	SB	CS	SPEED	AVG	OBP	SLG	MLVR	EQAVG	EQOBP	EQSLG	EQA	VORP	DEFENSE			
2005	JAM	A-	21	275	34	14	3	9	38	9	60	4	0	4.9	.300	.320	.479	.116	.228	.240	.343	.203	-25.5	25-3B	-6	23-RF	-3
2006	GRB	A	22	395	46	18	2	15	60	24	82	9	4	5.0	.245	.291	.428	.020	.200	.233	.331	.199	-38.8	73-RF	-7		
2007	FLO	MLB	23	388	29	18	1	7	38	15	92	4	2	4.7	.215	.249	.328	-.363	.216	.247	.332	.190	-22.5	93-RF	-5		

Breakout: 48% Improve: 59% Collapse: 33% Attrition: 16% Comparables: Brett Carroll, Terry Evans, Matt Carson, Brian Costello

Homers are pretty easy to come by in Greensboro, so don't drool over Harvey's slugging just yet; his rates translate to a 564 OPS, which doesn't signify a prospect. It's not surprising that the two positions he's tried thus far have been third and right field, because his best defensive weapon is a cannon arm that used to hit 97 when he pitched in college. He hasn't taken to the offensive side of the game, so it's still possible that he could end up a pitcher like his dad, Bryan, who closed for the inaugural 1993 Marlins.

Wes Helms — 1B/3B — Bats: R — Throws: R — Height: 6' 4" — Weight: 230 — Born: May 12, 1976 — Age: 31

YEAR	TEAM	LVL	AGE	PA	R	2B	3B	HR	RBI	BB	SO	SB	CS	SPEED	AVG	OBP	SLG	MLVR	EQAVG	EQOBP	EQSLG	EQA	VORP	DEFENSE			
2004	MIL	MLB	28	306	24	13	1	4	28	24	60	0	1	2.9	.263	.331	.361	-.064	.258	.325	.353	.239	-1.2	59-3B	-4		
2005	MIL	MLB	29	188	18	13	1	4	24	14	30	0	1	3.7	.298	.356	.458	.137	.299	.356	.473	.283	8.8	20-3B	2	13-1B	0
2006	FLO	MLB	30	278	30	19	5	10	47	21	55	0	4	4.4	.329	.390	.575	.387	.343	.400	.591	.321	26.3	48-1B	-4	10-3B	0
2007	PHI	MLB	31	242	31	14	1	8	34	20	44	1	1	3.9	.288	.356	.479	.084	.284	.352	.468	.278	9.3	60-1B	-2		

Breakout: 9% Improve: 25% Collapse: 41% Attrition: 45% Comparables: Brian Buchanan, Greg Colbrunn, David McCarty, Mike Marshall

The premise of *The Facts of Life* was that Mrs. Garrett was a housemother who was in charge of some much younger girls who were away from home for the fist time and mostly naïve about how the world worked. Cue Wes Helms, who was Mrs. Garrett with a .314 EqA and the fifth-highest VORP in the house on last year's Marlins. But just as Mrs. Garrett eventually left the house and started her own business, so Helms has left for Philadelphia. Helms creamed all comers last year, socking lefties for .333/.413/.505 rates and righties at a .331/.376/.646 clip. Of course, his career rates aren't anywhere near that good, particularly his unimpressive career record of .263/.316/.431 against right-handers. The Phillies will give Helms a chance to start at third base, and while he'll be far more rewarding than, say, Abraham Nunez, they may find that the world never seems to be living up to their dreams.

Jeremy Hermida   RF   **Bats: L**   **Throws: R**   Height: 6' 4"   Weight: 200   Born: January 30, 1984   Age: 23

YEAR	TEAM	LVL	AGE	PA	R	2B	3B	HR	RBI	BB	SO	SB	CS	SPEED	AVG	OBP	SLG	MLVR	EQAVG	EQOBP	EQSLG	EQA	VORP	DEFENSE	
2004	JUP	A+	20	393	53	17	1	10	50	42	73	10	3	5.2	.297	.377	.441	.235	.293	.355	.446	.278	13.7	73-RF	-8
2005	CAR	AA	21	507	77	29	2	18	63	111	89	23	2	5.6	.293	.457	.518	.367	.275	.418	.495	.318	41.4	113-RF	5
2005	FLO	MLB	21	47	9	2	0	4	11	6	12	2	0	5.1	.293	.383	.634	.435	.293	.383	.634	.330	6.1		
2006	FLO	MLB	22	348	37	19	1	5	28	33	70	4	1	5.1	.251	.332	.368	-.073	.261	.343	.384	.257	-0.2	77-RF	-5
2007	*FLO*	*MLB*	*23*	*456*	*70*	*25*	*2*	*15*	*57*	*57*	*82*	*10*	*2*	*5.4*	*.282*	*.376*	*.475*	*.108*	*.283*	*.374*	*.480*	*.292*	*21.9*	*108-RF*	*1*

Breakout: 25% Improve: 61% Collapse: 16% Attrition: 15%   Comparables: Clint Hurdle, Andy Van Slyke, John Hale, Steve Kemp

Hermida missed time early on with a hip flexor injury, then missed time late with an ankle injury, both of which confirmed the reputation for fragility he built up in the minors. In between, he rarely resembled the player he was supposed to be, even taking into account that there's disagreement about what he's supposed to be. PECOTA was a bit underwhelmed last year, comparing him to some recent slowpokes such as Jack Cust and Dee Brown. The comparables are even more pessimistic now, though Van Slyke was an excellent player, and Kemp was a very good one whose career was derailed by injuries. Hermida's really quite a bit more athletic than that, so although the evaporation of his minor league walk rate is discouraging, he's still young enough to be a great bounceback candidate.

Mike Jacobs   1B   **Bats: L**   **Throws: R**   Height: 6' 2"   Weight: 200   Born: October 30, 1980   Age: 26

YEAR	TEAM	LVL	AGE	PA	R	2B	3B	HR	RBI	BB	SO	SB	CS	SPEED	AVG	OBP	SLG	MLVR	EQAVG	EQOBP	EQSLG	EQA	VORP	DEFENSE			
2004	NOR	AAA	23	106	8	3	0	2	6	9	30	0	0	3.1	.177	.245	.271	-.394	.177	.245	.260	.185	-9.5	14-C	0		
2005	BIN	AA	24	482	66	37	2	25	93	35	94	1	2	2.9	.321	.376	.589	.368	.293	.342	.532	.291	31.3	52-1B	-3	41-C	-15
2005	NYN	MLB	24	112	19	7	0	11	23	10	22	0	0	2.8	.310	.375	.710	.520	.310	.381	.730	.344	14.8	27-1B	-3		
2006	FLO	MLB	25	520	54	37	1	20	77	45	105	3	0	3.7	.262	.325	.473	.065	.270	.335	.487	.279	12.2	110-1B	-8		
2007	*FLO*	*MLB*	*26*	*539*	*67*	*31*	*2*	*24*	*83*	*49*	*106*	*2*	*1*	*3.8*	*.271*	*.340*	*.490*	*.057*	*.272*	*.337*	*.496*	*.278*	*17.9*	*127-1B*	*-6*		

Breakout: 23% Improve: 50% Collapse: 21% Attrition: 13%   Comparables: Dick Nen, Tino Martinez, Adam LaRoche, Greg Walker

Jacobs didn't treat his .710 SLG in 2005 as a jumping-off point, but nobody really thought he'd pick up where he left off in New York anyway. He started the year slowly, finished it badly, and in between had a few months where he smoked the ball. In the Marlins' well-publicized quest to add a center fielder, Jacobs's name has come up as someone they might trade, which isn't a bad idea. He's not young, he needed to be platooned, and he has little positional flexibility. Though he has a little catcher in him, he's never actually caught in the majors, and if Josh Willingham couldn't get behind the plate last year, Jacobs has little chance of it. Then again, maybe new manager Fredi Gonzalez will be less of a catching snob than Joe Girardi was.

Bradley McCann   1B   **Bats: R**   **Throws: R**   Height: 6' 3"   Weight: 190   Born: December 9, 1982   Age: 24

YEAR	TEAM	LVL	AGE	PA	R	2B	3B	HR	RBI	BB	SO	SB	CS	SPEED	AVG	OBP	SLG	MLVR	EQAVG	EQOBP	EQSLG	EQA	VORP	DEFENSE	
2004	JAM	A-	21	123	16	6	2	3	13	7	16	0	1	4.4	.277	.328	.446	.087	.226	.262	.365	.214	-6.5	24-3B	-5
2005	GRB	A	22	527	67	35	2	28	106	37	97	1	1	2.6	.295	.355	.552	.283	.244	.285	.436	.243	-6.5	103-1B	-12
2006	JUP	A+	23	496	47	23	0	12	40	32	108	3	5	3.3	.231	.288	.360	-.018	.225	.272	.345	.215	-31.2	89-1B	-4
2007	*FLO*	*MLB*	*24*	*458*	*41*	*22*	*2*	*13*	*55*	*26*	*98*	*1*	*1*	*3.9*	*.239*	*.288*	*.389*	*-.193*	*.240*	*.286*	*.393*	*.228*	*-11.3*	*108-1B*	*-2*

Breakout: 37% Improve: 53% Collapse: 20% Attrition: 10%   Comparables: Charley Carter, Rusty Brown, Mike Eylward, Ben Jones

Quickly adopting the Jason Stokes career path, which isn't as promising a thing as it seemed in 2002, McCann failed to carry over any momentum from his breakout year in 2005. There's more hope here than with Stokes, but not much more, as McCann is a little old for where he's currently stationed.

Miguel Olivo   C   **Bats: R**   **Throws: R**   Height: 6' 0"   Weight: 220   Born: July 15, 1978   Age: 28

YEAR	TEAM	LVL	AGE	PA	R	2B	3B	HR	RBI	BB	SO	SB	CS	SPEED	AVG	OBP	SLG	MLVR	EQAVG	EQOBP	EQSLG	EQA	VORP	DEFENSE	
2004	CHA	MLB	25	156	21	7	2	7	26	10	29	5	4	6.9	.270	.316	.496	.017	.264	.316	.486	.263	5.8	30-C	2
2004	SEA	MLB	25	173	25	8	2	6	14	10	55	2	2	6.9	.200	.260	.388	-.217	.208	.267	.415	.230	-2.6	46-C	-5
2005	TAC	AAA	26	99	13	4	1	3	21	7	19	8	1	7.2	.233	.293	.400	-.137	.228	.280	.391	.244	-1.0	15-C	1
2005	SEA	MLB	26	157	14	4	0	5	18	4	49	1	1	5.1	.151	.172	.276	-.549	.127	.159	.247	.149	-14.6	46-C	-3
2005	SDN	MLB	26	124	16	7	1	4	16	4	31	6	1	6.3	.304	.341	.487	.196	.322	.358	.530	.301	11.0	32-C	0
2006	FLO	MLB	27	452	52	22	3	16	58	9	103	2	3	4.5	.263	.287	.440	-.046	.271	.296	.459	.252	5.9	110-C	4
2007	*FLO*	*MLB*	*28*	*413*	*48*	*20*	*3*	*15*	*53*	*20*	*97*	*8*	*4*	*5.4*	*.253*	*.294*	*.437*	*-.106*	*.254*	*.292*	*.442*	*.245*	*7.2*	*98-C*	*0*

Breakout: 31% Improve: 61% Collapse: 19% Attrition: 20%   Comparables: Ned Yost, Jim Hegan, Dante Bichette, Bill Haselman

Florida Marlins

Olivo has always had a bit of power, but, when the Baseball Fairy was handing out talent, she neglected to give little Miggy the ability to tell a ball from a strike from a duckbilled platypus. In 2006, Oliva became just one of a dozen players in the last half-century to come to the plate 400 or more times and failed to draw ten walks. Four of Oliva's nine walks were intentional, giving him an unintentional walk rate of one every 90.4 plate appearances. That's not quite as bad as Alfredo Griffin's 1984 (4 UIBB in 441 PA, or 110.3 UIBB/PA) or the immortal Whitey Alperman's two walks in 442 PA for the 1909 Dodgers, but it's still special. Olivo also seemed to fall victim to late-season LoDuca-itis, as he had a dreadful final two months. Without any secondary skills, he's not a good bet to build on his 2006 numbers. His nickname should be "Extra-Virgin."

Hanley Ramirez SS Bats: R Throws: R Height: 6' 3" Weight: 195 Born: December 23, 1983 Age: 23

YEAR	TEAM	LVL	AGE	PA	R	2B	3B	HR	RBI	BB	SO	SB	CS	SPEED	AVG	OBP	SLG	MLVR	EQAVG	EQOBP	EQSLG	EQA	VORP	DEFENSE	
2004	SAR	A+	20	263	33	8	4	1	24	17	39	12	7	6.4	.310	.364	.389	.118	.286	.328	.359	.244	5.9	60-SS	-7
2004	PME	AA	20	139	26	7	2	5	15	10	26	12	3	8.4	.310	.360	.512	.198	.277	.324	.454	.269	7.6	31-SS	0
2005	PME	AA	21	519	66	21	7	6	52	39	62	26	13	7.4	.271	.335	.385	.014	.250	.308	.356	.237	1.4	109-SS	-1
2006	FLO	MLB	22	700	119	46	11	17	59	56	128	51	15	8.0	.292	.353	.480	.150	.305	.366	.504	.294	54.9	149-SS	-4
2007	*FLO*	*MLB*	*23*	*663*	*104*	*36*	*8*	*15*	*66*	*52*	*102*	*47*	*17*	*7.1*	*.287*	*.349*	*.450*	*.034*	*.289*	*.347*	*.455*	*.276*	*37.7*	*155-SS*	*-1*

Breakout: 31% Improve: 54% Collapse: 12% Attrition: 0%   Comparables: Mariano Duncan, Ryne Sandberg, Paul Molitor, Barry Larkin

If not having a dominant season on your minor league resumé prevents you from having a good major league debut, someone forgot to tell Ramirez, who beat out Ryan Zimmerman for the NL Rookie of the Year Award. He posted his worst stolen base rate of the year in September (8-for-13), which hides how good he was on the bases for the first five months. He should develop some more power, which would make him a viable option further down in the order, but he's fine where he is right now. Ramirez is not the platonic ideal of the leadoff hitter, but with his speed and gap power there's nothing wrong with giving him the larger number of plate appearances the spot confers.

Kevin Randel 2B Bats: L Throws: R Height: 6' 1" Weight: 180 Born: June 11, 1981 Age: 26

YEAR	TEAM	LVL	AGE	PA	R	2B	3B	HR	RBI	BB	SO	SB	CS	SPEED	AVG	OBP	SLG	MLVR	EQAVG	EQOBP	EQSLG	EQA	VORP	DEFENSE			
2004	GRB	A	23	149	20	10	1	4	21	12	27	2	2	4.2	.299	.369	.478	.198	.257	.302	.400	.242	-0.5				
2005	JUP	A+	24	465	59	19	1	9	50	58	95	15	3	4.8	.285	.384	.407	.197	.275	.350	.389	.262	16.6	98-2B	-17		
2006	CAR	AA	25	389	54	26	2	12	57	47	87	3	3	4.1	.280	.376	.483	.239	.272	.350	.482	.282	27.6	64-2B	-5	15-3B	1
2007	*FLO*	*MLB*	*26*	*452*	*53*	*26*	*3*	*13*	*54*	*42*	*102*	*4*	*2*	*4.5*	*.259*	*.335*	*.432*	*-.038*	*.260*	*.332*	*.437*	*.262*	*15.3*	*107-2B*	*-6*		

Breakout: 8% Improve: 31% Collapse: 23% Attrition: 10%   Comparables: Jason Grabowski, Jake Gautreau, Kevin Burford, Brooks Conrad

A 2002 thirteenth-rounder out of Long Beach State, Randel has changed some things over the years: He used to play short, and he used to switch hit. The excitement over his Double-A debut vanishes when you see his birth date. At best, he could help a team as a spare part playing some second and third; he's your basic baseball rat, not a prospect.

Eric Reed CF Bats: L Throws: L Height: 5' 11" Weight: 170 Born: December 2, 1980 Age: 26

YEAR	TEAM	LVL	AGE	PA	R	2B	3B	HR	RBI	BB	SO	SB	CS	SPEED	AVG	OBP	SLG	MLVR	EQAVG	EQOBP	EQSLG	EQA	VORP	DEFENSE	
2004	CAR	AA	23	239	32	9	6	3	14	14	55	24	5	8.9	.306	.345	.441	.132	.293	.326	.418	.264	7.5	47-CF	-5
2005	CAR	AA	24	298	35	9	0	1	15	17	62	23	8	6.5	.255	.305	.299	-.188	.227	.266	.266	.202	-23.0	63-CF	5
2005	ABQ	AAA	24	181	19	5	4	1	20	3	31	17	7	7.2	.310	.335	.404	-.049	.264	.283	.345	.224	-4.7	37-CF	3
2006	ABQ	AAA	25	420	68	20	9	5	39	24	94	20	9	7.4	.303	.344	.438	-.009	.264	.301	.386	.239	-0.7	87-CF	12
2006	FLO	MLB	25	47	6	0	0	0	0	2	10	3	1	6.7	.098	.178	.098	-.803	.000	.087	.000	.081	-7.2	12-CF	2
2007	*FLO*	*MLB*	*26*	*408*	*47*	*17*	*6*	*5*	*33*	*20*	*87*	*20*	*7*	*7.1*	*.253*	*.293*	*.367*	*-.204*	*.254*	*.291*	*.371*	*.230*	*-4.2*	*97-CF*	*5*

Breakout: 32% Improve: 45% Collapse: 26% Attrition: 16%   Comparables: Elpidio Guzman, Quincy Foster, Dan McKinley, Rich Thompson

Reed is the kind of guy who doesn't need to own a glove or a bat, because his only real above-average contribution comes from what he does in cleats. His brief taste of the majors isn't an accurate representation of his skills, but it does nicely illustrate his offensive limitations. He's too old to turn into anything else.

Jason Restko   **LF**   **Bats: R**   **Throws: R**   Height: 6′ 5″   Weight: 190   Born: December 15, 1984   Age: 22

YEAR	TEAM	LVL	AGE	PA	R	2B	3B	HR	RBI	BB	SO	SB	CS	SPEED	AVG	OBP	SLG	MLVR	EQAVG	EQOBP	EQSLG	EQA	VORP	DEFENSE
2004	JAM	A-	19	312	40	11	1	6	46	16	74	0	2	3.8	.238	.285	.345	-.121	.189	.227	.264	.177	-69.7	66-1B -13
2005	GRB	A	20	476	69	22	3	15	70	53	91	3	0	4.2	.313	.414	.494	.304	.273	.344	.423	.267	5.3	60-LF -10
2006	JUP	A+	21	348	30	10	1	6	34	26	70	0	1	2.9	.255	.325	.350	.043	.265	.319	.368	.240	-9.2	53-LF -5
2007	FLO	MLB	22	416	39	19	1	9	45	29	92	0	0	4.1	.250	.311	.380	-.158	.251	.308	.384	.236	-6.3	99-LF -8

Breakout: 28%   Improve: 50%   Collapse: 22%   Attrition: 13%   Comparables: Jake Blalock, Matt Riordan, David Gibralter, Ronnie Hall

As Westley said in *The Princess Bride,* "get used to disappointment." Restko had a great 2005, but thanks to a number of nagging injuries, he had a mighty big regression last year. Big men have big strike zones, and Restko doesn't show much command over his. He spent a lot of time at first base in 2006, but didn't bring enough bat to make that a likely destination. There's still some hope here; he's got an awfully pretty swing, he's young, so he'll get another chance or two to prove 2005 wasn't a fluke.

Cody Ross   **LF**   **Bats: R**   **Throws: L**   Height: 5′ 9″   Weight: 205   Born: December 23, 1980   Age: 26

YEAR	TEAM	LVL	AGE	PA	R	2B	3B	HR	RBI	BB	SO	SB	CS	SPEED	AVG	OBP	SLG	MLVR	EQAVG	EQOBP	EQSLG	EQA	VORP	DEFENSE	
2004	LVG	AAA	23	259	44	17	2	14	49	18	43	2	0	5.3	.273	.328	.538	.022	.229	.282	.433	.243	-5.7	49-RF -5	
2005	LVG	AAA	24	448	79	21	4	22	63	49	103	4	2	5.3	.267	.348	.509	.028	.233	.306	.428	.251	-5.1	58-RF 4	47-CF -5
2006	LAN	MLB	25	14	4	1	1	2	9	0	2	1	0	8.1	.500	.500	1.143	1.677	.500	.500	.999	.470	5.9		
2006	LOU	AAA	25	64	11	1	0	3	6	13	12	0	2	2.8	.340	.484	.540	.513	.333	.469	.529	.333	9.4		
2006	FLO	MLB	25	279	30	11	1	11	37	22	61	0	1	3.4	.212	.284	.396	-.149	.220	.291	.412	.240	-5.7	25-RF -1	23-LF -1
2007	FLO	MLB	26	394	50	19	2	16	55	38	83	3	2	4.6	.255	.333	.460	-.007	.256	.330	.465	.268	8.9	94-RF -2	

Breakout: 37%   Improve: 71%   Collapse: 11%   Attrition: 30%   Comparables: Ozzie Timmons, Buddy Bradford, Jeffrey Hammonds, Ryan Ludwick

Quadruple-A type Ross bounced from team to team in 2006, going from the Dodgers to the Reds, before finally landing with the Marlins, something of a Quadruple-A team. A career .274/.344/.479 hitter in the minors, it was clear that Ross would be able to launch a few balls in the majors, but it seemed unlikely that he would be able to hit much more than .250, putting his performance in line with expectations. Nonetheless, he was a decent gamble for a Marlins team desperate for outfielders. His three-homer, seven-RBI game against the Mets in September is a happy memory, but he's a bit old for any real enthusiasm.

Jason Stokes   **1B**   **Bats: R**   **Throws: R**   Height: 6′ 4″   Weight: 225   Born: January 23, 1982   Age: 25

YEAR	TEAM	LVL	AGE	PA	R	2B	3B	HR	RBI	BB	SO	SB	CS	SPEED	AVG	OBP	SLG	MLVR	EQAVG	EQOBP	EQSLG	EQA	VORP	DEFENSE
2004	CAR	AA	22	441	66	26	0	23	78	42	121	5	0	5.0	.272	.345	.513	.198	.253	.315	.469	.266	8.0	103-1B 2
2005	ABQ	AAA	23	50	12	1	1	5	15	3	16	2	0	8.0	.283	.340	.674	.330	.255	.314	.574	.287	2.8	11-1B -1
2006	ABQ	AAA	24	274	39	13	2	7	34	35	85	2	1	4.4	.257	.350	.418	-.058	.225	.314	.367	.242	-7.3	63-1B 0
2007	FLO	MLB	25	380	47	18	2	16	52	36	120	8	1	4.9	.245	.323	.453	-.043	.246	.320	.458	.265	4.2	91-1B 1

Breakout: 28%   Improve: 61%   Collapse: 18%   Attrition: 15%   Comparables: Jayson Werth, Ryan Ludwick, Danny Peoples, Justin Sherrod

As a prospect, he's sort of a weird blend of Rob Stratton, Mike Aubrey, and Eric Crozier; he has the strikeout issues of the first, the injury problems of the second, and the stalled prospectdom of the third. Stokes really needed to stay healthy this year and get in some development time, but he hurt his back. His one real offensive skill—hitting for power—never really materialized, he was pull-happy when he did play, and he still has unresolved strike zone issues. Stokes turned 25 in January; let us not talk falsely now, the hour is getting late.

Matt Treanor   **C**   **Bats: R**   **Throws: R**   Height: 6′ 0″   Weight: 205   Born: March 3, 1976   Age: 31

YEAR	TEAM	LVL	AGE	PA	R	2B	3B	HR	RBI	BB	SO	SB	CS	SPEED	AVG	OBP	SLG	MLVR	EQAVG	EQOBP	EQSLG	EQA	VORP	DEFENSE
2004	ABQ	AAA	28	246	32	8	0	8	38	33	44	2	0	4.0	.258	.385	.419	-.075	.202	.313	.312	.232	-6.0	57-C 2
2004	FLO	MLB	28	61	7	2	0	0	1	4	13	0	0	3.4	.236	.311	.273	-.228	.236	.311	.273	.214	-1.5	20-C -4
2005	FLO	MLB	29	154	10	8	0	0	13	16	28	0	0	3.3	.201	.301	.261	-.266	.201	.301	.254	.207	-4.4	41-C -2
2006	FLO	MLB	30	185	12	6	1	2	14	19	34	0	1	3.7	.229	.328	.318	-.164	.241	.337	.329	.241	-2.8	49-C 6
2007	FLO	MLB	31	287	26	12	1	4	24	27	53	1	1	4.0	.225	.314	.325	-.238	.226	.312	.328	.224	-3.8	70-C 2

Breakout: 24%   Improve: 56%   Collapse: 21%   Attrition: 41%   Comparables: Dick Bertell, Alberto Castillo, Wiki Gonzalez, Jerry McNertney

Misty May's husband is pretty much your run-of-the-mill, nondescript backup catcher. Though Treanor was praised for working with a young, inexperienced staff in Miami, Scott Olsen was really the only pitcher he worked with regularly. His league-average OBP was boosted by four intentional walks and a decent amount of time batting eighth, where even the unintentional walks are somewhat intentional.

Dan Uggla · 2B · Bats: R · Throws: R · Height: 5' 11" · Weight: 200 · Born: March 11, 1980 · Age: 27

YEAR	TEAM	LVL	AGE	PA	R	2B	3B	HR	RBI	BB	SO	SB	CS	SPEED	AVG	OBP	SLG	MLVR	EQAVG	EQOBP	EQSLG	EQA	VORP	DEFENSE				
2004	LNC	A+	24	161	29	13	3	6	38	17	21	2	4	5.3	.336	.419	.600	.361	.259	.323	.435	.255	5.5	18-2B	2			
2004	ELP	AA	24	318	29	12	2	4	30	15	55	10	7	5.1	.258	.301	.353	-.141	.207	.241	.273	.186	-25.5	42-3B	-5	16-2B	1	
2005	TEN	AA	25	569	88	33	3	21	87	52	103	15	8	5.3	.297	.378	.502	.222	.263	.326	.445	.263	23.8	93-2B	-14	10-SS	-1	
2006	FLO	MLB	26	683	105	26	7	27	90	48	123	6	6	5.7	.282	.339	.480	.115	.292	.349	.500	.283	39.1	147-2B	11			
2007	*FLO*	*MLB*	*27*	*630*	*79*	*31*	*4*	*20*	*74*	*45*	*113*	*7*	*4*	*5.3*	*.268*	*.327*	*.443*	*-.030*	*.269*	*.324*	*.448*	*.261*	*20.9*	*147-2B*	*4*			

Breakout: 17% Improve: 43% Collapse: 21% Attrition: 5%   Comparables: Ty Wigginton, Don Money, Kelly Gruber, Jay Bell

Oops. Everything we assumed about Uggla coming in to 2006 turned out to be wrong. Everything. That he was old for his leagues up to that point didn't stop him, That he relied on batting average didn't stop him. That he was moving to a pitcher's park after years in a hitter's system didn't stop him. He was a terrific and unexpected story for most of 2006, quickly becoming a fan favorite and inspiring countless folks to research the Rule 5 Draft. In typical "what have you done for me lately" fashion, we now turn our attention to whether he can do it again. PECOTA thinks not; the four top comps you see above were wildly inconsistent and frequently disappointing.

Josh Willingham · LF · Bats: R · Throws: R · Height: 6' 1" · Weight: 200 · Born: February 17, 1979 · Age: 28

YEAR	TEAM	LVL	AGE	PA	R	2B	3B	HR	RBI	BB	SO	SB	CS	SPEED	AVG	OBP	SLG	MLVR	EQAVG	EQOBP	EQSLG	EQA	VORP	DEFENSE			
2004	CAR	AA	25	455	81	24	0	24	76	91	87	6	3	4.5	.281	.449	.565	.416	.252	.385	.482	.298	36.3	78-C	-1	17-1B	0
2004	FLO	MLB	25	29	2	0	0	1	1	4	8	0	0	2.5	.200	.310	.320	-.184	.200	.310	.320	.228	-0.7				
2005	ABQ	AAA	26	279	56	14	3	19	54	47	54	5	1	5.4	.324	.455	.676	.554	.271	.389	.537	.311	27.9	58-C	-12		
2005	FLO	MLB	26	28	3	1	0	0	4	2	5	0	0	2.9	.304	.407	.348	.082	.292	.393	.333	.267	1.4				
2006	CAR	AA	27	8	0	0	0	0	0	0	3	0	0	3.7	.250	.250	.250	-.263	.250	.250	.250	.158	-0.8				
2006	FLO	MLB	27	573	62	28	2	26	74	54	109	2	0	4.3	.277	.356	.496	.162	.287	.366	.515	.298	27.8	121-LF	-10		
2007	*FLO*	*MLB*	*28*	*562*	*81*	*28*	*3*	*24*	*81*	*68*	*109*	*3*	*1*	*4.5*	*.270*	*.368*	*.488*	*.101*	*.271*	*.365*	*.493*	*.290*	*25.6*	*132-LF*	*-6*		

Breakout: 8% Improve: 36% Collapse: 20% Attrition: 7%   Comparables: Ken Harrelson, Dwight Evans, Jeff Burroughs, Gary Matthews

On the whole it was a very satisfying year for Josh Willingham. He endured a long May slump and a brief stay on the DL with a sore left hand in June, but he slugged over .500 in April and from July to the end of the season. His home park didn't help him much—holding him to .243/.321/.425 with a home run every 22.5 AB—but he countered by being a force on the road, hitting .310/.389/.565 with a home run every 17 AB, and mashing lefties to the tune of .299/.411/.619. It's too late for him to have much of a real career, so this may be as good as it gets with him, but he can hit, draw a walk, and stand around in left field.

PITCHERS

Joe Borowski · Bats: R · Throws: R · Height: 6' 2" · Weight: 225 · Born: May 4, 1971 · Age: 36

YEAR	TEAM	LVL	AGE	W	L	SV	G	GS	IP	H	BB	SO	HR	GB%	BABIP	STUFF	WHIP	ERA	PERA	EQERA	EQH9	EQBB9	EQSO9	EQHR9	VORP	WXRL
2004	CHN	MLB	33	2	4	9	22	0	21¹	27	15	17	3	—	.348	-10	1.97	8.03	5.18	7.36	11.0	5.3	6.1	1.2	-5.3	-0.23
2005	CHN	MLB	34	0	0	0	11	0	11	12	1	11	5	48.6%	.233	2	1.18	6.55	7.49	6.55	9.8	0.8	8.2	4.1	-1.3	-0.19
2005	TBA	MLB	34	1	5	0	32	0	35¹	26	11	16	3	48.6%	.217	-10	1.05	3.82	4.34	3.44	5.9	2.7	3.9	0.7	7.5	1.04
2006	FLO	MLB	35	3	3	36	72	0	69²	63	33	64	7	34.3%	.284	8	1.38	3.74	4.02	3.89	7.8	3.6	7.4	0.8	14.6	2.82
2007	*CLE*	*MLB*	*36*	*3*	*4*	*13*	*52*	*0*	*59¹*	*63*	*26*	*43*	*9*	*40.0%*	*.294*	*-9*	*1.50*	*5.02*	*4.89*	*4.78*	*9.2*	*3.7*	*6.0*	*1.3*	*4.1*	*0.50*

Breakout: 13% Improve: 37% Collapse: 33% Attrition: 21%   Comparables: Don McMahon, Ray Moore, Doug Henry, Turk Wendell

For a guy who flunked out of Tampa, Borowski had himself a pretty good year in Miami, and on the cheap. His strikeout rate came back despite underwhelming stuff, and he led the staff in WXRL. He also reportedly failed an offseason physical with the Phillies before signing with the Indians, so it's possible that the Marlins got the last of Borowski. At first glance, his walk rate seems to have taken a serious turn for the worse in 2006, but Joe Girardi had him issue a career-high seven intentional walks.

Adam Bostick — Bats: L Throws: L Height: 6' 1" Weight: 220 Born: March 17, 1983 Age: 24

YEAR	TEAM	LVL	AGE	W	L	SV	G	GS	IP	H	BB	SO	HR	GB%	BABIP	STUFF	WHIP	ERA	PERA	EQERA	EQH9	EQBB9	EQSO9	EQHR9	VORP	WXRL
2005	JUP	A+	22	4	5	0	17	17	91¹	95	36	94	7	38.1%	.351	-4	1.43	3.84	5.60	5.91	10.2	4.6	5.8	1.4	-3.0	—
2005	CAR	AA	22	4	3	0	9	9	44¹	42	25	39	3	47.0%	.310	3	1.51	4.67	5.51	5.98	9.3	5.2	5.6	1.0	-1.8	—
2006	CAR	AA	23	8	7	0	22	22	115¹	100	67	109	7	42.2%	.301	8	1.45	3.52	5.61	5.42	8.8	5.4	5.9	1.0	2.3	—
2006	ABQ	AAA	23	1	2	0	5	5	27²	39	13	30	4	42.0%	.432	7	1.91	4.63	4.87	6.04	12.1	4.1	7.3	1.6	-1.4	—
2007	NYN	MLB	24	5	7	0	24	17	100²	100	63	80	15	41.0%	.287	0	1.62	5.29	5.92	5.76	8.9	5.0	6.4	1.2	0.8	0.80

Breakout: 16% Improve: 45% Collapse: 20% Attrition: 0%   Comparables: Tom Fordham, Brent Billingsley, Lindsay Gulin, Eric Cyr

He misses enough bats to be interesting, but remember, it's the K/BB ratio that's important. Bostick hides the ball well, but since he struggles to throw strikes, all the deception in the world isn't going to do him much good—it's not deception if the batter knows it probably won't be near the strike zone, which could be one reason why he was traded to the Mets with Jason Vargas for Henry Owens and Matt Lindstrom. With the Mets rotation in a state of flux, to say the least, there's a good chance Bostick will get to pitch in the majors at some point this season.

Jesus Delgado — Bats: R Throws: R Height: 6' 1" Weight: 200 Born: April 19, 1984 Age: 23

YEAR	TEAM	LVL	AGE	W	L	SV	G	GS	IP	H	BB	SO	HR	GB%	BABIP	STUFF	WHIP	ERA	PERA	EQERA	EQH9	EQBB9	EQSO9	EQHR9	VORP	WXRL
2004	AUG	A	20	1	5	0	21	16	58²	61	26	34	10	—	.280	-43	1.48	5.21	8.29	6.87	9.7	4.7	3.1	2.7	-8.1	—
2005	GRN	A	21	7	3	2	33	0	72	57	39	69	3	61.0%	.280	1	1.33	3.50	5.49	4.80	7.7	6.2	5.1	0.8	6.2	—
2006	JUP	A+	22	2	4	0	28	0	38	33	18	40	0	63.2%	.320	0	1.34	2.61	4.44	6.08	8.8	5.1	6.1	0.2	-2.0	—
2007	FLO	MLB	23	2	4	0	28	5	57¹	63	37	38	7	55.0%	.309	-11	1.75	5.84	6.21	6.11	9.7	5.0	5.3	0.9	-3.4	0.10

Breakout: 15% Improve: 41% Collapse: 25% Attrition: 17%   Comparables: Julio Depaula, Hugo Castellanos, Mark Michael, Christopher Malone

The Marlins are pretty high on Jesus, whom they acquired from Boston in the Beckett deal to maintain the organization's Delgado quota. A raw 23-year-old righty from Venezuela, Delgado allowed just one home run last year, though that might have something to do with the fact that his pitches aren't in the strike zone often enough for opposing batters to hit home runs.

Harvey Garcia — Bats: R Throws: R Height: 6' 2" Weight: 170 Born: March 16, 1984 Age: 23

YEAR	TEAM	LVL	AGE	W	L	SV	G	GS	IP	H	BB	SO	HR	GB%	BABIP	STUFF	WHIP	ERA	PERA	EQERA	EQH9	EQBB9	EQSO9	EQHR9	VORP	WXRL
2004	LOW	A-	20	4	6	0	14	14	61	61	30	54	8	—	.299	-36	1.49	5.16	10.11	7.36	11.6	6.7	4.4	3.4	-10.8	—
2005	GRN	A	21	3	5	6	32	0	44²	49	18	54	3	52.7%	.380	-7	1.50	2.01	5.39	4.78	11.2	4.6	6.4	1.2	3.9	—
2006	JUP	A+	22	0	7	21	55	0	64²	54	32	83	5	36.1%	.314	-2	1.34	2.94	5.50	5.14	9.1	5.4	7.6	1.5	3.1	—
2007	FLO	MLB	23	2	4	1	28	4	54	60	41	48	9	41.0%	.320	-6	1.86	6.05	7.08	6.09	9.8	5.8	7.2	1.4	-2.9	0.20

Breakout: 14% Improve: 42% Collapse: 31% Attrition: 21%   Comparables: William Fleck, Grant Balfour, Carlos Guevara, Richard Roberts

The Marlins hope that Garcia, a raw, 23-year-old Venezuelan, will making it to the rotation, but unlike his countryman Anibal Sanchez, he profiles better as a reliever, as he just doesn't have secondary pitches to succeed more than once through the order.

Jose Garcia — Bats: R Throws: R Height: 5' 11" Weight: 165 Born: January 7, 1985 Age: 22

YEAR	TEAM	LVL	AGE	W	L	SV	G	GS	IP	H	BB	SO	HR	GB%	BABIP	STUFF	WHIP	ERA	PERA	EQERA	EQH9	EQBB9	EQSO9	EQHR9	VORP	WXRL
2005	GRB	A	20	3	0	0	5	4	28¹	11	4	39	1	56.9%	.179	27	0.53	1.27	3.02	2.30	4.9	1.6	7.6	0.7	10.0	—
2006	JUP	A+	21	6	2	0	12	11	77	60	16	69	3	61.4%	.266	20	0.99	1.87	3.76	4.58	7.5	2.1	5.3	0.7	8.7	—
2006	CAR	AA	21	6	7	0	14	14	84²	78	25	87	10	46.5%	.302	5	1.22	3.42	5.40	4.66	9.3	2.6	6.6	1.8	8.7	—
2006	FLO	MLB	21	0	0	0	5	0	11	10	5	8	1	37.1%	.265	3	1.36	4.91	4.14	4.76	7.9	3.2	5.6	0.8	1.2	0.25
2007	FLO	MLB	22	8	9	1	35	19	138	135	47	110	17	46.0%	.289	12	1.32	4.41	4.51	4.55	8.6	2.6	6.4	1.0	16.7	2.50

Breakout: 14% Improve: 54% Collapse: 15% Attrition: 0%   Comparables: Dicky Gonzalez, Chin-Hui Tsao, Ian Snell, Anibal Sanchez

Garcia's a little guy who wouldn't look very intimidating if you ran into him in a bar. You could totally beat him up and steal his girlfriend. Not that we're advocating that; for one thing, he could be armed. Garcia's stature isn't a huge issue, as he doesn't throw hard enough to make his shoulder's explode from the effort of trying to get big velocity out of a small frame. Garcia can throw three pitches for strikes, and that's something the Marlins can use, as most of their other young options struggle to get the ball over the plate consistently. Last year he went from High-A all the way to Florida and didn't look out of place anywhere along the way.

Matt Herges Bats: L Throws: R Height: 6′ 0″ Weight: 210 Born: April 1, 1970 Age: 37

YEAR	TEAM	LVL	AGE	W	L	SV	G	GS	IP	H	BB	SO	HR	GB%	BABIP	STUFF	WHIP	ERA	PERA	EQERA	EQH9	EQBB9	EQSO9	EQHR9	VORP	WXRL
2004	SFN	MLB	34	4	5	23	70	0	65¹	90	21	39	8	—	.374	-14	1.70	5.24	4.47	5.75	11.9	2.5	4.7	0.9	-1.8	-0.37
2005	SFN	MLB	35	1	1	0	21	0	21	23	7	6	2	45.9%	.292	-27	1.43	4.71	4.78	4.57	9.6	2.5	2.5	0.8	2.1	0.10
2005	TUC	AAA	35	1	2	0	26	0	28²	39	8	29	3	49.4%	.434	-6	1.64	3.14	4.35	4.08	12.2	2.8	6.3	1.3	4.8	—
2006	FLO	MLB	36	2	3	0	66	0	71	94	28	36	5	47.5%	.353	-10	1.72	4.31	4.20	5.01	11.2	3.1	4.0	0.6	3.3	-0.95
2007	FLO	MLB	37	2	3	1	49	0	56²	72	23	31	7	47.0%	.328	-18	1.66	5.43	6.01	5.56	11.1	3.1	4.4	1.0	-0.1	0.00

Breakout: 21% Improve: 50% Collapse: 34% Attrition: 37%   Comparables: Jim Konstanty, Rick White, Clyde Shoun, Mike Maddux

Herges is the chain restaurant of the relief pitcher world. There are loads of pitchers just like him, he doesn't do any one thing particularly well, and teams always wind up settling for him rather than intentionally seeking him out. He's currently a free agent, and unlikely to thrive outside of a pitcher's park.

Gaby Hernandez Bats: R Throws: R Height: 6′ 3″ Weight: 210 Born: May 21, 1986 Age: 21

YEAR	TEAM	LVL	AGE	W	L	SV	G	GS	IP	H	BB	SO	HR	GB%	BABIP	STUFF	WHIP	ERA	PERA	EQERA	EQH9	EQBB9	EQSO9	EQHR9	VORP	WXRL
2005	HAG	A	19	6	1	0	18	18	92²	59	30	99	4	48.3%	.243	24	0.96	2.43	4.59	3.89	7.5	3.7	5.9	0.7	16.7	—
2005	SLU	A+	19	2	5	0	10	10	42¹	48	10	32	1	40.0%	.367	6	1.37	5.74	4.81	7.07	11.1	2.6	4.3	0.4	-6.9	—
2006	JUP	A+	20	9	7	0	21	20	120	120	35	115	7	44.7%	.330	11	1.29	3.68	4.85	5.70	10.0	3.0	5.7	1.1	-1.3	—
2007	FLO	MLB	21	6	9	0	26	20	121²	127	50	92	18	44.0%	.297	9	1.46	5.09	5.37	5.20	9.2	3.2	6.1	1.2	5.3	1.40

Breakout: 19% Improve: 56% Collapse: 11% Attrition: 1%   Comparables: Ricky Nolasco, Anthony Swarzak, Tony Armas, Kyle Davies

Hernandez took advantage of the reduced rates on the direct NYC-Miami flight from Omar Minaya Airlines and settled in for a full season of Florida State League action as a member of the Marlins system. After a rough FSL debut last year, he made some progress with both his breaking ball and changeup. You'd like to see him miss more bats before getting too worked up, but you can say that about a dozen guys who eventually will pick up a few extra Ks. Nevertheless, he is only 20 and will start 2007 in Double-A, so he's well worth keeping an eye on. Mets prospects tend to get a bit overhyped, but Hernandez looks like he's got a solid major league future ahead of him.

Josh Johnson Bats: L Throws: R Height: 6′ 7″ Weight: 240 Born: January 31, 1984 Age: 23

YEAR	TEAM	LVL	AGE	W	L	SV	G	GS	IP	H	BB	SO	HR	GB%	BABIP	STUFF	WHIP	ERA	PERA	EQERA	EQH9	EQBB9	EQSO9	EQHR9	VORP	WXRL
2004	JUP	A+	20	5	12	0	23	22	114¹	124	47	103	4	—	.345	11	1.50	3.39	4.43	6.29	10.2	4.1	5.4	0.7	-8.7	—
2005	CAR	AA	21	12	4	0	26	26	139²	139	50	113	4	53.1%	.325	19	1.35	3.87	3.86	5.05	9.2	3.2	5.1	0.5	8.5	—
2005	FLO	MLB	21	0	0	0	4	1	12¹	11	10	10	0	39.4%	.333	13	1.70	3.66	4.62	3.55	7.8	6.4	6.4	0.0	2.5	0.33
2006	FLO	MLB	22	12	7	0	31	24	157	136	68	133	14	46.7%	.284	25	1.30	3.10	3.91	3.52	7.5	3.4	6.8	0.7	40.2	4.54
2007	FLO	MLB	23	9	10	0	30	25	160²	157	67	137	15	48.0%	.302	19	1.39	4.26	4.49	4.40	8.6	3.2	6.9	0.8	21.7	3.40

Breakout: 18% Improve: 42% Collapse: 31% Attrition: 3%   Comparables: Mark Gubicza, Jim Gott, Carlos Zambrano, Jerry Reuss

Had he enough innings to qualify, Johnson would have been tied with Cy Young award winner Brandon Webb for third in the NL with his 3.10 ERA. He came up a few innings short for two reasons: He spent the first month of the year working out of the bullpen, then missed the last three weeks of the season after suffering a strained forearm, an injury he picked up after Joe Girardi sent him back into a game after a long rain delay. The media questioned Girardi's simultaneous firing/ Manager of the Year status, but that alone might have been a fireable offense right there. As Hank Greenberg said when he was general manager of the Indians, an organization invests a lot of time and money in developing a prospect, a manager can't just slag him on a whim. An ERA as low as Johnson's doesn't usually result from his peripherals, so don't expect him to build on that; start your 2007 expectations with an ERA around 4.00, and go from there.

Logan Kensing Bats: R Throws: R Height: 6′ 1″ Weight: 185 Born: July 3, 1982 Age: 24

YEAR	TEAM	LVL	AGE	W	L	SV	G	GS	IP	H	BB	SO	HR	GB%	BABIP	STUFF	WHIP	ERA	PERA	EQERA	EQH9	EQBB9	EQSO9	EQHR9	VORP	WXRL
2004	JUP	A+	22	6	7	0	23	23	127²	120	35	100	5	—	.302	11	1.21	2.96	4.44	4.77	9.0	2.8	4.7	0.8	11.6	—
2004	FLO	MLB	22	0	3	0	5	3	13²	19	9	7	5	—	.326	-26	2.05	9.85	8.72	10.29	12.2	5.1	3.9	3.2	-6.7	-0.41
2005	CAR	AA	23	4	1	0	7	7	39²	35	14	33	4	50.4%	.267	2	1.23	3.17	6.02	4.19	9.1	3.3	5.4	1.6	6.1	—
2006	ABQ	AAA	24	1	1	2	13	0	18	11	5	18	2	60.5%	.220	12	0.89	3.00	4.15	2.95	5.4	2.5	6.9	1.0	5.4	—
2006	FLO	MLB	24	1	3	1	36	0	37²	30	19	45	6	28.6%	.282	16	1.30	4.54	4.50	4.46	7.3	4.0	9.6	1.2	5.7	-0.09
2007	FLO	MLB	24	2	3	2	43	0	50¹	48	23	47	6	43.0%	.295	7	1.40	4.45	4.70	4.56	8.4	3.5	7.5	1.0	5.9	0.50

Breakout: 33% Improve: 68% Collapse: 14% Attrition: 36%   Comparables: Byron McLaughlin, Danny Frisella, Jorge Julio, Jim Crawford

(continued next page)

Logan Kensing *(continued)*

Converted to full-time relief for the first time, Kensing finally started missing bats with regularity. Good thing that took, because he didn't have a future in the rotation, not with the more promising relief prospects coming up behind him. Having blown out his elbow, he doesn't have an immediate future in the bullpen either; he'll miss 2007 following Tommy John surgery.

Carlos Martinez   Bats: R   Throws: R   Height: 6' 1"   Weight: 170   Born: May 26, 1982   Age: 25

YEAR	TEAM	LVL	AGE	W	L	SV	G	GS	IP	H	BB	SO	HR	GB%	BABIP	STUFF	WHIP	ERA	PERA	EQERA	EQH9	EQBB9	EQSO9	EQHR9	VORP	WXRL
2005	JUP	A+	23	4	5	22	47	0	60²	52	22	65	5	54.1%	.294	-17	1.22	3.11	6.00	5.15	8.9	4.5	5.8	1.6	2.9	—
2006	FLO	MLB	24	0	1	0	12	0	10¹	9	6	11	0	24.0%	.360	10	1.45	1.75	3.17	1.74	7.8	4.4	8.7	0.0	4.9	0.32
2007	FLO	MLB	25	3	3	1	40	3	54	55	27	44	8	40.0%	.294	-2	1.51	4.87	5.40	4.92	8.9	3.8	6.5	1.2	3.9	0.40

Breakout: 5%   Improve: 19%   Collapse: 52%   Attrition: 42%   Comparables: Rich Yett, Don Cooper, Jose Acevedo, Al Widmar

Another live arm who threw ten pretty inspiring major league innings before blowing out his elbow and getting Tommy John'd, Martinez's control was iffy to begin with, so his rehab may be particularly exciting for those with behind-the-backstop season tickets in Greensboro.

Randy Messenger   Bats: R   Throws: R   Height: 6' 6"   Weight: 245   Born: August 13, 1981   Age: 25

YEAR	TEAM	LVL	AGE	W	L	SV	G	GS	IP	H	BB	SO	HR	GB%	BABIP	STUFF	WHIP	ERA	PERA	EQERA	EQH9	EQBB9	EQSO9	EQHR9	VORP	WXRL
2004	CAR	AA	22	6	3	21	58	0	69²	67	29	71	4	—	.330	1	1.38	2.58	4.28	3.41	9.2	4.1	6.0	0.8	16.7	—
2005	ABQ	AAA	23	4	2	7	39	0	48²	46	17	35	5	57.3%	.287	-9	1.29	3.88	4.67	4.20	8.2	2.9	4.9	0.9	7.7	—
2005	FLO	MLB	23	0	0	0	29	0	37	39	30	29	5	49.1%	.312	-1	1.86	5.35	5.72	5.35	8.8	6.5	6.3	1.2	0.3	-0.40
2006	FLO	MLB	24	2	7	0	59	0	60¹	72	24	45	8	40.4%	.337	-8	1.59	5.67	4.42	5.78	10.1	3.0	6.1	1.0	-3.0	-0.76
2007	FLO	MLB	25	2	3	1	45	0	51¹	55	24	39	6	45.0%	.305	-4	1.53	5.01	5.28	5.15	9.3	3.6	6.1	1.0	2.4	0.20

Breakout: 14%   Improve: 42%   Collapse: 20%   Attrition: 41%   Comparables: Bo McLaughlin, Dave Lemanczyk, Barry Jones, Dave Stevens

If his control problems are more or less behind him, Messenger is a pretty average reliever, which isn't a bad thing, so don't shoot him.

Sergio Mitre   Bats: R   Throws: R   Height: 6' 4"   Weight: 210   Born: February 16, 1981   Age: 26

YEAR	TEAM	LVL	AGE	W	L	SV	G	GS	IP	H	BB	SO	HR	GB%	BABIP	STUFF	WHIP	ERA	PERA	EQERA	EQH9	EQBB9	EQSO9	EQHR9	VORP	WXRL
2004	IOW	AAA	23	6	4	1	18	15	102²	97	39	95	9	—	.314	18	1.32	2.98	4.40	3.30	8.2	3.6	6.4	0.9	26.5	—
2004	CHN	MLB	23	2	4	0	12	9	51²	71	20	37	6	—	.374	0	1.76	6.62	4.49	6.28	12.2	3.1	5.6	0.8	-4.6	0.46
2005	IOW	AAA	24	5	6	0	13	13	70²	72	22	55	5	62.9%	.313	12	1.33	4.33	3.92	4.11	8.6	2.6	5.2	0.7	12.0	—
2005	CHN	MLB	24	2	5	0	21	7	60¹	62	23	37	11	69.2%	.268	-16	1.41	5.37	5.66	5.28	9.2	3.1	5.0	1.6	0.5	0.41
2006	FLO	MLB	25	1	5	0	15	7	41	44	20	31	7	52.7%	.303	-8	1.56	5.71	5.64	5.74	9.6	3.8	6.2	1.3	-1.5	0.18
2007	FLO	MLB	26	4	5	1	36	10	80	88	35	55	9	53.0%	.312	-3	1.53	4.97	5.28	5.17	9.7	3.3	5.6	0.9	3.7	0.70

Breakout: 15%   Improve: 45%   Collapse: 13%   Attrition: 14%   Comparables: Sean Bergman, Jerry Johnson, Jason Davis, La Marr Hoyt

Shoulder inflammation limited Mitre to just three pitches on May 12 in what would be his final start of the season. He was limited to bullpen duty after returning from the 60-day DL in August. Even that proved to be too much: he sat out the rest of the season to save his shoulder. Mitre was quoted in the *Miami Herald* as saying "I've done the bullpen thing before, and it didn't go so well for me." Prior to this year's few starts, the rotation didn't go so well for him either.

Brian Moehler   Bats: R   Throws: R   Height: 6' 3"   Weight: 235   Born: December 31, 1971   Age: 35

YEAR	TEAM	LVL	AGE	W	L	SV	G	GS	IP	H	BB	SO	HR	GB%	BABIP	STUFF	WHIP	ERA	PERA	EQERA	EQH9	EQBB9	EQSO9	EQHR9	VORP	WXRL
2004	GRN	AA	32	3	9	0	20	20	108	113	27	57	8	—	.289	-19	1.30	4.17	5.21	6.60	9.6	2.7	2.8	1.1	-11.8	—
2005	FLO	MLB	33	6	12	0	37	25	158¹	198	42	95	16	45.4%	.349	4	1.52	4.55	4.16	4.53	10.4	2.1	4.8	0.9	13.4	2.70
2006	FLO	MLB	34	7	11	0	29	21	122	164	38	58	19	46.2%	.340	-17	1.66	6.57	5.03	6.48	11.3	2.4	3.8	1.3	-16.5	0.21
2007	FLO	MLB	35	5	8	0	37	16	117²	144	36	61	17	47.0%	.313	-11	1.53	5.39	5.76	5.51	10.7	2.4	4.1	1.2	0.5	0.70

Breakout: 16%   Improve: 51%   Collapse: 17%   Attrition: 24%   Comparables: Jack Billingham, Cal McLish, Bob Forsch, Aaron Sele

Scuffy lost his rotation spot to Anibal Sanchez, and, at the end of the year, said that he just doesn't have what it takes to be a starter any more. It's true. A free agent at this writing, he's unlikely ever to land a steady gig again.

Ricky Nolasco　　　**Bats: R Throws: R**　　　Height: 6' 2"　　Weight: 220　　Born: December 13, 1982　　Age: 24

YEAR	TEAM	LVL	AGE	W	L	SV	G	GS	IP	H	BB	SO	HR	GB%	BABIP	STUFF	WHIP	ERA	PERA	EQERA	EQH9	EQBB9	EQSO9	EQHR9	VORP	WXRL
2004	WTN	AA	21	6	4	0	19	19	107	104	37	115	13	—	.317	-1	1.32	3.70	5.52	5.23	10.0	3.4	6.4	1.7	4.2	—
2004	IOW	AAA	21	2	3	0	9	9	40²	68	16	28	7	—	.409	-16	2.06	9.29	5.97	9.07	14.5	3.7	4.8	1.5	-16.1	—
2005	WTN	AA	22	14	3	0	27	27	161²	151	46	173	13	46.2%	.320	16	1.22	2.89	4.57	3.82	9.5	2.6	6.9	1.3	31.2	—
2006	FLO	MLB	23	11	11	0	35	22	140	157	41	99	20	40.5%	.319	2	1.41	4.82	4.55	5.12	9.6	2.2	5.7	1.1	6.7	2.78
2007	*FLO*	*MLB*	*24*	*7*	*9*	*1*	*35*	*20*	*136¹*	*146*	*46*	*103*	*18*	*44.0%*	*.304*	*8*	*1.41*	*4.70*	*5.02*	*4.80*	*9.4*	*2.6*	*6.1*	*1.1*	*12.6*	*2.10*

Breakout: 20% Improve: 59% Collapse: 12% Attrition: 4%　　Comparables: *John Snyder, Buster Narum, Tom Morgan, Jeff Suppan*

Over the winter, a lot was made of the fact that Florida's rotation featured five pitchers who won more than ten games in 2006, four of whom were rookies. The raw win totals for the kids are Johnson 12, Olsen 12, Nolasco 11, and Sanchez 10. Though also a counting stat, SNLVAR shows that one of these things is not like the others: Sanchez 5.0, Johnson 4.7, Olsen 4.7, and Nolasco 2.3. The Nolasco Kid had a decent year overall, but lefties slugged .590 against him, and that's the sort of thing you fix, or the rotation might not be his home for much longer.

Scott Olsen　　　**Bats: L Throws: L**　　　Height: 6' 4"　　Weight: 200　　Born: January 12, 1984　　Age: 23

YEAR	TEAM	LVL	AGE	W	L	SV	G	GS	IP	H	BB	SO	HR	GB%	BABIP	STUFF	WHIP	ERA	PERA	EQERA	EQH9	EQBB9	EQSO9	EQHR9	VORP	WXRL
2004	JUP	A+	20	7	6	0	25	25	136¹	127	54	158	8	—	.335	16	1.33	2.97	4.74	4.96	9.5	4.1	7.1	1.2	9.4	—
2005	CAR	AA	21	6	4	0	14	14	80¹	75	27	94	7	52.1%	.343	18	1.27	3.92	4.59	4.83	9.5	3.1	7.6	1.4	6.7	—
2005	FLO	MLB	21	1	1	0	5	4	20¹	21	10	21	5	40.0%	.291	15	1.52	3.99	5.77	5.91	8.9	3.8	8.0	2.1	-0.9	0.54
2006	FLO	MLB	22	12	10	0	31	31	180²	160	75	166	23	46.0%	.285	22	1.30	4.03	4.22	4.48	7.7	3.2	7.4	1.0	24.3	4.70
2007	*FLO*	*MLB*	*23*	*10*	*10*	*0*	*28*	*28*	*174*	*166*	*72*	*164*	*19*	*45.0%*	*.300*	*24*	*1.36*	*4.24*	*4.53*	*4.34*	*8.4*	*3.2*	*7.6*	*0.9*	*24.8*	*3.90*

Breakout: 23% Improve: 59% Collapse: 11% Attrition: 1%　　Comparables: *Ken Holtzman, Jerry Reuss, Jim Kaat, Arthur Rhodes*

His spotty mechanics now more or less sorted out, Olsen became one of the more capable pitchers on the team last year with a nasty fastball-slider combo and a good changeup. Olsen also survived the indignity of not breaking camp with the team while other ball-throwing bipeds did. In 2005, it was a toss-up as to who had the better long-term outlook between Olsen and Jason Vargas. It's pretty clear who's on top now.

Yusmeiro Petit　　　**Bats: R Throws: R**　　　Height: 6' 0"　　Weight: 180　　Born: November 22, 1984　　Age: 22

YEAR	TEAM	LVL	AGE	W	L	SV	G	GS	IP	H	BB	SO	HR	GB%	BABIP	STUFF	WHIP	ERA	PERA	EQERA	EQH9	EQBB9	EQSO9	EQHR9	VORP	WXRL
2004	CMB	A	19	9	2	0	15	15	83	47	22	122	8	—	.234	32	0.83	2.39	4.71	3.86	6.8	2.8	8.1	1.5	15.3	—
2004	SLU	A+	19	2	3	0	9	9	44¹	27	14	62	0	—	.284	43	0.93	1.22	3.05	2.51	6.7	3.3	8.6	0.2	14.8	—
2004	BIN	AA	19	1	1	0	2	2	12	10	5	16	0	—	.345	12	1.25	4.50	2.95	5.40	8.5	3.9	8.5	0.0	0.3	—
2005	BIN	AA	20	9	3	0	21	21	117²	90	18	130	15	35.0%	.262	19	0.92	2.91	4.56	3.56	7.4	1.5	6.8	1.6	26.4	—
2005	NOR	AAA	20	0	3	0	3	3	14²	24	6	14	5	33.3%	.422	-5	2.04	9.18	7.97	11.30	15.7	3.8	6.9	3.8	-9.1	—
2006	ABQ	AAA	21	4	6	0	17	17	96²	101	20	68	14	42.5%	.295	-1	1.26	4.30	4.94	4.64	8.7	1.8	4.8	1.5	10.6	—
2006	FLO	MLB	21	1	1	0	15	1	26¹	46	9	20	7	31.6%	.429	-13	2.09	9.58	5.47	8.89	14.8	2.6	5.9	2.0	-11.1	-0.37
2007	*FLO*	*MLB*	*22*	*6*	*8*	*1*	*39*	*18*	*121²*	*123*	*37*	*95*	*20*	*38.0%*	*.283*	*7*	*1.32*	*4.62*	*4.92*	*4.66*	*8.9*	*2.3*	*6.3*	*1.4*	*13.1*	*1.90*

Breakout: 27% Improve: 76% Collapse: 3% Attrition: 0%　　Comparables: *Dicky Gonzalez, Tony Cloninger, Buddy Carlyle, Bob Kipper*

As Blaise Pascal once wrote, "We are not yet, we hope to be." Scouts and statheads disagree on Petit's long-term potential, so in 2007 the pitcher will serve as one more battlefield in the ongoing struggle between the Calculator and the Clipboard. Petit was his usual walk-stingy self before a May callup, but his strikeout rates have been declining. The theory is that pitchers such as Petit, who rely less on speed than on variety, deception, and movement, get exposed by major league hitters, who are a little harder to fool than their minor league brethren. That theory got a little fuel last year as Petit's BABIP (.429) and homers (translated rate of 2 per 9 IP) were not good. Petit throws four pitches for strikes, but he's going to have to get better at the art of prestidigitation and legerdemain if he's going to succeed in the majors.

Renyel Pinto
Bats: L Throws: L Height: 6' 4" Weight: 195 Born: July 8, 1982 Age: 24

YEAR	TEAM	LVL	AGE	W	L	SV	G	GS	IP	H	BB	SO	HR	GB%	BABIP	STUFF	WHIP	ERA	PERA	EQERA	EQH9	EQBB9	EQSO9	EQHR9	VORP	WXRL
2004	WTN	AA	21	11	8	0	25	25	141²	107	72	179	10	—	.301	25	1.26	2.92	4.78	4.03	8.1	5.0	7.7	1.0	23.8	—
2005	WTN	AA	22	10	3	0	22	21	129²	101	58	123	3	52.1%	.300	29	1.23	2.71	4.05	3.66	7.6	4.1	6.0	0.4	27.6	—
2005	IOW	AAA	22	1	2	0	6	6	22²	31	24	24	3	46.5%	.452	2	2.42	9.52	6.65	11.57	12.0	8.9	6.9	1.2	-15.5	—
2006	ABQ	AAA	23	8	2	0	18	18	95¹	82	47	96	8	49.2%	.297	18	1.36	3.41	4.98	3.55	7.8	4.3	6.9	0.8	21.9	—
2006	FLO	MLB	23	0	0	1	27	0	29²	20	27	36	3	46.4%	.258	31	1.58	3.03	4.73	3.52	6.2	7.0	9.7	0.9	7.4	0.30
2007	FLO	MLB	24	5	7	1	46	15	103¹	98	67	97	11	47.0%	.302	5	1.59	4.97	5.34	5.14	8.4	5.0	7.5	0.9	5.3	1.00

Breakout: 8% Improve: 20% Collapse: 51% Attrition: 4% Comparables: Mike Kilkenny, Micah Bowie, Doug Davis, Shawn Chacon

Though he only pitched out of the pen in Florida last year, Pinto's being ticketed for the rotation in the future. Indeed, he had a pretty good year as a starter in Albuquerque. He's still somewhat raw, though, as his consistently high walk totals suggest. It's not difficult to see how his fastball-slider combo from a low, three-quarters delivery might work out better in the bullpen, particularly if he's going to continue to struggle with his command.

Chris Resop
Bats: R Throws: R Height: 6' 3" Weight: 220 Born: November 4, 1982 Age: 24

YEAR	TEAM	LVL	AGE	W	L	SV	G	GS	IP	H	BB	SO	HR	GB%	BABIP	STUFF	WHIP	ERA	PERA	EQERA	EQH9	EQBB9	EQSO9	EQHR9	VORP	WXRL
2005	CAR	AA	22	3	2	24	43	0	49	47	16	56	2	50.7%	.331	13	1.29	2.57	3.42	3.33	9.2	3.0	7.2	0.6	12.3	—
2005	FLO	MLB	22	2	0	0	15	0	17	22	9	15	1	28.3%	.404	-5	1.82	8.47	3.97	8.15	11.2	4.1	7.1	0.5	-6.0	-0.03
2006	ABQ	AAA	23	4	0	2	40	0	49	49	15	43	4	46.4%	.315	2	1.31	3.86	4.00	3.58	8.4	2.7	5.9	0.9	11.3	—
2006	FLO	MLB	23	1	2	0	21	0	21¹	26	16	10	1	39.2%	.342	-14	1.97	3.38	5.00	3.63	10.5	5.6	3.6	0.4	5.1	-0.13
2007	LAA	MLB	24	3	4	2	84	1	74²	85	30	48	10	44.0%	.309	-7	1.53	4.98	5.09	4.87	10.1	3.4	5.4	1.1	4.9	0.40

Breakout: 6% Improve: 28% Collapse: 43% Attrition: 4% Comparables: Kevin Correia, Duaner Sanchez, Gary Ross, Elio Serrano

Resop used to try to hit spherical objects for a living, and when that didn't work, he tried to throw them. The problem is that all he's learned how to do is throw them really, really hard. He needs another pitch, but it'll be the Angels' job to teach him one, as he was sent westward for Kevin Gregg.

Anibal Sanchez
Bats: R Throws: R Height: 6' 0" Weight: 180 Born: February 27, 1984 Age: 23

YEAR	TEAM	LVL	AGE	W	L	SV	G	GS	IP	H	BB	SO	HR	GB%	BABIP	STUFF	WHIP	ERA	PERA	EQERA	EQH9	EQBB9	EQSO9	EQHR9	VORP	WXRL
2004	LOW	A-	20	4	4	0	15	15	76¹	43	29	101	3	—	.230	18	0.94	1.77	5.41	3.95	7.0	5.1	6.5	1.0	13.0	—
2005	WIL	A+	21	6	1	0	14	14	78²	53	24	95	7	47.9%	.253	18	0.98	2.40	4.73	3.57	7.6	3.1	6.9	1.3	17.1	—
2005	PME	AA	21	3	5	0	11	11	57¹	53	16	63	5	46.5%	.322	16	1.20	3.46	4.52	4.98	9.5	2.9	6.8	1.1	3.9	—
2006	CAR	AA	22	3	6	0	15	15	85	82	27	92	7	48.2%	.319	12	1.28	3.18	4.47	5.04	9.5	2.8	7.0	1.3	5.2	—
2006	FLO	MLB	22	10	3	0	18	17	114¹	90	46	72	9	43.1%	.243	20	1.19	2.83	4.19	3.00	6.8	3.2	5.1	0.6	36.2	4.81
2007	FLO	MLB	23	11	11	0	34	32	190	182	76	157	22	44.0%	.289	18	1.36	4.22	4.53	4.32	8.4	3.1	6.6	0.9	28.3	4.20

Breakout: 4% Improve: 24% Collapse: 40% Attrition: 0% Comparables: Joel Pineiro, Ned Garver, Tom Seaver, Frank Castillo

During his no-hitter in September, Sanchez was still hitting 95 MPH in the ninth inning. That is a bit more velocity than he was showing a few years ago, and it seems he owes his increased velocity to 2003 nerve transposition surgery. Lost in the giddiness of his first major league season was the fact that he lost about two strikeouts per nine innings from his 2005 rate. Given his ultra-low BABIP (.243) and the fact that he nearly cut his career home run rate in half last year, it's easy to see why he's a good candidate for some regression.

Taylor Tankersley
Bats: L Throws: L Height: 6' 1" Weight: 220 Born: March 7, 1983 Age: 24

YEAR	TEAM	LVL	AGE	W	L	SV	G	GS	IP	H	BB	SO	HR	GB%	BABIP	STUFF	WHIP	ERA	PERA	EQERA	EQH9	EQBB9	EQSO9	EQHR9	VORP	WXRL
2004	JAM	A-	21	1	1	0	6	6	26²	21	8	32	2	—	.275	-6	1.09	3.37	6.35	6.20	9.1	4.0	5.5	1.8	-1.6	—
2005	GRB	A	22	2	7	0	12	12	66	74	25	63	12	41.9%	.326	-38	1.50	5.18	8.89	7.63	12.5	4.7	5.0	3.5	-13.8	—
2005	JUP	A+	22	1	0	0	4	4	24	21	9	19	1	41.8%	.308	4	1.25	3.38	4.83	4.63	8.1	4.2	4.6	0.8	2.5	—
2006	CAR	AA	23	4	1	6	22	0	28²	11	14	40	0	49.1%	.229	27	0.89	0.96	3.30	1.98	4.6	4.6	8.9	0.3	11.0	—
2006	FLO	MLB	23	2	1	3	49	0	41	33	26	46	4	46.5%	.305	23	1.44	2.85	4.04	3.00	7.1	4.9	9.0	0.9	13.0	2.13
2007	FLO	MLB	24	2	2	3	55	0	47	44	30	45	5	41.0%	.297	2	1.57	4.64	5.18	4.73	8.3	4.8	7.6	0.9	4.3	0.40

Breakout: 14% Improve: 20% Collapse: 32% Attrition: 33% Comparables: Kent Mercker, Corey Thurman, Jim Crawford, Chuck McElroy

In his first full year of relief, Tankersley was one of the best relievers in baseball at keeping the ball out of play:

Reliever	IP	Pitches	Inplay	Inplay%
B. J. Ryan	71.0	1096	164	14.96%
Taylor Tankersley	40.0	702	105	14.96%
Kiko Calero	57.0	1013	150	14.81%
Joel Zumaya	83.1	1425	209	14.67%
Jonathan Broxton	75.2	1305	189	14.48%

Of course, you need a boatload of walks to really rank high on this list, and Tankersley had that. Tankersley fits the old Armando Reynoso scouting report: "3-2 on everybody." Bumped to the bullpen because he didn't have the durability or repertoire to challenge the surplus of young arms in the Florida system for a rotation spot, Tankersley can be a good, cheap, late-inning option for the Marlins if he can command his stuff better. Without that command, most of his appearances will be nailbiters.

Scott Tyler Bats: R Throws: R Height: 6' 5" Weight: 265 Born: August 20, 1982 Age: 24

YEAR	TEAM	LVL	AGE	W	L	SV	G	GS	IP	H	BB	SO	HR	GB%	BABIP	STUFF	WHIP	ERA	PERA	EQERA	EQH9	EQBB9	EQSO9	EQHR9	VORP	WXRL
2004	QUD	A	21	7	4	0	22	19	103²	73	64	132	3	—	.293	30	1.32	2.60	5.29	3.94	8.0	7.6	6.8	0.6	17.7	—
2005	FTM	A+	22	7	8	0	23	23	118¹	106	48	109	18	35.2%	.288	-37	1.30	3.96	7.97	5.95	9.9	4.9	5.4	2.8	-4.3	—
2006	CAR	AA	23	1	2	3	48	0	61	56	44	52	5	46.5%	.288	-11	1.64	3.69	6.45	5.22	9.0	6.6	5.2	1.3	2.5	—
2007	FLO	MLB	24	2	4	0	27	6	55¹	53	60	51	7	40.0%	.299	-11	2.03	6.12	7.09	6.23	8.4	8.3	7.4	1.0	-3.6	0.20

Breakout: 7% Improve: 17% Collapse: 46% Attrition: 17% Comparables: Frank Francisco, Scott Sobkowiak, Pat Collins, Kris Keller

By the time the pitching gods got to the T's, it had been a long day. They had endowed distinctive characteristics to the one they called Takatsu, and gave the Tavarezes, the Trachsels, and the Timlins some resiliency. But when there was just one name left on their list, they wanted to go home. They had no more ideas. "What is the most common young pitcher profile?" asked Walkmetheus, the God of Untranslated Walk Rates. "Why, a hard-throwing yet wild right-hander," answered Mechanicus. "Then let us make this Tyler one of those." "Shall we prepare his elbow for ruination, too?" asked Mechanicus. "No. Let's wait a while on that," said Walkmetheus on his way out the door. And lo, it was done.

Jason Vargas Bats: L Throws: L Height: 6' 0" Weight: 215 Born: February 2, 1983 Age: 24

YEAR	TEAM	LVL	AGE	W	L	SV	G	GS	IP	H	BB	SO	HR	GB%	BABIP	STUFF	WHIP	ERA	PERA	EQERA	EQH9	EQBB9	EQSO9	EQHR9	VORP	WXRL
2004	JAM	A-	21	3	1	0	8	8	41¹	35	13	41	2	—	.292	-3	1.16	1.96	5.84	4.99	8.6	4.3	4.5	1.1	2.7	—
2005	GRB	A	22	4	1	0	5	5	33²	16	10	33	1	35.4%	.188	15	0.77	0.80	4.48	1.95	5.3	3.6	5.0	0.6	13.1	—
2005	JUP	A+	22	2	3	0	9	9	55¹	47	14	60	6	36.8%	.287	2	1.10	3.42	5.75	5.09	8.8	3.1	6.1	2.0	3.0	—
2005	CAR	AA	22	1	0	0	3	3	19	13	7	25	3	41.9%	.256	18	1.05	2.84	6.13	3.50	8.0	3.5	8.5	2.5	4.2	—
2005	FLO	MLB	22	5	5	0	17	13	73²	71	31	59	4	31.4%	.302	21	1.38	4.03	3.78	4.24	8.1	3.4	6.5	0.5	10.8	1.77
2006	ABQ	AAA	23	3	6	0	13	13	69	98	28	51	11	37.6%	.395	-16	1.83	7.43	5.79	7.32	12.0	3.4	5.0	1.6	-13.6	—
2006	FLO	MLB	23	1	2	0	12	5	43	50	30	25	9	32.2%	.299	-17	1.86	7.33	6.85	7.66	10.1	5.4	4.6	1.6	-10.8	-0.54
2007	NYN	MLB	24	6	8	0	32	21	122²	126	56	79	21	38.0%	.276	-4	1.48	5.18	5.58	5.64	9.3	3.6	5.2	1.4	2.6	1.00

Breakout: 26% Improve: 61% Collapse: 13% Attrition: 0% Comparables: Mike McCormick, Michael Connolly, Josh Habel, Allen Watson

Even though the Marlins had a really nice date with him in 2005, Vargas found himself buried in the pitching staff's Little Black Book last year. So, whatever, he totally didn't need them, and if Florida did decide to call, he'd let it ring a few times before picking so as not to seem desperate. So what if he had a little walk trouble *this* year? Do you break up with someone over a few extra walks? *Do you?* And don't give him the whole "it's not you, it's us; we just need more time to think" thing. He totally tried to be himself last year, and if he came off as something other than what he was, then so what? That's not his fault, right? The Mets called and asked for him by name, so he's with them now. Only when the Marlins finally come to town, it's going to be, like, so awkward.

Chris Volstad   Bats: R Throws: R   Height: 6′ 7″   Weight: 190   Born: September 23, 1986   Age: 20

YEAR	TEAM	LVL	AGE	W	L	SV	G	GS	IP	H	BB	SO	HR	GB%	BABIP	STUFF	WHIP	ERA	PERA	EQERA	EQH9	EQBB9	EQSO9	EQHR9	VORP	WXRL
2005	JAM	A-	18	3	2	0	7	7	38	43	11	29	0	59.1%	.344	9	1.42	2.13	4.21	5.12	9.8	3.3	3.5	0.2	2.1	—
2006	GRB	A	19	11	8	0	26	26	152	161	36	99	12	61.4%	.314	-10	1.30	3.08	5.61	5.58	10.3	2.6	3.5	1.5	0.3	—
2007	FLO	MLB	20	6	10	0	25	22	128²	145	49	69	16	54.0%	.300	1	1.51	5.41	5.49	5.64	9.9	2.9	4.3	1.0	-1.2	0.80

Breakout: 16% Improve: 43% Collapse: 17% Attrition: 1%   Comparables: Michael Schlact, Dallas Trahern, Brandon League, Kyle Waldrop

Florida's Minor League Pitcher of the Year, Volstad is young and raw, but has good mechanics and an assortment that belies his youth. Although he has his struggles against lefties, Greensboro is a launching pad, and his home run rate was yeoman's work. Scouts like his ability to keep the ball on the ground, and everybody likes his ability to throw strikes with low-90s heat, curves, and changeups.

Dontrelle Willis   Bats: L Throws: L   Height: 6′ 4″   Weight: 240   Born: January 12, 1982   Age: 25

YEAR	TEAM	LVL	AGE	W	L	SV	G	GS	IP	H	BB	SO	HR	GB%	BABIP	STUFF	WHIP	ERA	PERA	EQERA	EQH9	EQBB9	EQSO9	EQHR9	VORP	WXRL
2004	FLO	MLB	22	10	11	0	32	32	197	210	61	139	20	—	.312	16	1.38	4.02	4.10	4.64	9.6	2.5	5.6	0.9	24.1	4.20
2005	FLO	MLB	23	22	10	0	34	34	236¹	213	55	170	11	46.0%	.290	33	1.13	2.63	3.24	3.09	7.5	1.9	5.8	0.4	65.2	8.61
2006	FLO	MLB	24	12	12	0	34	34	223¹	234	83	160	21	48.8%	.316	17	1.42	3.87	4.24	4.08	9.1	2.9	5.8	0.7	40.5	5.41
2007	FLO	MLB	25	12	11	0	32	32	208¹	214	66	157	21	48.0%	.302	17	1.34	4.06	4.45	4.16	9.0	2.4	6.1	0.8	34.4	5.00

Breakout: 12% Improve: 39% Collapse: 21% Attrition: 0%   Comparables: Jim Abbott, Jim Kaat, Mark Buehrle, C. C. Sabathia

Willis looked like a total mess in the World Baseball Classic, his mechanics were all out of whack, his velocity was down, and he was throwing batting practice fastballs with maximum effort. This sort of thing was one of the primary concerns about having the WBC played during spring training, and it looked like Willis would be one of the tournament's first casualties. Fortunately, he made some early-season corrections to his mechanics and recovered enough of his prior mojo to have a pretty good season. Of course, he let a few extra balls leave the yard, lost the gains in his control that helped make his 2005 such a great year, and has yet to repeat his rookie strikeout rate. Topping things off, some late-season injury trouble served as another reminder that throwing a baseball is a hazardous occupation, particularly when you throw like Willis.

Lineouts

PLAYER	TEAM	LVL	AGE	PA	R	2B	3B	HR	RBI	BB	SO	SB-CS	SPEED	AVG/OBP/SLG	MLVrEqAVG/EqOBP/EqSLG	EqA	VORP
RF C. Aguila	ABQ	AAA	27	333	53	15	3	11	61	26	54	7-3	6.0	.318/.369/.497	.123	.267/.314/.420	.254	-2.1
	FLO	MLB	27	104	5	8	1	0	7	9	26	2-1	3.8	.232/.298/.337	-.197	.232/.305/.337	.229	-3.1
OF A. De Aza*	CAR	AA	22	266	40	12	2	2	16	21	46	27-10	7.0	.278/.346/.374	.061	.282/.340/.395	.261	6.9
RF T. Hickman*	MRL	Rk	18	207	28	12	4	2	20	30	43	4-5	5.5	.263/.377/.411	.178	.243/.327/.395	.249	6.3
C P. Hoover	ABQ	AAA	30	343	38	21	1	6	41	33	71	3-2	4.4	.278/.351/.414	-.048	.225/.287/.331	.221	-10.1
3B L. Mitchell	CAR	AA	24	520	56	37	1	11	56	46	139	2-6	3.8	.253/.329/.409	.064	.246/.312/.412	.247	10.6
1B G. Sanchez	GRB	A	22	237	43	12	0	14	40	39	20	6-2	4.6	.317/.447/.603	.514	.265/.361/.485	.288	11.8
	JUP	A+	22	68	13	3	1	1	7	12	12	1-0	6.5	.182/.324/.327	-.033	.175/.294/.316	.231	-3.9
SS A. Septimo*	GRB	A	22	326	44	10	2	7	25	30	71	20-3	6.7	.263/.333/.384	.037	.227/.276/.323	.217	-10.6

PLAYER	TEAM	LVL	AGE	W	L	SV	IP	H	BB	SO	HR	GB%	BABIP	STUFF	WHIP	ERA	PERA	EqERA	EqH9	EqBB9	EqSO9	EqHR9	VORP
J. Fulchino	ABQ	AAA	26	6	10	0	140¹	144	56	109	12	—	.321	4	1.43	4.50	4.99	4.96	8.9	3.5	5.2	0.9	10.2
F. German	FLO	MLB	26	0	0	0	12	7	14	6	1	—	.176	-2	1.75	3.00	7.25	2.92	5.1	8.8	4.4	0.7	4.0
P. Mildren*	CAR	AA	22	10	10	0	167²	161	54	150	19	—	.307	-7	1.29	4.14	5.59	5.45	9.5	2.9	5.7	1.7	2.8
S. Nestor	JUP	A+	21	2	2	10	39²	19	26	48	0	—	.221	21	1.15	2.53	4.87	3.82	5.5	6.9	7.4	0.2	7.5
	CAR	AA	21	2	2	0	13¹	18	13	13	1	—	.386	-10	2.37	7.56	6.93	11.77	13.2	9.0	6.2	1.4	-8.9
A. Thompson*	GRB	A	19	8	8	0	134	139	35	114	12	—	.327	-8	1.30	3.63	5.75	5.80	10.6	2.8	4.6	1.7	-2.9
R. Tucker	GRB	A	19	7	13	0	131¹	123	67	133	14	—	.308	-18	1.45	5.01	7.22	7.24	10.3	5.7	5.6	2.1	-22.7
S. West*	GRB	A	20	8	5	0	120²	115	40	102	13	—	.304	-21	1.29	3.74	6.94	5.21	10.3	3.7	4.7	2.1	5.0

If **Chris Aguila** couldn't win a spot on the 2006 Marlins given the competition for his job, there's not much hope left for him. He doesn't hit for average or power, doesn't work the count, doesn't steal bases. Then again, he signed a minor league deal with Pirates, a team whose outfield is even thinner than that of the Marlins. At the plate, **Alejandro de Aza** is like the CGI Yoda in a lightsaber duel—swift, nimble, hyperkinetic, and never lays a good stroke on anything. **Thomas Hickman** was a two-way player in high school, though his future with the Marlins seems to be in right field. His pro debut was encouraging, but it's too early to get excited or cynical about the specifics. **Paul Hoover** finally got a chance to play when Matt Treanor reinjured his shoulder. Of course, he only wound up getting five plate appearances, but he still out-VORPed Treanor. **Lee Mitchell** was old for his league, and is only in the book because there are simply no other major-league ready position players to talk about in the Marlins' system. He can pick it at third, though. **Gaby Sanchez**'s season was truncated because of a broken hand and a broken toe, but he managed to hit well enough to be named the organization's Player of the Year. He's got a good eye, but no defensive value, and he's a bit old to still be awaiting his promotion to Double-A. **Agustin Septimo**'s translations have been unkind. Sure, he can run a little, and play a little defense, but he'd have to run a two-minute mile and be a literal vacuum at short to make up for his career-high EqA of .228.

A six-foot-five hulk out of UConn, **Jeff Fulchino** doesn't really have any plus stuff, just an occasionally good fastball. He seems a bit out of place in an organization otherwise populated with pitching prospects. **Franklyn German** was hampered by shoulder tendonitis as well as his usual control problems last year; he'll be in Rangers camp as a non-roster invitee. Though not one of the top arms in the system, Aussie **Paul Mildren** was added to the 40-man roster this winter anyway. He's still too accommodating to righties, but he throws strikes and earns the league minimum; that's all you need to be in Florida's bullpen mix nowadays. **Scott Nestor** is on a dedicated quest to let all batters reach base when he pitches. Another young 'un in the Sally League, **Aaron Thompson**'s stuff isn't nearly as good as Volstad's, West's, or Tucker's; he'll need better command if he's to succeed. **Ryan Tucker** has a live arm and a hard fastball, but struggles with his command and lacks a reliable second pitch. He's just 19, so we can cut him some slack for a year or three. **Sean West** is a tall lefty who'd better get used to the Randy Johnson comparisons, particularly since he has a live fastball, a three-quarters arm slot, and no real changeup.

Manager: Joe Girardi

Year	Team	W-L	Pythag +/-	Avg PC	100 +P	120 +P	QS	BQS	REL	REL w Zero R	IBB	SUBS	PH	PH Avg	PH HR	SB2	CS2	SB3	CS3	SAC Att	SAC %	POS SAC	Squeeze	Swing	In Play
2006	FLO	78-84	-2	94.9	74	3	86	9	436	270	58	96	247	.242	4	95	50	13	6	103	73.8%	42	4	145	104

Joe Girardi was let go after just one year, though it wasn't because of any on-field failures. That doesn't make the firing any less legitimate; in any enterprise, the middle manager's job is to successfully navigate between those below him and those above. Girardi apparently failed the latter part of the assignment, reportedly arguing with both the owner and general manager in a less than decorous manner. Unfortunately for Girardi, in this day of corporate ownership, fraternal George vs. Billy tussles are a thing of the past. If Girardi doesn't understand this, he's going to have problems in his next job, even if it's back in the Bronx as Joe Torre's successor. On the field, Girardi was a mixed bag. He got bonus points for leading his young team into a brief period of Wild Card contention. In particular—and this is something to keep an eye on with replacement Fredi Gonzalez—Girardi did a decent job of keeping the young pitchers out of harm's way: Florida starters went beyond 120 pitches just six times last year. All of those starts belonged to Dontrelle Willis, whom Girardi seemed to have mistaken for a fully-formed veteran because of his experience relative to the rest of the staff. The only other misstep was the bizarre decision to push Josh Johnson through a 1:22 rain delay. Girardi used more defensive subs than any other manager in baseball but was otherwise middle of the pack in most regards.

Gonzalez, who spent the last four seasons as Bobby Cox's third base coach, is the former skipper of the Florida State League Miami Miracle, which is what they'll call it if he's able to move the Marlins forward from their surprising showing last year. Another former catcher, Gonzalez will be expected to have a facility with the pitching staff, but will face a greater challenge in organizing an offense.

Houston Astros

Considering how many things went wrong in Houston in 2006, it might seem less than generous to call their fifth consecutive second-place finish in the NL Central it anything less than a success. That is until you consider that the Astros failed to make the playoffs after reaching the NLCS in consecutive years and winning the pennant in 2005. Just making it to the big dance would have provided a semblance of a happy ending to a team whose entire season had been held hostage to Roger Clemens's flirtation with retirement.

The Astros could have avoided shopping in the fairy tale aisle altogether if they'd just been more decisive than Clemens themselves. Over the past decade, the team has been held in stasis by a schizophrenic run of front office and ownership decisions. Houston's record over the last five years has been 434–376 (.536), and they have had some fine seasons in that time, but they've failed to build a ballclub that can keep up with the Cardinals, let alone consistently win the minimum 90 games it takes to have a solid shot at the playoffs each year. Caught between winning now and rebuilding, between spending big and crying mid-market poor, the Astros have been a winning team that lacks the internal coherence to evolve in any particular direction.

Despite their late run at the division title, the Astros climbed back down to .500 last year. Only the Cardinals' stretch-drive swoon generated any element of drama, this was a .500 team that played .500 ball. According to the Pythagenports (the number of wins expected from their runs scored and allowed), they were an 83-win team; adjusting for strength of schedule, they were an 80- or 81-win team. They weren't unlucky, they were mediocre. If they came up a game short, it was because they acquired mediocre talents such as Aubrey Huff to help them achieve their mediocre ambitions.

> ## ASTROS PROSPECTUS
>
> **2006 record:** 82–80; Second place, NL Central
>
> **Pythagenport record:** 82–80
>
> **Runs scored per game:** 4.54 (12th in NL)
>
> **Runs allowed per game:** 4.44 (2nd in NL)
>
> **Team EqA:** .254 (12th in NL)
>
> **2006 Batters Age:** 31.1 (3rd oldest in NL)
>
> **2006 Pitchers Age:** 30.2 (5th oldest in NL)
>
> **Ballpark:** Minute Maid Park; Neutral park; Park Factor of 1.005
>
> **2006:** A year spent with both legs caught in the "Popular Aging Veteran" trap.
>
> **2007:** Only one leg's caught in the "Popular Aging Veteran" trap, which means they can now run in circles.

The problem that prevented Tim Purpura from charting a bolder course in his second year as general manager arose at the December 2005 winter meetings. The team gave a press conference to announce that staff ace Roger Clemens would not be offered salary arbitration. The journalists in attendance alternately chuckled or groused about covering a formality; few realized that this decision would impact the Astros' season more than any other. Having not offered him arbitration, the Astros were barred from re-signing Clemens until May 1, a month after the start of the season. Clemens had offers from other teams, most notably the Texas Rangers, but few believed that he would pitch anywhere other than Houston.

The exasperating May 1 rule was not carried over to the new Collective Bargaining Agreement, making Clemens the last player and the Astros the last team to be seriously troubled by it. In originally bargaining for the rule, the Players Association was seeking a mechanism that would pressure teams to make a decision on their free agents. Given the Rocket's ambivalence about pitching in 2006, it's not clear that either party placed much importance on the May 1 penalty. For a second-place ballclub that had a lot of question marks, that was a crucial mistake. Despite not offering Clemens arbitration, the team still needed to reserve cash for the possibility of what some in the organization would later call Clemens's "budget-buster" contract. Doing so hindered the team's ability to re-arm for the coming season. With Clemens doing his Schrödinger's cat routine, the Astros became the idlers in their own diamond-minded drama, "Waiting for Rocket."

It's impossible to know if Clemens would have acted more decisively had the team offered him arbitration, but his enforced absence, however pleasant it may have been for him, wound up hurting the Astros badly. Rather than leap into action on May 1, when the club was only a half-game out of first place, Clemens equivocated until May 30, at which point he finally signed that anticipated big-money contract with the Astros. He then took a slow tour through the minor leagues. He had one start at each level, selling out each minor league stadium (including two in which he holds an ownership interest). You can forgive Astros fans for their frustration if, while Clemens took almost three weeks to "work himself into shape," they remembered that he'd had no problem taking the mound for Team USA back in March. After keeping pace with the Cardinals through May 5, the Astros fell into an 8–22 slump over the next month and were languishing a game below .500 when Clemens finally made his 2006 major league debut on June 22. During the seven weeks they waited for Clemens, Houston had fallen six games behind the Cardinals.

The Astros could have obviated the need for Clemens, or at least made that need not quite as urgent, had they had simply signed a worthwhile replacement or two back in December, rather than waiting around for a player who had long said he was retiring. Because they did not, the rotation was a jury-rigged contraption after Roy Oswalt and Andy Pettitte. Brandon Backe would fill the third slot, but the last two starters would be a pair of as-yet-undetermined youngsters. PECOTA projected just 33 wins coming from that front three; Clemens was needed to bring the rotation to a level that could support a contender.

This bad situation was made worse immediately after the season started when the team lost Backe to an elbow injury in mid-April. Rookies Fernando Nieve and Taylor Buchholz were suddenly pressed into a rotation already counting on the immortal Wandy Rodriguez. While Clemens was barnstorming, Buchholz was getting blitzed. While Clemens was in Round Rock, Rodriguez was not in Round Rock. The Astros overestimated their kids: PECOTA forecasted Fernando Nieve, Wandy Rodriguez, and Taylor Buchholz for VORP values of 8.6, –3.0, and –1.2, respectively; their actual VORP totals were 19.0, –4.3, and –3.6, with a lot of Nieve's value coming through his work in the pen after his elbow started causing problems. Rodriguez and Buchholz would wind up making 43 starts and were a combined one win below replacement-level. The youngsters weren't helping the team at all, they were hurting it.

Upon arrival, Clemens commenced mowing down hitters as he had the prior season. Despite an unimpressive 7–6 record, and an equally unimpressive 9–10 team record in his starts—both largely the result of poor run support—the Rocket was clearly one of the top pitchers in baseball. His 42.1 VORP suggests that if he had played a full season, which would have given him about a dozen more starts, the Astros could have picked up three more wins—enough

to consign the 2006 Cardinals to history's dustbin. It didn't happen, and instead it was the Astros who were tossed on the ash heap.

This winter, the Clemens scenario has already repeated itself, but the rules change in the CBA allows for a different outcome. The Astros again refused to offer Clemens arbitration, but under the new Agreement, all that means is that if Clemens chooses to sign elsewhere, the team won't receive a compensatory draft pick. The May 1 prohibition won't handicap anyone ever again.

Having already seen the "Waiting for Rocket" scenario consume his second season as general manager, Purpura sprung into action following the 2006 season, bolstering the Astros' flaccid outfield production by signing slugger Carlos Lee to a six-year, $100 million contract in late November. The hope is that Lee will be what Jeff Bagwell stopped being several years ago, providing the lineup with a reliable right-handed slugger who can protect Lance Berkman. Of course, the length of the deal is a concern. Lee will turn 31 this season, and he's already more than a little heavy, which suggests that he might have to move to first base before the end of his contract, which could have the added effect of pushing Berkman back to the outfield.

With Clemens idling and Andy Pettitte electing to go back to New York, Purpura responded to his suddenly even more acute need for starting pitching by trading his top pitching prospect, Jason Hirsh, starting center fielder Willy Taveras, and Buchholz to Colorado for one year of Jason Jennings, who will be eligible for free agency at the end of the season. If the Lee deal was supposed to represent a commitment to contending in the future, the Jennings trade made it clear that the future is very much right now. On the surface, the deal makes some sense—Jennings has survived Coors Field, so he should be at least as effective in Minute Made, a park that has juiced other moundsmen. It's also possible that Jennings will be signed to a multi-year deal, although after this winter's market mayhem, the Astros could end up paying top dollar for an ultimately middle-class talent, which is a bad strategy.

That very factor comes into play with Purpura's decision to lure 40-year-old Woody Williams away from the Padres with a two-year, $12.5-million deal. Jennings might replace Pettitte, but Williams is a fragile fly-ball pitcher who surrendered 4.9 runs per nine innings away from PETCO, logging only 5 quality starts in 14 on the road (against 6 in 11 in San Diego). Relocated to the Juice Box, Williams will only please that subsection of Astros fans who watch NASCAR for the crashes. Thus, despite Purpura's two additions, his staff's still one Rocket short of launching.

Unfortunately, neither Lee nor Jennings solves the Astros' most persistent offensive problem. We've picked on the decision to stick with Adam Everett and Brad Ausmus as everyday players before, and there's no reason to stop now. Playing in a bandbox in the non-DH league, Houston annually punts two lineup slots on players who aren't just defensive specialists, but are among the league's worst hitters at their positions. That places too much responsibility on the shoulders of Berkman and company—they have to come through virtually every time they have an opportunity in order for the Astros to win. Lee might be a major improvement on the likes of Preston Wilson or Jason Lane, but those are improvements by degrees in a lineup a third of which remains lethally unproductive.

In concert, these moves smack of a desperation to keep treading water and hope something else works out somehow. That's not exactly a plan. If anything, it's a reflec-tion of the "benefits" of playing in the NL Central—if nobody looks like a 90-game winner, you can wing it, punting anything resembling long-term planning, and stumble into your share of playoff spots. The Astros are left with a team built around Roy Oswalt, Lance Berkman, and Carlos Lee, none of whom is without his flaws, and the farm system isn't about to crank out a cheap, homegrown blue-chipper or two to help out. If, we note in Purpura's defense that he has basically had to play out somebody else's hand, we subsequently have to acknowledge that we have no more idea about his long-term abilities as a general manager two years later than we did when he took over from Gerry Hunsicker. We may never know more. The Astros remain a team without an author, waiting for some organizing current. It will be a long time in coming.

HITTERS

Josh Anderson — CF — Bats: L — Throws: R — Height: 6' 2" — Weight: 195 — Born: August 10, 1982 — Age: 24

YEAR	TEAM	LVL	AGE	PA	R	2B	3B	HR	RBI	BB	SO	SB	CS	SPEED	AVG	OBP	SLG	MLVR	EQAVG	EQOBP	EQSLG	EQA	VORP	DEFENSE
2004	LEX	A	21	342	69	12	3	4	31	33	47	48	9	8.3	.326	.403	.426	.178	.283	.340	.360	.259	4.2	73-CF -7
2004	SLM	A+	21	306	45	13	6	2	21	13	53	31	4	9.6	.268	.314	.379	-.002	.257	.291	.368	.238	-4.8	66-CF 5
2005	CCH	AA	22	573	67	17	9	1	26	29	80	50	19	7.9	.282	.329	.355	-.071	.268	.311	.334	.236	-9.2	125-CF -3
2006	CCH	AA	23	610	83	26	4	3	50	27	73	43	13	7.3	.308	.349	.385	.033	.296	.326	.364	.248	5.5	117-CF -12
2007	HOU	MLB	24	500	64	19	6	3	36	23	68	36	10	7.3	.270	.311	.356	-.175	.269	.309	.351	.237	-2.3	118-CF -3

Breakout: 11% Improve: 40% Collapse: 32% Attrition: 10% Comparables: Alex Sanchez, Rich Thompson, Brandon Watson, Jerry Owens

Anderson is crazy fast, so fast that no one seems to notice that he doesn't have any other skills; it's probably the blur from all that speed. Give Anderson a level piece of ground anywhere in the world and he's good to go. Anderson's numbers bounced back a bit with a repeat engagement in Double-A last year, but he's still only an aspiring fifth outfielder type. Did we mention he's fast?

Jonny Ash — 2B — Bats: L — Throws: R — Height: 5' 9" — Weight: 185 — Born: September 11, 1982 — Age: 24

YEAR	TEAM	LVL	AGE	PA	R	2B	3B	HR	RBI	BB	SO	SB	CS	SPEED	AVG	OBP	SLG	MLVR	EQAVG	EQOBP	EQSLG	EQA	VORP	DEFENSE
2004	TCV	A-	21	278	50	7	3	2	25	25	16	5	4	5.4	.297	.388	.377	.133	.253	.314	.320	.227	-6.5	36-3B -6 13-2B 2
2005	LEX	A	22	299	44	11	2	8	38	25	20	3	7	3.7	.320	.395	.473	.239	.269	.320	.380	.243	4.2	51-2B -6
2005	SLM	A+	22	248	32	19	2	1	25	14	15	3	5	4.5	.320	.365	.436	.142	.297	.327	.401	.251	8.1	56-2B -5
2006	CCH	AA	23	438	40	22	5	1	28	25	36	5	8	4.9	.314	.370	.403	.101	.301	.343	.380	.251	14.2	107-2B 1
2007	HOU	MLB	24	451	47	22	4	3	39	24	35	4	3	5.1	.275	.321	.368	-.137	.274	.320	.363	.236	3.3	107-2B -2

Breakout: 10% Improve: 38% Collapse: 39% Attrition: 10% Comparables: Jeff Pickler, Ismael Gallo, Joe Thurston, Dominic Rich

Ash is a small second basemen who knows how to make contact, but has very little in the way of secondary skills. He's a great makeup guy, and if he could play on the left side of the infield he'd make a nifty utility guy, but alas.

Brad Ausmus — C — Bats: R — Throws: R — Height: 5' 11" — Weight: 190 — Born: December 31, 1969 — Age: 38

YEAR	TEAM	LVL	AGE	PA	R	2B	3B	HR	RBI	BB	SO	SB	CS	SPEED	AVG	OBP	SLG	MLVR	EQAVG	EQOBP	EQSLG	EQA	VORP	DEFENSE
2004	HOU	MLB	35	448	38	14	1	5	31	33	56	2	2	4.0	.248	.306	.325	-.188	.239	.299	.313	.219	-6.9	114-C 1
2005	HOU	MLB	36	451	35	19	0	3	47	51	48	5	3	4.0	.258	.351	.331	-.075	.257	.351	.334	.247	7.1	120-C 9
2006	HOU	MLB	37	502	37	16	1	2	39	45	71	3	1	4.0	.230	.308	.285	-.265	.224	.305	.276	.216	-17.5	125-C 6
2007	HOU	MLB	38	406	34	16	1	3	32	32	55	4	2	4.2	.233	.299	.304	-.288	.232	.298	.300	.209	-9.4	97-C -1

Breakout: 8% Improve: 35% Collapse: 34% Attrition: 31% Comparables: Joe Girardi, Tony Pena, Bob Boone, Mike Guerra

Insiders continue to call Ausmus a winner who improves a pitching staff, but it's hard to believe he could retain many adherents after a season as bad as 2006. According to VORP, Ausmus had the 16th-worst offensive season of any player since 1960, but that's trivia. Last year the average catcher had an OBP of .330 and slugged .417. Say the Astros had A. J. Pierzynski, who had an OBP of .330 and a slugging percentage of .436. By our calculation, Ausmus created 38 runs of offense last year while using up 351 outs, while Pierzinsky would have created 68 runs while using up the same number of outs. Those additional 30 runs are worth roughly three wins in the standings. Knowing that, how much credit do you want to give Ausmus for the Astros staff? Did he improve them by one percent? Five? Ten? It stretches belief that Ausmus deserves credit for a twentieth or even a tenth of the success of Roger Clemens or Andy Pettitte, and there is no objective evidence that changing catchers would result in any penalty. For all of Ausmus's wizardry, the Astros haven't established a young pitcher since 2001. The Astros have been needlessly costing themselves wins in a competitive division; it's time to get over it.

| Lance Berkman | | 1B | | | Bats: S | | Throws: L | | Height: 6' 1" | | Weight: 220 | | Born: February 10, 1976 | | Age: 31 | |

YEAR	TEAM	LVL	AGE	PA	R	2B	3B	HR	RBI	BB	SO	SB	CS	SPEED	AVG	OBP	SLG	MLVR	EQAVG	EQOBP	EQSLG	EQA	VORP	DEFENSE	
2004	HOU	MLB	28	687	104	40	3	30	106	127	101	9	7	4.8	.316	.450	.566	.433	.311	.444	.562	.336	72.8	80-RF 7	56-LF -2
2005	HOU	MLB	29	565	76	34	1	24	82	91	72	4	1	4.3	.293	.411	.524	.305	.290	.410	.526	.317	46.9	83-1B 1	32-LF -2
2006	HOU	MLB	30	646	95	29	0	45	136	98	106	3	2	4.0	.315	.420	.621	.440	.311	.418	.615	.337	70.1	102-1B 3	34-RF -2
2007	*HOU*	*MLB*	*31*	*631*	*112*	*37*	*2*	*32*	*104*	*99*	*100*	*5*	*2*	*4.5*	*.308*	*.420*	*.573*	*.329*	*.307*	*.419*	*.565*	*.328*	*55.0*	*147-1B 0*	

Breakout: 10% Improve: 28% Collapse: 27% Attrition: 3% Comparables: Eddie Murray, Reggie Smith, Carlos Delgado, Todd Helton

If it weren't for Roger Clemens, Berkman would be the face of the Astros. He's one of the premier hitters in the game, and it will be interesting to see what having Lee around does for him. Without that kind of hitter behind him, Berkman was intentionally walked 22 times, but nevertheless finished tied with Brian McCann for second in the majors (behind Miguel Cabrera) by driving in 21.4 percent of the runners on base when he stepped in. He can still play an adequate outfield, but his knee problems make him a much better first baseman. Berkman would like everyone to know that he hates the "Fat Elvis" nickname some have tried to hang on him. He's right, too—fat Elvis didn't have this many hits.

| Craig Biggio | | 2B | | | Bats: R | | Throws: R | | Height: 5' 11" | | Weight: 185 | | Born: December 31, 1969 | | Age: 41 | |

YEAR	TEAM	LVL	AGE	PA	R	2B	3B	HR	RBI	BB	SO	SB	CS	SPEED	AVG	OBP	SLG	MLVR	EQAVG	EQOBP	EQSLG	EQA	VORP	DEFENSE	
2004	HOU	MLB	38	700	100	47	0	24	63	40	94	7	2	5.2	.281	.337	.469	.089	.277	.332	.465	.271	22.7	72-LF -8	58-CF 0
2005	HOU	MLB	39	651	94	40	1	26	69	37	90	11	1	6.0	.264	.325	.468	.070	.264	.323	.471	.271	29.5	132-2B -6	
2006	HOU	MLB	40	607	79	33	0	21	62	40	84	3	2	4.0	.246	.306	.422	-.075	.246	.306	.423	.250	8.3	118-2B -13	
2007	*HOU*	*MLB*	*41*	*521*	*62*	*26*	*2*	*15*	*74*	*41*	*70*	*5*	*2*	*4.7*	*.259*	*.327*	*.422*	*-.064*	*.258*	*.326*	*.416*	*.256*	*11.0*	*123-2B -5*	

Breakout: 17% Improve: 31% Collapse: 26% Attrition: 34% Comparables: Steve Finley, Minnie Minoso, Eddie Murray, Gary Gaetti

Bob Hope was a great comedian. The original "Rapid Robert," listening to his old radio shows or watching his early movies, one is struck by his quick timing and easy way with an adlib. Unfortunately, Hope kept performing into his nineties. Along the way he aged from a loose, funny comic into a stodgy old guy who was trying to be funny. The results were difficult to watch, particularly for anyone who had seen, say, *The Road to Morocco*. Craig Biggio, whom Bill James one argued was the best player in baseball, has undergone a very similar transformation. All of his production is now a product of Minute Maid; last season he hit .298/.346/.522 at home, but just .178/.253/.388 on the road. His speed has faded, and he's drawn fewer walks as he's gotten older. His glovework demonstrates why just three other players have logged even 100 games at second at his age; the only forty year olds to play as many games at the keystone as Biggio were Rabbit Maranville and Nap Lajoie. Biggio is not helping the Astros, instead he's playing to reach the individual milestone of 3,000 hits. With Biggio just 70 hits from his goal, if the ballclub is smart they'll space his work out rather than let him make his run at the mark as an everyday player.

| Eric Bruntlett | | UT | | | Bats: R | | Throws: R | | Height: 6' 0" | | Weight: 190 | | Born: March 29, 1978 | | Age: 29 | |

YEAR	TEAM	LVL	AGE	PA	R	2B	3B	HR	RBI	BB	SO	SB	CS	SPEED	AVG	OBP	SLG	MLVR	EQAVG	EQOBP	EQSLG	EQA	VORP	DEFENSE	
2004	NWO	AAA	26	380	50	12	4	6	37	35	72	14	4	6.5	.250	.331	.364	-.109	.241	.311	.332	.235	-2.4	64-SS -3	18-CF 0
2004	HOU	MLB	26	61	14	2	0	4	8	7	13	4	0	6.3	.250	.328	.519	.122	.250	.328	.519	.294	5.0	16-SS -3	
2005	HOU	MLB	27	121	19	5	2	4	14	10	25	7	2	7.5	.220	.292	.413	-.092	.220	.298	.440	.253	1.3	11-CF 5	
2006	ROU	AAA	28	93	11	3	1	1	7	17	13	3	2	5.6	.219	.380	.329	-.022	.221	.355	.325	.244	-2.6	13-LF -1	
2006	HOU	MLB	28	136	11	8	0	0	10	13	21	3	1	4.8	.277	.351	.345	-.077	.277	.356	.336	.253	2.0	16-SS 1	
2007	*HOU*	*MLB*	*29*	*273*	*33*	*12*	*2*	*5*	*26*	*26*	*48*	*6*	*3*	*5.6*	*.246*	*.327*	*.375*	*-.138*	*.245*	*.325*	*.370*	*.244*	*1.6*	*67-SS 1*	

Breakout: 12% Improve: 39% Collapse: 28% Attrition: 51% Comparables: Bill Pecota, John Kennedy, Connie Ryan, Dave Anderson

(continued next page)

Eric Bruntlett *(continued)*

It's ironic that PECOTA doesn't think much of a player whose best comp is Bill Pecota. Bruntlett is a useful player for a club with a variety of offensively weak parts. He's played every position on the field except catcher, and he isn't an automatic out (he even went 7-for-17 as a pinch-hitter last year), so he can be inserted into the game without completely sacrificing offense for versatility. When Phil Garner gets a bit grumpy with Everett's accumulating outs, Bruntlett's there to pick up some playing time. The two would be a nice platoon, with Bruntlett in behind the fly ball pitchers and Everett starting when the groundballers throw. Then again, the Astros could dump them both and find a shortstop that can actually hit.

Chris Burke 2B Bats: R Throws: R   Height: 5' 11" Weight: 180 Born: March 11, 1980   Age: 27

YEAR	TEAM	LVL	AGE	PA	R	2B	3B	HR	RBI	BB	SO	SB	CS	SPEED	AVG	OBP	SLG	MLVR	EQAVG	EQOBP	EQSLG	EQA	VORP	DEFENSE			
2004	NWO	AAA	24	560	93	33	6	16	52	55	76	37	14	7.3	.315	.396	.507	.297	.310	.380	.478	.294	49.9	117-2B	3		
2005	ROU	AAA	25	101	15	6	2	2	11	8	13	9	0	8.0	.311	.380	.489	.159	.293	.350	.446	.286	5.8	17-2B	2		
2005	HOU	MLB	25	359	49	19	2	5	26	23	62	11	6	6.3	.248	.309	.368	-.113	.249	.310	.377	.240	-5.2	72-LF	-1		
2006	HOU	MLB	26	413	58	23	1	9	40	27	77	11	1	5.7	.276	.347	.418	.016	.276	.345	.417	.269	15.3	38-2B	-4	32-CF	0
2007	*HOU*	*MLB*	*27*	*491*	*70*	*26*	*4*	*14*	*55*	*39*	*80*	*16*	*5*	*6.3*	*.278*	*.347*	*.451*	*.025*	*.277*	*.346*	*.445*	*.273*	*18.0*	*116-2B*	*-1*		

Breakout: 16% Improve: 44% Collapse: 21% Attrition: 17%   Comparables: Jackie Brandt, Mickey Brantley, Carl Furillo, Robby Thompson

Pushed from second base to the outfield by Biggio, Burke has adapted well enough to earn playing time and avoid wasting his career waiting around for the old man to retire. Biggio's re-signing means that Burke is unlikely to ever really establish himself as a second baseman, but, with Willy Taveras in Colorado, an opportunity has opened up for him in center. Burke hits enough to be a plus there for most teams, which is what he should be for the Astros after returning from shoulder surgery (he's expected to be ready by spring training).

Brooks Conrad 2B/3B Bats: S Throws: R   Height: 5' 11" Weight: 185 Born: January 16, 1980   Age: 27

YEAR	TEAM	LVL	AGE	PA	R	2B	3B	HR	RBI	BB	SO	SB	CS	SPEED	AVG	OBP	SLG	MLVR	EQAVG	EQOBP	EQSLG	EQA	VORP	DEFENSE			
2004	ROU	AA	24	561	84	39	6	13	83	63	105	8	7	5.4	.290	.365	.477	.163	.266	.329	.427	.262	20.2	123-2B	-4		
2005	CCH	AA	25	94	13	6	1	2	11	16	15	8	0	7.4	.234	.372	.416	.052	.225	.340	.400	.268	2.3	21-2B	1		
2005	ROU	AAA	25	483	84	22	3	21	57	52	104	12	3	6.2	.263	.347	.481	.044	.249	.322	.431	.261	14.2	107-2B	11		
2006	ROU	AAA	26	599	100	40	15	24	94	54	135	15	6	7.3	.267	.334	.534	.215	.261	.319	.510	.277	36.4	97-2B	7	37-3B	-3
2007	*HOU*	*MLB*	*27*	*495*	*67*	*32*	*5*	*17*	*63*	*44*	*109*	*9*	*4*	*5.8*	*.271*	*.341*	*.484*	*.051*	*.270*	*.339*	*.478*	*.275*	*24.9*	*117-2B*	*3*		

Breakout: 19% Improve: 50% Collapse: 16% Attrition: 8%   Comparables: Chase Lambin, Jose Valentin, Howard Johnson, Jim Morrison

Quick quiz: who led the minor leagues in extra-base hits last year? If you guessed some top prospect such as Alex Gordon, you're wrong, it was Conrad. One of those undersized, max-effort, low-tools/big-heart guys, all Conrad has done is hit at every level. He's still not a great prospect. A long swing means plenty of strikeouts and a low batting average, but he can play second and third base, switch hit, and he has some pop, so there's some sort of value here. The problem is that he's blocked by Biggio playing out the string at second, and Mike Lamb providing lefty sock at the corners from the bench.

Morgan Ensberg 3B Bats: R Throws: R   Height: 6' 2" Weight: 220 Born: August 26, 1975   Age: 31

YEAR	TEAM	LVL	AGE	PA	R	2B	3B	HR	RBI	BB	SO	SB	CS	SPEED	AVG	OBP	SLG	MLVR	EQAVG	EQOBP	EQSLG	EQA	VORP	DEFENSE	
2004	HOU	MLB	28	456	51	20	3	10	66	36	46	6	4	4.7	.275	.330	.411	-.005	.272	.328	.405	.254	4.8	98-3B	-11
2005	HOU	MLB	29	624	86	30	3	36	101	85	119	6	7	4.3	.283	.388	.557	.305	.282	.388	.569	.312	53.5	145-3B	9
2006	HOU	MLB	30	495	67	17	1	23	58	101	96	1	4	4.1	.235	.396	.463	.125	.234	.398	.462	.296	19.0	108-3B	6
2007	*HOU*	*MLB*	*31*	*489*	*72*	*23*	*2*	*21*	*67*	*71*	*90*	*4*	*2*	*4.5*	*.263*	*.375*	*.481*	*.097*	*.262*	*.373*	*.474*	*.289*	*25.3*	*115-3B*	*1*

Breakout: 7% Improve: 28% Collapse: 34% Attrition: 11%   Comparables: Sal Bando, Wayne Gross, Doug DeCinces, Tim Salmon

Ensberg started 2006 like a hyperactive three year old on triple-espresso shots and double-stuff epinephrine Oreos, hitting .329/.467/.765 with 9 home runs in 85 April at-bats. He hit another 8 bombs in May and had taken 40 walks by June 1, though his batting average was dropping rapidly. He was batting .241/.397/.511 on June 10 when he dove for a foul pop off the bat of Ryan Langerhans and damaged his shoulder. Ensberg played for another month before going on the DL, but his bat had gone deader than Joe Piscopo's career (.158/.422/.263 with one home run in 57 at-bats). Twenty days of healing and rehab didn't seem to help much, as Ensberg hit just one more home run during the month of August, but he finished strong, batting .273/.421/.477 with 3 homers in sporadic September playing time, leaving a ray of hope for the future. When healthy, Ensberg has used the Crawford Boxes—Minute Maid's short right-field porch—better than any other player, slugging 100 points better at home than on the road. He's neither a great defender nor a favorite of Phil Garner's, so he'll remain under threat of trade for the foreseeable future, but the team can't afford to part with the power production that a fully functional Ensberg provides.

Adam Everett SS Bats: R Throws: R Height: 6′ 0″ Weight: 170 Born: February 2, 1977 Age: 30

YEAR	TEAM	LVL	AGE	PA	R	2B	3B	HR	RBI	BB	SO	SB	CS	SPEED	AVG	OBP	SLG	MLVR	EQAVG	EQOBP	EQSLG	EQA	VORP	DEFENSE	
2004	HOU	MLB	27	435	66	15	2	8	31	17	56	13	2	7.2	.273	.317	.385	-.088	.270	.313	.386	.248	9.1	90-SS	3
2005	HOU	MLB	28	595	58	27	2	11	54	26	103	21	7	6.5	.248	.290	.364	-.145	.247	.289	.370	.233	2.2	146-SS	3
2006	HOU	MLB	29	566	52	28	6	6	59	34	71	9	6	5.9	.239	.290	.352	-.204	.236	.289	.348	.224	-8.7	142-SS	20
2007	HOU	MLB	30	507	56	24	4	10	47	29	73	11	5	6.1	.254	.303	.384	-.162	.253	.302	.379	.235	4.6	120-SS	6

Breakout: 22% Improve: 49% Collapse: 22% Attrition: 15% Comparables: Pokey Reese, Frank White, Julian Javier, Shawon Dunston

Some of what we said in the Brad Ausmus comment applies here as well. It's tough to be so good with the glove that your bat doesn't matter, and Everett is showing just how tough. Think of him as the reverse Jeter—he's got crazy skills with the leather, but can't hit enough to hold off even an average hitter such as Mark Bruntlett. There's simply no room in today's game for the new Mark Belanger, not at time when 12 teams are starting shortstops who outperformed the league average OPS last year, and especially not in a lineup in the non-DH league.

Hector Gimenez C Bats: S Throws: R Height: 5′ 10″ Weight: 180 Born: September 28, 1982 Age: 24

YEAR	TEAM	LVL	AGE	PA	R	2B	3B	HR	RBI	BB	SO	SB	CS	SPEED	AVG	OBP	SLG	MLVR	EQAVG	EQOBP	EQSLG	EQA	VORP	DEFENSE			
2004	ROU	AA	21	359	38	16	3	6	46	18	64	2	0	4.7	.245	.284	.366	-.161	.226	.260	.324	.208	-16.9	87-C	3		
2005	CCH	AA	22	498	47	19	1	12	58	32	88	2	3	2.6	.273	.322	.399	-.029	.255	.302	.367	.234	-1.6	86-C	10	15-1B	0
2006	ROU	AAA	23	302	31	8	0	8	37	24	42	2	3	4.0	.273	.331	.389	.006	.273	.327	.392	.248	6.8	62-C	2	10-1B	0
2007	HOU	MLB	24	385	37	18	1	9	42	26	64	2	1	4.2	.253	.306	.385	-.157	.252	.305	.380	.234	0.1	92-C	2		

Breakout: 36% Improve: 62% Collapse: 19% Attrition: 17% Comparables: Koyie Hill, Brian Luderer, Matt Curtis, Steve Torrealba

Of the two Venezuelan catchers battling to back up Brad Ausmus, Gimenez is both the younger one and the one who's been homegrown by the organization. He's also the one who needs more development time, although he's already better than the likes of Raul Chavez, for what little that's worth. Good at deterring the running game, he's a catch-and-throw guy, which is a polite, scouty way of saying he's not much of a hitter.

J. R. House C Bats: R Throws: R Height: 5′ 10″ Weight: 200 Born: November 11, 1979 Age: 27

YEAR	TEAM	LVL	AGE	PA	R	2B	3B	HR	RBI	BB	SO	SB	CS	SPEED	AVG	OBP	SLG	MLVR	EQAVG	EQOBP	EQSLG	EQA	VORP	DEFENSE			
2004	NAS	AAA	24	337	38	21	1	15	49	23	72	1	1	3.5	.288	.344	.508	.139	.272	.323	.458	.264	15.8	62-C	-10	15-1B	-2
2006	CCH	AA	26	423	58	23	2	10	69	32	44	2	2	4.3	.325	.376	.475	.226	.297	.334	.419	.260	18.0	65-C	-9	29-1B	-3
2006	ROU	AAA	26	128	25	15	0	5	36	9	15	0	0	3.7	.412	.445	.675	.787	.397	.426	.647	.349	22.6	24-1B	0		
2007	BAL	MLB	27	479	52	26	1	14	65	26	70	2	1	4.0	.279	.321	.435	-.033	.277	.325	.442	.268	12.3	113-C	-5		

Breakout: 20% Improve: 39% Collapse: 23% Attrition: 10% Comparables: John Gall, Julio Vinas, Mike Vento, Jason Alfaro

House's first attempt at baseball didn't work out, so the former West Virginia University quarterback went off to try football again. That didn't work out either, but rather than move on to rugby, or polo, or backgammon, he gave baseball another shot. Once a promising prospect, his career has been derailed by more injuries than Will Carroll could count. Signed to a minor league deal with the Orioles, House might be able to stick as one of the new breed of backup catchers, such as Eric Munson or Mike Rivera, who offer more at the plate than behind it.

Aubrey Huff 3B/OF/1B Bats: L Throws: R Height: 6′ 4″ Weight: 230 Born: December 20, 1976 Age: 30

YEAR	TEAM	LVL	AGE	PA	R	2B	3B	HR	RBI	BB	SO	SB	CS	SPEED	AVG	OBP	SLG	MLVR	EQAVG	EQOBP	EQSLG	EQA	VORP	DEFENSE			
2004	TBA	MLB	27	667	92	27	2	29	104	56	74	5	1	4.8	.297	.360	.493	.156	.299	.366	.503	.295	39.5	80-3B	-7	33-1B	0
2005	TBA	MLB	28	636	70	26	2	22	92	49	88	8	7	4.8	.261	.321	.428	-.005	.271	.339	.455	.269	8.7	90-RF	3	18-1B	-2
2006	TBA	MLB	29	256	26	15	1	8	28	24	25	0	0	3.7	.283	.348	.461	.062	.282	.355	.471	.283	9.4	55-3B	-2		
2006	HOU	MLB	29	261	31	10	1	13	38	26	39	0	0	3.5	.250	.341	.478	.066	.250	.338	.487	.280	7.5	29-RF	-6	24-3B	0
2007	BAL	MLB	30	524	66	25	1	18	73	43	68	3	2	4.5	.273	.337	.447	.004	.272	.340	.454	.278	14.6	123-3B	-4		

Breakout: 13% Improve: 38% Collapse: 26% Attrition: 9% Comparables: Dick Sisler, Pat Putnam, Sean Casey, Chris Chambliss

(continued next page)

Aubrey Huff *(continued)*

The Astros weren't expecting Huff to be the 2006 version of Carlos Beltran, swooping in and saving their season. He was supposed to be a solid hitter who could cover for the injured Ensberg and possibly make the streaky regular third baseman redundant. Instead, Huff was what he's been for the last few seasons—merely okay. Huff batted .312/.366/.540 from 2002 to 2003, but .276/.342/.463 over the last three seasons. Those numbers work coming from a third baseman, but Huff is a terrible fielder at the hot corner, and, as a first baseman, his bat is marginal to borderline unacceptable. Signed to a three-year deal by Baltimore, Huff could make himself very useful as a left-handed supersub for righties Millar, Mora, and Payton at first, third and left field respectively.

Charlton Jimerson OF **Bats: R** **Throws: R** Height: 6′ 3″ Weight: 210 Born: September 22, 1979 Age: 27

YEAR	TEAM	LVL	AGE	PA	R	2B	3B	HR	RBI	BB	SO	SB	CS	SPEED	AVG	OBP	SLG	MLVR	EQAVG	EQOBP	EQSLG	EQA	VORP	DEFENSE			
2004	ROU	AA	24	528	78	22	5	18	53	31	163	39	6	8.4	.238	.290	.414	-.089	.215	.257	.356	.220	-36.0	92-RF	3	30-CF	-1
2005	CCH	AA	25	467	67	24	3	16	44	29	145	27	10	7.4	.259	.317	.442	.011	.233	.283	.376	.232	-20.4	98-RF	-7	13-CF	3
2006	ROU	AAA	26	501	56	27	6	18	45	23	183	28	8	7.7	.247	.287	.445	-.012	.248	.282	.435	.246	-8.8	77-RF	6	40-CF	3
2006	HOU	MLB	26	6	2	0	0	1	1	0	3	2	0	7.6	.333	.333	.833	.658	.333	.333	.833	.362	1.8				
2007	HOU	MLB	27	431	49	21	3	16	51	20	154	22	7	6.6	.241	.282	.425	-.153	.240	.281	.420	.240	-5.3	102-RF	4		

Breakout: 28% Improve: 56% Collapse: 17% Attrition: 23% Comparables: Julio Ramirez, Jeremy Owens, Tim Unroe, Pete Whisenant

An impoverished man's Wily Mo Peña, Jimerson's first major league hit was a towering home run that broke up Cole Hamel's attempt at a perfect game. Many are convinced that will be his sole career highlight. He's strong, fast, powerful, and by all accounts a great guy, but the one thing he isn't is a prospect.

Mike Lamb 1B/3B **Bats: L** **Throws: R** Height: 6′ 1″ Weight: 190 Born: August 9, 1975 Age: 31

YEAR	TEAM	LVL	AGE	PA	R	2B	3B	HR	RBI	BB	SO	SB	CS	SPEED	AVG	OBP	SLG	MLVR	EQAVG	EQOBP	EQSLG	EQA	VORP	DEFENSE			
2004	HOU	MLB	28	312	38	14	3	14	58	31	63	1	1	4.9	.288	.356	.511	.191	.282	.350	.502	.287	18.4	53-3B	-6		
2005	HOU	MLB	29	349	41	13	5	12	53	22	65	1	1	5.1	.236	.284	.419	-.081	.234	.286	.425	.243	-2.9	48-1B	-2	12-3B	2
2006	HOU	MLB	30	421	70	22	3	12	45	35	55	2	4	4.7	.307	.361	.475	.147	.306	.363	.472	.282	16.9	56-1B	-2	28-3B	3
2007	HOU	MLB	31	382	49	19	3	13	52	32	60	2	2	4.9	.275	.338	.459	.016	.274	.336	.453	.268	9.7	91-1B	-1		

Breakout: 9% Improve: 34% Collapse: 35% Attrition: 26% Comparables: Irv Noren, Denny Walling, B. J. Surhoff, George Altman

Lamb spent 2003 stuck behind Hank Blalock. In 2004, he barely escaped being stuck behind Alex Rodriguez, then came to Houston and ended up stuck behind Morgan Ensberg. Instead of pouting, Lamb has become a very solid bench player. He's not an ideal everyday first baseman, but Jason Lane's sudden collapse pressed Lamb into action there a lot in 2006 (with Berkman playing a goodly amount of right). He subsequently had to help cover for Ensberg's extended absences at third. That sort of versatility has helped the Astros cover for the failures or limitations of others. Although playing Lamb regularly hasn't been a matter of design, he's been an asset as an insurance policy.

Jason Lane RF **Bats: R** **Throws: L** Height: 6′ 2″ Weight: 220 Born: December 22, 1976 Age: 30

YEAR	TEAM	LVL	AGE	PA	R	2B	3B	HR	RBI	BB	SO	SB	CS	SPEED	AVG	OBP	SLG	MLVR	EQAVG	EQOBP	EQSLG	EQA	VORP	DEFENSE			
2004	HOU	MLB	27	156	21	10	2	4	19	16	33	1	0	5.9	.272	.348	.463	.096	.265	.342	.456	.275	6.4	22-LF	-4	19-RF	-2
2005	HOU	MLB	28	561	65	34	4	26	78	32	105	6	2	5.3	.267	.316	.499	.102	.264	.315	.509	.274	20.5	126-RF	-6		
2006	HOU	MLB	29	345	44	10	0	15	45	49	75	1	2	3.7	.201	.318	.392	-.125	.199	.320	.383	.247	-6.0	75-RF	4		
2006	ROU	AAA	29	55	7	2	0	1	11	5	16	1	0	3.5	.261	.327	.370	-.038	.271	.321	.375	.252	0.3	12-CF	-3		
2007	HOU	MLB	30	375	48	19	2	17	52	38	79	3	2	4.9	.248	.330	.470	-.005	.247	.329	.464	.268	6.2	90-RF	-2		

Breakout: 28% Improve: 49% Collapse: 19% Attrition: 26% Comparables: Jermaine Dye, Carmelo Martinez, Tom Brunansky, Dustan Mohr

A pull hitter that can't hit sliders, Lane is emblematic of the franchise's struggles in moving their prospects into the lineup. Lane was expected to explode onto the scene four years ago, providing some right-handed power to pair up with Lance Berkman. Having been bounced back to Round Rock last year due to his poor performance, he's closer to imploding. Heading into his arbitration years at age 29, he's about to explode onto the journeyman outfielder scene.

Eric Munson   C   Bats: L   Throws: R   Height: 6' 3"   Weight: 220   Born: October 3, 1977   Age: 29

YEAR	TEAM	LVL	AGE	PA	R	2B	3B	HR	RBI	BB	SO	SB	CS	SPEED	AVG	OBP	SLG	MLVR	EQAVG	EQOBP	EQSLG	EQA	VORP	DEFENSE	
2004	DET	MLB	26	357	36	14	2	19	49	29	90	1	1	4.6	.212	.289	.445	-.095	.216	.297	.456	.253	-0.6	80-3B	4
2005	DUR	AAA	27	425	67	22	0	25	71	38	81	1	1	3.4	.285	.351	.539	.203	.254	.316	.472	.265	7.9	90-1B	-11
2006	HOU	MLB	28	156	10	6	0	5	19	11	32	0	0	3.3	.199	.269	.348	-.272	.191	.263	.326	.209	-5.9	31-C	-1
2007	HOU	MLB	29	274	31	12	1	12	40	24	56	0	0	3.9	.240	.314	.445	-.071	.239	.313	.439	.254	3.9	67-C	-2

Breakout: 24%   Improve: 54%   Collapse: 20%   Attrition: 36%   Comparables: Harry Anderson, Tim Laudner, Preston Ward, Marv Throneberry

There was a good instinct behind the Astros' decision to move Munson back to catcher, the position he played in college. Munson's not a great hitter, and his bat can't carry first or third base, but as a reserve catcher who bats lefty with home run power, he makes a nifty asset off the bench. The results weren't great, but it was definitely an experiment worth trying, and perhaps one that should be repeated in other organizations with their own suboptimal first and third basemen, in the same way that teams now habitually give poor hitters with good arms a chance to show that they can throw fastballs.

Orlando Palmeiro   PH   Bats: L   Throws: L   Height: 5' 11"   Weight: 185   Born: December 31, 1969   Age: 38

YEAR	TEAM	LVL	AGE	PA	R	2B	3B	HR	RBI	BB	SO	SB	CS	SPEED	AVG	OBP	SLG	MLVR	EQAVG	EQOBP	EQSLG	EQA	VORP	DEFENSE			
2004	HOU	MLB	35	156	19	5	0	3	12	18	19	2	1	4.9	.241	.344	.346	-.094	.239	.342	.336	.245	-0.4	11-LF	-1		
2005	HOU	MLB	36	231	22	17	2	3	20	15	23	3	1	5.3	.284	.341	.431	.057	.282	.336	.442	.269	7.3	21-LF	-3	17-RF	2
2006	HOU	MLB	37	128	12	6	1	0	17	6	17	0	1	4.6	.252	.294	.319	-.237	.242	.289	.300	.208	-3.8				
2007	HOU	MLB	38	67	7	3	0	1	7	5	9	0	0	4.9	.249	.309	.351	-.199	.248	.308	.346	.226	-1.3	21-DH			

Breakout: 0%   Improve: 25%   Collapse: 55%   Attrition: 56%   Comparables: Lenny Harris, Frank Baumholtz, B. J. Surhoff, Jose Vizcaino

Palmeiro's career pinch-hitting rates of .267/.338/.366 may not seem impressive, but he provides consistent value in a very difficult role. Among the 68 players who have had 300 or more pinch-hit plate appearances since 1960, Palmeiro's average ranks 19th. His main suitability for the role is that he makes contact and puts the ball in play. Palmeiro rarely plays the field and almost never bats against lefties, so his professional existence is dependent on his ability to deliver singles off righty pitchers. That's something, but it's a very narrow use of a precious roster spot.

Hunter Pence   OF   Bats: R   Throws: R   Height: 6' 4"   Weight: 220   Born: April 13, 1983   Age: 24

YEAR	TEAM	LVL	AGE	PA	R	2B	3B	HR	RBI	BB	SO	SB	CS	SPEED	AVG	OBP	SLG	MLVR	EQAVG	EQOBP	EQSLG	EQA	VORP	DEFENSE			
2004	TCV	A-	21	225	36	18	1	8	37	23	30	3	5	4.4	.296	.369	.518	.283	.243	.298	.417	.244	1.8	45-CF	1		
2005	LEX	A	22	341	59	14	3	25	60	38	53	8	3	5.0	.338	.413	.652	.521	.283	.340	.519	.286	25.9	42-CF	-2	27-LF	1
2005	SLM	A+	22	171	24	8	1	6	30	18	37	1	2	3.7	.305	.374	.490	.218	.288	.339	.442	.267	7.9	28-CF	-1		
2006	CCH	AA	23	592	97	31	8	28	95	60	109	17	4	7.2	.283	.357	.533	.236	.267	.331	.488	.278	18.7	105-RF	2	20-CF	-1
2007	HOU	MLB	24	529	74	29	4	22	74	42	103	10	4	5.5	.279	.340	.490	.065	.278	.338	.484	.277	19.0	125-RF	1		

Breakout: 26%   Improve: 49%   Collapse: 16%   Attrition: 4%   Comparables: Gabe Kapler, Danny Clyburn, Michael Cuddyer, Corey Hart

Pence is the best young hitter in an organization that would have trouble putting together enough position player prospects to play a game of bridge. He has real power, but it's not clear what kind of an average he'll hit for in the majors due to an uppercut swing. Pence has a semblance of strike zone judgment and possesses surprising speed for a big man. He's a good defender, but between an arm that isn't quite good enough for right field and range that's a bit short for center, he's destined for left field. Twenty-four in April, Pence is a bit old to develop into a star, but he should be a useful regular.

Humberto Quintero   C   Bats: R   Throws: R   Height: 5' 9"   Weight: 215   Born: August 2, 1979   Age: 27

YEAR	TEAM	LVL	AGE	PA	R	2B	3B	HR	RBI	BB	SO	SB	CS	SPEED	AVG	OBP	SLG	MLVR	EQAVG	EQOBP	EQSLG	EQA	VORP	DEFENSE	
2004	POR	AAA	24	274	36	25	0	5	30	8	18	0	0	3.6	.317	.348	.471	.104	.276	.304	.398	.242	3.8	61-C	14
2004	SDN	MLB	24	78	7	3	0	2	10	5	16	0	2	3.2	.250	.295	.375	-.110	.250	.295	.375	.226	-0.9	21-C	-1
2005	ROU	AAA	25	205	23	13	0	8	31	10	30	2	1	3.0	.288	.327	.482	.032	.263	.293	.428	.246	3.5	46-C	7
2005	HOU	MLB	25	57	6	1	0	1	8	1	10	0	0	4.7	.185	.200	.259	-.486	.145	.161	.218	.141	-4.7	14-C	-2
2006	ROU	AAA	26	322	39	21	2	4	37	19	48	4	0	4.4	.298	.352	.425	.117	.296	.342	.421	.267	14.6	78-C	8
2006	HOU	MLB	26	22	2	2	0	0	2	1	3	0	0	2.7	.333	.364	.429	.106	.333	.364	.429	.274	1.1		
2007	HOU	MLB	27	401	39	21	1	9	48	19	58	2	1	3.9	.265	.307	.397	-.130	.264	.306	.392	.238	3.8	96-C	8

Breakout: 17%   Improve: 40%   Collapse: 36%   Attrition: 14%   Comparables: Carlos Ruiz, Vance Wilson, Doc Edwards, Joe Azcue

(continued next page)

Humberto Quintero *(continued)*

Quintero is the quintessential backup catcher. He doesn't mind carrying his own bag, he's quiet, doesn't eat the last of the good salami from the postgame spread, and he showers regularly. What he can't do is play every day or hit enough to push even Brad Ausmus aside. Guys like Quintero don't dream of being Ivan Rodriguez someday; they dream of being Henry Blanco. One wonders if that fan club has a newsletter.

Michael Rodriguez　　**OF**　　**Bats: L**　**Throws: L**　Height: 5' 10"　Weight: 180　Born: October 15, 1980　Age: 26

YEAR	TEAM	LVL	AGE	PA	R	2B	3B	HR	RBI	BB	SO	SB	CS	SPEED	AVG	OBP	SLG	MLVR	EQAVG	EQOBP	EQSLG	EQA	VORP	DEFENSE			
2004	ROU	AA	23	451	59	23	5	4	53	39	55	16	10	6.3	.267	.331	.380	-.043	.248	.303	.346	.232	-19.8	70-LF	-9	24-CF	-4
2005	CCH	AA	24	456	51	16	9	5	50	47	50	25	7	7.3	.281	.359	.406	.049	.261	.330	.373	.254	-8.0	100-LF	5		
2006	ROU	AAA	25	501	70	16	7	6	38	51	55	28	6	6.7	.276	.352	.385	.040	.277	.344	.388	.263	11.7	91-CF	3	10-LF	0
2007	HOU	MLB	26	453	58	21	6	6	40	36	54	18	5	6.2	.265	.326	.391	-.104	.264	.325	.386	.250	2.6	107-CF	0		

Breakout: 16% Improve: 42% Collapse: 34% Attrition: 14%　　Comparables: Chris Prieto, Terrmel Sledge, McKay Christensen, Kevin Reese

Rodriguez is one of those guys who keeps moving up one rung at a time and keeps putting up decent numbers, the kind that don't get him cut, but don't get him shots at big league jobs either. He's a good fielder, he makes good contact, and he runs well. He also has little power and can't hit lefties. He could still reach the Show as a bench outfielder, especially after the Taveras trade, but offseason shoulder surgery doesn't help his cause.

Luke Scott　　**OF**　　**Bats: L**　**Throws: R**　Height: 6' 0"　Weight: 210　Born: June 25, 1978　Age: 29

YEAR	TEAM	LVL	AGE	PA	R	2B	3B	HR	RBI	BB	SO	SB	CS	SPEED	AVG	OBP	SLG	MLVR	EQAVG	EQOBP	EQSLG	EQA	VORP	DEFENSE			
2004	SLM	A+	26	287	45	20	1	8	35	41	58	6	1	5.5	.278	.376	.469	.221	.234	.306	.375	.240	-9.5	37-RF	-2	25-CF	-1
2004	ROU	AA	26	253	45	17	0	19	62	33	43	0	2	3.1	.298	.401	.654	.461	.249	.328	.511	.279	8.3	22-RF	0	21-LF	-2
2005	ROU	AAA	27	449	69	25	4	31	87	43	96	2	2	3.7	.286	.363	.603	.268	.265	.327	.527	.282	17.7	86-LF	8	11-RF	0
2005	HOU	MLB	27	89	6	4	2	0	4	9	23	1	1	6.6	.188	.270	.288	-.310	.175	.258	.275	.194	-5.7	17-LF	-2		
2006	ROU	AAA	28	381	63	15	1	20	63	52	66	6	1	5.4	.299	.400	.541	.361	.292	.376	.514	.301	24.2	82-LF	0		
2006	HOU	MLB	28	249	31	19	6	10	37	30	43	2	1	5.9	.336	.426	.622	.478	.332	.422	.617	.339	29.9	45-LF	-1		
2007	HOU	MLB	29	545	76	29	4	24	80	58	106	5	2	5.0	.269	.352	.498	.087	.268	.350	.491	.284	19.3	128-LF	-1		

Breakout: 10% Improve: 30% Collapse: 28% Attrition: 9%　　Comparables: Leon Durham, Ben Broussard, Paul O'Neill, Harry Anderson

Scott's late arrival in the big leagues is evidence of a pro career that started slowly after college ball at Oklahoma State. Coming over from the Indians with Taveras in the Jeriome Robertson deal, Scott's been a career .280/.366/.534 hitter in the minor leagues, which suggests he has something to contribute at the big league level. He's not the .336 hitter he was in 2006, but even as his bat cooled during everyday play in September he still hit .268/.375/.634. Scott loved Minute Maid, batting .375/.455/.813 with 8 of his 10 home runs there, but he was still productive on the road at .305/.403/.466. He has a solid (if short) future as a platoon outfielder.

Willy Taveras　　**CF**　　**Bats: R**　**Throws: R**　Height: 6' 0"　Weight: 160　Born: December 25, 1981　Age: 25

YEAR	TEAM	LVL	AGE	PA	R	2B	3B	HR	RBI	BB	SO	SB	CS	SPEED	AVG	OBP	SLG	MLVR	EQAVG	EQOBP	EQSLG	EQA	VORP	DEFENSE			
2004	ROU	AA	22	464	76	13	1	2	27	38	76	55	11	7.4	.335	.402	.386	.135	.318	.372	.366	.272	17.4	86-CF	0	11-LF	0
2005	HOU	MLB	23	635	82	13	4	3	29	25	103	34	11	7.5	.291	.325	.341	-.085	.290	.326	.346	.243	4.6	142-CF	15		
2006	HOU	MLB	24	587	83	19	5	1	30	34	88	33	9	7.3	.278	.333	.338	-.118	.279	.335	.341	.247	5.1	123-CF	17		
2007	COL	MLB	25	583	91	22	6	4	44	38	80	35	10	7.2	.305	.357	.395	-.013	.282	.338	.365	.252	7.3	137-CF	8		

Breakout: 17% Improve: 39% Collapse: 30% Attrition: 8%　　Comparables: Brian Hunter, Alan Wiggins, Juan Pierre, Jim Busby

He hits enough singles to give him a little bit of a batting average, and of course he's a fast runner, but as a regular, Taveras is something of a disaster. He has no power and little patience, and his occasional stolen bases do nothing to make up for that. Putting him in the everyday lineup and batting him leadoff or second, thereby giving him a higher percentage of the team's plate appearances, is just doing the opposing pitcher's work for him. Taveras's speed does make him a plus defender, something that will help cover the gaps at Coors, but he won't provide the Rockies with a top-of-the-order hitter any better-equipped to help them than Juan Pierre was.

Justin Towles   C   Bats: R   Throws: R   Height: 6′ 2″   Weight: 195   Born: February 11, 1984   Age: 23

YEAR	TEAM	LVL	AGE	PA	R	2B	3B	HR	RBI	BB	SO	SB	CS	SPEED	AVG	OBP	SLG	MLVR	EQAVG	EQOBP	EQSLG	EQA	VORP	DEFENSE	
2004	GRV	Rk	20	136	17	6	0	0	8	12	23	4	3	4.4	.243	.370	.297	-.027	.202	.265	.226	.185	-23.2	34-C	0
2005	LEX	A	21	193	35	14	2	5	23	16	29	11	7	6.9	.346	.436	.549	.421	.301	.360	.457	.276	13.0	36-C	0
2006	LEX	A	22	321	39	19	2	12	55	21	46	13	5	5.2	.317	.382	.525	.321	.275	.317	.440	.259	12.2	58-C	4
2007	*HOU*	*MLB*	*23*	*426*	*50*	*24*	*2*	*11*	*49*	*26*	*70*	*9*	*5*	*4.9*	*.267*	*.322*	*.421*	*-.069*	*.266*	*.321*	*.415*	*.252*	*10.3*	*101-C*	*2*

Breakout: 15% Improve: 43% Collapse: 26% Attrition: 9%   Comparables: Phil Avlas, John Pachot, Lou Palmisano, Chad Moeller

Towles has had an injury-plagued career so far—a broken finger here, a sore knee there. None of the injuries have been serious, but they've limited him to 165 games since being drafted in 2004. That's a shame, because when Towles is healthy, he's pretty damn good, with a career average of .311, 60 extra-base hits and very good defensive skills to boot. The only issue is that he turns 23 before spring training and has yet to get out of A-ball. He's an unproven commodity to be sure, but an interesting one.

PITCHERS

Matt Albers   Bats: L   Throws: R   Height: 6′ 0″   Weight: 205   Born: January 20, 1983   Age: 24

YEAR	TEAM	LVL	AGE	W	L	SV	G	GS	IP	H	BB	SO	HR	GB%	BABIP	STUFF	WHIP	ERA	PERA	EQERA	EQH9	EQBB9	EQSO9	EQHR9	VORP	WXRL
2004	LEX	A	21	8	3	0	22	21	111¹	95	57	140	3	—	.329	28	1.37	3.32	4.41	4.81	9.1	5.7	6.7	0.4	9.4	—
2005	SLM	A+	22	8	12	0	28	27	148²	161	62	146	15	55.1%	.349	-14	1.50	4.66	5.85	6.55	11.2	4.3	5.5	1.6	-15.1	—
2006	CCH	AA	23	10	2	0	19	19	116¹	96	47	95	4	53.5%	.277	20	1.23	2.17	4.35	3.58	7.8	3.8	5.2	0.5	26.0	—
2006	ROU	AAA	23	2	1	0	4	4	25²	24	10	26	2	40.2%	.304	19	1.35	3.93	4.38	4.32	9.4	3.6	7.2	1.1	3.6	—
2006	HOU	MLB	23	0	2	0	4	2	15	17	7	11	1	43.5%	.356	1	1.60	6.00	3.81	5.87	10.0	3.5	5.9	0.6	-0.2	-0.12
2007	*HOU*	*MLB*	*24*	*6*	*8*	*0*	*31*	*19*	*123*	*124*	*62*	*94*	*16*	*49.0%*	*.292*	*4*	*1.51*	*4.94*	*5.21*	*5.21*	*8.7*	*4.0*	*6.2*	*1.0*	*8.2*	*1.60*

Breakout: 11% Improve: 43% Collapse: 16% Attrition: 0%   Comparables: Rett Johnson, Russ Ortiz, Josh Hall, Pete Munro

It's always nice to see a hometown kid make it with the big club. It's also good to see a player overcome off-field problems (in Albers's case, some drinking issues he's already sorted out). Thus there were warm fuzzies all around when Albers was added to the bullpen in August, when the pen was at its most unstable. Unfortunately, he was unable to establish himself as a real option. Still, if he can't crack the rotation out of spring training, he may wind up back in the pen, which his stuff seems better suited for, even if his demeanor doesn't.

Ezequiel Astacio   Bats: R   Throws: R   Height: 6′ 3″   Weight: 150   Born: November 4, 1979   Age: 27

YEAR	TEAM	LVL	AGE	W	L	SV	G	GS	IP	H	BB	SO	HR	GB%	BABIP	STUFF	WHIP	ERA	PERA	EQERA	EQH9	EQBB9	EQSO9	EQHR9	VORP	WXRL
2004	ROU	AA	24	13	10	0	28	28	176	155	56	185	12	—	.307	5	1.20	3.89	4.81	5.81	8.8	3.5	6.2	1.1	-4.0	—
2005	ROU	AAA	25	4	4	1	13	12	65²	53	12	57	6	42.2%	.264	17	0.99	3.01	4.30	3.74	7.8	1.7	6.0	1.0	13.4	—
2005	HOU	MLB	25	3	6	0	22	14	81	100	25	66	23	37.6%	.317	-25	1.54	5.67	6.09	6.26	11.2	2.5	6.7	2.5	-5.7	0.41
2006	ROU	AAA	26	8	4	0	21	17	92²	95	43	76	15	45.9%	.289	-23	1.50	4.88	6.39	5.76	10.2	4.3	5.8	2.0	-1.6	—
2007	*COL*	*MLB*	*27*	*4*	*6*	*1*	*47*	*9*	*87¹*	*102*	*37*	*62*	*17*	*48.0%*	*.309*	*-7*	*1.58*	*5.80*	*5.39*	*5.19*	*9.5*	*3.5*	*5.7*	*1.4*	*5.5*	*0.80*

Breakout: 32% Improve: 69% Collapse: 11% Attrition: 2%   Comparables: Mel Bunch, Dan Murray, Rod Henderson, Clint Weibl

Part of the Billy Wagner deal, Astacio could still pay off the loss of the closer, but, for now, he's best known for giving up a World Series homer to Geoff Blum. He was completely unable to do anything in Houston and left his control somewhere on the trip to Round Rock. At 27, having a plus fastball isn't enough anymore.

Brandon Backe   Bats: R   Throws: R   Height: 6′ 0″   Weight: 195   Born: April 5, 1978   Age: 29

YEAR	TEAM	LVL	AGE	W	L	SV	G	GS	IP	H	BB	SO	HR	GB%	BABIP	STUFF	WHIP	ERA	PERA	EQERA	EQH9	EQBB9	EQSO9	EQHR9	VORP	WXRL
2004	NWO	AAA	26	6	5	0	19	9	64¹	57	26	74	7	—	.309	12	1.29	2.80	4.36	3.94	8.3	3.8	7.9	1.1	11.8	—
2004	HOU	MLB	26	5	3	0	33	9	67	75	27	54	10	—	.333	-2	1.52	4.30	4.56	4.17	9.5	3.1	6.3	1.2	9.6	1.60
2005	HOU	MLB	27	10	8	0	26	25	149¹	151	67	97	19	42.3%	.288	-1	1.46	4.76	4.95	5.00	9.3	3.7	5.4	1.1	10.4	2.64
2006	HOU	MLB	28	3	2	0	8	8	43	43	18	19	4	38.4%	.275	-3	1.42	3.77	4.86	3.71	9.1	3.3	3.7	0.8	10.6	1.28
2007	*HOU*	*MLB*	*29*	*5*	*6*	*0*	*35*	*14*	*95*	*101*	*42*	*58*	*14*	*44.0%*	*.287*	*-8*	*1.50*	*5.05*	*5.41*	*5.27*	*9.2*	*3.5*	*5.0*	*1.1*	*5.3*	*1.00*

Breakout: 6% Improve: 20% Collapse: 42% Attrition: 16%   Comparables: Ken Schrom, Joe Coleman, Armando Reynoso, Turk Lown

Having spend most of the 2006 season trying to avoid Tommy John surgery, Backe's another bullet point in the case that many hitter-to-pitcher conversion projects end up with elbow problems. He'll now spend most of 2007 rehabbing from what was, in the end, unavoidable. He's unlikely to pitch this season and may have pitched his last for the Astros.

Jimmy Barthmaier

Bats: R　Throws: R　　Height: 6' 4"　Weight: 210　Born: January 6, 1984　Age: 23

YEAR	TEAM	LVL	AGE	W	L	SV	G	GS	IP	H	BB	SO	HR	GB%	BABIP	STUFF	WHIP	ERA	PERA	EQERA	EQH9	EQBB9	EQSO9	EQHR9	VORP	WXRL
2004	GRV	Rk	20	4	3	0	13	13	69	70	22	65	3	—	.322	-10	1.33	3.78	5.32	6.47	10.6	4.3	3.7	1.0	-6.3	—
2005	LEX	A	21	11	6	0	25	25	134²	108	55	142	3	57.3%	.304	24	1.21	2.27	4.24	3.85	8.4	4.8	5.6	0.4	25.0	—
2006	SLM	A+	22	11	8	0	27	27	146¹	137	67	134	6	52.7%	.326	10	1.40	3.63	4.78	5.31	9.7	4.6	5.6	0.8	4.6	—
2007	HOU	MLB	23	6	8	0	25	20	117¹	121	62	82	15	51.0%	.294	3	1.56	5.25	5.47	5.56	8.9	4.2	5.7	1.0	2.9	1.10

Breakout: 9%　Improve: 27%　Collapse: 27%　Attrition: 0%　　Comparables: Kevin Hart, Jim Johnson, Rett Johnson, Alex Hart

An Astros executive says that Barthmaier's best skill is "missing bats." He also has some ground ball tendencies, a trait that helped him limit batters to just six home runs last year. Barthmaier doesn't have a third pitch beyond his low-90s heat and plus curveball, so he's likely bullpen material. Regardless, the Astros got great value for their thirteenth-round pick in 2003, having convinced Barthmaier that baseball was a better path than football.

Dave Borkowski

Bats: R　Throws: R　　Height: 6' 1"　Weight: 230　Born: February 7, 1977　Age: 30

YEAR	TEAM	LVL	AGE	W	L	SV	G	GS	IP	H	BB	SO	HR	GB%	BABIP	STUFF	WHIP	ERA	PERA	EQERA	EQH9	EQBB9	EQSO9	EQHR9	VORP	WXRL
2004	OTT	AAA	27	6	9	0	16	16	85¹	99	26	56	6	—	.332	2	1.47	4.85	4.54	5.42	10.0	3.0	4.4	0.7	1.7	—
2004	BAL	MLB	27	3	4	0	17	8	56	65	15	45	6	—	.339	11	1.43	5.14	3.76	5.25	9.9	2.2	6.6	0.8	2.8	0.85
2005	OTT	AAA	28	10	10	0	29	28	182²	217	38	104	18	47.7%	.327	-3	1.40	4.33	4.80	5.29	10.7	2.1	3.8	1.0	6.3	—
2006	HOU	MLB	29	3	2	0	40	0	71	70	23	52	8	49.1%	.292	2	1.31	4.69	3.94	4.48	8.7	2.5	6.0	0.9	9.9	0.59
2007	HOU	MLB	30	3	3	2	46	0	62²	68	21	41	9	48.0%	.298	-6	1.42	4.47	4.90	4.69	9.4	2.7	5.3	1.1	7.6	0.60

Breakout: 28%　Improve: 55%　Collapse: 18%　Attrition: 19%　　Comparables: Matt Whiteside, Luis Sanchez, Paul Reuschel, John Frascatore

While it wasn't one of the season's more exciting developments, Borkowski found a home doing middle relief work in the Astros bullpen in 2006, and acquitted himself nicely. He seemed to relish pitching at Minute Maid, holding hitters to .217/.266/.333 there against .289/.349/.526 on the road. As long as he continues to keep the ball down—only 20 percent of his pitches were above the belt last season—he should remain useful.

Taylor Buchholz

Bats: R　Throws: R　　Height: 6' 4"　Weight: 220　Born: October 13, 1981　Age: 25

YEAR	TEAM	LVL	AGE	W	L	SV	G	GS	IP	H	BB	SO	HR	GB%	BABIP	STUFF	WHIP	ERA	PERA	EQERA	EQH9	EQBB9	EQSO9	EQHR9	VORP	WXRL
2004	NWO	AAA	22	6	7	0	20	17	98	107	29	74	16	—	.295	-11	1.39	5.23	5.37	5.82	9.6	2.7	5.2	1.6	-2.4	—
2005	ROU	AAA	23	6	0	0	20	14	76²	79	27	45	14	47.8%	.285	-25	1.38	4.81	6.36	5.17	9.4	3.1	4.0	1.9	3.7	—
2006	ROU	AAA	24	1	3	0	7	7	44	47	17	37	2	42.6%	.345	10	1.45	4.91	3.83	6.34	10.0	3.5	5.9	0.6	-3.6	—
2006	HOU	MLB	24	6	10	0	22	19	113	107	34	77	21	45.5%	.258	-6	1.25	5.89	4.99	5.89	8.4	2.4	5.6	1.5	-3.6	1.40
2007	COL	MLB	25	6	10	0	34	22	135²	155	46	90	20	50.0%	.308	2	1.48	5.48	4.76	4.98	9.3	2.9	5.2	1.1	11.8	2.10

Breakout: 34%　Improve: 70%　Collapse: 6%　Attrition: 8%　　Comparables: Mark Clark, John Snyder, Dan Wright, Bob Heffner

Another bit of the Wagner bounty, if bounty's the right word. Buchholz generates a lot of fly balls with his curve/fastball mix. That's particularly dangerous in a hitter's park, as his home run rate attests, but Buchholz can't blame the Crawford Boxes for his gopher tendencies, as he gave up just as many long balls on the road. In other words, when he's bad, he's really bad, and when he's good, well . . . call us when you see what that looks like. In Colorado, this could get even worse. One small plus: he doesn't walk many.

Roger Clemens

Bats: R　Throws: R　　Height: 6' 4"　Weight: 235　Born: December 31, 1969　Age: 44

YEAR	TEAM	LVL	AGE	W	L	SV	G	GS	IP	H	BB	SO	HR	GB%	BABIP	STUFF	WHIP	ERA	PERA	EQERA	EQH9	EQBB9	EQSO9	EQHR9	VORP	WXRL
2004	HOU	MLB	41	18	4	0	33	33	214¹	169	79	218	15	—	.283	40	1.16	2.98	3.29	3.13	6.9	2.9	8.0	0.6	61.1	7.46
2005	HOU	MLB	42	13	8	0	32	32	211¹	151	62	185	11	50.3%	.248	41	1.01	1.87	3.10	2.41	6.7	2.4	7.2	0.5	80.2	9.40
2006	HOU	MLB	43	7	6	0	19	19	113¹	89	29	102	7	49.4%	.271	41	1.04	2.30	3.05	2.68	7.2	2.0	7.4	0.5	42.1	4.84
2007	HOU	MLB	44	11	6	0	27	24	155	127	50	140	13	48.0%	.269	22	1.15	3.02	3.17	3.22	7.1	2.6	7.4	0.7	42.4	5.70

Breakout: 33%　Improve: 33%　Collapse: 35%　Attrition: 6%　　Comparables: Nolan Ryan, Gaylord Perry, Phil Niekro, Hoyt Wilhelm

Clemens has retired more times than Evander Holyfield, but he's kept his fastball. About the only negative to his season was the Hamlet-y late start; as the narrator at the beginning of the 1948 Laurence Olivier version says, "This is the tragedy of a man who could not make up his mind." If Clemens wasn't as insanely dominant last year as he was in 2005, he was still twice as good as kids half his age. His ERA away from Minute Maid was 1.86. He did have to contend with the dicky groin that has been his *bete noir* of recent years, suggesting that when age finally does claim him other parts of the body will go before his arm does. Frighteningly, he may be able to do this awhile longer. The only question, unresolved at this writing, is whether or not he wants to.

Paul Estrada

Bats: R Throws: R   Height: 6′ 2″   Weight: 215   Born: September 10, 1982   Age: 24

YEAR	TEAM	LVL	AGE	W	L	SV	G	GS	IP	H	BB	SO	HR	GB%	BABIP	STUFF	WHIP	ERA	PERA	EQERA	EQH9	EQBB9	EQSO9	EQHR9	VORP	WXRL
2004	TCV	A-	21	5	1	8	23	0	41²	26	17	56	4	—	.247	-11	1.03	2.81	8.39	4.50	9.8	6.0	6.8	2.8	4.4	—
2005	LEX	A	22	6	7	3	46	3	90¹	65	34	94	6	53.0%	.266	-12	1.10	2.69	5.87	4.36	8.3	4.7	5.4	1.3	11.7	—
2006	CCH	AA	23	8	5	15	56	0	88²	61	37	134	10	54.0%	.296	13	1.11	3.06	4.56	3.89	7.6	4.0	9.9	1.5	16.3	—
2007	HOU	MLB	24	3	4	1	28	6	61¹	56	33	58	8	49.0%	.289	9	1.46	4.27	4.80	4.48	7.9	4.3	7.7	1.0	8.4	1.00

Breakout: 13% Improve: 31% Collapse: 31% Attrition: 15%   Comparables: Marc Kroon, Manny Delcarmen, Chad Harville, Bert Snow

Estrada finished second in the Double-A Texas League last year with 134 strikeouts. That might not sound overly impressive at first, but consider the fact that Estrada was the team's closer. With 13.6 strikeouts per nine innings and a .191 opponent's average, it's pretty evident that Estrada misses bats. His fastball is in the low-90s and is really just an average pitch, but he nukes hitters with a power slider that draws comparisons to K-Rod's. He could make some noise this year.

Juan Gutierrez

Bats: R Throws: R   Height: 6′ 3″   Weight: 200   Born: July 14, 1983   Age: 23

YEAR	TEAM	LVL	AGE	W	L	SV	G	GS	IP	H	BB	SO	HR	GB%	BABIP	STUFF	WHIP	ERA	PERA	EQERA	EQH9	EQBB9	EQSO9	EQHR9	VORP	WXRL
2004	GRV	Rk	20	8	2	0	13	13	65²	74	30	59	4	—	.357	-16	1.58	3.70	7.03	6.49	12.1	6.3	3.7	1.5	-6.0	—
2005	LEX	A	21	9	5	0	22	21	120²	106	43	100	10	45.7%	.287	-14	1.23	3.21	6.21	5.56	9.4	4.1	4.5	1.5	0.5	—
2006	CCH	AA	22	8	4	0	20	20	103	94	34	106	10	41.5%	.288	14	1.24	3.06	4.50	3.77	8.8	3.0	6.8	1.1	20.9	—
2007	HOU	MLB	23	5	8	0	26	18	106²	112	53	78	18	43.0%	.291	1	1.54	5.37	5.79	5.57	9.1	3.9	6.0	1.3	2.5	1.00

Breakout: 8% Improve: 30% Collapse: 33% Attrition: 1%   Comparables: Wascar Serrano, Ryan Vogelsong, Merkin Valdez, Dustin McGowan

The Astros have a number of strong-armed Latin imports in the system, with a particular concentration on Venezuelans. Gutierrez is the one who has gotten the best results. His mid-90s fastball and curveball are both above-average offerings, but he doesn't really have an effective off-speed pitch, leading many to project him as a reliever. He'll be at Triple-A to begin 2007, but he could get a look at some point during the season.

Jason Hirsh

Bats: R Throws: R   Height: 6′ 8″   Weight: 250   Born: February 20, 1982   Age: 25

YEAR	TEAM	LVL	AGE	W	L	SV	G	GS	IP	H	BB	SO	HR	GB%	BABIP	STUFF	WHIP	ERA	PERA	EQERA	EQH9	EQBB9	EQSO9	EQHR9	VORP	WXRL
2004	SLM	A+	22	11	7	0	26	23	130¹	128	57	96	8	—	.305	-8	1.42	4.01	5.85	5.80	9.1	4.8	4.4	1.1	-2.8	—
2005	CCH	AA	23	13	8	0	29	29	172¹	137	42	165	12	45.4%	.277	19	1.04	2.87	4.33	3.97	8.3	2.7	6.4	0.9	30.0	—
2006	ROU	AAA	24	13	2	0	23	23	137¹	94	51	118	5	40.8%	.245	29	1.06	2.10	3.83	3.05	6.8	3.3	6.1	0.4	38.4	—
2006	HOU	MLB	24	3	4	0	9	9	44²	48	22	29	11	32.5%	.264	-15	1.57	6.04	6.44	5.91	9.7	3.7	5.3	2.0	-1.8	0.68
2007	COL	MLB	25	6	10	0	32	26	135¹	145	58	105	20	45.0%	.304	6	1.50	5.43	4.75	4.90	8.8	3.6	6.1	1.1	13.1	2.30

Breakout: 8% Improve: 34% Collapse: 26% Attrition: 0%   Comparables: Scott Elarton, Rich Gale, John Maine, Sean Douglass

If the Astros had a young hurler who established himself as something more than back-of-the-rotation filler, it was Hirsh. He dominated the PCL and acquitted himself reasonably well when forced up to the big club to aid their late-season surge, running off four straight quality starts at one point. Although he also took his lumps in the Show, his lower home run rate in Triple-A is something you like to see from somebody who will have to pitch in a bandbox. Likely because of that, the Rockies coveted him and got him in the Jennings deal. With his height, you might think he's an intimidator on the mound, but he's more of a polished sinker-slider type than an imposing figure. The takeaway from his projection is that he can win enough battles at home plate to minimize the damage; if he gives up fewer cookies than he did in Houston, he'll be a solid replacement for Jennings.

Brad Lidge

Bats: R Throws: R   Height: 6′ 5″   Weight: 210   Born: December 23, 1976   Age: 30

YEAR	TEAM	LVL	AGE	W	L	SV	G	GS	IP	H	BB	SO	HR	GB%	BABIP	STUFF	WHIP	ERA	PERA	EQERA	EQH9	EQBB9	EQSO9	EQHR9	VORP	WXRL
2004	HOU	MLB	27	6	5	29	80	0	94²	57	30	157	8	—	.301	58	0.92	1.90	2.42	2.07	5.7	2.5	13.1	0.7	38.8	8.13
2005	HOU	MLB	28	4	4	42	70	0	70²	58	23	103	5	47.8%	.349	45	1.15	2.29	2.56	2.78	7.8	2.6	12.0	0.6	22.1	4.65
2006	HOU	MLB	29	1	5	32	78	0	75	69	36	104	10	46.2%	.335	24	1.40	5.28	3.68	5.07	8.6	3.8	11.2	1.1	3.6	0.81
2007	HOU	MLB	30	4	5	31	57	0	64¹	51	26	79	7	44.0%	.289	25	1.20	3.21	3.33	3.38	6.9	3.2	10.0	0.8	18.4	2.60

Breakout: 26% Improve: 56% Collapse: 11% Attrition: 5%   Comparables: Kyle Farnsworth, Lee Smith, Paul Shuey, Jeff Nelson

(continued next page)

Brad Lidge *(continued)*

The joke goes that the ball Albert Pujols hit off Brad Lidge in the 2005 NLCS still hasn't landed. If so, it appears to have taken Lidge's confidence along for the ride. Sabermetric orthodoxy would suggest that anyone can close, but Lidge never seemed to recover from that shot to the ego, flailing in the closer role last year. For those looking for a physical explanation for his poor showing, Lidge has a long history of arm and specifically elbow issues (as a starter in the low minors, he appeared in just 19 games from 1999 to 2001) owing to his violent mechanics. His struggles with his control last year just might be a portent of another date with the surgeon's table.

Mark McLemore Bats: L Throws: L Height: 6′ 2″ Weight: 220 Born: October 9, 1980 Age: 26

YEAR	TEAM	LVL	AGE	W	L	SV	G	GS	IP	H	BB	SO	HR	GB%	BABIP	STUFF	WHIP	ERA	PERA	EQERA	EQH9	EQBB9	EQSO9	EQHR9	VORP	WXRL
2004	SLM	A+	23	7	7	6	37	14	93¹	80	44	79	8	—	.269	-21	1.33	3.67	6.86	4.97	8.5	5.6	5.0	1.7	6.2	—
2005	CCH	AA	24	5	6	0	15	15	73²	59	34	65	5	37.9%	.273	6	1.26	2.81	5.38	5.04	8.3	5.4	5.7	1.0	4.3	—
2006	ROU	AAA	25	2	3	0	21	9	57	48	38	52	5	39.4%	.277	3	1.51	2.84	5.86	4.82	8.7	5.9	6.4	1.1	4.9	—
2007	HOU	MLB	26	3	5	0	28	10	72²	73	54	58	11	42.0%	.292	-8	1.75	5.61	6.29	5.80	8.7	6.0	6.5	1.2	-0.3	0.30

Breakout: 7% Improve: 28% Collapse: 40% Attrition: 3% Comparables: Tom Fordham, Adrian Burnside, Eric Cyr, Les Walrond

No, not *that* Mark McLemore. This is the other one. Even in Houston, the outfield situation wasn't quite that desperate, well . . . okay, yes it was, but this McLemore is a pitcher. Yes, "was" is the correct tense; McLemore didn't come all the way back to his previous levels after labrum surgery in 2005. Twenty-six years old and without his best stuff, McLemore might end up a popular guy at the Dell Diamond in Round Rock, but that's not exactly ambition of the highest level.

Trever Miller Bats: R Throws: L Height: 6′ 3″ Weight: 200 Born: May 29, 1973 Age: 34

YEAR	TEAM	LVL	AGE	W	L	SV	G	GS	IP	H	BB	SO	HR	GB%	BABIP	STUFF	WHIP	ERA	PERA	EQERA	EQH9	EQBB9	EQSO9	EQHR9	VORP	WXRL
2004	TBA	MLB	31	1	1	1	60	0	49	48	15	43	3	—	.319	14	1.29	3.12	3.30	3.60	8.8	2.5	7.4	0.5	13.1	0.85
2005	TBA	MLB	32	2	2	0	61	0	44¹	45	29	35	4	43.3%	.333	4	1.67	4.06	5.37	4.30	8.8	5.7	6.8	0.8	5.2	-0.89
2006	HOU	MLB	33	2	3	1	70	0	50²	42	13	56	7	34.4%	.282	21	1.09	3.02	3.67	2.82	7.6	1.9	9.0	1.1	17.0	1.65
2007	HOU	MLB	34	2	2	3	49	0	44¹	43	16	40	6	43.0%	.291	5	1.30	3.68	4.09	3.85	8.3	2.8	7.3	1.0	9.5	0.90

Breakout: 14% Improve: 32% Collapse: 33% Attrition: 17% Comparables: Paul Assenmacher, Alan Embree, Mike Stanton, Lance Painter

Miller is a LOOGY and nothing more. He missed a month in early 2006 with an elbow sprain, but, once activated, went right back to mowing down lefties in short stints. He's not exciting, but he's effective. Given that he's only 33, he still gets carded at the LOOGY Bar and Grill.

Fernando Nieve Bats: R Throws: R Height: 6′ 0″ Weight: 195 Born: July 15, 1982 Age: 24

YEAR	TEAM	LVL	AGE	W	L	SV	G	GS	IP	H	BB	SO	HR	GB%	BABIP	STUFF	WHIP	ERA	PERA	EQERA	EQH9	EQBB9	EQSO9	EQHR9	VORP	WXRL
2004	SLM	A+	21	10	6	0	24	24	149	136	40	117	9	—	.286	8	1.18	2.96	4.63	4.02	8.3	2.8	4.8	1.0	25.9	—
2004	ROU	AA	21	2	0	0	3	3	17¹	12	8	17	0	—	.267	17	1.16	1.56	4.03	2.65	6.9	4.8	6.4	0.0	5.6	—
2005	CCH	AA	22	4	3	0	14	14	85	62	29	96	7	42.2%	.276	25	1.07	2.65	4.36	3.42	7.7	3.6	7.8	1.1	19.8	—
2005	ROU	AAA	22	4	4	0	13	13	82	92	33	75	10	42.5%	.339	7	1.52	4.83	4.94	5.16	10.4	3.5	6.3	1.2	4.0	—
2006	HOU	MLB	23	3	3	0	40	11	96¹	87	41	70	18	41.7%	.254	-10	1.33	4.21	5.28	3.96	8.0	3.3	6.0	1.5	19.0	1.85
2007	HOU	MLB	24	5	6	1	43	12	101	99	40	78	15	42.0%	.280	3	1.38	4.58	4.81	4.78	8.5	3.2	6.3	1.2	11.6	1.60

Breakout: 4% Improve: 22% Collapse: 47% Attrition: 16% Comparables: Byron McLaughlin, Doug Drabek, Joe Presko, Steve Ridzik

Briefly plugged into the rotation in the wake of the disaster that befell Backe and the disasters called Wandy and Buchholz, Nieve remains a genuine prospect. His slider rates with the best in the organization, and his heater tops 90 MPH, but he's lost some of his dominance since hurting his elbow in 2004. He'll have to stay healthy and develop a changeup to combat opinions that he's better-suited for relief work.

Roy Oswalt Bats: R Throws: R Height: 6′ 0″ Weight: 185 Born: August 29, 1977 Age: 29

YEAR	TEAM	LVL	AGE	W	L	SV	G	GS	IP	H	BB	SO	HR	GB%	BABIP	STUFF	WHIP	ERA	PERA	EQERA	EQH9	EQBB9	EQSO9	EQHR9	VORP	WXRL
2004	HOU	MLB	26	20	10	0	36	35	237	233	62	206	17	—	.321	33	1.24	3.49	3.34	3.60	8.5	2.1	6.9	0.6	51.1	6.22
2005	HOU	MLB	27	20	12	0	35	35	241²	243	48	184	18	50.9%	.310	29	1.20	2.94	3.37	3.39	9.3	1.6	6.3	0.7	65.1	7.71
2006	HOU	MLB	28	15	8	0	33	32	220²	220	38	166	18	49.9%	.310	30	1.17	2.98	3.26	3.06	8.9	1.4	6.2	0.6	72.4	7.52
2007	HOU	MLB	29	14	10	0	32	32	214²	212	49	164	24	48.0%	.289	19	1.21	3.64	3.92	3.84	8.5	1.8	6.2	0.9	47.1	6.40

Breakout: 4% Improve: 24% Collapse: 37% Attrition: 1% Comparables: Frank Lary, Larry Jackson, Mike Garcia, Doug Drabek

Houston Astros

Oswalt signed a five-year contract in August. While such lengthy contracts for pitchers are seldom a good idea, Oswalt might be the exception to the rule. His workload during his team-controlled years has been heavy, but he's pitched effectively through the minor injuries. One of the best pitchers in the game, Oswalt's not the type to let his new contract do more than buy him some new bulldozers (seriously—you know boys and their toys). Most of the comparables PECOTA picked had seen their best days by the time they turned 30, but we expect Oswalt to hold his value for now.

Troy Patton Bats: S Throws: L   Height: 6' 1"   Weight: 185   Born: September 3, 1985   Age: 21

YEAR	TEAM	LVL	AGE	W	L	SV	G	GS	IP	H	BB	SO	HR	GB%	BABIP	STUFF	WHIP	ERA	PERA	EQERA	EQH9	EQBB9	EQSO9	EQHR9	VORP	WXRL
2004	GRV	Rk	18	2	2	0	6	6	28	23	5	32	1	—	.293	18	1.00	1.93	4.02	4.00	9.0	2.3	5.0	0.7	4.8	—
2005	LEX	A	19	5	2	0	15	15	78²	59	20	94	3	55.3%	.306	33	1.00	1.94	3.84	3.69	8.2	2.9	6.5	0.6	16.1	—
2005	SLM	A+	19	1	4	0	10	9	41	34	8	38	2	43.9%	.291	19	1.02	2.63	3.85	3.57	8.3	2.0	5.1	0.7	9.1	—
2006	SLM	A+	20	7	7	0	19	19	101	92	37	102	4	45.7%	.318	22	1.28	2.94	4.09	5.64	9.4	3.5	6.4	0.7	-0.4	—
2006	CCH	AA	20	2	5	0	8	8	45	48	13	37	6	36.1%	.327	7	1.36	4.40	5.31	5.40	10.0	2.6	5.4	1.6	1.0	—
2007	*HOU*	*MLB*	*21*	*7*	*8*	*0*	*28*	*21*	*129²*	*130*	*48*	*101*	*19*	*43.0%*	*.287*	*12*	*1.37*	*4.61*	*4.86*	*4.81*	*8.7*	*3.0*	*6.3*	*1.2*	*14.4*	*2.40*

Breakout: 19% Improve: 50% Collapse: 13% Attrition: 1%   Comparables: Ryan Ketchner, Randey Dorame, Chin-Hui Tsao, Andy Pratt

Patton has good velocity for a southpaw as well as a power curve, and showed considerable promise by forcing his way up to Double-A at midseason. He didn't dominate after the jump, but that's not a problem; at 21, he'll have the chance to repeat the level and stay on track. Assuming he can stay healthy with his choppy mechanics, the Texas lefty could compete for a rotation slot sometime in 2008.

Felipe Paulino del Guidice Bats: R Throws: R   Height: 6' 2"   Weight: 180   Born: October 5, 1983   Age: 23

YEAR	TEAM	LVL	AGE	W	L	SV	G	GS	IP	H	BB	SO	HR	GB%	BABIP	STUFF	WHIP	ERA	PERA	EQERA	EQH9	EQBB9	EQSO9	EQHR9	VORP	WXRL
2004	GRV	Rk	20	1	3	0	10	10	32	30	22	37	4	—	.321	-20	1.63	7.59	11.02	12.18	12.2	10.2	4.9	3.3	-20.0	—
2005	LEX	A	21	1	1	0	7	5	24¹	21	6	30	2	48.4%	.328	9	1.11	1.85	4.78	3.91	9.8	2.7	6.7	1.6	4.3	—
2005	TCV	A-	21	2	2	1	13	2	30²	21	11	34	2	47.4%	.253	-16	1.04	3.81	7.12	6.43	8.7	4.8	5.1	1.9	-2.6	—
2006	SLM	A+	22	9	7	0	27	26	126	119	59	91	13	45.2%	.285	-28	1.41	4.36	6.93	6.40	10.1	4.8	4.5	1.9	-10.8	—
2007	*HOU*	*MLB*	*23*	*3*	*7*	*0*	*25*	*14*	*85²*	*96*	*55*	*56*	*18*	*44.0%*	*.290*	*-14*	*1.77*	*6.60*	*7.09*	*6.81*	*9.7*	*5.1*	*5.3*	*1.7*	*-10.2*	*0.50*

Breakout: 18% Improve: 45% Collapse: 20% Attrition: 4%   Comparables: Elvin Nina, Kenneth Durost, Emar Fleming, Hal Garrett

Owner of the best arm in the Houston minor league system, Paulino touched 98 MPH last year and has lit up three digits on radar guns in the past. Unfortunately, he's just not a very good pitcher—his fastball is a little bit too true, his curveball is inconsistent, his changeup is just not good, and if all that wasn't enough, he has problems throwing strikes. Every once in a while, something clicks with pitchers who have this kind of talent, but more often than not it just proves the lesson that man cannot live by fastball alone.

Andy Pettitte Bats: L Throws: L   Height: 6' 5"   Weight: 225   Born: June 15, 1972   Age: 35

YEAR	TEAM	LVL	AGE	W	L	SV	G	GS	IP	H	BB	SO	HR	GB%	BABIP	STUFF	WHIP	ERA	PERA	EQERA	EQH9	EQBB9	EQSO9	EQHR9	VORP	WXRL
2004	HOU	MLB	32	6	4	0	15	15	83	71	31	79	8	—	.278	27	1.23	3.90	3.58	3.81	7.4	3.0	7.5	0.7	16.0	2.06
2005	HOU	MLB	33	17	9	0	33	33	222¹	188	41	171	17	51.4%	.272	31	1.03	2.39	3.27	2.93	7.8	1.5	6.4	0.7	72.1	8.55
2006	HOU	MLB	34	14	13	0	36	35	214¹	238	70	178	27	50.8%	.333	17	1.44	4.20	3.92	4.45	9.8	2.6	6.8	1.0	30.3	4.15
2007	*NYA*	*MLB*	*35*	*12*	*9*	*0*	*30*	*30*	*191²*	*201*	*54*	*140*	*23*	*49.0%*	*.300*	*14*	*1.33*	*4.20*	*4.06*	*4.07*	*9.3*	*2.4*	*6.1*	*1.0*	*29.7*	*4.50*

Breakout: 12% Improve: 36% Collapse: 18% Attrition: 3%   Comparables: Chuck Finley, David Wells, Frank Tanana, Gaylord Perry

Over his three years in Houston, Pettitte had one injury-plagued year, one middling year, and one great one that helped put his team in the World Series. On average, Pettitte pitched 173 innings a year with a 3.38 ERA. That might lead you to conclude that the Astros got a good return on his contract, but it doesn't tell the whole story. Judging the investment ultimately comes down to the difficult question of consistency versus peak value. Last year, Pettitte struggled with elbow tendonitis in the first, but appeared to recover after the break, posting a 2.80 ERA from then until the end of the season. Clearly consistency isn't his bag. Given his age, injury history, and move from the easy league to the DH league, his return to the Yankees will probably be quite similar to his stay in Houston—some good, some bad, and some time on the DL.

Chad Qualls
Bats: R Throws: R   Height: 6' 5"   Weight: 220   Born: August 17, 1978   Age: 28

YEAR	TEAM	LVL	AGE	W	L	SV	G	GS	IP	H	BB	SO	HR	GB%	BABIP	STUFF	WHIP	ERA	PERA	EQERA	EQH9	EQBB9	EQSO9	EQHR9	VORP	WXRL
2004	NWO	AAA	25	3	6	1	32	14	106²	134	30	72	8	—	.348	-3	1.54	5.57	4.34	6.15	11.0	2.7	4.7	0.7	-6.6	—
2004	HOU	MLB	25	4	0	1	25	0	33	34	8	24	3	—	.307	5	1.27	3.55	4.08	3.21	9.1	1.9	5.9	0.8	7.8	1.39
2005	HOU	MLB	26	6	4	0	77	0	79²	73	23	60	7	59.7%	.292	6	1.21	3.27	3.99	3.81	8.6	2.4	6.3	0.8	15.5	1.93
2006	HOU	MLB	27	7	3	0	81	0	88²	76	28	56	10	60.9%	.266	-2	1.17	3.75	4.44	3.61	7.7	2.5	5.2	0.9	21.8	2.93
2007	*HOU*	*MLB*	*28*	*4*	*3*	*2*	*61*	*1*	*71*	*73*	*24*	*47*	*7*	*55.0%*	*.294*	*-3*	*1.37*	*4.04*	*4.32*	*4.32*	*8.9*	*2.7*	*5.4*	*0.8*	*12.3*	*1.00*

Breakout: 15% Improve: 38% Collapse: 34% Attrition: 13%   Comparables: Antonio Alfonseca, Tim Crabtree, George Frazier, Braden Looper

Qualls didn't record any saves last year, but he was nearly as valuable as Dan Wheeler in the wake of Brad Lidge's wilting performance. Qualls's ability to grind grounders out of hitters and neutralize lefties has a particular value for a bullpen that doesn't always show up in the box score. If there's any worry, it's his workload. If he can avoid a meaningful decline after making 158 appearances over the last two seasons, he'll be on the short list of baseball's setup heroes.

Chad Reineke
Bats: R Throws: R   Height: 6' 6"   Weight: 210   Born: April 9, 1982   Age: 25

YEAR	TEAM	LVL	AGE	W	L	SV	G	GS	IP	H	BB	SO	HR	GB%	BABIP	STUFF	WHIP	ERA	PERA	EQERA	EQH9	EQBB9	EQSO9	EQHR9	VORP	WXRL
2004	TCV	A-	22	0	2	3	23	0	36²	27	23	52	0	—	.329	12	1.36	2.45	5.46	5.12	9.4	9.7	6.8	0.3	1.7	—
2005	LEX	A	23	10	8	4	42	11	102¹	84	49	108	5	52.7%	.312	-5	1.30	3.52	5.73	5.68	9.1	6.2	5.4	0.9	-0.8	—
2006	SLM	A+	24	6	5	0	17	17	99	82	29	87	5	52.9%	.275	1	1.12	3.00	4.84	5.59	8.9	3.1	5.1	1.0	0.1	—
2006	CCH	AA	24	1	3	0	15	4	44¹	33	26	45	3	45.6%	.264	9	1.34	3.06	5.30	4.22	7.4	5.9	6.3	0.8	6.5	—
2007	*HOU*	*MLB*	*25*	*4*	*6*	*0*	*27*	*13*	*87*	*91*	*52*	*64*	*12*	*47.0%*	*.298*	*-4*	*1.64*	*5.52*	*5.85*	*5.80*	*9.0*	*4.8*	*6.0*	*1.1*	*-0.3*	*0.50*

Breakout: 6% Improve: 34% Collapse: 24% Attrition: 4%   Comparables: Tom Davey, Kevin Beirne, John Sneed, Derrick Lewis

The Astros moved Reineke to the bullpen at the end of the season, and he flourished there, posting a 2.10 ERA in 25.2 innings to go along with 29 strikeouts and just 12 hits allowed. He's big (six-foot-six), he can get it up to 95 MPH when he's limited to an inning at a time, and his slider has the makings of a plus pitch. The organization is understandably excited about him.

Wandy Rodriguez
Bats: S Throws: L   Height: 5' 11"   Weight: 160   Born: January 18, 1979   Age: 28

YEAR	TEAM	LVL	AGE	W	L	SV	G	GS	IP	H	BB	SO	HR	GB%	BABIP	STUFF	WHIP	ERA	PERA	EQERA	EQH9	EQBB9	EQSO9	EQHR9	VORP	WXRL
2004	ROU	AA	25	11	6	0	26	25	142²	159	57	115	15	—	.326	-25	1.51	4.48	6.53	6.42	10.9	4.6	4.7	1.8	-12.5	—
2005	ROU	AAA	26	4	2	0	8	8	46¹	43	16	48	7	40.6%	.300	11	1.27	3.69	5.29	4.11	9.0	3.1	7.0	1.6	7.6	—
2005	HOU	MLB	26	10	10	0	25	22	128²	135	53	80	19	46.0%	.294	-9	1.46	5.52	5.31	5.80	9.7	3.4	5.1	1.3	-1.8	1.29
2006	ROU	AAA	27	2	2	0	5	5	26¹	32	13	13	2	43.6%	.333	-18	1.72	6.90	5.93	9.00	11.8	4.5	3.5	1.0	-9.8	—
2006	HOU	MLB	27	9	10	0	30	24	135²	154	63	98	17	47.1%	.329	0	1.60	5.64	4.62	5.89	10.1	3.6	5.8	1.0	-4.3	0.96
2007	*HOU*	*MLB*	*28*	*6*	*9*	*0*	*36*	*18*	*120*	*131*	*53*	*82*	*18*	*46.0%*	*.298*	*-3*	*1.53*	*5.30*	*5.56*	*5.55*	*9.4*	*3.5*	*5.5*	*1.2*	*2.8*	*1.00*

Breakout: 22% Improve: 53% Collapse: 12% Attrition: 23%   Comparables: Al Jackson, Nelson Figueroa, John Curtis, Rick Krivda

It's not a nickname or a diminutive—the man's real name is Wandy Fulton Rodriguez. That's an odd collection of names—an implement from the Harry Potter books, the inventor of the steamboat, and, mixing the exotic with the jejune, one of baseball's most common surnames. Even his son, Wadells, gets in on the name game. As for his pitching, he's a prototypical skinny Dominican without a dominant pitch. He's a swingman, if the swing referred to is the short trip from Houston to Round Rock.

Chris Sampson
Bats: R Throws: R   Height: 6' 1"   Weight: 190   Born: May 23, 1978   Age: 29

YEAR	TEAM	LVL	AGE	W	L	SV	G	GS	IP	H	BB	SO	HR	GB%	BABIP	STUFF	WHIP	ERA	PERA	EQERA	EQH9	EQBB9	EQSO9	EQHR9	VORP	WXRL
2004	SLM	A+	26	7	11	0	27	27	151²	170	26	101	8	—	.331	-6	1.29	3.80	4.78	5.75	10.2	2.0	3.7	1.0	-2.5	—
2005	CCH	AA	27	4	12	4	32	19	150	147	19	92	11	56.6%	.288	-6	1.11	3.12	4.48	5.25	9.8	1.5	3.8	1.1	5.7	—
2006	ROU	AAA	28	12	3	4	27	18	125	110	14	68	12	59.9%	.250	-5	0.99	2.52	4.53	4.67	8.5	1.0	3.7	1.2	12.7	—
2006	HOU	MLB	28	2	1	0	12	3	34	25	5	15	3	55.1%	.212	1	0.88	2.12	3.89	2.62	6.6	1.0	3.7	0.8	12.9	1.34
2007	*HOU*	*MLB*	*29*	*5*	*6*	*1*	*47*	*13*	*101*	*113*	*21*	*49*	*12*	*55.0%*	*.292*	*-8*	*1.32*	*4.49*	*4.60*	*4.80*	*9.6*	*1.7*	*3.9*	*1.0*	*11.4*	*1.50*

Breakout: 18% Improve: 41% Collapse: 24% Attrition: 7%   Comparables: Jim Acker, Mike Proly, Ramiro Mendoza, Pat Ahearne

Sampson is a Texas Tech product and Houston native, so his climb to the big club had a nice local touch. He's got nothing left to prove in the minors, and his cameo appearance last year may give him a better shot at cracking the rotation out of spring training. With plus-plus command of average-to-below stuff, he'll never be a star, but he could stick around a while.

Russ Springer Bats: R Throws: R   Height: 6' 4" Weight: 215 Born: December 31, 1969 Age: 38

YEAR	TEAM	LVL	AGE	W	L	SV	G	GS	IP	H	BB	SO	HR	GB%	BABIP	STUFF	WHIP	ERA	PERA	EQERA	EQH9	EQBB9	EQSO9	EQHR9	VORP	WXRL
2004	NWO	AAA	35	1	2	6	26	0	31	31	14	33	3	—	.337	-2	1.45	3.48	5.24	4.50	9.6	4.8	6.9	1.2	3.7	—
2004	HOU	MLB	35	0	1	0	16	0	13²	15	6	9	1	—	.318	-6	1.54	2.63	4.30	2.57	9.6	3.2	5.1	0.6	4.6	0.08
2005	HOU	MLB	36	4	4	0	62	0	59	49	21	54	9	40.1%	.253	1	1.19	4.73	4.63	5.16	7.9	2.9	7.6	1.4	1.9	0.76
2006	HOU	MLB	37	1	1	0	72	0	59²	46	16	46	10	27.9%	.222	0	1.04	3.47	4.72	3.28	7.0	2.1	6.3	1.3	17.0	0.62
2007	SLN	MLB	38	2	2	2	39	0	43¹	42	15	32	8	34.0%	.267	-8	1.31	4.23	4.73	4.48	9.1	2.7	5.8	1.5	6.3	0.50

Breakout: 15% Improve: 24% Collapse: 43% Attrition: 43%   Comparables: Aurelio Lopez, Don McMahon, Ted Power, Dennis Cook

Love him or hate him for throwing at Barry Bonds on "principle," Springer is a useful back-of-the-bullpen guy, even at 38. He held right-handers to a .187 average last year, and will try to do the same this year for the Cardinals.

Dan Wheeler Bats: R Throws: R   Height: 6' 3" Weight: 220 Born: December 10, 1977 Age: 29

YEAR	TEAM	LVL	AGE	W	L	SV	G	GS	IP	H	BB	SO	HR	GB%	BABIP	STUFF	WHIP	ERA	PERA	EQERA	EQH9	EQBB9	EQSO9	EQHR9	VORP	WXRL
2004	NYN	MLB	26	3	1	0	32	1	50²	65	17	46	9	—	.357	-2	1.62	4.79	4.43	4.88	11.3	2.6	7.1	1.4	3.2	0.21
2004	HOU	MLB	26	0	0	0	14	0	14¹	11	3	9	1	—	.244	3	0.98	2.52	3.74	2.45	6.8	1.8	4.9	0.6	5.1	0.27
2005	HOU	MLB	27	2	3	3	71	0	73¹	53	19	69	7	37.2%	.250	21	0.98	2.21	3.51	2.32	6.8	2.1	7.8	0.9	26.7	3.35
2006	HOU	MLB	28	3	5	9	75	0	71¹	58	24	68	5	37.9%	.279	22	1.15	2.52	3.23	2.61	7.3	2.6	7.8	0.5	26.0	3.88
2007	HOU	MLB	29	3	3	6	56	0	63¹	60	22	56	9	40.0%	.282	6	1.29	3.78	4.27	3.92	8.2	2.7	7.1	1.1	13.6	1.20

Breakout: 9% Improve: 17% Collapse: 57% Attrition: 9%   Comparables: Scott Sullivan, Todd Worrell, T. J. Mathews, Alejandro Pena

Wheeler functioned as the de facto closer during Brad Lidge's various mercy breaks and did a reasonable job. That says something about the way the "only certain pitchers have the fortitude to close" lobby has overstated its case; the Astros have gone through a series of closers and have never had the slightest problem promoting the next guy into the role. A more accurate truth would be that not all pitchers have the fortitude to close, but many do. Consider Wheeler one of baseball's best-kept secrets; since the Mets trade him to Houston for no-hit minor league outfielder Adam Seuss in August 2004, Wheeler has assembled the following line: 159 innings, 122 hits, 46 walks, 146 strikeouts, and a 2.38 ERA. Wheeler will likely close again sometime, especially if the Astros find someone willing to give Brad Lidge a change of scenery.

Lineouts

PLAYER	TEAM	LVL	AGE	PA	R	2B	3B	HR	RBI	BB	SO	SB-CS	SPEED	AVG/OBP/SLG	MLVr	EqAVG/OBP/SLG	EqA	VORP
3B K. Clemens	LEX	A	19	352	40	19	1	5	39	32	67	2-1	4.0	.229/.313/.346	-.074	.197/.257/.284	.196	-24.2
1B R. Huffman	ROU	AAA	29	412	62	25	2	10	59	50	73	3-2	4.3	.299/.396/.467	.252	.289/.367/.441	.280	16.3
OF E. Iorg	LEX	A	23	516	68	32	4	15	85	33	119	42-6	7.1	.256/.313/.437	.061	.212/.249/.342	.214	-42.1
UT J. McEwing	ROU	AAA	33	460	64	21	1	10	46	23	65	16-7	6.1	.315/.351/.441	.156	.288/.315/.380	.243	7.6
RF J. Parraz	TCV	A-	0	298	46	18	2	6	38	33	44	23-3	6.6	.336/.421/.494	.370	.295/.356/.455	.284	20.9
C L. Santangelo	SLM	A+	23	394	48	19	5	18	57	36	112	0-4	3.7	.241/.310/.473	.112	.218/.269/.411	.230	-4.5
C M. Sapp*	TCV	A-	18	189	20	9	0	1	20	22	37		3.7	.229/.317/.301	-.048	.186/.258/.250	.190	-30.1
1B O. Sheldon	LEX	A	23	291	46	27	0	4	32	43	43	7-3	4.7	.328/.436/.490	.355	.265/.344/.393	.260	1.8
	SLM	A+	23	197	19	6	0	1	24	31	32	2-1	3.1	.292/.421/.348	.155	.281/.376/.339	.257	1.1
2B D. Sutton#	SLM	A+	23	551	65	27	2	15	48	69	84	20-15	4.9	.263/.360/.430	.146	.247/.320/.396	.249	9.1

PLAYER	TEAM	LVL	AGE	W	L	SV	IP	H	BB	SO	HR	GB%	BABIP	STUFF	WHIP	ERA	PERA	EqERA	EqH9	EqBB9	EqSO9	EqHR9	VORP
P. Barzilla*	ROU	AAA	27	8	5	1	112²	114	48	80	5	—	.310	4	1.44	3.85	4.27	5.56	9.6	3.9	4.9	0.6	0.5
B. Bogusevic*	LEX	A	22	2	5	0	70	76	24	60	6	—	.330	-27	1.43	4.76	6.33	7.43	11.5	4.2	4.3	1.9	-13.6
	TCV	A-	22	0	0	0	11¹	10	5	6	1	—	.250	-30	1.35	4.05	11.59	11.57	12.5	7.7	2.9	3.9	-6.2
R. Diaz	LEX	A	22	8	5	0	99	84	35	107	8	—	.305	-16	1.20	2.36	6.31	4.47	9.8	4.3	5.6	1.7	11.6
	SLM	A+	22	3	2	0	43¹	42	13	29	2	—	.301	-2	1.28	3.55	4.88	5.36	9.9	3.0	4.1	0.9	1.1
C. Douglass	CCH	AA	22	7	8	0	161²	144	56	102	13	—	.281	2	1.24	3.52	5.04	3.94	8.2	3.1	4.2	0.9	29.9
T. Fairchild	LEX	A	22	10	3	0	108¹	90	19	98	5	—	.290	10	1.01	1.67	4.37	3.18	8.9	2.1	4.6	1.0	28.2
	SLM	A+	22	4	4	0	64	63	19	44	3	—	.299	0	1.28	3.80	4.59	6.03	9.8	2.9	4.2	0.9	-3.0
M. Gallo*	ROU	AAA	29	2	0	0	40¹	46	16	25	4	—	.336	-27	1.55	5.61	5.61	6.86	11.2	3.7	4.3	1.1	-5.5
	HOU	MLB	29	1	2	0	16¹	28	7	7	3	—	.417	-29	2.14	6.07	5.77	5.82	14.8	3.2	3.2	1.6	0.1
J. Peguero	CCH	AA	25	2	0	14	38²	18	16	48	0	—	.234	19	0.89	0.71	4.07	1.47	5.6	4.4	7.6	0.2	16.8
	ROU	AAA	25	1	2	1	36	34	18	30	3	—	.299	-8	1.44	3.50	4.93	5.30	9.1	4.5	5.8	1.0	1.2

Roger's kid, **Koby Clemens**, wasn't purely a nepotism pick, but he's struggled as a pro. He has a little power and a strong arm (no surprise), but his hitting skills, approach, and athleticism are all a little behind the curve. The experiment with making **Royce Huffman** a catcher was stillborn, making him an oxymoronic "utility tweener"—not enough glove to help up the middle, and not enough bat to help in the corners. **Eli Iorg**, son of Garth, was a first-round pick in 2005, but fell flat in his full-season debut. He was old when drafted because of a Mormon mission, and remains advanced in age as prospects go (he'll be 24 in March). Still, there's some skill base there. **Joe McEwing** continues to hang around on the off chance that he'll recapture some of he love that's being given to the other Bloomquist types. When the Astros selected **Jordan Parraz** in the third round of the 2004 draft, they knew he'd take a while. Indeed, he finally showed some major signs of life in 2006 with a monster season in the New York-Penn League. He's got more tools than Santa's elves, so keep an eye on his full-season debut. **Lou Santangelo** has two skills: he throws well and he can hit home runs. There's not much more to see here, but those two skills on their own are enough to give him a career as a backup. The team's first-round pick in 2006, **Max Sapp** is a left-handed-hitting catcher with power and a good throwing arm who was overmatched in the New York-Penn League while facing players who were generally three years older than he was. Give him a mulligan statistically, as he has a nice set of skills to build on. **Ole Sheldon** had a .430 on-base percentage in 2006, but he was also 24 years old, in A-ball, and has no power, not exactly what one looks for in a first baseman. **Drew Sutton** put up some nice numbers at High-A Salem, showing power, speed, an ability to take walks, and some pretty good defensive skills. At the same time, he belonged in Double-A. We're still waiting for him to get tested.

Philip Barzilla has a name built for marketing and fun headlines, but he's a career minor league lefty who depends on a good breaking ball to keep hitters off balance rather than a monster who blows them away with his heat ray. Sure, that big lizard keeps Tokyo off balance too, but not with finesse. **Brian Bogusevic** has been a disappointment since becoming the team's first-round pick in 2005. He's battled arm soreness since signing, though the team thinks he finally came around with a nice run of starts at the end of last year. He's a power lefty with a fastball-slider combination and will get lots of time to bounce back. **Raymar Diaz** is a six-foot-seven right-hander who can dial it up to 95 on occasion, but his secondary pitches are notable for their absence. He could have a future in the bullpen. **Chance Douglass** has had a decent minor league career by mixing up an average fastball, average slider, and average change. Average doesn't get you a whole lot of notice, but could get you a job in the back of a bullpen. **Tip Fairchild** is trying to discover just how far you can get if you have marginal stuff but never walk anybody. It worked in the Sally League, but his ERA more than doubled after jumping to High-A. A not-very-special lefty specialist who had a vaguely decent season in 2005, **Mike Gallo** was hammered early and demoted in June. He'll try to resuscitate his career with the Rockies. **Jailen Peguero** was an age-gate "victim" who gained about three years when his true identity was discovered, so now he's a 26 year old with just half a year of experience above Double-A. Nonetheless, he had a good enough season to be a late addition to the Astros' 40-man roster.

Manager: Phil Garner

ear	Team	W-L	Pythag +/-	Avg PC	100 +P	120 +P	QS	BQS	REL	REL w Zero R	IBB	SUBS	PH	PH Avg	PH HR	SB2	CS2	SB3	CS3	SAC Att	SAC %	POS SAC	Squeeze	Swing	In Play
2004	HOU	48-26	+2	91.9	30	3	28	3	241	155	24	52	138	.282	3	46	14	17	0	44	86.4%	20	2	63	37
2005	HOU	89-73	-2	96.2	69	5	96	7	434	293	29	87	250	.252	3	101	35	12	5	122	67.2%	47	9	142	117
2006	HOU	82-80	-1	93.8	61	4	83	13	497	326	65	72	286	.240	7	74	30	5	3	131	76.3%	45	5	137	110

It's hard to imagine a guy nicknamed "Scrap Iron" being too mellow, but that was one of the criticisms lobbed at Phil Garner in 2006. He spent most of the year looking for offense where there was none while babysitting a bullpen that was jumbled by the Lidge situation. Garner has a tendency to fall in love with certain players, especially ones that remind him of his playing days—get dirty, and Phil will find you a slot. While his patience with some of the kids in the rotation was frustrating, Garner handled his relief problems well, and he's nimble enough tactically to exploit some of the position flexibility that players such as Lamb, Berkman, Burke, and Bruntlett afford him. The key for Garner is to figure out how to make this team play in the first half like it does in the second. Given his results in his short tenure with the Astros, it might surprise some that Garner is on the hot seat, but if the Astros start slowly again . . .

Kansas City Royals

It's a well-rehearsed cliché to question the intelligence of baseball owners for some of the decisions they make, and certainly as a group they are prone to make some doozies, ranging from the creation and long defense of the color line to the 1995 replacement players. But you don't become wealthy enough to buy a major league baseball team without some business acumen. David Glass may be cheap, he may let his son stick his head into baseball affairs that are way over his head, but he isn't dumb. In 2006, with the Royals headed for their fourth 100-loss season in five years, he read the writing on the wall, calculated that public opinion had turned against him, and made the two best baseball decisions of his career: (1) He hired Dayton Moore to replace Allard Baird as General Manager. (2) He agreed to stay the heck out of Moore's way.

Dayton Moore wasn't unanimously considered the best potential GM in baseball, but he was certainly towards the top of everyone's short list. Moore had joined the Braves in 1994 as a scouting supervisor, and was promoted through the organization rapidly, rising to Director of Player Personnel (i.e. the Farm Director) in 2003. After that season, he was ranked the number-one general manager prospect in the game by Baseball America. He was later offered the Red Sox's position during Theo Epstein's brief sabbatical in 2005.

Like his mentor, John Schuerholz, Moore is not on the cutting edge of statistical analysis, but few organizations have done a better job of scouting and developing young talent over the last 15 years than the Braves. With more and more teams embracing the use of statistical analysis to complement traditional scouting, the argument can be made that teams can better exploit inefficiencies in the valuation of baseball players by out-scouting their opponents than by outdoing them on the analytical front. The

> ## ROYALS PROSPECTUS
>
> **2006 record:** 62–100; Fifth place, AL Central
>
> **Pythagenport record:** 61–101
>
> **Runs scored per game:** 4.67 (12th in AL)
>
> **Runs allowed per game:** 5.99 (14th in AL)
>
> **Team EqA:** .248 (13th in AL)
>
> **2006 Batters Age:** 30.2 (5th oldest in AL)
>
> **2006 Pitchers Age:** 28.4 (4th youngest in AL)
>
> **Ballpark:** Kauffman Stadium; Slight hitter's park; Park Factor of 1.017
>
> **2006:** The talent level was even lower than the payroll, and fan interest was lower still.
>
> **2007:** Gordon, Butler, and Hochevar provide an entirely new sense of crushable hope.

AL's reigning champions in Detroit were built in essentially that fashion by Dave Dombrowski. So long as Moore pays the same common-sense level of respect to baseball statistics that Dombrowski does, there's no reason he can't emulate that level of success.

The hiring of Moore in June jolted the Royals out of their freefall. The club hit rock bottom with a 16–47 record on June 13th, five days after Moore was introduced. Since 1900, only six teams had a worse record after 63 games. From that point on, the Royals did a shockingly good impersonation of a major league baseball team, going 46–53 the rest of the way. In the last 70 years, 27 teams have started 19–44 or worse. As table 1 shows, only one of those teams played better than the 2006 Royals from that point on.

If history is any guide, the Royals' turnaround over the last four months of the season is a meaningful development. The 1988 Padres finished over .500, and in 1989 the team went 89–73, which would have made them a wild card team under today's rules. San Diego's resurgence in 2003 led to even greater success: an 87-win team in 2004 and divisional crowns the last two seasons. The Tigers and Twins had less immediate success, but both teams reached .500 within two years, an exciting enough prospect for a Royals club that has had just one .500 season in the last dozen.

The Royals were a better team from mid-June on because they were a *different* team from mid-June on. Mark Teahen's reversal of fortune deserves a large amount credit, but the changes went beyond his career-saving turnaround. The team on the field in July was substantially different than the team in May, which in turn was substantially different from the team in September. Moore took over the reins on June 8th, and that same day the Royals released Seth Etherton and called up Kyle Snyder. The next

Table 1. Best Turnarounds, 1937–2006

Year	Team	Through 63 Games			Rest of Season			Entire Year		
		W	L	Pct.	W	L	Pct.	W	L	Pct.
1987	San Diego	17	46	.270	48	51	.485	65	97	.401
2006	Kansas City	16	47	.254	46	53	.465	62	100	.383
2003	San Diego	18	45	.286	46	53	.465	64	98	.395
1982	Minnesota	14	49	.222	46	53	.465	60	102	.370
1953	Detroit	18	45	.286	42	49	.462	60	94	.390

day Todd Wellemeyer was claimed off waivers and Steven Andrade was sent packing; two days later Snyder was cut in favor of Brandon Duckworth, and the pace had been set. Moore moved eight players off the 40-man roster in June alone. Five more followed in July as the trading deadline approached.

In December, after a lull leading up to the winter meetings, the Royals had a spasm of activity that added seven new players to the roster in the span of two weeks. Counting players on the 60-day DL, the Royals had 45 players on their roster when Moore took over. With the signing of David Riske on December 20th, only 19 of those players remained. Few teams have ever turned over their roster as violently and expeditiously as the Royals have in Moore's first six months. Of the 11 pitchers that broke camp with the Royals last April, just one (Jimmy Gobble) is likely to be on the Opening Day roster this year.

Taken individually, Moore's moves range from the inspired (Jeremy Affeldt and Denny Bautista for Ryan Shealy) to the shaky (J. P. Howell for Joey Gathright) to the just plain irrelevant (Ruben Gotay for Jeff Keppinger). As a whole, the Royals' transactions over Moore's first six months follow a few major themes:

It's better to trade a veteran for little in July than to walk away with nothing in October. Credit Moore with not hesitating to take the best offer on the table for his veterans at the trading deadline, even if it meant getting less than full value. Not every GM is willing to pull the trigger so readily. (Dave Littlefield, please pick up the white courtesy phone.) Before the deadline last July, Moore turned Tony Graffanino into a wild, but hard-throwing lefty (Jorge de la Rosa); Matt Stairs into a wild, but hard-throwing righty (Jose Diaz); and Mike MacDougal into a well-regarded pitching prospect (Tyler Lumsden) and another live arm (Daniel Cortes).

Sometimes the best way to improve the pitching is to improve the defense. While Moore went hard after pitching from Day One, he went against the grain with one of his first deals, trading former first-rounder J. P. Howell to Tampa Bay for Gathright. By moving David DeJesus to left field and Emil Brown to DH, the Royals ostensibly improved their defense at two outfield positions. The deal grades out poorly because Gathright simply doesn't hit enough to be a starting outfielder, but many instances of what we consider pitching breakthroughs were in fact the result of defensive improvements. Moore should know; his old boss Schuerholz did just that with the 1990–91 Braves.

Don't be afraid to get creative. Moore sent middle reliever Elmer Dessens to the Dodgers in exchange for Odalis Perez and as a pair of Grade C prospects in Blake Johnson and Julio Pimental. Perez is exactly the sort of gamble the Royals should be taking–a pitcher with a history of success whose basic skills are still intact, but who has so worn out his welcome with his current team that they're willing to eat part of his contract *and* give up prospects just to get rid of him. Perez enters the year as the Royals' number-two starter while earning a reasonable salary given the current market; if he turns it around, the Royals may be able to move him for even more prospects in July. This was one of Moore's most inspired deals.

Show no tolerance for underachievers. This is the defining principle that runs through all of Moore's transactions, and explains some of his more questionable moves. The Royals' pitching staff was chock-full of guys with better stuff than results. They occasionally showed glimpses of what they could be, but never with any kind of consistency. Moore cashiered every last one of them, almost immediately shipping out Jeremy Affeldt, the original underachiever, and Denny Bautista, who flings fastballs in the high-90s and racks up ERAs in the high-5.00s.

Scouts have labeled Howell a whiner since his collegiate days. Ambiorix Burgos is wild and has just one plus pitch; he was traded for Brian Bannister, whose fastball might lose a race to Burgos's splitter, but who moves the ball around effectively. Andy Sisco's height, velocity, and promising rookie season hid the fact that his work ethic has been questionable for years—there's a reason the Cubs left him unprotected in the 2004 Rule 5 draft. He was moved for Ross Gload, who's a decent bench player at best but is, in scouts' parlance, a gamer. Runelvys Hernandez started the 2006 season on the DL essentially because he was too fat to pitch; he was cut in December. Gotay, the one hitting prospect Moore traded, also had the whiff of unmet expectations about him, so he was moved for an older, less athletic player at the same position, only Keppinger has a reputation for being a heady player who gets the most out of his ability.

This is not to say that Moore was correct to trade these players, or even that these labels are entirely deserved. Many a team has given up on a player they perceived to be a head case, only to see him blossom (and peel off that label) with a change of scenery. The point is that Moore felt it wasn't enough to inject the team with talent—the team needed a full-scale institutional culture transplant. For years, the Royals, whether out of design or out of desperation, had accepted potential as a substitute for performance. Moore made it clear that those days are over, and didn't mind bleeding some talent to send that message.

The move that may ultimately come to symbolize the Moore administration is five-year, $55-million contract given to Gil Meche. Meche has never thrown 190 innings in a season, once missed two full seasons after labrum surgery, and is coming off a 4.48 ERA, which he posted in the AL's best pitchers park and also happened to be his best ERA since the Clinton administration. On the surface, the move appears crazy.

When you dig deeper, the signing of Meche actually proves to be as touched by madness as it first appeared. Meche is young, he's been more or less healthy in the short term, his strikeout rate jumped last season, and he has the stuff of a number-two or number-three starter. But that's his upside, and even that would make his contract only a fair deal. There's little chance he'll turn out to be a bargain, and an uncomfortably high chance he'll turn out to be an expensive disaster along the lines of Darren Dreifort.

In Moore's defense, he deserves credit for what he *didn't* do: He didn't spread that money around to four or five aging, slightly above-replacement level veterans, the way the Royals had the previous year. Moore and his front office identified Meche as the one player they wanted above all, and then set about getting him. They put too many years and too many dollars in the deal to get it done, but the strategy—sign one good player instead of five mediocrities—is sound. As analysts, we can be much more confident that Moore's economic strategy was correct than we

can be in our evaluation of Meche himself. Meche looks like a waste of money, but we can't be entirely sure he won't be the next Chris Carpenter or Jason Schmidt. We *can* be quite sure that spending the money on more Scott Elartons would have been a guaranteed disaster.

Defining the new Royals administration by the Meche signing, however, overlooks far more significant, if less publicized moves. Among the most significant are the decisions to add a seventh minor league team in the Appalachian League—the Mets are the only other organization with seven farm teams—and to move their high-A team out of the pinball machine environment of High Desert and back to the pitcher-friendly ballpark in Wilmington, Delaware. Even better, the Royals are opening a new Dominican academy this year. These organizational developments are not only likely to improve the Royals in player development, but they require a long-term commitment to bear fruit, something that was missing while the Glass family called the shots more directly.

The turnover at the major league level obscures the equally significant turnover at all levels of the front office. Before the 2006 season ended, Moore brought in a new assistant GM (Dean Taylor), a new assistant director of scouting (Steve Williams), and a new director (J. J. Piccolo) and assistant director (Scott Sharp) of player development. He also hired Rene Francisco away from the Braves to head up international scouting. In the offseason, the minor league staff and scouting departments saw similar upheaval.

The potential impact of the Royals' new brain trust was most evident in the Rule 5 draft. Although the potential talent available in the draft has been decimated by the new CBA, the Royals selected Joakim Soria from the Padres, who immediately created a minor buzz at the Winter Meetings when word of his low-90s velocity, command, and changeup circulated around Orlando—not every team had enough of a ground presence in Mexico to have a recent scouting report on him. In his first outing after the draft, Soria threw just the third perfect game in the history of the Mexican Pacific League, and already seems a lock for a roster spot.

The Royals are still the same team that lost 489 games over the last five years, but they suddenly have a hands-off owner who's expanding their budget, a well-respected, risk-taking GM heading up an overhauled front office, and over two dozen players who weren't on the roster last May. Whether the Royals are headed in the right direction remains to be seen, but they're definitely headed in a different direction. For now, that's enough.

HITTERS

Paul Bako   C   Bats: L   Throws: R   Height: 6' 2"   Weight: 215   Born: June 20, 1972   Age: 35

YEAR	TEAM	LVL	AGE	PA	R	2B	3B	HR	RBI	BB	SO	SB	CS	SPEED	AVG	OBP	SLG	MLVR	EQAVG	EQOBP	EQSLG	EQA	VORP	DEFENSE	
2004	CHN	MLB	32	157	13	8	0	1	10	15	29	1	0	4.0	.203	.288	.283	-.305	.187	.274	.252	.198	-6.2	42-C	2
2005	LAN	MLB	33	47	1	2	0	0	4	7	12	0	0	3.9	.250	.362	.300	-.086	.250	.362	.300	.245	0.6	12-C	1
2006	KCA	MLB	34	167	7	3	0	0	10	11	46	0	0	2.9	.209	.261	.229	-.488	.179	.242	.192	.168	-13.3	45-C	-1
2007	BAL	MLB	35	208	13	6	1	2	16	16	51	0	0	3.7	.208	.272	.275	-.381	.207	.275	.279	.195	-8.3	52-C	3

Breakout: 39% Improve: 57% Collapse: 37% Attrition: 53%   Comparables: Larry Haney, Greg Myers, Brent Mayne, Ron Tingley

A message to all you parents out there: if your son dreams of one day joining the International Brotherhood of Backup Catchers—hey, it's easier to join than the Priory of Sion—get him working on his left-handed swing. Bako has hit under .230 in five of the last seven years, he's hit one homer in the last four, yet he keeps finding teams interested in a left-handed stick to complement their right-handed starter. The latest is the Orioles, who are paying him $900,000 to impersonate a minimum-wage backup.

Angel Berroa   SS   Bats: R   Throws: R   Height: 6' 0"   Weight: 190   Born: January 27, 1978   Age: 29

YEAR	TEAM	LVL	AGE	PA	R	2B	3B	HR	RBI	BB	SO	SB	CS	SPEED	AVG	OBP	SLG	MLVR	EQAVG	EQOBP	EQSLG	EQA	VORP	DEFENSE	
2004	KCA	MLB	26	554	72	27	6	8	43	23	87	14	8	6.5	.262	.308	.385	-.107	.262	.311	.389	.243	10.2	127-SS	-7
2005	KCA	MLB	27	652	68	21	5	11	55	18	108	7	5	5.2	.270	.305	.375	-.113	.277	.320	.392	.246	8.1	156-SS	-12
2006	KCA	MLB	28	503	45	18	1	9	54	14	88	3	1	4.3	.234	.259	.333	-.332	.226	.259	.328	.209	-17.4	127-SS	-9
2007	KCA	MLB	29	464	45	19	2	7	43	17	76	7	3	5.3	.255	.289	.361	-.208	.246	.285	.362	.229	-1.6	110-SS	-6

Breakout: 34% Improve: 62% Collapse: 19% Attrition: 20%   Comparables: Rafael Ramirez, Pete Castiglione, Joe Demaestri, Frank Duffy

Since winning Rookie of the Year honors in 2003—yes, that actually happened—Berroa's OBP, SLG, and steals have declined for three straight years, and last season he had the lowest EqA (minimum 300 PA) in the American League. His defense, which was above-average as a rookie, has been well below-average each of the last three years. The simplest way for the Royals to find another three wins is to replace Berroa with another—any other—shortstop. With two years left on his contract and no ready in-house candidates, the Royals will have to wait until Dayton Moore swings a trade for his replacement.

Andres Blanco   SS   Bats: S   Throws: R   Height: 5' 10"   Weight: 185   Born: April 11, 1984   Age: 23

YEAR	TEAM	LVL	AGE	PA	R	2B	3B	HR	RBI	BB	SO	SB	CS	SPEED	AVG	OBP	SLG	MLVR	EQAVG	EQOBP	EQSLG	EQA	VORP	DEFENSE	
2004	WIC	AA	20	359	34	10	2	0	21	18	44	7	6	4.7	.247	.299	.290	-.223	.225	.268	.255	.192	-22.0	87-SS	5
2004	KCA	MLB	20	67	9	2	2	0	5	5	6	1	2	6.6	.317	.379	.417	.091	.317	.388	.417	.274	3.6	19-SS	0
2005	OMA	AAA	21	129	13	4	2	1	9	10	23	2	0	4.8	.254	.331	.351	-.156	.239	.305	.316	.227	-2.0	34-SS	5
2005	KCA	MLB	21	86	6	0	1	0	5	0	5	0	1	5.1	.215	.220	.241	-.506	.192	.207	.218	.164	-8.3	21-2B	2
2006	OMA	AAA	22	319	30	9	4	2	20	21	41	6	4	5.6	.237	.309	.318	-.188	.228	.288	.300	.213	-10.3	89-SS	10
2006	KCA	MLB	22	96	9	4	1	0	9	5	14	0	1	4.3	.241	.290	.310	-.301	.233	.290	.291	.208	-3.3	23-SS	1
2007	KCA	MLB	23	405	39	14	2	2	31	20	53	5	3	5.4	.254	.300	.324	-.239	.246	.296	.324	.222	-5.1	97-SS	5

Breakout: 68% Improve: 76% Collapse: 13% Attrition: 14%   Comparables: Abraham Nuñez, Guillermo Reyes, Danny Sandoval, Danny Bravo

Blanco still can't hit, not that such a thing would disqualify him from unseating Angel Berroa at shortstop. Unlike Berroa, he can at least field his position with some semblance of competence. Still, any player with a career .314 slugging average in the majors (and a .308 slugging average in the minors) is part of the problem, not the solution. A torn labrum suffered on a check swing late in the year should keep Blanco out for at least part of the season, allowing Berroa to hold on without a major challenge in the early going.

Emil Brown   OF   Bats: R   Throws: R   Height: 6' 2"   Weight: 210   Born: December 29, 1974   Age: 32

YEAR	TEAM	LVL	AGE	PA	R	2B	3B	HR	RBI	BB	SO	SB	CS	SPEED	AVG	OBP	SLG	MLVR	EQAVG	EQOBP	EQSLG	EQA	VORP	DEFENSE			
2004	MEM	AAA	29	63	7	3	0	0	4	5	9	1	1	4.1	.281	.349	.333	-.113	.259	.317	.293	.218	-3.3	13-RF	1		
2004	NWO	AAA	29	101	12	10	1	2	17	4	20	4	2	5.7	.337	.386	.533	.348	.319	.356	.468	.278	4.8	22-RF	-1		
2005	KCA	MLB	30	609	75	31	5	17	86	48	108	10	1	5.6	.286	.349	.455	.092	.291	.362	.478	.290	25.9	126-RF	-12		
2006	KCA	MLB	31	601	77	41	2	15	81	59	95	6	3	4.9	.287	.358	.457	.067	.285	.364	.460	.284	20.6	82-LF	0	47-RF	0
2007	KCA	MLB	32	548	71	30	2	14	68	47	90	7	3	4.9	.279	.346	.438	.014	.270	.342	.439	.276	9.1	129-RF	-4		

Breakout: 8% Improve: 35% Collapse: 35% Attrition: 10%   Comparables: Gary Ward, Gary Matthews, Glenallen Hill, Larry Herndon

(continued next page)

Emil Brown *(continued)*

The perception of Brown is that he is a Quadruple-A journeyman, no more than an adequate fourth outfielder, someone who lucked into regular playing time with the Royals the last two years and should have been non-tendered rather than taken to arbitration this winter. That's not entirely fair—the difference between Brown and a league-average corner outfielder is something on the order of half a win. Over the past two years he's been a better hitter than Craig Monroe, now considered an integral cog in the Tigers lineup. Likely to be overwhelmed by the hordes of young outfielders the Royals are bringing in, Brown could bring additional value to Kansas City via a trade to a contending team in need of a right-handed hitter off the bench.

John Buck — C — Bats: R — Throws: R — Height: 6' 3" — Weight: 220 — Born: July 7, 1980 — Age: 26

YEAR	TEAM	LVL	AGE	PA	R	2B	3B	HR	RBI	BB	SO	SB	CS	SPEED	AVG	OBP	SLG	MLVR	EQAVG	EQOBP	EQSLG	EQA	VORP	DEFENSE	
2004	NWO	AAA	24	254	31	11	0	12	35	21	39	0	1	2.9	.300	.368	.507	.227	.290	.350	.468	.277	17.0	58-C	-7
2004	KCA	MLB	24	258	36	9	0	12	30	15	79	1	1	4.5	.235	.280	.424	-.100	.233	.283	.428	.241	3.4	63-C	-4
2005	KCA	MLB	25	430	40	21	1	12	47	23	94	2	2	3.9	.242	.287	.389	-.139	.246	.301	.405	.242	2.4	112-C	-5
2006	KCA	MLB	26	409	37	21	1	11	50	26	84	0	2	3.4	.245	.306	.396	-.146	.243	.309	.395	.243	-1.0	106-C	-2
2007	KCA	MLB	26	413	43	20	1	13	53	28	85	1	1	4.0	.253	.310	.416	-.098	.244	.307	.416	.253	5.6	98-C	-4

Breakout: 31% Improve: 54% Collapse: 24% Attrition: 28% Comparables: Randy Knorr, Harry Chiti, Dan Walters, George Mitterwald

If nothing else, he's consistent—take a look at his major league EqAs. If you squint, though, you can see Buck making some slight progress. His walks went up, his strikeouts went down, and . . . okay, that's about all the progress he's made. He's a decent defensive catcher, and he turns 27 this summer, so there's some reason for a modest brand of optimism, even if he's disappointed thus far. Still, it's telling that the Royals spent $2.5 million to bring Jason LaRue in to challenge Buck the starter's job.

Billy Butler — OF — Bats: R — Throws: R — Height: 6' 2" — Weight: 225 — Born: November 30, 1999 — Age: 21

YEAR	TEAM	LVL	AGE	PA	R	2B	3B	HR	RBI	BB	SO	SB	CS	SPEED	AVG	OBP	SLG	MLVR	EQAVG	EQOBP	EQSLG	EQA	VORP	DEFENSE			
2004	IDA	Rk	0	323	74	22	3	10	68	57	63	5	0	5.6	.373	.486	.596	.486	.287	.362	.427	.276	33.4	47-3B	2		
2005	HDS	A+	0	430	70	30	2	25	91	42	80	0	0	2.6	.348	.419	.636	.463	.274	.334	.473	.274	24.0	40-3B	-6	34-LF	-4
2005	WIC	AA	0	119	14	9	0	5	19	7	18	0	0	2.3	.313	.353	.527	.248	.286	.328	.482	.271	3.6	25-LF	-6		
2006	WIC	AA	0	535	82	33	1	15	96	41	67	1	0	3.8	.331	.388	.499	.264	.309	.354	.464	.281	22.7	95-RF	-3	20-LF	-1
2007	KCA	MLB	21	526	62	32	1	14	70	37	78	0	0	4.2	.295	.347	.454	.051	.285	.343	.455	.279	14.4	124-RF	-6		

Breakout: 25% Improve: 52% Collapse: 19% Attrition: 4% Comparables: Vernon Wells, Michael Restovich, Joe Crede, Albert Pujols

The Robin to Alex Gordon's Batman, Butler makes a hell of a sidekick, and would be the best prospect in a number of organizations. Before leaving the Wichita a few weeks early to help the U.S. Olympic Team win the qualifier in Cuba, Butler won the Texas League batting title at age 20, and hit for good power (15 homers, 33 doubles) while striking out just 67 times. He may hit the ball too hard for his own good—his 25 GIDPs in 119 games conjures up memories of a late-career Jim Rice ending Red Sox rallies by the bushelful. Given that his defense has improved from "historically awful" all the way to "borderline playable," we may even get to enjoy him thundering around the outfield for a few years before he makes the inevitable transition to career DH. Lack of defensive value or not, he's a keeper.

Shane Costa — OF — Bats: L — Throws: R — Height: 6' 0" — Weight: 200 — Born: December 12, 1981 — Age: 25

YEAR	TEAM	LVL	AGE	PA	R	2B	3B	HR	RBI	BB	SO	SB	CS	SPEED	AVG	OBP	SLG	MLVR	EQAVG	EQOBP	EQSLG	EQA	VORP	DEFENSE			
2004	WIL	A+	22	500	70	20	4	7	60	32	43	9	4	5.5	.308	.364	.417	.148	.287	.330	.400	.254	-0.9	63-LF	-5	40-CF	-2
2005	WIC	AA	23	316	37	18	2	8	43	24	23	5	1	4.5	.282	.349	.448	.102	.266	.327	.429	.263	1.0	59-LF	-8	12-RF	0
2005	KCA	MLB	23	88	13	2	0	2	7	5	11	0	0	4.4	.235	.287	.333	-.228	.237	.299	.338	.225	-3.2	19-LF	-3		
2006	OMA	AAA	24	224	35	12	4	10	29	13	25	4	0	5.7	.342	.398	.593	.449	.333	.381	.583	.319	24.1	37-RF	-1	13-LF	-2
2006	KCA	MLB	24	252	23	20	1	3	23	6	29	2	0	4.7	.274	.304	.405	-.115	.272	.308	.413	.250	0.4	35-RF	-3	18-CF	-1
2007	KCA	MLB	25	435	54	25	2	11	54	23	47	4	1	5.1	.288	.331	.447	.009	.279	.327	.448	.272	8.9	103-RF	-4		

Breakout: 22% Improve: 55% Collapse: 20% Attrition: 21% Comparables: Mark Kotsay, Al Woods, Warren Cromartie, Don Mueller

For years, the knock on Costa was that he would never develop the power needed from a corner outfielder, so his offensive explosion in Triple-A last season is a welcome development. His four unintentional walks in 72 games with the Royals were not. Costa figures to be the player hurt most by the Royals determination not to resolve their outfield logjam. He's earned at least a platoon spot in left field, and, at 25, has considerable upside, but the Royals acquired Ross Gload for that role. Nevertheless, Costa still has options left, so if Moore maintains his hyperkinetic transaction pace, he should get another shot before year's end.

David DeJesus **OF** **Bats: L** **Throws: L** Height: 6' 0" Weight: 185 Born: December 20, 1979 Age: 27

YEAR	TEAM	LVL	AGE	PA	R	2B	3B	HR	RBI	BB	SO	SB	CS	SPEED	AVG	OBP	SLG	MLVR	EQAVG	EQOBP	EQSLG	EQA	VORP	DEFENSE			
2004	OMA	AAA	24	226	38	14	4	6	16	21	30	7	6	6.4	.315	.400	.518	.268	.294	.369	.463	.282	14.9	49-CF	-4		
2004	KCA	MLB	24	413	58	15	3	7	39	33	53	8	11	5.6	.287	.360	.402	.023	.287	.363	.409	.262	9.6	80-CF	3		
2005	KCA	MLB	25	523	69	31	6	9	56	42	76	5	5	5.6	.293	.359	.445	.097	.300	.374	.467	.287	25.2	115-CF	4		
2006	KCA	MLB	26	552	83	36	7	8	56	43	70	6	3	6.1	.295	.364	.446	.069	.294	.369	.449	.282	23.2	62-LF	2	55-CF	3
2007	KCA	MLB	27	591	82	31	5	10	60	49	79	7	4	6.0	.290	.357	.425	.024	.281	.353	.425	.277	16.6	138-CF	1		

Breakout: 6% Improve: 32% Collapse: 34% Attrition: 5% Comparables: Mark Kotsay, Del Unser, Marvin Benard, Wally Moon

The bad news is that DeJesus did not have the breakout season that many expected, and that he remained injury-prone, missing almost two months with a lame hamstring. The good news is that, even if he doesn't improve a whit, the long-term deal he signed in 2005 (five years, $13.8 million, with a $6-million option for 2011) makes him a bargain in this market. His value depends on whether the Royals admit their mistake with Joey Gathright and move DeJesus back to center field, where he was an average defender. Expect a power spike into the 13–17 homer range this season—PECOTA is being a wee bit conservative.

Adam Donachie **C** **Bats: R** **Throws: R** Height: 6' 1" Weight: 215 Born: March 3, 1984 Age: 23

YEAR	TEAM	LVL	AGE	PA	R	2B	3B	HR	RBI	BB	SO	SB	CS	SPEED	AVG	OBP	SLG	MLVR	EQAVG	EQOBP	EQSLG	EQA	VORP	DEFENSE	
2004	BUR	A	20	259	17	7	0	1	21	21	41	5	2	4.0	.189	.261	.232	-.298	.162	.220	.183	.160	-35.2	64-C	3
2005	HDS	A+	21	394	64	24	0	12	48	43	78	1	0	3.4	.294	.375	.467	.075	.224	.293	.342	.224	-8.6	92-C	12
2006	HDS	A+	22	250	32	12	0	6	21	31	46	0	1	3.0	.271	.365	.414	-.038	.215	.293	.329	.222	-7.2	61-C	5
2006	WIC	AA	22	114	21	5	0	2	10	19	20	0	1	5.2	.191	.325	.309	-.209	.165	.281	.258	.201	-7.8	29-C	0
2007	KCA	MLB	23	398	31	15	0	7	38	32	73	0	1	4.0	.221	.287	.323	-.282	.213	.284	.324	.216	-10.9	95-C	8

Breakout: 52% Improve: 68% Collapse: 18% Attrition: 11% Comparables: Brad Ramsey, Ryan Jorgensen, Justin Knoedler, David Parrish

A repeat year in High Desert seemed the perfect recipe for offensive hijinks, instead Donachie mustered a feeble 6 homers in 210 at-bats and a .414 slugging average, and then struggled mightily after a late promotion to Double-A. Donachie is an excellent defensive catcher, consistently nailing over 40 percent of attempted basestealers and controlling the strike zone well. None of that matters if he doesn't start hitting the ball with more authority. Taken by the Phillies in the Rule 5 draft, Donachie was immediately traded to Baltimore, where the ubiquitous Paul Bako stands in his way.

Joey Gathright **CF** **Bats: L** **Throws: R** Height: 5' 10" Weight: 170 Born: April 22, 1982 Age: 26

YEAR	TEAM	LVL	AGE	PA	R	2B	3B	HR	RBI	BB	SO	SB	CS	SPEED	AVG	OBP	SLG	MLVR	EQAVG	EQOBP	EQSLG	EQA	VORP	DEFENSE	
2004	MNT	AA	22	138	23	5	1	0	8	11	30	10	6	6.8	.341	.399	.397	.180	.328	.377	.375	.264	6.9	22-CF	0
2004	DUR	AAA	22	260	34	9	1	0	8	19	46	33	13	6.9	.326	.384	.373	.035	.298	.355	.336	.254	3.6	58-CF	-5
2004	TBA	MLB	22	57	11	0	0	0	1	2	14	6	1	6.9	.250	.316	.250	-.301	.250	.304	.250	.223	-1.4		
2005	DUR	AAA	23	260	46	10	5	1	18	29	47	31	8	9.3	.305	.388	.407	.102	.288	.367	.380	.273	8.6	50-CF	-6
2005	TBA	MLB	23	218	29	7	3	0	13	10	39	20	5	7.8	.276	.316	.340	-.132	.290	.340	.355	.256	2.2	58-CF	1
2006	DUR	AAA	24	40	5	2	0	0	1	6	3	6	2	6.8	.258	.410	.323	.046	.250	.385	.312	.261	0.3		
2006	TBA	MLB	24	182	25	6	0	0	13	20	30	12	3	7.3	.201	.305	.240	-.378	.197	.311	.230	.219	-7.9	50-CF	5
2006	KCA	MLB	24	263	34	6	3	1	28	22	45	10	6	7.3	.262	.332	.328	-.182	.265	.344	.332	.244	-2.1	66-CF	2
2007	KCA	MLB	26	459	67	14	4	3	30	37	78	32	10	7.6	.273	.340	.350	-.118	.264	.336	.351	.257	3.1	109-CF	-2

Breakout: 26% Improve: 40% Collapse: 24% Attrition: 24% Comparables: David Hulse, Curtis Goodwin, Chone Figgins, Billy North

You can see what Moore was thinking when he traded for Gathright; he might be the fastest player in the major leagues, and moving DeJesus to left field gave the Royals two-thirds of an excellent defensive outfield. The problem is that, for all his speed, Gathright is not a top-flight defensive player. He also can't hit. He makes for a good fifth outfielder, a saturated commodity in Kansas City these days.

Esteban German   UT   Bats: R   Throws: R   Height: 5' 9"   Weight: 165   Born: January 26, 1978   Age: 29

YEAR	TEAM	LVL	AGE	PA	R	2B	3B	HR	RBI	BB	SO	SB	CS	SPEED	AVG	OBP	SLG	MLVR	EQAVG	EQOBP	EQSLG	EQA	VORP	DEFENSE		
2004	SAC	AAA	26	259	33	8	4	2	29	19	28	18	2	7.3	.329	.380	.424	.103	.306	.353	.387	.270	9.9	40-2B	-4	13-SS -1
2004	OAK	MLB	26	65	9	1	1	0	7	4	13	0	1	6.4	.250	.297	.300	-.226	.233	.292	.283	.205	-2.2	12-3B	1	
2005	OKL	AAA	27	564	103	27	6	5	68	65	74	43	6	8.2	.313	.400	.423	.102	.296	.369	.386	.275	25.9	74-3B	-7	14-SS 1
2006	KCA	MLB	28	331	44	18	5	3	34	40	49	7	3	6.3	.326	.422	.459	.218	.324	.426	.465	.309	26.5	21-3B	0	19-2B -2
2007	KCA	MLB	29	396	57	17	3	4	32	37	54	14	4	6.4	.287	.361	.386	-.023	.278	.357	.387	.273	10.4	95-3B	-1	

Breakout: 4%   Improve: 26%   Collapse: 36%   Attrition: 28%   Comparables: Jeff Frye, Joe Koppe, Wally Backman, Ryan Freel

Sweet vindication! The number-eighteen prospect on our list back in 2000 finally got a full shot at the majors last year and was brilliant, playing six different positions while ranking fourth in the league in OBP among players with 300 plate appearances. German was over his head, but only a little. His minor league record has always been notable for plate discipline and speed, but his defense is shaky, which is why the Royals elected to re-sign Mark Grudzielanek and keep German in a super-utility role. You have to wonder how bad his defense at shortstop would have to be for him to not represent an upgrade over Berroa. Along with Gload and LaRue, he gives the Royals what is suddenly one of the better benches in the league.

Alex Gordon   3B   Bats: L   Throws: R   Height: 6' 1"   Weight: 220   Born: February 10, 1984   Age: 23

YEAR	TEAM	LVL	AGE	PA	R	2B	3B	HR	RBI	BB	SO	SB	CS	SPEED	AVG	OBP	SLG	MLVR	EQAVG	EQOBP	EQSLG	EQA	VORP	DEFENSE	
2006	WIC	AA	22	576	111	39	1	29	101	72	113	22	3	6.3	.325	.427	.588	.440	.302	.386	.538	.312	65.4	119-3B	6
2007	KCA	MLB	23	581	87	37	3	25	83	60	125	14	5	5.6	.282	.363	.509	.139	.273	.359	.510	.300	35.7	136-3B	8

Breakout: 10%   Improve: 35%   Collapse: 24%   Attrition: 1%   Comparables: Mark Teixeira, Kevin Mench, Jonny Gomes, Carlos Pena

The number-one prospect in baseball. After a stellar college career and a Golden Spikes award, Gordon went straight to Double-A in his pro debut and hit for average and power, commanded the strike zone, stole bases with both frequency and efficiency, and showed good defense at a key defensive position. The only drama left with Gordon is whether he will push Mark Teahen to the outfield on Opening Day, or if the Royals will let the Omaha native perform in front of the home-town crowd for a few months first. He's a lifelong Royals fan whose brother was named after George Brett, so this could be the start of a beautiful relationship.

Mark Grudzielanek   2B   Bats: R   Throws: R   Height: 6' 1"   Weight: 190   Born: June 30, 1970   Age: 37

YEAR	TEAM	LVL	AGE	PA	R	2B	3B	HR	RBI	BB	SO	SB	CS	SPEED	AVG	OBP	SLG	MLVR	EQAVG	EQOBP	EQSLG	EQA	VORP	DEFENSE	
2004	CHN	MLB	34	278	32	12	1	6	23	15	32	1	1	4.1	.307	.347	.432	.055	.301	.341	.421	.262	11.6	68-2B	1
2005	SLN	MLB	35	563	64	30	3	8	59	26	81	8	6	5.2	.294	.334	.407	.032	.295	.337	.413	.258	16.5	130-2B	3
2006	KCA	MLB	36	586	85	32	4	7	52	28	69	3	2	5.7	.297	.331	.409	-.041	.295	.336	.411	.259	18.2	126-2B	9
2007	KCA	MLB	37	514	61	27	4	6	51	28	68	5	3	5.6	.285	.327	.393	-.075	.276	.323	.393	.254	9.3	121-2B	-2

Breakout: 21%   Improve: 45%   Collapse: 22%   Attrition: 18%   Comparables: Alvin Dark, Jim Gantner, Tony Taylor, Dick Groat

It may have been a surprise to see Grudzielanek win his first Gold Glove at 36, but it's an accurate reflection of his defense. Few players in history have improved their defense in their thirties as much as Grudzielanek has; he's particularly adept on the deuce. Combined with his solid, if unspectacular bat, that defensive skill makes him a useful player at a favorable cost ($4 million). The Royals should aiming to use him as one of their trade chits at this summer's trade deadline.

Justin Huber   1B   Bats: R   Throws: R   Height: 6' 2"   Weight: 195   Born: July 1, 1982   Age: 24

YEAR	TEAM	LVL	AGE	PA	R	2B	3B	HR	RBI	BB	SO	SB	CS	SPEED	AVG	OBP	SLG	MLVR	EQAVG	EQOBP	EQSLG	EQA	VORP	DEFENSE		
2004	BIN	AA	22	295	44	16	1	11	33	46	57	2	2	4.0	.271	.414	.487	.237	.256	.376	.455	.286	19.2	61-C	-1	
2005	WIC	AA	23	396	68	22	3	16	74	51	70	7	3	5.1	.343	.432	.570	.455	.327	.407	.542	.319	42.6	67-1B	-10	
2005	OMA	AAA	23	131	19	6	1	7	23	16	33	3	0	4.6	.274	.374	.531	.199	.259	.344	.474	.280	4.5	32-1B	-1	
2005	KCA	MLB	23	85	6	3	0	0	6	5	20	0	0	3.5	.218	.271	.256	-.365	.208	.271	.247	.193	-6.1	16-1B	-3	
2006	OMA	AAA	24	398	47	22	2	15	44	40	94	2	2	3.9	.278	.358	.480	.155	.277	.349	.482	.280	14.9	68-LF	0	29-1B -5
2006	KCA	MLB	24	11	1	1	0	0	1	1	4	1	0	6.5	.200	.273	.300	-.363	.200	.273	.300	.226	-0.4			
2007	KCA	MLB	24	458	57	24	2	15	61	44	102	3	1	4.3	.271	.348	.452	.028	.262	.343	.453	.279	11.2	108-1B	-3	

Breakout: 10%   Improve: 41%   Collapse: 28%   Attrition: 11%   Comparables: Tom Evans, David Kelton, Ryan Ludwick, Michael Cuddyer

Sometimes a player and an organization just aren't a good match for each other. The Royals seem to be going out of their way to deny Huber opportunities to succeed. After winning the Texas League MVP in 2005, Huber started last season hitting .289/.413/.579 in Triple-A. When the inevitable Mike Sweeney injury cleared space on the roster, the Royals called him up on May 1 . . . and then gave him only 11 plate appearances over the better part of three weeks. He then returned to Omaha and was promptly moved to left field. Unsurprisingly, he went into a slump at that point, rebounding late in the year. Huber is now stuck behind Ryan Shealy at first and a small horde of young outfielders, and there's even talk of moving him back behind the plate. He's much more likely to be moved in trade at some point this year.

| Josh Johnson | | 2B | | Bats: S | | Throws: R | | Height: 5' 11" | | Weight: 170 | | Born: January 11, 1986 | | | Age: 21 |

YEAR	TEAM	LVL	AGE	PA	R	2B	3B	HR	RBI	BB	SO	SB	CS	SPEED	AVG	OBP	SLG	MLVR	EQAVG	EQOBP	EQSLG	EQA	VORP	DEFENSE	
2005	IDA	Rk	19	160	20	5	4	2	26	25	25	3	6	5.0	.240	.369	.388	-.057	.164	.258	.221	.185	-26.4	37-2B	-4
2006	BUR	A	20	497	59	8	5	3	40	93	72	18	9	5.9	.241	.391	.312	.079	.235	.349	.306	.244	-1.9	98-2B	13
2007	KCA	MLB	21	495	56	16	3	2	32	53	74	9	5	5.7	.248	.333	.315	-.192	.239	.329	.316	.239	-3.0	117-2B	5

Breakout: 42% Improve: 76% Collapse: 13% Attrition: 13%   Comparables: Albenis Machado, William Arroyo, Jose Contreras, Liu Rodriguez

Johnson is an interesting prospect, which is different from saying he's a good prospect. Johnson has several well-defined virtues (defensive ability at second base, a tremendous walk rate, speed, youth) coupled with a single, potentially fatal flaw: A lack of power so glaring that more advanced hurlers are likely to neutralize his ability to take pitches by simply pounding him with strikes. Scouts are confident that he will develop enough power as he matures to keep pitchers honest. It's likely to be a rocky road for him as he climbs the ladder, but there's not much difference between Johnson and Esteban German at the same age.

| Jeff Keppinger | | INF | | Bats: R | | Throws: R | | Height: 6' 0" | | Weight: 180 | | Born: April 21, 1980 | | | Age: 27 |

YEAR	TEAM	LVL	AGE	PA	R	2B	3B	HR	RBI	BB	SO	SB	CS	SPEED	AVG	OBP	SLG	MLVR	EQAVG	EQOBP	EQSLG	EQA	VORP	DEFENSE			
2004	ALT	AA	24	346	44	17	2	1	33	27	15	10	5	5.2	.337	.387	.413	.178	.316	.359	.381	.262	16.1	72-2B	3		
2004	BIN	AA	24	54	14	3	1	0	5	6	2	2	1	7.0	.362	.426	.468	.312	.333	.389	.438	.288	3.9				
2004	NYN	MLB	24	123	9	2	0	3	9	6	7	2	1	3.6	.284	.317	.379	-.055	.284	.317	.379	.244	2.2	30-2B	1		
2005	NOR	AAA	25	278	40	15	3	3	29	16	13	5	1	5.6	.337	.377	.455	.251	.342	.382	.459	.290	25.4	52-2B	5		
2006	NOR	AAA	26	366	36	13	0	2	26	28	21	0	4	3.7	.300	.353	.359	.105	.304	.354	.365	.253	12.5	54-2B	3	12-LF	0
2006	OMA	AAA	26	142	21	6	1	2	17	12	9	0	0	4.2	.354	.407	.465	.288	.341	.390	.450	.291	13.4	16-2B	-2		
2006	KCA	MLB	26	67	11	2	0	2	8	5	6	0	0	4.8	.267	.323	.400	-.090	.271	.338	.407	.259	0.0	12-3B	1		
2007	KCA	MLB	27	475	57	22	1	4	44	31	27	3	1	4.8	.311	.358	.396	.003	.300	.353	.397	.269	15.7	112-2B	5		

Breakout: 20% Improve: 47% Collapse: 18% Attrition: 9%   Comparables: Joey Amalfitano, Placido Polanco, Ted Sizemore, Aaron Ledesma

You rarely see challenge trades as minor as the Keppinger-for-Gotay swap of Triple-A second basemen that the Mets and Royals executed last summer. Keppinger is three years older, but the Royals had completely given up on Gotay's ability to play second, whereas Keppinger's skills can slot him into a utility role right away. Keppinger has batted over .300 at every minor-league stop since his first season thanks to one of the highest contact rates in baseball—last year he set a career high for strikeouts with 36. Unfortunately, all that contact from a right-handed ground-ball hitter leads to a ton of double plays; Keppinger has hit into eight in just 55 major league games. His lack of secondary skills keeps him from being a starter, but if you can play second base and hit .280, some team will find a place for you on their roster. That team might not be the Royals—Keppinger was designated for assignment in January to make room for David Riske.

| Chris Lubanski | | LF | | Bats: L | | Throws: L | | Height: 6' 3" | | Weight: 206 | | Born: March 24, 1985 | | | Age: 22 |

YEAR	TEAM	LVL	AGE	PA	R	2B	3B	HR	RBI	BB	SO	SB	CS	SPEED	AVG	OBP	SLG	MLVR	EQAVG	EQOBP	EQSLG	EQA	VORP	DEFENSE			
2004	BUR	A	19	537	64	26	7	9	56	43	104	16	11	5.7	.275	.336	.414	.114	.260	.308	.385	.241	0.4	117-CF	-13		
2005	HDS	A+	20	581	91	38	6	28	116	38	131	14	1	6.6	.301	.349	.554	.165	.238	.277	.413	.238	-4.8	121-CF	-6		
2006	WIC	AA	21	613	93	34	11	15	70	72	112	11	7	6.6	.282	.369	.475	.153	.265	.340	.439	.269	8.0	107-LF	-13	25-CF	-4
2007	KCA	MLB	22	563	67	31	4	15	65	42	112	8	3	5.7	.261	.319	.422	-.069	.252	.315	.422	.260	3.6	132-LF	-7		

Breakout: 22% Improve: 56% Collapse: 17% Attrition: 5%   Comparables: Grady Sizemore, Laynce Nix, Ryan Langerhans, Carlos Beltran

For the second straight year, Lubanski flashed a very promising mix of skills, and, for the second straight year, a slow start kept him from being recognized as a legitimate prospect. While his superficial numbers dropped a little in 2006, his performance was far more impressive than the year before given that he had moved to Double-A and away from one of the

(continued next page)

Chris Lubanski *(continued)*

best hitter's parks in the minor leagues in High Desert. Also note that he doubled his walk total while lowering his strike-outs. On the other hand, Lubanski's speed continued to decline, and his defense forced a move to left field last year. As a former fifth-overall pick, Lubanski has been considered a bit of a disappointment so far, but consider that, if he had gone to college, he would have been drafted last summer, and even first-round picks out of college are rarely able to hit at Double-A right away. He's risky, but he's also a breakout candidate.

Mitch Maier   **CF**   **Bats: L**   **Throws: R**   Height: 6′ 2″   Weight: 200   Born: June 30, 1982   Age: 25

YEAR	TEAM	LVL	AGE	PA	R	2B	3B	HR	RBI	BB	SO	SB	CS	SPEED	AVG	OBP	SLG	MLVR	EQAVG	EQOBP	EQSLG	EQA	VORP	DEFENSE			
2004	BUR	A	22	345	41	24	3	4	36	27	51	34	10	7.0	.300	.354	.432	.183	.278	.321	.395	.253	8.9	70-3B	2		
2004	WIL	A+	22	194	25	9	2	3	17	15	29	10	2	6.9	.264	.326	.391	.021	.247	.295	.371	.238	-1.0	48-3B	-2		
2005	HDS	A+	23	227	42	26	1	8	32	12	43	6	1	6.4	.336	.370	.583	.290	.256	.283	.428	.244	-3.9	41-RF	7		
2005	WIC	AA	23	342	55	21	5	7	49	15	47	10	3	7.8	.255	.289	.416	-.064	.238	.272	.390	.230	-7.0	76-CF	-3		
2006	WIC	AA	24	603	95	35	7	14	92	41	96	13	12	6.0	.306	.357	.473	.153	.284	.324	.433	.259	19.3	114-CF	6	20-RF	3
2006	KCA	MLB	24	15	3	0	0	0	0	2	4	0	0	3.9	.154	.267	.154	-.587	.077	.200	.077	.126	-1.8				
2007	*KCA*	*MLB*	*25*	*507*	*55*	*29*	*3*	*11*	*56*	*28*	*91*	*10*	*4*	*5.8*	*.256*	*.300*	*.399*	*-.136*	*.248*	*.296*	*.400*	*.246*	*-2.2*	*120-CF*	*3*		

Breakout: 15% Improve: 44% Collapse: 26% Attrition: 11%   *Comparables: Brian Gordon, Jorge Piedra, Chris Stowers, Nic Jackson*

Lubanski was moved to left field to make room for Maier in center, as the former collegiate catcher continued to impress with his defensive skills in the outfield. Maier's greatest strength is a lack of weaknesses; he hits for a good average with lots of doubles power, has an adequate walk rate, and runs about as well as can be expected from a former catcher. Conversely, his greatest weakness is a lack of any one obvious strength, limiting his projection to that of a fourth outfielder.

Doug Mientkiewicz   **1B**   **Bats: L**   **Throws: R**   Height: 6′ 2″   Weight: 205   Born: June 19, 1974   Age: 33

YEAR	TEAM	LVL	AGE	PA	R	2B	3B	HR	RBI	BB	SO	SB	CS	SPEED	AVG	OBP	SLG	MLVR	EQAVG	EQOBP	EQSLG	EQA	VORP	DEFENSE	
2004	MIN	MLB	30	328	34	18	0	5	25	38	38	2	2	3.6	.246	.340	.363	-.111	.241	.340	.358	.249	-2.6	75-1B	-2
2004	BOS	MLB	30	119	13	6	1	1	10	10	18	0	1	4.8	.215	.286	.318	-.305	.208	.286	.302	.211	-6.4	28-1B	1
2005	NYN	MLB	31	313	36	13	0	11	29	32	39	0	1	3.6	.240	.322	.407	-.030	.240	.324	.415	.255	-0.2	76-1B	-5
2006	KCA	MLB	32	360	37	24	2	4	43	35	50	3	0	5.0	.283	.359	.411	.005	.281	.365	.416	.277	6.2	82-1B	-5
2007	*NYA*	*MLB*	*33*	*263*	*29*	*13*	*1*	*5*	*30*	*26*	*38*	*1*	*1*	*4.4*	*.251*	*.328*	*.382*	*-.112*	*.249*	*.331*	*.387*	*.258*	*-1.7*	*65-1B*	*-2*

Breakout: 15% Improve: 40% Collapse: 28% Attrition: 41%   *Comparables: Greg Brock, Pete O'Brien, Mike Jorgensen, Tim McCarver*

Have glove, will travel. There's not much more to say about Eye Chart. Actually, it may be more accurate to say *had* glove, which means pretty soon he won't travel. Mienkiewicz's facility with the leather left him before he left Minnesota, and, now that he's coming off back surgery, he's more likely to be a liability in the field than an asset. The Yankees have postponed the inevitable for Minky by picking him up be the dominant half of their first-base platoon, thus sinking their production at the position into a deep, deep hole.

Angel Sanchez   **SS**   **Bats: R**   **Throws: R**   Height: 6′ 2″   Weight: 185   Born: September 20, 1983   Age: 23

YEAR	TEAM	LVL	AGE	PA	R	2B	3B	HR	RBI	BB	SO	SB	CS	SPEED	AVG	OBP	SLG	MLVR	EQAVG	EQOBP	EQSLG	EQA	VORP	DEFENSE	
2004	BUR	A	20	395	37	13	1	2	25	18	51	16	7	5.3	.252	.303	.311	-.093	.236	.272	.288	.205	-18.3	83-SS	-5
2005	HDS	A+	21	639	102	33	4	5	70	39	54	10	5	5.6	.313	.356	.409	-.031	.243	.280	.303	.210	-20.2	131-SS	10
2006	WIC	AA	22	612	105	24	1	4	57	44	63	8	9	5.4	.282	.339	.352	-.069	.262	.309	.323	.227	-4.3	132-SS	1
2006	KCA	MLB	22	28	2	0	0	0	1	0	4	0	0	4.9	.222	.214	.222	-.588	.148	.143	.148	.119	-2.7		
2007	*KCA*	*MLB*	*23*	*513*	*49*	*21*	*2*	*3*	*41*	*25*	*53*	*5*	*3*	*5.3*	*.261*	*.301*	*.330*	*-.225*	*.253*	*.297*	*.330*	*.224*	*-4.0*	*121-SS*	*3*

Breakout: 48% Improve: 67% Collapse: 13% Attrition: 9%   *Comparables: John McDonald, Willie Bloomquist, Jt Stotts, Eric Bruntlett*

By making his major league debut last September, Sanchez spared the Royals the humiliation of having their 2001 draft—the one made famous by drafting Colt Griffin and Roscoe Crosby in the first two rounds—fail to yield a single major league player, which has only happened four times in the draft's history. Sanchez is Puerto Rican, but his skills come straight out of central casting for a Dominican shortstop: Good defense, good contact skills, little plate discipline, and not a trace of power. His best asset—and the best reason to give him playing time this year—is that he is not Angel Berroa. See also: Faint praise, damning with.

Reggie Sanders RF   Bats: R   Throws: R   Height: 6' 1"   Weight: 205   Born: December 31, 1969   Age: 39

YEAR	TEAM	LVL	AGE	PA	R	2B	3B	HR	RBI	BB	SO	SB	CS	SPEED	AVG	OBP	SLG	MLVR	EQAVG	EQOBP	EQSLG	EQA	VORP	DEFENSE			
2004	SLN	MLB	36	487	64	27	3	22	67	33	118	21	5	7.1	.260	.315	.482	.067	.260	.315	.487	.271	15.5	72-RF	-1	32-LF	5
2005	SLN	MLB	37	329	49	14	2	21	54	28	75	14	1	6.2	.271	.340	.546	.205	.272	.343	.561	.301	23.1	71-LF	0		
2006	KCA	MLB	38	358	45	23	1	11	49	28	86	7	7	5.3	.246	.304	.425	-.106	.246	.313	.436	.252	-3.4	68-RF	3		
2007	KCA	MLB	39	380	49	22	2	14	50	31	91	10	4	5.5	.258	.321	.458	-.019	.249	.318	.459	.271	4.5	91-RF	-1		

Breakout: 19% Improve: 30% Collapse: 22% Attrition: 41%   Comparables: Steve Finley, Ellis Burks, Craig Biggio, Ruben Sierra

Sanders was injured for much of 2006, but he gets injured every year. The difference is he didn't hit when he was healthy for the first time since 2000. He bounced back last time; this time he's 39 years old and spending a second straight season with a non-contender for the first time since his early years with the Reds. Last year was also his first in the American League, and the higher quality of competition likely didn't help him any. He's due $5 million this year, and the Royals have to give him a chance to earn it in the hopes that they can flip him at the deadline.

Ryan Shealy 1B   Bats: R   Throws: R   Height: 6' 5"   Weight: 250   Born: August 29, 1979   Age: 27

YEAR	TEAM	LVL	AGE	PA	R	2B	3B	HR	RBI	BB	SO	SB	CS	SPEED	AVG	OBP	SLG	MLVR	EQAVG	EQOBP	EQSLG	EQA	VORP	DEFENSE	
2004	TUL	AA	24	552	88	32	3	29	99	61	123	1	1	3.8	.318	.411	.584	.417	.290	.363	.517	.295	38.0	124-1B	5
2005	CSP	AAA	25	468	85	30	2	26	88	41	81	4	0	4.7	.328	.393	.601	.315	.287	.345	.508	.288	25.1	101-1B	-1
2005	COL	MLB	25	104	14	7	0	2	16	13	22	1	0	3.3	.330	.413	.473	.239	.308	.394	.462	.298	7.4	17-1B	0
2006	CSP	AAA	26	248	37	16	1	15	55	20	34	0	0	3.5	.284	.351	.568	.194	.248	.309	.500	.271	6.1	44-1B	3
2006	KCA	MLB	26	210	29	10	1	7	36	15	50	1	1	4.5	.280	.338	.451	.014	.277	.343	.461	.273	3.2	52-1B	-6
2007	KCA	MLB	27	460	56	25	1	18	67	37	91	2	1	4.3	.269	.332	.467	.020	.260	.328	.467	.276	8.8	109-1B	-1

Breakout: 14% Improve: 38% Collapse: 22% Attrition: 11%   Comparables: Julio Zuleta, Matthew LeCroy, Bucky Jacobsen, Jason Lane

Dayton Moore's best move to date was acquiring this thumper for two of the most exasperating arms in the organization. Shealy isn't young, he isn't particularly deft afield, and he isn't Todd Helton, all traits which made him expendable in Colorado. For the Royals, though, he represents a cheap, prime-of-career source of power at first base, a commodity they will have control over until shortly after his 33rd birthday. He'll slug over .500 at some point in his career, making him a solid secondary cog in the lineup behind Gordon and Butler for the rest of the decade. Twenty-five years ago, the Royals took advantage of the Yankees' surplus of talent at first base to nab Steve Balboni—this trade looks even better than that.

Mike Sweeney DH   Bats: R   Throws: R   Height: 6' 3"   Weight: 220   Born: July 22, 1973   Age: 33

YEAR	TEAM	LVL	AGE	PA	R	2B	3B	HR	RBI	BB	SO	SB	CS	SPEED	AVG	OBP	SLG	MLVR	EQAVG	EQOBP	EQSLG	EQA	VORP	DEFENSE	
2004	KCA	MLB	30	452	56	23	0	22	79	33	44	3	2	4.0	.287	.347	.504	.146	.284	.347	.506	.286	25.4	55-1B	-4
2005	KCA	MLB	31	514	63	39	0	21	83	33	61	3	0	4.1	.300	.347	.517	.191	.305	.361	.541	.302	34.6	48-1B	-4
2006	KCA	MLB	32	252	23	15	0	8	33	28	48	2	0	3.7	.258	.349	.438	-.002	.252	.353	.439	.277	6.1		
2007	KCA	MLB	33	404	50	21	1	15	60	36	62	3	1	4.0	.274	.342	.465	.038	.265	.338	.465	.281	12.3	96-DH	

Breakout: 2% Improve: 25% Collapse: 34% Attrition: 27%   Comparables: Juan Gonzalez, Orlando Cepeda, Eric Karros, Richie Zisk

As fans, we may claim that we want our heroes to be as pristine off the field as they are productive on it. In reality, character is always trumped by results. Sweeney established a reputation as one of the nicest players in baseball a decade ago and has done nothing but add to it since. His stature in Kansas City only rose after he became the only homegrown player during their current run of losing to agree to a long-term deal. But, since his contract started in 2003, he has been troubled by a bad back that has forced him to miss more than 40 games in each year of the deal, and the fans have turned on him. Nobody loves a man who gets paid $11 million a year to hit .258/.349/.438, even if he is a Boy Scout. Sweeney is in the last year of his deal and probably won't be back, so it's time to remember the good. Over the last 21 seasons, Sweeney leads all Royals in games, at-bats, hits, homers, doubles, runs, RBI, and total bases, and by huge margins in most of those categories. Royals fans should wish him luck in his future endeavors and look forward to seeing him on Old Timer's Day.

Mark Teahen　　3B　　Bats: L　Throws: R　　Height: 6' 3"　　Weight: 220　　Born: September 6, 1981　　Age: 25

YEAR	TEAM	LVL	AGE	PA	R	2B	3B	HR	RBI	BB	SO	SB	CS	SPEED	AVG	OBP	SLG	MLVR	EQAVG	EQOBP	EQSLG	EQA	VORP	DEFENSE	
2004	MID	AA	22	229	31	15	4	6	36	29	44	0	0	4.5	.335	.419	.543	.375	.312	.384	.505	.301	23.8	52-3B	6
2004	SAC	AAA	22	81	9	8	0	0	10	11	22	0	1	3.3	.275	.383	.391	.012	.243	.346	.329	.244	0.4	20-3B	0
2004	OMA	AAA	22	274	33	15	1	8	31	21	69	0	0	3.6	.280	.344	.447	.025	.268	.325	.412	.255	8.1	65-3B	3
2005	KCA	MLB	23	491	60	29	4	7	55	40	107	7	2	5.8	.246	.309	.376	-.116	.250	.323	.389	.250	-1.7	123-3B	-2
2006	OMA	AAA	24	98	14	8	4	2	14	19	12	0	0	5.1	.380	.500	.658	.718	.383	.490	.667	.378	23.6	21-3B	-2
2006	KCA	MLB	24	439	70	21	7	18	69	40	85	10	0	7.4	.290	.357	.517	.151	.286	.362	.518	.298	27.9	105-3B	10
2007	KCA	MLB	25	537	77	30	4	18	70	53	110	9	3	5.6	.283	.357	.474	.084	.274	.353	.475	.289	25.5	126-3B	5

Breakout: 18%　Improve: 37%　Collapse: 18%　Attrition: 6%　　Comparables: Eric Hinske, Norm Siebern, Larry Walker, Mel Hall

Allard Baird's parting gift to the team was considerably more thoughtful than the traditional fruit basket. Baird made Teahen the centerpiece of the Carlos Beltran trade two years ago, going against the majority opinion in the game that Teahen would never develop the power necessary to be an impact talent. Teahen had an uninspiring rookie season, and started 2006 with a .195/.241/.351 line before being demoted to Omaha on May 4. He then went 2 for his first 23 in Triple-A; none of this was particularly helpful to Baird's job security. Then, after working with his Triple-A batting coach, Teahen morphed into George Brett for the rest of the year. He hit .500/.606/.875 in his next 17 games before returning to Kansas City on June 3, then hit .313/.384/.557 for the Royals until he was shut down in early September for shoulder surgery. He went from waiver bait to owning the second-highest EqA of any AL third baseman (behind Alex Rodriguez) in four months. Is he likely to keep it up? Great Leaps Forward are rare, but they're considerably less rare at age 24 than later in life. PECOTA is certainly optimistic, projecting him to keep most of his gains. The Royals now find themselves in the rare position of having arguably the best prospect in baseball trying to break in at the same position as a quality regular in his mid-20s. The solution that maximizes value to the Royals involves a trade, but the Royals are likely to send Teahen to one of the outfield corners as soon as Gordon is ready. It's a waste of his defensive value, but his bat should play in a corner. Keeping him means one more above-average bat in a lineup which is on the verge of sneaking into the league's top half.

PITCHERS

John Bale　　Bats: L　Throws: L　　Height: 6' 4"　　Weight: 210　　Born: May 22, 1974　　Age: 33

YEAR	TEAM	LVL	AGE	W	L	SV	G	GS	IP	H	BB	SO	HR	GB%	BABIP	STUFF	WHIP	ERA	PERA	EQERA	EQH9	EQBB9	EQSO9	EQHR9	VORP	WXRL
2004	HRO	JP	30	11	10	0	25	0	160¹	165	62	173	16	—	.326	20	1.42	4.21	4.22	4.74	9.0	4.0	7.0	0.7	15.1	—
2005	HRO	JP	31	2	1	24	51	0	53²	44	16	72	9	—	.282	10	1.12	3.18	4.31	4.08	7.6	3.1	9.0	1.5	9.0	—
2006	HRO	JP	32	1	2	6	30	5	43	45	11	46	5	—	.325	6	1.30	0.00	4.10	3.61	10.0	2.8	7.4	1.3	9.4	—
2007	KCA	MLB	33	3	6	5	47	7	75²	86	32	61	11	44.0%	.324	-1	1.56	5.23	5.07	4.70	9.4	3.6	6.7	1.1	4.7	0.70

Breakout: 12%　Improve: 33%　Collapse: 25%　Attrition: 16%　　Comparables: Chuck Cary, Mike Remlinger, Lance Painter, Joe Price

Prior to the 2002 season, Allard Baird traveled to Japan and signed left-hander Darrell May, who gave the Royals one good year sandwiched between two bad ones. This winter, Dayton Moore very quietly signed his own *gaijin* southpaw, John Bale, while the winter meetings were still abuzz over the Gil Meche deal. What the signing lacks in ambition, it makes up for in its risk aversion. It's hard to pan a two-year, $4-million contract for *any* free agent, and Bale's translated performance from Japan suggests a pitcher who can give the Royals an ERA around 4.00 with peripherals to match. While we don't have splits from Japan, Bale pitched 79 innings in the majors from 1999 to 2003 and completely neutralized left-handed hitters—their career line against him was .147/.253/.235. Dollar for dollar, he might wind up being one of the best signings of the winter.

Ryan Braun　　Bats: R　Throws: R　　Height: 6' 1"　　Weight: 215　　Born: July 29, 1980　　Age: 26

YEAR	TEAM	LVL	AGE	W	L	SV	G	GS	IP	H	BB	SO	HR	GB%	BABIP	STUFF	WHIP	ERA	PERA	EQERA	EQH9	EQBB9	EQSO9	EQHR9	VORP	WXRL
2004	WIL	A+	23	2	3	24	51	0	57	48	25	58	2	—	.289	-4	1.28	2.21	4.87	5.40	9.1	5.2	6.1	0.7	1.2	—
2006	WIC	AA	25	1	6	10	26	0	40²	30	16	58	2	48.9%	.322	15	1.14	2.24	3.99	3.23	8.1	4.2	8.8	0.7	10.3	—
2006	OMA	AAA	25	0	2	3	17	0	25¹	23	13	22	0	52.7%	.324	3	1.43	2.15	3.74	3.55	8.2	4.6	6.0	0.4	5.8	—
2006	KCA	MLB	25	0	1	0	9	0	10²	13	3	6	2	40.0%	.333	-14	1.50	6.73	4.93	5.56	9.5	2.4	4.8	1.6	-0.7	-0.34
2007	KCA	MLB	26	2	4	2	63	3	61	73	35	46	7	49.0%	.338	-8	1.77	5.81	5.55	5.30	9.9	4.9	6.2	0.9	-0.9	0.00

Breakout: 14%　Improve: 43%　Collapse: 28%　Attrition: 9%　　Comparables: Brandon Villafuerte, Shawn Camp, Jake Meyer, Josh Kinney

Not to be confused with the Brewers' prospect, Braun suffered a career-threatening shoulder injury in 2005 and missed most of the season. His full recovery was one of the bright spots for the Royals' farm system last year. He has the classic reliever repertoire of mid-90s fastball and hard-breaking slider. Braun was dominant in the high minors, was even more effective against left-handed hitters than right-handers, and wasn't overwhelmed in a September cup of coffee. At 26, his window is now—expect him to climb through it.

Billy Buckner   Bats: R Throws: R   Height: 6' 2"   Weight: 210   Born: August 27, 1983   Age: 23

YEAR	TEAM	LVL	AGE	W	L	SV	G	GS	IP	H	BB	SO	HR	GB%	BABIP	STUFF	WHIP	ERA	PERA	EQERA	EQH9	EQBB9	EQSO9	EQHR9	VORP	WXRL
2004	IDA	Rk	20	2	2	0	8	5	34^1	44	8	37	4	—	.392	-10	1.52	3.94	6.34	5.50	12.1	2.4	4.5	2.1	0.4	—
2005	BUR	A	21	3	7	0	11	11	60^1	66	17	60	9	50.0%	.322	-15	1.38	3.88	7.08	6.33	11.3	2.9	5.9	2.8	-4.7	—
2005	HDS	A+	21	5	6	0	17	17	94	105	46	92	10	58.4%	.357	2	1.61	5.36	5.44	5.72	9.4	4.8	5.6	1.2	-1.3	—
2006	HDS	A+	22	7	1	0	16	16	90^1	92	47	85	6	56.6%	.328	7	1.54	3.90	5.40	4.37	8.9	5.3	5.3	1.0	12.4	—
2006	WIC	AA	22	5	3	0	13	13	75^2	78	39	63	7	57.1%	.308	4	1.56	4.67	5.37	5.23	9.5	4.6	5.5	1.1	3.1	—
2007	KCA	MLB	23	5	10	0	25	22	119^1	145	64	72	16	53.0%	.323	-3	1.74	6.17	5.81	5.65	10.0	4.6	5.0	1.0	-7.4	0.20

Breakout: 10% Improve: 38% Collapse: 27% Attrition: 1%   Comparables: Matt Albers, Matt Wright, Zach Day, Zach Miner

In the two seasons that the Royals affiliated with High Desert, Buckner was their only starting pitcher to survive the experience without developing Post-Traumatic Stress Disorder. He was a wise use of a second-round pick; his stock fell before the draft after he came down with mono as a college junior. His control remains a major issue, but his other indicators, particularly his ability to induce ground balls, are all positive. His curveball is probably his best pitch, and, given the effects of altitude on breaking stuff, that's a good sign that his numbers may take a step forward at lower elevation.

Ambiorix Burgos   Bats: R Throws: R   Height: 6' 3"   Weight: 235   Born: April 19, 1984   Age: 23

YEAR	TEAM	LVL	AGE	W	L	SV	G	GS	IP	H	BB	SO	HR	GB%	BABIP	STUFF	WHIP	ERA	PERA	EQERA	EQH9	EQBB9	EQSO9	EQHR9	VORP	WXRL
2004	BUR	A	20	7	11	0	27	26	133^2	109	75	172	13	—	.309	-3	1.38	4.38	7.14	6.04	9.6	6.7	7.1	1.9	-6.0	—
2005	WIC	AA	21	1	1	1	12	0	12^2	8	8	19	1	50.0%	.259	12	1.26	4.96	4.98	5.84	6.6	6.6	10.2	0.7	-0.3	—
2005	KCA	MLB	21	3	5	2	59	0	63^1	60	31	65	6	47.1%	.321	21	1.44	3.98	4.08	3.80	7.6	4.2	8.7	0.8	11.6	0.57
2006	KCA	MLB	22	4	5	18	68	1	73^1	83	37	72	16	44.9%	.335	-4	1.64	5.53	5.54	5.31	9.4	4.1	8.1	1.7	1.2	-1.34
2007	NYN	MLB	23	3	3	4	53	0	61	54	28	58	7	45.0%	.285	9	1.35	3.81	4.24	4.22	8.0	3.7	7.6	0.9	10.4	1.00

Breakout: 35% Improve: 66% Collapse: 10% Attrition: 33%   Comparables: Jim Donohue, Mike Jackson, Ray Corbin, Neil Allen

Burgos may have exasperated the Royals with his inability or unwillingness to convert his stuff into results, but there are a number of reasons why they may live to regret exiling him to the Mets. It's not Burgos's fault he was promoted to the majors with less than a month's experience above the Midwest League—no one should be surprised that he has struggled with command in the majors, leading to both walks and gopher pitches. He still throws very, very hard, and he doesn't turn 23 until after the season begins. Burgos moves to the inferior league, against hitters not familiar with him, and Shea Stadium is a godsend for power pitchers. PECOTA's breakout forecast of 41 percent seems, if anything, a little low.

Daniel Christensen   Bats: L Throws: L   Height: 6' 1"   Weight: 205   Born: August 10, 1983   Age: 23

YEAR	TEAM	LVL	AGE	W	L	SV	G	GS	IP	H	BB	SO	HR	GB%	BABIP	STUFF	WHIP	ERA	PERA	EQERA	EQH9	EQBB9	EQSO9	EQHR9	VORP	WXRL
2005	BUR	A	21	3	7	1	26	21	109^1	100	53	110	9	40.0%	.302	-7	1.40	3.54	6.09	5.32	9.0	5.1	5.9	1.5	3.3	—
2006	HDS	A+	22	6	6	0	28	28	162	175	58	153	23	43.4%	.350	-20	1.44	4.89	6.55	5.11	9.9	3.6	5.3	2.1	8.8	—
2007	KCA	MLB	23	4	10	0	24	21	111	136	65	67	20	44.0%	.317	-8	1.81	6.73	6.38	6.06	10.1	5.0	5.0	1.4	-12.7	0.40

Breakout: 6% Improve: 28% Collapse: 32% Attrition: 1%   Comparables: Scott Wiggins, Brian Burres, Ryan Snare, Chris Narveson

A fourth-round pick in 2002 from that noted baseball hotbed, Brooklyn, Christensen's career turned around after Tommy John surgery in 2004. He returned with better velocity than before his injury, and, over the past two years, has struck out nearly a man an inning. Last year he had an excellent 153/58 strikeout-to-walk ratio, but posted a 4.89 ERA anyway thanks to his home park. He showed enough in the AFL (10 innings, 2 earned runs) to get added to the 40-man roster in November. Double-A will tell us more.

Luis Cota   **Bats: R Throws: R**   Height: 6′ 2″   Weight: 200   Born: August 19, 1985   Age: 21

YEAR	TEAM	LVL	AGE	W	L	SV	G	GS	IP	H	BB	SO	HR	GB%	BABIP	STUFF	WHIP	ERA	PERA	EQERA	EQH9	EQBB9	EQSO9	EQHR9	VORP	WXRL
2004	IDA	Rk	18	2	1	0	13	12	48	61	21	40	5	—	.366	-18	1.71	5.81	7.03	7.35	11.2	4.2	3.7	1.8	-9.5	—
2005	BUR	A	19	5	8	0	26	26	148	143	63	137	10	52.0%	.317	8	1.39	4.01	5.37	5.20	9.1	4.2	5.5	1.2	6.5	—
2006	HDS	A+	20	5	11	0	27	26	132	153	63	126	19	39.0%	.350	-21	1.64	7.09	6.71	7.24	10.5	4.6	5.5	2.0	-24.2	—
2007	KCA	MLB	21	4	9	0	24	20	108	131	56	68	20	44.0%	.315	-3	1.73	6.50	6.13	5.84	10.1	4.4	5.2	1.4	-9.3	0.10

Breakout: 30% Improve: 65% Collapse: 4% Attrition: 0% Comparables: Dennis Tankersley, Carlos Chantres, Jimmy Barrett, Chad Durbin

This is why no major league team wants High Desert as an affiliate. Cota was signed as a draft-and-follow for first-round money in 2004 and probably has the best arm in the system. He throws harder than all but a few starters in the minor leagues and had a promising season as a 19 year old for Burlington in 2005. All that is meaningless when you pitch in a shoe box—Cota had a 7.09 ERA despite striking out twice as many batters as he walked. The Royals will give him another shot as a starter in Wilmington, with the bullpen as a backup option.

Jorge de la Rosa   **Bats: L Throws: L**   Height: 6′ 1″   Weight: 210   Born: April 5, 1981   Age: 26

YEAR	TEAM	LVL	AGE	W	L	SV	G	GS	IP	H	BB	SO	HR	GB%	BABIP	STUFF	WHIP	ERA	PERA	EQERA	EQH9	EQBB9	EQSO9	EQHR9	VORP	WXRL
2004	IND	AAA	23	5	6	0	20	20	85²	80	36	86	9	—	.305	8	1.35	4.52	4.96	4.81	8.4	4.1	6.9	1.0	7.5	—
2004	MIL	MLB	23	0	3	0	5	5	22²	29	14	5	1	—	.318	-26	1.90	6.34	5.10	7.61	11.0	4.9	1.9	0.4	-5.9	-0.32
2005	MIL	MLB	24	2	2	0	38	0	42¹	48	38	42	1	52.4%	.382	19	2.03	4.47	4.10	4.74	10.1	7.2	8.0	0.2	2.8	-0.12
2006	HUN	AA	25	3	1	0	6	6	30	31	3	23	1	47.3%	.341	7	1.13	2.40	3.50	5.16	10.0	0.9	4.2	0.6	1.5	—
2006	MIL	MLB	25	2	2	0	18	3	30¹	32	22	31	4	44.3%	.333	6	1.78	8.32	4.80	7.67	9.1	5.4	8.2	1.1	-8.6	0.27
2006	KCA	MLB	25	3	4	0	10	10	48²	49	32	36	10	41.3%	.279	1	1.66	5.17	6.20	4.80	8.2	5.5	6.0	1.6	4.1	0.97
2007	KCA	MLB	26	4	7	1	44	13	97¹	111	56	72	12	44.0%	.323	-5	1.72	5.78	5.49	5.23	9.4	4.9	6.2	0.9	-0.7	0.40

Breakout: 27% Improve: 56% Collapse: 15% Attrition: 18% Comparables: Angel Miranda, Marcelino Lopez, Jim Shellenback, Dean Stone

De la Rosa is a hard-throwing Mexican lefty; arms like this don't grow on trees. He was a worthwhile flyer to take in exchange for three months of Tony Graffanino's career. He simply doesn't throw enough strikes to survive in a starting rotation. The Royals seem committed to proving that point experimentally; the sooner they accept the inevitable and give him a shot at being a power lefty out of the pen, the better.

Gabe DeHoyos   **Bats: R Throws: R**   Height: 5′ 11″   Weight: 226   Born: April 14, 1980   Age: 27

YEAR	TEAM	LVL	AGE	W	L	SV	G	GS	IP	H	BB	SO	HR	GB%	BABIP	STUFF	WHIP	ERA	PERA	EQERA	EQH9	EQBB9	EQSO9	EQHR9	VORP	WXRL
2004	BUR	A	24	1	2	5	16	0	23²	19	11	26	0	—	.317	-1	1.27	2.28	4.53	3.63	8.5	6.0	5.2	0.4	4.9	—
2005	BUR	A	25	4	1	3	28	3	69¹	51	27	81	2	54.0%	.290	8	1.13	1.56	4.17	4.28	7.4	4.4	6.3	0.5	9.9	—
2006	HDS	A+	26	3	1	13	28	0	28¹	13	14	37	0	71.9%	.232	13	0.96	2.56	3.94	3.33	4.7	5.7	7.0	0.3	6.8	—
2006	WIC	AA	26	2	1	7	22	0	33²	20	19	28	1	49.5%	.226	2	1.17	1.63	4.79	2.48	5.5	5.8	5.0	0.3	11.3	—
2007	KCA	MLB	27	2	4	1	28	5	57¹	60	43	42	5	50.0%	.310	-8	1.80	5.39	5.34	4.93	8.7	6.4	6.2	0.7	1.7	0.30

Breakout: 4% Improve: 13% Collapse: 65% Attrition: 14% Comparables: Santiago Ramirez, Todd Williams, Len Hart, J. J. Trujillo

You're always going to have trouble getting taken seriously as a prospect when your pro career begins with the Schaumburg Flyers, but DeHoyos has a shot at being one of the few Independent League alumni to make good in the major leagues. He's short and stocky, but throws a decent slider and a fastball around 90 MPH which is most notable for its sink. He's almost impossible to hit for power–counting the AFL, he surrendered just one homer in 76 innings last year while pitching in ballparks that ranged from unfriendly to pure evil. He's a long shot for major league success, but then he was a long shot to even to get to this point.

Scott Elarton   **Bats: R Throws: R**   Height: 6′ 7″   Weight: 255   Born: February 23, 1976   Age: 31

YEAR	TEAM	LVL	AGE	W	L	SV	G	GS	IP	H	BB	SO	HR	GB%	BABIP	STUFF	WHIP	ERA	PERA	EQERA	EQH9	EQBB9	EQSO9	EQHR9	VORP	WXRL
2004	BUF	AAA	28	1	1	0	3	3	20	19	5	10	1	—	.277	0	1.20	3.15	4.32	3.60	8.1	2.7	3.2	0.4	4.4	—
2004	COL	MLB	28	0	6	0	8	8	41¹	57	20	23	8	—	.343	-20	1.86	9.81	5.51	8.66	10.9	3.7	4.3	1.4	-13.8	-1.23
2004	CLE	MLB	28	3	5	0	21	21	117¹	107	42	80	25	—	.241	-8	1.27	4.53	5.62	4.38	7.6	2.9	5.6	1.7	19.0	2.44
2005	CLE	MLB	29	11	9	0	31	31	181²	189	48	103	32	33.8%	.274	-8	1.30	4.61	5.20	5.18	9.6	2.4	5.0	1.5	14.6	2.66
2006	KCA	MLB	30	4	9	0	20	20	114²	117	52	49	26	30.5%	.250	-27	1.47	5.34	6.73	4.96	8.2	3.8	3.5	1.7	5.4	1.36
2007	KCA	MLB	31	5	10	0	29	21	126²	152	49	68	25	36.0%	.298	-9	1.59	6.25	5.79	5.55	9.9	3.3	4.4	1.6	-6.3	0.30

Breakout: 5% Improve: 32% Collapse: 28% Attrition: 5% Comparables: Cal Eldred, Dennis Rasmussen, Andy Hawkins, Steve Renko

Wow, Scott Elarton hurt his shoulder—who saw that coming? If you're wondering why so many Royals fans are trying to defend the Gil Meche signing, consider that these are the kind of free agent signings they have grown accustomed to. Elarton might be back by midseason; if his fastball doesn't return with him, would anyone notice?

Brent Fisher   Bats: L Throws: L   Height: 6' 2"   Weight: 190   Born: August 6, 1987   Age: 19

YEAR	TEAM	LVL	AGE	W	L	SV	G	GS	IP	H	BB	SO	HR	GB%	BABIP	STUFF	WHIP	ERA	PERA	EQERA	EQH9	EQBB9	EQSO9	EQHR9	VORP	WXRL
2006	ROY	Rk	18	3	1	0	14	14	68^1	41	19	98	2	40.7%	.279	28	0.88	2.11	4.82	3.20	7.8	3.1	6.8	1.3	17.3	—
2007	KCA	MLB	19	6	8	1	30	20	120^2	129	50	100	21	42.0%	.301	12	1.48	4.94	5.06	4.37	8.8	3.5	6.9	1.4	12.5	2.00

Breakout: 0%   Improve: 14%   Collapse: 52%   Attrition: 1%   Comparables: Alan Webb, Rick Ankiel, Jake Peavy, Jake Stevens

The Royals' best pitching prospect in the low minors, Fisher struck out 69 batters in 50 innings in his pro debut in 2005. For some reason the Royals didn't feel that merited a promotion, so Fisher returned to the Arizona League last season and increased his strikeout rate to 12.9 per nine innings. He finally got called up to Idaho Falls in time for the playoffs, and, in two appearances, faced 22 hitters, allowed 2 to reach base, and struck out 13 of them. Fisher's stuff isn't as good as his numbers, but he's a lefty who touches 90 MPH, throws a hammer curve, and has a deceptive delivery which makes his stuff appear faster than it is. Note his age; he was just 17 when he was drafted. Also note the names of two of his comps. If he adds any velocity at all this season, he could be in Double-A before he turns 20, and you don't see that every day.

Jimmy Gobble   Bats: L Throws: L   Height: 6' 3"   Weight: 205   Born: July 19, 1981   Age: 25

YEAR	TEAM	LVL	AGE	W	L	SV	G	GS	IP	H	BB	SO	HR	GB%	BABIP	STUFF	WHIP	ERA	PERA	EQERA	EQH9	EQBB9	EQSO9	EQHR9	VORP	WXRL
2004	KCA	MLB	22	9	8	0	25	24	148	157	43	49	24	—	.262	-13	1.35	5.35	5.34	4.58	8.4	2.3	2.7	1.2	7.7	2.09
2005	OMA	AAA	23	2	7	0	12	12	58^1	76	21	45	8	43.8%	.360	-8	1.66	6.64	5.06	7.24	11.2	3.0	5.1	1.4	-10.9	—
2005	KCA	MLB	23	1	1	0	28	4	53^2	64	30	38	9	34.7%	.329	-8	1.75	5.70	5.52	4.92	9.4	4.8	6.0	1.4	0.3	0.93
2006	KCA	MLB	24	4	6	2	60	6	84	95	29	80	12	38.9%	.339	7	1.48	5.14	3.96	4.83	9.2	2.9	7.8	1.1	6.4	-0.24
2007	KCA	MLB	25	4	6	2	48	7	83^2	94	31	62	12	42.0%	.311	0	1.50	5.21	4.88	4.67	9.3	3.2	6.1	1.1	5.5	0.70

Breakout: 24%   Improve: 56%   Collapse: 8%   Attrition: 8%   Comparables: Bob Owchinko, Jerry Garvin, Dick Stigman, Bob Kipper

Ladies and gentlemen, your strikeout leader for the 2006 Kansas City Royals! Gobble led the team with 80–eighty, eight zero, *ochenta* (*ocho cero* if you're Chad Johnson). Since 1960, only three staff leaders have had a lower strikeout total in a non-strike season: Paul Splittorff with 61 for the 1983 Royals, Scott Schoeneweis with 78 for the 2000 Angels, and Carlos Reyes with 78 for the 1996 As. Gobble's strikeout rate last season (8.54 K/9) was more than double his previous career average (4.18) as the move to the bullpen added some life to his fastball, which, in turn, made his curveball more effective. A future as an effective, if homer-prone, lefty in the Jamie Walker mold is his upside.

Zack Greinke   Bats: R Throws: R   Height: 6' 2"   Weight: 185   Born: October 21, 1983   Age: 23

YEAR	TEAM	LVL	AGE	W	L	SV	G	GS	IP	H	BB	SO	HR	GB%	BABIP	STUFF	WHIP	ERA	PERA	EQERA	EQH9	EQBB9	EQSO9	EQHR9	VORP	WXRL
2004	OMA	AAA	20	1	1	0	6	6	28^2	25	6	23	2	—	.261	23	1.08	2.51	3.87	2.48	7.4	1.9	5.6	0.6	10.1	—
2004	KCA	MLB	20	8	11	0	24	24	145	143	26	100	26	—	.264	16	1.15	3.97	4.59	3.34	8.0	1.4	5.7	1.4	34.6	4.29
2005	KCA	MLB	21	5	17	0	33	33	183	233	53	114	23	40.0%	.340	9	1.56	5.80	4.53	5.13	10.0	2.5	5.3	1.0	-7.0	1.71
2006	WIC	AA	22	8	3	0	18	17	105	96	27	94	12	44.0%	.297	6	1.17	4.37	4.82	4.97	8.6	2.3	5.9	1.4	7.4	—
2006	KCA	MLB	22	1	0	0	3	0	6^1	7	3	5	1	35.0%	.316	3	1.58	4.29	4.77	4.05	9.4	4.1	6.8	1.4	1.3	0.17
2007	KCA	MLB	23	6	9	0	30	19	121	142	35	77	20	42.0%	.307	3	1.46	5.44	5.05	4.86	9.7	2.5	5.3	1.3	4.7	1.30

Breakout: 7%   Improve: 40%   Collapse: 24%   Attrition: 1%   Comparables: Jin Ho Cho, John Hudgins, Luke Prokopec, Ian Snell

The exact psychological diagnosis which put Greinke's career on hold has yet to be announced publicly, so it's not certain if the issues that he needed half a season to come to terms with will go away with treatment or are a part of who he is. The Royals were unusually understanding of his situation, refusing to discuss his diagnosis or treatment with the media and giving him all the time he needed to return. When he did, Greinke quietly had a strong half-season in Wichita and pitched out of the bullpen a few times in September. Consider that along with Buckner, Hochevar, and Lumsden, Greinke was part of an all-prospect rotation in the Texas League playoffs—and Greinke was the youngest of the quartet. Don't write him off yet.

Runelvys Hernandez
Bats: R Throws: R   Height: 6' 1"   Weight: 250   Born: April 27, 1978   Age: 29

YEAR	TEAM	LVL	AGE	W	L	SV	G	GS	IP	H	BB	SO	HR	GB%	BABIP	STUFF	WHIP	ERA	PERA	EQERA	EQH9	EQBB9	EQSO9	EQHR9	VORP	WXRL
2005	KCA	MLB	27	8	14	0	29	29	159²	172	70	88	18	38.4%	.298	0	1.52	5.52	4.96	4.79	8.4	3.8	4.7	0.9	2.5	1.06
2006	OMA	AAA	28	5	6	0	12	11	64²	65	27	43	6	42.0%	.295	-7	1.43	4.63	5.16	4.96	8.8	3.7	4.4	1.1	4.6	—
2006	KCA	MLB	28	6	10	0	21	21	109²	145	48	50	22	41.7%	.332	-26	1.76	6.48	6.05	6.24	10.7	3.6	3.7	1.6	-11.9	0.35
2007	BOS	MLB	29	6	8	0	31	19	113²	138	48	63	16	43.0%	.315	-7	1.63	5.82	5.47	5.30	9.4	3.6	4.6	1.0	-0.8	0.70

Breakout: 19% Improve: 51% Collapse: 23% Attrition: 14%   Comparables: Mike Scott, Galen Cisco, Dave Lemanczyk, Ken Schrom

This guy you can write off. The sinister Mr. Applegate negated his contract after Hernandez went 4–0 with a 1.36 ERA in April 2003, but the Royals stuck with him through Tommy John surgery and the David Wells Diet. At some point, even the Royals had to cry uncle; from May 1, 2003 until the end of the 2006 season, Hernandez put up a 6.11 ERA in 321 innings. Released, he was signed to a minor league deal by the Red Sox; apparently new Bosox assistant GM Allard Baird just can't let go.

Luke Hochevar
Bats: R Throws: R   Height: 6' 5"   Weight: 205   Born: September 15, 1983 Age: 23

YEAR	TEAM	LVL	AGE	W	L	SV	G	GS	IP	H	BB	SO	HR	GB%	BABIP	STUFF	WHIP	ERA	PERA	EQERA	EQH9	EQBB9	EQSO9	EQHR9	VORP	WXRL
2006	BUR	A	22	0	1	0	4	4	15	8	2	16	2	39.5%	.167	0	0.67	1.20	9.01	3.38	8.8	2.0	6.1	4.1	3.3	—
2007	KCA	MLB	23	6	8	0	30	19	115	129	32	73	33	40.0%	.266	-2	1.40	5.26	5.72	4.51	9.3	2.4	5.3	2.2	9.7	1.70

Breakout: 1% Improve: 11% Collapse: 68% Attrition: 5%   Comparables: Vladimir Nunez, Brian Rogers, Stephen Cowie, Mark Difelice

Most scouts felt that Andrew Miller was a better prospect than Hochevar on draft day, although Hochevar was a clear number-two to most draft experts. You have to hope the Royals weren't lying when they claimed they drafted Hochevar based purely on merit rather than his signability, given that Miller (drafted sixth overall by the Tigers) signed literally the day after Hochevar, and for about two percent more money. Hochevar dominated the Midwest League, then made two starts in the Texas League playoffs, one good, one bad. He threw eight ineffective innings in the AFL before his season ended with a minor shoulder strain. Despite his much-publicized draft drama from 2005, Hochevar gets high marks for his work ethic and dedication to the game. It will be a disappointment to the Royals if he doesn't crack their rotation at some point this year.

Luke Hudson
Bats: R Throws: R   Height: 6' 3"   Weight: 195   Born: May 2, 1977   Age: 30

YEAR	TEAM	LVL	AGE	W	L	SV	G	GS	IP	H	BB	SO	HR	GB%	BABIP	STUFF	WHIP	ERA	PERA	EQERA	EQH9	EQBB9	EQSO9	EQHR9	VORP	WXRL
2004	CHT	AA	27	7	7	0	16	16	86²	71	25	91	9	—	.284	-7	1.11	3.32	5.88	4.98	9.2	3.2	5.9	1.7	5.6	—
2004	LOU	AAA	27	2	1	0	3	3	19	15	5	17	2	—	.255	15	1.05	2.84	4.34	3.79	7.1	2.8	6.2	0.9	3.8	—
2004	CIN	MLB	27	4	2	0	9	9	48¹	36	25	38	3	—	.250	20	1.26	2.42	4.11	2.92	6.6	4.0	6.2	0.5	14.4	2.16
2005	CIN	MLB	28	6	9	0	19	16	84²	83	50	53	14	38.9%	.284	-12	1.57	6.38	6.41	6.11	8.3	4.7	5.0	1.4	-9.8	-0.13
2006	OMA	AAA	29	2	0	1	13	2	35¹	30	7	21	0	50.4%	.268	2	1.05	2.82	3.49	3.82	7.4	1.8	4.1	0.3	7.0	—
2006	KCA	MLB	29	7	6	0	26	15	102	109	38	64	7	50.8%	.315	10	1.44	5.12	3.98	4.81	8.6	3.0	5.1	0.5	8.0	2.21
2007	KCA	MLB	30	4	7	1	35	12	88²	104	37	55	13	45.0%	.312	-7	1.59	5.61	5.27	5.06	9.7	3.6	5.2	1.1	1.2	0.60

Breakout: 14% Improve: 36% Collapse: 27% Attrition: 12%   Comparables: Dick Starr, Dan Osinski, Eddie Solomon, Jesse Jefferson

Hudson was released by the Reds in spring training and designated for assignment by the Royals in early May before returning at the end of June. He was, nonetheless, the team's best pitcher in the second half of the season. His turnaround started when his father and brother watched him pitch in Omaha and noticed he was throwing from a different arm slot than usual. He had shown flashes of being an effective starter with the Reds in 2004 before shoulder woes wrecked the following season. If healthy, he's a cheap solution for the bottom of the rotation.

Blake Johnson
Bats: R Throws: R   Height: 6' 3"   Weight: 185   Born: November 30, 1999 Age: 22

YEAR	TEAM	LVL	AGE	W	L	SV	G	GS	IP	H	BB	SO	HR	GB%	BABIP	STUFF	WHIP	ERA	PERA	EQERA	EQH9	EQBB9	EQSO9	EQHR9	VORP	WXRL
2004	OGD	Rk	0	3	3	0	13	12	57	73	19	57	5	—	.400	-10	1.61	6.47	5.92	6.71	10.7	3.2	4.1	1.5	-7.3	—
2005	CGA	A	0	9	4	0	24	17	100	83	36	88	4	54.2%	.287	7	1.19	3.33	4.57	5.13	7.9	3.9	4.8	0.6	5.1	—
2006	VRO	A+	0	4	5	0	20	18	106	121	19	73	11	45.2%	.324	-13	1.32	4.92	5.56	4.74	10.1	1.8	3.9	1.7	10.3	—
2006	HDS	A+	0	1	1	0	3	2	11²	15	0	9	1	44.2%	.357	2	1.34	5.63	4.07	5.40	10.8	0.8	4.6	1.5	0.3	—
2007	KCA	MLB	22	4	9	0	25	19	108¹	135	36	53	19	46.0%	.309	-6	1.58	6.41	5.59	5.83	10.3	2.8	4.1	1.4	-9.2	0.10

Breakout: 7% Improve: 30% Collapse: 35% Attrition: 0%   Comparables: Jeff Karstens, Chris Mears, Dustin Moseley, Bob Keppel

Part of the swag the Royals got from the Dodgers in gratitude for taking Odalis Perez off their hands, Johnson is a very polished high school product who walked just 19 batters in 117 innings last season. His velocity is marginal, though he still has some projection left. After just three appearances with High Desert, he was shut down with a tender elbow. The biggest concern with Johnson is that Dodgers' scouting director Logan White is so good at identifying the impact players in the draft that you have to assume any player he's willing to give up must have something wrong with him.

Tyler Lumsden

Bats: L Throws: L   Height: 6' 4"   Weight: 215   Born: May 9, 1983   Age: 24

YEAR	TEAM	LVL	AGE	W	L	SV	G	GS	IP	H	BB	SO	HR	GB%	BABIP	STUFF	WHIP	ERA	PERA	EQERA	EQH9	EQBB9	EQSO9	EQHR9	VORP	WXRL
2004	WNS	A+	21	3	1	0	15	3	39^1	45	20	31	2	—	.333	-8	1.65	4.12	5.24	6.81	10.8	5.4	4.9	0.9	-5.1	—
2006	BIR	AA	23	9	4	0	20	20	123^2	114	40	72	9	58.6%	.283	-8	1.25	2.70	5.41	4.17	8.6	2.9	3.6	1.2	19.5	—
2006	WIC	AA	23	2	1	0	7	6	35^2	35	20	24	3	52.1%	.304	-1	1.56	3.07	5.98	3.57	9.2	5.3	4.3	1.0	8.0	—
2007	KCA	MLB	24	4	9	0	25	19	107^1	135	52	49	14	53.0%	.319	-11	1.74	6.36	5.82	5.84	10.4	4.1	3.8	1.0	-9.4	0.20

Breakout: 1% Improve: 9% Collapse: 56% Attrition: 0%   Comparables: Sean Henn, Jimmy Osting, Brian O'Connor, Kason Gabbard

The main prospect the Royals received for Mike MacDougal, Lumsden is the best prospect they acquired at the trading deadline. His numbers last season are superficially unimpressive, particularly the 96 whiffs in 159 innings, but Lumsden missed all of 2005 following surgery to remove a bone spur in his elbow, and went straight to Double-A on his return. More importantly, his stuff surpasses his statistics; he throws comfortably in the low-90s with an excellent curveball. He's likely to get an audition by mid-season.

Joe Nelson

Bats: R Throws: R   Height: 6' 1"   Weight: 210   Born: October 25, 1974   Age: 32

YEAR	TEAM	LVL	AGE	W	L	SV	G	GS	IP	H	BB	SO	HR	GB%	BABIP	STUFF	WHIP	ERA	PERA	EQERA	EQH9	EQBB9	EQSO9	EQHR9	VORP	WXRL
2004	PME	AA	29	3	2	13	25	0	30^1	16	15	49	1	—	.254	29	1.02	1.78	3.64	3.10	5.9	5.3	9.6	0.3	8.1	—
2004	PAW	AAA	29	0	0	0	16	0	21^1	27	9	31	1	—	.456	10	1.69	4.65	3.55	6.33	11.8	4.2	9.7	0.4	-1.7	—
2005	DUR	AAA	30	0	3	6	35	0	46	41	21	62	9	37.0%	.296	-1	1.35	4.11	5.97	5.16	8.3	4.6	8.9	2.2	2.2	—
2006	OMA	AAA	31	2	2	7	24	0	32	19	12	39	4	43.7%	.242	7	0.97	1.97	5.61	2.87	6.3	3.4	8.0	1.4	9.5	—
2006	KCA	MLB	31	1	1	9	43	0	44^2	37	24	44	5	35.0%	.278	14	1.37	4.43	4.25	3.91	6.8	4.5	8.2	0.8	8.6	1.78
2007	KCA	MLB	32	2	3	4	45	1	47^1	48	25	45	7	39.0%	.304	2	1.53	4.96	4.80	4.43	8.4	4.5	7.8	1.2	4.4	0.40

Breakout: 21% Improve: 41% Collapse: 31% Attrition: 30%   Comparables: John Wyatt, Aurelio Lopez, Ben Wade, Rich Delucia

If closing is such a mystical art capable of being performed by only a select few, how do you explain Nelson, a 31-year-old journeyman who had thrown less than five major league innings before 2006, getting thrust into the role out of desperation and going 9-for-10 in save opportunities? The irony is that all those opportunities came in August and September, when the shine wore off on the rookie; Nelson had a 1.35 ERA at the end of July and a 7.43 ERA thereafter. Even a pitcher with a 7.43 ERA can save 90 percent of save opportunities if he gets enough three-run leads. The saves notwithstanding, Nelson is still a journeyman pitcher best treated as the fungible asset he is. The Royals agree; their many bullpen acquisitions this winter mean Nelson will be fighting for a roster spot in March.

Chris Nicoll

Bats: R Throws: R   Height: 6' 2"   Weight: 190   Born: October 30, 1983   Age: 23

YEAR	TEAM	LVL	AGE	W	L	SV	G	GS	IP	H	BB	SO	HR	GB%	BABIP	STUFF	WHIP	ERA	PERA	EQERA	EQH9	EQBB9	EQSO9	EQHR9	VORP	WXRL
2005	IDA	Rk	21	0	3	0	7	7	27^1	26	9	34	4	38.0%	.333	-18	1.28	3.63	8.46	5.54	10.0	4.5	5.2	3.1	0.2	—
2006	BUR	A	22	4	9	0	23	23	134^2	105	40	140	13	36.5%	.266	-35	1.08	2.82	7.73	5.36	10.3	4.0	5.6	2.8	3.2	—
2006	HDS	A+	22	2	0	0	3	3	16^2	17	6	26	3	42.6%	.409	16	1.42	5.00	6.77	5.74	11.5	4.0	9.2	2.9	-0.2	—
2007	KCA	MLB	23	5	9	0	27	19	110	131	59	74	24	39.0%	.305	-5	1.72	6.27	6.35	5.52	9.8	4.6	5.6	1.7	-5.0	0.30

Breakout: 19% Improve: 43% Collapse: 23% Attrition: 2%   Comparables: Jeff Bruksch, Kevin Olore, Jeff Yoder, Danny Tamayo

A third-round pick in 2005 out of UC-Irvine, Nicoll was considered a very polished pitcher out of college, making curious the Royals' decision to leave him in the Midwest League most of last season. Nicoll pitched very well, and had little trouble in three late starts at High Desert, whiffing 26 in 17 innings. There are warning signs here; he throws three good pitches but no great ones and is a strong fly-ball pitcher, a tendency which is going to give him problems as he climbs the ladder.

Leo Nuñez
Bats: R　Throws: R　Height: 6' 1"　Weight: 165　Born: August 14, 1983　Age: 23

YEAR	TEAM	LVL	AGE	W	L	SV	G	GS	IP	H	BB	SO	HR	GB%	BABIP	STUFF	WHIP	ERA	PERA	EQERA	EQH9	EQBB9	EQSO9	EQHR9	VORP	WXRL
2004	HIC	A	20	10	4	1	27	20	144	121	46	140	16	—	.279	-5	1.16	3.13	5.91	4.00	8.8	3.4	5.3	1.7	24.8	—
2005	KCA	MLB	21	3	2	0	41	0	53²	73	18	32	9	37.9%	.354	-14	1.70	7.54	5.15	6.32	10.7	2.8	5.1	1.4	-10.5	-0.57
2006	WIC	AA	22	1	2	3	15	0	21²	18	12	22	3	47.4%	.278	3	1.42	4.25	6.08	4.64	8.0	5.1	6.8	1.7	2.3	—
2006	OMA	AAA	22	2	2	5	23	0	38²	37	13	33	5	35.7%	.299	-1	1.31	2.12	5.00	2.79	8.6	3.0	6.1	1.4	12.1	—
2006	KCA	MLB	22	0	0	0	7	0	13¹	15	5	7	2	46.5%	.317	-10	1.50	4.74	5.66	3.86	9.0	3.2	4.5	1.3	2.2	0.04
2007	KCA	MLB	23	2	4	2	70	0	65²	83	27	40	13	40.0%	.318	-14	1.68	6.37	6.08	5.66	10.4	3.6	5.1	1.5	-3.9	0.40

Breakout: 6%　Improve: 27%　Collapse: 45%　Attrition: 5%　　Comparables: Johann Lopez, Enmanuel Ulloa, Jason Anderson, Shane Bazzell

In 2005, Nuñez was inexplicably rushed to Kansas City with barely a month's experience above Low-A ball and was predictably abused by major league hitters. Last season, he had the luxury of competing at a level commensurate with his experience, pitching well enough in the high minors to warrant another look. He's got a string-bean physique, but has legitimate mid-90s heat and good control; think Julian Tavarez minus the anger management issues.

Joel Peralta
Bats: R　Throws: R　Height: 5' 11"　Weight: 180　Born: March 23, 1976　Age: 31

YEAR	TEAM	LVL	AGE	W	L	SV	G	GS	IP	H	BB	SO	HR	GB%	BABIP	STUFF	WHIP	ERA	PERA	EQERA	EQH9	EQBB9	EQSO9	EQHR9	VORP	WXRL
2004	SLC	AAA	28	4	2	1	39	0	56	64	18	68	6	—	.379	8	1.46	4.98	3.94	4.68	9.4	3.0	8.0	0.9	5.9	—
2005	SLC	AAA	29	4	1	10	19	0	20	11	6	18	0	34.0%	.216	7	0.85	2.70	3.85	2.70	4.9	2.7	5.8	0.0	6.4	—
2005	ANA	MLB	29	1	0	0	28	0	34²	28	14	30	6	33.7%	.239	3	1.21	3.89	4.87	4.04	7.1	3.5	7.6	1.5	7.1	0.85
2006	KCA	MLB	30	1	3	1	64	0	73²	74	17	57	10	32.1%	.299	4	1.24	4.40	3.99	3.99	8.1	1.9	6.5	1.1	13.4	0.76
2007	KCA	MLB	31	2	3	3	52	0	59²	64	18	46	9	38.0%	.299	0	1.38	4.69	4.45	4.16	8.9	2.6	6.4	1.2	7.5	0.60

Breakout: 20%　Improve: 41%　Collapse: 26%　Attrition: 20%　　Comparables: Luis Vizcaino, Shigetoshi Hasegawa, Cliff Politte, Nelson Cruz

You've heard of LOOGYs; Peralta is that much-rarer specimen, the ROOGY. Most right-handed, one-out guys are sidearmers, making them easy to identify. Peralta has gone under the radar in large part because he isn't a sidearmer; his platoon split is the result of the vicious slider he uses as his out-pitch. During his two-year career, righties have hit .219/.258/.376 against him, while lefties have hit .311/.387/.593. Peralta has faced right-handed hitters in 65 percent of his matchups, which is why his overall numbers appear so favorable, but he's a situational pitcher until he proves otherwise.

Odalis Perez
Bats: L　Throws: L　Height: 6' 0"　Weight: 220　Born: June 11, 1977　Age: 30

YEAR	TEAM	LVL	AGE	W	L	SV	G	GS	IP	H	BB	SO	HR	GB%	BABIP	STUFF	WHIP	ERA	PERA	EQERA	EQH9	EQBB9	EQSO9	EQHR9	VORP	WXRL
2004	LAN	MLB	27	7	6	0	31	31	196¹	180	44	128	26	—	.272	10	1.14	3.26	4.25	3.80	8.5	1.8	5.3	1.1	49.4	6.30
2005	LVG	AAA	28	1	0	0	4	4	14²	14	4	11	1	40.0%	.302	3	1.22	4.29	3.82	3.52	7.0	2.3	4.7	0.6	3.5	—
2005	LAN	MLB	28	7	8	0	19	19	108²	109	28	74	13	47.1%	.292	9	1.26	4.55	4.12	4.89	9.0	2.1	5.6	1.1	8.2	2.06
2006	LAN	MLB	29	4	4	0	20	8	59¹	89	13	33	9	50.4%	.372	-12	1.72	6.83	4.44	6.82	12.3	1.7	4.5	1.2	-9.4	-0.52
2006	KCA	MLB	29	2	4	0	12	12	67	80	18	48	9	43.0%	.332	10	1.46	5.64	4.11	5.14	9.6	2.2	5.9	1.0	1.9	0.68
2007	KCA	MLB	30	7	9	1	34	20	132¹	156	34	77	17	48.0%	.314	1	1.44	4.97	4.63	4.48	9.8	2.2	4.9	1.0	11.0	2.00

Breakout: 28%　Improve: 68%　Collapse: 12%　Attrition: 8%　　Comparables: Alex Kellner, Dave Lapoint, Paul Splittorff, Brian Bohanon

As a Dodger last season, Perez surrendered a whopping .372 batting average on balls in play. For all the explanations as to why he flunked his way off the team last year—he lost his stuff, had a bad attitude, was tanking—the explanation for which we have the most evidence was overlooked: He was simply horrendously unlucky on the mound. The Royals don't have All-Star aspirations for him; they're simply thrilled they've got a starting pitcher who can throw strikes.

Mark Redman
Bats: L　Throws: L　Height: 6' 5"　Weight: 245　Born: January 5, 1974　Age: 33

YEAR	TEAM	LVL	AGE	W	L	SV	G	GS	IP	H	BB	SO	HR	GB%	BABIP	STUFF	WHIP	ERA	PERA	EQERA	EQH9	EQBB9	EQSO9	EQHR9	VORP	WXRL
2004	OAK	MLB	30	11	12	0	32	32	191	218	68	102	28	—	.308	-4	1.50	4.71	4.92	4.95	10.0	2.9	4.4	1.1	23.4	3.63
2005	PIT	MLB	31	5	15	0	30	30	178¹	188	56	101	18	50.5%	.305	5	1.37	4.90	4.29	4.99	9.3	2.6	4.6	0.9	11.0	2.71
2006	KCA	MLB	32	11	10	0	29	29	167	202	63	76	19	46.1%	.324	-4	1.59	5.71	4.88	5.15	9.8	3.1	3.8	0.9	4.1	1.72
2007	KCA	MLB	33	7	11	0	29	26	148	183	54	73	21	47.0%	.315	-6	1.60	5.68	5.36	5.13	10.2	3.1	4.1	1.1	0.4	1.20

Breakout: 13%　Improve: 48%　Collapse: 24%　Attrition: 5%　　Comparables: Paul Splittorff, Bill Krueger, Charlie Leibrandt, Ron Villone

A finesse lefty with borderline velocity in his best years, Redman has lost what little margin for error he had. The Royals wanted him for the innings, and they got that, but, in the future, they might want to be a bit more particular on the quality of those innings. Redman's durability and portsidedness will get him another shot, but he'll need an airtight defense behind him to make good on it.

Andy Sisco | **Bats: L Throws: L** | Height: 6' 10" Weight: 270 Born: January 13, 1983 Age: 24

YEAR	TEAM	LVL	AGE	W	L	SV	G	GS	IP	H	BB	SO	HR	GB%	BABIP	STUFF	WHIP	ERA	PERA	EQERA	EQH9	EQBB9	EQSO9	EQHR9	VORP	WXRL
2004	DAY	A+	21	4	10	0	26	25	126	118	65	134	11	—	.325	-4	1.45	4.21	6.22	5.43	9.8	5.4	6.5	1.6	2.3	—
2005	KCA	MLB	22	2	5	0	67	0	75¹	68	42	76	6	42.2%	.313	25	1.46	3.11	3.94	2.96	7.1	4.8	8.5	0.7	21.3	0.22
2006	KCA	MLB	23	1	3	1	65	0	58¹	66	40	52	8	39.8%	.345	1	1.82	7.10	5.04	6.34	9.3	5.6	7.4	1.0	-7.1	-1.23
2007	CHA	MLB	24	3	3	2	56	0	56	54	32	54	7	41.0%	.300	8	1.52	4.57	4.31	4.19	8.5	4.7	8.2	1.0	8.3	0.70

Breakout: 33% Improve: 72% Collapse: 13% Attrition: 26%   Comparables: Dennys Reyes, Bart Johnson, Rich Gossage, Brian Bruney

Sisquatch had a sophomore season as disappointing as his rookie season was promising. His slider flattened out, he lost command of his fastball, and his ERA more than doubled. Lefties smacked him to the tune of .318/.430/.489, which for a southpaw with his height and arm angle is unforgivable. The Royals' frustration with Sisco was understandable, but so was the White Sox' interest. He still has three major assets: his physique, his stuff, and his youth. Now he's working with a pitching coach, Don Cooper, who has had success processing raw arms into finished pitchers. The Royals sent him to winter ball in Mexico as a starter, and the White Sox say they'll let Sisco decide which role suits him best.

Todd Wellemeyer | **Bats: R Throws: R** | Height: 6' 3" Weight: 205 Born: August 30, 1978 Age: 28

YEAR	TEAM	LVL	AGE	W	L	SV	G	GS	IP	H	BB	SO	HR	GB%	BABIP	STUFF	WHIP	ERA	PERA	EQERA	EQH9	EQBB9	EQSO9	EQHR9	VORP	WXRL
2004	IOW	AAA	25	1	1	0	14	4	23	24	12	23	2	—	.333	0	1.57	3.91	5.34	4.30	9.8	5.1	7.0	0.8	3.3	—
2004	CHN	MLB	25	2	1	0	20	0	24¹	27	20	30	1	—	.413	20	1.93	5.93	3.66	5.68	9.9	6.4	9.6	0.4	-0.3	0.46
2005	IOW	AAA	26	3	2	0	12	12	53²	47	25	48	2	37.0%	.300	16	1.34	3.02	3.94	3.48	7.6	4.0	6.0	0.3	12.8	—
2005	CHN	MLB	26	2	1	1	22	0	32¹	32	22	32	7	48.3%	.305	0	1.67	6.13	5.98	6.00	9.0	5.5	8.2	1.9	-3.1	0.41
2006	KCA	MLB	27	1	2	1	28	0	57	48	37	37	5	52.7%	.265	5	1.49	3.63	5.08	3.49	6.8	5.3	5.3	0.6	14.0	0.42
2006	FLO	MLB	27	0	2	0	18	0	21¹	20	13	17	1	45.9%	.317	1	1.55	5.49	4.24	5.32	8.2	4.5	6.5	0.4	0.9	-0.37
2007	KCA	MLB	28	3	4	2	47	1	67²	72	39	50	8	44.0%	.306	-6	1.63	5.12	4.96	4.62	8.7	4.9	6.2	0.9	4.8	0.40

Breakout: 16% Improve: 38% Collapse: 36% Attrition: 22%   Comparables: Dennis Higgins, Charlie Williams, Don Stanhouse, Jose Paniagua

Twenty different pitchers threw at least 15 innings for the Royals last year; Wellemeyer's ERA led them all by nearly a full run. The team shouldn't read too much into that, given that he walked as many as he struck out. They're talking about giving him a shot in the rotation in the spring, which is silly; Wellemeyer is still a thrower, not a pitcher, and he may never make the transition. His best chance would seem to be one inning at a time, not seven. Becoming the next Kyle Farnsworth is a best-case scenario.

Lineouts

PLAYER	TEAM	LVL	AGE	PA	R	2B	3B	HR	RBI	BB	SO	SB-CS	SPEED	AVG/OBP/SLG	MLVr	EqAVG/EqOBP/EqSLG	EqA	VORP
SS M. Aviles	OMA	AAA	25	502	52	21	3	8	47	28	48	14-5	5.5	.264/.307/.373	-.095	.252/.289/.353	.227	-7.2
SS J. Bianchi	ROY	Rk	19	54	13	4	0	2	6	9	3	1-1	4.7	.429/.537/.667	.821	.340/.418/.511	.317	14.6
OF D. Brown*	WIC	AA	28	422	56	22	0	16	78	24	64	0-0	4.0	.307/.346/.490	.161	.249/.275/.367	.225	-19.7
2B D. Murphy	WIC	AA	23	395	57	25	1	14	45	19	65	6-3	4.4	.249/.300/.437	-.044	.227/.265/.398	.227	-6.0
C P. Phillips	OMA	AAA	29	375	43	11	1	9	39	22	37	0-0	3.6	.243/.286/.359	-.167	.222/.259/.313	.203	-20.0
	KCA	MLB	29	69	8	3	0	1	5	1	8	0-0	5.2	.277/.284/.369	-.199	.266/.284/.344	.222	-1.2
1B M. Stodolka*	HDS	A+	24	513	81	33	2	11	67	78	103	4-3	4.8	.284/.396/.449	.067	.217/.307/.329	.229	-23.3
C M. Tupman*	WIC	AA	26	280	35	8	1	1	31	48	27	1-1	4.7	.305/.425/.364	.115	.277/.371/.328	.255	6.1
	OMA	AAA	26	81	9	0	0	0	4	8	6	0-0	3.7	.247/.321/.247	-.258	.230/.296/.230	.198	-5.2

PLAYER	TEAM	LVL	AGE	W	L	SV	IP	H	BB	SO	HR	GB%	BABIP	STUFF	WHIP	ERA	PERA	EqERA	EqH9	EqBB9	EqSO9	EqHR9	VORP
A. Bernero	SWB	AAA	29	1	1	0	25²	11	4	17	2	—	.138	9	0.60	1.79	4.73	2.96	5.2	1.5	4.4	1.1	7.1
	OMA	AAA	29	5	3	1	79¹	64	23	47	5	—	.253	4	1.10	2.84	4.47	3.26	7.0	2.6	3.9	0.8	20.8
	KCA	MLB	29	1	0	0	13	15	0	12	0	—	.366	13	1.15	1.38	2.13	1.35	9.4	0.7	7.4	0.0	6.8
S. Dohmann	COL	MLB	28	1	1	1	24²	26	15	22	4	—	.324	-3	1.66	6.19	5.24	5.61	9.1	4.6	7.0	1.1	-0.8
	KCA	MLB	28	1	3	0	23²	33	18	22	5	—	.412	-4	2.15	7.97	6.13	6.84	11.5	6.1	7.6	1.4	-4.6
B. Duckworth	IND	AAA	30	8	3	0	74	67	23	57	4	—	.292	10	1.22	2.43	4.43	3.86	9.0	3.2	5.1	0.7	14.0
	KCA	MLB	30	1	5	0	45²	62	24	27	3	—	.376	-1	1.88	6.11	4.40	6.14	11.0	4.3	4.8	0.6	-4.9
N. Musser*	TUC	AAA	25	1	3	0	36	44	24	18	4	—	.328	-17	1.89	5.50	6.82	6.38	10.8	5.9	3.4	1.2	-3.2
	WIC	AA	25	6	3	2	83	80	48	67	12	—	.294	-23	1.54	4.99	7.48	6.83	9.5	6.0	4.9	2.0	-11.0
J. Plummer	HDS	A+	22	11	5	10	95²	92	20	114	11	—	.331	-6	1.18	4.07	5.03	4.64	9.3	2.1	6.6	1.7	10.1
M. Wood	KCA	MLB	26	3	3	0	64²	86	23	29	10	—	.323	-20	1.69	5.70	5.53	6.12	10.9	2.9	3.7	1.2	-7.1

Former Division II Player of the Year **Mike Aviles** has topped out in Triple-A with a bat that's marginal for a shortstop and a glove that plays best at third base. The Royals' second-round pick in 2005, **Jeff Bianchi** has only played in 40 professional games in two seasons, having been hampered by a chronic shoulder problem that finally necessitated surgery last summer. He still ranks among the team's best prospects, because in that time he's hit .414/.500/.721. He's stretched at shortstop, and with the shoulder injury he's likely to end up at second, where some scouts project him as another Michael Young. He's on the short list of minor league breakout candidates this season. Former first-round pick and Top-20 prospect **Dee Brown** has seemingly regressed as a hitter every year since he turned 21; last year he was reduced to providing veteran lineup protection for Gordon and Butler in Double-A Wichita. He signed a minor league deal with the Diamondbacks. **Donald Murphy** is a second base prospect who has shown speed, power, plate discipline, and the ability to hit for average in his minor league career, but never any of them at the same time. Sold to the A's after the season; the fourth word of this sentence should make the Royals a little bit nervous that they missed something. **Paul Phillips** has stayed healthy the last three years, but his performance has declined in each of the last two. Taken off the 40-man after the season, his defense could make him a marginal backup somewhere. The fourth overall pick in the 2000 draft (probably the weakest draft class of the last 20 years), **Mike Stodolka**'s career as a pitcher was so fraught with failure that, in 2005, Baseball America named him the worst number-four pick of all time. That year, he was moved to first base; despite not swinging a bat in anger in nearly six years, Stodolka hit for a .339 average with 12 doubles that April. Any performance in High Desert has to be taken with a clump of salt, but there's a small chance he could develop. A left-handed hitter with a .425 OBP in Double-A would normally get your attention, but **Mat Tupman** has no power, is slower than the Middle East peace process, and he's already turned 27. The lefty bat will likely keep him stashed away in Triple-A as a team's emergency catcher for a long time to come.

The quintessential Quadruple-A pitcher, **Adam Bernero** has the stuff of an undrafted pitcher and the savvy of a pitcher who made it to the majors in barely a year anyway. He's another player Allard Baird lured to Boston after the season. **Scott Dohmann** was a throw-in in the Shealy trade because of his blazing fastball; only after you've seen the guy on a daily basis do you realize why his previous team was so willing to part with him: Dohmann has no secondary pitch, no command, and generally no clue on the mound. The Royals saw all of that and released him. Like Bernero, **Brandon Duckworth** is a non-drafted free agent who zoomed to the majors, and he's also marginally above replacement-level. If they both wind up pitching for the same team again, that team will probably lose 100 games, too. The most surprising addition to the Royals' 40-man roster, **Neil Musser**, is 26 and is in his third organization in barely a year. He held left-handers to just 2 hits in 26 at-bats in the AFL, and the Royals think he can be groomed as a future LOOGY. Acquired from the Dodgers in a low-level trade before last season began, **Jarod Plummer** deserves a medal for toiling in High Desert all year and compiling a K/BB ratio of nearly six. He may have a modest future in middle relief. Finesse right-hander **Mike Wood** is effective when he has pinpoint control and gets hammered when he doesn't. A back injury last summer didn't help; he's an NRI with the Rangers.

Manager: Buddy Bell

Year	Team	W-L	Pythag +/-	Avg PC	100 +P	120 +P	QS	BQS	REL	REL w Zero R	IBB	SUBS	PH	PH Avg	PH HR	SB2	CS2	SB3	CS3	SAC Att	SAC %	POS SAC	Squeeze	Swing	In Play
2005	KCA	43-69	+1	88.5	25	0	32	6	308	174	17	15	95	.183	1	32	12	2	2	40	77.5%	29	2	72	61
2006	KCA	62-100	+1	89.8	46	5	46	10	473	241	45	32	91	.250	1	55	30	10	4	76	68.4%	48	2	110	81

Last season there were over 8,000 words written in the Royals chapter of this book, and Buddy Bell's name appeared only once. This year, his name does not appear outside of this comment. There is a good reason for this: Bell is the perfect managerial cipher, a man who, at his best, makes no contribution to his team good or bad, and whose personality seems to take on the traits of whatever team he happens to be managing. This is not a flattering thing to say about a man whose teams have had a .416 winning percentage, but Bell has shown precious little talent for molding the young and building the squads he has been entrusted with into competitive teams. As a tactician, he is notable only for his lack of notability; he uses the bunt, the stolen base, pinch-hitters, defensive replacements, and so on about as often as his peers do on average. This is less a reflection of moderation on his part than a lack of ambition. Bell's teams don't appear to have a niche philosophy on how to win other than to do so on talent, which is hardly a sound strategy when your teams are routinely outmuscled on the talent front. Bell gets high marks for his character, his candor, and for a firm-yet-loving approach. His handling of Zack Greinke's personal difficulties was perhaps his finest hour last year. Bell left the team in late September to get the cancer in his throat removed. He needed neither radiation nor chemotherapy afterwards, and we all hope he will be 100 percent this spring. The Royals will eventually need a better in-game manager, but Bell is a perfectly harmless caretaker until the team is ready for the next step.

Los Angeles Angels of Anaheim

Having won the AL West in both 2004 and 2005, the Angels came into 2006 reasonably confident of their ability to repeat. The Rangers didn't seem poised for a 90-win season, the Mariners seemed comfortably mired in last place, and the A's were going to have to rely on their usual balance of retreads and homegrown talent, which might make them strong enough to challenge, but then again it might not. In contrast, the Angels had what looked to be a particularly potent rotation, one of the best bullpens in baseball, a lineup built around Vlad Guerrero, and one of the best tacticians in the game in Mike Scioscia skippering the club. Beyond the veteran talent, the Angels had so much young, improving, or nearly-ready new blood that the team could plausibly anticipate a mini-dynasty establishing itself. As master plans go, it's hard to criticize.

As so often happens, the Angels learned that what seems like a sure thing on paper doesn't respond to reality once you start playing the games (as Moltke the Elder said, no battle plan ever survives contact with the enemy). The A's got off to their typical slow start, but the Angels weren't in a position to take advantage due to debilitating problems in the rotation and the lineup. Three months into the season, the Angels' were languishing at 35–44, seven games behind the A's, and looking up at everyone, even the Mariners.

The rotation issues were particularly ugly in the early going. After shoulder trouble knocked him out of the 2005 playoffs, defending Cy Young winner Bartolo Colon clearly wasn't himself in the early going, making his decision to participate in the World Baseball Classic all the more

regrettable. Colon went on the DL after three April starts, and replacements Hector Carrasco and Kevin Gregg did little better in his place. Meanwhile, Jeff Weaver, a late-winter addition thought to be a solid one-year replacement for departed free agent Jarrod Washburn, made a run at stealing Losing Pitcher Mulcahy's nickname by tallying a 3–10 record over the season's first three months (see table 1).

Before the arrival of Jered Weaver, the Colon/Jeff Weaver slots of the rotation were generating "winnable" ballgames less than a third of the time, which is unacceptable for a fifth starter, let alone from two expensive veterans. None of the other three were able to pick up the slack (Santana caught fire with 5 quality stars in 5 attempts in June, but had just 4 quality starts in 11 attempts over the first two months). Hobbled by a lineup that wasn't delivering a ton of runs, the Angels were going to be hard-pressed to defend their division title while getting this sort of performance from their rotation.

Having witnessed three months of frustration, GM Bill Stoneman and Scioscia started making changes. After turning in quality starts in his first four major league games, Jered Weaver had been returned to Salt Lake City when Colon was activated in mid-June, but, by the end of the month, Stoneman and Scioscia had seen enough of his older brother, discarded their one Weaver too many, and plugged Weaver the Younger into the rotation to stay. Armed with a full rotation for the first time all year, the Angels rattled off a 13–1 record to open July, getting 11 quality starts in that 14-game stretch. Jered Weaver would give the team 10 quality starts (with two more blown) in his 15 appearances after being put into the rotation to stay.

ANGELS PROSPECTUS

2006 record: 89–73; Second place, AL West

Pythagenport record: 84–78

Runs scored per game: 4.73 (11th in AL)

Runs allowed per game: 4.52 (4th in AL)

Team EqA: .259 (7th in AL)

2006 Batters Age: 29.3 (7th youngest in AL)

2006 Pitchers Age: 28.5 (7th youngest in AL)

Ballpark: Angel Stadium; Moderate pitcher's park; Park Factor of .962

2006: Gaping holes in the lineup led to a regrouping season, while Oakland raced on ahead.

2007: The first year of the ill-advised Gary Matthews Jr. contract doesn't mask the arrival of some tremendous talent.

Table 1. Angel Rotation Performance, April–June

Starting Pitcher	QS	BQS	NonQS
John Lackey	10	0	6
Ervin Santana	9	0	7
Jeff Weaver	5	2	9
Kelvim Escobar	8	2	5
Bartolo Colon	1	0	5
Jered Weaver	4	0	0
Hector Carrasco	1	0	2
Kevin Gregg	1	0	2

NOTE: QS: Quality Starts; BQS: Blown Quality Starts; NonQS: Non-Quality Starts.

Colon gave the team three quality starts in July before breaking down for good in his fourth start, but his replacement, Joe Saunders, would make 8 quality starts in his 13. From July 1 to season's end, the Angels would go 54–29, a tremendous .651 pace that could have propelled the team into the playoffs but for the fact that Oakland had kick started their season a month earlier with an 18–8 record in June. The risk the A's had taken on Frank Thomas had paid off and once Milton Bradley made a triumphant return from the DL in mid-July, Oakland had an insurmountable advantage.

So what's the lesson here? Jeff Weaver's failings make for an easy target, but he had provided the Dodgers with two years of good work in 2004 and 2005, so you can't really blame Stoneman and Scioscia for trying to be patient with him. The more difficult problem was Colon. Considering his shoulder problems at the end of 2005 and the fact that conditioning was never the big man's strong suit, letting him participate in MLB's latest self-indulgent internationalist event was indefensible. Perhaps Colon's shoulder would have given out at some later date, but his responsibility should have been to the Angels' 2006 season. Instead, the Angels gambled with the $26 million they'd already committed to Colon for 2006 and 2007 and lost both financially and on the field. Happily, even without Colon, the Angels' rotation is set for the next three years with Lackey and Escobar under contract through 2009, and Weaver, Saunders, and Santana under team control for a few seasons beyond that.

The problems with the Angels' lineup are more involved. Since winning the World Series in 2002, the Angels, once a mid-pack team in overall attendance, have moved up into the paying-customer stratosphere, topping three million in attendance in each of the last four years. The Angels didn't just get the standard post-championship attendance spike; they've leveraged their crown into a full-fledged exploitation of the second-largest media market in the country, putting themselves in the big-spender category with the New York teams, the Dodgers, and the Red Sox, able to go toe-to-toe with them when bidding on any player.

The problem is how they've invested that capital. In the spring of 2004, following Garret Anderson's finest pair of seasons at the plate, the Angels gave him a four-year, $48-million contract extension. That extension reflects both an admirable loyalty to a homegrown player who now holds many of the team's all-time records and a poor investment strategy. The money spent on Anderson might have made sense if he had the broad base of skills that would have sustained his production through 2008. The problem is, he doesn't. Anderson hadn't been a quality center fielder since 1999, and was never much of a basepath commando, swiping bags at a harmful 61 percent success rate through 2001 (the last season he stole more than six bases). What that left was a DH or left fielder with an admirable ability to make contact with power and a powerful aversion to ball four, something short of a premium hitter at a premium power position.

At another premium power position, the club's inability to find a productive first baseman continues to cost them wins. To some extent, this problem goes back to the team being burned by its decision to sign Mo Vaughn to a big-money contract in 1999 (see table 2). Since their two seasons with the big man at first, the Angels have lurched from adequate temping by Scott Spiezio to popularity-contest casting with Darin Erstad. Last year promised to provide a change, as the organization felt that Casey Kotchman was finally ready to step in and provide quality offense at first base. Unfortunately, Kotchman contracted mononucleosis before the season and lost the year to his recovery. In his absence, the team tried three alternatives—calling up blue chip prospects Kendry Morales and Howie Kendrick as well as toying with a platoon of Dallas McPherson and Robb Quinlan. The problem was that none of these alternatives wound up being as attractive in reality as they might have seemed in the abstract. Morales floundered,

Table 2. Angel First Basemen: First is for Hitters?

Year	PA	AVG/OBP/SLG	MLV	VORP	20+ GS
2000	732	.271/.358/.498	14.6	12.4	Vaughn 147
2001	660	.273/.320/.435	-4.5	-9.2	Spiezio 88, Joyner 31
2002	670	.291/.373/.451	22.2	18.7	Spiezio 125, Fullmer 27
2003	665	.293/.362/.492	29.9	35.3	Spiezio 89, Wooten 27
2004	706	.280/.334/.378	-11.3	8.0	Erstad 124, Kotchman 27
2005	727	.271/.324/.379	-9.4	1.6	Erstad 144
2006	656	.255/.297/.367	-27.8	-17.7	Morales 49, Quinlan 46, Kendrick 42, Kotchman 22

natural second baseman Kendrick was obviously out of place, and McPherson's upside now seems to be teetering between overstated and nonexistent.

A similar problem has existed at third base for much of the last four years, beginning with the injury problems that contributed to Troy Glaus's decline and departure. Even moreso than first base, third base has cost the Angels runs at a premium offensive position. Because of the injury to Erstad last year, Chone Figgins ended up playing more center field than third base, forcing the club to review McPherson, Quinlan, and a washed-up Edgardo Alfonzo before resorting to Maicer Izturis. Although Izturis did an admirable job as fill-in, the Angels still didn't receive anything approaching the sort of production they got during Glaus's heyday (see table 3).

Table 3. Angel Third Base Production: Cooling Off the Hot Corner

Year	PA	AVG/OBP/SLG	MLV	VORP	20+ GS
2000	695	.281/.398/.605	49.4	74.0	Glaus 155
2001	717	.250/.367/.532	26.2	52.3	Glaus 158
2002	720	.256/.354/.462	16.0	39.2	Glaus 153
2003	672	.236/.314/.397	−11.4	13.7	Glaus 86, Spiezio 43
2004	675	.300/.359/.483	21.9	35.2	Figgins 80, Quinlan 28, Halter 22
2005	674	.244/.305/.387	−15.3	4.5	McPherson 55, Figgins 48, Quinlan 30, Izturis 26
2006	707	.265/.330/.405	−9.1	15.0	Izturis 78, Figgins 32, McPherson 25

Keep in mind, MLV (Marginal Lineup Value) is a metric that looks at value relative to an average player at a position, while VORP calculates a player's value compared to a replacement player. Some of the struggles at third base can be attributed to Glaus's injuries in 2003 and 2004, and some of the stronger numbers in the above chart reflect Mike Scioscia's admirable tactical flexibility in employing moving parts such as Figgins, Spiezio, and Quinlan where needed, but there comes a point at which being able to make do becomes less a virtue than a reflection of a basic weakness. First and third base are premium offensive positions and, between them, the 2006 Angels were down about ten wins from where they were in 2000 (according to MLV). Getting those wins back from up-the-middle positions and the pitching staff is no easy feat, but that's effectively what the Angels were forced to do. It's no surprise that they failed.

Fortunately, the Angels' lineup problems are well on their way to being sorted out, which is a credit to Stone-man's patience. The old homegrown core of the lineup, which was down to Anderson, Erstad, and Tim Salmon last year, is slowly being turned over to a new homegrown core, an impressive feat for any organization. Replacing Adam Kennedy with Kendrick should add runs to the lineup from second, and Brandon Wood will eventually take over at third base and give the team production not unlike what Glaus provided in his better seasons. Those improvements in performance should make it easier to afford the indulgence of carrying Anderson as the last formerly-famous Angel left standing.

Wood is merely the best of a host of shortstop prospects coming up through the system, but, because his bat will play well at third, he has a ready outlet for his ability at the major league level. The others are all going to have to wait out the last two years of Orlando Cabrera's four-year contract. For the younger talents deeper down in the system, players such as Sean Rodriguez or Hainley Statia, that's not the end of the world—they'll have mastered the upper levels (or not) by the time Cabrera's a free agent. More problematic is deciding what to do with Erick Aybar, who's about as ready for the major leagues as he's ever going to be. Offering Aybar in trade to get Miguel Tejada for last year's stretch drive made sense at the time, and that's probably Aybar's immediate utility to the ballclub—a prize to pitch for veteran players who might help secure a division title. The Angels could also invert the concept in the unlikely event that they flounder in 2007, peddling Cabrera to create an opportunity for Aybar; either way, the Angels have shortstops at a time when teams are overpaying for the services of Alex Gonzalez and resuscitating Royce Clayton.

Similarly, what the Angels' system lacks in depth amongst its pitching prospects, it makes up for in quality. Young hurlers such as Nick Adenhart, Stephen Marek, and Tommy Mendoza all have the kind of potential upside that make them plausible follow-ups to Lackey, Santana, Jered Weaver, and perhaps Joe Saunders. Churning out homegrown starting pitchers with that sort of ability spares you the expense of having to sign veterans like Bartolo Colon and Kelvim Escobar. That will be particularly important in the years to come should the market for free agent pitching escalate any further.

What remains is for the Angels to spend their money effectively to fix the problems the team still has. Unfortunately, the Angels aren't doing that. Rather than wait and see if either Kotchman or Morales can become a solid offensive contributor at first base, the Angels decided to hedge their bets against a repeat of 2006 by signing Shea Hillenbrand to a one-year, $6.5-million contract (with a club option for 2008). The potential for surprise here is almost entirely negative—Hillenbrand will either be mediocre or disappointing, and neither result really helps the team compete with the rest of the league at first base.

Even more disappointing is the decision to sign Gary Matthews Jr. to a five-year, $50-million deal. Not only is Matthews unlikely to repeat his nifty 2006 season, let alone build on it at the age of 32, the expenditure fixes a problem the Angels didn't really have. Even if Wood doesn't win the third base job until 2008, where does Chone Figgins go once Wood's up to stay? Figgy's offense is sufficient to be a regular in center, but for the money being paid to Matthews, Little Sarge is going to have to play. Stoneman would have been better off taking advantage of Figgins's flexibility and Wood's imminent arrival by striking a shorter deal for someone like Kenny Lofton.

The Angels have the talent and the financial muscle to win their division. It would be a pity if they lacked the brains to exploit those qualities, because what's at stake is more than just AL West bragging rights—this team could see attendance track its non-achievement, costing Arte Moreno millions in the process. Misfortunes such as what befell the team's 2006 Opening Day rotation can be considered coincidental for only so long, and the Matthews contract, like those of Anderson and the finally-off-the-books Erstad, will be a significant handicap for years to come. The rotation has the talent to deliver titles, but it's going to be up to Stoneman to make sure the team converts potential into victory by putting a lineup on the field that can score enough runs to turn winnable ballgames into wins. The early returns are inauspicious.

HITTERS

Garret Anderson   **LF**   **Bats: L**   **Throws: L**   Height: 6' 3"   Weight: 225   Born: June 30, 1972   Age: 35

YEAR	TEAM	LVL	AGE	PA	R	2B	3B	HR	RBI	BB	SO	SB	CS	SPEED	AVG	OBP	SLG	MLVR	EQAVG	EQOBP	EQSLG	EQA	VORP	DEFENSE	
2004	ANA	MLB	32	475	57	20	1	14	75	29	75	2	1	4.9	.301	.343	.446	.071	.305	.352	.453	.276	21.1	80-CF	0
2005	ANA	MLB	33	603	68	34	1	17	96	23	84	1	1	4.0	.283	.308	.435	.004	.290	.325	.456	.265	11.2	102-LF	-8
2006	ANA	MLB	34	588	63	28	2	17	85	38	95	1	0	4.2	.280	.323	.433	-.015	.283	.333	.445	.268	9.0	91-LF	3
2007	ANA	MLB	35	529	59	26	2	15	72	31	87	2	1	4.5	.275	.318	.427	-.053	.273	.321	.439	.265	7.5	124-LF	-3

Breakout: 15%   Improve: 39%   Collapse: 27%   Attrition: 15%   Comparables: B. J. Surhoff, Dante Bichette, Dave Parker, Brian Jordan

Honorary recipient of the scarlet letter from Erstad: M for "Millstone." He's not evil, and he's not terrible; the problem is that he's a professional hitter being paid a superstar's wage, and with Juan Rivera outshining him in every phase of the game, shunting Anderson off to the DH role only sticks the team with an unexceptional DH. He's due at least $26 million over the next two years, handicapping the team's ability to pay or play someone with more ability to hurt the other guys.

Erick Aybar   **SS**   **Bats: S**   **Throws: R**   Height: 5' 10"   Weight: 170   Born: January 14, 1984   Age: 23

YEAR	TEAM	LVL	AGE	PA	R	2B	3B	HR	RBI	BB	SO	SB	CS	SPEED	AVG	OBP	SLG	MLVR	EQAVG	EQOBP	EQSLG	EQA	VORP	DEFENSE	
2004	RCU	A+	20	627	102	25	11	14	65	26	66	51	36	7.3	.330	.370	.485	.209	.287	.317	.406	.249	20.8	132-SS	3
2005	ARK	AA	21	590	101	29	10	9	54	29	51	49	23	8.6	.303	.350	.445	.078	.271	.315	.400	.252	16.3	133-SS	-9
2006	SLC	AAA	22	368	63	20	3	6	45	21	36	32	18	7.0	.283	.327	.413	-.067	.251	.291	.370	.231	-0.2	80-SS	-6
2006	ANA	MLB	22	40	5	1	1	0	2	0	8	1	0	7.3	.250	.250	.325	-.337	.225	.225	.300	.189	-1.2		
2007	ANA	MLB	23	452	55	20	3	6	39	20	46	26	12	6.7	.266	.304	.372	-.158	.264	.307	.383	.248	6.5	107-SS	-1

Breakout: 23%   Improve: 57%   Collapse: 18%   Attrition: 6%   Comparables: Eider Torres, Kenny Perez, Anderson Hernandez, William Bergolla

Burgeoning with Web-Gemmy goodness, Aybar has all the tools to be a great defensive shortstop and relishes showing off his ability—that's not a sin, is it? For better and worse, his key offensive skill is aggressiveness. He's not a slapper at the plate, making strong contact with some amount of power. On the bases, his big caught-stealing totals are a reflection of a player and an organization testing his limits; unless he spits the bit, he should end up stealing fewer at a better clip at the major league level. As promising as Aybar is, he still needs to show improvement at the plate before he starts making Stoneman wonder about dealing Orlando Cabrera before the latter's contract ends after 2008.

Matt Brown **3B** **Bats: R** **Throws: R** Height: 6' 0" Weight: 200 Born: August 8, 1982 Age: 24

YEAR	TEAM	LVL	AGE	PA	R	2B	3B	HR	RBI	BB	SO	SB	CS	SPEED	AVG	OBP	SLG	MLVR	EQAVG	EQOBP	EQSLG	EQA	VORP	DEFENSE	
2004	CDR	A	21	490	67	20	4	23	82	33	126	6	6	4.9	.233	.303	.455	.036	.201	.254	.374	.217	-16.8	111-3B	-1
2005	RCU	A+	22	547	68	39	4	12	65	40	125	4	5	4.0	.262	.329	.432	-.092	.223	.274	.336	.215	-17.9	119-3B	0
2006	ARK	AA	23	576	77	41	3	19	79	47	108	7	6	4.6	.293	.362	.495	.129	.261	.318	.439	.259	21.1	128-3B	-11
2007	ANA	MLB	24	509	50	26	2	14	61	30	114	4	2	4.6	.240	.291	.392	-.173	.238	.294	.403	.244	-2.3	120-3B	-3

Breakout: 32% Improve: 61% Collapse: 16% Attrition: 7%   Comparables: Corey Erickson, Joe Dillon, Greg Sain, Andy Phillips

Brown is a solidly unspectacular third base type—he can play third well enough, but not so well he'll wow people, and his hitting is similarly adequate. His likely future is as a trade throw-in; between Aybar and Wood, it would take a very strange combination of events for him to wind up threatening anyone beyond Robb Quinlan. He was added to the 40-man roster as a ripple effect of the additional year of protection teams acquired for their prospects in the new CBA.

Orlando Cabrera **SS** **Bats: R** **Throws: R** Height: 5' 9" Weight: 180 Born: November 2, 1974 Age: 32

YEAR	TEAM	LVL	AGE	PA	R	2B	3B	HR	RBI	BB	SO	SB	CS	SPEED	AVG	OBP	SLG	MLVR	EQAVG	EQOBP	EQSLG	EQA	VORP	DEFENSE	
2004	MON	MLB	29	425	41	19	2	4	31	28	31	12	3	5.5	.246	.298	.336	-.164	.238	.292	.326	.224	0.5	94-SS	0
2004	BOS	MLB	29	248	33	19	1	6	31	11	23	4	1	5.7	.294	.320	.465	.016	.288	.319	.465	.270	12.0	53-SS	-5
2005	ANA	MLB	30	587	70	28	3	8	57	38	50	21	2	6.5	.257	.309	.365	-.115	.266	.328	.386	.256	12.8	137-SS	0
2006	ANA	MLB	31	675	95	45	1	9	72	51	58	27	3	6.6	.282	.335	.404	-.035	.285	.345	.417	.273	29.5	147-SS	-1
2007	ANA	MLB	32	589	71	29	2	8	54	40	54	15	5	5.9	.270	.322	.381	-.112	.268	.325	.391	.258	15.1	138-SS	-2

Breakout: 22% Improve: 45% Collapse: 22% Attrition: 5%   Comparables: Phil Garner, Phil Rizzuto, Eric Young, Johnny Logan

Okay, so he isn't the star player of 2003, but he did bounce back to post a year that more closely resembled his 2001 and 2002 run-up to greatness, and he's still a solid major league shortstop. Add in swiping bases at a 80 or 90 percent clip and spraying the ball around pretty nicely at the plate, and you get a nice little player in his good years. The danger is that if he falls back to what he did in 2005, you've got the same guy, only he's chewing through a lot of outs to give you some pretty meager counting stats.

Darin Erstad **CF/1B** **Bats: L** **Throws: L** Height: 6' 2" Weight: 215 Born: June 4, 1974 Age: 33

YEAR	TEAM	LVL	AGE	PA	R	2B	3B	HR	RBI	BB	SO	SB	CS	SPEED	AVG	OBP	SLG	MLVR	EQAVG	EQOBP	EQSLG	EQA	VORP	DEFENSE	
2004	ANA	MLB	30	543	79	29	1	7	69	37	74	16	1	6.5	.295	.346	.400	-.007	.299	.354	.404	.271	14.0	114-1B	15
2005	ANA	MLB	31	663	86	33	3	7	66	47	109	10	3	5.9	.273	.325	.371	-.071	.280	.343	.386	.257	-0.7	142-1B	15
2006	ANA	MLB	32	105	8	8	1	0	5	6	18	1	1	5.2	.221	.279	.326	-.291	.223	.288	.319	.218	-3.7	25-CF	2
2007	ANA	MLB	33	306	31	13	1	3	26	21	46	3	2	5.3	.242	.297	.324	-.249	.240	.300	.334	.227	-9.7	74-1B	3

Breakout: 10% Improve: 31% Collapse: 43% Attrition: 38%   Comparables: Chris Singleton, Lenny Harris, Hal Morris, George Altman

Erstad's the boyfriend you really shouldn't keep: he might be popular and talented, but he's bad news. He spends all your money and never really quite delivers on any of his promises. If you only think of him in terms of how good you feel around him, you miss out on the more basic things. You know, like runs. To his credit, he didn't embarrass himself in center, but it's his athleticism that had people mooning over him in the first place. A bad ankle kept him off the field for most of the year, sparing the Angels from having to bench him out of self-interest; offseason surgery is supposed to have him ship-shape for spring, but the Angels have finally moved on.

Terry Evans **OF** **Bats: R** **Throws: R** Height: 6' 3" Weight: 200 Born: January 19, 1982 Age: 25

YEAR	TEAM	LVL	AGE	PA	R	2B	3B	HR	RBI	BB	SO	SB	CS	SPEED	AVG	OBP	SLG	MLVR	EQAVG	EQOBP	EQSLG	EQA	VORP	DEFENSE			
2004	PEO	A	22	409	48	21	1	13	59	35	105	8	3	4.9	.222	.301	.392	-.031	.190	.249	.315	.201	-37.2	73-RF	-1	15-CF	0
2004	PMB	A+	22	64	7	4	0	2	7	4	16	1	0	4.2	.224	.281	.397	-.030	.203	.250	.356	.217	-5.1	18-RF	-2		
2005	PMB	A+	23	425	34	16	1	8	47	29	110	12	6	4.0	.221	.285	.330	-.157	.203	.254	.294	.200	-41.8	103-RF	-12		
2006	PMB	A+	24	263	43	10	1	15	45	20	50	21	1	5.8	.311	.373	.550	.393	.295	.342	.516	.293	15.1	41-RF	3	18-CF	1
2006	SFD	AA	24	84	13	4	0	7	20	3	21	5	1	6.3	.307	.369	.640	.432	.295	.333	.603	.301	6.9	21-RF	2		
2006	ARK	AA	24	213	48	9	2	11	22	18	56	11	6	6.9	.309	.385	.553	.257	.278	.338	.495	.279	13.4	44-CF	3		
2007	ANA	MLB	25	516	53	21	2	14	58	30	138	13	5	5.1	.236	.288	.374	-.204	.234	.291	.385	.240	-10.5	122-RF	1		

Breakout: 18% Improve: 42% Collapse: 27% Attrition: 7%   Comparables: Nelson Cruz, Kirk Asche, Pete Tucci, Jason Michaels

The payoff for sending Jeff Weaver to the Cardinals, Evans was probably the biggest surprise breakout in the minor leagues last year. While he made a point of crediting his faith for renewed focus, the practical change he made was to stop swinging at the pitcher's pitch. His long swing still doesn't get a lot of scouts excited, and his range won't play in center on an everyday basis, but if he keeps doing what he just did, he'll start winning converts.

Chone Figgins   UT   Bats: S   Throws: R   Height: 5' 7"   Weight: 180   Born: January 22, 1978   Age: 29

YEAR	TEAM	LVL	AGE	PA	R	2B	3B	HR	RBI	BB	SO	SB	CS	SPEED	AVG	OBP	SLG	MLVR	EQAVG	EQOBP	EQSLG	EQA	VORP	DEFENSE			
2004	ANA	MLB	26	638	83	22	17	5	60	49	94	34	13	7.8	.296	.350	.419	.022	.302	.361	.435	.276	22.6	76-3B	-7	41-CF	-7
2005	ANA	MLB	27	720	113	25	10	8	57	64	101	62	17	8.0	.290	.352	.397	.021	.303	.374	.422	.283	29.7	48-3B	-2	44-CF	2
2006	ANA	MLB	28	683	93	23	8	9	62	65	100	52	16	7.8	.267	.336	.376	-.083	.273	.350	.388	.265	14.2	92-CF	1	31-3B	-7
2007	ANA	MLB	29	622	87	23	7	9	46	59	86	40	13	8.0	.258	.331	.374	-.113	.256	.334	.385	.264	8.0	145-CF	-2		

Breakout: 2%   Improve: 17%   Collapse: 31%   Attrition: 6%   Comparables: Don Buford, Ray Durham, Ryan Freel, Vince Coleman

Much as we might wish it, he's not the kinder, gentler Tony Phillips for a new generation, he's just Figgy, pretty useful ballplayer. The drop-off last season wasn't an injury, he just got off to a slow start and didn't turn it around—he still walked as often, and had as much power, but he lost that proverbial extra gork per week that makes all the difference. He also hasn't done anything against lefties in the last couple of years, which eats into his utility as an everyday leadoff man. Unlike most speedsters, he's not some slap-hitter who can easily be overpowered with men on base. With Gary Matthews Jr. signed for way too much for way too long and Juan Rivera recovering from a broken leg, he'll be going back to roving, splitting time between third, left, center, second, and wherever else Scioscia decides to plug him in on a day-to-day basis.

Nick Gorneault   OF   Bats: R   Throws: R   Height: 6' 3"   Weight: 220   Born: April 19, 1979   Age: 28

YEAR	TEAM	LVL	AGE	PA	R	2B	3B	HR	RBI	BB	SO	SB	CS	SPEED	AVG	OBP	SLG	MLVR	EQAVG	EQOBP	EQSLG	EQA	VORP	DEFENSE			
2004	ARK	AA	25	554	91	28	4	21	81	45	128	7	5	5.4	.281	.341	.481	.099	.240	.287	.395	.235	-18.6	54-RF	1	51-LF	3
2005	SLC	AAA	26	555	106	26	11	26	108	58	119	7	6	6.6	.293	.366	.551	.137	.246	.312	.445	.257	-1.4	62-LF	-2	59-RF	0
2006	SLC	AAA	27	452	66	25	9	15	78	38	106	6	4	6.2	.283	.343	.499	.074	.246	.301	.430	.248	-4.8	81-RF	-4		
2007	ANA	MLB	28	407	43	19	2	10	46	25	101	4	2	5.4	.247	.297	.390	-.161	.245	.300	.401	.246	-6.7	97-RF	0		

Breakout: 22%   Improve: 48%   Collapse: 28%   Attrition: 13%   Comparables: Brian Buchanan, Todd Dunn, Emil Brown, Jeff Deardorff

Gorneault is one of a type the Angels seem to collect—decent enough athletes with very little up-side. Like a lot of them, Gorneault was the beneficiary last year of a ballpark that made him look a little more special than he is, as he slugged a hundred points better in Utah than elsewhere. Corner outfielders who slug less than .450 in the PCL don't have great futures, and Gorneault's not young. If more platoon jobs existed, he could fill one against lefties.

Vladimir Guerrero   RF   Bats: R   Throws: R   Height: 6' 3"   Weight: 235   Born: February 9, 1976   Age: 31

YEAR	TEAM	LVL	AGE	PA	R	2B	3B	HR	RBI	BB	SO	SB	CS	SPEED	AVG	OBP	SLG	MLVR	EQAVG	EQOBP	EQSLG	EQA	VORP	DEFENSE	
2004	ANA	MLB	28	680	124	39	2	39	126	52	74	15	3	5.4	.337	.391	.598	.389	.342	.399	.613	.331	77.4	137-RF	0
2005	ANA	MLB	29	594	95	29	2	32	108	61	48	13	1	5.6	.317	.394	.565	.360	.328	.412	.600	.335	63.7	115-RF	2
2006	ANA	MLB	30	665	92	34	1	33	116	50	68	15	5	5.1	.329	.382	.552	.310	.335	.394	.573	.319	63.9	122-RF	-11
2007	ANA	MLB	31	636	105	38	2	30	109	46	63	12	3	5.3	.326	.380	.557	.272	.323	.384	.572	.324	55.8	148-RF	-2

Breakout: 2%   Improve: 47%   Collapse: 32%   Attrition: 0%   Comparables: Dave Winfield, Orlando Cepeda, Bob Watson, Hank Bauer

People might focus on Big Papi, but Vladi's the guy pitchers really least liked to face with men on in the AL, as he led the AL in intentional walks for the second year in a row. It's not hard to understand why—he's the best contact-with-power hitter in the league, his wrists haven't slowed down with age, and he had the league's highest first-pitch swing percentage. It's sort of the Jorge Bell skill set with better results. Guerrero's getting to a difficult point in a career for his skills—it's going to be hard for him to maintain this kind of production while walking unintentionally fewer than 30 times per year, but continuing to DH every fifth day or so will help keep the nagging concerns about his back at bay.

Maicer Izturis　　　　**INF**　　　**Bats: S**　**Throws: R**　　Height: 5′ 8″　　Weight: 160　　Born: September 12, 1980　Age: 26

YEAR	TEAM	LVL	AGE	PA	R	2B	3B	HR	RBI	BB	SO	SB	CS	SPEED	AVG	OBP	SLG	MLVR	EQAVG	EQOBP	EQSLG	EQA	VORP	DEFENSE		
2004	EDM	AAA	23	443	65	19	2	3	36	57	30	14	12	5.1	.338	.428	.423	.162	.326	.408	.404	.285	37.8	84-SS	-5	
2004	MON	MLB	23	121	10	5	2	1	4	10	20	4	0	6.7	.206	.286	.318	-.248	.194	.275	.306	.217	-1.8	23-SS	-2	
2005	ANA	MLB	24	210	18	8	4	1	15	17	21	9	3	6.0	.246	.306	.346	-.156	.255	.325	.362	.247	-0.4	31-3B -3	24-SS	-2
2006	ANA	MLB	25	399	64	21	3	5	44	38	35	14	6	6.7	.293	.365	.412	.043	.299	.378	.425	.280	13.9	79-3B	-10	
2007	ANA	MLB	26	521	74	24	4	6	42	50	48	17	6	6.3	.277	.351	.386	-.048	.275	.355	.396	.273	14.9	123-3B	-3	

Breakout: 7%　Improve: 30%　Collapse: 24%　Attrition: 15%　　Comparables: Bill Doran, Jerry Browne, Brian Roberts, Horace Clarke

Bill Stoneman doesn't get a lot of credit for his role in running things—Arte Moreno's money bought Vladi, Mike Scioscia or Bud Black helped fix this guy or that, and so on. But in one of the better deals in recent years, Stoneman not only got Juan Rivera for persona non grata Jose Guillen (a swap that would have worked straight up), he managed to snag Izturis on the side. Although Izturis is never going to be a star, he's an underrated defender, and he can help a team caught without a good player at second, short, or third.

Howie Kendrick　　　　**2B**　　　**Bats: R**　**Throws: R**　　Height: 5′ 10″　Weight: 195　　Born: July 12, 1983　　　Age: 23

YEAR	TEAM	LVL	AGE	PA	R	2B	3B	HR	RBI	BB	SO	SB	CS	SPEED	AVG	OBP	SLG	MLVR	EQAVG	EQOBP	EQSLG	EQA	VORP	DEFENSE		
2004	CDR	A	20	337	66	24	6	10	49	12	41	15	6	7.4	.367	.398	.578	.449	.328	.352	.519	.290	34.5	62-2B	6	
2005	RCU	A+	21	304	69	23	6	12	47	14	42	13	4	8.9	.384	.421	.638	.524	.339	.366	.542	.304	35.2	59-2B	5	
2005	ARK	AA	21	204	35	20	2	7	42	6	20	12	4	7.3	.342	.382	.579	.352	.307	.343	.526	.291	19.1	46-2B	1	
2006	SLC	AAA	22	312	57	25	6	13	62	12	48	11	3	7.2	.369	.408	.631	.443	.330	.363	.568	.307	37.8	59-2B	7	
2006	ANA	MLB	22	283	25	21	1	4	30	9	44	6	0	5.5	.285	.314	.416	-.053	.287	.324	.426	.263	5.0	39-1B -5	25-2B	4
2007	ANA	MLB	23	548	76	35	3	17	74	21	75	12	4	6.1	.304	.338	.483	.083	.301	.341	.496	.290	30.4	129-2B	12	

Breakout: 16%　Improve: 44%　Collapse: 28%　Attrition: 8%　　Comparables: Raul Mondesi, Jeffrey Hammonds, Tommy Davis, Jose Ortiz

A bumpy transition to the majors might have dulled some of the anticipation, but make no mistake about it—there are batting titles in Kendrick's bat. He has tremendous plate coverage and whip-quick wrists even Vladi might envy. It won't all be singles, either: 35 to 40 doubles and 15 to 20 homers are already in the forecast, and he's still shy of 24. Just when you might be thinking we've got a latter-day Rogers Hornsby in the making, keep in mind he's actually a solid defender at the keystone. He used to have problems turning the deuce, but he's worked at it to the point that he'll be perfectly acceptable.

Adam Kennedy　　　　**2B**　　　**Bats: L**　**Throws: R**　　Height: 6′ 0″　　Weight: 185　　Born: January 10, 1976　　Age: 31

YEAR	TEAM	LVL	AGE	PA	R	2B	3B	HR	RBI	BB	SO	SB	CS	SPEED	AVG	OBP	SLG	MLVR	EQAVG	EQOBP	EQSLG	EQA	VORP	DEFENSE	
2004	ANA	MLB	28	533	70	20	5	10	48	41	92	15	5	6.2	.278	.351	.406	-.012	.285	.359	.418	.272	20.7	132-2B	10
2005	ANA	MLB	29	460	49	23	0	2	37	29	64	19	4	6.1	.300	.354	.370	.002	.312	.374	.393	.276	17.3	123-2B	9
2006	ANA	MLB	30	503	50	26	6	4	55	39	72	16	10	5.8	.273	.334	.384	-.073	.280	.348	.404	.261	10.9	127-2B	11
2007	SLN	MLB	31	460	60	22	4	7	41	35	65	14	6	6.0	.269	.333	.391	-.088	.274	.336	.405	.258	12.9	109-2B	2

Breakout: 4%　Improve: 25%　Collapse: 33%　Attrition: 17%　　Comparables: Mickey Morandini, Delino DeShields, Jerry Lumpe, Jim Gantner

A lot of his value offensively is in his line-drive stroke, and batting averages can move around, but he has a bit of doubles power, and he won't absolutely refuse to take a walk. His defensive skills are similarly understated but useful. What's a little more troubling is that Kennedy's going to be 31, and his PECOTA comparables are all guys whose careers fell apart around that age. Still, if he has years as good as Mickey Morandini did in 1997 and 1998 at ages 31 and 32 (.295/.376/.382 combined), you have to figure the Cardinals will take whatever they get in year three of his new deal.

Casey Kotchman　　　　**1B**　　　**Bats: L**　**Throws: L**　　Height: 6′ 3″　　Weight: 215　　Born: February 22, 1983　Age: 24

YEAR	TEAM	LVL	AGE	PA	R	2B	3B	HR	RBI	BB	SO	SB	CS	SPEED	AVG	OBP	SLG	MLVR	EQAVG	EQOBP	EQSLG	EQA	VORP	DEFENSE	
2004	ARK	AA	21	130	19	11	0	3	18	10	7	0	0	3.2	.368	.438	.544	.416	.314	.374	.475	.291	8.3	25-1B	2
2004	SLC	AAA	21	220	32	22	0	5	38	14	25	0	0	3.4	.372	.423	.558	.304	.302	.350	.450	.274	8.2	39-1B	0
2004	ANA	MLB	21	128	7	6	0	0	15	7	11	3	0	4.5	.224	.289	.276	-.333	.224	.289	.267	.211	-6.1	31-1B	1
2005	SLC	AAA	22	417	62	23	1	10	58	43	40	0	2	2.9	.289	.372	.441	-.009	.245	.319	.369	.241	-8.1	89-1B	3
2005	ANA	MLB	22	143	16	5	0	7	22	15	18	1	1	4.1	.278	.352	.484	.133	.282	.366	.508	.293	7.0	15-1B	1
2006	ANA	MLB	23	88	6	2	0	1	6	7	13	0	1	4.1	.152	.221	.215	-.600	.103	.186	.154	.138	-11.7	22-1B	2
2007	ANA	MLB	24	340	34	15	0	6	36	25	40	0	1	4.2	.256	.316	.364	-.154	.254	.319	.375	.246	-5.1	82-1B	3

Breakout: 37%　Improve: 57%　Collapse: 16%　Attrition: 28%　　Comparables: Pete LaCock, Tom O'Malley, Dave Hansen, Tom Satriano

Los Angeles Angels of Anaheim

It really seemed that Kotchman had turned the corner during the second half of 2005, but then he got mono and essentially lost all of 2006. The Angels still think he's the guy who helped them get to the playoffs in '05, and Morales's struggles and Erstad's likely departure should give them every opportunity to find out for certain. Because of the unusual circumstances in play, you might want to overlook that projection and play Rally Monkey-see, Rally Monkey-do in the hope that he'll turn in a season's worth of his 2005-level performance. He may lose time to the arrival of Shea Hillenbrand, but the veteran additon will also see time at third and DH.

Jeff Mathis C Bats: R Throws: R Height: 6′ 0″ Weight: 185 Born: March 31, 1983 Age: 24

YEAR	TEAM	LVL	AGE	PA	R	2B	3B	HR	RBI	BB	SO	SB	CS	SPEED	AVG	OBP	SLG	MLVR	EQAVG	EQOBP	EQSLG	EQA	VORP	DEFENSE	
2004	ARK	AA	21	494	57	24	3	14	55	49	102	2	1	4.2	.227	.310	.394	-.108	.196	.266	.331	.213	-23.4	102-C	-5
2005	SLC	AAA	22	479	78	26	3	21	73	42	85	4	3	4.7	.276	.340	.499	.003	.236	.294	.413	.242	3.0	94-C	2
2006	SLC	AAA	23	417	62	33	3	5	45	26	75	3	1	5.4	.289	.333	.430	-.029	.258	.300	.388	.239	1.8	83-C	3
2006	ANA	MLB	23	63	9	2	0	2	6	7	14	0	0	3.9	.145	.238	.291	-.463	.130	.238	.259	.187	-4.7	15-C	-4
2007	ANA	MLB	24	428	41	22	1	10	46	29	85	2	1	4.6	.236	.291	.375	-.197	.234	.294	.386	.239	-0.9	102-C	-2

Breakout: 34% Improve: 56% Collapse: 20% Attrition: 15% Comparables: Giuseppe Chiaramonte, Steve Torrealba, Brandon Inge, Ryan Christianson

The Angels expected Mathis to be their catcher by now, and gave him every opportunity last April to make the job his own. It's hard to see why they wouldn't rather have him in, say, Seattle. Although he's a smooth receiver, he's not a great arm behind the plate, and his track record as a hitter is just so much Salt Lake froth. Although young, he's just not going to develop into anything more than a nice reserve.

Dallas McPherson 3B/1B Bats: L Throws: R Height: 6′ 4″ Weight: 230 Born: July 23, 1980 Age: 26

YEAR	TEAM	LVL	AGE	PA	R	2B	3B	HR	RBI	BB	SO	SB	CS	SPEED	AVG	OBP	SLG	MLVR	EQAVG	EQOBP	EQSLG	EQA	VORP	DEFENSE			
2004	ARK	AA	23	302	53	17	6	20	69	34	74	6	5	6.1	.321	.404	.660	.473	.289	.360	.585	.305	37.2	56-3B	-4		
2004	SLC	AAA	23	284	54	19	8	20	57	23	95	6	3	7.0	.313	.370	.680	.322	.263	.319	.546	.283	21.6	60-3B	-11		
2004	ANA	MLB	23	43	5	1	0	3	6	3	17	1	0	5.2	.225	.279	.475	.163	.225	.279	.475	.255	2.4	12-3B	0		
2005	SLC	AAA	24	63	8	1	2	6	19	7	20	1	2	5.0	.278	.349	.704	.302	.255	.317	.618	.289	6.2	12-3B	0		
2005	ANA	MLB	24	220	29	14	2	8	26	14	64	3	3	5.3	.244	.295	.449	-.029	.252	.314	.470	.260	2.5	54-3B	-4		
2006	SLC	AAA	25	231	35	11	5	17	45	15	88	3	1	6.6	.250	.307	.596	.120	.223	.276	.521	.263	8.4	23-3B	0	15-1B	-4
2006	ANA	MLB	25	121	16	4	0	7	13	6	40	1	0	3.5	.261	.298	.478	-.013	.263	.306	.500	.269	2.5	26-3B	-3		
2007	ANA	MLB	26	412	50	19	2	21	63	33	131	4	3	5.2	.242	.308	.471	-.038	.240	.311	.484	.271	10.9	98-3B	-3		

Breakout: 12% Improve: 28% Collapse: 36% Attrition: 8% Comparables: Dave Kingman, Franklin Stubbs, Travis Hafner, Russ Branyan

Called up in May once the Angels got over their Edgardo Alfonzo experience, McPherson almost made the most of it, smacking his six homers in a little more than a month of part-time play. He then strained his back and went back down on a rehab assignment that never really ended because Izturis delivered in his absence. The future just went from now to then for McPherson; Brandon Wood's almost ready, and fragile sluggers with strikeout issues and defensive limitations generally don't live happily ever after.

Jose Molina C Bats: R Throws: R Height: 6′ 2″ Weight: 220 Born: June 3, 1975 Age: 32

YEAR	TEAM	LVL	AGE	PA	R	2B	3B	HR	RBI	BB	SO	SB	CS	SPEED	AVG	OBP	SLG	MLVR	EQAVG	EQOBP	EQSLG	EQA	VORP	DEFENSE	
2004	ANA	MLB	29	218	26	10	2	3	25	10	52	4	1	5.6	.261	.296	.374	-.176	.262	.304	.376	.239	-0.0	54-C	13
2005	ANA	MLB	30	203	14	4	0	6	25	13	41	2	0	3.5	.228	.286	.348	-.207	.232	.302	.365	.236	-1.5	53-C	16
2006	ANA	MLB	31	245	18	17	0	4	22	9	49	1	0	3.8	.240	.273	.369	-.234	.239	.278	.374	.229	-4.8	67-C	11
2007	ANA	MLB	32	292	26	14	1	6	31	15	60	3	1	4.3	.238	.283	.363	-.228	.237	.286	.373	.233	-2.5	71-C	6

Breakout: 27% Improve: 60% Collapse: 22% Attrition: 43% Comparables: Bob Montgomery, Andy Etchebarren, Mike Difelice, Phil Roof

¡Viva el último de los Molinas por los Angeles de Los Angeles! There can be only one! Jose is a decent enough reserve with some sock and an outstanding throwing arm. The pity of the matter is that his offensive skills only shadow instead of complement Napoli's. That doesn't make him any less useful as a backup backstop, of course.

Kendry Morales   1B   Bats: S   Throws: R   Height: 6' 1"   Weight: 220   Born: June 20, 1983   Age: 24

YEAR	TEAM	LVL	AGE	PA	R	2B	3B	HR	RBI	BB	SO	SB	CS	SPEED	AVG	OBP	SLG	MLVR	EQAVG	EQOBP	EQSLG	EQA	VORP	DEFENSE	
2004	Ind	CL	21	133	16	12	1	2	17	9	13	0	0	3.8	.358	.406	.520	.324	.344	.383	.512	.301	21.5		
2004	Ind	CL	21	133	16	12	1	2	17	9	13	0	0	3.8	.358	.406	.520	.324	.344	.383	.512	.301	549.1		
2005	RCU	A+	22	100	18	3	0	5	17	6	11	0	0	2.9	.344	.400	.544	.290	.301	.340	.452	.271	3.4	15-1B	-2
2005	ARK	AA	22	301	47	12	0	17	54	17	43	2	0	3.7	.306	.349	.530	.197	.270	.312	.472	.264	6.7	60-1B	-3
2006	SLC	AAA	23	273	41	13	1	12	52	14	40	0	3	3.6	.320	.359	.520	.163	.283	.319	.473	.265	7.7	50-1B	-5
2006	ANA	MLB	23	215	21	10	1	5	22	17	28	1	1	3.5	.234	.293	.371	-.198	.236	.302	.385	.238	-7.3	51-1B	4
2007	ANA	MLB	24	443	47	20	1	15	60	27	64	0	1	4.1	.262	.309	.423	-.084	.259	.312	.435	.259	0.3	105-1B	0

Breakout: 18%   Improve: 48%   Collapse: 25%   Attrition: 13%   Comparables: Ed Kranepool, Daryle Ward, John Ellis, Tony Horton

Morales is the latest example of a Cuban import being something less than advertised. He's not the athletic, young outfielder they thought they might have bought, but is instead a stiff, slow-footed first baseman, as well as an impatient, hack-happy hitter. He's still young enough that if he improves his pitch recognition, he could take a step forward and deliver a bit more power from his line-drive stroke, but he's behind Kotchman for now, and his ceiling is considerably more limited than the sunny wishcasts on the original date of purchase.

Tommy Murphy   CF   Bats: S   Throws: R   Height: 6' 0"   Weight: 185   Born: August 27, 1979   Age: 27

YEAR	TEAM	LVL	AGE	PA	R	2B	3B	HR	RBI	BB	SO	SB	CS	SPEED	AVG	OBP	SLG	MLVR	EQAVG	EQOBP	EQSLG	EQA	VORP	DEFENSE			
2004	ARK	AA	24	528	77	24	6	7	45	36	113	27	5	7.8	.260	.310	.379	-.105	.225	.268	.322	.216	-27.6	119-CF	-2		
2005	ARK	AA	25	557	85	24	11	17	76	43	97	26	12	7.9	.288	.346	.482	.110	.249	.300	.408	.246	-10.9	79-RF	6	49-CF	0
2006	SLC	AAA	26	310	43	16	3	7	36	19	62	6	13	5.8	.302	.351	.453	.041	.266	.311	.405	.239	3.4	54-CF	-3	12-RF	0
2006	ANA	MLB	26	77	12	4	1	1	6	5	21	4	1	8.9	.229	.276	.357	-.257	.232	.289	.362	.237	-1.5	16-CF	4		
2007	ANA	MLB	27	388	38	16	2	7	36	20	84	9	4	6.1	.234	.278	.351	-.255	.232	.280	.361	.228	-10.3	93-CF	2		

Breakout: 15%   Improve: 35%   Collapse: 34%   Attrition: 26%   Comparables: Chad Green, John Shelby, Chris Magruder, Mark Little

"Barely serviceable" sounds so harsh. Is a Yugo a car, or not? It most certainly is, and if you drive one, you're the proud owner of the finest in automotive technology from the former Socialist Federal Republic of Yugoslavia, and you have wheels. Similarly, Murphy's a fourth outfielder, and if you're not the sort who wants to live dangerously and just go entirely without one, he'll fulfill your fourth outfielder needs. So, let's try not to bring quality into it, okay?

Mike Napoli   C   Bats: R   Throws: R   Height: 6' 0"   Weight: 205   Born: October 31, 1981   Age: 25

YEAR	TEAM	LVL	AGE	PA	R	2B	3B	HR	RBI	BB	SO	SB	CS	SPEED	AVG	OBP	SLG	MLVR	EQAVG	EQOBP	EQSLG	EQA	VORP	DEFENSE			
2004	RCU	A+	22	585	94	29	4	29	118	88	166	9	5	4.8	.282	.394	.539	.274	.245	.337	.437	.267	22.5	72-C	8	34-1B	-4
2005	ARK	AA	23	541	96	22	2	31	99	88	140	12	4	5.6	.237	.372	.508	.140	.210	.333	.438	.267	16.8	103-C	4		
2006	SLC	AAA	24	90	12	6	0	3	10	8	29	1	1	5.1	.244	.344	.436	-.036	.213	.300	.375	.234	-0.8	17-C	3		
2006	ANA	MLB	24	325	47	13	0	16	42	51	90	2	3	4.1	.228	.360	.455	.039	.231	.372	.473	.286	13.0	80-C	2		
2007	ANA	MLB	25	441	57	19	1	20	60	53	119	5	2	4.5	.236	.337	.450	-.020	.234	.340	.463	.281	17.7	105-C	6		

Breakout: 19%   Improve: 63%   Collapse: 18%   Attrition: 19%   Comparables: Jim Pagliaroni, Tom Haller, Earl Battey, Darren Daulton

Stepping in for Mathis in May, Napoli proved both his defenders and critics correct. He surprised the league at first, hitting .286/.412/.579 between his May callup and the All-Star break, then pitchers caught up to him and held him to .164/.303/.320 in the second half, inducing a 4-for-54 homerless slump (with 13 walks) from mid-July to mid-August. Hence PECOTA's strange spread of optimism and fear—players whose skills are entirely tied up in secondary offensive attributes such as power and patience can disappear almost as quickly as they arrive. As long as Napoli's hidden from guys with overpowering heat, his all-or-nothing approach should serve against the nibblers as he works counts for a cookie. Whereas he was once seen as a relatively iffy defender, hard work has helped him improve against the running game; he threw out 31 percent of would-be thieves as an Angel last year. He'll never be a star, but he contributes in all phases of the game.

Aaron Peel   OF   Bats: R   Throws: R   Height: 6′ 0″   Weight: 195   Born: February 8, 1983   Age: 24

YEAR	TEAM	LVL	AGE	PA	R	2B	3B	HR	RBI	BB	SO	SB	CS	SPEED	AVG	OBP	SLG	MLVR	EQAVG	EQOBP	EQSLG	EQA	VORP	DEFENSE			
2004	CDR	A	21	233	25	6	1	9	24	17	66	4	4	4.2	.216	.289	.385	-.085	.186	.240	.307	.196	-23.9	20-RF	-2	19-LF	-1
2005	CDR	A	22	216	31	13	0	8	34	21	46	6	4	3.3	.308	.407	.511	.315	.263	.333	.433	.262	1.5	23-LF	-6		
2005	RCU	A+	22	248	46	12	4	11	35	15	57	1	2	5.6	.311	.375	.550	.214	.274	.319	.452	.261	3.1	19-RF	-3	16-LF	2
2006	ARK	AA	23	548	67	37	4	16	66	28	105	13	11	5.2	.285	.344	.473	.062	.255	.299	.420	.245	-9.1	111-LF	-9		
2007	*ANA*	*MLB*	*24*	*481*	*48*	*24*	*1*	*13*	*56*	*23*	*105*	*6*	*3*	*4.6*	*.246*	*.292*	*.393*	*-.166*	*.244*	*.295*	*.404*	*.245*	*-7.5*	*114-LF*	*-4*		

Breakout: 27%   Improve: 49%   Collapse: 23%   Attrition: 7%   Comparables: Mike Vento, Dave Kim, Dustan Mohr, Mario Valenzuela

Sort of like Gorneault, Peel's an outfield prospect with limits, but he's still young enough to change people's minds. Peel struggled in his first couple of months in Double-A last year, but, from June 1 on, he hit .304/.355/.554. He's got his Don Baylor routine down, taking 18 pitches for the team; he was also plunked 20 times in 2005, so that's part of his skillset, and an important one given how infrequently he'll work his way on with a walk. He'll have to show that his in-season improvement is for real for him to challenge for a reserve role, because he's not really a gifted fielder or a plus runner. His nickname should be "Mrs."

Robb Quinlan   1B/3B   Bats: R   Throws: R   Height: 6′ 1″   Weight: 200   Born: March 17, 1977   Age: 30

YEAR	TEAM	LVL	AGE	PA	R	2B	3B	HR	RBI	BB	SO	SB	CS	SPEED	AVG	OBP	SLG	MLVR	EQAVG	EQOBP	EQSLG	EQA	VORP	DEFENSE			
2004	SLC	AAA	27	122	15	9	1	2	17	14	14	1	1	4.3	.296	.377	.454	.003	.236	.311	.345	.233	-4.2	23-1B	1		
2004	ANA	MLB	27	177	23	14	0	5	23	14	26	3	1	5.0	.344	.401	.525	.315	.352	.412	.547	.323	16.9	23-3B	-1	12-1B	1
2005	SLC	AAA	28	62	13	6	0	1	4	2	8	0	0	4.1	.383	.403	.533	.270	.311	.323	.426	.255	1.9				
2005	ANA	MLB	28	143	17	8	0	5	14	7	26	0	1	4.1	.231	.273	.403	-.144	.235	.287	.417	.238	-2.4	27-3B	-3		
2006	ANA	MLB	29	244	28	11	1	9	32	7	28	2	1	4.6	.321	.344	.491	.150	.323	.352	.504	.288	12.5	43-1B	3	15-3B	-2
2007	*ANA*	*MLB*	*30*	*288*	*35*	*15*	*1*	*8*	*38*	*16*	*41*	*2*	*1*	*4.8*	*.284*	*.328*	*.436*	*-.017*	*.281*	*.331*	*.448*	*.272*	*7.0*	*70-1B*	*1*		

Breakout: 20%   Improve: 40%   Collapse: 26%   Attrition: 32%   Comparables: Ron Jackson, Rondell White, Alex Johnson, Ron Coomer

Quinlan's one of the few lefty-mashing platoon players with staying power, having slugged .561 against lefties and .387 against right-handers over the last three years. It probably helps that he's a good fastball hitter, which helps him come in cold off the bench. He's no great shakes at third, but Izturis, McPherson, and Figgins are all less effective against southpaws. Unfortunately, he's probably the player hurt most by Juan Rivera's broken leg (other than Rivera himself, of course); the decision to sign Shea Hillenbrand puts a veteran player in his space, and once Rivera heals up, someone's going to have to go.

Juan Rivera   OF   Bats: R   Throws: R   Height: 6′ 2″   Weight: 205   Born: July 3, 1978   Age: 28

YEAR	TEAM	LVL	AGE	PA	R	2B	3B	HR	RBI	BB	SO	SB	CS	SPEED	AVG	OBP	SLG	MLVR	EQAVG	EQOBP	EQSLG	EQA	VORP	DEFENSE			
2004	MON	MLB	26	426	48	24	1	12	49	34	45	6	2	4.6	.307	.364	.465	.173	.302	.361	.460	.281	23.7	80-RF	2	10-CF	-1
2005	ANA	MLB	27	376	46	17	1	15	59	23	44	1	9	3.4	.271	.316	.454	.030	.282	.337	.483	.265	4.8	33-LF	1	26-RF	-3
2006	ANA	MLB	28	494	65	27	0	23	85	33	59	0	4	3.3	.310	.362	.525	.218	.314	.371	.546	.302	33.5	53-LF	8	27-RF	-3
2007	*ANA*	*MLB*	*28*	*488*	*65*	*26*	*1*	*17*	*72*	*35*	*59*	*2*	*3*	*4.4*	*.296*	*.350*	*.477*	*.087*	*.294*	*.354*	*.490*	*.291*	*21.2*	*115-LF*	*0*		

Breakout: 12%   Improve: 43%   Collapse: 27%   Attrition: 11%   Comparables: Rondell White, Bob Watson, George Hendrick, Craig Monroe

The Angels had a top-ten finisher in RBI percentage last year, but it wasn't Vladi—Rivera drove in more than 20 percent of the runners on-base when he came to the plate in 2006, good for ninth in all of baseball among hitters with 200 or more plate appearances. Mini-Vlad has a similar ability to make contact with authority. If there's one complaint, it's the minor one that he can't really play center, which means he's basically sharing the corners and the DH job with Vladi and Garret Anderson. Keep in mind he's no spring chicken—he'll turn 29 before the All-Star break, so he's as good as he'll ever get right now. Another strike against him is that the time he'll lose to the leg he broke in winter ball forced the Angels to go out and sign Shea Hillenbrand.

Sean Rodriguez   SS   **Bats: R   Throws: R**   Height: 6′ 1″   Weight: 198   Born: April 26, 1985   Age: 22

YEAR	TEAM	LVL	AGE	PA	R	2B	3B	HR	RBI	BB	SO	SB	CS	SPEED	AVG	OBP	SLG	MLVR	EQAVG	EQOBP	EQSLG	EQA	VORP	DEFENSE	
2004	CDR	A	19	224	35	8	4	4	17	18	54	14	4	8.2	.250	.333	.393	.014	.225	.287	.353	.230	-4.9	25-2B	2
2004	PRO	Rk	19	292	64	14	4	10	55	51	62	9	3	6.0	.338	.486	.569	.457	.263	.353	.396	.263	22.0	59-SS	2
2005	CDR	A	20	546	86	29	3	14	45	78	85	27	11	6.3	.250	.371	.422	.098	.218	.312	.362	.240	0.8	84-SS -5	15-CF 5
2006	RCU	A+	21	523	78	29	5	24	77	47	124	15	3	5.3	.301	.377	.545	.278	.273	.330	.480	.276	33.8	113-SS	9
2006	ARK	AA	21	79	16	5	0	5	9	11	18	0	3	4.0	.354	.462	.662	.557	.324	.418	.603	.322	13.3	19-SS	2
2007	*ANA*	*MLB*	*22*	*563*	*67*	*28*	*2*	*17*	*66*	*46*	*125*	*10*	*4*	*5.1*	*.253*	*.319*	*.418*	*-.080*	*.251*	*.322*	*.430*	*.265*	*18.0*	*132-SS*	*5*

Breakout: 20% Improve: 48% Collapse: 18% Attrition: 4%   *Comparables: Chin-Feng Chen, Michael Cuddyer, Shawn Gallagher, Andy Marte*

His comps aren't really helpful as far as conjuring up a mental image—try to think of him as a Ronnie Belliard type, and happily one without the tongue gymnastics. Like Belliard back in the day, he's sort of squat and not especially athletic, so he's not a scout's prospect. Although Rodriguez has the arm to make a play from the hole, questions about his range are expected to drive him to second. He got homer-happy last summer, a consequence of hitting in the always-cozy Epicenter in Rancho Cucamonga. In the rest of the hitter-friendly Cal League, Rodriguez hit a less-exciting .256/.360/.433. He's young and provides power at positions where it's hard to come by, but in this organization, he's blocked. Sprung, he could have a career as nifty as Belliard's or better.

Tim Salmon   DH   **Bats: R   Throws: R**   Height: 6′ 3″   Weight: 235   Born: December 31, 1969   Age: 38

YEAR	TEAM	LVL	AGE	PA	R	2B	3B	HR	RBI	BB	SO	SB	CS	SPEED	AVG	OBP	SLG	MLVR	EQAVG	EQOBP	EQSLG	EQA	VORP	DEFENSE
2004	ANA	MLB	35	206	15	7	0	2	23	14	41	1	0	4.2	.253	.306	.323	-.217	.254	.311	.330	.232	-5.0	
2006	ANA	MLB	37	244	30	8	2	9	27	29	44	0	2	3.5	.265	.361	.450	.068	.269	.373	.466	.286	8.4	

Despite the injuries that repeatedly marred his career, Salmon is the franchise's all-time home run leader with 299. Most of the power categories in franchise history are his or Garret Anderson's, with Salmon also holding the team records for slugging (.498), walks, strikeouts, and runs, while Anderson leads in games, hits, at-bats, total bases, doubles, and RBIs. The debate over the greatest Angel hitter ever won't be an easy one to settle; historically, the franchise has made turnover its watchword. It's probably Salmon, and not Anderson, Brian Downing, or Rod Carew, and if that's something still short of the Hall of Fame, it was nice to see him go out on his shield instead of on a stretcher.

Hainley Statia   SS   **Bats: S   Throws: R**   Height: 5′ 11″   Weight: 160   Born: January 19, 1986   Age: 21

YEAR	TEAM	LVL	AGE	PA	R	2B	3B	HR	RBI	BB	SO	SB	CS	SPEED	AVG	OBP	SLG	MLVR	EQAVG	EQOBP	EQSLG	EQA	VORP	DEFENSE
2005	RCU	A+	19	112	12	2	0	1	8	5	13	6	3	5.4	.245	.286	.292	-.399	.213	.241	.250	.185	-9.8	22-2B 3
2005	ORM	Rk	19	308	44	17	6	2	41	23	40	12	10	6.0	.300	.360	.426	.055	.256	.293	.329	.219	-8.1	65-SS 8
2006	CDR	A	20	480	68	31	1	1	38	52	54	23	15	5.5	.297	.379	.384	.126	.261	.325	.342	.237	4.2	107-SS 9
2006	RCU	A+	20	70	8	2	1	0	8	8	7	1	1	4.9	.300	.386	.367	.038	.274	.333	.339	.240	0.9	15-SS 1
2007	*ANA*	*MLB*	*21*	*520*	*51*	*23*	*2*	*3*	*39*	*33*	*62*	*12*	*6*	*5.7*	*.243*	*.293*	*.321*	*-.261*	*.241*	*.296*	*.330*	*.225*	*-5.2*	*122-SS 8*

Breakout: 28% Improve: 54% Collapse: 26% Attrition: 6%   *Comparables: Guillermo Reyes, Alejandro Machado, Callix Crabbe, Carlos Leon*

An immigrant from Curacao snagged in the ninth round in 2004, Statia's an old-school shortstop prospect, a ballplayer instead of an all-tools athlete. His power isn't going to blossom the way one might think looking at last year's doubles tally—he's not driving balls to the gaps, but trying to slip them down the lines. At the same time, he's more a line-drive hitter than a slapper. Defensively, Statia is sound, not especially gifted, but good. With the organization's crowd at shortstop, he's young enough for the Angels to take their time with him, and talented enough to plausibly be offered up in place of Aybar in a bit of bait-and-switch at the trade deadline.

Reggie Willits   CF   **Bats: S   Throws: R**   Height: 5′ 11″   Weight: 185   Born: May 30, 1981   Age: 26

YEAR	TEAM	LVL	AGE	PA	R	2B	3B	HR	RBI	BB	SO	SB	CS	SPEED	AVG	OBP	SLG	MLVR	EQAVG	EQOBP	EQSLG	EQA	VORP	DEFENSE	
2004	RCU	A+	23	625	99	17	5	5	52	73	112	45	15	6.9	.285	.374	.365	.005	.246	.315	.300	.230	-18.4	124-CF	5
2005	ARK	AA	24	561	75	23	6	2	46	54	78	40	14	7.2	.304	.377	.388	.047	.267	.333	.339	.247	-1.5	79-CF -3	34-RF 4
2006	SLC	AAA	25	437	85	18	4	3	39	77	50	31	15	6.9	.327	.448	.426	.182	.285	.400	.373	.280	20.8	75-CF 5	19-LF 2
2006	ANA	MLB	25	58	12	1	0	0	2	11	10	4	3	7.4	.267	.411	.289	-.053	.273	.429	.295	.265	0.8	13-CF	0
2007	*ANA*	*MLB*	*26*	*460*	*57*	*16*	*3*	*4*	*34*	*43*	*69*	*17*	*6*	*6.4*	*.249*	*.324*	*.332*	*-.185*	*.247*	*.328*	*.342*	*.248*	*-3.3*	*109-CF 3*	

Breakout: 11% Improve: 32% Collapse: 43% Attrition: 21%   *Comparables: Donzell McDonald, Darren Lewis, Chris Prieto, Nick Punto*

Although "Whatchu Talkin' 'Bout" Willits has a better arm than most of his fourth/fifth outfielder ilk, he's pretty much your standard slap-and-sprint example of the type. The minefield most of these guys have to run to actually make it and stick isn't too dissimilar from salmon trying to slip past all those bears on their way to the spawning. Happily, Willits doesn't have to worry about turning an unfashionable shade of red, let alone being eaten, but whether or not he actually produces a big league career is more in the hands of Scioscia and Stoneman than his own.

Bobby Wilson   C   Bats: R   Throws: R   Height: 6' 0"   Weight: 205   Born: April 8, 1983   Age: 24

YEAR	TEAM	LVL	AGE	PA	R	2B	3B	HR	RBI	BB	SO	SB	CS	SPEED	AVG	OBP	SLG	MLVR	EQAVG	EQOBP	EQSLG	EQA	VORP	DEFENSE		
2004	CDR	A	21	441	45	23	0	8	64	30	55	4	2	3.7	.268	.320	.386	-.002	.224	.266	.322	.210	-20.4	69-C	11	12-3B -1
2005	RCU	A+	22	501	66	32	1	14	77	30	61	2	1	3.3	.290	.333	.453	-.029	.243	.279	.359	.222	-10.3	102-C	2	
2006	ARK	AA	23	418	45	26	0	9	53	33	47	1	6	3.3	.286	.350	.428	.012	.248	.303	.381	.235	0.6	80-C	0	
2007	ANA	MLB	24	422	36	18	1	8	45	23	55	0	1	4.0	.244	.289	.356	-.221	.243	.292	.366	.231	-3.5	100-C	2	

Breakout: 43%   Improve: 64%   Collapse: 18%   Attrition: 11%   Comparables: Chris Stewart, Jason Phillips, Brian Luderer, Javier Cardona

A high school teammate of Casey Kotchman's, Wilson's a decent enough catching prospect, and he swings a quick bat that generates a lot of liners. He's that odd rarity, a catcher who can throw well, but is sort of rough behind the plate; anybody remember Mike Heath? He won't be a major improvement on Napoli or anyone else, just something different, and a plausible half of a job-sharing arrangement.

Brandon Wood   SS/3B   Bats: R   Throws: R   Height: 6' 3"   Weight: 185   Born: March 2, 1985   Age: 22

YEAR	TEAM	LVL	AGE	PA	R	2B	3B	HR	RBI	BB	SO	SB	CS	SPEED	AVG	OBP	SLG	MLVR	EQAVG	EQOBP	EQSLG	EQA	VORP	DEFENSE	
2004	CDR	A	19	535	65	30	5	11	64	46	117	21	5	6.4	.251	.322	.404	.011	.222	.276	.350	.223	-11.9	124-SS	-19
2005	RCU	A+	20	595	109	51	4	43	115	48	128	7	3	5.0	.321	.383	.672	.423	.271	.320	.531	.282	47.7	123-SS	-7
2006	ARK	AA	21	522	74	42	4	25	83	54	149	19	3	5.4	.276	.355	.552	.178	.247	.315	.486	.273	29.3	115-SS	10
2007	ANA	MLB	22	512	59	29	2	20	69	38	138	15	4	5.0	.239	.300	.436	-.098	.237	.304	.449	.264	16.3	121-SS	2

Breakout: 22%   Improve: 45%   Collapse: 28%   Attrition: 6%   Comparables: Chris Young, Jason Regan, Jonny Gomes, David Kelton

The team's star of the future, Wood generates tremendous power with his bat, but it all comes out of his forearms and quick wrists; he's not a hulking slugger. Critics might note that he could stand to shorten his swing, but that's not his game. The Angels are going to move him to third, not because he can't play short, but because it's the logical application of a talented player to a position that needs a long-term solution. He has the arm to make the throw from the hot corner, and his power profiles perfectly well for the position. The Angels might take the heat off of him by letting him get his feet wet at third in Triple-A for a month or two, but his successful jump to Double-A pretty much guarantees he'll be up sometime this year.

PITCHERS

Nick Adenhart   Bats: R   Throws: R   Height: 6' 3"   Weight: 185   Born: August 24, 1986   Age: 20

YEAR	TEAM	LVL	AGE	W	L	SV	G	GS	IP	H	BB	SO	HR	GB%	BABIP	STUFF	WHIP	ERA	PERA	EQERA	EQH9	EQBB9	EQSO9	EQHR9	VORP	WXRL
2006	CDR	A	19	10	2	0	16	16	106	84	26	99	2	52.5%	.283	31	1.04	1.95	3.75	4.11	8.1	2.8	5.1	0.4	17.1	—
2006	RCU	A+	19	5	2	0	9	9	52	51	16	46	1	57.8%	.331	24	1.29	3.81	3.66	4.27	8.9	2.9	5.1	0.3	7.8	—
2007	ANA	MLB	20	9	9	0	28	24	149²	157	54	91	15	50.0%	.293	10	1.41	4.53	4.34	4.51	9.3	3.1	5.1	0.8	16.1	2.70

Breakout: 5%   Improve: 32%   Collapse: 25%   Attrition: 1%   Comparables: Ricky Nolasco, Troy Patton, Abel Moreno, Junior Herndon

Adenhart was considered one of the top high school pitchers in the country in 2004, rivaling Homer Bailey, but he blew out his elbow just before the draft. The Angels took a chance that they could convince him to skip college, drafting him in the fourteenth round and then paying him what it took to make the pick stick. The gamble is already paying off. Adenhart started off his pro career in 2005, and made his full-season debut last year. He consistently throws in the low-90s, and supplements it with a good curve and a remarkably polished change. Adenhart isn't perfect; he still has mechanical issues. Nevertheless, considering his assortment and that he didn't even blink at facing advanced competition in High-A Rancho Cucamonga, he's a comer—one of the twenty best young arms in the minor leagues.

Jose Arredondo   Bats: R Throws: R   Height: 6' 0"   Weight: 170   Born: March 30, 1984   Age: 23

YEAR	TEAM	LVL	AGE	W	L	SV	G	GS	IP	H	BB	SO	HR	GB%	BABIP	STUFF	WHIP	ERA	PERA	EQERA	EQH9	EQBB9	EQSO9	EQHR9	VORP	WXRL
2005	ORM	Rk	21	5	0	0	15	13	68²	76	20	60	4	50.2%	.355	-20	1.40	4.19	5.88	6.82	11.0	3.8	3.5	1.2	-8.9	—
2006	RCU	A+	22	5	6	0	15	15	90	62	35	115	4	39.4%	.299	29	1.08	2.30	4.17	3.27	7.2	4.0	7.3	0.7	22.8	—
2006	ARK	AA	22	2	3	0	11	11	60¹	80	22	48	8	45.9%	.367	-8	1.70	6.59	5.24	7.01	11.5	3.2	5.1	1.5	-9.7	—
2007	ANA	MLB	23	6	8	0	25	20	117²	131	55	79	18	42.0%	.305	2	1.58	5.63	5.47	5.51	9.9	4.0	5.7	1.3	-2.2	0.70

Breakout: 5%   Improve: 39%   Collapse: 17%   Attrition: 0%   Comparables: Aaron Cames, Juan Rincon, Wascar Serrano, Ian Snell

Another shortstop-turned-hurler, Arredondo, like many of his breed, has a plus fastball despite not having the big frame typical flamethrowers. Little more than two years into the conversion, the slight Dominican has a lot of the problems you'd expect—poor control, no reliable second pitch, and no real touch when it comes to changing speeds. It probably didn't help matters that the Angels pushed him up to Double-A prematurely, but with his fastball topping out at 97 MPH, we could see Arredondo panning out as a reliever.

Hector Carrasco   Bats: R Throws: R   Height: 6' 2"   Weight: 220   Born: December 31, 1969   Age: 37

YEAR	TEAM	LVL	AGE	W	L	SV	G	GS	IP	H	BB	SO	HR	GB%	BABIP	STUFF	WHIP	ERA	PERA	EQERA	EQH9	EQBB9	EQSO9	EQHR9	VORP	WXRL
2004	OSA	JP	34	8	8	5	53	0	76	74	37	70	12	—	.282	-13	1.46	5.57	5.54	6.14	8.7	4.3	6.7	1.5	-4.7	—
2005	WAS	MLB	35	5	4	2	64	5	88¹	59	38	75	6	44.2%	.236	16	1.10	2.04	3.99	2.61	6.2	3.5	7.0	0.6	30.5	2.40
2006	ANA	MLB	36	7	3	1	56	3	100¹	93	27	72	10	51.5%	.278	9	1.20	3.41	3.96	3.69	8.2	2.3	6.1	0.8	25.3	2.22
2007	ANA	MLB	37	4	4	2	55	2	78	82	27	54	9	45.0%	.298	-4	1.39	4.26	4.34	4.19	9.4	2.9	5.9	1.0	11.4	1.00

Breakout: 19%   Improve: 39%   Collapse: 33%   Attrition: 12%   Comparables: Steve Reed, Tim Worrell, Steve Bedrosian, Dave Burba

The erstwhile utility pitcher was initially tabbed to replace the ailing Colon in the rotation, but a couple of weak efforts and a tough loss pushed him back into the pen. He spent the rest of the year there mopping up and pitching in middle relief and thrived in the role, giving the Angels old-fashioned relief succor in the form of multi-inning outings and stranded inherited runners. That sort of multi-inning role is one other teams could probably stand to create within their own pens.

Bartolo Colon   Bats: R Throws: R   Height: 5' 11"   Weight: 250   Born: May 24, 1973   Age: 34

YEAR	TEAM	LVL	AGE	W	L	SV	G	GS	IP	H	BB	SO	HR	GB%	BABIP	STUFF	WHIP	ERA	PERA	EQERA	EQH9	EQBB9	EQSO9	EQHR9	VORP	WXRL
2004	ANA	MLB	31	18	12	0	34	34	208¹	215	71	158	38	—	.288	2	1.37	5.01	4.85	4.97	8.6	2.8	6.3	1.5	22.7	3.51
2005	ANA	MLB	32	21	8	0	33	33	222²	215	43	157	26	41.6%	.285	19	1.16	3.48	3.82	3.82	8.4	1.7	6.1	1.0	49.1	6.71
2006	ANA	MLB	33	1	5	0	10	10	56¹	71	11	31	11	41.3%	.316	-6	1.46	5.12	5.15	5.90	10.9	1.7	4.7	1.6	-1.7	0.20
2007	ANA	MLB	34	7	8	0	30	19	121²	135	32	72	18	42.0%	.295	-1	1.38	4.74	4.67	4.63	9.9	2.3	5.0	1.2	11.3	1.90

Breakout: 14%   Improve: 49%   Collapse: 18%   Attrition: 5%   Comparables: Pete Harnisch, Don Robinson, Burt Hooton, Bobby Witt

There was no time during 2006 at which the AL's defending Cy Young winner was healthy. He was trying to work through shoulder trouble before he ever decided to light out and pitch for the Dominican Republic in the ill-considered World Baseball Classic. The shoulder never got better, and he was on the DL before April was through. He came back to pitch in June and July, only to break down again. He's busily rehabbing a partially torn rotator cuff through the winter, but there's no real timetable for his return. The Angels have five other solid starters without bum wings or conditioning issues, and this is the walk year of Colon's four-year, $51-million contract, so what's going to happen is anyone's guess.

Brendan Donnelly   Bats: R Throws: R   Height: 6' 3"   Weight: 240   Born: July 4, 1971   Age: 35

YEAR	TEAM	LVL	AGE	W	L	SV	G	GS	IP	H	BB	SO	HR	GB%	BABIP	STUFF	WHIP	ERA	PERA	EQERA	EQH9	EQBB9	EQSO9	EQHR9	VORP	WXRL
2004	ANA	MLB	33	5	2	0	40	0	42	34	15	56	5	—	.319	34	1.17	3.00	3.12	2.91	7.1	2.9	11.0	1.0	15.4	0.75
2005	ANA	MLB	34	9	3	0	66	0	65¹	60	19	53	9	32.1%	.277	3	1.21	3.72	4.25	4.16	8.1	2.6	7.1	1.2	11.5	0.62
2006	ANA	MLB	35	6	0	0	62	0	64	58	28	53	8	46.6%	.276	1	1.34	3.94	4.64	4.29	8.0	3.7	7.1	1.0	10.9	1.12
2007	BOS	MLB	35	3	3	2	51	0	57²	59	23	49	7	42.0%	.301	2	1.42	4.50	4.26	4.09	7.9	3.5	7.0	0.9	8.3	0.70

Breakout: 25%   Improve: 45%   Collapse: 24%   Attrition: 13%   Comparables: Don McMahon, Tim Worrell, Al Worthington, Juan Berenguer

Regardless of whether he's just not the same pitcher since Frank Robinson (and former teammate Jose Guillen) so publicly outed him as a cheat, Donnelly did manage to retain some measure of his value last year. That said, he was almost seven runs worse with inherited runners on in 2006 than he had been in 2005, and his sneaky delivery isn't quite so sneaky now that the movement on his pitches has flattened out a bit. He still has value as a right-handed situational guy, so, to an extent, he'll be stepping into Chad Bradford's old role with Boston, having been dealt straight up for lefty Phil Seibel.

Kelvim Escobar

Bats: R Throws: R   Height: 6' 1"   Weight: 230   Born: April 11, 1976   Age: 31

YEAR	TEAM	LVL	AGE	W	L	SV	G	GS	IP	H	BB	SO	HR	GB%	BABIP	STUFF	WHIP	ERA	PERA	EQERA	EQH9	EQBB9	EQSO9	EQHR9	VORP	WXRL
2004	ANA	MLB	28	11	12	0	33	33	208¹	192	76	191	21	—	.298	29	1.29	3.93	3.73	3.77	7.8	2.9	7.6	0.8	53.2	6.33
2005	ANA	MLB	29	3	2	1	16	7	59²	45	21	63	4	46.1%	.273	36	1.11	3.02	3.15	3.25	6.6	3.1	9.1	0.6	17.2	2.60
2006	ANA	MLB	30	11	14	0	30	30	189¹	192	50	147	17	46.1%	.311	25	1.28	3.61	3.58	4.23	8.8	2.2	6.6	0.7	33.9	4.83
2007	*ANA*	*MLB*	*31*	*11*	*9*	*0*	*29*	*28*	*180¹*	*176*	*57*	*142*	*19*	*45.0%*	*.292*	*19*	*1.29*	*3.94*	*3.87*	*3.89*	*8.7*	*2.7*	*6.6*	*0.9*	*31.8*	*4.70*

Breakout: 10% Improve: 54% Collapse: 9% Attrition: 9% Comparables: Andy Messersmith, Kevin Appier, Bartolo Colon, Burt Hooton

Escobar's arguably the best transformer this side of the summer multiplex—he really can be an effective closer, or a quality starter. Starting has allowed Escobar to show off his broad assortment, as he will spring a splitter or cutter on hitters that he rarely used when he only had to deliver his mid-90s heat out of the pen. After working through a DL stint and some shoulder and elbow woes, Escobar delivered down the stretch, posting 9 quality starts in his last 13 before being shut down with knee trouble. Managed carefully, he should be able to continue to deliver. In a solid bit of anticipation of where the market was headed, Stoneman got Escobar under contract for three more years for $28.5 million.

Nick Green

Bats: R Throws: R   Height: 6' 4"   Weight: 180   Born: August 20, 1984   Age: 22

YEAR	TEAM	LVL	AGE	W	L	SV	G	GS	IP	H	BB	SO	HR	GB%	BABIP	STUFF	WHIP	ERA	PERA	EQERA	EQH9	EQBB9	EQSO9	EQHR9	VORP	WXRL
2004	PRO	Rk	19	4	3	0	17	10	51¹	55	20	44	4	—	.329	-17	1.46	3.86	6.02	5.57	9.6	4.0	3.7	1.4	0.2	—
2005	CDR	A	20	3	3	2	26	8	100²	95	14	74	11	37.1%	.283	-14	1.08	3.57	5.38	4.80	9.2	1.4	4.4	1.8	8.8	—
2006	RCU	A+	21	5	3	0	11	11	65²	77	19	57	9	41.6%	.342	-8	1.47	4.14	6.03	4.57	11.2	2.9	5.1	2.1	7.4	—
2006	ARK	AA	21	8	5	0	17	17	112¹	115	21	77	23	30.9%	.280	-21	1.21	4.42	6.34	5.10	9.2	1.7	4.5	2.3	6.3	—
2007	*LAA*	*MLB*	*22*	*6*	*9*	*0*	*26*	*22*	*127²*	*149*	*36*	*69*	*29*	*37.0%*	*.285*	*-2*	*1.45*	*5.67*	*5.65*	*5.42*	*10.4*	*2.4*	*4.6*	*1.9*	*-0.9*	*0.90*

Breakout: 4% Improve: 32% Collapse: 20% Attrition: 0% Comparables: Rich Fischer, Jarod Plummer, Jason Ryan, Jamie Shields

Usually, when a guy gets picked in the 35th round, there's a temptation to think he's a draft-and-follow. Not Green; he got picked in 2004, signed in 2004, and has advanced quickly since, though not because of any extraordinary ability. Green's best pitch is his change, and his other offerings are pretty average. His best virtue is also a vice: Green throws strikes so often it turns to disadvantage, as he makes too many mistakes within the strike zone. Nevertheless, this system's so thin on pitching talent that he warrants a mention.

Kevin Gregg

Bats: S Throws: R   Height: 6' 6"   Weight: 235   Born: June 20, 1978   Age: 29

YEAR	TEAM	LVL	AGE	W	L	SV	G	GS	IP	H	BB	SO	HR	GB%	BABIP	STUFF	WHIP	ERA	PERA	EQERA	EQH9	EQBB9	EQSO9	EQHR9	VORP	WXRL
2004	ANA	MLB	26	5	2	1	55	0	87²	86	28	84	6	—	.322	23	1.29	4.21	3.19	4.17	8.3	2.6	7.9	0.5	18.5	0.85
2005	SLC	AAA	27	3	1	0	7	6	34²	36	10	36	2	46.4%	.362	21	1.33	3.89	3.53	3.53	8.6	2.5	6.8	0.5	8.2	—
2005	ANA	MLB	27	1	2	0	33	2	64¹	70	29	52	8	47.1%	.316	-1	1.52	5.04	4.63	5.18	9.5	4.0	7.1	1.1	3.6	-0.26
2006	ANA	MLB	28	3	4	0	32	3	78¹	88	21	71	10	35.8%	.335	12	1.39	4.14	3.78	4.50	9.8	2.2	7.7	1.0	11.5	0.17
2007	*FLO*	*MLB*	*29*	*5*	*5*	*2*	*44*	*5*	*87²*	*85*	*31*	*78*	*10*	*42.0%*	*.297*	*9*	*1.32*	*4.17*	*4.38*	*4.25*	*8.5*	*2.7*	*7.2*	*0.9*	*13.7*	*1.40*

Breakout: 33% Improve: 52% Collapse: 21% Attrition: 10% Comparables: Bobby Howry, Tom Acker, Jose Mesa, Dan Wheeler

A perfectly respectable swingman of the old-school sort: Gregg lasted more than two innings in a dozen relief appearances last year. He's been dealt to the Marlins to give them some veteran gravitas in whatever role they need filled; the Angels received Chris Resop in return. Miami's thick air and near-sea-level altitude will help ameliorate the souvenir-generating potential of Gregg's fly-ball tendencies. He was much better in the second half, and if he can get back to spotting his splitter more effectively, he could surprise people.

Greg Jones

Bats: R Throws: R   Height: 6' 2"   Weight: 195   Born: November 15, 1976   Age: 30

YEAR	TEAM	LVL	AGE	W	L	SV	G	GS	IP	H	BB	SO	HR	GB%	BABIP	STUFF	WHIP	ERA	PERA	EQERA	EQH9	EQBB9	EQSO9	EQHR9	VORP	WXRL
2004	SLC	AAA	27	1	4	3	36	0	53¹	63	19	43	11	—	.325	-24	1.54	5.74	6.04	5.53	9.3	3.3	5.4	1.8	0.4	—
2005	SLC	AAA	28	1	2	10	23	0	25¹	20	6	25	3	38.2%	.262	6	1.03	3.20	4.08	3.12	6.6	2.1	6.2	1.0	7.2	—
2006	SLC	AAA	29	5	6	17	47	0	55²	52	19	45	7	38.5%	.279	-15	1.29	4.24	5.24	4.69	8.4	3.1	5.3	1.5	5.6	—
2006	ANA	MLB	29	0	0	0	5	0	6	8	2	1	1	45.5%	.333	-41	1.67	6.00	5.72	7.11	11.4	2.8	1.4	1.4	-1.0	-0.04
2007	*ANA*	*MLB*	*30*	*3*	*3*	*2*	*58*	*3*	*59*	*64*	*20*	*36*	*11*	*39.0%*	*.282*	*-12*	*1.43*	*4.97*	*5.07*	*4.80*	*9.7*	*2.9*	*5.1*	*1.5*	*4.1*	*0.50*

Breakout: 26% Improve: 56% Collapse: 16% Attrition: 23% Comparables: Clint Weibl, Bob Priddy, Aquilino Lopez, Calvin Maduro

Because of service time, Jones may no longer technically be a rookie, but he's 30 years old and hasn't thrown 40 career innings in the major leagues. He's been on the 40-man for years, quite an investment of organizational management capital, and while he does have a nice fastball-slider combo, so do a lot of people. He'll be battling for Chris Resop for one of the last spots in the pen.

John Lackey — Bats: R Throws: R — Height: 6' 6" Weight: 235 Born: October 23, 1978 Age: 28

YEAR	TEAM	LVL	AGE	W	L	SV	G	GS	IP	H	BB	SO	HR	GB%	BABIP	STUFF	WHIP	ERA	PERA	EQERA	EQH9	EQBB9	EQSO9	EQHR9	VORP	WXRL
2004	ANA	MLB	25	14	13	0	33	32	198¹	215	60	144	22	—	.321	16	1.41	4.67	4.04	4.64	9.1	2.4	6.0	0.9	26.6	3.63
2005	ANA	MLB	26	14	5	0	33	33	209	208	71	199	13	46.1%	.328	38	1.33	3.44	3.32	3.74	8.8	3.0	8.3	0.5	49.1	5.50
2006	ANA	MLB	27	13	11	0	33	33	217²	203	72	190	14	44.6%	.304	34	1.26	3.56	3.40	3.93	8.2	2.8	7.4	0.5	47.1	5.43
2007	ANA	MLB	28	14	10	0	32	32	211	207	63	176	20	45.0%	.299	23	1.28	3.83	3.77	3.79	8.7	2.6	7.0	0.8	41.0	5.80

Breakout: 22% Improve: 67% Collapse: 6% Attrition: 1% Comparables: Bob Rush, Ben McDonald, Freddy Garcia, Aaron Sele

"Capitalist" Lackey is no man's running dog—he is unleashed power, set loose to liquidate bats and downsize offenses. Until or unless Jered Weaver can show that he can reliably post ERAs in the twos, Lackey's the Angels' true ace, though one could argue that an ace would pitch better within in the division—although he owns rival Oakland, weaker sisters Texas and Seattle have Lackey's number. Having mastered using his off-speed stuff to neutralize lefties, he'll be entering his fifth full season with perhaps only one little thing to work on—holding baserunners. Give the man some luck with run support and he'd be a favorite for the Cy Young in the non-Johan Santana category. Stoneman wisely signed last spring to a three-year extension that, with a $9 million club option for 2009, will keep Lackey in place for four years at below-market rates.

Stephen Marek — Bats: R Throws: R — Height: 6' 2" Weight: 200 Born: September 3, 1983 Age: 23

YEAR	TEAM	LVL	AGE	W	L	SV	G	GS	IP	H	BB	SO	HR	GB%	BABIP	STUFF	WHIP	ERA	PERA	EQERA	EQH9	EQBB9	EQSO9	EQHR9	VORP	WXRL
2005	ORM	Rk	21	1	3	0	15	14	66	74	25	55	7	55.0%	.351	-37	1.50	4.50	7.94	7.55	11.6	5.1	3.5	2.5	-13.4	—
2006	CDR	A	22	10	2	0	19	19	119²	95	24	100	8	49.0%	.262	-11	1.00	1.96	5.89	3.43	8.9	2.6	4.3	1.8	27.2	—
2006	RCU	A+	22	2	3	0	6	6	32	26	13	33	4	45.2%	.289	2	1.22	3.94	6.60	4.35	8.4	4.4	5.8	2.0	4.3	—
2007	ANA	MLB	23	5	9	0	26	20	116	141	52	59	22	46.0%	.301	-10	1.66	6.19	6.20	6.01	10.8	3.8	4.3	1.6	-9.6	0.10

Breakout: 2% Improve: 10% Collapse: 57% Attrition: 0% Comparables: Anastacio Martinez, Mark Roberts, Ryan Cummings, Arnold Gooch

A Texas juco reliever, Marek was picked by the Angels as a draft-and-follow in 2004 and came on strong in his full-season debut last year. An intimidator in the making, Marek's the sort that pumps the hard stuff with a loud grunt. He consistently delivers heat in the low-90s (topping out at 95), and supplements it with a nice curve and change, though his delivery needs work. He has work to do—he won't be able to overpower people as easily in Double-A—but he's among the organization's best pitching prospects.

Tommy Mendoza — Bats: R Throws: R — Height: 6' 2" Weight: 195 Born: August 18, 1987 Age: 19

YEAR	TEAM	LVL	AGE	W	L	SV	G	GS	IP	H	BB	SO	HR	GB%	BABIP	STUFF	WHIP	ERA	PERA	EQERA	EQH9	EQBB9	EQSO9	EQHR9	VORP	WXRL
2005	RCU	A+	17	1	0	0	1	2	1	10	4	0	12	0	28.6%	.190	10	0.40	0.00	2.15	0.93	3.7	0.9	7.4	0.0	5.0	—
2006	CDR	A	18	11	6	0	27	27	170¹	169	32	134	15	44.6%	.309	-11	1.18	4.18	6.08	6.20	10.7	2.2	4.3	2.0	-10.8	—
2007	ANA	MLB	19	7	10	0	29	24	143	166	39	77	28	42.0%	.289	1	1.43	5.42	5.35	5.24	10.3	2.3	4.5	1.7	2.3	1.30

Breakout: 35% Improve: 78% Collapse: 1% Attrition: 0% Comparables: Gil Meche, Zach Miner, Justin Germano, Mike Nannini

Subtlety is often lost on the young, but that doesn't mean they don't have aptitude for it. A 2005 fourth-rounder out of a Florida high school, Mendoza tried to blow away the Midwest League in his full-season debut and got belted around for the first two months. Having seen for himself that his moving, low-90s heat wasn't going to provide consistent results by itself, he learned to weave in his off-speed stuff more effectively and started generating more groundouts. Gifted with good mechanics, if he continues to improve his touch on his curve and change, he'll stick as a starter. He'll be one of the youngest starting pitchers in the Cal League this season, so he has year to iron things out.

Dustin Moseley

Bats: R Throws: R Height: 6' 4" Weight: 190 Born: December 26, 1981 Age: 25

YEAR	TEAM	LVL	AGE	W	L	SV	G	GS	IP	H	BB	SO	HR	GB%	BABIP	STUFF	WHIP	ERA	PERA	EQERA	EQH9	EQBB9	EQSO9	EQHR9	VORP	WXRL
2004	CHT	AA	22	3	2	0	8	8	47¹	33	10	40	4	—	.230	11	0.91	2.66	4.66	3.94	7.3	2.2	5.1	1.2	8.4	—
2004	LOU	AAA	22	2	4	0	12	12	71²	78	34	48	7	—	.318	2	1.56	4.64	5.39	4.73	9.5	4.6	4.6	1.0	7.0	—
2005	SLC	AAA	23	4	6	0	17	17	82¹	102	30	38	11	48.7%	.327	-17	1.60	5.03	5.59	4.88	9.6	3.0	3.0	1.2	6.9	—
2006	SLC	AAA	24	13	8	0	26	26	149¹	164	51	114	18	52.7%	.318	-3	1.44	4.71	5.07	5.22	9.7	3.0	5.3	1.3	6.4	—
2006	ANA	MLB	24	1	0	0	3	2	11	22	2	3	3	38.3%	.432	-31	2.18	9.00	5.89	8.49	17.0	1.5	2.3	2.3	-3.8	-0.33
2007	*ANA*	*MLB*	*25*	*5*	*8*	*0*	*31*	*17*	*111*	*132*	*42*	*57*	*17*	*47.0%*	*.304*	*-8*	*1.56*	*5.57*	*5.47*	*5.47*	*10.5*	*3.2*	*4.3*	*1.3*	*-1.4*	*0.60*

Breakout: 15% Improve: 41% Collapse: 21% Attrition: 0% Comparables: Shawn Sedlacek, Mickey Callaway, Jason Young, Ben Hendrickson

When you were a freshman in college, did you have a classmate who, doomed by genetics, lost all of his hair before the year was out? Think about him—already carrying the mark of an older man by his nineteenth birthday. Moseley's lot is much like that of someone with a prematurely exposed pate: Lacking any particularly reliable out-pitch, Moseley's destiny is to be a Quadruple-A hurler, casting about for emergency starts and the off chance that some really bad ballclub will somehow back into having him on their roster. It's the sort of thing that ought to encourage a guy to look up Mike Scott and ask for a tip or two on how to conjure up an unhittable forkball.

Francisco Rodriguez

Bats: R Throws: R Height: 6' 0" Weight: 180 Born: January 7, 1982 Age: 25

YEAR	TEAM	LVL	AGE	W	L	SV	G	GS	IP	H	BB	SO	HR	GB%	BABIP	STUFF	WHIP	ERA	PERA	EQERA	EQH9	EQBB9	EQSO9	EQHR9	VORP	WXRL
2004	ANA	MLB	22	4	1	12	69	0	84	51	33	123	2	—	.286	62	0.99	1.82	2.07	2.20	5.3	3.1	12.1	0.2	37.1	5.09
2005	ANA	MLB	23	2	5	45	66	0	67¹	45	32	91	7	46.1%	.259	41	1.14	2.67	3.25	2.77	5.9	4.2	11.9	0.9	22.9	5.62
2006	ANA	MLB	24	2	3	47	69	0	73	52	28	98	6	39.2%	.288	42	1.10	1.73	2.82	2.07	6.3	3.3	11.3	0.7	33.4	7.30
2007	*ANA*	*MLB*	*25*	*5*	*5*	*38*	*54*	*0*	*61²*	*44*	*25*	*79*	*6*	*41.0%*	*.275*	*33*	*1.12*	*2.62*	*2.67*	*2.57*	*6.4*	*3.4*	*10.8*	*0.8*	*22.4*	*3.60*

Breakout: 21% Improve: 27% Collapse: 46% Attrition: 18% Comparables: Ugueth Urbina, Al Hrabosky, Armando Benitez, Mark Littell

If we earned a wag of the finger anywhere in last year's book, it was in anticipating a career-altering injury for K-Rod. Having come up a save short of Bryan Harvey's club saves record in 2005, Rodriguez set the new record in 2006; he also led MLB in WXRL. Rodriguez logged 22 saves in the season's final two months—impressive, but also a reflection on how hot the Angels were. It also demonstrated why it won't be easy to top Bobby Thigpen's single-season saves record of 57. You not only need a team that can win ballgames, you need a team that doesn't win too many games by too large a margin; the Angels are pretty close to that, and it would still take a lot of things going K-Rod's way for him to have a shot at Thiggy. This winter, the Angels signed Justin Speier for $18 million over four years; you can understand how that contract might create problems with K-Rod two years away from free agency and about to re-enter arbitration.

J. C. Romero

Bats: S Throws: L Height: 5' 11" Weight: 205 Born: June 4, 1976 Age: 31

YEAR	TEAM	LVL	AGE	W	L	SV	G	GS	IP	H	BB	SO	HR	GB%	BABIP	STUFF	WHIP	ERA	PERA	EQERA	EQH9	EQBB9	EQSO9	EQHR9	VORP	WXRL
2004	MIN	MLB	28	7	4	1	74	0	74¹	61	38	69	4	—	.290	19	1.34	3.51	3.73	3.40	7.0	4.1	7.6	0.5	19.9	2.19
2005	MIN	MLB	29	4	3	0	68	0	57	50	39	48	6	57.0%	.277	10	1.56	3.47	5.37	3.88	8.1	6.1	7.4	0.9	9.5	0.81
2006	ANA	MLB	30	1	2	0	65	0	48¹	57	28	31	3	59.4%	.344	-8	1.76	6.71	4.39	7.07	10.3	4.9	5.4	0.5	-7.9	0.11
2007	*BOS*	*MLB*	*31*	*2*	*2*	*1*	*51*	*0*	*47*	*50*	*25*	*36*	*4*	*54%*	*.317*	*-4*	*1.59*	*4.65*	*4.51*	*4.32*	*8.3*	*4.6*	*6.4*	*0.6*	*5.5*	*0.4*

Breakout: 33% Improve: 64% Collapse: 18% Attrition: 19% Comparables: Darold Knowles, Jamie Easterly, Terry Forster, Paul Mirabella

Before 2006, Scioscia had been a little haphazard about getting with the situational program and employing lefty specialists with any regularity. To his credit, he seemed to recognize there are better ways to use the last spot in a bullpen during the regular season. This year was different, as the Angels made a point of going out and getting Romero from the Twins. He succeeded as the team's token situational lefty, holding southpaws to .202/.298/.303. Unfortunately, even with that going for him, he got beaten up a little too regularly and fell out of favor before the All-Star break. His walk rate, already a barely-tenable four unintentionals per nine innings from 2003 to 2005, spiked to almost five. Discarded, Romero signed up with the Red Sox. In his place the Angels have added lefties Darren Oliver, through free agency, and Phil Seibel, via trade Boston.

Ervin Santana
Bats: R Throws: R   Height: 6′ 2″   Weight: 160   Born: January 10, 1983   Age: 24

YEAR	TEAM	LVL	AGE	W	L	SV	G	GS	IP	H	BB	SO	HR	GB%	BABIP	STUFF	WHIP	ERA	PERA	EQERA	EQH9	EQBB9	EQSO9	EQHR9	VORP	WXRL
2004	ARK	AA	21	2	1	0	8	8	43²	41	18	48	3	—	.319	16	1.35	3.30	4.83	4.19	9.0	4.2	6.9	1.0	6.7	—
2005	ARK	AA	22	5	1	0	7	7	39	34	15	32	2	36.3%	.288	12	1.26	2.31	4.47	3.26	7.9	4.0	5.6	0.7	10.1	—
2005	SLC	AAA	22	1	0	0	3	3	19¹	19	2	17	2	33.3%	.315	20	1.09	4.20	3.94	4.58	8.2	0.9	5.9	0.9	2.2	—
2005	ANA	MLB	22	12	8	0	23	23	133²	139	47	99	17	35.8%	.300	12	1.39	4.64	4.57	4.93	9.2	3.2	6.4	1.1	11.9	2.94
2006	ANA	MLB	23	16	8	0	33	33	204	181	70	141	21	38.9%	.272	16	1.23	4.28	4.32	4.46	7.8	2.9	5.9	0.8	30.2	4.12
2007	ANA	MLB	24	11	11	0	30	30	189¹	193	68	140	26	39.0%	.290	15	1.38	4.61	4.48	4.50	9.1	3.1	6.2	1.1	20.3	3.50

Breakout: 16%   Improve: 49%   Collapse: 17%   Attrition: 0%   Comparables: Gary Gentry, Tom Brewer, Kyle Lohse, Bob Welch

Santana ran off seven quality starts in eight appearances from June into July, then trade deadline rumors started to swirl and he was a little too publicly held up as one of the plums. There's no shame in having to keep him—he might not have the same upside Lackey had after two years, but he's not far behind. Watch him pitch if you want to see how a right-handed fly ball/strikeout guy can keep big league hitters from teeing off—he'll "miss" inside against right-handers every so often, pushing them off the inside corner, and preventing them from digging in to get something extra on their swing.

Joe Saunders
Bats: L Throws: L   Height: 6′ 3″   Weight: 210   Born: June 16, 1981   Age: 26

YEAR	TEAM	LVL	AGE	W	L	SV	G	GS	IP	H	BB	SO	HR	GB%	BABIP	STUFF	WHIP	ERA	PERA	EQERA	EQH9	EQBB9	EQSO9	EQHR9	VORP	WXRL
2004	RCU	A+	23	9	7	0	19	19	105²	106	23	76	13	—	.291	-32	1.22	3.41	6.74	5.28	9.9	2.6	3.9	2.2	3.6	—
2004	ARK	AA	23	4	3	0	8	8	39	51	14	25	5	—	.357	-21	1.67	5.77	6.80	6.23	11.8	3.7	3.9	1.8	-2.7	—
2005	ARK	AA	24	7	4	0	18	18	105²	107	32	80	9	52.3%	.308	-4	1.32	3.49	5.09	5.28	9.3	3.5	4.8	1.1	3.7	—
2005	SLC	AAA	24	3	3	0	9	9	55	65	21	29	3	54.9%	.341	-1	1.56	4.58	4.25	5.43	9.0	3.1	3.4	0.5	1.1	—
2006	SLC	AAA	25	10	4	0	21	20	135²	117	38	97	12	53.6%	.268	11	1.15	2.66	4.41	3.01	7.5	2.4	4.9	1.0	39.5	—
2006	ANA	MLB	25	7	3	0	13	13	70²	71	29	51	6	48.2%	.307	13	1.42	4.71	4.03	5.10	8.7	3.5	6.1	0.7	4.8	2.13
2007	ANA	MLB	26	8	10	0	32	28	151	170	55	87	20	47.0%	.301	1	1.49	5.06	4.93	5.00	10.0	3.1	4.9	1.1	6.9	1.80

Breakout: 11%   Improve: 43%   Collapse: 26%   Attrition: 0%   Comparables: Alex Graman, Steve Trout, Joe Kennedy, John Curtis

Saunders was the other rookie star in the Angels rotation in 2006, and the hope is that he will be a solid fourth starter from here on out; he can mix up sinkers, cutters, and running fastballs to hide a merely adequate curve. The one warning sign is that the league might have seen what he has to offer and come away unimpressed—in his first start against a given opponent, Saunders allowed 2.8 runs per nine inning, but in four subsequent matchups against teams that had already seen him, he allowed a staggering 16.34. Saunders missed 2003 with a shoulder injury, which he rehabbed instead of having it cut, and he's been reliably healthy since.

Steven Shell
Bats: R Throws: R   Height: 6′ 5″   Weight: 190   Born: March 10, 1983   Age: 24

YEAR	TEAM	LVL	AGE	W	L	SV	G	GS	IP	H	BB	SO	HR	GB%	BABIP	STUFF	WHIP	ERA	PERA	EQERA	EQH9	EQBB9	EQSO9	EQHR9	VORP	WXRL
2004	RCU	A+	21	12	7	0	28	28	165¹	151	40	190	19	—	.317	1	1.16	3.59	5.70	4.78	9.5	2.7	6.7	1.9	14.6	—
2005	ARK	AA	22	10	8	0	27	27	159²	175	58	126	18	46.3%	.331	-5	1.46	4.56	5.51	5.57	10.0	3.8	5.3	1.4	0.5	—
2006	ARK	AA	23	1	2	0	3	3	18	20	4	10	1	51.7%	.322	-3	1.33	4.00	4.23	6.38	9.3	2.0	3.4	0.5	-1.6	—
2006	SLC	AAA	23	5	9	0	24	22	122²	156	32	82	16	38.9%	.357	-11	1.54	6.19	5.26	6.62	11.2	2.2	4.6	1.4	-14.2	—
2007	ANA	MLB	24	5	7	0	27	16	100²	119	34	58	17	42.0%	.304	-4	1.52	5.69	5.51	5.54	10.5	2.9	4.8	1.4	-2.2	0.40

Breakout: 18%   Improve: 56%   Collapse: 11%   Attrition: 0%   Comparables: Jason Olsen, Paul Stewart, Bronson Arroyo, Gary Glover

A middling talent, "Snail" Shell throws relatively average velocity, but with good movement and mixes in a solid curve. Shell might be the bomb, but that's only because he's always ticking towards an eventual explosion—he frustrates insiders with a tendency to get intimidated in jams and attempt to pitch around trouble before detonating. With runners on base last year, Shell got tattooed for a .349 average and .540 SLG, the sort of mark you regret the morning after, whatever body part it's been inked on. He has a good frame and decent stuff, but he's clearly going to have to become some pitching coach's special project if he's going to pan out.

Scot Shields   Bats: R   Throws: R   Height: 6' 1"   Weight: 170   Born: July 22, 1975   Age: 31

YEAR	TEAM	LVL	AGE	W	L	SV	G	GS	IP	H	BB	SO	HR	GB%	BABIP	STUFF	WHIP	ERA	PERA	EQERA	EQH9	EQBB9	EQSO9	EQHR9	VORP	WXRL
2004	ANA	MLB	28	8	2	4	60	0	105¹	97	40	109	6	—	.312	30	1.30	3.33	3.08	3.48	7.9	3.1	8.5	0.4	31.4	4.74
2005	ANA	MLB	29	10	11	7	78	0	91²	66	37	98	5	55.4%	.270	33	1.12	2.75	3.09	3.28	6.4	3.6	9.4	0.5	25.3	4.53
2006	ANA	MLB	30	7	7	2	74	0	87²	70	24	84	8	53.4%	.270	23	1.07	2.87	3.26	3.02	7.0	2.3	8.1	0.7	29.1	3.73
2007	ANA	MLB	31	4	3	5	63	0	74²	67	24	69	6	50.0%	.292	15	1.21	3.14	3.13	3.13	7.9	2.7	7.8	0.6	22.4	1.80

Breakout: 24%   Improve: 53%   Collapse: 15%   Attrition: 4%   Comparables: Jason Isringhausen, Gene Garber, Jeff Montgomery, Jim Mecir

Sometimes the setup guy becomes a closer—Mariano Rivera, J. J. Putz, and K-Rod himself are good examples—and sometimes he doesn't. It's a sabermetric canard that anyone with ability can close. Shields has been fine in limited engagements, but he's not your typical fire-belching relief ace. Rather, he's the reigning example of a rubber-armed reliever, mixing in curves, sliders, and changes for strikes along with his plus fastball. Shields can do whatever is asked of him; now that he's into his arbitration eligibility, it's up to the Angels to keep him well-paid to compensate for K-Rod getting to hog the fanthead stat.

Jered Weaver   Bats: R   Throws: R   Height: 6' 7"   Weight: 205   Born: October 4, 1982   Age: 24

YEAR	TEAM	LVL	AGE	W	L	SV	G	GS	IP	H	BB	SO	HR	GB%	BABIP	STUFF	WHIP	ERA	PERA	EQERA	EQH9	EQBB9	EQSO9	EQHR9	VORP	WXRL
2005	RCU	A+	22	4	1	0	7	7	33	25	7	49	3	29.7%	.314	27	0.97	3.82	3.78	5.01	7.8	2.2	8.4	1.1	2.1	—
2005	ARK	AA	22	3	3	0	8	8	43	43	19	46	5	31.5%	.314	13	1.44	3.98	5.14	5.10	9.4	4.7	7.2	1.5	2.4	—
2006	SLC	AAA	23	6	1	0	12	11	77¹	63	10	93	7	32.6%	.308	41	0.95	2.10	3.16	2.33	7.6	1.2	8.4	0.9	28.1	—
2006	ANA	MLB	23	11	2	0	19	19	123	94	33	105	15	31.6%	.239	29	1.03	2.56	3.86	2.66	6.7	2.3	7.2	1.0	46.5	5.11
2007	ANA	MLB	24	14	10	0	34	34	205²	194	56	177	27	34.0%	.281	25	1.21	3.76	3.75	3.64	8.4	2.3	7.3	1.1	44.7	6.00

Breakout: 5%   Improve: 17%   Collapse: 51%   Attrition: 0%   Comparables: Dennis Eckersley, Scott Elarton, Don Wilson, Scott Sanderson

Score one for the statheads, at least for the time being. Many scouty types were dubious about how effective Weaver's stuff would be in the majors, but to be fair, nobody thought he wouldn't make it, and pitchers who give up as many long flies as Weaver does can give anybody the willies. Keep that in mind while looking at that "collapse" rate—that collapse is relative to Weaver's extraordinary rookie campaign, not a suggestion that he's got a 50 percent shot at being terrible. He's going to settle in as a solid second or third starter, sort what his brother has been at the best of times, while being every bit as much of a high-intensity moundsman with excellent command of a broad assortment of pitches.

Lineouts

PLAYER	TEAM	LVL	AGE	PA	R	2B	3B	HR	RBI	BB	SO	SB-CS	SPEED	AVG/OBP/SLG	MLVrEqAVG/EqOBP/EqSLG	EqA	VORP
OF P. Bourjos	ORM	Rk	19	279	42	16	7	5	28	22	67	13-5	7.3	.292/.354/.472	.246	.267/.304/.401 .243	3.2
C R. Budde	SLC	AAA	26	244	32	15	0	8	33	22	55	1-1	3.1	.233/.324/.414	-.106	.195/.275/.350 .218	-8.1
C M. Collins	RCU	A+	21	543	61	29	1	7	82	29	74	9-9	4.2	.291/.371/.400	.053	.261/.311/.361 .235	0.1
SS R. Mount*	ORM	Rk	19	319	54	14	2	9	38	36	67	10-3	5.8	.285/.370/.448	.227	.259/.314/.379 .244	9.5
LF C. Pride*	SLC	AAA	37	331	54	18	0	8	44	54	75	21-6	6.0	.311/.424/.465	.182	.235/.327/.329 .241	-13.1
	ANA	MLB	37	33	6	2	0	1	2	6	8	0-0	4.5	.222/.364/.407	-.024	.222/.364/.407 .272	0.6
OF D. Toussaint	RCU	A+	23	419	47	25	1	12	42	35	119	2-2	3.4	.242/.325/.411	-.050	.207/.267/.336 .212	-30.6

PLAYER	TEAM	LVL	AGE	W	L	SV	IP	H	BB	SO	HR	GB%	BABIP	STUFF	WHIP	ERA	PERA	EqERA	EqH9	EqBB9	EqSO9	EqHR9	VORP
R. Aldridge	CDR	A	22	2	3	24	57²	34	21	81	4	—	.259	-5	0.96	2.36	6.34	4.01	8.2	4.9	7.5	1.9	9.1
J. Bulger	SLC	AAA	27	2	2	4	34¹	30	15	44	0	—	.353	16	1.32	4.75	3.42	4.81	8.6	4.0	8.8	0.3	3.0
M. Gonzalez	RCU	A+	22	1	0	1	26	17	2	24	2	—	.208	7	0.73	1.73	4.18	2.10	6.7	0.7	5.3	1.1	10.0
	ARK	AA	22	0	2	4	53²	41	17	38	8	—	.226	-15	1.09	3.89	5.82	3.86	6.7	2.9	4.7	1.7	10.4
K. Lynch	RCU	A+	23	2	3	1	56	41	25	53	3	—	.263	-6	1.18	2.41	5.23	3.46	7.2	4.8	5.1	0.8	13.0
W. Madrigal	ANG	Rk	22	2	1	5	12²	11	3	13	0	—	.355	-16	1.15	3.69	3.92	5.11	9.5	2.9	4.4	0.0	0.7
R. Mosebach	CDR	A	21	10	6	0	159¹	166	29	97	5	—	.318	2	1.23	3.05	4.49	5.81	10.1	2.1	3.2	0.7	-3.6
	RCU	A+	21	1	1	0	22²	23	8	15	1	—	.301	-5	1.40	6.49	5.13	7.15	9.5	3.6	4.0	0.8	-3.9
R. Rodriguez	RCU	A+	21	3	0	0	17¹	15	2	20	0	—	.341	17	0.99	0.53	2.66	1.06	8.5	1.1	6.9	0.0	8.6
	ARK	AA	21	5	10	0	133	175	55	83	28	—	.339	-39	1.73	6.63	7.17	7.45	11.6	3.7	4.1	2.4	-27.8
R. Thompson	ARK	AA	22	3	4	10	66	52	27	60	13	—	.235	-20	1.20	5.18	6.90	5.32	7.5	3.7	6.0	2.3	2.1

Peter Bourjos is an athletic, toolsy center fielder picked up in the tenth round of the 2005 draft who just made his pro debut; he'll need to show better hitting skills, but it's still very early. Before the Phillies signed Rod Barajas, they snagged **Ryan Budde** through the Rule 5 draft as a potential third-catcher candidate. Aussie import **Michael Collins** is neither the father of the Irish Republic, nor the *Apollo 11* astronaut who drew the short straw, but he's shown some power potential, however scruffy around the edges he is in all phases of the game. **Ryan Mount** is a strong-armed shortstop (yes, another one) with the power potential to make him a prospect at second or third, but he's very unpolished. **Curtis Pride** has had something less than a full major league career, and the way he swings the bat keeps us wondering why not. At one point, **Drew Toussaint** was seen as a top prospect, but if you can't hit in Rancho Cucamonga, managing a Denny's looks like a more likely prospect for your future than the major leagues.

Richard Aldridge torched the kiddies with the best slider in the Midwest League, but he was older than the competition; it remains to be seen if that plus his average fastball will play well at higher levels. **Jason Bulger** was the unique talent the Halos acquired from Arizona to get Alberto Callaspo out of their hair simply because they seemed to have too many middle infielders; Bulger got designated for assignment after only a year in the organization. An undrafted amateur who's pitched well enough to attract notice is a pretty rare thing, but **Miguel Gonzalez** has pulled it off in only two years as a pro despite a relatively modest assortment. **Kevin Lynch** is a product of Florida State, so the fact that he held his own in the Cal League was expected; he won't overpower people, but he will fool a few with some good breaking stuff. **Warner Madrigal** played in the outfield to start the year, but the Angels made him a pitcher and he flashed 97 MPH on the speed gun. The Angels draft a goodly number of finesse right-handers, but **Robert Mosebach** complements an adequate fastball with a pretty good slider, and he's good at keeping the ball on the ground. Dominican project pitcher **Rafael Rodriguez** throws in the low-90s and is something of an organizational favorite, but despite entering his sixth season with the organization, he's still a long way off and struggling to find a repeatable delivery. **Richard Thompson** is another one of the organization's Australians with a familiar name, but his modest assortment isn't the sort of thing that's going to shoot out the lights.

Manager: Mike Scioscia

Year	Team	W-L	Pythag +/-	Avg PC	100 +P	120 +P	QS	BQS	REL	REL w Zero R	IBB	SUBS	PH	PH Avg	PH HR	SB2	CS2	SB3	CS3	SAC Att	SAC %	POS SAC	Squeeze	Swing	In Play
2004	ANA	92-70	0	97.1	82	3	77	7	343	212	27	57	91	.260	2	123	42	19	3	77	72.7%	54	5	188	131
2005	ANA	95-67	0	97.2	76	1	93	7	377	246	24	49	90	.234	1	149	47	12	8	65	66.2%	42	3	171	137
2006	ANA	89-73	+4	97.3	83	2	86	11	380	231	27	50	101	.171	4	123	45	23	6	42	73.8%	29	2	189	154

There are few active managers more capable than Scioscia. He's flexible with his lineups, and not simply because he has Chone Figgins. He's equally flexible with his roster management, coordinating with GM Bill Stoneman to make sure the roster's never lacking for arms or the right reserves during any one series. He's also the closest thing to Whitey Herzog we have these days, as he pushes the running game and the hit-and-run more than any of his peers. His MLB-leading 13-for-13 success rate on double-steals last year was a nice turn. In the pen, Scioscia is again something of a throwback, showing a remarkable willingness to use relievers for multi-inning outings, and generally eschewing the situational overmanagement that consumes so many of his peers. Although he might miss both his pitching coach (Bud Black, now managing the Padres) and bench coach (Joe Maddon, still with the D-Rays), Scioscia should be able to move on without them and lead yet another aggressively well-run club with his mastery of in-game tactical detail and attentive roster management.

Los Angeles Dodgers

The popular fable of the 2006 Dodgers is that, after two years in thrall to Paul "Google Boy" DePodesta and his *Moneyball*-driven pocket-protector geekery, the team returned to its winning ways thanks to the decisive moves and old-school baseball sense of new General Manager Ned Colletti. It makes for a tidy story arc, but, in reality, the Dodgers' run to the NL Wild Card last year owed less to Colletti's occasionally frenetic deck-shuffling than to the foundation laid by DePodesta and the organization's thriving player development system.

Chaos reigned after the 2005 Dodgers led the majors in salary spent on disabled players en route to a dismal 71–91 campaign. Disappointed that five years of solid performance didn't merit an extension, Manager Jim Tracy exercised an out-clause in his contract and departed shortly after season's end. The replacement DePodesta settled on was team Director of Player Development Terry Collins. The choice of Collins, notorious for managing late-season collapses in Houston and Anaheim, didn't sit well with owner Frank McCourt or Special Advisor Tommy Lasorda, and DePodesta was fired by the end of October, just as the business of the offseason began.

A veteran of nine years as the Giants' Assistant GM under Brian Sabean, Colletti was hired two weeks later. Despite fears that he'd mimic his mentor's don't-trust-anyone-under-35 approach and strip mine the prospect-rich system's bluest chips, Colletti initially took a conservative tack, signing a handful of free agents to short deals to bridge the gap to the up-and-coming prospects. He quickly gave the team that had, after all, won the NL West in 2004 a solid shot at recapturing a weak division while preserving the bulk of its future talent base. Thus constructed, the 2006 Dodgers

surged and slumped with alarming regularity. After a 46–42 first half, they started the second half 1–12, only to win 11 straight games, kicking off a 41–19 finish that left them second to the Padres only via a head-to-head tiebreaker.

Given that he won the Wild Card in Year One, it's tempting to give Colletti a pass, but, in actuality, his moves were a mixed bag. Nate Silver's Marginal value Over Replacement Player formula (MORP) accounts for the non-linearity in the market price of baseball talent in order to produce a monetary valuation for players that more closely reflects their actual contributions. Using MORP, we can see the disconnect between the Dodger free agents' pay and production (see table 1):

Among Colletti's signings, two big hits offset several less successful moves. Rafael Furcal—the only player Colletti signed for more than two years—put up a near-MVP-caliber season at shortstop, while 36-year-old Japanese import Takashi Saito turned in an Eric Gagne-like performance as closer. Elsewhere, returns were less flattering. Kenny Lofton proved an adequate hired gun, and Aaron Sele and Joe Beimel climbed off the scrapheap with pockets full of smoke and mirrors, but, despite a hot first half, Nomar Garciaparra's injuries and second-half slump made his incentive-based contract a losing proposition. In addition, Brett Tomko was bumped from the rotation after the midseason cavalry arrived, and though his shift to the bullpen began successfully, the returns soon diminished, while Bill Mueller's knees forced him to the DL after one month and into retirement at season's end, making nearly all of his $9.5-million, two-year deal a sunk cost.

To offset some of those shortcomings, Colletti traded vigorously, and though enough injuries and ineffectiveness befell the ex-Dodgers to suggest a gypsy curse, the deals

---

DODGERS PROSPECTUS

2006 record: 88–74; Second place, NL West; Lost to Mets in Division Series

Pythagenport record: 87–75

Runs scored per game: 5.06 (4th in NL)

Runs allowed per game: 4.64 (4th in NL)

Team EqA: .268 (2nd in NL)

2006 Batters Age: 30.4 (4th oldest in NL)

2006 Pitchers Age: 30.6 (2nd oldest in NL)

Ballpark: Dodger Stadium; Neutral park; Park Factor of .993

2006: Clearly, the 88 wins were the responsibility of Tommy Lasorda, while the NLDS loss was rightfully placed at the feet of Paul DePodesta.

2007: With this much pitching depth, even signing Juan Pierre won't be enough to keep them out of contention in the NL West.

Table 1. How the West Wasn't Won With a Few Dollars More

Player	WARP1	2006 Salary ($)	MORP	+/– ($)
Furcal	7.9	9,000,000	17,637,060	8,637,060
Garciaparra	3.6	8,500,000*	4,870,360	–3,629,640
Mueller	0.5	4,250,000	621,500	–3,628,500
Lofton	3.0	4,000,000*	3,724,000	-276,000
Tomko	2.2	3,600,000	2,437,440	–1,162,560
Sele	2.3	700,000	2,583,140	1,883,140
Saito	6.9	500,000	13,955,260	13,455,260
Beimel	2.4	380,500	2,733,160	2,352,660
Total	**28.8**	**$30,930,500**	**$48,561,920**	**$17,631,420**

NOTE: MORP = 485,000 × WARP + 216,000 × (WARP^2) + 325,000.

*Includes PA-based incentives attained.

were often counterproductive. In the end, only two of the dozen players obtained accumulated more than 2.0 WARP in Dodger blue (see table 2).

Why Colletti believed Mark Hendrickson had suddenly transformed into a league-average starter despite peripherals that said otherwise was but one mystery. Why Odalis Perez so needed exile that he required an escort by two warm bodies and a dowry exceeding $10 million was another. Only the wintertime trade of Milton Bradley (whose off-field issues made him untenable), the deadline grab of Greg Maddux (a legitimately great move), and the August 31 pickup of Marlon Anderson had more than a marginal impact on the team's run. The acquisitions of Wilson Betemit and Julio Lugo, though providing manager Grady Little with the flexibility to patch an infield worn down by injuries, were undone by post-trade slumps which Colletti couldn't have predicted at the time.

The moves cost the team several tainted but nonetheless talented prospects. Joel Guzman had seen his stock plummet due to a shift across the defensive spectrum and

weak performances at Triple-A Las Vegas. Dioner Navarro had shown promise at the plate, but struggled to contain the running game. Edwin Jackson had regressed since his tantalizing 2003 debut. Willy Aybar had performed somewhat over his head, but the net cost of trading him, Jackson, and Chuck Tiffany for Betemit and four months of Baez was steep.

Remaining in the fold were even more prospects assembled under the front office's true superstar, Director of Amateur Scouting (now Assistant GM, Scouting) Logan White. Many made positive contributions to the 2006 team. Catcher Russell Martin, who spent just a month at Triple-A, quickly bypassed Navarro not only as the team's backstop of the future, but of the present. Smoke-throwing Jonathan Broxton carved a niche as the team's top setup man. Chad Billingsley and Hong-Chi Kuo stabilized the rotation in the second half after Hendrickson proved a bust and Sele flamed out. James Loney hit .328/.381/.741 spotting for Garciaparra over the final two months. Matt Kemp provided an initial burst of power before his hacktastic ways got the better of him.

Bill Plaschke may have rushed to celebrate the affable Colletti's superiority over his reserved predecessor, but DePodesta's signings provided the Dodgers with their butter and egg men (as Vin Scully, reaching back for a Roaring Twenties Broadway locution, likes to put it). Derek Lowe and Brad Penny led the pitching staff, and J. D. Drew and Jeff Kent provided much of the offensive muscle. Just as DePodesta's victorious 2004 squad owed a great deal to his predecessor Dan Evans's groundwork, Colletti's winner had an estranged parent in DePo.

Colletti's 2006–2007 offseason moves are again a hodgepodge. Former Giant Jason Schmidt's three-year, $47-million deal rates among the winter's best, and follows Colletti's best practice of the previous winter, paying more for a shorter deal. While no longer a true ace, Schmidt rebounded nicely from a down 2005, and his PECOTA fore-

Table 2. Colletti's Trades

Player(s) Acquired (WARP1)	Player(s) Dealt (WARP 1)
Andre Ethier (2.9)	Milton Bradley (2.8) and Antonio Perez (– 0.9)
Jae Seo (0.6) and Tim Hamulack (0.1)	Duaner Sanchez (2.5), Steve Schmoll
Danny Baez (1.8) and Lance Carter (– 0.1)	Edwin Jackson (0.2), Chuck Tiffany
Mark Hendrickson (1.0), Toby Hall (0.7)	Dioner Navarro (1.1), Jae Seo (1.7)
Elmer Dessens (0.4)	Odalis Perez (1.0), Julio Pimentel, Blake Johnson, and $10.1 million
Wilson Betemit (0.5)	Danny Baez (0.2), Willy Aybar (0.2)
Julio Lugo (0.0)	Joel Guzman, Sergio Pedroza
Greg Maddux (2.6)	Cesar Izturis (– 0.2)
Marlon Anderson (1.1)	Jhonny Nunez
Total: 12 players, 11.6 WARP1	**8.2 WARP1 + four Top 50 prospects + $10.1 million**

casts a weighted mean ERA of 4.12. Former Phillie Randy Wolf (one year, $8 million) had a rough return from Tommy John surgery, but further time to heal and an escape from Citizens Bank Park should aid his recovery; at the very least he provides enough depth that the team can explore trading Penny, Tomko, or Hendrickson. Saito, re-signed for a mere $1 million, may be the game's best closer on a per-dollar basis.

The offense's outlook is less rosy. Garciaparra netted a two-year, $18.5-million return engagement, a move driven less by baseball reasons than by the need for positive PR in the wake of J. D. Drew's decision to opt out of his contract. Former Diamondback Luis Gonzalez likely won't generate enough offense to fill Drew's shoes or justify his $7.35 million salary. The *coup de grâce* is the appalling five-year, $44-million deal handed to Juan Pierre, a below-average hitter (EqAs of .257 and .255 the past two years) whose entirely speed-based game is unlikely to age well; the team already has an excellent leadoff hitter in Furcal and a potential long-term centerfield solution in Kemp. The Dodgers could have instead matched the $6 million Texas is paying Lofton, who even at 40 has a rosier PECOTA (.302/.362/.398, an MLVr of −.003) than the 29-year-old Pierre (.292/.339/.374,

an MLVr of −.083). The wretched Pierre deal rates among the winter's worst; it won't help an offense already hard-pressed to match last year's 820 runs. Gonzo's limited to left, Nomar to first, creating a logjam in right—Loney, Kemp, and Ethier—that will leave ready-now young talent waiting around.

Still, the organizational bounty of prospects and financial resources remains, as does Colletti's ultimate commitment to a youth movement. Andy LaRoche should eventually take over third base and provide ample offense and defense, converting Betemit back to his supersub role, if not trade bait. Jonathan Meloan could join Broxton as another power arm in the bullpen. If they pitch up to their late-season efforts, Billingsley and Kuo offer significant upgrades over their predecessors over the course of a full season. Kemp could deliver on his sizable upside after shoring up his plate discipline in Las Vegas. Drew's departure frees up room for this big-market team to add to its relatively modest payroll, one that should remain in check due to the cheap young talent at hand. The winter's machinations have yet to produce a clear-cut favorite in the NL West, so for all of Colletti's stumbles, time remains on the Dodgers' side.

HITTERS

Tony Abreu 2B Bats: R Throws: R Height: 5' 9" Weight: 185 Born: November 13, 1984 Age: 22

YEAR	TEAM	LVL	AGE	PA	R	2B	3B	HR	RBI	BB	SO	SB	CS	SPEED	AVG	OBP	SLG	MLVR	EQAVG	EQOBP	EQSLG	EQA	VORP	DEFENSE
2004	CGA	A	19	383	50	21	8	8	54	8	59	16	12	6.9	.302	.327	.472	.131	.275	.291	.414	.239	5.6	91-2B -10
2004	VRO	A+	19	47	8	3	1	0	3	1	8	4	1	7.6	.419	.435	.535	.486	.386	.404	.523	.319	7.4	10-SS -1
2005	VRO	A+	20	421	54	23	7	4	43	15	56	14	10	6.1	.327	.356	.452	.193	.291	.318	.407	.250	12.9	83-2B 4
2005	JAX	AA	20	102	10	3	2	0	9	4	21	0	2	4.9	.250	.284	.323	-.178	.227	.255	.278	.192	-6.9	20-2B -3
2006	JAX	AA	21	509	66	24	3	6	55	33	69	8	4	5.1	.287	.343	.392	.098	.288	.337	.415	.262	20.2	110-2B 5
2007	*LAN*	*MLB*	*22*	*509*	*60*	*28*	*3*	*8*	*53*	*26*	*70*	*9*	*4*	*5.6*	*.279*	*.323*	*.408*	*-.075*	*.281*	*.322*	*.410*	*.250*	*13.8*	*120-2B 0*

Breakout: 19% Improve: 44% Collapse: 24% Attrition: 2%   Comparables: Luis Gonzalez, Jerry Hairston, Jack Wilson, Dan Cey

Don't be fooled by the raw rate stats; the 2005 Florida State League batting champ continued his steady development as he progressed up the ladder. Most notably, he improved his plate discipline, lowering his strikeouts per unintentional walk from a scary 3.94 to a workable 2.22. He has no one outstanding skill, but is solid to above-average across the board, and his keystone pairing with Chin-Lung Hu gets raves for its double-play acrobatics. As the duo graduates to Las Vegas, perhaps they could book an act at Circus Circus.

Marlon Anderson 2B/OF Bats: L Throws: R Height: 5' 11" Weight: 200 Born: January 6, 1974 Age: 33

YEAR	TEAM	LVL	AGE	PA	R	2B	3B	HR	RBI	BB	SO	SB	CS	SPEED	AVG	OBP	SLG	MLVR	EQAVG	EQOBP	EQSLG	EQA	VORP	DEFENSE	
2004	SLN	MLB	30	271	31	12	0	8	28	12	38	6	2	5.4	.237	.269	.379	-.171	.234	.266	.377	.225	-4.7	26-2B -2	21-LF 2
2005	NYN	MLB	31	260	31	9	0	7	19	18	45	6	1	5.7	.264	.316	.391	-.047	.267	.322	.394	.254	3.0	18-1B 0	16-2B 1
2006	WAS	MLB	32	239	31	13	2	5	23	18	41	2	4	5.4	.274	.331	.423	.015	.284	.342	.447	.265	6.1	26-2B -1	
2006	LAN	MLB	32	73	12	3	2	7	15	7	8	2	2	5.0	.375	.431	.813	.800	.375	.431	.812	.362	13.6	13-LF -2	
2007	*LAN*	*MLB*	*33*	*274*	*37*	*14*	*2*	*9*	*36*	*21*	*43*	*4*	*2*	*5.6*	*.278*	*.336*	*.456*	*.012*	*.280*	*.335*	*.458*	*.268*	*9.8*	*67-DH*	

Breakout: 15% Improve: 37% Collapse: 27% Attrition: 31%   Comparables: Todd Hollandsworth, Lee Maye, Gates Brown, Marvin Benard

When the Dodgers traded for Anderson on August 31, they were simply adding depth, and hoping they'd added a solid pinch-hitter who could spot in both the infield and the outfield. Surprisingly, Anderson quickly won favor with Grady Little and soon edged out a slumping Andre Ethier for the starting job in left, whereupon he went on a rampage. He homered

(continued next page)

Marlon Anderson *(continued)*

seven times in just 64 at-bats, including twice in the September 18 four-consecutive-homer epic. All told, his impact on the NL West race guarantees a permanent spot in both Dodger lore and the annals of great deadline pickups. That said, Little should avoid becoming too enamored of his services (which the Dodgers retained for $925,000); there's no earthly reason to crowd Ethier out of the lineup on a regular basis. Anderson's a fantastic pinch-hitter (.291/.358/.437 in 206 career AB) whose profile complements Olmedo Saenz in that he's a lefty who can play beyond the corner infield spots.

Wilson Betemit   INF   Bats: S   Throws: R   Height: 6' 3"   Weight: 200   Born: November 2, 1981   Age: 25

YEAR	TEAM	LVL	AGE	PA	R	2B	3B	HR	RBI	BB	SO	SB	CS	SPEED	AVG	OBP	SLG	MLVR	EQAVG	EQOBP	EQSLG	EQA	VORP	DEFENSE			
2004	RIC	AAA	22	391	48	24	2	13	59	32	99	3	3	4.3	.278	.336	.466	.076	.263	.321	.431	.257	14.2	79-3B	-6	15-SS	-2
2004	ATL	MLB	22	52	2	0	0	0	3	4	16	0	1	4.4	.170	.231	.170	-.562	.085	.154	.085	.108	-5.9				
2005	ATL	MLB	23	274	36	12	4	4	20	22	55	1	3	5.5	.305	.359	.435	.110	.305	.362	.447	.274	11.5	48-3B	-6	15-SS	0
2006	ATL	MLB	24	219	30	16	0	9	29	19	57	2	1	4.1	.281	.344	.497	.136	.281	.347	.487	.281	12.4	23-3B	-1	10-SS	0
2006	LAN	MLB	24	193	19	7	0	9	24	17	45	1	0	3.4	.241	.306	.437	-.056	.243	.311	.428	.255	0.5	44-3B	-4		
2007	LAN	MLB	25	431	52	17	2	15	56	37	94	5	3	4.9	.257	.324	.434	-.056	.258	.323	.436	.258	10.0	102-3B	-1		

Breakout: 12%   Improve: 35%   Collapse: 28%   Attrition: 19%   Comparables: Carlos Guillen, Dave Hollins, Billy Smith, Mark Whiten

Illegally signed out of the Dominican Republic at the tender age of 14, Betemit endured a rocky relationship with the Braves as the shine wore off his star prospect status. Honored as a minor league All-Star from 1999 to 2001, Betemit's career stalled at Triple-A, where he made almost 1,300 plate appearances over three seasons; he made the big club in 2005 partly because he was out of options. Despite hitting well above expectations that year, he was consigned to fill-in status; the Braves refused to move Chipper Jones off third base and decided that Betemit's body had thickened too much to merit his taking over shortstop. Still a reserve as 2006 dawned, Betemit hit well when Jones was sidelined in April and July, but scrambled for at-bats in between. Desperate for relievers, the Braves sent him to L.A. for Danny Baez and Willy Aybar, a younger and less-heralded, but essentially comparable player. The Dodgers hoped Betemit would solve their third-base vacancy, but he ran hot and cold. He's still the starter, but Ned Colletti openly trawled for upgrades over the winter, leaving open the question of how committed the team is to Betemit despite his youth and low salary.

Jose Cruz Jr.   OF   Bats: S   Throws: R   Height: 6' 0"   Weight: 210   Born: April 19, 1974   Age: 33

YEAR	TEAM	LVL	AGE	PA	R	2B	3B	HR	RBI	BB	SO	SB	CS	SPEED	AVG	OBP	SLG	MLVR	EQAVG	EQOBP	EQSLG	EQA	VORP	DEFENSE			
2004	TBA	MLB	30	636	76	25	8	21	78	76	117	11	6	6.1	.242	.333	.433	-.027	.244	.340	.439	.269	8.8	143-RF	-10		
2005	ARI	MLB	31	245	23	9	0	12	28	42	54	0	1	2.7	.213	.347	.436	.017	.209	.347	.438	.270	5.3	46-CF	-9		
2005	LAN	MLB	31	179	23	14	2	6	22	23	43	0	1	4.3	.301	.391	.532	.305	.303	.397	.548	.313	14.3	42-RF	3		
2006	LAN	MLB	32	273	34	16	1	5	17	43	54	5	1	5.3	.233	.353	.381	-.049	.233	.358	.390	.269	1.9	31-LF	0	16-RF	2
2007	SDN	MLB	33	344	47	18	2	11	42	49	68	4	2	5.1	.243	.354	.438	-.009	.249	.357	.452	.277	9.4	83-RF	-3		

Breakout: 20%   Improve: 45%   Collapse: 23%   Attrition: 36%   Comparables: Jim Russell, Roger Maris, Dan Pasqua, Merv Rettenmund

After hitting well in a late-season stint with the 2005 Dodgers, Cruz had the odd distinction of re-signing during the interim between Paul DePodesta's firing and Ned Colletti's hiring. As such, he had no real champion within the organization, but, thanks to injuries, he found playing time at all three outfield spots prior to the arrival of rookies Andre Ethier and Matt Kemp. He showed his usual plate discipline, but his power has drained away, and the Dodgers decided they needed the roster spot more than the player at the trade deadline. He didn't catch on elsewhere, waiting until December to sign a one-year deal with the Padres. He's barely hanging on as a fourth outfielder.

Travis Denker   2B   Bats: R   Throws: R   Height: 5' 9"   Weight: 170   Born: August 5, 1985   Age: 21

YEAR	TEAM	LVL	AGE	PA	R	2B	3B	HR	RBI	BB	SO	SB	CS	SPEED	AVG	OBP	SLG	MLVR	EQAVG	EQOBP	EQSLG	EQA	VORP	DEFENSE	
2004	OGD	Rk	18	254	44	17	1	12	43	24	52	2	3	3.9	.311	.372	.556	.180	.222	.256	.351	.213	-17.8	46-2B	1
2005	CGA	A	19	434	65	23	1	21	68	67	78	2	5	2.5	.310	.417	.556	.386	.275	.357	.474	.282	31.8	68-2B	10
2005	VRO	A+	19	125	14	3	0	2	9	15	26	1	2	3.4	.185	.296	.269	-.232	.162	.256	.234	.183	-12.3	27-2B	4
2006	CGA	A	20	320	47	11	1	11	45	65	37	2	1	4.2	.268	.420	.452	.236	.240	.359	.397	.269	11.2	64-2B	-4
2006	VRO	A+	20	220	24	6	0	5	25	24	36	0	2	3.4	.220	.309	.330	-.111	.194	.268	.291	.203	-13.8	40-3B	-3
2007	LAN	MLB	21	510	53	22	1	12	54	53	80	1	1	4.3	.241	.324	.376	-.145	.242	.323	.378	.242	3.4	120-2B	1

Breakout: 28%   Improve: 62%   Collapse: 15%   Attrition: 10%   Comparables: Pat Manning, Juan Espinal, Joe Lawrence, Adam Morrissey

Despite tearing up the Sally League in 2005, Denker struggled in a late-season promotion to Vero Beach. Given his age and the sample size, that hardly caused alarm. A repeat go at Vero—this time playing third base so Blake DeWitt could test out second—went almost as badly, and by mid-June Denker was back in Columbus and at the keystone. While he didn't replicate his 2005 showing there, at the lower level he's shown outstanding plate discipline and excellent power for a middle infielder, drawing comparisons to Marcus Giles (especially due to his size), but a lack of range and fringe-average arm suggest he'll resume his journey down the defensive spectrum. An outfield corner is a possible home, but if Denker can't crack the code of High-A pitching, it will hardly matter.

Blake DeWitt   3B/2B   Bats: L   Throws: R   Height: 5' 11"   Weight: 175   Born: August 20, 1985   Age: 21

YEAR	TEAM	LVL	AGE	PA	R	2B	3B	HR	RBI	BB	SO	SB	CS	SPEED	AVG	OBP	SLG	MLVR	EQAVG	EQOBP	EQSLG	EQA	VORP	DEFENSE		
2004	OGD	Rk	18	332	61	19	3	12	47	28	78	1	1	4.6	.284	.350	.488	.013	.199	.232	.290	.186	-46.3	65-3B	-13	
2005	CGA	A	19	522	61	31	3	11	65	34	79	0	1	3.0	.283	.333	.428	.072	.247	.285	.359	.224	-8.2	110-3B	-11	
2006	VRO	A+	20	478	61	18	1	18	61	45	79	8	5	4.5	.268	.339	.442	.103	.244	.305	.415	.248	7.8	90-2B	-10	16-3B 1
2006	JAX	AA	20	112	6	1	0	1	6	8	21	0	1	3.0	.183	.241	.221	-.332	.181	.232	.219	.164	-12.1	24-3B	0	
2007	LAN	MLB	21	517	51	24	1	13	59	35	86	3	2	4.3	.249	.303	.387	-.161	.250	.302	.389	.235	0.6	122-2B	-6	

Breakout: 55%   Improve: 75%   Collapse: 14%   Attrition: 5%   Comparables: Ivanon Coffie, Scott Hodges, Donnie Murphy, Nick Leach

The 28th pick of the 2004 draft, DeWitt was widely considered the best high school hitter available at the time. Despite a sweet, left-handed swing, he has yet to live up to the scouts' expectations of his raw power potential (he slugged just .397 away from hitter-friendly Vero Beach) or knowledge of the strike zone, but at least the translated stats indicate steady progress on both fronts. Some of his difficulties as a hitter in 2005 can be traced to the Dodgers discovering that he had astigmatism but initially failing to outfit him with the correct contact lens prescription. With third baseman Andy LaRoche now the system's top hitting prospect, the Dodgers shifted DeWitt to second base last year; while he has the raw tools to handle the move, the initial results didn't draw raves. Whether he stays there or returns to the hot corner, there's no sense in rushing him given his tender age and the depth of the system.

J. D. Drew   RF   Bats: L   Throws: R   Height: 6' 1"   Weight: 200   Born: November 20, 1975   Age: 31

YEAR	TEAM	LVL	AGE	PA	R	2B	3B	HR	RBI	BB	SO	SB	CS	SPEED	AVG	OBP	SLG	MLVR	EQAVG	EQOBP	EQSLG	EQA	VORP	DEFENSE		
2004	ATL	MLB	28	645	118	28	8	31	93	118	116	12	3	6.8	.305	.436	.570	.403	.301	.433	.566	.335	69.5	128-RF	4	
2005	LAN	MLB	29	311	48	12	1	15	36	51	50	1	1	4.8	.286	.412	.520	.306	.291	.415	.546	.323	26.9	43-RF	-2	27-CF -1
2006	LAN	MLB	30	594	84	34	6	20	100	89	106	2	3	5.2	.283	.393	.498	.210	.285	.396	.504	.305	34.9	125-RF	13	
2007	BOS	MLB	31	504	80	28	3	15	63	73	92	4	2	5.7	.284	.391	.473	.139	.271	.384	.467	.302	20.6	119-RF	3	

Breakout: 4%   Improve: 21%   Collapse: 33%   Attrition: 10%   Comparables: Bobby Abreu, Von Hayes, Johnny Briggs, Jim Edmonds

After an injury-marred inaugural season as a Dodger, not to mention a pair of offseason surgeries (wrist and knee), Drew put the lie to his critics in 2006. Despite aches and pains, he avoided the DL all season and reached a career high in games played; ten pinch-hit appearances padded the total, but credit Grady Little with successfully managing his workload. Though a midsummer power outage saw him go eight weeks without a homer, Drew rediscovered his stroke in September and helped key the Wild Card run, hitting .317/.462/.683 with six home runs for the month. As the season wound down, Drew spoke of declining to exercise an opt-out clause in his five-year, $55-million contract, noting he liked living in L.A., but boom times signaled by the early resolution of labor negotiations changed the landscape enough for the Scott Boras client to reconsider. Ned Colletti's hurt feelings aside, that should have generated sighs of relief; Drew's propensity for injury would have inevitably bitten the Dodgers. As if to underscore the point, the five-year, $70-million deal Boras hammered out with the Red Sox required restructuring after Drew failed his physical because of a bum shoulder.

Cory Dunlap   1B   Bats: L   Throws: L   Height: 6' 1"   Weight: 205   Born: November 30, 1999   Age: 23

YEAR	TEAM	LVL	AGE	PA	R	2B	3B	HR	RBI	BB	SO	SB	CS	SPEED	AVG	OBP	SLG	MLVR	EQAVG	EQOBP	EQSLG	EQA	VORP	DEFENSE	
2004	OGD	Rk	0	317	57	18	1	7	53	68	40	0	0	3.2	.351	.492	.518	.360	.261	.363	.360	.261	1.5	48-1B	-5
2005	VRO	A+	0	505	61	25	0	7	77	65	64	5	2	3.3	.291	.382	.398	.129	.246	.327	.341	.241	-14.2	98-1B	-12
2006	VRO	A+	0	380	43	15	0	14	47	88	69	0	1	2.5	.261	.435	.461	.253	.234	.387	.421	.287	13.0	72-1B	-9
2007	LAN	MLB	23	487	58	22	0	13	56	70	83	0	0	3.9	.261	.370	.414	.001	.262	.369	.416	.274	9.3	115-1B	-7

Breakout: 30%   Improve: 57%   Collapse: 16%   Attrition: 9%   Comparables: Steve Cox, Mark Johnson, Brad Wilkerson, Jeremy Brown

A gargantuan prospect who weighed nearly 300 pounds as a high school senior, Dunlap has been fighting the Battle of the Bulge since before he was drafted out of Contra Costa Community College in 2004. Skipped up from rookie ball to High-A in 2005, Dunlap repeated the level last year and showed considerable progress, though, like most Vero Beach players, his home/road splits (.524 SLG home, .396 SLG road) reveal that his home park overstated his power. He's an extremely patient hitter—we'll hesitate to praise his "plate discipline" in this case—who struggles with maintaining his balance and has yet to convert his bulk into power on a consistent basis. Unsurprisingly, his physique hampers him in the field as well. The Dodgers have helped Dunlap with diet and conditioning, but he'll have to take control of the situation himself before it stalls his progress.

Andre Ethier   **OF**   **Bats: L**   **Throws: L**   Height: 6′ 1″   Weight: 210   Born: April 10, 1982   Age: 25

YEAR	TEAM	LVL	AGE	PA	R	2B	3B	HR	RBI	BB	SO	SB	CS	SPEED	AVG	OBP	SLG	MLVR	EQAVG	EQOBP	EQSLG	EQA	VORP	DEFENSE			
2004	MOD	A+	22	471	72	23	5	7	53	45	64	2	5	4.1	.313	.383	.442	.157	.275	.333	.377	.247	6.1	68-CF	-7	17-LF	-1
2005	MID	AA	23	572	104	30	3	18	80	48	93	1	4	4.0	.319	.385	.497	.248	.296	.357	.462	.280	21.0	69-LF	-2	46-RF	8
2006	LVG	AAA	24	103	15	4	3	1	12	14	16	2	1	6.3	.349	.447	.500	.296	.318	.408	.466	.303	7.1	20-RF	0		
2006	LAN	MLB	24	441	50	20	7	11	55	34	77	5	5	5.2	.308	.365	.477	.162	.310	.367	.480	.287	19.1	99-LF	-4		
2007	LAN	MLB	25	477	66	24	3	14	61	41	77	5	3	5.2	.289	.356	.461	.062	.290	.355	.464	.278	16.9	113-LF	-1		

Breakout: 19%   Improve: 45%   Collapse: 27%   Attrition: 21%   Comparables: Bruce Boisclair, Chris Chambliss, Mike Darr, Bruce Bochte

Despite winning the 2005 Texas League MVP, Ethier appeared to be a tweener—lacking the speed for center field or the power for a corner spot—an underwhelming return in the Milton Bradley-Antonio Perez trade. Then Ethier stepped into the left field breach upon being called up on May 1 and helped the stumbling Dodgers turn things around. He hit .324/.395/.577 in May while the team went 18–10, and carried a similarly torrid pace through August. He was still hitting .335/.376/.528 when Ned Colletti traded for Marlon Anderson, but, when Grady Little started mixing Anderson into the lineup, Ethier's production went south. He sulked through a 2-for-34 slump, and, though Little excused him for mental exhaustion, Ethier publicly voiced concerns about his future with the team. Colletti reassured the youngster of his place in their plans, but the situation took the luster off an otherwise stellar rookie campaign. Ethier flat-out nailed his 90th percentile PECOTA projection (.306/.374/.474, .290 EqA); while his performance certainly raises the bar a bit, expecting a repeat would be asking a lot.

Rafael Furcal   **SS**   **Bats: S**   **Throws: R**   Height: 5′ 8″   Weight: 195   Born: October 24, 1977   Age: 29

YEAR	TEAM	LVL	AGE	PA	R	2B	3B	HR	RBI	BB	SO	SB	CS	SPEED	AVG	OBP	SLG	MLVR	EQAVG	EQOBP	EQSLG	EQA	VORP	DEFENSE	
2004	ATL	MLB	26	632	103	24	5	14	59	58	71	29	6	7.3	.279	.345	.414	.027	.275	.341	.413	.268	31.0	121-SS	12
2005	ATL	MLB	27	689	100	31	11	12	58	62	78	46	10	7.9	.284	.348	.429	.067	.283	.349	.436	.277	42.3	147-SS	23
2006	LAN	MLB	28	736	113	32	9	15	63	73	98	37	13	7.0	.300	.369	.445	.115	.302	.375	.452	.286	46.9	153-SS	9
2007	LAN	MLB	29	668	98	24	8	11	58	65	82	35	9	7.3	.275	.349	.401	-.043	.276	.348	.403	.266	27.1	156-SS	8

Breakout: 4%   Improve: 23%   Collapse: 39%   Attrition: 2%   Comparables: Ray Durham, Kazuo Matsui, Bump Wills, Don Buford

Furcal was the first of Ned Colletti's free agent signings, and the best despite a rocky start. Furcal underwent knee surgery in early January, but his slow April (.198/.306/.219) had more to do with a late-spring back strain. Once healthy, he surpassed expectations, hitting a robust .338/.402/.545 after July 1, including a September off the back of Albert Pujols's baseball card (.369/.424/.622). Overall, his .372 OBP out of the leadoff spot was .0005 from leading all NL leadoff hitters with over 400 plate appearances. The performance was somewhere between his 75th and 90th percentile PECOTA projections, so you can expect he'll fall off a bit, but it's possible that he's found an especially comfortable niche in L.A. (he hit .333/.426/.529 at home); maintaining this level isn't out of the question given that he won't turn 30 until late October.

Nomar Garciaparra   **1B**   **Bats: R**   **Throws: R**   Height: 6′ 0″   Weight: 190   Born: July 23, 1973   Age: 33

YEAR	TEAM	LVL	AGE	PA	R	2B	3B	HR	RBI	BB	SO	SB	CS	SPEED	AVG	OBP	SLG	MLVR	EQAVG	EQOBP	EQSLG	EQA	VORP	DEFENSE			
2004	BOS	MLB	30	169	24	7	3	5	21	8	16	2	0	5.3	.321	.367	.500	.158	.314	.361	.487	.290	13.7	32-SS	-4		
2004	CHN	MLB	30	185	28	14	0	4	20	16	14	2	1	4.7	.297	.364	.455	.096	.289	.357	.440	.275	10.6	35-SS	-1		
2005	CHN	MLB	31	247	28	12	0	9	30	12	24	0	0	4.1	.283	.320	.452	.050	.279	.319	.450	.263	8.9	33-3B	-5	23-SS	-1
2006	LAN	MLB	32	523	82	31	2	20	93	42	30	3	0	5.0	.303	.367	.505	.199	.303	.368	.506	.296	27.6	114-1B	-8		
2007	LAN	MLB	33	484	64	26	2	15	68	35	38	3	1	4.7	.289	.346	.463	.047	.290	.345	.465	.275	16.3	114-1B	-4		

Breakout: 10%   Improve: 35%   Collapse: 24%   Attrition: 19%   Comparables: Vic Power, Andy Pafko, Steve Garvey, George Kell

Banished from Boston and the shortstop position, limited by injury to just 143 games combined in 2004 and 2005, the Garciaparra who signed with the Dodgers in December 2005 was a shadow of the player who gained fame as a member of the late-nineties trinity of great AL shortstops. PECOTA foretold a meager .273/.324/.427 line with just 329 plate appearances, and, when Garciaparra started the season on the DL with an oblique strain, even that seemed optimistic. But, once activated, he conjured up his old greatness, hitting .358/.426/.578 in the first half, including a 22-game hitting streak. The second half wasn't so sunny, as a prolonged slump (.229/.286/.408) was accompanied by knee and quad strains. The former required another stint on the DL, the latter preceded a pair of dramatic walk-off blasts in the season's penultimate week which kickstarted the team's Wild Card run—high drama, fantastic theater, comeback hits from the NL Comeback Player of the Year on the league's comeback team. Sentiment and J. D. Drew's departure precipitated a return engagement, as the Dodgers signed him for two more years at $18.5 million; with James Loney in tow, the team at least has the depth to withstand the deal's probable downside.

Toby Hall   **C**   **Bats: R**   **Throws: R**   Height: 6' 3"   Weight: 240   Born: October 21, 1975   Age: 31

YEAR	TEAM	LVL	AGE	PA	R	2B	3B	HR	RBI	BB	SO	SB	CS	SPEED	AVG	OBP	SLG	MLVR	EQAVG	EQOBP	EQSLG	EQA	VORP	DEFENSE	
2004	TBA	MLB	28	441	35	21	0	8	60	24	41	0	2	2.2	.255	.300	.366	-.162	.257	.305	.374	.237	-0.9	115-C	0
2005	TBA	MLB	29	463	28	20	0	5	48	16	39	0	0	2.9	.287	.315	.368	-.082	.296	.333	.386	.253	9.5	121-C	3
2006	TBA	MLB	30	234	15	13	0	8	23	8	17	0	2	2.3	.231	.261	.398	-.233	.228	.265	.393	.224	-6.1	57-C	-11
2006	LAN	MLB	30	60	2	4	0	0	8	2	5	0	0	3.2	.368	.383	.439	.204	.368	.383	.421	.283	4.4	14-C	1
2007	CHA	MLB	31	362	28	17	0	8	42	15	33	0	1	3.1	.253	.287	.372	-.199	.247	.286	.366	.229	-3.4	87-C	-3

Breakout: 11%   Improve: 37%   Collapse: 43%   Attrition: 35%   Comparables: Ben Molina, Brian Johnson, John Bateman, John Flaherty

Hall's bat never lived up to the modest expectations set for it in Tampa Bay. The new regime in Tampa didn't take long to identify his position as one in desperate need of an upgrade ("1. Complete purchase of team; 2. New catcher; 3. Get some pitching!!!"), so, when Ned Colletti came sniffing around for Mark Hendrickson, the D-Rays happily included Hall to nab Dioner Navarro. Confined to a backup role in L.A. by the emergence of Russell Martin, Hall illustrated Jazayerli's Law of Backup Catchers, hitting surprisingly well in extremely limited duty. Non-tendered by the Dodgers, he signed a two-year, $3.65-million deal with the White Sox. His ability to hit lefties (.297/.334/.436 over the past three years, compared to .258/.290/.355 vs. righties) will complement A. J. Pierzynski's weakness against same.

Chin-Lung Hu   **SS**   **Bats: R**   **Throws: R**   Height: 5' 9"   Weight: 150   Born: February 2, 1984   Age: 23

YEAR	TEAM	LVL	AGE	PA	R	2B	3B	HR	RBI	BB	SO	SB	CS	SPEED	AVG	OBP	SLG	MLVR	EQAVG	EQOBP	EQSLG	EQA	VORP	DEFENSE	
2004	CGA	A	20	368	58	15	4	6	25	20	50	17	7	6.8	.298	.342	.422	.079	.275	.306	.377	.239	5.6	80-SS	10
2004	VRO	A+	20	83	12	4	1	0	10	5	6	3	1	6.3	.307	.350	.387	.064	.273	.309	.351	.233	0.5	18-SS	2
2005	VRO	A+	21	505	80	29	1	8	56	19	40	23	6	6.6	.313	.347	.430	.137	.273	.303	.384	.241	8.4	114-SS	8
2006	JAX	AA	22	556	71	20	2	5	34	49	63	11	5	5.6	.254	.326	.334	-.022	.251	.315	.343	.235	0.9	119-SS	-2
2007	LAN	MLB	23	501	57	23	2	5	43	30	51	10	4	5.9	.274	.324	.369	-.131	.275	.323	.371	.242	10.3	118-SS	3

Breakout: 25%   Improve: 54%   Collapse: 20%   Attrition: 4%   Comparables: Gary Cates, Jerry Hairston, Chris Burke, Jack Wilson

The tiny Taiwanese doesn't just draw praise for his fielding, he's widely considered the best defensive shortstop in the minors and a future Gold Glove winner. Though Hu's arm isn't especially strong, he combines speed, first-step quickness, and excellent instincts to produce unequalled range afield. His bat, however, is a work in progress, as his power takes an electron microscope to measure. His plate discipline has improved markedly, and his 2006 walk total nearly topped the previous three seasons combined. He may never be an above-average hitter, but his age-23 translations bear far more resemblance to Omar Vizquel (.266/.316/.331) than Cesar Izturis (.256/.286/.321), to cherry-pick a couple of similarly-sized, slick-fielding shortstops. Not too shabby.

Matt Kemp   **CF**   **Bats: R**   **Throws: R**   Height: 6' 2"   Weight: 230   Born: September 23, 1984   Age: 22

YEAR	TEAM	LVL	AGE	PA	R	2B	3B	HR	RBI	BB	SO	SB	CS	SPEED	AVG	OBP	SLG	MLVR	EQAVG	EQOBP	EQSLG	EQA	VORP	DEFENSE			
2004	CGA	A	19	458	67	22	8	17	66	24	100	8	7	5.8	.288	.330	.499	.160	.263	.293	.430	.243	-5.3	99-RF	5		
2004	VRO	A+	19	42	5	5	0	1	9	4	12	2	1	4.6	.351	.405	.568	.417	.316	.357	.500	.285	2.8	12-RF	0		
2005	VRO	A+	20	454	76	21	4	27	90	25	92	23	6	7.1	.306	.349	.569	.323	.274	.311	.509	.274	26.3	66-CF	1	34-RF	-2
2006	JAX	AA	21	224	38	15	2	7	34	20	38	11	2	6.0	.327	.402	.528	.387	.332	.397	.559	.318	28.8	44-CF	0		
2006	LVG	AAA	21	202	37	14	6	3	36	17	26	14	3	7.8	.368	.428	.560	.371	.330	.386	.508	.306	20.3	36-CF	2		
2006	LAN	MLB	21	166	30	7	1	7	23	9	53	6	0	7.6	.253	.289	.448	-.053	.255	.295	.444	.259	3.2	20-CF	-6		
2007	LAN	MLB	22	579	86	35	4	23	82	38	115	21	7	6.2	.294	.346	.504	.109	.296	.345	.507	.285	32.0	136-CF	-2		

Breakout: 16%   Improve: 56%   Collapse: 18%   Attrition: 3%   Comparables: Juan Encarnacion, Michael Coleman, Sammy Sosa, Ruben Mateo

Coming into last year, the 2003 sixth-rounder had scouts raving about his athleticism, but his approach at the plate—particularly the 4.1 K/UIBB ratio he put up over 2004 and 2005—was raw enough to generate concern, while Vero Beach–inflated stats (.749 SLG, 22 HR at home, .372, 5 HR on the road) kept many from fully endorsing his future stardom. Kemp started slowly in his introduction to Double-A, but soon reeled off a 16-game hitting streak while showing considerably better plate discipline. When the Dodgers promoted him at the end of May, Kemp made a quick impression, homering in his first three games at Dodger Stadium and going yard seven times through his first 18 games. For all of his advances, Kemp struggled with major league breaking balls, so, after seven weeks, the Dodgers sent him to Triple-A. Kemp fared well in Vegas, but mostly rusted in a September return that saw him limited to 16 at-bats over the last three weeks. He's still very much in the big club's picture, but he'll need to rein in his free-swinging ways to avoid becoming *le Francoeur des Dodgers*. To that end, the Dodgers intend to keep him in Las Vegas for a good chunk of the year.

Jeff Kent **2B** **Bats: R** **Throws: R** Height: 6' 1" Weight: 210 Born: December 31, 1969 Age: 39

YEAR	TEAM	LVL	AGE	PA	R	2B	3B	HR	RBI	BB	SO	SB	CS	SPEED	AVG	OBP	SLG	MLVR	EQAVG	EQOBP	EQSLG	EQA	VORP	DEFENSE	
2004	HOU	MLB	36	606	96	34	8	27	107	49	96	7	3	5.5	.289	.348	.531	.208	.284	.343	.525	.290	47.7	124-2B	15
2005	LAN	MLB	37	637	100	36	0	29	105	72	85	6	2	4.3	.289	.377	.512	.246	.294	.381	.532	.306	52.8	137-2B	5
2006	LAN	MLB	38	473	61	27	3	14	68	55	69	1	2	4.2	.292	.385	.477	.179	.293	.386	.480	.296	32.8	99-2B	11
2007	LAN	MLB	39	350	51	19	2	13	46	39	52	3	1	4.7	.282	.370	.481	.106	.283	.369	.484	.290	26.8	84-2B	-1

Breakout: 12%　Improve: 36%　Collapse: 27%　Attrition: 31%　　Comparables: *Mike Schmidt, Moises Alou, Randy Velarde, Jeff Conine*

The Milton Bradley incident aside, Kent was one of the few bright spots of the Dodgers' dismal 2005 season, but the injuries he avoided then found him last year. Beaned by Brad Hennessey on April 17, he sustained a concussion and struggled with blurred vision that sapped his productivity; he hit just .183/.310/.244 for the month. He was sidelined by a wrist strain in late May, and was dogged by a grade-two oblique strain that limited him to 25 at-bats in July. He returned to the lineup on August 7 and hit .327/.407/.515 the rest of the way. You can't ask for much more than that from a 38-year-old second baseman, so it's tough to begrudge Ned Colletti granting him an $11.5-million extension for 2007 with a $9-million club option for 2008 that vests with 550 plate appearances. Kent holds the all-time record for homers by a second baseman, and he's now topped 100 WARP (103.9); by the end of this contract his Cooperstown credentials should be unassailable.

Andy LaRoche **3B** **Bats: R** **Throws: R** Height: 6' 1" Weight: 215 Born: September 13, 1983 Age: 23

YEAR	TEAM	LVL	AGE	PA	R	2B	3B	HR	RBI	BB	SO	SB	CS	SPEED	AVG	OBP	SLG	MLVR	EQAVG	EQOBP	EQSLG	EQA	VORP	DEFENSE	
2004	CGA	A	20	285	52	20	0	13	42	29	30	12	5	5.7	.283	.375	.525	.253	.246	.311	.449	.260	9.6	61-3B	1
2004	VRO	A+	20	243	26	13	0	10	35	17	42	2	3	3.6	.233	.290	.429	-.018	.200	.248	.373	.214	-9.8	53-3B	-8
2005	VRO	A+	21	271	54	14	1	21	51	19	38	6	1	5.5	.333	.380	.651	.504	.294	.336	.575	.298	31.4	55-3B	-5
2005	JAX	AA	21	264	41	12	0	9	43	32	54	2	2	3.7	.273	.367	.445	.145	.258	.337	.425	.263	10.4	58-3B	-2
2006	JAX	AA	22	277	42	13	0	9	46	41	32	6	3	5.4	.309	.419	.483	.334	.302	.401	.498	.307	29.7	60-3B	3
2006	LVG	AAA	22	230	35	14	1	10	35	25	32	3	2	4.5	.322	.400	.550	.267	.288	.361	.502	.289	19.5	52-3B	2
2007	LAN	MLB	23	524	73	27	1	21	74	48	79	6	2	4.8	.282	.353	.481	.077	.283	.352	.484	.282	27.3	123-3B	-1

Breakout: 18%　Improve: 45%　Collapse: 16%　Attrition: 4%　　Comparables: *Michael Cuddyer, Carlos Quentin, Garrett Atkins, Brendan Harris*

Helped by what was largely a Vero Beach-driven power spike, Son of LaLob enjoyed a breakout campaign in 2005, winning the team's Minor League Player of the Year award. A slow start in Jacksonville in 2006 generated told-you-so's, but LaRoche soon heated up and earned a promotion to Las Vegas on June 11. Within a week, he suffered a partially torn labrum in his throwing shoulder while diving for a ground ball, but came back strong after missing just two weeks, forestalling surgery until October. With the graduation of so many blue-chippers to the big league club, he's easily the organization's top prospect down on the farm. The presence of Wilson Betemit may indicate a position change in someone's future, but it seems unlikely that it will be LaRoche who's going to move.

Kenny Lofton **CF** **Bats: L** **Throws: L** Height: 5' 11" Weight: 190 Born: December 31, 1969 Age: 40

YEAR	TEAM	LVL	AGE	PA	R	2B	3B	HR	RBI	BB	SO	SB	CS	SPEED	AVG	OBP	SLG	MLVR	EQAVG	EQOBP	EQSLG	EQA	VORP	DEFENSE	
2004	NYA	MLB	37	313	51	10	7	3	18	31	27	7	3	7.3	.275	.346	.395	-.040	.277	.353	.398	.265	6.2	65-CF	-1
2005	PHI	MLB	38	406	67	15	5	2	36	32	41	22	3	7.9	.335	.392	.420	.158	.332	.391	.416	.290	28.2	84-CF	8
2006	LAN	MLB	39	522	79	15	12	3	41	45	42	32	5	7.5	.301	.360	.403	.043	.301	.364	.407	.278	26.1	107-CF	-7
2007	TEX	MLB	40	490	75	18	9	4	38	37	43	18	6	7.2	.300	.355	.407	.003	.291	.351	.401	.272	12.1	116-CF	-2

Breakout: 3%　Improve: 21%　Collapse: 37%　Attrition: 31%　　Comparables: *Brett Butler, Otis Nixon, Enos Slaughter, B. J. Surhoff*

Joining his eighth team since 2001, Lofton functioned well as one of Ned Colletti's short-term, contention-ready patches. Hitting out of the number-two spot, he acted as a second leadoff man, getting on base frequently and advancing himself liberally. Not only does he still have his speed, he's developed that late-period Davey Lopes aura of the base thief emeritus, with an 87 percent success rate over the past two years. Alas, his power is going, going, gone, and his defense in centerfield is best termed "adventurous," but, at 40, Lofton is a battle-tested vet who can advance the cause of a contender. The Rangers signed him to a one-year, $6-million deal; PECOTA thinks he'll be within four runs of Gary Matthews's VORP at the same 2007 price, but without the extra $44 million over four more years.

James Loney

1B **Bats: L** **Throws: L** Height: 6′ 2″ Weight: 220 Born: May 7, 1984 Age: 23

YEAR	TEAM	LVL	AGE	PA	R	2B	3B	HR	RBI	BB	SO	SB	CS	SPEED	AVG	OBP	SLG	MLVR	EQAVG	EQOBP	EQSLG	EQA	VORP	DEFENSE	
2004	JAX	AA	20	442	39	19	2	4	35	42	75	6	5	4.4	.238	.314	.327	-.103	.226	.290	.303	.213	-29.9	98-1B	3
2005	JAX	AA	21	572	74	31	2	11	65	59	87	1	4	3.0	.284	.357	.419	.102	.271	.332	.411	.257	4.5	130-1B	7
2006	LVG	AAA	22	406	64	33	2	8	67	32	34	9	5	5.1	.380	.426	.546	.363	.338	.382	.503	.300	33.2	77-1B	-4
2006	LAN	MLB	22	111	20	6	5	4	18	8	10	1	0	5.3	.284	.342	.559	.209	.284	.348	.569	.301	6.5	25-1B	-3
2007	LAN	MLB	23	537	71	33	3	16	73	42	65	5	3	4.7	.294	.352	.469	.071	.296	.351	.472	.278	19.0	126-1B	2

Breakout: 32% Improve: 59% Collapse: 11% Attrition: 3% *Comparables: Ed Kranepool, Adrian Gonzalez, Daryle Ward, Justin Morneau*

Loney looked poised for big things in the spring of 2004 when the 2002 first-round pick was the talk of Dodgertown and won an award as the team's top rookie. A wrist injury shot that season to hell, but a repeat engagement in Double-A stabilized his development. His 2006 was a story of elevation. At high-altitude, hitter-friendly Las Vegas, Loney led the minor leagues in batting average, but remained more of an underpowered, contact-oriented hitter than is desirable from a corner player. He hit reasonably well in three separate stints spotting for the delicate Nomar Garciaparra, including a two-homer, nine-RBI effort at Colorado in a key game on September 28. Remove that big day and his line comes out to .261/.320/.489, perhaps a more realistic gauge of his progress. J. D. Drew's departure triggered the return of Garciaparra and the addition of Luis Gonzalez, leaving Loney to split time backing up both positions.

Julio Lugo

SS **Bats: R** **Throws: R** Height: 6′ 1″ Weight: 175 Born: November 16, 1975 Age: 31

YEAR	TEAM	LVL	AGE	PA	R	2B	3B	HR	RBI	BB	SO	SB	CS	SPEED	AVG	OBP	SLG	MLVR	EQAVG	EQOBP	EQSLG	EQA	VORP	DEFENSE			
2004	TBA	MLB	28	655	83	41	4	7	75	54	106	21	5	6.6	.275	.338	.396	-.047	.279	.345	.404	.266	24.5	139-SS	6		
2005	TBA	MLB	29	690	89	36	6	6	57	61	72	39	11	7.0	.295	.362	.403	.059	.309	.383	.424	.286	42.8	153-SS	19		
2006	TBA	MLB	30	322	53	17	1	12	27	27	47	18	4	6.4	.308	.373	.498	.184	.308	.379	.503	.301	31.3	71-SS	-1		
2006	LAN	MLB	30	164	16	5	1	0	10	12	29	6	5	6.3	.219	.278	.267	-.348	.212	.276	.253	.197	-10.3	18-2B	2	13-3B	0
2007	BOS	MLB	31	538	75	30	3	8	52	44	75	19	6	6.5	.283	.346	.406	-.025	.271	.340	.401	.268	17.2	126-SS	4		

Breakout: 3% Improve: 20% Collapse: 40% Attrition: 13% *Comparables: Barry Larkin, Bob Dillinger, Dave Concepcion, Ed Charles*

The timing of Lugo's departure from the Devil Rays had been the subject of speculation for more than a year. Given the injury concerns about the entire Dodger infield, going out and getting him was an entirely reasonable move on Ned Colletti's part, even if he did part with former top prospect Joel Guzman to do it. Playing out of position at second, third, and in the outfield and hampered by an injured finger, Lugo didn't hit, and he certainly didn't embrace his utility role. None of that meant much in December, when Boston signed him to a four-year, $36-million deal to be their everyday shortstop.

Russell Martin

C **Bats: R** **Throws: R** Height: 5′ 10″ Weight: 210 Born: February 15, 1983 Age: 24

YEAR	TEAM	LVL	AGE	PA	R	2B	3B	HR	RBI	BB	SO	SB	CS	SPEED	AVG	OBP	SLG	MLVR	EQAVG	EQOBP	EQSLG	EQA	VORP	DEFENSE	
2004	VRO	A+	21	505	74	24	1	15	64	72	54	9	5	5.0	.250	.366	.421	.092	.218	.314	.377	.246	0.0	100-C	7
2005	JAX	AA	22	505	83	17	1	9	61	78	69	15	7	5.0	.311	.430	.423	.243	.297	.399	.417	.289	36.8	112-C	6
2006	LVG	AAA	23	91	14	9	0	0	9	13	11	0	2	4.3	.297	.389	.419	.056	.250	.341	.342	.244	0.6	22-C	6
2006	LAN	MLB	23	468	65	26	4	10	65	45	57	10	5	5.5	.282	.355	.436	.062	.283	.358	.437	.275	18.5	113-C	11
2007	LAN	MLB	24	520	69	25	2	11	57	53	65	10	4	5.2	.270	.351	.409	-.030	.271	.350	.411	.265	18.2	122-C	9

Breakout: 13% Improve: 36% Collapse: 30% Attrition: 7% *Comparables: Ben Petrick, Ramon Hernandez, Bill Freehan, Butch Wynegar*

Martin drew an Honorable Mention on our Top-50 Prospects list last year after an excellent season in Jacksonville, but with just three years of catching under his belt and young Dioner Navarro in place, he appeared ticketed for Triple-A in 2006. When a bone bruise felled Navarro in early May, Martin got the call, and the result marked the turning point of the team's season. The Dodgers won 16 of Martin's first 18 starts; Navarro was Wally Pipped out of a job and dealt to Tampa Bay. By season's end, the Dodgers were 71–43 in games Martin started. There is little not to like about Martin's game; he showed durability, solid on-base skills, developing power, above-average speed for a backstop, adept handling of pitchers, and excellent defense. He threw out 31 percent of attempted thieves and averaged 0.27 non-stealing assists per game; the team's other backstops cut down just 13 percent and averaged 0.14 assists per game. The Dodgers have themselves a long-term asset at a key position—but what an ill-starred lot of comparables PECOTA came up with, undone by a plane crash, Parkinson's, and Pete Rose. Martin might want to take out an insurance policy or three.

Ramon Martinez INF **Bats: R** **Throws: R** Height: 6' 0" Weight: 190 Born: October 10, 1972 Age: 34

YEAR	TEAM	LVL	AGE	PA	R	2B	3B	HR	RBI	BB	SO	SB	CS	SPEED	AVG	OBP	SLG	MLVR	EQAVG	EQOBP	EQSLG	EQA	VORP	DEFENSE			
2004	CHN	MLB	31	298	22	15	1	3	30	26	40	1	0	3.7	.246	.313	.346	-.168	.240	.307	.335	.232	-2.0	63-SS	-1	19-3B	-3
2005	DET	MLB	32	62	4	1	0	0	5	3	4	0	0	3.7	.268	.300	.286	-.252	.273	.317	.291	.224	-1.4	10-SS	-1		
2005	PHI	MLB	32	65	7	2	0	1	9	3	7	0	0	3.1	.286	.317	.375	-.076	.286	.312	.375	.250	-0.1				
2006	LAN	MLB	33	194	20	7	1	2	24	15	20	0	0	3.9	.278	.339	.364	-.070	.278	.342	.364	.249	2.4	28-2B	0		
2007	LAN	MLB	34	243	24	11	1	3	25	18	27	1	0	4.3	.266	.326	.366	-.137	.267	.325	.368	.241	2.0	60-2B	0		

Breakout: 18% Improve: 39% Collapse: 30% Attrition: 47%   Comparables: Chris Gomez, Glenn Beckert, Tommy Helms, Mark Grudzielanek

This Colletti pick-up didn't bring anything to the Dodgers aside from wistful memories of his namesake's years in Dodger blue. A .328/.397/.418 first half made it difficult to complain about Grady Little's sudden fetish for Martinez's services, but even Colletti knew that was too good to be true, dealing for Julio Lugo. Martinez's playing time dried up (just 24 at-bats after July 31), and it's fair to wonder if the team could have better employed the roster spot. Still, Martinez shouldn't be confused with Neifi Perez. He's hardly an automatic out—his .252 career EqA compares favorably to any utility infielder you'd care to name—and he won't embarrass himself at second, short, or third base. The Dodgers re-signed him to a reasonable $800,000 deal with a club option.

Anthony Raglani LF **Bats: L** **Throws: L** Height: 6' 2" Weight: 215 Born: April 6, 1983 Age: 24

YEAR	TEAM	LVL	AGE	PA	R	2B	3B	HR	RBI	BB	SO	SB	CS	SPEED	AVG	OBP	SLG	MLVR	EQAVG	EQOBP	EQSLG	EQA	VORP	DEFENSE			
2005	VRO	A+	22	491	82	20	5	19	77	60	98	9	2	5.8	.289	.383	.496	.255	.259	.338	.446	.271	7.2	54-LF	3	47-RF	-1
2006	VRO	A+	23	74	10	4	1	1	7	10	10	0	1	4.1	.317	.419	.460	.273	.292	.378	.431	.276	2.8	13-LF	-1		
2006	JAX	AA	23	386	49	25	0	9	40	44	88	6	2	5.0	.244	.339	.399	.072	.239	.324	.411	.255	-4.1	56-LF	0	31-RF	0
2007	LAN	MLB	24	469	61	25	3	16	61	47	100	6	3	5.2	.260	.341	.452	.000	.261	.340	.455	.270	10.1	111-LF	0		

Breakout: 28% Improve: 57% Collapse: 13% Attrition: 9%   Comparables: Jason Cooper, Ryan Langerhans, John-Ford Griffin, Trot Nixon

A fifth-round 2004 pick out of George Washington, Raglani struggled in his initial taste of Double-A ball last year and was demoted in early June while hitting .217/.323/.342. Three weeks at Vero Beach helped, and Rags hit .275/.354/.462 upon returning to Jacksonville in early July. Despite drawing a reasonable number of walks, Raglani has never been noted for working the count. Since hitting is his ticket to The Show—he lacks speed and is nothing special afield—he'll have to do better with the bat. Expect him to start 2007 with a repeat engagement in Jacksonville.

Jason Repko CF **Bats: R** **Throws: R** Height: 5' 10" Weight: 190 Born: December 27, 1980 Age: 26

YEAR	TEAM	LVL	AGE	PA	R	2B	3B	HR	RBI	BB	SO	SB	CS	SPEED	AVG	OBP	SLG	MLVR	EQAVG	EQOBP	EQSLG	EQA	VORP	DEFENSE			
2004	JAX	AA	23	207	26	11	2	6	19	13	43	10	5	6.4	.291	.341	.466	.167	.280	.320	.440	.262	1.6	32-LF	-2		
2004	LVG	AAA	23	326	55	26	4	7	41	18	57	13	5	7.1	.311	.355	.493	.044	.269	.311	.420	.251	5.6	64-CF	3		
2005	LAN	MLB	24	301	43	15	3	8	30	16	80	5	0	6.8	.221	.281	.384	-.141	.224	.286	.394	.238	-3.6	41-CF	2	24-RF	-1
2006	LAN	MLB	25	150	21	5	1	3	16	15	24	10	4	6.9	.254	.345	.377	-.057	.260	.349	.382	.259	2.2	24-CF	0		
2007	LAN	MLB	26	290	39	15	2	9	34	21	54	12	4	6.5	.263	.326	.431	-.051	.264	.325	.434	.261	6.5	71-CF	1		

Breakout: 27% Improve: 65% Collapse: 20% Attrition: 30%   Comparables: Hal Jeffcoat, Carmen Castillo, Jeffrey Hammonds, Larry Herndon

Exposed as replacement-level fodder by the team's injury situation in 2005, Repko was again pressed into service when Kenny Lofton began the year on the DL. Having apparently sold his soul in exchange for one hot month, Repko hit a ridiculous .328/.414/.574 with 6 steals in April. The devil got his due when Repko suffered a high ankle sprain on May 9 after digging his left foot into fence padding in an attempt to snag a home run. He didn't return until late July, and, shorn of his lone asset, speed, hit a useless .197/.290/.213 the rest of the way. If he's healed, his defensive ability and the off chance that he's actually learned to hit make him an acceptable choice as a fifth outfielder, but that's a low ceiling to work with.

Olmedo Saenz 1B **Bats: R** **Throws: R** Height: 5' 11" Weight: 220 Born: October 8, 1970 Age: 36

YEAR	TEAM	LVL	AGE	PA	R	2B	3B	HR	RBI	BB	SO	SB	CS	SPEED	AVG	OBP	SLG	MLVR	EQAVG	EQOBP	EQSLG	EQA	VORP	DEFENSE			
2004	LAN	MLB	33	128	17	1	0	8	22	12	33	0	0	2.8	.279	.352	.505	.167	.279	.352	.514	.292	7.5	16-1B	1		
2005	LAN	MLB	34	351	39	24	0	15	63	27	63	0	1	3.0	.263	.325	.480	.094	.267	.330	.500	.277	11.6	54-1B	-5	14-3B	-2
2006	LAN	MLB	35	204	30	15	0	11	48	14	47	0	0	3.7	.296	.363	.564	.265	.296	.360	.559	.304	15.8	18-1B	-1		
2007	LAN	MLB	36	263	34	15	0	14	46	22	55	0	0	3.5	.271	.342	.516	.096	.272	.341	.519	.285	13.7	65-DH			

Breakout: 16% Improve: 33% Collapse: 30% Attrition: 41%   Comparables: Glenallen Hill, Willie Horton, Donn Clendenon, Joe Adcock

A predictable pleasure of watching the Dodgers is the consistency with which Vin Scully marvels at the reasoning of any pitcher who dares offer this professional hitter some heat: "Why in the world would you ever throw Olmedo Saenz a fast-ball?" he'll say, as Saenz rips another shot to left-centerfield. A Jim Tracy/Paul DePodesta favorite, Saenz survived the regime change with his playing time scaled back to more appropriate levels. Whether in the lineup (.330/.398/.643 in 112 AB at first and third base) or off the bench (.263/.333/.491 in 57 pinch at-bats), he raked. Concerns about his glove and durability, not to mention the tactical value of using him in high-leverage spots late in the game, ensure that the Dodgers will at least get their money's worth from him as a bench player.

Jayson Werth   OF   Bats: R   Throws: R   Height: 6' 4"   Weight: 210   Born: May 20, 1979   Age: 28

YEAR	TEAM	LVL	AGE	PA	R	2B	3B	HR	RBI	BB	SO	SB	CS	SPEED	AVG	OBP	SLG	MLVR	EQAVG	EQOBP	EQSLG	EQA	VORP	DEFENSE			
2004	LVG	AAA	25	60	13	2	1	5	20	8	10	2	0	5.9	.412	.500	.784	.807	.365	.450	.673	.360	11.6				
2004	LAN	MLB	25	326	56	11	3	16	47	30	85	4	1	6.7	.262	.338	.486	.106	.265	.340	.498	.282	10.1	61-LF	5	11-RF	-1
2005	LVG	AAA	26	64	9	0	0	3	10	13	17	6	1	4.4	.367	.516	.551	.454	.333	.460	.471	.330	6.0	15-LF	-1		
2005	LAN	MLB	26	395	46	22	2	7	43	48	114	11	2	5.7	.234	.338	.374	-.043	.238	.342	.387	.262	3.4	39-LF	4	33-RF	3
2007	PHI	MLB	28	356	54	16	2	15	46	38	86	10	2	6.3	.272	.357	.480	.074	.268	.354	.469	.283	14.7	86-LF	2		

Breakout: 14%   Improve: 40%   Collapse: 26%   Attrition: 19%   Comparables: Joe Gaines, Chuck Hinton, Cliff Mapes, Earl Robinson

The nightmare continues. Werth broke his left wrist in the 2005 spring-training opener, and when he was finally able to play, the injury hampered him significantly. After the season, doctors discovered that he'd also torn a ligament in the wrist. He had surgery, but his rehab went poorly, and he went under the knife again in August. Non-tendered by the Dodgers, he signed on to be the Phillies' fourth outfielder, reuniting with Pat Gillick, who was GM in Baltimore when the Orioles made Werth their 1997 first-round pick. At this writing, Werth has yet to resume baseball activities, including a hoped-for stint in winter ball. With luck he'll recover to build on his promising 2004 campaign, but that seems unlikely.

Delwyn Young   RF   Bats: S   Throws: R   Height: 5' 8"   Weight: 210   Born: June 30, 1982   Age: 25

YEAR	TEAM	LVL	AGE	PA	R	2B	3B	HR	RBI	BB	SO	SB	CS	SPEED	AVG	OBP	SLG	MLVR	EQAVG	EQOBP	EQSLG	EQA	VORP	DEFENSE			
2004	VRO	A+	22	540	76	36	3	22	85	57	134	11	4	5.4	.281	.364	.511	.224	.253	.321	.467	.268	26.0	114-2B	-19		
2005	JAX	AA	23	406	52	25	1	16	62	27	86	1	3	2.8	.297	.346	.499	.210	.280	.320	.481	.269	23.0	88-2B	-11		
2005	LVG	AAA	23	170	23	12	0	4	14	8	35	0	0	2.8	.325	.361	.475	.056	.272	.306	.389	.240	1.9	36-2B	2		
2006	LVG	AAA	24	583	76	42	1	18	98	42	104	3	4	4.3	.273	.326	.457	-.015	.236	.286	.403	.237	-17.4	89-RF	-1	34-LF	-7
2007	LAN	MLB	25	464	47	20	1	16	61	31	98	2	1	4.4	.241	.296	.405	-.155	.242	.296	.407	.238	-4.1	110-RF	-5		

Breakout: 11%   Improve: 33%   Collapse: 44%   Attrition: 15%   Comparables: Roosevelt Brown, Matt Curtis, Johnny Isom, Matt Craig

Another year older and even less likely to be confused with Devil Rays prospect Delmon Young, Delwyn made his long-awaited transition from second base, where his glove had proven inadequate, to the outfield corners while playing in Las Vegas. Despite superficially attractive Triple Crown numbers, his stat line was inflated by the PCL. Young is what he is: a slow, unathletic hacker whose difficulty with lefties (.198/.235/.325 in 126 AB) dispels the notion that he's a switch hitter. Unless he shows more at Triple-A, he's most likely a lefty bat off of the bench.

PITCHERS

Brian Akin   Bats: R   Throws: R   Height: 6' 3"   Weight: 185   Born: October 13, 1981   Age: 25

YEAR	TEAM	LVL	AGE	W	L	SV	G	GS	IP	H	BB	SO	HR	GB%	BABIP	STUFF	WHIP	ERA	PERA	EQERA	EQH9	EQBB9	EQSO9	EQHR9	VORP	WXRL
2004	OGD	Rk	22	1	1	0	21	0	47²	65	22	63	3	—	.446	-19	1.82	6.04	5.88	7.17	12.5	5.1	5.1	1.1	-8.3	—
2005	CGA	A	23	1	4	2	35	1	72¹	77	31	54	8	56.8%	.319	-42	1.49	4.36	7.84	6.19	10.9	5.4	3.7	2.2	-4.5	—
2006	VRO	A+	24	3	3	7	22	0	35¹	23	16	48	2	57.8%	.266	6	1.11	1.79	5.18	4.32	7.0	5.4	7.6	1.1	4.7	—
2006	JAX	AA	24	2	1	6	20	0	36²	25	22	46	2	52.7%	.302	10	1.30	2.98	5.07	4.19	8.4	6.0	7.9	1.0	5.4	—
2007	LAN	MLB	25	3	4	1	28	6	61²	68	41	49	9	53.0%	.316	-7	1.76	5.56	6.25	5.62	10.1	5.2	6.4	1.2	0.0	0.20

Breakout: 17%   Improve: 37%   Collapse: 35%   Attrition: 10%   Comparables: Monte Mansfield, Jordan De Jong, Scotty Layfield, Marty Janzen

After adjusting his mechanics under the tutelage of Rick Honeycutt, this fourteenth-round 2004 pick out of Davidson College took a solid leap forward last year. He raised his arm angle, making it tougher for hitters to recognize his pitches, and thus missed more bats and significantly cut his home run rate. His repertoire—low-90s fastball, plus slider, changeup—is a bit better than the typical mid-range prospect's. As a groundballer, Akin might run the Las Vegas gauntlet better than a flyballer such as Mark Alexander and put himself in line for a promotion to L.A.

Mark Alexander

Bats: R Throws: R　　Height: 5′ 10″　Weight: 190　Born: December 6, 1980　Age: 26

YEAR	TEAM	LVL	AGE	W	L	SV	G	GS	IP	H	BB	SO	HR	GB%	BABIP	STUFF	WHIP	ERA	PERA	EQERA	EQH9	EQBB9	EQSO9	EQHR9	VORP	WXRL
2004	OGD	Rk	23	4	1	9	25	0	34	30	8	37	4	—	.295	-24	1.12	2.65	7.06	2.94	8.6	2.7	4.3	2.4	10.0	—
2005	VRO	A+	24	5	4	23	52	0	65¹	64	23	91	6	41.5%	.379	-13	1.33	3.03	5.53	4.75	11.0	4.6	7.6	1.8	5.7	—
2006	JAX	AA	25	3	2	26	40	0	47²	26	13	72	2	35.7%	.269	23	0.83	0.95	3.44	2.64	7.3	2.8	9.1	0.8	14.6	—
2006	LVG	AAA	25	2	1	1	12	0	14	11	10	13	0	33.3%	.289	6	1.50	3.21	4.61	3.86	7.1	6.4	6.4	0.0	2.7	—
2007	LAN	MLB	26	3	4	1	29	6	62	61	28	56	10	41.0%	.291	6	1.43	4.51	5.01	4.48	9.1	3.6	7.3	1.3	8.0	1.00

Breakout: 9%　Improve: 20%　Collapse: 50%　Attrition: 8%　　Comparables: Jimmy Serrano, Eduardo Rodriguez, Keith Troutman, Kazuhito Tadano

A college closer and a twentieth-round pick out of Missouri in 2004, Alexander doesn't get much love from prospect mavens due to his size, but he's made quick progress through the system, blowing hitters away at every stop thanks to an excellent slider. He was especially dominant in Jacksonville last year, stringing together a 25.2-inning scoreless streak that was interrupted by his promotion to Las Vegas. He won the organization's Minor League Pitcher of the Year award, and, considering the competition, that ain't hay. If he can survive Las Vegas, he may find a spot in the Dodger bullpen.

Joe Beimel

Bats: L Throws: L　　Height: 6′ 2″　Weight: 215　Born: April 19, 1977　Age: 30

YEAR	TEAM	LVL	AGE	W	L	SV	G	GS	IP	H	BB	SO	HR	GB%	BABIP	STUFF	WHIP	ERA	PERA	EQERA	EQH9	EQBB9	EQSO9	EQHR9	VORP	WXRL
2004	ROC	AAA	27	2	4	2	49	1	62	83	24	44	12	—	.341	-40	1.73	6.97	6.42	7.80	11.8	3.9	4.8	2.0	-15.2	—
2005	DUR	AAA	28	1	2	0	48	0	52²	58	21	36	3	59.3%	.322	-12	1.50	3.93	4.39	4.31	8.8	3.8	4.5	0.7	7.8	—
2005	TBA	MLB	28	0	0	0	7	0	11	15	4	3	1	43.2%	.326	-24	1.73	3.27	4.76	3.09	10.8	3.1	2.3	0.8	3.0	0.02
2006	LVG	AAA	29	3	0	0	10	0	13¹	9	4	9	0	61.1%	.265	0	0.99	1.37	3.39	1.35	6.1	2.7	4.7	0.0	6.3	—
2006	LAN	MLB	29	2	1	2	62	0	70	70	21	30	7	58.2%	.274	-11	1.30	2.96	4.35	3.11	8.2	2.4	3.5	0.7	20.9	2.44
2007	LAN	MLB	30	2	3	2	57	0	53¹	62	20	28	7	53.0%	.305	-16	1.54	4.87	5.36	4.95	10.7	3.0	4.2	1.1	3.8	0.30

Breakout: 10%　Improve: 28%　Collapse: 41%　Attrition: 34%　　Comparables: Ricky Horton, John O'Donoghue, Fred Scherman, Dave Tomlin

That Beimel went from being an obscure spring NRI to a critical relief asset was one of the more remarkable stories of the Dodgers' 2006 season. Promoted from Las Vegas in May, Beimel quickly earned Grady Little's trust by retiring Barry Bonds twice in a pair of wins and soon became the team's top lefty reliever. Little generally used Beimel for one or two innings at a time rather than as a LOOGY, with impressive results; Beimel's ability to generate ground balls helped him place second on the staff in both double play percentage (21.3) and WXRL. His success against Bonds also held up (1-for-10 with a homer and two walks). Alas, on the eve of the Division Series against the Mets, Beimel cut his pitching hand, maintaining he'd done so in his hotel room; only later did he concede that it happened in a bar after curfew. Given the tightness of the series and the Mets' vulnerability to lefties, it's no stretch to say his injury played a big role in swinging the balance in New York's favor. Nobody would have been surprised if the Dodgers told Beimel to pound sand, but the pitcher took unusual steps to show contrition, including a temperance pledge and a broken heart tattoo, and the Dodgers agreed to give him a second chance.

Chad Billingsley

Bats: R Throws: R　　Height: 6′ 0″　Weight: 245　Born: July 29, 1984　Age: 22

YEAR	TEAM	LVL	AGE	W	L	SV	G	GS	IP	H	BB	SO	HR	GB%	BABIP	STUFF	WHIP	ERA	PERA	EQERA	EQH9	EQBB9	EQSO9	EQHR9	VORP	WXRL
2004	VRO	A+	19	7	4	0	18	18	92	68	49	111	6	—	.278	23	1.27	2.35	5.34	3.89	8.0	5.5	7.5	1.2	16.7	—
2004	JAX	AA	19	4	0	0	8	8	42¹	32	22	47	1	—	.301	28	1.28	2.98	4.03	4.14	7.4	5.0	6.5	0.2	6.7	—
2005	JAX	AA	20	13	6	0	28	26	146	116	50	162	12	47.3%	.284	18	1.14	3.51	4.62	4.45	8.3	3.2	7.2	1.3	18.1	—
2006	LVG	AAA	21	6	3	0	13	13	70	57	32	78	7	47.8%	.289	23	1.27	3.99	4.53	3.82	7.4	3.9	7.6	1.0	14.0	—
2006	LAN	MLB	21	7	4	0	18	16	90	92	58	59	7	49.1%	.313	16	1.67	3.90	4.70	4.02	8.5	4.9	5.2	0.6	17.0	2.68
2007	LAN	MLB	22	9	11	0	34	30	168²	161	88	149	20	48.0%	.293	15	1.47	4.52	4.82	4.58	8.8	4.1	7.1	1.0	21.2	3.30

Breakout: 6%　Improve: 28%　Collapse: 31%　Attrition: 0%　　Comparables: Richard Dotson, Ben Sheets, Alex Fernandez, Dave Morehead

The Dodgers got a good inkling that their top pitching prospect—the 24th pick in the 2003 draft out of Defiance, Ohio—was nearly ready for the big time when he tossed five scoreless innings against the Angels in the Freeway Series finale at Dodger Stadium on April 2. Nonetheless, Billingsley began the season in Las Vegas, where he survived the pitching thresher, dominating righties (.174/.259/.273) and relying on ground balls to pitch better at home (1.81 G/F, 3.48 ERA) than on the road (0.66, 4.60). The Dodgers promoted him in mid-June and he got by, generally firing his hundred bullets in five innings, and overcoming an inordinate number of walks by pitching particularly well with runners in scoring position (.191/.311/.255). Just as he found his groove, he strained an oblique and missed three weeks, and pitched poorly thereafter. With three plus pitches (92 to 95 MPH fastball, curveball, slider) he's expected to develop into a frontline starter, and while he's not there yet, he should be a productive member of the rotation in 2007.

Yhency Brazoban **Bats: R Throws: R** Height: 6′ 0″ Weight: 240 Born: June 11, 1980 Age: 27

YEAR	TEAM	LVL	AGE	W	L	SV	G	GS	IP	H	BB	SO	HR	GB%	BABIP	STUFF	WHIP	ERA	PERA	EQERA	EQH9	EQBB9	EQSO9	EQHR9	VORP	WXRL
2004	JAX	AA	24	4	4	13	37	0	51	38	22	61	4	—	.286	-2	1.18	2.65	5.16	4.25	8.0	4.6	6.7	1.1	7.3	—
2004	LAN	MLB	24	6	2	0	31	0	32²	25	15	27	2	—	.271	7	1.22	2.48	3.70	2.76	7.2	3.6	6.6	0.6	11.6	0.94
2005	LAN	MLB	25	4	10	21	74	0	72²	70	32	61	11	40.0%	.296	-9	1.40	5.32	5.07	5.59	8.9	3.5	6.9	1.3	-2.4	0.92
2007	*LAN*	*MLB*	*27*	*2*	*3*	*1*	*40*	*1*	*50*	*51*	*22*	*41*	*8*	*38.0%*	*.294*	*-2*	*1.46*	*4.83*	*5.11*	*4.81*	*9.4*	*3.4*	*6.6*	*1.3*	*4.4*	*0.40*

Breakout: 19% Improve: 36% Collapse: 28% Attrition: 35% Comparables: Dan Miceli, Bob Moorhead, Dan Wheeler, Bill Simas

Since coming over in the Kevin Brown-Jeff Weaver deal, the Dodgers have treated this converted outfielder to a workload seemingly designed by Tommy "Torquemada" Lasorda and his pitching coach, the Marquis de Sade. After 152 appearances and 168⅔ innings at all levels in 2004 and 2005 combined—not to mention a lot of deep counts—the Dodgers allowed Brazoban to throw 27 innings in the Dominican Winter League to aid him in his quest to find a changeup. Soon after reporting to Vero Beach, he developed a sore shoulder, and, during the second week of the season, suffered an avulsion of his UCL—the ligament tore away a fragment of bone. He underwent Tommy John surgery and should be able to participate in spring training, but the odds he'll ever deliver on the promise that he showed down the stretch in 2004 have gotten longer.

Jonathan Broxton **Bats: R Throws: R** Height: 6′ 3″ Weight: 290 Born: June 16, 1984 Age: 23

YEAR	TEAM	LVL	AGE	W	L	SV	G	GS	IP	H	BB	SO	HR	GB%	BABIP	STUFF	WHIP	ERA	PERA	EQERA	EQH9	EQBB9	EQSO9	EQHR9	VORP	WXRL
2004	VRO	A+	20	11	6	0	23	23	128¹	110	43	144	7	—	.311	22	1.19	3.23	4.40	4.13	8.9	3.5	6.9	1.0	20.3	—
2005	JAX	AA	21	5	3	5	33	13	96²	79	31	107	4	45.1%	.307	23	1.14	3.16	3.54	4.09	8.2	2.9	7.1	0.7	15.9	—
2005	LAN	MLB	21	1	0	0	14	0	13²	13	12	22	0	16.1%	.419	14	1.83	5.91	3.32	7.07	9.0	7.1	12.9	0.0	-3.0	-0.13
2006	LAN	MLB	22	4	1	3	68	0	76¹	61	33	97	7	40.5%	.303	35	1.23	2.60	3.11	2.76	6.9	3.3	10.2	0.7	26.2	2.30
2007	*LAN*	*MLB*	*23*	*4*	*4*	*5*	*57*	*1*	*68²*	*61*	*30*	*75*	*7*	*42.0%*	*.297*	*17*	*1.31*	*3.84*	*3.89*	*3.89*	*8.1*	*3.4*	*8.7*	*0.9*	*13.3*	*1.30*

Breakout: 11% Improve: 30% Collapse: 30% Attrition: 20% Comparables: Andrew Sisco, Dennys Reyes, Scott Elarton, Edwin Nunez

When the Dodgers shifted this behemoth from the rotation to the bullpen in Double-A two years ago, his fastball jumped from the 93 to 95 MPH rage to as high as 99. He wound up tantalizing the big club during a pair of second-half stints in 2005. Wisely, the team stuck with this Paul DePodesta-brand experiment despite the regime change. Broxton rained down a hail of zeroes on the PCL last April, earning a promotion at the end of the month. He immediately began blowing hitters away and emerged as the team's top right-handed setup option. Notably, he didn't show any loss of stamina late in the season; his K-rate was higher in the second half (12.2 per nine innings) than the first (10.7) and peaked in September (13.8). His other peripherals followed that pattern, as well. If the Dodgers were nonchalant about the departure of Eric Gagne, it's because they know they've got a future closer right here.

Giovanni Carrara **Bats: R Throws: R** Height: 6′ 2″ Weight: 230 Born: December 31, 1969 Age: 39

YEAR	TEAM	LVL	AGE	W	L	SV	G	GS	IP	H	BB	SO	HR	GB%	BABIP	STUFF	WHIP	ERA	PERA	EQERA	EQH9	EQBB9	EQSO9	EQHR9	VORP	WXRL
2004	IOW	AAA	36	1	2	1	20	0	28¹	29	8	23	3	—	.325	-11	1.31	3.82	5.26	4.13	9.2	2.9	5.1	1.3	4.6	—
2004	LVG	AAA	36	0	1	2	11	0	14¹	11	8	15	1	—	.256	10	1.33	2.52	4.79	2.51	6.3	5.7	6.3	0.6	4.9	—
2004	LAN	MLB	36	5	2	2	42	0	53²	46	20	48	1	—	.294	20	1.23	2.18	2.95	2.85	8.2	3.0	7.2	0.2	18.8	1.67
2005	LAN	MLB	37	7	4	0	72	0	75²	65	38	56	6	42.9%	.286	2	1.36	3.92	4.58	4.23	8.0	4.1	6.1	0.7	10.5	1.08
2006	IND	AAA	38	1	1	0	9	1	15	8	5	14	1	25.0%	.219	-3	0.87	3.00	5.54	3.86	6.4	3.9	6.4	1.3	2.7	—
2006	LVG	AAA	38	2	1	4	21	0	25²	23	12	19	3	48.7%	.270	-15	1.39	4.64	6.19	4.68	8.3	4.7	4.7	1.4	2.6	—
2006	LAN	MLB	38	0	1	1	25	0	27²	27	7	25	5	34.9%	.282	7	1.23	4.55	4.36	4.13	8.3	1.9	7.3	1.3	4.4	-0.20
2007	*LAN*	*MLB*	*39*	*1*	*2*	*1*	*32*	*0*	*33¹*	*36*	*15*	*25*	*5*	*41.0%*	*.301*	*-11*	*1.52*	*5.32*	*5.44*	*5.35*	*10.0*	*3.4*	*6.1*	*1.4*	*1.0*	*0.10*

Breakout: 4% Improve: 7% Collapse: 68% Attrition: 54% Comparables: Don McMahon, Tim Worrell, Steve Reed, Grant Jackson

Stapled inside the cover of the office copy of *Dodger General Management for Dummies* is a coffee-stained business card with Carrara's phone number. After toiling in obscurity for more than a decade, the Venezuelan journeyman turned up on Kevin Malone's watch, and he's now pitched intermittently during the Dan Evans, Paul DePodesta, and Ned Colletti regimes, enjoying a success in Dodger Blue he's never found anywhere else. Maybe it's the Dodger Dogs. Carrara might not make the team out of spring training, but as his K/BB ratio suggests, he can still contribute in the middle of the bullpen.

Lance Carter

Bats: R Throws: R Height: 6' 1" Weight: 190 Born: December 18, 1974 Age: 32

YEAR	TEAM	LVL	AGE	W	L	SV	G	GS	IP	H	BB	SO	HR	GB%	BABIP	STUFF	WHIP	ERA	PERA	EQERA	EQH9	EQBB9	EQSO9	EQHR9	VORP	WXRL
2004	TBA	MLB	29	3	3	0	56	0	80¹	77	23	36	12	—	.246	-16	1.22	3.47	4.95	3.29	8.5	2.3	3.7	1.2	25.2	0.79
2005	DUR	AAA	30	1	5	0	8	7	35	40	12	30	8	42.7%	.320	-17	1.49	5.14	6.72	6.11	9.7	3.3	5.6	2.5	-2.0	—
2005	TBA	MLB	30	1	2	1	39	0	57	61	15	22	9	39.1%	.277	-22	1.33	4.89	5.26	4.22	8.7	2.3	3.3	1.4	5.1	-0.47
2006	LVG	AAA	31	2	4	13	45	0	57²	58	16	51	7	45.2%	.321	-10	1.29	3.93	4.87	4.06	9.1	2.7	5.8	1.4	9.9	—
2006	LAN	MLB	31	0	1	0	10	0	11²	17	8	5	1	47.7%	.372	-27	2.14	8.46	5.11	8.03	11.7	5.1	3.6	0.7	-3.2	-0.04
2007	LAN	MLB	32	2	3	2	51	0	56¹	63	22	33	9	43.0%	.293	-16	1.51	5.25	5.59	5.26	10.4	3.1	4.8	1.4	2.3	0.20

Breakout: 6% Improve: 28% Collapse: 46% Attrition: 17% Comparables: Bryan Corey, Bob Humphreys, Juan Acevedo, Jim Slaton

The trade that brought Carter and Danny Baez to the Dodgers for Edwin Jackson and Chuck Tiffany was sold to the public as the acquisition of a pair of All-Star relievers for a couple of prized prospects. The reality was much more pedestrian; Carter's stint as the Rays' closer earned him token honors in 2003, but he'd long since fallen out of favor, and it didn't take long for him to descend even further once he got to L.A. He ratcheted up his ERA nearly every time he took the hill, and, by May, was banished to Las Vegas. Though he pitched well there, a pair of unimpressive appearances in a brief recall prevented a longer look either in L.A. or points beyond. Still a free agent at this writing, he's a good bet to grace some camp as a non-roster invitee.

Elmer Dessens

Bats: R Throws: R Height: 5' 11" Weight: 200 Born: January 13, 1972 Age: 36

YEAR	TEAM	LVL	AGE	W	L	SV	G	GS	IP	H	BB	SO	HR	GB%	BABIP	STUFF	WHIP	ERA	PERA	EQERA	EQH9	EQBB9	EQSO9	EQHR9	VORP	WXRL
2004	ARI	MLB	32	1	6	2	38	9	85¹	107	23	55	11	—	.332	-4	1.52	4.75	4.17	4.58	10.5	2.1	5.0	1.0	1.7	0.63
2004	LAN	MLB	32	1	0	0	12	1	19²	16	8	18	4	—	.231	5	1.22	3.20	5.15	3.20	7.8	3.2	7.3	1.8	5.3	-0.18
2005	LAN	MLB	33	1	2	0	28	7	65²	63	19	37	6	52.3%	.271	-2	1.25	3.56	4.16	4.18	8.6	2.4	4.6	0.8	10.1	1.26
2006	KCA	MLB	34	5	7	2	43	0	54	63	13	36	4	45.0%	.335	4	1.41	4.50	3.50	4.47	9.4	1.9	5.4	0.6	5.8	-0.67
2006	LAN	MLB	34	0	1	0	19	0	23	23	9	16	4	45.2%	.275	-8	1.39	4.70	4.98	4.18	8.4	3.0	5.7	1.5	3.3	0.86
2007	LAN	MLB	36	3	4	2	53	1	70²	76	22	46	9	49.0%	.295	-7	1.38	4.38	4.57	4.45	9.9	2.5	5.2	1.1	9.5	0.80

Breakout: 19% Improve: 41% Collapse: 35% Attrition: 17% Comparables: Terry Leach, Steve Reed, Dave Giusti, Dick Drago

After a season and a half as the Dodgers' swingman, Dessens was forced to make an unsexy choice between the Rockies and Royals as a free agent last winter. He chose K.C., going so far as to secure a no-trade clause prohibiting him from being sent to Colorado. By mid-May, Dessens was the Royals' nominal closer, but a pair of bombings ended that. The Dodgers reacquired him in late July in a deal designed primarily to dump some of Odalis Perez' salary; the Royals picked up Dessens's remaining salary for 2006 and 2007. As a Dodger, he didn't pitch as badly as his ERA would indicate, but neither did he earn Grady Little's trust, and he pitched sparingly after an ankle sprain cost him half of August. He'll return in a middle relief role.

Scott Elbert

Bats: L Throws: L Height: 6' 2" Weight: 190 Born: November 30, 1999 Age: 21

YEAR	TEAM	LVL	AGE	W	L	SV	G	GS	IP	H	BB	SO	HR	GB%	BABIP	STUFF	WHIP	ERA	PERA	EQERA	EQH9	EQBB9	EQSO9	EQHR9	VORP	WXRL
2004	OGD	Rk	0	2	3	0	12	12	49²	47	30	45	5	—	.298	-12	1.55	5.25	7.50	5.54	8.0	5.9	3.9	1.8	0.3	—
2005	CGA	A	0	8	5	0	25	24	115	83	57	128	8	48.6%	.269	12	1.22	2.66	5.74	3.76	7.6	5.6	6.1	1.2	22.5	—
2006	VRO	A+	0	5	5	0	17	15	83¹	57	41	97	4	46.8%	.275	27	1.18	2.38	4.86	3.40	6.6	5.0	6.9	0.8	20.0	—
2006	JAX	AA	0	6	4	0	11	11	62	40	44	76	11	32.9%	.254	8	1.35	3.63	8.18	4.78	8.3	6.6	8.2	2.9	5.3	—
2007	LAN	MLB	21	6	7	0	28	18	107²	99	76	99	17	42.0%	.280	6	1.63	5.12	5.71	5.12	8.5	5.6	7.4	1.3	6.5	1.40

Breakout: 2% Improve: 16% Collapse: 55% Attrition: 2% Comparables: Wilfredo Rodriguez, Travis Blackley, Carlos Hernandez, Rob Burger

Chosen seventeenth in the 2004 draft, Elbert is the Next Big Thing among Dodger pitching prospects, and some consider him the top left-handed pitching prospect in the minors. He's a true power lefty, with a 90 to 93 MPH fastball, workable changeup, and big-breaking slider that he occasionally has trouble throwing for strikes. He blazed through the Florida State League, struggling with his control at times, but avoiding the home run ball even in a park heavily favoring hitters. Promoted to Jacksonville, Elbert took his lumps; his walk and homer rates were unsightly, and he gave up far more fly balls than at the lower level, something which may cause grief when he reaches Las Vegas. For all of his control issues—none of which are out of the ordinary for lefty pitching prospects—batters still had a very tough time making contact against him, hitting just .192/.313/.312 for the year. Mechanical tweaks Elbert made in the Instructional League may smooth out his delivery, making him even more effective. Rumors of a shift to the bullpen continue to follow him, but, for now, he'll remain a starter.

Eric Gagne

Bats: R Throws: R   Height: 6' 0"   Weight: 245   Born: January 7, 1976   Age: 31

YEAR	TEAM	LVL	AGE	W	L	SV	G	GS	IP	H	BB	SO	HR	GB%	BABIP	STUFF	WHIP	ERA	PERA	EQERA	EQH9	EQBB9	EQSO9	EQHR9	VORP	WXRL
2004	LAN	MLB	28	7	3	45	70	0	82¹	53	22	114	5	—	.276	47	0.91	2.19	2.49	2.74	6.5	2.2	11.2	0.5	27.8	8.00
2005	LAN	MLB	29	1	0	8	14	0	13¹	10	3	22	2	53.6%	.308	13	0.98	2.71	2.69	2.70	6.8	2.0	13.5	1.4	4.0	1.09
2007	TEX	MLB	31	4	4	33	49	0	53¹	39	14	68	4	43.0%	.278	36	0.98	2.34	2.07	2.11	6.1	2.2	10.7	0.6	20.0	3.50

Breakout: 35% Improve: 57% Collapse: 24% Attrition: 23%   Comparables: Bryan Harvey, Trevor Hoffman, Rich Gossage, Duane Ward

The Dodgers received a return on their investment on Gagne that must have made them long for the reliable bargain that was Darren Dreifort—15 ⅓ innings over the life of Gagne's two-year, $19-million deal. Once the league's most dominant closer, Gagne self-inflicted a cascade injury in 2005 by pitching through a knee sprain. After missing the season's first six weeks and making just 14 appearances, he underwent elbow surgery—not for his second UCL replacement, as planned, but to relocate a peripheral sensory nerve entrapped by scar tissue. One spring training later, the nerve continued to cause irritation due to a benign tumor, so Gagne went back under the knife in April. He returned in early June, but, after two appearances, went back to the DL with more elbow trouble; amid that setback, a herniated disc precipitated surgery and ended his season. With no guarantee Gagne would regain his old form, the Dodgers declined his $12-million option, hoping to work out an incentive-based deal. Instead, Scott Boras steered his client to Texas, where he signed an incentive-laden, one-year deal for a guaranteed $6 million. To the Rangers, we say "good luck."

Tim Hamulack

Bats: R Throws: L   Height: 6' 2"   Weight: 220   Born: November 14, 1976   Age: 30

YEAR	TEAM	LVL	AGE	W	L	SV	G	GS	IP	H	BB	SO	HR	GB%	BABIP	STUFF	WHIP	ERA	PERA	EQERA	EQH9	EQBB9	EQSO9	EQHR9	VORP	WXRL
2004	PME	AA	27	2	0	0	7	0	15¹	16	7	16	0	—	.364	2	1.50	3.53	3.87	4.20	9.6	4.8	6.0	0.0	2.3	—
2004	PAW	AAA	27	7	4	2	35	0	29²	44	19	25	4	—	.396	-20	2.12	6.97	6.21	8.19	13.3	6.4	5.8	1.5	-8.5	—
2005	BIN	AA	28	2	2	6	21	0	28²	20	6	27	0	66.7%	.250	3	0.91	1.25	3.18	2.86	6.4	2.5	5.1	0.3	8.6	—
2005	NOR	AAA	28	3	1	6	28	0	35¹	20	9	34	1	59.6%	.224	16	0.82	1.02	3.18	1.82	5.7	2.6	6.5	0.3	14.6	—
2006	LVG	AAA	29	0	1	3	28	0	38¹	30	26	44	1	52.2%	.322	20	1.47	1.42	4.17	2.13	7.3	6.2	7.6	0.2	14.7	—
2006	LAN	MLB	29	0	3	0	33	0	34	36	22	34	7	49.0%	.305	-3	1.71	6.35	5.59	6.62	9.2	4.8	7.9	1.5	-5.2	-0.50
2007	LAN	MLB	30	2	3	2	57	0	49¹	50	29	43	5	50.0%	.308	-4	1.59	4.92	5.12	5.03	9.3	4.6	6.9	0.9	3.2	0.30

Breakout: 28% Improve: 56% Collapse: 11% Attrition: 31%   Comparables: Mike Munoz, Dennis Higgins, Bill Scherrer, Willard Hunter

The hard-throwing Hamulack toiled in obscurity for a decade after being picked in the 32nd round by the Astros back in 1995. Scalded by his late-season cup of coffee with the Mets in 2005 and sent to the Dodgers in the Jae Seo-Duaner Sanchez deal, Hamulack began the year as the team's top lefty reliever, but soon fell behind Joe Beimel and spent much of the summer in Las Vegas. As with Beimel, Grady Little used Hamulack to start an inning more than twice as often as bringing him in mid-frame, but the results were backwards; lefties hit him much harder than righties, which is no way to go through life if you have aspirations of big league success as a southpaw.

Joel Hanrahan

Bats: R Throws: R   Height: 6' 3"   Weight: 215   Born: October 6, 1981   Age: 25

YEAR	TEAM	LVL	AGE	W	L	SV	G	GS	IP	H	BB	SO	HR	GB%	BABIP	STUFF	WHIP	ERA	PERA	EQERA	EQH9	EQBB9	EQSO9	EQHR9	VORP	WXRL
2004	LVG	AAA	22	7	7	0	25	22	119¹	128	75	97	22	—	.299	-9	1.70	5.05	6.70	5.15	8.8	5.7	5.5	1.6	6.1	—
2005	VRO	A+	23	1	0	0	5	5	21¹	25	11	25	5	34.4%	.357	-15	1.69	5.92	10.33	8.05	13.7	6.6	6.6	4.7	-5.2	—
2005	JAX	AA	23	9	8	0	23	21	111²	118	55	102	17	44.1%	.323	-36	1.55	4.91	7.19	6.98	11.0	4.8	5.8	2.5	-16.4	—
2006	JAX	AA	24	7	2	0	12	12	66	49	38	67	4	46.7%	.288	12	1.32	2.59	5.62	3.90	8.7	5.8	6.2	1.0	11.8	—
2006	LVG	AAA	24	4	3	0	14	14	74¹	70	39	46	7	41.2%	.276	-4	1.47	4.49	5.52	5.33	8.1	4.5	4.3	0.9	2.3	—
2007	WAS	MLB	25	5	7	0	25	16	96	100	58	68	15	42.0%	.288	-6	1.64	5.54	6.45	5.97	9.3	4.8	5.7	1.3	-3.5	0.30

Breakout: 4% Improve: 31% Collapse: 24% Attrition: 2%   Comparables: Luther Hackman, Ray Ricken, Brian Slocum, Kevin Beirne

This 2000 second round pick reached Las Vegas late in 2003 and spent all of 2004 there while getting bombed like a groom-to-be. He then slid back down the ladder while wrestling with control problems and shoulder weakness. Though still walking too many hitters, Hanrahan otherwise pitched well enough at Jacksonville to earn a return to Vegas; he survived the stint but didn't miss many bats. Unable to justify a spot for him on the big league roster, the Dodgers let him depart as a six-year minor league free agent; he signed a big league deal with the Nationals in early November, ensuring he'll never summer in Vegas again.

Mark Hendrickson   Bats: L Throws: L   Height: 6' 9" Weight: 230 Born: June 23, 1974   Age: 33

YEAR	TEAM	LVL	AGE	W	L	SV	G	GS	IP	H	BB	SO	HR	GB%	BABIP	STUFF	WHIP	ERA	PERA	EQERA	EQH9	EQBB9	EQSO9	EQHR9	VORP	WXRL
2004	TBA	MLB	30	10	15	0	32	30	183¹	211	46	87	21	—	.300	1	1.40	4.81	4.40	5.00	10.2	2.1	4.0	0.9	12.0	2.76
2005	TBA	MLB	31	11	8	0	31	31	178¹	227	49	89	24	45.6%	.329	-4	1.55	5.91	4.62	5.56	10.4	2.4	4.3	1.1	-12.8	0.79
2006	TBA	MLB	32	4	8	0	13	13	89²	81	34	51	10	48.8%	.258	8	1.28	3.81	4.62	3.46	7.1	3.2	4.7	0.9	18.6	2.55
2006	LAN	MLB	32	2	7	0	18	12	75	92	28	48	7	49.6%	.336	4	1.60	4.68	4.10	4.96	10.2	2.9	5.1	0.7	4.8	0.48
2007	LAN	MLB	33	8	11	0	34	25	159²	176	55	96	22	48.0%	.297	-2	1.45	5.09	5.09	5.18	10.2	2.7	4.8	1.2	7.8	2.00

Breakout: 8% Improve: 37% Collapse: 28% Attrition: 4%   Comparables: Bill Krueger, Marvin Freeman, Mike Smithson, Jason Johnson

One of the sillier notions that stuck in Ned Colletti's bonnet last year was the idea that, after three-plus seasons of 5.20 ERA pitching, Mark Hendrickson could be the solution to the Dodgers' rotation problems. Sure, his ERA looked respectable at the time, but his peripherals said otherwise; a higher walk rate offset the increase in strikeouts, and he was basically just hit-lucky. Colletti nevertheless sent Jae Seo and Dioner Navarro to the D-Rays for Hendrickson and Toby Hall. Hendrickson returned to his usual level of ineptitude, and was pitching out of the bullpen by September. Though his good results out of the pen—six hits, two runs, 12 strikeouts in 11 ⅔ innings—may vanish with more exposure, they do provide a broad hint to the Dodgers as to how they might get value out of him in the future.

Clayton Kershaw   Bats: L Throws: L   Height: 6' 3" Weight: 210 Born: March 19, 1988   Age: 19

YEAR	TEAM	LVL	AGE	W	L	SV	G	GS	IP	H	BB	SO	HR	GB%	BABIP	STUFF	WHIP	ERA	PERA	EQERA	EQH9	EQBB9	EQSO9	EQHR9	VORP	WXRL
2006	DGR	Rk	18	2	0	1	10	8	37	28	5	54	0	51.5%	.357	35	0.89	1.95	2.51	3.82	9.2	1.5	7.6	0.3	7.0	—
2007	LAN	MLB	19	8	7	1	31	18	124	121	30	116	16	46.0%	.298	24	1.21	3.86	3.99	3.89	9.0	1.9	7.5	1.1	25.5	3.30

Breakout: 23% Improve: 39% Collapse: 25% Attrition: 0%   Comparables: Yusmeiro Petit, Alan Webb, Craig Anderson, Joel Zumaya

With the seventh pick in the 2006 draft, Logan White had the run of the entire prep ranks, and he chose this lefty. Kershaw's clean mechanics and excellent command of a 92 to 94 MPH fastball and a plus curveball draw raves. He made mincemeat out of GCL hitters, and may have the highest ceiling of any Dodger pitching prospect; our own Kevin Goldstein rated him as the number-two southpaw starter in the minors back in August.

Hong-Chih Kuo   Bats: L Throws: L   Height: 6' 0" Weight: 235 Born: July 23, 1981   Age: 25

YEAR	TEAM	LVL	AGE	W	L	SV	G	GS	IP	H	BB	SO	HR	GB%	BABIP	STUFF	WHIP	ERA	PERA	EQERA	EQH9	EQBB9	EQSO9	EQHR9	VORP	WXRL
2005	VRO	A+	23	1	1	0	11	3	26	19	10	42	2	45.3%	.340	14	1.12	2.08	5.21	3.38	9.0	4.9	9.0	1.5	5.9	—
2005	JAX	AA	23	1	1	3	17	0	28¹	22	11	44	1	48.4%	.350	25	1.17	1.91	3.13	2.96	8.6	3.6	9.9	0.7	8.0	—
2006	LVG	AAA	24	4	3	1	23	9	53¹	52	22	63	5	45.7%	.356	12	1.39	3.05	3.96	3.83	8.7	3.5	8.2	1.0	10.6	—
2006	LAN	MLB	24	1	5	0	28	5	59²	54	33	71	3	45.3%	.347	30	1.46	4.22	3.14	4.21	7.7	4.2	9.4	0.4	9.9	1.04
2007	LAN	MLB	25	6	6	2	50	13	99¹	93	48	105	12	45.0%	.307	14	1.42	4.23	4.49	4.27	8.7	3.8	8.4	1.0	16.4	2.00

Breakout: 19% Improve: 37% Collapse: 33% Attrition: 9%   Comparables: Tug McGraw, Arthur Rhodes, Erik Bedard, Dick Stigman

Sidelined by two Tommy John surgeries and limited to 42 ⅓ pro innings from 2001 to 2004, this Taiwanese native dazzled once he was healthy, lighting up radar guns with 99 MPH heat out of the bullpen, rare for a southpaw. He made the Dodgers out of spring training but struggled with his control, walking 24 in 27 ⅓ innings while bouncing between the City of Angels and Sin City. In mid-July, he was converted back to starting at Triple-A, and the results were revelatory. Despite earning just one win after being recalled, he was arguably the team's top starter in September (29 ⅓ IP, 3.07 ERA, 35 K, 7 BB, 1 HR) and didn't embarrass himself in his postseason start either. Stamina is his biggest issue; if he can increase his, he's clearly got the stuff to succeed in the big leagues.

Derek Lowe   Bats: R Throws: R   Height: 6' 6" Weight: 230 Born: June 1, 1973   Age: 34

YEAR	TEAM	LVL	AGE	W	L	SV	G	GS	IP	H	BB	SO	HR	GB%	BABIP	STUFF	WHIP	ERA	PERA	EQERA	EQH9	EQBB9	EQSO9	EQHR9	VORP	WXRL
2004	BOS	MLB	31	14	12	0	33	33	182²	224	71	105	15	—	.333	6	1.61	5.42	4.19	6.08	10.6	3.1	4.8	0.6	-8.0	1.36
2005	LAN	MLB	32	12	15	0	35	35	222	223	55	146	28	64.3%	.286	8	1.25	3.61	4.33	4.59	9.0	2.0	5.4	1.1	22.5	3.84
2006	LAN	MLB	33	16	8	0	35	34	218	221	55	123	14	67.8%	.293	20	1.27	3.63	3.62	3.72	8.4	2.0	4.6	0.5	49.3	6.60
2007	LAN	MLB	34	11	11	0	31	29	186	200	56	113	16	61.0%	.304	7	1.38	4.31	4.39	4.47	9.9	2.4	4.9	0.7	24.8	3.90

Breakout: 18% Improve: 51% Collapse: 6% Attrition: 0%   Comparables: Mark Gubicza, Mike Morgan, John Denny, Larry Jackson

When the Fourth Estate mob who helped drive Paul DePodesta out of town reckon with Google Boy's contributions to the Dodgers, they'll be forced to admit that his choice of Lowe among the 2004 free agent starters was one of his best moves. Within that class, Lowe ranks first in innings, second to Pedro Martinez in SNLVAR and ERA, third behind Martinez and

Kevin Millwood in VORP, and miles beyond the Matt Clement/Eric Milton/Carl Pavano/Jaret Wright/Russ Ortiz dreck that's done little but stink up the joint since then. Brad Penny may have gotten the All-Star Game start, but this worm-killing machine (he led the majors in ground-ball percentage) was the Dodgers' most reliable and durable starter, routinely lasting into the seventh inning. He was especially effective after the trading deadline (75 ⅓ IP, 2.76 ERA, 41/13 K/BB), apparently benefiting from the opportunity to pick Greg Maddux's brain on the art of efficiency (13.8 pitches per inning during that stretch, compared to 15.8 before). A dominant, strikeout-oriented ace in front of him in the rotation would be nice, but, as it is, Lowe has become a solid staff leader who's lived up to his end of the deal.

Greg Maddux **Bats: R Throws: R** Height: 6' 0" Weight: 180 Born: December 31, 1969 Age: 41

YEAR	TEAM	LVL	AGE	W	L	SV	G	GS	IP	H	BB	SO	HR	GB%	BABIP	STUFF	WHIP	ERA	PERA	EQERA	EQH9	EQBB9	EQSO9	EQHR9	VORP	WXRL
2004	CHN	MLB	38	16	11	0	33	33	212²	218	33	151	35	—	.294	8	1.18	4.02	4.38	4.21	9.1	1.3	5.7	1.3	34.8	4.55
2005	CHN	MLB	39	13	15	0	35	35	225	239	36	136	29	54.4%	.299	8	1.22	4.24	4.20	4.41	9.5	1.3	5.0	1.1	28.6	4.13
2006	CHN	MLB	40	9	11	0	22	22	136¹	153	23	81	14	51.7%	.313	15	1.29	4.69	3.64	4.28	9.7	1.3	4.9	0.8	14.0	1.90
2006	LAN	MLB	40	6	3	0	12	12	73²	66	14	36	6	54.7%	.263	13	1.09	3.30	3.70	3.57	7.3	1.4	3.9	0.6	18.7	2.51
2007	SDN	MLB	41	12	10	0	31	29	190	198	40	103	21	52.0%	.283	4	1.25	3.88	4.31	4.32	9.4	1.6	4.4	0.9	28.9	4.60

Breakout: 7% Improve: 37% Collapse: 16% Attrition: 5% Comparables: Bert Blyleven, Dennis Martinez, Don Sutton, Warren Spahn

Maddux spent much of 2006 inducing goose bumps as he displayed the artistry which will one day make him a first-ballot Hall of Famer, but he spent nearly as much time reminding followers that he's a 40-year-old legend whose best years are behind him. After a fantastic April (5–0, 1.35 ERA), he rode the down escalator as the Cubs' season collapsed, yielding a 5.77 ERA over the next three months. Nonetheless, Ned Colletti liberated Maddux from Chicago just moments before the trade deadline. Maddux tossed six no-hit innings in his first start in Dodger blue, and chased no-hitters two other times, at one point retiring 32 straight hitters for a "hidden perfect game." His acquisition bolstered the staff, and much was made of his imparting pitching wisdom to his new teammates. Although Grady Little kept Maddux on an even shorter leash than Dusty Baker had (go figure), Maddux still tossed more innings over the entire season than any Dodger starter other than Derek Lowe; he made his bullets count, which is part of the reason why a plaque in Cooperstown awaits. Bet on him to continue doing so in San Diego, where he signed a one-year, $10-million deal.

Jonathan Meloan **Bats: R Throws: R** Height: 6' 3" Weight: 225 Born: July 11, 1984 Age: 22

YEAR	TEAM	LVL	AGE	W	L	SV	G	GS	IP	H	BB	SO	HR	GB%	BABIP	STUFF	WHIP	ERA	PERA	EQERA	EQH9	EQBB9	EQSO9	EQHR9	VORP	WXRL
2005	OGD	Rk	20	0	2	1	16	6	39	30	18	54	4	55.4%	.306	-6	1.23	3.69	7.40	4.54	9.1	6.1	6.1	2.0	4.2	—
2006	CGA	A	21	1	1	1	12	0	23	9	7	41	2	61.1%	.212	21	0.70	1.57	4.98	2.95	5.9	3.4	9.7	1.7	6.3	—
2006	VRO	A+	21	1	0	0	4	3	18¹	15	4	27	2	67.9%	.346	18	1.05	2.49	4.81	3.57	8.7	2.5	8.7	2.0	4.0	—
2006	JAX	AA	21	1	0	0	5	0	10¹	3	5	23	1	43.8%	.214	9	0.79	1.78	3.57	2.89	5.8	4.8	15.4	1.9	2.8	—
2007	LAN	MLB	22	3	4	1	25	7	63	56	33	63	9	51.0%	.283	12	1.41	4.17	4.65	4.21	8.2	4.1	8.0	1.1	9.6	1.20

Breakout: 11% Improve: 21% Collapse: 43% Attrition: 23% Comparables: Francisco Liriano, Mike Meyers, Don Cardwell, Franklyn German

Another Logan White find, this fifth-round 2005 pick out of the University of Arizona has rocketed through the system with impressive results at every stop; through 91 pro innings he's struck out 145, walked just 34, and yielded a 2.67 ERA. Despite missing the first five weeks of 2006 with elbow soreness and being handled with kid gloves all year (generally pitching a couple innings every fifth day), Meloan dominated hitters with a 92 to 94 MPH fastball that touched 97 and a monster curveball. Given that he's got no third pitch, he's likely to stay in the bullpen, where some feel he has closer potential. The next step will be showing he can hold up once the Dodgers loosen the reins a bit.

Greg Miller **Bats: L Throws: L** Height: 6' 5" Weight: 220 Born: November 3, 1984 Age: 22

YEAR	TEAM	LVL	AGE	W	L	SV	G	GS	IP	H	BB	SO	HR	GB%	BABIP	STUFF	WHIP	ERA	PERA	EQERA	EQH9	EQBB9	EQSO9	EQHR9	VORP	WXRL
2006	JAX	AA	21	1	0	1	11	0	22¹	12	13	24	0	85.5%	.222	19	1.13	0.81	4.24	4.29	6.4	5.6	7.3	0.4	3.1	—
2006	LVG	AAA	21	3	0	0	33	0	37	33	33	32	1	65.7%	.311	9	1.78	4.38	5.42	4.26	7.8	7.6	5.9	0.2	5.7	—
2007	LAN	MLB	22	3	4	0	26	6	56	52	51	51	3	62.0%	.311	-1	1.84	5.04	5.51	5.27	8.5	7.2	7.3	0.4	2.1	0.40

Breakout: 4% Improve: 16% Collapse: 56% Attrition: 24% Comparables: Jimmy Anderson, Ben Hendrickson, Adam Harben, Tommie Sisk

Once upon a time, Miller was considered the top lefty pitching prospect in the minors; he was number 33 on our 2003 Top-50 Prospect List on the basis of his age-18 season at Vero Beach and Jacksonville (142 ⅓ IP, 151 K, 2.21 ERA). Shoulder woes requiring two uncommon surgeries (a removal of the bursa sac and a shaving of the tip of the shoulder blade) cost him all of 2004; since coming back, he's switched to the bullpen and dropped to a three-quarters arm angle to avoid impingement.

(continued next page)

Greg Miller *(continued)*

He made it through 2006 in one piece, a victory in itself, but only with a significant amount of babying—he pitched back-to-back days just twice, and missed half of July with a minor shoulder flare-up. His velocity can still reach the low- to mid-90s, and he does a great job of generating ground balls, but as those walk rates illustrate, his control hasn't been the same. Still, even in his diminished form, it's too early to give up on him.

T. J. Nall Bats: R Throws: R   Height: 6′ 1″   Weight: 207   Born: November 4, 1980   Age: 26

YEAR	TEAM	LVL	AGE	W	L	SV	G	GS	IP	H	BB	SO	HR	GB%	BABIP	STUFF	WHIP	ERA	PERA	EQERA	EQH9	EQBB9	EQSO9	EQHR9	VORP	WXRL
2004	JAX	AA	23	8	9	1	32	20	143¹	146	36	123	19	—	.303	-21	1.27	4.15	5.86	5.53	9.9	2.5	4.9	1.9	1.1	—
2005	LVG	AAA	24	6	7	0	29	15	108	154	47	96	20	49.5%	.394	-21	1.86	7.17	5.76	6.51	11.5	3.6	5.8	1.7	-11.5	—
2006	JAX	AA	25	10	7	2	29	19	140¹	116	30	155	10	52.6%	.292	5	1.04	2.83	4.43	4.96	9.7	2.2	6.6	1.3	9.4	—
2007	WAS	MLB	26	5	7	1	31	13	97	106	30	69	13	47.0%	.305	2	1.40	4.83	5.29	5.28	9.8	2.5	5.8	1.1	4.1	0.90

Breakout: 23% Improve: 59% Collapse: 11% Attrition: 0%   Comparables: Geoff Geary, Steve Watkins, Chad Durbin, Eric Schmitt

A 1999 eighth-round high school pick, Nall has pitched impressively at Jacksonville, but has never been able to get over the hump at Las Vegas. That's no crime; even relative to other PCL parks, Cashman Field is capable of making a pitcher's ERA look like the next Boeing product. A groundballer such as Nall ought to fare better there, unless it's actually the fact that he's got no real out-pitch that's vexing him. The Dodgers felt that was the case, opting to let him depart at the end of the year as a minor league free agent. He signed with the Nationals in the same dragnet that ensnared Joel Hanrahan and former Dodger prospect Joe Thurston.

Brad Penny Bats: R Throws: R   Height: 6′ 4″   Weight: 260   Born: May 24, 1978   Age: 29

YEAR	TEAM	LVL	AGE	W	L	SV	G	GS	IP	H	BB	SO	HR	GB%	BABIP	STUFF	WHIP	ERA	PERA	EQERA	EQH9	EQBB9	EQSO9	EQHR9	VORP	WXRL
2004	FLO	MLB	26	8	8	0	21	21	131¹	124	39	105	10	—	.298	27	1.24	3.15	3.54	3.59	8.5	2.4	6.4	0.6	32.3	3.95
2004	LAN	MLB	26	1	2	0	3	3	11²	6	6	6	2	—	.129	-2	1.03	3.08	6.25	3.86	4.6	3.9	3.9	1.5	2.2	0.53
2005	LAN	MLB	27	7	9	0	29	29	175¹	185	41	122	17	47.9%	.307	17	1.29	3.90	3.80	4.04	9.5	1.9	5.7	0.9	29.6	4.42
2006	LAN	MLB	28	16	9	0	34	33	189	206	54	148	19	44.8%	.327	20	1.38	4.33	3.78	4.14	9.2	2.2	6.3	0.8	32.8	4.56
2007	LAN	MLB	29	11	10	0	29	29	181²	190	50	139	23	47.0%	.300	15	1.32	4.28	4.49	4.32	9.6	2.2	6.1	1.1	26.4	4.20

Breakout: 4% Improve: 31% Collapse: 20% Attrition: 6%   Comparables: Chris Bosio, Mark Clark, Freddy Garcia, Larry Christenson

The last man standing from the most controversial trade in the team's recent history—the Paul Lo Duca-Hee Seop Choi deal with the Marlins—Penny signed a three-year, $25.5-million extension on Paul DePodesta's watch in the summer of 2005. He began 2006 looking as though he might make the deal seem like a bargain, earning a starting nod for the All-Star Game thanks to a 10–2, 2.91 ERA first half. It was downhill from there, as "Bad Penny" kept turning up to slog his way through to a second-half ERA of 6.25. Reasons for the decline were unclear; in late May, Penny erupted after being pulled, then complained he'd been pitching through a sore shoulder. The problem was determined to be mechanical, and he didn't even miss a turn. Down the stretch, he attempted to pitch through lower back tightness and was often hit hard, but, even with eleven starters in reserve, the team didn't skip his turn until the postseason, when Grady Little split the difference by using Penny in relief during Game One of the Division Series; Penny surrendered a lead and took the loss. Penny's shown a disturbing trend towards wearing down as the season goes on: 6.2 IP/GS, 3.16 ERA, 0.6 HR/9 before the break in 2005 and 2006, against 5.4 IP/GS, 5.38 ERA, 1.3 HR/9 after. The Dodgers would do well to ensure that he's in top shape and prevent him from pitching when he's less than healthy in order to maximize the return on their investment.

Takashi Saito Bats: L Throws: R   Height: 6′ 2″   Weight: 200   Born: November 30, 1999   Age: 37

YEAR	TEAM	LVL	AGE	W	L	SV	G	GS	IP	H	BB	SO	HR	GB%	BABIP	STUFF	WHIP	ERA	PERA	EQERA	EQH9	EQBB9	EQSO9	EQHR9	VORP	WXRL
2004	YKO	JP	0	2	5	0	16	0	44¹	64	13	37	12	—	.352	-24	1.74	7.72	5.92	7.98	12.3	3.1	5.3	2.0	-11.6	—
2005	YKO	JP	0	3	4	0	21	16	106	111	29	93	12	—	.306	8	1.32	3.82	4.20	4.31	9.9	2.8	5.9	1.0	14.9	—
2006	LAN	MLB	0	6	2	24	72	0	78¹	48	23	107	3	36.6%	.280	53	0.91	2.07	2.15	2.14	5.4	2.2	11.0	0.3	33.6	5.47
2007	LAN	MLB	37	3	4	21	46	0	56	53	21	58	7	41.0%	.304	10	1.33	3.85	4.19	3.86	8.8	3.0	8.2	1.1	11.4	1.60

Breakout: 25% Improve: 40% Collapse: 30% Attrition: 9%   Comparables: Rudy Seanez, Jay Howell, Trevor Hoffman, Steve Bedrosian

After 14 years with the Yokohama BayStars of the Japanese Central League, mainly as a starter, Saito desired to emulate former high school, college, and BayStars teammate Kazuhiro Sasaki and prove himself stateside while he still had the stuff (namely a 93 MPH fastball and a devastating slider). Signed to a minor league deal, he was guaranteed nothing but an opportunity; by mid-May he was sharing closer duties with Danny Baez. He gained sole possession of the job following Eric Gagne's disappointing cameo and was nothing short of season-saving brilliant, particularly down the stretch when he was scored upon in just three of his final 28 appearances and struck out 14 men in his last 7 ⅓ innings while walking just one. Overall, he led major league relievers in strikeouts, finished third in the NL in WXRL, didn't allow a homer after May 15, and skinned right-handers alive (.129/.205/.193). Rather than overpay for damaged goods in Eric Gagne, the Dodgers persuaded Saito to remain stateside with a one-year, $1-million deal, providing considerably better bang for their buck.

Aaron Sele   **Bats: R Throws: R**   Height: 6′ 3″   Weight: 220   Born: June 25, 1970   Age: 37

YEAR	TEAM	LVL	AGE	W	L	SV	G	GS	IP	H	BB	SO	HR	GB%	BABIP	STUFF	WHIP	ERA	PERA	EQERA	EQH9	EQBB9	EQSO9	EQHR9	VORP	WXRL
2004	ANA	MLB	34	9	4	0	28	24	132	163	51	51	16	—	.324	-13	1.66	5.05	5.03	5.41	10.3	3.1	3.2	1.0	5.2	1.61
2005	SEA	MLB	35	6	12	0	21	21	116	147	41	53	18	42.0%	.326	-16	1.62	5.66	5.40	5.81	11.2	3.2	4.0	1.4	-3.4	1.72
2006	LVG	AAA	36	3	0	0	5	5	29	25	5	28	1	45.8%	.296	25	1.03	2.48	3.17	2.79	7.8	1.6	5.9	0.3	9.1	—
2006	LAN	MLB	36	8	6	0	28	15	103¹	120	30	57	11	45.9%	.315	0	1.45	4.53	4.18	4.54	9.6	2.3	4.5	0.8	12.2	1.84
2007	LAN	MLB	37	5	7	0	32	15	103²	121	36	57	15	45.0%	.303	-11	1.51	5.16	5.45	5.19	10.8	2.7	4.4	1.3	5.1	1.10

Breakout: 16%   Improve: 46%   Collapse: 22%   Attrition: 18%   Comparables: Bob Forsch, Rick Mahler, Paul Splittorff, Sid Hudson

Sele ignored the Grim Forksman's suggestion that he was done after being released twice in 2005 by accepting an assignment to Las Vegas after a spring-training invite panned out. He dominated in Triple-A and was recalled in early May, when, in his first-ever taste of NL action, he offered a primer on the relative strength of the two leagues. As much as rookies such as Russell Martin and Andre Ethier, Sele helped turn the Dodgers' season around. He was 6–2 with a 2.91 ERA at the break, but things unraveled from there, and he earned a trip to the pen in early August when the team feared he was gassed; he gave the Dodgers little help in the second half (7.28 ERA). The Dodgers made nice work in pulling Sele off the scrap heap, but they'd be better off finding the next useful NRI than expecting a repeat performance here.

Eric Stults   **Bats: L Throws: L**   Height: 6′ 0″   Weight: 215   Born: December 9, 1979   Age: 27

YEAR	TEAM	LVL	AGE	W	L	SV	G	GS	IP	H	BB	SO	HR	GB%	BABIP	STUFF	WHIP	ERA	PERA	EQERA	EQH9	EQBB9	EQSO9	EQHR9	VORP	WXRL
2005	JAX	AA	25	4	3	0	12	12	68	73	14	58	6	44.3%	.319	-7	1.28	3.31	4.97	5.89	10.8	2.1	4.9	1.5	-2.1	—
2005	LVG	AAA	25	3	7	0	15	14	78	107	24	60	15	43.3%	.358	-15	1.68	6.58	5.47	5.60	10.8	2.5	5.0	1.8	0.0	—
2006	LVG	AAA	26	10	11	0	26	26	153¹	153	68	128	10	46.8%	.330	12	1.44	4.23	4.39	4.79	8.7	3.9	5.7	0.7	14.0	—
2006	LAN	MLB	26	1	0	0	6	2	17²	17	7	5	4	40.7%	.236	-31	1.36	5.59	6.65	5.40	7.9	2.9	2.5	2.0	-0.2	0.26
2007	LAN	MLB	27	5	8	0	34	15	105¹	120	44	68	16	46.0%	.305	-6	1.55	5.45	5.66	5.51	10.5	3.3	5.2	1.3	1.5	0.80

Breakout: 8%   Improve: 35%   Collapse: 27%   Attrition: 0%   Comparables: Mike Mason, Ted Bowsfield, Bob Shirley, John Curtis

Stults, a 2002 pick out of Bethel College, is no sort of prospect, but he is a lefty. He took a great leap forward in his second tour of duty at Las Vegas, earning a September recall. He gave the Dodgers two respectable starts, the better of which was a key six-inning, two-hit effort at Shea Stadium on September 10. With an 88 to 92 MPH fastball, a plus changeup, and an average cutter, he generates enough ground balls that he could find a spot in the bullpen.

Brett Tomko   **Bats: R Throws: R**   Height: 6′ 2″   Weight: 225   Born: April 7, 1973   Age: 34

YEAR	TEAM	LVL	AGE	W	L	SV	G	GS	IP	H	BB	SO	HR	GB%	BABIP	STUFF	WHIP	ERA	PERA	EQERA	EQH9	EQBB9	EQSO9	EQHR9	VORP	WXRL
2004	SFN	MLB	31	11	7	0	32	31	194	196	64	108	19	—	.283	8	1.34	4.04	4.20	4.36	8.7	2.6	4.4	0.8	26.5	3.84
2005	SFN	MLB	32	8	15	1	33	30	190²	205	57	114	20	40.1%	.301	7	1.37	4.48	4.34	4.62	9.5	2.5	4.9	0.9	19.3	2.47
2006	LAN	MLB	33	8	7	0	44	15	112¹	123	29	76	17	39.2%	.300	-4	1.35	4.73	4.37	4.89	9.1	2.0	5.4	1.2	8.4	1.05
2007	LAN	MLB	34	5	7	1	38	13	103²	113	32	66	16	42.0%	.292	-6	1.40	4.84	5.00	4.85	10.0	2.4	5.1	1.3	9.6	1.50

Breakout: 13%   Improve: 35%   Collapse: 26%   Attrition: 8%   Comparables: Don Robinson, Pete Harnisch, Bobby Witt, Johnny Sain

Tomko won no friends with his criticism of the staff in San Francisco, so it was surprising when Ned Colletti inked him to a two-year, $8.7-million deal shortly after he hung out his shingle. Tomko got off to an excellent start—coming off five consecutive quality starts on May 15 he stood at 5–1 with a 2.88 ERA. Five bombings in a row nearly doubled that ERA before he missed five weeks with an oblique strain. Displaced by Greg Maddux, he handled his shift to the bullpen with surprising grace. Initial returns were positive—20 appearances, 20 innings, 13 hits allowed, 19/6 K/BB—but by September he'd lost velocity and worn out his welcome. He finished with just 0.03 WXRL, and led the Dodger bullpen in entry-induced groans from the crowd. Still, for a guy who doesn't inspire much enthusiasm as a starter because of his low strikeout rate, Tomko adapted well to the pen. That may not be worth $4.1 million, but it's something.

Dequam Wright

Bats: R Throws: L   Height: 5′ 11″   Weight: 160   Born: January 28, 1985   Age: 22

YEAR	TEAM	LVL	AGE	W	L	SV	G	GS	IP	H	BB	SO	HR	GB%	BABIP	STUFF	WHIP	ERA	PERA	EQERA	EQH9	EQBB9	EQSO9	EQHR9	VORP	WXRL
2004	OGD	Rk	19	3	3	0	17	2	44¹	56	23	66	3	—	.434	-6	1.78	6.30	5.27	8.80	11.7	5.3	6.3	1.2	-15.6	—
2005	CGA	A	20	1	5	1	30	0	60²	38	33	68	2	50.7%	.252	14	1.17	1.93	5.33	4.03	6.7	6.2	6.2	0.6	10.1	—
2006	VRO	A+	21	3	3	0	26	0	42	29	23	51	0	42.4%	.302	22	1.24	1.50	3.98	2.81	6.5	5.6	7.1	0.2	12.9	—
2006	JAX	AA	21	1	1	1	15	0	21	14	11	28	2	42.9%	.273	12	1.19	4.71	5.59	6.86	8.2	5.0	9.2	1.4	-2.8	—
2007	LAN	MLB	22	2	4	0	27	6	54¹	54	40	48	7	43.0%	.304	-3	1.74	5.60	5.95	5.66	9.2	5.8	7.1	1.1	-0.1	0.20

Breakout: 13% Improve: 37% Collapse: 33% Attrition: 26%   Comparables: Damian Moss, Horacio Estrada, Wilfredo Rodriguez, Tyler Johnson

Another undersized, unheralded Dodger pitching prospect, if nothing else, DeQuam LaWesley Wright might have the best name in the entire organization. Drafted out of an Alabama high school in 2003, the southpaw has made solid progress through the system, struggling with control issues, but missing a good number of bats. He bounced between Vero Beach and Jacksonville last year and should return to Double-A to start 2007.

Lineouts

PLAYER	TEAM	LVL	AGE	PA	R	2B	3B	HR	RBI	BB	SO	SB-CS	SPEED	AVG/OBP/SLG	MLVr	EqAVG/EqOBP/EqSLG	EqA	VORP
C J. Apodaca	CGA	A	19	217	23	8	0	1	22	25	35	1-0	3.8	.249/.336/.307	-.079	.214/.281/.250	.198	-14.3
	VRO	A+	19	124	17	5	0	4	14	13	23	3-1	3.7	.257/.341/.413	.061	.232/.306/.375	.238	-0.3
3B J. Bell#	OGD	Rk	19	276	45	17	3	12	53	23	72	4-0	5.3	.308/.367/.544	.248	.245/.283/.406	.237	1.0
SS I. De Jesus	CGA	A	19	563	65	17	2	1	44	63	85	16-5	5.3	.277/.361/.327	.001	.252/.315/.294	.225	-9.3
SS P. Mattingly	DGR	Rk	18	199	22	12	3	1	29	9	39	12-3	6.6	.290/.322/.403	.118	.268/.288/.379	.234	2.5
OF X. Paul*	VRO	A+	21	520	62	23	3	13	49	38	114	22-15	5.4	.285/.343/.430	.105	.265/.314/.408	.247	-4.8
2B O. Robles*	LVG	AAA	30	316	29	10	0	0	28	36	20	0-1	3.7	.287/.366/.324	-.114	.230/.299/.251	.205	-16.0
	LAN	MLB	30	39	6	0	1	0	0	5	5	0-0	7.2	.152/.263/.212	-.481	.121/.237/.182	.165	-3.2

PLAYER	TEAM	LVL	AGE	W	L	SV	IP	H	BB	SO	HR	GB%	BABIP	STUFF	WHIP	ERA	PERA	EqERA	EqH9	EqBB9	EqSO9	EqHR9	VORP
A. Bastardo*	CGA	A	22	3	1	0	32	22	14	33	2	—	.253	7	1.13	1.41	6.29	3.26	7.4	5.3	5.3	1.5	7.9
	VRO	A+	22	5	5	0	93	97	47	105	12	—	.339	-18	1.55	4.55	7.18	5.88	10.5	5.5	6.5	2.3	-2.8
Z. Hammes	VRO	A+	22	6	3	1	91	95	46	90	9	—	.335	-18	1.55	4.35	6.49	5.02	9.8	5.4	5.6	1.7	5.8
D. J. Houlton	LVG	AAA	26	9	11	0	162¹	180	60	132	25	—	.318	-14	1.48	5.61	5.72	6.07	9.8	3.3	5.5	1.7	-8.6
E. Hull	LVG	AAA	26	2	4	2	73¹	54	43	78	6	—	.271	9	1.33	4.19	5.00	4.54	6.9	5.3	7.2	0.9	8.6
S. Lundberg	JAX	AA	29	15	2	0	150²	124	42	110	3	—	.283	17	1.11	2.28	3.80	4.34	8.8	2.9	4.3	0.4	20.3
	LVG	AAA	29	0	4	0	21²	38	5	14	3	—	.422	-12	2.03	7.22	5.12	7.77	15.1	2.0	4.1	1.6	-5.3
M. Megrew*	VRO	A+	22	2	3	0	53	44	44	62	5	—	.302	7	1.66	3.57	7.69	4.62	8.3	9.1	6.9	1.6	5.5
M. Merricks*	VRO	A+	23	0	3	0	35²	29	17	48	4	—	.325	1	1.31	4.09	7.20	6.75	9.2	5.7	7.6	2.2	-4.3
A. Morris	OGD	Rk	19	4	5	0	59	64	40	79	3	—	.386	9	1.76	5.19	5.85	7.49	10.3	7.5	6.4	1.1	-12.1
J. Orenduff	JAX	AA	0	4	2	0	50	40	19	54	4	—	.286	6	1.18	3.42	4.98	5.85	9.3	3.6	7.0	1.3	-1.3
F. Osoria	LVG	AAA	24	2	2	2	51	81	21	28	2	—	.407	-15	2.00	4.41	4.46	5.20	13.1	3.5	3.7	0.3	2.4
	LAN	MLB	24	0	2	0	17²	27	9	13	4	—	.397	-17	2.04	7.12	5.75	6.27	12.5	3.9	5.8	1.9	-2.3

With the trade of Dioner Navarro, the most promising backstop in the system is **Juan Apodaca**, an undersized Venezuelan. He's got some plate discipline, but not much power, and his skills as a catch-and-throw guy are well-regarded. He's a long way off. Senioritis helped the Dodgers nab **Josh Bell**, a massive, athletic high schooler in the fourth round of the 2005 draft. He's got a long swing and thus strikes out way too often and doesn't walk enough, but his raw power is impressive. Son of the former major leaguer of the same name, **Ivan De Jesus** is a wiry 2005 second round high school pick who has above-average defensive skills, speed, and a mature approach at the plate, but almost no power. Donnie Baseball's kid, **Preston Mattingly** isn't the pure hitter his father was, but he's a bigger, better athlete whose stock skyrocketed just before the draft; the Dodgers took him with a supplemental pick at number 31. Having not seen much pitching outside of Indiana, he took his lumps in his debut, but his plate coverage and wrist speed draw praise. Nobody's fond of his defense, so first base or leftfield might be his ultimate home. **Xavier Paul** offers athleticism, speed, some power, and the best outfield arm in the system, but his approach at the plate remains fairly raw. He fared well in a repeat at Vero Beach, but that kind of success isn't without its caveats. **Oscar Robles** knocked around the minors for eleven years before getting a shot in the bigs, but he lost his utility job to Ned Colletti's man, Ramon Martinez. In a world in which Neifi Perez remains gainfully employed, this guy deserves a better shot.

A smallish lefty, **Alberto Bastardo** was pried from the Orioles during the minor league phase of last year's Rule 5 draft. He's got decent stuff and good command, projecting as a back-end starter in the majors. Cracks about being a corn-fed monster might be inevitable for a six-foot-six hulk from Iowa, but **Zach Hammes** was rated high enough to be a second-round pick in 2001, and he's on the 40-man now. A Rule 5 pick who lasted the full year with the Dodgers in 2005, **D. J. Houlton** was sent back to Las Vegas last year, hell on earth for a fly ball pitcher with his middling skills. Yet another undersized non-prospect who keeps climbing the ladder, **Eric Hull** survived both an introduction to the rough justice of the PCL and a conversion to the bullpen. He also showed an interesting reverse platoon split (.207/.329/.298 vs. lefties, .241/.347/.383 vs. Righties). Certainly not a prospect, but you have to tip your cap to **Spike Lundberg** for completing his tenth year in the minors. Briefly taken away by the Marlins in the 2005 Rule 5 draft after he had missed much of the previous season recovering from Tommy John surgery, **Mike Megrew** was returned to the Dodgers in mid-April, and still looked raw after recovering from new problems with his shoulder. On the 40-man, for reasons only Ned Colletti can explain. Like Mike McGrew, **Matt Merricks** is another Rule 5'd lefty still hoping to be thought of as an injured starter instead of LOOGY bait. **Avery Morris** didn't sign with the Devil Rays as a draft-and-follow in 2005, so the Dodgers tabbed him with the number 26 pick after he'd spent one year in a Tennessee junior college. He's got a mid-90s fastball and one of the better curves in the 2006 class, but he underwent Tommy John surgery after the season. A 2004 first-rounder, sinkerballer **Justin Orenduff** was building on a productive 2005 when he was felled by shoulder impingement problems and underwent surgery in August. Wait and see before expecting a big future—shoulder issues are career-threatening. Skinny six-fingered sinkerballer **Franquelis Osoria** got a long look with the 2005 Dodgers, but fell out of favor with the new regime; judging by his line, Las Vegas played without an infield when he pitched (.410 BABIP, but just .096 ISO). Lost in a roster crunch, he'll rejoin Jim Tracy in Pittsburgh.

Manager: Grady Little

Year	Team	W-L	Pythag +/-	Avg PC	100 +P	120 +P	QS	BQS	REL	REL w Zero R	IBB	SUBS	PH	PH Avg	PH HR	SB2	CS2	SB3	CS3	SAC Att	SAC %	POS SAC	Squeeze	Swing	In Play
2006	LAN	88-74	0	91.6	54	1	75	4	454	278	40	58	285	.195	7	116	42	12	5	86	76.7%	27	2	157	125

If the knock on Grady Little's Red Sox tenure was that he couldn't run a pitching staff—going an inning too far with Pedro Martinez, letting chaos reign in a closerless bullpen—he undermined that reputation nicely in his first season at the Dodger helm. The rotation was so unstable it was deemed radioactive—ten pitchers made at least 5 starts, but just two managed more than 16. In response, Little showed one of the quickest hooks of any NL manager; Dodgers starters threw the second-fewest pitches per start (91.6), and logged the fewest blown quality starts. Little spread the bullpen workload around, so despite ranking fifth in relief innings, the pen was third-to-last in total relievers used, and fifth-to-last in consecutive-day usage. As a result of this more old-fashioned pattern of usage, Little was rewarded with a pen that ranked fifth in WXRL even with Eric Gagne's injury, helping the team finish fourth in fewest runs allowed. On the other side of the ball, Little took advantage of his roster's flexibility to navigate around a gimpy infield, and, far from bridling at the youth movement or the dictates of upper management, gave rookies Russell Martin, Andre Ethier, Willy Aybar, and Matt Kemp every chance to hold down jobs, with the notable exception of playing hot hand Marlon Anderson over the slumping Ethier in September. Tactically, he ran a great deal (third in the NL in stolen base attempts, second in hit-and-run attempts) but didn't overdo the sac bunting (twelfth in non-pitcher sacrifice attempts), again showing that he may have actually learned a lesson or two in Boston.

Milwaukee Brewers

The Brewers have been mouthing the empty promise of "wait 'til next year" since, well, forever. In the franchise's 37-year history the team has finished first exactly once, and that came back in 1982. They've finished as high as second just once since then, and since moving to the National League they've never finished higher than third.

In 2005, the Brewers posted a .500 record for the first time since 1992. An encore was eagerly awaited, and most trends pointed northward. They had a GM who cleaned house and rebuilt from within. There were no more Seligs on premises. They had a good training staff, a newish stadium, and one of the better starting pitchers in the game. They had young, cheap players who projected to be stars. They also had young, cheap players who projected to be around league-average, so they didn't need to overpay for veteran reserves to fill out the roster. They rented what veterans they needed with the intention (and flexibility) of moving them for spare parts, and were keeping positions open so that their younger, better players had jobs waiting for them once they were promoted. They were doing all the right things.

Unfortunately, things went very, very wrong, for the Brewers as much as for everyone else in the NL Central division someone was required to win. Table 1 shows the adjusted standings of the 2006 NL Central, with each team ranked by its third-order won-loss record (Pythagenport record based on equivalent runs, which are adjusted for the quality of opponent's pitching and defense, rather than actual runs); the third column is the difference between their actual and third-order won-loss records.

With the exception of the Houston-St. Louis flip-flop, the division is unchanged. Whether you look at actual

BREWERS PROSPECTUS

2006 record: 75–87; Fourth place, NL Central

Pythagenport record: 70–92

Runs scored per game: 4.51 (14th in NL)

Runs allowed per game: 5.14 (14th in NL)

Team EqA: .254 (11th in NL)

2006 Batters Age: 29.2 (7th youngest in NL)

2006 Pitchers Age: 28.5 (4th youngest in NL)

Ballpark: Miller Park; Neutral park; Park Factor of 1.007

2006: A mediocre team with some exciting young players that could turn into something … didn't. Yet.

2007: Much more of the same; the fixable holes have been ignored, while the front office's attention was on rotation depth. The division is still there to be taken.

record, in which the Brewers trailed the eventual World Champs by 8 games, or third-order record, in which they trailed the hard-luck Astros by 7.3 games, the Brewers were never in this race. Third-order wins, however, reveal the Brewers regression to be even more severe than it initially appeared. Instead of their real-world decline from 81 wins to 75, the Brewers, judging by their underlying performance and strength of schedule, fell from 82.4 wins in 2005 to a mere 73.2 last year. Failing to build on an 81-win season is one thing, but taking more than nine steps back in the process is quite another.

One of the higher-profile reasons for the Brewers' failure to make good was the absence of Ben Sheets, who missed nearly two and a half months between a pair of DL stints. Of course, there's no way that the injuries to Sheets alone could have accounted for the drop, particularly as Sheets was also plagued by injury in 2005. Instead it was a combination of events that sabotaged the Brewers attempt to surge forward into contention, though most of them were indeed injury related.

Baseball Prospectus tracks Disabled List information and organizes it by dollars lost to the DL, days lost to the DL, and percentage of payroll lost to the DL. Where the Brewers are concerned, it tells a pretty good story (see table 2). There are a few misleading aspects of this list. First, Milwaukee's DL day total has a whole lot of Vince Perkins on it, a pitcher who didn't figure to get any real innings in 2006. Saying that his injury hurt the team is not quite accurate—stowed on the 60-day DL, he didn't even take up a spot on the 40-man roster. Conversely, the Brewers had a few injuries in September (Gabe Gross and Laynce Nix), but because they occurred after rosters

Table 1. 2006 Adjusted NL Central Standings

Team	W	L	W3	L3	Diff
Astros	82	80	80.5	81.5	−1.5
Cardinals	83	78	75.8	85.2	−7.2
Reds	80	82	75.2	86.8	−4.8
Brewers	75	87	73.2	88.8	−1.8
Cubs	66	96	70.7	91.3	4.7
Pirates	67	95	66.8	95.2	−0.2

Table 2. The Bandaged Band: Brewer Days Lost to the DL

Player	Days on DL	Player	Days on DL
Vince Perkins	171	Rick Helling	71
J. J. Hardy	138	Rickie Weeks	65
Ben Sheets	107	Matt Wise	49
Corey Koskie	79	Jorge de la Rosa	47
Tomo Ohka	77	Jose Capellan	16
		Total	820 (13th in MLB)

expanded, there was no need for the team to place them on the DL.

This is precisely why we follow salary lost to the DL as well. Perkins's days on the DL may inflate the overall total without really harming the team proportionally, but his lost league minimum salary doesn't matter all that much in the grand scheme of things, even if the Brewers did "lose" 100 percent of it (see table 3). Despite negating Perkins's time on the DL due to his low salary, this table actually suggests that the Brewers were hit harder by injuries than their gross days on the DL did. Reality was worse than that, still. Shortstop J. J. Hardy also made roughly the league minimum last year, so his 138 days are underrepresented in Table Three, meaning the impact of injuries on the Brewers last year was even greater than it appears here.

Clearly the 2006 Brewers were damaged beyond repair by injuries. In addition to their 28-year-old ace Sheets, both halves of the Brewers' young keystone combo spent

Table 3. MLB Dollars Lost to the DL, 2006

Rnk	Team	% of Payroll	Rnk	Team	% of Payroll
1	Atlanta	33.37	6	Houston	27.14
2	Washington	33.32	7	Milwaukee	23.33
3	Kansas City	28.76	8	L.A. Dodgers	21.10
4	San Diego	28.71	9	Boston	17.59
5	Chicago Cubs	28.70			

significant time on the DL last year. Getting Hardy and second baseman Rickie Weeks established was deemed pivotal for any impending Brewer competitiveness, but the Hardy-Weeks-Fielder infield of the future was only on the field together for 25 games last year, and, even then, they weren't all productive at the same time.

Hardy's sprained ankle was a fluke, but his lost development time raises a legitimate question about whether the Brewers really need to replace Bill Hall, who has established himself as a strong player while management was looking in the other direction.

One key to the franchise's short term future will be how they utilize Hall in the coming year. There's a good chance that the team will elect to shoot itself in the foot. The Brewers have an overabundance of talented young players, which is typically deemed "a good problem to have." Of course, even good problems require good solutions or they remain problems. The Brewers have two players for shortstop, Hall and Hardy. Third baseman Ryan Braun, the organization's top offensive prospect, is just about ready to go. Between he and Corey Koskie—assuming Koskie is healthy, and Braun's weak defensive skills allow him to play third in the majors rather than force a move to the outfield—that position is blocked. The Brewers have also retained utility man Tony Graffanino, who filled in for the injured Weeks at second over the season's final two months after coming over from the Royals for Jorge de la Rosa, and signed free agent middle infielder Craig Counsell, who was the Brew Crew's starting shortstop in 2004.

The outfield is more complicated. By the end of the season, the Brewers had accumulated a plethora of options, some with high upsides, some of the head-scratching variety. The Carlos Lee trade brought Kevin Mench and Laynce Nix. Corey Hart, a prospect the Brewers had seemingly been kicking around since the Seattle Pilots days, finally got consistent playing time in September, mostly in left field, and hit .287/.333/.525—a fair representation of his skills. Anthony Gwynn got some regular time in center field over the last two weeks of the season. Gabe Gross showed he could contribute in a platoon/fourth outfielder role. Finally, center field and right field incumbents Brady Clark and Geoff Jenkins are still with the club. That's seven outfielders for three positions. Include Braun as a potential outfielder and that's eight. There's a ninth candidate too—Hall. The Brewers plan to move him to left or center field so Hardy can play short.

J. J. Hardy has now played 159 major league games, or about one full season's worth. In 566 plate appearances he's batted .246/.319/.388 with 27 doubles, 1 triple, and 14 home runs. He's walked 54 times, struck out 71 times. He's stolen one base in two attempts. He has a higher upside than this; though constant injuries have cost him valuable development time, he's just 24, so it's still possible he could turn into a .275/.330/.440 shortstop.

That upside would normally make it worth staying with Hardy and gambling that he will overcome his injuries and grow with experience. The problem is that that the Brewers have Hall, and he's already better than that. Over the last two seasons, Hall has hit .280/.344/.525 with 52 home runs in 1038 at-bats. Reports on Hall's defense vary. Old school measures, such as range factor, don't rate him highly; basic Zone Rating sees him as middle of the pack, and our own Davenport Translations take a similarly jaundiced view. Conversely, David Pinto's Probabilistic Model of Range and the plus/minus system developed by Baseball Info Solutions place him among the best field shortstops in the majors. The definitive opinion, because it's the only one that will directly effect Hall's future at the position, is that of Brewers General Manager Doug Melvin. Melvin revealed his estimation of Hall's defense at short by telling the *Milwaukee Journal-Sentinel* in November, "I think there's probably a pretty good chance he'll move to the outfield. I personally think he's better suited to left field."

Despite typical sportscaster hyperbole about this shortstop or another being able to save a run or two a game with his glove, the spread from the best defensive shortstop to an average one, or even the worst acceptable shortstop, is not nearly so large. There are a limited number of baseballs hit to shortstop in any given season, and, of those, a good portion are of the type that any barely competent shortstop can turn into outs. There are only so many that are hit in the no man's lands of the third base hole or the second base bag. That means that, in the interplay between bat and glove, the good bat/average glove player is always going to be more valuable than the poor bat/great glove player.

Consider this hypothetical: Let's throw out the more positive assessments of Hall's glove and take the 9 fielding runs below average evaluation of the Davenport Translations as gospel. Say he'll contribute about 90 runs of offense, consistent with 2006. That gives him a net 81 runs. We'll also assume that J. J. Hardy will hit consistent with his PECOTA projection (.264/.331/.416) and have the same amount of playing time as Hall, in which case he would contribute about 70 runs of offense. The Davenport Translations see Hardy as having been about 7 runs above average with the glove in his 151 career games at shortstop. That's also a fair estimate for a healthy Hardy in 2007. Add those seven runs to his total and he still trails Hall 81–77.

Looking at that four run difference, it's not unreasonable to reason that these measures are imprecise enough that the difference might be closer to zero or even favorable to Hardy. Hall could be a little worse than advertised, Hardy a little better, and maybe the upgrade to Hardy in the field would have an elevating effect on the whole pitching staff. The problem is that bumping Hall to the outfield has other consequences, specifically substituting Hardy's bat for that of the outfielders Hall's replacing. Even though some of the outfielders are unlikely to be far above average, the exchange still works out badly for the Brewers. Table 4 contains the PECOTA projected rates for Hardy, Craig Counsell (since he too could play if Hardy gets hurt and the Brewers insist on keeping Hall in the pasture), Hall, and the eight outfield candidates.

Table 4. Hall Monitor—Where To?

Player	Pos	PECOTA Rates
J. J. Hardy	SS	.264/.331/.416
Craig Counsell	SS	.267/.342/.363
Bill Hall	SS/OF	.277/.345/.520
Brady Clark	CF	.274/.350/.381
Anthony Gwynn	CF	.253/.318/.349
Laynce Nix	CF	.264/.312/.444
Ryan Braun	OF	.284/.344/.496
Corey Hart	OF	.289/.354/.522
Kevin Mench	OF	.279/.346/.472
Geoff Jenkins	RF	.268/.345/.445
Gabe Gross	OF	.265/.359/.447

The Brewer center fielders are such a weak offensive bunch that, if Hall were to play center, the loss created by the displacement of a center fielder for Hardy might not be that big a loss. However, with Hall slated for left, he's certain to displace a better bat. The change in runs scored will almost certainly be a net loss for the Brewers despite whatever increase in defense Hardy might provide. If the at-bats come at the expense of Hart, or, down the road, Braun, they'll have the additional consequence of stunting the growth of a young player.

Since the end of the 2006 season, the annual NL Central frontrunners have been going backwards. At the same time, the Brewers have made some positive moves, adding catching depth with Johnny Estrada and adding a decent second-line starter (while subtracting the same from the Cardinals) in Jeff Suppan. There are also more prospects set to arrive in late 2007 or early 2008, such as Braun and pitchers Yovani Gallardo and Will Inman. It's not all rosy, however. Estrada cost the Brewers Doug Davis, which negates the addition of Suppan. The organization took a hit when they traded Carlos Lee at the dealine last year for of a collection of mediocrities, blowing an easy chance to better themselves. However they resolve the Hall/Hardy situation, they have a glut of outfielders, and are unlikely to find a taker for Geoff Jenkins, suddenly an expensive reserve on a team that could use the financial flexibility. Brewer fans are used to waiting another year; it's what they do. But it might not be quite as easy to do it again, not if the team blows this latest chance at a return to respectability.

HITTERS

David Bell — 3B — Bats: R — Throws: R — Height: 5' 10" — Weight: 195 — Born: September 14, 1972 — Age: 34

YEAR	TEAM	LVL	AGE	PA	R	2B	3B	HR	RBI	BB	SO	SB	CS	SPEED	AVG	OBP	SLG	MLVR	EQAVG	EQOBP	EQSLG	EQA	VORP	DEFENSE	
2004	PHI	MLB	31	603	67	33	1	18	77	57	75	1	1	3.9	.291	.363	.458	.122	.288	.360	.457	.281	23.6	136-3B	6
2005	PHI	MLB	32	617	53	31	1	10	61	47	69	0	1	3.4	.248	.310	.361	-.119	.243	.307	.358	.234	-7.5	146-3B	7
2006	PHI	MLB	33	365	39	17	2	6	34	32	38	1	0	4.2	.278	.345	.398	-.020	.275	.344	.401	.262	3.4	87-3B	8
2006	MIL	MLB	33	201	21	10	2	4	29	18	30	2	1	4.4	.256	.323	.400	-.065	.257	.328	.402	.255	-0.4	49-3B	6
2007	MIL	MLB	34	493	54	24	2	10	53	45	65	3	1	4.4	.263	.335	.391	-.089	.263	.332	.389	.250	4.7	116-3B	3

Breakout: 21% Improve: 43% Collapse: 28% Attrition: 26% Comparables: Joe Randa, Billy Johnson, Clete Boyer, Buddy Bell

Bell was picked up at the July deadline, when the Brewers were beginning to wonder about Cirillo's return, but were still entertaining wild card hopes. About the only thing he does that's above-average is field, but he did a nice enough Albert Pujols impression over the final ten games, hitting .378/.452/.703. For the other 152, he was David Bell. A free agent, he'll hang around as a wandering third baseman whose upside is a .260 EqA, though, at 34, he's likely to find that mark forever beyond his grasp.

Ryan Braun — 3B? — Bats: R — Throws: R — Height: 6' 2" — Weight: 200 — Born: November 17, 1983 — Age: 23

YEAR	TEAM	LVL	AGE	PA	R	2B	3B	HR	RBI	BB	SO	SB	CS	SPEED	AVG	OBP	SLG	MLVR	EQAVG	EQOBP	EQSLG	EQA	VORP	DEFENSE	
2005	HEL	Rk	21	47	6	2	1	2	10	2	6	2	1	4.9	.341	.383	.585	.403	.273	.298	.432	.260	0.8		
2005	WVA	A	21	166	21	16	2	8	35	9	34	2	4	3.9	.355	.396	.645	.538	.314	.345	.545	.290	18.1	34-3B	-6
2006	BRV	A+	22	260	34	12	2	7	37	23	54	14	4	6.3	.274	.346	.438	.146	.270	.328	.442	.267	12.5	58-3B	-3
2006	HUN	AA	22	257	42	19	1	15	40	21	46	12	0	6.6	.303	.367	.589	.380	.294	.350	.596	.310	32.3	57-3B	-12
2007	MIL	MLB	23	523	75	32	4	21	72	38	105	18	6	5.5	.283	.341	.504	.089	.282	.337	.501	.281	28.2	123-3B	-9

Breakout: 13% Improve: 37% Collapse: 34% Attrition: 3% Comparables: Gabe Kapler, David Kelton, Jim Chamblee, Scott Hairston

So, we have another Braun who can deliver moon shots, as those who followed his 2006 Arizona Fall League service (6 home runs in 92 at bats) can attest. His strike zone judgment didn't improve as he climbed the ladder, and despite comparisons to a young Scott Rolen, he now looks destined for a corner outfield spot. His bat should play anywhere, but it would look a lot better at the hot corner in a homegrown (and cheap) Braun-Hardy-Weeks-Fielder formation. He's ticketed for a final year in the minors, but if he has to wait until September for a callup it would be a disappointment.

Lorenzo Cain — OF — Bats: R — Throws: R — Height: 6' 2" — Weight: 165 — Born: April 13, 1986 — Age: 21

YEAR	TEAM	LVL	AGE	PA	R	2B	3B	HR	RBI	BB	SO	SB	CS	SPEED	AVG	OBP	SLG	MLVR	EQAVG	EQOBP	EQSLG	EQA	VORP	DEFENSE	
2006	WVA	A	20	603	91	36	4	6	60	58	104	34	11	6.0	.307	.384	.425	.175	.275	.329	.382	.252	-5.5	123-RF	7
2007	MIL	MLB	21	537	62	29	4	6	44	37	100	16	7	5.5	.261	.318	.373	-.146	.260	.314	.371	.237	-9.0	126-RF	7

Breakout: 28% Improve: 55% Collapse: 24% Attrition: 7% Comparables: Juan Piniella, Angel Mendoza, Milton Bradley, Manny Lopez

A tall, scrawny outfielder, Cain led the Sally League in hits. His bat doesn't really fit at a corner, but so long as he's Darren Ford's teammate, he's in right. A prospect, he's projected to have better power once he fills out, he swings a quick bat, and he runs well. If he survives the Florida State League, Milwaukee's got something.

Jeff Cirillo　　3B/1B　　Bats: R　Throws: R　Height: 6' 1"　Weight: 200　Born: December 31, 1969　Age: 37

YEAR	TEAM	LVL	AGE	PA	R	2B	3B	HR	RBI	BB	SO	SB	CS	SPEED	AVG	OBP	SLG	MLVR	EQAVG	EQOBP	EQSLG	EQA	VORP	DEFENSE				
2004	SDN	MLB	34	81	12	3	0	1	7	5	14	0	0	5.4	.213	.259	.293	-.311	.200	.247	.267	.188	-4.5					
2005	MIL	MLB	35	219	29	15	0	4	23	23	22	4	2	5.4	.281	.373	.427	.090	.282	.372	.431	.278	8.7	41-3B	1			
2006	MIL	MLB	36	290	33	16	0	3	23	21	33	1	1	4.0	.319	.369	.414	.083	.319	.372	.414	.275	11.1	31-3B	5	11-1B	1
2007	MIN	MLB	37	213	24	11	1	3	23	15	27	1	1	4.6	.278	.331	.383	-.087	.271	.329	.384	.255	1.0					

Breakout: 18%　Improve: 35%　Collapse: 36%　Attrition: 41%　　Comparables: Bubba Morton, Lou Piniella, Tommy Davis, Ken Boyer

Cirillo has fallen a long way since his first go-round in Milwaukee, but in the right role, he can still contribute. That role is lefty-killer. Last year, he pasted lefties at a .413/.451/.493 clip, but suffered a 200-plus-point drop in OPS against righties, who turned him into a punchless league-average infielder. Cirillo saw time at all four infield positions in 2006. A free agent, he moved one state to the west and signed a one-year deal with the Twins. Career rates with the Brewers: .307/.383/.449. Career rates with everyone else: .283/.343/.404.

Brady Clark　　CF　　Bats: R　Throws: R　Height: 6' 2"　Weight: 205　Born: April 18, 1973　Age: 34

YEAR	TEAM	LVL	AGE	PA	R	2B	3B	HR	RBI	BB	SO	SB	CS	SPEED	AVG	OBP	SLG	MLVR	EQAVG	EQOBP	EQSLG	EQA	VORP	DEFENSE	
2004	MIL	MLB	31	419	41	18	1	7	46	53	48	15	8	5.0	.280	.385	.397	.094	.280	.384	.401	.277	14.5	97-RF	-1
2005	MIL	MLB	32	674	94	31	1	13	53	47	55	10	13	4.2	.306	.372	.426	.120	.308	.375	.434	.275	29.0	144-CF	11
2006	MIL	MLB	33	482	51	14	2	4	29	43	60	3	4	4.2	.263	.348	.335	-.106	.266	.349	.344	.249	0.3	104-CF	-5
2007	MIL	MLB	34	434	54	18	2	7	42	39	53	5	4	4.9	.269	.346	.384	-.074	.269	.342	.382	.252	5.2	103-CF	0

Breakout: 8%　Improve: 28%　Collapse: 50%　Attrition: 27%　　Comparables: Gino Cimoli, Harvey Kuenn, Gary Ward, Jim Piersall

We've noted before that Clark's been a pretty decent player despite taking a long while to get his career going, but he failed to live up to even modest expectations in 2006, turning in his worst season as a Brewer. Clark still gets on base enough to be an asset, but he's not getting any younger and his precipitous power drop is worrisome. The Brewers have made it known that they're looking for a center fielder; with Clark set to earn almost $4 million in 2007, the Brewers may have an expensive backup. If he has a hot first half, he could be dealt to play a Chad Curtis role on a contender.

Callix Crabbe　　2B　　Bats: S　Throws: R　Height: 5' 7"　Weight: 171　Born: February 14, 1983　Age: 23

YEAR	TEAM	LVL	AGE	PA	R	2B	3B	HR	RBI	BB	SO	SB	CS	SPEED	AVG	OBP	SLG	MLVR	EQAVG	EQOBP	EQSLG	EQA	VORP	DEFENSE	
2004	HDS	A+	21	614	89	26	11	7	62	59	64	37	11	7.2	.291	.366	.419	-.016	.229	.291	.324	.225	-17.8	132-2B	-19
2005	HUN	AA	22	475	42	15	4	1	33	65	65	18	6	5.3	.243	.354	.310	-.109	.221	.315	.282	.225	-15.7	104-2B	5
2006	HUN	AA	23	571	59	18	2	5	46	71	62	32	13	6.3	.267	.368	.345	.046	.258	.348	.348	.255	8.5	127-2B	12
2007	MIL	MLB	24	549	70	23	4	3	38	54	61	27	8	6.1	.257	.337	.342	-.154	.257	.333	.340	.244	6.5	129-2B	0

Breakout: 26%　Improve: 56%　Collapse: 23%　Attrition: 10%　　Comparables: Nick Punto, David Eckstein, Joe Espada, Bernie Castro

If you've ever wondered what that dry, spidery-looking connective tissue is on the stem-end of your eggplant, it's called a calyx. A Calix Crabbe sounds like a parasite that infests such bits of vegetable matter, but, in fact, it's a diminutive, speedy, switch-hitting infielder native to the Virgin Islands. Crabbe has what might be called "infield power," which doesn't project too well; if you don't slug, pitchers aren't afraid to throw you strikes, which means you won't walk either.

Alcides Escobar　　SS　　Bats: R　Throws: R　Height: 6' 1"　Weight: 155　Born: December 16, 1986　Age: 20

YEAR	TEAM	LVL	AGE	PA	R	2B	3B	HR	RBI	BB	SO	SB	CS	SPEED	AVG	OBP	SLG	MLVR	EQAVG	EQOBP	EQSLG	EQA	VORP	DEFENSE	
2004	HEL	Rk	17	261	38	8	0	2	24	20	44	20	9	6.3	.281	.345	.342	-.150	.220	.249	.240	.183	-35.9	65-SS	2
2005	WVA	A	18	562	80	25	8	2	36	20	90	30	13	8.5	.271	.305	.362	-.073	.233	.255	.295	.201	-30.2	120-SS	-3
2006	BRV	A+	19	386	47	9	1	2	33	19	56	28	8	7.0	.257	.296	.306	-.116	.244	.277	.291	.213	-16.9	79-SS	-14
2007	MIL	MLB	20	459	49	15	3	2	28	19	63	27	10	6.9	.248	.283	.314	-.299	.247	.280	.312	.210	-9.0	109-SS	-1

Breakout: 50%　Improve: 75%　Collapse: 10%　Attrition: 5%　　Comparables: Willy Taveras, Ruddy Yan, Pedro Lopez, Joaquin Arias

Still just 19 years old, Escobar only managed 12 extra base hits all year, and didn't do a whole lot of walking either. He's young enough to still be all over the map with his PECOTA comps, but he's also failed to demonstrate a basic competency with a bat. Scouts still love his tools, but he needs to start building something with them soon.

Charlie Fermaint   OF   Bats: R   Throws: R   Height: 5' 9"   Weight: 180   Born: October 11, 1985   Age: 21

YEAR	TEAM	LVL	AGE	PA	R	2B	3B	HR	RBI	BB	SO	SB	CS	SPEED	AVG	OBP	SLG	MLVR	EQAVG	EQOBP	EQSLG	EQA	VORP	DEFENSE
2004	HEL	Rk	18	245	30	14	2	5	39	19	83	8	2	5.8	.229	.300	.381	-.219	.151	.185	.181	.144	-68.8	58-CF -10
2005	HEL	Rk	19	149	46	9	2	12	32	15	28	11	2	8.2	.364	.419	.744	.726	.301	.342	.551	.296	23.4	27-CF -2
2005	WVA	A	19	124	18	7	0	5	17	8	39	4	2	5.3	.248	.301	.442	.014	.207	.244	.345	.206	-7.5	26-CF 5
2006	BRV	A+	20	479	67	20	4	7	33	42	119	27	14	6.0	.276	.349	.392	.092	.269	.328	.386	.251	7.0	109-CF -4
2007	*MIL*	*MLB*	*21*	*498*	*59*	*25*	*3*	*13*	*50*	*37*	*126*	*17*	*8*	*5.7*	*.248*	*.309*	*.405*	*-.129*	*.247*	*.306*	*.402*	*.243*	*1.8*	*118-CF -1*

Breakout: 38%   Improve: 63%   Collapse: 13%   Attrition: 5%   Comparables: Cody Ross, Chris Young, Mike Vento, Andy Burress

Fermaint has been a work in progress, but his fourth year as a pro saw him finally start to come into his own at the plate in his first full season playing full-season ball. His bat is the last tool to show up—he has plus range in center, outstanding speed, and an arm that won't get taken advantage of. The jump to Double-A at 21 might make for a slow start, but if he adapts, he'll be able to work his way into the Brewers' center-field picture in another year or two.

Prince Fielder   1B   Bats: L   Throws: R   Height: 6' 0"   Weight: 260   Born: May 9, 1984   Age: 23

YEAR	TEAM	LVL	AGE	PA	R	2B	3B	HR	RBI	BB	SO	SB	CS	SPEED	AVG	OBP	SLG	MLVR	EQAVG	EQOBP	EQSLG	EQA	VORP	DEFENSE
2004	HUN	AA	20	577	70	29	1	23	78	65	93	11	7	4.5	.272	.366	.473	.163	.246	.324	.422	.257	1.6	132-1B -19
2005	NAS	AAA	21	441	68	21	0	28	86	54	93	8	5	3.7	.291	.388	.569	.308	.274	.360	.514	.292	26.6	91-1B -8
2005	MIL	MLB	21	62	2	4	0	2	10	2	17	0	0	3.0	.288	.306	.458	.044	.288	.306	.441	.255	2.0	
2006	MIL	MLB	22	648	82	35	1	28	81	59	125	7	2	4.3	.271	.347	.483	.098	.271	.347	.486	.283	20.0	150-1B 4
2007	*MIL*	*MLB*	*23*	*585*	*89*	*33*	*2*	*28*	*94*	*62*	*99*	*7*	*3*	*4.3*	*.292*	*.375*	*.529*	*.186*	*.292*	*.371*	*.526*	*.300*	*33.8*	*137-1B 3*

Breakout: 44%   Improve: 81%   Collapse: 10%   Attrition: 12%   Comparables: Boog Powell, Kent Hrbek, David Ortiz, Chris Chambliss

Fielder is now the Brewers' record holder for home runs by a rookie. Coming up in the Year of the Rookie meant he received just two third-place votes for NL Rookie of the Year for his efforts, but his debut was nothing to sneeze at. He'll have to listen to weight comments for his entire career, but he did steal seven bases, so he's not as immobile as his weight and the 18 double plays he hit into might suggest. With old-player skills at a relatively young age, Fielder doesn't promise to have a long career, but the next five or six years should provide all sorts of fun.

Tony Graffanino   2B/3B   Bats: R   Throws: R   Height: 6' 1"   Weight: 190   Born: June 6, 1972   Age: 35

YEAR	TEAM	LVL	AGE	PA	R	2B	3B	HR	RBI	BB	SO	SB	CS	SPEED	AVG	OBP	SLG	MLVR	EQAVG	EQOBP	EQSLG	EQA	VORP	DEFENSE			
2004	KCA	MLB	32	314	37	11	0	3	26	27	38	10	2	5.8	.263	.332	.335	-.137	.261	.333	.330	.245	4.1	75-2B	4		
2005	KCA	MLB	33	217	29	5	2	3	18	22	28	3	1	5.4	.298	.377	.393	.060	.303	.391	.415	.285	8.5	19-2B	-2	15-3B	-1
2005	BOS	MLB	33	200	39	12	1	4	20	9	23	4	1	5.7	.319	.355	.457	.124	.319	.365	.470	.287	12.1	48-2B	-1		
2006	KCA	MLB	34	250	34	16	0	5	32	25	31	3	4	5.1	.268	.346	.409	-.033	.267	.354	.415	.263	3.1	25-3B	2	11-1B	-1
2006	MIL	MLB	34	261	34	17	3	2	27	20	37	2	0	5.0	.280	.345	.403	-.004	.280	.345	.403	.263	9.0	55-2B	-11		
2007	*MIL*	*MLB*	*35*	*428*	*56*	*22*	*3*	*8*	*43*	*38*	*58*	*7*	*3*	*5.6*	*.276*	*.345*	*.410*	*-.036*	*.276*	*.342*	*.408*	*.259*	*11.5*	*102-2B*	*-4*		

Breakout: 17%   Improve: 36%   Collapse: 33%   Attrition: 24%   Comparables: Johnny Temple, Craig Biggio, Ed Charles, Cookie Rojas

A sensible midseason acquisition to bolster a suddenly gimpy Milwaukee infield, Graffanino's not much of a slugger, but he puts the ball in play, knows how to take a walk, and he can fill in around the infield. Graffanino accepted arbitration from the Brewers, but with Craig Counsell on the roster, he'll have some competition for bench primacy, but he is the superior hitter and has the advantage of being a right-handed hitter on a team that needs to platoon lefty Corey Koskie at third base.

Gabe Gross   OF   Bats: L   Throws: R   Height: 6' 3"   Weight: 210   Born: October 21, 1979   Age: 27

YEAR	TEAM	LVL	AGE	PA	R	2B	3B	HR	RBI	BB	SO	SB	CS	SPEED	AVG	OBP	SLG	MLVR	EQAVG	EQOBP	EQSLG	EQA	VORP	DEFENSE			
2004	SYR	AAA	24	433	52	29	2	9	54	53	81	4	5	4.1	.294	.381	.454	.121	.274	.359	.421	.271	7.8	24-LF	1		
2004	TOR	MLB	24	148	18	4	0	3	16	19	31	2	2	5.0	.209	.311	.310	-.277	.203	.311	.297	.221	-8.5	38-LF	3		
2005	SYR	AAA	25	449	64	29	4	6	46	52	83	14	2	6.4	.297	.380	.438	.100	.273	.353	.400	.268	3.0	58-LF	-1	38-RF	2
2005	TOR	MLB	25	102	11	4	1	1	7	10	21	1	1	4.3	.250	.324	.348	-.133	.253	.340	.352	.245	-1.8	16-RF	0	11-LF	1
2006	MIL	MLB	26	252	42	15	0	9	38	36	60	1	0	4.8	.274	.382	.476	.151	.274	.384	.471	.296	15.7	29-CF	1	14-LF	4
2007	*MIL*	*MLB*	*27*	*299*	*41*	*16*	*1*	*9*	*35*	*37*	*62*	*4*	*1*	*5.1*	*.261*	*.356*	*.444*	*.015*	*.261*	*.352*	*.441*	*.273*	*9.1*	*73-DH*			

Breakout: 11%   Improve: 35%   Collapse: 24%   Attrition: 41%   Comparables: Jeromy Burnitz, Duke Carmel, Len Gabrielson, Johnny Lewis

Finally freed from a Blue Jays organization that seemed determined to avoid giving him a fair shake, Gross managed the fifth-highest VORP among Brewers hitters last year despite being strictly used as a platoon player. He doesn't have much in the way of breakout potential, but as the long side of a platoon and an adequate defender in all three pastures, he's a pretty useful player to keep around.

Anthony Gwynn OF Bats: L Throws: R Height: 6' 0" Weight: 185 Born: October 4, 1982 Age: 24

YEAR	TEAM	LVL	AGE	PA	R	2B	3B	HR	RBI	BB	SO	SB	CS	SPEED	AVG	OBP	SLG	MLVR	EQAVG	EQOBP	EQSLG	EQA	VORP	DEFENSE			
2004	HUN	AA	21	598	74	20	5	2	37	53	95	35	16	7.0	.243	.318	.311	-.139	.223	.285	.280	.211	-36.9	135-CF	-9		
2005	HUN	AA	22	601	83	21	5	1	41	76	75	34	15	6.7	.271	.370	.338	-.030	.246	.330	.311	.236	-11.1	130-CF	-7		
2006	NAS	AAA	23	494	73	21	5	4	42	42	84	30	11	6.7	.300	.360	.396	.053	.292	.346	.392	.262	14.6	91-CF	4	11-LF	0
2006	MIL	MLB	23	80	5	2	1	0	4	2	15	3	1	5.3	.260	.275	.312	-.274	.247	.262	.299	.206	-2.5	15-CF	2		
2007	MIL	MLB	24	479	59	20	5	4	35	40	76	21	7	6.4	.253	.319	.351	-.178	.253	.316	.349	.235	-3.6	113-CF	-1		

Breakout: 21% Improve: 44% Collapse: 28% Attrition: 12%   Comparables: McKay Christensen, Kennard Jones, Peter Bergeron, Mike Rodriguez

Gywnn is technically in the mix for the center field job, but his inauspicious major league debut and limited offensive skills will keep him pretty far down on the list of options. He did start hitting to the opposite field more, but his strike zone judgment got worse and his isolated power was below .100 yet again; without some power to frighten opposing pitchers, he'll need his singles to fall in at a pretty high rate to be of much use. He might make a good backup/pinch runner, but Milwaukee has a lot of outfield candidates and not enough surplus offense to start worrying about getting fancy with their roster construction.

Bill Hall SS/OF? Bats: R Throws: R Height: 6' 0" Weight: 210 Born: December 28, 1979 Age: 27

YEAR	TEAM	LVL	AGE	PA	R	2B	3B	HR	RBI	BB	SO	SB	CS	SPEED	AVG	OBP	SLG	MLVR	EQAVG	EQOBP	EQSLG	EQA	VORP	DEFENSE			
2004	MIL	MLB	24	415	43	20	3	9	53	20	119	12	6	6.5	.238	.276	.374	-.158	.233	.273	.367	.222	-2.6	47-2B	-6	37-SS	5
2005	MIL	MLB	25	546	69	39	6	17	62	39	103	18	6	6.3	.291	.342	.495	.156	.289	.342	.499	.283	36.2	56-SS	5	49-3B	2
2006	MIL	MLB	26	608	101	39	4	35	85	63	162	8	9	5.3	.270	.345	.553	.189	.271	.350	.557	.293	44.3	124-SS	-9		
2007	MIL	MLB	27	589	86	34	5	28	83	53	140	12	6	6.0	.277	.345	.520	.114	.277	.342	.517	.284	38.8	138-SS	-1		

Breakout: 19% Improve: 48% Collapse: 13% Attrition: 6%   Comparables: Max Alvis, Jim Morrison, Sammy Sosa, Ty Wigginton

Hall didn't have a position to start the year, but, thanks to a slew of injuries, Ned Yost didn't have to get too creative to find him some playing time. You'd think that being the most productive Brewer would solidify his standing with the team, but that's not so. Still positionless, he's the early leader for the starting job in left field, and that's a worrisome position switch. As an infielder, Hall's bat is well above-average. As a corner outfielder, it's somewhat less exotic. He's not a perfect shortstop, but the move is a symptom of a J. J. Hardy infatuation that should have run its course by now. Hall was always panned as a no-patience, free-swinging guy, but his development into a fine player (seeing 4.15 pitches per plate appearance last year) is a nice bit of evidence that young players with his profile shouldn't be dismissed without examination.

J. J. Hardy SS Bats: R Throws: R Height: 6' 2" Weight: 190 Born: August 19, 1982 Age: 24

YEAR	TEAM	LVL	AGE	PA	R	2B	3B	HR	RBI	BB	SO	SB	CS	SPEED	AVG	OBP	SLG	MLVR	EQAVG	EQOBP	EQSLG	EQA	VORP	DEFENSE	
2004	IND	AAA	21	112	17	10	0	4	20	9	8	0	0	4.1	.277	.330	.495	.091	.248	.304	.436	.252	3.5	24-SS	0
2005	MIL	MLB	22	427	46	22	1	9	50	44	48	0	0	4.2	.247	.327	.384	-.059	.246	.329	.393	.253	8.8	106-SS	3
2006	MIL	MLB	23	139	13	5	0	5	14	10	23	1	1	3.7	.242	.295	.398	-.123	.244	.302	.394	.240	0.4	29-SS	3
2007	MIL	MLB	24	384	43	19	1	11	44	33	49	2	1	4.5	.263	.329	.419	-.061	.263	.326	.417	.254	13.0	92-SS	4

Breakout: 24% Improve: 56% Collapse: 14% Attrition: 22%   Comparables: Kevin Elster, Jose Valdivielso, Chris Gomez, Jack Lohrke

Originally expected to miss two to six weeks after a May ankle injury, Hardy instead missed the rest of the year. He also failed to build on his strong second half in 2005, as he could only muster a .234 EqA before hitting the DL. Hardy's injuries so far (shoulder, ankle) are unrelated and fluky, not the kind of thing you can prevent, but his fragility is becoming awfully suspicious. Coupled with his minor league shoulder injury, he's missed a lot of development time in his young career, and it's not at all clear that once-generous projections still apply.

Corey Hart OF Bats: R Throws: R Height: 6' 6" Weight: 215 Born: March 24, 1982 Age: 25

YEAR	TEAM	LVL	AGE	PA	R	2B	3B	HR	RBI	BB	SO	SB	CS	SPEED	AVG	OBP	SLG	MLVR	EQAVG	EQOBP	EQSLG	EQA	VORP	DEFENSE		
2004	IND	AAA	22	491	68	29	8	15	67	42	92	17	7	7.0	.282	.344	.486	.107	.262	.324	.440	.263	4.0	91-RF	-8	
2005	NAS	AAA	23	489	85	29	9	17	69	48	88	31	7	8.5	.308	.377	.536	.262	.295	.355	.493	.290	24.8	71-RF	2	29-LF 1
2005	MIL	MLB	23	63	9	2	1	2	7	6	11	2	0	6.4	.193	.270	.368	-.216	.193	.270	.368	.228	-1.4	11-CF	-3	
2006	NAS	AAA	24	115	19	10	1	4	21	12	25	11	2	6.3	.320	.391	.560	.356	.314	.379	.539	.309	9.4	17-LF	-2	
2006	MIL	MLB	24	256	32	13	2	9	33	17	58	5	8	5.1	.283	.328	.468	.060	.284	.332	.479	.263	4.2	30-RF	3	19-LF 0
2007	MIL	MLB	25	445	69	26	4	19	63	38	85	17	6	6.2	.288	.352	.518	.131	.288	.349	.514	.289	21.7	105-RF	1	

Breakout: 18% Improve: 57% Collapse: 10% Attrition: 15% Comparables: Felipe Alou, Charlie Spikes, Ivan Calderon, Dave Engle

The big feller did all right, and now that he's beyond the experimenting with making him a corner infielder, he seems prepped to become the club's top outfield bopper. PECOTA gave a weighted-mean projection of .276/.338/.487, and Hart delivered a .283/.328/.468 performance, albeit in less than half the at-bats that PECOTA suggested he'd get. Both Geoff Jenkins and Kevin Mench are being dangled in various deals, and Hart's the best choice for the regular job in right. There's still plenty of a upside here if the Brewers will give him a chance.

Geoff Jenkins RF Bats: L Throws: R Height: 6' 1" Weight: 210 Born: July 21, 1974 Age: 32

YEAR	TEAM	LVL	AGE	PA	R	2B	3B	HR	RBI	BB	SO	SB	CS	SPEED	AVG	OBP	SLG	MLVR	EQAVG	EQOBP	EQSLG	EQA	VORP	DEFENSE	
2004	MIL	MLB	29	681	88	36	6	27	93	46	152	3	1	4.8	.264	.325	.473	.083	.261	.320	.468	.267	14.6	152-LF	1
2005	MIL	MLB	30	618	87	42	1	25	86	56	138	0	0	3.8	.292	.375	.513	.235	.290	.372	.517	.300	40.9	140-RF	7
2006	MIL	MLB	31	555	62	26	1	17	70	56	129	4	1	4.5	.271	.357	.434	.048	.271	.359	.437	.277	14.6	125-RF	2
2007	MIL	MLB	32	473	60	24	2	16	62	43	101	3	1	4.5	.268	.343	.449	.007	.267	.340	.447	.268	8.2	112-RF	0

Breakout: 1% Improve: 21% Collapse: 39% Attrition: 19% Comparables: Mike Easler, Walt Moryn, Dick Sisler, Dave Clark

While it's not on the order of Arizona's decision to let Luis Gonzalez slip away, the decision to bench Jenkins in favor of the kids did represent something of an end of an era in Milwaukee, considering that Jenkins has spent nine years here. He's had some solid seasons, but when Troy O'Leary starts showing up on your aging outfielder's list of PECOTA comps, the canary in this coal mine just fell of its perch. That being said, Jenkins is not without value as a platoon player—despite being eased out of the lineup, he hit .306/.381/.490 against righties last year, and his 2005 split was even better.

Corey Koskie 3B Bats: L Throws: R Height: 6' 3" Weight: 220 Born: June 28, 1973 Age: 34

YEAR	TEAM	LVL	AGE	PA	R	2B	3B	HR	RBI	BB	SO	SB	CS	SPEED	AVG	OBP	SLG	MLVR	EQAVG	EQOBP	EQSLG	EQA	VORP	DEFENSE	
2004	MIN	MLB	31	488	68	24	2	25	71	49	103	9	3	5.3	.251	.342	.495	.100	.248	.342	.495	.283	21.8	113-3B	-12
2005	TOR	MLB	32	404	49	20	0	11	36	44	90	4	1	4.2	.249	.337	.398	-.042	.247	.345	.399	.263	5.6	76-3B	6
2006	MIL	MLB	33	289	29	23	0	12	33	29	58	1	2	3.6	.261	.343	.490	.092	.262	.344	.500	.280	9.5	69-3B	9
2007	MIL	MLB	34	375	50	19	1	14	52	41	75	4	1	4.5	.258	.346	.457	.014	.258	.343	.454	.271	12.1	90-3B	-1

Breakout: 4% Improve: 32% Collapse: 27% Attrition: 32% Comparables: Dale Long, Robin Ventura, Lee Stevens, Sid Bream

Koskie's season ended in early July thanks to post-concussion syndrome. In late August, MLB.com reported that Koskie had, "been urged by physicians to limit his mental activity as much as possible." One imagines Koskie spending eight to ten hours a day watching *Gilligan's Island* episodes and reading lad magazines. The injury itself was no joke, as Koskie suffered from constant dizziness, nausea, and fatigue. As with Hardy's ankle, Koskie's concussion, the result of striking his head on the ground while diving for a pop-up, wasn't something that he or the training staff could have prevented. If healthy, he's a decent producer against right-handers.

David Krynzel CF Bats: L Throws: L Height: 6' 1" Weight: 180 Born: November 7, 1981 Age: 25

YEAR	TEAM	LVL	AGE	PA	R	2B	3B	HR	RBI	BB	SO	SB	CS	SPEED	AVG	OBP	SLG	MLVR	EQAVG	EQOBP	EQSLG	EQA	VORP	DEFENSE		
2004	IND	AAA	22	292	36	10	4	6	26	20	63	10	8	6.5	.271	.327	.411	-.034	.260	.314	.385	.242	1.1	61-CF	1	
2004	MIL	MLB	22	47	6	1	0	0	3	3	15	0	0	5.2	.220	.319	.244	-.255	.195	.298	.220	.197	-2.1			
2005	NAS	AAA	23	511	71	25	7	11	51	43	138	24	8	7.8	.256	.324	.416	-.063	.247	.304	.384	.244	-2.1	106-CF	-15	
2006	NAS	AAA	24	416	49	17	4	7	40	42	107	23	4	6.8	.231	.314	.359	-.131	.228	.302	.356	.240	-18.1	43-LF	1	35-CF -2
2007	ARI	MLB	25	426	54	20	5	10	43	33	110	18	6	6.4	.254	.318	.412	-.098	.244	.310	.392	.245	0.3	101-CF	-2	

Breakout: 23% Improve: 52% Collapse: 21% Attrition: 17% Comparables: Kory DeHaan, Tarrik Brock, Jon Hamilton, Alexis Gomez

(continued next page)

David Krynzel (*continued*)

Krynzel started the year hurt, after breaking his right clavicle in a mini-bike accident, and ended it by being traded to Arizona. In between, he was pretty dreadful at the plate, good defensively, and great on the basepaths—pretty much what he's always offered. As ever, the problem is that he doesn't reach base enough to put his speed to good use. Arizona has some depth in the outfield, so his lot in life has improved only insofar as his offensive numbers will look better in Tucson, even if his game hasn't improved. He's out of options, so he'll wind up elsewhere if he doesn't make the team.

Kevin Mench OF **Bats: R** **Throws: R** Height: 6' 0" Weight: 225 Born: January 7, 1978 Age: 29

YEAR	TEAM	LVL	AGE	PA	R	2B	3B	HR	RBI	BB	SO	SB	CS	SPEED	AVG	OBP	SLG	MLVR	EQAVG	EQOBP	EQSLG	EQA	VORP	DEFENSE			
2004	TEX	MLB	26	481	69	30	3	26	71	33	63	0	0	4.7	.279	.335	.539	.112	.269	.331	.524	.284	20.9	58-RF	3	40-LF	-2
2005	TEX	MLB	27	615	71	33	3	25	73	50	68	4	3	4.7	.264	.328	.469	.042	.263	.337	.476	.274	15.2	110-LF	1	35-RF	-7
2006	TEX	MLB	28	349	36	18	1	12	50	23	42	1	0	4.3	.284	.338	.459	.023	.274	.337	.454	.271	9.2	55-RF	2	15-LF	-4
2006	MIL	MLB	28	133	9	6	1	1	18	4	17	0	0	4.4	.230	.248	.317	-.336	.216	.241	.304	.195	-9.3	32-LF	1		
2007	*MIL*	*MLB*	*29*	*483*	*64*	*26*	*2*	*20*	*70*	*40*	*63*	*1*	*1*	*4.6*	*.279*	*.343*	*.486*	*.065*	*.278*	*.339*	*.483*	*.276*	*15.7*	*114-LF*	*-2*		

Breakout: 25% Improve: 52% Collapse: 15% Attrition: 9%   *Comparables: Ivan Calderon, Jason Lane, Shane Spencer, Ron Jackson*

It was widely felt that GM Doug Melvin came out way behind in the Carlos Lee trade. Consider Mench's career home/road splits as a Ranger:

Park	PA	AVG/OBP/SLG
Home	1061	.284/.353/.503
Road	931	.263/.314/.454

Mench wasn't all Texas cooking, but outfielder-wise, he was more hat than cattle. Remove Lone Star inflation from the picture, and you get a player with middling offensive skills who also happens to be one of the worst defensive outfielders in the game—his comps afield include Jack Black, a gouty Persian housecat named Puddles, and the Oxford English Dictionary. It's not clear why Melvin felt that this combination of skills would be an asset to the team, especially when he had more interesting outfielders in his own system. Mench's overall career batting line is now .271/.329/.469, which is a few extra slugging points from being league average. He's not as bad as his Milwaukee line showed, but that's small consolation, as Melvin's now in danger of having to dump the guy he overvalued, reducing the return on the Lee deal even further.

Damian Miller C **Bats: R** **Throws: R** Height: 6' 3" Weight: 220 Born: December 31, 1969 Age: 37

YEAR	TEAM	LVL	AGE	PA	R	2B	3B	HR	RBI	BB	SO	SB	CS	SPEED	AVG	OBP	SLG	MLVR	EQAVG	EQOBP	EQSLG	EQA	VORP	DEFENSE	
2004	OAK	MLB	34	442	39	25	0	9	58	39	87	0	1	2.5	.272	.339	.403	-.038	.269	.341	.406	.260	12.0	102-C	13
2005	MIL	MLB	35	431	50	25	1	9	43	37	94	0	1	3.7	.273	.340	.413	.029	.271	.340	.419	.263	17.0	103-C	0
2006	MIL	MLB	36	376	34	28	0	6	38	33	86	0	0	3.5	.251	.322	.390	-.089	.251	.323	.396	.252	2.0	95-C	0
2007	*MIL*	*MLB*	*37*	*399*	*39*	*24*	*1*	*8*	*42*	*36*	*85*	*0*	*1*	*3.6*	*.250*	*.324*	*.391*	*-.118*	*.250*	*.320*	*.389*	*.244*	*4.4*	*95-C*	*-2*

Breakout: 6% Improve: 42% Collapse: 35% Attrition: 28%   *Comparables: Terry Steinbach, Elston Howard, Joe Girardi, Jamie Quirk*

Miller exercised his player option to return to Milwaukee just a few weeks before the Brewers traded for Johnny Estrada, which relegated Miller to reserve status right quick. If they so choose, the Brewers can put out a reasonably productive tandem, but the real advantage to having a pair like this is that if the team is out of it by the end of July, they can deal one to a contender without having to start Mike Rivera or J. D. Closser.

Laynce Nix CF **Bats: L** **Throws: L** Height: 6' 0" Weight: 200 Born: October 30, 1980 Age: 26

YEAR	TEAM	LVL	AGE	PA	R	2B	3B	HR	RBI	BB	SO	SB	CS	SPEED	AVG	OBP	SLG	MLVR	EQAVG	EQOBP	EQSLG	EQA	VORP	DEFENSE			
2004	TEX	MLB	23	400	58	20	4	14	46	23	113	1	1	5.7	.248	.293	.437	-.131	.239	.291	.424	.243	-0.8	95-CF	-3		
2005	TEX	MLB	24	240	28	12	3	6	32	9	45	2	0	6.3	.240	.267	.397	-.180	.236	.275	.404	.234	-2.9	59-CF	-2		
2006	OKL	AAA	25	314	39	14	1	10	55	18	77	4	1	5.1	.269	.323	.430	.043	.271	.315	.436	.259	8.4	43-CF	-5	22-RF	1
2006	TEX	MLB	25	34	1	1	0	0	4	0	17	0	0	4.5	.094	.118	.125	-.965	.000	.029	.000	.042	-6.4				
2006	NAS	AAA	25	73	16	5	1	7	13	4	18	0	0	5.8	.412	.452	.824	.960	.406	.446	.812	.386	20.0				
2006	MIL	MLB	25	36	2	1	0	1	6	0	11	0	0	3.0	.229	.250	.343	-.291	.229	.250	.343	.204	-1.4				
2007	*MIL*	*MLB*	*26*	*438*	*51*	*22*	*4*	*16*	*59*	*25*	*112*	*3*	*2*	*5.3*	*.260*	*.308*	*.450*	*-.059*	*.260*	*.305*	*.447*	*.252*	*7.5*	*104-CF*	*-4*		

Breakout: 18% Improve: 42% Collapse: 30% Attrition: 13%   *Comparables: Brian Gordon, Matt Cepicky, Scott Krause, Jorge Piedra*

Nix didn't play past September 4 after succumbing to turf toe and undergoing surgery. He claimed the toe had been bothering him for two years, which was probably meant to help explain his stalled development; the problem is that he's been stagnating for four years, not just two. He is what he is at this point, but he has a shot at winning the center field job, if only because the team might mistake spring performance for a less likely turnaround.

Mike Rivera   **C**   **Bats: R**   **Throws: R**   Height: 6′ 0″   Weight: 210   Born: September 8, 1976   Age: 30

YEAR	TEAM	LVL	AGE	PA	R	2B	3B	HR	RBI	BB	SO	SB	CS	SPEED	AVG	OBP	SLG	MLVR	EQAVG	EQOBP	EQSLG	EQA	VORP	DEFENSE	
2004	SAC	AAA	27	184	12	7	2	5	20	10	34	1	1	3.8	.224	.262	.376	-.296	.192	.228	.285	.186	-14.4	43-C	3
2005	NAS	AAA	28	228	34	12	1	16	43	9	37	3	1	4.2	.285	.320	.575	.199	.261	.288	.500	.261	9.7	55-C	-2
2006	NAS	AAA	29	236	30	11	0	10	46	13	40	3	3	4.1	.296	.339	.488	.147	.266	.304	.427	.251	5.4	51-C	0
2006	MIL	MLB	29	158	16	9	0	6	24	10	21	0	0	3.0	.268	.325	.458	.029	.268	.325	.458	.267	5.3	40-C	-1
2007	MIL	MLB	30	373	35	17	1	12	45	19	67	1	1	3.7	.243	.289	.402	-.170	.243	.286	.400	.231	-0.2	89-C	0

Breakout: 21%   Improve: 44%   Collapse: 30%   Attrition: 27%   Comparables: Brian Johnson, Rod Barajas, Izzy Molina, Todd Greene

Prior to the season, Rivera was a career emergency catcher with a .218/.255/.315 batting line. Called up because the Brewers finally gave up on Chad Moeller, Rivera responded to his first big league service time since 2003 by showing the pop he can deliver when he's at his best. With Miller and Estrada around, Rivera won't get a chance to show that wasn't a fluke unless someone gets injured or traded.

Angel Salome   **C**   **Bats: R**   **Throws: R**   Height: 5′ 7″   Weight: 190   Born: June 8, 1986   Age: 21

YEAR	TEAM	LVL	AGE	PA	R	2B	3B	HR	RBI	BB	SO	SB	CS	SPEED	AVG	OBP	SLG	MLVR	EQAVG	EQOBP	EQSLG	EQA	VORP	DEFENSE	
2005	HEL	Rk	19	175	34	17	0	8	50	15	16	6	2	4.0	.415	.469	.673	.759	.327	.362	.497	.292	29.0	19-C	-9
2005	WVA	A	19	126	15	7	1	4	21	8	17	1	0	4.1	.254	.302	.432	.006	.217	.254	.358	.215	-5.3	15-C	-1
2006	WVA	A	20	467	63	31	2	10	85	39	63	7	3	4.4	.292	.349	.447	.143	.255	.299	.394	.242	2.7	76-C	2
2007	MIL	MLB	21	469	48	26	1	10	49	28	68	4	3	4.5	.257	.303	.391	-.150	.257	.300	.389	.234	2.4	111-C	1

Breakout: 16%   Improve: 40%   Collapse: 35%   Attrition: 5%   Comparables: Humberto Cota, Jeff Mathis, Ryan Lehr, Justin Huber

Born in the Dominican Republic but a resident of New York City from age 12 on, Salome is a squat and bubbly catcher. He's still learning the position, but has a great arm from behind the plate, and, in his first full season, he showed excellent power for his age, so he's no Spanky Lavalliere in the making. A dislocated ankle ended his season in mid-August, but he should be fine in camp.

Rickie Weeks   **2B**   **Bats: R**   **Throws: R**   Height: 6′ 0″   Weight: 205   Born: September 13, 1982   Age: 24

YEAR	TEAM	LVL	AGE	PA	R	2B	3B	HR	RBI	BB	SO	SB	CS	SPEED	AVG	OBP	SLG	MLVR	EQAVG	EQOBP	EQSLG	EQA	VORP	DEFENSE	
2004	HUN	AA	21	568	67	35	6	8	42	55	107	11	12	5.2	.259	.366	.407	.072	.242	.326	.374	.246	5.8	128-2B	-17
2005	NAS	AAA	22	249	43	14	9	12	48	28	51	10	1	7.0	.320	.435	.655	.541	.311	.407	.613	.333	36.0	54-2B	-9
2005	MIL	MLB	22	414	56	13	2	13	42	40	96	15	2	5.8	.239	.333	.394	-.036	.238	.332	.407	.262	9.9	94-2B	-13
2006	MIL	MLB	23	413	73	15	3	8	34	30	92	19	5	6.8	.279	.363	.404	.022	.282	.362	.412	.274	18.5	90-2B	-8
2007	MIL	MLB	24	533	79	27	4	16	61	46	104	15	6	5.9	.275	.358	.456	.046	.274	.354	.453	.277	25.9	125-2B	-6

Breakout: 18%   Improve: 43%   Collapse: 21%   Attrition: 15%   Comparables: Ken Boyer, Carney Lansford, Ron Gant, Scott Hairston

Weeks spent the majority of his time hitting leadoff, where his .360 OBP was put to its best use, and no one really minded that he wasn't driving pitchers in from first base due to less power output than had been expected. A word of warning: his high OBP wasn't the product of any advanced walk-drawing ability. He was hit by 19 pitches, behind only Toronto's Reed Johnson (21) for the major league lead. Weeks missed August and September after an injury to a tendon in his right wrist required surgery. Quite often, hitters don't come out of wrist surgery, particularly a soft-tissue surgery, with the same snap that they had when they went in; if you remember what happened to Brent Gates after a promising rookie season and a wrist injury, you're appropriately concerned. The other open-ended question about Weeks results from his defense, which has opened the possibility of a move to another position. He's still an intriguing player, but his career could head in all sorts of directions, not all of them good. The comparison to Gant, who also had to move off second to really blossom as a hitter, is suggestive.

PITCHERS

David Bush

Bats: R Throws: R   Height: 6' 2"   Weight: 210   Born: November 9, 1979   Age: 27

YEAR	TEAM	LVL	AGE	W	L	SV	G	GS	IP	H	BB	SO	HR	GB%	BABIP	STUFF	WHIP	ERA	PERA	EQERA	EQH9	EQBB9	EQSO9	EQHR9	VORP	WXRL
2004	SYR	AAA	24	6	6	0	16	16	99²	108	20	88	7	—	.329	22	1.28	4.06	3.70	4.65	9.7	2.0	6.1	0.7	10.6	—
2004	TOR	MLB	24	5	4	0	16	16	97²	95	25	64	11	—	.282	16	1.23	3.68	4.13	3.86	8.3	2.1	5.5	0.9	22.1	2.27
2005	SYR	AAA	25	2	2	0	9	9	55	65	9	40	6	49.2%	.343	8	1.35	4.42	4.24	4.50	10.3	1.6	5.0	1.1	6.8	—
2005	TOR	MLB	25	5	11	0	25	24	136¹	142	29	75	20	46.4%	.282	0	1.25	4.49	4.88	4.64	9.3	1.9	4.8	1.2	16.2	2.63
2006	MIL	MLB	26	12	11	0	34	32	210	201	38	166	26	48.4%	.289	22	1.14	4.41	3.90	4.14	8.2	1.4	6.4	1.0	30.9	4.12
2007	*MIL*	*MLB*	*27*	*12*	*10*	*0*	*29*	*29*	*191²*	*194*	*46*	*138*	*23*	*47.0%*	*.290*	*17*	*1.25*	*4.01*	*4.17*	*4.10*	*8.8*	*1.8*	*5.8*	*1.0*	*34.3*	*5.00*

Breakout: 19% Improve: 56% Collapse: 7%   Attrition: 0%   Comparables: Dick Bosman, Frank Castillo, Mike Garcia, Brian Lawrence

Of the many Bushes plying their trade in public these days, this one is by far the most productive, and he was only league-average last year. A college closer turned starting pitcher, Bush arrived from Toronto and was slotted into the rotation, where he put his groundballing ways to work. Bush's already great control improved even more, and he even found a few extra strikeouts. Ned Yost's comparisons to Chris Carpenter might be a bit premature, but Bush has become a steady, productive rotation regular. Those PECOTA comps are a scary bunch; Garcia had a solid run of about a decade, but the other three had a useful lifespan of about two seasons apiece.

Jose Capellan

Bats: R Throws: R   Height: 6' 4"   Weight: 235   Born: January 13, 1981   Age: 26

YEAR	TEAM	LVL	AGE	W	L	SV	G	GS	IP	H	BB	SO	HR	GB%	BABIP	STUFF	WHIP	ERA	PERA	EQERA	EQH9	EQBB9	EQSO9	EQHR9	VORP	WXRL
2004	MYR	A+	23	5	1	0	8	8	46¹	27	11	62	0	—	.260	36	0.82	1.94	3.00	3.27	6.8	2.9	7.8	0.2	11.4	—
2004	GRN	AA	23	5	1	0	9	8	50¹	53	19	53	1	—	.359	18	1.43	2.50	3.50	3.62	10.0	3.8	6.0	0.4	10.9	—
2004	RIC	AAA	23	4	2	0	7	7	43	33	15	37	0	—	.273	23	1.12	2.51	3.32	3.16	7.0	3.4	6.1	0.2	11.6	—
2004	ATL	MLB	23	0	1	0	3	2	8	14	5	4	2	—	.414	-35	2.38	11.25	6.51	10.80	15.1	5.4	4.3	2.2	-4.8	-0.22
2005	NAS	AAA	24	5	3	6	36	12	90²	88	42	76	4	44.0%	.319	9	1.43	3.87	4.01	3.98	8.4	3.9	5.6	0.4	16.7	—
2005	MIL	MLB	24	1	1	0	17	0	15²	17	5	14	1	34.1%	.372	10	1.40	2.87	3.24	3.38	9.6	2.8	7.3	0.6	3.6	-0.49
2006	MIL	MLB	25	4	2	0	61	0	71²	65	31	58	11	33.2%	.274	-3	1.34	4.39	4.78	4.15	7.7	3.3	6.5	1.2	11.2	1.94
2007	*MIL*	*MLB*	*26*	*3*	*3*	*2*	*52*	*0*	*61²*	*58*	*28*	*50*	*8*	*41.0%*	*.278*	*0*	*1.40*	*4.40*	*4.55*	*4.48*	*8.2*	*3.5*	*6.5*	*1.1*	*8.6*	*0.70*

Breakout: 18% Improve: 41% Collapse: 34%   Attrition: 14%   Comparables: Turk Farrell, Bill Simas, Shawn Hillegas, Mike Garman

When shoulder soreness moved in, it looked like the Capellan-Kolb deal would be a bust all around. But, after a DL stint, Capellan recovered his velocity and eventually settled in as a late-inning flamethrower. His strikeout and walk rates moved in the wrong directions, and you'd like to see him be less generous with the long ball, but he proved to be Milwaukee's most effective pitcher out of the pen last year (by WXRL). His days as a starter help make him the sort of reliever who can throw more than an inning per appearance now that the Brewers have committed to keeping him in the pen.

Chris Capuano

Bats: L Throws: L   Height: 6' 2"   Weight: 220   Born: August 19, 1978   Age: 28

YEAR	TEAM	LVL	AGE	W	L	SV	G	GS	IP	H	BB	SO	HR	GB%	BABIP	STUFF	WHIP	ERA	PERA	EQERA	EQH9	EQBB9	EQSO9	EQHR9	VORP	WXRL
2004	MIL	MLB	25	6	8	0	17	17	88¹	91	37	80	18	—	.304	-1	1.45	4.99	5.28	5.28	9.2	3.3	7.2	1.6	1.0	1.49
2005	MIL	MLB	26	18	12	0	35	35	219	212	91	176	31	39.5%	.292	8	1.38	3.99	4.85	4.24	8.8	3.4	6.6	1.3	31.5	4.05
2006	MIL	MLB	27	11	12	0	34	34	221¹	229	47	174	29	41.2%	.303	19	1.25	4.03	3.89	3.84	8.8	1.7	6.3	1.0	41.1	4.86
2007	*MIL*	*MLB*	*28*	*11*	*11*	*0*	*30*	*30*	*194²*	*198*	*56*	*151*	*27*	*43.0%*	*.292*	*16*	*1.31*	*4.32*	*4.56*	*4.38*	*8.8*	*2.2*	*6.3*	*1.1*	*29.4*	*4.40*

Breakout: 5%   Improve: 44% Collapse: 15%   Attrition: 0%   Comparables: Alex Kellner, Woodie Fryman, Denny Neagle, Nate Robertson

Capuano was an All-Star in 2006, but only after Tom Glavine bowed out. Capuano deserved it anyway as he never missed a start and turned in 24 quality starts out of 34. It's always hard to know when to treat one-year improvements as the start of a trend and when to treat them as one-year flukes. Capuano's control took a huge step forward last year, which helped hide his declining strikeout rate. While you might expect him to give some of it back next year, PECOTA's relatively optimistic that he's becoming a reliable asset.

Francisco Cordero Bats: R Throws: R   Height: 6' 2"   Weight: 235   Born: May 11, 1975   Age: 32

YEAR	TEAM	LVL	AGE	W	L	SV	G	GS	IP	H	BB	SO	HR	GB%	BABIP	STUFF	WHIP	ERA	PERA	EQERA	EQH9	EQBB9	EQSO9	EQHR9	VORP	WXRL
2004	TEX	MLB	29	3	4	49	67	0	71²	60	32	79	1	—	.317	36	1.29	2.13	2.68	2.08	7.2	3.5	9.2	0.1	31.2	5.97
2005	TEX	MLB	30	3	1	37	69	0	69	61	30	79	5	44.5%	.316	28	1.32	3.39	3.35	3.27	7.3	3.8	9.8	0.6	16.8	3.49
2006	TEX	MLB	31	7	4	6	49	0	48²	48	16	54	5	45.0%	.341	21	1.32	4.80	3.42	4.47	8.2	2.7	9.1	0.7	6.5	-0.94
2006	MIL	MLB	31	3	1	16	28	0	26²	20	16	30	2	34.4%	.290	24	1.35	1.69	3.56	1.63	6.5	4.6	9.1	0.7	12.9	1.72
2007	MIL	MLB	32	4	5	27	53	0	59¹	50	26	65	6	43.0%	.292	17	1.29	3.30	3.74	3.35	7.3	3.4	8.9	0.8	16.3	2.30

Breakout: 12% Improve: 32% Collapse: 35% Attrition: 10%   Comparables: Roberto Hernandez, Eric Plunk, Jason Isringhausen, Don Aase

Don't let the high ERA in Texas fool you; park effects, bad defense, and very strong peripherals argue it should have been about a run lower. After arriving in Milwaukee, Cordero stepped in as closer, allowed one run in his first 23⅔ innings despite control problems, and was promptly rewarded after the season by having his option picked up for the low, low price of $5.4 million. That's a bit on the steep side, but he's been a reliable reliever for six years running, and he'll keep Derrick Turnbow away from save situations. Ask a Brewer fan how much that's worth in white-knuckle currency.

Doug Davis Bats: R Throws: L   Height: 6' 4"   Weight: 210   Born: September 21, 1975 Age: 31

YEAR	TEAM	LVL	AGE	W	L	SV	G	GS	IP	H	BB	SO	HR	GB%	BABIP	STUFF	WHIP	ERA	PERA	EQERA	EQH9	EQBB9	EQSO9	EQHR9	VORP	WXRL
2004	MIL	MLB	28	12	12	0	34	34	207¹	192	79	166	14	—	.298	27	1.31	3.39	3.69	3.53	8.2	3.0	6.3	0.6	46.3	6.49
2005	MIL	MLB	29	11	11	0	35	35	222²	196	93	208	26	45.9%	.283	22	1.30	3.84	4.13	4.10	8.0	3.4	7.7	1.0	35.6	5.00
2006	MIL	MLB	30	11	11	0	34	34	203¹	206	102	159	19	45.9%	.314	17	1.51	4.91	4.21	4.58	8.6	3.9	6.3	0.7	18.8	3.01
2007	ARI	MLB	31	10	12	0	30	30	186¹	190	77	141	21	49.0%	.298	11	1.43	4.63	4.50	4.45	8.5	3.4	6.1	0.9	25.7	4.00

Breakout: 8% Improve: 31% Collapse: 17% Attrition: 0%   Comparables: Rudy May, Gary Peters, Brian Bohanon, Chuck Finley

Davis has been durable, and manager Ned Yost and pitching coach Mike Maddux have handled him well, keeping his pitches per start at an acceptable level. Ironically, Davis's durability, coupled with his challenge-everybody approach, has resulted in a lot of pitches thrown. From 2004 through 2006, Davis ranked twentieth, third, and tenth in the majors in total pitches thrown, respectively. The confluence of these factors—the regression in his rate stats, his mileage, and, most of all, his arbitration eligibility—encouraged the Brewers to pack him off to Arizona in November. He's a lefty without dominating stuff coming to a park that's even more generous to right-handed power than Miller Park. His unintentional walks per nine innings have gone from 3.3 to 3.6 to 4.5 over the last three years, and, during that same time, he gave up 3.6 runs per nine innings in Milwaukee against 5.1 on the road. So, he's leaving the park that helped him, his control's slipping, and he's entering one of the game's best hitter's parks. Durability is an important quality, to be sure, but if he posts another ERA a half-run higher than league-average in this year, the Snakes should be satisfied.

Dana Eveland Bats: L Throws: L   Height: 6' 1"   Weight: 250   Born: October 29, 1983   Age: 23

YEAR	TEAM	LVL	AGE	W	L	SV	G	GS	IP	H	BB	SO	HR	GB%	BABIP	STUFF	WHIP	ERA	PERA	EQERA	EQH9	EQBB9	EQSO9	EQHR9	VORP	WXRL
2004	BLT	A	20	9	6	2	22	16	117¹	108	24	119	8	—	.307	7	1.13	2.84	4.67	4.87	9.9	2.3	5.4	1.3	9.1	—
2004	HUN	AA	20	0	2	0	4	4	23²	23	4	14	0	—	.291	12	1.14	2.28	3.48	3.47	8.9	1.5	3.5	0.4	5.5	—
2005	HUN	AA	21	10	4	0	18	18	109	96	38	98	4	61.7%	.304	26	1.23	2.72	3.92	3.67	7.6	3.1	5.6	0.6	23.7	—
2005	MIL	MLB	21	1	1	1	27	0	31²	40	18	23	2	53.4%	.376	-5	1.83	5.96	4.25	5.79	11.3	4.7	5.8	0.6	-1.6	0.68
2006	NAS	AAA	22	6	5	0	20	19	105²	71	41	110	4	55.1%	.275	35	1.06	2.74	3.71	3.72	6.8	3.5	7.4	0.4	21.7	—
2006	MIL	MLB	22	0	3	0	9	5	27²	39	16	32	4	47.7%	.427	11	1.99	8.12	4.67	7.14	12.4	4.3	9.0	1.2	-6.0	-0.95
2007	MIL	MLB	23	7	8	1	38	22	126	124	53	108	12	52.0%	.303	13	1.40	4.29	4.52	4.44	8.5	3.2	6.9	0.8	18.1	2.60

Breakout: 27% Improve: 63% Collapse: 4%   Attrition: 0%   Comparables: Jeremy Affeldt, Tommy John, Jaret Wright, Phil Norton

It was the best of pitches, it was the worst of pitches, it was the age of success, it was the age of failure, it was proof of competence, it was proof of incompetence. Eveland's Triple-A success will ensure Eveland gets more major league trials, but they'll now happen in Arizona. Milwaukee may regret giving up a 23-year-old power lefty arm who throws heat in the 90s and plus breaking stuff with reliable command. However, monitoring his weight was a bit of a distraction; if he doesn't take his conditioning seriously, it won't make it any easier for him to realize his promise.

Yovani Gallardo

Bats: R Throws: R   Height: 6' 3"   Weight: 215   Born: February 27, 1986   Age: 21

YEAR	TEAM	LVL	AGE	W	L	SV	G	GS	IP	H	BB	SO	HR	GB%	BABIP	STUFF	WHIP	ERA	PERA	EQERA	EQH9	EQBB9	EQSO9	EQHR9	VORP	WXRL
2005	WVA	A	19	8	3	1	26	18	121¹	100	51	110	5	52.9%	.297	12	1.24	2.75	5.00	4.35	8.2	4.7	5.0	0.7	16.4	—
2006	BRV	A+	20	6	3	0	13	13	77¹	54	23	103	4	58.8%	.298	37	1.00	2.10	3.92	3.60	7.6	3.1	7.9	0.8	16.7	—
2006	HUN	AA	20	5	2	0	13	13	77	50	28	85	2	42.6%	.268	42	1.01	1.64	3.34	2.83	6.5	3.2	7.1	0.4	23.5	—
2007	MIL	MLB	21	7	8	0	29	21	133	123	65	124	15	48.0%	.291	18	1.41	4.35	4.63	4.46	8.0	3.8	7.5	0.9	18.5	2.80

Breakout: 6% Improve: 25% Collapse: 31% Attrition: 0%   Comparables: Kyle Davies, Chad Billingsley, Jake Peavy, Clint Nageotte

The minor league leader in strikeouts with 188, Gallardo has shot up prospect lists after his 2006 season. He has three solid pitches: A plus fastball, a sweeping slider, and a nice, diving curve. The only downside is that some scouts don't think his ceiling is very high, but he'll fit into the front end of a big league rotation, and that'll go over nicely enough, thank you. Mark Rogers and Gallardo went one-two in Milwaukee's 2004 draft, and Gallardo has already passed Rogers as the better prospect—something that was true even before Rogers got hurt. Gallardo still has some time before he hits the majors, but Milwaukee's got a good one here.

Geremi Gonzalez

Bats: R Throws: R   Height: 6' 0"   Weight: 220   Born: January 8, 1975   Age: 32

YEAR	TEAM	LVL	AGE	W	L	SV	G	GS	IP	H	BB	SO	HR	GB%	BABIP	STUFF	WHIP	ERA	PERA	EQERA	EQH9	EQBB9	EQSO9	EQHR9	VORP	WXRL
2004	TBA	MLB	29	0	5	0	11	8	50¹	72	20	22	9	—	.356	-21	1.83	6.98	5.59	6.75	12.6	3.3	3.6	1.4	-7.3	0.05
2005	BOS	MLB	30	2	1	0	28	3	56	64	16	28	7	39.2%	.305	-13	1.43	6.11	4.67	5.52	9.4	2.5	4.3	1.1	-2.7	0.10
2006	NYN	MLB	31	0	0	0	3	3	14	21	6	8	4	28.0%	.370	-18	1.93	7.71	6.41	7.53	13.2	3.1	4.4	2.5	-2.9	0.10
2006	MIL	MLB	31	4	2	0	21	1	42	50	17	36	6	31.8%	.349	0	1.60	5.14	4.38	5.77	10.1	3.1	6.8	1.0	-2.5	0.12
2007	MIL	MLB	32	4	5	1	38	7	81¹	87	31	56	13	39.0%	.290	-6	1.45	5.14	5.33	5.19	9.3	2.9	5.5	1.3	4.4	0.70

Breakout: 27% Improve: 54% Collapse: 16% Attrition: 19%   Comparables: Terry Mathews, Juan Acevedo, Mark Gardner, Carl Willey

The Mets called Gonzalez up in May after three-fifths of their rotation hit the DL simultaneously. That's what it takes for Gonzalez to get a shot these days; he sits in a cabinet wearing a sign that says, "break glass in case of abject desperation." He didn't pitch well, and the Mets moved on to younger hurlers. Sent to Milwaukee for Mike Adams, he found his strike-outs in Dairyland and kept a few more balls in the yard. His arm was ruined by a UCL injury back in 1998, so his best use is as someone who gives you four weeks of emergency work, which is what he'll hope to do for the Blue Jays, who invited him to camp.

Rick Helling

Bats: R Throws: R   Height: 6' 3"   Weight: 255   Born: December 15, 1970   Age: 36

YEAR	TEAM	LVL	AGE	W	L	SV	G	GS	IP	H	BB	SO	HR	GB%	BABIP	STUFF	WHIP	ERA	PERA	EQERA	EQH9	EQBB9	EQSO9	EQHR9	VORP	WXRL
2005	NAS	AAA	34	9	3	0	21	21	130²	128	50	105	12	42.9%	.303	-1	1.36	4.13	5.15	5.40	8.9	3.7	5.0	1.0	2.9	—
2005	MIL	MLB	34	3	1	0	15	7	49	39	18	42	2	30.9%	.276	23	1.16	2.39	3.31	2.52	7.2	3.1	7.0	0.4	17.5	2.21
2006	MIL	MLB	35	0	2	0	20	2	35	25	15	32	6	30.4%	.221	7	1.14	4.11	4.67	3.79	6.1	3.3	7.3	1.3	6.6	0.84
2007	MIL	MLB	36	4	5	1	38	8	81²	86	36	58	14	37.0%	.286	-8	1.49	5.14	5.58	5.15	9.2	3.4	5.7	1.4	4.5	0.70

Breakout: 6% Improve: 36% Collapse: 38% Attrition: 25%   Comparables: Hideo Nomo, Steve Renko, Cal Eldred, Tim Stoddard

After returning from an early-season elbow injury, Helling bombed in two starts and was relegated to the bullpen. He did exceptionally well there, with a 2.43 ERA over 29 innings, many of them meaningful. It was the same role he thrived in with the Marlins during their second World Series run, so, if he ever gets over wanting to start, he just might have a career waiting for him.

Ben Hendrickson

Bats: R Throws: R   Height: 6' 4"   Weight: 190   Born: February 4, 1981   Age: 26

YEAR	TEAM	LVL	AGE	W	L	SV	G	GS	IP	H	BB	SO	HR	GB%	BABIP	STUFF	WHIP	ERA	PERA	EQERA	EQH9	EQBB9	EQSO9	EQHR9	VORP	WXRL
2004	IND	AAA	23	11	3	0	21	21	125	114	26	93	6	—	.290	27	1.12	2.02	3.44	2.47	7.6	2.0	5.1	0.5	44.3	—
2004	MIL	MLB	23	1	8	0	10	9	46¹	58	20	29	6	—	.342	-5	1.68	6.22	5.01	6.04	11.0	3.4	4.9	0.9	-4.7	0.07
2005	NAS	AAA	24	6	12	0	28	27	155²	176	58	122	17	51.3%	.343	0	1.50	4.97	4.77	5.43	9.7	3.2	5.3	1.1	3.0	—
2006	NAS	AAA	25	9	8	0	23	23	139	121	46	97	9	55.6%	.288	11	1.20	3.37	4.33	4.36	8.3	2.9	4.9	0.8	19.1	—
2006	MIL	MLB	25	0	2	0	4	3	12	21	9	8	0	55.3%	.447	-17	2.50	12.00	4.09	11.37	14.9	5.7	5.0	0.0	-9.3	-0.41
2007	MIL	MLB	26	5	8	0	31	16	110¹	121	45	71	14	51.0%	.302	-1	1.50	5.21	5.24	5.39	9.5	3.1	5.2	1.0	3.6	1.00

Breakout: 16% Improve: 43% Collapse: 19% Attrition: 1%   Comparables: Sean Bergman, Jay Tibbs, Pete Munro, Glen Hobbie

Roger Angell once wrote about pitchers, "Once the game begins he is (in concert with his catcher) the only man on the field who knows what is meant to happen next." Hendrickson could very well know what is meant to happen before each of his pitches gets thrown, and he has a minor league track record that suggests he can actualize this intention with some regularity, but in his major league career he has been suspiciously unable to control the outcome of a plate appearance. His future has gotten much bleaker since a strong 2004 campaign in Indianapolis started tantalizing prospect-watchers. If you want to see his pretty curve with any regularity, get thee to Nashville, because, at this point, he's an emergency starter.

Will Inman **Bats: R Throws: R** Height: 6' 0" Weight: 200 Born: February 6, 1987 Age: 20

YEAR	TEAM	LVL	AGE	W	L	SV	G	GS	IP	H	BB	SO	HR	GB%	BABIP	STUFF	WHIP	ERA	PERA	EQERA	EQH9	EQBB9	EQSO9	EQHR9	VORP	WXRL
2005	HEL	Rk	18	6	0	1	13	5	45	29	11	58	5	55.9%	.250	10	0.89	2.00	6.40	2.98	7.9	3.0	6.0	2.1	12.3	—
2006	WVA	A	19	10	2	0	23	20	110	75	24	134	3	42.6%	.279	40	0.90	1.72	3.57	2.61	7.5	2.4	6.6	0.5	35.5	—
2007	MIL	MLB	20	7	7	1	29	19	125	119	47	106	18	44.0%	.282	16	1.32	4.08	4.58	4.12	8.3	2.8	6.9	1.1	22.1	3.10

Breakout: 0% Improve: 6% Collapse: 73% Attrition: 2% Comparables: Jake Peavy, Troy Patton, Sean Gallagher, John Stephens

A high school hurler picked in the third round of the 2005 draft, Inman led the Sally League with a 1.77 ERA thanks to some filthy strikeout numbers. He's not overpowering, instead relying on plus control, a hard curve, and a willingness to go after hitters. He had some shoulder trouble last year that shut him down for a month, and was monitored closely afterwards, and some fret he doesn't have the big frame you want, but this kind of dominance is hard to ignore.

Zach Jackson **Bats: L Throws: L** Height: 6' 5" Weight: 220 Born: May 13, 1983 Age: 24

YEAR	TEAM	LVL	AGE	W	L	SV	G	GS	IP	H	BB	SO	HR	GB%	BABIP	STUFF	WHIP	ERA	PERA	EQERA	EQH9	EQBB9	EQSO9	EQHR9	VORP	WXRL
2005	DUN	A+	22	8	1	0	10	10	59¹	56	6	48	3	59.8%	.301	12	1.05	2.88	3.74	4.73	8.8	1.2	4.4	0.8	5.7	—
2005	NHP	AA	22	4	3	0	9	9	54	57	12	43	3	53.8%	.338	10	1.28	4.00	4.05	5.50	9.8	2.3	4.8	0.7	0.6	—
2005	SYR	AAA	22	4	4	0	8	8	47¹	61	21	33	3	48.1%	.379	1	1.73	5.14	4.51	6.14	11.0	4.1	4.8	0.6	-2.9	—
2006	NAS	AAA	23	4	6	0	18	18	107²	106	44	58	11	51.2%	.286	-11	1.40	4.11	5.62	5.13	9.3	3.6	3.8	1.2	5.6	—
2006	MIL	MLB	23	2	2	0	8	7	38¹	48	14	22	6	47.1%	.323	-4	1.62	5.40	5.20	5.22	10.7	2.7	4.5	1.1	0.0	-0.06
2007	MIL	MLB	24	6	10	0	29	25	127²	142	54	75	18	49.0%	.298	-2	1.53	5.46	5.54	5.62	9.6	3.2	4.8	1.1	0.8	1.00

Breakout: 13% Improve: 44% Collapse: 23% Attrition: 0% Comparables: Derrin Ebert, Randy Lerch, Jimmy Osting, Mike Gosling

The big lefty spent a few weeks in the majors last year, but between that and an underwhelming Triple-A performance, he hasn't done anything to muscle his way into the 2007 rotation plans. He throws hard enough to avoid the finesse label, but doesn't miss enough bats. He's mostly a sinker/cutter pitcher who needs to keep the ball down. He'll be in the mix for some innings next year, but whether they're meaningful or mop-up innings depends upon his strikeout rate.

Danny Kolb **Bats: R Throws: R** Height: 6' 4" Weight: 210 Born: March 29, 1975 Age: 32

YEAR	TEAM	LVL	AGE	W	L	SV	G	GS	IP	H	BB	SO	HR	GB%	BABIP	STUFF	WHIP	ERA	PERA	EQERA	EQH9	EQBB9	EQSO9	EQHR9	VORP	WXRL
2004	MIL	MLB	29	0	4	39	64	0	57¹	50	15	21	3	—	.247	-9	1.13	2.98	4.09	3.24	7.6	2.2	2.9	0.5	13.8	3.01
2005	ATL	MLB	30	3	8	11	65	0	57²	78	29	39	5	53.5%	.378	-12	1.87	5.93	4.38	6.03	11.8	4.1	5.4	0.8	-4.6	-2.02
2006	MIL	MLB	31	2	2	1	53	0	48¹	53	20	26	4	54.3%	.310	-11	1.51	4.84	4.30	4.50	9.2	3.2	4.3	0.7	4.6	0.02
2007	MIL	MLB	32	2	3	1	45	0	51¹	58	21	29	5	53.0%	.307	-14	1.54	4.96	5.18	5.15	9.8	3.2	4.5	0.8	2.9	0.20

Breakout: 16% Improve: 28% Collapse: 37% Attrition: 30% Comparables: Mike Barlow, Tom Timmermann, Jim Todd, Ben Weber

Having gone pumpkin in 2005 when his ground-ball voodoo didn't work in Atlanta, Kolb is now generally recognized as not the kind of pitcher to be trusted with men on base. After taking a second look, the Brewers rightly let him walk. Kolb remains unsigned at this writing, but someone will give him a shot at an eleventh- or twelfth-man spot in their pen; his days of protecting late leads should be over.

Tomo Ohka

Bats: S Throws: R   Height: 6' 1"   Weight: 200   Born: March 18, 1976   Age: 31

YEAR	TEAM	LVL	AGE	W	L	SV	G	GS	IP	H	BB	SO	HR	GB%	BABIP	STUFF	WHIP	ERA	PERA	EQERA	EQH9	EQBB9	EQSO9	EQHR9	VORP	WXRL
2004	MON	MLB	28	3	7	0	15	15	84²	98	20	38	11	—	.299	-2	1.39	3.40	4.54	3.96	10.1	1.9	3.5	1.0	12.6	1.83
2005	WAS	MLB	29	4	3	0	10	9	54	44	27	17	6	42.5%	.220	-13	1.31	3.33	5.77	4.09	7.2	4.1	2.6	1.0	9.9	1.20
2005	MIL	MLB	29	7	6	0	22	20	126¹	145	28	81	16	41.8%	.313	7	1.37	4.35	4.19	4.53	10.1	1.8	5.2	1.1	13.6	2.15
2006	MIL	MLB	30	4	5	0	18	18	97	98	35	50	12	41.7%	.280	-1	1.37	4.82	4.83	4.61	8.6	2.8	4.2	1.0	7.5	1.76
2007	MIL	MLB	31	6	9	0	30	20	127	141	44	69	19	44.0%	.290	-5	1.45	5.04	5.32	5.12	9.6	2.6	4.4	1.2	7.8	1.70

Breakout: 2%   Improve: 24%   Collapse: 35%   Attrition: 9%   Comparables: Jim Slaton, Armando Reynoso, James Baldwin, Duane Pillette

Shoulder and hamstring injuries derailed his season and ended his Brewers tenure, but Ohka was a solid citizen in the rotation prior to that, which is about what his upside is: Non-descript, mid-rotation innings-muncher. The highlight of his year didn't come on the mound at all, but in a *SportsCenter*-ready four-RBI performance at the plate against the Rockies on August 24 during which he suddenly began switch-hitting.

Manny Parra

Bats: L Throws: L   Height: 6' 3"   Weight: 200   Born: October 30, 1982   Age: 24

YEAR	TEAM	LVL	AGE	W	L	SV	G	GS	IP	H	BB	SO	HR	GB%	BABIP	STUFF	WHIP	ERA	PERA	EQERA	EQH9	EQBB9	EQSO9	EQHR9	VORP	WXRL
2004	HDS	A+	21	5	2	0	13	12	67¹	76	19	64	3	—	.351	13	1.41	3.48	4.03	4.76	8.7	3.0	5.1	0.6	6.5	—
2005	HUN	AA	22	5	6	0	16	16	91	111	21	86	4	59.0%	.374	21	1.45	3.96	3.54	4.65	10.5	2.0	5.8	0.7	9.8	—
2006	BRV	A+	23	1	3	0	15	14	54²	47	32	61	4	53.1%	.319	1	1.46	2.99	6.49	6.31	9.3	6.8	6.3	1.4	-4.0	—
2006	HUN	AA	23	3	0	0	6	6	31²	26	8	29	0	54.0%	.370	17	1.09	2.88	3.32	4.94	8.1	2.3	5.8	0.3	2.3	—
2007	MIL	MLB	24	5	7	0	25	17	102	106	52	77	12	53.0%	.304	4	1.55	5.25	5.30	5.46	9.0	3.9	6.1	0.9	2.6	1.00

Breakout: 11%   Improve: 36%   Collapse: 18%   Attrition: 3%   Comparables: Charlie Manning, Scott Downs, Mike Bynum, Josh Kalinowski

Health is a skill, and Parra doesn't have it. He had arthroscopic shoulder surgery in August 2005 and again failed to pitch a full season after his recovery. He's been overtaken by Gallardo and Inman in the organization, even though Parra's got good stuff. It's tempting to still try to get him to hold up for six or seven innings a night, but he's never done it, and getting him for an inning or two in relief would be better than nothing at all.

Dennis Sarfate

Bats: R Throws: R   Height: 6' 4"   Weight: 210   Born: April 9, 1981   Age: 26

YEAR	TEAM	LVL	AGE	W	L	SV	G	GS	IP	H	BB	SO	HR	GB%	BABIP	STUFF	WHIP	ERA	PERA	EQERA	EQH9	EQBB9	EQSO9	EQHR9	VORP	WXRL
2004	HUN	AA	23	7	12	0	28	25	129	128	78	113	12	—	.316	-7	1.60	3.98	6.44	5.73	10.0	6.2	5.2	1.3	-1.8	—
2005	HUN	AA	24	9	9	0	24	24	130	120	59	110	13	42.5%	.292	-15	1.38	3.88	6.55	5.02	8.8	4.5	5.0	1.6	8.2	—
2006	NAS	AAA	25	10	7	0	34	21	125¹	125	78	117	7	51.6%	.340	15	1.62	3.67	4.71	4.84	9.6	5.6	6.5	0.6	10.5	—
2006	MIL	MLB	25	0	0	0	8	0	8¹	9	4	11	0	30.4%	.391	9	1.56	4.34	2.53	4.15	9.3	4.2	10.4	0.0	1.6	0.05
2007	MIL	MLB	26	3	6	0	34	9	79¹	82	56	64	11	43.0%	.300	-7	1.74	5.76	6.25	5.85	9.0	5.4	6.5	1.1	-1.5	0.20

Breakout: 2%   Improve: 30%   Collapse: 39%   Attrition: 8%   Comparables: Chris Clemons, Joaquin Benoit, Jon Leicester, Ray Ricken

Poet Jack Spicer wrote about a changeup that "at the last second, doesn't change." At one time, that essentially described Sarfate, who really only had one pitch, a fastball, and it never changed. Happily, he's since refined his curveball enough that it's a useful complementary pitch. Sarfate still walks almost six batters per nine innings, but, as he's out of options, he should get a long look for one of the bullpen openings.

Ben Sheets

Bats: R Throws: R   Height: 6' 1"   Weight: 220   Born: July 18, 1978   Age: 28

YEAR	TEAM	LVL	AGE	W	L	SV	G	GS	IP	H	BB	SO	HR	GB%	BABIP	STUFF	WHIP	ERA	PERA	EQERA	EQH9	EQBB9	EQSO9	EQHR9	VORP	WXRL
2004	MIL	MLB	25	12	14	0	34	34	237	201	32	264	25	—	.292	44	0.98	2.70	2.85	3.16	7.6	1.1	8.9	0.9	65.0	7.71
2005	MIL	MLB	26	10	9	0	22	22	156²	142	25	141	19	38.3%	.281	28	1.07	3.33	3.48	3.74	8.1	1.3	7.4	1.1	32.1	4.13
2006	MIL	MLB	27	6	7	0	17	17	106	105	11	116	9	42.1%	.342	47	1.09	3.82	2.56	3.57	8.5	0.8	8.9	0.7	24.0	3.24
2007	MIL	MLB	28	12	8	0	28	28	177¹	160	29	171	21	44.0%	.284	32	1.07	3.35	3.34	3.42	7.8	1.3	7.8	1.0	44.1	6.00

Breakout: 16%   Improve: 49%   Collapse: 8%   Attrition: 6%   Comparables: Juan Marichal, Turk Farrell, Fergie Jenkins, Shane Reynolds

One of the only two holdovers from the pre-Melvin years (the other being Geoff Jenkins), Sheets is supposed to be the kind of pitcher you build a contender around. Various maladies have prevented him from throwing more than 157 innings in either of the last two seasons, so his dependability is always questioned, one of those "he's good, *but...*" sorts of players. You just cannot ignore how good he is when he takes the mound, though. He'd always had great control before, but last year's equivalent walk rate of 0.8 per nine innings is approaching the reliability you get with a pitching machine. Next year—if healthy—he could easily be one of the best starters in the league.

Brian Shouse

Bats: L **Throws: L**   Height: 5′ 11″ Weight: 190   Born: December 31, 1969   Age: 38

YEAR	TEAM	LVL	AGE	W	L	SV	G	GS	IP	H	BB	SO	HR	GB%	BABIP	STUFF	WHIP	ERA	PERA	EQERA	EQH9	EQBB9	EQSO9	EQHR9	VORP	WXRL
2004	TEX	MLB	35	2	0	0	53	0	44¹	36	18	34	3	—	.260	9	1.17	2.23	3.71	2.17	6.9	3.4	6.3	0.6	19.5	1.51
2005	TEX	MLB	36	3	2	0	64	0	53¹	55	18	35	7	54.7%	.291	-9	1.37	5.23	4.68	5.34	8.4	2.9	5.7	1.1	-2.0	0.16
2006	TEX	MLB	37	0	0	0	6	0	4¹	6	1	3	1	37.5%	.333	-7	1.62	4.19	5.06	4.15	12.5	2.1	6.2	2.1	1.0	-0.29
2006	MIL	MLB	37	1	3	2	59	0	34	34	17	20	3	53.2%	.292	-12	1.50	3.97	5.12	3.82	8.7	3.8	4.6	0.8	6.9	0.36
2007	MIL	MLB	38	2	2	2	46	1	42	44	18	23	4	52.0%	.286	-14	1.46	4.20	4.61	4.34	9.1	3.3	4.5	0.8	6.3	0.60

Breakout: 17% Improve: 40% Collapse: 31% Attrition: 47%   Comparables: Rheal Cormier, Al Brazle, Darold Knowles, Steve Howe

Righties hit .309/.427/.515 against Shouse, which means he should never, ever face a righty. Ever. But he wasn't as effective against lefties in 2006 as he'd been in previous years, so maybe the logical next step is that he shouldn't pitch against anyone. The Brewers are hoping for a comeback, re-signing Shouse for 2007 for just shy of a million dollars. Among relievers with more than 30 appearances in 2006, Shouse had the fifth-lowest innings-per-appearance figure, on a list populated by lefty specialists such as Mike Myers, Randy Choate, Scott Sauerbeck, George Sherrill, and the man himself. In addition to slowing up the game, promoting inferior pitchers ahead of superior ones, and, in many cases, provoking matchups that are the precise opposite of what the manager on defense intended, these pitchers put a disproportionate burden on the rest of the staff by taking up a roster spot without absorbing sufficient playing time. Other than that, though, they're a great idea.

Derrick Turnbow

Bats: R **Throws: R**   Height: 6′ 3″ Weight: 210   Born: January 25, 1978   Age: 29

YEAR	TEAM	LVL	AGE	W	L	SV	G	GS	IP	H	BB	SO	HR	GB%	BABIP	STUFF	WHIP	ERA	PERA	EQERA	EQH9	EQBB9	EQSO9	EQHR9	VORP	WXRL
2004	SLC	AAA	26	2	6	6	46	3	74²	75	42	56	8	—	.300	-8	1.57	5.06	5.54	4.77	7.7	5.1	5.0	0.9	7.1	—
2004	ANA	MLB	26	0	0	0	4	0	6¹	2	7	3	0	—	.125	5	1.42	0.00	6.41	0.00	2.8	8.5	4.3	0.0	4.4	0.05
2005	MIL	MLB	27	7	1	39	69	0	67¹	49	24	64	5	51.1%	.249	21	1.08	1.74	3.41	2.11	6.6	2.9	7.8	0.7	26.2	4.66
2006	MIL	MLB	28	4	9	24	64	0	56¹	56	39	69	8	44.4%	.336	11	1.69	6.87	4.59	7.25	8.8	5.2	9.7	1.1	-12.8	-1.24
2007	MIL	MLB	29	2	3	3	48	0	52¹	47	30	51	6	47.0%	.289	5	1.47	4.44	4.60	4.58	7.8	4.4	7.8	0.8	6.5	0.60

Breakout: 31% Improve: 52% Collapse: 16% Attrition: 24%   Comparables: Billy Koch, Jerry Johnson, Dave Sisler, Hal Reniff

While Dana Eveland may have gotten the "Tale of Two Pitchers" treatment, Turnbow probably had a stronger claim to the reference. Looking at his post-All-Star break performance (18.1 IP, 11.29 ERA, 23/17 K/BB), it's easy to forget that Turnbow actually did attend the All-Star Game itself, as a participant, due in no small part to his accumulation of saves rather than any actual effective pitching. Self-reported information is usually pretty unreliable, but he chalked his struggles up to losing his slider, without which he's a one-pitch pitcher. He was still missing bats in the second half, so there's some reason for optimism, but the closer's job is Cordero's, and Turnbow's going to have to earn Ned Yost's trust if he wants to be the primary setup man.

Carlos Villanueva

Bats: R **Throws: R**   Height: 6′ 2″ Weight: 190   Born: November 28, 1983   Age: 23

YEAR	TEAM	LVL	AGE	W	L	SV	G	GS	IP	H	BB	SO	HR	GB%	BABIP	STUFF	WHIP	ERA	PERA	EQERA	EQH9	EQBB9	EQSO9	EQHR9	VORP	WXRL
2004	BLT	A	20	8	8	1	25	21	114²	102	30	113	20	—	.259	-46	1.15	3.77	8.34	6.69	10.7	3.1	5.4	3.3	-12.9	—
2005	BRV	A+	21	8	1	0	21	21	112¹	78	32	124	11	41.6%	.252	3	0.98	2.32	5.46	3.48	8.0	3.3	6.6	1.7	25.0	—
2005	HUN	AA	21	1	3	0	4	4	20²	21	9	14	3	30.0%	.277	-14	1.45	7.39	7.17	7.84	9.1	3.9	4.4	2.2	-5.2	—
2006	HUN	AA	22	4	5	0	11	10	62¹	60	14	59	6	48.6%	.303	8	1.19	3.77	4.67	5.46	9.6	2.1	6.0	1.5	0.9	—
2006	NAS	AAA	22	7	1	0	11	9	66²	42	26	61	6	41.4%	.210	19	1.03	2.72	4.61	3.02	6.3	3.4	6.4	1.1	18.8	—
2006	MIL	MLB	22	2	2	0	10	6	53²	43	11	39	8	44.4%	.230	18	1.01	3.69	4.40	3.29	6.9	1.6	5.9	1.2	14.1	1.42
2007	MIL	MLB	23	8	9	0	35	25	143²	142	51	109	25	42.0%	.274	8	1.34	4.73	4.98	4.76	8.6	2.7	6.1	1.4	15.1	2.50

Breakout: 8% Improve: 28% Collapse: 24% Attrition: 1%   Comparables: Kiko Calero, Mark Brownson, John Hudgins, Justin Duchscherer

Have you ever stopped to translate Spanish names into English? Jose Mesa becoming Joe Table is a good one, but "Charles Newtown" doesn't quite have the same zip. As with a lot of finesse pitchers, scouts don't like his chances to maintain his strikeout rates as he pitches at more advanced levels. He'll be in the mix for the fifth starter job in 2007, but there are cautions about his ability to keep his rookie-year success going. His control isn't nearly as good as it appeared last year, and, given his .230 BABIP, his chances to maintain his low ERA with those peripherals are mighty poor.

Matt Wise　　Bats: R　Throws: R　　Height: 6' 4"　Weight: 200　Born: November 18, 1975　Age: 31

YEAR	TEAM	LVL	AGE	W	L	SV	G	GS	IP	H	BB	SO	HR	GB%	BABIP	STUFF	WHIP	ERA	PERA	EQERA	EQH9	EQBB9	EQSO9	EQHR9	VORP	WXRL
2004	IND	AAA	28	1	0	0	7	1	20	12	4	20	3	—	.200	13	0.80	1.80	5.03	2.25	5.4	1.8	6.8	1.8	7.4	—
2004	MIL	MLB	28	1	2	0	30	3	52²	51	15	30	3	—	.284	0	1.25	4.44	3.75	4.36	8.6	2.3	4.5	0.5	5.4	0.90
2005	MIL	MLB	29	4	4	1	49	0	64¹	37	25	62	6	42.0%	.190	18	0.96	3.36	3.87	3.46	5.4	3.2	7.9	0.8	14.3	1.42
2006	MIL	MLB	30	5	6	0	40	0	44¹	45	14	27	6	46.1%	.289	-8	1.33	3.86	4.61	4.14	8.5	2.4	4.9	1.0	5.9	0.80
2007	MIL	MLB	31	2	2	1	36	0	44¹	45	16	29	6	46.0%	.282	-6	1.37	4.31	4.53	4.42	8.8	2.8	5.3	1.0	6.2	0.50

Breakout: 14%　Improve: 38%　Collapse: 39%　Attrition: 30%　　Comparables: Bert Roberge, Tim Burke, Dave Smith, Larry Andersen

"I was going after a salad" is one of the odder explanations for how one wound up on the DL, but it's true, as Wise cut his finger on salad tongs in June. He also finished the year on the 60-day DL after undergoing elbow surgery; he had complained of a "zinging" sensation in his fingers. That injury was unrelated to leafy greens or twisting one's body unnaturally to get around the sneeze guard. When healthy, Wise throws a bajillion changeups, which we should avoid calling his off-speed pitches, since you generally need on-speed pitches to make the term apt. He'll be healthy in time for spring training.

Lineouts

PLAYER	TEAM	LVL	AGE	PA	R	2B	3B	HR	RBI	BB	SO	SB-CS	SPEED	AVG/OBP/SLG	MLVr	EqAVG/EqOBP/EqSLG	EqA	VORP
OF D. Anderson*	HUN	AA	25	452	60	24	4	6	43	39	80	17-8	6.4	.291/.359/.415	.138	.278/.333/.409	.258	0.6
	NAS	AAA	25	69	15	5	1	1	9	2	12	3-1	7.6	.333/.348/.492	.208	.323/.338/.477	.276	2.8
SS C. Barnwell	NAS	AAA	27	440	46	18	2	4	37	38	60	16-6	5.1	.300/.375/.389	.069	.284/.347/.368	.256	14.6
SS B. Brewer	BRR	Rk	18	201	25	3	6	3	22	16	53	10-0	6.5	.264/.328/.396	.007	.214/.248/.312	.201	-25.8
1B C. Errecart	HEL	Rk	21	313	49	16	0	13	61	25	56	5-3	3.8	.316/.406/.518	.338	.263/.310/.413	.247	-2.3
3B M. Gamel*	WVA	A	20	555	65	28	5	17	88	52	81	9-2	5.2	.288/.359/.469	.180	.253/.306/.408	.247	9.3
OF B. Katin	BRV	A+	23	496	64	34	3	13	75	34	112	4-6	4.2	.289/.349/.464	.197	.274/.321/.439	.257	5.0
	HUN	AA	23	60	11	2	0	4	8	1	11	0-0	5.1	.224/.250/.466	.002	.224/.250/.466	.233	-0.7
C C. Moeller	MIL	MLB	31	104	9	3	0	2	5	4	26	0-0	3.2	.184/.231/.276	-.450	.163/.212/.245	.166	-8.4
	NAS	AAA	31	154	10	6	0	2	18	15	28	0-2	3.0	.220/.307/.311	-.216	.190/.261/.255	.190	-11.6
UT V. Rottino	NAS	AAA	26	452	55	25	2	7	42	40	74	12-7	5.2	.314/.379/.440	.160	.302/.359/.423	.270	26.3

PLAYER	TEAM	LVL	AGE	W	L	SV	IP	H	BB	SO	HR	GB%	BABIP	STUFF	WHIP	ERA	PERA	EqERA	EqH9	EqBB9	EqSO9	EqHR9	VORP
C. Demaria	NAS	AAA	25	4	0	1	51²	48	17	50	4	—	.305	4	1.27	2.99	4.08	3.88	9.0	3.0	6.7	0.9	9.7
	MIL	MLB	25	0	1	0	13²	10	9	11	4	—	.171	-9	1.39	5.91	7.84	6.43	6.4	5.1	6.4	2.6	-1.8
T. Dillard	HUN	AA	22	10	7	0	163²	167	36	108	10	—	.301	4	1.24	3.14	4.38	5.29	9.6	1.9	4.2	0.9	5.6
R. Hinton	BRV	A+	21	5	4	2	89²	88	26	95	6	—	.336	1	1.28	3.33	4.58	4.91	9.8	3.0	6.2	1.1	6.7
J. Jeffress	BRR	Rk	18	2	5	0	33	30	25	37	0	—	.316	2	1.67	6.00	5.95	7.99	9.1	8.0	5.2	0.3	-8.7
M. Jones	BRV	A+	23	0	2	0	54¹	45	27	30	1	—	.262	-8	1.33	2.83	5.26	4.25	7.5	5.6	3.1	0.3	8.0
J. Lehr	NAS	AAA	28	4	7	0	112¹	120	31	90	15	—	.307	-7	1.35	3.93	5.21	4.80	10.4	2.5	5.4	1.6	9.8
	MIL	MLB	28	2	1	0	15²	24	7	12	2	—	.431	-14	1.98	8.60	4.43	8.10	13.0	3.2	5.9	1.1	-5.4
M. Rogers	BRV	A+	20	1	2	0	71²	68	53	96	6	—	.371	16	1.70	5.06	6.29	6.98	10.0	7.9	8.2	1.4	-10.5
C. Spurling	TOL	AAA	29	1	4	5	66²	61	10	34	4	—	.281	-12	1.07	2.04	4.42	4.11	8.9	1.5	3.4	0.8	10.9
	DET	MLB	29	0	0	0	11¹	13	4	4	2	—	.282	-24	1.50	3.19	5.70	3.18	10.3	3.2	3.2	1.6	3.7
	MIL	MLB	29	0	0	0	10	12	4	3	3	—	.250	-38	1.60	7.20	7.25	6.10	9.6	3.5	2.6	2.6	-1.3

Drew Anderson isn't a prospect. He's been groomed as a fourth outfielder since his days at Nebraska, but a suddenly-crowded Milwaukee outfield will keep him in Triple-A. Minor league veteran **Chris Barnwell** got to step in as an emergency player last year, but he could be sitting on two career singles for an awfully long time. **Brent Brewer** is raw, sashimi raw. Also recruited as a wide receiver, he's young, athletic, and toolsy. It's far too early to worry about baseball-specific things, though he's clearly in the right organization. **Chris Errecart** was picked out of Cal in the fifth round last summer; his bat's his only tool, and, while it's the best one to have, he's limited to first or left defensively. Though we should discount his .469 SLG a little bit since it came in the offense-happy Sally League, **Mat Gamel** still put his line-drive swing to good use. Hopefully he'll be a bit more selective as he advances and pitchers start to respect his batting stroke. A teammate of Ryan Braun's at the University of Miami, muscular **Brendan Katin** had a nice year beating up on less polished players in the Florida State League. **Chad Moeller** posted a park-inflated age-27 season line of .286/.385/.467 with Arizona in 2002; it's been all downhill from there. He signed a one-year deal with the Reds to be their third catcher. **Vinny Rottino** doesn't really have a position. He spent time as a catcher in the AFL, but can't really catch, and he's a bit old to be a real prospect.

A changeup artist, **Chris Demaria** is proof that not everyone has Doug Jones's mastery of the craft. **Tim Dillard** isn't seen as a top prospect, but he's got a nifty sinker and easy, repeatable mechanics. If he masters some off-speed stuff, he could make it to a big league rotation. One of a dying breed—the new CBA eliminated the draft-and-follow—**Robert Hinton** has a nice power fastball-slider mix. Yes, **Jeremy Jeffress** was incredibly wild in his pro debut, but cut the kid some slack. Less than a year ago he was still thinking about matching a corsage to his prom date's dress, so don't look for polish on his resume quite yet. He had a 0.19 ERA during his senior year of high school, thanks in part to a nearly triple-digit fastball. "**Mike Jones**" isn't the name of a pitcher. It's the name of a friend of a friend who crashed on your couch in college some weekend, a guy about whom you remember nothing except that he ate all the pizza without chipping in for the delivery. This Jones missed 2005 after labrum surgery, struggled with his command upon returning to the mound in 2006. As a former first-rounder, he'll get every opportunity to regain the spark he had in high school, but it's a long road back. **Justin Lehr** opened the year in the Brewer bullpen, but pitched his way down to Nashville after two months, only to be promoted to starting. The converted catcher isn't making headway. In December it was announced that **Mark Rogers** would undergo shoulder surgery to alleviate the soreness that plagued him throughout 2006; he's expected to miss most or all of 2007. His triple-digit heat hasn't translated into great results as yet, but Rogers is young enough to come back. **Chris Spurling** was claimed off of waivers from the Tigers, but not because he may be a hidden gem. His low ERAs hide the fact that big league hitters just don't swing and miss at his pitches all that often. That's not hyperbole: Only seven relievers allowed a higher percent of balls in play than Spurling did.

Manager: Ned Yost

Year	Team	W-L	Pythag +/-	Avg PC	100 +P	120 +P	QS	BQS	REL	REL w Zero R	IBB	SUBS	PH	PH Avg	PH HR	SB2	CS2	SB3	CS3	SAC Att	SAC %	POS SAC	Squeeze	Swing	In Play
2004	MIL	67-94	+1	93.4	60	9	78	7	423	246	27	41	280	.205	7	124	35	14	2	78	71.8%	28	5	157	101
2005	MIL	81-81	-3	99.5	86	4	87	11	395	238	52	43	255	.245	6	68	30	11	3	97	68.0%	41	5	135	100
2006	MIL	75-87	+5	94.6	67	3	77	13	427	257	34	20	235	.267	4	60	33	10	4	84	69.1%	20	1	134	96

Former catchers dominated the managerial ranks last season, with 12 out of 30 skippers formerly wearing the tools of ignorance. Since then, the total has risen by one, with Joe Girardi being replaced by Fredi Gonzalez and Bob Geren joining the ranks Bob Geren and Fredi Gonzalez joining the ranks. Yost is one of the more conservative coaches in the business, making relatively few moves. He's not particularly worried about platoon matchups on either offense or defense, and as a result doesn't use a lot of lineups or go to the bullpen a million times a game; he pinch-hits infrequently for an NL manager, but gets decent results when he does. Yost isn't overly fond of the bunt, and the Brewers don't do it very well, but he does have a fondness for the squeeze play. He also likes the running game—another thing his Brewers haven't been particularly adept at—and the hit-and-run. With a young team that may soon deliver on its power-hitting potential, better Yost continues to observe his stay-the-course tendencies than give in to the smallball manager that's trying to break out.

Minnesota Twins

If Tigers can change their stripes—and did—perhaps we have to torture some other metaphor where the Twins are concerned. After years of apparently settling, of not making that extra effort to field a team that could do more than just win the AL Central, Terry Ryan has been shaken out of his reverie. Watching the White Sox win the division and the World Series in 2005 must have been a rude awakening, but having the Indians slip by them as well that year made it clear that the status quo in the Central was a thing of the past.

Unfortunately, those events weren't enough in themselves. Despite having come up short in 2005, Ryan settled for modest fixes once again in the winter of 2005–06, his pick up of speedy second baseman Luis Castillo in a nice little deal with the Marlins being the lone exception. Ryan added geezers Tony Batista, Rondell White, Ruben Sierra, and Juan Castro without recognizing that none of them were significantly useful players, let alone fixes for the team's production problems in the outfield or at DH. Those four were portrayed as players the Twins could afford, but for more than $5 million combined, they were being paid far more than they'd be worth. Perhaps this approach came of the confidence that springs from having both the best pitcher and best young hitter in baseball (the Twins will be built around Johan Santana and Joe Mauer through 2008 at the very least). Perhaps it came from the cautious, reasonable expectation that better things were ahead for Justin Morneau and Michael Cuddyer—the pace of player development being blissfully divorced from the day-to-day panics of the 24/7 news cycle or fant-head desperation. If so, Ryan would have been better served skipping the geezers altogether in favor of his existing in-house fixes, as the 2006 season would soon prove.

Six weeks into the season, the Twins were down more than eight games in the standings as the Tigers and White Sox were both playing .600 ball. The lineup was busted in at least four spots, and the rotation had seen three starters do bellyflops. Ryan recognized that things weren't going well, and, while it would be easy to be snarky and say that this was pretty obvious, other general managers have let these sorts of things slide, either hopelessly hoping that things would look up, or looking on with flat-footed desperation, flabbergasted that their master plan has failed (shades of Bill Bavasi's zombified shock over how things turned out in Anaheim in 1999).

One of the most fundamental problems was that this fundamentals-first ballclub was doing a bad job on the pitching-and-defense side of the equation. Two months into the season, the Twins' defense was last in the majors in Defensive Efficiency (or DER)—the rate at which a team turns balls in play into outs (see table 1). The major-league average at that point of the year was .690; with a DER of .644, the Twins were giving up 7 percent more baserunners on balls in play than anyone else in the league. That alone understates the magnitude of the problem, as the Twins' rotation at that point had more defense-dependent pitchers than most. As a staff, the Twins were third in MLB in the percentage of their outs recorded via strikeouts (26.8 percent), but, while there are times when Johan Santana seems like he could leave everyone but the catcher in the dugout, that's not true of pitchers such as Carlos Silva or Brad Radke. Take away Santana and the rest of the Twins' starters were getting only 13.9 percent of their outs on strikeouts at a time when 23.7 percent of all major league outs were being made on third strikes. The result was and increased dependence on a defense that wasn't getting the job done. The results were horrendous.

Part of the reason for the defense's poor performance was that Luis Castillo's range on turf left a lot to be desired.

TWINS PROSPECTUS

2006 record: 96–66; First place, AL Central; Lost to Athletics in Division Series

Pythagenport record: 93–69

Runs scored per game: 4.94 (8th in AL)

Runs allowed per game: 4.22 (2nd in AL)

Team EqA: .260 (6th in AL)

2006 Batters Age: 28.8 (3rd youngest in AL)

2006 Pitchers Age: 27.3 (2nd youngest in AL)

Ballpark: Metrodome; Neutral park; Park Factor of .999

2006: A quick course correction helped the game's highest high-end talents put the Twins back in the postseason.

2007: Johan and the Johettes won't be enough to keep the offense in the running with the Indians.

Table 1. The Best Defense is a Good Defense: Best and Worst Defensive Efficiency, Opening Day through 5/31

1	Cardinals	.719	26	Reds	.675
2	Padres	.718	27	Brewers	.673
3	Cubs	.712	28	Phillies	.672
4	Tigers	.715	29	Pirates	.666
5	Giants	.711	30	Twins	.644

The Twins also learned by hard experience that Castillo's not good around the bag on the deuce. Elsewhere, Shannon Stewart and Rondell White showed their ages in left, and Batista's reflexes at third were shot. To some extent this explains why the Twins felt the need to employ defensive specialist Juan Castro as their everyday shortstop, but with Batista, White, and Lew Ford also sapping the offense, they couldn't carry his slack stick.

Things finally started to change on May 15 (see table 2). The Twins woke up that day with a 17–20 record, already 7.5 games behind in the Central and falling further amid five consecutive loses to the division leading White Sox and Tigers. With Johan Santana off to his customary underwhelming start, the Twins' starters had assembled a 6.44 ERA to that point, far and away the worst in baseball, outuglying the Orioles' rotation by more than half a run. Two of the major props behind Santana had collapsed as dramatically, as we warned was possible last year. Kyle Lohse demonstrated what happens when fourth starters go bad, while Carlos Silva's extreme dependence on defensive support had tilted to untenable. On May 15, Ryan and Gardenhire finally addressed the situation. Carlos Silva, who had allowed 8 runs in 3 ⅓ in a loss to the White Sox the nights before, was sent to the bullpen. Two days later Lohse, who allowed five Tiger runs in just 2 ⅔ innings in a loss on the 16th, was sent to Rochester. Into their places went two-thirds of the Pierzynski heist—rookies Boof Bonser and fearsome lefty Francisco Liriano. Both were hard throwers with higher strikeout rates than the men they replaced.

Still, the club entered June 10.5 games back, at which point the failures of another rookie starter, Scott Baker, necessitated Silva's return to the rotation following four scoreless relief appearances out of five. The temporizing path of the past wasn't going to cut it, and the lineup needed fixing as well. On June 11, Tony Batista played his last game; the next day marked Castro's last in a Twins uni. On June 14, Nick Punto and Jason Bartlett started their first game together as the left side of the Twins infield, and both proved adequate afield and perhaps more than that at the plate. Michael Cuddyer had already taken over for Lew Ford as the regular in right a week and a half before the initial rotation shake-up, but the team's outfield and DH production spiked when Jason Kubel was briefly healthy enough to help replace the equally fragile White and Stewart, hitting .333/.365/.580 for the month. When Ruben Sierra came off of the DL, he got only two starts before being discarded. And if Castillo wasn't going to become radically better afield, he was at least helping the team score runs.

Having replaced nearly half of their lineup and rotation, the Twins started winning games. A 36–10 run through July 31 propelled them into the wild-card hunt alongside both brands of Sox. The offense, such a disaster in the early going in 2006 and for all of 2005, finished comfortably in baseball's middle class, smack-dab in the center of an 18-team pack that sat below the Yankees and Indians in team Equivalent Average. Before ditching Batista and Castro, they'd averaged 4.6 runs per game in their first 63 contests; they averaged 5.2 per over the remaining 99.

In a league in which teams averaged almost five runs per game, the Twins had found the difference between bad teams and good. Although Kubel would falter, the key components for a top offense were there—Joe Mauer, Justin Morneau, Michael Cuddyer, and Torii Hunter are the core of a young and talented lineup. Swapping out the broken bits for ones that worked well enough provided the support that core needed, it also put a radically better defensive unit on the field; from June 1 till season's end, the Twins were second in MLB in Defensive Efficiency (.703).

Table 2. How Fargo the Twins?—Pieces for the Woodchipper, 6/1

Player	Solution
SS Juan Castro .238/.265/.313	Traded 6/15
3B Tony Batista .250/.308/.417	Designated for assignment 6/13
DH Rondell White .195/.211/.232	Benched 6/18; DL 6/30-7/15 and 8/9-23
OF Lew Ford .234/.307/.315	Lost RF job in early May; Only 11 starts after 7/1
SP Kyle Lohse 8.92 ERA in eight starts (3 QS)	Optioned to Rochester 5/17; traded to the Reds 7/31
SP Carlos Silva 8.80 ERA in eight starts (1 QS)	Two weeks in the pen
SP Scott Baker 6.06 ERA in nine starts (2 QS)	Optioned to Rochester 5/31

Identifying and fixing the problems seem obvious in the abstract, given that the players who were flailing were so absolutely terrible. Nevertheless, a team is a human thing, and deciding to break things up isn't necessarily an easy decision. To Terry Ryan's credit, he had his Branch Rickey moment of clarity, deciding he really preferred winning to the alternative. We've been hard on the Twins in years past, and there are still things to complain about. Players such as Punto or Jason Tyner—who filled in for an injured Hunter in center, White in left, and Kubel at DH, picking up 58 starts in the second half—shouldn't be seen as long-term solutions at any position. Real life isn't a lab experiment, though, and real teams generally don't feature All-Stars at every position. Ryan and Gardenhire fixed things on the fly instead of waiting around, and it made a substantive difference in nearly every aspect of the team's performance.

The fixes applied to the pitching staff succeeded in spectacular and unlikely fashion. The team finished with one of the ten best rotations in Support-Neutral statistics despite the horrendous start and the ongoing uncertainty of Brad Radke, guttily pitching through a career-ending shoulder injury, and Carlos Silva, whose ERA dropped under 6.00 only because of a three-quality-start streak in September. In large part, the difference was attributable to Liriano, who exploded on the league like a bombshell—once he got his arm limber enough to work deeper into games (it took two starts), he mowed down hitters at a pace that ranked with Santana's. With that one-two punch and workmanlike goodness from Radke and Bonser, the rotation was in good shape for two months. Unfortunately, the season added an additional wrinkle as July turned to August. First Liriano's elbow started giving him trouble, forcing him to the DL one start into the month. Little more than two weeks later, Radke's shoulder finally gave out. Once again, Ryan patched things up well enough in-house, first calling up former Fresno State star (and 2005 first-round pick) Matt Garza, then turning back to Baker. Sucked into the breach, both top prospects reflected well on the organization's exceptional pitching depth by keeping the team in games.

It helped that, by this point, the Twins had one consistent asset they could rely on—the best bullpen in the league. The bullpen ranked second overall (behind the Mets) in WXRL, and first in Adjusted Runs Prevented. The late-inning handoff remained the same, with Juan Rincon setting up Joe Nathan, both enjoying seasons almost as good as their initial 2004 hookup. Jesse Crain slipped into a middle relief role that was slightly less intense, joining Matt Guerrier in giving the Twins an excellent bridge between the starters and the late-inning relievers. The

Twins also wound up with one of the best situational tandems in the game, neither of whom cost them much. After arriving with all sorts of the promise with the Dodgers, hefty lefty Dennys Reyes had been reduced to roster flotsam, bobbing through six organizations in four years before landing in Minnesota and enjoying the best season of his career; he limited lefty hitters to .148/.219/.205. From the other side, homegrown sidearmer Pat Neshek was added to the pen before the All-Star break, and his particularly wicked offerings emasculated right-handers (.140/.159/.221). As potentially unreliable as reliever performance can be season to season, this is a talented sextet, and one in which everyone's roles are defined in a way that plays to their strengths. The Twins might be able to keep this group together through 2008, and while there's always the potential for injury, there's a reasonable shot this group will continue to rank among baseball's best pens over the next two years.

Combined, that pen, the patched-together rotation, the team's young offensive core, and the in-house replacements that shored up the offense and defense were able to catch the Tigers and win the division. Given how much of a scramble it had been to get that far, you can forgive the Twins if their postseason ended on a down note, with a quick three-and-out against the A's. The question is whether or not that holds any portent for their 2007 season. Liriano's out for the year, recovering from Tommy John surgery; Radke's out forever. Although some of the basic elements for the team's success in 2006 are in place—the pen, the quartet of offensive stars, Jonah Santana—the rotation will almost certainly be filled out with last year's expediencies. Full years from some combination of Bonser, Baker, Garza, and Glen Perkins will almost certainly deliver uneven results as the Twins sort out which of them will stick behind Santana and Liriano in 2008.

Perhaps that explains why it might seem that Ryan may again prove willing to settle rather than aggressively try to improve upon players such as Punto, Tyner, or Rondell White. To no small extent, the club's immediate future is dependent on what they'll get out of the rotation, and expecting to coast to another 96-win season on the arms of three pitchers experiencing their first full seasons in the Show would be overly optimistic. Ideally, two of that group of starters will step forward. Ideally, Kubel will finally be ready to play almost every day.

The talent involved is worth betting on, but the frustration for Twins fans might be that this year's step back might prefigure further disappointments. That would be unfair as well as premature—it's a year of reloading, not settling (as 2005 was). If that means that the Twins might not be able to defend their division title as aggressively as some might like, it also means that what they learn about their prospects will prepare them that much more for a run at the whole thing come 2008. In the meantime, they'll make things difficult for the White Sox, Tigers, and Indians, and, if none of them is a 95-win team, perhaps even pull off another come-from-behind surprise.

HITTERS

Jason Bartlett SS Bats: R Throws: R Height: 6' 0" Weight: 180 Born: October 30, 1979 Age: 27

YEAR	TEAM	LVL	AGE	PA	R	2B	3B	HR	RBI	BB	SO	SB	CS	SPEED	AVG	OBP	SLG	MLVR	EQAVG	EQOBP	EQSLG	EQA	VORP	DEFENSE	
2004	ROC	AAA	24	313	54	15	7	3	29	33	37	7	3	6.9	.331	.415	.472	.236	.308	.386	.436	.288	25.5	65-SS	6
2005	ROC	AAA	25	269	41	10	2	5	33	29	34	2	2	4.4	.332	.405	.459	.205	.309	.379	.429	.284	20.8	60-SS	3
2005	MIN	MLB	25	252	33	10	1	3	16	21	37	4	0	5.3	.241	.316	.335	-.163	.240	.324	.335	.240	1.6	65-SS	11
2006	ROC	AAA	26	250	42	23	3	1	20	10	28	6	3	7.1	.306	.336	.443	.116	.294	.321	.434	.260	12.4	57-SS	0
2006	MIN	MLB	26	372	44	18	2	2	32	22	46	10	5	5.6	.306	.364	.390	.005	.306	.369	.391	.270	16.2	99-SS	1
2007	MIN	MLB	27	486	65	25	4	7	47	36	62	10	4	6.1	.285	.344	.408	-.025	.278	.343	.408	.269	18.9	115-SS	5

Breakout: 14% Improve: 42% Collapse: 28% Attrition: 9% Comparables: Edgar Renteria, Jerry Coleman, Joey Amalfitano, Dave Concepcion

See what happens when you give a guy a chance? Just one of many who played a huge role in Minnesota's second-half surge, Bartlett could have been helping the team all along if the Twins weren't bigger skeptics than Penn and Teller when it comes to their own young players. Until mid-June, the Twins kept Bartlett at the urgent task of proving that he could hit Triple-A pitching for the third straight season. Like Lewis Carroll's White Queen, apparently the Twins can believe as many as six impossible things before breakfast—among them that Juan Castro's ten seasons weren't sufficient evidence that he was a thoroughly miserable player. Bartlett's not really a .309 hitter in the big leagues, but he's a capable fielder and a better bat than the Castros of the world, and that's all that really matters.

Alexi Casilla 2B/SS Bats: S Throws: R Height: 5' 9" Weight: 160 Born: July 20, 1984 Age: 22

YEAR	TEAM	LVL	AGE	PA	R	2B	3B	HR	RBI	BB	SO	SB	CS	SPEED	AVG	OBP	SLG	MLVR	EQAVG	EQOBP	EQSLG	EQA	VORP	DEFENSE			
2005	CDR	A	20	347	62	11	3	3	17	29	31	47	12	8.0	.325	.392	.409	.172	.285	.336	.361	.255	9.3	41-SS	-2	35-2B	-1
2005	ARK	AA	20	21	4	0	0	0	4	2	3	1	1	6.2	.211	.286	.211	-.398	.158	.238	.158	.174	-3.1				
2005	SLC	AAA	20	46	3	0	0	0	1	3	6	1	1	3.2	.256	.310	.256	-.403	.220	.273	.220	.190	-3.4	10-2B	0		
2006	FTM	A+	21	359	56	12	6	0	33	30	36	31	6	7.4	.331	.390	.406	.206	.315	.366	.397	.274	20.1	43-2B	0	36-SS	-2
2006	NBR	AA	21	199	28	10	1	1	13	18	20	19	4	7.6	.294	.375	.382	.108	.284	.354	.375	.266	8.1	45-SS	5		
2007	MIN	MLB	22	556	84	27	5	3	42	37	56	36	11	7.4	.304	.355	.393	-.011	.296	.353	.394	.273	24.2	131-SS	3		

Breakout: 33% Improve: 61% Collapse: 16% Attrition: 1% Comparables: Alejandro Machado, Rafael Furcal, Ramon Santiago, Ruddy Yan

Who wants to be the next Luis Castillo? No, it's not the latest reality show on Fox, but if it was, here's your favorite to win the big prize. Casilla is a small, switch-hitting speedster, and he understands his strengths—making contact, legging out hits, and stealing second base when the opportunity presents itself. The one big difference between Castillo and Casilla is that the latter can play both middle infield positions. Bonus!

Luis Castillo 2B Bats: S Throws: R Height: 5' 11" Weight: 190 Born: September 12, 1975 Age: 31

YEAR	TEAM	LVL	AGE	PA	R	2B	3B	HR	RBI	BB	SO	SB	CS	SPEED	AVG	OBP	SLG	MLVR	EQAVG	EQOBP	EQSLG	EQA	VORP	DEFENSE	
2004	FLO	MLB	28	649	91	12	7	2	47	75	68	21	4	6.8	.291	.373	.348	.011	.296	.377	.352	.269	25.4	144-2B	6
2005	FLO	MLB	29	524	72	12	4	4	30	65	32	10	7	5.7	.301	.391	.374	.081	.312	.404	.391	.282	21.4	114-2B	7
2006	MIN	MLB	30	652	84	22	6	3	49	56	58	25	11	6.7	.296	.358	.370	-.042	.295	.364	.368	.261	21.2	140-2B	-7
2007	MIN	MLB	31	611	94	19	3	4	43	61	54	20	7	6.5	.301	.372	.373	-.011	.293	.370	.373	.273	20.8	143-2B	4

Breakout: 23% Improve: 46% Collapse: 18% Attrition: 6% Comparables: Maury Wills, Bip Roberts, Steve Sax, Mark McLemore

Give Castillo this much—he's remarkably consistent, putting up EqAs between .266 and .282 in each of the last five seasons. That said, the .266 mark came last year, and plenty of trends are headed downwards. Castillo has clearly lost a step or two, ankle and knee problems having worn away at this speed. He's no longer a huge threat on the basepaths, and while he's a dependable gloveman, his range is slipping as well. PECOTA thinks there's more good stuff to come with the bat, but, with players such as Castillo, the line between being an offensive positive and being something less than that is exceedingly thin.

Mike Cuddyer RF **Bats: R** **Throws: R** Height: 6′ 2″ Weight: 220 Born: March 27, 1979 Age: 28

YEAR	TEAM	LVL	AGE	PA	R	2B	3B	HR	RBI	BB	SO	SB	CS	SPEED	AVG	OBP	SLG	MLVR	EQAVG	EQOBP	EQSLG	EQA	VORP	DEFENSE			
2004	MIN	MLB	25	382	49	22	1	12	45	37	74	5	5	4.3	.263	.339	.440	.003	.258	.339	.436	.264	8.8	33-3B	-5	31-2B	4
2005	MIN	MLB	26	470	55	25	3	12	42	41	93	3	4	3.9	.263	.330	.422	-.004	.265	.343	.439	.267	8.1	90-3B	-8	18-RF	0
2006	MIN	MLB	27	635	102	41	5	24	109	62	130	6	0	6.1	.284	.362	.504	.144	.279	.365	.506	.296	36.3	138-RF	-8		
2007	MIN	MLB	28	585	80	32	3	21	81	55	118	7	3	5.2	.272	.347	.465	.046	.265	.345	.466	.284	15.6	137-RF	-4		

Breakout: 5% Improve: 33% Collapse: 21% Attrition: 7% Comparables: Ivan Calderon, Ellis Burks, Marty Cordova, Jermaine Dye

Well, that certainly took a while. Cuddyer was the club's first-round pick in 1997, but he waited until 2006 to finally live up to expectations. Perhaps one key to his success was finally getting out of the infield, where he always struggled. The Twins certainly seemed to think so, because, when the Tony Batista experiment went sour, Gardenhire made sure that everybody knew that Cuddyer was *not* an option to fill the open slot at the hot corner. Cuddyer has finally arrived, and in his case "arrived" means "he's all here." Given his age, this is the start of him being what he is—not a star, but a very good player.

Lew Ford OF **Bats: R** **Throws: R** Height: 6′ 0″ Weight: 200 Born: August 12, 1976 Age: 30

YEAR	TEAM	LVL	AGE	PA	R	2B	3B	HR	RBI	BB	SO	SB	CS	SPEED	AVG	OBP	SLG	MLVR	EQAVG	EQOBP	EQSLG	EQA	VORP	DEFENSE			
2004	MIN	MLB	27	658	89	31	4	15	72	67	75	20	2	6.0	.299	.381	.446	.136	.295	.380	.445	.292	36.3	81-LF	-2	42-CF	-5
2005	MIN	MLB	28	590	70	30	4	7	53	45	85	13	6	6.0	.264	.338	.377	-.048	.268	.350	.388	.261	7.7	61-CF	-3	15-RF	-1
2006	MIN	MLB	29	255	40	6	1	4	18	16	43	9	1	6.4	.227	.287	.312	-.307	.220	.290	.302	.221	-11.1	36-LF	0	19-RF	6
2007	MIN	MLB	30	333	42	14	2	6	32	27	49	7	3	5.7	.266	.334	.382	-.090	.259	.333	.383	.259	0.5	80-LF	2		

Breakout: 10% Improve: 39% Collapse: 28% Attrition: 30% Comparables: Calvin Murray, Al Cowens, Raul Gonzalez, Jacob Brumfield

Splat. Ford has gone downhill in a big way since 2004, though his numbers last year where brought down when injuries elsewhere in the outfield forced him to play through a strained oblique. He's no more than an extra outfielder at this point, but he has enough skills to be better than this, and still of value to the Twins.

Torii Hunter CF **Bats: R** **Throws: R** Height: 6′ 2″ Weight: 215 Born: July 18, 1975 Age: 31

YEAR	TEAM	LVL	AGE	PA	R	2B	3B	HR	RBI	BB	SO	SB	CS	SPEED	AVG	OBP	SLG	MLVR	EQAVG	EQOBP	EQSLG	EQA	VORP	DEFENSE	
2004	MIN	MLB	28	569	79	37	0	23	81	40	101	21	7	5.4	.271	.330	.475	.039	.267	.330	.474	.274	23.4	115-CF	2
2005	MIN	MLB	29	416	63	24	1	14	56	34	65	23	7	6.8	.269	.337	.452	.055	.273	.349	.467	.281	19.4	90-CF	1
2006	MIN	MLB	30	611	86	21	2	31	98	45	108	12	6	5.1	.278	.336	.490	.073	.276	.342	.497	.281	32.6	139-CF	2
2007	MIN	MLB	31	537	75	28	2	20	77	40	93	15	5	5.4	.280	.338	.470	.045	.272	.337	.471	.283	22.1	126-CF	-2

Breakout: 11% Improve: 38% Collapse: 31% Attrition: 9% Comparables: Glenallen Hill, Gary Ward, Emil Brown, Brian Jordan

The Twins picked up Hunter's 2007 option for $12 million, and, between the explosion of free agent compensation and the absence of a replacement in the system who could come even close to replacing him, it was a good move. Hunter established a career high in home runs last year, and is still a good center fielder, though a bit overrated. He's also been around long enough to provide leadership in a very young lineup. If Hunter has another good year, it will almost certainly mark the end of his Minnesota tenure, because he will have finally priced himself out of the Twins' budget.

Garrett Jones 1B **Bats: L** **Throws: L** Height: 6′ 4″ Weight: 245 Born: June 21, 1981 Age: 26

YEAR	TEAM	LVL	AGE	PA	R	2B	3B	HR	RBI	BB	SO	SB	CS	SPEED	AVG	OBP	SLG	MLVR	EQAVG	EQOBP	EQSLG	EQA	VORP	DEFENSE			
2004	FTM	A+	23	70	6	5	0	1	6	4	19	2	0	4.4	.242	.286	.364	-.066	.224	.257	.328	.203	-5.6	19-1B	-1		
2004	NBR	AA	23	493	68	33	2	30	92	28	98	11	4	5.0	.311	.356	.593	.346	.293	.331	.547	.290	34.1	120-1B	-1		
2005	ROC	AAA	24	527	71	22	2	24	72	36	109	5	1	4.9	.244	.297	.445	-.071	.225	.279	.405	.234	-16.5	120-1B	-2		
2006	ROC	AAA	25	582	72	32	3	21	92	49	121	3	4	4.9	.238	.302	.430	-.003	.224	.286	.414	.239	-14.2	119-1B	8	20-RF	-3
2007	MIN	MLB	26	455	47	22	1	15	63	31	99	2	1	4.6	.241	.295	.409	-.142	.235	.294	.409	.246	-8.5	108-1B	2		

Breakout: 22% Improve: 51% Collapse: 23% Attrition: 10% Comparables: Brooks Kieschnick, Kevin Witt, Jason Cooper, Derek Michaelis

Jones is a massive individual with an equally massive swing. He can hit the ball a mile when he gets a hold of one, but he doesn't get hold of one often enough. His kind of left-handed power is hard to come by, so he could get some cups of coffee before all is said and done.

Jason Kubel

LF   **Bats: L**   **Throws: R**   Height: 5' 11"   Weight: 200   Born: May 25, 1982   Age: 25

YEAR	TEAM	LVL	AGE	PA	R	2B	3B	HR	RBI	BB	SO	SB	CS	SPEED	AVG	OBP	SLG	MLVR	EQAVG	EQOBP	EQSLG	EQA	VORP	DEFENSE	
2004	NBR	AA	22	159	25	14	4	6	29	19	19	0	2	4.8	.377	.453	.667	.656	.355	.425	.617	.336	25.3	35-RF	-1
2004	ROC	AAA	22	390	71	28	0	16	71	34	40	16	3	6.3	.343	.398	.560	.343	.310	.367	.511	.298	26.0	75-RF	6 10-LF 1
2004	MIN	MLB	22	67	10	2	0	2	7	6	9	1	1	5.0	.300	.358	.433	.246	.305	.373	.441	.281	3.9		
2006	ROC	AAA	24	134	18	7	2	4	22	12	23	2	0	5.1	.283	.343	.475	.150	.275	.336	.483	.280	4.5	22-RF	-3
2006	MIN	MLB	24	235	23	8	0	8	26	12	45	2	0	3.2	.241	.279	.386	-.207	.235	.280	.387	.232	-6.0	23-LF	-5
2007	*MIN*	*MLB*	*25*	*405*	*55*	*21*	*2*	*13*	*56*	*32*	*62*	*6*	*2*	*5.1*	*.287*	*.344*	*.465*	*.053*	*.279*	*.343*	*.465*	*.283*	*13.7*	*97-DH*	

Breakout: 24% Improve: 54% Collapse: 13% Attrition: 16%   *Comparables: Terry Whitfield, Leron Lee, Bruce Bochte, Todd Hollandsworth*

In 2004, Kubel tore through the Twins system and looked to be an early favorite for Rookie of the Year honors in 2005. Then he destroyed his left knee in a freak collision early in the Arizona Fall League season; this was not your standard miss-the-season injury, doctors described it as the kind of damage you normally see in car accidents. The knee continued to bother him in 2006, and then the right one flared up, requiring minor surgery for a torn meniscus after the season ended. PECOTA thinks he can bounce back, and the Twins do as well.

Erik Lis

1B   **Bats: L**   **Throws: L**   Height: 6' 1"   Weight: 220   Born: March 8, 1984   Age: 23

YEAR	TEAM	LVL	AGE	PA	R	2B	3B	HR	RBI	BB	SO	SB	CS	SPEED	AVG	OBP	SLG	MLVR	EQAVG	EQOBP	EQSLG	EQA	VORP	DEFENSE	
2005	ELZ	Rk	21	180	29	12	1	10	41	9	35	0	0	3.2	.315	.356	.577	.335	.249	.276	.399	.229	-11.7	38-1B	0
2006	BLT	A	22	465	69	37	3	16	70	51	83	4	3	4.7	.326	.402	.547	.399	.286	.345	.477	.277	20.9	74-1B	-13 12-LF -2
2007	*MIN*	*MLB*	*23*	*512*	*59*	*33*	*2*	*14*	*67*	*36*	*105*	*2*	*2*	*4.6*	*.274*	*.328*	*.441*	*-.017*	*.266*	*.326*	*.442*	*.268*	*5.2*	*121-1B*	*-5*

Breakout: 26% Improve: 52% Collapse: 18% Attrition: 4%   *Comparables: Jay Gibbons, Kevin Barker, Aaron Rifkin, Larry Broadway*

Here's a difficult one. Lis led the Midwest League in all three triple-crown rate stats in 2006, but he's not considered much of a prospect. Lis was also 22 last year, so he was old for a Low-A league. His bat is really his only tool, as he's not even a good enough athlete to be a decent first baseman. You know those chocolates that look really good out of the box, but when you bite into then you realize that they're filled with some sort of disgusting unidentifiable Technicolor cream? They make better photographs than food. Lis is kind of like that.

Joe Mauer

C   **Bats: L**   **Throws: R**   Height: 6' 4"   Weight: 220   Born: April 19, 1983   Age: 24

YEAR	TEAM	LVL	AGE	PA	R	2B	3B	HR	RBI	BB	SO	SB	CS	SPEED	AVG	OBP	SLG	MLVR	EQAVG	EQOBP	EQSLG	EQA	VORP	DEFENSE	
2004	MIN	MLB	21	122	18	8	1	6	17	11	14	1	0	5.4	.308	.369	.570	.273	.302	.369	.557	.309	12.6	27-C	3
2005	MIN	MLB	22	554	61	26	2	9	55	61	64	13	1	5.7	.294	.372	.411	.080	.295	.383	.418	.286	34.7	111-C	11
2006	MIN	MLB	23	608	86	36	4	13	84	79	54	8	3	5.0	.347	.429	.507	.325	.342	.433	.510	.324	66.9	119-C	9
2007	*MIN*	*MLB*	*24*	*638*	*110*	*39*	*3*	*17*	*82*	*75*	*61*	*12*	*3*	*5.3*	*.329*	*.410*	*.502*	*.248*	*.320*	*.408*	*.503*	*.320*	*60.0*	*149-C*	*7*

Breakout: 23% Improve: 55% Collapse: 16% Attrition: 0%   *Comparables: Carlos May, B. J. Surhoff, Thurman Munson, Kent Hrbek*

Mauer is the best position player on the Twins, and one of the best in all of baseball. The scary thing is that he's probably only going to get better from here: the 36 doubles and 13 home runs he hit last year are going to slowly morph into something more like 25/25 over the next few years, and that batting average is anything but a fluke. Oh yeah, and we haven't even mentioned how good he is defensively. We're guessing all that talk about the Twins making a mistake by taking the hometown boy over Mark Prior with the first pick of the 2001 draft has calmed down a bit.

Justin Morneau

1B   **Bats: L**   **Throws: R**   Height: 6' 4"   Weight: 225   Born: May 15, 1981   Age: 26

YEAR	TEAM	LVL	AGE	PA	R	2B	3B	HR	RBI	BB	SO	SB	CS	SPEED	AVG	OBP	SLG	MLVR	EQAVG	EQOBP	EQSLG	EQA	VORP	DEFENSE	
2004	ROC	AAA	23	326	51	23	0	22	63	32	47	1	1	3.6	.306	.377	.615	.343	.276	.347	.555	.296	22.6	68-1B	4
2004	MIN	MLB	23	312	39	17	0	19	58	28	54	0	0	3.7	.271	.340	.536	.135	.266	.340	.536	.290	15.7	56-1B	2
2005	MIN	MLB	24	543	62	23	4	22	79	44	94	0	2	3.9	.239	.304	.437	-.047	.239	.313	.448	.259	0.2	129-1B	-7
2006	MIN	MLB	25	661	97	37	1	34	130	53	93	3	3	4.3	.321	.375	.559	.283	.316	.378	.566	.311	52.0	152-1B	6
2007	*MIN*	*MLB*	*26*	*621*	*88*	*34*	*2*	*30*	*105*	*58*	*95*	*2*	*1*	*4.3*	*.292*	*.361*	*.524*	*.163*	*.284*	*.359*	*.524*	*.302*	*30.7*	*145-1B*	*2*

Breakout: 18% Improve: 44% Collapse: 22% Attrition: 5%   *Comparables: Kent Hrbek, Greg Walker, Ryan Klesko, Wally Joyner*

Look, it's not his fault the voters got it wrong. He definitely had a fantastic season, so don't let your anger over somebody else's opinion of him erode that fact that he's still pretty damn good. One disturbing thing: his PECOTA comps have a scary number of big, Stiffly Stifferson first basemen who stopped hitting in their early thirties. The good news is that Morneau is at least one big free agent contract away from reaching the point where that's a concern, and he has a good chance of putting up the kind of numbers over the next five years that will keep him in the picture for a more legitimate MVP award.

Matt Moses 3B Bats: L Throws: R Height: 6'' 0'' Weight: 210 Born: February 20, 1985 Age: 22

YEAR	TEAM	LVL	AGE	PA	R	2B	3B	HR	RBI	BB	SO	SB	CS	SPEED	AVG	OBP	SLG	MLVR	EQAVG	EQOBP	EQSLG	EQA	VORP	DEFENSE	
2004	QUD	A	19	125	16	7	0	3	14	12	25	0	0	3.6	.223	.304	.366	-.060	.191	.256	.304	.197	-8.1	13-3B	-3
2005	FTM	A+	20	298	37	16	1	7	42	28	59	13	4	4.9	.306	.376	.453	.213	.284	.342	.424	.267	15.8	57-3B	3
2005	NBR	AA	20	204	25	9	1	6	30	14	51	3	2	5.2	.210	.275	.366	-.148	.197	.255	.330	.207	-10.5	47-3B	4
2006	NBR	AA	21	516	47	16	2	15	72	35	113	2	2	4.1	.249	.303	.386	-.025	.240	.289	.380	.231	-3.2	101-3B	3
2007	MIN	MLB	22	498	50	24	2	12	59	32	105	4	2	4.6	.251	.303	.392	-.144	.244	.302	.392	.244	-1.8	118-3B	2

Breakout: 50% Improve: 72% Collapse: 12% Attrition: 4%   Comparables: Scott Hodges, Brad Nelson, Ivanon Coffie, Pete LaForest

Many of the Twins' top hitting prospects had disappointing seasons, and Moses leads that particular pack. Always in possession of one of the prettiest swings, Moses used to have excuses revolving around injuries or being rushed, but he was healthy the whole year, belonged in Double-A in his third full season, and he failed all the same. As long as we're hitting a guy when he's down, he's not a really good third baseman either.

Phil Nevin 1B/OF Bats: R Throws: R Height: 6' 3'' Weight: 220 Born: January 19, 1971 Age: 36

YEAR	TEAM	LVL	AGE	PA	R	2B	3B	HR	RBI	BB	SO	SB	CS	SPEED	AVG	OBP	SLG	MLVR	EQAVG	EQOBP	EQSLG	EQA	VORP	DEFENSE	
2004	SDN	MLB	33	623	78	31	1	26	105	66	121	0	0	3.7	.289	.368	.492	.206	.298	.375	.510	.300	36.8	128-1B	5
2005	SDN	MLB	34	306	31	11	1	9	47	19	67	1	0	4.9	.256	.301	.399	-.047	.265	.310	.416	.252	-0.4	68-1B	-1
2005	TEX	MLB	34	108	15	5	0	3	8	8	30	2	0	4.7	.182	.250	.323	-.342	.173	.257	.306	.206	-5.4		
2006	TEX	MLB	35	199	26	8	0	9	31	21	39	0	0	3.4	.216	.307	.415	-.141	.207	.307	.414	.248	-2.2		
2006	CHN	MLB	35	197	26	4	0	12	33	17	52	0	0	4.0	.274	.335	.497	.097	.270	.335	.494	.279	6.5	32-1B	3
2006	MIN	MLB	35	54	2	1	0	1	4	10	15	0	0	3.9	.190	.340	.286	-.245	.171	.340	.268	.236	-2.0		
2007	MIN	MLB	36	381	41	16	1	13	51	35	88	1	1	4.1	.242	.315	.409	-.107	.236	.313	.410	.255	-1.4	91-1B	-2

Breakout: 12% Improve: 28% Collapse: 38% Attrition: 39%   Comparables: Deron Johnson, Joe Adcock, Gil Hodges, Joe Torre

It's been a strange career for Nevin. Picked first overall in the 1992 draft by the Astros, Nevin began his career in Triple-A, was a bit overmatched, and just never did much to excite anyone. He went to the Tigers and Angels in minor deals, was even converted to catcher for a while, but didn't come around until he landed in San Diego, where, for whatever reason, everything worked out and at the age of 28 he was suddenly a very good player. It didn't last very long. In 2006 he played the role of power-hitting journeyman bench player. After slugging 22 home runs in 397 at-bats, someone somewhere will be interested in obtaining similar services this year.

Trent Oeltjen RF Bats: L Throws: L Height: 6' 1'' Weight: 190 Born: February 28, 1983 Age: 24

YEAR	TEAM	LVL	AGE	PA	R	2B	3B	HR	RBI	BB	SO	SB	CS	SPEED	AVG	OBP	SLG	MLVR	EQAVG	EQOBP	EQSLG	EQA	VORP	DEFENSE			
2004	FTM	A+	21	360	45	8	5	2	28	18	61	25	8	7.4	.278	.337	.352	.020	.269	.310	.349	.238	-4.0	55-CF	-6	13-RF	0
2005	FTM	A+	22	395	44	17	4	4	43	26	77	21	9	5.9	.287	.369	.396	.113	.270	.330	.372	.250	-6.8	77-LF	-1		
2006	NBR	AA	23	464	61	16	10	3	44	36	58	23	11	7.3	.299	.378	.411	.153	.290	.355	.408	.268	8.1	60-RF	4	30-LF	-4
2007	MIN	MLB	24	492	65	23	6	6	44	28	75	19	7	6.8	.282	.332	.395	-.066	.274	.330	.396	.261	2.0	116-RF	0		

Breakout: 16% Improve: 54% Collapse: 20% Attrition: 13%   Comparables: David Miller, Chris Duffy, Nathan Haynes, Josh Anderson

Oeltjen is an Australian outfielder with big league bench potential. He runs well, makes good contact, and he can play all three outfield positions, but he lacks the power or patience for everyday play. As career prospects go, it might not beat alligator wrestling, but no worries.

Trevor Plouffe SS Bats: R Throws: R Height: 6' 1'' Weight: 175 Born: June 15, 1986 Age: 21

YEAR	TEAM	LVL	AGE	PA	R	2B	3B	HR	RBI	BB	SO	SB	CS	SPEED	AVG	OBP	SLG	MLVR	EQAVG	EQOBP	EQSLG	EQA	VORP	DEFENSE			
2004	ELZ	Rk	18	264	29	7	2	4	28	19	34	3	1	4.3	.283	.340	.380	.046	.234	.267	.286	.200	-27.2	50-SS	0		
2005	BLT	A	19	532	58	18	0	13	60	50	78	8	4	3.4	.223	.300	.345	-.132	.186	.246	.275	.192	-37.2	123-SS	-12		
2006	FTM	A+	20	524	60	26	4	4	45	58	93	8	5	4.9	.246	.333	.347	-.013	.238	.310	.340	.232	-2.3	93-SS	0	23-3B	-1
2007	MIN	MLB	21	487	44	22	1	7	43	33	83	4	2	4.9	.236	.292	.340	-.243	.230	.291	.340	.224	-6.3	115-SS	0		

Breakout: 48% Improve: 71% Collapse: 19% Attrition: 8%   Comparables: Luis Montanez, Jayson Nix, Tomas de la Rosa, Tripper Johnson

A first-round pick in 2004, Plouffe has had two eerily similar seasons over the past two years. He's very good defensively, with nice range to both sides and a plus arm, but, if he can't hit better than he has, it just doesn't matter. Plouffe hits the occasional home run and draws a decent number of walks, so, in another era, he could have been the next Dick Schofield. Unfortunately, this is not that era. In certain advanced cooking circles, "Plouffe" is the sound a soufflé makes when it falls, and it is considered very bad luck even to say the word.

Nick Punto INF **Bats: S** **Throws: R** Height: 5′ 9″ Weight: 185 Born: November 8, 1977 Age: 29

YEAR	TEAM	LVL	AGE	PA	R	2B	3B	HR	RBI	BB	SO	SB	CS	SPEED	AVG	OBP	SLG	MLVR	EQAVG	EQOBP	EQSLG	EQA	VORP	DEFENSE			
2004	MIN	MLB	26	103	17	0	0	2	12	12	19	6	0	5.4	.253	.340	.319	-.163	.244	.340	.322	.252	2.0	12-2B	1		
2005	MIN	MLB	27	439	45	18	4	4	26	36	86	13	8	5.8	.239	.301	.335	-.196	.240	.313	.346	.234	-7.1	63-2B	2	27-SS	2
2006	MIN	MLB	28	524	73	21	7	1	45	47	68	17	5	7.0	.290	.352	.373	-.055	.288	.359	.372	.264	9.1	86-3B	0	17-SS	0
2007	MIN	MLB	29	505	69	23	4	5	41	50	73	18	7	6.5	.270	.344	.372	-.084	.262	.342	.372	.261	7.9	119-3B	0		

Breakout: 27% Improve: 59% Collapse: 20% Attrition: 13% Comparables: Bump Wills, Len Randle, Julio Cruz, Quilvio Veras

Punto entered the year as a utility player, but became the everyday third baseman when the Twins cut bait on Tony Batista. He did yeoman's work there, playing good defense, slapping ground balls through the holes, and reaching base at a decent clip. He has no power, a troubling platoon split that leaves him only marginally effective against righties, and a track record that argues that his 2006 performance, just okay at best, isn't sustainable. He'll keep his starting job to begin 2007, but the Twins brought in Jeff Cirillo as a backup plan just in case.

Josh Rabe LF **Bats: R** **Throws: R** Height: 6′ 3″ Weight: 215 Born: October 15, 1978 Age: 28

YEAR	TEAM	LVL	AGE	PA	R	2B	3B	HR	RBI	BB	SO	SB	CS	SPEED	AVG	OBP	SLG	MLVR	EQAVG	EQOBP	EQSLG	EQA	VORP	DEFENSE			
2004	ROC	AAA	25	481	54	27	0	7	45	40	76	26	5	6.3	.263	.333	.375	-.090	.233	.300	.329	.232	-25.6	60-LF	-8	34-CF	-5
2005	ROC	AAA	26	321	50	17	0	11	49	29	57	5	2	5.3	.239	.313	.414	-.086	.208	.278	.349	.222	-20.3	47-LF	-6	14-CF	-2
2006	ROC	AAA	27	398	51	20	1	6	47	35	37	7	4	5.2	.299	.362	.411	.106	.279	.337	.393	.256	-1.1	82-LF	-2	11-RF	1
2006	MIN	MLB	27	51	8	1	0	3	7	2	11	0	1	3.5	.286	.314	.490	.039	.286	.327	.490	.267	0.9				
2007	MIN	MLB	28	415	41	18	1	8	43	27	63	6	2	4.8	.244	.296	.359	-.206	.237	.295	.359	.233	-11.3	99-LF	-2		

Breakout: 22% Improve: 38% Collapse: 30% Attrition: 13% Comparables: Emil Brown, Virgil Chevalier, John Gall, Chad Mottola

Rabe was spending his fourth season at Triple-A Rochester, doing what he does best—hit line drives, run a little, and act as an expert guide for the rare Rochester tourist—when the injury bug hit Minnesota, giving Rabe his first taste of the big leagues. It's always fun to root for the guys who keep at it and finally achieve their dream, but Rabe will more than likely return to Triple-A this April, waiting for another invitation to the land of nice planes and big per diems.

Mike Redmond C **Bats: R** **Throws: R** Height: 5′ 11″ Weight: 200 Born: May 5, 1971 Age: 36

YEAR	TEAM	LVL	AGE	PA	R	2B	3B	HR	RBI	BB	SO	SB	CS	SPEED	AVG	OBP	SLG	MLVR	EQAVG	EQOBP	EQSLG	EQA	VORP	DEFENSE	
2004	FLO	MLB	33	273	19	15	0	2	25	14	28	1	0	3.6	.256	.315	.341	-.128	.258	.314	.339	.233	0.3	73-C	-6
2005	MIN	MLB	34	159	17	9	0	1	26	6	14	0	0	3.1	.311	.350	.392	.021	.315	.363	.404	.268	7.1	42-C	3
2006	MIN	MLB	35	191	20	13	0	0	23	4	19	0	0	3.5	.339	.363	.411	.065	.337	.368	.427	.277	9.4	43-C	5
2007	MIN	MLB	36	311	28	17	0	2	33	12	31	0	0	3.9	.290	.324	.372	-.106	.282	.322	.373	.248	3.9	75-C	1

Breakout: 7% Improve: 37% Collapse: 22% Attrition: 49% Comparables: Jerry Grote, Brian Harper, Don Slaught, Bob Scheffing

Good catchers are harder to find than single women at a comic book store. There are 30 major league starting jobs out there, but not 30 guys with enough talent to fill them. Given the paucity of viable candidates, it's surprising that Redmond has never gotten the opportunity to start four or five times a week. Not that he'd be Johnny Bench or anything, but he's a solid defender who has hit .300 or higher as a backup in six of the last nine years. The Twins were smart enough to realize what a nice thing that had in Redmond and lock him up for two more years with an option for 2009, giving them, by far, the best catching corps in baseball.

Luis Rodriguez INF Bats: S Throws: R Height: 5′ 9″ Weight: 190 Born: June 27, 1980 Age: 27

YEAR	TEAM	LVL	AGE	PA	R	2B	3B	HR	RBI	BB	SO	SB	CS	SPEED	AVG	OBP	SLG	MLVR	EQAVG	EQOBP	EQSLG	EQA	VORP	DEFENSE			
2004	ROC	AAA	24	565	73	33	1	5	52	53	49	3	3	4.3	.286	.353	.389	-.019	.259	.327	.345	.241	1.4	110-2B	-9		
2005	ROC	AAA	25	157	19	10	0	1	17	16	14	0	1	2.9	.304	.381	.399	.060	.271	.346	.343	.243	2.2	25-2B	2		
2005	MIN	MLB	25	203	21	10	2	2	20	18	23	2	2	5.2	.269	.335	.383	-.060	.273	.350	.390	.259	2.1	24-2B	2	22-3B	-2
2006	MIN	MLB	26	132	11	4	0	2	6	14	16	0	0	3.1	.235	.315	.322	-.231	.230	.323	.310	.232	-3.3	21-3B	2		
2007	MIN	MLB	27	259	28	13	1	3	25	24	28	1	1	4.5	.273	.341	.379	-.077	.265	.340	.380	.259	4.4	64-2B	0		

Breakout: 31% Improve: 70% Collapse: 13% Attrition: 38% Comparables: Bryan Little, Bobby Hill, Mark Lemke, Felipe Crespo

Rodriguez has spent much of the last two years as the Twins' secondary utility player, backing up all over the infield. While the versatility is nice, the ability to coax of few walks here and there his only real skill. The Twins like versatility and they like stability, so while Rodriguez went non-tendered at the end of the year, the Twins quickly signed him to a non-guaranteed deal.

Alex Romero OF Bats: L Throws: R Height: 6′ 0″ Weight: 190 Born: September 9, 1983 Age: 23

YEAR	TEAM	LVL	AGE	PA	R	2B	3B	HR	RBI	BB	SO	SB	CS	SPEED	AVG	OBP	SLG	MLVR	EQAVG	EQOBP	EQSLG	EQA	VORP	DEFENSE			
2004	FTM	A+	20	447	59	21	2	6	42	54	47	6	4	4.7	.292	.387	.405	.175	.276	.351	.390	.261	2.7	67-RF	5	13-CF	2
2005	NBR	AA	21	560	65	31	2	15	77	36	69	12	11	4.2	.301	.354	.458	.164	.285	.335	.437	.262	8.4	120-LF	7	12-CF	2
2006	NBR	AA	22	200	29	11	2	5	16	26	19	15	7	7.0	.281	.384	.461	.209	.273	.365	.465	.284	7.6	44-LF	-1		
2006	ROC	AAA	22	262	20	8	2	0	26	15	22	6	2	4.5	.250	.300	.301	-.167	.235	.283	.286	.211	-20.6	43-LF	2	22-RF	2
2007	MIN	MLB	23	449	55	24	2	7	47	34	49	10	5	5.0	.278	.336	.398	-.057	.270	.335	.398	.262	1.6	107-LF	2		

Breakout: 30% Improve: 63% Collapse: 16% Attrition: 10% Comparables: Rafael Alvarez, Roberto Vaz, Shane Costa, Terrmel Sledge

Everything seemed to be coming together for Romero after a solid year at Double-A in 2005, but it all went backward last year. He got off to a horrible start at Triple-A and was sent back to the Eastern League as much for his attitude as his poor play. He recovered a bit during the summer months and hit almost .300 after his return to Triple-A, but his gap power and patient approach disappeared. Romero could be a fourth outfielder in the majors, but it's not going to happen in 2007 without a return to his previous form.

Denard Span CF Bats: L Throws: L Height: 6′ 0″ Weight: 190 Born: February 27, 1984 Age: 23

YEAR	TEAM	LVL	AGE	PA	R	2B	3B	HR	RBI	BB	SO	SB	CS	SPEED	AVG	OBP	SLG	MLVR	EQAVG	EQOBP	EQSLG	EQA	VORP	DEFENSE	
2004	QUD	A	20	282	29	4	3	0	14	34	49	15	8	5.8	.267	.363	.308	-.013	.244	.319	.276	.221	-11.2	62-CF	-5
2005	FTM	A+	21	212	38	3	3	1	19	22	25	13	4	7.4	.339	.410	.403	.224	.316	.376	.384	.272	11.1	47-CF	-9
2005	NBR	AA	21	304	47	6	5	0	26	22	41	10	8	7.4	.285	.355	.345	.004	.270	.331	.325	.237	-2.6	65-CF	1
2006	NBR	AA	22	597	80	16	6	2	45	40	78	24	11	6.7	.285	.340	.349	.007	.272	.321	.338	.236	-5.2	128-CF	-3
2007	MIN	MLB	23	498	62	15	4	1	32	31	68	17	7	6.7	.279	.328	.338	-.151	.272	.327	.339	.243	-1.7	117-CF	-2

Breakout: 34% Improve: 59% Collapse: 13% Attrition: 8% Comparables: Joey Gathright, Jason Tyner, Brandon Watson, Alex Sanchez

Like Matt Moses and Trevor Plouffe, Span is a former first-round prep pick who has hit a wall. He's a career .287 hitter in the minors and a very good runner with outstanding range in center field, but he offers little in the way of power or on-base skills and has yet to figure out how to use his speed to steal bases. The Twins were hoping that Span could step in when Torii Hunter took off for greener pastures after the 2007 season, but it's looking less and less likely that Span will be up to the challenge.

Shannon Stewart LF Bats: R Throws: R Height: 5′ 11″ Weight: 210 Born: February 25, 1974 Age: 33

YEAR	TEAM	LVL	AGE	PA	R	2B	3B	HR	RBI	BB	SO	SB	CS	SPEED	AVG	OBP	SLG	MLVR	EQAVG	EQOBP	EQSLG	EQA	VORP	DEFENSE	
2004	MIN	MLB	30	430	46	17	2	11	47	47	44	6	3	4.7	.304	.380	.447	.112	.299	.380	.448	.288	16.4	63-LF	-8
2005	MIN	MLB	31	599	69	27	3	10	56	34	73	7	5	5.0	.274	.323	.388	-.052	.276	.334	.401	.256	1.7	123-LF	0
2006	MIN	MLB	32	190	21	5	1	2	21	14	19	3	1	4.5	.293	.347	.368	-.070	.291	.353	.366	.257	0.6	32-LF	-1
2007	MIN	MLB	33	387	45	16	2	6	40	29	45	4	2	5.0	.276	.332	.384	-.086	.268	.330	.384	.256	-0.6	92-LF	-4

Breakout: 8% Improve: 33% Collapse: 43% Attrition: 25% Comparables: Gary Ward, Brady Clark, Tommy Davis, Ken Berry

Stewart was limited to 44 games last year by a partially torn plantar fascia in his left foot, and he's looking for a deal in 2007 despite the fact that nobody, including Stewart, seems to be able to guarantee his health. From 1998 to 2004, Stewart was an underappreciated, dynamic talent, hitting .305/.371/.452 while doing a little bit of everything—hit for average, hit for power, run the bases, and show good patience. Oddly, he rarely did all of them at the same time. Those days are over thanks to injuries. Stewart never was a great outfielder, and the injuries have further diminished him in that regard, making him a problematic fourth outfielder. No doubt someone will give him a shot in the hopes of recapturing the past, but it's getting very near the end.

Terry Tiffee **3B** **Bats: S Throws: R** Height: 6' 3" Weight: 215 Born: April 21, 1979 Age: 28

YEAR	TEAM	LVL	AGE	PA	R	2B	3B	HR	RBI	BB	SO	SB	CS	SPEED	AVG	OBP	SLG	MLVR	EQAVG	EQOBP	EQSLG	EQA	VORP	DEFENSE	
2004	ROC	AAA	25	342	42	26	3	12	68	21	26	0	0	3.8	.307	.357	.522	.188	.277	.327	.462	.267	17.7	67-3B -11	
2004	MIN	MLB	25	48	7	4	0	2	8	3	3	0	0	4.3	.273	.333	.500	.120	.273	.333	.477	.273	2.3	10-3B -2	
2005	ROC	AAA	26	252	33	11	1	10	39	15	24	0	1	3.4	.266	.313	.454	-.011	.242	.289	.407	.238	1.2	44-3B -5	
2005	MIN	MLB	26	159	9	8	1	1	15	8	15	1	0	3.5	.207	.245	.293	-.368	.196	.245	.284	.192	-10.2	20-3B -2	
2006	ROC	AAA	27	331	37	20	0	4	38	20	50	1	0	4.3	.273	.314	.377	-.031	.243	.284	.340	.220	-7.9	59-3B -13	
2006	MIN	MLB	27	49	4	1	0	2	6	4	8	0	1	2.9	.244	.306	.400	-.132	.244	.320	.400	.243	-0.9		
2007	BAL	MLB	28	379	29	13	1	6	40	20	51	0	1	4.0	.223	.268	.319	-.323	.221	.271	.325	.207	-14.6	91-3B -7	

Breakout: 21% Improve: 32% Collapse: 52% Attrition: 20%   Comparables: Donny Leon, Andy Barkett, Brian Rios, Jose Leon

The Twins thought they had something when Tiffee was an Eastern League All-Star in 2003, but he's spent the last three seasons at Triple-A Rochester only filling in with the Twins here and there. His performance has degraded with each year, including a disturbing loss of power. Tiffee signed as a six-year free agent with the Orioles, where he'll likely spend the year at Triple-A Norfolk and fill in with the Orioles here and there. It will be just like before, except the owner speaks Greek now.

Steven Tolleson **2B** **Bats: R Throws: R** Height: 5' 10" Weight: 180 Born: November 1, 1983 Age: 23

YEAR	TEAM	LVL	AGE	PA	R	2B	3B	HR	RBI	BB	SO	SB	CS	SPEED	AVG	OBP	SLG	MLVR	EQAVG	EQOBP	EQSLG	EQA	VORP	DEFENSE	
2005	ELZ	Rk	21	73	18	6	1	2	8	11	4	2	1	6.1	.321	.457	.571	.466	.258	.343	.419	.261	6.8	12-SS -2	
2005	BLT	A	21	125	16	2	0	3	10	17	23	3	0	4.1	.176	.311	.284	-.213	.148	.246	.213	.181	-12.7	25-2B 0	
2006	BLT	A	22	204	23	8	2	2	16	27	34	7	9	5.2	.287	.390	.392	.154	.250	.328	.333	.235	-0.3	17-3B 1	16-2B -2
2006	FTM	A+	22	186	23	8	1	4	23	22	24	3	1	4.2	.268	.353	.408	.107	.259	.333	.414	.262	6.0	27-2B 2	
2007	MIN	MLB	23	450	46	21	2	7	43	36	72	5	3	4.9	.246	.312	.362	-.170	.239	.311	.362	.242	-1.0	107-2B 0	

Breakout: 40% Improve: 55% Collapse: 21% Attrition: 8%   Comparables: Brian Benefield, Vicente Garcia, Carlos Villalobos, Craig Stansberry

Wayne's kid is very similar to his father: He's a gritty little infielder who can play all over the infield, hit a bit, and draw some walks. Daddy turned it into a ten-year career with a couple of starting jobs here and there, and Steven has a decent shot at doing the same.

Jason Tyner **OF** **Bats: L Throws: L** Height: 6' 1" Weight: 175 Born: April 23, 1977 Age: 30

YEAR	TEAM	LVL	AGE	PA	R	2B	3B	HR	RBI	BB	SO	SB	CS	SPEED	AVG	OBP	SLG	MLVR	EQAVG	EQOBP	EQSLG	EQA	VORP	DEFENSE	
2004	RIC	AAA	27	269	40	12	1	1	16	15	22	18	6	7.2	.288	.346	.358	-.048	.267	.318	.328	.236	-10.9	39-LF 4	12-CF 0
2004	BUF	AAA	27	166	25	4	1	0	16	18	15	5	0	5.8	.345	.417	.388	.158	.322	.390	.357	.276	6.9	28-CF -5	
2005	ROC	AAA	28	591	81	18	2	1	36	48	57	18	6	5.9	.286	.351	.334	-.093	.256	.316	.293	.224	-18.2	93-CF -6	31-LF 2
2005	MIN	MLB	28	60	8	1	1	0	5	4	4	2	0	6.0	.321	.367	.375	.040	.327	.383	.382	.278	2.2	10-LF -1	
2006	ROC	AAA	29	352	52	14	5	0	22	25	39	8	2	6.7	.329	.379	.405	.148	.302	.349	.377	.258	9.5	77-CF -5	
2006	MIN	MLB	29	232	29	5	2	0	18	11	18	4	2	5.5	.312	.345	.353	-.079	.310	.349	.352	.249	1.2	32-LF 9	17-CF 0
2007	MIN	MLB	30	439	53	14	3	0	33	29	43	9	3	6.1	.281	.331	.337	-.147	.273	.330	.337	.243	-3.0	104-CF 2	

Breakout: 26% Improve: 55% Collapse: 26% Attrition: 26%   Comparables: Milt Thompson, Adrian Brown, Omar Ramirez, Dave Roberts

Tyner was having a fine season at Triple-A Rochester, but with Lew Ford, Shannon Stewart, and Rondell White all suffering through various injuries, the little speedster got another shot. His virtues shined through, the both of them—hitting for average and running. As the only Twin other than Hunter who can really play center, he'll likely break camp in the big leagues for the first time since 2002. His middle name is Renyt, which is Tyner backwards. His Earth-2 incarnation is named Nosaj Tyner Renyt. He's very, very slow, and is teammates with a pitcher named Foob.

Kevin West   OF   Bats: R   Throws: R   Height: 6' 2"   Weight: 225   Born: January 1, 1980   Age: 27

YEAR	TEAM	LVL	AGE	PA	R	2B	3B	HR	RBI	BB	SO	SB	CS	SPEED	AVG	OBP	SLG	MLVR	EQAVG	EQOBP	EQSLG	EQA	VORP	DEFENSE		
2004	NBR	AA	24	490	68	35	1	25	87	41	98	2	3	3.6	.293	.359	.551	.271	.265	.320	.483	.269	12.0	61-RF	-3	
2004	ROC	AAA	24	85	10	8	0	4	22	4	19	0	0	3.3	.278	.306	.532	.090	.241	.271	.456	.246	-0.0			
2005	ROC	AAA	25	485	60	26	1	20	64	45	94	2	2	3.1	.271	.355	.478	.093	.245	.322	.428	.258	-0.6	61-RF	6	23-LF 0
2006	ROC	AAA	26	289	34	9	1	11	41	20	69	0	2	3.7	.246	.318	.418	.011	.239	.302	.417	.245	-4.7	27-RF	-1	
2007	MIN	MLB	27	374	35	16	1	13	50	26	86	0	1	3.7	.236	.295	.399	-.159	.230	.294	.399	.243	-8.8	90-RF	0	

Breakout: 12%   Improve: 34%   Collapse: 36%   Attrition: 15%   Comparables: Ryan Ludwick, Marcus Thames, Mike Hessman, Jon Knott

West had established himself as a pretty decent minor league slugger, the kind that would have gotten a chance given the MASH unit that was the Twins outfield situation last year. Instead, he tore up his knee playing in Venezuela over the previous winter, wasn't available until June, and was a shell of himself when he returned. If he gets another chance, it will come elsewhere, as the Twins let him go as a minor league free agent at the end of the year.

Rondell White   DH   Bats: R   Throws: R   Height: 6' 1""   Weight: 225   Born: February 23, 1972   Age: 35

YEAR	TEAM	LVL	AGE	PA	R	2B	3B	HR	RBI	BB	SO	SB	CS	SPEED	AVG	OBP	SLG	MLVR	EQAVG	EQOBP	EQSLG	EQA	VORP	DEFENSE	
2004	DET	MLB	32	498	76	21	2	19	67	39	77	1	2	4.5	.270	.337	.453	.037	.276	.345	.471	.277	10.9	60-LF	-1
2005	DET	MLB	33	400	49	24	3	12	53	17	48	1	0	5.0	.313	.348	.489	.173	.321	.363	.514	.296	24.3	60-LF	-1
2006	MIN	MLB	34	355	32	17	1	7	38	11	54	1	1	3.6	.246	.276	.365	-.241	.240	.276	.362	.222	-13.1	32-LF	-2
2007	MIN	MLB	35	341	35	17	1	8	46	16	52	1	1	4.3	.265	.304	.405	-.115	.258	.302	.406	.248	-1.4	82-DH	

Breakout: 13%   Improve: 31%   Collapse: 38%   Attrition: 33%   Comparables: Wayne Nordhagen, Dante Bichette, Andy Pafko, Ted Kluszewski

White was one of worst hitters in the majors during the first half of last year, battling hamstring issues and hitting just .182/.209/.215 at the All-Star break. He didn't get healthy until the end of the year, but, when he did, he was pivotal in the team's September surge, slugging .538 after the break. It was enough to convince the team to bring him back in 2007. He still has value as a fourth outfielder/occasional starter if his legs hold up.

David Winfree   3B   Bats: R   Throws: R   Height: 6' 3"   Weight: 215   Born: August 5, 1985   Age: 21

YEAR	TEAM	LVL	AGE	PA	R	2B	3B	HR	RBI	BB	SO	SB	CS	SPEED	AVG	OBP	SLG	MLVR	EQAVG	EQOBP	EQSLG	EQA	VORP	DEFENSE		
2004	ELZ	Rk	18	241	31	8	0	8	37	18	51	1	1	3.3	.286	.349	.433	.137	.237	.274	.325	.210	-18.1	41-3B	-6	12-1B -2
2005	BLT	A	19	601	80	31	5	16	101	22	93	3	2	3.9	.294	.329	.452	.111	.260	.283	.398	.234	1.2	133-3B	-18	
2006	FTM	A+	20	287	43	13	2	13	48	19	59	2	0	4.8	.276	.328	.490	.185	.260	.306	.460	.260	11.1	27-3B	-2	17-1B -1
2007	MIN	MLB	21	446	44	22	1	13	58	21	89	1	1	4.4	.255	.295	.408	-.133	.248	.294	.408	.245	-2.0	106-3B	-7	

Breakout: 39%   Improve: 64%   Collapse: 15%   Attrition: 6%   Comparables: Joe Crede, Jeff Francoeur, Rolando Segura, Mike Morse

Winfree led the Midwest League in hits, total bases, and RBIs in 2005, but 2006 started off tough as a shoulder injury hampered him in spring training. Then things got just plain weird. Winfree spent a week in the Florida State League before walking away from the game for two and a half months while questioning his commitment. The good news is that, when he returned, he was as good as ever—a big third baseman with decent defensive skills who can really put a charge into the ball. He'll likely start the 2007 season in Double-A; the Twins hope he stays with the team this time, because the talent is there to succeed.

PITCHERS

Scott Baker
Bats: R Throws: R Height: 6' 4" Weight: 210 Born: September 19, 1981 Age: 25

YEAR	TEAM	LVL	AGE	W	L	SV	G	GS	IP	H	BB	SO	HR	GB%	BABIP	STUFF	WHIP	ERA	PERA	EQERA	EQH9	EQBB9	EQSO9	EQHR9	VORP	WXRL
2004	FTM	A+	22	4	2	0	7	7	45	40	6	37	1	—	.291	20	1.02	2.40	3.21	3.40	8.2	1.4	4.8	0.4	11.0	—
2004	NBR	AA	22	5	3	0	10	10	70¹	44	13	72	2	—	.225	39	0.81	2.43	3.11	3.34	6.2	1.8	6.7	0.4	17.6	—
2004	ROC	AAA	22	1	3	0	9	9	54¹	65	15	36	3	—	.339	9	1.47	4.97	4.12	5.07	10.3	2.6	4.6	0.5	3.2	—
2005	ROC	AAA	23	5	8	0	22	22	134²	123	26	107	15	36.6%	.280	13	1.11	3.01	4.38	3.52	8.2	1.9	5.5	1.1	31.3	—
2005	MIN	MLB	23	3	3	0	10	9	53²	48	14	32	5	34.7%	.265	13	1.16	3.35	3.91	3.62	7.9	2.3	5.3	0.8	13.5	1.66
2006	ROC	AAA	24	5	4	0	12	12	84¹	77	25	68	4	42.4%	.303	19	1.21	2.68	3.98	3.46	8.9	2.8	5.6	0.6	19.8	—
2006	MIN	MLB	24	5	8	0	16	16	83¹	114	16	62	17	34.8%	.355	-3	1.56	6.37	4.67	6.31	11.3	1.6	6.1	1.6	-7.1	0.10
2007	MIN	MLB	25	8	9	0	31	26	146¹	164	38	96	21	40.0%	.303	9	1.38	4.85	4.64	4.72	9.2	2.2	5.6	1.1	13.3	2.40

Breakout: 13% Improve: 46% Collapse: 16% Attrition: 1%   Comparables: Brett Tomko, Chad Ogea, Bob Heffner, Eric Rasmussen

This is not a case of how the mighty have fallen, but not so very long ago, Baker was one of the organization's top pitching prospects. He's now been passed by a pre-injury Fransisco Liriano, Boof Bonser, and Matt Garza, and there are more arms coming through the system that will slide by him soon enough. As the numbers show, Baker throws strikes, just too many of them; he doesn't have a strong enough repertoire to fool batters into chasing stuff outside the strike zone. The Twins were vocal in their frustration with Baker, and, despite some openings in the rotation, he's low on the totem pole as far as getting a chance to fill them.

Boof Bonser
Bats: R Throws: R Height: 6' 4" Weight: 260 Born: October 14, 1981 Age: 25

YEAR	TEAM	LVL	AGE	W	L	SV	G	GS	IP	H	BB	SO	HR	GB%	BABIP	STUFF	WHIP	ERA	PERA	EQERA	EQH9	EQBB9	EQSO9	EQHR9	VORP	WXRL
2004	NBR	AA	22	12	9	0	27	27	154¹	160	56	146	22	—	.317	-7	1.40	4.37	5.51	5.63	9.9	3.4	6.2	1.7	-0.5	—
2005	ROC	AAA	23	11	9	0	28	28	160¹	153	57	168	22	39.8%	.312	9	1.31	3.99	4.73	4.56	8.7	3.4	7.3	1.4	18.5	—
2006	ROC	AAA	24	6	4	0	14	14	86¹	68	35	83	4	38.3%	.272	24	1.20	2.82	4.05	3.83	7.8	3.9	6.8	0.6	16.7	—
2006	MIN	MLB	24	7	6	0	18	18	100¹	104	24	84	18	43.1%	.299	11	1.28	4.22	4.33	4.15	8.5	2.0	6.9	1.4	17.8	2.36
2007	MIN	MLB	25	9	10	0	33	28	158²	165	60	126	22	41.0%	.300	13	1.42	4.70	4.60	4.57	8.5	3.2	6.7	1.1	16.4	2.80

Breakout: 13% Improve: 39% Collapse: 23% Attrition: 4%   Comparables: Steve Renko, Ron Schueler, Tommy Greene, Ryan Rupe

Bonser was filling in here and there before taking over Liriano's rotation spot at the end of the year. He pitched well enough to start Game Two of the ALDS and has pretty much guaranteed a spot for himself in the rotation on Opening Day. He's a solid all-around pitcher—his fastball, curveball, changeup, and control are all pretty good—but he lacks that one swing-and-miss offering that would allow us to project him as a star. He also has some troubles with the long ball, but there's no reason he can't be a solid innings-eater for a long time. Last time we looked, those guys make $10 million a year, so it's nice work if you can get it.

Jesse Crain
Bats: R Throws: R Height: 6' 1" Weight: 205 Born: July 5, 1981 Age: 25

YEAR	TEAM	LVL	AGE	W	L	SV	G	GS	IP	H	BB	SO	HR	GB%	BABIP	STUFF	WHIP	ERA	PERA	EQERA	EQH9	EQBB9	EQSO9	EQHR9	VORP	WXRL
2004	ROC	AAA	23	3	2	19	41	0	50²	38	17	64	5	—	.277	19	1.08	2.49	3.83	3.58	7.0	3.2	8.8	1.1	11.3	—
2004	MIN	MLB	23	3	0	0	22	0	27	17	12	14	2	—	.194	-5	1.08	2.00	4.54	1.93	5.1	3.5	4.2	0.6	11.6	0.14
2005	MIN	MLB	24	12	5	1	75	0	79²	61	29	25	6	49.2%	.222	-16	1.13	2.71	5.02	3.24	7.0	3.2	2.8	0.7	23.1	3.83
2006	MIN	MLB	25	4	5	1	68	0	76²	79	18	60	6	57.0%	.309	14	1.27	3.52	3.36	3.40	8.5	1.9	6.5	0.6	21.1	0.59
2007	MIN	MLB	25	3	3	3	56	1	66	65	21	45	6	50.0%	.288	3	1.30	3.70	3.62	3.70	8.0	2.7	5.8	0.7	15.7	1.20

Breakout: 7% Improve: 27% Collapse: 38% Attrition: 11%   Comparables: Clay Carroll, Ron Davis, Bob Wickman, Steve Foucault

The comedian Lewis Black has a bit about the Clinton-Lewinsky madness of the late nineties: He's flipping between two channels, one of which is showing Clinton's videotaped testimony, the broadcasting a live shot of Clinton acting as president, addressing the United Nations. Black becomes flabbergasted at how different the two are and finally shouts, "Which one is real?" That's how one feels when looking at Crain's numbers over the last two seasons. In 2005, he suddenly stopped striking batters out, yet he was strangely effective. Last year, the strikeouts returned, but his hit rate and ERA shot up. Which one is real? Likely 2006, as his season was better than the numbers suggest; he overcame a horrible start to post a 1.68 ERA after June 1. His track record supports that answer, though his freakish 2005 likely threw off PECOTA too, allowing him to confuse both man and machine.

J. D. Durbin   Bats: R   Throws: R   Height: 6' 0"   Weight: 210   Born: February 24, 1982   Age: 25

YEAR	TEAM	LVL	AGE	W	L	SV	G	GS	IP	H	BB	SO	HR	GB%	BABIP	STUFF	WHIP	ERA	PERA	EQERA	EQH9	EQBB9	EQSO9	EQHR9	VORP	WXRL
2004	NBR	AA	22	4	1	0	13	13	64¹	62	22	53	4	—	.302	11	1.31	2.52	4.39	3.36	9.0	3.2	5.3	0.7	16.0	—
2004	ROC	AAA	22	3	2	0	7	7	35²	49	16	38	4	—	.421	6	1.82	4.54	4.59	6.75	12.2	4.2	7.2	1.2	-4.6	—
2005	ROC	AAA	23	5	5	0	22	19	104	97	51	90	8	48.5%	.309	12	1.42	4.33	4.78	4.57	8.4	4.7	6.0	0.8	11.9	—
2006	ROC	AAA	24	4	3	0	16	16	89	67	50	81	3	42.0%	.270	28	1.31	2.33	4.53	3.29	7.4	5.4	6.4	0.4	22.5	—
2007	MIN	MLB	25	5	7	0	28	16	101	111	60	74	12	45.0%	.312	0	1.68	5.55	5.44	5.44	8.9	4.9	6.2	0.9	-0.1	0.60

Breakout: 1%   Improve: 15%   Collapse: 59%   Attrition: 1%   Comparables: Matt Perisho, Ray Culp, Juan Dominguez, Jimmy Journell

Earlier in the decade, Durbin was one of the system's shining stars, but shoulder surgery and arm soreness have prevented him from throwing more than 110 innings in any of the last three seasons. It's a shame, because he's still pretty good. Durbin still throws hard, his curveball has blossomed into a true big league offering, and his bulldog demeanor is the kind of thing scouts love, but his control has gone backwards, and that pesky annual trip to the disabled list keeps holding him back. Durbin is in line for a fourth year at Triple-A, but could fill in as a starter or reliever should the need arise.

Willie Eyre   Bats: R   Throws: R   Height: 6' 2"   Weight: 205   Born: July 21, 1978   Age: 28

YEAR	TEAM	LVL	AGE	W	L	SV	G	GS	IP	H	BB	SO	HR	GB%	BABIP	STUFF	WHIP	ERA	PERA	EQERA	EQH9	EQBB9	EQSO9	EQHR9	VORP	WXRL
2004	ROC	AAA	25	6	7	4	36	21	136	131	53	91	13	—	.282	-6	1.35	3.64	5.05	4.02	8.4	3.8	4.6	1.0	24.0	—
2005	ROC	AAA	26	10	3	7	56	0	82²	79	28	74	3	60.7%	.322	11	1.29	2.72	3.64	3.47	8.6	3.3	6.1	0.3	19.6	—
2006	MIN	MLB	27	1	0	0	42	0	59¹	75	22	26	8	47.5%	.321	-21	1.63	5.31	5.37	5.11	10.7	3.1	3.6	1.0	4.2	0.21
2007	MIN	MLB	28	3	3	1	41	0	56	63	22	32	7	47.0%	.302	-9	1.52	4.67	4.81	4.59	9.2	3.3	4.8	0.9	5.9	0.50

Breakout: 15%   Improve: 41%   Collapse: 25%   Attrition: 33%   Comparables: John Frascatore, Jim Hearn, Mike Garman, Guillermo Mota

After toiling away as just another organizational arm for seven years, Scott's younger brother got hot at the right time—spring training—and broke camp with the big league club. He somehow stayed in the bigs all year as the last arm out of the bullpen despite pitching well enough to get released when the season was over. He'll now try to earn a similar job with the Rangers.

Matt Garza   Bats: R   Throws: R   Height: 6' 4"   Weight: 185   Born: November 11, 1983   Age: 23

YEAR	TEAM	LVL	AGE	W	L	SV	G	GS	IP	H	BB	SO	HR	GB%	BABIP	STUFF	WHIP	ERA	PERA	EQERA	EQH9	EQBB9	EQSO9	EQHR9	VORP	WXRL
2005	BLT	A	21	3	3	0	10	10	56	53	15	64	5	46.7%	.338	11	1.21	3.54	5.24	4.53	10.2	2.9	6.7	1.7	6.4	—
2005	ELZ	Rk	21	1	1	0	4	4	19²	14	6	25	3	50.0%	.262	-12	1.02	3.65	9.90	6.88	10.6	5.3	5.3	3.7	-2.4	—
2006	FTM	A+	22	5	1	0	8	8	44	27	11	53	3	46.8%	.231	20	0.86	1.43	4.54	3.61	7.0	2.8	7.0	1.3	9.4	—
2006	NBR	AA	22	6	2	0	10	10	57	40	14	68	2	39.9%	.271	34	0.95	2.53	3.23	4.13	7.0	2.4	7.5	0.5	9.3	—
2006	ROC	AAA	22	3	1	0	5	5	34	20	7	33	1	51.8%	.235	34	0.79	1.85	3.28	2.41	6.1	1.9	6.7	0.3	11.9	—
2006	MIN	MLB	22	3	6	0	10	9	50	62	23	38	6	38.1%	.346	7	1.70	5.76	4.35	5.54	10.2	3.8	6.2	0.9	0.8	0.65
2007	MIN	MLB	23	9	10	0	35	28	156¹	163	58	124	23	42.0%	.298	13	1.41	4.80	4.64	4.67	8.5	3.1	6.7	1.1	14.7	2.60

Breakout: 17%   Improve: 47%   Collapse: 12%   Attrition: 1%   Comparables: Dennis Tankersley, Kurt Ainsworth, Ralph Terry, Mike Meyers

Garza began the year in the Florida State League as the incumbent first-round pick and a pitcher that the team was pretty excited about, but nobody expected this. Garza suddenly gained a couple ticks on his fastball without losing any of his outstanding control, and all of his secondary pitchers (two breaking balls and a changeup) took a step forward as well; he cruised through the minors in short order. What you saw at the end of the year in Minnesota was a tired pitcher, and he's expected to be much better to start 2007. The Twins are comfortable enough with him to hand him a rotation job. It won't be a huge surprise if he's soon the team's best starter after Santana.

Matt Guerrier   Bats: R   Throws: R   Height: 6' 3"   Weight: 194   Born: August 2, 1978   Age: 28

YEAR	TEAM	LVL	AGE	W	L	SV	G	GS	IP	H	BB	SO	HR	GB%	BABIP	STUFF	WHIP	ERA	PERA	EQERA	EQH9	EQBB9	EQSO9	EQHR9	VORP	WXRL
2004	MIN	MLB	25	0	1	0	9	2	19	22	6	11	5	—	.288	-16	1.47	5.68	6.19	5.49	9.6	2.7	4.6	1.8	0.2	-0.14
2005	MIN	MLB	26	0	3	0	43	0	71²	71	24	46	6	48.2%	.293	3	1.33	3.39	4.08	3.56	8.8	2.9	5.6	0.7	18.1	0.44
2006	MIN	MLB	27	1	0	1	39	1	69²	78	21	37	9	47.2%	.305	-9	1.42	3.36	4.49	3.59	9.0	2.5	4.5	1.0	18.3	0.77
2007	MIN	MLB	28	3	3	2	45	2	68²	76	23	40	8	46.0%	.300	-6	1.44	4.47	4.56	4.38	9.0	2.8	5.0	0.9	9.2	0.80

Breakout: 9%   Improve: 28%   Collapse: 40%   Attrition: 14%   Comparables: John Frascatore, Travis Harper, Randy Moffitt, Jim Hearn

As a rookie in 2005, Guerrier was a serviceable reliever—nothing spectacular, but he got the job done more often than not. Last year, his hit rate went up and his strikeout rate dropped to borderline unacceptable. At 28, it's not like he's going to get better, and, while he's not yet in danger of needing to look for another job, if he takes even the smallest step backward, he'll probably need to update his résumé.

Francisco Liriano

Bats: L Throws: L   Height: 6' 2" Weight: 200 Born: October 26, 1983   Age: 23

YEAR	TEAM	LVL	AGE	W	L	SV	G	GS	IP	H	BB	SO	HR	GB%	BABIP	STUFF	WHIP	ERA	PERA	EQERA	EQH9	EQBB9	EQSO9	EQHR9	VORP	WXRL
2004	FTM	A+	20	6	7	0	21	21	117	118	43	125	6	—	.350	16	1.38	4.00	4.37	5.32	9.8	3.8	6.4	1.0	3.6	—
2004	NBR	AA	20	3	2	0	7	7	39²	45	17	49	4	—	.369	26	1.56	3.17	4.60	3.66	11.0	4.1	8.0	1.1	8.5	—
2005	NBR	AA	21	3	5	0	13	13	76²	70	26	92	6	60.4%	.335	22	1.25	3.64	4.21	4.94	9.3	3.5	7.5	1.0	5.5	—
2005	ROC	AAA	21	9	2	0	14	14	91	56	24	112	4	55.1%	.259	54	0.88	1.78	2.79	2.69	5.8	2.5	8.7	0.4	29.2	—
2005	MIN	MLB	21	1	2	0	6	4	23²	19	7	33	4	47.2%	.306	24	1.10	5.70	3.31	5.25	7.1	2.6	12.4	1.5	0.3	0.25
2006	MIN	MLB	22	12	3	1	28	16	121	89	32	144	9	56.9%	.285	54	1.00	2.16	2.63	2.25	6.2	2.2	9.9	0.6	51.0	5.09
2007	MIN	MLB	23	10	7	1	32	22	149	131	50	148	11	50.0%	.296	31	1.22	3.29	3.18	3.28	7.2	2.8	8.4	0.6	38.7	5.00

Breakout: 17% Improve: 43% Collapse: 13% Attrition: 6%   Comparables: Dave Righetti, Don Newcombe, Vida Blue, Dennis Bennett

For half a season, he was easily one of the most exciting pitchers in all of baseball. The good news is that the recovery rate for Tommy John surgery continues to improve; the bad news is that there are no guarantees the Liriano that emerges will be the same one we saw in 2006. He looked like a once-per-generation talent, like the only man capable of making Johan Santana a number-two starter. We just hope it all comes back, because you didn't have to be a Twins fan to love watching him pitch. We probably won't know until sometime in 2008.

Eduardo Morlan

Bats: R Throws: R   Height: 6' 2" Weight: 178 Born: March 1, 1986   Age: 21

YEAR	TEAM	LVL	AGE	W	L	SV	G	GS	IP	H	BB	SO	HR	GB%	BABIP	STUFF	WHIP	ERA	PERA	EQERA	EQH9	EQBB9	EQSO9	EQHR9	VORP	WXRL
2005	BLT	A	19	4	4	0	10	10	51¹	39	31	55	5	39.3%	.266	12	1.36	4.39	6.80	4.93	8.4	6.2	6.6	1.6	3.7	—
2005	ELZ	Rk	19	2	0	0	4	4	22	6	6	30	0	52.4%	.146	20	0.55	0.82	4.82	1.80	4.9	4.1	5.8	0.4	8.4	—
2006	BLT	A	20	5	5	2	28	18	106	78	38	125	6	36.1%	.281	4	1.09	2.29	5.36	3.79	8.5	4.2	6.6	1.4	20.1	—
2007	MIN	MLB	21	5	7	0	27	16	100¹	104	55	82	18	37.0%	.290	5	1.58	5.19	5.45	4.96	8.4	4.6	6.9	1.4	5.9	1.20

Breakout: 4% Improve: 13% Collapse: 55% Attrition: 6%   Comparables: Ubaldo Jimenez, Anibal Sanchez, John Patterson, Wilfredo Rodriguez

The Twins certainly seem to grow young arms on trees, don't they? Morlan is one of the better ones at the lower levels, and he's a pretty nice story as well: Morlan's family escaped from Cuba in the late-nineties; their initial destination was Spain, one of the few countries that gives refugee status to Cubans, but they moved to Florida so the kid could play baseball. Morlan has grown a bit since being a third-round pick in 2004, and now touches 97 MPH with his fastball while also throwing it for strikes. If he can find another pitch, he could be pretty good, and, even if not, the fastball is sufficient for late-inning relief work.

Joe Nathan

Bats: R Throws: R   Height: 6' 4" Weight: 220 Born: November 22, 1974 Age: 32

YEAR	TEAM	LVL	AGE	W	L	SV	G	GS	IP	H	BB	SO	HR	GB%	BABIP	STUFF	WHIP	ERA	PERA	EQERA	EQH9	EQBB9	EQSO9	EQHR9	VORP	WXRL
2004	MIN	MLB	29	1	2	44	73	0	72¹	48	23	89	3	—	.273	45	0.98	1.62	2.43	1.70	5.7	2.6	10.2	0.4	37.1	7.72
2005	MIN	MLB	30	7	4	43	69	0	70	46	22	94	5	37.6%	.270	47	0.97	2.70	2.45	2.79	6.0	2.8	11.8	0.6	22.9	4.39
2006	MIN	MLB	31	7	0	36	64	0	68¹	38	16	95	3	37.2%	.246	58	0.79	1.58	1.97	1.56	4.8	1.9	11.7	0.4	34.5	6.58
2007	MIN	MLB	32	5	4	38	56	0	61²	46	16	81	5	36.0%	.287	37	1.01	2.18	2.20	2.14	6.0	2.2	11.1	0.6	23.6	4.20

Breakout: 25% Improve: 49% Collapse: 31% Attrition: 18%   Comparables: Rich Gossage, John Wetteland, Tom Henke, Trevor Hoffman

One of the best closers around, Nathan started off beautifully in 2004 and has made tiny, incremental improvements since then. When you add it all up, he's become downright scary. His ERA as a Twin is 1.97, and he's blown just 10 saves in 133 chances. Thanks to his dominance and some favorable luck on balls in play, Nathan allowed a career-low five hits per nine innings last year. While he doesn't show up on Nathan's PECOTA comp list, his 2006 season resembles a vintage Dennis Eckersley year. Eck didn't start having those years until he was in his mid-30s; Nathan has a nice head start.

Pat Neshek　　Bats: S　Throws: R　　Height: 6' 3"　Weight: 205　Born: September 4, 1980　Age: 26

YEAR	TEAM	LVL	AGE	W	L	SV	G	GS	IP	H	BB	SO	HR	GB%	BABIP	STUFF	WHIP	ERA	PERA	EQERA	EQH9	EQBB9	EQSO9	EQHR9	VORP	WXRL
2004	FTM	A+	23	0	1	10	16	0	18¹	16	2	19	2	—	.269	-6	0.98	2.95	5.65	4.58	9.7	1.0	5.6	2.5	2.0	—
2004	NBR	AA	23	2	1	2	26	0	35¹	34	18	38	2	—	.327	3	1.47	3.82	4.48	4.41	9.3	4.9	6.7	0.8	4.6	—
2005	NBR	AA	24	6	4	24	55	0	82¹	69	21	95	9	42.4%	.297	-9	1.09	2.19	5.01	3.66	8.9	3.0	6.8	1.6	17.0	—
2006	ROC	AAA	25	6	2	14	33	0	60	41	14	87	7	50.8%	.276	24	0.92	1.95	3.97	2.47	7.4	2.3	10.2	1.5	20.3	—
2006	MIN	MLB	25	4	2	0	32	0	37	23	6	53	6	33.3%	.236	38	0.78	2.19	2.78	2.15	5.3	1.4	11.9	1.2	16.2	1.46
2007	MIN	MLB	26	4	4	7	81	1	78¹	74	22	76	11	39.0%	.293	16	1.23	3.67	3.69	3.56	7.7	2.3	8.2	1.0	18.3	1.70

Breakout: 17%　Improve: 26%　Collapse: 52%　Attrition: 11%　　Comparables: Ron Davis, Kerry Ligtenberg, Mark Davis, John Wetteland

It took the Twins awhile to trust a sidewinder in their bullpen, but, when they did, Neshek paid big dividends. In today's version of baseball, with expanded bullpens and overly specialized left-handers, it was inevitable that we would one day see the ROOGY, the Righty One-Out GuY; Neshek is just that. Right-handers simply can't pick up the ball out of his hand, and the fact that he can deliver a pitch with that motion in the low-90s makes him nearly impossible to hit, as evidenced by the .140/.159/.221 line righties put up against him in 86 at-bats. On the other hand, lefties slugged .511 off him. If you know how to use him, there's a lot of high-leverage value here.

Glen Perkins　　Bats: L　Throws: L　　Height: 5' 11"　Weight: 200　Born: March 2, 1983　Age: 24

YEAR	TEAM	LVL	AGE	W	L	SV	G	GS	IP	H	BB	SO	HR	GB%	BABIP	STUFF	WHIP	ERA	PERA	EQERA	EQH9	EQBB9	EQSO9	EQHR9	VORP	WXRL
2005	FTM	A+	22	3	2	0	10	9	55	41	13	66	2	43.5%	.295	26	0.98	2.13	3.57	3.23	8.0	2.7	6.8	0.7	14.0	—
2005	NBR	AA	22	4	4	0	14	14	79	80	35	67	4	40.2%	.326	9	1.46	4.90	4.88	5.91	9.7	4.6	5.2	0.7	-2.7	—
2006	NBR	AA	23	4	11	0	23	23	117²	109	45	131	11	36.8%	.320	0	1.31	3.92	5.16	5.40	9.3	3.9	6.8	1.4	2.6	—
2006	ROC	AAA	23	0	1	0	1	1	4²	6	5	3	0	47.7%	.279	4	2.62	2.14	6.25	4.15	12.5	10.4	4.2	0.0	0.7	—
2006	MIN	MLB	23	0	0	0	4	0	5²	3	0	6	0	21.4%	.214	6	0.53	1.58	1.69	1.59	4.8	0.0	9.5	0.0	2.9	0.17
2007	MIN	MLB	24	5	8	0	32	17	108²	119	50	80	16	40.0%	.306	3	1.56	5.37	5.23	5.20	8.9	3.9	6.2	1.1	3.1	1.00

Breakout: 10%　Improve: 37%　Collapse: 26%　Attrition: 1%　　Comparables: Brandon Claussen, Tom Gorzelanny, Mario Ramos, Brent Billingsley

The Twins love drafting local talent, and Perkins is from St. Paul and pitched for the Gophers in college. More important than the local angle is that he's pitched extremely well as a pro and will go into spring training with an outside shot at winning the number-five slot in the rotation. His curve and fastball are both above-average pitches, and the only real knock against him is his short, squat body. As we've all been taught since childhood, appearances can be deceiving; never judge a book by its short, squat body. Though Perkins doesn't look the part, he's one of the better starting pitching prospects in the system.

Brad Radke　　Bats: R　Throws: R　　Height: 6' 2"　Weight: 185　Born: October 27, 1972　Age: 34

YEAR	TEAM	LVL	AGE	W	L	SV	G	GS	IP	H	BB	SO	HR	GB%	BABIP	STUFF	WHIP	ERA	PERA	EQERA	EQH9	EQBB9	EQSO9	EQHR9	VORP	WXRL
2004	MIN	MLB	31	11	8	0	34	34	219²	229	26	143	23	—	.296	22	1.15	3.48	3.52	3.33	8.7	1.0	5.4	0.8	59.6	7.46
2005	MIN	MLB	32	9	12	0	31	31	200²	214	23	117	33	43.6%	.284	4	1.18	4.04	4.46	4.38	9.5	1.0	5.1	1.4	31.8	3.70
2006	MIN	MLB	33	12	9	0	28	28	162¹	197	32	83	24	43.4%	.324	0	1.41	4.33	4.44	4.58	9.9	1.7	4.3	1.2	23.3	3.17

Somehow, Brad Radke pitched 162 ⅓ innings in 2006 without a shoulder. He didn't do anything in his non-baseball life with his right arm—eat, change channels on the TV, nothing—but every five days he'd take the mound and gut it out. He got the win in Game Three of the ALDS and hung 'em up at the end of the year, done at 34. It wasn't a great career, but it certainly was an admirable one. He pitched 200 or more innings in nine of the last eleven years, had an ERA better than the league average in ten of them, and his career walk rate of 1.63 ranks ninth all-time among pitchers with at least 1,500 innings pitched and is the second-best rate of the last 75 years. Consistent and dependable pitchers are hard to find. Radke will be missed.

Dennys Reyes　　Bats: R　Throws: L　　Height: 6' 3"　Weight: 245　Born: April 19, 1977　Age: 30

YEAR	TEAM	LVL	AGE	W	L	SV	G	GS	IP	H	BB	SO	HR	GB%	BABIP	STUFF	WHIP	ERA	PERA	EQERA	EQH9	EQBB9	EQSO9	EQHR9	VORP	WXRL
2004	KCA	MLB	27	4	8	0	40	12	108	114	50	91	12	—	.325	8	1.52	4.75	4.21	4.53	8.7	3.7	6.8	0.9	9.7	0.99
2005	SDN	MLB	28	3	2	0	36	1	43²	57	32	35	3	67.1%	.378	0	2.04	5.15	4.61	6.15	11.3	5.8	6.6	0.6	-3.1	-0.41
2006	MIN	MLB	29	5	0	0	66	0	50²	35	15	49	3	72.1%	.254	28	0.99	0.89	2.89	1.38	5.7	2.4	8.1	0.5	26.5	2.14
2007	MIN	MLB	30	4	3	3	56	3	66²	68	27	56	5	57.0%	.316	6	1.43	3.77	4.00	3.77	8.4	3.4	7.1	0.6	14.3	1.30

Breakout: 17%　Improve: 43%　Collapse: 14%　Attrition: 6%　　Comparables: Andy Hassler, Bob Wickman, Ray King, Mike Timlin

After bouncing through seven organizations in five years, Reyes landed in Minnesota, providing the Twins a much-needed LOOGY. Lefthanders hit .148 against Reyes, who pounds the inside half with an effective cutter and solid curveball. The key to his breakthrough was a much lower walk rate, which seems to happen to anyone who puts on a Twins cap. We also like him for his physical resemblance to Rich Garces. *¡Viva El Guapo!*

Juan Rincon   Bats: R   Throws: R   Height: 5' 11"   Weight: 205   Born: January 23, 1979   Age: 28

YEAR	TEAM	LVL	AGE	W	L	SV	G	GS	IP	H	BB	SO	HR	GB%	BABIP	STUFF	WHIP	ERA	PERA	EQERA	EQH9	EQBB9	EQSO9	EQHR9	VORP	WXRL
2004	MIN	MLB	25	11	6	2	77	0	82	52	32	106	5	—	.270	44	1.05	2.63	2.68	2.68	5.5	3.1	10.7	0.4	28.5	2.82
2005	MIN	MLB	26	6	6	0	75	0	77	63	30	84	2	48.7%	.313	36	1.21	2.45	2.78	2.99	7.5	3.4	9.5	0.2	23.4	3.37
2006	MIN	MLB	27	3	1	1	75	0	74¹	76	24	65	2	51.6%	.344	23	1.35	2.91	2.98	3.39	8.5	2.7	7.2	0.2	20.6	3.20
2007	MIN	MLB	28	3	3	4	55	0	61	56	24	58	5	49.0%	.301	14	1.32	3.59	3.49	3.59	7.5	3.3	8.0	0.6	14.3	1.20

Breakout: 17%   Improve: 30%   Collapse: 39%   Attrition: 9%   Comparables: Eddie Watt, Billy Koch, Greg McMichael, Dave Righetti

He wasn't as good as he was in 2005, when he wasn't as good as he was in 2004, but all in all, he was still pretty good. There are few things more volatile in this world than non-closing relievers, and even closers aren't exactly all that stable. Despite that, Rincon put up his third straight year with a sub-3.00 ERA, but every trend that matters is going in the wrong direction.

Johan Santana   Bats: L   Throws: L   Height: 6' 0"   Weight: 210   Born: March 13, 1979   Age: 28

YEAR	TEAM	LVL	AGE	W	L	SV	G	GS	IP	H	BB	SO	HR	GB%	BABIP	STUFF	WHIP	ERA	PERA	EQERA	EQH9	EQBB9	EQSO9	EQHR9	VORP	WXRL
2004	MIN	MLB	25	20	6	0	34	34	228	156	54	265	24	—	.252	50	0.92	2.61	2.98	2.58	5.9	1.9	9.6	0.8	89.9	9.51
2005	MIN	MLB	26	16	7	0	33	33	231²	180	45	238	22	40.5%	.265	45	0.97	2.87	2.90	2.97	6.9	1.7	9.0	0.8	73.0	7.64
2006	MIN	MLB	27	19	6	0	34	34	233²	186	47	245	24	41.5%	.273	44	1.00	2.77	3.02	2.92	6.6	1.7	8.7	0.8	79.6	8.38
2007	MIN	MLB	28	16	8	0	32	32	221	188	48	223	24	42.0%	.278	37	1.07	2.91	2.88	2.85	6.9	1.8	8.5	0.8	69.4	8.80

Breakout: 30%   Improve: 53%   Collapse: 25%   Attrition: 2%   Comparables: Tom Seaver, Steve Carlton, Sandy Koufax, Mario Soto

What does one say here? We could stick with the basic stats and point out that Santana hasn't missed a start for three years, pitching 228 innings or more each season. We could point out that, over those three years, he's led the league in ERA twice, finished second once, and led the league each year in hits per nine innings, WHIP, strikeouts per nine innings, and total strikeouts. But what purpose would that or any of our fancy-ass stats serve? You don't need us to tell you that Johan Santana is the best pitcher in baseball.

Carlos Silva   Bats: R   Throws: R   Height: 6' 4"   Weight: 245   Born: April 23, 1979   Age: 28

YEAR	TEAM	LVL	AGE	W	L	SV	G	GS	IP	H	BB	SO	HR	GB%	BABIP	STUFF	WHIP	ERA	PERA	EQERA	EQH9	EQBB9	EQSO9	EQHR9	VORP	WXRL
2004	MIN	MLB	25	14	8	0	33	33	203	255	35	76	23	—	.320	2	1.43	4.21	4.26	3.86	10.3	1.4	3.1	0.9	38.1	4.79
2005	MIN	MLB	26	9	8	0	27	27	188¹	212	9	71	25	50.7%	.295	1	1.17	3.44	4.19	4.19	10.0	0.4	3.3	1.1	38.4	4.03
2006	MIN	MLB	27	11	15	0	36	31	180¹	246	32	70	38	45.6%	.320	-25	1.54	5.94	5.47	6.21	11.2	1.5	3.2	1.7	-7.6	1.34
2007	MIN	MLB	28	9	11	0	37	26	173¹	216	30	70	24	47.0%	.309	-3	1.42	4.93	4.87	4.83	10.2	1.5	3.4	1.1	12.7	2.50

Breakout: 17%   Improve: 59%   Collapse: 16%   Attrition: 2%   Comparables: Vern Law, Bill Gullickson, Brian Meadows, Carl Pavano

The weak link in the Twins rotation, Silva's game has always revolved around throwing a lot of strikes (in 2005 he walked 0.43 batter per nine innings, the lowest rate in modern history) and hoping nothing gets hit too hard. Last year those hopes were frustrated. Despite great control, Silva doesn't have the kind of extreme ground-ball tendencies necessary to survive striking out so few batters. The Twins picked up his option for 2007, but that's just because, with Liriano hurt and Radke retired, they had to ensure the requisite number of warm bodies for the rotation. After logging only 11 quality starts (1 blown) in 31 attempts last year, he'll be on a very short leash this year.

Kevin Slowey   Bats: R   Throws: R   Height: 6' 3"   Weight: 190   Born: May 4, 1984   Age: 23

YEAR	TEAM	LVL	AGE	W	L	SV	G	GS	IP	H	BB	SO	HR	GB%	BABIP	STUFF	WHIP	ERA	PERA	EQERA	EQH9	EQBB9	EQSO9	EQHR9	VORP	WXRL
2005	BLT	A	21	3	2	0	13	9	64¹	42	8	69	4	37.8%	.242	23	0.78	2.24	3.95	3.18	7.1	1.3	6.4	1.2	16.8	—
2006	FTM	A+	22	4	2	0	14	14	89	52	9	99	2	42.5%	.230	41	0.69	1.01	2.88	2.78	6.4	1.1	6.4	0.4	27.4	—
2006	NBR	AA	22	4	3	0	9	9	59²	50	13	52	6	39.4%	.265	9	1.06	3.19	4.89	3.97	8.1	2.1	5.5	1.4	10.7	—
2007	MIN	MLB	23	9	8	0	29	23	148¹	150	29	105	21	38.0%	.280	17	1.20	4.15	3.86	4.05	8.2	1.6	6.0	1.1	25.4	3.60

Breakout: 4%   Improve: 6%   Collapse: 61%   Attrition: 0%   Comparables: John Maine, Steve Woodard, Andrew Sonnanstine, Justin Verlander

(continued next page)

Kevin Slowey *(continued)*

Slowey was drafted one round after Garza and is moving almost as quickly through the system. A strikeout-to-walk ratio of nearly 7:1 tends to get one ahead. Nobody preaches control more, or teaches it better, than the Twins, and Slowey is their prize pupil. There are some worries that he'll struggle as he moves up; his raw stuff isn't overwhelming, and he already got hit hard a few times at Double-A. Some adjustments will be needed before he gets to the big leagues, but he could get a look at some point this year.

| Alexander Smit | | | | | | **Bats: L** | **Throws: L** | | | | Height: 6' 4" | | Weight: 205 | | Born: October 2, 1985 | | | Age: 21 |

YEAR	TEAM	LVL	AGE	W	L	SV	G	GS	IP	H	BB	SO	HR	GB%	BABIP	STUFF	WHIP	ERA	PERA	EQERA	EQH9	EQBB9	EQSO9	EQHR9	VORP	WXRL
2004	ELZ	Rk	18	1	1	0	6	5	28¹	25	10	43	0	—	.397	27	1.24	2.54	3.83	4.05	9.8	4.4	6.4	0.3	4.6	—
2005	BLT	A	19	1	9	0	14	10	49²	58	28	54	9	41.3%	.345	-17	1.73	5.98	8.26	8.23	12.6	5.9	6.7	3.3	-13.7	—
2005	ELZ	Rk	19	6	1	3	21	0	45²	25	12	86	3	43.2%	.314	17	0.81	1.97	4.93	3.57	8.9	4.0	8.0	1.6	9.1	—
2006	BLT	A	20	7	2	0	34	13	108²	77	53	141	6	37.0%	.297	8	1.20	2.99	5.56	5.36	8.3	5.9	7.3	1.3	2.7	—
2007	MIN	MLB	21	4	6	0	26	12	76	85	51	67	15	37.0%	.312	0	1.79	6.07	6.44	5.75	9.1	5.6	7.4	1.5	-2.8	0.10

Breakout: 10% Improve: 36% Collapse: 25% Attrition: 10%   Comparables: Ryan Hannaman, Cedrick Bowers, Chris Mowday, Tyler Johnson

While Bert Blyleven's status as the finest Dutch-born pitcher in Twins history is not in any jeopardy, Smit has the distinction of having grown up in Holland, as opposed to Rikalbert, who was born there but raised in Southern California. After some early struggles, Smit thrived after a move to the rotation at the end of June, putting up a 2.43 ERA in 13 starts while allowing just 44 hits in 74 innings and striking out 98. His fastball is outstanding, but his secondary stuff isn't, so, to most observers, he looks like a future power reliever. There are precious few left-handers who answer to that description.

| Anthony Swarzak | | | | | | **Bats: R** | **Throws: R** | | | | Height: 6' 3" | | Weight: 195 | | Born: September 10, 1985 | | Age: 21 |

YEAR	TEAM	LVL	AGE	W	L	SV	G	GS	IP	H	BB	SO	HR	GB%	BABIP	STUFF	WHIP	ERA	PERA	EQERA	EQH9	EQBB9	EQSO9	EQHR9	VORP	WXRL
2005	BLT	A	19	9	5	0	18	18	91¹	81	32	101	7	49.2%	.318	15	1.24	4.04	5.10	5.28	9.3	3.6	6.7	1.3	3.2	—
2005	FTM	A+	19	3	4	0	10	10	59	72	11	55	3	44.7%	.379	20	1.41	3.66	3.86	4.94	11.7	2.0	5.4	0.8	4.3	—
2006	FTM	A+	20	11	7	0	27	27	145¹	131	60	131	8	40.2%	.300	9	1.32	3.29	4.84	4.37	9.0	4.3	5.4	1.0	19.4	—
2007	MIN	MLB	21	6	8	0	26	20	117²	132	55	81	19	41.0%	.304	4	1.59	5.49	5.44	5.32	9.1	3.9	5.8	1.2	1.6	1.00

Breakout: 4% Improve: 32% Collapse: 33% Attrition: 0%   Comparables: Bubba Nelson, Francisco Cruceta, Mike Meyers, Fernando Cabrera

A high school draftee, Swarzak hasn't moved through the system with the speed of some of the college arms in the organization, but that doesn't mean the Twins don't love his potential. Given the team's approach to raising pitchers, it's easy to assume they have nothing but control specialists, but Swarzak is more of a pure power pitcher. Swarzak can get the ball into the mid-90s at times and has a solid breaking ball and changeup. He won't be ready for a look until 2008 at the earliest, but only Garza has a higher ceiling among the Twins' coming crop of young arms.

| Kyle Waldrop | | | | | | **Bats: R** | **Throws: R** | | | | Height: 6' 4" | | Weight: 190 | | Born: October 27, 1985 | | Age: 21 |

YEAR	TEAM	LVL	AGE	W	L	SV	G	GS	IP	H	BB	SO	HR	GB%	BABIP	STUFF	WHIP	ERA	PERA	EQERA	EQH9	EQBB9	EQSO9	EQHR9	VORP	WXRL
2004	ELZ	Rk	18	2	0	0	4	4	25	21	3	25	1	—	.290	18	0.96	3.24	4.06	4.74	8.4	1.5	4.0	0.7	2.4	—
2005	BLT	A	19	6	11	0	27	27	151²	182	23	108	17	57.0%	.329	-12	1.35	4.98	5.64	6.03	11.8	1.5	4.3	1.9	-7.1	—
2006	BLT	A	20	6	3	0	18	18	110¹	110	17	62	8	62.4%	.287	-17	1.15	3.84	6.15	5.80	10.3	1.8	3.0	1.7	-2.4	—
2006	FTM	A+	20	3	2	0	8	7	45	48	17	25	4	52.2%	.297	-15	1.44	3.60	6.02	6.50	10.2	3.9	3.2	1.6	-4.4	—
2007	MIN	MLB	21	6	10	0	27	21	127	157	35	51	21	51.0%	.302	-6	1.51	5.92	5.44	5.84	10.1	2.3	3.4	1.3	-6.5	0.30

Breakout: 13% Improve: 61% Collapse: 14% Attrition: 0%   Comparables: Gary Galvez, Dario Ferrand, James Tiller, Jeff Bennett

When the Twins selected Waldrop with a first-round pick in 2004, he seemed like the kind of strike-throwing control artist they love. While he didn't throw exceptionally hard, there was reason to expect an increase in velocity given that Waldrop is roughly the size of an NBA shooting guard. Unfortunately, Waldrop has not gained a single tick on the heater, rarely touching 90 MPH. That makes him a control specialist who can't miss bats, and the last thing the Twins need is another Carlos Silva.

Lineouts

PLAYER	TEAM	LVL	AGE	PA	R	2B	3B	HR	RBI	BB	SO	SB-CS	SPEED	AVG/OBP/SLG	MLVr	EqAVG/EqOBP/EqSLG	EqA	VORP
3B T. Batista	MIN	MLB	32	195	24	12	0	5	21	15	27	0-1	3.9	.236/.303/.388	-.166	.233/.308/.381	.238	-4.0
RF D. Deeds*	NBR	AA	25	521	71	35	3	14	72	70	107	4-3	5.0	.282/.383/.470	.220	.262/.346/.431	.270	11.1
C C. Heintz	ROC	AAA	31	406	46	22	0	3	39	23	63	0-4	4.0	.286/.323/.369	-.017	.245/.280/.314	.209	-15.2
SS P. Kelly	BLT	A	19	423	58	22	4	3	48	32	60	4-5	4.7	.280/.352/.384	.087	.253/.304/.347	.229	-1.0
RF C. Parmelee*	TWI	Rk	18	179	29	7	4	8	32	23	47	3-3	5.1	.279/.369/.532	.329	.248/.313/.478	.264	6.8
1B B. Peterson	FTM	A+	22	500	65	21	4	21	75	40	93	6-6	4.6	.291/.356/.497	.245	.278/.331/.479	.272	18.0
3B W. Robbins*	BLT	A	21	140	12	9	1	3	26	22	17	1-0	4.3	.304/.421/.482	.320	.277/.367/.445	.284	9.2
CF B. Roberts*	FTM	A+	21	313	40	12	1	3	34	20	43	27-7	6.7	.316/.370/.396	.153	.299/.345/.388	.263	9.3
	SAR	A+	21	273	40	5	1	1	15	16	39	23-7	7.4	.267/.325/.308	-.079	.245/.290/.285	.217	-14.2
3B G. Williams#	ROC	AAA	28	414	37	20	4	7	36	36	84	3-1	4.5	.257/.326/.389	-.007	.239/.303/.370	.236	-1.1

PLAYER	TEAM	LVL	AGE	W	L	SV	IP	H	BB	SO	HR	GB%	BABIP	STUFF	WHIP	ERA	PERA	EqERA	EqH9	EqBB9	EqSO9	EqHR9	VORP
R. Barrett*	ROC	AAA	25	5	1	1	47	31	26	49	0	—	.274	19	1.21	3.45	3.73	4.70	6.7	5.5	7.2	0.2	4.6
J. DePaula	FTM	A+	23	1	1	3	15²	8	6	10	1	—	.159	-16	0.92	0.00	6.08	3.68	5.5	4.3	3.7	1.2	3.1
	NBR	AA	23	2	2	7	66	58	27	43	1	—	.274	-3	1.29	2.59	4.43	3.93	7.9	4.1	3.9	0.3	12.3
B. Duensing*	BLT	A	23	2	3	0	70	68	14	55	3	—	.314	-4	1.17	2.96	4.88	4.95	9.9	2.5	3.9	1.1	4.9
	FTM	A+	23	2	5	0	40²	47	8	33	4	—	.352	-11	1.37	4.25	5.52	7.32	11.9	2.3	4.6	1.8	-7.5
	NBR	AA	23	1	2	0	49¹	51	18	30	6	—	.304	-22	1.41	3.67	6.38	5.92	9.6	3.7	3.7	1.8	-1.7
J. Jones*	FTM	A+	21	1	3	0	53¹	72	22	32	3	—	.369	-19	1.77	5.25	5.53	8.15	12.7	4.2	3.6	1.0	-15.0
	NBR	AA	21	2	2	0	27²	30	15	29	0	—	.385	13	1.65	3.31	4.26	5.27	10.5	5.3	6.6	0.3	1.0
J. Mijares*	FTM	A+	21	3	5	0	63	52	27	77	10	—	.301	-15	1.25	3.57	7.56	5.19	9.8	4.6	7.6	2.9	2.7
J. Miller*	ROC	AAA	23	3	8	1	99²	101	36	87	10	—	.320	-8	1.38	3.81	5.02	5.05	9.9	3.5	6.2	1.4	6.0
Y. Pino	BLT	A	22	14	2	3	94¹	69	20	99	4	—	.257	-4	0.95	1.91	4.54	3.73	8.2	2.7	5.3	1.1	18.6
E. Simonitsch*	NBR	AA	23	8	14	0	148	186	39	89	19	—	.337	-28	1.52	4.50	5.97	5.89	11.5	2.7	3.6	1.8	-4.8
M. Smith	ROC	AAA	28	11	5	0	150	152	57	110	12	—	.306	-6	1.39	3.90	5.24	5.50	9.9	3.8	5.0	1.1	1.6
O. Sosa	BLT	A	20	9	7	0	117²	102	36	95	1	—	.296	24	1.18	2.76	3.90	4.62	8.4	3.5	4.3	0.2	12.5
	FTM	A+	20	4	1	0	34²	23	18	27	1	—	.241	13	1.20	2.11	4.83	4.01	6.4	5.3	4.8	0.5	6.0
Z. Ward	DYT	A	22	7	0	0	114	74	37	95	2	—	.243	14	0.97	2.29	4.91	4.15	7.0	4.2	4.2	0.4	17.4
	BLT	A	22	1	4	0	30¹	29	11	23	1	—	.295	-13	1.33	5.98	5.80	8.48	10.0	4.7	3.8	0.9	-9.2

With the wide-open stance and the swinging from his heels, **Tony Batista** used to crank out enough home runs to mitigate, though not fully compensate for, on-base percentages that regularly dipped below .300. That clearly wasn't happening in 2006. After the Twins released him in mid-June, nobody called. **Doug Deeds** is one of those polished college hitters with good plate discipline but only doubles power and not enough athleticism to play anywhere but first base or left field. Not a thrilling combination. An eleven-year minor league veteran who got one at-bat in the big leagues last year, catcher **Chris Heintz** will be hard pressed to get another one. A second-round pick in 2005, **Paul Kelly** had a solid but unspectacular full-season debut that was cut short by a minor knee injury. He's still all potential at this point, but the Twins like him. The Twins' first-round pick last June, **Chris Parmalee** was one of the best high school sluggers available. The Minnesota system is desperate for power, so he's a perfect fit. Parmelee was even better than advertised is his debut, as his raw power showed up in game situations surprisingly fast. **Brock Peterson** put up some nice numbers in the Florida State League, leading the circuit with 21 home runs and finishing second in slugging percentage, but he was old for the league, is a bit stiff athletically, and nobody is going to believe in him until he shows he can do it at Double-A. A fourth-round pick out of Georgia Tech in 2006, **Whit Robbins** had a breakout final season with the Yellow Jackets, and his season-long hot streak continued in his pro debut at Low-A Beloit. He doesn't have the standard power profile one expects in a third baseman, but he can hit. **Brandon Roberts** came over from the Reds in a mid-season deal for Juan Castro. He's a Tyner type with plenty of speed, the ability to play center, and very little in the way of power or well-rounded on-base skills. Thirteen years ago, the Braves gave 16-year-old Australian **Glenn Williams** $850,000, which remains the bonus record for an amateur from down under. He's still trucking away in the minor leagues, hitting a little bit here and there, so you have to give him credit for tenacity if nothing else.

Lefthander **Ricky Barrett** is short and doesn't have much of a breaking ball, but he can bring it with a low-90s fastball and could have LOOGY potential after limiting Triple-A lefty hitters to a 5-for-40 (.125) line with 16 strikeouts. **Julio DePaula** has put up some decent ERAs in the minors thanks to an excellent changeup, but if he doesn't start missing bats soon, it's not going to matter. Southpaw **Brian Duensing** moved from Low-A to Double-A in one year, but as a 23 year old, he probably belonged in Double-A in the first place. That said, he's a command and control lefty who depends on changing speeds, the kind of pitcher who has a hard time succeeding in the big leagues. Once a ballyhooed prospect with the Cubs, **Justin Jones** has rarely been healthy or in shape, and he's almost out of chances after being removed from the Twins' 40-man roster. **Jose Mijares** is a left-handed reliever who averaged 11 strikeouts per nine innings in the Florida State League thanks to an outstanding fastball-slider combination. He might become something interesting if he ever gets in shape. Right now, he's just a fat guy with a good arm. **Jason Miller** is an organizational lefty who has spent seven years in the system without a sniff of the big leagues. He has a very good curve and little else, but he is left-handed. Right-hander **Yohan Pino** put up great numbers at Low-A as both a starter and reliever, and concerns about his marginal fastball have been lessened a bit by an outstanding performance against more advanced hitters in the Venezuelan Winter League. **Jay Rainville** was one of the better young arms in the system, but he missed all of 2006 recovering from surgery to fix a nerve problem in his shoulder. The Twins insist he'll be fine. Everything was going just dandy for **Errol Simonitsch** until he got to Double-A. Then things stopped going well, and there's no reason to think they'll start up again. He's yet another strike thrower in a system full of them. **Mike Smith** is an organizational right-hander with a decent slider-fastball combo and has put up decent numbers. Is he decent enough to get a few more emergency starts in the big leagues? The chances are decent. **Oswaldo Sosa** has a power pitcher's build, a nasty fastball-slider combination, and gets plenty of groundballs when he's not striking people out. He's a future big league reliever at the very least. Acquired from the Reds for Kyle Lohse, **Zach Ward** put up some nice numbers in the Midwest League. His best pitch is a slider, though his fastball is good enough to set it up effectively. He projects as a bullpen arm.

Manager: Ron Gardenhire

Year	Team	W-L	Pythag +/-	Avg PC	100 +P	120 +P	QS	BQS	REL	REL w Zero R	IBB	SUBS	PH	PH Avg	PH HR	SB2	CS2	SB3	CS3	SAC Att	SAC %	POS SAC	Squeeze	Swing	In Play
2004	MIN	92-70	+4	94.1	63	1	79	11	435	273	27	39	125	.257	6	97	39	19	6	64	71.9%	44	3	155	107
2005	MIN	83-79	-1	92.1	45	0	84	14	396	273	38	35	104	.259	2	85	39	17	4	70	60.0%	40	3	141	116
2006	MIN	96-66	+2	90.1	43	0	71	5	421	287	25	35	93	.143	2	88	36	13	6	59	52.5%	28	0	177	146

For the first six weeks of the season, Gardenhire was hammered by beat writers and analysts alike for questionable lineup moves and rotation choices. These went a long way towards making the Twins the comeback story of the year; if Gardenhire and partner in malpractice Terry Ryan hadn't been so stubbornly wrongheaded at the beginning of the year, the Twins might not have *needed* to come back. Confronted with a 25–33 record a week into June, Gardenhire was man enough to abandon his plans and start making the changes that revived the team—something that required not only awareness and humility, but a high level of clubhouse diplomacy, something we should never underestimate. Gardenhire is brilliant with his bullpen usage, but other aspects of in-game strategy are a bit sketchy. Gardenhire can stay too long with his starting pitcher; while he doesn't hesitate to hook a pitcher he thinks is struggling, if a pitcher is doing well he will sometimes stay with him until he isn't doing well anymore. He used to be one of the AL's more bunt-happy managers, but Ozzie Guillen, Jim Leyland, and others have surpassed him. He continues to love the hit-and-run, and favors players who have more going on with the glove than with the bat—players of the type he was himself.

New York Mets

In 2006, the Mets dominated the National League East, tied for the major league lead in wins, and finally ended the Atlanta Braves dynasty after eleven years. Their young shortstop went from caterpillar to butterfly, transforming from a player projected for future stardom into an actual star. Their expensive center fielder had an MVP season. Their expensive first baseman gave them production at first base like they hadn't had in years. Their expensive closer saved games. They whipped the Dodgers in the Division Series. They played a seven-game Championship Series with the Cardinals...and that's where the fairy tale comes to an abrupt end.

Along the way, the Mets did something that hadn't been done before in the entire history of baseball. They went into the postseason with just one of their top three starting pitchers available to pitch. Typically, when 40 percent of a team's rotation goes down at midseason, that team doesn't survive to play in October, but the Mets saved their injuries for the very end. Staff ace Pedro Martinez and postseason superstar Orlando Hernandez actually started consecutive games on September 27 and 28 before determining they'd be unable to go in the postseason due to a torn rotator cuff and calf respectively.

Teams in the postseason have always been affected by injuries. A severely infected left arm held Babe Ruth to only one at-bat in the last three games of the 1921 World Series. Herb Pennock, the left-handed ace of the 1928 Yankees, was diagnosed with "neuritis" in his arm late in the season, had four teeth extracted trying to fix it the problem ("That won't do him any good," his manager, Miller Huggins complained. "He doesn't pitch with his teeth. He doesn't even catch with 'em."), but missed the World Series anyway. More recently, Reggie Jackson tore a hamstring and missed the 1972 World Series. Jim Rice missed the 1975 World Series with a broken hand. Cardinals' leadoff man Vince Coleman got eaten by a tarp rolling machine during the 1985 NLCS and missed the World Series. Two years later, the Cards had to do without their sole slugger, Jack Clark, who sat out the World Series with torn ankle ligaments.

Sometimes teams have intentionally avoided their ace starter in the postseason. In 1929, Connie Mack of the A's had Lefty Grove, the best pitcher in baseball, but looked at the overwhelmingly right-handed lineup of his World Series opponent, the Cubs, and decided that Grove wouldn't be starting in the Series. This would be tantamount to Ron Gardenhire benching Johan Santana in the postseason, something that would probably get him fired on the spot. Fortunately for Mack, he owned part of the team—and he won the World Series.

The Mets have their own special way of suffering injuries that have hurt them in the postseason. Perhaps the most dramatic example occurred on the eve of the 1988 playoffs, when lefty starter Bobby Ojeda amputated the top of his left middle finger with his electric hedge clippers. Ojeda was only a little better than league average in 1988, and, in his absence, the Mets still had a playoff rotation of Dwight Gooden, David Cone, Ron Darling, and Sid Fernandez. That should have been good enough, but the Dodgers were especially vulnerable to lefty pitching that year, and Ojeda's absence probably negated some of New York's edge.

The Mets would top that bad break in 2006, but it was a matter of disaster becoming the residue of design. In January, Omar Minaya had dealt Kris Benson to the Orioles for pitchers Jorge Julio and John Maine. While Benson was far from an ace, he was a known quantity with a mediocre

---

METS PROSPECTUS

2006 record: 97–65; First place, NL East; Lost to Cardinals in Championship Series

Pythagenport record: 91–71

Runs scored per game: 5.15 (3rd in NL)

Runs allowed per game: 4.51 (3rd in NL)

Team EqA: .270 (1st in NL)

2006 Batters Age: 30.3 (5th oldest in NL)

2006 Pitchers Age: 32.7 (Oldest in NL)

Ballpark: Shea Stadium; Moderate pitcher's park; Park Factor of .966

2006: The portrait in Tom Glavine's study had a rough year; Jose Reyes's excitement-to-performance ratio came into balance a bit.

2007: Mets will have to put some runs on the board to win with a spotty rotation, but David Wright & Co. are fully capable of doing that.

consistency. Julio was a career reliever, while Maine, a starter, was not slotted to go right into the rotation but was instead acquired for organizational depth.

The move gave the Mets an Opening Day rotation of Tom Glavine, Pedro Martinez, Steve Trachsel, rookie Brian Bannister, and Victor Zambrano. Bannister and Zambrano were both lost to injuries by the first week of May, and the Mets reacted by adding Orlando Hernandez, putting the top four spots in the Mets rotation in the hands of a 40-year-old (Glavine), a 34-year-old (Martinez), a 35-year-old (Trachsel), and another 40-year-old (Hernandez) who might not actually have been 40 but was more likely somewhere between 40 and the fall of the Roman Empire.

There's nothing inherently wrong with having an old starting rotation. Some teams have been quite successful with graying rotations. The pennant-winning 1928 Cardinals had a rotation of Pete Alexander (41), Clarence Mitchell (37), Jesse Haines (34), Bill Sherdel (31), and Flint Rhem (27); that staff was second in the league in ERA. At times during the 1947 season the Phillies had a rotation of Oscar Judd (39), Dutch Leonard (38), Schoolboy Rowe (37), Bill Donnelly (33), and Ken Heintzelman (31). The staff was above average, but the team lost 92 games because it couldn't hit.

The real problem with an AARP rotation is that the chances of multiple injuries increase. A year after spending most of the season recovering from back surgery, Trachsel made it through 30 starts, despite various aches and pains. In contrast, Glavine, Martinez, and Hernandez failed to make it all the way through to the end of the campaign without interruption.

What happened to the Mets was very similar to the experience of the 2004 Yankees. Like the Mets, those Yankees were never really threatened on their way to the division title. They too had an elderly rotation—Kevin Brown (39), Orlando Hernandez (38 going on 100), Mike Mussina (35), Jon Lieber (34), Jose Contreras (32ish), and Javier Vazquez (28); Contreras was later traded for Esteban Loaiza, also 32. Lieber was on the disabled list through May recovering from Tommy John surgery. Mussina spent six weeks on the DL at midseason with elbow problems. Brown's back caused him to miss 44 games starting in mid-June; he also missed most of September after a self-inflicted broken hand. El Duque was on the shelf through mid-July, the continuation of the shoulder problems that caused him to miss the entire 2003 season.

The difference between the 2004 Yankees and the 2006 Mets was that the former team had the good sense to bunch its injuries away from the playoffs. By the time the playoffs rolled around, all of their pitchers (save perhaps Brown, who pitched anyway) were healthy, though not particularly effective. Like the Mets, the Yankees made it to Game Seven of the Championship Series. Unlike the Mets, the reasons for their failure were systemic rather the result of the decimated pitching staff. Because of the late-season injuries to Martinez and Hernandez, the Mets were left with Glavine, Trachsel, Maine, and trading deadline reclamation project Oliver Perez to carry their banner into October. The Mets had managed to stitch together a championship-class pitching staff during the regular season, but by October they had run out of patches.

The problem of age also afflicts the team's position players. While Jose Reyes and David Wright are still quite young, and Carlos Beltran is in the prime of his career, the rest of the lineup is in a dangerous place. Catcher Paul Lo Duca will turn 35 in April. Carlos Delgado will reach that same milestone in June. Shawn Green, 34, is finished as a productive everyday player. Jose Valentin is 37, and, should he stumble, the player first in line to replace him, Damion Easley, is 37 as well.

The moves the Mets made over the winter did little to address this problem. Left fielder Cliff Floyd was replaced by Moises Alou, who will turn 41 in July. Alou is still a fine hitter, but he's fragile and has as much range as Tony Danza. The only potential successor to Lo Duca in the organization, Jesus Flores, was spirited away by the Nationals in the Rule 5 draft (as he has yet to play in Double-A, there's a good chance he'll be back). Trachsel was allowed to leave as a free agent, but both Glavine and Hernandez were re-signed.

The pitching staff should nevertheless get younger. With Martinez, who went under the knife just as the playoffs began, out for at least half the season, and Trachsel not replaced by a veteran (at least not yet), the rotation will have to be rounded out by Maine and at least two pitchers from a group that includes Perez, Mike Pelfrey, Phillip Humber, Alay Soler, and Jason Vargas (acquired in a November trade with the Marlins).

In contrast, their crop of position player prospects is weak. Despite his rumored inclusion in every trade going back to Koosman-Orosco, the Mets still possess Lastings Milledge; he remains a fine prospect. Carlos Gomez, another outfielder, may be close to contributing. After that, there is precious little in the way of depth. If injuries hit, or any of the thirtysomething (or fortysomething) regulars reach obsolescence on a slightly accelerated schedule, the team will have a tough time patching in-house, and Minaya would be forced to go shopping.

All of this adds up to a National League East is not in the grips of a new dynasty. The Mets may be able to hold on to the division for another year. If the young pitchers are phased in without too much trouble the horizon could extend further, but, for now, the team's position is tenuous.

The Mets may have finally gotten out from under the Braves only to find that they've already peaked.

HITTERS

Michel Abreu — 1B — Bats: R — Throws: R — Height: 6' 0" — Weight: 220 — Born: January 2, 1979 — Age: 32

YEAR	TEAM	LVL	AGE	PA	R	2B	3B	HR	RBI	BB	SO	SB	CS	SPEED	AVG	OBP	SLG	MLVR	EQAVG	EQOBP	EQSLG	EQA	VORP	DEFENSE	
2006	BIN	AA	31	450	62	26	1	17	70	45	87	0	0	3.9	.332	.404	.530	.360	.280	.333	.430	.262	8.3	94-1B	1
2007	NYN	MLB	32	409	44	23	1	11	52	27	93	0	1	4.1	.270	.322	.427	-.060	.273	.324	.440	.258	4.0	98-1B	3

Breakout: 23% Improve: 38% Collapse: 35% Attrition: 31% Comparables: Ryan Thompson, Gene Schall, Chris Saunders, Bobby Smith

A Cuban import who hit well at Double-A last year, but whether you choose to believe that he's 27, as the Mets have, or 32, as the Red Sox claimed when they voided his first MLB contract, the upside is pretty much non-existent.

Carlos Beltran — CF — Bats: S — Throws: R — Height: 6' 1" — Weight: 200 — Born: April 24, 1977 — Age: 30

YEAR	TEAM	LVL	AGE	PA	R	2B	3B	HR	RBI	BB	SO	SB	CS	SPEED	AVG	OBP	SLG	MLVR	EQAVG	EQOBP	EQSLG	EQA	VORP	DEFENSE	
2004	KCA	MLB	27	309	51	19	2	15	51	37	44	14	3	6.9	.278	.367	.534	.206	.273	.369	.534	.304	26.6	69-CF	4
2004	HOU	MLB	27	399	70	17	7	23	53	55	57	28	0	8.7	.258	.368	.559	.239	.251	.361	.542	.310	38.9	86-CF	3
2005	NYN	MLB	28	650	83	34	2	16	78	56	96	17	6	6.0	.266	.330	.414	.013	.269	.335	.429	.265	17.6	146-CF	3
2006	NYN	MLB	29	617	127	38	1	41	116	95	99	18	3	6.4	.275	.388	.594	.332	.280	.394	.609	.328	68.5	132-CF	15
2007	NYN	MLB	30	622	102	31	4	31	91	80	98	17	4	6.3	.282	.377	.529	.181	.286	.380	.546	.309	51.6	145-CF	4

Breakout: 10% Improve: 42% Collapse: 12% Attrition: 4% Comparables: Tom Tresh, Ray Lankford, Kirk Gibson, Reggie Smith

Three things kept Carlos Beltran from enjoying a better showing than fourth place in the MVP balloting last year: he didn't hit for average at home (though he was still quite productive at .224/.368/.487), he didn't hit in September (.203/.365/.413—the result of a strained left quadriceps and a bruised left knee), and crediting the best player on the best team in the league just might be too subtle for most of the voters. That aside, Beltran blew away memories of his disappointing 2005 with the best season of his career and one of the top five seasons in team history, which included tying the Mets franchise record for home runs. He shouldn't be expected to match it, but there's still plenty o' goodness to come, maybe not in 2010 or 2011, but between now and then.

Mike Carp — 1B — Bats: L — Throws: R — Height: 6' 2" — Weight: 205 — Born: June 30, 1986 — Age: 21

YEAR	TEAM	LVL	AGE	PA	R	2B	3B	HR	RBI	BB	SO	SB	CS	SPEED	AVG	OBP	SLG	MLVR	EQAVG	EQOBP	EQSLG	EQA	VORP	DEFENSE	
2005	HAG	A	19	375	49	12	1	19	63	35	96	2	2	2.9	.249	.358	.476	.161	.227	.295	.409	.242	-7.7	77-1B	-9
2006	SLU	A+	20	573	69	27	1	17	88	51	107	2	1	3.5	.287	.379	.450	.212	.275	.344	.443	.272	15.8	134-1B	3
2007	NYN	MLB	21	526	55	27	1	16	63	42	105	0	1	3.8	.256	.326	.424	-.066	.260	.329	.437	.260	4.5	124-1B	0

Breakout: 22% Improve: 54% Collapse: 23% Attrition: 3% Comparables: Justin Morneau, Adrian Gonzalez, Scott Thorman, Andy Marte

Carp was the Mets' ninth-round pick two years ago. He failed to live up to that high honor in his first two professional seasons, but last year he started hitting the ball to all fields, boosting his average. He also goosed his OBP by getting in front of 25 pitches, giving him a total of 46 HBPs over the last two years. Carp still has some work to do against his fellow lefties. He has time. Though his 2006 was a good season in the context of his league, it represents the beginning of prospect-dom, not the end.

Ramon Castro — C — Bats: R — Throws: R — Height: 6' 3" — Weight: 235 — Born: March 1, 1976 — Age: 31

YEAR	TEAM	LVL	AGE	PA	R	2B	3B	HR	RBI	BB	SO	SB	CS	SPEED	AVG	OBP	SLG	MLVR	EQAVG	EQOBP	EQSLG	EQA	VORP	DEFENSE	
2004	FLO	MLB	28	108	9	3	0	3	8	11	30	0	0	3.4	.135	.231	.260	-.454	.115	.213	.229	.167	-8.4	29-C	0
2005	NYN	MLB	29	240	26	16	0	8	41	25	58	1	0	3.5	.244	.321	.435	.006	.244	.322	.445	.265	8.8	65-C	2
2006	NYN	MLB	30	144	13	7	0	4	12	15	40	0	0	3.7	.238	.322	.389	-.083	.238	.326	.397	.253	1.0	34-C	4
2007	NYN	MLB	31	333	34	16	1	11	37	32	83	1	0	3.9	.226	.305	.398	-.159	.230	.308	.411	.246	3.4	80-C	1

Breakout: 13% Improve: 41% Collapse: 20% Attrition: 36% Comparables: Tim Laudner, Mark Parent, Doug Mirabelli, Rich Rowland

Castro did a great job of subbing for Mike Piazza in 2005, but last year he careened from one disaster to another. Lo Duca being more durable than Piazza, Castro was already in for a reduction in playing time, but nature took him all the way to

(continued next page)

Ramon Castro *(continued)*

the limit. After a strained left quad put him on the DL, Castro tore up a knee while preparing for a rehab appearance. He underwent surgery, missing just over eight weeks. Castro is eligible for free agency after this season; some team may yet be tempted enough by his power to offer him a starting job.

Endy Chavez OF Bats: L Throws: L Height: 6' 0" Weight: 165 Born: February 7, 1978 Age: 29

YEAR	TEAM	LVL	AGE	PA	R	2B	3B	HR	RBI	BB	SO	SB	CS	SPEED	AVG	OBP	SLG	MLVR	EQAVG	EQOBP	EQSLG	EQA	VORP	DEFENSE		
2004	MON	MLB	26	547	65	20	6	5	34	30	40	32	7	7.8	.277	.318	.371	-.073	.272	.314	.365	.245	7.5	122-CF	-7	
2005	WAS	MLB	27	12	2	1	0	0	1	3	1	0	1	4.8	.222	.417	.333	.039	.222	.417	.333	.252	-0.2			
2005	PHI	MLB	27	118	17	3	3	0	10	4	13	2	1	7.7	.215	.243	.299	-.363	.209	.243	.291	.194	-7.3	13-CF	1	
2006	NYN	MLB	28	390	48	22	5	4	42	24	44	12	3	6.6	.306	.348	.431	.074	.311	.356	.437	.275	15.3	35-RF	0	29-CF 5
2007	*NYN*	*MLB*	*29*	*348*	*45*	*15*	*4*	*2*	*26*	*22*	*35*	*13*	*4*	*6.9*	*.280*	*.329*	*.373*	*-.112*	*.284*	*.331*	*.385*	*.252*	*3.0*	*84-CF*	*1*	

Breakout: 11% Improve: 36% Collapse: 20% Attrition: 25%   Comparables: Marv Rackley, Lance Johnson, Jose Tartabull, Rudy Law

Chavez is on the short list of 2006 Stars/2007 Minor Leaguers. Writing about Endy in the 2005 edition of this book, we said, "This is a dangerous player. His batting average is high enough that he looks like a good enough hitter. He'll steal enough bases that you'll want him for that...Managers bite on these kinds of players, and suddenly they're at the top of the lineup every day. As a result, guys like Chavez have the potential to wreak havoc on a team far out of proportion to their modest talents." This is doubly true now that Chavez has had a year at the top end of his range, because he's unlikely to get there again. The acquisition of Ben Johnson from the Padres gives the Mets a good alternative to pushing their luck.

Carlos Delgado 1B Bats: L Throws: R Height: 6' 3" Weight: 240 Born: June 25, 1972 Age: 35

YEAR	TEAM	LVL	AGE	PA	R	2B	3B	HR	RBI	BB	SO	SB	CS	SPEED	AVG	OBP	SLG	MLVR	EQAVG	EQOBP	EQSLG	EQA	VORP	DEFENSE	
2004	TOR	MLB	32	551	74	26	0	32	99	69	115	0	1	3.1	.269	.372	.535	.167	.262	.368	.527	.301	32.1	113-1B	7
2005	FLO	MLB	33	616	81	41	3	33	115	72	121	0	0	3.6	.301	.399	.582	.396	.313	.408	.618	.335	62.2	136-1B	-14
2006	NYN	MLB	34	618	89	30	2	38	114	74	120	0	0	4.1	.265	.361	.548	.221	.270	.366	.559	.306	35.2	139-1B	-7
2007	*NYN*	*MLB*	*35*	*554*	*79*	*27*	*1*	*29*	*87*	*66*	*113*	*0*	*0*	*3.8*	*.269*	*.363*	*.513*	*.124*	*.273*	*.366*	*.529*	*.298*	*28.6*	*130-1B*	*-5*

Breakout: 1% Improve: 17% Collapse: 45% Attrition: 9%   Comparables: Boog Powell, Jim Thome, George Crowe, Willie McCovey

As with Beltran, the home fans didn't see the best of Delgado last year—he batted .304/.390/.608 on tour but just .226/.331/.487 in soon-to-be dismantled Shea Stadium. The Marlins kick in $2 million of his $13.5-million salary this year, and $4 million of his $16 million in 2008, so although the contract was designed to be backloaded, it doesn't work out that way for the Mets. Delgado's season was terrific by the standards of Mets first basemen in the post-John Olerud era, but a bit less than his best. Delgado's 2006 level of play seems representative of his true level of ability, making a reversion to his 2003/2005 form unlikely. That should nevertheless be enough for the Mets over the final two years of his contract.

Jesus Flores C Bats: R Throws: R Height: 6' 1" Weight: 180 Born: October 26, 1984 Age: 21

YEAR	TEAM	LVL	AGE	PA	R	2B	3B	HR	RBI	BB	SO	SB	CS	SPEED	AVG	OBP	SLG	MLVR	EQAVG	EQOBP	EQSLG	EQA	VORP	DEFENSE	
2005	HAG	A	20	337	34	18	0	7	42	12	90	2	2	3.5	.216	.250	.339	-.219	.169	.193	.228	.155	-45.2	70-C	-9
2006	SLU	A+	21	480	66	32	0	21	70	28	127	2	0	4.4	.266	.335	.487	.181	.251	.303	.466	.259	17.2	102-C	13
2007	*WAS*	*MLB*	*22*	*549*	*49*	*29*	*1*	*18*	*68*	*29*	*146*	*2*	*1*	*4.1*	*.228*	*.279*	*.397*	*-.206*	*.232*	*.283*	*.409*	*.232*	*2.9*	*129-C*	*2*

Breakout: 37% Improve: 63% Collapse: 18% Attrition: 8%   Comparables: Craig Stone, Vic Valencia, Jeff Mathis, Jeff Bailey

The Mets ended the season with few position-playing prospects, but after the 2006 Rule 5 draft, they had one less. The Nationals grabbed Flores, who tied for the Florida State League lead in home runs last year. The most likely outcomes are that Flores gets returned to the Mets or the Nats keep him but stunt his development; his offensive game is not polished enough for the majors.

Cliff Floyd LF Bats: L Throws: R Height: 6' 4" Weight: 230 Born: December 5, 1972 Age: 34

YEAR	TEAM	LVL	AGE	PA	R	2B	3B	HR	RBI	BB	SO	SB	CS	SPEED	AVG	OBP	SLG	MLVR	EQAVG	EQOBP	EQSLG	EQA	VORP	DEFENSE	
2004	NYN	MLB	31	457	55	26	0	18	63	47	103	11	4	5.1	.260	.352	.462	.097	.262	.352	.469	.281	12.2	89-LF	0
2005	NYN	MLB	32	626	85	22	2	34	98	63	98	12	2	5.9	.273	.358	.505	.190	.277	.363	.523	.297	37.4	143-LF	13
2006	NYN	MLB	33	376	45	19	1	11	44	29	58	6	0	5.5	.244	.324	.407	-.045	.249	.327	.414	.260	1.3	85-LF	-5
2007	*NYN*	*MLB*	*34*	*435*	*60*	*21*	*2*	*17*	*59*	*42*	*75*	*8*	*2*	*5.1*	*.263*	*.342*	*.457*	*.011*	*.266*	*.345*	*.471*	*.278*	*13.1*	*103-LF*	*-2*

Breakout: 12% Improve: 32% Collapse: 28% Attrition: 25%   Comparables: Kirk Gibson, Gates Brown, Leon Wagner, Chris Chambliss

Pancho Villa's last words were reportedly, "Don't let it end this way. Tell them I said something." Floyd expressed similar sentiments, not wanting a literally lame ending to his Mets phase. Sadly, the only word he could get out was, "Ouch." In 2005, a Willy Randolph pep talk on fortitude in the face of pain resulted in Floyd making it through a full season for just the third time in his career. Last year, the spirit may still have been willing, but his Achilles tendon was weak. Floyd never got his bat going in a meaningful way between DL stints. A free agent, he's a good candidate for one of those make-good, incentive-laden one-year deals.

Julio Franco   **PH**   **Bats: R**   **Throws: R**   Height: 6' 1″   Weight: 210   Born: December 31, 1969   Age: 47

YEAR	TEAM	LVL	AGE	PA	R	2B	3B	HR	RBI	BB	SO	SB	CS	SPEED	AVG	OBP	SLG	MLVR	EQAVG	EQOBP	EQSLG	EQA	VORP	DEFENSE	
2004	ATL	MLB	45	361	37	18	3	6	57	36	68	4	2	4.9	.309	.378	.441	.146	.306	.375	.438	.282	17.0	65-1B	-1
2005	ATL	MLB	46	265	30	12	1	9	42	27	57	4	0	4.8	.275	.348	.451	.092	.272	.347	.457	.279	10.2	48-1B	-1
2006	NYN	MLB	47	179	14	10	0	2	26	13	49	6	1	3.9	.273	.330	.370	-.068	.274	.335	.372	.253	1.5	21-1B	-1
2007	NYN	MLB	48	203	34	9	1	3	20	17	50	6	2	4.7	.253	.318	.372	-.120	.256	.321	.383	.246	-0.4		

Breakout: N/A   Improve: N/A   Collapse: N/A   Attrition: N/A   Comparables: Satchel Paige, Strom Thurmond, George Blanda, Harriet the Galapagos Tortoise

Restricted to a pinch-hitting role for the first time in his career, Franco struggled to find consistency, although it could have been that 47-year-olds just aren't consistent. As the year dragged on, Willie Randolph found fewer reasons to use Franco and his averages declined. Scientists are still unsure whether Franco's career will end before the catastrophic effects of global warming flood Shea Stadium, but this season's small numbers and reduced role suggest that the seas will rise slightly sooner for Franco than they will for the rest of us. Still, Eisenhower-baby Franco batted .250 in his 66 pinch-hitting appearances, far better than Nixon-baby Ricky Ledee, so anything is possible. PS: Wouldja believe the Mets worked Franco out at second base last August?

Carlos Gomez   **RF**   **Bats: R**   **Throws: R**   Height: 6' 2″   Weight: 175   Born: December 4, 1985   Age: 21

YEAR	TEAM	LVL	AGE	PA	R	2B	3B	HR	RBI	BB	SO	SB	CS	SPEED	AVG	OBP	SLG	MLVR	EQAVG	EQOBP	EQSLG	EQA	VORP	DEFENSE			
2004	KNG	Rk	18	163	24	10	4	1	20	5	29	8	1	7.6	.287	.333	.427	.082	.236	.258	.331	.209	-24.2	32-RF	-3		
2005	HAG	A	19	539	75	13	6	8	48	32	88	64	24	8.0	.275	.331	.376	.005	.245	.282	.318	.221	-35.3	59-RF	-7	53-CF	5
2006	BIN	AA	20	486	53	24	8	7	48	27	97	41	9	7.5	.281	.350	.423	.108	.275	.329	.427	.267	15.0	115-CF	5		
2007	NYN	MLB	21	523	70	25	5	9	44	28	92	41	13	6.9	.264	.315	.393	-.122	.268	.317	.405	.254	6.8	123-CF	3		

Breakout: 30%   Improve: 63%   Collapse: 11%   Attrition: 8%   Comparables: Rocco Baldelli, Lastings Milledge, Frank Diaz, Hanley Ramirez

Gomez is a mixed bag—he has great tools and succeeded at Double-A at age 20, but it's still not clear what that will add up to. His plate judgment is a work in progress, as he doesn't walk much, instead spiking his OBP with 20 HBPs. He has great speed, but is more suited to right field than center, but currently lacks the power to be a suitable regular in an outfield corner. Youth is on Gomez's side with that, as with everything. If he doesn't develop much from where he is now, he'll be a very useful fourth outfielder. If he keeps on growing, look out.

Ruben Gotay   **2B**   **Bats: S**   **Throws: R**   Height: 5' 11″   Weight: 190   Born: December 25, 1982   Age: 24

YEAR	TEAM	LVL	AGE	PA	R	2B	3B	HR	RBI	BB	SO	SB	CS	SPEED	AVG	OBP	SLG	MLVR	EQAVG	EQOBP	EQSLG	EQA	VORP	DEFENSE	
2004	WIC	AA	21	476	71	22	6	9	68	51	60	9	10	5.5	.289	.373	.440	.141	.270	.338	.406	.257	16.1	105-2B	-8
2004	KCA	MLB	21	166	17	7	3	1	16	9	36	0	1	4.5	.270	.315	.375	-.085	.272	.321	.377	.244	2.5	36-2B	-1
2005	KCA	MLB	22	317	32	14	2	5	29	22	51	2	2	5.4	.227	.288	.344	-.214	.231	.300	.361	.234	-7.2	76-2B	0
2005	WIC	AA	22	122	22	8	0	3	15	12	13	0	2	4.2	.245	.320	.400	-.041	.207	.279	.333	.216	-4.5	25-2B	0
2006	OMA	AAA	23	374	45	16	2	9	43	26	67	7	1	4.9	.264	.322	.404	-.024	.262	.315	.408	.252	7.9	80-2B	-6
2006	NOR	AAA	23	169	19	12	1	3	21	10	29	4	5	5.7	.266	.317	.416	.099	.284	.329	.452	.261	8.9	37-2B	-2
2007	NYN	MLB	24	477	53	21	3	11	50	36	82	6	4	5.1	.249	.311	.393	-.139	.253	.314	.405	.246	7.5	113-2B	-5

Breakout: 17%   Improve: 51%   Collapse: 27%   Attrition: 12%   Comparables: Brooks Conrad, Ian Kinsler, Josh McKinley, Ronnie Merrill

The Mets acquired Gotay, defrocked Royals second baseman of the future, in July in exchange for Jeff Keppinger. It was a trade of a second baseman the Mets didn't want for one that, with the emergence of Jose Valentin, they didn't need. Still, the Mets got three years younger in the deal, and Gotay, once a valued prospect, played quite well at Norfolk. With Valentin almost guaranteed to regress this season, there may yet be a second act to the Gotay story.

Shawn Green   RF   Bats: L   Throws: L   Height: 6′ 4″   Weight: 210   Born: November 10, 1972   Age: 34

YEAR	TEAM	LVL	AGE	PA	R	2B	3B	HR	RBI	BB	SO	SB	CS	SPEED	AVG	OBP	SLG	MLVR	EQAVG	EQOBP	EQSLG	EQA	VORP	DEFENSE		
2004	LAN	MLB	31	671	92	28	1	28	86	71	114	5	2	4.7	.266	.352	.459	.101	.268	.353	.464	.279	24.0	102-1B	6	46-RF -4
2005	ARI	MLB	32	656	87	37	4	22	73	62	95	8	4	5.3	.286	.355	.477	.139	.279	.350	.476	.281	29.4	115-RF	3	35-CF -1
2006	ARI	MLB	33	462	59	22	3	11	51	37	64	4	4	4.9	.283	.348	.429	.024	.276	.344	.421	.263	7.0	96-RF	-9	11-1B 0
2006	NYN	MLB	33	126	14	9	0	4	15	8	18	0	0	2.8	.257	.325	.442	.011	.265	.333	.460	.271	2.0	28-RF	-4	
2007	NYN	MLB	34	502	65	24	2	13	59	46	77	5	2	4.9	.270	.342	.418	-.034	.274	.345	.431	.267	8.0	118-RF	-4	

Breakout: 17% Improve: 40% Collapse: 31% Attrition: 20%   Comparables: Jim Northrup, Ken Griffey, Andy Van Slyke, B. J. Surhoff

The Mets will only regret acquiring Green one time, and that's constantly. Since turning 30, Green has batted .277/.351/.458. That looks acceptable, in a bare minimum sort of way, until you consider that his getting to play in Faceless Banking Services Conglomerate Ballpark in Phoenix had been contributing more than a little bit. A slight slip further downward in 2007, and he'll be a major impediment to the Mets if they insist keeping him as their everyday right fielder.

Anderson Hernandez   2B   Bats: S   Throws: R   Height: 5′ 9″   Weight: 170   Born: October 30, 1982   Age: 24

YEAR	TEAM	LVL	AGE	PA	R	2B	3B	HR	RBI	BB	SO	SB	CS	SPEED	AVG	OBP	SLG	MLVR	EQAVG	EQOBP	EQSLG	EQA	VORP	DEFENSE		
2004	LAK	A+	21	106	14	3	3	0	9	6	19	5	0	7.8	.289	.327	.381	.028	.273	.305	.364	.240	1.0	26-SS	4	
2004	ERI	AA	21	440	65	19	3	5	29	26	89	17	6	6.8	.274	.326	.376	-.067	.252	.296	.342	.228	-3.6	97-SS	-2	
2005	BIN	AA	22	296	46	14	1	7	24	14	58	11	9	6.1	.326	.360	.462	.181	.304	.339	.435	.264	17.9	54-SS	-3	
2005	NOR	AAA	22	293	34	6	4	2	30	22	46	24	9	7.3	.303	.354	.379	.065	.311	.361	.379	.268	12.4	36-2B	2	29-SS -4
2006	NOR	AAA	23	444	44	11	4	0	23	21	70	15	5	6.5	.249	.285	.295	-.136	.264	.301	.317	.223	-6.4	70-SS	-4	30-2B 4
2006	NYN	MLB	23	67	4	1	1	1	3	1	12	0	0	4.8	.152	.164	.242	-.625	.076	.090	.136	.091	-7.5	12-2B	0	
2007	NYN	MLB	24	415	45	14	4	4	31	22	70	13	5	6.5	.254	.296	.345	-.228	.257	.299	.355	.228	0.0	99-SS	-1	

Breakout: 24% Improve: 44% Collapse: 36% Attrition: 14%   Comparables: Alfredo Amezaga, Carlos Leon, Bernie Castro, Nelson Liriano

The glove is still there, but the bat done died. Hernandez is still on the 40-man, and the second base situation has its share of questions, but when you get oversloughed by the likes of Ruben Gotay, people start to talk.

Ricky Ledee   PH   Bats: L   Throws: L   Height: 6′ 1″   Weight: 225   Born: November 22, 1973   Age: 33

YEAR	TEAM	LVL	AGE	PA	R	2B	3B	HR	RBI	BB	SO	SB	CS	SPEED	AVG	OBP	SLG	MLVR	EQAVG	EQOBP	EQSLG	EQA	VORP	DEFENSE		
2004	PHI	MLB	30	145	19	7	0	7	26	22	27	2	0	4.1	.285	.393	.512	.235	.276	.386	.488	.301	10.9	13-CF	3	
2004	SFN	MLB	30	60	6	2	0	0	4	5	20	1	0	5.2	.113	.200	.151	-.669	.019	.117	.019	.089	-7.8			
2005	LAN	MLB	31	266	31	16	1	7	39	20	55	0	0	4.2	.278	.335	.443	.078	.281	.336	.455	.273	8.6	44-LF	-10	10-RF 0
2006	LAN	MLB	32	55	4	5	0	1	8	2	10	1	0	3.6	.245	.273	.396	-.166	.245	.273	.377	.227	-0.3			
2006	NYN	MLB	32	36	4	1	0	1	1	4	6	0	0	5.5	.094	.194	.219	-.617	.062	.167	.188	.140	-4.1			
2007	NYN	MLB	33	176	19	9	1	4	20	15	35	1	1	4.5	.243	.311	.381	-.159	.246	.314	.393	.243	-0.5	45-DH		

Breakout: 30% Improve: 55% Collapse: 22% Attrition: 54%   Comparables: Bill Renna, Mark Smith, Harry Spilman, Tito Francona

He batted .151 as a pinch-hitter, which is kind of an occupational hazard; even renowned pinch-hitters such as Smoky Burgess had years like that, though in Smoky's case he was 40 and took it as a sign that he should retire. With visits to the DL in each of the last three seasons, Ledee has been a more consistent patient than hitter. In 2006, he missed a good deal of time with a strained groin. It's just as well; he shouldn't be a candidate for anything greater than the 150 to 200-at-bat role his injuries have limited him to, if that.

Paul Lo Duca   C   Bats: R   Throws: R   Height: 5′ 10″   Weight: 185   Born: April 12, 1972   Age: 35

YEAR	TEAM	LVL	AGE	PA	R	2B	3B	HR	RBI	BB	SO	SB	CS	SPEED	AVG	OBP	SLG	MLVR	EQAVG	EQOBP	EQSLG	EQA	VORP	DEFENSE	
2004	LAN	MLB	32	381	41	18	1	10	49	22	27	2	4	3.5	.301	.351	.444	.101	.306	.355	.454	.273	17.3	79-C	-1
2004	FLO	MLB	32	213	27	11	1	3	31	14	22	2	1	5.1	.258	.314	.376	-.088	.265	.318	.381	.248	1.9	38-C	4
2005	FLO	MLB	33	496	45	23	1	6	57	34	31	4	3	4.3	.283	.334	.380	-.001	.292	.342	.400	.260	15.9	116-C	-5
2006	NYN	MLB	34	551	80	39	1	5	49	24	38	3	0	4.9	.318	.355	.428	.095	.323	.360	.438	.277	27.2	114-C	-7
2007	NYN	MLB	35	506	58	28	2	6	51	28	39	3	2	4.8	.287	.331	.395	-.073	.291	.334	.407	.255	14.6	119-C	-3

Breakout: 7% Improve: 30% Collapse: 40% Attrition: 17%   Comparables: Vic Power, Jerry Grote, Don Slaught, Felipe Alou

Lo Duca wouldn't have been blamed if he had done his traditional second-half fade last year, or even a first-half fade, given that his marriage imploded in full view of the public when his wife filed for divorce and his affair with a 19 year old hit the tabloids. Instead, Lo Duca seemed to thrive on the adversity, "enjoying" his most consistent season since 2001. Reversing his historical pattern, he was actually better in the second half, batting .338/.369/.450 after the break versus .302/.343/.409 before it. Defensively, Lo Duca has some problems. Catchers' fielding percentages are misleading because they receive a putout for each strikeout caught, thereby disguising their rate of errors on plays in which they actually are active participants. With the strikeouts removed, the fielding percentage for all catchers who caught 100 or more innings last year was .919. Lo Duca made 10 errors in 80 chances for a .875 percentage, which ranked 59th in a group of 72. Limit that group to catchers with 400 or more innings caught and he was 29th out of 33. Over the last three seasons, the "true" fielding percentage of catchers with more than 1000 innings caught was .933; Lo Duca's .920 ranked 27th of 36. Lo Duca's contract is up at the end of the year, and given his age and the weakness of his game beyond batting average, the Mets should be considering possible replacements.

Eli Marrero — UT — Bats: R — Throws: R — Height: 6' 1" — Weight: 180 — Born: November 17, 1973 — Age: 33

YEAR	TEAM	LVL	AGE	PA	R	2B	3B	HR	RBI	BB	SO	SB	CS	SPEED	AVG	OBP	SLG	MLVR	EQAVG	EQOBP	EQSLG	EQA	VORP	DEFENSE			
2004	ATL	MLB	30	280	37	18	1	10	40	23	50	4	1	5.4	.320	.374	.520	.260	.316	.369	.520	.301	19.1	44-LF	1	22-RF	-1
2005	KCA	MLB	31	100	11	4	0	4	9	7	18	1	0	4.7	.159	.222	.341	-.373	.151	.224	.326	.202	-6.8				
2005	BAL	MLB	31	56	8	3	2	3	10	4	20	0	0	5.3	.220	.268	.540	.021	.224	.286	.551	.275	1.4				
2006	COL	MLB	32	72	7	3	0	4	10	11	16	3	0	4.9	.217	.347	.467	.012	.200	.333	.433	.272	2.1				
2006	NYN	MLB	32	41	4	1	0	2	5	4	15	2	0	5.9	.182	.282	.394	-.187	.176	.275	.382	.243	-0.2				
2007	NYN	MLB	33	219	29	11	1	9	30	23	53	6	2	5.3	.246	.331	.456	-.023	.249	.334	.471	.274	6.5				

Breakout: 23% Improve: 54% Collapse: 11% Attrition: 36% Comparables: Eric Davis, Ted Savage, Pat Mullin, Adrian Garrett

The Mets' "reward" for ridding themselves of Kaz Matsui, Marrero was waived in early August and vanished without a trace. A career .233/.289/.391 hitter versus right-handed pitching, he's not quite Eduardo Perez against lefties, so playing him in a pure platoon role isn't all that useful. Marrero is valuable only in a very limited set of circumstances, say for a team with a predominately left-handed lineup that also has light-hitting catchers. Enter the Cardinals, who got Marrero on a minor league deal, so Marrero gets a chance to be the new Scott Hemond, or, since he played that role for LaRussa as recently as 2003, the old Eli Marrero.

Fernando Martinez — CF — Bats: L — Throws: R — Height: 6' 0" — Weight: 185 — Born: October 10, 1988 — Age: 18

YEAR	TEAM	LVL	AGE	PA	R	2B	3B	HR	RBI	BB	SO	SB	CS	SPEED	AVG	OBP	SLG	MLVR	EQAVG	EQOBP	EQSLG	EQA	VORP	DEFENSE	
2006	HAG	A	17	211	24	14	2	5	28	15	36	7	4	5.1	.333	.389	.505	.355	.313	.351	.480	.282	16.1	43-CF	-5
2006	SLU	A+	17	130	18	4	2	5	11	6	24	1	1	6.0	.193	.254	.387	-.119	.180	.223	.352	.198	-9.6	27-CF	0
2007	NYN	MLB	18	463	50	27	3	10	46	21	74	6	4	5.3	.258	.296	.406	-.143	.261	.299	.418	.241	3.6	110-CF	-3

Breakout: 35% Improve: 61% Collapse: 15% Attrition: 6% Comparables: Alex Fernandez, Josh Hamilton, Miguel Cabrera, Kimani Newton

After years of failing to develop any outfielders of note, the Mets have a few coming. They signed Dominican teen titan Martinez for $1.4 million, then sent him to the full-season Sally League at the tender age of 17. He acquitted himself beautifully, though advanced A-ball proved to be too much, too soon—in part due to knee and wrist injuries. It's early, but at this stage you'd have to say the sky's the limit.

Lastings Milledge — OF — Bats: R — Throws: R — Height: 6' 1" — Weight: 185 — Born: April 5, 1985 — Age: 22

YEAR	TEAM	LVL	AGE	PA	R	2B	3B	HR	RBI	BB	SO	SB	CS	SPEED	AVG	OBP	SLG	MLVR	EQAVG	EQOBP	EQSLG	EQA	VORP	DEFENSE			
2004	CMB	A	19	294	66	22	1	13	58	17	53	23	6	7.6	.340	.399	.580	.423	.307	.345	.511	.288	23.6	56-CF	-9		
2004	SLU	A+	19	93	6	6	2	2	8	9	21	3	2	5.7	.235	.319	.432	.050	.214	.283	.381	.230	-2.3	21-CF	2		
2005	SLU	A+	20	269	48	15	0	4	22	19	41	18	13	6.6	.302	.385	.418	.168	.273	.335	.388	.249	5.1	59-CF	-2		
2005	BIN	AA	20	214	33	17	0	4	24	14	47	11	5	5.9	.337	.392	.487	.270	.306	.357	.454	.280	13.3	41-CF	-3		
2006	NOR	AAA	21	367	52	21	4	7	36	43	67	13	10	6.3	.277	.388	.440	.250	.300	.398	.492	.299	35.7	54-CF	-1	21-LF	1
2006	NYN	MLB	21	185	14	7	2	4	22	12	39	1	2	4.0	.241	.310	.380	-.118	.246	.314	.401	.243	-3.8	23-RF	-4	21-LF	1
2007	NYN	MLB	22	562	82	31	3	16	62	47	100	17	10	5.8	.284	.356	.457	.052	.288	.359	.471	.281	24.5	132-CF	-2		

Breakout: 18% Improve: 48% Collapse: 20% Attrition: 5% Comparables: Jack Clark, Adrian Beltre, Cody Ross, Carney Lansford

(continued next page)

Lastings Milledge *(continued)*

Milledge acts like he's the second coming of Deion Sanders, Rickey Henderson, and Madonna combined, not exactly the best way to win friends and influence people. Statistical comparisons to Jack Clark or Adrian Beltre aside, a more instructive comparison might be to Rondell White or Brian Jordan. That ain't bad—prior to turning 30, White was a career .295/ .351/.484 hitter, while Jordan finished his peak period at .291/.339/.474—but it doesn't make you a star or even an All-Star in most seasons (White and Jordan made one All-Star team each). Given Milledge's youth, significant growth is still possible, but, for now, the disconnect between Milledge's self-regard and his actual abilities is the reason the Mets haven't wholly committed to him.

Jose Reyes　　　　　**SS**　　　**Bats: S**　**Throws: R**　　Height: 6' 0"　Weight: 175　Born: June 11, 1983　　Age: 24

YEAR	TEAM	LVL	AGE	PA	R	2B	3B	HR	RBI	BB	SO	SB	CS	SPEED	AVG	OBP	SLG	MLVR	EQAVG	EQOBP	EQSLG	EQA	VORP	DEFENSE	
2004	NYN	MLB	21	229	33	16	2	2	14	5	31	19	2	8.5	.255	.271	.373	-.171	.252	.269	.369	.234	2.4	39-2B	1
2005	NYN	MLB	22	733	99	24	17	7	58	27	78	60	15	8.7	.273	.300	.386	-.068	.277	.307	.399	.252	22.4	158-SS	-11
2006	NYN	MLB	23	703	122	30	17	19	81	53	81	64	17	8.6	.300	.354	.487	.161	.307	.363	.502	.294	58.8	147-SS	-16
2007	NYN	MLB	24	662	98	29	10	14	59	38	70	58	17	8.2	.287	.330	.436	-.017	.291	.333	.450	.272	36.1	154-SS	-2

Breakout: 18%　Improve: 32%　Collapse: 22%　Attrition: 0%　　Comparables: Jimmy Rollins, Bert Campaneris, Cristian Guzman, Luis Aparicio

Speaking of Rickey, the Greatest Leadoff Hitter of All Time worked with Reyes during spring training trying to impart a greater appreciation of the strike zone. This would seem akin to bringing Babe Ruth to camp to reveal the virtues of power-hitting to Joey Gathright, and, indeed, these sorts of interventions rarely amount to much. It would seem at first as though the message got through, but this would be misunderstanding Reyes's transformation from out-machine to useful offensive player. Reyes's unintentional walk rate increased from 4 percent of his plate appearances to 7 percent, but he actually saw fractionally fewer pitches per trip, 3.60 in 2006 versus 3.62 the year before. Simultaneously, Reyes's isolated power increased from .114 to .187, which largely reflects his home run rate increasing from one every 99 at-bats to one every 34. Reyes did *not* become more selective in the sense of working the count; rather, his pitch recognition improved, leading to his guessing correctly on a greater percentage of the pitches that he saw. The results represent the maturation of a ballplayer rather than a one-year change of philosophy, and are thus much more likely to be sustained.

Jose Valentin　　　　**2B**　　　**Bats: S**　**Throws: R**　　Height: 5' 10"　Weight: 190　Born: December 31, 1969　Age: 37

YEAR	TEAM	LVL	AGE	PA	R	2B	3B	HR	RBI	BB	SO	SB	CS	SPEED	AVG	OBP	SLG	MLVR	EQAVG	EQOBP	EQSLG	EQA	VORP	DEFENSE				
2004	CHA	MLB	34	504	73	20	3	30	70	43	139	8	6	5.8	.216	.287	.473	-.119	.213	.289	.474	.254	7.6	117-SS	9			
2005	LAN	MLB	35	184	17	4	2	2	14	31	38	3	1	5.7	.170	.326	.265	-.229	.170	.326	.265	.229	-6.9	25-3B	-2	18-LF	-1	
2006	NYN	MLB	36	432	56	24	3	18	62	37	71	6	2	5.4	.271	.330	.490	.095	.273	.335	.495	.280	23.6	86-2B	15			
2007	NYN	MLB	37	336	44	15	2	13	43	34	61	5	2	5.4	.250	.330	.446	-.036	.253	.333	.460	.269	12.6	81-2B	3			

Breakout: 26%　Improve: 51%　Collapse: 19%　Attrition: 30%　　Comparables: Gary Redus, Ron Gant, Ryne Sandberg, Hank Bauer

Valentin's first season in New York made for a nice comeback story for both player and team. After missing two-thirds of the 2005 season with a knee injury, Valentin signed with the Mets for less than $1 million. Valentin was strictly a fill-in during the first month, but after everyone this side of Rod Kanehl failed at second base, Randolph gave Valentin a shot at the position, which the former shortstop and occasional third baseman and outfielder had last played 11 years earlier. Valentin responded with what was arguably the best season of his career. After, the Mets re-signed Valentin to a one-year, $4-million deal that will turn into a two-year, $8-million deal if Valentin receives 400 plate appearances. Valentin is 37, needs to be platooned (he's a career .208/.284/.309 hitter against lefties and even briefly stopped switch-hitting with the White Sox), finished the season in a slump, and has no recent record of hitting this well. Valentin's deal was by no means the wackiest handed out during the off-season, but the odds are against the Mets getting value from this one.

Chris Woodward　　　　**INF**　　　**Bats: R**　**Throws: R**　　Height: 6' 0"　Weight: 190　Born: June 27, 1976　　Age: 31

YEAR	TEAM	LVL	AGE	PA	R	2B	3B	HR	RBI	BB	SO	SB	CS	SPEED	AVG	OBP	SLG	MLVR	EQAVG	EQOBP	EQSLG	EQA	VORP	DEFENSE				
2004	TOR	MLB	28	232	21	13	4	1	24	14	46	1	2	5.3	.235	.283	.347	-.271	.226	.281	.335	.217	-5.3	57-SS	-2			
2005	NYN	MLB	29	192	16	10	0	3	18	13	46	0	0	3.8	.283	.337	.393	.008	.283	.340	.393	.258	3.1	23-1B	-2			
2006	NYN	MLB	30	253	25	10	1	3	25	23	55	1	1	4.7	.216	.289	.311	-.260	.215	.291	.305	.217	-8.4	33-2B	3	11-SS	0	
2007	NYN	MLB	31	284	29	13	2	5	27	22	57	2	2	4.9	.242	.304	.363	-.196	.246	.307	.374	.234	-0.8	69-2B	1			

Breakout: 25%　Improve: 50%　Collapse: 26%　Attrition: 43%　　Comparables: Pokey Reese, Dave Campbell, Steve Dillard, Alex Grammas

One of the Mets' cadre of failed second basemen, Woodward played far more often last year than was useful despite not hitting at all, attempting (and failing) to provide Valentin with a platoon partner. In 40 games after the All-Star break, Woodward batted .200/.268/.291. This was subsequently blamed on a torn labrum in his left shoulder, for which Woodward had surgery after the season. A free agent, Woodward has versatility in his favor, but so do the rest of the blunt tools in the utility closet. Free agent signee Damion Easley takes his place in Queens, while Woodward moves to the Braves on a one-year contract. If it matters much, the Mets came out ahead.

David Wright			3B				Bats: R		Throws: R			Height: 6' 0"		Weight: 200		Born: December 20, 1982			Age: 24	

YEAR	TEAM	LVL	AGE	PA	R	2B	3B	HR	RBI	BB	SO	SB	CS	SPEED	AVG	OBP	SLG	MLVR	EQAVG	EQOBP	EQSLG	EQA	VORP	DEFENSE	
2004	BIN	AA	21	272	44	27	0	10	40	39	41	20	6	5.8	.363	.467	.619	.572	.329	.421	.558	.327	38.9	57-3B	-2
2004	NOR	AAA	21	134	18	8	0	8	17	16	19	2	4	3.6	.298	.388	.579	.388	.293	.373	.552	.296	15.4	31-3B	1
2004	NYN	MLB	21	283	41	17	1	14	40	14	40	6	0	5.5	.293	.332	.525	.176	.293	.332	.532	.290	17.0	67-3B	-7
2005	NYN	MLB	22	657	99	42	1	27	102	72	113	17	7	5.3	.306	.388	.523	.291	.311	.394	.543	.312	57.2	159-3B	4
2006	NYN	MLB	23	661	96	40	5	26	116	66	113	20	5	5.8	.311	.381	.531	.278	.316	.387	.541	.312	54.3	152-3B	10
2007	NYN	MLB	24	633	107	37	3	29	94	72	99	18	6	5.5	.301	.385	.540	.226	.306	.388	.557	.314	58.1	148-3B	4

Breakout: 14% Improve: 53% Collapse: 21% Attrition: 1%   Comparables: Jim Ray Hart, Gil McDougald, Frank Robinson, Gary Sheffield

Last year our weighted mean PECOTA prediction for the Wright Stuff called for him to hit .299/.385/.530 with 40 doubles and 29 home runs; nice shootin'. While it's notable that among his most comparable players are guys such as Frank Robinson and Gary Sheffield, it's troubling that his most comparable player was Jim Ray Hart, a terrific hitter and defensive nightmare whose career floundered at age 26 amidst injuries and off-field problems. Relax, pilgrims, statistical models aren't destiny. That being said, there was some serious weirdness afoot in Wright's season. After hitting 20 dingers in 339 first-half at-bats, his home run stroke went Gary Gaetti 1984 in the second half, with no long balls from July 29 to August 29, a span of 100 at-bats. Seven days into the dry spell, Wright signed a six-year, $55-million contract extension (which, after baseball's WHEEEEE! MONEY! offseason, is a bargain—Aramis Ramirez got $75 million for five years from the Cubs). This was given as a reason for the slump, as were those other old favorites, altering one's swing for the home-run derby, too much off-field activity, and the later films of Woody Allen. Unless Wright opens the season in another .305/.375/.469 "slump" we can probably chalk this up to an aberrant couple of months in the life of a young player.

PITCHERS

Brian Bannister				Bats: R	Throws: R			Height: 6' 2"		Weight: 200		Born: February 28, 1981			Age: 26	

YEAR	TEAM	LVL	AGE	W	L	SV	G	GS	IP	H	BB	SO	HR	GB%	BABIP	STUFF	WHIP	ERA	PERA	EQERA	EQH9	EQBB9	EQSO9	EQHR9	VORP	WXRL
2004	SLU	A+	23	5	7	0	20	20	110¹	111	27	106	6	—	.329	-1	1.25	4.24	4.94	6.77	10.4	2.7	5.4	1.2	-13.8	—
2004	BIN	AA	23	3	3	0	8	8	44¹	45	17	28	2	—	.321	-4	1.40	4.06	4.56	5.98	9.9	3.7	4.1	0.6	-1.8	—
2005	BIN	AA	24	9	4	0	18	18	109	91	27	94	11	49.2%	.278	-2	1.08	2.56	5.36	3.52	8.0	2.8	4.9	1.3	24.8	—
2005	NOR	AAA	24	4	1	0	8	8	45¹	48	13	48	0	45.9%	.369	28	1.35	3.18	2.94	4.40	10.0	2.8	7.4	0.2	6.0	—
2006	NOR	AAA	25	3	3	0	6	6	30²	34	5	24	4	41.4%	.319	0	1.29	3.87	5.15	4.99	10.0	1.5	5.3	1.8	2.1	—
2006	NYN	MLB	25	2	1	0	8	6	38	34	22	19	4	43.9%	.252	-3	1.47	4.26	5.34	4.19	8.1	4.7	4.2	0.9	6.8	1.02
2007	KCA	MLB	26	5	8	0	35	17	107²	130	45	60	15	44.0%	.314	-8	1.62	5.77	5.41	5.20	10.0	3.6	4.6	1.1	-0.5	0.60

Breakout: 11% Improve: 38% Collapse: 34% Attrition: 7%   Comparables: Skip Lockwood, Brad Hennessey, Dave Sisler, John Stuper

Bannister beat out Aaron Heilman for the fifth rotation spot in spring training and moved up when Victor Zambrano was called back to Mars. Then, only five starts in, Bannister blew a hammy. Supposedly the strain was mild, and he was schedule to start a rehab assignment forthwith, but, on the verge of returning, he re-aggravated the injury and disappeared onto the 60-day DL until August. Even with the rotation shredded into teeny little pieces by that point, the team didn't seem particularly eager to give him back his spot. Bannister's stuff isn't great, and he really wasn't fooling anyone; he was extremely lucky on balls in play. He might need to give hitters a new look; he experimented with different changeups in spring training. Traded to the Royals for Ambiorix Burgos, it's doubtful that Bannister will get the kind of support from his new organization that he needs to succeed.

Heath Bell
Bats: R Throws: R Height: 6' 3" Weight: 225 Born: September 29, 1977 Age: 29

YEAR	TEAM	LVL	AGE	W	L	SV	G	GS	IP	H	BB	SO	HR	GB%	BABIP	STUFF	WHIP	ERA	PERA	EQERA	EQH9	EQBB9	EQSO9	EQHR9	VORP	WXRL
2004	NOR	AAA	26	3	1	16	45	0	55²	42	24	69	4	—	.295	16	1.18	3.23	4.17	3.95	7.4	4.3	8.6	0.8	10.0	—
2004	NYN	MLB	26	0	2	0	17	0	24¹	22	6	27	5	—	.309	18	1.15	3.33	4.25	3.33	8.1	1.8	8.9	1.8	6.3	0.41
2005	NOR	AAA	27	1	0	6	13	2	26²	15	5	29	1	63.5%	.233	24	0.75	1.69	2.76	2.42	5.5	1.7	7.6	0.3	9.2	—
2005	NYN	MLB	27	1	3	0	42	0	46²	56	13	43	3	46.2%	.373	10	1.48	5.59	3.17	5.85	10.8	2.3	7.6	0.6	-2.0	-0.01
2006	NOR	AAA	28	3	3	12	30	0	35¹	27	8	56	1	54.5%	.356	35	1.00	1.28	2.41	2.60	7.5	2.3	10.6	0.5	11.6	—
2006	NYN	MLB	28	0	0	0	22	0	37	51	11	35	6	52.9%	.398	3	1.68	5.11	3.98	5.68	12.1	2.4	7.6	1.2	-0.6	0.29
2007	*SDN*	*MLB*	*29*	*3*	*2*	*4*	*48*	*0*	*49¹*	*49*	*17*	*47*	*5*	*48%*	*.312*	*10*	*1.33*	*3.83*	*4.36*	*4.22*	*9.0*	*2.7*	*7.8*	*0.8*	*9.0*	*0.8*

Breakout: 35% Improve: 68% Collapse: 15% Attrition: 20% Comparables: Mike Stanton, Dick Tidrow, Luis Sanchez, Mike Timlin

Bell spent eight years in the Mets' system and all or parts of the last five years at Norfolk. His line there over the last three years is 117.1 innings pitched, 84 hits, 5 home runs, 37 walks, and 153 strikeouts, plus 34 of those save baubles, so it's safe to say the lad can pitch. And yet, there are mysteries. Bell appears to have a reverse platoon—righties have hit 13 of the 14 home runs he's allowed in the majors—and his major league BABIPs has been consistently, weirdly high, though they should come down. The Bell now toils for the Padres, having been traded with Royce Ring for Ben Johnson and Jon Adkins. He should get an opportunity to set up Trevor Hoffman.

Chad Bradford
Bats: R Throws: R Height: 6' 5" Weight: 205 Born: September 14, 1974 Age: 32

YEAR	TEAM	LVL	AGE	W	L	SV	G	GS	IP	H	BB	SO	HR	GB%	BABIP	STUFF	WHIP	ERA	PERA	EQERA	EQH9	EQBB9	EQSO9	EQHR9	VORP	WXRL
2004	OAK	MLB	29	5	7	1	68	0	59	51	24	34	5	—	.257	-8	1.27	4.42	4.57	4.65	7.8	3.3	4.8	0.6	9.6	0.80
2005	BOS	MLB	30	2	1	0	31	0	23¹	29	4	10	1	68.7%	.341	-7	1.41	3.86	3.82	3.28	10.2	1.5	3.6	0.4	5.1	0.35
2006	NYN	MLB	31	4	2	2	70	0	62	59	13	45	1	65.8%	.312	18	1.16	2.90	2.67	3.16	8.5	1.7	6.0	0.1	19.2	1.83
2007	*BAL*	*MLB*	*32*	*3*	*2*	*3*	*50*	*0*	*53²*	*59*	*13*	*32*	*3*	*61.0%*	*.313*	*-1*	*1.33*	*3.61*	*3.62*	*3.41*	*10.0*	*2.0*	*5.0*	*0.5*	*11.7*	*1.00*

Breakout: 34% Improve: 52% Collapse: 20% Attrition: 15% Comparables: Mike Timlin, Mark Eichhorn, Bob Locker, Dale Mohorcic

Last year saw a strong rebound from Chad Bradford. He got his usual allotment of groundballs, did well with lefties when forced to face them, and avoided high cholesterol foods, a problem for Mississippi natives who generally take their oysters fried. Just 10 of 53 baserunners Bradford inherited came home. Did the magic come from being reunited with old A's pitching coach Rick Peterson? Bradford signed a three-year deal to pitch for the Orioles, so he's going to find out if a different pitching guru can pilot his submarine.

Pedro Feliciano
Bats: L Throws: L Height: 5' 10" Weight: 185 Born: August 25, 1976 Age: 30

YEAR	TEAM	LVL	AGE	W	L	SV	G	GS	IP	H	BB	SO	HR	GB%	BABIP	STUFF	WHIP	ERA	PERA	EQERA	EQH9	EQBB9	EQSO9	EQHR9	VORP	WXRL
2004	NOR	AAA	27	4	3	2	32	0	35²	35	15	25	4	—	.277	-22	1.40	5.29	5.93	6.88	9.2	4.3	4.8	1.3	-5.0	—
2004	NYN	MLB	27	1	1	0	22	0	18¹	14	12	14	2	—	.235	-1	1.42	5.41	5.26	5.79	7.2	5.3	6.3	1.0	-0.3	0.34
2005	FKU	JP	28	3	2	0	37	0	37	30	13	36	5	—	.250	-6	1.16	3.89	5.06	5.00	7.8	3.8	7.0	1.5	2.4	—
2006	NYN	MLB	29	7	2	0	64	0	60¹	56	20	54	4	51.7%	.310	18	1.26	2.09	3.37	2.21	8.6	2.7	7.4	0.6	25.2	1.27
2007	*NYN*	*MLB*	*30*	*3*	*2*	*3*	*61*	*0*	*56¹*	*54*	*24*	*45*	*6*	*47.0%*	*.290*	*-1*	*1.38*	*3.90*	*4.46*	*4.32*	*8.7*	*3.4*	*6.5*	*0.8*	*9.4*	*0.80*

Breakout: 7% Improve: 25% Collapse: 41% Attrition: 16% Comparables: Steve Mingori, Dave Hamilton, Darold Knowles, Rich Rodriguez

Feliciano followed up a season pitching for the Fukuoka Softbank Hawks by riding a non-roster spring training invite to what was nearly his first full season of major league work. With Darren Oliver doing long work, Feliciano took on the spot lefty job. He fit the bill, holding left-handed batters to .231/.272/.316. As is typically the case, righties found him easier to deal with, batting .266/.354/.349; Feliciano did his best to pitch around them. He also wasn't much good at stranding inherited baserunners, saying, "be my guest" to 12 of the 39 guys he was supposed to strand. Still, that's not a bad breakthrough for a 1995 31st-round pick and former *gaijin*.

Tom Glavine
Bats: L Throws: L Height: 6' 0" Weight: 185 Born: December 31, 1969 Age: 41

YEAR	TEAM	LVL	AGE	W	L	SV	G	GS	IP	H	BB	SO	HR	GB%	BABIP	STUFF	WHIP	ERA	PERA	EQERA	EQH9	EQBB9	EQSO9	EQHR9	VORP	WXRL
2004	NYN	MLB	38	11	14	0	33	33	212¹	204	70	109	20	—	.270	7	1.29	3.60	4.28	3.76	8.5	2.6	4.1	0.8	40.4	4.97
2005	NYN	MLB	39	13	13	0	33	33	211¹	227	61	105	12	48.7%	.308	14	1.36	3.54	3.81	3.89	9.6	2.3	4.1	0.5	42.4	5.44
2006	NYN	MLB	40	15	7	0	32	32	198	202	62	131	22	46.2%	.299	12	1.33	3.82	4.17	4.17	9.2	2.5	5.4	0.9	37.1	4.98
2007	*NYN*	*MLB*	*41*	*12*	*10*	*0*	*30*	*30*	*190²*	*195*	*60*	*108*	*21*	*50.0%*	*.282*	*2*	*1.34*	*4.05*	*4.47*	*4.53*	*9.2*	*2.5*	*4.6*	*0.9*	*26.7*	*4.30*

Breakout: 0% Improve: 33% Collapse: 28% Attrition: 3% Comparables: Kenny Rogers, Warren Spahn, Jerry Koosman, Jamie Moyer

Between the 2005 and 2006 All-Star breaks, Glavine made 34 starts. His line over that stretch was 228.1 innings, 211 hits, 56 walks, 141 strikeouts, and an ERA of 2.88—it was 1992 and 1993 all over again. Then came numbness in his ring finger and fears of a major blood clot. Thankfully for Glavine and fans of future Hall of Famers, these proved to be unfounded. Upon returning from the clot scare (he missed two weeks between the initial investigation and the need to let the incision from the angiogram heal), he was himself again, posting a 3.38 ERA in six September starts. However, those all came on six days' rest as the Mets looked to keep their most effective ambulatory pitcher upright for the playoffs. All together, Glavine posted his highest strikeout rate since 1998(!), and seems like a safe bet for at least one more year. After apparently agonizing over a return to Atlanta, Glavine re-upped with the Mets for a one-year deal worth $10.5 million with a 2008 option that vests if he pitches 160 innings this year. Like his Bronx borough counterpart, Mike Mussina, Glavine spared his team from the inflationary wave that struck the pitching market this offseason.

Aaron Heilman   Bats: R   Throws: R   Height: 6' 5"   Weight: 220   Born: November 12, 1978   Age: 28

YEAR	TEAM	LVL	AGE	W	L	SV	G	GS	IP	H	BB	SO	HR	GB%	BABIP	STUFF	WHIP	ERA	PERA	EQERA	EQH9	EQBB9	EQSO9	EQHR9	VORP	WXRL
2004	NOR	AAA	25	7	10	0	26	26	151²	156	66	123	15	—	.307	1	1.46	4.33	5.22	5.67	9.5	4.3	5.6	1.1	-1.2	—
2004	NYN	MLB	25	1	3	0	5	5	28	27	13	22	4	—	.291	6	1.43	5.46	4.72	5.34	8.5	3.8	6.3	1.3	0.7	0.41
2005	NYN	MLB	26	5	3	5	53	7	108	87	37	106	6	46.8%	.290	29	1.15	3.17	3.27	3.47	7.5	2.8	8.1	0.5	25.9	3.30
2006	NYN	MLB	27	4	5	0	74	0	87	73	28	73	5	46.5%	.286	18	1.16	3.62	3.30	3.70	7.7	2.6	6.9	0.5	20.6	3.27
2007	NYN	MLB	28	4	3	3	59	1	74¹	69	29	61	7	47.0%	.285	4	1.32	3.81	4.12	4.25	8.4	3.2	6.7	0.8	13.4	1.20

Breakout: 21%   Improve: 39%   Collapse: 32%   Attrition: 11%   Comparables: Mike Henneman, Ken Forsch, Jay Powell, Barry Jones

No one's fool, Willie Randolph looked at Heilman's 5.88 ERA in 25 starts over the last three years and decided that he belonged in the bullpen, no matter how the former first-round pick felt about it. The results were somewhat disappointing given how well Heilman had done in the pen in 2005—his strikeout rate fell, and he allowed 7 of his 14 inherited baserunners to score while leaving a few messes of his own for other relievers to clean up. As a result, his Fair Run Average (like RA but adjusted to reflect inherited and bequeathed baserunners) was 4.14. To date, the Mets have resisted all trade entreaties for Heilman, but, in truth, they overvalue him a bit.

Orlando Hernandez   Bats: R   Throws: R   Height: 6' 2"   Weight: 220   Born: December 31, 1969   Age: 37

YEAR	TEAM	LVL	AGE	W	L	SV	G	GS	IP	H	BB	SO	HR	GB%	BABIP	STUFF	WHIP	ERA	PERA	EQERA	EQH9	EQBB9	EQSO9	EQHR9	VORP	WXRL
2004	NYA	MLB	34	8	2	0	15	15	84²	73	36	84	9	—	.286	30	1.29	3.29	3.92	3.09	7.4	3.4	8.2	0.8	27.6	3.24
2005	CHA	MLB	35	9	9	1	24	22	128¹	137	50	91	18	40.0%	.306	3	1.46	5.12	5.00	5.12	10.0	3.5	6.3	1.2	6.9	1.43
2006	ARI	MLB	36	2	4	0	9	9	45²	52	20	52	8	31.7%	.373	19	1.58	6.11	4.43	5.51	9.9	3.4	9.1	1.3	-0.4	0.75
2006	NYN	MLB	36	9	7	0	20	20	116²	103	41	112	14	36.4%	.287	25	1.23	4.09	3.98	4.27	8.2	2.7	7.9	1.0	19.4	3.37
2007	NYN	MLB	37	10	9	0	30	26	166	157	61	146	22	39.0%	.285	14	1.31	4.18	4.57	4.56	8.5	3.0	7.1	1.1	22.7	3.60

Breakout: 12%   Improve: 49%   Collapse: 15%   Attrition: 2%   Comparables: Charlie Hough, Tim Wakefield, Mark Gardner, Tom Candiotti

Omar Minaya is a capital O optimist. Having signed El Duque to a two-year, $13-million contract, he must be optimistic that Hernandez will be 37 next year, not 41. Having seen El Duque sidelined for two weeks by a "tired arm," then knocked out of the playoffs by a torn right calf muscle, as well as missing time with a sore back while with Arizona, he must be optimistic that Hernandez will show more durability at his advanced age—whatever it is—than he has at any point in a major league career that has included seven DL stays in eight seasons. Having watched Hernandez post an ERA of 5.40 with the White Sox and Diamondbacks, he must hope that his Mets ERA was for real. It seems unlikely that all of those wishes will come true, but here's hoping that they do—the majors are a more colorful place with El Duque in them.

Roberto Hernandez   Bats: R   Throws: R   Height: 6' 4"   Weight: 245   Born: November 11, 1964   Age: 41

YEAR	TEAM	LVL	AGE	W	L	SV	G	GS	IP	H	BB	SO	HR	GB%	BABIP	STUFF	WHIP	ERA	PERA	EQERA	EQH9	EQBB9	EQSO9	EQHR9	VORP	WXRL
2004	PHI	MLB	39	3	5	0	63	0	56²	66	29	44	9	53%	.337	-14	1.68	4.76	5.04	6.05	10.4	4.0	6.2	1.2	-3.1	-1.3
2005	NYN	MLB	40	8	6	4	67	0	69²	57	28	61	5	41%	.283	14	1.22	2.58	3.70	2.80	7.5	3.3	7.3	0.6	22.3	2.6
2006	PIT	MLB	41	0	3	2	46	0	43	46	24	33	3	49%	.312	0	1.63	2.93	4.09	4.37	8.7	4.2	6.0	0.6	4.9	-0.3
2006	NYN	MLB	41	0	0	0	22	0	20²	15	8	15	2	42%	.236	1	1.11	3.48	4.04	3.48	6.5	3.0	6.1	0.9	5.7	0.4
2007	CLE	MLB	42	3	3	2	53	0	59¹	64	25	40	7	47%	.302	-10	1.50	4.89	4.62	4.74	9.3	3.6	5.6	1.0	4.2	0.4

Breakout: 3%   Improve: 22%   Collapse: 33%   Attrition: 25%   Comparables: Rich Gossage, Woodie Fryman, Mike Morgan, Don McMahon

(continued next page)

Roberto Hernandez *(continued)*

Now, this guy we know is 42. The great thing about Hernandez's 15-year career is that it almost didn't happen at all—blood clots nearly took him off the board before his major league debut. From now until the end of his career, he'll be working on a series of one-year contracts. But then, aren't we all? Top five seasons by a 40-plus relievers according to Wins Above Replacement (WARP): 1. Doug Jones, 1997 (9.1), 2. Dutch Leonard, 1952 (7.1), 3. Hoyt Wilhelm, 1964 (7.6), 4. Hoyt Wilhelm, 1965 (6.6), 5. Roberto Hernandez, 2005 (5.5). Signed by the Indians to help fill a wide-open bullpen, Hernandez could do anything from setting up, to closing now and again, to acting his age and getting released.

Philip Humber Bats: R Throws: R   Height: 6' 4"   Weight: 210   Born: December 21, 1982   Age: 24

YEAR	TEAM	LVL	AGE	W	L	SV	G	GS	IP	H	BB	SO	HR	GB%	BABIP	STUFF	WHIP	ERA	PERA	EQERA	EQH9	EQBB9	EQSO9	EQHR9	VORP	WXRL
2005	SLU	A+	22	2	6	0	14	14	70¹	74	18	65	6	45.2%	.340	-7	1.31	4.99	5.59	6.45	10.7	3.0	5.1	1.4	-6.5	—
2006	SLU	A+	23	3	1	0	7	7	38¹	24	9	36	4	53.4%	.211	-1	0.87	2.36	6.48	4.04	7.8	2.8	5.3	2.0	6.2	—
2006	BIN	AA	23	2	2	0	6	6	34	25	10	36	4	41.9%	.239	10	1.03	2.91	5.57	4.09	8.2	3.0	6.5	1.6	5.5	—
2007	NYN	MLB	24	6	7	0	30	16	110²	112	44	78	17	43.0%	.280	1	1.41	4.82	5.27	5.27	9.1	3.2	5.7	1.3	7.1	1.40

Breakout: 10% Improve: 40% Collapse: 20% Attrition: 0%   Comparables: Jason Bell, Eric Schmitt, Todd Wellemeyer, Kenny Baugh

Humber, the third overall pick in the 2004 draft, missed almost a year recovering from Tommy John surgery, but returned in June and pitched quite well. His fastball was still reaching 90 to 94 MPH, his curve still looked great, and his changeup was sharp. He had about the best recovery from surgery that one could have. The only discordant note was some shoulder tendonitis that got Humber pulled from the Arizona Fall League after two innings, but he's expected to be ready to compete for a rotation spot in the spring. Phillip Humber's nickname should be "Humber"; baseball needs more Nabokov references.

Matt Lindstrom Bats: R Throws: R   Height: 6' 4"   Weight: 210   Born: February 11, 1980   Age: 27

YEAR	TEAM	LVL	AGE	W	L	SV	G	GS	IP	H	BB	SO	HR	GB%	BABIP	STUFF	WHIP	ERA	PERA	EQERA	EQH9	EQBB9	EQSO9	EQHR9	VORP	WXRL
2004	CMB	A	24	3	2	0	12	11	56	47	10	64	3	—	.301	6	1.02	3.21	4.23	5.47	8.8	2.2	5.5	1.0	0.8	—
2004	SLU	A+	24	5	5	0	14	14	79²	83	20	50	5	—	.306	-19	1.29	3.73	5.56	6.75	10.2	2.9	3.4	1.4	-9.9	—
2005	BIN	AA	25	2	5	0	35	10	73¹	90	55	58	11	55.6%	.345	-35	1.98	5.40	8.80	8.70	11.8	9.0	4.5	2.2	-23.9	—
2006	SLU	A+	26	1	0	2	11	0	18²	14	7	16	2	68.6%	.250	-21	1.15	2.47	7.11	4.76	9.0	4.8	4.8	2.1	1.6	—
2006	BIN	AA	26	2	4	11	35	0	40²	42	14	54	2	54.7%	.392	0	1.39	3.81	4.38	5.35	11.4	4.0	7.7	0.7	1.1	—
2007	FLO	MLB	27	3	4	1	28	6	58¹	65	36	43	8	52%	.314	-9	1.72	5.61	6.25	5.87	9.8	4.7	5.9	1.1	-1.4	0.1

Breakout: 36% Improve: 59% Collapse: 19% Attrition: 17%   Comparables: Rodney Ormond, Ben Shaffar, Kevin Gryboski, Josh Kinney

Lindstrom got a late start on his career due to religious commitments. He could earn a bullpen spot with a fastball that reaches triple-digits, but he doesn't have a second pitch to rely on, and the heater is as straight as an arrow. He was shipped to the Marlins as the second player (with Henry Owens) in the Vargas deal.

John Maine Bats: R Throws: R   Height: 6' 4"   Weight: 205   Born: May 8, 1981   Age: 26

YEAR	TEAM	LVL	AGE	W	L	SV	G	GS	IP	H	BB	SO	HR	GB%	BABIP	STUFF	WHIP	ERA	PERA	EQERA	EQH9	EQBB9	EQSO9	EQHR9	VORP	WXRL
2004	BOW	AA	23	4	0	0	5	5	28	16	7	34	1	—	.227	28	0.82	2.25	3.09	3.25	5.9	2.6	7.8	0.3	7.2	—
2004	OTT	AAA	23	5	7	0	22	22	119²	123	52	105	12	—	.316	8	1.46	3.91	4.90	4.34	9.0	4.2	6.1	1.0	16.8	—
2005	OTT	AAA	24	6	11	0	23	23	128¹	128	42	111	13	41.3%	.307	7	1.33	4.56	4.53	5.19	9.1	3.2	6.0	1.1	5.8	—
2005	BAL	MLB	24	2	3	0	10	8	40	39	24	24	8	45.1%	.248	-10	1.58	6.30	6.58	6.15	8.3	5.3	5.3	1.8	-4.4	0.15
2006	NOR	AAA	25	3	5	0	10	10	56¹	55	20	48	2	52.3%	.317	14	1.34	3.53	3.73	4.74	8.4	3.3	5.8	0.5	5.4	—
2006	NYN	MLB	25	6	5	0	16	15	90	69	33	71	15	40.4%	.225	9	1.13	3.60	4.82	3.87	6.9	2.9	6.5	1.4	19.3	2.38
2007	NYN	MLB	26	8	8	0	34	22	137¹	129	57	103	17	41.0%	.275	6	1.35	4.33	4.62	4.77	8.5	3.3	6.1	1.0	16.7	2.60

Breakout: 11% Improve: 40% Collapse: 21% Attrition: 1%   Comparables: Jack Armstrong, Paul Moskau, Charlie Lea, Mac Suzuki

State O' Maine salvaged the Kris & Anna Benson deal for the Mets, just barely. Maine didn't make the Mets' rotation out of spring training, but was called up to replace the injured Bannister. Maine's first few starts were rough, but after an injury timeout for an inflamed middle finger (no gags, please), he was a consistent part of the rotation. He also pitched well in two of three postseasons starts, though Randolph kept him on as short a leash as he did throughout the season. Indeed, Randolph showed little confidence in Maine at times, and, until every other member of the starting rotation ate the salmon mousse, he planned to put him in the bullpen for the postseason. Maine was especially tough on righties, though what they did hit went for distance. The key to his success was limiting hitters to a .225 average on balls in play, the lowest against any pitcher in baseball with 70 or more innings pitched. Lady Luck is certain to be less kind this year.

Pedro Martinez
Bats: R Throws: R   Height: 5′ 11″ Weight: 180   Born: October 25, 1971   Age: 35

YEAR	TEAM	LVL	AGE	W	L	SV	G	GS	IP	H	BB	SO	HR	GB%	BABIP	STUFF	WHIP	ERA	PERA	EQERA	EQH9	EQBB9	EQSO9	EQHR9	VORP	WXRL
2004	BOS	MLB	32	16	9	0	33	33	217	193	61	227	26	—	.299	35	1.17	3.90	3.57	3.68	7.9	2.3	8.7	0.9	54.4	6.27
2005	NYN	MLB	33	15	8	0	31	31	217	159	47	208	19	40.1%	.253	39	0.95	2.82	3.19	3.05	6.8	1.8	7.9	0.8	64.8	7.62
2006	NYN	MLB	34	9	8	0	23	23	132²	108	39	137	19	36.5%	.266	26	1.11	4.48	3.99	4.65	7.6	2.3	8.5	1.1	15.4	3.11
2007	NYN	MLB	35	12	6	0	26	26	167¹	134	46	164	20	39.0%	.258	27	1.07	2.98	3.31	3.27	7.2	2.2	7.9	1.0	47.3	6.20

Breakout: 35% Improve: 61% Collapse: 6%   Attrition: 6%   Comparables: Early Wynn, Tom Seaver, Mike Mussina, Don Sutton

Three years ago, the Red Sox made an eminently sane, restrained decision not to offer Pedro Martinez the sort of multi-year contract it would have taken to keep him in Boston. That they would later abandon all restraint and sanity in pursuing Daisuke Matsuzaka does not alter the rationality of the earlier decision. The nexus of Martinez's contract demands and increasing risk of breakdown made him a poor risk for a long-term deal. Even the Mets knew it would be all fun and games until Martinez got hurt, which was exactly what happened. That doesn't make their decision wrong; it just means they placed less of an emphasis on the fun/dollars ratio than the Sox did. Martinez was his old self through the end of May, posting a 2.50 ERA and an 88-17 strikeout-to-walk ratio in 75.2 innings. Even then, though, his season was one long medical report, as Martinez was slowed early on by his right big toe, an injury carried over from 2005. He then had two long DL stays as the result of an inflamed hip (the result of a clubhouse fall) and a strained right calf. When he returned from a month away, he was relentlessly hammered, posting an 11.81 ERA in three September starts, and appeared to be emotionally distraught. Further examinations revealed a torn left calf, but more seriously, Martinez had also suffered a torn rotator cuff, perhaps the result of altering his motion to compensate for the other injuries. After October surgery, Martinez raised the possibility of retirement; he won't be back until the All-Star break at earliest. Given his age and increasing fragility, what we see when he pitches again may be different than what came before. Pedro the Hall of Famer may have exited for good in May, 2006.

Guillermo Mota
Bats: R Throws: R   Height: 6′ 4″   Weight: 210   Born: July 25, 1973   Age: 33

YEAR	TEAM	LVL	AGE	W	L	SV	G	GS	IP	H	BB	SO	HR	GB%	BABIP	STUFF	WHIP	ERA	PERA	EQERA	EQH9	EQBB9	EQSO9	EQHR9	VORP	WXRL
2004	LAN	MLB	30	8	4	1	52	0	63	51	27	52	4	—	.280	12	1.24	2.14	3.76	2.43	7.7	3.4	6.7	0.6	24.8	2.93
2004	FLO	MLB	30	1	4	3	26	0	33²	24	10	33	4	—	.241	13	1.01	4.81	3.91	4.81	6.7	2.4	8.0	1.1	2.8	0.87
2005	FLO	MLB	31	2	2	2	56	0	67	65	32	60	5	42.3%	.314	7	1.45	4.70	3.85	5.19	8.2	3.8	7.3	0.6	1.8	1.45
2006	CLE	MLB	32	1	3	0	34	0	37²	45	19	27	9	30.6%	.313	-19	1.70	6.21	6.04	5.95	9.6	4.1	5.9	1.8	-2.0	-0.18
2006	NYN	MLB	32	3	0	0	18	0	18	10	5	19	2	47.7%	.190	18	0.83	1.00	3.29	1.00	5.0	2.0	8.5	1.0	10.0	0.83
2007	NYN	MLB	33	3	3	2	53	0	62²	62	25	50	9	40.0%	.286	-3	1.38	4.33	4.73	4.75	8.9	3.2	6.4	1.1	7.3	0.60

Breakout: 8% Improve: 32% Collapse: 32% Attrition: 20%   Comparables: Tim Worrell, Doug Henry, Bill Campbell, Bobby Bolin

After a rough patch with the Indians, Mota turned his season around in New York. Apparently performance-enhancing drugs had something to do with it, as he's been suspended for the first 50 games of the 2007 season. Minaya decided to make it a paid vacation, re-signing Mota to a two-year, $5-million dollar contract. It was Dwight Gooden's misfortune not to have this kind of forgiving enabler in the front office in the mid-nineties.

Darren Oliver
Bats: R Throws: L   Height: 6′ 2″   Weight: 220   Born: October 6, 1970   Age: 36

YEAR	TEAM	LVL	AGE	W	L	SV	G	GS	IP	H	BB	SO	HR	GB%	BABIP	STUFF	WHIP	ERA	PERA	EQERA	EQH9	EQBB9	EQSO9	EQHR9	VORP	WXRL
2004	FLO	MLB	33	2	3	0	18	8	58²	75	17	33	13	—	.328	-24	1.57	6.44	5.64	6.79	11.3	2.3	4.5	1.8	-6.8	-0.46
2004	HOU	MLB	33	1	0	0	9	2	14	12	4	13	1	—	.306	14	1.14	3.86	3.15	3.77	7.5	2.5	7.5	0.6	2.8	0.67
2006	NYN	MLB	35	4	1	0	45	0	81	70	21	60	13	50.2%	.248	-1	1.12	3.44	4.55	3.64	7.8	2.1	6.1	1.3	21.0	1.36
2007	NYN	MLB	36	4	3	2	52	1	70²	76	22	46	7	47.0%	.301	-6	1.38	4.05	4.68	4.49	9.6	2.5	5.3	0.9	10.2	0.90

Breakout: 33% Improve: 56% Collapse: 17% Attrition: 20%   Comparables: Giovanni Carrara, Rick White, Alan Embree, Tom Burgmeier

For the first time since 1994, Oliver's manager left him in the pen. There were constant temptations to start him, just as there were with Heilman, but Randolph, proving that inflexibility can sometimes be an asset—did not budge. Oliver's August and September ERA was 6.75, but he came back to pitch six shutout innings in Game Three of the NLCS—pretty impressive given that Oliver retired in May 2005 after posting a 9.38 ERA for two minor league teams. Not to be a broken record about this whole BABIP thing, but you see the ".248" under that heading? Yeah, that's not happening again. Oliver signed a one-year deal with the Angels for 2007. They'll find out.

Henry Owens **Bats: R Throws: R** Height: 6' 3" Weight: 230 Born: April 23, 1979 Age: 28

YEAR	TEAM	LVL	AGE	W	L	SV	G	GS	IP	H	BB	SO	HR	GB%	BABIP	STUFF	WHIP	ERA	PERA	EQERA	EQH9	EQBB9	EQSO9	EQHR9	VORP	WXRL
2004	LYN	A+	25	3	4	4	39	0	54²	46	26	49	4	—	.280	-19	1.32	4.28	6.72	5.65	9.0	5.8	5.1	1.6	-0.3	—
2005	SLU	A+	26	2	5	4	38	1	54¹	49	24	74	2	43.8%	.351	3	1.34	3.15	4.90	6.39	9.9	5.7	7.3	0.7	-4.5	—
2006	BIN	AA	27	2	2	20	37	0	40¹	19	10	74	1	42.4%	.281	36	0.72	1.57	2.74	2.89	6.5	2.9	10.8	0.5	11.2	—
2007	FLO	MLB	28	2	3	1	24	2	43	42	24	43	5	43%	.315	8	1.53	4.84	5.06	4.99	8.6	4.2	8.1	0.9	3.2	0.4

Breakout: 25% Improve: 48% Collapse: 26% Attrition: 30%　　Comparables: Paul Shuey, Hector Mercado, John Wyatt, Mike Adams

Owens is a converted catcher with an unorthodox motion—he throws to the plate as if he were still a catcher trying to nail a baserunner. The Mets snagged him from the Pirates with a minor league Rule 5 pick in 2004. He missed some time last year with a small tear in his ulnar collateral ligament, but should be okay. He's a bit old to be considered a solid gold prospect, but dig those crazy strikeout rates. Traded to the Marlins with Matt Lindstrom for Adam Bostic and Jason Vargas, he should have a good chance to land a job in Florida's wide open bullpen.

Mike Pelfrey **Bats: R Throws: R** Height: 6' 7" Weight: 210 Born: November 30, 1999 Age: 23

YEAR	TEAM	LVL	AGE	W	L	SV	G	GS	IP	H	BB	SO	HR	GB%	BABIP	STUFF	WHIP	ERA	PERA	EQERA	EQH9	EQBB9	EQSO9	EQHR9	VORP	WXRL
2006	SLU	A+	0	2	1	0	4	4	22²	17	2	26	1	64.7%	.327	22	0.86	1.62	3.31	2.91	8.3	0.8	6.6	0.8	6.5	—
2006	BIN	AA	0	4	2	0	12	12	66¹	60	26	77	2	49.7%	.347	28	1.30	2.72	3.68	3.74	9.3	3.9	7.3	0.4	13.4	—
2006	NOR	AAA	0	1	0	0	2	2	8²	4	5	6	1	33.3%	.150	6	1.10	2.20	7.16	3.24	4.3	5.4	5.4	2.2	2.2	—
2006	NYN	MLB	0	2	1	0	4	4	21¹	25	12	13	1	49.3%	.353	0	1.73	5.49	4.56	5.73	10.6	4.5	4.9	0.4	-0.0	0.15
2007	NYN	MLB	23	8	8	0	35	24	137	134	61	112	14	49.0%	.297	10	1.43	4.38	4.79	4.87	8.9	3.6	6.6	0.8	15.0	2.40

Breakout: 7% Improve: 24% Collapse: 28% Attrition: 0%　　Comparables: Jason Young, Pete Munro, Josh Karp, Kris Benson

The towering Wichita State alum was the ninth overall pick in the 2005 draft, but didn't get around to signing until 2006. He made a fast trip to the majors, but that was more because of the Mets' unraveling rotation than his own readiness. Pelfrey throws a mid-90s sinking fastball, but his off-speed offerings aren't anything special right now, so much so that he junked his curve for a slider during a brief AFL stint. Pelfrey missed the end of the regular season with a strained back and ended his AFL tour early due to "general soreness." He'll compete for a rotation spot in spring training, but, unless his secondary offerings have improved, Triple-A seems more likely.

Oliver Perez **Bats: L Throws: L** Height: 6' 3" Weight: 210 Born: August 15, 1981 Age: 25

YEAR	TEAM	LVL	AGE	W	L	SV	G	GS	IP	H	BB	SO	HR	GB%	BABIP	STUFF	WHIP	ERA	PERA	EQERA	EQH9	EQBB9	EQSO9	EQHR9	VORP	WXRL
2004	PIT	MLB	22	12	10	0	30	30	196	145	81	239	22	—	.280	43	1.15	2.98	3.61	3.25	6.7	3.3	9.6	0.9	52.8	6.58
2005	PIT	MLB	23	7	5	0	20	20	103	102	70	97	23	32.2%	.297	-4	1.67	5.85	6.46	5.83	9.1	5.5	7.7	2.0	-4.4	0.56
2006	PIT	MLB	24	2	10	0	15	15	76	88	51	61	13	32.2%	.336	0	1.83	6.63	5.51	6.72	9.4	5.0	6.3	1.3	-12.4	0.27
2006	IND	AAA	24	1	3	0	6	6	32¹	28	11	34	6	33.7%	.275	-2	1.21	5.61	6.77	7.04	9.4	3.5	7.6	2.6	-4.9	—
2006	NOR	AAA	24	1	2	0	4	4	19²	18	12	26	4	44.7%	.333	12	1.56	6.09	7.74	7.23	9.6	6.3	9.6	2.9	-3.4	—
2006	NYN	MLB	24	1	3	0	7	7	36²	41	17	41	7	31.4%	.358	16	1.58	6.38	4.77	6.03	10.4	3.6	9.2	1.4	-1.9	0.40
2007	NYN	MLB	25	8	8	0	29	23	132	117	70	127	18	37.0%	.278	15	1.41	4.46	4.87	4.85	8.0	4.3	7.8	1.1	14.6	2.40

Breakout: 30% Improve: 59% Collapse: 8% Attrition: 13%　　Comparables: Arthur Rhodes, Tom Griffin, Ray Culp, Al Downing

It could be that the answer to the Oliver Perez mystery is that 2004 was just a massive fluke. Set that one season aside and you have a pitcher who has posted a career 4.89 ERA. The consensus is that Perez's stuff is just fine, but his approach to pitching is poorly conceived. He pitches up in the zone despite poor control and the result is a lot of walks and home runs. When behind in the count, Perez would rather challenge a hitter with a fastball down the middle than try to work out of trouble some other way. The hitters know this, so when a Perez Special comes down the pike, they don't miss. Pittsburgh, being baseball's most expert franchise at not knowing anything, wasn't able to help Perez find a better way. Lending credence to the notion that Perez might find salvation in Queens is that, though he continued to be gamahuched as a member of the Mets, he was significantly better. From September 1 through and including the postseason, Perez's line was 40⅓ innings, 40 hits, 13 walks, 39 strikeouts, and a 4.50 ERA. That's the good; the bad and the ugly are the eight homers he allowed over that span.

Royce Ring

Bats: L Throws: L   Height: 6′ 0″   Weight: 220   Born: December 21, 1980   Age: 26

YEAR	TEAM	LVL	AGE	W	L	SV	G	GS	IP	H	BB	SO	HR	GB%	BABIP	STUFF	WHIP	ERA	PERA	EQERA	EQH9	EQBB9	EQSO9	EQHR9	VORP	WXRL
2004	BIN	AA	23	2	2	1	19	0	28²	25	11	23	5	—	.250	-21	1.25	3.76	6.89	4.88	9.1	3.9	5.2	2.3	2.2	—
2004	NOR	AAA	23	3	1	0	29	0	34²	37	12	22	5	—	.294	-20	1.41	3.63	5.62	4.15	9.6	3.4	4.4	1.6	5.6	—
2005	NOR	AAA	24	3	0	2	33	0	38²	34	13	26	2	56.7%	.281	-8	1.21	3.26	4.33	4.46	8.2	3.3	4.7	0.5	4.9	—
2005	NYN	MLB	24	0	2	0	15	0	10²	10	10	8	0	53.1%	.313	0	1.88	5.05	4.78	5.06	9.3	7.6	5.9	0.0	0.4	0.12
2006	NOR	AAA	25	2	2	11	36	0	39	30	15	40	2	66.3%	.286	5	1.15	3.00	4.26	4.15	7.2	3.7	6.9	0.7	6.3	—
2006	NYN	MLB	25	0	0	0	11	0	12²	7	3	8	2	62.2%	.143	3	0.79	2.13	4.59	2.08	4.8	2.1	4.8	1.4	5.4	0.18
2007	SDN	MLB	26	3	3	3	56	2	50¹	46	22	36	4	53%	.275	-1	1.34	3.72	4.17	4.17	8.3	3.3	5.9	0.7	10.2	0.9

Breakout: 18%   Improve: 39%   Collapse: 43%   Attrition: 21%   Comparables: Mike Beard, Steve Kline, Marc Wilkins, C. J. Nitkowski

Ring was a Met long enough to have been traded for Roberto Alomar. The team never showed much interest in using the former first-round pick as a situational lefty despite some decent minor league results—this year, lefties hit .140/.204/.140 against him, albeit in a small sample. Shipped to the Padres in the Ben Johnson deal, he should get more of an opportunity.

Duaner Sanchez

Bats: R Throws: R   Height: 6′ 2″   Weight: 210   Born: October 14, 1979   Age: 27

YEAR	TEAM	LVL	AGE	W	L	SV	G	GS	IP	H	BB	SO	HR	GB%	BABIP	STUFF	WHIP	ERA	PERA	EQERA	EQH9	EQBB9	EQSO9	EQHR9	VORP	WXRL
2004	LAN	MLB	24	3	1	0	67	0	80	81	27	44	9	—	.287	-11	1.35	3.38	4.78	4.15	9.5	2.7	4.5	0.9	16.3	0.97
2005	LAN	MLB	25	4	7	8	79	0	82	75	36	71	8	46.6%	.299	6	1.35	3.73	4.17	4.00	8.3	3.6	7.1	0.9	13.6	1.72
2006	NYN	MLB	26	5	1	0	48	0	55¹	43	24	44	3	54.4%	.274	11	1.21	2.60	3.80	3.07	7.3	3.4	6.6	0.5	17.7	2.80
2007	NYN	MLB	27	3	3	2	55	0	66	67	27	48	7	48.0%	.295	-2	1.42	3.99	4.65	4.44	9.1	3.3	5.9	0.9	10.2	0.90

Breakout: 3%   Improve: 24%   Collapse: 42%   Attrition: 18%   Comparables: Jay Powell, Pete Mikkelsen, Albie Lopez, Mike Garman

As Casey Stengel said when Don Larsen crashed his car in the predawn hours, the man was either out too late or out too early. Of course, Sanchez was a passenger in a Miami taxi, apparently out looking for a post-midnight snack. The munchies cost Sanchez a severely separated shoulder and the last two months of the season. They also cost the Mets Xavier Nady, as Minaya instantaneously dealt for Roberto Hernandez and Oliver Perez. We'll see what Sanchez has when he comes back, but heretofore he's been a useful setup man. Even healthy, that's probably his ceiling. Lefty hitters like him a little too much (.290/.357/.455 over the last three years), and pitching away from home makes him twitchy; his 0.85 home/4.94 road ERA split is merely an extreme version of what he's been doing all along. Perhaps, as Sanchez traveled America's lonely highways, he had a premonition of being T-boned while questing for chivo liniero and casabe.

Alay Soler

Bats: R Throws: R   Height: 6′ 1″   Weight: 240   Born: October 9, 1979   Age: 27

YEAR	TEAM	LVL	AGE	W	L	SV	G	GS	IP	H	BB	SO	HR	GB%	BABIP	STUFF	WHIP	ERA	PERA	EQERA	EQH9	EQBB9	EQSO9	EQHR9	VORP	WXRL
2006	SLU	A+	26	2	0	0	6	6	30²	13	9	33	0	44.1%	.191	20	0.73	0.60	3.44	1.55	5.3	3.4	5.9	0.3	13.1	—
2006	BIN	AA	26	1	0	0	3	3	19²	16	3	22	0	46.2%	.320	19	0.99	2.81	2.72	3.79	8.5	1.9	6.2	0.5	3.8	—
2006	NOR	AAA	26	1	1	0	2	2	10¹	13	4	12	0	50.0%	.448	10	1.68	6.24	3.09	7.84	11.3	3.5	7.8	0.0	-2.6	—
2006	NYN	MLB	26	2	3	0	8	8	45	50	21	23	7	42.8%	.283	-12	1.58	6.00	5.40	6.46	9.8	3.7	4.1	1.2	-3.2	0.56
2007	NYN	MLB	27	6	7	0	35	18	116	117	48	78	16	43.0%	.282	-2	1.42	4.79	5.07	5.28	9.1	3.3	5.4	1.1	7.1	1.40

Breakout: 18%   Improve: 47%   Collapse: 22%   Attrition: 15%   Comparables: Gary Knotts, Craig Swan, Runelvys Hernandez, Eli Grba

That almost worked out. Cuban refugee Soler was signed back in August 2004, but visa problems kept him out of the country until November 2005. Soler spent about two minutes in the minors, jumping from Double-A to the majors. Rick Peterson must have sensed that Soler felt intimidated, because prior to his first start he cautioned, "It's good to have butterflies, as long as they fly in formation to the plate." Really, no pressure, kid. But Soler felt it, and there were subsequent mumblings from the Mets that he was afraid to challenge hitters. Soler put together three consecutive strong starts in June, then was bombed in his next three and got sent down. After that, Soler was shut down with a strained right calf. With Soler's stuff and slider, there's still a high upside here. As we've seen with other Cuban imports, finding his comfort level might just be a process of acculturation. Keep in mind that he's 28 if we credit his listed age, so this is it.

Steve Trachsel
Bats: R Throws: R   Height: 6' 4"   Weight: 205   Born: October 31, 1970   Age: 36

YEAR	TEAM	LVL	AGE	W	L	SV	G	GS	IP	H	BB	SO	HR	GB%	BABIP	STUFF	WHIP	ERA	PERA	EQERA	EQH9	EQBB9	EQSO9	EQHR9	VORP	WXRL
2004	NYN	MLB	33	12	13	0	33	33	202²	203	83	117	25	—	.282	1	1.41	4.00	4.85	4.37	9.0	3.3	4.6	1.0	24.8	4.10
2005	NYN	MLB	34	1	4	0	6	6	37	37	12	24	6	41.4%	.282	2	1.32	4.14	5.10	5.02	9.1	2.6	5.3	1.4	3.0	0.66
2006	NYN	MLB	35	15	8	0	30	30	164²	185	78	79	23	43.4%	.299	-12	1.60	4.97	5.29	4.98	10.0	3.7	3.9	1.1	14.9	2.89
2007	NYN	MLB	36	9	10	0	30	27	161	172	69	88	23	43.0%	.282	-6	1.49	4.89	5.45	5.37	9.6	3.4	4.4	1.2	8.7	2.10

Breakout: 11% Improve: 26% Collapse: 42% Attrition: 7%   Comparables: Bob Welch, Bob Forsch, Jim Palmer, Mike Torrez

Entry #365,983 in the "Wins Are An Overrated Stat" casebook, Trachsel posted a Quality Start in just 13 of 30 starts, a 43 percent rate which ranked 116th among major league pitchers with 10 or more starts (the top ten ranged from Roy Oswalt at 78 percent to Tom Glavine at 69 percent), yet he tied for 20th in the majors with 15 wins. Over six runs of support a game (6.61, most in the league) can get one out of a lot of trouble. A free agent, Trachsel is unsigned at this writing. It's not clear how much he has left at age 35, but given the kind of rewards less accomplished pitchers have been receiving, Trachsel will probably be given his own island. Is that socialism?

Billy Wagner
Bats: L Throws: L   Height: 5' 11"   Weight: 205   Born: July 25, 1971   Age: 35

YEAR	TEAM	LVL	AGE	W	L	SV	G	GS	IP	H	BB	SO	HR	GB%	BABIP	STUFF	WHIP	ERA	PERA	EQERA	EQH9	EQBB9	EQSO9	EQHR9	VORP	WXRL
2004	PHI	MLB	32	4	0	21	45	0	48¹	31	6	59	5	—	.243	36	0.77	2.42	2.71	2.98	6.0	0.9	9.9	0.9	14.6	3.14
2005	PHI	MLB	33	4	3	38	75	0	77²	45	20	87	6	44.9%	.218	35	0.84	1.51	2.95	2.08	5.5	2.1	9.2	0.7	30.8	3.79
2006	NYN	MLB	34	3	2	40	70	0	72¹	59	21	94	7	53.4%	.308	36	1.11	2.24	2.92	2.71	7.6	2.2	10.6	0.7	26.0	5.95
2007	NYN	MLB	35	4	4	36	58	0	57	43	17	62	4	48.0%	.270	21	1.04	2.32	2.57	2.61	6.8	2.3	8.8	0.6	21.2	3.30

Breakout: 31% Improve: 46% Collapse: 27% Attrition: 6%   Comparables: Jim Brewer, Paul Assenmacher, Mike Remlinger, Gary Lavelle

Though he blew a few saves in dramatic fashion, Wagner was everything the Mets expected, at least until the NLCS. In Game Two, Wagner turned a 6–6, ninth-inning tie into a 9–6 loss (a home run by So Taguchi was the big hit), and he also pitched poorly in the team's Game Six win. As a result, Willie Randolph didn't go to Wagner in the ninth inning of Game Seven's 1–1 tie, letting Heilman go an extra inning and take the loss. After Wagner's strong regular season, there's little reason to think that he was experiencing anything more than postseason jitters. The only discordant note in his 2006 record was his hits allowed per nine innings, which was his worst outside of his injury-shortened 2000. Then again, the Mets didn't do an especially good job of catching the ball when he was on the mound. The only lefty to hit a home run off of Wagner last year? Barry Bonds, in a pinch-hit job on April 26.

Dave Williams
Bats: L Throws: L   Height: 6' 3"   Weight: 230   Born: March 12, 1979   Age: 28

YEAR	TEAM	LVL	AGE	W	L	SV	G	GS	IP	H	BB	SO	HR	GB%	BABIP	STUFF	WHIP	ERA	PERA	EQERA	EQH9	EQBB9	EQSO9	EQHR9	VORP	WXRL
2004	NAS	AAA	25	6	2	0	21	21	116²	113	33	103	10	—	.299	17	1.25	3.47	4.05	4.00	8.1	2.6	6.0	0.8	21.2	—
2004	PIT	MLB	25	2	3	0	10	6	38²	31	13	33	4	—	.255	14	1.14	4.42	4.12	4.81	7.1	2.7	6.9	0.9	2.7	0.49
2005	PIT	MLB	26	10	11	0	25	25	138²	137	58	88	20	39.8%	.281	-4	1.41	4.41	5.27	4.71	8.9	3.4	5.2	1.3	12.6	2.45
2006	CIN	MLB	27	2	3	0	8	8	40	54	16	16	9	32.9%	.315	-24	1.75	7.20	6.35	6.43	11.1	3.0	3.2	1.7	-6.6	-0.20
2006	NOR	AAA	27	2	2	0	7	6	36²	33	10	17	3	41.5%	.250	-13	1.19	3.73	5.52	5.40	7.9	2.7	3.2	1.2	0.8	—
2006	NYN	MLB	27	3	1	0	6	5	29	39	4	16	5	35.6%	.354	-2	1.48	5.59	4.70	5.52	12.0	1.2	4.6	1.5	1.2	0.73
2007	NYN	MLB	28	7	8	0	31	20	124¹	133	40	72	17	42.0%	.285	-2	1.38	4.58	5.08	5.02	9.6	2.6	4.7	1.2	11.5	2.00

Breakout: 16% Improve: 50% Collapse: 16% Attrition: 12%   Comparables: Paul Splittorff, Dave Dravecky, Bob Milacki, Woodie Fryman

From the Pirates to the Reds to New York . . . who knew the Ohio River emptied into Flushing Bay? Williams is a fly-balling lefty who hasn't done much since his rookie year of 2001. To put it in basic medical terms, labrum surgery is a drag. Williams missed most of 2002 and 2003 because of the procedure, and the pitcher he might have been before is still missing and unlikely to be found. His walk and strikeout rates are below average, he allows a ton of home runs, and even lefty hitters have hit .282/.356/.519 against him. There's very little upside here.

Victor Zambrano

Bats: S Throws: R   Height: 6' 0"   Weight: 205   Born: August 6, 1974   Age: 31

YEAR	TEAM	LVL	AGE	W	L	SV	G	GS	IP	H	BB	SO	HR	GB%	BABIP	STUFF	WHIP	ERA	PERA	EQERA	EQH9	EQBB9	EQSO9	EQHR9	VORP	WXRL
2004	TBA	MLB	29	9	7	0	23	22	128	107	96	109	13	—	.273	24	1.59	4.43	5.39	4.33	7.8	6.1	7.1	0.8	20.0	3.05
2004	NYN	MLB	29	2	0	0	3	3	14	12	6	14	0	—	.300	14	1.29	3.86	2.92	5.79	8.4	3.2	8.4	0.0	-0.0	0.49
2005	NYN	MLB	30	7	12	0	31	27	166¹	170	77	112	12	53.0%	.304	12	1.48	4.17	4.50	4.63	9.4	3.8	5.5	0.6	18.3	3.21
2006	NYN	MLB	31	1	2	0	5	5	21¹	25	11	15	5	29.6%	.303	-11	1.69	6.76	6.01	6.65	10.4	4.2	5.8	2.1	-2.4	0.11
2007	*NYN*	*MLB*	*31*	*6*	*7*	*0*	*32*	*17*	*115*	*114*	*56*	*80*	*13*	*45.0%*	*.285*	*-2*	*1.48*	*4.73*	*5.13*	*5.23*	*9.0*	*3.9*	*5.6*	*1.0*	*7.8*	*1.50*

Breakout: 4%   Improve: 28%   Collapse: 26%   Attrition: 13%   Comparables: Pat Rapp, Ray Moore, Jim Bullinger, Stan Bahnsen

Rick Peterson's "I can fix him in ten minutes" line (later disavowed) may go down in history with General Sedgwick's "They couldn't hit an elephant at this dis . . ." in the ill-considered braggadocio department. Of course, he couldn't have seen that Zambrano would suffer a physical breakdown as well as a mechanical one. Zambrano underwent Tommy John surgery, his second, in mid-May. He also had bone chips removed and a damaged flexor tendon repaired. He might be back in spring training, but more realistic is a later return with a slight chance of never.

Lineouts

PLAYER	TEAM	LVL	AGE	PA	R	2B	3B	HR	RBI	BB	SO	SB-CS	SPEED	AVG/OBP/SLG	MLVr	EqAVG/EqOBP/EqSLG	EqA	VORP
INF C. Basak	NOR	AAA	27	417	53	22	3	8	36	39	76	17-3	6.7	.267/.345/.407	.131	.279/.347/.434	.272	25.8
OF A. Concepcion	SLU	A+	22	316	38	21	2	1	33	25	67	18-9	5.7	.287/.343/.387	.078	.266/.310/.352	.234	-3.3
	BIN	AA	22	235	24	11	1	3	29	7	57	11-2	6.4	.261/.291/.362	-.071	.248/.275/.347	.225	-13.4
C M. Difelice	BIN	AA	37	134	9	7	0	1	19	15	24	0-0	3.2	.277/.373/.366	.068	.227/.299/.286	.215	-5.4
	NYN	MLB	37	30	3	1	0	0	1	5	10	0-0	5.3	.080/.233/.120	-.663	.000/.167/.000	.099	-3.8
SS C. Ragsdale	BIN	AA	23	487	47	19	3	10	37	40	182	12-9	5.7	.204/.274/.330	-.171	.198/.262/.313	.206	-23.7
C K. Stinnett	NYA	MLB	36	87	6	3	0	1	9	5	29	0-0	4.3	.228/.282/.304	-.316	.218/.282/.282	.206	-3.3
	NYN	MLB	36	12	0	0	0	0	0	0	4	0-0	3.8	.083/.083/.083	-1.028	.000/.000/.000	.031	-2.5
LF M. Tucker*	NOR	AAA	35	333	44	18	2	6	33	49	45	10-3	5.4	.265/.381/.411	.193	.252/.339/.372	.254	-5.2
	NYN	MLB	35	74	3	4	0	1	6	16	14	2-0	3.4	.196/.378/.321	-.085	.196/.378/.321	.270	0.2

PLAYER	TEAM	LVL	AGE	W	L	SV	IP	H	BB	SO	HR	GB%	BABIP	STUFF	WHIP	ERA	PERA	EqERA	EqH9	EqBB9	EqSO9	EqHR9	VORP
E. Camacho*	BIN	AA	23	3	4	1	79	71	25	61	6	—	.277	-16	1.22	3.65	4.90	5.00	9.0	3.3	4.8	1.2	5.2
M. Devaney	SLU	A+	23	8	3	0	94²	63	35	86	4	—	.241	11	1.04	1.62	5.12	3.61	7.5	4.3	5.1	0.8	19.8
	BIN	AA	23	4	2	0	53¹	39	35	43	5	—	.248	3	1.39	3.05	6.91	4.09	7.6	6.9	5.2	1.4	8.5
D. Guerra	HAG	A	17	6	7	0	81	59	37	64	3	—	.259	11	1.19	2.22	5.22	3.45	7.5	5.1	4.4	0.8	18.7
J. Lima	NOR	AAA	33	7	8	0	140²	140	20	88	15	—	.293	-15	1.14	3.92	5.48	4.99	9.1	1.5	3.9	1.7	9.5
	NYN	MLB	33	0	4	0	17¹	25	10	12	3	—	.361	-19	2.02	9.88	5.72	11.21	13.2	4.6	5.6	1.5	-10.8
K. Mulvey	BIN	AA	21	0	1	0	13	10	5	10	1	—	.257	1	1.15	1.38	4.97	3.46	7.6	3.5	4.8	1.4	3.1
J. Niese*	HAG	A	19	11	9	0	123	121	62	132	7	—	.342	4	1.49	3.95	5.68	6.29	10.6	5.6	5.9	1.2	-9.0
	SLU	A+	19	0	2	0	10	8	5	10	0	—	.296	8	1.30	4.50	4.04	9.31	8.4	5.6	5.6	0.0	-4.0
S. Schmoll	NOR	AAA	26	5	4	0	55	56	19	42	4	—	.323	-14	1.36	4.75	4.71	5.82	8.9	3.2	5.2	1.0	-1.4
J. Smith	BRO	A-	22	0	1	9	20	10	3	28	0	60%	.233	10	0.65	0.45	3.75	2.89	7.2	2.4	6.8	0.5	5.6
	BIN	AA	22	0	2	0	12²	12	11	12	1	54%	.344	-3	1.89	5.90	6.79	6.75	9.8	9.0	6.0	1.5	-1.5

Chris Basak could have done better than Chris Woodward in a reserve role, but if he didn't get the call last year, you have to figure it isn't going to come in this organization. **Ambiorix Concepcion** has some tools, but has so little patience he would struggle to post a .275 OBP in the majors. The Mets signed **Mike DiFelice** to work with Pelfrey, then fell back on him when Castro went down. His future is in coaching or aluminum siding. The year in Mets prospectdom was particularly embittering; take **Corey Ragsdale**. Once seen as a toolsy talent, a full year at Double-A only resurrected speculation that he might be better off as a pitcher. As a Yankee, **Kelly Stinnett** struck out in more than a third of his at-bats, and the results of his short-lived stint as Randy Johnson's personal catcher weren't anything to brag about. Released in July, the Mets signed him to replace Castro temporarily. He stayed just long enough to earn his second release of the season at the end of September. Veteran outfielder **Michael Tucker** was released by the Nats during spring training, signed with Norfolk, and, though he didn't show much life, got called up in August when Cliff Floyd bowed out.

Eddie Camacho is a possible heir to Royce Ring's 26th-man LOOGY role. His lack of a quality breaking pitch limits him to spot work. **Mike Devaney** was the Mets' 23rd-round pick in 2004. He doesn't have great velocity, but with height and a good curveball he could fit in the back end of someone's rotation. **Deolis Guerra** has yet to take a legal drink, but his changeup and 86 to 91 MPH fastball, good for his age, encouraged the Mets to push him up to the FSL for his last pair of starts. From 2005 to 2006, **Jose Lima** made 36 starts and went 5-20 with a 7.26 ERA. Sui generis, thank God. **Kevin Mulvey** made it to Double-A in his first year on his Villanova polish; at the moment, he's got a fastball that averages in the low-90s, and his slider, curve, and changeup are already solid. Still, that was a bit aggressive on the part of the organization, and Mulvey could have a lower posting at the start of this season. **John Niese**, teen lefty, already throws in the 90s. He's still working on control and off-speed stuff, but this is a very promising start. In 99 2/3 innings split between Triple-A and the majors, **Juan Padilla** posted an ERA of 1.44. Unfortunately, that was 2005, and, thanks to Tommy John surgery, he hasn't pitched since. He'll be back this year, still trying to establish himself at age 30. In case the Mets find themselves pining for Chad Bradford's submarining goodness, they could turn to **Steve Schmoll**, although he failed to impress in his first year in the system after coming over in the Jae Seo trade. **Joe Smith** is another sidearmer; this genus is typically stunning in the low minors and gradually less so as they climb the ladder; he allowed two runs in his first game in the City of Churches, then didn't allow another until he reached Double-A.

Manager: Willie Randolph

ear	Team	W-L	Pythag +/-	Avg PC	100 +P	120 +P	QS	BQS	REL	REL w Zero R	IBB	SUBS	PH	PH Avg	PH HR	SB2	CS2	SB3	CS3	SAC Att	SAC %	POS SAC	Squeeze	Swing	In Play
2005	NYN	83-79	-7	97.3	73	4	93	9	392	250	43	65	220	.291	5	121	34	31	6	94	73.4%	39	1	129	104
2006	NYN	97-65	+5	96.0	79	1	78	4	473	330	39	32	246	.187	3	119	33	27	2	105	73.3%	38	1	127	101

You might say that Willie Randolph, at least in baseball circles, is the Decider, because Randolph decides things, and then he holds to his decisions. Once he has established in his mind what a player's proper role should be, Randolph is extremely reluctant to reevaluate that judgment. Perhaps as a result of that, the man who was the quiet, unprepossessing member of the Bronx Zoo Yankees (maybe the only one) can be defensive or snappish with the media when they question his decisions—he's already dealt with that issue and, satisfied with his own reasoning, going over it again seems like a waste of time. As we said above, inflexibility can be an asset at times; it won't hurt a manager who has a team of strong starting players and is picking between good player A and good player B. It's when the team has more gray areas, and the decision-making process requires a more nuanced approach, that skippers who never think twice can run into trouble. Randolph successfully tangled with unstable situations in both outfield corners and second base in 2006, but it's the nature of baseball that a patch that worked once won't necessarily work twice (read: Endy Chavez, Jose Valentin). The Decider may be challenged to undecide his decisions and invent new solutions for a new year. The question is, will he?

New York Yankees

You might have missed the 2006 Yankees season. The New York media did, which means to a large extent New York itself did too. It's possible that the Yankees played it and lived through it and missed it too.

There were any number of storylines weaving through what was, on the whole, a very successful season. The on-field story was one of conquest in the face of adversity. Despite early injuries that took Hideki Matsui and Gary Sheffield off the board for nearly the entire season, a starting rotation long on age and short on results, and a bullpen that, at times, became so overly reliant on Scott Proctor that it seemed as if he was being called out of the bullpen in relief of himself, the Yankees pulled into Boston on August 18 and swept a five-game series, knocking the Red Sox out of the race. The American League East race was effectively won on August 21; the Yankees would ultimately finish with a ten-game lead on second-place Toronto, who snuck past the Boston in the season's final week. That the Yankees folded quickly and relatively quietly in the ALDS against the Tigers doesn't diminish what came before.

The bigger story took place off the field, though it had a direct impact on the way the race played out. General manager Brian Cashman's contract ran out at the end of the 2005 season. Amidst speculation that he would be leaving due to frustration with George Steinbrenner's meddlesome Tampa-based cabal and despite feelers from other clubs, Cashman opted to stay, but only in exchange for a promise of greater autonomy.

Yankee Kremlinology is a difficult topic at the best of times. Ironically, even those on the inside sometimes deliver conflicting versions of which side is winning in the endless

> ## YANKEES PROSPECTUS
>
> **2006 record:** 97–65; First place, AL East; Lost to Tigers in Division Series
>
> **Pythagenport record:** 95–67
>
> **Runs scored per game:** 5.74 (1st in AL)
>
> **Runs allowed per game:** 4.73 (6th in AL)
>
> **Team EqA:** .280 (1st in AL)
>
> **2006 Batters Age:** 31.5 (Oldest in AL)
>
> **2006 Pitchers Age:** 32.9 (Oldest in AL)
>
> **Ballpark:** Yankee Stadium; Slight pitcher's park; Park Factor of .976
>
> **2006:** Frustrations focused on their best player, continuing a long, proud MLB tradition.
>
> **2007:** Younger by a little, fortified with talent from overseas, they'll put runs on the board and still be the target for the rest of the East.

New York-Tampa power struggle. It appears, though, that Cashman did win at least a window of time in which he could operate according to his own philosophy. The change evidenced itself multiple times throughout the season. Rather than panic and trade for a veteran outfielder such as Reggie Sanders (a possibility frequently mentioned in the press), he waited a very long time before making a move. First Melky Cabrera was given a chance to replace Matsui, and acquitted himself well. Simultaneously, Cashman endured miserable right field production and defense from Bernie Williams until the price on Bobby Abreu dropped to almost nothing and Cory Lidle was thrown in. Before the season, Cashman took a similar tack with Johnny Damon, repeatedly telling the press that he would be entirely comfortable with Bubba Crosby as his starting center fielder, while waiting for Damon to get nervous.

For the first time in years, the Yankees made astute waiver claims, grabbing Darrell Rasner from the Nationals and Brian Bruney from the Diamondbacks. Phil Hughes, the team's top pitching prospect, was not dealt for Preston Wilson or some other mediocrity. During the offseason that followed, Cashman acted contrary to traditional Yankees practice by dealing three players close to the end of their careers—Jaret Wright, Gary Sheffield, and Randy Johnson—for young players. It used to be that those young players would be headed in the other direction.

That change of tactics, combined with Senior Vice-President/Director of Scouting Damon Oppenheimer running two consecutive productive drafts, constituted an abandonment of the way the Yankees had done business since 1973. It was as if the departure of Roger Clemens,

Andy Pettitte, and David Wells after the 2003 season was Cashman's road-to-Damascus moment. When the three veteran pitchers left, it revealed the Yankees as a team that had amassed a $200-million payroll yet was bankrupt of starting pitching. Over the next two years, the Yankees would be forced to make increasingly desperate moves for starting pitchers, compelled simultaneously to purchase expensive non-functional ornaments such as Jaret Wright and Carl Pavano, and go dumpster-diving for Shawn Chacon, Aaron Small, Tim Redding, Darrell May, Tanyon Sturtze, and Donovan Osborne, not to mention past-expiration versions of Al Leiter and Kevin Brown (and possibly Randy Johnson). Cashman's behavior since suggests that he resolved not to be put in that position again.

Cashman's power grab, accompanied by the team's unlikely division title, was the story of the year, but, if you weren't looking closely, you missed it, because the overwhelming focus was on one player, one personality, and his place on the team. From beginning to end, 2006 was the Year of Alex Rodriguez.

Having gone 2-for-15 in the Yankees' 2005 ALDS loss to the Angels—concluding his performance by grounding into a double play while representing the tying run in the ninth inning of the decisive fifth game—Rodriguez confirmed his New York rep as the game's highest-paid choker. He carried that weight through the 2006 season, enduring constant hostility from the home crowds. By the end of the year, various Yankees were even endorsing the view in a devastating *Sports Illustrated* article by Tom Verducci. Rodriguez appeared to prove his critics right by going 1-for-14 in another ALDS loss, with the added indignity of Joe Torre dropping him to eighth in the Yankee order in the final game.

On the surface, Rodriguez's "clutch" numbers actually look quite good. In 2006, Mr. Rod came to bat with 534 runners on base, the most in the majors, and plated 16.1 percent of them; the average for AL players with 300 or more plate appearances was 15.3 percent. For the season, he hit .302/.431/.508 with runners in scoring position and .293/.404/.534 with runners on base. In part, the "unclutch" rap was an issue of selective memory. Rodriguez played in a high-powered offense and had multiple chances to be the hero and the goat, and was often both in the same game.

Despite those nice numbers, a consensus point of view developed that Rodriguez was a front-runner, a hitter who, coming to bat with the bases loaded, would strike out if the Yankees were trailing 2–1 but hit a grand slam if they were up 9–1. For once, the conventional wisdom had a point. Baseball Prospectus's Keith Woolner has developed the concept of Win Expectancy for both hitters and pitchers. Win Expectancy depicts a team's chances of winning at any point of the game. These chances, expressed mathematically, rise or fall during a given game situation. As Woolner wrote in the 2006 edition of this book:

> To determine the WX [Win Expectation] of a batter's plate appearance, we simply take the difference between the win probabilities immediately before and immediately after the pitch that ends his plate appearance. The difference is the win value created by the batter. For example, when David Ortiz came to bat with two outs in the top of the eight inning with a runner on first in a tie game versus Toronto on September 14, the Red Sox had a 43.95% chance of winning the game. After Ortiz clubbed a two-run home run, the Red Sox had an 83.42% chance of winning the game. The 39.37% difference in win probability is credited to Ortiz as .3937 WX.

An important aspect of win expectancy is leverage. As Woolner explained:

> Each plate appearance has a certain leverage depending on the inning, baserunners, and current score. If a team plays a lot of close games, the batter will, on average, have more opportunity to affect the probability of winning each time they come to the plate . . . It's important to emphasize that leverage says nothing about the hitter's actual performance. It is almost completely beyond his control. It's a measure of the circumstances he batted in . . . A hitter with high average leverage had a proportionately greater opportunity to influence the outcomes of games than a hitter with low average leverage, but the low-average hitter could have been significantly better.

In 2006, Rodriguez didn't do as well in game-changing situations as his closest group of peers—in this case, players with 200 or more plate appearances and an OPS (on-base plus slugging) within 20 points of A-Rod's .914. In table 1 the group is ranked by WX per plate appearance, to account for discrepancies in playing time.

Rodriguez is second-to-last in the group, though it is important to note that he batted in fewer high leverage situations than anyone in the group save Sizemore. The median WX/PA for the group was .0046; had Rodriguez performed at that level over his 674 plate appearances, he would have generated an additional 1.71 WX (or a smidge less accounting for his below-average leverage). This is roughly equivalent to A-Rod being so "unclutch" that his production in those situations cost the Yankees nearly two wins. Another way of considering Rodriguez's WX is that the shortfall rendered him the equivalent of a player of normal clutch ability, but who had 17 fewer runs of VORP. That's not the same thing as saying that Rodriguez was not valuable to the Yankees—even penalizing him for his lack of big hits, he was still a four or five-win player.

So the critics were right, at least insofar as 2006 is concerned. There is evidence that last year was an aberration—

Table 1. Win Expectancy for the Big Boppers, 2006

Name	PA	AVG	OBP	SLG	OPS	WX	WX/PA	LEV
Derek Jeter	715	.343	.417	.483	900	5.91	.0083	1.01
Josh Bard	284	.333	.404	.522	926	2.37	.0083	1.22
Justin Morneau	661	.321	.375	.559	934	5.14	.0078	1.00
David Wright	661	.311	.381	.531	912	4.78	.0072	1.02
Frank Thomas	559	.270	.381	.545	926	3.65	.0065	1.02
Moises Alou	378	.301	.352	.571	923	2.39	.0063	1.11
Ray Durham	555	.293	.360	.538	898	3.31	.0060	1.07
Vladimir Guerrero	665	.329	.382	.552	934	3.82	.0057	1.10
Chase Utley	739	.309	.379	.527	906	4.19	.0057	1.08
Carlos Delgado	618	.265	.361	.548	909	3.05	.0049	1.03
Carlos Guillen	622	.320	.400	.519	920	3.00	.0048	1.06
Olmedo Saenz	204	.296	.363	.564	927	.950	.0046	1.06
Bill Hall	608	.270	.345	.553	899	2.79	.0046	1.06
Brad Hawpe	575	.293	.383	.515	898	2.52	.0044	1.12
David Ross	296	.255	.353	.579	932	1.25	.0042	1.09
Grady Sizemore	751	.290	.375	.533	907	2.96	.0039	0.94
Aramis Ramirez	660	.291	.352	.561	912	2.34	.0035	1.04
Carlos Lee	695	.300	.355	.540	895	2.45	.0035	1.03
Paul Konerko	643	.313	.381	.551	932	2.22	.0035	1.04
Adam LaRoche	557	.285	.354	.561	915	1.89	.0034	1.02
Alfonso Soriano	728	.277	.351	.560	911	2.42	.0033	1.06
David Dellucci	301	.292	.369	.530	899	.880	.0029	1.05
Vernon Wells	677	.303	.357	.542	899	1.96	.0029	1.00
Greg Norton	335	.296	.374	.520	895	.780	.0023	1.09
Alex Rodriguez	674	.290	.392	.523	914	1.39	.0021	0.99
Jason Bay	689	.286	.396	.532	928	1.41	.0020	1.12

Table 2. The Few, The Proud, The Best, 2005

Name	PA	AVG	OBP	SLG	OPS	WX	WX/PA	LEV
Alex Rodriguez	715	.321	.421	.610	1031	6.19	.0087	0.92
Albert Pujols	700	.330	.430	.609	1039	4.28	.0061	0.96

Table 3. Win Expectancy for the Boppers, 2004

Name	PA	AVG	OBP	SLG	OPS	WX	WX/PA	LEV
Mark Sweeney	215	.266	.377	.508	885	2.24	.0104	1.17
Miguel Cabrera	685	.294	.366	.512	879	4.29	.0063	0.97
Eli Marrero	280	.320	.374	.520	894	1.67	.0060	0.95
Paul Konerko	634	.279	.360	.540	899	3.64	.0057	1.02
Troy Glaus	238	.246	.353	.562	915	1.16	.0049	1.02
Eric Chavez	573	.275	.398	.502	900	2.78	.0049	1.16
Alex Rodriguez	693	.289	.378	.517	895	3.23	.0047	1.01
Mark Loretta	707	.335	.391	.495	886	3.27	.0046	1.00
Hideki Matsui	675	.298	.388	.518	906	3.03	.0045	0.96
Miguel Tejada	725	.311	.360	.534	894	3.19	.0044	1.05
Carlos Delgado	551	.269	.372	.535	907	2.42	.0044	1.07
Jason Bay	472	.282	.358	.550	907	1.76	.0037	1.04
Jose Hernandez	238	.289	.370	.540	910	.83	.0035	1.08
Jorge Posada	543	.270	.400	.481	881	1.8	.0033	0.98
Carlos Lee	649	.309	.371	.533	904	1.57	.0024	1.02
Aaron Rowand	530	.308	.360	.542	902	1.25	.0024	1.00
Jeff Kent	606	.289	.348	.531	880	1.08	.0018	0.95
Ivan Rodriguez	575	.334	.383	.510	893	.84	.0015	1.08

Table 4. Sluggers' Win Expectancy, 2003

Name	PA	AVG	OBP	SLG	OPS	WX	WX/PA	LEV
Alex Rodriguez	715	.298	.396	.600	995	5.03	.0070	0.99
Manny Ramirez	679	.325	.427	.587	1014	4.23	.0062	1.03
Jim Edmonds	531	.275	.385	.617	1002	3.28	.0062	1.04
Vladimir Guerrero	467	.33	.426	.586	1012	2.28	.0049	1.06

at least as far as the regular season is concerned. Rodriguez's overall hitting game was so good in 2005 that there was only one player within 20 points of his OPS, and A-Rod outperformed him in high-leverage situations (see table 2). In 2004, he was middle of the pack (see table 3), and back in 2003, his final campaign with the Rangers and his previous MVP season, he led the small group of players who had comparable statistics (see table 4).

The evidence suggests that Rodriguez is not chronically unclutch, which also should mean that he'll revert to form in 2007. His postseason appearances would seem to be damning, but those samples are small, consisting of 29 at-bats split over the space of 12 months. Unless Rodriguez has developed a psychosis about high-leverage situations—not impossible given the kind of negative reinforce-ment he's received from fans, media, teammates, and manager—he should be back to making hits that count.

The need for those hits is underscored by the unfortunate decision to sign Doug Mientkiewicz to be the dominant half of a first-base platoon with the winner of this spring's Josh Phelps-Andy Phillips steel cage match. Jason Giambi's injuries and declining mobility may have necessitated the need for the Yankees to acquired another first baseman, but, in signing Minky, the Yankees have overestimated the importance of first-base defense (as well as how much of it Mientkiewicz has left to offer) while underrating the importance of first-base offense. One of the ironic aspects of the Yankees in the Cashman/Torre era is that as much offense as they've had (from 1996 through 2006, the Yankees led all AL teams in runs scored, and led the majors in runs scored in 1998, 2002, and 2006), they've given away a good deal more.

The Torre teams have always had unusually strong offensive players up the middle, including Derek Jeter, Bernie Williams, Jorge Posada, Chuck Knoblauch, Johnny Damon, and Robinson Cano. Simultaneously, they tended to put below-average performers first base, third base, left field, right field, and designated hitter, enduring the decline phases of Knoblauch (in left), Scott Brosius, Tino Martinez, and Paul O'Neill, as well as disappointing years from Cecil Fielder, Chad Curtis, Rondell White, and others. It's one of the reasons that, as good as the Yankees have been, they haven't been unstoppable, and that other weaknesses, more difficult to correct, have been able to undermine them over the last five years.

It just goes to show that however much the Yankees have learned about running their baseball team over the last few years, there is still more learning to be done.

HITTERS

Bobby Abreu RF **Bats: L** **Throws: R** Height: 6' 0" Weight: 210 Born: March 11, 1974 Age: 33

YEAR	TEAM	LVL	AGE	PA	R	2B	3B	HR	RBI	BB	SO	SB	CS	SPEED	AVG	OBP	SLG	MLVR	EQAVG	EQOBP	EQSLG	EQA	VORP	DEFENSE	
2004	PHI	MLB	30	713	118	47	1	30	105	127	116	40	5	6.8	.301	.428	.544	.349	.298	.424	.542	.330	73.5	151-RF	3
2005	PHI	MLB	31	719	104	37	1	24	102	117	134	31	9	6.4	.286	.405	.474	.217	.282	.403	.479	.306	47.0	154-RF	-5
2006	PHI	MLB	32	438	61	25	2	8	65	91	86	20	4	5.8	.277	.427	.434	.167	.270	.424	.430	.309	25.5	95-RF	-3
2006	NYA	MLB	32	248	37	16	0	7	42	33	52	10	2	5.7	.330	.419	.507	.298	.330	.427	.515	.323	23.5	50-RF	3
2007	NYA	MLB	33	635	104	31	2	18	74	94	120	25	7	6.0	.274	.385	.442	.081	.272	.389	.448	.302	24.2	148-RF	1

Breakout: 0% Improve: 13% Collapse: 27% Attrition: 3% Comparables: John Kruk, Von Hayes, Kenny Lofton, Carl Yastrzemski

Abreu seemed lethargic in Philly—always a selective hitter, he was looking at more pitches than ever before, leading the majors with 4.45 pitches per plate appearance in the first half. The deep counts led to lots of walks (his Philadelphia rate of .208 walks per plate appearance would have led the majors over the full season), but not much else. Abreu was just as selective in New York, but once in a while he took the bat off his shoulder and swung. The results of the changed approach speak for themselves. Asked to explain the decline of his power numbers a year after winning the All-Star Game Home Run Derby, Abreu said, "I don't ever get any elevation on the ball." But he did get some in New York, hitting more flies and line drives than he had as a Phillie. The Gotham Abreu was reminiscent of his mid-twenties incarnation, a big change from the month before his arrival, when some pundits were speculating he was done.

Melky Cabrera LF **Bats: S** **Throws: L** Height: 5' 11" Weight: 170 Born: August 11, 1984 Age: 22

YEAR	TEAM	LVL	AGE	PA	R	2B	3B	HR	RBI	BB	SO	SB	CS	SPEED	AVG	OBP	SLG	MLVR	EQAVG	EQOBP	EQSLG	EQA	VORP	DEFENSE	
2004	BCR	A	19	188	35	16	3	0	16	15	23	7	2	7.1	.333	.383	.462	.260	.303	.344	.411	.266	7.5	41-CF	1
2004	TAM	A+	19	364	48	20	3	8	51	23	59	3	1	5.0	.288	.341	.438	.144	.274	.316	.424	.253	9.1	80-CF	-4
2005	TRN	AA	20	464	57	22	3	10	60	28	72	11	2	5.8	.275	.322	.411	.030	.268	.311	.399	.249	4.3	103-CF	7
2005	COH	AAA	20	112	15	3	0	3	17	9	15	2	0	4.6	.248	.309	.366	-.118	.235	.297	.343	.229	-2.8	14-CF	2
2005	NYA	MLB	20	19	1	0	0	0	0	0	2	0	0	4.6	.211	.211	.211	-.549	.105	.105	.105	.085	-1.9		
2006	COH	AAA	21	135	19	6	2	4	24	10	9	3	1	5.1	.385	.430	.566	.541	.385	.430	.590	.340	23.6	27-CF	-4
2006	NYA	MLB	21	525	75	26	2	7	50	56	60	12	5	6.0	.280	.360	.390	-.013	.281	.369	.398	.270	7.8	112-LF	7
2007	NYA	MLB	22	575	75	27	3	10	60	45	66	10	4	5.9	.281	.340	.406	-.038	.278	.343	.411	.269	9.0	135-LF	1

Breakout: 18% Improve: 46% Collapse: 24% Attrition: 11% Comparables: Rick Manning, Carlos Beltran, Alfredo Griffin, Roberto Alomar

Before the season, Baseball America listed Cabrera as a player for whom "time is running out for." Little did the know that, by late May, "Got Melky?" T-shirts would be spotted around the Big Apple. The lesson, of course, is that when evaluating a player you should never end a sentence with a preposition. They actually weren't that far off base; in his brief 2005 audition, Cabrera had seemed tentative and intimidated, swinging at everything at the plate and dropping flies in the outfield. After that, the only thing still in his favor was youth. Melky 2.0 had exactly one day like that—his first. Thereafter he was a defensive asset, displaying a cannon arm; at the plate he showed surprising patience and an ability to hit for average, if not for power. Still, he blew hot and cold, spoiling his numbers with an artic September. The overall package doesn't quite add up to a starting corner outfielder—yet.

Miguel Cairo

INF **Bats: R** **Throws: R** Height: 6' 1" Weight: 210 Born: May 4, 1974 Age: 33

YEAR	TEAM	LVL	AGE	PA	R	2B	3B	HR	RBI	BB	SO	SB	CS	SPEED	AVG	OBP	SLG	MLVR	EQAVG	EQOBP	EQSLG	EQA	VORP	DEFENSE			
2004	NYA	MLB	30	408	48	17	5	6	42	18	49	11	3	6.2	.292	.346	.417	.006	.299	.353	.432	.275	17.1	92-2B	0		
2005	NYN	MLB	31	367	31	18	0	2	19	19	31	13	3	5.6	.251	.296	.324	-.191	.254	.299	.329	.232	-6.0	74-2B	6		
2006	NYA	MLB	32	244	28	12	3	0	30	13	31	13	1	8.0	.239	.280	.320	-.294	.237	.286	.315	.228	-4.5	36-2B	7	11-SS	1
2007	NYA	MLB	33	295	33	12	2	2	24	14	34	12	4	6.1	.258	.300	.344	-.208	.256	.303	.349	.239	-1.7	72-2B	0		

Breakout: 20% Improve: 45% Collapse: 28% Attrition: 42%   Comparables: Royce Clayton, Lenny Harris, Bob Bailor, Craig Shipley

The best evidence that a million dollars means less to the Yankees than it does to normal people. What differentiates Cairo from a hundred minor leaguers with his skill set is Yankee management's peculiar ability to see value in him that isn't there. He can't hit, but, for what it's worth, he did have a good baserunning year. The Yankees decided to wring a final drop of blood from the Cairo stone and brought him back for another season.

Robinson Cano

2B **Bats: L** **Throws: R** Height: 6' 0" Weight: 190 Born: October 22, 1982 Age: 24

YEAR	TEAM	LVL	AGE	PA	R	2B	3B	HR	RBI	BB	SO	SB	CS	SPEED	AVG	OBP	SLG	MLVR	EQAVG	EQOBP	EQSLG	EQA	VORP	DEFENSE	
2004	TRN	AA	21	323	43	20	8	7	44	24	40	2	4	5.5	.301	.356	.497	.211	.290	.336	.468	.270	19.6	66-2B	1
2004	COH	AAA	21	240	22	9	2	6	30	18	27	0	1	3.4	.259	.316	.403	-.059	.248	.305	.385	.240	1.0	59-2B	-2
2005	COH	AAA	22	114	19	8	3	4	24	6	13	0	0	5.5	.333	.368	.574	.357	.324	.360	.556	.300	13.2	21-2B	0
2005	NYA	MLB	22	551	78	34	4	14	62	16	68	1	3	4.9	.297	.320	.458	.054	.305	.338	.479	.274	21.2	129-2B	2
2006	NYA	MLB	23	508	62	41	1	15	78	18	54	5	2	4.7	.342	.365	.525	.252	.344	.373	.537	.304	49.1	113-2B	15
2007	NYA	MLB	24	584	77	36	3	16	82	30	66	5	3	5.1	.307	.345	.472	.083	.304	.349	.478	.287	33.6	137-2B	7

Breakout: 20% Improve: 46% Collapse: 22% Attrition: 8%   Comparables: Carlos Baerga, Rod Carew, Ken Boswell, Ron Hunt

Early in the season, Cano earned plaudits for his improved defense, but his bat was a disappointment—through May, he had hit just two home runs. He continued to be among the game's most impatient hitters, inevitably swinging at the first pitch and sometimes a fluttering hot dog wrapper or passing pigeon. The result was .293/.318/.383—a batting average full of empty calories—and nary a hit with runners on. Cano got hot in June, but the month ended abruptly with a pulled hamstring, putting the question of whether this was a new Cano on hold for six weeks. The answer was yes—once he returned, Cano batted .365/.380/.635. Even if he settles in at his career rates (.319/.342/.490), the Yankees have an immensely valuable property on their hands, but, below that, his lack of patience will start to tell.

Bubba Crosby

CF **Bats: L** **Throws: L** Height: 5' 11" Weight: 190 Born: August 11, 1976 Age: 30

YEAR	TEAM	LVL	AGE	PA	R	2B	3B	HR	RBI	BB	SO	SB	CS	SPEED	AVG	OBP	SLG	MLVR	EQAVG	EQOBP	EQSLG	EQA	VORP	DEFENSE			
2004	NYA	MLB	27	58	8	2	0	2	7	2	13	2	0	7.1	.151	.196	.302	-.532	.132	.179	.283	.178	-5.1	12-RF	-4		
2005	NYA	MLB	28	103	15	0	1	1	6	4	14	4	1	7.3	.276	.304	.327	-.174	.281	.324	.333	.238	-1.4	16-CF	6	11-RF	1
2006	NYA	MLB	29	96	9	3	1	1	6	4	21	3	1	7.2	.207	.258	.299	-.390	.198	.258	.291	.204	-5.5	13-CF	0	10-RF	-1
2007	CIN	MLB	30	154	19	6	1	3	14	11	27	4	2	6.1	.249	.315	.376	-.156	.247	.312	.372	.238	0.3	40-CF	1		

Breakout: 35% Improve: 55% Collapse: 25% Attrition: 38%   Comparables: Herm Winningham, Catfish Metkovich, Mike Kingery, Jim Gosger

Surprisingly, the Yankees got some mileage out of the Robin Ventura deal with the Dodgers, trading the tired last games of the third baseman's career for Crosby and Scott Proctor. Crosby is a slightly better hitter than he's shown in his sporadic major league playing time, but not so much that you would want to give him a greater role than fifth outfielder/first man back to the minors when a roster spot is needed. With Cabrera, Damon, and Abreu giving the Yankees their best defensive outfield in years, the need for Crosby's skills was diminished; signed by the Reds, he'll presumably caddy for Junior Griffey—if he makes the team.

Johnny Damon

CF **Bats: L** **Throws: L** Height: 6' 2" Weight: 205 Born: November 5, 1973 Age: 33

YEAR	TEAM	LVL	AGE	PA	R	2B	3B	HR	RBI	BB	SO	SB	CS	SPEED	AVG	OBP	SLG	MLVR	EQAVG	EQOBP	EQSLG	EQA	VORP	DEFENSE	
2004	BOS	MLB	30	702	123	35	6	20	94	76	71	19	8	6.8	.304	.380	.477	.140	.297	.380	.471	.292	42.7	141-CF	10
2005	BOS	MLB	31	688	117	35	6	10	75	53	69	18	1	7.4	.316	.366	.439	.115	.316	.376	.450	.292	40.9	139-CF	-2
2006	NYA	MLB	32	671	115	35	5	24	80	67	85	25	10	7.1	.285	.359	.482	.118	.287	.368	.497	.291	42.3	122-CF	-6
2007	NYA	MLB	33	647	97	31	5	18	76	65	79	15	6	6.6	.288	.361	.453	.067	.285	.365	.459	.291	31.9	151-CF	-1

Breakout: 9% Improve: 28% Collapse: 35% Attrition: 5%   Comparables: Andy Van Slyke, Jose Cruz, Enos Slaughter, Steve Finley

(continued next page)

Johnny Damon (*continued*)

As predicted, Damon left some batting average at Fenway Park, but he compensated by adding power. Increasingly burdened by a variety of dings and dents, including a broken sesamoid bone in his foot suffered early in the year, Damon appeared to be tired in September, and his abysmal final month (.205/.286/.307) diminished what had been a strong season to that point. Damon was never the Yankees' best choice of leadoff man, and even if he gets back to hitting .300 he still won't be. Unfortunately, images die hard in the Bronx. The Yankees can only hope that Damon has moved into the Steve Finley Phase II/unexpected power stage of his career, because even at his peak Damon was never a consistent .300 hitter, and he doesn't walk enough to be interesting with a lower batting average.

Eric Duncan   **3B**   **Bats: L**   **Throws: R**   Height: 6′ 3″   Weight: 195   Born: December 7, 1984   Age: 22

YEAR	TEAM	LVL	AGE	PA	R	2B	3B	HR	RBI	BB	SO	SB	CS	SPEED	AVG	OBP	SLG	MLVR	EQAVG	EQOBP	EQSLG	EQA	VORP	DEFENSE	
2004	BCR	A	19	333	52	23	2	12	57	38	84	7	1	5.7	.260	.351	.479	.175	.237	.309	.421	.252	6.6	75-3B	-4
2004	TAM	A+	19	209	24	20	2	4	26	31	47	0	2	3.9	.254	.364	.458	.173	.235	.325	.415	.255	5.7	46-3B	-6
2005	TRN	AA	20	520	60	15	3	19	61	59	136	9	3	4.8	.235	.326	.408	.006	.233	.314	.397	.249	6.3	115-3B	-19
2006	COH	AAA	21	122	7	3	1	0	6	9	24	0	1	3.4	.209	.279	.255	-.254	.207	.270	.252	.194	-11.8	19-1B	-1
2006	TRN	AA	21	242	32	15	2	10	29	32	38	0	0	4.1	.248	.355	.485	.220	.251	.346	.498	.284	10.4	44-1B	-3
2007	NYA	MLB	22	465	53	23	1	16	60	43	98	2	1	4.5	.249	.322	.421	-.074	.246	.325	.427	.264	4.5	110-3B	-5

Breakout: 35% Improve: 60% Collapse: 10% Attrition: 7%   Comparables: Joey Votto, Richard Brown, Travis Ishikawa, Carlos Pena

Duncan now seems likely to go down as a busted first-round pick, though, at 22, there is still time for him to sort things out. Duncan had an indifferent, injury-plagued season at Trenton in 2005, but after an MVP campaign in the Arizona Fall League, the Yankees rewarded him with a promotion to Columbus. Lower back problems and the unreality of AFL accomplishments sent him back to the Garden State, where he was somewhat better when not dealing with the back. In his short career, Duncan has gone from third base to first base and back again, and next year the Yankees may try him at short toaster, pinch-brigand, or designated grysbok. Duncan's ultimate destination had better be third, or the bat won't keep him in the lineup, if the bad back doesn't keep him out anyway.

Brett Gardner   **CF**   **Bats: L**   **Throws: L**   Height: 5′ 10″   Weight: 180   Born: August 24, 1983   Age: 23

YEAR	TEAM	LVL	AGE	PA	R	2B	3B	HR	RBI	BB	SO	SB	CS	SPEED	AVG	OBP	SLG	MLVR	EQAVG	EQOBP	EQSLG	EQA	VORP	DEFENSE			
2005	STA	A-	21	335	62	9	1	5	32	39	49	19	3	7.0	.284	.377	.376	.179	.265	.321	.338	.240	-5.9	67-CF	3		
2006	TAM	A+	22	278	46	12	5	0	22	43	51	30	7	7.9	.323	.433	.418	.282	.317	.410	.421	.298	22.8	48-CF	-1	12-LF	0
2006	TRN	AA	22	251	41	4	3	0	13	27	39	28	5	8.5	.272	.352	.318	.019	.276	.344	.317	.254	-0.9	51-CF	3		
2007	NYA	MLB	23	538	76	21	5	5	38	47	92	31	11	7.3	.273	.340	.365	-.098	.271	.343	.370	.263	7.5	126-CF	3		

Breakout: 19% Improve: 49% Collapse: 23% Attrition: 11%   Comparables: Michael Bourn, Jamal Strong, Mike Curry, Victor Hall

One of the few Yankees prospects last year who moved up a level and didn't completely fall apart, Gardner is one of the game's fastest runners. He can't hit the light switch and be under the covers before the room gets dark, as used to be said of Cool Papa Bell, but with the delayed brightening of energy-efficient bulbs, Gardner can hit the switch and be out of bed before the room gets light. Gardner knows his job is to get on base and is happy to take a walk. He's still working on outfield routes, but his speed compensates for that. Gardner's main shortcoming is a lack of power. He'll need to keep up his average and patience if he wants to avoid getting slapped with a Jason Tyner label.

Jason Giambi   **DH**   **Bats: L**   **Throws: R**   Height: 6′ 3″   Weight: 230   Born: January 8, 1971   Age: 36

YEAR	TEAM	LVL	AGE	PA	R	2B	3B	HR	RBI	BB	SO	SB	CS	SPEED	AVG	OBP	SLG	MLVR	EQAVG	EQOBP	EQSLG	EQA	VORP	DEFENSE	
2004	NYA	MLB	33	322	33	9	0	12	40	47	62	0	1	3.4	.208	.342	.379	-.095	.214	.349	.389	.262	-0.7	39-1B	3
2005	NYA	MLB	34	545	74	14	0	32	87	108	109	0	0	3.5	.271	.440	.535	.332	.280	.455	.569	.345	50.6	63-1B	-8
2006	NYA	MLB	35	579	92	25	0	37	113	110	106	2	0	3.6	.253	.413	.558	.281	.255	.421	.568	.331	47.4	54-1B	-8
2007	NYA	MLB	36	551	92	22	0	31	88	111	108	2	1	4.0	.255	.417	.526	.221	.253	.421	.532	.331	36.9	129-DH	

Breakout: 15% Improve: 38% Collapse: 30% Attrition: 22%   Comparables: Willie McCovey, Jack Clark, Harmon Killebrew, Frank Thomas

Runs and fields like a 45 played at 33 ⅓. Those who grew up in the compact disc era won't get that reference, but, trust us, it's slow. He can't avoid running, but it seems likely that Giambi's time in the field is done after too many nagging injuries last year. The days of hitting .300 are also gone, but with his great patience and power Giambi will be an offensive asset even as his averages continue to decline. It's hard to believe, but the Yankees will pay Giambi at least another $47 million (two guaranteed years plus an all-but-certain $5 million buyout of 2009). That's a lot of moolah for a player who will spend the next two years praying that his bat doesn't slow as much as his body already has.

New York Yankees

Aaron Guiel   RF   Bats: L   Throws: R   Height: 5' 10"   Weight: 200   Born: October 5, 1972   Age: 34

YEAR	TEAM	LVL	AGE	PA	R	2B	3B	HR	RBI	BB	SO	SB	CS	SPEED	AVG	OBP	SLG	MLVR	EQAVG	EQOBP	EQSLG	EQA	VORP	DEFENSE	
2004	KCA	MLB	31	157	15	4	0	5	13	17	42	1	1	4.1	.156	.263	.296	-.387	.149	.258	.284	.200	-13.0	38-LF	-1
2005	KCA	MLB	32	121	18	5	0	4	7	6	21	1	0	3.5	.294	.355	.450	.101	.296	.364	.472	.288	6.4	21-CF	-1
2006	KCA	MLB	33	59	9	3	0	3	7	7	11	0	0	3.9	.220	.339	.460	-.016	.220	.350	.440	.273	1.2		
2006	NYA	MLB	33	92	16	3	0	4	11	7	20	2	1	5.0	.256	.337	.439	-.010	.259	.348	.432	.269	1.6	12-RF	0
2007	NYA	MLB	34	350	38	15	1	12	45	33	76	1	1	4.2	.228	.312	.396	-.137	.226	.316	.402	.254	-3.1	84-RF	0

Breakout: 21%   Improve: 43%   Collapse: 34%   Attrition: 43%   Comparables: Walt Moryn, Warren Newson, Joe Collins, Richie Hebner

Claimed off of waivers on July 5, Guiel seemed like the foundation of a passable right field platoon with Bernie Williams, but the acquisition of Abreu put an end to that. Guiel found himself in the minors for the next three weeks, returning as part of an ill-defined first-base rotation with Giambi and Craig Wilson. A left-hander with a bit of pop and versatile enough that the Yankees used him at all three outfield positions and first base, Guiel could be useful in a fifth outfielder/pinch-hitting role for another year or two. The Yankees' sole non-tender in December, he's joined the Yakult Swallows for 2007.

Derek Jeter   SS   Bats: R   Throws: R   Height: 6' 3"   Weight: 195   Born: June 26, 1974   Age: 33

YEAR	TEAM	LVL	AGE	PA	R	2B	3B	HR	RBI	BB	SO	SB	CS	SPEED	AVG	OBP	SLG	MLVR	EQAVG	EQOBP	EQSLG	EQA	VORP	DEFENSE	
2004	NYA	MLB	30	721	111	44	1	23	78	46	99	23	4	6.2	.292	.352	.471	.099	.298	.358	.486	.289	52.0	150-SS	-5
2005	NYA	MLB	31	752	122	25	5	19	70	77	117	14	5	6.0	.309	.389	.450	.169	.318	.407	.474	.304	59.3	153-SS	12
2006	NYA	MLB	32	715	118	39	3	14	97	69	102	34	5	6.8	.344	.417	.483	.276	.346	.425	.494	.320	80.5	145-SS	7
2007	NYA	MLB	33	685	114	33	4	13	72	62	98	24	7	6.1	.324	.392	.453	.148	.321	.396	.459	.306	57.3	159-SS	4

Breakout: 8%   Improve: 39%   Collapse: 21%   Attrition: 2%   Comparables: Julio Franco, Paul Molitor, Roberto Alomar, Carney Lansford

Derek Jeter is your AL VORP leader, regardless of MVP controversies, and, less convincingly, the AL's Gold Glove shortstop for 2006. An argument can be made that Jeter's 2006 was even better than his shoulda-been-MVP 1999 because he was more problematic defensively in the earlier season. Metrics that once condemned Jeter are more complimentary now, though the initial edition of John Dewan's *Fielding Bible* made a convincing case that the statistical progress has not been mirrored in Jeter's real-world performance. A more intriguing question, and one more easily answered, is, do we expect an encore from a player who will turn 33 this year and just had his second-best season? From 2003 to 2005, Jeter batted .307/.377/.458, in line with his career statistics to that point (.314/.386/.461). He'll be closer to that level this year. Jeter's a strange case; most players gain power and lose batting average as they age, but he seems to be doing the opposite.

Hideki Matsui   LF   Bats: L   Throws: R   Height: 6' 2"   Weight: 230   Born: June 12, 1974   Age: 33

YEAR	TEAM	LVL	AGE	PA	R	2B	3B	HR	RBI	BB	SO	SB	CS	SPEED	AVG	OBP	SLG	MLVR	EQAVG	EQOBP	EQSLG	EQA	VORP	DEFENSE			
2004	NYA	MLB	30	680	109	34	2	31	108	88	103	3	0	5.0	.298	.390	.522	.239	.301	.397	.532	.314	44.4	151-LF	-2		
2005	NYA	MLB	31	703	108	45	3	23	116	63	78	2	2	4.8	.305	.367	.496	.198	.314	.384	.519	.305	43.9	111-LF	2	25-CF	-3
2006	NYA	MLB	32	201	32	9	0	8	29	27	23	1	0	4.0	.302	.393	.494	.208	.300	.398	.494	.307	13.3	32-LF	6		
2007	NYA	MLB	33	407	60	20	1	14	58	50	50	2	1	4.6	.288	.376	.474	.119	.285	.380	.480	.302	21.8	97-LF	0		

Breakout: 1%   Improve: 23%   Collapse: 32%   Attrition: 15%   Comparables: Paul O'Neill, Ryan Klesko, Cliff Floyd, Larry Walker

Hideki Matsui long prided himself on never missing a game, but not even Lou Gehrig could have played through a snapped wrist. He spent four months healing and rehabbing, then came back and hit like Hideki Ted Williams for two weeks, batting .412/.484/.608 with three home runs in 51 at-bats. Matsui isn't the rangiest or most instinctive outfielder, though he's passable. Still, the first time a ball goes over his head, and one will, the Yankees will be pressured to get Cabrera back out on defense.

Andy Phillips   1B   Bats: R   Throws: R   Height: 6' 0"   Weight: 205   Born: April 6, 1977   Age: 30

YEAR	TEAM	LVL	AGE	PA	R	2B	3B	HR	RBI	BB	SO	SB	CS	SPEED	AVG	OBP	SLG	MLVR	EQAVG	EQOBP	EQSLG	EQA	VORP	DEFENSE			
2004	COH	AAA	27	493	82	19	6	25	84	51	61	2	1	5.1	.316	.386	.560	.328	.293	.358	.505	.291	30.6	83-1B	6		
2005	COH	AAA	28	340	60	14	1	22	54	36	61	2	0	4.4	.300	.379	.573	.332	.282	.353	.518	.292	29.3	28-3B	1	26-1B	0
2005	NYA	MLB	28	41	7	4	0	1	4	1	13	0	0	5.0	.150	.171	.325	-.494	.128	.171	.256	.154	-3.9				
2006	NYA	MLB	29	263	30	11	3	7	29	15	56	3	2	5.0	.240	.281	.394	-.186	.239	.289	.403	.237	-7.5	60-1B	-5		
2007	NYA	MLB	30	343	40	16	2	12	49	24	65	2	1	4.7	.260	.314	.441	-.053	.257	.317	.447	.266	3.2	83-1B	-1		

Breakout: 21%   Improve: 49%   Collapse: 24%   Attrition: 30%   Comparables: Mike Ivie, Hal Breeden, Deron Johnson, Candy Maldonado

(continued next page)

Andy Phillips (*continued*)

Phillips got several chances to grab the first base job last year and failed despite defense that was vastly superior to Giambi's—according to some Yankees broadcasters, that made Phillips the new Stuffy McInnis, though in truth he fell far short of greatness. Phillips's average suffered due to a lack of plate judgment that stuck out badly on this highly selective club; he swung at everything, and, as old timers will tell you, "everything" is a broad, amorphous concept that is very difficult to conceive, let alone make contact with. He also struggled against lefties (.195/.233/.244), making even a platoon role problematic. Phillips had his best minor league seasons under new Yankees hitting coach Kevin Long, so there's a faint hope for improvement—if he beats out Josh Phelps and makes the team. Unproven players his age don't tend to get second chances.

Jorge Posada   C   Bats: S   Throws: R   Height: 6' 2"   Weight: 205   Born: August 17, 1971   Age: 35

YEAR	TEAM	LVL	AGE	PA	R	2B	3B	HR	RBI	BB	SO	SB	CS	SPEED	AVG	OBP	SLG	MLVR	EQAVG	EQOBP	EQSLG	EQA	VORP	DEFENSE	
2004	NYA	MLB	32	547	72	31	0	21	81	88	92	1	3	3.1	.272	.400	.481	.180	.276	.408	.493	.307	41.4	128-C	-1
2005	NYA	MLB	33	546	67	23	0	19	71	66	94	1	0	4.5	.262	.352	.430	.047	.268	.368	.451	.284	26.8	122-C	-1
2006	NYA	MLB	34	544	65	27	2	23	93	64	96	3	0	4.4	.278	.375	.494	.154	.279	.383	.504	.303	38.0	118-C	13
2007	NYA	MLB	35	493	66	22	1	17	66	67	87	3	1	4.2	.256	.363	.439	.026	.254	.367	.445	.289	22.9	116-C	-1

Breakout: 5%   Improve: 23%   Collapse: 48%   Attrition: 16%   Comparables: Mike Piazza, Jeff Bagwell, Ken Caminiti, Jim Hickman

Posada quietly had a great year. While postseason talking heads spent October smooching Pudge Rodriguez's overrated fundament, they missed that, for the sixth year in a row, Posada left him in the dust. Since 2000, BP's translated batting stats have Posada hitting .283/.395/.506 with a .307 EqA, while Rodriguez has hit .314/.358/.524 with a .296 EqA. In addition to the huge lead in OBP, Posada also led Pudge in isolated power .210 to .198. (He also outproduced Mike Piazza's translated .291/.369/.535, .302 EqA over that span.) Posada caught up defensively this year as well. Coach Tony Peña tweaked Posada's throwing mechanics, and the result was a career high in runners caught stealing (though his passed ball tendencies persisted). Posada will remain valuable for at least another year or two.

Alex Rodriguez   3B   Bats: R   Throws: R   Height: 6' 3"   Weight: 225   Born: July 27, 1975   Age: 31

YEAR	TEAM	LVL	AGE	PA	R	2B	3B	HR	RBI	BB	SO	SB	CS	SPEED	AVG	OBP	SLG	MLVR	EQAVG	EQOBP	EQSLG	EQA	VORP	DEFENSE	
2004	NYA	MLB	28	698	112	24	2	36	106	80	131	28	4	6.0	.286	.375	.512	.212	.290	.382	.524	.308	53.7	152-3B	-3
2005	NYA	MLB	29	715	124	29	1	48	130	91	139	21	6	5.8	.321	.421	.610	.449	.332	.439	.643	.350	91.0	157-3B	-5
2006	NYA	MLB	30	674	113	26	1	35	121	90	139	15	4	5.1	.290	.392	.523	.234	.292	.401	.535	.315	51.6	145-3B	-16
2007	NYA	MLB	31	663	110	30	2	34	105	85	133	15	4	5.1	.287	.384	.528	.201	.284	.388	.535	.318	51.4	154-3B	-3

Breakout: 4%   Improve: 16%   Collapse: 44%   Attrition: 3%   Comparables: Ken Boyer, Eddie Mathews, Kirk Gibson, Ryan Klesko

Take some notable failures to come through in big situations including three straight postseason series, a case of the fielding yips, a West Coast road trip that included 14 strikeouts in 20 at-bats, a team captain who is permanently aggrieved about some comments you made in a magazine interview a hundred years ago, a manager sick of answering the same questions about you, and a fan base that can't seem to forget your salary. Compound this with postgame commentary that was either obtuse or self-aggrandizing, and you have the formula for making yourself unpopular despite winning and MVP and batting an aggregate .299/396/.549 over three seasons. It's not fair—Rodriguez certainly didn't lose those playoff series by himself—but that's life in the big city. More troubling was a defensive decline that that may signal that Rodriguez will sooner move to first base than back to shortstop.

Gary Sheffield   RF   Bats: R   Throws: R   Height: 6' 0"   Weight: 215   Born: December 31, 1969   Age: 38

YEAR	TEAM	LVL	AGE	PA	R	2B	3B	HR	RBI	BB	SO	SB	CS	SPEED	AVG	OBP	SLG	MLVR	EQAVG	EQOBP	EQSLG	EQA	VORP	DEFENSE	
2004	NYA	MLB	35	684	117	30	1	36	121	92	83	5	6	4.5	.290	.393	.534	.272	.295	.401	.548	.316	54.1	121-RF	4
2005	NYA	MLB	36	675	104	27	0	34	123	78	76	10	2	5.3	.291	.379	.512	.225	.300	.396	.538	.314	47.5	124-RF	-3
2006	NYA	MLB	37	166	22	5	0	6	25	13	16	5	1	4.9	.298	.355	.450	.079	.302	.367	.470	.290	7.0	19-RF	-1
2007	DET	MLB	38	397	55	16	1	12	49	37	43	9	3	4.9	.276	.347	.433	.007	.273	.350	.443	.282	8.6	95-RF	-4

Breakout: 0%   Improve: 12%   Collapse: 55%   Attrition: 23%   Comparables: Felipe Alou, Al Kaline, Moises Alou, Dave Winfield

Sheffield wore number 11 on his back in New York so everyone could be doubly sure who he looks out for. Sheffield is right to want to wring every dollar from the short career of the pro athlete, but, at this late stage, he's made well over $100 million, and the constant carping about his contracts (the most recent of which he negotiated himself) is spectacularly tedious.

This is a man who, when St. Peter welcomes him to heaven, will bitch that he didn't get another three-year extension tagged onto the end of his lifespan. An April 29 collision with Shea Hillenbrand at first base inflicted soft tissue damage to Sheffield's left wrist, largely wiping out the rest of his season. When Sheffield returned, the acquisition of Bobby Abreu had made his Skylab-like routes unwelcome in the outfield. A rushed move to first base didn't pan out; it was ironic that the man who once asserted that he intentionally threw balls over his first baseman's head was now missing them from the opposite side of the equation. Traded to Detroit, he'll get into the Tigers' outfield/DH mix and try to make a living out of hitting Johan Santana. The Tigers extended his deal by two years, which means the bitching won't start until sometime in 2008.

Jose Tabata   RF   Bats: R   Throws: R   Height: 5' 11"   Weight: 160   Born: August 12, 1988   Age: 18

YEAR	TEAM	LVL	AGE	PA	R	2B	3B	HR	RBI	BB	SO	SB	CS	SPEED	AVG	OBP	SLG	MLVR	EQAVG	EQOBP	EQSLG	EQA	VORP	DEFENSE
2006	CSC	A	17	363	50	22	1	5	51	30	66	15	5	5.4	.298	.377	.420	.178	.269	.322	.377	.247	-5.7	68-RF -1
2007	NYA	MLB	18	476	52	23	2	7	43	24	73	14	6	5.6	.255	.298	.362	-.190	.253	.301	.367	.239	-11.8	113-RF -2

Breakout: 25%   Improve: 54%   Collapse: 26%   Attrition: 8%   Comparables: Kimani Newton, Domingo Cuello, Eduardo Nunez, Jose Reyes

A jammed thumb limited him to two games in the second half, but his bat had quieted before that and had largely gone dead in July (.222/.386/.333). The power is supposed to develop, but that doesn't mean it will. Tabata is so very young—in a baseball sense he has yet to complete puberty—that it's difficult to say what kind of player he'll grow up to be. If you talk to the Yankees, they'll tell you they don't know where he's going to hit in the end, but they expect it to be somewhere between second and fifth in the batting order.

Marcos Vechionacci   3B   Bats: S   Throws: R   Height: 6' 2"   Weight: 170   Born: August 7, 1986   Age: 20

YEAR	TEAM	LVL	AGE	PA	R	2B	3B	HR	RBI	BB	SO	SB	CS	SPEED	AVG	OBP	SLG	MLVR	EQAVG	EQOBP	EQSLG	EQA	VORP	DEFENSE		
2004	TAM	A+	17	4	1	0	0	0	0	0	0	0	0	4.9	.250	.250	.250	-.280	.250	.250	.250	.165	-0.4			
2004	STA	A-	17	84	13	5	0	0	8	11	13	0	0	3.8	.292	.393	.361	.196	.280	.349	.333	.242	2.4	10-3B -1		
2005	CSC	A	18	558	83	26	8	2	62	43	83	16	2	7.9	.252	.314	.348	-.090	.220	.264	.285	.202	-34.0	65-3B 1	61-SS -2
2006	CSC	A	19	429	56	15	6	7	44	55	52	7	4	5.3	.255	.357	.386	.073	.229	.305	.340	.230	-6.4	92-3B -8		
2006	TAM	A+	19	149	15	3	1	1	15	11	29	1	2	3.9	.178	.242	.237	-.331	.168	.221	.219	.163	-17.8	35-3B -5		
2007	NYA	MLB	20	495	43	17	3	5	38	33	72	4	2	5.5	.223	.278	.303	-.325	.221	.281	.307	.208	-20.0	117-3B -1		

Breakout: 43%   Improve: 59%   Collapse: 21%   Attrition: 4%   Comparables: Kenny Perez, Elliot Johnson, Asdrubal Cabrera, Aaron Capista

After two disappointing seasons in a row, Vechionacci's status as a top prospect has to be questioned at least a little bit, though, in fairness to him, it must be said that the Yankees were pushing things by asking him to master the Florida State League at 20. Busted back down Charleston, he showed initial improvement, but finished the year in a slump. Right now we're talking about a player who, whatever his defensive capabilities, has to show an unlikely amount of offensive growth before he can play a corner in the majors. The Yankees believe it will happen.

Bernie Williams   OF   Bats: S   Throws: R   Height: 6' 2"   Weight: 205   Born: December 31, 1969   Age: 38

YEAR	TEAM	LVL	AGE	PA	R	2B	3B	HR	RBI	BB	SO	SB	CS	SPEED	AVG	OBP	SLG	MLVR	EQAVG	EQOBP	EQSLG	EQA	VORP	DEFENSE		
2004	NYA	MLB	35	651	105	29	1	22	70	85	96	1	5	3.9	.262	.360	.435	.027	.264	.369	.441	.278	19.0	88-CF -3		
2005	NYA	MLB	36	546	53	19	1	12	64	53	75	1	2	3.7	.249	.321	.367	-.101	.256	.338	.384	.254	0.8	98-CF -2		
2006	NYA	MLB	37	462	65	29	0	12	61	33	53	2	0	4.7	.281	.332	.436	-.000	.282	.341	.451	.273	11.8	48-RF -2	22-CF -5
2007	NYA	MLB	38	403	45	18	1	9	47	33	53	2	1	4.8	.256	.319	.387	-.119	.253	.322	.392	.254	0.6	96-CF -7		

Breakout: 2%   Improve: 28%   Collapse: 45%   Attrition: 28%   Comparables: Ruben Sierra, Paul O'Neill, Ken Griffey, Hank Bauer

As has been the case for most of his career, Williams continued to sock lefties last year, batting .323/.387/.549 against them. Unfortunately, most of his playing time came against the other guys, who dominated him (.261/.305/.383). In the post-Sheffield, pre-Abreu period, he played lots of right field and looked like a Gold Glover—that is, he looked like he was clanking around an actual Gold Glove award on his hand instead of a mitt. If the Yankees wanted to carry a right-handed half of a DH platoon, Williams might be worth a spot. Unfortunately, Joe Torre can't be counted on to be disciplined in the way he uses Williams, so the return wouldn't justify the expense, and rosters are too small to throw away a spot on such a limited player. As such, it's time—*again*—to say goodbye.

Craig Wilson 1B Bats: R Throws: R Height: 6' 2" Weight: 220 Born: November 30, 1976 Age: 30

YEAR	TEAM	LVL	AGE	PA	R	2B	3B	HR	RBI	BB	SO	SB	CS	SPEED	AVG	OBP	SLG	MLVR	EQAVG	EQOBP	EQSLG	EQA	VORP	DEFENSE			
2004	PIT	MLB	27	644	97	35	5	29	82	50	169	2	2	4.9	.264	.354	.499	.158	.264	.349	.501	.285	30.8	71-RF	1	53-1B	-3
2005	PIT	MLB	28	238	23	14	1	5	22	30	69	3	0	4.5	.264	.387	.421	.118	.268	.387	.439	.291	9.9	27-RF	0	16-LF	1
2006	PIT	MLB	29	286	38	11	2	13	41	24	88	1	0	4.7	.267	.339	.478	.077	.267	.339	.486	.280	8.3	41-1B	-3	22-RF	0
2006	NYA	MLB	29	109	15	4	0	4	8	4	34	0	0	4.2	.212	.248	.365	-.313	.204	.248	.350	.206	-6.1	26-1B	-2		
2007	NYA	MLB	30	354	42	16	1	15	49	30	99	2	1	4.6	.242	.319	.440	-.060	.240	.322	.446	.269	2.2	85-1B	-3		

Breakout: 8% Improve: 28% Collapse: 41% Attrition: 32% Comparables: Pete Incaviglia, Nate Colbert, Rick Reichardt, Bill Renna

Craig Wilson is a reflection of current events—sometimes liberation just doesn't work out the way you think it will. Despite his good power, the Pirates spent years keeping Wilson in a semi-regular role before dumping him on the Yankees for Shawn Chacon. As a Yankee, Wilson struck out at his usual high rates, but didn't do much else to compensate, and quickly lost Joe Torre's confidence. By the playoffs, he was at best the team's fourth choice to play first, after Sheffield, Phillips, and Giambi, and didn't even make the ALDS roster. A free agent at this writing, Wilson will recover to be a useful five-day-a-week starter for someone.

PITCHERS

T. J. Beam Bats: R Throws: R Height: 6' 7" Weight: 215 Born: August 28, 1980 Age: 26

YEAR	TEAM	LVL	AGE	W	L	SV	G	GS	IP	H	BB	SO	HR	GB%	BABIP	STUFF	WHIP	ERA	PERA	EQERA	EQH9	EQBB9	EQSO9	EQHR9	VORP	WXRL
2005	CSC	A	24	3	3	2	35	2	59²	45	18	78	2	42.3%	.312	2	1.06	1.66	4.03	3.49	8.4	3.8	6.5	0.6	13.3	—
2005	TAM	A+	24	1	1	1	12	0	17¹	14	7	27	2	34.2%	.333	-1	1.21	3.12	6.40	5.17	9.8	5.2	8.6	2.3	0.8	—
2006	TRN	AA	25	4	0	3	18	0	42²	26	12	34	1	36.6%	.231	1	0.90	0.85	3.83	2.23	6.9	3.1	4.7	0.4	15.1	—
2006	COH	AAA	25	2	0	1	19	0	31²	16	13	37	1	50.0%	.221	24	0.93	1.73	3.36	2.30	4.9	4.0	8.0	0.6	11.5	—
2006	NYA	MLB	25	2	0	0	20	0	18	26	6	12	5	27.7%	.350	-23	1.78	8.50	6.40	8.20	12.5	2.9	5.8	2.4	-5.1	-0.71
2007	NYA	MLB	26	3	4	2	70	2	70	75	29	51	14	37.0%	.283	-7	1.48	5.23	5.27	4.90	9.4	3.5	6.2	1.7	3.9	0.40

Breakout: 21% Improve: 48% Collapse: 22% Attrition: 10% Comparables: Josue Matos, Chris Gissell, Justin Speier, Chris Knapp

After each shelling, Torre would tell Beam, "We believe in you, we need you. *I* need you." It was like a musical, or one of those disturbingly homoerotic things that Kirk would sometimes say to Spock on Star Trek. The lanky Ole Miss product has a good fastball but—shades of early Scott Proctor—it doesn't move much. Beam's minor league line strongly argues that he can do this pitching thing, but, as with Proctor, he's going to need to develop a reliable off-speed pitch to set up the cheese.

Colter Bean Bats: L Throws: R Height: 6' 6" Weight: 255 Born: January 16, 1977 Age: 30

YEAR	TEAM	LVL	AGE	W	L	SV	G	GS	IP	H	BB	SO	HR	GB%	BABIP	STUFF	WHIP	ERA	PERA	EQERA	EQH9	EQBB9	EQSO9	EQHR9	VORP	WXRL
2004	COH	AAA	27	9	3	1	53	0	82²	61	23	109	3	—	.309	33	1.02	2.29	3.11	2.98	7.2	2.8	9.0	0.4	23.8	—
2005	COH	AAA	28	4	7	0	65	0	71²	60	39	82	5	52.3%	.309	11	1.38	3.01	4.85	4.58	8.0	5.5	7.8	0.8	8.0	—
2006	COH	AAA	29	9	2	0	47	6	88²	61	53	116	2	49.0%	.311	34	1.29	2.65	4.31	3.44	6.9	6.0	8.9	0.3	20.7	—
2007	NYA	MLB	30	3	3	1	28	5	57²	56	40	58	6	45.0%	.316	6	1.65	4.91	4.92	4.74	8.6	5.8	8.4	0.8	4.2	0.60

Breakout: 7% Improve: 21% Collapse: 53% Attrition: 16% Comparables: Wayne Twitchell, Mark Clear, Jason Christiansen, Bart Miadich

Bean's career minor league line: 459.2 innings, 337 hits, 204 walks, 587 strikeouts, 20 home runs allowed, 2.69 ERA. Fans reacted badly to Bean during his brief call-up—he's heavy and his stuff is unimpressive. There's an obvious downside to having radar gun readings in your stadium; everybody's a scout. If Chad Bradford could have a career, so could Bean.

Brian Bruney Bats: R Throws: R Height: 6' 2" Weight: 245 Born: February 17, 1982 Age: 25

YEAR	TEAM	LVL	AGE	W	L	SV	G	GS	IP	H	BB	SO	HR	GB%	BABIP	STUFF	WHIP	ERA	PERA	EQERA	EQH9	EQBB9	EQSO9	EQHR9	VORP	WXRL
2004	TUC	AAA	22	2	0	5	31	0	38	18	20	42	1	—	.198	27	1.00	1.18	3.77	1.64	4.0	4.9	7.5	0.2	16.9	—
2004	ARI	MLB	22	3	4	0	30	0	31¹	20	27	34	2	—	.257	24	1.50	4.31	4.51	4.22	5.9	6.8	8.4	0.6	3.9	0.38
2005	ARI	MLB	23	1	3	12	47	0	46	56	35	51	6	41.2%	.385	7	1.98	7.43	5.12	6.94	10.5	6.0	8.8	1.1	-10.2	-0.62
2006	COH	AAA	24	1	1	3	11	0	14	10	8	22	2	33.3%	.296	14	1.29	3.21	5.51	4.61	7.2	5.3	11.2	2.0	1.5	—
2006	NYA	MLB	24	1	1	0	19	0	20²	14	15	25	1	34.7%	.271	21	1.40	0.87	3.78	0.86	6.0	6.0	10.3	0.4	12.0	0.51
2007	NYA	MLB	25	2	2	1	40	1	44	41	30	45	5	39.0%	.302	5	1.62	5.01	4.95	4.79	8.3	5.8	8.6	1.0	3.0	0.30

Breakout: 13% Improve: 34% Collapse: 24% Attrition: 43% Comparables: Eric Plunk, Matt Anderson, Sammy Stewart, Chuck McElroy

To paraphrase the cover of Detective Comics #38, the *sensational* character find of 2006. Bruney went from Arizona's closer in mid-2005 to waiver bait in May 2006. What happened in between was a whole lot of bad pitching and some stretched elbow ligaments. Credit Brian Cashman and Yankees' scouting for figuring that a 24-year-old who throws 95 MPH is worth trying to fix. The Bruney that emerged from the Yankees' minor league counseling seemed to have better command than his Arizona incarnation, even if he did walk nearly seven batters per nine innings. That high walk rate means that the old Bruney could resurface at any time. Still, Bruney's ability to keep the ball in the park makes him a less frightening setup man than Kyle "Cape Canaveral" Farnsworth.

Tyler Clippard								**Bats: R Throws: R**				Height: 6' 4"		Weight: 170		Born: February 14, 1985				Age: 22	
YEAR	TEAM	LVL	AGE	W	L	SV	G	GS	IP	H	BB	SO	HR	GB%	BABIP	STUFF	WHIP	ERA	PERA	EQERA	EQH9	EQBB9	EQSO9	EQHR9	VORP	WXRL
2004	BCR	A	19	10	10	0	26	25	149	153	32	145	12	—	.323	3	1.24	3.44	5.38	5.33	10.0	2.4	5.0	1.5	4.4	—
2005	TAM	A+	20	10	9	0	26	25	147¹	118	34	169	12	39.3%	.296	17	1.03	3.18	4.78	4.11	8.4	2.6	6.7	1.4	23.6	—
2006	TRN	AA	21	12	10	0	28	28	166	118	55	175	14	44.4%	.258	13	1.04	3.36	5.06	5.11	8.3	3.3	6.8	1.2	8.6	—
2007	*NYA*	*MLB*	*22*	*7*	*8*	*0*	*27*	*21*	*127¹*	*138*	*49*	*97*	*21*	*40.0%*	*.299*	*10*	*1.46*	*5.22*	*5.02*	*4.96*	*9.6*	*3.2*	*6.4*	*1.4*	*6.2*	*1.50*

Breakout: 15% Improve: 51% Collapse: 16% Attrition: 1%   Comparables: Chin-Hui Tsao, Brandon Knight, Ervin Santana, Jason Grilli

With a fastball that hovers between 88 and 91 MPH, Clippard doesn't through hard, but he's got the deception thing down. He looks like the real deal, but pitchers like him have been known to lose a lost of their luster as they move up the ladder. That seemed to be the case during the first half of 2006—Clippard opened the season in a slump, and, by June, was 2–9 with a 5.69 ERA. He found his control in July and turned his season around, posting a 2.08 ERA after the break and throwing a no-hitter in August. Clippard is the kind of pitcher who will continually have to prove himself, and may well have adjustment problems when first reaching the majors. He should eventually settle in as a back of rotation starter, though that estimate may prove to be conservative.

J. B. Cox								**Bats: L Throws: R**				Height: 6' 3"		Weight: 205		Born: May 13, 1984				Age: 23	
YEAR	TEAM	LVL	AGE	W	L	SV	G	GS	IP	H	BB	SO	HR	GB%	BABIP	STUFF	WHIP	ERA	PERA	EQERA	EQH9	EQBB9	EQSO9	EQHR9	VORP	WXRL
2005	TAM	A+	21	1	2	0	16	0	27²	20	5	27	1	64.8%	.275	8	0.90	2.60	3.90	3.67	7.3	2.0	5.7	0.7	5.8	—
2006	TRN	AA	22	6	2	3	41	0	77¹	54	24	60	2	64.7%	.244	7	1.01	1.75	3.78	3.60	7.4	3.1	4.9	0.4	16.7	—
2007	*NYA*	*MLB*	*23*	*3*	*3*	*1*	*29*	*6*	*63²*	*68*	*23*	*37*	*7*	*56.0%*	*.296*	*-3*	*1.43*	*4.66*	*4.36*	*4.59*	*9.5*	*3.1*	*4.8*	*0.9*	*5.7*	*0.80*

Breakout: 3% Improve: 19% Collapse: 52% Attrition: 19%   Comparables: James Vermilyea, Scott Feldman, Richard Gardner, Ryan Brannan

There's a lot to like here. Cox set up for Huston Street at the University of Texas, and closed after Street left, and is being groomed as a big league setup man. He throws from a low-three-quarter angle and gets the ball to the plate in the high-80s to low-90s; batters pound it into the ground roughly three times as often as they hit it in the air. Normally, Cox's approach would let lefties feast, but he held them to .154/.248/.231 with Trenton last year. Cox says he pitches angry "half the time." This gives him the flexibility to be angry in his spare time, something he'll need when he reaches the majors and discovers that Joe Torre considers "young pitcher" and "bad pitcher" to be interchangeable terms.

Octavio Dotel								**Bats: R Throws: R**				Height: 6' 0"		Weight: 210		Born: November 25, 1973				Age: 33	
YEAR	TEAM	LVL	AGE	W	L	SV	G	GS	IP	H	BB	SO	HR	GB%	BABIP	STUFF	WHIP	ERA	PERA	EQERA	EQH9	EQBB9	EQSO9	EQHR9	VORP	WXRL
2004	HOU	MLB	30	0	4	14	32	0	34²	27	15	50	4	—	.315	32	1.21	3.11	3.22	3.82	7.1	3.3	11.5	1.0	6.9	0.52
2004	OAK	MLB	30	6	2	22	45	0	50²	41	18	72	9	—	.305	31	1.16	4.08	3.67	3.66	7.3	2.8	11.8	1.4	12.8	2.50
2005	OAK	MLB	31	1	2	7	15	0	15¹	10	11	16	2	26.3%	.222	15	1.37	3.53	5.03	3.52	6.5	6.5	9.4	1.2	3.8	0.09
2006	NYA	MLB	32	0	0	0	14	0	10	18	11	7	2	37.5%	.421	-18	2.90	10.80	6.89	11.32	15.7	9.6	6.1	1.7	-6.4	-0.43
2007	*NYA*	*MLB*	*33*	*2*	*2*	*2*	*37*	*0*	*40¹*	*39*	*20*	*41*	*7*	*35.0%*	*.296*	*5*	*1.47*	*4.85*	*4.73*	*4.58*	*8.7*	*4.2*	*8.5*	*1.4*	*4.0*	*0.30*

Breakout: 31% Improve: 74% Collapse: 17% Attrition: 37%   Comparables: Rich Delucia, Aurelio Lopez, Wes Stock, Doug Bair

This was a strange deal. When the Yankees signed Jon Lieber while he was recovering from Tommy John surgery, they made sure it was a two-year deal, and it worked out reasonably well. The Yankees paid Lieber to rehab, then he paid them back with a year of solid work. The Dotel deal was exactly the same, except it left out the second year. The Yankees paid Dotel to rehab from Tommy John surgery. Period. They gambled he would recover quickly enough to help them in 2006, and it didn't happen. Dotel's fastball came around, but his slider caused him discomfort, continually setting him back. If things go the way TJ aftermaths usually do, Dotel should be a more complete pitcher this year. It's sobering to realize that

(continued next page)

Octavio Dotel *(continued)*

he's now 33, closer to the end than the beginning, and that the heart of his career was 2001 to 2003 in Houston. The Royals signed Dotel to a one-year, incentive-rich deal that may be worth as much as $7.5 million. Perhaps they signed him to flip him to a contender at the deadline, or hoped that he'll pitch so well that he'll be a Type-A free agent and yield a draft pick. Maybe, laughable as it is, they thought that Dotel would offer a distraction as the Royals attempt to traverse the gap between mediocrity and sub-mediocrity. If it's not any of those things, we're out of guesses; the Royals need Dotel like a fern needs earmuffs.

Kyle Farnsworth   Bats: R   Throws: R   Height: 6' 4"   Weight: 240   Born: April 14, 1976   Age: 31

YEAR	TEAM	LVL	AGE	W	L	SV	G	GS	IP	H	BB	SO	HR	GB%	BABIP	STUFF	WHIP	ERA	PERA	EQERA	EQH9	EQBB9	EQSO9	EQHR9	VORP	WXRL
2004	CHN	MLB	28	4	5	0	72	0	66²	67	33	78	10	—	.335	8	1.50	4.72	4.22	5.00	9.0	4.0	9.2	1.2	4.0	0.47
2005	DET	MLB	29	1	1	6	46	0	42²	29	20	55	1	46.9%	.295	42	1.15	2.32	2.58	2.70	6.0	4.2	11.2	0.2	15.2	2.22
2005	ATL	MLB	29	0	0	10	26	0	27¹	15	7	32	4	36.1%	.193	27	0.80	1.98	3.89	1.98	5.3	2.0	9.9	1.3	10.7	2.06
2006	NYA	MLB	30	3	6	6	72	0	66	62	28	75	8	36.7%	.314	17	1.36	4.36	3.69	4.41	8.3	3.6	9.5	0.9	10.5	1.92
2007	NYA	MLB	31	3	3	5	53	0	58²	55	24	61	7	41.0%	.302	14	1.34	3.95	3.93	3.77	8.3	3.5	8.8	1.0	12.0	1.10

Breakout: 31%   Improve: 55%   Collapse: 20%   Attrition: 4%   Comparables: Lee Smith, Eric Plunk, Ron Davis, Roberto Hernandez

There must be easier pitchers to manage. Farnsworth is good for only one inning at a time, no matter how few pitches he throws, and he can't pitch on consecutive days, nor on days when his back locks up. Torre actually let the Farns pitch on consecutive days eleven times through early August, including two streaks of pitching on three consecutive days, with less than disastrous results (9 ⅔ innings, 2 runs). On August 9, Farnsworth pitched to the White Sox for the second day in a row and gave up a solo homer to Tad Iguchi and a three-run shot to Joe Crede in two-thirds of an inning. Torre swore off Farnsworth encores after that, returning to him on consecutive days just once over the rest of the season. Farnsworth lost that game.

Philip Hughes   Bats: R   Throws: R   Height: 6' 5"   Weight: 220   Born: June 24, 1986   Age: 21

YEAR	TEAM	LVL	AGE	W	L	SV	G	GS	IP	H	BB	SO	HR	GB%	BABIP	STUFF	WHIP	ERA	PERA	EQERA	EQH9	EQBB9	EQSO9	EQHR9	VORP	WXRL
2005	CSC	A	19	7	1	0	12	12	68²	46	16	72	1	49.4%	.269	36	0.90	1.97	3.32	3.48	6.8	2.5	5.6	0.3	15.9	—
2005	TAM	A+	19	2	0	0	5	4	17²	8	4	21	0	45.9%	.222	17	0.68	3.05	3.56	3.71	5.3	2.6	6.9	0.0	3.6	—
2006	TAM	A+	20	2	3	0	5	5	30²	19	2	30	0	51.9%	.247	30	0.70	1.79	2.58	3.00	6.3	0.6	5.7	0.3	8.7	—
2006	TRN	AA	20	10	3	0	21	21	116¹	73	32	138	5	52.8%	.266	42	0.90	2.25	3.39	3.30	7.3	2.7	7.7	0.6	28.5	—
2007	NYA	MLB	21	10	7	0	30	22	148	136	49	127	14	47.0%	.286	24	1.25	3.70	3.51	3.59	8.1	2.8	7.2	0.8	32.0	4.20

Breakout: 8%   Improve: 28%   Collapse: 35%   Attrition: 2%   Comparables: Brad Penny, Jake Peavy, Edwin Jackson, Yusmeiro Petit

Baby New Year, 2007. There is little doubt that Hughes could have succeeded at Triple-A or the majors in the second half 2006, but the Yankees were determined not to push their luck after just about half the system pancaked upon promotion. He was also on strict pitch counts late in the year and shut down early, just to be on the safe side after his first two seasons ended in soreness timeouts. Times have changed: In 1995, Paul Wilson made 26 minor league starts and threw 186.2 innings. Hughes should probably send Wilson, the Curt Flood of Injured Pitching Prospects, a thank-you note. Regardless of what happens in spring training, Hughes will probably head to Triple-A, but when May comes around and ballclubs reach for fifth starters, look out.

Kei Igawa   Bats: L   Throws: L   Height: 6' 1"   Weight: 205   Born: July 13, 1979   Age: 27

YEAR	TEAM	LVL	AGE	W	L	SV	G	GS	IP	H	BB	SO	HR	GB%	BABIP	STUFF	WHIP	ERA	PERA	EQERA	EQH9	EQBB9	EQSO9	EQHR9	VORP	WXRL
2004	HNS	JP	24	14	11	0	29	0	200¹	190	54	228	29	—	.302	18	1.22	3.73	4.17	4.54	8.4	2.8	7.4	1.1	23.1	—
2005	HNS	JP	25	13	9	0	27	27	172¹	199	60	145	23	—	.321	-2	1.50	3.87	4.84	5.44	10.3	3.5	5.6	1.3	3.1	—
2006	HNS	JP	26	14	9	0	29	29	209	180	49	194	17	—	.273	20	1.10	0.26	4.01	4.08	8.1	2.6	6.5	0.9	34.6	—
2007	NYA	MLB	27	12	10	0	30	30	186¹	197	61	137	24	44.0%	.300	15	1.38	4.47	4.35	4.29	9.4	2.8	6.2	1.1	24.4	3.90

Breakout: 25%   Improve: 59%   Collapse: 10%   Attrition: 1%   Comparables: Jim Rooker, Denny Neagle, Alex Kellner, Randy Wolf

At this writing, before Igawa has pitched to even a single major league batter in an intra-squad game, it isn't clear how good he actually is. His strikeout rates have been quite good, but he has also allowed a great many home runs, particularly in 2004 and 2005. His 2006 was far more impressive. Igawa adjusted his style last year, using his 90-MPH fastball to set up his off-speed stuff, and his walk and homer rates dropped and his strikeout rate went up. Igawa will initially benefit from his status as an unknown, but may receive a more lasting benefit from pitching in a large park in front of a major league defense. If the Yankees guessed right, they'll have added a solid, experienced fourth starter.

Randy Johnson **Bats: R Throws: L** Height: 6' 10" Weight: 230 Born: December 31, 1969 Age: 43

YEAR	TEAM	LVL	AGE	W	L	SV	G	GS	IP	H	BB	SO	HR	GB%	BABIP	STUFF	WHIP	ERA	PERA	EQERA	EQH9	EQBB9	EQSO9	EQHR9	VORP	WXRL
2004	ARI	MLB	40	16	14	0	35	35	245²	177	44	290	18	—	.269	54	0.90	2.60	2.60	2.93	6.4	1.4	9.4	0.6	71.1	7.75
2005	NYA	MLB	41	17	8	0	34	34	225²	207	47	211	32	45.2%	.288	27	1.13	3.79	3.86	3.98	7.9	1.8	8.1	1.2	43.8	5.63
2006	NYA	MLB	42	17	11	0	33	33	205	194	60	172	28	42.6%	.288	17	1.24	5.00	4.20	5.25	8.4	2.5	7.1	1.1	12.3	2.42
2007	*ARI*	*MLB*	*43*	*7*	*6*	*0*	*19*	*19*	*111¹*	*105*	*34*	*102*	*14*	*44%*	*.287*	*19*	*1.24*	*3.97*	*3.90*	*3.77*	*7.9*	*2.5*	*7.3*	*1.0*	*23.6*	*3.3*

Breakout: 43% Improve: 66% Collapse: 17% Attrition: 47% Roger Clemens, Phil Niekro, Gaylord Perry, Nolan Ryan

Johnson underwent surgery for a herniated disc after the season. He's expected to be pitching during spring training, but the exact timing of his return isn't set in stone. The disc surgery raises a number of interesting questions about Johnson's 2006. Johnson often had good velocity on his fastball, but his signature slider had disappeared, and he was unable to finish off hitters. Was Johnson ever truly healthy? Will the surgery help restore him to his old form, make no difference, or further diminish him? Or is it just that this is what a 43-year-old future Hall of Famer pitches like? Johnson is a unique specimen, but past experience with the entire lineage of pitchers suggests that, whether the pitcher be a knuckleballer or flame-thrower, 43 is the undiscovered country from whose bourn no traveler returns. Having reacquired Johnson in a five-player trade and extended his contract through 2008, the Diamoandbacks are about to go there with him.

Jeffrey Karstens **Bats: R Throws: R** Height: 6' 3" Weight: 175 Born: September 24, 1982 Age: 24

YEAR	TEAM	LVL	AGE	W	L	SV	G	GS	IP	H	BB	SO	HR	GB%	BABIP	STUFF	WHIP	ERA	PERA	EQERA	EQH9	EQBB9	EQSO9	EQHR9	VORP	WXRL
2004	TAM	A+	21	6	9	0	24	24	138²	151	31	116	11	—	.325	-5	1.31	4.02	5.09	5.98	11.2	2.4	5.2	1.5	-5.7	—
2005	TRN	AA	22	12	11	0	28	27	169	192	42	147	16	47.7%	.344	3	1.38	4.15	4.60	5.56	10.5	2.6	5.3	1.2	0.7	—
2006	TRN	AA	23	6	0	0	11	11	74²	54	14	67	4	46.9%	.248	19	0.92	2.30	3.94	3.64	8.0	2.0	5.5	0.9	15.6	—
2006	COH	AAA	23	5	5	0	14	14	73²	80	30	48	9	35.6%	.303	-16	1.50	4.30	5.99	5.45	9.6	3.9	4.5	1.7	1.2	—
2006	NYA	MLB	23	2	1	0	8	6	42²	40	10	16	6	33.6%	.238	-6	1.17	3.79	4.97	4.33	8.0	2.1	3.1	1.2	8.6	0.86
2007	*NYA*	*MLB*	*24*	*7*	*9*	*0*	*34*	*26*	*137¹*	*160*	*44*	*79*	*24*	*42.0%*	*.298*	*-2*	*1.48*	*5.58*	*5.24*	*5.32*	*10.3*	*2.7*	*4.8*	*1.5*	*0.3*	*1.00*

Breakout: 7% Improve: 37% Collapse: 18% Attrition: 0% Comparables: Travis Harper, Matt Wise, Ryan Nye, Mark Brownson

Karstens's fastball is strictly Wal-Mart, but his curve and change, which he throws with excellent control, make him a viable pitcher anyway. As with many curveballers, Karstens's curve tends to go airborne when hit. Combine this with few strikeouts and you have a recipe for a lot of home runs. He nevertheless pitched quite well in his brief tour with the Yankees, but a more complete tour around the league will likely bring more equivocal results.

Mike Mussina **Bats: L Throws: R** Height: 6' 2" Weight: 190 Born: December 31, 1969 Age: 38

YEAR	TEAM	LVL	AGE	W	L	SV	G	GS	IP	H	BB	SO	HR	GB%	BABIP	STUFF	WHIP	ERA	PERA	EQERA	EQH9	EQBB9	EQSO9	EQHR9	VORP	WXRL
2004	NYA	MLB	35	12	9	0	27	27	164²	178	40	132	22	—	.317	18	1.32	4.59	3.86	4.47	8.9	1.9	6.6	1.1	22.1	3.21
2005	NYA	MLB	36	13	8	0	30	30	179²	199	47	142	23	44.9%	.328	17	1.37	4.41	4.06	4.48	9.4	2.3	6.8	1.1	22.9	3.40
2006	NYA	MLB	37	15	7	0	32	32	197¹	184	35	172	22	42.5%	.285	30	1.11	3.51	3.40	3.94	8.1	1.5	7.3	0.9	44.9	5.07
2007	*NYA*	*MLB*	*38*	*12*	*9*	*0*	*29*	*29*	*183²*	*191*	*46*	*145*	*24*	*44.0%*	*.300*	*17*	*1.29*	*4.24*	*4.06*	*4.07*	*9.2*	*2.1*	*6.7*	*1.1*	*29.3*	*4.30*

Breakout: 14% Improve: 56% Collapse: 8% Attrition: 3% Comparables: Don Sutton, Gaylord Perry, Early Wynn, Kevin Brown

In a spring training intra-squad game, Jorge Posada smoked a Mussina change-up like he knew it was coming. In fact, he *did* know it was coming; Mussina was tipping the pitch. The Moose revised his grip, and, suddenly, he was a new pitcher—for a while. His line for April and May was 81.2 innings, 65 hits, 13 walks, and 70 Ks with a 2.53 ERA. After that, Mussina's groin began troubling him and he reverted to his 2004-to-2005, 4.50-ERA form, though he looked better in September after a DL stay put the groin back in working order. Mussina's peripherals remain strong, and his control is impeccable. The Yankees took a good risk in turning Mussina's one-year option into a discounted two-year extension.

Mike Myers **Bats: L Throws: L** Height: 6' 3" Weight: 220 Born: June 26, 1969 Age: 37

YEAR	TEAM	LVL	AGE	W	L	SV	G	GS	IP	H	BB	SO	HR	GB%	BABIP	STUFF	WHIP	ERA	PERA	EQERA	EQH9	EQBB9	EQSO9	EQHR9	VORP	WXRL
2004	SEA	MLB	35	4	1	0	50	0	27²	29	17	23	3	47%	.333	1	1.66	4.87	4.85	4.76	9.5	5.1	7.0	1.0	4.0	0.4
2004	BOS	MLB	35	1	0	0	25	0	15	16	6	9	2	60%	.286	-11	1.47	4.20	4.67	3.52	9.4	3.5	5.3	1.2	3.7	-0.0
2005	BOS	MLB	36	3	1	0	65	0	37¹	30	13	21	3	55%	.245	-5	1.15	3.14	4.34	3.23	6.5	3.0	4.8	0.7	10.1	1.2
2006	NYA	MLB	37	1	2	0	62	0	30²	29	11	22	3	48%	.277	-2	1.30	3.22	4.40	4.02	8.3	3.2	6.0	0.9	6.6	1.0
2007	*NYA*	*MLB*	*38*	*2*	*1*	*1*	*35*	*0*	*29²*	*33*	*10*	*19*	*3*	*48%*	*.305*	*-9*	*1.45*	*4.30*	*4.47*	*4.14*	*9.7*	*3.0*	*5.4*	*1.0*	*4.3*	*0.4*

Breakout: 14% Improve: 36% Collapse: 34% Attrition: 49% Comparables: Hank Aguirre, Mark Guthrie, Kent Mercker, Roberto Hernandez

(continued next page)

Mike Myers (continued)

Southpaw specialist Myers pitched only 30.2 not particularly high-leverage innings last year. Add in that inherited runners had an easy time scoring with him on the mound—more than one-third of the 18 hits he allowed to lefties went for extra bases—and some desultory work against righties resulting in a .345 OBP, and the Yankees didn't get a whole lot of bang for their buck beyond a pitcher who handicaps the roster with his limitations. With three strong righties to close out games, Myers proved to be a luxury the Yankees didn't need, and maybe nobody does.

Carl Pavano   Bats: R Throws: R   Height: 6' 5"   Weight: 240   Born: January 8, 1976   Age: 31

YEAR	TEAM	LVL	AGE	W	L	SV	G	GS	IP	H	BB	SO	HR	GB%	BABIP	STUFF	WHIP	ERA	PERA	EQERA	EQH9	EQBB9	EQSO9	EQHR9	VORP	WXRL
2004	FLO	MLB	28	18	8	0	31	31	222¹	212	49	139	16	—	.287	21	1.17	3.00	3.71	3.45	8.6	1.8	5.0	0.6	60.6	7.05
2005	NYA	MLB	29	4	6	0	17	17	100	129	18	56	17	50.7%	.333	-5	1.47	4.77	4.92	5.62	11.0	1.6	4.8	1.4	-1.8	0.95
2007	NYA	MLB	31	7	7	0	27	19	121	139	26	66	15	51.0%	.304	2	1.36	4.58	4.39	4.44	10.2	1.8	4.6	1.1	13.7	2.20

Breakout: 9%　Improve: 41%　Collapse: 25%　Attrition: 8%　Comparables: Bill Wegman, Ron Reed, Mark Clark, Bob Forsch

When it was revealed in late August that Pavano had busted a couple of ribs in a car accident, derailing his umpteenth comeback from bruised buttocks, bone chips, arm soreness, back stiffness, rotator cuff tendonitis, humerus pain, therapy to even the length of his legs, and dandruff, Derek Jeter cracked, "It's not a letdown if you weren't counting on it," and Johnny Damon said he hoped that the car was okay. Yankees sources were quoted as disparaging Pavano's "apparent indifference...he has been a regular on the massage table and is often seen munching candy bars." Having cemented his rep as the world's most expensive escapee from the Island of Misfit Toys (the Yankees have paid him close to $17 million so far and are in for another $23 million before they're done), Pavano will attempt to come back from nearly two years off. What the Yankees will get if he remains healthy is anyone's guess—Pavano was never that good in the first place.

Scott Proctor   Bats: R Throws: R   Height: 6' 1"   Weight: 200   Born: January 2, 1977   Age: 30

YEAR	TEAM	LVL	AGE	W	L	SV	G	GS	IP	H	BB	SO	HR	GB%	BABIP	STUFF	WHIP	ERA	PERA	EQERA	EQH9	EQBB9	EQSO9	EQHR9	VORP	WXRL
2004	COH	AAA	27	2	3	4	35	0	44	37	18	42	4	—	.277	0	1.25	2.86	4.68	3.30	7.6	4.1	6.6	1.0	11.2	—
2004	NYA	MLB	27	2	1	0	26	0	25	29	14	21	5	—	.316	-8	1.72	5.40	5.36	5.81	9.6	4.4	6.8	1.7	-0.3	0.19
2005	COH	AAA	28	6	1	14	35	1	42²	47	11	54	8	42.7%	.368	0	1.36	4.22	5.24	4.68	10.6	2.6	8.5	2.1	4.3	—
2005	NYA	MLB	28	1	0	0	29	1	44²	46	17	36	10	30.8%	.271	-11	1.41	6.04	5.69	6.07	8.8	3.3	7.0	2.0	-3.4	-0.33
2006	NYA	MLB	29	6	4	1	83	0	102¹	89	33	89	12	35.0%	.273	11	1.19	3.52	3.89	3.54	7.6	2.8	7.3	0.9	28.2	1.83
2007	NYA	MLB	30	4	3	3	67	0	75	77	26	61	12	38.0%	.291	1	1.37	4.43	4.44	4.20	9.1	2.9	6.9	1.3	11.1	0.90

Breakout: 20%　Improve: 47%　Collapse: 23%　Attrition: 8%　Comparables: John Johnstone, Cliff Politte, Vicente Romo, Dave Tobik

The Yankees went into spring training 2006 with the idea that Proctor could try starting, something he did in the minors through 2002. Although they ultimately chose to keep him in relief, the experiment was a great success, forcing Proctor to develop his curveball to the point where he could deploy it alongside his hard but straight fastball. The new and improved Proctor pitched well in April and Joe Torre fell in love—Proctor led the American League in games pitched and the majors in relief innings. Though Proctor actually pitched quite well in the second half, the workload did tell at times. With relievers often needing a refractory year after heavy usage, there's a good chance that Proctor won't be up for an encore. Trading Jaret Wright for Chris Britton seems to have been intended to insure the Yankees against that possibility. The team is again considering starting Proctor—if 100 innings didn't kill him, maybe 200 will do the trick.

Darrell Rasner   Bats: R Throws: R   Height: 6' 3"   Weight: 210   Born: January 13, 1981   Age: 26

YEAR	TEAM	LVL	AGE	W	L	SV	G	GS	IP	H	BB	SO	HR	GB%	BABIP	STUFF	WHIP	ERA	PERA	EQERA	EQH9	EQBB9	EQSO9	EQHR9	VORP	WXRL
2004	BRV	A+	23	6	5	0	22	21	119¹	133	31	88	6	—	.332	-7	1.37	3.17	5.04	5.62	11.2	2.9	4.1	1.1	-0.3	—
2004	HAR	AA	23	1	1	0	5	5	29²	21	9	15	1	—	.233	4	1.01	1.21	4.44	1.80	6.3	3.0	3.0	0.3	12.7	—
2005	HAR	AA	24	6	7	0	27	26	150¹	150	29	96	10	52.5%	.297	-1	1.19	3.59	4.71	4.64	9.2	2.2	3.6	0.9	15.9	—
2006	TAM	A+	25	0	0	0	2	2	7	12	3	6	0	38.5%	.480	-15	2.14	2.57	4.67	5.14	16.7	5.1	3.9	0.0	0.4	—
2006	COH	AAA	25	4	0	0	10	10	58²	60	11	47	4	44.3%	.316	14	1.22	2.78	3.92	3.79	8.9	1.8	5.5	0.9	11.9	—
2006	NYA	MLB	25	3	1	0	6	3	20¹	18	5	11	2	40.0%	.254	0	1.13	4.43	4.21	4.35	7.8	2.2	4.8	0.9	3.7	0.84
2007	NYA	MLB	26	6	7	0	33	15	109	132	31	56	17	46.0%	.308	-6	1.49	5.50	5.18	5.29	10.7	2.4	4.3	1.3	0.7	0.70

Breakout: 6%　Improve: 24%　Collapse: 39%　Attrition: 0%　Comparables: Jason Rakers, Shawn Sedlacek, Travis Thompson, Vicente Padilla

There is no truth to the rumor that the Nats, a team without any semblance of pitching, placed Rasner on waivers because his inflexible adherence to the Hollow Earth theory was disrupting clubhouse chemistry. It was just another inscrutable Jim Bowden move, sacrificing a viable arm to make room for Matt LeCroy on the roster. The Yankees reeled in the sinker-slider pitcher on a waiver claim, and Rasner pitched extremely well at Columbus. He was called up to pitch in middle relief, pitched 1 ⅔ innings and promptly disappeared onto the 60-day DL with shoulder soreness. Returning in September, Rasner pitched well enough to be a dark horse candidate for the 2007 rotation.

Mariano Rivera
Bats: R Throws: R   Height: 6′ 2″   Weight: 195   Born: December 31, 1969   Age: 37

YEAR	TEAM	LVL	AGE	W	L	SV	G	GS	IP	H	BB	SO	HR	GB%	BABIP	STUFF	WHIP	ERA	PERA	EQERA	EQH9	EQBB9	EQSO9	EQHR9	VORP	WXRL
2004	NYA	MLB	34	4	2	53	74	0	78²	65	20	66	3	—	.282	27	1.08	1.94	3.01	1.88	7.0	2.0	7.0	0.3	37.9	7.46
2005	NYA	MLB	35	7	4	43	71	0	78¹	50	18	80	2	56.2%	.239	42	0.87	1.38	2.47	2.13	5.5	2.0	8.9	0.2	32.2	5.18
2006	NYA	MLB	36	5	5	34	63	0	75	61	11	55	3	58.0%	.269	24	0.96	1.80	2.98	2.01	7.2	1.3	6.3	0.4	34.9	5.33
2007	NYA	MLB	37	4	4	27	51	0	59	57	13	48	5	54.0%	.295	9	1.18	2.76	3.06	2.67	8.5	1.9	6.8	0.6	18.8	2.90

Breakout: 13% Improve: 16% Collapse: 61% Attrition: 15%   Comparables: Larry Andersen, Chris Hammond, Buddy Groom, Bob Locker

Rivera hasn't posted an ERA as high as 2.00 since 2002. His line from 2003 to 2006 is 302.2 innings, 237 hits, 59 walks (or 1.75 per nine), 264 strikeouts, and a 1.69 ERA. The amazing thing about Rivera is that he's maintained effectiveness as he's gotten older. The 2003-to-2006 timeframe, from ages 33 to 36, has been the most successful of his career, but only fractionally. It's not so much that he's getting better, but that he's been consistent at a very high level, something that can be said of very few relievers. When you add his continued excellence in the face of the increasing fragility that afflicts most pitchers in their mid-30s, Rivera's consistency becomes almost unprecedented—the notable exception being Hoyt Wilhelm, who like Rivera had one special pitch and used it to effect. Rivera wants to pitch until the new Yankee Stadium opens in 2009; he'll be 39. The greatest impediment to that plan may not be the erosion of his pitching ability, but of his ability to be healthy enough to be the fulltime closer—a strained right elbow limited him to four games in September.

Jose Veras
Bats: R Throws: R   Height: 6′ 5″   Weight: 230   Born: October 20, 1980   Age: 26

YEAR	TEAM	LVL	AGE	W	L	SV	G	GS	IP	H	BB	SO	HR	GB%	BABIP	STUFF	WHIP	ERA	PERA	EQERA	EQH9	EQBB9	EQSO9	EQHR9	VORP	WXRL
2004	MNT	AA	23	1	0	0	3	3	10	10	7	6	2	—	.258	-19	1.70	6.30	9.65	7.45	9.3	7.4	3.7	2.8	-2.0	—
2004	DUR	AAA	23	6	5	0	30	10	84¹	101	33	63	9	—	.341	-12	1.59	5.34	5.16	5.95	10.7	3.8	5.2	1.1	-3.3	—
2005	OKL	AAA	24	3	5	24	57	0	61²	63	33	72	4	48.5%	.366	11	1.56	3.79	3.98	4.14	9.0	4.6	7.9	0.6	10.2	—
2006	COH	AAA	25	5	3	21	50	0	59	49	19	68	3	46.5%	.311	16	1.15	2.44	3.50	3.19	7.6	3.0	7.9	0.8	15.9	—
2006	NYA	MLB	25	0	0	1	12	0	11	8	5	6	2	31.3%	.200	-17	1.18	4.09	5.95	4.09	6.5	4.1	4.9	1.6	2.4	0.22
2007	NYA	MLB	26	3	3	2	37	2	60	63	26	45	9	44.0%	.296	-1	1.48	4.77	4.76	4.57	9.3	3.7	6.4	1.2	5.8	0.60

Breakout: 24% Improve: 52% Collapse: 28% Attrition: 13%   Comparables: Chad Ricketts, Eric Weaver, Bill Simas, Bart Miadich

"I feel proud that the Yankees have signed me to help set the table for Mariano Rivera," Veras said after joining the Yankees as a minor league free agent. "That's something very important to me." As it turned out, Veras would have had a better chance of table-setting for Mo if he had moonlighted as a waiter at Rivera's new restaurant. The good news is that Veras has a good fastball and seemed to put his command problems behind him at Columbus, dropping his walk rate to 2.9 per nine innings. He could be an option for the Yankees pen, should the organization learn to trust relievers under 30.

Ron Villone
Bats: L Throws: L   Height: 6′ 3″   Weight: 245   Born: January 16, 1970   Age: 37

YEAR	TEAM	LVL	AGE	W	L	SV	G	GS	IP	H	BB	SO	HR	GB%	BABIP	STUFF	WHIP	ERA	PERA	EQERA	EQH9	EQBB9	EQSO9	EQHR9	VORP	WXRL
2004	SEA	MLB	34	8	6	0	56	10	117	102	64	86	12	—	.264	4	1.42	4.08	4.97	4.68	8.0	4.4	6.2	0.8	15.5	2.20
2005	SEA	MLB	35	2	3	1	52	0	40¹	33	23	41	2	46.7%	.301	22	1.39	2.46	4.05	3.29	7.5	5.0	9.0	0.4	11.4	-0.17
2005	FLO	MLB	35	3	2	0	27	0	23²	24	12	29	2	40.3%	.367	11	1.52	6.84	3.74	7.77	8.9	4.1	10.0	0.7	-6.0	-0.05
2006	NYA	MLB	36	3	3	0	70	0	80¹	75	51	72	9	32.9%	.301	7	1.57	5.16	4.84	5.16	8.3	5.4	7.6	0.9	4.9	0.74
2007	NYA	MLB	37	3	3	2	64	0	67²	70	33	56	10	41.0%	.300	-4	1.52	4.91	4.89	4.68	9.2	4.2	7.0	1.2	5.6	0.50

Breakout: 28% Improve: 59% Collapse: 25% Attrition: 22%   Comparables: Don McMahon, Jose Mesa, Kent Mercker, Al Worthington

Villone was pretty much the best Villone he can be in the first half (2.27 ERA), but, by the break, he had already pitched 44.2 innings. At that point he either (A) Wore out from overuse; (B) Reverted to being Ron Villone; (C) Both. Regardless, his second-half ERA ballooned to 8.35. Villone really is quite good against lefties and would probably excel in a LOOGY role, but that assumes that he has anything left after his implosion (which, to be fair, was helped along by subsequent relievers waiving Villone's leftovers home), and that his manager can leave well enough alone.

Chien-Ming Wang   Bats: R Throws: R   Height: 6' 3" Weight: 220 Born: March 31, 1980   Age: 27

YEAR	TEAM	LVL	AGE	W	L	SV	G	GS	IP	H	BB	SO	HR	GB%	BABIP	STUFF	WHIP	ERA	PERA	EQERA	EQH9	EQBB9	EQSO9	EQHR9	VORP	WXRL
2004	TRN	AA	24	6	5	0	18	18	109	112	26	90	6	—	.320	13	1.27	4.05	4.02	4.76	8.6	2.3	4.8	0.7	10.4	—
2004	COH	AAA	24	5	1	0	6	5	40¹	31	8	35	3	—	.262	24	0.97	2.01	3.70	2.23	6.7	2.0	6.0	0.7	15.1	—
2005	COH	AAA	25	2	1	0	6	6	34	40	6	21	4	66.1%	.333	1	1.35	4.24	4.51	4.41	10.1	1.6	4.2	1.3	4.6	—
2005	NYA	MLB	25	8	5	0	18	17	116¹	113	32	47	9	65.7%	.270	6	1.25	4.02	4.39	4.26	8.2	2.5	3.5	0.7	16.8	2.12
2006	NYA	MLB	26	19	6	1	34	33	218	233	52	76	12	63.8%	.293	9	1.31	3.63	3.87	3.95	9.2	2.0	2.9	0.4	54.6	5.68
2007	NYA	MLB	27	12	10	0	31	31	195²	221	52	83	18	59.0%	.299	3	1.40	4.29	4.21	4.22	10.0	2.3	3.6	0.8	27.5	4.20

Breakout: 12% Improve: 44% Collapse: 19% Attrition: 0%   Comparables: Dennis Lamp, Brian Lawrence, Kevin Brown, John Doherty

Wang shouldn't work. Though he gets his fastball into the mid-90s, Wang struck out just 3.14 batters per nine innings last year. A pitcher who allows that many balls in play should, according to the physical laws of the universe, get killed—if not all the time, then often—because many of those balls will fall in. What makes Wang the great exception to the rule is that batters can't lift his heavy stuff—among pitchers with at least 150 innings pitched, only Derek Lowe and Brandon Webb allowed a lower percentage of fly balls. Some of Wang's grounders do go for singles, but he mitigates those by being stingy with walks and extra-base hits—he led the majors in fewest home runs allowed per nine innings pitched (0.5), and in lowest isolated power allowed (.098). Restricted to advancing one base at a time, the opposition has to shoot a lot of balls in a row past a diving Derek Jeter to have a big inning. As long as Wang's sinker is as good as it is, there's no reason to think he can't keep this up.

Jaret Wright   Bats: R Throws: R   Height: 6' 2" Weight: 230 Born: December 29, 1975 Age: 31

YEAR	TEAM	LVL	AGE	W	L	SV	G	GS	IP	H	BB	SO	HR	GB%	BABIP	STUFF	WHIP	ERA	PERA	EQERA	EQH9	EQBB9	EQSO9	EQHR9	VORP	WXRL
2004	ATL	MLB	28	15	8	0	32	32	186¹	168	70	159	11	—	.300	30	1.28	3.29	3.43	3.84	8.0	3.0	6.8	0.5	39.9	5.56
2005	NYA	MLB	29	5	5	0	13	13	63²	81	32	34	8	47.1%	.336	-9	1.77	6.08	5.51	6.82	10.9	4.4	4.6	1.1	-10.0	0.08
2006	NYA	MLB	30	11	7	0	30	27	140¹	157	57	84	10	39.5%	.319	9	1.52	4.49	4.23	4.76	9.8	3.4	5.1	0.6	18.1	3.48
2007	BAL	MLB	31	7	9	0	32	21	131¹	145	53	80	16	45%	.301	-2	1.51	4.92	4.79	4.73	10.0	3.4	5.1	1.1	9.0	1.9

Breakout: 10% Improve: 43% Collapse: 27% Attrition: 23%   Kent Bottenfield, Stan Bahnsen, Russ Ortiz, Mike Scott

In his second year in New York, Wright was a league-average, five-inning starter. It wasn't what the Yankees had in mind what they signed him (Lord knows what that was) but it wasn't disastrous—at least not until the playoffs, where there was a collective cry of, "Whoa! This guy is our fourth starter?" from Yankees fans and personnel alike. Wright was subsequently traded to the Orioles for Chris Britton. While Leo Mazzone will try to help Wright recapture that 2004 feeling, Wright's five-and-out tendencies make dealing a reliever for him like trashing your sprinkler system before setting the house on fire. For the Yankees, having Wright on the mound meant the almost certain use of four relievers every five days. And whaddya know, the O's followed the Wright deal by signing Jamie Walker, Denys Baez, Chad Bradford, and Scott Williamson—ladies and gentlemen, we give you Jaret Wright and the Wrightettes.

Lineouts

PLAYER	TEAM	LVL	AGE	PA	R	2B	3B	HR	RBI	BB	SO	SB-CS	SPEED	AVG/OBP/SLG	MLVr	EqAVG/EqOBP/EqSLG	EqA	VORP
SS A. Cannizaro	COH	AAA	27	487	69	32	1	3	32	51	59	6-5	5.1	.276/.367/.380	.094	.272/.352/.378	.257	18.3
C S. Fasano	PHI	MLB	34	149	9	8	0	4	10	5	47	0-1	3.2	.243/.284/.386	-.172	.241/.282/.383	.226	-2.6
	NYA	MLB	34	57	3	4	0	1	5	2	14	0-0	3.0	.143/.222/.286	-.510	.122/.218/.245	.178	-4.7
2B N. Green	TBA	MLB	27	45	4	0	0	0	0	6	11	0-3	4.5	.077/.200/.077	-.848	.000/.152/.000	.086	-9.1
	NYA	MLB	27	82	8	5	0	2	4	5	29	1-1	4.2	.240/.296/.387	-.166	.243/.309/.378	.238	-0.6
CF A. Jackson	CSC	A	19	611	90	24	5	4	47	61	151	37-12	6.6	.260/.340/.346	-.001	.237/.295/.309	.221	-24.5
RF T. Long*	COH	AAA	30	280	29	13	1	10	38	19	53	0-0	4.0	.277/.329/.450	.129	.266/.313/.433	.253	-0.6
	NYA	MLB	30	40	6	1	0	0	2	4	8	0-0	5.9	.167/.250/.194	-.567	.111/.200/.139	.138	-4.3
C W. Nieves	COH	AAA	28	348	29	13	0	5	34	18	29	2-1	3.8	.259/.298/.346	-.073	.240/.278/.320	.214	-12.8
LF K. Reese*	COH	AAA	28	240	30	8	2	5	21	15	37	4-6	5.1	.283/.354/.410	.120	.282/.342/.421	.259	2.6
RF B. Sardinha*	TRN	AA	23	373	47	10	1	10	40	34	78	0-2	4.1	.254/.324/.380	.045	.260/.322/.393	.248	-4.2
	COH	AAA	23	211	27	10	5	6	27	23	36	3-2	5.6	.286/.365/.492	.246	.296/.370/.532	.300	15.8
RF K. Thompson	COH	AAA	26	416	69	22	5	9	44	44	63	17-7	7.2	.265/.345/.428	.115	.264/.337/.436	.268	14.9
	NYA	MLB	26	37	5	3	0	1	6	6	9	2-0	5.9	.300/.417/.500	.258	.300/.417/.500	.320	3.5

PLAYER	TEAM	LVL	AGE	W	L	SV	IP	H	BB	SO	HR	GB%	BABIP	STUFF	WHIP	ERA	PERA	EqERA	EqH9	EqBB9	EqSO9	EqHR9	VORP
D. Betances	YAN	OR	18	0	1	0	23	14	7	27	1	—	.271	19	0.91	1.17	5.40	2.95	8.0	3.8	6.3	1.7	6.3
S. Henn*	COH	AAA	25	3	1	0	42²	44	20	33	1	—	.341	-1	1.52	4.05	4.16	4.57	8.9	4.4	5.2	0.4	5.0
	NYA	MLB	25	0	1	0	9¹	11	5	7	2	—	.321	-8	1.71	4.84	6.30	4.82	10.6	4.8	6.8	1.9	1.4
J. Kennard	TAM	A+	24	3	0	2	27	17	9	19	0	—	.230	-7	0.96	1.33	4.49	2.39	6.5	3.8	3.8	0.3	9.4
	TRN	AA	24	3	6	1	54	51	21	58	5	—	.327	-13	1.33	3.33	5.68	5.86	10.8	4.3	6.6	1.6	-1.5
G. Kontos	STA	A-	21	7	3	0	78¹	64	19	82	3	—	.317	-7	1.06	2.65	5.78	5.50	9.9	3.5	5.2	1.6	0.8
S. Ponson	SLN	MLB	29	4	4	0	68²	82	29	33	7	—	.332	-5	1.62	5.24	4.76	5.12	10.5	3.3	4.0	0.8	3.8
	NYA	MLB	29	0	1	0	16¹	26	7	15	3	—	.411	-7	2.02	10.49	4.54	10.59	13.8	3.7	7.4	1.6	-9.0
A. Small	COH	AAA	34	2	4	0	41²	64	12	17	4	—	.370	-30	1.84	5.68	5.73	6.43	13.3	3.0	2.6	1.5	-3.9
	NYA	MLB	34	0	3	0	27²	42	12	12	9	—	.324	-43	1.95	8.45	7.46	9.21	13.0	3.8	3.8	2.5	-10.7
T. Sturtze	NYA	MLB	35	0	0	0	10²	17	6	6	3	—	.359	-35	2.16	7.57	7.11	8.18	13.9	4.9	4.9	2.5	-2.9
S. White	TRN	AA	25	4	1	0	68¹	52	28	45	0	—	.267	11	1.17	2.11	4.63	3.62	8.4	4.7	3.9	0.3	14.2
	COH	AAA	25	4	9	0	107¹	100	42	88	8	—	.312	4	1.33	4.71	4.85	5.42	8.3	3.8	5.6	1.0	2.2
C. Wright*	TAM	A+	23	12	3	0	119	95	43	100	1	—	.281	14	1.16	1.89	3.93	3.47	7.7	4.1	4.6	0.2	27.6

Andy Cannizaro is an organizational guy with career minor league rates of .274/.350/.351 and nine homers in 2,105 at-bats. Naturally, he hit one in eight major league at-bats last September. **Sal Fasano** displayed a winning personality with the Yankees, but little else of merit; Posada has been exceptionally durable, missing time only for scheduled days off and minor injuries since 2001. Still, that accounts for 25 to 31 games caught by backups each year. In that time, the reserves have hit roughly .219/.253/.340 in 810 plate appearances. There has got to be a better way. **Nick Green** is one of the more bland alternatives to Miguel Cairo available; whatever it takes to keep Cairo in demand, it seems. **Austin Jackson** was all about basketball until the Yankees used an above-slot bonus to banish thoughts of hoops and baggy shorts from his mind. As such, he's still very raw, even for his age, but his willingness to take a walk is a good sign. Watch his speed, because, if he ends up in left rather than center, he might not hit enough. When **Terrence Long** was called up, Torre said, "He brings us experience and has base-stealing ability. He's got some things that can probably help us." Torre had gotten Terrence confused with *Herman* Long of the Boston Beaneaters. T-Long packed a lot of not hitting and poor fielding into 12 games. Herman, being quite dead, would have done less harm. **Wil Nieves** made the Opening Day roster because the Yankees were worried about losing him on waivers if they sent him down; replacement-level catchers turned out to be in greater supply than they thought. Compare Nieves's .244/.271/.308 PECOTA to the line in the Fasano comment above, then consider that the man he'll be battling for the backup catcher spot this spring is his top PECOTA comp, Raul Chavez. It doesn't matter who wins, nothing ever changes. **Kevin Reese** should have sued Brian Cashman for malpractice after the organization decided to demote him in favor of T-Long. A separated shoulder ended his season in July. **Bronson Sardinha** hit well in a smallish sample at Triple-A, the first positive thing he'd done in years. If he can keep it up, he'll have a future in the utility trade. **Kevin Thompson** outperformed Bubba Crosby in every way during the fifth-outfielder derby in spring training, except the crucial category of Torre-toadying. He was sent down, then hit well in three brief call-ups, but his season at Columbus, like the last, was uninspiring.

Dellin Betances is a great big guy (6′8″ and still growing) the Yankees kept out of college by paying above slot. Betances throws hard, looked good doing it, and could move quickly—or his arm could fall off. All the usual caveats apply. **Sean Henn** never rebounded from 2001 Tommy John surgery, or maybe he did but he's just not very good. The Yankees gave Henn a then-record $1.7 million as a draft-and-follow; the new labor agreement eliminates the DFE, so they won't be making that mistake again. **Jeff Kennard** made the 40-man for the first time this winter; he's been in the system since the Civil War, but the Yankees only just figured him out, dropping his arm angle to make his straight, mid-90s fastball a bit more mysterious. The Yankees took **Ian Kennedy** with their first-round draft pick in 2006. He throws only 88 to 92, but is said to have a good feel for pitching. The Yankees liked him because the USC product is already close to his (low) ceiling. **George Kontos** got hammered as a college senior, so, despite his good stuff, the Yankees were able to pick him up in the fifth round of last year's draft. They made some mechanical adjustments and he immediately looked better. Stay tuned. **Jeff Marquez** is a righty with a sinking fastball hoping to Wang his way to fame and fortune. He cut his walk rate last year, heretofore an impediment. **Sidney Ponson** brought dishonor on the House of Fat Pitchers. He may get bigger, but not better. **Aaron Small**: Attention, one-year wonder! At the sound of the bell, your year is up. *Ding!* **Tanyon Sturtze** underwent surgery for a small tear in his rotator cuff and missed the bulk of the season. There wasn't all that much there when he was healthy, so a comeback seems unlikely. The Braves gambled a guaranteed $750,000 plus incentives anyway. Injuries held **Steven White** back in 2005; poor performance at Triple-A held him back in 2006. Without a good secondary pitch, White will be coming to a bullpen near you. **Chase Wright**, FSL pitcher of the year, has a great curve and little else. He's bullpen bound.

Manager: Joe Torre

ear	Team	W-L	Pythag +/-	Avg PC	100 +P	120 +P	QS	BQS	REL	REL w Zero R	IBB	SUBS	PH	PH Avg	PH HR	SB2	CS2	SB3	CS3	SAC Att	SAC %	POS SAC	Squeeze	Swing	In Play
2004	NYA	101-61	+12	93.9	71	2	70	13	436	262	32	55	86	.308	5	67	25	16	8	48	77.1%	36	0	137	99
2005	NYA	95-67	+5	95.8	74	8	78	5	417	240	25	58	94	.244	2	67	20	17	7	43	65.1%	28	0	148	119
2006	NYA	97-65	+1	90.7	44	1	74	8	488	297	41	79	106	.231	0	121	30	18	4	50	68.0%	33	0	140	99

Going into the twelfth, and possibly last, season of the Joe Torre experience, what he brings to a team is no mystery. He's a weak in-game tactician, especially when it comes to handling the bullpen. Whereas, in years past, Torre demonstrated good instincts when it came to organizing his pen into a useful whole, he's now less patient, and will pick one or two pitchers to line up behind Mariano Rivera and ride them mercilessly, as he did with Scott Proctor in 2006, Tanyon Sturtze and Tom Gordon in 2005, or Gordon and Paul Quantrill in 2004. He also oversubscribes to the roles that he creates, forgetting that they are quite arbitrary and preferring, for example, to put his weakest pitcher into a ninth-inning tie on the road rather than use Rivera without a lead. Though Torre still fancies himself a National League manager, he doesn't make a fetish of one-run strategies. He bunts perhaps more often than he should given his lineup, but, compared to his fellow American League managers, he's been conservative. Similarly, over the last five years, the Yankees have made 672 stolen base attempts and succeeded 75 percent of the time, which just misses being the top success rate in baseball over that span. Ten teams made more attempts, but just one, the Mets, had a better success rate. Teams such as the White Sox and Twins, which supposedly know more than the Yankees about "small ball" ran into many more outs—for Torre, speed is a tool, not a suicide pact. His only real strategic hobbyhorse is the hit-and-run; Torre likes to keep the runners in motion to stay out of the double play. He also worries about platoon match-ups on both sides of the ball as much as any manager in baseball. Torre's main strength is the atmosphere of professionalism that he maintains, though this skill failed him in 2006 once he let the Alex Rodriguez situation get out of hand. Ironically, the calm that Torre brought to the Yankees, a countervailing force to George Steinbrenner's pressure tactics, may be less essential than heretofore as the aging Steinbrenner disengages from the team.

Oakland Athletics

By one measure—postseason success—the Athletics of 2006 became the most accomplished squad of General Manager Billy Beane's tenure as general manager. Finally, after all those first-round wipeouts, Beane's A's won a postseason series, sweeping the favored Twins. That's a *result,* and most fans and writers and broadcasters value results over performance. Product over process. Results can fool you, though. Smart people like Billy Beane know this, which is why he worries more about the process than the product. And in terms of pure, fundamental *performance,* the Athletics of 2006 were Beane's worst since 1999.

Yes, the A's did win 93 games last season, but they needed a great deal of good fortune to do that. Based purely on their runs scored (771) and allowed (727), the Athletics' expected winning percentage was just .527, which works out to (roughly) 85 wins and 77 losses. If we drill a bit deeper, the A's look even worse. According to third-order wins and losses—Pythagenport record derived from run elements rather than actual runs and adjusted for the quality of opponent's pitching and defense—the A's played like an 83–79 team, third-best in their division. Their fundamental performance was fully 10 games worse than their actual results. And this was not a single-season anomaly. From 2001 through 2003 the A's averaged 98 Pythagenport wins; from 2004 through 2006 they averaged only 88. In some important way, the A's have declined.

When Michael Lewis's *Moneyball* became a huge bestseller, there was, of course, a backlash, and not just the weekly backhanded slap from Joe Morgan. The most substantive (if not wholly accurate) criticism of the book was that Lewis paid little attention to Oakland's three excellent starting pitchers—Tim Hudson, Mark Mulder, and Barry Zito—without whom Lewis wouldn't have had any reason to write about the A's in the first place. By extension, this criticism was applied to Beane as well. Sure, on-base percentage is fine, and who doesn't want to exploit inefficiencies in the market if other teams aren't attaching enough value to OBP? But the A's simply wouldn't have reached the playoffs four straight times without their three aces. While Beane certainly had plenty to do with their drafting and development, he also was lucky. Hudson was a sixth-rounder in 1997, Mulder and Zito first-rounders in 1998 and 1999, respectively. Mulder was the second overall pick, Zito the ninth, and both were regarded as premier talents by plenty of people in the game. But many, many pitchers drafted in those slots don't become Cy Young candidates within a few years of signing.

Does Beane deserve credit for those three? Of course he does. But it's telling that, since those three, the A's haven't come up with even one pitcher as good. Rich Harden might have been as good, and might yet, but he keeps getting hurt. Jeremy Bonderman might yet be nearly that good, but the A's traded him (and today all they've got to show for that deal is Bobby Kielty and a 26-year-old Triple-A outfielder who didn't even make this book). Joe Blanton, who was part of the *Moneyball* draft, might have been that good, except it turns out he's not. It isn't that the A's have done anything wrong. Most teams would be thrilled to come up with Harden and Blanton within a few seasons. But Harden and Blanton haven't come close to replacing the brilliance of Hudson and Mulder.

Not that we should have expected them to. What the A's got from Hudson, Mulder, and Zito, with all three of them reaching the majors and almost immediately pitching

ATHLETICS PROSPECTUS

2006 record: 93–69; First place, AL West; Lost to Tigers in Championship Series

Pythagenport record: 85–77

Runs scored per game: 4.76 (9th in AL)

Runs allowed per game: 4.49 (3rd in AL)

Team EqA: .257 (11th in AL)

2006 Batters Age: 30.2 (5th oldest in AL)

2006 Pitchers Age: 27.6 (3rd youngest in AL)

Ballpark: McAfee Coliseum; Slight pitcher's park; Park Factor of .984

2006: Beane and Forst continue to find inefficiencies in the market, don't give a damn 'bout your bad reputation.

2007: A lot is riding on Harden and Crosby getting healthy to make up for the loss of Zito and Thomas.

effectively within the same two seasons (1999 and 2000), well, that just doesn't happen. As ESPN.com's David Schoenfield wrote in 2002, "The A's produced three star starters in a two-year span; no other team has done that and only the Braves with John Smoltz, Tom Glavine and Steve Avery did it in a three-year span." As Schoenfield concluded, "Billy Beane is a rare mastermind. He'd be the first GM I would hire to run a team. But Barry Zito, Tim Hudson and Mark Mulder—a trio of freaks—are even more rare." Throughout this book, you will see us returning to variations on the adage, "Luck is the residue of design"; if Baseball Prospectus had a company motto, that would very likely be it. Though Beane deserves much of the credit he's been given over the years, in this case, to a certain extent, genius was the residue of luck.

In 1990, long before Beane was running things, the A's owned the 14th, 26th, 34th, and 36th picks in the June draft. They used all of them to select pitchers: schoolboy Todd Van Poppel, universally regarded as the best pitcher in the draft, and three college pitchers: Don Peters, David Zancanaro, and Kirk Dressendorfer. Immediately they became known, at least to Baseball America readers and A's fans, as "the Four Aces." As it turned out, the A's would have gotten the same results if they had drafted the Four Tenors. The organization might reasonably have hoped (if not expected) that at least two of those young men would become valuable major leaguers, but the phenoms didn't phenominate. Dressendorfer debuted in the majors roughly 10 months after the draft, won three of his seven starts, and was never seen again. Van Poppel started one game for the A's when he was 19, returned to the majors two years later, but in 1996 the A's lost him to the Tigers via waivers. He was 24, and, in 407 major-league innings, he'd posted a 5.75 ERA. Neither Peters nor Zancanaro ever reached the majors.

One of those guys should have done better, probably. But the most that any team can reasonably hope for (then or now) is that one of four such prospects actually becomes a good major leaguer, and perhaps another makes some small contribution. Oakland's bad luck in 1990 underscores their outrageous good fortune in 1999. Some franchises struggle for years to come up with a winning starting rotation, the A's among them in the years prior to the arrival of the Big Three. The A's of Hudson's rookie season were long past the steroidal glory days of the Tony La Russa-Bash Brothers three-time pennant winners. The team hadn't posted a winning record since 1992, and in the three years prior to Hudson's arrival had run through 24 starting pitchers. One of them, Kenny Rogers, was actually pretty good, but the rest were ephemeral in the emerald and gold (see table 1).

Some of those pitchers were veterans, but many more were busted prospects, such as Karsay. Their broken bodies testify to just how hard it is to come up with one ace, let alone three. Once the A's were no longer able to afford their Big Three, there simply wasn't any way for the A's to adequately duplicate them.

Which is not to suggest the A's should have kept Hudson and Mulder, even given the financial wherewithal to keep them. In the two years since Beane traded Mulder to the Cardinals and Hudson to the Braves, those two have combined for 49 wins while sucking up nearly $24 million in salaries (and that latter figure would be a great deal higher if Hudson's contract with the Braves wasn't back-loaded). Meanwhile, Dan Haren, who came to the A's in the Mulder trade, has won 28 games all by himself while earning less than a million bucks over the two seasons. In the same deal, the A's picked up their number-one prospect (Daric Barton) and one of their top relievers (Kiko Calero). Beane didn't do nearly as well in the Hudson deal—hasn't done well at all, come to think of it—but then nobody wins all of them. And now Zito's gone, headed across the Bay for a contract that the A's couldn't have paid and nobody *should* have paid.

Table 1. With Neither Genius nor Luck: A'S Starting Pitching, 1996–1998

Pitcher	GS	IP	W	L	ERA
Jimmy Haynes	46	267.2	14	15	4.91
Mike Oquist	46	282.2	11	17	5.76
Ariel Prieto	45	259	12	16	4.83
Don Wengert	37	295.1	12	22	5.79
Dave Telgheder	35	200.1	8	14	5.26
Kenny Rogers	34	238.2	16	8	3.17
Tom Candiotti	33	201	11	16	4.84
Steve Karsay	24	132.2	3	12	5.77
Willie Adams	24	134.2	6	9	5.81
Doug Johns	23	158	6	12	5.98
John Wasdin	21	131.1	8	7	5.96
Blake Stein	20	117.1	5	9	6.37
Steve Wojciechowski	17	90	5	7	5.90
Carlos Reyes	16	199.2	10	14	5.18
Brad Rigby	14	77.2	1	7	4.87
Bobby Chouinard	11	59	4	2	6.10
Mike Mohler	10	243.2	10	16	4.65
Gil Heredia	6	42.2	3	3	2.74
Andrew Lorraine	6	29.2	3	1	6.37
Todd Van Poppel	6	63	1	5	7.71
Eric Ludwick	5	24	1	4	8.25
Aaron Small	3	161.1	11	9	5.63
Jay Witasick	3	51	2	4	6.18
Buddy Groom	1	3.1	0	0	8.11

No, the point isn't that the A's should have kept their three aces, or tried to. The point is that they were lucky to have all three of them for as long as they did, and that virtually any franchise would find them irreplaceable, let alone a franchise with Oakland's limited financial resources. The question wasn't whether the A's would fall, upon losing that amazing group of homegrown starters; the question was how far. From 2001 through 2003, the A's won 301 games. That wasn't quite tops in the majors. Thanks to their amazing 2001, the Mariners won 302 games over that span. But the A's won, and they did that while spending significantly less money than any of their rivals (which is why it's called *Money*ball). Meanwhile, from 2004 through 2006 the A's won 272 games. Four teams—the Yankees (293), Cardinals (288), Red Sox (279) and Angels (276)—fared better. All those teams vastly outspent the A's, and, among MLB's competitive franchises, only the Twins have approached Oakland's combination of economy and performance. It's been an admirable performance, and should only serve to burnish Beane's reputation even further. (See Sidebar: Marginal Dollars per Marginal Win.)

Today, Beane continues to combine economy and performance, but the performance isn't what it once was. It's been said the problem isn't that the A's have gotten dumber, but that the other teams have gotten smarter, thus making it harder for Beane to exploit inefficiencies in the market, as he so famously did earlier in the decade. Beane himself has espoused this theory while shifting financial resources to defense (Mark Kotsay, Jason Kendall) and mid-level pitching (Mark Redman, Esteban Loaiza), markets that supposedly were undervalued.

There might be something to that. Certainly, the average general manager today has more book-learning than he did even five years ago. There simply isn't the low-hanging fruit there was when Allard Baird and Chuck LaMar were running franchises into the ground. But Oakland's real problem is both simpler and more traditional: their player-development machine isn't working as well as it once did. In 2003, the last year of their brilliant three-season run, the A's featured five legitimate superstars, all of them homegrown: the three aces, Eric Chavez, and Miguel Tejada. Today only Chavez remains, and his stock has dropped precipitously. Meanwhile, Tejada's homegrown replacement, Bobby Crosby, hasn't been able to stay in the lineup, and neither has the latest homegrown ace, Harden, who has started just 28 games over the last two seasons. What's more, first Bonderman and now both Mark Teahen and Andre Ethier are making their bones elsewhere, after being traded by the A's in pursuit of that still-elusive penant. It's not that the A's system has failed, per se, but that it's straining against the nigh-impossible task of providing a constant flow of players so good that they completely mitigate the team's budgetary handicap.

Moneyball is fantastic. We love the book, we love the guy who wrote it, we love the guy who became MLB's marquee general manager because of it. Mostly, though, we love the guiding principles. But Moneyball (the principles, not the book) is a little bit like baserunning and hitting behind the runner and all those other neat things the broadcasters adore: you're not going to win many pennants simply by exploiting market inefficiencies. You win a pennant by putting premier talent on the field. If a low-revenue franchise such as the Athletics is to be consistently successful, it must draft, develop, and graduate a significant amount of that talent. Otherwise, even the most brilliant practitioner of Moneyball is like a little boy trying to plug holes in the dike until the new dike is built in Fremont. At this point one can't help but wonder if Billy Beane is running out of fingers.

MARGINAL DOLLARS PER MARGINAL WIN

The ratio of marginal dollars per marginal win depicts how efficient a team was in spending its money. The concept was developed by the late, greatly missed Baseball Prospectus author Doug Pappas. Pappas calculated the bare minimum that a team could spend on payroll. Using the minimum major league salary of $300,000, in effect until revised by the recently concluded Collective Bargaining Agreement, Pappas assumed each team would carry 25 players and have an additional three players on the disabled list, making the baseline payroll 28 x $300,000, or $8.4 million. Pappas figured this team, with its cheap, replacement-level players, would have a .300 winning percentage. Thus any wins over 48.6 are marginal, an achievement over the minimum. The ratio of marginal dollars divided by marginal wins shows how much a team spent for each win over the basic 49 victories and $8.4-million expenditure.

Marginal Dollars per Marginal Wins 2001–2003

TM	W	L	Payroll	WINP	MargW	MargPay	M$/MW
OAK	301	185	$124,075,751	0.619	51.7	$115,675,751.00	$2,236,000.34
MIN	269	216	$120,060,000	0.555	41.3	$111,660,000.00	$2,706,807.62
FLO	246	240	$127,192,417	0.506	33.4	$118,792,417.00	$3,556,659.19
MON/WAS	234	252	$125,778,500	0.481	29.4	$117,378,500.00	$3,992,465.99
SEA	302	184	$241,962,669	0.621	52.1	$233,562,669.00	$4,485,838.71
PHI	252	233	$170,398,832	0.520	35.6	$161,998,832.00	$4,553,957.78
SFN	285	199	$224,432,169	0.589	46.8	$216,032,169.00	$4,616,805.75
HOU	264	222	$195,101,084	0.543	39.4	$186,701,084.00	$4,738,606.19
CHA	250	236	$173,716,500	0.514	34.7	$165,316,500.00	$4,759,592.13
ANA	251	235	$188,288,501	0.516	35.1	$179,888,501.00	$5,129,900.22
SLN	275	211	$236,985,874	0.566	43.1	$228,585,874.00	$5,307,721.53
KCA	210	276	$123,197,500	0.432	21.4	$114,797,500.00	$5,364,369.16
SDN	209	277	$125,817,833	0.430	21.1	$117,417,833.00	$5,573,631.31
ATL	290	194	$291,050,200	0.599	48.5	$282,650,200.00	$5,831,913.61
TOR	244	242	$205,029,332	0.502	32.7	$196,629,332.00	$6,007,006.07
ARI	274	212	$268,559,998	0.564	42.7	$260,159,998.00	$6,087,987.47
CIN	213	273	$153,392,057	0.438	22.4	$144,992,057.00	$6,472,859.69
CHN	243	243	$220,274,999	0.500	32.4	$211,874,999.00	$6,539,351.82
PIT	209	276	$154,896,861	0.431	21.2	$146,496,861.00	$6,906,870.57
CLE	233	253	$220,646,284	0.479	29.1	$212,246,284.00	$7,302,051.06
NYA	299	184	$390,965,540	0.619	51.7	$382,565,540.00	$7,401,765.56
BOS	270	215	$318,348,393	0.557	41.6	$309,948,393.00	$7,453,268.41
COL	220	266	$195,572,044	0.453	24.7	$187,172,044.00	$7,567,602.86
LAN	263	223	$309,529,526	0.541	39.1	$301,129,526.00	$7,708,093.67
MIL	192	294	$134,801,666	0.395	15.4	$126,401,666.00	$8,207,900.39
TBA	180	305	$110,990,000	0.371	11.5	$102,590,000.00	$8,902,513.87
BAL	201	284	$201,970,527	0.414	18.5	$193,570,527.00	$10,441,742.36
NYN	223	261	$304,684,450	0.461	26.0	$296,284,450.00	$11,377,834.41
TEX	216	270	$297,651,289	0.444	23.4	$289,251,289.00	$12,361,166.20
DET	164	321	$157,632,167	0.338	6.2	$149,232,167.00	$24,150,017.02

Marginal Dollars per Marginal Wins 2004–2006

TM	W	L	Payroll	WINP	MargW	MargPay	M$/MW
FLO	244	242	$117,223,376	0.502	32.7	$108,823,376.00	$3,324,543.05
CLE	251	235	$131,853,300	0.516	35.1	$123,453,300.00	$3,520,531.37
MIN	271	215	$173,167,006	0.558	41.7	$164,767,006.00	$3,948,091.20
OAK	272	214	$177,094,508	0.560	42.1	$168,694,508.00	$4,010,170.55
MIL	223	262	$125,031,666	0.460	25.9	$116,631,666.00	$4,505,484.51
SDN	257	229	$188,571,807	0.529	37.1	$180,171,807.00	$4,860,750.19
TBA	198	287	$94,153,701	0.408	17.5	$85,753,701.00	$4,890,128.75
TEX	248	238	$179,128,079	0.510	34.1	$170,728,079.00	$5,011,587.45
TOR	234	251	$167,101,500	0.482	29.6	$158,701,500.00	$5,368,642.50
SLN	288	197	$264,226,537	0.594	47.6	$255,826,537.00	$5,374,739.89
PIT	206	279	$117,078,679	0.425	20.2	$108,678,679.00	$5,377,936.88
CHA	272	214	$243,141,167	0.560	42.1	$234,741,167.00	$5,580,217.92
CIN	229	257	$169,417,352	0.471	27.7	$161,017,352.00	$5,805,914.13
MON/WAS	219	267	$152,622,000	0.451	24.4	$144,222,000.00	$5,910,737.70
HOU	263	223	$240,870,435	0.541	39.1	$232,470,435.00	$5,950,608.40
DET	238	248	$198,536,866	0.490	30.7	$190,136,866.00	$6,186,665.92
ATL	265	221	$266,796,678	0.545	39.7	$258,396,678.00	$6,503,272.10
ANA	276	210	$298,874,489	0.568	43.4	$290,474,489.00	$6,692,960.58
COL	211	275	$154,517,167	0.434	21.7	$146,117,167.00	$6,723,182.53
PHI	259	227	$276,714,500	0.533	37.7	$268,314,500.00	$7,110,808.30
BAL	222	264	$198,123,248	0.457	25.4	$189,723,248.00	$7,469,419.21
LAN	252	234	$274,388,188	0.519	35.4	$265,988,188.00	$7,513,790.62
SFN	242	243	$262,275,085	0.499	32.2	$253,875,085.00	$7,876,250.00
BOS	279	207	$370,903,449	0.574	44.4	$362,503,449.00	$8,164,492.09
NYN	251	235	$299,051,754	0.516	35.1	$290,651,754.00	$8,288,548.12
CHN	234	252	$272,017,432	0.481	29.4	$263,617,432.00	$8,966,579.32
ARI	204	282	$191,794,142	0.420	19.4	$183,394,142.00	$9,453,306.29
SEA	210	276	$257,230,001	0.432	21.4	$248,830,001.00	$11,627,570.14
NYA	293	193	$587,163,846	0.603	49.1	$578,763,846.00	$11,795,458.82
KCA	176	310	$131,784,000	0.362	10.1	$123,384,000.00	$12,256,688.74

HITTERS

Daric Barton   1B   Bats: L   Throws: R   Height: 6' 0"   Weight: 225   Born: August 16, 1985   Age: 21

YEAR	TEAM	LVL	AGE	PA	R	2B	3B	HR	RBI	BB	SO	SB	CS	SPEED	AVG	OBP	SLG	MLVR	EQAVG	EQOBP	EQSLG	EQA	VORP	DEFENSE	
2004	PEO	A	18	393	63	23	0	13	77	69	44	4	4	3.6	.313	.445	.511	.394	.279	.384	.459	.290	30.2	51-C	-3
2005	STO	A+	19	361	60	16	2	8	52	62	49	0	1	3.1	.318	.438	.469	.257	.284	.383	.392	.277	10.1	58-1B	-9
2005	MID	AA	19	249	38	20	1	5	37	35	30	1	1	3.7	.316	.410	.491	.274	.292	.378	.454	.287	12.8	54-1B	-7
2006	SAC	AAA	20	180	25	6	4	2	22	32	26	1	0	5.2	.259	.389	.395	.092	.260	.378	.400	.279	4.3	36-1B	2
2007	OAK	MLB	21	402	53	21	2	9	43	50	56	2	1	4.9	.272	.364	.422	.019	.269	.366	.429	.285	11.1	96-1B	-2

Breakout: 23%   Improve: 43%   Collapse: 17%   Attrition: 10%   Comparables: Johnny Briggs, Cory Dunlap, Kila Kaaihue, Dernell Stenson

A year ago, Barton was listed as the A's top prospect and not just by geeks like us, but by our friends at Baseball America, too. It's hard to not love a 20-year-old former first-round pick with a .431 career OBP in the minors. Though Barton had played only 56 games above A-ball, and though we did express a touch of skepticism in this space a year ago, there was reasonable speculation that he'd be playing for the big club by the middle of last season. It didn't happen. First Barton didn't hit for any power—as the skeptics predicted—and then, in late May, he suffered a broken elbow that essentially ended his season. Barton did recover in time to put up a good showing in Dominican winter ball.

Hiram Bocachica   OF   Bats: R   Throws: R   Height: 5' 11"   Weight: 195   Born: March 4, 1976   Age: 31

YEAR	TEAM	LVL	AGE	PA	R	2B	3B	HR	RBI	BB	SO	SB	CS	SPEED	AVG	OBP	SLG	MLVR	EQAVG	EQOBP	EQSLG	EQA	VORP	DEFENSE			
2004	TAC	AAA	28	167	22	5	1	10	25	17	36	12	3	6.3	.287	.393	.559	.312	.273	.358	.490	.289	7.2	26-RF	-3		
2004	SEA	MLB	28	107	9	5	0	3	6	12	27	5	4	5.3	.244	.337	.400	-.055	.256	.352	.433	.265	0.7	21-CF	0		
2006	SAC	AAA	30	344	61	15	3	19	60	43	55	18	3	6.3	.326	.422	.595	.483	.308	.385	.540	.312	28.5	22-RF	-6	19-CF	-3
2006	OAK	MLB	30	16	3	0	0	0	0	3	4	1	0	6.7	.231	.375	.231	-.207	.231	.375	.231	.251	0.0				
2007	OAK	MLB	31	415	55	21	2	15	55	35	85	11	4	5.5	.262	.332	.453	-.004	.258	.334	.461	.279	11.2	99-CF	-7		

Breakout: 4%   Improve: 21%   Collapse: 44%   Attrition: 22%   Comparables: Hensley Meulens, Ray Montgomery, Joel Youngblood, Ivan Calderon

Welcome back, Hiram! After a year away from *Baseball Prospectus*, we're absolutely thrilled to see you again. We hated to leave one of organized baseball's best names out of last year's book, but when a 30-year-old outfielder with a .217 lifetime batting average misses almost an entire season . . . well, we hope you understood. After posting those monster numbers with Sacramento, you've certainly bought yourself another precious slot in our book, not to mention another few summers of baseball in the finest cities north of Mexico that Triple-A can offer.

Milton Bradley   RF   Bats: S   Throws: R   Height: 6' 0"   Weight: 190   Born: April 15, 1978   Age: 29

YEAR	TEAM	LVL	AGE	PA	R	2B	3B	HR	RBI	BB	SO	SB	CS	SPEED	AVG	OBP	SLG	MLVR	EQAVG	EQOBP	EQSLG	EQA	VORP	DEFENSE			
2004	LAN	MLB	26	597	72	24	0	19	67	71	123	15	11	4.9	.267	.362	.424	.066	.272	.366	.432	.273	17.1	90-CF	2	31-RF	1
2005	LAN	MLB	27	315	49	14	1	13	38	25	47	6	1	5.8	.290	.350	.484	.160	.292	.357	.504	.292	20.1	71-CF	5		
2006	OAK	MLB	28	405	53	14	2	14	52	51	65	10	2	5.6	.276	.370	.447	.082	.275	.378	.454	.290	17.9	90-RF	-2		
2007	OAK	MLB	29	469	66	19	2	14	56	49	82	11	5	5.7	.273	.352	.433	.013	.269	.354	.440	.282	12.5	111-RF	1		

Breakout: 13%   Improve: 45%   Collapse: 24%   Attrition: 13%   Comparables: Wes Parker, Ron Roenicke, Randy Winn, Tom Tresh

The conventional wisdom before the season was that while yes, Milton Bradley certainly has some problems and might become a distraction, if there's a clubhouse in which he'd fit, it was Oakland's. As it often is, the CW was correct: Bradley did sometimes lose his temper, but there weren't any public dust-ups with teammates, and he played well enough and often enough to make his $3 million salary look like one of the better bargains in the league. The A's obviously would have been better off if Bradley had been healthy all season, but his various injuries mean his raise this winter will be relatively small. As long as he's reasonably healthy and relatively happy, he'll be worth whatever the A's are paying him.

Jeremy Brown   C   Bats: R   Throws: R   Height: 5' 10"   Weight: 225   Born: October 25, 1979   Age: 27

YEAR	TEAM	LVL	AGE	PA	R	2B	3B	HR	RBI	BB	SO	SB	CS	SPEED	AVG	OBP	SLG	MLVR	EQAVG	EQOBP	EQSLG	EQA	VORP	DEFENSE	
2004	MID	AA	24	526	59	27	0	6	49	71	80	2	1	3.5	.256	.361	.357	-.033	.214	.303	.296	.219	-18.7	85-C	3
2005	MID	AA	25	462	65	27	1	20	72	52	88	0	0	3.0	.261	.359	.487	.142	.228	.311	.412	.250	5.9	100-C	-12
2006	SAC	AAA	26	306	41	14	0	13	40	23	60	0	0	4.0	.255	.317	.447	.036	.239	.293	.414	.244	2.0	64-C	6
2006	OAK	MLB	26	11	1	2	0	0	0	1	1	0	0	4.5	.300	.364	.500	.190	.300	.364	.500	.291	0.7		
2007	OAK	MLB	27	365	31	15	0	9	41	28	73	0	0	3.7	.229	.294	.361	-.215	.226	.296	.367	.235	-3.1	88-C	1

Breakout: 27%   Improve: 52%   Collapse: 30%   Attrition: 23%   Comparables: Jonathan Aceves, Jim Foster, Henry Blanco, Keith McDonald

After three seasons in the Texas League, Brown finally moved to the Pacific Coast League, where he played like a Triple-A catcher. The A's recalled Brown four times during the year to serve as a place-holder; he didn't bat during his first three big league tours. He's still behind Kendall and Melhuse on the depth chart, and as soon as 2007 he might find himself behind Kurt Suzuki. But a catcher who can stay healthy, get along with his managers, and throw reasonably well can make a good living in this game. Sal Fasano doesn't look good in jeans, either, but he's been kicking around in the majors for more than a decade now. The margin between having a Fasano-like career and being an organizational soldier is paper thin; Brown will have to catch a few breaks to achieve that modest dream.

Travis Buck — OF — Bats: L — Throws: R — Height: 6' 2" — Weight: 205 — Born: November 18, 1983 — Age: 23

YEAR	TEAM	LVL	AGE	PA	R	2B	3B	HR	RBI	BB	SO	SB	CS	SPEED	AVG	OBP	SLG	MLVR	EQAVG	EQOBP	EQSLG	EQA	VORP	DEFENSE	
2005	VAN	A-	21	41	7	1	0	2	9	5	8	1	1	3.7	.361	.439	.556	.542	.342	.390	.526	.297	8.5		
2005	KNC	A	21	144	17	13	0	1	22	19	19	3	1	2.7	.341	.427	.472	.321	.289	.361	.406	.270	2.8	31-RF	-1
2006	STO	A+	22	145	24	17	3	3	26	14	18	2	1	5.9	.349	.400	.603	.486	.323	.366	.546	.303	11.7	34-LF	0
2006	MID	AA	22	238	32	22	1	4	22	22	39	9	1	5.6	.302	.376	.472	.161	.276	.340	.429	.269	2.8	50-LF	4
2007	OAK	MLB	23	491	64	36	2	11	61	39	80	9	4	4.9	.290	.348	.459	.054	.286	.350	.466	.286	16.8	116-LF	3

Breakout: 18% Improve: 59% Collapse: 14% Attrition: 3%   Comparables: Rafael Alvarez, Jeremy Giambi, Doug Deeds, Kevin Burford

Barton wasn't the only Oakland prospect to miss significant time with an injury; in fact, most of their young hitters got hurt last season, Buck among them. A supplemental first-round pick out of Arizona State in 2005, Buck batted .346 in his first pro season (albeit without many homers, again like Barton). He moved up a level last spring, then another, and kept hitting all the while before suffering a torn abdominal muscle in mid-July. He didn't heal as expected and finally had surgery in early November; the A's expect him to be ready for spring training. Buck's arm and speed limit him to left field, so he's going to have to play at the top of his game to provide enough offense to start in the bigs.

Eric Chavez — 3B — Bats: L — Throws: R — Height: 6' 1" — Weight: 210 — Born: December 7, 1977 — Age: 29

YEAR	TEAM	LVL	AGE	PA	R	2B	3B	HR	RBI	BB	SO	SB	CS	SPEED	AVG	OBP	SLG	MLVR	EQAVG	EQOBP	EQSLG	EQA	VORP	DEFENSE	
2004	OAK	MLB	26	577	87	20	0	29	77	95	99	6	3	3.9	.276	.397	.501	.199	.274	.401	.502	.308	37.1	120-3B	19
2005	OAK	MLB	27	694	92	40	1	27	101	58	129	6	0	5.4	.269	.329	.466	.059	.272	.341	.479	.281	26.4	151-3B	3
2006	OAK	MLB	28	576	74	24	2	22	72	84	100	3	0	4.4	.241	.351	.435	-.001	.238	.358	.441	.279	12.9	130-3B	17
2007	OAK	MLB	29	583	78	26	2	23	81	74	105	4	1	4.7	.261	.357	.460	.047	.258	.359	.468	.291	25.3	136-3B	5

Breakout: 11% Improve: 32% Collapse: 28% Attrition: 7%   Comparables: Darrell Evans, Pete Ward, Corey Koskie, Wayne Gross

It's easy to look at Eric Chavez's 2006 and wonder what was wrong with him. There's certainly been no secret about his forearm injury. Really, though, the only significant difference between 2006 and 2005 was a few games and a relatively insignificant drop in batting average. He nailed his career OBP, and given another hundred at-bats he'd have approximated 2005's doubles and homers. Which isn't to say Chavez is just a bit of luck from being "himself" again, because maybe this current version is "himself." From 2001 through 2003, Chavez probably was one of the five best players in the American League, and, considering that he was only 25 in 2003, it really didn't seem all that crazy when Billy Beane compared him to Barry Bonds, and didn't seem all that crazy to think Chavez would become a perennial MVP candidate. Now it seems crazy. Whether it's the injuries or something else, the further we get from 2003, the less we should expect great things. He's still a good player, of course (especially if he continues to earn the Gold Gloves he's apparently going to win every season), which is a good thing, as the A's still owe him nearly $50 million.

Bobby Crosby — SS — Bats: R — Throws: R — Height: 6' 3" — Weight: 215 — Born: January 12, 1980 — Age: 27

YEAR	TEAM	LVL	AGE	PA	R	2B	3B	HR	RBI	BB	SO	SB	CS	SPEED	AVG	OBP	SLG	MLVR	EQAVG	EQOBP	EQSLG	EQA	VORP	DEFENSE	
2004	OAK	MLB	24	623	70	34	1	22	64	58	141	7	3	4.4	.239	.319	.426	-.069	.238	.321	.426	.259	17.2	149-SS	8
2005	OAK	MLB	25	371	66	25	4	9	38	35	54	0	0	5.7	.276	.346	.456	.079	.281	.362	.471	.285	21.5	83-SS	6
2006	OAK	MLB	26	398	42	12	0	9	40	36	76	8	1	5.1	.229	.298	.338	-.245	.224	.301	.331	.230	-4.1	92-SS	-10
2007	OAK	MLB	27	470	56	22	2	13	54	44	88	7	3	4.9	.253	.327	.407	-.081	.250	.329	.413	.264	14.6	111-SS	-2

Breakout: 30% Improve: 55% Collapse: 23% Attrition: 16%   Comparables: Morgan Ensberg, Scott Leius, Kevin Elster, Mike Cuddyer

We'll venture a guess: before 2006, Bobby Crosby had never struggled like this. He starred at Long Beach State, was a first-round draft pick, ripped through the minors, and was Rookie of the Year in 2004. Even in 2005, despite being limited to 84 games by injuries, his hitting and fielding were better than the year before. Crosby's 2006, though, was an unmitigated

(continued next page)

Bobby Crosby *(continued)*

disaster. At 26, he was supposed to be a little better and a lot healthier; instead he was a lot worse and nearly as unhealthy. In '05 the injuries were a broken rib and a broken ankle (in separate incidents); in '06, it was a strained lower back that didn't heal the way it was supposed to. At this point, we can't expect Crosby to become a star, but the A's certainly can expect to get more from him this season than they have in either of the last two. PECOTA's top four comps, above, could all be loosely classified as "late bloomers."

Mark Ellis   **2B**   **Bats: R**   **Throws: R**   Height: 5' 11"   Weight: 195   Born: June 6, 1977   Age: 30

YEAR	TEAM	LVL	AGE	PA	R	2B	3B	HR	RBI	BB	SO	SB	CS	SPEED	AVG	OBP	SLG	MLVR	EQAVG	EQOBP	EQSLG	EQA	VORP	DEFENSE
2005	OAK	MLB	28	486	76	21	5	13	52	44	51	1	3	5.0	.316	.384	.477	.203	.321	.397	.496	.302	36.0	109-2B 11
2006	OAK	MLB	29	500	64	25	1	11	52	40	76	4	0	5.0	.249	.319	.385	-.124	.248	.323	.390	.253	7.2	119-2B 4
2007	OAK	MLB	30	559	72	29	3	14	66	50	78	5	3	5.3	.277	.348	.435	.012	.274	.351	.442	.280	23.7	131-2B 3

Breakout: 19% Improve: 46% Collapse: 24% Attrition: 8%   Comparables: Ron Hunt, Ryne Sandberg, Junior Spivey, Joe Randa

With a year of hindsight, we may confidently assume that Ellis's .316 batting average—and similarly impressive on-base percentage—in 2005 was a statistical outlier. He's a good fielder, of course, but not good enough to play every day if his numbers in 2006 and 2003 accurately represent his true hitting ability. He's not young anymore, so it's likely that waiting for the big comeback is an unsupported act of optimism.

Javier Herrera   **CF**   **Bats: R**   **Throws: R**   Height: 5' 11"   Weight: 210   Born: April 9, 1985   Age: 22

YEAR	TEAM	LVL	AGE	PA	R	2B	3B	HR	RBI	BB	SO	SB	CS	SPEED	AVG	OBP	SLG	MLVR	EQAVG	EQOBP	EQSLG	EQA	VORP	DEFENSE	
2004	VAN	A-	19	293	50	15	4	12	47	24	59	23	1	7.8	.331	.392	.555	.435	.295	.332	.465	.277	27.3	36-CF -5	28-RF -4
2005	KNC	A	20	422	70	18	2	13	62	47	110	26	5	6.8	.275	.374	.444	.151	.241	.315	.384	.250	0.1	88-CF -4	
2005	SAC	AAA	20	15	5	1	0	1	3	1	1	1	0	5.6	.417	.533	.750	.890	.385	.467	.692	.387	2.8		
2007	OAK	MLB	22	389	48	18	1	11	42	28	94	15	2	6.3	.255	.316	.409	-.096	.252	.317	.416	.264	5.7	93-CF -3	

Breakout: 14% Improve: 46% Collapse: 24% Attrition: 5%   Comparables: Tydus Meadows, Gavin Wright, Ben Francisco, Brendan Harris

First, the 50-game suspension for failing a drug test prior to the 2005 season. Then, the Tommy John surgery in March 2006, which cost Herrera the entire season. At press time, he was expected to be ready for spring training. Herrera still has a high upside as an above-average power-speed combination in center field.

D'Angelo Jimenez   **2B**   **Bats: S**   **Throws: R**   Height: 6' 0"   Weight: 215   Born: December 21, 1977   Age: 29

YEAR	TEAM	LVL	AGE	PA	R	2B	3B	HR	RBI	BB	SO	SB	CS	SPEED	AVG	OBP	SLG	MLVR	EQAVG	EQOBP	EQSLG	EQA	VORP	DEFENSE
2004	CIN	MLB	26	652	76	28	3	12	67	82	99	13	7	5.0	.270	.364	.394	.053	.270	.364	.397	.268	27.4	142-2B 2
2005	CIN	MLB	27	119	14	7	0	0	5	14	23	2	1	5.2	.229	.319	.295	-.190	.219	.317	.276	.220	-2.3	24-2B 0
2005	CHT	AA	27	399	55	20	0	9	45	69	34	16	4	4.9	.278	.401	.422	.152	.221	.316	.325	.235	-3.9	69-SS 6
2006	TEX	MLB	28	68	7	3	0	1	8	10	6	0	0	3.9	.211	.328	.316	-.222	.196	.328	.304	.233	-0.8	15-2B -4
2006	SAC	AAA	28	151	30	8	1	4	23	24	14	2	4	5.3	.304	.413	.480	.287	.295	.387	.465	.288	12.5	23-2B -3
2006	OAK	MLB	28	20	1	0	0	0	0	6	7	0	0	2.1	.071	.350	.071	-.493	.000	.300	.000	.168	-1.5	
2007	WAS	MLB	29	266	31	12	1	5	25	32	37	3	1	4.9	.238	.335	.365	-.140	.243	.339	.377	.251	6.0	65-2B 0

Breakout: 21% Improve: 45% Collapse: 36% Attrition: 34%   Comparables: Chris Clapinski, Luis Alicea, Turner Ward, Adam Melhuse

Like Bocachica, Jimenez played well in Sacramento, but wasn't rewarded with much action in the majors despite all the injuries on the big club. When he finally did get a chance to play—thanks to Ellis's Division Series injury—he managed just two singles in a dozen ALCS at-bats. Jimenez will hang around for a few more years as a Quadruple-A utility infielder, but it's now hard to remember that he once was considered a better prospect than Alfonso Soriano. Having signed a minor league deal with the Nats, he'll be a stalking horse for Felipe Lopez as the latter tries to claim the spot vacated by Jose Vidro.

Dan Johnson   **1B**   **Bats: L**   **Throws: R**   Height: 6' 2"   Weight: 225   Born: August 10, 1979   Age: 27

YEAR	TEAM	LVL	AGE	PA	R	2B	3B	HR	RBI	BB	SO	SB	CS	SPEED	AVG	OBP	SLG	MLVR	EQAVG	EQOBP	EQSLG	EQA	VORP	DEFENSE	
2004	SAC	AAA	24	640	95	29	5	29	111	89	93	0	1	3.7	.299	.403	.535	.276	.280	.374	.479	.292	33.1	92-1B -6	14-LF -2
2005	SAC	AAA	25	217	36	17	0	8	41	32	24	0	1	2.7	.324	.424	.549	.333	.294	.385	.481	.295	13.4	43-1B -2	
2005	OAK	MLB	25	434	54	21	0	15	58	50	52	0	1	3.2	.275	.355	.451	.089	.277	.366	.470	.288	14.5	99-1B -2	
2006	SAC	AAA	26	209	34	13	1	7	44	32	27	0	1	3.8	.314	.426	.523	.376	.305	.402	.503	.307	16.9	38-1B 5	
2006	OAK	MLB	26	331	30	13	1	9	37	40	45	0	0	4.0	.234	.323	.381	-.131	.230	.329	.387	.254	-5.5	80-1B 8	
2007	OAK	MLB	27	454	57	23	1	15	61	55	65	0	0	4.1	.270	.361	.449	.045	.267	.363	.456	.289	13.7	108-1B 3	

Breakout: 19% Improve: 47% Collapse: 23% Attrition: 8%   Comparables: Nick Johnson, Ed Bouchee, Erubiel Durazo, Kent Hrbek

Upon finally earning a regular job with the Oakland in 2005, Johnson hit exactly as his minor-league stats said he would and provided plenty of bang for the A's buck as a minimum-wage player in a low-revenue lineup. It was shocking, then, when Johnson completely collapsed last spring; he got off to a 0-for-30 start, batted .196 with two homers in April and May combined, and, despite a solid June, was dispatched to Sacramento when Milton Bradley came off the disabled list on July 15. Johnson did well back in Triple-A—no surprise, considering he was PCL MVP in 2004—and again hit like himself upon returning to the A's in September. It looks like his terrible "season" was really just a two-month blip, the sort of thing that's occasionally going to happen to an average player (a year ago, PECOTA pegged his "collapse" chance at 22 percent). With the departure of Jay Payton, Nick Swisher is slated for left field, leaving first base available for Johnson's comeback attempt. The A's signed Erubiel Durazo to provide competition this spring, but Johnson should be able to take him.

Jason Kendall C **Bats: R** **Throws: R** Height: 6' 0" Weight: 205 Born: June 26, 1974 Age: 33

YEAR	TEAM	LVL	AGE	PA	R	2B	3B	HR	RBI	BB	SO	SB	CS	SPEED	AVG	OBP	SLG	MLVR	EQAVG	EQOBP	EQSLG	EQA	VORP	DEFENSE
2004	PIT	MLB	30	658	86	32	0	3	51	60	41	11	8	4.9	.319	.399	.390	.135	.319	.397	.391	.279	39.3	143-C 10
2005	OAK	MLB	31	676	70	28	1	0	53	50	39	8	3	4.6	.271	.345	.321	-.104	.278	.358	.332	.252	10.5	144-C -4
2006	OAK	MLB	32	626	76	23	0	1	50	53	54	11	5	4.7	.295	.367	.342	-.058	.297	.375	.346	.261	13.2	140-C 5
2007	OAK	MLB	33	538	63	21	1	1	43	46	43	8	4	4.9	.274	.346	.333	-.129	.271	.348	.339	.253	6.2	126-C 0

Breakout: 10% Improve: 39% Collapse: 37% Attrition: 14% Comparables: John Wathan, Paul Lo Duca, Brad Ausmus, Joe Girardi

Let's first dispense with the obvious: Kendall wasn't worth his $11.5-million salary in 2006, and he really won't be worth his $13-million salary in 2007, the last season covered by his six-year, $60-million contract. On the plus side, the Pirates are on the hook for a good chunk ($5 million) of Kendall's '07 income, his .367 on-base percentage last season ranked fourth among the nine MLB catchers who played enough to qualify for the batting title, and the A's rave about Kendall's work behind the plate. That isn't to say Kendall is worth even the $8 million the A's will spend on him this season. His OPS ranked ninth among those nine regular catchers, he threw out only 24 percent of larcenous baserunners, and he's totaled exactly one home run in the last two seasons. The day his contract expires should be one of relief in the Oakland front office.

Bobby Kielty OF **Bats: S** **Throws: R** Height: 6' 1" Weight: 220 Born: August 5, 1976 Age: 30

YEAR	TEAM	LVL	AGE	PA	R	2B	3B	HR	RBI	BB	SO	SB	CS	SPEED	AVG	OBP	SLG	MLVR	EQAVG	EQOBP	EQSLG	EQA	VORP	DEFENSE	
2004	OAK	MLB	27	278	29	14	1	7	31	35	47	1	0	4.3	.214	.321	.370	-.153	.212	.322	.364	.245	-5.3	41-LF -1	13-RF 0
2005	OAK	MLB	28	433	55	20	0	10	57	50	67	3	2	4.2	.263	.350	.395	-.003	.267	.364	.415	.272	6.8	51-LF 2	36-RF 0
2006	OAK	MLB	29	297	35	20	1	8	36	22	49	2	0	4.7	.270	.329	.441	-.011	.270	.336	.446	.269	5.4	38-LF 0	29-RF 0
2007	OAK	MLB	30	377	44	17	1	10	44	39	70	2	1	4.5	.255	.336	.405	-.066	.252	.338	.412	.267	2.1	90-LF -1	

Breakout: 14% Improve: 40% Collapse: 25% Attrition: 33% Comparables: Mark Whiten, Gary Matthews, Turner Ward, Gene Larkin

Kielty was the odd man in the outfield picture when the season opened, but as something of a lefty-killer—he entered 2006 with an 886 career OPS against southpaws—Kielty figured to work his way into the lineup at least a third of the time. He actually played more than that, thanks to all the injuries, and gave the A's exactly the sort of production you'd want from your fourth outfielder. Kielty's never going to hit as many homers as you'd expect from a 220-pound gardener, but as long as he hits .260 or .270 he'll have a job as some team's "professional hitter." It probably would help if he'd just stop switch-hitting, as he's batting just .230/.333/.350 in his career from the left side of the plate.

Mark Kotsay CF **Bats: L** **Throws: L** Height: 6' 0" Weight: 205 Born: December 2, 1975 Age: 31

YEAR	TEAM	LVL	AGE	PA	R	2B	3B	HR	RBI	BB	SO	SB	CS	SPEED	AVG	OBP	SLG	MLVR	EQAVG	EQOBP	EQSLG	EQA	VORP	DEFENSE
2004	OAK	MLB	28	673	78	37	3	15	63	55	70	8	5	4.9	.314	.370	.459	.122	.313	.374	.461	.286	36.8	139-CF 13
2005	OAK	MLB	29	629	75	35	1	15	82	40	51	5	5	4.7	.280	.325	.421	.000	.285	.340	.434	.264	15.4	132-CF 2
2006	OAK	MLB	30	558	57	29	3	7	59	44	55	6	3	4.9	.275	.332	.386	-.078	.274	.339	.391	.257	9.8	117-CF -8
2007	OAK	MLB	31	563	69	30	3	11	62	42	57	5	3	5.2	.283	.338	.416	-.027	.279	.340	.423	.270	15.1	132-CF -2

Breakout: 17% Improve: 51% Collapse: 23% Attrition: 11% Comparables: Joe Orsulak, Dale Mitchell, Willard Marshall, Ted Uhlaender

Eyebrows lifted and brows furrowed in 2005, when the A's signed Kotsay to a two-year, $15-million contract extension that would carry him through 2008. Oakland's rationale was that Kotsay wasn't a *bad* hitter and he was a *good* centerfielder. It now looks like they were wrong on both counts, and at 32, Kotsay's in the decline phase of his career. The A's are stuck with him, and though he's not the worst player in the world, he must be balanced by somebody better somewhere else on the roster.

Adam Melhuse   **C**   **Bats: S**   **Throws: R**   Height: 6′ 2″   Weight: 210   Born: March 27, 1972   Age: 35

YEAR	TEAM	LVL	AGE	PA	R	2B	3B	HR	RBI	BB	SO	SB	CS	SPEED	AVG	OBP	SLG	MLVR	EQAVG	EQOBP	EQSLG	EQA	VORP	DEFENSE
2004	OAK	MLB	32	231	23	11	0	11	31	16	47	0	1	3.3	.257	.309	.463	-.038	.255	.313	.462	.260	5.8	58-C -4
2005	OAK	MLB	33	102	11	7	0	2	12	5	28	0	0	5.0	.247	.284	.381	-.150	.250	.301	.406	.242	0.1	18-C 1
2006	OAK	MLB	34	139	10	8	0	4	18	9	34	0	1	2.6	.219	.273	.375	-.246	.213	.273	.378	.223	-4.3	22-C 3
2007	OAK	MLB	35	224	19	10	0	7	30	14	57	0	0	3.6	.229	.282	.384	-.207	.226	.283	.391	.235	-2.2	56-C 0

Breakout: 15%   Improve: 31%   Collapse: 35%   Attrition: 54%   Comparables: Phil Roof, Del Rice, Mickey Grasso, Jeff Newman

Melhuse has only been kicking around the bigs since 2000, so it's a bit shocking to realize he'll be 35 when Opening Day rolls around. That's because he didn't make it to the Show until he was 28. Because of those 11 homers Melhuse popped as a part-timer in 2004, he gives the frisson of being a bit better than he is. He does have good power for a catcher, but you can't play five games per week with a sub-.300 OBP unless you're a defensive wiz—and that's not Melhuse.

Kevin Melillo   **2B**   **Bats: L**   **Throws: R**   Height: 5′ 11″   Weight: 185   Born: May 14, 1982   Age: 25

YEAR	TEAM	LVL	AGE	PA	R	2B	3B	HR	RBI	BB	SO	SB	CS	SPEED	AVG	OBP	SLG	MLVR	EQAVG	EQOBP	EQSLG	EQA	VORP	DEFENSE
2004	VAN	A-	22	109	22	11	2	2	21	11	16	2	1	6.5	.340	.422	.564	.496	.277	.327	.416	.258	6.4	20-2B 1
2005	KNC	A	23	342	47	18	3	8	36	53	40	10	4	4.8	.286	.399	.457	.213	.242	.326	.379	.248	3.9	64-2B -11
2005	STO	A+	23	104	21	7	1	9	23	12	18	2	0	4.5	.400	.471	.800	.921	.351	.404	.660	.346	18.6	21-2B -3
2005	MID	AA	23	147	33	10	0	7	34	14	23	9	2	7.2	.282	.347	.519	.184	.248	.311	.459	.269	5.2	32-2B -4
2006	MID	AA	24	581	73	31	3	12	73	68	98	14	7	5.5	.280	.367	.426	.065	.252	.325	.370	.247	5.5	130-2B -12
2007	OAK	MLB	25	480	53	26	2	9	52	39	87	7	3	5.2	.254	.318	.387	-.122	.250	.320	.394	.254	6.9	113-2B -7

Breakout: 17%   Improve: 52%   Collapse: 25%   Attrition: 9%   Comparables: Kevin Randel, Warren Morris, Brooks Conrad, Jason Grabowski

A fifth-round pick in 2004, Melillo took a medium-sized step backward last season. After leading the system with 24 home runs in 2005, his first full season, Melillo spent all of 2006 in the Texas League and hit only 12 bombs. He'll turn 25 this spring and he's not known for his defense, so he has to hit, and he has to hit right now if he's going to become a better option than Mark Ellis.

Jermaine Mitchell   **CF**   **Bats: L**   **Throws: L**   Height: 6′ 0″   Weight: 200   Born: November 2, 1984   Age: 22

YEAR	TEAM	LVL	AGE	PA	R	2B	3B	HR	RBI	BB	SO	SB	CS	SPEED	AVG	OBP	SLG	MLVR	EQAVG	EQOBP	EQSLG	EQA	VORP	DEFENSE
2006	VAN	A-	21	163	23	7	2	3	23	22	27	14	6	6.3	.362	.460	.507	.504	.342	.411	.479	.304	32.6	32-CF -4
2007	OAK	MLB	22	520	72	27	5	7	47	40	101	21	11	6.3	.287	.346	.411	-.016	.284	.348	.418	.272	15.6	122-CF -4

Breakout: 2%   Improve: 15%   Collapse: 59%   Attrition: 10%   Comparables: Tyrell Godwin, Chris Duffy, Matt Meath, Curtis Granderson

In his first game as a pro, Mitchell went 3-for-4, and he never stopped hitting after that. He put together a 22-game hitting streak in August, and finished the 2006 season with a .362 batting average. Unfortunately, like almost every other A's prospect he spent some time recuperating, in his case from a broken foot that cost him five weeks prior to his hitting streak. The A's feel they got a steal in Mitchell, a fifth-round pick out of North Carolina-Greensboro, seeing him as a potential power/speed dynamo.

Jay Payton   **OF**   **Bats: R**   **Throws: R**   Height: 5′ 10″   Weight: 185   Born: November 22, 1972   Age: 34

YEAR	TEAM	LVL	AGE	PA	R	2B	3B	HR	RBI	BB	SO	SB	CS	SPEED	AVG	OBP	SLG	MLVR	EQAVG	EQOBP	EQSLG	EQA	VORP	DEFENSE		
2004	SDN	MLB	31	511	57	17	4	8	55	43	56	2	0	4.9	.260	.326	.367	-.066	.266	.331	.379	.251	3.1	121-CF 10		
2005	BOS	MLB	32	144	24	7	0	5	21	10	14	0	0	4.8	.263	.313	.429	-.033	.260	.319	.435	.258	1.7	21-RF 4		
2005	OAK	MLB	32	291	38	9	1	13	42	14	33	0	1	4.4	.269	.302	.451	-.007	.273	.316	.465	.263	4.6	46-LF 3	24-CF 1
2006	OAK	MLB	33	588	78	32	3	10	59	22	52	8	4	5.7	.296	.325	.418	-.027	.298	.333	.423	.261	10.7	51-LF 4	43-CF -5
2007	BAL	MLB	34	421	51	20	2	9	48	22	43	5	2	5.6	.281	.322	.408	-.067	.279	.326	.414	.261	4.2	100-CF 0		

Breakout: 22%   Improve: 48%   Collapse: 30%   Attrition: 23%   Comparables: Dan Gladden, Gerald Williams, Brian Jordan, Vic Power

Most of the writers in this book have something of a man-crush on Billy Beane. That's probably no secret. Simultaneously, most of us can't figure out what Beane saw in Jay Payton. In July 2005, the A's received Payton and cash when they sent Chad Bradford to the Red Sox. Payton did hit 13 homers in 69 games with the A's, balancing (somewhat) his .302 on-base percentage. With his speed and his decent defense, Payton's not a bad fourth outfielder, but he's not good enough to play in 142 games for a good team. With Bradley and Kotsay frequently unavailable, that's just what he did last year for the A's. Payton signed with the Orioles in November, which is just so Orioles-ish, isn't it?

Antonio Perez INF Bats: R Throws: R Height: 5' 11" Weight: 175 Born: January 26, 1980 Age: 27

YEAR	TEAM	LVL	AGE	PA	R	2B	3B	HR	RBI	BB	SO	SB	CS	SPEED	AVG	OBP	SLG	MLVR	EQAVG	EQOBP	EQSLG	EQA	VORP	DEFENSE			
2004	LVG	AAA	24	554	92	24	6	22	88	61	87	23	12	6.6	.296	.379	.511	.096	.251	.330	.414	.258	19.1	73-SS	-10	44-2B	5
2005	LAN	MLB	25	287	28	13	2	3	23	21	61	11	4	6.1	.297	.360	.398	.071	.305	.367	.417	.275	12.1	31-3B	-2	21-2B	-1
2006	OAK	MLB	26	109	10	5	1	1	8	10	44	0	1	6.9	.102	.185	.204	-.712	.041	.139	.082	.104	-15.9	21-3B	1		
2007	OAK	MLB	27	281	32	13	1	7	30	24	68	5	2	5.8	.234	.304	.382	-.167	.231	.306	.388	.247	-0.6	69-DH			

Breakout: 42% Improve: 59% Collapse: 21% Attrition: 38%   Comparables: Russ Davis, Larry Burright, Andy Sheets, Jack Heidemann

Having batted .297 for the Dodgers as a part-timer in 2005, Perez was seen as yet another solid role player on what looked like a bench full of them. At least that was the plan. But Perez went hitless in his first 25 at-bats, and while that's not necessarily a season-killer, he batted only .137 after that terrible start. Amazingly, the A's never did completely lose their patience with Perez, who kept his spot on the roster until October.

Landon Powell C Bats: S Throws: R Height: 6' 3" Weight: 240 Born: March 19, 1982 Age: 25

YEAR	TEAM	LVL	AGE	PA	R	2B	3B	HR	RBI	BB	SO	SB	CS	SPEED	AVG	OBP	SLG	MLVR	EQAVG	EQOBP	EQSLG	EQA	VORP	DEFENSE	
2004	VAN	A-	22	163	24	6	1	3	19	26	22	0	0	4.3	.244	.368	.370	.064	.192	.270	.247	.194	-22.2	19-C	2
2006	STO	A+	24	375	44	12	0	15	47	43	77	0	0	3.1	.264	.350	.439	.072	.229	.296	.359	.230	-5.3	82-C	6
2006	MID	AA	24	45	4	0	0	1	4	3	12	0	0	2.2	.268	.333	.341	-.117	.238	.289	.310	.218	-1.5	12-C	1
2007	OAK	MLB	25	408	27	11	1	8	40	28	89	0	0	3.7	.209	.267	.303	-.354	.206	.268	.308	.202	-16.3	97-C	6

Breakout: 38% Improve: 46% Collapse: 33% Attrition: 13%   Comparables: Dennis Anderson, Keith McDonald, Ryan Jorgensen, Rob Bowen

Powell was the A's number-one draft pick in 2004, didn't do much as a first-year pro, and missed all of 2005 after tearing an ACL while working out in the off-season. Nice start, huh? We'd like to report a happy ending, or at least the beginning of a happy ending. Can't do it, though: Powell turns 25 before Opening Day, he's barely escaped Class A, and he's never looked like anything but an adequate minor league hitter. He's also in danger of eating himself out of whatever career he has left. He'll get plenty of chances because of a big bonus. Let's hope he hasn't spent all of it on food, which, given his size in the Arizona Fall League, he very well might have.

Danny Putnam OF Bats: L Throws: L Height: 5' 10" Weight: 200 Born: September 17, 1982 Age: 23

YEAR	TEAM	LVL	AGE	PA	R	2B	3B	HR	RBI	BB	SO	SB	CS	SPEED	AVG	OBP	SLG	MLVR	EQAVG	EQOBP	EQSLG	EQA	VORP	DEFENSE			
2004	VAN	A-	21	52	10	2	0	2	3	14	8	1	0	4.2	.289	.481	.500	.434	.256	.385	.372	.273	0.9	11-LF	1		
2004	KNC	A	21	199	30	5	2	7	28	30	42	0	0	4.4	.220	.348	.402	.040	.197	.296	.341	.227	-11.4	50-LF	-2		
2005	STO	A+	22	594	97	37	3	15	100	66	92	1	3	3.4	.307	.388	.479	.167	.273	.338	.402	.258	0.0	102-LF	-7	25-RF	-2
2006	STO	A+	23	46	7	2	0	1	9	6	8	0	0	4.4	.375	.457	.500	.443	.341	.413	.463	.307	4.4				
2006	MID	AA	23	254	33	13	2	8	37	23	37	2	1	5.3	.244	.317	.427	-.045	.221	.281	.377	.229	-12.0	32-LF	-3	25-RF	0
2007	OAK	MLB	24	430	41	21	1	8	46	33	78	1	1	4.7	.241	.303	.365	-.185	.238	.305	.371	.241	-10.3	102-LF	-5		

Breakout: 25% Improve: 48% Collapse: 35% Attrition: 10%   Comparables: Brett Roneberg, Nick Leach, John-Ford Griffin, Jorge Cortes

Putnam played for Billy Beane's high school coach, and then he spent three years at Stanford, so perhaps the A's simply had to draft him with the 36th overall pick in 2004. He did well in his first full season of High-A ball, but struggled in the Texas League last year. He's built like Matt Stairs, and similarly limited to left field or first base, and if he doesn't start hitting he'll soon be considered a suspect rather than a prospect.

Richie Robnett OF Bats: L Throws: L Height: 5' 10" Weight: 200 Born: September 17, 1983 Age: 23

YEAR	TEAM	LVL	AGE	PA	R	2B	3B	HR	RBI	BB	SO	SB	CS	SPEED	AVG	OBP	SLG	MLVR	EQAVG	EQOBP	EQSLG	EQA	VORP	DEFENSE			
2004	VAN	A-	20	195	26	14	1	4	36	28	43	1	2	4.0	.299	.395	.470	.282	.263	.328	.389	.251	4.6	35-CF	-6		
2005	STO	A+	21	519	77	30	0	20	74	56	151	8	4	4.6	.243	.324	.440	-.074	.204	.272	.340	.218	-34.0	99-RF	-2	13-CF	-2
2006	STO	A+	22	307	46	8	2	11	38	35	73	4	3	5.2	.266	.358	.434	.081	.245	.318	.386	.246	1.0	38-CF	0	28-RF	-3
2006	MID	AA	22	19	5	1	0	1	2	4	4	0	0	5.6	.357	.474	.643	.595	.333	.450	.600	.355	2.9				
2006	SAC	AAA	22	11	0	1	0	0	0	0	3	0	0	1.9	.091	.091	.182	-.860	.000	.000	.000	.032	-3.7				
2007	OAK	MLB	23	413	40	18	1	11	45	33	108	4	2	4.9	.229	.294	.369	-.206	.226	.295	.376	.237	-9.5	98-RF	-3		

Breakout: 34% Improve: 57% Collapse: 28% Attrition: 14%   Comparables: Juan Camilo, Carlos Sosa, Luke Grayson, Jon Hamilton

After a so-so 2005 in the California League, Robnett returned to Stockton last spring and showed virtually no progress; the power remained, but so did the strikeouts. Nevertheless, the A's pushed him to Sacramento (briefly) and Midland. Things

(continued next page)

Richie Robnett

went swimmingly for a few games, then Robnett fractured a hamate bone and was out for the season. He was back in action for the Instructional League and Arizona Fall League. A first-round draft pick in 2004, he's now 23, and the bloom is nearly off the rose.

Marco Scutaro　　　　　**2B/SS**　　**Bats: R**　**Throws: R**　　Height: 5' 10"　Weight: 190　Born: October 30, 1975　　Age: 31

YEAR	TEAM	LVL	AGE	PA	R	2B	3B	HR	RBI	BB	SO	SB	CS	SPEED	AVG	OBP	SLG	MLVR	EQAVG	EQOBP	EQSLG	EQA	VORP	DEFENSE			
2004	OAK	MLB	28	477	50	32	1	7	43	16	58	0	0	4.0	.273	.297	.393	-.138	.270	.299	.389	.237	3.4	101-2B	-5	13-SS	0
2005	OAK	MLB	29	423	48	22	3	9	37	36	48	5	2	5.5	.247	.310	.391	-.094	.251	.325	.404	.253	6.3	74-SS	3	30-2B	3
2006	OAK	MLB	30	423	52	21	6	5	41	50	66	5	1	5.7	.266	.350	.397	-.032	.264	.357	.403	.270	14.7	64-SS	-11	34-2B	0
2007	OAK	MLB	31	421	46	21	2	6	41	36	59	4	2	5.0	.256	.321	.373	-.132	.253	.323	.379	.252	6.1	100-SS	-2		

Breakout: 12%　Improve: 40%　Collapse: 31%　Attrition: 25%　　Comparables: Frank Bolling, Jim Davenport, Dickie Thon, Kevin Seitzer

At 30, Scutaro finally gave the A's the .350 on-base percentage they'd been expecting when they signed him out of the Mets organization as a six-year free agent three years ago. Just in time, too—with Ellis and Crosby limping through the season, the A's wouldn't have won the West without Scooter. With some big hits in the A's Division Series win against the Twins, he got into the running for the Scrappiest Player Alive award, if only temporarily; with the A's getting swept by the Tigers, and the Cardinals making their improbable run, David Eckstein retained his title with a World Series knockout.

Justin Sellers　　　　　**SS**　　　**Bats: R**　**Throws: R**　　Height: 5' 10"　Weight: 160　Born: February 1, 1986　　Age: 21

YEAR	TEAM	LVL	AGE	PA	R	2B	3B	HR	RBI	BB	SO	SB	CS	SPEED	AVG	OBP	SLG	MLVR	EQAVG	EQOBP	EQSLG	EQA	VORP	DEFENSE	
2005	VAN	A-	19	207	31	8	1	0	13	19	24	8	3	5.9	.274	.369	.331	.064	.246	.307	.289	.220	-8.7	47-SS	-2
2006	KNC	A	20	495	75	21	2	5	46	58	65	17	5	6.3	.241	.346	.338	-.031	.205	.285	.288	.213	-20.5	116-SS	-5
2007	OAK	MLB	21	461	44	20	2	4	34	32	60	8	4	5.9	.232	.292	.316	-.277	.228	.294	.321	.222	-7.2	109-SS	1

Breakout: 46%　Improve: 67%　Collapse: 17%　Attrition: 6%　　Comparables: Tomas de la Rosa, Gookie Dawkins, Maikell Diaz, Mike Peeples

Scouts like everything about Sellers but his size; though five-foot-ten isn't terribly small for a shortstop, Sellers's frame isn't expected to carry much more weight as he matures than his listed 160 pounds. He's regarded as an excellent defender and will have to continue to earn that reputation on the field while improving his hitting in order to move through the system.

Matt Sulentic　　　　　**OF**　　　**Bats: L**　**Throws: R**　　Height: 5' 10"　Weight: 170　Born: October 6, 1987　　Age: 19

YEAR	TEAM	LVL	AGE	PA	R	2B	3B	HR	RBI	BB	SO	SB	CS	SPEED	AVG	OBP	SLG	MLVR	EQAVG	EQOBP	EQSLG	EQA	VORP	DEFENSE	
2006	KNC	A	18	113	12	4	1	1	13	12	19	1	2	4.8	.235	.327	.327	-.076	.206	.274	.294	.205	-9.8	28-LF	-2
2006	VAN	A-	18	162	24	10	1	2	22	14	30	3	4	4.6	.354	.409	.479	.398	.342	.381	.463	.286	19.5	36-RF	-6
2007	OAK	MLB	19	490	50	28	3	6	44	28	90	5	5	5.1	.267	.312	.380	-.132	.264	.314	.387	.247	-6.0	116-RF	-6

Breakout: 31%　Improve: 50%　Collapse: 30%　Attrition: 8%　　Comparables: Dave Krynzel, Felix Pie, Melky Cabrera, Milton Bradley

Scouting director Eric Kubota compared Sulentic, the A's third-round pick in last June's draft, to Lenny Dykstra; that must warm the cockles of Billy Beane's heart, as he was a minor-league teammate of Dykstra's. "He's not the most physically imposing guy," Kubota said, "but just a very good baseball player." Appropriately enough, Sulentic put up numbers evocative of a young Dykstra in his first pro experience. The comparison to Dykstra ends there—he lacks Nails's speed and will be limited to an outfield corner. He struggled after a promotion, but he's only 19 and has plenty of time to figure out the Midwest League.

Kurt Suzuki　　　　　**C**　　　**Bats: R**　**Throws: R**　　Height: 6' 0"　Weight: 205　Born: October 4, 1983　　Age: 23

YEAR	TEAM	LVL	AGE	PA	R	2B	3B	HR	RBI	BB	SO	SB	CS	SPEED	AVG	OBP	SLG	MLVR	EQAVG	EQOBP	EQSLG	EQA	VORP	DEFENSE	
2004	VAN	A-	20	211	27	10	3	3	31	18	26	0	1	4.4	.297	.394	.440	.239	.260	.314	.359	.238	0.3	25-C	0
2005	STO	A+	21	523	85	26	5	12	65	63	61	5	3	5.1	.277	.378	.440	.062	.241	.322	.359	.243	0.8	103-C	-7
2006	MID	AA	22	444	64	26	1	7	55	58	50	5	3	4.5	.285	.392	.415	.097	.260	.351	.376	.258	11.4	87-C	3
2007	OAK	MLB	23	458	48	23	1	7	45	40	59	3	2	4.6	.252	.325	.362	-.143	.248	.327	.369	.250	3.9	109-C	1

Breakout: 27%　Improve: 56%　Collapse: 17%　Attrition: 13%　　Comparables: Russell Martin, Phil Avlas, Robinson Cancel, Gerald Laird

It was an up-and-down season for the former second-round pick, as Suzuki batted .362 in April, .238 in May, .341 in June, .215 in July, and then .333 in five August games before leaving to play for Team USA. He's still on schedule to take over from Jason Kendall in 2008, which is particularly appropriate given Suzuki's tendencies to draw walks, make a lot of contact, and hit the ball over the fence just occasionally. He made great strides throwing out baserunners this year. If the A's are fated to have a Kendall-type backstop, at least he'll be a *cheap* Kendall-type backstop.

Oakland Athletics

Nick Swisher   OF/1B   Bats: S   Throws: L   Height: 6' 0"   Weight: 215   Born: November 25, 1980   Age: 26

YEAR	TEAM	LVL	AGE	PA	R	2B	3B	HR	RBI	BB	SO	SB	CS	SPEED	AVG	OBP	SLG	MLVR	EQAVG	EQOBP	EQSLG	EQA	VORP	DEFENSE			
2004	SAC	AAA	23	554	109	28	2	29	92	103	109	3	3	4.6	.269	.406	.537	.253	.246	.373	.466	.288	31.2	101-CF	-6	10-RF	0
2004	OAK	MLB	23	71	11	4	0	2	8	8	11	0	0	3.9	.250	.352	.417	-.035	.250	.361	.400	.271	0.4	11-LF	-1		
2005	OAK	MLB	24	522	66	32	1	21	74	55	110	0	1	3.9	.236	.322	.446	-.005	.240	.335	.459	.270	6.8	115-RF	-2	13-1B	-1
2006	OAK	MLB	25	672	106	24	2	35	95	97	152	1	2	4.2	.254	.372	.493	.122	.251	.378	.499	.297	28.1	78-1B	1	73-LF	8
2007	OAK	MLB	26	650	88	27	2	31	94	87	138	2	2	4.4	.248	.355	.473	.050	.244	.357	.481	.292	20.1	152-1B	2		

Breakout: 13%   Improve: 37%   Collapse: 28%   Attrition: 3%   Comparables: Tim Salmon, Harmon Killebrew, Andre Thornton, Lance Berkman

Swisher's already something of a folk hero in Oakland, but the open question is whether or not his performance is ever going to match his enthusiasm. Not that there's anything wrong with a guy who can play first base and left field and hit 35 homers and draw 100 walks, not at all. But when you strike out nearly once per game, it's not easy to be *great*. It's been a while since the A's developed a great player. Given their pre-Fremont payroll, they simply have to come up with their own great players every so often if they're going to continue to contend for a spot in the World Series Derby every season. That's not Swisher's fault—he doesn't run the scouting department, the statistical research department, or whatever Moneyball-ish amalgam of the two the A's are using these days.

Frank Thomas   DH   Bats: R   Throws: R   Height: 6' 5"   Weight: 275   Born: December 31, 1969   Age: 39

YEAR	TEAM	LVL	AGE	PA	R	2B	3B	HR	RBI	BB	SO	SB	CS	SPEED	AVG	OBP	SLG	MLVR	EQAVG	EQOBP	EQSLG	EQA	VORP	DEFENSE
2004	CHA	MLB	36	311	53	16	0	18	49	64	57	0	2	3.9	.271	.434	.563	.309	.265	.434	.555	.330	29.1	
2005	CHA	MLB	37	124	19	3	0	12	26	16	31	0	0	2.9	.219	.315	.590	.148	.214	.323	.602	.297	7.4	
2006	OAK	MLB	38	559	77	11	0	39	114	81	81	0	0	2.4	.270	.381	.545	.224	.267	.386	.552	.313	41.3	
2007	TOR	MLB	39	578	88	19	1	40	105	85	102	1	0	3.3	.262	.376	.554	.199	.253	.371	.537	.311	36.1	135-DH

Breakout: 9%   Improve: 28%   Collapse: 17%   Attrition: 6%   Comparables: Cliff Johnson, Darrell Evans, Frank Robinson, Mike Schmidt

Signing Thomas was perhaps the best $500,000 gamble ever; that's all Thomas was guaranteed when he signed a one-year deal with the A's last winter. He wound up earning more than $3 million after cashing in most of his bonus clauses (except for the $50,000 Gold Glove bonus, which must have been somebody's idea of a joke, and a pretty good one). More lucratively, Thomas cashed in after the season with a new deal with the Blue Jays that guarantees him $18 million over the next two seasons, which probably tells you most of what you'd want to know about the financial divide separating the A's from most of their competitors.

PITCHERS

Joe Blanton   Bats: R   Throws: R   Height: 6' 3"   Weight: 240   Born: December 11, 1980   Age: 26

YEAR	TEAM	LVL	AGE	W	L	SV	G	GS	IP	H	BB	SO	HR	GB%	BABIP	STUFF	WHIP	ERA	PERA	EQERA	EQH9	EQBB9	EQSO9	EQHR9	VORP	WXRL
2004	SAC	AAA	23	11	8	0	28	26	176¹	199	34	143	13	—	.332	21	1.32	4.19	3.65	4.61	9.0	1.7	5.4	0.7	20.2	—
2004	OAK	MLB	23	0	0	0	3	0	8	6	2	6	1	—	.231	8	1.29	5.63	3.89	5.62	6.8	2.2	6.8	1.1	-0.6	-0.07
2005	OAK	MLB	24	12	12	0	33	33	201¹	178	67	116	23	45.1%	.252	7	1.22	3.53	4.58	4.00	8.3	3.0	5.2	1.0	44.4	5.67
2006	OAK	MLB	25	16	12	0	32	31	194¹	241	58	107	17	44.8%	.341	10	1.54	4.82	4.05	4.60	10.4	2.5	4.6	0.7	19.7	2.90
2007	OAK	MLB	26	11	11	0	30	30	187	208	56	111	24	45.0%	.300	8	1.41	4.64	4.57	4.48	9.5	2.6	5.0	1.0	20.2	3.50

Breakout: 14%   Improve: 48%   Collapse: 17%   Attrition: 0%   Comparables: Bobby Jones, Danny Cox, Doc Medich, Carl Pavano

A control pitcher like Blanton will always be highly subject to the vagaries of luck on balls in play, and, over the last two seasons, Blanton's luck has swung from one extreme to the other. As long as he can keep his walks down, limit home runs, and stay healthy, he'll be a league-average starting pitcher, and at his salary there's absolutely nothing wrong with that. Actually, these days there would be absolutely nothing wrong with that if he were making twenty times his salary. It's funny to see Carl Pavano among Blanton's comparables, above—Blanton works for a living.

Kiko Calero Bats: R Throws: R Height: 6' 1" Weight: 200 Born: January 9, 1975 Age: 32

YEAR	TEAM	LVL	AGE	W	L	SV	G	GS	IP	H	BB	SO	HR	GB%	BABIP	STUFF	WHIP	ERA	PERA	EQERA	EQH9	EQBB9	EQSO9	EQHR9	VORP	WXRL
2004	SLN	MLB	29	3	1	2	41	0	45^1	27	10	47	5	—	.218	24	0.82	2.78	3.29	3.00	5.8	1.8	8.4	1.0	14.5	2.27
2005	OAK	MLB	30	4	1	1	58	0	55^2	45	18	52	6	37.2%	.260	16	1.13	3.23	3.68	3.21	7.6	2.9	8.4	1.0	15.7	1.36
2006	OAK	MLB	31	3	2	2	70	0	58	50	24	67	4	33.6%	.317	28	1.28	3.41	3.01	3.17	7.4	3.5	9.7	0.6	17.3	2.40
2007	OAK	MLB	32	3	2	4	50	0	53^1	49	20	57	6	38.0%	.301	17	1.28	3.56	3.63	3.41	7.9	3.2	9.1	0.9	12.4	1.20

Breakout: 19% Improve: 43% Collapse: 28% Attrition: 20% Comparables: Troy Percival, Alejandro Pena, Roberto Hernandez, Enrique Romo

If Calero had been all the Athletics got from the Cardinals in the Mulder deal, it would have been a good trade for the A's. Of course, Calero was essentially a throw-in after Dan Haren and Daric Barton. Unlike pen-mate Jason Duchscherer, Calero relies on only two pitches—a fastball and slider. The pair give the A's one of the most reliable one-two righty setup punches around.

Santiago Casilla Bats: R Throws: R Height: 6' 0" Weight: 200 Born: June 25, 1980 Age: 27

YEAR	TEAM	LVL	AGE	W	L	SV	G	GS	IP	H	BB	SO	HR	GB%	BABIP	STUFF	WHIP	ERA	PERA	EQERA	EQH9	EQBB9	EQSO9	EQHR9	VORP	WXRL
2004	KNC	A	24	1	0	16	25	0	30	16	6	49	0	—	.291	19	0.73	0.30	3.32	1.59	7.0	2.5	7.9	0.3	12.6	—
2004	MID	AA	24	2	0	2	13	0	18	10	15	32	0	—	.313	17	1.39	1.50	4.77	2.16	6.5	9.7	10.8	0.5	6.4	—
2004	SAC	AAA	24	1	2	1	11	0	13^2	10	9	21	1	—	.333	14	1.39	3.94	3.88	3.95	6.6	5.9	10.5	0.7	2.5	—
2005	MID	AA	25	0	0	6	10	0	16^2	9	9	30	1	56.7%	.286	16	1.08	1.08	4.13	2.30	6.3	6.3	11.5	1.1	5.8	—
2005	SAC	AAA	25	3	6	20	44	0	48^1	45	20	73	6	43.2%	.358	14	1.35	4.47	3.94	5.59	8.8	3.5	10.2	1.3	0.1	—
2006	SAC	AAA	26	2	0	4	25	0	33^1	25	10	24	2	45.7%	.264	7	1.06	3.26	3.91	3.78	6.8	2.7	6.5	0.8	6.7	—
2007	OAK	MLB	27	3	3	2	52	3	54^1	54	26	46	7	40.0%	.293	1	1.46	4.85	4.61	4.68	8.5	4.1	7.1	1.1	4.4	0.50

Breakout: 17% Improve: 38% Collapse: 31% Attrition: 28% Comparables: Mike Corkins, Bob Hall, Doug Bochtler, Charlie Hough

This is the same guy who used to be named Jairo Garcia and born in 1983. You see the new name and the new birthday, and you can guess what happened. He was doing well in Sacramento until June 14, when he went down with a sore shoulder. The doctors never did find anything worth operating on, so Casilla spent the autumn rehabbing and was expected to pitch winter ball in his native Dominican Republic. Whatever else happens, he'll always have that 2004 stat line from Kane County. That was almost certainly his professional peak, it just happened at the wrong time and place. Think about how frightening it must be to know that. Say you're 20 years old, or 30, and you somehow find out that you will never achieve more or be happier than when you were 15. What would you do then?

Justin Duchscherer Bats: R Throws: R Height: 6' 3" Weight: 200 Born: November 19, 1977 Age: 29

YEAR	TEAM	LVL	AGE	W	L	SV	G	GS	IP	H	BB	SO	HR	GB%	BABIP	STUFF	WHIP	ERA	PERA	EQERA	EQH9	EQBB9	EQSO9	EQHR9	VORP	WXRL
2004	OAK	MLB	26	7	6	0	53	0	96^1	85	32	59	13	—	.255	-5	1.21	3.27	4.74	3.29	7.9	2.7	5.1	1.1	29.4	2.10
2005	OAK	MLB	27	7	4	5	65	0	85^2	67	19	85	7	43.4%	.274	30	1.00	2.21	2.99	2.71	7.4	2.0	8.8	0.7	30.0	3.25
2006	OAK	MLB	28	2	1	9	53	0	55^2	52	9	51	4	39.5%	.304	24	1.10	2.91	2.84	2.68	7.9	1.4	7.7	0.6	19.6	3.57
2007	OAK	MLB	29	4	3	8	52	0	62^2	62	16	52	7	43.0%	.297	10	1.25	3.51	3.65	3.37	8.5	2.2	7.1	0.9	15.6	1.50

Breakout: 12% Improve: 33% Collapse: 44% Attrition: 10% Comparables: Mike Schooler, Dave Veres, Rick Aguilera, Greg McMichael

Since becoming a full-time reliever in 2004, Duchscherer's posted a 2.80 ERA and filled in reliably as closer when Huston Street has been wounded. He seems to have the stuff and repertoire of a decent starting pitcher, but during the last three seasons he hasn't started at all, while Shane Komine, Jason Windsor, Seth Etherton, Ryan Glynn, Brad Halsey, and (especially) Kirk Saarloos have. So it seems the A's have made up their minds about Duchscherer: He's a fireman, and a good one.

Ron Flores Bats: L Throws: L Height: 5' 11" Weight: 200 Born: August 9, 1979 Age: 27

YEAR	TEAM	LVL	AGE	W	L	SV	G	GS	IP	H	BB	SO	HR	GB%	BABIP	STUFF	WHIP	ERA	PERA	EQERA	EQH9	EQBB9	EQSO9	EQHR9	VORP	WXRL
2004	SAC	AAA	24	4	3	1	55	0	53	59	18	55	4	—	.340	6	1.45	3.74	3.63	4.25	9.0	3.1	7.0	0.7	8.3	—
2005	SAC	AAA	25	5	3	3	52	0	60^1	46	30	66	5	39.7%	.283	11	1.26	2.39	4.21	2.82	6.8	4.3	7.4	0.9	18.7	—
2005	OAK	MLB	25	0	0	0	11	0	8^2	8	0	6	1	25.0%	.259	9	0.92	1.03	3.32	1.04	8.3	1.0	6.2	1.0	4.6	0.13
2006	SAC	AAA	26	5	5	2	26	0	25	25	14	27	0	45.8%	.362	0	1.56	6.48	3.72	7.36	8.8	4.9	7.4	0.4	-5.0	—
2006	OAK	MLB	26	1	2	1	25	0	29^2	28	10	20	3	33.3%	.287	1	1.28	3.33	4.01	2.93	7.9	2.9	5.6	0.9	9.0	-0.06
2007	OAK	MLB	27	2	2	3	56	1	48^1	51	19	39	7	37.0%	.297	0	1.44	4.52	4.60	4.29	9.0	3.5	6.8	1.2	6.2	0.60

Breakout: 8% Improve: 24% Collapse: 48% Attrition: 32% Comparables: Bob McClure, Steve Wilson, Craig Lefferts, Chuck McElroy

If you have trouble keeping St. Louis's Randy Flores and Oakland's Ron Flores straight, don't feel bad; their mom probably does, too. They're roughly the same size, they're both left-handed relief pitchers, and, of course, they're brothers. Both have marginal stuff and will last exactly as long as they can consistently retire left-handed batters. Ron should be sure to sit close to new pen-mate Alan Embree this summer in the hope that some of that veteran LOOGY-ness will rub off.

Chad Gaudin

Bats: R **Throws: R** Height: 5' 11" Weight: 165 Born: March 24, 1983 Age: 24

YEAR	TEAM	LVL	AGE	W	L	SV	G	GS	IP	H	BB	SO	HR	GB%	BABIP	STUFF	WHIP	ERA	PERA	EQERA	EQH9	EQBB9	EQSO9	EQHR9	VORP	WXRL
2004	DUR	AAA	21	1	3	2	17	7	47²	48	17	52	8	—	.325	6	1.36	4.72	5.30	4.94	9.3	3.4	7.6	1.7	3.5	—
2004	TBA	MLB	21	1	2	0	26	4	42²	59	16	30	4	—	.390	0	1.76	4.85	4.22	5.15	12.4	3.1	6.0	0.8	2.2	0.68
2005	SYR	AAA	22	9	8	0	23	23	150¹	140	35	113	12	45.8%	.296	18	1.16	3.35	4.10	3.67	8.2	2.2	5.2	0.8	32.6	—
2005	TOR	MLB	22	1	3	0	5	3	13	31	6	12	6	40.7%	.521	-17	2.85	13.15	7.48	12.51	20.4	4.0	7.9	4.0	-10.6	-0.50
2006	SAC	AAA	23	3	0	0	4	4	24¹	14	8	26	0	56.1%	.255	24	0.91	0.37	2.83	2.62	5.2	3.0	7.5	0.4	7.9	—
2006	OAK	MLB	23	4	2	2	55	0	64	51	42	36	3	40.7%	.251	4	1.45	3.09	4.72	3.14	6.7	5.5	4.8	0.4	19.3	1.59
2007	OAK	MLB	24	4	4	2	45	5	72	75	33	52	9	43.0%	.297	-2	1.50	4.71	4.72	4.54	8.9	4.0	6.1	1.0	7.6	0.80

Breakout: 11% Improve: 39% Collapse: 33% Attrition: 18% Comparables: Dick Selma, Eduardo Rodriguez, Larry Demery, Oscar Villarreal

As Gaudin was tearing through the Devil Rays' system and making his MLB debut at 20, there was talk about his slider already ranking among the very best in the game. Things didn't work out with Tampa Bay, and Gaudin lasted just one year with the Blue Jays despite a solid season with Syracuse. He seems to have found a home in the Oakland bullpen despite his brilliant numbers as a starter with Sacramento, but a note of caution considering his awful K/BB ratio is definitely in order. We can't take that 3.09 ERA seriously, but Gaudin still has that good slider, and he doesn't turn 24 until this spring, so he figures to be a capable back-of-the-bullpen guy in 2007, with possibilities beyond.

Brad Halsey

Bats: L **Throws: L** Height: 6' 1" Weight: 185 Born: February 14, 1981 Age: 26

YEAR	TEAM	LVL	AGE	W	L	SV	G	GS	IP	H	BB	SO	HR	GB%	BABIP	STUFF	WHIP	ERA	PERA	EQERA	EQH9	EQBB9	EQSO9	EQHR9	VORP	WXRL
2004	COH	AAA	23	11	4	0	24	23	144	128	37	109	8	—	.278	23	1.15	2.63	3.87	3.09	7.7	2.5	5.2	0.6	40.6	—
2004	NYA	MLB	23	1	3	0	8	7	32	41	14	25	4	—	.352	2	1.72	6.47	4.48	6.68	10.7	3.5	6.4	1.1	-4.3	0.04
2005	ARI	MLB	24	8	12	0	28	26	160	191	39	82	20	42.2%	.320	0	1.44	4.61	4.62	4.87	10.0	1.9	4.1	1.0	-0.5	2.00
2006	OAK	MLB	25	5	4	0	52	7	94¹	108	46	53	11	45.7%	.312	-12	1.63	4.68	5.09	4.52	9.7	4.1	4.7	0.9	10.5	1.25
2007	OAK	MLB	26	5	6	1	50	10	98²	113	36	53	13	45.0%	.300	-9	1.50	5.01	4.90	4.84	9.8	3.2	4.5	1.1	6.0	1.00

Breakout: 15% Improve: 37% Collapse: 31% Attrition: 13% Comparables: Don Hood, Jerry Augustine, Scott Bailes, John Curtis

When you look at Halsey's EqERAs, you see only one good number, his solid campaign three years ago with the Yankees' Triple-A farm club. That's true even if you go back to 2003 (not pictured here). The A's could use a reliable LOOGY, but Halsey doesn't seem particularly suited to that role; lefties have hit .273/.338/.427 against him in the major leagues. Halsey's a lefty, and he can give you five or six innings in a pinch, so he's got some value, but if he can't improve his slider or develop a good curveball, he's not going to be around much longer.

Rich Harden

Bats: L **Throws: R** Height: 6' 1" Weight: 195 Born: November 30, 1981 Age: 25

YEAR	TEAM	LVL	AGE	W	L	SV	G	GS	IP	H	BB	SO	HR	GB%	BABIP	STUFF	WHIP	ERA	PERA	EQERA	EQH9	EQBB9	EQSO9	EQHR9	VORP	WXRL
2004	OAK	MLB	22	11	7	0	31	31	189²	171	81	167	16	—	.295	30	1.33	3.99	3.71	3.99	8.0	3.5	7.3	0.6	42.3	5.00
2005	OAK	MLB	23	10	5	0	22	19	128	93	43	121	7	43.3%	.257	44	1.06	2.53	3.09	3.08	6.9	3.0	8.4	0.5	40.7	5.17
2006	OAK	MLB	24	4	0	0	9	9	46²	31	26	49	5	44.2%	.241	33	1.22	4.24	4.15	3.94	5.6	4.7	8.8	0.9	9.2	1.35
2007	OAK	MLB	25	8	6	0	27	19	122¹	105	52	121	11	45.0%	.287	26	1.29	3.78	3.51	3.69	7.4	3.7	8.4	0.7	27.1	3.40

Breakout: 24% Improve: 39% Collapse: 16% Attrition: 8% Comparables: Ernie Broglio, Jim Maloney, Juan Guzman, Andy Messersmith

It was another rough year for Harden, as the supposed future Cy Young candidate managed only four wins. He missed five weeks with a strained muscle in his back, and then—more seriously—three and a half months with a strained elbow ligament. He did return to the rotation in September and looked healthy if somewhat erratic. An optimistic A's fan will argue that the loss of Zito will be balanced by a healthy Harden, but a pessimistic, or perhaps a realistic, one might argue that Harden has started only 28 games over the last two seasons and is unlikely to come anywhere near Zito's annual 34 or 35 starts.

Dan Haren   Bats: R Throws: R   Height: 6' 5"   Weight: 220   Born: September 17, 1980   Age: 26

YEAR	TEAM	LVL	AGE	W	L	SV	G	GS	IP	H	BB	SO	HR	GB%	BABIP	STUFF	WHIP	ERA	PERA	EQERA	EQH9	EQBB9	EQSO9	EQHR9	VORP	WXRL
2004	MEM	AAA	23	11	4	0	21	21	128	137	33	150	19	—	.351	17	1.33	4.15	4.28	4.30	9.4	2.4	8.1	1.5	18.7	—
2004	SLN	MLB	23	3	3	0	14	5	46	45	17	32	4	—	.306	4	1.35	4.50	4.13	4.89	9.2	2.9	5.7	0.8	6.0	0.45
2005	OAK	MLB	24	14	12	0	34	34	217	212	53	163	26	47.2%	.290	18	1.22	3.73	3.96	4.27	9.2	2.2	6.6	1.0	39.5	5.25
2006	OAK	MLB	25	14	13	0	34	34	223	224	45	176	31	45.3%	.292	19	1.21	4.12	4.02	4.00	8.5	1.7	6.6	1.1	41.4	5.29
2007	OAK	MLB	26	13	10	0	31	31	203	211	47	152	24	46.0%	.299	20	1.27	4.08	3.92	3.95	8.9	2.0	6.3	1.0	35.2	5.10

Breakout: 21%   Improve: 60%   Collapse: 6%   Attrition: 1%   Comparables: Frank Sullivan, Freddy Garcia, Erik Hanson, Ben McDonald

If not for J. J. Hardy, Dan Haren would follow Rich Harden in an alphabetical register of 2006 major leaguers, and that's probably how most fans think of them: Harden, then Haren. But while Harden has totaled 175 innings over the last two seasons, Haren has established himself as one of the more durable starters in the majors, making 34 starts in both seasons. He's otherwise consistent, too, with 14 wins in each season and virtually identical numbers down the line. Haren has just one weakness: Home runs. Last season only six American League pitchers gave up more dingers than Haren. If he can solve that problem—or get just a few extra dollops of luck—fans will figure out that Haren comes before Harden in the only way that matters.

Joe Kennedy   Bats: R Throws: L   Height: 6' 4"   Weight: 245   Born: May 24, 1979   Age: 28

YEAR	TEAM	LVL	AGE	W	L	SV	G	GS	IP	H	BB	SO	HR	GB%	BABIP	STUFF	WHIP	ERA	PERA	EQERA	EQH9	EQBB9	EQSO9	EQHR9	VORP	WXRL
2004	COL	MLB	25	9	7	0	27	27	162¹	163	67	117	17	—	.304	16	1.42	3.66	4.36	3.31	8.3	3.2	5.6	0.8	41.3	4.48
2005	COL	MLB	26	4	8	0	16	16	92	128	44	52	12	48.0%	.364	-9	1.87	7.04	5.17	6.75	11.2	3.8	4.4	1.0	-20.5	-1.48
2005	OAK	MLB	26	4	5	0	19	8	60²	64	20	45	8	40.5%	.299	3	1.38	4.45	4.34	4.84	9.8	2.9	6.6	1.2	6.3	0.33
2006	OAK	MLB	27	4	1	1	39	0	35	34	13	29	1	49.5%	.317	14	1.34	2.31	3.15	2.48	8.2	3.0	6.9	0.2	13.7	1.97
2007	OAK	MLB	28	4	4	1	38	7	68¹	76	26	47	8	47.0%	.312	-2	1.50	4.74	4.74	4.59	9.6	3.3	5.8	0.9	6.6	0.90

Breakout: 15%   Improve: 38%   Collapse: 28%   Attrition: 19%   Comparables: Lou Brissie, Dave LaPoint, Dennys Reyes, Stan Williams

For the first time in his career, Kennedy didn't start even a single game, and he took to his new role well, posting the lowest ERA (and the lowest PERA) of his career by a healthy margin. Most impressively, Kennedy gave up just one homer all year. Still, the season was hardly an unqualified success; Kennedy missed the middle three months with a shoulder injury. With the exception of one game, he pitched brilliantly after coming off the DL in mid-August, so there's no reason to worry about his arm in the immediate future. Kennedy will eventually become a LOOGY, but he's still young, and, right now, more valuable to the A's in a larger role, which is why they'll try to convert him back to starting this spring despite the fact that his career ERA as a starter is twice what it's been out of the pen.

Shane Komine   Bats: R Throws: R   Height: 5' 9"   Weight: 175   Born: October 18, 1980   Age: 26

YEAR	TEAM	LVL	AGE	W	L	SV	G	GS	IP	H	BB	SO	HR	GB%	BABIP	STUFF	WHIP	ERA	PERA	EQERA	EQH9	EQBB9	EQSO9	EQHR9	VORP	WXRL
2004	MID	AA	23	4	5	0	17	17	94¹	103	28	65	10	—	.305	-19	1.39	4.77	5.76	6.27	10.0	3.1	4.1	1.5	-6.9	—
2005	MID	AA	24	2	1	0	5	5	31¹	27	7	33	5	47.6%	.286	7	1.09	3.16	6.15	4.15	8.6	2.7	6.8	2.1	4.9	—
2006	SAC	AAA	25	11	8	0	24	22	140	145	38	116	13	42.7%	.319	9	1.31	4.05	4.40	4.47	8.9	2.3	5.6	1.1	18.0	—
2006	OAK	MLB	25	0	0	0	2	2	9	10	8	1	3	36.1%	.212	-32	2.00	5.00	10.01	4.82	9.6	7.7	1.0	2.9	1.0	0.23
2007	OAK	MLB	26	6	7	0	30	16	106¹	125	36	64	17	42.0%	.307	-3	1.51	5.39	5.28	5.15	10.0	2.9	5.1	1.3	2.5	0.90

Breakout: 15%   Improve: 39%   Collapse: 26%   Attrition: 1%   Comparables: Evan Thomas, Felipe Lira, Mike Saipe, Tim Redding

Komine (pronounced KO-min-ay), "The Hawaiian Punch-Out," was making steady progress through the system before Tommy John surgery cost him big chunks of two seasons. He got back on track in late 2005 with solid stints in the Texas League and the Arizona Fall League, then zipped right along in his first Triple-A season. At five-foot-nine in his spikes, Komine's always going to be on a (pardon the pun) short leash, but he throws reasonably hard and features one of the best curveballs in the system—he's sort of a poor man's young Tom Gordon. He's part of the back-up plan should Kennedy not transition well back into starting. That's appropriate, given that Komine profiles as something of a Saarloos-type pitcher. Still, if he achieves that much, he'll have exceeded expectations.

Esteban Loaiza

Bats: R Throws: R   Height: 6′ 3″   Weight: 215   Born: December 31, 1971   Age: 35

YEAR	TEAM	LVL	AGE	W	L	SV	G	GS	IP	H	BB	SO	HR	GB%	BABIP	STUFF	WHIP	ERA	PERA	EQERA	EQH9	EQBB9	EQSO9	EQHR9	VORP	WXRL
2004	CHA	MLB	32	9	5	0	21	21	140²	156	45	83	23	—	.298	-2	1.43	4.86	4.79	4.73	9.5	2.6	4.9	1.2	18.9	1.92
2004	NYA	MLB	32	1	2	0	10	6	42¹	61	26	34	9	—	.377	-10	2.06	8.51	5.78	8.46	12.1	4.8	6.4	1.6	-14.0	-0.53
2005	WAS	MLB	33	12	10	0	34	34	217	227	55	173	18	45.3%	.322	25	1.30	3.77	3.53	4.02	9.3	2.1	6.5	0.7	39.4	5.26
2006	OAK	MLB	34	11	9	0	26	26	154²	179	40	97	17	43.1%	.320	11	1.42	4.89	4.08	4.78	9.7	2.1	5.2	0.9	11.9	2.24
2007	OAK	MLB	35	9	10	0	29	26	163¹	184	46	100	22	44.0%	.304	5	1.41	4.77	4.65	4.59	9.6	2.5	5.2	1.1	14.5	2.70

Breakout: 22% Improve: 54% Collapse: 13% Attrition: 5%   Comparables: *Doyle Alexander, Rick Rhoden, John Burkett, Dave Stewart*

A year ago, PECOTA projected that, among the seven free-agent pitchers who signed contracts worth at least $10 million last winter, Loaiza would wind up representing the most value in terms of dollars per win. Hey, it could have worked out that way, but, thanks to a trapezius injury more serious than initially thought, Loaiza's ERA stood at 6.72 when August opened and he was on the verge of losing his job. From his next start on August 2 through the end of the season, Loaiza went 7–2 with a 3.16 ERA and a 6:1 K/BB ratio. Even in the postseason, when he got cuffed around pretty good, Loaiza walked just one batter in 11 innings. No, the A's didn't get their money's worth in 2006, but, considering how he finished the season and the sky-rocketing costs of decent and durable starting pitchers, Loiaza still figures to be worth the $14.5 million the A's owe him over the next two seasons.

Marcus McBeth

Bats: R Throws: R   Height: 6′ 2″   Weight: 183   Born: August 23, 1980   Age: 26

YEAR	TEAM	LVL	AGE	W	L	SV	G	GS	IP	H	BB	SO	HR	GB%	BABIP	STUFF	WHIP	ERA	PERA	EQERA	EQH9	EQBB9	EQSO9	EQHR9	VORP	WXRL
2005	KNC	A	24	1	2	1	16	0	19²	20	13	21	2	29.8%	.340	-13	1.68	5.03	7.35	6.27	10.6	7.7	5.8	1.9	-1.4	—
2006	STO	A+	25	0	0	7	8	0	8²	1	2	14	0	30.8%	.077	8	0.37	0.00	2.43	1.12	2.2	2.2	9.0	0.0	4.0	—
2006	MID	AA	25	3	2	25	45	0	54¹	43	20	65	4	42.9%	.287	3	1.16	2.50	4.26	3.40	7.8	3.7	7.3	1.0	13.0	—
2006	SAC	AAA	25	0	1	0	6	0	7	7	6	7	3	18.2%	.211	-13	1.86	11.57	13.25	11.57	10.3	7.7	6.4	5.1	-4.6	—
2007	OAK	MLB	26	3	4	1	29	6	62	62	33	50	11	38.0%	.284	-2	1.54	5.05	5.21	4.78	8.6	4.7	6.8	1.4	4.3	0.60

Breakout: 12% Improve: 31% Collapse: 31% Attrition: 9%   Comparables: *Paul Bush, Brian Bevil, Jim Mann, Chris Schroder*

The A's fourth-round draft pick in 2001—that's the year before the *Moneyball* draft—Marcus "The Scottish Play" McBeth batted .233 in three seasons as a center fielder, so in 2005 he made the logical switch from the garden to the hill. He's had his ups and downs as a reliever, but in 2006 it was mostly up, and he's a prospect as long as he maintains that strikeout rate (or something close to it). McBeth gets his fastball into the mid-90s and he's working on a slider, but it's his changeup that everybody talks about. He's ticketed for Sacramento this spring.

Dan Meyer

Bats: R Throws: L   Height: 6′ 3″   Weight: 220   Born: July 3, 1981   Age: 25

YEAR	TEAM	LVL	AGE	W	L	SV	G	GS	IP	H	BB	SO	HR	GB%	BABIP	STUFF	WHIP	ERA	PERA	EQERA	EQH9	EQBB9	EQSO9	EQHR9	VORP	WXRL
2004	GRN	AA	23	6	3	0	14	13	65	50	12	86	1	—	.314	41	0.95	2.22	2.67	3.11	7.9	1.8	7.9	0.1	17.6	—
2004	RIC	AAA	23	3	3	0	12	11	61¹	62	25	60	6	—	.322	13	1.42	2.79	4.50	3.67	9.2	4.0	6.8	1.0	13.1	—
2005	SAC	AAA	24	2	8	0	19	17	89	101	43	63	15	39.1%	.313	-20	1.62	5.36	6.07	6.03	9.7	4.1	4.7	1.7	-4.3	—
2006	SAC	AAA	25	3	3	0	10	10	49¹	63	20	29	10	37.7%	.329	-29	1.69	5.13	7.03	5.90	11.1	3.6	4.1	2.3	-1.7	—
2007	OAK	MLB	25	5	7	0	28	15	95¹	116	42	53	19	38.0%	.303	-11	1.66	6.25	6.18	5.90	10.4	3.9	4.7	1.6	-6.7	0.10

Breakout: 3% Improve: 26% Collapse: 41% Attrition: 1%   Comparables: *Cory Stewart, Brian McNichol, Brent Billingsley, Eric Cyr*

As well as the Mark Mulder trade worked out, the Tim Hudson deal worked out just as badly (notwithstanding the slough-ing of Hudson's salary). Juan Cruz never earned Billy Beane's trust and was traded to Arizona. Charles Thomas washed out. Dan Meyer hasn't looked good for more than a few seconds at a time. Two winters ago, Meyer apparently worked out too much and hurt his shoulder, which destroyed his 2005. Meyer was supposed to be ready to pitch last spring, but when his fastball topped out in the high-80s it was obvious that he wasn't anything close to right. After 10 starts with Sacramento, the A's shut him down, even though nobody could figure out exactly what was wrong. Finally, Meyer's fourth doctor real-ized that a piece of his shoulder blade had broken off and become lodged somewhere inconvenient; this "impediment" was removed in mid-July. Shoulder injuries are notoriously problematic, and, if Meyer doesn't make it back, the A's will wind up having traded Tim Hudson for Brad Halsey.

Jason Ray

Bats: R Throws: R Height: 5' 11" Weight: 195 Born: July 14, 1984 Age: 22

YEAR	TEAM	LVL	AGE	W	L	SV	G	GS	IP	H	BB	SO	HR	GB%	BABIP	STUFF	WHIP	ERA	PERA	EQERA	EQH9	EQBB9	EQSO9	EQHR9	VORP	WXRL
2005	VAN	A-	20	0	1	0	20	0	29²	17	23	56	1	43.1%	.340	25	1.35	2.12	6.37	3.91	8.9	11.0	9.9	1.1	4.8	—
2006	KNC	A	21	6	1	0	13	13	65²	48	35	68	1	44.3%	.276	20	1.27	3.04	5.13	5.37	7.5	6.5	5.5	0.4	1.6	—
2006	STO	A+	21	5	5	0	18	7	60¹	59	33	48	9	36.6%	.306	-23	1.53	4.94	7.95	5.82	9.0	5.4	4.6	2.2	-1.5	—
2007	OAK	MLB	22	4	6	0	24	15	84	91	70	59	14	39.0%	.298	-12	1.92	6.52	6.63	6.21	9.3	7.3	6.0	1.3	-8.2	0.30

Breakout: 5% Improve: 25% Collapse: 42% Attrition: 5% Comparables: Ben Howard, Brad Baker, Alberto Garza, Lesli Brea

As a first-year pro in 2005, Ray struck out 32 batters in his last 14 innings (over 10 games) thanks to his mid-90s fastball and hard curve. That earned him a spot on prospect lists. He got roughed up some after a mid-2006 promotion to the fast California League, mostly because his homer rate skyrocketed. That's a hitter's league, of course, and Ray's got time on his side.

Connor Robertson

Bats: R Throws: R Height: 6' 2" Weight: 215 Born: September 10, 1981 Age: 25

YEAR	TEAM	LVL	AGE	W	L	SV	G	GS	IP	H	BB	SO	HR	GB%	BABIP	STUFF	WHIP	ERA	PERA	EQERA	EQH9	EQBB9	EQSO9	EQHR9	VORP	WXRL
2005	KNC	A	23	2	2	1	20	0	27²	23	14	47	0	55.6%	.442	22	1.34	2.92	3.99	4.15	9.7	5.9	9.3	0.3	4.2	—
2005	STO	A+	23	5	2	1	32	0	42¹	37	23	68	1	41.7%	.387	22	1.42	2.77	3.92	4.14	8.5	6.1	8.7	0.2	6.7	—
2006	MID	AA	24	7	2	6	55	0	83	73	22	97	1	48.8%	.362	24	1.14	2.82	2.85	3.69	8.2	2.6	7.0	0.1	17.6	—
2007	OAK	MLB	25	3	3	1	28	6	61¹	65	27	50	7	45.0%	.313	6	1.50	4.65	4.63	4.50	9.0	3.9	6.9	0.9	6.3	0.80

Breakout: 13% Improve: 30% Collapse: 43% Attrition: 11% Comparables: Kevin Frederick, Luke Anderson, Chad Ricketts, Scott Henderson

Robertson is a power pitcher without much power. His sinker-slider combination isn't anything special, but his deceptive peek-a-boo delivery makes all his pitches tough to read, and it's a good sinker; in 194 professional innings, he's given up only five homers. He's 25 and not the sort of pitcher who's going to move anywhere quickly—he spent all of last season in the Texas League—but if he can maintain those numbers with Sacramento this spring, the A's won't be able to ignore him.

Kirk Saarloos

Bats: R Throws: R Height: 6' 0" Weight: 185 Born: May 23, 1979 Age: 28

YEAR	TEAM	LVL	AGE	W	L	SV	G	GS	IP	H	BB	SO	HR	GB%	BABIP	STUFF	WHIP	ERA	PERA	EQERA	EQH9	EQBB9	EQSO9	EQHR9	VORP	WXRL
2004	OAK	MLB	25	2	1	0	6	5	24¹	27	12	10	4	—	.284	-19	1.60	4.44	6.06	4.68	9.7	4.0	3.6	1.4	4.1	0.55
2005	OAK	MLB	26	10	9	0	29	27	159²	170	54	53	11	56.8%	.291	-1	1.40	4.17	4.70	4.54	10.2	3.1	3.0	0.6	27.8	3.97
2006	OAK	MLB	27	7	7	2	35	16	121¹	149	53	52	19	55.1%	.315	-22	1.66	4.75	5.54	4.64	10.2	3.6	3.6	1.2	12.0	1.67
2007	OAK	MLB	28	7	8	1	36	17	120¹	143	45	55	14	53.0%	.308	-10	1.56	5.07	5.03	4.95	10.1	3.3	3.9	0.9	5.8	1.30

Breakout: 13% Improve: 37% Collapse: 21% Attrition: 11% Comparables: Al Fitzmorris, Jimmy Jones, Don August, Jim McGlothlin

Saarloos has put Billy Beane in an awkward spot. Beane loved Saarloos's college stats, and he loved his minor league stats, and, eventually, he pried him away from the Astros. Since then, Saarloos has posted a winning record and a decent ERA with the A's while costing the club essentially nothing. Yet, Beane knows that a pitcher who walks as many batters as he strikes out is always walking a tightrope. Most teams will give a player with some history of success enough rope to hang himself, but given the A's thin margin between success and failure, if the A's do that, they might be hanging themselves, too. Don't be surprised if Saarloos turns into a pumpkin and costs the A's a few games before he's sent away.

Scott Sauerbeck

Bats: R Throws: L Height: 6' 3" Weight: 200 Born: November 9, 1971 Age: 35

YEAR	TEAM	LVL	AGE	W	L	SV	G	GS	IP	H	BB	SO	HR	GB%	BABIP	STUFF	WHIP	ERA	PERA	EQERA	EQH9	EQBB9	EQSO9	EQHR9	VORP	WXRL
2005	CLE	MLB	33	1	0	0	58	0	35²	35	16	35	4	52.0%	.323	8	1.43	4.03	4.39	4.71	9.2	4.0	8.7	1.0	4.3	0.15
2006	CLE	MLB	34	0	1	0	24	0	13	9	9	11	2	37.1%	.212	5	1.38	6.23	5.94	6.08	6.1	6.1	7.4	1.4	-0.3	-0.34
2006	OAK	MLB	34	0	0	0	22	0	12¹	13	9	6	1	50.0%	.293	-21	1.78	3.66	7.72	5.11	10.2	6.6	4.4	0.7	0.4	0.23
2007	OAK	MLB	35	2	2	1	51	0	43¹	44	24	32	5	44.0%	.294	-11	1.57	5.07	4.91	4.92	8.8	4.9	6.2	1.0	2.2	0.20

Breakout: 23% Improve: 51% Collapse: 18% Attrition: 32% Comparables: Joe Gibbon, Norm Charlton, Mike Myers, Doug Henry

Leaving aside Sauerbeck's scrap with Johnny Law in late May (when he was still with the Indians), you have to look at his 2006 stats and wonder: "What's the point?" In 46 games, Sauerbeck faced only 121 batters, which is an odd ratio even for a LOOGY, and he wasn't good against lefties, which might be why he's still looking for work at this writing. He'll be back because he's held left-handed hitters to a .199 batting average on his career, and if he can limit the drinking and driving and hiding in bushes to maybe once every other season or so he'll still be pitching in five years.

Huston Street

Bats: R Throws: R   Height: 6' 0"   Weight: 190   Born: August 2, 1983   Age: 23

YEAR	TEAM	LVL	AGE	W	L	SV	G	GS	IP	H	BB	SO	HR	GB%	BABIP	STUFF	WHIP	ERA	PERA	EQERA	EQH9	EQBB9	EQSO9	EQHR9	VORP	WXRL
2005	OAK	MLB	21	5	1	23	67	0	78¹	53	26	72	3	43.8%	.253	35	1.01	1.72	2.97	2.05	6.5	3.0	8.1	0.3	33.3	4.36
2006	OAK	MLB	22	4	4	37	69	0	70²	64	13	67	4	39.1%	.303	30	1.09	3.31	2.74	3.24	7.7	1.5	8.0	0.5	19.7	3.26
2007	OAK	MLB	23	4	5	28	57	0	63²	59	18	57	7	42.0%	.286	15	1.21	3.29	3.32	3.17	7.9	2.5	7.6	0.9	16.8	2.50

Breakout: 19% Improve: 36% Collapse: 37% Attrition: 21%   Comparables: Brian Fisher, Chad Cordero, Scott Williamson, Elias Sosa

Despite two separate and unrelated 15-day DL stints, Street's sophomore season must be considered a success, as he maintained his strikeout rate, cut his walk rate in half, and racked up 37 saves. He did give up more hits, but he'd been hit-lucky in 2005, so that shouldn't have surprised anybody. The only item of concern was Street's 11 blown saves, which is a lot; the only other major leaguer with more than 10 blown saves was Kansas City's Ambiorix Burgos, who shouldn't have been in a position to blow saves in the first place. Looking at all of Street's numbers, though, there's every reason to think all those blown saves were as much due to bad luck as anything else, and he figures to rank among the league's better closers this season.

Jason Windsor

Bats: R Throws: R   Height: 6' 2"   Weight: 235   Born: July 16, 1982   Age: 24

YEAR	TEAM	LVL	AGE	W	L	SV	G	GS	IP	H	BB	SO	HR	GB%	BABIP	STUFF	WHIP	ERA	PERA	EQERA	EQH9	EQBB9	EQSO9	EQHR9	VORP	WXRL
2005	STO	A+	22	2	2	0	10	10	55¹	52	8	64	5	38.4%	.326	19	1.08	3.58	3.96	4.63	8.3	1.4	6.4	1.1	6.1	—
2005	MID	AA	22	3	6	0	11	11	56²	69	23	39	5	37.1%	.348	-7	1.62	5.71	5.35	6.63	10.6	4.1	4.6	1.1	-6.5	—
2006	MID	AA	23	4	1	0	6	6	33¹	27	10	35	2	48.2%	.305	21	1.12	2.99	3.68	3.82	7.6	2.7	6.8	0.8	6.5	—
2006	SAC	AAA	23	13	1	0	20	20	118	128	32	123	7	46.2%	.356	29	1.36	3.81	3.39	4.24	9.3	2.3	7.1	0.7	18.3	—
2006	OAK	MLB	23	0	1	0	4	3	13²	21	5	6	2	42.0%	.396	-19	1.90	6.57	4.95	6.91	12.6	3.1	3.8	1.3	-3.1	-0.21
2007	OAK	MLB	24	7	8	0	30	18	120²	133	40	85	16	43.0%	.308	7	1.44	5.02	4.70	4.85	9.4	2.9	6.0	1.0	7.4	1.50

Breakout: 17% Improve: 50% Collapse: 15% Attrition: 1%   Comparables: John Stephens, Sidney Ponson, Kelvim Escobar, Don Aase

Windsor's stuff has been described as "fringe-average," a term that doesn't seem particularly specific but doesn't exactly suggest future greatness. Nevertheless, his stats have been fine and he reached the majors just a bit more than two years after the A's drafted him. He was on a short leash, and returned to Sacramento after a couple of July starts. He did get another quick shot in September, but struggled again. Windsor earned some goodwill with that 13–1 record in the PCL, and he's got a good a chance to overtake Kirk Saarloos as the team's shaky-but-cheap swingman.

Jay Witasick

Bats: R Throws: R   Height: 6' 4"   Weight: 240   Born: August 28, 1972   Age: 34

YEAR	TEAM	LVL	AGE	W	L	SV	G	GS	IP	H	BB	SO	HR	GB%	BABIP	STUFF	WHIP	ERA	PERA	EQERA	EQH9	EQBB9	EQSO9	EQHR9	VORP	WXRL
2004	SDN	MLB	31	0	1	1	44	0	61²	57	26	57	8	—	.290	4	1.35	3.21	4.30	4.31	8.3	3.3	7.3	1.1	10.1	-0.20
2005	COL	MLB	32	0	4	0	32	0	35²	27	12	40	2	53.9%	.287	29	1.09	2.52	3.08	2.43	6.3	2.7	9.0	0.5	11.4	0.91
2005	OAK	MLB	32	1	1	1	28	0	27²	26	17	33	2	47.4%	.324	24	1.55	3.25	3.99	4.88	9.1	5.5	10.7	0.7	2.7	0.19
2006	OAK	MLB	33	1	0	0	20	0	22²	25	21	23	3	45.5%	.349	11	2.03	6.74	5.59	6.17	9.6	7.7	8.5	1.2	-1.7	0.21
2007	OAK	MLB	34	2	2	1	37	0	42	41	22	36	4	46.0%	.298	0	1.48	4.33	4.32	4.21	8.2	4.5	7.2	0.8	6.0	0.50

Breakout: 31% Improve: 56% Collapse: 19% Attrition: 21%   Comparables: Don Larsen, Don McMahon, Tim Stoddard, Danny Cox

Witasick's 2006 was wiped out by a couple of long DL stints due to an injured left ankle. When he did pitch, he was awful. Still, Witasick's arm is fine, and there are a lot of teams that could find a place in the bullpen for a pitcher with his track record.

Barry Zito

Bats: L Throws: L   Height: 6' 4"   Weight: 210   Born: May 13, 1978   Age: 29

YEAR	TEAM	LVL	AGE	W	L	SV	G	GS	IP	H	BB	SO	HR	GB%	BABIP	STUFF	WHIP	ERA	PERA	EQERA	EQH9	EQBB9	EQSO9	EQHR9	VORP	WXRL
2004	OAK	MLB	26	11	11	0	34	34	213	216	81	163	28	—	.299	12	1.39	4.48	4.42	4.58	9.0	3.1	6.4	1.0	32.5	4.64
2005	OAK	MLB	27	14	13	0	35	35	228¹	185	89	171	26	42.0%	.249	15	1.20	3.86	4.55	4.20	7.8	3.5	6.7	1.0	41.1	5.48
2006	OAK	MLB	28	16	10	0	34	34	221	211	99	151	27	39.8%	.287	9	1.40	3.83	4.89	3.68	8.2	3.8	5.7	1.0	49.9	6.07
2007	SFN	MLB	29	11	11	0	30	30	194	187	76	154	22	42.0%	.287	14	1.36	4.20	4.60	4.45	8.2	3.1	6.3	0.9	28.5	4.40

Breakout: 2% Improve: 28% Collapse: 22% Attrition: 1%   Comparables: Chuck Finley, Wilson Alvarez, Vinegar Bend Mizell, John Smiley

Zito has become the mound version of Derek Jeter: Overrated by some, underrated by many others. Zito started 34 or 35 games in each of the last six seasons, and his ERA has been well below the league average in five of those six. Zito would be the best or second-best starter on a fair number of teams. That said, his curveball isn't what it once was, and he certainly has benefited from his home ballpark and, in recent seasons, Oakland's solid defense behind him. Zito signed a seven-year deal with the Giants in December, with a club option for 2014. While it's clear what Zito was thinking—stay in the Bay Area while still making lots of money—it's less obvious what the Giants were trying to accomplish by adorning their aging roster with this good but hardly destiny-altering pitcher.

Lineouts

PLAYER	TEAM	LVL	AGE	PA	R	2B	3B	HR	RBI	BB	SO	SB-CS	SPEED	AVG/OBP/SLG	MLVr	EqAVG/EqOBP/EqSLG	EqA	VORP
3B J. Baisley	KNC	A	23	545	86	35	1	22	110	62	86	6-1	4.3	.298/.382/.519	.275	.240/.302/.415	.248	7.7
OF D. Clark*	SAC	AAA	30	574	93	22	2	15	67	57	104	25-8	6.3	.287/.366/.431	.125	.273/.336/.398	.259	-1.4
1B B. Colamarino*	MID	AA	25	568	69	35	8	17	91	60	109	2-2	4.8	.285/.364/.491	.154	.252/.315/.418	.254	-1.2
INF M. Kiger	MID	AA	26	283	43	12	3	6	20	30	58	7-2	6.3	.307/.379/.450	.142	.266/.323/.367	.244	3.3
	SAC	AAA	26	216	34	8	0	3	14	30	47	4-1	5.6	.233/.348/.330	-.087	.224/.324/.317	.236	-1.5
3B S. McClain	SAC	AAA	34	605	84	33	0	28	107	48	117	7-4	4.4	.252/.313/.466	.054	.207/.253/.349	.210	-24.9
SS C. Pennington#	STO	A+	22	202	36	7	0	2	21	24	35	7-1	5.7	.203/.302/.277	-.284	.175/.252/.224	.182	-17.8
INF G. Petit	STO	A+	21	576	71	25	7	8	63	38	96	22-13	6.0	.256/.310/.378	-.092	.234/.275/.333	.217	-19.0
LF B. Stavisky*	MID	AA	26	399	60	22	2	6	49	64	53	3-1	4.6	.316/.429/.450	.231	.282/.375/.392	.273	6.5
	SAC	AAA	26	126	16	6	0	2	8	16	23	0-0	3.9	.239/.333/.349	-.085	.225/.310/.315	.225	-6.9
CF C. Thomas*	SAC	AAA	27	434	58	8	2	9	43	38	77	8-9	5.2	.274/.350/.376	.010	.270/.334/.369	.244	4.1

PLAYER	TEAM	LVL	AGE	W	L	SV	IP	H	BB	SO	HR	GB%	BABIP	STUFF	WHIP	ERA	PERA	EqERA	EqH9	EqBB9	EqSO9	EqHR9	VORP
D. Braden*	ATH	Rk	22	2	0	0	21²	12	3	36	0	—	.364	20	0.71	0.85	2.69	1.77	7.1	1.8	7.1	0.4	8.6
	STO	A+	22	2	0	0	13	12	5	17	3	—	.300	0	1.31	6.23	9.20	7.30	10.2	4.4	7.3	3.6	-2.3
T. Cahill	ATH	Rk	18	0	0	0	9	2	7	11	0	—	.118	9	1.00	3.00	5.67	5.19	2.1	8.3	5.2	0.0	0.4
C. Italiano	KNC	A	19	0	1	0	18²	18	9	23	1	—	.378	9	1.48	3.46	6.08	7.27	10.9	5.7	6.7	1.0	-3.2
R. Keisler*	SAC	AAA	30	9	5	0	103	107	47	82	2	—	.333	15	1.50	3.84	4.04	4.97	8.8	4.1	5.1	0.3	7.4
	OAK	MLB	30	0	0	0	10	14	2	5	3	—	.344	-19	1.60	4.50	6.15	4.35	11.3	1.7	4.4	2.6	1.8
J. Lansford	KNC	A	19	11	6	0	104¹	87	42	50	1	—	.271	8	1.24	2.85	5.12	4.81	7.4	4.5	2.5	0.2	9.0
	STO	A+	19	0	1	0	11	23	5	9	4	—	.422	-29	2.55	13.09	11.19	17.18	19.6	4.1	4.9	5.7	-14.2
V. Mazzaro	KNC	A	19	9	9	0	119²	146	42	81	7	—	.363	-17	1.58	5.06	5.95	8.08	11.7	4.0	3.6	1.3	-32.2
M. Roney	SAC	AAA	26	4	3	6	58²	58	19	65	4	—	.351	10	1.32	2.94	3.85	4.25	8.9	2.9	7.6	0.8	8.9
B. Ziegler	MID	AA	26	9	6	0	141²	151	37	88	17	—	.307	-19	1.33	3.38	5.84	4.67	9.8	2.6	3.7	1.6	14.5
	SAC	AAA	26	0	1	0	21¹	32	5	11	3	—	.387	-15	1.75	5.97	5.54	7.06	12.9	2.1	3.3	1.7	-3.5

Jeff Basiley led the Midwest League in total bases, runs, and RBIs, but he also turned 24 in December. We've seen performances like that from older college players in Low-A before, and usually very little comes of it. **Doug Clark**, all 30 years of him, picked up his first major league hit (a single up the middle off Clay Hensley) and his first major league stolen base on June 28. Both were also his last of the season, and quite likely of his major league career. **Brant Colamarino**, five-foot-ten and 220-some pounds, is yet another of the Athletics' young prospective DHs who've yet to distinguish themselves in the minors. Having made his big-league debut in postseason play, **Mark Kiger** secured his place in trivia history, but he'll be hard-pressed to give you a second reason to remember him. **Scott McClain** hit 28 homers with Sacramento last year, giving him 302 as a professional—all 302 of them coming in the minors or Japan. He's probably tired of smart-alecks like us calling him "Crash." Signed by San Francisco and invited to spring training, he's just 34, which will make him the fresh-faced kid in the Giants' elderly clubhouse. **Cliff Pennington**, was the 21st overall pick in the 2005 draft out of Texas A&M, and held his own that summer in the Midwest League. Last year he hit just .203 in the California League and saw his season derailed by a bad hamstring. **Gregorio Petit** is an outstanding defender at any infield position and just might have enough bat in the end to be a solid utility player. **Brian Stavisky** is sort of an older, poor man's Daric Barton. He has a .404 career OBP in the minors, but he can't run, he can't throw, he turns 27 this July, and his power is not impressive for an older player whose only tool is his bat. **Charles Thomas** probably won't get much space when Billy Beane writes his autobiography as Beane was apparently fooled by the only good season of Thomas's professional career.

With the retirement of Jim Mecir in 2005, it seemed that we had seen the last of the screwball pitchers, but **Dallas Braden** is just such a rare creature. Sadly, he's coming off shoulder surgery, and the pitch is really his only plus offering, so the breed remains on the endangered species list. Just as they did in 2005, the A's went against their supposed type and used a number of their early draft picks to select high school players last June. Their first pick—the 66th overall because, also against type, they surrendered their first-rounder by signing Esteban Loaiza—was young **Trevor Cahill**, who threw 84-mile-per-hour fastballs as a high-school junior, but somehow added ten ticks to his heater as a senior. In addition to the fastball, Cahill throws a knucklecurve, a changeup, and a slider, but, like most hard-throwing high schoolers, he's never had to worry much about off-speed stuff. The first of the many high school pitchers the A's took in the 2005 draft, **Craig Italiano** threw as hard as anybody in high school that spring, but fell to the second round because of a supposedly minor shoulder injury and worries about his mechanics. The logical conclusion to the first part of his professional career came last May, when doctors operated on his labrum. Italiano was throwing again this winter and is expected back for spring training, but at this point his future probably lies in the bullpen. **Randy Keisler** has to be a left-handed pitcher, doesn't he? Can you imagine somebody named "Randy Keisler" playing shortstop, or center field? Anyway, he's made for Triple-A and he's signed with the Cardinals. The son of former A's star Carney, **Jared Lansford** limited opposing batters to a .236 average in the Midwest League and even spun a seven-inning no-hitter, but his disturbingly low strikeout rate has given concern to both scouts and analysts alike. One of the prep draftees from 2005, **Vince Mazzaro**'s raw numbers fail to impress, but he was the rawest of the bunch, and he induced a lot of ground balls with a sinker-curve mix. Since moving to the bullpen full-time in 2005, **Matt Roney**'s Triple-A ERA has been 2.50 in 119 innings. Given his stuff, one wonders how Roney does as well as he does, but adequate tools and good smarts play well in the minors. Signed as a minor league free agent by the Blue Jays, he'll compete for the eleventh or twelfth spot on their staff this spring. Picked up in 2004 off the indy league scrapheap, **Brad Ziegler** has put up some decent numbers in the minors. The A's are trying to turn him into the next Chad Bradford with a conversion to throwing submarine style.

Manager: Ken Macha

Year	Team	W-L	Pythag +/-	Avg PC	100 +P	120 +P	QS	BQS	REL	REL w Zero R	IBB	SUBS	PH	PH Avg	PH HR	SB2	CS2	SB3	CS3	SAC Att	SAC %	POS SAC	Squeeze	Swing	In Play
2004	OAK	91-71	+5	101.3	96	9	78	10	414	279	49	26	120	.182	3	41	19	6	2	35	71.4%	25	0	95	73
2005	OAK	88-74	-4	97.2	71	4	87	8	410	258	42	15	82	.157	0	29	20	2	1	34	55.9%	18	0	117	91
2006	OAK	93-69	+7	98.6	78	6	75	5	444	285	47	29	62	.154	1	56	19	4	1	32	78.1%	22	0	121	97

Ken Macha was fired shortly after the A's were knocked out of the postseason by the Twins. According to the San Francisco Chronicle's Susan Slusser, "Macha's problems communicating with players, along with what injured players have described as a callous attitude toward them," provoked the move. Backup catcher Adam Melhuse must be thrilled that Bob Geren is Macha's successor. Not only was Geren a backup catcher himself, but Melhuse was one of Macha's most vocal post-firing critics. Was the switch all about personal management style? Most likely. Tactically, Macha managed like Oakland's manager is expected to manage. The A's ranked 12th in the AL in stolen-base attempts, third in stolen-base percentage, and 13th in sacrifice-hit attempts. He also did a good job adjusting to the injuries that hobbled Rich Harden, Justin Duchscherer, and various key hitters last year, and won nearly 57 percent of his games over four seasons. His firing was all about keeping the players happy. What does Bob Geren know about managing? From 1989 through 1991, he played for Dallas Green, Bucky Dent, and Stump Merrill, who presided over the Yankees' worst three-season stretch since Wally Pipp was a rookie. In 1992 with San Diego, Geren played for Jim Riggleman. Maybe he learned what *not* to do. Prior to joining the A's major-league staff, Geren managed in the minor leagues for seven seasons, and his teams won 54 percent of their games. Here's something you probably don't know, and probably should forget immediately: Geren shares a birthday with Bob Lemon, Tommy Lasorda, and Larry Dierker. Here's something you probably know, and will be told again a few hundred times this season: Geren, a San Diego native, played baseball against Billy Beane in high school, and the two have been friends for many years. One wonders if Beane, when the time comes, will be as willing to send Geren away as he was Art Howe and Macha.

Philadelphia Phillies

Pat Gillick has earned his reputation as one of the best front office honchos of his generation. His signal achievement was guiding the Blue Jays for 17 years, elevating them from expansion laughingstock to repeat world champs. He followed that with gigs in Baltimore and Seattle, in both places helping talented teams achieve their unrealized potential, reaching the playoffs in each of his first two years at the helm of both teams.

Success bred expectations. In each case, Gillick elected to take a step back. He fulfilled the third year of his contract with the Orioles, then put Clan Angelos in his rearview mirror. He stepped down after four years as Mariners general manager to take on an advisory role. In each instance, Gillick was reverting to what might be seen as his first love, player development, reflecting his status as one of the game's definitive "baseball men." Having been spurned in his attempt to land the Nationals job and end his latest semi-retirement, Gillick was signed on with the Phillies in November 2005.

The Phillies were in need of a man of Gillick's broad experience as both a player development guru and a Billy Martin of the boardroom who could deliver immediate success. Picking Gillick as general manager also prevented the organization from having to make the uncomfortable choice between its two well-regarded Assistant General Managers, Mike Arbuckle and Ruben Amaro. Picking one might have cost them the services of the other, and there's more than enough work to be done to make the resulting brain drain all the more regrettable. Gillick was one of the few executives available from the outside who was long enough in the tooth to not kill off either man's ambitions, but also had the track record required to lead them.

> ## PHILLIES PROSPECTUS
>
> **2006 record:** 85–77; Second place, NL East
>
> **Pythagenport record:** 85–77
>
> **Runs scored per game:** 5.34 (1st in NL)
>
> **Runs allowed per game:** 5.01 (12th in NL)
>
> **Team EqA:** .268 (3rd in NL)
>
> **2006 Batters Age:** 29.7 (8th youngest in NL)
>
> **2006 Pitchers Age:** 30.5 (3rd oldest in NL)
>
> **Ballpark:** Citizens Bank Park; Moderate hitter's park; Park Factor of 1.031
>
> **2006:** Ryan Howard makes an entire league look like Jose Lima.
>
> **2007:** Some faceless lineup members are going to have to step up to help a balanced but unspectacular team win the division.

Three weeks into the job, Gillick solved the club's most pressing issue, picking the first baseman the organization had developed over the star his predecessor had signed. Nevertheless, trading Jim Thome was not necessarily an indicator that Gillick was predisposed to tear this team down—the acquisition of Aaron Rowand from the defending World Champion White Sox was intended to fill vacancy in center field that had existed more or less since injuries brought an early end to Lenny Dykstra's career. Rowand also gave the Phillies a center fielder who could help cover the gaps, all the more important in an outfield in which neither Bobby Abreu nor Pat Burrell was known for his glove-work (Abreu was felt to be wall-shy, while Burrell's range was so limited that the wall was more likely to come to him than he was to go to it).

Rowand was an appropriate addition to a team with a core of talent that really wasn't all that young. Abreu had been a Philly regular for eight years, Burrell had been the same for six, and "new kid" Jimmy Rollins already had five full seasons to his credit. Even the team's less experienced cornerstones—Brett Myers, Ryan Madson, Chase Utley, and Ryan Howard—were in the act of passing out of their baseball youth and/or already had a couple of seasons under their belts. Despite the effort the organization had put into overhauling its player development system, there weren't many players close to joining the homegrown Rollins-Burrell-Utley-Howard core. The list of top-flight prospects began and ended with Cole Hamels, and even he seemed to be as fragile as a debutante on her first date.

Confronted by the reality of a team with limited horizons, Gillick decided to give former GM Ed Wade's charges another shot. Rather than attempt an overhaul, he settled for a few discrete additions. To the bullpen he added former Mariner starter Ryan Franklin and a pair of veteran relievers, closer-to-be Flash Gordon and lefty Arthur Rhodes. To the bench he added utility infielder Abraham Nuñez, and outfielder David Dellucci. Other than Rhodes, who was acquired from the Indians for displaced platoon center fielder Jason Michaels, all were free agents signings. Other than Gordon, only major change to the roster was the addition of Rowand via Gillicks resolution of the first base situation. Believing that he had bolstered the team for contention, Gillick talked about the two things no Phillie team had done since the 1993 pennant winners: winning 90 games and making the playoffs.

It all sounded plausible and of a part with his previous pair of quick franchise fix-ups. A little more than two months into the year, it seemed to be working out well enough—after completing its first West Coast swing, the team was 32–27, only 3.5 games behind the Mets, and in the middle of the pack in the wild card hunt. Unfortunately, it was at this point that the rotation went to pieces when Jon Lieber hit the DL with a strained groin, and Brett Myers was deactivated after being arrested for attacking his wife. Hamels was called up, but got cuffed around, and the experiment with making Ryan Madson a starter resulted in exasperating inconsistency. As July began they were completing an ugly six-series run against the Mets and the AL East in which they went 4–14. Pat Gillick was getting ready to call it quits on the Phillies' fortunes. The team had fallen to seven games under .500 after interleague play; three weeks later, that was down to eight games under. Ninety wins and the playoffs seemed unlikely. Somewhere around this point, priorities shifted, and trading Bobby Abreu became Gillick's most important task.

Dealing the team's biggest star made sense in that it could benefit the team one of two ways—either a return in talent or in the financial flexibility that would allow Gillick to make more significant upgrades in the pursuit of the 2007 postseason. As is often the case for the latter, the Yankees proved the best match—they took almost $34 million off of the Phillies books, and threw the Phillies a quartet of forget-me-nots whose contributions to the franchise's fortunes seem mostly notional. In the last week of July, Gillick dealt Abreu as well as David Bell, Rheal Cormier, and Sal Fasano, or his right fielder and number-three hitter, his third baseman, his best lefty reliever, and his backup catcher. Those are the sorts of players contenders acquire, not deal away. Indeed, Fasano preceded Abreu in the Yankee clubhouse. As Gillick said at the time, "This group had an opportunity to win here for a period of time, but it didn't work out. The other thing is, we want to give some people opportunities to play, people we haven't gotten a real good look at." The ensuing weeks proved that Gillick had been referring to

players such as his offseason signings David Dellucci and Abraham Nuñez—not exactly a youth movement.

As the lights dimmed on the games of July 31, the standings in the National League were a model of agglutination. Beyond the Mets (63–41) and Cardinals (58–46), twelve teams were clumped between 47 and 55 wins. With 49 victories, the Phillies were towards the bottom of the pile, but still viable. At that moment, the Phillies offense caught fire—something it might just as easily have done with Abreu still there, though we'll never know—while the field suddenly started wiping itself out in head-to-head play. Gillick came to recognize that with everyone else falling out of the race, his team was still effectively in it. In a radical change of course, just nineteen days after cleaning house, Gillick shored up the club, adding Jamie Moyer to stabilize the rotation, Jeff Conine to compensate for Rowand's season-ending ankle injury, and utility man Jose Hernandez to add some right-handed pinch-hitting pop to the bench. The Phillies clambered back up to .500 by the end of August.

The Phillies' sudden turn is a portent of the possibilities in the wild-card era: dumping is not defeat; there is no such thing as a white flag trade. The simple dichotomy of contending or dumping is, for midmarket ballclubs, a mirage. This is particularly true if the year happens to be one of parity, which was certainly true of the National League in 2006. No team was great (not even the Mets). No team was extremely bad. The 1906 Cubs did not bestride the landscape, dominating all. Instead, a sudden hot or cold streak took on unusual importance. Ten days of good play could rewrite the entire race.

For the Phillies, the high-water mark came on September 23, after they had completed a sweep of the Marlins and stood only a half-game behind the Dodgers for the wild card with seven games to play. Unfortunately, a suddenly-necessary makeup-date loss to the Astros, followed by the team dropping two out of three to the Nationals, halted their momentum and killed off their belated dreams of grandeur. The Phillies posted the league's fourth-best record, but they were done.

Historically, Gillick's decision to deal Abreu is comparable to Bing Devine's famous decision to deal Ernie Broglio to the Cubs for Lou Brock. When Devine pulled the trigger on that deal on June 15, 1964 (then the trading deadline), the Cardinals were seemingly mired in eighth place (out of ten teams) at 28–30. Broglio was an established ace and the club's Opening Day starter. The Cubs were ahead of St. Louis in the standings, and Devine was only two months away from a decision to resign in the face of Branch Rickey's attempts to take the general manager's chair one last time. No one could have expected Brock to be part of a 65–39 run that elevated the Cardinals to the pennant and then a World Series win. The difference between the two deals isn't limited to the distinction that the 1964 Cardinals won the World Series, while the 2006 Phillies missed out on October baseball. In "dumping" Broglio, the Cardinals got Brock, who, freed from the Friendly Confines, terrorized the National League by hitting .348/.387/.527 for the rest of the season. In two-thirds of a season, Brock was easily the Cardinals' best hitter, and the team found ways to replace Broglio in the rotation sufficient to keep their bid for greatness going.

That wasn't the way dealing Abreu worked out, but it also wasn't the objective in dealing him. The nature of the competitive environment has changed; Gillick was buying flexibility for 2007, not swapping pros for prospects. He couldn't have known that his team was going to be one of the ones that would break out of the pack. While you could argue that the unhappy coincidences of a rough part of the schedule and seeing his rotation go to pieces in June were unusually discouraging, and that Gillick could have kept faith that things would bounce back, he made a tough call.

The only way to evaluate that decision fairly is to examine what he's done with the financial muscle dealing Abreu gave him. However many times the old man says he loves player development best, he knows that his stack of tomorrows isn't much higher than Rollins's or Utley's or Howard's. To his credit, Gillick has exploited this newfound strength, and the Phillies' winter has been exceptionally busy. He's signed Adam Eaton and re-upped Jamie Moyer

to help fill out the rotation, and dealt for Freddy Garcia (taking on somebody else's salary dump) to front it. With those three added to incumbents Myers and Lieber, the Phillies could have the best rotation in the league, though the expectation is that one starter (probably the slothful Lieber) will be dealt to make sure there's space for Hamels. On offense, he's settled for modest patching so far, signing Rod Barajas to replace Mike Lieberthal, and Wes Helms to give the team an upgrade on David Bell at third; the lineup will, at the very least, hold its ground in both spots, though the chances of improvement are slight.

The business left undone is replacing Abreu himself. Having lost Dellucci to free agency and dealt the 40-year-old Conine to Cincinnati, the Phillies are still short a right fielder as we go to press. Gillick initially played for high stakes, trying to acquire Manny Ramirez from the Red Sox. Even that would be a zero-sum exercise, as the various iterations of the deal would have involved sending Pat Burrell to Boston, leaving Philly still short one starting outfielder. That really leaves the starter-for-an-outfielder scenario, especially since the Abreu dividend seems spent. Gillick could always option Hamels to the minors and see whether or not his team can get by with Shane Victorino or Jayson Werth; if not, finding a rental veteran outfielder coming to the end of a contract is one of the easier things a GM can pull off at the trading deadline. Regardless, the rotation Gillick has assembled should provide the club the kind of platform with which to unseat the Mets. That's the gamble Gillick took last July, and it looks to pay out this year.

HITTERS

Welinson Baez   3B   **Bats: R**   **Throws: R**   Height: 6' 3"   Weight: 190   Born: July 7, 1984   Age: 22

YEAR	TEAM	LVL	AGE	PA	R	2B	3B	HR	RBI	BB	SO	SB	CS	SPEED	AVG	OBP	SLG	MLVR	EQAVG	EQOBP	EQSLG	EQA	VORP	DEFENSE	
2005	BAT	A-	20	196	34	14	1	6	37	22	45	2	1	4.3	.324	.408	.524	.394	.283	.340	.444	.268	21.3	24-SS	-5
2006	LWD	A	21	478	48	34	3	6	51	41	158	5	5	4.4	.232	.305	.368	-.008	.215	.267	.321	.208	-21.6	118-3B	9
2007	PHI	MLB	22	445	41	26	2	11	48	30	141	3	3	4.5	.233	.289	.389	-.195	.230	.287	.380	.226	-6.8	106-3B	4

Breakout: 33%   Improve: 55%   Collapse: 28%   Attrition: 10%   Comparables: Lee Mitchell, Josh Bonifay, Kevin Eberwein, Jeff Baker

Baez had enormous problems with off-speed pitches at the start of 2006, swinging far too often at pitches out of the strike zone. By mid-summer, he started to lay off them, and the results were dramatic; after hitting .194/.254/.287 with a 37 percent strikeout rate through the first three months of 2006, he hit .286/.363/.478 the rest of the way, cutting his strikeout rate to 30 percent. That's still too often, but does get him back in line with what he did in 2005. He's a gifted third baseman, with an arm that almost made him a pitcher.

Michael Bourn — CF — Bats: L — Throws: R — Height: 5' 11" — Weight: 180 — Born: December 27, 1982 — Age: 24

YEAR	TEAM	LVL	AGE	PA	R	2B	3B	HR	RBI	BB	SO	SB	CS	SPEED	AVG	OBP	SLG	MLVR	EQAVG	EQOBP	EQSLG	EQA	VORP	DEFENSE			
2004	LWD	A	21	510	92	20	14	5	53	85	88	58	6	9.0	.315	.431	.467	.342	.303	.394	.437	.300	37.8	55-CF	0	49-RF	-3
2005	REA	AA	22	614	80	18	8	6	44	63	123	38	12	7.9	.268	.348	.364	.003	.255	.328	.346	.245	-2.9	78-CF	7	52-RF	3
2006	REA	AA	23	361	62	5	6	4	26	36	67	30	4	8.2	.274	.350	.365	.054	.269	.337	.361	.258	3.1	78-CF	0		
2006	SWB	AAA	23	174	34	5	7	1	15	20	33	15	1	8.3	.283	.368	.428	.142	.288	.368	.458	.293	11.7	27-CF	2		
2006	PHI	MLB	23	11	2	0	0	0	0	1	3	1	2	5.2	.125	.222	.125	-.669	.111	.200	.111	.141	-2.4				
2007	PHI	MLB	24	492	73	18	9	7	39	47	94	30	8	7.9	.270	.344	.401	-.055	.266	.341	.392	.261	8.6	116-CF	2		

Breakout: 7% Improve: 35% Collapse: 27% Attrition: 14% Comparables: Adam Greenberg, Mike Curry, Jeff Duncan, Tim Raines

Bourn is a fairly typical center field prospect with blazing speed and little power. He does well when he sticks to things within his skill-set—working a walk, taking a single—but has a tendency to think he's Ryan Howard when he comes up with men on base. After July, his schedule was interrupted by three separate call-ups to the majors (where he was rarely used) and by a stint on the United States's Olympic qualifying team. He could stand a full year at Triple-A, but could also step in as a reserve outfielder right away.

Pat Burrell — LF — Bats: R — Throws: R — Height: 6' 4" — Weight: 235 — Born: October 10, 1976 — Age: 30

YEAR	TEAM	LVL	AGE	PA	R	2B	3B	HR	RBI	BB	SO	SB	CS	SPEED	AVG	OBP	SLG	MLVR	EQAVG	EQOBP	EQSLG	EQA	VORP	DEFENSE	
2004	PHI	MLB	27	534	66	17	0	24	84	78	130	2	0	4.0	.257	.365	.455	.096	.253	.361	.454	.283	13.1	118-LF	4
2005	PHI	MLB	28	669	78	27	1	32	117	99	160	0	0	3.2	.281	.389	.504	.222	.275	.386	.504	.303	41.3	146-LF	-3
2006	PHI	MLB	29	567	80	24	1	29	95	98	131	0	0	3.6	.258	.388	.502	.176	.251	.385	.492	.300	27.5	109-LF	-2
2007	PHI	MLB	30	554	82	24	1	31	88	85	128	1	0	3.9	.261	.377	.522	.151	.257	.373	.511	.298	27.3	130-LF	-4

Breakout: 21% Improve: 45% Collapse: 20% Attrition: 6% Comparables: Greg Luzinski, Jay Buhner, Tom Brunansky, Tim Salmon

Fans and management alike jumped on Burrell for hitting just .222 with runners in scoring position last year. Never mind that that it isn't so far removed from his normal batting average—given 153 AB with RISP, we're talking about four, count 'em, four hits worth of difference. Burrell is not a high-average player in *any* situation. If there are men on base, especially late in a game, he's never going to face a left-handed pitcher, which is particularly notable since he has an unusually high platoon split for a righty. Using a low-average/high-strikeout hitter to protect Ryan Howard is the manager's failure, not Burrell's. The Zeno's Paradox Outfielder, in that no matter how close he seems to be to catching the ball, he's still only halfway there.

Adrian Cardenas — SS — Bats: L — Throws: R — Height: 6' 0" — Weight: 185 — Born: October 10, 1987 — Age: 18

YEAR	TEAM	LVL	AGE	PA	R	2B	3B	HR	RBI	BB	SO	SB	CS	SPEED	AVG	OBP	SLG	MLVR	EQAVG	EQOBP	EQSLG	EQA	VORP	DEFENSE	
2006	PHL	Rk	18	177	22	5	4	2	21	17	28	13	3	6.1	.318	.384	.442	.266	.292	.339	.422	.267	28.1	41-SS	-9

Cardenas was the 37th pick in last year's draft, a supplemental first-rounder from a Miami high school. His makeup couldn't be more different from his fellow first-rounders; Cardenas graduated near the top of his class and entertained guests at his draft party by playing Liszt and Gershwin on the piano. He also led his high school team to the state championship by hitting .647 and slugging 1.319, earning Baseball America's High School Player of the Year award, and finished up by raking in the GCL. He's an outstanding hitting prospect who will probably move to second in the future.

Jeff Conine — 1B/OF — Bats: R — Throws: R — Height: 6' 1" — Weight: 225 — Born: December 31, 1969 — Age: 41

YEAR	TEAM	LVL	AGE	PA	R	2B	3B	HR	RBI	BB	SO	SB	CS	SPEED	AVG	OBP	SLG	MLVR	EQAVG	EQOBP	EQSLG	EQA	VORP	DEFENSE			
2004	FLO	MLB	38	579	55	35	1	14	83	48	78	5	5	4.0	.280	.340	.432	.062	.286	.345	.441	.269	10.3	83-LF	12	56-1B	3
2005	FLO	MLB	39	384	42	20	2	3	33	38	58	2	0	4.7	.304	.374	.403	.115	.314	.384	.422	.286	15.5	29-LF	2	26-1B	-2
2006	BAL	MLB	40	432	43	20	3	9	49	35	53	3	2	4.5	.265	.325	.401	-.079	.266	.334	.409	.258	-1.7	51-1B	2	49-LF	-6
2006	PHI	MLB	40	107	11	6	1	1	17	5	12	0	0	5.0	.280	.327	.390	-.047	.280	.327	.390	.249	0.3	19-RF	-2		
2007	CIN	MLB	41	433	52	21	3	9	48	39	55	4	2	4.3	.268	.336	.403	-.068	.267	.333	.399	.253	0.4	103-LF	0		

Breakout: 4% Improve: 39% Collapse: 40% Attrition: 28% Comparables: B. J. Surhoff, Wade Boggs, Lou Piniella, Eddie Murray

The Phillies picked up the former Mr. Marlin to split time with David Dellucci in right after Shane Victorino was pressed into the center field job following a season-ending injry to Aaron Rowand in late August. While his batting average looks acceptable, without much in the way of walks or power he really didn't help. Conine's contract with the Orioles had a $2-million

(continued next page)

Jeff Conine *(continued)*

option for 2007 that vested when he reached 450 plate appearances, but Gillick avoided getting stuck with him by unloading him on the Reds. Conine will end up platooning with Scott Hatteberg at first when he isn't spot-starting for one of the outfield regulars.

Michael Costanzo   3B   **Bats: L**   **Throws: R**   Height: 6′ 3″   Weight: 215   Born: September 9, 1983   Age: 23

YEAR	TEAM	LVL	AGE	PA	R	2B	3B	HR	RBI	BB	SO	SB	CS	SPEED	AVG	OBP	SLG	MLVR	EQAVG	EQOBP	EQSLG	EQA	VORP	DEFENSE	
2005	BAT	A-	21	323	47	17	3	11	50	35	89	0	1	3.7	.274	.356	.473	.214	.232	.285	.374	.228	-6.9	68-3B	4
2006	CLR	A+	22	593	72	33	1	14	81	74	133	3	2	4.2	.258	.364	.411	.094	.236	.324	.384	.249	7.8	131-3B	4
2007	*PHI*	*MLB*	*23*	*502*	*56*	*27*	*2*	*15*	*62*	*46*	*124*	*2*	*2*	*4.4*	*.249*	*.323*	*.418*	*-.085*	*.245*	*.320*	*.408*	*.249*	*4.4*	*118-3B*	*3*

Breakout: 36% Improve: 66% Collapse: 17% Attrition: 7%   Comparables: Christian Snavely, Brett Bonvechio, Daryl Clark, Shawn McCorkle

A lifetime Phillie fan with the good fortune to have been drafted by them in the first round of the 2005 draft, Costanzo struggled through the first half of the season before finishing strong at Clearwater. Like Welinson Baez, he's a good, strong-armed defender at third; whereas Baez was nearly a pitcher, Costanzo really was one, at least in college. Offense is the problem; he's been a total bust against lefties in two years as a pro, and he hasn't hit righties enough to make up for it.

Chris Coste   C   **Bats: R**   **Throws: R**   Height: 6′ 1″   Weight: 200   Born: February 4, 1973   Age: 34

YEAR	TEAM	LVL	AGE	PA	R	2B	3B	HR	RBI	BB	SO	SB	CS	SPEED	AVG	OBP	SLG	MLVR	EQAVG	EQOBP	EQSLG	EQA	VORP	DEFENSE			
2004	IND	AAA	31	290	34	21	1	2	26	21	37	2	3	4.1	.296	.358	.408	.034	.252	.304	.327	.225	-4.7	29-3B	-3	27-C	-1
2005	SWB	AAA	32	562	73	26	1	20	89	40	85	3	4	3.4	.292	.351	.466	.110	.252	.300	.376	.235	0.3	91-3B	3	26-1B	-1
2006	SWB	AAA	33	161	12	8	0	2	14	9	28	1	1	4.5	.177	.236	.272	-.333	.113	.161	.120	.118	-35.5	25-1B	2	12-C	0
2006	PHI	MLB	33	213	25	14	0	7	32	10	31	0	0	3.5	.328	.376	.505	.233	.323	.371	.490	.292	16.5	49-C	-8		
2007	*PHI*	*MLB*	*34*	*352*	*31*	*16*	*1*	*8*	*40*	*19*	*61*	*0*	*1*	*3.7*	*.249*	*.298*	*.378*	*-.183*	*.245*	*.295*	*.370*	*.227*	*-3.5*	*85-C*	*-2*		

Breakout: 41% Improve: 57% Collapse: 25% Attrition: 35%   Comparables: Mike Matheny, Pat Borders, Brook Fordyce, Tom Pagnozzi

Coste ranks right up there with the Tigers as one of the feel-good stories of 2006. Undrafted out of college, Coste spent four years in the Northern League and didn't play his first game in the minors until age 27. He's bounced around constantly since then, both from team to team and around the field (he's played everywhere but center field). He's done whatever it took to keep playing baseball, including writing a book about his long minor league odyssey; a second tome is on its way. At the risk of spoiling the fairy tale, Coste has never been nearly as a good a hitter in the minors as he was for Philadelphia last year, and cannot be expected to repeat his performance.

David Dellucci   OF   **Bats: L**   **Throws: L**   Height: 5′ 11″   Weight: 195   Born: October 31, 1973   Age: 33

YEAR	TEAM	LVL	AGE	PA	R	2B	3B	HR	RBI	BB	SO	SB	CS	SPEED	AVG	OBP	SLG	MLVR	EQAVG	EQOBP	EQSLG	EQA	VORP	DEFENSE			
2004	TEX	MLB	30	387	59	13	1	17	61	47	88	9	4	5.5	.242	.342	.441	-.044	.231	.337	.426	.264	1.3	79-LF	-5		
2005	TEX	MLB	31	518	97	17	5	29	65	76	121	5	3	5.9	.251	.367	.513	.149	.248	.375	.519	.299	28.2	43-LF	-1		
2006	PHI	MLB	32	301	41	14	5	13	39	28	62	1	3	5.7	.292	.369	.530	.215	.288	.365	.527	.294	17.7	31-LF	0	21-RF	-3
2007	*CLE*	*MLB*	*33*	*258*	*36*	*12*	*1*	*10*	*34*	*30*	*57*	*3*	*1*	*5.9*	*.251*	*.346*	*.450*	*.006*	*.248*	*.347*	*.460*	*.283*	*6.2*				

Breakout: 6% Improve: 26% Collapse: 35% Attrition: 21%   Comparables: John Lowenstein, Ray Lankford, Jim Dwyer, Charlie Keller

This was a bit of an odd exchange for the Phillies, and a tough one for Dellucci to adjust to. He went from being Texas's primary DH to pinch-hitting. He rotted on the bench for the first four months of the season, unable to get any regular playing time until after Bobby Abreu was traded to the Yankees at the deadline. Once he was turned loose, he hit just as well as he had in 2005, and his hot streak was part of what kick-started the team's return to contention. He's with the Indians this year on a fresh three-year contract as their presumptive regular left fielder, although probably in a platoon with fellow former Phillie Jason Michaels.

Greg Golson   CF   **Bats: R**   **Throws: R**   Height: 6′ 0″   Weight: 190   Born: September 17, 1985   Age: 21

YEAR	TEAM	LVL	AGE	PA	R	2B	3B	HR	RBI	BB	SO	SB	CS	SPEED	AVG	OBP	SLG	MLVR	EQAVG	EQOBP	EQSLG	EQA	VORP	DEFENSE	
2005	LWD	A	19	409	51	19	8	4	27	26	106	25	9	8.2	.264	.322	.389	.036	.246	.285	.345	.224	-12.2	89-CF	-7
2006	LWD	A	20	419	56	15	4	7	31	19	107	23	7	7.8	.220	.258	.333	-.138	.204	.231	.290	.191	-36.5	92-CF	-5
2006	CLR	A+	20	174	31	11	2	6	17	11	53	7	3	7.1	.264	.324	.472	.118	.247	.299	.444	.252	2.8	37-CF	3
2007	*PHI*	*MLB*	*21*	*490*	*50*	*23*	*4*	*10*	*46*	*22*	*124*	*15*	*8*	*6.6*	*.235*	*.275*	*.369*	*-.247*	*.232*	*.272*	*.361*	*.216*	*-12.6*	*116-CF*	*1*

Breakout: 45% Improve: 67% Collapse: 16% Attrition: 7%   Comparables: Julio Ramirez, Chris Aguila, Tim Lemon, Reggie Taylor

In a nutshell, everything about being a baseball player that comes from athletic ability is something Golson has; everything else is missing. He has bat speed, power, a strong throwing arm, and runs well, all pluses. Unfortunately, he doesn't recognize pitches, has no concept of the strike zone, has a mechanically awful swing, can't read a pitcher's move so as to leverage his speed into stolen bases, and takes bad routes in the outfield. He's young enough to harness his raw talent, but that's quite the bronco for him to have to bust.

C. J. Henry   **SS**   **Bats: R**   **Throws: R**   Height: 6' 3"   Weight: 205   Born: May 31, 1986   Age: 20

YEAR	TEAM	LVL	AGE	PA	R	2B	3B	HR	RBI	BB	SO	SB	CS	SPEED	AVG	OBP	SLG	MLVR	EQAVG	EQOBP	EQSLG	EQA	VORP	DEFENSE	
2006	CSC	A	20	316	35	19	3	2	33	32	86	14	4	5.9	.240	.330	.353	-.019	.220	.283	.314	.216	-10.1	56-SS	-5
2006	LWD	A	20	99	13	3	4	1	16	7	25	1	0	5.8	.253	.313	.407	.071	.245	.283	.372	.225	-0.5	25-SS	-6
2007	*PHI*	*MLB*	*21*	*517*	*54*	*25*	*6*	*6*	*42*	*31*	*129*	*13*	*6*	*6.0*	*.240*	*.289*	*.356*	*-.235*	*.236*	*.286*	*.348*	*.218*	*-1.4*	*122-SS*	*-9*

Breakout: 47% Improve: 66% Collapse: 18% Attrition: 14%   *Comparables: Dennis Abreu, Enrique Cruz, Irwin Centeno, Bryan Bass*

Henry was the Yankees' 2005 first-rounder, and, on paper, he's the prize from the Abreu trade. He's very much the kind of prospect Gillick is excited by: Fast, strong-armed, rangy, and still pretty far from growing up to be a baseball player. His full-season debut in the Sally League was disappointing, and he's unreliable in the field, but he's supposed to have the physical tools to be a good shortstop. It remains to be seen if he'll ever be able to hit a quality breaking pitch. Gillick's betting on his athleticism—if it works, Henry's sort of a bigger Jimmy Rollins, and if it doesn't, Gillick got bupkis for a star.

Jose Hernandez   **1B**   **Bats: R**   **Throws: R**   Height: 6' 1"   Weight: 190   Born: December 31, 1969   Age: 37

YEAR	TEAM	LVL	AGE	PA	R	2B	3B	HR	RBI	BB	SO	SB	CS	SPEED	AVG	OBP	SLG	MLVR	EQAVG	EQOBP	EQSLG	EQA	VORP	DEFENSE			
2004	LAN	MLB	34	238	32	12	1	13	29	26	61	3	1	5.0	.289	.370	.540	.256	.289	.370	.550	.304	21.3	39-2B	-3		
2005	CLE	MLB	35	256	28	7	0	6	31	14	60	1	3	3.6	.231	.277	.338	-.224	.235	.292	.348	.223	-10.4	38-1B	0	18-3B	0
2006	PIT	MLB	36	132	8	2	1	2	12	11	29	0	0	3.9	.267	.328	.350	-.115	.267	.333	.350	.242	-0.7	11-1B	0		
2006	PHI	MLB	36	34	4	2	0	1	7	1	11	0	0	3.7	.250	.273	.406	-.143	.250	.273	.406	.230	-0.4				
2007	*PIT*	*MLB*	*37*	*113*	*10*	*4*	*1*	*2*	*13*	*9*	*28*	*1*	*0*	*4.2*	*.239*	*.299*	*.357*	*-.216*	*.234*	*.295*	*.355*	*.223*	*-1.4*				

Breakout: 11% Improve: 23% Collapse: 55% Attrition: 46%   *Comparables: Hubie Brooks, Jim Piersall, Joel Youngblood, Hank Majeski*

Hernandez used to be able to play anywhere, but he's been shifted to the corners with age. He used to be able to provide a power bat for those willing to overlook his strikeouts, but has only slugged .347 over the last two years. He might find a team for 2007, and maybe he can still shock us like he did in 2004, but you'd have to be high on Pop Rocks to bet on it.

Ryan Howard   **1B**   **Bats: L**   **Throws: L**   Height: 6' 4"   Weight: 250   Born: November 19, 1979   Age: 27

YEAR	TEAM	LVL	AGE	PA	R	2B	3B	HR	RBI	BB	SO	SB	CS	SPEED	AVG	OBP	SLG	MLVR	EQAVG	EQOBP	EQSLG	EQA	VORP	DEFENSE	
2004	REA	AA	24	433	73	18	1	37	102	46	129	1	2	3.5	.297	.386	.647	.417	.275	.348	.575	.299	34.8	97-1B	2
2004	SWB	AAA	24	127	21	10	0	9	29	14	37	0	0	3.6	.270	.362	.604	.286	.250	.339	.554	.290	7.7	28-1B	0
2004	PHI	MLB	24	42	5	5	0	2	5	2	13	0	0	3.3	.282	.333	.564	.237	.282	.333	.538	.287	2.9		
2005	SWB	AAA	25	257	38	19	0	16	54	39	66	0	0	2.1	.371	.467	.690	.676	.355	.446	.645	.356	43.5	57-1B	-5
2005	PHI	MLB	25	348	52	17	2	22	63	33	100	0	1	4.6	.288	.356	.567	.265	.284	.356	.568	.302	23.5	80-1B	4
2006	PHI	MLB	26	704	104	25	1	58	149	108	181	0	0	3.9	.313	.425	.659	.492	.306	.420	.646	.344	81.5	157-1B	-15
2007	*PHI*	*MLB*	*27*	*660*	*110*	*33*	*1*	*47*	*130*	*82*	*175*	*0*	*1*	*3.8*	*.297*	*.391*	*.612*	*.326*	*.293*	*.388*	*.598*	*.322*	*55.8*	*154-1B*	*-6*

Breakout: 16% Improve: 37% Collapse: 19% Attrition: 0%   *Comparables: Mo Vaughn, Travis Hafner, Mike Epstein, Boog Powell*

Ryan Howard is a big, really big, reason why the Phillies need to go for broke in the short term. Historically, players like Howard, big-bodied guys with limited defensive skills such as Mo Vaughn and Boog Powell, tended to have high but brief peak periods. Their legs just couldn't carry that much mass for very long, and around 30 their defense plummeted, their playing time dropped due to nagging injuries, and their singles dried up and disappeared. The Phillies should have a three-year window in which they can expect this kind of production from Howard, but should not plan beyond that. He'll be fun to watch in the meantime.

Jason Jaramillo   C   Bats: S   Throws: R   Height: 6' 0"   Weight: 200   Born: October 9, 1982   Age: 24

YEAR	TEAM	LVL	AGE	PA	R	2B	3B	HR	RBI	BB	SO	SB	CS	SPEED	AVG	OBP	SLG	MLVR	EQAVG	EQOBP	EQSLG	EQA	VORP	DEFENSE	
2004	BAT	A-	21	127	11	5	0	1	14	12	27	0	1	3.0	.232	.307	.304	-.087	.198	.252	.241	.180	-21.5	18-C	-3
2005	LWD	A	22	496	46	28	4	8	63	44	72	2	3	2.7	.304	.368	.438	.210	.279	.325	.384	.246	10.2	102-C	-11
2006	REA	AA	23	364	35	25	1	6	39	32	55	0	1	3.5	.248	.320	.388	.021	.242	.303	.382	.239	0.2	81-C	1
2007	PHI	MLB	24	411	33	20	1	6	41	28	66	0	1	3.6	.243	.298	.347	-.230	.239	.295	.339	.217	-6.1	98-C	-3

Breakout: 19% Improve: 35% Collapse: 47% Attrition: 10%   Comparables: Josh Bard, Koyie Hill, Andy Kropf, Jed Morris

Mike Lieberthal's departure creates a long-term catching void, one that management hoped would be filled by Jaramillo. It still may be, but not in 2007. Jaramillo was aggressively pushed up two levels last year, and his offense suffered, although the bruised hand that cost him three weeks early on didn't help. Defensively solid, his lack of speed means he'll need to make plenty of solid contact to get hits, something he did in college with metal bats but hasn't done as a pro.

Mike Lieberthal   C   Bats: R   Throws: R   Height: 6' 0"   Weight: 190   Born: January 18, 1972   Age: 35

YEAR	TEAM	LVL	AGE	PA	R	2B	3B	HR	RBI	BB	SO	SB	CS	SPEED	AVG	OBP	SLG	MLVR	EQAVG	EQOBP	EQSLG	EQA	VORP	DEFENSE	
2004	PHI	MLB	32	529	58	31	1	17	61	37	69	1	1	3.1	.271	.335	.447	.047	.270	.333	.449	.267	20.5	117-C	0
2005	PHI	MLB	33	443	48	25	0	12	47	35	35	0	0	4.1	.263	.336	.418	.017	.261	.334	.425	.264	16.3	113-C	-4
2006	PHI	MLB	34	230	22	14	0	9	36	8	19	0	0	3.7	.273	.316	.469	.025	.269	.311	.458	.261	7.1	54-C	10
2007	LAN	MLB	35	327	34	18	0	9	42	21	35	0	0	3.9	.265	.322	.415	-.079	.266	.321	.417	.252	7.3	79-C	1

Breakout: 10% Improve: 28% Collapse: 34% Attrition: 37%   Comparables: Bo Diaz, John Flaherty, Jerry McNertney, Mike Macfarlane

This is what typically happens to veteran catchers; injuries devour their playing time. For Lieberthal, the knee, hip, back, and abdominal injuries he suffered in 2006 had him thinking about retirement, but he's reached an agreement with the Dodgers to play a reserve role. He was still effective between his DL stints, and should have a better chance to stay healthy playing two days a week instead of five.

Lou Marson   C   Bats: R   Throws: R   Height: 6' 1"   Weight: 195   Born: June 26, 1986   Age: 21

YEAR	TEAM	LVL	AGE	PA	R	2B	3B	HR	RBI	BB	SO	SB	CS	SPEED	AVG	OBP	SLG	MLVR	EQAVG	EQOBP	EQSLG	EQA	VORP	DEFENSE	
2005	BAT	A-	19	252	25	11	3	5	25	27	52	0	1	3.2	.245	.329	.391	.047	.203	.260	.303	.202	-26.9	55-C	-8
2006	LWD	A	20	410	44	16	5	4	39	49	82	4	0	4.8	.243	.343	.351	.038	.234	.307	.330	.228	-7.6	100-C	10
2007	PHI	MLB	21	440	39	18	2	7	42	31	88	2	2	4.4	.234	.291	.342	-.254	.230	.289	.334	.213	-8.9	104-C	6

Breakout: 39% Improve: 56% Collapse: 28% Attrition: 6%   Comparables: Max St-Pierre, Manuel Ramirez, John Buck, Jeremy Hill

Another contender, along with Jaramillo and Ruiz, for future Philly catching jobs, Marson only converted to catcher after being drafted—his best high school position was quarterback, but an injury cost him his chance at gridiron glory. Marson made a dramatic improvement in his K/BB ratio within the season, from 52:19 in the first half to 28:29 in the second, and, with that, he gained in average (from .210 to .267) and power (from .276 to .428). It's that second-half kick that puts him on the radar.

Tim Moss   2B   Bats: R   Throws: R   Height: 5' 9"   Weight: 150   Born: January 26, 1982   Age: 24

YEAR	TEAM	LVL	AGE	PA	R	2B	3B	HR	RBI	BB	SO	SB	CS	SPEED	AVG	OBP	SLG	MLVR	EQAVG	EQOBP	EQSLG	EQA	VORP	DEFENSE	
2004	LWD	A	22	312	31	15	1	2	28	24	75	10	8	4.5	.256	.342	.341	-.018	.243	.296	.312	.217	-9.0	77-2B	-3
2005	CLR	A+	23	536	87	30	5	17	61	45	129	28	10	7.6	.269	.348	.463	.129	.241	.304	.410	.249	6.7	117-2B	-6
2006	CLR	A+	24	300	43	12	6	6	38	20	66	20	4	7.1	.284	.353	.443	.137	.258	.306	.404	.250	4.2	65-2B	1
2006	REA	AA	24	230	23	5	6	7	23	16	82	6	2	6.8	.180	.242	.364	-.172	.171	.224	.333	.201	-16.6	58-2B	-2
2007	PHI	MLB	25	515	59	24	5	12	52	32	140	19	7	5.9	.245	.300	.394	-.160	.241	.297	.385	.237	3.2	121-2B	-2

Breakout: 28% Improve: 58% Collapse: 25% Attrition: 5%   Comparables: Mo Bruce, Jose Morban, Rayner Bautista, Blake Whealy

While generally liking what he had done in 2005, scouts questioned Moss's contact skills and ability to improve as he moved up. Score one for them, because Double-A pitchers, particularly left-handers, ate him alive. He did a little better after he was sent back to the FSL, but even that comes with an asterisk in the form of an unusually large home-road split. He should come off of everybody's lists until he shows us something outside of Clearwater.

Abraham Nuñez 3B   Bats: S   Throws: R   Height: 5' 11"   Weight: 190   Born: March 16, 1976   Age: 31

YEAR	TEAM	LVL	AGE	PA	R	2B	3B	HR	RBI	BB	SO	SB	CS	SPEED	AVG	OBP	SLG	MLVR	EQAVG	EQOBP	EQSLG	EQA	VORP	DEFENSE			
2004	PIT	MLB	28	195	17	9	0	2	13	10	36	1	3	4.0	.236	.275	.319	-.251	.230	.268	.311	.201	-7.2	26-2B	0		
2005	SLN	MLB	29	467	64	13	2	5	44	37	63	0	1	4.9	.285	.343	.361	-.033	.286	.348	.369	.252	5.0	81-3B	8	15-2B	-2
2006	PHI	MLB	30	369	42	10	2	2	32	41	58	1	0	5.0	.211	.303	.273	-.299	.199	.296	.258	.208	-18.2	70-3B	5		
2007	*PHI*	*MLB*	*31*	*323*	*32*	*10*	*2*	*2*	*26*	*27*	*50*	*2*	*2*	*5.2*	*.245*	*.312*	*.314*	*-.245*	*.241*	*.309*	*.307*	*.214*	*-7.6*	*78-3B*	*2*		

Breakout: 16%   Improve: 38%   Collapse: 36%   Attrition: 37%   Comparables: Al Newman, Ted Kubiak, Jeff McKnight, Chico Ruiz

When David Bell was traded to the Brewers at the deadline, the Phillies gave Nuñez the full-time third-base job. It was more by default than by choice, since Nuñez was only hitting .162, albeit in extremely limited playing time. He pulled it together with regular play, hitting and fielding like he had done in St. Louis the year before. The Phils will have interesting offense/defense and righty/lefty choices with Nuñez and Wes Helms at the position this year.

Chris Roberson OF   Bats: S   Throws: R   Height: 6' 2"   Weight: 180   Born: August 23, 1979   Age: 27

YEAR	TEAM	LVL	AGE	PA	R	2B	3B	HR	RBI	BB	SO	SB	CS	SPEED	AVG	OBP	SLG	MLVR	EQAVG	EQOBP	EQSLG	EQA	VORP	DEFENSE			
2004	CLR	A+	24	345	52	13	6	9	38	27	71	16	12	6.9	.307	.371	.473	.232	.276	.324	.424	.254	10.4	77-CF	-7		
2005	REA	AA	25	611	90	24	8	15	70	40	112	34	14	7.7	.311	.365	.465	.193	.285	.332	.417	.261	5.0	72-RF	1	62-CF	2
2006	SWB	AAA	26	316	44	14	2	1	17	23	57	25	9	6.9	.292	.349	.366	.040	.282	.335	.355	.250	2.4	63-CF	-2		
2006	PHI	MLB	26	43	9	0	1	0	1	0	9	3	0	9.1	.195	.214	.244	-.519	.167	.186	.214	.166	-3.2				
2007	*PHI*	*MLB*	*27*	*375*	*48*	*17*	*3*	*6*	*34*	*22*	*75*	*20*	*7*	*6.6*	*.270*	*.319*	*.388*	*-.116*	*.266*	*.316*	*.380*	*.244*	*-0.1*	*90-CF*	*-1*		

Breakout: 13%   Improve: 31%   Collapse: 31%   Attrition: 25%   Comparables: Gene Kingsale, Jerry Mumphrey, Jesus Tavarez, Andres Torres

Roberson was called up to Philadelphia four different times in 2007, finally sticking after the trade deadline, but was never used as anything other than a pinch-hitter or pinch-runner after July and would have been better off with regular playing time in Scranton. He's a late bloomer who's learned to hit for a respectable average and steal a base or three; he'll be a fine, cheap reserve outfielder for a team that doesn't overemphasize the need for major league experience among its reserves.

Jimmy Rollins SS   Bats: S   Throws: R   Height: 5' 8"   Weight: 170   Born: November 27, 1978   Age: 28

YEAR	TEAM	LVL	AGE	PA	R	2B	3B	HR	RBI	BB	SO	SB	CS	SPEED	AVG	OBP	SLG	MLVR	EQAVG	EQOBP	EQSLG	EQA	VORP	DEFENSE	
2004	PHI	MLB	25	725	119	43	12	14	73	57	73	30	9	8.0	.289	.348	.455	.090	.287	.346	.452	.275	43.1	152-SS	-11
2005	PHI	MLB	26	732	115	38	11	12	54	47	71	41	6	8.0	.290	.338	.431	.056	.286	.337	.434	.272	42.5	153-SS	-10
2006	PHI	MLB	27	758	127	45	9	25	83	57	80	36	4	7.5	.277	.334	.478	.072	.273	.331	.471	.278	45.2	154-SS	9
2007	*PHI*	*MLB*	*28*	*711*	*104*	*39*	*8*	*17*	*72*	*54*	*76*	*32*	*8*	*7.3*	*.290*	*.347*	*.453*	*.036*	*.285*	*.344*	*.442*	*.273*	*38.3*	*162-SS*	*3*

Breakout: 9%   Improve: 40%   Collapse: 21%   Attrition: 0%   Comparables: Rafael Furcal, Ray Durham, Brian Roberts, Bert Campaneris

Rollins entered 2006 on a 36-game hitting streak, but only managed to extend it by two games before falling into a slump that dragged on until the end of May. Although his batting average never completely recovered, his power soared to new heights, essentially doubling his normal homer output. Still, his overall value didn't appreciably change. Any further increase in power should push him away from the leadoff spot, something his low on-base percentage has been arguing for years only to lose the debate to the powerful counter-argument made by his speed.

Aaron Rowand CF   Bats: R   Throws: R   Height: 6' 0"   Weight: 200   Born: August 29, 1977   Age: 29

YEAR	TEAM	LVL	AGE	PA	R	2B	3B	HR	RBI	BB	SO	SB	CS	SPEED	AVG	OBP	SLG	MLVR	EQAVG	EQOBP	EQSLG	EQA	VORP	DEFENSE	
2004	CHA	MLB	26	534	94	38	2	24	69	30	91	17	5	6.7	.310	.361	.544	.196	.307	.360	.545	.300	42.0	115-CF	2
2005	CHA	MLB	27	640	77	30	5	13	69	32	116	16	5	6.0	.270	.329	.407	-.031	.270	.336	.417	.263	14.7	150-CF	5
2006	PHI	MLB	28	445	59	24	3	12	47	18	76	10	4	5.6	.262	.321	.425	-.040	.262	.318	.429	.256	8.8	101-CF	0
2007	*PHI*	*MLB*	*29*	*499*	*67*	*28*	*3*	*15*	*62*	*27*	*84*	*11*	*4*	*6.0*	*.280*	*.333*	*.457*	*.010*	*.276*	*.330*	*.446*	*.265*	*15.3*	*118-CF*	*1*

Breakout: 15%   Improve: 32%   Collapse: 28%   Attrition: 16%   Comparables: Brian Jordan, Larry Herndon, Roberto Kelly, Jim Busby

Rowand may be a hard-nosed guy, but when his nose challenged the center-field fence, the nose lost. It was a heck of a catch, and arguably proved to be a game-winner; surprisingly enough it only cost him two weeks. He couldn't come back from the broken ankle he suffered in a collision with Chase Utley in August, though; the break was bad enough that he'll be closely watched in the spring. His aggressiveness, however inspirational in the field, unfortunately carries over to the plate, where he also tends to chase balls despite not being allowed to roam outside of the batter's box. He's a decent player reaching the point at which the injuries resulting from his reckless style of play could entirely derail his career.

Carlos Ruiz C **Bats: R Throws: R** Height: 5' 10" Weight: 200 Born: January 22, 1979 Age: 28

YEAR	TEAM	LVL	AGE	PA	R	2B	3B	HR	RBI	BB	SO	SB	CS	SPEED	AVG	OBP	SLG	MLVR	EQAVG	EQOBP	EQSLG	EQA	VORP	DEFENSE	
2004	REA	AA	25	383	45	15	2	17	50	22	37	8	4	4.6	.284	.338	.484	.118	.251	.292	.413	.242	3.4	86-C	6
2005	SWB	AAA	26	388	50	25	9	4	40	30	48	4	5	5.8	.300	.354	.458	.111	.279	.332	.419	.259	14.2	55-C	3
2006	SWB	AAA	27	423	56	25	0	16	69	42	56	4	3	3.4	.307	.389	.505	.293	.288	.362	.491	.288	35.2	78-C	8
2006	PHI	MLB	27	78	5	1	1	3	10	5	8	0	0	3.4	.261	.316	.435	-.033	.257	.312	.429	.255	1.4	19-C	-1
2007	PHI	MLB	28	441	52	22	2	13	57	31	57	3	2	4.0	.276	.335	.436	-.019	.272	.332	.427	.259	13.9	105-C	3

Breakout: 12% Improve: 43% Collapse: 24% Attrition: 11% Comparables: Rick Cerone, Joe Azcue, Terry Steinbach, Michael Barrett

Given a second shot at Triple-A, Ruiz cranked up his hitting, just as he had done in second tries in Double-A and High-A ball. He did the same thing in miniature in the majors, going 5-for-35 with no extra base hits in his first call-up in May, and then hitting .379/.455/.793 in his subsequent trips to the bigs. The only thing not to like about him is that he's already 28. That would normally elicit a comment about this being as good he gets, but there's something about his pattern of improvement that cautions against taking a normal career path for granted.

Jeremy Slayden LF **Bats: L Throws: R** Height: 6' 0" Weight: 185 Born: July 28, 1982 Age: 23

YEAR	TEAM	LVL	AGE	PA	R	2B	3B	HR	RBI	BB	SO	SB	CS	SPEED	AVG	OBP	SLG	MLVR	EQAVG	EQOBP	EQSLG	EQA	VORP	DEFENSE	
2005	BAT	A-	22	229	35	11	0	9	36	28	45	1	0	3.3	.268	.373	.464	.220	.211	.275	.330	.216	-29.5	48-LF	-9
2006	LWD	A	23	454	65	44	3	10	81	41	89	5	0	4.6	.310	.381	.510	.361	.282	.328	.446	.266	6.5	74-LF	-3
2007	PHI	MLB	24	524	54	34	3	14	66	33	122	3	1	4.3	.252	.305	.422	-.108	.249	.302	.413	.243	-1.4	123-LF	-4

Breakout: 24% Improve: 41% Collapse: 34% Attrition: 7% Comparables: Eddie Rivero, Ben Candelaria, Greg Dobbs, Jayson Drobiak

Slayden established himself as a power hitter early in his college career, which got him drafted even after a torn rotator cuff and other injuries shut him down. Healthy last season, Slayden showed he had plenty of sock left, ripping 44 doubles in only 400 at-bats, a feat made both more and less impressive by the fact that he almost never played against left-handed pitchers. That, age, and being a defensive liability are all working against him.

Joe Thurston 2B **Bats: L Throws: R** Height: 5' 11" Weight: 190 Born: September 29, 1979 Age: 27

YEAR	TEAM	LVL	AGE	PA	R	2B	3B	HR	RBI	BB	SO	SB	CS	SPEED	AVG	OBP	SLG	MLVR	EQAVG	EQOBP	EQSLG	EQA	VORP	DEFENSE	
2004	LVG	AAA	24	360	38	17	3	4	23	20	46	7	2	5.1	.284	.356	.394	-.118	.240	.304	.323	.227	-7.0	82-2B	5
2005	LVG	AAA	25	286	32	10	2	6	35	13	36	4	5	4.1	.288	.326	.412	-.128	.245	.278	.343	.218	-7.1	64-2B	0
2005	COH	AAA	25	118	13	3	3	2	7	7	19	2	2	6.4	.234	.287	.374	-.159	.222	.276	.343	.217	-3.6	27-2B	-4
2006	SWB	AAA	26	544	74	29	9	9	55	43	65	20	10	7.0	.282	.349	.436	.124	.275	.336	.434	.264	24.5	118-2B	7
2006	PHI	MLB	26	20	3	1	0	0	0	1	2	0	0	5.5	.222	.300	.278	-.285	.222	.300	.278	.211	-0.8		
2007	WAS	MLB	27	495	56	23	5	7	47	28	62	11	6	5.7	.262	.313	.384	-.138	.267	.318	.396	.245	9.2	117-2B	3

Breakout: 20% Improve: 49% Collapse: 29% Attrition: 11% Comparables: Jason Conti, Kevin Reese, Paul Ottavinia, Fernando Vina

The former Second Baseman of the Future for the Dodgers rediscovered his bat last year, but didn't have a prayer of taking the second base job away from Utley. He signed with Washington after the season. Since they've dealt Jose Vidro, he'll find himself in a much more winnable competition against the likes of Felipe Lopez and Bernie Castro. That leaves the important distinction between his winning a job and being good at it, the latter of which is less likely.

Chase Utley 2B **Bats: L Throws: R** Height: 6' 1" Weight: 185 Born: December 17, 1978 Age: 28

YEAR	TEAM	LVL	AGE	PA	R	2B	3B	HR	RBI	BB	SO	SB	CS	SPEED	AVG	OBP	SLG	MLVR	EQAVG	EQOBP	EQSLG	EQA	VORP	DEFENSE			
2004	SWB	AAA	25	144	23	8	1	6	25	18	29	4	2	5.7	.285	.368	.512	.188	.272	.352	.488	.283	10.4	33-2B	2		
2004	PHI	MLB	25	287	36	11	2	13	57	15	40	4	1	5.6	.266	.308	.468	.018	.262	.304	.461	.260	9.2	42-2B	5	12-1B	0
2005	PHI	MLB	26	628	93	39	6	28	105	69	109	16	3	6.3	.291	.376	.540	.260	.287	.373	.545	.307	54.9	135-2B	1		
2006	PHI	MLB	27	739	131	40	4	32	102	63	132	15	4	6.2	.309	.379	.527	.244	.304	.376	.519	.302	65.2	152-2B	-11		
2007	PHI	MLB	28	668	105	37	5	31	99	67	113	11	5	5.8	.287	.366	.524	.160	.283	.362	.512	.294	46.0	156-2B	-4		

Breakout: 9% Improve: 35% Collapse: 21% Attrition: 2% Comparables: Willie Upshaw, Gil McDougald, Richie Hebner, Jorge Orta

In our 2006 edition, we used this space to talk about how Utley needed to be given a chance hit against left-handers in order to learn how to hit them. The previous season had been the first when he was allowed to play regularly against lefties, and we weren't worried that he only hit .219 against them; it was a learning experience. Utley proved to be a good student, hitting .301 off of them last year and filling in the last hole in his game. He didn't have quite the same power against them as he did against right-handers, which explains the slight drop in his slugging average, but you can safely buckle up and enjoy several seasons' worth of stardom from here on out. The inheritor of Mark Grace's slow white guy/smart baserunner mantle, you won't see him make many mistakes as far as the chances he takes.

Shane Victorino CF **Bats: S** **Throws: R** Height: 5' 9" Weight: 180 Born: November 30, 1980 Age: 26

YEAR	TEAM	LVL	AGE	PA	R	2B	3B	HR	RBI	BB	SO	SB	CS	SPEED	AVG	OBP	SLG	MLVR	EQAVG	EQOBP	EQSLG	EQA	VORP	DEFENSE			
2004	JAX	AA	23	329	70	13	7	16	43	20	65	9	7	7.6	.327	.373	.582	.410	.318	.355	.553	.297	35.3	66-CF	7		
2004	LVG	AAA	23	216	28	9	1	3	20	11	37	7	2	6.3	.235	.278	.335	-.387	.193	.235	.262	.185	-19.9	50-CF	3		
2005	SWB	AAA	24	559	93	25	16	18	70	51	74	17	9	7.4	.310	.377	.534	.264	.293	.358	.499	.288	42.6	120-CF	12		
2005	PHI	MLB	24	19	5	0	0	2	8	0	3	0	0	5.9	.294	.263	.647	.224	.294	.263	.647	.293	1.5				
2006	PHI	MLB	25	462	70	19	8	6	46	24	54	4	3	6.3	.287	.346	.414	.017	.286	.343	.414	.261	12.1	61-CF	6	17-RF	3
2007	PHI	MLB	26	526	74	25	7	13	59	36	70	10	5	6.7	.292	.349	.457	.047	.287	.345	.447	.271	18.6	124-CF	9		

Breakout: 16% Improve: 54% Collapse: 17% Attrition: 11% Comparables: Dave Martinez, Coco Crisp, Devon White, Brian McRae

Rowand's injury and Abreu's trade gave Victorino the chance to play regularly last year, and he made the most of it. Despite only stealing four bases—he batted ahead of Utley and Howard and was understandably red-lighted—speed is a vital part of his game, whether he's slashing across the outfield or taking extra bases with abandon. Rowand shouldn't assume that his center field job is uncontested.

PITCHERS

Eude Brito **Bats: L** **Throws: L** Height: 5' 11" Weight: 160 Born: August 19, 1978 Age: 28

YEAR	TEAM	LVL	AGE	W	L	SV	G	GS	IP	H	BB	SO	HR	GB%	BABIP	STUFF	WHIP	ERA	PERA	EQERA	EQH9	EQBB9	EQSO9	EQHR9	VORP	WXRL
2004	REA	AA	25	8	6	4	43	7	97²	95	41	84	10	—	.294	-22	1.39	4.42	5.82	6.16	9.6	4.5	5.1	1.4	-5.9	—
2005	SWB	AAA	26	6	2	0	28	15	98¹	97	39	76	13	46.6%	.304	-16	1.38	4.85	5.70	5.79	9.0	3.9	5.3	1.4	-2.1	—
2005	PHI	MLB	26	1	2	0	6	5	22	20	11	15	2	46.2%	.286	1	1.41	3.68	4.86	3.63	8.5	4.0	5.6	0.8	4.7	0.70
2006	SWB	AAA	27	10	8	1	26	23	147²	116	55	103	11	40.5%	.245	-2	1.16	3.18	5.02	4.87	8.3	3.7	4.9	1.1	11.5	—
2006	PHI	MLB	27	1	2	0	5	2	18¹	21	12	9	2	35.5%	.317	-15	1.80	7.38	5.41	6.52	9.3	5.1	3.7	0.9	-2.8	-0.15
2007	PHI	MLB	28	5	7	0	32	15	99¹	108	48	63	16	44.0%	.289	-9	1.57	5.54	5.69	5.45	9.5	3.9	5.1	1.3	1.8	0.80

Breakout: 16% Improve: 42% Collapse: 18% Attrition: 0% Comparables: Randy Flores, Matt White, Roger Deago, Jeffrey Williams

Brito got a taste of the major leagues after a good 2005 in Triple-A, and his 2006 repeater season in Scranton was even better. Called up for two starts in June, he was shelled in both; called back up in September, he pitched long relief. He's an extreme example of how different a pitcher can be depending on his usage—for one inning of work he can throw 95 MPH, but force him to go longer and he can barely make 90. On the other hand, when he tires, his breaking pitches have more movement. Brito really has to overwhelm people in Triple-A if he's going to get another chance at starting.

Carlos Carrasco **Bats: R** **Throws: R** Height: 6' 3" Weight: 180 Born: March 21, 1987 Age: 20

YEAR	TEAM	LVL	AGE	W	L	SV	G	GS	IP	H	BB	SO	HR	GB%	BABIP	STUFF	WHIP	ERA	PERA	EQERA	EQH9	EQBB9	EQSO9	EQHR9	VORP	WXRL
2005	LWD	A	18	1	7	0	13	13	62²	78	28	46	11	43.5%	.333	-35	1.69	7.03	9.16	9.30	13.1	5.1	4.1	3.2	-24.7	—
2005	BAT	A-	18	0	3	0	4	4	15¹	29	5	12	8	34.9%	.389	-61	2.22	13.53	26.93	21.00	29.2	4.5	4.5	16.5	-20.5	—
2006	LWD	A	19	12	6	0	26	26	159¹	103	65	159	6	50.4%	.254	21	1.06	2.26	4.93	4.22	7.4	4.5	5.5	0.8	23.2	—
2007	PHI	MLB	20	6	9	0	24	21	117	124	59	86	22	45.0%	.288	3	1.57	5.63	5.95	5.49	9.3	4.0	5.9	1.5	1.6	1.00

Breakout: 36% Improve: 70% Collapse: 9% Attrition: 3% Comparables: Kris Honel, Ervin Santana, Chad Durbin, Gavin Floyd

There is a tendency for us here at BP to emphasize the physical and tangible over the mental. Carrasco started 2005 in the Sally League and got his head handed to him in his first couple of starts. The result was that he stopped believing in his stuff, tried to throw everything harder and harder, and reaped increasingly poor results. Last year he got off to a good start, pitched within his ability, and succeeded. The only tangible difference in 2006 was the addition of an improved curve to his low-90s fastball and excellent changeup. Scouts love his frame, and expect the skinny Venezuelan to fill out and get stronger.

Fabio Castro

Bats: L **Throws: L** Height: 5' 7" Weight: 175 Born: January 20, 1985 Age: 22

YEAR	TEAM	LVL	AGE	W	L	SV	G	GS	IP	H	BB	SO	HR	GB%	BABIP	STUFF	WHIP	ERA	PERA	EQERA	EQH9	EQBB9	EQSO9	EQHR9	VORP	WXRL
2004	KAN	A	19	4	0	3	37	0	51	44	23	44	2	—	.282	-3	1.31	3.00	4.85	4.14	8.5	4.7	4.7	0.5	8.1	—
2005	WNS	A+	20	5	5	6	53	0	79	58	37	75	7	45.2%	.262	-5	1.20	2.28	5.66	3.12	7.0	4.6	5.3	1.3	21.5	—
2006	FRI	AA	21	0	1	0	5	4	13²	14	8	10	1	45.5%	.302	-4	1.67	2.05	5.15	4.61	9.2	5.3	4.6	0.7	1.5	—
2006	TEX	MLB	21	0	0	0	4	0	8¹	6	7	5	0	48.0%	.240	9	1.56	4.34	4.93	5.19	6.2	7.3	5.2	0.0	0.8	0.02
2006	PHI	MLB	21	0	1	1	16	0	23¹	12	6	13	1	39.7%	.177	9	0.77	1.55	3.67	1.50	4.1	1.9	4.5	0.4	11.7	-0.58
2007	PHI	MLB	22	3	4	1	35	4	59¹	60	29	44	8	45.0%	.286	-3	1.49	4.84	5.08	4.77	8.8	4.0	5.9	1.1	5.3	0.70

Breakout: 0%   Improve: 7%   Collapse: 82%   Attrition: 46%   Comparables: Eduardo Rodriguez, Ray Sadecki, Oscar Villarreal, Bill Champion

Castro was a Rule 5 pick last year, taken from the White Sox by the Royals, immediately traded to the Rangers, and then traded in-season to the Phillies for a decent starting prospect, Daniel Haigwood. As so often happens with Rule 5 guys, any excuse for injury was taken to put him on the DL and send him to the minors on rehab for as long as possible. Featuring a low-90s fastball, a curve, and a slider, he pitched well when given a chance, holding lefties to 2 hits in 27 at bats and even getting a couple of shots at closing. Castro was a nifty pickup by Gillick and the sort of talent the Phillies should be making space for on an otherwise sparse 40-man roster.

Clay Condrey

Bats: R **Throws: R** Height: 6' 3" Weight: 195 Born: November 19, 1975 Age: 31

YEAR	TEAM	LVL	AGE	W	L	SV	G	GS	IP	H	BB	SO	HR	GB%	BABIP	STUFF	WHIP	ERA	PERA	EQERA	EQH9	EQBB9	EQSO9	EQHR9	VORP	WXRL
2004	SWB	AAA	28	9	9	0	27	27	155	206	34	70	23	—	.324	-27	1.55	5.46	5.65	6.78	11.9	2.2	3.0	1.6	-20.4	—
2005	SWB	AAA	29	7	8	0	25	24	132¹	159	29	74	13	52.4%	.330	-7	1.42	4.15	4.65	5.24	10.4	2.1	3.7	1.1	5.4	—
2006	SWB	AAA	30	4	2	6	39	0	51¹	41	15	28	1	57.2%	.267	-7	1.10	1.94	4.10	3.26	8.2	3.1	3.6	0.4	12.9	—
2006	PHI	MLB	30	2	2	0	21	0	28²	35	9	16	3	47.9%	.352	-6	1.53	3.14	4.08	3.00	9.9	2.4	4.5	0.9	8.2	0.03
2007	PHI	MLB	31	2	3	2	52	1	53¹	61	17	29	6	52.0%	.302	-12	1.46	4.45	4.87	4.40	9.9	2.6	4.4	1.0	6.8	0.70

Breakout: 32%   Improve: 59%   Collapse: 21%   Attrition: 36%   Comparables: Chuck Taylor, Tom Tellmann, Alan Levine, A. J. Sager

After four years as a starter, Condrey went back to relieving last year and had something of a fluke season with Triple-A Scranton. Typically, anything Condrey throws gets hit, frequently hard, but he did an exceptional job of suppressing extra-base hits with men on base last year in both Triple-A and the majors, preventing opponents from scoring nearly as many runs off of him as they should have at either level. That seems unlikely to happen again. A nine-year minor league veteran, Condrey's not just a retread, but one with a bent rim and a nail and two pieces of glass embedded in the sidewall. Somehow he's still holding air.

Gavin Floyd

Bats: R **Throws: R** Height: 6' 4" Weight: 220 Born: January 27, 1983 Age: 24

YEAR	TEAM	LVL	AGE	W	L	SV	G	GS	IP	H	BB	SO	HR	GB%	BABIP	STUFF	WHIP	ERA	PERA	EQERA	EQH9	EQBB9	EQSO9	EQHR9	VORP	WXRL
2004	REA	AA	21	6	6	0	20	20	119	93	46	94	5	—	.255	22	1.17	2.57	4.33	3.34	7.4	3.6	5.2	0.5	29.8	—
2004	SWB	AAA	21	1	3	0	5	5	30²	39	9	18	4	—	.333	-4	1.56	4.98	5.51	6.16	11.7	2.9	4.1	1.5	-1.9	—
2004	PHI	MLB	21	2	0	0	6	4	28¹	25	16	24	1	—	.304	19	1.45	3.50	4.38	3.45	8.5	4.4	6.9	0.3	6.9	0.73
2005	SWB	AAA	22	6	9	0	24	23	137¹	155	66	97	11	49.3%	.338	1	1.61	6.16	5.33	7.20	10.1	4.5	4.9	0.8	-24.7	—
2005	PHI	MLB	22	1	2	0	7	4	26	30	16	17	5	40.4%	.298	-17	1.77	10.04	6.56	10.80	10.5	5.1	5.4	1.7	-14.9	0.02
2006	PHI	MLB	23	4	3	0	11	11	54¹	70	32	34	14	36.7%	.322	-18	1.88	7.29	6.63	6.95	10.6	4.4	4.9	1.9	-10.9	-0.20
2006	SWB	AAA	23	7	4	0	17	17	115	117	38	85	9	42.1%	.320	2	1.35	4.23	4.95	5.64	10.6	3.2	5.2	1.0	-0.5	—
2007	CHA	MLB	24	6	9	0	35	21	124	150	60	76	25	45%	.309	-9	1.70	6.55	5.88	5.96	10.8	4.0	5.1	1.7	-8.7	-0.1

Breakout: 25%   Improve: 60%   Collapse: 14%   Attrition: 15%   Comparables: Brian Reith, Gary Glover, Allen Levrault, John Ennis

He's got the size, he's got the pitches, but he never got the results, and the Phillies have given up, sending him to the White Sox for Freddy Garcia. His fastball and curve both rate as excellent pitches, but he does pitch up in the zone, after which hilarity ensues—if you find gopher balls funny. All of the reports and statements seem to add up to the dreaded diagnosis of "head case," sufferers of which sometimes fail to recover and sometimes turn into Curt Schilling. Heaven help you if you're the GM who trades away the next Schilling, but guess which outcome happens more often.

Aaron Fultz
Bats: L Throws: L   Height: 6' 0"   Weight: 210   Born: September 4, 1973   Age: 33

YEAR	TEAM	LVL	AGE	W	L	SV	G	GS	IP	H	BB	SO	HR	GB%	BABIP	STUFF	WHIP	ERA	PERA	EQERA	EQH9	EQBB9	EQSO9	EQHR9	VORP	WXRL
2004	MIN	MLB	30	3	3	1	55	0	50	50	23	37	5	—	.310	-3	1.42	5.04	4.24	4.50	8.3	3.6	6.1	0.7	9.1	-0.19
2005	PHI	MLB	31	4	0	0	62	0	72¹	47	23	54	6	40.2%	.212	10	0.97	2.24	4.04	2.71	6.2	2.6	6.2	0.7	23.5	0.62
2006	PHI	MLB	32	3	1	0	66	1	71¹	80	28	62	7	38.9%	.349	7	1.51	4.54	3.78	4.38	9.4	3.0	6.9	0.7	9.4	0.48
2007	*CLE*	*MLB*	*33*	*3*	*3*	*2*	*59*	*0*	*59²*	*64*	*23*	*44*	*7*	*43%*	*.303*	*-3*	*1.45*	*4.47*	*4.45*	*4.28*	*9.2*	*3.3*	*6.2*	*1.0*	*7.7*	*0.7*

Breakout: 8%   Improve: 37%   Collapse: 37%   Attrition: 25%   *Comparables: Chuck McElroy, Arnold Earley, Lance Painter, Tony Castillo*

If Fultz pitched on a team with a well-stocked bullpen, he'd be a situational lefty and have an ERA about a run lower. Reserving him for his best matchups was a luxury the lackluster Philly pen didn't have last year, so Fultz was merely alright, reversing his BABIP luck from the year before. The free agent took his arm to Cleveland, where he'll try to shore up a bullpen that ranked among the majors' worst in WXRL last year.

Geoff Geary
Bats: R Throws: R   Height: 6' 0"   Weight: 175   Born: August 26, 1976   Age: 30

YEAR	TEAM	LVL	AGE	W	L	SV	G	GS	IP	H	BB	SO	HR	GB%	BABIP	STUFF	WHIP	ERA	PERA	EQERA	EQH9	EQBB9	EQSO9	EQHR9	VORP	WXRL
2004	PHI	MLB	27	1	0	0	33	0	44²	52	16	30	8	—	.314	-16	1.52	5.44	5.29	5.76	10.5	2.8	5.4	1.4	-0.7	0.52
2005	PHI	MLB	28	2	1	0	40	0	58	54	21	42	5	47.2%	.287	1	1.29	3.72	3.97	4.58	8.4	2.9	5.9	0.8	6.9	0.11
2006	PHI	MLB	29	7	1	1	81	0	91¹	103	20	60	6	51.2%	.331	11	1.35	2.96	3.51	2.95	9.4	1.7	5.2	0.5	27.6	1.84
2007	*PHI*	*MLB*	*30*	*3*	*3*	*2*	*59*	*0*	*67²*	*76*	*22*	*44*	*9*	*49.0%*	*.307*	*-7*	*1.44*	*4.43*	*4.83*	*4.36*	*9.8*	*2.6*	*5.2*	*1.0*	*10.0*	*0.80*

Breakout: 10%   Improve: 38%   Collapse: 43%   Attrition: 11%   *Comparables: Mark Williamson, Mike Maddux, Mike Perez, Luis Aponte*

Geary's been a BP fave for awhile, the kind of guy who succeeds in spite of the scouting reports. Pitching on a wing and a prayer, Geary survived a brief trip to Triple-A (he had an option left) to emerge at the end of the year as the Phils' best reliever. Geary is a bullpen version of Josh Towers, and he's going to be in serious trouble if his control wavers by even the slightest bit.

Justin Germano
Bats: R Throws: R   Height: 6' 3"   Weight: 205   Born: August 6, 1982   Age: 23

YEAR	TEAM	LVL	AGE	W	L	SV	G	GS	IP	H	BB	SO	HR	GB%	BABIP	STUFF	WHIP	ERA	PERA	EQERA	EQH9	EQBB9	EQSO9	EQHR9	VORP	WXRL
2004	MOB	AA	21	2	1	0	5	5	32¹	31	7	20	3	—	.286	1	1.18	2.51	5.05	3.98	9.4	2.0	3.7	1.1	5.7	—
2004	POR	AAA	21	9	5	0	20	20	122²	113	25	98	12	—	.277	20	1.12	3.37	4.11	3.60	8.4	1.9	5.6	1.0	27.3	—
2004	SDN	MLB	21	1	2	0	7	5	21¹	31	14	16	2	—	.397	-9	2.11	8.87	4.56	10.48	12.5	5.2	5.6	0.8	-9.0	-0.30
2005	POR	AAA	22	7	6	0	19	19	112	111	32	100	13	44.6%	.311	12	1.28	3.70	4.47	4.46	8.9	2.5	6.1	1.2	14.3	—
2005	LOU	AAA	22	3	2	0	8	8	49¹	62	5	38	7	46.3%	.359	9	1.36	4.02	4.68	4.97	10.8	0.9	5.3	1.4	3.5	—
2006	LOU	AAA	23	8	6	0	19	18	117²	124	22	67	11	53.1%	.309	-5	1.25	3.69	5.08	5.06	9.9	1.8	4.0	1.3	7.0	—
2006	SWB	AAA	23	2	0	0	6	6	38	40	2	25	2	60.5%	.322	15	1.11	2.84	3.39	4.54	10.5	0.5	4.5	0.7	4.4	—
2006	CIN	MLB	23	0	1	0	2	1	6²	8	3	8	1	63.2%	.389	7	1.65	5.37	4.32	5.14	10.3	3.9	9.0	1.3	0.5	-0.03
2007	*PHI*	*MLB*	*24*	*6*	*8*	*1*	*35*	*17*	*120²*	*138*	*30*	*76*	*17*	*52%*	*.306*	*2*	*1.39*	*4.98*	*4.97*	*4.95*	*9.9*	*2.0*	*5.1*	*1.2*	*8.5*	*1.6*

Breakout: 16%   Improve: 45%   Collapse: 17%   Attrition: 14%   *Comparables: Charles Nagy, Paul Thormodsgard, Matt Belisle, Mike Wood*

Germano is a borderline-interesting starting prospect, with a slightly below-average fastball and a slightly above-average curveball. He's just tantalizing enough to keep showing up in deals at the trade deadline, going for Rheal Cormier last year and for Joe Randa the year before that. The Phillies have a rotation built around win-now veterans, so Germano will slot into Triple-A for a fourth year, competing with Brito in the injury call-up sweepstakes.

Gio Gonzalez
Bats: R Throws: L   Height: 5' 11"   Weight: 185   Born: September 19, 1985   Age: 21

YEAR	TEAM	LVL	AGE	W	L	SV	G	GS	IP	H	BB	SO	HR	GB%	BABIP	STUFF	WHIP	ERA	PERA	EQERA	EQH9	EQBB9	EQSO9	EQHR9	VORP	WXRL
2004	KAN	A	18	1	2	0	8	8	40²	39	20	34	1	—	.297	11	1.45	3.76	4.47	4.95	9.2	5.2	4.5	0.4	2.9	—
2004	BRI	Rk	18	1	2	0	7	6	24	17	8	36	0	—	.327	22	1.04	2.25	3.64	4.43	8.5	4.0	6.4	0.4	2.9	—
2005	KAN	A	19	5	3	0	11	10	57²	36	22	84	3	48.8%	.277	36	1.01	1.87	4.28	3.33	7.7	4.3	8.2	1.0	13.6	—
2005	WNS	A+	19	8	3	0	13	13	73¹	61	25	79	5	40.1%	.304	23	1.17	3.56	4.37	4.58	7.9	3.3	6.1	1.0	8.2	—
2006	REA	AA	20	7	12	0	27	27	154	140	81	166	24	42.9%	.293	-11	1.44	4.68	7.00	6.24	10.0	5.3	7.0	2.3	-10.5	—
2007	*CHA*	*MLB*	*21*	*6*	*9*	*0*	*23*	*23*	*117*	*131*	*71*	*95*	*26*	*41%*	*.301*	*4*	*1.73*	*6.22*	*6.02*	*5.57*	*9.9*	*5.0*	*6.9*	*1.9*	*-2.5*	*0.6*

Breakout: 18%   Improve: 57%   Collapse: 15%   Attrition: 8%   *Comparables: Andy Pratt, Onan Masaoka, Matt Chico, Chuck Tiffany*

(continued next page)

Gio Gonzalez *(continued)*

Gio's first taste of Double-A got rough, particularly in the middle of the season, when he over-compensated for control problems and started handing out homers like they were flags at a Fourth of July game. He's still an excellent prospect; there aren't many 20-year-old lefties who can strike out a batter an inning in Double-A. The main prospect acquired in the Jim Thome trade, he was returned to the White Sox in the Freddy Garcia trade.

Tom Gordon Bats: R Throws: R   Height: 5' 10" Weight: 195 Born: December 31, 1969 Age: 39

YEAR	TEAM	LVL	AGE	W	L	SV	G	GS	IP	H	BB	SO	HR	GB%	BABIP	STUFF	WHIP	ERA	PERA	EQERA	EQH9	EQBB9	EQSO9	EQHR9	VORP	WXRL
2004	NYA	MLB	36	9	4	4	80	0	89²	56	23	96	5	—	.242	40	0.87	2.21	2.60	2.25	5.3	2.1	8.9	0.5	38.9	6.31
2005	NYA	MLB	37	5	4	2	79	0	80²	59	29	69	8	52.3%	.238	14	1.09	2.57	3.79	2.82	6.2	3.1	7.4	0.9	26.6	3.28
2006	PHI	MLB	38	3	4	34	59	0	59¹	53	22	68	9	46.5%	.293	19	1.26	3.34	3.79	3.10	7.5	2.8	9.1	1.2	17.1	3.39
2007	PHI	MLB	39	3	4	24	49	0	55²	47	21	54	6	49.0%	.276	10	1.22	3.33	3.33	3.32	7.3	3.0	7.8	0.8	14.5	2.10

Breakout: 4% Improve: 23% Collapse: 37% Attrition: 13% Comparables: Hoyt Wilhelm, Stu Miller, Jesse Orosco, Al Worthington

Back in a regular closing role for the first time since 2001, Gordon turned in a standout season; the only blemish being a dead arm in August, which got him rocked two nights in a row and resulted in a three-week rest on the DL, none of which was particularly surprising given his injury history and the 159 times Joe Torre called his number over the previous two seasons. The Phils should probably be a little more careful about using him on consecutive days, particularly given the fact that he's signed through 2008, but otherwise there's no reason not to trust Flash with closing again this year.

Cole Hamels Bats: L Throws: L   Height: 6' 4" Weight: 195 Born: December 27, 1983 Age: 23

YEAR	TEAM	LVL	AGE	W	L	SV	G	GS	IP	H	BB	SO	HR	GB%	BABIP	STUFF	WHIP	ERA	PERA	EQERA	EQH9	EQBB9	EQSO9	EQHR9	VORP	WXRL
2006	LWD	A	22	0	0	0	1	1	5¹	3	2	3	1	50.0%	.154	-26	0.98	1.76	13.40	4.15	8.3	6.2	4.2	4.2	0.7	—
2006	CLR	A+	22	1	1	0	4	4	20	16	9	29	0	53.1%	.327	19	1.25	1.80	3.36	4.74	9.0	5.2	8.5	0.5	1.8	—
2006	SWB	AAA	22	2	0	0	3	3	23	10	1	36	0	39.0%	.244	22	0.48	0.39	1.45	0.82	5.3	0.4	11.0	0.0	11.7	—
2006	PHI	MLB	22	9	8	0	23	23	132¹	117	48	145	19	41.7%	.298	32	1.25	4.08	3.79	3.96	7.5	2.8	8.8	1.1	23.1	3.43
2007	PHI	MLB	23	12	8	0	29	29	177²	151	66	180	21	43.0%	.278	30	1.22	3.66	3.69	3.61	7.4	3.0	8.1	0.9	39.5	5.50

Breakout: 18% Improve: 49% Collapse: 11% Attrition: 2% Comparables: Dave Righetti, Dennis Bennett, Don Wilson, Vida Blue

Faberge eggs, china dolls, ice sculptures, Cole Hamels. If this were that pyramid gameshow, the category would be, "beautiful things that are fragile." Hamels pitched a full season last year for the first time ever, starting 31 games. No young pitcher is totally in the clear, but most of Hamels's injuries haven't been from pitching: he broke his arm in high school playing football, and broke his hand defending a teammate in a fight prior to 2005. The bulging disk in his back is more worrisome, but he was able to work around it all year. Missing out on the minor league innings may be a developmental negative and a health positive; like Chris Capuano, Hamels matured physically with less wear and tear on his arm. PECOTA's comparables are cold. Righetti's career as a starter ended after 76 starts due to a move to the bullpen; Bennett had a short and mostly ineffective career; Blue was terrific early but burned out quickly due to overuse and drug abuse; Wilson pitched two no-hitters for the Astros but killed himself on the eve of his 30th birthday. We imagine the Phillies would be more than happy if Hamels were to equal Blue's three 20-win seasons by age 25. Hamels is 23 now, so he'd better get started.

J. A. Happ Bats: L Throws: L   Height: 6' 5" Weight: 205 Born: October 19, 1982 Age: 24

YEAR	TEAM	LVL	AGE	W	L	SV	G	GS	IP	H	BB	SO	HR	GB%	BABIP	STUFF	WHIP	ERA	PERA	EQERA	EQH9	EQBB9	EQSO9	EQHR9	VORP	WXRL
2004	BAT	A-	21	1	2	0	11	11	35²	22	18	37	1	—	.247	6	1.12	2.02	6.32	3.24	6.5	7.0	4.9	0.8	8.7	—
2005	LWD	A	22	4	4	0	14	12	72¹	57	26	70	3	46.5%	.278	4	1.15	2.37	5.12	4.80	8.2	4.4	4.9	0.8	6.2	—
2006	CLR	A+	23	3	7	0	13	13	80¹	63	19	77	9	47.5%	.255	-12	1.02	2.81	6.20	5.21	9.0	2.7	5.4	2.1	3.3	—
2006	REA	AA	23	6	2	0	12	12	74¹	58	29	81	2	41.2%	.298	25	1.17	2.67	3.79	4.38	8.2	4.0	6.8	0.4	9.8	—
2006	SWB	AAA	23	1	0	0	1	1	6	3	1	4	1	38.9%	.118	6	0.67	1.50	7.36	1.59	6.4	1.6	4.8	1.6	2.5	—
2007	PHI	MLB	24	6	8	0	26	21	120¹	124	58	86	20	44.0%	.286	2	1.52	5.31	5.45	5.23	9.0	3.9	5.8	1.3	5.4	1.40

Breakout: 4% Improve: 28% Collapse: 31% Attrition: 0% Comparables: Micah Bowie, Eric Cyr, Josh Kalinowski, Cory Stewart

Happ cleared two levels in 2006 and finished the year by pitching in the Arizona Fall League. His stuff is unimpressive—a fastball that generally stays below 90 and a slider that's too frequently a slurve. What he does have is control, a deceptive delivery that makes his fastball look faster than it really is, a good changeup, and an intelligent, polished approach to pitching. That's good and bad—learning how to pitch effectively is where a lot of minor league pitchers develop, so it is difficult to see where and how he's going to improve.

Jon Lieber **Bats: L Throws: R** Height: 6' 2" Weight: 235 Born: April 2, 1970 Age: 37

YEAR	TEAM	LVL	AGE	W	L	SV	G	GS	IP	H	BB	SO	HR	GB%	BABIP	STUFF	WHIP	ERA	PERA	EQERA	EQH9	EQBB9	EQSO9	EQHR9	VORP	WXRL
2004	NYA	MLB	34	14	8	0	27	27	176²	216	18	102	20	—	.329	14	1.32	4.33	3.64	4.20	10.0	0.8	4.7	0.9	26.1	3.15
2005	PHI	MLB	35	17	13	0	35	35	218¹	223	41	149	33	46.5%	.285	6	1.21	4.21	4.38	4.56	9.2	1.5	5.6	1.3	30.1	4.18
2006	PHI	MLB	36	9	11	0	27	27	168	196	24	100	27	44.4%	.309	4	1.31	4.93	4.34	4.66	9.6	1.1	4.8	1.2	13.6	2.67
2007	PHI	MLB	37	10	10	0	29	27	167¹	188	28	98	24	48.0%	.297	5	1.29	4.48	4.55	4.42	9.8	1.4	4.7	1.2	22.6	3.60

Breakout: 15% Improve: 63% Collapse: 12% Attrition: 1%   *Comparables: Doyle Alexander, Ken Forsch, Bob Tewksbury, Tim Belcher*

Lieber had trouble getting untracked last year. He had an awful April and just as he began to settle down in May he pulled a groin muscle while covering first. That's where age and a flabby physique took its toll: What was initially thought to be a quick 15-day DL stay dragged out over seven weeks, forcing the Phils to improvise in the rotation. When Lieber finally returned to action, it was April all over again, and getting back on track took another month. He's starting to lose his fastball, and, when he starts out behind in the count, hitters tee off; their OPS after a 1-0 count was 769 in 2004, 807 in 2005, and 875 last year. Addressing the media at the winter meetings, Charlie Manuel said, "I think at times Jon could definitely have had better conditioning." Skipping a few of Philadelphia's fabled three-cheesesteak lunches might not help him recover his lost velocity, but it might keep him on the mound for a few extra turns.

Ryan Madson **Bats: L Throws: R** Height: 6' 6" Weight: 195 Born: August 28, 1980 Age: 26

YEAR	TEAM	LVL	AGE	W	L	SV	G	GS	IP	H	BB	SO	HR	GB%	BABIP	STUFF	WHIP	ERA	PERA	EQERA	EQH9	EQBB9	EQSO9	EQHR9	VORP	WXRL
2004	PHI	MLB	23	9	3	1	52	1	77	68	19	55	6	—	.276	11	1.13	2.34	3.74	2.78	8.1	2.0	5.7	0.6	26.0	2.75
2005	PHI	MLB	24	6	5	0	78	0	87	84	25	79	11	49.0%	.312	6	1.25	4.14	4.11	4.60	8.9	2.4	7.5	1.1	9.7	0.95
2006	PHI	MLB	25	11	9	2	50	17	134¹	176	50	99	20	43.9%	.364	-5	1.68	5.70	4.65	5.39	11.0	2.8	5.8	1.2	-1.0	1.26
2007	PHI	MLB	26	6	8	2	52	12	114¹	127	40	84	15	48.0%	.310	1	1.45	4.80	4.96	4.76	9.7	2.8	5.9	1.1	11.1	1.50

Breakout: 18% Improve: 49% Collapse: 18% Attrition: 7%   *Comparables: Sean Bergman, Jose Silva, Mike Parrott, Bob Anderson*

Working as a reliever, Madson's 2006 stats were pretty similar to his 2004 numbers; it was the time he spent starting that made his season look like a train wreck. Starting was what he wanted to do, and he won a rotation spot out of spring, lost it when Hamels came off the DL in May, and then regained it when Hamels went back on in June. Madson had ongoing problems with his curve last year, leaving him with just two pitches—an okay fastball and killer change. Only a few pitchers can go through a lineup more than once on only two pitches. Madson's not one of them.

Matt Maloney **Bats: L Throws: L** Height: 6' 4" Weight: 220 Born: January 16, 1984 Age: 23

YEAR	TEAM	LVL	AGE	W	L	SV	G	GS	IP	H	BB	SO	HR	GB%	BABIP	STUFF	WHIP	ERA	PERA	EQERA	EQH9	EQBB9	EQSO9	EQHR9	VORP	WXRL
2005	BAT	A-	21	2	1	0	8	8	37	38	15	36	2	31.7%	.364	-13	1.43	3.89	6.36	7.07	10.1	5.3	4.3	1.5	-5.8	—
2006	LWD	A	22	16	9	0	27	27	168¹	120	73	180	5	46.2%	.267	18	1.15	2.03	5.00	4.63	8.2	5.3	5.5	0.7	17.0	—
2007	PHI	MLB	23	5	9	0	22	22	115²	122	70	87	19	43.0%	.294	2	1.66	5.86	6.04	5.77	9.2	4.9	6.0	1.3	-2.0	0.70

Breakout: 6% Improve: 24% Collapse: 38% Attrition: 1%   *Comparables: Ken Holubec, J. A. Happ, Cory Stewart, Cory Vance*

Like Happ, Maloney is a big lefty who doesn't have the fastball you'd expect from a pitcher his size, and instead has to rely on a mix of pitches led by a good changeup. In the Sally League, that was overwhelming—he nearly won the pitching Triple Crown for the league, losing the ERA title on the final weekend when another pitcher made the innings threshhold. His ERA title would have been tainted anyway, since a whopping 30 percent of his runs allowed were unearned, nearly twice the league and team average. As with Happ, there are worries about how Maloney can improve as he moves up given his style and assortment.

Scott Mathieson **Bats: R Throws: R** Height: 6' 3" Weight: 190 Born: February 27, 1984 Age: 23

YEAR	TEAM	LVL	AGE	W	L	SV	G	GS	IP	H	BB	SO	HR	GB%	BABIP	STUFF	WHIP	ERA	PERA	EQERA	EQH9	EQBB9	EQSO9	EQHR9	VORP	WXRL
2004	LWD	A	20	8	9	0	25	25	131¹	130	50	112	7	—	.306	3	1.37	4.32	4.95	6.25	9.5	4.0	4.5	0.8	-9.4	—
2005	CLR	A+	21	3	8	0	23	23	121²	111	34	118	17	39.6%	.289	-20	1.19	4.14	6.63	5.19	9.2	3.1	5.6	2.3	5.4	—
2006	REA	AA	22	7	2	0	14	14	92	73	29	99	8	40.8%	.290	14	1.11	3.23	4.83	4.35	8.6	3.1	6.9	1.2	12.4	—
2006	SWB	AAA	22	3	1	0	5	5	34	26	10	36	2	37.4%	.276	25	1.06	3.97	3.74	5.18	8.2	3.0	7.6	0.8	1.5	—
2006	PHI	MLB	22	1	4	0	9	8	37¹	48	16	28	8	35.7%	.339	-6	1.71	7.48	5.32	7.55	10.5	3.2	5.9	1.6	-10.5	-0.55
2007	PHI	MLB	23	7	10	0	31	26	137²	145	56	106	25	40.0%	.290	5	1.46	5.42	5.44	5.31	9.2	3.3	6.2	1.5	5.1	1.50

Breakout: 22% Improve: 70% Collapse: 4% Attrition: 0%   *Comparables: Aaron Myette, Adam Johnson, Kiko Calero, Mike Meyers*

(continued next page)

Scott Mathieson *(continued)*

The good news is that Mathieson finally harnessed his talent, adding a slider to his power fastball, and jumping into the major league rotation for a spell. The bad news is that he blew out his elbow in September, and the resultant TJ surgery will cost him all or most of 2007. Mathieson has a fair number of "extra" innings on his arm—he logged time in the AFL in 2005 and also pitched in three international tournaments for Canada in 2005 and 2006.

Jamie Moyer   Bats: L Throws: L   Height: 6' 0" Weight: 180 Born: December 31, 1969 Age: 44

YEAR	TEAM	LVL	AGE	W	L	SV	G	GS	IP	H	BB	SO	HR	GB%	BABIP	STUFF	WHIP	ERA	PERA	EQERA	EQH9	EQBB9	EQSO9	EQHR9	VORP	WXRL
2004	SEA	MLB	41	7	13	0	34	33	202	217	63	125	44	—	.275	-13	1.39	5.21	5.67	5.43	9.5	2.5	5.2	1.7	9.4	2.14
2005	SEA	MLB	42	13	7	0	32	32	200	225	52	102	23	37.8%	.301	4	1.39	4.28	4.51	4.42	9.9	2.3	4.5	1.0	27.8	3.67
2006	SEA	MLB	43	6	12	0	25	25	160	179	44	82	25	38.8%	.296	-4	1.39	4.39	4.91	4.47	9.4	2.3	4.3	1.3	20.6	2.67
2006	PHI	MLB	43	5	2	0	8	8	51¹	49	7	26	8	50.3%	.255	5	1.09	4.04	4.54	3.93	7.9	1.0	4.1	1.2	9.3	1.20
2007	*PHI*	*MLB*	*44*	*8*	*12*	*0*	*32*	*27*	*168²*	*203*	*50*	*101*	*32*	*43.0%*	*.307*	*-5*	*1.50*	*5.40*	*5.72*	*5.26*	*10.5*	*2.4*	*4.8*	*1.5*	*6.2*	*1.90*

Breakout: 5%   Improve: 18%   Collapse: 24%   Attrition: 13%   Comparables: Warren Spahn, Phil Niekro, Charlie Hough, Gaylord Perry

In order to get Moyer to waive his no-trade clause and cross the country, the Phillies had to extend his contract into 2007. They liked what they got so much that they reworked it after the year was out, piling on more money and extending him into 2008. Former Mariner's GM Gillick is clearly counting on Moyer's junk working as well in Philly as it did in Safeco, which isn't going to happen if he keeps generating grounders only 40 percent of the time as he did in Seattle the last three years; curiously enough, he was up to 50 percent after moving over to the weaker league.

Brett Myers   Bats: R Throws: R   Height: 6' 4" Weight: 240 Born: August 17, 1980 Age: 26

YEAR	TEAM	LVL	AGE	W	L	SV	G	GS	IP	H	BB	SO	HR	GB%	BABIP	STUFF	WHIP	ERA	PERA	EQERA	EQH9	EQBB9	EQSO9	EQHR9	VORP	WXRL
2004	PHI	MLB	23	11	11	0	32	31	176	196	62	116	31	—	.299	-7	1.47	5.52	5.14	5.78	10.0	2.8	5.2	1.4	0.0	1.15
2005	PHI	MLB	24	13	8	0	34	34	215¹	193	68	208	31	47.2%	.282	21	1.21	3.72	4.24	3.93	8.3	2.6	8.0	1.2	41.6	4.92
2006	PHI	MLB	25	12	7	0	31	31	198	194	63	189	29	46.7%	.307	23	1.30	3.91	3.92	3.74	8.2	2.5	7.7	1.1	40.7	5.42
2007	*PHI*	*MLB*	*26*	*12*	*10*	*0*	*31*	*31*	*200²*	*194*	*63*	*178*	*25*	*48.0%*	*.293*	*23*	*1.28*	*4.09*	*4.17*	*4.05*	*8.4*	*2.5*	*7.1*	*1.0*	*36.1*	*5.20*

Breakout: 22% Improve: 57% Collapse: 5%   Attrition: 1%   Comparables: Freddy Garcia, Andy Benes, Ben McDonald, Pete Vuckovich

Bret Myers established himself as one of the game's class acts by physically assaulting his own wife on a Boston street in late June. In a just world that act would condemn him to eternal public scorn, but he'll probably have to live with it only as long as it takes him to throw a no-hitter, win a World Series game, or post a Cy Young-worthy season. Myers was allowed to take his scheduled turn on national television the day after, only to have public outrage prompt the Phillies to give him a three-week time-out to think about what he'd done. Had Myers not been the Phillies only reliable starter at the time, building on his 2005 breakthrough, things might have gone a bit differently. America, actions such as Myers's should bother you far more than the use of performance enhancing drugs.

Josh Outman   Bats: L Throws: L   Height: 6' 1" Weight: 180 Born: September 14, 1984 Age: 22

YEAR	TEAM	LVL	AGE	W	L	SV	G	GS	IP	H	BB	SO	HR	GB%	BABIP	STUFF	WHIP	ERA	PERA	EQERA	EQH9	EQBB9	EQSO9	EQHR9	VORP	WXRL
2005	BAT	A-	20	2	1	0	11	4	29¹	23	14	31	1	58.0%	.278	-5	1.26	2.76	5.87	6.11	8.0	5.8	4.8	1.0	-1.6	—
2006	LWD	A	21	14	6	0	27	27	155¹	119	75	161	5	47.4%	.288	17	1.25	2.96	5.11	5.29	8.6	5.6	5.6	0.7	5.0	—
2007	*PHI*	*MLB*	*22*	*5*	*9*	*0*	*23*	*21*	*115*	*120*	*72*	*85*	*16*	*47.0%*	*.296*	*2*	*1.66*	*5.73*	*5.81*	*5.70*	*9.1*	*5.0*	*5.9*	*1.1*	*-1.1*	*0.80*

Breakout: 13% Improve: 35% Collapse: 24% Attrition: 0%   Comparables: Neal Cotts, Jared Doyle, Cory Vance, Pete Zamora

A tenth-round pick in 2005, Outman finished the year strongly, allowing no runs in five of his last seven starts. He started 2006 as essentially a one-pitch pitcher—a fastball he dials up to 95 MPH—but improved with his changeup and slider as the year went on. Outman originally pitched with an extremely strange motion designed by his father to take stress off his shoulder, and there is some thought that he is still learning to pitch conventionally, causing some of his control problems. Even if his secondary pitches don't develop, his fastball alone might be enough for him to make it as a power lefty out of the pen. Imagine the marketability of "Out-Man," superhero closer.

Arthur Rhodes   Bats: L Throws: L   Height: 6' 2"   Weight: 210   Born: December 31, 1969   Age: 37

YEAR	TEAM	LVL	AGE	W	L	SV	G	GS	IP	H	BB	SO	HR	GB%	BABIP	STUFF	WHIP	ERA	PERA	EQERA	EQH9	EQBB9	EQSO9	EQHR9	VORP	WXRL
2004	OAK	MLB	34	3	3	9	37	0	38²	46	21	34	9	—	.330	-9	1.75	5.12	5.57	4.95	10.4	4.3	7.2	1.8	4.4	0.43
2005	CLE	MLB	35	3	1	0	47	0	43¹	33	12	43	2	43.6%	.270	27	1.04	2.08	2.78	2.86	7.0	2.5	8.8	0.4	14.5	1.56
2006	PHI	MLB	36	0	5	4	55	0	45²	47	29	48	2	38.6%	.346	16	1.66	5.32	3.60	4.72	8.7	4.9	8.3	0.4	3.9	0.95
2007	PHI	MLB	37	2	3	3	48	0	47	50	22	42	7	44.0%	.312	-2	1.52	4.74	5.09	4.66	9.2	3.7	7.2	1.2	4.8	0.50

Breakout: 18% Improve: 35% Collapse: 35% Attrition: 26%   Comparables: Kent Mercker, Mark Guthrie, Diego Segui, John Hiller

The Phillies brought Rhodes in to be the primary setup man for Tom Gordon, trading Jason Michaels to get him, and were so committed to that idea that they kept using him in the role long after it was clear he wasn't filling it. Rhodes's control deserted him last year. While his walk total doesn't look too bad, he started more than half the hitters he faced with a ball, which meant hitters could forget the slider and sit dead red. His season was mercifully ended by a strained elbow in September. He's since filed for free agency.

Brian Sanches   Bats: R Throws: R   Height: 6' 0"   Weight: 190   Born: August 8, 1978   Age: 28

YEAR	TEAM	LVL	AGE	W	L	SV	G	GS	IP	H	BB	SO	HR	GB%	BABIP	STUFF	WHIP	ERA	PERA	EQERA	EQH9	EQBB9	EQSO9	EQHR9	VORP	WXRL
2004	REA	AA	25	4	2	3	41	0	69²	55	25	60	10	—	.241	-26	1.15	2.71	6.64	3.63	8.2	3.9	5.2	2.0	14.7	—
2005	SWB	AAA	26	5	3	1	51	2	83	81	27	75	9	39.8%	.317	-5	1.30	3.69	4.92	4.23	9.0	3.1	6.2	1.1	12.6	—
2006	SWB	AAA	27	3	2	19	36	0	43²	24	13	52	2	45.9%	.239	21	0.86	1.88	3.37	2.59	6.3	3.0	8.4	0.6	13.9	—
2006	PHI	MLB	27	0	0	0	18	0	21¹	23	14	22	5	28.6%	.310	6	1.73	5.92	5.63	5.24	8.9	4.8	8.1	1.6	0.4	-0.12
2007	PHI	MLB	28	2	3	3	52	1	51	51	23	43	8	40.0%	.290	-2	1.46	4.74	5.12	4.62	8.8	3.6	6.8	1.3	5.6	0.50

Breakout: 12% Improve: 26% Collapse: 41% Attrition: 40%   Comparables: Dave Tobik, Mike Armstrong, Al Reyes, Mel Queen

A second-round pick by the Royals in the last millennium, Sanches was just another pitcher with a mediocre fastball knocking around the minor leagues until he developed a splitter. That gave him the out-pitch he'd lacked, and you can trace its impact in his translated strikeout numbers; he terrorized Triple-A hitters last year. To use it most effectively, though, he needs to get to two strikes, and major league hitters pounded his get-it-over-to-get-ahead offerings.

Matt Smith   Bats: L Throws: L   Height: 6' 5"   Weight: 225   Born: June 15, 1979   Age: 28

YEAR	TEAM	LVL	AGE	W	L	SV	G	GS	IP	H	BB	SO	HR	GB%	BABIP	STUFF	WHIP	ERA	PERA	EQERA	EQH9	EQBB9	EQSO9	EQHR9	VORP	WXRL
2004	TRN	AA	25	4	4	0	14	11	61²	67	31	56	5	—	.346	-3	1.59	4.96	5.48	5.69	9.5	5.3	5.3	1.2	-0.6	—
2005	TRN	AA	26	3	4	2	22	4	54²	46	23	59	2	56.6%	.317	5	1.26	2.80	4.28	5.13	8.2	5.0	6.0	0.5	2.8	—
2005	COH	AAA	26	2	0	1	25	0	27²	24	13	33	3	43.2%	.300	8	1.34	2.60	4.99	3.29	8.2	4.6	8.2	1.3	7.0	—
2006	COH	AAA	27	0	1	0	24	0	26	27	8	22	3	51.3%	.316	-11	1.35	2.08	5.41	3.81	9.3	3.1	5.5	1.7	5.2	—
2006	NYA	MLB	27	0	0	0	12	0	12	4	8	9	0	41.4%	.138	12	1.00	0.00	4.04	0.00	2.9	5.8	6.6	0.0	8.2	0.06
2006	SWB	AAA	27	0	0	4	9	0	9¹	5	6	6	1	51.9%	.167	-3	1.21	1.98	7.91	3.12	6.2	6.2	4.2	2.1	2.4	—
2006	PHI	MLB	27	0	1	0	14	0	8²	3	4	12	0	53.3%	.200	9	0.81	2.07	2.26	2.08	3.1	4.2	11.4	0.0	3.8	0.68
2007	PHI	MLB	28	2	3	2	62	1	50¹	51	27	41	6	49.0%	.300	-4	1.53	4.62	4.96	4.58	8.8	4.3	6.5	0.9	5.7	0.60

Breakout: 7% Improve: 19% Collapse: 62% Attrition: 30%   Comparables: Gene Walter, Ron Villone, Hector Mercado, Ray King

The token big-leaguer in the Abreu trade, Smith actually has a decent amount of value. Not Abreu-level value, of course, but he's a lefty with good velocity for a southpaw (cracking 90 MPH now and again), and he's got a sharp slider. He should be a lock to step into the primary LOOGY role, barring a late addition. He's more than ready, and he'll be good in the job.

Rick White   Bats: R Throws: R   Height: 6' 4"   Weight: 240   Born: December 31, 1969   Age: 38

YEAR	TEAM	LVL	AGE	W	L	SV	G	GS	IP	H	BB	SO	HR	GB%	BABIP	STUFF	WHIP	ERA	PERA	EQERA	EQH9	EQBB9	EQSO9	EQHR9	VORP	WXRL
2004	CLE	MLB	35	5	5	1	59	0	78¹	88	29	44	15	—	.305	-25	1.51	5.29	5.48	5.40	9.3	3.0	4.6	1.5	1.9	0.54
2005	PIT	MLB	36	4	7	2	71	0	75	90	29	40	3	55.6%	.349	-3	1.59	3.72	3.94	4.68	10.6	3.2	4.3	0.4	6.7	0.72
2006	CIN	MLB	37	1	0	1	26	0	27¹	34	5	17	5	62.2%	.341	-12	1.43	6.26	4.65	6.35	10.2	1.3	5.1	1.3	-4.1	-0.63
2006	PHI	MLB	37	3	1	0	38	0	37¹	38	15	23	3	64.7%	.310	-6	1.42	4.34	4.20	4.42	8.6	3.0	4.9	0.7	4.2	0.63
2007	PHI	MLB	38	2	3	1	46	1	56²	68	20	31	7	56.0%	.311	-16	1.55	4.95	5.28	4.94	10.4	2.9	4.3	1.0	4.4	0.40

Breakout: 24% Improve: 45% Collapse: 32% Attrition: 27%   Comparables: Roberto Hernandez, Dennis Lamp, Jim Hearn, Al Benton

The aging reliever added to his frequent-flier miles, joining his seventh major league organization in the last four years when the Phils claimed him off waivers from the Reds in late June. They then assigned him to mop-up duty for the rest of the year. He's been a free agent after each of the last five seasons, and has always taken until the last few weeks before spring training starts to latch on with someone new. This winter is no exception.

Randy Wolf

Bats: L Throws: L Height: 6' 0" Weight: 205 Born: August 22, 1976 Age: 30

YEAR	TEAM	LVL	AGE	W	L	SV	G	GS	IP	H	BB	SO	HR	GB%	BABIP	STUFF	WHIP	ERA	PERA	EQERA	EQH9	EQBB9	EQSO9	EQHR9	VORP	WXRL
2004	PHI	MLB	27	5	8	0	23	23	136²	145	36	89	20	—	.293	4	1.32	4.28	4.56	4.87	9.5	2.1	5.2	1.2	15.2	2.31
2005	PHI	MLB	28	6	4	0	13	13	80	87	26	61	14	35.9%	.312	3	1.41	4.39	5.14	4.56	10.0	2.7	6.3	1.6	10.1	1.43
2006	PHI	MLB	29	4	0	0	12	12	56²	63	33	44	13	39.0%	.305	-6	1.69	5.56	6.01	5.16	9.3	4.4	6.2	1.7	1.1	0.97
2007	LAN	MLB	30	5	7	1	34	15	98	106	43	74	16	40.0%	.299	-3	1.52	5.17	5.53	5.15	10.0	3.5	6.0	1.4	5.0	1.10

Breakout: 13% Improve: 39% Collapse: 31% Attrition: 15%   Comparables: Pete Falcone, Juan Pizarro, Don Carman, Bob Shirley

Wolf's 2005 season ended with Tommy John surgery, and it took him until after the All-Star break last year to get back onto a major league diamond. He demonstrated that he was pretty much the same pitcher he had been the previous three years, absent some control—common enough after TJ and the sort of thing that can be expected to improve as he gets further into his recovery. The downside is that the name Randy Wolf still conjures notions of the pitcher he was from 2000 to 2002, not the average guy he's been since. The Dodgers shelled out $7.5 million hoping to get the former; the change in parks will work in their favor.

Lineouts

PLAYER	TEAM	LVL	AGE	PA	R	2B	3B	HR	RBI	BB	SO	SB-CS	SPEED	AVG/OBP/SLG	MLVr	EqAVG/EqOBP/EqSLG	EqA	VORP
C J. Gosewisch	CLR	A+	22	339	32	14	0	9	39	24	55	1-0	3.2	.252/.318/.387	-.007	.224/.278/.353	.222	-9.2
SS B. Harman	CLR	A+	20	482	59	19	1	2	25	48	102	6-2	5.1	.241/.322/.305	-.109	.221/.291/.281	.210	-19.2
3B B. King	SWB	AAA	25	392	40	25	2	12	48	20	69	5-0	4.5	.261/.302/.440	.041	.255/.294/.441	.251	9.4
2B H. Made	TAM	A+	21	334	37	22	2	3	28	13	42	6-8	5.0	.286/.312/.397	.051	.274/.298/.384	.232	2.0
	CLR	A+	21	107	5	2	0	1	4	2	22	0-0	3.1	.212/.226/.260	-.334	.183/.198/.221	.155	-13.1
C J. Sanchez	YAN	Rk	18	104	10	5	0	0	10	9	19	3-0	4.2	.269/.346/.323	.032	.237/.288/.289	.211	-12.9
	PHL	Rk	18	29	1	2	0	0	1	1	8	1-0	1.9	.192/.241/.269	-.219	.148/.172/.185	.140	-14.4
INF D. Sandoval#	SWB	AAA	27	368	31	17	1	2	39	14	50	1-1	4.2	.255/.288/.328	-.133	.239/.271/.305	.206	-14.6
	PHI	MLB	27	43	1	1	0	0	4	4	3	0-0	2.9	.211/.279/.237	-.393	.184/.256/.211	.181	-2.3
PH R. Simon*	TIJ	MX	31	270	46	13	0	18	69	29	18	1-0	4.1	.348/.422/.635	.468	.300/.363/.554	.305	28.4
	OKL	AAA	31	72	3	5	0	1	7	7	7	0-0	2.7	.317/.389/.444	.221	.292/.356/.400	.267	2.3
	PHI	MLB	31	23	0	0	0	0	2	2	6	0-0	3.8	.238/.304/.238	-.327	.190/.261/.190	.172	-0.8
OF M. Spidale	LWD	A	24	361	58	19	3	1	37	37	33	29-4	6.9	.345/.418/.435	.340	.314/.361/.387	.270	14.5

PLAYER	TEAM	LVL	AGE	W	L	SV	IP	H	BB	SO	HR	GB%	BABIP	STUFF	WHIP	ERA	PERA	EqERA	EqH9	EqBB9	EqSO9	EqHR9	VORP
K. Drabek	PHL	Rk	18	1	3	0	23¹	33	11	14	2	—	.408	-29	1.90	7.79	8.64	9.93	13.9	5.6	3.2	2.8	-10.9
E. Garcia	BAT	A-	18	3	5	0	66²	62	10	46	5	—	.279	-19	1.09	2.99	7.39	5.66	11.0	2.0	3.6	2.9	-0.4
K. Kendrick	LWD	A	21	3	2	0	46²	34	15	54	0	—	.291	23	1.06	2.14	3.57	4.30	8.4	3.7	6.1	0.2	6.4
	CLR	A+	21	9	7	0	130²	117	37	79	15	—	.260	-24	1.18	3.53	6.47	5.24	9.1	3.0	3.6	2.0	5.1
B. Mazone*	REA	AA	29	1	3	0	37	32	7	26	3	—	.264	-1	1.05	2.43	4.93	3.75	9.0	2.0	4.0	1.2	7.4
	SWB	AAA	29	13	3	0	128	108	36	85	6	—	.269	11	1.13	2.04	4.22	4.05	8.7	2.9	4.5	0.7	21.4
Z. Segovia	CLR	A+	23	5	1	0	49¹	39	12	41	2	—	.278	9	1.04	2.20	4.66	3.78	8.3	2.8	4.5	0.8	9.6
	REA	AA	23	11	5	0	107²	90	24	75	8	—	.259	0	1.06	3.11	4.97	4.99	8.7	2.3	4.3	1.1	7.1

Tuffy Gosewisch threw out 43 would-be basestealers last year, the third-best total in pro ball. The two players ahead of him were lower in the minors, caught more innings, and allowed more stolen bases. He started hitting the ball with authority in the second half, but that's probably a fleeting thing; he still profiles as a defensive backup. **Brad Harman**, Australia's WBC shortstop, was awful after a breakthrough 2005; his father's illness may have taken his mind off of baseball. **Brennan King** is a veteran minor leaguer who has made slooooow progress, and has re-signed with Philadelphia; the relative vacuum at third may give him a chance to sneak in. **Hector Made** was the second baseman acquired from Yankees for Sal Fasano so the Phillies could claim they weren't just giving him away for free. One of three minor leaguers the Yankees gave up to get Bobby Abreu, the 19-year-old **Jesus Sanchez** is already considered to be an elite defender with a quick release and a strong arm, but has a long way to go as a hitter. **Danny Sandoval**, slick-fielding infielder, played like himself when given a shot at the majors. From childhood we're taught to be ourselves, but what if one's self isn't very interesting? **Randall Simon** went down to the Mexican League to prove he could still be a line-drive machine; that done, Texas signed him, then sold him to the Phillies. He might hack his way back into a regular pinch-hitting job. Its nice to win a batting title, but, come on—**Mike Spidale** was a 24-year-old with Double- and Triple-A experience playing in the Sally League.

Kyle Drabek slipped to eighteenth in last year's draft on the basis of personal issues, not baseball talent or pedigree (he's Doug's son). His fastball can run into the upper-90s, his curve was one the of the best in the draft, and he could have been drafted as a shortstop if he wasn't such a good pitcher. Some of his off-field behavior can be explained by more or less normal adolescent immaturity. He got his butt kicked in the GCL, and didn't handle failure well at all; how he responds in the coming year will tell whether he's got the attitude to match his aptitude. **Edgar Garcia** is a Dominican with a tremendous upside, boasting a nifty curve and low-90s velocity. While he's a long way off, he probably has the best ceiling of anyone not named Hamels in the organization. A former high school quarterback, **Kyle Kendrick** made improvements in his off-speed stuff to complement a good moving fastball. You want heartache? Spend nine years in the minors, get called in for an emergency start, and have it rain. **Brian Mazone** didn't get another chance. A 2002 second-rounder and top high school pitcher, **Zach Segovia** finally came all the way back from his 2004 Tommy John surgery last year. He may be chunkier than you'd like, but if he has some more years like this and he'll be back on the prospect path.

Manager: Charlie Manuel

Year	Team	W-L	Pythag +/-	Avg PC	100 +P	120 +P	QS	BQS	REL	REL w Zero R	IBB	SUBS	PH	PH Avg	PH HR	SB2	CS2	SB3	CS3	SAC Att	SAC %	POS SAC	Squeeze	Swing	In Play
2005	PHI	88-74	-2	93.1	58	3	80	8	441	281	51	46	263	.233	4	99	26	17	1	92	67.4%	25	0	111	83
2006	PHI	85-77	+1	93.0	56	2	68	7	500	323	63	77	296	.209	3	87	25	5	0	82	69.5%	28	0	105	69

As Bill James observed, teams that have had managers with intense, high-pressure personalities tend to hire mellow, easygoing managers as an antidote. Manuel followed the amped-to-11 Larry Bowa, coming with a reputation as a players' manager and an endorsement from the team's star slugger and former Manuel hitting pupil Jim Thome. There's little doubt the Phillies players have appreciated the cooler clubhouse atmosphere, but the downside to the "let 'em play" approach is that, while it works well with a deep team that requires little in the way of John McGraw-style coaching, on a flawed team such as the Phillies, it can seem like drift. Manuel uses fewer lineups than any manager in baseball, picking one batting order and staying with it. He's extremely conservative with the hit-and-run, reluctant to bunt with a non-pitcher, and his team hasn't pulled off a squeeze play in the last two years. The Phillies bullpen has been a constant sore spot; as with his lineups, Manuel establishes pitchers in roles and then leaves them there whether they're performing or not. Manuel is unequivocally a great teacher of hitting; the list of hitters who improved with Manuel as their coach or manager is long, and even good hitters tend to perk up in his care. Given his mix of skills and strategic tendencies, Manuel is probably the greatest A's manager Billy Beane has never hired.

Pittsburgh Pirates

Since the end of their 1990-to-1992 run of National League East Championships under Jim Leyland, the Pirates have been consistently competitive, although their brand of competition has been a little different from everyone else's. The Pirates fight not to win their division, now the NL Central, but to not lose 100 games, not to slip from the advanced mediocrity of their current position to the abject misery of the Kansas City Royals.

It's an unnatural state of affairs. It's worth remembering just how far this franchise has fallen since its 1979 "We are Family" Championship. Times were different then, but not too different; Pittsburgh still hasn't led the National League in attendance since 1925. At no time during the franchise's run of great teams in the 1970s (see table 1) did the club rank higher than fifth. Attendance in the championship season of 1979 ranked tenth in a twelve-team league. As a city, Pittsburgh's population was already declining, falling to 423,938 by 1980, down by over 250,000 from the city's 1950 peak.

Though Pittsburgh has continued to hemorrhage population in the ensuing decades, the population in its metropolitan area (as reckoned by the US Census Bureau's July 2005 estimate of Metropolitan Statistical Areas) has been falling at a slower rate, dropping roughly 2 percent since the 2000 census. Pittsburgh's MSA, while small at an estimated 2.38 million, is by no means the smallest on the major league circuit, ranking ahead of Denver, Cleveland, Cincinnati, Kansas City, and Milwaukee (see table 2).

Pittsburgh is indisputably a small-market club, though it's clear that they could be doing a better job of exploiting the market that they have. Even the opening of PNC Park provided little more than a momentary spike in attendance. The contract between the consumer and this purveyor of entertainment has been broken. After fourteen straight losing seasons, the fans are saying, as the stock policeman character does in many a film, move along folks, there's nothing to see here. That decision, to stay away in droves (as Yogi Berra would say), locks the Pirates into a self-sustaining cycle of failure. As the product declines and stagnates, the fans stay away, withholding the money the team needs to improve the product.

There is a question of whether the Pirates would know what to do with the money if the fans gave it to them. The administration of former General Manager Cam Bonifay (1993–2001) has already become legendary for its incompetence, but after four and a half years under Bonifay's replacement, Dave Littlefield, little has changed. This is particularly apparent in the organization's minor league operations.

The first year of the Bonifay era was the last time the Pirates drafted out of the top 20 in June. They've twice had the number one pick in that time. Excluding the 2004 to 2006 drafts, which may yet yield a few usable players, the Pirates fumbled ten consecutive amateur classes (see table 3).

The Pirates have spent ten years drafting conservatively, taking low-ceiling college player after low-ceiling college player, and getting very little in return. Paul Maholm is exactly what he was expected to be coming out of college, a back-of-the-rotation starter. Last year's fourth-overall pick, Brad Lincoln, is the same kind of pitcher. They've avoided high-risk/high-impact players, but they are so poor at developing players that even their low-risk/low-impact draft choices generally fail to develop. This stands in very direct contras to the Brewers, who have remade themselves in part by picking players with up-side and radically making over the organization since the Seligs finally sold the franchise.

PIRATES PROSPECTUS

2006 record: 67–95; Fifth place, NL Central

Pythagenport record: 70–92

Runs scored per game: 4.27 (16th in NL)

Runs allowed per game: 4.90 (8th in NL)

Team EqA: .249 (16th in NL)

2006 Batters Age: 28.2 (3rd youngest in NL)

2006 Pitchers Age: 26.9 (2nd youngest in NL)

Ballpark: PNC Park; Neutral park; Park Factor of 1.006

2006: A team unburdened by excessive talent, excitement, or promise tries not to distract from a peach of a ballpark.

2007: If everything possible breaks their way, they will still win only 76 games.

Table 1. The Greatest Hits of Disco: Top Teams, 1970–1979

Wins	Team	W	L	PCT	DIV	PEN	WS
1	Reds	953	657	.592	6	4	2
2	Orioles	944	656	.590	5	3	1
3	Pirates	916	695	.569	6	2	2
4	Dodgers	910	701	.565	3	3	0
5	Red Sox	895	714	.556	1	1	0
6	Yankees	891	715	.555	3	2	2
7	Royals	851	760	.528	3	0	0
8	A's	838	772	.520	5	3	3
9	Twins	812	794	.506	1	0	0
10	Phillies	812	801	.503	3	0	0

Note: Div: Division Titles; PEN: League Pennants; WS: World Series Win.

The Pirates are lost in limbo, neither signing star free agents nor building from within, and the result is a deep and unyielding malaise.

This is a shame, because the NL Central has not always been the most demanding of divisions. In five of eleven seasons since 1995, the division winner has won fewer than 94 games (and fewer than 90 in four of those). One of those seasons was 2006, a year in which the Cardinals needed just 83 wins to reach the postseason. Even so, the Pirates never had a chance. In spite of bothering some contenders down the stretch, they finished right back where they started, matching their 2005 record. It is not unheard of for a 67-win team with a third-order win projection five wins better—which describes the 2005 Pirates—to improve by 10 or 12

Table 2. Pittsburghers, Take to Your Beds! Estimated Metropolitan Area Populations, July 2005

MSA	Pop	Per Capita Personal Income (Dollars)*	2006 Attendance
New York-Northern New Jersey-Long Island, NY-NJ-PA	18,747,320	45,570	Mets: 3,379,535 / Yankees: 4,248,067
Los Angeles-Long Beach-Santa Ana, CA	12,923,547	36,917	Dodgers: 3,758,545 / Angels: 3,406,790
Chicago-Naperville-Joliet, IL-IN-WI	9,443,356	38,439	Cubs: 3,123,215 / White Sox: 2,957,414
Philadelphia-Camden-Wilmington, PA-NJ-DE-MD	5,823,233	40,468	Phillies: 2,701,815
Dallas-Fort Worth-Arlington, TX	5,819,475	37,075	Rangers: 2,388,757
Miami-Fort Lauderdale-Miami Beach, FL	5,422,200	36,293	Marlins: 1,164,134
Toronto, Ontario†	5,304,100	46,352	Blue Jays: 2,302,212
Houston-Sugar Land-Baytown, TX	5,280,077	39,052	Astros: 3,022,763
Washington-Arlington-Alexandria, DC-VA-MD-WV	5,214,666	49,530	Nationals: 2,153,056
Atlanta-Sandy Springs-Marietta, GA	4,917,717	35,009	Braves: 2,550,524
Detroit-Warren-Livonia, MI‡	4,488,335	37,694	Tigers: 2,595,937
Boston-Cambridge-Quincy, MA-NH	4,411,835	48,158	Red Sox: 2,930,588
Phoenix-Mesa-Scottsdale, AZ	3,865,077	32,536	Diamondbacks: 2,091,685
Seattle-Tacoma-Bellevue, WA	3,203,314	41,661	Mariners: 2,481,165
Minneapolis-St. Paul-Bloomington, MN-WI	3,142,779	42,083	Twins: 2,285,018
San Diego-Carlsbad-San Marcos, CA§	2,933,462	39,880	Padres: 2,659,757
St. Louis, MO-IL	2,778,518	36,174	Cardinals: 3,407,104
Baltimore-Towson, MD	2,655,675	40,846	Orioles: 2,153,139
Tampa-St. Petersburg-Clearwater, FL	2,647,658	33,008	Devil Rays: 1,368,950
Pittsburgh, PA	2,386,074	36,208	Pirates: 1,861,549
Denver-Aurora, CO	2,359,994	42,574	Rockies: 2,104,362
Cleveland-Elyria-Mentor, OH	2,126,318	35,542	Indians: 1,997,995
Cincinnati-Middletown, OH-KY-IN	2,070,441	35,618	Reds: 2,134,607
Kansas City, MO-KS	1,947,694	35,859	Royals: 1,372,638
Milwaukee-Waukesha-West Allis, WI	1,512,855	37,862	Brewers: 2,335,643

*Projected 2005 as of September 2006. Source: US Bureau of Economic Analysis.

†2001 Census, Statistics Canada. Does not include the Buffalo-Niagara, NY area, which would add an additional 1.1 million. Income data approximate based on exchange rate as of January 2004.

‡Does not include nearby Canadian population.

§Does not include nearby Mexican population.

Table 3. Alert the Flying Spaghetti Monster—We're Short of Pirates

Year	Draft Pos.	#1 Pick	Principal Major Leaguers (Games with Pirates)
1994	11	Mark Farris, SS	Jimmy Anderson (102)
1995	10	Chad Hermansen, SS	Chad Hermansen (139), Bronson Arroyo (53), Alex Hernandez (27), Brian O'Connor (6)
1996	1	Kris Benson, RHP	Rob Mackowiak (593), Tike Redman (392), Kris Benson (126), Carlos Rivera (85)
1997	8	J. J. Davis, OF	John Grabow (208)*, Mike Gonzalez (168)*, J. J. Davis (53)
1998	15	Clint Johnson, LHP/OF	David Williams (66), Mike Johnston (25)
1999	8	Bobby Bradley, RHP	Ryan Doumit (136)*, J. R. House (6)
2000	19	Sean Burnett, LHP	Jose Bautista (151)*, Nate McLouth (147)*, Sean Burnett (13)
2001	8	John Van Benschoten, RHP/1B	Chris Duffy (123)*, Zach Duke (48)*, Rajai Davis (20)*, John Van Benschoten (6)
2002	1	Bryan Bullington, RHP	Matt Capps (89)*, Brad Eldred (55), Bryan Bullington (1)
2003	8	Paul Maholm, LHP	Paul Maholm (36)*, Tom Gorzelanny (14)*, Josh Sharpless (14)*

*Active with Pirates in 2006.

real games the following year, get a little lucky in a couple others, and end up with a 15-game increase. While not routine, such scenarios come nowhere near qualifying as "miracle team" showings. Had the Pirates done just that in 2006, they would have won the division and, given the nature of things in October, perhaps more. In other words, the trip from last place in 2005 to the division title in 2006 was not an especially long one, but it was a trip the Pirates came nowhere near being able to navigate.

The veterans that general manager David Littlefield brought in the previous offseason spent the first portion of 2006 proving what even the most unsophisticated blogger could see: that their days of helping teams win baseball games were behind them. Joe Randa's return to Pittsburgh was predictably uninspired. Jeromy Burnitz's $6-million salary produced a sub-replacement-level performance (–4.5 VORP), and Sean Casey's limited home run power evaporated even further in the black and gold.

None of these players' 2006 campaigns can be classified as disappointing, as there were no realistic expectations that they were going to do anything other than continue the decline phases of their respective careers. It's troubling to think that those expectations may have existed in the Pirates front office. It's one thing to bring in a player at the top of his game and have him take an uncharacteristic powder. It's another to bring him in after he's already demonstrated that he's taking on water and watch him continue to sink.

The continuing decay of the aging new hires coupled with the collapse of the team defense, which resulted in a bevy of pitchers getting killed by high opponent batting averages on balls in play (BABIP), the continued mismanagement and eventual dismissal of Craig Wilson via trade, and the generally woeful state of the offense doomed the team to another miserable year. Despite another good year from Jason Bay (though not the equal of his 2005), the surprise season by Freddy Sanchez, and a nice rookie turn by Ronny Paulino, Pittsburgh was last in the league in runs scored. This condition can only partly be attributed to playing in a pitcher's park, as five teams scored fewer runs at home than the Buccos did, including the Cubs and Astros, who play in hitter's havens. On the road, their shortcomings with the bat were truly exposed: No team came within 30 runs of their league-worst road total of 311.

It is important to note just how obtuse the management of personnel in this organization can be. Freddy Sanchez's rise was only made possible by the stress fracture in Joe Randa's foot that knocked the veteran off his pins in early May. Sanchez immediately got hot, quickly interjecting himself among the National League batting leaders. Throughout this period, Littlefield was insistent that Randa would send Sanchez back to the bench when he returned. It was only in early June, when Sanchez had raised his batting average to .358 and took over the league lead, that Littlefield conceded that this 28-year-old who was blossoming before his eyes should perhaps stay in the lineup over a gimpy 36-year-old on the edge of retirement.

A few days after the season ended, the team's board of directors had an opportunity to replace CEO Kevin McClatchy and declined to do so. An ownership restructuring in January that put chairman Robert Nutting in charge of the team at McClatchy's expense served as a second missed opportunity. Nutting, just as he had in October, pledged his support to McClatchy and Littlefield. "The board and the partnership group are completely supportive of Kevin and his executive team," Nutting told MLB.com. "We have great confidence in this group and are especially pleased to have Kevin as our managing general partner and CEO. He will continue in that position as long as he desires." In October, Nutting told the Associated Press that he and the board were, "extremely encouraged by the team's performance in the second half of the season." Indeed, the Pirates were 37–35 after the All-Star break, but half a season of mild success does not outweigh ten and a half years of abject failure.

In any case, the Pirates didn't get hot after the middle of July, they got the law of averages. Through the break, the Pirates were just 8–25 in one-run games. Afterwards, they came at 16–6 in the close shaves. Maintaining a .250 winning percentage for an entire season in games that could go either way is no easy task. Even the 1962 Mets, a team infamous for its failures in the close ones, still managed to win over a third of them. It was likely that the Pirates would experience a leveling out as the season wore on. This change in their fortunes had little too do with the men running the show, and everything to do with a few more balls bouncing favorably than they had in the first part of the season.

Anticipating a carryover effect to 2007 is appealing in the abstract. It sounds reasonable that a team that improves in the latter stages of one season will continue to do so in the next, having finally "figured things out." Unfortunately, this doesn't jibe with the Pirates' reality. The human mind strains to summon cause and effect where there isn't any. It must be especially tempting to do so in a place like Pittsburgh, where any hint of hope, however unfounded, is grounds for celebration.

After being renewed by the board, McClatchy, Littlefield, and their cohort were so excited by their new mandate that they rushed right out and did absolutely nothing. Randa retired and Burnitz was allowed to leave, but, otherwise, the cast of characters for 2007 is exactly the same. There is not even a pretense of trying, perhaps not even of caring. The organization is a hollow shell, extant only because of a few age-old reasons: Baseball has roots in this city going back to the 1880s, the league requires an even number of teams to keep the schedule manageable, and someone was dumb enough to build them a stadium. The only rational response to the Pirates' apathy is apathy.

HITTERS

Jose Bautista OF/3B **Bats: R** Throws: R Height: 6' 0" Weight: 190 Born: October 19, 1980 Age: 26

YEAR	TEAM	LVL	AGE	PA	R	2B	3B	HR	RBI	BB	SO	SB	CS	SPEED	AVG	OBP	SLG	MLVR	EQAVG	EQOBP	EQSLG	EQA	VORP	DEFENSE		
2005	ALT	AA	24	507	63	27	1	23	90	48	101	7	3	3.8	.283	.364	.503	.233	.266	.335	.466	.272	27.8	113-3B -14		
2005	IND	AAA	24	55	6	3	0	1	4	4	10	1	1	4.1	.255	.309	.373	-.119	.235	.291	.333	.218	-1.3	13-3B 0		
2005	PIT	MLB	24	31	3	1	0	0	1	3	7	1	0	5.1	.143	.226	.179	-.544	.107	.194	.143	.147	-3.1			
2006	IND	AAA	25	119	12	9	0	2	9	14	19	2	1	3.2	.277	.370	.426	.148	.265	.347	.422	.271	5.3	23-3B 0		
2006	PIT	MLB	25	469	58	20	3	16	51	46	110	2	4	4.1	.235	.335	.420	-.033	.236	.334	.425	.260	4.4	47-CF 3	30-3B -1
2007	PIT	MLB	26	510	61	27	2	16	62	48	111	4	3	4.4	.259	.338	.436	-.028	.253	.333	.434	.262	10.3	120-3B -3		

Breakout: 34% Improve: 62% Collapse: 15% Attrition: 14%   Comparables: Gary Gaetti, Brook Jacoby, Doug DeCinces, Lou Clinton

If there's a record for most big league stops in a two-year period without a decent showing in any of them, Bautista must have set it over the 2004 and 2005 seasons. It was a different story when he was called up in May of 2006. Through the end of July, he was golden, hitting .362/.485/.847. One heck of a course correction was coming up: Bautista hit .215/.323/.316 in August and .167/.278/.346 in September. A player with that kind of first-half production who can play all three outfield positions and third base would be a handy fellow to have around, but sadly he's not going to do that again. A hallmark of bad teams is that they take the players who would be perfect complementary parts on a contender and stretch them into starting roles. Here's exhibit A.

Jason Bay OF **Bats: R Throws: R** Height: 6' 2" Weight: 205 Born: September 20, 1978 Age: 28

YEAR	TEAM	LVL	AGE	PA	R	2B	3B	HR	RBI	BB	SO	SB	CS	SPEED	AVG	OBP	SLG	MLVR	EQAVG	EQOBP	EQSLG	EQA	VORP	DEFENSE	
2004	PIT	MLB	25	472	61	24	4	26	82	41	129	4	6	4.9	.282	.358	.550	.249	.283	.355	.553	.295	26.6	114-LF 3	
2005	PIT	MLB	26	707	110	44	6	32	101	95	142	21	1	6.7	.306	.402	.559	.350	.305	.403	.574	.328	72.6	134-LF 7	25-CF -3
2006	PIT	MLB	27	689	101	29	3	35	109	102	156	11	2	5.2	.286	.396	.532	.257	.284	.395	.527	.313	49.7	155-LF 12	
2007	PIT	MLB	28	652	107	34	5	34	103	86	142	12	4	5.4	.283	.383	.544	.210	.277	.378	.541	.307	40.5	152-LF 5	

Breakout: 5% Improve: 21% Collapse: 36% Attrition: 4%   Comparables: Tim Salmon, Dale Murphy, Eric Davis, Jesse Barfield

It wasn't a subtle visual pun, but then puns are rarely subtle. In some forgotten 1970s issue of *The Incredible Hulk,* there is a splash page of the Hulk, backed up against the edge of a dock, the sea to his back. A helicopter spotlight shines down from above. Pursuers close in from all sides. The caption says, "The Hulk at Bay!" Like Marvel's Bruce Banner, Jason Bay

(continued next page)

Jason Bay *(continued)*

is a Hulk at bay, a powerful presence cornered by the brutish, unthinking mediocrity of those around him. As was the case with Ralph Kiner in the late 1940s, he's the sole star on a team seemingly unable to develop more than one player at a time. When Branch Rickey came to the Pirates, he believed that the team could be jump-started by trading Kiner for a package of talent. Ownership dithered, and, by the time Rickey was allowed to pull off a deal, Kiner had declined and the Buccos didn't get a whole lot back. The current Pirates aren't in the same position—moving Bay would probably destroy what little credibility they have. However, it's important to note that Bay got a late start on the major league portion of his career, that his offense dropped considerably in 2006, from a VORP of 72.6 the year before down to 49.7, and that his PECOTA comparables didn't have great second acts to their careers.

Brian Bixler   **SS**   **Bats: R   Throws: R**   Height: 6' 1"   Weight: 190   Born: October 22, 1982   Age: 24

YEAR	TEAM	LVL	AGE	PA	R	2B	3B	HR	RBI	BB	SO	SB	CS	SPEED	AVG	OBP	SLG	MLVR	EQAVG	EQOBP	EQSLG	EQA	VORP	DEFENSE		
2004	WPT	A-	21	250	40	7	4	0	21	15	51	14	5	7.5	.276	.321	.342	.011	.248	.281	.295	.210	-17.4	58-SS	-4	
2005	HIC	A	22	557	74	23	2	9	50	38	134	21	10	5.6	.281	.343	.388	.036	.244	.285	.319	.216	-14.7	125-SS	-11	
2006	LYN	A+	23	317	46	16	2	5	33	35	58	18	7	6.1	.303	.402	.434	.217	.283	.354	.403	.265	16.4	71-SS	-1	
2006	ALT	AA	23	253	36	13	1	3	19	16	57	6	2	6.1	.301	.363	.407	.133	.299	.349	.420	.269	15.0	56-SS	-6	
2007	PIT	MLB	24	509	57	25	4	6	45	31	116	13	6	5.8	.261	.313	.372	-.155	.255	.309	.370	.236	5.4	120-SS	-3	

Breakout: 14% Improve: 42% Collapse: 30% Attrition: 8%   Comparables: Mo Bruce, Richard Lewis, Michael Young, Caonabo Cosme

A decent hitter with good speed, Bixler impressed at Lynchburg and carried on in the same vein after a promotion to Altoona in the Eastern League. He's 24 now, so it's time for him to take Triple-A by storm and start that major league career sooner rather than later. A slide over to second base seems inevitable at this point, especially with Brent Lillibridge in the van.

Jeromy Burnitz   **RF**   **Bats: L   Throws: R**   Height: 6' 0"   Weight: 210   Born: December 31, 1969   Age: 38

YEAR	TEAM	LVL	AGE	PA	R	2B	3B	HR	RBI	BB	SO	SB	CS	SPEED	AVG	OBP	SLG	MLVR	EQAVG	EQOBP	EQSLG	EQA	VORP	DEFENSE			
2004	COL	MLB	35	606	94	30	4	37	110	58	124	5	6	5.1	.283	.356	.559	.179	.267	.342	.528	.285	31.7	62-RF	1	54-CF	-5
2005	CHN	MLB	36	671	84	31	2	24	87	57	109	5	4	4.7	.258	.322	.435	.013	.254	.321	.437	.259	8.3	153-RF	9		
2006	PIT	MLB	37	342	35	12	0	16	49	22	74	1	1	3.5	.230	.289	.422	-.116	.231	.290	.423	.243	-4.5	73-RF	-7		
2007	PIT	MLB	38	336	38	15	1	13	48	25	71	2	1	4.4	.252	.311	.435	-.081	.246	.307	.433	.251	-0.4	81-RF	-4		

Breakout: 12% Improve: 31% Collapse: 38% Attrition: 49%   Comparables: George Crowe, Brian Jordan, John Vander Wal, Dave Parker

It is tough being a living emblem of everything that is wrong with an organization, or at least sharing that distinction with Sean Casey and Joe Randa. "Veteran stopgap" can be a lucrative gig, but you have to produce enough so that you can continue being one. Burnitz didn't in 2006 and could be in jeopardy of making the leap from veteran stopgap to just plain stopped. It seems like we say this every year, but many believed that Burnitz was overdrafted as the Mets first-round pick (17th overall) in 1990. Dallas Green didn't think he could play, and he didn't get a chance to play regularly until he was 28. Despite those obstacles, he still hit over 300 home runs in the big leagues. We don't know how he feels about it, but we're satisfied.

Michael Carlin   **1B/LF**   **Bats: R   Throws: R**   Height: 6' 0"   Weight: 205   Born: July 6, 1981   Age: 25

YEAR	TEAM	LVL	AGE	PA	R	2B	3B	HR	RBI	BB	SO	SB	CS	SPEED	AVG	OBP	SLG	MLVR	EQAVG	EQOBP	EQSLG	EQA	VORP	DEFENSE			
2004	WPT	A-	23	136	19	7	1	6	22	15	22	4	1	5.1	.274	.353	.504	.263	.236	.294	.423	.248	-3.8	14-1B	-2		
2005	HIC	A	24	354	53	21	4	16	65	29	70	6	1	5.3	.318	.398	.568	.393	.269	.319	.446	.262	5.3	74-1B	4		
2006	HIC	A	25	69	12	8	1	2	10	3	15	0	1	5.9	.359	.391	.609	.527	.318	.333	.500	.276	3.9	16-1B	-1		
2006	LYN	A+	25	495	70	23	6	13	74	51	78	11	4	5.7	.274	.357	.449	.147	.247	.306	.395	.245	-12.3	58-LF	6	45-1B	-1
2007	PIT	MLB	25	484	55	27	4	12	57	34	96	5	3	5.1	.258	.316	.417	-.092	.252	.312	.416	.248	-2.3	114-1B	4		

Breakout: 11% Improve: 42% Collapse: 25% Attrition: 5%   Comparables: Brandon Berger, Mike Vento, Ryan Mulhern, Andy Wilson

He made the jump from High-A this season and held his own at Altoona, but it's probably a case of too little, too late. Carlin will turn 26 in the middle of the 2007 season, and there are first basemen his age and younger winning major league MVP trophies. First on the list of Seven Things Carlin Can't Do on a Baseball Field: Hit right-handers with authority.

Jose Castillo   2B   Bats: R   Throws: R   Height: 6' 0"   Weight: 210   Born: March 19, 1981   Age: 26

YEAR	TEAM	LVL	AGE	PA	R	2B	3B	HR	RBI	BB	SO	SB	CS	SPEED	AVG	OBP	SLG	MLVR	EQAVG	EQOBP	EQSLG	EQA	VORP	DEFENSE	
2004	PIT	MLB	23	414	44	15	2	8	39	23	92	3	2	4.8	.256	.298	.368	-.128	.252	.296	.361	.229	-0.1	106-2B	-3
2005	PIT	MLB	24	398	49	16	3	11	53	23	59	2	3	4.6	.268	.307	.416	-.028	.266	.309	.429	.251	5.8	95-2B	-7
2006	PIT	MLB	25	562	54	25	0	14	65	32	98	6	4	4.2	.253	.299	.382	-.136	.251	.299	.381	.237	-0.1	139-2B	-23
2007	*PIT*	*MLB*	*26*	*485*	*54*	*23*	*2*	*12*	*54*	*30*	*79*	*5*	*3*	*4.9*	*.264*	*.314*	*.406*	*-.105*	*.258*	*.310*	*.404*	*.244*	*6.8*	*115-2B*	*-5*

Breakout: 28%   Improve: 49%   Collapse: 28%   Attrition: 18%   Comparables: Michael Young, Reno Bertoia, Charlie Hayes, Carlos Garcia

Oh, for May. In that one month, Castillo hit half his of 14 home runs and piled on a good deal of whatever other meat his statistical plate contained last year, hitting .366/.413/.634. That proves that just about anybody can be Albert Pujols for four weeks. As for the rest of 2006, he put up sub-replacement-level numbers, and a knee injury has severely inhibited his mobility. After three years of waiting for something more than a .301 OBP from Castillo, it's time for the Pirates to consider moving on.

Humberto Cota   C   Bats: R   Throws: R   Height: 5' 11"   Weight: 215   Born: February 7, 1979   Age: 28

YEAR	TEAM	LVL	AGE	PA	R	2B	3B	HR	RBI	BB	SO	SB	CS	SPEED	AVG	OBP	SLG	MLVR	EQAVG	EQOBP	EQSLG	EQA	VORP	DEFENSE	
2004	PIT	MLB	25	70	10	1	1	5	8	3	20	0	0	5.5	.227	.271	.500	-.013	.227	.271	.500	.253	1.9	15-C	-1
2005	PIT	MLB	26	320	29	20	1	7	43	17	80	0	0	3.3	.242	.285	.387	-.122	.240	.287	.389	.234	1.6	77-C	-3
2006	PIT	MLB	27	110	5	1	0	0	5	8	26	0	0	3.6	.190	.248	.200	-.516	.140	.209	.150	.145	-10.4	28-C	-1
2007	*PIT*	*MLB*	*28*	*269*	*25*	*12*	*1*	*7*	*31*	*19*	*63*	*0*	*1*	*3.9*	*.243*	*.300*	*.379*	*-.183*	*.238*	*.296*	*.377*	*.230*	*-1.2*	*66-C*	*-1*

Breakout: 54%   Improve: 72%   Collapse: 14%   Attrition: 49%   Comparables: Bob Montgomery, Randy Knorr, Steve Swisher, Phil Roof

Cota had just one double to show for 110 plate appearances last year. It was a fluke, of course; Cota hit 20 the year before. Cota's production is all too typical for Pirate catchers; Don Slaught would probably make a list of the team's top-five all-time offensive catchers. For a franchise with a history going back to the nineteenth century, that's amazing. Given the same number of at-bats next year—about all he can expect—if nothing else, Cota should double his doubles several times over.

Rajai Davis   CF   Bats: R   Throws: R   Height: 5' 11"   Weight: 195   Born: October 19, 1980   Age: 26

YEAR	TEAM	LVL	AGE	PA	R	2B	3B	HR	RBI	BB	SO	SB	CS	SPEED	AVG	OBP	SLG	MLVR	EQAVG	EQOBP	EQSLG	EQA	VORP	DEFENSE			
2004	LYN	A+	23	574	91	27	7	5	38	59	60	57	15	8.2	.314	.388	.424	.190	.284	.343	.387	.261	14.8	115-CF	-7		
2005	ALT	AA	24	561	82	22	5	4	34	43	76	45	9	8.3	.281	.351	.369	.036	.266	.327	.348	.248	-1.4	115-CF	-4		
2006	IND	AAA	25	417	53	17	1	2	21	27	59	45	13	7.3	.283	.335	.348	-.004	.279	.329	.351	.249	0.9	75-CF	3	17-LF	-2
2006	PIT	MLB	25	17	1	1	0	0	0	2	3	1	3	5.7	.143	.250	.214	-.506	.143	.250	.214	.147	-2.8				
2007	*PIT*	*MLB*	*26*	*418*	*61*	*20*	*4*	*4*	*33*	*28*	*56*	*35*	*10*	*7.0*	*.280*	*.334*	*.382*	*-.092*	*.274*	*.329*	*.380*	*.254*	*5.4*	*100-CF*	*0*		

Breakout: 21%   Improve: 49%   Collapse: 22%   Attrition: 16%   Comparables: Carlos Valderrama, Tyrell Godwin, Tim Raines, Peter Bergeron

After a none-too-scintillating year at Triple-A, Davis is beginning to look like Chris Duffy Lite, a strange kind of dietetic beer diluted with the waters of the toxic Monongehela. That's not the ideal label for a 26-year-old with just 14 major league at-bats to his credit. He'll get some more time before he's done, but the minor leagues brew this brand by the case.

Yurendell DeCaster   3B   Bats: R   Throws: R   Height: 6' 1"   Weight: 205   Born: September 26, 1979   Age: 27

YEAR	TEAM	LVL	AGE	PA	R	2B	3B	HR	RBI	BB	SO	SB	CS	SPEED	AVG	OBP	SLG	MLVR	EQAVG	EQOBP	EQSLG	EQA	VORP	DEFENSE			
2004	ALT	AA	24	358	53	18	1	14	40	22	78	4	2	4.9	.274	.328	.463	.099	.257	.302	.425	.249	8.0	84-3B	-7		
2005	IND	AAA	25	462	60	31	4	11	61	37	103	7	5	5.2	.280	.346	.453	.074	.265	.328	.418	.256	1.0	48-RF	4	23-3B	-2
2006	IND	AAA	26	462	47	22	3	11	51	35	100	7	7	4.6	.273	.330	.418	.074	.271	.323	.427	.255	17.0	52-3B	-4	32-1B	3
2007	*PIT*	*MLB*	*27*	*413*	*45*	*22*	*2*	*10*	*48*	*26*	*94*	*6*	*3*	*4.8*	*.260*	*.313*	*.406*	*-.111*	*.255*	*.309*	*.404*	*.243*	*-0.3*	*98-3B*	*-1*		

Breakout: 16%   Improve: 34%   Collapse: 36%   Attrition: 16%   Comparables: Casey Blake, Mike Neal, Robb Quinlan, Mike Bell

DeCaster's second full season at Indianapolis was remarkably similar to his first, though he seemed to regress slightly in every phase of the game. It's as if someone made a second-generation cassette tape copy of his 2005 season and simply played it back last year. His PECOTA comparables suggest that there could be some corner-position utility work in his future, but he'll have to catch a few breaks to get even that far, such as finding someone who will let him use their CD burner.

Ryan Doumit   C/1B   Bats: S   Throws: R   Height: 6' 1"   Weight: 215   Born: April 3, 1981   Age: 26

YEAR	TEAM	LVL	AGE	PA	R	2B	3B	HR	RBI	BB	SO	SB	CS	SPEED	AVG	OBP	SLG	MLVR	EQAVG	EQOBP	EQSLG	EQA	VORP	DEFENSE			
2004	ALT	AA	23	255	31	20	0	10	34	21	49	0	1	3.0	.262	.343	.489	.146	.241	.309	.447	.257	7.1	25-C	-4		
2005	IND	AAA	24	188	41	11	0	12	35	16	36	1	3	4.3	.345	.415	.630	.496	.329	.394	.593	.317	26.6	35-C	-3		
2005	PIT	MLB	24	257	25	13	1	6	35	11	48	2	1	4.7	.255	.324	.398	-.029	.258	.320	.412	.253	6.1	48-C	2		
2006	PIT	MLB	25	178	15	9	0	6	17	15	42	0	0	3.4	.208	.322	.389	-.113	.212	.320	.397	.252	-2.2	23-1B	-2	10-C	0
2007	PIT	MLB	26	317	38	16	1	11	45	23	61	1	1	4.0	.269	.342	.458	.018	.263	.338	.456	.270	11.0	77-C	0		

Breakout: 32%   Improve: 57%   Collapse: 11%   Attrition: 35%   Comparables: Ben Davis, Dave Hollins, Randy Knorr, Todd Benzinger

Ronny Paulino had already established himself at catcher by the time Doumit's left hamstring forced him onto the disabled list in June. When Doumit came back two months later, there wasn't a lot of playing time available. A position switch seems inevitable, but Doumit's bat would be less exceptional at first base than it is behind the plate. If Doutmit can stay healthy for more than two minutes at a time, he might have more value to the Pirates as a trading chit in a thin catching market. Who are we kidding? The Pirates don't upgrade through trades. Come to think of it, they don't upgrade.

Chris Duffy   CF   Bats: L   Throws: L   Height: 5' 9"   Weight: 190   Born: April 20, 1980   Age: 27

YEAR	TEAM	LVL	AGE	PA	R	2B	3B	HR	RBI	BB	SO	SB	CS	SPEED	AVG	OBP	SLG	MLVR	EQAVG	EQOBP	EQSLG	EQA	VORP	DEFENSE	
2004	ALT	AA	24	509	84	23	6	8	41	33	77	32	8	7.6	.309	.378	.439	.176	.296	.349	.411	.267	20.2	111-CF	5
2005	IND	AAA	25	340	55	13	7	7	31	16	57	17	9	8.3	.308	.358	.464	.137	.295	.339	.439	.267	14.6	71-CF	-3
2005	PIT	MLB	25	136	22	4	2	1	9	7	22	2	2	6.6	.341	.385	.429	.181	.349	.397	.437	.285	8.2	28-CF	2
2006	IND	AAA	26	118	18	7	2	2	19	10	13	13	3	7.6	.349	.415	.509	.388	.346	.407	.533	.317	15.4	24-CF	1
2006	PIT	MLB	26	348	46	14	3	2	18	19	71	26	1	8.0	.255	.317	.338	-.164	.256	.317	.338	.248	3.8	76-CF	-6
2007	PIT	MLB	27	462	67	21	5	7	41	26	76	26	9	7.1	.293	.343	.415	-.020	.287	.338	.413	.263	13.2	109-CF	-1

Breakout: 10%   Improve: 35%   Collapse: 31%   Attrition: 18%   Comparables: Alex Sanchez, Russ Snyder, David Hulse, Cory Sullivan

Duffy started in center field on Opening Day, having won a part in a time-share with Nate McLouth. In direct contrast to his hot 2005 debut, Duffy opened the 2006 season in a slump, batting .194/.255/.276 over his first 98 at-bats. On May 14, the Pirates sent Duffy to Triple-A; he didn't report. Gripped by a crisis of confidence and apparently disenchanted with the coaching staff, instead he went home. He stayed there nearly a month before agreeing to return. He then spent two and a half weeks in extended spring training before finally arriving in Indy. He played well there, and, to their credit the Pirates brought him back in August—and played him—rather than blackballing him. In what was left of the season, Duffy had a very bad August (.229/.286/.275) and a terrific September (.336/.403/.458). Combined, his post-return rates were .282/.345/.366. With his speed, if he can hit somewhere between those rates and those projected in his PECOTA above, he can be a useful fourth outfielder or even a starter on some teams, such as this one. Unfortunately, Duffy's speed somehow hasn't translated into great center field defense as of yet.

Brad Eldred   1B   Bats: R   Throws: R   Height: 6' 5"   Weight: 275   Born: July 12, 1980   Age: 25

YEAR	TEAM	LVL	AGE	PA	R	2B	3B	HR	RBI	BB	SO	SB	CS	SPEED	AVG	OBP	SLG	MLVR	EQAVG	EQOBP	EQSLG	EQA	VORP	DEFENSE	
2004	LYN	A+	23	388	54	22	1	21	77	35	97	5	2	4.2	.310	.397	.570	.393	.280	.344	.509	.285	21.1	88-1B	-3
2004	ALT	AA	23	158	24	9	0	17	60	6	51	0	0	2.7	.279	.329	.687	.416	.267	.304	.640	.298	13.4	37-1B	3
2005	ALT	AA	24	93	22	6	0	13	27	8	25	1	1	4.5	.333	.387	.869	.810	.306	.355	.765	.339	15.5	19-1B	-1
2005	IND	AAA	24	214	31	13	1	15	48	14	57	4	0	4.8	.282	.336	.590	.250	.265	.318	.546	.287	10.7	37-1B	3
2005	PIT	MLB	24	208	23	9	0	12	27	13	77	1	1	3.3	.221	.279	.458	-.055	.222	.280	.466	.249	-1.2	46-1B	-6
2006	IND	AAA	25	71	10	7	0	3	10	8	18	1	1	3.9	.226	.310	.484	.092	.194	.282	.452	.249	-1.3	13-1B	0
2007	PIT	MLB	26	317	40	15	1	18	53	28	88	4	2	3.9	.245	.319	.497	.010	.240	.315	.494	.270	8.5	77-1B	-1

Breakout: 12%   Improve: 32%   Collapse: 42%   Attrition: 16%   Comparables: J. J. Davis, Juan Diaz, Ryan Ludwick, Cecil Fielder

Eldred is on a tough run that includes losing most of last season to a thumb injury, a rough go in the AFL, and striking out in over half his at-bats in winter ball. He's just young enough that there's time to recover and forge a short big league career, but anyone with his weak sense of the strike zone is more likely to break hearts than deliver souvenirs as regularly as his power might seem to promise.

Jody Gerut OF **Bats: L** **Throws: L** Height: 6′ 0″ Weight: 220 Born: September 18, 1977 Age: 29

YEAR	TEAM	LVL	AGE	PA	R	2B	3B	HR	RBI	BB	SO	SB	CS	SPEED	AVG	OBP	SLG	MLVR	EQAVG	EQOBP	EQSLG	EQA	VORP	DEFENSE			
2004	CLE	MLB	26	548	72	31	5	11	51	54	59	13	6	6.1	.252	.334	.405	-.053	.259	.345	.418	.266	5.0	111-RF	0	10-CF	-1
2005	CLE	MLB	27	157	12	9	1	1	12	18	14	1	1	4.4	.275	.357	.377	.010	.287	.376	.390	.272	2.7	20-RF	-1	16-LF	-2
2005	CHN	MLB	27	16	1	1	0	0	0	2	3	0	0	5.0	.071	.188	.143	-.684	.000	.125	.000	.078	-2.3				
2005	PIT	MLB	27	18	2	1	0	0	2	0	3	0	0	5.1	.222	.222	.278	-.422	.167	.167	.222	.140	-1.6				
2007	*PIT*	*MLB*	*29*	*337*	*46*	*18*	*2*	*7*	*37*	*33*	*37*	*5*	*2*	*5.5*	*.278*	*.353*	*.425*	*.000*	*.271*	*.349*	*.424*	*.268*	*6.1*	*81-RF*	*-3*		

Breakout: 11% Improve: 35% Collapse: 32% Attrition: 26% Comparables: Raul Ibanez, Mike Greenwell, Ed Kranepool, Joe Orsulak

Gerut endured a lost season at a time in his career when that was the last thing he needed. It didn't help that the Players Association had to file a grievance just to get the Pirates to agree that Gerut had a knee injury. The Pirates don't know much about baseball, but, when it comes to medicine, well, they know even less. He's still on the 40-man, and with Nady's issues against right-handed pitching, he might yet get his career back on track.

Javier Guzman 2B/SS **Bats: S** **Throws: R** Height: 6′ 0″ Weight: 170 Born: May 4, 1984 Age: 22

YEAR	TEAM	LVL	AGE	PA	R	2B	3B	HR	RBI	BB	SO	SB	CS	SPEED	AVG	OBP	SLG	MLVR	EQAVG	EQOBP	EQSLG	EQA	VORP	DEFENSE			
2004	HIC	A	20	505	75	20	12	2	63	20	78	31	14	8.1	.306	.334	.413	.052	.267	.287	.350	.226	-3.8	123-SS	-13		
2005	LYN	A+	21	279	40	13	7	5	35	20	41	13	5	7.5	.324	.374	.488	.247	.293	.327	.430	.263	14.1	68-SS	-4		
2005	ALT	AA	21	279	27	9	1	3	24	10	46	8	5	5.6	.236	.262	.312	-.218	.223	.253	.295	.199	-15.1	69-SS	10		
2006	*ALT*	*AA*	*22*	*524*	*57*	*23*	*5*	*7*	*40*	*25*	*64*	*12*	*8*	*5.3*	*.268*	*.307*	*.379*	*-.008*	*.252*	*.286*	*.358*	*.226*	*-4.1*	*68-SS*	*-10*	*56-2B*	*-4*

Breakout: 0% Improve: 0% Collapse: 0% Attrition: 0% Comparables:

Strong-armed and athletic, Javier Guzman joins a gaggle of good gloves in the middle infield for an organization already paying top dollar for Jack Wilson in addition to employing Jose Castillo and Freddy Sanchez, both of whom really should be second basemen. What little up-side Guzman has as a hitter is tied up in his age, but he didn't show much grown in a second season at Double-A.

Brent Lillibridge SS **Bats: R** **Throws: R** Height: 5′ 11″ Weight: 180 Born: September 18, 1983 Age: 23

YEAR	TEAM	LVL	AGE	PA	R	2B	3B	HR	RBI	BB	SO	SB	CS	SPEED	AVG	OBP	SLG	MLVR	EQAVG	EQOBP	EQSLG	EQA	VORP	DEFENSE	
2005	WPT	A-	21	191	19	12	4	4	18	14	35	10	3	7.3	.243	.305	.432	.059	.192	.234	.316	.199	-21.3	41-SS	3
2006	HIC	A	22	333	59	18	5	11	43	51	61	29	8	7.1	.299	.414	.522	.366	.271	.355	.460	.281	24.1	72-SS	7
2006	LYN	A+	22	252	47	10	3	2	28	36	43	24	5	7.5	.313	.426	.423	.245	.299	.385	.402	.283	17.6	54-SS	0
2007	*ATL*	*MLB*	*23*	*616*	*90*	*34*	*7*	*12*	*57*	*56*	*119*	*30*	*11*	*6.4*	*.276*	*.349*	*.429*	*-.003*	*.272*	*.344*	*.427*	*.267*	*30.0*	*144-SS*	*7*

Breakout: 22% Improve: 57% Collapse: 26% Attrition: 7% Comparables: Joe Jester, Ed Maysonet, Scott Pratt, Jose Morban

Lillibridge made a fairly seamless midseason jump from Hickory to High-A Lynchburg. However, his power didn't make the trip with him. Still, his speed and selectivity at the plate should have him in Pittsburgh sooner rather than later. He has above average range, good hands, and a strong arm to go with his patience and gap power. With Lillibridge possibly starting 2007 at Double-A, the Pirates will soon get the chance to see if they have a better shortstop than Jack Wilson, and might thereby improve their lot my moving their current regular. We'll all be waiting to see them take that chance.

Carlos Maldonado C **Bats: R** **Throws: R** Height: 6′ 1″ Weight: 245 Born: January 3, 1979 Age: 28

YEAR	TEAM	LVL	AGE	PA	R	2B	3B	HR	RBI	BB	SO	SB	CS	SPEED	AVG	OBP	SLG	MLVR	EQAVG	EQOBP	EQSLG	EQA	VORP	DEFENSE	
2004	BIR	AA	25	448	48	30	1	12	68	52	81	0	3	2.9	.265	.353	.441	.124	.236	.306	.373	.236	-1.1	60-C	3
2005	ALT	AA	26	321	27	14	0	7	34	35	63	0	1	1.7	.252	.339	.378	.007	.219	.292	.309	.215	-11.6	77-C	-2
2006	IND	AAA	27	384	37	18	0	6	47	36	67	2	0	3.9	.283	.354	.390	.081	.266	.331	.377	.252	6.9	95-C	-3
2006	PIT	MLB	27	20	0	0	0	0	0	1	10	1	0	5.4	.105	.150	.105	-.861	.000	.050	.000	.062	-3.2		
2007	*PIT*	*MLB*	*28*	*382*	*29*	*16*	*1*	*7*	*38*	*29*	*79*	*1*	*1*	*3.5*	*.231*	*.294*	*.340*	*-.253*	*.226*	*.290*	*.339*	*.216*	*-6.8*	*91-C*	*-1*

Breakout: 24% Improve: 41% Collapse: 33% Attrition: 25% Comparables: Keith McDonald, Tim Laker, Jonathan Aceves, Robert Machado

With Chris Coste having made it to the major leagues and found a certain amount of success, players such as Carlos Maldonado have renewed hope. Like Coste, Maldonado didn't start playing professionally until he was 23. While he hasn't raked in the minors the way Coste did, he had a pretty decent year at Indianapolis in 2006. In the midst of his prime years now, he'd be as good a backup catcher as any for about half the teams in the majors.

Andrew McCutchen   CF   Bats: R   Throws: R   Height: 5' 11"   Weight: 170   Born: October 10, 1986   Age: 20

YEAR	TEAM	LVL	AGE	PA	R	2B	3B	HR	RBI	BB	SO	SB	CS	SPEED	AVG	OBP	SLG	MLVR	EQAVG	EQOBP	EQSLG	EQA	VORP	DEFENSE	
2005	WPT	A-	18	62	12	3	1	0	5	8	6	4	1	7.0	.346	.443	.442	.347	.304	.361	.393	.267	4.5	13-CF	0
2006	HIC	A	19	503	77	20	4	14	62	42	91	22	7	5.9	.291	.356	.446	.183	.267	.313	.404	.250	6.3	113-CF	-1
2006	ALT	AA	19	87	12	4	0	3	12	8	20	1	1	4.4	.308	.379	.474	.249	.304	.368	.494	.287	7.0		
2007	*PIT*	*MLB*	*20*	*533*	*65*	*30*	*4*	*12*	*57*	*33*	*95*	*12*	*6*	*5.6*	*.273*	*.323*	*.422*	*-.062*	*.267*	*.318*	*.420*	*.252*	*8.9*	*125-CF*	*2*

Breakout: 25% Improve: 56% Collapse: 20% Attrition: 4%   Comparables: Franklin Gutierrez, Lastings Milledge, Melky Cabrera, Carlos Gonzalez

The crown jewel in the tarnished tiara that is the Pirates farm system, McCutchen is the real thing: A five-tool player with no weaknesses. The whole workbench is already showing up in games, too, including power, speed, and a good approach at the plate. It's probably already time to start thinking of a Toy Cannon-type nickname for the somewhat undersized prospect. In tribute to Tiny Tim and the crippled state of the Pirates' organization, we suggest "Crutch" McCutchen. He'll start 2007 at Double-A; the Pirates aren't going to risk rushing him.

Nate McLouth   OF   Bats: L   Throws: R   Height: 5' 11"   Weight: 185   Born: October 28, 1981   Age: 25

YEAR	TEAM	LVL	AGE	PA	R	2B	3B	HR	RBI	BB	SO	SB	CS	SPEED	AVG	OBP	SLG	MLVR	EQAVG	EQOBP	EQSLG	EQA	VORP	DEFENSE			
2004	ALT	AA	22	592	93	40	4	8	73	48	62	31	7	6.9	.322	.384	.462	.230	.312	.364	.442	.282	24.0	98-RF	-12	21-CF	2
2005	IND	AAA	23	455	64	20	3	5	39	39	58	34	8	7.4	.297	.364	.401	.049	.286	.350	.386	.267	1.2	73-LF	2	27-CF	0
2005	PIT	MLB	23	120	20	6	0	5	12	3	20	2	0	5.7	.257	.305	.450	.003	.255	.303	.464	.262	3.1	19-CF	-4		
2006	PIT	MLB	24	297	50	16	2	7	16	18	59	10	1	6.8	.233	.293	.385	-.158	.232	.292	.391	.242	-1.0	39-CF	-4	19-RF	-4
2007	*PIT*	*MLB*	*25*	*388*	*55*	*22*	*2*	*9*	*43*	*28*	*59*	*15*	*4*	*6.3*	*.283*	*.343*	*.442*	*.010*	*.277*	*.339*	*.440*	*.270*	*11.5*	*93-CF*	*-4*		

Breakout: 28% Improve: 57% Collapse: 17% Attrition: 21%   Comparables: Dave Martinez, Tommy McCraw, Denny Walling, Steve Hovley

The Pirates have corned the market on FOGies—Fourth Outfielder Guys. Their farm system is practically the Fourth Outfielder Factory. If a young outfielder is just good enough to not start, the Pirates will sniff him out and make sure he stays that way. You can buy just one or you can buy them in bulk at a discount. McLouth? Duffy? McDuffy? Butter or no butter, salted or unsalted, cinnamon and sour cream varieties, frozen and unfrozen. Move away from Pittsburgh? They'll ship a case to you so you never have to feel lonely. McLouth isn't quite as good as Duffy. He plated only 6.3 percent of the men on base when he batted (the worst mark in baseball among hitters with 150 plate appearances), and he can't really play center either. No matter how scrappy you are, people notice when you do this little with that much playing time.

Xavier Nady   RF   Bats: R   Throws: R   Height: 6' 2"   Weight: 205   Born: November 14, 1978   Age: 28

YEAR	TEAM	LVL	AGE	PA	R	2B	3B	HR	RBI	BB	SO	SB	CS	SPEED	AVG	OBP	SLG	MLVR	EQAVG	EQOBP	EQSLG	EQA	VORP	DEFENSE			
2004	POR	AAA	25	320	52	19	1	22	70	22	42	3	0	4.5	.333	.394	.632	.451	.308	.363	.563	.306	26.9	39-RF	-3	18-CF	0
2004	SDN	MLB	25	84	7	4	0	3	9	5	13	0	0	2.9	.247	.301	.416	-.082	.256	.310	.410	.247	-0.8				
2005	SDN	MLB	26	356	40	15	2	13	43	22	67	2	1	5.0	.261	.321	.439	.046	.273	.334	.466	.271	8.7	33-1B	-1	27-CF	-6
2006	NYN	MLB	27	292	37	15	1	14	40	19	51	2	1	4.4	.264	.326	.487	.084	.272	.333	.502	.279	9.5	69-RF	-4		
2006	PIT	MLB	27	220	20	13	0	3	23	11	34	1	2	3.9	.300	.352	.409	.029	.304	.355	.417	.263	2.6	27-1B	2	26-RF	1
2007	*PIT*	*MLB*	*28*	*530*	*68*	*31*	*2*	*18*	*77*	*33*	*88*	*4*	*2*	*4.6*	*.286*	*.340*	*.471*	*.045*	*.280*	*.335*	*.468*	*.271*	*13.3*	*125-RF*	*-4*		

Breakout: 10% Improve: 41% Collapse: 24% Attrition: 8%   Comparables: Ollie Brown, Rip Repulski, Rondell White, Craig Monroe

Nady's numbers look better in translation, understandable because the two ballparks he called home in 2006 aren't among the friendliest. It's too bad there aren't more lefthanders in the world—Nady's been pretty hard on them over the last three years (.331/.409/.506). Against righties, though, he doesn't reach base even 30 percent of the time; their majority status in our species has really held Xavier back. Since the Buccos like left-handed power hitters in their system to take advantage of their short porch in right, Nady is just the sort of player they weren't looking for. Of course, a perfect fit was not on their minds when they went to unload Oliver Perez. When a team on its way to the postseason is willing to discard their starting right fielder for a 41-year-old reliever and a starter with an ERA of 6.63 that says something—Nady's a platoon player at best.

Ron Paulino   C   Bats: R   Throws: R   Height: 6' 2"   Weight: 240   Born: April 21, 1981   Age: 26

YEAR	TEAM	LVL	AGE	PA	R	2B	3B	HR	RBI	BB	SO	SB	CS	SPEED	AVG	OBP	SLG	MLVR	EQAVG	EQOBP	EQSLG	EQA	VORP	DEFENSE	
2004	ALT	AA	23	404	54	23	2	15	58	32	61	3	2	4.4	.285	.345	.482	.162	.270	.322	.445	.262	16.9	80-C	5
2005	ALT	AA	24	184	24	6	0	6	20	15	30	3	0	4.0	.292	.350	.435	.128	.271	.326	.400	.254	4.6	40-C	3
2005	IND	AAA	24	302	49	18	2	13	42	26	48	3	0	5.1	.315	.372	.538	.270	.299	.358	.504	.291	26.1	63-C	4
2006	PIT	MLB	25	481	37	19	0	6	55	34	79	0	0	3.2	.310	.360	.394	.033	.308	.362	.395	.266	16.4	119-C	1
2007	*PIT*	*MLB*	*26*	*490*	*58*	*28*	*2*	*12*	*62*	*36*	*78*	*3*	*1*	*4.2*	*.289*	*.344*	*.440*	*.014*	*.283*	*.340*	*.439*	*.267*	*19.8*	*116-C*	*3*

Breakout: 25% Improve: 49% Collapse: 31% Attrition: 11%   *Comparables: Ray Fosse, Ramon Hernandez, Javy Lopez, Doc Edwards*

Paulino was lost in the great flood of quality rookies in 2006, but he posted a WARP3 of 4.9, good enough for third among National League catchers behind sophomore Brian McCann of the Braves and fellow rookie Russell Martin of the Dodgers. Paulino is two years older than Martin and three years older than McCann, but there's nothing new about a catcher getting a late entry into the big leagues. He's a plus guy behind the plate but his lack of noticeable secondary offensive skills (.050 on-base and .084 slugging) are a bit worrisome in a regular; a batting average collapse would take his whole offensive game down with it.

Steven Pearce   1B   Bats: R   Throws: R   Height: 5' 11"   Weight: 200   Born: April 13, 1983   Age: 24

YEAR	TEAM	LVL	AGE	PA	R	2B	3B	HR	RBI	BB	SO	SB	CS	SPEED	AVG	OBP	SLG	MLVR	EQAVG	EQOBP	EQSLG	EQA	VORP	DEFENSE	
2005	WPT	A-	22	312	48	26	0	7	52	35	43	2	4	3.3	.301	.381	.474	.269	.229	.282	.337	.217	-31.6	69-1B	1
2006	HIC	A	23	179	35	13	1	12	38	15	32	1	3	4.7	.288	.363	.606	.401	.246	.296	.485	.255	2.4	39-1B	0
2006	LYN	A+	23	377	48	27	1	14	60	34	65	7	5	3.6	.265	.348	.482	.170	.233	.290	.419	.243	-7.1	86-1B	-3
2007	*PIT*	*MLB*	*24*	*491*	*49*	*29*	*1*	*14*	*63*	*32*	*91*	*2*	*3*	*4.0*	*.250*	*.305*	*.416*	*-.118*	*.245*	*.301*	*.414*	*.242*	*-6.4*	*116-1B*	*2*

Breakout: 41% Improve: 57% Collapse: 17% Attrition: 7%   *Comparables: Tagg Bozied, Andy Wilson, Jason Lane, Jeremy West*

Pearce hit just enough between Hickory and Lynchburg last year to keep himself on the periphery of the Pirates' plans. He stayed hot immediately after his promotion, but cooled considerably in the second half. He has the reputation of being a bit clumsy, and his 10-for-22 career stolen base record is an indication that, once on board, he best stay where he is and let somebody else move him around. Given his age, rate of progress and accomplishment, and how hard it is to make it as a major league first baseman, there's a good chance that this listing is purely a courtesy.

Freddy Sanchez   INF   Bats: R   Throws: R   Height: 5' 10"   Weight: 185   Born: December 21, 1977   Age: 29

YEAR	TEAM	LVL	AGE	PA	R	2B	3B	HR	RBI	BB	SO	SB	CS	SPEED	AVG	OBP	SLG	MLVR	EQAVG	EQOBP	EQSLG	EQA	VORP	DEFENSE			
2004	NAS	AAA	26	140	10	7	1	1	11	11	17	4	1	4.8	.264	.326	.360	-.142	.250	.307	.336	.232	-1.8	18-2B	0		
2004	PIT	MLB	26	20	2	0	0	0	2	0	3	0	0	5.8	.158	.158	.158	-.734	.000	.000	.000	.025	-2.9				
2005	PIT	MLB	27	492	54	26	4	5	35	27	36	2	2	5.2	.291	.336	.400	.016	.294	.340	.408	.259	11.7	54-3B	7	44-2B	-4
2006	PIT	MLB	28	632	85	53	2	6	85	31	52	3	2	4.7	.344	.378	.473	.207	.343	.378	.468	.292	43.3	92-3B	15	27-SS	2
2007	*PIT*	*MLB*	*29*	*614*	*76*	*38*	*4*	*9*	*63*	*36*	*55*	*5*	*3*	*5.1*	*.298*	*.344*	*.425*	*-.001*	*.292*	*.339*	*.423*	*.262*	*19.7*	*144-3B*	*7*		

Breakout: 11% Improve: 38% Collapse: 28% Attrition: 5%   *Comparables: Cookie Rojas, Glenn Beckert, Eddie Kasko, Mark Grudzielanek*

One of the nicest surprises of the 2006 season, Sanchez went from an injury-wrecked Triple-A season to National League batting champion in two years. Not to rain too hard on the happy parade, but he is 29 already, doesn't hit the long ball, doesn't walk, and doesn't steal. He's good in the field, though, and if he were the team's shortstop we'd be that much more excited about him. Sanchez is the kind of player who can hit .300 and not be all that productive. Given his age, those kinds of years are already rushing up on him.

Neil Walker   C   Bats: S   Throws: R   Height: 6' 2"   Weight: 215   Born: September 10, 1985   Age: 21

YEAR	TEAM	LVL	AGE	PA	R	2B	3B	HR	RBI	BB	SO	SB	CS	SPEED	AVG	OBP	SLG	MLVR	EQAVG	EQOBP	EQSLG	EQA	VORP	DEFENSE	
2004	WPT	A-	18	35	2	3	0	0	7	2	1	1	2	3.7	.313	.343	.406	.154	.273	.306	.333	.221	-1.6		
2005	HIC	A	19	518	78	33	2	12	68	20	71	7	4	5.1	.301	.332	.452	.123	.265	.284	.388	.232	-1.3	80-C	-2
2005	LYN	A+	19	45	4	2	1	0	12	0	12	0	0	5.1	.262	.244	.357	-.218	.238	.222	.310	.194	-3.7		
2006	LYN	A+	20	294	32	22	1	3	35	19	41	3	5	3.9	.284	.345	.409	.083	.266	.308	.391	.240	3.4	53-C	-1
2006	ALT	AA	20	32	5	0	0	2	3	1	4	0	0	4.3	.161	.188	.355	-.289	.161	.188	.355	.180	-3.3		
2007	*PIT*	*MLB*	*21*	*430*	*44*	*24*	*2*	*10*	*52*	*18*	*62*	*3*	*2*	*4.5*	*.271*	*.307*	*.412*	*-.105*	*.265*	*.303*	*.410*	*.241*	*6.3*	*102-C*	*1*

Breakout: 48% Improve: 67% Collapse: 13% Attrition: 5%   *Comparables: Ryan Doumit, A. J. Pierzynski, Jose Morales, Miguel Montero*

(continued next page)

Neil Walker *(continued)*

The Joe Mauer trajectory of local catcher making good isn't going as planned so far for Neil Walker. Injuries (wrist surgery), illness (a viral infection), and uninspired production have the Pirates talking about moving him to third base. Ironically that will make him even less of a prospect because, as is often the case, a strong bat for a catcher is a weak bat elsewhere around the diamond. Walker didn't hit well in the Arizona Fall League (.291/.306/.397), which is like being on the faculty at Bordello University and not being able to score with a co-ed.

Jack Wilson SS **Bats: R** **Throws: R** Height: 6' 0" Weight: 185 Born: December 29, 1977 Age: 29

YEAR	TEAM	LVL	AGE	PA	R	2B	3B	HR	RBI	BB	SO	SB	CS	SPEED	AVG	OBP	SLG	MLVR	EQAVG	EQOBP	EQSLG	EQA	VORP	DEFENSE	
2004	PIT	MLB	26	693	82	41	12	11	59	26	71	8	4	6.1	.308	.335	.459	.109	.305	.333	.456	.269	42.8	148-SS	20
2005	PIT	MLB	27	639	60	24	7	8	52	31	58	7	3	5.7	.257	.299	.363	-.126	.258	.301	.371	.235	3.3	153-SS	22
2006	PIT	MLB	28	594	70	27	1	8	35	33	65	4	3	4.5	.273	.316	.370	-.108	.272	.317	.367	.240	4.6	127-SS	8
2007	PIT	MLB	29	584	68	29	5	8	53	33	60	7	3	5.6	.279	.324	.394	-.093	.273	.320	.392	.246	13.1	137-SS	8

Breakout: 18% Improve: 51% Collapse: 16% Attrition: 7%   *Comparables: Bill Russell, Mark Grudzielanek, Gary DiSarcina, Carlos Garcia*

As each year passes, 2004 will protrude further and further above the normal Wilsonian landscape, a promontory in a plain of unrelenting near-adequacy. Naturally, because we're talking Pirate-brand luck, that was the season that got him paid. Still not 30, he's the kind of player that would get a lot more attention for his fielding if he were surrounded by a team of real hitters. Signed through 2009 with an $8.4-million option for 2010, or a $600,000 buyout; that will be the best six-hundred grand the Pirates ever spent.

PITCHERS

Jonah Bayliss **Bats: R** **Throws: R** Height: 6' 2" Weight: 200 Born: August 13, 1980 Age: 26

YEAR	TEAM	LVL	AGE	W	L	SV	G	GS	IP	H	BB	SO	HR	GB%	BABIP	STUFF	WHIP	ERA	PERA	EQERA	EQH9	EQBB9	EQSO9	EQHR9	VORP	WXRL
2004	WIL	A+	23	6	6	0	24	24	110¹	117	44	78	11	—	.307	-36	1.46	4.90	7.15	7.69	11.4	4.8	4.2	2.0	-23.9	—
2005	WIC	AA	24	1	2	8	30	0	57	43	26	63	5	32.4%	.273	4	1.21	2.84	5.46	3.79	7.4	5.3	7.1	1.2	11.0	—
2005	KCA	MLB	24	0	0	0	11	0	11²	7	4	10	2	25.0%	.167	7	0.94	4.62	5.56	4.50	5.2	3.0	7.5	1.5	1.5	-0.02
2006	IND	AAA	25	3	3	23	46	0	58¹	37	28	67	4	41.3%	.248	13	1.12	2.17	4.63	3.04	6.9	4.8	8.1	1.0	16.0	—
2006	PIT	MLB	25	1	1	0	11	0	14²	13	11	15	1	35.9%	.316	15	1.64	4.29	4.30	4.11	7.6	5.9	8.2	0.6	2.8	0.01
2007	PIT	MLB	26	3	4	4	69	2	68¹	66	37	60	10	39.0%	.286	-2	1.50	4.86	5.11	4.84	8.2	4.5	7.1	1.1	6.2	0.60

Breakout: 24% Improve: 53% Collapse: 24% Attrition: 9%   *Comparables: Todd Wellemeyer, Scott Dunn, Jim Mann, Aaron Myette*

Acquired from the Royals in the Mark Redman deal, Bayliss began closing for Wichita in 2005 and continued in that role for Indianapolis in 2006. He really ramped up his strikeouts last year, but needs to get his walk rate under control if he's going to make impression enough to land a full-time major league job. He hasn't allowed too many home runs to this point in his career, but it's hard to believe he can keep that up with his unfavorable groundball-to-flyball ratio, however much movement he has on his fastball; his slider is just average.

Bryan Bullington **Bats: R Throws: R** Height: 6' 5" Weight: 220 Born: September 30, 1980 Age: 26

YEAR	TEAM	LVL	AGE	W	L	SV	G	GS	IP	H	BB	SO	HR	GB%	BABIP	STUFF	WHIP	ERA	PERA	EQERA	EQH9	EQBB9	EQSO9	EQHR9	VORP	WXRL
2004	ALT	AA	23	12	7	0	26	26	145	160	47	100	18	—	.307	-17	1.43	4.10	5.82	5.65	10.6	3.2	4.4	1.6	-0.8	—
2005	IND	AAA	24	9	5	0	18	18	109¹	104	26	82	11	53.8%	.290	8	1.19	3.38	4.40	4.39	8.9	2.3	5.3	1.1	14.6	—
2007	PIT	MLB	26	3	5	1	26	8	65²	77	24	42	9	48.0%	.314	-5	1.53	5.40	5.53	5.45	10.0	3.0	5.1	1.1	1.3	0.40

Breakout: 8% Improve: 33% Collapse: 27% Attrition: 36%   *Comparables: Jerry Johnson, Doug Brocail, Vladimir Nunez, Ed Lynch*

The Pirates have the poor man's version of the Cubs oft-shelved Kerry Wood-Mark Prior duo in the persons of Bryan Bullington and John van Benschoten. After missing all of 2006, Bullington is expected to be at 100 percent by the time pitchers and catchers report. Whether he can continue the progress he showed in 2005 seems like an afterthought compared to his health issues, and he still has to show the velocity he used to have in college. Indianapolis beckons—at least for a few months—but a strong spring could land him a spot in the rotation.

Matt Capps

Bats: R Throws: R   Height: 6' 2"   Weight: 240   Born: September 3, 1983   Age: 23

YEAR	TEAM	LVL	AGE	W	L	SV	G	GS	IP	H	BB	SO	HR	GB%	BABIP	STUFF	WHIP	ERA	PERA	EQERA	EQH9	EQBB9	EQSO9	EQHR9	VORP	WXRL
2004	HIC	A	20	2	3	0	12	8	42	82	16	27	8	—	.425	-46	2.33	10.07	7.55	14.14	18.4	3.9	3.4	2.8	-39.9	—
2004	WPT	A-	20	3	5	0	11	11	65	84	4	33	7	—	.336	-34	1.35	4.85	6.91	9.62	13.5	0.9	2.4	2.7	-28.0	—
2005	HIC	A	21	3	4	14	35	0	53²	47	5	39	0	54.9%	.297	2	0.97	2.51	3.22	3.69	8.2	1.0	3.7	0.3	11.4	—
2005	ALT	AA	21	0	2	7	17	0	20	21	1	26	2	51.7%	.339	20	1.10	2.70	3.30	4.05	10.4	0.4	7.7	1.4	3.4	—
2006	PIT	MLB	22	9	1	1	85	0	80²	81	12	56	12	41.9%	.292	2	1.15	3.79	4.10	3.67	8.1	1.2	5.6	1.2	17.3	0.74
2007	*PIT*	*MLB*	*23*	*3*	*3*	*3*	*58*	*0*	*63¹*	*73*	*14*	*37*	*8*	*47.0%*	*.306*	*-4*	*1.37*	*4.40*	*4.65*	*4.42*	*9.8*	*1.8*	*4.7*	*1.0*	*9.1*	*0.70*

Breakout: 48% Improve: 86% Collapse: 1% Attrition: 26%   Comparables: Joe Moeller, Esteban Yan, Carlos Silva, Julian Tavarez

Capps did a nice job of keeping opponents off the bases, a good thing since he was taken downtown 12 times in his 80+ innings of work. He wasn't as effective in the second half, suggesting that 85 appearances might have been a bit much for a rookie whose minor league high was 56. Those 85 games were the third-most ever for a rookie behind Sean Runyan (88 for the 1998 Tigers) and Oscar Villarreal (86 for the 2003 Diamondbacks). Runyan's follow-up was oblivion and, until a nice turn last year, so was Villarreal's.

Shawn Chacon

Bats: R Throws: R   Height: 6' 3"   Weight: 220   Born: December 23, 1977   Age: 29

YEAR	TEAM	LVL	AGE	W	L	SV	G	GS	IP	H	BB	SO	HR	GB%	BABIP	STUFF	WHIP	ERA	PERA	EQERA	EQH9	EQBB9	EQSO9	EQHR9	VORP	WXRL
2004	COL	MLB	26	1	9	35	66	0	63¹	71	52	52	12	—	.314	-10	1.94	7.11	6.34	6.35	9.3	6.3	6.3	1.4	-8.0	-1.68
2005	COL	MLB	27	1	7	0	13	12	72²	69	36	39	7	36.7%	.283	3	1.44	4.09	5.27	3.55	7.8	3.9	4.3	0.8	13.7	1.31
2005	NYA	MLB	27	7	3	0	14	12	79	66	30	40	7	42.7%	.240	7	1.22	2.85	4.82	2.99	7.2	3.3	4.4	0.8	25.0	3.24
2006	NYA	MLB	28	5	3	0	17	11	63	77	36	35	11	33.8%	.313	-20	1.79	7.00	6.15	7.52	10.7	4.9	4.7	1.4	-13.1	-0.01
2006	PIT	MLB	28	2	3	0	9	9	46	47	27	27	12	34.9%	.261	-17	1.61	5.48	7.18	5.59	8.4	4.5	4.7	2.0	-1.0	0.65
2007	*PIT*	*MLB*	*29*	*5*	*8*	*0*	*36*	*16*	*113*	*122*	*53*	*72*	*16*	*41.0%*	*.292*	*-7*	*1.55*	*5.24*	*5.50*	*5.23*	*9.2*	*3.9*	*5.1*	*1.1*	*5.3*	*1.20*

Breakout: 20% Improve: 52% Collapse: 22% Attrition: 12%   Comparables: Juan Eichelberger, Tony Cloninger, Tom Griffin, Jeff Robinson

As long as Chacon keeps having stretches of pitching lucidity, he can keep his mediocre career running indefinitely; he's due for his next stretch in 2008. Run out of New York when his Emperor-has-no-strikeouts act of 2005 was found out, he's broken even on his strikeout-to-walk ratio in two of the past three years. The days of being successful as a 1:1 man are decades in the past.

Zach Duke

Bats: L Throws: L   Height: 6' 2"   Weight: 220   Born: April 19, 1983   Age: 24

YEAR	TEAM	LVL	AGE	W	L	SV	G	GS	IP	H	BB	SO	HR	GB%	BABIP	STUFF	WHIP	ERA	PERA	EQERA	EQH9	EQBB9	EQSO9	EQHR9	VORP	WXRL
2004	LYN	A+	21	10	5	0	17	17	97	73	20	106	3	—	.278	37	0.96	1.39	3.38	2.95	7.6	2.2	6.8	0.6	27.9	—
2004	ALT	AA	21	5	1	0	9	9	51¹	41	10	36	2	—	.262	20	0.99	1.58	3.53	2.63	7.4	1.8	4.6	0.5	16.9	—
2005	IND	AAA	22	12	3	0	16	16	108	108	23	66	8	53.0%	.302	12	1.21	2.92	4.05	3.83	9.1	2.0	4.2	0.8	21.2	—
2005	PIT	MLB	22	8	2	0	14	14	84²	79	23	58	3	50.0%	.303	33	1.20	1.81	3.22	2.29	8.3	2.2	5.6	0.3	32.7	3.98
2006	PIT	MLB	23	10	15	0	34	34	215¹	255	68	117	17	53.9%	.336	13	1.50	4.47	3.99	4.19	9.5	2.4	4.3	0.6	28.5	3.80
2007	*PIT*	*MLB*	*24*	*11*	*12*	*0*	*31*	*31*	*198²*	*216*	*60*	*125*	*20*	*52.0%*	*.304*	*11*	*1.39*	*4.24*	*4.49*	*4.31*	*9.2*	*2.5*	*5.1*	*0.8*	*31.0*	*4.60*

Breakout: 10% Improve: 28% Collapse: 34% Attrition: 0%   Comparables: Jim Abbott, Bruce Ruffin, Steve Trout, Danny Jackson

Duke had the third-highest hit rate in the National League in 2006 thanks to the NL's highest BABIP (.336). The Pirates managed to place three qualifying starters among the ten worst BABIP rates in the league, the first time that's happened since 1995 when Astros' Doug Drabek, Shane Reynolds and Greg Swindell pulled the trick—or, rather, had the trick pulled on them by the seven guys behind them. Those BABIP rankings are a consequence of Pittsburgh's last-in-the-majors defensive efficiency rating (DER); no team was less successful at turning balls in play into outs last year. In fact, Pittsburgh's .676 DER misses being the lowest rate since 1960 by just one percentage point (.01). In Duke's case, the Pirates' defensive shortcomings were compounded by his own declining strikeout rate, which dropped to dangerous levels. About the worst thing that could happen for a pitcher whose defense is allowing a third of the balls in play to fall for hits is to allow more balls in play than ever before. Amazingly, he was able to keep the ball in the park and around the plate often enough to post a league-average ERA despite it all.

Mike Gonzalez

Bats: R Throws: L   Height: 6′ 2″   Weight: 220   Born: May 23, 1978   Age: 29

YEAR	TEAM	LVL	AGE	W	L	SV	G	GS	IP	H	BB	SO	HR	GB%	BABIP	STUFF	WHIP	ERA	PERA	EQERA	EQH9	EQBB9	EQSO9	EQHR9	VORP	WXRL
2004	NAS	AAA	26	2	0	2	14	0	20	12	7	35	0	—	.375	20	0.95	0.90	2.13	1.35	5.8	3.2	11.7	0.0	9.4	—
2004	PIT	MLB	26	3	1	1	47	0	43¹	32	6	55	2	—	.294	44	0.88	1.25	2.09	1.65	6.6	1.0	10.1	0.4	20.3	1.14
2005	PIT	MLB	27	1	3	3	51	0	50	35	31	58	2	50.8%	.280	33	1.32	2.70	3.38	2.82	6.5	4.9	9.5	0.4	15.5	2.42
2006	PIT	MLB	28	3	4	24	54	0	54	42	31	64	1	39.1%	.311	35	1.35	2.17	2.98	2.09	6.6	4.3	9.5	0.2	23.3	3.49
2007	ATL	MLB	29	4	4	28	57	0	54²	47	29	61	4	46%	.301	16	1.38	3.22	3.88	3.30	7.5	4.2	9.0	0.6	15.8	2.2

Breakout: 2%   Improve: 9%   Collapse: 82%   Attrition: 12%   Breakout: Rob Murphy, Francisco Cordero, Al Holland, Jim Kern

After blowing the first three save opportunities in his career in 2004, Gonzalez has converted his last 28. He doesn't just give lefties the fits (.176/.260/.218 over the past three seasons), right-handers have hit just .217/.310/.291 against him over the same span. If it weren't for his generosity with walks, he'd be getting into household name territory—at least households in western Pennsylvania. Households that don't nail the doors shut when the Pirates get mentioned. At any rate, Gonzalez missed the final month of the season with elbow tendonitis, but was the subject of myriad trade rumors in the offseason anyway. He hasn't been moved as we go to press, but it seems only a matter of time.

Tom Gorzelanny

Bats: L Throws: L   Height: 6′ 2″   Weight: 210   Born: July 12, 1982   Age: 24

YEAR	TEAM	LVL	AGE	W	L	SV	G	GS	IP	H	BB	SO	HR	GB%	BABIP	STUFF	WHIP	ERA	PERA	EQERA	EQH9	EQBB9	EQSO9	EQHR9	VORP	WXRL
2004	HIC	A	21	7	2	0	16	15	93	63	34	106	9	—	.245	4	1.04	2.23	5.68	3.67	7.6	4.1	6.0	1.5	18.9	—
2004	LYN	A+	21	3	5	0	10	10	55²	54	19	61	6	—	.329	3	1.31	4.85	5.91	6.08	10.3	3.7	6.9	1.9	-2.8	—
2005	ALT	AA	22	8	5	0	23	23	129²	114	46	124	6	47.7%	.306	20	1.23	3.26	4.10	4.07	8.3	3.6	5.9	0.6	21.8	—
2006	IND	AAA	23	6	5	0	16	16	99	67	27	94	4	48.2%	.254	32	0.95	2.36	3.45	3.32	6.8	2.6	6.6	0.6	24.8	—
2006	PIT	MLB	23	2	5	0	11	11	61²	50	31	40	3	50.8%	.264	16	1.31	3.79	4.16	3.80	6.6	3.8	5.2	0.4	12.1	1.76
2007	PIT	MLB	24	8	11	0	32	28	154²	156	66	121	17	48.0%	.298	11	1.43	4.67	4.67	4.75	8.6	3.5	6.3	0.9	16.1	2.80

Breakout: 6%   Improve: 27%   Collapse: 36%   Attrition: 1%   Comparables: Chris Capuano, Bob Knepper, Brandon Claussen, Dean Stone

Gorzelanny was placed on the 15-day disabled list on the same day for the same problem as Mike Gonzalez. Unlike Gonzalez, he came back after the minimum and looked none the worse for wear, pitching well enough to put the Pirates in a position to win in his last eight starts. With proper support, he's got the potential to post the kind of won-loss record that would put him on the baseball map. It should be noted, however, that his BABIP was exceedingly low for a pitcher having to cope with the Pirates defense. That number will rise in 2007 as more balls evade Pirate leather and roll, unmolested, to a gentle stop somewhere in the grass. That's why PECOTA is predicting Gorzelanny to add nearly a run to his ERA.

John Grabow

Bats: L Throws: L   Height: 6′ 2″   Weight: 210   Born: November 4, 1978   Age: 28

YEAR	TEAM	LVL	AGE	W	L	SV	G	GS	IP	H	BB	SO	HR	GB%	BABIP	STUFF	WHIP	ERA	PERA	EQERA	EQH9	EQBB9	EQSO9	EQHR9	VORP	WXRL
2004	PIT	MLB	25	2	5	1	68	0	61²	81	28	64	8	—	.408	3	1.77	5.11	3.96	5.37	11.3	3.5	8.1	1.0	-0.7	-0.08
2005	PIT	MLB	26	2	3	0	63	0	52	46	25	42	6	47.0%	.276	-3	1.37	4.85	4.65	5.26	8.0	3.9	6.6	1.0	0.7	1.00
2006	PIT	MLB	27	4	2	0	72	0	69²	68	30	66	7	52.0%	.323	11	1.41	4.13	3.86	3.86	8.1	3.2	7.6	0.7	13.0	1.25
2007	PIT	MLB	28	3	3	3	63	1	63²	67	28	54	6	50.0%	.320	2	1.50	4.50	4.74	4.57	9.0	3.7	6.9	0.8	8.1	0.70

Breakout: 27%   Improve: 47%   Collapse: 25%   Attrition: 14%   Comparables: Mike Myers, Mark Guthrie, Paul Assenmacher, Scott Ruskin

You can make a strong argument that no team needs a LOOGY. Mike Scioscia won 92 games and a division title in 2004 without having a lefty reliever on his team. LOOGies do more harm than good because they end up facing just as many righties than lefties as a result of walks and pinch-hitters, and take up precious roster space without providing enough innings. Whether you buy that or not, a team going nowhere has little need for a specialized tactical weapon; it's like Liechtenstein developing a SEAL team. Contenders are always on the lookout for situational lefties, though and have been known to make some spectacularly lopsided trades in order to acquire them, so that might their greatest value to a team like the Pirates, as bargaining chips. Grabow's been in the LOOGY role for three years, and Littlefield has yet to leverage him into anything of value. Grabow's strikeout rate spiked in 2006, but he's not very good at retiring lefties; over the last three years they've hit .282/338/.440 against him.

Brad Lincoln
Bats: L Throws: R Height: 5′ 11″ Weight: 180 Born: May 25, 1985 Age: 22

YEAR	TEAM	LVL	AGE	W	L	SV	G	GS	IP	H	BB	SO	HR	GB%	BABIP	STUFF	WHIP	ERA	PERA	EQERA	EQH9	EQBB9	EQSO9	EQHR9	VORP	WXRL
2006	PIR	Rk	21	0	0	0	2	2	7²	6	1	9	0	31.6%	.333	7	0.97	0.00	2.75	2.45	8.6	1.2	6.1	0.0	2.6	—
2006	HIC	A	21	1	2	0	4	4	16¹	25	6	10	2	55.9%	.411	-32	1.93	6.71	7.62	10.57	15.8	4.1	3.5	2.9	-8.4	—
2007	PIT	MLB	22	3	7	0	29	12	83²	113	33	48	16	50.0%	.334	-12	1.74	6.84	6.93	6.87	11.5	3.3	4.6	1.5	-11.3	0.70

Breakout: 39% Improve: 65% Collapse: 8% Attrition: 3% Comparables: Jesse Chavez, Walker Chapman, Ramon Mora, Vince Lacorte

The fourth overall pick in last year's draft, Lincoln turned on the juice in his last year at the University of Houston and got himself noticed. He's already been promoted once and appears to be on the kind of career trajectory that will have him making multiple stops until he tops out in Pittsburgh as early as next year. He throws 91 to 95 MPH, with a max of 97, and possess a plus curve and excellent command. He's the great pitching hope of the system, which is an indicator the Pirates need to find some star potential in this year's draft, as well. There's nothing wrong with coming up with solid, mid-rotation pitchers, but if that's all you've got, the future is going to be a dark place. It's not polite to mention his size, but Lincoln is a bit height-challenged for a right-hander.

Paul Maholm
Bats: L Throws: L Height: 6′ 2″ Weight: 230 Born: June 25, 1982 Age: 25

YEAR	TEAM	LVL	AGE	W	L	SV	G	GS	IP	H	BB	SO	HR	GB%	BABIP	STUFF	WHIP	ERA	PERA	EQERA	EQH9	EQBB9	EQSO9	EQHR9	VORP	WXRL
2005	ALT	AA	23	6	2	0	16	16	81²	73	26	75	5	63.7%	.308	8	1.21	3.19	4.45	4.26	8.5	3.4	5.5	0.8	12.0	—
2005	IND	AAA	23	1	1	0	6	6	35²	40	12	21	2	55.5%	.325	1	1.46	3.53	4.25	5.30	10.1	3.3	4.0	0.5	1.2	—
2005	PIT	MLB	23	3	1	0	6	6	41¹	31	17	26	2	58.2%	.242	17	1.16	2.18	4.10	2.36	6.9	3.4	5.1	0.4	15.7	1.94
2006	PIT	MLB	24	8	10	0	30	30	176	202	81	117	19	55.0%	.334	8	1.61	4.76	4.62	4.39	9.4	3.5	5.3	0.8	20.7	3.09
2007	PIT	MLB	25	9	11	0	28	28	166²	178	72	117	15	55.0%	.310	11	1.50	4.52	4.81	4.61	9.1	3.6	5.7	0.7	19.9	3.30

Breakout: 8% Improve: 35% Collapse: 23% Attrition: 3% Comparables: Andy Hassler, Jason Jennings, Dave LaPoint, Bob Hendley

Maholm is a pitch-to-contact, ground-ball lefty. In last year's book, PECOTA named Danny Jackson as Maholm's top comp. This year it says Andy Hassler. The former won 23 games in 1988; the latter never won 10. We didn't tell PECOTA that Maholm finished the season with a supposedly harmless sore rotator cuff, but the program reads extensively in its spare time, so that could be what was on its mind. If not for the medical news, Maholm's second half would have rated a thumbs up as he overcame a rough first half and the Pirates nightmarish defense to post a 4.28 second-half ERA.

Damaso Marte
Bats: L Throws: L Height: 6′ 2″ Weight: 210 Born: February 14, 1975 Age: 32

YEAR	TEAM	LVL	AGE	W	L	SV	G	GS	IP	H	BB	SO	HR	GB%	BABIP	STUFF	WHIP	ERA	PERA	EQERA	EQH9	EQBB9	EQSO9	EQHR9	VORP	WXRL
2004	CHA	MLB	29	6	5	6	74	0	73²	56	34	68	10	—	.257	8	1.23	3.42	4.44	3.11	6.7	3.7	7.6	1.1	24.0	2.43
2005	CHA	MLB	30	3	4	4	66	0	45¹	45	33	54	5	40.2%	.342	24	1.72	3.77	4.57	3.91	9.2	6.5	10.4	1.0	8.2	1.14
2006	PIT	MLB	31	1	7	0	75	0	58¹	51	31	63	5	37.7%	.326	17	1.41	3.70	3.82	4.15	7.4	4.0	8.6	0.6	9.3	-0.05
2007	PIT	MLB	32	2	3	4	58	0	53	49	26	54	6	43.0%	.302	8	1.41	3.92	4.28	3.92	7.9	4.0	8.2	0.8	10.1	0.90

Breakout: 16% Improve: 46% Collapse: 26% Attrition: 20% Comparables: Jesse Orosco, Bill Kennedy, Jim Brewer, Mike Myers

The champagne from Chicago's championship had barely dried on his uniform when Damaso Marte was shipped to Pittsburgh for utility man Rob Mackowiak. His wildness in 2005 helped make him expendable and, though his control improved in Pittsburgh, his 2006 season was hardly a unqualified success. Over the past three seasons, Marte has pitched much better before the All-Star break, suggesting that his workloads have been a bit much for him. Fact: If a serious team such as the White Sox is dealing away relievers such as Marte for fungible players such as Mackowiak, that should tell you something about Marte. Fact Two: As we observed with Grabow above, this is the sort of player the Pirates should be dealing away, not collecting. That should tell you something about the Pirates.

Juan Perez
Bats: R Throws: L Height: 6′ 0″ Weight: 170 Born: September 3, 1978 Age: 28

YEAR	TEAM	LVL	AGE	W	L	SV	G	GS	IP	H	BB	SO	HR	GB%	BABIP	STUFF	WHIP	ERA	PERA	EQERA	EQH9	EQBB9	EQSO9	EQHR9	VORP	WXRL
2006	NOR	AAA	27	0	1	0	43	0	63²	65	34	55	4	44.4%	.337	-3	1.57	2.85	5.11	4.24	9.0	5.2	5.8	0.8	9.6	—
2007	PIT	MLB	28	2	4	1	34	4	57¹	63	35	41	7	47.0%	.313	-10	1.72	5.33	5.88	5.36	9.4	5.1	5.8	0.9	1.7	0.30

Breakout: 2% Improve: 18% Collapse: 54% Attrition: 20% Comparables: Ricardo Jordan, Tim Adkins, Jason Jimenez, Matt Williams

It's been a long time since Juan Perez was an 18 year old striking out 13.8 batters per nine innings in rookie league, or maybe that's just the time displacement one feels when three years get added to a player's age by exposing his sketchy birth certificate. We're not saying Perez is old, but that's him standing next to Juan Marichal in his high school team photo. Relieving since Double-A, he's been walking too many batters of late. Possessed of a decent breaking ball, his left-handedness will give him chances regardless of his age.

Todd Redmond **Bats: R Throws: R** Height: 6′ 3″ Weight: 185 Born: May 17, 1985 Age: 22

YEAR	TEAM	LVL	AGE	W	L	SV	G	GS	IP	H	BB	SO	HR	GB%	BABIP	STUFF	WHIP	ERA	PERA	EQERA	EQH9	EQBB9	EQSO9	EQHR9	VORP	WXRL
2005	WPT	A-	20	1	2	0	15	14	72²	62	21	63	2	47.3%	.297	2	1.14	1.98	4.93	4.46	9.7	3.7	4.1	0.8	8.7	—
2006	HIC	A	21	13	6	0	27	27	160²	137	33	148	13	39.8%	.280	-7	1.06	2.75	5.83	4.85	9.5	2.3	4.9	1.7	12.8	—
2007	PIT	MLB	22	6	10	0	26	22	126²	143	45	82	22	43.0%	.299	3	1.48	5.42	5.62	5.39	9.6	2.9	5.2	1.3	3.8	1.30

Breakout: 3% Improve: 30% Collapse: 31% Attrition: 0% Comparables: Justin Duchscherer, Fredy Deza, Ronald Bay, Mike Nannini

Redmond had a very effective first full pro season at Hickory after being taken in the 39th round as a draft-and-follow in 2005. He has more command than stuff, throwing a fastball, curve, and changeup for strikes at any point in the count. He profiles as a back of the rotation starter or middle reliever, which makes him one of the better talents in the organization.

Brian Rogers **Bats: R Throws: R** Height: 6′ 4″ Weight: 190 Born: July 17, 1982 Age: 24

YEAR	TEAM	LVL	AGE	W	L	SV	G	GS	IP	H	BB	SO	HR	GB%	BABIP	STUFF	WHIP	ERA	PERA	EQERA	EQH9	EQBB9	EQSO9	EQHR9	VORP	WXRL
2004	WMI	A	21	6	8	0	25	25	142¹	163	44	120	9	—	.345	-11	1.45	4.55	5.46	6.68	11.6	3.7	4.3	1.2	-16.5	—
2005	LAK	A+	22	4	1	2	52	1	65²	50	21	65	2	51.1%	.284	2	1.08	2.05	4.15	3.30	8.2	3.7	5.6	0.6	16.0	—
2006	ERI	AA	23	3	2	1	37	0	64¹	49	14	69	7	45.8%	.268	-1	0.98	2.39	4.89	3.45	7.8	2.3	6.6	1.6	15.0	—
2006	IND	AAA	23	1	1	1	7	0	8	2	1	8	1	50.0%	.059	8	0.38	1.13	4.81	1.17	3.5	1.2	7.0	1.2	3.8	—
2006	PIT	MLB	23	0	0	0	10	0	8²	11	2	7	2	33.3%	.360	-4	1.50	8.28	5.21	7.00	11.0	2.0	6.0	2.0	-2.3	0.12
2007	PIT	MLB	24	3	4	1	38	2	62²	71	23	45	10	45.0%	.312	-3	1.50	5.19	5.46	5.19	9.7	3.1	5.8	1.2	3.2	0.30

Breakout: 19% Improve: 38% Collapse: 16% Attrition: 12% Comparables: Pat Neshek, Scott Henderson, Heath Bost, Jeff Harris

Rogers left starting behind in Low-A ball, and it's too bad because it would have been a real feather in David Littlefield's cap if he had been able to flip Sean Casey for a useful starting pitcher. Instead, he got this slider/command guy who had an 89:19 K/BB ratio in 85 innings at three levels last year. His lack of velocity (topping out in the high-80s) puts him in the marginal category. Take our word for it: when they gather around the Hot Photon Stove to talk baseball decades from now, they're not going to be reminiscing about the time ol' Littlefield fleeced the Tigers back in 'aught-six.

Victor Santos **Bats: R Throws: R** Height: 6′ 2″ Weight: 205 Born: October 2, 1976 Age: 30

YEAR	TEAM	LVL	AGE	W	L	SV	G	GS	IP	H	BB	SO	HR	GB%	BABIP	STUFF	WHIP	ERA	PERA	EQERA	EQH9	EQBB9	EQSO9	EQHR9	VORP	WXRL
2004	MIL	MLB	27	11	12	0	31	28	154	169	57	115	18	—	.319	7	1.47	4.97	4.35	5.21	9.7	2.9	5.9	0.9	1.4	2.77
2005	MIL	MLB	28	4	13	0	29	24	141²	153	60	89	20	43.3%	.289	-7	1.50	4.57	5.10	5.34	9.6	3.4	5.2	1.2	1.7	0.91
2006	PIT	MLB	29	5	9	0	25	19	115¹	150	42	81	16	44.8%	.362	1	1.66	5.70	4.46	5.43	10.6	2.8	5.6	1.0	-2.0	0.94
2007	CIN	MLB	30	5	7	0	29	13	98	111	37	69	15	44%	.309	-1	1.51	5.26	5.42	5.12	10.4	3.0	5.7	1.3	5.3	1.0

Breakout: 23% Improve: 46% Collapse: 27% Attrition: 24% Comparables: Harry Byrd, R. A. Dickey, Don Nottebart, Jesse Jefferson

Another Bucs hurler with a crazy-high BABIP. You had to be at PNC Park last year to see the way the Pirates fielders reacted with lightning indifference to the crack of the bat. Some of them specialized at being motionless, while others were merely inert. Among pitchers who logged over 100 innings, only Ryan Madson of the Phillies successfully combined pitching ineptitude with defensive non-support to post a BABIP higher than Santos's. Santos isn't actually all that good, but he could do a better impression of competent defensive work behind him. He continues to operate with a reverse platoon split, which indicates how well right-handed batters have hit him. Designated for assignment in October, he signed a minor league deal with the Reds in January. He's unlikely to provide much more than organizational depth.

Josh Sharpless **Bats: R Throws: R** Height: 6′ 5″ Weight: 235 Born: January 26, 1981 Age: 26

YEAR	TEAM	LVL	AGE	W	L	SV	G	GS	IP	H	BB	SO	HR	GB%	BABIP	STUFF	WHIP	ERA	PERA	EQERA	EQH9	EQBB9	EQSO9	EQHR9	VORP	WXRL
2004	HIC	A	23	6	2	5	44	0	74¹	42	55	109	4	—	.271	17	1.31	3.03	6.45	4.41	7.1	9.2	7.5	0.9	8.9	—
2005	LYN	A+	24	3	0	5	17	0	27	7	11	46	0	37.5%	.175	25	0.67	0.00	3.18	1.08	4.3	4.7	9.0	0.4	12.6	—
2006	ALT	AA	25	2	0	8	14	0	21²	8	9	30	0	39.0%	.200	20	0.80	0.85	3.40	1.80	4.9	4.9	8.1	0.4	8.4	—
2006	IND	AAA	25	1	1	1	23	0	33²	32	15	30	1	37.6%	.320	3	1.42	2.44	3.83	3.82	9.3	4.4	6.3	0.5	6.5	—
2006	PIT	MLB	25	0	0	0	14	0	12	7	11	7	0	36.4%	.212	8	1.50	1.50	5.01	1.42	5.0	7.1	4.3	0.0	6.1	0.19
2007	PIT	MLB	26	3	3	2	58	3	60²	52	49	56	6	38.0%	.280	-4	1.67	4.66	5.18	4.66	7.4	6.7	7.4	0.7	6.5	0.70

Breakout: 2% Improve: 8% Collapse: 85% Attrition: 13% Comparables: Kevin Barry, Brian Bowles, Aaron Myette, Brad Voyles

Sharpless authored last season's most self-deprecating quote. After spraining his ankle trying to field a ball hit by Houston's Brad Ausmus, he told the Pittsburgh Post-Gazette, "I'm a non-athletic guy trying to make an athletic play. It doesn't work." He's sprained his various ankles six times and broken them once each in his young life. A local product who went to the College Formerly Known as Beaver before being drafted by the Pirates, he's progressed nicely up the organizational ladder. Never a control freak in his dealing one nasty slider after another, he's averaged five walks per nine in his minor league career which, oddly, is nearly as many hits as he's allowed (5.23 H/9 to 5.05 BB/9).

Ian Snell　　　　**Bats: R Throws: R**　　　Height: 5' 11"　Weight: 190　Born: October 30, 1981　Age: 25

YEAR	TEAM	LVL	AGE	W	L	SV	G	GS	IP	H	BB	SO	HR	GB%	BABIP	STUFF	WHIP	ERA	PERA	EQERA	EQH9	EQBB9	EQSO9	EQHR9	VORP	WXRL
2004	ALT	AA	22	11	7	0	26	26	151	147	40	142	16	—	.311	10	1.24	3.16	4.61	3.79	9.4	2.5	6.1	1.3	30.1	—
2004	PIT	MLB	22	0	1	0	3	1	12	14	9	9	2	—	.333	-3	1.92	7.50	5.80	7.30	10.2	5.8	5.8	1.5	-2.5	-0.10
2005	IND	AAA	23	11	3	0	18	18	112	90	23	104	14	43.4%	.255	14	1.01	3.70	4.28	4.31	7.7	2.0	6.6	1.3	15.9	—
2005	PIT	MLB	23	1	2	0	15	5	42	43	24	34	5	37.8%	.311	3	1.60	5.14	4.83	5.23	9.2	4.6	6.7	1.0	0.7	0.22
2006	PIT	MLB	24	14	11	0	32	32	186	198	74	169	29	43.2%	.327	14	1.46	4.74	4.32	4.45	8.7	3.0	7.2	1.2	21.5	3.49
2007	PIT	MLB	25	10	11	0	29	29	178²	179	63	152	22	44.0%	.298	19	1.35	4.35	4.49	4.37	8.5	2.9	6.9	1.0	26.3	4.00

Breakout: 18% Improve: 51% Collapse: 15% Attrition: 0%　　Comparables: Wade Miller, Lynn McGlothen, Russ Meyer, Adam Eaton

Lefties munched this control artist pretty good last year, belting him around at a .305/.380/.526 clip. As long as they treat him with so little regard, he's never going to get to make much progress. Not all of that is attributable to poor defensive support; he was nearly twice as likely to walk a lefty batter as he was a right-hander. Still, all told it was a decent first full season. The Pirates were one of only six teams in the National League to have three starting pitchers posting a VORP of at least 20, and all three are fairly young. While that doesn't make them the Marlins, it's certainly a positive.

Wardell Starling　　　　**Bats: R Throws: R**　　　Height: 6' 4"　Weight: 205　Born: March 14, 1983　Age: 24

YEAR	TEAM	LVL	AGE	W	L	SV	G	GS	IP	H	BB	SO	HR	GB%	BABIP	STUFF	WHIP	ERA	PERA	EQERA	EQH9	EQBB9	EQSO9	EQHR9	VORP	WXRL
2004	HIC	A	21	11	8	0	26	26	140	133	51	114	10	—	.292	-9	1.31	4.11	5.68	6.50	9.5	3.9	4.2	1.1	-13.7	—
2005	LYN	A+	22	10	10	0	28	28	153¹	168	55	102	18	52.0%	.311	-29	1.45	5.23	6.52	7.06	10.5	3.7	3.7	1.7	-24.4	—
2006	LYN	A+	23	4	4	0	13	13	73¹	53	17	45	3	52.7%	.234	-1	0.96	3.20	4.74	6.03	7.3	2.4	3.6	0.8	-3.4	—
2006	ALT	AA	23	6	5	0	15	15	86¹	81	27	42	6	51.5%	.266	-12	1.25	2.82	5.30	5.12	9.3	3.2	3.0	1.1	4.5	—
2007	PIT	MLB	24	4	9	0	26	17	104¹	123	44	53	15	51.0%	.304	-10	1.61	6.17	5.96	6.28	10.1	3.5	4.1	1.2	-7.5	0.10

Breakout: 16% Improve: 45% Collapse: 15% Attrition: 0%　　Comparables: Jared Wells, Mickey Callaway, Trevor Hutchinson, Derrick Cook

Starling throws in the 88 to 91 MPH range, but can get it up to 94 when the situation demands it. He has a plus curve and a decent change, but has seen his strikeout rates drop steadily as he's risen through the minors. This is fairly typical except it has slipped to the point where, if it had a fuel gauge, the "fill tank" light would have come on by now. Goes in the baseball aviary with Dean Crow, Chicken Stanley, Doug Bird, Birdie Cree, Robin Roberts, Hawk Harrelson, Goose Gossage, Ducky Medwick, Ed Crane, and Phil "The Vulture" Regan.

Salomon Torres　　　　**Bats: R Throws: R**　　　Height: 5' 11"　Weight: 210　Born: March 11, 1972　Age: 35

YEAR	TEAM	LVL	AGE	W	L	SV	G	GS	IP	H	BB	SO	HR	GB%	BABIP	STUFF	WHIP	ERA	PERA	EQERA	EQH9	EQBB9	EQSO9	EQHR9	VORP	WXRL
2004	PIT	MLB	32	7	7	0	84	0	92	87	22	62	6	—	.298	10	1.18	2.64	3.64	3.16	8.2	1.9	5.4	0.5	24.6	2.95
2005	PIT	MLB	33	5	5	3	78	0	94²	76	36	55	7	51.2%	.246	0	1.18	2.76	4.36	3.27	7.3	3.1	4.8	0.7	23.7	1.69
2006	PIT	MLB	34	3	6	12	94	0	93¹	98	38	72	6	57.0%	.329	11	1.46	3.28	3.79	3.61	8.7	3.1	6.1	0.5	20.8	4.62
2007	PIT	MLB	35	3	4	6	65	0	72¹	78	29	48	6	54.0%	.309	-7	1.47	4.35	4.52	4.47	9.2	3.3	5.4	0.7	9.8	0.90

Breakout: 7% Improve: 19% Collapse: 54% Attrition: 10%　　Comparables: Dave Giusti, Mike Timlin, Clay Carroll, Jim Mecir

As the 2006 season was getting underway, Torres was signed to a lucrative two-year extension with a club option for 2009. Jim Tracey then proceeded to use him like he was on a week-to-week contract. Torres appeared in the second-most games in baseball history behind Mike Marshall's 104 in 1974, tying former Pirate Kent Tekulve's 1979 mark of 94, thus becoming the first pitcher to crack 90 appearances since Tekulve in 1987. In the process, his RA jumped from the twin 3.23 figures of 2004 and 2005 to 4.05. The first figure was unsustainably low; the law of averages and Pirates defense took care of the rest. If you've been reading straight through, you've probably guessed that the Pirates defense was a real problem.

John Van Benschoten　　Bats: R　Throws: R　　Height: 6′ 4″　Weight: 215　Born: April 14, 1980　　Age: 27

YEAR	TEAM	LVL	AGE	W	L	SV	G	GS	IP	H	BB	SO	HR	GB%	BABIP	STUFF	WHIP	ERA	PERA	EQERA	EQH9	EQBB9	EQSO9	EQHR9	VORP	WXRL
2004	NAS	AAA	24	4	11	0	23	23	131²	135	49	101	16	—	.295	-1	1.40	4.72	5.21	4.96	8.6	3.4	5.2	1.1	9.6	—
2004	PIT	MLB	24	1	3	0	6	5	28²	33	19	18	3	—	.337	-6	1.81	6.90	5.33	8.19	10.0	5.2	4.9	0.9	-9.2	-0.51
2006	IND	AAA	26	1	1	0	3	3	11	10	7	13	2	32.3%	.286	11	1.55	5.73	7.22	6.75	9.3	5.9	8.4	2.5	-1.4	—
2007	PIT	MLB	27	4	6	0	25	13	85²	88	43	63	12	46.0%	.290	-2	1.53	5.35	5.39	5.40	8.7	4.2	5.9	1.1	2.3	0.80

Breakout: 27%　Improve: 63%　Collapse: 12%　Attrition: 34%　　Comparables: Tim Van Egmond, Gary Knotts, Joaquin Benoit, David West

Van Benschoten's recovery from labrum and rotator cuff surgeries has been a long time in coming. He missed all of 2005 and spent last season pitching sparingly at three different minor league levels. The word is that he will be good to go by spring, but the list of pitchers who've made successful comebacks from labrum surgery is quite short. Had things progressed according to plan, Van Bencshoten would have put the Pirates' decision to make him a pitcher instead of a hitter behind him years ago. Instead, it's the only aspect of his career likely to be of continuing interest.

Shane Youman　　Bats: L　Throws: L　　Height: 6′ 4″　Weight: 220　Born: October 11, 1979　　Age: 27

YEAR	TEAM	LVL	AGE	W	L	SV	G	GS	IP	H	BB	SO	HR	GB%	BABIP	STUFF	WHIP	ERA	PERA	EQERA	EQH9	EQBB9	EQSO9	EQHR9	VORP	WXRL
2004	LYN	A+	24	4	2	2	47	0	74	67	35	62	5	—	.286	-19	1.38	3.16	6.24	4.65	9.2	5.8	4.8	1.4	7.4	—
2005	ALT	AA	25	8	6	2	44	5	101	102	48	77	10	52.1%	.299	-25	1.49	3.92	6.43	5.94	9.7	5.6	4.3	1.5	-3.7	—
2006	ALT	AA	26	7	2	1	23	11	95	70	20	64	4	60.7%	.235	2	0.95	1.52	4.16	3.90	7.6	2.3	3.8	0.7	17.4	—
2006	IND	AAA	26	4	0	0	8	7	42¹	42	10	19	2	56.2%	.284	-6	1.24	4.06	4.20	5.57	9.2	2.4	3.0	0.6	0.1	—
2006	PIT	MLB	26	0	2	0	5	3	21²	15	10	5	1	58.6%	.203	-16	1.15	2.90	4.73	2.42	5.2	3.6	2.0	0.4	7.6	1.14
2007	PIT	MLB	27	4	7	0	35	12	93	110	40	49	12	53.0%	.309	-13	1.61	5.50	5.70	5.60	10.0	3.6	4.2	1.0	0.4	0.50

Breakout: 4%　Improve: 19%　Collapse: 56%　Attrition: 3%　　Comparables: Derek Lee, Kelly Wunsch, John O'Donoghue, J. D. Arteaga

This tall lefty doesn't have blow-away stuff, but throws strikes, throws downhill, has a good sinker, and gets plenty of ground balls. After proving he didn't need that second year in Double-A, he was promoted to Indianapolis, where he pitched just well enough to earn three starts for the pitching-starved Pirates. His strikeouts per nine innings went from 6 to 4 to 2 in his three 2006 stops, so if he wants in on the Pittsburgh rotation, something will need to be done about that. Then again, maybe he fits right in.

Lineouts

PLAYER	TEAM	LVL	AGE	PA	R	2B	3B	HR	RBI	BB	SO	SB-CS	SPEED	AVG/OBP/SLG	MLVrEqAVG/EqOBP/EqSLG	EqA	VORP
OF A. Boeve	ALT	AA	26	162	26	7	2	3	24	18	35	3-2	6.0	.333/.407/.478	.315	.315/.370/.455	.286	8.1
	IND	AAA	26	352	32	20	0	6	37	28	81	24-5	5.5	.269/.339/.389	.047	.257/.322/.382	.253	-5.8
OF W. Corley	HIC	A	22	575	87	32	2	16	100	18	109	9-3	5.2	.281/.323/.438	.118	.250/.275/.379	.225	-25.1
UT M. Edwards	IND	AAA	29	359	40	21	3	3	29	27	48	5-4	5.3	.258/.320/.369	-.016	.246/.301/.353	.229	-15.8
	PIT	MLB	29	18	1	0	0	0	0	1	5	0-0	2.9	.188/.235/.188	-.560	.118/.167/.118	.115	-1.8
OF N. Morgan*	LYN	A+	26	274	43	7	3	0	22	20	40	38-11	8.1	.303/.390/.360	.099	.271/.322/.312	.237	-4.8
	ALT	AA	26	244	39	6	5	1	10	15	28	21-11	8.4	.306/.359/.393	.113	.280/.325/.356	.243	-5.7
2B C. Stansberry	ALT	AA	24	297	46	18	3	10	30	31	62	8-3	5.8	.258/.345/.465	.149	.248/.321/.444	.261	10.7
	IND	AAA	24	238	30	10	2	3	25	35	35	10-3	6.0	.223/.345/.340	-.034	.225/.339/.355	.252	1.7

PLAYER	TEAM	LVL	AGE	W	L	SV	IP	H	BB	SO	HR	GB%	BABIP	STUFF	WHIP	ERA	PERA	EqERA	EqH9	EqBB9	EqSO9	EqHR9	VORP
D. Davidson*	HIC	A	22	2	1	0	56¹	39	21	72	2	—	.294	5	1.07	1.93	4.74	4.27	8.2	4.6	6.7	0.9	7.8
	ALT	AA	22	1	1	0	11²	8	10	13	0	—	.237	11	1.61	2.41	4.93	4.09	7.4	9.0	7.4	0.0	1.8
M. Felix*	WPT	A-	20	1	6	0	48¹	41	33	49	3	—	.311	-9	1.54	3.56	9.63	6.91	11.0	10.2	5.6	2.6	-6.1
M. McLeary	IND	AAA	31	3	4	2	104²	96	33	115	6	—	.327	13	1.24	2.68	3.89	3.73	9.4	3.3	7.3	0.9	21.0
	PIT	MLB	31	2	0	0	17²	17	6	8	1	—	.281	-2	1.30	2.03	3.90	2.45	7.9	2.5	3.4	0.5	6.8
J. Shortslef*	ALT	AA	24	6	2	0	60²	62	13	50	4	—	.339	-3	1.25	4.49	4.44	6.60	10.6	2.3	4.9	1.1	-6.5
J. Vaclavik	HIC	A	22	4	2	18	51	44	21	59	6	—	.299	-26	1.27	3.18	7.74	5.40	10.6	5.2	6.2	2.7	1.0
R. Vogelsong	PIT	MLB	28	0	0	0	38	44	16	27	2	—	.359	0	1.58	6.39	4.21	5.62	9.7	3.2	5.6	0.4	-1.2
	IND	AAA	28	4	5	0	67²	54	12	43	5	—	.244	5	0.98	2.68	4.65	4.21	8.0	1.8	4.3	1.1	10.2

You can't take **Adam Boeve** seriously as a prospect; he's been old for his levels all along, and hasn't really shown all that much power since pounding the Sally League as a 24-year-old graybeard back in 2004. Probably overdrafted in the second round of the 2005 draft, **Brad Corley** didn't exactly dominate in his full-season debut, showing little more than a wee bit of power and a decent arm. Without a better approach against more advanced pitching than he saw in Low-A Hickory, he won't make it. **Mike Edwards** hasn't done enough in his minor league career to recommend him for anything other than furthering his minor league career; he struck Jim Tracy's fancy back in their Dodger days, just not so much as to get a chance in 2007. If you were hoping that the Pirates had a solution to their center field problem that involved an aging single-slappy speedster, meet **Nyjer Morgan**, the answer to your prayers; you really should have asked for more. Recently seen as a prospect with some power for a second sacker, the Pirates got frustrated that **Craig Stansberry** didn't shine in his second season above A-ball, put him on waivers in December, and lost him to the Padres.

A Canadian import drafted in the tenth round of the 2002 draft, **David Davidson** was added to the 40-man this winter after overpowering everyone everywhere, including the AFL; he's not just a LOOGY in the making. It's going to be a while before you see 2006 second-rounder **Mike Felix** in Pittsburgh unless he gets his control under control. **Yoslan Herrera** is a defector from Castro-country who's been on the shelf for the last 18 months; signed by the Pirates in December, the 25-year-old Cuban will bring his promising splitter, plus-90 velocity, and offspeed stuff to Indianapolis this spring with hopes that he'll be able to make it to the majors during the summer. The aging **Marty McLeary**'s second cup of coffee was much nicer than his first. In and of itself, it was probably not enough to keep his dream alive, although his K/BB ratio at Indy was pretty sweet. **Josh Shortslef** finally made the 40-man roster after seven seasons, which might make some of you wonder if any part of that is a typo. A strained arm cut his season short, but he's tough on lefties and keeps the ball in the infield; John Grabow might need to start worrying. **Justin Vaclavik** was a closer at the University of Houston and in his first two years in the low minors, but that's probably not his big league fate given his underwhelming skills and repertoire. Once seen as possibly being the prize in the deal that made Jason Schmidt a Giant, **Ryan Vogelsong**'s now 28 years old with a career ERA of 5.86. He has never pitched well, and the Pirates could never really figure out what he was for—starting, relieving, or getting coffee. Fortunately for everyone involved, the mystery's hit the road as a free agent.

Manager: Jim Tracy

Year	Team	W-L	Pythag +/-	Avg PC	100 +P	120 +P	QS	BQS	REL	REL w Zero R	IBB	SUBS	PH	PH Avg	PH HR	SB2	CS2	SB3	CS3	SAC Att	SAC %	POS SAC	Squeeze	Swing	In Play
2004	LAN	93-69	+3	89.8	46	4	82	9	458	307	47	33	286	.211	9	91	35	10	3	81	85.2%	36	7	121	89
2005	LAN	71-91	-2	92.0	55	6	73	12	457	278	34	62	298	.231	4	54	33	4	2	81	70.4%	19	3	132	95
2006	PIT	67-95	-2	94.5	58	2	67	6	503	313	62	35	261	.227	5	63	18	5	3	87	71.3%	32	3	113	81

Jim Tracy clearly subscribes to the concept that it is better to have any major league managing job than to not have one at all. Otherwise, what possible motivation could have had for taking on the unenviable task of caretaking a sub-.500 run that dates back to the inaugural year of the Clinton administration? There exists the notion that success here could lead to accolades not available in a more nurturing environment, but that's just the problem in Pittsburgh: There is so little nurturing from above that success is measured by accomplishments such as avoiding 90 losses or not finishing last. The best a Pirates manager can hope for is something like what Tracy got in 2006, a good second half that secures his job for the following season. Tracy is no offensive noodler; the Pirates were fourteenth in the National League in stolen base attempts, eleventh in sacrifice attempts, and held similarly low positions in swings with runners going and substitutions. On the mound, his starting pitcher workloads were about average, and he was one of the five NL managers to motion to the pen 500 or more times. Tracy does not appear to feel the need to put his personal stamp on every game the way Little or Dusty Baker seem to. This stands in contrast to his predecessor, Lloyd McClendon, who was not one to lose idly. In the end, the debate about these divergent approaches comes down to this: on a team such as the Pirates, should the rare baserunner be used as a gambling chit, or treated as a sacred commodity? Tracy's approach is the more aesthetically pleasing for the stathead crowd, but it won't have a major impact in the standings until there are enough Pirates on base for this philosophical split to matter.

St. Louis Cardinals

So, now the Cardinals are world champions, and what comes to mind is John Milton noting that "luck is the residue of design" a few centuries before Branch Rickey appropriated the line. (Another pretty nifty pickup by the Mahatma, although to be fair, we don't know what Milton got in the deal.) Applying that quote to the Cardinals might seem like a left-handed compliment, especially considering how handily they beat the Tigers in the World Series. Let's face it, the term "luck" in itself is considered something of a dirty word in some circles, and not just among math-heads twitting over statistical destinies. To the average fan, saying that a World Series crown is a matter of luck is to lump it in with an improbable event such as Ozzie Smith's left-handed home run off of Tom Niedenfuer in the 1985 NLCS. In summoning up the old poet and pondering the Cardinals' paradise found, our intent is not to focus on luck. Rather, the operative word in that comment is "design."

Design reflects intent; in this case the tireless industry of Walt Jocketty and Tony La Russa in operating a team that has made six playoff appearances in the last seven years, won two pennants in the last three, and capped those accomplishments off with last October's demolition of a far less probable pennant winner from Detroit. Rather than attempt to find the perfect solution for every roster need, an impossible task even for the richest of clubs, Jocketty was pragmatic enough to employ usable players where necessary, knowing he could trust La Russa to use their specific abilities to effect, and trusting his two superstars, Albert Pujols and Chris Carpenter, to carry the day given a just-good-enough supporting cast.

Indeed, if you look at the number of things that went wrong for the 2006 Cardinals, it might be more appropriate to describe them as *unlucky*. Seemingly reasonable solutions to their holes at second base, left field and right field didn't work out. At the keystone, Junior Spivey failed to make the team or hit in Triple-A. In left, Larry Bigbie lost time to a broken foot in April, didn't hit in May, and had his season ended in June by an umbilical hernia. In right field, mid-market free agent Juan Encarnacion only proved to be a drain on the offense. Their closer, Jason Isringhausen, melted down due to a career-threatening hip injury, and their top lefty situational guy, Ricardo Rincon, blew out his shoulder in April. The rotation seemed to go to pieces at mid-season as June saw Mark Mulder break down and Sidney Ponson pitch his way off the team, reducing La Russa and Jocketty to calling in Jeff Weaver, who had been discarded by the Angels. All the while, Jason Marquis continued to rap out a maddening tattoo of decent and horrendous starts. Indeed, Marquis was one of the risks taken by the Cardinals teams of recent years that finally backfired in 2006— David Eckstein's hitting and Jim Edmonds's health being others.

As improbably or lucky as the 83-win World Champion Cardinals of 2006 might have seemed, they were the direct descendants of the 100- and 105-win teams of 2004 and 2005, two teams for whom the balance of risk and reward that was part of Jocketty's active design which tipped much further in the direction of the latter.

With all of that, it's no surprise that last year's Cardinals slipped in the standings in the second half, at one point looking like they were about to join the 1964 Phillies on the list of all-time collapses. Credit Jocketty with being able to mitigate a great deal of the disasters above to keep his team afloat. Some of it was a matter of staying the course: in the rotation, Jeff Suppan made 10 quality starts in his 15 after the All-Star break, providing the club a reliable

---

CARDINALS PROSPECTUS

2006 record: 83–78; First place, NL Central; Beat Tigers in World Series, 4–1

Pythagenport record: 82–80

Runs scored per game: 4.85 (6th in NL)

Runs allowed per game: 4.73 (5th in NL)

Team EqA: .262 (8th in NL)

2006 Batters Age: 30.2 (6th oldest in NL)

2006 Pitchers Age: 29.2 (7th youngest in NL)

Ballpark: Busch Stadium; Neutral park; Park Factor of .994

2006: Bad luck during the regular season in exchange for good luck in October was a trade they were happy to make.

2007: Tony La Russa's mission, if he decides to accept it, is to get through the season with less than 14 starting pitchers.

number two. Weaver righted his ship in August, and rookie Anthony Reyes stepped in for Mulder, albeit with mixed results. Absent the famous people in the pen, La Russa and pitching coach Dave Duncan made do with an underrated collection of youngsters that was mostly homegrown, and fronted by prospect Adam Wainwright. The lineup got its own reinforcement from the farm system in Chris Duncan, and, though he might be hard-pressed for an encore, for two months he gave the Cards a lefty power bat every bit as potent as that of a healthy Jim Edmonds. Adding Ronnie Belliard and Preston Wilson might not have been deadline masterstrokes, but both provided the Cards with small improvements that, in the end, proved critical. These patches were matters of adatptation, if a bit of design-on-the-fly; some of it contingency planning, and some of it crisis management. It might have been fortunate that, having made it into the postseason, both Jeff Weaver and Anthony Reyes reminded people that they can pitch a little bit, but that's also why they were starting games in the first place.

When statheads talk about unlucky teams, one thing we focus on is a team's one-run record, which can often be seen as the residue of luck given its tendency to fluctuate seemingly at random from year to year, averaging out around .500. The 2006 Cardinals were also unlucky by this standard, finishing four games under .500 in one-run games.

Curiously, the 100-win Cardinals of the year before weren't much luckier, finishing five under. Seeing as the Cardinals posted winning records in both seasons despite those poor one-run showings, they find themselves in pretty rare company. Since 1960, the only eight teams (nine if you count the 1962–1964 Twins twice) had a larger differential over a two year span between their winning percentages in one-run games and in games decided by more than one run than the 2005–2006 Cardinals (see table 1). If anything, this goes to show that the Cardinals have won despite their luck, not because of it.

What table 1 reveals, beyond one-run records and winning percentage differentials, is these teams' fates in games decided by more than one run. If a team's one-run record is the residue of luck, then it would follow that multi-run record is where design manifests itself most completely. Among the ten teams listed above (again counting the Twins twice), only one saw a bigger drop in its multi-run record from one season to the next. That team is the 2005–2006 Indians. This striking similarity between one of the most disappointing teams of 2006 and the one covered in champagne at the end of October should serve as both a sign of hope for the former, but also as a warning for the latter.

Table 2 shows the largest one-year declines in multi-run-game winning percentage among teams that never-

Table 1. There But for the Grace of Casey Stengel Go Us—Two-Year One-Run Differential

	Team	Year	One-Run W–L	Multi-Run W–L	One-Run W%	Multi-Run W%	Diff
Year 1	Minnesota	1962	21–25	70–46			
Year 2	Minnesota	1963	13–26	78–44	.400	.622	.222
Year 1	Minnesota	1963	13–26	78–44			
Year 2	Minnesota	1964	28–38	51–45	.390	.592	.201
Year 1	Cleveland	2005	22–36	71–33			
Year 2	Cleveland	2006	18–26	60–58	.392	.590	.198
Year 1	Boston	1988	19–26	70–47			
Year 2	Boston	1989	13–25	70–54	.386	.581	.195
Year 1	Boston	2001	19–23	63–56			
Year 2	Boston	2002	13–23	80–46	.410	.584	.173
Year 1	Kansas City	1971	18–30	67–45			
Year 2	Kansas City	1972	22–31	54–47	.396	.568	.172
Year 1	NY Mets	1989	22–30	65–45			
Year 2	NY Mets	1990	23–28	68–43	.437	.602	.165
Year 1	LA Dodgers	1980	31–33	61–38			
Year 2	LA Dodgers	1981	16–21	47–26	.465	.628	.163
Year 1	Houston	1993	18–25	66–52			
Year 2	Houston	1994	13–17	53–32	.425	.586	.162
Year 1	St. Louis	2005	21–25	79–37			
Year 2	St. Louis	2006	22–27	61–51	.453	.614	.161

theless managed to finish above .500 in both seasons, as well as their assorted destinies. In most cases, these teams went from a happy place involving postseason glory to disappointment the following season. In the first year, these ten averaged 100 wins; in the second, 86 (factoring in the 1981 Orioles projected over a full 162-game season). The Cardinals are one of only two teams to make the playoffs in Year Two and are the only team who achieved more in the second season listed than in the first.

A season in which a new stadium is launched, 3.5 million people come through the turnstiles, and a championship is won has be considered a success. The Cardinals aren't a team that can rest on its laurels, however. Though they have Pujols and Carpenter to build around, the Cardinals have lost ground. If they want to keep ahead of their neighbors in the NL Central, they cannot afford to take a victory lap this season. That means using last year's success as a springboard for a necessary reshuffling. It is a reflection on the sound judgment of the Cardinals' brass that they have not let the events of October go to their collective heads, and are doing as much rearming as they can within the room they have to maneuver.

The lion's share of the Cardinals' payroll has already been invested in keeping the offensive core of Pujols, Edmonds, and Rolen together. While Jocketty could have settled for picking up Edmonds's $10 million option for 2007, he elected to take a chance and lock up the injury-prone center fielder for an additional season, replacing the option with a two-year, $16-million extension with an additional $3 million to be paid out over ten years starting in 2010. Thirty-seven and more than a little banged-up, Edmonds is not guaranteed to remain the third wheel that drives the club's offense, but in a market in which teams are paying Gary Matthews Jr. and Juan Pierre $9 or $10 million annually, rolling the dice on getting some shadow of Edmonds's former greatness is as good a gamble as any.

The most significant position player addition the Cardinals made over the winter was signing Adam Kennedy, the man they once traded to get Edmonds, to a three-year contract, thereby reuniting him with fellow 2002 Angels Scott Spiezio and David Eckstein. Beyond the good-vibes boost, a lot of veterans seem to enjoy working with La Russa and in front of the best fans in baseball. Kennedy will also benefit from not having to play half his game at Angel Stadium, as he's been a much more productive road player the past three seasons. While Kennedy should solidify second base, a position that was a defensive liability and a drag on the Cardinal offense in 2006, any serious hope for offensive breakout potential in 2007 is invested in the wishcast that Chris Duncan can be the player who hit

Table 2. One of These Things Is Not Like the Others—Two-Year Non-One-Run Differential (with Consecutive Winning Seasons)

	Year	Team	Win%	Wins	Multi-Run W–L	Multi-Run Win%	Diff	Notes
Year 1	1980	Baltimore	.617	100	72–39	.649		2nd in AL East
Year 2	1981	Baltimore	.562	59	38–39	.494	.155	2nd overall AL East, missed playoffs amid strike-season shenanigans
Year 1	1973	Baltimore	.599	97	74–41	.643		ALCS loss
Year 2	1974	Baltimore	.562	91	51–50	.505	.139	ALCS loss
Year 1	1961	Detroit	.620	101	78–40	.661		2nd place
Year 2	1962	Detroit	.528	85	57–52	.523	.138	4th place
Year 1	1979	Pittsburgh	.601	98	68–38	.642		World Champs
Year 2	1980	Pittsburgh	.512	83	51–50	.505	.137	3rd place
Year 1	2005	St. Louis (N)	.617	100	79–37	.681		NLCS loss
Year 2	2006	St. Louis (N)	.516	83	61–51	.545	.136	World Champs
Year 1	1978	Kansas City	.568	92	68–43	.613		ALCS loss
Year 2	1979	Kansas City	.525	85	51–55	.481	.131	2nd place
Year 1	1986	NY Mets	.667	108	79–34	.699		World Champs
Year 2	1987	NY Mets	.568	92	63–47	.573	.126	2nd place
Year 1	2002	Arizona	.605	98	75–44	.630		NL West champs
Year 2	2003	Arizona	.519	84	54–53	.505	.126	3rd place
Year 1	1990	Oakland	.613	103	78–46	.629		World Series loss
Year 2	1991	Oakland	.519	84	62–60	.508	.121	4th place
Year 1	1984	Detroit	.642	104	79–47	.627		World Champs
Year 2	1985	Detroit	.522	84	55–53	.509	.118	3rd place

.330/.393/.634 in his first couple of months, and not the one who hit .213/.300/.494 in their increasingly desperate September.

In putting together a staff for the future, Jocketty's taken a similar approach, mixing big-dollar investments on big-game talent with risks born of the experience that, as hard as pitching might be to conjure up, the La Russa–Duncan combo has as strong a track record as anybody's when it comes to getting mileage out of veterans. On the high end, after getting tremendous work from Chris Carpenter as a reward for investing in him when he was injured and no sure thing, Jocketty made the commitment to him as a staff ace that he'd sensibly ducked with Matt Morris, giving the Cardinal rotation frontman a multi-year extension that keeps him locked in through 2011.

Wisely saving his money for top-shelf talent such as Carpenter, Jocketty assessed the market for free agent pitching this winter and chose to let three of his starters walk out the door rather than pay them champions' wages for middling performance. Jeffs Suppan and Weaver and Jason Marquis each dove into the pool seeking their fortunes (with Suppan and Marquis having already emerged much wealthier men). Although the team pursued Jason Schmidt, Randy Wolf, and Miguel Batista, all three chases came to naught. Instead, to fill out their rotation behind Carpenter and Anthony Reyes, the Cardinals have settled for re-upping Mark Mulder on an incentive-laden deal, and landing Kip Wells and Ryan Franklin to round it out.

Wells and Franklin aren't world-beaters, but Wells has a combination that suggests he could be under the right circumstances. With quality breaking stuff and low-90s velocity, the talent's there, and the two injuries that wrecked his 2006 season—surgically repairing a clogged artery that cost him three months at the start, and a torn-up foot that ended his season six weeks early—aren't of the sort that would hinder his ability to sling pills for strikes once healed. There's a reasonable possibility that he'll be a bargain not unlike previous Cardinal retreadings. If Wells is more towards the Chris Carpenter end of the spectrum (he's just a year older than Carpenter was when he threw his first Cardinal pitch), Franklin can hope to be the new Kent Bottenfield, perhaps, a solid enough utility pitcher.

Mulder had had rotator cuff surgery this past September, and isn't expected to be back until July, so there's still a bit of a problem finding enough bodies to fill out the staff in the near term, and the lack of minor league candidates for the rotation has led to offseason talk about moving Braden Looper and/or Adam Wainwright to starting roles. All of which promises an active camp with some hard choices for La Russa and Duncan.

While Cardinals fans might have spent the winter fretting because the team reached the New Year with a three-man starting rotation (the Mulder and Franklin deals were both been finalized on January 10), one would assume by now that Jocketty knows what he is doing. Just as understands that 83 wins won't bag this particular division a second time, he recognizes that, the massive expenditures of the Cubs and the Astros notwithstanding, it probably won't take 100 to ice it either. The product of Jocketty's design is a division winner buttressed against misfortune. If the 2006 Cardinals taught us anything, it's that, as the popular lottery slogan goes, "you've got to be in it to win it." Had Branch Rickey lived to see baseball's three-tiered playoff system, he'd surely have slapped his name on that quote as well. Getting to the dance is the greater part of the struggle; the rest can, and often does, take care of itself.

HITTERS

Bryan Anderson — C — Bats: L — Throws: R — Height: 6' 1" — Weight: 200 — Born: December 16, 1986 — Age: 19

YEAR	TEAM	LVL	AGE	PA	R	2B	3B	HR	RBI	BB	SO	SB	CS	SPEED	AVG	OBP	SLG	MLVR	EQAVG	EQOBP	EQSLG	EQA	VORP	DEFENSE	
2005	JCY	Rk	18	176	28	8	1	6	36	15	29	6	1	4.9	.331	.383	.513	.278	.265	.303	.377	.240	1.2	36-C	-8
2006	QUD	A	19	431	50	29	3	3	51	42	66	2	6	3.5	.302	.377	.417	.186	.277	.333	.386	.249	10.8	89-C	-6
2007	SLN	MLB	20	520	52	31	2	9	53	36	83	3	2	4.4	.260	.314	.387	-.134	.265	.318	.400	.245	11.7	122-C	-1

Breakout: 35% Improve: 53% Collapse: 30% Attrition: 4%   Comparables: Brian McCann, Justin Huber ,Jeff Mathis, Jarrod Saltalamacchia

At 19, Anderson was among the younger set in the Midwest League last year, but he didn't play like a naïf. Doors can open pretty fast for left-handed hitting catchers, even ones who are still developing their defensive games, as Anderson is. He began the season with an invite to the big league training camp, so he's a pretty big blip on the Cardinals radar.

Ron Belliard — 2B — Bats: R — Throws: R — Height: 5' 8" — Weight: 195 — Born: April 7, 1975 — Age: 32

YEAR	TEAM	LVL	AGE	PA	R	2B	3B	HR	RBI	BB	SO	SB	CS	SPEED	AVG	OBP	SLG	MLVR	EQAVG	EQOBP	EQSLG	EQA	VORP	DEFENSE	
2004	CLE	MLB	29	663	78	48	1	12	70	60	98	3	2	3.9	.282	.348	.426	.037	.288	.359	.439	.276	29.9	140-2B	4
2005	CLE	MLB	30	587	71	36	1	17	78	35	72	2	2	4.4	.284	.325	.450	.052	.293	.344	.475	.278	24.0	139-2B	8
2006	CLE	MLB	31	379	43	21	0	8	44	21	45	2	0	4.4	.291	.337	.420	.000	.295	.347	.431	.270	15.9	87-2B	1
2006	SLN	MLB	31	211	20	9	1	5	23	15	36	0	3	3.5	.237	.295	.371	-.166	.237	.299	.366	.227	-3.1	50-2B	-4
2007	SLN	MLB	32	513	58	26	2	11	58	38	69	2	2	4.4	.271	.328	.407	-.073	.276	.332	.422	.257	16.1	121-2B	-1

Breakout: 10% Improve: 31% Collapse: 25% Attrition: 7%   Comparables: Joe Randa, Gil McDougald, Frank Malzone, Hank Majeski

Yes, appearances do count in the work world, even in a job in which one wears a birdy on one's chest. Even when you're kicking ass like Manny Ramirez, the contrived sloppy look will earn you a few detractors, and when you play like Belliard did after coming to St. Louis, the appearance tends to be interpreted literally. PECOTA doesn't see him ever getting back to where he was with Cleveland in 2005. He was a walking machine when he first came up but his patience has gone the way of his ability to tuck in a shirt.

Gary Bennett — C — Bats: R — Throws: R — Height: 6' 0" — Weight: 210 — Born: April 17, 1972 — Age: 35

YEAR	TEAM	LVL	AGE	PA	R	2B	3B	HR	RBI	BB	SO	SB	CS	SPEED	AVG	OBP	SLG	MLVR	EQAVG	EQOBP	EQSLG	EQA	VORP	DEFENSE	
2004	MIL	MLB	32	246	18	14	0	3	20	22	32	1	0	3.6	.224	.297	.329	-.190	.215	.289	.315	.219	-3.3	64-C	-6
2005	WAS	MLB	33	228	11	7	0	1	21	21	37	0	1	2.8	.221	.298	.271	-.253	.221	.300	.276	.213	-6.6	58-C	-3
2006	SLN	MLB	34	170	13	5	0	4	22	11	30	0	0	3.5	.223	.274	.331	-.269	.217	.272	.312	.208	-6.2	44-C	-10
2007	SLN	MLB	35	252	19	9	0	4	24	18	43	0	0	3.6	.225	.285	.324	-.294	.229	.289	.335	.213	-4.3	62-C	-3

Breakout: 25% Improve: 51% Collapse: 31% Attrition: 53%   Comparables: Danny Sheaffer, Ray Murray, Mike Difelice, Joe Oliver

Bennett's lone plate appearance in 16 postseason games is a testament to the otherworldliness of Yadier Molina's October effort, but also speaks to the fate of the backup catchers whose managers are afraid to use them for fear of being left catcher-less should an injury occur. He gets the same playoff share as everybody else though, and quite possibly another season in the bigs. Given his level of accomplishment at his age, that's no small thing.

Chris Duncan — LF/1B — Bats: L — Throws: R — Height: 6' 5" — Weight: 210 — Born: May 5, 1981 — Age: 26

YEAR	TEAM	LVL	AGE	PA	R	2B	3B	HR	RBI	BB	SO	SB	CS	SPEED	AVG	OBP	SLG	MLVR	EQAVG	EQOBP	EQSLG	EQA	VORP	DEFENSE			
2004	TEN	AA	23	455	57	23	0	16	65	64	94	8	4	4.4	.289	.393	.473	.206	.261	.351	.426	.270	9.8	74-1B	-5	14-RF	1
2005	MEM	AAA	24	500	57	21	2	21	73	63	104	1	3	2.3	.265	.358	.469	.047	.257	.338	.434	.266	8.2	99-1B	-5	17-RF	-4
2006	MEM	AAA	25	206	23	11	0	7	31	25	53	1	2	3.2	.271	.359	.448	.133	.266	.345	.440	.267	4.0	27-RF	-4	14-LF	-6
2006	SLN	MLB	25	314	60	11	3	22	43	30	69	0	0	5.4	.293	.363	.589	.292	.294	.366	.591	.312	24.8	37-LF	1	16-RF	1
2007	SLN	MLB	26	450	62	20	2	20	66	49	99	2	1	4.3	.272	.356	.486	.080	.277	.360	.503	.289	20.8	107-LF	-3		

Breakout: 24% Improve: 61% Collapse: 13% Attrition: 16%   Comparables: Mike Epstein, Carlos Pena, Jason Thompson, Willie Aikens

Is Chris Duncan the single worst defensive outfielder in modern memory? One usually needs to go to the stockyards to witness his brand of advanced butchery. The misplaced first baseman's one true destiny is obvious: Lefty-mashing designated hitter, and there's no time like the present to get him moving toward that end. As awkward as it might be to deal the pitching coach's son, his trade value is probably as high as it will ever get—there is nothing in his minor league record to suggest that he's really a .290 hitter. Having said all that, he was a shot in the arm when St. Louis desperately needed it.

David Eckstein   **SS**   **Bats: R**   **Throws: R**   Height: 5' 7"   Weight: 165   Born: January 20, 1975   Age: 32

YEAR	TEAM	LVL	AGE	PA	R	2B	3B	HR	RBI	BB	SO	SB	CS	SPEED	AVG	OBP	SLG	MLVR	EQAVG	EQOBP	EQSLG	EQA	VORP	DEFENSE	
2004	ANA	MLB	29	637	92	24	1	2	35	42	49	16	5	6.0	.276	.339	.332	-.157	.281	.346	.342	.249	6.9	122-SS	2
2005	SLN	MLB	30	713	90	26	7	8	61	58	44	11	8	5.4	.294	.363	.395	.058	.296	.365	.407	.269	32.4	150-SS	-1
2006	SLN	MLB	31	552	68	18	1	2	23	31	41	7	6	4.8	.292	.350	.344	-.067	.295	.352	.345	.248	8.5	117-SS	-1
2007	SLN	MLB	32	549	67	20	3	3	40	37	40	8	4	5.8	.276	.336	.346	-.139	.281	.340	.358	.245	12.5	129-SS	2

Breakout: 10%   Improve: 31%   Collapse: 39%   Attrition: 9%   Comparables: Roberto Pena, Rey Sanchez, Felix Millan, Phil Rizzuto

Career lows in doubles-plus-triples (19), steals (7), and—most disturbingly for a leadoff hitter—walks (31) are not good signs at age 32. Eckstein hit a soft .297 through June, at which point he went into a six-week slump that was only halted by a left oblique injury. He was on the shelf for a month, hit well when he returned, and, of course, was elevated to folk hero status by Games Four and Five of the World Series. He's signed through this season. Both Tyler Greene and Brendan Ryan took a step back last year, so the Cards will have to give serious consideration to diving into the free agent market after Carlos Guillen this offseason. Re-upping Eckstein, whose margin of success and failure is already razor thin, would be a mistake.

Jim Edmonds   **CF**   **Bats: L**   **Throws: L**   Height: 6' 1"   Weight: 210   Born: June 27, 1970   Age: 37

YEAR	TEAM	LVL	AGE	PA	R	2B	3B	HR	RBI	BB	SO	SB	CS	SPEED	AVG	OBP	SLG	MLVR	EQAVG	EQOBP	EQSLG	EQA	VORP	DEFENSE	
2004	SLN	MLB	34	612	102	38	3	42	111	101	150	8	3	5.6	.301	.418	.643	.480	.302	.417	.646	.342	81.2	134-CF	14
2005	SLN	MLB	35	567	88	37	1	29	89	91	139	5	5	4.7	.263	.385	.533	.253	.265	.387	.544	.308	44.2	129-CF	19
2006	SLN	MLB	36	408	52	18	0	19	70	53	101	4	0	3.9	.257	.350	.471	.079	.256	.352	.466	.283	20.0	90-CF	1
2007	SLN	MLB	37	433	62	19	1	21	65	59	104	5	2	4.6	.253	.358	.482	.062	.258	.362	.498	.290	22.4	103-CF	0

Breakout: 1%   Improve: 23%   Collapse: 54%   Attrition: 24%   Comparables: Ken Griffey, Reggie Jackson, Eddie Mathews, Fred Lynn

Bothered by a sore right shoulder, Edmonds couldn't get it going last year, hitting just .265/.362/.423 through June 21 when he crashed into the wall at the Cell in Chicago. He left that game with dizziness and blurred vision, but his bat came alive with a .276/.373/.655 July. He continued to play regularly through mid-August, up until he was diagnosed with post-concussion syndrome. Edmonds made just four more starts after being diagnosed, appearing in just six other games as a pinch-hitter and/or defensive replacement. He then started every game in the postseason despite getting cortisone injections in his foot, though the rust showed on his bat. In the offseason, he went under the knife to fix the shoulder (supposedly a minor clean-up) and the foot (a hammer toe). The former still isn't right, however, and could keep the 36-year-old Edmonds out of action into April, making the Cardinals decision to give him a new two-year, $19-million extension around the time of the surgery look all the more blindly optimistic.

Juan Encarnacion   **RF**   **Bats: R**   **Throws: R**   Height: 6' 3"   Weight: 215   Born: March 8, 1976   Age: 31

YEAR	TEAM	LVL	AGE	PA	R	2B	3B	HR	RBI	BB	SO	SB	CS	SPEED	AVG	OBP	SLG	MLVR	EQAVG	EQOBP	EQSLG	EQA	VORP	DEFENSE			
2004	FLO	MLB	28	182	21	12	1	3	19	17	33	2	1	5.3	.238	.320	.381	-.070	.242	.324	.385	.249	-0.8	48-RF	-1		
2004	LAN	MLB	28	350	42	18	1	13	43	21	53	3	3	4.7	.235	.289	.417	-.095	.238	.289	.423	.240	-4.8	72-RF	0		
2005	FLO	MLB	29	563	59	27	3	16	76	41	104	6	5	5.0	.287	.349	.447	.120	.296	.358	.471	.281	20.7	125-RF	-11		
2006	SLN	MLB	30	598	74	25	5	19	79	30	86	6	5	5.2	.278	.317	.443	.003	.279	.319	.443	.259	8.8	111-RF	4	25-CF	-7
2007	SLN	MLB	31	523	65	26	3	16	62	33	79	5	4	5.2	.271	.322	.435	-.047	.276	.326	.450	.261	7.8	123-RF	-5		

Breakout: 15%   Improve: 39%   Collapse: 33%   Attrition: 13%   Comparables: Al Cowens, Derek Bell, Barry Bonnell, Mickey Stanley

Winning a World Series can salve a whole lot of bum decisions, but in the end you're still stuck with the consequences of your actions. In Encarnacion, the Cards signed a thoroughly mediocre player to a three-year contract. Tony La Russa used Encarnacion's experience as a center fielder to paper over Edmonds's long absences, but, if anything, the move exacerbated things; Encarnacion batted .233/.273/.320 as a center fielder and played defense with the speed and agility of a garbage truck. In right, the team had a better option—John Rodriguez had the same VORP in about a third as many plate appearances. Encarnacion's disappearing act in the postseason finally drove Tony La Russa to bench him. Normally that might signal the beginning of the end of his time in St. Louis, but he's signed for another two long seasons.

Tyler Greene SS **Bats: R** **Throws: R** Height: 6' 2" Weight: 185 Born: August 17, 1983 Age: 22

YEAR	TEAM	LVL	AGE	PA	R	2B	3B	HR	RBI	BB	SO	SB	CS	SPEED	AVG	OBP	SLG	MLVR	EQAVG	EQOBP	EQSLG	EQA	VORP	DEFENSE
2005	NWJ	A-	21	159	28	12	0	1	18	15	37	13	1	7.6	.261	.352	.370	.047	.211	.269	.279	.205	-15.4	34-SS -2
2005	PMB	A+	21	92	17	4	0	2	5	5	28	6	0	6.8	.271	.326	.388	.016	.253	.301	.356	.241	-0.0	20-SS -1
2006	QUD	A	22	256	42	8	3	15	47	20	65	11	0	5.8	.287	.375	.552	.342	.255	.312	.481	.271	13.6	56-SS -6
2006	PMB	A+	22	303	38	10	1	5	19	29	90	22	3	6.2	.224	.308	.325	-.070	.229	.297	.338	.233	-4.3	72-SS -3
2007	SLN	MLB	23	567	63	26	4	13	56	37	156	20	7	5.6	.238	.296	.376	-.197	.242	.299	.389	.237	9.0	133-SS -4

Breakout: 34% Improve: 48% Collapse: 32% Attrition: 4%   Comparables: Kelly Dransfeldt, John Nelson, Corey Ragsdale, Jose Morban

Greene fished his 2005 debut in the Florida State League, where he played well, and he returned there for his full-season debut last year. Things started off poorly and stayed that way; he was striking out a ton and making an error every three games. In June, Greene was shipped down to the Midwest League and found it more to his liking. The power he showed in college returned, and he got back into the prospect groove. The ship has been righted, for now, but the stormy weather of Florida is calling once again. Greene will still have to prove himself at the higher level.

Cody Haerther LF **Bats: L** **Throws: R** Height: 6' 1" Weight: 198 Born: July 14, 1983 Age: 23

YEAR	TEAM	LVL	AGE	PA	R	2B	3B	HR	RBI	BB	SO	SB	CS	SPEED	AVG	OBP	SLG	MLVR	EQAVG	EQOBP	EQSLG	EQA	VORP	DEFENSE
2004	PEO	A	20	366	48	20	2	5	45	32	59	7	3	4.8	.316	.383	.436	.216	.289	.341	.396	.258	1.0	50-LF -1
2005	PMB	A+	21	192	29	8	7	8	30	17	31	8	3	6.7	.318	.380	.584	.395	.301	.354	.540	.295	13.8	16-LF 0
2005	SFD	AA	21	219	30	10	1	10	37	9	44	0	1	3.2	.298	.333	.500	.153	.282	.315	.469	.262	3.7	30-LF -5
2006	SFD	AA	22	452	56	27	3	11	52	37	59	4	4	4.3	.277	.336	.437	.057	.263	.313	.408	.247	-5.8	92-LF -5
2007	SLN	MLB	23	473	56	26	3	12	57	33	76	4	2	4.7	.276	.329	.429	-.038	.281	.333	.444	.263	9.2	112-LF -4

Breakout: 19% Improve: 59% Collapse: 16% Attrition: 6%   Comparables: Michael Ryan, Mike Frank, Andre Ethier, Joe Pomierski

One of the few current ballplayers with whom you can do a Six Degrees of Kevin Bacon thread, Haerther has a screen credit in the 1995 Patrick Swayze vehicle *Three Wishes*. He played an "additional ballplayer." If Haerther wants to be more than an extra in the Cardinals' plans he's going to have to show better progress than he did at Springfield in 2006. At best it could be said that he made some adjustments and saved his season with a pretty good second half. An outfielder who shows something in this system has plenty of opportunities at the top. As for those six degrees, we can do it in three: *Three Wishes* co-starred Mary Elizabeth Mastrantonio, who was in *The Color of Money* with Tom Cruise, who was in *A Few Good Men* with Kevin Bacon.

Jonathan Jay LF **Bats: L** **Throws: L** Height: 6' 0" Weight: 200 Born: March 15, 1985 Age: 22

YEAR	TEAM	LVL	AGE	PA	R	2B	3B	HR	RBI	BB	SO	SB	CS	SPEED	AVG	OBP	SLG	MLVR	EQAVG	EQOBP	EQSLG	EQA	VORP	DEFENSE
2006	QUD	A	21	268	42	13	3	3	45	28	27	9	4	6.0	.342	.416	.462	.328	.313	.369	.436	.281	10.3	49-LF -6
2007	SLN	MLB	22	482	69	29	4	7	49	36	52	12	6	5.9	.299	.354	.435	.032	.305	.359	.450	.276	18.3	114-LF -3

Breakout: 20% Improve: 45% Collapse: 23% Attrition: 4%   Comparables: Mike Darr, Brandon Jones, Shin-Soo Choo, Cody Haerther

There's a place awaiting him on the All-Founding Fathers Team alongside John Quincy Adams Strick (Louisville, 1882), Benjamin Franklin Callahan (Oakland, 1982), Thomas Jefferson Bridges (Detroit, 1930–1946), George Washington "Zip" Zabel (Chicago Cubs, 1913–1915), Patrick Henry "Cozy" Dolan (various, 1895–1906) and James Madison Pearce (Washington and Cincinnati, 1949–1955). Jay went straight from college to lead the Swing of the Quad Cities in OBP (.416). That .383 BABIP will be hard for Jay to maintain, but without power or speed he's going to have to if he wants to play every day in a corner.

Aaron Miles 2B **Bats: S** **Throws: R** Height: 5' 8" Weight: 175 Born: December 15, 1976 Age: 30

YEAR	TEAM	LVL	AGE	PA	R	2B	3B	HR	RBI	BB	SO	SB	CS	SPEED	AVG	OBP	SLG	MLVR	EQAVG	EQOBP	EQSLG	EQA	VORP	DEFENSE	
2004	COL	MLB	27	566	75	15	3	6	47	29	53	12	7	5.6	.293	.329	.368	-.117	.279	.316	.351	.236	1.0	114-2B -10	
2005	COL	MLB	28	347	37	12	3	2	28	8	38	4	2	5.7	.281	.306	.355	-.146	.271	.298	.345	.226	-3.3	69-2B 6	
2006	SLN	MLB	29	471	48	20	5	2	30	38	42	2	1	5.1	.263	.324	.347	-.129	.261	.326	.341	.238	1.4	73-2B -6	33-SS -1
2007	SLN	MLB	30	413	38	13	3	2	31	23	43	4	2	5.5	.236	.284	.303	-.319	.241	.287	.313	.206	-9.8	98-2B -1	

Breakout: 12% Improve: 25% Collapse: 55% Attrition: 20%   Comparables: Larry Milbourne, Sandy Alomar, Abraham Nunez, Denny Doyle

Miles actually had a better offensive season in 2006 than he did in his two years playing in Colorado. It still wasn't good enough to keep the Cardinals from looking elsewhere for a second baseman to carry them down the stretch run; enter Ronnie Belliard. Already moving toward professional marginalization, if Miles had a better fielding reputation he could delay that particular fate for several years. However, with no bat and a glove inadequate for short, he's unlikely to stick as a reserve infielder.

Yadier Molina   C   Bats: R   Throws: R   Height: 5′ 11″   Weight: 225   Born: July 13, 1982   Age: 24

YEAR	TEAM	LVL	AGE	PA	R	2B	3B	HR	RBI	BB	SO	SB	CS	SPEED	AVG	OBP	SLG	MLVR	EQAVG	EQOBP	EQSLG	EQA	VORP	DEFENSE	
2004	MEM	AAA	21	150	19	6	0	1	14	17	14	0	0	3.5	.302	.387	.372	.040	.290	.362	.344	.255	3.8	36-C	7
2004	SLN	MLB	21	151	12	6	0	2	15	13	20	0	1	3.0	.267	.329	.356	-.086	.265	.327	.360	.241	0.8	42-C	1
2005	SLN	MLB	22	421	36	15	1	8	49	23	30	2	3	4.3	.252	.295	.358	-.142	.251	.297	.362	.229	-1.1	108-C	18
2006	SLN	MLB	23	461	29	26	0	6	49	26	41	1	2	3.3	.216	.274	.321	-.287	.211	.269	.321	.209	-19.7	117-C	18
2007	SLN	MLB	24	428	39	20	1	6	44	29	40	1	2	4.1	.249	.306	.354	-.201	.254	.309	.366	.232	0.2	102-C	9

Breakout: 40% Improve: 68% Collapse: 11% Attrition: 28%   Comparables: Ramon Hernandez, Mike Sweeney, Mike Heath, Michael Barrett

Molina's blistering postseason erased one of the twenty worst VORP showings of the expansion era from short-term memory. That's a fancy way of saying he was a historically bad hitter, settling in at number nine between the pre-Operation Shutdown (but still just as miserable) Derek Bell of the 1999 Astros and Jerry Morales of the 1979 Tigers. If Molina could just hit at replacement level, he'd be an extremely valuable commodity, since his defense last year was nothing short of superb.

Albert Pujols   1B   Bats: R   Throws: R   Height: 6′ 3″   Weight: 225   Born: January 16, 1980   Age: 27

YEAR	TEAM	LVL	AGE	PA	R	2B	3B	HR	RBI	BB	SO	SB	CS	SPEED	AVG	OBP	SLG	MLVR	EQAVG	EQOBP	EQSLG	EQA	VORP	DEFENSE	
2004	SLN	MLB	24	692	133	51	2	46	123	84	52	5	5	4.6	.331	.415	.657	.535	.332	.415	.662	.342	92.3	150-1B	10
2005	SLN	MLB	25	700	129	38	2	41	117	97	65	16	2	5.6	.330	.430	.609	.484	.329	.430	.620	.345	88.3	152-1B	5
2006	SLN	MLB	26	634	119	33	1	49	137	92	50	7	2	4.7	.331	.431	.671	.548	.331	.433	.671	.353	85.4	140-1B	17
2007	SLN	MLB	27	655	126	37	3	38	116	93	63	9	2	5.2	.327	.428	.609	.410	.333	.433	.630	.348	75.8	153-1B	10

Breakout: 10% Improve: 32% Collapse: 15% Attrition: 7%   Comparables: Jeff Bagwell, Frank Robinson, Orlando Cepeda, Eddie Murray

Very few players burst on the majors as fully-formed Hall of Famers. As this book was being written, Cal Ripken and Tony Gwynn were elected to the Hall of Fame. While it's possible there were some observers who felt certain by, say, 1983 or 1984 that they were looking at Hall of Famers in the making, there were undoubtedly just as many who saw Gwynn as a singles hitter with a bad body and Ripken as a guy who was too big for shortstop and would almost certainly be kicked over to third base as soon as someone better like Juan Bell came along. With Pujols it was clear almost right away what kind of player he was, which is why so many people expressed disbelief: They were seeing a player who, if he never grew, if he never peaked, if he just stayed right where he was, was going to be an annual MVP candidate. That's almost exactly what happened, except that Pujols has been improving slightly each season. He had his best year yet in 2006, posting a career high WARP (12.9) despite missing 19 games with an oblique strain and other minor scrapes. That total is boosted by his stellar defense at first, an underrated aspect of his skill set. Perhaps the only question left to answer is whether or not he can take one more step forward and have a couple of otherworldly, inner-circle Hall of Fame seasons like those enjoyed by Lou Gehrig and Jimmie Foxx. If it's going to happen, it will be in the next few years.

Colby Rasmus   CF   Bats: L   Throws: L   Height: 6′ 1″   Weight: 175   Born: August 11, 1986   Age: 20

YEAR	TEAM	LVL	AGE	PA	R	2B	3B	HR	RBI	BB	SO	SB	CS	SPEED	AVG	OBP	SLG	MLVR	EQAVG	EQOBP	EQSLG	EQA	VORP	DEFENSE	
2005	JCY	Rk	18	244	47	16	5	7	27	21	73	13	3	8.0	.296	.362	.514	.215	.229	.272	.348	.220	-20.5	58-CF	2
2006	QUD	A	19	341	49	22	3	11	50	29	55	17	5	6.5	.310	.373	.512	.310	.281	.328	.463	.270	15.9	73-CF	-8
2006	PMB	A+	19	225	22	4	5	5	35	27	35	11	3	5.6	.254	.351	.404	.119	.251	.332	.402	.258	4.2	51-CF	-7
2007	SLN	MLB	20	539	69	29	5	14	59	39	102	18	8	6.1	.261	.319	.431	-.066	.265	.322	.446	.261	15.0	127-CF	-4

Breakout: 43% Improve: 68% Collapse: 11% Attrition: 6%   Comparables: Chris Lubanski, Carlos Gonzalez, Nate McLouth, Franklin Gutierrez

Rasmus made the mid-year leap to High-A after earning his way at Quad Cities. The casualty of the transition was a drop in power (which comes with the territory in the Florida State League), but Rasmus compensated with increased plate discipline. He uncorks from the outfield in the mid-90s, which is about half again as fast as Johnny Damon. A toolsy top pick who should continue to rung it to St. Louis on the double quick.

John Rodriguez　　　OF　　　Bats: L　　Throws: L　　Height: 6' 0"　　Weight: 205　　Born: January 20, 1978　　Age: 29

YEAR	TEAM	LVL	AGE	PA	R	2B	3B	HR	RBI	BB	SO	SB	CS	SPEED	AVG	OBP	SLG	MLVR	EQAVG	EQOBP	EQSLG	EQA	VORP	DEFENSE			
2004	COH	AAA	26	437	78	29	10	16	69	48	82	9	3	7.3	.300	.388	.557	.309	.281	.362	.508	.293	34.3	93-CF	-11		
2005	BUF	AAA	27	196	25	13	3	5	23	15	40	5	0	6.8	.247	.323	.447	-.019	.224	.287	.385	.238	-3.2	23-CF	0	16-RF	-1
2005	MEM	AAA	27	137	24	5	0	17	47	13	28	1	1	2.1	.342	.419	.808	.722	.331	.394	.718	.342	22.6	16-RF	-2	12-CF	-1
2005	SLN	MLB	27	176	15	6	0	5	24	19	45	2	0	4.9	.295	.382	.436	.148	.293	.379	.440	.288	8.8	32-LF	3		
2006	MEM	AAA	28	76	10	4	1	3	7	11	18	0	0	4.3	.266	.373	.500	.225	.258	.347	.485	.284	2.7	18-RF	2		
2006	SLN	MLB	28	212	31	12	3	2	20	21	45	0	0	4.9	.301	.374	.432	.105	.301	.374	.432	.284	8.8	26-LF	2		
2007	SLN	MLB	29	291	40	14	2	9	37	28	62	3	1	5.4	.277	.352	.460	.044	.282	.356	.476	.283	14.2	71-DH			

Breakout: 8%　Improve: 36%　Collapse: 28%　Attrition: 26%　　Comparables: Todd Hollandsworth, Bill Howerton, Mitchell Page, Geoff Jenkins

Rodriguez possesses one of the strangest batting setups of recent times; it's entertaining, but more importantly, it works. In fact, Rodriguez is a better hitter than a lot of his better-compensated major league colleagues, and it would be nice to see him get more playing time so both he and the Cards could reap the benefits. Rodriguez has been used almost exclusively against right-handers, but it's not like he's proven himself a failure against his own kind, going .300/.451/.450 in the 50 chances he's been given at the big league level. No one has ever believed in Rodriguez—the Yankees washed their hands of him, and maybe the Cards don't quite buy him either. Better they wake up and give him a chance to get 400 at-bats as the strong side of a platoon than they keep punishing themselves with the likes of Encarnacion.

Scott Rolen　　　3B　　　Bats: R　　Throws: R　　Height: 6' 4"　　Weight: 240　　Born: April 4, 1975　　Age: 32

YEAR	TEAM	LVL	AGE	PA	R	2B	3B	HR	RBI	BB	SO	SB	CS	SPEED	AVG	OBP	SLG	MLVR	EQAVG	EQOBP	EQSLG	EQA	VORP	DEFENSE	
2004	SLN	MLB	29	593	109	32	4	34	124	72	92	4	3	5.1	.314	.409	.598	.425	.315	.408	.601	.330	65.0	140-3B	16
2005	SLN	MLB	30	223	28	12	1	5	28	25	28	1	2	4.5	.235	.323	.383	-.063	.236	.327	.395	.249	-0.5	55-3B	9
2006	SLN	MLB	31	594	94	48	1	22	95	56	69	7	4	5.1	.296	.369	.518	.210	.297	.370	.522	.299	36.6	137-3B	12
2007	SLN	MLB	32	560	84	34	2	23	81	60	74	5	3	5.1	.283	.366	.504	.131	.288	.371	.521	.298	38.3	131-3B	9

Breakout: 12%　Improve: 42%　Collapse: 31%　Attrition: 4%　　Comparables: Cal Ripken, Kevin McReynolds, Edgar Martinez, Mike Lowell

The player with whom Scott Rolen is most often compared is Mike Schmidt. Through the age of 31, Rolen has amassed a WARP of 89.3. Through the same age, Schmidt was at 94.9. Even if Rolen can stay healthy, he probably will not equal Schmidt's final total of 161.3; Schmidt had a very good attendance record. More importantly, Schmidt was a more rounded player, with greater patience and power and a batting average that was, in its time, in the same neighborhood as Rolen's. Even if the Michael Jack comparison isn't apt, Rolen is a very good player in his own right, and close enough to his Phillies forebear that he'll find himself on a podium in upstate New York reading a prepared statement about 15 years from now. His was a nice comeback season that will, at the very minimum, be matched in 2007. Note that despite the age and injuries, the great glove still endures.

Scott Spiezio　　　UT　　　Bats: S　　Throws: R　　Height: 6' 2"　　Weight: 220　　Born: September 21, 1972　Age: 34

YEAR	TEAM	LVL	AGE	PA	R	2B	3B	HR	RBI	BB	SO	SB	CS	SPEED	AVG	OBP	SLG	MLVR	EQAVG	EQOBP	EQSLG	EQA	VORP	DEFENSE			
2004	SEA	MLB	31	415	38	12	3	10	41	36	60	4	1	4.7	.215	.288	.346	-.232	.220	.295	.357	.233	-13.0	61-3B	12	33-1B	1
2005	SEA	MLB	32	51	2	1	0	1	1	4	18	0	0	2.2	.064	.137	.149	-.809	.000	.098	.000	.066	-8.6				
2006	SLN	MLB	33	321	44	15	4	13	52	37	66	1	0	5.6	.272	.366	.496	.151	.272	.368	.496	.294	16.3	25-LF	-2	23-3B	0
2007	SLN	MLB	34	326	40	14	2	11	42	33	65	2	1	4.9	.236	.321	.421	-.094	.240	.325	.435	.259	4.2	79-3B	0		

Breakout: 21%　Improve: 41%　Collapse: 27%　Attrition: 44%　　Comparables: Franklin Stubbs, Chuck Hinton, Raul Mondesi, Walt Moryn

Back from his Ballplayer of the Living Dead experience in Seattle, Spiezio was arguably the best bench player among the eight teams in the 2006 playoffs. The hits he got in key spots could very well buy him Jeff Conine-B. J. Surhoff-style longevity. Having the electric-red facial hair hook doesn't hurt, either. Ostensibly a switch-hitter, he continues to handle right-handers better than left, which is a positive thing since there are so many more of them.

Nick Stavinoha　　　RF　　　Bats: R　　Throws: R　　Height: 6' 2"　　Weight: 225　　Born: May 3, 1982　　Age: 25

YEAR	TEAM	LVL	AGE	PA	R	2B	3B	HR	RBI	BB	SO	SB	CS	SPEED	AVG	OBP	SLG	MLVR	EQAVG	EQOBP	EQSLG	EQA	VORP	DEFENSE			
2005	QUD	A	23	279	54	9	2	14	53	23	25	4	0	5.1	.344	.398	.564	.414	.300	.339	.477	.279	11.0	53-RF	0		
2006	SFD	AA	24	453	55	26	3	12	73	28	81	2	1	4.5	.297	.340	.460	.117	.280	.313	.424	.253	0.2	84-RF	-6	13-LF	-3
2007	SLN	MLB	25	447	48	22	2	12	56	25	77	2	1	4.5	.264	.309	.415	-.103	.268	.312	.430	.251	0.6	106-RF	-2		

Breakout: 12%　Improve: 40%　Collapse: 33%　Attrition: 9%　　Comparables: Rob Cosby, Jorge Toca, Kevin West, Dee Haynes

An old senior at LSU, Stavinoha was 23 during his last year there and it's put him behind the eight ball age-wise. Had he torched the Texas League last year like he did the Midwest League in 2005, his ascension would be more clear-cut. A pedestrian walk rate and a somewhat disturbing jump in strikeouts suggest he was overmatched at this level and could stand some more time there. Time, unfortunately, is not on his side. But then, time isn't really on anyone's side, is it?

So Taguchi   LF   **Bats: R**   **Throws: R**   Height: 5' 10"   Weight: 165   Born: December 31, 1969   Age: 37

YEAR	TEAM	LVL	AGE	PA	R	2B	3B	HR	RBI	BB	SO	SB	CS	SPEED	AVG	OBP	SLG	MLVR	EQAVG	EQOBP	EQSLG	EQA	VORP	DEFENSE			
2004	SLN	MLB	35	206	26	10	2	3	25	12	23	6	3	6.1	.291	.337	.419	.012	.293	.342	.418	.263	3.3	26-LF	-2	24-CF	-2
2005	SLN	MLB	36	424	45	21	2	8	53	20	62	11	2	5.8	.288	.322	.412	.013	.286	.323	.415	.258	9.7	36-RF	3	31-LF	1
2006	SLN	MLB	37	361	46	19	1	2	31	32	48	11	3	5.9	.266	.335	.351	-.100	.266	.339	.348	.249	0.2	41-LF	6	40-CF	-4
2007	*SLN*	*MLB*	*37*	*319*	*38*	*15*	*2*	*4*	*29*	*23*	*44*	*8*	*3*	*5.9*	*.266*	*.323*	*.369*	*-.138*	*.270*	*.326*	*.382*	*.247*	*0.5*	*77-LF*	*-2*		

Breakout: 15%   *Improve: 27%*   *Collapse: 36%*   *Attrition: 34%*   *Comparables: Al Bumbry, Rich Amaral, Dave Philley, Willie McGee*

Taguchi doesn't have the bearing of a player who will turn 38 at mid-season, but there he is, just 12 years from being eligible for AARP membership, or its Japanese equivalent. He wasn't quite as productive as he had been in the past, although he made up for it in a few playoff instances. Never a great hitter, he doesn't offer much. Over the last three years he's hit .275/.320/.393 against left-handers, so he doesn't even warrant use in a platoon. There are, at minimum, 50 right-handed Triple-A outfielders who could give the Cardinals more in the same role.

Preston Wilson   LF   **Bats: R**   **Throws: R**   Height: 6' 2"   Weight: 215   Born: July 19, 1974   Age: 32

YEAR	TEAM	LVL	AGE	PA	R	2B	3B	HR	RBI	BB	SO	SB	CS	SPEED	AVG	OBP	SLG	MLVR	EQAVG	EQOBP	EQSLG	EQA	VORP	DEFENSE			
2004	COL	MLB	29	222	24	11	0	6	29	17	49	2	1	3.7	.248	.315	.391	-.131	.233	.302	.371	.235	-2.1	48-CF	-1		
2005	COL	MLB	30	296	39	15	1	15	47	25	77	3	2	4.8	.258	.322	.491	.049	.248	.315	.485	.268	9.5	66-CF	-10		
2005	WAS	MLB	30	280	34	14	1	10	43	20	71	3	4	4.4	.261	.329	.443	.062	.269	.336	.470	.269	8.2	54-CF	-7	10-LF	-1
2006	HOU	MLB	31	417	40	22	2	9	55	22	94	6	2	4.7	.269	.309	.405	-.073	.268	.312	.410	.250	-2.6	91-LF	-4		
2006	SLN	MLB	31	120	18	3	0	8	17	7	27	6	0	6.0	.243	.300	.486	.007	.243	.306	.486	.273	3.7	17-RF	-1		
2007	*SLN*	*MLB*	*32*	*488*	*58*	*23*	*2*	*14*	*62*	*34*	*111*	*8*	*4*	*4.7*	*.263*	*.320*	*.421*	*-.076*	*.268*	*.323*	*.435*	*.257*	*6.3*	*115-LF*	*-7*		

Breakout: 24%   *Improve: 55%*   *Collapse: 23%*   *Attrition: 19%*   *Comparables: Derek Bell, Larry Herndon, Cleon Jones, Jerry Martin*

Wilson's been reduced to replacement level against right-handers in recent years, and his defense long ago ceased to be adequate for center, if it ever was. He still handles lefties well enough, but teams are going to have to start looking at him as something less than a full-time player if they want to get value out of him. Unfortunately, a player with as undisciplined a swing as Wilson's isn't a natural fit for bench work; managers like to see their reserve hitters make a bit of contact. A free-agent this winter, Wilson didn't have a job at press time.

PITCHERS

Chris Carpenter   **Bats: R**   **Throws: R**   Height: 6' 6"   Weight: 230   Born: April 27, 1975   Age: 32

YEAR	TEAM	LVL	AGE	W	L	SV	G	GS	IP	H	BB	SO	HR	GB%	BABIP	STUFF	WHIP	ERA	PERA	EQERA	EQH9	EQBB9	EQSO9	EQHR9	VORP	WXRL
2004	SLN	MLB	29	15	5	0	28	28	182	169	38	152	24	—	.282	20	1.14	3.46	3.95	4.01	8.8	1.7	6.7	1.1	40.5	5.22
2005	SLN	MLB	30	21	5	0	33	33	241²	204	51	213	18	55.4%	.285	36	1.06	2.83	3.12	3.37	7.8	1.7	7.3	0.7	67.8	8.62
2006	SLN	MLB	31	15	8	0	32	32	221²	194	43	184	21	54.7%	.278	32	1.07	3.09	3.40	3.17	7.8	1.5	6.8	0.8	67.8	7.35
2007	*SLN*	*MLB*	*32*	*14*	*9*	*0*	*31*	*31*	*211*	*198*	*49*	*171*	*20*	*51.0%*	*.287*	*21*	*1.17*	*3.31*	*3.66*	*3.62*	*8.8*	*1.9*	*6.5*	*0.8*	*51.6*	*6.80*

Breakout: 8%   *Improve: 41%*   *Collapse: 25%*   *Attrition: 2%*   *Comparables: Gaylord Perry, Roger Clemens, Esteban Loaiza, Fergie Jenkins*

PECOTA likes him, it really likes him. Carpenter's top comps include three Hall of Famers and Esteban Loaiza—just to keep it real. One misconception that probably hurt him in the Cy Young voting last year was that his 2006 wasn't nearly as good as his 2005, but aside from the drop from 21–5 to 15–8 in won-loss record, they were fairly comparable efforts. He rebounded well from the heaviest workload of his career in 2005, though he did have a quick DL stint due to shoulder bursitis. He was unstoppable at home, posting a 1.81 ERA in St. Louis.; the downside of that dominance was an untidy 4.70 ERA on the road, where he was more vulnerable to giving up the longball. In early December, the Cards signed Carpenter to a five-year, $65-million contract extension. That's a long time to be on the hook for any pitcher, particularly one already into his thirties, but at least St. Louis is starting with one at the top of his game, if not *the* game.

Randy Flores
Bats: L Throws: L Height: 6′ 0″ Weight: 180 Born: July 31, 1975 Age: 31

YEAR	TEAM	LVL	AGE	W	L	SV	G	GS	IP	H	BB	SO	HR	GB%	BABIP	STUFF	WHIP	ERA	PERA	EQERA	EQH9	EQBB9	EQSO9	EQHR9	VORP	WXRL
2004	MEM	AAA	28	5	7	2	36	15	122²	115	46	99	10	—	.294	1	1.31	3.81	4.52	4.63	8.0	3.5	5.4	0.8	13.4	—
2004	SLN	MLB	28	1	0	0	9	1	14	13	3	7	0	—	.310	-2	1.14	1.93	4.02	2.57	9.6	1.9	3.9	0.0	5.9	0.27
2005	SLN	MLB	29	3	1	1	50	0	41²	37	13	43	5	42.3%	.302	12	1.20	3.45	3.91	4.93	8.4	2.6	8.6	1.1	3.3	0.70
2006	SLN	MLB	30	1	1	0	65	0	41²	49	22	40	5	40.3%	.355	-1	1.70	5.61	4.20	5.70	10.5	4.0	7.8	0.8	-1.0	1.07
2007	*SLN*	*MLB*	*31*	*2*	*2*	*2*	*49*	*0*	*45*	*45*	*19*	*36*	*5*	*44.0%*	*.297*	*-3*	*1.42*	*4.43*	*4.79*	*4.81*	*9.4*	*3.4*	*6.5*	*1.0*	*4.9*	*0.40*

Breakout: 28% Improve: 56% Collapse: 20% Attrition: 31% Comparables: Aaron Fultz, Frank DiPino, Arnold Earley, Yorkis Perez

Flores continues to pitch often, if briefly. Among relievers with at least 40 appearances last year, he had the fifth-lowest innings-per-game average behind only fellow LOOGies Mike Myers, Scott Sauerbeck, George Sherrill, and Brian Shouse. His teammate, Tyler Johnson, came in sixth, so that's two roster spots eating less than nine games worth of innings. Right-handed batters really battered him last year (.329/.416/.556), and while he handled lefthanders well enough (.258/.337/.355), it was nothing like his performance in 2005. He's fungible, and with Ricky Rincon due back, up against the wall.

Jaime Garcia
Bats: L Throws: L Height: 6′ 1″ Weight: 200 Born: July 8, 1986 Age: 19

YEAR	TEAM	LVL	AGE	W	L	SV	G	GS	IP	H	BB	SO	HR	GB%	BABIP	STUFF	WHIP	ERA	PERA	EQERA	EQH9	EQBB9	EQSO9	EQHR9	VORP	WXRL
2006	QUD	A	19	5	4	0	13	13	77²	67	18	80	1	64.1%	.313	33	1.10	2.91	3.38	4.66	8.8	2.6	5.6	0.4	7.9	—
2006	PMB	A+	19	5	4	0	12	12	77¹	84	16	51	3	60.8%	.337	14	1.30	3.85	4.00	4.98	9.8	2.1	3.8	0.7	5.4	—
2007	*SLN*	*MLB*	*20*	*9*	*10*	*0*	*36*	*24*	*159*	*167*	*53*	*96*	*16*	*56%*	*.294*	*5*	*1.38*	*4.52*	*4.69*	*5.00*	*9.8*	*2.7*	*4.8*	*0.9*	*12.9*	*2.5*

Breakout: 8% Improve: 42% Collapse: 21% Attrition: 8% Comparables: Brandon League, Bobby Livingston, Sean Burnett, Cesar Jimenez

It's exciting to glance at the birth years of a high minor league team and find in their midst a relative babe. That will be Garcia at Double-A Springfield this year. Just 20 and on the fast track to NeoBusch, Garcia lacks projection, but he throws a hard sinker that had them killing grubs galore in the low minors.

Josh Hancock
Bats: R Throws: R Height: 6′ 3″ Weight: 205 Born: April 11, 1978 Age: 29

YEAR	TEAM	LVL	AGE	W	L	SV	G	GS	IP	H	BB	SO	HR	GB%	BABIP	STUFF	WHIP	ERA	PERA	EQERA	EQH9	EQBB9	EQSO9	EQHR9	VORP	WXRL
2004	SWB	AAA	26	8	7	0	18	18	107²	107	21	65	10	—	.283	3	1.19	4.01	4.35	4.76	8.9	1.9	4.1	1.0	10.1	—
2004	CIN	MLB	26	5	1	0	12	9	54²	60	25	31	14	—	.263	-23	1.55	4.44	6.58	5.08	9.2	3.7	4.4	2.1	-0.2	1.07
2005	LOU	AAA	27	1	2	0	11	8	44	59	17	38	5	55.9%	.394	-8	1.73	5.93	5.00	6.85	11.7	3.8	5.8	1.2	-6.2	—
2005	CIN	MLB	27	1	0	0	11	0	14	11	1	5	1	35.4%	.213	-7	0.86	1.93	3.65	2.51	6.3	0.6	3.1	0.6	4.6	0.05
2006	SLN	MLB	28	3	3	1	62	0	77	70	23	50	9	41.9%	.263	-2	1.21	4.09	4.17	4.04	8.1	2.3	5.3	0.9	14.7	0.52
2007	*SLN*	*MLB*	*29*	*3*	*3*	*2*	*50*	*1*	*64²*	*65*	*22*	*41*	*8*	*44.0%*	*.279*	*-8*	*1.35*	*4.24*	*4.64*	*4.59*	*9.4*	*2.8*	*5.0*	*1.1*	*8.6*	*0.70*

Breakout: 16% Improve: 49% Collapse: 20% Attrition: 26% Comparables: Guillermo Mota, Jeff Shaw, Bob Chakales, Tom Buskey

Hancock bounced back from an injury-plagued 2005 to post a nice K/BB ratio in middle relief. A starter in over 80 percent of his professional appearances prior to last year, one would like to think he'd get one more shot at a rotation spot before he's pigeon-holed for life. Not that it's a bad life to have.

Jason Isringhausen
Bats: R Throws: R Height: 6′ 3″ Weight: 230 Born: September 7, 1972 Age: 34

YEAR	TEAM	LVL	AGE	W	L	SV	G	GS	IP	H	BB	SO	HR	GB%	BABIP	STUFF	WHIP	ERA	PERA	EQERA	EQH9	EQBB9	EQSO9	EQHR9	VORP	WXRL
2004	SLN	MLB	31	4	2	47	74	0	75¹	55	23	71	5	—	.250	21	1.04	2.87	3.22	3.46	7.0	2.5	7.6	0.6	20.1	4.98
2005	SLN	MLB	32	1	2	39	63	0	59	43	27	51	4	51.9%	.247	12	1.19	2.14	3.79	2.43	6.8	3.8	7.1	0.6	22.0	3.72
2006	SLN	MLB	33	4	8	33	59	0	58¹	47	38	52	10	45.0%	.247	2	1.46	3.55	5.54	3.62	7.2	5.1	7.2	1.4	14.1	1.06
2007	*SLN*	*MLB*	*34*	*3*	*4*	*20*	*52*	*0*	*58¹*	*52*	*30*	*49*	*6*	*45.0%*	*.276*	*-2*	*1.39*	*3.77*	*4.34*	*4.09*	*8.3*	*4.1*	*6.7*	*0.8*	*11.1*	*1.40*

Breakout: 6% Improve: 27% Collapse: 53% Attrition: 15% Comparables: Don Larsen, Dick Tidrow, Don McMahon, Bill Campbell

It's got to hurt a hell of a lot to chuck a ball 90 miles an hour and land hard on a leg that's connected to a hip made faulty by arthritis and an impingement. Isringhausen opted for surgery in September, choosing it over a less-aggressive scoping. When he'll be back to full capability will be determined in spring training. A full recovery has got to be defined as something beyond what he showed prior to going down in 2006, otherwise he's not going to be a closer for much longer. Izzie's stuff seemed to have declined badly over the last couple of years, but it's tough to evaluate a pitcher's arm when he's working on one leg.

Tyler Johnson

Bats: S Throws: L   Height: 6' 2"   Weight: 180   Born: June 7, 1981   Age: 26

YEAR	TEAM	LVL	AGE	W	L	SV	G	GS	IP	H	BB	SO	HR	GB%	BABIP	STUFF	WHIP	ERA	PERA	EQERA	EQH9	EQBB9	EQSO9	EQHR9	VORP	WXRL
2004	TEN	AA	23	2	2	4	53	0	56¹	48	37	77	4	—	.333	8	1.51	4.80	5.37	6.04	9.2	6.7	8.0	1.0	-2.6	—
2005	MEM	AAA	24	2	1	7	57	0	59	51	26	77	6	45.1%	.328	11	1.31	4.27	4.13	4.70	8.0	3.8	8.9	1.1	5.9	—
2006	SLN	MLB	25	2	4	0	56	0	36¹	33	23	37	5	40.8%	.301	7	1.54	4.96	4.97	4.82	8.4	4.8	8.2	1.0	3.3	0.07
2007	SLN	MLB	26	2	2	2	52	0	44²	42	25	43	5	44.0%	.300	3	1.50	4.49	4.90	4.87	8.8	4.5	7.7	1.0	4.4	0.40

Breakout: 27% Improve: 50% Collapse: 17% Attrition: 44%   Comparables: Grant Jackson, Chuck McElroy, Jesus Colome, Mike Wallace

Johnson had a decent debut last year as a tyro LOOGY, striking out 24 southpaws in 77 at-bats. One problem he had was, when lefties did touch him, the ball traveled well; portsiders had a .195 isolated power against him, including three home runs. Two of the other extra-base hits off of him by lefties were triples, possibly symptomatic of the poor defensive outfield the Cardinals played last year, as well as Johnson's pronounced fly-ball tendency. As a youngish lefty spot man Johnson could pitch forever—with Jesse Orosco-like longevity we could still be talking about him in the 2027 edition of this book—but nothing tends to kill a short reliever's career faster than an inclination towards giving up home runs.

Josh Kinney

Bats: R Throws: R   Height: 6' 1"   Weight: 195   Born: March 31, 1979   Age: 28

YEAR	TEAM	LVL	AGE	W	L	SV	G	GS	IP	H	BB	SO	HR	GB%	BABIP	STUFF	WHIP	ERA	PERA	EQERA	EQH9	EQBB9	EQSO9	EQHR9	VORP	WXRL
2004	TEN	AA	25	3	8	4	50	0	55²	67	34	48	6	—	.355	-28	1.81	5.49	7.07	8.03	12.1	6.8	4.8	1.7	-14.2	—
2005	SFD	AA	26	5	2	11	32	0	42	28	12	42	2	54.1%	.243	3	0.95	1.29	3.95	2.66	6.6	3.3	6.2	0.7	13.3	—
2005	MEM	AAA	26	1	2	0	26	0	25²	40	19	25	4	43.8%	.429	-16	2.30	7.35	6.25	7.18	13.7	6.5	6.5	1.7	-4.6	—
2006	MEM	AAA	27	2	2	3	51	0	71¹	46	29	76	2	56.8%	.260	20	1.05	1.52	3.61	2.42	6.2	3.7	7.3	0.4	25.0	—
2006	SLN	MLB	27	0	0	0	21	0	25	17	8	22	3	57.4%	.215	12	1.00	3.24	3.97	3.20	6.0	2.5	7.1	1.1	7.8	0.62
2007	SLN	MLB	28	3	4	3	75	2	69²	70	33	54	7	52.0%	.299	-5	1.48	4.44	4.91	4.86	9.4	3.9	6.1	0.9	7.1	0.70

Breakout: 6% Improve: 25% Collapse: 36% Attrition: 7%   Comparables: Greg Aquino, Shawn Camp, Jim Winn, Hal Reniff

Fished out of the Frontier League in mid-2001, Kinney endured six seasons in the Cards system and one shoulder surgery before finally getting the call last July. The results weren't bad. A low-velocity, sinker-slider type, he'll battle for a bullpen spot this spring as something slightly more useful than a righty situational guy. Not many from among the competition will have 6⅓ scoreless innings in the postseason to their credit.

Chris Lambert

Bats: R Throws: R   Height: 6' 1"   Weight: 205   Born: March 8, 1983   Age: 24

YEAR	TEAM	LVL	AGE	W	L	SV	G	GS	IP	H	BB	SO	HR	GB%	BABIP	STUFF	WHIP	ERA	PERA	EQERA	EQH9	EQBB9	EQSO9	EQHR9	VORP	WXRL
2004	PEO	A	21	1	1	0	9	9	38¹	31	24	46	2	—	.305	13	1.44	2.58	6.08	4.84	9.2	7.6	6.4	1.0	3.0	—
2005	PMB	A+	22	7	1	0	10	10	54²	53	15	46	4	44.8%	.310	-2	1.24	2.63	5.47	4.42	9.8	3.2	4.8	1.4	6.9	—
2005	SFD	AA	22	3	8	0	18	18	85	97	48	69	10	41.7%	.343	-10	1.71	6.35	6.69	8.06	11.0	6.0	5.6	1.5	-22.6	—
2006	SFD	AA	23	10	9	0	23	23	120²	126	63	113	20	44.1%	.314	-21	1.57	5.32	6.76	7.00	10.2	4.9	6.1	2.1	-18.4	—
2007	SLN	MLB	24	4	7	0	27	15	95²	102	56	72	16	42.0%	.298	-5	1.65	5.71	6.33	6.10	10.0	4.7	6.0	1.4	-3.7	0.20

Breakout: 24% Improve: 66% Collapse: 10% Attrition: 3%   Comparables: Joel Hanrahan, Ryan Cameron, Justin Echols, Claudio Vargas

Wasn't he the star of "Highlander?" Lambert has now made 41 starts at Double-A over the last two seasons and it looks like he could use some more. A 5.00-plus ERA with impractical walk rates might make one a multi-millionaire at the big league level, but another year of that in the high minors is going to dead-end the former first-round pick in a hurry. He might be better off returning to the jungle and flirting with a young Andie MacDowell.

Braden Looper

Bats: R Throws: R   Height: 6' 3"   Weight: 220   Born: October 28, 1974   Age: 32

YEAR	TEAM	LVL	AGE	W	L	SV	G	GS	IP	H	BB	SO	HR	GB%	BABIP	STUFF	WHIP	ERA	PERA	EQERA	EQH9	EQBB9	EQSO9	EQHR9	VORP	WXRL
2004	NYN	MLB	29	2	5	29	71	0	83¹	86	16	60	5	—	.314	14	1.22	2.70	3.25	2.99	9.3	1.5	5.8	0.5	24.5	3.65
2005	NYN	MLB	30	4	7	28	60	0	59¹	65	22	27	7	53.5%	.282	-21	1.47	3.95	5.26	4.77	10.0	3.0	3.7	1.0	4.8	-0.17
2006	SLN	MLB	31	9	3	0	69	0	73¹	76	20	41	3	51.9%	.317	5	1.31	3.56	3.44	3.50	9.2	2.2	4.6	0.4	19.1	1.59
2007	SLN	MLB	32	7	10	0	36	22	141¹	174	40	71	17	51.0%	.317	-8	1.51	4.99	5.60	5.42	11.5	2.3	4.0	1.1	5.0	1.50

Breakout: 2% Improve: 8% Collapse: 76% Attrition: 16%   Comparables: Ron Kline, Paul Quantrill, Clay Carroll, Phil Regan

Here's to souvenir-free pitching, as year one of Looper's three-year deal turned out rather nicely. He kept the ball in the yard, joining Juan Rincon, Takashi Saito, Mariano Rivera, and B. J. Ryan as the pitchers who had thrown at least 65 innings who were least likely to give up a home run. Looper jumped from being ranked 546th in WXRL up to 62nd, so getting him

(continued next page)

Braden Looper *(continued)*

out of the closing role turned out to be a clever idea on the Cardinals' part. Now they're pushing the cleverness envelope again, considering him for the starting rotation. It's not the worst idea in the world—if it doesn't work, Looper can head back to the pen, and if it does, it isn't like they'll be missing an irreplaceable reliever.

Jason Marquis Bats: L Throws: R Height: 6' 1" Weight: 210 Born: August 21, 1978 Age: 28

YEAR	TEAM	LVL	AGE	W	L	SV	G	GS	IP	H	BB	SO	HR	GB%	BABIP	STUFF	WHIP	ERA	PERA	EQERA	EQH9	EQBB9	EQSO9	EQHR9	VORP	WXRL
2004	SLN	MLB	25	15	7	0	32	32	201¹	215	70	138	26	—	.305	7	1.42	3.71	4.60	4.37	10.0	2.8	5.5	1.1	36.7	4.84
2005	SLN	MLB	26	13	14	0	33	32	207	206	69	100	29	53.1%	.269	-9	1.33	4.13	5.15	5.22	9.2	2.8	4.0	1.3	18.2	4.23
2006	SLN	MLB	27	14	16	0	33	33	194¹	221	75	96	35	43.7%	.294	-16	1.52	6.02	5.71	5.90	10.1	3.0	4.0	1.5	-5.7	2.12
2007	CHN	MLB	28	7	10	0	35	22	143¹	161	53	82	21	48%	.297	-4	1.50	5.14	5.33	5.28	9.7	2.9	4.6	1.2	8.1	1.8

Breakout: 14% Improve: 50% Collapse: 26% Attrition: 26% Comparables: Josh Fogg, Stan Bahnsen, Jeff Suppan, Russ Kemmerer

You're a starter on a mediocre team starved for pitchers and, even with that, they don't see you as a candidate to make the postseason roster. Regardless, instead of having to have your agent beg for a spring training invite for the following season, you get a three-year, $20-million deal from the Cubs. It's as if starting 32-plus games three years in a row obligates baseball to make you rich, regardless of your ability to prevent runs. Note the four PECOTA comps above. You might recall Hawkins as an especially pathetic Yankees signing in the days when they would sign anyone with the "free agent" designation before their names, regardless of talent. Fogg impressed by being average as a rookie and has been decidedly less so ever since. Bahnsen, too, will be remembered by some as a Rookie of the Year who burned out quickly. That leaves Herman Ralph Wehmeier, who pitched in the bigs from 1945 to 1958, mostly for the Reds. From 1948 through 1954, he had an ERA of 5.06 against a league average of 4.01. In 1950 he pitched 230 innings with an ERA of 5.67. In 1953, he pitched 82 innings with an ERA of 7.13. Wehmeier was a bad pitcher, and this is probably the only time even the most dedicated of baseball aficionados will think of him this year. We just wanted to give him his due among the Marquis Parade of Mediocrities. To Marquis's credit, at least the man can hit, with 19 doubles and 26 RBI in 310 career at-bats. He'll need to keep helping himself if the Cubs are going to get value from his contract.

Mark McCormick Bats: R Throws: R Height: 6' 2" Weight: 195 Born: October 15, 1983 Age: 22

YEAR	TEAM	LVL	AGE	W	L	SV	G	GS	IP	H	BB	SO	HR	GB%	BABIP	STUFF	WHIP	ERA	PERA	EQERA	EQH9	EQBB9	EQSO9	EQHR9	VORP	WXRL
2005	QUD	A	21	1	2	0	9	9	42²	41	28	45	4	53.8%	.327	2	1.62	5.48	7.28	6.75	10.8	7.2	6.3	1.8	-5.1	—
2006	QUD	A	22	2	4	0	11	11	52²	38	38	63	3	55.4%	.297	11	1.46	3.79	8.15	6.26	9.0	10.0	6.7	1.6	-3.4	—
2007	SLN	MLB	23	3	6	0	24	14	78¹	82	77	63	11	48%	.309	-14	2.03	6.22	7.51	6.67	9.8	8.0	6.4	1.2	-7.5	-0.3

Breakout: 10% Improve: 46% Collapse: 33% Attrition: 15% Comparables: Rob Caputo, Matthew Durkin, Alberto Garza, Jay O'Shaughnessy

The Bird with the Blur, McCormick is a power pitcher capable of nearing the century mark when he dials it up. His innings-pitched total wasn't dialed up to the century mark last year due to shoulder soreness. The speed thing he's got down, it's the rest of the pitching experience that needs work; until he gets his control under control, the heat alone isn't going to be enough to get the more advanced players out.

Mark Mulder Bats: L Throws: L Height: 6' 6" Weight: 215 Born: August 5, 1977 Age: 29

YEAR	TEAM	LVL	AGE	W	L	SV	G	GS	IP	H	BB	SO	HR	GB%	BABIP	STUFF	WHIP	ERA	PERA	EQERA	EQH9	EQBB9	EQSO9	EQHR9	VORP	WXRL
2004	OAK	MLB	26	17	8	0	33	33	225²	223	83	140	25	—	.290	9	1.34	4.43	4.49	4.48	8.8	3.0	5.2	0.9	40.1	4.73
2005	SLN	MLB	27	16	8	0	32	32	205	212	70	111	19	60.9%	.299	6	1.38	3.64	4.47	4.34	9.5	2.8	4.5	0.8	37.0	5.31
2006	SLN	MLB	28	6	7	0	17	17	93¹	124	35	50	19	55.6%	.339	-21	1.70	7.14	5.64	6.94	11.6	2.9	4.3	1.6	-14.9	0.22
2007	SLN	MLB	29	7	9	0	31	21	132¹	146	51	74	15	54.0%	.299	-4	1.49	4.79	5.27	5.25	10.3	3.1	4.5	1.0	7.6	1.70

Breakout: 15% Improve: 51% Collapse: 24% Attrition: 4% Comparables: Joe Magrane, Brian Bohanon, Dave LaPoint, Dan Petry

In the end, Billy Beane kept the right one. Faced with losing all or some of his Big Three starters after 2004, Beane kept Barry Zito and dispatched Tim Hudson and Mulder. Dan Haren and Kiko Calero have given the A's a great deal since coming over in the Mulder trade, and the meter hasn't even started running yet on Daric Barton. As for Mulder himself, things started to go bad in late May when his left shoulder quit, and he was forced to undergo surgery to repair a partial thickness tear of his rotator cuff. His last starts were like something out of the oeuvre of Irwin Allen. Predictably, more than a handful of teams were ready to gamble—albeit at reduced stakes—that Mulder is capable of being effective again. He eventually decided to return to St. Louis, where he'll pitch the next two years on a $13-million contract with games-started incentives that could expand it to three years, $45 million.

St. Louis Cardinals

Anthony Reyes   **Bats: R** **Throws: R**   Height: 6' 2"   Weight: 215   Born: October 16, 1981   Age: 25

YEAR	TEAM	LVL	AGE	W	L	SV	G	GS	IP	H	BB	SO	HR	GB%	BABIP	STUFF	WHIP	ERA	PERA	EQERA	EQH9	EQBB9	EQSO9	EQHR9	VORP	WXRL
2004	PMB	A+	22	2	0	0	6	6	30²	32	7	36	3	—	.367	6	1.27	4.40	5.40	6.91	11.9	2.5	7.2	2.2	-4.2	—
2004	TEN	AA	22	6	2	0	12	12	74¹	62	13	102	3	—	.339	41	1.01	3.03	3.01	3.98	8.7	1.7	8.2	0.5	13.0	—
2005	MEM	AAA	23	7	6	0	23	23	128²	105	34	136	13	36.3%	.283	24	1.08	3.64	3.92	3.82	7.3	2.3	7.2	1.0	25.7	—
2005	SLN	MLB	23	1	1	0	4	1	13¹	6	4	12	2	36.4%	.129	13	0.75	2.71	4.41	2.70	4.1	2.7	7.4	1.4	4.2	0.28
2006	MEM	AAA	24	6	1	0	13	13	84	70	11	82	9	42.0%	.270	22	0.96	2.57	3.90	3.21	7.7	1.2	6.9	1.3	22.3	—
2006	SLN	MLB	24	5	8	0	17	17	85¹	84	34	72	17	36.1%	.289	1	1.38	5.06	5.30	4.66	8.9	3.1	6.8	1.6	9.8	1.92
2007	SLN	MLB	25	10	9	0	32	28	164¹	153	50	140	21	39.0%	.279	18	1.23	3.89	4.20	4.17	8.7	2.5	6.8	1.1	29.5	4.20

Breakout: 13%   Improve: 44%   Collapse: 13%   Attrition: 3%   Comparables: Bob Sebra, Ron Schueler, Brett Tomko, Eric Rasmussen

Reyes seemed like somebody who was going to hit the ground running once he landed in the majors. That it didn't quite happen that way is no reason to think he won't pick up speed after a not-too-exhilarating 2006. The extent of his struggles was reflected in the Cardinals' decision to ship him to Memphis despite having to cope with a rotation that included the overly-generous Marquis and the damaged Mulder. To keep expectations realistic, imagine the 2007 version of Reyes to be something between the pitcher who only got past the sixth inning in three of his 17 starts and the man who shut the Tigers down in Game One of the World Series.

Ricardo Rincon   **Bats: L** **Throws: L**   Height: 5' 9"   Weight: 190   Born: April 13, 1970   Age: 37

YEAR	TEAM	LVL	AGE	W	L	SV	G	GS	IP	H	BB	SO	HR	GB%	BABIP	STUFF	WHIP	ERA	PERA	EQERA	EQH9	EQBB9	EQSO9	EQHR9	VORP	WXRL
2004	OAK	MLB	34	1	1	0	67	0	44	45	22	40	3	—	.316	7	1.52	3.68	3.70	4.20	9.2	4.0	7.6	0.6	9.0	1.24
2005	OAK	MLB	35	1	1	0	67	0	37¹	34	20	27	7	42.3%	.260	-7	1.45	4.34	5.93	4.58	8.7	4.8	6.5	1.7	5.0	0.46
2006	SLN	MLB	36	0	0	0	5	0	3¹	6	4	6	1	50.0%	.556	4	3.00	10.91	6.73	12.27	14.7	9.8	12.3	2.5	-1.7	0.15
2007	SLN	MLB	37	1	1	1	30	0	27²	27	16	26	3	46.0%	.307	-3	1.55	4.46	5.20	4.81	9.3	4.6	7.5	1.0	2.9	0.20

Breakout: 25%   Improve: 51%   Collapse: 20%   Attrition: 52%   Comparables: John Hiller, Doug Bair, Blix Donnelly, Kent Mercker

Rincon's spring training began with a visa hassle that delayed his entry by two weeks. Considering what happened next, he would have been better off staying home: No sooner was the season underway than he was under the blade with both TJ and labrum surgery. To paraphrase Barry McGuire, he's on the eve of personal destruction. Fortunately for the Cards, with Flores and Johnson the team is stocked with the requisite number of lefty specialists, even if Tony La Russa might only feel truly comfortable with three, or even four.

Jorge Sosa   **Bats: R** **Throws: R**   Height: 6' 2"   Weight: 175   Born: April 28, 1977   Age: 30

YEAR	TEAM	LVL	AGE	W	L	SV	G	GS	IP	H	BB	SO	HR	GB%	BABIP	STUFF	WHIP	ERA	PERA	EQERA	EQH9	EQBB9	EQSO9	EQHR9	VORP	WXRL
2004	TBA	MLB	27	4	7	1	43	8	99¹	100	54	94	17	—	.302	-1	1.55	5.53	4.88	5.49	8.9	4.4	7.9	1.3	1.0	2.00
2005	ATL	MLB	28	13	3	0	44	20	134	122	64	85	12	36.6%	.269	4	1.39	2.55	4.48	3.01	7.9	3.9	5.2	0.8	41.3	4.98
2006	ATL	MLB	29	3	10	3	26	13	87¹	105	32	58	20	36.7%	.310	-21	1.57	5.46	5.55	5.66	9.9	2.8	5.4	1.8	-3.4	-0.95
2006	SLN	MLB	29	0	1	1	19	0	30²	33	8	17	10	34.0%	.247	-24	1.34	5.28	6.83	4.94	9.3	2.0	4.6	2.6	2.7	0.07
2007	SLN	MLB	30	5	7	3	49	9	102	105	38	70	17	39.0%	.281	-6	1.40	4.61	5.18	4.92	9.6	3.0	5.5	1.4	9.4	1.30

Breakout: 14%   Improve: 36%   Collapse: 36%   Attrition: 12%   Comparables: Todd Burns, Jim Coates, Paul Byrd, Victor Santos

Jorge Sosa may have been the last pitcher to benefit from the Mazzone Effect in Atlanta, though his peripherals from 2005 suggest his success was more a case of great fortune than great coaching. Both went away in 2006 and, by the end of July, he had regressed to the point that Atlanta designated him for assignment. It was then that St. Louis hooked Sosa from Atlanta for the price of reliever Rich Scalamandre, (who, for whatever it's worth, has crafted a 23–5 won-loss record in five minor league seasons). Sosa surrendered a whopping 10 home runs in a mere 30⅔ innings for the Birds. Needless to say, he'll be wearing a different uniform this year.

Jeff Suppan   **Bats: R** **Throws: R**   Height: 6' 2"   Weight: 220   Born: January 2, 1975   Age: 32

YEAR	TEAM	LVL	AGE	W	L	SV	G	GS	IP	H	BB	SO	HR	GB%	BABIP	STUFF	WHIP	ERA	PERA	EQERA	EQH9	EQBB9	EQSO9	EQHR9	VORP	WXRL
2004	SLN	MLB	29	16	9	0	31	31	188	192	65	110	25	—	.283	0	1.37	4.16	4.83	5.06	9.6	2.8	4.7	1.1	20.4	3.80
2005	SLN	MLB	30	16	10	0	32	32	194¹	206	63	114	24	47.2%	.298	2	1.38	3.57	4.69	4.68	9.8	2.7	4.9	1.1	27.5	4.32
2006	SLN	MLB	31	12	7	0	32	32	190	207	69	104	21	47.0%	.299	4	1.45	4.12	4.55	4.45	9.6	2.8	4.5	0.9	27.0	4.35
2007	MIL	MLB	32	9	11	0	31	28	172¹	192	62	99	24	48.0%	.296	0	1.47	4.95	5.25	5.06	9.6	2.8	4.6	1.1	12.0	2.50

Breakout: 9%   Improve: 36%   Collapse: 25%   Attrition: 1%   Comparables: Jaime Navarro, Steve Trachsel, Dock Ellis, Walt Terrell

(continued next page)

Jeff Suppan (continued)

Ever since his first full season as a starter for the Royals in 1999, Jeff Suppan has been alarmingly consistent and decidedly league-average. There's certainly value in that, though perhaps not the $42 million over four years the Brewers seem to think it's worth. Worse for Milwaukee, PECOTA seems to think the bubble's about to burst. Suppan's overly reliant on his defense, seemed to get a mighty boost from his team's new park last year (5.36 road ERA vs. 3.18 at home), and his walk rate is trending upwards toward his poor strikeout rate. It all makes you ask yourself to what degree the Brewers' funding stemmed from his foxy postseason performance.

Brad Thompson
Bats: R Throws: R Height: 6' 1" Weight: 190 Born: January 31, 1982 Age: 25

YEAR	TEAM	LVL	AGE	W	L	SV	G	GS	IP	H	BB	SO	HR	GB%	BABIP	STUFF	WHIP	ERA	PERA	EQERA	EQH9	EQBB9	EQSO9	EQHR9	VORP	WXRL
2004	TEN	AA	22	8	2	0	13	12	72¹	56	11	57	6	—	.248	10	0.93	2.37	4.85	3.06	7.8	1.5	4.7	1.1	20.0	—
2004	MEM	AAA	22	1	0	0	3	3	14²	20	3	10	3	—	.347	-2	1.56	5.51	5.49	5.87	11.2	1.8	4.7	1.8	-0.5	—
2005	MEM	AAA	23	2	1	0	9	0	13²	12	7	11	1	65.9%	.289	0	1.39	3.28	4.92	3.29	7.9	4.6	5.3	0.7	3.5	—
2005	SLN	MLB	23	4	0	1	40	0	55	46	15	29	5	58.7%	.243	-5	1.11	2.95	4.47	4.07	8.0	2.3	4.4	0.8	11.5	1.58
2006	MEM	AAA	24	2	0	0	14	5	42¹	36	6	33	3	60.8%	.282	11	1.00	2.14	3.74	2.76	7.7	1.3	5.5	0.9	13.3	—
2006	SLN	MLB	24	1	2	0	43	1	56²	58	20	32	4	56.2%	.298	-2	1.38	3.33	4.20	3.41	9.2	2.8	4.7	0.6	15.0	0.72
2007	SLN	MLB	25	4	4	2	49	4	75²	78	23	45	7	54.0%	.288	-4	1.33	3.98	4.33	4.39	9.6	2.5	4.8	0.8	12.5	1.20

Breakout: 6%   Improve: 15%   Collapse: 59%   Attrition: 18%   Comparables: Roger McDowell, Hipolito Pichardo, Ron Davis, Brad Clontz

For the second year in a row, Thompson had considerably more success at home than on the road. It's hard to call a sophomore season that included two demotions to the minors a success, but Thompson only earned the first and pitched very well after returning. The line one always hears about sinkerball pitchers is that they need to be tired to be effective. Contrary to that theory, Thompson's best efforts in the past two seasons has come in his first 15 pitches (.226/.291/.301). Beyond that, his OPS jumps 250 points.

Adam Wainwright
Bats: R Throws: R Height: 6' 7" Weight: 205 Born: August 30, 1981 Age: 25

YEAR	TEAM	LVL	AGE	W	L	SV	G	GS	IP	H	BB	SO	HR	GB%	BABIP	STUFF	WHIP	ERA	PERA	EQERA	EQH9	EQBB9	EQSO9	EQHR9	VORP	WXRL
2004	MEM	AAA	22	4	4	0	12	12	63²	68	28	64	12	—	.306	-3	1.51	5.37	5.89	6.72	9.4	4.1	7.0	1.8	-8.0	—
2005	MEM	AAA	23	10	10	0	29	29	182	204	51	147	18	46.8%	.333	11	1.40	4.40	4.26	4.54	9.5	2.4	5.4	1.0	21.9	—
2006	SLN	MLB	24	2	1	3	61	0	75	64	22	72	6	49.0%	.290	22	1.15	3.12	3.31	2.96	7.7	2.2	7.8	0.6	24.3	2.84
2007	SLN	MLB	25	9	9	0	29	24	148²	151	50	119	19	44.0%	.297	13	1.35	4.44	4.70	4.81	9.5	2.7	6.4	1.1	15.3	2.70

Breakout: 5%   Improve: 23%   Collapse: 45%   Attrition: 18%   Comparables: Randy Moffitt, Adrian Devine, Turk Farrell, Ron Davis

Without qualification, 2006 was a very successful year for rookie Adam Wainwright. Wainwright allowed multiple runs in just three of his 61 appearances, and followed that with an exemplary postseason performance. Over the course of 16 October appearances, he pitched the equivalent of a complete game shutout, striking out 15 batters while walking just two and allowing seven hits (although he did blow a save in Game Four of the World Series by allowing an inherited runner to score). Wainwright started 135 of his 137 minor league games, so the Cardinals have the option of using him where most needed this year, be it in the still-understaffed rotation, or as the closer should Isringhausen not make a complete recovery.

Jeff Weaver
Bats: R Throws: R Height: 6' 5" Weight: 200 Born: August 22, 1976 Age: 30

YEAR	TEAM	LVL	AGE	W	L	SV	G	GS	IP	H	BB	SO	HR	GB%	BABIP	STUFF	WHIP	ERA	PERA	EQERA	EQH9	EQBB9	EQSO9	EQHR9	VORP	WXRL
2004	LAN	MLB	27	13	13	0	34	34	220	219	67	153	19	—	.299	17	1.30	4.01	4.03	4.49	9.4	2.4	5.6	0.7	35.2	5.11
2005	LAN	MLB	28	14	11	0	34	34	224	220	43	157	35	41.9%	.278	6	1.17	4.22	4.74	4.49	9.0	1.6	5.8	1.4	27.0	4.20
2006	ANA	MLB	29	3	10	0	16	16	88²	114	21	62	18	40.1%	.332	-7	1.52	6.29	5.02	6.63	11.2	2.0	5.8	1.7	-9.2	-0.22
2006	SLN	MLB	29	5	4	0	15	15	83¹	99	26	45	16	43.1%	.305	-11	1.50	5.19	5.47	4.98	10.5	2.4	4.4	1.5	7.0	1.51
2007	SLN	MLB	30	10	10	0	29	28	177	184	50	117	24	42.0%	.287	8	1.32	4.36	4.75	4.69	9.7	2.3	5.3	1.2	21.3	3.50

Breakout: 23%   Improve: 60%   Collapse: 9%   Attrition: 3%   Comparables: Steve Trachsel, Jim Clancy, Ray Burris, Ismael Valdez

Not only was F. Scott Fitzgerald wrong about there not being second acts in life in American lives, there are often more than the Shakespearean standard of five. Weaver is living proof of that, having journeyed through a season that moved him from the rocky shores of humiliation to the beaches of redemption. The displacement-by-sibling in Anaheim and October heroics in St. Louis aside, there is still the matter of his pitching. Prior to 2006, Weaver had only allowed more than a hit per inning once, but safeties were falling much more frequently in both stops last year. He's become a lot more susceptible to the long ball over the past two seasons as well. Still, something seemed to click once Dave Duncan got a hold of him—Weaver sported a 6.71 ERA on the season after his fourth Cardinal start, then dropped it a run by posting a 4.18 mark over his final eleven. That was followed by his 2.43 ERA in five postseason starts, capped by his gem in the World Series clincher. Weaver was 29 last year, the same age as Dave Stewart and Chris Carpenter when they first came under Duncan's tutelage. We're not saying that Weaver will win 20 games if he comes back to St. Louis, but he might want to give it some serious thought. Otherwise, he's at least guaranteed to eat innings, and when teams are casting about for back-of-the-rotation guys, that sometimes counts as much as results.

Lineouts

PLAYER	TEAM	LVL	AGE	PA	R	2B	3B	HR	RBI	BB	SO	SB-CS	SPEED	AVG/OBP/SLG	MLVr	EqAVG/EqOBP/EqSLG	EqA	VORP
LF L. Bigbie*	SLN	MLB	28	28	2	1	0	0	1	3	9		2.6	.240/.321/.280	-.235	.240/.321/.280	.221	-1.0
OF J. Gall	MEM	AAA	28	324	31	13	2	6	34	28	36	3-4	4.1	.287/.361/.408	.096	.280/.342/.399	.257	0.8
OF R. Gorecki	SFD	AA	25	381	56	21	2	16	51	42	80	17-9	6.2	.251/.340/.474	.092	.226/.297/.406	.244	-1.4
	MEM	AAA	25	87	7	4	0	1	9	9	21	3-3	5.4	.162/.256/.257	-.393	.158/.241/.237	.182	-8.9
C M. Hernandez	MEM	AAA	27	321	24	10	1	2	28	27	29	3-1	4.0	.274/.336/.337	-.062	.268/.320/.330	.234	-1.8
SS J. Nelson	MEM	AAA	27	475	55	16	2	21	48	42	153	12-2	5.7	.215/.291/.411	-.082	.208/.272/.377	.228	-7.4
OF T. Perez*	MEM	AAA	31	296	42	16	2	13	41	21	27	4-2	5.4	.295/.349/.515	.239	.276/.317/.465	.264	4.3
	SLN	MLB	31	35	3	1	0	1	3	3	4	0-0	4.5	.194/.286/.323	-.275	.194/.286/.323	.217	-1.4
LF S. Schumaker*	MEM	AAA	26	403	47	13	3	3	27	23	48	11-4	5.4	.306/.348/.382	.052	.301/.337/.371	.252	7.4
	SLN	MLB	26	60	3	1	0	1	2	5	6	2-1	4.7	.185/.254/.259	-.428	.167/.237/.241	.182	-5.0

PLAYER	TEAM	LVL	AGE	W	L	SV	IP	H	BB	SO	HR	GB%	BABIP	STUFF	WHIP	ERA	PERA	EqERA	EqH9	EqBB9	EqSO9	EqHR9	VORP
T. Cate*	PMB	A+	25	2	2	1	41¹	19	13	58	3	—	.211	6	0.78	1.53	5.14	2.82	6.1	3.8	7.7	1.4	11.8
	SFD	AA	25	1	1	1	15²	5	6	20	1	—	.129	15	0.72	0.59	4.53	1.84	4.3	4.3	8.0	0.6	6.1
A. Cavazos	SFD	AA	25	2	2	0	20²	6	12	19	0	—	.133	12	0.89	0.45	4.54	1.37	3.2	5.9	5.5	0.5	9.3
	MEM	AAA	25	1	5	4	56	47	16	55	2	—	.302	13	1.13	3.54	3.20	3.97	7.6	2.5	6.7	0.5	10.3
D. Dove	PMB	A+	24	3	3	4	51²	38	13	56	3	—	.292	-9	1.00	2.81	4.89	5.14	8.1	2.9	5.9	1.1	2.5
	SFD	AA	24	0	3	0	14	18	8	15	6	—	.300	-46	1.86	9.00	12.97	11.48	14.2	6.1	6.8	6.1	-8.7
B. Falkenborg	MEM	AAA	28	4	5	16	51	51	15	53	6	—	.326	-5	1.29	4.24	4.51	5.47	9.4	2.6	7.1	1.4	0.7
B. Hawksworth	PMB	A+	23	7	2	0	83	75	19	55	0	—	.301	14	1.13	2.49	3.96	3.70	8.5	2.5	3.6	0.3	17.5
	SFD	AA	23	4	2	0	79²	72	31	66	8	—	.296	1	1.30	3.41	5.22	4.35	8.6	3.7	5.4	1.3	10.9
C. Narveson*	PMB	A+	24	0	0	0	17²	9	1	13	2	—	.156	3	0.58	2.09	6.19	3.24	5.9	0.5	4.3	2.2	4.4
	MEM	AAA	24	8	5	0	80²	70	33	58	9	—	.269	-3	1.28	2.81	5.36	3.22	7.9	3.6	5.0	1.3	21.4
	SLN	MLB	24	0	0	0	9¹	6	5	12	1	—	.238	10	1.18	4.84	3.82	4.66	6.5	3.7	10.2	0.9	1.3
A. Ottavino	SCO	A-	20	2	2	0	28²	23	13	26	1	—	.262	1	1.28	3.19	6.59	5.81	8.9	6.2	4.8	1.4	-0.6
	QUD	A	20	2	3	0	36¹	28	19	38	3	—	.295	-1	1.30	3.49	7.67	7.09	9.3	6.5	6.0	1.9	-5.5
C. Perez	QUD	A	21	2	0	12	29	20	19	32	0	—	.296	11	1.34	1.86	5.62	3.95	7.6	7.9	6.3	0.3	5.0

The last thing a player in **Larry Bigbie**'s situation needed was a hernia, but that's what he got, and it severely limited his playing time in a season in which a corner outfielder on the make could have gone places with the Cardinals. **John Gall**'s top four PECOTA comparisons have combined for 570 major league plate appearances and a WARP of 1.9. For a 29-year-old corner man with lead-glove fielding skills, that's not good news. Outfielder **Reid Gorecki** created some early-season buzz with 9 home runs and a .306 batting average in April, but he hit just .211 with 8 jacks for the remainder of the season; talk about buzz-kill. **Michel Hernandez** is definitely in the right organization; in St. Louis, catch-and-throw guys are the rule, not the avoidable exception. He's in line for third catcher duties and the emergency call-ups that involves. A shortstop who pops 21 homers at Triple-A should be exciting, but there isn't a whole lot else going on with **John Nelson**. Serious contact problems, advancing age, and poor defense are his various Waterloos. **Timo Perez** was easily one of the worst players in the bigs in 2004 and 2005, but avoided that tag in 2006 by spending the year in Triple-A and playing pretty well. Having found his proper level, he should finish his career there, but some general manager is bound to tab him as a fill-in at some point just because he's been there before. He's in camp with the Tigers. **Skip Schumaker** didn't show much at Memphis last year—certainly not enough to be forcing himself onto a big league roster, even as a fifth outfielder.

In an organization in which the manager at the top of the pyramid loves his situational lefties, it's a good thing to be a situational lefty. Enter Mariner discard **Troy Cate**, who might have the smoke and mirrors thing down well enough to graduate to the Show someday. **Andy Cavazos** entered the season as an organizational arm, but has an outside shot to pitch out of the Cardinal pen at some point in 2007 thanks to a low-90s fastball and decent slider. **Dennis Dove** is a strong-armed right-hander who looked good in a conversion to the bullpen until he moved up to Double-A, where he learned that he needs a second pitch. **Brian Falkenborg** is another TJ survivor who had his fourth cup of big league joe with his fourth different team last year. He was up and back down by Memorial Day, though, and will have to battle to get another shot. **Blake Hawksworth** has made some nice strides since labrum surgery in 2004, but his strikeout rate hasn't come all the way back just yet. He's got a good curve and change and lots of movement on his fastball. **Chris Narveson** should get a shot at the Cards' half-full rotation, but another year in Triple-A seems more likely as he continues on his seemingly endless hamster-wheel trip back from the Tommy John surgery he had five years ago. The team's first-round pick last June, **Adam Ottavino** is a power righty who was able to succeed in a full-season league during his pro debut. **Chris Perez** was one of the better college relievers in last year's draft. He pitched well in his debut and should move quickly, but his ceiling is probably setup man.

Manager: Tony La Russa

Year	Team	W-L	Pythag +/-	Avg PC	100 +P	120 +P	QS	BQS	REL	REL w Zero R	IBB	SUBS	PH	PH Avg	PH HR	SB2	CS2	SB3	CS3	SAC Att	SAC %	POS SAC	Squeeze	Swing	In Play
2004	SLN	105-57	+3	97.6	82	6	87	9	469	336	24	99	272	.262	6	96	41	15	5	85	85.9%	43	5	178	118
2005	SLN	100-62	0	96.6	62	1	92	6	436	298	27	78	265	.226	6	69	28	13	4	104	74.0%	47	15	173	145
2006	SLN	83-78	+1	92.7	55	2	74	5	468	294	35	69	271	.235	7	53	26	6	5	93	76.3%	32	4	135	110

Tony La Russa has a shot at finishing his career with more wins than any other non-self-employed manager in history. There even exists a small possibility of besting that pillar of managerial job security himself, Connie Mack, a man who kept his job about twenty years past his expiration date because he also owned the team. Already the manager with the third-highest win total, La Russa needs another 466 wins to pass number two, John J. McGraw. At a rate of 90 wins a season (which means no more 83-win clubs, championship or not), he would need just over five years to surpass the Little Napoleon. That would leave him just 968 wins—a whole career's worth for most managers—away from breaking the record the Tall Tactician built in his senescent golden years. La Russa would have to keep winning into his seventies, something that few managers have been able to do, but given recent skippering stints by septuagenarians such as Jack McKeon and Frank Robinson it's not altogether impossible. Long considered a genius by the mainstream media because he has a law degree and occasionally wears glasses, La Russa has never been held in overly high regard in the stathead community. He still has a maddening tendency to insert himself into every late-inning at-bat via excessive matchup-influenced pitching changes. Yet, he was not especially meddlesome in 2006. In any number of categories that indicate a manager's desire to put his own imprint on the game, La Russa was either in the middle of the pack or close to the bottom, including pitchouts, sacrifice attempts, and stolen base attempts. He and pitching coach Dave Duncan showed restraint with their starters as well; St. Louis ranked 14th in the league in 100-plus pitch counts. That was in part a function of making do with starters such as Sidney Ponson, Jason Marquis, and the injury-afflicted Mark Mulder, all of whose performances demanded quick exits, but also a function of La Russa simply knowing when to make his move. Over the last three seasons, the Cardinals have blown just 20 of 273 possible quality starts, the second-best rate in baseball. They have the eighth-highest pinch-hit average over that span, and the sixth-most pinch-hit home runs. In those three seasons, the Cardinals have also pulled off the most squeeze plays (24) and rank second to Mike Scioscia's Angels in hit-and-run attempts. All of this speaks to LaRussa's actively swimming in a game's ebb and flow, and his justified belief that he is a master of timing.

San Diego Padres

Marx had it all wrong. In San Diego it was farce that preceded tragedy. The team won an excuse-me division title in 2005; they didn't get the memo that the point of the NL West that year was have everyone finish below .500 and make people wonder if the six-division format was such a good idea after all. Although the Pads hummed a few bars, they ultimately tired of playing along and seized the glory of an 82-win division title, then had the good taste to go three and out against the Cardinals in the Divisional Series.

In contrast, the 2006 team was good enough to win—good enough to have beaten anybody else in the injury-wracked National League field, certainly. That's why they play the games, though, and, in an immensely frustrating Division Series rematch with the Cardinals, a talented, balanced Padre ballclub was outplayed and outpitched in three of four games.

While it's important to give Tony LaRussa's charges credit for their execution, the Padres probably lost the series as a result of the schedule, which allowed the Cardinals to start Chris Carpenter on a full four days of rest between Games One and Four. There's nothing especially humiliating about losing to the best starter on any NL playoff team twice, provided it's actually that starter who beats you. When your virtues disappear when you need them most, though, you have to wonder.

The 2006 Padres' best assets were their rotation, bullpen, and defense, three elements generally considered fundamental to postseason success. In Support-Neutral Lineup-adjusted Value above Average (SNLVA), a stat designed to convey starter quality independent of run support, the Padres were the best team in the NL. With Chris Young, Jake Peavy, and Clay Hensley, they had three of the top twenty starting pitchers in baseball, and, in Woody Williams and later David Wells, they had veterans who had enjoyed playoff success in the past. The Padres would finish tied for second in the NL in quality starts (behind the Marlins), a measure of how reliably their starters could deliver a game that, with an average amount of offense, a team should be able to win.

Unfortunately, they didn't take full advantage of that strength in the postseason. Hensley went to the pen for the playoffs, and Woody Williams, perhaps the weakest of their regular starters, was put on the mound for Game Four with the Padres down 1–2 in the best of five series. At this stage of his career, Williams was very much a pitcher whose shortcomings were being masked by PETCO Park; on the road, he threw only five quality starts in 14, a sub-par performance even for a fifth starter, and a particularly ominous statistic heading into a playoff game in St. Louis. Nevertheless, Williams pitched into the sixth inning of Game Four having allowed only two runs through five. That proved to be his limit. With the game tied 2–2 in the bottom of the sixth, Williams walked Albert Pujols, got Jim Edmonds to fly out, then surrendered the go-ahead run on a triple down the right field line by Juan Encarnacion.

Bruce Bochy turned to his bullpen, a cause for very literal relief throughout the season. Even before Cla Meredith was called up in July, Bochy had the game's late-game tandem *par excellence*, with Scott Linebrink putting up zeroes in the eighth to make sure that Trevor Hoffman got the glory stat in the ninth. Meredith's arrival shortened ballgames against the Padres considerably; three innings against some combination of Meredith, Linebrink, veteran

---

PADRES PROSPECTUS

2006 record: 88–74; First place, NL West; Lost to Cardinals in Division Series

Pythagenport record: 86–76

Runs scored per game: 4.51 (13th in NL)

Runs allowed per game: 4.19 (1st in NL)

Team EqA: .266 (6th in NL)

2006 Batters Age: 31.2 (2nd oldest in NL)

2006 Pitchers Age: 30.5 (3rd oldest in NL)

Ballpark: Petco Park; Severe pitcher's park; Park Factor of .928

2006: A pretty good run behind some very hot bullpen streaks, but the rest of the division's getting serious.

2007: A deep rotation and shored-up power in the lineup could be enough to blow it wide open. Several projects, but good options if they don't work out.

---

lefty Alan Embree, and Hoffman made it especially difficult for opponents to come from behind. Collectively, Padres relievers were the second-best unit in the league in both WXRL and Fair Run Average (a metric that accounts for how the pen handled inherited runners), trailing the Mets in both categories.

Here, the Padres were already down, but, whereas almost every team has some trouble with the mid-inning transition from a flagging starter to the pen, Bochy had handled his charges particularly skillfully in this particularly delicate phase of the game (see table 1). Nobody outperformed Bochy and his relief crew in shutting the door

Table 1. Transition Innings—Team Runs Allowed in a Starter's Last Inning (Relievers' Runs Allowed Included)

Rnk	Team	R	RA/9	Rnk	Team	R	RA/9
1	Padres	124	6.89	26	Phillies	187	10.45
2	Reds	144	8.00	27	Rangers	192	10.67
3	Yankees	146	8.11	28	Nationals	206	11.44
4	Athletics	148	8.22	29	Royals	213	11.83
5	Braves	149	8.28	30	Orioles	233	13.02
6	White Sox	151	8.39				
7	D'backs	154	8.56				
8	Brewers	155	8.66				
9	Red Sox	156	8.67				
10	Pirates	157	8.72				

and getting his starters out of games with the least amount of damage done. In this case, Meredith came in for Williams down 2-3 with one out and a man on third. Perhaps Meredith was worn out from having to pitch nearly every other day over the preceding three months—there was some disagreement on the subject in-house, but Meredith had a rough couple of days just before the postseason. Nevertheless, this was something the Padres did better than anybody—until now. Meredith plunked Ronnie Belliard on a 2-2 pitch to make it first-and-third, then after initially getting ahead 0-2 on Scott Spiezio, lost him on a single to center that put the Padres down by two. Meredith then allowed a single to Yadier Molina to load up the bases and bring the pitcher, Carpenter, to the plate.

The third pillar of Pad power had been their skill afield; they ranked first in Defensive Efficiency, converting 71.8 percent of balls in play into outs. Even allowing for the lower-offense environment of their home park, that's impressive. In Mike Cameron and Dave Roberts, they had two centerfield-quality fielders running down fly balls, and, in Adrian Gonzalez, Josh Barfield, and Khalil Greene, they had a trio of young, light-footed infielders who cov-

ered a good amount of space. But a defense is also more than the sum of its parts, and however strong the Padres were as a unit, they were a club with a few glaring defensive weaknesses, especially going into October.

Losing Greene, their slick-fielding shortstop, to a finger injury that kept him from being able to swing a bat was the biggest blow. During the frantic stretch run, the Padres couldn't afford to have Greene play through the injury for his glove alone, and he was limited to bench duty in the NLDS, forcing Geoff Blum into action in his stead. The left side of the infield was weaker still because third base was manned by clearly incapable fielders Russell Branyan and Todd Walker doing what they could. Making matters worse, the Padres were the worst team in baseball at stopping the opposing running game, allowing 150 stolen bases at an 85 percent success rate. While these were manageable problems over the long season, in a short series, in which runs are more likely to be scarce, these defects are magnified. In the sixth inning of Game Four, Carpenter hit the ball to the Padres' equivalent of the "don't hit it to me" kid by grounding towards third. Branyan had the time to get Belliard at home, but his rushed, wild throw pulled Josh Bard off the plate. The Cards scored their third run of the inning and led 5–2. David Eckstein's textbook suicide squeeze scored a fourth run, and the season was done.

It had to be a galling way to lose; the team's weaknesses had shown up on schedule and done their worst, but the team's best elements had let down too. Worse, the club's offense had completely disappeared in the short series, scoring only six runs in four games. At first glance this seems unsurprising; they had to face Carpenter twice, and they were only 13th in the league in runs scored. But that total overlooks the way playing in PETCO muted their attack. Stripping away park illusions reveals that the Padres ranked among the National League's better lineups. The Padres were sixth in the NL with a .271 team Equivalent Average, while the league-leading Mets clocked in at .273, just a couple of ticks ahead. They had the second-best running game in the league, behind those same Mets, and they were sixth in the league in unintentional walks drawn. Patience travels with you wherever you go; the Pads drew the exact same number of walks on the road as at home. Scoring runs wasn't that much of a problem during the season.

The one element of their offensive game in which the Padres did indeed come up short was power. Isolated Power (ISO) is a simple enough stat—subtract batting average from slugging, and you've got an easy yardstick of how much power a team has. The Padres ranked 15th in the National League in Isolated Power, ahead of only the Pirates. It's reasonable to suspect that PETCO had something to do with that, but it wasn't the case. The Padres' ISO on the road would have been good for eighth in the league, a big step, but definitely mediocre in a 16-team league. This wasn't something that General Manager Kevin Towers failed to notice—he went out and made late-season deals to bring in players with some pop such as Walker and Branyan, even if it meant enduring their indifferent defense.

Walker and Branyan weren't simply being brought in to replace Vinny Castilla's dead stick, they were brought in to help compensate for a lineup that wasn't getting the power from its corner outfielders you normally associate with right and left fields. Part of that was expected given the presence of Dave Roberts in left. Part of it wasn't. Prior to the season, the Padres bet $30 million that Brian Giles would be a continuing source of power in right field, but over the past three seasons, Giles's power production has slowly deflated. Since 2004, Giles's home runs have dropped from 23 to 15 to 14, while his ISO has declined from .191 to .182 to an unacceptable .134. Giles is also among the team's defensive liabilities, and his contract handicaps Towers's ability to add hitting talent.

Given those financial limitations, Towers has to be creative. This winter he tried to fix two problems at once by acquiring a third baseman who was also a right-handed power source, thereby staffing the position and compensating for Mike Piazza's departure. Dealing Josh Barfield to the Indians to get Kevin Kouzmanoff was expensive in terms of talent, but the Padres had little else they could

afford to deal. The gamble is that Kouzmanoff plus free agent second baseman Marcus Giles will produce as much power or more than the combination of Barfield and Piazza, and that one from a crowd of lefty power bats that includes Jose Cruz Jr., Terrmel Sledge, Jack Cust, and Paul McAnulty can step into left field to provide more power than departed free agent Dave Roberts.

Towers may well have over-corrected—there's no obvious candidate to bat leadoff, and the team's speed left town with Roberts and Barfield. How well new manager Bud Black adjusts to this kind of lineup coming from Mike Scioscia's tactically aggressive Angels makes for a particularly interesting leitmotif. In Towers's defense, there's no strong offensive centerpiece upon which he can stake his club's immediate future, and the farm system has no impact player on the way to help retrieve the situation. His other major offseason move, swapping out Woody Williams to bring in Greg Maddux, merely puts an exclamation point on his team's reliance on the quality of its rotation. The result is a team with strong starting pitching, a bullpen anchored on an incomparable trio of relievers, some defensive virtues, and power throughout the lineup. If that sounds familiar, it should—it worked pretty nicely for the White Sox and Tigers the last two years. If Adrian Gonzalez or Kouzmanoff break out, the Padres might even have their offensive centerpieces. As confections go, this might not be a team built to last, but it's a solid adaptation to an improving division.

HITTERS

Josh Bard   **C**   **Bats: S**   Throws: R   Height: 6' 3"   Weight: 210   Born: March 30, 1978   Age: 29

YEAR	TEAM	LVL	AGE	PA	R	2B	3B	HR	RBI	BB	SO	SB	CS	SPEED	AVG	OBP	SLG	MLVR	EQAVG	EQOBP	EQSLG	EQA	VORP	DEFENSE	
2004	BUF	AAA	26	169	25	10	0	4	18	11	23	0	0	4.4	.263	.310	.404	-.077	.229	.278	.344	.220	-4.9	31-C	0
2004	CLE	MLB	26	23	5	2	0	1	4	3	0	0	0	5.6	.421	.478	.684	.958	.421	.478	.684	.381	3.8		
2005	CLE	MLB	27	95	6	4	0	1	9	9	11	0	0	3.6	.193	.266	.277	-.345	.185	.269	.272	.203	-3.9	25-C	1
2006	BOS	MLB	28	21	2	1	0	0	0	3	3	0	0	4.5	.278	.381	.333	-.063	.278	.381	.333	.261	0.4		
2006	SDN	MLB	28	263	28	19	0	9	40	27	39	1	0	3.7	.338	.406	.537	.364	.346	.416	.545	.325	29.7	55-C	3
2007	SDN	MLB	29	362	42	19	1	8	43	37	50	1	1	4.1	.269	.345	.408	-.043	.275	.348	.422	.265	12.8	87-C	0

Breakout: 8%   *Improve: 28%*   *Collapse: 35%*   *Attrition: 28%*   *Comparables: Jason Varitek, Ron Hassey, Dwight Lowry, Mitch Meluskey*

After Bard took to being knuckleballer Tim Wakefield's personal catcher like a duck takes to being repeatedly poked with a fork, the Red Sox panicked and flipped him to San Diego for his predecessor, Doug Mirabelli. They never could have anticipated he'd hit like he did in San Diego, just as there's no reason for the Padres to expect him to do it again. Still, Bard's a true switch-hitter, solid against both righties and lefties, and PECOTA expects him to maintain his newfound plate discipline, so he'll still be one of the better players at his position. Although properly considered the better-throwing alternative to Mike Piazza on last year's Pads, Bard didn't surpass him by much. Throwing out only 18 percent of opposing baserunners isn't very special, but, in Bard's defense, he's done better before; perhaps Pads pitchers need to work on holding runners as much as their catchers need to work on throwing.

Josh Barfield 2B Bats: R Throws: R Height: 6′ 0″ Weight: 190 Born: December 17, 1982 Age: 24

YEAR	TEAM	LVL	AGE	PA	R	2B	3B	HR	RBI	BB	SO	SB	CS	SPEED	AVG	OBP	SLG	MLVR	EQAVG	EQOBP	EQSLG	EQA	VORP	DEFENSE	
2004	MOB	AA	21	581	79	28	3	18	90	48	119	4	2	5.0	.248	.313	.417	-.003	.229	.284	.374	.229	-8.8	136-2B	9
2005	POR	AAA	22	578	74	25	1	15	72	52	108	20	5	5.0	.310	.370	.450	.115	.295	.348	.415	.268	27.3	135-2B	7
2006	SDN	MLB	23	578	72	32	3	13	58	30	81	21	5	6.5	.280	.318	.423	-.002	.290	.329	.442	.267	21.8	139-2B	10
2007	CLE	MLB	24	578	71	31	2	16	66	37	93	12	4	5.6	.267	.316	.422	-.068	.264	.318	.432	.264	15.5	135-2B	5

Breakout: 23% Improve: 53% Collapse: 18% Attrition: 11% Comparables: Bill Mazeroski, Davey Johnson, Ron Gant, Robin Yount

In an otherwise nifty rookie season, Barfield drew walks (the unintentional kind) in fewer than 4 percent of his plate appearances. After it, he was dealt to Cleveland for Kevin Kouzmanoff and Andrew Brown. The Indians hope Barfield's solid but unexceptional glovework will shore up the right side of the infield. At the plate, his splits suggest all sorts of happy or unhappy possibilities: he struggled in PETCO (.241/.279/.361) and against right-handers (.266/.299/.376), but thrived on the road (.319/.355/.484) and against lefties (.331/.378/.587). You can understand why PECOTA posted a modest median projection, but with Barfield freed from PETCO and put into a lineup slot where he won't be forced to hack as much (he was in the eight-hole almost all year), he'll outhit it.

Mark Bellhorn INF Bats: S Throws: R Height: 6′ 1″ Weight: 205 Born: August 23, 1974 Age: 32

YEAR	TEAM	LVL	AGE	PA	R	2B	3B	HR	RBI	BB	SO	SB	CS	SPEED	AVG	OBP	SLG	MLVR	EQAVG	EQOBP	EQSLG	EQA	VORP	DEFENSE			
2004	BOS	MLB	29	620	93	37	3	17	82	88	177	6	1	5.6	.264	.373	.444	.047	.257	.372	.438	.284	30.0	114-2B	9	16-3B	0
2005	BOS	MLB	30	335	41	20	0	7	28	49	109	3	0	5.2	.216	.328	.360	-.126	.212	.337	.360	.253	1.0	81-2B	2		
2005	NYA	MLB	30	20	2	0	0	1	2	3	3	0	0	4.6	.118	.250	.294	-.393	.118	.250	.294	.198	-1.2				
2006	SDN	MLB	31	288	26	11	2	8	27	32	90	0	0	4.4	.190	.285	.344	-.230	.194	.292	.357	.229	-10.3	36-3B	-2	11-1B	0
2007	SDN	MLB	32	294	38	15	1	11	36	40	83	2	1	4.7	.231	.341	.439	-.039	.236	.344	.453	.271	10.5	72-2B	0		

Breakout: 48% Improve: 73% Collapse: 5% Attrition: 67% Comparables: John Vander Wal, Jim Russell, Dan Pasqua, Bob Robertson

Bellhorn has had a nifty little career; he has a ring and had two great years, 2002 as the Cubs' primary third baseman and 2004 as Boston's second sacker. Having survived the worst that Art Howe and Dusty Baker could do, though, Bellhorn appears to be done. His defense was never great, and a utility man who can't get the ball in play off the bench or pinch-run would have to find a manager who's pretty walks-obsessed to get a job. And nobody—not even us—is that obsessed with walks.

Kyle Blanks 1B Bats: R Throws: R Height: 6′ 6″ Weight: 270 Born: September 11, 1986 Age: 20

YEAR	TEAM	LVL	AGE	PA	R	2B	3B	HR	RBI	BB	SO	SB	CS	SPEED	AVG	OBP	SLG	MLVR	EQAVG	EQOBP	EQSLG	EQA	VORP	DEFENSE	
2006	FTW	A	19	359	41	20	0	10	52	36	79	2	0	3.8	.292	.382	.455	.259	.269	.334	.424	.263	4.8	51-1B	-1
2007	SDN	MLB	20	471	47	21	1	13	54	36	106	1	1	4.0	.248	.314	.396	-.131	.254	.317	.409	.247	-3.0	111-1B	1

Breakout: 8% Improve: 39% Collapse: 28% Attrition: 12% Comparables: Aaron McNeal, Leo Daigle, Nate Rolison, Adam Dunn

A huge first baseman with a good approach at the plate, Blanks isn't really 270 pounds—people who see him say he's closer to three bills. He's surprisingly athletic for a big man, enough so that the Pads haven't ruled out trying him in left, and he's nimble with soft hands at first. Men this large typically provide tons of leverage in their swings, so the hope is that his power potential will flower as he gets more experience, but he really should try to get back down to 270, and, as Prince Fielder did, accept the challenge of making himself a major leaguer through conditioning.

Geoff Blum INF Bats: S Throws: R Height: 6′ 3″ Weight: 205 Born: April 26, 1973 Age: 34

YEAR	TEAM	LVL	AGE	PA	R	2B	3B	HR	RBI	BB	SO	SB	CS	SPEED	AVG	OBP	SLG	MLVR	EQAVG	EQOBP	EQSLG	EQA	VORP	DEFENSE			
2004	TBA	MLB	31	369	38	21	0	8	35	24	58	2	3	4.4	.215	.266	.348	-.285	.214	.270	.344	.215	-15.3	44-3B	-3	37-2B	1
2005	SDN	MLB	32	252	26	13	1	5	22	24	28	3	2	4.7	.241	.321	.375	-.057	.251	.331	.399	.253	1.9	26-3B	3	18-2B	0
2005	CHA	MLB	32	99	6	2	1	1	3	4	15	0	1	4.6	.200	.232	.274	-.425	.170	.220	.245	.167	-8.3				
2006	SDN	MLB	33	299	27	17	1	4	34	17	51	0	1	3.8	.254	.293	.366	-.151	.258	.300	.378	.236	-2.7	43-SS	4	22-3B	-2
2007	SDN	MLB	34	288	29	15	1	6	33	22	45	1	1	4.6	.242	.303	.377	-.179	.248	.306	.389	.237	0.8	70-SS	0		

Breakout: 36% Improve: 56% Collapse: 25% Attrition: 41% Comparables: Doug Strange, Paul Popovich, Thomas Howard, Gene Michael

As utility infielders go, Blum's a pretty rare bird. He's a good enough fielder to plug into any of the four infield positions, but he also provides slightly more power than most glovely spare parts. He struggles with lefties, though, so ideally, he'd be paired up with a righty-hitting infield reserve such as Luis Cruz, but Cruz isn't quite ready yet.

Rob Bowen   **C**   **Bats: S**   **Throws: R**   Height: 6' 3"   Weight: 225   Born: February 24, 1981   Age: 26

YEAR	TEAM	LVL	AGE	PA	R	2B	3B	HR	RBI	BB	SO	SB	CS	SPEED	AVG	OBP	SLG	MLVR	EQAVG	EQOBP	EQSLG	EQA	VORP	DEFENSE	
2004	NBR	AA	23	285	28	10	0	9	24	31	76	3	0	4.0	.197	.292	.345	-.185	.180	.263	.302	.206	-18.4	66-C	2
2004	MIN	MLB	23	32	1	0	0	1	2	4	10	0	0	2.1	.111	.226	.222	-.595	.074	.194	.185	.155	-3.2	10-C	-3
2005	ROC	AAA	24	303	38	13	2	6	25	37	68	0	2	3.4	.267	.366	.401	.010	.253	.347	.381	.255	7.6	63-C	4
2006	SDN	MLB	25	110	22	5	0	3	13	13	26	0	1	5.4	.245	.339	.394	-.035	.255	.355	.426	.269	1.8	22-C	0
2007	SDN	MLB	26	326	36	16	1	8	37	35	76	3	2	4.3	.237	.326	.388	-.128	.243	.329	.400	.251	4.7	79-C	1

Breakout: 36%   Improve: 62%   Collapse: 13%   Attrition: 35%   Comparables: Ben Davis, Alan Ashby, Stan Lopata, Jason Varitek

Once seen as a top catching prospect in the Twins' system, Bowen's managed to outlive the disappointment of not panning out. Given a third catcher with ability last year, former backstop Bruce Bochy couldn't resist carving out a role for Bowen, even after the club lifted Bard from Boston. Bowen wound up getting a lot of work caddying for Make Piazza late in games so that Bard didn't have to catch when Piazza came out, but with both Bochy and Piazza gone, he should settle into a more typical backup role this year.

Russ Branyan   **4C**   **Bats: L**   **Throws: R**   Height: 6' 3"   Weight: 195   Born: December 19, 1975   Age: 31

YEAR	TEAM	LVL	AGE	PA	R	2B	3B	HR	RBI	BB	SO	SB	CS	SPEED	AVG	OBP	SLG	MLVR	EQAVG	EQOBP	EQSLG	EQA	VORP	DEFENSE			
2004	BUF	AAA	28	366	58	16	2	25	75	42	102	5	2	5.0	.288	.374	.591	.308	.265	.342	.517	.287	18.0	33-1B	1	28-3B	0
2004	MIL	MLB	28	182	21	11	1	11	27	20	68	1	0	5.0	.234	.324	.525	.127	.228	.319	.513	.278	8.1	43-3B	1		
2005	MIL	MLB	29	242	23	11	0	12	31	39	80	1	0	3.5	.257	.378	.490	.178	.252	.376	.485	.294	14.6	52-3B	0		
2006	TBA	MLB	30	193	23	10	0	12	27	19	62	2	0	4.4	.201	.286	.473	-.101	.198	.292	.479	.260	0.2	41-RF	-2		
2006	SDN	MLB	30	89	14	1	0	6	9	15	27	0	0	4.6	.292	.416	.556	.333	.306	.433	.583	.339	8.1	20-3B	-3		
2007	SDN	MLB	31	322	44	14	1	18	51	42	95	3	1	4.5	.239	.344	.495	.044	.244	.348	.511	.286	14.1	78-3B	-3		

Breakout: 13%   Improve: 35%   Collapse: 25%   Attrition: 35%   Comparables: Roger Repoz, Dan Pasqua, Henry Rodriguez, Darryl Strawberry

Consider calling him a "4C" for the four corner positions where he'll be used: first, third, right and left. Having being fished out of the bargain bin, the left-handed Branyan probably won't be used in a true platoon with Kevin Kouzmanoff at third, but he'll make up for it by getting at-bats at the other three positions. Branyan remains the leader in Three True Outcome percentage since 1969 (min. of 1000 PA) having delivered a homer, walk, or whiff an amazing 52.3 percent of his plate appearances. Rounding out the top ten: Rob Deer 49.1, Adam Dunn 49, Mel Nieves 49, Jim Thome 47.5, Ryan Howard 47.4, Mark Bellhorn 45.7, Mark McGwire 45.6, Bo Jackson 45, and Bobby Estalella 44.3. Ten years ago, the list would have had names like Mickey Tettleton, Sam Horn, and Ken Phelps—you know, DHs. It's an interesting reflection on how much the game has changed, as the benefits of trying to get your cookie and make it into your meal ticket seem pretty well understood among the beefier set.

Mike Cameron   **CF**   **Bats: R**   **Throws: R**   Height: 6' 2"   Weight: 200   Born: January 8, 1973   Age: 34

YEAR	TEAM	LVL	AGE	PA	R	2B	3B	HR	RBI	BB	SO	SB	CS	SPEED	AVG	OBP	SLG	MLVR	EQAVG	EQOBP	EQSLG	EQA	VORP	DEFENSE	
2004	NYN	MLB	31	562	76	30	1	30	76	57	143	22	6	6.4	.231	.319	.479	.039	.233	.320	.482	.272	19.9	134-CF	1
2005	NYN	MLB	32	343	47	23	2	12	39	29	85	13	1	6.5	.273	.342	.477	.127	.276	.347	.497	.289	17.6	67-RF	-6
2006	SDN	MLB	33	634	88	34	9	22	83	71	142	25	9	6.6	.268	.355	.482	.135	.280	.367	.505	.294	39.8	138-CF	3
2007	SDN	MLB	34	545	78	27	6	22	74	60	125	19	7	6.3	.256	.346	.474	.034	.262	.349	.489	.283	25.0	128-CF	-3

Breakout: 9%   Improve: 33%   Collapse: 27%   Attrition: 15%   Comparables: Reggie Sanders, Bobby Bonds, Hank Bauer, Ellis Burks

Despite starting the season on the DL with a strained oblique and then putting up a really ugly first two months (.239/.323/.310), Cameron enjoyed his best season since 2001. In so doing, he dispatched fears of any lingering effects from his frightening outfield collision with Carlos Beltran in 2005; he also proved he's still got it in center field. With only one year left on his contract, he presents an interesting problem for management—he's aging well, but if he loses a step and moves to a corner after 2007, he'll go from offensive asset to offensive problem. On the other hand, the organization has nobody ready to take his place, which means they'll still be in the market if they let him walk.

Luis Cruz   SS   Bats: R   Throws: R   Height: 6' 1"   Weight: 180   Born: February 10, 1984   Age: 23

YEAR	TEAM	LVL	AGE	PA	R	2B	3B	HR	RBI	BB	SO	SB	CS	SPEED	AVG	OBP	SLG	MLVR	EQAVG	EQOBP	EQSLG	EQA	VORP	DEFENSE			
2004	LEL	A+	20	551	75	35	3	8	72	24	56	3	7	4.1	.277	.310	.404	-.052	.238	.266	.330	.208	-17.1	112-SS	4		
2005	MOB	AA	21	164	14	2	1	3	6	9	31	0	1	3.6	.159	.215	.245	-.468	.123	.166	.149	.127	-28.4	37-SS	0		
2005	MCD	MX	21	239	29	15	3	4	23	10	26	4	1	6.0	.283	.315	.429	-.232	.222	.247	.335	.204	-14.9	35-2B	2	16-3B	-1
2006	MOB	AA	22	539	65	35	3	12	65	29	62	8	4	5.5	.261	.302	.415	.039	.257	.293	.434	.247	10.7	81-2B	12	36-SS	-4
2007	SDN	MLB	23	484	45	25	3	9	50	24	61	4	2	5.0	.246	.287	.372	-.213	.251	.290	.384	.228	0.7	114-2B	4		

Breakout: 48% Improve: 68% Collapse: 17% Attrition: 5%   Comparables: Josh Wilson, Javier Colina, Keith Luuloa, Jayson Nix

Like Blum, Cruz is a good defender at either short or second, and he has a little pop in his bat. After he struggled at Mobile at the start of 2005, the Padres loaned him to the Mexico City Red Devils in May rather than ride it out and see if he'd adjust to Double-A pitching. Maybe it was the home cooking (Cruz was born in Navojoa, Mexico), but the move seemed to give him the confidence to make the jump in his second try at BayBears baseball. Despite taking the long way around, he's still quite young, and should be in the picture as an alternative to Blum whenever Khalil Greene's latest injury forces him out of the lineup.

Jack Cust   LF   Bats: L   Throws: R   Height: 6' 1"   Weight: 230   Born: January 16, 1979   Age: 28

YEAR	TEAM	LVL	AGE	PA	R	2B	3B	HR	RBI	BB	SO	SB	CS	SPEED	AVG	OBP	SLG	MLVR	EQAVG	EQOBP	EQSLG	EQA	VORP	DEFENSE
2004	OTT	AAA	25	413	55	15	1	17	55	65	127	4	0	4.8	.235	.358	.433	.015	.217	.332	.386	.255	-8.2	31-LF -3
2005	SAC	AAA	26	600	95	28	1	19	75	115	153	2	4	3.1	.257	.402	.438	.080	.240	.367	.389	.268	2.1	75-LF -7
2006	POR	AAA	27	591	97	23	0	30	77	143	124	0	3	3.1	.293	.467	.549	.421	.276	.432	.509	.322	48.2	117-LF -10
2007	SDN	MLB	28	506	69	21	1	20	65	88	127	1	0	3.8	.250	.385	.454	.072	.256	.389	.469	.295	22.1	119-LF -7

Breakout: 16% Improve: 45% Collapse: 26% Attrition: 13%   Comparables: Graham Koonce, Randy Milligan, Jeremy Giambi, Otto Velez

Not to go on about the Three True Outcomes as much as we do about, say, batting average on balls in play, but it's something you have to bring up when discussing Cust given his career TTO percentage of 47.8 percent (major and minor leagues combined). He's probably the hitter most likely to let you pitch around him as all 143 of his walks have been unintentional. He probably doesn't help himself with his indifferent fielding—it isn't that he's simply bad; it's that he doesn't seem to care. Nevertheless, he has an actual shot at a big league job; if he manages to outshine Terrmel Sledge and Jose Cruz Jr. in camp, he might earn a share of the playing time in left.

Brian Giles   RF   Bats: L   Throws: L   Height: 5' 10"   Weight: 205   Born: January 20, 1971   Age: 36

YEAR	TEAM	LVL	AGE	PA	R	2B	3B	HR	RBI	BB	SO	SB	CS	SPEED	AVG	OBP	SLG	MLVR	EQAVG	EQOBP	EQSLG	EQA	VORP	DEFENSE		
2004	SDN	MLB	33	711	97	33	7	23	94	89	80	10	3	5.9	.284	.374	.475	.186	.294	.383	.495	.300	40.2	157-RF -12		
2005	SDN	MLB	34	674	92	38	8	15	83	119	64	13	5	5.9	.301	.423	.483	.302	.317	.437	.517	.328	55.8	136-RF -3	15-CF	-2
2006	SDN	MLB	35	717	87	37	1	14	83	104	60	9	4	4.5	.263	.374	.397	.050	.273	.385	.413	.282	17.7	155-RF -10		
2007	SDN	MLB	36	654	104	35	4	18	78	98	62	10	4	5.3	.280	.392	.459	.112	.287	.395	.474	.299	32.1	152-RF -6		

Breakout: 12% Improve: 43% Collapse: 17% Attrition: 3%   Comparables: Enos Slaughter, Carl Yastrzemski, Gene Woodling, Brady Anderson

While so many other things took a turn for the better as the Padres' season unfolded, one thing lost in the shuffle was Giles's disappearing power. It wasn't all PETCO; he slugged a still-weak .410 on the road. Making matters worse, he noticed the problem, started overswinging, and hurt his OBP in the process. Compounding those offensive issues, he's gotten crab-like on the bases and in the outfield, and his arm is well short of the standard in right. That he hit into 21 doubleplays last year suggests he's no longer viable in the middle of the order, and with Dave Roberts's departure, the Padres might want to bat him leadoff where he can focus on getting on base rather than trying to drive the ball. It's probably the only way the Padres are going to be able to get anything close to value for the $9 million they have to pay him in each of the next two seasons.

Adrian Gonzalez   1B   Bats: L   Throws: L   Height: 6' 2"   Weight: 220   Born: May 8, 1982   Age: 25

YEAR	TEAM	LVL	AGE	PA	R	2B	3B	HR	RBI	BB	SO	SB	CS	SPEED	AVG	OBP	SLG	MLVR	EQAVG	EQOBP	EQSLG	EQA	VORP	DEFENSE	
2004	OKL	AAA	22	508	61	28	3	12	88	39	73	1	1	3.9	.304	.364	.457	.107	.287	.341	.415	.263	8.3	122-1B	8
2004	TEX	MLB	22	44	7	3	0	1	7	2	6	0	0	5.8	.238	.273	.381	-.111	.214	.250	.333	.203	-0.2		
2005	OKL	AAA	23	368	61	17	1	18	65	32	44	0	0	3.0	.338	.399	.561	.328	.323	.377	.524	.304	29.9	82-1B	4
2005	TEX	MLB	23	162	17	7	1	6	17	10	37	0	0	3.7	.227	.272	.407	-.164	.224	.280	.422	.239	-2.7		
2006	SDN	MLB	24	631	83	38	1	24	82	52	113	0	1	3.2	.304	.362	.500	.204	.313	.372	.518	.300	32.8	148-1B	13
2007	SDN	MLB	25	606	76	33	2	22	89	52	93	1	1	4.1	.287	.353	.477	.077	.294	.356	.492	.285	25.0	142-1B	9

Breakout: 21% Improve: 55% Collapse: 18% Attrition: 5%   Comparables: Chris Chambliss, Bob Chance, Wally Joyner, Kent Hrbek

We've been hearing about Gonzalez for so long that it's important to remember he's really only just getting started. He won't turn 25 until five weeks into the season, and he's still a couple of years removed from arbitration eligibility, let alone free agency. In a lineup with so many other patient hitters, he makes for a necessary contact-with-power supplement. He's also particularly gambit-proof, in that he can hit lefties, and he can go with a pitch and drive it. Add in that he's a mobile, slick-fielding first baseman, and you've got an almost-complete ballplayer. The lone negatives are the things that don't show up readily in box scores—he hits into a lot of double-plays, and he's particularly prone to baserunning errors, getting caught leaning or thrown out trying to force plays he shouldn't. Note that he hit .311/.378/.527 away from PETCO.

Khalil Greene   SS   Bats: R   Throws: R   Height: 5' 11"   Weight: 195   Born: October 21, 1979   Age: 27

YEAR	TEAM	LVL	AGE	PA	R	2B	3B	HR	RBI	BB	SO	SB	CS	SPEED	AVG	OBP	SLG	MLVR	EQAVG	EQOBP	EQSLG	EQA	VORP	DEFENSE	
2004	SDN	MLB	24	554	67	31	4	15	65	53	94	4	2	5.2	.273	.349	.446	.095	.283	.357	.463	.282	31.5	129-SS	-1
2005	SDN	MLB	25	476	51	30	2	15	70	25	93	5	0	5.4	.250	.296	.431	-.019	.260	.306	.460	.262	15.5	115-SS	-12
2006	SDN	MLB	26	460	56	26	2	15	55	39	87	5	1	4.4	.245	.320	.427	-.020	.255	.329	.450	.267	14.2	111-SS	6
2007	SDN	MLB	27	516	65	27	3	18	66	44	92	6	2	5.0	.260	.331	.452	-.016	.266	.334	.467	.271	25.0	122-SS	1

Breakout: 21% Improve: 51% Collapse: 23% Attrition: 13%   Comparables: Dale Berra, Ty Wigginton, Gary Gaetti, Kevin Elster

The disconnect between a more tools-oriented appreciation of Greene's glovework and statistical analysis seems to have finally resolved itself, with the systems belatedly agreeing with the scouts that he's a plus defender. This merely highlights the need to use as many metrics as possible—whether you like Dave Pinto's Probabilistic Model of Range, John Dewan's plus/minus system, or our own Clay Davenport's Fielding Translations, the best way to use these different metrics are in concert and in addition to scouting reports and other analytical tools. All three systems concur that Greene's 2006 was his best year afield yet, and while there's an ingrained tendency to think of fielding as more of a fixed quality that changes gradually over time, Greene's numbers have shifted radically while the scouting reports remain essentially the same. On a more pragmatic level, the Padres are focused on seeing if he can avoid a fourth consecutive season with an exasperating injury of some sort, because Greene's value as a shortstop with some sock isn't easily replaced.

Chase Headley   3B   Bats: S   Throws: R   Height: 6' 2"   Weight: 195   Born: May 9, 1984   Age: 23

YEAR	TEAM	LVL	AGE	PA	R	2B	3B	HR	RBI	BB	SO	SB	CS	SPEED	AVG	OBP	SLG	MLVR	EQAVG	EQOBP	EQSLG	EQA	VORP	DEFENSE	
2005	EUG	A-	21	259	29	14	3	6	33	34	48	1	1	3.5	.268	.375	.441	.158	.223	.297	.343	.226	-9.0	57-3B	-12
2006	LEL	A+	22	571	79	33	0	12	73	74	96	4	5	3.9	.291	.389	.434	.135	.256	.336	.384	.252	12.8	124-3B	-17
2007	SDN	MLB	23	491	52	25	2	11	53	48	90	2	2	4.4	.248	.326	.389	-.119	.254	.329	.401	.250	5.7	116-3B	-9

Breakout: 42% Improve: 59% Collapse: 13% Attrition: 8%   Comparables: Drew Sutton, Adam Leggett, Corey Smith, Jack Hannahan

The Padres' second-round pick in 2005 out of the University of Tennessee, Headley's seen by his boosters as a Bill Mueller type. He's not a toolsy player at third, but he's considered competent, and the organization loves his intelligent yet instinctual approach to the game. He'll have to show considerably more power to pan out. Like the next guy, he's a top prospect in an organization without top prospects.

Nick Hundley   C   Bats: R   Throws: R   Height: 6' 1"   Weight: 210   Born: September 8, 1983   Age: 23

YEAR	TEAM	LVL	AGE	PA	R	2B	3B	HR	RBI	BB	SO	SB	CS	SPEED	AVG	OBP	SLG	MLVR	EQAVG	EQOBP	EQSLG	EQA	VORP	DEFENSE	
2005	EUG	A-	21	184	30	7	1	7	22	33	35	1	0	4.0	.250	.391	.453	.183	.208	.310	.352	.237	-4.4	40-C	-5
2006	FTW	A	22	248	29	19	0	8	44	25	45	1	1	3.6	.274	.355	.474	.234	.240	.301	.418	.247	3.2	57-C	6
2006	LEL	A+	22	200	18	13	0	3	23	20	44	1	1	3.4	.278	.357	.403	.027	.242	.305	.352	.233	-1.9	41-C	-3
2007	SDN	MLB	23	446	43	21	1	12	49	39	97	2	2	4.1	.232	.304	.376	-.186	.237	.307	.388	.238	2.0	106-C	1

Breakout: 32% Improve: 56% Collapse: 16% Attrition: 11%   Comparables: Justin Knoedler, Corky Miller, Javi Herrera, David Ross

(continued next page)

Nick Hundley (*continued*)

The organization's Catcher of the Future, because dealing George Kottaras erased the only other aspirant. Hundley is a big, strapping guy with power, a long swing, and a good arm. He's not perfect—his throws need to be sped up, and, as a former college player at the University of Arizona, hitting in the Cal League in his full-season debut should be a matter of course, not an achievement. If he makes the jump to Double-A in 2007, the Padres have got something.

Ben Johnson   **LF**   **Bats: R**   **Throws: R**   Height: 6' 1"   Weight: 220   Born: June 18, 1981   Age: 26

YEAR	TEAM	LVL	AGE	PA	R	2B	3B	HR	RBI	BB	SO	SB	CS	SPEED	AVG	OBP	SLG	MLVR	EQAVG	EQOBP	EQSLG	EQA	VORP	DEFENSE			
2004	MOB	AA	23	545	80	28	6	23	85	55	136	5	6	5.3	.251	.335	.480	.115	.233	.303	.431	.251	-6.9	89-RF	-6	33-LF	-3
2005	POR	AAA	24	472	79	27	0	25	83	51	88	6	1	4.1	.312	.394	.558	.318	.291	.364	.504	.293	27.6	64-RF	-4	42-CF	-8
2005	SDN	MLB	24	88	10	8	1	3	13	11	23	0	2	4.3	.213	.310	.467	.019	.227	.322	.507	.268	0.5				
2006	POR	AAA	25	227	35	11	1	7	22	23	55	7	1	5.9	.263	.344	.434	.048	.252	.325	.416	.262	4.2	42-CF	0		
2006	SDN	MLB	25	135	19	5	2	4	12	14	36	3	0	6.2	.250	.333	.425	.008	.258	.346	.458	.278	3.5	19-LF	4	12-CF	2
2007	NYN	MLB	26	387	50	19	2	14	49	36	88	5	3	5.2	.254	.329	.446	-.033	.258	.332	.460	.268	11.9	93-CF	0		

Breakout: 17%   Improve: 43%   Collapse: 25%   Attrition: 17%   Comparables: Dave Henderson, Marcus Thames, Andy Thompson, Ryan Ludwick

Johnson bounced between the majors and minors all season, which didn't help him get into a groove, but he still showed the various talents that make him interesting. He's athletic, has more pop than most of your low-end center field types, and he's worked hard to improve his command of the strike zone. Traded to the Mets, Johnson will have to battle Endy Chavez and Shawn Green for playing time, but, even if he doesn't win a job outright, he'll be able to snag a goodly amount of playing time as a right-handed-hitting alternative.

Ryan Klesko   **1B**   **Bats: L**   **Throws: L**   Height: 6' 3"   Weight: 220   Born: June 12, 1971   Age: 36

YEAR	TEAM	LVL	AGE	PA	R	2B	3B	HR	RBI	BB	SO	SB	CS	SPEED	AVG	OBP	SLG	MLVR	EQAVG	EQOBP	EQSLG	EQA	VORP	DEFENSE			
2004	SDN	MLB	33	480	58	32	2	9	66	73	67	3	2	4.7	.291	.399	.448	.197	.301	.407	.465	.302	23.3	77-LF	-6	17-1B	1
2005	SDN	MLB	34	520	61	19	1	18	58	75	80	3	4	4.1	.248	.358	.418	.068	.261	.371	.447	.281	12.6	103-LF	-1		
2007	SFN	MLB	36	289	37	15	1	7	33	42	47	2	1	4.1	.264	.372	.415	.010	.262	.370	.419	.275	6.7	71-LF	-3		

Breakout: 14%   Improve: 34%   Collapse: 36%   Attrition: 40%   Comparables: J. T. Snow, Chris Chambliss, Johnny Grubb, Dave Bergman

Klesko spent almost the entire season on the DL recovering from shoulder surgery, but even though he could only pinch-hit, the Padres included him on their postseason roster. He had given the club six full seasons beforehand, and he was the only player who provided either the Padres or the Braves with much value from deal that sent the Klesko and Bret Boone to San Diego for Wally Joyner, Reggie Sanders, and Quilvio Veras before the 2000 season. Signed to a one-year deal with the Giants, Klesko is expected to be the left side of a platoon at first base. Don't expect his power to return—in 2005, he slugged .438 in PETCO, and only .400 on the road.

Jon Knott   **1B/OF**   **Bats: R**   **Throws: R**   Height: 6' 3"   Weight: 220   Born: August 4, 1978   Age: 28

YEAR	TEAM	LVL	AGE	PA	R	2B	3B	HR	RBI	BB	SO	SB	CS	SPEED	AVG	OBP	SLG	MLVR	EQAVG	EQOBP	EQSLG	EQA	VORP	DEFENSE			
2004	POR	AAA	25	508	79	22	3	26	85	58	110	5	3	4.8	.290	.376	.533	.218	.270	.348	.465	.278	13.9	99-LF	-2		
2005	POR	AAA	26	577	81	34	4	25	78	55	112	1	0	3.8	.251	.333	.483	.039	.230	.298	.422	.247	-12.2	66-LF	-1	38-1B	-2
2006	POR	AAA	27	544	80	32	6	32	113	52	103	3	3	4.2	.280	.353	.572	.270	.262	.325	.524	.281	23.4	69-1B	-1	31-RF	-4
2007	SDN	MLB	28	453	52	22	2	18	64	41	99	1	1	4.0	.248	.323	.446	-.048	.254	.326	.461	.265	6.4	107-1B	-2		

Breakout: 19%   Improve: 39%   Collapse: 28%   Attrition: 17%   Comparables: Adam Hyzdu, Marcus Thames, Andy Phillips, Nick Esasky

Knott came into the game as an undrafted free agent out of Mississippi State, and his four straight seasons with 25 or more homers certainly suggest that teams can benefit from finding the guys that those who grab only the low-hanging fruit miss out on. Still, Knott's prospectdom is summed up by his name; signed to a minor-league deal by Baltimore, Orioles fans might be forgiven if they see Marcus Thames's amongst Knott's comparables and let their hearts go pitter-pat. With Jay Payton and Aubrey Huff already joining Kevin Millar, the odds of Knott being anything more than Norfolk's cleanup hitter seem pretty remote.

San Diego Padres

Justin Leone **3B** **Bats: R** **Throws: R** Height: 6' 1" Weight: 210 Born: March 9, 1977 Age: 30

YEAR	TEAM	LVL	AGE	PA	R	2B	3B	HR	RBI	BB	SO	SB	CS	SPEED	AVG	OBP	SLG	MLVR	EQAVG	EQOBP	EQSLG	EQA	VORP	DEFENSE			
2004	TAC	AAA	27	286	56	10	5	21	51	26	82	5	6	6.9	.269	.344	.597	.261	.247	.311	.510	.269	16.1	44-3B	-7	11-SS	1
2004	SEA	MLB	27	115	15	5	0	6	13	9	32	1	0	5.2	.216	.298	.441	-.084	.225	.307	.471	.263	0.5	28-3B	1		
2005	TAC	AAA	28	370	51	19	2	7	38	51	93	5	2	4.7	.243	.351	.383	-.038	.228	.317	.330	.233	-4.3	64-3B	-9	10-SS	1
2006	POR	AAA	29	524	66	20	0	20	73	61	106	4	4	3.4	.260	.353	.437	.066	.236	.313	.385	.244	3.8	85-3B	-3	16-2B	-3
2007	SDN	MLB	30	413	44	17	2	13	50	39	108	4	2	4.4	.234	.313	.396	-.143	.240	.315	.409	.248	3.1	99-3B	-2		

Breakout: 31% Improve: 56% Collapse: 16% Attrition: 16% Comparables: *Mike Coolbaugh, Scott Sheldon, Dave Silvestri, Joe Dillon*

We probably didn't need to give you a full-length comment on Leone. He's not about to become somebody's regular third baseman, he's not a prospect, and, unless you're playing in a PCL fantasy league, you probably aren't overly invested in his fate. He's here to show off his PECOTA and his comparables, because, like everyone in that crew, he can play, just not quite well enough to be more than a big league spare part.

Paul McAnulty **1B/LF** **Bats: L** **Throws: R** Height: 5' 10" Weight: 220 Born: February 24, 1981 Age: 26

YEAR	TEAM	LVL	AGE	PA	R	2B	3B	HR	RBI	BB	SO	SB	CS	SPEED	AVG	OBP	SLG	MLVR	EQAVG	EQOBP	EQSLG	EQA	VORP	DEFENSE			
2004	LEL	A+	23	591	98	36	3	23	87	88	106	3	1	4.3	.297	.404	.521	.291	.252	.338	.417	.263	0.8	57-LF	0	26-1B	-2
2005	MOB	AA	24	341	39	17	2	10	42	34	66	5	2	4.0	.282	.364	.453	.135	.257	.323	.414	.256	-2.2	66-LF	4		
2005	POR	AAA	24	168	27	15	0	6	27	16	29	0	0	2.8	.344	.405	.563	.384	.314	.369	.497	.294	11.7	21-1B	0		
2005	SDN	MLB	24	29	4	0	0	0	0	3	7	1	0	6.2	.208	.321	.208	-.301	.200	.310	.200	.207	-1.1				
2006	POR	AAA	25	552	76	34	5	19	79	62	79	1	2	4.1	.310	.388	.521	.284	.298	.370	.506	.296	36.2	68-1B	-5	47-3B	-6
2006	SDN	MLB	25	15	3	1	0	1	3	2	4	0	0	5.5	.231	.333	.538	.127	.231	.333	.538	.287	1.1				
2007	SDN	MLB	26	501	62	28	2	18	69	52	89	2	1	4.3	.267	.348	.459	.027	.273	.351	.474	.279	18.5	118-1B	-4		

Breakout: 18% Improve: 48% Collapse: 23% Attrition: 10% Comparables: *Dan Johnson, Robin Jennings, Brian Daubach, Ryan Church*

A squat gamer, McAnulty's another polished hitter off of Long Beach State's factory line. After last year's failed experiment with making him a third baseman, the Padres plan to make him the notional youngster in the fight for the club's open outfield job in left, but he's not really that young, and his ceiling as a prospect isn't especially high. His power is all against right-handers (he hit 18 of his 19 Portland taters against them), so he might make a better fit in a platoon with Jose Cruz Jr. than either Sledge or Cust.

Colt Morton **C** **Bats: R** **Throws: R** Height: 6' 5" Weight: 230 Born: April 10, 1982 Age: 25

YEAR	TEAM	LVL	AGE	PA	R	2B	3B	HR	RBI	BB	SO	SB	CS	SPEED	AVG	OBP	SLG	MLVR	EQAVG	EQOBP	EQSLG	EQA	VORP	DEFENSE	
2004	FTW	A	22	146	10	5	1	4	11	16	45	0	0	2.9	.150	.260	.299	-.234	.105	.185	.165	.138	-23.9	36-C	0
2004	EUG	A-	22	285	43	13	0	17	45	33	75	2	0	4.2	.239	.340	.502	.143	.172	.234	.305	.193	-39.9	46-C	-4
2005	FTW	A	23	265	27	15	0	10	46	35	57	0	0	1.2	.261	.362	.464	.177	.226	.299	.383	.238	-1.1	59-C	-4
2005	LEL	A+	23	113	19	4	0	9	19	14	30	0	1	1.9	.323	.407	.646	.424	.280	.345	.520	.287	8.9	23-C	-4
2006	LEL	A+	24	222	30	15	0	5	22	36	44	0	1	2.4	.227	.374	.398	.011	.180	.293	.291	.213	-10.1	45-C	4
2006	MOB	AA	24	152	15	10	0	6	21	11	44	0	0	3.2	.266	.329	.468	.149	.255	.309	.454	.256	5.4	37-C	3
2007	SDN	MLB	25	399	29	14	0	12	46	35	107	0	0	3.3	.202	.277	.342	-.298	.207	.280	.353	.215	-8.7	95-C	3

Breakout: 34% Improve: 50% Collapse: 30% Attrition: 13% Comparables: *David Ross, Vito Chiaravalloti, Jimmy Gonzalez, Greg Sain*

Morton's a monster-sized backstop who's surprisingly decent behind the plate and can throw. If you remember the debate over whether or not Jayson Werth would stick as a catcher because he was so much larger than most—as it turned out, he didn't—Morton is even larger than Werth. There's something to be said for the theory that a large human being is ill-suited for the squatting that catching requires; it's like asking an especially beefy Scotsman to toss the caber 160 times in three hours—then bat and run the bases. Appropriately for someone so Bunyanesque, what he hits goes *really* far when he connects, but his approach is Kingman-esque; he swings at everything and hopes for the best. He's not a prospect, but if you like your players improbable and unique, you should root for him.

Mike Piazza   **C**   **Bats: R**   **Throws: R**   Height: 6' 3"   Weight: 215   Born: December 31, 1969   Age: 38

YEAR	TEAM	LVL	AGE	PA	R	2B	3B	HR	RBI	BB	SO	SB	CS	SPEED	AVG	OBP	SLG	MLVR	EQAVG	EQOBP	EQSLG	EQA	VORP	DEFENSE			
2004	NYN	MLB	35	528	47	21	0	20	54	68	78	0	0	3.1	.266	.362	.444	.098	.266	.362	.451	.281	22.2	53-1B	-5	37-C	-5
2005	NYN	MLB	36	442	41	23	0	19	62	41	67	0	0	3.6	.251	.326	.452	.050	.252	.328	.466	.269	20.0	91-C	-7		
2006	SDN	MLB	37	439	39	19	1	22	68	34	66	0	0	3.2	.283	.342	.501	.153	.292	.352	.519	.291	26.7	79-C	-18		
2007	OAK	MLB	38	372	40	17	1	14	57	29	58	0	0	3.4	.263	.323	.443	-.031	.259	.325	.451	.270	11.2	89-C	-9		

Breakout: 12%   Improve: 27%   Collapse: 37%   Attrition: 33%   Comparables: Walker Cooper, Joe Adcock, Tony Perez, Cliff Johnson

It might have seemed like the old Mike Piazza was back last year, freed from his Big Apple-flavored prison, but he basically just hit for a better average, perhaps the benefit of Bochy giving him regular rest. He hit much better away from PETCO (.332/.372/.564), and quite poorly against right-handers (.257/.314/.449), which hardly profiles well for an everyday cleanup hitter. Piazza's been inked by Oakland to be their DH and, given the A's in-game passivity, you might wonder if he's in danger of grounding into some astronomical number of double-plays. The man Piazza is replacing, Frank Thomas, couldn't run a lick last year and hit into a double play in 14 percent of his opportunities, while Piazza's mark with the Padres was 15.2 percent. The trick is that Thomas had the sixth-highest fly ball rate among hitters with 300 plate appearances, leaving him with just 24.8 percent ground balls compared to Piazza's 40.2 percent. Still, Piazza has a long way to go to match the DP rate of 2006 Padre team leader Adrian Gonzalez, whose 21.9 percent was one of the twenty worst marks on the season for MLB players with 150 or more PA.

Dave Roberts   **CF**   **Bats: L**   **Throws: L**   Height: 5' 10"   Weight: 180   Born: May 31, 1972   Age: 35

YEAR	TEAM	LVL	AGE	PA	R	2B	3B	HR	RBI	BB	SO	SB	CS	SPEED	AVG	OBP	SLG	MLVR	EQAVG	EQOBP	EQSLG	EQA	VORP	DEFENSE			
2004	LAN	MLB	32	270	45	4	7	2	21	28	31	33	1	9.1	.253	.340	.356	-.071	.252	.336	.355	.271	6.7	41-LF	1	16-CF	1
2004	BOS	MLB	32	101	19	10	0	2	14	10	17	5	2	7.0	.256	.330	.442	-.039	.247	.330	.447	.273	1.5	13-RF	0		
2005	SDN	MLB	33	480	65	19	10	8	38	53	59	23	12	7.3	.275	.356	.428	.087	.290	.372	.464	.283	19.7	100-CF	-10		
2006	SDN	MLB	34	566	80	18	13	2	44	51	61	49	6	8.6	.293	.360	.393	.038	.304	.371	.410	.286	22.2	108-LF	9	11-CF	1
2007	SFN	MLB	35	526	86	20	10	3	36	48	63	42	13	8.2	.295	.364	.404	.004	.293	.361	.409	.274	14.1	124-LF	0		

Breakout: 8%   Improve: 38%   Collapse: 35%   Attrition: 17%   Comparables: Al Bumbry, Kenny Lofton, Lou Brock, Bill Bruton

Roberts is a wonderful little ballplayer. Kevin Towers deserves credit for stealing two years of Roberts from the Red Sox for Dave Pauley, Ramon Vazquez, and a year in the life of Jay Payton. Playing Roberts in left might seem like a bad gambit in terms of VORP, but real teams don't work that way—Cameron's the better center fielder, and Roberts's first responsibility was batting leadoff. He'll be playing in center every day for the Giants for the next three years (for $18 million), which won't exactly help them that much defensively—Randy Winn's rag arm will just get run on when balls are hit to right, and Roberts isn't exactly Andruw Jones out there himself. As a center fielder for the Giants, his projected VORP would be 28.4.

Terrmel Sledge   **LF**   **Bats: L**   **Throws: L**   Height: 6' 0"   Weight: 185   Born: March 18, 1977   Age: 30

YEAR	TEAM	LVL	AGE	PA	R	2B	3B	HR	RBI	BB	SO	SB	CS	SPEED	AVG	OBP	SLG	MLVR	EQAVG	EQOBP	EQSLG	EQA	VORP	DEFENSE			
2004	MON	MLB	27	446	45	20	6	15	62	40	66	3	3	5.6	.269	.336	.462	.082	.265	.334	.458	.267	10.8	66-LF	1	32-RF	3
2005	WAS	MLB	28	46	7	0	1	1	8	7	8	2	1	6.0	.243	.348	.378	-.005	.243	.348	.378	.265	0.6				
2006	POR	AAA	29	434	69	18	5	24	73	59	75	5	3	5.1	.311	.402	.583	.392	.285	.364	.517	.297	25.7	52-RF	-8	24-CF	-3
2006	SDN	MLB	29	78	7	3	0	2	7	8	17	0	0	4.1	.229	.308	.357	-.164	.229	.308	.343	.230	-1.7				
2007	SDN	MLB	30	441	61	21	4	15	57	49	80	5	3	5.4	.267	.351	.457	.030	.274	.354	.472	.279	15.9	105-RF	-1		

Breakout: 14%   Improve: 40%   Collapse: 26%   Attrition: 18%   Comparables: Randy Bush, Jim Edmonds, Jose Cruz, Brian Myrow

Although you might still think of Sledge as a prospect, he's about to get his last best shot at regular work in the major leagues just in time for his 30th birthday. It helps that the organization likes him, but he isn't really what statheads would call a Ken Phelps All-Star, an unrecognized star in the minors; he can play, but so can McAnulty or even Cust. What might help is that, with Roberts gone, nobody on the team is a prototypical leadoff hitter, and Sledge might bear the closest passing resemblance to one. With his power and ability to make contact, he'd be the sort of leadoff hitter who can deliver after a pitcher bunts the runners over.

Will Venable   **OF**   **Bats: L**   **Throws: L**   Height: 6' 2"   Weight: 205   Born: October 29, 1982   Age: 24

YEAR	TEAM	LVL	AGE	PA	R	2B	3B	HR	RBI	BB	SO	SB	CS	SPEED	AVG	OBP	SLG	MLVR	EQAVG	EQOBP	EQSLG	EQA	VORP	DEFENSE	
2005	EUG	A-	22	156	17	5	2	2	14	14	38	2	1	5.0	.216	.295	.324	-.144	.159	.212	.207	.162	-45.9	26-LF	-4
2006	FTW	A	23	541	86	34	5	11	91	55	81	18	5	6.3	.314	.389	.477	.317	.283	.336	.423	.266	5.1	112-LF	0
2007	SDN	MLB	24	498	55	26	4	8	49	34	92	8	3	5.6	.254	.310	.381	-.155	.260	.312	.393	.242	-4.5	117-LF	0

Breakout: 35%   Improve: 51%   Collapse: 22%   Attrition: 6%   Comparables: Stephen Larkin, Ron Calloway, Kyle Logan, Jess Graham

Not your average tools guy, Venable's an Ivy Leaguer with skills (assuming Princeton's cranking out better products than Woodrow Wilson these days). Developmentally, Venable's still a bit on the raw side for a guy who's already 24, but he focused on hoops in college and has already made fast progress. In Fort Wayne, he had the pleasure of having his dad (Max, the former big league outfielder) as his hitting coach, but, from here on out, he won't get to hang around one level; the Pads want to see him move up fast. He might get caught as a tweener, because he probably doesn't have the instincts or arm to stick in center, but if he makes the jump to Double-A this summer and keeps hitting, he'll get onto big-league radars.

Todd Walker   **1B/2B**   **Bats: L**   **Throws: R**   Height: 6' 0"   Weight: 185   Born: May 25, 1973   Age: 34

YEAR	TEAM	LVL	AGE	PA	R	2B	3B	HR	RBI	BB	SO	SB	CS	SPEED	AVG	OBP	SLG	MLVR	EQAVG	EQOBP	EQSLG	EQA	VORP	DEFENSE			
2004	CHN	MLB	31	424	60	19	4	15	50	43	52	0	3	4.9	.274	.352	.468	.091	.269	.347	.460	.274	19.8	78-2B	0		
2005	CHN	MLB	32	433	50	25	3	12	40	31	40	1	1	4.8	.305	.355	.474	.155	.301	.354	.480	.283	25.9	90-2B	-5		
2006	CHN	MLB	33	362	38	16	1	6	40	38	27	0	1	3.8	.277	.352	.390	-.016	.271	.351	.388	.261	5.5	37-2B	-2	35-1B	1
2006	SDN	MLB	33	142	18	6	1	3	13	17	11	2	0	5.2	.282	.366	.419	.080	.293	.380	.431	.287	6.1	17-3B	-2	12-2B	1
2007	SDN	MLB	34	434	53	21	2	9	48	44	41	2	2	4.7	.268	.345	.401	-.053	.274	.348	.414	.263	11.7	103-2B	-2		

Breakout: 9%   Improve: 32%   Collapse: 26%   Attrition: 20%   Comparables: Bill Spiers, Eddie Waitkus, Phil Cavarretta, Don Mattingly

Besides not being a supermodel, or a doctor, or a caped crusader, Todd Walker isn't a third baseman. As much as the Padres wished it was so, and as dutifully as he tried to fulfill those wishes, it wasn't so. With the additions of Kouzmanoff and Marcus Giles, he'll be reduced to a Keith Lockhart-like reserve role, spot-starting at second, first, and even third, but mostly giving new manager Bud Black a dangerous lefty stick with which to pinch-hit.

PITCHERS

Jon Adkins   **Bats: L**   **Throws: R**   Height: 6' 0"   Weight: 200   Born: August 30, 1977   Age: 29

YEAR	TEAM	LVL	AGE	W	L	SV	G	GS	IP	H	BB	SO	HR	GB%	BABIP	STUFF	WHIP	ERA	PERA	EQERA	EQH9	EQBB9	EQSO9	EQHR9	VORP	WXRL
2004	CHA	MLB	26	2	3	0	50	0	62	75	20	44	13	—	.328	-14	1.53	4.65	5.07	4.64	10.4	2.5	5.9	1.5	9.6	-0.29
2005	CHR	AAA	27	4	9	0	23	21	127¹	148	43	92	20	45.2%	.329	-18	1.50	5.37	5.68	5.84	10.3	3.3	4.9	1.6	-3.4	—
2006	SDN	MLB	28	2	1	0	55	0	54¹	55	20	30	3	43.4%	.306	-5	1.38	3.98	3.91	4.42	9.3	2.9	4.6	0.5	9.7	0.87
2007	SDN	MLB	29	2	2	2	46	0	51¹	54	20	33	6	46.0%	.292	-8	1.43	4.18	4.93	4.59	9.6	2.9	5.2	1.0	6.7	0.50

Breakout: 22%   Improve: 60%   Collapse: 14%   Attrition: 36%   Comparables: Bobby Hogue, Matt Whiteside, John Frascatore, Mike DeJean

Adkins's role in both of his major league seasons has been middle-inning mop-up work. He's diddled around with other possibilities, switching back and forth between starting and relieving in the minors, but, in the end and like his comps, he's just going to have to get over the unbearable lightness of being Warren Brusstar. Reunited with fellow Oakland refugee Rick Peterson in New York, he might have an inside track on a back of the bullpen job.

Manny Ayala   **Bats: R**   **Throws: R**   Height: 6' 3"   Weight: 225   Born: November 6, 1984   Age: 22

YEAR	TEAM	LVL	AGE	W	L	SV	G	GS	IP	H	BB	SO	HR	GB%	BABIP	STUFF	WHIP	ERA	PERA	EQERA	EQH9	EQBB9	EQSO9	EQHR9	VORP	WXRL
2006	LEL	A+	21	5	4	0	23	12	91¹	90	12	71	8	43.2%	.309	-2	1.12	4.05	4.63	4.61	9.1	1.3	4.5	1.3	10.1	—
2007	SDN	MLB	22	5	7	0	29	14	98¹	107	24	59	18	42.0%	.281	-1	1.33	4.93	5.37	5.34	9.8	1.9	4.9	1.5	4.4	1.00

Breakout: 15%   Improve: 37%   Collapse: 25%   Attrition: 5%   Comparables: Cha-Seung Baek, Shaun Stokes, Jamie Shields, Jonathan Albaladejo

Perhaps the weirdest of San Diego's indy league pickups, Ayala pitched in the Golden League after a college baseball scholarship fell through, then signed with the Pads. He's hardly the most scouty of pitching prospects, in that he's sort of a beefy guy with an average fastball and plus changeup, but he might make it in a relief role.

Cesar Carrillo

Bats: R Throws: R   Height: 6' 3"   Weight: 175   Born: April 29, 1984   Age: 23

YEAR	TEAM	LVL	AGE	W	L	SV	G	GS	IP	H	BB	SO	HR	GB%	BABIP	STUFF	WHIP	ERA	PERA	EQERA	EQH9	EQBB9	EQSO9	EQHR9	VORP	WXRL
2005	LEL	A+	21	1	2	0	7	7	25²	30	9	29	3	62.0%	.360	1	1.52	7.00	5.32	7.36	10.9	3.5	6.7	1.4	-5.0	—
2005	MOB	AA	21	4	0	0	5	5	30²	23	7	35	2	45.6%	.276	30	0.98	3.22	3.81	3.56	7.1	2.1	7.1	0.9	6.9	—
2006	MOB	AA	22	1	3	0	9	9	50²	45	15	43	5	57.8%	.286	3	1.20	3.05	5.52	4.74	9.1	2.7	5.5	1.5	4.7	—
2007	SDN	MLB	23	6	8	0	25	19	117²	115	49	88	15	49.0%	.284	9	1.39	4.64	5.02	5.13	8.8	3.2	6.1	1.0	8.4	1.70

Breakout: 12% Improve: 49% Collapse: 11% Attrition: 0%   Comparables: Pete Munro, Mark Brownson, Kurt Ainsworth, Michael Hinckley

The franchise's best (and perhaps only) real pitching prospect, Carrillo was a first-round pick in 2005 after serving as the staff ace at the University of Miami, where he was worked like a galley slave. That last bit is what has kept everyone waiting for more, because, while Carrillo's plus fastball-curve-change mix seems geared for big-league success, his elbow gave out in June. The Padres are hoping rest will do the trick, and that he'll be ready to get back on the accelerated timetable they had planned for him in the spring. If he's sound, he'll almost certainly show up in the Padres rotation at some point this summer.

Scott Cassidy

Bats: R Throws: R   Height: 6' 2"   Weight: 180   Born: October 3, 1975   Age: 31

YEAR	TEAM	LVL	AGE	W	L	SV	G	GS	IP	H	BB	SO	HR	GB%	BABIP	STUFF	WHIP	ERA	PERA	EQERA	EQH9	EQBB9	EQSO9	EQHR9	VORP	WXRL
2004	PAW	AAA	28	5	3	1	28	12	80²	72	38	72	10	—	.281	-5	1.36	3.46	5.68	4.20	8.4	4.8	6.1	1.4	12.3	—
2005	PAW	AAA	29	6	3	0	26	3	60	54	23	66	5	34.8%	.325	6	1.28	4.05	4.24	5.01	8.3	3.8	7.4	0.9	3.9	—
2005	POR	AAA	29	0	1	11	17	0	19	10	7	19	2	47.9%	.186	4	0.89	1.89	4.82	2.41	5.3	3.4	6.8	1.0	6.6	—
2005	SDN	MLB	29	1	1	0	10	0	12¹	15	3	12	3	32.4%	.353	1	1.46	6.59	5.17	7.11	10.7	2.1	7.8	2.1	-2.6	0.42
2006	POR	AAA	30	3	1	9	17	0	20²	21	6	23	0	36.8%	.382	13	1.34	2.67	2.84	3.05	9.1	2.6	7.4	0.4	5.9	—
2006	SDN	MLB	30	6	4	0	42	0	42²	39	19	49	8	35.2%	.310	11	1.36	2.53	4.51	3.74	8.5	3.5	9.3	1.5	9.8	-0.60
2007	SDN	MLB	31	2	2	2	41	1	47¹	44	21	43	7	37.0%	.282	2	1.38	4.33	4.84	4.69	8.4	3.5	7.4	1.2	5.7	0.50

Breakout: 14% Improve: 36% Collapse: 31% Attrition: 31%   Comparables: Mike Hartley, Elmer Singleton, Rich Delucia, Matt Mantei

When not fending off lonely fortysomething women clutching Partridge Family LPs, Cassidy provides an object lesson in the dangers of seeing an ERA and not looking beyond it. While Cassidy's raw ERA was nice enough last year, a third of his runs allowed were unearned, and his fly-ball tendencies delivered a few too many souvenirs despite benefits of pitching in PETCO. The Padres got understandably frustrated, demoting Cassidy in mid-July and only bringing him back when rosters expanded, which reflects on how insecure his future, with this or any team, remains.

Michael Ekstrom

Bats: R Throws: R   Height: 6' 0"   Weight: 185   Born: August 30, 1983   Age: 23

YEAR	TEAM	LVL	AGE	W	L	SV	G	GS	IP	H	BB	SO	HR	GB%	BABIP	STUFF	WHIP	ERA	PERA	EQERA	EQH9	EQBB9	EQSO9	EQHR9	VORP	WXRL
2004	EUG	A-	20	3	1	0	12	7	39	38	10	42	1	—	.330	4	1.23	3.69	4.16	5.26	10.0	3.1	5.0	0.5	1.4	—
2004	FTW	A	20	0	2	0	3	3	14¹	21	3	10	1	—	.385	-13	1.68	8.18	4.85	9.42	13.2	2.5	3.8	1.3	-6.1	—
2005	FTW	A	21	13	6	0	28	28	167²	167	36	112	11	51.1%	.296	-2	1.21	3.70	4.94	4.87	9.4	2.2	3.8	1.2	13.5	—
2006	LEL	A+	22	7	4	0	14	14	82²	76	21	68	2	55.2%	.318	19	1.18	2.30	3.86	4.01	8.3	2.6	4.6	0.3	14.7	—
2006	MOB	AA	22	3	7	0	14	14	84	87	19	49	2	55.9%	.301	13	1.26	3.86	3.64	5.08	9.3	2.0	3.7	0.3	4.9	—
2007	SDN	MLB	23	6	9	0	26	21	126	135	41	71	16	50.0%	.288	1	1.39	5.02	5.15	5.59	9.7	2.5	4.6	1.1	2.3	1.10

Breakout: 3% Improve: 26% Collapse: 33% Attrition: 0%   Comparables: Mike Lincoln, Steven Kelly, Brian Lawrence, Lance Cormier

Ekstrom is your standard shortish command-and-control right-hander and someone whose average to below-average velocity wouldn't light up your typical scout's eyes. He does have a tasty sinker, however, and keeping the ball in the infield can lead to opportunities to transcend the excitement of that Quadruple-A, Kevin Jarvis lifestyle.

Alan Embree

Bats: L Throws: L   Height: 6' 2"   Weight: 190   Born: January 23, 1970   Age: 37

YEAR	TEAM	LVL	AGE	W	L	SV	G	GS	IP	H	BB	SO	HR	GB%	BABIP	STUFF	WHIP	ERA	PERA	EQERA	EQH9	EQBB9	EQSO9	EQHR9	VORP	WXRL
2004	BOS	MLB	34	2	2	0	71	0	52¹	49	11	37	7	—	.268	0	1.15	4.13	3.98	4.36	8.0	1.7	5.9	1.0	9.3	1.98
2005	BOS	MLB	35	1	4	1	43	0	37²	42	11	30	8	41.5%	.309	-10	1.41	7.64	5.07	7.09	9.2	2.5	6.9	1.8	-8.3	-1.00
2005	NYA	MLB	35	1	1	0	24	0	14¹	20	3	8	2	43.4%	.353	-18	1.60	7.55	4.53	8.40	12.0	1.8	4.8	1.2	-4.9	-0.51
2006	SDN	MLB	36	4	3	0	73	0	52¹	50	15	53	4	44.6%	.319	20	1.24	3.27	3.00	3.59	8.9	2.2	8.4	0.7	13.4	1.40
2007	OAK	MLB	37	2	2	2	52	0	47	53	12	34	6	43%	.312	-2	1.37	4.42	4.41	4.31	9.6	2.2	6.2	1.1	6.1	0.5

Breakout: 41% Improve: 60% Collapse: 23% Attrition: 27%   Comparables: Bob Patterson, Darren Holmes, Sparky Lyle, Rich Rodriguez

Having earned the mutual enmity of equally rabid Red Sox and Yankees fans, Embree sensibly took his act to the Left Coast, where his better-than-average velocity (for a southpaw) and strike-throwing might found new life. Although he surprisingly struggled in PETCO, he was the untouted fourth man who helped make the Padre pen so dominating. He's scooted to Oakland, where his presence will allow Joe Kennedy to move back into the rotation.

Clay Hensley   Bats: R Throws: R
Height: 5' 11" Weight: 190 Born: August 31, 1979 Age: 27

YEAR	TEAM	LVL	AGE	W	L	SV	G	GS	IP	H	BB	SO	HR	GB%	BABIP	STUFF	WHIP	ERA	PERA	EQERA	EQH9	EQBB9	EQSO9	EQHR9	VORP	WXRL
2004	MOB	AA	24	11	10	0	27	27	159	167	48	125	14	—	.319	-13	1.35	4.30	5.42	6.31	10.7	3.2	4.4	1.3	-12.0	—
2005	POR	AAA	25	2	2	0	15	14	90¹	63	22	71	8	58.4%	.228	17	0.94	2.99	4.13	3.29	6.3	2.1	5.4	0.9	23.2	—
2005	SDN	MLB	25	1	1	0	24	1	47²	33	17	28	0	56.7%	.234	8	1.05	1.70	3.39	2.42	6.1	3.0	4.8	0.2	16.8	1.97
2006	SDN	MLB	26	11	12	0	37	29	187	174	76	122	15	55.0%	.285	13	1.34	3.71	4.07	4.05	8.6	3.2	5.4	0.7	40.8	5.39
2007	SDN	MLB	27	9	9	0	29	25	158¹	160	60	103	16	52.0%	.289	8	1.39	4.25	4.69	4.73	9.1	2.9	5.3	0.8	18.2	3.00

Breakout: 5% Improve: 21% Collapse: 28% Attrition: 1%   Comparables: Chuck Rainey, Walt Terrell, Ernie McAnally, Paul Wagner

The bias against short pitchers being what it is, Hensley's not going to catch a lot of breaks, but he remains a steal, having been acquired straight-up for Matt Herges back in 2003. That said, it took Padre coaching to get him to lower his arm slot and bring his pitches down in the zone. If they hadn't, perhaps Hensley never would have been a viable major leaguer. Making that change in 2005 made his sinker-slider mix that much more difficult to pick up or hit with any lift. He didn't pitch in college until his senior year, which means he's a unique talent without a lot of mileage on his arm.

Trevor Hoffman   Bats: R Throws: R
Height: 6' 0" Weight: 215 Born: December 31, 1969 Age: 39

YEAR	TEAM	LVL	AGE	W	L	SV	G	GS	IP	H	BB	SO	HR	GB%	BABIP	STUFF	WHIP	ERA	PERA	EQERA	EQH9	EQBB9	EQSO9	EQHR9	VORP	WXRL
2004	SDN	MLB	36	3	3	41	55	0	54²	42	8	53	5	—	.262	24	0.91	2.30	2.93	2.60	6.8	1.1	7.6	0.8	20.1	4.36
2005	SDN	MLB	37	1	6	43	60	0	57²	52	12	54	3	37.7%	.299	22	1.11	2.96	2.81	3.66	7.8	1.7	7.6	0.5	11.2	3.71
2006	SDN	MLB	38	0	2	46	65	0	63	48	13	50	6	33.2%	.236	14	0.97	2.14	3.45	2.44	7.2	1.6	6.6	0.9	25.7	6.00
2007	SDN	MLB	39	3	4	26	46	0	51	47	12	40	6	37.0%	.271	2	1.16	3.45	3.78	3.77	8.3	1.9	6.3	1.0	10.8	1.80

Breakout: 7% Improve: 18% Collapse: 62% Attrition: 18%   Comparables: Ellis Kinder, Chris Hammond, Steve Reed, Doug Jones

Last year, Hoffman pitched in his highest number of games since 2000 and threw his most innings since 1999. Now that he's tacked on 130 saves since his surgery, it might seem that not all shoulder surgeries are created equal, and that not all former position players are doomed to career-altering arm problems. Of course, it helps that Hoffman is someone who doesn't take his role or his craft for granted. He found a way to pitch through the shoulder problems that sapped the moving fastball that used to be his signature pitch in the mid-nineties, adapting by mastering the changeup that's now his weapon of choice. It's that improbable transition that will make him an easy pick for the Hall of Fame.

Scott Linebrink   Bats: R Throws: R
Height: 6' 2" Weight: 200 Born: August 4, 1976 Age: 30

YEAR	TEAM	LVL	AGE	W	L	SV	G	GS	IP	H	BB	SO	HR	GB%	BABIP	STUFF	WHIP	ERA	PERA	EQERA	EQH9	EQBB9	EQSO9	EQHR9	VORP	WXRL
2004	SDN	MLB	27	7	3	0	73	0	84	61	26	83	8	—	.264	21	1.04	2.14	3.55	2.66	6.6	2.4	7.9	0.9	30.6	3.56
2005	SDN	MLB	28	8	1	1	73	0	73²	55	23	70	4	38.9%	.270	26	1.06	1.83	3.02	2.27	6.5	2.5	7.8	0.5	27.4	3.73
2006	SDN	MLB	29	7	4	2	73	0	75²	70	22	68	9	40.5%	.289	10	1.22	3.57	3.72	3.79	8.6	2.2	7.5	0.9	18.9	3.99
2007	SDN	MLB	30	3	3	4	55	0	63	59	21	54	8	38.0%	.278	5	1.26	3.67	4.27	3.98	8.4	2.6	7.0	1.1	13.0	1.10

Breakout: 9% Improve: 23% Collapse: 54% Attrition: 7%   Comparables: Mike Trombley, T. J. Mathews, Jeff Reardon, Guillermo Mota

There are some whose destiny it is to be Robin to somebody else's Batman, and even if Linebrink never graduates to the closer's role, his three-year run has given Trevor Hoffman the most reliable setup man he's ever had. Linebrink's run accounts for three of the top five single-season WXRL totals by Padre setup men during Hoffman's career; the other two are Akinori Otsuka's 2004 season and Cla Meredith's 2006. In terms of his stuff, he mixes mid-90s fastballs with a splitter that makes him especially tough on lefties; right-handers can sit dead-red and get a cookie a little too often, though.

Cla Meredith
Bats: R Throws: R Height: 6' 0" Weight: 180 Born: June 4, 1983 Age: 24

YEAR	TEAM	LVL	AGE	W	L	SV	G	GS	IP	H	BB	SO	HR	GB%	BABIP	STUFF	WHIP	ERA	PERA	EQERA	EQH9	EQBB9	EQSO9	EQHR9	VORP	WXRL
2004	AUG	A	21	1	0	6	13	0	15¹	8	3	18	0	—	.222	15	0.72	0.00	3.37	0.60	6.0	2.4	6.0	0.0	8.3	—
2004	SAR	A+	21	0	2	12	16	0	16¹	15	3	16	0	—	.333	8	1.10	2.21	3.16	2.81	9.0	1.7	6.2	0.0	5.0	—
2005	PME	AA	22	1	0	9	12	0	15	5	3	12	0	75.0%	.143	9	0.53	0.00	3.36	0.61	3.7	1.8	4.9	0.0	8.2	—
2005	PAW	AAA	22	2	5	10	40	0	48¹	63	12	42	6	55.9%	.370	-6	1.55	5.59	4.39	5.66	11.3	2.4	6.0	1.3	-0.3	—
2006	PAW	AAA	23	0	0	0	8	0	13	16	5	14	1	68.3%	.395	-2	1.62	5.54	4.14	6.92	11.1	3.5	7.6	0.7	-1.9	—
2006	POR	AAA	23	3	0	2	24	0	32	26	4	24	2	66.3%	.264	9	0.94	1.41	3.36	1.64	6.5	1.1	5.2	0.8	14.5	—
2006	SDN	MLB	23	5	1	0	45	0	50²	30	6	37	3	69.8%	.199	22	0.71	1.07	2.99	1.25	5.7	0.9	6.1	0.5	27.9	3.76
2007	*SDN*	*MLB*	*24*	*3*	*2*	*3*	*52*	*0*	*49²*	*48*	*14*	*35*	*3*	*61.0%*	*.289*	*5*	*1.23*	*3.18*	*3.59*	*3.60*	*8.7*	*2.1*	*5.8*	*0.5*	*11.7*	*1.10*

Breakout: 10% Improve: 17% Collapse: 54% Attrition: 31%   Comparables: *Brad Thompson, Willie Hernandez, Bill Castro, Elias Sosa*

As if the panic in Beantown wasn't rewarding enough in that it turned Doug Mirabelli into Josh Bard, the Padres managed to get Meredith as a throw-in in the deal. We can all snigger about how Meredith was a symptom of what seemed like a sudden industry-wide drive to draft, develop, or dig up the next Chad Bradford—echoing the unfortunate tendency to try to draft "the next Michael Jordan" in the NBA twenty years ago, or "the next Kellen Winslow" in the NFL—but Meredith looks like the real deal, a guy with a tricky delivery and a particularly nasty sinker. It's pretty easy to say that nobody can sustain a level of play that included a 34-inning scoreless streak, but he's in the right park, and it's unlikely he'll be asked to appear in 44 games in three months again.

Jose Oyervidez
Bats: R Throws: R Height: 5' 11" Weight: 195 Born: February 18, 1982 Age: 25

YEAR	TEAM	LVL	AGE	W	L	SV	G	GS	IP	H	BB	SO	HR	GB%	BABIP	STUFF	WHIP	ERA	PERA	EQERA	EQH9	EQBB9	EQSO9	EQHR9	VORP	WXRL
2005	MOB	AA	23	7	9	0	27	27	153²	129	82	130	16	53.7%	.275	-10	1.37	3.81	6.58	5.14	8.1	5.0	5.3	1.7	7.7	—
2006	MOB	AA	24	6	12	0	28	28	149¹	146	75	131	11	56.6%	.317	-6	1.48	3.92	5.80	5.83	9.9	4.9	5.3	1.2	-3.7	—
2007	*SDN*	*MLB*	*25*	*5*	*8*	*0*	*25*	*18*	*107*	*110*	*60*	*75*	*15*	*49.0%*	*.289*	*-2*	*1.59*	*5.30*	*5.89*	*5.84*	*9.3*	*4.4*	*5.7*	*1.1*	*-1.2*	*0.60*

Breakout: 14% Improve: 43% Collapse: 24% Attrition: 0%   Comparables: *Ricky Stone, Clay Hensley, Nelson Figueroa, Steve Green*

A short Texas juco vet who went undrafted, Oyervidez survived 2004 Tommy John surgery on his elbow and jumped directly to Double-A in 2005, but he's not gifted with any real upside. His best features are that he throws strikes with three different pitches and he goes after hitters, but, like a lot of people in the pitching-friendly Southern League, he's about to learn a few hard lessons in the PCL.

Chan Ho Park
Bats: R Throws: R Height: 6' 2" Weight: 210 Born: June 30, 1973 Age: 34

YEAR	TEAM	LVL	AGE	W	L	SV	G	GS	IP	H	BB	SO	HR	GB%	BABIP	STUFF	WHIP	ERA	PERA	EQERA	EQH9	EQBB9	EQSO9	EQHR9	VORP	WXRL
2004	TEX	MLB	31	4	7	0	16	16	95²	105	33	63	22	—	.301	-11	1.50	5.45	6.01	5.00	9.5	2.8	5.5	1.7	0.7	0.32
2005	TEX	MLB	32	8	5	0	20	20	109²	130	54	80	8	50.1%	.352	17	1.68	5.66	4.26	5.01	9.7	4.3	6.3	0.5	2.3	1.28
2005	SDN	MLB	32	4	3	0	10	9	45²	50	26	33	3	48.3%	.326	6	1.66	5.91	4.60	6.46	9.5	4.6	5.9	0.6	-6.3	0.22
2006	SDN	MLB	33	7	7	0	24	21	136²	146	44	96	20	43.9%	.299	3	1.39	4.81	4.73	5.36	9.9	2.5	5.8	1.2	8.0	1.99
2007	*SDN*	*MLB*	*34*	*8*	*9*	*0*	*29*	*21*	*140²*	*146*	*51*	*94*	*17*	*45.0%*	*.291*	*3*	*1.40*	*4.59*	*5.00*	*5.05*	*9.4*	*2.8*	*5.5*	*1.0*	*11.2*	*2.10*

Breakout: 25% Improve: 57% Collapse: 11% Attrition: 2%   Comparables: *Bobby Witt, Ron Darling, Ed Whitson, Tim Leary*

It's been a strange career already, but, between losing parts of two seasons to a back injury and parts of a third to a hamstring, this year's life-threatening intestinal problems only made it plain that lightning can strike repeatedly in the same place. Currently a free agent, it's hard to guess who would want to take a flier on a fifth starter so ill-starred, and his reputation as a headhunter doesn't help. As recently as five years ago, Park was an unexceptional workhorse starter who looked like a potential ace to some due to the forgiving nature of Dodger Stadium. When life stripped away that veneer, it did so with a vengeance.

Jake Peavy
Bats: R Throws: R Height: 6' 1" Weight: 180 Born: May 31, 1981 Age: 26

YEAR	TEAM	LVL	AGE	W	L	SV	G	GS	IP	H	BB	SO	HR	GB%	BABIP	STUFF	WHIP	ERA	PERA	EQERA	EQH9	EQBB9	EQSO9	EQHR9	VORP	WXRL
2004	SDN	MLB	23	15	6	0	27	27	166¹	146	53	173	13	—	.307	40	1.20	2.27	3.39	2.93	8.0	2.6	8.3	0.6	56.0	6.47
2005	SDN	MLB	24	13	7	0	30	30	203	162	50	216	18	46.0%	.281	41	1.04	2.88	3.19	3.31	7.1	2.0	8.7	0.8	53.1	6.56
2006	SDN	MLB	25	11	14	0	32	32	202¹	187	62	215	23	39.3%	.307	33	1.23	4.09	3.47	4.15	8.7	2.4	8.7	0.9	39.2	5.86
2007	*SDN*	*MLB*	*26*	*14*	*8*	*0*	*30*	*30*	*206¹*	*175*	*57*	*212*	*22*	*42.0%*	*.280*	*34*	*1.12*	*3.15*	*3.45*	*3.46*	*7.7*	*2.1*	*8.4*	*0.9*	*52.9*	*7.00*

Breakout: 22% Improve: 63% Collapse: 8% Attrition: 3%   Comparables: *Pedro Martinez, Don Sutton, Javier Vazquez, Tom Seaver*

Twenty-two quality starts in 32 is supposed to generate better results in terms of wins and losses, but Peavy was the second-most unlucky starter in baseball when you compare his performance to his actual won-loss record. He pitched well enough for the Padres to have gone 18–14 in his starts, instead they went 15–17. With normal support, Peavy's record would have been 14–10. Peavy's better than this, just look at those comparable pitchers above. He has four pitches he can throw for strikes, plus heat, and the ability to dominate. Intriguingly, he became slightly wilder in the second half (walking 3 per nine innings versus 1.6 before the break), but started seeing better results, giving up fewer hits and homers, and logging 10 quality starts in his last 13 to help put the Pads in the postseason.

Rudy Seanez — Bats: R Throws: R — Height: 5' 11" Weight: 200 Born: December 31, 1969 Age: 38

YEAR	TEAM	LVL	AGE	W	L	SV	G	GS	IP	H	BB	SO	HR	GB%	BABIP	STUFF	WHIP	ERA	PERA	EQERA	EQH9	EQBB9	EQSO9	EQHR9	VORP	WXRL
2004	KCA	MLB	35	0	1	0	16	0	23	21	11	21	0	—	.323	13	1.39	3.91	3.12	3.38	7.5	3.8	7.5	0.4	5.8	-0.62
2004	FLO	MLB	35	3	1	0	23	0	23	18	8	25	3	—	.263	18	1.13	2.74	3.73	3.13	7.0	2.7	8.6	1.2	7.3	0.15
2005	SDN	MLB	36	7	1	0	57	0	60¹	49	22	84	4	37.2%	.338	40	1.18	2.69	2.70	3.06	7.3	2.9	11.2	0.6	17.3	1.68
2006	BOS	MLB	37	2	1	0	41	0	46²	51	26	48	6	31.4%	.336	10	1.65	4.82	4.32	4.81	8.9	4.6	8.5	0.9	4.0	-1.16
2006	SDN	MLB	37	1	2	0	8	0	6¹	7	6	6	2	38.1%	.263	-3	2.05	5.71	7.61	5.40	9.4	6.8	8.1	2.7	0.2	-0.85
2007	SDN	MLB	38	2	2	2	36	0	43	39	20	40	6	39.0%	.282	3	1.37	3.96	4.55	4.31	8.2	3.6	7.6	1.1	7.0	0.60

Breakout: 18% Improve: 30% Collapse: 28% Attrition: 36% — Comparables: Don McMahon, Mike Remlinger, Mark Leiter, Dennis Cook

"Traction Action" has long been a house fave hereabouts. It's not a Goth thing because he's seemingly deathless, but more a matter of his outlasting failed expectations of greatness to become a reliably unreliable commodity. You never know when Seanez will be healthy enough to help, but, for a few weeks at a time, he can show up, pump gas, and help a team win. Joining the Padres for a fourth tour in his third trading deadline team change in the last six years (no, really), he's now made the playoffs in two different stints two different teams (the other being the Braves).

Joakim Soria — Bats: R Throws: R — Height: 6' 2" Weight: 170 Born: May 18, 1984 Age: 23

YEAR	TEAM	LVL	AGE	W	L	SV	G	GS	IP	H	BB	SO	HR	GB%	BABIP	STUFF	WHIP	ERA	PERA	EQERA	EQH9	EQBB9	EQSO9	EQHR9	VORP	WXRL
2005	MCD	MX	21	5	0	0	30	5	66¹	75	31	60	7	39.2%	.352	15	1.60	4.48	4.28	3.71	8.3	3.8	7.7	0.9	14.8	—
2006	MCD	MX	22	0	0	15	39	0	37	37	11	30	2	49.6%	.325	12	1.30	3.89	3.49	3.49	7.4	2.6	7.0	0.7	9.1	—
2006	FTW	A	22	1	0	0	7	0	11¹	5	2	11	1	48.4%	.207	-8	0.63	2.43	6.81	4.35	6.1	2.6	5.2	2.6	1.4	—
2007	KCA	MLB	23	3	4	1	26	5	54²	58	22	41	8	44.0%	.298	2	1.46	4.84	4.69	4.34	8.7	3.5	6.2	1.1	5.4	0.70

Breakout: 12% Improve: 26% Collapse: 40% Attrition: 24% — Comparables: P. J. Bevis, Jesse Carlson, Scott Williamson, Matt Anderson

When contemplating Mexican League statistics, it's important to remember three things: 1) While ostensibly a Triple-A league, the level of competition actually falls between Double-A and High-A; 2) The league, as a whole, is a tremendous hitters league, even more so than the old PCL; 3) There is tremendous variation in altitude between teams, which makes park effects extremely relevant. The first two points make it virtually impossible for hitters to cross the Rio Grande, but the third makes the adjustment for some pitchers surprisingly easy. Soria played in Mexico City, which at 7,300 feet is 2,000 feet higher than Denver. As a result, his translated ERAs are actually *better* than his actual ERAs. He was drafted based on a scouting impression, but his statistical impression is just as good. Having been stealthily scouted and snagged by the Royals in the Rule 5 draft, Soria is slated for middle relief, but could well emerge as a mid-rotation starter in the not-too-distant future.

Tim Stauffer — Bats: R Throws: R — Height: 6' 1" Weight: 205 Born: June 2, 1982 Age: 25

YEAR	TEAM	LVL	AGE	W	L	SV	G	GS	IP	H	BB	SO	HR	GB%	BABIP	STUFF	WHIP	ERA	PERA	EQERA	EQH9	EQBB9	EQSO9	EQHR9	VORP	WXRL
2004	LEL	A+	22	2	0	0	6	6	35¹	28	9	30	0	—	.277	15	1.05	1.78	3.63	3.12	7.5	2.9	4.7	0.3	9.6	—
2004	MOB	AA	22	3	2	0	8	8	51¹	56	13	33	3	—	.327	4	1.35	2.63	4.22	3.91	10.3	2.5	3.7	0.7	9.5	—
2004	POR	AAA	22	6	3	0	14	14	81¹	83	26	50	15	—	.267	-15	1.34	3.54	6.10	5.07	9.1	3.0	4.3	1.8	4.8	—
2005	POR	AAA	23	3	5	0	13	13	75¹	90	17	64	5	45.1%	.362	17	1.42	5.14	3.72	5.66	10.6	1.9	5.8	0.7	-0.5	—
2005	SDN	MLB	23	3	6	0	15	14	81	92	29	49	10	41.4%	.312	-1	1.49	5.33	4.74	5.29	9.8	2.9	5.0	1.1	-0.2	0.66
2006	POR	AAA	24	7	12	0	28	26	153¹	199	52	89	20	43.4%	.349	-18	1.64	5.53	5.58	5.97	10.9	2.9	3.9	1.4	-6.5	—
2007	SDN	MLB	25	5	7	1	38	12	100²	112	37	59	15	45.0%	.296	-8	1.48	5.31	5.76	5.82	10.1	2.9	4.8	1.2	-0.8	0.40

Breakout: 12% Improve: 36% Collapse: 32% Attrition: 0% — Comparables: Tim Drew, Jeff Austin, Mickey Callaway, Luis Delossantos

(continued next page)

Tim Stauffer *(continued)*

It wasn't very long ago that Stauffer was seen as a top prospect, coming out of the University of Richmond to become the fourth-overall pick in the 2003 draft. Unfortunately, he's no longer the guy who used to touch 95 MPH in college, as a bum shoulder has prevented him from getting out of the 80s on more than rare occasions. This sort of fundamental change in self-image can be more than a little difficult for a guy who's still relatively young. Stauffer's going to have to become something more subtle than the big man on campus, and, while that isn't inconceivable, it's also really difficult to achieve.

Brian Sweeney   **Bats: R Throws: R**   Height: 6' 2" Weight: 200 Born: June 13, 1974   Age: 33

YEAR	TEAM	LVL	AGE	W	L	SV	G	GS	IP	H	BB	SO	HR	GB%	BABIP	STUFF	WHIP	ERA	PERA	EQERA	EQH9	EQBB9	EQSO9	EQHR9	VORP	WXRL
2004	POR	AAA	30	11	4	0	24	23	138²	130	42	110	16	—	.272	1	1.24	3.83	4.81	4.46	8.7	3.0	5.2	1.2	17.4	—
2004	SDN	MLB	30	1	0	0	7	2	14¹	20	2	10	1	—	.380	1	1.53	5.66	3.17	5.52	12.3	1.2	5.5	0.6	0.1	-0.04
2005	POR	AAA	31	4	5	0	20	16	110²	121	16	72	15	38.4%	.308	-8	1.24	3.98	4.96	4.54	9.8	1.3	4.1	1.5	13.1	—
2005	DUR	AAA	31	3	4	0	10	10	51	70	20	39	5	39.2%	.392	-6	1.76	4.06	5.01	4.99	11.4	4.0	4.8	1.0	3.5	—
2006	POR	AAA	32	2	1	0	7	5	30	33	7	22	3	44.3%	.323	-4	1.33	4.80	4.64	5.34	9.5	2.1	4.7	1.2	0.9	—
2006	SDN	MLB	32	2	0	2	37	0	56¹	53	16	23	6	41.6%	.255	-14	1.22	3.20	4.56	3.81	8.6	2.2	3.3	1.0	15.2	0.31
2007	*SDN*	*MLB*	*33*	*3*	*4*	*2*	*41*	*3*	*63²*	*71*	*22*	*35*	*9*	*42.0%*	*.292*	*-13*	*1.44*	*4.73*	*5.34*	*5.16*	*10.0*	*2.6*	*4.5*	*1.1*	*4.3*	*0.40*

Breakout: 12% Improve: 28% Collapse: 45% Attrition: 21%   Comparables: *Al Papai, Jerry Reed, John Montague, George Zuverink*

Sweeney was one of the survivors from the slag pits of the Mariners' farm system; unlike the more prized prospects who withered before the whips and cudgels of M's coaching, Sweeney was an undrafted free agent who just kept poking along. Thrown into the 2004 Jeff Cirillo deal, Sweeney spent the first three months of 2006 in the Pads' pen before going back down to gear up for starting, ultimately waiting for an emergency call that never came. He was signed by the Hokkaido Fighters for 2007, so here's to a guy who managed to hang on and cash in somehow.

Mike Thompson   **Bats: R Throws: R**   Height: 6' 4" Weight: 200 Born: November 6, 1980   Age: 26

YEAR	TEAM	LVL	AGE	W	L	SV	G	GS	IP	H	BB	SO	HR	GB%	BABIP	STUFF	WHIP	ERA	PERA	EQERA	EQH9	EQBB9	EQSO9	EQHR9	VORP	WXRL
2004	MOB	AA	23	10	2	0	35	18	121¹	129	31	69	13	—	.304	-26	1.32	3.41	5.85	4.90	10.6	2.6	3.3	1.5	9.2	—
2005	MOB	AA	24	6	6	0	18	18	114²	116	27	68	6	46.8%	.307	0	1.25	3.22	4.67	4.55	8.9	2.3	3.5	0.9	13.4	—
2005	POR	AAA	24	4	2	0	9	9	60	58	13	25	6	49.0%	.268	-4	1.18	3.15	4.66	3.54	8.1	1.9	2.8	1.0	14.0	—
2006	POR	AAA	25	6	1	0	13	13	69	69	20	41	4	46.2%	.300	6	1.29	3.78	4.32	3.80	8.2	2.5	4.1	0.6	14.2	—
2006	SDN	MLB	25	4	5	0	19	16	92	103	30	35	13	50.0%	.288	-17	1.45	4.99	5.35	5.63	10.4	2.6	3.1	1.2	4.5	1.20
2007	*SDN*	*MLB*	*26*	*6*	*8*	*0*	*34*	*19*	*120²*	*132*	*38*	*59*	*16*	*46.0%*	*.286*	*-7*	*1.41*	*4.72*	*5.17*	*5.20*	*9.9*	*2.4*	*3.9*	*1.1*	*7.2*	*1.50*

Breakout: 11% Improve: 32% Collapse: 28% Attrition: 15%   Comparables: *Lerrin Lagrow, Ed Lynch, Bob Shaw, Terry Mulholland*

Although basically an organizational guy, Thompson rose to the occasion when pressed into the rotation at the end of May, logging four quality starts (one subsequently blown) in his first eight, and then three more from the end of July into August. Apparently it wasn't enough to let him call dibs on the fifth starter's slot—there's talk of bringing Park back for another go-round—but he's likely to be in the same role this year, coming up once one of the old timers falls down and can't get up.

Sean Thompson   **Bats: L Throws: L**   Height: 5' 11" Weight: 170 Born: October 13, 1982   Age: 24

YEAR	TEAM	LVL	AGE	W	L	SV	G	GS	IP	H	BB	SO	HR	GB%	BABIP	STUFF	WHIP	ERA	PERA	EQERA	EQH9	EQBB9	EQSO9	EQHR9	VORP	WXRL
2004	FTW	A	21	9	6	0	27	27	148	125	57	157	15	—	.289	-16	1.23	3.10	6.77	4.76	9.1	4.6	5.5	2.1	13.1	—
2005	LEL	A+	22	4	1	0	6	6	33¹	26	13	45	4	38.0%	.293	19	1.17	2.16	5.36	4.18	8.1	4.2	7.8	1.7	5.1	—
2005	MOB	AA	22	4	5	0	20	20	113²	127	55	94	10	47.4%	.357	-6	1.60	4.67	5.55	5.76	10.1	4.3	5.2	1.3	-2.0	—
2006	MOB	AA	23	6	10	0	27	27	154²	148	46	134	18	51.1%	.304	-14	1.26	3.85	5.80	5.32	9.7	2.7	5.4	1.9	4.7	—
2007	*SDN*	*MLB*	*24*	*6*	*8*	*0*	*26*	*19*	*112²*	*116*	*52*	*80*	*18*	*45.0%*	*.286*	*2*	*1.49*	*5.09*	*5.72*	*5.54*	*9.3*	*3.5*	*5.8*	*1.3*	*2.6*	*1.10*

Breakout: 10% Improve: 33% Collapse: 18% Attrition: 1%   Comparables: *Andy Beal, Steve Smyth, Charlie Manning, Lindsay Gulin*

Thompson's a little lefty who's light on his toes and athletic, and armed with a plus curve but a pedestrian heater. That's all pretty straightforward, but Thompson unfortunately seems to harbor hopes of being a power pitcher and gets a bit wound up when occasionally confronted with the more disappointing reality. Can you blame the kid for wanting to be Billy Wagner? Even if letting go of certain dreams is harder for some than others, he's still got good enough command to still fulfill a future at the back end of a rotation, and the stuff to stick in a situational role if all else fails.

San Diego Padres

David Wells

Bats: L **Throws: L** Height: 6' 3" Weight: 250 Born: December 31, 1969 Age: 44

YEAR	TEAM	LVL	AGE	W	L	SV	G	GS	IP	H	BB	SO	HR	GB%	BABIP	STUFF	WHIP	ERA	PERA	EQERA	EQH9	EQBB9	EQSO9	EQHR9	VORP	WXRL
2004	SDN	MLB	41	12	8	0	31	31	195²	203	20	101	23	—	.281	8	1.14	3.73	3.96	4.12	9.0	0.8	4.1	1.0	37.0	5.55
2005	BOS	MLB	42	15	7	0	30	30	184	220	21	107	21	50.3%	.324	14	1.31	4.45	3.86	4.19	9.8	1.0	5.0	0.9	25.1	3.65
2006	BOS	MLB	43	2	3	0	8	8	47	64	8	24	10	48.8%	.333	-5	1.53	4.98	5.02	4.93	10.8	1.5	4.2	1.6	2.0	0.64
2006	SDN	MLB	43	1	2	0	5	5	28¹	33	4	14	1	51.5%	.327	11	1.31	3.50	3.06	3.77	10.7	1.3	4.1	0.3	7.7	1.04
2007	*SDN*	*MLB*	*44*	*8*	*8*	*0*	*29*	*22*	*136²*	*151*	*28*	*79*	*17*	*50.0%*	*.297*	*0*	*1.31*	*4.27*	*4.77*	*4.71*	*10.0*	*1.6*	*4.7*	*1.0*	*16.0*	*2.60*

Breakout: 0% Improve: 34% Collapse: 17% Attrition: 17% Comparables: Gaylord Perry, Warren Spahn, Tommy John, Jamie Moyer

Boomer's hefty lefty-ness and goofball charm no doubt helped him win friends and influence people in ways Denny Neagle probably should have taken notes on. Still, Wells has moved into the purely mercenary phase of a certain kind of veteran's career, in which, with the right enticements, he'll agree to be part of a big-name ensemble cast so that he can still be seen with the right sorts of people. Call it the Shelley Winters career path. Wells insisted he was retiring at the end of the 2006 season, but he's being wooed with an incentive-laden deal to pitch for his hometown Pads in 2007. He seems to be listening, and he probably should. In uniform, he's a quirky celebrity. Out of uniform, he's one of a million unkempt fat guys.

Jared Wells

Bats: R **Throws: R** Height: 6' 4" Weight: 200 Born: October 31, 1981 Age: 25

YEAR	TEAM	LVL	AGE	W	L	SV	G	GS	IP	H	BB	SO	HR	GB%	BABIP	STUFF	WHIP	ERA	PERA	EQERA	EQH9	EQBB9	EQSO9	EQHR9	VORP	WXRL
2004	FTW	A	22	4	6	0	14	14	81¹	91	19	72	6	—	.336	-11	1.35	4.10	5.43	5.67	10.9	2.8	4.2	1.5	-0.6	—
2004	LEL	A+	22	4	6	0	13	12	71²	81	30	38	5	—	.313	-17	1.55	4.52	5.99	6.40	10.1	4.9	2.9	1.2	-6.2	—
2005	LEL	A+	23	11	3	0	19	19	120¹	116	26	80	6	51.2%	.301	8	1.18	3.44	4.38	4.20	8.3	2.3	3.5	0.7	19.0	—
2005	MOB	AA	23	2	5	0	7	7	43	51	16	22	3	45.0%	.340	-13	1.56	4.40	5.23	5.77	10.1	3.5	3.1	1.0	-0.8	—
2006	MOB	AA	24	4	3	0	12	12	61	53	27	49	4	48.1%	.283	-2	1.31	2.66	5.63	3.79	8.8	4.2	4.9	1.1	11.9	—
2006	POR	AAA	24	2	9	0	15	15	73	87	46	55	8	46.5%	.342	-10	1.82	7.27	6.04	8.04	10.2	5.4	5.2	1.2	-20.3	—
2007	*SDN*	*MLB*	*25*	*5*	*7*	*0*	*25*	*16*	*98¹*	*105*	*48*	*59*	*14*	*46.0%*	*.288*	*-6*	*1.55*	*5.40*	*5.92*	*5.92*	*9.7*	*3.8*	*4.9*	*1.2*	*-2.0*	*0.50*

Breakout: 10% Improve: 39% Collapse: 25% Attrition: 1% Comparables: Steve Watkins, Willie Eyre, Brian Slocum, Josh Karp

A big, rangy former football player, Wells is a good example of why a speed gun reading alone shouldn't automatically earn one a "power pitcher" label. He can dial it up into the mid-90s, but his fastball comes in straight and he makes mistakes with it high; the most you can say for his secondary pitches is that they exist. The flip thing to suggest would be that he should learn a splitter and have a career, but he doesn't throw as hard as guys such as Mike Scott or Dave Stewart—they were good enough to make it first, and then adapt to the majors with a new weapon. Wells isn't so good that he's an automatic bet to make it past the PCL.

Woody Williams

Bats: R **Throws: R** Height: 6' 0" Weight: 200 Born: December 31, 1969 Age: 40

YEAR	TEAM	LVL	AGE	W	L	SV	G	GS	IP	H	BB	SO	HR	GB%	BABIP	STUFF	WHIP	ERA	PERA	EQERA	EQH9	EQBB9	EQSO9	EQHR9	VORP	WXRL
2004	SLN	MLB	37	11	8	0	31	31	189²	193	58	131	20	—	.296	13	1.32	4.18	4.18	4.74	9.6	2.5	5.6	0.9	26.5	3.96
2005	SDN	MLB	38	9	12	0	28	28	159²	174	51	106	24	35.9%	.299	-2	1.41	4.85	4.86	5.05	9.4	2.6	5.4	1.4	3.1	2.24
2006	SDN	MLB	39	12	5	0	25	24	145¹	152	35	72	21	37.3%	.275	-3	1.29	3.65	4.82	4.38	9.7	1.9	4.1	1.2	27.3	3.59
2007	*HOU*	*MLB*	*40*	*8*	*9*	*0*	*30*	*23*	*142²*	*156*	*43*	*77*	*23*	*41.0%*	*.281*	*-6*	*1.39*	*4.87*	*5.14*	*5.07*	*9.4*	*2.4*	*4.4*	*1.3*	*11.0*	*2.20*

Breakout: 3% Improve: 32% Collapse: 33% Attrition: 28% Comparables: Tom Candiotti, Danny Darwin, Joe Niekro, Don Sutton

Williams is not a good choice for the front half of a rotation—he's fragile, and he needs a big park and/or a great lineup to succeed. Signed to a two-year, $12.5-million deal by the Astros, he's a fly ball pitcher going to the Non-Carbonated Fruit Beverage House of Pain for Pitchers, and, outside of PETCO, hitters pasted him at a .295/.341/.476 clip. Still, he wanted to pitch at home, and, let's face it, the guy's a former 28th-round pick who didn't become a rotation regular until he was 30, he's 40 now, and he has 120 career wins—it isn't like he just threw away his shot at the Hall of Fame by heading to Texas. What he might cost the Astros is a different story.

Chris Young   Bats: R Throws: R   Height: 6' 10" Weight: 260 Born: May 25, 1979   Age: 28

YEAR	TEAM	LVL	AGE	W	L	SV	G	GS	IP	H	BB	SO	HR	GB%	BABIP	STUFF	WHIP	ERA	PERA	EQERA	EQH9	EQBB9	EQSO9	EQHR9	VORP	WXRL
2004	FRI	AA	25	6	5	0	18	18	88¹	94	31	75	9	—	.315	-23	1.42	4.48	6.20	6.45	11.2	4.1	4.9	1.7	-7.9	—
2004	OKL	AAA	25	3	0	0	5	5	30¹	20	9	34	2	—	.254	30	0.96	1.49	3.30	2.37	5.9	2.7	7.7	0.6	10.9	—
2004	TEX	MLB	25	3	2	0	7	7	36¹	36	10	27	7	—	.264	9	1.27	4.71	4.88	4.30	8.4	2.2	6.2	1.4	5.6	0.59
2005	TEX	MLB	26	12	7	0	31	31	164²	162	45	137	19	34.3%	.294	22	1.26	4.26	3.86	4.03	8.0	2.4	7.1	0.9	24.1	3.57
2006	SDN	MLB	27	11	5	0	31	31	179¹	134	69	164	28	26.8%	.232	16	1.13	3.46	4.54	3.65	7.1	3.0	7.6	1.3	45.8	6.50
2007	SDN	MLB	28	11	9	0	29	28	176	154	65	157	24	34.0%	.265	20	1.24	4.00	4.33	4.33	7.9	2.9	7.3	1.2	28.5	4.20

Breakout: 0%   Improve: 27%   Collapse: 17%   Attrition: 2%   Comparables: Dennis Rasmussen, Ed Halicki, Blake Stein, Rick Sutcliffe

Peavy might be the more famous name at the moment, but it's Young who's developing into the staff's best starter. That said, even with the advantage in leverage granted by his height boosted even further by an over-the-top delivery and a power assortment, he's a pretty extreme fly-ball pitcher, so he'd be hard-pressed to blossom anywhere else as fully as he has in San Diego. Back trouble nipped into the tail end of his season, and he allowed 12 homers in his last 69⅔ innings. When you're as tall as Young, that's no small thing. If he can't bring his pitches down, he'll have to live dangerously in the high end of the strike zone, but if he's healthy, the home run rate will come down as he'll be able to work in the lower half of the zone. If he does that, we've got a right-handed answer to Randy Johnson, albeit with Nolan Ryan's indifference to baserunners (thieves stole 41 bases against four times caught last year).

Lineouts

PLAYER	TEAM	LVL	AGE	PA	R	2B	3B	HR	RBI	BB	SO	SB-CS	SPEED	AVG/OBP/SLG	MLVr	EqAVG/EqOBP/EqSLG	EqA	VORP
INF M. Alexander	POR	AAA	35	472	78	21	0	7	37	35	58	14-4	5.9	.265/.323/.363	-.087	.214/.258/.273	.195	-27.8
	SDN	MLB	35	39	2	1	1	0	4	2	5	0-1	5.9	.176/.216/.265	-.489	.171/.211/.257	.172	-3.9
INF M. Antonelli	EUG	A-	21	245	38	12	1	0	22	46	31	9-1	5.6	.286/.426/.360	.165	.243/.348/.296	.244	-2.3
1B T. Brown*	LEL	A+	23	532	74	37	1	10	75	79	90	4-1	3.8	.299/.428/.460	.242	.263/.360/.396	.268	7.4
OF K. Burke*	PDR	Rk	18	192	24	3	4	1	15	26	56	1-3	4.1	.209/.313/.294	-.192	.143/.208/.143	.142	-83.1
SS M. Bush	FTW	A	20	78	8	3	0	0	7	6	13	2-1	3.6	.268/.333/.310	-.016	.247/.295/.288	.210	-2.5
3B D. Freese	EUG	A-	23	71	19	8	0	5	26	7	12	0-0	4.5	.379/.465/.776	.813	.312/.366/.594	.310	14.0
	FTW	A	23	230	27	13	3	8	44	21	44	1-1	4.7	.299/.374/.510	.328	.268/.320/.441	.259	9.1
2B B. Hill#	POR	AAA	28	373	55	23	0	4	33	48	67	0-1	3.9	.282/.396/.395	.100	.252/.349/.352	.252	5.4
OF C. Huffman	EUG	A-	21	244	41	17	1	9	40	25	34	2-3	4.5	.343/.439/.576	.489	.301/.365/.505	.294	24.4
OF C. Hunter*	PDR	Rk	18	262	46	13	4	1	44	40	22	17-5	5.7	.371/.467/.484	.420	.309/.370/.399	.275	29.2
LF V. Sinisi*	FRI	AA	24	75	9	2	1	0	9	6	11	2-2	6.0	.309/.373/.368	.021	.286/.342/.343	.244	-0.8
	MOB	AA	24	439	52	33	1	7	48	50	71	7-2	5.0	.269/.349/.417	.114	.260/.329/.420	.261	-0.2

PLAYER	TEAM	LVL	AGE	W	L	SV	IP	H	BB	SO	HR	GB%	BABIP	STUFF	WHIP	ERA	PERA	EqERA	EqH9	EqBB9	EqSO9	EqHR9	VORP
M. Adams	NAS	AAA	27	1	1	2	16	17	8	18	2	—	.357	2	1.56	3.38	5.00	5.06	10.1	4.5	7.9	1.7	1.0
	NOR	AAA	27	0	0	0	14¹	13	7	12	0	—	.317	-6	1.42	5.11	3.93	6.43	8.4	5.1	5.8	0.0	-1.3
	POR	AAA	27	0	2	0	23¹	29	7	15	1	—	.346	-13	1.56	4.29	3.80	5.70	10.3	2.7	4.2	0.4	-0.3
J. Anderson	POR	AAA	27	5	2	4	79	74	29	62	8	—	.289	-11	1.30	3.30	4.96	3.81	8.1	3.2	5.3	1.1	16.0
D. Brazelton	SDN	MLB	26	0	2	0	18	28	9	9	6	—	.344	-47	2.06	12.00	7.34	12.76	13.7	3.9	3.9	2.9	-14.4
	POR	AAA	26	5	7	0	91²	100	25	53	15	—	.293	-23	1.37	4.54	6.07	4.71	9.2	2.4	3.9	1.8	9.3
D. Brocail	SDN	MLB	39	2	2	0	28¹	27	8	19	1	—	.299	1	1.24	4.77	3.12	5.34	8.8	2.2	5.7	0.3	2.7
S. Estes*	SDN	MLB	33	0	1	0	6	5	3	4	0	—	.263	6	1.33	4.50	4.23	4.50	9.0	4.5	6.0	0.0	0.8
N. Jamison	LEL	A+	22	5	6	31	65¹	63	15	62	10	—	.296	-27	1.20	3.32	6.48	4.66	9.8	2.4	5.4	2.4	6.7
C. Ramos*	LEL	A+	22	7	8	0	141²	161	44	70	9	—	.321	-13	1.45	3.70	5.27	5.26	9.9	3.1	2.7	1.0	5.4

If you didn't like **Manny Alexander** juiced, chances are your palate's discriminating enough to not like the dried-out version either. A first-rounder picked out of Wake Forrest last summer, **Matt Antonelli** has a good eye and quick hands; if he pans out, his upside is as a good-hitting second baseman. One of the organization's many independent league finds, **Tim Brown** washed out of the Pirates' organization, but put in a year in the Frontier League that earned his resurrection. He's not a prospect, but he is a survivor. A tools-minded pick in the first round of the 2006 draft, **Kyler Burke** is a Tennessee high schooler long on potential, but with an equally long list of things to work on, such as his approach at the plate and his fielding. After injuries derailed **Matt Bush** in 2006, his outside chance at being the new Royce Clayton got a little more outside; he could always go back to the mound, where he was projected as a second-round talent coming out of high school. The team's eighth-rounder in 2006, University of Alabama star **David Freese** signed quickly and continued to terrorize pitchers wherever he played. Although he's already 24, if he hits his way to Double-A, he might make it. At this late date, **Bobby Hill**'s ship isn't only unlikely to come in, it may never have been launched in the first place. His good deed for 2006 was playing on the US Olympic team. **Chad Huffman** was picked in the second round last summer, after Burke, and is his antithesis: A polished college hitter out of Texas Christian. If more likely than Burke to bop in the minors, he also has less upside. Georgia prep talent **Cedric Hunter** was the club's third-round pick in last year's draft and had one of the best debuts of any 2006 selection. He might not stick in center, though, and, without power, he might wind up lost in the tweener triangle. Acquired in a minor deal with the Rangers a month into the season, **Vince Sinisi**'s power never really showed up, so he has yet to turn into Don Mattingly the way some thought he would coming out of college.

After flitting through three organizations last summer, **Mike Adams** might seem like the ultimate roster hot potato, but anyone with his kind of mid-90s heat will elicit interest. Claimed off of waivers from the Yankees before the season, **Jason Anderson** still throws hard and might yet stick in a bullpen someday. Keats highlighted mystery, uncertainty, and doubt in his "Ode to a Grecian Urn," which might also speak to pondering the tantalizing, unrealized greatness of **Dewon Brazelton**. Not that the D-Rays did him any favors, but, if truth is beauty, and beauty truth, Brazelton's future seems as truly ugly as his past, however many shots he gets. A nice human interest story after fighting his way back after two offseason angioplasties, **Doug Brocail** missed out on his first-ever shot at playoff baseball by severely tearing a hamstring in September. He'll be back in San Diego for his twentieth year as a pro, twenty-second if you count the two years he spent rehabbing his elbow. **Shawn Estes** missed nearly all of the 2006 season with elbow trouble that culminated in Tommy John surgery in June; while he re-signed for 2007, don't expect to see him before August, if then. As a closer at Long Beach State, **Neil Jamison** posted a 0.00 ERA in his last year of college in 2005. How far he goes will depend on his plus slider and his knowing how to pitch; his fastball's marginal. **Cesar Ramos** is a lefty who pitches a lot like Mario (Ramos, not the *Donkey Kong* character). He relies on good location, a decent change, and his defense. He's a hard-worker and an energetic bulldog, but, without a real fastball, he's a longshot.

Manager: Bruce Bochy

Year	Team	W-L	Pythag +/-	Avg PC	100 +P	120 +P	QS	BQS	REL	REL w Zero R	IBB	SUBS	PH	PH Avg	PH HR	SB2	CS2	SB3	CS3	SAC Att	SAC %	POS SAC	Squeeze	Swing	In Play
2004	SDN	87-75	-1	92.4	44	2	75	6	436	271	39	68	249	.203	5	45	20	7	5	71	73.2%	22	0	114	91
2005	SDN	82-80	+6	94.4	59	2	75	7	456	295	45	72	274	.209	4	94	36	4	6	97	74.2%	36	0	141	118
2006	SDN	88-74	+1	95.8	66	5	83	9	475	320	63	82	258	.260	8	111	26	12	4	79	74.7%	19	1	157	114

Twelve years, four division titles, one pennant . . . not too shabby for a guy who got sucked into the job Jim Riggleman didn't want. A manager has a lot of discretion in his bullpen usage and construction, and, while you can wrestle with chicken-egg questions over whether or not being spotted a Trevor Hoffman makes it easy to look brilliant, Bochy has found ways to get good mileage out of all sorts of relief sidekicks. He also has knack for issuing intentional walks. Over the last three years, there have been an increasing number of occasions in which Bochy has held up four fingers. He called for 39 free passes in 2004 (17th among all managers), 45 in 2005 (9th), and 63 in 2006 (6th). Jake Peavy ranked fourth in the league last year with 11 free passes—how many aces get asked to issue *eleven* free passes? Yet there was a method to Bochy's madness; 5 of the 11 intentional walks Peavy handed out brought up the pitcher, and on all 5 occasions the opposition failed to score. Indeed, opponents converted on only 2 of those 11 passes. One was when Peavy intentionally walked Luis Gonzalez to load the bases and get to Conor Jackson; Jackson cleared the bases. The other was when Peavy walked Miguel Cabrera with a man in scoring position to get to Cody Ross with two outs; Ross went yard, but Bochy was clearly putting kids on the spot both times. As much as he may like to take the bat out of the hands of his opposition, he doesn't do it to his own players very often as he's one of the few managers in the NL who understands you shouldn't bunt with your position players—he was 28th in baseball and least-likely of any NL manager to ask a hitter to bunt. Few managers would run a lineup built on patience and speed that way. It would seem he'd be very well-suited to managing a lineup with Barry Bonds in it, assuming they ever finalize the language in Bonds's contract.

San Francisco Giants

Sorry to have to bring this up again, Giant fans, but it really is unavoidable. Your lineup is old. Not "aging," or "experienced," or "proven," or "youth-challenged," or whatever euphemism might be in vogue this week. The Giants lineup is older than the hills, dirt, and Methuselah put together, or at least older than any team of hitters ever assembled.

It isn't just the 2006 Giants that were unusually old; most of the recent history of the Giants franchise is represented on a list of the oldest teams in history (see table 1). The squads from 2002, 2003, and 2005 all make the top ten. Beyond the top ten, the 2004 Giants currently rank 21st on the all-time list of most aged teams weighted by plate appearances; the 2001 group is 25th. As for first place, they hold it by a mile, with a lead to rival Secretariat or Bob Beamon.

Other teams near the top also come in clusters. You can see the 1998–99 Orioles at numbers two and three, but their bookends from 1997 and 2000 both make the top 25 (at numbers 24 and 12, respectively). You can see the Angels of 1982 and 1985; expand the list to 30 teams and you'll also pick up 1983 (30), 1984 (18), and 1986 (19). In other words, fully half of the 30 oldest teams come from three player cores. There are several other pairs of teams in the top 30, including the Tigers of 1944 and 1945, the Yankees of 2004 and 2005, and the Diamondbacks of 2001 and 2002.

That said, it's worth noting how many of these teams come from the last decade. There is no question that baseball players, like the US population, are skewing older. The average plate-appearance-weighted age of the major leagues since 2000 is 29.18, the first time that the average has ever broken the threshold of 29. The average age in the 1990s was 28.67, which was the prevailing record at the time. The trend has multiple sources:

Health: Modern medicine is able to return players to the field who would have been forced into retirement in years past. Tommy John surgery is the best-known single example, but practically any of today's medical procedures is simpler, safer, and more likely to fix the problem than anything that went before.

Maintenance/Prevention: Aside from being better able to fix problems, knowledge of how to prevent problems is far more expansive and more frequently applied. Nutrition, year-round training regimens, and the widespread availability of training equipment have made it possible to get players into top condition and keep them there.

Money: The salary difference between the major and minor leagues (or retail sales) is larger than it has ever been before. That lends unprecedented incentive to the competition for jobs, which, in turn, drives the perseverance in training. It also means that, regardless of how much today's players might have in the bank, the financial hit of not squeezing every available pitch or at-bat from ones body is technically greater than ever before. Also, one shouldn't ignore the manner in which the change in salary over the length of a major league career shapes player's perceptions. Mike Stanton, for example, earned $1 million last year and $4 million in 2005. When he debuted in the majors in August 1989, the highest salary in baseball belonged to Orel Hershiser, whose three-year, $7.9-million deal worked out to a little over $2.6 million per year. An even dozen Giants earned that much last year. That $4 million is a lot more money from Stanton's perspective than it is to, say, Pedro Feliz, who will make $5.1 million this year

---

GIANTS PROSPECTUS

2006 record: 76–85; Third place, NL West

Pythagenport record: 76–86

Runs scored per game: 4.63 (9th in NL)

Runs allowed per game: 4.91 (9th in NL)

Team EqA: .254 (13th in NL)

2006 Batters Age: 34.5 (Oldest in NL)

2006 Pitchers Age: 29.0 (6th youngest in NL)

Ballpark: AT&T Park; Neutral park; Park Factor of 1.002

2006: The AARP Gang: A bad, boring, old team with the ballpark and the swirl of controversy as the draws.

2007: A lot like last year, but with some dispiriting finales from a team with no shortage of elder statesmen and mid-career nonentities.

Table 1. The New Senior League—Average Age of Team Roster, Weighted by Plate Appearances

1	2006 San Francisco NL	34.53
2	1998 Baltimore AL	33.32
3	1999 Baltimore AL	32.56
4	1982 California AL	32.46
5	1985 California AL	32.44
6	2005 San Francisco NL	32.43
7	1945 Detroit AL	32.42
8	2002 San Francisco NL	32.30
9	2003 San Francisco NL	32.30
10	2005 New York AL	32.24

and made his major league debut just months before Alex Rodriguez signed with the Rangers for a quarter of a billion dollars.

Game Style: The modern game emphasizes power over speed. There is a distinct correlation between the relative value of the running game and age. Speed is a young player skill, power hitting is an old player skill. During periods in which stolen base totals climbed—the 1910s, 1960s, and 1970s—average ages dropped into the 27s. Reduce that emphasis, let power take over, and ages go up.

That's only the short list. There's also a demographic component, as the American population cycles through the coming of age of the Baby Boomers, then the Baby Busters, then the children of the Baby Boomers. There's the possibility—which does not show up in the statistics, although the error bars on such studies are wide enough that you cannot rule it out conclusively—that because of football, basketball, video games, or the general decline of Western Civilization, the players coming up now aren't as good as the 23-year-olds of the past, and aren't able to push their elders. While not numerous, Japanese imports are almost always older than the players who might otherwise have had their roster spot. And maybe the clampdown in security since 9/11 has forced everyone into divulging their real ages, breaking a pattern of age-shaving that had persisted for a hundred years, making this an artifact of record-keeping instead of actual aging.

Whatever the cause of the overall aging trend, Brian Sabean has led the Giants to the pinnacle of this self-defeating mountain. Make no mistake, the decisions of the Giant front office brought the team here as surely as if going grey was their ultimate goal. The farm system has been unable to produce a hitter of any note–Pedro Feliz is an object of almost singular pride–and no one noteworthy is ready to step forward now. It is ironic that the Giants

should have won the bidding on one Angel Villalona, a Dominican man-child who's been hitting 400-foot home runs with wooden bats for the last three years, giving him a $2.1-million bonus three days after his 16th birthday. It's like one of those supermarket tabloid headlines: 95-YEAR-OLD GREAT-GRANDMOTHER PREGNANT! In the context of the Giants, it's so incongruous that it automatically seems unlikely to work out. Like parenting, raising a ballplayer requires practice, a nurturing instinct, and skill.

Given the moves made this off-season, it does not appear that Sabean considers age to be a significant problem. The roster as currently constructed would seem to have a good chance of breaking last year's mark, as they employ an even older lineup (see table 2). The only spot where the team got younger was center field, but even though the change saves them six years, the 35-year-old Roberts is a long way from draft day. Catcher could go either way; Alfonzo split time with two 35-year-olds last year (Greene and Matheny), and the mix between Molina and the now-28 Alfonzo will determine how the arrow of time pierces the position. In the meantime, the six returning players are all a year older (as are all of their backups, you, the authors of this book, Queen Elizabeth II, and the guy who comes to read your gas meter), and Aurilia and Klesko add an average of seven years to the three-headed monster they and returning head Mark Sweeney replace at first.

Table 2. How Long in the Tooth Can They Get? The Giants Aging Lineup

Pos	2006	2007
C	Eliezer Alfonzo, 27	Bengie Molina, 32
1B	Shea Hillenbrand, 30	Rich Aurilia, 35
	Lance Niekro, 27	Ryan Klesko, 36
	Mark Sweeney, 36	Mark Sweeney, 37
2B	Ray Durham, 34	Ray Durham, 35
SS	Omar Vizquel, 39	Omar Vizquel, 40
3B	Pedro Feliz, 31	Pedro Feliz, 32
LF	Barry Bonds, 41	Barry Bonds, 42
CF	Steve Finley, 41	Dave Roberts, 35
RF	Randy Winn, 32	Randy Winn, 33

Fortunately for the Giants, the pitching staff is in far better shape, not to mention younger. Free agent addition Barry Zito is the nominal ace of the staff, replacing Jason Schmidt (five years Zito's senior), but expectations are that 22-year-old Matt Cain will be the real ace after a dominating second half last season. Matt Morris and Noah Lowry return to man the third and fourth slots, with the fifth is a mystery in mid-January. Jonathan Sanchez, who finished

2006 in the rotation, is perhaps the leading candidate going in to spring training. Brad Hennessey has a shot, as does 2006 first-rounder Tim Lincecum—assuming he isn't pressed into service to shore up a weak bullpen.

The Giants also become younger in the dugout, with 52-year-old Bruce Bochy taking over from 71-year-old Felipe Alou. In doing so, they have removed an obstacle to their future success—Bochy is almost certainly not going to let Cain throw as many pitches as Alou did, and figures to be similarly restrained with Lincecum should the prospect get brought up to The Show as a starter.

The Giants' shot at success this year depends on the old hitters taking their Boniva regularly and not falling apart on them. While Barry Bonds remains a force in the lineup—health and the US Justice Department permit-

ting—no one else provides any serious punch. The Giants were tenth in the league in runs scored last year, and there's no reason to believe the 2007 squad will do any better; if they lose Bonds for any reason, or if he finally shows his age at the plate, their offense will be anemic.

Meanwhile, their division rivals have been active. The Dodgers have added Jason Schmidt, Luis Gonzalez, Randy Wolf, and Juan Pierre, the Padres signed Marcus Giles and Greg Maddux, and the Diamondbacks have brought back Randy Johnson and added Doug Davis to complement first full seasons from Stephen Drew, Chris Young, and Carlos Quentin. While stranger things have happened, the Giants' sub-par offense will make a .500 season an accomplishment. A playoff berth would be an unlikely miracle, tantamount to discovering the Fountain of Youth.

HITTERS

Eliezer Alfonzo   C   Bats: R   Throws: R   Height: 6' 0"   Weight: 225   Born: February 7, 1979   Age: 28

YEAR	TEAM	LVL	AGE	PA	R	2B	3B	HR	RBI	BB	SO	SB	CS	SPEED	AVG	OBP	SLG	MLVR	EQAVG	EQOBP	EQSLG	EQA	VORP	DEFENSE	
2005	SJO	A+	26	217	35	16	0	13	45	11	49	1	3	2.4	.357	.410	.638	.466	.298	.329	.463	.267	12.1	47-C	8
2005	NRW	AA	26	189	30	9	0	9	31	8	39	1	0	3.8	.313	.355	.517	.272	.285	.317	.458	.263	9.1	36-C	1
2006	NRW	AA	27	74	8	3	0	0	7	7	16	1	0	5.2	.277	.351	.323	.053	.269	.315	.299	.223	-1.6	15-C	-2
2006	FRE	AAA	27	87	5	0	1	2	6	4	18	0	0	4.6	.189	.282	.297	-.294	.179	.253	.282	.200	-5.7	20-C	-6
2006	SFN	MLB	27	309	27	17	2	12	39	9	74	1	0	3.6	.266	.302	.465	-.002	.267	.301	.472	.260	8.3	79-C	2
2007	SFN	MLB	28	418	42	20	2	13	53	20	98	3	1	4.0	.250	.297	.414	-.135	.248	.294	.419	.241	3.9	99-C	0

Breakout: 21%   Improve: 46%   Collapse: 27%   Attrition: 26%   Comparables: John Bateman, Brian Johnson, Joe Oliver, Nelson Santovenia

Alfonzo was called up in early June to replace the concussed Matheny, and held on to the job until September, when a concussion of his own forced him to the bench. Alfonzo started hitting really well for the first time in his career in 2005, and the Giants were planning on calling him up, but he was suspended for a substance abuse violation in the minors. He almost won the backup job coming out of spring training last year, but lost it to Todd Greene. Job well done, but he figures to regress in 2007.

Moises Alou   OF   Bats: R   Throws: R   Height: 6' 3"   Weight: 225   Born: December 31, 1969   Age: 40

YEAR	TEAM	LVL	AGE	PA	R	2B	3B	HR	RBI	BB	SO	SB	CS	SPEED	AVG	OBP	SLG	MLVR	EQAVG	EQOBP	EQSLG	EQA	VORP	DEFENSE			
2004	CHN	MLB	38	675	106	36	3	39	106	68	80	3	0	4.8	.293	.361	.557	.243	.285	.355	.545	.299	40.2	146-LF	-4		
2005	SFN	MLB	39	490	67	21	3	19	63	56	43	5	1	4.9	.321	.400	.518	.303	.320	.400	.527	.315	41.9	65-LF	-4	46-RF	-1
2006	SFN	MLB	40	378	52	25	1	22	74	28	31	2	1	4.1	.301	.352	.571	.257	.300	.354	.574	.304	27.9	73-RF	-3		
2007	NYN	MLB	40	328	46	17	1	13	48	31	32	3	1	4.1	.287	.355	.484	.089	.291	.358	.499	.289	17.0	79-RF	-3		

Breakout: 5%   Improve: 29%   Collapse: 47%   Attrition: 27%   Comparables: Dave Winfield, Hank Aaron, Harold Baines, Lou Piniella

The 40-year-old Alou is still a dangerous hitter, especially against southpaws. Last year, the Mets were vulnerable to lefties being brought in to face Beltran and Delgado, each of whom lost about 220 points of OPS against them. Adding a lefty-killer to slot between them was just what they needed. They signed Alou to a one-year-plus-team-option deal. As bad as Alou is with the glove at this point, he's replacing Cliff Floyd, so the Mets won't be taking a defensive hit.

Barry Bonds
LF   **Bats: L**   **Throws: L**   Height: 6' 2"   Weight: 230   Born: December 31, 1969   Age: 42

YEAR	TEAM	LVL	AGE	PA	R	2B	3B	HR	RBI	BB	SO	SB	CS	SPEED	AVG	OBP	SLG	MLVR	EQAVG	EQOBP	EQSLG	EQA	VORP	DEFENSE	
2004	SFN	MLB	39	617	129	27	3	45	101	232	41	6	1	5.2	.362	.609	.812	.929	.356	.605	.799	.456	132.0	117-LF	4
2005	SFN	MLB	40	52	8	1	0	5	10	9	6	0	0	2.5	.286	.404	.667	.468	.286	.404	.667	.341	6.4	11-LF	-1
2006	SFN	MLB	41	493	74	23	0	26	77	115	51	3	0	3.8	.270	.454	.545	.352	.268	.454	.541	.340	46.6	99-LF	-6
2007	SFN	MLB	42	585	104	25	1	29	95	129	77	8	1	4.0	.254	.431	.515	.226	.252	.428	.521	.326	41.1	137-LF	-9

Breakout: 2%   Improve: 2%   Collapse: 72%   Attrition: 17%   Comparables: Stan Musial, Carlton Fisk, Dave Winfield, Willie McCovey

Twenty-one more home runs will give him 755, and 22 will make him the all-time home run leader. He played the entire 2006 season with bone chips in his elbow that had him swinging one-handed at times; those were taken out after the season ended. The balky knee that cost him almost all of 2005 was still a problem, costing him a game here and five there throughout the season, although he did avoid the DL. The knee is still a risk going forward, as are his legal issues, with the government pursuing a perjury charge for testifying that he never knowingly took steroids; some elements of that case could conceivably wind up before the Supreme Court. As we were going to press, it was alleged that Bonds had failed an amphetamine test last season. While failing one test doesn't trigger a suspension (if he did indeed fail it) it does cast further doubt upon Bonds's protestations of innocence in other, more sinister, areas.

Emmanuel Burriss
SS   **Bats: S**   **Throws: R**   Height: 6' 0"   Weight: 170   Born: January 17, 1985   Age: 21

YEAR	TEAM	LVL	AGE	PA	R	2B	3B	HR	RBI	BB	SO	SB	CS	SPEED	AVG	OBP	SLG	MLVR	EQAVG	EQOBP	EQSLG	EQA	VORP	DEFENSE	
2006	SLO	A-	21	293	50	8	2	1	27	27	22	35	11	7.8	.307	.384	.366	.152	.273	.325	.318	.238	0.6	59-SS	0

A supplemental first-round pick from Kent State, Burriss is a leadoff hitter all the way. He has no power at all and isn't expected to develop any, but, unlike a lot of similarly-skilled players, he knows it and doesn't swing for the fences. He's a contact hitter who will take a single or a walk and then use his speed to get to second—his 35 steals led the league by 13. No one doubts that he has the range to play shortstop. The questions all have to do with strength-whether he'll ever be strong enough to keep the bat from being knocked out of his hands or to make throws from the hole.

Benjamin Copeland
OF   **Bats: L**   **Throws: L**   Height: 6' 1"   Weight: 195   Born: December 17, 1983   Age: 23

YEAR	TEAM	LVL	AGE	PA	R	2B	3B	HR	RBI	BB	SO	SB	CS	SPEED	AVG	OBP	SLG	MLVR	EQAVG	EQOBP	EQSLG	EQA	VORP	DEFENSE	
2005	SLO	A-	21	133	25	5	4	4	23	11	25	2	1	6.8	.306	.364	.512	.275	.264	.308	.416	.245	-2.8	22-LF	0
2006	AUG	A	22	610	90	29	12	5	71	73	90	30	21	7.0	.281	.368	.410	.173	.261	.324	.372	.244	-13.4	125-LF	-6
2007	SFN	MLB	23	532	69	29	9	6	46	42	91	13	9	6.1	.271	.331	.406	-.070	.269	.329	.410	.252	2.1	125-LF	-3

Breakout: 36%   Improve: 70%   Collapse: 17%   Attrition: 7%   Comparables: Ethan Faggett, Mike Rodriguez, Kory DeHaan, Jason Conti

Copeland was the Giants' top draft pick in 2005, albeit from the fourth round—that's what you get when you sign free agents and don't lose any. He's a polished college outfielder with a line-drive swing and gap power and has adjusted easily to wooden bats. He started 2006 ice-cold and didn't get his batting average above .200 until the first week of May, but hit .298 from then on. He draws walks and steals bases, but that's not something that one expects from a corner outfielder, and Copeland can't play center.

Ray Durham
2B   **Bats: S**   **Throws: R**   Height: 5' 8"   Weight: 190   Born: November 30, 1971   Age: 35

YEAR	TEAM	LVL	AGE	PA	R	2B	3B	HR	RBI	BB	SO	SB	CS	SPEED	AVG	OBP	SLG	MLVR	EQAVG	EQOBP	EQSLG	EQA	VORP	DEFENSE	
2004	SFN	MLB	32	542	95	28	8	17	65	57	60	10	4	6.8	.282	.364	.484	.143	.279	.360	.480	.286	33.9	109-2B	-10
2005	SFN	MLB	33	560	67	33	0	12	62	48	59	6	3	4.3	.290	.356	.429	.086	.289	.357	.434	.275	25.4	128-2B	-14
2006	SFN	MLB	34	555	79	30	7	26	93	51	61	7	2	5.5	.293	.360	.538	.219	.292	.362	.541	.300	47.9	129-2B	-14
2007	SFN	MLB	35	477	74	28	3	16	66	45	56	7	3	5.2	.304	.374	.501	.158	.301	.371	.506	.296	36.9	113-2B	-8

Breakout: 14%   Improve: 47%   Collapse: 16%   Attrition: 12%   Comparables: Roberto Alomar, Bill Mueller, Bret Boone, Craig Biggio

Last year was the first of Durham's career in which his team never tried to bat him leadoff, a long overdue acknowledgement that that his leadoff days are behind him. Durham thrived when initially put in the five-hole in 2005 and, returning to it last year, he was even better, muscling up for a career-best 26 homers. He's a good enough hitter to make his lost range at second affordable as tradeoffs go. PECOTA expects him to lose some playing time to age this year, but otherwise predicts that his Indian summer will last another season.

Jason Ellison OF **Bats: R Throws: R** Height: 5' 10" Weight: 180 Born: April 4, 1978 Age: 29

YEAR	TEAM	LVL	AGE	PA	R	2B	3B	HR	RBI	BB	SO	SB	CS	SPEED	AVG	OBP	SLG	MLVR	EQAVG	EQOBP	EQSLG	EQA	VORP	DEFENSE			
2004	FRE	AAA	26	552	90	32	7	9	40	40	66	27	12	7.1	.315	.368	.459	.095	.283	.331	.396	.253	11.4	114-CF	6		
2005	SFN	MLB	27	386	49	18	2	4	24	24	44	14	6	6.4	.264	.316	.361	-.100	.266	.319	.370	.243	-1.0	66-CF	6	19-RF	0
2006	FRE	AAA	28	211	41	18	2	1	18	14	20	7	4	6.1	.406	.452	.536	.522	.388	.427	.515	.318	24.8	26-RF	3	18-CF	1
2006	SFN	MLB	28	91	14	5	1	2	4	5	14	2	2	6.5	.222	.273	.383	-.202	.232	.289	.390	.230	-3.4	13-LF	-1		
2007	SFN	MLB	29	404	50	22	3	5	36	24	50	10	4	6.0	.280	.329	.391	-.088	.277	.326	.395	.250	3.1	96-CF	3		

Breakout: 5% Improve: 18% Collapse: 40% Attrition: 21% Comparables: Pablo Ozuna, Garey Ingram, Chad Meyers, Dave Gallagher

For the first two months of 2006, Ellison played nearly every day and still had only 25 at bats—such is the life of the man who will one day be remembered as "Barry Bonds's Legs." The Giants eventually decided to let him play full-time in Fresno, and, while he rocked the PCL, there was no indication in September or since that he's being considered for anything other than a reprise of his fifth outfielder role.

Pedro Feliz 3B **Bats: R Throws: R** Height: 6' 1" Weight: 210 Born: April 27, 1977 Age: 32

YEAR	TEAM	LVL	AGE	PA	R	2B	3B	HR	RBI	BB	SO	SB	CS	SPEED	AVG	OBP	SLG	MLVR	EQAVG	EQOBP	EQSLG	EQA	VORP	DEFENSE			
2004	SFN	MLB	27	531	72	33	3	22	84	23	85	5	2	5.1	.276	.305	.485	.040	.273	.303	.484	.263	12.9	62-1B	-2	40-3B	2
2005	SFN	MLB	28	615	69	30	4	20	81	38	102	0	2	4.1	.250	.295	.422	-.056	.247	.296	.428	.246	-1.0	69-LF	-5	66-3B	4
2006	SFN	MLB	29	644	75	35	5	22	98	33	112	1	1	4.4	.244	.281	.428	-.110	.243	.284	.425	.241	-8.2	155-3B	10		
2007	SFN	MLB	32	552	62	29	3	18	75	35	92	2	2	4.4	.261	.311	.440	-.067	.259	.308	.444	.253	8.0	130-3B	0		

Breakout: 24% Improve: 56% Collapse: 20% Attrition: 11% Comparables: Tim Wallach, Charlie Hayes, Chris Sabo, Frank Thomas

Determined to pay more attention to Feliz's power than his total inability to get to first base, the Giants have re-hired him for 2007. No team in baseball got less offense (.234 EqA) from their third basemen last year than the Giants, because no other set of third basemen were within 30 points of the dreadful .277 OBP put up by the Giants contingent. When the worst hitter at a given position files for free agency, you should let him go. By definition, there are better options. That's the 1951 to 1966 Frank Thomas that PECOTA is comparing Feliz to, not the modern day DH; think of him as Frank Thomas the Lesser.

Steve Finley CF **Bats: L Throws: L** Height: 6' 2" Weight: 195 Born: December 31, 1969 Age: 42

YEAR	TEAM	LVL	AGE	PA	R	2B	3B	HR	RBI	BB	SO	SB	CS	SPEED	AVG	OBP	SLG	MLVR	EQAVG	EQOBP	EQSLG	EQA	VORP	DEFENSE	
2004	ARI	MLB	39	456	61	16	1	23	48	40	52	8	4	5.1	.275	.338	.490	.095	.266	.330	.478	.273	20.0	99-CF	-3
2004	LAN	MLB	39	250	31	12	0	13	46	21	30	1	3	3.8	.263	.324	.491	.093	.267	.327	.498	.271	9.1	51-CF	5
2005	ANA	MLB	40	440	41	20	3	12	54	26	71	8	4	5.7	.222	.271	.374	-.194	.228	.289	.396	.238	-8.1	99-CF	-2
2006	SFN	MLB	41	481	66	21	12	6	40	46	55	7	0	7.3	.246	.320	.394	-.084	.245	.322	.395	.253	6.5	110-CF	1
2007	SFN	MLB	42	371	46	16	5	6	40	36	47	9	2	6.3	.243	.320	.371	-.155	.241	.318	.375	.243	0.2	89-CF	-4

Breakout: 12% Improve: 31% Collapse: 34% Attrition: 50% Comparables: Bob Thurman, Rickey Henderson, Enos Slaughter, Dave Philley

Consolation prize: In 2006, Finley became just the second player to hit 12 triples at age 41 or older (Honus Wagner hit 17 in 1915 at the same age), but that came as much from outfielders losing respect for his power and playing him in as it did from his skills. Center field was almost as unproductive for the Giants last year as third base; they were 27th in EqA at the position, and the Marlins were the only NL team that was worse. The Giants went out of their way to re-sign their third baseman; here they went out of their way to buy out Finley's option and send him on his way. It was the right thing to do.

Kevin Frandsen 2B **Bats: R Throws: R** Height: 6' 0" Weight: 175 Born: May 24, 1982 Age: 25

YEAR	TEAM	LVL	AGE	PA	R	2B	3B	HR	RBI	BB	SO	SB	CS	SPEED	AVG	OBP	SLG	MLVR	EQAVG	EQOBP	EQSLG	EQA	VORP	DEFENSE			
2004	SLO	A-	22	112	22	5	0	3	14	9	9	0	1	4.5	.296	.369	.439	.155	.238	.277	.324	.208	-7.1	19-2B	2		
2005	SJO	A+	23	335	57	22	3	2	40	26	22	13	11	6.1	.351	.429	.467	.232	.325	.378	.407	.273	21.3	60-2B	-2	14-SS	0
2005	NRW	AA	23	142	22	8	0	2	20	4	14	7	3	6.6	.287	.336	.395	.055	.273	.312	.386	.246	1.9	26-2B	1		
2005	FRE	AAA	23	98	18	10	1	2	16	2	5	1	1	5.1	.351	.378	.543	.314	.326	.340	.505	.283	8.2	20-2B	1		
2006	FRE	AAA	24	328	46	25	3	3	30	12	30	7	4	5.8	.304	.358	.440	.121	.299	.343	.445	.270	17.6	46-2B	2	12-3B	-2
2006	SFN	MLB	24	102	12	4	0	2	7	3	14	0	1	4.1	.215	.284	.323	-.265	.213	.275	.309	.205	-3.6	19-2B	-3		
2007	SFN	MLB	25	433	52	24	2	6	41	18	39	9	4	5.2	.285	.330	.400	-.069	.283	.328	.405	.252	11.5	103-2B	0		

Breakout: 15% Improve: 38% Collapse: 28% Attrition: 14% Comparables: Jeff Keppinger, Bobby Richardson, Felix Millan, Luis Maza

The good health of Ray Durham and, to a lesser extent, Omar Vizquel made it difficult for Frandsen to break into the Giants lineup for any stretch of time last year, and the broken jaw he suffered from an errant pitch in August didn't help. A native of the Bay Area, Frandsen attended San Jose State, so he's hardly spent any time playing far from home. The team loves his attitude, so he'll probably be given more chances to establish himself than other players of his approximate skills. He hit well in the minors the last two years and in the AFL, making his SF line from last year, assembled from four different stints, the outlier.

Todd Greene   C   **Bats: R**   **Throws: R**   Height: 5' 10"   Weight: 210   Born: May 8, 1971   Age: 36

YEAR	TEAM	LVL	AGE	PA	R	2B	3B	HR	RBI	BB	SO	SB	CS	SPEED	AVG	OBP	SLG	MLVR	EQAVG	EQOBP	EQSLG	EQA	VORP	DEFENSE	
2004	COL	MLB	33	209	23	14	0	10	35	13	38	0	0	2.6	.282	.325	.508	.055	.267	.311	.472	.263	8.8	45-C	-7
2005	COL	MLB	34	134	10	4	0	7	23	7	21	0	0	2.4	.254	.299	.452	-.031	.238	.289	.429	.243	3.5	30-C	-12
2006	SFN	MLB	35	170	16	12	2	2	17	10	45	0	0	5.4	.289	.335	.428	.023	.289	.339	.428	.264	5.5	36-C	-2
2007	SFN	MLB	36	230	24	12	1	7	29	14	52	1	0	4.0	.256	.306	.423	-.103	.254	.303	.428	.247	3.2	57-C	-5

Breakout: 7%   Improve: 32%   Collapse: 31%   Attrition: 60%   Comparables: Kelly Stinnett, Mike Heath, Joe Oliver, Jerry McNertney

If you pick Greene's spots carefully, sending him up against pitchers who will have to come to him with a fastball, he can still be a good hitter. Of course, given his relative noodle of an arm, you also need to schedule him against teams that don't run. There's a reason he's averaged less than 50 games a season, and never played 100.

Shea Hillenbrand   1B   **Bats: R**   **Throws: R**   Height: 6' 1"   Weight: 210   Born: July 27, 1975   Age: 31

YEAR	TEAM	LVL	AGE	PA	R	2B	3B	HR	RBI	BB	SO	SB	CS	SPEED	AVG	OBP	SLG	MLVR	EQAVG	EQOBP	EQSLG	EQA	VORP	DEFENSE			
2004	ARI	MLB	28	604	68	36	3	15	80	24	49	2	0	4.6	.310	.348	.464	.116	.301	.338	.452	.271	24.5	126-1B	-11	13-3B	1
2005	TOR	MLB	29	645	91	36	2	18	82	26	79	5	1	4.8	.291	.343	.449	.070	.291	.349	.462	.278	23.3	66-1B	3	51-3B	0
2006	TOR	MLB	30	319	40	15	1	12	39	14	40	1	2	3.6	.301	.342	.480	.078	.294	.340	.478	.274	11.4	16-1B	-1	14-3B	-3
2006	SFN	MLB	30	247	33	12	0	9	29	7	40	0	0	3.9	.248	.275	.415	-.136	.249	.276	.416	.236	-6.3	51-1B	3		
2007	ANA	MLB	31	517	57	25	1	14	67	23	67	2	1	4.3	.277	.317	.419	-.064	.275	.320	.431	.263	4.5	122-1B	-2		

Breakout: 16%   Improve: 44%   Collapse: 28%   Attrition: 17%   Comparables: Ron Coomer, Lou Piniella, Tommy Davis, Herb Perry

The Giants were desperate for a first baseman in mid-summer, and, lo and behold, a dilly of a fight in Toronto dropped a first baseman in their lap. Unfortunately, whether it was due to the after-effects of his hurt feelings or the gamma rays that bathed everyone who tried to play first for the Giants last year, Hillenbrand stopped hitting when he got to the NL, so they were no better off with him than they had been without him. He decided to return to the AL in the off-season, signing a deal with the Angels, who were just as desperate for a first baseman—the Giants and Angels ranked 29th and 30th in first base EqA last year. Hillenbrand's lack of power and patience make him an impediment to his team if he hits under .300. If you happen to run into him, try to break the news gently; fiercely proud and a bit obtuse, he thinks he's something of a star.

Brian Horwitz   OF   **Bats: R**   **Throws: R**   Height: 6' 1"   Weight: 180   Born: November 7, 1982   Age: 24

YEAR	TEAM	LVL	AGE	PA	R	2B	3B	HR	RBI	BB	SO	SB	CS	SPEED	AVG	OBP	SLG	MLVR	EQAVG	EQOBP	EQSLG	EQA	VORP	DEFENSE	
2004	SLO	A-	21	300	41	24	1	2	44	21	34	3	3	4.2	.347	.407	.466	.294	.283	.314	.360	.236	-12.7	49-RF	-2
2005	AUG	A	22	535	77	38	4	2	88	50	39	6	6	4.2	.349	.415	.460	.326	.312	.357	.403	.267	11.7	114-RF	-13
2006	SJO	A+	23	244	26	11	2	2	31	30	23	0	2	2.7	.324	.414	.425	.275	.313	.381	.401	.276	7.9	37-RF	-5
2006	NRW	AA	23	307	23	9	1	2	29	31	35	3	3	3.4	.286	.365	.349	.116	.299	.365	.365	.261	1.6	42-LF	5
2007	SFN	MLB	24	502	51	27	2	4	46	36	53	2	2	4.3	.277	.334	.374	-.105	.275	.331	.377	.245	-3.0	118-RF	-3

Breakout: 12%   Improve: 37%   Collapse: 43%   Attrition: 4%   Comparables: Robb Quinlan, Curt Fiore, Jose Amado, Travis Chapman

Horwitz wasn't drafted out of college. He doesn't run well thanks to an old knee injury. He doesn't throw well. He doesn't have power. What he does have is an uncanny ability to spray line drives around a park, a skill that's earned him two minor league batting titles. If he keeps hitting for translated .300 averages (his numbers from Norwich, a pitcher's park, just miss at .299/.365/.365), he'll force his way up, regardless of the scouting consensus, and have a career as a fourth outfielder/pinch-hitter.

Travis Ishikawa   1B   Bats: L   Throws: L   Height: 6' 3"   Weight: 210   Born: September 24, 1983   Age: 23

YEAR	TEAM	LVL	AGE	PA	R	2B	3B	HR	RBI	BB	SO	SB	CS	SPEED	AVG	OBP	SLG	MLVR	EQAVG	EQOBP	EQSLG	EQA	VORP	DEFENSE	
2004	HAG	A	20	416	59	19	2	15	54	45	110	10	5	5.0	.257	.357	.447	.105	.231	.303	.378	.239	-11.8	93-1B	-1
2004	SJO	A+	20	68	10	7	0	1	10	10	16	0	0	3.6	.232	.353	.411	.040	.186	.279	.305	.209	-4.9	16-1B	1
2005	SJO	A+	21	516	87	28	7	22	79	70	129	1	4	4.5	.282	.387	.532	.179	.260	.343	.444	.270	11.9	125-1B	11
2006	NRW	AA	22	340	33	13	4	10	42	35	88	0	0	4.4	.232	.316	.403	.070	.244	.318	.426	.257	0.2	79-1B	7
2006	SFN	MLB	22	25	1	3	1	0	4	1	6	0	0	4.5	.292	.320	.500	.095	.292	.320	.500	.273	0.8		
2007	SFN	MLB	23	440	50	22	3	13	53	45	116	2	1	4.4	.249	.330	.423	-.065	.247	.328	.428	.258	1.2	104-1B	5

Breakout: 15%   Improve: 50%   Collapse: 18%   Attrition: 9%   Comparables: Eric Munson, Kevin Burns, Daryl Clark, Nate Dishington

The organization was excited about Ishikawa's 2005 being the start of a breakout, but success was fleeting. Part of the problem was Connecticut's Thomas Dodd Stadium, which was a brutal hitting environment; part was that he failed to hit even .200 against lefties, after hitting .317 off them the prior year. The bigger, perhaps unassailable problem, though, is his swing. It has holes, leading to strikeouts, and has a pronounced uppercut, leading to lots of fly-ball outs since he isn't strong enough to drive pitches over the wall consistently. The combination of a fly-ball swing, warning-track power, and strikeouts is a sure recipe for a low batting average and feelings of inadequacy.

Justin Knoedler   C   Bats: R   Throws: R   Height: 6' 2"   Weight: 210   Born: July 17, 1980   Age: 26

YEAR	TEAM	LVL	AGE	PA	R	2B	3B	HR	RBI	BB	SO	SB	CS	SPEED	AVG	OBP	SLG	MLVR	EQAVG	EQOBP	EQSLG	EQA	VORP	DEFENSE	
2004	NRW	AA	23	454	64	28	3	9	47	32	98	5	3	5.2	.274	.335	.423	.054	.264	.314	.400	.248	8.0	100-C	2
2005	FRE	AAA	24	327	35	19	1	4	32	26	61	5	5	3.8	.272	.345	.387	-.063	.258	.320	.359	.239	1.1	77-C	5
2006	NRW	AA	25	76	7	6	0	1	8	4	24	1	1	4.1	.211	.263	.338	-.113	.208	.260	.319	.202	-4.2	21-C	-4
2006	FRE	AAA	25	261	32	13	4	4	27	22	58	4	0	6.0	.253	.319	.395	-.053	.245	.305	.376	.240	-0.0	63-C	-1
2007	SFN	MLB	26	373	38	19	2	7	37	24	83	4	2	4.7	.241	.298	.368	-.201	.239	.296	.372	.228	-1.9	90-C	0

Breakout: 14%   Improve: 39%   Collapse: 39%   Attrition: 28%   Comparables: A. J. Hinch, Henry Blanco, Blake Barthol, Gerald Laird

Knoedler and Alfonzo shared the catching duties at Fresno last year, and, while Knoedler hit better there, it was Alfonzo who was called up to replace Matheny. Knoedler gets high marks for his arm and game-calling skills—he was actually drafted as a pitcher, so he has some firsthand knowledge of what goes on out there on the mound—but hasn't shown any kind of batting aptitude. Signing Bengie Molina led to Knoedler's being DFAed in January.

Fred Lewis   OF   Bats: L   Throws: R   Height: 6' 2"   Weight: 190   Born: December 9, 1980   Age: 26

YEAR	TEAM	LVL	AGE	PA	R	2B	3B	HR	RBI	BB	SO	SB	CS	SPEED	AVG	OBP	SLG	MLVR	EQAVG	EQOBP	EQSLG	EQA	VORP	DEFENSE			
2004	SJO	A+	23	541	88	20	11	8	57	84	109	33	14	7.3	.301	.424	.451	.280	.281	.372	.398	.273	22.2	113-CF	-8		
2004	FRE	AAA	23	29	3	1	0	1	2	5	5	1	1	3.9	.304	.429	.478	.223	.292	.414	.458	.292	2.2				
2005	NRW	AA	24	594	79	28	7	7	47	69	124	30	13	7.3	.273	.361	.396	.087	.263	.340	.378	.256	9.3	63-CF	-6	62-LF	-3
2006	FRE	AAA	25	517	85	20	11	12	56	68	105	18	8	6.8	.276	.375	.453	.141	.268	.357	.440	.276	11.5	85-LF	0	20-CF	0
2006	SFN	MLB	25	11	5	1	0	0	2	0	3	0	0	5.8	.455	.455	.545	.555	.455	.455	.545	.343	1.6				
2007	SFN	MLB	26	472	66	23	6	8	45	48	101	14	6	6.2	.270	.349	.417	-.025	.268	.346	.421	.266	9.9	112-LF	-2		

Breakout: 14%   Improve: 40%   Collapse: 30%   Attrition: 10%   Comparables: Mark Budzinski, Jeff Duncan, Terrmel Sledge, Rick Miller

A second-round pick in 2002, Lewis is an outstanding athlete whose baseball tools are still trying to catch up to his body. He has good patience and speed, but his batting average and power are a little on the low side. He's fast enough to play center, but doesn't judge the ball well, which limits him to the corners where his offensive deficiencies become less excusable. That certainly sounds like the profile of a fourth outfielder, doesn't it?

Todd Linden   OF   Bats: S   Throws: R   Height: 6' 3"   Weight: 220   Born: June 30, 1980   Age: 27

YEAR	TEAM	LVL	AGE	PA	R	2B	3B	HR	RBI	BB	SO	SB	CS	SPEED	AVG	OBP	SLG	MLVR	EQAVG	EQOBP	EQSLG	EQA	VORP	DEFENSE			
2004	FRE	AAA	24	567	93	28	2	23	75	63	149	8	6	5.2	.260	.349	.466	.017	.238	.320	.407	.251	-6.2	101-RF	-2	14-LF	1
2004	SFN	MLB	24	40	6	1	0	0	1	5	7	0	0	5.8	.156	.289	.188	-.475	.121	.256	.152	.170	-4.0				
2005	FRE	AAA	25	415	81	25	4	30	80	62	97	6	2	5.2	.321	.437	.682	.567	.301	.402	.605	.328	45.5	86-RF	-7		
2005	SFN	MLB	25	187	20	8	0	4	13	10	54	3	0	5.0	.216	.280	.333	-.218	.209	.273	.331	.216	-6.7	36-RF	5		
2006	FRE	AAA	26	221	31	11	3	5	23	29	44	5	0	6.1	.278	.385	.449	.154	.266	.360	.422	.277	4.3	41-RF	4		
2006	SFN	MLB	26	89	15	4	2	2	5	9	20	1	0	5.8	.273	.356	.455	.079	.269	.360	.449	.280	3.4	15-LF	1		
2007	SFN	MLB	27	406	56	22	2	14	51	42	100	6	2	5.1	.266	.352	.462	.037	.264	.349	.467	.278	12.0	97-RF	1		

Breakout: 17%   Improve: 44%   Collapse: 24%   Attrition: 15%   Comparables: Abraham Nunez, Bobby Kielty, Jimmy Hurst, Jon Knott

Linden swapped jobs with Ellison in July, sending Ellison to Fresno while he started baby-sitting Bonds's knees on an everyday basis—"Barry Bonds's *Other* Legs?" The good news is that he did hit a little this time up, although not nearly enough to gainsay everybody who labeled him as a Quadruple-A player. With the Giants looking like they will have Bonds around in 2007, they are going to need one out of the group of Linden, Ellison, or Lewis around to sub on defense, plus another one to be a normal backup outfielder. It's a competition Linden should win.

Eddy Martinez-Esteve LF   Bats: R   Throws: R   Height: 6' 2"   Weight: 215   Born: July 14, 1983   Age: 23

YEAR	TEAM	LVL	AGE	PA	R	2B	3B	HR	RBI	BB	SO	SB	CS	SPEED	AVG	OBP	SLG	MLVR	EQAVG	EQOBP	EQSLG	EQA	VORP	DEFENSE	
2004	SLO	A-	20	42	5	4	0	0	2	6	7	0	0	3.4	.286	.405	.400	.149	.211	.286	.263	.204	-5.4		
2004	HAG	A	20	56	4	1	1	1	11	8	8	1	1	4.2	.217	.339	.348	-.076	.204	.286	.327	.219	-2.8		
2004	SJO	A+	20	74	11	7	2	0	14	4	9	0	1	4.9	.420	.446	.580	.663	.400	.419	.529	.314	10.5		
2005	SJO	A+	21	579	89	44	3	17	94	89	82	4	2	3.7	.313	.427	.524	.269	.287	.379	.451	.289	35.2		
2006	NRW	AA	22	105	8	10	0	2	11	9	14	0	0	3.2	.272	.324	.446	.172	.269	.314	.452	.266	0.7	25-LF	0
2007	*SFN*	*MLB*	*23*	*363*	*42*	*23*	*1*	*10*	*45*	*34*	*54*	*1*	*0*	*4.0*	*.275*	*.346*	*.442*	*.007*	*.273*	*.343*	*.447*	*.270*	*8.4*	*87-LF*	*-1*

Breakout: 9%   Improve: 37%   Collapse: 31%   Attrition: 19%   Comparables: Bob Watson, Michael Aubrey, Conor Jackson, Juan Tejeda

Martinez-Esteve is a terrific hitter, but that's about all you can say for him. He's fragile, averaging a surgery a year (last year it was a torn labrum in his non-throwing shoulder). Hamstring injuries have taken his legs, while shoulder injuries have sapped his arms. Guys who can't run or throw are generally not good fielders; add in that he doesn't seem to care and you have a frightening defensive spectacle. That leads us to his attitude, which has been a turn-off for everyone associated with him in the minors. The Giants almost have to trade him to an AL team, assuming any of them want their DH young, surly, and fragile.

Mike Matheny C   Bats: R   Throws: R   Height: 6' 3"   Weight: 225   Born: September 22, 1970 Age: 36

YEAR	TEAM	LVL	AGE	PA	R	2B	3B	HR	RBI	BB	SO	SB	CS	SPEED	AVG	OBP	SLG	MLVR	EQAVG	EQOBP	EQSLG	EQA	VORP	DEFENSE	
2004	SLN	MLB	33	419	28	22	1	5	50	23	83	0	2	3.2	.247	.292	.348	-.171	.243	.290	.346	.223	-5.5	106-C	13
2005	SFN	MLB	34	485	42	34	0	13	59	29	91	0	2	2.8	.242	.295	.406	-.084	.239	.293	.413	.241	5.7	126-C	5
2006	SFN	MLB	35	177	10	8	0	3	18	9	30	0	0	2.7	.231	.276	.338	-.256	.230	.278	.335	.219	-6.0	44-C	0
2007	*SFN*	*MLB*	*36*	*335*	*26*	*17*	*0*	*7*	*36*	*18*	*56*	*0*	*1*	*3.2*	*.236*	*.282*	*.368*	*-.234*	*.234*	*.280*	*.372*	*.220*	*-4.0*	*81-C*	*2*

Breakout: 16%   Improve: 34%   Collapse: 28%   Attrition: 47%   Comparables: Ray Murray, Bill Haselman, Sandy Alomar, Bob Boone

On May 31, in the second inning of a 6–1 win over the Marlins, Matheny took a foul tip off his face mask. That event, though routine for a catcher, may have ended his career. The dizziness that typically follows a hit like that didn't go away, not the next inning, not the next day, not the next month. That last hit to the head was the proverbial straw breaking the camel's back, not so impressive in itself, but the latest in a cumulative series of blows sustained by one of the toughest backstops in the game. It is hard to imagine him getting clearance to resume play given how long his symptoms persisted.

Michael McBryde CF   Bats: R   Throws: R   Height: 6' 1"   Weight: 170   Born: March 20, 1985   Age: 22

YEAR	TEAM	LVL	AGE	PA	R	2B	3B	HR	RBI	BB	SO	SB	CS	SPEED	AVG	OBP	SLG	MLVR	EQAVG	EQOBP	EQSLG	EQA	VORP	DEFENSE	
2006	SLO	A-	21	255	38	9	5	3	34	22	59	16	4	7.7	.276	.344	.400	.116	.248	.298	.346	.231	-10.1	62-CF	5
2007	*SFN*	*MLB*	*22*	*461*	*51*	*19*	*5*	*5*	*34*	*30*	*107*	*17*	*8*	*6.6*	*.247*	*.301*	*.354*	*-.212*	*.245*	*.298*	*.357*	*.228*	*-6.4*	*109-CF*	*8*

Breakout: 28%   Improve: 53%   Collapse: 24%   Attrition: 14%   Comparables: Todd Donovan, Chris Rahl, Matt Forbes, Billy Brown

McBryde missed all but three games of his last year at college with a hamstring injury, but was able to play in Salem after being drafted. He's a fast runner with outstanding center-field range and a rocket arm—in college he was also his team's closer. McBryde should be a future Gold Glover; he and Burriss were key parts of a Salem-Keizer team that rated +41 in fielding runs, far and away the best per-game rate in professional baseball last season. The question is whether or not he'll hit; he has good bat speed and projectable power, but his approach and swing mechanics are bad.

Lance Niekro　　　　1B　　Bats: R　Throws: R　Height: 6' 3"　Weight: 225　Born: January 29, 1979　Age: 28

YEAR	TEAM	LVL	AGE	PA	R	2B	3B	HR	RBI	BB	SO	SB	CS	SPEED	AVG	OBP	SLG	MLVR	EQAVG	EQOBP	EQSLG	EQA	VORP	DEFENSE	
2004	SJO	A+	25	64	13	7	1	1	14	2	5	0	0	5.5	.311	.328	.508	.220	.258	.277	.387	.228	-2.0	15-1B	0
2004	FRE	AAA	25	258	42	21	4	12	47	14	32	1	1	5.2	.298	.337	.566	.181	.266	.305	.488	.263	5.8	33-1B -2	19-3B 2
2005	SFN	MLB	26	302	32	16	3	12	46	17	53	0	2	3.9	.252	.295	.460	-.002	.250	.295	.467	.255	2.0	59-1B	2
2006	FRE	AAA	27	152	27	7	0	14	34	7	23	0	0	3.7	.319	.349	.660	.448	.297	.322	.607	.300	13.2	34-1B	-5
2006	SFN	MLB	27	210	27	9	2	5	31	11	32	0	0	4.8	.246	.286	.387	-.157	.242	.286	.379	.229	-6.3	49-1B	3
2007	SFN	MLB	28	341	39	19	2	13	49	19	53	1	1	4.4	.267	.311	.461	-.033	.265	.308	.466	.258	4.0	82-1B	1

Breakout: 23%　Improve: 43%　Collapse: 30%　Attrition: 32%　　Comparables: Wes Chamberlain, Butch Huskey, Ricky Jordan, Andy Kosco

Niekro had his chance, breaking spring training with the starting first-base job, but, once again, he flubbed it. He hit marginally well through June, then got sharply worse after coming back from a stint on the DL caused by a groin pull. Demoted, he hit .382 and slugged over .800 in the two weeks after he was sent down, taking out his frustrations on the PCL. His only remaining value is as the poor side of a platoon. PECOTA thinks about statistics rather than history, but it is perhaps not a coincidence that all four of the comparables listed above were at one time thought by to be promising prospects, only to prove those predictions wrong when they reached the majors. That's Niekro's story too.

Dan Ortmeier　　　　OF　　Bats: S　Throws: L　Height: 6' 4"　Weight: 215　Born: May 11, 1981　Age: 26

YEAR	TEAM	LVL	AGE	PA	R	2B	3B	HR	RBI	BB	SO	SB	CS	SPEED	AVG	OBP	SLG	MLVR	EQAVG	EQOBP	EQSLG	EQA	VORP	DEFENSE	
2004	NRW	AA	23	439	55	23	6	10	48	47	110	18	2	7.0	.252	.353	.424	.069	.247	.332	.407	.261	-1.6	98-RF	5
2005	NRW	AA	24	575	85	23	6	20	79	48	115	35	12	7.6	.274	.360	.463	.172	.265	.334	.439	.268	7.8	124-RF	2
2006	NRW	AA	25	189	17	9	1	2	11	17	38	7	4	4.7	.252	.328	.353	.039	.257	.317	.357	.239	-1.2	34-CF	-4
2006	FRE	AAA	25	283	37	14	3	6	33	16	40	8	6	6.4	.244	.293	.389	-.113	.230	.272	.362	.221	-9.0	45-CF -8	16-LF 1
2007	SFN	MLB	26	420	53	23	3	10	44	30	87	13	5	5.8	.263	.324	.419	-.072	.261	.321	.423	.255	4.7	100-CF	-1

Breakout: 28%　Improve: 50%　Collapse: 15%　Attrition: 14%　　Comparables: Fletcher Bates, Brian Simmons, Shawn Garrett, Doug Devore

Hard-nosed and oft-injured, Ortmeier excited the Giants when he hit .274/.360/.463 with 20 home runs and 35 stolen bases at Norwich in 2005. He started 2006 in Fresno but played himself down back to Norwich. His timing couldn't have been worse. Going on 26, he's near the end of the line.

Nate Schierholtz　　　RF　　Bats: L　Throws: R　Height: 6' 2"　Weight: 215　Born: February 15, 1984　Age: 23

YEAR	TEAM	LVL	AGE	PA	R	2B	3B	HR	RBI	BB	SO	SB	CS	SPEED	AVG	OBP	SLG	MLVR	EQAVG	EQOBP	EQSLG	EQA	VORP	DEFENSE	
2004	HAG	A	20	261	41	22	0	15	54	19	52	1	0	3.6	.298	.356	.583	.324	.255	.299	.486	.264	11.6	54-3B	-2
2004	SJO	A+	20	281	39	18	9	3	31	15	41	3	1	6.2	.295	.338	.469	.156	.273	.306	.413	.246	6.1	35-3B 0	15-RF -2
2005	SJO	A+	21	548	83	37	8	15	86	32	132	5	7	5.3	.319	.363	.514	.150	.300	.334	.450	.266	14.1	108-RF	3
2006	NRW	AA	22	510	55	25	7	14	54	27	81	8	3	5.3	.270	.325	.443	.169	.285	.331	.472	.271	15.8	112-RF	-13
2007	SFN	MLB	23	518	63	31	4	14	66	29	99	5	2	5.0	.281	.326	.451	-.009	.278	.324	.456	.262	9.0	122-RF	-1

Breakout: 12%　Improve: 45%　Collapse: 24%　Attrition: 3%　　Comparables: Cody Haerther, Alex Fernandez, Jeff Key, Aaron Rowand

Schierholtz has a ton of power, but he hasn't been able to show it off in games. The Giants worked hard on getting him to shorten his ridiculously long swing. It took him a while to settle in with the changes, hitting just .223/.281/.350 through the end of June; then he got hot, going on a 25-game hitting streak and hitting 8 of his 14 homers in the last month of the season. Drafted as a third baseman, he looks bad in the outfield despite a good arm and decent speed.

Sharlon Schoop　　　SS　　Bats: R　Throws: R　Height: 6' 0"　Weight: 160　Born: April 15, 1987　Age: 20

YEAR	TEAM	LVL	AGE	PA	R	2B	3B	HR	RBI	BB	SO	SB	CS	SPEED	AVG	OBP	SLG	MLVR	EQAVG	EQOBP	EQSLG	EQA	VORP	DEFENSE	
2006	GIA	Rk	19	160	29	7	1	1	21	26	15	8	3	5.0	.310	.437	.405	.214	.250	.329	.314	.236	-0.7	27-SS	3
2007	SFN	MLB	20	390	37	15	1	2	26	33	38	5	3	5.0	.238	.308	.301	-.274	.236	.306	.304	.214	-6.4	93-SS	11

Breakout: 21%　Improve: 47%　Collapse: 40%　Attrition: 24%　　Comparables: Luis Dominguez, Jose Martinez, Justin Sellers, Michael Sandoval

If baseball had offensive and defensive teams like the NFL, then this 18-year-old kid from Curacao might already be playing shortstop in the majors. Since the Players Association hasn't yet won the battle for 50-man rosters, he'll have to learn to hit along the way. Thus far he's shown good bat control and contact skills. Whether he ever develops power or not is only relevant to whether he becomes a star—he could hit like Rey Ordoñez and reach the majors with his glove. He's only 20 years old, so it's going to be awhile before any of his talents are set in stone; his hitting could prove to be better than Ordonez's, his fielding could be worse. What we know for certain is that the ability to be that kind of defender is there. His nickname should be "Chicken."

Mark Sweeney | PH | **Bats: L** | **Throws: L** | Height: 6' 1" | Weight: 215 | Born: December 31, 1969 | Age: 37

YEAR	TEAM	LVL	AGE	PA	R	2B	3B	HR	RBI	BB	SO	SB	CS	SPEED	AVG	OBP	SLG	MLVR	EQAVG	EQOBP	EQSLG	EQA	VORP	DEFENSE				
2004	COL	MLB	34	215	25	12	2	9	40	32	51	1	0	4.9	.266	.377	.508	.136	.249	.361	.486	.291	10.8	15-RF	2	11-1B	-1
2005	SDN	MLB	35	267	31	12	1	8	40	40	58	4	0	4.8	.294	.395	.466	.231	.309	.408	.495	.315	19.3	38-1B	-2		
2006	SFN	MLB	36	291	32	15	2	5	37	28	50	0	1	4.3	.251	.330	.382	-.077	.252	.331	.391	.251	-2.9	45-1B	3	13-LF	-2
2007	*SFN*	*MLB*	*37*	*259*	*33*	*13*	*1*	*6*	*31*	*28*	*48*	*2*	*1*	*4.5*	*.267*	*.352*	*.419*	*-.018*	*.265*	*.349*	*.424*	*.267*	*5.0*				

Breakout: 9% Improve: 30% Collapse: 38% Attrition: 45%   *Comparables: Dale Long, Chris Chambliss, David Segui, Richie Hebner*

Sweeney is a player who needs to be kept in a strict platoon role; letting him bat at a disadvantage even 14 percent of the time, as he did last year, is a mistake. That was easy to do all the years he spent as a pinch-hitter, but the Giants expect him to play semi-regularly at first base or left field, where it's harder to manage. The decisions to sign Klesko and Aurilia should force him back into a reserve role.

Omar Vizquel | SS | **Bats: S** | **Throws: R** | Height: 5' 9" | Weight: 175 | Born: December 31, 1969 | Age: 40

YEAR	TEAM	LVL	AGE	PA	R	2B	3B	HR	RBI	BB	SO	SB	CS	SPEED	AVG	OBP	SLG	MLVR	EQAVG	EQOBP	EQSLG	EQA	VORP	DEFENSE	
2004	CLE	MLB	37	651	82	28	3	7	59	57	62	19	6	6.2	.291	.353	.388	-.025	.298	.365	.401	.273	26.3	131-SS	8
2005	SFN	MLB	38	651	66	28	4	3	45	56	58	24	10	6.2	.271	.341	.350	-.075	.273	.345	.358	.251	12.3	145-SS	12
2006	SFN	MLB	39	659	88	22	10	4	58	56	51	24	7	6.6	.295	.361	.389	.016	.297	.364	.393	.270	28.0	145-SS	0
2007	*SFN*	*MLB*	*40*	*578*	*81*	*25*	*7*	*6*	*46*	*52*	*50*	*16*	*8*	*6.1*	*.284*	*.353*	*.396*	*-.035*	*.282*	*.350*	*.400*	*.262*	*19.7*	*135-SS*	*1*

Breakout: 18% Improve: 45% Collapse: 35% Attrition: 28%   *Comparables: Maury Wills, Ozzie Smith, Barry Larkin, Otis Nixon*

Last year, at age 39, Vizquel hit 10 triples for the first time in his career, tying Joe Start for the record of oldest player to hit 10 or more triples in a season. Don't remember Joe Start? He was the first baseman for the Providence Grays in 1882. Vizquel also stole 24 bases for the second year in a row, hit for the third-highest average of his career, and picked up his eleventh Gold Glove, the kind of accomplishments you might expect from someone who's 29, not 39. People started mentioning Vizquel for the Hall of Fame a few years ago based on a perceived similarity to Ozzie Smith with both the bat and the glove. That's a flawed argument given that Smith's career took place in a much more difficult offensive environment than has Vizquel's. Still, as Vizquel continues to play surprisingly well at an advanced age, however, his case takes on greater merit. Smith's translated rates are .277/.355/.365, with an EqA of .263; Vizquel's are .281/.349/.373 with an EqA of .258. Of course, that's only half the battle. Vizquel, while good, has never been Smith's equal in the field—no one has.

Randy Winn | OF | **Bats: S** | **Throws: R** | Height: 6' 2" | Weight: 195 | Born: June 9, 1974 | Age: 33

YEAR	TEAM	LVL	AGE	PA	R	2B	3B	HR	RBI	BB	SO	SB	CS	SPEED	AVG	OBP	SLG	MLVR	EQAVG	EQOBP	EQSLG	EQA	VORP	DEFENSE				
2004	SEA	MLB	30	703	84	34	6	14	81	53	98	21	7	6.3	.286	.346	.427	.035	.295	.357	.445	.279	25.0	120-CF	0	35-LF	-1
2005	SFN	MLB	31	247	39	22	5	14	26	11	38	7	5	6.7	.359	.391	.680	.559	.358	.392	.694	.335	37.7	55-CF	8		
2005	SEA	MLB	31	436	46	25	1	6	37	37	53	12	6	5.6	.275	.342	.391	-.007	.289	.364	.421	.273	7.0	90-LF	5		
2006	SFN	MLB	32	635	82	34	5	11	56	48	63	10	8	5.4	.262	.324	.396	-.062	.264	.327	.398	.250	0.8	74-RF	9	50-CF	3
2007	*SFN*	*MLB*	*33*	*583*	*82*	*33*	*5*	*11*	*62*	*43*	*69*	*12*	*6*	*5.9*	*.297*	*.353*	*.443*	*.038*	*.294*	*.350*	*.447*	*.273*	*19.4*	*137-CF*	*4*		

Breakout: 11% Improve: 42% Collapse: 22% Attrition: 7%   *Comparables: Stan Javier, Devon White, Jerry Mumphrey, Ken Griffey*

The acquisition of Dave Roberts will give Winn the chance to move over to right field and stay there, rather than shifting back and forth trying to cover for Finley and Alou. Winn repaid the three-year, $23-million extension he received last spring by disappearing for the last three months of the year, hitting just .246 with no power after July 1. He fouled a ball off his knee in May, which apparently led to bruising and stiffness that never really healed during the season, but the timing of that injury makes attributing his second half swoon to it look like wishful thinking on the part of the Giants.

PITCHERS

Brian Anderson　　　　**Bats: R Throws: R**　　　Height: 6′ 3″　Weight: 210　Born: May 25, 1983　　Age: 24

YEAR	TEAM	LVL	AGE	W	L	SV	G	GS	IP	H	BB	SO	HR	GB%	BABIP	STUFF	WHIP	ERA	PERA	EQERA	EQH9	EQBB9	EQSO9	EQHR9	VORP	WXRL
2005	SLO	A-	22	3	1	19	27	0	27²	16	3	42	2	43.1%	.255	2	0.69	1.95	5.08	3.55	8.5	1.4	6.8	1.8	5.8	—
2006	SJO	A+	23	1	1	37	54	0	67	44	17	85	5	42.0%	.270	2	0.91	1.88	4.55	2.81	7.5	2.8	7.0	1.3	19.8	—
2007	SFN	MLB	24	3	4	2	27	5	60²	61	21	49	11	39.0%	.282	4	1.35	4.20	4.96	4.37	8.5	2.8	6.3	1.3	8.7	1.10

Breakout: 2%　Improve: 9%　Collapse: 76%　Attrition: 14%　Comparables: Pat Neshek, Doug Sessions, John Birtwell, Jared Blasdell

One of the problems with pitching translations is that the stats only show us that a pitcher is overwhelming the competition; it doesn't show how. Anderson—who is neither the former fourth starter for the 2001 World Champion Diamondbacks, nor the White Sox's current center fielder—is a college pitcher with a fringy fastball that usually doesn't break 90 MPH, a sharp slider, and great control. He knows more than the hitters he's facing about setting them up and finishing them off. He's dominated so far in his pro career with a 127:20 strikeout-to-walk ratio, a 1.90 ERA, and a California League-record 37 saves. The question remains, without dominant stuff, how is he going to stay ahead of the hitters as they get smarter?

Armando Benitez　　　　**Bats: R Throws: R**　　　Height: 6′ 4″　Weight: 260　Born: November 3, 1972　Age: 34

YEAR	TEAM	LVL	AGE	W	L	SV	G	GS	IP	H	BB	SO	HR	GB%	BABIP	STUFF	WHIP	ERA	PERA	EQERA	EQH9	EQBB9	EQSO9	EQHR9	VORP	WXRL
2004	FLO	MLB	31	2	2	47	64	0	69²	36	21	62	6	—	.178	21	0.82	1.29	3.44	1.67	4.8	2.4	7.2	0.8	32.8	6.19
2005	SFN	MLB	32	2	3	19	30	0	30	25	16	23	5	32.6%	.247	-8	1.37	4.50	5.43	4.99	7.3	4.4	6.2	1.5	1.5	0.66
2006	SFN	MLB	33	4	2	17	41	0	38¹	39	21	31	6	33.0%	.303	-3	1.57	3.52	4.94	3.20	8.9	4.3	6.6	1.1	10.7	0.03
2007	SFN	MLB	34	2	3	12	30	0	35²	32	15	28	5	34.0%	.262	-4	1.32	4.05	4.41	4.25	7.5	3.4	6.2	1.0	6.0	0.80

Breakout: 4%　Improve: 9%　Collapse: 60%　Attrition: 23%　Comparables: Don Larsen, Tim Stoddard, Dick Tidrow, Tim Worrell

You could say that one off year was bad luck, but, after two years, it's fair to conclude that Benitez's was a bad contract. After missing most of 2005 with a hamstring injury, Benitez fought arthritic knees throughout the 2006 season. Those knees kept him from pitching effectively, and they aren't likely to heal. His ERA may have improved over 2005, but his pitching didn't thanks to too many walks, too few strikeouts, and eight blown saves in 25 opportunities. He thinks a trade to a warmer clime, such as Miami, would help, although the evidence shows that he actually pitched better at home each of the last two years.

Matt Cain　　　　**Bats: R Throws: R**　　　Height: 6′ 3″　Weight: 235　Born: October 1, 1984　Age: 22

YEAR	TEAM	LVL	AGE	W	L	SV	G	GS	IP	H	BB	SO	HR	GB%	BABIP	STUFF	WHIP	ERA	PERA	EQERA	EQH9	EQBB9	EQSO9	EQHR9	VORP	WXRL
2004	SJO	A+	19	7	1	0	13	13	72²	58	17	89	5	—	.301	30	1.03	1.86	4.34	3.99	8.5	2.7	7.2	1.2	12.5	—
2004	NRW	AA	19	6	4	0	15	15	86	73	40	72	7	—	.264	13	1.31	3.35	5.09	5.34	8.4	4.5	5.5	1.0	2.4	—
2005	FRE	AAA	20	10	5	0	26	26	145²	118	73	176	22	32.7%	.280	19	1.31	4.39	5.16	4.66	7.8	4.3	8.3	1.5	15.1	—
2005	SFN	MLB	20	2	1	0	7	7	46¹	24	19	30	4	28.7%	.160	23	0.93	2.33	4.33	2.49	4.6	3.3	5.4	0.8	17.0	2.11
2006	SFN	MLB	21	13	12	0	32	31	190²	157	87	179	18	37.8%	.272	33	1.28	4.15	3.86	3.99	7.5	3.6	7.7	0.7	34.9	4.76
2007	SFN	MLB	22	10	10	0	28	28	176²	158	75	167	20	39.0%	.283	24	1.32	4.18	4.36	4.44	7.5	3.4	7.5	0.9	26.9	4.00

Breakout: 12%　Improve: 33%　Collapse: 23%　Attrition: 1%　Comparables: John Smoltz, Jim Maloney, Pete Broberg, Jim Nash

Cain went into the 2006 season as one of the game's top-rated prospects—we called him the twelfth-best pitching prospect in the game, Baseball America said tenth-best, John Sickels said third. After a full season in the majors, he was no longer a prospect, but, if anything, his reputation had risen even further. That outcome didn't seem likely at mid-season. He carried a 5.12 ERA into the break, undone by persistent control problems. Over his next 12 starts, he was the dominant ace of which every team dreams, winning seven decisions and pitching four straight games without allowing a run. The down side was that he was doing this in the heat of a pennant race and racked up some high pitch counts for a 21-year-old; he had a three-game count of 360 Pitcher Abuse Points during that stretch, the highest in the majors in 2006 (see Keith Woolner's essay on Pitcher Abuse Points in the back of this book). By the end he was apparently fatigued, as he got rocked in his last three starts.

Vinny Chulk
Bats: R **Throws: R**   Height: 6' 1"   Weight: 195   Born: December 19, 1978   Age: 28

YEAR	TEAM	LVL	AGE	W	L	SV	G	GS	IP	H	BB	SO	HR	GB%	BABIP	STUFF	WHIP	ERA	PERA	EQERA	EQH9	EQBB9	EQSO9	EQHR9	VORP	WXRL
2004	SYR	AAA	25	4	2	3	18	0	28²	27	11	26	5	—	.272	-10	1.32	2.82	5.92	4.13	8.6	3.8	6.4	1.9	4.6	—
2004	TOR	MLB	25	1	3	2	47	0	56	59	27	44	6	—	.315	0	1.54	4.66	4.27	4.19	9.0	3.9	6.5	0.8	9.9	0.18
2005	TOR	MLB	26	0	1	0	62	0	72	68	26	39	9	43.9%	.269	-12	1.31	3.88	4.80	4.03	8.3	3.2	4.8	1.0	13.7	1.94
2006	TOR	MLB	27	1	0	0	20	0	24	29	5	18	4	43.2%	.325	-2	1.42	5.25	4.55	5.55	10.7	1.8	6.3	1.5	0.5	0.04
2006	SYR	AAA	27	3	2	1	19	0	32	20	14	43	4	50.7%	.239	15	1.06	2.25	5.43	2.87	6.6	4.3	9.2	1.7	9.5	—
2006	SFN	MLB	27	0	3	0	28	0	22¹	17	15	25	2	44.6%	.278	20	1.43	5.25	4.08	4.70	7.0	5.1	9.0	0.8	2.1	0.08
2007	SFN	MLB	28	3	3	2	52	2	60²	59	27	50	6	43.0%	.294	0	1.41	4.31	4.67	4.60	8.2	3.5	6.5	0.8	8.1	0.70

Breakout: 17%   Improve: 33%   Collapse: 33%   Attrition: 22%   Comparables: Bob Chakales, Jeff Brantley, Mike Corkins, Jerry Johnson

The Incredible Chulk spent the first half of the season running back and forth between Toronto and Syracuse due to an overly generous impulse when handing out gopher balls. The Jays gave up on him, sending him to the Giants with Shea Hillenbrand, which means the Giants get something longer-lasting than three months from the trade. Chulk's top PECOTA comp above, Bob Chakales, wasn't a great pitcher but he wasn't a bad hitter, hitting .271 in 96 lifetime at-bats with three seasons over .300 in small samples. When your top pitching comp isn't known for his pitching, you could be in trouble.

Kevin Correia
Bats: R **Throws: R**   Height: 6' 3"   Weight: 200   Born: August 24, 1980   Age: 26

YEAR	TEAM	LVL	AGE	W	L	SV	G	GS	IP	H	BB	SO	HR	GB%	BABIP	STUFF	WHIP	ERA	PERA	EQERA	EQH9	EQBB9	EQSO9	EQHR9	VORP	WXRL
2004	FRE	AAA	23	3	7	0	29	16	105¹	118	35	70	12	—	.310	-8	1.45	4.53	4.87	5.08	9.2	3.0	4.5	1.1	6.2	—
2004	SFN	MLB	23	0	1	0	12	1	19	25	10	14	3	—	.379	-18	1.84	8.05	5.24	8.84	11.6	4.2	6.1	1.4	-8.0	-0.37
2005	FRE	AAA	24	3	2	7	31	3	46	50	23	35	6	40.5%	.310	-21	1.59	6.07	5.46	7.19	9.7	4.3	5.2	1.4	-8.2	—
2005	SFN	MLB	24	2	5	0	16	11	58¹	61	31	44	12	35.8%	.293	-9	1.58	4.63	6.21	4.70	9.6	4.4	6.2	1.8	5.2	0.80
2006	SFN	MLB	25	2	0	0	48	0	69²	64	22	57	5	36.1%	.291	15	1.23	3.49	3.48	3.17	8.2	2.4	6.7	0.5	19.9	1.83
2007	SFN	MLB	26	3	4	2	47	3	72	71	29	55	10	40.0%	.284	-1	1.39	4.37	4.82	4.61	8.3	3.2	6.1	1.0	9.3	0.90

Breakout: 22%   Improve: 46%   Collapse: 21%   Attrition: 12%   Comparables: Dave Stewart, Bobby Thigpen, Shawn Boskie, Mark Grant

Correia was demoted to Fresno out of spring training, but he was called up before the Triple-A season even started and never went back. The Giants used him in low-leverage situations last year—such as when the starting pitcher had been chased before the fourth inning and the team was looking at a 17-run deficit. The PA announcer saying, "Now pitching, Kevin Correia," rapidly became a kind of folk code for, "If you head for your car now you might beat the traffic out of the parking lot." The Giants were only 2–14 in games in which they used Correia in April and May, but, as he continued to pitch well, they started using him in more competitive games. Further development is unlikely.

Adam Cowart
Bats: R **Throws: R**   Height: 6' 2"   Weight: 190   Born: August 18, 1983   Age: 22

YEAR	TEAM	LVL	AGE	W	L	SV	G	GS	IP	H	BB	SO	HR	GB%	BABIP	STUFF	WHIP	ERA	PERA	EQERA	EQH9	EQBB9	EQSO9	EQHR9	VORP	WXRL
2006	SLO	A-	22	10	1	0	15	15	83²	51	8	55	2	63.7%	.202	9	0.71	1.08	4.07	3.47	7.2	1.2	3.1	0.7	19.0	—

Cowart was a 35th-round draft pick last year who became a submariner after a long battle with a staph infection in his leg caused him to miss a year at Kansas State. When he returned, he found that the year off had had negatively affected his velocity. He throws a fastball and a slider with impeccable control, but, even on a friendly gun, only reaches the mid-80s. He didn't strike many out, but Low-A hitters who may have never seen a sidearmer before tended to beat his pitches weakly into the ground. Cowart led the Northwest League in wins and ERA, but isn't expected to be able to get more advanced hitters out.

Brad Hennessey
Bats: R **Throws: R**   Height: 6' 2"   Weight: 195   Born: February 7, 1980   Age: 27

YEAR	TEAM	LVL	AGE	W	L	SV	G	GS	IP	H	BB	SO	HR	GB%	BABIP	STUFF	WHIP	ERA	PERA	EQERA	EQH9	EQBB9	EQSO9	EQHR9	VORP	WXRL
2004	NRW	AA	24	5	5	0	18	18	101	106	34	55	8	—	.295	-13	1.39	3.56	5.32	5.00	10.2	3.5	3.4	1.1	6.6	—
2004	FRE	AAA	24	4	1	0	5	5	35²	26	15	16	2	—	.214	1	1.15	2.02	4.75	2.23	5.7	4.0	3.0	0.5	13.6	—
2004	SFN	MLB	24	2	2	0	7	7	34¹	42	15	25	2	—	.345	6	1.66	4.99	3.68	6.06	10.6	3.5	5.6	0.5	-1.7	0.10
2005	FRE	AAA	25	4	2	0	11	11	67²	75	22	46	7	49.3%	.315	0	1.43	5.18	4.84	5.24	9.8	2.8	4.6	1.0	2.7	—
2005	SFN	MLB	25	5	8	0	21	21	118¹	127	52	64	15	49.5%	.294	-6	1.51	4.64	5.14	4.67	9.5	3.6	4.5	1.1	10.4	2.55
2006	SFN	MLB	26	5	6	1	34	12	99¹	92	42	42	12	44.0%	.256	-15	1.35	4.26	5.43	4.28	8.4	3.3	3.5	1.0	13.6	1.32
2007	SFN	MLB	27	5	7	1	38	13	105¹	113	43	55	13	47.0%	.287	-10	1.48	4.88	5.24	5.22	9.1	3.3	4.1	0.9	6.3	1.10

Breakout: 8%   Improve: 30%   Collapse: 37%   Attrition: 11%   Comparables: Steve Comer, Ken Clay, Dick Pole, Cloyd Boyer

(continued next page)

Brad Hennessey *(continued)*

Hennessey lost the springtime battle for a rotation spot to Jamey Wright, then briefly claimed the spot in August before being pushed out by Jonathan Sanchez. In between, he functioned as the team's emergency starter, taking over for brief injuries and retreating to the pen for long relief after the dust settled. He had a sparkling 2.43 ERA entering August, but a 5.26 mark afterwards that was more in keeping with his peripheral stats and his history.

Steve Kline Bats: R Throws: L   Height: 6' 1" Weight: 210 Born: August 22, 1972   Age: 34

YEAR	TEAM	LVL	AGE	W	L	SV	G	GS	IP	H	BB	SO	HR	GB%	BABIP	STUFF	WHIP	ERA	PERA	EQERA	EQH9	EQBB9	EQSO9	EQHR9	VORP	WXRL
2004	SLN	MLB	31	2	2	3	67	0	50¹	37	17	35	3	—	.245	6	1.07	1.79	3.90	2.50	7.2	2.7	5.5	0.5	19.7	1.54
2005	BAL	MLB	32	2	4	0	67	0	61	59	30	36	11	57.2%	.262	-18	1.44	4.28	5.84	4.60	8.3	4.3	5.2	1.6	4.8	-0.84
2006	SFN	MLB	33	4	3	1	72	0	51²	53	26	33	3	47.5%	.318	-4	1.53	3.66	4.06	3.74	9.0	3.9	5.1	0.5	10.6	1.56
2007	SFN	MLB	34	2	2	2	52	0	46²	50	22	31	4	49.0%	.301	-12	1.53	4.66	5.08	5.02	9.0	3.8	5.2	0.7	3.8	0.30

Breakout: 2% Improve: 12% Collapse: 64% Attrition: 26%   Comparables: Steve Barber, Paul Lindblad, Darold Knowles, Dave Righetti

Kline bounced back from his utterly awful season in Baltimore, giving the Giants the better side of the LaTroy Hawkins trade. Still, his 2006 wasn't up to the standards Kline set for himself in St. Louis, as batters from both sides found him easier to hit. It's unlikely he'll be revisiting those golden years, but he was old enough for Brian Sabean's team, and was re-signed for two more years.

Tim Lincecum Bats: L Throws: R   Height: 5' 11" Weight: 160 Born: June 15, 1984   Age: 23

YEAR	TEAM	LVL	AGE	W	L	SV	G	GS	IP	H	BB	SO	HR	GB%	BABIP	STUFF	WHIP	ERA	PERA	EQERA	EQH9	EQBB9	EQSO9	EQHR9	VORP	WXRL
2006	SJO	A+	22	2	0	0	6	6	27	13	12	48	3	50.0%	.246	25	0.93	2.00	5.33	3.24	6.8	4.7	10.4	1.8	6.6	—
2007	SFN	MLB	23	7	6	1	23	17	110	81	51	138	12	42.0%	.271	36	1.20	3.18	3.58	3.36	6.2	3.7	9.9	0.8	32.5	3.80

Breakout: 8% Improve: 36% Collapse: 35% Attrition: 13%   Comparables: Jose Deleon, Kerry Wood, Mickey McDermott, Dave Boswell

The last six times the Giants have had a first-round pick—they didn't have one in 2004 or 2005—they've chosen a right-handed pitcher. Lincecum joins David Aardsma, Matt Cain, Brad Hennessey, Boof Bonser, and Kurt Ainsworth as Giant first-rounders, but Cain is the only one who should be considered a true peer to Lincecum. Lincecum had the best stuff of any pitcher in last year's draft, with a mid- to upper-90s fastball and an absolute top-of-the-line curve; he led NCAA Division I in both total strikeouts and strikeouts per nine innings. He could have stepped straight into the majors, but the Giants decided to let him get acquainted with pro ball and rest up after his college season. There are two knocks on him: He's small (the height listed above may be generous), and his control can quit on him at times. With health, he and Cain could easily be a dominating duo for the next half-decade. Some scouts see him as a right-handed Billy Wagner, but the Giants have decided not to go in that direction for now.

Noah Lowry Bats: R Throws: L   Height: 6' 2" Weight: 200 Born: October 10, 1980   Age: 26

YEAR	TEAM	LVL	AGE	W	L	SV	G	GS	IP	H	BB	SO	HR	GB%	BABIP	STUFF	WHIP	ERA	PERA	EQERA	EQH9	EQBB9	EQSO9	EQHR9	VORP	WXRL
2004	FRE	AAA	23	7	5	0	17	17	89¹	98	28	73	9	—	.320	7	1.41	4.13	4.21	5.20	9.1	2.8	5.6	1.0	4.1	—
2004	SFN	MLB	23	6	0	0	16	14	92	91	28	72	10	—	.300	19	1.29	3.82	3.83	3.93	8.6	2.4	6.2	0.9	18.3	2.32
2005	SFN	MLB	24	13	13	0	33	33	204²	193	76	172	21	41.1%	.295	21	1.31	3.78	4.06	4.01	8.5	3.0	6.9	0.9	36.5	4.90
2006	SFN	MLB	25	7	10	0	27	27	159¹	166	56	84	21	37.5%	.288	-1	1.39	4.75	4.81	4.49	9.2	2.8	4.3	1.1	17.7	4.12
2007	SFN	MLB	26	8	10	0	28	26	155²	159	55	106	20	42.0%	.287	9	1.37	4.41	4.83	4.66	8.6	2.8	5.4	1.0	19.3	3.10

Breakout: 11% Improve: 35% Collapse: 31% Attrition: 0%   Comparables: Alex Kellner, Sterling Hitchcock, Bob Ojeda, Scott Karl

Lowry pulled up in the second inning of his first start with a strained oblique. He missed the next month despite some advanced techniques used by the Giants medical staff to pinpoint the parts of the muscle that actually needed treatment. He then picked up where he left off, but had some troubling (for a team that just signed him to a four-year deal) dead-arm periods in July and again in September, the latter accompanied by elbow soreness. His last five starts cost him a full run on his seasonal ERA. Lowry's fly-ball rates are somewhat disturbing given his low strikeout rates.

Pat Misch

Bats: R Throws: L   Height: 6' 2"   Weight: 195   Born: August 18, 1981   Age: 25

YEAR	TEAM	LVL	AGE	W	L	SV	G	GS	IP	H	BB	SO	HR	GB%	BABIP	STUFF	WHIP	ERA	PERA	EQERA	EQH9	EQBB9	EQSO9	EQHR9	VORP	WXRL
2004	NRW	AA	22	7	6	0	26	26	159	138	35	123	13	—	.271	12	1.09	3.00	4.26	4.19	8.5	2.1	5.1	1.0	24.5	—
2005	NRW	AA	23	4	2	0	9	9	61¹	63	7	43	7	45.1%	.306	-1	1.14	3.52	5.03	4.43	9.7	1.2	4.1	1.5	7.9	—
2005	FRE	AAA	23	3	9	0	19	19	102	135	40	69	18	42.9%	.357	-24	1.72	6.35	5.98	6.95	11.7	3.3	4.6	1.7	-15.6	—
2006	NRW	AA	24	5	4	0	18	17	103	95	24	79	7	48.5%	.294	0	1.16	2.27	4.98	3.83	9.2	2.5	4.5	1.1	19.9	—
2006	FRE	AAA	24	4	2	0	10	10	65²	74	11	57	7	42.7%	.342	13	1.30	4.00	3.98	4.32	9.9	1.5	5.9	1.2	9.5	—
2007	SFN	MLB	25	6	8	0	30	18	116²	128	36	71	17	44.0%	.295	0	1.41	4.84	5.23	5.13	9.3	2.4	4.8	1.1	8.2	1.60

Breakout: 5%   Improve: 32%   Collapse: 25%   Attrition: 0%   Comparables: Paul Ahyat, Jason Stanford, Justin Atchley, Mike Kusiewicz

A lefty junkball artist, Misch might have an outside shot at the fifth starter's job. He's not going to overpower anybody, but he spins a nice enough curve. Every organization has a lefty like this, but with Russ Ortiz and Jamey Wright in camp, the Giants could probably end up using theirs.

Matt Morris

Bats: R Throws: R   Height: 6' 5"   Weight: 220   Born: August 9, 1974   Age: 32

YEAR	TEAM	LVL	AGE	W	L	SV	G	GS	IP	H	BB	SO	HR	GB%	BABIP	STUFF	WHIP	ERA	PERA	EQERA	EQH9	EQBB9	EQSO9	EQHR9	VORP	WXRL
2004	SLN	MLB	29	15	10	0	32	32	202	205	56	131	35	—	.281	-4	1.29	4.72	4.96	5.52	9.5	2.2	5.2	1.4	10.7	3.13
2005	SLN	MLB	30	14	10	0	31	31	192²	209	37	117	22	50.2%	.303	8	1.28	4.11	4.15	5.14	10.0	1.6	5.0	1.0	18.3	2.97
2006	SFN	MLB	31	10	15	0	33	33	207²	218	63	117	22	47.3%	.291	8	1.35	4.98	4.39	4.77	9.4	2.4	4.6	0.9	16.0	3.13
2007	SFN	MLB	32	10	12	0	31	29	185¹	202	51	105	23	47.0%	.293	4	1.36	4.58	4.83	4.90	9.2	2.2	4.5	1.0	17.6	3.20

Breakout: 18%   Improve: 55%   Collapse: 8%   Attrition: 2%   Comparables: Don Newcombe, Steve Trachsel, Jim Lonborg, Aaron Sele

Morris has had extra difficulty pitching from the stretch since undergoing shoulder surgery in 2003, a problem that has translated into about 30 more runs than you would have expected over the last three years, adding almost half a run to his ERA. In a generally mediocre season, Morris had a sensational run from the end of May through the beginning of July (seven straight quality starts, 2.50 ERA) and a hideous run in September (20 runs allowed over three starts); it was later discovered that he had broken a rib sometime before those September games. He'll chew up innings for the next two years of his contract, but that's all. He won't go back to being what he was four years ago, let alone eight to ten.

Scott Munter

Bats: R Throws: R   Height: 6' 6"   Weight: 260   Born: March 7, 1980   Age: 27

YEAR	TEAM	LVL	AGE	W	L	SV	G	GS	IP	H	BB	SO	HR	GB%	BABIP	STUFF	WHIP	ERA	PERA	EQERA	EQH9	EQBB9	EQSO9	EQHR9	VORP	WXRL
2004	NRW	AA	24	2	4	3	42	0	65	63	22	30	4	—	.280	-23	1.31	2.35	5.14	3.68	9.3	3.5	2.8	0.8	13.6	—
2004	FRE	AAA	24	1	1	1	13	0	15²	20	4	5	1	—	.317	-25	1.53	3.44	4.34	4.41	9.9	2.2	2.2	0.6	2.2	—
2005	FRE	AAA	25	1	3	0	12	0	12¹	17	4	5	0	71.1%	.405	-25	1.71	5.12	3.86	5.68	11.4	2.8	2.8	0.0	-0.1	—
2005	SFN	MLB	25	2	0	0	45	0	38²	40	12	11	1	64.4%	.298	-17	1.34	2.56	3.97	3.66	9.2	2.5	2.3	0.2	8.7	0.85
2006	NRW	AA	26	1	4	1	28	0	40	45	15	22	1	65.9%	.336	-24	1.50	4.73	4.68	6.81	10.2	4.1	3.2	0.5	-5.3	—
2006	SFN	MLB	26	0	1	0	27	0	22²	30	18	7	1	56.0%	.392	-27	2.12	8.72	5.52	7.71	12.0	6.2	2.3	0.4	-6.5	0.00
2007	SFN	MLB	27	2	3	1	50	1	52²	62	25	19	4	59.0%	.306	-23	1.64	4.99	5.42	5.48	9.9	3.7	2.9	0.6	1.4	0.20

Breakout: 14%   Improve: 37%   Collapse: 28%   Attrition: 44%   Comparables: Mark Lee, Heathcliff Slocumb, Steve Shields, Jim Acker

Munter throws a sinker that terrorizes miners, sewermen, Morlocks, CHUDs... but that's all he throws, again and again. Munter never strikes anyone out; he just wants you to beat the pitch into the ground, preferably by chasing a pitch that's already *on* the ground. That works if he gets you to two strikes and you have to swing, but hitters quickly learned to take those pitches for balls and force him to come up in the zone.

Nick Pereira

Bats: R Throws: R   Height: 6' 0"   Weight: 190   Born: September 22, 1982   Age: 24

YEAR	TEAM	LVL	AGE	W	L	SV	G	GS	IP	H	BB	SO	HR	GB%	BABIP	STUFF	WHIP	ERA	PERA	EQERA	EQH9	EQBB9	EQSO9	EQHR9	VORP	WXRL
2005	SLO	A-	22	5	3	0	14	9	50¹	54	14	41	0	60.8%	.351	-13	1.35	3.04	4.31	6.84	10.5	3.7	3.5	0.4	-6.7	—
2006	SJO	A+	23	7	1	0	13	13	78¹	65	16	76	1	55.0%	.296	27	1.04	2.07	3.18	3.49	8.0	2.2	5.2	0.2	18.1	—
2006	FRE	AAA	23	4	3	0	15	15	79	87	48	60	10	42.4%	.321	-6	1.71	5.92	6.11	6.14	9.7	5.2	5.2	1.5	-4.8	—
2007	SFN	MLB	24	5	8	0	27	18	109	117	52	75	13	47.0%	.302	0	1.55	5.29	5.56	5.67	9.1	3.8	5.4	0.9	0.9	0.80

Breakout: 7%   Improve: 33%   Collapse: 24%   Attrition: 0%   Comparables: Brian Bannister, Josh Fogg, Rodrigo Lopez, Vinnie Chulk

Pereira's a University of San Francisco product and the Giants skipped him over Connecticut to keep him close to home. He's got a slider that was wiping right-handed hitters off the plate in San Jose, but PCL hitters waited it out, knowing that his fastball wasn't a real threat. His control deteriorated as the season wore on; he walked at least two batters in each of his last twelve games and walked four or more in six of them. The current list of PECOTA comparables is less than hopeful.

David Quinowski   Bats: L   Throws: L   Height: 5′ 10″   Weight: 170   Born: April 23, 1986   Age: 21

YEAR	TEAM	LVL	AGE	W	L	SV	G	GS	IP	H	BB	SO	HR	GB%	BABIP	STUFF	WHIP	ERA	PERA	EQERA	EQH9	EQBB9	EQSO9	EQHR9	VORP	WXRL
2005	SLO	A-	19	2	1	0	19	0	14	12	14	19	1	40.6%	.355	10	1.86	3.21	9.29	6.57	10.2	13.1	7.3	1.5	-1.3	—
2006	AUG	A	20	4	2	4	44	0	75²	36	24	76	1	38.9%	.196	17	0.80	1.44	3.67	2.70	5.2	3.4	5.5	0.2	23.6	—
2007	SFN	MLB	21	3	4	1	28	6	60	55	33	47	9	39.0%	.267	0	1.47	4.48	5.11	4.71	7.8	4.4	6.3	1.1	6.8	0.90

Breakout: 0%   Improve: 9%   Collapse: 73%   Attrition: 15%   Comparables: Fabio Castro, Chad Gaudin, Ryan Ketchner, David Martinez

The Giants altered Quinowski's delivery into a funky sort of sidestep that hides the ball and, despite a fastball that only reaches 90 MPH when a stiff breeze blows in from center field, hitters can't make solid contact, producing anemic hit totals (including a .144 opponents' batting average). He went up against better competition in the Hawaiian Winter League and still held hitters to a .200 average. Lefty, righty, it doesn't matter; no one can pick the ball up off of him. He's another pitcher for whom high fly-ball rates in the minors could transform into high home-run rates in the majors. Giants pitchers allowed the highest percentage of fly balls in the National League last year (29.6 percent) and had the 14th-lowest rate of grounders (43.6 percent), which, in turn, led to the 13th-lowest rate of turning double plays (11.2 percent). Clearly the Giants encourage their pitchers to work up in the zone in order to take advantage of Pac Bell's fly-deadening ways, but there are consequences to this strategy that could work against them.

Billy Sadler   Bats: R   Throws: R   Height: 6′ 0″   Weight: 190   Born: September 21, 1981   Age: 25

YEAR	TEAM	LVL	AGE	W	L	SV	G	GS	IP	H	BB	SO	HR	GB%	BABIP	STUFF	WHIP	ERA	PERA	EQERA	EQH9	EQBB9	EQSO9	EQHR9	VORP	WXRL
2004	SJO	A+	22	2	2	0	30	3	56²	29	40	66	1	—	.220	23	1.22	2.38	5.56	3.57	5.4	8.5	6.8	0.3	12.0	—
2004	NRW	AA	22	0	3	0	17	0	30¹	22	18	24	3	—	.226	-8	1.32	3.86	6.36	5.46	7.6	5.8	5.2	1.2	0.5	—
2005	NRW	AA	23	6	5	5	47	0	84¹	64	33	81	4	44.1%	.269	2	1.15	3.31	4.91	4.50	7.7	4.3	5.8	0.7	10.0	—
2006	NRW	AA	24	4	3	20	44	0	45¹	23	29	67	1	48.9%	.247	27	1.15	2.59	4.41	4.04	6.2	7.2	8.9	0.4	7.3	—
2006	FRE	AAA	24	2	0	1	7	0	10¹	5	2	12	1	45.0%	.211	10	0.69	1.78	3.55	1.80	4.5	1.8	8.1	0.9	4.2	—
2007	SFN	MLB	25	3	3	1	31	3	55	48	41	51	5	44.0%	.286	0	1.63	4.63	5.28	4.94	7.4	6.0	7.3	0.7	4.8	0.60

Breakout: 10%   Improve: 33%   Collapse: 37%   Attrition: 14%   Comparables: Jim Sak, Allan Simpson, Brad Voyles, Jeremy Hill

In his third year at Double-A, Sadler was given the closer's role and started pitching just one inning at a time. His tailing fastball proved tougher than ever to hit, but the big step forward was due to his curveball becoming a plus pitch that is just as tough to hit, though even tougher for Sadler to control. He had silly hits-to-innings-pitched ratios and found himself enjoying September by the Bay. While he didn't look good in the majors, he still made a name for himself in the fall by holding hitters in the notoriously hit-happy Arizona Fall League to a .184 average.

Jonathan Sanchez   Bats: L   Throws: L   Height: 6′ 2″   Weight: 165   Born: November 19, 1982   Age: 24

YEAR	TEAM	LVL	AGE	W	L	SV	G	GS	IP	H	BB	SO	HR	GB%	BABIP	STUFF	WHIP	ERA	PERA	EQERA	EQH9	EQBB9	EQSO9	EQHR9	VORP	WXRL
2004	SLO	A-	21	2	1	0	6	6	22¹	16	19	34	3	—	.289	12	1.57	4.84	10.74	6.98	9.8	11.6	7.4	3.3	-3.0	—
2005	AUG	A	22	5	7	0	25	25	125²	122	39	166	8	47.5%	.373	3	1.28	4.08	4.90	5.74	10.1	3.7	6.7	1.2	-1.9	—
2006	NRW	AA	23	2	1	2	13	3	31²	14	9	46	0	49.2%	.250	30	0.74	1.15	2.80	2.97	5.3	3.0	8.9	0.3	8.9	—
2006	FRE	AAA	23	2	2	0	6	6	23¹	13	13	28	1	38.9%	.235	23	1.13	3.90	4.10	3.91	5.5	5.1	8.6	0.4	4.3	—
2006	SFN	MLB	23	3	1	0	27	4	40	39	23	33	2	36.6%	.306	5	1.55	4.95	4.13	5.27	9.0	4.4	6.6	0.4	1.0	0.23
2007	SFN	MLB	24	4	6	1	40	11	77¹	75	43	71	9	41.0%	.299	3	1.52	4.99	5.31	5.30	8.2	4.4	7.2	0.9	3.8	0.80

Breakout: 17%   Improve: 34%   Collapse: 31%   Attrition: 25%   Comparables: Ron Moeller, Kent Mercker, Frank Bertaina, Tim Conroy

Sanchez lasted until the 27th round in the 2004 draft. The Giants thought he had bad mechanics that could be fixed, and they've turned out to be right. He swung between the pen and rotation last year as the team wrestled with short-term (he could come up and help in relief right now) versus long-term (he'd be more valuable as a starter). His performance—2.91 ERA in relief, 7.36 as a starter—gives the short-term hawks a lead, but the long-term doves will see that he gets more chances. His fastball and changeup are good, but he's had trouble with overthrowing his curve. Top PECOTA comp Ron Moeller was a 1956 Baltimore Bonus Baby whose career never happened; Frank Bertaina had one good season in a six-year career; Conroy had potential but never mastered his control. That leaves veteran lefty swinger Mercker as the high upside.

Jason Schmidt **Bats: R Throws: R** Height: 6' 5" Weight: 210 Born: January 29, 1973 Age: 34

YEAR	TEAM	LVL	AGE	W	L	SV	G	GS	IP	H	BB	SO	HR	GB%	BABIP	STUFF	WHIP	ERA	PERA	EQERA	EQH9	EQBB9	EQSO9	EQHR9	VORP	WXRL
2004	SFN	MLB	31	18	7	0	32	32	225	165	77	251	18	—	.268	44	1.08	3.20	3.11	3.36	6.6	2.7	8.8	0.6	62.1	7.72
2005	SFN	MLB	32	12	7	0	29	29	172	160	85	165	16	40.1%	.306	25	1.42	4.40	4.04	4.61	8.4	4.0	7.8	0.8	17.5	3.02
2006	SFN	MLB	33	11	9	0	32	32	213¹	189	80	180	21	38.3%	.283	25	1.26	3.59	3.84	3.61	7.9	2.9	6.9	0.8	49.4	5.89
2007	LAN	MLB	34	12	10	0	30	30	192¹	177	73	177	25	41.0%	.283	19	1.30	4.10	4.21	4.13	8.5	3.0	7.4	1.1	32.8	4.90

Breakout: 6% Improve: 35% Collapse: 21% Attrition: 1% Comparables: Hideo Nomo, Jack Morris, Early Wynn, Dave Burba

For the first three months of 2007, Schmidt was right there with the best pitchers in baseball, owning a 2.78 ERA after 115 innings. After the All-Star break, his ERA went up nearly two runs to 4.76, driven by an opposition batting average 50 points higher. Yes, he was worked hard in May and June—eight straight starts over 110 pitches, four of them over 120—but he wasn't pushed radically harder than younger pitchers such as Bronson Arroyo and Carlos Zambrano. Even when going well, he wasn't getting the strikeouts he did in the past. The Dodgers signed him to a three-year, $47-million contract, which seems more than fair given the expensive environment this off-season; holding the deal to three years was a victory.

Mike Stanton **Bats: L Throws: L** Height: 6' 1" Weight: 215 Born: December 31, 1969 Age: 40

YEAR	TEAM	LVL	AGE	W	L	SV	G	GS	IP	H	BB	SO	HR	GB%	BABIP	STUFF	WHIP	ERA	PERA	EQERA	EQH9	EQBB9	EQSO9	EQHR9	VORP	WXRL
2004	NYN	MLB	37	2	6	0	83	0	77	70	33	58	6	—	.277	3	1.34	3.16	4.01	3.68	8.2	3.4	6.0	0.7	16.5	1.21
2005	NYA	MLB	38	1	2	0	28	0	14	17	6	12	1	37.8%	.364	-3	1.64	7.07	3.66	6.91	10.7	3.8	7.5	0.6	-2.1	-0.29
2005	WAS	MLB	38	2	1	0	30	0	27²	31	9	14	2	44.6%	.322	-12	1.45	3.57	4.02	4.40	9.7	2.5	4.1	0.6	3.4	1.12
2005	BOS	MLB	38	0	0	0	1	0	1	1	0	1	0	100.0%	.500	1	1.00	0.00	2.04	0.00	9.0	0.0	9.0	0.0	0.6	0.01
2006	WAS	MLB	39	3	5	0	56	0	44¹	47	21	30	1	43.2%	.333	0	1.53	4.47	3.56	4.14	9.1	3.7	5.5	0.2	7.3	0.31
2006	SFN	MLB	39	4	2	8	26	0	23¹	23	6	18	1	44.1%	.328	10	1.24	3.09	3.13	2.66	8.7	1.9	6.5	0.4	7.7	1.30
2007	CIN	MLB	40	2	3	3	50	0	47²	57	20	33	7	45.0%	.320	-14	1.61	5.37	5.58	5.26	11.0	3.3	5.5	1.3	1.6	0.10

Breakout: 9% Improve: 25% Collapse: 67% Attrition: 28% Comparables: Buddy Groom, Jeff Fassero, Mike Flanagan, Harry Gumbert

Stanton passed Dan Plesac, Kent Tekulve, Hoyt Wilhelm, and Dennis Eckersley on the career games pitched list last year, and now stands third behind John Franco and Jesse Orosco. His resurgence with San Francisco, taking over as closer and picking up eight saves while Benitez was down, all but guarantees him a shot at the 11 games he'll need to pass Franco. Stanton is the only pitcher in the top 15 in games pitched who has less than 139 saves; last year's eight gives him 84 for his career. The Reds signed him to a two-year deal with plans to use him as, at minimum, a co-closer; if he can stay healthy for both years he'll be closing in on Orosco (142 games away) for the all-time lead.

Jack Taschner **Bats: L Throws: L** Height: 6' 3" Weight: 210 Born: April 21, 1978 Age: 29

YEAR	TEAM	LVL	AGE	W	L	SV	G	GS	IP	H	BB	SO	HR	GB%	BABIP	STUFF	WHIP	ERA	PERA	EQERA	EQH9	EQBB9	EQSO9	EQHR9	VORP	WXRL
2004	NRW	AA	26	3	1	0	14	10	58	47	16	55	5	—	.264	2	1.09	2.48	4.67	3.70	8.5	3.1	5.6	1.3	11.8	—
2004	FRE	AAA	26	4	7	0	18	9	53¹	71	32	44	14	—	.329	-34	1.93	9.29	7.74	9.67	11.5	5.7	5.7	2.5	-24.4	—
2005	FRE	AAA	27	3	0	10	44	0	49¹	30	24	62	3	46.9%	.250	23	1.10	1.64	3.78	1.85	6.1	4.3	8.5	0.6	20.3	—
2005	SFN	MLB	27	2	0	0	24	0	22²	15	13	19	0	30.6%	.242	13	1.24	1.59	3.55	1.96	6.3	4.7	7.0	0.0	8.8	0.58
2006	FRE	AAA	28	6	7	14	45	0	49	49	17	68	5	43.1%	.389	13	1.35	3.67	4.00	4.07	9.6	3.1	9.4	1.3	8.3	—
2006	SFN	MLB	28	0	1	0	24	0	19¹	31	7	15	4	29.3%	.380	-19	1.97	8.39	5.21	9.45	13.9	2.7	6.3	1.8	-9.7	-0.17
2007	SFN	MLB	29	2	3	4	65	1	52²	51	23	47	7	38.0%	.293	1	1.40	4.53	4.88	4.78	8.2	3.4	7.0	1.0	5.7	0.60

Breakout: 36% Improve: 68% Collapse: 7% Attrition: 28% Comparables: Alan Embree, Mike Myers, Jason Christiansen, Gary Wayne

Taschner opened 2006 with the Giants, but when he retired just seven of the first 21 batters he faced, he was sent to the Valley. Things were better after that; Taschner posted a 3.65 ERA in Fresno, and then a 4.20 after his August recall. Better isn't the same as good; Taschner failed to pitch as well as he had in 2005, when he finally proved himself healthy after years of injuries. If you can endure our making one more remark about high fly-ball rates, check out Taschner's. Right-handed hitters batted .400/.456/.760 with four home runs in 50 at-bats against him; between his inability to keep the ball down and the natural advantage that righties have over lefties, Taschner turned every righty who faced him into Jimmie Foxx on a hot streak. On the—pardon the expression—other hand, Taschner limited fellow lefties to .275/.318/.275. Though this would tend to paint Taschner as a future LOOGY, this is all small-sample stuff. He had a reverse split in another small major league sample in 2005, and another at Fresno in 2006. Crafting a role for him is going to be difficult.

Brian Wilson **Bats: R Throws: R**   Height: 6′ 1″   Weight: 205   Born: March 16, 1982   Age: 25

YEAR	TEAM	LVL	AGE	W	L	SV	G	GS	IP	H	BB	SO	HR	GB%	BABIP	STUFF	WHIP	ERA	PERA	EQERA	EQH9	EQBB9	EQSO9	EQHR9	VORP	WXRL
2004	HAG	A	22	2	5	3	23	3	57¹	63	22	41	7	—	.316	-35	1.48	5.34	7.20	6.63	10.7	4.4	3.6	2.1	-6.4	—
2005	AUG	A	23	5	1	13	26	0	33	23	7	30	0	70.7%	.253	-5	0.91	0.82	3.92	3.03	6.9	2.5	4.4	0.3	9.3	—
2005	NRW	AA	23	0	0	8	15	0	15²	6	5	22	0	50.0%	.200	15	0.70	0.57	3.07	1.20	4.8	3.6	8.4	0.0	7.3	—
2005	FRE	AAA	23	1	1	0	9	0	11¹	8	8	13	0	29.0%	.276	11	1.42	3.98	3.91	5.56	6.4	6.4	7.9	0.0	0.1	—
2006	FRE	AAA	24	1	3	7	24	0	28¹	20	14	30	2	51.4%	.269	10	1.21	2.88	4.34	3.18	6.7	4.4	7.3	1.0	7.6	—
2006	SFN	MLB	24	2	3	1	31	0	30	32	21	23	1	47.3%	.344	3	1.77	5.40	4.13	4.99	9.7	5.6	6.2	0.3	1.1	0.09
2007	SFN	MLB	25	2	3	2	48	1	51¹	50	29	42	5	48.0%	.300	-3	1.54	4.69	4.96	5.06	8.3	4.4	6.4	0.7	3.8	0.40

Breakout: 12% Improve: 33% Collapse: 31% Attrition: 31%   Comparables: Phil Hennigan, Jay Powell, Ron Willis, Gene Pentz

Wilson is a flamethrower with an upper-90s fastball and a hard slider. He has fought control problems his entire career, and has usually lost. The Giants sent him to winter ball to work on closing, and, aside from more control problems (nine walks in 14 innings through Christmas-time in Puerto Rico), he was spectacular, allowing just five hits, no runs, and earning 11 saves in those 14 innings. With Benitez's future in doubt, Wilson may emerge as the default closer candidate, but anticipate some ugly lines in the box score as a result.

Jamey Wright **Bats: R Throws: R**   Height: 6′ 6″   Weight: 235   Born: December 24, 1974   Age: 32

YEAR	TEAM	LVL	AGE	W	L	SV	G	GS	IP	H	BB	SO	HR	GB%	BABIP	STUFF	WHIP	ERA	PERA	EQERA	EQH9	EQBB9	EQSO9	EQHR9	VORP	WXRL
2004	OMA	AAA	29	8	6	0	18	18	104²	111	35	70	13	—	.296	-8	1.39	4.21	5.60	5.04	9.3	3.2	4.4	1.3	6.6	—
2004	COL	MLB	29	2	3	0	14	14	78²	82	45	41	8	—	.286	3	1.61	4.12	5.30	3.84	8.6	4.5	4.1	0.8	14.4	2.13
2005	COL	MLB	30	8	16	0	34	27	171¹	201	81	101	22	54.0%	.322	-6	1.65	5.46	5.28	5.35	9.6	3.8	4.7	1.0	-7.1	0.68
2006	SFN	MLB	31	6	10	0	34	21	156	167	64	79	16	58.9%	.303	-3	1.48	5.19	4.75	4.91	9.5	3.2	4.1	0.8	10.0	1.73
2007	SFN	MLB	32	6	9	0	36	18	129	143	55	73	13	52.0%	.302	-8	1.53	5.04	5.35	5.44	9.3	3.4	4.5	0.8	4.3	1.20

Breakout: 7% Improve: 27% Collapse: 33% Attrition: 9%   Comparables: Jaime Navarro, Dan Petry, Jason Johnson, Dock Ellis

Wright pitched well for about three months; a good March got him the fifth starter's job, and a very respectable 3.84 ERA through his first eight starts justified the decision. He then posted a 6.49 ERA with more walks than strikeouts over his next twelve before Alou finally decided he'd seen enough and yanked Wright in favor of Hennessey. He's a non-roster invitee to Giant camp this spring.

Lineouts

PLAYER	TEAM	LVL	AGE	PA	R	2B	3B	HR	RBI	BB	SO	SB-CS	SPEED	AVG/OBP/SLG	MLVr	EqAVG/EqOBP/EqSLG	EqA	VORP
SS T. de la Rosa	FRE	AAA	28	335	43	21	2	8	43	23	45	8-5	5.0	.293/.352/.457	.124	.276/.322/.422	.255	13.1
2B M. Minicozzi	SJO	A+	23	558	70	23	2	4	77	44	87	2-4	4.1	.282/.345/.360	.017	.270/.315/.331	.230	-3.9
RF M. Mooney	AUG	A	23	557	82	28	7	11	74	44	115	38-10	6.8	.287/.355/.439	.200	.263/.306/.385	.245	-12.6
RF A. Nunez#	FRE	AAA	29	326	44	19	3	12	57	41	65	5-3	5.4	.279/.368/.495	.191	.258/.333/.447	.268	4.6
CF A. Richardson#	AUG	A	22	493	78	17	4	2	28	54	73	66-9	7.7	.292/.381/.366	.142	.276/.337/.342	.255	1.2
SS M. Sanders	SJO	A+	20	246	39	9	1	0	17	25	43	24-5	8.0	.213/.302/.265	-.254	.205/.273/.247	.207	-15.4
1B C. Santos*	FRE	AAA	25	381	40	18	1	14	70	24	86	0-0	3.5	.261/.307/.436	-.009	.250/.291/.416	.241	-5.8

PLAYER	TEAM	LVL	AGE	W	L	SV	IP	H	BB	SO	HR	GB%	BABIP	STUFF	WHIP	ERA	PERA	EqERA	EqH9	EqBB9	EqSO9	EqHR9	VORP
K. Acosta	SJO	A+	21	0	1	0	9²	10	4	11	2	—	.333	-11	1.52	6.85	8.19	9.35	11.4	4.2	7.3	3.1	-3.6
J. Hedrick	SJO	A+	24	6	4	6	85	53	30	110	3	—	.280	12	0.98	2.01	3.92	2.99	6.9	4.0	7.0	0.7	23.6
M. Kinney	FRE	AAA	29	8	7	0	153¹	158	53	127	23	—	.297	-16	1.38	4.82	5.72	5.45	9.3	3.2	5.5	1.8	2.6
O. Matos	AUG	A	21	7	3	13	61	42	12	81	3	—	.277	12	0.89	1.77	3.84	3.09	8.0	2.3	7.1	1.1	16.3
	NRW	AA	21	0	0	2	9²	11	2	5	0	—	.324	-13	1.41	3.91	3.42	4.66	10.2	1.9	2.8	0.0	1.0
E. Threets*	FRE	AAA	24	2	1	0	62²	51	44	51	4	—	.270	3	1.53	2.89	5.52	3.84	7.2	6.1	5.7	0.7	12.4
M. Valdez	FRE	AAA	23	0	4	5	49	52	39	48	6	—	.329	-9	1.86	5.88	6.47	7.61	9.8	6.9	6.7	1.4	-11.1
B. Villafuerte	FRE	AAA	30	2	5	2	66²	60	18	60	2	—	.320	8	1.18	4.62	3.50	4.84	8.1	2.6	5.9	0.4	5.7

Tomas de la Rosa is a veteran player best stashed at Triple-A and used only in emergencies. Mark Minicozzi has played full-time at both second and third base; last year his hitting was inflated by a huge home-field advantage. Mike Mooney has the best outfield arm in the system, but his league-leading 15 assists came with a league-leading 12 errors. A local kid from San Francisco, Mooney doesn't have the bat for right, and he was old for the Sally League. Abraham Nuñez—the former Royals outfielder, not the current Phillies infielder—hit .223 and slugged .419 in Fresno before serving a 50-game suspension for taking performance-enhancing drugs. He then hit .341 and slugged .578 after coming back, which isn't what you'd expect given that his batteries had been taken out. Antoan Richardson's 66 stolen bases were the fourth-best total in pro ball last year, but only third in the Sally League. Unfortunately, speed and a good eye are about all the pint-sized Richardson has going for him. Another speedster, Marcus Sanders was a shell of himself last year after having offseason shoulder surgery. He appeared to be a good leadoff prospect in 2005, but his arm is so bad that he can't play short or centerfield. That limits him to second base and only second base. If his bat doesn't recover to levels approximating the .300/.400/.407 he put up in the Sally League in 2005, he'll be out of baseball in a hurry. The fact that the Giants called up Chad Santos at all shows just how desperate they were for first base help last year.

It remains to be seen if Kelyn Acosta is still a hard-throwing comer given that he missed much of the last two years with elbow problems. Old for A-ball, Justin Hedrick set up for Brian Anderson at San Jose last year and was his near equal in dominance; unfortunately he's also Anderson's near equal in raw stuff. Anyone in Triple-A, especially if they have major league experience, is a candidate to be called up in a desperate situation, no matter how bad they are. That said, Matt Kinney is in Triple-A. Osiris Matos's switch to closing worked wonders for him; he was especially effective against left-handed hitters, and impressed enough to be added to the 40-man roster. Having survived shoulder surgery, Erick Threets is a little too wild to make a reliable lefty specialist, but he's that rare Giant farmhand who keeps the ball on the ground. Merkin Valdez threw 99 MPH last spring, but with the control of a bat-spun drunk. He had already been demoted from being Fresno's closer when he blew out his elbow; he will miss the 2007 season. Brandon Villafuerte pitched unusually poorly with men on base last year, but could still get a shot from a club with a weak bullpen.

Manager: Felipe Alou

Year	Team	W-L	Pythag +/-	Avg PC	100 +P	120 +P	QS	BQS	REL	REL w Zero R	IBB	SUBS	PH	PH Avg	PH HR	SB2	CS2	SB3	CS3	SAC Att	SAC %	POS SAC	Squeeze	Swing	In Play
2004	SFN	91-71	+2	98.8	78	13	79	8	521	291	35	86	235	.293	4	36	20	7	2	101	91.1%	48	1	131	103
2005	SFN	75-87	+5	98.3	93	7	72	12	509	319	42	72	238	.252	3	56	30	13	2	116	78.5%	52	5	137	108
2006	SFN	76-85	0	99.6	91	9	74	7	438	255	37	75	210	.225	3	47	22	10	3	103	77.7%	36	2	134	109

The Giants learned an important lesson last year. Just a few managers have worked into their 70s, let alone past 65. The septuagenarian group includes Connie Mack, who won his last pennant at 68; Casey Stengel, who turned 70 in 1960, the year of his last pennant; Jack McKeon, the great outlier, who won a World Series with the Marlins at 72; Frank Robinson, who appears to be through at 71; and Felipe Alou, who managed his last two seasons with the Giants at ages 70 and 71. Alou had little chance of winning with this shallow, aged squad, but the best way he could think of to try was to overwork the team's only long-term asset, its pitching. It was time for a younger man, and Bruce Bochy takes over a very different team than the one he had in San Diego. Bochy likes to be aggressive, attempting steals and hit-and-runs more than an average manager, which will endear him to fantasy owners of Omar Vizquel and Dave Roberts. His teams have been among the best in terms of stolen base percentage, and they rarely bunt (aside from the pitchers), though with an offense as weak as the Giants' appears to be, he may be tempted to try.

Seattle Mariers

On June 30, the AL West looked like it could be in the Mariners' grasp. Sure, they opened the day only one game over .500, but they were in second place, two games behind the Oakland A's, and in the midst of a five-game winning streak. That day they completed a deal for Eduardo Perez, the right-handed half of the Cleveland Indians' first-base platoon to address their 8–16 record against left-handed starters. That weakness addressed, Bill Bavasi's team was ready to make its charge.

Unfortunately, the Mariners had already peaked. After completing a sweep of the Angels on June 11, the Mariners were themselves swept by Oakland. It was the second time that the A's had taken a three-game set from Seattle. The Mariners would not win another game against their division for more than two months. In 20 intra-division games between June 12 and August 20, the Mariners were outscored, 137–65, having been held to two or fewer runs 12 times, including four shutouts. On August 20, the M's had lost 11 games in a row and were 12 games out of the division lead. They threw in the towel, dealing Jamie Moyer to the Philadelphia Phillies for two right-handed relief prospects. This ended Moyer's ten-year association with Seattle, a span that saw him become the franchise's leader in innings pitched (2,093) and wins (145). Moyer was the last link to the late nineties Mariner teams of Ken Griffey Jr., Randy Johnson, and Alex Rodriguez.

The intra-division losing streak was broken little more than a week later, at home against the Angels, with Felix Hernandez pitching his first career shutout. A month after that, the M's got their first win of the season against Oakland, staging a three-run, ninth-inning comeback to beat them 10–9 in extra innings, and break a string of 15 con-secutive losses to the division leaders. The feeling of achievement was short-lived. The next night, the A's would beat them and clinch the division title. It was only right that it was the Mariners who were forced to watch the Athletics celebrate—with a 17–1 record against Seattle, Oakland had made the playoffs on the Mariners' backs.

Overall, the Mariners played well over .500 (59–46) against non-AL West opponents, which, sadly, is not an indication that they were a better team than their record suggests. Their third-order won-lost record—that's the number of games the Mariners could have been expected to win based on adjusted runs scored and allowed—indicates that, if the Mariners underperformed, it was only by a couple of games. Still, starting with a near-.500 team isn't the end of the world in their division. The A's offense is still weak, and made weaker by the loss of Frank Thomas; the Angels' big move was to sign Gary Matthews Jr.; the Rangers lost Matthews and Carlos Lee. Based upon the major league talent at hand, none of those teams looks like a prohibitive favorite in 2007.

The opportunity was there this winter for Bavasi to steal a march on his opponents by making bold, aggressive, talent-grabbing moves. Instead, he went about acquiring mediocre veterans Jose Guillen, Miguel Batista, Horacio Ramirez, Chris Reitsma, and Jose Vidro. As wrong-headed as that approach may seem, there may have been a very good reason for it. The Mariners had a paid attendence of about 2.5 million in 2006. That was good enough for sixth in the American League, but continued a steady decline of about a quarter of a million tickets per season from the franchise's all-time attendance high point in 2002. While the M's couldn't have expected much coming off of con-secutive seasons of more than 90 losses, the erosion of

---

MARINERS PROSPECTUS

2006 record: 78–84; Fourth place, AL West

Pythagenport record: 77–85

Runs scored per game: 4.67 (13th in AL)

Runs allowed per game: 4.89 (9th in AL)

Team EqA: .256 (12th in AL)

2006 Batters Age: 29.1 (5th youngest in AL)

2006 Pitchers Age: 28.6 (6th oldest in AL)

Ballpark: Safeco Field; Severe pitcher's park; Park Factor of .949

2006: Still awaiting the coronation of King Fleix, the M's become impatient with the rest of their prospects.

2007: Concerned about the instability of his team's mediocrity, Bavasi shores it up with mediocre vets.

their ticket base would be of serious concern to any franchise (with the possible exception of the Pirates).

Some of the veteran hands brought on to make the M's respectable—or at least interesting—make a bit more sense than the others. Giving outfielder Jose Guillen a one-year, $5.5-million contract with incentives looks like a good gamble. Guillen was available at a steep discount because of the 2006 surgery on his throwing elbow, and, to a lesser extent, his cheerful personality. Guillen was a fair hitter prior to his injury (batting .295/.349/.513 from 2003 through 2005) and, if healthy, should do a good job holding down right field until Adam Jones is ready.

After being rebuffed in their latest attempt at geographical nepotism when Washington-state native Jason Schmidt signed with the Dodgers, the M's picked up a couple of finesse ground-ball pitchers in Ramirez and Batista. Both pitchers have spent time near the top of the leaderboard in double plays induced, Batista finishing third in the majors last year and Ramirez finishing second in 2005. Notionally Bavasi had assembled complementing skill sets, with the infield glovework of Adrian Beltre, Yunieski Betancourt, and Jose Lopez ready to make Ramirez and Batista look brilliant. However, despite the reputations of some of the Mariners' defenders, this is not a good defensive ballclub—ranking only 24th in the majors in park-adjusted defensive efficiency (the rate at which teams turn balls in play into outs)—so the net results of Ramirez and Batista putting a ton of balls in play might be disappointing.

Perhaps the most perplexing acquisition of the off-season was the new designated hitter, Jose Vidro. Vidro was a coveted commodity back when the Nationals were still the Montreal Expos, but the past three years haven't been kind to the 32-year-old second baseman. Vidro's Equivalent Average has declined each of the past three seasons. Averaging only 109 games played per year over that span, Vidro's one of the few players whose propensity for injury approaches that of one of the players he was traded for, Chris Snelling. (When Snelling was called up from Triple-A last year, he famously managed to injure himself sometime between hearing the news of his promotion and actually suiting up with the varsity.) After spending much of 2005 hobbled by ankle, quad, and knee problems in his right leg, Vidro lost time in 2006 to a left hamstring injury. He was hardly a speedster to begin with, so this spate of leg injuries doesn't portend good things for the future.

The argument in favor of acquiring Vidro rests on the fact that RFK Stadium was eating him alive. In two seasons in the nation's capital, Vidro hit .254/.324/.354 at home (394 PA), and .308/.360/.450 on the road (464 PA). As with other acquisitions during his tenure, it appears that Bavasi is counting on salvaging a player's value based on their road performance by removing them from a broken home. Still, any advantage these numbers might imply is offset by the fact that Safeco isn't exactly a hitter's paradise, either, and by the positional change that Vidro is making from the middle infield to DH. While Vidro may experience health benefits from a shift to DH, removing him from the middle infield also removes much of his value. A second baseman sporting Vidro's road average would be a special guy; a DH with that same production is pretty mediocre—and that's pretty close to a best-case scenario.

Bavasi didn't only acquire questionable players, he gave up talent to get them. While Guillen and Batista were Type B free agents, which require no compensation from their new teams under the new Collective Bargaining Agreement, Ramirez came to the Mariners at the cost of Rafael Soriano, a young right-hander who returned from surgery to be one of the top 25 relievers in the majors last year (by WXRL). Usually, a trade of a starting pitcher for a reliever is a positive move, because starters pitch more innings and are harder to come by. However, Soriano was a former top prospect with great stuff, while Ramirez is a pedestrian finesse lefty. In exchange for Vidro, Bavasi sent the Nationals Snelling and promising right-hander Emiliano Fruto. There is a very real possibility that Snelling will outperform Vidro in 2007, straight up, and for a fraction of Vidro's salary of $12 million over the next two years.

The losses of Snelling and Fruto, as well as Asdrubal Cabrera (traded for Perez) and Shin Soo Choo (traded for Ben Broussard), have thinned out the ranks of the team's most advanced prospects. At the same time that the organization is cashing in its prospects for veterans, there is concern about the development of many of the players remaining in the Mariners' system. Mariners position player prospects were below the average team age level at every minor league level above rookie ball. The effect is less pronounced among the M's pitching prospects, but falls into place at the higher levels. The Mariners featured the youngest teams in the Pacific Coast and Texas Leagues by a wide margin.

There are a number of factors that could help explain this phenomenon, including the Mariners' extensive efforts in signing foreign amateurs, who typically join the organization at an earlier age than a U.S. draftee would. However, case after case points to the Mariners rushing their highly regarded prospects through the minors. Some prospects, such as Jones, seemed to handle the sprint through the minors pretty well, while others, such as Jeff Clement, Rob Johnson, and Matt Tuiasosopo, wilted under the pressure. On the pitching side, the Mariners brought three pitchers (Mark Lowe, Travis Chick, and Mark Feierabend) to the majors directly from Double-A last year, and brought up another (Eric O'Flaherty) with all of two Pacific Coast League appearances under his belt. One has to wonder whether such an aggressive promotion scheme will hurt the development of these prospects. Putting a prospect in a position to struggle as the youngest player in his league (as happened to Cabrera prior to the Perez deal) is counterproductive and has been damaging to the Mariners so far.

Naturally the front office will have to take risks as Bavasi tries to squeeze a winning season out of this organization. Perhaps the Mariners' prospects won't be perma-

nently damaged by hop-scotching through the minors. Maybe Vidro will rediscover his health and potency now that he's removed from the keystone, and maybe Soriano's shoulder will blow up on the Braves, leaving everyone in the Pacific Northwest happy that the team got some return for him before it happened. An unexpected playoff run can plaster over a number of self-inflicted cuts, as the Tigers showed last season. But if this new, veteran ballclub doesn't jump into contention, and quickly, Mariners fans will have to live with the consequences far longer than Bavasi will.

HITTERS

Yuniesky Betancourt   SS   Bats: R   Throws: R   Height: 5' 10"   Weight: 190   Born: January 31, 1982   Age: 25

YEAR	TEAM	LVL	AGE	PA	R	2B	3B	HR	RBI	BB	SO	SB	CS	SPEED	AVG	OBP	SLG	MLVR	EQAVG	EQOBP	EQSLG	EQA	VORP	DEFENSE	
2005	SAN	AA	23	239	25	10	3	5	20	9	18	12	7	6.5	.273	.301	.410	-.003	.264	.296	.392	.239	3.2	51-SS	0
2005	TAC	AAA	23	194	13	9	6	2	30	6	14	7	5	5.9	.295	.323	.443	.044	.290	.311	.425	.250	7.4	48-SS	13
2005	SEA	MLB	23	228	24	11	5	1	15	11	24	1	3	6.2	.256	.296	.370	-.135	.269	.319	.389	.242	0.2	52-SS	-4
2006	SEA	MLB	24	584	68	28	6	8	47	17	54	11	8	6.1	.289	.310	.403	-.071	.295	.324	.418	.252	13.6	154-SS	-11
2007	SEA	MLB	25	578	67	28	5	9	57	22	53	12	7	6.2	.278	.307	.397	-.110	.277	.309	.408	.251	13.2	135-SS	0

Breakout: 31%   Improve: 56%   Collapse: 17%   Attrition: 14%   Comparables: Bill Russell, Rafael Ramirez, Orlando Cabrera, Dickie Thon

Despite Betancourt's agility, good footwork, and preternatural ability to make strong, accurate throws on the move, our Davenport Translations show his defensive performance to be seriously sub-par for the second straight season. The statistical evaluation of defense is far from perfect, and its best to get a consensus of different measures. Most other methods—including play-by-play measures based on Zone Rating—seem to be less than excited by Betancourt's range. Of course, a bad defensive season—or even the 210-game sample we have for Betancourt at the major league level—is not the last word on a player's defensive ability, just as a single bad season with the bat isn't the last word on a player's ability to hit. To go with one high-shelf example, in Dave Concepcion's first two seasons—a 205-game sample—he was a combined 13 runs below average at shortstop, but he would soon break out as an elite defender, averaging over 20 Fielding Runs Above Average per season from 1974 to 1977. Still, if Betancourt's numbers don't come around, he could take Derek Jeter's place as the shortstop fueling the fielding statistics debate.

Willie Bloomquist   UT   Bats: R   Throws: R   Height: 5' 11"   Weight: 195   Born: November 27, 1977   Age: 29

YEAR	TEAM	LVL	AGE	PA	R	2B	3B	HR	RBI	BB	SO	SB	CS	SPEED	AVG	OBP	SLG	MLVR	EQAVG	EQOBP	EQSLG	EQA	VORP	DEFENSE			
2004	SEA	MLB	26	201	27	10	0	2	18	10	48	13	2	7.3	.245	.283	.330	-.247	.246	.288	.332	.232	-3.4	26-3B	1	16-SS	-2
2005	SEA	MLB	27	267	27	15	2	0	22	11	38	14	1	7.0	.257	.289	.333	-.197	.265	.308	.347	.243	-0.4	29-2B	0	20-SS	-4
2006	SEA	MLB	28	283	36	6	2	1	15	24	40	16	3	7.5	.247	.320	.299	-.233	.254	.335	.306	.243	-2.4	36-CF	0	14-2B	-4
2007	SEA	MLB	29	306	35	11	2	2	22	19	48	13	4	6.9	.250	.303	.331	-.227	.249	.304	.340	.236	-3.8	74-CF	-3		

Breakout: 21%   Improve: 39%   Collapse: 27%   Attrition: 40%   Comparables: Jolbert Cabrera, Darren Lewis, Adrian Brown, Hank Allen

It's important to note that, in most cases, when we express exasperation over the performance of a player such as Bloomquist, it's not really the player that has upset us. Most of these scrappy out-machines give their all on the diamond. As long as he's doing his best, you can't blame a player for taking the field when his name's penciled into the lineup. Bloomquist didn't force Mike Hargrove to write his .243 EqA into the starting lineup 66 times last year—48 of them starts in the outfield. Bloomquist didn't force Bill Bavasi to extend his contract through 2008. While current management is in place, we can look forward to two more seasons of Bloomquist being applied as the all-healing balm for anything that ails the Mariners lineup, but that's not his fault. Then again, refusing the contract for the good of the team would have been a terrifically noble gesture.

Ben Broussard **DH** **Bats: L** **Throws: L** Height: 6′ 2″ Weight: 220 Born: September 24, 1976 Age: 30

YEAR	TEAM	LVL	AGE	PA	R	2B	3B	HR	RBI	BB	SO	SB	CS	SPEED	AVG	OBP	SLG	MLVR	EQAVG	EQOBP	EQSLG	EQA	VORP	DEFENSE		
2004	CLE	MLB	27	485	57	28	5	17	82	52	95	4	2	5.2	.275	.370	.488	.138	.284	.380	.510	.300	24.2	117-1B	-1	
2005	CLE	MLB	28	505	59	30	5	19	68	32	98	2	2	5.4	.255	.307	.464	.023	.264	.325	.492	.273	9.2	117-1B	0	
2006	CLE	MLB	29	288	44	14	0	13	46	17	58	0	1	4.3	.321	.361	.519	.219	.325	.372	.532	.301	18.3	65-1B	-2	
2006	SEA	MLB	29	177	17	7	0	8	17	9	45	2	0	4.1	.238	.282	.427	-.132	.241	.294	.438	.251	-1.3			
2007	*SEA*	*MLB*	*30*	*425*	*55*	*22*	*2*	*18*	*62*	*34*	*86*	*3*	*2*	*4.8*	*.269*	*.333*	*.473*	*.029*	*.268*	*.334*	*.485*	*.282*	*12.6*	*101-1B*	*-1*	

Breakout: 14% Improve: 34% Collapse: 30% Attrition: 15% Comparables: *Leon Durham, Raul Ibanez, Pat Putnam, Dale Long*

The on-base ability Broussard showed in 2004 proved to be a fluke, attributable to 12 hit-by-pitches and a momentary spike in his walk rate. Broussard was having the best season of his career when the M's picked him up in late July of last year, but his two months with the Mariners were ugly. Safeco is the biggest strikeout park in the majors, and Broussard's strikeout rate rose by 25 percent as a Mariner, with most of those extra Ks coming at home. Even if Broussard can adjust to life in the Pacific Northwest, given his age and track record, his upside—we've said it before, but the comparison still holds—is Paul Sorrento.

Yung-Chi Chen **2B** **Bats: R** **Throws: R** Height: 5′ 11″ Weight: 170 Born: July 13, 1983 Age: 23

YEAR	TEAM	LVL	AGE	PA	R	2B	3B	HR	RBI	BB	SO	SB	CS	SPEED	AVG	OBP	SLG	MLVR	EQAVG	EQOBP	EQSLG	EQA	VORP	DEFENSE				
2004	EVE	A-	20	222	37	13	1	3	34	16	36	25	3	7.9	.300	.353	.420	.072	.244	.279	.330	.225	-12.0	26-3B	2	20-2B	-3
2005	WIS	A	21	549	77	27	7	7	80	37	76	15	6	6.2	.292	.339	.416	.081	.267	.303	.378	.238	3.2	77-3B	8	35-2B	2
2006	SBR	A+	22	309	49	17	3	5	48	22	40	21	7	7.0	.342	.388	.478	.265	.315	.351	.437	.276	18.9	61-2B	-5		
2006	SAN	AA	22	174	22	9	2	3	22	18	23	5	3	6.3	.295	.365	.443	.158	.292	.349	.429	.270	9.3	34-2B	-3		
2007	*SEA*	*MLB*	*23*	*517*	*59*	*27*	*3*	*8*	*47*	*28*	*78*	*15*	*5*	*6.0*	*.266*	*.308*	*.382*	*-.137*	*.265*	*.310*	*.393*	*.250*	*6.2*	*122-2B*	*0*		

Breakout: 18% Improve: 46% Collapse: 26% Attrition: 4% Comparables: *Marco Scutaro, Chris Burke, Jack Wilson, Luis Maza*

Chen started the year with a bang, hitting a grand slam in Taiwan's WBC face-off against mainland China. He continued to rake in the California and Texas Leagues on his way to what was easily his best season as a pro. Chen's value is in his batting average and his versatility, but with a crowded field ahead of him for the utility slot—including Bloomquist, Mike Morse, and Michael Garciaparra—he can't afford to slack off at Tacoma in 2007.

Jeff Clement **C** **Bats: L** **Throws: R** Height: 6′ 1″ Weight: 210 Born: August 21, 1983 Age: 23

YEAR	TEAM	LVL	AGE	PA	R	2B	3B	HR	RBI	BB	SO	SB	CS	SPEED	AVG	OBP	SLG	MLVR	EQAVG	EQOBP	EQSLG	EQA	VORP	DEFENSE	
2005	WIS	A	21	127	17	5	0	6	20	12	25	1	2	1.9	.319	.386	.522	.320	.291	.339	.479	.275	8.4	20-C	-1
2006	SAN	AA	22	70	7	6	1	2	10	7	8	0	0	4.6	.288	.386	.525	.301	.290	.366	.516	.294	6.5	12-C	0
2006	TAC	AAA	22	272	23	10	0	4	32	16	53	0	2	3.2	.257	.321	.347	-.082	.253	.306	.337	.227	-3.5	36-C	0
2007	*SEA*	*MLB*	*23*	*401*	*36*	*18*	*1*	*10*	*46*	*26*	*80*	*0*	*1*	*3.7*	*.248*	*.305*	*.381*	*-.157*	*.247*	*.306*	*.392*	*.245*	*2.5*	*96-C*	*-2*

Breakout: 28% Improve: 48% Collapse: 25% Attrition: 16% Comparables: *Ryan Christianson, Mike Jacobs, Jed Morris, Javier Cardona*

Clement wasn't the same after undergoing knee and elbow surgery in May. It didn't help that the Mariners inexplicably promoted him directly to Triple-A after the injury. With Johjima backstopping at the major league level, there should have been no pressure to rush the third-overall pick from the 2005 draft. The trouble Clement had at Tacoma he carried over to the Hawaiian Winter League, where the young catcher finished under the Mendoza line. He'll have to work hard to reclaim the mantle of top Mariners prospect from Adam Jones.

Carl Everett **Nuisance** **Bats: S** **Throws: R** Height: 6′ 0″ Weight: 220 Born: June 3, 1971 Age: 35

YEAR	TEAM	LVL	AGE	PA	R	2B	3B	HR	RBI	BB	SO	SB	CS	SPEED	AVG	OBP	SLG	MLVR	EQAVG	EQOBP	EQSLG	EQA	VORP	DEFENSE			
2004	MON	MLB	33	141	8	10	0	2	14	8	19	0	0	2.5	.252	.319	.378	-.063	.250	.312	.375	.241	-1.1	15-LF	-3	14-RF	2
2004	CHA	MLB	33	169	21	7	1	5	21	8	26	1	0	5.0	.266	.320	.422	-.080	.266	.320	.422	.257	1.3				
2005	CHA	MLB	34	547	58	17	2	23	87	42	99	4	5	4.3	.251	.311	.435	-.033	.249	.318	.444	.260	6.3	13-LF	-2		
2006	SEA	MLB	35	343	37	8	0	11	33	29	57	1	3	3.6	.227	.297	.360	-.201	.230	.309	.368	.236	-9.9				
2007	*SEA*	*MLB*	*36*	*245*	*25*	*9*	*1*	*7*	*30*	*20*	*40*	*1*	*1*	*4.4*	*.236*	*.302*	*.378*	*-.173*	*.235*	*.304*	*.389*	*.245*	*-2.1*				

Breakout: 27% Improve: 42% Collapse: 37% Attrition: 48% Comparables: *Ted Simmons, Bob Jones, Gates Brown, Eric Karros*

(continued next page)

Carl Everett *(continued)*

The wit and wisdom of Carl Everett: "I've been booed here. I enjoy it. I don't mind the boos. You get booed when you can play." Well, sometimes they boo you when you *can't* play, too. Everett was brought in on a series of false assumptions—the front office counted his switch-hitting as an asset, even though he hadn't done anything from the right side of the plate since 1999, and they thought he'd be a good influence on his teammates, despite his well-known tendency to rebel against management when deprived of playing time. Who'd have imagined that this wouldn't work out well? If this is the end for Jurassic Carl, we wish him well and give him thanks for all the interesting moments of anger and philosophy he brought us over his 14-year career.

Raul Ibañez — LF — Bats: L — Throws: R — Height: 6' 2" — Weight: 220 — Born: June 2, 1972 — Age: 35

YEAR	TEAM	LVL	AGE	PA	R	2B	3B	HR	RBI	BB	SO	SB	CS	SPEED	AVG	OBP	SLG	MLVR	EQAVG	EQOBP	EQSLG	EQA	VORP	DEFENSE	
2004	SEA	MLB	32	524	67	31	1	16	62	36	72	1	2	4.0	.304	.353	.472	.150	.312	.365	.485	.288	22.5	100-LF	7
2005	SEA	MLB	33	690	92	32	2	20	89	71	99	9	4	5.3	.280	.355	.436	.088	.291	.375	.464	.289	29.3	53-LF	-2
2006	SEA	MLB	34	699	103	33	5	33	123	65	115	2	4	4.6	.289	.353	.516	.171	.296	.368	.536	.299	37.8	156-LF	-4
2007	*SEA*	*MLB*	*35*	*621*	*84*	*32*	*3*	*22*	*88*	*57*	*99*	*4*	*2*	*4.9*	*.282*	*.350*	*.470*	*.066*	*.281*	*.352*	*.483*	*.289*	*23.4*	*145-LF*	*-4*

Breakout: 12%   Improve: 33%   Collapse: 24%   Attrition: 5%   Comparables: B. J. Surhoff, Larry Walker, Dave Parker, Jim Northrup

BP 2004: "The Mariners are going to be staring at a lot of wasted salary by the end of his awful three-year, $13-million contract." BP 2007: Oops. Ibañez looked like he had started to decline in 2003 after a modest peak during his time in Kansas City. Instead, he decided to take a junior version of the Luis Gonzalez career path, by which a formerly mediocre left fielder goes on an unexpected tear in his early 30s. As for how much salary Seattle "wasted," Ibañez was worth nearly fourteen wins over replacement over the course of the contract. As measured by Marginal Value Above Replacement, his 2006 season alone was worth $10.4 million. Far from asking for their money back, the Mariners extended Ibañez's contract through 2008. As to what we said about Ibanez in 2004, well, um . . . the guy who wrote that isn't with us anymore.

Kenji Johjima — C — Bats: R — Throws: R — Height: 6' 0" — Weight: 200 — Born: June 8, 1976 — Age: 31

YEAR	TEAM	LVL	AGE	PA	R	2B	3B	HR	RBI	BB	SO	SB	CS	SPEED	AVG	OBP	SLG	MLVR	EQAVG	EQOBP	EQSLG	EQA	VORP	DEFENSE	
2004	FKU	JP	28	497	91	25	1	36	91	49	45	6	0	5.0	.338	.433	.655	.517	.334	.412	.519	.315	56.9		
2005	FKU	JP	29	444	70	22	4	24	57	33	32	3	4	5.1	.309	.360	.557	.290	.313	.372	.488	.292	37.7		
2006	SEA	MLB	30	542	61	25	1	18	76	20	46	3	1	4.2	.291	.332	.451	.039	.297	.343	.468	.276	24.0	131-C	3
2007	*SEA*	*MLB*	*31*	*496*	*64*	*26*	*2*	*12*	*61*	*32*	*45*	*3*	*1*	*4.6*	*.296*	*.350*	*.441*	*.038*	*.294*	*.351*	*.453*	*.282*	*23.5*	*117-C*	*1*

Breakout: 9%   Improve: 30%   Collapse: 31%   Attrition: 10%   Comparables: Thurman Munson, Paul Lo Duca, Del Crandall, Terry Steinbach

PECOTA had this Japanese import pegged. The catcher was one of the hardest batters to strike out in the AL, leading all batting-title qualifiers by striking out in only 8.49 percent of his plate appearances. That's free swinging by Johjima's standards; in 2003 he struck out in just 15 of 604 plate appearances (2.48 percent) with Fukuoka. With Johjima signed for two more years (a bargain at just over $5 million per) and Clement and Rob Johnson in the queue, the M's should have the catching position covered for the forseeable future.

Rob Johnson — C — Bats: R — Throws: R — Height: 6' 1" — Weight: 200 — Born: July 22, 1983 — Age: 23

YEAR	TEAM	LVL	AGE	PA	R	2B	3B	HR	RBI	BB	SO	SB	CS	SPEED	AVG	OBP	SLG	MLVR	EQAVG	EQOBP	EQSLG	EQA	VORP	DEFENSE	
2004	EVE	A-	20	84	17	3	1	1	7	4	10	6	2	8.3	.234	.286	.338	-.189	.162	.190	.188	.153	-24.0		
2005	WIS	A	21	335	41	19	1	9	51	20	31	10	3	4.7	.272	.319	.430	.053	.243	.277	.383	.231	-4.0	75-C	2
2005	SBR	A+	21	86	15	3	0	2	12	10	14	2	0	4.8	.314	.381	.443	.070	.288	.345	.397	.269	2.9	19-C	2
2006	TAC	AAA	22	359	28	9	4	4	33	13	74	14	7	6.1	.231	.261	.318	-.257	.235	.261	.314	.206	-17.5	71-C	4
2007	*SEA*	*MLB*	*23*	*375*	*34*	*15*	*2*	*5*	*34*	*14*	*69*	*10*	*5*	*5.2*	*.239*	*.270*	*.334*	*-.290*	*.238*	*.271*	*.343*	*.218*	*-9.1*	*90-C*	*6*

Breakout: 51%   Improve: 68%   Collapse: 17%   Attrition: 22%   Comparables: Yorvit Torrealba, Joe Azcue, Juan Brito, Josh Paul

In the mad rush to get their catching prospects to the majors, the Mariners made Johnson—with all of 80 High-A plate appearances under his belt—skip Double-A altogether and spend all of 2006 in Tacoma. Guess what? It was hard! Johnson's a good catch-and-throw guy, but his bat is going to take some time to develop. Tacoma might not be big enough for Johnson and Clement to both get the playing time they need.

Adam Jones CF Bats: R Throws: R Height: 6' 2" Weight: 200 Born: August 1, 1985 Age: 21

YEAR	TEAM	LVL	AGE	PA	R	2B	3B	HR	RBI	BB	SO	SB	CS	SPEED	AVG	OBP	SLG	MLVR	EQAVG	EQOBP	EQSLG	EQA	VORP	DEFENSE		
2004	WIS	A	18	559	76	23	7	11	72	33	124	8	4	5.8	.267	.314	.404	.030	.241	.278	.354	.223	-8.8	112-SS	-16	
2005	SBR	A+	19	315	43	20	5	8	46	29	64	4	5	5.2	.295	.374	.494	.114	.259	.319	.401	.250	8.1	64-SS	-8	
2005	SAN	AA	19	257	33	10	3	7	20	22	48	9	4	5.8	.298	.365	.461	.199	.293	.354	.444	.275	17.8	59-SS	-1	
2006	TAC	AAA	20	416	69	19	4	16	62	28	78	13	4	6.1	.287	.345	.484	.184	.291	.341	.488	.281	26.7	83-CF	-1	12-RF 1
2006	SEA	MLB	20	76	6	4	0	1	8	2	22	3	1	5.3	.216	.237	.311	-.405	.205	.237	.288	.192	-4.1	22-CF	5	
2007	SEA	MLB	21	520	63	26	3	14	59	34	107	12	5	5.7	.263	.317	.418	-.076	.262	.318	.430	.263	12.1	122-CF	0	

Breakout: 24% Improve: 62% Collapse: 15% Attrition: 6%   Comparables: Brandon Phillips, Elijah Dukes, Franklin Gutierrez, Chet Lemon

Another prospect the M's just couldn't wait for, the toolsy Jones adapted well to a move from shortstop to center field last year, didn't let the position change affect his development with the bat, and got his first taste of the Show in July—all that without being able to have a legal drink until August. Now that Ichiro's in center and Jose Guillen is on board as the new right fielder, Jones could stand to return to Triple-A to work on his plate discipline and his fly-catching.

Bryan LaHair 1B Bats: L Throws: R Height: 6' 5" Weight: 215 Born: November 5, 1982 Age: 24

YEAR	TEAM	LVL	AGE	PA	R	2B	3B	HR	RBI	BB	SO	SB	CS	SPEED	AVG	OBP	SLG	MLVR	EQAVG	EQOBP	EQSLG	EQA	VORP	DEFENSE		
2004	WIS	A	21	280	30	24	0	5	29	16	66	0	6	2.8	.279	.323	.427	.084	.237	.272	.357	.214	-14.8	41-1B	-1	30-LF -1
2005	SBR	A+	22	569	81	28	2	22	113	51	125	0	1	2.5	.310	.373	.503	.140	.278	.329	.421	.258	6.4	116-1B	3	
2006	SAN	AA	23	252	22	12	0	6	30	24	52	0	0	3.6	.293	.371	.428	.144	.285	.347	.412	.264	4.9	57-1B	2	
2006	TAC	AAA	23	230	36	10	0	10	44	23	49	3	0	4.8	.327	.393	.525	.364	.332	.391	.532	.313	22.6	52-1B	5	
2007	SEA	MLB	24	489	51	24	1	14	61	35	112	1	1	4.0	.265	.319	.418	-.071	.264	.321	.429	.262	1.7	115-1B	2	

Breakout: 15% Improve: 48% Collapse: 25% Attrition: 11%   Comparables: Tim Giles, Chris Duncan, Scott Thorman, Kevin Burns

A 39th-round pick in 2002, LaHair was old for his level in 2005, but caught up by playing well at two levels last year. Big and slow with old-player skills, he's running out of time if he wants to avoid the dreaded Quadruple-A tag. It doesn't help that he's blocked by Sexson and Broussard at the big league level.

Jose Lopez 2B Bats: R Throws: R Height: 6' 0" Weight: 200 Born: November 24, 1983 Age: 23

YEAR	TEAM	LVL	AGE	PA	R	2B	3B	HR	RBI	BB	SO	SB	CS	SPEED	AVG	OBP	SLG	MLVR	EQAVG	EQOBP	EQSLG	EQA	VORP	DEFENSE		
2004	TAC	AAA	20	303	40	19	0	13	39	16	30	6	2	4.7	.295	.342	.505	.151	.272	.315	.448	.261	13.9	42-SS	0	20-3B -2
2004	SEA	MLB	20	218	28	13	0	5	22	8	31	0	1	4.7	.232	.263	.367	-.240	.233	.267	.364	.217	-3.1	54-SS	-8	
2005	TAC	AAA	21	194	29	19	0	5	31	8	25	2	3	4.0	.319	.354	.505	.227	.297	.326	.459	.261	10.3	44-2B	-5	
2005	SEA	MLB	21	203	18	19	0	2	25	6	25	4	2	4.9	.247	.282	.379	-.149	.257	.299	.401	.242	-1.1	50-2B	2	
2006	SEA	MLB	22	655	78	28	8	10	79	26	80	5	2	5.7	.282	.319	.405	-.058	.289	.331	.424	.260	18.3	148-2B	-18	
2007	SEA	MLB	23	590	68	31	3	12	64	26	69	7	3	5.5	.279	.317	.415	-.067	.278	.319	.426	.261	16.0	138-2B	-7	

Breakout: 31% Improve: 55% Collapse: 14% Attrition: 9%   Comparables: Bill Mazeroski, Rennie Stennett, Bobby Valentine, Tommy Davis

Jose Lopez finished the season with a performance that was achingly similar to that of his double-play partner, Betancourt, right down to the disappointing defensive numbers. Lopez's power disappeared after the All-Star break; his second-half isolated power was a mere .051 compared to .174 prior to the midsummer classic. That finish gave him the distinction of concluding the season with the lowest WARP total of any Mariner All-Star ever. The only man who came close to Lopez's 2.0 WARP was Jeffrey Leonard, who posted a 2.5 WARP in 1989, when his gaudy home run and RBI totals at the half convinced Tony La Russa to put the DH with a .319 OBP on the squad, even though Leonard's teammate Alvin Davis had a better slugging percentage and an OBP more than 100 points higher. Lopez's EqA was the lowest for a Mariner All-Star since Harold Reynolds (.246) in 1987. On the positive side, Lopez just turned 23 in November, so there's still a chance for him to develop into a legitimate All-Star.

Michael Morse   UT   Bats: R   Throws: R   Height: 6' 4"   Weight: 225   Born: March 22, 1982   Age: 25

YEAR	TEAM	LVL	AGE	PA	R	2B	3B	HR	RBI	BB	SO	SB	CS	SPEED	AVG	OBP	SLG	MLVR	EQAVG	EQOBP	EQSLG	EQA	VORP	DEFENSE			
2004	BIR	AA	22	226	30	9	5	11	38	15	46	0	3	4.8	.287	.336	.536	.246	.269	.313	.481	.264	13.5	47-SS	-7		
2004	SAN	AA	22	173	18	10	1	6	33	9	27	0	2	3.1	.274	.326	.465	.133	.267	.306	.447	.254	7.2	40-SS	0		
2005	TAC	AAA	23	203	20	12	2	4	23	16	36	1	0	3.6	.253	.317	.407	-.063	.247	.300	.382	.239	1.6	49-SS	2		
2005	SEA	MLB	23	258	27	10	1	3	23	18	50	3	1	3.9	.278	.349	.370	-.010	.291	.368	.396	.272	9.1	51-SS	-9		
2006	TAC	AAA	24	228	23	15	1	5	34	14	46	0	1	3.4	.248	.300	.403	-.048	.254	.298	.416	.244	3.5	15-3B	0	14-1B	1
2006	SEA	MLB	24	48	5	5	0	0	11	3	7	1	0	3.9	.372	.396	.488	.287	.381	.417	.500	.322	4.6				
2007	SEA	MLB	25	432	42	22	2	10	52	25	86	1	1	4.1	.255	.304	.396	-.134	.254	.305	.407	.250	3.6	103-SS	-1		

Breakout: 18% Improve: 41% Collapse: 27% Attrition: 14% Comparables: Jeff Baker, Corey Myers, Brennan King, Wes Helms

Morse started his inexorable slide down the defensive spectrum in 2006, getting playing time at third base, left field, and first base in addition to his usual position of shortstop. That versatility will increase his chances of sticking with the big club, but since he's right-handed, gravitating toward the corners, and never walks, he'll have to show more power than we've seen to this point. He'll also have to shake the "fragile" label—tough to do after losing another month of his career to knee surgery last year.

Eduardo Perez   1B   Bats: R   Throws: R   Height: 6' 4"   Weight: 240   Born: December 31, 1969   Age: 37

YEAR	TEAM	LVL	AGE	PA	R	2B	3B	HR	RBI	BB	SO	SB	CS	SPEED	AVG	OBP	SLG	MLVR	EQAVG	EQOBP	EQSLG	EQA	VORP	DEFENSE	
2004	TBA	MLB	34	42	2	2	0	1	7	4	9	0	0	3.2	.211	.286	.342	-.266	.211	.286	.342	.221	-1.8		
2005	TBA	MLB	35	190	23	6	0	11	28	26	30	0	2	2.3	.255	.368	.497	.163	.264	.387	.522	.302	9.3	37-1B	-4
2006	CLE	MLB	36	108	16	9	0	8	22	5	11	0	0	3.3	.303	.343	.636	.340	.306	.352	.653	.320	10.1	22-1B	0
2006	SEA	MLB	36	102	6	1	0	1	11	13	22	0	1	2.9	.195	.304	.241	-.372	.186	.304	.233	.204	-7.2		
2007	SEA	MLB	37	311	35	14	0	11	44	29	53	0	1	3.1	.258	.332	.433	-.033	.257	.334	.444	.271	5.4	75-DH	

Breakout: 4% Improve: 19% Collapse: 36% Attrition: 50% Comparables: Joe Adcock, Bob Watson, Walt Dropo, Cliff Johnson

The other half of the magical Cleveland first base platoon that was traded to the Mariners, Perez, like Broussard, found life in Safeco not worth living. Perez has quietly made a 13-year career out of one skill, the ability to mash lefties—in nearly 1,000 plate appearances against them, he's hit .265/.362/.501, more than 200 OPS points higher than he's hit against right-handed pitchers. Now a free agent, someone is certain to see some value in what Perez brings to the table.

Guillermo Quiroz   C   Bats: R   Throws: R   Height: 6' 1"   Weight: 200   Born: November 29, 1981   Age: 25

YEAR	TEAM	LVL	AGE	PA	R	2B	3B	HR	RBI	BB	SO	SB	CS	SPEED	AVG	OBP	SLG	MLVR	EQAVG	EQOBP	EQSLG	EQA	VORP	DEFENSE	
2004	SYR	AAA	22	288	32	19	1	8	32	28	54	0	0	3.7	.227	.309	.404	-.120	.206	.285	.366	.228	-6.1	71-C	-5
2004	TOR	MLB	22	57	2	2	0	0	6	2	8	1	0	3.9	.212	.263	.250	-.449	.192	.246	.231	.184	-3.6	12-C	-1
2005	DUN	A+	23	43	4	1	0	2	6	2	8	0	0	1.6	.237	.326	.421	.007	.225	.279	.400	.225	-0.9		
2005	SYR	AAA	23	94	11	3	0	6	18	9	19	0	0	2.2	.229	.309	.482	-.019	.202	.284	.405	.237	-0.8	23-C	-1
2005	TOR	MLB	23	39	3	2	0	0	4	2	13	0	0	4.8	.194	.256	.250	-.417	.167	.250	.222	.177	-2.4		
2006	TAC	AAA	24	153	15	8	0	3	28	11	29	0	0	3.4	.304	.359	.428	.143	.300	.346	.421	.268	7.5	29-C	3
2006	SAN	AA	24	68	5	3	0	3	9	3	15	0	0	2.8	.188	.235	.375	-.257	.154	.191	.277	.170	-8.0	15-C	-1
2007	TEX	MLB	25	289	23	11	0	7	32	16	61	0	0	3.7	.225	.275	.344	-.275	.218	.273	.339	.214	-8.7	71-C	-2

Breakout: 31% Improve: 44% Collapse: 38% Attrition: 20% Comparables: Pat Cline, Jason Dewey, Dan Conway, Ryan Jorgensen

Picked up on waivers from Toronto, Quiroz saw just how much his stock dropped when the Mariners sent him down to Double-A in July. Still, he showed a little life with the bat at Triple-A, and his defensive reputation remains intact. A free agent, he signed a one-year major league contract with the Rangers; he'll compete with Miguel Ojeda for the backup job behind Gerald Laird.

Jeremy Reed

CF **Bats: L** **Throws: L** Height: 6' 0" Weight: 200 Born: June 15, 1981 Age: 26

YEAR	TEAM	LVL	AGE	PA	R	2B	3B	HR	RBI	BB	SO	SB	CS	SPEED	AVG	OBP	SLG	MLVR	EQAVG	EQOBP	EQSLG	EQA	VORP	DEFENSE	
2004	CHR	AAA	23	324	44	14	1	8	37	36	34	12	7	5.6	.275	.357	.420	.039	.261	.341	.396	.259	7.2	65-CF	0
2004	TAC	AAA	23	259	40	10	5	5	36	23	22	14	2	7.6	.305	.366	.455	.129	.292	.349	.415	.271	10.5	60-CF	5
2004	SEA	MLB	23	66	11	4	0	0	5	7	4	3	1	5.3	.397	.470	.466	.387	.414	.493	.483	.345	7.3	16-CF	0
2005	SEA	MLB	24	544	61	33	3	3	45	48	74	12	11	5.5	.254	.322	.352	-.108	.267	.344	.377	.251	-2.0	131-CF	-3
2006	SEA	MLB	25	229	27	6	5	6	17	11	31	2	3	6.5	.217	.260	.377	-.257	.219	.269	.395	.225	-6.5	57-CF	-5
2007	*SEA*	*MLB*	*26*	*388*	*51*	*18*	*3*	*7*	*38*	*33*	*47*	*9*	*4*	*6.3*	*.267*	*.333*	*.396*	*-.075*	*.266*	*.334*	*.407*	*.264*	*7.8*	*93-CF*	*-1*

Breakout: 38% Improve: 60% Collapse: 14% Attrition: 28%   *Comparables: Hosken Powell, Steve Hovley, Steve Lyons, Joe Orsulak*

Injuries derailed Reed's season and, at age 26, with no positive major league track record to speak of, he's past his prospect expiration date. The Mariners have moved on, installing Ichiro as the centerfielder for 2007 and grooming Adam Jones as the Center Fielder of the Future. The question is, do the Mariners cut bait on Reed, or do they keep him around, hoping that some other team will take a look at his .327/.401/.478 career minor league line and want to take a whiff of the milk carton? Top PECOTA comp Hosken Powell had a .334 average in the minor leagues from 1975 to 1977, but hit .259 in the majors from 1978 to 1983. He and the other comparables are PECOTA code for, "I wash my hands of him."

Rene Rivera

C **Bats: R** **Throws: R** Height: 5' 10" Weight: 210 Born: July 31, 1983 Age: 23

YEAR	TEAM	LVL	AGE	PA	R	2B	3B	HR	RBI	BB	SO	SB	CS	SPEED	AVG	OBP	SLG	MLVR	EQAVG	EQOBP	EQSLG	EQA	VORP	DEFENSE	
2004	SBR	A+	20	424	41	22	1	6	53	28	70	0	1	2.9	.235	.300	.346	-.175	.196	.246	.265	.187	-33.8	97-C	23
2005	SAN	AA	21	221	20	14	1	2	21	7	35	1	0	3.4	.278	.305	.382	-.033	.269	.299	.368	.233	-0.4	56-C	3
2005	TAC	AAA	21	51	3	3	0	1	6	2	12	0	1	2.3	.204	.235	.327	-.387	.184	.216	.286	.177	-4.6	13-C	0
2005	SEA	MLB	21	50	3	3	0	1	6	1	11	0	0	3.4	.396	.408	.521	.423	.404	.429	.532	.325	7.1	13-C	-2
2006	SEA	MLB	22	106	8	4	0	2	4	3	29	1	0	4.8	.152	.184	.253	-.621	.122	.165	.214	.148	-11.5	30-C	2
2007	*SEA*	*MLB*	*23*	*323*	*26*	*14*	*1*	*6*	*34*	*15*	*70*	*2*	*1*	*4.2*	*.231*	*.271*	*.347*	*-.275*	*.230*	*.272*	*.356*	*.220*	*-6.5*	*78-C*	*4*

Breakout: 59% Improve: 69% Collapse: 16% Attrition: 35%   *Comparables: Joe Azcue, Fred Kendall, Terry Humphrey, Javier Valentin*

On a per-at-bat basis, Rivera had one of the worst-hitting seasons in the American League last year—right up there with Edgardo Alfonso, Kevin Witt, and Antonio Perez. Some credit should go to the Mariners' pizza-delivery development program, which saw Rivera as a full-time backup despite having fewer than 70 career plate appearances at Triple-A. Note to Bill Bavasi: You don't get your players in 30 minutes or less. You get them when they're ready.

Richie Sexson

1B **Bats: R** **Throws: R** Height: 6' 8" Weight: 235 Born: December 29, 1974 Age: 32

YEAR	TEAM	LVL	AGE	PA	R	2B	3B	HR	RBI	BB	SO	SB	CS	SPEED	AVG	OBP	SLG	MLVR	EQAVG	EQOBP	EQSLG	EQA	VORP	DEFENSE	
2004	ARI	MLB	29	104	20	4	0	9	23	14	21	0	0	4.4	.233	.337	.578	.174	.222	.327	.556	.288	5.6	23-1B	0
2005	SEA	MLB	30	656	99	36	1	39	121	89	167	1	1	3.6	.263	.369	.541	.235	.275	.389	.577	.318	45.7	148-1B	10
2006	SEA	MLB	31	663	75	40	0	34	107	64	154	1	1	3.1	.264	.338	.504	.103	.269	.350	.524	.291	24.9	147-1B	12
2007	*SEA*	*MLB*	*32*	*647*	*85*	*32*	*1*	*32*	*100*	*76*	*158*	*0*	*1*	*3.7*	*.256*	*.348*	*.489*	*.064*	*.255*	*.350*	*.502*	*.292*	*22.0*	*151-1B*	*5*

Breakout: 2% Improve: 22% Collapse: 34% Attrition: 2%   *Comparables: Jose Canseco, Dale Murphy, Cecil Fielder, Frank Howard*

After absolutely killing the M's in the first half of last season, Sexson came on like gangbusters in the last two months, salvaging his season numbers, but perhaps not the affection of the franchise's fans. He gained 91 points of EqA in the second half, the fourth-largest increase in the majors after Rondell White, Kaz Matsui, and Ryan Howard (one of these things is not like the others). Unlike Betancourt, Sexson's Defensive Translations seem to be refuted by all other metrics available, as well as the naked eye. It's possible that our system is giving him credit at the cost of a too-negative evaluation of Lopez, his partner on the right side of the infield. The Mariners shopped him in the offseason but asked for a starting ace in return; with $28 million left on Sexson's contract, they're certain to try again at the trading deadline.

Chris Snelling

OF **Bats: L** **Throws: L** Height: 5' 10" Weight: 205 Born: December 3, 1981 Age: 25

YEAR	TEAM	LVL	AGE	PA	R	2B	3B	HR	RBI	BB	SO	SB	CS	SPEED	AVG	OBP	SLG	MLVR	EQAVG	EQOBP	EQSLG	EQA	VORP	DEFENSE			
2005	TAC	AAA	23	291	50	17	2	8	46	36	43	2	3	3.8	.370	.452	.553	.527	.369	.440	.536	.330	35.7	41-RF	-6	11-LF	-1
2005	SEA	MLB	23	35	4	2	0	1	1	5	2	0	2	3.9	.276	.382	.448	.122	.286	.412	.464	.281	0.5				
2006	TAC	AAA	24	290	36	13	1	5	39	31	60	4	2	4.4	.216	.326	.340	-.109	.226	.321	.359	.243	-8.5	31-RF	3		
2006	SEA	MLB	24	119	14	6	1	3	8	13	38	2	1	6.4	.250	.360	.427	.023	.263	.377	.442	.285	3.2	26-RF	-4		
2007	*WAS*	*MLB*	*25*	*439*	*57*	*23*	*3*	*12*	*53*	*47*	*89*	*4*	*4*	*4.7*	*.265*	*.355*	*.441*	*.014*	*.270*	*.360*	*.455*	*.278*	*13.1*	*104-RF*	*-5*		

Breakout: 11% Improve: 33% Collapse: 26% Attrition: 10%   *Comparables: Rob Ryan, Paul McAnulty, Darrell Evans, Kevin Burford*

(continued next page)

Chris Snelling *(continued)*

Life doesn't have to be like a hamster wheel; you can make forward progress if you try. For example, if you have a promising young player such as Snelling, a fellow who can hit but breaks something every time he takes the field, you could: (A) install him as your DH, confident that he'll hit enough to be productive at the position and will stay relatively healthy having been restricted from all that exercise that outfielders are forced to get, or (B) you can trade for Jose Vidro, an old, more expensive DH who is almost certain not to out-hit Snelling and is not guaranteed to be healthy either. Vidro is the hamster wheel. From Snelling's perspective, the move to Washington is a positive because he should have a clear shot at playing time, but a negative because, in the National League, he'll have to run and jump and hop and skip and contend with some of the worst traffic problems in the nation—the perfect recipe for more trips to the 60-Day DL.

Ichiro Suzuki   **OF**   **Bats: L   Throws: R**   Height: 5' 9"   Weight: 170   Born: October 22, 1973   Age: 33

YEAR	TEAM	LVL	AGE	PA	R	2B	3B	HR	RBI	BB	SO	SB	CS	SPEED	AVG	OBP	SLG	MLVR	EQAVG	EQOBP	EQSLG	EQA	VORP	DEFENSE	
2004	SEA	MLB	30	762	101	24	5	8	60	49	63	36	11	6.6	.372	.414	.455	.284	.383	.428	.471	.314	68.7	158-RF	5
2005	SEA	MLB	31	739	111	21	12	15	68	48	66	33	8	7.8	.303	.350	.436	.097	.317	.372	.466	.291	34.1	158-RF	9
2006	SEA	MLB	32	752	110	20	9	9	49	49	71	45	2	7.7	.322	.370	.416	.088	.329	.383	.426	.293	46.4	119-RF	2 38-CF 4
2007	SEA	MLB	33	654	94	23	5	6	54	40	59	20	7	6.5	.310	.354	.398	-.003	.308	.355	.409	.274	13.8	152-RF	0

Breakout: 6%   Improve: 10%   Collapse: 35%   Attrition: 12%   Comparables: Lance Johnson, Matty Alou, Mickey Rivers, Lou Brock

Ichiro finally made the shift to center field in August, just in time to enter the walk year of his contract; his projected VORP for 2007 would jump up from 13.8 as a right fielder (as shown above) to 27.0 as a center fielder. It's almost inconceivable that Seattle wouldn't keep Suzuki on for the three additional years it will probably take for him to reach 2,000 hits in his major league career. In 2007 he will pass 3,000 hits for his combined career in Japan and the United States. PECOTA's pessimism is based on the fact that some of Ichiro's comps have lost their wheels at this age, but it's hard to imagine Suzuki slowing down after enjoying one of the best basestealing seasons in history. Ichiro's 95.7 percent stolen base success rate in 2006 is the all-time high for anyone who's attempted 40 steals. In addition, the threat of Ichiro's speed led to four botched pickoff attempts, tied with Scott Podsednik and Willy Taveras for most in the majors.

Matt Tuiasosopo   **SS**   **Bats: R   Throws: R**   Height: 6' 2"   Weight: 210   Born: May 10, 1986   Age: 21

YEAR	TEAM	LVL	AGE	PA	R	2B	3B	HR	RBI	BB	SO	SB	CS	SPEED	AVG	OBP	SLG	MLVR	EQAVG	EQOBP	EQSLG	EQA	VORP	DEFENSE	
2004	EVE	A-	18	123	20	6	1	3	17	11	38	4	3	6.2	.255	.350	.415	.027	.211	.266	.325	.209	-12.9		
2005	WIS	A	19	464	72	21	3	6	45	44	96	8	5	5.1	.276	.359	.386	.059	.254	.313	.353	.234	2.2	76-SS -17	
2006	SBR	A+	20	253	31	14	0	1	34	14	58	5	6	4.2	.306	.359	.379	.032	.276	.313	.339	.228	0.9	39-SS -4	15-3B 1
2006	SAN	AA	20	241	16	4	0	1	10	20	64	2	1	4.0	.185	.259	.218	-.432	.181	.242	.204	.170	-26.4	56-3B -10	
2007	SEA	MLB	21	440	36	16	1	5	35	24	106	4	3	4.9	.231	.279	.313	-.307	.230	.280	.321	.211	-13.1	105-3B -9	

Breakout: 43% Improve: 60% Collapse: 23% Attrition: 10%   Comparables: Dennis Abreu, Chris Patten, Chuck Klee, Papo Bolivar

Stop us if you've heard this one before: Baby Tui was rushed to Double-A. Rushed, as in, he was the youngest player in the Texas League aside from a couple of kids who got one-game shots of espresso. Among the whippersnappers who got substantial playing time, Tuiasosopo was 22 days younger than the next youngest guy, Wichita's Billy Butler. This illustrates the problem in the Mariners system: Butler was young for Double-A as well, but he had the distinction of having hit very well at every stop along the way—whipping the Pioneer League and overpowering the California League with a .348 batting average and 25 homers—earning his promotion. In contrast, the Mariners ignored Tuiasosopo's double-digit isolated power at Inland Empire (.073), blindly kicking him up to San Antonio based on an empty .300 batting average. Beyond the M's questionable player development policies, there are plenty of questions about whether Tuiasosopo has the basic baseball talent to justify the money the team spent to keep him away from football.

Luis Valbuena   **2B**   **Bats: L   Throws: R**   Height: 5' 10"   Weight: 160   Born: November 30, 1985   Age: 21

YEAR	TEAM	LVL	AGE	PA	R	2B	3B	HR	RBI	BB	SO	SB	CS	SPEED	AVG	OBP	SLG	MLVR	EQAVG	EQOBP	EQSLG	EQA	VORP	DEFENSE
2005	EVE	A-	19	325	47	10	3	12	51	31	37	14	6	6.5	.261	.333	.443	.072	.211	.265	.342	.217	-23.3	72-2B -6
2006	WIS	A	20	373	45	16	6	3	38	44	44	21	7	6.5	.286	.371	.400	.154	.264	.330	.377	.252	6.9	80-2B 1
2006	SBR	A+	20	181	18	10	1	2	10	14	26	1	3	4.7	.252	.315	.362	-.114	.228	.275	.323	.209	-6.9	28-2B -2
2007	SEA	MLB	21	524	57	25	3	7	45	37	69	11	5	5.6	.251	.306	.357	-.185	.250	.308	.366	.241	0.8	123-2B -1

Breakout: 49% Improve: 72% Collapse: 12% Attrition: 8%   Comparables: Nate Spears, Ramon Vazquez, Callix Crabbe, Mike Peeples

Calling someone a second base prospect might be an oxymoron. After all, most of the players who wind up at the keystone at the major league level were shortstops in the minors, at least for a time. Valbuena's got some speed, some on-base ability, and a bit of gap power, but he's nowhere close to the majors.

PITCHERS

Cha-Seung Baek
Bats: R Throws: R   Height: 6' 4"   Weight: 220   Born: May 29, 1980   Age: 27

YEAR	TEAM	LVL	AGE	W	L	SV	G	GS	IP	H	BB	SO	HR	GB%	BABIP	STUFF	WHIP	ERA	PERA	EQERA	EQH9	EQBB9	EQSO9	EQHR9	VORP	WXRL
2004	TAC	AAA	24	5	4	0	14	14	72²	85	24	56	7	—	.329	3	1.50	4.21	4.44	5.11	10.1	3.0	5.4	1.0	4.0	—
2004	SEA	MLB	24	2	4	0	7	5	31	35	11	20	5	—	.297	-4	1.48	5.52	5.03	6.47	9.8	2.8	5.3	1.4	-2.0	0.34
2005	TAC	AAA	25	8	8	0	25	21	113²	147	36	73	19	47.8%	.340	-29	1.61	6.41	5.59	7.53	11.5	2.7	4.3	1.7	-24.6	—
2006	TAC	AAA	26	12	4	0	24	24	147²	133	37	103	17	49.6%	.269	-2	1.15	3.00	5.10	4.01	8.1	2.2	4.8	1.4	26.1	—
2006	SEA	MLB	26	4	1	0	6	6	34¹	26	13	23	6	44.1%	.208	6	1.14	3.67	5.50	3.82	6.4	3.1	5.6	1.5	7.9	1.20
2007	*SEA*	*MLB*	*27*	*6*	*9*	*0*	*34*	*22*	*123*	*140*	*41*	*72*	*19*	*45.0%*	*.300*	*-3*	*1.48*	*5.38*	*5.12*	*5.25*	*9.9*	*2.7*	*4.9*	*1.3*	*1.8*	*1.00*

Breakout: 10%   Improve: 43%   Collapse: 18%   Attrition: 0%   Comparables: Eric Rasmussen, Shane Bowers, Amaury Telemaco, Ron Kline

Things finally clicked for Baek on his third go-around in Tacoma. A big-bonus prospect out of Korea all the way back in the twentieth century, Baek posted a 12–4 record at Triple-A last year before the Jamie Moyer trade got him a promotion to Seattle. He made six starts for the Mariners—three of them quality—before triceps tendonitis ended his season. If healthy, he will be in the scrum for a rotation spot in spring training.

Yorman Bazardo
Bats: R Throws: R   Height: 6' 2"   Weight: 220   Born: July 11, 1984   Age: 22

YEAR	TEAM	LVL	AGE	W	L	SV	G	GS	IP	H	BB	SO	HR	GB%	BABIP	STUFF	WHIP	ERA	PERA	EQERA	EQH9	EQBB9	EQSO9	EQHR9	VORP	WXRL
2004	JUP	A+	19	5	9	0	25	25	154¹	161	30	95	3	—	.304	20	1.24	3.27	3.81	5.62	9.4	2.0	3.7	0.3	-0.3	—
2005	CAR	AA	20	8	7	0	19	19	108¹	108	36	73	12	56.8%	.294	-13	1.33	3.99	6.14	5.77	9.8	3.1	4.3	1.7	-2.0	—
2005	SAN	AA	20	3	1	0	6	6	33²	38	11	26	4	41.3%	.343	5	1.45	4.27	5.34	5.08	10.2	3.5	5.1	1.6	1.9	—
2006	SAN	AA	21	6	5	0	25	25	138¹	144	45	80	10	43.3%	.309	1	1.37	3.65	4.85	4.51	9.3	2.9	3.8	0.9	16.9	—
2007	*SEA*	*MLB*	*22*	*5*	*9*	*0*	*26*	*19*	*114¹*	*135*	*43*	*57*	*18*	*47.0%*	*.301*	*-5*	*1.56*	*5.86*	*5.45*	*5.75*	*10.3*	*3.0*	*4.2*	*1.3*	*-5.4*	*0.30*

Breakout: 8%   Improve: 33%   Collapse: 19%   Attrition: 0%   Comparables: Mickey Callaway, Dustin Moseley, Darvin Withers, William Martinez

Bazardo's a hard thrower whose fastball is as straight as a rail. His strikeout rate is in free-fall, his control is good, but not great, and he doesn't compensate by getting a lot of ground balls. He's only 22, though, and he's got a great name, so life could be worse. Bazardo was used as a reliever in winter ball; that might be a role to which he's better suited.

Travis Blackley
Bats: L Throws: L   Height: 6' 3"   Weight: 200   Born: November 4, 1982   Age: 24

YEAR	TEAM	LVL	AGE	W	L	SV	G	GS	IP	H	BB	SO	HR	GB%	BABIP	STUFF	WHIP	ERA	PERA	EQERA	EQH9	EQBB9	EQSO9	EQHR9	VORP	WXRL
2004	TAC	AAA	21	8	6	0	19	18	110¹	100	47	80	14	—	.275	1	1.33	3.84	5.44	4.05	7.9	4.0	5.0	1.2	19.1	—
2004	SEA	MLB	21	1	3	0	6	6	26	35	22	16	9	—	.310	-16	2.19	10.04	8.59	10.46	11.8	6.8	5.1	2.7	-13.7	-0.48
2006	SAN	AA	23	8	11	0	25	25	144²	139	45	100	18	38.8%	.283	-14	1.28	4.06	6.00	5.34	9.2	3.0	4.5	1.6	4.1	—
2006	TAC	AAA	23	1	1	0	2	2	11	10	5	5	2	34.2%	.222	-18	1.36	4.09	7.20	4.76	7.9	4.0	3.2	2.4	1.1	—
2007	*SEA*	*MLB*	*24*	*4*	*9*	*0*	*27*	*18*	*106*	*121*	*49*	*59*	*22*	*39.0%*	*.286*	*-9*	*1.60*	*6.04*	*5.95*	*5.79*	*9.9*	*3.7*	*4.7*	*1.7*	*-5.5*	*0.20*

Breakout: 18%   Improve: 46%   Collapse: 19%   Attrition: 2%   Comparables: Chris Narveson, Phil Seibel, Mike Matthews, Damaso Marte

Blackley is a lefty control guy from Down Under who missed 2005 due to shoulder surgery and hasn't been the same since. Sent back down to San Antonio—a level he dominated three years ago—Blackley was able to hold his own. Rushed his first time up the ladder, he'll now attempt to repeat the trip with greatly diminished stuff and lowered expectations for his future.

Jorge Campillo
Bats: R Throws: R   Height: 6' 1"   Weight: 190   Born: November 30, 1999   Age: 28

YEAR	TEAM	LVL	AGE	W	L	SV	G	GS	IP	H	BB	SO	HR	GB%	BABIP	STUFF	WHIP	ERA	PERA	EQERA	EQH9	EQBB9	EQSO9	EQHR9	VORP	WXRL
2005	TAC	AAA	0	4	1	0	12	12	66¹	63	18	43	5	53.9%	.297	7	1.22	2.71	4.13	3.38	8.4	2.4	4.3	0.8	16.5	—
2007	*SEA*	*MLB*	*28*	*3*	*5*	*0*	*28*	*9*	*74²*	*89*	*20*	*35*	*11*	*45.0%*	*.300*	*-10*	*1.45*	*5.22*	*5.03*	*5.09*	*10.4*	*2.1*	*3.9*	*1.2*	*2.5*	*0.60*

Breakout: 6%   Improve: 11%   Collapse: 62%   Attrition: 27%   Comparables: Ray Semproch, Cisco Carlos, Brian Tollberg, Vern Ruhle

Campillo is an import from the Mexican Leagues. He signed with the Mariners in 2005 at the age of 27, much later than the usual prospect. At the time, he was expected to compete immediately for a position in the rotation. Instead, he wound up competing immediately to get a priority appointment for Tommy John surgery. Campillo came back from surgery earlier than most, but didn't look ready. Seattle took him off the 40-man in November, but it remains to be seen if they've truly given up on him.

Travis Chick   **Bats: R Throws: R**   Height: 6′ 3″   Weight: 215   Born: June 10, 1984   Age: 23

YEAR	TEAM	LVL	AGE	W	L	SV	G	GS	IP	H	BB	SO	HR	GB%	BABIP	STUFF	WHIP	ERA	PERA	EQERA	EQH9	EQBB9	EQSO9	EQHR9	VORP	WXRL
2004	FTW	A	20	5	0	0	7	7	42¹	32	9	55	4	—	.283	22	0.97	2.13	5.17	3.54	8.4	2.4	6.9	1.8	9.3	—
2005	CHT	AA	21	2	2	0	8	8	46¹	47	27	21	5	40.3%	.284	-15	1.60	4.86	6.90	5.21	8.9	5.2	2.9	1.5	2.0	—
2005	MOB	AA	21	2	9	0	19	19	97¹	107	40	92	12	39.5%	.339	-13	1.51	5.27	5.92	6.52	10.3	3.7	6.0	1.9	-9.9	—
2006	CHT	AA	22	4	5	0	16	16	84	79	36	77	12	42.8%	.294	-18	1.37	4.61	6.64	5.82	9.8	3.8	5.9	2.2	-2.0	—
2006	SAN	AA	22	4	2	0	11	11	67¹	57	37	44	3	46.8%	.269	12	1.40	3.22	4.88	3.72	7.6	4.9	4.3	0.5	14.1	—
2007	SEA	MLB	23	4	9	0	31	17	108	121	63	71	19	41.0%	.296	-7	1.69	6.19	6.02	5.98	9.7	4.7	5.5	1.4	-8.2	0.10

Breakout: 8%   Improve: 39%   Collapse: 28%   Attrition: 1%   Comparables: Rafael Medina, Aaron Myette, Joel Hanrahan, Matt Peterson

Chick was the return the Mariners got for trading Eddy Guardado to the Reds. Drafted in 2002 and on his fourth major league organization, he's gotten off to a start that would make Mike Morgan proud. In the 2005 edition of this book we praised Chick as "a pitcher who scouts compare to Curt Schilling and statheads adore for his 4.6:1 K:BB ratio." That ratio flattened out to 1.5:1 in 2006, and took much of our interest with it.

Renee Cortez   **Bats: R Throws: R**   Height: 6′ 4″   Weight: 180   Born: December 9, 1982   Age: 24

YEAR	TEAM	LVL	AGE	W	L	SV	G	GS	IP	H	BB	SO	HR	GB%	BABIP	STUFF	WHIP	ERA	PERA	EQERA	EQH9	EQBB9	EQSO9	EQHR9	VORP	WXRL
2004	SAN	AA	21	2	5	3	36	0	52²	61	24	46	7	—	.346	-22	1.61	4.44	6.64	5.71	10.9	4.7	5.5	2.1	-0.6	—
2005	SAN	AA	22	5	3	10	44	1	63²	61	23	62	4	43.3%	.326	1	1.32	3.96	4.18	5.26	8.7	3.7	6.5	0.9	2.4	—
2006	TAC	AAA	23	5	3	5	31	0	51	61	28	50	3	43.2%	.382	1	1.75	4.24	4.19	5.54	10.6	4.7	6.8	0.7	0.3	—
2007	SEA	MLB	24	2	4	1	31	5	61¹	72	31	44	9	45.0%	.323	-5	1.68	5.87	5.81	5.71	10.2	4.1	6.1	1.2	-2.4	0.10

Breakout: 20%   Improve: 50%   Collapse: 28%   Attrition: 12%   Comparables: Jeff Verplancke, Shane Bazzell, Chris Fussell, Andy Shipman

Cortez is probably best known for the steroid suspension he drew at the beginning of the 2005 season. He's a righty relief prospect with a big fastball that he can crank into the mid-90s, but no effective secondary pitch and not much command. He was taken off the 40-man roster in November and re-signed to a minor league deal.

Francisco Cruceta   **Bats: R Throws: R**   Height: 6′ 2″   Weight: 215   Born: July 4, 1981   Age: 25

YEAR	TEAM	LVL	AGE	W	L	SV	G	GS	IP	H	BB	SO	HR	GB%	BABIP	STUFF	WHIP	ERA	PERA	EQERA	EQH9	EQBB9	EQSO9	EQHR9	VORP	WXRL
2004	AKR	AA	23	4	8	0	15	15	88²	89	33	45	11	—	.269	-19	1.38	5.28	5.95	5.62	8.7	3.5	3.3	1.4	-0.2	—
2004	BUF	AAA	23	6	5	0	14	14	83	78	36	62	6	—	.295	12	1.37	3.25	4.56	4.10	8.1	4.2	5.2	0.8	13.9	—
2005	BUF	AAA	24	6	4	0	30	13	102¹	123	32	92	16	36.6%	.350	-11	1.52	5.19	5.16	5.64	10.6	3.0	6.2	1.6	-0.5	—
2006	TAC	AAA	25	13	9	0	28	28	160¹	150	76	185	25	41.8%	.314	0	1.41	4.38	5.59	5.02	9.0	4.2	8.1	1.8	10.3	—
2006	SEA	MLB	25	0	0	0	4	1	6²	10	6	2	2	36.0%	.348	-45	2.40	10.75	8.88	9.45	13.5	8.1	2.7	2.7	-3.6	-0.24
2007	TEX	MLB	25	5	6	1	32	13	96	106	46	77	16	41%	.310	3	1.58	5.50	5.25	4.93	9.2	4.1	6.7	1.3	3.9	0.9

Breakout: 26%   Improve: 59%   Collapse: 16%   Attrition: 23%   Comparables: Don Robinson, Dustin Hermanson, Todd Wellemeyer, Lynn McGlothen

Cruceta's 185 strikeouts for Tacoma were the second most in all the minors last year, which speaks well of his deep repertoire—a fastball that creeps up into the mid-90s, as well as a sinker, curve, and split. His Kryptonite is the gopherball—he allowed 27 in 167 innings last year. Claimed off waivers by the Rangers, Cruceta's unlikely to find the former Ballpark at Arlington to be his Fortress of Solitude.

Ryan Feierabend   **Bats: L Throws: L**   Height: 6′ 3″   Weight: 190   Born: August 22, 1985   Age: 21

YEAR	TEAM	LVL	AGE	W	L	SV	G	GS	IP	H	BB	SO	HR	GB%	BABIP	STUFF	WHIP	ERA	PERA	EQERA	EQH9	EQBB9	EQSO9	EQHR9	VORP	WXRL
2004	WIS	A	18	9	7	0	26	26	161	158	44	106	17	—	.285	-16	1.25	3.63	6.60	4.93	9.3	3.1	3.4	1.9	11.8	—
2005	SBR	A+	19	8	7	0	29	29	150²	186	51	122	16	44.6%	.368	1	1.57	3.88	5.27	4.68	10.1	3.3	4.6	1.3	15.9	—
2006	SAN	AA	20	9	12	0	28	28	153	156	55	127	16	38.7%	.317	4	1.38	4.29	5.06	5.52	9.5	3.2	5.5	1.3	1.4	—
2006	SEA	MLB	20	0	1	0	4	2	17	15	7	11	3	38.9%	.235	9	1.29	3.71	5.39	3.63	7.3	3.6	5.7	1.6	4.5	0.19
2007	SEA	MLB	21	6	10	0	34	20	128²	143	53	79	21	43.0%	.294	0	1.52	5.33	5.29	5.15	9.6	3.3	5.2	1.3	3.6	1.20

Breakout: 9%   Improve: 44%   Collapse: 18%   Attrition: 0%   Comparables: Michael Connolly, Chris Seddon, Craig Anderson, Derrick Van Dusen

Saying someone is a lefty without overwhelming stuff is rarely much of an endorsement, but Feierabend is a sleeper. A 20-year-old at Double-A last season, he's been young for his level every step along the way and has held his own. A low-three-quarters delivery and sweeping breaking ball make him ideally suited for a relief role, but his arsenal might be deep enough for a back-of-the-rotation starter or swing man—something along the lines of a John Halama.

Emiliano Fruto
Bats: R Throws: R   Height: 6' 3"   Weight: 235   Born: June 6, 1984   Age: 23

YEAR	TEAM	LVL	AGE	W	L	SV	G	GS	IP	H	BB	SO	HR	GB%	BABIP	STUFF	WHIP	ERA	PERA	EQERA	EQH9	EQBB9	EQSO9	EQHR9	VORP	WXRL
2004	SAN	AA	20	3	3	1	43	1	68¹	77	37	56	6	—	.336	-16	1.67	5.67	6.10	6.88	10.3	5.4	5.2	1.3	-9.7	—
2005	SAN	AA	21	2	3	12	40	0	66²	56	22	63	6	41.5%	.289	3	1.17	2.56	4.70	3.56	7.8	3.4	6.4	1.1	14.9	—
2005	TAC	AAA	21	1	2	0	9	0	11	11	11	12	1	38.7%	.357	-5	2.00	13.09	6.99	13.91	9.8	9.0	7.4	0.8	-10.2	—
2006	TAC	AAA	22	1	3	10	28	0	45¹	33	21	55	1	51.4%	.302	21	1.20	3.19	3.61	5.00	7.2	4.0	8.6	0.2	3.0	—
2006	SEA	MLB	22	2	2	1	23	0	36	34	24	34	4	37.5%	.300	11	1.61	5.50	4.87	5.59	8.3	5.6	7.8	1.0	-0.1	0.54
2007	*WAS*	*MLB*	*23*	*2*	*3*	*3*	*41*	*1*	*48*	*43*	*23*	*47*	*5*	*42%*	*.289*	*10*	*1.36*	*4.13*	*4.38*	*4.54*	*8.0*	*3.8*	*7.9*	*0.8*	*6.3*	*0.6*

Breakout: 37% Improve: 59% Collapse: 17% Attrition: 31%   Comparables: Ryan Wagner, Neil Allen, Lance McCullers, Tom Griffin

Scouts love Fruto's stuff—the mid-90s heat, the big changeup, the plus curve. With King Felix in the major league rotation, Fruto might have been the best arm the Mariners had in the high minors last year. Still, Fruto showed very little command of his pitches in an extended tryout with the big league club, and there were grumblings about his makeup. Thrown into the Vidro-Snelling trade, Fruto will get a new start with the Nationals.

Sean Green
Bats: R Throws: R   Height: 6' 6"   Weight: 230   Born: April 20, 1979   Age: 28

YEAR	TEAM	LVL	AGE	W	L	SV	G	GS	IP	H	BB	SO	HR	GB%	BABIP	STUFF	WHIP	ERA	PERA	EQERA	EQH9	EQBB9	EQSO9	EQHR9	VORP	WXRL
2004	TUL	AA	25	4	3	2	52	0	77¹	63	29	50	5	—	.252	-24	1.19	3.03	6.02	5.18	8.6	4.4	3.8	1.1	3.4	—
2005	SAN	AA	26	0	1	14	21	0	24¹	17	8	18	1	67.1%	.225	-12	1.03	2.96	4.68	5.32	6.5	3.8	4.6	0.8	0.7	—
2005	TAC	AAA	26	4	2	1	33	0	49¹	40	29	44	1	63.6%	.287	8	1.40	3.65	4.30	4.56	7.7	5.1	6.0	0.2	5.7	—
2006	TAC	AAA	27	4	1	5	15	0	24	18	11	12	0	64.8%	.265	-11	1.21	2.25	4.67	2.62	6.8	4.1	3.4	0.4	7.9	—
2006	SEA	MLB	27	0	0	0	24	0	32	34	13	15	2	59.8%	.305	-13	1.47	4.50	4.49	4.13	9.1	3.6	3.9	0.6	5.5	-0.04
2007	*SEA*	*MLB*	*28*	*2*	*3*	*1*	*46*	*2*	*56*	*61*	*27*	*29*	*4*	*59.0%*	*.301*	*-13*	*1.57*	*4.63*	*4.66*	*4.64*	*9.5*	*3.9*	*4.3*	*0.6*	*4.8*	*0.50*

Breakout: 8% Improve: 31% Collapse: 28% Attrition: 35%   Comparables: Greg Booker, Mark Lee, Brandon Puffer, Rich Loiselle

When you're emptying out your minor league pitching staffs *en route* to using 24 pitchers on the season, you don't want anyone to feel left out. Everyone else was pitching for the big league club, so why not Sean Green? Green came over from the Rockies' organization in 2004. His age and disconcerting tendency to walk almost as many guys as he strikes out don't recommend him, though he does get more than his share of ground balls.

Felix Hernandez
Bats: R Throws: R   Height: 6' 3"   Weight: 230   Born: April 8, 1986   Age: 21

YEAR	TEAM	LVL	AGE	W	L	SV	G	GS	IP	H	BB	SO	HR	GB%	BABIP	STUFF	WHIP	ERA	PERA	EQERA	EQH9	EQBB9	EQSO9	EQHR9	VORP	WXRL
2004	SBR	A+	18	9	3	0	16	15	92	85	26	114	5	—	.345	38	1.21	2.74	4.22	3.67	8.9	3.1	7.1	0.9	19.5	—
2004	SAN	AA	18	5	1	0	10	10	57¹	47	21	58	3	—	.282	31	1.19	3.30	4.45	4.29	7.8	3.7	6.4	0.8	8.3	—
2005	TAC	AAA	19	9	4	0	19	14	88	62	48	100	3	56.6%	.277	45	1.25	2.25	3.70	2.76	6.8	4.7	7.8	0.3	27.8	—
2005	SEA	MLB	19	4	4	0	12	12	84¹	61	23	77	5	68.2%	.257	55	1.00	2.67	3.05	2.93	6.4	2.4	8.0	0.5	28.1	3.10
2006	SEA	MLB	20	12	14	0	31	31	191	195	60	176	23	58.9%	.315	33	1.34	4.52	3.84	4.68	8.8	2.6	7.7	1.0	22.1	3.70
2007	*SEA*	*MLB*	*21*	*13*	*10*	*0*	*31*	*31*	*202*	*186*	*77*	*182*	*13*	*57.0%*	*.301*	*30*	*1.30*	*3.55*	*3.50*	*3.55*	*8.0*	*3.1*	*7.6*	*0.5*	*45.1*	*6.10*

Breakout: 33% Improve: 80% Collapse: 8%   Attrition: 6%   Comparables: Bob Moose, Bert Blyleven, Don Drysdale, Milt Pappas

King Felix's early performance—he had a 5.78 ERA at the end of May—drove Mariners' fans to analyze video of his starts with a level of scrutiny usually reserved for presidential assassinations. Hernandez came around, but, overall, the season was a disappointment. Still, there's been no change in his stuff—that fastball has so much movement it looks like something out of RBI Baseball on Super Nintendo—his strikeout and walk rates held steady, and he remained one of the top-ten groundball pitchers in the majors. That 91 percent improve rate is incredibly high for a guy who didn't exactly stink up the joint last year. To paraphrase Alex Rodriguez's favorite movie, "Blue Horseshoe *loves* Felix Hernandez."

Jonathan Huber **Bats: R Throws: R** Height: 6' 2" Weight: 195 Born: July 7, 1981 Age: 25

YEAR	TEAM	LVL	AGE	W	L	SV	G	GS	IP	H	BB	SO	HR	GB%	BABIP	STUFF	WHIP	ERA	PERA	EQERA	EQH9	EQBB9	EQSO9	EQHR9	VORP	WXRL
2004	LEL	A+	23	8	6	0	20	20	107	107	44	100	9	—	.321	-7	1.41	3.70	5.90	5.24	9.9	4.8	5.3	1.5	4.1	—
2004	SBR	A+	23	4	1	0	7	5	32¹	42	14	38	4	—	.396	-8	1.73	6.13	6.66	8.04	12.6	5.2	6.6	2.0	-8.5	—
2005	SAN	AA	24	7	8	0	26	26	148	159	49	112	11	45.8%	.326	-2	1.41	4.74	4.90	6.32	9.6	3.6	5.0	1.0	-11.7	—
2006	SAN	AA	25	0	3	11	21	0	24	30	4	19	0	53.1%	.395	-6	1.42	4.88	3.21	5.55	11.5	1.5	4.8	0.4	0.1	—
2006	TAC	AAA	25	3	1	12	29	0	41²	46	10	38	3	48.4%	.350	5	1.36	2.62	3.92	3.43	10.1	2.1	6.4	0.9	10.1	—
2006	SEA	MLB	25	2	1	0	16	0	16²	10	6	11	0	53.2%	.213	7	0.96	1.08	3.24	1.59	5.3	3.2	5.8	0.0	8.3	0.80
2007	SEA	MLB	25	3	4	3	70	2	65¹	76	28	45	10	47.0%	.315	-7	1.58	5.41	5.35	5.28	10.1	3.4	5.8	1.2	0.7	0.10

Breakout: 17% Improve: 46% Collapse: 19% Attrition: 9% Comparables: Ricky Stone, Manny Barrios, Jose Paniagua, Bill Stafford

Acquired from the Padres for Dave Hansen back in 2004, Huber was a starter until this season. The shift to relief seems to agree with him, and his improved command earned him a successful September call-up. Huber's out-pitch is a hard-breaking curve, which complements his low-90s fastball. He should be in the middle relief mix this spring.

Cesar Jimenez **Bats: L Throws: L** Height: 5' 11" Weight: 180 Born: November 12, 1984 Age: 22

YEAR	TEAM	LVL	AGE	W	L	SV	G	GS	IP	H	BB	SO	HR	GB%	BABIP	STUFF	WHIP	ERA	PERA	EQERA	EQH9	EQBB9	EQSO9	EQHR9	VORP	WXRL
2004	SBR	A+	19	6	7	6	43	2	85¹	80	18	80	3	—	.314	16	1.15	2.32	3.78	3.66	8.3	2.3	5.2	0.5	18.5	—
2005	SAN	AA	20	3	5	4	45	1	68²	64	24	54	3	50.5%	.307	7	1.28	2.62	4.16	3.41	8.1	3.7	5.2	0.5	16.7	—
2006	SAN	AA	21	0	2	0	3	3	16²	10	5	10	0	69.6%	.217	9	0.93	2.78	3.79	3.31	5.5	2.8	3.9	0.0	4.1	—
2006	TAC	AAA	21	5	10	3	24	19	107	107	55	66	8	49.9%	.302	-2	1.51	4.37	5.21	5.04	8.8	4.5	4.2	0.8	6.8	—
2006	SEA	MLB	21	0	0	0	4	1	7¹	13	4	3	4	29.0%	.333	-42	2.32	14.79	10.15	14.09	15.3	4.7	3.5	4.7	-7.4	-0.37
2007	SEA	MLB	22	4	8	0	32	14	94²	110	46	52	13	48.0%	.305	-8	1.64	5.78	5.56	5.68	10.1	3.9	4.6	1.1	-3.5	0.20

Breakout: 9% Improve: 36% Collapse: 30% Attrition: 5% Comparables: Clayton Andrews, Jonathan Connolly, Derrick Van Dusen, Macay McBride

Jimenez is a lefty out of Venezuela who's pretty young despite being a five-year veteran of the organization. He has an average fastball, but his best pitch might well be a changeup that's more effective against right-handed hitters. He's a decent relief prospect, but one who might not fit comfortably if pressed into a LOOGY role.

Bobby Livingston **Bats: L Throws: L** Height: 6' 3" Weight: 195 Born: September 3, 1982 Age: 24

YEAR	TEAM	LVL	AGE	W	L	SV	G	GS	IP	H	BB	SO	HR	GB%	BABIP	STUFF	WHIP	ERA	PERA	EQERA	EQH9	EQBB9	EQSO9	EQHR9	VORP	WXRL
2004	SBR	A+	21	12	6	0	28	27	186²	187	30	141	15	—	.303	0	1.16	3.57	4.84	5.07	8.8	1.7	4.3	1.3	11.1	—
2005	SAN	AA	22	8	4	0	18	18	116¹	103	27	78	7	50.6%	.282	12	1.12	2.86	4.18	4.17	7.7	2.4	4.5	0.8	18.5	—
2005	TAC	AAA	22	6	2	0	10	10	51²	53	15	41	2	49.1%	.317	14	1.32	4.70	3.44	5.85	9.1	2.4	5.3	0.3	-1.5	—
2006	TAC	AAA	23	8	11	0	23	22	135¹	165	36	69	18	45.8%	.328	-17	1.49	4.60	5.45	5.49	10.6	2.3	3.5	1.6	1.7	—
2007	CIN	MLB	24	5	8	0	34	16	111	128	38	64	18	47%	.300	-6	1.50	5.64	5.51	5.55	10.6	2.7	4.7	1.4	0.1	0.7

Breakout: 26% Improve: 59% Collapse: 14% Attrition: 23% Comparables: Derrin Ebert, Eddie Priest, Charlie Leibrandt, Trever Miller

Once considered a top prospect, Livingston's a lefty soft-tosser with a low (and declining) strikeout rate. The Mariners' designated him for assignment in December. After some trade shenanigans between the Devil Rays and Phillies resulted in Tampa's waiver claim on him being nullified by the league, Livingston wound up in Cincinnati. He'll get his chances with the Reds, but he's not a great fit for the ballpark.

Mark Lowe **Bats: R Throws: R** Height: 6' 3" Weight: 190 Born: June 7, 1983 Age: 24

YEAR	TEAM	LVL	AGE	W	L	SV	G	GS	IP	H	BB	SO	HR	GB%	BABIP	STUFF	WHIP	ERA	PERA	EQERA	EQH9	EQBB9	EQSO9	EQHR9	VORP	WXRL
2004	EVE	A-	21	1	2	7	18	3	38¹	42	14	38	4	—	.336	-28	1.46	4.93	7.33	7.07	12.4	4.8	4.5	2.3	-5.8	—
2005	WIS	A	22	6	6	0	22	22	103²	107	49	72	12	48.4%	.295	-41	1.50	5.47	8.04	8.12	10.8	5.3	4.0	2.3	-27.6	—
2006	SBR	A+	23	1	0	2	13	2	29¹	14	11	46	0	60.0%	.233	25	0.86	1.86	3.20	3.95	5.9	4.3	8.9	0.3	5.0	—
2006	SAN	AA	23	0	2	4	11	0	16	14	3	14	1	50.0%	.289	4	1.06	2.25	3.65	2.81	7.9	1.7	5.6	0.6	5.0	—
2006	SEA	MLB	23	1	0	0	15	0	18²	12	9	20	1	46.5%	.262	19	1.13	1.93	3.69	1.93	5.8	4.3	9.2	0.5	8.6	1.63
2007	SEA	MLB	24	3	4	2	63	2	65	71	34	49	9	48.0%	.310	-5	1.61	5.31	5.39	5.18	9.5	4.2	6.3	1.1	1.5	0.20

Breakout: 24% Improve: 66% Collapse: 10% Attrition: 7% Comparables: Manny Delcarmen, Gary Majewski, Jeff Bennett, Duaner Sanchez

Seattle's fifth-round pick in 2004, Lowe impressed the Mariners with a big fastball that touches triple digits and tore through the Cal and Texas leagues prior to landing in Seattle. Then came the arm pain, not surprising given the organization's track record with young pitchers. "Minor" arthroscopic elbow surgery after the season turned out to be more substantial than expected, as Lowe had microfracture surgery to help generate new cartilage in the joint. There's no telling if he'll be ready to start the season, and, even if he is, if he'll live up to the potential he showed in 2006.

Julio Mateo   **Bats: R Throws: R**   Height: 6' 0"   Weight: 220   Born: August 2, 1977   Age: 29

YEAR	TEAM	LVL	AGE	W	L	SV	G	GS	IP	H	BB	SO	HR	GB%	BABIP	STUFF	WHIP	ERA	PERA	EQERA	EQH9	EQBB9	EQSO9	EQHR9	VORP	WXRL
2004	SEA	MLB	26	1	2	1	45	0	57²	56	16	43	11	—	.266	-7	1.25	4.68	5.13	4.42	8.7	2.3	6.3	1.5	9.3	0.20
2005	SEA	MLB	27	3	6	0	55	1	88¹	79	17	52	12	32.4%	.249	-3	1.09	3.06	4.64	3.29	8.1	1.7	5.2	1.2	23.9	1.21
2006	SEA	MLB	28	9	4	0	48	0	53²	62	22	31	6	27.5%	.326	-11	1.57	4.19	4.78	4.23	9.9	3.4	4.9	1.0	8.6	-0.58
2007	*SEA*	*MLB*	*29*	*3*	*3*	*2*	*47*	*1*	*60¹*	*66*	*17*	*37*	*10*	*37.0%*	*.284*	*-7*	*1.37*	*4.34*	*4.61*	*4.15*	*9.5*	*2.3*	*5.1*	*1.4*	*8.8*	*0.80*

Breakout: 13% Improve: 37% Collapse: 32% Attrition: 26%   *Comparables: Pete Ladd, Dave Heaverlo, Keith Atherton, John Frascatore*

Mateo's 2006 season ended when he broke his left hand in a weight-lifting accident. Other than blowing his chances at a Bowflex endorsement, the injury cut short an awful season. Mateo's numbers may look decent on the surface, but our reliever metrics show that he was a master of allowing other pitchers' runners to score, thus leaving a game in worse condition he found it. With Rafael Soriano gone, Mateo stands to get even more high-leverage innings in 2007. Check this space next year for a discussion of whether pitchers such as Mateo just have one-year runs of bad luck with runners on or its a chronic condition attributable to some childhood trauma.

Gil Meche   **Bats: R Throws: R**   Height: 6' 3"   Weight: 220   Born: September 8, 1978   Age: 28

YEAR	TEAM	LVL	AGE	W	L	SV	G	GS	IP	H	BB	SO	HR	GB%	BABIP	STUFF	WHIP	ERA	PERA	EQERA	EQH9	EQBB9	EQSO9	EQHR9	VORP	WXRL
2004	TAC	AAA	25	1	3	0	10	10	57	55	27	45	8	—	.275	-2	1.44	5.05	5.67	5.97	8.5	4.4	5.5	1.4	-2.4	—
2004	SEA	MLB	25	7	7	0	23	23	127²	139	47	99	21	—	.300	4	1.45	5.00	4.76	4.95	9.6	3.0	6.5	1.3	11.8	2.24
2005	SEA	MLB	26	10	8	0	29	26	143¹	153	72	83	18	41.1%	.296	-4	1.57	5.09	5.19	5.69	9.4	4.5	5.1	1.1	-1.8	1.42
2006	SEA	MLB	27	11	8	0	32	32	186²	183	84	156	24	45.0%	.298	13	1.43	4.48	4.58	4.84	8.5	3.8	7.0	1.0	18.0	3.44
2007	*KCA*	*MLB*	*28*	*8*	*12*	*0*	*29*	*29*	*171²*	*194*	*72*	*125*	*22*	*44.0%*	*.316*	*10*	*1.54*	*5.37*	*4.98*	*4.86*	*9.3*	*3.6*	*6.1*	*1.0*	*6.7*	*2.00*

Breakout: 21% Improve: 61% Collapse: 13% Attrition: 1%   *Comparables: Joey Jay, James Baldwin, Kevin Gross, Moe Drabowsky*

Gil Meche leaves town with his commemorative "I Survived Being A Mariners Pitching Prospect and All I Got Was This Lousy Arm Surgery" t-shirt, which, on the back, lists a partial roster of his fallen comrades, fellows such as Ryan Anderson, Jeff Heaverlo, Matt Thornton, Ken Cloude, and Bobby Madritsch. Well, he also gets a five-year, $55-million contract from the Royals. That works out to a guaranteed million dollars for each one of Meche's career wins. The buyers should beware of his home-road splits: 3.76 ERA, with 8.93 K/9, 3.35 BB/9 and 0.91 HR/9 at cushy Safeco in 2006; 5.14 ERA, 6.24 K/9, 4.68 BB/9, and 1.38 HR/9 on the road, and that road ERA doesn't count his 10 unearned runs allowed.

Brandon Morrow   **Bats: R Throws: R**   Height: 6' 3"   Weight: 175   Born: July 26, 1984   Age: 22

YEAR	TEAM	LVL	AGE	W	L	SV	G	GS	IP	H	BB	SO	HR	GB%	BABIP	STUFF	WHIP	ERA	PERA	EQERA	EQH9	EQBB9	EQSO9	EQHR9	VORP	WXRL
2006	MRN	Rk	21	0	2	0	7	4	13²	10	9	13	0	58.1%	.323	-6	1.44	2.73	5.91	4.26	7.1	8.5	4.3	0.7	1.9	—
2007	*SEA*	*MLB*	*22*	*3*	*6*	*0*	*24*	*14*	*79²*	*78*	*74*	*58*	*9*	*48.0%*	*.289*	*-9*	*1.89*	*5.93*	*5.92*	*5.84*	*8.5*	*7.5*	*6.1*	*0.9*	*-4.1*	*0.00*

Breakout: 1% Improve: 1% Collapse: 95% Attrition: 11%   *Comparables: Vince Perkins, Manuel Esquivia, Jerome Gamble, David Wolensky*

Morrow didn't put it together at Cal until 2006, the first time in his college career he was able to hold down a spot in the rotation. That was good enough to raise him from a 2003 fortieth-rounder to the fifth overall pick in the 2006 draft. Morrow's fastball is consistently in the high-90s, and his splitter and slider are plus pitches. It speaks volumes about the Mariners' luck with young pitchers that, when a local columnist wrote a satirical piece claiming Morrow hurt his arm answering the telephone on draft day, plenty of people thought it was for real.

Clint Nageotte

Bats: R Throws: R   Height: 6' 3"   Weight: 225   Born: October 25, 1980   Age: 26

YEAR	TEAM	LVL	AGE	W	L	SV	G	GS	IP	H	BB	SO	HR	GB%	BABIP	STUFF	WHIP	ERA	PERA	EQERA	EQH9	EQBB9	EQSO9	EQHR9	VORP	WXRL
2004	TAC	AAA	23	6	6	0	14	14	80²	78	35	63	9	—	.290	3	1.40	4.46	5.25	4.76	8.5	4.0	5.4	1.1	7.6	—
2004	SEA	MLB	23	1	6	0	12	5	36²	48	27	24	3	—	.372	-3	2.05	7.36	5.26	7.11	11.6	5.9	5.4	0.7	-6.6	-0.09
2005	TAC	AAA	24	2	1	2	19	0	34	21	22	35	2	62.4%	.232	13	1.26	2.65	4.58	4.50	5.8	5.6	7.1	0.5	4.2	—
2006	TAC	AAA	25	7	7	0	19	19	89¹	102	53	51	6	58.3%	.332	-7	1.74	5.76	5.51	7.02	10.0	5.1	3.9	0.8	-14.4	—
2007	SEA	MLB	26	4	7	0	30	13	88²	102	55	50	9	53.0%	.314	-12	1.76	6.00	5.68	5.98	10.0	5.0	4.7	0.8	-6.8	0.20

Breakout: 32%   Improve: 65%   Collapse: 10%   Attrition: 2%   Comparables: Jason Standridge, Scott Randall, J. J. Putz, Mike Dunne

Three years ago, we deemed Nageotte the 37th-fairest prospect in the whole land. Back then, his slider was as sharp as a straight razor. Now it's almost as straight as one. Nageotte looked like he'd grow up to be an elite strikeout pitcher, but now he can't crack an unadjusted strikeout rate of five per nine innings, and he's walking just as many. A minor league free agent, it's now doubtful he'll even have a major league career.

Eric O'Flaherty

Bats: L Throws: L   Height: 6' 2"   Weight: 195   Born: February 5, 1985   Age: 22

YEAR	TEAM	LVL	AGE	W	L	SV	G	GS	IP	H	BB	SO	HR	GB%	BABIP	STUFF	WHIP	ERA	PERA	EQERA	EQH9	EQBB9	EQSO9	EQHR9	VORP	WXRL
2004	WIS	A	19	3	3	0	12	10	57¹	83	23	38	3	—	.388	-12	1.85	6.13	5.33	7.29	12.6	4.3	3.4	0.9	-10.9	—
2005	WIS	A	20	4	4	13	45	0	69²	73	30	51	2	54.0%	.324	-7	1.48	3.74	4.53	5.56	9.7	4.3	4.4	0.5	0.3	—
2006	SBR	A+	21	0	1	1	16	0	28¹	31	6	33	1	60.5%	.417	12	1.32	3.52	3.46	3.86	10.6	2.2	6.8	0.6	5.4	—
2006	SAN	AA	21	2	2	7	25	0	39	45	15	36	0	56.4%	.391	9	1.54	1.15	3.70	2.75	10.8	3.4	6.2	0.2	12.4	—
2006	SEA	MLB	21	0	0	0	15	0	11	18	6	6	2	38.6%	.381	-24	2.18	4.09	5.61	7.15	13.5	4.8	4.8	1.6	-1.7	-0.42
2007	SEA	MLB	22	3	4	2	86	2	68²	85	31	41	9	49.0%	.328	-11	1.68	5.86	5.65	5.76	10.7	3.6	5.0	1.0	-3.2	0.20

Breakout: 7%   Improve: 36%   Collapse: 31%   Attrition: 11%   Comparables: Ryan Cullen, Benito Baez, John Grabow, Daniel Freeman

The Mariners hop-scotched this lefty across four levels in 2006, culminating in an August call-up to the Show, all at the tender age of 21. O'Flaherty's not a future star, so he could probably use a little more time in the minors to practice trying to retire the right-handed batters that even the most dedicated of lefty specialists must sometimes face.

Joel Pineiro

Bats: R Throws: R   Height: 6' 1"   Weight: 200   Born: September 25, 1978 Age: 28

YEAR	TEAM	LVL	AGE	W	L	SV	G	GS	IP	H	BB	SO	HR	GB%	BABIP	STUFF	WHIP	ERA	PERA	EQERA	EQH9	EQBB9	EQSO9	EQHR9	VORP	WXRL
2004	SEA	MLB	25	6	11	0	21	21	140²	144	43	111	21	—	.299	11	1.33	4.67	4.35	4.75	9.1	2.5	6.6	1.2	18.7	2.97
2005	SEA	MLB	26	7	11	0	30	30	189	224	56	107	23	46.1%	.326	2	1.48	5.62	4.53	5.50	10.4	2.6	4.9	1.0	2.3	1.43
2006	SEA	MLB	27	8	13	1	40	25	165²	209	64	87	23	48.7%	.331	-13	1.65	6.35	5.14	6.21	10.8	3.3	4.4	1.1	-14.4	0.63
2007	BOS	MLB	28	7	9	1	41	19	135²	168	41	77	17	48%	.325	-2	1.54	5.36	5.05	4.90	9.7	2.6	4.8	0.9	5.1	1.4

Breakout: 40% Improve: 67% Collapse: 12% Attrition: 23%   Comparables: Stan Bahnsen, Livan Hernandez, Dick Drago, Jack Fisher

Piniero had the worst ERA of any pitcher who qualified for the ERA title in 2006, showing that special mix of suckitude and resilience that makes things really ugly. His ERA rose each month except for September, when his 7.78 ERA couldn't top August's 9.43 mark. Piniero was arbitration-eligible at year's end. The decision not to offer a player like this arbitration was so simple that it should be incorporated into the field sobriety test given to drivers who've been pulled over. Bottoms up in Boston, where he was signed to a one-year, $4-million deal with thoughts of making him the closer.

J. J. Putz

Bats: R Throws: R   Height: 6' 5"   Weight: 250   Born: February 22, 1977   Age: 30

YEAR	TEAM	LVL	AGE	W	L	SV	G	GS	IP	H	BB	SO	HR	GB%	BABIP	STUFF	WHIP	ERA	PERA	EQERA	EQH9	EQBB9	EQSO9	EQHR9	VORP	WXRL
2004	SEA	MLB	27	0	3	9	54	0	63	66	24	47	10	—	.304	-8	1.43	4.71	4.98	4.76	9.4	3.1	6.3	1.3	8.4	1.04
2005	SEA	MLB	28	6	5	1	64	0	60	58	23	45	8	56.3%	.286	-3	1.35	3.60	4.64	4.11	8.5	3.4	6.6	1.2	10.9	0.75
2006	SEA	MLB	29	4	1	36	72	0	78¹	59	13	104	4	52.5%	.311	52	0.92	2.30	2.05	2.37	6.6	1.4	11.2	0.5	32.6	5.64
2007	SEA	MLB	30	4	6	33	62	0	68¹	63	21	73	7	50.0%	.305	21	1.22	3.35	3.30	3.31	8.0	2.4	9.0	0.8	17.7	2.60

Breakout: 20% Improve: 68% Collapse: 13% Attrition: 10%   Comparables: Roberto Hernandez, Jeff Nelson, Mike Schooler, Jose Mesa

Always a hard thrower, but never much of a success, Putz learned a new grip on his splitfinger fastball from former Mariners closer Eddie Guardado and credited the pitch for the great leap forward he made in 2006. As measured by WXRL, Putz had the best relief season for a Mariner reliever since Bill Caudill in 1982. Whenever someone feels like overpaying for a "proven" free agent closer, they should remember what Putz, Takashi Saito, and Akinori Otsuka did in 2006, or Bobby Jenks and Derrick Turnbow did in 2005—guys who weren't necessarily considered closers on Opening Day, but who grew into the role as the season progressed.

Seattle Mariners

George Sherrill

Bats: L **Throws: L** **Height:** 6' 0" **Weight:** 225 **Born:** April 18, 1977 **Age:** 30

YEAR	TEAM	LVL	AGE	W	L	SV	G	GS	IP	H	BB	SO	HR	GB%	BABIP	STUFF	WHIP	ERA	PERA	EQERA	EQH9	EQBB9	EQSO9	EQHR9	VORP	WXRL
2004	TAC	AAA	27	4	2	13	36	0	50¹	42	9	62	4	—	.309	24	1.01	2.33	3.03	2.68	7.7	1.8	8.4	0.7	16.3	—
2004	SEA	MLB	27	2	1	0	21	0	23²	24	9	16	3	—	.284	-6	1.39	3.80	4.56	4.44	8.9	3.0	5.5	1.1	4.0	0.52
2005	TAC	AAA	28	1	3	7	22	0	23²	19	6	38	0	52.8%	.358	23	1.05	2.28	2.12	3.09	8.1	2.3	10.8	0.4	6.5	—
2005	SEA	MLB	28	4	3	0	29	0	19	13	7	24	3	39.5%	.250	19	1.05	5.21	3.95	5.59	6.1	3.3	11.2	1.4	-0.0	0.95
2006	SEA	MLB	29	2	4	1	72	0	40	30	27	42	0	31.3%	.303	24	1.43	4.28	3.48	3.98	6.6	5.8	8.9	0.2	7.7	1.35
2007	*SEA*	*MLB*	*30*	*2*	*2*	*4*	*55*	*0*	*44¹*	*42*	*21*	*47*	*5*	*39.0%*	*.309*	*13*	*1.41*	*4.39*	*4.15*	*4.28*	*8.2*	*3.8*	*9.0*	*1.0*	*6.1*	*0.50*

Breakout: 17% Improve: 41% Collapse: 27% Attrition: 19%   Comparables: Al Holland, Brian Fuentes, Randy Myers, Rob Murphy

Sherrill and Safeco are a match made in heaven—Safeco is a lefty-stiffling environment with a big outfield, and Sherrill is a lefty-killing extreme fly ball pitcher. He held southpaw swingers to .143/.230/.182 last year. Those rates include three extra-base hits, all doubles. Righties were a different matter, hitting .297/.446/.359 as, like most lefty specialists, he tended to pitch around batters who didn't hit from the approved side of the box. Significantly, righties also failed to knock one out of the park against Sherrill. This is what we call good luck; normally a pitcher who allows as many fly balls as Sherrill does would have some go out as a matter of course, but, in his 40 innings last year, it just happened that the fly balls always went to the deepest part of the park on cold nights when the wind was blowing in at 30 MPH. In his previous 42⅔ career innings, Sherrill allowed 6 home runs, which is a more realistic total, albeit one suppressed by Safeco, where he has a career ERA of 3.98 (against 4.77 on the road). The steady supply of lefty relief prospects in the system could make him expendable come the trade deadline.

Rafael Soriano

Bats: R **Throws: R** **Height:** 6' 1" **Weight:** 220 **Born:** December 19, 1979 **Age:** 27

YEAR	TEAM	LVL	AGE	W	L	SV	G	GS	IP	H	BB	SO	HR	GB%	BABIP	STUFF	WHIP	ERA	PERA	EQERA	EQH9	EQBB9	EQSO9	EQHR9	VORP	WXRL
2006	SEA	MLB	26	1	2	2	53	0	60	44	21	65	6	28.5%	.262	26	1.08	2.25	3.44	2.35	6.3	2.9	9.1	0.9	25.3	3.19
2007	*ATL*	*MLB*	*27*	*3*	*3*	*4*	*50*	*0*	*56²*	*51*	*22*	*57*	*7*	*37.0%*	*.288*	*13*	*1.28*	*3.66*	*4.08*	*3.70*	*8.0*	*3.0*	*8.2*	*1.0*	*13.0*	*1.20*

Breakout: 6% Improve: 23% Collapse: 53% Attrition: 11%   Comparables: Trevor Hoffman, T. J. Mathews, Ricky Bottalico, Bobby Howry

After pitching a grand total of 13 games between 2004 and 2005, Soriano made a triumphant return from Tommy John surgery in 2006—at least until he got brained by a Vlad Guerrero line drive in late August. Until that point, he rivaled Putz as the best reliever on the team. After some late-season speculation that he might be granted a rotation spot in 2007, Soriano was dealt away for middling lefty starter Horacio Ramirez. In Atlanta, Soriano will be in line to take over the closer's role during Bob Wickman's yearly DL trip. In Seattle, Ramirez will get in line at Pike's Place market for fresh asparagus.

Jarrod Washburn

Bats: L **Throws: L** **Height:** 6' 1" **Weight:** 190 **Born:** August 13, 1974 **Age:** 32

YEAR	TEAM	LVL	AGE	W	L	SV	G	GS	IP	H	BB	SO	HR	GB%	BABIP	STUFF	WHIP	ERA	PERA	EQERA	EQH9	EQBB9	EQSO9	EQHR9	VORP	WXRL
2004	ANA	MLB	29	11	8	0	25	25	149¹	159	40	86	20	—	.287	4	1.33	4.64	4.47	4.66	8.9	2.2	4.8	1.0	22.6	3.36
2005	ANA	MLB	30	8	8	0	29	29	177¹	184	51	94	19	41.2%	.296	8	1.33	3.20	4.50	3.46	9.1	2.6	4.6	0.9	47.7	5.67
2006	SEA	MLB	31	8	14	0	31	31	187	198	55	103	25	40.9%	.284	2	1.35	4.67	4.73	4.63	9.0	2.5	4.6	1.1	20.6	3.05
2007	*SEA*	*MLB*	*32*	*9*	*12*	*0*	*30*	*28*	*172*	*192*	*54*	*96*	*25*	*42.0%*	*.293*	*2*	*1.43*	*4.85*	*4.84*	*4.69*	*9.7*	*2.5*	*4.7*	*1.2*	*14.3*	*2.70*

Breakout: 10% Improve: 34% Collapse: 28% Attrition: 0%   Comparables: Bud Black, Mike Flanagan, Shane Rawley, Ken Raffensberger

If Washburn were a big-box superstore, his motto would be "A Quality Provider of League-Average Innings Since 1998!" When you shop at Washburn's, you know what you're getting. To see part of the reason why the M's disregarded the sign at the door, let's play a little Player A/Player B:

	IP	H	ER	HR	BB	K	ERA
Player A	90.1	109	59	15	25	43	5.88
Player B	96.2	89	38	10	30	60	3.54

When the M's signed Washburn, he had one of the larger home-road splits in baseball. Over eight seasons as an Angel, Washburn was 31–34 with a 4.61 ERA in Anaheim, 47–24 with a 3.31 ERA on the road. The question was, if removed from Anaheim, would Washburn bloom into the kind of player he had been on the road? Player A, who has Washburn's road numbers in 2006, says no. Player B possesses his numbers at home. Player B's performance matches Washburn's career numbers at Safeco coming into 2006. Transported into the friendly confines of a ballpark suited to left-handed fly-ball pitchers, Washburn went from road warrior to stay-at-home dad, and the Mariners remain a team looking for an ace pitcher to take the pressure off Felix Hernandez.

Jake Woods

Bats: L Throws: L Height: 6′ 1″ Weight: 190 Born: September 3, 1981 Age: 25

YEAR	TEAM	LVL	AGE	W	L	SV	G	GS	IP	H	BB	SO	HR	GB%	BABIP	STUFF	WHIP	ERA	PERA	EQERA	EQH9	EQBB9	EQSO9	EQHR9	VORP	WXRL
2004	ARK	AA	22	9	2	0	14	14	90	86	19	60	5	—	.287	12	1.17	2.70	4.26	3.05	8.2	2.1	4.0	0.8	25.9	—
2004	SLC	AAA	22	6	4	0	15	14	83	108	42	60	13	—	.343	-9	1.81	6.07	5.84	6.10	10.0	4.6	4.9	1.3	-4.8	—
2005	SLC	AAA	23	3	1	0	15	5	36²	50	17	36	7	37.6%	.371	-10	1.83	5.89	5.66	5.87	11.3	3.8	6.6	1.6	-1.1	—
2005	ANA	MLB	23	1	1	0	28	0	27²	30	8	20	7	38.5%	.274	-10	1.37	4.55	6.10	5.72	9.5	2.5	6.4	2.2	-0.5	0.08
2006	SEA	MLB	24	7	4	1	37	8	105	115	53	66	12	43.1%	.307	-3	1.60	4.20	4.86	4.15	9.3	4.2	5.2	0.9	18.9	1.51
2007	*SEA*	*MLB*	*25*	*4*	*7*	*2*	*48*	*9*	*100*	*109*	*42*	*67*	*14*	*43.0%*	*.298*	*-3*	*1.51*	*4.98*	*4.98*	*4.83*	*9.5*	*3.4*	*5.6*	*1.2*	*6.9*	*0.90*

Breakout: 12% Improve: 35% Collapse: 32% Attrition: 13%   Comparables: Bob Owchinko, Bud Black, Scott Bailes, Mike Kekich

Woods was acquired on waivers from the Angels and enjoyed a nice—if a bit fluky—2006 campaign in the Pacific Northwest. Woods's best pitch is his curve when he can get it over the plate. One of the long list of Mariners lefties with bad strikeout rates hoping to inherit the mantle of Jamie Moyer, Woods needs to improve his control if he hopes to have a lasting career in the Moyer mold or any other.

Lineouts

PLAYER	TEAM	LVL	AGE	PA	R	2B	3B	HR	RBI	BB	SO	SB-CS	SPEED	AVG/OBP/SLG	MLVr	EqAVG/EqOBP/EqSLG	EqA	VORP
RF T. Bohn	TAC	AAA	26	419	53	20	1	9	43	33	81	15-3	5.5	.283/.345/.413	.077	.284/.337/.414	.263	4.0
	SEA	MLB	26	16	2	0	0	1	2	2	8		4.9	.143/.250/.357	-.350	.143/.250/.357	.212	-0.9
3B G. Dobbs*	TAC	AAA	28	421	60	19	3	9	55	37	58	14-5	5.6	.314/.375/.451	.214	.309/.361/.439	.278	28.9
	SEA	MLB	28	28	4	3	1	0	3	0	4	0-1	6.9	.370/.393/.556	.382	.370/.393/.556	.302	2.8
2B M. Garciaparra	SAN	AA	23	121	13	3	1	1	16	8	21	1-1	4.6	.305/.375/.381	.094	.312/.364/.385	.263	5.7
	TAC	AAA	23	162	26	5	0	1	10	22	26	3-3	4.6	.316/.422/.375	.186	.324/.416/.396	.285	13.0
CF M. Lawton*	SEA	MLB	34	29	5	0	0	0	1	2	2		5.9	.259/.310/.259	-.310	.259/.310/.259	.208	-1.2
LF J. Nelson	SAN	AA	26	174	23	10	1	5	18	6	54	3-1	5.9	.245/.293/.411	-.057	.220/.247/.333	.203	-14.9
	TAC	AAA	26	292	43	15	4	14	46	12	83	3-3	5.3	.284/.332/.524	.220	.287/.325/.516	.278	12.0
DH R. Petagine*	TAC	AAA	35	10	1	0	0	0	0	4	1		4.2	.167/.500/.167	.026	.143/.400/.143	.248	-0.5
	SEA	MLB	35	32	3	2	0	1	2	4	10		4.4	.185/.313/.370	-.191	.185/.312/.370	.241	-0.3
RF M. Wilson#	SBR	A+	23	226	38	15	3	9	38	22	59	4-6	5.7	.315/.389/.555	.350	.285/.341/.483	.276	8.6
	SAN	AA	23	283	32	12	1	12	43	28	85	1-1	3.6	.245/.336/.446	.067	.246/.318/.438	.257	-0.6

PLAYER	TEAM	LVL	AGE	W	L	SV	IP	H	BB	SO	HR	GB%	BABIP	STUFF	WHIP	ERA	PERA	EqERA	EqH9	EqBB9	EqSO9	EqHR9	VORP
A. Baldwin	CLR	A+	23	8	8	0	147	164	22	100	11	—	.330	-13	1.27	4.04	5.07	6.61	11.2	1.7	3.7	1.4	-16.2
	SBR	A+	23	2	1	0	22¹	12	2	13	1	—	.225	10	0.63	0.81	4.31	1.64	5.3	0.8	3.3	0.8	9.7
A. Butler*	EVE	A-	18	1	2	0	42	23	25	52	2	—	.233	26	1.14	2.79	6.10	4.31	6.4	7.0	6.6	1.1	5.7
J. Foppert	TAC	AAA	25	0	1	0	10¹	10	14	11	0	—	.385	10	2.38	7.13	7.51	9.90	9.9	12.6	7.2	0.0	-4.8
J. Harris	TAC	AAA	32	0	3	0	31	43	7	13	6	—	.319	-41	1.61	5.52	7.04	7.47	12.4	2.0	2.6	2.3	-6.5
	SEA	MLB	32	0	0	0	3¹	3	0	1	0	—	.273	-9	0.90	5.45	2.92	2.70	8.1	0.0	2.7	0.0	0.2
S. Kahn	SBR	A+	22	2	0	8	27	16	15	35	1	—	.250	16	1.15	2.00	4.54	2.77	6.6	5.9	7.6	0.7	8.2
	SAN	AA	22	1	3	0	39¹	50	31	33	3	—	.385	-8	2.07	6.21	5.86	7.49	11.6	7.0	5.4	0.9	-8.3
C. Tillman	EVE	A-	18	1	3	0	19¹	25	15	29	4	—	.477	3	2.09	8.01	11.91	9.72	16.7	10.3	8.6	4.9	-7.6

A good defender at the outfield corners, **T. J. Bohn** was claimed off waivers by the Braves. Cornerman **Greg Dobbs**'s qualifications for a major league job all come down to one thing: "Bats left-handed," and not well enough at that. After a big rebound in 2006, Nomar's little brother, **Michael Garciaparra**, comes into 2007 with a decent shot at a utility infield job despite having worse range than the giant bronze mitt outside the stadium. To everyone's surprise, **Matt Lawton** found someone who would accept him in 2006, steroid suspension and all; to no one's surprise, he didn't hit and was shipped out soon after serving that suspension. **Jon Nelson** is a big right-handed-hitting first baseman and corner outfielder whose good power is offset by horrible plate discipline; he struck out nearly eight times for each walk last season. At this point it's safe to say that the story of **Roberto Petagine**'s career in the U.S. was that he was repeatedly picked up by franchises that then found absolutely no use for him; at 36, he's likely done. **Mike Wilson**'s a big, athletic corner outfielder who might be a late bloomer—your classic lottery-ticket prospect.

Andy Baldwin was part of the M's return for Jamie Moyer, a fringe relief prospect with the Phillies who showed signs he may yet reach his potential with a new organization. It's early yet, and he's still raw, but 2006 high school draftee **Tony Butler** is a six-foot-seven lefty with legitimate mid-90s heat and a plus curve. Left off the 40-man after the season, **Jesse Foppert** was re-signed to a minor league deal, perhaps in the hope that he can salvage something like Meche's career in Seattle, Meche's K.C. deal having made the former Mariner into the new junk-into-jewelry baseball alchemical icon. An organizational soldier who didn't stick with the team despite 47 decent innings in 2005, **Jeff Harris** is now gone to Indians, jiggety-jig. **Stephen Kahn**, a relief prospect with a great fastball but not much command, needs to cut his walk rate before he's considered a top prospect. As James T. Kirk said to Kahn's namesake, "Like a poor marksman, you just keep missing the target!" **Chris Tillman**, another 2006 prep pick, is Butler's right-handed bookend, another kid who runs the fastball up to 95 MPH, but is still miles away from the Show.

Manager: Mike Hargrove

Year	Team	W-L	Pythag +/-	Avg PC	100 +P	120 +P	QS	BQS	REL	REL w Zero R	IBB	SUBS	PH	PH Avg	PH HR	SB2	CS2	SB3	CS3	SAC Att	SAC %	POS SAC	Squeeze	Swing	In Play
2005	SEA	69-93	-6	96.6	74	1	71	10	432	270	32	23	121	.214	1	87	42	13	4	69	53.6%	34	1	152	123
2006	SEA	78-84	+1	98.5	86	3	71	6	429	263	50	25	117	.206	2	90	34	16	3	48	79.2%	34	2	130	92

Part of the Human Rain Delay's appeal to the Mariners is his reputation for working with young players, a reputation forged during his time with the Indians in the early nineties. Whatever truth it holds, that reputation seems increasingly irrelevant as the Mariners have insisted on trading away their prospects for veterans. On the positive side, Hargrove was scrupulous about imposing limitations on Felix Hernandez's usage (though overall he is one of the slowest managers in baseball to rescue a starting pitcher who is in trouble), holding him to predetermined pitches-per-start and innings-per-season limits. As an in-game tactician, he is derided in Seattle for his ill-timed decisions on when to bunt or issue an intentional walk. His poor record with pinch-hitters supports the notion of a timing problem. Hargrove pinch-hits less often than most American League managers but the results are also poorer than most. Hargrove hasn't managed a team to a winning record since 1999. After a year in which there were no in-season managerial changes, Hargrove should head-line the list of skippers unlikely to make it through 2007.

Tampa Bay Devil Rays

In the 1966 camp classic *Batman,* the feature film version of the television series of the same name, Batman finds himself scurrying about the Gotham City docklands trying to dispose of a bomb. He's a man in a blue scalloped cape, running down a pier in broad daylight holding a giant, cartoon-style black sphere with a lit fuse. No one seems overly concerned. Husbands stroll along hand in hand with their wives, mothers push babies in carriages. Batman needs to throw the thing somewhere, but the seemingly narcotized citizenry won't get clear. Finally, he has a bright idea. He's at the water's edge, so he'll just lean over and toss the bomb into the sea. He goes to do it, but, just then, a mother duck and her brood of fuzzy yellow chicks swim by. Batman just can't bring himself to do it. Frustrated, he drops his shoulders, and, fuse still sizzling, looks at the camera. "Some days," he says, "you just can't get rid of a bomb."

Let's not beat around the bush: clearly we're going for the tried-and-true Adam West-bomb-as-metaphor-for-some-unwanted-aspect-of-the-Devil-Rays-franchise trick, a favored device of sportswriters of a certain age. We can identify many Devil Rays as being or having bombed. The list is practically endless. Could it be Elijah Dukes, emblematic of a player development program that has trouble getting it all right? Travis Lee, the unproductive first baseman who was always somehow deemed good enough? Or could it be the franchise and its sorry history under Vince Naimoli and Chuck LaMar? With the Tampa Bay Devil Rays, there are a lot of bombs to choose from.

Going into the 2006 season, the Devil Rays had been around for eight years, and had never come within hailing

DEVIL RAYS PROSPECTUS
2006 record: 61–101; Fifth place, AL East
Pythagenport record: 64–98
Runs scored per game: 4.25 (14th in AL)
Runs allowed per game: 5.28 (12th in AL)
Team EqA: .246 (14th in AL)
2006 Batters Age: 27.8 (Youngest in AL)
2006 Pitchers Age: 27.2 (Youngest in AL)
Ballpark: Tropicana Field; Neutral park; Park Factor of .993
2006: What was perceived as poor planning and poorer decisions was largely bad luck with injuries.
2007: Worth the price of admission just to watch the outfield; won't contend, but the building blocks are impressive.

distance of a winning record. By the end of their ninth season, they had lost 100 games for the third time in franchise history. That perennial futility marks them as special, even as expansion clubs go (see table 1).

There's a line between the Astros and Expos, in that between the expansion that brought in Houston and the Mets and the later one that enlisted Montreal and San Diego we had the advent of the amateur draft, which began in 1965. Between the 1969 expansion and that of 1977, we had a similar industry-changing event, the arrival of free agency. These are important demarcation points in evaluating the first nine years of Devil Rays baseball. The early expansion clubs faced severely restricted expansion drafts that granted them access to has-beens and never-weres. For the first several years of their existence, they also did not have access to the leveling aspects of the minor league draft or free agency. Consider that Tom Seaver, the key player in the turnaround of the Mets, became available to them due to the draft; the Padres later picked Dave Winfield, but it was only when free agency allowed them to sign Gene Tenace, Oscar Gamble, Gaylord Perry, and Rollie Fingers that they finished a season over .500. The Devil Rays had these options available to them from the outset, and yet their record is the worst of any expansion franchise except the Padres and the Mets.

In 2006, at long last the Rays started over. LaMar was fired on October 6, 2005, the same day that Stuart Sternberg became the team's principal owner. Over the next six weeks, Sternberg assembled his management team. Matthew Silverman, like Sternberg a Wall Street veteran, became team president. Andrew Friedman, another captain of finance, was named Executive Vice President of Baseball Opera-

Table 1. Progress is Not the Passage of Time: Expansion Club Performance

Expansion Club	First Year	First Winning Record	Record Through Nine Seasons	Seasons with ≥ 100 Losses
L.A. Angels	1961	1962, 2nd season	685–770 (.471)	0
Washington/Texas	1961	1969, 9th season	607–844 (.418)	4
New York Mets	1962	1969, 8th season	577–878 (.397)	5
Houston	1962	1972, 11th season	634–822 (.435)	0
Montreal/Washington	1969	1979, 11th season	629–821 (.434)	2
San Diego	1969	1978, 10th season	567–881 (.392)	4
Seattle/Milwaukee	1969	1978, 10th season	614–836 (.423)	0
Kansas City	1969	1971, 3rd season	743–706 (.513)	0
Seattle Mariners	1977	1991, 15th season	574–829 (.409)	3
Toronto	1977	1983, 7th season	625–774 (.447)	3
Colorado	1993	1995, 2nd season	667–728 (.478)	0
Florida	1993	1997, 5th season	627–764 (.451)	1
Tampa Bay	1998	? ≥ 10th Season	579–876 (.398)	3
Arizona	1998	1999, 2nd season	728–730 (.499)	1

tions. As a counterweight to the baseball novices that populated the front office, former Mets and Astros general manager Gerry Hunsicker was added as Senior Vice President of Baseball Operations. Finally, Joe Maddon, longtime Angels bench coach, was named manager.

In the early going, the team's moves were modest. Pitcher Dewon Brazelton was dealt to the Padres for third baseman Sean Burroughs in an exchange of failed prospects. Minor leaguer Travis Schlichting was dealt to the Angels for reserve catcher Josh Paul. On January 11, 2006, the Rays won the bidding for Japanese all-star reliever Shinji Mori. Other free agent signings during January included relievers Shawn Camp and Dan Miceli and infielder Ty Wigginton. To repopulate the system, twenty minor league free agents were signed, some of whom would prove to be useful, such as pitcher Ruddy Lugo, third baseman Russ Branyan, and four-corner reserve Greg Norton.

On January 14, the Rays initiated what would be a very productive trading relationship with the Dodgers, sending relievers Danys Baez and Lance Carter westward for pitchers Edwin Jackson and Chuck Tiffany. As the summer dragged on for the losing ballclub, the trades came with increasing frequency as the team distanced itself from the old regime's players. Joey Gathright and Fernando Cortez were dealt to the Royals for pitcher J. P. Howell. Two of the team's icons of ineffectiveness, Toby Hall and Mark Hendrickson, were transformed from overextended regulars to supporting players in Los Angeles in exchange for Dioner Navarro and Jae Seo. Aubrey Huff, rumored to be trade bait for so long that Jacob Ruppert once offered $100,000 for him, was finally packed off to the Astros for

Ben Zobrist and Mitch Talbot. The Dodgers came through for the third time on the year, handing over Joel Guzman and Sergio Pedroza for Julio Lugo. Finally, Russ Branyan was sent to the Padres for Evan Meek.

This flurry of moves proved a number of things. First, day-old sushi doesn't sell, no matter how much you cut the price, and especially if you don't. The Rays actually got a surprisingly good return on Huff and Lugo despite the old regime's inability to unclench and let them go. Huff's value was down after an off year, and both he and Lugo were in the last year of their contracts. Yet, among all of the trading above, the Rays received Navarro, a promising catcher, and Zobrist, who should establish himself as a useful regular at shortstop for at least as long as it takes top prospect Reid Brignac to reach the majors.

As the Yankees proved with their own damaged-goods trades this past winter of Gary Sheffield, Jaret Wright, and Randy Johnson, a team has to trade top-tier talent to receive top-tier talent. Aside from the occasional Jeff Bagwell-for-Larry Andersen deal (and those are so rare that nearly 17 years later we're still using it as a benchmark), trades have a certain balance, especially in an era where payroll is a fundamental concern. Banjo-hitting Joey Gathright was unlikely to land the Rays the top-level offensive prospects they needed to change the outcome of the 2006 or 2007 season; you have to trade something worth a Brandon Wood to get a Brandon Wood.

Third, and perhaps most importantly, the new administration proved it would deal on a timely basis. LaMar had become legendary for his outrageous trade demands and inability to commit to a deal. In contrast, Friedman and

Hunsicker, lacking LaMar's inexplicable affection for mediocrities, were able to move anything that wasn't worth keeping.

As this was going on, the Rays received a few strong performances. Carl Crawford had another strong season, and Rocco Baldelli showed that his long layoff hadn't ruined him. Jonny Gomes crushed the ball and Scott Kazmir pitched very much like an ace, although both went down with injuries. The organization also finally committed to top prospects B. J. Upton and Delmon Young, rather than keeping them on the farm because they couldn't afford the plane fare to the majors.

Yet the Devil Rays went backwards as they were going forwards, losing 100 games for the first time since 2002. In fairness to the new regime, they had lost over 90 games in all three seasons between the two century marks. When a team is that bad, all it takes is a small streak of bad luck—such as the injuries that befell Gomes, Kazmir, and Jorge Cantu, not to mention Huff and Lugo before they were dealt—to push them over the 100 mark. Still, there is no way to bill what happened as straightforward progress.

The killer was replacement and sub-replacement-level players. Even as the Rays were clearing out LaMar's minions for whatever return they could get, they weren't creating enough depth fast enough to withstand the injuries the team suffered or cover for the turnover. It's judging the new regime too quickly to call the long rope given to poor players complacency (as it clearly was with the LaMar gang), but players such as Damon Hollins, Travis Lee, and Tomas Perez are known commodities, yet all received a good deal more playing time than the should have.

As we have shown in the past, playing even one replacement-level player can undo a team in a close race. Playing multiple replacement-level players will kill a team dead. Table 2 shows the percentage of total team plate appearances each American League club devoted to players below replacement level as per VORP, excluding players with fewer than 10 plate appearances.

The sub-par performers on the Rays were not starters gone bad or rookies that didn't perform as expected, as with the three White Sox, above. They were discretionary players, second-liners that were well established as such from the very beginning. It's not that the Rays were surprised when they went bad—they probably weren't—it's that they didn't react. Pitching was similar. The Devil Rays have a lot of evidence that Seth McClung can't help them, but he's not only still around, he may be in line for the closer's job this year.

An underappreciated part of building a team is developing depth. That doesn't just mean having a healthy minor league system—the Rays are on their way to that. It also means using it, and not settling for the worst players your organization has to offer. A great deal changed for the better in Tampa Bay in 2006, but letting go of that old LaMarian passivity, that has yet to come. That's the one cartoon bomb they have yet to get rid of. As Burt Ward/Robin said to Batman in a similar situation, "Holy finishing touches!"

Table 2. More Pointless Than the Royals

Team	% of PA, Negative VORP	Chief Offenders
Tigers	8.9	Dmitri Young, Sean Casey
Blue Jays	11.1	Russ Adams, John McDonald
Angels	14.1	Jose Molina, Kendry Morales
Red Sox	14.2	Alex Cora, Doug Mirabelli
Yankees	15.2	Andy Phillips, Miguel Cairo
Athletics	15.8	Bobby Crosby, Don Johnson
Rangers	17.6	Brad Wilkerson, Phil Nevin
Orioles	19	Jeff Conine, David Newhan, Luis Matos
Mariners	22.6	Willie Bloomquist, Jeremy Reed, Carl Everett
Twins	23.6	Rondell White, Lew Ford, Jason Kubel
White Sox	26.8	Juan Uribe, Scott Podsednik, Brian Anderson
Indians	27	Jason Michaels, Aaron Boone
Royals	31.9	John Buck, Reggie Sanders, Angel Berroa
Devil Rays	46.3	Too many to mention

HITTERS

Rocco Baldelli **CF** **Bats: R** **Throws: R** Height: 6' 4" Weight: 200 Born: September 25, 1981 Age: 25

YEAR	TEAM	LVL	AGE	PA	R	2B	3B	HR	RBI	BB	SO	SB	CS	SPEED	AVG	OBP	SLG	MLVR	EQAVG	EQOBP	EQSLG	EQA	VORP	DEFENSE	
2004	TBA	MLB	22	565	79	27	3	16	74	30	88	17	4	6.2	.280	.326	.436	-.007	.283	.330	.444	.268	18.3	121-CF	6
2006	TBA	MLB	24	387	59	24	6	16	57	14	70	10	1	7.5	.302	.339	.533	.171	.302	.344	.546	.297	33.1	86-CF	-2
2007	TBA	MLB	25	550	81	31	4	21	72	30	91	14	4	6.3	.299	.342	.501	.110	.296	.344	.503	.293	31.3	129-CF	0

Breakout: 12% Improve: 42% Collapse: 20% Attrition: 7% Comparables: Garry Maddox, Rondell White, Roberto Kelly, Ellis Burks

After missing all of 2005 because of elbow and knee surgeries, Baldelli strained his left hamstring and missed the first two months of the 2006 season. When he finally returned, the Devil Rays didn't know what they were going to get, as 221 games had passed since his last appearance. Fortunately, he remembered how to to play baseball, and didn't lose his speed on the bases (despite hurting his other hamstring later in the year). Despite staying upright for just 364 at-bats, he tied his previous high with 16 home runs, and his isolated power jumped from .156 in 2004 to .231. Given the poor history of young players who had missed as much time as Baldelli had, this was a stunningly good result. Where the year off did hurt him was in the patience and pitch-recognition department. In his rookie year, Baldelli had drawn one unintentional walk per 24.5 plate appearances; in 2004, he improved to one per 20.2 PA. Last year, he regressed past his starting point, drawing just one unintentional walk per 29.8. Baldelli was one of the players most sought-after in trades this offseason, in no small part because of his reasonable contract, made even more reasonable by the fact that didn't reach his escalators in 2006; he's set to earn just $750,000 in 2007. Baldelli's improving power gives hope that his production will survive any disruptions in his batting average in the future, hope that didn't exist before his injuries.

Wes Bankston			**1B**			**Bats: R**		**Throws: R**			Height: 6' 4"		Weight: 200		Born: November 23, 1983		Age: 23	
YEAR	TEAM	LVL	AGE	PA	R	2B	3B	HR	RBI	BB	SO	SB	CS	SPEED	AVG	OBP	SLG	MLVR	EQAVG	EQOBP	EQSLG	EQA	VORP	DEFENSE
2004	CSC	A	20	551	82	30	3	23	101	73	104	9	0	5.2	.289	.390	.513	.288	.265	.341	.446	.272	13.6	90-1B	-4
2005	VIS	A+	21	78	15	4	1	3	23	15	17	0	2	4.3	.387	.513	.629	.645	.354	.455	.538	.331	10.5	15-1B	1
2005	MNT	AA	21	337	42	17	2	12	47	30	64	3	3	3.6	.292	.362	.482	.185	.276	.334	.461	.269	10.3	66-1B	-2
2006	MNT	AA	22	183	20	7	1	4	19	12	37	4	1	4.7	.263	.322	.389	.065	.260	.311	.402	.249	3.4	29-3B	-4
2006	DUR	AAA	22	207	22	13	0	5	29	10	40	0	1	4.0	.297	.333	.441	.100	.277	.314	.431	.254	1.7	46-1B	-8
2007	TBA	MLB	23	440	50	22	1	14	52	32	89	3	1	4.5	.258	.316	.425	-.073	.255	.317	.426	.261	1.4	105-1B	-6

Breakout: 18% Improve: 46% Collapse: 28% Attrition: 9%   Comparables: Juan Tejeda, David Kelton, Shawn Gallagher, Garrett Atkins

Going into 2006, the Devil Rays were in desperate need of a first baseman, as has been the case since Fred McGriff was traded to the Cubs in 2001. The Rays' primary post-Crime Dog first basemen have ranged from inadequate to mediocre, as they've moved from Steve Cox to Travis Lee to Tino Martinez and back to Lee, ever getting quality work from any of them. Bankston was the closest thing the Devil Rays had to a projectable young first baseman heading into last year, but rather than recognize that and get him moving towards the major leagues, the Rays took the one-time outfielder and moved him to third base, a move which necessitated a return to Double-A to open the season, and seems to have negatively affected his hitting. While the Rays had other candidates for third base such as B. J. Upton, they had no other candidate for first. Bankston is almost certainly not a future All-Star: His offensive skills have regressed as he's climbed the ladder, and he's failed to keep himself in great shape. Still, he and Joel Guzman currently represent the organization's best chances of breaking the club's reliance on stopgaps at the cool corner.

Reid Brignac			**SS**			**Bats: L**		**Throws: R**			Height: 6' 3"		Weight: 170		Born: January 16, 1986		Age: 21	
YEAR	TEAM	LVL	AGE	PA	R	2B	3B	HR	RBI	BB	SO	SB	CS	SPEED	AVG	OBP	SLG	MLVR	EQAVG	EQOBP	EQSLG	EQA	VORP	DEFENSE
2004	PRI	Rk	18	109	16	4	2	1	25	9	10	2	1	5.0	.361	.413	.474	.284	.284	.315	.373	.241	4.6	24-SS	-2
2005	SWM	A	19	565	77	29	2	15	61	40	131	5	5	3.9	.264	.319	.416	.006	.230	.270	.357	.219	-11.9	124-SS	-14
2006	VIS	A+	20	455	82	26	3	21	83	35	82	12	6	6.0	.326	.382	.557	.331	.294	.338	.493	.279	35.4	97-SS	-7
2006	MNT	AA	20	121	18	6	2	3	16	7	31	3	0	6.7	.300	.355	.473	.250	.304	.347	.500	.289	11.4	28-SS	-5
2007	TBA	MLB	21	556	64	32	3	17	66	34	114	6	4	5.2	.260	.309	.437	-.065	.257	.311	.439	.261	17.8	131-SS	-5

Breakout: 33% Improve: 64% Collapse: 23% Attrition: 4%   Comparables: Brandon Wood, Josh Barfield, Chris Lubanski, Eric Chavez

At the end of the 2005 season, Brignac was a six-foot-one, 185-pound shortstop. At the beginning of the 2006 season, he'd sprouted up to six-foot-three and 200 pounds—and it all came from cleaning living and organic, BGH-free whole milk. We often talk about young prospects "growing into their bodies," and Brignac's a pretty good illustration of how much growth there is left in some of these kids. There's a possibility that he's grown himself right out of the shortstop position; even as a smaller guy, his range wasn't terribly great, and it doesn't figure to improve now that he has to haul more of himself around out there. But no matter, his bat looks good at any position. The good news about his added bulk is that it came with extra power, which helped him earn a late-season promotion to Double-A. The main flaw in his batting game is patience, but he's one of those players for whom patience should develop later as pitchers start to respect his bat and throw him stuff he can't drive. This is a small matter given just how good the overall picture is.

Jorge Cantu **2B** **Bats: R** **Throws: R** Height: 6' 1" Weight: 185 Born: January 30, 1982 Age: 25

YEAR	TEAM	LVL	AGE	PA	R	2B	3B	HR	RBI	BB	SO	SB	CS	SPEED	AVG	OBP	SLG	MLVR	EQAVG	EQOBP	EQSLG	EQA	VORP	DEFENSE			
2004	DUR	AAA	22	392	57	33	1	22	80	16	64	3	0	4.8	.302	.335	.576	.213	.268	.304	.509	.271	22.5	43-2B	6	36-SS	-4
2004	TBA	MLB	22	185	25	20	1	2	17	9	44	0	0	4.7	.301	.341	.462	.124	.302	.346	.465	.276	11.6	30-2B	0	11-3B	0
2005	TBA	MLB	23	630	73	40	1	28	117	19	83	1	0	3.5	.286	.311	.497	.095	.294	.327	.520	.282	31.4	76-2B	-8	57-3B	-8
2006	TBA	MLB	24	448	40	18	2	14	62	26	91	1	1	3.4	.249	.295	.404	-.144	.248	.301	.407	.245	3.0	102-2B	-10		
2007	TBA	MLB	25	560	61	29	2	21	79	29	97	1	1	4.1	.265	.307	.449	-.050	.262	.308	.450	.263	14.4	131-2B	-6		

Breakout: 17% Improve: 46% Collapse: 21% Attrition: 11% Comparables: Joe Crede, Jim Presley, Adrian Beltre, Don Money

An injury-wracked season may have ended on a slight up note, but a year after a great season at the plate, Cantu's position appears to be far from secure. Add in that Cantu's fielding, never great, went backwards, and you have a player whose hold on his job is quite tenuous. With Elliot Johnson pressing him on one side and Akinori Iwamura on the other, Cantu is going to have to have a good spring training and a better April, hence the D-Rays' willingness to dangle him in deals this winter.

Carl Crawford **LF** **Bats: L** **Throws: L** Height: 6' 2" Weight: 220 Born: August 5, 1981 Age: 25

YEAR	TEAM	LVL	AGE	PA	R	2B	3B	HR	RBI	BB	SO	SB	CS	SPEED	AVG	OBP	SLG	MLVR	EQAVG	EQOBP	EQSLG	EQA	VORP	DEFENSE			
2004	TBA	MLB	22	672	104	26	19	11	55	35	81	59	15	8.8	.296	.331	.450	.041	.300	.339	.459	.279	24.6	114-LF	15	24-CF	2
2005	TBA	MLB	23	687	101	33	15	15	81	27	84	46	8	8.6	.301	.331	.469	.101	.312	.350	.497	.291	37.3	142-LF	1		
2006	TBA	MLB	24	652	89	20	16	18	77	37	85	58	9	8.4	.305	.348	.482	.113	.305	.356	.491	.293	41.1	144-LF	-6		
2007	TBA	MLB	25	658	103	30	11	16	67	37	76	44	10	8.0	.309	.350	.472	.093	.305	.352	.474	.293	29.1	153-LF	1		

Breakout: 18% Improve: 51% Collapse: 14% Attrition: 1% Comparables: Willie Wilson, Gates Brown, Marquis Grissom, Ken Griffey

One of the most exciting players in the league, Crawford declared he wanted to be the best fantasy player ever, and delivered for both ballclub and fantheads alike. He was the team VORP leader (41.1, sixth among major league left fielders, second to Manny Ramirez among the American League variety) and finally got his on-base percentage above league-average with a career-best walk rate. Rumors regularly circulate that Crawford will be traded, but the Rays would be unwise to do so without a stunning offer; he's signed through 2010 at salaries that have become almost cruelly low given the current compensation environment, and he has many good years ahead of him.

Elijah Dukes **OF** **Bats: R** **Throws: R** Height: 6' 2" Weight: 225 Born: June 26, 1984 Age: 23

YEAR	TEAM	LVL	AGE	PA	R	2B	3B	HR	RBI	BB	SO	SB	CS	SPEED	AVG	OBP	SLG	MLVR	EQAVG	EQOBP	EQSLG	EQA	VORP	DEFENSE			
2004	CSC	A	20	185	26	12	2	2	15	18	47	14	1	7.2	.288	.368	.423	.133	.266	.324	.379	.255	-3.3	30-LF	1		
2004	BAK	A+	20	244	44	16	2	8	34	26	50	16	7	6.5	.332	.416	.540	.390	.300	.365	.468	.285	10.9	31-LF	3	24-CF	2
2005	MNT	AA	21	498	73	21	5	18	73	45	83	19	9	6.2	.287	.355	.478	.164	.270	.327	.462	.268	22.1	79-CF	-3	24-LF	-2
2006	DUR	AAA	22	334	58	15	5	10	50	44	47	9	4	6.2	.293	.401	.488	.254	.282	.383	.484	.296	18.6	39-LF	-5	26-RF	0
2007	TBA	MLB	23	495	72	25	3	15	57	43	85	12	4	5.9	.284	.351	.460	.055	.281	.353	.461	.286	18.3	117-LF	-1		

Breakout: 21% Improve: 48% Collapse: 18% Attrition: 4% Comparables: Matt Holliday, Brian Anderson, Jack Clark, Dee Brown

Dukes endured multiple suspensions last year after run-ins with his manager, coaches, teammates, and umpires both on and off the field. By August, the Rays were sick of it, suspending him and telling him to go home. Dukes had football aspirations at one time, and responded to his predicament by questioning whether or not he'd even stay in baseball. He's a tremendous outfield talent who improved across the board at Double-A and again at Triple-A, but if he can't control his emotions, his major league career could be over before it starts.

Jonny Gomes **DH** **Bats: R** **Throws: R** Height: 6' 1" Weight: 205 Born: November 22, 1980 Age: 26

YEAR	TEAM	LVL	AGE	PA	R	2B	3B	HR	RBI	BB	SO	SB	CS	SPEED	AVG	OBP	SLG	MLVR	EQAVG	EQOBP	EQSLG	EQA	VORP	DEFENSE			
2004	DUR	AAA	23	470	73	27	1	26	78	51	136	8	5	4.9	.257	.368	.532	.162	.236	.336	.479	.277	8.9	100-LF	-6		
2005	DUR	AAA	24	202	34	13	0	14	46	30	44	7	1	4.4	.321	.446	.660	.540	.301	.416	.614	.336	22.9	23-LF	-3	22-RF	-5
2005	TBA	MLB	24	407	61	13	6	21	54	39	113	9	5	5.7	.282	.372	.534	.239	.294	.389	.574	.315	31.1	33-RF	-1	13-LF	0
2006	TBA	MLB	25	461	53	21	1	20	59	61	116	1	5	3.0	.216	.325	.431	-.075	.216	.332	.442	.263	-0.4				
2007	TBA	MLB	26	535	74	23	2	28	74	65	132	6	3	4.5	.237	.342	.478	.026	.234	.344	.480	.286	16.5	126-DH			

Breakout: 9% Improve: 30% Collapse: 38% Attrition: 15% Comparables: Don Lock, Greg Vaughn, Bob Robertson, Tim Salmon

Gomes had a big April (.305/.453/.732 with 11 home runs), and that was it. He hurt his shoulder and struggled through the rest of the year before finally electing to have surgery on it in September. Rehab has been going well, and he's reportedly trying to slim down. He's crowded out of the outfield picture, but since he's not thrilled about becoming a DH, he'll be working out at first base to keep himself in the lineup. Gomes has already had to make his own breaks throughout his career, so don't bet against him.

Joel Guzman   1B   Bats: R   Throws: R   Height: 6′ 6″   Weight: 250   Born: November 24, 1984   Age: 22

YEAR	TEAM	LVL	AGE	PA	R	2B	3B	HR	RBI	BB	SO	SB	CS	SPEED	AVG	OBP	SLG	MLVR	EQAVG	EQOBP	EQSLG	EQA	VORP	DEFENSE			
2004	VRO	A+	19	356	52	22	8	14	51	21	78	8	5	6.7	.307	.347	.550	.279	.278	.313	.504	.271	26.8	82-SS	8		
2004	JAX	AA	19	200	25	11	3	9	35	13	44	1	2	4.8	.280	.325	.522	.210	.270	.308	.492	.267	12.6	43-SS	-7		
2005	JAX	AA	20	496	63	31	2	16	75	42	128	7	3	4.3	.287	.351	.475	.174	.277	.328	.465	.271	30.1	92-SS	4	18-3B	-2
2006	LVG	AAA	21	352	44	16	2	11	55	26	72	9	5	4.8	.297	.353	.464	.058	.265	.318	.421	.256	-1.5	39-LF	1	24-1B	-1
2006	LAN	MLB	21	23	2	0	0	0	3	3	2	0	0	2.7	.211	.348	.211	-.295	.211	.348	.211	.219	-1.2				
2006	DUR	AAA	21	92	7	5	0	4	9	4	23	0	0	2.5	.193	.228	.386	-.207	.170	.207	.341	.188	-7.3	12-3B	-3	12-LF	0
2007	TBA	MLB	22	475	55	24	2	17	61	31	111	6	3	4.7	.261	.314	.438	-.057	.258	.315	.439	.264	8.6	112-SS	0		

Breakout: 24%   Improve: 65%   Collapse: 15%   Attrition: 8%   Comparables: Matt Holliday, Austin Kearns, Oscar Salazar, Michael Restovich

Guzman has bounced all over the field since the Dodgers decided he had grown too large to play short, and—coincidentally or not—his bat atrophied along the way. Traded to the Rays for Julio Lugo, Guzman has gone from top prospect to something of an afterthought. As a first baseman, his bat is the blandest flavor of stale vanilla. Fortunately for him, the team has an opening at the position and a history of not being discriminating about whom they put there.

Damon Hollins   OF   Bats: R   Throws: L   Height: 5′ 11″   Weight: 180   Born: June 12, 1974   Age: 33

YEAR	TEAM	LVL	AGE	PA	R	2B	3B	HR	RBI	BB	SO	SB	CS	SPEED	AVG	OBP	SLG	MLVR	EQAVG	EQOBP	EQSLG	EQA	VORP	DEFENSE			
2004	RIC	AAA	30	386	50	26	2	20	67	24	57	5	3	4.6	.301	.341	.553	.230	.267	.305	.464	.259	3.7	93-RF	-3	10-CF	0
2004	ATL	MLB	30	23	3	2	0	0	5	0	4	0	0	5.1	.364	.364	.455	.081	.348	.348	.435	.268	0.6				
2005	DUR	AAA	31	99	11	5	0	2	17	15	17	3	2	3.5	.296	.414	.432	.173	.247	.343	.353	.250	-1.7	13-RF	1		
2005	TBA	MLB	31	369	44	17	1	13	46	23	63	8	1	5.2	.249	.296	.418	-.072	.256	.313	.440	.261	4.8	71-CF	-5	19-RF	0
2006	TBA	MLB	32	355	37	20	0	15	33	19	64	3	3	4.7	.228	.269	.423	-.181	.228	.278	.432	.238	-7.1	53-RF	3	24-CF	-4
2007	TBA	MLB	33	371	41	18	1	12	47	22	67	3	2	4.6	.250	.299	.417	-.119	.247	.300	.418	.251	-1.8	89-RF	-2		

Breakout: 15%   Improve: 43%   Collapse: 28%   Attrition: 28%   Comparables: Mike Devereaux, Dick Williams, Dan Ford, Hoot Evers

Hollins again got off to a hot start, at least by his standards, batting .253/.297/.440 through the end of May. He then faded badly, hitting just .203/.249/.385 after June 1. That he saw time at all three outfield positions might suggest he has some defensive versatility, but his fielding might best be described as "creative." He can hit a home run or two off lefties, but there are many righty-swinging outfielders who can do the same thing while doing a better job of getting on base.

Akinori Iwamura   3B   Bats: L   Throws: R   Height: 5′ 9″   Weight: 175   Born: February 9, 1979   Age: 28

YEAR	TEAM	LVL	AGE	PA	R	2B	3B	HR	RBI	BB	SO	SB	CS	SPEED	AVG	OBP	SLG	MLVR	EQAVG	EQOBP	EQSLG	EQA	VORP	DEFENSE	
2004	YKL	JP	25	607	99	19	0	44	103	70	173	9	0	5.4	.300	.386	.583	.314	.297	.378	.446	.285	38.9		
2005	YKL	JP	26	611	83	31	4	30	102	63	146	6	3	5.7	.319	.390	.555	.337	.307	.382	.469	.295	45.7		
2006	YKL	JP	27	621	84	27	2	32	77	70	128	8	1	5.7	.311	.389	.544	.327	.298	.381	.460	.293	47.5		
2007	TBA	MLB	28	578	80	27	5	17	64	61	124	7	3	5.2	.274	.352	.448	.033	.271	.354	.449	.283	22.1	135-3B	-1

Breakout: 7%   Improve: 37%   Collapse: 27%   Attrition: 1%   Comparables: Lou Whitaker, Billy Klaus, Gil McDougald, Steve Braun

Iwamura has put up some big numbers in Japan, but is even better known for his glove work, winning five Gold Gloves at third base in his home country. While it seems strange to see the Devil Rays sign him when they have a few good third basemen in the system, Iwamura can fill in at second base and all three outfield slots, so he's not going to be blocking any deserving prospects. The general line of thinking is that players coming over from Japan have an easier time maintaining their batting average than their power, and PECOTA agrees.

John Jaso   C   Bats: L   Throws: R   Height: 6′ 2″   Weight: 205   Born: September 19, 1983   Age: 23

YEAR	TEAM	LVL	AGE	PA	R	2B	3B	HR	RBI	BB	SO	SB	CS	SPEED	AVG	OBP	SLG	MLVR	EQAVG	EQOBP	EQSLG	EQA	VORP	DEFENSE			
2004	HUD	A-	20	225	34	17	2	2	35	22	32	1	0	4.7	.302	.378	.437	.243	.282	.338	.403	.257	15.8	24-C	3	14-1B	1
2005	SWM	A	21	386	61	25	1	14	50	42	53	3	1	3.6	.307	.383	.515	.269	.269	.329	.451	.267	17.9	27-C	4		
2006	VIS	A+	22	406	58	22	0	10	55	31	48	1	2	3.5	.309	.362	.451	.126	.269	.310	.396	.246	5.8	21-C	-4		
2007	TBA	MLB	23	435	45	21	1	12	50	29	64	1	1	4.2	.257	.310	.404	-.111	.254	.311	.405	.252	5.7	103-C	1		

Breakout: 27%   Improve: 52%   Collapse: 23%   Attrition: 12%   Comparables: Jacob Fox, Mike Jacobs, Ryan Christianson, Phil Avlas

Jaso followed up his breakout 2005 with a .309/.362/.451 line for Visalia in High-A ball. Careful, though—everyone hits in the Cal League. If he doesn't stick behind the plate—Jaso's defense gets an "e" for effort—he doesn't have enough bat to be an asset at first or DH.

Elliot Johnson   **2B**   **Bats: S**   **Throws: R**   Height: 6' 0"   Weight: 171   Born: March 9, 1984   Age: 23

YEAR	TEAM	LVL	AGE	PA	R	2B	3B	HR	RBI	BB	SO	SB	CS	SPEED	AVG	OBP	SLG	MLVR	EQAVG	EQOBP	EQSLG	EQA	VORP	DEFENSE	
2004	CSC	A	20	574	92	22	7	6	41	54	91	43	15	7.9	.262	.339	.370	-.005	.239	.296	.326	.226	-14.1	120-2B	13
2005	VIS	A+	21	256	42	10	3	8	33	24	49	28	5	8.3	.273	.350	.449	-.016	.235	.295	.363	.243	-3.0	54-2B	-10
2005	MNT	AA	21	283	31	9	6	3	21	13	68	15	5	7.7	.261	.305	.375	-.078	.249	.283	.368	.230	-4.0	59-2B	-4
2006	MNT	AA	22	542	69	21	10	15	50	39	122	20	18	6.8	.281	.335	.455	.183	.283	.330	.481	.269	35.3	112-2B	12
2007	TBA	MLB	23	516	64	29	5	10	48	31	104	17	7	6.7	.268	.315	.413	-.081	.265	.317	.415	.259	12.1	122-2B	2

Breakout: 28%   Improve: 59%   Collapse: 13%   Attrition: 6%   Comparables: Brooks Conrad, Angel Santos, Santiago Perez, Julio Lugo

Johnson was added to the 40-man roster after being named Player of the Year at Double-A Montgomery last year. While his OBP looks like an improvement over what he managed in his first exposure to Double-A pitching in 2005, it's amazing what 20 extra points of batting average will do for your image. He did draw a few extra walks, but not enough to say that he's successfully climbed Mt. Plate Discipline. Johnson's real gains in 2006 were in the power department. His prospects for leveraging that into plate discipline are still up in the air. He has improved on defense as well, and if Jorge Cantu can't rediscover his 2005 stroke, Johnson will be right behind him.

Evan Longoria   **3B**   **Bats: R**   **Throws: R**   Height: 6' 2"   Weight: 180   Born: October 7, 1985   Age: 21

YEAR	TEAM	LVL	AGE	PA	R	2B	3B	HR	RBI	BB	SO	SB	CS	SPEED	AVG	OBP	SLG	MLVR	EQAVG	EQOBP	EQSLG	EQA	VORP	DEFENSE	
2006	HUD	A-	20	39	5	1	1	4	11	5	5	1	0	5.4	.424	.487	.879	1.102	.400	.450	.829	.393	21.4		
2006	VIS	A+	20	128	22	8	0	8	28	13	19	1	1	4.0	.327	.402	.618	.448	.289	.346	.526	.288	10.9	22-3B	3
2006	MNT	AA	20	109	14	5	0	6	19	1	20	2	1	5.6	.267	.266	.486	.119	.257	.257	.495	.253	3.1	25-3B	5
2007	TBA	MLB	21	482	60	26	2	21	70	29	80	7	3	4.7	.272	.317	.480	.015	.269	.319	.481	.276	17.7	114-3B	12

Breakout: 9%   Improve: 38%   Collapse: 30%   Attrition: 1%   Comparables: Brandon Wood, Andy Marte, Ryan Zimmerman, Jeff Fiorentino

Ordinarily, we limit same-year draft picks to a Lineout because they only had enough professional experience to warrant a token mention of their short-season professional debut. Not so with Longoria, where he hit at every level, earning quick promotions. There are small sample size issues at each level, but scouts liked what they saw, and the quick ascent was seen as warranted. B. J. Upton's defense better improve in a hurry, because Longoria might be competing for his job very soon.

Dioner Navarro   **C**   **Bats: S**   **Throws: R**   Height: 5' 9"   Weight: 215   Born: February 9, 1984   Age: 23

YEAR	TEAM	LVL	AGE	PA	R	2B	3B	HR	RBI	BB	SO	SB	CS	SPEED	AVG	OBP	SLG	MLVR	EQAVG	EQOBP	EQSLG	EQA	VORP	DEFENSE	
2004	TRN	AA	20	292	32	14	1	3	29	33	44	1	0	3.9	.271	.354	.369	.007	.262	.336	.354	.246	3.2	50-C	4
2004	COH	AAA	20	155	18	8	2	1	16	14	17	1	0	5.2	.250	.316	.360	-.124	.241	.308	.343	.235	-1.8	39-C	8
2005	LVG	AAA	21	286	31	12	0	6	29	38	24	2	2	2.7	.266	.366	.390	-.101	.219	.312	.320	.229	-6.0	64-C	4
2005	LAN	MLB	21	199	21	9	0	3	14	20	21	0	0	4.1	.273	.354	.375	.016	.278	.362	.381	.263	7.6	49-C	0
2006	LAN	MLB	22	86	5	2	0	2	8	11	18	1	0	3.7	.280	.372	.387	.028	.280	.372	.387	.272	3.1	22-C	-6
2006	TBA	MLB	22	216	23	7	0	4	20	20	33	1	1	3.3	.244	.316	.342	-.191	.241	.321	.346	.237	-2.6	53-C	1
2007	TBA	MLB	23	401	46	20	1	9	43	40	55	3	1	4.5	.265	.341	.402	-.054	.262	.343	.403	.267	11.8	96-C	2

Breakout: 70%   Improve: 94%   Collapse: 2%   Attrition: 24%   Comparables: Butch Wynegar, Biff Pocoroba, Glenn Borgmann, Dave Nilsson

The Devil Rays acquired Navarro in a mid-season, four-player, C-grade challenge trade with the Dodgers that mercifully released Toby Halls's grip on the catching position and banished Mark Hendrickson to the other side of the country. In Navarro, they picked up a player that still has some upside, though for the moment it all seems to be tied up in his plate discipline. His defense in Los Angeles was problematic, and his power simply hasn't materialized. Still, he is just 23, and will be the best catcher in the franchise's short history if he matches that projection.

Greg Norton   **UT**   **Bats: S**   **Throws: R**   Height: 6' 1"   Weight: 200   Born: July 6, 1972   Age: 34

YEAR	TEAM	LVL	AGE	PA	R	2B	3B	HR	RBI	BB	SO	SB	CS	SPEED	AVG	OBP	SLG	MLVR	EQAVG	EQOBP	EQSLG	EQA	VORP	DEFENSE			
2004	TOL	AAA	32	209	26	6	1	4	16	24	48	1	1	4.6	.207	.297	.315	-.234	.180	.257	.243	.186	-18.0	51-3B	3		
2004	DET	MLB	32	99	9	1	0	2	2	12	21	0	0	2.7	.174	.276	.256	-.409	.165	.276	.247	.197	-7.2	11-3B	-1		
2005	CHR	AAA	33	381	57	19	1	17	56	47	67	0	2	3.1	.285	.374	.503	.184	.240	.317	.396	.248	5.5	42-3B	-5	10-1B	1
2006	TBA	MLB	34	335	47	15	0	17	45	35	69	1	5	3.5	.296	.374	.520	.205	.297	.383	.531	.298	20.9	24-RF	-6	20-1B	-2
2007	TBA	MLB	34	383	46	19	1	13	52	40	82	1	1	3.9	.259	.339	.443	-.007	.256	.341	.444	.275	7.6	92-DH			

Breakout: 31%   Improve: 62%   Collapse: 19%   Attrition: 34%   Comparables: Carl Everett, Roy Smalley, J. T. Snow, Walt Moryn

Going into 2006, Norton was a career .245/.326/.419 utility man who, despite having good pop for a versatile guy, couldn't find a major league job in 2005. Thanks to the always-fluid Rays roster, he was able to play himself into regular work in the second half and responded with a terrific two-month hot streak, batting .302/.392/.553 after the All-Star break. Norton is already in late middle-age as baseball players go, so his season doesn't signify anything more than the great dice-roller in the sky finding the sweet spot on Norton's Strat card for a while. Still, the Rays re-signed him to a one-year deal with an option for the second. They plan to begin the year with Norton in something more than a utility role, but for the good of the organization that will have to change quickly.

Tomas Perez INF Bats: S Throws: R Height: 5' 11" Weight: 195 Born: December 29, 1973 Age: 33

YEAR	TEAM	LVL	AGE	PA	R	2B	3B	HR	RBI	BB	SO	SB	CS	SPEED	AVG	OBP	SLG	MLVR	EQAVG	EQOBP	EQSLG	EQA	VORP	DEFENSE			
2004	PHI	MLB	30	190	22	13	2	6	21	9	44	0	0	5.5	.216	.257	.415	-.181	.215	.255	.407	.225	-3.4	12-2B	1	11-3B	0
2005	PHI	MLB	31	176	17	7	0	0	22	11	27	1	0	4.3	.233	.289	.277	-.283	.219	.280	.256	.200	-7.8	17-1B	2		
2006	TBA	MLB	32	254	31	12	0	2	16	5	44	1	0	5.6	.212	.224	.286	-.476	.193	.213	.265	.176	-19.5	33-SS	1	19-3B	-1
2007	TBA	MLB	33	249	23	15	1	4	24	10	43	1	1	5.1	.245	.278	.366	-.229	.242	.279	.367	.227	-3.5	62-SS	-2		

Breakout: 66% Improve: 78% Collapse: 16% Attrition: 45% Comparables: Jose Uribe, Paul Popovich, Al Weis, Rob Wilfong

The Devil Rays got exactly what they should have expected from Perez, a utility player who isn't utilitarian. Giving this much time to so futile a player sends a message to the fans: We're not serious about winning, and we don't intend to entertain you, either.

Shawn Riggans C Bats: R Throws: R Height: 6' 2" Weight: 190 Born: July 25, 1980 Age: 26

YEAR	TEAM	LVL	AGE	PA	R	2B	3B	HR	RBI	BB	SO	SB	CS	SPEED	AVG	OBP	SLG	MLVR	EQAVG	EQOBP	EQSLG	EQA	VORP	DEFENSE	
2004	BAK	A+	23	144	20	11	0	5	22	15	23	0	1	2.7	.346	.417	.551	.425	.303	.354	.470	.277	10.7	26-C	-2
2005	MNT	AA	24	350	40	21	0	8	53	26	69	1	2	2.5	.310	.365	.454	.166	.280	.325	.416	.257	11.8	66-C	-3
2006	DUR	AAA	25	453	43	26	2	11	54	27	88	2	2	4.0	.293	.341	.444	.111	.282	.330	.442	.262	21.1	85-C	-5
2006	TBA	MLB	25	33	3	1	0	0	1	4	7	0	0	3.1	.172	.273	.207	-.501	.138	.242	.172	.164	-2.8		
2007	TBA	MLB	26	425	40	20	1	12	50	26	91	0	1	3.7	.252	.304	.399	-.132	.249	.305	.400	.248	3.7	101-C	0

Breakout: 15% Improve: 33% Collapse: 35% Attrition: 20% Comparables: Mike Macfarlane, Geronimo Gil, Julio Vinas, Jody Davis

Riggans is a good defensive catcher who's a bit long in the tooth to be a real prospect. He won't get much better than he is now, but he's a contact hitter who has added a bit of power as he's matured. He's a better option than Josh Paul right now, and, with Paul arbitration-eligible, it's worth a gamble to see if a Navarro-Riggans tandem can outperform a Navarro-Paul one.

B. J. Upton 3B Bats: R Throws: R Height: 6' 3" Weight: 180 Born: August 21, 1984 Age: 22

YEAR	TEAM	LVL	AGE	PA	R	2B	3B	HR	RBI	BB	SO	SB	CS	SPEED	AVG	OBP	SLG	MLVR	EQAVG	EQOBP	EQSLG	EQA	VORP	DEFENSE			
2004	MNT	AA	19	120	21	7	1	2	15	14	28	3	0	6.0	.327	.407	.471	.279	.318	.387	.458	.296	12.4	23-SS	-2		
2004	DUR	AAA	19	313	65	17	1	12	36	42	72	17	5	7.1	.311	.411	.519	.262	.284	.381	.463	.293	27.6	66-SS	-10		
2004	TBA	MLB	19	177	19	8	2	4	12	15	46	4	1	6.3	.258	.324	.409	-.040	.259	.330	.411	.260	4.4	15-SS	-2		
2005	DUR	AAA	20	631	98	36	6	18	74	78	127	44	13	7.6	.303	.392	.490	.218	.282	.368	.451	.286	45.9	130-SS	-23		
2006	DUR	AAA	21	470	72	18	4	8	41	65	89	46	17	7.2	.269	.374	.394	.081	.264	.364	.403	.272	25.0	84-SS	-6	18-3B	-2
2006	TBA	MLB	21	189	20	5	0	1	10	13	40	11	3	6.8	.246	.302	.291	-.291	.243	.307	.283	.223	-7.6	46-3B	-8		
2007	TBA	MLB	22	574	87	26	4	13	50	60	117	38	14	6.7	.268	.348	.413	-.025	.265	.350	.414	.276	20.8	134-SS	-9		

Breakout: 17% Improve: 35% Collapse: 24% Attrition: 7% Comparables: Carlos Febles, Jim Fregosi, Willie Randolph, Delino Deshields

Joe Maddon has hinted that Upton's future might not be at third anymore, leaving the outfield a likely destination. As has been the case for at least the last two years, it's time for the franchise to stop pushing Upton to do things he can't and start figuring out what he *can* do. That task has now become more complicated because Upton's bat died last year. That's now the first mystery to be solved. After that, whether Upton becomes a left fielder, a center fielder, an unconventional Darin Erstad-style first baseman, or the world's fastest DH, it's time to stop asking him to throw the baseball across the infield. It's stunting his growth worse than cigarettes.

Ty Wigginton　　　　**2B**　　**Bats: R**　**Throws: R**　　Height: 6' 0"　　Weight: 225　　Born: October 11, 1977　　Age: 29

YEAR	TEAM	LVL	AGE	PA	R	2B	3B	HR	RBI	BB	SO	SB	CS	SPEED	AVG	OBP	SLG	MLVR	EQAVG	EQOBP	EQSLG	EQA	VORP	DEFENSE			
2004	NYN	MLB	26	339	46	23	2	12	42	23	48	6	1	5.6	.285	.334	.487	.125	.285	.334	.494	.281	17.0	54-3B	-6	19-2B	2
2004	PIT	MLB	26	206	17	7	0	5	24	22	34	1	0	3.6	.220	.306	.341	-.159	.214	.301	.341	.229	-4.8	51-3B	-4		
2005	IND	AAA	27	328	53	18	0	14	52	45	56	8	5	4.6	.293	.390	.507	.233	.263	.354	.442	.274	17.9	51-3B	1		
2005	PIT	MLB	27	171	20	9	1	7	25	14	30	0	1	4.5	.258	.324	.465	.060	.258	.327	.477	.269	4.7	34-3B	-4		
2006	TBA	MLB	28	486	55	25	1	24	79	32	97	4	3	3.8	.275	.330	.498	.074	.276	.337	.510	.281	20.5	38-1B	-2	38-2B	2
2007	TBA	MLB	29	463	60	23	2	19	63	40	88	4	2	4.7	.269	.335	.466	.024	.265	.337	.467	.280	16.6	110-3B	-2		

Breakout: 12% Improve: 47% Collapse: 21% Attrition: 7%　　Comparables: Doug Rader, Sean Berry, Benny Agbayani, Deron Johnson

Wigginton went from prospect flop to adequate placeholder in just a few years, which is another nice reminder that lacking plate discipline at an early age isn't a career death sentence. He's versatile, seeing time at five different positions last year, and whips lefties, though he also hit for power against normal people in 2006. He'll likely start the season at first base, for which his bat is not qualified at any level lower than last year's peak. He's best used as a rover whose bat can keep the team above replacement level wherever there's an injury.

Delmon Young　　　　**RF**　　**Bats: R**　**Throws: R**　　Height: 6' 3"　　Weight: 205　　Born: September 14, 1985　Age: 21

YEAR	TEAM	LVL	AGE	PA	R	2B	3B	HR	RBI	BB	SO	SB	CS	SPEED	AVG	OBP	SLG	MLVR	EQAVG	EQOBP	EQSLG	EQA	VORP	DEFENSE	
2004	CSC	A	18	578	95	26	5	25	116	53	120	21	6	6.0	.322	.388	.538	.352	.298	.346	.475	.280	24.0	113-RF	5
2005	MNT	AA	19	370	59	13	4	20	71	25	66	25	8	7.0	.336	.386	.582	.407	.317	.357	.556	.303	31.7	78-RF	-5
2005	DUR	AAA	19	234	33	13	3	6	28	4	33	7	4	7.0	.285	.303	.447	-.004	.263	.282	.412	.236	-5.3	50-RF	-8
2006	DUR	AAA	20	370	50	22	4	8	59	15	65	22	4	6.7	.316	.341	.474	.170	.308	.332	.481	.281	14.7	83-RF	-5
2006	TBA	MLB	20	131	16	9	1	3	10	1	24	2	2	6.1	.317	.336	.476	.094	.320	.344	.480	.273	5.2	28-RF	-4
2007	TBA	MLB	21	553	78	31	4	17	68	27	97	20	7	6.3	.296	.334	.471	.054	.293	.336	.473	.282	17.1	130-RF	-3

Breakout: 22% Improve: 50% Collapse: 14% Attrition: 6%　　Comparables: Ruben Mateo, Cesar Cedeno, Tommy Davis, Rocco Baldelli

Delmon Young threw a bat at an umpire last April and earned an indefinite suspension. After returning, he threw his bat at a whole lot of baseballs and earned a promotion. Young doesn't walk a whole lot (just 16 times in 501 plate appearances between Triple-A and the majors last year), but boy howdy he can hit. Over 30 games with the Rays, Young hit almost exactly as well as he did at Durham, which is a helluva thing for a 20-year-old to do in his major league debut. Young is the kind of player the Rays can afford to let grow in the majors. That is, if he does wind up growing; judging by the comparable players above, PECOTA isn't so sure. Maybe Vlad Guerrero can get away with swinging from his heels at everything he sees, and maybe Young can cover the plate in a way that reminds us of the Impaler, but, for now, Young is just a kid who needs to learn that, if he wants to get ahead, he's going to have to stop throwing his bat at everything that comes near home plate.

Ben Zobrist　　　　**SS**　　**Bats: S**　**Throws: R**　　Height: 6' 3"　　Weight: 200　　Born: May 26, 1981　　　Age: 26

YEAR	TEAM	LVL	AGE	PA	R	2B	3B	HR	RBI	BB	SO	SB	CS	SPEED	AVG	OBP	SLG	MLVR	EQAVG	EQOBP	EQSLG	EQA	VORP	DEFENSE	
2004	TCV	A-	23	310	50	14	3	4	45	43	31	15	4	6.0	.339	.438	.463	.338	.279	.347	.373	.258	19.4	65-SS	4
2005	LEX	A	24	310	45	17	2	2	32	47	35	16	5	5.9	.304	.415	.413	.177	.243	.320	.310	.235	-2.9	63-SS	5
2005	SLM	A+	24	180	25	12	1	3	13	37	17	2	1	3.6	.333	.475	.496	.400	.303	.408	.428	.293	17.1	36-SS	3
2006	CCH	AA	25	381	57	25	6	3	30	55	46	9	5	6.2	.327	.434	.473	.316	.306	.392	.433	.288	33.1	79-SS	2
2006	DUR	AAA	25	82	12	3	1	0	6	10	9	4	1	6.9	.304	.400	.377	.122	.282	.378	.352	.270	3.6	18-SS	-4
2006	TBA	MLB	25	198	10	6	2	2	18	10	26	2	3	4.8	.224	.260	.311	-.358	.215	.260	.298	.199	-9.7	50-SS	0
2007	TBA	MLB	26	504	64	28	3	5	41	45	65	8	4	5.5	.274	.342	.381	-.072	.271	.344	.382	.262	15.2	119-SS	2

Breakout: 14% Improve: 47% Collapse: 20% Attrition: 12%　　Comparables: Jolbert Cabrera, D'Angelo Jimenez, Don Kelly, Kevin Stocker

Part of the payoff for Aubrey Huff, Zobrist is less the Shortstop of the Future then the shortstop of right now. Too old to be considered a high-ceiling prospect, he's still a solid player with great command of the strike zone. He doesn't have much power to speak of, but if he can catch the ball and get on base, he'll be plenty serviceable for the time being.

PITCHERS

Shawn Camp
Bats: R Throws: R   Height: 6' 1"   Weight: 200   Born: November 18, 1975   Age: 31

YEAR	TEAM	LVL	AGE	W	L	SV	G	GS	IP	H	BB	SO	HR	GB%	BABIP	STUFF	WHIP	ERA	PERA	EQERA	EQH9	EQBB9	EQSO9	EQHR9	VORP	WXRL
2004	OMA	AAA	28	1	1	1	15	0	22	26	6	21	2	—	.348	-2	1.45	5.32	4.08	5.64	10.5	2.4	6.4	0.8	-0.1	—
2004	KCA	MLB	28	2	2	2	42	0	66²	74	16	51	10	—	.320	2	1.33	3.91	4.30	4.26	9.2	1.9	6.2	1.2	10.7	1.19
2005	OMA	AAA	29	3	6	1	21	7	67²	71	22	42	9	48.6%	.300	-18	1.37	3.86	5.55	4.87	9.1	2.9	4.1	1.4	5.5	—
2005	KCA	MLB	29	1	4	0	29	0	49	69	13	28	4	57.2%	.369	-6	1.67	6.43	4.05	5.85	11.2	2.2	4.8	0.7	-8.8	-1.39
2006	TBA	MLB	30	7	4	4	75	0	75	93	19	53	9	57.8%	.357	-1	1.49	4.68	4.27	4.25	10.1	2.1	5.9	0.9	7.8	0.75
2007	TBA	MLB	31	3	3	3	58	0	67¹	77	19	41	7	53.0%	.315	-4	1.43	4.46	4.42	4.12	9.5	2.4	5.2	0.8	8.7	0.70

Breakout: 35%   Improve: 63%   Collapse: 21%   Attrition: 24%   Comparables: Bill Fischer, Rodney Myers, Scott Terry, Donn Pall

Camp's your basic veteran bullpen arm, a strike-thrower with good command who shows up, keeps the ball down, and goes home. In fact, he was roughly league average in just about every way possible last year. There was but one exceptional thing about him: He set the Devil Rays' franchise record for pitching appearances in a single season with 75. Thrilling.

Marcos Carvajal
Bats: R Throws: R   Height: 6' 4"   Weight: 175   Born: August 19, 1984   Age: 22

YEAR	TEAM	LVL	AGE	W	L	SV	G	GS	IP	H	BB	SO	HR	GB%	BABIP	STUFF	WHIP	ERA	PERA	EQERA	EQH9	EQBB9	EQSO9	EQHR9	VORP	WXRL
2004	CGA	A	19	4	2	1	36	0	72	50	35	72	2	—	.264	12	1.18	1.88	4.64	3.07	7.0	5.1	5.4	0.4	19.8	—
2005	COL	MLB	20	0	2	0	39	0	53	52	21	47	8	51.3%	.301	10	1.38	5.09	4.65	4.39	8.0	3.1	7.2	1.3	4.1	-0.17
2006	MNT	AA	21	2	2	0	39	0	72	66	39	69	7	41.6%	.292	-9	1.46	3.88	5.80	5.27	9.8	4.9	6.2	1.5	2.6	—
2007	TBA	MLB	22	3	4	1	35	6	65¹	73	39	48	10	44.0%	.309	-6	1.71	6.01	5.85	5.52	9.3	5.0	6.2	1.2	-2.7	0.10

Breakout: 7%   Improve: 23%   Collapse: 54%   Attrition: 8%   Comparables: Johann Lopez, Kris Honel, Ismael Villegas, P. J. Bevis

Designated for assignment by Seattle right before the season began, Carvajal was snapped up by Tampa and enjoyed a solid year in Montgomery. Despite not getting the call all year during the D-Rays open auditions for their bullpen spots, Carvajal has both "success as a Rule 5 pick" and "can pitch in Coors Field" on his resume. He should be in the bullpen mix in 2007.

Tim Corcoran
Bats: R Throws: R   Height: 6' 2"   Weight: 205   Born: April 15, 1978   Age: 29

YEAR	TEAM	LVL	AGE	W	L	SV	G	GS	IP	H	BB	SO	HR	GB%	BABIP	STUFF	WHIP	ERA	PERA	EQERA	EQH9	EQBB9	EQSO9	EQHR9	VORP	WXRL
2004	MNT	AA	26	0	1	0	6	2	16¹	14	3	12	2	—	.273	-14	1.04	2.76	6.19	3.94	8.4	2.2	3.9	1.7	3.0	—
2004	DUR	AAA	26	3	3	0	33	0	50²	46	33	40	4	—	.290	-1	1.56	3.91	5.65	4.14	8.1	6.5	5.4	0.9	8.1	—
2005	DUR	AAA	27	5	1	0	29	0	56	49	22	49	3	38.8%	.286	4	1.27	2.89	4.11	3.47	7.3	3.8	5.8	0.5	13.5	—
2005	TBA	MLB	27	0	0	0	10	1	22²	19	12	13	1	40.8%	.257	-5	1.37	5.95	4.45	5.40	6.9	4.6	5.0	0.4	-0.7	0.08
2006	DUR	AAA	28	5	1	1	19	3	37	30	9	32	2	40.6%	.272	5	1.05	1.95	3.76	3.38	7.0	2.4	5.8	0.7	9.2	—
2006	TBA	MLB	28	5	9	0	21	16	90¹	92	48	59	10	42.1%	.304	6	1.55	4.39	4.96	3.99	8.2	4.4	5.4	0.9	12.9	2.08
2007	TBA	MLB	29	5	8	1	41	17	107	120	50	67	15	44.0%	.303	-7	1.58	5.46	5.28	5.02	9.3	3.9	5.3	1.1	1.8	0.80

Breakout: 5%   Improve: 14%   Collapse: 57%   Attrition: 14%   Comparables: Ken Schrom, Pat Rapp, Luke Hudson, Roric Harrison

Corcoran was outrighted off of the 40-man roster early in the season, but was an emergency callup just a few days later. He looked solid in relief in his first few appearances and appeared to be a good veteran find, but he had more failures than successes after being inserted into the rotation. His virtues are a good Irish surname and his ability to throw a baseball sixty-odd feet when asked.

Wade Davis
Bats: R Throws: R   Height: 6' 5"   Weight: 220   Born: September 7, 1985   Age: 21

YEAR	TEAM	LVL	AGE	W	L	SV	G	GS	IP	H	BB	SO	HR	GB%	BABIP	STUFF	WHIP	ERA	PERA	EQERA	EQH9	EQBB9	EQSO9	EQHR9	VORP	WXRL
2004	PRI	Rk	18	3	5	0	13	13	57²	71	19	38	8	—	.326	-35	1.56	5.93	8.18	6.95	11.2	3.9	2.7	2.7	-8.6	—
2005	HUD	A-	19	7	4	0	15	15	86	75	23	97	5	56.1%	.320	6	1.14	2.72	5.49	5.05	9.7	3.2	5.5	1.5	5.0	—
2006	SWM	A	20	7	12	0	27	27	146²	124	64	165	5	50.1%	.330	19	1.29	3.02	4.93	4.76	8.8	5.1	6.2	0.8	13.1	—
2007	TBA	MLB	21	5	9	0	25	21	117²	136	63	80	19	48.0%	.312	1	1.69	6.06	5.85	5.61	9.6	4.5	5.8	1.3	-6.8	0.20

Breakout: 9%   Improve: 38%   Collapse: 31%   Attrition: 0%   Comparables: Matt Wright, Adam Harben, Grant Roberts, Brian Rogers

Davis led the NY-Penn League in strikeouts in 2005, so expectations were high that he'd keep it going in the Midwest League. In April, May, and August, he looked like he was well on his way to being a premium young pitcher, dominating hitters by throwing in the high-90s and showing great command of his curveball. In June and July, he looked like a completely different pitcher, putting up ERAs of 5.59 and 5.29 and seeing his walk rate climb to almost 5 per nine innings pitched. He'll get to follow this up with a trip to the Cal League; if he emerges from that in one piece, we may have something here.

Casey Fossum
Bats: L Throws: L Height: 6' 1" Weight: 160 Born: January 9, 1978 Age: 29

YEAR	TEAM	LVL	AGE	W	L	SV	G	GS	IP	H	BB	SO	HR	GB%	BABIP	STUFF	WHIP	ERA	PERA	EQERA	EQH9	EQBB9	EQSO9	EQHR9	VORP	WXRL
2004	ARI	MLB	26	4	15	0	27	27	142	171	63	117	31	—	.334	-11	1.65	6.65	5.61	6.07	10.4	3.5	6.4	1.7	-19.0	0.18
2005	TBA	MLB	27	8	12	0	36	25	162²	170	60	128	21	39.3%	.304	8	1.41	4.92	4.73	5.11	8.8	3.2	6.8	1.1	4.1	1.33
2006	TBA	MLB	28	6	6	0	25	25	130	136	63	88	18	46.9%	.289	1	1.53	5.33	5.32	5.17	8.6	4.0	5.6	1.1	-1.3	2.03
2007	*TBA*	*MLB*	*29*	*7*	*10*	*0*	*31*	*23*	*139²*	*153*	*57*	*97*	*18*	*45.0%*	*.305*	*5*	*1.50*	*5.07*	*4.88*	*4.67*	*9.1*	*3.4*	*5.8*	*1.0*	*8.5*	*1.80*

Breakout: 38% Improve: 66% Collapse: 10% Attrition: 3%   Comparables: Dave Koslo, Al Downing, Shane Rawley, Omar Daal

Fossum hurt his groin, shin, shoulder, and foot at differing points during the year; three he hurt while pitching, and one he hurt while climbing out of a hot tub. He's a slender reed of a guy who doesn't resemble the pitcher the Red Sox were reluctant to include in so many rumored deals a few years ago, and surgery to fix a frayed labrum merely highlights a concern we've heard about him all along: He's not durable enough to withstand a starter's workload. Shoulder rehab isn't an exact enough science to suggest what the Rays will be getting once he does return, but when he does it will almost certainly be in a relief role, which may have been where he belonged the whole time.

Jason Hammel
Bats: R Throws: R Height: 6' 6" Weight: 200 Born: September 2, 1982 Age: 24

YEAR	TEAM	LVL	AGE	W	L	SV	G	GS	IP	H	BB	SO	HR	GB%	BABIP	STUFF	WHIP	ERA	PERA	EQERA	EQH9	EQBB9	EQSO9	EQHR9	VORP	WXRL
2004	CSC	A	21	4	7	0	18	18	94²	94	27	88	7	—	.309	-3	1.28	3.23	4.92	6.22	9.7	3.1	4.8	1.2	-6.4	—
2004	BAK	A+	21	6	2	0	11	11	71¹	52	20	65	4	—	.262	16	1.01	1.89	4.68	2.93	6.8	3.1	5.2	0.9	21.0	—
2005	MNT	AA	22	8	2	0	12	12	81¹	70	19	76	5	43.6%	.300	20	1.09	2.66	4.01	3.44	8.0	2.1	5.9	0.9	19.4	—
2005	DUR	AAA	22	3	2	0	10	10	54²	57	27	48	8	45.0%	.306	3	1.54	4.11	5.80	4.85	8.7	4.7	6.0	1.5	4.6	—
2006	DUR	AAA	23	5	9	0	24	24	127¹	133	36	117	11	47.8%	.335	9	1.33	4.25	4.49	5.23	9.2	2.7	6.3	1.1	5.3	—
2006	TBA	MLB	23	0	6	0	9	9	44	61	21	32	7	43.7%	.375	-3	1.86	7.77	4.95	6.56	11.0	3.9	6.0	1.2	-8.4	-0.27
2007	*TBA*	*MLB*	*24*	*6*	*10*	*0*	*31*	*26*	*135²*	*151*	*52*	*96*	*20*	*46.0%*	*.306*	*6*	*1.49*	*5.41*	*4.99*	*5.01*	*9.2*	*3.3*	*6.0*	*1.1*	*2.6*	*1.20*

Breakout: 21% Improve: 56% Collapse: 13% Attrition: 0%   Comparables: Don Aase, Matt Bruback, John Maine, Sean Douglass

Fans shouldn't be too concerned about Hammel's rough introduction to major league hitting. His PERA (ERA based on his equivalent peripherals) was much stronger than his actual ERA, suggesting that his struggles were more a product of some ill-timed events and not a wholesale failure to execute his program, a suggestion supported by his .375 BABIP. PERA also tends to predict future ERA more accurately than raw ERA does. Hammel throws hard and has an assortment of complementary pitches; he may not be a star, but he's far more desirable than the Doug Waechters of the world.

Travis Harper
Bats: L Throws: R Height: 6' 4" Weight: 190 Born: May 21, 1976 Age: 31

YEAR	TEAM	LVL	AGE	W	L	SV	G	GS	IP	H	BB	SO	HR	GB%	BABIP	STUFF	WHIP	ERA	PERA	EQERA	EQH9	EQBB9	EQSO9	EQHR9	VORP	WXRL
2004	TBA	MLB	28	6	2	0	52	0	78²	69	23	59	8	—	.269	8	1.19	3.89	4.08	3.83	8.0	2.4	6.3	0.8	14.3	2.24
2005	TBA	MLB	29	4	6	0	52	0	73¹	88	24	40	14	32.1%	.315	-26	1.54	6.75	5.44	6.22	9.9	2.8	4.7	1.5	-11.7	-0.58
2006	TBA	MLB	30	2	0	0	30	0	42	62	13	32	6	37.0%	.400	-3	1.79	4.93	4.30	4.63	11.7	2.4	6.2	1.0	1.3	-0.52
2007	*TBA*	*MLB*	*31*	*3*	*3*	*1*	*41*	*2*	*61¹*	*71*	*19*	*41*	*9*	*42.0%*	*.311*	*-4*	*1.46*	*5.01*	*4.89*	*4.55*	*9.6*	*2.6*	*5.6*	*1.2*	*4.5*	*0.40*

Breakout: 31% Improve: 53% Collapse: 26% Attrition: 32%   Comparables: Doug Bird, Jim Coates, Ron Kline, Bobby Howry

Harper was shut down for the year with shoulder trouble following a pretty terrible performance against the Tigers on August 1. This particular writing has been on the wall for a while; his innings totals have been decreasing steadily since 2003, and his training wheels went back on, as he again saw a lot of low-leverage action. He was released, ostensibly to free up a roster spot for Akinori Iwamura. Harper is a Devil Rays rarity: A player of whom you can say "he spent his entire career with the Devil Rays," and have it refer to more than three or four seasons.

J. P. Howell
Bats: L Throws: L Height: 6' 0" Weight: 175 Born: November 30, 1999 Age: 24

YEAR	TEAM	LVL	AGE	W	L	SV	G	GS	IP	H	BB	SO	HR	GB%	BABIP	STUFF	WHIP	ERA	PERA	EQERA	EQH9	EQBB9	EQSO9	EQHR9	VORP	WXRL
2004	IDA	Rk	0	3	1	0	6	4	26	16	12	38	1	—	.288	13	1.08	2.77	5.22	3.65	6.9	5.1	6.2	0.7	5.4	—
2005	HDS	A+	0	3	1	0	8	8	46	33	24	48	2	68.7%	.274	24	1.24	1.96	4.85	3.15	6.3	5.5	5.9	0.6	12.4	—
2005	WIC	AA	0	2	0	0	3	3	18	12	5	23	2	63.4%	.256	17	0.94	2.50	4.54	3.12	6.7	3.1	8.8	1.6	4.8	—
2005	OMA	AAA	0	3	1	0	7	7	37²	40	19	29	1	56.6%	.355	11	1.56	4.06	3.94	4.42	9.1	4.2	5.1	0.2	5.1	—
2005	KCA	MLB	0	3	5	0	15	15	72²	73	39	54	9	54.3%	.299	8	1.54	6.19	5.18	5.99	8.0	4.6	6.3	1.1	-7.9	0.07
2006	OMA	AAA	0	3	2	0	8	8	36²	39	14	33	3	61.1%	.360	8	1.46	4.72	4.21	4.62	9.2	3.4	6.3	1.0	4.0	—
2006	DUR	AAA	0	5	3	0	10	10	55¹	53	15	49	2	49.4%	.333	23	1.23	2.61	3.66	3.20	8.3	2.6	6.1	0.5	15.0	—
2006	TBA	MLB	0	1	3	0	8	8	42¹	52	14	33	4	47.4%	.366	16	1.56	5.11	3.98	4.47	9.9	2.6	6.5	0.8	3.5	0.91
2007	*TBA*	*MLB*	*24*	*8*	*10*	*0*	*30*	*29*	*151²*	*159*	*65*	*118*	*16*	*51.0%*	*.310*	*14*	*1.48*	*4.71*	*4.53*	*4.38*	*8.7*	*3.6*	*6.5*	*0.8*	*14.9*	*2.70*

Breakout: 28% Improve: 53% Collapse: 15% Attrition: 1%   Comparables: Tom Underwood, Danny Jackson, Shawn Estes, Tommy John

That Tampa was able to acquire Howell for Joey Gathright and Fernando Cortez was pretty amazing. Cortez still doesn't hit, and Gathright was quickly being squeezed out of the outfield picture, so Tampa essentially got Howell for nothing. He was rushed in Kansas City, but he settled down in 2006 and had a nice season at Durham and Tampa after the trade. Perhaps Howell can slide in behind Kazmir for the next few years; he has nothing left to prove at Triple-A. One of his problems in Kansas City was that he knew it.

Edwin Jackson
Bats: R Throws: R Height: 6' 3" Weight: 190 Born: September 9, 1983 Age: 23

YEAR	TEAM	LVL	AGE	W	L	SV	G	GS	IP	H	BB	SO	HR	GB%	BABIP	STUFF	WHIP	ERA	PERA	EQERA	EQH9	EQBB9	EQSO9	EQHR9	VORP	WXRL
2004	LVG	AAA	20	6	4	0	19	19	90²	90	55	70	4	—	.310	19	1.60	5.85	4.92	5.61	8.0	5.5	5.2	0.4	-0.1	—
2004	LAN	MLB	20	2	1	0	8	5	24²	31	11	16	7	—	.308	-11	1.70	7.29	6.57	7.56	11.5	3.6	5.0	2.5	-4.1	0.27
2005	JAX	AA	21	6	4	0	11	11	62	52	18	44	7	47.7%	.249	-6	1.13	3.48	5.93	5.55	8.6	2.7	4.7	1.8	0.3	—
2005	LVG	AAA	21	3	7	0	12	11	55¹	76	37	33	13	37.6%	.339	-27	2.04	8.63	7.76	8.33	10.8	5.6	3.9	2.2	-17.7	—
2005	LAN	MLB	21	2	2	0	7	6	28²	31	17	13	2	33.7%	.293	-11	1.67	6.27	5.03	6.75	9.8	4.9	3.7	0.6	-4.6	0.07
2006	DUR	AAA	22	3	7	5	22	13	73¹	84	35	66	7	47.6%	.352	-6	1.63	5.54	5.26	7.05	10.1	4.5	6.2	1.2	-11.9	—
2006	TBA	MLB	22	0	0	0	23	1	36¹	42	25	27	2	52.1%	.348	5	1.84	5.45	4.44	5.63	9.2	5.6	6.1	0.5	-2.4	-0.59
2007	*TBA*	*MLB*	*23*	*4*	*7*	*1*	*42*	*13*	*92*	*107*	*54*	*60*	*15*	*45.0%*	*.312*	*-11*	*1.75*	*6.45*	*6.05*	*5.97*	*9.7*	*4.9*	*5.5*	*1.2*	*-9.7*	*0.50*

Breakout: 31% Improve: 64% Collapse: 14% Attrition: 1%   *Comparables: Rafael Medina, Mike Moore, William Martinez, Donnie Bridges*

Jackson is the B. J. Upton of pitching; he's bad and no one could figure out why. The one-time Dodgers prospect had himself a mighty underwhelming year at Durham, and the only thing he did well in Tampa was keep the ball in the park. The glass-half-full sect would argue that, for as long as he's been mentioned in prospect circles, he's still just 23. The glass-half-empty contingent would point out that, outside of his four-game major league debut at age 19, he's never pitched well above Double-A. One of the side effects of the Dodgers rushing him up to the majors at such a young age is that he's now out of options, so he may get a bullpen job regardless of whether or not he deserves one. He could very easily put it all together and post an ERA of 2.75 next season, but PECOTA sees Jackson's glass as half empty.

Scott Kazmir
Bats: L Throws: L Height: 6' 0" Weight: 190 Born: January 24, 1984 Age: 23

YEAR	TEAM	LVL	AGE	W	L	SV	G	GS	IP	H	BB	SO	HR	GB%	BABIP	STUFF	WHIP	ERA	PERA	EQERA	EQH9	EQBB9	EQSO9	EQHR9	VORP	WXRL
2004	SLU	A+	20	1	2	0	11	11	50	49	22	51	3	—	.326	8	1.42	3.42	4.96	4.62	9.8	4.4	6.3	1.1	5.3	—
2004	BIN	AA	20	2	1	0	4	4	26	16	9	29	0	—	.276	25	0.96	1.73	3.46	2.49	6.8	3.2	7.5	0.4	8.7	—
2004	MNT	AA	20	1	2	0	4	4	25	14	11	24	0	—	.230	22	1.00	1.44	3.93	3.33	5.5	4.4	5.9	0.4	6.1	—
2004	TBA	MLB	20	2	3	0	8	7	33¹	33	21	41	4	—	.345	34	1.62	5.68	4.16	5.29	9.0	5.0	10.3	1.1	1.9	0.69
2005	TBA	MLB	21	10	9	0	32	32	186	172	100	174	12	41.6%	.316	38	1.46	3.77	3.96	4.10	7.7	4.7	8.1	0.5	29.4	4.49
2006	TBA	MLB	22	10	8	0	24	24	144²	132	52	163	15	43.3%	.314	43	1.27	3.23	3.32	3.29	7.4	3.0	9.3	0.8	38.7	4.80
2007	*TBA*	*MLB*	*23*	*10*	*10*	*0*	*28*	*28*	*173²*	*163*	*74*	*174*	*19*	*43.0%*	*.302*	*29*	*1.37*	*4.20*	*4.02*	*3.87*	*7.8*	*3.6*	*8.4*	*0.9*	*27.8*	*4.20*

Breakout: 12% Improve: 46% Collapse: 22% Attrition: 5%   *Comparables: Curt Simmons, Vida Blue, Billy Pierce, Pedro Martinez*

PECOTA's pessimistic view of Kazmir's walk rate last year was based on a very limited data set; we probably shouldn't have been so surprised when he cut if from near five per nine innings to near league average. This was a critical improvement; it's hard to get innings under your belt when it takes you about 20 pitches to get through just one, particularly when you're a young arm with whose pitch counts are monitored closely. A few weeks after the All-Star break, Kazmir started experiencing arm trouble. He was placed on the DL with a sore shoulder twice—once in July, and then again in August—and was completely shut down in September after continuing to complain of discomfort. Credit the Devil Rays for not taking any chances with their young ace. They know that the first competitive Rays' squad will need Kazmir at the front of the rotation. Health permitting, he's one of the best pitchers in the AL.

Ruddy Lugo
Bats: R Throws: R Height: 6' 0" Weight: 190 Born: May 22, 1980 Age: 27

YEAR	TEAM	LVL	AGE	W	L	SV	G	GS	IP	H	BB	SO	HR	GB%	BABIP	STUFF	WHIP	ERA	PERA	EQERA	EQH9	EQBB9	EQSO9	EQHR9	VORP	WXRL
2004	JUP	A+	24	1	7	11	31	0	39¹	42	15	33	4	—	.319	-42	1.45	5.27	7.62	9.57	11.5	4.7	4.7	2.5	-16.2	—
2004	CAR	AA	24	0	1	0	8	1	14²	16	9	6	3	—	.255	-46	1.70	4.90	10.29	7.71	10.9	6.4	2.6	3.2	-3.3	—
2005	MNT	AA	25	1	1	2	26	0	40¹	25	23	48	1	46.0%	.242	14	1.19	1.12	4.47	3.49	6.3	5.8	7.0	0.5	9.1	—
2006	TBA	MLB	26	2	4	0	64	0	85	75	37	48	4	44.2%	.272	3	1.32	3.81	4.19	3.45	7.0	3.7	4.7	0.4	18.7	0.87
2007	*TBA*	*MLB*	*27*	*3*	*3*	*2*	*54*	*1*	*68²*	*72*	*32*	*45*	*9*	*45.0%*	*.290*	*-7*	*1.50*	*4.86*	*4.66*	*4.47*	*8.6*	*3.9*	*5.5*	*1.0*	*5.9*	*0.50*

Breakout: 18% Improve: 37% Collapse: 33% Attrition: 18%   *Comparables: Steve Ridzik, Ron Willis, Vinny Chulk, Alan Mills*

Do you remember the season of *The Real World* in which a cast member from Brooklyn was dating a blonde woman who was substantially taller than he was? Lugo went to the same high school as that guy. He's bounced around quite a bit since then, but after landing with his brother Julio's team last year, got a chance in Tampa's wide-open bullpen. He did surprisingly

(continued next page)

Ruddy Lugo *(continued)*

well for himself, cutting his walks and doing an exceptional job of keeping the ball in the ballpark, and was crowned the best reliever on the team by WXRL. We hope he enjoyed it, because his BABIP will be bouncing upwards this year, and his ERA will go with it. The real world, it's a harsh place.

Seth McClung　　　　　Bats: R　Throws: R　　　Height: 6' 6"　Weight: 250　Born: February 7, 1981　Age: 26

YEAR	TEAM	LVL	AGE	W	L	SV	G	GS	IP	H	BB	SO	HR	GB%	BABIP	STUFF	WHIP	ERA	PERA	EQERA	EQH9	EQBB9	EQSO9	EQHR9	VORP	WXRL
2005	DUR	AAA	24	2	0	0	6	3	18¹	23	6	19	1	50.9%	.393	8	1.58	3.93	3.60	5.30	10.6	2.9	7.2	0.5	0.6	—
2005	TBA	MLB	24	7	11	0	34	17	109¹	106	62	92	20	35.9%	.274	-5	1.55	6.59	5.79	6.51	8.1	5.0	7.2	1.5	-15.4	0.49
2006	DUR	AAA	25	1	0	5	14	0	16¹	16	2	26	1	35.0%	.385	16	1.12	2.24	2.89	3.38	9.6	1.1	11.2	0.6	3.9	—
2006	TBA	MLB	25	6	12	6	39	15	103	120	68	59	14	39.5%	.316	-10	1.83	6.29	5.68	5.65	9.3	5.4	4.7	1.1	-7.3	0.41
2007	*TBA*	*MLB*	*26*	*4*	*7*	*2*	*44*	*11*	*92²*	*97*	*48*	*66*	*14*	*40.0%*	*.291*	*-5*	*1.57*	*5.59*	*5.19*	*5.14*	*8.7*	*4.4*	*6.0*	*1.2*	*0.3*	*0.50*

Breakout: 34%　Improve: 60%　Collapse: 12%　Attrition: 17%　　Comparables: Blake Stein, Rick Sutcliffe, Dan Wright, Jason Johnson

McClung broke camp with the big club as the number-two starter, but was positively awful in the rotation; he was eventually demoted to Triple-A Durham, but not before he posted a 6.81 ERA and walked five batters for every four he struck out. Sent to Durham to work in long relief, he looked like a totally different pitcher, but after earning an invite back to Tampa, he immediately reprised his role in *Ball Four: The Musical,* though in fewer innings since he was kept in the pen. Though the Devil Rays haven't named a closer for 2007, McClung figures to get a look. If he earns 25 saves this year, he'll become the all-time save leader among West Virginia natives.

Brian Meadows　　　　　Bats: R　Throws: R　　　Height: 6' 3"　Weight: 240　Born: November 21, 1975　Age: 31

YEAR	TEAM	LVL	AGE	W	L	SV	G	GS	IP	H	BB	SO	HR	GB%	BABIP	STUFF	WHIP	ERA	PERA	EQERA	EQH9	EQBB9	EQSO9	EQHR9	VORP	WXRL
2004	PIT	MLB	28	2	4	1	68	0	78	76	19	46	7	—	.288	-2	1.22	3.58	3.81	4.39	8.2	1.9	4.6	0.7	8.6	0.23
2005	PIT	MLB	29	3	1	0	65	0	74²	84	21	44	8	47.8%	.315	-9	1.41	4.58	4.16	5.07	9.9	2.2	4.8	0.9	3.3	0.22
2006	TBA	MLB	30	3	6	8	53	0	69²	90	16	35	14	39.9%	.318	-22	1.52	5.29	5.13	4.40	10.1	1.8	4.2	1.6	3.0	0.50
2007	*TBA*	*MLB*	*31*	*3*	*4*	*4*	*52*	*1*	*70*	*80*	*17*	*35*	*9*	*45.0%*	*.297*	*-10*	*1.39*	*4.73*	*4.48*	*4.33*	*9.5*	*2.1*	*4.2*	*1.0*	*7.1*	*0.70*

Breakout: 27%　Improve: 52%　Collapse: 21%　Attrition: 25%　　Comparables: Rod Beck, Jose Bautista, Reggie Cleveland, Ron Kline

Meadows allowed a ton of balls in play to complement his eight saves, so he's not really a different pitcher than when he first failed out of Florida, San Diego, Pittsburgh, and Kansas City. Tampa wasn't fooled and cut him loose. He could very well have been the most least likely source of saves for fantasy owners since Tim Wakefield—just another example of how fantasy value and real world utility are totally different things.

Evan Meek　　　　　Bats: R　Throws: R　　　Height: 6' 1"　Weight: 190　Born: May 12, 1983　Age: 24

YEAR	TEAM	LVL	AGE	W	L	SV	G	GS	IP	H	BB	SO	HR	GB%	BABIP	STUFF	WHIP	ERA	PERA	EQERA	EQH9	EQBB9	EQSO9	EQHR9	VORP	WXRL
2004	ELZ	Rk	21	1	2	0	11	3	21¹	18	23	21	1	—	.288	-13	1.92	8.45	12.38	15.50	10.0	16.5	4.5	1.5	-19.8	—
2005	BLT	A	22	0	1	0	13	0	18	15	36	11	0	58.6%	.278	3	2.83	10.00	12.69	15.19	8.4	24.2	3.9	0.6	-17.0	—
2006	LEL	A+	23	6	6	0	26	25	119	136	62	113	5	58.7%	.370	3	1.66	4.99	5.14	6.90	10.7	5.6	5.1	0.7	-16.9	—
2007	*TBA*	*MLB*	*24*	*3*	*7*	*0*	*26*	*14*	*79*	*88*	*76*	*55*	*7*	*54.0%*	*.324*	*-15*	*2.07*	*7.14*	*6.52*	*6.82*	*9.2*	*8.1*	*5.9*	*0.7*	*-15.4*	*1.10*

Breakout: 39%　Improve: 67%　Collapse: 9%　Attrition: 15%　　Comparables: Lenny DiNardo, Randi Mallard, Darin Moore, Anderson Garcia

On one hand, a guy who used to have success is probably preferable to a guy who's never had it. On the other hand, how many guys with walk trouble does one organization need? Meek's problems are out of the purview of performance analysis; mental/concentration struggles left him unsure of his curveball prior to last year, effectively turning him into a one-pitch pitcher. He seemed to get it back under control in 2006, going from a pitcher who could not find the strike zone to one who is merely very wild. In context, that's a very encouraging development.

Dan Miceli　　　　　Bats: R　Throws: R　　　Height: 6' 0"　Weight: 225　Born: September 9, 1970　Age: 36

YEAR	TEAM	LVL	AGE	W	L	SV	G	GS	IP	H	BB	SO	HR	GB%	BABIP	STUFF	WHIP	ERA	PERA	EQERA	EQH9	EQBB9	EQSO9	EQHR9	VORP	WXRL
2004	HOU	MLB	33	6	6	2	74	0	77²	74	27	83	10	—	.311	14	1.30	3.59	3.76	3.73	8.2	2.7	8.4	1.0	15.0	1.69
2005	COL	MLB	34	1	2	0	19	0	18¹	19	13	19	1	39.2%	.360	14	1.75	5.90	4.10	5.21	8.5	5.7	8.5	0.5	-0.2	-0.08
2006	TBA	MLB	35	1	2	4	33	0	32	25	20	18	4	45.4%	.226	-10	1.41	3.94	5.74	4.05	6.2	5.1	4.6	1.1	4.7	-0.14
2007	*TBA*	*MLB*	*36*	*2*	*2*	*2*	*32*	*0*	*36¹*	*38*	*17*	*27*	*5*	*45.0%*	*.293*	*-7*	*1.50*	*4.71*	*4.73*	*4.31*	*8.6*	*4.0*	*6.2*	*1.1*	*3.9*	*0.30*

Breakout: 24%　Improve: 50%　Collapse: 35%　Attrition: 36%　　Comparables: Don McMahon, Turk Lown, Juan Berenguer, Jose Mesa

Miceli missed nearly three months with shoulder trouble last year. He still throws hard enough to be worth a flyer, but his upside remains what it's always been: League-average relief. His strikeout-to-walk ratio was a disturbing negative in 2006, but that seems to have been an artifact of his injury. He reversed it after he came off the DL.

Tampa Bay Devil Rays

Shinji Mori

Bats: L Throws: R   Height: 6' 2"   Weight: 195   Born: September 12, 1974   Age: 32

YEAR	TEAM	LVL	AGE	W	L	SV	G	GS	IP	H	BB	SO	HR	GB%	BABIP	STUFF	WHIP	ERA	PERA	EQERA	EQH9	EQBB9	EQSO9	EQHR9	VORP	WXRL
2004	SEI	JP	29	0	4	4	34	0	49	50	38	49	5	—	.315	4	1.80	4.59	5.23	6.34	9.2	6.9	7.2	0.9	-4.1	—
2005	SEI	JP	30	2	2	5	48	0	49	44	19	60	5	0.0%	.310	9	1.29	4.22	4.11	5.03	8.2	4.1	8.8	1.1	3.1	—
2007	TBA	MLB	32	2	2	1	30	2	39	41	25	37	5	43.0%	.318	0	1.67	5.55	5.34	5.12	8.6	5.4	8.1	1.1	0.3	0.10

Breakout: 18% Improve: 61% Collapse: 13% Attrition: 43%   Comparables: Sam McDowell, Dave Hamilton, George Frazier, Sammy Stewart

Twenty years from now, we'll be looking at labrum tears differently than we do now: The diagnosis will be cleaner, the surgery will be better, the rehab will be faster, and, hopefully, the chances of regaining effectiveness will be far greater. For now, torn labrums are all but career-ending. Mori elected to not have surgery and has been rehabbing in Japan since spring training of 2006. He'll be fighting against an awful lot of history.

Jeff Niemann

Bats: R Throws: R   Height: 6' 9"   Weight: 260   Born: February 28, 1983   Age: 24

YEAR	TEAM	LVL	AGE	W	L	SV	G	GS	IP	H	BB	SO	HR	GB%	BABIP	STUFF	WHIP	ERA	PERA	EQERA	EQH9	EQBB9	EQSO9	EQHR9	VORP	WXRL
2005	VIS	A+	22	0	1	0	5	5	20^1	12	10	28	3	38.6%	.220	20	1.08	3.99	6.65	4.58	5.9	5.5	7.8	1.8	2.2	—
2005	MNT	AA	22	0	1	0	6	3	10^1	7	5	14	0	45.8%	.292	10	1.17	4.37	3.15	7.20	7.2	4.5	9.0	0.0	-1.8	—
2006	MNT	AA	23	5	5	0	14	14	77^2	56	29	84	6	45.7%	.255	11	1.10	2.68	5.18	3.77	8.4	3.5	6.9	1.3	15.0	—
2007	TBA	MLB	24	6	8	0	27	19	116	120	57	92	18	43.0%	.295	8	1.52	5.21	5.08	4.78	8.6	4.1	6.7	1.2	5.8	1.40

Breakout: 12% Improve: 22% Collapse: 35% Attrition: 5%   Comparables: John Sneed, Gene Conley, Jason Hirsh, Jon Rauch

It's risky enough having one of Rice's mistletoe-pierced Balders in your system, but the D-Rays have two. Niemann is further along on the development curve than Wade Townsend, though both have missed considerable time due to injuries to the part of their body with which they hope to make their livings. Niemann didn't make his first appearance last year until June, having had to recover from minor shoulder surgery first, but, to his credit, he was quite good after that. That he has a less-than-graceful command of his large body doesn't help the injury concerns.

Chad Orvella

Bats: R Throws: R   Height: 5' 11"   Weight: 190   Born: October 1, 1980   Age: 26

YEAR	TEAM	LVL	AGE	W	L	SV	G	GS	IP	H	BB	SO	HR	GB%	BABIP	STUFF	WHIP	ERA	PERA	EQERA	EQH9	EQBB9	EQSO9	EQHR9	VORP	WXRL
2004	CSC	A	23	1	0	4	22	0	47^1	28	5	76	4	—	.273	16	0.70	1.33	4.05	2.64	7.7	1.2	7.9	1.4	14.6	—
2004	BAK	A+	23	0	1	4	15	0	17^2	13	4	24	2	—	.268	0	0.96	3.05	5.75	4.76	8.5	2.6	7.4	2.1	1.6	—
2005	MNT	AA	24	0	0	9	16	0	25	15	6	29	0	42.6%	.250	19	0.84	0.36	2.82	1.11	5.9	2.2	7.0	0.4	12.1	—
2005	TBA	MLB	24	3	3	1	37	0	50	47	23	43	4	35.1%	.299	10	1.38	3.60	3.91	4.33	7.8	4.0	7.4	0.7	6.8	0.80
2006	DUR	AAA	25	4	0	1	27	0	38^1	31	9	55	2	37.1%	.337	31	1.05	1.89	2.87	3.08	7.6	2.1	9.9	0.7	10.6	—
2006	TBA	MLB	25	1	5	0	22	0	24^1	36	20	17	6	36.8%	.370	-18	2.30	7.41	7.38	7.36	12.3	6.7	5.6	1.8	-6.5	-0.77
2007	TBA	MLB	26	2	2	2	46	1	49^2	49	19	43	7	41.0%	.289	6	1.36	4.31	4.30	3.91	8.2	3.3	7.2	1.1	7.8	0.70

Breakout: 39% Improve: 67% Collapse: 11% Attrition: 25%   Comparables: Trevor Hoffman, Jim Ray, Mark Brandenburg, Keith Foulke

A successful position player-to-pitcher conversion case, Orvella's performances in the minors conjure memories of a young Troy Percival. Given that, his major league debut in 2005 was somewhat disappointing, but still suggested that the Rays had a useful reliever on their hands. Last spring, Joe Maddon and his coaches decided that Orvella's delivery time to the plate was poor enough that it necessitated reworking his mechanics, despite the risk that the young pitcher, more inexperienced than most of his peers, might not take well to learning how to pitch *again*. The Rays got what they wanted, but lost what they had, as the new-look Orvella couldn't get anyone out. Given the various handicaps under which the Rays operate, these kinds of self-defeating moves are just gratuitous. Orvella's 2006 at Durham strongly suggests that he could be a successful major league pitcher if he could just get free of the masochists.

Jeff Ridgway

Bats: R Throws: L   Height: 6' 3"   Weight: 189   Born: August 17, 1980   Age: 26

YEAR	TEAM	LVL	AGE	W	L	SV	G	GS	IP	H	BB	SO	HR	GB%	BABIP	STUFF	WHIP	ERA	PERA	EQERA	EQH9	EQBB9	EQSO9	EQHR9	VORP	WXRL
2004	BAK	A+	23	2	3	1	15	1	35	32	19	27	0	—	.305	-4	1.46	2.31	5.36	5.35	8.3	6.7	4.3	0.3	0.9	—
2005	VIS	A+	24	3	4	0	24	0	45	43	36	56	2	48.8%	.376	8	1.76	5.20	6.12	6.65	8.7	9.3	6.6	0.6	-5.1	—
2006	MNT	AA	25	1	0	2	16	0	19^1	10	7	29	1	73.2%	.250	16	0.89	2.36	4.39	3.57	7.1	4.1	9.2	1.0	4.0	—
2006	DUR	AAA	25	1	4	0	34	0	38^1	35	13	38	3	56.6%	.302	1	1.26	3.07	4.46	3.99	8.2	3.3	6.8	0.9	6.9	—
2007	TBA	MLB	26	3	4	1	27	6	56^1	58	36	45	5	53.0%	.311	0	1.66	5.03	4.98	4.70	8.5	5.4	6.8	0.7	3.3	0.50

Breakout: 31% Improve: 54% Collapse: 21% Attrition: 17%   Comparables: Mike Bynum, Sean Fesh, Travis Miller, Matt Smith

(continued next page)

Jeff Ridgway *(continued)*

Ridgway put in a nice season in Triple-A last year, and was rewarded with a 40-man roster spot seven years after being drafted. We're somewhat conditioned to think "LOOGY" when guys like this get promoted, but Ridgway handles both kinds of hitters pretty well. On this team, with this bullpen, he's got his best shot at proving he can stay.

Juan Salas Bats: R Throws: R   Height: 6' 2"   Weight: 210   Born: November 7, 1978   Age: 28

YEAR	TEAM	LVL	AGE	W	L	SV	G	GS	IP	H	BB	SO	HR	GB%	BABIP	STUFF	WHIP	ERA	PERA	EQERA	EQH9	EQBB9	EQSO9	EQHR9	VORP	WXRL
2005	VIS	A+	26	2	1	1	25	0	38¹	30	18	47	6	45.3%	.279	-12	1.25	3.52	7.62	4.86	7.8	5.4	6.6	2.2	3.0	—
2005	MNT	AA	26	1	0	0	15	0	22	25	12	18	2	54.2%	.333	-21	1.68	3.68	6.86	5.91	11.0	5.5	4.6	1.7	-0.7	—
2006	MNT	AA	27	3	0	14	23	0	34¹	13	14	52	0	56.1%	.197	30	0.79	0.00	3.11	1.97	5.3	4.2	9.0	0.3	12.9	—
2006	DUR	AAA	27	1	1	3	27	0	28²	15	11	33	3	44.1%	.185	12	0.92	1.60	5.12	2.25	5.1	3.9	8.0	1.3	10.4	—
2006	TBA	MLB	27	0	0	0	8	0	10	13	3	8	1	44.4%	.343	1	1.60	5.40	3.64	5.23	10.5	2.6	7.0	0.9	-0.2	0.08
2007	*TBA*	*MLB*	*28*	*2*	*4*	*2*	*57*	*3*	*58¹*	*63*	*32*	*49*	*11*	*44.0%*	*.305*	*-5*	*1.63*	*5.63*	*5.68*	*5.13*	*9.0*	*4.7*	*7.1*	*1.4*	*0.3*	*0.10*

Breakout: 9%   Improve: 24%   Collapse: 57%   Attrition: 14%   Comparables: Tom Shearn, Kane Davis, Mark Corey, Aaron Rakers

Salas's control has gotten better as he's advanced, but it's hard to tell whether that's meaningful or a statistical trinket given his innings pitched totals. He allowed 28 hits in 63 innings between Double-A and Triple-A before appearing in Tampa's bullpen, which is insanely low, especially for someone who just finished his second full year of pitching. His BABIPs were also astoundingly low, as if he had Ozzie Smith, Tris Speaker, and Mercury playing behind him. It's unlikely that his one-pitch plan of attack will work in the majors, but he's out of options and it can't hurt to find out.

Chris Seddon Bats: L Throws: L   Height: 6' 3"   Weight: 190   Born: October 13, 1983   Age: 23

YEAR	TEAM	LVL	AGE	W	L	SV	G	GS	IP	H	BB	SO	HR	GB%	BABIP	STUFF	WHIP	ERA	PERA	EQERA	EQH9	EQBB9	EQSO9	EQHR9	VORP	WXRL
2004	BAK	A+	20	5	0	0	7	7	41¹	30	8	41	0	—	.278	34	0.92	0.65	3.20	1.54	6.8	2.2	5.7	0.2	18.5	—
2004	MNT	AA	20	9	10	0	21	21	119	129	44	102	19	—	.318	-20	1.45	4.39	6.68	5.94	10.5	3.6	5.1	2.2	-4.4	—
2005	MNT	AA	21	6	1	0	10	10	52¹	58	20	46	4	47.6%	.351	3	1.49	4.82	4.81	6.02	10.1	3.4	5.5	1.2	-2.4	—
2005	DUR	AAA	21	4	9	0	19	19	95²	114	43	70	11	37.6%	.337	-6	1.64	5.45	5.64	6.39	9.9	4.2	4.9	1.1	-8.7	—
2006	DUR	AAA	22	9	9	0	28	28	154²	168	46	108	20	41.1%	.309	-13	1.39	4.73	5.68	5.34	9.5	2.8	4.8	1.7	4.5	—
2007	*TBA*	*MLB*	*23*	*4*	*8*	*0*	*23*	*17*	*97*	*120*	*40*	*56*	*21*	*41.0%*	*.307*	*-6*	*1.65*	*6.54*	*6.23*	*5.95*	*10.2*	*3.5*	*4.9*	*1.6*	*-9.8*	*0.30*

Breakout: 11%   Improve: 37%   Collapse: 28%   Attrition: 2%   Comparables: Chris Narveson, Benj Sampson, Greg Miller, Doug Waechter

Though added to the 40-man roster in 2004, Seddon has yet to make his big league debut, and with good reason, as he hasn't improved as he's advanced. His profile is fairly common, and it's not one that PECOTA is particularly kind to.

Jae Seo Bats: R Throws: R   Height: 6' 0"   Weight: 230   Born: May 24, 1977   Age: 30

YEAR	TEAM	LVL	AGE	W	L	SV	G	GS	IP	H	BB	SO	HR	GB%	BABIP	STUFF	WHIP	ERA	PERA	EQERA	EQH9	EQBB9	EQSO9	EQHR9	VORP	WXRL
2004	NYN	MLB	27	5	10	0	24	21	117²	133	50	54	17	—	.310	-15	1.56	4.89	5.31	4.80	10.0	3.4	3.7	1.2	7.0	1.92
2005	NYN	MLB	28	8	2	0	14	14	90¹	84	16	59	9	38.5%	.282	19	1.11	2.59	3.75	2.86	8.4	1.5	5.4	0.9	29.8	3.54
2006	LAN	MLB	29	2	4	0	19	10	67	75	25	49	14	42.3%	.303	-10	1.49	5.78	5.26	5.58	9.3	2.9	5.8	1.7	-0.7	0.72
2006	TBA	MLB	29	1	8	0	17	16	90	122	31	39	17	33.0%	.335	-18	1.70	5.00	5.59	4.34	10.7	2.8	3.5	1.4	4.2	1.54
2007	*TBA*	*MLB*	*30*	*6*	*10*	*0*	*35*	*20*	*133¹*	*159*	*45*	*77*	*23*	*41.0%*	*.305*	*-5*	*1.53*	*5.48*	*5.42*	*4.96*	*9.9*	*2.8*	*4.9*	*1.4*	*3.0*	*1.10*

Breakout: 8%   Improve: 34%   Collapse: 28%   Attrition: 7%   Comparables: Wayne Garland, Andy Hawkins, Early Wynn, Jim Colborn

Sometimes you need a little finesse, sometimes you need a lot. Seo arrived from L.A. and had a rotation spot waiting for him, but promptly lost his command and his ability to miss bats—and he didn't have a lot of room for error in either department to begin with. It worked out in the end, but his low ERA hid some nasty peripherals. Seo benefited greatly from a bullpen which did a commendable job of stranding his baserunners when he was lifted from games in mid-inning; his Fair RA, which factors in bequeathed runners, checks in at a hefty 5.80, making his combined 2006 ERA of 5.33 look good, and that's not good.

James Shields   **Bats: R Throws: R**   Height: 6' 4"   Weight: 215   Born: December 20, 1981   Age: 25

YEAR	TEAM	LVL	AGE	W	L	SV	G	GS	IP	H	BB	SO	HR	GB%	BABIP	STUFF	WHIP	ERA	PERA	EQERA	EQH9	EQBB9	EQSO9	EQHR9	VORP	WXRL
2004	BAK	A+	22	8	5	0	20	20	117	120	33	92	13	—	.307	-21	1.31	4.23	6.46	5.56	9.7	3.2	4.4	1.9	0.5	—
2004	MNT	AA	22	0	3	0	4	4	18^1	24	8	14	4	—	.345	-24	1.75	7.87	7.94	9.17	12.7	4.1	4.6	3.1	-7.0	—
2005	MNT	AA	23	7	5	0	17	16	109^1	95	31	104	6	50.5%	.318	17	1.15	2.80	4.29	3.67	8.2	2.7	5.8	0.8	23.2	—
2006	DUR	AAA	24	3	2	0	10	10	61^1	60	6	64	3	53.3%	.352	34	1.08	2.65	2.95	3.77	8.6	0.9	7.1	0.6	12.6	—
2006	TBA	MLB	24	6	8	0	21	21	124^2	141	38	104	18	43.5%	.334	16	1.44	4.84	4.24	4.21	9.1	2.5	6.8	1.1	14.6	2.17
2007	*TBA*	*MLB*	*25*	*9*	*11*	*0*	*32*	*29*	*169^2*	*187*	*49*	*124*	*23*	*45.0%*	*.308*	*14*	*1.39*	*4.70*	*4.55*	*4.31*	*9.1*	*2.4*	*6.2*	*1.1*	*17.9*	*3.10*

Breakout: 17%   Improve: 54%   Collapse: 16%   Attrition: 2%   Comparables: Bob Sebra, Doc Medich, Bob Heffner, John Lackey

Shields was named Tampa's top rookie by the Baseball Writers Association of America, capping a strong two-year run. He began appearing on prospect lists after a strong 2005 at Double-A and in the Arizona Fall League, then kept his command-and-prosper act going in Triple-A last year, earning a big league callup at the end of May. No one's ever going to stop and admire one of Shields's pitches, but he stays low in the strike zone, throws a sinker to get ground balls, and mixes in some decent off-speed stuff to keep hitters honest. It's not always pretty, but it works.

Andrew Sonnanstine   **Bats: L Throws: R**   Height: 6' 3"   Weight: 185   Born: March 18, 1983   Age: 24

YEAR	TEAM	LVL	AGE	W	L	SV	G	GS	IP	H	BB	SO	HR	GB%	BABIP	STUFF	WHIP	ERA	PERA	EQERA	EQH9	EQBB9	EQSO9	EQHR9	VORP	WXRL
2004	CSC	A	21	2	0	0	8	5	30^2	18	7	42	0	—	.269	29	0.81	0.59	2.85	2.15	6.8	2.5	7.4	0.3	11.2	—
2004	HUD	A-	21	3	1	1	9	2	27	18	3	24	0	—	.234	5	0.78	1.00	3.20	2.77	7.3	1.4	4.2	0.3	8.2	—
2005	SWM	A	22	10	4	0	18	18	116^2	103	11	103	10	44.6%	.281	-1	0.98	2.54	4.81	4.58	9.7	1.0	5.0	1.6	12.7	—
2005	VIS	A+	22	4	1	0	10	10	64	71	7	75	5	34.4%	.375	25	1.22	3.80	3.47	3.95	9.4	1.1	6.4	1.0	12.1	—
2006	MNT	AA	23	15	8	0	28	28	185^1	151	34	153	15	45.0%	.276	5	1.00	2.67	4.64	4.22	8.7	1.7	5.2	1.3	27.4	—
2007	*TBA*	*MLB*	*24*	*7*	*9*	*0*	*28*	*22*	*136^1*	*158*	*30*	*83*	*24*	*43.0%*	*.301*	*7*	*1.38*	*5.14*	*4.90*	*4.69*	*9.6*	*1.9*	*5.2*	*1.4*	*8.3*	*1.80*

Breakout: 8%   Improve: 25%   Collapse: 30%   Attrition: 0%   Comparables: Jin Cho, Josh Banks, Shaun Marcum, Justin Germano

We always grumble when promising minor league arms are brought up too quickly and the increased workloads predictably proves to be too much. In Sonnanstine's case, he logged the second-highest innings-pitched total in the minor leagues last year, and is very close to making a good, reliable addition to the major-league rotation without any jarring workload owies. Like Shields, his raw stuff won't win any skills competitions, but he uses it all well. No, he doesn't miss bats, but he doesn't miss the strike zone, either; his K/BB ratio is what's important here, and his command is major league-ready now. This isn't a pitcher who projects to be star, but if he can handle the International League in the first half 2007, he'll fit in as a back-of-the-rotation guy.

Brian Stokes   **Bats: R Throws: R**   Height: 6' 1"   Weight: 205   Born: September 7, 1979   Age: 27

YEAR	TEAM	LVL	AGE	W	L	SV	G	GS	IP	H	BB	SO	HR	GB%	BABIP	STUFF	WHIP	ERA	PERA	EQERA	EQH9	EQBB9	EQSO9	EQHR9	VORP	WXRL
2005	VIS	A+	25	1	2	0	4	4	17	15	5	21	3	37.8%	.293	0	1.18	4.24	6.45	4.32	8.6	3.2	6.5	2.2	2.4	—
2005	MNT	AA	25	4	6	0	16	16	93^1	82	28	70	8	40.9%	.277	-12	1.18	3.47	5.66	4.45	8.4	3.1	4.4	1.5	11.6	—
2006	DUR	AAA	26	7	7	0	29	23	133	134	49	103	8	48.0%	.312	3	1.38	4.13	4.62	5.25	8.6	3.5	5.2	0.8	5.3	—
2006	TBA	MLB	26	1	0	0	5	4	24	31	9	15	2	42.7%	.363	5	1.67	4.88	4.12	3.91	10.3	3.2	5.0	0.7	3.2	0.75
2007	*TBA*	*MLB*	*27*	*5*	*8*	*0*	*34*	*18*	*104*	*120*	*41*	*63*	*17*	*44.0%*	*.302*	*-6*	*1.54*	*5.68*	*5.36*	*5.22*	*9.6*	*3.3*	*5.1*	*1.3*	*-0.8*	*0.50*

Breakout: 7%   Improve: 28%   Collapse: 28%   Attrition: 0%   Comparables: Bryan Wolff, Kerry Taylor, Greg Keagle, Julio Santana

All organizations have guys like this: Promising pitchers at one time who have repeated a level, need to work on a third pitch, and look more like middle relievers in the making than starters. Stokes has a spot on the 40-man roster to call his own, so he'll get a few more looks.

Jon Switzer   **Bats: L Throws: L**   Height: 6' 3"   Weight: 190   Born: August 13, 1979   Age: 27

YEAR	TEAM	LVL	AGE	W	L	SV	G	GS	IP	H	BB	SO	HR	GB%	BABIP	STUFF	WHIP	ERA	PERA	EQERA	EQH9	EQBB9	EQSO9	EQHR9	VORP	WXRL
2005	MNT	AA	25	3	1	0	6	6	31^1	33	5	20	2	37.1%	.307	-4	1.21	3.45	5.40	4.99	10.0	1.8	3.8	1.2	2.1	—
2005	DUR	AAA	25	0	5	0	17	8	44^1	64	22	28	6	40.7%	.379	-22	1.94	7.11	6.27	6.85	11.9	4.7	4.3	1.4	-6.4	—
2006	DUR	AAA	26	3	0	3	26	0	31	22	13	29	1	38.4%	.247	9	1.13	0.87	3.91	1.72	6.0	4.0	6.3	0.3	13.5	—
2006	TBA	MLB	26	2	2	0	40	0	33^2	38	19	18	5	50.0%	.297	-17	1.69	4.54	5.67	4.33	8.9	4.6	4.3	1.3	3.7	-0.07
2007	*TBA*	*MLB*	*27*	*2*	*2*	*1*	*55*	*0*	*46^1*	*53*	*22*	*30*	*6*	*44.0%*	*.308*	*-11*	*1.62*	*5.24*	*5.24*	*4.79*	*9.4*	*4.1*	*5.4*	*1.0*	*2.0*	*0.20*

Breakout: 20%   Improve: 40%   Collapse: 30%   Attrition: 41%   Comparables: John Cummings, Don Hood, Bob MacDonald, Daryl Patterson

(continued next page)

Jon Switzer (*continued*)

Switzer recovered from labrum trouble well enough to have a nice season with Durham, then ended the year with 33 uninspiring innings in the bigs. He was a command lefty way back when, but hasn't regained any of the stuff that he had prior to missing 2004. Righties torched him, so whatever future he has in the big leagues is probably as a lefty specialist.

Mitch Talbot Bats: R Throws: R Height: 6' 2" Weight: 175 Born: October 17, 1983 Age: 23

YEAR	TEAM	LVL	AGE	W	L	SV	G	GS	IP	H	BB	SO	HR	GB%	BABIP	STUFF	WHIP	ERA	PERA	EQERA	EQH9	EQBB9	EQSO9	EQHR9	VORP	WXRL
2004	LEX	A	20	10	10	0	27	27	152²	145	49	115	16	—	.279	-13	1.27	3.83	6.04	5.30	9.5	3.4	4.0	1.6	5.0	—
2005	SLM	A+	21	8	11	0	27	27	151¹	169	46	100	15	58.1%	.316	-16	1.42	4.34	5.65	6.60	10.9	3.0	3.8	1.5	-16.5	—
2006	CCH	AA	22	6	4	1	18	17	90	94	29	96	4	52.5%	.360	25	1.37	3.40	3.56	5.16	9.7	2.9	7.0	0.5	4.4	—
2006	MNT	AA	22	4	3	0	10	10	66	51	18	59	2	51.8%	.277	26	1.05	1.91	3.68	3.06	8.1	2.5	5.7	0.4	18.3	—
2007	TBA	MLB	23	7	10	0	34	21	135²	155	50	91	17	51.0%	.315	5	1.51	5.18	4.96	4.81	9.5	3.1	5.6	1.0	5.7	1.50

Breakout: 22% Improve: 53% Collapse: 12% Attrition: 7% Comparables: Pete Munro, Grant Roberts, Richard Gardner, Ryan Madson

Talbot took a huge step forward this year, mostly in the strikeout department, but it's always hard to separate the guys who have figured things out from the guys who get lucky for a year. Still, Talbot has become less of an extreme ground-baller as his strikeout rate has improved, suggesting a conscious change in approach away from his previous pitch-to-contact style, yet he's still managed to keep his home-run rate very low. Talbot has very clean mechanics and finally added a breaking pitch, though it's really more of a slurve, which is often perceived as a poor man's curve ball. Still, if last year represents a new level of ability, it means the Rays received a bigger bounty for Aubrey Huff than we thought.

Wade Townsend Bats: R Throws: R Height: 6' 4" Weight: 230 Born: February 22, 1983 Age: 24

YEAR	TEAM	LVL	AGE	W	L	SV	G	GS	IP	H	BB	SO	HR	GB%	BABIP	STUFF	WHIP	ERA	PERA	EQERA	EQH9	EQBB9	EQSO9	EQHR9	VORP	WXRL
2005	HUD	A-	22	0	4	0	12	10	39¹	44	24	33	4	44.5%	.325	-33	1.73	5.50	10.27	9.00	12.9	8.7	3.9	3.1	-13.2	—
2007	TBA	MLB	24	2	4	0	19	9	53²	56	51	31	8	45.0%	.281	-24	1.99	7.35	6.55	6.90	8.7	8.0	4.9	1.2	-10.2	0.90

Breakout: 48% Improve: 56% Collapse: 19% Attrition: 21% Comparables: Brandon Luna, Scotty Layfield, Dustin Craig, Marcus Moseley

Two and a half years removed from his final pitch at Rice, Townsend has just 39 ⅓ innings on his professional résumé, all of them coming in 2005. Prior to that, he had not played competitive baseball from June 2004 until his 2005 stint in the NY-Penn League because of a holdout/re-enrollment debacle with the Orioles. His rehab from Tommy John surgery is now complete, and after some instructional league appearances he reported that his elbow is pain-free. He'll start 2007 in the Sally League. As with most things in life, if you lower your expectations, you'll either be proven right, or you'll be pleasantly surprised. It's win-win!

Lineouts

PLAYER	TEAM	LVL	AGE	PA	R	2B	3B	HR	RBI	BB	SO	SB-CS	SPEED	AVG/OBP/SLG	MLVrEqAVG/EqOBP/EqSLG	EqA	VORP
CF S. Cumberland*	VIS	A+	21	574	86	18	3	16	98	42	133	29-9	6.6	.258/.319/.396	-.071	.230/.278/.345	.223	-32.2
1B T. Lee*	TBA	MLB	31	388	35	11	2	11	31	42	73	5-2	4.6	.224/.312/.364	-.183	.221/.317/.369	.242	-11.4
C J. Paul	TBA	MLB	31	165	15	9	0	1	8	14	39	1-2	4.2	.260/.327/.342	-.161	.264/.340/.354	.243	-1.5
CF F. Perez	VIS	A+	23	641	123	19	9	4	56	78	134	33-16	7.7	.307/.398/.397	.107	.275/.346/.349	.251	5.9

PLAYER	TEAM	LVL	AGE	W	L	SV	IP	H	BB	SO	HR	GB%	BABIP	STUFF	WHIP	ERA	PERA	EqERA	EqH9	EqBB9	EqSO9	EqHR9	VORP
S. Dunn	DUR	AAA	28	4	2	0	66²	57	28	70	2	—	.309	14	1.28	2.72	3.67	3.36	7.5	4.0	7.0	0.4	16.7
C. Harville	TBA	MLB	29	0	2	1	41	44	22	30	5	—	.315	-4	1.61	5.93	4.72	5.02	8.6	4.4	6.1	1.0	0.6
J. Hellickson	HUD	A-	19	4	3	0	77	55	16	96	3	—	.280	17	0.92	2.45	5.08	4.48	8.7	2.7	6.6	1.5	9.0
J. McGee*	SWM	A	19	7	9	0	134	103	65	171	7	—	.311	18	1.25	2.96	5.47	4.71	8.5	5.8	7.1	1.2	12.5
D. Waechter	DUR	AAA	25	1	12	0	79	129	24	45	7	41.5%	.407	-20	1.94	8.32	4.75	8.60	13.4	2.8	3.7	1.1	-27.6
	TBA	MLB	25	1	4	0	53	67	19	25	6	34.0%	.330	-6	1.62	6.62	4.98	5.34	10.2	2.9	3.9	0.8	-4.3
T. Walker	TBA	MLB	30	1	3	10	20	18	7	16	0	—	.305	8	1.25	4.95	2.97	4.29	7.3	3.0	6.4	0.0	2.5

Shaun Cumberland started off the year on fire, but faded to the line above. Twenty-two-year-old left-handed hitters who post .223 EqAs in the Cal League aren't prospects; if they can't hit there, they can't hit anywhere. In 2006, **Travis Lee** realized the ultimate baseball humiliation: Being released by a last-place team that may not have anyone better to play your position after you're gone. Because athletes can rarely bring themselves to admit that they're no good, Lee was shocked, *shocked* at the turn life had taken. Lee's career began with great expectations; it's a bit sad to think he still has them. Very few teams carry three catchers, but, when they do, one of them is usually someone like **Josh Paul**. **Fernando Perez** is a speed-and-defense centerfielder with a high average and high OBP, but his .397 SLG in the Cal League (padded by nine triples) is troubling.

The Rays had a revolving door bullpen, but **Scott Dunn** couldn't squeeze back in after an abysmal April. He had another high-walk, high-strikeout year at Durham after his demotion. The A's will take a one-year gamble on him, like the D-Rays did. **Chad Harville** was designated for assignment just 15 days before rosters expanded. He publicly blasted the organization and stated that he had no desire to be with them any longer. Apparently he forgot that he's Chad Harville; Tampa gave him his wish and released him. For the second year in a row, a Devil Ray led the NY-Penn League in strikeouts. This year it was **Jeremy Hellickson**, who had notably good command as well. Unfortunately, he had neither the size nor stuff of Wade Davis, who preceded him. **Jacob McGee** made his full-season debut in the Midwest League and led the league with 171 strikeouts in 134 innings. He added some velocity, refined his slow curveball, and should keep right on advancing. He's a sleeper. Even when he was healthy, **Doug Waechter** never looked like the kind of pitcher who could do more than just throw a baseball and hope for the best. Since he added labrum surgery to his list of offseason plans, it's even less likely he'll ever amount to much; released. **Matt Walker** was another promising starter in Southwest Michigan's rotation. His curveball is advanced, but he still needs to control it better. Tampa bought low on **Tyler Walker**, who was designated for assignment by the Giants after a terrible April, and fell into a temp job as the Rays' closer. He blew out his elbow, got Tommy John'd, and signed a minor league deal with the Giants.

Manager: Joe Maddon

Year	Team	W-L	Pythag +/-	Avg PC	100 +P	120 +P	QS	BQS	REL	REL w Zero R	IBB	SUBS	PH	PH Avg	PH HR	SB2	CS2	SB3	CS3	SAC Att	SAC %	POS SAC	Squeeze	Swing	In Play
2006	TBA	61-101	-3	93.0	49	1	62	5	444	228	39	68	80	.225	1	109	45	24	7	64	54.7%	32	4	153	112

For the Devil Rays, much of last year's managerial drama happened in Triple-A Durham, but now that Upton and Young have reached the majors, Joe Maddon will have to play father figure and head-shrinker. That's just one of the many reasons why this mellow anti-Piniella was hired. On the field, his tactics were anti-Piniellan, as well. He kept a tight rein on his rotation, asking them to throw more than 120 pitches just once, which is admirable considering that Tampa's about to become awfully reliant on its youngsters. Of course, one could argue that Maddon had no earthly reason to push his rotation, since the pitchers that comprised it (sans Kazmir) weren't likely to get that deep into a ballgame to start off with. Similarly, pointing out that only five quality starts were blown on Maddon's watch misses some important context: There weren't very many to blow. Not getting enough innings from his starters meant that Maddon went to his bullpen more often than Piniella did, which would have been the second half of a good pitching management strategy had the bullpen been an asset. It wasn't, and the pen's unreliability remained a problem for the entire year. It's not surprising that Maddon called for the second-highest number of stolen bases in the game with Carl Crawford on hand, but, given the number of injuries and weak hitters he had to deal with, Maddon didn't have the depth to do many other sorts of in-game maneuvering. Maddon's main task in the seasons to come won't be stealing bases or sending in pinch-hitters, but helping the organization's young players get established in the majors. Not every manager can do that, or is willing to. Maddon's just beginning down that path now; we'll see how he takes to the task.

Texas Rangers

At first glance, it would seem that a team in the American League West's short stack has a relatively easy task: simply beat out three other teams, then bounce into the roulette wheel that is the postseason. Surely that's nothing compared to having to unseat the twin behemoths of New York and Boston in the East.

Or is it? The West actually has its own pair of behemoths in the A's and Angels, two teams that have combined to win the last five AL West titles as well as one wild card over that span. A monolithic empire might be expected to crumble, even if after a long while, but having two teams locked in a multi-year death match creates a savage competitive dynamic that doesn't make it easy to butt in as a third wheel.

Compounding the stifling effect of those twin titans, the AL West lacks one ticket to victory that the other two American League divisions enjoy—a patsy bad enough to consistently fall short of 70 wins. Since 1998, the Mariners of 2004 and 2005 have been the only AL West teams that have failed to win at least 70 games in a season. The East and the Central, meanwhile, have had at least one sub-70 win team in every one of those nine seasons (in 1999 the Central had *three*). While the Mariners have taken themselves out of the AL West equation and probably won't be back in it until Bill Bavasi is assigned other duties, they still managed to win 78 games in 2006 and look to be more of a mediocrity than an embarrassment in the coming years.

Thus, the issue of intra-division competition is not one of quantity, but of quality. Since 2001, the West has amassed a greater cumulative record than either of the other two American League divisions. It's not even close: The West clocks in at a .534 cumulative winning percentage, the East at .498, and the Central at .480.

RANGERS PROSPECTUS

2006 record: 80–82; Third place, AL West

Pythagenport record: 85–77

Runs scored per game: 5.15 (4th in AL)

Runs allowed per game: 4.84 (8th in AL)

Team EqA: .258 (10th in AL)

2006 Batters Age: 28.9 (4th youngest in AL)

2006 Pitchers Age: 28.5 (7th youngest in AL)

Ballpark: Ameriquest Field; Moderate hitter's park; Park Factor of 1.034

2006: The pitching pick-ups worked pretty well for once; Blalock and Wilkerson didn't.

2007: A rebound by Blalock and Teixeira could make this the best team in the division after the McCarthy trade.

The Rangers face other challenges, among them their ballpark. Team construction in an extreme hitter's park is no easy task. It can warp perceptions of fans and the media, not to mention of the people responsible for assessing talent. Take the perception that Rangers pitching is consistently terrible. There have been years in which the Rangers' pitchers were just that without any help from their home environment. The 2001 and 2003 clubs conjured up images of the hapless 1930 Phils staff serving up easy pickings at the Baker Bowl, another extreme hitter's park. That wasn't the case last year. The average American League team plated 4.86 runs per game in 2006, while the Rangers allowed 4.84. Considering that they play half their games in a launching pad, being a couple of ticks above league average in the run prevention department is something special. On the road last year, the Rangers held opponents to a mere 4.58 runs per game, which would have been good for fourth in the league. In 2004, the Rangers ranked fifth in the league in runs allowed per game. Taken together, those strong performances in two of the last three years represent a great leap forward from the regrettable staffs of the early part of the decade.

Those achievements have come despite the Rangers' home field, but the ballpark has its advantages as well, primarily the fact that it tends to be well populated. The Rangers have a loyal fan base, drawing more than 2 million fans every year since 1989 with the exception of strike-shortened 1995 (but *including* the even shorter 1994), and have been in the top half of the league in attendance every year since 1988. While these numbers are not spectacular—they've never been higher than third in the league or broken three million in attendance—they are steady, and illustrate that the team's fan base is solid and unwavering despite the fact that the Rangers have finished above .500 just once in the last seven years. That the team has never bottomed out has been its saving grace. There's no need for Texas to "win back" the fans; the majority have never left.

Despite those solid attendance figures, the Rangers still can't outspend the Angels. In fact, the Rangers have barely outspent *Oakland* over the past three years. The difference between the Rangers' and A's combined payrolls from 2004 to 2006 amounts to less than a two percent accounting in Texas's favor. That is quite a change from earlier in the decade, when the Rangers boasted one of the largest payrolls in baseball, in no small part due to the generosity shown to Alex Rodriguez. From 2001 to 2003, the Rangers ranked seventh, third, and fifth in payroll among MLB's 30 teams. In the three years since then, they've dropped to the 18-to-20 range. Meanwhile, the on-field results have headed in the other direction—they've jumped to a three-year average of 83 wins per season versus the 72 they averaged while spending nearly twice as much money. This relative success can create an environment in which big spending can be viewed as going hand-in-hand with failure. The miscalculations that previous General Manager John Hart made with Rodriguez and Chan Ho Park have thus ensured that Jon Daniels and his staff will have to make do with less, which means the best way for the team to improve itself in the short term is through trades.

Thus far things haven't gone particularly well for Daniels on that front. With Ian Kinsler ready to take over at second base and Alfonso Soriano about to enter his walk year, Daniel's first big move after being hired in October of 2005 was the one that still defines his tenure in Texas. At the time, it looked brilliant. Daniels traded one year of Soriano, a bad defender who didn't get on base and had seemingly become entirely dependent on the Rangers' home park (he hit .224/.265/.374 on the road in 2005), to Washington for Brad Wilkerson, a younger, defensively versatile on-base machine who was likely to benefit greatly from a move to the former Ballpark at Arlington. Daniels also got a lefty power bat for the bench and a young pitcher for the system thrown in. Unfortunately, Soriano thrived in Washington, playing a strong left field and mashing both on the road and in his pitcher-friendly new home park. Wilkerson worked out about as well as the last batch of players to arrive in Arlington from the nation's capital, Bob Short's Senators. In Wilkerson's case the problem was a sore shoulder that sapped his production and ended his season in early August.

Daniels immediately followed the Soriano deal by taking Terrmel Sledge, the lefty bench bat acquired from the Nationals, and flipping him along with pitcher Chris Young and first baseman Adrian Gonzalez to the Padres for starter Adam Eaton, reliever Akinori Otsuka, and a teenage minor league catcher. Young was an emerging pitcher, but he had a nasty fly-ball rate, a recipe for disaster in slugger-friendly Texas. Gonzalez failed to hit in a brief stint with the Rangers, and Sledge was, and is, a Quadruple-A hitter. Once again, the deal blew up in Daniels's face. While Otsuka excelled (eventually assuming the closer's role), Eaton underwent hand surgery in April, didn't pitch until July, was terrible, then departed as a free agent. Meanwhile, both Young and Gonzalez emerged as stars in San Diego, helping the Padres to their second consecutive division title.

With his two big offseason acquisitions fighting injuries, the players he sent away making headlines, and his team falling out of contention, Daniels kept at it, making a big splash at last year's trading deadline by sending four players—including a starting outfielder, his deposed closer, the team's former Center Fielder of the Future, and a low-minors reliever—to Milwaukee for Nelson Cruz and a two-month rental on Carlos Lee. It all amounted to a lot of noise, a last throw to try to salvage the season. Cruz likely replaces Kevin Mench directly, while Lee departed for a big-money free-agent deal with that other Texas team after the Rangers' lease was up.

However disappointing the Soriano and Lee deals were in the short term, they may wind up having very little impact at all. Soriano left Washington for a historic payday, just as he would have left Texas. So, ultimately, the verdict on the Soriano trade comes down to a question of preference—the compensation picks the team would have received for Soriano, or Wilkerson. Given their financial restrictions on the free agent market, the Rangers are probably better off taking real major league talent when they can get it to support the offensive core of Mark Teixeira, Michael Young, Hank Blalock, and Kinsler. If he enters the 2007 season healthy, Wilkerson could change a lot of minds about the trade. As for the Lee deal, the players sent to Milwaukee won't be missed, and Cruz will be under team control for longer than Mench, giving the Rangers a small net gain of a few arbitration years on one of their starting outfielders.

The Eaton-Young deal is a tougher proposition to defend. Daniels was probably right to doubt Young's ability to succeed as an extreme fly-ball pitcher in Arlington, no matter how good he looks in the comfort of PETCO. Gonzalez was blocked by Teixeira at first base, and, while Daniels could have had him share the DH and first base playing time with Teixeira, you can also understand the incentive to use excess talent at one position to improve another. Otsuka wound up to be a significant upgrade in the closer role over Francisco Cordero, who finally became too unpredictable for the job. Yet, there's still a strong possibility that Otsuka's quirky delivery won't fool American League hitters a second time around, which seems to be what happened to him in the NL. It's hard to list this one as a positive for Daniels, but it's not quite as bad as it might look given the relative performances of the two starting pitchers involved. Similarly, the $60 million, five-year contract Daniels gave to free agent Kevin Millwood prior to 2006 looked excessive at the time, but it fits this offseasons inflated pitching market. The common thread to Daniels's moves seems to be that they're built on a solid bed of logic. Even though the walls seemed to cave in time and again, a defensible foundation for how to build up the ballclub remains.

Beyond those three big splashes (four counting Millwood), Daniels has made a number of small moves for pitching. The goal last winter was to shore up the rotation behind Millwood, but Daniels has made a bit more noise this winter by acquiring longtime White Sox untouchable Brandon McCarthy from Chicago for a trio of young hurlers. Previously, Daniels had flipped hitting for pitching knowing that, with his ballpark, he could always find players to put runs on the board, but with the McCarthy deal he traded away his own young arms for someone else's. McCarthy seems an odd fit for Texas; he was very prone to the longball in Chicago. In Texas, he may be a back-of-the-rotation starter at best, while John Danks (the best of the three pitching prospects sent to Chicago) is projected to be a better pitcher than McCarthy. Kenny Williams always said he wasn't going to trade McCarthy unless he was blown away by the offer. When Williams said "yes," Daniels should have known he was giving up too much.

Despite making four major trades in the past year and a half, it doesn't appear that Jon Daniels has made any significant improvements to his ballclub. The lineup is still highly dependent on Teixeira, Young, and some combination of the fading Blalock and the emerging Kinsler. Free-agent additions Frank Catalanotto and Kenny Lofton are role players rather than difference makers, and Cruz and Wilkerson remain question marks due to inexperience and injury respectively. The pitching staff is largely unchanged from last year, although McCarthy replaces Eaton and his placeholders, and Daniels has taken a flier on former Dodgers' megastar-turned-medical freak show Eric Gagne in the bullpen. For all of the work Daniels has done to shake things up, the Rangers look destined for yet another worms-eye view of the A's and Angels.

HITTERS

Joaquin Arias   SS   **Bats: R**   **Throws: R**   Height: 6' 1"   Weight: 165   Born: September 21, 1984   Age: 22

YEAR	TEAM	LVL	AGE	PA	R	2B	3B	HR	RBI	BB	SO	SB	CS	SPEED	AVG	OBP	SLG	MLVR	EQAVG	EQOBP	EQSLG	EQA	VORP	DEFENSE
2004	STO	A+	19	543	77	20	8	4	62	31	53	30	14	6.8	.300	.344	.396	.027	.268	.303	.342	.230	-1.1	112-SS -17
2005	FRI	AA	20	526	65	23	8	5	56	17	46	20	10	6.6	.315	.335	.423	.063	.290	.314	.390	.246	14.2	117-SS -4
2006	OKL	AAA	21	525	56	14	10	4	49	19	64	26	10	7.1	.268	.296	.361	-.106	.270	.294	.366	.234	1.7	122-SS -4
2006	TEX	MLB	21	12	4	1	0	0	1	1	0	0	1	6.4	.545	.583	.636	1.069	.545	.583	.636	.380	2.8	
2007	TEX	MLB	22	485	58	23	5	6	42	18	53	15	6	6.4	.277	.307	.387	-.125	.268	.304	.381	.244	7.3	115-SS -1

Breakout: 35%   Improve: 55%   Collapse: 16%   Attrition: 7%   Comparables: William Bergolla, Luis Ordaz, Chin Lung Hu, Jack Wilson

Part of the very light payoff for Alex Rodriguez, Joaquin Arias has the physical tools to be a fine shortstop. That doesn't mean he's going to be a useful major league player—he hasn't developed even rudimentary selectivity at the plate and lacks consistency on defense. He's young enough to develop further, but given the distance he has to travel, we may be asking the impossible. With Michael Young around, Arias will eventually be tried out at second, the first step toward a few years in the bigs as a reserve middle infielder.

Rod Barajas   C   **Bats: R**   **Throws: R**   Height: 6' 2"   Weight: 230   Born: September 5, 1975   Age: 31

YEAR	TEAM	LVL	AGE	PA	R	2B	3B	HR	RBI	BB	SO	SB	CS	SPEED	AVG	OBP	SLG	MLVR	EQAVG	EQOBP	EQSLG	EQA	VORP	DEFENSE
2004	TEX	MLB	28	389	50	26	1	15	58	13	63	0	1	4.7	.249	.276	.453	-.141	.242	.270	.441	.241	1.5	103-C 1
2005	TEX	MLB	29	449	53	24	0	21	60	26	70	0	0	3.5	.254	.306	.466	-.014	.252	.315	.473	.266	16.1	115-C 8
2006	TEX	MLB	30	371	49	20	0	11	41	17	51	0	0	4.1	.256	.298	.410	-.139	.247	.298	.406	.242	0.6	93-C 2
2007	PHI	MLB	31	364	40	19	1	15	52	22	54	0	1	3.9	.255	.308	.452	-.061	.251	.305	.442	.252	9.5	87-C 0

Breakout: 22%   Improve: 48%   Collapse: 23%   Attrition: 30%   Comparables: Joe Oliver, Jeff Newman, Brian Johnson, Kevin Young

Offense in baseball is pretty basic. If you don't make outs, you get to keep hitting. If you get to keep hitting, you get more chances to get hits and walks. If you get more hits and walks, you'll probably score more runs. Forget stolen bases, squeeze plays, smallball, Moneyball, medicine ball, or any other ball you can think of—scoring runs in baseball is about reaching base, and Barajas is one of the worst in the game at it. Despite playing in an extremely generous hitter's park over the last three years, his OBP during that time was just .294. Over that same period, the average American League hitter's OBP was .336. The average catcher, a group which includes Barajas, had a .325 OBP during that time. Barajas hits a few home runs, and they're legit—his power isn't just a gift from the ballpark. If the Rangers had no alternative to Barajas in the organization, that would have been an adequate consolation prize. The Rangers had Gerald Laird, though, so that excuse doesn't wash. Finally wising up with the departure of Buck Showalter, the Rangers let Barajas leave as a free agent. He signed with Philadelphia, where he'll once again block a better player in Carlos Ruiz.

Hank Blalock   3B   Bats: L   Throws: R   Height: 6' 1"   Weight: 200   Born: November 21, 1980   Age: 26

YEAR	TEAM	LVL	AGE	PA	R	2B	3B	HR	RBI	BB	SO	SB	CS	SPEED	AVG	OBP	SLG	MLVR	EQAVG	EQOBP	EQSLG	EQA	VORP	DEFENSE	
2004	TEX	MLB	23	713	107	38	3	32	110	75	149	2	2	4.3	.276	.355	.500	.097	.265	.350	.485	.283	30.1	154-3B	11
2005	TEX	MLB	24	705	80	34	0	25	92	51	132	1	0	3.9	.263	.318	.431	-.026	.261	.328	.439	.263	11.4	155-3B	-3
2006	TEX	MLB	25	646	76	26	3	16	89	51	98	1	0	4.5	.266	.325	.401	-.093	.257	.325	.394	.251	0.0	120-3B	-13
2007	TEX	MLB	26	635	79	32	2	21	81	56	110	2	1	4.4	.270	.337	.445	.000	.261	.334	.438	.272	15.7	148-3B	-1

Breakout: 25% Improve: 55% Collapse: 12% Attrition: 3%   Comparables: Roy Howell, Pete Ward, Jason Giambi, Scott Cooper

"You are a waste of talent," Rangers batting coach Rudy Jaramillo told Blalock on the final day of the season, and, though he was just trying to motivate the young man, he wasn't far off. Of the 87 big leaguers entrusted with 600 or more plate appearances last year, only Pedro Feliz (–8.2) and Jeff Francoeur (–1.0) had a lower value over replacement than Blalock's definitively replacement-level 0.0. Blalock looked like a terrific all-around hitter coming out of the minors and early on in the majors, but he's been relentlessly headed backwards ever since. At this point, he's a captive of his limitations, unable to hit lefties (.232/.286/.372 over the last three seasons) or away from the comforts of home (.241/.303/.391). In his defense, Blalock started 2006 like gangbusters (.344/.411/.542 in April) but began a sharp decline in May and by July was complaining of a shoulder injury which would require arthroscopic surgery after the season. Showalter had begun to see Blalock as a platoon player, but new manager Ron Washington is going to play him every day.

Jason Botts   DH   Bats: S   Throws: R   Height: 6' 5"   Weight: 250   Born: July 26, 1980   Age: 26

YEAR	TEAM	LVL	AGE	PA	R	2B	3B	HR	RBI	BB	SO	SB	CS	SPEED	AVG	OBP	SLG	MLVR	EQAVG	EQOBP	EQSLG	EQA	VORP	DEFENSE			
2004	FRI	AA	23	573	85	25	3	24	92	77	126	7	4	4.5	.293	.399	.507	.261	.269	.357	.460	.280	21.5	127-1B	-16		
2005	OKL	AAA	24	589	93	31	7	25	102	67	152	2	4	4.3	.286	.375	.522	.172	.278	.355	.486	.283	22.9	81-LF	-9		
2005	TEX	MLB	24	30	4	0	0	0	3	3	13	0	0	3.9	.296	.367	.296	-.088	.259	.355	.259	.231	-0.0				
2006	OKL	AAA	25	259	43	19	1	13	39	31	61	6	0	5.2	.309	.398	.582	.422	.311	.388	.582	.321	26.7	24-LF	0	18-1B	1
2006	TEX	MLB	25	60	8	4	0	1	6	8	18	0	0	4.1	.220	.317	.360	-.207	.204	.317	.327	.238	-1.4				
2007	TEX	MLB	26	436	55	23	1	16	58	42	110	3	1	4.6	.258	.334	.447	-.011	.250	.331	.440	.272	6.0	104-LF	-5		

Breakout: 7% Improve: 22% Collapse: 48% Attrition: 16%   Comparables: Jon Knott, Bucky Jacobsen, Ryan Shealy, Tydus Meadows

Although Botts hit well at Triple-A for the second year in a row, he's a bit of a Vasco de Gama in the outfield, and an honorary member of the Giambi clan at first base. As a switch-hitter on a team on which there are plenty of players who need protection from lefty pitchers, he should get a chance at a platoon job at the very least. The rest will depend on the disposition of the other outfielders, particularly Brad Wilkerson and Nelson Cruz. Botts batted .365/.400/.635 against southpaws at Oklahoma City (albeit in a small sample), which is a positive sign. His season was cut short by a fractured hamate bone in his right hand, so the caution flag will waive until he shows himself to have fully recovered.

Nelson Cruz   RF   Bats: R   Throws: R   Height: 6' 3"   Weight: 225   Born: July 1, 1980   Age: 26

YEAR	TEAM	LVL	AGE	PA	R	2B	3B	HR	RBI	BB	SO	SB	CS	SPEED	AVG	OBP	SLG	MLVR	EQAVG	EQOBP	EQSLG	EQA	VORP	DEFENSE			
2004	MOD	A+	24	290	54	27	1	11	52	24	73	8	4	5.2	.345	.407	.582	.434	.294	.341	.472	.275	9.3	47-LF	5	23-RF	0
2004	MID	AA	24	289	51	14	2	14	46	26	69	8	3	5.8	.313	.377	.542	.290	.285	.341	.487	.280	11.5	53-RF	4		
2005	HUN	AA	25	286	45	19	0	16	54	31	71	10	3	4.8	.306	.388	.577	.345	.270	.338	.508	.285	12.5	65-RF	-5		
2005	NAS	AAA	25	246	33	13	0	11	27	30	62	9	4	4.4	.269	.382	.490	.164	.252	.350	.435	.270	4.0	53-RF	4		
2006	NAS	AAA	26	423	68	22	1	20	73	42	100	17	6	5.6	.302	.378	.528	.271	.288	.356	.500	.290	22.1	86-RF	2		
2006	TEX	MLB	26	138	15	3	0	6	22	7	32	1	0	4.8	.223	.261	.385	-.260	.209	.254	.364	.216	-5.1	35-RF	2		
2007	TEX	MLB	26	475	60	24	1	19	65	37	120	9	4	5.0	.256	.319	.451	-.033	.248	.316	.444	.267	2.4	112-RF	2		

Breakout: 14% Improve: 33% Collapse: 37% Attrition: 10%   Comparables: Jason Lane, Jon Knott, Dave Henderson, Scott Morgan

(continued next page)

Nelson Cruz *(continued)*

Cruz has been through four organizations—the Mets, A's, Brewers, and now Rangers. He's been traded for Jorge Velandia, Keith Ginter, and a package of players including Laynce Nix, Kevin Mench, and Fracisco Cordero. At least he was a throw-in on a prestige deal this time around—constantly being traded for fringe reserve infielders can sap a guy's confidence. He'll have a solid shot at the starting right field job this spring. With four assists in just 38 games in right for the Rangers, he made a case that he's the best defensive fit for the job, but his bat may prove to be a bit light for a right fielder in Texas's low-gravity ballpark. As with Botts, Cruz's immediate future may depend on whether Wilkerson has a comeback season in him.

Mark DeRosa　　2B　　Bats: R　Throws: R　Height: 6' 1"　Weight: 205　Born: February 2, 1975　Age: 32

YEAR	TEAM	LVL	AGE	PA	R	2B	3B	HR	RBI	BB	SO	SB	CS	SPEED	AVG	OBP	SLG	MLVR	EQAVG	EQOBP	EQSLG	EQA	VORP	DEFENSE		
2004	ATL	MLB	29	345	33	16	0	3	31	23	53	1	3	4.0	.239	.293	.320	-.222	.232	.288	.313	.215	-13.7	64-3B	-7	
2005	TEX	MLB	30	166	26	5	0	8	20	16	35	1	0	3.8	.243	.325	.439	-.015	.240	.335	.452	.270	3.7	21-RF	0	
2006	TEX	MLB	31	572	78	40	2	13	74	44	102	4	4	4.8	.296	.357	.456	.065	.290	.357	.453	.277	21.9	58-RF	5	39-3B -4
2007	CHN	MLB	32	409	55	22	2	11	50	34	73	3	3	4.8	.282	.347	.448	.022	.277	.341	.435	.265	13.3	97-RF	-2	

Breakout: 14%　Improve: 42%　Collapse: 32%　Attrition: 25%　　Derek Bell, Larry Herndon, Gary Ward, Cleon Jones

After missing most of April with a sprained ankle, DeRosa came back swinging the bat like hitting the baseball would scratch an itch he hadn't reached in years. At the close of June he was batting .346/.401/.514. Sure as the Good Lord failed to give polar bears water wings, he didn't program man so that 31-year-old infielders could turn into Ty Cobb-like right fielders overnight. Inexorably, DeRosa came back down to earth, batting a more DeRosa-like .265/.333/.423 the rest of the way. The Tribune Company went for the okeydoke on the May-June surge, buying in for three years and $13 million. They've upgraded on Todd Walker, but they won't get the instant Cuppa-Cobb guy.

Victor Diaz　　OF　　Bats: R　Throws: R　Height: 6' 0"　Weight: 200　Born: December 10, 1981　Age: 25

YEAR	TEAM	LVL	AGE	PA	R	2B	3B	HR	RBI	BB	SO	SB	CS	SPEED	AVG	OBP	SLG	MLVR	EQAVG	EQOBP	EQSLG	EQA	VORP	DEFENSE		
2004	NOR	AAA	22	578	81	31	1	24	94	31	133	6	8	4.4	.292	.332	.491	.164	.290	.329	.475	.270	18.1	125-RF	2	
2004	NYN	MLB	22	53	8	3	0	3	8	1	15	0	0	3.3	.294	.321	.529	.175	.294	.321	.510	.276	2.8	13-RF	-1	
2005	NOR	AAA	23	184	30	11	0	10	34	14	47	6	2	5.3	.300	.353	.541	.297	.300	.353	.524	.291	12.8	25-1B	1	11-RF 1
2005	NYN	MLB	23	313	41	17	3	12	38	30	82	6	2	5.3	.257	.329	.468	.081	.258	.332	.487	.276	10.1	74-RF	-4	
2006	NOR	AAA	24	411	30	16	0	8	38	25	99	5	5	3.9	.224	.276	.330	-.117	.234	.284	.350	.221	-22.8	82-RF	-7	
2006	NYN	MLB	24	11	0	1	0	0	2	0	5	0	0	3.8	.182	.182	.273	-.534	.091	.091	.091	.076	-1.2			
2006	OKL	AAA	24	15	1	0	0	0	2	1	6	0	0	4.0	.385	.400	.385	.217	.462	.467	.462	.320	2.3			
2007	NYN	MLB	25	393	42	16	1	12	48	27	97	5	3	4.4	.246	.302	.402	-.145	.250	.305	.415	.244	-3.9	94-RF	-2	

Breakout: 7%　Improve: 36%　Collapse: 33%　Attrition: 23%　　Comparables: Ray Sadler, David Kelton, Josh Bonifay, Jason Michaels

Disastrous defensively and impatient at the plate, Diaz is no use at all if he doesn't hit .290. The Mets cut bait and sent him to Texas for catch-and-throw catcher Mike Nickeas. The Rangers have the right park for a player of his skills, but they also have outfielders ahead of him, even if he does rediscover his swing.

Freddy Guzman　　CF　　Bats: S　Throws: R　Height: 5' 10"　Weight: 165　Born: January 20, 1981　Age: 26

YEAR	TEAM	LVL	AGE	PA	R	2B	3B	HR	RBI	BB	SO	SB	CS	SPEED	AVG	OBP	SLG	MLVR	EQAVG	EQOBP	EQSLG	EQA	VORP	DEFENSE	
2004	MOB	AA	23	157	21	5	2	1	7	16	28	17	5	7.8	.283	.359	.370	.033	.261	.325	.331	.246	-1.8	33-CF	3
2004	POR	AAA	23	300	48	12	4	1	19	30	46	48	5	8.5	.292	.365	.379	-.027	.275	.342	.349	.267	2.2	63-CF	5
2004	SDN	MLB	23	80	8	3	0	0	5	3	13	5	2	7.0	.211	.250	.250	-.390	.197	.237	.237	.181	-5.2	17-CF	0
2006	POR	AAA	25	139	15	7	2	2	14	14	19	11	3	6.9	.274	.348	.411	.032	.262	.331	.397	.259	2.3	29-CF	2
2006	OKL	AAA	25	293	45	9	2	1	14	36	36	31	9	7.1	.282	.375	.345	.025	.280	.361	.342	.261	4.7	67-CF	-7
2006	TEX	MLB	25	9	1	0	0	0	0	1	1	0	0	4.5	.286	.444	.286	.003	.286	.444	.286	.285	0.3		
2007	TEX	MLB	26	436	66	18	4	3	30	34	62	40	11	7.3	.275	.335	.365	-.105	.266	.332	.360	.260	4.3	103-CF	0

Breakout: 16%　Improve: 45%　Collapse: 21%　Attrition: 16%　　Comparables: Andres Torres, Chone Figgins, Roger Cedeno, Chris Prieto

Guzman missed all of 2005 after undergoing Tommy John surgery, then got swiped away from the Padres in a minor deal. Healed up, Guzman picked up where he left off in 2004, stealing bases, showing decent plate discipline, and exhibiting no pop whatsoever. He'll fill somebody's fourth or fifth outfielder needs for at least a year or two before he's done, but in this year's camp, he'll be going *mano y mano* with Marlon Byrd for the job of Kenny Lofton's defensive replacement in center.

Jerry Hairston Jr. **2B/OF** **Bats: R** **Throws: R** Height: 5' 10" Weight: 185 Born: May 29, 1976 Age: 31

YEAR	TEAM	LVL	AGE	PA	R	2B	3B	HR	RBI	BB	SO	SB	CS	SPEED	AVG	OBP	SLG	MLVR	EQAVG	EQOBP	EQSLG	EQA	VORP	DEFENSE			
2004	BAL	MLB	28	334	43	19	1	2	24	29	29	13	8	6.3	.303	.378	.397	.027	.308	.384	.402	.277	9.3	25-RF	2	13-CF	1
2005	CHN	MLB	29	430	51	25	2	4	30	31	46	8	9	5.4	.261	.336	.368	-.058	.263	.337	.378	.246	0.5	43-CF	-2	37-2B	-1
2006	CHN	MLB	30	92	8	3	0	0	4	4	14	3	0	5.8	.207	.253	.244	-.438	.190	.244	.226	.185	-6.0	17-2B	-2		
2006	TEX	MLB	30	100	17	3	1	0	6	9	20	2	2	6.2	.205	.286	.261	-.400	.184	.276	.241	.193	-7.4	16-LF	3		
2007	*TEX*	*MLB*	*31*	*253*	*31*	*11*	*1*	*3*	*21*	*18*	*34*	*6*	*3*	*6.1*	*.256*	*.320*	*.352*	*-.162*	*.248*	*.317*	*.347*	*.241*	*-3.1*	*62-2B*	*2*		

Breakout: 23% Improve: 52% Collapse: 28% Attrition: 33%   Comparables: Bill Sample, Bob Bailor, Keith Miller, Jerry Royster

Acquired from the Cubs in the Phil Nevin bake sale, Hairston batted .206/.270/.253 between the two clubs. With his production plummeting like an elevator with a snapped cable, a career of similar longevity to his pop's seems increasingly unlikely. No speed, no power, no patience, no batting average, no defense . . . no point. Hairston was released after the season ended in order to make room for Mike Wood, an excellent indication of his current perceived value. Texas gave him a one-year contract to come back and try again.

Ian Kinsler **2B** **Bats: R** **Throws: R** Height: 6' 0" Weight: 200 Born: June 22, 1982 Age: 25

YEAR	TEAM	LVL	AGE	PA	R	2B	3B	HR	RBI	BB	SO	SB	CS	SPEED	AVG	OBP	SLG	MLVR	EQAVG	EQOBP	EQSLG	EQA	VORP	DEFENSE	
2004	CLN	A	22	259	52	30	1	11	53	26	37	16	6	6.3	.401	.465	.687	.716	.343	.394	.576	.319	41.0	56-SS	4
2004	FRI	AA	22	326	51	21	1	9	46	32	47	7	4	4.8	.300	.400	.480	.233	.273	.351	.436	.271	18.6	71-SS	-6
2005	OKL	AAA	23	597	102	28	2	23	94	53	89	19	5	6.2	.274	.348	.464	.031	.259	.322	.423	.259	16.6	126-2B	-7
2006	OKL	AAA	24	41	7	3	0	2	6	2	5	1	1	5.3	.256	.293	.487	.064	.231	.268	.436	.235	-0.5		
2006	TEX	MLB	24	474	65	27	1	14	55	40	64	11	4	5.1	.286	.347	.454	.036	.278	.347	.450	.275	24.3	117-2B	-4
2007	*TEX*	*MLB*	*25*	*590*	*84*	*34*	*2*	*21*	*79*	*45*	*81*	*12*	*5*	*5.2*	*.284*	*.345*	*.475*	*.066*	*.275*	*.342*	*.467*	*.283*	*28.2*	*138-2B*	*-2*

Breakout: 20% Improve: 57% Collapse: 10% Attrition: 5%   Comparables: Denis Menke, Wil Cordero, Davey Johnson, Don Money

Higher on-base percentage than Alfonso Soriano? Check. Better defense? Check. Was the overall package superior to the Texas edition of Soriano? Well, no, but it was close enough; the Washington Nationals' Soriano is a different matter, but that's not what the Rangers had when they dealt him. As measured by Wins Above Replacement (WARP), which considers both hitting and fielding, Soriano was worth 4.0 WARP in 2005, while Kinsler was worth 3.5 in only 75 percent as much playing time (he missed a month and a half early in the season with a dislocated thumb). Kinsler's season left some question marks for 2007, among them if he can hit on the road, and if his second-half slowdown (.267/.329/.399 vs. .320/.379/.553 in the first half) means the league is catching up to him or can be chalked up to rookie inconsistency.

Gerald Laird **C** **Bats: R** **Throws: R** Height: 6' 1" Weight: 225 Born: November 13, 1979 Age: 27

YEAR	TEAM	LVL	AGE	PA	R	2B	3B	HR	RBI	BB	SO	SB	CS	SPEED	AVG	OBP	SLG	MLVR	EQAVG	EQOBP	EQSLG	EQA	VORP	DEFENSE	
2004	TEX	MLB	24	168	20	6	0	1	16	12	35	0	1	4.0	.224	.287	.286	-.367	.205	.274	.253	.199	-8.5	46-C	6
2005	OKL	AAA	25	317	51	12	4	17	55	28	61	12	2	6.4	.310	.380	.562	.264	.295	.353	.510	.292	25.7	72-C	11
2005	TEX	MLB	25	42	7	2	0	1	4	2	7	0	0	5.1	.225	.262	.350	-.259	.231	.286	.359	.224	-0.9	11-C	0
2006	TEX	MLB	26	260	46	20	1	7	22	12	54	3	1	5.4	.296	.332	.473	.051	.287	.332	.471	.273	12.2	66-C	8
2007	*TEX*	*MLB*	*27*	*327*	*40*	*18*	*2*	*10*	*39*	*23*	*64*	*4*	*2*	*4.9*	*.264*	*.321*	*.435*	*-.046*	*.255*	*.318*	*.428*	*.263*	*8.2*	*79-C*	*5*

Breakout: 18% Improve: 41% Collapse: 28% Attrition: 26%   Comparables: Ron Karkovice, Harry Chiti, Dave Roberts, Bill Haselman

We sometimes find ourselves in danger of overusing the term "lefty-masher," but Laird deserved that sobriquet in 2006, pounding southpaws for 34 hit in 85 at-bats for .400/.414/.600 rates. His performance against right-handers was a mirror image at .241/.291/.405. As this suggests, Laird is the kind of hitter who would greatly benefit from being a little less eager to chase bad pitches, because the overall offensive package isn't going to carry him past the point of being a poor man's Paul Lo Duca. He's a good defender, and, with Barajas out of the way, he'll finally get a shot at regular play, but as long as he's so dependent on batting average and on seeing the right pitchers, he's always going to be pushed towards a reserve role as soon as someone flashier catches his manager's eye.

Carlos Lee LF Bats: R Throws: R Height: 6' 2" Weight: 240 Born: June 20, 1976 Age: 31

YEAR	TEAM	LVL	AGE	PA	R	2B	3B	HR	RBI	BB	SO	SB	CS	SPEED	AVG	OBP	SLG	MLVR	EQAVG	EQOBP	EQSLG	EQA	VORP	DEFENSE	
2004	CHA	MLB	28	658	103	37	0	31	99	54	86	11	5	4.8	.305	.366	.525	.208	.300	.366	.523	.298	38.5	138-LF	17
2005	MIL	MLB	29	688	85	41	0	32	114	57	87	13	4	5.4	.265	.324	.487	.097	.263	.324	.491	.276	24.7	158-LF	-5
2006	MIL	MLB	30	435	60	18	0	28	81	38	39	12	2	4.7	.286	.347	.549	.202	.285	.349	.552	.299	27.2	95-LF	-12
2006	TEX	MLB	30	260	42	19	1	9	35	20	26	7	0	5.7	.322	.369	.525	.222	.313	.369	.519	.304	20.0	48-LF	-5
2007	HOU	MLB	31	632	96	35	2	31	102	54	73	12	4	5.1	.293	.357	.526	.155	.292	.356	.519	.293	33.2	148-LF	-6

Breakout: 17% Improve: 45% Collapse: 28% Attrition: 4%   Comparables: Kevin McReynolds, Ivan Calderon, Kevin Young, Eric Karros

As the Lyle Lovett song says, "That's right, you're not from Texas, but Texas wants you anyway." The Rangers dealt for Lee, and not to be one-upped, the Astros signed him to a six-year, $100 million deal. Lee's home run power didn't show up quite so much in Texas, where it was assumed that the ballpark would liberate him, but he still enjoyed one of the most productive stretches of his career thanks to an uncharacteristically high batting average. Note the top PECOTA comp, Kevin McReynolds, another outfielder who ate himself out of a good career; originally a good defensive outfielder, McReynolds came to resemble a bleached Grimmace and his career quickly faded. This is a danger for Lee—if at some point during the season the Astros suddenly and unexpectedly put Chris Burke on the DL, it might not be that he's hurt, but that Lee ate him.

Gary Matthews Jr. CF Bats: S Throws: R Height: 6' 3" Weight: 225 Born: August 25, 1974 Age: 32

YEAR	TEAM	LVL	AGE	PA	R	2B	3B	HR	RBI	BB	SO	SB	CS	SPEED	AVG	OBP	SLG	MLVR	EQAVG	EQOBP	EQSLG	EQA	VORP	DEFENSE			
2004	OKL	AAA	29	171	33	9	4	9	36	23	29	4	1	6.8	.324	.409	.628	.464	.287	.360	.520	.298	13.6	18-CF	-1	13-LF	-2
2004	TEX	MLB	29	317	37	17	1	11	36	33	64	5	1	5.4	.275	.350	.461	.034	.264	.347	.444	.275	10.8	52-RF	3	26-CF	2
2005	TEX	MLB	30	526	72	25	5	17	55	47	90	9	2	6.1	.255	.320	.436	-.023	.253	.330	.445	.267	11.6	95-CF	-2	21-RF	2
2006	TEX	MLB	31	690	102	44	6	19	79	58	99	10	7	5.8	.313	.371	.495	.164	.306	.371	.493	.292	50.0	139-CF	-6		
2007	ANA	MLB	32	606	80	29	3	15	69	53	95	9	4	5.7	.273	.339	.422	-.024	.271	.342	.434	.275	17.2	142-CF	-3		

Breakout: 1% Improve: 18% Collapse: 38% Attrition: 9%   Comparables: Jerry Mumphrey, Ken Griffey, Fred Valentine, Gary Ward

Kudos to the Rangers for not getting caught up in the moment and signing Matthews to a long-term deal. Two of the Rangers five most-productive players last year happened to be career reserves who defied the norm and put together career years at the age of 31. The temptation to reward Matthews and Mark DeRosa would have been too much for some clubs, but the Rangers did the right thing in both cases by bidding them fond adieus. You've got to be happy for Matthews, the patent holder on the $50 Million Catch, but that doesn't make the Angels any less crazy.

John Mayberry OF Bats: R Throws: R Height: 6' 6" Weight: 230 Born: December 21, 1983 Age: 23

YEAR	TEAM	LVL	AGE	PA	R	2B	3B	HR	RBI	BB	SO	SB	CS	SPEED	AVG	OBP	SLG	MLVR	EQAVG	EQOBP	EQSLG	EQA	VORP	DEFENSE			
2005	SPO	A-	21	302	51	16	0	11	26	26	71	7	3	5.3	.253	.341	.438	.071	.194	.249	.312	.201	-50.6	60-RF	-8		
2006	CLN	A	22	533	77	26	4	21	77	59	117	9	3	5.2	.268	.358	.479	.196	.233	.300	.407	.244	-12.5	90-RF	-7	25-LF	0
2007	TEX	MLB	23	485	51	25	2	14	55	33	117	5	3	5.0	.234	.292	.390	-.178	.226	.289	.384	.237	-14.2	115-RF	-5		

Breakout: 45% Improve: 65% Collapse: 19% Attrition: 3%   Comparables: Shelley Duncan, Joe Mather, Steve Smitherman, Marcus Thames

By the time Mayberry's father was this age, he had played 281 games at Triple-A and another 105 in the majors; the son has yet to play a game in High-A. If this sounds like an argument against staying in school, it really isn't, especially if you get a Stanford education out of the deal. Mayberry initially had a rough year at Clinton, but he did have a solid second half and had an outstanding season in the in the Hawaiian Winter League (.321/.394/.548 in 84 at-bats), where he led a pitcher's league in slugging.

Miguel Ojeda C Bats: R Throws: R Height: 6' 1" Weight: 230 Born: January 29, 1975 Age: 32

YEAR	TEAM	LVL	AGE	PA	R	2B	3B	HR	RBI	BB	SO	SB	CS	SPEED	AVG	OBP	SLG	MLVR	EQAVG	EQOBP	EQSLG	EQA	VORP	DEFENSE	
2004	SDN	MLB	29	174	23	3	0	8	26	15	34	0	0	4.2	.256	.322	.429	.011	.263	.328	.436	.263	5.6	42-C	-1
2005	SDN	MLB	30	83	6	3	1	0	6	9	21	1	1	5.7	.137	.232	.205	-.494	.110	.207	.164	.150	-7.4	14-C	-2
2005	SEA	MLB	30	37	2	0	0	1	3	6	3	0	1	4.2	.172	.314	.276	-.300	.179	.343	.286	.230	-1.8	11-C	1
2006	COL	MLB	31	82	5	3	0	2	11	8	16	0	0	2.3	.230	.305	.351	-.194	.216	.293	.324	.219	-1.5	20-C	0
2006	TEX	MLB	31	13	0	2	0	0	4	0	3	0	0	3.9	.308	.308	.462	.006	.308	.308	.462	.258	0.5		
2007	TEX	MLB	32	353	36	14	1	8	36	29	65	2	1	4.3	.236	.304	.365	-.188	.229	.301	.359	.236	-3.4	85-C	0

Breakout: 27% Improve: 46% Collapse: 31% Attrition: 25%   Comparables: Tim Laker, Haywood Sullivan, Chris Widger, Mike Hubbard

Ojeda has a contract for the 2007 season, a triumph given that after last season's spring training NRI the Rockies were so enamored with him they loaned him out to the Mexican League. He's currently slotted in to back up Laird behind the plate. There is little to distinguish him in the parade of reserve catchers.

Taylor Teagarden   **C**   **Bats: R**   **Throws: R**   Height: 6' 1"   Weight: 200   Born: December 21, 1983   Age: 23

YEAR	TEAM	LVL	AGE	PA	R	2B	3B	HR	RBI	BB	SO	SB	CS	SPEED	AVG	OBP	SLG	MLVR	EQAVG	EQOBP	EQSLG	EQA	VORP	DEFENSE	
2005	SPO	A-	21	122	23	5	4	7	16	23	32	1	1	5.3	.281	.426	.635	.445	.212	.320	.433	.260	5.0	20-C	-1
2006	RNG	Rk	22	29	4	0	0	0	1	9	7	1	0	3.4	.050	.345	.050	-.467	.042	.233	.042	.137	-15.5		
2007	TEX	MLB	23	239	21	8	1	5	20	31	69	1	1	4.4	.171	.282	.288	-.361	.166	.279	.284	.202	-10.4	59-C	0

Breakout: 39%   Improve: 53%   Collapse: 35%   Attrition: 38%   Comparables: Josh Glassey, Heath Wilson, Matt Gajewski, Dominick Lombardi

The great-grand nephew of classic jazz trombonist Jack Teagarden had a difficult full season debut, missing most of it after undergoing Tommy John surgery. He entered the year as a top prospect, highly regarded on both sides of the ball. With the TJ procedure, his ability to cut down the running game is thrown into question, but he's a very good handler of pitchers, so he still has something to offer behind the plate. It's the lost development time that's going to be most difficult to recover from. That first full year out of college is crucial to a prospect's development. The majors look forward to "Swingin' on a Teagarden Gate."

Mark Teixeira   **1B**   **Bats: S**   **Throws: R**   Height: 6' 3"   Weight: 220   Born: April 11, 1980   Age: 27

YEAR	TEAM	LVL	AGE	PA	R	2B	3B	HR	RBI	BB	SO	SB	CS	SPEED	AVG	OBP	SLG	MLVR	EQAVG	EQOBP	EQSLG	EQA	VORP	DEFENSE	
2004	TEX	MLB	24	625	101	34	2	38	112	68	117	4	1	5.2	.281	.370	.560	.197	.269	.363	.541	.300	41.5	139-1B	-8
2005	TEX	MLB	25	730	112	41	3	43	144	72	124	4	0	4.8	.301	.379	.575	.300	.298	.386	.584	.319	61.9	153-1B	4
2006	TEX	MLB	26	727	99	45	1	33	110	89	128	2	0	4.2	.282	.371	.514	.160	.273	.371	.506	.298	37.4	158-1B	10
2007	TEX	MLB	27	685	106	39	2	34	111	76	123	3	1	4.6	.289	.373	.534	.193	.280	.370	.526	.308	37.5	159-1B	2

Breakout: 8%   Improve: 36%   Collapse: 23%   Attrition: 0%   Comparables: Dave Hollins, Eddie Murray, Bobby Bonilla, Lance Berkman

Seen in the context of his 2005 breakout, Teixeira's 2006 was a disappointment. He had a very slow start, particularly in the power department; through the end of June he had numbers that looked like something out of the Travis Lee Catalog, .273/.355/.438 with eight home runs in 320 at-bats. He snapped back after that, batting .291/.394/.604 after the break with 24 home runs in 275 at-bats. Teixeira felt that his swing had gotten out of whack, corrected the problem, and got back on the future-MVP track. PECOTA sees another year like this in his future, but he could blow that projection away if he takes better advantage of his friendly home park; he hit just .266/.336/.455 at home in 2006. If he can mate some approximation of 2005's home numbers—.334/.411/.698, with 30 home runs—with 2006's road numbers—.298/.406/.577 with 21 home runs—look out. His glove remains an asset no matter how he hits.

Brad Wilkerson   **OF**   **Bats: L**   **Throws: L**   Height: 6' 0"   Weight: 205   Born: June 1, 1977   Age: 30

YEAR	TEAM	LVL	AGE	PA	R	2B	3B	HR	RBI	BB	SO	SB	CS	SPEED	AVG	OBP	SLG	MLVR	EQAVG	EQOBP	EQSLG	EQA	VORP	DEFENSE			
2004	MON	MLB	27	688	112	39	2	32	67	106	152	13	6	5.6	.255	.374	.498	.184	.251	.370	.490	.291	37.0	75-1B	4	48-LF	1
2005	WAS	MLB	28	661	76	42	7	11	57	84	147	8	10	5.1	.248	.351	.405	.036	.255	.359	.423	.268	13.2	84-CF	0	32-LF	-1
2006	TEX	MLB	29	365	56	15	2	15	44	37	116	3	2	5.5	.222	.306	.422	-.134	.215	.309	.421	.250	-5.3	75-LF	2		
2007	TEX	MLB	30	454	61	22	3	18	55	52	115	5	3	5.7	.242	.334	.448	-.024	.234	.331	.441	.271	4.9	108-LF	-1		

Breakout: 14%   Improve: 37%   Collapse: 31%   Attrition: 23%   Comparables: Willie Kirkland, Ray Lankford, Pete Ward, Roger Repoz

Well, that didn't work out as planned. The prize for Alfonso Soriano came with a bum shoulder that thwarted the basic formulation of, "Wilkerson, good hitter + good hitters' park = big year." After fighting the injury most of the season, Wilkerson finally bowed out in mid-August and went under the knife. Despite regressing in all phases with the bat, Wilkerson actually led the team in home runs for awhile, though that might speak more to the problems of teammates such as Teixeira and Blalock. The shoulder was also a problem in 2005, so it's been a long time since we've seen the real Wilkerson, and there's a good possibility that the 27-year-old slugger of 2004 is gone for good. Even if healthy, he's going to have to hit well enough to keep his job despite the presence of Catalanotto, Botts, Cruz, and new center fielder Kenny Lofton.

Eric Young　　OF　　Bats: R　Throws: R　Height: 5′ 9″　Weight: 185　Born: December 31, 1969　Age: 40

YEAR	TEAM	LVL	AGE	PA	R	2B	3B	HR	RBI	BB	SO	SB	CS	SPEED	AVG	OBP	SLG	MLVR	EQAVG	EQOBP	EQSLG	EQA	VORP	DEFENSE		
2004	TEX	MLB	37	402	55	25	2	1	27	43	28	14	9	5.3	.288	.377	.381	-.019	.281	.373	.371	.265	6.2	34-LF -3	19-2B -4
2005	SDN	MLB	38	163	22	9	0	2	12	18	12	7	6	5.7	.275	.356	.380	.025	.294	.377	.406	.265	2.3	19-LF 3	10-2B 0
2006	SDN	MLB	39	147	19	5	0	3	13	13	16	8	2	5.6	.203	.281	.313	-.277	.211	.293	.336	.232	-6.4	27-LF -2	
2006	TEX	MLB	39	12	1	1	1	0	2	1	1	0	0	4.3	.200	.273	.500	-.105	.200	.273	.500	.256	0.1		
2007	TEX	MLB	40	221	28	10	2	3	21	19	22	7	5	5.6	.251	.323	.374	-.133	.243	.320	.368	.246	-2.7	55-LF -3	

Breakout: 8%　Improve: 32%　Collapse: 20%　Attrition: 34%　　Comparables: Minnie Minoso, Pee Wee Reese, Barry Larkin, Wally Moses

One of the most prominent athletes to come out of Rutgers University prior to running back Ray Rice entering the national consciousness in 2006, Young now nears the end of the line after a career of which it can be said that he got the most out of his skills. That sounds like a faint compliment, but there are many athletes who do less. A free agent, at press time he had no takers.

Mike Young　　SS　　Bats: R　Throws: R　Height: 6′ 1″　Weight: 200　Born: October 19, 1976　Age: 30

YEAR	TEAM	LVL	AGE	PA	R	2B	3B	HR	RBI	BB	SO	SB	CS	SPEED	AVG	OBP	SLG	MLVR	EQAVG	EQOBP	EQSLG	EQA	VORP	DEFENSE
2004	TEX	MLB	27	739	114	33	9	22	99	44	89	12	3	6.2	.313	.353	.483	.103	.302	.348	.473	.280	51.9	151-SS -11
2005	TEX	MLB	28	732	114	40	5	24	91	58	91	5	2	5.0	.331	.385	.513	.257	.329	.393	.524	.309	72.4	153-SS -14
2006	TEX	MLB	29	748	93	52	3	14	103	48	96	7	3	4.8	.314	.356	.459	.086	.306	.355	.454	.278	46.0	154-SS 21
2007	TEX	MLB	30	673	96	38	4	17	79	50	84	7	3	5.3	.304	.357	.461	.084	.294	.354	.454	.285	39.7	157-SS 1

Breakout: 14%　Improve: 39%　Collapse: 28%　Attrition: 1%　　Comparables: Alvin Dark, Johnny Logan, Jeff Cirillo, Derek Jeter

Our Davenport Translations reversed field on Young after years of deploring his work with the glove, a change which is reflected, at least to some degree, in other fielding metrics as well. The sad truth is that until baseball has some kind of GPS chip implanted on every fielder, we're not really going to know precisely just how far each player travels from point A to point B in pursuit of the ball. Young's bat took a little step back last year after three seasons of rising production, but was still plenty good when combined with his improved glove. Texas has a 2008 option on Young for $4 million; if there's any question of whether or not they'll be picking that up, keep in mind that's less than Kenny Lofton will make this year.

PITCHERS

Rick Bauer　　Bats: R　Throws: R　Height: 6′ 6″　Weight: 225　Born: January 10, 1977　Age: 30

YEAR	TEAM	LVL	AGE	W	L	SV	G	GS	IP	H	BB	SO	HR	GB%	BABIP	STUFF	WHIP	ERA	PERA	EQERA	EQH9	EQBB9	EQSO9	EQHR9	VORP	WXRL
2004	OTT	AAA	27	3	5	0	11	11	63	69	19	42	3	—	.325	9	1.40	4.00	4.15	3.96	9.5	3.0	4.5	0.6	11.6	—
2004	BAL	MLB	27	2	1	0	23	2	53²	49	20	37	4	—	.273	5	1.29	4.69	4.04	4.69	7.8	2.9	5.7	0.6	7.0	1.08
2005	OTT	AAA	28	3	8	1	30	10	74¹	84	35	43	12	49.8%	.312	-30	1.60	4.00	6.60	5.01	10.3	4.8	3.9	1.7	4.8	—
2005	BAL	MLB	28	0	0	0	5	0	8¹	13	4	5	2	45.2%	.379	-26	2.04	9.76	6.18	8.31	13.5	4.2	5.2	2.1	-3.9	-0.07
2006	TEX	MLB	29	3	1	2	58	1	71	73	25	35	4	54.5%	.301	-3	1.38	3.55	4.14	3.54	8.4	2.9	4.2	0.5	17.7	1.71
2007	TEX	MLB	30	3	3	1	46	0	56²	67	24	32	7	51.0%	.314	-12	1.60	5.03	4.95	4.58	9.8	3.6	4.8	0.9	4.7	0.40

Breakout: 17%　Improve: 38%　Collapse: 33%　Attrition: 21%　　Comparables: Greg Booker, Jay Powell, Bob Lee, Cecil Upshaw

Relievers are a volatile lot. Maybe it's that luck plays a bigger hand in their results given the small sample sizes of their annual workloads, maybe it's that it's more difficult to maintain all the different mechanical aspects of pitching when you only throw so many pitches at a time, or perhaps that lack of consistency is what put many relievers in the pen in the first place. Bauer is actually one of the more consistent relievers within his range; he's been a more or less league-average pitcher since 2001. He also has a strikeout-free approach, which explains why the normally feckless Orioles didn't hesitate to cut bait in 2005. Bauer adjusted to pitching in Texas by kicking up his ground-ball rate; he only allowed one home run in Arlington in 146 batters faced. PECOTA sees his unimpressive K/BB rate catching up with him in 2007.

Joaquin Benoit
Bats: R Throws: R   Height: 6' 3"   Weight: 220   Born: July 26, 1977   Age: 29

YEAR	TEAM	LVL	AGE	W	L	SV	G	GS	IP	H	BB	SO	HR	GB%	BABIP	STUFF	WHIP	ERA	PERA	EQERA	EQH9	EQBB9	EQSO9	EQHR9	VORP	WXRL
2004	TEX	MLB	26	3	5	0	28	15	103	113	31	95	19	—	.323	6	1.40	5.68	4.54	4.89	9.4	2.4	7.6	1.4	7.7	0.84
2005	TEX	MLB	27	4	4	0	32	9	87	69	38	78	9	31.5%	.251	18	1.23	3.72	4.06	3.59	6.5	3.8	7.7	0.8	18.0	1.92
2006	TEX	MLB	28	1	1	0	56	0	79²	68	38	85	5	39.0%	.296	24	1.33	4.86	3.41	4.92	7.1	3.9	8.9	0.4	5.9	0.19
2007	TEX	MLB	29	3	4	2	50	1	70²	72	31	67	10	39.0%	.309	7	1.45	4.82	4.43	4.36	8.5	3.7	7.9	1.1	8.3	0.70

Breakout: 26% Improve: 56% Collapse: 19% Attrition: 10%   Comparables: Alejandro Pena, Steve Bedrosian, Don Aase, Scott Linebrink

Benoit had the best strikeout rate on the team once Francisco Cordero was shipped to Milwaukee. He was also the unluckiest reliever in the American League in terms of bequeathed runners prevented, with seven more runners crossing the plate than would have been expected had he received typical support from the pitchers that followed him. Benoit was used in a lot of low-leverage situations, so the hurlers that came after him weren't exactly Billy Wagner and Mariano Rivera. A fly-ball pitcher in a park that frowns on such tendencies, Benoit cut his home run rate down last year while actually raising the number of fly balls he allowed. Without any indication it isn't just smoke and mirrors, his home run rate will go up, his fortunes down.

John Danks
Bats: L Throws: L   Height: 6' 1"   Weight: 200   Born: April 15, 1985   Age: 22

YEAR	TEAM	LVL	AGE	W	L	SV	G	GS	IP	H	BB	SO	HR	GB%	BABIP	STUFF	WHIP	ERA	PERA	EQERA	EQH9	EQBB9	EQSO9	EQHR9	VORP	WXRL
2004	CLN	A	19	3	2	0	14	8	49²	38	14	64	4	—	.279	16	1.05	2.17	4.99	4.02	8.6	3.3	6.9	1.5	8.3	—
2004	STO	A+	19	1	4	0	13	13	55	62	26	48	5	—	.345	-7	1.60	5.24	6.06	7.26	11.0	5.4	5.1	1.5	-9.8	—
2005	BAK	A+	20	3	3	0	10	10	57²	50	16	53	5	48.8%	.280	17	1.14	2.50	4.62	3.12	8.0	2.8	5.3	1.1	15.9	—
2005	FRI	AA	20	4	10	0	18	17	98¹	117	34	85	12	43.5%	.354	-2	1.54	5.49	5.45	6.52	10.7	3.6	5.8	1.5	-10.0	—
2006	FRI	AA	21	5	4	0	13	13	69	74	22	82	11	39.2%	.354	11	1.39	4.17	5.13	5.06	10.0	2.9	7.8	1.8	4.2	—
2006	OKL	AAA	21	4	5	0	14	13	70²	67	34	72	11	39.2%	.299	2	1.44	4.36	5.75	5.76	9.0	4.2	7.2	1.8	-1.2	—
2007	CHA	MLB	22	6	7	0	21	21	113	124	52	90	22	42%	.302	11	1.55	5.52	5.21	4.98	9.8	3.8	6.7	1.6	5.6	1.4

Breakout: 20% Improve: 60% Collapse: 9% Attrition: 9%   Comparables: Cedrick Bowers, Scott Olsen, Odalis Perez, Andy Pratt

The ninth player taken in the 2003 draft, Danks was shipped Chicago-ward in exchange for Brandon McCarthy, breaking up the much-heralded DVD trio of pitching prospects and leaving the Rangers with just VD. Danks might not be able to fill McCarthy's shoes right away, but the White Sox believe he'll be the better pitcher in the long run. He has above-average velocity for a lefthander, but his curveball is his best offering. He also has an annoying habit of needing more time than most to adjust to a new level, so expect some early adjustment blues when he gets the call.

Thomas Diamond
Bats: R Throws: R   Height: 6' 3"   Weight: 245   Born: April 6, 1983   Age: 24

YEAR	TEAM	LVL	AGE	W	L	SV	G	GS	IP	H	BB	SO	HR	GB%	BABIP	STUFF	WHIP	ERA	PERA	EQERA	EQH9	EQBB9	EQSO9	EQHR9	VORP	WXRL
2004	CLN	A	21	1	0	0	7	7	30²	18	8	42	1	—	.262	23	0.85	2.05	3.81	3.38	7.1	3.1	7.1	0.6	7.2	—
2004	SPO	A-	21	0	2	1	5	3	15¹	13	5	26	0	—	.419	14	1.18	2.35	3.57	4.40	10.0	4.4	7.5	0.6	1.9	—
2005	BAK	A+	22	8	0	0	14	14	81¹	53	31	101	3	48.1%	.289	32	1.03	1.99	4.13	2.61	6.8	4.1	7.1	0.5	26.3	—
2005	FRI	AA	22	5	4	0	14	14	69	66	38	68	8	35.8%	.307	5	1.51	5.35	6.10	6.12	8.8	5.9	6.8	1.5	-3.9	—
2006	FRI	AA	23	12	5	0	27	27	129	104	78	145	14	39.8%	.285	9	1.41	4.26	5.66	4.85	7.7	5.7	7.2	1.3	10.7	—
2007	TEX	MLB	24	5	7	0	26	18	105¹	111	66	86	17	42.0%	.300	3	1.68	5.86	5.47	5.30	8.7	5.4	6.8	1.3	-0.3	0.70

Breakout: 10% Improve: 25% Collapse: 39% Attrition: 1%   Comparables: Dennis Tankersley, Eric Gagne, Matt Kinney, Jose Capellan

The "D" left in "VD," and even if was still "DVD," with Blue-Ray and HD-DVD, plain ol' DVD might not cut it. In fact, the way Diamond's development has slowed, VD might soon be down to just "V," or, failing that, "Betamax." A first-round pick in 2004, he can launch his fastball up to 97 MPH when he has to, although he's usually in the 92 to 94 range. He's got a good changeup as well, but he's struggled to find a breaking ball, and the whispers about a move to the bullpen are getting louder. That might not be the end of the world; with his velocity, Diamond has definite closer possibilities. Note the high walk rate; that may be the result of being forced to throw a curve whether he has a feel for it or not; a move to the bullpen would obviate the need for the pitch and the walk rate would (theoretically) come down.

Adam Eaton

Bats: R Throws: R Height: 6′ 2″ Weight: 200 Born: November 23, 1977 Age: 29

YEAR	TEAM	LVL	AGE	W	L	SV	G	GS	IP	H	BB	SO	HR	GB%	BABIP	STUFF	WHIP	ERA	PERA	EQERA	EQH9	EQBB9	EQSO9	EQHR9	VORP	WXRL
2004	SDN	MLB	26	11	14	0	33	33	199^1	204	52	153	28	—	.300	9	1.28	4.61	4.39	5.29	9.1	2.1	6.1	1.2	11.6	3.03
2005	SDN	MLB	27	11	5	0	24	22	128^2	140	44	100	14	41.3%	.319	12	1.43	4.27	4.21	4.88	9.4	2.7	6.3	0.9	8.0	2.27
2006	TEX	MLB	28	7	4	0	13	13	65	78	24	43	11	37.6%	.324	-2	1.57	5.12	5.13	4.66	9.8	3.1	5.5	1.3	6.4	0.71
2007	PHI	MLB	29	6	8	0	30	19	116^2	126	38	83	18	43.0%	.297	3	1.41	5.00	5.08	4.91	9.4	2.6	5.7	1.3	9.1	1.70

Breakout: 17% Improve: 43% Collapse: 19% Attrition: 6%   Comparables: Frank Castillo, Dan Spillner, John Montefusco, Ron Darling

If the Duke of Wellington had been a talking head on ESPN, he might have quipped that Eaton met his Waterloo on the playing fields of Arlington. As for Eaton himself, he received a multi-year contract from the Phillies—not a bad reward for 65 innings of work. Eaton underwent surgery on his right middle finger in April, resolving an injury that went back to the year before. Given Eaton's injury record, if it hadn't been that, it would have been something else. He didn't take the mound until late July, and given the results, it might have been better if he had rehabbed for awhile longer. Lefties in particular troubled him, battering his offerings for .320/.393/.592 rates with eight home runs in 125 at-bats. This is a move Pat Gillick is likely to regret.

Scott Feldman

Bats: L Throws: R Height: 6′ 6″ Weight: 225 Born: February 7, 1983 Age: 24

YEAR	TEAM	LVL	AGE	W	L	SV	G	GS	IP	H	BB	SO	HR	GB%	BABIP	STUFF	WHIP	ERA	PERA	EQERA	EQH9	EQBB9	EQSO9	EQHR9	VORP	WXRL
2005	FRI	AA	22	1	2	14	46	0	61	43	23	41	3	63.4%	.237	-4	1.08	2.36	4.47	3.10	5.9	3.8	4.6	0.6	16.9	—
2005	TEX	MLB	22	0	1	0	8	0	9^1	9	2	4	0	54.8%	.290	-2	1.18	0.97	3.32	0.93	7.4	1.9	3.7	0.0	5.0	0.11
2006	OKL	AAA	23	2	2	4	23	0	27	20	9	24	2	53.3%	.254	3	1.07	2.00	4.55	3.33	7.0	3.0	6.3	1.0	6.8	—
2006	TEX	MLB	23	0	2	0	36	0	41^1	42	10	30	4	60.2%	.306	6	1.26	3.92	3.99	3.80	8.4	2.1	6.1	0.8	9.5	-0.01
2007	TEX	MLB	24	3	3	2	48	1	53^2	58	18	39	5	56.0%	.314	4	1.40	4.14	3.93	3.82	9.0	2.8	6.0	0.7	9.8	0.90

Breakout: 13% Improve: 28% Collapse: 45% Attrition: 18%   Comparables: Kameron Loe, Ryan Madson, Terry Adams, Elias Sosa

Rangers pitchers must all have Tommy John baseball cards in the spokes of their bicycles. Another survivor of the procedure, Feldman has regained his control. His approach is so basic you'd think anyone could do it; using a sidearm delivery, he gets his sinkers into the low-90s, and he mixes in a sweeping slider. The result is a high ground-ball rate, a real plus given the place his team calls home. Despite this, Feldman wasn't used in too many pressure situations. Perhaps his manager feared what good lefty hitters could do to him, and rightly so. Still, Chad Bradford has shown the world how valuable this kind of pitcher can be if deployed carefully. All that remains is for Ron Washington to figure that out.

Eric Hurley

Bats: R Throws: R Height: 6′ 4″ Weight: 195 Born: September 17, 1985 Age: 21

YEAR	TEAM	LVL	AGE	W	L	SV	G	GS	IP	H	BB	SO	HR	GB%	BABIP	STUFF	WHIP	ERA	PERA	EQERA	EQH9	EQBB9	EQSO9	EQHR9	VORP	WXRL
2004	SPO	A-	18	0	2	0	8	6	28^1	31	6	21	6	—	.294	-22	1.31	5.41	9.61	7.18	12.3	2.4	3.8	4.1	-4.6	—
2005	CLN	A	19	12	6	0	28	28	155^1	135	59	152	11	38.7%	.300	13	1.25	3.77	5.16	4.84	8.7	3.8	5.9	1.2	12.9	—
2006	BAK	A+	20	5	6	0	18	18	100^2	92	32	106	12	41.5%	.308	-2	1.24	4.13	5.70	5.56	8.5	3.1	6.1	1.8	0.4	—
2006	FRI	AA	20	3	1	0	6	6	37^2	21	11	31	4	44.2%	.189	20	0.86	1.94	5.22	2.41	5.3	2.7	5.5	1.2	13.2	—
2007	TEX	MLB	21	6	9	0	27	21	121^1	138	50	85	27	40.0%	.293	3	1.54	5.91	5.56	5.26	9.4	3.5	5.9	1.7	0.2	0.90

Breakout: 4% Improve: 39% Collapse: 23% Attrition: 0%   Comparables: Ubaldo Jimenez, John Patterson, Neal Frendling, Tyler Clippard

A high school teammate of Billy Butler's, Hurley is beginning to look a lot like the real thing. His fastball is in the 92 to 95 MPH zone and he moves it around with aplomb. His slider works well and, when he gets the changeup worked out, he'll be better armed for the continued climb upwards. It wouldn't be surprising to see him in Arlington as a late-season call-up this year, and battling for a rotation spot in 2008. If that changeup doesn't happen, he could find a home in the pen as a power reliever/guy who tells stories about how Butler's defense was even worse when he was 16.

John Koronka

Bats: L Throws: L Height: 6′ 1″ Weight: 180 Born: July 3, 1980 Age: 26

YEAR	TEAM	LVL	AGE	W	L	SV	G	GS	IP	H	BB	SO	HR	GB%	BABIP	STUFF	WHIP	ERA	PERA	EQERA	EQH9	EQBB9	EQSO9	EQHR9	VORP	WXRL
2004	IOW	AAA	24	12	9	0	29	23	153^1	164	65	116	19	—	.305	-3	1.49	4.34	5.20	4.85	9.1	3.9	5.2	1.2	13.0	—
2005	IOW	AAA	25	9	11	0	23	21	136	135	48	96	12	46.1%	.307	7	1.35	4.24	4.47	4.08	8.4	3.0	4.7	0.8	23.5	—
2005	CHN	MLB	25	1	2	0	4	3	15^2	19	8	10	2	43.9%	.309	-12	1.72	7.45	4.96	7.31	10.7	3.9	5.1	1.1	-3.3	-0.12
2006	TEX	MLB	26	7	7	0	23	23	125	145	47	61	17	44.3%	.308	-7	1.54	5.69	5.03	5.17	9.4	3.1	4.1	1.0	6.0	1.87
2007	TEX	MLB	26	7	9	0	32	22	133^2	161	50	74	20	45.0%	.311	-4	1.58	5.64	5.19	5.11	10.0	3.2	4.6	1.2	2.5	1.20

Breakout: 17% Improve: 41% Collapse: 23% Attrition: 7%   Comparables: Paul Kilgus, Bobby Jones, Ted Bowsfield, Wandy Rodriguez

Koronka was doing a credible job as a back-end rotation man until the All-Star break when the wheels came off the cart. Several rough outings got him sent back to the OKC. Koronka hasn't been much better against lefties than righties, so a bullpen specialist role is right out. What seems more likely is trash time middle relief and Kevin Jarvis-style work as a desperation starter. Anything he does beyond acting as a placeholder would be gravy. Still, he'll get a shot at the rotation again in 2007.

Wes Littleton   Bats: R Throws: R   Height: 6' 2"   Weight: 210   Born: September 2, 1982   Age: 24

YEAR	TEAM	LVL	AGE	W	L	SV	G	GS	IP	H	BB	SO	HR	GB%	BABIP	STUFF	WHIP	ERA	PERA	EQERA	EQH9	EQBB9	EQSO9	EQHR9	VORP	WXRL
2004	STO	A+	21	8	10	0	30	23	141	139	56	72	7	—	.284	-11	1.38	4.15	5.62	5.83	9.0	4.4	3.0	0.8	-3.6	—
2005	FRI	AA	22	2	3	3	48	0	81²	93	24	71	9	56.0%	.354	-10	1.43	3.97	4.97	4.50	10.1	3.1	5.8	1.3	10.0	—
2006	FRI	AA	23	3	0	3	17	0	27²	13	7	25	1	64.3%	.174	13	0.74	0.66	3.64	1.32	4.3	2.3	5.9	0.3	13.0	—
2006	OKL	AAA	23	4	1	2	13	0	16	14	5	15	3	65.2%	.262	0	1.19	2.25	5.90	2.81	8.4	2.8	6.8	2.2	5.0	—
2006	TEX	MLB	23	2	1	1	33	0	36¹	23	13	17	2	71.4%	.204	-4	0.99	1.74	4.30	1.69	5.1	2.9	3.9	0.5	17.8	1.58
2007	TEX	MLB	24	3	3	2	49	1	52¹	55	21	32	5	55.0%	.297	-5	1.47	4.41	4.22	4.06	8.8	3.5	5.1	0.8	7.7	0.70

Breakout: 11%   Improve: 37%   Collapse: 32%   Attrition: 30%   Comparables: Ricky Trlicek, Ron Davis, Brad Thompson, Ron Willis

Littleton kept the ball on the ground—and then some. He led the club with a 3.75 groundball-to-flyball ratio, making him the poster child of the Rangers keep-it-earthbound movement. Another sidearmer, right-handers couldn't touch him, batting just .157/.222/.193. Many of those outs were made on balls in play; that .204 BABIP is going to be impossible to maintain. Still, if he can continue to keep the ball low and stay away from the evil lefties, he should be useful reliever for a while.

Kameron Loe   Bats: R Throws: R   Height: 6' 7"   Weight: 240   Born: September 10, 1981   Age: 25

YEAR	TEAM	LVL	AGE	W	L	SV	G	GS	IP	H	BB	SO	HR	GB%	BABIP	STUFF	WHIP	ERA	PERA	EQERA	EQH9	EQBB9	EQSO9	EQHR9	VORP	WXRL
2004	FRI	AA	22	7	7	0	19	19	113¹	122	29	97	5	—	.344	19	1.33	3.10	3.93	4.19	10.5	2.6	5.4	0.6	17.5	—
2004	OKL	AAA	22	5	2	0	8	8	52¹	52	13	42	6	—	.309	13	1.24	3.27	4.46	3.74	8.7	2.4	5.6	1.0	11.0	—
2005	OKL	AAA	23	2	1	0	5	5	28¹	32	10	23	5	46.2%	.314	0	1.48	5.09	5.48	5.59	9.6	3.1	5.6	1.9	0.0	—
2005	TEX	MLB	23	9	6	1	48	8	92	89	31	45	7	59.7%	.272	-1	1.30	3.42	4.24	3.55	7.8	2.9	4.2	0.7	17.4	1.36
2006	FRI	AA	24	0	1	0	2	2	7²	8	4	4	1	62.5%	.304	-17	1.67	5.00	7.13	6.14	9.8	4.9	3.7	1.2	-0.4	—
2006	OKL	AAA	24	1	2	1	13	3	22¹	32	13	21	3	58.8%	.392	-20	2.04	9.37	5.68	10.07	13.3	5.2	6.4	1.6	-11.1	—
2006	TEX	MLB	24	3	6	0	15	15	78¹	105	22	34	10	52.5%	.331	-7	1.62	5.86	4.57	5.57	10.8	2.3	3.6	1.0	-0.0	0.62
2007	TEX	MLB	25	6	7	0	38	17	113	136	39	60	14	54.0%	.317	-5	1.55	5.27	4.85	4.85	10.0	2.9	4.5	1.0	6.1	1.20

Breakout: 16%   Improve: 50%   Collapse: 16%   Attrition: 6%   Comparables: Sean Bergman, Chris Reitsma, Bob Anderson, Danny Cox

After a nice turn in late 2005, Loe began the year in the Texas rotation and alternated decent starts with disastrous ones as if on a schedule to do so. He got off the seesaw in June with three consecutive bad starts and was placed on the disabled list with a bruised elbow soon thereafter. That marked the end of the big league portion of his 2006 season. His strikeout rate is deep in the danger zone (3.9), although that can work for him as long as he continues to keep the hitters on the ground; his strikeout rate wasn't that much better in 2005 when he pitched his way into the Rangers plans.

Ron Mahay   Bats: L Throws: L   Height: 6' 2"   Weight: 190   Born: June 28, 1971   Age: 36

YEAR	TEAM	LVL	AGE	W	L	SV	G	GS	IP	H	BB	SO	HR	GB%	BABIP	STUFF	WHIP	ERA	PERA	EQERA	EQH9	EQBB9	EQSO9	EQHR9	VORP	WXRL
2004	TEX	MLB	33	3	0	0	60	0	67	60	29	54	5	—	.281	11	1.33	2.55	3.78	2.60	7.7	3.5	6.6	0.5	24.8	1.21
2005	TEX	MLB	34	0	2	1	30	0	35²	47	16	30	8	50.0%	.348	-12	1.74	6.81	5.39	6.21	10.5	3.8	7.2	1.7	-4.3	-0.31
2006	TEX	MLB	35	1	3	0	62	0	57	54	28	56	7	42.5%	.307	10	1.44	3.95	4.07	4.25	7.7	4.1	8.0	0.9	9.2	0.25
2007	TEX	MLB	36	2	2	2	49	0	48¹	48	22	45	5	45.0%	.309	5	1.44	4.43	4.09	4.04	8.2	3.9	7.8	0.9	7.1	0.60

Breakout: 34%   Improve: 55%   Collapse: 23%   Attrition: 20%   Comparables: Dennis Cook, Arthur Rhodes, Mark Guthrie, Ricardo Rincon

Mahay first reached the majors a decade ago. In the intervening time, he has managed to spend one full year in the majors, that being 2004. Until last year, his stints were either excellent or disastrous, but like a pendulum winding down he seems to slowly be discovering the center. Mahay handles lefties and righties about equally well and, at 35, posted one of his best strikeout rates ever in 2006, although his walk rate didn't do him any favors. You have to admire his stick-to-itiveness, especially since he's still widely known for crossing the line in 1995 when his team insisted the then-converted outfielder do so to avoid a release.

Kevin Millwood

Bats: R Throws: R   Height: 6' 4"   Weight: 230   Born: December 24, 1974   Age: 32

YEAR	TEAM	LVL	AGE	W	L	SV	G	GS	IP	H	BB	SO	HR	GB%	BABIP	STUFF	WHIP	ERA	PERA	EQERA	EQH9	EQBB9	EQSO9	EQHR9	VORP	WXRL
2004	PHI	MLB	29	9	6	0	25	25	141	155	51	125	14	—	.337	20	1.46	4.85	3.88	5.15	10.0	2.9	7.0	0.8	9.6	1.48
2005	CLE	MLB	30	9	11	0	30	30	192	182	52	146	20	47.0%	.286	22	1.22	2.86	3.84	3.61	8.7	2.5	6.7	0.9	50.4	5.71
2006	TEX	MLB	31	16	12	0	34	34	215	228	53	157	23	45.6%	.311	20	1.31	4.52	3.74	4.27	8.7	2.1	6.0	0.8	32.9	4.12
2007	*TEX*	*MLB*	*32*	*11*	*10*	*0*	*31*	*31*	*190²*	*216*	*53*	*137*	*25*	*47.0%*	*.315*	*13*	*1.41*	*4.67*	*4.44*	*4.23*	*9.4*	*2.4*	*6.0*	*1.0*	*24.5*	*3.90*

Breakout: 14% Improve: 55% Collapse: 18% Attrition: 0%   Comparables: Jim Clancy, Gaylord Perry, Kevin Gross, Chris Bosio

The 2005 American League ERA champion had a predictable rise in that department with the move to Arlington—except that only tells part of the story. While his home ERA nearly doubled, his road number jumped by nearly a run as well. The real difference wasn't that pronounced, however; his Defense-Adjusted ERA (DERA) was only about three-quarters of a run worse than in 2005. His Ranger-mates got him about a run and a half more offensive support per game than did his fellow Indians the previous year, so the window dressing looked a lot better. His deal with the Rangers is looking like a bargain compared to what came this past offseason—especially if his elbow continues to hold up.

Akinori Otsuka

Bats: R Throws: R   Height: 6' 0"   Weight: 210   Born: January 13, 1972   Age: 35

YEAR	TEAM	LVL	AGE	W	L	SV	G	GS	IP	H	BB	SO	HR	GB%	BABIP	STUFF	WHIP	ERA	PERA	EQERA	EQH9	EQBB9	EQSO9	EQHR9	VORP	WXRL
2004	SDN	MLB	32	7	2	2	73	0	77¹	56	26	87	6	—	.265	30	1.06	1.75	3.03	2.18	6.5	2.6	9.0	0.7	32.5	5.06
2005	SDN	MLB	33	2	8	1	66	0	62²	55	34	60	3	51.4%	.302	16	1.42	3.59	3.67	4.18	7.7	4.3	7.8	0.4	9.2	1.54
2006	TEX	MLB	34	2	4	32	63	0	59²	53	11	47	3	53.2%	.294	21	1.07	2.11	2.81	2.32	7.1	1.6	6.5	0.4	23.9	2.67
2007	*TEX*	*MLB*	*35*	*3*	*2*	*4*	*49*	*0*	*53¹*	*52*	*18*	*43*	*5*	*50.0%*	*.298*	*5*	*1.32*	*3.79*	*3.54*	*3.47*	*8.2*	*2.9*	*6.8*	*0.7*	*11.6*	*1.10*

Breakout: 8% Improve: 25% Collapse: 42% Attrition: 14%   Comparables: Steve Farr, Dave Smith, Bob Wickman, Jay Howell

Last year we suggested that a change of leagues was just the thing for a pitcher with Otsuka's unorthodox way of throwing, in that, once such a pitcher's quirks become familiar, they become hittable. That proved to be good advice, as Otsuka rebounded strongly after moving over to the junior circuit, even assuming the job of Rangers' closer. PECOTA sees another 2005-like downturn coming next year, though. Now that he's done both Japanese leagues and both American leagues, where else can he go that they've never seen his act? The Rangers had this in mind when they signed Eric Gagne with the intention of pushing Otsuka back into a setup role.

Vicente Padilla

Bats: R Throws: R   Height: 6' 2"   Weight: 220   Born: September 27, 1977   Age: 29

YEAR	TEAM	LVL	AGE	W	L	SV	G	GS	IP	H	BB	SO	HR	GB%	BABIP	STUFF	WHIP	ERA	PERA	EQERA	EQH9	EQBB9	EQSO9	EQHR9	VORP	WXRL
2004	PHI	MLB	26	7	7	0	20	20	115¹	119	36	82	16	—	.297	6	1.34	4.53	4.73	4.94	9.4	2.5	5.7	1.2	10.9	1.72
2005	PHI	MLB	27	9	12	0	27	27	147	146	74	103	22	46.2%	.284	-2	1.50	4.71	5.42	4.82	9.1	4.1	5.8	1.3	13.2	2.85
2006	TEX	MLB	28	15	10	0	33	33	200	206	70	156	21	45.1%	.310	20	1.38	4.50	4.23	4.35	8.6	2.9	6.5	0.8	29.2	4.19
2007	*TEX*	*MLB*	*29*	*11*	*10*	*0*	*30*	*30*	*185²*	*202*	*66*	*133*	*25*	*46.0%*	*.304*	*12*	*1.44*	*4.71*	*4.46*	*4.27*	*9.0*	*3.0*	*6.0*	*1.0*	*23.3*	*3.80*

Breakout: 19% Improve: 67% Collapse: 2% Attrition: 0%   Comparables: Pete Vuckovich, James Baldwin, Steve Trachsel, Pedro Astacio

Texas picked up Padilla for Ricardo Rodriguez, who hasn't been seen since; it's possible not even the Phillies remember his name. Padilla improved his control last year, which meant he was pitching ahead of more batters and getting more strikeouts. It was a nice little year that looks even better once you give Padilla credit for pitching in a bandbox. He was re-signed to a three-year, $33.75-million deal to be Texas's number-two, or whatever passes for that kind of pitcher in Texas these days. The 1977 Rangers had Bert Blyleven, Gaylord Perry, Doyle Alexander, and Dock Ellis; the 1978 crew had Alexander, Ellis, Jon Matlack, Fergie Jenkins, and Doc Medich. The Rangers haven't had four "name" pitchers in the rotation in a long time.

John Rheinecker

Bats: L Throws: L   Height: 6' 2"   Weight: 230   Born: May 29, 1979   Age: 28

YEAR	TEAM	LVL	AGE	W	L	SV	G	GS	IP	H	BB	SO	HR	GB%	BABIP	STUFF	WHIP	ERA	PERA	EQERA	EQH9	EQBB9	EQSO9	EQHR9	VORP	WXRL
2004	SAC	AAA	25	11	9	0	28	27	172¹	194	51	129	22	—	.317	0	1.42	4.44	5.13	4.90	9.2	2.7	5.0	1.2	13.8	—
2005	SAC	AAA	26	4	0	0	7	7	45²	29	14	24	0	58.0%	.213	11	0.94	1.77	3.99	2.74	5.5	2.7	3.5	0.2	14.6	—
2006	OKL	AAA	27	4	5	0	15	15	93	93	24	68	5	58.3%	.319	17	1.26	2.52	3.84	3.54	8.9	2.3	4.9	0.7	21.5	—
2006	TEX	MLB	27	4	6	0	21	13	70²	104	19	28	6	58.9%	.371	-8	1.74	5.86	4.24	5.33	12.0	2.2	3.3	0.6	2.9	1.04
2007	*TEX*	*MLB*	*28*	*8*	*10*	*0*	*35*	*27*	*151²*	*184*	*48*	*76*	*17*	*55.0%*	*.318*	*-3*	*1.53*	*5.06*	*4.75*	*4.66*	*10.1*	*2.7*	*4.2*	*0.9*	*11.1*	*2.20*

Breakout: 19% Improve: 46% Collapse: 16% Attrition: 0%   Comparables: Zane Smith, Dave Roberts, Frank Baumann, Bill Lee

Texas Rangers

Lefties were just about worthless against Rheinecker in 2006, but righties dominated him, hitting .392/.425/.552, and he saw a lot more of them than he did the lefties. In spite of being unmercifully creamed by the majority of hitters, he managed to pitch well at home, posting a 3.24 ERA under the Texas lights. A leveling off of his .371 BABIP is going to make him look better in 2007. As a 28-year old lefty, it's not too late for Rheinecker to cobble together a big league career.

Josh Rupe   **Bats: R Throws: R**   Height: 6' 2"   Weight: 210   Born: August 18, 1982   Age: 24

YEAR	TEAM	LVL	AGE	W	L	SV	G	GS	IP	H	BB	SO	HR	GB%	BABIP	STUFF	WHIP	ERA	PERA	EQERA	EQH9	EQBB9	EQSO9	EQHR9	VORP	WXRL
2004	STO	A+	21	2	0	0	4	3	18¹	12	4	14	0	—	.226	11	0.87	0.98	4.12	2.50	6.5	2.5	4.5	0.5	6.2	—
2004	SPO	A-	21	2	0	0	4	3	18	14	3	19	1	—	.271	7	0.94	1.50	5.01	2.65	9.0	2.1	4.8	1.1	5.6	—
2004	FRI	AA	21	2	2	0	7	6	37	41	16	16	5	—	.277	-25	1.54	4.38	7.65	7.00	11.0	4.5	2.8	2.0	-5.6	—
2005	FRI	AA	22	4	3	0	11	10	65	64	26	55	7	63.2%	.311	3	1.38	3.74	5.60	4.48	9.0	4.2	5.7	1.4	8.0	—
2005	OKL	AAA	22	6	7	0	17	17	93²	116	38	62	12	51.8%	.341	-12	1.64	6.24	5.52	7.45	10.4	3.4	4.4	1.3	-19.9	—
2005	TEX	MLB	22	1	0	0	4	1	9²	7	4	6	0	61.5%	.269	2	1.14	2.78	4.41	3.60	6.3	3.6	5.4	0.0	2.3	0.19
2006	OKL	AAA	23	1	1	2	12	0	13	13	6	4	0	68.2%	.295	-29	1.46	3.46	5.24	4.15	9.0	4.2	2.1	0.0	2.1	—
2006	TEX	MLB	23	0	1	0	16	0	29	33	9	14	2	67.3%	.313	-6	1.45	3.10	4.05	3.26	9.2	2.7	3.9	0.6	8.8	-0.16
2007	TEX	MLB	24	3	3	1	42	2	54¹	61	23	29	6	56.0%	.301	-11	1.54	4.84	4.65	4.44	9.3	3.6	4.4	0.9	5.4	0.50

Breakout: 32%   Improve: 63%   Collapse: 11%   Attrition: 42%   *Comparables: Randy Moffitt, Ricky Trlicek, Tom Hausman, Al Fitzmorris*

Along with Scott Feldman and Wes Littleton, Rupe was one of the Rangers pitchers who did the best job of keeping the ball on the ground in 2006. Nonetheless, this was probably about as good as it's going to get for him. That means an evening out of his splits and a far higher ERA.

Rob Tejeda   **Bats: R Throws: R**   Height: 6' 3"   Weight: 230   Born: March 24, 1982   Age: 25

YEAR	TEAM	LVL	AGE	W	L	SV	G	GS	IP	H	BB	SO	HR	GB%	BABIP	STUFF	WHIP	ERA	PERA	EQERA	EQH9	EQBB9	EQSO9	EQHR9	VORP	WXRL
2004	REA	AA	22	8	14	0	27	26	150¹	148	59	133	29	—	.274	-24	1.38	5.15	6.77	5.95	9.6	3.8	5.8	2.3	-5.8	—
2005	SWB	AAA	23	2	0	0	5	5	28¹	21	13	28	0	32.9%	.300	26	1.20	2.23	3.49	2.89	6.8	4.5	7.1	0.3	8.4	—
2005	PHI	MLB	23	4	3	0	26	13	85²	67	51	72	5	35.7%	.270	21	1.38	3.57	4.43	3.83	7.4	4.9	6.9	0.5	17.7	2.78
2006	OKL	AAA	24	6	2	0	15	15	80	61	42	79	7	42.0%	.265	16	1.29	3.15	4.90	3.71	7.2	4.6	6.9	1.0	16.8	—
2006	TEX	MLB	24	5	5	0	14	14	73²	83	32	40	10	39.1%	.307	-4	1.56	4.27	5.12	4.34	9.2	3.6	4.5	1.1	10.1	1.60
2007	TEX	MLB	25	7	8	0	33	23	125²	137	58	92	20	39.0%	.301	2	1.56	5.40	5.07	4.85	9.1	4.0	6.1	1.3	6.9	1.50

Breakout: 12%   Improve: 33%   Collapse: 40%   Attrition: 6%   *Comparables: Shawn Hillegas, Eric Gagne, Roger Salkeld, Bob Walk*

After a 2005 that showed much promise, Tejeda was inexplicably cast off by the Phillies, in part because they had to make room for Ryan Franklin, of all people. Tejeda's 2006 turned out to be a year of marking time. He's only 25, though, so there are a few more years where that came from. On the bright side, his DERA was really only about a half-run higher than it was the year before, and he did show fairly well when relegated to Oklahoma City and even better when he returned late in the season. He's not penciled into the rotation but could end up on its backend before the season is out.

Edinson Volquez   **Bats: R Throws: R**   Height: 6' 0"   Weight: 200   Born: July 3, 1983   Age: 23

YEAR	TEAM	LVL	AGE	W	L	SV	G	GS	IP	H	BB	SO	HR	GB%	BABIP	STUFF	WHIP	ERA	PERA	EQERA	EQH9	EQBB9	EQSO9	EQHR9	VORP	WXRL
2004	CLN	A	21	4	4	3	22	15	91	83	30	77	8	—	.285	-17	1.24	4.05	6.01	6.24	9.3	3.8	4.5	1.6	-6.3	—
2004	STO	A+	21	4	1	0	8	8	39²	31	14	34	6	—	.234	-7	1.13	2.95	7.72	4.34	8.4	4.1	5.1	2.7	5.2	—
2005	BAK	A+	22	5	4	0	11	11	66²	64	12	77	9	49.2%	.327	14	1.14	4.18	5.06	4.91	9.5	1.8	6.8	1.6	5.1	—
2005	FRI	AA	22	1	5	0	10	10	58²	58	17	49	6	47.2%	.306	8	1.28	4.14	4.86	4.78	8.8	3.1	5.7	1.2	5.3	—
2005	TEX	MLB	22	0	4	0	6	3	12²	25	10	11	3	43.1%	.458	-17	2.76	14.17	6.59	14.49	15.8	6.6	7.2	2.0	-13.1	-0.89
2006	OKL	AAA	23	6	6	0	21	21	120²	86	72	130	9	46.2%	.270	28	1.31	3.22	4.74	4.11	6.8	5.2	7.6	0.9	19.9	—
2006	TEX	MLB	23	1	6	0	8	8	33¹	52	17	15	7	43.8%	.366	-23	2.07	7.30	6.09	6.88	12.5	4.1	3.6	1.5	-5.0	-0.12
2007	TEX	MLB	23	6	9	0	33	24	122¹	139	62	89	20	46.0%	.311	1	1.64	5.86	5.44	5.32	9.5	4.3	6.1	1.3	-0.7	0.80

Breakout: 31%   Improve: 63%   Collapse: 6%   Attrition: 0%   *Comparables: Mike Judd, Herm Wehmeier, Russ Ortiz, Dennis Tankersley*

The "V" you've been waiting for, the one in DVD. Whatever else it stands for, it ain't "Victory," as Volquez has been unmercifully pounded at the big league level. He's been so bad his PECOTA comps include Dennis Tankersley, who tanked, and an always-exciting Herm Wehmeier appearance in this book. Volquez looked good at Triple-A last year, but that may not mean anything—there are, on rare occasions, pitchers who can't pull it together emotionally. Think Salomon Torres, who did, albeit years later, and Scott Ruffcorn, who didn't.

Kip Wells

Bats: R Throws: R   Height: 6' 3"   Weight: 205   Born: April 21, 1977   Age: 30

YEAR	TEAM	LVL	AGE	W	L	SV	G	GS	IP	H	BB	SO	HR	GB%	BABIP	STUFF	WHIP	ERA	PERA	EQERA	EQH9	EQBB9	EQSO9	EQHR9	VORP	WXRL
2004	PIT	MLB	27	5	7	0	24	24	138¹	145	66	116	14	—	.321	16	1.53	4.56	4.29	4.43	9.1	3.7	6.6	0.8	16.0	3.42
2005	PIT	MLB	28	8	18	0	33	33	182	186	99	132	23	45.2%	.300	2	1.57	5.09	5.22	5.61	9.2	4.4	6.0	1.1	-3.2	2.66
2006	PIT	MLB	29	1	5	0	7	7	36¹	46	18	16	3	52.3%	.344	-10	1.76	6.69	4.98	5.87	10.3	3.8	3.5	0.7	-3.0	0.14
2006	TEX	MLB	29	1	0	0	2	2	8	15	3	4	0	54.5%	.455	-11	2.25	6.75	3.56	6.48	15.1	3.2	4.3	0.0	-0.5	0.14
2007	*SLN*	*MLB*	*30*	*5*	*7*	*0*	*31*	*15*	*104¹*	*110*	*46*	*66*	*12*	*47.0%*	*.295*	*-5*	*1.50*	*4.78*	*5.26*	*5.20*	*9.9*	*3.6*	*5.1*	*1.0*	*6.7*	*1.30*

Breakout: 15% Improve: 43% Collapse: 18% Attrition: 11%   *Comparables: Stan Bahnsen, Jaret Wright, Neil Allen, Jim Hannan*

No sooner had recovered from getting an artery replaced in the spring and escaped the Pirates gulag in a deadline deal than Wells sprained his foot and landed on the DL. At the time, it seemed as if there was some sort of chance that Wells might bounce back to his good run of 2002–04, and it cost the Rangers little to risk finding out. Healthy or otherwise, he's struggled with his control, so if Dave Duncan can get that rectified to some extent, Wells will be an asset for the Cardinals.

C. J. Wilson

Bats: L Throws: L   Height: 6' 1"   Weight: 215   Born: November 18, 1980   Age: 26

YEAR	TEAM	LVL	AGE	W	L	SV	G	GS	IP	H	BB	SO	HR	GB%	BABIP	STUFF	WHIP	ERA	PERA	EQERA	EQH9	EQBB9	EQSO9	EQHR9	VORP	WXRL
2005	BAK	A+	24	0	1	0	4	4	13²	10	4	14	2	56.4%	.216	-7	1.02	3.28	6.30	4.05	7.4	3.4	5.4	2.0	2.3	—
2005	FRI	AA	24	0	4	0	12	12	44²	51	14	43	7	55.1%	.349	-19	1.45	4.43	6.47	7.48	11.0	3.5	6.0	2.1	-9.0	—
2005	TEX	MLB	24	1	7	1	24	6	48	63	18	30	5	61.4%	.360	-8	1.69	6.94	4.37	6.22	10.7	3.2	5.3	0.9	-7.0	-0.23
2006	TEX	MLB	25	2	4	1	44	0	44¹	39	18	43	7	52.4%	.274	7	1.29	4.06	4.80	4.14	7.5	3.4	8.1	1.2	7.5	0.19
2007	*TEX*	*MLB*	*26*	*3*	*3*	*2*	*50*	*2*	*55*	*56*	*23*	*44*	*6*	*51.0%*	*.301*	*3*	*1.43*	*4.47*	*4.15*	*4.09*	*8.5*	*3.5*	*6.7*	*0.9*	*8.0*	*0.80*

Breakout: 48% Improve: 71% Collapse: 8% Attrition: 23%   *Comparables: Steve Kline, Mike Magnante, Ricky Horton, Fred Scherman*

We're going to count this one as a plus in Wilson's ledger. Good hit and strikeout rates made for some very competent pitching in 2006. He held lefties to a .155 average, though he did allow them four home runs in just 71 at-bats. He had the lefty spot-man's usual difficulties with righties. With health he'll stay around forever, though that BABIP rate will be heading northward again this year, and with it his ERA.

Lineouts

PLAYER	TEAM	LVL	AGE	PA	R	2B	3B	HR	RBI	BB	SO	SB-CS	SPEED	AVG/OBP/SLG	MLVrEqAVG/EqOBP/EqSLG	EqA	VORP
CF A. Brown#	OKL	AAA	32	142	15	4	1	1	11	17	18	11-1	5.5	.295/.379/.369	.075	.276/.340/.339 .252		-3.3
	TEX	MLB	32	40	6	1	0	0	2	2	9	1-0	5.4	.194/.231/.222	-.570	.167/.205/.194 .167		-3.7
1B C. Davis*	SPO	A-	20	280	38	18	1	15	42	23	65	2-3	3.6	.277/.343/.534	.228	.230/.279/.437 .239		-13.4
SS M. Lemon*	RNG	Rk	18	101	16	4	2	0	9w	16	10	11-2	6.1	.310/.420/.405	.190	.264/.337/.341 .246		4.2
INF D. Meyer*	OKL	AAA	24	403	37	14	4	2	28	27	91	9-11	5.4	.228/.278/.305	-.249	.230/.276/.300 .206		-19.0
C C. Tracy	SPO	A-	21	283	41	14	1	11	35	23	46	4-1	4.5	.262/.339/.456	.117	.221/.272/.384 .226		-9.9
LF A. Webster*	FRI	AA	23	239	37	10	4	5	19	18	25	3-5	6.0	.310/.364/.463	.142	.285/.332/.421 .257		2.4
	OKL	AAA	23	265	30	15	2	3	19	13	36	16-4	6.8	.269/.317/.384	-.035	.267/.309/.381 .247		-6.4

PLAYER	TEAM	LVL	AGE	W	L	SV	IP	H	BB	SO	HR	GB%	BABIP	STUFF	WHIP	ERA	PERA	EqERA	EqH9	EqBB9	EqSO9	EqHR9	VORP
A. Alfonseca	TEX	MLB	34	0	0	0	16	23	7	5	3	—	.345	-35	1.88	5.63	5.86	5.29	11.6	3.7	2.6	1.6	0.9
J. Bannister	BAK	A+	22	5	8	0	96	109	53	109	9	—	.380	-4	1.69	5.91	6.18	7.06	10.6	5.6	6.3	1.5	-15.5
F. Francisco	FRI	AA	26	0	0	0	14	10	4	22	1	—	.300	14	1.00	1.93	3.41	2.63	7.2	2.6	9.2	0.7	4.5
	TEX	MLB	26	0	1	0	7¹	8	2	6	2	—	.273	-2	1.36	4.93	5.58	4.91	8.6	2.5	7.4	2.5	0.9
A. Galarraga	FRI	AA	24	1	6	0	41	56	13	38	5	—	.398	-12	1.68	5.49	5.63	8.06	12.6	3.0	5.7	1.5	-11.3
K. Kiker*	SPO	A-	18	0	7	0	52	44	35	51	5	—	.291	-8	1.52	4.15	8.33	6.70	8.3	8.0	5.3	2.2	-6.1
N. Masset	FRI	AA	24	2	2	0	48²	38	20	40	0	—	.275	16	1.20	2.05	4.00	3.35	7.1	4.1	5.0	0.2	12.1
	OKL	AAA	24	4	5	3	67	79	28	65	4	—	.373	3	1.60	4.84	4.01	6.72	10.5	3.6	6.6	0.7	-8.5
	TEX	MLB	24	0	0	0	8²	9	2	4	0	—	.346	-9	1.27	4.14	4.35	4.15	9.3	2.1	4.2	0.0	2.0
J. Wasdin	OKL	AAA	33	3	3	0	63²	52	17	62	2	—	.299	22	1.09	1.99	3.41	3.86	7.7	2.6	6.3	0.4	12.2
	TEX	MLB	33	2	2	0	30	33	13	16	6	—	.265	-16	1.53	5.10	6.42	4.94	9.3	3.5	4.4	1.5	1.8

Adrian Brown made it back to the bigs last year and was worse than ever. At 33, his unholy triumvirate of comparable players are Darren Lewis, Brian Hunter, and Calvin Murray. **Chris Davis** is a hulking first baseman who was among the Northwest leaders in home runs. He'll have to keep it up to move up because that's all he does well. **Richard Hidalgo** took 2006 off despite auditions with the Orioles and Yankees. He'll try to make a comeback at 31 with his original club, the Astros, but his 2004 to 2005 line was .232/.297/.433, and it's hard to see that getting better after a year off. Still, if any club is desperate for outfielders, it's the Astros. **Marcus Lemon** is Chet's kid. Like dad, he's a fantastic defender, only this time the position is shortstop, not center field. It cost the Rangers a million dollars to buy him away from college, and he rewarded them with better than expected batting. **Drew Meyer** got what 95 percent of the minor leaguers who show as little as he has in the minors never do: A cup of coffee. Despite the team's efforts to salvage him by turning him into a utility player, he simply can't hit. Pirates manager Jim Tracy's son, **Chad Tracy** was the best offensive catcher in the 2006 draft, but he might move to first base due to defensive weakness. **Anthony Webster** is an athletic outfielder who has been slow to translate his skills; he might make it as a fourth outfielder.

Antonio Alfonseca pitched just 50 professional innings over the past two seasons after his elbow busted on him. He'll surface in the bigs again if only because he's been there before. **John Bannister** put up a good strikeout rate in the California League and throws a nifty curveball, but it's his only plus pitch; he was far too hittable. You know it's been one of those careers when your most well-known throw involved a piece of furniture rather than a baseball. **Frank Francisco**'s late 2004 results were tantalizing, but that was before the Tommy John surgery and his proving himself to be an idiot. A highly regarded right-hander when he came over in the Brad Wilkerson-Alfonso Soriano deal, **Armando Galarraga**, lost a season due to elbow problems. The Rangers remain guardedly optimistic. The team's first-round pick in 2006, **Kasey Kiker** is a short left-hander who touched 98 MPH in high school, drawing some early Billy Wagner comparisons. It's too soon to be thinking that way, but he has the potential. A hard thrower, **Nick Masset** has both started and relieved in his minor league career. His safest bet for landing a job after going to the White Sox as part of the Brandon McCarthy deal will be in their bullpen. A year at Triple-A is more likely. **John Wasdin** continues to pitch just at or below league average, and one supposes that could go on indefinitely if allowed to.

Manager: Buck Showalter

Year	Team	W-L	Pythag +/-	Avg PC	100 +P	120 +P	QS	BQS	REL	REL w Zero R	IBB	SUBS	PH	PH Avg	PH HR	SB2	CS2	SB3	CS3	SAC Att	SAC %	POS SAC	Squeeze	Swing	In Play
2004	TEX	89-73	+2	92.4	47	3	59	7	468	289	29	39	85	.167	1	64	32	5	4	33	69.7%	22	1	128	87
2005	TEX	79-83	-2	92.6	66	2	61	6	454	250	31	19	57	.241	3	61	14	6	1	11	81.8%	9	0	125	92
2006	TEX	80-82	-6	91.2	47	0	68	7	489	307	18	30	39	.171	0	47	23	6	1	33	54.6%	15	0	109	83

Despite having some managerial experience with Class-A Columbia in the Mets system in 1993 and 1994, Ron Washington made his reputation as a coach with the A's, where he spent the last eleven seasons, ten as the third base coach. You might recall Washington's appearance in *Moneyball*—he was the infield coach with the A's who was charged with turning Scott Hatteberg into a first baseman. Eric Chavez also gives Washington credit for turning him into a Gold Glove winner. Rangers' owner Tom Hicks seems more focused on Washington's abilities as a clubhouse diplomat and straight talker. "He's a baseball guy and he's a winner," Hicks told MLB.com. "Oakland has been winning for so long with different managers . . . something has kept that clubhouse effective. I think Ron has played a big part in that." It's not surprising that Hicks would be focused on personality; Washington is to be the cool jazz antidote to Buck Showalter's marching-band stridence. Washington had an unusual career as a player. A native of New Orleans, he entered baseball through the Royals' famous Baseball Academy, and began his career as a catcher before shifting over to shortstop at 21. He never did hit much, and didn't get a cup of coffee until he was 25. It took him another four years to secure his return to the bigs with a Twins team that was rebuilding from the ground up and, having traded its starting shortstop to the Yankees without getting another in return, was desperate for help. Washington started for that team, the 1982 Twins. They lost 97 games that year, but had a historic team nonetheless, bringing together Kent Hrbek, Gary Gaetti, Tom Brunansky, and Frank Viola, the heart of what would be a very good ballclub. If Washington took anything away from his career, you'd hope it was the lesson of 1982: Let the kids play, teach them well, and someday great rewards will follow.

Toronto Blue Jays

On the first day of September in the first year of the current decade, Rogers Communications, Canada's largest telecommunications company, purchased a majority interest in the Toronto Blue Jays. This was back during the heady days of the dot-com boom, and companies such as Rogers, with their interests in hot sectors such as wireless phones and digital cable, were leading the way; Rogers's stock price had climbed more than 400 percent in the past 24 months alone. The buzzwords of the hour were "synergy" and "bundling," and while the Blue Jays reported themselves to be a money-losing franchise, Rogers expected to recoup its investment through cross-platform programming. There was talk of wired-in fans catching Jays games on their cell phones, and of families checking a box on their cable bill to purchase season tickets.

The Jays were quiet in that winter's free agent market, but the team's payroll increased by more than $30 million as established stars such as Carlos Delgado and Raul Mondesi began to earn out the expensive years of their back-loaded contracts, and younger talent such as Jose Cruz Jr. and Tony Batista hit their arbitration paydays. The Jays did not gain in the standings in 2001, and the market was crashing. Shortly after the September 11 attacks, Rogers's price was down to $6.19 per share, barely half of what it had been when it purchased the Jays. "Bundled" became "overextended" in the lexicon of Wall Street, and Rogers promised to cut costs.

One of those costs, evidently, was the Blue Jays. J. P. Ricciardi was hired in November 2001 and charged with reducing payroll, which he did by trading Billy Koch to the A's, letting Alex Gonzalez go to the Cubs, and bidding good riddance to Joey Hamilton. Chris Carpenter got hurt, the bullpen imploded, and Toronto finished at 78–84. Rogers,

> ## BLUE JAYS PROSPECTUS
>
> **2006 record:** 87–75; Second place, AL East
>
> **Pythagenport record:** 86–76
>
> **Runs scored per game:** 4.99 (7th in AL)
>
> **Runs allowed per game:** 4.65 (5th in AL)
>
> **Team EqA:** .266 (3rd in AL)
>
> **2006 Batters Age:** 29.2 (6th youngest in AL)
>
> **2006 Pitchers Age:** 28.4 (4th youngest in AL)
>
> **Ballpark:** Rogers Centre; Moderate hitter's park; Park Factor of 1.026
>
> **2006:** Burnett and Wells refused to shine during the same half of the season.
>
> **2007:** If healthy, they'll erroneously be mentioned as dark horses again in the AL East.

meanwhile, continued to slump. By the end of the 2002 baseball season, its stock price was as low as it had been since 1998.

The 2003 season went better; Roy Halladay won the Cy Young Award, Vernon Wells broke through, and the team ended the year at 87 wins. Ricciardi appeared to be fulfilling his promise as the protégé of Billy Beane. But Jays fans, who once had filled the Skydome at a rate of 4 million per season, were not impressed by this version of Moneyball, as attendance remained sluggish and ranked just 22nd in the league. The next year, 2004, was the last year of Carlos Delgado's contract and would be the key test for Ricciardi's Jays.

They failed it rather miserably. Young players such as Alex Rios and Eric Hinske did not meet expectations, the bullpen was a continued source of problems, and the Jays tallied 94 losses, their worst showing since 1980. That winter they made no serious attempt to re-sign Delgado, ultimately failing to offer him arbitration; he was lost to the Mets. They spent 2005 adrift around the .500 mark, a Moneyball-branded franchise that was neither making money nor playing compelling baseball.

Meanwhile, Rogers had become hot property again. It added more than $5 billion to its market capitalization during 2005 as its wireless service exploded and the Canadian dollar continued its recovery. The word "bundle" and its variants appeared 26 times in its annual report. It poured money into the Blue Jays franchise, authorizing a massive increase in payroll, with Ricciardi responding by investing a collective $147 million in A. J. Burnett, B. J. Ryan, and Troy Glaus. The Moneyball days were over (former Baseball Prospectus author and special assistant to Ricciardi, Keith Law, parted ways with the club in May), the team was front-page news again in 2006, and attendance recovered to 2.3 million at the re-dubbed Rogers Centre, its highest mark in nearly a decade. Then in December, the team announced that it had signed Vernon Wells to a seven-year, $126 million extension, the sixth-richest contract in baseball history. The damage from punting Delgado had been undone, and the Canadian flag would fly proudly atop the American League East standings for many years to come...

*   *   *

That should bring us more or less up to speed. This is a book about baseball; we don't mean to bore you with talk of tech bubbles and synergies and annual reports. But, in this era of corporate ownership, there's no way to talk about baseball without talking about those things, and there's no better evidence of that than the Blue Jays. The ESPN framing of this story is that J. P. Ricciardi went crazy, turning his back on his cost-cutting roots, throwing his autographed copy of *Moneyball* in the trash, and spending wildly on any pitcher with an injury history and two initials in place of a first name. The CNBC framing is that Rogers Communications was responding to the streaks and slumps in its share price, treating the Blue Jays as it would any other investment, and letting middle manager Ricciardi do the dirty work.

Which story is right? It's the economic one, stupid. As you can see from our little fairy tale, the correlation between Rogers Communications's stock price and the Blue Jays' payroll has been nearly perfect since the former took over the franchise. The general manager of a baseball team is a very important person, but, with rare exception, general managers have little say in determining team payroll. If Fred Wilpon decided to cut the Mets' payroll by $50 million, or Kevin McClatchy's Pirates decided to double theirs, Omar Minaya and Dave Littlefield would suddenly develop very different reputations as GMs.

In 2005, Rogers reported revenues of $6.36 billion dollars. The Blue Jays, whose annual revenues are a hair over $100 million, represent somewhere around two percent of this total. In other words, there is no shortage of capital that might be spent on the Blue Jays, and there never really has been. If Rogers decides to cut payroll, that should be because they think the loss in attendance and media revenues will be less than their cost savings; if it decides to raise payroll, the opposite is true.

The problem with corporate ownership of baseball teams is that corporations tend to apply old economy thinking to a new economy business. Baseball teams are managed as a line item on a profit-and-loss statement. If there is shareholder pressure to cut costs, then the ball-club's payroll will be slashed, even if this might lead to a loss in net profits. If the company is awash in cash, on the other hand, then the team's budget will be increased, even if it is unlikely to recoup its investment. Rogers has done each of these things in the six years that they've managed the Blue Jays. Were they closer to getting it right before, when the Blue Jays were operating on a $50 million payroll, or are they getting it right now?

One of the false associations that a reader of *Moneyball* might make is that a statistically-oriented approach is the exclusive domain of team on a tight payroll. Both of these things describe the A's, after all: they don't spend much on payroll, and they're oriented toward analysis in their decision making.

In fact, a team's place in the market has little to do with its mode of decision making (see table 1). There are big-budget teams such as the Red Sox that hire a kitchen cabinet of statistical advisors, and downmarket teams such as the Twins that rely almost entirely on scouting and development. Teams can switch decision-making paradigms when they switch general managers—the Dodgers and Devil Rays are two recent examples—without switching payroll brackets, or, like the Blue Jays, they can aim for a different point on the revenue curve without a paradigm shift.

What this all boils down to, however, is comparative advantage. Baseball is a tough business: Teams are applying an effectively unlimited resource (cash from rich investors or corporations) to secure an inherently limited one (the 1,215 regular season wins, eight playoff spots, and one championship available in the major leagues each season). If a team doesn't do *some* things better than most of its 29 counterparts, it's going to have trouble competing.

A highly abbreviated list of some of these potential advantages is provided in table 2. Although there is perhaps some relationship between the items placed in different bundles—teams that draft well *generally* develop players well too—there are plenty of examples of teams selecting from this menu a la carte. Kenny Williams's White Sox tend

Table 1. Who Uses What They've Got, and How?

Team Type	Analysis-Oriented	Balanced	Scouting-Oriented
Up-market	Red Sox, Dodgers (DePodesta)	Yankees	Cubs, Dodgers (Colletti)
Mid-market	Rangers, Padres	Astros, Tigers	Cardinals, Mariners
Down-market	A's, Devil Rays (Friedman)	Brewers	Twins, Devil Rays (LaMar)

Table 2. Competencies Within Approaches

Analytically-Oriented Competencies

- Statistically-based projection models
- Understanding of relationship between statistical inputs (walks, HR, etc.) and key outputs (runs, wins)
- Understanding of relationship between wins, revenues, and expenditures.
- Exploitation of market dynamics and inefficiencies

Scouting-Oriented Competencies

- Effective scouting of amateur and international talent
- Development of minor league talent
- Major league scouting
- Hiring of effective managers and coaches
- Understanding of personality-based influences on performance

to be strong in evaluating established major league talent (a skill on the scouting side) and market timing (on the analysis side), but have drafted poorly and are prone to overrate players with skills such as baserunning speed. The Rangers have pretty good Latin American pipelines and a keen sense for what statistical components win ballgames, but struggle with developing pitchers and with finding the right payroll. Some teams, such as the A's and the Braves, are competent at a great number of these things, while others such as the Pirates do very few of them well. And any of these combinations can be permuted further with a high-budget or low-budget payroll. Thus the dynamic is three- not two-dimensional.

Where do the Blue Jays' competencies lie? Still mostly on the analytical side. Ricciardi has a superb understanding of the value of on-base percentage and the relationship between offense and defense. The Blue Jays are ahead of the curve in looking at things such as ground-ball percentage to evaluate their pitchers. They've been good at procuring and exploiting cheaply-available talent, such as Reed Johnson and much of the bullpen.

The Jays have also had problems, however, particularly with the amateur draft. Specifically, they sometimes seem to be exploiting a market inefficiency that no longer exists. It once was the case that college draft picks produced much better returns than players from high schools, but were underdrafted. With teams such as the A's, Diamondbacks and Padres picking extremely heavily from the college ranks in recent years in addition to the Blue Jays, that edge has largely disappeared.

What's more, Toronto seems to be selecting the *wrong* college players. The Blue Jays have an exceptionally large number of players in their system that fall into one of two categories: hitters that draw walks but have little power or athleticism, and pitchers that throw strikes but lack stuff. Sophisticated projection systems such as PECOTA are starting to show what the scouts were telling us all along: these groups of players can *not* expect the same growth as some of their counterparts. The result is a lot of fifth starters and fourth outfielders, which is what the Blue Jay's farm system has come up with.

The Blue Jays minor league drought is beginning to show some signs of improvement. They have two very bright outfield prospects in Travis Snider (selected from the high school ranks last June) and Adam Lind, while other players such as Curtis Thigpen and Ricky Romero should become solid major league contributors. Still, their four draft classes from 2000 through 2003 were nearly complete failures, and this has produced some huge gaps in their system.

This plays into the relationship between wins, revenues, and expenditures. As we found in *Baseball Between the Numbers,* there are strong incentives for a team to position itself to the point where it is at least competing for the playoffs; the benefit from a single playoff appearance can be as much as $25 million. It is hard enough to compete for the playoffs on a $50 million payroll, but it becomes nearly impossible if the farm system is not pulling its weight.

The Jays initially did well on a limited payroll, as internally-developed players like Wells and Halladay, selected out of high school in the Gord Ash regime, began to pay dividends. But they were expecting further help from the farm system that never came. Mediocrities like Russ Adams were gobbling up playing time, while the Blue Jays were producing almost nothing on the pitching side, leaving the back end of the bullpen and the rotation in shambles. Replicating the success of the A's would not be on the agenda, particularly not in a division that included the Red Sox and the Yankees.

So the Jays were faced with a choice of lingering around the .500 mark for the remainder of the 'aughts, or upping payroll and trying to come up with a winner. This choice rested not with J. P. Ricciadi, but with Ted Rogers Sr., the magnate of Rogers Communications.

Rogers decided to increase payroll, perhaps for reasons that had more to do with the success of his other businesses than any specific goals for the Blue Jays. Still, while the payroll increase might have come about for the wrong rationale, it was probably the right decision. Attendance improved by 300,000 last season, while Rogers reported that TV ratings had increased by nearly 40 percent. Rogers is particularly well-positioned to capture any marginal increase in revenues, since they own many of the communications channels on which Blue Jays games are broadcast.

A final consideration is Canadian pride. Canada lost the Expos, and it has increasingly been losing its national sport of hockey, with no Canadian team winning the Stanley Cup since the 1992–93 Montreal Canadiens. The last thing that Canadians want to be told is that they are second-class, particularly when it comes from the intensely patriotic Ted Rogers. Their Blue Jays resigning themselves to a limited payroll and a permanent position in third place made them feel exactly that way. Conversely, the mere pretense of competing may be worth more in Toronto than it would be in other locales.

Whether Ricciardi has executed well on his increased payroll is another question, but the early returns haven't been bad. Of the team's three major acquisitions last winter, Troy Glaus and B. J. Ryan had outstanding seasons, while A. J. Burnett performed well when he was healthy. The Blue Jays clearly benefited from the decision to delve into the market a year before the Collective Bargaining Agreement expired, as contracts such as Burnett's, which seemed expensive a year ago, now look like comparative bargains.

Ryan, Burnett, Glaus, and Lyle Overbay—who was signed to a four-year, $24-million extension as we went to press—have a collective 15 years remaining on their contracts, and the impact of the Vernon Wells's extension and the Frank Thomas singing have yet to be seen. But if there's one principle that Ricciardi has carried forward from his sabermetric days, it's not to spend big money on marginal talent. All of these players are among the best at their positions when healthy, and thus the Blue Jays have the front-line talent in place to challenge the Red Sox and Yankees in years in which enough other things go their way. The Jays have been penny-foolish in places, perhaps, but they are increasingly pound-wise.

Ricciardi's ultimate test, however, will be the degree to which he is able to resurrect the farm system. The Blue Jays might be willing to spend $80 million, but they have the misfortune of competing in a division with two teams that are willing to spend twice that amount. Their fans are mollified for now, but another few years without a playoff appearance could reverse that momentum. With the constant threat that Rogers's share price could tank again, causing the company to reverse course, the Blue Jays may think they can't afford to invest in scouting and development, but, in fact, they can't afford not to.

HITTERS

Russ Adams — SS — Bats: L — Throws: R — Height: 6' 0" — Weight: 195 — Born: August 30, 1980 — Age: 26

YEAR	TEAM	LVL	AGE	PA	R	2B	3B	HR	RBI	BB	SO	SB	CS	SPEED	AVG	OBP	SLG	MLVR	EQAVG	EQOBP	EQSLG	EQA	VORP	DEFENSE	
2004	SYR	AAA	23	540	58	37	3	5	54	45	62	6	2	4.8	.288	.351	.408	.004	.265	.327	.372	.247	11.5	118-SS -14	
2004	TOR	MLB	23	78	10	2	1	4	10	5	5	1	0	4.0	.306	.359	.528	.180	.292	.354	.514	.292	7.1	17-SS -3	
2005	TOR	MLB	24	545	68	27	5	8	63	50	57	11	2	6.5	.256	.325	.383	-.082	.254	.334	.388	.258	13.3	123-SS -21	
2006	SYR	AAA	25	179	21	9	3	0	15	17	23	3	2	5.1	.311	.374	.404	.105	.290	.352	.383	.256	6.5	37-2B 1	
2006	TOR	MLB	25	280	31	14	1	3	28	22	41	1	2	4.4	.219	.282	.319	-.320	.210	.282	.306	.211	-10.1	37-2B 0	31-SS -5
2007	TOR	MLB	26	371	43	18	2	6	35	33	48	4	2	5.3	.260	.328	.382	-.106	.251	.324	.370	.250	4.7	89-SS -6	

Breakout: 16% Improve: 48% Collapse: 22% Attrition: 28%   Comparables: Mike Phillips, Wayne Causey, Jerry Lumpe, Bernie Allen

Perhaps no player better represents the failures of the SABRJays than Russ Adams. Taken with the fourteenth pick in the 2002 draft—the players selected immediately after him were Scott Kazmir, Nick Swisher, and Cole Hamels—Adams was widely regarded as a safe, low-upside pick. That's exactly what he's been. One of the things that scouts intuited before statheads is that walk rate is highly related to power: it's hard to draw free passes if pitchers have no disincentive to challenge you. Thus Adams, who doesn't hit for power, drew walks in 16.5 percent of his plate appearances in his final year at UNC, but has walked in only 8.5 percent of his PAs in his major league career. Without power or a plus walk rate, you pretty much have to hit .285 with good defense to make a viable major league regular, and Adams has done neither of those things. He's on the outs with the organization and will need some luck to get another 500 at bats in the Show.

Chip Cannon — 1B — Bats: L — Throws: R — Height: 6' 5" — Weight: 225 — Born: November 30, 1981 — Age: 25

YEAR	TEAM	LVL	AGE	PA	R	2B	3B	HR	RBI	BB	SO	SB	CS	SPEED	AVG	OBP	SLG	MLVR	EQAVG	EQOBP	EQSLG	EQA	VORP	DEFENSE
2004	AUB	A-	22	238	33	15	1	10	41	22	55	0	0	3.7	.271	.338	.495	.208	.225	.274	.394	.232	-16.7	43-1B -1
2005	LNS	A	23	191	22	9	2	11	36	20	47	0	0	2.6	.268	.351	.542	.252	.227	.286	.438	.247	-2.8	30-1B 2
2005	DUN	A+	23	129	28	4	2	14	39	16	32	0	1	4.3	.384	.465	.830	.855	.336	.403	.698	.343	22.0	15-1B 1
2005	NHP	AA	23	181	15	13	1	7	23	10	58	2	0	3.4	.247	.293	.459	.027	.246	.291	.450	.250	-0.6	29-1B 1
2006	NHP	AA	24	539	78	25	1	27	69	51	158	0	2	4.2	.248	.335	.476	.154	.242	.314	.462	.261	6.6	114-1B -7
2007	TOR	MLB	25	487	53	22	1	22	73	36	142	0	1	4.1	.239	.300	.441	-.094	.230	.296	.427	.251	-6.4	115-1B 0

Breakout: 9% Improve: 36% Collapse: 34% Attrition: 10%   Comparables: Kevin Witt, Ryan Howard, Jason Cooper, Derek Michaelis

(continued next page)

Chip Cannon *(continued)*

Scouts sometimes deride a prospect that runs poorly by saying that he's club-footed. Chip Cannon actually has two club feet, but that's how he came out of the womb. Numerous childhood operations reduced the problem to something manageable, but he can't be counted on for anything that requires speed or mobility, so he's pretty much limited to hitting for power and playing a mediocre first base. Fortunately, the power is for real, but in spite of inspiring PECOTA comparable Ryan Howard, he has an uphill battle ahead of him, something Cannon surely knows a thing or two about.

Frank Catalanotto LF **Bats: L** **Throws: R** Height: 6' 0" Weight: 195 Born: April 27, 1974 Age: 33

YEAR	TEAM	LVL	AGE	PA	R	2B	3B	HR	RBI	BB	SO	SB	CS	SPEED	AVG	OBP	SLG	MLVR	EQAVG	EQOBP	EQSLG	EQA	VORP	DEFENSE
2004	TOR	MLB	30	274	27	19	1	1	26	17	33	1	0	4.2	.293	.344	.390	-.053	.290	.344	.383	.258	1.4	36-LF -1
2005	TOR	MLB	31	475	56	29	5	8	59	37	53	0	2	4.4	.301	.367	.451	.115	.300	.375	.458	.287	19.9	85-LF 3
2006	TOR	MLB	32	499	56	36	2	7	56	52	37	1	3	4.1	.300	.376	.439	.085	.292	.378	.434	.282	17.4	86-LF 6
2007	TEX	MLB	33	463	61	26	2	7	47	43	43	2	2	4.7	.290	.361	.413	.015	.281	.358	.407	.274	8.6	110-LF -1

Breakout: 5% Improve: 31% Collapse: 31% Attrition: 15% Comparables: Barney McCosky, Russ Snyder, Rusty Greer, Ken Griffey

This longtime BP favorite has made a nice career for himself, but any corner outfielder that does not hit for power needs to do a lot of other things well to be worth putting in the lineup five times a week. While Frankie the Cat will be drawing walks long into the McCain/Obama administration, a slow thirtysomething that relies on hitting .300 has more yellow flags than a NASCAR race. The Blue Jays are waving a red one at the right time.

Robinzon Diaz C **Bats: R** **Throws: R** Height: 5' 11" Weight: 210 Born: September 19, 1983 Age: 23

YEAR	TEAM	LVL	AGE	PA	R	2B	3B	HR	RBI	BB	SO	SB	CS	SPEED	AVG	OBP	SLG	MLVR	EQAVG	EQOBP	EQSLG	EQA	VORP	DEFENSE
2004	CWV	A	20	450	62	20	2	2	42	27	31	10	4	5.2	.287	.342	.361	-.012	.254	.291	.314	.216	-13.4	81-C 1
2005	DUN	A+	21	414	47	17	6	1	65	15	28	5	2	5.1	.294	.325	.376	-.012	.255	.282	.327	.216	-12.0	84-C 0
2006	DUN	A+	22	447	59	21	1	3	44	20	37	8	1	5.1	.306	.341	.383	.047	.272	.303	.350	.230	-2.8	88-C 2
2007	TOR	MLB	23	437	40	19	2	3	38	15	37	3	1	4.9	.259	.288	.335	-.242	.250	.284	.325	.215	-9.9	104-C 4

Breakout: 34% Improve: 52% Collapse: 24% Attrition: 11% Comparables: Brayan Pena, Juan Brito, Yorvit Torrealba, Chris Walther

Diaz is a little bit of an anomaly: A catcher who hits like a middle infielder, with good contact-hitting ability, a very low strikeout rate, and above-average speed. His defense is quite good, and repeating the level can't be held against him because the organization gave priority to Curtis Thigpen. Still, the toll of the catching position is going to make it hard for him to keep legging out base hits, so there may not be much development in his bat.

Troy Glaus 3B **Bats: R** **Throws: R** Height: 6' 5" Weight: 240 Born: August 3, 1976 Age: 30

YEAR	TEAM	LVL	AGE	PA	R	2B	3B	HR	RBI	BB	SO	SB	CS	SPEED	AVG	OBP	SLG	MLVR	EQAVG	EQOBP	EQSLG	EQA	VORP	DEFENSE
2004	ANA	MLB	27	242	47	11	1	18	42	31	52	2	3	4.6	.251	.355	.575	.179	.257	.364	.592	.305	14.1	16-3B -1
2005	ARI	MLB	28	634	78	29	1	37	97	84	145	4	2	4.4	.258	.363	.522	.186	.252	.359	.521	.294	37.5	141-3B -11
2006	TOR	MLB	29	634	105	27	0	38	104	86	134	3	2	3.5	.252	.355	.513	.104	.244	.356	.505	.289	29.3	133-3B 5
2007	TOR	MLB	30	597	90	28	1	37	103	80	132	3	1	4.3	.259	.362	.540	.155	.250	.357	.523	.301	33.9	140-3B -1

Breakout: 17% Improve: 45% Collapse: 19% Attrition: 6% Comparables: Scott Rolen, Mike Schmidt, Greg Luzinski, Richie Sexson

Even after a year that lived up to any reasonable expectation, Glaus has had to endure some of the Adam Dunn stigma as a big, goofy-looking guy who doesn't hit for average. Unlike Dunn, Glaus's defense is actually acceptable; he played shortstop in college and, while he doesn't have much of that mobility left, he's good moving in on balls and can be nimble enough when his knees allow him. Glaus probably isn't helped by his soft-spoken demeanor, which is described as humility when he's hitting well and narcissism when he's not. Either way, he's still a championship-caliber ballplayer.

Aaron Hill 2B **Bats: R** **Throws: R** Height: 5' 11" Weight: 195 Born: March 21, 1982 Age: 25

YEAR	TEAM	LVL	AGE	PA	R	2B	3B	HR	RBI	BB	SO	SB	CS	SPEED	AVG	OBP	SLG	MLVR	EQAVG	EQOBP	EQSLG	EQA	VORP	DEFENSE	
2004	NHP	AA	22	564	78	26	2	11	80	63	61	3	2	4.3	.280	.369	.411	.103	.270	.346	.394	.262	23.2	135-SS -9	
2005	SYR	AAA	23	168	22	11	0	5	18	4	17	2	0	4.0	.301	.339	.468	.074	.272	.308	.430	.253	5.8	39-SS 1	
2005	TOR	MLB	23	407	49	25	3	3	40	34	41	2	1	5.3	.274	.342	.385	-.038	.273	.350	.394	.263	7.2	32-3B 2	20-2B 4
2006	TOR	MLB	24	606	70	28	3	6	50	42	66	5	2	4.8	.291	.349	.386	-.047	.285	.349	.383	.259	18.7	103-2B 17	49-SS -10
2007	TOR	MLB	25	602	75	30	3	12	64	46	65	5	2	4.9	.282	.342	.414	-.023	.272	.338	.401	.264	15.8	141-2B 3	

Breakout: 23% Improve: 53% Collapse: 15% Attrition: 11% Comparables: Gary Sutherland, Damion Easley, Buddy Bell, Cass Michaels

Toronto Blue Jays

The big difference between Aaron Hill and Russ Adams is that Hill has learned to become more of an early-count hitter, which allows him to cut down on his strikeouts and leverage his contact-hitting ability. The club thinks that his transition to second base, where his defense is quite good, will allow him to concentrate on his work at the plate, though he actually hit better at shortstop last year. PECOTA agrees that he'll add a few home runs, making him a tolerable replacement for Orlando Hudson.

Reed Johnson   **OF**   **Bats: R**   **Throws: R**   Height: 5' 10"   Weight: 180   Born: December 8, 1976   Age: 30

YEAR	TEAM	LVL	AGE	PA	R	2B	3B	HR	RBI	BB	SO	SB	CS	SPEED	AVG	OBP	SLG	MLVR	EQAVG	EQOBP	EQSLG	EQA	VORP	DEFENSE			
2004	TOR	MLB	27	582	68	25	2	10	61	28	98	6	3	4.8	.270	.320	.380	-.128	.267	.319	.379	.244	-6.7	53-LF	1	43-RF	-1
2005	TOR	MLB	28	439	55	21	6	8	58	22	82	5	6	5.9	.269	.332	.412	-.019	.270	.339	.422	.260	3.6	66-LF	4	28-RF	-1
2006	TOR	MLB	29	517	86	34	2	12	49	33	81	8	2	5.6	.317	.388	.477	.173	.311	.386	.479	.297	32.5	72-LF	7	28-RF	5
2007	TOR	MLB	30	470	59	24	3	11	53	27	77	6	3	5.3	.275	.330	.420	-.042	.266	.325	.407	.260	1.0	111-LF	2		

Breakout: 7%   Improve: 20%   Collapse: 44%   Attrition: 19%   Comparables: Jay Payton, Tsuyoshi Shinjo, Roberto Kelly, Alex Ochoa

Johnson's BABIP jumped from .321 in 2005 to .367 in 2006, which accounts for almost the all of the increase in his offensive output. Though BABIP doesn't have the same importance for hitters that it does for pitchers, it can still indicate a lucky season, and Johnson simply hit it where they weren't more often than he usually does. Johnson's a perfect fourth outfielder because he plays good defense and his contact-hitting ability lends itself well to pinch hitting, but the impression created by his 2006 campaign is unrealistic. The sooner the Jays give his job to Adam Lind, the better their pennant chances will be.

Ryan Klosterman   **SS**   **Bats: R**   **Throws: R**   Height: 5' 11"   Weight: 185   Born: May 28, 1982   Age: 25

YEAR	TEAM	LVL	AGE	PA	R	2B	3B	HR	RBI	BB	SO	SB	CS	SPEED	AVG	OBP	SLG	MLVR	EQAVG	EQOBP	EQSLG	EQA	VORP	DEFENSE			
2004	AUB	A-	22	302	50	13	4	5	32	22	55	16	2	7.3	.275	.346	.409	.112	.235	.281	.335	.221	-12.4	63-SS	-3		
2005	LNS	A	23	530	85	26	4	13	69	62	99	30	4	7.6	.241	.343	.403	.034	.205	.278	.323	.221	-17.6	125-SS	-3		
2006	DUN	A+	24	354	55	27	3	12	64	24	78	19	0	6.8	.287	.350	.502	.198	.255	.302	.442	.257	12.2	85-SS	-3		
2006	NHP	AA	24	165	22	5	0	4	16	17	37	7	3	5.7	.248	.358	.372	.060	.245	.331	.378	.253	3.6	25-SS	0	18-2B	-1
2007	TOR	MLB	25	478	54	24	3	13	52	30	109	12	4	5.9	.241	.297	.399	-.153	.233	.293	.386	.242	2.9	113-SS	0		

Breakout: 28%   Improve: 60%   Collapse: 19%   Attrition: 4%   Comparables: Josh Wilson, J. J. Furmaniak, Chris Basak, Dave Matranga

Klosterman fits into the Russ Adams mold of a polished college player who doesn't have enough juice in his bat to project for much upside. His shortstop defense is fine, though more based on solid fundamentals than plus range. He runs well enough to make it as a utility player, but he's been old for his levels and needs another good year to remain on the organizational radar. That's a lot of qualifiers, which is what you're going to get with Blue Jays prospects.

Adam Lind   **LF**   **Bats: L**   **Throws: L**   Height: 6' 2"   Weight: 195   Born: July 17, 1983   Age: 23

YEAR	TEAM	LVL	AGE	PA	R	2B	3B	HR	RBI	BB	SO	SB	CS	SPEED	AVG	OBP	SLG	MLVR	EQAVG	EQOBP	EQSLG	EQA	VORP	DEFENSE	
2004	AUB	A-	20	295	43	23	0	7	50	24	36	1	0	4.0	.308	.367	.474	.251	.260	.306	.407	.247	-9.4	58-LF	-4
2005	DUN	A+	21	554	80	42	4	12	84	49	77	2	1	4.1	.313	.375	.487	.222	.281	.336	.446	.268	9.8	119-LF	-16
2006	NHP	AA	22	378	43	24	0	19	71	25	87	2	1	3.8	.310	.357	.543	.328	.302	.344	.538	.292	25.0	78-LF	-6
2006	SYR	AAA	22	137	20	7	0	5	18	23	18	1	0	4.0	.395	.496	.596	.589	.369	.467	.577	.353	20.3	33-LF	7
2006	TOR	MLB	22	65	8	8	0	2	8	5	12	0	0	4.5	.367	.415	.600	.464	.356	.415	.610	.336	8.4		
2007	TOR	MLB	23	572	75	34	2	22	84	46	105	2	1	4.5	.287	.346	.490	.089	.277	.341	.474	.284	18.6	134-LF	-2

Breakout: 13%   Improve: 46%   Collapse: 20%   Attrition: 3%   Comparables: Jay Gibbons, Gabe Kapler, Brad Hawpe, Mark Quinn

Adam Lind is as low-risk a prospect as you'll find. He has nothing left to prove after demolishing his way through two minor league levels last season and has the sort of natural left-handed swing that scouts love. He's an instinct hitter who doesn't get cute at the plate, but he knows how to distinguish balls from strikes and his walk rate should improve. The question is whether he'll be great or merely good. His secondary traits such as speed and defense aren't particularly impressive, which may be what leads PECOTA to conclude that he'll have an early peak.

Dustin Majewski　　　　**CF**　　　　**Bats: L**　**Throws: L**　　Height: 5' 11"　Weight: 205　Born: August 16, 1981　　Age: 25

YEAR	TEAM	LVL	AGE	PA	R	2B	3B	HR	RBI	BB	SO	SB	CS	SPEED	AVG	OBP	SLG	MLVR	EQAVG	EQOBP	EQSLG	EQA	VORP	DEFENSE		
2004	KNC	A	22	521	75	23	2	12	62	48	105	20	6	6.1	.274	.339	.409	.070	.241	.291	.349	.228	-13.2	119-CF	-5	
2005	STO	A+	23	605	91	43	3	20	73	60	130	13	7	5.5	.272	.348	.477	.053	.229	.289	.368	.231	-12.5	119-CF	-11	12-RF -1
2006	DUN	A+	24	274	38	16	2	7	41	49	39	3	3	4.2	.271	.398	.457	.195	.237	.341	.397	.259	5.0	63-CF	5	
2006	NHP	AA	24	291	44	8	1	13	33	51	56	1	1	3.9	.233	.372	.441	.154	.225	.345	.426	.268	8.5	36-CF	4	14-RF -1
2007	TOR	MLB	25	496	54	23	2	12	55	47	102	4	2	4.7	.237	.312	.380	-.153	.229	.308	.368	.242	-5.7	117-CF	0	

Breakout: 23%　Improve: 49%　Collapse: 30%　Attrition: 8%　　Comparables: Jeff Salazar, Eric Valent, Brian Sellier, John-Ford Griffin

Another oddball skill set: Majewski is extremely patient at the plate, drawing 100 walks between two levels last year, can hit for a little bit of power, and combines that with plus defense in center field. The rest of the profile is lacking—he doesn't hit for contact, nor is he athletic enough to steal bases. Players with offensive profiles that don't match their positional prototypes are probably working against some inherent bias, though PECOTA is pessimistic about Majewski too.

John McDonald　　　　**SS**　　　　**Bats: R**　**Throws: R**　　Height: 5' 11"　Weight: 185　Born: September 24, 1974　Age: 32

YEAR	TEAM	LVL	AGE	PA	R	2B	3B	HR	RBI	BB	SO	SB	CS	SPEED	AVG	OBP	SLG	MLVR	EQAVG	EQOBP	EQSLG	EQA	VORP	DEFENSE	
2004	CLE	MLB	29	100	17	5	1	2	7	4	11	0	0	6.1	.204	.237	.344	-.343	.204	.245	.344	.206	-3.6	25-SS	-2
2005	DET	MLB	30	78	10	3	1	0	4	5	12	1	1	5.5	.260	.308	.329	-.160	.264	.321	.333	.231	-0.3	17-SS	3
2005	TOR	MLB	30	106	8	3	0	0	12	6	12	5	0	5.0	.290	.340	.323	-.128	.286	.350	.319	.256	2.4	25-SS	0
2006	TOR	MLB	31	286	35	7	3	3	23	16	41	7	2	6.8	.223	.271	.308	-.349	.210	.268	.292	.207	-10.4	75-SS	-5
2007	TOR	MLB	32	305	32	11	3	3	24	17	41	6	3	5.9	.247	.293	.335	-.240	.238	.289	.325	.221	-4.3	74-SS	-2

Breakout: 31%　Improve: 55%　Collapse: 35%　Attrition: 47%　　Comparables: Frank Taveras, Stan Rojek, Frank Duffy, Joe McEwing

It's generally not a good sign when your club allows a 31-year-old utility infielder to set his career high in plate appearances. McDonald doesn't profess to be anything that he's not. The Jays' staff generates a lot of ground balls, which he's particularly adept at turning into outs, but he's also about 20 runs per season below replacement level at the plate, and it's nearly impossible to make up that difference with a good glove alone. He's been re-signed to be the root canal to Royce Clayton's molar extraction.

Bengie Molina　　　　**C**　　　　**Bats: R**　**Throws: R**　　Height: 5' 11"　Weight: 225　Born: July 20, 1974　　Age: 32

YEAR	TEAM	LVL	AGE	PA	R	2B	3B	HR	RBI	BB	SO	SB	CS	SPEED	AVG	OBP	SLG	MLVR	EQAVG	EQOBP	EQSLG	EQA	VORP	DEFENSE	
2004	ANA	MLB	29	363	36	13	0	10	54	18	35	0	1	2.9	.276	.313	.404	-.083	.281	.321	.415	.254	6.0	86-C	-4
2005	ANA	MLB	30	449	45	17	0	15	69	27	41	0	2	3.0	.295	.336	.446	.072	.303	.353	.474	.281	23.6	97-C	-4
2006	TOR	MLB	31	458	44	20	1	19	57	19	47	1	1	3.1	.284	.319	.467	.008	.277	.320	.469	.266	15.5	96-C	-7
2007	SFN	MLB	32	437	45	21	1	13	59	26	44	0	1	3.4	.277	.323	.430	-.048	.274	.320	.435	.256	12.0	104-C	-5

Breakout: 8%　Improve: 32%　Collapse: 32%　Attrition: 22%　　Comparables: Del Crandall, Bob Boone, Sandy Alomar, Terry Steinbach

Molina broke up the family when he departed from Anaheim a year ago, but now that he's off on his solo career, he's singing a different tune than his brothers. While Molina hit more home runs last season than Jose and Yadier have in their entire respective careers, his defense has gone the other way. Bengie allowed 68 of 83 baserunners to steal successfully last season, something that was not helpful to a pitching staff that gives up more than its share of baserunners. He'll probably lose some power in San Francisco's home park next season, but now that he's turned 32, the Giants probably figured they could afford to gamble.

Lyle Overbay　　　　**1B**　　　　**Bats: L**　**Throws: L**　　Height: 6' 2"　Weight: 235　Born: January 28, 1977　　Age: 30

YEAR	TEAM	LVL	AGE	PA	R	2B	3B	HR	RBI	BB	SO	SB	CS	SPEED	AVG	OBP	SLG	MLVR	EQAVG	EQOBP	EQSLG	EQA	VORP	DEFENSE	
2004	MIL	MLB	27	668	83	53	1	16	87	81	128	2	1	4.2	.301	.385	.478	.222	.296	.381	.476	.295	42.6	151-1B	3
2005	MIL	MLB	28	622	80	34	1	19	72	78	98	1	0	4.2	.276	.367	.449	.123	.273	.368	.452	.284	23.5	143-1B	3
2006	TOR	MLB	29	640	82	46	1	22	92	55	96	5	3	4.1	.312	.372	.508	.185	.303	.372	.507	.296	36.3	140-1B	5
2007	TOR	MLB	30	601	83	34	2	20	84	62	97	3	1	4.4	.289	.364	.471	.096	.279	.359	.457	.287	17.7	141-1B	2

Breakout: 7%　Improve: 32%　Collapse: 25%　Attrition: 6%　　Comparables: Bruce Bochte, Norm Siebern, Dick Sisler, Eddie Robinson

Overbay is a known commodity and had a typically good year with the Jays last year, reversing a longstanding pattern of declining in the second half, and providing good defense around the first-base bag. Still, he's a reminder that problems with player development tend to compound like credit card debt. The Jays traded for Overbay because they weren't satisfied with Eric Hinske's progress. As a result, they're missing David Bush, and may need to move more young talent to fill the hole in their rotation.

Ryan Patterson   **OF**   **Bats: R**   **Throws: R**   Height: 5' 11"   Weight: 210   Born: May 2, 1983   Age: 24

YEAR	TEAM	LVL	AGE	PA	R	2B	3B	HR	RBI	BB	SO	SB	CS	SPEED	AVG	OBP	SLG	MLVR	EQAVG	EQOBP	EQSLG	EQA	VORP	DEFENSE		
2005	AUB	A-	22	306	52	23	4	13	65	21	53	5	2	5.5	.339	.386	.595	.468	.279	.308	.456	.259	18.4	36-CF	-6	15-LF 0
2006	DUN	A+	23	380	65	25	0	19	69	20	61	2	4	4.8	.288	.327	.520	.192	.251	.286	.465	.249	-2.5	62-LF	-7	15-CF -1
2006	NHP	AA	23	205	19	14	1	6	20	13	50	2	0	4.2	.257	.310	.439	.078	.258	.304	.447	.255	-0.6	40-LF	-4	
2007	TOR	MLB	24	498	55	29	2	18	69	25	101	2	2	4.7	.260	.300	.451	-.064	.250	.296	.437	.254	-0.7	118-LF	-7	

Breakout: 30%   Improve: 47%   Collapse: 26%   Attrition: 5%   Comparables: Pete Tucci, Mike Vento, Kevin West, Kevin Mench

Patterson had a three-homer day at Dunedin in June, shortly after which he was promoted. The last Dunedin Blue Jay to manage that feat was Josh Phelps, who makes a good comparable for Patterson: Both are strong guys who hit for a lot of power, and both have significant problems with their plate approach. The concern here, as with many Blue Jay prospects, is development. Although Patterson's untranslated numbers overstate the effect, he hasn't shown much growth as he's moved up the system, and he hasn't been young for his levels.

Alex Rios   **RF**   **Bats: R**   **Throws: R**   Height: 6' 5"   Weight: 195   Born: February 18, 1981   Age: 26

YEAR	TEAM	LVL	AGE	PA	R	2B	3B	HR	RBI	BB	SO	SB	CS	SPEED	AVG	OBP	SLG	MLVR	EQAVG	EQOBP	EQSLG	EQA	VORP	DEFENSE		
2004	SYR	AAA	23	195	14	10	1	3	23	9	30	2	1	3.8	.259	.292	.373	-.170	.238	.276	.341	.216	-7.3	30-CF	2	15-RF 0
2004	TOR	MLB	23	460	55	24	7	1	28	31	84	15	3	6.5	.286	.338	.383	-.075	.281	.338	.376	.255	4.1	106-RF	1	
2005	TOR	MLB	24	519	71	23	6	10	59	28	101	14	9	6.6	.262	.306	.397	-.088	.262	.316	.404	.248	-3.4	118-RF	6	
2006	TOR	MLB	25	498	68	33	6	17	82	35	89	15	6	6.5	.302	.349	.516	.149	.294	.349	.517	.290	29.0	108-RF	8	
2007	TOR	MLB	26	523	72	29	5	15	64	37	93	15	6	6.2	.279	.332	.455	.011	.269	.327	.441	.271	6.2	123-RF	4	

Breakout: 22%   Improve: 52%   Collapse: 21%   Attrition: 8%   Comparables: Larry Herndon, Al Cowens, Lee Walls, Bill Robinson

Rios started out the year on fire, finally responding to years of Blue Jay instruction trying to get him to pull the ball. By the time a staph infection forced him to the DL in late June, he had 15 home runs, almost all of which were to left or left-center. When he came back, he had reverted to the old Rios, slapping at the ball and hitting for little more than doubles power. It should be fairly easy for Mickey Brantley to show him videotape and make him understand the error of his ways, in which case he'll soundly beat his PECOTA projection. It might be in someone else's uniform, though. Rios is a very tradable commodity and, in a Pareto-optimal world would be playing center field instead of left.

Ryan Roberts   **2B**   **Bats: R**   **Throws: R**   Height: 5' 11"   Weight: 190   Born: September 19, 1980   Age: 26

YEAR	TEAM	LVL	AGE	PA	R	2B	3B	HR	RBI	BB	SO	SB	CS	SPEED	AVG	OBP	SLG	MLVR	EQAVG	EQOBP	EQSLG	EQA	VORP	DEFENSE
2004	CWV	A	23	290	38	9	0	13	39	55	50	0	0	2.5	.284	.441	.498	.317	.245	.359	.396	.266	10.3	66-2B -3
2004	DUN	A+	23	246	29	1	1	7	25	36	51	0	3	3.2	.239	.350	.356	-.015	.215	.305	.318	.222	-6.8	59-2B -4
2005	DUN	A+	24	192	33	9	0	9	35	24	27	6	1	5.0	.287	.380	.506	.230	.240	.316	.421	.257	4.2	40-2B -5
2005	NHP	AA	24	399	54	19	3	15	44	55	94	5	1	4.8	.272	.379	.479	.205	.262	.354	.447	.277	22.9	90-2B 4
2006	SYR	AAA	25	403	44	28	1	10	49	30	86	5	3	4.8	.273	.330	.439	.057	.255	.309	.422	.250	8.7	76-2B 10
2006	TOR	MLB	25	14	1	0	0	1	1	1	4	0	0	1.9	.077	.143	.308	-.677	.077	.143	.308	.158	-1.6	
2007	TOR	MLB	26	414	44	20	2	12	49	37	94	2	1	4.3	.247	.317	.403	-.107	.238	.313	.390	.250	3.5	99-2B -1

Breakout: 17%   Improve: 45%   Collapse: 28%   Attrition: 16%   Comparables: Jay Canizaro, Gabe Alvarez, Marshall McDougall, Rob Sasser

Undersized college prospect who draws walks but has been old for his levels. Undersized college prospect who draws walks but has been old for his levels. All work and no play makes Jack a dull boy. All walks and no prospects make Toronto a dull . . . Where were we? Roberts got a cup of coffee last season and would be an intriguing outside-the-box solution at shortstop, but he's played just one game at the position since being drafted out of UT Arlington in 2003.

Travis Snider   **OF**   **Bats: L**   **Throws: L**   Height: 5' 11"   Weight: 245   Born: February 2, 1988   Age: 19

YEAR	TEAM	LVL	AGE	PA	R	2B	3B	HR	RBI	BB	SO	SB	CS	SPEED	AVG	OBP	SLG	MLVR	EQAVG	EQOBP	EQSLG	EQA	VORP	DEFENSE
2006	PUL	Rk	18	226	36	12	1	11	41	30	47	6	3	5.4	.325	.412	.567	.380	.257	.317	.432	.257	0.2	43-RF 2
2007	TOR	MLB	19	493	56	27	2	14	54	34	100	6	4	5.1	.256	.308	.416	-.098	.247	.304	.403	.248	-7.2	116-RF 5

Breakout: 28%   Improve: 52%   Collapse: 17%   Attrition: 9%   Comparables: Ian Stewart, Vernon Wells, Ben Johnson, Jeff Francoeur

The Blue Jays went back to the high school ranks in last June's draft to nab Snider and were rewarded with a fine debut at Pulaski, where Snider led the Appy League in slugging percentage. It's that power, generated by his prodigious bat speed, that will be Snider's calling card, but his pitch recognition is also advanced, and his makeup is considered excellent. Snider's a big guy, which can be a favorable indicator for a power hitter, but he will need to watch his weight, especially if he wants to play outfield rather than first base. The upside here is very high.

Curtis Thigpen C **Bats: R Throws: R** Height: 5' 10" Weight: 185 Born: April 19, 1983 Age: 24

YEAR	TEAM	LVL	AGE	PA	R	2B	3B	HR	RBI	BB	SO	SB	CS	SPEED	AVG	OBP	SLG	MLVR	EQAVG	EQOBP	EQSLG	EQA	VORP	DEFENSE	
2004	AUB	A-	21	196	34	11	2	7	29	23	32	1	1	4.7	.301	.388	.518	.326	.263	.327	.434	.260	13.3	30-C	3
2005	LNS	A	22	352	41	18	2	5	35	54	34	5	0	3.7	.287	.397	.413	.166	.260	.344	.370	.255	7.4	58-C	5
2005	NHP	AA	22	157	18	8	0	4	15	9	19	0	0	2.7	.284	.340	.426	.085	.271	.323	.417	.254	4.8	30-C	7
2006	NHP	AA	23	373	49	25	5	5	36	52	61	5	1	5.5	.259	.370	.421	.144	.261	.357	.428	.274	18.8	73-C	-4
2006	SYR	AAA	23	56	3	3	0	1	9	2	9	0	1	4.1	.264	.304	.377	-.069	.226	.268	.321	.207	-2.5	14-C	-4
2007	TOR	MLB	24	461	53	26	2	10	51	42	71	3	1	4.7	.255	.328	.402	-.082	.246	.324	.390	.255	6.5	109-C	1

Breakout: 12% Improve: 39% Collapse: 30% Attrition: 14% Comparables: Justin Towle, Jon Schaeffer, Joe Lawrence, Juan Tejeda

Thigpen mostly played first base at Texas in college behind Taylor Teagarden, but since going pro has gone from being a bit of novelty to an organizational favorite. His defense is surprisingly well-regarded, and, while the home runs haven't come yet, he's hit for enough doubles to project for 10–15 homers annually in the big leagues to go with a decent OBP. He's not a future All-Star, but could be a future big league regular, and, given the lack of catching depth in Toronto, that chance could come sooner rather than later.

Vernon Wells CF **Bats: R Throws: R** Height: 6' 1" Weight: 225 Born: December 8, 1978 Age: 28

YEAR	TEAM	LVL	AGE	PA	R	2B	3B	HR	RBI	BB	SO	SB	CS	SPEED	AVG	OBP	SLG	MLVR	EQAVG	EQOBP	EQSLG	EQA	VORP	DEFENSE	
2004	TOR	MLB	25	590	82	34	2	23	67	51	83	9	2	5.3	.272	.337	.472	.032	.267	.338	.466	.275	23.2	129-CF	4
2005	TOR	MLB	26	678	78	30	3	28	97	47	86	8	3	4.9	.269	.320	.463	.031	.267	.328	.469	.271	23.8	152-CF	3
2006	TOR	MLB	27	677	91	40	5	32	106	54	90	17	4	6.0	.303	.357	.542	.200	.295	.357	.538	.299	58.9	146-CF	-5
2007	TOR	MLB	28	640	93	35	3	27	98	54	88	13	4	5.2	.286	.347	.495	.098	.276	.343	.480	.287	29.0	149-CF	-2

Breakout: 11% Improve: 45% Collapse: 17% Attrition: 5% Comparables: Carlos Lee, Kevin McReynolds, Ivan Calderon, Jermaine Dye

Being a franchise player means a lot of different things. Wells is 557 RBI behind Carlos Delgado on the Blue Jays' all-time leaderboard, and 650 base hits behind Tony Fernandez. He should have no trouble surpassing those marks by the time his $126-million contract extension has expired in 2014, which means that, in some tangible sense, he'll be the most important Blue Jay in history. But was Wells appointed to the franchise player role, or did he earn it? He has had two great seasons in his past four years along with two merely good ones; although he was injured for parts of 2004, there's no reason to reject the Occam's Razor conclusion that the truth is somewhere in between. Fortunately, he has a much larger margin of error because of his fine defense, to which our Davenport Translations aren't doing justice. Wells is from the Andruw Jones school, in that his defense is based more on great positioning and a great jump than a ton of raw speed, which could make it relatively age-proof. Still, investing $126 million in what any human being is going to be doing eight years from now is a risky proposition.

Gregg Zaun C **Bats: S Throws: R** Height: 5' 10" Weight: 190 Born: April 14, 1971 Age: 36

YEAR	TEAM	LVL	AGE	PA	R	2B	3B	HR	RBI	BB	SO	SB	CS	SPEED	AVG	OBP	SLG	MLVR	EQAVG	EQOBP	EQSLG	EQA	VORP	DEFENSE	
2004	TOR	MLB	33	392	46	24	0	6	36	47	61	0	2	3.5	.269	.367	.393	-.020	.265	.367	.390	.267	11.9	94-C	-8
2005	TOR	MLB	34	512	61	18	1	11	61	73	70	2	3	3.8	.251	.355	.373	-.038	.249	.365	.376	.264	14.4	122-C	-3
2006	TOR	MLB	35	339	39	19	0	12	40	41	42	0	2	3.0	.272	.363	.462	.070	.266	.366	.458	.283	15.3	61-C	-1
2007	TOR	MLB	36	389	48	20	1	9	47	50	55	1	1	4.0	.266	.364	.417	.008	.257	.360	.404	.275	11.7	93-C	-3

Breakout: 18% Improve: 42% Collapse: 27% Attrition: 37% Comparables: Johnny Roseboro, Rick Dempsey, Alan Ashby, Rick Cerone

Not since Danny Noonan has someone done more to prove that sometimes the caddy is better than the guy whose clubs he's carrying. The Blue Jays caught a break when Rod Barajas's reneged on their contract offer, which allowed them to keep the more valuable player in Zaun. Expect some decline in the home run output, but Zaun can handle a pitching staff, and he treats his at-bats like he's getting residuals from the Brotherhood of Backup Catchers for every pitch he sees.

PITCHERS

Jeremy Accardo

Bats: R Throws: R Height: 6' 2" Weight: 190 Born: December 8, 1981 Age: 25

YEAR	TEAM	LVL	AGE	W	L	SV	G	GS	IP	H	BB	SO	HR	GB%	BABIP	STUFF	WHIP	ERA	PERA	EQERA	EQH9	EQBB9	EQSO9	EQHR9	VORP	WXRL
2004	SJO	A+	22	1	2	27	50	0	55	57	15	43	3	—	.310	-18	1.31	4.25	4.68	5.80	9.6	3.1	4.3	1.0	-1.2	—
2005	FRE	AAA	23	2	0	3	25	0	32¹	25	10	30	0	47.7%	.287	14	1.08	1.95	3.01	2.23	7.0	2.8	6.4	0.3	12.1	—
2005	SFN	MLB	23	1	5	0	28	0	29²	26	9	16	2	41.7%	.255	-6	1.18	3.94	4.00	3.86	7.7	2.4	4.5	0.6	5.0	-0.01
2006	SFN	MLB	24	1	3	3	38	0	40¹	38	11	40	2	44.7%	.321	20	1.21	4.91	2.81	4.61	8.6	2.2	8.1	0.4	3.9	0.54
2006	TOR	MLB	24	1	1	0	27	0	28²	38	9	14	5	43.7%	.337	-21	1.64	5.96	5.06	5.46	11.2	2.7	3.9	1.2	0.5	-0.92
2007	TOR	MLB	25	3	3	3	54	1	63¹	67	21	48	8	47.0%	.299	3	1.37	4.50	4.01	4.30	8.6	2.7	6.3	1.0	9.6	0.80

Breakout: 24% Improve: 56% Collapse: 13% Attrition: 21% Comparables: Tom Walker, Brad Clontz, Donnie Moore, Mike Garman

Accardo's strikeout rate halved after he came into the American League, providing yet another data point for the huge disparity in league strength. We reviewed video of some of Accardo's appearances both with the Giants and with the Jays and detected no decline in velocity. It may have been that changing location with his mid-90s fastball was plenty enough to fool senior circuit hitters, but his lack of a secondary pitch really hurt him against their savvier American League counterparts. With that caveat in mind, he's been victimized by some high BABIPs, and is a good bet to be at least a league-average middle reliever.

Josh Banks

Bats: R Throws: R Height: 6' 3" Weight: 215 Born: July 18, 1982 Age: 24

YEAR	TEAM	LVL	AGE	W	L	SV	G	GS	IP	H	BB	SO	HR	GB%	BABIP	STUFF	WHIP	ERA	PERA	EQERA	EQH9	EQBB9	EQSO9	EQHR9	VORP	WXRL
2004	DUN	A+	21	7	1	0	11	11	60	49	8	60	4	—	.280	20	0.95	1.80	4.13	3.22	8.1	1.4	6.1	1.2	15.5	—
2004	NHP	AA	21	6	6	0	18	17	91¹	89	28	76	15	—	.278	-15	1.28	5.03	5.92	6.42	10.2	3.0	5.6	2.0	-8.0	—
2005	NHP	AA	22	8	12	0	27	27	162¹	159	11	145	18	44.7%	.307	8	1.05	3.83	4.17	5.13	9.3	0.7	5.5	1.4	8.4	—
2006	SYR	AAA	23	10	11	0	29	29	170¹	184	28	126	35	38.9%	.278	-31	1.25	5.19	6.60	6.15	10.1	1.6	5.1	2.7	-10.4	—
2007	TOR	MLB	24	6	7	0	29	17	109	129	24	65	25	40.0%	.292	-1	1.40	5.83	5.22	5.37	9.7	1.8	5.0	1.8	1.5	0.80

Breakout: 16% Improve: 56% Collapse: 7% Attrition: 2% Comparables: D. J. Houlton, Ryan Nye, Mark Brownson, Carlos Castillo

Minor league pitching prospects that post fantastic strikeout-to-walk ratios generally fall into one of two categories: Those that are merely biding time on the farm until they emerge as a superstar and those that have little in the way of raw stuff but are adept at exploiting the weaknesses of minor league hitters. One relatively reliable way to distinguish between the two is to look at home run rate. What happens when the pitcher does make a mistake or when he faces a hitter as talented as Delmon Young or Alex Gordon? On that score, Josh Banks is in a lot of trouble: You don't give up 35 home runs in Syracuse and go on to have a meaningful big league career.

A. J. Burnett

Bats: R Throws: R Height: 6' 4" Weight: 230 Born: January 3, 1977 Age: 30

YEAR	TEAM	LVL	AGE	W	L	SV	G	GS	IP	H	BB	SO	HR	GB%	BABIP	STUFF	WHIP	ERA	PERA	EQERA	EQH9	EQBB9	EQSO9	EQHR9	VORP	WXRL
2004	FLO	MLB	27	7	6	0	20	19	120	102	38	113	9	—	.291	34	1.17	3.68	3.39	3.87	7.8	2.5	7.5	0.6	25.1	3.55
2005	FLO	MLB	28	12	12	0	32	32	209	184	79	198	12	59.8%	.304	35	1.26	3.44	3.36	4.26	7.5	3.0	7.6	0.5	30.5	4.60
2006	TOR	MLB	29	10	8	0	21	21	135²	138	39	118	14	52.8%	.317	27	1.30	3.98	3.75	4.02	8.9	2.4	7.3	0.8	25.3	3.05
2007	TOR	MLB	30	11	8	0	30	28	174¹	175	58	137	17	52.0%	.301	19	1.34	3.98	3.75	3.81	8.2	2.8	6.5	0.7	35.8	4.90

Breakout: 21% Improve: 64% Collapse: 6% Attrition: 3% Comparables: Jim Beattie, Dave Goltz, Aaron Sele, Bob Rush

The first reaction that most people will have to A. J. Burnett's 2006 is: "see, he got hurt again." Still, there's a lot to like about what he accomplished. He kept his ERA under 4.00, which is no small feat pitching in Rogers Centre against AL East opponents. His control numbers were the best of his career. And his mechanics improved in the second half, as he had more time to work with pitching coach Brad Arnsberg. Considering the inflation in the system, Burnett could well provide as much value over the remaining four years of his deal as any pitcher that was on this winter's market. What, you'd rather have Gil Meche's contract?

Gustavo Chacin   Bats: L   Throws: L   Height: 5' 11"   Weight: 195   Born: December 4, 1980   Age: 26

YEAR	TEAM	LVL	AGE	W	L	SV	G	GS	IP	H	BB	SO	HR	GB%	BABIP	STUFF	WHIP	ERA	PERA	EQERA	EQH9	EQBB9	EQSO9	EQHR9	VORP	WXRL
2004	NHP	AA	23	16	2	0	25	25	141²	113	49	109	15	—	.244	-6	1.14	2.92	5.48	4.36	8.6	3.5	5.0	1.4	18.8	—
2004	TOR	MLB	23	1	1	0	2	2	14	8	3	6	0	—	.190	11	0.79	2.57	3.53	2.57	5.1	1.9	3.9	0.0	5.7	0.66
2005	TOR	MLB	24	13	9	0	34	34	203	213	70	121	20	40.2%	.304	11	1.39	3.72	4.36	3.98	9.3	3.1	5.2	0.8	39.3	4.98
2006	TOR	MLB	25	9	4	0	17	17	87¹	90	38	47	19	37.1%	.261	-20	1.47	5.05	6.34	4.72	8.9	3.7	4.5	1.7	8.7	1.47
2007	TOR	MLB	26	7	8	0	31	21	124¹	142	50	74	20	43.0%	.300	-2	1.55	5.37	5.08	5.01	9.4	3.3	5.0	1.3	7.3	1.60

Breakout: 12% Improve: 28% Collapse: 40% Attrition: 10% Comparables: Ross Baumgarten, Alex Kellner, Bob Ojeda, Trevor Wilson

Chacin's elbow wasn't right for much of the season. When injury is accompanied by poor performance, there are two ways to look at the problem: "He pitched poorly *but* he was hurt," or "he pitched poorly *and* he was hurt." In Chacin's case, we're inclined toward the latter framing. Relying on a cutter that's just average and a deceptive delivery, Chacin has little margin for error when it comes to losing anything further off his stuff. When coupled with concerns about his health and his propensity for giving up the longball, that will keep him on a short leash this year.

Chi-Hung Cheng   Bats: L   Throws: L   Height: 6' 1"   Weight: 200   Born: June 20, 1980   Age: 22

YEAR	TEAM	LVL	AGE	W	L	SV	G	GS	IP	H	BB	SO	HR	GB%	BABIP	STUFF	WHIP	ERA	PERA	EQERA	EQH9	EQBB9	EQSO9	EQHR9	VORP	WXRL
2004	PUL	Rk	24	4	1	0	14	14	60²	47	35	74	4	—	.297	1	1.35	2.82	7.21	5.34	8.9	7.6	5.2	1.5	1.6	—
2005	LNS	A	25	7	6	0	26	25	137	109	72	142	8	0.0%	.273	15	1.32	3.15	5.32	4.78	8.1	5.3	6.3	1.0	12.2	—
2006	LNS	A	26	11	5	0	28	28	143¹	129	68	154	5	50.8%	.340	12	1.38	2.70	5.29	5.11	9.4	5.8	5.7	0.9	7.4	—
2007	TOR	MLB	22	5	8	0	25	20	108	120	77	78	19	47.0%	.304	-4	1.82	6.12	6.02	5.70	9.1	5.9	6.0	1.3	-3.0	0.50

Breakout: 5% Improve: 28% Collapse: 34% Attrition: 1% Comparables: Corwin Malone, Neal Cotts, Tyler Johnson, Phil Dumatrait

Cheng is a southpaw with a nifty curveball who limited opposing lefties to a .306 slugging average in Lansing last year. He has his share of issues—his fastball isn't much, he sometimes looks lost on the mound, and he had minor shoulder surgery at the end of the season—but in an organization that's bereft of guys with plus pitches, he rates as mild sleeper. He's most likely to emerge as a good arm out of the bullpen.

Scott Downs   Bats: L   Throws: L   Height: 6' 2"   Weight: 190   Born: March 17, 1976   Age: 31

YEAR	TEAM	LVL	AGE	W	L	SV	G	GS	IP	H	BB	SO	HR	GB%	BABIP	STUFF	WHIP	ERA	PERA	EQERA	EQH9	EQBB9	EQSO9	EQHR9	VORP	WXRL
2004	EDM	AAA	28	10	6	0	22	22	135¹	143	26	67	16	—	.283	-6	1.25	3.53	4.93	4.09	8.6	1.8	3.2	1.2	23.3	—
2004	MON	MLB	28	3	6	0	12	12	63	79	23	38	9	—	.337	-6	1.62	5.14	4.87	6.30	11.1	2.9	4.8	1.1	-7.3	1.03
2005	SYR	AAA	29	2	3	0	7	7	39¹	45	3	35	5	53.7%	.339	12	1.22	4.81	3.96	4.99	10.2	0.7	5.9	1.4	2.7	—
2005	TOR	MLB	29	4	3	0	26	13	94	93	34	75	12	54.1%	.289	9	1.35	4.31	4.41	4.39	8.8	3.2	7.0	1.0	12.2	1.88
2006	TOR	MLB	30	6	2	1	59	5	77	73	30	61	9	56.5%	.287	3	1.34	4.09	4.23	4.00	8.2	3.3	6.6	0.9	14.8	0.80
2007	TOR	MLB	31	4	4	2	58	3	72²	80	27	49	9	50.0%	.308	-5	1.47	4.86	4.50	4.63	9.1	3.1	5.7	1.0	7.5	0.80

Breakout: 17% Improve: 49% Collapse: 22% Attrition: 15% Comparables: Bob Kuzava, Paul Lindblad, Joe Gibbon, Cliff Chambers

Scott Downs's modus operandi is pretty transparent: Pound everything down and in and see how long you can get away with it. Lately, he's been getting away with it more often than not, keeping lefties to a .232/.298/.379 batting line last season and limiting the damage against righties by generating ground balls. Sometimes, the scouting reports can catch up with a guy like this, otherwise there's no reason to expect a significant change in performance.

Jason Frasor   Bats: R   Throws: R   Height: 5' 10"   Weight: 170   Born: August 9, 1977   Age: 29

YEAR	TEAM	LVL	AGE	W	L	SV	G	GS	IP	H	BB	SO	HR	GB%	BABIP	STUFF	WHIP	ERA	PERA	EQERA	EQH9	EQBB9	EQSO9	EQHR9	VORP	WXRL
2004	TOR	MLB	26	4	6	17	63	0	68¹	64	36	54	4	—	.305	10	1.46	4.08	3.90	3.57	8.0	4.2	6.5	0.5	17.8	2.58
2005	TOR	MLB	27	3	5	1	67	0	74²	67	28	62	8	50.7%	.294	8	1.27	3.25	4.10	3.54	8.0	3.3	7.3	0.8	18.3	2.88
2006	TOR	MLB	28	3	2	0	51	0	50	47	17	51	8	44.4%	.291	12	1.28	4.32	4.17	3.88	8.3	2.8	8.6	1.2	10.3	0.72
2007	TOR	MLB	29	3	3	2	54	0	58²	59	26	54	7	45.0%	.307	7	1.44	4.31	4.16	4.07	8.2	3.7	7.7	0.9	10.5	0.90

Breakout: 11% Improve: 35% Collapse: 32% Attrition: 12% Comparables: Doug Bair, Curt Leskanic, Mike Marshall, Darren Holmes

Frasor is not overpowering, but he shaved enough off his walk rate last year to become another cog in the Jays' deep bullpen. The problem is that there seems to be an inverse correlation between his walk rate and his home run rate, so that when he challenges hitters more, he often pays the price. Frasor should continue to post an ERA in the low 4.00s or high 3.00s, but is not a good breakout candidate for that reason.

Roy Halladay **Bats: R Throws: R** Height: 6' 6" Weight: 225 Born: May 14, 1977 Age: 30

YEAR	TEAM	LVL	AGE	W	L	SV	G	GS	IP	H	BB	SO	HR	GB%	BABIP	STUFF	WHIP	ERA	PERA	EQERA	EQH9	EQBB9	EQSO9	EQHR9	VORP	WXRL
2004	TOR	MLB	27	8	8	0	21	21	133	140	39	95	13	—	.313	20	1.35	4.20	3.73	3.93	8.9	2.4	5.9	0.7	28.2	3.37
2005	TOR	MLB	28	12	4	0	19	19	141²	118	18	108	11	61.5%	.264	37	0.96	2.41	3.17	2.55	7.5	1.1	6.7	0.6	53.3	6.03
2006	TOR	MLB	29	16	5	0	32	32	220	208	34	132	19	59.1%	.279	23	1.10	3.19	3.54	3.20	8.1	1.3	5.1	0.7	68.0	6.45
2007	*TOR*	*MLB*	*30*	*14*	*8*	*0*	*30*	*30*	*203¹*	*210*	*40*	*130*	*18*	*57.0%*	*.295*	*16*	*1.23*	*3.58*	*3.36*	*3.48*	*8.5*	*1.6*	*5.3*	*0.7*	*50.4*	*6.60*

Breakout: 6% Improve: 31% Collapse: 19% Attrition: 0% Comparables: *Rick Reuschel, Kevin Brown, Dave Goltz, Charles Nagy*

Halladay is one of the best pitchers of his generation, but there's room for concern about his declining strikeout rate, which is now decidedly below league average. The Blue Jays' explain that this is the result of coaching—Halladay has been instructed to keep his pitch counts down and take advantage of his relatively good defense. There are good reasons to buy into the Jays' explanation: There's been little visual degradation in Halladay's stuff, he's able to pitch very deep into ballgames, and his results speak for themselves. Still, some of the same things were said about Tim Hudson before his career went belly-up.

Casey Janssen **Bats: R Throws: R** Height: 6' 4" Weight: 205 Born: September 17, 1981 Age: 25

YEAR	TEAM	LVL	AGE	W	L	SV	G	GS	IP	H	BB	SO	HR	GB%	BABIP	STUFF	WHIP	ERA	PERA	EQERA	EQH9	EQBB9	EQSO9	EQHR9	VORP	WXRL
2004	AUB	A-	22	3	1	0	10	10	50	46	10	43	2	—	.301	-9	1.12	3.60	5.05	6.00	9.6	2.8	3.8	1.1	-2.1	—
2005	LNS	A	23	4	0	0	7	7	46	27	4	38	0	59.2%	.231	24	0.67	1.37	2.98	2.58	5.8	1.0	4.4	0.2	15.2	—
2005	DUN	A+	23	6	1	0	10	10	59²	46	12	51	2	54.3%	.275	13	0.97	2.26	3.99	3.39	7.6	2.5	4.5	0.6	14.3	—
2005	NHP	AA	23	3	3	0	9	9	43	49	4	47	3	54.8%	.383	16	1.23	2.93	3.52	5.27	11.0	1.1	6.5	0.8	1.6	—
2006	SYR	AAA	24	1	5	0	9	9	42¹	47	8	32	3	55.9%	.336	5	1.31	4.92	4.07	5.23	9.8	1.7	5.2	0.8	1.8	—
2006	TOR	MLB	24	6	10	0	19	17	94	103	21	44	12	54.1%	.285	-3	1.32	5.07	4.70	5.14	9.5	1.9	3.9	1.0	6.1	1.19
2007	*TOR*	*MLB*	*25*	*8*	*8*	*0*	*34*	*22*	*137²*	*157*	*34*	*74*	*18*	*53.0%*	*.301*	*2*	*1.38*	*4.77*	*4.27*	*4.57*	*9.4*	*2.0*	*4.5*	*1.0*	*16.4*	*2.40*

Breakout: 21% Improve: 59% Collapse: 13% Attrition: 6% Comparables: *Don August, Bob Forsch, Vern Ruhle, Jim Barr*

Think Brian Lawrence. Janssen is not a stuff guy, but he can be perfectly acceptable in front of a good infield defense, avoiding walks and generating enough ground balls to be a league-average starter. The Jays were a bit quick to pull the plug on him last year, demoting him to Syracuse after a series of frustrating outings in July. Guys like Janssen that pitch to contact are always going to have their ups and downs, like buoys bobbing on Lake Ontario.

Brandon League **Bats: R Throws: R** Height: 6' 2" Weight: 195 Born: March 16, 1983 Age: 24

YEAR	TEAM	LVL	AGE	W	L	SV	G	GS	IP	H	BB	SO	HR	GB%	BABIP	STUFF	WHIP	ERA	PERA	EQERA	EQH9	EQBB9	EQSO9	EQHR9	VORP	WXRL
2004	NHP	AA	21	6	4	2	41	10	104	92	41	90	3	—	.302	14	1.28	3.38	4.00	4.71	9.1	3.8	5.8	0.4	10.0	—
2005	SYR	AAA	22	4	4	0	19	10	63	78	18	35	7	56.4%	.333	-14	1.52	5.71	5.03	6.16	10.6	2.7	3.8	1.1	-4.0	—
2005	TOR	MLB	22	1	0	0	20	0	35²	42	20	17	8	57.4%	.298	-25	1.74	6.55	6.97	6.44	10.4	5.0	4.2	2.0	-3.7	0.08
2006	SYR	AAA	23	3	2	8	31	1	54²	57	15	43	0	78.4%	.343	9	1.33	2.16	3.32	3.58	9.1	2.6	5.4	0.2	12.4	—
2006	TOR	MLB	23	1	2	1	33	0	42²	34	9	29	3	76.2%	.244	10	1.01	2.53	3.61	3.32	7.1	1.9	5.8	0.6	12.1	0.54
2007	*TOR*	*MLB*	*24*	*4*	*4*	*3*	*81*	*1*	*84*	*93*	*30*	*49*	*6*	*63.0%*	*.311*	*-4*	*1.45*	*4.42*	*4.00*	*4.33*	*9.0*	*2.9*	*4.9*	*0.5*	*12.4*	*1.10*

Breakout: 18% Improve: 53% Collapse: 13% Attrition: 11% Comparables: *Bill Swift, Beau Kemp, Terry Adams, Fred Newman*

Brandon League's groundball-to-flyball ratio last season was 5.71; by way of comparison, Brandon Webb, the most extreme groundball pitcher among qualifiers for the ERA title, was at 4.06. League throws from a low arm angle, but still delivers the ball on a sharp downward plane, which sometimes creates the illusion that the ball never gets above the hitter's knees. Instead of throwing down in the dirt when ahead in the count, which hitters are expecting from him anyway, he'll sometimes do the opposite, getting the pitch up, but employing enough sink that it gets grounded safely to the second baseman. It's a pretty unique approach, and one that PECOTA isn't terribly well equipped to deal with, but it's hard to say how well it will hold up when he gets around the league a couple more times. In any event, the Jays will be counting on League to replace Justin Speier as B. J. Ryan's primary set-up man.

Ted Lilly **Bats: L Throws: L** Height: 6' 1" Weight: 190 Born: January 4, 1976 Age: 31

YEAR	TEAM	LVL	AGE	W	L	SV	G	GS	IP	H	BB	SO	HR	GB%	BABIP	STUFF	WHIP	ERA	PERA	EQERA	EQH9	EQBB9	EQSO9	EQHR9	VORP	WXRL
2004	TOR	MLB	28	12	10	0	32	32	197¹	171	89	168	26	—	.264	18	1.32	4.06	4.42	3.67	7.4	3.6	7.0	1.0	46.8	5.65
2005	TOR	MLB	29	10	11	0	25	25	126¹	135	58	96	23	38.9%	.296	-4	1.53	5.56	5.33	5.29	9.4	4.1	6.6	1.5	4.0	1.69
2006	TOR	MLB	30	15	13	0	32	32	181²	179	81	160	28	38.6%	.292	12	1.43	4.31	4.62	4.35	8.6	3.7	7.4	1.2	26.4	3.85
2007	*CHN*	*MLB*	*31*	*10*	*10*	*0*	*30*	*28*	*174¹*	*159*	*72*	*150*	*23*	*42.0%*	*.275*	*16*	*1.32*	*4.19*	*4.26*	*4.30*	*7.9*	*3.2*	*6.9*	*1.1*	*29.7*	*4.40*

Breakout: 13% Improve: 52% Collapse: 15% Attrition: 3% Comparables: *Rudy May, Mark Langston, Gary Peters, Jack Harshman*

(continued next page)

Ted Lilly *(continued)*

People remember Ted Lilly's run-in with manager John Gibbons, which came in the third inning of the Jays' August 21 home game against the A's. Lilly was pulled over his objection after he'd given up five runs against one out and still had two men on base. What they might not remember is that the Blue Jays were actually ahead 8–5 at the time, having teed off on Dan Haren. We aren't lip-readers, and we aren't privy to the exact words that Lilly and Gibbons exchanged on the mound or in the dugout tunnel, but it doesn't take a genius to figure that Lilly may have wanted to go five innings to get a win on his resume with his free agency pending at the end of the season. Lilly and Gibbons were able to patch things up to the point at which Lilly strongly considered returning to the Blue Jays this winter before departing for Chicago. At least this sort of thing won't be a problem with the Cubs, who would never have gotten Lilly eight runs of support to begin with. All kidding aside, the Cubs got one of the better pitching deals of the winter, provided they remember Lilly is a high-pitch-count guy and often needs bullpen help by the sixth or seventh inning.

Jesse Litsch — **Bats: R Throws: R** — Height: 6′ 1″ — Weight: 205 — Born: March 9, 1985 — Age: 22

YEAR	TEAM	LVL	AGE	W	L	SV	G	GS	IP	H	BB	SO	HR	GB%	BABIP	STUFF	WHIP	ERA	PERA	EQERA	EQH9	EQBB9	EQSO9	EQHR9	VORP	WXRL
2005	PUL	Rk	20	5	1	0	11	11	65²	51	10	67	6	55.7%	.268	-7	0.93	2.74	6.34	4.48	8.8	2.3	3.9	1.9	7.8	—
2005	AUB	A-	20	0	1	0	4	3	10	11	6	7	0	54.1%	.324	-14	1.70	3.60	5.45	10.24	10.2	7.4	2.8	0.0	-5.0	—
2006	DUN	A+	21	6	6	0	16	15	89¹	94	8	81	5	58.6%	.333	18	1.14	3.54	3.77	4.48	9.7	0.9	5.3	0.9	11.2	—
2006	NHP	AA	21	3	4	0	12	12	69¹	85	13	54	6	53.3%	.367	2	1.42	5.08	4.70	6.59	11.5	1.8	4.8	1.2	-7.7	—
2007	TOR	MLB	22	7	8	0	27	21	131	155	31	70	21	51.0%	.302	3	1.42	5.31	4.74	5.03	9.7	2.0	4.4	1.3	7.5	1.70

Breakout: 22% Improve: 68% Collapse: 8% Attrition: 0% Comparables: Matt Belisle, Justin Germano, Yorman Bazardo, Mike Wood

The Blue Jays tend to teach their farmhands to pitch to contact, and Litsch has posted some outstanding control numbers on top of a reasonable groundball rate. He might be better served, though, by trying to get his slider to break out of the strike zone, because his average fastball is getting hit more and more as he moves up the ladder, leading to some very high BABIP totals. Just like plate discipline sometimes means swinging at a good pitch rather than taking a bad one, good command sometimes means trying to get a hitter to swing through a pitch outside of the strike zone, rather than grooving one down the middle.

Shaun Marcum — **Bats: R Throws: R** — Height: 6′ 0″ — Weight: 190 — Born: December 14, 1981 — Age: 25

YEAR	TEAM	LVL	AGE	W	L	SV	G	GS	IP	H	BB	SO	HR	GB%	BABIP	STUFF	WHIP	ERA	PERA	EQERA	EQH9	EQBB9	EQSO9	EQHR9	VORP	WXRL
2004	CWV	A	22	7	4	0	13	13	79	64	16	83	7	—	.271	2	1.01	3.19	4.97	4.88	8.8	2.4	5.2	1.5	6.1	—
2004	DUN	A+	22	3	2	0	12	12	69¹	74	4	72	6	—	.343	10	1.13	3.12	4.53	4.76	10.7	0.7	6.1	1.7	6.3	—
2005	NHP	AA	23	7	1	0	9	9	53¹	44	10	40	5	44.2%	.265	5	1.01	2.53	4.89	3.44	7.9	2.1	4.5	1.2	12.6	—
2005	SYR	AAA	23	6	4	0	18	18	103²	112	18	90	17	43.4%	.309	0	1.25	4.95	4.86	5.07	9.6	1.6	6.0	1.6	6.2	—
2006	SYR	AAA	24	4	0	0	18	5	52¹	48	9	60	6	49.6%	.316	14	1.09	3.45	4.13	3.83	8.7	1.6	8.0	1.6	10.2	—
2006	TOR	MLB	24	3	4	0	21	14	78¹	87	38	65	14	36.8%	.313	-1	1.60	5.06	5.21	4.57	9.6	4.0	6.9	1.3	9.4	1.69
2007	TOR	MLB	25	6	7	1	41	16	110¹	121	35	82	18	43.0%	.301	5	1.41	4.82	4.56	4.50	9.0	2.7	6.2	1.2	13.7	1.90

Breakout: 12% Improve: 42% Collapse: 21% Attrition: 10% Comparables: Bob Sebra, Albie Lopez, Gil Meche, Reggie Cleveland

Marcum has a soft-touch repertoire with command of a high-80s fastball that gets pretty good sink and three average secondary pitches that he throws perhaps more often than he should. PECOTA thinks he'll hold up pretty well, and he should certainly be better than a lot of the fourth- and fifth-starters that teams are running out there every day. As with many pitchers in this system, however, his gaudy minor league K/BB ratios cannot be taken at face value.

Dustin McGowan — **Bats: R Throws: R** — Height: 6′ 2″ — Weight: 215 — Born: March 24, 1982 — Age: 25

YEAR	TEAM	LVL	AGE	W	L	SV	G	GS	IP	H	BB	SO	HR	GB%	BABIP	STUFF	WHIP	ERA	PERA	EQERA	EQH9	EQBB9	EQSO9	EQHR9	VORP	WXRL
2004	NHP	AA	22	2	0	0	6	6	31	24	15	29	4	—	.241	9	1.26	4.06	5.83	4.85	8.5	4.9	6.4	1.5	2.5	—
2005	DUN	A+	23	0	1	0	5	5	21	21	5	20	2	49.2%	.311	-8	1.24	4.29	5.90	6.64	10.2	3.1	5.3	1.8	-2.3	—
2005	NHP	AA	23	0	2	0	6	6	35	35	10	33	6	43.3%	.309	-4	1.29	3.34	6.50	5.03	10.1	3.2	5.6	2.4	2.2	—
2005	TOR	MLB	23	1	3	0	13	7	45¹	49	17	34	7	47.6%	.309	0	1.46	6.36	5.29	6.22	9.9	3.3	6.6	1.4	-4.3	0.20
2006	SYR	AAA	24	4	5	1	23	13	84	77	39	86	7	55.2%	.303	6	1.38	4.39	4.81	5.25	8.5	4.4	7.1	1.1	3.3	—
2006	TOR	MLB	24	1	2	0	16	3	27¹	35	25	22	2	44.1%	.363	3	2.20	7.25	5.34	8.04	11.2	7.7	6.8	0.6	-8.5	-0.14
2007	TOR	MLB	25	4	6	1	45	11	85¹	96	47	62	13	47.0%	.312	-6	1.68	6.05	5.40	5.70	9.2	4.6	6.1	1.2	-2.4	0.10

Breakout: 30% Improve: 62% Collapse: 12% Attrition: 1% Comparables: Ryan Glynn, Wynn Hawkins, Dan Spillner, Tom Shearn

McGowan was the opposite of many Blue Jays prospects in that his scouting reports generally ran ahead of his stats. Now, following a truly ugly series of outings in Toronto, there's nobody that's all that high on him. McGowan does throw pretty hard, and there are days when his secondary pitches are working for him and he looks like a good pitcher, but there are literally hundreds of pitchers throughout the PECOTA database with this same basic profile, and perhaps only a couple dozen of them broke through to have significant major league careers.

Davis Romero   **Bats: L Throws: L**   Height: 5' 10"   Weight: 170   Born: March 30, 1983   Age: 24

YEAR	TEAM	LVL	AGE	W	L	SV	G	GS	IP	H	BB	SO	HR	GB%	BABIP	STUFF	WHIP	ERA	PERA	EQERA	EQH9	EQBB9	EQSO9	EQHR9	VORP	WXRL
2004	CWV	A	21	5	4	1	32	14	103¹	78	30	108	6	—	.271	5	1.05	2.53	4.46	4.06	7.9	3.2	5.5	0.9	17.1	—
2005	DUN	A+	22	9	6	1	34	18	124²	133	34	136	10	52.9%	.360	-5	1.34	3.46	4.80	5.30	10.7	3.2	6.1	1.3	4.0	—
2006	NHP	AA	23	6	5	0	12	12	73¹	57	19	70	3	54.2%	.277	21	1.04	2.95	3.76	4.23	7.6	2.6	5.7	0.6	11.0	—
2006	SYR	AAA	23	4	4	1	18	3	44²	46	7	36	3	62.2%	.319	3	1.20	3.87	4.15	5.44	9.5	1.4	5.6	0.8	0.8	—
2006	TOR	MLB	23	1	0	0	7	0	16¹	19	6	10	1	57.4%	.340	-1	1.53	3.87	4.01	3.78	10.3	3.2	5.4	0.5	4.1	0.10
2007	*TOR*	*MLB*	*24*	*5*	*6*	*1*	*49*	*11*	*95¹*	*109*	*33*	*63*	*14*	*50.0%*	*.311*	*-2*	*1.49*	*5.14*	*4.75*	*4.86*	*9.4*	*2.8*	*5.5*	*1.1*	*7.5*	*1.10*

Breakout: 10%   Improve: 37%   Collapse: 16%   Attrition: 3%   Comparables: Michael Tejera, Mike Caldwell, Ray Aguilar, Dave McNally

This is one of those names that would work better the other way around; Romero Davis sounds like the backup point guard for the Denver Nuggets. There's a fair amount to like in the *zurdo* from Panama: Romero throws strikes and changes speeds, keeps the ball down, and his performance has held up across all levels of the system. He's of small stature, and that contributes to the perception that he'll have to work out of the bullpen, but there's an argument for letting him fight for a rotation job in March.

Ricky Romero   **Bats: R Throws: L**   Height: 6' 1"   Weight: 200   Born: November 6, 1984   Age: 22

YEAR	TEAM	LVL	AGE	W	L	SV	G	GS	IP	H	BB	SO	HR	GB%	BABIP	STUFF	WHIP	ERA	PERA	EQERA	EQH9	EQBB9	EQSO9	EQHR9	VORP	WXRL
2005	DUN	A+	20	1	0	0	8	8	30²	36	7	22	2	46.7%	.330	-2	1.40	3.81	4.58	4.45	10.7	2.7	4.2	1.2	3.9	—
2006	DUN	A+	21	2	1	0	10	10	58	48	14	61	5	41.8%	.291	15	1.07	2.48	4.78	3.30	8.2	2.5	6.1	1.4	14.6	—
2006	NHP	AA	21	2	7	0	12	12	67	65	26	41	7	47.7%	.282	-16	1.36	5.10	5.93	6.62	9.0	3.8	3.8	1.5	-7.6	—
2007	*TOR*	*MLB*	*22*	*6*	*8*	*0*	*25*	*20*	*116¹*	*134*	*49*	*68*	*22*	*44.0%*	*.294*	*-2*	*1.57*	*5.88*	*5.43*	*5.47*	*9.4*	*3.5*	*4.9*	*1.5*	*0.1*	*0.90*

Breakout: 7%   Improve: 37%   Collapse: 25%   Attrition: 0%   Comparables: Andy Pratt, Randey Dorame, Chris Narveson, Noah Lowry

The Blue Jays bypassed players such as Troy Tulowitzki, Mike Pelfry, and Cameron Maybin to take Romero with the sixth pick in the 2005 draft, and there's a lot of organizational pride tied into how well he develops as a pitcher. If the Jays are expecting a number-two starter, they'll probably be disappointed, as his average fastball has resulted in predictably average strikeout rates. On the other hand, Romero is a better prospect than the Davenport Translations indicate. It looks like he lost a ton of momentum upon being promoted to New Hampshire, but, after getting hit hard in his first few starts at the level, he settled down for four quality starts in his last five outings. He's also got a bulldog demeanor on the mound and a reputation for hard work off of it, which should help him to make the most of his opportunities.

B. J. Ryan   **Bats: L Throws: L**   Height: 6' 6"   Weight: 260   Born: December 28, 1975   Age: 31

YEAR	TEAM	LVL	AGE	W	L	SV	G	GS	IP	H	BB	SO	HR	GB%	BABIP	STUFF	WHIP	ERA	PERA	EQERA	EQH9	EQBB9	EQSO9	EQHR9	VORP	WXRL
2004	BAL	MLB	28	4	6	3	76	0	87	64	35	122	4	—	.309	51	1.14	2.28	2.39	2.33	6.5	3.2	11.6	0.4	37.5	5.00
2005	BAL	MLB	29	1	4	36	69	0	70¹	54	26	100	4	45.6%	.321	49	1.14	2.43	2.46	2.62	6.8	3.2	12.4	0.5	24.9	3.37
2006	TOR	MLB	30	2	2	38	65	0	72¹	42	20	86	3	38.9%	.245	47	0.86	1.37	2.29	1.47	5.2	2.3	10.1	0.4	37.4	5.97
2007	*TOR*	*MLB*	*31*	*5*	*4*	*38*	*60*	*0*	*59*	*45*	*18*	*75*	*4*	*42.0%*	*.293*	*33*	*1.08*	*2.39*	*2.35*	*2.27*	*6.3*	*2.6*	*10.5*	*0.6*	*23.4*	*3.80*

Breakout: 24%   Improve: 27%   Collapse: 51%   Attrition: 15%   Comparables: Rich Gossage, Duane Ward, Robb Nen, Jim Kern

If Ryan isn't the best relief pitcher in baseball, he at least belongs in the conversation. He traded some strikeouts for a lower walk rate last year, but that's probably a good exchange. The Blue Jays just need to do a better job of creating high-leverage situations for him. On account of their all-or-nothing starting pitching, the Jays would sometimes go days on end without a save situation, so Ryan made 10 appearances when Toronto was ahead by at least four runs, and another 7 when they trailed by two or more. This problem may resolve itself next year, but if it doesn't, John Gibbons will need to be more creative about deploying his relief ace.

Justin Speier
Bats: R Throws: R   Height: 6' 4"   Weight: 205   Born: November 6, 1973   Age: 33

YEAR	TEAM	LVL	AGE	W	L	SV	G	GS	IP	H	BB	SO	HR	GB%	BABIP	STUFF	WHIP	ERA	PERA	EQERA	EQH9	EQBB9	EQSO9	EQHR9	VORP	WXRL
2004	TOR	MLB	30	3	8	7	62	0	69	61	25	52	8	—	.272	3	1.25	3.91	4.34	3.68	7.7	2.9	6.2	0.9	17.1	-0.17
2005	TOR	MLB	31	3	2	0	65	0	66²	48	15	56	10	33.3%	.216	11	0.95	2.56	4.18	2.65	6.5	2.0	7.4	1.2	23.0	0.96
2006	TOR	MLB	32	2	0	0	58	0	51¹	47	21	55	5	31.7%	.300	20	1.32	3.16	3.49	3.08	8.0	3.4	8.9	0.7	16.1	1.35
2007	ANA	MLB	33	3	3	3	53	0	60	59	20	50	9	35.0%	.285	4	1.31	4.04	4.12	3.91	8.7	2.8	7.1	1.2	10.6	0.90

Breakout: 5%   Improve: 27%   Collapse: 41%   Attrition: 13%   Comparables: Moe Drabowsky, Turk Wendell, Steve Reed, Keith Foulke

Speier is one of the flyballing-est fly-ball pitchers around, and, while he'd learned to pitch well at Rogers Centre, it was probably a good idea for him to get out of there before those long flies started bouncing off the hotel windows. He'd be a standard-issue righty reliever all the way, with a fastball-slider repertoire and the requisite facial scruff, if not for his forkball, which sets him ahead of the Scott Williamsons of the world. He might beat that PECOTA, but the Angels' giving him four years was a little silly, since relief pitcher is the one position that's known for its inconsistency.

Brian Tallet
Bats: L Throws: L   Height: 6' 6"   Weight: 215   Born: September 21, 1977   Age: 29

YEAR	TEAM	LVL	AGE	W	L	SV	G	GS	IP	H	BB	SO	HR	GB%	BABIP	STUFF	WHIP	ERA	PERA	EQERA	EQH9	EQBB9	EQSO9	EQHR9	VORP	WXRL
2005	BUF	AAA	27	6	5	0	22	17	97²	98	25	61	17	40.7%	.271	-24	1.26	4.05	5.95	4.76	8.8	2.5	4.2	1.8	9.2	—
2006	SYR	AAA	28	1	2	3	20	0	25	32	10	21	4	44.6%	.368	-25	1.68	5.76	6.83	6.84	11.9	4.0	5.8	2.2	-3.4	—
2006	TOR	MLB	28	3	0	0	44	1	54¹	45	31	37	5	42.1%	.272	2	1.40	3.81	4.90	3.56	7.3	4.9	5.7	0.6	13.2	1.46
2007	TOR	MLB	29	3	3	1	56	1	56	61	26	38	9	44.0%	.296	-9	1.55	4.97	4.96	4.64	9.0	3.9	5.6	1.2	5.7	0.50

Breakout: 18%   Improve: 42%   Collapse: 17%   Attrition: 33%   Comparables: Ken Patterson, Gary Wayne, Bob MacDonald, Dennis Higgins

Several of marginal Blue Jays prospects that we've talked about in this chapter might wind up with a career a lot like Brian Tallet's, who finally got his first real taste of the big leagues at age 29 after having been acquired last January for someone named Bubbie Buzachero. Unfortunately Tallet, who was once a bit of a stathead favorite before Tommy John surgery limited him to the bullpen, might find that this major league tenure is short-lived, as he lacks Scott Downs's big splits against lefties or Davis Romero's fresh-faced upside.

Ty Taubenheim
Bats: R Throws: R   Height: 6' 6"   Weight: 250   Born: November 17, 1982   Age: 24

YEAR	TEAM	LVL	AGE	W	L	SV	G	GS	IP	H	BB	SO	HR	GB%	BABIP	STUFF	WHIP	ERA	PERA	EQERA	EQH9	EQBB9	EQSO9	EQHR9	VORP	WXRL
2004	BLT	A	21	5	3	12	47	0	90¹	78	17	106	10	—	.300	-20	1.05	3.59	5.84	5.31	10.2	2.3	6.2	2.1	2.7	—
2005	BRV	A+	22	10	2	0	16	16	106	86	26	75	7	45.4%	.262	-3	1.06	2.63	5.40	4.32	8.6	2.9	4.0	1.1	14.5	—
2005	HUN	AA	22	2	6	0	11	11	64	64	24	44	7	44.2%	.305	-10	1.38	4.36	5.89	5.04	8.8	3.4	4.3	1.7	4.0	—
2006	SYR	AAA	23	2	4	0	18	14	75¹	75	18	48	9	49.4%	.287	-9	1.24	2.88	5.45	3.45	8.9	2.3	4.4	1.5	18.1	—
2006	TOR	MLB	23	1	5	0	12	7	35	40	18	26	5	47.4%	.315	-1	1.66	4.89	5.36	5.05	10.1	4.3	6.3	1.0	2.1	0.52
2007	TOR	MLB	24	6	8	0	33	20	112²	129	42	68	21	45.0%	.296	-4	1.52	5.74	5.18	5.37	9.4	3.1	5.1	1.4	1.5	0.90

Breakout: 4%   Improve: 20%   Collapse: 41%   Attrition: 1%   Comparables: Gary Glover, John Ennis, Taylor Buchholz, Allen Levrault

Taubenheim was the extra chip the Blue Jays got back in the Lyle Overbay-David Bush trade, and he responded with a competent performance as an emergency starter at intervals throughout the season. He was also the second Blue Jay to wind up on the DL with a staph infection (the other was Alex Rios), which calls into question the stereotype of Canadian cleanliness. Maybe they keep their country so clean by licking the dirt off it. If so, it's a task the Blue Jay players best leave to the natives in the future. Taubenheim doesn't have much in the way of stuff, and he's the sort of pitcher your major league team won't need if its season is going well.

Josh Towers
Bats: R Throws: R   Height: 6' 1"   Weight: 180   Born: February 26, 1977   Age: 30

YEAR	TEAM	LVL	AGE	W	L	SV	G	GS	IP	H	BB	SO	HR	GB%	BABIP	STUFF	WHIP	ERA	PERA	EQERA	EQH9	EQBB9	EQSO9	EQHR9	VORP	WXRL
2004	SYR	AAA	27	3	1	0	6	5	36	33	7	25	5	—	.267	5	1.11	2.50	4.97	3.00	8.0	2.0	4.8	1.5	10.4	—
2004	TOR	MLB	27	9	9	0	21	21	116¹	148	26	51	16	—	.322	-4	1.50	5.11	4.74	4.77	10.8	1.8	3.7	1.0	12.1	2.19
2005	TOR	MLB	28	13	12	0	33	33	208²	237	29	112	24	45.2%	.306	11	1.27	3.71	3.96	4.28	10.0	1.2	4.7	1.0	35.2	4.24
2006	SYR	AAA	29	5	5	0	15	15	101	121	11	76	12	48.3%	.345	-6	1.31	4.01	4.96	5.31	11.0	1.1	5.0	1.6	3.3	—
2006	TOR	MLB	29	2	10	0	15	12	62	93	17	35	17	40.7%	.347	-28	1.77	8.42	6.04	8.30	12.8	2.2	4.8	2.1	-18.9	-0.73
2007	TOR	MLB	30	9	9	0	34	26	149	174	29	80	24	45.0%	.298	1	1.36	4.83	4.45	4.55	9.5	1.6	4.5	1.2	17.2	2.80

Breakout: 34%   Improve: 78%   Collapse: 4%   Attrition: 0%   Comparables: Ray Washburn, Early Wynn, Dennis Martinez, Travis Driskill

Towers doesn't really have an out-pitch or much trickery up his sleeve, so it was probably a matter of time before hitters keyed into his strategy of just throwing strikes and hoping for the best. The regression in his ground-ball rate didn't help either, which may indicate that Towers is losing what little stuff he had. He might be a candidate for the number-five spot in Dunedin, but this type of profile has very little hope for redemption.

Kyle Yates

Bats: R Throws: R Height: 5′ 11″ Weight: 190 Born: January 8, 1983 Age: 24

YEAR	TEAM	LVL	AGE	W	L	SV	G	GS	IP	H	BB	SO	HR	GB%	BABIP	STUFF	WHIP	ERA	PERA	EQERA	EQH9	EQBB9	EQSO9	EQHR9	VORP	WXRL
2005	LNS	A	22	4	3	0	14	14	81¹	82	19	81	6	48.1%	.342	1	1.24	4.43	5.14	5.81	10.4	2.5	5.6	1.4	-1.8	—
2005	DUN	A+	22	7	3	0	14	14	75¹	69	19	67	4	54.8%	.304	7	1.17	1.91	4.45	4.52	8.8	2.9	5.0	0.9	8.8	—
2006	DUN	A+	23	2	0	0	4	2	14²	8	0	13	0	54.1%	.222	14	0.56	0.63	2.60	1.26	5.0	0.6	5.0	0.0	6.9	—
2006	NHP	AA	23	6	9	1	28	18	127¹	118	38	102	10	41.4%	.294	-6	1.23	3.75	5.03	5.16	9.0	3.0	4.9	1.1	6.1	—
2007	TOR	MLB	24	5	7	0	27	15	94	112	37	56	18	45.0%	.303	-6	1.58	6.02	5.49	5.61	9.8	3.3	5.0	1.5	-1.6	0.40

Breakout: 8% Improve: 27% Collapse: 32% Attrition: 1% Comparables: Josh Fogg, Vinnie Chulk, Rodrigo Lopez, Robert Brownlie

Yates is another guy who doesn't crack six-feet or 90 miles per hour on the radar gun, but his curve is considered the best in the organization, and he impressed Arizona Fall League observers with a 1.13 ERA over six starts. Although he may ultimately end up as a reliever, he has a good head on his shoulders, is liked by the organization, and could be a dark-horse candidate for rotation time this season.

Lineouts

PLAYER	TEAM	LVL	AGE	PA	R	2B	3B	HR	RBI	BB	SO	SB-CS	SPEED	AVG/OBP/SLG	MLVrEqAVG/EqOBP/EqSLG	EqA	VORP
3B R. Cosby	SYR	AAA	25	486	54	24	1	18	66	21	97	1-3	3.8	.252/.293/.428	-.028	.232/.273/.408	.230	-2.4
LF J. Griffin*	SYR	AAA	26	249	30	19	0	6	22	19	59	2-0	5.0	.225/.289/.388	-.103	.197/.258/.355	.215	-18.4
INF A. Hatch*	LNS	A	22	278	46	23	3	9	37	35	37	5-1	6.2	.314/.406/.548	.407	.280/.349/.488	.283	21.4
3B J. Hattig#	SYR	AAA	26	413	48	30	1	4	36	35	108		4.1	.276/.341/.394	.019	.257/.319/.374	.242	4.4
	TOR	MLB	26	29	2	1	0	0	3	5	8		2.1	.333/.448/.375	.172	.292/.414/.333	.278	1.8
OF W. Lydon#	SYR	AAA	25	580	80	16	12	9	46	53	120	26-10	7.5	.263/.335/.394	-.000	.250/.319/.387	.248	3.0
C J. Phillips	SYR	AAA	29	281	31	11	0	7	40	22	43	1-1	3.2	.273/.341/.402	.025	.239/.301/.361	.233	-2.5
	TOR	MLB	29	51	4	6	0	0	6	1	5	0-1	3.6	.250/.275/.375	-.227	.229/.255/.333	.203	-2.0
SS S. Santos	SYR	AAA	23	509	48	24	1	5	38	24	96	1-3	3.9	.214/.254/.299	-.276	.195/.237/.277	.183	-38.1

PLAYER	TEAM	LVL	AGE	W	L	SV	IP	H	BB	SO	HR	GB%	BABIP	STUFF	WHIP	ERA	PERA	EqERA	EqH9	EqBB9	EqSO9	EqHR9	VORP
B. Magee	AUB	A-	22	3	1	0	52¹	51	19	40	1	—	.320	-10	1.34	3.11	5.60	6.84	10.5	5.4	3.7	0.7	-6.7
D. Purcey*	NHP	AA	24	4	5	0	88	101	44	81	9	—	.351	-15	1.65	5.63	6.68	7.62	11.6	5.4	5.4	1.6	-19.1
	SYR	AAA	24	2	7	0	51²	49	38	45	7	—	.290	-5	1.70	5.45	7.18	7.82	8.9	7.1	6.2	1.8	-12.5
F. Rosario	SYR	AAA	25	0	3	1	42	29	13	50	2	—	.281	24	1.00	2.79	3.79	3.46	6.9	3.0	8.2	0.6	9.9
	TOR	MLB	25	1	2	0	23	24	16	21	4	—	.303	5	1.74	6.26	5.58	5.70	9.1	5.7	7.6	1.5	-0.1
P. Walker	TOR	MLB	37	1	1	1	30	37	13	27	5	—	.344	-3	1.67	5.40	4.49	6.39	10.5	3.5	7.5	1.2	-3.1

Organizational soldier **Rob Cosby** could not build momentum from an intriguing year in New Hampshire in 2005. He has age and an unrefined plate approach working against him. This was **John-Ford Griffin**'s last chance to make it after a 30-homer campaign in 2005 put him back on prospect lists, but he got hurt and couldn't hit when he played. He's going to that place where prospects go to die. On the bright side, that can't be too much of a downgrade from Syracuse. **Anthony Hatch** is such a deep sleeper that he's probably been approached to pitch one of those infomercial mattresses. After having had surgery on both his wrists during the off-season, he posted some gaudy, well-rounded numbers in Lansing. He's been tried everywhere in the infield, and the Blue Jays will need to settle on a position for him, but he's someone worth checking up on over the course of the season. **John Hattig** is the first player from Guam to make it to the majors; the island territory of 170,000 thus beat Brazil, Russia, and the entire continent of Africa to the big leagues. That's really the most noteworthy thing about John Hattig; his offensive development flatlined a couple of years ago. **Wayne Lydon** was signed away from the Mets as a minor league free agent. He no longer steals 70 bases a year, but he accumulated 37 extra-base hits last season, his highest total in six years. Every once and again, a player like this demonstrates some late growth and turns into Randy Winn, but Lydon's future is probably contingent on his finding a fit on a club with less outfield depth. Baseball's most famous aging hipster, **Jason Phillips**'s big season with the Mets in 2003 now looks like a one-year fluke; there hasn't been much evidence before or since that he can hit better than your usual backup catcher. He's been re-signed for next year as the primary backup to Gregg Zaun. Some scouts attribute it to a hitch in his swing, others to filling out too much and losing flexibility in his body, either way **Sergio Santos** ain't hit a lick since he was promoted to Triple-A two years ago. This is a make-or-break year for him, if he isn't already broken.

Brandon Magee's numbers don't translate well; a 22-year-old pitching in short-season A-ball should be striking out at least a batter an inning if he has major league aspirations. That said, Magee came out of a small college program (Bradley University) and may require more ramping up than someone with an SEC or Pac-10 pedigree. His ground-ball rate has been very strong, at least. The Blue Jays tried to get **David Purcey** to dial down a bit and concentrate on throwing strikes, but all that happened was that his strikeout rate went down while his command problems remained stubbornly intact. He's a huge guy who is prone to mechanical inconsistencies, so the next step may be to send him to the bullpen, let him go full throttle for short-inning bursts, and see what happens. Once considered a high-upside guy, **Francsico Rosario** has had his share of arm troubles and has gotten older without the upside coming around, but he could be salvaged as a decent arm out of the bullpen if he maintains the uptick in control he experienced with Syracuse last year. **Pete Walker**'s late-summer rotator-cuff surgery might have doomed a lesser pitcher, but this man has been to Japan and back to keep his major league career alive, so it wouldn't be surprising to see him in a Devil Ray or Nationals uniform at some point next year. On the other hand, his strikeout rate was uncharacteristically good last season, so perhaps the very last drop of juice has been squeezed out of this particular orange.

Manager: John Gibbons

Year	Team	W-L	Pythag +/-	Avg PC	100 +P	120 +P	QS	BQS	REL	REL w Zero R	IBB	SUBS	PH	PH Avg	PH HR	SB2	CS2	SB3	CS3	SAC Att	SAC %	POS SAC	Squeeze	Swing	In Play
2004	TOR	20-30	-1	90.0	16	2	19	2	130	69	11	6	41	.229	3	19	10	3	2	2	100%	2	0	52	37
2005	TOR	80-82	-9	90.6	45	1	76	8	432	278	29	59	144	.306	3	58	32	13	2	32	65.6%	20	2	157	118
2006	TOR	87-75	0	90.2	54	2	63	9	480	282	56	59	112	.240	2	53	26	12	7	25	64.0%	16	3	164	140

It's impossible to talk about John Gibbons without talking about his widely-reported confrontations with Ted Lilly and Shea Hillenbrand. Some managers have gone decades without any such incident; Gibbons had two in the span of less than a month. There are extenuating circumstances in both cases. Lilly, who generally had a good relationship with Gibbons, was operating under the pressures of a contract year and was thus loathe to be taken out of a ballgame in which he might have accumulated a win. Hillenbrand can be self-righteous and unprofessional; he was the guy who called Theo Epstein a "faggot" on drive-time radio after he was traded from Boston to Arizona. But just as surely, Gibbons's immediate reactions were unacceptable. He should not have followed Lilly down into the dugout tunnel in the middle of a ballgame, and he should not have played down to Hillenbrand's level by challenging him to a fight. The "stathead" way to look at the problem is this: It might have been coincidence, but it's improbable that Gibbons had two such incidents in one season without some fundamental lack of people skills. Besides that, what is Gibbons's upside, anyway? He certainly doesn't seem to be Earl Weaver when it comes to strategy, or Ozzie Guillen when it comes to motivating his players. But that isn't quite fair, either to Gibbons or to the politics of the situation. If ownership had fired Gibbons after either of these incidents, then they have created the perception that the inmates ran the asylum. That is no way to run a business or a baseball team. The Blue Jays' choice of Gibbons is not arbitrary. They think he is a good man who generally runs a good clubhouse, and they think that he will learn from his mistakes. Certainly, there have been notations made on his permanent record, and they could come into play relatively quickly if the Blue Jays get off to a disappointing start. But now is not the time to dismiss him.

Washington Nationals

Getting the question of who owns the team out of the way was long overdue, but it's done now, with the Lerner family, their various in-laws and hangers-on, a few thoughtfully-recruited African-American businessmen with minority stakes, and team president and part-owner Stan Kasten all tastefully celebrating their victory. Ticket prices were rolled back, and impromptu fan-friendly events hosted. Customer service—a bit on the sketchy side in the team's first 18 months of existence—was made a new priority, just in case anyone ambivalent about the club might have become less favorably so after an initial visit to RFK Stadium.

The big winners seem pretty obvious. Bud Selig's promise to his peers that the franchise would sell for $300 million proved to be true—the Lerners and their cohorts ponied up $450 million for the privilege after a spirited bidding and selection process. That price tag for this club might seem a surprise, because not every team would command that kind of dough on the open market, but the Expos came with benefits, among them a stadium deal strong-armed out of a particularly choice local market and a few specific eager-to-please local pols. They also weren't overly burdened with local history or tradition, which meant that buying the team, while not quite the same as investing in an expansion franchise, involved the same sort of freedom of action that starting from scratch would.

Not all of it was by design or particularly productive—whether you want to talk about the ransacking of the franchise by the kleptomaniac Loria clan before they lit out for Miami, or caretaker GM Omar Minaya's self-glorifying slash-and-burn approach to organizational management—the Nationals-to-be were the industry's redheaded stepchild from the moment the 29 co-conspirators

> ## NATIONALS PROSPECTUS
>
> **2006 record:** 71–91; Fifth place, NL East
>
> **Pythagenport record:** 68–94
>
> **Runs scored per game:** 4.60 (11th in NL)
>
> **Runs allowed per game:** 5.38 (16th in NL)
>
> **Team EqA:** .264 (7th in NL)
>
> **2006 Batters Age:** 29.0 (5th youngest in NL)
>
> **2006 Pitchers Age:** 29.4 (8th oldest in NL)
>
> **Ballpark:** RFK Stadium; Severe pitcher's park; Park Factor of .958
>
> **2006:** Mercifully, the season was finite, even if the fans' suffering might not have been.
>
> **2007:** Nationals' marketing department reaches out to NASCAR fans, hoping to draw them with inevitable gruesome Chris Snelling/Nick Johnson pile-up.

assumed control of the franchise. Regardless of intent or efficiency, the owners' cannibalistic feast has fed them well, as the industry as a whole has gained a better market, while winning friends and influencing people on Capitol Hill makes for a nice side benefit. Thus, another brick in the foundation of Czar Bud's historic legacy of inspired and expansive stewardship gets mortared into place. Omar Minaya wound up another winner; his audition for a better opportunity served his ambitions quite nicely.

Are the new owners going to similarly come out ahead? It would be hard for them not to, considering the sweetheart stadium deal and virtually nonexistent expectations regarding the team on the field. They'll play the 2007 RFK nostalgia card for whatever it might be worth—even the Giants did with Candlestick/3Com before moving into Pac Bell/SBC/Telecommunications MegaCorp Sportsplex.

The Lerners have exploited a friendly local media, portraying themselves as the happy, lucky new guys, so in love with their new toy that they've even gone so far as to invest $10 to 30 million in the club's new ballpark. It doesn't hurt the franchise that this money gets deducted from their revenue-sharing, or that the money they'll receive from the enhanced luxury suites, the expanded restaurant, or the ads that will run on the now more ginormous snootling Jumbotron will all go back into their own pockets. The Lerners aren't dumb, and they're not going to make the mistake the White Sox did when they moved into their new ballpark—with the park as yet unfinished, now is the time to do whatever it takes to help make the ballpark a cash cow and a fan favorite, not years after moving into the premises. Owners investing in their own product might not seem like cause for celebration, but set against the brass-knuckled approach MLB took towards achieving its goals in Washington, or even Dan Snyder's fractious, fatuous machinations with the Redskins, the Lerners get to play white knights.

The Lerners will have to enjoy that status while it lasts. They should also do whatever they can to disassociate themselves from the terms of MLB's stadium deal with the District of Columbia. That's because there will be disappointments come 2008. MLB's inflexibility and the city's often-clumsy management have produced sub-optimal solutions for parking and public transportation, and already-spoiled promises about how the surrounding neighborhood will be developed. Add in the city's innumerable financial problems and the frustrating recognition that the new stadium exists for the entertainment of suburban residents who aren't helping pay for the park with their taxes, and you have a formula for resentment and an easily-ruined relationship.

With a new team on their hands, former Atlanta Braves, Hawks, and Thrashers President Stan Kasten started making changes. Many from among the skeleton crew that had been operating the organization in MLB's name were purged, with the survivors coming from amongst General Manager Jim Bowden's Reds connection and from the ranks of scouting director Dana Brown's productive little player development cadre. Bowden's survival might have been a surprise to some, especially given his aggressive attempts to land a job in another team's front office over the preceding winter, and especially in light of Kasten's wooing Diamondbacks' Vice President of Scouting Mike Rizzo away from Arizona. Rizzo was brought aboard in late July, around the same time that the Lerners officially assumed control of the franchise, and, given his presence on a lot of insider's "future GM" lists, Bowden seemed to be on his way out.

For the time being, that doesn't seem to be the case. Part of the reason is that, although many of Bowden's deals didn't work out, several of them worked out spectacularly well. There are still some unhappy reminders, of course, such as the four-year deals given to Cristian Guzman and Brian Schneider, but adding Alfonso Soriano turned out better than anyone expected, and, on the player development front, the decision to pick up Ryan Zimmerman in the first round in 2005 has given the current administration an instant homegrown star of their own making.

Just before and immediately after the Lerners's takeover and Rizzo's arrival, a couple of masterstrokes helped shore up Bowden's position, regardless of what was happening on the diamond. First, his All-Star break robbery of his former franchise, the Reds, provided the Nats with a pair of solid big league regulars who represent significant upgrades in the middle infield and outfield. That adding Austin Kearns and Felipe Lopez only cost the club one particularly good young reliever in Bill Bray, one overworked mediocrity in Gary Majewski, a couple of bit parts, and eleven weeks of Royce Clayton was nothing short of brilliant. Beyond the merits of the talent, that Bowden was able to improve the team through barter, as he had with Soriano, quelled any immediate concerns about the team's need to compete on the free agent market. Instead of having to bid against 29 rivals during the winter, Bowden only had to convince one man of the merits of the deal. Having made the sale, Bowden not only added good offensive players at positions at which the Nats had nothing on the way, he acquired them at a point in their careers at which they're still a couple of seasons shy of free agency.

Bowden followed his Reds heist by making a deal with Rizzo's former club, dealing Livan Hernandez with a year left on his contract to the Snakes for two particularly promising arms, Matt Chico and Garrett Mock. By early August, the Nats were better off making news off the field than try to entertain fans on it, and the exchange with Arizona highlighted the need to discard the last remnants of the ephemeral achievements of the Minaya era. The swap also highlighted the prospective virtues of a Bowden-Rizzo-Brown partnership, the wheeler-dealer working hand-in-glove with a talented group of bush-beating prospect hounds to accelerate the restocking of a farm system starving for funds, talents, and attention. The subsequent deal to make gimpy veteran second baseman Jose Vidro a DH with the Mariners, thus clearing salary while adding a pair of high-risk, high-reward prospects (the oft-injured Chris Snelling and flamethrower Emiliano Fruto), marked a similarly inspired break from the past.

Getting two prospects for every veteran unlikely to be a major part of the first good Nats team sounds great in the abstract, but, unfortunately, there weren't that many desirable veterans to deal. Otherwise, this might have been a rebuilding project achieved as quickly as what's already happened twice in Florida. Instead, the Nats will be forced to try to get by, in the lineup, on the bench, but particularly on the pitching staff.

We've been critical of Bowden before for his seemingly non-discriminating tastes in journeyman hurlers, particularly when it involved discarding semi-useful guys such as Tomo Ohka and Claudio Vargas in favor of the likes of Zach Day or Ryan Drese. As badly as things melted down with last year's pitching staff, it was a bad situation made worse by losing first Brian Lawrence (who had been acquired for Vinny Castilla) in spring training, then John Patterson. Left with Livan Hernandez pitching through knee trouble and four guys who couldn't reliably get into the sixth inning (and later deleting Livan from that equation), the Nats finished third in MLB in total relief innings pitched, behind only the Royals and Cubs. For a staff working in one of the game's best pitcher's parks, that's plainly unacceptable.

Faced with this year's challenge of summoning up a pitching staff amid a pitching market gone mistral-mad in its mayhem, Bowden's rapacious taste for hurlers of almost any stripe is exactly what the Nats need right now. He's been admirably aggressive in assembling a group of Loaiza wannabes. Guys such as Tim Redding, Joel Hanrahan, Jerome Williams, Jim Magrane, and Brandon Claussen aren't just part of an ensemble cast from an indie film called *Once Were Prospects,* they're pitchers that Baseball Prospectus or Baseball America were touting not so very long ago, with performance records to match. As we go to press, there's even talk of bringing Ohka back. There's no reason to believe that Randy St. Claire can fix any of these guys—there are good reasons why they're all available, after all—but the dead air of RFK will only help, and if the Nats retread any of them successfully, they'll have gotten something for nothing (or at least very little).

On the other side of the equation, even with Lopez moving across the bag to start a new career as a second baseman, and Kearns in place in right field, this won't be a good offensive ballclub, even after making allowances for the difficulty of scoring runs in RFK. New manager Manny Acta has already indicated that he favors playing the light-hitting Nook Logan in center over Ryan Church, putting the team back on the same merry-go-round they rode trying to pick between Church and Endy Chavez, and between Brad Wilkerson and Chavez before that. Like Wilkerson, Church can be moved to a corner, but, in a lineup already handicapped by Schneider and Guzman, the decision to carry Logan will help ensure that the Nats wind up in the bottom quartet in the NL in run-scoring. It also sets up a three-way fight for the job in left between Church, Snelling, and Kory Casto, which seems incongruous given the team's overall shortage of talent.

Going into 2007, the only keeper component on the big-league roster is Zimmerman, but that's not the end of the world. Everyone else has to be seen as trade bait on the hoof, the raw material with which the front office can try to rebuild a franchise. Few general managers have Bowden's energy for trying to put together deals, and fewer still his creativity. The opportunity is here for him to break from the tail-chasing non-progress that typified his leadership in Cincinnati and even his first year in Washington. Instead, he's poised to become the leader of a front office that can follow up on the promising deals from last summer and winter, one that should be devoted to assembling the talent that can claim the title "America's Team" for itself.

HITTERS

Tony Blanco　　　　**1B**　　　　**Bats: R**　　**Throws: R**　　Height: 6' 1"　　Weight: 175　　Born: November 10, 1981　　Age: 25

YEAR	TEAM	LVL	AGE	PA	R	2B	3B	HR	RBI	BB	SO	SB	CS	SPEED	AVG	OBP	SLG	MLVR	EQAVG	EQOBP	EQSLG	EQA	VORP	DEFENSE			
2004	POT	A+	22	258	42	10	0	17	47	27	66	2	0	3.9	.306	.403	.588	.405	.282	.357	.542	.298	18.3	34-1B	-4	12-LF	-3
2004	CHT	AA	22	237	25	8	1	12	31	15	53	0	0	3.4	.245	.300	.455	.012	.224	.270	.399	.227	-11.0	45-LF	-5		
2005	NWO	AAA	23	68	7	4	0	2	14	2	13	1	0	3.2	.281	.294	.438	-.100	.277	.290	.415	.245	1.1	15-3B	1		
2005	WAS	MLB	23	65	7	3	0	1	7	2	19	1	0	6.2	.177	.215	.274	-.424	.161	.200	.242	.165	-4.9				
2006	POT	A+	24	214	24	13	0	8	32	14	61	3	0	4.4	.255	.313	.444	.071	.222	.260	.379	.221	-8.8				
2006	HAR	AA	24	34	2	1	0	2	8	2	11	0	0	2.6	.290	.353	.516	.246	.281	.343	.500	.284	2.1				
2007	WAS	MLB	25	351	30	14	1	11	42	20	107	3	1	4.2	.221	.272	.374	-.255	.226	.276	.386	.223	-8.8				

Breakout: 17%　Improve: 36%　Collapse: 43%　Attrition: 19%　　Comparables: Donnie Hood, T. R. Marcinczyk, Juan Silvestre, Josh Bonifay

Getting picked in the Rule 5 draft was probably the worst thing that could have happened to a player like Blanco. A marginal slugging prospect, he should have spent 2005 sorting out how to hit breaking stuff at Double-A rather than idling away on the Nationals bench. Instead, the Reds' failure to protect him set him back to where he was in 2004. If he'd been left alone, he might have graduated to Triple-A by now and have a more polished approach as well as some resolution as to which position he should play (it'll be first base). Instead, he's now 25, hasn't established himself at Double-A, and might never. That's a pretty steep price to pay for getting picked by your former GM.

Larry Broadway — 1B — Bats: L — Throws: L — Height: 6' 4" — Weight: 230 — Born: December 17, 1980 — Age: 26

YEAR	TEAM	LVL	AGE	PA	R	2B	3B	HR	RBI	BB	SO	SB	CS	SPEED	AVG	OBP	SLG	MLVR	EQAVG	EQOBP	EQSLG	EQA	VORP	DEFENSE	
2004	HAR	AA	23	552	69	20	0	22	71	68	102	2	3	3.2	.271	.362	.452	.109	.250	.332	.413	.258	2.3	119-1B	1
2005	HAR	AA	24	207	29	14	0	12	24	17	37	0	0	2.8	.269	.329	.538	.190	.234	.290	.463	.255	-0.3	45-1B	-5
2005	NWO	AAA	24	64	4	3	0	0	5	7	17	2	0	3.5	.193	.281	.246	-.460	.190	.266	.224	.184	-7.3	15-1B	-1
2006	NWO	AAA	25	499	60	25	2	15	78	45	116	5	1	4.5	.288	.353	.455	.156	.293	.348	.461	.278	20.0	113-1B	9
2007	WAS	MLB	26	452	47	21	1	14	58	40	105	3	1	4.0	.246	.316	.408	-.112	.251	.320	.421	.253	-0.5	107-1B	2

Breakout: 16% Improve: 41% Collapse: 36% Attrition: 15% Comparables: Kevin Burns, Damon Minor, Ray Brown, Brooks Kieschnick

Welcome to the life of a minor league slugger in the making. Broadway can crush, especially soft junk, but how many first basemen can't you say that about? He's 26 and not clear of Triple-A, so he likely has dibs on the best locker and preferred spots on the bench in New Orleans. At this stage, he's playing for injury-created gigs—which can happen, this being Nick Johnson's team—and cameos that might translate into a solid-money offer play in Japan.

Marlon Byrd — CF — Bats: R — Throws: R — Height: 6' 0" — Weight: 235 — Born: August 30, 1977 — Age: 29

YEAR	TEAM	LVL	AGE	PA	R	2B	3B	HR	RBI	BB	SO	SB	CS	SPEED	AVG	OBP	SLG	MLVR	EQAVG	EQOBP	EQSLG	EQA	VORP	DEFENSE	
2004	PHI	MLB	26	378	48	13	2	5	33	22	68	2	2	5.0	.228	.287	.321	-.239	.221	.280	.310	.210	-13.3	78-CF	-2
2005	PHI	MLB	27	15	0	0	0	0	0	1	3	0	0	3.9	.308	.400	.308	.015	.308	.400	.308	.263	0.4		
2005	WAS	MLB	27	244	20	15	2	2	26	18	47	5	1	5.0	.264	.318	.380	-.050	.272	.326	.401	.258	1.3	43-LF	5
2006	WAS	MLB	28	228	28	8	1	5	18	22	47	3	3	4.6	.223	.317	.350	-.152	.234	.326	.376	.245	-3.1	45-CF	-3
2007	WAS	MLB	29	302	35	15	2	7	35	22	53	4	2	4.9	.258	.321	.407	-.095	.263	.326	.420	.256	5.2	74-CF	-2

Breakout: 20% Improve: 41% Collapse: 23% Attrition: 33% Comparables: Wendell Magee, Tracy Jones, Gabe Kapler, Glenn Braggs

Byrd led the Nats in starts in center field last year despite being cut at the All-Star break. He's a center fielder who can't play center and a right-handed hitter who's not especially hard on lefties and doesn't hit for power or average or get on base. If Terrence Long was looking for a platoon partner, Byrd would be perfect. The Platoon of Doom, perhaps. Signed with Texas, he's presumably going to be Kenny Lofton's legs. Don't hold your breath expecting him to live up to even that limited role.

Kory Casto — 3B — Bats: L — Throws: R — Height: 6' 1" — Weight: 195 — Born: December 8, 1981 — Age: 25

YEAR	TEAM	LVL	AGE	PA	R	2B	3B	HR	RBI	BB	SO	SB	CS	SPEED	AVG	OBP	SLG	MLVR	EQAVG	EQOBP	EQSLG	EQA	VORP	DEFENSE				
2004	SAV	A	22	526	67	35	4	16	88	31	70	1	2	3.7	.286	.337	.474	.153	.253	.288	.400	.235	2.2	110-3B	-22			
2005	POT	A+	23	594	86	36	4	22	90	84	98	6	3	4.5	.290	.394	.510	.263	.255	.334	.425	.263	22.3	131-3B	15			
2006	HAR	AA	24	590	84	24	6	20	80	81	104	6	5	5.0	.272	.379	.468	.206	.261	.351	.453	.276	34.5	89-3B	6	47-LF	3	
2007	WAS	MLB	25	513	58	25	3	14	62	48	89	2	2	4.5	.255	.329	.415	-.074	.261	.333	.428	.260	10.2	121-3B	1			

Breakout: 10% Improve: 42% Collapse: 23% Attrition: 7% Comparables: Jason Grabowski, Eric Gillespie, Eric Valent, Trot Nixon

Casto had an excellent little breakthrough season in Double-A last year, marred by the fact that he didn't do much against lefties (.189/.311/.273). Of course, the flip side of that is that he mashed against right-handers (.303/.405/.541). He also slumped in the last month, but that hasn't set him back in the organization. Although he made himself into a pretty solid third baseman, he was an outfielder in college, and Zimmerman skipping ahead of him necessitated a change of position. He doesn't have a high ceiling, but opportunity is a big part of prospectdom, and Casto won't have to worry about wilting on the vine in this sparse farm system. He'll get every opportunity to win the left field job in camp.

Bernie Castro — 2B/OF — Bats: S — Throws: R — Height: 5' 10" — Weight: 165 — Born: July 14, 1979 — Age: 27

YEAR	TEAM	LVL	AGE	PA	R	2B	3B	HR	RBI	BB	SO	SB	CS	SPEED	AVG	OBP	SLG	MLVR	EQAVG	EQOBP	EQSLG	EQA	VORP	DEFENSE				
2004	POR	AAA	24	334	38	8	1	0	20	22	30	17	9	6.1	.263	.310	.295	-.287	.244	.288	.267	.206	-16.7	62-2B	-10			
2005	OTT	AAA	25	559	81	21	5	1	36	42	50	41	6	7.9	.315	.364	.382	.021	.290	.339	.349	.256	9.0	117-2B	1			
2005	BAL	MLB	25	89	14	3	1	0	7	9	10	6	2	8.1	.288	.360	.350	-.023	.291	.371	.354	.264	2.6	11-2B	-1			
2006	NWO	AAA	26	292	36	5	3	2	25	18	34	22	2	7.2	.284	.329	.347	-.049	.278	.318	.333	.243	-1.0	49-2B	-9	10-CF	-2	
2006	WAS	MLB	26	120	18	1	3	0	10	9	18	7	2	8.5	.227	.286	.291	-.285	.227	.292	.300	.221	-3.1	25-2B	-2			
2007	WAS	MLB	27	384	43	10	3	0	23	25	42	22	7	6.6	.247	.299	.294	-.294	.252	.303	.304	.220	-7.6	92-2B	-2			

Breakout: 9% Improve: 26% Collapse: 49% Attrition: 23% Comparables: Maury Wills, Elvis Pena, Alfredo Amezaga, Mike Metcalfe

What generally separates a lot of Triple-A second basemen from major league utility jobs is their inability to run and spot in the outfield. If you can do that, you get opportunities. Though not a prospect by any means, Castro can do that. Of course, it doesn't hurt that he's playing for a GM and assistant GM who once thought that keeping Wilton Guerrero around was a good idea.

Ryan Church CF Bats: L Throws: L Height: 6' 1" Weight: 220 Born: October 14, 1978 Age: 28

YEAR	TEAM	LVL	AGE	PA	R	2B	3B	HR	RBI	BB	SO	SB	CS	SPEED	AVG	OBP	SLG	MLVR	EQAVG	EQOBP	EQSLG	EQA	VORP	DEFENSE			
2004	EDM	AAA	25	408	74	29	8	17	79	51	62	0	1	5.0	.346	.430	.622	.460	.324	.400	.552	.318	40.7	75-RF	-2		
2004	MON	MLB	25	71	6	1	0	1	6	7	16	0	0	3.6	.175	.257	.238	-.426	.143	.229	.206	.166	-6.4				
2005	WAS	MLB	26	301	41	15	3	9	42	24	70	3	2	5.7	.287	.353	.466	.157	.295	.359	.496	.288	15.3	37-LF	1	15-RF	2
2006	NWO	AAA	27	206	29	6	0	7	29	25	41	5	1	4.1	.246	.345	.400	.026	.244	.329	.389	.254	2.0	27-CF	-1	13-RF	2
2006	WAS	MLB	27	230	22	17	1	10	35	26	60	6	1	4.8	.276	.366	.526	.215	.284	.373	.543	.307	18.5	41-CF	-1	11-RF	-2
2007	WAS	MLB	28	366	49	18	3	14	49	38	76	6	3	5.0	.265	.347	.465	.032	.271	.352	.480	.281	16.0	88-CF	-1		

Breakout: 15% Improve: 34% Collapse: 26% Attrition: 22% Comparables: Roger Repoz, Len Gabrielson, Ryan Klesko, Geoff Jenkins

It's usually a hallmark of badly-run ballclubs that they don't pick the easy solution to a lingering problem, preferring instead the comfort of carping. However, despite appearances, that's not what's happened here. Church has found ways to keep himself out of the team's good graces, all the more frustrating because they need him and he needs a job. A far from perfect player; he doesn't have the range to the gaps you want in a center fielder, and he can be a bit of a streak hitter. The good news is that Church gets a clean slate with a new manager in 2007, and new managers can mean new opportunities for everybody. It would be easy to suggest that Church should be in some sort of platoon with Escobar, but also lazy—Church hasn't struggled against lefties in his brief big league career (.286/.350/.462 in 105 PA).

Ian Desmond SS Bats: R Throws: R Height: 6' 2" Weight: 185 Born: September 20, 1985 Age: 21

YEAR	TEAM	LVL	AGE	PA	R	2B	3B	HR	RBI	BB	SO	SB	CS	SPEED	AVG	OBP	SLG	MLVR	EQAVG	EQOBP	EQSLG	EQA	VORP	DEFENSE	
2005	SAV	A	19	320	37	10	2	4	23	13	60	20	6	7.0	.247	.291	.334	-.135	.217	.244	.280	.194	-21.9	72-SS	-4
2005	POT	A+	19	248	37	13	3	3	15	21	53	13	6	8.4	.256	.325	.384	-.042	.229	.282	.322	.217	-6.8	54-SS	-7
2006	POT	A+	20	408	50	20	2	9	45	29	79	14	8	5.5	.244	.313	.384	-.020	.232	.280	.369	.226	-4.3	89-SS	-14
2006	HAR	AA	20	132	8	4	1	0	3	5	35	4	1	6.0	.182	.214	.231	-.394	.169	.202	.210	.163	-16.3	36-SS	-6
2007	WAS	MLB	21	465	43	21	3	7	42	23	94	11	6	5.5	.229	.274	.346	-.284	.234	.277	.357	.216	-4.8	110-SS	-6

Breakout: 52% Improve: 75% Collapse: 14% Attrition: 14% Comparables: Luis Montanez, Alejandro Ahumada, Angel Chavez, Jesus Medrano

Maybe it was a matter of trying to keep up with the Joneses—the local soccer team, D.C. United, has teen phenom Freddy Adu, so the Nats just had to have someone young and gifted that they could hype up to appeal to…well, whoever gets worked up about these things. Unfortunately, Desmond is terribly unready for the limelight. Though the Nats started him off in Double-A, they quickly recognized that was a reach. He has the physical tools to be a good shortstop, including a strong arm, but he's not fundamentally sound. His hitting is similarly sketchy—he simply lacks anything resembling pitch recognition, and, although he has some strength, he's easily carved up by pitchers who can bust him inside or get him to go fishing. Most likely, he'll flop, and it doesn't help that the team is talking about getting him back up to Double-A without a solid season at A-ball.

Alex Escobar OF Bats: R Throws: R Height: 6' 1" Weight: 190 Born: September 6, 1978 Age: 28

YEAR	TEAM	LVL	AGE	PA	R	2B	3B	HR	RBI	BB	SO	SB	CS	SPEED	AVG	OBP	SLG	MLVR	EQAVG	EQOBP	EQSLG	EQA	VORP	DEFENSE			
2004	BUF	AAA	25	69	10	5	0	4	10	4	15	0	1	3.6	.286	.348	.556	.217	.250	.304	.484	.260	1.9				
2004	CLE	MLB	25	179	20	8	2	1	12	23	42	1	1	5.9	.211	.318	.309	-.244	.212	.328	.311	.233	-6.1	21-CF	1	16-RF	2
2006	HAR	AA	27	150	21	11	0	5	26	20	23	2	2	4.4	.311	.440	.525	.388	.267	.360	.443	.277	4.2	19-RF	-3		
2006	WAS	MLB	27	99	14	3	2	4	18	8	18	2	0	5.8	.356	.394	.575	.427	.372	.408	.593	.336	13.3	20-CF	0		
2007	WAS	MLB	28	397	49	20	2	10	45	37	75	4	2	5.0	.264	.341	.421	-.038	.269	.345	.434	.267	11.1	95-CF	1		

Breakout: 7% Improve: 26% Collapse: 34% Attrition: 17% Comparables: Terrell Lowery, Cliff Brumbaugh, Chris Sheff, Darren Burton

When Escobar slugged .584 as a 19-year-old in the Sally League back in the sunny summer of 1998, so many things seemed possible; if nothing else, the young man was on the fast track. He then missed all but three games of 1999, all of 2002 and 2005, and large parts of 2004 and 2006 due to injury. Suddenly he's Roy Hobbs. Nats fans got to see little of him last year before he strained a hamstring, got an infected knee, and tore up a shoulder—all in little more than a month. What they did see gave them a peek into his tremendous ability—the man can cover ground, and has a quick swing and excellent power. If some heroes have feet of clay, Escobar's appear to be made out of porcelain. Given his obvious fragility, a role as the fourth outfielder and defensive replacement in center, allowing him to be swapped in on double-switches for Snelling or Church, would provide solid tactical value while making sure he gets playing time.

Robert Fick C/1B **Bats: L** **Throws: R** Height: 6' 1" Weight: 205 Born: March 15, 1974 Age: 33

YEAR	TEAM	LVL	AGE	PA	R	2B	3B	HR	RBI	BB	SO	SB	CS	SPEED	AVG	OBP	SLG	MLVR	EQAVG	EQOBP	EQSLG	EQA	VORP	DEFENSE			
2004	TBA	MLB	30	238	12	5	2	6	26	20	32	0	0	3.3	.201	.273	.327	-.307	.198	.277	.325	.215	-12.2	11-LF	-1		
2004	SDN	MLB	30	15	2	0	0	0	0	2	4	0	0	5.2	.167	.333	.167	-.360	.167	.333	.167	.206	-0.9				
2005	SDN	MLB	31	260	25	10	2	3	30	26	33	0	2	4.4	.265	.340	.365	-.017	.275	.351	.389	.259	2.9	22-1B	1	21-C	-4
2006	WAS	MLB	32	141	14	4	0	2	9	10	24	1	1	3.7	.266	.324	.344	-.120	.271	.333	.341	.239	-1.1	19-C	-6		
2007	WAS	MLB	33	212	22	8	1	4	22	20	32	2	1	4.4	.248	.323	.371	-.147	.253	.328	.383	.246	0.4	53-DH			

Breakout: 19% Improve: 42% Collapse: 27% Attrition: 38% Comparables: Tim McCarver, J. C. Martin, Tito Francona, Catfish Metkovich

One of the game's most time-honored grievances is that you can never find enough catchers. Like light bulbs and paper towels, you never know how much you need some things until you run out of them. That's what keeps guys such as Ken Huckaby and Alberto Castillo in clover despite their lack of obvious utility. One of the more interesting recent developments has been the increased willingness of teams to punt defense from their backup catchers and just take what they can get. It brought back Todd Greene and gave new leases on life to guys such as Eric Munson, Mike Rivera, and Fick. Fick's not a great match for Schneider, in that he's a fellow lefty hitter, but he might stick in a role that combines the responsibilities of a third catcher, backup first baseman, and pinch-hitter with power.

Jose Guillen RF **Bats: R** **Throws: R** Height: 5' 11" Weight: 195 Born: May 17, 1976 Age: 31

YEAR	TEAM	LVL	AGE	PA	R	2B	3B	HR	RBI	BB	SO	SB	CS	SPEED	AVG	OBP	SLG	MLVR	EQAVG	EQOBP	EQSLG	EQA	VORP	DEFENSE	
2004	ANA	MLB	28	620	88	28	3	27	104	37	92	5	4	4.9	.294	.352	.497	.139	.300	.359	.513	.291	25.8	126-LF	6
2005	WAS	MLB	29	611	81	32	2	24	76	31	102	1	1	4.4	.283	.338	.479	.140	.290	.342	.505	.285	26.6	132-RF	-4
2006	WAS	MLB	30	268	28	15	1	9	40	15	48	1	0	4.2	.216	.276	.398	-.168	.224	.280	.415	.240	-6.6	61-RF	5
2007	SEA	MLB	31	405	47	20	1	14	55	22	71	2	1	4.6	.262	.312	.437	-.060	.261	.314	.448	.265	2.7	97-RF	0

Breakout: 12% Improve: 35% Collapse: 31% Attrition: 21% Comparables: Rip Repulski, Jerry Martin, Sam Mele, Willie Horton

Shocking nobody, the abrasive Guillen, who has never played three full seasons with any one team, wore out his welcome in his second year in Washington. To make matters worse, he stumbled through an injury-plagued season before being shut down for keeps in July with a bum elbow. This winter he signed a one-and-one contract with the Mariners with $5 million due in 2007 and a $9-million mutual option (or a $500,000 buyout) for 2008; we all know how that's going to wind up. Guillen could potentially earn another $3 million in incentives; presumably none of them involve starting a brawl with the Angels and his old pal Mike Scioscia. There's a good chance Guillen has very little left, but, if nothing else, the AL West just got a little more interesting.

Cristian Guzman SS **Bats: S** **Throws: R** Height: 6' 0" Weight: 195 Born: March 21, 1978 Age: 29

YEAR	TEAM	LVL	AGE	PA	R	2B	3B	HR	RBI	BB	SO	SB	CS	SPEED	AVG	OBP	SLG	MLVR	EQAVG	EQOBP	EQSLG	EQA	VORP	DEFENSE	
2004	MIN	MLB	26	624	84	31	4	8	46	30	64	10	5	6.1	.274	.309	.384	-.131	.271	.310	.382	.242	8.6	142-SS	13
2005	WAS	MLB	27	492	39	19	6	4	31	25	76	7	4	5.9	.219	.260	.314	-.270	.217	.262	.317	.206	-14.9	129-SS	-13
2007	WAS	MLB	29	343	34	13	2	3	28	18	42	6	2	6.0	.243	.286	.332	-.271	.248	.290	.343	.218	-2.5	83-SS	-1

Breakout: 26% Improve: 50% Collapse: 30% Attrition: 31% Comparables: Garry Templeton, Larry Milbourne, Roger Metzger, Chico Ruiz

Hmmm, these two entries back-to-back might make for Jim Bowden's least-favorite corner of the book. Guillen and Guzman were supposed to be building blocks for the new, exciting Nationals franchise. We'll wait until you're done laughing . . . There's no way to know what the Nats will get from Guzman now that he's coming back from shoulder surgery—will he get in shape and come back with some element of the power and speed he once flashed as a Twin, or will he come back just enough to keep collecting a paycheck? The trade of Jose Vidro to the Mariners gets Guzman his job back, but that just re-starts the countdown for Nats fans hoping Bowden will make him somebody else's problem. Two years and counting, folks.

Brandon Harper C **Bats: R** **Throws: R** Height: 6' 4" Weight: 200 Born: April 29, 1976 Age: 31

YEAR	TEAM	LVL	AGE	PA	R	2B	3B	HR	RBI	BB	SO	SB	CS	SPEED	AVG	OBP	SLG	MLVR	EQAVG	EQOBP	EQSLG	EQA	VORP	DEFENSE	
2004	ERI	AA	28	188	26	12	0	9	29	16	31	2	1	3.8	.289	.372	.524	.215	.224	.282	.374	.226	-3.1	41-C	1
2004	TOL	AAA	28	68	10	0	0	3	7	6	10	0	1	4.2	.190	.294	.345	-.210	.167	.250	.267	.191	-5.4	19-C	-4
2005	TOL	AAA	29	290	33	14	1	6	34	28	36	4	0	4.4	.246	.334	.381	-.034	.232	.306	.344	.233	-3.9	69-C	-1
2006	NWO	AAA	30	143	18	10	0	2	11	15	21	3	1	5.3	.292	.394	.425	.186	.270	.350	.373	.256	3.7	31-C	-1
2006	WAS	MLB	30	47	6	3	0	2	6	4	4	0	0	3.9	.293	.362	.512	.215	.293	.362	.488	.291	3.6	12-C	-3
2007	WAS	MLB	31	323	31	15	1	6	31	24	49	3	1	4.2	.234	.304	.351	-.217	.238	.308	.362	.233	-1.3	78-C	-1

Breakout: 8% Improve: 32% Collapse: 35% Attrition: 31% Comparables: Charlie O'Brien, Darron Cox, Ernie Whitt, Tim Laker

A minor league veteran in his third organization, Harper's a hopeful story for every ham-'n-egger backstop hoping to catch a break and get some big league service time. Although credited with a solid throwing arm, Harper didn't catch any of the nine big league base thieves who ran on him last year, thus invalidating one of his calling cards. His bid for a roster spot probably depends more on Rule 5 pick Jesus Flores's spring training performance than his own.

Damian Jackson UT — Bats: R Throws: R Height: 5' 11" Weight: 185 Born: August 16, 1973 Age: 33

YEAR	TEAM	LVL	AGE	PA	R	2B	3B	HR	RBI	BB	SO	SB	CS	SPEED	AVG	OBP	SLG	MLVR	EQAVG	EQOBP	EQSLG	EQA	VORP	DEFENSE			
2004	CHN	MLB	30	18	1	0	0	1	1	3	6	0	0	3.8	.067	.222	.267	-.504	.067	.222	.267	.183	-1.6				
2004	KCA	MLB	30	16	1	2	0	0	2	1	6	0	0	4.9	.133	.188	.267	-.584	.067	.125	.133	.107	-1.6				
2005	SDN	MLB	31	313	44	9	0	5	23	30	45	15	2	5.9	.255	.335	.342	-.068	.268	.349	.366	.262	6.1	30-2B	4	21-SS	-4
2006	WAS	MLB	32	135	16	6	1	4	10	12	39	1	3	5.6	.198	.295	.371	-.179	.212	.306	.407	.238	-3.2	16-CF	-3		
2007	LAN	MLB	33	187	24	8	1	6	22	20	41	3	2	5.8	.244	.336	.419	-.063	.245	.336	.422	.259	7.5	48-CF	-2		

Breakout: 20% Improve: 42% Collapse: 38% Attrition: 35% Comparables: Eddie Pellagrini, Lonnie Smith, Reggie Sanders, Juan Samuel

Jackson played everywhere but first and catcher last year. As last-man utility types go, he's an odd sort. He has more power than most speed guys, and more speed than the power guys, all without having much power or speed. He's sort of the other choice for your in-flight meal—if you're asked "chicken or pasta," and you somehow wind up with inedible tofu that tastes vaguely like peanut butter and wallpaper glue, you've got the Damian Jackson Special. It isn't like anything else, and you have to wonder how you got so lucky. Naturally, the Dodgers couldn't resist and signed him to a minor league deal.

Nick Johnson 1B — Bats: L Throws: L Height: 6' 3" Weight: 225 Born: September 19, 1978 Age: 28

YEAR	TEAM	LVL	AGE	PA	R	2B	3B	HR	RBI	BB	SO	SB	CS	SPEED	AVG	OBP	SLG	MLVR	EQAVG	EQOBP	EQSLG	EQA	VORP	DEFENSE	
2004	MON	MLB	25	295	35	16	0	7	33	40	58	6	3	4.8	.251	.359	.398	.034	.247	.356	.386	.262	5.9	70-1B	0
2005	WAS	MLB	26	547	66	35	3	15	74	80	87	3	8	4.0	.289	.408	.479	.258	.300	.417	.508	.310	34.1	122-1B	13
2006	WAS	MLB	27	628	100	46	0	23	77	110	99	10	3	4.9	.290	.428	.520	.317	.300	.437	.540	.331	51.0	142-1B	4
2007	WAS	MLB	28	599	97	32	3	21	78	93	96	9	5	4.9	.278	.398	.481	.150	.284	.404	.497	.307	33.7	140-1B	5

Breakout: 8% Improve: 34% Collapse: 36% Attrition: 7% Comparables: John Mayberry, Leon Durham, Norm Siebern, Steve Kemp

If more people had gotten to see Nats games on television the last two years—nationally or locally—Johnson might have been get recognized as one of the most underrated players in the game. He's got a smooth swing and a Hrbek-like agility around the bag. The fifteen intentional walks he drew all came in the last four months—once Soriano was put into the leadoff spot to stay; opposing teams weren't much frightened by what a banged-up Guillen or Vidro might do to them, and they were willing to take their chances with Kearns. Although Johnson has logged nearly two full seasons of playing time, his reputation for fine-boned fragility is no thing of the past—a late-season collision with Kearns broke his leg, and he's still limping in January, creating concern that he won't be ready by Opening Day. Although the Nationals took a good risk in signing Johnson to a three-year, $16.5-million contract through 2009, his durability issues should encourage them to start entertaining offers should someone try to knock their socks off while trying to pick up a bat for a stretch run.

Austin Kearns RF — Bats: R Throws: R Height: 6' 3" Weight: 235 Born: May 20, 1980 Age: 27

YEAR	TEAM	LVL	AGE	PA	R	2B	3B	HR	RBI	BB	SO	SB	CS	SPEED	AVG	OBP	SLG	MLVR	EQAVG	EQOBP	EQSLG	EQA	VORP	DEFENSE	
2004	LOU	AAA	24	104	19	7	1	2	15	19	16	3	1	5.7	.337	.471	.518	.394	.318	.442	.482	.320	9.8	22-RF	2
2004	CIN	MLB	24	246	28	10	2	9	32	28	71	2	1	4.6	.230	.321	.419	-.009	.230	.321	.415	.254	2.5	51-RF	-1
2005	LOU	AAA	25	123	24	15	1	7	21	11	30	0	0	4.7	.342	.407	.685	.555	.321	.387	.643	.331	16.3	26-RF	-2
2005	CIN	MLB	25	448	62	26	1	18	67	48	107	0	0	4.4	.240	.333	.452	.042	.238	.330	.456	.270	9.1	101-RF	8
2006	CIN	MLB	26	368	53	21	1	16	50	35	85	7	1	4.8	.274	.351	.492	.111	.269	.348	.485	.284	15.7	84-RF	8
2006	WAS	MLB	26	261	33	12	1	8	36	41	50	2	3	4.6	.250	.381	.429	.088	.259	.391	.453	.290	7.8	55-RF	0
2007	WAS	MLB	27	591	83	31	3	23	82	69	129	7	3	4.9	.265	.361	.473	.065	.270	.365	.488	.289	23.2	138-RF	2

Breakout: 25% Improve: 54% Collapse: 14% Attrition: 8% Comparables: Bob Allison, Dale Murphy, Ivan Calderon, Dwight Evans

It took five years, but Kearns finally showed what he could do as an everyday player last year, and it was solid stuff, even despite his post-deal slump. The comparisons to Dewey Evans, above, seems more apt than Dale Murphy—Kearns isn't on the cusp of winning an MVP award, and, however much some might wish he was a center fielder, he really isn't. Like Dewey, he's relatively athletic for a big guy, and, if his arm is somewhat less legendary, it's still effective. The question remains: Is he worth signing to a multi-year extension before he reaches free agency, or does he want to get out of Dodge? The Nats need to get the answer before the July trade deadline and act accordingly.

Nook Logan CF **Bats: S Throws: R** Height: 6′ 3″ Weight: 180 Born: November 28, 1979 Age: 27

YEAR	TEAM	LVL	AGE	PA	R	2B	3B	HR	RBI	BB	SO	SB	CS	SPEED	AVG	OBP	SLG	MLVR	EQAVG	EQOBP	EQSLG	EQA	VORP	DEFENSE		
2004	TOL	AAA	24	462	67	14	9	2	27	23	95	38	11	9.2	.263	.303	.352	-.136	.259	.299	.340	.235	-10.1	102-CF	-3	
2004	DET	MLB	24	152	12	5	2	0	10	13	24	8	2	6.2	.278	.340	.346	-.195	.280	.347	.348	.257	-1.2	46-CF	-1	
2005	DET	MLB	25	356	47	12	5	1	17	21	52	23	6	8.1	.258	.305	.335	-.181	.269	.327	.351	.248	-2.2	99-CF	8	
2006	ERI	AA	26	88	14	2	1	0	2	11	23	9	3	7.5	.247	.341	.299	-.068	.228	.307	.278	.224	-4.3	17-CF	-2	
2006	TOL	AAA	26	76	9	2	1	0	4	9	18	3	2	7.5	.185	.284	.246	-.250	.197	.284	.258	.198	-5.3	19-CF	-1	
2006	WAS	MLB	26	99	13	3	1	1	8	6	20	2	1	6.4	.300	.337	.389	-.013	.311	.347	.400	.263	2.5	25-CF	-6	
2007	WAS	MLB	27	346	41	13	4	2	23	25	68	19	5	7.6	.246	.304	.334	-.233	.251	.308	.345	.234	-3.7	83-CF	0	

Breakout: 16% Improve: 39% Collapse: 25% Attrition: 21% Comparables: Greg Martinez, Gene Kingsale, Jesus Tavarez, Andres Torres

If the Nats wischcast Endy Chavez's 2006 season into an everyday job for Nook in 2007, they'll wind up with the Endy model they've already discarded—the one that spends lots of time in the dugout during offensive innings, instead of on base. The fascination with finding the next fifth outfielder who might grow up to be Tom Goodwin has to come to an end—some quests have unworthy objects.

Felipe Lopez 2B **Bats: S Throws: R** Height: 6′ 1″ Weight: 185 Born: May 12, 1980 Age: 27

YEAR	TEAM	LVL	AGE	PA	R	2B	3B	HR	RBI	BB	SO	SB	CS	SPEED	AVG	OBP	SLG	MLVR	EQAVG	EQOBP	EQSLG	EQA	VORP	DEFENSE			
2004	LOU	AAA	24	326	50	11	3	9	43	25	71	2	2	5.3	.273	.329	.423	-.022	.251	.307	.376	.240	3.3	62-SS	-8		
2004	CIN	MLB	24	295	35	18	2	7	31	25	81	1	1	5.4	.242	.314	.405	-.049	.242	.313	.404	.247	4.3	44-SS	1	23-3B	-2
2005	CIN	MLB	25	648	97	34	5	23	85	57	111	15	7	6.4	.291	.352	.486	.159	.291	.354	.497	.286	45.8	134-SS	-14		
2006	CIN	MLB	26	394	55	14	1	9	30	47	66	23	6	6.4	.268	.356	.394	-.018	.263	.355	.383	.266	14.9	82-SS	-5		
2006	WAS	MLB	26	320	43	13	2	2	22	34	60	21	6	6.9	.281	.362	.365	-.007	.293	.377	.377	.273	12.9	68-SS	-11		
2007	WAS	MLB	27	656	92	32	5	14	64	65	116	26	10	6.4	.269	.345	.419	-.029	.275	.350	.432	.271	30.7	153-SS	-6		

Breakout: 14% Improve: 44% Collapse: 20% Attrition: 7% Comparables: Bump Wills, Bill Doran, D'Angelo Jimenez, Ray Durham

Three franchises have now struggled with the dilemma of what to do with him, but Felipe Lopez is a second baseman from here on out, as dealing Vidro allows the Nats to slip Lopez across the keystone. It's just as well—he was terrible coming across the bag on the deuce and lacked the arm strength to make plays from the hole. There's no guarantee that he'll be able to handle the pivot from second either, but his limitations won't be quite as difficult to put up with at his new position. The real problem is that he's about to take a big step back in the world, going from what might be seen as a premium hitter at short to an Eckstein-type at second (as a second baseman, his VORP drops to 26.9). Of his 11 bombs last year, five were hit in his 186 plate appearances in the Gap, and none in RFK, his new home park. On his career, he's hit a home run every 31.8 PA in Cincinnati and one every 50.8 everywhere else. As long as he's in RFK, you can expect that 23-homer 2005 season to remain a matter of memory.

Brian Schneider C **Bats: L Throws: R** Height: 6′ 1″ Weight: 195 Born: November 26, 1976 Age: 30

YEAR	TEAM	LVL	AGE	PA	R	2B	3B	HR	RBI	BB	SO	SB	CS	SPEED	AVG	OBP	SLG	MLVR	EQAVG	EQOBP	EQSLG	EQA	VORP	DEFENSE	
2004	MON	MLB	27	488	40	20	3	12	49	42	63	0	1	3.9	.257	.325	.399	-.031	.251	.321	.390	.247	10.5	123-C	13
2005	WAS	MLB	28	408	38	20	1	10	44	29	48	1	0	3.9	.268	.330	.409	.018	.274	.337	.425	.264	15.9	103-C	11
2006	WAS	MLB	29	455	30	18	0	4	55	38	67	2	2	3.6	.256	.320	.329	-.153	.262	.328	.337	.237	-4.9	112-C	5
2007	WAS	MLB	30	434	42	18	2	7	43	33	60	2	1	4.0	.255	.317	.367	-.159	.260	.321	.378	.241	4.5	103-C	4

Breakout: 22% Improve: 41% Collapse: 33% Attrition: 19% Comparables: Johnny Oates, Jake Gibbs, Brent Mayne, Bill Fahey

Schneider endured a street-pizza season at the plate, but at least he retained his defensive value, doing a particularly good job of deterring and controlling the running game. As far as his hitting, it wasn't a platoon thing or an RFK thing; Schneider slugged a feeble .333 against right-handers and .313 on the road. Nor was it a matter of playing him too much; Schneider handled just under 70 percent of the team's playing time behind the plate. Instead, the Nats are confronted with the very real likelihood that they got Schneider's peak performance within the normal range of a player's best seasons, and, now that he's left his age-26, 27 and 28 seasons behind him, they're on the hook for $13.3 million for three years of this sort of production. Consider this another Jim Bowden gamble that turned out exceptionally badly.

Alfonso Soriano   LF   Bats: R   Throws: R   Height: 6' 1"   Weight: 180   Born: January 7, 1978   Age: 31

YEAR	TEAM	LVL	AGE	PA	R	2B	3B	HR	RBI	BB	SO	SB	CS	SPEED	AVG	OBP	SLG	MLVR	EQAVG	EQOBP	EQSLG	EQA	VORP	DEFENSE	
2004	TEX	MLB	26	658	77	32	4	28	91	33	121	18	5	6.0	.280	.324	.484	.023	.271	.319	.476	.270	31.5	134-2B	-3
2005	TEX	MLB	27	682	102	43	2	36	104	33	125	30	2	7.2	.268	.309	.512	.074	.266	.317	.517	.283	39.5	152-2B	-20
2006	WAS	MLB	28	728	119	41	2	46	95	67	160	41	17	7.0	.277	.351	.560	.236	.288	.363	.585	.304	48.2	156-LF	9
2007	CHN	MLB	31	676	109	40	3	41	115	51	133	32	11	6.3	.285	.347	.565	.184	.280	.341	.548	.294	41.8	157-LF	-3

Breakout: 16% Improve: 45% Collapse: 27% Attrition: 0%   Comparables: Andre Dawson, Paul Blair, Jeff Kent, Leon Wagner

Soriano's 2006 was a strange, fun, and interesting season from a strange, fun, and interesting player, but it's hard to expect him to provide value on his eight-year, $136-million contract with the Cubs. Challenged to make a move to the outfield, Soriano adapted, if at first indifferently, eventually showing good range and an infielder's instincts for staying in the action. Last year's 22 assists were more a matter of runners learning what he could do than a testament to a shoulder-mounted howitzer—10 came on batters trying to take an extra base, six on fly-out doubleplays in which baserunners were caught taking big leads on balls Soriano caught, and two on lineout doubleplays in which, again, the runners were leaning; in other words, he played aggressively in response to some aggressive baserunning. Having made his bones with third base coaches around the league last year, deterrence should be in place from here on out. That he set a career high in walks last year was also impressive (his previous was 38), but keep in mind that he was issued 16 intentionals. His actual jump was from a pre-2006 career average of drawing an unintentional walk in four percent of his plate appearances to doing so in seven percent of his PAs last year; positive, just not as positive. It remains to be seen how much of this spike was a product of poor lineup protection versus a newly-developed skill, though the fact that he was put on first intentionally to bring up Royce Clayton five times in little more than a month serves as some indication. With the Cubs, he'll be better protected unless Lou Piniella bats Cesar Izturis second, but our uncertainty about whether that will be a positive (better pitches to hit), a negative (fewer walks), or ultimately irrelevant reflects how little we really know about the tactical impact of lineup protection.

Jose Vidro   2B   Bats: S   Throws: R   Height: 5' 11"   Weight: 195   Born: August 27, 1974   Age: 32

YEAR	TEAM	LVL	AGE	PA	R	2B	3B	HR	RBI	BB	SO	SB	CS	SPEED	AVG	OBP	SLG	MLVR	EQAVG	EQOBP	EQSLG	EQA	VORP	DEFENSE	
2004	MON	MLB	29	467	51	24	0	14	60	49	43	3	1	4.1	.294	.367	.454	.149	.288	.363	.450	.281	31.0	99-2B	-9
2005	WAS	MLB	30	347	38	21	2	7	32	31	30	0	0	3.9	.275	.339	.424	.057	.279	.346	.438	.272	13.3	74-2B	0
2006	WAS	MLB	31	511	52	26	1	7	47	41	48	1	0	4.2	.289	.348	.395	.011	.297	.357	.403	.267	17.3	102-2B	-4
2007	SEA	MLB	32	421	47	19	1	6	42	37	42	1	1	4.3	.273	.339	.381	-.080	.272	.340	.391	.262	9.9	100-2B	-4

Breakout: 13% Improve: 31% Collapse: 30% Attrition: 19%   Comparables: Johnny Ray, Tom Herr, Todd Walker, Kevin Seitzer

Ping-ponging back to the positive, credit Jim Bowden for making Omar Minaya's ridiculously generous four-year, $30-million extension for Vidro go away. Between the knee injuries and the bulky build that kept him from ever being a scouts' fave, he's failed to play a full season in any of the last four. As a second baseman, he's one step from done, and as a DH, he's a completely appropriate choice to replicate Carl Everett's punchless contributions to last year's Mariners, even if you accept that his .304/.361/.424 road rates from 2006 will portage over perfectly to Safeco and the superior league, which they won't.

Josh Whitesell   1B   Bats: L   Throws: L   Height: 6' 3"   Weight: 220   Born: April 14, 1982   Age: 25

YEAR	TEAM	LVL	AGE	PA	R	2B	3B	HR	RBI	BB	SO	SB	CS	SPEED	AVG	OBP	SLG	MLVR	EQAVG	EQOBP	EQSLG	EQA	VORP	DEFENSE	
2004	SAV	A	22	444	56	29	0	16	54	58	91	0	1	2.7	.250	.352	.453	.116	.211	.288	.362	.228	-21.4	104-1B	-14
2005	POT	A+	23	474	59	32	2	18	66	74	125	1	1	2.8	.293	.416	.524	.318	.264	.357	.443	.275	14.6	86-1B	-6
2006	HAR	AA	24	467	47	11	0	19	56	53	125	2	6	2.3	.264	.354	.433	.121	.254	.330	.419	.257	3.0	84-1B	-7
2007	WAS	MLB	25	447	45	19	1	15	57	45	117	0	1	3.6	.244	.325	.411	-.095	.249	.329	.424	.257	1.0	106-1B	-4

Breakout: 18% Improve: 55% Collapse: 24% Attrition: 11%   Comparables: Chris Duncan, John-Ford Griffin, Chris Haas, Eric Munson

One of the bigger disappointments in a system in which expectations rot on the vine, Whitesell was seen as a power prospect. It's easy to understand why; he drives the ball well when he gets his arms extended. Unfortunately, he also gets pull-conscious, his long swing can get diced up, and he seems to make few adjustments when down to his last strike. He'll be 25 this spring, and first base is no place for late learners with basic adaptation issues.

Ryan Zimmerman   **3B**   **Bats: R**   **Throws: R**   Height: 6' 3"   Weight: 210   Born: September 28, 1984 Age: 22

YEAR	TEAM	LVL	AGE	PA	R	2B	3B	HR	RBI	BB	SO	SB	CS	SPEED	AVG	OBP	SLG	MLVR	EQAVG	EQOBP	EQSLG	EQA	VORP	DEFENSE	
2005	HAR	AA	20	252	40	20	0	9	32	15	34	1	5	3.5	.326	.371	.528	.293	.294	.337	.481	.272	17.8	53-3B	2
2005	WAS	MLB	20	62	6	10	0	0	6	3	12	0	0	3.8	.397	.419	.569	.550	.397	.419	.552	.329	9.3	12-3B	2
2006	WAS	MLB	21	682	84	47	3	20	110	61	120	11	8	4.7	.287	.351	.471	.123	.296	.363	.486	.286	26.9	155-3B	9
2007	WAS	MLB	22	662	95	43	4	23	93	55	101	13	9	5.1	.298	.359	.498	.124	.304	.363	.513	.291	44.3	154-3B	7

Breakout: 26% Improve: 53% Collapse: 14% Attrition: 2%   *Comparables: Carney Lansford, Bob Bailey, David Wright, Travis Fryman*

Zimmerman is a tremendous ballplayer. Losing the Rookie of the Year award to Hanley Ramirez doesn't mean he won't have the better career. Some nervous nellies started tearing out their hair over a few early errors afield, but Zimmerman's range, touch, soft hands, and on-field anticipation rate with the best in the league. Add in that he was the Nats' best hitter when it came to plating runners (scoring 18.8 percent of the men on base when he batted), and you've got the face of the franchise, for at least as long as the Lerners decide to afford him.

PITCHERS

Tony Armas   **Bats: R** **Throws: R**   Height: 6' 3"   Weight: 225   Born: April 29, 1978   Age: 29

YEAR	TEAM	LVL	AGE	W	L	SV	G	GS	IP	H	BB	SO	HR	GB%	BABIP	STUFF	WHIP	ERA	PERA	EQERA	EQH9	EQBB9	EQSO9	EQHR9	VORP	WXRL
2004	MON	MLB	26	2	4	0	16	16	72	66	45	54	13	—	.265	-3	1.54	4.88	6.00	4.79	8.3	4.9	5.9	1.5	4.2	1.77
2005	WAS	MLB	27	7	7	0	19	19	101¹	100	54	59	16	37.4%	.268	-12	1.51	4.98	5.95	5.23	8.9	4.4	4.8	1.4	5.2	1.74
2006	WAS	MLB	28	9	12	0	30	30	154	167	64	97	19	40.1%	.307	1	1.50	5.03	4.87	5.11	9.4	3.2	5.1	1.0	5.8	2.80
2007	WAS	MLB	29	7	9	0	30	22	134¹	141	54	87	17	41.0%	.290	0	1.45	4.76	5.34	5.17	9.4	3.2	5.3	1.1	7.4	1.70

Breakout: 15% Improve: 51% Collapse: 23% Attrition: 6%   *Comparables: Jason Johnson, James Baldwin, Mike Scott, Ed Whitson*

Armas is having a rough go of it as a free agent, which isn't surprising. He has a hard time getting past five innings per start despite pitching in the league without DHs and in one of the best pitcher's parks in baseball. He's a fly-ball pitcher, which will mean especially bad news almost anywhere outside of RFK, and he's five years removed from his last uninterrupted season in a major league rotation. Even in this winter's Crazy Eddie pitching market, no one is this insane.

Pedro Astacio   **Bats: R** **Throws: R**   Height: 6' 2"   Weight: 210   Born: December 31, 1969 Age: 37

YEAR	TEAM	LVL	AGE	W	L	SV	G	GS	IP	H	BB	SO	HR	GB%	BABIP	STUFF	WHIP	ERA	PERA	EQERA	EQH9	EQBB9	EQSO9	EQHR9	VORP	WXRL
2004	BOS	MLB	34	0	0	0	5	1	8²	13	5	6	2	—	.367	-24	2.08	10.34	5.90	9.00	13.0	5.0	6.0	2.0	-2.9	0.04
2005	TEX	MLB	35	2	8	0	12	12	67	79	11	45	13	44.7%	.310	3	1.34	6.04	4.61	5.09	9.4	1.4	5.7	1.5	-0.3	0.65
2005	SDN	MLB	35	4	2	0	12	10	59²	54	26	33	4	39.8%	.275	5	1.34	3.17	4.34	3.23	7.8	3.5	4.5	0.6	14.4	2.13
2006	WAS	MLB	36	5	5	0	17	17	90¹	109	31	42	14	37.5%	.310	-13	1.55	5.98	5.05	5.69	10.2	2.7	3.8	1.3	-5.3	0.70
2007	WAS	MLB	37	5	7	0	26	15	94²	111	30	48	14	41.0%	.299	-11	1.48	5.22	5.74	5.66	10.5	2.5	4.1	1.2	-0.1	0.60

Breakout: 4% Improve: 37% Collapse: 45% Attrition: 21%   *Comparables: Bob Welch, Jim Perry, Bob Forsch, Bob Buhl*

One of the bargain-bin pickups, Astacio strained his forearm at the end of camp, which cost him the first three months of the season. He was willing to take advantage of RFK's thick air by challenging hitters, but still lost often enough to allow 11·home runs in 59 home innings. On the road, he averaged more than ten runs per nine innings. A last-hurrah complete game shutout of the Braves aside, there's more here that's done than still juicy.

Luis Ayala   **Bats: R** **Throws: R**   Height: 6' 2"   Weight: 185   Born: January 12, 1978   Age: 29

YEAR	TEAM	LVL	AGE	W	L	SV	G	GS	IP	H	BB	SO	HR	GB%	BABIP	STUFF	WHIP	ERA	PERA	EQERA	EQH9	EQBB9	EQSO9	EQHR9	VORP	WXRL
2004	MON	MLB	26	6	12	2	81	0	90¹	92	15	63	6	—	.314	14	1.18	2.69	3.36	2.86	9.2	1.4	5.6	0.5	26.5	0.21
2005	WAS	MLB	27	8	7	1	68	0	71	75	14	40	7	41.9%	.316	-3	1.25	2.66	4.28	3.11	9.5	1.6	4.6	0.9	18.8	2.22
2007	WAS	MLB	29	2	2	1	38	1	50	58	12	29	6	48.0%	.311	-7	1.40	4.18	5.09	4.53	10.4	1.9	4.7	0.9	6.2	0.60

Breakout: 1% Improve: 8% Collapse: 76% Attrition: 31%   *Comparables: Paul Quantrill, John Habyan, Chuck Crim, Bill Castro*

Another victim of the ill-considered World Baseball Classic, Ayala sacrificed a year of his career for the greater glory of Mexico in a series with less cachet than most Olympic qualifying games. One sprained elbow-cum-ligament transplant surgery later, the Nats are hoping they'll have their primary setup man back . . . at some point. To be fair, Ayala seemed to be wearing down under the heavy workloads of seasons past, and there's a lot we don't know about relief workloads. Do fewer games and more innings make more sense than more games and fewer innings? At what age? How much does the type of pitches a reliever throws matter? What about their varying abilities to work from the stretch? What we do know is that Ayala did too much, and that the Nats were out one strike-throwing sinker-slider guy.

Collin Balester

Bats: R Throws: R   Height: 6' 5"   Weight: 190   Born: June 6, 1986   Age: 21

YEAR	TEAM	LVL	AGE	W	L	SV	G	GS	IP	H	BB	SO	HR	GB%	BABIP	STUFF	WHIP	ERA	PERA	EQERA	EQH9	EQBB9	EQSO9	EQHR9	VORP	WXRL
2005	SAV	A	19	8	6	0	24	23	125	105	42	95	11	43.1%	.257	-11	1.18	3.67	6.10	5.94	8.9	3.8	4.2	1.6	-4.5	—
2006	POT	A+	20	4	5	0	23	22	117²	126	53	87	12	43.9%	.325	-19	1.53	5.22	6.32	6.25	10.2	4.2	4.6	1.8	-8.4	—
2006	HAR	AA	20	1	0	0	3	3	19²	15	6	10	0	45.8%	.273	7	1.09	1.88	4.26	2.75	6.9	2.7	3.2	0.0	6.2	—
2007	WAS	MLB	21	5	8	0	23	19	108¹	114	49	70	19	40.0%	.279	0	1.49	5.43	5.98	5.86	9.4	3.6	5.3	1.5	-2.6	0.50

Breakout: 16%   Improve: 49%   Collapse: 19%   Attrition: 1%   Comparables: Chris Gissell, Fernando Cabrera, Ryan Madson, Matt DeWitt

A rangy, long-limbed young surfer dude from SoCal, Balester didn't embarrass himself in either the Carolina League or Double-A once he ironed out some early mechanical problems. Already dealing in the low-90s with solid command, he's still working on making a potentially plus curve a more reliable change of pace. He'll repeat Double-A, probably for a full season, but if he pitches through the next three or four years without injury, he could mature into a solid mid-rotation starter.

Jason Bergmann

Bats: R Throws: R   Height: 6' 4"   Weight: 190   Born: September 25, 1981   Age: 25

YEAR	TEAM	LVL	AGE	W	L	SV	G	GS	IP	H	BB	SO	HR	GB%	BABIP	STUFF	WHIP	ERA	PERA	EQERA	EQH9	EQBB9	EQSO9	EQHR9	VORP	WXRL
2004	SAV	A	22	3	7	0	13	13	65	67	34	58	6	—	.316	-14	1.55	4.85	7.00	7.26	10.7	6.1	4.5	1.6	-11.4	—
2004	BRV	A+	22	3	2	8	24	0	31²	20	18	28	0	—	.235	4	1.20	1.14	4.93	2.97	6.5	6.2	5.3	0.3	8.9	—
2005	HAR	AA	23	2	0	5	21	0	37	27	16	37	3	35.1%	.255	2	1.16	1.22	5.36	2.27	7.3	4.8	6.1	1.0	13.2	—
2005	NWO	AAA	23	3	2	2	20	0	37	26	13	39	5	40.0%	.250	6	1.05	3.16	5.05	3.93	6.9	2.9	7.4	1.5	6.8	—
2005	WAS	MLB	23	2	0	0	15	1	19²	14	11	21	1	32.7%	.271	20	1.27	2.74	3.83	3.15	6.8	4.5	8.6	0.4	5.8	0.52
2006	NWO	AAA	24	8	2	4	26	4	60²	54	20	62	5	28.5%	.318	10	1.23	3.29	3.99	3.58	8.4	2.8	7.2	0.9	13.5	—
2006	WAS	MLB	24	0	2	0	29	6	64²	81	27	54	12	32.0%	.356	-9	1.67	6.68	5.16	6.21	10.9	3.2	6.8	1.5	-6.7	-0.22
2007	WAS	MLB	25	4	5	2	48	8	83²	84	34	65	12	37.0%	.288	0	1.41	4.65	5.18	5.01	9.0	3.2	6.4	1.2	6.3	0.90

Breakout: 20%   Improve: 46%   Collapse: 15%   Attrition: 26%   Comparables: Rich Yett, Kevin Correia, Renie Martin, Pat Mahomes

Bergmann's projection depends on how much you're willing to overlook to see the promise of a big guy with three quality pitches. In a mop-up relief role, Bergmann got thoroughly crisped, allowing 64 baserunners in 34 innings (not including five free passes). Tried out as a starter, he got belted around five times and posted a quality start in the second game of a double-header. The Nats need players who can do anything, but the problem here might be one of having a guy who could do anything, but needs to be asked to do something, which is a wee bit more specific. He throws in the low-90s, and both his slider and curve fool people; given some direction, he could settle into a useful career.

Chris Booker

Bats: R Throws: R   Height: 6' 3"   Weight: 235   Born: December 9, 1976   Age: 29

YEAR	TEAM	LVL	AGE	W	L	SV	G	GS	IP	H	BB	SO	HR	GB%	BABIP	STUFF	WHIP	ERA	PERA	EQERA	EQH9	EQBB9	EQSO9	EQHR9	VORP	WXRL
2004	CHT	AA	27	2	0	5	28	0	39	26	25	57	0	—	.302	23	1.31	1.38	4.39	2.23	7.7	7.2	8.2	0.2	13.6	—
2004	LOU	AAA	27	0	1	0	7	0	12	10	10	9	2	—	.235	-7	1.67	4.50	7.94	4.63	7.7	8.5	5.4	1.5	1.3	—
2005	LOU	AAA	28	8	4	20	59	0	65	45	28	91	2	33.6%	.312	31	1.12	2.49	3.10	3.08	6.6	4.3	9.5	0.3	18.0	—
2006	CLR	A+	29	0	0	0	6	0	10²	7	2	20	2	18.8%	.357	9	0.88	5.29	7.19	6.75	10.6	1.9	10.6	3.9	-1.2	—
2006	SWB	AAA	29	0	0	0	6	0	7²	4	3	7	1	31.3%	.200	-3	0.97	1.25	6.38	2.57	6.4	3.9	6.4	2.6	2.4	—
2006	NWO	AAA	29	2	2	0	15	0	16²	14	13	29	0	34.4%	.467	16	1.67	3.89	3.43	4.50	9.0	7.3	11.8	0.0	2.0	—
2006	WAS	MLB	29	0	0	0	10	0	7¹	5	1	7	1	21.1%	.222	7	0.82	3.70	3.32	3.68	6.1	1.2	7.4	1.2	1.8	0.19
2007	WAS	MLB	30	2	2	2	39	2	41¹	37	24	42	6	33%	.286	2	1.49	4.86	5.31	5.24	8.1	4.7	8.2	1.1	2.1	0.2

Breakout: 40%   Improve: 65%   Collapse: 21%   Attrition: 32%   Comparables: Dwayne Henry, Armando Almanza, Roger Mason, Mike Armstrong

In a ten-month stretch, Booker bounced from the Reds to the Nats to the Tigers to the Phillies to the Royals and back to the Nats, with a minor league contract, the Rule 5 draft, a sale, and a couple of waiver claims involved. In each case, a team was drawn in by Booker's speed-gun readings, only to become disenchanted by the absence of movement on those fastballs and his lack of a secondary pitch to set it up. As long as Booker keeps popping gloves, he'll keep getting passed around.

Micah Bowie

Bats: L Throws: L   Height: 6' 4"   Weight: 205   Born: November 10, 1974   Age: 32

YEAR	TEAM	LVL	AGE	W	L	SV	G	GS	IP	H	BB	SO	HR	GB%	BABIP	STUFF	WHIP	ERA	PERA	EQERA	EQH9	EQBB9	EQSO9	EQHR9	VORP	WXRL
2005	HAR	AA	30	1	1	1	10	0	16¹	16	3	19	1	66.7%	.349	1	1.17	4.42	3.69	5.17	9.8	2.3	6.3	1.1	0.8	—
2006	NWO	AAA	31	2	0	1	31	0	42¹	33	24	57	0	45.6%	.337	23	1.35	3.85	3.74	5.05	8.1	5.5	9.0	0.2	2.5	—
2006	WAS	MLB	31	0	1	0	15	0	19²	11	7	11	1	35.7%	.182	1	0.92	1.37	3.78	1.37	5.0	2.7	4.6	0.5	10.1	0.68
2007	WAS	MLB	32	2	3	2	59	2	52	50	25	44	6	44.0%	.294	-2	1.45	4.36	4.97	4.75	8.6	3.9	6.9	0.9	5.2	0.50

Breakout: 2%   Improve: 10%   Collapse: 72%   Attrition: 28%   Comparables: Bill Kennedy, Frank Papish, Trever Miller, Lance Painter

(continued next page)

Micah Bowie *(continued)*

Proof that anybody can come back, Bowie is one of a generation's worth of Brave pitching prospect flops and threw less than 40 innings from 2003 to 2005. After missing all of 2004, Bowie worked his way back through the Nationals' system over the last two seasons to earn a shot as a lefty reliever. He doesn't throw anything in particular that might floor you, but strikes are good, and he's already shown some moxie by trying to get back into things, even if he did finish the year on the DL once again.

Bret Campbell Bats: R Throws: R Height: 6' 0" Weight: 170 Born: October 17, 1981 Age: 25

YEAR	TEAM	LVL	AGE	W	L	SV	G	GS	IP	H	BB	SO	HR	GB%	BABIP	STUFF	WHIP	ERA	PERA	EQERA	EQH9	EQBB9	EQSO9	EQHR9	VORP	WXRL
2004	VER	A-	22	0	1	0	11	0	22	24	10	25	3	—	.344	-26	1.55	4.09	10.13	7.91	13.5	7.0	5.6	4.2	-5.0	—
2005	SAV	A	23	4	2	19	36	0	48	28	15	50	2	52.5%	.218	-7	0.90	1.69	4.87	3.20	6.8	4.0	5.2	0.8	12.0	—
2005	POT	A+	23	0	2	1	12	0	15	21	10	13	3	54.7%	.375	-34	2.07	9.60	10.08	13.50	14.8	7.7	4.5	3.2	-12.3	—
2006	POT	A+	24	3	1	8	19	0	22	22	2	27	3	38.7%	.333	-4	1.09	2.45	6.24	3.92	11.3	0.9	7.4	2.6	3.9	—
2006	HAR	AA	24	0	3	8	13	0	14	16	11	20	0	36.8%	.421	12	1.93	3.21	4.52	4.72	11.5	8.8	8.8	0.0	1.3	—
2006	NWO	AAA	24	0	1	0	15	0	20¹	14	11	19	1	43.6%	.241	3	1.24	4.03	4.25	4.50	6.3	4.9	6.8	0.4	2.4	—
2006	WAS	MLB	24	0	0	0	4	0	4¹	4	2	4	1	16.7%	.273	-1	1.38	10.47	6.34	6.23	8.3	4.2	8.3	2.1	-2.0	-0.09
2007	WAS	MLB	25	3	4	1	33	4	60	64	32	45	10	40.0%	.296	-7	1.60	5.35	6.25	5.74	9.6	4.3	6.2	1.4	-0.6	0.10

Breakout: 19% Improve: 44% Collapse: 34% Attrition: 13% Comparables: Paul Bush, Alfredo Gonzalez, Isauro Pineda, Pat Flury

A true 34th-rounder in the 2004 draft (as opposed to a draft-and-follow), Campbell's already exceeded expectations by making it to the majors. Work with minor league pitching coordinator Bret Strom armed him with a pretty decent splitter, and he mixes his pitches well enough that he might stick as a serviceable guy in the back end of a big league bullpen.

Matt Chico Bats: L Throws: L Height: 5' 11" Weight: 200 Born: June 10, 1983 Age: 24

YEAR	TEAM	LVL	AGE	W	L	SV	G	GS	IP	H	BB	SO	HR	GB%	BABIP	STUFF	WHIP	ERA	PERA	EQERA	EQH9	EQBB9	EQSO9	EQHR9	VORP	WXRL
2004	SBN	A	21	8	5	0	14	14	87²	59	27	89	9	—	.229	-10	0.98	2.57	6.66	3.83	7.9	3.7	5.2	2.1	16.2	—
2004	ELP	AA	21	3	7	0	14	12	62¹	82	36	59	7	—	.375	-6	1.89	5.78	6.05	7.39	11.1	5.7	5.8	1.6	-12.6	—
2005	TEN	AA	22	1	7	0	10	10	52²	75	15	35	8	36.1%	.379	-22	1.71	5.98	6.41	7.64	12.7	2.5	4.2	2.2	-12.0	—
2005	LNC	A+	22	7	2	0	18	18	110	101	39	102	13	43.4%	.293	-2	1.27	3.76	5.50	3.90	7.9	3.7	5.2	1.4	20.9	—
2006	LNC	A+	23	3	4	0	10	10	50²	48	11	49	5	43.5%	.293	-1	1.18	3.76	5.12	4.59	8.3	2.3	5.1	1.6	5.7	—
2006	TEN	AA	23	7	2	0	13	13	81¹	62	21	63	6	40.6%	.249	6	1.02	2.22	4.69	3.15	7.4	2.4	4.8	1.2	21.8	—
2006	HAR	AA	23	2	0	0	4	4	22²	28	8	13	3	46.7%	.347	-14	1.62	3.24	6.81	4.09	11.9	3.7	3.7	2.0	3.7	—
2007	WAS	MLB	24	6	8	0	26	19	113	118	47	72	20	41.0%	.276	-2	1.46	5.20	5.82	5.60	9.3	3.4	5.2	1.5	0.7	0.90

Breakout: 3% Improve: 13% Collapse: 44% Attrition: 2% Comparables: Ryan Snare, Michael Connolly, Brent Billingsley, Phil Seibel

Chico has had a bumpy road by prospect standards. A top amateur in high school, he passed up pro money from the Red Sox to play at USC, couldn't hack the coursework, drifted out of sight and into a SoCal semi-pro league, then got rediscovered by the D'backs in 2003. They taught him how to use a decent curve and change to support his low-90s heat; he's not a reliever in the making. Although it took him three years to get past Double-A, the first time was an aggressive late-season promotion from Low-A in only his first full season as a pro, and the second came when he started off at that level and proved he really did need to get in some time at High-A. He's been challenged by his parent organization, and the challenges have made him a better prospect for the long haul. He'll come into camp with an outside shot at winning a job in the rotation, but it's more likely that he'll get some extra seasoning in Triple-A to show he's the real Tabasco, then get the call in June or July after the veterans have flopped.

Chad Cordero Bats: R Throws: R Height: 6' 0" Weight: 200 Born: March 18, 1982 Age: 25

YEAR	TEAM	LVL	AGE	W	L	SV	G	GS	IP	H	BB	SO	HR	GB%	BABIP	STUFF	WHIP	ERA	PERA	EQERA	EQH9	EQBB9	EQSO9	EQHR9	VORP	WXRL
2004	MON	MLB	22	7	3	14	69	0	82²	68	43	83	8	—	.278	18	1.34	2.94	3.96	3.00	7.5	4.2	7.9	0.8	23.6	4.55
2005	WAS	MLB	23	2	4	47	74	0	74¹	55	17	61	9	37.3%	.221	10	0.97	1.82	3.96	3.11	6.7	1.9	6.8	1.1	20.7	4.61
2006	WAS	MLB	24	7	4	29	68	0	73¹	59	22	69	13	37.1%	.240	6	1.10	3.19	4.49	3.13	7.0	2.3	7.6	1.4	21.5	3.88
2007	WAS	MLB	25	4	5	24	53	0	61	54	22	53	8	36.0%	.267	7	1.24	3.69	4.08	3.98	7.9	2.9	7.1	1.0	12.6	1.60

Breakout: 4% Improve: 22% Collapse: 55% Attrition: 11% Comparables: Frank Smith, Mike Jackson, Steve Foucault, Cecilio Guante

He still tries to get righties to chase high heat. It works often enough; all sorts of hitters want to be heroes and go yard, and Cordero happily logs a fair number of fly-ball outs. Unfortunately, he also ends up regretting this approach more than you'd like to see from a premium closer. It's hard to know what to expect—he could keep doing this for a few more years—but it would be nice to see him try to cut back on the deep flies. That said, his raw numbers from 2006 underrate his performance—he gave up 10 of his 27 runs and 4 of his 13 home runs in just two blown save losses. However deflating those days at the office may have been, the games don't get any more lost, and Cordero has demonstrated that crucial ability to forget about his bad days.

Shawn Hill
Bats: R Throws: R   Height: 6' 2"   Weight: 185   Born: April 28, 1981   Age: 26

YEAR	TEAM	LVL	AGE	W	L	SV	G	GS	IP	H	BB	SO	HR	GB%	BABIP	STUFF	WHIP	ERA	PERA	EQERA	EQH9	EQBB9	EQSO9	EQHR9	VORP	WXRL
2004	HAR	AA	23	5	7	0	17	17	87²	90	20	53	4	—	.312	7	1.25	3.39	4.11	4.38	9.2	2.2	3.8	0.5	12.0	—
2004	MON	MLB	23	1	2	0	3	3	9	17	7	10	1	—	.533	-7	2.67	16.00	4.64	15.43	16.4	5.8	8.7	1.0	-10.6	-0.49
2006	HAR	AA	25	3	3	0	10	10	50	46	5	32	2	63.0%	.275	5	1.02	2.70	3.79	4.29	8.4	1.1	3.6	0.5	7.3	—
2006	WAS	MLB	25	1	3	0	6	6	36²	43	12	16	2	50.4%	.323	3	1.50	4.66	4.14	4.26	9.9	2.6	3.6	0.5	4.3	0.94
2007	WAS	MLB	26	8	9	0	32	25	141²	156	41	71	13	54.0%	.296	0	1.38	4.46	4.85	4.96	9.8	2.3	4.1	0.8	11.7	2.10

Breakout: 26% Improve: 61% Collapse: 14% Attrition: 0%   Comparables: Jake Westbrook, Rick Matula, Chris Begg, Jared Gothreaux

Having missed 2005 after TJ surgery on his elbow, Hill's 2006 was supposed to be a simple season devoted to recovering his command. Instead, he got pressed into action as the Nats' pitching staff started going to pieces. He's something of a finesse guy, relying on a sinker and hoping he can fool the occasional lefty with a curve or change, but it doesn't happen as often as he might like. Given the team's general desperation for pitching of any type, Hill has a good shot at the back of the rotation.

Brian Lawrence
Bats: R Throws: R   Height: 6' 0"   Weight: 195   Born: May 14, 1976   Age: 31

YEAR	TEAM	LVL	AGE	W	L	SV	G	GS	IP	H	BB	SO	HR	GB%	BABIP	STUFF	WHIP	ERA	PERA	EQERA	EQH9	EQBB9	EQSO9	EQHR9	VORP	WXRL
2004	SDN	MLB	28	15	14	0	34	34	203	226	55	121	26	—	.313	3	1.38	4.12	4.51	4.65	9.8	2.2	4.7	1.1	25.4	4.49
2005	SDN	MLB	29	7	15	0	33	33	195²	211	57	109	18	47.8%	.298	7	1.37	4.83	4.37	4.65	9.3	2.4	4.5	0.8	12.3	3.74
2007	WAS	MLB	31	4	6	0	26	12	85²	96	27	48	11	48.0%	.300	-5	1.43	4.71	5.32	5.15	10.1	2.5	4.6	1.0	4.9	1.00

Breakout: 9% Improve: 32% Collapse: 33% Attrition: 13%   Comparables: John Buzhardt, Rick Camp, Danny Graves, Ray Washburn

The straight-up exchange of Vinny Castilla for Lawrence seemed like a steal for the Nats at the time, but it was discovered in camp that Lawrence had a torn labrum and rotator cuff and wouldn't be able to pitch all year. Discarded by the Nats after the season, his four years as a rotation regular for the Pads are enough for several teams to bid on the privilege to see if he can be retreaded. He was always a finesse guy, so he might adapt well enough, but his decline before injury was already discouraging. If he does sign with the Rockies, as was rumored as we went to press, they might as well try to retread Fred Flintstone's feet.

Anastacio Martinez
Bats: R Throws: R   Height: 6' 2"   Weight: 180   Born: November 3, 1978   Age: 28

YEAR	TEAM	LVL	AGE	W	L	SV	G	GS	IP	H	BB	SO	HR	GB%	BABIP	STUFF	WHIP	ERA	PERA	EQERA	EQH9	EQBB9	EQSO9	EQHR9	VORP	WXRL
2004	PAW	AAA	25	3	3	1	38	0	67¹	73	31	57	5	—	.325	-4	1.55	3.74	4.68	5.21	9.8	4.5	5.9	0.8	2.9	—
2004	BOS	MLB	25	2	1	0	11	0	10²	13	6	5	2	—	.289	-32	1.78	8.41	6.42	7.36	10.6	4.9	4.1	1.6	-2.3	-0.19
2005	PAW	AAA	26	3	4	1	35	6	58²	74	27	46	4	48.5%	.359	-12	1.72	5.98	4.63	6.83	11.1	4.4	5.3	0.8	-8.1	—
2006	HAR	AA	27	2	0	0	2	2	12¹	10	3	11	1	55.9%	.273	5	1.07	3.72	5.31	4.63	8.5	3.1	5.4	1.5	1.3	—
2006	NWO	AAA	27	5	11	0	24	24	128²	121	58	115	13	45.5%	.305	0	1.40	4.49	5.34	5.41	8.9	4.1	6.1	1.2	2.7	—
2007	WAS	MLB	28	5	7	0	32	16	97¹	105	46	71	12	45.0%	.304	-3	1.54	5.35	5.75	5.86	9.6	3.8	5.9	1.0	-2.3	0.40

Breakout: 14% Improve: 35% Collapse: 15% Attrition: 3%   Comparables: Dave Stevens, Ryan Dempster, Storm Davis, Erv Palica

The former Red Sox prospect still throws a mid-90s fastball with tailing action, and just as certainly still has nothing to offer where his secondary stuff is concerned. As a result, he's essentially unarmed against lefties (.303/.417/.488 in New Orleans), but can be very tough on right-handed hitters (.214/.285/.338). Even then, the lack of a viable second pitch can make sitting on his fastball a solid guess, which makes his chances to thrive in anything more than a secondary bullpen role slim.

Shairon Martis
Bats: R Throws: R   Height: 6' 1"   Weight: 175   Born: March 30, 1987   Age: 20

YEAR	TEAM	LVL	AGE	W	L	SV	G	GS	IP	H	BB	SO	HR	GB%	BABIP	STUFF	WHIP	ERA	PERA	EQERA	EQH9	EQBB9	EQSO9	EQHR9	VORP	WXRL
2006	AUG	A	19	6	4	0	15	15	76¹	76	21	66	3	35.5%	.322	9	1.27	3.67	4.45	6.60	9.8	3.0	4.7	0.8	-8.3	—
2006	SAV	A	19	1	1	0	4	4	21²	23	4	14	2	33.8%	.323	-1	1.27	3.82	5.76	4.64	10.1	2.1	3.4	1.7	2.3	—
2006	POT	A+	19	0	2	0	2	2	12²	9	3	7	0	36.1%	.250	11	0.98	2.95	3.80	4.26	6.4	2.1	3.6	0.0	1.9	—
2006	HAR	AA	19	0	1	0	1	1	5²	8	3	1	4	22.7%	.222	-51	2.12	12.12	24.34	14.40	16.2	5.4	1.8	10.8	-4.9	—
2007	WAS	MLB	20	6	8	0	24	19	113²	121	43	74	20	36.0%	.283	2	1.44	5.30	5.75	5.68	9.6	3.0	5.3	1.4	-0.5	0.80

Breakout: 28% Improve: 68% Collapse: 6% Attrition: 4%   Comparables: James Parr, Jarod Matthews, Tyler Clippard, Chad Durbin

(continued next page)

Shairon Martis *(continued)*

"Dutch ace" sounds like a cheap brand of rotgut or a particularly nasty cigarette, but Martis put himself on prospect radars with a fine performance in the World Baseball Classic, shutting out Panama over seven innings. He's a stringbean with reliable low-90s heat and a hard curve. Once he masters a changeup, he might start fooling more people, but he needs to learn to work lower in the zone. Thrown to the Nats in exchange for Mike Stanton at the deadline, the native of the Dutch Antilles immediately became one of the best prospects in the organization. He won't be pitching in Double-A by his 20th birthday, but he joins Balester to give the organization a pair of young, hard-throwing tyros.

Garrett Mock — Bats: R Throws: R — Height: 6' 4" — Weight: 215 — Born: April 25, 1983 — Age: 24

YEAR	TEAM	LVL	AGE	W	L	SV	G	GS	IP	H	BB	SO	HR	GB%	BABIP	STUFF	WHIP	ERA	PERA	EQERA	EQH9	EQBB9	EQSO9	EQHR9	VORP	WXRL
2004	YAK	A-	21	2	0	0	5	5	23¹	18	4	14	1	—	.243	-8	0.94	1.55	4.68	3.86	6.6	1.9	2.7	0.8	4.5	—
2004	SBN	A	21	3	2	0	8	8	54	49	12	37	2	—	.281	2	1.13	3.00	4.48	4.89	8.6	2.5	3.4	0.7	4.2	—
2005	LNC	A+	22	14	7	0	28	28	174¹	202	33	160	19	50.8%	.344	5	1.35	4.18	4.67	4.57	9.7	1.9	5.0	1.3	20.5	—
2006	TEN	AA	23	4	8	0	23	23	131¹	144	50	117	14	50.6%	.339	-16	1.48	4.94	5.83	6.70	10.8	3.5	5.5	1.7	-15.8	—
2006	HAR	AA	23	0	4	0	4	4	16	29	5	9	2	42.6%	.422	-32	2.13	10.69	6.16	12.67	16.5	3.3	3.3	1.7	-12.8	—
2007	WAS	MLB	24	6	8	0	27	18	114	125	42	71	17	46.0%	.295	-1	1.46	5.30	5.67	5.79	9.8	3.0	5.1	1.2	-1.8	0.60

Breakout: 23% Improve: 55% Collapse: 12% Attrition: 0% Comparables: Josh Hancock, Jason Olsen, Brian Reith, Dan Perkins

Mock is among the most frustrating promising arms in any organization, which is why he was available (with Chico) for Livan Hernandez. Scouts see a power pitcher's body, low- to mid-90s velocity, a good changeup, and two breaking pitches he can throw for strikes. Stuff and command? Sounds great! Except that he keeps turning out to be much more hittable than you'd expect. There's nothing that anybody has picked up on mechanically that's begging for an easy correction, and no indication that he's tipping his pitches. It wouldn't be crazy to suggest that he'll suddenly figure it out and become a potentially solid third-starter in the major leagues; it also wouldn't be crazy to think he'll just continue to be maddening. Either way, he's something the Nats should want a piece of, because his chances of panning out are a risk they need to take.

Michael O'Connor — Bats: L Throws: L — Height: 6' 3" — Weight: 170 — Born: August 17, 1980 — Age: 26

YEAR	TEAM	LVL	AGE	W	L	SV	G	GS	IP	H	BB	SO	HR	GB%	BABIP	STUFF	WHIP	ERA	PERA	EQERA	EQH9	EQBB9	EQSO9	EQHR9	VORP	WXRL
2004	BRV	A+	23	8	8	0	26	14	103	98	42	104	5	—	.324	-3	1.36	4.11	5.15	5.99	10.1	4.7	5.8	1.0	-4.2	—
2005	POT	A+	24	10	11	0	26	26	167²	144	48	158	14	46.9%	.285	-8	1.14	3.54	5.29	5.30	8.9	3.2	4.9	1.3	5.4	—
2006	NWO	AAA	25	1	0	0	6	6	26¹	21	11	28	2	45.6%	.292	15	1.23	2.76	4.39	3.81	8.0	3.8	7.6	1.0	5.2	—
2006	WAS	MLB	25	3	8	0	21	20	105	96	44	59	15	38.6%	.254	-6	1.33	4.80	5.29	4.76	7.9	3.3	4.6	1.2	7.6	2.47
2007	WAS	MLB	26	6	8	0	34	20	123¹	128	52	83	17	41.0%	.287	-1	1.45	4.89	5.38	5.31	9.3	3.4	5.5	1.1	4.9	1.30

Breakout: 14% Improve: 34% Collapse: 27% Attrition: 8% Comparables: Brandon Claussen, Frank Kreutzer, Bobby Jones, Jorge Sosa

Sometimes organizational soldiers just have to do as they're told. O'Connor really had no business starting 20 games in the majors last year, but he was only following orders. A local product out of George Washington University, O'Connor's performance was gutty for a guy with a modest assortment of junk and who'd never pitched above A-ball coming into the season, but offseason elbow surgery might keep him out of the running for another shot at the rotation to start 2007.

Ramon Ortiz — Bats: R Throws: R — Height: 6' 0" — Weight: 175 — Born: March 23, 1973 — Age: 34

YEAR	TEAM	LVL	AGE	W	L	SV	G	GS	IP	H	BB	SO	HR	GB%	BABIP	STUFF	WHIP	ERA	PERA	EQERA	EQH9	EQBB9	EQSO9	EQHR9	VORP	WXRL
2004	ANA	MLB	31	5	7	0	34	14	128	139	38	82	18	—	.306	0	1.38	4.43	4.50	4.26	9.1	2.4	5.3	1.1	25.0	1.33
2005	CIN	MLB	32	9	11	0	30	30	171¹	206	51	96	34	44.9%	.312	-16	1.50	5.36	5.60	5.23	9.8	2.4	4.5	1.7	-3.4	1.35
2006	WAS	MLB	33	11	16	0	33	33	190²	230	64	104	31	40.7%	.311	-8	1.54	5.57	5.29	5.41	10.5	2.6	4.4	1.3	-2.6	2.38
2007	WAS	MLB	34	9	11	0	33	26	168	187	48	91	24	42.0%	.292	-2	1.40	4.76	5.32	5.15	10.0	2.3	4.4	1.2	9.3	2.10

Breakout: 11% Improve: 53% Collapse: 17% Attrition: 5% Comparables: Willie Blair, Johnny Sain, Sid Hudson, Scuffy Moehler

How bad did things get in the Nats' rotation last summer? By August, Ortiz was getting top billing in local media coverage, but only because he was the veteran still standing that nobody else would trade for. He provided leadership of a sort, tying with Jason Marquis for the league lead in losses and finishing behind only Dontrelle Willis with 18 hit batsmen (you can't blame him for being grumpy under the circumstances). His slider doesn't fool people all that frequently, and his flat fastball and relatively short stature make for a pitcher without a lot of ability to attack hitters from different planes, so everyone hits him, and everyone can drive balls for power off of him. If he wasn't good enough to get by in RFK last year, he probably can't contribute anywhere in the majors. The Nats are trying to bring him back; they have need, but he needs them every bit as much.

John Patterson

Bats: R Throws: R Height: 6' 5" Weight: 210 Born: January 30, 1978 Age: 29

YEAR	TEAM	LVL	AGE	W	L	SV	G	GS	IP	H	BB	SO	HR	GB%	BABIP	STUFF	WHIP	ERA	PERA	EQERA	EQH9	EQBB9	EQSO9	EQHR9	VORP	WXRL
2004	MON	MLB	26	4	7	0	19	19	98¹	100	46	99	18	—	.306	6	1.48	5.04	5.08	4.95	9.3	3.7	8.0	1.4	4.0	1.55
2005	WAS	MLB	27	9	7	0	31	31	198¹	172	65	185	19	31.5%	.287	30	1.19	3.13	3.68	3.44	7.8	2.7	7.6	0.8	50.9	6.67
2006	WAS	MLB	28	1	2	0	8	8	40²	36	9	42	4	31.8%	.302	32	1.11	4.42	3.28	4.35	7.8	1.7	8.5	0.9	5.7	1.08
2007	WAS	MLB	29	8	7	0	27	21	127¹	119	40	115	17	35.0%	.282	18	1.25	3.99	4.37	4.30	8.3	2.5	7.3	1.1	20.5	2.90

Breakout: 8% Improve: 36% Collapse: 22% Attrition: 14% Comparables: Tim Belcher, Bob Johnson, Turk Farrell, Andy McGaffigan

More than any other pitcher on the staff, Patterson will be the one to watch this spring. Everyone will be hoping the elbow and forearm problems that shut him down early last year will be behind him, because losing him on top of Esteban Loaiza fundamentally altered the way the rest of the staff functioned last year; the pen flamed out trying to cover for a staff that was down to Livan Hernandez and four guys who couldn't consistently get to the sixth inning. The combination of his power fastball-curve mix and RFK's forgiving dimensions should be enough to make him the team's best starter, not that there's any competition. If healthy, his 2007 won't quite be like Steve Carlton's 1972 (the year Carlton won 27 of the Phillies' 59 games), but it won't be that much unlike it, either.

Beltran Perez

Bats: R Throws: R Height: 6' 2" Weight: 180 Born: October 24, 1981 Age: 25

YEAR	TEAM	LVL	AGE	W	L	SV	G	GS	IP	H	BB	SO	HR	GB%	BABIP	STUFF	WHIP	ERA	PERA	EQERA	EQH9	EQBB9	EQSO9	EQHR9	VORP	WXRL
2004	ELP	AA	22	2	6	3	37	8	104	102	46	77	14	—	.286	-27	1.42	4.41	6.75	4.63	8.3	4.4	4.5	1.8	11.3	—
2005	VRO	A+	23	3	2	0	19	0	33¹	31	15	33	3	41.1%	.329	-14	1.38	3.78	6.60	5.46	9.8	5.7	5.5	1.7	0.5	—
2005	JAX	AA	23	2	3	3	17	1	31	22	16	32	1	49.4%	.273	7	1.23	2.90	4.35	4.20	7.2	4.8	6.6	0.6	4.7	—
2006	HAR	AA	24	8	6	1	31	16	121¹	127	40	107	8	46.6%	.330	-5	1.38	3.12	4.90	4.75	10.1	3.5	5.1	1.0	11.3	—
2006	WAS	MLB	24	2	1	0	8	3	21	16	13	9	3	36.5%	.217	-12	1.38	3.86	5.99	3.74	6.6	5.0	3.3	1.2	4.9	0.59
2007	WAS	MLB	25	4	6	0	32	12	92²	101	45	58	15	42.0%	.290	-9	1.57	5.42	6.18	5.85	9.7	3.9	5.0	1.3	-2.1	0.30

Breakout: 2% Improve: 19% Collapse: 53% Attrition: 0% Comparables: Jason Secoda, Brian Slocum, Kip Bouknight, Rodrigo Rosario

To the 29 better-stocked organizations, Jim Bowden made this basic request, "Send these, the homeless, tempest-tost to me." Hoping for one Lazarus-like reincarnation after another, he instead wound up with a pile of corpses. Among those who registered a pulse was former Snakes prospect Perez, who previously survived nearly three years in the plane of pitcher's hell known as El Paso. Perez has always thrown strikes with a fastball-slider-change combo and might be the best choice on the staff for a utility pitcher role, starting in the emergencies that will come and manning the long innings that will come free when the non-Patterson starters get knocked out of the box.

Jon Rauch

Bats: R Throws: R Height: 6' 11" Weight: 260 Born: September 27, 1978 Age: 28

YEAR	TEAM	LVL	AGE	W	L	SV	G	GS	IP	H	BB	SO	HR	GB%	BABIP	STUFF	WHIP	ERA	PERA	EQERA	EQH9	EQBB9	EQSO9	EQHR9	VORP	WXRL
2004	CHA	MLB	25	1	1	0	2	2	8²	16	4	4	0	—	.485	-13	2.31	6.21	3.84	6.00	16.0	4.0	4.0	0.0	0.4	0.07
2004	MON	MLB	25	3	0	0	9	2	23¹	14	7	18	1	—	.213	18	0.90	1.55	3.14	1.54	5.4	2.3	6.2	0.4	10.8	1.23
2005	WAS	MLB	26	2	4	0	15	1	30	24	11	23	3	25.3%	.250	5	1.17	3.60	4.22	3.82	7.0	2.9	6.2	0.9	6.1	0.44
2006	WAS	MLB	27	4	5	2	85	0	91¹	78	36	86	13	31.7%	.272	7	1.25	3.35	4.23	3.47	7.4	3.1	7.6	1.2	23.5	1.71
2007	WAS	MLB	28	4	3	4	63	0	74¹	68	27	66	9	35.0%	.277	6	1.27	3.74	4.31	4.00	8.1	2.9	7.2	1.0	14.2	1.20

Breakout: 12% Improve: 34% Collapse: 44% Attrition: 16% Comparables: Todd Worrell, Bobby Howry, Bill Dawley, Jeff Nelson

Statheads can paint with broad strokes. Everybody prefers balls in play to be earthbound, but pitchers this tall, such as the Padres' Chris Young and Arizona's Randy Johnson—but Rauch, especially, because of his over-the-top delivery—bring pitches boring in on the plate at such a steep angle that it's almost impossible for a hitter to put them on the ground. So they get pop outs and fly balls, and a few of the latter go over the wall, but, rather than get worked up over it, we should recognize that Rauch is part of a rare group of hard-throwing giants, who just so happens to be in one of the best possible places for someone with his fly-ball tendencies to succeed. It's to the Nats' credit that they've exploited their circumstances to benefit from this sort of rare bird; assuming his arm doesn't fall off from overwork, of course. If Manny Acta puts him in another 85 games, we might as well be talking about the deadly virtues of the marsupial wolf.

Saul Rivera

Bats: S Throws: R Height: 5' 11" Weight: 150 Born: December 7, 1977 Age: 29

YEAR	TEAM	LVL	AGE	W	L	SV	G	GS	IP	H	BB	SO	HR	GB%	BABIP	STUFF	WHIP	ERA	PERA	EQERA	EQH9	EQBB9	EQSO9	EQHR9	VORP	WXRL
2004	HAR	AA	26	0	2	3	18	0	20²	27	12	15	3	—	.353	-33	1.88	7.83	7.39	10.80	12.6	6.3	4.5	1.8	-11.6	—
2004	HUN	AA	26	2	1	1	26	0	33¹	30	16	25	1	—	.302	-11	1.38	1.62	4.80	3.66	8.7	5.3	3.9	0.6	6.9	—
2005	HAR	AA	27	3	3	9	40	0	76²	72	20	70	3	66.1%	.309	-1	1.20	2.46	4.04	4.44	9.0	3.0	5.0	0.6	9.7	—
2006	NWO	AAA	28	1	1	1	12	2	28²	25	12	25	1	58.3%	.300	4	1.31	1.60	4.42	2.54	8.3	3.8	6.0	0.3	9.6	—
2006	WAS	MLB	28	3	0	1	54	0	60¹	59	33	41	4	46.2%	.288	1	1.52	3.43	4.40	3.90	8.5	4.2	5.5	0.6	12.0	1.11
2007	WAS	MLB	29	2	3	1	46	1	56	61	26	36	5	50.0%	.304	-10	1.54	4.58	5.31	5.04	9.7	3.8	5.3	0.8	4.0	0.30

Breakout: 10% Improve: 25% Collapse: 48% Attrition: 30% Comparables: Dick Hyde, John Riedling, Marc Valdes, Ken Trinkle

Sometimes, the guy who keeps taking the ball under any circumstance catches a break. Rivera's a small slip of a pitcher by major league standards, he'll never overpower anybody, and he'd be a poor choice as a last man in the pen for most teams, but, when everybody else floundered last year, it was the little journeyman who kept plugging along. He's a symptom of a broken staff, and someone Nats fans should think kindly of while looking forward to a better ballclub.

Felix Rodriguez

Bats: R Throws: R Height: 6' 1" Weight: 210 Born: September 9, 1972 Age: 34

YEAR	TEAM	LVL	AGE	W	L	SV	G	GS	IP	H	BB	SO	HR	GB%	BABIP	STUFF	WHIP	ERA	PERA	EQERA	EQH9	EQBB9	EQSO9	EQHR9	VORP	WXRL
2004	SFN	MLB	31	3	5	0	53	0	44²	43	19	31	7	—	.269	-11	1.39	3.42	5.37	3.57	8.7	3.4	5.6	1.2	10.7	0.65
2004	PHI	MLB	31	2	3	1	23	0	21	18	10	28	1	—	.347	21	1.33	3.00	2.93	3.00	8.1	3.9	10.7	0.4	6.2	1.03
2005	NYA	MLB	32	0	0	0	34	0	32¹	33	20	18	2	42.1%	.295	-8	1.64	5.02	4.99	4.81	8.6	5.3	4.8	0.5	2.7	-0.01
2006	WAS	MLB	33	1	1	0	31	0	29¹	32	16	15	5	35.4%	.287	-26	1.64	7.68	6.30	6.82	9.5	4.2	4.2	1.5	-5.8	-0.09
2007	FLO	MLB	34	1	2	0	27	0	30	32	18	21	4	41%	.294	-15	1.65	5.33	5.84	5.42	9.3	4.7	5.6	1.1	0.5	0.0

Breakout: 14% Improve: 42% Collapse: 34% Attrition: 23% Comparables: Terry Mathews, Ricky Bottalico, Alan Mills, Johnny Klippstein

F-Rod was supposed to provide some sort of experienced know-how in a setup role in last year's pen. He started with the best of intentions; after watching Pedro Martinez pelt Jose Guillen twice, he tried to step up and answer in kind by beaning Paul Lo Duca. This got him suspended for three games, but it was probably the closest he came to providing veteran leadership, as he subsequently strained a forearm, then hurt his shoulder. He then did something else veterans do, skedaddling to Florida on a minor league deal. He might stick, but he's a couple of years removed from success.

Chris Schroder

Bats: R Throws: R Height: 6' 3" Weight: 210 Born: August 20, 1978 Age: 28

YEAR	TEAM	LVL	AGE	W	L	SV	G	GS	IP	H	BB	SO	HR	GB%	BABIP	STUFF	WHIP	ERA	PERA	EQERA	EQH9	EQBB9	EQSO9	EQHR9	VORP	WXRL
2004	HAR	AA	25	2	2	11	32	0	48¹	39	17	51	3	—	.290	-1	1.16	2.42	4.80	3.09	8.3	3.9	6.4	0.8	13.0	—
2004	EDM	AAA	25	2	1	0	17	1	26²	24	15	32	3	—	.318	11	1.46	4.38	4.90	4.39	8.1	5.4	8.4	1.0	3.6	—
2005	HAR	AA	26	2	3	0	16	0	23	20	11	28	4	33.3%	.308	-9	1.35	4.70	7.71	6.33	9.7	5.9	7.2	2.5	-1.7	—
2005	NWO	AAA	26	2	0	4	19	0	23	21	15	29	6	34.4%	.283	-10	1.57	7.83	8.26	8.46	9.7	6.0	8.9	2.8	-7.1	—
2006	HAR	AA	27	2	0	1	9	0	14	18	6	13	2	42.6%	.356	-22	1.71	5.14	6.80	6.75	12.8	4.7	5.4	2.0	-1.7	—
2006	NWO	AAA	27	2	1	1	28	0	47¹	25	16	60	2	44.4%	.223	29	0.87	1.53	3.29	2.14	5.4	3.1	8.7	0.6	17.8	—
2006	WAS	MLB	27	0	2	0	21	0	28¹	23	15	39	7	29.7%	.281	15	1.34	6.36	5.65	6.21	7.8	4.0	11.2	1.9	-2.4	-0.36
2007	WAS	MLB	28	3	4	3	72	1	70²	66	32	67	11	36.0%	.284	3	1.40	4.64	5.17	4.98	8.4	3.7	7.7	1.3	5.9	0.50

Breakout: 25% Improve: 50% Collapse: 22% Attrition: 8% Comparables: Mike Armstrong, Scott Dohmann, Robinson Checo, Cecilio Guante

After a few ownership and management changes, you have to figure that something would be left behind that nobody had noticed before. There are very few survivors from the Expos' 2001 draft—top pick Josh Karp is long gone, and Mike Hinckley never panned out, though Josh Labandeira's probably in a file box around here somewhere—but their 19th-rounder from that year, Schroder, just might be a guy who sticks. He's never been considered a prospect, but he lives and dies at home plate as much as people with much better stuff, posting an impressive 423:159 K/BB ratio in 357⅔ pro innings despite a modest moving fastball and an even more nondescript slider. He has always been a reliever, which demonstrates that they can come from the strangest places, including minor league bullpens.

Billy Traber

Bats: L Throws: L Height: 6' 5" Weight: 200 Born: September 18, 1979 Age: 27

YEAR	TEAM	LVL	AGE	W	L	SV	G	GS	IP	H	BB	SO	HR	GB%	BABIP	STUFF	WHIP	ERA	PERA	EQERA	EQH9	EQBB9	EQSO9	EQHR9	VORP	WXRL
2005	KIN	A+	25	2	2	0	4	4	21²	19	6	13	2	55.9%	.266	-20	1.15	4.98	5.88	6.86	8.6	3.0	3.0	1.7	-2.9	—
2005	AKR	AA	25	3	2	0	5	5	34	25	5	27	2	48.0%	.235	9	0.88	2.65	4.13	4.13	7.7	1.7	4.4	0.8	5.3	—
2005	BUF	AAA	25	3	7	0	19	12	76²	96	30	55	7	52.4%	.346	-9	1.64	5.75	4.70	6.89	10.7	3.7	4.8	0.9	-11.2	—
2006	NWO	AAA	26	7	7	0	21	21	124¹	143	26	102	8	56.5%	.352	17	1.36	4.06	3.96	4.74	10.5	1.9	5.6	0.8	12.0	—
2006	WAS	MLB	26	4	3	0	15	8	43¹	53	14	25	5	46.4%	.329	-8	1.55	6.44	4.95	6.25	10.9	2.4	4.6	1.0	-4.8	0.30
2007	*WAS*	*MLB*	*27*	*7*	*9*	*1*	*35*	*21*	*126*	*139*	*37*	*77*	*15*	*49.0%*	*.301*	*0*	*1.39*	*4.67*	*5.06*	*5.14*	*9.9*	*2.4*	*5.0*	*1.0*	*7.2*	*1.50*

Breakout: 28% Improve: 66% Collapse: 6% Attrition: 2% Comparables: Randy Lerch, Trever Miller, Steve Avery, Terry Mulholland

Another survivor of the Nats wide-open casting call that left them overstocked with tweeners, Traber's your basic lefty strike-thrower, delivering please-don't-hurt-me, not-in-the-face junk. He used to throw with much more velocity in his days as a top Mets and Indians prospect, but he's one of the guys who had elbow surgery and didn't come back all better—you know, the ones you never hear about. He was tough on lefties in New Orleans, and he can keep the ball in the infield, but the Nats still aren't sure how to use him.

Ryan Wagner

Bats: R Throws: R Height: 6' 4" Weight: 225 Born: July 15, 1982 Age: 24

YEAR	TEAM	LVL	AGE	W	L	SV	G	GS	IP	H	BB	SO	HR	GB%	BABIP	STUFF	WHIP	ERA	PERA	EQERA	EQH9	EQBB9	EQSO9	EQHR9	VORP	WXRL
2004	LOU	AAA	21	1	0	1	15	0	16²	13	9	19	0	—	.295	16	1.32	2.69	3.57	2.76	7.2	5.5	8.3	0.0	5.1	—
2004	CIN	MLB	21	3	2	0	49	0	51²	59	27	37	7	—	.317	-8	1.66	4.70	5.01	4.89	9.8	4.1	5.6	1.0	0.5	-0.35
2005	CIN	MLB	22	3	2	0	42	0	45²	56	17	39	4	63.7%	.366	4	1.60	6.11	4.00	6.04	10.2	3.0	6.8	0.8	-4.7	-0.49
2006	LOU	AAA	23	1	3	1	35	0	38²	55	14	28	3	61.9%	.403	-21	1.81	6.36	4.68	8.15	13.0	3.5	5.1	1.2	-11.0	—
2006	WAS	MLB	23	3	3	0	26	0	30²	36	15	20	3	63.1%	.330	-11	1.66	4.69	4.61	5.68	10.2	3.7	5.1	0.9	-0.6	-0.64
2007	*WAS*	*MLB*	*24*	*3*	*4*	*3*	*85*	*0*	*81¹*	*89*	*35*	*55*	*7*	*54.0%*	*.313*	*-6*	*1.52*	*4.83*	*5.26*	*5.37*	*9.8*	*3.4*	*5.5*	*0.8*	*2.6*	*0.20*

Breakout: 32% Improve: 56% Collapse: 17% Attrition: 6% Comparables: Yoel Hernandez, Sergio Mitre, Randy Moffitt, Pete Vuckovich

Wagner might be the anti-Schroder—he's never been anything but a prospect, and he came into the game with a slider that was once graded a 70 to 80 on a scouting scale. Unfortunately, it's now more likely to grade around a 50, and, although he still throws hard, he's lost ground there as well. The extreme problems he's had learning to repeat his delivery and show his stuff with any consistency drove the Reds to distraction. It also created questions of whether Wagner was pitching scared. Thrown into the Kearns-Lopez deal, he has a new lease on life. If pitching coach Randy St. Claire can fix him, it will make a sweet deal that much sweeter for the Nats.

Lineouts

PLAYER	TEAM	LVL	AGE	PA	R	2B	3B	HR	RBI	BB	SO	SB-CS	SPEED	AVG/OBP/SLG	MLVr	EqAVG/EqOBP/EqSLG	EqA	VORP
OF R. Bernadina*	POT	A+	22	504	60	19	3	6	42	56	98	28-11	6.1	.270/.355/.369	.045	.259/.325/.358	.244	-0.5
CF F. Diaz	HAR	AA	22	428	44	17	1	9	50	19	59	5-5	4.1	.259/.296/.373	-.044	.247/.281/.365	.224	-10.5
SS M. Dorta	HAR	AA	24	442	54	15	3	5	30	30	34	33-10	7.2	.257/.307/.347	-.062	.239/.284/.322	.223	-11.4
	WAS	MLB	24	20	3	1	0	0	0	1	2	0-2	6.9	.211/.250/.263	-.404	.158/.200/.211	.135	-2.5
C D. Ivany	POT	A+	23	482	62	19	3	6	55	25	64	12-3	5.5	.262/.311/.359	-.043	.242/.273/.327	.213	-18.2
3B B. Larson	NWO	AAA	30	422	58	17	1	20	76	38	101	4-3	4.3	.268/.336/.476	.140	.254/.308/.429	.251	10.8
OF C. Marrero	NAT	Rk	18	91	10	9	0	0	16	8	19		3.6	.309/.374/.420	.218	.274/.319/.369	.241	-5.4
OF J. Maxwell	SAV	A	22	68	8	2	2	1	7	8	23	1-0	5.2	.172/.294/.328	-.142	.131/.221/.230	.175	-9.1
	VER	A-	22	306	36	11	3	4	33	27	61	20-5	6.6	.269/.346/.376	.104	.233/.288/.339	.227	-19.8
OF P. Redman	HAR	AA	26	342	40	22	1	11	45	38	63	8-8	4.8	.286/.374/.478	.223	.256/.327/.422	.257	0.5
	MEM	AAA	26	60	6	3	0	1	8	4	15	1-0	5.0	.268/.317/.375	-.047	.263/.311/.351	.232	-1.0

PLAYER	TEAM	LVL	AGE	W	L	SV	IP	H	BB	SO	HR	GB%	BABIP	STUFF	WHIP	ERA	PERA	EqERA	EqH9	EqBB9	EqSO9	EqHR9	VORP
C. Everts	POT	A+	21	5	10	0	90¹	96	53	92	11	—	.326	-17	1.65	5.99	6.82	8.08	10.6	5.6	6.4	2.1	-24.2
M. Hinckley*	POT	A+	23	6	8	0	148	178	63	79	18	—	.326	-49	1.63	5.53	7.69	7.45	11.6	4.4	3.1	2.4	-29.8
T. Hughes	NWO	AAA	28	2	6	4	73¹	50	41	87	3	—	.275	21	1.24	2.34	4.04	4.23	6.7	5.1	8.1	0.5	11.0
	WAS	MLB	28	0	0	0	11¹	13	6	4	2	—	.306	-32	1.68	6.37	7.23	5.40	10.0	3.9	3.1	1.5	-0.5
J. Nunez	DGR	Rk	20	6	0	0	57¹	35	19	56	0	—	.242	22	0.95	1.58	3.99	3.13	7.1	3.8	5.1	0.3	15.0
Z. Zinicola	VER	A-	21	0	0	4	9¹	6	1	10	0	—	.261	7	0.77	0.00	2.99	1.04	7.3	1.0	5.2	0.0	4.4
	POT	A+	21	3	0	3	13²	11	3	13	0	—	.314	11	1.06	2.05	2.89	2.70	7.4	2.0	6.1	0.0	4.3
	HAR	AA	21	1	1	5	10¹	11	11	8	0	—	.314	3	2.18	2.67	6.15	6.30	9.9	10.8	5.4	0.0	-0.8

Almost six years since his being signed, Dutch Antilles import **Rogearvin Bernadina** is still seen as someone with promise despite poor instincts that no amount of speed seems to make up for. If **Frank Diaz** was supposed to be a prospect, his introduction to Double-A had all the drama of *Bambi Meets Godzilla*. He's still young enough to recover a career as a fourth outfielder. A jump-out-of-his-shoes free swinger, **Melvin Dorta** is probably ruing his poor fortunes to have arrived on the scene so many years after the sexual revolution. At the plate, he's a threat to no one but himself. **Esmailyn Gonzalez** will have to show that he's more than a propaganda victory after signing out of the Dominican Republic for $1.4 million. He's tremendously athletic and has the physical tools to be a top-shelf glove, but nobody's sure what sort of hitter the 17-year-old will grow up to be. **Devin Ivany** isn't really a prospect, but we wanted to include a certain number of Nats, and guys who wear the tools of ignorance have it rough. To Ivany's credit, he's a smooth receiver and throws well, gunning down 35 percent of attempting base stealers. Another Red refugee who didn't quite turn out the way people hoped, **Brandon Larson**'s now just another Trotskyite on the lam, hoping that whatever power he shows in more obscure circumstances will win him some small amount of favor. The club's first round pick in 2006, Chris Marrero was seen as one of the best high school hitters on the board. Athletic with plus power and quick wrists, he's young, raw, and understandably on the slow boat instead of the express that brought guys such as Cordero, Zimmerman, and Bray up so quickly. Athletic yet injury-prone, **Justin Maxwell** has the basic attributes that excite scouts (power, speed, and a plus arm), but he's going to have to start convincing people that those tools will wind up on the diamond instead of the trainer's table. **Prentice Redman** had the poor fortune to be associated with a particularly awful edition of the Mets, but his performances since suggest he might still make a fine fourth or fifth outfielder for somebody.

Clint Everts came into the game spinning one of the prettiest curves you probably never did see; he's never really made it back from Tommy John surgery, so be skeptical whenever you hear that the procedure turns hurlers into supermen. Once seen as one of the organization's best hurlers, **Michael Hinckley** has completely lost his command over the last two years, gutting his prospect status. That **Travis Hughes** somehow got discarded by organizations as pitching-desperate as the Rangers and now the Nats should set off some alarm bells, but Boston signed him for 2007, figuring he throws hard and has some off-speed stuff that wiggles. If the other shoe drops and he turns out to be an axe murderer or something, I guess we'll hear all about it. **Jhonny Nunez** came over from the Dodgers in exchange for Marlon Anderson's services after posting a dominating season in the Gulf Coast League. The Nats pounced when University of Arizona reliever **Zech Zinicola** fell to them in the sixth round of last summer's draft; with a low-90s fastball and a hard slider he might move up fast, and he has that unflappable quality teams like in relievers.

Manager: Frank Robinson

Year	Team	W-L	Pythag +/-	Avg PC	100 +P	120 +P	QS	BQS	REL	REL w Zero R	IBB	SUBS	PH	PH Avg	PH HR	SB2	CS2	SB3	CS3	SAC Att	SAC %	POS SAC	Squeeze	Swing	In Play
2004	MON	67-95	+1	92	67	13	66	13	463	276	78	37	249	.190	2	88	34	21	3	121	82.6%	49	1	164	123
2005	WAS	81-81	+4	97.1	80	16	83	6	469	313	77	68	266	.199	2	34	36	11	7	125	72.8%	47	2	136	101
2006	WAS	71-91	+2	90.2	49	3	63	7	515	322	93	49	312	.263	8	104	43	19	19	105	72.4%	37	2	152	127

The great man didn't leave on his own terms, and there were clearly aspects of the job—and perhaps this particular job—that he wasn't thrilled about. His getting worked up over pulling Matt LeCroy mid-game was touching, but also more than a little mawkish—LeCroy couldn't stop the opposing running game, and pulling him mid-inning while protecting a lead when the opposition was running wild was not humiliating, it was a matter of trying to win the game. And the Nats did win, that time. In many ways, Robinson was something of a leftover—more involved tactically than most of his peers, both offensively (with the bunt and the hit-and-run), and defensively—Robinson was more likely to issue an intentional walk than almost anyone else in the game the last few years, even making allowances for the staff's 2006 meltdown.

In Robinson's place is one of his former coaches, Manny Acta, who coached third for the Expos from 2002–2004. At the tender age of 38, he's the youngest manager in the majors. Acta comes back after coaching third for the Mets in the interim. His managerial experience mostly comes from eight years in the Astros' system in the nineties, four in the New York–Penn League, one in the Midwest, and three in the Florida State League, all levels at which a manager is under pretty strict guidelines and has to observe player development goals more than pursue tactical or operational trickery for fun and profit. Acta also managed the Dominican Republic in the World Baseball Classic and has a bunch of winter league experience.

You've Got the Brawn, I've Got the Brains, Let's Make Lots of Money

Neil de Mause and Maury Brown

If 2006 didn't see much in the way of on-field historic moments—no sox of any color breaking postseason curses, just the Cardinals' World Championship odometer turning over from nine to ten—it was a watershed for MLB's business side. In the spring, funding was approved for four new stadiums, in Washington and Minnesota, and for both New York teams, a flurry of construction activity that, by 2009, will have all but six teams playing in stadiums built within the last 20 years. In the fall, a largely forgettable World Series was interrupted by the startling announcement that baseball's owners and players had agreed to a new Collective Bargaining Agreement two months before the old one was to expire, leading to much talk of a new era of labor-management cooperation. Add in continuing changes in the way tickets are sold (and resold) and how fans follow their teams via television and the Internet, and it was definitely a year of major transition for baseball as an industry.

The following are some the top off-the-field developments from the year just past:

The New Collective Bargaining Agreement

Bud Selig has always insisted that no major announcements should be allowed to upstage the World Series, but this year he broke his own rule. On October 24, before the Cardinals and Tigers faced off for Game Three of the Fall Classic, Selig and Major League Baseball Players Association chief Donald Fehr announced that the league and the union had approved a new collective bargaining agreement two months before the previous labor pact was set to expire. By the time the new CBA ends on December 11, 2011, baseball will have experienced an unprecedented 16 years without a work stoppage.

The new agreement is not a major departure from the previous pact, with the largest adjustments being made to baseball's revenue-sharing formula and the competitive balance tax, more commonly known as the "luxury tax." Other changes affect baseball's amateur draft, minimum salary, draft choice compensation, and key free agency dates. MLB's testing program for steroids and other performance enhancing drugs was also incorporated into the CBA for the first time.

The revenue-sharing changes are designed to make the system more equitable, while still transferring roughly the same total amount of revenues from high-revenue clubs to low-revenue ones. The old system included two components. The first was a "straight pool" whereby each club was taxed 34 percent of its net local revenues (defined as a club's gross baseball revenues, not counting revenues from national broadcast deals and other central MLB sources, and minus stadium development expenses), which was then distributed evenly to all 30 clubs. The second was a "split pool" that taxed only clubs above the median revenue, with that money going solely to clubs below the median based on how far below the median they fell.

There was one big problem with this system. When the effects of the straight pool and split pool were combined, low-revenue clubs ended up paying a higher marginal tax rate (48 percent) than their high-revenue competitors (40 percent). (The marginal tax rate is the share of each new dollar of income that one pays in taxes. Anyone who has paid income taxes should be familiar with the concept: If you're in the 25 percent bracket, you don't pay 25 percent of your total income in taxes, but for every $1,000 your income rises, your tax bill goes up by $250.) While low-revenue teams didn't pay into the split pool, their revenue-sharing checks shrunk as their revenues increased. As a result, if a team such as the Kansas City Royals were to increase its local income by $10 million, it would end up seeing a $4.8 million drop in its revenue-sharing receipts. This created a rather large disincentive for these clubs to reinvest in player payroll, since a big chunk of any new money they brought in would go straight back to the league.

In the new revenue sharing system, the "straight pool" is reduced to 31 percent of net local revenues, while the "split-pool" component is now based on a club's past revenues, not its current ones, and teams below the league median in revenues will now all receive equal amounts (with the caveat that no amount can push a team over the median). Put it all together, and the result is that while the same total dollar amount will change hands via revenue-sharing ($326 million, the same as in 2006), the effective marginal tax rate for all teams is significantly reduced to 31 percent—something that it is hoped will provide an incentive for clubs to increase their revenues, since they will be allowed to keep more of each new dollar earned.

Will the new rules stop the perception that some clubs are pocketing their revenue-sharing dollars instead of reinvesting them in their ballclubs? While the details are still being negotiated at press time, the new pact is likely to contain similar language to the old CBA, requiring that each team use its revenue-sharing funds "in an effort to improve its performance on the field." However, there is nothing that states unequivocally that the money must be spent directly on MLB player payroll or such things as player development and scouting. Although this past winter's orgy of free-agent spending indicates the drop in the marginal tax rate loosened many teams' purse strings, it's done more to encourage high-revenue teams such as the Cubs to spend even more than low-revenue teams to start throwing money around; outside of Gil Meche's big Kansas City payday, all of this winter's big-money signings involved teams in the major media markets.

As for the other CBA provisions, the luxury tax remains in place, with minor adjustments. The threshold for paying the tax will jump from $136.5 million in team payroll to $148 million in 2007, $155 million in 2008, $162 million in 2009, $170 million in 2010 and $178 million in 2011, an increase of approximately five percent a year. Clubs that exceed those figures would be hit with a tax of 22.5 percent for first-time violations, 30 percent for going over the threshold a second time, and 40 percent for surpassing it more than twice during the current labor agreement. Finally, any clubs that paid luxury tax in 2006 will be accessed a 40 percent tax rate should they exceed the threshold again in 2007, a provision that would affect only the Yankees and Red Sox (see table 1).

The major-league minimum salary will increase from the current $327,000 in the prior agreement to $380,000 in 2007, with cost-of-living adjustments each year until 2011. If the new minimum salary had been in place in 2006, when Florida had seventeen players on their 25-man roster earning the minimum, the Marlins would have been on the hook for an additional $901,000 in salary—which, while it may not look like much in baseball terms, would have represented six percent of the team's total payroll.

Despite rumors that the new CBA would end the system of using draft picks to compensating teams that lose free agents, that did not happen, but there were several adjustments. For Type A free agents—formerly the top 30 percent of major-league players as defined by MLB's rating system, now the top 20 percent per the new CBA—the club that loses the player will receive the first-round pick of the team that signed him, plus an extra "sandwich" pick from the supplemental round between the first and second rounds. Type B players (now defined as the next 21 to 40 percent of players at each position, down from 31 to 50 percent under the old CBA) no longer cost teams a draft pick; instead, the team that loses the player will receive a sandwich pick. Compensation for Type C free agents has been eliminated. All of these changes went into effect for the 2006–07 free agent season, something that no doubt contributed to the lucrative offers received by Frank Thomas, Juan Pierre, Ted Lilly, and other Type B's, since these players suddenly cost only cash, not picks.

Free agency dates have been changed in the new agreement, as well. Under the old CBA, any free agent not offered arbitration by his former team was ineligible to re-sign with that team until May 1. Under the new rules, they may re-sign with their old club at any time, regardless of the arbitration offer. The salary arbitration deadlines also moved slightly: The date to offer arbitration to free agents moves from December 7 to December 1, the deadline for players to accept offers moves from December 19 to December 7, and the tender date is now December 12.

Lastly, some 40 grievances have been settled in the new CBA, some of which dealt with union charges that management colluded to keep player salaries down following the 2002 and 2003 seasons by setting up a central database to compile teams' contract offers to free agents. In settling these latest collusion grievances, management

Table 1. Luxury Tax Figures During 2003–2006 CBA

Club	2003	2004	2005	2006	Total
NY Yankees	$11,798,357	$25,964,060	$33,978,702	$26,009,039	$97,750,158
Red Sox	—	$3,148,962	$4,148,981	$497,549	$7,795,492
Angels	—	$927,059	—	—	$927,059
Total	**$11,798,357**	**$30,040,081**	**$38,127,683**	**$26,506,587**	**$106,472,706**

You've Got the Brawn, I've Got the Brains, Let's Make Lots of Money

made no admissions of guilt, and agreed to pay players just $12 million, compared with the $280 million that owners had to cough up in the 1980s when arbitrators found MLB guilty of colluding to keep player payroll down.

All in all, the new agreement works to address some of the shortcomings of the 2003–2006 CBA. With Bud Selig having announced that he will be retiring when his contract expires in 2009, it will be interesting to see how a new commissioner approaches the next labor agreement when this one expires in 2011.

Four Teams Get New Stadiums (and the Royals Get a Rehabbed One)

After a five-year span in which only one new baseball stadium was approved—the Cardinals' Busch Stadium III, which broke ground in 2004 and opened last spring—2006 saw the logjam burst, with new homes approved for the Washington Nationals, New York Mets, New York Yankees, and Minnesota Twins, and a large-scale renovation for the Kansas City Royals.

The first project to get the go-ahead was the as-yet unnamed Nationals stadium, which received final approval from the Washington, D.C., city council in March, 18 months after it was first proposed by Mayor Anthony Williams. In that time, the stadium's price tag had risen from $440 million to $611 million, thanks largely to an initial estimate that had, according to a *Washington Post* investigation, purposely lowballed contingency costs in order to make the plan more palatable to the city council. Of the total cost, the vast majority would be paid for by D.C. taxpayers: The Nationals owners would be responsible for just $5.5 million a year in rent, plus $20 million toward a parking garage, while collecting all stadium revenues from ticket sales, concessions, parking fees, and naming rights.

The Washington stadium is set to open in 2008, with a glass-and-steel design that, depending on your perspective, is either refreshingly modern or disturbingly reminiscent of a suburban office park. One remaining uncertainty is how fans will get there: The council rejected a parking-garage plan that would have required raising the stadium spending limit yet again, instead approving a scaled-back plan that will provide just 1,225 of the 9,000 parking spaces that the district had hoped for. The nearby Navy Yard Metro station will be expanded with $20 million in federal money, though even then it will only match the capacity of the often-overwhelmed RFK station that currently serves D.C. baseball fans.

After Washington, Kansas City was the next to approve public funds for its baseball team. On April 4, vot-ers in Missouri's Jackson County narrowly approved (53–47 percent) a plan to raise sales taxes three-eighths of a percentage point for the next 25 years, generating $425 million to be used on renovations to both the Royals' Kauffman Stadium and the neighboring Arrowhead Stadium, home of the NFL's Chiefs. (Among the K.C. baseball greats who had stumped on behalf of the stadium referendum were the late Buck O'Neil and George Brett.) The cash will help pay for what the Royals promise will be a "360-degree entertainment atmosphere" at the 33-year-old stadium, including new restaurants and concessions concourses, plus 2,500 "fountain seats" to be installed around Kauffman Stadium's iconic outfield fountains.

Both Kansas City teams had "state-of-the-art" clauses in their leases that would have allowed them to relocate if the upgrades were not approved. (Though Royals executives had been careful not to threaten to leave town, the Kansas City Star made the case for them, running an article the week before election day that began: "Imagine the Portland Royals. Or the Charlotte Royals.") With the renovations approved, the Royals are now committed to stay put for 25 years, with the power to tap additional public funds for future renovations to ensure that their stadium remains "first class."

One day after the Royals vote, New York's city council acted to approve its own stadium deal, okaying a new home for the Yankees that will cost about $1.3 billion total; the Mets had their own $600-million-plus stadium project approved later that month. Thus ended, depending on how you count, either one of the most drawn-out or one of the shortest stadium battles in history. Talk of a new Yankees stadium, either in the Bronx or Manhattan, had been kicking around since the eighties, while the Mets had proudly announced plans for an "Ebbets Field with a roof" in April 1998. Yet the official plans for the latest incarnations of these stadiums—both to be built adjacent to the teams' current homes, and both shorn of their originally planned roofs—were not publicly disclosed until June 2005. After a whirlwind ten months of public hearings (one development expert remarked that the stadiums had moved "at warp speed" compared to the typical city construction project), both had been approved.

The deal marks the end of the line for both Yankee Stadium, which will be torn down in 2009 to make way for new public ballfields (initial plans to retain a small piece of the grandstand and the playing field were quietly scrapped in late 2005), and Shea Stadium, which will become the parking lot for the Mets' new home. It also marks the demise of Macombs Dam Park, the century-old city park that stood just north of the House that Ruth Built; by the end of last summer, its ballfields and running track had been torn up, and construction crews were busily sinking the foundation of the Yankees' new home. Neighborhood residents filed a lawsuit to block the taking of their parkland—as one had declared at a press conference, "If they're not allowed to build a stadium in Central Park, why should they be allowed to build in our park?"—but it was dismissed in October.

While the New York teams touted their new stadiums as "privately financed," the reality was more complex. The Mets and Yankees will be responsible for paying off the stadium construction bonds, but they will also receive a series of tax and rent breaks that will ease their fiscal burden; the city, for example, is spending $160 million on new recreational facilities to replace those demolished for the Yanks' stadium, while the Mets will get a bigger cut of parking revenues in their new home than they did at Shea. Counting both direct subsidies and tax breaks, city and state taxpayers will contribute just under $700 million to the two stadiums—just a hair less than the two teams themselves will spend after accounting for both the value of tax breaks and the value of being able to deduct stadium expenses from their revenue-sharing payments to MLB.

In May, a team that had been plotting for a new stadium almost as long as the Mets and Yankees saw its plans come to fruition, as the Minnesota state legislature approved plans for a $522-million Twins stadium after eleven years of public battles. The breakthrough came when the board of commissioners of Hennepin County, which includes Minneapolis, hit upon a clever ploy by which the county would raise $373 million in public funds for the stadium via a sales-tax increase; state legislators would need to vote to lift the requirement for a public referendum on any tax hikes, but would not have kick in any state funds. As a result, the stadium funding was able to be approved by the vote of just four of seven county legislators. The new park, which is set to open in 2010, will be open-air (a controversial move in wintry Minneapolis), and tucked into a smallish plot of land near the Target Center, home to the NBA's Timberwolves.

Though this year's stadium crop included many different funding strategies, it continued a trend among owners to prefer asking for indirect public subsidies rather than straight cash contributions—in part prompted by the 2002 change to MLB's revenue-sharing formula that allowed clubs to deduct stadium construction costs, but not rent or taxes paid. New York's financing was the most creative, having the teams issue their stadium bond payments as "payments in lieu of taxes," enabling them to take advantage of city-issued triple-tax-exempt bonds. Since bondholders don't have to pay city, state, or federal taxes on their bond

payments, this allows the teams to pay a much lower interest rate than they would with regular private bonds—effectively pushing hundreds of millions of dollars of the construction cost onto federal taxpayers. (The Yankees' groundbreaking, in fact, was held up for several months while the IRS ruled on the legality of the scheme.)

Another clear preference among MLB owners is the downsizing of capacity. D.C.'s as-yet-unnamed home will hold just 41,000, compared to RFK Stadium's 46,000. (The last row of seats at the new stadium will still be farther from the field than at RFK, though.) The new Twins park will hold 40,000, down from 45,000 at the Metrodome. The Mets' new CitiField, as it will be dubbed thanks to a $20-million-a-year naming-rights deal with CitiGroup, will be significantly scaled down from Shea's 55,000 capacity to a mere 44,000, 2,500 of which will be standing room. The Yankees' new stadium will be a few thousand seats shy of their old one as well. Reducing capacity enables teams to drive up demand, and thereby sell fewer tickets for a higher price: Average Yankees ticket prices are projected to rise from $27 to $57 in the new stadium, according to city economic consultants.

The next stadium plan on the horizon looks to be cognizant of all these trends. In November, A's owner Lew Wolff announced preliminary plans for a new stadium in the East Bay city of Fremont, about 25 miles south of Oakland, as part of a larger condo development. The new facility is set to hold as little as 30,000 fans, which would make it baseball's smallest stadium since the Expos' days in Parc Jarry. As for funding, while Wolff declared that the A's would pay construction costs, a team press release stated that the team planned to use tax "benefits generated solely by the development" and "other aspects of public-private cooperation that will stand the test of public acceptance." Any reports of the death of the publicly subsidized stadium, it's clear, have been greatly exaggerated.

The New National Television Agreement With Fox and Turner Sports

On July 11, MLB announced that a new national television contract had been reached that retained Fox as baseball's sole over-the-air broadcast partner, while, for the first time, adding Turner Sports to the cable mix.

Under the new agreement, which runs through 2013, Fox will pay approximately $257 million a year for the rights to the World Series, the All-Star Game, one League Championship Series, and 26 Saturday Games of the Week. Turner will pay about $104 million a year for the other LCS and exclusive rights to League Division Series games—

meaning that the first round of baseball's postseason will, for the first time, be solely available on pay TV—plus a new national Sunday afternoon broadcast during the regular season. Starting in 2008, Turner Sports will also air any tiebreaker games and the All-Star Game selection show, rights formerly held by ESPN. When the Fox and Turner Sports television revenues are added to the separate ESPN television deal brokered in 2005, MLB will pull in nearly $660 million a year in national television rights fees. Tim Brosnan, MLB's executive vice president of business, has projected that baseball's total national television revenues will increase by 19 percent under the new agreement.

Starting in 2007, the League Championship Series will flip-flop between channels, with TBS getting the NLCS in 2007, 2009, 2011, and 2013, and the ALCS in even-numbered years. Overflow programming—such as one of two Division Series games being played simultaneously—and the All-Star Game selection show will be shown on TNT.

Though the shift to cable-only broadcasts for the Division Series (and one LCS) represents a potential loss of visibility to MLB, it should only be a small one: Currently, 91 million of the 111 million TV households in the U.S. (82 percent) have cable or satellite hookups, and that figure continues to grow. With *Monday Night Football* and the NBA conference finals moving to cable, the departure of much of the baseball postseason to pay TV may have been inevitable.

As part of the deal, Fox's Saturday Game of the Week will air 26 weeks a year, up from 18 currently, and start time will move from 1:00 pm to 3:30 pm Eastern. TBS will air 26 Sunday Games of the Week. At the same time, the superstation is relinquishing its 30-year-long role as the national home of Braves telecasts in 2008 to focus on more lucrative ventures such as airing reruns of *Seinfeld* and *Friends,* though some games will continue to air on WTBS, the local Atlanta affiliate.

Baseball fans will get a bit more stability out of the new TV deal: Instead of viewers needing to flip back and forth among five channels—Fox, ESPN, Fox Family, ABC Family, and FX—as they have in recent years, all postseason games will now air on one of three stations, Fox, TBS, or TNT. There could be more flipping during the games themselves, though: As part of the new deal, Fox gets expanded commercial time between half-innings.

Fantasy Sports Company Wins First Round In Court

As court decisions go, it was hardly *Brown v. Board of Education,* or even *Flood v. Kuhn.* But, when the ruling in *CBC Distribution and Marketing Inc. v. MLBAM* was handed down in August, it was nonetheless closely watched by baseball fans and industry execs alike for its far-reaching implications: the future of fantasy baseball games, and, more broadly, what uses can be freely made of baseball statistics.

The roots of the case go back to February 2005, when MLB Advanced Media—MLB's internet marketing arm, which had bought the rights to license player names for fantasy purposes from the players' union for $10 million a year a month earlier—decided to dramatically scale back the number of companies that it would license to operate fantasy games. Previously, anyone who coughed up a fee would be granted a license, but MLBAM put out word that henceforth it would make only a limited number of licenses available. (Artificially creating scarcity to drive up prices is clearly not limited to stadium-capacity decisions.) Everyone else, except for tiny services with fewer than 5,000 customers apiece, would have to close up shop.

One of the companies that was being locked out was CDM, which ran fantasy baseball games for USA Today and The Sporting News, among others. "On Friday [February 4] we get an e-mail back from them that they're not going to grant us a license to operate fantasy baseball games this year," CDM Vice President Charlie Wiegert told Baseball Prospectus at the time. "The only option that they gave us was we could send our customers to them, and if our customers signed up to play their games, they'd give us a 10 percent royalty."

CDM promptly filed suit, with the aid of a lawyer who'd successfully defended a client who'd published his own phone book by copying names and numbers out of a competitor's white pages (CBC Distribution, the official plaintiff, was the umbrella corporation that owned CDM), and it continued running its fantasy games, operating without a license.

While much of the news coverage made the resulting legal battle seem like one over who owns baseball statistics—"Baseball Is a Game of Numbers, But Whose Numbers Are They?" asked one New York Times headline—the actual point of contention was a far narrower one. CDM argued that it was simply reporting game results, no different than when a newspaper publishes box scores of the day's games. MLBAM countered that allowing anyone to run fantasy baseball without a license would infringe on the players' "right of publicity"—the same privacy right that prohibits you from putting out a breakfast cereal called "Jolie-O's" and slapping Mrs. Pitt's face on the box to boost sales. The first case to establish a right of publicity was, in fact, the 1953 case in which Bowman successfully sued Topps for issuing baseball cards in violation of its exclusive license to use players' names and images.

The question before the court, then, was, when you join a fantasy league, are you paying for a stat service, or for the right to play a made-up game involving real-life human beings?

Each side had case law it could cite in its defense. CDM's lawyers pointed to *NBA v. Motorola and Stats Inc.*, a 1997 case over the stat service paying reporters to provide live updates of basketball game scores that would be beamed to customers' pagers. (The NBA lost, clearing the way for the Gamecast-type services that proliferate today.) MLBAM, for its part, pointed to a long history of legal rulings indicating that athletes, like other celebrities, have a right to control the use of their names or likenesses, and further noted that both fantasy sports companies and others that used sports statistics in their products, such as manufacturers of baseball cards and table games, had always paid license fees. When fantasy-sports operators insisted that they had just as much of a right to use player names as Trivial Pursuit does to write trivia questions about celebrities, MLBAM lawyer Lee Goldsmith countered that CDM was not selling merely facts or statistics, but, "the ability to buy, sell, draft, and cut Derek Jeter, Alex Rodriguez, Albert Pujols. And part and parcel of the reason that people are willing to pay for that ability is the persona of Jeter, of Rodriguez, of Pujols."

The long-awaited court case, though, was over before it even got out of the first inning. Before the trial had begun, federal district judge Mary Ann Medler issued a summary judgment in favor of CDM, ruling that, "players do not have a right of publicity in their names and playing records as used in CBC's fantasy games," on the grounds that the fantasy game company was not trying to gain a commercial advantage through use of the names, since, "there is nothing about CBC's fantasy games which suggests that any Major League baseball player is associated with CBC's games or that any player endorses or sponsors the games in any way." Further, Medler wrote that, even if the players did have a right of publicity, "the First Amendment takes precedence over such a right," just as it does for newspapers that print player names and statistics as part of box scores.

MLBAM promptly appealed Judge Medler's ruling; the Eighth Circuit federal court of appeals is expected to hear the case sometime in 2007. In the meantime, despite panicked predictions by baseball officials that a ruling for the plaintiffs would lead to companies issuing bootleg baseball card sets without paying for player names and team logos, things remain more or less business as usual— at least until both sides have resolved all their appeals.

MLB Advanced Media Continues to Grow

In June 2000, MLB.com was launched, bringing what had been 30 independent team websites under one umbrella, with the expenses—and profits—evenly split among ballclubs. Each club was to invest $1 million a year over four years. The cost was targeted at $120 million. To the joy of the owners, MLB.com started generating a profit in only its second year.

Since that time, MLB Advanced Media, the company set up to oversee baseball's Internet presence, has become a revenue-making juggernaut. In 2005 alone, MLBAM accounted for $265 million in total revenues for Major League Baseball, a 92 percent increase from the year prior. At last count, MLBAM was projected to pull in more than $600 million in revenues for 2006, a figure that is expected to grow as MLB.com runs more advertising, which currently accounts for about 10 percent of all of MLBAM's revenues. MLBAM also announced this year that it sold a record 20 million tickets online through MLB.com. (MLBAM bought Tickets.com for $66 million in 2005 to be its ticket-sales arm.)

MLBAM also introduced new streaming audio and video options in 2006, such as MLB.TV's "Mosaic," which allows users to watch up to six games simultaneously, pull up stats from a customized player list, and get alerts on games around the league. MLBAM has begun using this technology for other sports and entertainment as well, such as streaming video of such musicians as Earth, Wind & Fire and the New Cars with Todd Rundgren performing at their rehearsal space. MLBAM also owns a 10 percent share of the World Championship Sports Network, which provides netcasts of sports such as track and field, rowing, wrestling, and gymnastics. All told, non-baseball MLBAM revenues are projected to be $40 million for 2006.

There is also a continuing push to provide more Spanish-language MLB websites. At the beginning of the 2006 season, the sites of the San Francisco Giants, Houston Astros, and Los Angeles Dodgers, as well as MLB.com's central site, were available in Spanish. By the end of the 2006 season, those teams were joined by New York Yankees, Chicago White Sox, San Diego Padres, and Arizona Diamondbacks in offering Spanish-language content.

The still-uncertain legal climate around new media rights could end up greatly influencing the future of baseball's online marketing. For example, depending on the final outcome of the *CBC v. MLBAM* "fantasy stats" case, MLBAM may have to revisit its $50 million deal for fantasy rights with the Players Association. MLBAM has also declared that it will seek to force a licensing agreement on

Sling Media Inc., the makers of the popular Slingbox device that allows users to watch local television stations from anywhere in the world via computer, a technology dubbed "place shifting." MLBAM claims that the technology is in violation of MLB's cable and satellite user agreements, since it allows game broadcasts to be viewed outside of the geographic region for which it has been licensed.

Ticket Resales Become Big Business

If baseball's s-word for 2005 was "steroids," for 2006 it might well have been "StubHub." The online ticket-resale site, founded in 2000, saw its revenues double to nearly $100 million last year. Estimates of the overall size of the "secondary ticket market" vary widely, with published reports placing it anywhere from $2 billion to $25 billion in annual sales.

While many in the general public may lump StubHub (and other secondary ticket brokers such as RazorGator) together with ticket scalping, there's a significant logistical—and legal—distinction. For starters, these brokers neither buy nor sell tickets: They're just a virtual "auction house" where ticket buyers and sellers can meet online to conduct deals. Someone with extra tickets for sale posts an ad on StubHub giving the game, the general seating location (and sometimes individual seat numbers), and their requested selling price; the first buyer to bite has the tickets sent to them. StubHub collects a 15 percent fee from the seller in exchange for providing the site, guaranteeing ticket authenticity, and mediating disputes—if a seller backs out on a sale, for example, the service will try to find the buyer comparable seats.

It's a "peer-to-peer" service, in other words, operating in the same legal gray area as eBay and Craigslist—which also serve as conduits for ticket resales, though neither tracks baseball-specific sales. Another parallel, though, might be Napster, whose arms-length distancing from sellers didn't save it from litigation.

Several teams have already set up their own secondary-tickets markets, generally charging fees equal to about 20 percent of the total transaction, plus handling charges and sales tax. In a twist on the usual ticket-scalping laws that set maximum resale prices to protect buyers from price-gouging, most teams set minimum prices on resales, to ensure that fans don't dump unwanted tickets for below face value, and compete with the team's sales of its own unsold tickets.

At the same time, many franchises are starting to crack down on unauthorized ticket resales—not by going after StubHub and its ilk, but by threatening to revoke the ticket rights of season-ticket or mini-plan holders who resell their tickets through unauthorized channels. (The Yankees began notifying ticketholders that they would pull tickets of anyone caught selling on StubHub or eBay, even though the team's own planned "Pinstripe Marketplace" has yet to open for business.) Some teams can even revoke individual tickets that they find to have been resold by invalidating the barcodes before game day, providing a nasty surprise for those who are turned away unexpectedly from the turnstiles.

One sports franchise has already taken legal action against independent secondary-ticket sales. In November, the New England Patriots sued StubHub in Massachusetts state court, charging it with violating state ticket-scalping laws, facilitating the unauthorized resale of its tickets (which by team policy may only be resold through its own Ticketmaster-run website), and misappropriating the team's name without permission. Shortly thereafter, the team rescinded 38 season tickets held by former player Fred Smerlas, charging he had violated his contract by reselling them through his own company.

Some industry observers predict it's only a matter of time before baseball sets up its own league-wide resale agency, much as MLBAM centralized baseball's Internet presence a couple of years back. With billions of dollars changing hands, but only a thin trickle going to teams—MLB.com told the Washington Post last summer that baseball teams' take from ticket resales is less than $10 million per year—there's a huge incentive to expand baseball's control over this growing industry. MLBAM spokesperson Jim Gallagher says there are no plans for a league-wide ticket resale agency, at least at the moment, but does note that the MLBAM-owned Tickets.com already performs resales for several big-league teams, splitting the ticket-fee proceeds between the service and the individual team.

Why the Sale of the Braves has not Been Completed

For the past year, the sale of the Atlanta Braves has lingered in the background of MLB's business dealings. Time Warner, which has owned the team since buying Turner Broadcasting in 1995, announced plans in May to sell the team to Colorado-based Liberty Media, but by year's end the deal had not yet been consummated.

The holdup is a complicated stock-swap scheme designed to allow both Time Warner and Liberty Media to dodge approximately $700 million in taxes. The deal would create a newly formed Time Warner subsidiary that would own the team and $1.35 billion in cash, which would then be transferred to Liberty Media. Liberty, in turn, would send about $1.84 billion worth of Time Warner shares it currently holds back to Time Warner. If Time Warner were to sell the Braves directly to Liberty Media for, say, $450 million, it would have to pay $175 million of federal and state income taxes. Instead, under what's known as a "cash-rich split-off," established under Section 355 of the Tax Increase Prevention and Reconciliation Act of 2005, neither side will pay any income taxes on the deal.

The Braves deal must be reviewed not only by the IRS, but also by MLB, which wishes to retain a local ownership face to the Braves. Liberty Media CEO Greg Maffei, speaking to an investor conference in December, referred to the Braves as a "little operating asset" that came along with the 355 deal, leading MLB to worry that Liberty Media sees the Braves only as a widget in the larger tax-shelter deal, and will likely turn the team around for resale once the five-year ownership period required by Section 355 expires. Baseball's owners have held off on voting on the Braves sale until they can ensure that Liberty intends to run the club in line with MLB's interest, and not merely as the booby prize in a tax-dodge deal.

A Peek at the Future

Looking ahead to next year, we'll likely be talking about the end of media-conglomerate ownership with the sale of the Braves and the Cubs, stadium debates for the A's and Marlins, and maybe, just maybe, final legal decisions on not just the fantasy baseball case, but the Los Angeles Angels of Anaheim name dispute as well. Also, by 2008 we should know whether the CBA-fueled salary inflation of this winter was a one-year bubble, or a sign that the leveling off of payrolls from 2002 to 2006 was a mere lull. Scott Boras, no doubt, will be waiting with bated breath.

Green-Lighting Environmental Change: How Baseball Is Shifting Its Outlook

Will Weiss

Energy politics experienced a watershed year in 2006. In his State of the Union address, President Bush admitted that the U.S. population was "addicted to oil." If that didn't get our attention, the subsequent hike in gas and oil prices, numerous new reports describing the reduction of the Greenland ice sheet and its effect on rising ocean temperatures, the British study on global warming suggesting that we're headed for a natural armageddon, and the success of Al Gore's bestselling book and documentary, *An Inconvenient Truth* all should have.

Global warming was discussed as frequently and fervently in the media as baseball's steroid scandle. For every story with scientific evidence to support the phenomenon, there seemed to be another debunking it. Like any good baseball-related debate, numbers can help put matters into context. The basic fact behind global warming is that when high carbon dioxide levels exist in the atmosphere, global mean temperature rises. The Energy Information Administration, a statistical and analytical organization within the U.S. Department of Energy, noted in preliminary data for 2005 that carbon dioxide equivalent (CO_2 Eq., a combination of carbon dioxide, methane, nitrous oxide, hydrofluorocarbons, perfluorocarbons, and sulfur hexafluoride) greenhouse gas emissions in the United States had increased 17 percent from 1990, when global warming was just beginning to enter public consciousness.

"Right now, it's fair to say there's a consensus that something is happening in the atmosphere due to global warming," said Dr. Allen Hershkowitz, a senior scientist at the Natural Resources Defense Council (NRDC), a leading independent environmental organization. "I don't know precisely what our contribution is or precisely how to resolve it."

The Sierra Club's "Cool Cities" program lists the cities and counties in the United States that have passed legislation to curb their impacts on global warming. In addition, the site describes the specific measures each city is planning to employ or has already put into motion. At press time, per the Cool Cities website, mayors in 21 of the 27 domestic MLB cities had signed the U.S. Mayors Climate Protection Agreement, a national bill calling for mayors across the country to develop more eco-friendly practices in their respective cities, with Boston, Chicago, New York, and Seattle taking the lead in aggressively enforcing environmental legislation. Policies in each metropolis range from new construction complying with the U.S. Green Building Council's Leadership in Energy and Environmental Design (LEED) standards to expanding the number of hybrid vehicles in their taxi and bus fleets. Houston and Pittsburgh, which have not yet signed the agreement, are working with local environmental groups to plan initiatives to alter their practices and become more active in climate protection measures.

Although Major League Baseball, with its pastoral roots, isn't the first industry that comes to mind when you think of energy concerns, it is directly and indirectly energy-intensive, and has a high environmental impact. The lights that power the stadium, the materials used to maintain the fields, the water used in restrooms and clubhouses and by vendors and groundskeepers, the air used to provide a climate-controlled setting in a dome, and the millions of gallons of gas consumed by the millions of patrons driving to the ballparks all contribute to the current state of affairs. Statistics gathered by NRDC estimate that Major League Baseball generated 72 million pounds of solid waste, used 1.2 billion gallons of water, and 93,000 kilowatt hours (kWh) of electricity per game for the 2005 regular season (April 3 through October 2). Powering a stadium for a baseball game requires the emission of approximately 154,000 pounds of CO_2. The total weight of CO_2 emissions produced by electricity use for the '05 regular season was thus roughly 374 million pounds, or 170,000 metric tons (the units in which the EIA presents its figures). That doesn't include transportation emissions for the roughly 75 million patrons who attended games in '05. NRDC research fellow Jack Murphy said the metric tonnage of CO_2 emissions would double if transportation was included in the EIA's figures.

Carbon dioxide is not federally regulated, and companies are not required to report their emissions. However, many provide their shareholders with sustainability reports, which contain information on their environmental impacts and practices. For example, companies such as Ford Motor Company and General Motors, with large manufacturing plants around the globe, emit nearly 3 million and 12 million metric tons of carbon dioxide, respectively (information based on each company's 2004–05 sustainability reports).

When compared to some of the country's most recognized commercial industries, Major League Baseball's emissions seem small. Overall, MLB's total emissions accounted for only 1.6 percent of the 1.0609 billion metric tons of carbon dioxide emitted by commercial operations in 2005. A reduction in these emissions on the league's part would make an almost negligible contribution to the effort to halt the global warming trend.

That's the macro outlook, though. On the micro level, within their respective cities baseball teams are major generators of pollution and waste. Since sports teams can be influential members of their communities, we wanted to know if the teams and MLB were aware of all this? If so, have they been doing anything about it?

The Commissioner's Initiative on Sustainable Stadium Operations and Team Practices

In November 2005, Robert Fisher, a board member of the Oakland A's and a NRDC trustee, approached his principal owner, Lewis Wolff, and Commissioner Bud Selig about improving environmental practices among the 30 teams. Over the course of the past year, continued discussions between NRDC representatives and John McHale, Jr., MLB's executive vice president of operations, have led to a league-wide initiative between the league and NRDC that unofficially went into effect in late August of 2006.

To start the initiative, NRDC issued a league-wide environmental performance survey to gather information on existing practices among the 30 teams. None of the teams are required to participate; teams can respond to the survey or discuss their efforts separately with MLB or NRDC at their discretion. At press time, 11 teams had completed the survey, and all of those teams were engaging in some form of environmentally-conscious practices.

The survey, which teams can access and complete online, covers topics ranging from paper use and recycling to waste management. There are also questions on water treatment and energy consumption: Specifically, if teams are exploring renewable energy or non-fossil fuel options to power their operations.

Many questions and comment options within the survey are listed in a comprehensive outline NRDC devised specifically for baseball. The most prominent feature of the outline is a top-five list of steps for teams to incorporate greener operating procedures: calling an energy audit provider and asking for a free energy audit, calling a printer or paper supplier and asking about recycled paper options, reducing office paper through double-sided printing, implementing recycling programs for bottles and cans during games, and educating fans about environmental issues.

Of the 11 teams that have responded to the survey, many have already incorporated some of the aforementioned steps. Some have even gone beyond the basics and are developing more innovative programs.

"We wanted to find out what clubs were doing because we had a sense there were a lot of forward-thinking environmental practices being pursued among our clubs, and we thought it would be a good idea to create a clearing house and to advise other clubs of what the best practices were," McHale said.

The following are preliminary results of the survey, per NRDC documents:

- All 11 teams had assigned purchasing priority to environmentally superior products, such as cleaning materials and compostable cups.

- Seven teams provide fans with recycling opportunities for plastic cups, bottles, and/or metal cans.

- Six teams are attempting to reduce paper consumption through recycling and less paper-intensive office practices.

- Nine teams are attempting to reduce energy consumption by auditing stadium energy use, adjusting energy management practices, and installing more efficient devices. Examples include water conservation measures such as using low-flow devices for toilets, transportable water treatment plants to reuse roof-cleaning wastewater, high-efficiency ballast (a device that maintains current at a constant voltage) in light fixtures, and time schedules for exterior and field lighting.

- Four teams are exploring the possibilities of renewable energy (wind, solar, geothermal hydro energy, etc.).

- Eight teams have reduced toxic chemical use by purchasing environmentally preferable chemicals for cleaning and field treatment, and changing general maintenance practices.

Green-Lighting Environmental Change

- Two teams are providing employees with reimbursement incentives for using public transportation to get to work.

For participating teams, MLB is leaving it up to the individual franchises to determine whether they want to announce their participation in the joint directive, or if they want to publicize their work with NRDC. It is the intention of both the league and NRDC to provide a non-political and non-judgmental approach to the initiative.

"The last thing we want to do is be seen as preaching or developing some sort of political position that certain clubs are not comfortable with," McHale said. "Our approach has been to make this as low-key and long-term a project as possible."

The league is trying to set an example for its member organizations by changing its practices in its New York headquarters and the rest of its national and international operating offices. The first priority, which should come as no surprise, is saving money. The best place to start, according to Dr. Hershkowitz, is cutting back on paper.

NRDC estimates that paper accounts for 50 to 90 percent of all office waste; it is also the third-largest industrial contributor to global warming. Printing double-sided or using vendors who supply recycled-content paper are just some of the ways teams can curb paper waste and cut costs. Due to supply contracts, however, some teams may be unable to change their paper policy for five to eight years. Others can do so immediately at no cost.

Teams changing their lighting to more energy-efficient bulbs will be able to save money on their electric bills within a year and a half. Total savings on energy reduction could reach 40 percent or more.

"We're not looking [to ask clubs] to change their vendors, we're looking to change practices. Then, the marketplace will change," Dr. Hershkowitz said. "We have built up the infrastructure for the supply chain of our economy over centuries. It doesn't change overnight, but it's starting to change.

"These guys aren't in the business of saving the planet, they're in the business of getting into the World Series and providing good entertainment. The fact that they're taking on these issues is all we can ask."

Making Green from Greening

One goal of the Commissioner's Initiative is to use green strategies as another means for teams to generate revenue. NRDC has experience greening the operations of professional sports franchises and helping them in this manner. The body consults for several National Basketball Association teams and is pushing to launch a league-wide directive with Commissioner David Stern on greening the NBA's arenas, but its work with the National Football League's Philadelphia Eagles can perhaps provide the closest parallel to how baseball teams can implement and market their respective programs.

The Eagles and NRDC began their partnership in 2003, not long after construction of Lincoln Financial Field and its adjacent practice facility were completed. First, an energy audit was conducted. From there, the Eagles and NRDC developed "Go Green," which in addition to serving as a rallying cry for the team (green is the Eagles' dominant team color), is a program designed to limit greenhouse gas emissions. Now in its fourth year, "Go Green" has been made part of the franchise's modus operandi. The program is heavily publicized; in addition to a "Go Green" microsite on philadelphiaeagles.com, the Eagles have "Go Green" advertisements posted throughout their stadium, and, according to Eagles director of marketing, Mike Malo, "You can't walk around our stadium without seeing a recycling receptacle."

The Eagles are setting the standard for green practices among sports teams. They purchase 25 percent of their energy from clean sources, use recycled, chlorine-free paper in their offices and publications, and non-toxic cleaning and maintenance supplies for their offices and fields. The Eagles are also exploring the feasibility of converting the cooking fat used in kitchens and concessions into the low-pollution fuel bio-diesel, which would be used to power stadium vehicles.

To date, the "Go Green" program has saved 139 million metric tons of greenhouse gas, 5.6 billion BTUs of energy, and 214 tons of wood by recycling and buying recycled paper, which has saved 450,000 trees. In addition, the Eagles have recycled 150 tons of paper, cardboard, and plastic beverage containers. The Eagles have saved a total of 6.4 million pounds of pollutants and 7.1 million miles of auto travel over the four-year life of the program. Information on financial savings resulting from the program's efforts was unavailable.

"This is not an effort of saving money for the organization, this is a commitment to being responsible to the environment," Malo said. "By setting an example of how to practice conservation, use renewable energy products—to set an example to make it more mainstream—we can go to our fans and say, 'We've made this commitment, and you can too.'

"Maybe where we haven't done our job," Malo added, "is telling our fans how to do more; educate our fans that there are options; encourage them to follow our lead."

Malo said "Go Green" is now entering its second phase, which involves broader incentive-based programs for both Eagles employees and fans. In one opportunity run through the Philadelphia area's utility company (PECO), Eagles employees can buy wind energy at a charge of 25 cents per day, which the organization will then reimburse. At the Eagles' regular-season finale last New Year's Eve, fans were presented with opportunities to make a New Year's resolution to join the "Go Green" program, and also to buy wind energy.

Another plan for the 2007 season has fans and businesses participating in a conservation contest, with each entity posting the results of their efforts to recycle and/or reduce pollutants online at the Eagles' "Go Green" microsite. The Eagles will recognize the efforts of one fan and one business each month, and award prizes. The contest is scheduled to run through the end of the 2007 regular season, culminating in a "Go Green"-themed game, complete with ads, literature, multimedia presentations, and an in-game awards presentation to the top conservationists.

The Eagles took four years to develop the breadth of their "green" operation, and only plan to launch two to three programs per year. NRDC won't be able to tailor programs for Major League Baseball teams until it gets more responses to its survey. However, the council and MLB are examining incentives for fans such as preferential parking for stadium patrons who drive hybrid cars and branded in-stadium presentations such as a "Recycled Play of the Day," in which a highlight from a past season gets broadcast on the jumbotron.

"The startup is the hardest part, getting the teams bought into changing their standard operating procedures to incorporate these new criteria," Dr. Hershkowitz said. "But in the long run, it's really important—baseball is really known as a civic, virtuous institution."

GreenMark Sports, an environmentally-focused sports marketing company based in Minneapolis, looks to link teams and their facilities with sponsorship partners across a number of environmental platforms. Through software called the EcoBrand Suite, which contains a database of 1,100 companies, teams can create a specific marketing strategy and match themselves with a corresponding company to sponsor a green program. The sponsor would not only have its name associated with the program, it would provide the technology for it. A hypothetical example would be if Cisco, which is paying $4 million a year for the next 30 years to have its name associated with the Oakland Athletics' stadium in Fremont, Calif., provided the information technology for all aspects of the ballpark in addition to the naming rights.

"We're looking at the whole building as a marketing opportunity—to sponsor the guts of the building and pub-licize those as positive improvements," said Mark Andrew, president of GreenMark Sports.

Similarly, NRDC suggests teams screen sponsors based on environmental performance.

MLB and Green Construction

Greening an operation isn't relegated to simply conserving paper or energy, or purchasing more eco-friendly products. The number of teams working with their architecture and design companies, builders and subcontractors, and their local governmental officials to green their stadiums is increasing.

The U.S. Green Building Council, a nonprofit organization founded in 1993, is a leader in this area. Through its Leadership in Energy and Environmental Design (LEED) ratings system, USGBC awards points to facilities meeting certain criteria in categories such as sustainable site (minimizing impact on the immediate surroundings via erosion and sediment control, stormwater management, etc.), water efficiency, energy and atmosphere considerations, materials and resources, indoor environmental quality, and an innovative category for exceptional items used in the greening process. Buildings must achieve 26 points on the 69-point scale to become LEED certified; USGBC awards a silver, gold, or platinum rating for scores higher than 26.

USGBC uses its ratings system to identify what should be done on a project basis for any given element of the ratings system. It does not certify building materials, however. The cost of going green depends on a number of factors; some materials are extremely expensive, such as countertops made from recycled glass and, depending on the state, Forest Stewardship Council-certified lumber. Items such as carpeting are more affordable.

"We look at a broad spectrum of impact in the materials sector that goes back into the supply chain," said Kimberly Hosken, USGBC's director of LEED new construction. "That's where a lot of the manufacturers are starting to work with us and talk to us about what they can do to their products and their processes to be more environmentally friendly.

"The green evolution is sort of at a tipping point right now, with everybody trying to figure out what they can do to their products, their process, and their design."

That is especially true for the Washington Nationals, who are collaborating with the architecture and design firm HOK Sport, USGBC, and the D.C. Council on LEED upgrades for their stadium, which is set to open in April 2008. According to Hosken, the Nationals are using recycled glass products as a base for the field itself as opposed to manufactured rock from a plant, and using energy-efficient lighting throughout the stadium. Nancy Stoner, director of NRDC's Clean Water project, added that wash-down water—water used by cleanup crews to hose down seats, aisles, parking lots, etc.—will be transported to a sanitary treatment plant so the dirty water doesn't flow into the already heavily-polluted Anacostia River. There is also a motion to recycle water used to treat the field itself for irrigation purposes.

The relationship between the stadium and the river is perhaps the greatest challenge facing builders, government officials and green advocates. In urban areas there are no filtration systems in place to prevent rainwater or melted snow from carrying contaminants into adjacent waterways, thereby polluting them. LEED standards for stormwater runoff are generally lower than the standards for energy. Thus, groups like NRDC have presented possibilities such as permeable pavement and planting rain gardens (areas with soil, plants, and trees to collect water) to assist in cleaning the stormwater runoff and decreasing the stadium's direct pollution impact on the river.

"The prerequisite for having an erosion control plan during construction is how the project protects the river," USGBC's Hosken said. "Usually codes help enforce the practices, but that sometimes depends on where you are in the country. The USGBC identifies how any project can implement a plan to avoid runoff events during construction that would carry contaminants off-site."

The most ambitious idea proposed was a green roof, specifically in the areas above concessions and luxury boxes, where the roofs are flat. In a green roof, a permeable lining with a soil median would be used to trap and filter stormwater. The Nationals' stadium would have been the first major sports stadium to have a green roof, and it would have been the largest on the East Coast. However, the proposal was rejected.

"One of the reasons we're interested in these green roofs is because there will be so many people who'll see them, either because they would attend the baseball games or because they would see them on TV," Stoner said.

The concept of green construction for the stadium originated in the D.C. Council, but the measures met opposition from the D.C. Sports and Entertainment Commission, which is supervising the construction project. The DCSEC cited financial concerns. The project is costing $631 million: $611 million public money and $20 million from Major League Baseball in the 2007 fiscal year (an extra $20 million is being contributed for ballpark development). Within those figures, $2 million—0.3 percent of the $611 million—was to be allocated for green components,

but, to date, only $1.2 million has been spent on eco-friendly provisions.

"The general feeling was that it should be doable [to implement $2 million worth of green construction]," said Ed Lazere, executive director of the D.C. Fiscal Policy Institute, one of the groups opposed the public financing of the stadium. "The people building the stadium were reluctant to go all the way with the $2 million environmental investment."

"[The D.C. Sports and Entertainment Commission] didn't say, 'We hate it,' but they haven't decided to make it a priority and do it," Stoner said. "We also talked to the Lerners [the new owners]. . . . They have gone back to the D.C. Council for various things—to put additional money in for other things, but they haven't decided to put it into [greening]."

Calls placed to the D.C. Sports and Entertainment Commission and the Anacostia Waterfront Corporation, a government-sponsored organization that supervises land development and restoration of the riverfront area and is responsible for paying for cost overruns on the stadium, were not retuned before press time.

In late 2006, then-Washington mayor Anthony A. Williams signed a green building bill into legislation, but the major components of the act won't go into effect until 2008, 2009, and 2012. By then, the stadium will be fully operational.

"You can write the best bill in the world, but we're not putting enough pressure on the District to implement it that quickly," said Christopher Weiss, director of Friends of the Earth, a Washington-based environmental advocacy group.

Despite the continued legal wrangling, the D.C. Council, Clark Construction, Hunt Construction Group, and Smoot Construction—the Clark/Hunt/Smoot Joint Venture is responsible for building the stadium—are continuing the effort to make the Nationals' stadium the first LEED-certified stadium in baseball. But that is not enough to appease those who believe the stadium could be even more environmentally friendly than it will be.

"We're glad that we will have LEED standards at the baseball stadium," Weiss said. "But I suspect there'll be some problems before we finish and that we may not get as much as we think we're going to get now. But it'll be something."

*   *   *

The Minnesota Twins and the New York Mets, with the help of USGBC, are also researching LEED possibilities for their new stadiums. Like the Nationals, the Twins have placed a heavy emphasis on water treatment in their greening plans. In addition to water considerations, the franchise is exploring the viability of renewing some of the methane gas produced at a waste facility adjacent to the ballpark site to power certain stadium operations. Details of the Mets' greening plans were not available at press time.

The Milwaukee Brewers, who opened Miller Park in 2001, are consulting with USGBC on upgrades to get the stadium fully LEED certified. So far, only the Utah Olympic Oval, which hosted speed skating in the 2002 Winter Olympics in Salt Lake City, and the Detroit Lions' Head-quarters and Training Facility in Allen Park, Michigan, have become accredited. The University of Connecticut is awaiting LEED certification results on the Burton Family Football Complex and the Mark R. Shenkman Training Center. Numerous other sports projects are awaiting USGBC LEED approval.

The challenge, Hosken said, is for the teams to continue operating the stadiums green after construction is complete.

"There's a disconnect because it's a different group of people that operate the buildings than the group that design and build it," Hosken says. "It's making that con-nection at an owner level."

Convincing team owners, local politicians and sta-dium operators that they could reap more benefits and save in the long term by spending more in the short term, as the case appears to be with the Nationals, could be the way to go.

"By getting LEED certified, operational costs drop dramatically," Andrew said. "The average LEED-certified building realizes savings 10 times the expenditure to get it energy efficient."

NRDC hopes to educate teams and bridge the per-ceived disconnect between teams and the designers and builders by meeting with MLB stadium operators every two years. The first of these meetings will take place this year.

What's Next?

The Commissioner's Initiative, much like any program so broad in scope and magnitude, is a long-term project. The Natural Resources Defense Council and Major League Baseball recognize that. The response has been good, despite the initiative being in the nascent stage. The trick will be getting the program to stick, and for the teams par-ticipating now and in the future to realize that the benefits, in some cases, may not come immediately.

"The teams need to be reassured that doing a little bit now will help in the long run," Dr. Hershkowitz said.

There's still a lot of convincing taking place: NRDC and MLB are pitching teams to change practices and edu-cate the public to do the same, getting cooperating spon-sors and, in general, making the concept stick.

There is not one particular remedy to global warming or many of the other environmental impacts to which we all contribute. Elizabeth Kolbert's three-part series pub-lished in the *New Yorker* two years ago and subsequent book, *Field Notes from a Catastrophe,* surmised that the damage already done is irreversible. Yet it is possible to reduce contributions to global warming on an individual basis, and perhaps powerful, high-profile sporting entities such as Major League Baseball can lead the way in main-streaming that mentality.

"This particular institution, Major League Baseball, really is the pinnacle of cultural influence." Dr. Her-shkowitz said. "That and the movies . . . will bring about a huge shift in education, baseball, in particular, because of the children and how the sports deal with youth. We're not going to be able to do everything, but baseball is going to be able to influence the fan. The fan that goes to the sta-dium will see a recycling bin and act accordingly. Maybe they'll get a bracelet that says 'Stop Global Warming.' Maybe the next time they go to buy a car they'll think about global warming. They won't say, 'I learned about it at a baseball game,' but maybe they will."

If the don't learn, Dr. Hershkowitz cautioned, "There might not be an atmosphere where they'll be able to play baseball."

Playing Naked: The Non-Impact of Baseball's Amphetamines Ban

Will Carroll with Jay Jaffe

I epected more.

When I wrote *The Juice* in late 2004, the steroid hysteria was at its height, but I felt so strongly about one point that I convinced my publisher to adjust the subtitle accordingly: "The Real Story of Baseball's Drug Problems"—not "Problem," but the plural. Baseball has never just had a steroid problem. Throughout the juiced era, and actually much further back in the game's history, baseball has quietly dealt with another, larger problem: the use of amphetamines.

Amphetamines had been in the game since the late forties, and connected to some of its greatest players. Some point to Ted Williams and other pilots returning from World War II as the first users; the Army Air Corps used amphetamines and other substances to keep pilots awake and alert on long flights. From Since the fifties on, the "bottle of greenies" had been a fixture in locker rooms. In 1979, Pete Rose admitted to using greenies in an interview with *Playboy*. The use and abuse of amphetamines was a part of the game's fabric. Even the Pittsburgh cocaine scandal of 1985 had an amphetamine abuse angle. Those players had used cocaine, a potent "upper," in place of amphetamines in large part due its to easy availability and "less jitters."

The problem continued to fester beneath the surface into the 21st century. While most of the media was pointing to the bottle of steroid precursor androstenedione in Mark McGwire's locker or what Victor Conte had in his U-Store-It unit, amphetamine use continued. In the affidavit filed after the search and interview with former pitcher Jason Grimsley, IRS Special Agent Jeff Novitzky stated that Grimsley told him about the "player's coffee." This idea of mixing uppers with one pot of coffee was hardly a new concept. Jim Bouton referred to it in his classic *Ball Four*, and Tony Gwynn mentioned it in his famous *Outside the Lines* interview. I can testify myself. In 2003, a friendly player who knew of my love for coffee asked if I wanted a cup. I had no idea he was going to hand me the "player's coffee." After that experience, even today, with the ban in place, you won't find me drinking the coffee in any locker room.

When baseball's drug policy was tightened in 2005 after Congressional scrutiny, I noted that there was no "giveback" to the MLBPA in return for yet again re-opening the Agreement. I now believe that amphetamines were the giveback, in that the players agreed to more steroid testing, something they knew was of concern to only a very small percentage of players, in order to keep their greenies. When amphetamines finally were banned for the 2006 season, I expected some effect. I was hardly alone. Longtime pitching coach Joe Kerrigan told the *Boston Globe*, "[A]mphetamines might be the next bomb that goes off in baseball." At a speech I gave in late 2005, I estimated the occasional use of amphetamines by players at 50 percent. Immediately, a team staffer in the audience said "higher."

To the casual fan, the amphetamine ban appeared to have no effect. Part of this was due to the testing program. Anticipating the possibility of high usage, the agreement between the Players Association and Major League Baseball put amphetamine use on a different track than steroids or other illegal or banned drugs. The penalties were lighter, and, more importantly, the first offense would not be made public.

It's known that some number of players tested positive for amphetamines during the 2006 season. No sources could confirm the exact count, but reports ranged from two to fifty. Meanwhile, no player drew the 25-game suspension mandated by a second offense. For the first year of the ban, the number was surprisingly low, even lower than steroid usage in its first year of survey testing (five to seven percent). I'd expected at least ten percent. Baseball players are creatures of habit. Wade Boggs famously ate chicken before every ball game. Stories about superstitions and routines are part of baseball lore. If players were used to playing "beaned up," but were now "playing naked," the change was going to involve some sort of cost.

Or was it? Jay Jaffe, who examined the statistical evidence of the effect of steroids in *The Juice,* searched for statistical evidence of the amphetamine ban's impact. What he found was stunning to me. With just a single year of the amphetamine ban under its collective belt, Major League Baseball as a whole didn't exhibit any statistical pattern that would suggest a league-wide effect, at least with regards to a few places we looked.

For starters, offensive levels rose, a result that doesn't particularly jibe with our notion of players trudging around the basepaths with less chemically-induced spring in their steps. Combining the two leagues, scoring rose by .27 runs per game (5.8 percent), home runs per game rose by 7.4 percent, batting average rose by five points, slugging percentage by 13 points, isolated power by nine points. Scoring, batting average, and slugging percentage were all at their highest levels since 2000 (see table 1).

Looking at recent history, it was 2005—the year steroid hysteria took over—that was the anomaly, not 2006. In 2005, scoring, batting average, slugging percentage, isolated power, home runs per game and per plate appearance were all down from 2004, supposedly a result of more stringent testing. The differences between 2004 and 2006 levels are very small, and in the context of the past 14 seasons, would barely rate a passing mention if they were consecutive years given some of the other fluctuations.

We examined a couple of other areas where it's been suggested that effects of the ban might show up. Since the supplements were purportedly often taken to counteract the effect of the previous night's action—both on the field and on the town—we'd expect to see fewer players in the lineups for day games after night games who had also played the night before (see table 2).

By way of explanation, DNG is the number of times teams played day games after night games. STARTS is the number of hitters in the starting lineups appearing in both

games, PER is the per-game average of players from both teams who played in both games and %CHG is the percentage change over the previous year. The number of players starting in both games fell by just about half a percent last year... to exactly the 2004 level, following a slight rise in 2005. In magnitude, the change was the seventh-largest of the past 14 seasons, but piddling in comparison to the changes which happened in 1997, 2002, and 2003. Again, there's no evidence here of the effects of the ban.

Since amphetamines were also purportedly taken to help players stay in the lineup, we examined the number of players playing in streaks of consecutive games, using 10-game increments as markers. Streaks were only counted based on the highest number of games played; that is, a 29-game streak was credited under the 20 category, and credited only once instead of nine times for the overlapping streaks (games 1–20, 2–21, etc.). Since MLB limits the number of consecutive days a team can be scheduled to play at 20 in a row, off days were ignored to allow for longer streaks; the point was to track players' availability to their teams, not whether they were sleeping in late enough. Also, because of the fact that, at any given moment, teams may have played differing numbers of ballgames, streaks interrupted by in-season trades and other transactions were ignored. Table 3 shows the data going back to 1998, when the leagues expanded to 30 teams, creating a player pool that's the same size as today's:

There's not much rhyme or reason here. Twenty-game, 30-game, and 100-game streaks were up in 2006, but every other category was down; still, the differences at the highest levels were small enough to have been obscured by players

Table 1. Year-to-Year Changes on Offense

Year	R/G	%chg	AVG	SLG	ISO	HR/PA	HR/G	%chg
1993	4.60	11.7%	.265	.403	.138	2.37%	0.89	23.1%
1994	4.92	7.1%	.270	.424	.155	2.72%	1.03	16.3%
1995	4.85	-1.5%	.267	.417	.150	2.67%	1.01	-2.1%
1996	5.04	3.9%	.270	.427	.157	2.87%	1.09	8.2%
1997	4.77	-5.3%	.267	.419	.152	2.71%	1.02	-6.4%
1998	4.79	0.5%	.266	.420	.154	2.76%	1.04	1.7%
1999	5.08	6.2%	.271	.434	.163	2.99%	1.14	9.3%
2000	5.14	1.1%	.270	.437	.167	3.07%	1.17	2.9%
2001	4.78	-7.1%	.264	.427	.163	3.00%	1.12	-4.1%
2002	4.62	-3.3%	.261	.417	.155	2.78%	1.04	-7.2%
2003	4.73	2.4%	.264	.422	.158	2.85%	1.07	2.8%
2004	4.81	1.8%	.266	.428	.162	2.97%	1.12	4.8%
2005	4.59	-4.6%	.264	.419	.154	2.76%	1.03	-8.1%
2006	4.86	5.8%	.269	.432	.163	2.94%	1.11	7.4%

Table 2. Getting Out of Bed and Into the Lineup

Year	DNG	STARTS	PER	%CHG
1993	501	6173	12.32	-0.17%
1994	365	4541	12.44	0.97%
1995	444	5554	12.51	0.55%
1996	518	6479	12.51	-0.01%
1997	537	6456	12.02	-3.88%
1998	528	6347	12.02	-0.01%
1999	540	6504	12.04	0.20%
2000	545	6687	12.27	1.87%
2001	544	6717	12.35	0.63%
2002	545	6527	11.98	-3.01%
2003	553	6810	12.31	2.83%
2004	544	6713	12.34	0.21%
2005	574	7121	12.41	0.53%
2006	578	7131	12.34	-0.55%

Table 3. Player Consecutive Games-Played Endurance

Year	10	20	30	40	50	60	70	80	90	100
1998	907	366	190	107	67	41	33	19	15	11
1999	908	355	182	106	66	44	26	20	12	9
2000	892	351	189	114	73	51	33	26	19	18
2001	955	366	178	105	70	47	26	19	15	11
2002	913	353	170	92	56	38	27	17	12	9
2003	947	361	187	98	57	35	25	20	15	11
2004	957	375	191	104	67	41	22	15	12	9
2005	922	365	173	115	77	49	37	23	15	8
2006	920	385	196	105	64	35	27	19	13	10
Avg	925	362	183	105	67	43	29	20	14	11

changing teams. In any event, the totals seen last year were within five of the 1998–2005 average, with the exception of the 20- and 30-game streaks (more of them) and the 60-game streaks (less of them). Once more, there is nothing here to indicate that the ban had any effect on performance.

Upon examining this information, about the only thing that is clear is that one of two possibilities is in play—either players did not use amphetamines at the levels that were widely assumed, or they were able to switch to other, non-banned products without any cost to their games. After speaking with players and other team officials, I believe the latter is the case.

"We spent twice as much on coffee," one clubhouse attendant told me. "I never had much to do with it. It was hands-off for me. Don't ask, don't tell. Now, we run out and I have to order more." Instead of hidden bottles of greenies, players now have mini-fridges of protein shakes and Red Bull in their lockers. A long-time minor league player—and, remember, the minor leaguers have been tested for amphetamines for years—told me that in the first year that minor leaguers were tested, he noticed more sleep. "Guys would sleep on the bus. Guys would sleep before games. I didn't see much partying in spring training, so I think the [big league players] had to go natural."

There are two ways that players could switch from presumably high-powered amphetamines to legal, available alternatives. For occasional users, a Red Bull or a strong two-shot latte before the game might be enough. Not the same, to be sure, but enough. Heavy users would likely try to find a legal or untestable variant. There was

quite a bit of this, with a record number of requests for a "Therapeutic Use Waiver" in the season preceding the ban. This waiver allows those that have real, verifiable medical needs to use the drugs. The best-known example is players that take Ritalin or similar drugs to treat Attention Deficit Disorder. For some, such as Scott Eyre or Adam LaRoche, the need is real and the condition was diagnosed many years ago. For others, Ritalin is a nice substitute for amphetamines. It has the same properties, giving players a quick rush and helping them feel "locked in."

However, Ritalin as a drug is actually primitive. Much as the now-banned anabolic steroids are three generations back from what players are using to beat the system, the prescription drug Provigil, designed to treat sleep disorders, is now the fastest growing drug of its type. Sports fans might recognize the generic name for Provigil—modafinil, the same drug used by many of the BALCO athletes, and one that has an incredible effect. It could easily be described as amphetamines without any of the side effects. Even more, it is not believed to be on the list of MLB banned substances, though it is on the more stringent Olympic list. Major League Baseball had to institute new policies to combat the abuse of the therapeutic waiver. It remains to be seen whether it will be effective. Certainly, the leaked positive test for Barry Bonds brings even more attention to this subject, opening baseball up to more oversight and calls for transparency.

It appears then, from statistical and anecdotal evidence, that the amphetamine problem was as overstated as the steroid problem, while being fraught with the same types of replacement issues. Abuse was a problem, though likely not in the extremely high numbers estimated even by those close to the game. Players feared the public scrutiny and financial penalties associated with a positive test and found alternatives or, in many cases, simply "went naked." If the mere existence of a testing policy has all but eliminated amphetamines from baseball, the policy was successful. The root of the problem, however, remains: Players will always seek an edge, legal or illegal, in a sport in which millions of dollars are on the line. Declaring victory would be premature; Bud Selig would be standing under a "Mission Accomplished" banner if Major League Baseball did not keep its eyes open and build on its early success.

Pitch Counts and PAP Revisited

Keith Woolner

The standardized, careful collection of baseball statistics has come a long way from the mere box score. Over the past several decades, several organizations, including Project Scoresheet, Total Sports, STATS, MLB Advanced Media, 24 × 7 Baseball, Baseball Information Solutions, and Retrosheet have continually upped the ante for the level of detail and quality of data collected, and baseball fans around the world have benefited. One remarkable accomplishment is that after the 2007 season we will have a nearly complete collection of data recording each pitch thrown in the majors over a 20 year span. In honor of this remarkable achievement to be, we're revisiting one of Baseball Prospectus' most popular contributions to sabermetrics—Pitcher Abuse Points.

Background

Following pioneering work done by Craig Wright in *The Diamond Appraised* in 1988, Baseball Prospectus's Rany Jazayerli introduced the concept of Pitcher Abuse Points (PAP) to measure pitcher workload in 1998. Jazayerli's hypothesis was that it was pitching while tired that posed the greatest risk, and that that risk increased the longer a pitcher threw while tired. This led to the first iteration of PAP, which established some of the key features of the system—a baseline of 100 pitches under which no PAP is charged, and an increasing marginal cost per pitch as the pitch count in a single start increased beyond that baseline. In *Baseball Prospectus 2001*, I modified the formula for marginal cost beyond the baseline based on my research of actual declines in pitcher effectiveness following high-pitch-count starts and differences in injury rates among pitchers based on the shape of their workload. My research indicated a cubic relationship between pitches above 100 and the risk of workload-induced decline afterwards. Because of this, the system was dubbed PAP^3 (or PAP3), and later just PAP as it replaced the older system.

PAP version 1:

$$PAP(NP) = \int \begin{matrix} \text{if } NP \le 100 \text{ then } 0 \\ \text{else } \sum_{x=100}^{NP} (X-100) \end{matrix}$$

PAP^3:

$$PAP(NP) = \int \begin{matrix} \text{if } NP \le 100 \text{ then } 0 \\ \text{else } (NP-100)^3 \end{matrix}$$

NP: Number of Pitches

Pitch Count Trends

One trend in the historical data caught my eye—pitch counts have been steadily rising over time. The average number of pitches per game rose about 7% from 272 in 1988 to 291 in 2006. Plate appearances per game have also risen over that span (the higher on-base percentages of recent years mean more batters are coming to the plate per out), but only by 2%, so some of the increase must be coming from batters seeing increased numbers of pitches per plate appearance. Sure enough, checking the data confirms that the average number of pitches per batter in 1988 was 3.585; in 2006 it was 3.833, up 6.9%. Some of this can be attributed to the overall increase in strikeouts and walks, as those plate appearances tend to have more pitches than PA in which the ball is batted into play. However, the change in strikeouts and walks can only explain so much. The total percentage of plate appearances ending in a strikeout, walk, or hit-by-pitch increased from 23.3% in 1988 to 26.2% in 2006. This trend by itself explains only 0.038 pitches, or about 15% of the increase. The rest seems to be part of an overall trend of rising pitch counts.

Since the data we have is mostly complete only since 1988, we start there. I charted the average number of pitches per PA for each of the following batting outcomes: strikeout, walk, HBP, ball in play, HR. For example, in 2006 the average PA that ended with a strikeout took about 4.8 pitches. Plotting each pitch count average over time shows a distinct rising trend (see figure 1).

This establishes that there's been a gradual increase over the past 20 years or so, but what about further back in time? Fortunately, the amazing folks over at Retrosheet (www.retrosheet.org) have been able to compile pitch counts for a handful of games in the 1960s and 1970s. Together those roughly 1,100 games add up to about 45% of a single 30-team season, but if we combine all of them,

Figure 1. Average Pitches Thrown per Event, 1988–2006

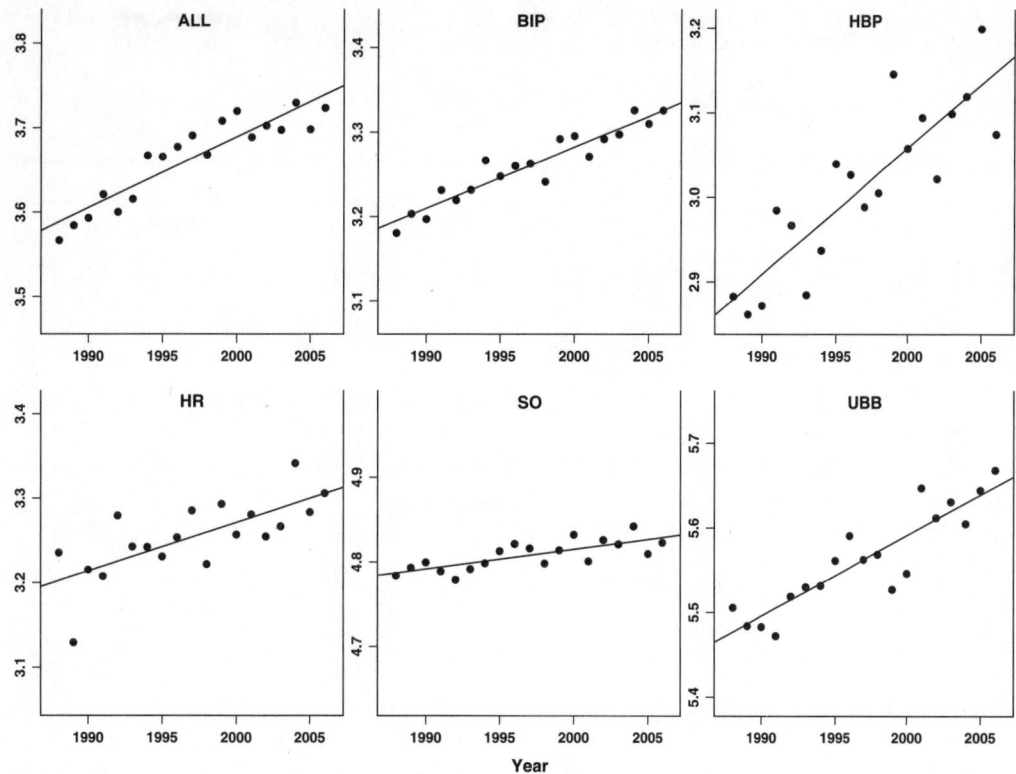

averaging the year component, and treat it as another data point, we can see that the increasing trend is supported by the available data. In doing so, we see evidence of a long-trend—over the past 46 years, pitch counts per outcome have risen about 4% per plate appearance, independent of outcome. (See figure 2.)

Pitch Counts As a Chronological Phenomenon

Having determined that there is a trend of rising pitch counts, a natural question is whether the increase in pitches is attributable to the overall increase in offense between the 1960s and today, or is it truly a chronological phenomenon. To investigate this, I looked at several different changes in the game over time—overall offense (runs per 9 innings, or RA), strikeout rate (SO/PA), unintentional base on balls rate (UBB / PA = (BB − IBB) / PA), batting average on balls in play (BABIP = (H − HR) / (AB − HR − SO)), and the percentage of plate appearances with balls hit into play (BIP rate or BIPr = (AB − SO − HR) / PA), and ran a regression of each variable against pitch count per plate appearance to see which was most closely correlated. All were significantly correlated, as expected, but year was slightly more highly correlated, explaining more of the variance seen in the data. Furthermore, after accounting

for the effect of offense level, there was a still a decent (though lower) correlation with year, indicating that offense level did not fully capture the time-based relationship. In statistical terms, the residuals after regressing pitch count per plate appearance with RA, for instance, were still noticeably correlated with year, but when regressing on year, none of the other variables were statistically significant (and usually not particularly close, many with p > 0.7). We therefore conclude that the trend is a true evolution of the game over time, rather than being driven by swings in offensive level.

Regression

Variable	Year	BABIP	BIPr	RA	SO/PA	UBB/PA
Year	0.000	0.066	−0.141	0.116	0.180	0.032
BABIP	0.411	0.000	−0.272	−0.020	0.135	−0.184
BIPr	0.397	0.183	0.000	0.066	−0.033	−0.014
RA	0.509	0.099	−0.270	0.000	0.160	−0.180
SO	0.584	0.297	−0.259	0.225	0.000	0.152
UBB	0.731	0.450	−0.582	0.378	0.496	0.000

(Correlation values range between +1 and −1. Values near 0 indicate little relationship. Values near +1 indicate a strong direct relationship. Values near −1 indicate a strong inverse relationship.)

Figure 2. Average Pitches Thrown per Event, 1960–2006

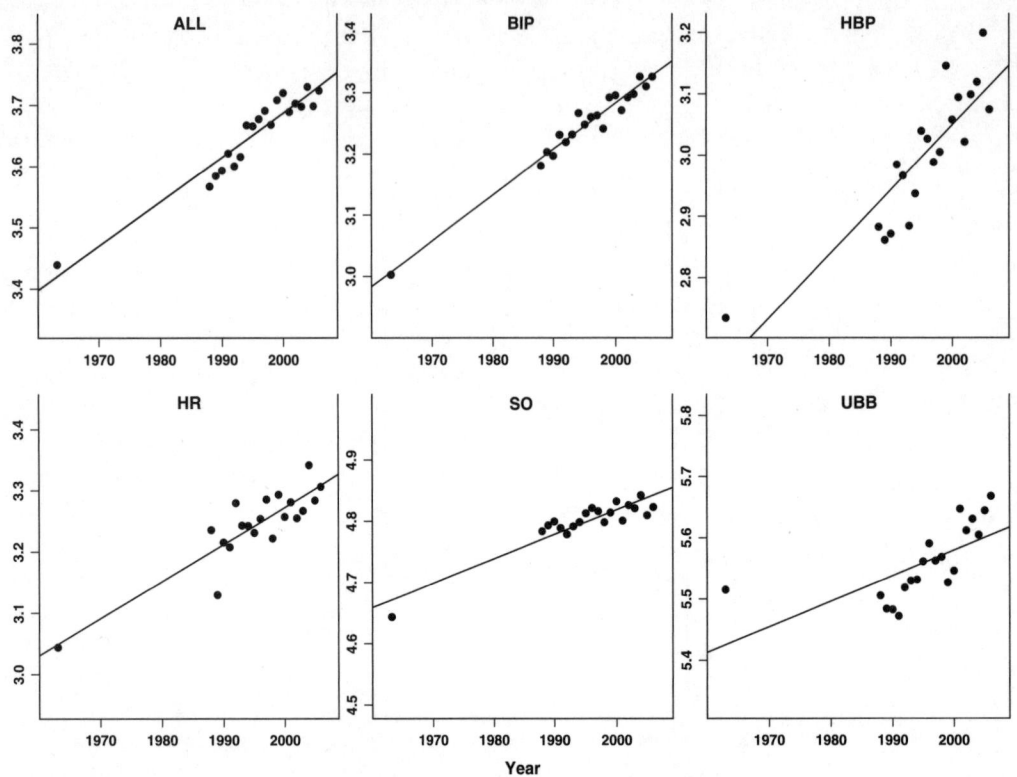

Formula for Estimating Pitches in an Appearance

To estimate historical pitch count data for years we don't have actual data for, we need a formula to relate what statistics we do have to pitch counts. Such statistics include those typically found in a pitching line: innings pitched, hits, walks, and strikeouts. For most games of the past 50 years, Retrosheet has play by play (if not pitch-by-pitch) data available, and we can use such data to add home runs, hit by pitch, and plate appearances to our estimating formula. And, as we've seen above, the year in which the game occurred carries some information about how many pitches were likely to be thrown as well. While there are a variety of pitch count estimators available and in use, none that I'm aware of explicitly takes into account this year-based trend.

One step in the process is to estimate the number of batting outs from a pitching line. Though a pitcher may record 20 outs (6⅔ innings), not all of those outs are necessarily recorded from retiring 20 batters. Some of those outs may be recorded in other ways, such as double plays, caught stealing, and runners out on base. All of these will reduce the number of batting outs a pitcher records.

Regressing batting outs versus innings pitched, we find that each third of an inning (out recorded) is equal to about 0.93 batting outs.

The formula we use is:

$$NP = 10.26 +$$
$$2.733 \times BIP +$$
$$4.482 \times SO +$$
$$5.538 \times UBB +$$
$$4 \times IBB +$$
$$2.390 \times HR +$$
$$2.431 \times HBP +$$
$$0.004885 \times pa \times adj\_yr$$

Where

BIP = OUTS_IN_PLAY + (H-HR)
OUTS_IN_PLAY = 0.93 × (3 × IP – SO)
PA = BIP + SO + UBB + HR + HBP (if not directly known)
ADJ_YEAR = MAX(YEAR – 1960,0) (thus 0 if YEAR – 1960 is a negative number)
0.004885 is the average increase of pitches per plate appearance per year regardless of outcome

If you don't have IBB treat all walks as unintentional, let HBP = 0 or HR = 0 if you don't have HBP or HR data, respectively. Note that, since our current pitch count data can not be validated back earlier than 1960, we are conservatively assuming that the rising pitch count trend begins that year. If additional pitch count data for earlier eras becomes available through Retrosheet, the formula can be adjusted to account for any trends that emerge in older seasons.

One interesting thing to note about this formula is that it contains an intercept term, the result of the best-case linear regression fit to the existing data. In principle, this tells us that, even if a pitcher had a pitching line of straight zeros (0 IP, 0 H, 0 BB, 0 SO, 0 HBP), that we would still estimate that he threw 10 pitches. While this is counterintuitive, recall that this formula has been built solely on starting pitching lines, not of reliever lines, and that the regression is designed to minimize overall error, not to provide maximum accuracy at the extremes. We could design a no-intercept formula that estimated zero pitches for a all-zero pitching line, but we would sacrifice accuracy in the more frequent cases of starts in the 80–150 pitch range.

PAP Study Design and Changes from Original Study

In revisiting the pitch count analysis, a few changes in methodology were made. To begin with, with the wealth of additional data available today, and with faster computers to process it, we can analyze a much larger sample than was previously possible. For this study, I included actual pitch counts from 1988 to 2006, and estimated pitch counts, using the formula presented earlier, for years 1960 to 1987.

In addition to increasing the years analyzed, I've also increased the population of pitchers within each year who were considered. The original PAP study I conducted in 2001 divided pitchers into two groups, based on whether they were above or below average in endurance (as measured by their median pitch count in games started). The focus of the study was on the "high endurance" group pitchers—those regularly asked to throw a lot of pitches, meaning those whose median pitch count was above the major league median.

For my current research, pitchers in each season were divided into four quartiles, based on each one's median number of pitches thrown. That is, I looked at the median number of pitches each starting pitcher threw (e.g. a pitcher who had three starts of 60, 80, and 140 pitches would have a median start of 80 pitches), and ranked all pitchers in order by that median value. The bottom 25 percent of the list formed quartile #1, pitchers in the range of 26 to 50 percent formed quartile #2, those ranking between 51 to 75 percent formed quartile #3, and the top 25 percent (76 to 100 percent) were quartile #4. Unlike the prior study, all quartiles were analyzed, rather than just those above the median.

Another change from the 2001 study is in how we measure the baseline that post-start performance was benchmarked against. In the prior articles, the previous 21 days of performance was used to establish a "snapshot" of how the pitcher was performing prior to a high pitch count start. Subsequent analysis showed that this was biased. Pitchers allowed to throw a lot of pitches had done somewhat better in their recent starts than they did earlier in the season, or over the entire season. This makes some intuitive sense—managers are more likely to let a guy who has been throwing well in recent weeks go deeper into the game. However, as a result of this, the baseline that subsequent performance was being gauged against was skewed high, making any pitch-count related declines seem somewhat more pronounced than they should have been. The post-high-pitch-count decline was still there, but its magnitude was overestimated as a result of the selection bias in using the prior 3 weeks to establish a baseline.

To correct this, I used the following approach. To see how well a pitcher fared following a high-pitch-count start, I computed the full-season stats (in games started), minus the stats from the high pitch count game itself. This gives the full season (but one) stats for the pitcher, or exactly what your expectation would be in rates of production for a random start selected from the N − 1 remaining starts.

This is perhaps better explained with an example:

Freddy Fingertips made 30 starts, threw 210 innings, allowed 105 runs, for an RA of 4.50.

We want to see how well he did following a game on July 15 when he threw a complete game shutout of 125 pitches.

Full season	30 GS	210 IP	105 R	4.50 RA
Start	1 GS	9 IP	0 R	0.00 RA
Rest of season	29 GS	201 IP	105 R	4.70 RA

For any of the remaining 29 starts, we'd expect a 4.70 RA. If his performance is systematically worse than a 4.70 RA after throwing 125 pitches, then there's evidence for the PAP hypothesis (higher pitch counts lead to a bigger decline in subsequent performance). If his post-shutout performance is no worse than 4.70 RA, then he is not suffering any ill effects from the high pitch outing. Furthermore, if the decline is larger following starts with more than 125 pitches than with fewer, than the marginally increasing risk per pitch portion of the PAP hypothesis is supported.

The bias in the prior study would be that in the 3 weeks prior to July 15, Freddy (and similar pitchers) would often have had a streak of better than typical starts, perhaps giving the manager confidence to let Freddy complete the shutout. Had we been comparing his performance to a 3-week sample of, say, 4.00 RA instead of 4.70 RA, the magnitude of any decline would have been exaggerated.

All of the new analyses presented in this article use the full "rest of season" baseline rather than the 21-day baseline.

Analysis of Rate Components

First, we look at the change in RA following a high-pitch count start. As will be the case in many of the following charts, we are grouping starts into 10-pitch wide clusters (80–89, 90–99, 100–109, 110–119, 120–129, etc), and charting starting from the 80–89 pitch group (starts below this level are relatively rare, and may indicate something physically wrong with the pitcher during the game, and as such we want to discount those from our study).

We also look at trends in strikeout rate, walk rate, batting average on balls in play, SNLVAR, home run rate, batting average allowed, OBP allowed, and SLG allowed.

Two of the statistics mentioned may not be well known to some readers, so we'll describe them briefly. Batting average on balls in play, or BABIP, measures how often a ball put in play by the batter turned into a hit. Home runs are excluded, as fielders generally have no chance to influence those outcomes. BABIP is often used to measure the overall fielder performance of a team, since its inverse, 1-BABIP, or Defensive Average, indicates the percentage of balls in play that were turned into outs by the defense. BABIP came to prominence when Voros McCracken published his controversial but revolutionary theory that pitchers had, at best, a minimal range of influence on whether or not batted balls are turned into outs.

SNLVAR is a mouthful of an acronym standing for Support-Neutral Lineup-adjusted, Value Added over Replacement. One of Baseball Prospectus' unique pitching metrics, SNLVAR measures how much chance a pitcher gave his team to win the game compared to a "replacement level" pitcher (such as a typical fifth or sixth starter, a "Quadruple-A" journeyman, or other fringe major leaguer—an in depth treatment of replacement level is presented in *Basbeall Prospectus 2002*. Computed for each pitcher's start individually, this metric takes into account innings pitched, runs allowed, baserunners left on when departing the game (regardless of whether subsequent pitchers actually allowed them to score or not), equalizes offensive and bullpen support (Support Neutral), and adjusts for park and league offensive context (Lineup-adjusted) in one nice, neat, all-inclusive number.

Results:

- Increasing with pitch count: RA, AVG, BABIP, HR rate
- Decreasing with pitch count: SNLVAR, UBB rate
- No effect from pitch count: SO rate

Note that a decrease in SNLVAR indicates a decline in performance, as opposed to RA, AVG, BABIP and HR for which increasing values indicate poorer pitching performance. The other statistics shown give some indication of how and why SNLVAR trends downward. While strikeout and walk rate are relatively unaffected, it is the outcomes on batted balls that seem to get a pitcher into trouble. Batting average itself rises significantly, driven by increasing rates in home runs surrendered and in hits on balls in play. One potential explanation for this is that pitchers, rather than losing raw velocity, lose their command within the strike zone. To compensate for the loss of control, more pitches are thrown in the "fat" part of the plate, a change in approach that garners no more walks overall, but leads to more hittable pitches.

What are striking are the differences in performance for each workload quartile. The group with the lowest median workload performed noticeably worse in virtually every measure, and at virtually every pitch count level. Furthermore, the decreases in performance were sharper at higher pitch counts for the lowest quartile than for higher workload pitchers. Conversely, the quartile with the highest workload showed much flatter trends in performance as pitch count increased. In other words, the PAP effect was far greater for different classes of pitcher workloads. Certainly, part of this is biased because we are investigating how workload affects pitchers, but grouping pitchers according to how much they have been worked. There's a confusion of cause and effect. The pronounced differences in the magnitude of effect for the lowest quartile vs. the highest quartile suggest that managers are doing a fair job identifying what pitchers are capable of handling a heavier load and which lack the endurance to throw deep into a game. Those regularly asked to throw deep into the game show less of a dropoff following a long start than others (although this is offset by the fact that their baseline for comparison includes a higher percentage of games thrown following a high pitch count game), while those who go deep less often are far more likely to suffer in subsequent weeks after being pushed deep into a game. (See figures 3 through 9.)

Figure 3. HR Performance Trend in Next 30 Days by Pitch Count, 1960–2006

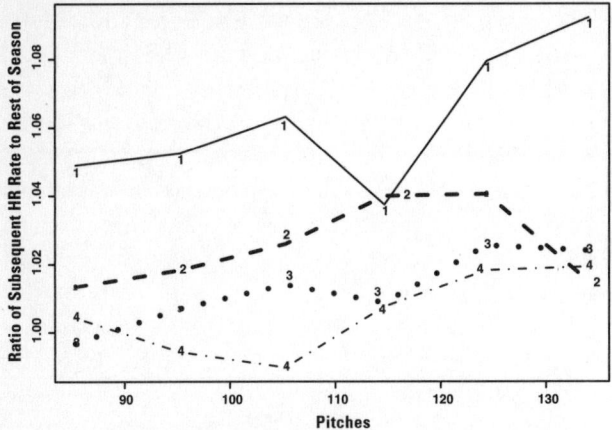

Pitchers grouped into workload based quartiles:1 = lowest quartile, 4 = highest quartile

Figure 4. Strikeout Rate Performance Trend in Next 30 Days by Pitch Count, 1960–2006

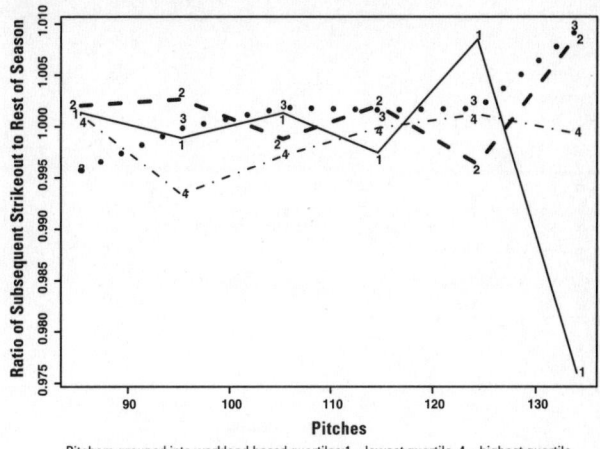

Pitchers grouped into workload based quartiles:1 = lowest quartile, 4 = highest quartile

Figure 5. RA Performance Trend in Next 30 Days by Pitch Count, 1960–2006

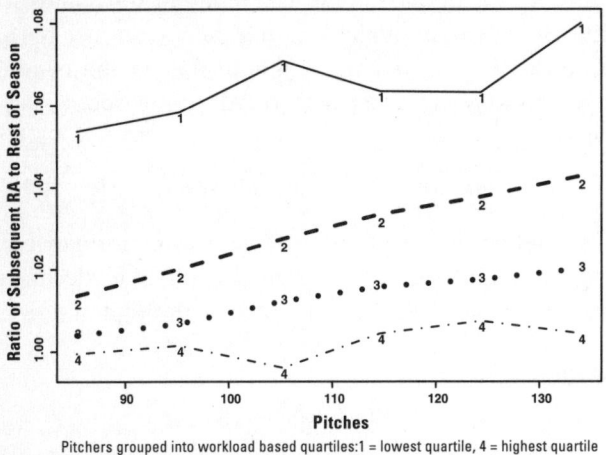

Pitchers grouped into workload based quartiles:1 = lowest quartile, 4 = highest quartile

Figure 6. SNLVAR Performance Trend in Next 30 Days by Pitch Count, 1960–2006

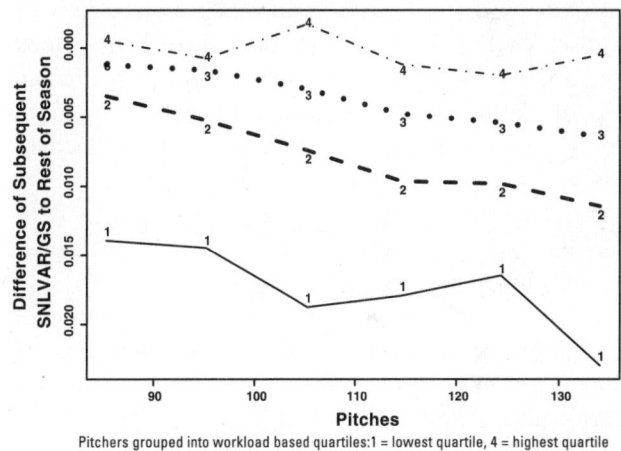

Pitchers grouped into workload based quartiles:1 = lowest quartile, 4 = highest quartile

Figure 7. Walk Rate Performance Trend in Next 30 Days by Pitch Count, 1960–2006

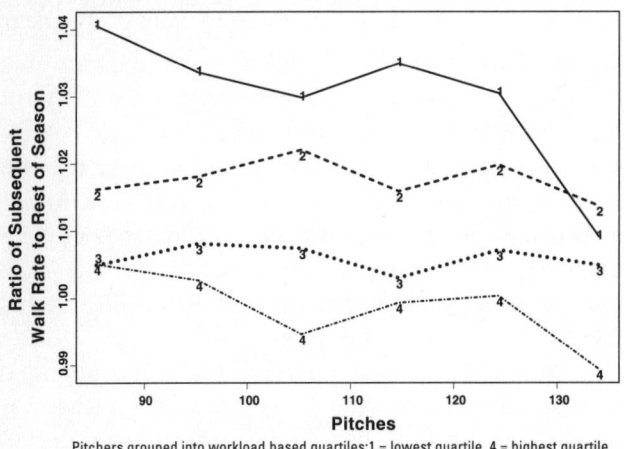

Pitchers grouped into workload based quartiles:1 = lowest quartile, 4 = highest quartile

Figure 8. AVG Performance Trend in Next 30 Days by Pitch Count, 1960–2006

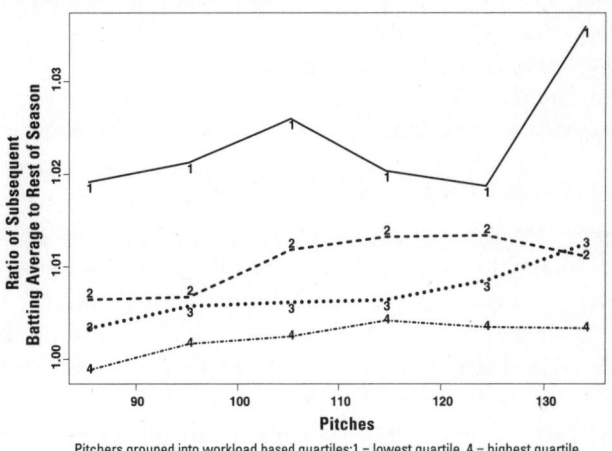

Pitchers grouped into workload based quartiles:1 = lowest quartile, 4 = highest quartile

Figure 9. BABIP Performance Trend in Next 30 Days by Pitch Count, 1960–2006

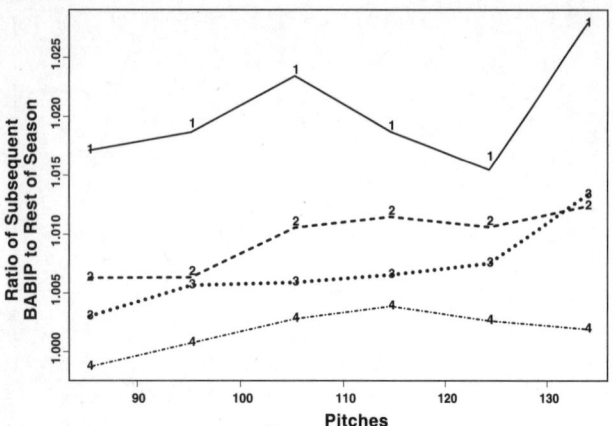

Pitchers grouped into workload based quartiles:1 = lowest quartile, 4 = highest quartile

Figure 10. SNLVAR Performance Trend Averaged Across Workload Groups, 1960–2006

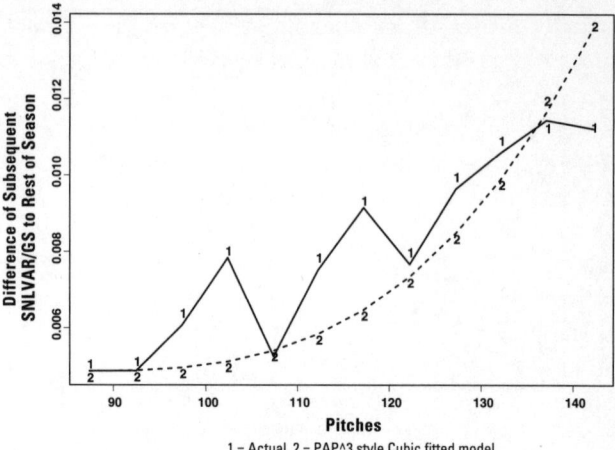

1 = Actual, 2 = PAP^3 style Cubic fitted model

The PAP Formula

The original PAP^3 research fit the abuse-point allocation to a trend line that was a composite of various pitching rate statistics. We have better tools in our sabermetric toolbox today than we did then, and one of them in particular, SNLVAR, captures nearly everything we were trying to do with the composite line. SNLVAR captures both effectiveness and endurance, and directly relates to the probability of a team winning a game. The pitching rate charts above show us "how" performance declines. SNLVAR encapsulates how much that decline costs.

One problem arises in using the entire population of pitchers is that the contributions from different type of pitchers are different at different pitch counts. The top quartile in pitcher workload contributes a disproportionate number of starts to the 120 and higher pitch ranges than they do at lower levels. To balance this, we are taking the change for each workload group, and averaging them, thus forcing equal contribution from each group of pitchers at each pitch count level. In addition, we've also flipped the SNLVAR change around to rise as pitch counts grow, for visual simplicity. (See figure 10.)

We've plotted a cubic function, very similar to PAP^3 against the actual data. As shown, the cubic relationship tracks the decline in SNLVAR conservatively. That is, given the fluctuation in the actual data, the fitted function tracks the lowest points on the curve, achieving particularly good fits to 5 of the points across the range of values. It errs on the side of underestimating pitch count related decline.

Interestingly, this curve actually plots PAP^3 using an 85 pitch baseline, rather than a 100 pitch baseline. This suggests that the impact of pitch counts may be felt even earlier than the 100 pitches. This is perhaps not surprising, given that we are analyzing a wider range of pitchers, particularly those with lower endurance and performance levels. It may be possible to use different thresholds for different classes of pitchers, rather than a one size fits all formula. We'll be looking at this further in the coming year, and may make changes to PAP to incorporate new findings.

$$PAP = MAX(0, NP - 85)^3 \text{ instead of } PAP = MAX(0, NP - 100)^3$$

Another lesson from the analysis of performance by pitcher workload is that the amount of observed decline is larger for less heavily worked pitchers (lower quartiles).

Beyond 150 Pitches

One valid criticism of the original PAP formula is that it was too open-ended given the range of pitch counts it was validated against. The cubic formula continued to rise faster and faster as pitch counts rose from 100 to 150 to 200 pitches, but in the sample of years studied there were only a handful of starts in the 150–170 range, and none above it, certainly not enough to justify an ever-increasing damage estimate. Indeed, PAP^3 said that a 200-pitch start would be more than 27 times more damaging than a 133-pitch start, which is the low-end of Category V—starts considered most risky. A factor of 27 probably means that a pitcher's arm spontaneously combusts. At even higher pitch counts, such as Tom Cheney's 228 pitches on September 12, 1962 when he struck out 21 batters in 16 innings, PAP^3 would have suggested that all life in a 100 mile radius would have been vaporized.

Clearly, the runaway nature of PAP^3, unsupported by sufficient statistical sample sizes above 150 pitches was not warranted. But with our pitch-count estimator, and the available seasons worth of data going back to 1960, it is possible to investigate with a larger sample of starts.

However, pitchers who throw 150-plus pitches are distinctly different from other pitchers. To begin with, such starts only represent 0.3 percent of all starts since 1960, and those high pitch count starts are not evenly distributed among the starting pitcher population. To ensure we are getting a proper representation of these elite pitchers, we will consider statistics only from those pitchers who threw at least 150 pitches in a start, and only those seasons from such pitchers that contain at least one start in that range. That is, Tim Wakefield threw 168 pitches in a 1997 start, so we will include Wakefield's 1997 season in our sample, but not his 2006 season in which he peaked at 116 pitches. In all, this exclusive club contains 505 seasons (only about 4.3 percent of the pitcher-seasons containing at least 1 start) from 272 different pitchers (out of 2,633 different pitchers who've made a start since 1960). Even with this larger sample, the available data shrinks dramatically as we get above 150 pitches:

NP Range	GS	%
150–154	301	45.1%
155–159	158	23.7%
160–164	96	14.4%
165–169	48	7.2%
170–174	28	4.2%
175–179	12	1.8%
180–184	6	0.9%
185–189	7	1.0%
190–194	4	0.6%
195–199	3	0.4%
200–204	1	0.1%
205–210	2	0.3%
225–229	2	0.3%

In figures 11 through 17 we see the same set of performance indicators shown before. The sample size problems, particularly above 180 pitches, cause wild fluctuations towards the far right side charts, which obscures the fact that we see the continuation of some trends we saw earlier, namely that strikeout rate remains flat and all other performance indicators are negative (for the pitcher) until around 170 pitches. This is most noticeable on the SNLVAR chart.

However, the charts also flatten out to a great degree above 150 pitches (prior to the huge fluctuations, of course), indicating that there is not an increasing degradation of performance above 150 pitches as PAP^3 would have had us believe per the doomsday scenarios mentioned above. Thus, it seems reasonable to cap our penalty for pitch counts above that level. We'll modify the PAP^3 formula to a maximum of 150 pitches for now. If future pitch count data for even older seasons allow further refinement, we can consider adjusting the cap, or modifying the formula to a different shape.

Figure 11. Strikeout Rate Performance Trend in Next 30 Days by Pitch Count, 1960–2006

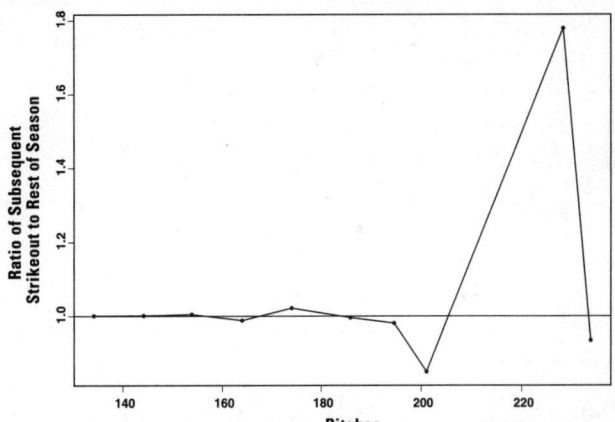

Pitcher seasons containing at least one start of 150 or more pitches

Figure 12. RA Performance Trend in Next 30 Days by Pitch Count, 1960–2006

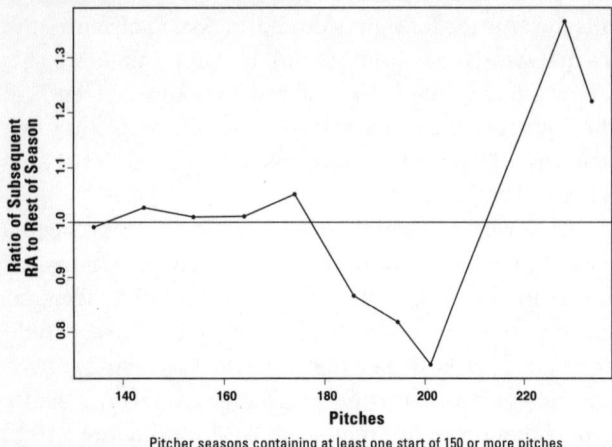

Pitcher seasons containing at least one start of 150 or more pitches

Figure 13. SNLVAR Performance Trend in Next 30 Days by Pitch Count, 1960–2006

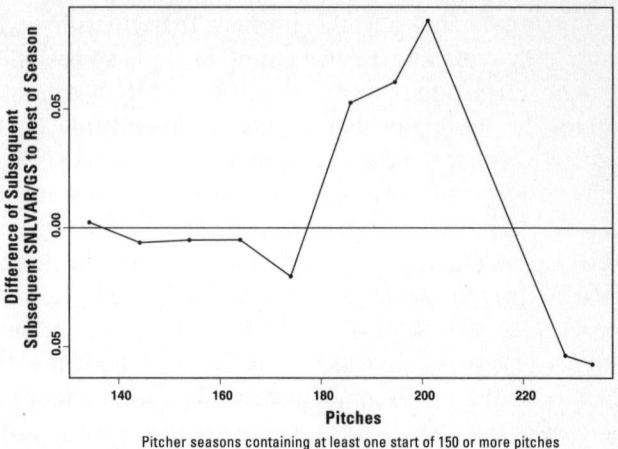

Pitcher seasons containing at least one start of 150 or more pitches

Figure 14. Walk Rate Performance Trend in Next 30 Days by Pitch Count, 1960–2006

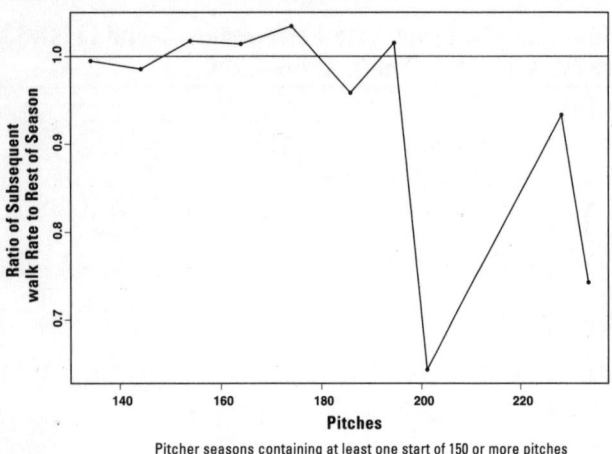

Pitcher seasons containing at least one start of 150 or more pitches

Figure 15. AVG Performance Trend in Next 30 Days by Pitch Count, 1960–2006

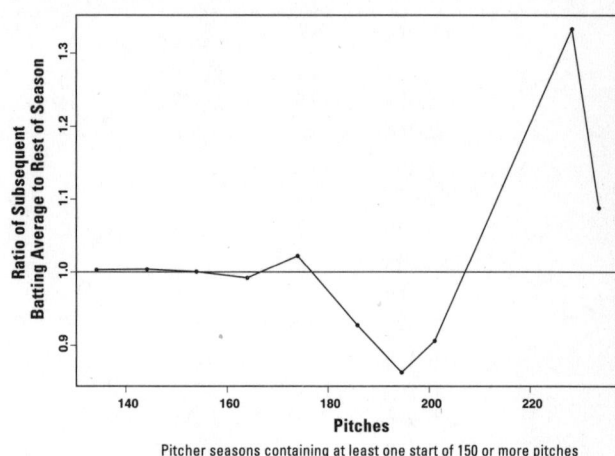

Pitcher seasons containing at least one start of 150 or more pitches

Figure 16. BABIP Performance Trend in Next 30 Days by Pitch Count, 1960–2006

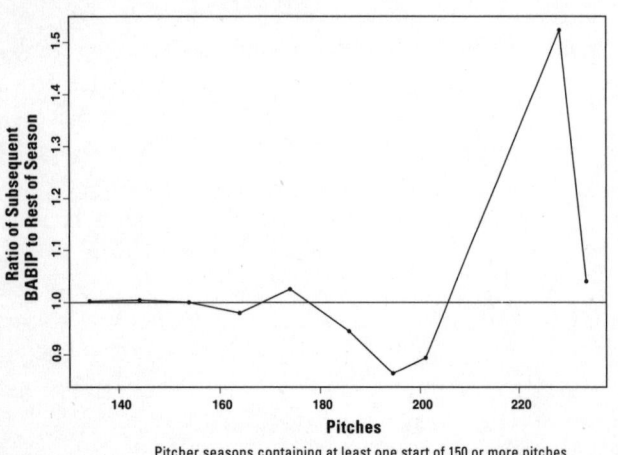

Pitcher seasons containing at least one start of 150 or more pitches

Figure 17. HR Performance Trend in Next 30 Days by Pitch Count, 1960–2006

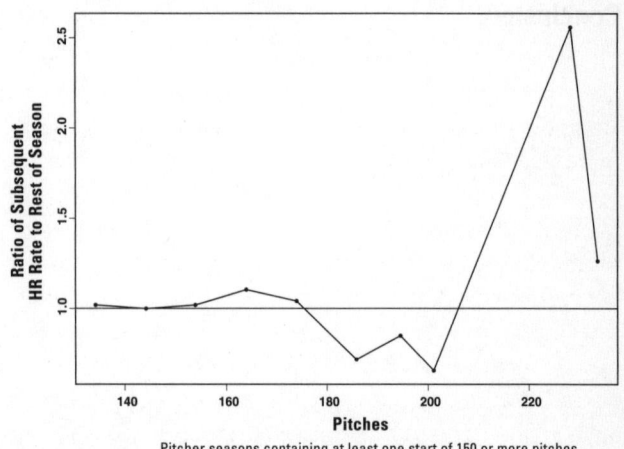

Pitcher seasons containing at least one start of 150 or more pitches

Pitch Counts and PAP Revisited

Backcasting PAP for Historical Data

With our estimated pitch count formula, the long-term trend in pitcher usage can be shown using the PAP formula. One of the most remarkable trends is the near-extinction of the Category V start (133-plus pitches) since 1990. The Category II start (101–109 pitches) has nearly doubled in frequency since the 1960s, gaining even more additional "market share" than the lowest category (up to 100 pitches) has. Some degree of standardization in pitcher usage has taken hold.

Years	STRESS	CAT1	CAT2	CAT3	CAT4	CAT5	Years	STRESS	CAT1	CAT2	CAT3	CAT4	CAT5
1960	71.8	50.5%	13.6%	16.4%	9.6%	5.9%	1984	43.4	52.2%	16.0%	15.8%	8.2%	2.9%
1961	72.0	49.1%	13.8%	16.5%	10.8%	5.4%	1985	43.1	52.6%	15.0%	16.6%	7.8%	3.0%
1962	74.2	49.1%	14.1%	16.8%	9.7%	5.7%	1986	49.3	50.7%	16.6%	16.0%	7.2%	3.8%
1963	67.9	51.4%	13.3%	16.9%	8.9%	5.1%	1987	49.7	53.8%	14.5%	15.3%	7.7%	3.6%
1964	66.0	53.1%	13.0%	15.3%	9.0%	4.9%	1988	50.5	54.3%	17.2%	16.5%	7.9%	4.1%
1965	55.6	54.0%	13.3%	16.0%	8.1%	3.9%	1989	44.5	58.2%	15.8%	15.0%	7.7%	3.1%
1966	47.5	54.7%	14.5%	15.3%	7.3%	3.0%	1990	40.2	61.0%	15.5%	13.3%	7.1%	2.8%
1967	60.1	52.4%	13.6%	17.0%	7.9%	4.4%	1991	31.9	58.7%	17.2%	15.4%	6.6%	1.9%
1968	56.5	48.5%	14.4%	18.2%	8.5%	4.2%	1992	36.2	57.6%	17.0%	15.6%	6.8%	2.6%
1969	75.7	48.8%	12.4%	17.4%	10.2%	6.4%	1993	35.6	56.7%	17.6%	16.0%	7.1%	2.4%
1970	68.8	47.4%	13.7%	17.9%	9.5%	5.2%	1994	38.0	53.3%	17.7%	17.5%	9.1%	2.3%
1971	68.4	47.0%	13.8%	18.3%	10.5%	5.0%	1995	32.9	58.2%	16.8%	15.8%	7.0%	1.9%
1972	66.0	46.8%	13.4%	19.0%	10.9%	4.4%	1996	30.1	55.4%	17.9%	17.4%	7.4%	1.5%
1973	77.7	44.0%	13.9%	18.1%	11.5%	6.3%	1997	24.3	55.9%	19.0%	17.9%	5.9%	0.9%
1974	79.6	45.0%	13.3%	18.4%	10.5%	6.6%	1998	28.1	56.6%	18.8%	16.6%	5.9%	1.8%
1975	76.0	45.9%	12.9%	19.4%	10.6%	6.1%	1999	25.1	55.6%	20.2%	17.0%	5.9%	1.3%
1976	64.6	48.0%	13.6%	18.7%	9.1%	4.9%	2000	23.6	53.1%	20.3%	19.6%	6.2%	0.9%
1977	65.8	51.4%	13.2%	16.2%	9.3%	4.9%	2001	13.6	59.5%	21.0%	15.9%	3.3%	0.3%
1978	59.0	48.5%	14.5%	18.2%	8.9%	4.1%	2002	12.8	59.1%	21.9%	15.7%	3.2%	0.2%
1979	51.9	50.2%	14.2%	17.6%	8.0%	3.8%	2003	11.9	59.8%	22.5%	14.8%	2.7%	0.2%
1980	50.0	51.3%	15.4%	16.7%	7.6%	3.6%	2004	11.1	57.9%	24.0%	15.5%	2.5%	0.2%
1981	45.0	55.5%	14.4%	14.8%	7.0%	3.2%	2005	9.1	57.9%	25.2%	15.2%	1.6%	0.1%
1982	48.3	53.9%	14.0%	16.1%	7.4%	3.4%	2006	7.5	60.1%	25.3%	13.2%	1.4%	0.1%
1983	48.4	51.9%	14.3%	16.3%	8.9%	3.1%							

Category	Pitch Range
I	0–100
II	101–109
III	110–121
IV	122–132
V	133+

Conclusion

The wealth of play-by-play data now available has enabled deeper research into pitcher usage patterns in different eras. We've documented trends that batters are seeing more and more pitches per plate appearance, regardless of outcome, over the past four decades. With that insight, we've built a pitch-count estimator that is sensitive to the era a pitcher played in. From there, we've explored the relationship between high pitch counts and performance for different categories of pitcher and found that the costliness of a high pitch count varies widely depending on the category of pitcher. Furthermore, existing usage patterns seems to separate pitchers correctly in that those pitchers more regularly worked hard show less decline as a result of high pitch counts than the most lightly used pitchers. We've shown that a cap on the existing pitch count formula was needed to deal with ultra-high pitch counts seen in earlier eras that were not part of the original PAP research, and documented the trends towards standardization of pitch counts over the past two decades, as awareness of the importance of pitch counts and pitcher fatigue have penetrated every level of organized baseball. Lastly, we've seen some evidence that the baseline from which PAP accumulates may vary according to other identifiable pitcher characteristics, setting the stage for the next iteration in pitcher usage research to further refine how to quantify pitcher usage.

The Baseball Prospectus Top 100 Prospects

Kevin Goldstein

Welcome to Baseball Prospectus' first ever Top 100 Prospects list. We've limited our list to the Top 50 in the past, but we want the book to be twice as good this year, or, failing that, twice as long. Ranking prospects properly involves a lot of ingredients, and since I was brought on from *Baseball America* to give BP a full-time guy on the minor league beat, I've worked to combine our statistical tools with the performance side of evaluating prospects. In constructing these rankings, we spoke with scouts and other baseball decision-makers about each player, measured actual performance, and considered what PECOTA had to say about them, as well. No one aspect takes precedence over any other. The trick, if there is one, is to combine a player's projected peak with the odds that he'll reach it—which takes a little bit of intuition informed by years of experience, too.

1. Alex Gordon, 3B, Royals, 23

The remarkable season Gordon had at Double-A in his pro debut last year has been well documented, but here's the twist: The reason Gordon hit *only* .325/.427/.588 is that he played through a wrist injury in June. Gordon hit .359 after July 1 with 19 home runs (.687 slugging) and 34 walks in 230 at-bats. While not nearly as good with the glove, on the offensive side, he falls somewhere between Scott Rolen on the low end and Mike Schmidt on the high.

2. Philip Hughes, RHP, Yankees, 21

He was nearly flawless on a statistical level in 2006, and his remarkable numbers at Double-A become more impressive when one realizes he was just 19. He has a prototypical power pitcher's build and the stuff to match, which he combines with the control and command of a surgeon. The Yankees insist he'll start the year at Triple-A, but chances are his performance there will force a call-up before the All-Star break.

3. Delmon Young, OF, Devil Rays, 21

Young has been compared to Albert Belle since high school. They're similar in stature, and Young's swing evokes Belle's, including the pronounced load and his lead foot "stepping in the bucket." Unfortunately the Belle comparisons extended to his behavior in 2006. As any modern sports fan knows by now, talent overrides everything, and the bat-throwing incident is just a bump in the road to stardom. He's going to be tremendous.

4. Homer Bailey, RHP, Reds, 21

If Hughes is the #1 pitching prospect in baseball, then Bailey is #1A. While Bailey lacks Hughes' command, he makes up for it with slightly better stuff. Bailey is the latest in a long line of Texas-born flamethrowers and is equally capable of chucking mid-90s heat and making hitters look silly with one of two breaking balls—a slow, Zito-esque curve and a hard slider, neither of which is touchable when he's on. As with Hughes and the Yankees, the parent club is aware that they have something special in their midst and are proceeding with caution.

5. Brandon Wood, SS, Angels, 22

Yes, he hit just .276 last year, but 2005's .321 mark happened in the southern half of the hitting-friendly California League. Given his high strikeout rate, he wasn't expected to sustain that high average. He doesn't walk like Eddie Yost, his 2006 rate was acceptable and an improvement from the year before. During the last two seasons, Wood has averaged 61 doubles, 6 triples, and 44 home runs per 162 games. Now you know why you're reading about him so early.

6. Tim Lincecum, RHP, Giants, 23

Scouts call him "Seabiscuit." You'll find bigger kids in the Little League World Series, but when Lincecum starts his bizarre motion and his left leg kicks way up in the air and his torso twists and his pitching hand drops to the point of almost scraping the pitching mound, wonderful things happen. His mid- to upper-90s fastball isn't even his best pitch; his curveball is already one of the best in baseball at any level. The nine teams that picked ahead of the Giants in 2006 and passed on Lincecum because they feared what they did not understand will rue the day.

7. Cameron Maybin, OF, Tigers, 20

Welcome to the Land of Tools, boys and girls, now step right up and see our main attraction. Many scouts expected Maybin to struggle in his pro debut. Not that they didn't like him, they just thought his adjustment to the pros would take awhile. Instead, he had an excellent year that was even better than it looks; he raked at a .333/.416/.517 clip away from West Michigan's pitcher's haven of a home park. He doesn't have a ceiling, he has a stratosphere.

8. Chris Young, OF, Diamondbacks, 23

Pure center fielder with 30/30 potential who's ready for the big leagues? Sign us up. Something strange happened with Young in 2006—not bad, mind you, but strange. His biggest issue had always been high strikeout totals. In 2005, he struck out once every 3.6 at-bats. At Triple-A last year he dropped that all the way to one per 5.7 at-bats, but nothing else changed. There were no gains in batting average and no loss of power, just more batted balls resulting in outs. Logically, dividends on the improvement will be paid out eventually.

9. Jay Bruce, OF, Reds, 20

In 2005, Bruce transformed from a nice high school outfielder to a top-10 pick. In 2006, he went from a top-10 pick to a top-10 prospect. Some observers believe he has at least one more great leap forward left. Despite missing 23 games with minor here-and-there injuries, Bruce led the Midwest League with 63 extra-base hits, and everything from his power to his left-handed swing to his surprising speed brings to mind the next Larry Walker.

10. Evan Longoria, 3B, Devil Rays, 21

Longoria was universally considered the best college hitter in the country in 2006, but he really didn't have much competition for that honor in a weak class. The skeptics vanished after his pro debut. Reaching Double-A and slugging 18 home runs in your first 248 professional at-bats can change people's opinions pretty quickly. He's one of the best infield power prospects in the game.

11. Reid Brignac, SS, Devil Rays, 21

Take one raw high school hitter who made dramatic strides in his full-season debut, place him in the California League, and Presto! Instant breakout. Two things about Brignac's season that really stand out beyond the numbers: He kept up the pace when promoted to Double-A, and his defensive reviews changed from, "He has to move to third base," to "He *might* have to move to third base." The last thing the Devil Rays need right now is another third baseman, but nobody is going to complain about having yet another infielder in the system who could hit 30 home runs in the big leagues.

12. Ryan Bruan, 3B, Brewers, 23

In 165 minor league games, Braun has 200 hits, 87 of them for extra bases—and he's just coming into his wooden-bat power. Braun played just 59 games for Huntsville, but nonetheless finished tied for eighth in the pitching-friendly Southern League with 15 home runs in 231 at-bats. He also has a career 30 stolen bases with a 77 percent success rate. The Brewers need him to improve defensively and avoid having to move to the outfield as the real organizational need is at the hot corner. Offensively, he'll be a star no matter where he ends up.

13. Matt Garza, RHP, Twins, 23

Sometimes it just happens: Guys start throwing two or three miles per hour harder than the year before. Sometimes their decent breaking pitches become bendy monsters. Sometimes they suddenly start locating, not just throwing more strikes, but better ones. All of those things happened for Garza in 2006. Nobody saw it coming. The Twins are desperate for starting pitchers, and Garza is ready to contribute.

14. Yovani Gallardo, RHP, Brewers, 21

Throughout the 2006 season, Gallardo paralleled Hughes and Bailey. The trio began the year in the High Class A Florida State League, dominated, moved up to Double-A, and didn't miss a beat. Gallardo's statistics rank right with the big two, but his projection does not. He's a little smaller than the pair, and his stuff is just a tick behind them as well. Hughes and Bailey each have an elite facet to their game, while Gallardo is simply very good all-around. Being ranked 14th in this group is no insult.

15. Andrew McCutchen, OF, Pirates, 20

Like Maybin, McCutchen was an outstanding athlete who was expected to struggle as he acclimated to pro baseball. Wrong. McCutchen immediately showed a well-rounded set of skills, putting an exclamation mark on the season with an impressive 20-game Double-A stint before his 20th birthday. His size prevents him from having Maybin's projection, but the fact that he has no glaring statistical weaknesses and plenty of room to improve makes him very exciting.

16. Clayton Kershaw, LHP, Dodgers, 19

It's dangerous to read too much into Gulf Coast League stats, but Kershaw's numbers are hard to ignore. In 37 innings, the only extra-base hits he allowed were a pair of doubles. On a scouting level, his photo is in the dictionary next to the entry for "Perfect Teenage Lefty." His fastball already gets into the mid-90, his curveball is devastating, and his mechanics are nearly flawless. At some point in the next 12 to 24 months, people will be talking about Kershaw the way they do about Hughes and Bailey.

17. Andrew Miller, LHP, Tigers, 22

Miller has a few flaws. During his college career his control would sometimes falter, or his slider would flatten out. In the end he was the guy everybody wanted but was afraid to pick because of signability concerns, but left-handers with his size and stuff are a rare commodity.

18. Fernando Martinez, OF, Mets, 18

There's no road map to go on here, no Rosetta stone. Most players who fit Martinez's profile play as 17-year-olds in the Dominican Summer League or spend half the year acclimating to *los Estados Unidos* before getting one or two hundred plate appearances in a short-season rookie league. As such, what Martinez did at his age—starting out in the full-season Sally League and earning a promotion to High-A—is pretty special. The only issue is trying to figure out what he will become. We don't know where he'll hit in the lineup, or where he'll play in the outfield, we just know he'll be good.

19. Adam Miller, RHP, Indians, 22

When you're given lemons, make lemonade. That just what Miller did when arm soreness limited his fastball in 2005. Forced to work more on his secondary offerings and command, Miller emerged as a more complete pitcher last year. He'll start 2007 at Triple-A, but could steal the title of Indians' ace away from C. C. Sabathia at any time.

20. Andy LaRoche, 3B, Dodgers, 23

LaRoche is not a pure power hitter. He's not going to hear "oohs" from the crowd as he stands there admiring a majestic moon shot. His primary offensive skills are hitting for average and getting on-base. LaRoche's contact rates and hand-eye coordination make it easy to project him as a .300 hitter in the big leagues, but what makes him special is that he hits everything so squarely that 20 to 25 of his screaming line drives are going to leave the park annually.

21. Billy Bulter, OF, Royals, 21

When your PECOTA comps include Albert Pujols, something good is going on. Butler's home run and walk rates took significant dips in 2006, but that's to be expected when one leaves the comfy confines of High Desert for Double-A before being of legal drinking age. They may have to invent a new defensive position for him, something like "chair." Third base was a cruel joke, and he hasn't been much better in the outfield. Athletically, Butler's about as gifted as a wounded moose, but he sure can hit.

22. Jose Tabata, OF, Yankees, 18

Tabata and Fernando Martinez are going to be linked for years. The top hitting prospects of the two New York teams,

they're both high-ceiling Latin American outfielders with batting skills that belie the fact that each of them would have been high school seniors had they been born in the U.S. Martinez might have slightly more power, Tabata slightly better hitting skills. The debate over which teenager is better is a lot like the upcoming presidential election: There's already a lot of yelling going on, but we won't know anything until the end of 2008.

23. Luke Hochevar, RHP, Royals, 23

When players sit out a year or more due to draft negotiation hijinks, the primary risk is atrophy. However, for the last three big-name players to do so (all advised by Scott Boras), it's been a non-issue. Both Stephen Drew and Jered Weaver reached the major leagues last year as future stars, and Hochevar could follow as early as this year. Some scouts said he looked better in his indy league stint than he ever did in college, which might show what a little rest can do for young arms.

24. Troy Tulowitzki, SS, Rockies, 22

The next in the line of the big, athletic, modern shortstops, Tulowitzki had a strong full-season debut in the Texas League, hitting for average, for power, getting on base, and playing a good shortstop. He does everything well enough right now for the Rockies to be comfortable with him as their starting shortstop, and he's only going to get better.

25. Jeff Niemann, RHP, Devil Rays, 24

Due to a chronically sore shoulder, Niemann has pitched only 108 innings since being drafted in 2004, but surgery to remove an impingement seems to have done the trick. He looked outstanding during the season's second half once the team extended his pitch count and is almost to the point at which we can say he's cleared the injury nexus. At six-foot-nine and 260-plus pounds, he resembles a right-handed Randy Johnson with a food addiction. With a mid-90s fastball and a big league slider, he almost has the stuff to match.

26. Philip Humber, RHP, Mets, 24

In 2004, Rice's big three—Humber, Jeff Niemann, and Wade Townsend— were all selected within the first eight picks of the June draft. They all had disturbing workloads in college, and now they've had two Tommy John surgeries (Humber, Townsend) and a series of shoulder problems requiring minor surgery (Niemann). Humber's return from the procedure was nothing short of remarkable, but if I had a kid with a million dollar arm who insisted on going to college, he sure wouldn't go to Rice.

27. Brandon Erbe, RHP, Orioles, 19

No older than most high school draftees last year, Erbe shone is his full-season debut with nearly as many strikeouts as base runners allowed, flashing a power arsenal and command beyond his years. There are some mechanical issues here, some fly-ball tendencies there, and the need for a third pitch in whatever the third place is, but this is clearly a special arm.

28. Nick Adenhart, RHP, Angels, 21

Prospect lists today contain player after player who has had some kind of major surgical procedure. It's a tribute to modern medicine; a generation ago, Adenhart would have been done before he even begun. Instead, undergoing Tommy John surgery in high school was no more than a delay in his progression. He's still on track to be the stud right-handed starter he was projected to be before he felt that sickening pop in his elbow.

29. Justin Upton, OF, Diamondbacks, 19

Upton entered 2006 as one of the top two or three prospects in the game, but his pro debut was disappointing. Oddly, though he failed to live up to expectations, there was no giant hole in his game that needed filling. He kept his strike-outs down, hit for power, and drew walks, he just didn't do any of those things enough. Scouts still love his tools, but they were disappointed by the effort made. Here's hoping that failing to live up to expectations isn't genetic.

30. Mike Pelfrey, RHP, Mets, 23

Arguably the top college pitcher in the 2005 draft, Pelfrey has an outstanding fastball. Heaters tend to have great velocity or great movement, but Pelfrey's has both, reaching the mid-90s with tremendous sink. He needs a breaking ball, but only a usable one. People seem to think he's taken a step backwards because of his struggles in the big leagues, but let's all calm down a bit. Last year was his pro debut and he's still ahead of the curve.

31. Carlos Gonzalez, OF, Diamondbacks, 21

Gonzalez is a multi-faceted threat with a lightening-quick bat, power, good outfield instincts, and an outstanding arm. In any other system, he might be a household name by now, but he's been buried in what has been a stacked Arizona system over the past few years. At times, he can be guilty of putting it into cruise control, but even a Porsche going 35 MPH is something to behold.

32. Scott Elbert, LHP, Dodgers, 21

Elbert is at the stage in his career at which he does two things remarkably well and needs to add a third. He strikes batters out (10.7 K/9) and doesn't give up hits (6.0 H/9), but he walks too many guys (5.2 BB/9). This happens with power lefthanders quite often in the minor leagues. If the control improves, he'll be great. Even if it doesn't, with those rates to build on, he'll at least be pretty good.

33. Franklin Morales, LHP, Rockies, 21

Any pitcher who can sit in the mid-90s, touch 98, and back it all up with a knee-buckling curve is special. To find a lefty who can do it is like stumbling across the Hope Diamond. No southpaw in the minors can beat Morales on a pure stuff level. That said, his control is a problem. With 89 walks and 24 wild pitches last year, Morales has a little bit of LaLoosh in him. He should try breathing through his eyelids.

34. Carlos Gomez, OF, Mets, 21

To rank this high with a good-not-great .281/.359/.423 line at Double-A means "Tools City and plenty to dream on," as the scouting lingo goes. This isn't just any old dream, this is a Technicolor masterpiece with cupcakes and puppy dogs and some other things we probably shouldn't talk about in a family publication. There are those in the Mets organization who think he's the team's best prospect, envisioning another Jose Reyes, but in center field. Plenty to dream on, indeed.

35. Chuck Lofgren, LHP, Indians, 22

The best thing about Lofgren is that there are no glaring weakness in his game and he's not even out of A-ball yet. He has a full arsenal; all of his pitches are good or better, and he throws strikes. While he's only 21 years old, it's already easy to project him as a number-three starter—and that's at the bare minimum. Any improvement he makes between now and getting the big call will raise the ceiling.

36. Donald Veal, LHP, Cubs, 22

Veal is another one of those pure power lefties with control problems, but it doesn't matter, because nobody's found a way to consistently get hits off his heavy fastball. Last year, he gave up just 91 safeties in 154 ⅓ innings, which made his 82 walks much easier to swallow. He's a huge guy with an equally huge upside, but his size is walking that thin line between a point in his favor and a conditioning issue.

37. Carlos Carrasco, RHP, Phillies, 20

Carrasco needed two attempts to master the Low Class-A South Atlantic League. He passed his second test with flying colors at the age of 19. He's your classic high-upside Latin American arm—tall and skinny with a whip-like arm action that gets him into the low-90s and offers plenty of projection. What separates him from most teenagers is his changeup, a very good one. Carrasco is good now and is going to get better.

38. Eric Hurley, RHP, Rangers, 21

For the last couple of years, you couldn't talk about the Rangers' system without bringing up "DVD," the young pitching trio of Danks, Volquez and Diamond. Now, Hurley has come along and messed everything up by passing all three. A tall power pitcher with mid-90s heat and a wicked slider, Hurley might not be a Texan, but he sure pitches like one. A high school teammate of Billy Butler, Hurley had no problems winning at Double-A as a 21-year-old, always an encouraging sign.

39. Dexter Fowler, OF, Rockies, 21

Every team has that ultra-athletic tools guy in their system, and every year two or three of them make that sudden jump from athlete to baseball player. Fowler was the Rockies' 2006 winner. He drew walks, stole bases, hit a bunch of doubles that should become home runs in the bigs, and hit for average thanks to a pleasantly surprising contact rate. In his 2005 debut, Fowler whiffed 73 times in 220 at-bats. Last year, he had just 6 more strikeouts in 405 at-bats. That's a mammoth improvement, one that he's capable of making in other aspects of his game.

40. Travis Snider, OF, Blue Jays, 19

Snider was the best high school hitter in the 2006 draft. Scouts were concerned that he'd need an adjustment period, but he won Appy League MVP honors in his pro debut. Snider isn't anything but a bat, as he's built like a fire plug and limited to first base or left field. At the same time, he's already shown a keen eye, and there's no need to talk about power potential because his power is already showing up in games. The Blue Jays finally stopped taking safe, low-ceiling college players with every top pick they had, and Snider was their instant reward.

41. Clay Buchholz, RHP, Red Sox, 22

Buchholz entered the year as a standard, decent righty, the kind every system has three or four of. He looked good early in the year, looked a little better by midseason, and by the end of the year looked like the best prospect the Red Sox have. With three plus or better pitches and matching command, Buchholz has quickly transformed from a solid all-around package into the total package.

42. Felix Pie, OF, Cubs, 22

Pie's Triple-A campaign was classified as a disappointment by some, but when you consider his age and strong second half, he stood still more than he stepped back. Pie still needs to refine his approach and learn how to leverage his speed, but his hitting skills, particular his power, continue to develop rapidly. Alfonso Soriano's time in center field will be brief; he'll slide over to left once Pie is ready, probably at some point in 2007.

43. Adam Lind, OF, Blue Jays, 23

Lind is not a very good left fielder. He's not a very good runner, as evidenced by 6 career stolen bases in 339 professional games. His is a very good hitter, and, in his 60 at-bat audition with Toronto last year, he proved he can hit big

league pitching. Lind has never batted lower than .310 at any stop, including the majors, and his power output has nearly doubled in each of his last two seasons. He doesn't have a ton of upside, but is a nice Rookie of the Year dark horse for 2007.

44. Adam Jones, OF, Mariners, 21

The Mariners are making it hard to evaluate their prospects of late by pushing players through the system faster than is necessary. In his first full year as a center fielder, the ultra-athletic Jones found himself in Triple-A and then the majors before his 21st birthday. While he struggled in the big leagues, his Triple-A performance included improved power, a better contact rate, and a surprisingly quick adaptation to his new position. If he had been playing at the level at which he belonged, everyone would be talking about him.

45. Jacob McGee, LHP, Devil Rays, 20

Beyond the high-end hitting prospects and near-ready starters such as Young and Niemann, the Devil Rays have a number of exciting younger arms. McGee leads the pack. He gained 1 to 2 miles per hour on his fastball in each of the last two years; it's now a low- to mid-90s monster. His control could use improvement, as could his other pitches, but the ingredients for great success are all there.

46. Jason Hirsh, RHP, Rockies, 25

Hirsh was the best pitcher in the Double-A Texas League in 2005, and the best in the Triple-A Pacific Coast League last year. The prospect prize of the Jason Jennings deal, Hirsh is expected to take Jennings's spot in the rotation. While people much smarter than you and I have tried to figure out what kind of pitcher can succeed Coors Field, Hirsh's size and stuff make him look like a right-handed Jeff Francis, and Francis has worked out pretty well so far.

47. Hunter Pence, OF, Astros, 24

With Hirsh gone, Pence becomes the Astros' best prospect, though there are many who felt that was the case before the deal. Scouts didn't trust Pence's 2005 performance in A-ball because of his age, the way he chokes up on the bat, and his loopy swing. His power surge continued at Double-A and silenced many of his critics. His home run power is a proven commodity, but questions persist about his ability to hit for average or play center field well enough to stay there.

48. Jacoby Ellsbury, OF, Red Sox, 23

Ellsbury reached Double-A in his first full season and has already shown the ability to hit for average, get on base via the walk, wreck havoc on the basepaths, and use his speed as an asset in center field. What he doesn't have is much power or one overwhelming skill. The good news is that crystal-balling him as an above-average outfielder and leadoff man is a no-brainer.

49. Chris Iannetta, C, Rockies, 24

The Rockies have spent the majority of their existence without a decent catcher, but Iannetta has arrived to save the day. Beyond being an excellent defender and a natural on-field leader, Iannetta came into his own offensively in 2006, hitting for a decent average and a bit of power while drawing walks like they're going out of style. Imagine Kevin Youkilis with the ability to play behind the plate. Pretty cool, huh?

50. Colby Rasmus, OF, Cardinals, 20

In a system desperate for anything resembling a position player prospect, the 2005 first-round pick did it all in his full-season debut. With 17 home runs, 28 stolen bases, 56 walks and excellent defensive skills, Rasmus has an excellent base to build on, and his skinny frame means there is more power to come. With Jim Edmonds locked up for two more years, Rasmus' advancement through the minors could time perfectly with when the need for him arrives.

51. Jarrod Saltalamacchia, C, Braves, 22

Saltalamacchia entered 2006 as the game's top catching prospect. While his 2006 season was a flop, there are some gold nuggets in the dirt. Salty cranked up the offense after recovering from wrist problems and he didn't take his struggles with him behind the plate, where he made some big-time improvements. He's blocked with the Braves, but that doesn't diminish his potential and rather increases his desirability to other clubs.

52. Kevin Kouzmanoff, 3B, Padres, 25

Kouzmanoff is one of those guys who hits, but scouts don't like him. Then he hits again, and scouts still don't like him. Then he keeps on hitting to the point at which teams are forced to give him a big league shot, and the scouts go get a beer. With the Padres after the Josh Barfield trade, chances are good that he'll keep on hitting.

53. Joey Votto, 1B, Reds, 23

A big, hulking Canadian first baseman in the style of Justin Morneau, Votto fell just short of winning the Southern League Triple Crown. On the downside, he doesn't quite have Morneau's power, and the offensive expectations for that position are enormous.

54. James Loney, 1B/OF, Dodgers, 23

Loney has finally become the hitter everyone thought he could be. Though he's proven himself to be big league-ready, the Dodgers brought Nomar Garciaparra back to play first base. The good news is that Loney will get some long stints as the starter when Nomar is diagnosed with an ingrown rib cage or dislocated sinus cavity. Loney will hit for a high average, but not the power one normally expects at first base.

55. Billy Rowell, 3B, Orioles, 18

The first high school hitter taken in the 2006 draft (ninth overall pick), Rowell did everything in his pro debut but hit home runs—though, with 19 doubles in 195 at-bats and a gargantuan six-foot-five frame, the power is going to come. He's awful at third base, and there's little reason to think he'll get better, so we're likely looking at a Richie Sexson-esque first baseman.

56. Joba Chamberlain, RHP, Yankees, 21

Chamberlain entered 2006 as one of the better college arms out there, but some ill-timed arm soreness and concerns about his size kept him on the board until the Yankees took him with the 41st pick. He could end up being one of the steals of the draft. He signed too late to debut, but was outstanding in the Hawaiian Winter League, showing impressive command of a mid-90s fastball, a put-away slider, and no rust.

57, Troy Patton, LHP, Astros, 21

The Astros have a number of impressive arms at the upper levels, but Patton's youth, polish, and left-handedness put him well ahead of the others. He has moved quickly through the system, but would be best served with a bit of a slowdown at Double-A as he figures out how to best use his above-average stuff and command.

58. John Danks, LHP, White Sox, 22

When the White Sox traded Brandon McCarthy to the Rangers, they got a new number-one prospect in return. Danks had a troubling habit of struggling at each new level, but hit the ground running at Triple-A last year. While he's not ready to take over for McCarthy just yet, his long-term value should be greater.

59. Jeff Clement, C, Mariners, 24

What Seattle did with Clement in 2006 was absolutely nonsensical. They pushed him to Double-A, then moved him to Triple-A *after* minor surgery. Worse, they had him split time between catcher and DH despite the fact that his defense is what needs the most work. All that jerking around clearly affected Clement at the plate, but he'll bounce back if the Mariners will let him.

60. Trevor Crowe, OF, Indians, 23

As a pure leadoff man, Crowe did it all in his pro debut, putting together a .449 on-base percentage and 29 stolen bases in 60 games at High Class-A Kinston, where he spent the majority of the season. The only problem is how to fit him into the modern game. His mediocre defense limits him to left field. While that was a common position for players like Crowe in the 1980s, it's a pure power position now, thus putting Crowe there requires finding mashers at other positions. Grady Sizemore in center might give the Indians some leeway there.

61. Edinson Volquez, RHP, Rangers, 23

Volquez has become troublesome for the Rangers. Scouts have been excited enough by the skinny Dominican's mid-90s fastball and outstanding change to throw out Pedro Martinez comparisons. At the same time, all of the things he's needed to do to become that kind of pitcher, specifically finding a breaking ball and better command, just haven't happened. There's still time.

62. Daric Barton, 1B, Athletics, 21

If anyone could afford a lost season, it was Barton. His 2006 season was limited to just 45 games because of a broken bone in his elbow, but he'll still start 2007 as a 21-year-old in Triple-A, still well ahead of the standard development curve. He can hit with anyone and draws a ton of walks, so his value at the big league level is nearly guaranteed. If he develops the 20-plus home run power the A's think he will, he'll be John Olerud II.

63. Sean West, RHP, Marlins, 21

He's raw, but all of the ingredients going into the oven are top-notch. At six-foot-eight and a good 30 to 40 pounds heavier than his listed weight of 200, West is an imposing presence on the mound. He sits in the low-90s with a power sinker that generates plenty of ground balls—when batters make contact at all. His ceiling is higher than many ranked ahead of him, but he's still a long way from reaching it.

64. Angel Villalona, 3B, Giants, 16

That Villalona ranks in the top two-thirds of the prospect list despite being just 16 and never having played a professional inning suggests he's something special. The Giants paid Villalona more money ($2.1 million) than they paid for Lincecum, and other teams were offering up to $3 million. According to everyone who's seen him, he's the real deal with outstanding hitting skills and tremendous raw power, but we really won't now what the weaknesses are until they are exposed.

65. Humberto Sanchez, RHP, Yankees, 24

The Tigers collect power arms the way a philatelist collects stamps, so it wasn't tough for them to deal one of their better ones for Gary Sheffield. Sanchez is huge and throws hard, but he also has a complete arsenal and great command. His injury history and conditioning are troubling; he'd rank much high if he could get through just one season without a trip to the disabled list.

66. Ubaldo Jimenez, RHP, Rockies, 23

Colorado has a number of hard-throwing Latin Americans in their system, and Ubaldo is the best right-handed example thanks to a mid-90s fastball and one of the best curveballs in the organization. His violent mechanics and lack of a decent changeup might lead to the bullpen, but the Rockies need starters, so for now that's what he'll continue to do.

67. Travis Buck, OF, Athletics, 23

Before being sidelined, Buck was doing his best impression of Earl Webb, smacking 39 doubles in 338 at-bats while also batting .319. The standard logic is that doubles turn into home runs eventually. That may not be the case with Buck given his line drive approach, but the batting average is real.

68. Ryan Tucker, RHP, Marlins, 20

The Marlins' rotation at Low Class-A Greensboro consisted of four first-round picks. Tucker is the one with the most gas. He's touched 98 MPH several times and sits comfortably at 92 to 95, but everything else needs a lot of work. The best news is that his walk rate dropped throughout the season, setting him up for a possible breakout if his slider comes around.

69. Ryan Sweeney, OF, White Sox, 22

Sweeney has been rushed through the system, but he's usually held his own. The White Sox insist that his power will eventually come. Sweeney nearly doubled his career-high with 13 jacks in 2006, a step in the right direction, but he's still a long way from where he needs to be.

70. Ian Stewart, 3B, Rockies, 22

How the mighty have fallen. After hitting .319/.398/.594 in his full-season debut, the tenth overall pick in the 2003 draft quickly became the flavor of the month, but that flavor has soured. Offensively, Stewart has regressed in nearly every way, but he shows just enough each year to keep scouts expressing vague interest. In many ways, this will be a make or break year.

71. Chris Volstad, RHP, Marlins, 20

Yet another of the Marlins young guns, Volstad nearly matches Sean West in height at six-foot-seven, but he's not yet a true power pitcher. He's still looking for a real out-pitch, but for now he's had plenty of success with a low-90s sinker that hitters pound into the ground. With his size, more velocity is going to come, and when it does, look out.

72. Josh Fields, 3B, White Sox, 24

Fields was better known at Oklahoma State as a star quarterback, but finally came into his own as a baseball player last year, finishing among the International League's top five in batting average and slugging. He's eerily similar to the incumbent, Joe Crede, but only on the offensive side of things.

73. Jonathan Sanchez, LHP, Giants, 24

Sanchez is one of the best pitchers in college history—okay, NAIA college history. After spending all of 2005 in Low-A, Sanchez reached the majors last year thanks to a fastball-changeup combination that keeps opposing hitters off balance. Some see him as a bullpen arm, but the Giants think he can succeed in as a starter with more work at Triple-A.

74. Brandon Morrow, RHP, Mariners, 22

Scouts have always been enamored with Morrow's arm, but he didn't start throwing strikes until this year. He's touched 99 MPH with his fastball while mixing in a splitter and a hard curve, and those same scouts now see him as a future closer.

75. Will Inman, RHP, Brewers, 20

On a pure numbers level, Inman is a monster. On a scouting level, he's only pretty good. An undersized right-hander who rarely tops 90 MPH, Inman has remarkable command and control, not just throwing strikes, but consistently painting the corners at will. It's hard to project players with his skill set as stars, but his location really is special.

76. Miguel Montero, C, Diamondbacks, 23

Short and squat, Montero's lack of stature certainly doesn't disqualify him from his position. He has a unique combination of decent power and above-average contact skills, a combination that nearly always indicates future success. He'll be a quality, everyday big league catcher.

77. Wade Davis, RHP, Devil Rays, 21

When he's on, Davis is a top-50 prospect, blowing away hitters with three plus pitches, including a mid-90s fastball that gets into the 96 to 98 MPH range and arrives on a downhill plane thanks to Davis's six-foot-five frame. He had a disturbing dead-arm period during the 2006 season in which he lost control and velocity, leaving many to want a full-season of shiny goodness before he gets anointed as the next big thing.

78. Erick Aybar, SS, Angels, 23

Aybar is spectacular to watch in the field and on the basepaths, but there's been a disappointing lack of progress in his overall game. He needs to become more patient, learn how to steal bases, and prove he can be a consistent defender as well as a flashy one. All the tools are there, but he's stalled for now.

79. Matt Harrison, RHP, Braves, 21

Normally a big, athletic lefty like Harrison with low- to mid-90s heat and outstanding control would rank higher, but his stats currently don't match his stuff. He gives up too many hits and doesn't record enough strikeouts, but, to most, it's a matter of learning how to pitch; the necessary tools for the job are there.

80, Brett Lillibridge, SS, Pirates, 23

The little engine that could. Short and skinny, Lillibridge is not a player your eyes lock onto when he takes the field, but he's quick to sell you with his all-around game. He hits for average, draws walks, steals bases, plays a legitimate big league shortstop, and has a little juice in his bat. He does nothing exceptionally well, but everything well enough that the whole is mightier than the sum of its parts.

81. Glenn Perkins, LHP, Twins, 24

Destined to be a fan favorite, the St. Paul native has two plus pitches, a low-90s fastball and a hard-breaking curve. He's a tad on the small side, and his fly-ball tendencies are a little scary, but he keeps enough balls out of the air with his high strikeout rate that its not too bothersome.

82. Sean Gallagher, RHP, Cubs, 21

It was a frustrating year for Gallagher, always overshadowed by the triumvirate of Hughes, Bailey and Gallardo in both the Florida State and Southern Leagues. It's a shame, as Gallagher had a very good season. Scouts warmed up to him thanks to a fastball that gained two or three ticks over previous years.

83. Brad Lincoln, RHP, Pirates, 22

It looked as if the Pirates finally understood this whole drafting thing when they selected toolsy McCutchen in 2005, but it was back to old habits in 2006 as the Bucs took the safe Lincoln as opposed to higher-upside arms such as Kershaw and Lincecum. Nothing against Lincoln, who should quickly become a middle-rotation workhorse, but the draft is the only place for small market teams to find impact talent. The Pirates seem to have forgotten that.

84. Kevin Slowey, RHP, Twins, 23

It looks like a season out of Johan Santana's resume: 220⅔ innings, 146 hits, 30 walks, and 235 strikeouts. That's Slowey's career minor league line. The bad news is that he's right handed and his stuff is nothing like Santana's. While it's hard to get excited by finesse pitchers, Slowey has refined his craft to the point that, once he gets to the upper levels, he should be able to leap over the wall that many with his profile run into face first.

85. Sean Rodriguez, SS, Angels, 22

While Rodriguez hit just .250 in 2005, there were still reasons to be excited, such as his 14 home runs, 78 walks, and 27 stolen bases. His hitting skills took a slight step forward in 2006. If scouts liked him at shortstop, he'd rank far higher, but even on the other side of the second base bag, his secondary skills are a rare treat.

86. Michael Bowden, RHP, Red Sox, 20

The Red Sox selected Buchholz and Bowden with two of their three supplemental picks in 2005, and both exceeded expectations in their full-season debuts. Though a teenager, Bowden showed the control of a grizzled veteran, so look out if, as happens often with prodigious young arms, his already above-average stuff takes a step forward,.

87. Jeremy Jeffress, RHP, Brewers, 19

Yes, Jeffress hit 100 MPH in high school. No, he's not the second coming of Colt Griffin, no matter what the numbers from his pro debut might suggest. Jeffress's mechanics are every bit as smooth as Griffin's were violent, and his development should be much smoother as well.

88. Hank Conger, C, Angels, 19

As a child, Hyun Choi Conger was nicknamed "Hank" by his grandfather in tribute to Hank Aaron, and the kid's destiny was set. It will be hard to live up to the Hammer's standards, but Conger's power bat will be that much more valuable if he can stay at catcher.

89. Cesar Carrillo, RHP, Padres, 23

The Padres have a terrible system largely due to some nightmarish first-round picks. There have been some plain-awful selections (hello, Matt Bush), and then there are the injured pitchers, Carrillo among them. While Carrillo avoided surgery last year, that's often just delaying the inevitable. It's a shame, as he had a rare combination of power and control before going all ouchy.

90. Chris Parmelee, OF, Twins, 19

While Parmelee's 8 home runs in 154 at-bats look good, they're even better than that. That rate was actually the second best in the Gulf Coast League, and Parmelee is a good a power prospect. He'll have to keep it up, as his other tools lag behind.

91. Alberto Callaspo, 2B, Diamondbacks, 24

Callaspo finished second in the PCL batting race last year, but that wasn't a huge surprise as everyone has liked his bat for years. It was his suddenly patient approach (.404 OBP) and defensive versatility that has the Diamondbacks toying with the though of trading Orlando Hudson to upgrade the team elsewhere.

92. Dellin Betances, RHP, Yankees, 19

Part New York legend and part real deal, Betences was a six-foot-eight beanpole dealing mid-90s heat as a Brooklyn high schooler, but, when scouts tracked him down early in 2006, they saw a crude arm with command troubles who epito-mized the term "project." By the end of the season, his velocity had improved, he had added a power curve, and the Yankees gave him $1 million to keep him away from Vanderbilt.

93. Chris Marrero, OF, Nationals, 18

Marrero was the nation's best high school hitter entering the season, but some health problems and a case of draftitis dropped him to the Nationals in the middle of the first round. He looked good in a pro debut that came to a premature end due to viral meningitis. The Nats are envisioning a homemade power threat—something the former Montreal franchise hasn't developed for eons.

94. Brett Sinkbeil, RHP, Marlins, 22

After using all four of their first-round picks on pitchers in 2005, the Marlins spent their top pick in 2006 on another pitcher. The 2005 group was all teenagers, but Sinkbeil was a college arm whom the Marlins feel could move quickly. His name is fitting; Sinkbeil's best pitch is a low-90s sinker that induces many a grounder, when batters aren't simply missing his slider, that is.

95. Cedric Hunter, OF, Padres, 19

Cedric the Entertainer had a stunning pro debut, reaching base at a .458 clip by batting .364 and drawing 41 walks in 228 at-bats. Scouts are cautiously impressed, hedging because hitting singles and drawing walks seems to be the limit of his abilities.

96. Pedro Beato, RHP, Orioles, 20

A New Yorker who spent a year in junior college after the Mets couldn't sign him, Beato is a powerfully-built fastball machine who can get into the mid-90s and also subtract a bit of heat for a power sinker. His curve gives him a third plus pitch. The Orioles' stocking of impressive young arms continues.

97. Javier Herrera, OF, Athletics, 22

Herrera missed all of 2006 recovering from Tommy John surgery, but the end result shouldn't have any effect on his remarkable tools. He was already young for the levels at which he was playing, and, at 22, he has plenty of time to reach his potential.

98. Neftali Feliz, RHP, Braves, 19

The Braves are well known for their ability to draft and develop pitchers, but they rarely delve into the international market to find young arms. Feliz, a teenage Dominican right-hander, struck out 42 in 29 innings during his stateside debut by pumping 98 MPH gas. The Braves tend to focus on pitchers with complete arsenals and excellent command, so it will be interesting to see how they develop a raw, pure power arm like this one.

99. Kyle Drabek, RHP, Phillies, 19

Makeup is a funny thing, and athletically gifted teenagers with attitude problems, such as Drabek, are nothing new. That said, Kyle is the son of a big leaguer, and, ironically, those are the kids scouts prefer for the maturity and professionalism they show. Drabek had the talent to be a top-eight pick last June, and that's why he's ranked here for now.

100. Elijah Dukes, OF, Devil Rays, 23

On pure talent, Dukes would rank much higher, easily in the top 50. Unfortunately, he seems to be focused on self-destruction, with a variety of suspensions and other incidents that all result from an inability to control his emotions. By all accounts, Dukes is a hard worker who wants to get better, and his upbringing was a Dickensian nightmare in modern dress. It's not that he lacks for understanding supporters, but that baseball is a microcosm of society with its own standards of deportment and mores. If Dukes can't train himself to meet those standards the way he's trained himself to excel on the ballfield, his talent will come to nothing.

Ten Who Just Barely Missed the Cut, and Why

Brian Barton, OF, Indians: Despite great numbers, his age is a factor, as are his struggles against left-handers and poor strikeout and walk rates. **Alexi Casilla, INF, Twins:** A little dynamo who will reach base at a .350-plus clip, play good defense at second and short, and steal a ton of bases, he'll be lucky to get 25 extra-base hits annually. **Tyler Clippard, RHP, Yankees:** His statistics are very good, but scouts are unimpressed with any right-hander who works in the upper-80s. When you look at the track record for players with this profile, the lack of velocity tends to catch up to them eventually. **Chris Lubanski, OF, Royals:** Lubanski had yet another Jekyll-and-Hyde year in 2006. The numbers were good, but his speed has regressed to the point at which he's limited to left field, where his power ceiling and inability to hit southpaws become major weaknesses. **Eric Patterson, 2B, Cubs:** Corey's younger brother has a much better approach at the plate, but lacks his older brother's power while sharing the same long swing. Defensive struggles don't help his cause. **Dustin Pedroia, 2B, Red Sox:** Pedroia can't play shortstop, but remains a decent offensive player. He's a second baseman now, which affects his projection, and his big league debut revealed some exploitable holes that need to be addressed. **Radhames Liz, RHP, Orioles:** One of the hardest throwers around is also a one-pitch arm whose destiny is the bullpen. He needs to find a consistent secondary pitch to succeed even there. **Drew Stubbs, OF, Reds:** The highest drafted position player (eighth overall) from the 2006 first round to not be ranked above, Stubbs did little in his pro debut to quell concerns about his ability to make consistent contact. **Kurt Suzuki, C, Athletics:** The former College World Series hero made great strides last year both offensively and in cutting down the running game, but his lack of power and deficient receiving skills balance out those improvements. **Neil Walker, C, Pirates:** The 2004 first-round pick has failed to develop any sort of secondary skills, and defensive struggles have brought about discussions of a move to third base, where the offensive expectations are even greater.

Team, League, and Level Key and Park Factors

Clay Davenport

Teams

Abrev	Fullname	Lgeague (2006)	Level	2004	2005	2006	Abrev	Fullname	Lgeague (2006)	Level	2004	2005	2006
ABE	Aberdeen	NYP	A-	972	976	994	CGA	Columbus GA	SAL	A	972	983	986
ABQ	Albuquerque	PCL	AAA	1117	1117	1118	CHA	Chicago (AL)	AL	MLB	1026	1025	1028
AGU	Aguascaliente	MEX	MEX	1082	1080	1082	CHB	Chiba	JPL	JPL	931	915	913
AKR	Akron	EAS	AA	1036	1028	1017	CHN	Chicago (NL)	NL	MLB	1008	1017	1026
ALT	Altoona	EAS	AA	973	986	1006	CHR	Charlotte	INT	AAA	999	1007	1013
ANA	Anaheim	AL	MLB	963	961	962	CHT	Chattanooga	SOU	AA	1025	1027	1009
ANG	AZL Angels	AZL	Rk	—	—	1000	CHU	Chunichi	JCL	JPL	943	935	928
ARI	Arizona	NL	MLB	1048	1046	1048	CIN	Cincinnati	NL	MLB	1001	1018	1038
ARK	Arkansas	TXS	AA	1033	1039	1056	CLE	Cleveland	AL	MLB	961	953	961
ASH	Asheville	SAL	A	1120	1121	1110	CLN	Clinton	MDW	A	1024	1020	1025
ATH	AZL Athletics	AZL	Rk	—	—	1000	CLR	Clearwater	FSL	A+	1007	1023	1032
ATL	Atlanta	NL	MLB	993	1000	995	CMB	Capitol City	SAL	A	993	—	—
AUB	Auburn	NYP	A-	1002	993	993	Cmg	Camaguey	CBA	Ind	984	988	979
AUG	Augusta	SAL	A	974	960	935	CMP	Campeche	MEX	MEX	914	927	931
BAK	Bakersfield	CLF	A+	952	947	948	COH	Columbus OH	INT	AAA	983	972	965
BAL	Baltimore	AL	MLB	993	985	985	COL	Colorado	NL	MLB	1104	1093	1083
BAT	Batavia	NYP	A-	972	972	976	CSC	Charleston SC	SAL	A	972	980	992
BCR	Battle Creek	MDW	A	977	—	—	CSP	Colorado Springs	PCL	AAA	1065	1053	1067
BIL	Billings	PIO	Rk	962	968	979	CUB	AZL Cubs	AZL	Rk	—	—	1000
BIN	Binghamton	EAS	AA	1008	1027	1028	CWV	Charleston WV	SAL	A	999	—	—
BIR	Birmingham	SOU	AA	976	976	958	DAY	Daytona	FSL	A+	1040	1035	1045
BLT	Beloit	MDW	A	1026	1019	1009	DEL	Delmarva	SAL	A	984	991	986
BLU	Bluefield	APL	Rk	1051	1031	1026	DET	Detroit	AL	MLB	965	974	981
BNC	Burlington NC	APL	Rk	987	976	971	DGR	GCL Dodgers	GCL	Rk	—	—	1000
BOI	Boise	NWN	A-	1049	1048	1033	DNV	Danville	APL	Rk	910	897	902
BOS	Boston	AL	MLB	1030	1026	1017	DUN	Dunedin	FSL	A+	1040	1046	1052
BOW	Bowie	EAS	AA	954	962	984	DUR	Durham	INT	AAA	1036	1028	1027
BRA	GCL Braves	GCL	Ind	—	—	1000	DYT	Dayton	MDW	A	1046	1027	1020
BRI	Bristol	APL	Rk	949	984	997	EDM	Edmonton	PCL	AAA	935	—	—
BRO	Brooklyn	NYP	A-	986	994	975	ELP	El Paso	TXS	AA	1109	—	—
BRR	AZL Brewers	AZL	Rk	—	—	1000	ELZ	Elizabethton	APL	Rk	960	973	968
BRV	Brevard County	FSL	A+	967	977	981	ERI	Erie	EAS	AA	1038	1026	1004
BUF	Buffalo	INT	AAA	998	1024	1046	EUG	Eugene	NWN	A-	1001	1011	1016
BUR	Burlington IA	MDW	A	951	941	931	EVE	Everett	NWN	A-	1049	1049	1052
CAR	Carolina	SOU	AA	996	999	1014	FKU	Fukuoka/SoftBank	JPL	JPL	953	952	919
CAS	Casper	PIO	Rk	1016	1025	1032	FLO	Florida	NL	MLB	943	943	944
CCH	Corpus Christi	TXS	AA	—	966	962	FRD	Frederick	CRL	A+	1025	1025	1033
CCN	Cancun	MEX	MEX	878	869	—	FRE	Fresno	PCL	AAA	983	967	970
CDR	Cedar Rapids	MDW	A	1032	1033	1027	FRI	Frisco	TXS	AA	996	997	1004
Cfg	Cienfuegos	CBA	Ind	936	913	901	FTM	Ft Myers	FSL	A+	975	986	989

brev	Fullname	Lgeague (2006)	Level	2004	2005	2006	brev	Fullname	Lgeague (2006)	Level	2004	2005	2006
FTW	Ft Wayne	MDW	A	957	958	958	MIS	Mississippi	SOU	AA	—	962	965
GIA	AZL Giants	AZL	Rk	—	—	1000	MNT	Montgomery	SOU	AA	979	991	1008
GRB	Greensboro	SAL	A	1008	1029	1039	MOB	Mobile	SOU	AA	1006	1005	1011
GRF	Great Falls	PIO	Rk	954	959	970	MOD	Modesto	CLF	A+	974	979	983
GRN	Greenville	SAL	AA	1016	1019	1016	MON	Montreal	NL	MLB	1013	—	—
GRV	Greeneville	APL	Rk	942	942	936	MRL	GCL Marlins	GCL	Rk	—	—	1000
Gtm	Guantanamo	CBA	Ind	1108	1133	1134	MRN	AZL Mariners	AZL	Rk	—	—	1000
Hab	La Habana	CBA	Ind	1004	985	966	MSO	Missoula	PIO	Rk	990	1000	1014
HAG	Hagerstown	SAL	A	997	977	966	MTR	Monterrey	MEX	MEX	977	970	975
HAR	Harrisburg	EAS	AA	1011	1017	1014	MTS	GCL Mets	GCL	Rk	—	—	1000
HDS	High Desert	CLF	A+	1106	1109	1114	Mtz	Matanzas	CBA	Ind	1055	1073	1095
HEL	Helena	PIO	Rk	952	970	979	MYR	Myrtle Beach	CRL	A+	940	960	982
HIC	Hickory	SAL	A	1014	993	977	NAS	Nashville	PCL	AAA	934	952	976
HNS	Hanshin	JCL	JPL	982	983	988	NAT	GCL Nationals	GCL	Rk	—	—	1000
HOU	Houston	NL	MLB	1009	1002	1005	NBR	New Britain	EAS	AA	990	999	1018
HRO	Hiroshima	JCL	JPL	1053	1076	1091	NHP	New Hampshire	EAS	AA	968	968	985
HUD	Hudson Valley	NYP	A-	955	961	946	NIP	Nippon Ham	JPL	JPL	1012	996	981
HUN	Huntsville	SOU	AA	1014	1026	1019	NOR	Norfolk	INT	AAA	927	916	903
IDA	Idaho Falls	PIO	Rk	1057	1045	1024	NRW	Norwich CT	EAS	AA	973	978	907
IDN	GCL Indians	GCL	Rk	—	—	1000	NWJ	New Jersey	NYP	A-	991	979	
IJv	Isla Juventud	CBA	Ind	1020	1023	1022	NWO	New Orleans	PCL	AAA	899	913	924
Ind	Industriales	CBA	Ind	924	920	931	NYA	New York (AL)	AL	MLB	975	981	976
IND	Indianapolis	INT	AAA	1006	995	981	NYN	New York (NL)	NL	MLB	970	973	966
IOW	Iowa	PCL	AAA	975	983	970	OAK	Oakland	AL	MLB	998	988	984
JAM	Jamestown	NYP	A-	1089	1100	1107	OAX	Oaxaca	MEX	MEX	1030	1019	1025
JAX	Jacksonville	SOU	AA	968	973	990	OGD	Ogden	PIO	Rk	1053	1061	1064
JCY	Johnson City	APL	Rk	1023	1030	1006	OKL	Oklahoma	PCL	AAA	944	948	933
JUP	Jupiter	FSL	A+	942	918	889	OMA	Omaha	PCL	AAA	951	967	967
KAN	Kannapolis	SAL	A	993	995	1001	ONE	Oneonta	NYP	A-	1056	1051	1064
KCA	KansasCity	AL	MLB	1022	1009	1017	ORM	Orem	PIO	Rk	—	896	892
KIN	Kinston	CRL	A+	979	983	982	ORX	Orix	JPL	JPL	1073	1003	991
KNC	Kane County	MDW	A	1014	1049	1065	OSA	Osaka	JPL	JPL	987	—	—
KNG	Kingsport	APL	Rk	995	1013	1032	OTT	Ottawa	INT	AAA	1018	1017	1025
LAA	Los Angeles(AL)	AL	MLB	960	959	957	PAW	Pawtucket	INT	AAA	992	1010	1020
LAK	Lakeland	FSL	A+	1016	1022	1038	PdR	Pinar Del Rio	CBA	Ind	931	906	881
LAN	Los Angeles(NL)	NL	MLB	960	975	993	PEO	Peoria	MDW	A	990	999	989
LEL	Lake Elsinore	CLF	A+	970	979	980	PHI	Philadelphia	NL	MLB	996	1023	1031
LEX	Lexington	SAL	A	1035	1024	1011	PHL	GCL Phillies	GCL	Rk	—	—	1000
LKC	Lake County	SAL	A	1001	1011	1032	PIR	GCL Pirates	GCL	Rk	—	—	1000
LNC	Lancaster	CLF	A+	1090	1091	1096	PIT	Pittsburgh	NL	MLB	993	998	1006
LNS	Lansing	MDW	A	984	983	990	PMB	Palm Beach	FSL	A+	955	949	943
LOU	Louisville	INT	AAA	1019	997	972	PME	Portland ME	EAS	AA	1041	1026	1026
LOW	Lowell	NYP	A-	1023	1006	977	POR	Portland OR	PCL	AAA	953	962	976
LTU	Las Tunas	CBA	Ind	1188	1181	1158	POT	Potomac	CRL	A+	1012	995	977
LVG	Las Vegas	PCL	AAA	1074	1081	1084	PRI	Princeton	APL	Rk	1057	1039	1048
LWD	Lakewood	SAL	A	933	924	925	PRO	Provo	PIO	Rk	1039	—	—
LYN	Lynchburg	CRL	A+	995	984	993	PUE	Puebla	MEX	MEX	1059	1045	1046
MCD	Mexico City	MEX	MEX	1107	1089	1088	PUL	Pulaski	APL	Rk	1042	1065	1075
MCL	Monclova	MEX	MEX	984	989	1002	PZA	Poza Rica	MEX	MEX	—	—	905
MCT	Tigres-Angelopolis	MEX	MEX	1100	1098	1094	QUD	Quad Cities	MDW	A	993	993	998
MEM	Memphis	PCL	AAA	924	924	931	RAK	Rakuten	JPL	JPL	—	1015	1021
MET	Metropolitans	CBA	Ind	983	977	969	RCU	Rancho Cucamonga	CLF	A+	982	982	986
MHV	Mahoning Valley	NYP	A-	1017	1013	1023	RDS	GCL Reds	GCL	Rk	—	—	1000
MID	Midland	TXS	AA	1005	1003	1008	REA	Reading	EAS	AA	1019	1006	986
MIL	Milwaukee	NL	MLB	1003	1007	1007	RIC	Richmond	INT	AAA	986	1003	1011
MIN	Minnesota	AL	MLB	1012	1007	999	RNG	AZL Rangers	AZL	Rk	—	—	1000

Team, League, and Level Key and Park Factors

brev	Fullname	Lgeague (2006)	Level	2004	2005	2006	brev	Fullname	Lgeague (2006)	Level	2004	2005	2006
ROC	Rochester	INT	AAA	1023	1025	1023	TBA	TampaBay	AL	MLB	983	986	993
ROM	Rome	SAL	A	938	936	950	TCV	Tri-City	NYP	A-	1024	1031	1043
ROU	Round Rock	PCL	AA	961	944	927	TEN	Tennessee	SOU	AA	1032	1025	1021
ROY	AZL Royals	AZL	Rk	—	—	1000	TEX	Texas	AL	MLB	1059	1044	1034
RSX	GCL RedSox	GCL	Rk	—	—	1000	TGR	GCL Tigers	GCL	Rk	—	—	1000
SAC	Sacramento	PCL	AAA	955	951	945	TIJ	Tijuana	MEX	MEX	1045	1024	998
SAN	San Antonio	TXS	AA	916	934	931	TOL	Toledo	INT	AAA	960	944	934
SAR	Sarasota	FSL	A+	999	1001	1014	TOR	Toronto	AL	MLB	1035	1031	1026
SAV	Savannah	SAL	A	973	974	981	TRI	Tri-City	NWN	A-	915	909	895
SBN	South Bend	MDW	A	966	960	970	TRN	Trenton	EAS	AA	978	964	947
SBR	Inland Empire	CLF	A+	952	958	960	TUC	Tucson	PCL	AAA	1089	1073	1047
SCO	State College	NYP	A-	—	982	972	TUL	Tulsa	TXS	AA	985	1003	1004
SCu	SantiagoCuba	CBA	Ind	1036	1013	994	TWI	GCL Twins	GCL	Rk	—	—	1000
SDN	San Diego	NL	MLB	919	921	928	VAN	Vancouver	NWN	A-	934	933	943
SEA	Seattle	AL	MLB	950	953	949	VAQ	Vaqueros Laguna	MEX	MEX	1128	1114	1079
SEI	Seibu	JPL	JPL	992	999	996	VCI	Villa Clara	CBA	Ind	950	956	962
SFD	Springfield	TXS	AA	—	969	965	VER	Vermont	NYP	A-	999	1019	1030
SFN	San Francisco	NL	MLB	1001	1004	1002	VIS	Visalia	CLF	A+	1003	999	987
SJO	San Jose	CLF	A+	912	897	886	VRC	Veracruz	MEX	MEX	917	915	900
SLC	Salt Lake	PCL	AAA	1090	1087	1087	VRO	Vero Beach	FSL	A+	1045	1040	1036
SLM	Salem VA	CRL	A+	967	954	950	WAS	Washington	NL	MLB	—	952	958
SLN	St Louis	NL	MLB	976	990	994	WIC	Wichita	TXS	AA	976	984	988
SLO	Salem-Keizer	NWN	A-	994	976	974	WIL	Wilmington	CRL	A+	983	982	977
SLP	San Luis Potosi	MEX	MEX	1047	1046	1039	WIS	Wisconsin	MDW	A	997	989	983
SLT	Saltillo	MEX	MEX	1047	1036	1030	WMI	WesternMichigan	MDW	A	972	979	979
SLU	St Lucie	FSL	A+	1004	999	990	WNS	Winston-Salem	CRL	A+	1047	1055	1048
SPO	Spokane	NWN	A-	1028	1049	1065	WPT	Williamsport	NYP	A-	969	978	985
SSp	Sancti Spiritus	CBA	Ind	982	1014	1018	WTN	West Tennessee	SOU	AA	992	993	996
STA	Staten Island	NYP	A-	901	890	878	WVA	West Virginia	SAL	A	—	999	1027
STO	Stockton	CLF	A+	954	957	955	YAK	Yakima	NWN	A-	995	979	960
SWB	Scranton/W-B	INT	AAA	1000	998	996	YAN	GCL Yankees	GCL	Rk	—	—	1000
SWM	SW Michigan	MDW	A	—	1024	1027	YKL	Yakult	JCL	JPL	1012	1037	1063
SYR	Syracuse	INT	AAA	1025	1035	1054	YKO	Yokohama	JCL	JPL	1068	1077	1076
TAB	Tabasco	MEX	MEX	842	854	861	YOM	Yomiuri	JCL	JPL	961	950	952
TAC	Tacoma	PCL	AAA	921	914	923	YUC	Yucatan	MEX	MEX	890	883	874
TAM	Tampa	FSL	A+	985	992	981							

Leagues

AL:	American League
APL:	Appalachian League
AZL:	Arizonal League
CBA:	Cuban League
CLF:	Califonia League
CRL:	Carolina League
EAS:	Eastern League
FSL:	Florida State League
GCL:	Gulf Coast League
INT:	International League
JCL:	Japanese Central League
JPL:	Japanese Pacific League
MDW:	Midwest League
MEX:	Mexican League
NL:	National League
NWN:	Northwest League
NYP:	New York-Penn League
PCL:	Pacific Coast League
PIO:	Pioneer League
SAL:	South Atlantic League
SOU:	Southern League
TXS:	Texas League

Levels

MLB:	Major League Baseball
AAA:	Triple-A
JPL:	Japanese Leagues
MEX:	Mexican League
AA:	Double-A
A+:	Full-season High-A-ball
A:	Full-season A-ball
A-:	Short-Season A-Ball
Ind:	Independent
Rk:	Rookie Ball

Team, League, and Level Key and Park Factors

Index

Biographies

Jim Baker has been with Baseball Prospectus since 2004 and is the author of the "Prospectus Matchups" column on BP.com. He is also a frequent contributor to ESPN.com's Page 2. Prior to that, he was a regular columnist on ESPN's baseball and Insider pages. He has contributed to such books as *The Baseball Abstract, The Bill James Historical Baseball Abstract, Mind Game,* and *Rob Neyer's Big Book of Baseball Blunders,* and has been anthologized in the *Fireside Book of Baseball.* Originally from Piscataway, New Jersey, he lives in Austin, Texas with his daughters Victoria and Olivia.

Maury Brown is the creator and editor of www.Bizof-Baseball.com. He's blessed beyond words to have his wife, Glenna, and sons Tyler and Travis, who let him be an obsessive/compulsive when it comes to all manner of baseball and sports business. He lives in Portland, Oregon.

Will Carroll is a writer for Baseball Prospectus and ESPN.com. His particular area of expertise is player injuries; his baseball column "Under The Knife" is the "industry standard" according to Peter Gammons while his football column is "a f**king nightmare" according to Patriots coach Bill Belichick. He won the 2005 SABR Research Award for his book, *The Juice* and Fantasy Article of the Year from the Fantasy Sports Trade Association. He was seen on ESPN TV last year as part of *The Fantasy Show* and is a regular guest on WGN Radio, ESPN News, and over 30 other media outlets. Will lives in Indianapolis, where he teaches the gyroball and really doesn't sleep. He dedicates his contributions to this year's book to his mom, Anne Carroll.

Clay Davenport was born and raised in Virginia; his earliest baseball memories are the bitter disappointment of the Orioles losing the 1971 World Series to the Pirates. He began developing his translations of player statistics in the late 1980s, and led a popular effort to distribute Davenport Translations and commentary for all teams through the rec.sport.baseball newsgroup—efforts from which today's Baseball Prospectus sprang. Outside of baseball, he works as a meteorologist, developing techniques to estimate and track precipitation from satellite, with a primary goal of making more timely and accurate flash-flood warnings. He lives in Maryland with his wife, Susan, and their daughter.

Neil deMause is a lifelong New Yorker who has personally witnessed seven World Series games and two no-hitters, but has yet to catch a foul ball. Neil is co-author of the book *Field of Schemes: How the Great Stadium Swindle Turns Public Money Into Private Profit* (scheduled for re-release in 2008 by the University of Nebraska Press in an expanded edition), is a former sports business columnist for SportsJones.com, and has written for publications ranging from the *Village Voice* to *ESPN The Magazine.* He lives in Brooklyn with his partner, Mindy, and their son, Jordan.

John Erhardt lives with his wife Cheryl in Canandaigua, New York. For employment, he sits in a cubicle and stares at XML files for a Rochester-based instructional design company. Beyond this year's annual, he's also a contributor to the forthcoming *It Ain't Over.* His

non-baseball passions include Mediterranean cooking, fingerstyle guitar, philosophy, and Trappist beer.

Dan Fox just completed his first season as a regular columnist at baseballprospectus.com, doing his best to entertain readers with a variety of sabermetric analyses in his column, "Schrödinger's Bat." Dan also works part-time as a stats stringer for Major League Baseball Advanced Media, and is the author of the blog Dan Agonistes (danagonistes.blogspot.com), where he struggles with baseball and other topics. A graduate of Iowa State University, when not crunching the numbers Dan works as a Software Architect for Compassion International in Colorado Springs, where he lives with his wife and two daughters.

Steven Goldman is the creator of the long-running "Pinstriped Bible" column and companion "Pinstriped Blog" at yesnetwork.com, the "You Could Look It Up" column for baseballprospectus.com, and is a baseball columnist for the New York Sun. Steven is also the author of the biography *Forging Genius: The Making of Casey Stengel,* the editor of Baseball Prospectus's book *Mind Game,* and a contributor to BP's *Baseball Between the Numbers.* This is the second edition of the Baseball Prospectus annual he has co-edited with Christina Kahrl. Immediately after completing his stint as co-editor of this book, Steven will begin work on BP's next book, *It Ain't Over.* Steven lives in New Jersey with his wife, Stefanie, daughter, Sarah, and son, Clemens.

Kevin Goldstein covers the minor leagues, prospects, player development, scouting and the draft for Baseball Prospectus. Following the independent publication of *The Prospect Report,* which gained national recognition from Peter Gammons and others, Kevin spent three years with Baseball America before joining Baseball Prospectus in the spring of 2006 to lead their coverage of baseball below the major league level. He lives in Chicago with his unindicted co-conspirator and love, Margaret, her children Xander and Cameron on weekends, as well as a pair of tabby cats, Henry and Pickles, and Otto the Pit Bull.

Derek Jacques is an attorney residing in New York City, where he works with his wife, Paula, running a freelance editing business. He sometimes rues the day in high school when Joe Sheehan said to him "Hey, you! You look like you don't have anything to do on evenings or weekends. Want to join a Strat-O-Matic league?"—even though there's a pretty straight line from that conversation to his contributing to this book. Derek also writes his own blog, www.weblogthatderekbuilt.blogspot.com.

Jay Jaffe is the founder of the six-year-old Futility Infielder website (www.futilityinfielder.com), one of the oldest baseball blogs. In addition to covering the annual Hall of Fame ballot for BP, he writes the weekly "Prospectus Hit List" during the season. In recent years he's contributed work to *Mind Game,* Will Carroll's *The Juice, Bombers Broadside 2007, Fantasy Baseball Index,* and BP's forthcoming *It Ain't Over.* A graduate of Brown University who works as a graphic designer in New York City, he's married to Andra, the most supportive gal in the world, and once came in third in the famous Milwaukee Brewers sausage race.

Rany Jazayerli, 31, was a first-year medical student when he became part of the original team that founded Baseball Prospectus 11 winters ago. He is now a dermatologist in private practice in the western suburbs of Chicago. He lives with his wife of nearly 10 years, Belsam, and daughters Cedra and Jenna.

Christina Kahrl is one of the founding five members of Baseball Prospectus, and is one of three who has been involved in the creation of all twelve editions of the annual. Beyond her regular "Transaction Analysis" column at BP.com (entering its twelfth year this spring), she's written about baseball and football for *Playboy, The New York Sun,* Salon.com, Slate.com, SportsIllustrated.com, and ESPN.com, and contributed to *Mind Game, The ESPN Pro Football Encyclopedia,* and the forthcoming *It Ain't Over.* She also published a few dozen cutting-edge books on almost every sport imaginable during her five years as Sports Acquisitions Editor at Brassey's/ Potomac Books, helping launch the careers of several of her contemporaries. A graduate of the University of Chicago with a Master's degree from Loyola University (she went into the lucrative field of History for both), she now lives in the Washington, DC metro area with somebody else's dog, and roots to this day for the team of her childhood, the Oakland A's.

Ben Murphy has been with Baseball Prospectus since early 2004, doing technical work and writing about various statistical topics. His baseball interests include player salaries, fantasy baseball, and the scheduling problem, which was the subject of his Master's thesis for his degree in Operations Research. Ben runs the fantasy Scoresheet league, Kings, which uses the Scoresheet Sports simulation system. Each year, Baseball Prospectus donates $1000 to the charity of the winners' choice. Ben has helped with the Baseball Prospectus annual for the past two years, wrote a piece for *Mind Game,* and helped with Dayn Perry's book *Winners* as a research

assistant doing statistical research. He works doing data processing and statistical analysis, forecasting and modeling for a regional bank in North Carolina with his loving wife Kristen and dogs Spud and Coda.

Rob Neyer has been writing about baseball on ESPN.com for eleven years, and hopes to make it twelve.

Marc Normandin is a student at Merrimack College, majoring in communication. This is his first year at Baseball Prospectus, as well as his first contributing to the annual. He lives outside of Boston, where he roots for the Red Sox and the cross-country San Diego Padres.

Nate Silver is the Executive Vice President of Baseball Prospectus and the creator of the PECOTA system. In addition to his duties for BP, Nate has written for *Sports Illustrated,* ESPN.com, and Slate.com. Nate lives in Chicago and claims that rooting for the White Sox, Cubs and Tigers is no greater a sin than wearing unmatching socks.

Will Weiss, formerly the senior editor of YESNetwork.com, is the Director of Ad Operations for Broadband Enterprises. He lives on Long Island with his wife, Toni.

Keith Woolner lives in Cary, North Carolina with his wife and son, and works in the software industry. A lifelong Red Sox fan, he has been analyzing and writing about baseball for over 15 years. He earned undergraduate degrees from M.I.T. in Mathematics, Computer Science, and Management, and a Master's degree from Stanford University in Decision Analysis. While best known for inventing VORP (Value Over Replacement Player), Keith has written numerous research articles on topics such as catcher game-calling, replacement level theory, the effects of high pitch counts, win expectancy, and revenue sharing. As head of Baseball Prospectus's R&D, he developed and maintains the huge database of statistics that powers the BP website's stat reports.

Acknowledgments

As an organization in the business of providing you with the best content on baseball, we'd fall well short of that without the help, insight, contributions, or observations of people both in- and outside the baseball industry. Although this list is by no means comprehensive, we'd like to thank Sandy Alderson, Jeff Angus, Dan Arey, Mark Armour, Chuck Armstrong, Doug Atterbury, Andrew Baharlias, Tyler Barnes, Allen Barra, Jeff Barton, Buzzie Bavasi, John Beamer, Billy Beane, Louie Belina, Alex Belth, Craig Birkemeier, Tyler Bleszinski, Chaim Bloom, Howard Bloom, Ronald Blum, John Blundell, Lawrence Boes, Dean Bonham, Kent Bonham, Brian Borawski, Greg Bouris, Jim Bowdon of ESPN, Josh Boyd, J.C. Bradbury, John Brattain, John Buccigross, Steve Bunin, Rich Burk and everyone with the Portland Beavers, Larry Burke, William Burke, John Burnson, Jack Cain, Jim Callis, Steve Canter, Mike Carminati, Alex Carnevale, Chuck Carree, Jay Catalano, Jim Charlton, Steven Charnick, Ben Cherington, Richard Chow, Alex Ciepley, Devin Clancy, Fred Claire, James Click, Dave Cokin, John Coniff, John Coppolella, Cleve Corner, Dick Cramer, Jerry Crasnick, Kimball Crosley, Kevin Cuddihy, John Dewan, Nando Di Fino, Scott Drucker, Bob Dutton, Michael Epstein, Jeff Erickson, Bill Felber, Mike Ferrin, Adam Fisher, Eric Fisher, Dan Evans, Tom Fontaine, Sean Forman, David Forst, Rod Fort, Geoff Foster, Ted Frank, Meyer Freeman and Drew Mahalic with the Oregon Sports Authority, Peter Friberg, Lee Froehlich, Bill Frucht, Carter Gaddis, Jim Gallagher, Brent Gambill, Jeff Gambino, Peter Gammons, David Gassko, Jim Gates, Sam Geaney, Charles Gearing, Steve Gietschier, Bill Gilbert, Gary Gillette, Tom Gisriel, Aaron Gleeman, the clan Goldman (Stefanie, Sarah, Clemens, Reuven, and Eliane), Alexander Gomez, Tom Gorman, Andrew Grant, Rick Hahn, Joe Hamrahi, Virginia Harmon, Fred Harner, Louis Hau, John Heer, Lynn Henning, A.J. Hinch, Alan and Alexandra Houghton, Gary Huckabay, Kurt Hunzeker and the South Coast League, Rick Hurd, Toby Hyde, Tatsuya Ishida, Chris Isidore, Chris Jaffe, Bill James, Dwight

Jaynes, David Kahn, Justin Kahrl, Dave Kaplan, Jason Karegeannes, Stan Kasten, King Kaufman, Brian Kenny, Bill Kent and everyone at Sports Management Worldwide, Jonah Keri, Peter King, Chris Kline, Sydelle Kramer, Eric Kubota, Bowie Kuhn, Duane Kurisu, Deric Ladnier, Jon Lalonde, Mark Lamster, Dr. Lynn Lashbrook, David Laurila, Keith Law, Tony LeCava, Rich Lederer, Kevin Lee, Ian Lefkowitz, Tim Lemke, Keith Lieppman, Jeff Lissack, Jacob Luft, Carlos Lugo, Freddie Lutz, Steve Lyons, Jeff Ma, Norman Macht, Paul Mahler, Tim Marchman, Greg Marzullo, Rob McMillin, Paul Merzlak, Chris Metz, Dave Metz, Russ Meyer, Bernie Miklasz, Alan Miller, Rob Miller, Omar Minaya, John Mirabelli, Dr. Richard Mohring, Adam Morris, Kristen Murphy, Alan Nero, Bob Neumeier, Margaret Nissen, Kojo Nnamdi, Roger Noll, Vincent Novicki, Bill Nowlin, Patrick K. O'Donnell, Oz Ocampo, Matt Oshinsky, Jeanette Mott Oxford, Nick Padgett, Pete Palmer, Jason Pare, Brian Parker, Jeff Passan, Sean Passanisi, Dave Pease, John Perrotto, David Pinto, Bob Plapinger, Joe Posnanski, Peter Quadrino, Todd Radom, Atif Rafiq, Joshua Raisen, Nate Ravitz, Josh Rawitch, Geoff Reiss, Alex Riethmiller, Mike Rizzo, Issac Ropp, Dave Rolf, Ken Rosenthal, Darren Rovell, Jeff Sackmann, Anthony Salazar, David Samson, Earl Santee, Aaron Schatz, Keith Scherer, David Schoenfield, Chris Schofield, Peter Schoenke, Annie Schultz, Cory Schwartz, Alan Schwarz, Dan Scotto, Melissa Segura, Mark Shapiro, Stu Shea, Mike Siano, Matt Silverman, Michael Silverman, Eric Simon, Greg Simons, Allan Simpson, Bryan Smith, Janet Marie Smith, Mike Smith, Paul Smith, Tal Smith, Greg Spira, Jayson Stark, Dan Steinberg, Chris Stone, Nick Stone, Dave Studenmund, Paul Swangard, Brendan Sweeney, Chris Talbott, Cecilia Tan, Dr. David Tate, Bruce Taylor, John Thorn, Neal Traven, Fay Vincent, Darren "Repoz" Viola, Diane Vogel, Tom Waddle, Franklin Wagner, Childs Walker, Don Walker, Sam Walker, John Walsh, Al and Suiling Weed, Jon Weisman, Jared Weiss, Charlie Wilmoth, Chuck Wilson, Mary Wisniewski, Kathy Woolner, Josh Yates, Farhan Zaidi, Brad Ziegler, Andrew Zimbalist, Herbie Zucker, and Derek Zumsteg.